The Oxford Crossword Dictionary

SECOND EDITION

The Oxford Crossword Dictionary

SECOND EDITION

Compiled by
Market House Books Ltd

OXFORD
UNIVERSITY PRESS

OXFORD
UNIVERSITY PRESS

Great Clarendon Street, Oxford OX2 6DP

Oxford University Press is a department of the University of Oxford.
It furthers the University's objective of excellence in research, scholarship,
and education by publishing worldwide in

Oxford New York

Athens Auckland Bangkok Bogotá Buenos Aires Calcutta
Cape Town Chennai Dar es Salaam Delhi Florence Hong Kong Istanbul
Karachi Kuala Lumpur Madrid Melbourne Mexico City Mumbai
Nairobi Paris São Paulo Singapore Taipei Tokyo Toronto Warsaw

with associated companies in Berlin Ibadan

Published in the United States
by Oxford University Press Inc., New York

First published 1998
First published in paperback 2000
This edition first published 2001

British Library Cataloguing in Publication Data
Data available

Library of Congress Cataloging in Publication Data
Data available

ISBN 0–19–866265–3

1 3 5 7 9 10 8 6 4 2

Typeset in Times and Univers
by Market House Books Ltd
Printed in Great Britain
by Clays Ltd, St Ives plc

PREFACE

The *Oxford Crossword Dictionary* is the ideal resource for anyone who enjoys solving crosswords or playing word games. The dictionary comprises two sections:

- an informative introduction by Michael Macdonald-Cooper on the history of crossword puzzles and the types of cryptic clue used by crossword compilers;
- lists of words arranged according to the number of letters they contain;
- a reference section, comprising thematic lists, including biographical and geographical information.

The word lists provide the reader with a much quicker, easier, and clearer way of finding words of a given length than a traditional dictionary. The listing of words and phrases by the number of letters they contain enables the reader to look for words with the required number of letters, rather than painstakingly picking out words of the appropriate length from a purely alphabetical sequence. The removal of all definitions and explanations means that the reader can locate words at a glance and can scan the lists for particular letter combinations. Within each numerical group the words are arranged alphabetically.

The word lists were created by a series of computer programs, using electronic versions of the *New Shorter Oxford English Dictionary* and the *Concise Oxford Dictionary*. Variant spellings, such as *judgement* and *judgment*, have been included where possible, as have irregular inflections of verbs and plural forms of nouns. Some regular plurals or inflections have also been included when the correct form may not be immediately obvious, e.g. *alibis* has been included to show that the plural of *alibi* is not *alibies*. Orthographic variants, including capitalized and lower case forms (e.g. *Post Office* and *post office*), hyphenated, solid, and broken forms (e.g. *rally-cross* and *rallycross*, *shut down* and *shutdown*) also appear in the lists to allow for the different rules and regulations of various word games and to help crossword solvers who are looking for multiple-word phrases rather than single words. Widely used and well-known abbreviations, such as *AIDS*, appear in the word lists – a detailed list of abbreviations appears at the end of the book. For completeness, formal, informal, taboo, dialect, archaic, and derogatory words have been included – but without labels, as these would have made the lists difficult to read. However, foreign words are printed in italics. The source dictionaries provide information about the meaning and usage of the listed words.

The encyclopedic section contains information compiled to provide answers to general-knowledge crossword clues and quiz questions, but is also useful in a wide variety of games. It includes lists in tabular form, such as *Capital Cities* and *Planets and their Satellites*, and thematic lists, such as *Fish, Musical Instruments,* and *Sporting Terms*. To help the reader locate a particular subject, the thematic section has been divided into a number of broad categories: **History, Politics, and War**; **Religion and Mythology**; **Geography and Transport**; **Science and Technology**; **Medicine**; **Animals**; **Plants**; **Art, Music, and Entertainment**; **Literature**; **Sport and Games**; **Food and Drink**; **Miscellaneous**; **Names**; **Abbreviations**.

A number of biographical lists are located in the appropriate thematic categories. These include both tabular lists with additional information, such as *Presidents of the USA* with dates in office, and alphabetical lists, such as *People in the Arts*. The abbreviations, arranged alphabetically, have been selected from the *Oxford Dictionary of Abbreviations* and brief definitions and explanations have been provided.

The editors believe that the *Oxford Crossword Dictionary* will be an invaluable reference source for all crossword solvers and word-game enthusiasts.

CONTENTS

Contents

ACKNOWLEDGEMENTS

Editor
Fran Alexander (First Edition)
John Daintith (Second Edition)

Contributing Editors
Anna Berry
Peter Blair
Jonathan Law
Mark Salad

Compiled and Typeset by
Market House Books Ltd., Aylesbury

Source Dictionaries
The New Shorter Oxford English Dictionary
The Concise Oxford Dictionary
The Oxford Dictionary of Abbreviations

INTRODUCTION

History of the Crossword Puzzle

Word games of various sorts go back a very long way. We do not know at what point the gradual progress of literacy inspired people to make the mental leap from the utilitarian representation of speech by written characters to the conceptually different process of playing with the characters themselves to produce other effects. What is beyond doubt, however, is that word games, in the modern world of widespread literacy, are now inextricably woven into our use of language, artistically, recreationally and commercially.

The ubiquitous **acronym** so beloved of commercial organizations and pressure groups alike can be traced at least as far back as Christians of the first century AD. Members of early Christian communities used the symbol and the word for 'fish' as a mutually intelligible means of identification, based on the fact that the five initial letters of the Greek words for Jesus Christ Son of God Saviour spell out the word for fish, ΙΧΘΥΣ.

Acrostics were used in ancient and medieval texts, often in order to incorporate a dedication or a special message. **Ciphers** and rumours of ciphers found their way into Shakespearean exegesis and the prophecies of Nostradamus. **Anagrams** featured in 17th-century accounts of the exploits of the Swedish king Gustavus Adolphus, whose first name (with U written as V, as in Latin inscriptions) was seen as a version of *Augustus*. In the 18th century the pseudonym *Voltaire* (made from the letters of *Arovet* – or *Arouet* – *le jeune*, abbreviated *L, I*) gives us a further example.

It was not until the early 20th century, however, that the crossword puzzle as such made its first appearance. Arthur Wynne, a native of Liverpool working as a journalist in New York, published a lozenge-shaped grid whose squares were to contain answers to clues, with letters of answers running horizontally contributing to the formation of answers running vertically down the grid. This puzzle appeared on 21 December 1913, in a newspaper publication – the 'Fun' supplement of *New York World*.

After the 1914-18 war the American partnership of Simon and Schuster published crossword puzzles in book form, which were phenomenally successful. During the twenties the new craze swept across North America, and newspapers, journals and magazines began to feature crossword puzzles regularly.

It was not long before the English-language crossword puzzle crossed the Atlantic in the early twenties and was taken up by newspapers and magazines in the British Isles. After ignoring the popular trend for a while, *The Times* eventually succumbed to the inevitable and published its first crossword in 1930.

Crossword puzzles now appear in many languages, and are, interestingly enough, used as a language-teaching tool. Thus the frivolous offspring of language, for long castigated as a time-wasting diversion, has now surprised its parent by landing a proper job. Crosswords are seen not only as a useful resource in helping young people to augment linguistic skills in an entertaining way, but as a valuable bulwark against the decline and loss of linguistic skill in the elderly, who, if they are regular crossword solvers, appear less likely to succumb to the deterioration of some mental functions which may afflict people of advanced years.

The American Crossword

Arthur Wynne's original puzzle had features which are now generally to be found in many modern American crosswords. The grid used is a symmetrical one; apart from the first and last letters of the words at the points of the lozenge shape, all letters contribute to an across and a down word; and the clues are more or less definitions or descriptions of the answers to be found.

Crosswords such as those appearing in the *New York Times* and in other American newspapers generally share these features. Crosswords are now often composed on a much larger scale than Wynne's initial offering. The artistry of the setter is shown in part by the variety of elegant grid designs with symmetrical arrangement of black squares at the corners, sides, or centre. As a rule all letters contribute to both an across and a down word. Consequently it is often quite likely that the solver will find some answers already completed from intersecting letters, without the need to solve every clue.

Clues in American crosswords tend in the main to be very concise. Most will be definitions, though sometimes the setter will deliberately choose items which can be defined succinctly in a potentially ambiguous way. Groups of letters which form abbreviations, and even straightforward alphabetical letter sequences such as MNO and RST have been used as the answers to clues. Answers consisting of more than one word are not usually signposted as such, a fact which British solvers tackling American puzzles must allow for.

Because of the range of words and names deemed suitable for legitimate inclusion in crosswords of the *New York Times* variety, the solver may require knowledge of recondite facts about players in baseball teams, minor film and television performers, musicians of various kinds, and many other fields of popular culture, as well as a wide-ranging general knowledge of United States and world geography, to take but a few areas.

Sometimes American crosswords will be partly thematic in terms of the mode of entry of some of the answers. For instance, the device of replacing a given group of letters with a symbol each time it occurs, in both the across and down aspects, has more than once produced considerable bafflement amongst solvers. A typical example of this device might consist of the substitution of an Arabic numeral 8 every time the letter sequence -EIGHT- occurs in a word, and I recall one clever puzzle of this type which contrived to have substitutions of all 'numbers' from ONE to NINE. Since the solver is unaware at the outset that this device is being used, or even that the puzzle has thematic features of any kind, mystification can be quite prolonged.

Crosswords have an enormous following in the United States, as even a British traveller on a holiday cruise ship cannot help being aware, when the daily faxes of popular American crosswords (with previous day's solution) are made available for collection by passengers sailing the remotest parts of the world's oceans.

British Crosswords

Definition crosswords

When the crossword puzzle first crossed the Atlantic the fairly simple methods of providing definitional clues which characterized the American crossword were adopted in Britain. These methods are still to be found in more or less unchanged form in the type of daily newspaper crossword which is designated 'quick' or 'concise'.

A change has occurred, however, in the way in which crossword grids are constructed for most puzzles of the concise type, as well as for many of the cryptic varieties. Instead of having every letter of across answers contribute to a down answer and vice versa, grids are designed with an arrangement of black squares which, typically, allows alternate letters of across answers to coincide with those belonging also to down words. In consequence, the solver must read and solve every clue in order to complete the diagram successfully.

Because the clues are of the 'concise' type, often consisting of a single word (e.g. animal, bird, fish) there may be several possible answers which would fit a space of given length, particularly if the word is a shortish one of, say, four or five letters. The solver may therefore need to think of a likely answer to the clue and test this by solving one or more of the clues to intersecting words, in order to find an answer which fits without clashing. There is thus an element of the jigsaw puzzle (which word will fit here?) entailed in the solving of many 'quick' or 'concise' crosswords.

In most crossword puzzles of this type the setter will still tend to use a grid pattern which is symmetrical (a mainly aesthetic consideration), though this is not invariably true. Because there is no need for the double (across and down) use of every letter, this type of grid is somewhat easier for the setter to fill with suitable words. Therefore the practice of using arbitrary letter sequences or even well-attested abbreviations – necessary standbys of the American setter – tends to be frowned on as unfair or unnecessary in the British concise crossword. Arcane or obscure items are still to be found within this type of puzzle, particularly in those designated as general knowledge crosswords, often a regular feature of some newspapers. Even at the level of 'everyday' vocabulary, it is clear that some words with which everybody is now familiar, such as YAK, ENNUI, EMU and OASIS, are encountered far more often in the squares of crossword puzzles than ever in real life.

Cryptic crosswords

Origins

A major change which distinguishes British crosswords from American ones, apart from the differences in crossword grids, has been the gradual development of the cryptic crossword.

The earliest departures from purely definitional clueing, in the 1920s and 1930s, did not extend to complete sets of cryptic clues for a whole puzzle, but rather used just a few examples of, for instance, anagrams, reversals, or other devices, along with many clues still consisting of definitions. Where anagrams did feature, it often happened that no definition of the final answer was indicated, and even that no instruction to rearrange the letters in the clue word was given.

Gradually, however, the cryptic crossword began to assume something like its traditional form. From 1926 dates the regular appearance of crosswords composed by setters of an academic cast of mind, beginning with Torquemada (Edward Powys Mather) in *The Observer*. Graham Greene, in his autobiography *A Sort of Life*, refers to the fact that two of his Berkhamsted schoolmasters used, after their retirement, to join forces every Sunday to tackle these crosswords. At first, to be sure, some of the clues were scarcely cryptic ones in the modern sense, consisting, perhaps, of a slightly oblique reference to an extremely obscure fact, or offering imperfect and incomplete instruction to the solver as to how the elements in the clue should be treated.

What eventually emerged from these tentative beginnings, however, appeared to be the propensity of members of the solving public who shared with the setters a certain sort of education and a similar cultural background to be able to trace a path through the conscious obscurity of the clueing to the intended answers. Yet the esoteric nature of many of the references (which would be condemned by many of today's crossword setters as offering merely a 'clue to a clue', rather than a satisfactory and *ultimately* unambiguous steer to the required answer) meant that the general reader still found such puzzles rather inaccessible.

The credit for making the cryptic crossword a much more reliable vehicle for the journey from initial bafflement to the enlightenment which culminates in a correct solution arrived at with certainty belongs to A. F. Ritchie (Afrit of *The Listener*, and in real life the headmaster of Wells Cathedral School). Active in the 1930s and 1940s, Ritchie was the first to advance the dictum that the composer of the cryptic clue need not mean what he says, but must say what he means. Thus, although the cryptic clue may have an ostensible, surface meaning which may be amusingly misleading, it must also contain precise instructions, when properly understood, for reaching the answer the setter intends.

Derrick Macnutt, classics master at Christ's Hospital, took the name Ximenes (like Torquemada, a pseudonym from the Spanish Inquisition) when he became the regular setter of *The Observer*'s difficult cryptic crossword. Ximenes endorsed wholeheartedly what Afrit had said about precision and fairness in clue writing. Indeed, Macnutt went further, and in a most practical way. Whereas observations and theoretical canons about fairness in cryptic clues had rarely appeared, if at all, outside the prefaces to crossword anthologies, the Ximenes puzzle became the vehicle for a regular competition amongst readers to see who could produce the best cryptic clue to a given word. The entries to this competition, good, bad, and indifferent, offered pegs on which Macnutt could hang a variety of musings, injunctions, and strictures in the notes accompanying his adjudications of prizewinning clues – notes sent to all solvers who wished to have them (with the commendation that they were 'especially helpful to less experienced competitors').

Gradually Macnutt's musings and strictures developed into something like a systematic theory of crossword clues. Eventually the book *Ximenes on the Art of the Crossword* (co-authored by Macnutt and Alec Robins, author of the Everyman puzzle in *The Observer*, and contributor, as Custos, of many crosswords published in *The Guardian*) set out the Ximenean canons of clue writing.

The participative and dialogue features of the clue-writing competition initiated by Ximenes are maintained by Jonathan Crowther (Azed), who succeeded Ximenes at *The Observer* almost thirty years ago. More recently the advent of dedicated crossword subscription magazines such as *Crossword* and the existence of newsgroups on the Internet have enabled many more crossword enthusiasts to read and to offer comment about clues from the aspects of fairness, style, humour, etc.

Such democratic feedback as that facilitated by Internet newsgroups and other more traditional sources can be extremely valuable to setters as well as solvers of crossword puzzles. As indicated above, the early pioneers of the British cryptic crossword were setters who had a particular sort of education and a certain view of what areas of knowledge ought fairly to be assumed to exist amongst the cohort of solvers. As the crossword has become more popular and setters more numerous there has undoubtedly been change and development in the range of references deemed to be fair to the solver. References to Shakespeare, classical mythology, the Bible, characters from classic novels, and similar sources are still encountered, but far less (absolutely and proportionally) than in earlier times; it is salutary to be reminded by honest expressions of bemusement that not everyone nowadays knows (if ever they did) the story of Uriah the Hittite, or who Jocasta was, or that Cloud-cuckoo-land features in *The Birds* by Aristophanes.

Solving cryptic crosswords

Virtually all British daily newspapers, almost all weekly papers, and a very wide range of magazines feature a cryptic crossword. Probably the best-known examples are to be found in the five London-based broadsheet newspapers, *The Daily Telegraph*, *The Financial Times*, *The Guardian*, *The Independent* and *The Times*; but most newspapers now in tabloid format, as well as Irish, Scottish, Welsh, and English regional papers, will have crosswords of a similar type. Sunday papers tend to have not only a cryptic crossword similar to or perhaps a little harder than those featured in the dailies, but also a more challenging barred-grid puzzle such as *The Observer*'s Azed Crossword, the *Independent on Sunday*'s Beelzebub, or *The Sunday Times*'s Mephisto. Some may also have a general knowledge crossword, which, without being cryptic in its clueing style, may demand knowledge of or reliable references to a remarkably wide range of factual information of the sort provided by the category lists in this book.

The defining feature of the cryptic crossword puzzle is its use of language in clues initially to mislead, though in a way which will subsequently clinch beyond reasonable doubt the word sought. Because of this characteristic there are, indeed, some people who maintain that cryptic clues are generally easier to solve than many non-cryptic ones. The cryptic clue, with one or two important exceptions, will offer two ways of getting to the answer – a definition, and a set of cryptic indications hinting at the composition of the word the solver must find; whereas the definition-only crossword requires the solver to find the answer from only the former indication, helped if necessary by letters from intersecting words. Even more help is available to the solver of the cryptic clue by the convention that the definition (of one word or more) appears as the first or the last element of the clue.

The better sort of cryptic clue is one which purports to offer an imaginably real or surreal scenario – couched often in a sort of condensed journalese typical, perhaps, of newspaper headlines or sets of everyday instructions.

To take an example:

With iodine, clean out wound to guard against infection (9)

This clue is intended to lead to the answer INOCULATE, by the following processes:

I, the chemical symbol for the element *iodine*, supplies the first letter;

the two words *clean out* provide an anagram of the remaining eight letters, and the indication that they should be used to make an anagram is offered, misleadingly, by the word *wound* – not, in this case a noun defining an injury, but the past participle of the verb 'to wind';

finally, the definition of INOCULATE is offered by the last four words of the clue, *to guard against infection.*

Such a clue, to my eye, offers a more satisfactory challenge to the solver than the type, still to be found in some quarters, which simply throws three or four elements together without attempting to produce any sort of sense. The result is often irresistibly reminiscent of Chomsky's famous example of a grammatical and at the same time meaningless sentence: "Colourless green ideas sleep furiously."

Is it important that a clue should have an ostensible meaning, as well as the necessary components to lead to the answer? I would answer 'yes' to this, on two counts. Firstly, for the relatively new solver, the clue will then paint a mental picture which holds the imagination for a moment or longer, until it has become evident that this plain reading of the clue does not by itself yield an answer; and secondly, because it may serve to suggest that perhaps one or other of its elements has been deliberately chosen by the setter because it is not, in its cryptic reading, the same word, or the same part of speech, as it appeared in the plain reading (as in the example *wound* in the clue quoted above).

Even very experienced solvers, who from habit are more likely to make a rapid progression from the ostensible to the cryptic reading of the clue, find that it is far more satisfying aesthetically to dissect a sentence which does appear to mean something, if only to demonstrate that in reality it means nothing of the kind. And such solvers, too, whatever they may say publicly, are not infrequently helped by the knowledge that they have to mistrust, at times, even the most innocent and transparent-looking elements in a well-constructed cryptic clue.

The amusement generated by the sudden realisation that, for instance, parts of speech have after all changed identities with each other is almost reminiscent of the apocryphal wartime newspaper headline 'Allies Push Bottles Up Germans', where the casual omission of an apostrophe at the end of the first word has the potentially hilarious effect of transposing the grammatical status of the second and third words.

Types of cryptic clues

double (or multiple) definition

A double definition clue takes two possible definitions of the answer and juxtaposes them, ideally in such a way as to create a two-word phrase suggestive of a different idea altogether from the associations offered by either of the component parts.

For example, the clue:

Soft furnishing (8)

is meant to lead to the answer YIELDING, since 'yielding' in a mainly adjectival sense can be defined as *soft*, whilst the present participle of the verb 'to yield' can be construed as 'supplying' or 'providing' in the same sense as the present participle of the verb 'to furnish'. A misleading effect is produced by the fact that *furnishing* can also be a noun, one apt potentially to be associated with the adjective *soft*.

Sometimes three or four consecutive definitions for the same word may be found and run together with some semblance of meaning, as in, e.g.:

Just show beautiful blonde (4)

leading in four different ways to the answer FAIR.

hidden

In a 'hidden' clue, the word to be found is indicated by consecutive letters in one (longer) word, or in a consecutive group of letters taken from a sequence of two or more words in the clue. The clue must also, of course, supply a definition of the word sought, tell the solver how to find the answer, and, according to purists, otherwise contain no extraneous words not required to cover the letter sequence of the hidden indication.

For instance:

Start of mission in Zagreb, last of five (5-3)

is intended to lead to the answer BLAST-OFF, and although four words are used to contain the necessary letter sequence, there is no redundant word in the clue. Note that the 'process' whereby the clue yields its answer must be indicated, and that this function is fulfilled by the word *in* in the present example.

charades

The type of clue referred to as a charade is comparable with the party game of the same name, in that the answer is hinted at by consecutive indications of its component parts.

In the example:

Vegetable extract sustains soldier (9)

the word MANGETOUT is suggested by the use of 'get out' (verb, transitive) positioned (in this case in a down clue) beneath the word 'man' for *soldier* (several meanings of common words such as 'man' will be found in crossword clues, with the setter usually choosing one which best fits the context), so that 'man' is *sustained* by the words 'get out', fulfilling the 'process' of the clue. MANGETOUT itself is probably not the first name of a vegetable likely to come to the solver's mind unbidden, as it were; but with help from the given word length, and eventually from intersecting letters in other answers, the solution to this clue can be found.

reversals

A fair number of words in English, especially among the shorter ones, will produce another valid word when the order of letters is reversed.

An example:

Horse-drawn vehicle in which constituent's driven back (4)

should lead the solver to the answer TRAP, because this *vehicle* consists of the letters of the word 'part' (defined by *constituent*) with their order exactly reversed. The example given here is suitable for an across or a down entry, since we may think of the answer produced in horizontal aspect by the clue on the page, before being entered in an across or a down space. If, however, the setter had so wished, he could have made the clue only suitable for a down entry, by changing *back* to 'up'.

In the case of reversal clues in particular setters will sometimes, deliberately or unconsciously, write a clue which retains some ambiguity until intersecting letters from other answers have been determined. Such an ambiguity would exist if the clue example given above were altered slightly to read:

Constituent driven back in horse-drawn vehicle (4)

The solver may legitimately take the clue to indicate that a word for *constituent* must be found, which, when *driven back*, will give a word for a *horse-drawn vehicle* as the answer to the clue, as in our original example; or that the definition *constituent* is to be answered by a word ('part') which would be found to be *driven back* in a word meaning *horse-drawn vehicle* ('trap'). Either way of looking at the clue is possible, and only when help is at hand from intersecting words in the diagram will it be clear beyond doubt which answer is required.

containers

Some words will be found on close examination to consist of the letters of one word, in their correct order, surrounding the letters of another. This type of 'container' or 'container-and-contents' clue may be exemplified by:

Sentimental work penned by secret agent (5)

leading to the answer SOPPY (defined by the first word *sentimental*), since the word 'spy' is *penning* the expression 'op', a musical *work*. The setter takes the opportunity of introducing a somewhat misleading element in the shape of the word *penned* – whose meaning here must be 'enclosed', in order to indicate the 'process' required in the clue, though it reads aptly in the ostensible meaning which suggests that the agent has written the sentimental work.

anagrams

One of the easier ways for a setter to give a cryptic indication of the word required is to produce a rearrangement of its letters, in the shape of one word or several. Because the setter has a much freer hand in the choice of words used to form the anagram of the answer than in the more restricting format of a reversal or a container clue, he should normally be able to contrive a pleasingly apposite scenario in a good anagram clue.

Example:

Repel savage brute (5)

leads without too much difficulty to the answer REBUT, formed from the letters of *brute*, the process being hinted at by the word *savage* (supplying the 'anagram indicator'), and the definition of the answer required being given by *repel*.

To take another instance:

Pipe replaced in a trench (7)

has nothing to do with the renewal of old and corroded gas mains, but instead should lead the solver to CHANTER, the melody pipe of the bagpiper.

Setters who are fond of anagrams, which with experience are quite easy to handle, often take pride in being able to use the words of the anagram ingredients along with other elements in the clue to produce a cleverly misleading picture, all the more amusing when correctly solved.

homophones

Some English words are identical to others in pronunciation, or virtually so, although their respective meanings are quite disparate.

For instance:

Charming musical composition we listen to (5)

should enable the solver to arrive at the answer SWEET (*charming*), which sounds to most of us indistinguishable from 'suite' (*musical composition*). As with other types of cryptic clue, the homophone clue is obliged to offer an indication of the process by which it leads to the answer, which in this case is conveyed by the phrase *we listen to*, itself apposite in the context of the ostensible reading of the clue.

Homophone indicators commonly consist of phrases such as 'we hear', 'we're told', 'they say', or, slightly more obliquely, 'when broadcast' or 'on the phone'.

The fairness of some homophone clues is sometimes a controversial matter, perhaps more so than in the case of other common types of cryptic clue. Although people in many parts of Britain would not nowadays distinguish between the pronunciations of 'Wales' and 'whales', received pronunciation, as well as most contemporary Scottish usage, for instance, would do so. One fair way to indicate homophones in clues where there is, perhaps, a regional variation in pronunciation, or a difference associated with e.g. dissimilar social backgrounds, may be to use a phrase such as 'some say' instead of one or other of the indicators suggested in the previous paragraph.

Even such a device, however, does not to my mind justify the implied use of elements constituting part-homophones, which some setters occasionally adopt, where the totality of the indicators does not add up to the answer. Consider a clue such as:

Provides drink before story's told (8)

intending the answer SUPPLIES. The definition *provides* is fair enough, but in offering the charade indicator 'sup' for *drink*, to be followed by the homophone 'lie's' (*story's*) the setter has not merely failed to indicate the second 'p' in the answer, he has specifically excluded it by asking the solver only to substitute for the first syllable a word meaning *drink*. The setter has been seduced into believing that his homophone indicator governs the sounds of both syllables, whereas strictly understood it can only govern the second one.

Note that this is quite different in principle from the frequently encountered interchangeable homophones 'analyst' and 'annalist', for instance. Despite the existence of double 'n' in one of the words and single 'n' in the other, the solver will usually have been asked to arrive at one complete word which is an exact homophone of the other, and which thus follows a perfectly valid process in the working of a clue of this type.

subtractions

Some words in effect have the same form as other words minus the first letter, the last letter or the middle letter, or some other component which can be identified in the clue and removed, leaving the shorter word as the answer. The setter must give the solver a definition of the answer, and an indication of the word to be mutilated together with fair instructions as to how the subtraction is to be done.

An example which involves subtracting the initial letter is:

Losing head in panic, make mistake (5)

which leads to ERROR, by the simple expedient of taking away the 't' from 'terror'.

In the next example, it is the final letter which is removed:

Theatre mostly for men only (4)

in which the word 'stage', used abstractly as a substitute for *theatre*, loses its last letter to become STAG, meaning *for men only*.

An example of the omission of a middle letter is:

Seasonal fare offered by heartless gaoler (6)

in which the dropping of the 'n' from 'turnkey' leaves TURKEY as the answer to the definition *seasonal fare*.

cryptic definitions

Instead of giving indications suggesting how the word answering the definition is made up, setters will sometimes use the device of cryptic definition. In this type of clue, lateral thinking is demanded from setter and solver. The clue consists of an apparently plausible message in which, however, a key word (or several) must be taken in a sense quite different from the ostensible meaning.

For example:

Unsuitable subject for oral examination? (4,5)

may at first make the solver think of academic examinations involving, or not, the speaking of e.g. a foreign language; however, the real way to look at the clue is to consider the popular adage "Don't look a GIFT HORSE in the mouth", whose fourth and fifth words provide the answer.

Similarly:

Little Italian blown down in high wind (7)

is not a reference to a diminutive southern European's mishap in the course of a freak storm, but a cryptic definition of PICCOLO (a flute which is *blown down* by the player, in the *upper* reaches of the orchestral wood*wind* section), supplemented by the indication present, for those who recognise it, in the fact that PICCOLO is an Italian word for *little.*

The use of an already established phrase as a cryptic definition when opportunity permits can also be satisfying, provided too much violence is not done to the ordinary meanings of words.

The clue:

Lap of the gods? (6)

as a cryptic definition of NECTAR just escapes this charge, since the *Oxford English Dictionary* offers one possible definition of the noun 'lap' as a slang term for drink or liquor of any description.

Some cryptic definitions first seen many years ago have become famous as clever examples of the use of lateral thinking:

Die of cold? (3,4)

leads the successful solver to ICE CUBE, just as

Jammed cylinder? (5,4)

provides a lovely definition of SWISS ROLL.

A particular feature of cryptic definition clues is that they are intrinsically humorous. In order to amuse the solver, setters will therefore try as far as possible to ensure that their crosswords contain at least a proportion of cryptic definition clues.

Compound clues

The list of basic clue types given above offers solvers a simple guide to the basic ingredients which setters use. In many real examples of crossword clues, however, a combination of some of these elements will be found together. In the clue:

Work of art featuring bowl, endlessly attractive (7)

the answer WOODCUT is reached by means of a charade which incorporates a subtraction: 'wood' is defined by *bowl*, in the sense of the object rolled across a bowling-green, and 'cut' is derived from 'cute', meaning *attractive*, here rendered *endlessly*, having undergone a subtractive treatment of its last letter.

An example combining an anagram with a subtraction is provided by:

   Log showing odd tree rings – deficiency of nitrogen (8)

in which the answer REGISTER, defined by *log* (as either a verb or a noun, in both cases), is made from the rearranged letters of *tree rings*, subtracting the letter 'N', the chemical symbol for *nitrogen*.

A combination of a hidden element and a reversal is to be found in a clue such as:

   Skilful backing section in steel band (4)

Leading to the answer ABLE, defined by *skilful*, and indicated as a hidden item by the use of *section in*, with reversal implied by *backing*.

The '& lit.' clue

A special type of clue, and one which can be very pleasing to solve, is the type often referred to as '& lit.', implying that the statement in the clue, whilst relying on one (or more) of the cryptic clue devices listed above, is at the same time literally true.

In the example:

   A square always has one (4)

there are three ways of arriving at the answer AREA, one of them admittedly rather minimalist. The abbreviation A may be used for area, and the letters of AREA may also be found hidden in the words *square always*. The third way is the literally true statement contained in the entire sentence which forms the clue. This last, when it is taken in isolation, is not in fact a cryptic clue at all – the sentence would not actually be out of place in a crossword whose clues were purely definitional. The coexistence of the genuinely cryptic hidden section, together, in this case, with the abbreviation A, renders beyond doubt the fact that the literal non-cryptic statement offered by the clue is to be taken as defining AREA, and not, for instance (were the word length to be different), 'perimeter'.

Letter indications in clue construction

By no means all words used as answers can be made to lend themselves neatly to one or more of the treatments so far outlined without the need for some additional fine tuning.

Sometimes, as we have seen, this can be provided by an instruction to remove a letter from another word hinted at or actually used elsewhere in the clue, such as an initial or final letter. Often, however, the setter will need a much wider range of indications of single letters or small groupings of letters, whether these are to be removed or, as will equally often be the case, included.

In one of the examples of a compound clue given earlier, the abbreviation N for the chemical element nitrogen was found as an indication of a letter to be subtracted from an anagram. There are over 100 elements in the periodic table, mostly designated by one or two letters, and compounds of these elements are also sometimes convenient. Commonly known elements include oxygen (O), carbon (C), and hydrogen (H) whilst amongst compounds, that for common salt or sodium chloride (NaCl) is surprisingly usable in such a clue as:

Salt consumed by simple aquatic creature (8)

in which 'NaCl' *consumed* by 'bare' leads to the answer BARNACLE.

Fun can also be had with the designations of chemical elements in clues where their function is disguised, as in:

He's a gas! (6)

leading to the element HELIUM as the actual answer (*He* being the chemical symbol for this gas), or the subtle:

As I say… (8)

in which *As* is the symbol for arsenic, *I* that for iodine, and *say* roughly the equivalent of 'to give a couple of examples'; the answer to this clue is therefore ELEMENTS.

Besides chemical elements, another large and user-friendly resource bank for the cryptic crossword setter is provided by the Greek alphabet, many of whose characters have names of two or three letters in modern English usage.

For example:

Hobby Greek character's adopted recently (9)

links the letter 'phi' with 'lately' in the answer PHILATELY.

Similarly:

Liable to change name of Greek character on list (7)

leads to a joining of 'mu' and 'table' in MUTABLE.

International vehicle registrations generally consist of one, two or three letters, as in D for Germany, MA for Morocco and EAU for Uganda. The appeal of indicators like these probably lies partly in the fact that countries as such are fairly large, unspecific entities and offer few restrictions in the creation of believable (or even surreal) scenarios conjured up by a clue which incorporates a country's indication in this way.

Short groups of letters constituting foreign words from other languages which are reasonably well-known are used by many setters. Elements from French, Italian, Spanish, and German, such as definite and indefinite articles (*le, la, les, un, une, il, los, las, el, der, die, das, ein* and *eine*) are often used, given indications such as 'the French', or 'European article'.

The familiar Roman numerals I, V, X, L, C, D, and M, and their various allowable combinations, are also frequently found as elements contributing to solutions.

Musical keys A, B, C, D, E, F and G, as well as the tonic sol-fa names of notes 'do', 're', 'me', etc., are sometimes very convenient indicators of single letters or short groups. Among some setters and solvers there is, however, a tendency to frown on single-letter indications which are general rather than specific, since in the former example 'note' or 'key' could imply any of he first seven letters of the alphabet.

Zip code abbreviations of American states such as WA, ND, ME and so on offer further scope to the inventive setter, as do the shortened forms of well-known cities such as LA and NY.

We have thus moved gradually from letters or letter-combinations with a symbolic value, as in the case of the elements, to abbreviations pure and simple. Most good dictionaries will include a wealth of abbreviations ranging from designations of degrees (MA, BA, BEd, etc.), through private and public organisations (ICI, MOD, RN), musical instructions (p, ff), compass points (N, S, E, W – also bridge players), linguistic etymologies (E, It, Ir, Sp) to the now conventional and almost hackneyed equivalences such as L for 'learner', 'pupil', 'student', 'beginner' and AB for 'sailor', with many other categories along the way.

A comparatively recent development among some setters of my acquaintance is to use the actual name of a letter from the phonetic alphabet (Delta, November, Oscar, Romeo, Tango, etc.). As with some other categories, this can be satisfying when done misleadingly, with an apparently plausible context, as perhaps in:

Arrived to collect Oscar for character role in film (5)

in which *arrived* suggests 'came', which, with 'O' for *Oscar*, gives the answer CAMEO.

Because the avowed purpose of the phonetic alphabet is primarily to represent letters unambiguously, with no subsidiary meaning such as letters used in abbreviations would have, it would be wrong, I feel, to use this device other than sparingly.

Indications of clue 'processes'

Except in the case of **double or multiple definition** clues and some **charade** clues, the setter must take care to supply, as well as the components to be used in the creation of the solution word, a valid and fair indication of what is to be done with these in order to form the answer.

In the case of **hidden** items, the process indication can be extremely simple, often consisting of no more than 'in', or 'part of':

Salad ingredient – bit of celeriac, ostensibly (3)

leads easily enough to COS.

When the general context of the clue does not permit one of these usages without uncomfortably straining the surface sense of the words used, the setter may give the word(s) hiding the group of letters which forms the answer, and the definition (in either order, of course), to be followed by 'to a certain extent', or something similar, by way of indication that only a section of the letters will supply the answer.

A variation on the hiding theme is to be found in clues which offer the letters of the answer not as a continuous sequence, but as specified (e.g. initial or final) letters in a particular sequence of words. For example:

Non-striker stands clear as bowler starts (4)

requires the first letters of *stands clear as bowler* to be used to form SCAB, a *non-striker* in the industrial action rather than the cricket context.

There is sometimes disagreement about satisfactory ways of indicating **reversals**, deriving from the evident difference in the entry of across and down answers. In general it would be fair to say, however, that reversals affecting answers for entry in either the across or down aspect are valid if they indicate that the letters given are to be taken in the opposite order, by some overt indication such as 'backing' or 'in turn' or 'on reflection'.

For example:

Hurry, having taken wrong turning (4)

In which *wrong* ('tort') when *turning* leads to the answer TROT.

The solution arrived at by means of reversing the necessary components in the horizontal mode (in which the clue itself is presented) can be entered in a downward direction without doing undue violence to the implied instruction to reverse.

Some forms of wording, however, belong properly only to down answers, in cases where there is an indication that the clue should be written, as it were, 'upwards'. This is the case when the reversal instruction is contained in words such as 'turned up' or 'turning up', which cannot properly be taken as an instruction to make a reversal in a horizontal plane.

Hence in:

Flowering tree – phone up about one (5)

The answer LILAC is arrived at by writing the letters of 'call' (for *phone*) *up*wards in the grid, around the Roman numeral 'I', for *one*, and must therefore be seen as a down entry in the context of the clue given.

Occasionally the instruction to reverse may be couched in slightly oblique terms, such as 'westwards', in order to indicate that the letters are to be read in the order right to left, as though in the westward direction on a conventional map.

Thus:

Oriental coming westwards encounters respect (6)

in which 'E' (for *oriental*, not itself affected by the reversal instruction) is followed by a westward-running 'meets' (for *encounters*), leading to the answer ESTEEM. Note that the *coming westwards* is placed ahead of the word *encounters*, which it has the effect of reversing, simply in order to make the sentence read satisfactorily.

This example would only do, however, for an across entry, since the instruction is referring so explicitly to the mode of entry of the word per se, rather than to the mental process entailed in solving the clue. The corresponding instruction in a down entry would properly be conveyed by having the clue read:

Oriental moving northwards encounters respect

Ways of indicating **container** clues are mostly quite straightforward, as in:

Brag about medical degree in pompously inflated language (7)

in which *about* provides the process indication to write 'boast' around MB to give BOMBAST.

Occasionally, however, a clue of the container type may be slightly elliptical in its language, without being unsound.

In the clue:

See people must have eaten fruit (5)

it is important to appreciate that the word implied by *see* ('lo') stands in a particular relationship to the phrase *people must have eaten* which could be expressed by inserting the word 'which' between *see* and *people*; hence we arrive at 'lo [which] men must have eaten', giving us the answer MELON.

Anagram indications are probably the most widely varying of all forms of process descriptions. Almost any verb participle, present or past, implying movement, whether vigorous or aimless; almost any adverb or adjective suggestive of confusion, incorrectness, or difference; as well as noun phrases referring to mishap, repair, reorganisation, and many other states or processes conveying unorthodoxy or instability, for instance, will serve as anagram indicators.

Clever setters will often try to conceal their anagram indicators by making them look like something else.

Consider:

Total ban, I fancy, for body of soldiers (9)

in which *fancy* is not a verb with subject *I*, but rather an adjective which applies to the nine letters of the three words preceding it, requiring them to be rearranged to form the answer BATTALION.

Likewise in:

Holds on to retsina supply (7)

the word *supply* is not to be read as a noun, but as an adverb, indicating that if *retsina* is spelled in a supple manner it will yield the answer RETAINS.

Mention has been made earlier of the common indicators for **homophone** clues, such as 'we hear', 'we're told', 'it's said', 'they say'. Sometimes a single adverb such as 'reportedly' will suffice. Occasionally it is possible to achieve a nice ambiguity by using a verbal past participle such as 'broadcast', which, as hinted earlier, can suggest the homophone type of clue relying on sound, as on the radio. It can also, however, call to mind the action of sowing seed by hand using the broadcast method, in which case the same cryptic indicator could serve as an instruction to make an anagram rather than find a homophone.

All forms of 'process' instruction in cryptic clues are, and should be, subject to evolution. If anagrams could only be legitimately indicated by a description such as 'confused' or one of its near synonyms, for instance, the phraseology of cryptic clues would very soon become extremely hackneyed. Happily those who write the most inventive clues are always apt to be influenced by the connotations of the words they are clueing, and to seek indications to describe the processes they variously require which sit appositely in context.

Advanced cryptic barred-grid and thematic crosswords

History

Although for most solvers of cryptic crosswords the blocked-grid 15 × 15 variety appearing on the back page of a daily newspaper is the kind normally thought of when crosswords are discussed, it is perhaps useful to say a little about other, somewhat harder, puzzles.

If we go back to the early history of the crossword in Britain, the pioneering puzzles of Torquemada were typically of the barred-grid type. Such puzzles consist of a square or, in the early days (and occasionally still) a rectangular grid in which every individual square contains a letter when the crossword has been successfully completed. The end of each answer, where this occurs other than at the edge of the crossword square, is marked by a thick line or bar.

Early puzzles of this type were often asymmetrical in their pattern of internal bars, and sometimes bore witness to the difficulty the setter had with grid construction; the occasional answer would be entered backwards, some – even quite short – words would be split between two locations, and the same short word or letter combination might appear more than once in the same crossword.

Gradually the setters of barred-grid cryptic crosswords became more proficient. Ximenes, mentioned earlier, succeeded Torquemada as the setter of *The Observer*'s regular barred-grid cryptic crosswords, and he, together with Afrit and other *Listener* setters of the 1940s and 1950s, introduced a more disciplined approach to grid construction in which it was considered normal to have a symmetrical arrangement of bars, except where the puzzle embodied a particular theme which necessitated a departure from this.

Soon the *Sunday Times Magazine* began its own series of Mephisto crosswords which still continues, although the persona of Mephisto changed in 1973, and again in 1995 following the untimely death of Richard Whitelegg (Mephisto II). Currently three setters in rotation contribute to the Mephisto series.

Since Ximenes's death in the early 1970s the current *Observer* setter Azed continues to entertain Ximenes's loyal cohort of solvers, and early in 2001 arrived at the milestone of the 1500th Azed puzzle.

In more recent years the *Independent on Sunday* has entered the scene with its Beelzebub crossword, started in 1990 by Richard Whitelegg (who thus for several years produced two barred-grid puzzles every week, as well as a considerable output of blocked-grid crosswords), and now continued by two setters who alternate.

Regular 'plain' crosswords

The Azed, Beelzebub, and Mephisto crosswords usually feature a 12 × 12 symmetrical grid, though Azed occasionally uses 11 × 13 rectangular grids. Usually the crossword contains 36 answers in a symmetrical arrangement, though sometimes slightly more or slightly fewer than this.

In constructing a barred-grid puzzle it is normal to have a greater proportion of letters cross-checked by those in intersecting answers than is usually possible in British blocked-grid crosswords. In the latter case a six-letter entry, for instance, would typically have only three of its letters cross-checked, whereas in a barred-grid puzzle this figure would rise to four or five.

A consequence of this generous level of checking is that suitable words which will fit a barred grid are somewhat farther to seek, and many words which would be considered unusual or even obscure in a daily newspaper puzzle (which the solver may tackle on the train or in a break during the working day) are to be found in the so-called **advanced cryptic crosswords** of the **barred-grid** type.

By way of compensation, setters of advanced cryptic barred-grid crosswords see themselves as having a responsibility to offer a level of precision in their clues which often exceeds that normally found in blocked-grid puzzles. Although many of the clue types described earlier as featuring in normal daily crosswords are the same as those which will be found in barred-grid cryptic crosswords, the cryptic definition, in particular, is not seen as sufficient by itself to convey the setter's intention. Cryptic definitions – some, indeed, very clever – will be found in barred-grid puzzles, but always supplemented by an indication of the component parts of the word sought. In the case of these and other clue types used in advanced puzzles of this sort, most setters choose to follow Ximenes, who made it a personal rule to give relatively straightforward clues for obscure and unusual words, and to reserve complex clues (possibly relying on obscure components) for only the more well-known words.

Although the solution grids of advanced barred-grid puzzles often look daunting and obscure to those coming to them for the first time (many solvers, like myself, have found that at first it is quite difficult to see how the clue and the answer are connected even when looking at the published solution), a typical crossword of this sort normally contains a majority of words which are well-known. Something between a quarter and (up to) a half of the entries may be found to be words for which reference to a dictionary is necessary. The pages of this book are extremely useful in checking for the existence of words both obscure and familiar, since the word length is the prime determinant of what will fit at a given place in the grid. When checking the actual meanings of difficult words against the possible definition element in the clue, a comprehensive dictionary of the normal sort is indispensable.

Before leaving the topic of reference books, let me try to dispose of the notion that the solver is somehow cheating if recourse is had to a dictionary, an atlas, an encyclopaedia, or any comparable source. The setter of the puzzle will have used reference books, or should have, because not to do so is to show an arrogance which runs the risk of letting down the solver from time to time by inaccurate definition. The crossword editor certainly has a responsibility to check the accuracy of the clues in the puzzles he is publishing, for the same reason, and will often have to make a judgement after comparison of several reference sources. There is therefore no reason whatever (except, naturally, in the course of certain sorts of competitions) for the solver to abstain from reference books at any level of crossword solving.

Themes

The three regular puzzles referred to above are usually described as 'plain' puzzles, because, with the exception of occasional Azed crosswords, they do not usually incorporate a theme. Once the clues are solved, the puzzle is solved.

In parallel with these developments in Sunday newspapers, however, other setters (sometimes, indeed, the same setters under different guises) have pursued what may be thought of as the apotheosis of the crossword, the **thematic advanced cryptic puzzle.**

Thematic barred-grid puzzles can be seen as the most highly developed form of the challenge of the crossword. Their special nature lies not, primarily, in their difficulty (though some are very difficult), but in their incorporation and treatment of their chosen theme.

At the most straightforward level this may consist purely of references to and works by, for instance, a particular writer, composer, or other well-known figure, often designed to appear on a relevant anniversary. The solver may be given special indications as to the nature of the theme, as, for instance, by means of messages spelled out in clue order by a series of deliberate misprints, typically one per clue; or, more simply, by having to guess the thematic answers, themselves left unclued, from the letters contributed by intersecting answers.

Sometimes the theme of the puzzle is designed to have a special effect on the way the answers are to be entered into the grid, and since the solver is not always explicitly told that this is the case there will often be some initial bafflement. Eventually, perhaps, enough of the puzzle will appear to make some sort of sense, when considered in the light of the slightly cryptic instructions conveyed by the preamble, to enable the solver to embark on the filling of the grid.

Two examples of this type come to mind, both from *The Listener* between ten and fifteen years ago. In the first, the solvers were advised that answers were to be entered in accordance with the theme, which would affect across answers in two ways, but down answers only in one. It gradually became clear that the entries could only be made to intersect properly if all vowels were omitted, and if the across entries (consonants only) were made to run from right to left. The theme of the puzzle thus finally revealed itself as *Hebrew* – in the written form which omits vowels and, at least when written horizontally, runs the opposite way to Western script.

In the second instance, the solver had to discover by trial and error (quite a lot of the latter) that the answers would only intersect if entered *boustrophedon*, that is, in the route taken by ploughing oxen – first across row left to right, second row right to left, third row left to right, etc.; then, first down column, top to bottom, second 'down' column, bottom to top, third down column, top to bottom, etc. Even when this had been done, it was found that seven answers were each one letter too short for their spaces, so that seven squares in the grid remained empty. Returning to the extremely cryptic preamble, the solver was just able to deduce that the setter required each of the remaining empty squares to be filled with a star. When this was done, light truly dawned, for the resulting arrangement of stars exactly corresponded with the positions in the night sky of the stars of the Plough, giving a wonderfully neat tie-in with the mode of entry of the answers.

Although I have instanced these two puzzles to show what can be achieved by an ingenious setter, it should be stressed that many advanced barred-grid cryptic crosswords are nowhere near so difficult to get started, or, indeed, to finish. What they tend to have in common is that they offer a longer-lasting entertainment – more a feature-length film than a half-hour sitcom. Most people attempting to solve puzzles of this sort would not finish them in a single session, so the setter has an intrinsic need to make the puzzle interesting enough for the solver to want to come back to.

Crosswords of this type appeared in *The Listener* for decades until the unfortunate demise of that publication in 1991 (an event which sparked off questions in Parliament specifically on the subject of the *Listener* crossword!). Since 1991 a home has been found for the *Listener* crossword in the Saturday edition of *The Times*.

Other magazines such as *New Statesman* and *The Spectator* were early in the field with thematic barred-grid puzzles, and the dedicated magazine *Crossword*, organ of the Crossword Club, began to publish very difficult thematic puzzles a little over twenty years ago.

In 1988 the *Independent Saturday Magazine* became the first regular newspaper vehicle for thematic barred-grid cryptic puzzles. These were deliberately designed to be of an easier and more accessible level than *The Listener* Crossword, at that time still appearing in *The Listener* itself. It is still fair to say that the Saturday Magazine puzzle in *The Independent* is, usually, the least difficult of the weekend's now regular batch of barred-grid thematic puzzles, though it has become a little harder over recent years.

Since 1992 a series of barred-grid thematic crosswords has appeared under the general title 'Enigmatic Variations', initially in the Saturday edition of *The Daily Telegraph*, migrating later to the *Sunday Telegraph* on the launch of the Sunday title.

Many of the setters who contribute puzzles of this type appear regularly in all three of the above series, with appropriate adjustment of themes and levels of difficulty, and occasionally using different pseudonyms.

Conclusions

I hope that this introduction, necessarily limited in scope, will have given the interested solver and would-be solver some indication of the aims and techniques of those who produce crosswords, especially cryptic crosswords as they have developed in the British Isles over much of the last century.

In describing and attempting to define clue types, and in passing occasional judgements on what should be thought of as fair and unfair dealing on the part of the setter, one cannot afford to forget that the real test of a clue and a puzzle is whether or not the solver manages to get to the answer the setter intends. If most people manage to get the right answer to a clue, it may matter to us aesthetically if its wording is inelegant or its process suspect – but it matters less. If, on the other hand, the clue is eminently justifiable in accordance with the best canons of fairness and soundness, but is not actually solved by anyone reading it, then the setter has failed. For the aim of the crossword setter is not to establish some kind of superiority over the solver by making clues too obscure to solve, but rather to produce clues which will yield their answers readily, preferably evoking amusement and delight, once they have engaged interest and the right level of attention.

One must also not lose sight of the fact that crosswords are by and large ephemeral productions, appearing as they do in daily and weekly news organs which will find their way to recycling centres before too long.

Nevertheless for those who do become addicted to this peculiar interest, there is little doubt that it offers a regular source of pleasure and fufilment. Many participants in TV quiz programmes – not only those based on crossword-like activities – give crossword solving a place amongst their three or four favourite pastimes. Crosswords are solved at office desks, on the daily journey to and from work, in lectures, in pubs and tearooms, and in the comfort of the armchair at home. To those who have retired from regular employment and now enjoy the freedom to relax in ways no longer circumscribed by the exigencies of earning a livelihood, crosswords offer a pleasurable way of continuing to take mental exercise.

The satisfaction afforded to regular solvers of crosswords is much missed when any unfortunate accident or production error interferes with their daily or weekly 'fix'. Nothing is as likely to provoke an outraged response simultaneously from so large a cohort of readers as a serious mistake or omission in a newspaper's crossword puzzle. The reason for this, I am sure, is that the crossword is virtually the sole part of the paper which is interactive, and with which the reader engages so totally. We *read* the news, the weather, the sports reports, the features, our horoscopes, perhaps – but we *do* the crossword.

Michael Macdonald-Cooper

WORD LISTS

TWO LETTERS

aa	ax	dy	fe	hy	ky	na	om	po	te	wa
ab	ay	ea	fo	id	la	ne	on	pu	ti	we
ac	ba	ee	fu	ie	le	né	oo	qi	to	wo
ad	be	ef	fy	if	li	ni	op	ra	ug	wy
ae	bi	eh	ga	in	lo	no	or	re	uh	xi
af	bo	el	ge	io	lü	nu	os	ri	um	xu
ah	bu	em	go	is	ly	ob	ot	sa	un	ya
ai	by	en	gy	it	ma	od	ou	se	up	yd
ak	ca′	er	ha	iv	me	oe	ow	sh	ur	ye
am	ce	es	he	ja	mi	of	ox	si	us	yi
an	da	et	He	jo	mo	oh	oy	so	ut	yo
ar	de	ew	hi	ka	Mr	oi	oz	st	uz	yu
as	di	ex	hm	ki	Ms	OK	pa	su	va	za
at	do	ey	ho	ko	mu	ol′	pe	sy	vi	zi
aw	Dr	fa	hu	ku	my	ol	pi	ta	vo	zo

THREE LETTERS

aam	asp	bro	cut	dos	erm	fud	hab	I Am	jut
aba	ass	bub	cwm	do's	ern	fug	had	ice	kab
abb	ate	bud	dab	DOS	err	fum	hae	icy	kae
a-be	Ate	bug	dad	dot	ess	fun	hag	ide	kai
abo	auk	bum	dae	DoT	est	fur	hah	iff	kat
aby	aul	bun	dag	dow	eta	gab	haj	ike	kay
ace	aum	bur	dah	Dow	eth	gad	ham	ilk	kea
ach	ava	bus	dai	dry	eve	gag	han	ill	ked
act	ave	but	dak	dub	ewe	gah	hào	I'll	kef
add	awa'	buy	dal	dud	eye	gal	hap	imp	keg
ado	awe	bye	dam	due	fab	gam	has	inf	kel
aft	awl	cab	dam'	dug	fad	gap	hat	ink	ken
aga	awn	cad	dan	dun	fag	gar	hau	inn	kep
Aga	axe	caf	Dan	duo	fah	gas	haw	ion	ket
age	aye	cal	Dao	dup	fam	gat	hay	IOU	kex
ago	baa	Cal	dap	dux	fan	gay	he'd	ire	key
agy	bab	cam	das	dye	far	ged	heh	irk	kid
aha	bad	can	dat	dyn	fat	gee	hem	ism	kif
aid	bag	cap	DAT	dzo	fax	gel	hen	ist	kin
ail	bah	car	daw	ean	fay	gem	hep	ita	kip
aim	bal	cat	day	ear	fed	gen	her	it'd	Kir
air	bam	caw	deb	eat	fee	geo	he's	ite	kit
ais	ban	cay	dee	eau	fei	get	het	it's	koa
ait	bap	cel	def	ebb	fem	gey	hew	its	kob
aka	bar	cep	del	ecu	fen	ghi	hex	I've	KO'd
ake	bat	cha	dem	écu	fes	gib	hey	ivi	koi
à la	baw	chi	den	edh	fet	gid	hic	ivy	kop
ala	bay	CIA	dew	eel	feu	gie	hid	jab	kos
alb	bed	CID	dey	Eem	few	gif	hie	jag	kou
ale	bee	cig	dha	e'en	fey	gig	him	Jah	kra
all	beg	clo'	dib	e'er	fez	gim	hin	jak	kya
alp	bel	clo	did	eff	fib	gin	hip	jam	kyd
alt	ben	cob	die	eft	fid	gio	his	Jap	kye
aly	ber	cod	dif	egg	fie	gip	hit	jar	kyu
amp	bet	cog	dig	ego	fig	git	hmm	jat	lab
amu	bey	col	dim	eid	fin	gnu	hob	jaw	lac
ana	bib	con	din	Eid	Fin	goa	hoc	jay	lad
and	bid	coo	dip	eik	fip	gob	hod	jee	lag
ane	big	cop	dis	eke	fir	god	hoe	jer	lah
ani	Bim	coq	dit	eld	fit	God	hog	jes	lai
ann	bin	cor	div	elf	fix	gog	hom	jet	lam
an't	bio	cos	dix	elk	fiz	gom	hon	Jew	lap
ant	bit	cot	DIY	ell	flu	goo	hoo	jib	lar
any	biz	cow	diz	elm	fly	gos	hop	jig	lat
A-OK	boa	cox	dob	eme	fob	got	hot	jit	lav
ape	bob	coy	doc	emu	foe	goy	how	job	law
aps	bod	coz	dod	end	fog	gra	hoy	Job	lax
apt	bog	cro	doe	ene	foh	gul	hub	jod	lay
arb	boh	cru	dog	Eno	fop	gum	hud	joe	lea
arc	boo	cry	doh	ens	for	gun	hue	Joe	led
ard	bop	cub	dol	eon	fou	gup	hug	jog	lee
are	bot	cud	dom	ept	fox	gur	huh	jot	leg
ark	bow	cue	Dom	era	foy	gut	hui	jow	lei
arm	Bow	cum	don	ere	Fra	guv	hum	joy	lek
art	box	cun	doo	erf	fro	guy	hun	jug	Leo
ash	boy	cup	dop	erg	fry	gym	hup	jun	lep
ask	bra	cur	dor	erk	fub	gyp	hut	jus	les

let	met	new	ole	pic	raw	saj	spy	tog	vav	wyn
leu	meu	nib	olm	pie	rax	sal	sty	tom	vee	yad
lev	mew	nid	one	pig	ray	sam	sub	Tom	veg	yag
lew	mho	nig	oof	pik	reb	san	sud	ton	vet	yah
ley	mic	nil	ooh	pin	rec	sap	sue	too	vex	yak
lez	mid	nim	ook	pip	red	sat	sug	top	via	yam
lib	mig	nip	ope	pir	ree	sav	suh	tor	vic	yap
lid	mil	nis	opp	pit	ref	saw	suk	tot	vie	yar
lie	mim	nit	opt	*più*	reg	sax	sul	tou	vim	yas
lig	min	nix	ora	pix	rei	say	sum	tow	VIP	yaw
lil	Min	noa	orb	ply	rem	sea	sun	toy	vis	yay
lin	Mir	nob	orc	poa	rep	sec	sup	tri	viz	yea
lip	mis	nod	ore	pod	res	see	suq	try	voe	yed
lis	mit	nog	øre	poh	ret	seg	sus	tsk	vol	yeh
lit	mix	Noh	öre	poi	rev	sei	swy	tsu	vow	yen
loa	miz	nor	orf	pol	Rev	sem	tab	tub	vox	yeo
lob	Mme	nor'	org	pom	rew	sen	tad	tue	vug	yep
lod	moa	not	ork	Pom	*Rex*	ser	tag	tug	vum	yer
log	mob	now	orl	poo	rhe	set	tai	tui	wad	yes
loo	moc	nox	oss	pop	rho	sew	taj	tum	wag	yet
lop	mod	noy	ouf	Pop	ria	sex	tam	tun	wai	yew
lor	Mod	nth	our	pot	rib	sey	tan	tup	wan	yex
lot	mog	nub	out	pou	rid	sez	Tao	tur	wap	yez
low	moi	nud	ova	pow	rig	she	tap	tut	war	Yid
lox	mol	nug	owe	pox	rim	sho	tar	tux	was	yin
loy	mom	num	owl	pre	rin	shy	tat	twa	wat	yip
lud	mon	nun	own	pro	rio	sib	tau	two	wau	yiz
lug	moo	nut	owt	pry	rip	*sic*	tav	tye	waw	yob
lum	mop	nye	pac	psi	ris	sif	taw	uff	wax	yod
lur	mor	oaf	pad	pst	rit	sig	tax	ufo	way	yoi
luv	mos	oak	pah	pub	riu	sin	taz	UFO	web	yok
lux	*mot*	OAP	pal	pud	rob	sip	tea	ugg	we'd	yon
lye	MOT	oar	pan	pug	roc	sir	tec	ugh	wed	you
maa	mou	oat	pap	pul	rod	sis	ted	uke	wee	yow
mab	mow	oba	par	pun	roe	sit	Ted	uki	wem	yuh
mac	moz	obe	pas	pup	rog	six	tee	ule	wen	yuk
mad	Mrs	obi	pat	pus	ROM	ska	teg	ult	wet	Yuk
mag	mud	obo	pav	put	roo	ski	tej	ulu	wey	yum
mah	mug	obs	paw	puy	rot	sky	ten	ump	who	yup
mai	mum	oca	pax	pya	rov	sly	ter	umu	why	yus
mam	mun	och	pay	pye	row	sny	tew	uni	wig	zac
man	mux	odd	pea	pyx	rub	sob	tex	unk	win	zad
map	mya	OD'd	peb	qat	rud	soc	tha	ure	wis	zag
mar	nab	ode	pec	Qin	rue	sod	the	uri	wit	zap
mas	nae	OD's	ped	qua	rug	soe	tho	urn	wiv	zat
mat	nag	o'er	pee	Qum	rum	sog	tho'	urs	wiz	zax
maw	nah	off	peg	rab	run	soh	thy	use	woa	zea
max	nan	oft	Peg	rad	rut	sol	tic	ush	woe	zed
may	nap	oga	pen	rag	rux	Sol	tid	uta	wog	zee
May	nar	ogi	pep	rah	rya	son	tie	ute	wok	zek
med	nat	ohm	PEP	rai	rye	sop	tig	uva	won	Zen
Med	naw	oho	per	raj	ryo	SOS	til	Uzi	woo	zho
mee	nay	oik	pes	Raj	ryu	sot	Tim	vac	wop	zig
meg	neb	oil	pet	ram	sab	sou	tin	vag	wot	zip
Meg	ned	oka	pew	ran	sac	sov	tip	van	wow	zit
mel	née	OK'd	phi	rap	sad	Sov	tit	var	woy	ziz
mem	neg	oke	pho	ras	sae	sow	tiz	vas	wro	zoa
men	nek	OKs	pia	rat	sag	sox	toa	vat	wry	zoo
Meo	nep	OK's		rav	sah	soy	tod	VAT	wuz	zug
mer	net	old			sai	spa	toe	vau	wye	

FOUR LETTERS

abba	aiel	anna	auto	bare	beta	blow	boun	bund
Abba	aile	anoa	Avar	barf	bevy	blub	bout	bung
abbé	Aino	anon	aven	bark	Bhil	blue	bove	bunk
abed	ain't	ansa	aver	barm	bhoy	blur	bowl	bunt
abet	Ainu	anta	avid	barn	bias	Boal	boxy	buoy
Abib	airt	ante	avow	Bart	bibb	boar	boyo	BUPA
able	airy	anti	away	base	bibi	boat	boza	burb
ably	aith	anus	a wee	bash	bice	bock	bozo	burd
abob	ajar	aoul	awny	bask	bide	bode	brab	bure
Abos	ajee	apex	AWOL	bass	bidi	body	brad	burg
abox	ajog	APEX	awry	bast	bien	Boer	brae	burh
abri	Akan	apse	axal	bate	bier	boff	brag	burk
ABTA	akee	apso	axel	bath	biff	bogy	brak	burl
abut	akin	Apus	axes	bats	biga	boho	bran	burn
ACAS	alan	aqua	axil	batt	bigg	Bohr	bras	burp
acer	Alan	aquo	axis	batz	bike	boil	brat	burr
ache	alap	Arab	axle	baud	bile	boke	braw	buru
achy	alar	arak	axon	bawd	bilk	boko	bray	bury
acid	Alar	Aran	ayah	bawl	bill	bola	bred	bush
acme	alas	arch	ayle	bawn	Bill	bold	bree	busk
acne	alba	area	ay me	baze	bind	bole	brei	buss
acre	alec	ared	ayre	bead	bine	bolk	bren	bust
acyl	alee	areg	azan	beak	bing	boll	Bren	busy
Adam	aley	Argo	baa'd	beal	bink	bolo	brer	butt
Adar	alfa	Argy	Baal	beam	bint	bolt	bret	buys
a-day	alga	aria	baas	bean	biog	boma	brew	buzz
adit	alit	arid	baba	bear	bird	bomb	brey	byes
adry	alky	aril	babe	be at	biri	bond	Brie	BYOB
adze	ally	army	Babi	beat	birk	bone	brig	byre
aeon	alma	arow	babu	beau	birl	bong	brim	byte
aery	alme	arra	baby	beck	biro	bonk	brio	caba
afar	alms	arse	bach	Bedu	Biro	bony	brit	cack
Afar	alod	arty	Bach	Beeb	birr	boob	Brit	cade
affy	aloe	arum	back	beef	bise	book	brod	cadi
Afro	alow	arvo	bade	been	bish	bool	brog	cady
agal	also	aryl	bael	beep	bisk	boom	broo	cafe
agar	alti	asci	baff	beer	bite	boon	brow	café
agba	alto	asea	baft	beet	bitt	boor	brrr	caff
aged	alum	ashy	baht	Befa	blab	boos	Brum	cage
agee	amah	as if	bail	bego	blad	boot	brut	cagy
agen	Amal	as is	bait	bein	blae	bora	Brut	caid
ager	ambo	as of	bake	Beja	blag	Bora	Bual	cain
agey	amel	Asti	bald	belk	blah	bord	bubo	Cain
agha	amen	as to	bale	bell	blat	bore	buck	cake
agin	Amex	atap	balk	belt	blay	born	bude	caky
agio	amid	at it	ball	bema	bleb	bort	buer	calf
aglu	amil	atom	balm	be me	bled	bosa	buff	calk
agma	amir	atop	Balt	Bemi	blee	bose	buhl	call
agog	ammo	A to Z	banc	bend	bleu	bosh	buhr	calm
agon	amok	atta	band	bene	blew	bosk	buit	calx
agro	Amoy	atwo	bane	bent	bley	bo's'n	bulb	came
ague	amyl	aula	bang	be of	blik	boss	bulk	camp
ahem	anal	auld	bani	bere	blin	bote	bull	cane
ahey	anew	aune	bank	berg	blip	both	bult	cang
ahoy	anil	aung	barb	berk	blob	bott	bumf	cant
aide	anis	aunt	Barb	berm	bloc	bouk	bump	can't
AIDS	ankh	aura	bard	best	blot	boul	Buna	cany

cape	choc	coin	crag	dade	deli	dive	dowd	duro
cap'n	chon	coir	cram	dado	dell	divi	dowf	dusk
capo	chop	coke	cran	daff	deme	dizz	dowl	dust
carb	chou	Coke	crap	daft	demi	doab	down	duty
card	Chou	cola	craw	dago	demn	doat	dowt	dyad
care	chow	cold	cray	Dáil	demo	dobe	doxy	Dyak
carf	chub	cole	cred	dais	Demo	do by	doze	dyer
cark	chug	coli	cree	dale	demy	doby	dozy	dyke
carl	chum	colk	Cree	dalt	dene	dock	drab	dyne
carp	Chün	coll	crew	Dama	denn	doct	drac	dyss
carr	chut	colt	crib	dame	dent	dodo	drag	dzho
cart	ciao	Colt	crim	damn	deny	doek	dram	each
case	ciel	coly	crin	damp	dere	doer	drap	earl
cash	cill	coma	crip	Dane	derm	does	drat	earn
cask	cine	comb	cris	dang	dern	doff	draw	ease
cass	cinq	come	crit	dank	derv	doge	dray	east
cast	cion	comp	croc	daps	desk	dogy	dree	easy
cate	ciré	coms	croo	Dard	dewy	do in	dreg	eath
cauk	cist	cone	crop	dare	dexy	do it	drek	eats
caul	cite	coni	crow	darg	dhak	doit	drew	eaux
cava	city	conk	crub	dark	dhal	dojo	drey	eave
cave	cive	conn	crud	darl	dhan	doke	drib	ebon
cavy	clad	cony	crue	darn	dhar	dole	drie	ecad
cawk	clag	coof	crum	dart	dhol	dolk	drip	ecce
cawl	clam	cook	crus	dash	dhow	doll	drog	echo
caza	clan	cool	crut	data	DHSS	dolt	drop	*echt*
cede	clap	coom	crux	date	dial	dome	drow	ecru
cedi	claw	coon	cube	dato	Dian	domy	drub	ecus
ceil	clay	co-op	cuck	daub	dibs	dona	drug	Edam
cell	cled	coop	cued	daud	dice	done	drum	Edda
celt	clee	coos	cues	daut	dick	dong	duab	eddo
Celt	clef	coot	cuff	davy	Dick	donk	duad	eddy
cent	cleg	cope	Cuff	Davy	dict	don't	dual	Eden
cere	clem	cops	cuke	dawg	dido	dool	duan	edge
CERN	clew	Copt	cull	dawk	didy	doom	duar	edgy
cero	clip	copy	culm	dawn	died	do on	dubs	edit
cert	clit	cord	cult	dawt	dies	door	duce	eely
cess	clod	core	Cuna	days	diet	dopa	Duce	Efik
cest	clog	corf	cunt	daze	diff	dope	duck	EFTA
cete	clop	cork	curb	dazy	digs	dopy	duct	egad
chad	clot	corm	curd	D-Day	dika	doré	dude	eggy
Chad	*clou*	corn	cure	dead	dike	dork	duel	egos
chah	clow	cose	curé	deaf	dikh	dorm	duet	eigh
chak	cloy	cosh	curf	deal	dill	dorp	duff	eild
chal	club	coss	curl	dean	dime	dorr	duke	eith
cham	clue	cost	curn	dear	dine	dort	dukw	ekka
chap	coak	cosy	curr	deas	ding	dory	dule	elan
char	coal	cote	curt	debt	dink	dose	dull	élan
chat	coat	coth	cush	deck	dint	dosh	duly	elft
chaw	coax	Coué	cusk	deco	diol	doss	duma	elhi
chay	cobb	coul	cusp	Deco	dire	dost	Duma	elks
chef	coca	coup	cuss	deed	dirk	dote	dumb	elmy
chew	cock	cove	cute	deem	dirl	doth	dump	else
chez	coco	cowl	cyan	deep	dirt	do to	dune	Elul
chic	coda	cowp	cyma	deer	disa	doty	dung	emic
chid	code	cowy	cyme	deft	disc	douc	dunk	emir
chin	coed	coxa	cyst	defy	dish	doum	dunt	emit
Chin	coff	Cox's	cyul	degu	disk	do up	duos	Emmy
chip	coft	coxy	czar	deid	diss	doup	dupe	empt
chir	coho	coze	dace	deil	dita	dour	dura	enol
chit	coif	cozy	dada	dele	dite	dout	dure	enow
chiv	coil	crab	Dada	delf	diva	dove	durn	envy

eoan	fall	filé	foil	fuzz	genu	gnar	Gram	hadj
épée	falx	fill	foin	fyke	germ	gnat	gran	haem
epic	fame	film	fold	fyrd	gest	gnaw	gray	haet
epos	fane	filo	folk	gaby	geta	GNVQ	Gray	haff
EPOS	fang	fils	fond	gade	gett	goad	gree	haft
ergo	Fang	find	font	gaed	geum	goaf	grew	ha-ha
ergs	fard	fine	food	Gael	ghan	goal	grex	haik
eria	fare	fink	fool	gaff	ghap	Goan	grey	hail
erne	farl	Finn	foot	gaga	ghat	go at	grid	hain
Eros	farm	fino	forb	gage	ghee	goat	grig	hair
Erse	faro	fire	ford	Gaia	Gheg	gobo	grim	hait
erst	fart	firk	fore	gain	gibe	go by	grin	haji
Esau	fash	firm	fork	gait	gift	go-by	grip	hajj
Esky	fast	firn	form	gala	GIFT	goby	grit	haka
esne	fate	fisc	fort	gale	GIGO	goer	grog	hake
esox	faun	fish	foss	gall	Gila	goes	grok	hale
espy	faux	fisk	foul	galt	gild	goff	grot	half
ESRC	fave	fist	four	gamb	gill	go-go	grow	hall
etch	fawn	fitz	fowl	game	Gill	Gogo	grub	halm
etic	faze	five	foxy	gamp	gilt	go in	grue	halo
etin	feak	fixt	frab	gamy	gimp	go it	grum	halt
etna	feal	fizz	frae	gang	ging	goky	Grus	hame
Eton	fear	flab	frap	gant	gink	gola	guan	hand
etui	feat	flag	frat	gaol	gird	Gola	guar	hang
étui	feck	flak	Frau	gaon	girl	gold	gufa	hank
euge	feeb	flam	fray	gape	girn	golf	guff	Hans
euro	fee'd	flan	free	garb	giro	Gond	guga	hapu
Euro	feed	flap	fret	gare	girr	gone	guib	hard
even	feel	flat	frib	gari	girt	gong	guid	hare
ever	feer	flaw	frig	garn	gise	gonk	gula	hark
evil	feet	flax	frim	Garo	gism	gony	gule	harl
evoe	fegs	flay	frit	gash	gist	good	gulf	harm
ewer	fehi	flea	friz	gasp	gîte	goof	gull	haro
ewry	Fehm	fled	froe	gate	gith	goog	gulp	harp
exam	feis	flee	frog	gatt	give	gook	gump	harr
exec	fell	fleg	from	GATT	givy	gool	gunk	hart
exes	felt	Flem	frot	gaud	gizz	go on	Gunn	hash
exit	feme	flet	frow	gauk	glad	goon	Günz	hask
exon	fend	flew	frug	Gaul	glam	goop	gurk	hasp
Expo	fent	flex	frum	gaum	gled	goor	gurl	hast
exta	feod	fley	fruz	gaup	glee	gore	gurn	hate
eyas	fere	flic	FT–SE	gaur	gleg	gorm	guru	hath
eyed	ferk	flim	fuci	gave	glei	gorp	gush	haul
eyer	fern	flip	fuck	Gawd	glen	gory	gust	haut
eyes	fess	flit	fuel	gawk	glet	gosh	guts	have
eyot	fest	flix	fuff	gawn	glew	goss	guze	hawk
eyra	feta	floc	fufu	gawp	gley	Goss	gwan	haze
eyre	fête	floe	fugu	gaze	glia	gote	gybe	hazy
face	feud	flog	full	GCHQ	glib	Goth	gyle	head
fack	feus	flop	fume	GCSE	glim	go to	gymp	heal
fact	Fian	flot	fumy	gean	glit	go up	gyne	heap
facy	fiar	flow	fund	gear	glob	gour	gypo	hear
fade	fiat	flub	funk	geck	glom	gout	gyps	heat
fado	fice	flue	furl	geed	glop	gove	gyre	hebe
fady	fico	flus	fury	geek	glow	gowk	gyri	Hebe
faff	Fido	flux	fusc	Geez	glue	gowl	gyro	heck
faik	fief	flys	fuse	geld	glug	gown	gyte	heed
fail	fiel	foal	fusk	gelt	glum	goys	gyve	heel
fain	FIFA	foam	fuss	gena	glut	grab	haaf	heft
fair	fife	foci	fust	gene	G-man	grad	haar	he he
fake	fike	fogy	futz	gens	G-men	Graf	hack	heil
fa-la	file	föhn	fuze	gent	gnap	gram	hade	heir

heit	hoki	hurr	info	jawy	jube	keno	knot	lady
HeLa	hoky	hurt	in it	jazz	juck	kent	know	laen
held	hold	hush	Inka	jean	judo	Kent	knub	Lahu
hele	hole	husk	inky	jeep	Judy	kepi	knur	laic
he'll	Holi	huso	inly	Jeep	juga	kept	knut	laid
hell	holl	huss	in on	jeer	ju-ju	kerb	koan	laik
helm	holm	hutt	in re	Jeez	juju	kerf	kobo	lain
help	holp	Hutu	INRI	jeff	juke	kern	koel	lair
heme	hols	huzz	inro	Jehu	July	kero	kohl	Laïs
hemp	holt	hwyl	inti	jell	jump	kest	koji	lait
hent	holy	Hyde	into	jeon	june	keta	koko	lake
herb	homa	hyla	Inuk	jerk	June	kewl	kola	lakh
herd	home	hyle	iota	jert	junk	kexy	Koli	laky
here	homo	hymn	ipoh	jess	Juno	keys	kolm	la-la
herl	Homo	hyne	IRBM	jest	jupe	khad	kolo	lall
herm	homy	hype	irid	Jesu	Jura	khan	Koma	lama
hern	hone	hypo	iris	jeté	jury	khat	Komi	lamb
hero	hong	hyst	iron	Jewy	just	khet	kona	lame
Herr	honk	hyte	I say	jiao	jute	khor	Kond	lamé
hers	hood	IAEA	ISBN	jibe	Jute	khud	kono	lamp
hest	hoof	iamb	ISDN	jiff	juve	kibe	Kono	land
hewn	hook	Iban	I see	jill	jynx	kiby	kook	Land
hick	hoon	ibex	isel	Jill	kade	kick	kopi	lane
hide	hoop	ibis	isle	jilt	kadi	kief	kora	lank
hied	hoot	IBRD	isn't	jimp	kagu	kier	Kora	lant
hies	hope	ICBM	I spy	Jina	Kahn	kike	kore	lanx
hi-fi	Hopi	iced	itch	jing	kaid	kill	kori	Lapp
high	hopo	icky	item	jink	kail	kiln	koru	lard
hike	hora	icon	iter	jinn	kaim	kilo	kosh	lare
hila	Hori	idea	Itie	jinx	kain	kilt	koto	larf
hili	horn	idee	itis	jism	kaka	kina	krab	lari
hill	hose	idem	it'll	jist	kaki	kind	Krag	lark
hilo	hoss	ides	itty	jiva	kale	kine	kran	larm
hilt	host	idle	iwis	jive	kali	king	kray	larn
himp	hour	idli	ixia	jizz	kama	kink	Krio	lary
hind	Hova	idly	izba	Joan	Kama	kino	kris	lase
hing	hove	idol	izle	jock	kame	kips	Kroo	lash
hint	howe	idyl	Ivan	Jock	kana	kirk	krug	lask
hipe	howk	iffy	jack	Jodo	kang	kirn	Kuan	lass
hire	howl	if so	Jack	jods	kans	kish	Kuba	last
hish	hoya	Igbo	jacu	joes	kaon	kiss	kudo	late
hisn	huck	iiwi	jade	joey	kapa	kist	kudu	lath
hiss	huer	ikat	jady	Joey	karo	kite	kuei	lati
hist	huff	ikey	jail	john	kart	kith	kuge	laud
hive	huge	ikky	Jain	John	kati	kiva	kuki	Laue
hiya	Hugo	ikon	jake	join	kava	kive	Kuki	lava
hizz	huhu	ilea	jama	joke	kaya	kiwi	kuku	lave
HMSO	huia	ilex	jamb	joky	kayo	ki-yi	kula	lawk
hoar	huke	ilia	jams	jole	kaza	Klan	Kuna	lawn
hoax	hula	ilka	jane	jolt	keck	klep	kura	laws
hobo	hule	illy	Jane	Joly	keek	klik	Kurd	laxy
hock	hulk	ilot	jann	jong	keel	klip	kuri	laze
hoed	hull	imam	jape	jook	keen	klop	kuru	Laze
hoer	huma	IMAX	jarl	joro	keep	knab	kuta	lazy
hoes	hump	imfe	jasp	josh	keif	knag	kyat	lead
hoey	hung	immy	jati	joss	keld	knap	kyle	leaf
hogg	hunk	impi	jato	joub	kell	knar	kype	leak
hogo	hunt	in at	jauk	jouk	kelp	knee	kyte	leal
ho ho	Hupa	Inca	jaup	jour	kelt	knew	lace	leam
hoik	hupp	inch	Java	Jove	Kelt	knit	lack	lean
hoit	hure	indy	Jawi	jowl	kemb	knob	lacy	leap
hoke	hurl	Indy	jawp	juba	kemp	knop	lade	lear

leat	limn	lord	lyse	matt	midi	moko	mums	Nara
lech	limo	lore	ma'am	maty	Midi	Moko	mu-mu	narc
Lech	limp	lorn	maar	maud	MIDI	mola	mung	nard
lect	limy	lors	maas	maul	mids	mold	muni	nare
leek	line	lory	mace	maum	mien	mole	munt	nark
leep	ling	lose	Mace	maun	miff	moll	muon	narp
leer	link	losh	Mach	maux	mike	molt	mura	narr
lees	linn	loss	mack	mawk	Mike	moly	mure	nary
leet	lino	lost	made	mawm	mild	mome	murk	NASA
left	lint	lote	mado	maxi	mile	Momi	murl	NATO
legh	liny	loth	Maga	maya	milk	mona	murr	nave
Lego	lion	loti	mage	Maya	mill	Mond	musa	navy
lehr	lira	loto	magg	mayo	milo	mong	muse	naze
leir	lire	loud	magi	maze	milt	monk	mush	Nazi
lekë	lirk	loup	maid	mazy	mime	mono	musk	neal
Lekh	liry	lour	mail	MDMA	mimi	mons	muso	neap
lend	lisk	lout	maim	mead	mimp	mood	muss	near
lene	lisp	love	main	meal	mina	Moog	must	neat
leno	Lisp	lowe	mair	mean	mind	mool	muta	neck
lens	liss	lown	majo	mear	mine	moon	mute	need
lent	list	lowy	make	meat	ming	Moon	muti	Néel
Lent	Lisu	Loxa	mako	mech	Ming	moop	mutt	neem
Leos	lite	Lozi	male	Mede	mini	moor	muzz	neep
lere	Lite	luau	mali	meed	mink	Moor	myal	ne'er
lerp	lith	Luba	Mali	meek	mint	moos	myna	neif
lese	live	lube	mall	meet	minx	moot	myst	nema
less	load	luce	malm	mega	miny	mope	myth	nemo
lest	loaf	luck	malt	mela	mire	mopy	myxa	nene
let's	loam	lucy	Malt	meld	mirk	mora	myxo	neon
Lett	loan	ludo	mama	mell	mirl	more	myxy	nerd
leud	lobe	lues	mamo	melo	mirr	morn	naam	nerf
leva	lobo	luff	mana	melt	miry	Moro	naan	nerk
levi	loch	luge	mane	meme	mise	mort	naat	nese
levs	loci	luke	mani	memo	miso	moss	nabe	nesh
levy	lock	lull	mank	mend	miss	most	nabi	ness
lewd	loco	lulu	Manu	meng	mist	mosy	nabs	nest
liar	lode	lump	Manx	meno	misy	mota	naff	nete
lias	lodh	luna	many	menu	mite	mote	naga	nett
lice	lo-fi	lune	mape	meow	mitt	moth	Naga	neum
lich	loft	lung	mara	merc	mity	moto	Nago	névé
lick	loge	lunk	Mara	merd	mixy	mott	naib	news
Lide	logo	lunt	marc	mere	Mizo	Motu	naïf	newt
lido	logy	luny	mard	Meru	Mlle	moue	naik	newy
lied	loid	lure	mare	mesa	m'lud	moul	nail	next
lief	loin	lurk	marg	mese	Mmes	moup	nain	nibs
lien	loir	lush	Mari	mesh	moan	move	naio	nice
lier	loll	lusk	mark	mess	moar	mown	Nair	Nice
lies	Lolo	lust	marl	meta	moas	moxa	naïs	nick
lieu	loma	lute	marm	Meta	moat	moya	nait	Nick
life	Loma	luth	Mars	mete	mock	moze	Naja	nide
lift	lone	lutz	mart	meth	moco	mozz	nake	nidi
Lifu	long	luxe	marv	meum	mode	Mr Lo	nala	nief
like	Lonk	lwei	Mary	mewl	Mods	much	Nama	niet
lila	loof	lyam	mase	mews	mogo	muck	name	Nife
lill	look	lych	mash	mewt	Moho	muff	nana	niff
Lilo	loom	lyke	mask	mezz	Mohs	muga	nant	nigh
Li-lo	loon	lyme	mass	mhos	moil	mugo	naoi	Nile
lilt	loop	Lyme	Mass	Miao	moit	muid	naos	nill
lily	loot	lynx	mast	mias	mojo	mule	naow	nimb
Lima	lope	Lyon	mate	mica	moke	muli	napa	nine
limb	lora	lyra	maté	mice	moki	mull	Napa	nipa
lime		lyre	math	mick		mump	nape	nisi

nite	Nyon	omen	ouph	parp	perp	pirn	Pong	prut
Noah	oafo	omer	ourn	parr	Perp	pirr	pons	psst
noax	oafs	omie	ours	pars	pert	pish	pont	ptui
nock	oaky	omit	oust	part	perv	piss	pony	puce
noda	oary	omul	outa	pash	peso	pita	poof	puck
node	oast	once	outy	pass	pess	pith	pooh	pudu
nodi	oath	oner	ouzo	past	pest	pito	pook	puer
noel	oaty	one's	oval	pata	Pete	pity	pool	puff
Noel	obbo	on it	oven	pate	peth	pium	poon	puha
Noël	obex	only	over	pâté	pevy	pivo	poop	puja
noem	obey	on to	ovum	path	pewl	pixy	poor	puka
noes	Obie	onto	Owen	paua	pewy	pize	pope	puke
nogg	obis	on to	owly	Paul	pfft	plan	pops	puku
no go	obit	onus	oxen	pave	pfui	plap	pore	pula
noia	oboe	onyx	oxer	pavé	phew	plat	pork	pule
noil	obol	oo-er	oxic	Pavo	Phil	play	porn	puli
noir	obus	oofy	Oxon	pavy	phit	plea	Poro	pulk
noll	oche	ooid	oyer	pawa	phiz	pleb	porr	pull
nolt	odal	ooky	oyes	pawk	phon	pled	port	pulp
noma	Oddi	oons	oyez	pawl	phoo	plet	pory	puly
nome	odds	oont	paca	pawn	phos	plew	pose	puma
none	odea	oops	pace	PAYE	phot	plié	posé	pump
nong	odic	Oort	pack	PCAS	phut	plim	posh	puna
no-no	odor	ooze	paco	peag	piai	plod	poss	pung
non-U	odyl	oozy	pact	peai	pial	plop	post	punk
nook	OECD	opah	pacu	peak	pian	plot	posy	punt
noon	ofay	opal	pacy	peal	Piat	plow	pote	puny
noop	offa	OPEC	pada	pean	pica	ploy	pott	pupa
nope	off'n	Op-Ed	padi	pear	pice	plud	Pott	pure
nork	o for	open	paff	peat	pick	plug	pouf	puri
norm	ogam	oppo	page	peba	pict	plum	poui	purl
Norn	ogee	opry	paha	peck	Pict	plup	pour	purr
nose	Ogen	opto	paho	pect	pied	plus	pout	purt
nosh	ogle	opus	paid	pede	pier	pneu	pouw	push
nosy	Ogpu	oral	paik	peed	piet	pnyx	poxy	puss
nota	ogre	orby	pail	peek	piff	pobs	prad	pute
note	ohia	orca	pain	peel	pika	pock	pram	putt
not-I	OHMS	ordo	pair	peen	pike	poco	prat	putz
nott	oh-oh	Oreo	pais	peep	piki	podo	prau	puya
noun	oh-so	orey	Paki	peer	piky	poem	pray	pyet
nous	oick	orfe	pala	pees	pile	poet	pree	pyot
nova	OIEO	orgy	pale	pego	pili	poge	preg	pyre
nown	oily	orle	pali	Pegu	pill	pogo	prem	pyro
nowt	oink	orlo	Pali	pein	Pils	pogy	prep	qadi
nowy	oint	or no	pall	peke	pily	poil	pres	Qing
noxa	OIRO	orra	palm	pele	Pima	poke	prex	quab
Nuba	okay	or so	palp	Pele	pimp	poky	Prex	quad
nubk	Okie	oryx	paly	pelf	piña	pole	prey	quag
nude	okra	osar	pamé	pell	pind	Pole	prez	quai
Nuer	okta	ossa	pand	Pell	pine	polk	prig	quar
nuff	Okun	Ossa	pane	pelt	ping	poll	prim	quat
nuke	olam	osse	Pane	pend	pink	Poll	proa	quay
null	olde	otic	pang	penk	Pink	polo	prob	quel
numb	olea	otto	Pano	pent	pint	polt	prod	quey
nunk	oleo	Otto	pant	peon	piny	poly	Prod	quid
NUPE	olid	ouch	papa	pepo	pion	Poma	prof	quim
nurd	olim	oued	para	perc	pipa	pome	prog	quin
nurk	olio	ough	Pará	père	pipe	Pomo	prom	quip
nurl	olla	ould	pard	peri	pipi	pomp	prop	quit
nuts	olpe	ouma	pare	perk	pipy	pond	pros	quiz
Nuzi	Oman	oung	park	perm	pire	pone	Prot	quod
nyet	omee	oupa	parm	pern	pirl	pong	prow	quop

raad	reel	roar	ruds	sapo	self	shor	skil	snod
race	reem	robe	rued	sard	sell	shot	skim	snog
rack	reen	rock	rues	Sard	sema	show	skin	snot
racy	reft	rode	ruff	sari	seme	shox	skip	snow
RADA	rego	roed	ruga	sark	semé	Shri	skis	snub
raff	reif	roid	ruin	Sart	semi	*shul*	skit	snug
Rafi	Reil	roil	rukh	sash	semp	shun	*skol*	snum
raft	rein	roke	rule	sass	sena	shut	skua	snye
raga	rely	roky	ruly	sate	send	shwa	skun	soak
rage	rems	role	rump	saté	sene	sial	Skye	soam
ragi	rend	rôle	rune	sati	senn	sice	slab	soap
raia	reng	Rolf	rung	Sauk	sent	sich	slag	soar
raid	rent	roll	runo	save	seps	sick	slam	so as
raik	repo	Roma	runt	sawn	sept	sida	slap	Soay
rail	repp	Rome	rupp	saxe	sera	side	slat	soba
rain	rerd	romp	rupt	Saxe	Serb	sidi	Slav	soca
rait	rere	rond	rurp	SAYE	SERC	SIDS	slaw	sock
raja	rest	rone	ruru	says	sere	sidy	slay	soda
rake	rete	Rong	rusa	scab	serf	sies	sled	sody
raki	reub	rood	ruse	scad	Seri	sift	slew	sofa
raku	re-up	roof	rush	scag	sesh	sigh	sley	soft
rale	rhea	rook	rusk	scam	sess	sign	slid	soga
rame	rhus	room	Russ	scan	seta	sijo	slim	soho
rami	rial	roon	rust	scar	SETI	sika	slip	Soho
ramp	RIBA	roop	ruth	scat	Seto	sike	slit	soil
rams	rice	root	rutt	scaw	sett	Sikh	slob	soke
Rana	rich	rope	ryot	scob	sewn	sild	sloe	sola
rand	rick	ropy	rype	scop	sext	sile	slog	sold
rang	ride	ro-ro	sabe	scot	sexy	silk	slop	sole
rani	riel	rort	sack	Scot	SGML	sill	slot	soli
rank	rife	Rory	sade	scow	shab ·	silo	slow	solo
rant	riff	rose	safe	scry	shad	silt	slub	Solo
rape	Riff	rosé	saga	scud	shag	sima	slud	soma
rapt	rift	ross	sage	scug	shah	simi	slue	some
rare	riga	Ross	SAGE	scum	sham	simp	slug	sone
rase	Riga	rosy	sago	scun	shan	sind	slum	song
rash	rile	Rosy	sagy	scur	Shan	sine	slup	Song
rasp	rill	rota	sa-ha	scut	shat	sing	slur	sook
rass	rima	rote	Saho	scye	shaw	sinh	slut	sool
rata	rime	roti	saic	SDLP	shay	sink	smay	soon
rate	rimu	roto	said	seah	Shay	sion	smew	soop
rath	rimy	roué	sail	seal	shea	Sion	smig	soor
rauk	rind	rouf	sain	seam	she'd	sipe	smir	soot
rave	rine	rouk	sais	sean	shed	sire	smit	sope
rayl	ring	roun	Saka	SEAQ	shen	sisi	smog	soph
raze	rink	roup	sake	sear	shep	siss	smon	sora
razz	riot	rous	saki	seat	she's	sist	smug	sorb
read	ripe	Rous	sala	seau	shew	site	smur	Sorb
real	rise	rout	sale	seax	shhh	sith	smut	sord
ream	risk	roux	salp	sect	Shi'a	sitt	snab	sore
rean	risp	rove	salt	seed	Shia	Siva	snag	sori
reap	Riss	rown	SALT	seek	shim	size	snap	sorn
rear	rite	rowy	same	seel	shin	sizy	snax	sort
reck	ritz	RSPB	Sami	seem	Shin	sizz	sneb	so so
reco	riva	RSVP	samp	seen	ship	skag	sned	soss
rect	rive	rube	sand	seep	shit	skat	sneg	SOSs
redd	riza	ruby	sane	seer	shiv	sked	snew	Soto
rede	RNLI	ruck	sang	sego	shod	skeg	snib	souk
redo	RNZN	rudd	sank	seif	shoe	skeo	snig	soul
reed	road	Rudd	sans	seir	shog	skep	snip	soum
reef	roam	rude	Sant	Sekt	shoo	skew	snit	soup
reek	roan		sapa	sele	shop	skid	snob	sour

sowl	stut	syne	T-bar	tiao	toga	tram	tute	upgo
sown	stye	syph	tcha	tiar	to go	trap	tutu	up in
sowp	Styx	taal	tea'd	tice	togt	tray	Tuva	up on
soya	suba	tabi	teak	tich	to-ho	tree	TVEI	upon
spad	such	tabl	teal	tick	toil	tref	twat	upta
Spad	suck	tabu	team	Tico	toit	trek	tway	up to
spae	sudd	tach	tear	tide	Tojo	trem	twee	UPVC
spag	suds	tack	teat	tidy	toke	tret	twig	upya
spam	sued	taco	tech	tied	toki	trey	twin	ural
Spam	suer	tact	teed	tief	toko	Trib	twit	Ural
span	sues	ta-da	teem	t'ien	tola	trie	twos	urao
spar	suet	tael	teen	tier	told	trig	tyee	urbs
spat	Sufi	Taff	teer	tiff	tole	trim	tyer	Urdu
spay	sugi	taft	tees	tift	toll	trin	tyke	urdy
spaz	suid	tahr	teff	tige	tolt	trio	tyle	urea
spec	suit	Taig	TEFL	tika	tolu	trip	tymp	urge
sped	suke	tail	tegu	tike	tomb	tris	tyne	uric
spet	sukh	tait	tehr	tiki	tome	trod	type	uroo
spew	sulk	taka	teil	tile	tomo	trog	typo	Ursa
spey	sull	take	tele	till	tone	tron	tyre	Uruk
spic	Sulu	tala	tell	tilt	tong	trot	tyro	urus
spin	sumi	talc	temp	time	toni	Trot	tzar	used
spit	sumo	tale	tend	tind	tonk	trow	UB40	user
spiv	sump	tali	tent	tine	tony	troy	UCAS	USSR
spot	sung	talk	tepa	ting	Tony	trub	UCCA	utas
SPQR	Sung	tall	term	t'ing	tooa	true	ucky	uvea
spry	suni	tame	tern	Ting	took	trug	udad	uver
spud	sunk	tamp	terp	tink	tool	tsar	udal	vade
spue	sunn	tana	terr	tint	toom	tsps	udon	vagi
spun	sunt	tang	TESL	tiny	toon	tsun	Uduk	vail
spur	supe	Tang	Teso	tipi	toot	tuan	UEFA	vain
SSSI	supp	tanh	test	tipt	tope	tuba	ufer	vair
stab	sura	tank	tête	tire	toph	tube	ufos	vale
stac	surd	tant	Teut	tirl	topi	tuck	UFOs	vamp
stad	sure	Taos	Tewa	tiro	topo	tuel	Ugli	vane
stag	surf	tapa	text	tirr	tops	tufa	ugly	vang
stap	suss	tape	Thai	tite	tora	tuff	uh-uh	vara
star	susu	tapu	than	titi	torc	tuft	ukky	vari
stat	Susu	ta-ra	thar	tivy	tore	tule	ulli	vary
stay	Svan	tara	that	Tiwa	tori	tulp	ulna	vasa
steg	swab	tare	thaw	Tiwi	torn	Tulu	ulto	vase
stem	swad	tarn	thee	tizz	toro	tu-mo	ulva	vast
Sten	swag	taro	the I	toad	torp	tump	umbo	veal
step	swam	tarp	them	to a T	torr	tuna	umph	Veda
stet	swan	tars	then	Toba	tort	tunc	umps	veed
stew	swap	tart	thet	tobe	Tory	tund	unal	veep
stey	swat	tash	thew	to-be	tosa	tune	unau	veer
stim	Swat	task	they	toby	Tosa	tung	unbe	vega
stir	sway	tass	thig	Toc H	tosh	tunk	unci	veil
stoa	swee	Tass	thin	tock	Tosk	tuny	unco	vein
stob	swig	ta-ta	thir	toco	toss	Tupi	undo	vela
stød	swim	tate	this	Toda	tost	turb	undy	Vela
stog	swiz	tatu	thon	to-do	tote	turd	unio	veld
stop	swob	taum	thou	tody	toto	turf	unis	vell
stot	Swoe	taut	thow	toea	toup	turk	unit	vena
stow	swop	tave	thra	toed	tour	Turk	Unix	vend
stub	swot	tawa	thro	toes	tout	turm	unky	vent
stuc	swum	tawm	thru	toey	town	turn	unto	veny
stud	syce	tawn	thud	toff	towy	turr	upas	verb
stug	syed	taws	thug	toft	toze	tush	up at	verd
stum	syke	taxa	thus	Toft	trac	tusk	up-by	vers
stun	sync	taxi	tial	tofu	trad	tuss	up-do	vert

very	voom	warp	wept	will	worn	yare	yoga	zarf
Very	vote	wart	we're	wilt	wort	yark	yogh	Zarp
vest	vour	wary	were	wily	wove	yarm	yogi	Z-bar
veto	vril	wase	wert	wimp	WRAC	yarn	yo-ho	Z-bed
vial	vuln	wash	west	WIMP	WRAF	yate	yoke	zeal
vibe	Waac	wasm	weta	wind	wrap	yaup	yole	zebu
vice	Waaf	wasp	we've	wine	wraw	yawl	yolk	zein
Vici	waal	WASP	Weyl	wing	wray	yawn	yomp	zeme
vide	wack	wast	wham	wink	wree	yawp	yond	Zend
vier	wade	wath	whap	wino	wren	yaws	yoni	zerk
Viet	wadi	watt	what	winy	Wren	yawy	yont	zero
view	wady	waul	whau	wipe	wrig	Y-cut	yoop	zest
viff	waff	waur	whee	wire	writ	yeah	yopo	zeta
viga	waft	wave	when	wiry	WRNS	yean	yore	Zeus
vila	wage	wavy	whet	wise	wrot	year	york	zeze
vild	waif	wa-wa	whew	wish	wuff	yech	York	zhos
vile	wail	wawl	whey	wisp	wump	yeep	yote	Zhou
vill	wain	waxy	whid	wist	Würm	yegg	you'd	ziff
vina	wait	weak	whig	wite	wuss	yeld	your	zinc
vine	waka	weal	Whig	with	wych	yelk	yous	zine
vink	wake	wean	whim	wive	wynd	yell	yowe	zing
vino	wald	wear	whin	wi-wi	wynn	yelm	yowl	zino
vint	wale	weed	whio	woad	wype	yelp	yo-yo	Zion
viny	walk	week	whip	wo ho	wyte	yeow	yuan	zipp
viol	wall	weel	whir	woke	X-cut	yere	Yuan	zita
virl	walm	ween	whit	wold	Xmas	yerk	yuca	ziti
visa	walt	weep	Whit	wolf	x-ray	yern	yuck	zizz
vise	waly	weer	whiz	womb	xylo	yesk	Yüeh	zoco
visé	wame	weet	whoa	wong	yaas	yeso	yuft	zoea
viss	wand	weft	who'd	wonk	yack	yest	Yugo	zoic
vita	wane	weid	whom	wont	yagé	yeti	Yuit	zoid
Vita	wang	weil	whoo	won't	Yagi	yett	yuke	zona
viva	wank	weir	whop	wood	yair	yeuk	Yuki	zone
vive	want	weka	whys	Wood	Yakö	yé-yé	yuky	zonk
vizy	wa'n't	weld	wich	woof	Yale	yike	yule	zoom
vlei	waqf	welk	wick	wool	y'all	yill	Yule	zoon
voce	warb	we'll	wide	woon	Yami	yips	Yuma	zoot
vogt	ward	well	Wien	woos	Yana	yite	yump	zori
void	ware	wels	wife	wops	yang	ylem	yuro	zouk
vola	wari	welt	wift	word	yank	ylid	yurt	zubr
vole	wark	wely	wild	wore	Yank	YMCA	YWCA	Zulu
volk	warm	wend	wile	work	yapp	yock	zack	Zuñi
volt	warn	went	wili	worm	yard	yodh	zany	zyme

FIVE LETTERS

abaca	acrid	afore	akkra	aloha	anent	après	arsis
abaci	acrow	afoul	aknee	alone	angel	April	arson
aback	act as	afrit	alack	along	anger	apron	*artel*
abaft	actin	Afros	aland	aloof	angle	apsis	Artex
abaht	act on	after	alant	aloud	Angle	aptly	artic
abase	acton	again	alarm	alpha	Anglo	araba	artsy
abash	actor	agama	alary	altar	angon	Araby	arval
abask	act up	agami	alate	alter	angry	arage	arvos
abate	acute	agape	album	altho'	angst	arain	Aryan
abaya	adage	agasp	alcid	altos	anigh	arbor	asail
Abaza	adapt	agate	aldea	altus	anile	arced	ASCII
abbey	a-days	agave	alder	alula	anima	archy	ascon
abbot	addax	agaze	Aldis	alure	anile	arder	ascot
abeam	added	agent	aldol	alway	animé	aread	ascus
abear	adder	agger	aleck	amain	anion	areal	asdic
abeat	add in	aggri	aleft	amand	anise	arear	Asdic
abele	addle	aggro	aleph	amang	anker	areca	ASEAN
abeng	add-on	aggry	alert	amasi	ankle	arena	as for
aberr	add to	agila	Aleut	amass	ankus	arene	ashen
abhor	add up	agile	alfin	Amati	annal	aren't	ashet
abide	adeem	aging	algae	amaze	annex	arête	as how
abled	adept	agios	algal	amber	annoy	argal	Asian
abler	à deux	agist	algid	ambit	annul	argan	aside
abnet	ad hoc	aglet	algin	amble	anode	Argie	A-side
abode	adieu	agley	Algol	ambon	anole	argil	asile
aboil	adios	agloo	algum	ambos	anomy	argle	asker
A-bomb	ad lib	aglow	alias	ambry	antae	argol	askew
aboon	adman	Agnus	alibi	ameba	anted	argon	Aslef
abord	admen	a gogo	Alice	ameer	anter	argot	as-new
abort	admin	à gogo	alick	amend	antes	argue	asoak
about	admit	agone	a lick	amene	antic	Argus	aspen
above	admix	agony	alien	ament	anti-g	Arhat	asper
ab ovo	adobe	agora	align	amice	antis	Arian	as per
Abram	adopt	agree	alike	amide	antra	ariel	aspic
abrim	adore	agrin	aline	amigo	antre	Aries	aspre
abrin	adorn	agued	A-line	amine	antsy	arise	assai
Abuna	adown	aguti	alive	amino	anvil	Arita	Assam
abune	adoze	ahead	alkie	Amish	Anzac	arity	assay
abura	adrad	aheap	alkyd	amiss	Anzus	arjun	asses
abuse	ad rem	ahigh	alkyl	amity	aorta	arles	asset
abuzz	adrip	ahind	Allah	amnia	apace	Armco	as sin
abysm	aduki	ahold	allay	amnio	apart	armed	assot
abyss	adult	ahull	allel	amole	apeak	armet	aster
acari	adunc	ahunt	Allen	among	apert	armil	astir
accra	adust	aider	alley	amora	apery	armor	Astis
ace it	adyta	aimer	all in	amort	aphid	aroar	as was
acerb	aegis	aioli	allis	amour	aphis	aroid	asway
acidy	aerie	aïoli	allod	amper	apian	aroma	as who
acini	afanc	airer	allot	ample	apish	arose	aswim
ackee	afara	aisle	allow	amply	a-poop	arrah	as yet
acned	afear	aitch	alloy	ampul	aport	arras	asyle
acock	affix	aiver	all up	amuck	a-pout	array	at all
acold	afire	Akali	allus	amuse	appal	arrha	ataxy
acone	aflat	akara	allyl	ancon	apple	arris	at bat
acorn	aflow	akela	almah	and if	apply	arrow	at bay
acral	afoam	Akela	almug	anear	appro	arsed	A-team
acred	afoot	Akita	aloft	anele	appui	arses	A tent

athel	awful	balmy	beach	bench	binal	bloom	boosa
atilt	awing	baloo	beady	bendy	Binet	bloop	boost
atlas	awned	balsa	beaky	benet	binge	blore	boosy
at law	awner	Balti	be-all	Benin	bingo	blown	booth
atman	awoke	banal	beamy	benne	bingy	blowy	boots
atole	awork	banco	beano	benni	binit	blued	booty
atoll	axial	bandy	beard	benny	biome	bluer	booza
atomy	axile	bangy	beast	benty	biota	blues	booze
at one	axing	bania	beath	be off	biped	bluet	boozy
atone	axiom	banjo	beaty	beray	birch	bluey	Borah
atony	axion	banky	beaus	beret	birle	bluff	borak
atopy	axled	banns	beaut	bergy	biros	blunt	borax
atour	ayont	Bantu	beaux	berob	birse	blurb	boree
at par	Azeri	barbe	bebop	beroe	birth	blurt	borel
atria	azide	bardi	bedad	berry	bison	blush	borer
atrip	azine	bardy	beddy	berth	bitch	board	boric
at sea	azoic	barge	bedel	beryl	biter	boart	borne
attap	azole	barky	bedew	besaw	bitsy	boast	*borné*
attar	azote	barmy	bedim	besee	bitts	bobac	boron
atter	azoth	baron	bedip	beset	bitty	bobak	boser
attic	Aztec	barre	bedye	besom	bivvy	bobby	bosey
Attic	azuki	barré	beech	besot	bixin	bob of	boshy
at war	azure	barry	beedi	betel	black	bocca	bosie
aucht	azury	barse	beefs	Betsy	Black	Boche	bosky
audio	azyme	basal	beefy	Betty	blade	boden	bosom
audit	baaed	basan	beery	bevel	blady	boder	boson
augen	Baath	bases	beeve	bever	blahs	bodge	bossy
auger	babby	basha	befit	bevil	blain	bodin	bo'sun
Auger	babel	basho	befog	bevvy	blame	bodle	bosun
aught	babul	basic	be for	bewet	bland	Boehm	botch
augur	bacca	BASIC	befur	bewig	blank	boffo	botel
aulic	bacco	basil	begad	bewit	blare	bogey	bothy
aumil	baccy	basin	begah	bezel	blart	boggy	botty
aunty	backy	basis	began	B-film	blasé	bogie	bouge
aurae	bacon	bason	begat	B flat	blast	bogle	bough
aural	baddy	basse	begem	bhaji	blate	bogue	boule
auras	badge	bassi	beget	bhang	blatt	bogus	boult
auric	badly	basso	begin	Bheel	blaud	bohea	bound
aurin	bad of	baste	begob	Bhora	blaze	bohos	bourd
autos	BAFTA	basto	begot	bhusa	bleak	boier	bourg
auxin	bagel	Batak	begum	Bible	blear	boing	bourn
avail	baggy	batch	begun	bicky	bleat	boist	bouse
avast	bags I	bated	beige	biddy	bleck	bokay	bovid
avens	bag up	batey	being	bidet	bleed	bolar	bowel
avert	Baha'i	bathe	beisa	bidri	bleep	bolas	bower
avgas	Ba-ila	baths	bejel	bid up	blend	boldo	bowet
avian	bairn	batik	belah	bield	blent	bolus	bowie
avine	baity	baton	belap	bifid	bless	*bombe*	Bowie
aviso	baize	Batta	belar	bigha	blest	bonce	bow-on
avoid	Bajan	batty	belay	bight	blimp	boned	bowse
awabi	Bajau	Batwa	belch	bigly	blind	boner	boxen
AWACS	bajra	bauch	belee	bigot	blink	bongo	boxer
await	baked	bauds	belie	*bijou*	bliny	bonny	Boxer
awake	baken	baulk	belle	biker	blirt	bonus	boyar
awald	baker	Baumé	belly	bikie	bliss	bonze	boyer
award	balao	bavin	below	bikky	blite	booay	boyos
aware	balas	bawdy	bemad	bilbo	blitz	booby	bozos
awash	baldy	bayed	be man	bilby	bloat	booed	braai
aways	baler	bayou	Bemba	bilge	block	booer	brace
a week	balky	bazan	Bembo	bilgy	bloke	booky	brach
aweel	balls	bazil	be mum	billy	blond	boomy	brack
aweto	bally	bazoo	benab	bimbo	blood	boong	bract

Bragg	brugh	busby	calla	catch	chase	cholo	clart
braid	Bruin	buses	calmy	cater	chasm	chomp	clary
brail	bruit	bushy	Calor	catty	chawl	chook	clash
brain	brume	busky	calve	cauda	cheap	choom	clasp
brake	brung	bussu	calyx	cauld	cheat	chopt	class
braky	brunt	busty	caman	caulk	check	chord	clast
brand	brush	butch	camas	cause	cheek	chore	clave
brank	brusk	butea	camel	caval	cheep	chose	clead
brant	brute	butle	cameo	cavea	cheer	chota	cleam
brash	B-side	butte	campo	cavel	Cheka	chott	clean
brass	B-tree	butty	campy	caver	chela	chout	clear
brast	bubal	butut	CAMRA	cavie	chelp	choux	cleat
brava	bubby	butyl	camus	cavil	chena	chowk	cleck
brave	buchu	buxom	canal	C clef	chert	choya	cleed
bravo	bucko	buyer	can-do	CD-ROM	chess	Chubb	cleek
brawl	budda	buy-in	candy	cease	chest	chuck	cleft
brawn	buddy	buy it	caner	cebid	chevy	chufa	cleik
braxy	budge	buy up	canid	cecum	chewy	chuff	clepe
braze	buffe	buzzy	Canis	cedar	Chian	chula	clerk
bread	buffo	bwana	canna	cedis	chica	chump	cleuk
break	buffy	by air	canny	ceiba	chich	chunk	cleve
bream	buggy	by-end	canoe	celeb	chick	churl	click
breck	bught	by far	canon	cella	chide	churn	cliff
brede	Bugis	by gad	cañon	cello	chief	churr	clift
breed	bugle	by God	canst	celom	child	chuse	climb
breek	build	by gum	canto	cense	chile	chute	clime
breme	built	by hap	canty	cento	Chile	chyle	cline
brent	buist	by-law	caped	ceorl	chili	chyme	cling
brerd	bulge	by sea	caper	ceral	Chili	cibol	clink
Brett	bulgy	byssi	caple	cerci	chill	cicad	clint
breve	bulky	byway	capon	ceric	chimb	cicer	clipe
briar	bulla	Caaba	capos	cerin	chime	cider	clipt
bribe	Bulli	cabal	capot	certy	chimp	cigar	cloak
brick	bully	caban	cappa	ceryl	china	ciggy	cloam
bride	bumbo	cabas	Capri	Cetus	China	cilia	clock
brief	bumph	cabby	capsa	cetyl	chine	cimex	cloff
brier	bumpy	caber	capul	chace	chiné	cinch	cloke
brill	Buna N	cabin	caput	chack	Ching	cinct	cloky
brine	bunce	cable	carat	chaco	chink	circa	clomb
bring	bunch	cabob	cardi	chafe	Chink	Circe	clomp
brink	bunco	cabri	cardo	chaff	chino	circs	clone
briny	bundu	cacao	cardy	chaft	Chips	cirri	clonk
brish	bungy	cache	carer	Chaga	chirk	cisco	cloop
brisk	bunko	cacky	caret	chain	chirl	cissy	cloot
britt	bunny	cacti	carex	chair	chirm	citer	close
broad	bunty	caddy	carga	chalk	chirp	civet	closh
Broca	bunya	cadet	cargo	chama	chirr	civic	clote
broch	buran	Cadet	Carib	champ	chirt	civil	cloth
brock	burgh	cadew	carle	chang	chiru	civvy	cloud
broil	burin	cadge	carny	chank	chive	clack	clour
broke	burka	cadgy	carob	chant	chivy	clade	clout
brome	burke	cadre	carol	chaos	chizz	claes	clove
bromo	burly	Cafod	carom	chape	chock	claik	clown
bronc	burnt	cagey	carpi	chaps	choco	claim	cloze
Bronx	buroo	cahow	carry	chara	choga	clame	cluck
brood	burra	caird	carse	chard	choil	clamp	clued
brook	burro	cairn	carsy	chare	choir	clang	clues
brool	burru	cajan	carte	chark	choke	clank	clump
broom	burry	Cajun	carve	charm	choko	clapt	clung
brose	bursa	calid	caser	charr	choky	Clare	clunk
broth	burse	calif	casse	chart	chola	Clark	Cluny
brown	burst	calix	caste	chary	choli	claro	clype

coach	*conte*	cower	crone	cuppy	dandy	Dehua	dicky
coact	Conté	cowey	cronk	curby	Danic	de-ice	dicot
coaly	conto	cowle	crony	curch	danio	deify	dicta
coapt	conus	cowry	crood	curdy	danky	deign	dicty
coarb	cooed	coxae	crook	curer	dante	deism	diddy
coast	cooee	coxal	croon	curia	Darby	deist	didn't
coath	cooer	coyer	cropt	Curia	darcy	deity	didos
coati	coo-er	coyly	crore	curie	dared	dekko	didst
cobby	cooey	coypu	cross	curio	darer	delay	die-in
cobia	cooky	cozen	croup	curly	daric	deled	diene
coble	cooly	crack	crove	curny	Darii	delft	Digby
COBOL	coomb	craft	crowd	curry	darky	delis	dight
cobra	coomy	craig	crown	curse	dashy	delph	dig in
cocci	co-opt	crake	croze	curst	datal	delta	digit
cocky	co-own	cramp	cruck	curve	dated	delve	dig up
cocoa	copal	crane	crude	curvy	dater	demit	dildo
cocos	copek	crang	cruel	cusec	datok	demob	dilly
cocus	copen	crank	cruet	cushy	datuk	demoi	dilse
coder	coper	crape	crumb	cutch	datum	demon	dimer
codex	cop it	craps	crump	cutey	daube	demos	dimly
codon	copra	crapy	crums	cutie	dauby	demur	dimmy
cogie	copse	crare	crunk	cut-in	dault	denar	dimps
cogue	copsy	crash	crunt	cutin	daunt	de-net	dinar
cohoe	coque	crass	crura	cut in	Davis	denim	diner
cohog	corah	crate	cruse	cutis	davit	dense	dinge
coiff	coral	crave	crush	cutty	Dayak	den up	dingo
coign	cordy	crawk	crust	cut up	dayan	depel	dingy
coker	corer	crawl	crwth	cuvée	dealt	depot	Dinka
cokey	corgi	craze	cryer	cycad	deary	depth	dinky
coley	corks	crazy	crypt	cycle	death	deray	dinna
colic	corky	creak	cry up	cycli	deave	Derby	dioch
colin	corno	cream	CS gas	cyder	debag	de-rig	diode
colly	cornu	credo	Cuban	cylix	debar	derma	dippy
colon	corny	creed	cubby	cymar	debby	derry	dipso
color	corps	creek	cubeb	cynic	debel	desai	dirge
colsa	corse	Creek	cuber	Czech	debit	desex	dirty
colza	Corso	creel	cubic	dabby	debug	de-sex	disco
comae	Corti	creep	cubit	dacha	debus	deter	dishy
comas	cosec	Crees	cucuy	dachs	debut	detin	disna
combe	coset	crêpe	cuddy	daddy	début	detox	dital
combi	costa	crêpé	cueca	dados	Debye	detur	ditch
combo	Costa	crept	cue in	daffy	decad	deuce	ditsy
combs	cothe	crêpy	Cuffy	Daffy	decaf	devel	ditto
comby	cotta	cress	Cufic	dagga	Decaf	devil	ditty
comer	couac	crest	cuing	daggy	decal	Devon	ditzy
comes	couba	crève	cuish	Dagon	decan	*dévot*	divan
comet	couch	cribo	culch	dagos	decay	dewan	divas
comfy	coudé	crick	culet	daily	decky	dewar	dived
comic	cough	cried	culex	dairi	decor	Dewar	diver
comma	could	crier	cully	dairy	décor	Dewey	Dives
Commo	count	cries	*culpa*	daisy	decoy	dexie	divot
compo	coupe	crime	Cuman	daker	decry	dhand	divvy
Comus	coupé	crimp	cumin	Dakin	decus	dhobi	dixie
conch	coups	crine	cumly	dalek	decyl	dhole	Dixie
condo	court	crisp	cunet	dally	dedal	dhoon	dizen
coney	couth	croak	cu-nim	Dally	deedy	dhoti	dizzy
conga	coven	Croat	cunit	daman	deevy	dhyal	djinn
congé	cover	croci	cunny	damme	defat	Diana	D-mark
congo	covet	crock	cupel	damna	defer	diary	do-all
Congo	covey	croft	Cupid	dampy	degas	diazo	doaty
conic	covin	cromb	cupie	dam up	degum	dicer	dobby
conky	cowan	crome	cuppa	dance	degut	dicey	dobey

dobie	douar	drive	duple	effer	enact	essay	faced
dobro	Douay	droit	duply	E flat	enarm	Essex	facer
doddy	doubt	droke	duppy	egall	ender	ester	facet
dodge	douce	droll	dural	egest	end on	estoc	facia
dodgy	dough	drome	Durex	eggar	endow	estop	facta
dodos	douro	drone	Duroc	egger	endue	ethel	facty
doest	douse	drong	duroy	egret	end up	ether	faddy
doeth	dover	drony	durra	eider	enema	ethic	faded
do for	dovey	droob	durst	eight	enemy	ethos	fader
dogan	dowar	droog	durum	eigne	Enets	ethyl	fadge
doggo	dowdy	drook	durzi	eject	engem	etrog	fados
doggy	dowel	drool	dusky	eking	enjoy	Etrog	faery
dogie	dower	droop	dusty	ekker	ennew	ettle	faggy
dog it	dowie	dropt	Dusun	elain	ennit	étude	Fagin
dogma	dowly	dross	dutch	Elami	ennui	etwee	fagot
Dogra	Down's	drouk	Dutch	eland	enorm	etyma	faint
doily	downy	drove	duvet	elate	enrol	Euler	fairy
doing	dowry	drowk	dwale	elbow	ensky	Eupad	faith
dojos	dowse	drown	dwalm	elder	ensue	euros	faker
Dolby	doyen	Druid	dwang	elect	enter	eurus	fakir
dolce	doylt	drunk	dwarf	elegy	entia	Eusol	false
doler	doyly	drupe	dweeb	eleme	entry	evade	famed
dolia	dozed	druse	dwell	elemi	enure	evens	fanal
dolly	dozen	Druse	dwelt	elfin	enurn	event	fanam
dolma	dozer	drusy	dwile	Elian	envoi	evert	Fanar
dolor	draba	druxy	dwine	elide	envoy	every	fancy
dolos	drabi	Druze	dyery	elint	Enzed	Evian	fango
dolus	drach	dryad	dying	Elint	eosin	evict	fanny
domal	drack	dryas	dyker	elite	epact	evite	fanon
domed	Draco	dryer	dykey	élite	ephah	evoke	Fante
dompt	draff	dryly	dzong	elmen	ephod	ewery	Fanti
domus	draft	dryth	eager	elope	ephor	ewest	farad
donah	drail	dry up	eagle	elpee	epiky	ewhow	farce
Donau	drain	dubba	eagre	Elsan	epoch	Ewing	farcy
donee	drake	dubby	eared	elsin	epode	exact	farer
doner	drama	ducal	early	elude	epopt	exalt	Farsi
doney	drang	ducat	EAROM	elute	epoxy	excel	Fasti
donga	drank	duces	earth	elvan	EPROM	ex-con	fatal
donna	drant	duchy	easel	elven	Epsom	excur	fated
donné	drape	ducks	easer	elver	eptly	ex div	Fatha
donor	drave	ducky	eaten	elves	equal	exeat	fatly
donut	drawk	duddy	eater	e-mail	equid	exert	fatso
do off	drawl	duggy	eat-in	email	equip	exies	Fatso
dooms	drawn	dulce	eat up	embar	erase	exile	fatty
doomy	dread	dulia	eaved	embay	erbia	exine	fatwa
Doòna	dream	dully	eaves	embed	erect	exist	faugh
do out	drear	dulse	Eblis	ember	ergot	exite	fault
doozy	dreck	dumbo	E-boat	Ember	erica	exode	fauna
doper	dreed	dumka	ebony	embog	eriff	expat	faust
dopey	dreep	dummy	echoy	embow	Ernie	expel	fauve
doria	drees	dumps	éclat	embox	erode	expos	favic
Doric	dreng	dumpy	edder	embus	erose	extol	favor
dormy	dress	dunam	Eddic	emcee	error	extra	favus
dorsa	dried	dunce	edema	emend	eruca	extry	faxed
dorse	drier	dunch	edged	emery	eruct	exude	faxer
dorty	dries	dunga	edger	emmer	erump	exult	fayre
doser	drift	dungy	edict	emmet	erupt	exurb	F clef
dotal	drill	dunno	edify	Emmys	erven	exute	feast
doter	drily	dunny	educe	emony	eskar	eying	feaze
dotey	dring	duomo	educt	emote	esker	eyrie	fecal
dotty	D-ring	duper	eejit	emove	esraj	fabby	feces
Douai	drink		eerie	empty	esrog	fable	fedai

fedan	filch	flews	foody	fritt	F-word	gawky	ghyll
fed up	filer	flick	foots	fritz	fytte	gayal	giant
feely	filet	flier	footy	Fritz	gabby	gayer	gibby
feeze	filly	flies	foram	frizz	gable	gayly	gibel
feign	filmy	fling	foray	frock	gadid	gazar	giber
feint	filth	flint	forby	frond	gadso	gazer	gibli
feist	final	flipe	force	frons	gaffe	gazob	gibus
felid	finch	flirt	forcy	front	Gaian	gazoo	giddy
fella	finer	flisk	fordo	froom	gaily	G clef	gigot
felly	finew	flite	forel	frore	galah	gebur	gigue
felon	Fingo	float	forex	frory	galax	gecko	GI Joe
felty	finif	flock	forge	frosh	galbe	gee-ho	gilet
femic	finis	flong	forgo	frosk	galea	geeky	gilly
femur	finny	flood	forky	frost	Galen	geese	gilpy
fence	finos	floor	forma	froth	Galla	gee-up	gimme
fendy	fiord	flora	forme	frown	Galle	geeze	gimpy
fenks	firer	flory	formé	frowy	gally	gekko	ginep
fenny	firry	flosh	formy	froze	galon	gelid	ginny
feoff	first	floss	forte	fruit	galop	gelly	ginzo
feral	firth	flota	forth	frump	galvo	gemel	gipon
feria	fishy	flour	forty	frush	Gamay	gemma	gippo
Ferio	fiste	flout	forum	fryer	gamba	gemmy	gippy
ferly	fisty	flown	fossa	fry up	gambe	gemot	gipsy
fermi	fitch	flued	fosse	f-stop	gambo	genal	girba
Fermi	fit in	fluey	fossé	fubar	gamel	genco	girly
ferns	fitly	fluff	found	fubby	gamer	genet	giros
ferny	fit on	fluid	fount	fubsy	gamey	genic	girse
ferry	fitty	fluke	fouth	fucus	gamic	genie	girsh
fesse	fit-up	fluky	fouty	fudge	gamin	genii	girth
festa	fiver	flume	fovea	fudgy	gamma	genin	gismo
fetal	fives	flump	fowls	fugal	gammy	genip	given
fetch	fixed	flung	foxie	fuggy	gamut	genoa	giver
fetid	fixer	flunk	foyer	fugie	Gamza	Genoa	givey
fetor	fixit	fluor	frack	fugle	ganch	genre	gizmo
fetta	fix on	flurr	frail	fugue	ganga	genty	glacé
fetus	fix up	flush	frame	Fulah	gange	genus	glade
fetwa	fizzy	flute	franc	Fulbe	ganja	geode	glady
feuar	fjeld	fluty	frank	fully	ganzy	geoid	glaik
feued	fjord	fly at	Frank	fulth	gaper	gerah	glair
fever	flack	fly-by	frape	fumer	gappy	gerbe	gland
feyly	flail	flyer	frass	fumet	garbo	germy	glans
f-hole	flair	fly in	frate	fundi	Garda	gesso	glare
Fiann	flake	fly on	frati	Fundi	gardy	geste	glary
fiant	flaky	flype	fraud	fungi	garri	Getae	glass
fiber	flame	flyte	frayn	fungo	garth	Getan	glaum
fibre	flamy	foamy	freak	funky	garum	get at	glaze
fibro	flane	focal	freck	funny	gases	get by	glazy
fibry	flank	focus	freer	furan	gassy	Getic	gleam
fiche	flare	fodge	fremd	furca	gatch	get in	glean
fichu	flary	foehn	freon	furor	gated	get it	gleba
ficus	flash	fogey	Freon	furry	Gatha	get on	glebe
fidge	flask	foggy	frere	furyl	gator	get to	gleby
field	flawn	fogle	fresh	furze	Gatso	get up	gleed
fiend	flaxy	fogou	friar	furzy	gaudy	ghast	gleek
fiery	flead	foist	fried	fusee	gauge	ghazi	gleet
fifer	fleam	folia	frier	fusil	gault	Ghazi	glent
Fifer	fleay	folic	fries	fusky	gaumy	Ghent	gleyd
fifth	fleck	folie	frill	fussy	gaunt	ghoor	glial
fifty	fleed	folio	frisé	fusty	gauss	ghost	glide
figgy	fleer	folks	frisk	futon	gauze	ghoul	gliff
fight	fleet	folky	frist	fuzee	gauzy	Ghuzz	glint
filar	flesh	folly	frith	fuzzy	gavel		glisk

          Five Letters

gliss	golpe	grave	guess	hadal	harle	hemic	H-iron
glist	go mad	gravy	guest	hadda	harpy	hem in	hirst
glitz	gonad	graze	guide	Hades	harre	hemin	hi-spy
gloam	go nap	great	guige	hadji	Harri	hempy	hissy
gloat	Gondi	grebe	guild	hadn't	harry	hence	hitch
globe	goner	grebo	guile	hadst	Harry	henge	hithe
globi	gonna	grece	guilt	had to	harsh	Henle	hit in
globy	gonys	greed	guimp	hafiz	harsk	henna	hit it
glode	gonzo	Greek	guira	haggy	hashy	henny	hit on
glome	goodo	green	guiro	haham	Hasid	henry	hit up
gloom	goody	greet	guise	haick	hasky	Henry	hives
gloop	gooey	grège	guize	Haida	hasn't	he-oak	Hizen
glore	go off	grego	Gulag	haiku	haste	hepar	hoard
glory	goofy	Grepo	gular	haily	hasty	Herat	hoary
gloss	gooly	grice	gulch	hairy	hatch	herby	hoast
glost	goopy	gride	gules	haith	hater	herit	hobby
glout	goose	grief	gulfy	hajji	Hatti	heroa	hobos
glove	goosy	griff	gulix	hakea	haugh	heron	hoboy
gloze	go out	grift	gully	hakim	haulm	herse	hocus
gluck	gopak	grike	gulpy	Hakka	haunt	hertz	hodad
glued	gorah	grill	gumbo	halal	Hausa	Hertz	Hodge
gluer	goral	grime	gumly	halch	hause	het up	hoe in
glues	goree	grimy	gumma	haldi	haute	heuch	hogan
gluey	gorge	grind	gummy	haldu	haven	heugh	hogen
glugg	gorgy	griot	gumph	haler	haver	hevea	ho-hum
glume	gormy	gripe	gum up	halfa	havoc	hewed	hoick
glump	gorry	grist	Gumza	halgh	hawse	hewer	hoise
gluon	gorse	grith	gundi	hallo	hazan	hexad	hoist
glyde	gorsy	grits	gundy	halma	hazel	hexon	Hokan
glyph	gotta	groan	gunge	halon	hazer	hexyl	hokey
gnarl	Gouda	groat	gungy	halos	hazle	hey-ho	hokku
gnarr	Goudy	grody	gunny	halva	H-bomb	H-hour	hokum
gnash	gouge	groin	guppy	halve	heady	hiant	holed
gnaur	goura	groof	Gupta	Haman	heald	hiawa	holer
gnawn	gourd	groom	gurge	hamba	heapy	hided	holey
gnome	gouty	groop	gurly	hamel	heard	hider	holla
go ape	gowan	groot	gurry	hames	heart	hield	hollo
goaty	goyal	grope	gushy	hammy	heath	hi-fis	holly
goave	goyim	gross	gusle	hamza	heave	Higgs	holme
go bad	goyle	group	gussy	hanap	heavy	hight	homer
gobby	grace	grout	gusto	hance	hebra	hi-hat	homey
go big	gracy	grove	gusty	handy	heder	hijra	homie
Gödel	grade	grovy	gutsy	hangi	hedge	Hijra	homos
godet	graff	growl	gutta	hanif	hedgy	hiker	honda
godly	graft	grown	gutty	hanky	heeze	hilar	honey
go dry	grail	gruel	guyot	Hansa	heezy	hillo	honky
goest	Grail	gruff	gwely	hanse	hefty	hilly	honor
goeth	grain	gruft	gwine	Hanse	Heian	hilsa	hooch
goety	graip	grume	gynae	Hants	heiau	hilum	hooer
go far	grama	grump	gynie	hantu	heigh	hilus	hooey
gofer	grame	grunt	gyppo	haoma	heist	himbo	hoofs
go for	gramp	grush	gyppy	haori	heize	hinau	hoofy
gofor	grana	gryke	gypsy	hapax	hekte	Hindi	hoo-ha
go-get	grand	G-suit	gyral	haply	helio	Hindu	Hooke
going	grane	guaap	gyron	happi	helix	Hiney	hooky
golah	grant	guaca	gyros	happy	hello	hinge	hooly
Golah	grape	guaco	gyrus	haram	helly	hinny	Hoopa
goldy	graph	guana	gyver	hards	helot	hippo	hoose
golem	grapy	guano	habit	hardy	helve	hipps	hoosh
goles	grasp	guara	habra	harem	hemal	hippy	hoots
Golgi	grass	guard	háček	harif	he-man	hired	hoove
golly	grate	guava	hacky	harka	he-men	hirer	hooze

hoped	husky	ilium	inked	IUPAC	jeton	julep	kavir
hoper	hussy	illth	inken	ivied	jetty	julio	kayak
hop in	hutch	Iloco	inker	ivies	jewel	julus	Kayan
hop it	hutia	image	in key	ivory	Jewry	Julys	Kazak
Hoppo	Hutus	imago	inkle	ivvyed	jezia	jumar	kazoo
hoppy	huzza	Imari	in-law	ixora	jheel	jumbo	kbyte
horae	huzzy	imbed	inlaw	Iyyar	jhula	jumby	kebab
horah	Hydah	imbue	in lay	izard	jibba	jumma	kedge
horal	hydel	I mean	inlay	jabot	jiffy	jumpy	keech
horde	hydra	imide	inlet	J acid	jihad	junco	keely
horme	hydro	imine	in-lot	Jacko	jildi	jundy	keeve
horny	hyena	immer	in mew	Jacky	jimmy	junky	kefir
horse	hying	immie	inmix	Jacob	Jimmy	junta	kelch
horst	hyleg	immit	inner	jaded	jingo	junto	Kelim
horsy	hylic	immix	innit	Jaffa	jings	jupon	Kelly
hosen	hymen	impel	in-off	jäger	jinny	jural	kelpy
hosta	Hymie	impis	in one	jaggy	jippo	jurat	keltz
hotch	hyoid	imply	inorb	jagir	jirga	juror	kempt
hotel	hyper	impro	in pay	jakes	jiver	jutka	kempy
hotly	hypha	imshi	in pig	Jakun	jivey	jutty	kenaf
hotty	hypna	inact	in pod	jalap	jiwan	juvia	kench
hough	hypos	inajá	in pop	jamah	jizya	juvie	kendo
hound	hyrax	inaka	in pup	jaman	jnani	Kaaba	kente
houri	hyson	in all	input	jambe	Jocko	kaama	Kenya
house	Hy-spy	inane	inrun	jambo	jodel	kacha	kepis
hovel	hythe	inapt	inset	jambu	joeys	Kadet	Kerch
hoven	iambi	inarm	in sum	James	johar	Kafir	kêrel
hover	I-beam	in bad	inter	jamma	Johne	Kajar	Keres
how do	Iblis	in bed	intro	jammy	joint	kakar	kerne
howdy	icaco	in bud	intue	jam-up	joist	kakas	Kerry
howel	ichor	in-bye	in two	janty	jokee	kakur	ketal
howff	icier	Incan	Inuit	Janus	joker	kalij	ketch
how so	icily	in-car	inula	japan	jokey	kalpa	ketol
how-to	icing	incog	inure	Japan	jokul	Kamba	ketyl
hoyle	icker	incur	inurn	japer	jollo	kamik	kevel
Hoyle	ickle	incus	Invar	jarul	jolly	kanga	kevir
huaca	ictal	incut	in wed	jasey	Jolly	kango	keyed
huaco	ictic	index	inwit	jaspé	jolty	kanji	keyer
hubby	ictus	India	iodic	jatos	Jomon	Kansa	key up
huffy	idea'd	Indic	ionic	jaunt	Jonah	kanzu	khair
huh-uh	ideal	indie	Ionic	Javan	Jones	kapok	khaki
hulan	ident	Indio	Iowan	javel	jonga	kappa	khama
hulky	idiom	indri	ipiti	jawan	jonty	kapur	Khasi
hullo	idiot	indue	ippon	jawar	joree	kaput	khaya
hulwa	idler	Indus	irade	jawed	jorum	karat	kheda
human	idola	inept	Iraqi	jazzy	jotty	karee	Khmer
humic	idryl	inert	irate	jeans	jougs	Karen	Khond
humid	idyll	in fee	Irgun	jebel	joule	karma	khoum
humor	ier-oe	infer	Irish	jehad	joust	Karok	kiaat
humph	i' fegs	in feu	iroko	jelab	jowar	Karoo	kiack
humpy	if not	in few	irony	jello	jowel	karri	kiang
humus	Igbos	infix	ishan	Jell-O	jower	karst	kiawe
hunch	igloo	in for	Isiac	jelly	jowly	karsy	kicky
hunks	ileac	infra	Islam	jemmy	jubba	karzy	kiddo
hunky	ileal	in fun	islet	jenny	Judas	Kasha	kiddy
hurly	ileum	ingan	islot	jerid	judge	katel	kikar
Huron	ileus	ingem	Isnik	jerky	jugal	kathi	kikoi
Hurri	iliac	Ingin	issue	jerry	juger	katil	kilim
hurry	Iliad	ingle	istle	Jerry	jugum	katti	Kilim
hurst	Ilian	ingot	itchy	Jesse	juice	katun	kilos
husht	Iliat	inion	I-Thou	Jessy	juicy	kauch	kinda
huske		Injun	iulus	Jesus	juldy	kauri	kindy

kinep	kofta	kungu	laree	leash	level	lingo	loner
kingy	kohua	Kuo-yu	lares	least	lever	lingy	lones
kinin	koine	Kuril	large	leath	levin	linin	longe
kinky	kojic	kurta	largo	leave	levir	links	long s
kinos	kokam	kurus	larin	leavy	Levis	linky	looby
Kioko	koker	kvass	larix	Leber	lewis	linos	looey
kiore	kokko	kvell	larky	leche	Lewis	linty	looie
kiosk	kokum	kweek	larry	ledge	lewth	linum	looky
Kiowa	Kolam	kwela	Larry	ledgy	lexis	lipid	loony
kipsy	Kolbe	kyack	larum	ledum	lezzy	lippy	loopy
Kirby	Koman	kyang	larva	leech	Lhasa	lisle	loose
kirri	kombé	kyats	laser	Leeds	L-head	lispy	loper
kirsh	kombu	kyles	Lassa	lee ho	liana	liter	loppy
kisan	konak	kylie	lassi	leeky	liane	lithe	loral
Kisii	Kongo	kylin	lasso	leery	liang	litho	loran
Kissi	kooka	kylix	lassy	lefty	liard	lithy	lordy
kissy	kooky	kyloe	lasya	legal	libel	litre	Lordy
Kiswa	kopek	kyped	latch	leger	liber	litui	lored
Kitab	kopje	Kyrie	lated	Leger	Libra	lit up	loris
kithe	koppa	kythe	laten	leggo	licca	lived	lorry
kitty	Koran	laari	later	leggy	licit	liven	lorum
kiver	korin	label	lates	leg it	lidar	liver	losel
kiwis	Korku	labia	latex	legit	lidos	lives	loser
Kizil	korma	labor	lathe	leg-up	lie by	livid	lossy
kleft	Korwa	labra	lathi	lehua	liege	livor	lotic
klick	kotal	laced	laths	leigh	lie in	livre	lotos
klieg	kotos	lacet	lathy	leman	lie to	llama	lotsa
Kling	kotow	lacis	Latin	lemel	lie up	llano	lotta
klong	koura	laddo	laton	lemma	lifer	loach	lotto
kloof	kovsh	laden	latus	lemme	lifey	loamy	Lotto
klops	kraal	lader	lauan	lemna	ligan	loath	lotus
klunk	kraft	Ladik	lauds	lemon	liger	lobar	lough
klutz	krait	Ladin	laugh	lemur	light	lobby	louis
knack	Krama	ladle	laund	lenes	liken	lobed	Louis
knape	krans	lagan	laval	lenis	liker	local	loupe
knarl	kraut	lagen	laver	lenos	Likud	lo-cal	lourd
knaur	Kraut	lager	lavvy	lente	lilac	loche	loure
knave	kreef	lahar	lawdy	lento	Li-los	lochi	louro
knead	kreng	laich	lawks	leone	liman	lochy	loury
kneed	krill	laigh	lawny	leper	limax	locie	louse
kneel	kriti	laika	lawsy	lepid	limba	locky	lousy
knees	Kromo	laird	laxly	lepra	Limba	locos	lovat
knell	krona	lairy	lay at	lepta	limbi	locum	lover
knelt	krone	laity	lay-by	Lepus	limbo	locus	lovey
knick	kroon	laker	layer	lered	Limbu	loden	lowan
knife	Krupp	lakin	lay in	lerky	limen	lodge	lower
knish	kudos	lamba	lay on	lesbo	limer	loess	lowly
knive	kudzu	Lamba	lay to	lesed	limes	lofty	low on
knock	Kufic	lamel	lay up	lessy	Limey	logan	Lowry
Knole	kugel	lamia	lazar	leste	limit	loggy	loxia
knoll	kukri	lamin	Lazic	let at	limma	logia	loyal
Knoop	kukui	Lamut	l-dopa	let be	limos	logic	lozen
knorr	kulah	lanai	leach	letch	linac	logie	lubra
knosp	Kulah	lance	Leach	let go	linch	log in	Lucan
knout	kulak	Langi	leady	Lethe	Linde	logit	Lucas
knowe	kulan	Lango	leafy	let in	lindy	log on	Lucca
known	Kulin	lanky	leaky	let on	lined	logos	lucet
knuck	Kuman	lapel	leant	letty	linen	Logos	lucid
knurl	kumis	lappa	leapt	let up	liner	Lohan	lucky
knurr	Kumyk	lapse	learn	levan	liney	Loire	lucre
koala	kunai	larch	leary	levas	linga	lokey	ludic
Kodak	kunbi	lardy	lease	levee	linge	lolly	Ludic

luffa	madar	manse	mavis	merit	minae	moist	motel
Luger	madge	manta	mawky	merle	mince	molal	motet
Lugol	madia	manto	maxim	meros	miner	molar	motey
Luing	madid	manul	Maxim	merou	minge	moldy	mothy
lulav	madly	man up	maxis	merry	mingy	Moler	motif
lulla	maedi	manus	Mayan	mesad	Minié	moley	moton
lumen	Mafia	Maori	Mayas	meshy	minim	molly	motor
lumme	mafic	mapau	maybe	mesic	minis	molto	motte
lummy	mafoo	maple	mayer	meslé	minke	momma	motto
lumpy	Magar	mapou	mayn't	mesne	minol	momme	motty
lunar	magic	mappy	mayor	meson	minor	mommy	mouch
lunch	magma	maqui	mayst	messy	minty	Momus	mould
Lunda	magot	marae	mazar	metae	minus	monad	Mouli
lunel	magus	marah	mazer	metal	MIRAS	monal	moult
lunge	mahal	maral	mazey	metel	mired	monas	mouly
lungi	Mahdi	march	mazut	meter	mirex	mondo	mound
lungy	mahoe	March	Mbuti	metho	mirid	Monel	mount
lupin	mahua	mardy	McCoy	Metho	mirky	money	mourn
lupus	maidy	Maree	mealy	meths	mirth	mongo	mouse
lurch	maiko	mares	means	metic	misdo	Mongo	mousy
lurer	maint	marge	meant	metif	miser	monic	mouth
lurex	maire	margo	meany	metis	misgo	monos	mover
Lurex	maize	maria	mease	Metis	missy	monte	movie
Lurgi	major	Maria	meaty	metol	misty	month	mowed
lurgy	makai	marid	mebbe	me-too	mitch	monty	mower
lurid	makar	marie	mebos	metre	miter	mooch	mowra
lurky	maker	marly	Mecca	metro	mitre	moody	moxie
lurry	makos	marra	medal	meuse	mitry	mooed	moyen
lushy	malar	marri	media	mezzo	Mitty	mooey	Mr Big
lusky	Malay	marry	medic	miaow	mivvy	mooli	M-roof
lusty	maleo	Marse	Medic	miasm	Miwok	moony	Mrs Lo
lusus	Maler	marsh	medio	miaul	mixed	moory	msasa
luter	malic	Marsh	Medoc	micky	mixen	moose	MS-DOS
luton	malik	Marsi	Médoc	micro	mixer	moosh	mtepe
luvvy	malis	marum	meech	Midas	mix in	moped	muchi
lyart	malmy	Marys	meeja	middy	mixis	moper	mucho
lycée	Malta	Masai	meese	midge	mix it	moppy	mucic
lycid	Malto	maser	Meiji	midis	mix up	mopsy	mucid
Lycra	malty	masha	meith	mid-on	mizen	mop up	mucin
lygus	Malvi	mason	melam	midst	Mlles	mopus	mucky
lying	mamba	Massa	Melba	miffy	mneme	moral	mucor
lymph	mambo	massé	melch	might	mobby	morat	mucro
lynch	mamey	massy	mêlée	migma	moble	moray	mucus
Lyons	mamma	masty	melic	migod	mocha	moree	mudar
lyric	mammy	matai	meloe	mikan	Mocha	morel	muddy
Lyrid	Mande	match	melon	mikva	mocky	mores	mufti
lyses	mandy	mater	melos	Milan	modal	morne	muggy
lysin	maneb	matey	melsh	milch	model	morné	mug-up
lysis	maned	mathe	melty	milds	modem	moron	Mujur
Lysol	manes	maths	memos	miler	modii	Moros	mukim
lyssa	manga	matie	menad	miles	Modoc	morph	mukti
lythe	mange	matin	mench	milia	modom	morra	mulch
lytic	mango	matje	Mende	milko	moggy	morse	mulct
lytta	mangy	matlo	Mendi	milky	mogra	Morse	muled
macaw	mania	matra	mends	mille	mogul	Mosan	Mules
macca	manic	matte	mensa	Mills	Mogul	Mosel	muley
macer	manis	matzo	mense	milpa	mohel	Moses	mulga
macho	manky	mauby	mensh	miltz	mohur	mosey	mully
macle	manly	mauma	mento	mimeo	mohwa	Mossi	mulsh
Mâcon	manna	maund	mercy	mimer	Moine	mosso	mummy
macro	manny	mauve	merel	mimic	moire	mossy	mumps
madam	manor	maven	merge	mimsy	moiré	moted	mumsy

munch	nadir	Ndama	nieve	no joy	nudge	offer	on ice
Munda	naevi	neath	niffy	nokes	nudie	OFFER	onion
munga	Naffy	neato	nifle	no kid	Nujol	off of	onium
mungo	naggy	nebel	nifty	nolle	nulla	Ofgas	onlap
mungy	nagor	neddy	Niger	nomad	nullo	of his	onlay
munja	nahal	needs	nigga	no man	nully	of kin	on lee
Munro	naiad	needy	night	no-mar	numby	Oflag	onlie
mural	naice	ne'er a	nigra	nomen	numen	of old	on-off
murex	naieo	neeze	nigua	nomic	Numic	Oftel	on-set
Muria	naily	neger	nikau	nomos	nummy	often	onset
murid	naira	Negri	nilas	nonce	numps	oftly	ontal
murky	naive	negro	Nilot	nonda	nunky	ofuro	on tap
murly	naïve	Negro	nimbi	nones	nuque	Ofwat	ontic
Murmi	naked	negus	Nimby	nonet	nurse	ogee'd	on top
murra	naker	Negus	ninja	nonic	nutso	ogeed	oojah
murre	naled	Nehru	ninny	no-nos	nutsy	oggin	ooloo
Murut	NALGO	neigh	ninon	nonyl	nutty	ogham	oomph
musae	Namas	nelia	ninth	nooky	nyala	Oghuz	ootid
Musca	namer	nelly	Niobe	no one	Nyasa	ogive	op-amp
muser	namma	nemic	niopo	noose	nylon	ogler	op art
muset	nance	neoza	nippy	nopal	nymph	ogmic	opepe
musha	nancy	neper	Nippy	noria	nyssa	oh boy	opera
mushy	Nandi	neral	NIREX	Noric	Nzima	Ohian	opihi
music	Nanga	neram	Nisan	norma	oaken	ohmic	opine
musky	nanna	nerdy	nisei	Norna	oakum	ohone	opium
musos	nanny	nerka	nisin	Norse	oared	oidia	oppos
mussy	Nants	nerol	Niska	Norsk	oasis	oiled	opsin
musth	Nantz	nerts	Nissl	north	oaten	oiler	optic
musty	napoh	nerve	nisus	nosed	oater	oil in	opt in
mutch	napoo	nervy	nital	noser	oaths	oil up	orach
muted	nappa	net of	nitch	nosey	Obaku	ojime	oracy
mutha	Nappa	netty	niter	noshi	obang	okapi	orage
mutic	nappe	neuma	nitid	no sir	obeah	OK'ing	orang
muton	nappy	neume	niton	no-sky	obeli	oktas	orans
muzak	naras	nevel	nitre	notae	obese	olate	Oraon
Muzak	narco	never	nitro	notal	obley	olden	orate
muzzy	nares	nevus	nitta	notam	obole	older	orbed
mvule	narks	nevvy	nitty	notch	Occam	oldie	orbic
Mwami	narky	Newar	nival	noted	occur	oldly	orbit
myall	narra	newel	nixie	noter	ocean	oleic	orcin
my eye	nasal	newie	nix on	not-go	ocher	olein	order
my God	Nasca	newly	Nizam	not on	ochre	olent	oread
my hat	Nasho	newsy	nobby	notum	ochry	oleum	orful
Mylar	Nasik	nexal	Nobel	nouny	ocker	oleyl	organ
my man	nassa	nexus	noble	nouse	ocote	olios	orgic
mynah	nasty	ngaio	nobly	novae	ocrea	oliva	orgie
myoma	nasus	Ngala	no bon	novas	octad	olive	orgue
myope	natal	Ngoko	nocht	novel	octal	Olmec	oribi
myopy	Natal	Ngoni	nodal	no way	octet	ology	oriel
my own	natch	Nguni	noddy	noway	octic	Omaha	O-ring
myrrh	nates	ngwee	nodum	nowed	octyl	Omani	Orion
mysid	nathe	niata	nodus	nowel	oculi	omasa	Oriya
mysis	natty	nicad	noema	Nowel	oddly	ombre	Orlon
my son	naunt	Nicam	noeme	no-win	odeon	ombré	orlop
mythi	naval	nicey	no end	noxal	odeum	omega	ormer
NAAFI	navel	niche	Nogai	noyau	OD'ing	ommin	orpin
nabal	navew	nicol	Nogay	NSPCC	odist	oncer	orris
nabla	navvy	Nicol	no-hit	n-type	odium	on cue	ortet
nabob	nawab	nidge	nohow	nubby	odour	on dit	ortho
nache	nazar	nidor	noint	nubia	of all	on end	or two
nacho	Nazca	nidus	noise	nucha	offal	one-up	Osage
nacre	Nazis	niece	noisy	nuddy	offen	ongon	Oscan

Oscar	Ozark	pared	peace	pesta	pilei	plate	pokie
osier	ozena	paren	peach	pesto	piler	Platt	Polab
osmic	ozone	parer	péage	pesty	piles	platy	polar
osmol	Ozzie	pareu	peaky	petal	pilot	playa	poler
osone	pacay	parge	Peano	peter	pilus	plaza	poley
ossia	pacer	pargo	pearl	petit	Piman	plead	polio
Ossie	pacey	Paris	peart	petre	pinax	pleat	polis
ostia	pacha	parka	pease	petty	pinch	plebe	polje
otary	paddy	parky	peasy	Peulh	pinda	pleck	polka
other	Paddy	parle	peaty	pewee	piner	plene	pollo
Otomi	padge	parma	pecan	pewit	piney	pleon	polly
otter	padre	Parma	pecia	phage	pingo	plica	Polly
oubit	paean	parol	pecky	phare	pinic	plied	polyp
ouens	paeon	parry	pedal	phase	pinko	plier	polys
ought	pagan	parse	pedee	phasm	pinky	plies	Pomak
Ouija	paged	Parsi	pedes	pheer	pinna	pliés	pommé
oumer	pager	party	pedia	pheme	pinny	plink	pommy
ounce	Paget	pasan	pedon	phene	piñon	ploce	Pommy
ourie	pagle	Pasch	pedro	pheno	Pinot	plock	Ponca
ousel	pagne	paseo	pee em	pheon	pinta	plonk	ponce
out-by	paint	pasha	peent	phial	pinto	plore	poncy
outdo	paisa	pashm	peeoy	phlox	pin-up	plosh	Pondo
outen	paise	pasmo	peepy	phoca	pious	plote	pondy
outer	Pakis	passé	peery	phone	pipal	Plott	ponga
outgo	pa-kua	pasta	peeve	phono	piped	plotz	pongo
outly	palae	paste	peggy	phony	piper	plout	pongy
out of	palar	pasty	peg on	phoss	pipit	pluck	ponor
outré	palas	patas	peise	photo	pippy	pluff	ponty
outro	palea	patch	pekan	phwat	pique	plumb	pooch
outta	paled	pated	pekea	phyla	piqué	plume	pooey
out to	palla	patée	Pekin	phyle	piqui	plump	poofy
ouzel	pally	patel	pekoe	piani	pirog	plumy	pooja
ouzos	palmy	paten	pelta	piano	Pisan	plunk	pooka
ovary	palpi	pater	penal	pians	pisco	plush	Poole
ovate	palps	paths	pence	Piast	pissy	plute	pooly
overt	palsa	patil	penes	piccy	piste	Pluto	Poona
ovest	palsy	patio	pengö	pichi	pitch	poach	poopy
ovine	pamby	patly	penis	picky	pithy	pobby	pooty
ovism	panch	Patna	penne	picot	piton	pocan	poove
ovist	panda	patsy	penni	pi-dog	pitot	poché	poppa
ovoid	pandy	patty	penny	piece	pitso	pocky	poppy
ovoli	Pandy	Pauli	pensy	pietà	pitta	podal	popsy
ovolo	panel	pause	peola	Pietà	piuri	poddy	pop-up
ovule	panga	pauxi	peony	piety	pivot	podex	poral
o' will	panic	pavan	pepos	piezo	pixel	podge	porch
owing	panji	paven	peppy	piggy	pixie	podgy	pored
owler	panne	paver	Pepsi	pight	Piyut	podia	porer
owlet	pansy	pavia	perai	pig it	pizer	poena	porge
owner	panto	pavid	perch	piani	pizza	poesy	porgy
ownio	pants	pavis	Percy	pigmy	place	pogey	poria
own up	panty	pavvy	perdu	pi jaw	plack	pogge	porin
owzat	paolo	paw at	peril	pikau	plage	pogos	porky
ox-bot	papal	pawky	peris	piked	plaid	pogue	porno
oxbow	papas	pawne	perky	pikel	Plaid	poilu	porny
ox-eye	papaw	payas	perle	piker	plain	poind	porta
Oxfam	Papaw	payed	perry	pikey	plait	point	Porte
oxide	paper	payee	per se	pikia	plane	poire	porty
oxime	pappi	payer	perse	pilaf	plank	poise	posca
oxine	pappy	pay in	perve	pilau	plano	pokal	posed
oxlip	parch	payor	pervy	pilaw	plant	poked	poser
ox-ray	parcy	pay up	pesky	pilch	plash	poker	posey
oxter	pardi	p-code	pesos	pilea	plasm	pokey	posho

posit	prion	pulao	quack	racon	rauli	reest	retia
Posix	prior	puler	Quadi	radar	raupo	reeve	retie
posse	prise	pulik	quaff	radii	ravel	refan	re-tin
possy	prism	pulka	quail	radio	raven	refer	re-tip
posty	priss	pulli	quake	radix	raver	reffo	retro
potch	privy	pulpy	quaky	radly	ravin	refit	retry
poter	prize	pulse	quale	radon	rawin	refix	reune
pot on	pro-am	pulza	qualm	raffy	rawky	refry	reuse
potoo	probe	Punan	quant	rafty	rawly	regal	revel
potro	proby	punch	quare	ragee	rayed	Regge	revet
potsy	prodd	punga	quark	rager	rayon	reggo	revue
potto	proem	pungy	quarl	ragga	razee	regma	re-wet
potty	proke	Punic	quart	raggy	razer	regur	re-win
pot up	prole	punji	quash	rainy	razoo	rehab	rhamn
pouch	proly	punky	quasi	raise	razor	Reich	rheid
poulp	promo	punny	quass	raita	razzo	reify	rheme
poult	prone	punto	quave	rajah	R-boat	reign	rheum
pound	prong	punty	quawk	Rakah	reach	reink	rhine
pouty	pronk	pupae	quean	rakel	react	reins	Rhine
powan	proof	pupal	queen	raker	re-act	reive	rhino
power	proot	pupil	queer	rakis	ready	rejig	rhodo
pozzy	prore	puppy	quell	ralli	realm	rekey	rhody
praam	prosa	purau	queme	rally	Realo	relax	rhomb
prahu	prose	purée	quere	ramal	reamy	relay	Rhône
praia	pross	purge	querl	Raman	rearm	re-lay	rhumb
prana	prosy	Purim	quern	rambo	re-ask	relet	rhyme
prang	proud	purry	query	Rambo	reasy	re-let	rhyta
prank	prove	purse	quest	ramen	reata	relic	riant
p'raps	provo	pursy	queue	ramet	reate	relit	riata
prase	Provo	purty	quick	ramie	reave	reman	ribby
prate	prowl	Purum	quies	ramin	rebab	remen	ribes
pratt	proxy	pushy	quiet	rammy	reban	remex	ribit
Pratt	prude	pussy	quiff	ramon	re-bar	remit	ricer
prawn	prune	put at	quile	ramps	rebbe	remix	ricey
praya	prunt	put by	quill	ramus	rebec	renal	richy
predy	pryan	putid	quilt	rance	rebel	renew	ricin
preen	pryce	put in	quina	ranch	rebid	renga	rided
prego	pryse	put on	quint	R and R	rebud	renin	ridel
preon	psalm	putti	quipu	randy	rebus	repat	rider
pre-op	pseud	putto	quire	ranee	rebut	repay	ridge
press	pshaw	put to	quirk	range	rebuy	repel	ridgy
prest	psoas	putto	quirl	rangé	recap	repin	riffy
prexy	psora	putty	quirt	rangy	recce	repla	rifle
Prexy	psych	put-up	quite	ranid	recco	reply	rifty
prial	P trap	pygal	quits	ranny	recon	repot	right
prian	p-type	pygmy	quoin	ranty	recta	repro	rigid
price	pubes	pylon	quoit	raper	recti	reran	rigol
prick	pubic	pylor	quoll	raphe	recto	re-row	rigor
pricy	pubis	pyoid	Quorn	rapid	recur	rerun	riley
pride	pucka	pyral	quota	rarer	recut	resam	Riley
pridy	puddy	pyran	quote	Rarey	redan	resat	rille
pried	pudge	Pyrex	quoth	raspy	reddy	resaw	rilly
prier	pudgy	pyrus	Qur'an	rasse	redia	resee	rimed
pries	pudic	pyxie	Quran	Rasta	redid	reset	rimer
prill	pudor	pyxis	qursh	ratal	redly	resew	rindy
prima	pudsy	pzazz	rabat	ratan	redox	Resht	riner
prime	puffy	Qajar	rabbi	ratch	red 'un	resin	ringe
primi	puggy	Qiana	rabic	ratel	redux	resit	ringy
primo	pugil	qibla	rabid	rater	reedy	resol	Rinne
primp	puker	qibli	Racah	rathe	reefy	resow	rinse
prink	pukey	qirsh	racer	ratio	reeky	resty	Rioja
print	pukka	Q-ship	rache	ratty	reely	retch	ripen

rip up	roral	rumbo	sakes	saraf	scalp	scrod	señor
risen	rorty	rumen	sakis	Saran	scaly	scrog	sensa
riser	rosed	rumex	Sakta	saree	scamp	scrow	sense
rishi	roset	rum go	Sakti	sarge	Scand	scrub	sente
risky	Roshi	rummy	salad	sargo	scant	scrum	sepal
rithe	Rosie	rumor	salal	Sarik	scape	scuba	sepia
ritzy	rosin	rumpo	Salem	sarin	scapi	scudo	Sepik
rival	RoSPA	rumpy	salep	saris	scare	scuff	sepoy
rived	rotal	run at	salic	sarky	scarf	scull	septa
rivel	roter	runch	Salic	Sarn't	scari	sculp	serac
riven	rotge	runic	salie	sarod	scarn	scurf	serai
river	roton	run in	Salii	saron	scarp	scuse	seral
rivet	rotor	runny	salix	saros	scart	scuta	Serax
riyal	rotta	run on	salle	sarpo	SCART	scute	Seres
RNase	Rouen	runot	sally	sarsa	scary	scuzz	serge
roach	rouge	run to	Sally	Sarsi	scaum	Scyth	Seric
roast	rough	runty	salmi	Sarum	scaup	seamy	serif
robed	rouky	run up	salol	sarus	scaur	Sebat	serin
robin	round	rupee	salon	Saryk	*scena*	Sebei	serir
roble	roupy	rupia	salpa	sarza	scend	sebum	seron
robot	rouse	rural	salsa	Sasak	scene	secco	serow
robur	roust	rusha	salse	sasin	scent	secko	SERPS
roche	route	rushy	salta	sassy	schiz	sedan	serra
Roche	routh	rusma	salto	satai	schmo	Seder	serry
rocky	rover	rusty	salty	Satan	schol	sedge	serum
rodeo	rowan	rutin	salud	satay	schwa	sedgy	serve
rofia	rowdy	rutty	salve	satem	sci-fi	sedra	servo
rogan	rowed	ruvid	salvo	satin	scion	sedum	setae
roger	rowel	rymer	Salvo	satis	scoff	seech	setal
Roger	rowen	Saale	salvy	satyr	scoke	seedy	set by
rogue	rower	sabal	samaj	sauba	scold	see-er	set in
rohun	rowet	saber	Samal	sauce	scone	seege	set on
roily	row in	sabin	saman	sauch	scoop	see-ho	seton
roker	rowty	Sabir	samba	saucy	scoot	seely	set to
rolag	royal	sable	sambo	Saudi	scopa	see to	set up
roleo	royet	sably	Sambo	saugh	scope	segar	seven
rolly	RSPCA	sabot	samel	sault	scops	segos	sever
romal	ruana	sabra	samey	sauna	scopy	segue	Sevin
roman	rubby	sabre	samfu	saury	score	Sehna	sevum
Roman	rub in	sacky	sammo	sauté	scorn	seine	sewan
Romeo	rubio	sacra	sammy	saver	scorp	seise	sewed
romer	ruble	sacre	Sammy	savin	scote	seism	Sewee
rompy	rub on	sadhu	Samos	savor	Scots	seity	sewen
ronde	rubor	sadic	sampi	savoy	scoup	Seitz	sewer
rondo	rub up	sadly	sanad	Savoy	scour	seize	sewin
Roneo	ruche	sadza	sanct	savvy	scout	selah	sew-on
Ronga	rucky	Sagan	Sande	sawed	scove	Selah	sew up
ronge	rudas	sagey	sandy	sawer	scowl	selch	sexed
ronin	ruddy	saggy	Sandy	Saxon	scrab	selfs	sexer
Ronuk	rudie	sagos	sanga	sayer	scrag	selky	sexto
roofs	Rufai	sagum	Sanga	say no	scram	sella	seyal
roofy	ruffe	sahel	Sango	say on	scran	selva	shack
rooky	ruffy	sahib	Sanio	says I	scrap	selve	shade
roomy	rugal	Sahli	Sanka	say-so	scrat	semée	shads
roosa	rugby	saiga	sanko	S-band	scraw	semen	shady
roose	Rugby	saint	Sansi	S-bend	scray	semic	shaft
roost	ruggy	Saite	Santa	scads	scree	semis	shahi
roots	ruing	saith	santo	scaff	screw	semon	shail
rooty	ruise	Saiva	sapan	scala	scrib	semul	shake
roper	ruler	Sakai	sapid	scald	scrim	sengi	shako
ropey	rumal	Sakel	sapor	scale	scrin	senna	shaky
roque	rumba	saker	sappy	scall	scrip	Senoi	shale

shall	shirr	shuck	sisal	Skoda	slopy	sneap	solen
shalt	shirt	shude	sisel	skoob	slosh	sneck	soler
shaly	shish	shuka	sissy	skosh	slote	sneer	soles
shama	shite	shunt	sitar	skulk	sloth	snell	sol-fa
shame	shiur	shura	sit by	skull	slove	snick	solid
Shang	shiva	shush	sitch	skunk	sloyd	snide	solod
shank	Shiva	shute	sited	skyer	sluff	snidy	Solon
shan't	shive	shuto	sithe	skyey	sluit	sniff	solos
shant	shlub	shyer	sit in	slack	slump	snift	solum
shape	Shluh	shyly	Sitka	slade	slung	snipe	solus
shard	shmoo	siafu	sit on	slaik	slunk	snipy	solve
share	shoad	sibyl	sit-up	slain	slurb	snirt	solvi
shark	shoal	Sican	situs	slake	slurp	snite	somal
sharm	shoat	sicca	Sivan	slaky	slush	snock	Soman
sharn	shoch	Sicel	sixer	slamp	slyer	snoek	somma
sharp	shock	sicko	sixmo	slane	slyly	snoff	sonar
shave	shode	sicle	sixte	slang	slype	snoke	sonde
shawl	shoed	sided	sixth	slank	smack	snood	sonic
shawm	shoer	sider	sixty	slant	smaik	snook	sonly
shchi	shoes	Sidhe	sizar	slash	small	snool	Sonne
sheaf	shoey	sidle	sized	slate	smalt	snoop	sonny
shear	shogi	sidra	sizer	slath	smarm	snoot	sonse
sheat	shoji	Sidur	skaff	slaty	smart	snore	sonsy
sheel	shola	siege	skail	slave	smash	snork	sooey
sheen	sholt	Siena	skald	slawk	smaze	snort	soosy
sheep	sholy	sieur	skank	slead	smear	snous	sooth
sheer	Shona	sieve	skarn	sleak	smeek	snout	sooty
sheet	shone	sight	skate	slean	smell	snowy	Sophy
sheik	shonk	sigil	skean	sleat	smelt	snuck	sopor
sheld	shood	sigla	skeel	sleck	smift	snuff	soppy
shelf	shook	sigma	skeer	sleek	smile	snurt	soral
she'll	shool	siket	skeet	sleep	S-mine	soapy	Sorbo
shell	shoon	Silbo	skein	sleet	smirk	soave	sorel
shelt	shoos	silen	skelf	slent	smirr	Soave	sorgo
Shema	shoot	silex	skell	slept	smite	sobby	sorry
shend	Shope	silky	skelm	slice	smith	sober	sorus
sheng	shore	silly	skelp	slick	smock	socii	sorva
shent	Shore	silos	skelt	slide	smoke	socko	sotch
Sheol	shorn	silty	skene	slied	smoko	socks	Sotho
sherd	short	silva	Skene	slift	smoky	socle	sotie
sheth	shots	silyl	skerm	slily	smolt	sodar	sotol
sheva	shott	simar	skete	slime	smoor	soddy	sough
shewa	shout	simba	skewy	slimy	smoot	sodic	souly
shewt	shove	simpy	skice	sline	smore	Sodom	sound
Shias	Showa	simul	skied	sling	smote	soe'er	soupy
shice	shown	since	skier	slink	smout	sofa'd	souse
shick	showy	sinew	skies	slipe	smush	so far	south
shide	shoyu	singe	skiff	slish	snack	Sofar	sowar
shied	Shqip	Singh	skift	slite	snafu	softa	sowed
shiel	shrab	Sinic	skill	slive	snail	softy	sowel
shies	shrag	sinky	skimp	slize	snake	soggy	sower
shift	shram	Sinon	skink	slock	snaky	soily	sowff
Shiga	shrap	sinus	skint	sloff	snape	soken	sowth
shiko	shred	Sioux	skire	sloid	snaps	Sokol	space
shill	shrew	sipid	skirl	sloka	snare	solah	spack
Shina	shrim	siree	skirp	sloke	snarf	solan	spacy
shine	shrip	siren	skirr	slomo	snark	solar	spade
shiny	shrub	sirex	skirt	slonk	snarl	Solas	spahi
shipo	shrug	sirih	skish	sloom	snash	soldi	spake
shire	shtik	siris	skite	sloop	snath	soldo	spald
shirk	shtup	siroc	skive	sloot	snead	solea	spale
shirl	shuba	sirup	*skoal*	slope	sneak	soled	spall

spalt	spitz	stagy	still	strut	sump'n	swipe	Tajik
spane	Spitz	staid	stilt	stuck	sumpy	swire	taken
spang	splat	stain	stime	study	sum up	swirl	taker
spank	splay	stair	stimy	stufa	sunck	swish	takht
spare	splet	stake	sting	stuff	sunly	Swiss	takin
spari	splib	stale	stink	Stuka	Sunna	swith	takyr
spark	splif	stalk	stint	stull	Sunni	swive	talak
spart	split	stall	stipe	stulm	sunny	swizz	talaq
spasm	Spode	stamp	stire	stuma	sunup	swoln	talar
spate	spoil	stand	stirk	stumm	sun-up	swoof	talcy
spath	spoke	stang	stirp	stump	super	swoon	talea
spaug	spoky	stank	stith	stung	supra	swoop	tales
spave	spong	staph	stive	stunk	surah	sword	talha
spawl	spoof	stare	stivy	stunt	surai	swore	talik
spawn	spook	stark	stoai	stupa	sural	sworn	talky
spazz	spool	Stark	stoas	stupe	Surat	swung	tally
speak	spoom	starn	stoat	sturb	surfy	sybow	talma
spean	spoon	starr	stock	sture	surge	sycee	talon
spear	spoor	start	stoep	sturt	surgy	sycon	talpa
speck	spore	START	stogy	stuss	surly	Sylow	taluk
specs	Spork	stary	Stoic	styan	surma	sylph	taluq
spect	sport	stash	stoit	styca	surra	sylva	talus
speed	s'pose	Stasi	stoke	styes	sushi	synch	tambo
speel	sposh	state	stola	style	sussy	synod	tamer
speer	spout	stats	stole	styli	sutra	synth	Tamil
speir	sprag	stave	stolo	stylo	Sutra	Syrah	Tamla
speld	sprat	stead	stoma	styme	swack	syrma	tammy
spele	spray	steak	stomp	suade	swage	syrop	tanga
spelk	spree	steal	stone	suant	swain	syrup	tangi
spell	spret	steam	stonk	suave	swale	sysop	tango
spelt	sprew	stean	stony	subah	swami	tabac	tangy
spend	sprig	stech	stood	subby	swamp	tabby	tania
spent	sprit	steed	stook	suber	swamy	tabes	tanka
speos	sprod	steek	stool	Subud	swang	tabid	Tanka
sperm	sprog	steel	stoop	sucky	swank	tabla	tanky
spewy	sprot	steen	stoor	sucre	Swapo	table	tanna
sphex	sprue	steep	stope	Sudan	sward	taboo	tansy
spial	spule	steer	store	Sudra	sware	tabor	tante
spica	spume	stegh	stork	sudsy	swarf	tabun	tanto
spice	spumy	stein	storm	suede	swarm	Tabun	tanya
spick	spunk	stela	story	Suess	swart	tabus	tapas
spicy	spurn	stele	stoss	suety	swash	tacan	taper
spied	spurt	stelk	stoun	Sueve	swath	tacet	tapet
spiel	sputa	stell	stoup	Sufic	Swati	tache	tapia
spier	squab	stend	stour	Sufis	swats	tacho	tap-in
spies	squad	steno	stout	sugan	Swazi	tacit	tapir
spiff	squat	stent	stove	sugar	sweal	tacky	tapis
spike	squaw	stere	Strad	suing	swear	tacos	tapit
spiky	squeg	stern	stram	suint	sweat	taddy	tappa
spile	squib	stewy	strap	suite	Swede	taele	tapul
spill	squid	Steyr	straw	suity	sweep	taffy	tap up
spilt	squit	stich	stray	sukey	sweer	Taffy	tardy
spina	squiz	stick	strep	sulci	sweet	tafia	tarfa
spine	squop	Stick	strew	sulfa	swell	Tafia	targa
spink	sqush	stied	stria	sulky	swelt	tagma	taroc
spiny	srang	sties	strid	sulla	swept	tagua	taros
spire	sruti	stife	strig	sully	swift	taiga	tarot
spirt	stack	stiff	strip	sumac	swill	taiko	tarry
spiry	stade	Stift	strop	sumen	swine	Taino	tarse
spiss	stadt	Stijl	strow	sumi-e	swing	taint	tarsi
spite	staff	stilb	stroy	summa	Swing	taipo	tarse
spits	stage	stile	strum	sumph	swink	Taita	tarty

tarve	telic	thack	Thule	tipsy	tonto	toyte	trite
Taser	telly	thaft	thumb	tip-up	ton-up	trace	troat
tasse	tembe	Thais	thump	tired	tonus	track	Troic
tasso	tembo	thali	thunk	tiros	tooth	tract	troll
taste	Tembu	thana	thuya	tirve	toots	trade	tromp
tasto	Temne	thane	Thyad	Tisri	to pay	tragi	trona
tasty	Tempe	thang	thyme	tisso	topaz	traik	tronc
Tatar	tempi	thank	thymi	Titan	topee	trail	tronk
tater	tempo	tharm	thymy	titar	toper	train	troop
tatie	tempt	that's	tiang	titch	topgi	trait	trope
tatou	temse	thawy	tiara	titer	tophe	tra-la	tropo
tatty	tenas	thebe	tiare	tithe	tophi	trama	troth
taula	tench	theca	Tibet	titis	topic	tramp	trout
taunt	tendo	theek	tibia	title	topis	trank	trove
tauon	tenet	theft	tical	titre	topoi	trans	truce
taupe	tenia	thegn	ticca	titty	topos	trant	truck
tavel	tenko	theik	ticer	ti-tzu	toppy	trape	trued
Tavel	tenné	their	ticky	tizzy	topsy	trapp	truer
Tavgi	tenno	theme	tidal	tjalk	top up	traps	trues
tawer	tenny	theor	tiddy	toado	toque	tra-ra	truff
tawie	tenon	theow	tided	toady	Torah	trash	trull
tawny	Tenon	there	tidge	toast	torba	trass	truly
tawse	tenor	therm	tie-in	tober	torch	tratt	trump
taxed	tenpo	these	tie-on	today	toric	trave	trunk
taxer	tense	thesp	tie to	toddy	torii	trawl	truss
taxes	tenth	theta	tie-up	todea	torma	tread	trust
taxis	tenty	thete	tiffy	to-dos	torni	treat	truth
taxol	tepal	thewy	tifle	toe-in	torry	treed	try in
taxon	tepee	they'd	tiger	toffy	torse	treen	tryma
taxor	tepid	thick	tiggy	to-fro	torsk	trees	try me
tayra	terai	thief	tight	toga'd	torso	treet	try-on
tazza	terap	thigh	tigon	toged	torte	treey	tryst
T-bone	terce	thilk	Tigre	toggy	torus	trefa	tsama
tbsps	Terek	thill	Tigua	toghe	torve	treff	tsine
T-cell	teres	thine	tikka	togue	to see	trend	Tsing
tchin	tereu	thing	tilak	toich	toshy	tress	T-stop
teach	terga	Thing	tilde	toile	tosyl	trest	tsung
teaed	terna	think	tiled	toils	total	trete	tuart
teals	terne	thiol	tiler	toise	totem	trews	tubae
teart	terra	third	tilly	tokay	toter	treys	tubal
teary	terry	thirl	tilma	Tokay	totsy	triac	tubas
tease	terse	thoft	tilth	token	totty	triad	tubby
teasy	tesla	thole	timar	tokus	totum	trial	tubed
Tebet	TESOL	tholi	timbo	Tolai	touch	trian	tuber
techy	TESSA	thong	timer	to let	tough	trias	tucum
Tecla	testa	thorn	times	tolyl	tourn	tribe	Tudeh
teddy	testy	thorp	timid	toman	touse	trice	Tudor
teend	tetch	those	Timon	tombo	tousy	trich	tufty
teens	tetel	thous	timor	tommy	towai	trick	tuggy
teeny	Teton	thraw	Timor	Tommy	towan	tried	tuile
teeth	tetra	three	timps	tonal	to wed	trier	tuism
teety	tetty	threw	tinct	tondi	towel	tries	tukul
tee up	tetur	thrid	tinea	tondo	tower	trifa	tulip
te-hee	tevel	thrin	tined	toned	to wit	trike	tulle
Tê-hua	Tevet	thrip	tinge	tonel	towny	trill	tulsi
Teian	tewel	throb	tinny	toner	towse	trine	tuman
teind	tewit	throe	tinto	toney	towsy	Trini	tumbu
tekke	te-wit	throw	tinty	tonga	towzy	trink	tumid
Tekke	tewly	thrum	tip-in	Tonga	toxic	triol	tummy
telco	Texan	thuck	tip-it	tongs	toxin	trios	tumor
telex	Texas	thuja	tiple	tonic	toyer	tripe	tumpy
telia	Texel	thula	tippy	tonne	toyon	trist	tunal

tunas	typer	undig	upcut	vacat	venue	viva'd	wahey
tuner	typey	undub	up-dip	vaccy	Venus	vivas	wahoo
tuney	typha	undue	updry	vacky	Verel	vivat	waily
tunic	typic	undug	upend	vacua	verge	vivax	waist
tunku	typos	unfed	up-end	vagal	Verné	viver	waive
tunny	tyred	unfit	up for	vague	verse	vives	waked
tupan	Tyson	unfix	uplay	vagus	verso	vivid	waken
tupik	Ubaid	ungag	upled	vairy	verst	vixen	waker
Tupis	U-bend	ungay	upped	vakky	vertu	vizor	wakon
tuque	ubity	unget	upper	valet	verve	VJ day	waldo
turba	U-boat	ungod	uppie	valid	Vesak	Vlach	waler
turbo	Ubykh	ungot	upset	valor	Vespa	V-moth	Waler
turca	UCATT	ungum	upter	valse	vesta	V-neck	walia
turco	Uchee	unhad	uptie	value	vetch	vocab	walla
Turco	udder	unhat	up top	valva	veuve	vocal	wally
turfs	Ugric	unhid	uraei	valve	vexed	vodka	walty
turfy	uh-huh	unhip	urali	vampy	vexer	vodun	waltz
Turki	uhlan	unhit	urari	vanda	viand	vogie	wamus
turps	Uhuru	unify	urate	vaned	vibes	vogue	wanax
tusky	Uigur	union	urban	vapid	vibex	Vogul	wandy
tutee	UKAEA	unite	urbic	vapor	vicar	voice	waned
tutor	ukase	unity	urdee	vappa	Vicat	voile	waney
Tutsi	ukeke	unjam	ureal	vardo	Vichy	volar	wanga
tutti	ukemi	unkey	uredo	vardy	vicus	volet	wanky
tutty	ulcer	unkid	urent	varec	video	volta	wanle
twain	ulema	unkie	ure-ox	vario	viewy	volte	Wan-Li
Twana	ulmic	unlap	urger	varix	vigia	volva	wanly
twang	ulmin	unlaw	urial	varna	vigil	volve	wanna
twank	ulnae	unlay	uriei	varus	vigor	vomer	wanst
tweak	ulnar	unled	urine	varve	villa	vomit	wanta
tweed	ulnas	unlet	urisk	vasal	ville	votal	wanty
tweek	ultra	unlid	urnal	vased	villi	voter	wanze
tweel	ululu	unlit	urned	vasty	vinal	Votic	Warao
Tween	umbel	unman	Urnes	Vater	vinca	vouch	Waraw
tweer	umber	unmet	ursal	vates	Vinča	vowed	warby
tweet	umbos	unmix	ursid	vatic	vinea	vowel	waree
twerp	umbra	unpeg	urson	vatje	viner	vower	warth
twice	umbre	unpen	urubu	vaude	vinew	vozhd	warty
twick	umiak	unpin	urucu	vault	vinic	vraic	Washo
twill	umpty	unput	usage	vaunt	vinny	vroom	washy
twine	Unami	unray	usen't	V belt	vinyl	vrouw	wasn't
twing	Unani	unrig	use up	vealy	viola	V-sign	waspy
twink	unapt	unrip	Ushak	vease	viper	vuggy	WASPy
twiny	unarm	unsaw	usher	VE day	viral	vulgo	waste
twire	unary	unsay	usine	Vedda	vireo	vulva	wasty
twirk	unbag	unsee	us lot	Vedic	virga	vurry	watap
twirl	unban	unset	usnea	vedro	Virgo	vygie	watch
twirp	unbar	unsew	usnic	veena	virid	vying	water
twist	unbed	unsex	usnin	veery	virtu	wacke	waugh
twite	unbid	unshy	ustad	vegan	virus	wacko	waulk
twoer	unbit	unsin	usual	vegie	visa'd	wacky	waved
two-up	unbox	unson	usurp	Vehme	visas	waddy	wavel
twyer	uncap	untie	usury	veiny	visit	wader	waver
tyger	uncia	until	uteri	velar	visna	wadge	Waves
tyhee	uncle	unuse	utile	veldt	visne	wadis	wavey
tying	uncos	unweb	utrum	velic	vison	wafer	waxed
tyled	uncus	unwed	utter	velly	visor	wafty	waxen
tyler	uncut	unwet	U-turn	velum	vista	waged	waxer
typal	undam	unwig	uvala	venal	vital	wagel	way in
type A	undee	unwon	uveal	Venda	vitex	wager	way-up
type B	under	unzip	uvula	venge	vitry	Wagga	wazir
typed	undid	upbow	Uzbek	venom	vitta	wagon	Wazir

weaky	wheal	widdy	wodge	wrest	yahoo	yojan	Z-axis
weald	wheat	widen	wodgy	wrick	yajna	yoked	zazzy
Weald	wheek	widow	woe to	wride	yakka	yokel	Z-bend
we-all	wheel	width	woken	wrier	Yakut	yoker	zebec
weany	wheen	wield	Wolff	wrily	Yalie	yokes	zebra
weary	wheep	wifey	wolfy	wring	yandy	yolky	zendo
weave	wheft	wifie	wolly	wrist	yaply	Yomud	Zener
webby	whelk	Wigan	Wolof	write	yapok	yonks	zero G
weber	whelm	wiggy	wolve	wroke	yapon	you'll	zeros
Weber	whelp	wight	woman	wrong	yappy	young	zeste
wedge	where	wilco	womby	wrote	Yaqui	you're	zesty
wedgy	whewl	wildy	women	wroth	yarak	yourn	zibet
weeds	which	wilga	womyn	wrung	yauld	yours	zibib
weedy	whiff	willi	wonga	wryer	yawny	yourt	Ziehl
weeny	whift	willy	wongi	wryly	Y-axis	youse	zilch
weepy	while	Wilms	wonky	wumph	yayla	youth	Zimba
weese	whimp	wimpy	wonts	wurra	Yayoi	you've	zinco
weest	whine	Wimpy	woody	wurst	yclad	yowie	zineb
weeze	whing	wince	wooed	Wurtz	yealm	yowza	Zingg
wefty	whiny	winch	wooer	wussy	yearn	yo-yos	zingo
weigh	whirl	windy	woofy	wuzzy	yeast	ypent	zingy
weird	whirr	wined	woold	Wyatt	yechy	yrast	Zippo
weism	whish	winer	wooly	X-acto	yedda	ytter	zippy
welch	whisk	winey	woopy	X-axis	yeddo	yucca	zip-up
Welch	whisp	wingy	woosh	xebec	Yeddo	Yuchi	ziram
welly	whiss	winky	wootz	xenia	yeeow	yucky	zizel
welsh	whist	winny	woozy	xenic	Yekke	yukky	zizzy
Welsh	white	winos	wordy	xenon	yelek	Yukon	Z line
wench	White	winze	worky	Xeres	Yenan	yulan	zloty
wenge	whity	wiped	world	xeric	yenta	yuloh	zocle
wen li	whizz	wiper	wormy	Xerox	yentz	Yuman	zoeal
wenny	whole	wired	worry	Xhosa	yerba	yummy	Zohar
wersh	whomp	wirer	worse	xoana	yerra	Yunca	zoite
Wesak	whoof	wirey	worst	xylan	yerse	Yupik	zonal
westy	whoom	wirra	worth	xylem	yes-no	yuppy	zonda
wetly	whoop	wiser	wough	xylol	yesty	Yurak	zoned
wevet	whore	wisha	would	xylyl	yeuch	Yurok	zoner
whack	whorl	wisht	wound	xysma	yewen	Yuruk	zonky
whale	whort	wispy	woven	xysti	yield	yusho	zooid
whame	whory	witan	wowee	yabba	yikes	zabra	zooks
whang	whose	witch	wrack	yabby	yipes	Zahal	zoomy
whare	whoso	withe	wramp	ya boo	yoaks	zaire	zooty
wharf	whuff	withy	wrang	yaboo	yobbo	zakat	zoris
wharl	whump	witty	wrapt	yacca	yobby	zaman	zorro
whata	whush	wives	wrath	yacht	yodel	zambo	zowie
what'n	why so	Wiyot	wrawl	yacka	yogic	zamia	Z-plan
whaup	Wicca	wizen	wreak	yager	yogin	Zande	zygal
wheak	Widal	wizzo	wreck	yagna	yogis	zappy	zymin

SIX LETTERS

abacus	accrue	Adonai	agaric	alanna	all-red	amtrac	anonym
abanet	accuse	Adonic	agedly	alarum	all set	amtrak	anorak
abaser	acedia	Adonis	age gap	Alaska	all the	amulet	anoxia
abater	acetal	adoral	ageing	alated	allude	amusee	anoxic
abatis	acetic	adorer	ageism	albata	allure	amuser	answer
abator	acetyl	adream	ageist	albedo	all wet	Amytal	anthem
abbacy	achate	adrift	agency	albeit	Almain	anabas	anther
abbate	achene	adroit	agenda	albert	Almayn	anadem	antler
abbess	achkan	adsorb	age-old	albino	almery	anally	antlia
abbeys	Acholi	adsuki	aghast	Albion	almond	analog	antral
abduce	acidic	advect	aglare	albite	almost	ananas	antrum
abduct	acidly	advene	agleam	albugo	alnage	anarch	anuran
abeigh	acinar	advent	aglyph	alcade	alpaca	anatta	anuria
abelia	acinus	Advent	agnail	alcaic	alpeen	anatto	anuric
abided	ack-ack	adverb	agnate	alcove	alphin	anbury	any day
abider	ackers	advert	agnise	Aldine	alpine	anchor	anyhow
a bit of	acmite	advice	agnize	aldose	Alpine	Ancona	anyone
abject	acquit	advise	agogic	aldrin	alsike	and all	any way
abjure	acrawl	adviso	agonal	alegar	Altaic	Andean	anyway
Abkhaz	acrook	advoke	agones	alerce	altern	and how	Aonian
ablate	across	adytum	agonic	A level	aludel	Andrew	aorist
ablaut	act for	adzuki	agorot	alevin	alumna	aneath	aortal
ablaze	acting	aecial	agouti	alexia	alumni	anemia	aortas
ablest	action	aecium	agreed	alexic	alvine	anemic	aortic
ablins	active	aedile	agreer	alexin	always	anergy	aoudad
ablism	actory	Aegean	agrees	Alfvén	alwise	angary	Apache
abloom	act out	Aeolic	agrimi	algate	amadou	angely	apathy
ablush	actual	aeonic	aguila	Al-Hadj	amatol	angili	apeman
ablute	acuate	aerate	aguish	alhagi	amazed	angina	apemen
Abnaki	acuity	aerial	ahimsa	alhaji	Amazon	angled	aperçu
aboard	acumen	aerobe	a-horse	Al-Hajj	ambari	angler	A per se
aboral	acuter	aerugo	aidant	alibis	ambash	Anglic	apexes
aborti	adagio	aether	aidful	alible	ambler	Anglos	apheta
abound	Adamic	affair	aiglet	aliene	ambury	angola	aphony
abrade	adance	affect	aikido	alight	ambush	angora	aphtha
abrase	adatom	affeer	ailing	alisma	amebic	anicut	apiary
abroad	addend	affine	aimful	alkali	amends	anilic	apical
abrook	addict	affirm	air bag	alkane	amenta	animal	apices
abrupt	addled	afflux	air-bed	alkene	aments	animus	apiece
abseil	adduce	afford	Airbus	alkies	amerce	anisic	aplite
absent	adduct	affray	air-dry	alkine	amical	anisyl	aplomb
absorb	Adélie	affuse	airgun	alkyne	amidic	anklet	apnoea
absurd	adhere	Afghan	airier	all but	amidst	anlace	apodal
abulia	adhort	afield	airily	all-day	amigos	anlage	apodan
abuser	adieus	aflame	airing	allege	ammine	anlaut	apogee
abzyme	adieux	aflare	airish	allele	amnion	annals	apolar
acacia	adipic	afloat	airman	allene	amnios	annate	aporia
acajou	adject	afocal	airmen	allers	amoeba	anneal	appale
acarid	adjoin	afraid	air sac	alleys	amomum	annexe	appeal
acarus	adjure	A-frame	airway	all for	amoral	annual	appear
accede	adjust	afreet	aisled	allice	amount	annuli	append
accent	adless	afresh	aixies	allied	ampere	anodal	apples
accept	admass	afront	akasha	allies	ampler	anodic	applot
access	admire	afters	ake-ake	allium	ampule	anoint	apport
accloy	adnate	Agadic	aketon	all one	amrita	anomer	appose
accord	adnexa	agamic	akimbo	all out	amster	anomic	apsara
accost	adoing	agamid	alalia	all-pro	amtman	anomie	aquake

Aquila	arolla	aspect	athrob	auntly	Azeris	bajada	bare of
aquose	aromal	aspire	at last	au pair	azo dye	bakery	barfam
Arabic	around	asport	atlatl	aurata	azolla	baking	barfly
arabis	arouse	asquat	at most	aurate	azonal	Balaam	bargee
arable	aroynt	assail	at need	aureus	azonic	balata	barish
Arahat	arpent	assart	at odds	aurify	azygos	balboa	barite
aralia	arrack	asself	atomic	Auriga	babaco	baldie	barium
Aranda	arrand	assent	atonal	aurist	babble	baldly	barken
Aranta	arrant	assert	at once	aurora	babied	baleen	barker
Arawak	arrear	assess	atoner	aurous	babies	Balkan	barkey
arbour	arrect	assify	atonic	Aussie	babify	balk of	barkle
arbute	arrent	assign	atopic	Auster	babish	ballad	barkum
arcade	arrest	assish	at outs	Austin	Babism	ballan	barley
Arcady	arride	assist	at play	auteur	Babist	baller	barlow
arcana	arrive	assize	at rest	author	Babite	ballet	barman
arcane	arroba	assoil	atrial	autism	babool	ballot	barmen
archei	arrowy	assort	at risk	autumn	baboon	ballsy	barnet
archer	arroyo	as such	atrium	avania	babyfy	Balmer	barney
Arches	arshin	assume	Atsina	avatar	baccer	Baloch	Barnum
Archie	arsine	assure	at stud	avaunt	backed	balsam	Baroco
archil	artery	astare	at suck	avener	backen	balter	Barolo
archly	artful	astart	attach	avenge	backer	Baltic	barony
archon	artify	asteer	attack	avenue	backet	bamboo	barque
arcing	artist	astern	attain	averse	back of	banana	barras
Arctic	Arunta	as that	atteal	Avesta	back up	banate	barred
arcual	as a man	asthma	attend	aviary	backup	bandar	barrel
ardent	Asante	astony	attent	aviate	backus	bander	barren
ardour	ascend	astoop	attery	avidin	badass	bandit	barret
areola	ascent	astral	attest	avidly	badder	bandog	barrio
areole	aseity	astray	at that	avocet	baddie	banger	barrow
argali	as from	astrut	attire	avouch	bad egg	banghy	Barsac
Argand	as good	astute	at tops	avowal	badger	bangle	barter
argent	a shade	aswarm	attorn	avower	bad hat	bang on	barton
Argive	ashake	asweat	attrit	avowry	badian	bang-up	bar two
argosy	ashame	as well	attune	avoyer	Badian	banian	baryon
argued	A sharp	aswing	atwain	avulse	bad job	banish	baryta
arguer	ash-bin	aswirl	atweel	awaken	bad law	banjax	baryte
argues	ashcan	aswoon	atween	awaker	bad lot	banjos	basalt
argufy	as hell	asylum	at will	aweary	badman	banker	basely
argute	ashery	atabal	atwist	aweigh	baetyl	banket	bashaw
argyle	ashine	at a jar	atwixt	awheel	baffle	bank on	basher
aridly	ash-key	ataman	at work	awheto	bagful	bannat	basket
aright	ashlar	ataunt	atypia	awhile	bagged	banned	basnet
ariose	ashore	atavic	aubade	awhirl	bagger	banner	Basque
arioso	ashpan	ataxia	auburn	awmous	baggit	bantam	basset
arisen	ash-pit	ataxic	aucuba	awning	bag job	banter	bassus
arista	ashram	at best	audile	awoken	bagman	Bantus	basten
aristo	Ashura	at call	audion	awrong	bagmen	banyan	baster
arkite	asilid	at cost	au fait	axeman	bag-net	banzai	baston
arkose	asilus	at ease	au fond	axemen	bagnio	baobab	basuco
armada	as it is	a tempo	Augean	axenic	bag-wig	barbal	Basuto
armful	askant	at foot	augend	axiate	bahada	barbed	batata
armies	askari	at full	augite	axilla	Baha'is	barbel	batboy
arming	asking	at gaze	augury	axonal	Bahasa	barber	batchy
armlet	ask out	at hack	august	axonic	Bahutu	barbet	bateau
armory	a skull	athame	August	axopod	bailee	barbie	bather
armour	aslant	at hand	auklet	axtree	bailer	Barcoo	bathos
armpit	asleep	at heel	aumail	axunge	bailey	bardee	bating
armure	aslope	Athoan	aumbry	aye aye	bailie	bardic	batman
Arnaut	as many	at home	auncel	Aymara	bailor	bareca	batmen
arnica	asmoke	athort	aunter	azalea	Bairam	barège	batoon
aroint	as much	at host	auntie	Azande	baiter	barely	battel

batten	bedaub	behoof	berlin	biceps	birder	blowen	boiled
batter	bedaze	behove	Berlin	bicker	birdie	blower	boiler
battle	bedbug	behung	bertha	bidden	bireme	blow in	boil-up
battue	bedded	beigel	Bertha	bidder	birkie	blow on	bolden
bauble	bedder	bejant	besang	bide by	birley	blowse	boldly
bauera	bedeck	bekiss	beseem	bident	birsle	blowth	bolero
baulky	bedell	beknow	beseen	biding	bisect	blow up	bolide
bauson	bedene	belate	beside	bieldy	bishop	blowze	bollen
bawbee	bed-hop	belaud	besing	Bielid	bisket	blowzy	bollix
bawdry	bedlam	beldam	besmut	biface	bisque	bludge	bollux
bawler	bedlar	belfry	besnow	biffin	bister	bluely	Bolshy
bawley	bedpan	Belgae	besoil	bifold	bistre	bluest	bolson
bawson	bedral	Belgic	bespot	biform	bistro	bluesy	boltel
baxter	bedrid	Belgie	bestar	bigamy	bitchy	blueys	bolter
bayard	bedrop	Belial	bested	Big Ben	biting	bluggy	bolt on
bayman	bedsit	belief	bester	big bud	bitmap	bluing	bombax
bay rum	Beduin	belier	bestir	big bug	bitten	bluish	bombed
bazaar	bedull	belike	bestow	big cat	bitter	bluism	bomber
bazoom	bedust	belive	bestud	big end	biuret	blunge	bombyx
bazuco	beebee	belled	besung	biggen	bivium	blurry	bon-bon
beachy	beechy	bellow	be sure	bigger	blacky	blusht	bonded
beacon	beefer	bellum	betake	biggie	bladed	blushy	bonder
beaded	bee-fly	be long	bethel	biggin	blague	B-movie	bonduc
beadle	beef up	belong	betide	big gun	blakey	boatel	boneen
beagle	bee-gum	belord	bêtise	big lie	blamed	boater	bone up
beaked	bee man	belote	betony	big pot	blamer	boatie	bongos
beaker	been-to	belove	betook	big toe	blanch	bobbed	bonham
be a man	beeper	belted	betrap	big top	blanco	bobber	bonier
beamed	beer-up	belter	betray	bigwig	blanky	bobbin	bonify
beamer	beesty	belt up	betrim	Bihari	blasty	bobble	boning
beanie	beetle	beluga	betted	bikini	blatta	bobbly	bonism
beanos	beeves	be made	better	bilbos	blazed	bobcat	bonist
be a pup	beezer	bemata	bettor	bilker	blazer	bob-fly	bonito
beardy	befall	bemaul	beurré	billed	blazon	bob for	bon mot
bearer	befell	bemean	bevies	billet	bleach	boblet	bonnet
bear on	befile	bemire	bewail	billie	bleaky	bob-wig	bonnie
bear up	befoam	bemist	beware	billon	bleary	bocage	bonobo
beaten	befool	bemoan	beweep	billow	blebby	bodach	bonsai
beater	before	bemock	bewest	billy-o	blench	bodega	bonxie
beat in	befoul	bemoil	Bewick	bimbos	blende	bodger	bonzer
beat it	befrog	bemuse	be with	bimeby	blenny	bodgie	boo-boo
beat-up	beggar	bender	bewrap	binant	blerry	bodice	booboo
Beaumé	begged	Bengal	bewray	binary	blight	bodied	boodie
Beaune	begift	benign	beylik	binate	blimey	bodies	boodle
beauty	begild	bennet	beyond	bin-bag	blinis	bodily	boogie
beaver	begird	benumb	bezant	binder	blirry	boding	boohai
Beaver	begirt	benzil	bezoar	bindle	blirty	bodkin	boohoo
be away	begnaw	benzin	bezzle	bind up	blithe	Bodley	boojum
becall	beg off	benzol	bhajis	bin-end	blivit	Bodoni	booker
becalm	be gone	benzyl	bharal	bingee	blobby	boffin	bookie
became	begone	be on at	bhisti	binghi	blocky	Bofors	book in
becard	be good	be on to	bhoosa	bingle	blodge	bogeys	booksy
becket	begunk	bepelt	Bhotia	biniou	blonde	bog fir	book up
beckon	behalf	bepity	Bhutia	binman	bloody	bogged	boomer
beclad	behang	bepuff	biased	binmen	blooey	boggle	booted
beclip	Behari	be pulp	bibbed	binned	bloomy	bogies	bootee
beclog	behave	berate	bibber	biogas	blooth	bog oak	Boötes
become	behead	Berber	bibble	bionic	blotch	bog off	boozed
becurl	beheld	bereft	bibira	biopic	blotto	bogong	boozer
bedaff	behest	Bergan	biblic	biopsy	blotty	bog ore	bo-peep
bedark	behind	Bergen	biblus	biotic	blouse	Bohora	bopped
bedash	behold	berime	bicarb	biotin	blowed	bohunk	

bopper	bow out	bridge	budget	burden	buttie	caddie	camois
borage	bow-saw	bridle	budgie	bureau	butt in	caddis	camper
borane	bowsaw	briery	budlet	burgee	buttle	caddle	cample
borate	bowser	brieve	buffed	burger	button	caddow	campoo
bordar	bow tie	bright	buffel	burgle	butyne	cadent	campus
bordel	bow-wow	brigue	buffer	burgoo	buying	cadger	Canaan
border	bowyer	brimmy	buffet	burgul	buy off	caecal	Canada
boreal	boxcar	briony	buffle	burhel	buyout	caecum	canapé
borean	boxful	brisky	buffos	burial	buy out	Caelum	canard
Boreas	box-gum	britch	bugged	Buriat	buyout	Caesar	canary
boreen	boxier	Briton	bugger	buried	buzzer	cafard	canaut
boride	boxing	broach	bugler	burier	by-blow	caffle	cancan
boring	box pew	broché	buglet	buries	bye-bye	Caffre	cancel
borish	boyish	brogan	bugong	burlap	bye-law	cafila	cancer
borrel	boyism	brogue	bukshi	burler	by fits	caftan	candid
borrow	bracer	broken	bulbar	burley	by-form	cagier	candle
borsch	bracky	broker	bulbed	Burley	bygone	cagily	canful
borzoi	brahma	brolga	bulbil	Burman	by half	cagmag	cangia
bosbok	Brahma	brolly	bulbul	burned	by hand	cahoot	cangue
bosher	Brahmi	bromic	bulgar	burner	by Jove	cahoun	canine
bosker	Brahmo	bronco	Bulgar	burnet	by land	caiman	caning
bosket	Brahui	bronze	bulgur	burn in	by-lane	caique	canker
bosomy	brainy	bronzy	bulked	burn up	byline	cajang	canned
bosset	braird	brooch	bulker	bur oak	by much	cajole	cannel
Boston	braise	broody	bulkin	burpee	by name	calalu	canner
botany	branch	broomy	bulk up	burras	byname	calash	cannon
Botany	brandy	broose	buller	burros	bypass	calcar	cannot
botchy	branks	brothy	bullet	burrow	bypast	calces	canoed
botfly	branle	brough	bullsh	bursae	bypath	calcic	canoes
bother	branny	browed	bumbag	bursal	byplay	calean	canola
bothie	brashy	browis	bum-bee	bursar	by post	calice	canopy
botony	brassy	browny	bumble	bursas	byrlaw	calico	Cantab
bo tree	bratty	browse	bumboy	burton	byrnie	caliph	cantal
bottle	braver	browst	bumkin	Buryat	by road	calker	Cantal
bottom	bravos	browsy	bummed	busbar	byroad	calkin	cantar
boucan	brawly	brucia	bummel	busboy	by-room	callee	canter
bouclé	brawny	bruise	bummer	bushed	by rote	caller	canthi
boudin	brayer	brumal	bumper	bushel	by rule	callet	cantle
bouget	brazen	brumby	bump up	busher	byssal	call in	cantly
bought	brazil	Brummy	bum rap	bushie	byssus	call on	canton
bougie	Brazil	brunch	bunchy	bushwa	by tale	calloo	cantor
boules	breach	brunet	buncos	busier	by-talk	callop	cantos
boulle	breast	brushy	bunder	busily	by-time	callow	Canuck
bounce	breath	brutal	bundle	busker	by-walk	call up	canvas
bouncy	breech	Brutus	bundly	buskin	by wire	callus	canyon
bounty	breedy	bryony	bungee	busman	byword	calmer	canzon
bourne	breeks	bubble	bung-ho	busmen	by-work	calmly	capful
bourse	breeze	bubbly	bungle	bussed	byzant	calory	capias
bouton	breezy	buboes	bunion	busses	cabala	calpac	capite
bovate	bregma	buccal	bunker	busted	Cabala	calque	Caplet
bovine	Brehon	buccan	bunkie	bustee	cabana	caltha	caplin
Bovril	Breton	buccra	bunkum	buster	cabane	calved	capote
bovver	brevet	bucked	bunk-up	bustle	cabbie	calver	capped
bow-arm	brevit	bucker	Bunsen	bust up	cabler	calves	capper
bowery	brewer	bucket	buntal	busway	cablet	camail	capric
bowfin	brewis	buckie	bunter	but and	cabman	camber	caprid
bowing	brew up	buckle	Bunter	butane	cabmen	cambia	Capris
bowler	Briard	buckra	bunton	butene	cacaos	cameos	capryl
bowman	bribee	budded	bunyip	but for	cachet	camera	capsid
bowmen	briber	Buddha	buppie	butler	cachou	camion	captor
bow-net	bricky	buddle	burble	but one	cackle	camise	carafe
bow oar	bridal	budger	burbot	butter	cactus	camlet	carama

carapa	cassab	celled	chappy	chicly	chosen	citrus	*cloqué*
carbon	cassia	cellos	charas	chided	chough	cityfy	closed
carboy	cassie	Celtic	charge	chider	chouse	civics	closen
cardan	cassis	cembra	chargé	chield	chowry	civism	closer
carder	caster	cement	charka	chigoe	chowse	claggy	closet
cardia	castle	ceneme	Charon	chi-ike	chrism	clammy	clothe
cardie	cast on	censer	charro	chikan	Christ	clamor	cloths
careen	castor	censor	charry	childe	chroma	clanny	clotty
career	cast up	census	charta	Childe	chrome	claque	cloudy
care of	casual	cental	chaser	chiles	chromo	claret	clough
caress	catalo	center	Chasid	chilli	chubby	clarty	cloven
carfax	catchy	centos	chasmy	chilly	chucky	classy	clover
carfox	catena	centra	*chasse*	chimer	chuddy	clatch	Clovis
carful	catery	centre	chassé	chinar	chuffy	clause	clubby
cargos	catgut	centum	chaste	chinch	chukar	clavel	clucky
carhop	Cathar	cerate	chatty	Chinee	chukka	claver	clue in
Carian	Cathay	cercal	chat up	chinky	chumar	clavis	cluing
caribe	cat-ice	cercus	chauki	Chinky	chummy	clavus	clumps
caries	cation	cereal	chaung	chinny	chum up	clawed	clumpy
carina	catkin	cereus	chaunt	chinos	chunam	clawer	clumse
caring	cat-lap	ceriph	chavel	chinse	chunky	clayen	clumsy
Carley	catnap	cerise	chawer	chintz	church	clayey	clunch
carman	catnip	cerite	chaw up	chin up	churel	cleach	clunky
carnac	catsup	cerium	chazan	chip in	chutty	cleave	clutch
carnal	catted	cermet	Chazar	chippy	chylde	cledge	clypei
carnet	cattle	ceroon	cheapo	chiral	chypre	cledgy	coachy
carney	Cauchy	cerous	checky	chi-rho	cicada	cleeve	coaita
Carnic	caucus	certes	cheder	chirpy	cicala	clench	coaler
carnie	caudal	certie	cheeky	chisel	cicely	cleome	coarse
Carnot	caudex	cerule	cheepy	chital	cicuta	clergy	coated
caroon	caudle	ceruse	cheero	chitin	cidery	cleric	coatee
carpal	caught	cervid	cheers	chiton	cierge	clerid	coatis
carpel	caules	cervix	cheery	chitty	cigala	cletch	coaxer
carper	caulis	Cesare	cheese	chiule	cigary	cleuch	cobalt
carpet	Caurus	cesium	cheesy	chivvy	cilery	clever	cobber
carpus	causal	cesser	chelae	choana	cilice	clevis	cobble
carrel	causer	cestus	chelas	choate	cilium	cliche	cobbly
carrom	causey	cetane	chemic	chocho	cimbia	cliché	cobbra
carrot	cautel	Ceylon	chemmy	chocka	cinder	clicky	cobnut
carsey	cauter	cha-cha	chenar	choice	cinema	client	Coburg
cartel	cavass	chacma	cheque	choise	cingle	cliffy	cobweb
carter	caveat	chadar	chequy	choker	cinque	clifty	coccal
cartle	cave in	Chadic	cherry	chokey	cipher	climax	coccid
carton	cavern	chador	cherty	chokos	cippus	clinal	coccus
carval	caviar	chaeta	cherub	chokra	circar	clinch	coccyx
carvel	cavies	chafer	chesil	choler	circle	clingy	Cochin
carven	caving	chaffy	chesty	cholic	circus	clinic	cockal
carver	cavity	chagal	chetty	cholis	cirque	clinty	cocker
Carver	cavort	chagan	chevet	cholla	cirrus	clip-on	Cocker
carzey	cayman	Chagga	chevin	chomer	cisoid	clippy	cocket
casbah	Cayuga	chaise	chevra	choola	cistus	clique	cockle
casein	Cayuse	chakra	chèvre	choose	citess	clitch	cockly
casern	ceboid	chalan	chewer	choosy	cither	clitic	cocksy
cashel	cecity	chalet	chew on	chopin	citied	clivia	cock up
cashew	cedarn	chalky	chiack	choppy	cities	cloaca	cocoas
cash in	cedent	chalon	chiaus	chop up	citify	cloche	cocoon
cash up	cedrat	chamar	chibol	choral	citole	cloddy	codded
casing	Ceefax	chance	chic-er	chorda	citral	cloggy	codder
casino	Cefaut	chancy	chicha	chorea	citric	clonal	coddle
casket	celery	change	chichi	choree	citril	clonic	codger
Caslon	celiac	chanty	chi-chi	choric	citrin	clonus	codify
casque	cellar	chapel	chicle	chorus	citron	cloose	codlin

cod war	comfit	coolie	corves	cowman	creeve	cruxes	cupule
coelom	Comice	cool it	corvid	cowmen	creish	cry aim	curacy
coerce	coming	coolly	Corvus	co-work	cremor	crying	curare
coeval	comity	coolth	corymb	cow-pad	crenel	cry off	curate
coffee	commie	cooper	coryza	cow-pat	creole	crypta	curbed
coffer	Commie	cooter	cosher	cowpea	Creole	crypto	curber
coffin	commis	cootie	cosier	cow pen	crêpey	C sharp	curded
coffle	commit	copalm	cosily	cowpox	crépon	C sol fa	curdle
cogent	commix	copeck	cosine	cowrie	cresol	cuatro	curdly
cogged	common	copied	cosmea	cow-run	cresyl	cubage	cure of
cogger	commot	copier	cosmic	cowson	Cretan	cubbed	curfew
coggie	comose	copies	cosmos	coydog	cretic	cubica	curial
coggle	comous	coping	cosset	coyest	cretin	cubism	Curial
coggly	compel	copita	cossid	coyish	crewel	cubist	curing
cogito	comply	cop out	cossie	coynye	cribos	cuboid	curios
cognac	compos	copped	costae	coyote	crikey	cuckoo	curist
co-head	Comsat	copper	costal	coypus	crimes	cucujo	curium
coheir	concha	copple	co-star	cozzie	crimpy	cudden	curled
cohere	conche	copter	costed	crabby	crinal	cuddie	curler
cohorn	conchs	Coptic	coster	cracky	crined	cuddle	curlew
cohort	conchy	copula	costly	cradle	crinet	cuddly	curl up
cohosh	concur	coquet	costus	crafty	cringe	cudgel	curple
cohune	condom	corban	coteau	craggy	cripes	cue-bid	cursed
coiffé	condor	corbel	cotext	crakow	crises	cueing	curser
coiled	condos	corbie	cotise	crambo	crisis	cueist	cursor
coiner	coneys	corbin	cotman	cram in	crispy	cue-owl	cursus
coin-op	confab	cordax	cotset	crampy	crista	cuesta	curtal
coital	confer	corded	cottar	crance	critic	cuffed	curtly
coitus	confix	corder	cotted	cranch	croaky	Cuffee	curtsy
coldly	conga'd	cordia	cotter	crania	croche	cuffer	curule
coleta	congas	cordon	cottid	cranky	crocin	cuffin	curved
coleus	congee	coreal	cotton	cranny	crocus	cuisse	curvet
coleys	conger	corgis	cotwal	crants	croove	cuiter	cuscus
collar	congou	corial	coucal	crappy	croppy	cuivré	cushat
collet	conies	corium	couché	crases	crop up	culbut	cushaw
collie	coning	corked	couchy	crasis	crosse	Culdee	cusped
collop	conium	corker	cougar	cratch	crotal	culler	cuspid
collow	conjee	corkir	coulée	crater	crotch	cullet	cuspis
Colmar	conker	cornea	coulie	craton	crotey	cullis	cussed
colony	conman	corned	coulis	cravat	croton	culmen	custom
coloss	conmen	cornel	county	craven	Croton	cultch	custos
colour	conned	corner	coupee	craver	crouch	cultic	cutcha
colter	conner	cornet	coupla	crawly	croupy	cultus	cutely
colugo	connex	cornua	couple	crayer	crouse	culver	cutesy
column	conoid	cornus	coupon	crayon	crowdy	cumber	cut ice
colure	con-rod	corody	courge	crazed	crowed	cumbia	cutler
co-mate	consol	corona	course	crazia	cruces	cumble	cutlet
combat	consul	Corona	cousin	creagh	cruche	cumbly	cut-off
combed	contra	corozo	coutel	creaky	cruddy	cumene	cut-out
comber	conure	corpse	couter	creamy	cruise	cummer	cutted
combie	convex	corpsy	coutil	crease	cruive	cummin	cuttee
combos	convey	corpus	co-vary	creasy	crumbs	cumuli	cutter
come at	convoy	corral	covent	create	crumby	cuneal	cuttle
come by	conyza	corrie	covert	creave	crumen	cunjee	cuttoe
comedo	coobah	corsac	covess	crèche	crummy	cunjie	cyanic
comedy	cooeed	corsak	coveys	credal	crunch	cunner	cyanin
come in	cooees	corser	coving	credit	crural	cupful	cyathi
comely	cookee	corset	cowage	credos	crusie	cupola	cyborg
come of	cooker	Cortes	coward	creeky	Crusoe	cupped	cyclas
come on	cookie	cortex	cowboy	creepy	crusta	cupper	cycler
come to	cook up	corvée	cowish	creese	crusty	cupric	cyclic
come up	cooler	corver	cowled	creesh	crutch	cup-tie	cyclin

Cyclon
Cyclop
cyclus
cygnet
Cygnus
cymbal
cymene
cymoid
cymose
Cymric
cynism
cyphel
cypher
cy pres
cypris
cystic
cystid
cytase
cytoid
dabbed
dabber
dabble
daboia
da capo
Dacian
dacite
dacker
dacoit
Dacron
dactyl
dadder
daddle
daedal
daemon
daffle
daftie
daftly
dag-boy
dagesh
dagged
dagger
daggle
daggly
dagoba
dagoes
dahlia
daidle
daiker
daimio
daimon
daimyo
dainty
dakhma
Dakota
dalasi
dalles
dalton
damage
Damara
damask
dammar
dammed

dammer
dammit
damned
damner
damnum
dampen
damper
damply
damsel
damson
danaid
dancer
dander
Dandie
dandle
danger
dangle
dangly
Daniel
Danish
Danism
Danite
Danzig
daphne
dapped
dapper
dapple
Dardan
Dardic
daring
darken
darkey
darkie
darkle
darkly
darned
darnel
darner
daroga
darter
dartle
dartos
dartre
Darwin
dashed
dasher
dassen
dassie
dastur
datary
datcha
dating
dation
Datisi
dative
datura
dauber
dauncy
Davies
dawdle
dawing

day-bed
daybed
day-boy
day-fly
Day-Glo
day off
day out
day owl
dazzle
deacon
deaden
deadly
dead on
deafen
deafly
dealer
deaner
dearie
dearly
dear me
dearth
deasil
deathy
debark
debase
debate
debeak
debile
deblur
debord
debris
debtee
debtor
debunk
decade
decaff
decamp
decane
decani
decant
deceit
decent
decern
Decian
decide
decile
decima
decked
decker
deckie
deckle
decoct
decode
decoke
decore
decree
decury
dedans
deduce
deduct
deejay
deemer

deener
deepen
deepie
deeply
deeshy
deface
defalk
defame
defang
defeat
defect
defend
defial
defied
defier
defies
defile
define
deflex
deform
defray
deftly
defuse
dégagé
degras
degree
degust
dehair
dehorn
dehort
de-icer
deific
deisal
deixis
deja vu
déjà vu
deject
de jure
dekink
dekkos
delate
delect
delete
Delian
delict
delire
delish
delope
Delphi
delude
deluge
de luxe
delver
demand
demark
demean
dement
demise
demiss
demist
démodé
demote

demure
denary
denest
dengue
denial
denied
denier
denies
denned
dennet
denote
depark
depart
depend
deperm
depict
deploy
depone
deport
depose
depure
depute
deputy
derail
derate
deride
derive
dermal
dermic
dermis
derout
derris
desalt
descry
deseed
desert
design
desire
desist
desize
desman
desmid
desorb
despan
despin
despot
despun
des res
detach
detail
detain
detant
detect
detent

détenu
detest
detour
de trop
Dettol
detune
deuced
deutan
devall
devast
devein
devest
device
devise
devoid
devoir
devote
devour
devout
Dewali
dewani
dewbow
dew-cup
dewier
dewily
De-Witt
dewlap
deworm
dew-ret
dexter
Dexter
dhaman
dhamma
dhania
dharma
dharna
Dharuk
dhobey
dhobis
dholak
dholuk
dhoney
dhotis
dhurna
dhurra
dhyana
diacid
diadem
diadic
dialer
dialog
dial up
diaper
diapir
diarch
diatom
dibbed
dibber
dibble
dibbuk
dicast
dicier

dicken
dicker
dickey
dickin
dictum
didder
diddle
didoes
didric
die off
die out
diesel
diesis
dieted
dieter
dietic
differ
digamy
digest
digger
diglot
dig out
digram
digyny
diiamb
dik-dik
dikkop
diktat
dilate
dildos
dilogy
dilute
dimble
dimity
dimmed
dimmer
dim out
dimple
dimply
dimpsy
dim sim
dim sum
dim-wit
dimwit
din-din
dindle
dinero
dinful
dinger
dinges
dinghy
dingle
dingly
dingos
dingus
dining
dinkel
dinkey
dinkie
dinkly
dinkum
dinned

dinner
diodon
dioecy
diosma
diotic
dioxan
dioxin
diplex
diploe
dip-net
dipody
dipole
dip out
dipped
dip pen
dipper
dipsas
dipsos
diquat
dirdum
direct
direly
dirham
dirndl
disard
disarm
disbar
disbud
discal
discos
discus
disdar
disher
dish up
dismal
disman
dismay
disome
disorb
disour
disown
dispel
dissed
distad
distal
distil
disuse
diswig
ditchy
dither
ditone
dittay
dittos
Divali
dive in
divers
divert
divest
divide
divine
diving
Diwali

diwani	doline	dorsel	draunt	dry-ski	durant	ectype	eldern
djibba	dolium	dorser	drawee	dry way	durbar	eczema	eldest
D-layer	dollar	Dorset	drawer	duadic	duress	Eddaic	elding
doable	dollop	dorsum	draw in	dually	durgah	eddied	elegit
do a guy	dolman	dorter	drawly	dubash	Durham	eddies	elenge
do alms	dolmas	dosage	draw on	dubbed	durian	eddish	eleven
doater	dolmen	do-se-do	draw up	dubber	during	eddoes	elevon
do a ton	dolose	do-si-do	dreamt	dubbin	durned	Edenic	elfish
do away	dolour	dossal	dreamy	ducape	durrie	edge-on	elicit
dobbed	dolous	dossel	dreary	ducker	durwan	edgier	elisor
dobber	domain	dosser	dredge	duckie	durzis	edgily	elixir
dobbie	doment	dossil	dreepy	duck up	dusken	edging	El Niño
dobbin	domett	dotage	dreggy	ductor	duskly	edible	elodea
dobson	domina	dotard	dreich	ductus	dustak	Edipal	Elohim
Doccia	domine	dotate	dreigh	dudeen	duster	edited	eloign
docent	domino	do time	drench	dudess	dust-up	editor	eloper
Docete	domite	dotish	dressy	dudish	Dutchy	Edward	Elster
docile	donary	dotkin	dretch	dueful	dutied	eejity	eluant
docity	donate	dot-map	driech	duello	duties	eelery	eluate
docken	dongle	dotted	driegh	duende	duyker	Eemian	eluder
docker	donjon	dottel	driest	duenna	dwarfs	eerier	eluent
docket	donkey	dotter	drieth	duetto	dwarfy	eerily	elvish
doctor	donned	dottle	drifty	duffel	dweeby	efface	elytra
dodder	donnée	douane	drinky	duffer	dyadic	effect	embale
doddie	donner	double	drippy	duffle	dybbuk	effeir	emball
doddle	donnot	doubly	drivel	duff up	dyeing	effete	embalm
dodgem	donsie	doucet	driven	dufter	dynamo	effigy	embank
Dodgem	donzel	douche	driver	dugong	dynast	effing	embark
dodger	doocot	doucin	drogue	dugout	dynode	efflux	embind
dodkin	doodad	dought	drolly	duiker	dyvour	efform	emblem
dodman	doodah	doughy	dromic	duk-duk	eaglet	effort	emblic
dodoes	doodle	dourly	dromoi	dukely	earful	effund	embody
do down	doofer	dourra	dromos	dukery	earing	effuse	emboli
doesn't	Doolan	douser	droner	dulcet	ear-lap	efreet	emboly
doffer	doolie	douter	drongo	dulcin	earlet	EFTPOS	emboss
dogana	doomer	dovish	drooby	dumble	earner	egally	embrue
dogate	doonga	do-well	droopy	dumbly	earthy	Egeria	embrya
dog box	doored	do with	drop in	dumbos	earwax	egesta	embryo
dogdom	doovah	dowlas	drop it	dumb ox	earwig	egg-box	emceed
dog-ear	do over	downed	drop on	dumdum	ease in	eggcup	emcees
dog-end	doo-wop	downer	droppy	dum-dum	easier	eggery	em dash
dog-fly	doozer	down to	dropsy	dummel	easily	eggier	emerge
dog-fox	doozie	dowser	drop to	dumper	eassel	eggler	emerse
dogged	dopant	dowset	drossy	dump on	easter	egg-nog	emesis
dogger	dopier	doxies	drouth	dumpty	Easter	egoism	emetic
doggie	dopily	doyley	drover	dun-bar	easy on	egoist	emigre
dog-leg	Dopper	dozier	drowse	Dundee	eatage	egoity	émigré
dogleg	doppie	dozily	drowsy	dunder	eatery	egress	emigré
dogman	dorado	dozzle	drudge	dunite	eathly	eident	emodin
dogmen	dor-bee	drabby	druggy	dunker	eating	eidola	emoter
dog-nap	dor-bug	drably	drumly	Dunker	eat off	eighth	empale
do-good	Dorcas	drachm	drummy	dunlin	eat out	eighty	empery
do gree	dor-fly	draffy	drum up	Dunlop	eaving	either	empest
Dogrib	Dorian	drafty	drupel	dunned	écarté	ejecta	empire
dog tag	dories	dragée	dry-bob	dunner	echini	eke out	employ
doiled	Dorise	draggy	dry fly	dunter	echium	ektene	emptin
doited	Dorism	drag in	dry ice	duomos	echoer	elance	Empusa
do kief	Dorize	dragon	drying	dupery	echoes	elapid	em quad
dolcan	dormer	drag up	dryish	dupion	echoey	elapse	em rule
dolent	dormie	Dralon	dry out	duplet	echoic	elater	emu-bob
doless	dorsad	draper	dry rot	duplex	éclair	E-layer	emulge
dolina	dorsal	dratch	dry run	durain	ectene	elchee	enable

enamel	enough	epoché	étrier	exogen	faffle	fasola	Fenian
enamor	en quad	eponym	etymon	exoner	fag end	fasten	fenman
enarch	enrage	epopee	Euboic	exonic	fagged	faster	fennec
en bloc	enrank	epulis	euchre	exonym	fagger	fastly	fennel
encage	enrapt	equant	Euclid	exopod	faggot	fat cat	fenner
encamp	enrich	equate	eucone	exotic	fag hag	fat hen	ferash
encase	enring	equine	Eudist	expand	fagoty	father	ferfel
encash	enrobe	equity	eulogy	expect	failed	fathom	ferial
encave	enroot	eraser	eunomy	expede	failer	Fatiha	ferine
encell	en rule	erbium	eunuch	expend	faille	fatism	ferity
encode	enseal	erenow	eureka	expert	fainly	fatist	ferlie
encoop	enseam	ere yet	Euro-MP	expire	faints	fatted	Fermat
encore	enserf	Erinys	Europe	expiry	fainty	fatten	fermis
encyst	ensete	erlang	eutaxy	expone	fairly	fatter	ferrel
end-all	ensign	ermine	evader	export	fajita	faucal	Ferrel
en dash	ensile	Erotes	evanid	expose	fakery	fauces	ferret
endear	ensoul	erotic	eve-jar	exposé	falces	faucet	ferric
ending	ensued	errand	even as	ex post	falcon	faulty	ferula
endite	ensuer	errant	evener	exsect	fal-lal	faunal	ferule
endive	ensues	errata	evenly	exsert	fallen	faunas	fervid
end-man	ensure	ersatz	even so	extant	faller	fausen	fervor
endrin	entail	erucic	even up	extend	fall in	fautor	Fesapo
end run	entame	eryngo	everly	extent	fall on	favela	fescue
Endura	entera	Esalen	ever so	extern	Fallot	favism	festal
endure	entice	escape	evilly	extine	fallow	favour	fester
enduro	entify	escarp	evince	extirp	fall to	fawner	fetial
enemas	entire	eschar	Evipan	extort	falset	fawn on	fetish
energy	entity	eschew	evoker	extund	falter	fealty	fetter
enerve	entoil	escort	evolve	ex-voto	famble	feared	fettle
enface	entomb	escrod	evulse	eye-cup	family	fearer	feudal
en fête	entone	escrow	evzone	eyecup	famine	featly	feuing
enfile	entrap	escudo	Evzone	eyeful	famish	fecial	fewmet
enfold	entrée	Eskies	ewerer	eyeing	famose	fecket	fewter
engage	enurny	Eskimo	exacta	eyelet	famous	feckly	fezzed
engagé	enveil	espial	examen	eyelid	famuli	fecula	fezzes
engaol	envein	espied	ex ante	eye-pit	fandom	fecund	fiacre
engild	envied	espies	exarch	Eyetie	fanega	fedora	fiancé
engine	envier	esprit	excamb	Fabian	fanged	feeble	fiants
engird	envies	essart	excave	fabism	fangle	feebly	fiasco
engirt	enwall	Essene	exceed	fabled	fan-jet	feeder	fibbed
englut	enwind	essive	except	fabler	fanned	feed up	fibber
englyn	enwomb	essoin	excess	Fablon	fanner	feeler	fibred
engore	enwood	estate	excide	fabric	fantad	feerie	fibril
engram	enwrap	esteem	excise	facade	fan-tan	fegary	fibrin
engulf	enzyme	estral	excite	façade	Fantis	feijoa	fibros
enhalo	Eocene	estray	excuse	facete	fantod	Feinne	fibula
enigma	eolian	estrin	excyst	facial	faquir	feints	fiches
enisle	Eolian	etalon	exedra	facies	farcer	feirie	fickle
enjail	eolith	etaoin	exempt	facile	far cry	feisty	fickly
enjamb	Eonism	etcher	exequy	facing	farded	feline	fiddle
enjoin	Eonist	eterne	exergy	factor	fardel	fellah	fiddly
enknot	eparch	ethane	Exeter	factum	farina	feller	fidfad
enlace	epaule	ethene	exeunt	facula	faring	felloe	fidget
enlink	épéist	ethics	exhale	faculd	farman	fellow	fie-fie
enlist	ephebe	ethide	exhort	facund	farmer	felony	fierce
enlock	ephyra	ethine	exhume	faddle	far-off	felsic	fiesta
enmesh	epical	Ethiop	exilic	fade-in	far out	felter	Figaro
enmity	epilog	ethnic	exited	fading	farrow	female	figged
ennead	epimer	ethrog	exitus	faecal	farter	femora	fighty
enolic	epipod	ethyne	Exmoor	faeces	fasces	femurs	figura
enosis	Epirot	etoile	Exocet	Faenza	fascet	fencer	figure
enotic	epizoa	etrier	exodus	faerie	fascia	fender	Fijian

filaze	fitted	floose	folate	fortes	frisée	funker	galega
filial	fitten	floozy	folder	fortis	Frisic	funkia	galena
filing	fitter	floppy	fold in	forwhy	frisky	funnel	Galibi
filled	fitton	florae	fold up	fossae	frivel	fun run	galiot
filler	fixate	floral	foliar	fossed	frivol	furcal	galium
fillet	fixing	floras	folios	fossil	frizzy	furfur	galled
fill in	fixity	floret	foliot	fossor	Fröbel	furied	gallet
fillip	fixure	florid	folium	foster	froggy	furies	galley
fillis	fizgig	florin	folkie	fother	froise	furner	gallic
fill-up	fizzer	flossy	folksy	fought	frolic	furore	Gallic
filmic	fizzle	flotel	folles	Foulah	frosty	furphy	Gallio
filter	flabby	floury	follis	foully	frothy	furred	gallon
filthy	fladge	flower	follow	foul-up	frough	furrin	gallop
fimble	flaggy	flow-on	Folsom	fourth	froust	furrow	gallus
finale	flagon	fluent	foment	fouter	frowst	fusain	Galois
finder	flaked	fluffy	fondle	foutre	frowsy	fusile	galoot
find up	flaker	fluked	fondly	foveae	frowzy	fusion	galore
finely	flambé	flunky	fondue	foveal	frozen	fusoid	galosh
finery	flamen	flurry	fonduk	fowler	frugal	fusser	galpon
fine up	flamer	flushy	fontal	foxery	fruity	fustet	Galton
finger	flanch	fluted	foodie	fox-fur	frumpy	fustic	gamash
finial	flange	fluter	foo-foo	foxier	frushy	futile	gambit
finick	flappy	flutey	footed	foxily	frusta	futtah	gamble
finify	flaser	fly ash	footer	foxing	frutex	future	gambol
fining	flashy	fly boy	footie	Foxite	frypan	fu yung	gamely
finish	flatly	fly cop	foot it	fox-red	fry-pan	fuzzle	gamete
finite	flatty	flyest	footle	fracas	F sharp	fylfot	gamgee
finity	flatus	fly-fan	foozle	fraena	fucate	gabbed	gamier
finkle	flaunt	flying	forage	fraise	fucker	gabber	gamily
finlet	flavin	flyman	for aye	framed	fuck up	gabble	gamine
finnan	flavor	fly-net	forbad	framer	fucoid	gabbro	gaming
finned	flawed	fly-nut	forbid	*frappé*	fuddle	gabion	gammer
finner	flaxen	fly off	forbye	fratch	fuffle	gabled	gammon
Finnic	flayer	fly out	forced	frater	fugato	gablet	gamont
finnip	F-layer	fly-rod	forcer	fratry	fugged	Gaboon	ganbei
finnoc	*flèche*	flysch	foredo	Frauen	fuggle	gadbee	gander
finnow	fledge	flyter	forego	fraxin	fugued	gadded	gangan
fin-ray	fledgy	fly-tip	forest	frazil	fugues	gadder	ganger
Finsen	fleece	flyway	forfex	freaky	führer	gadfly	gangle
finsko	fleech	foamed	for fun	freath	Fulani	gadget	gangly
fiorin	fleecy	fobbed	forger	freely	fulcra	gadman	gangue
fipple	flench	fob off	forget	freest	fulfil	gadoid	gang up
fire up	flense	fo'c'sle	forgot	free up	fulgid	Gaelic	gannet
firing	fleshy	fo'c's'le	forint	freeze	fulgor	gaffer	ganoid
firker	fletch	fodder	forked	freezy	Fulham	gaffle	ganoin
firkin	fleury	fodgel	forker	French	fuller	gagaku	gansel
firlot	flewed	foeman	formal	frenum	full up	gag-bit	gansey
firman	flewet	foetal	format	frenzy	fulmar	gagged	gantry
firmly	flexed	foetid	formée	fresco	fulvid	gagger	gaoler
fiscal	flexor	foetor	former	fretty	fulyie	gaggie	gaping
fiscus	flight	foetus	formic	friary	fumado	gaggle	gapped
fisgig	flimsy	fog-bow	formol	fribby	fumage	gag man	garage
fisher	flinch	fog-dog	formyl	Friday	fumble	gaiety	Garand
fishes	flinty	fogeys	fornix	fridge	fumish	gaijin	garble
fissle	flirty	fogged	for now	friend	fumose	gainer	*garçon*
fisted	flisky	fogger	forold	frieze	fumous	gainly	garden
fistic	flitch	fogies	for one	friezy	fundal	gainst	gardie
fistle	floaty	fogman	forpet	fright	fundus	gaited	garget
fitché	flocci	fogram	forpit	frigid	funest	gaiter	gargle
fitchy	flocht	foible	forrel	frilly	fungal	galago	garish
fitful	flocky	foison	forrit	fringe	fungic	galaxy	garled
fit out	floody	foisty	forset	fringy	fungus	galeae	garlic

garner	gee-hup	gherao	glacis	gneeve	goniff	goyish	Griqua
garnet	geeing	ghetto	gladly	gneiss	gonion	grabby	grisly
Garnet	geelum	ghibli	glaire	gnomic	gonoph	graben	grison
garret	geezer	Ghilji	glairy	gnomon	goober	graced	gritty
garron	geggie	gholam	glaive	gnosis	gooder	gradal	grivet
garrya	geisha	ghoont	glance	goalie	goodie	grade A	Grizel
garter	gelada	ghosty	glassy	goanna	goodly	graded	groats
garuda	gelate	ghurry	glaver	goatee	good-oh	grader	Gro-bag
gasbag	gelder	*giaour*	glazed	go at it	good on	gradin	grocer
Gascon	gelled	gibber	glazen	go away	goofer	gradus	groggy
gas gun	Gemara	gibbet	glazer	go awry	goof-up	Graham	groomy
gashed	Gemini	gibbon	gleamy	go back	goofus	graine	groose
gashly	gemmae	gibier	glease	go bail	googly	grainy	groove
gasify	gemman	giblet	gledge	go bang	googol	graith	groovy
gasket	gemmed	Gibson	gleety	gobang	goo-goo	gramma	groper
gaskin	gemmen	giddap	glegly	gobbed	gooier	gramme	groser
gaslit	gemmer	giddup	gleyde	gobbet	gooily	Grammy	groset
gasman	gender	Gideon	gleyed	gobble	goolie	grampy	grossy
gasmen	geneat	gidgee	glibly	gobdaw	goonda	grange	grotto
gas oil	genera	gifted	glider	gobies	gooney	granma	grotty
gasper	geneva	giftie	glioma	gobiid	gooroo	granny	grouch
gassed	Geneva	gigged	glissé	goblet	gooses	Granth	ground
gasser	genial	giggle	glitch	goblin	goosey	granum	grouse
gasses	Genist	giggly	glitzy	gobony	go over	grapey	grouty
gaster	genius	giglet	global	go bung	gopher	graphy	groved
gateau	genned	gigman	globed	go bush	go phut	grappa	grovel
gather	gennel	gigolo	globin	go bust	gopura	grassy	grovet
Gathic	gennet	gilded	globus	go-cart	Gordon	grater	growan
gating	Genoan	gilder	glomus	God-box	gorged	gratin	grower
gatten	genome	gilgai	gloomy	goddam	gorger	gratis	growly
gatter	gentes	gilguy	gloopy	godkin	gorget	graved	grow on
gauche	gentil	gilled	gloppy	godlet	Gorgio	gravel	growth
gaucho	gentle	giller	gloria	God-man	gorgon	graven	grow up
gauger	gently	gillie	Gloria	go down	gorier	graver	groyne
Gaulic	gentoo	Gilyak	glossy	godown	gorily	graves	grubby
gaulin	Gentoo	gimbal	glover	godson	goring	Graves	grub up
gaulty	gentry	gimbri	glower	godwit	gosain	gravid	grudge
gaupus	genual	gimlet	glucan	God wot	Goshen	grazer	gruffy
gavage	geodic	gimmal	gluier	go easy	go sick	grazet	grugru
gavial	geonim	gimmer	gluily	goetic	go slow	grease	grumly
gawker	George	ginger	gluing	goffer	go some	greasy	grumph
gawper	gerbil	gingko	gluino	goggie	go sour	greave	grumpy
gawpus	gerent	ginkgo	gluish	goggle	gospel	grebos	Grundy
gay cat	german	ginned	glulam	goggly	gossan	greedy	grunge
gay dog	German	ginnel	glumly	goglet	gossip	greeny	grungy
gaydom	germen	ginner	glummy	go gold	gotcha	greety	Grunth
gayest	germin	gipser	glumpy	go hang	Gotham	gregal	grutch
gayety	germon	girded	glunch	go home	Gothic	greyly	guaiac
Gay Lib	gersum	girder	glutch	Goidel	Goidel	gricer	guanay
gazabo	gerund	girdle	glutei	go into	go to it	griece	guango
gazebo	gestic	girlie	gluten	goitre	gotten	grieve	guanos
gazook	get gay	girnel	glycan	go-kart	gouger	griffe	guardo
gazump	get his	giroes	glycin	golden	goujon	gri-gri	guardy
geared	get off	girran	glycol	golfer	go upon	grille	guarea
gear up	get-out	gismos	glycyl	go live	gourbi	grillo	guarri
geason	getter	gitana	gnamma	gollan	gousty	grilse	gubbin
gebang	get wet	gitano	gnap at	gollop	goutte	grimly	Gubbio
geckos	gewgaw	Giunta	gnarly	golosh	govern	gringa	gubble
gedact	geyser	give in	gnatoo	gomuti	gowany	gringo	guddle
geddit	gharry	give me	gnatty	go near	go well	griper	Guebre
geed-up	ghazal	give up	gnawed	gone on	go west	grippe	Guelph
gee-gee	Ghazis	giving	gnawer	gonger	gowpen	grippy	guemal

guenon	gusset	halawi	harass	header	hepcat	Higher	hoeing
guffaw	gustos	halely	harbor	head-on	hepped	highly	hogged
guffer	gutful	haleru	hard by	head up	hepper	high-up	hogger
guggle	Gutian	halide	harden	healer	heptad	hijack	hogget
guglia	gut-rot	halite	harder	health	heptyl	Hilary	hoggin
guider	gutser	hallal	hardly	heaped	herald	hilted	hog gum
Guider	gutted	halloo	hard on	heaper	Herati	hinaki	hognut
guidon	gutter	hallos	hard up	hearer	herbal	hincty	hog-pen
guilty	gut-tie	hallow	hareld	hearse	herbed	hinder	hog-tie
guimpe	guttle	hallux	harken	hearst	herber	Hindki	hoicks
guinea	guttur	haloes	harker	hearth	herder	Hindoo	hokier
Guinea	guttus	halter	Harlem	hearty	herdic	Hindus	holcus
guinep	gutzer	halvah	harlot	heated	hereat	hinged	hold by
guinzo	guvner	halver	harman	heater	hereby	hingle	holden
guiser	guyver	halves	harmel	heathy	herein	hinnie	holder
guitar	guzzle	hamada	harper	heaume	hereof	hinoki	hold in
guiver	gymnic	hamate	Harris	heaved	hereon	hint at	hold it
gulden	gympie	hamble	harrow	heaven	Herero	hinter	hold on
Gullah	gypped	Hamite	hartal	heaver	heresy	hip-cat	hold up
gullet	gypsum	hamlet	Harvey	hebete	hereto	hip hop	hole up
gulley	gyrase	Hamlet	haslet	hebona	heriot	hipped	holier
gulose	gyrate	hammal	Hassid	Hebrew	hermit	hipper	holily
gulper	gyrene	hammam	hassle	Hebrid	hernia	hippic	holing
gulpin	gyrine	hammed	hasten	Hecate	heroes	hippie	holism
Gumban	gyrose	hammer	hatbox	heckle	heroic	hippos	holist
gumbos	gyrous	hammle	hatful	hectic	heroin	hippus	holla'd
gum-gum	gyttja	hamose	hatpin	hector	herola	Hirado	hollas
gum ivy	habara	hamous	hatred	heddle	heroon	Hirato	holler
gum lac	habile	hamper	hatted	hedger	her own	hirmos	hollin
gumlah	hab-nab	hamsin	hatter	hee-haw	herpes	hirola	holloa
gummas	haboob	hamuli	Hattic	heeled	Herren	hirple	hollos
gummed	hachis	Hanafi	haught	heeler	Hesped	hirsel	hollow
gummer	hackee	handed	Hau Hau	hegira	Hesper	hirsle	holmia
gunate	hacker	hander	hauler	Hegira	Hesvan	his own	holoku
gun dog	hackia	hand-in	haunch	he-goat	hetero	hispid	holpen
gung-ho	hackie	handle	Hausas	heifer	hetman	hisser	homage
gunite	hackle	hand on	hausen	height	hetmen	hister	hombre
gunman	hackly	hangar	haüyne	heimin	heurte	hi-tech	homely
gunmen	hadada	hang-by	Havana	Heinie	hewgag	hither	homier
gunned	haddie	hanged	have it	hejira	hexane	Hitler	homily
gunnel	Hadean	hanger	haven't	Hejira	hexite	hit man	homing
gunner	Hadith	hangie	have on	heliac	hexode	hit men	hominy
gunnis	hadron	hang in	have to	heling	hexone	hit-out	homish
gun-pit	haemal	hang me	have up	helion	hexose	hitter	honcho
gunsel	haemic	hang on	havier	helium	hey-day	hive up	honest
gun-shy	haemin	hangul	having	heller	heyday	hoagie	honeys
Gunter	haffet	hang up	haw-haw	helluo	hiaqua	hoarse	honied
gunyah	hafter	haniwa	hawked	helmed	hiatal	hoaxer	honker
guppie	hagged	hanjar	hawker	helmet	hiatus	hobbit	honour
gurges	haggis	hanjee	hawkit	helper	hiccup	hobble	Honved
gurgle	haggle	hanker	hawser	help up	hickey	hobday	hooded
gurgly	Haidas	hankie	haybag	hemina	hickle	hob-nob	hoodie
gurjun	haikal	hansel	haybox	hemmed	hidage	hobnob	hoodoo
Gurkha	hailer	Hansen	haymow	hemmel	hidden	hoboes	hoofed
gurner	hairdo	hansom	hayrif	hemmer	hi-de-hi	hocket	hoofer
gurnet	haired	hantle	hazard	hempen	hi-de-ho	hockey	hoof it
gurney	hairen	happed	hazier	henbit	hide up	hodden	hoo-hoo
gurrag	hairif	happen	hazily	hen-egg	hiding	ho-de-ho	hookah
gurrah	hajeen	happis	hazing	Henoch	hieing	hodful	hooked
Gurung	hakama	hapten	hazzan	hen-run	hiemal	hodman	hooker
gusher	hakeem	haptic	H-block	henrys	higgle	hodmen	hookey
guslar	halala	hapuku	headed	hep-cat	higher	hoeful	Hookey

hook it	hourly	hunsup	ibexes	I'm easy	incend	in form	in-milk
hook-up	housel	hunted	Ibibio	imidic	incept	inform	in mode
Hoolee	housey	hunter	ibises	immane	incest	infula	inmost
hooley	howdah	hunt up	Ibizan	immerd	inched	in full	in name
hooped	howdie	hunyak	Icarus	immesh	incher	infuse	innate
hooper	howe'er	hurdie	ice age	immote	incide	in gage	in need
hoop-la	how far	hurdle	ice axe	immund	incise	ingaol	inness
hoopla	howish	hurkle	ice-bag	immune	incite	ingate	inning
hoopoe	howler	hurler	icebox	immure	inclip	in gear	in nuce
hooray	howlet	Hurler	ice cap	impack	income	in germ	Innuit
hooroo	how now	hurley	ice fog	impact	incubi	ingest	inogen
hootch	how way	hurrah	iceman	impair	incult	ingine	inosic
hooter	howzat	hurray	icemen	impala	in curl	in goal	inower
hooved	hoyden	hurroo	Icenic	impale	incuse	in good	in pain
Hoover	hoyman	hurter	ice pan	impall	incyst	ingram	in pale
hooves	Hubble	hurtle	I Ching	impark	indaba	in gree	in part
hop-dog	hubbub	hushed	icicle	imparl	indart	ingulf	in pawn
hop-fly	hub-cap	hush up	iciest	impart	indebt	Ingush	in pile
hop off	hubcap	husked	iconic	impave	indeed	inhale	in play
hopped	hubris	husker	Idaean	impawn	indeed	in hand	in rags
hopper	huchen	huskie	ideate	impede	indene	inhaul	inroad
hoppet	huckle	huspil	idiocy	impend	indent	in heat	inroot
hopple	huddle	hussar	idlest	impest	Indian	inhell	inrush
Hoppus	huerta	hustle	idolum	imphee	indict	inhere	in salt
hop toy	huffer	hutted	i' faith	impish	Indies	in hock	insane
horary	huffle	hutung	iffier	import	indign	inhume	insect
horkey	hugely	Huxham	iffish	impose	indigo	inimic	in seed
hormic	hugged	huzoor	if only	impost	indite	inisle	insert
horned	hugger	Hyades	if that	impros	indium	injail	in show
hornen	huggle	hyaena	ignify	improv	in dock	inject	in-side
horner	Hughie	hya-hya	ignite	impugn	indole	in jest	inside
hornet	huldee	hyalin	ignomy	impure	indoor	in-joke	in silk
horn in	hulver	hybrid	ignore	impute	indraw	injure	insist
horrid	humane	hybris	iguana	in a fog	indrew	injury	in situ
horror	humate	hydria	I guess	in a hat	indris	ink-cap	insole
horsey	humble	hydric	llamba	in a low	induce	inkier	insoul
horsie	humbly	hydrol	llanun	inanga	induct	in kind	inspan
hortal	humbug	hydros	Il Duce	inarch	indult	inkish	instal
hosier	Humean	Hydrus	Illano	in arms	induna	inknot	instar
hostel	humect	hyemal	ill-got	in a row	inface	inkosi	in step
hostie	humeri	hygeen	illipe	in a rut	in fact	ink out	instep
hot air	humhum	Hygeia	illish	in a way	infall	ink-pad	instil
hotbed	Humian	Hyksos	illite	in banc	infame	inkpot	in suit
hotcha	humify	hymnal	I'll say	in bank	infamy	inlaid	insula
hot dog	Humism	hymner	I'll see	in bend	infant	in-lamb	insult
hotdog	Humist	hymnic	illude	inbent	infare	inland	insure
hot key	humite	hymnum	illume	inbind	in fawn	in lane	in sync
Hotnot	humlie	hyphae	illupi	in bond	infect	inlaut	intact
hotpot	hummed	hyphal	ill use	inborn	infeed	in leaf	in tail
hot rod	hummel	hyphen	imaged	inbred	infeft	inleak	intake
hot tap	hummer	hypnum	imager	in bulk	in fess	inlier	intend
hotted	hummum	hypoid	imagic	Incaic	infest	in lieu	intent
hotter	hummus	hypped	imagos	in calf	in file	in life	intern
hottie	humour	Hyrcan	imaret	incall	infill	in-line	in that
hot tip	humous	hyssop	imbark	incame	in fine	inlook	intill
hot tub	humped	hyther	imbibe	incant	infirm	in love	intima
hot war	humper	iambic	imbibe	in care	in fits	in luck	in time
Houdan	humpty	iambus	imbrex	incarn	inflow	in mask	intine
hougan	hunger	Iatmul	imbrue	in case	in flue	in mass	in-toed
houp-la	hungry	iatric	imbued	incase	influx	inmate	intone
houred	hunker	Ibanag	imbues	in cash	in foal	inmeat	in toto
houris	hunkey	iberis	imbuya	incede	infold	in mesh	in-town

in-tray	Irishy	jaguar	jet set	join up	jump on	Kansan	kelter
in trim	iritic	Jahveh	jet ski	jojoba	jump to	Kansas	Keltic
intron	iritis	jailer	jetted	Jokari	jump up	kantar	kelvin
intros	irokos	Jaipur	jetton	jokery	juncos	kanuka	Kelvin
intuit	ironed	jalopy	Jetway	jokily	jungle	Kanuri	kempas
in tune	ironen	jam jar	Jew boy	jokist	jungly	kaolin	kemper
in turn	ironer	jammed	Jewess	jolley	Junian	kaonic	Kendal
inturn	ironic	jammer	Jewish	Jollof	junior	Kaposi	keneme
in tway	iron-on	jamoon	Jewism	jollop	junker	kappie	Kenite
in type	irrupt	jampan	jezail	jolter	junket	karaka	kenned
inulin	Isabel	jangle	jibbah	jonick	junkie	karamu	kennel
inunct	Isaian	jangly	jibbed	jonnop	jupati	karana	kentia
Inupik	isatin	janker	jibber	jordan	jurant	karate	kentum
invade	ischia	jansky	jib-guy	Jordan	juried	karaya	Kenyah
in vain	island	japery	jicama	jorram	juries	karela	Kenyan
invein	isobar	japish	jiffle	Joseph	juring	karkun	kephir
invent	isogam	jarful	jigged	josher	jurist	Karman	Kepler
invert	isogon	jargle	jigger	Joshua	just as	karmic	kereru
invest	isohel	jargon	jigget	joskin	just it	kaross	kerfed
in view	isolex	jarool	jiggle	josser	justle	karree	Kerman
invite	isolog	jarrah	jiggly	jostle	justly	Karren	kermes
in vivo	isolux	jarred	jig-jig	jotted	just so	karris	kermis
invoke	isomer	jarvey	jigman	jotter	Jutish	Karroo	kerned
in-wale	isopod	jasmin	jigsaw	jounce	jutted	karsey	kernel
inwall	Israel	jasper	jillet	joundy	jyrene	kartel	kernos
inward	issued	jaspis	Jiminy	journo	Kabaka	kasbah	kerria
inwarp	issuer	jassid	jimjam	jovial	kabane	Kashan	kersey
in wear	issues	Jataka	jimply	Jovian	kabuki	Kathak	Kertch
inwick	isthmi	jaunce	jimson	jowari	Kabuli	katipo	ketene
inwind	italic	jaunty	jingle	jowled	Kabyle	kauris	ketone
in wine	Italic	javver	jingly	jowler	Kachin	kausia	kettle
in with	it says	jaw-jaw	jinker	joyant	Kaffir	kavass	Keuper
inwith	itself	Jaycee	jinnee	joyful	kaftan	kawass	Kevlar
inwork	itzebu	jazzbo	jipper	joyous	kahili	kayles	kewpie
inwove	ivy-tod	jazzer	jirene	joy-pop	kahuna	kayoed	keyaki
inwrap	ixodid	jazz up	jirine	Judaic	kaikai	kayoes	key man
inyala	Izarra	J-cloth	jitney	judder	kainga	Kazakh	key map
inyoke	Izzara	J-curve	jitter	Judean	kainic	Kazan	keypad
iodate	izzard	jeaned	Jivaro	judger	kaiser	kebbie	key-way
iodide	jabbed	jeerer	joanna	Judies	Kaiser	keckle	keyway
iodine	jabber	jeerga	jobbed	judoka	k'ai shu	keddah	khadar
iodise	jabble	Jeeves	jobber	jugate	kaizen	keeker	khadir
iodism	jabers	jejune	jobbie	jugful	kajang	keeled	khakis
iodize	jabiru	Jekyll	jobble	jugged	kakaki	keeler	khalif
iolite	jacana	jelick	job lot	juggle	kakapo	keelie	khalsa
ion gun	jaçana	Jemima	job off	jug-jug	kaleej	Keemun	khanda
Ionian	jacent	jennet	Jocism	juglet	kalgan	keener	khanga
ionise	jackal	jerbil	Jocist	juiced	kalmia	keenly	Khanty
Ionism	jacked	jerboa	jocker	juicer	Kalmyk	keen on	khanum
ionium	jacker	jereed	jockey	jujube	kalong	keep at	khapra
ionize	jacket	jerker	jocose	Julian	kamahi	keeper	kharif
Ionize	Jackey	jerkin	jocund	jumart	kamala	keep in	Kharri
ionone	jack in	jerque	jogged	jumbal	kamash	keep on	Khatti
ipecac	jacksy	jersey	jogger	jumbie	kameez	keep to	Khazar
Iranic	jack-up	Jersey	joggle	jumble	kanaka	keep up	Khlyst
Iraqis	Jacobi	jessed	joggly	Jumble	kanari	Keftiu	Khotan
ireful	jadish	Jessie	jog-jog	jumbly	kanban	kegler	Khurri
irenic	jaeger	jester	johnny	jumbos	Kanjar	Kekchi	Khyber
iridal	Jaeger	Jesuit	Johnny	jument	kankar	Kekulé	kiaugh
irides	jagged	jet age	joiner	jump at	kankie	keloid	kibble
iridic	jagger	jet lag	join in	jumped	kanoon	kelper	kibitz
irised	jaggie	jetsam	jointy	jumper	kan-pei	kelson	kiblah

kiboko	kit-car	kopeck	laagte	lament	laster	lazuli	leguan
kibosh	kit-cat	koppel	labakh	lamina	Lastex	leachy	legume
kickee	Kit-cat	koppie	labial	lamish	lastly	leaded	lemans
kicker	kit-fox	Korana	labile	lamium	lateen	leaden	lemony
kick in	kitful	kordax	labium	Lammas	lately	leader	Lenape
kick on	kitsch	Korean	lablab	lammed	La Tène	lead-in	lenate
kick up	kitset	korero	labour	lammie	latent	lead on	lender
kidang	kitted	korkir	labral	Lamout	latest	lead up	length
kidded	kittel	koruna	labret	lampas	lathen	leafed	Lengua
kidder	kitten	Koryak	labrum	lamper	lather	leafit	lenify
kiddie	kittle	kosher	labrys	lanate	lathis	league	lenite
kiddle	kittly	kotuku	lac-dye	lanced	Latian	leaker	lenity
kiddos	kittul	kotwal	lacery	lancer	latigo	leally	lensed
kidlet	klatch	koulan	lace-up	lances	Latina	lealty	Lenten
kidnap	klaxon	kouros	laches	lancet	latine	leaned	lentic
kidney	Klaxon	kowhai	lacier	landau	Latino	leaner	lentil
kidult	klepht	kowtow	lacily	landed	latish	leanly	lentor
kidvid	klepto	kraken	lacing	lander	lative	lean on	Leonid
kiekie	klippe	kramat	lacker	Länder	latomy	lean-to	leopon
kierie	klooch	kronen	lackey	land on	latoun	leap at	Lepcha
Kievan	kludge	kroner	lactam	Landry	latria	leaped	lepper
kijang	klutzy	kronor	lactic	land to	latron	leaper	lepton
Kikuyu	Kluxer	kronur	lactim	land up	latten	learnt	lerret
kilhig	K-meson	K-shell	lactol	langur	latter	leasee	lesbic
kilian	knacky	kubong	lactyl	lankly	lauder	leaser	lesion
killas	knaggy	Ku Klux	lacuna	lanner	Laufen	leasor	lessee
killer	knarry	kukris	lacune	lanose	laughy	leasow	lessen
kilted	knawel	kukupa	ladang	lanugo	launce	leaved	lesser
kilter	Kneipp	Kullah	ladder	lap-dog	launch	leaven	lesses
kiltie	knevel	*Kultur*	laddie	lapdog	laurel	leaver	less of
kimchi	knicks	kumara	la-di-da	lapful	lauric	leaves	lesson
kim-kam	knifer	kumbuk	ladies	lapiés	lauryl	lebbek	lessor
kimmer	knifey	kumera	ladify	Lapita	lauter	leccer	let fly
kimnel	knifie	kumiss	lading	Lapith	lavabo	lecher	lethal
kimono	knight	kumkum	ladino	lap-lap	lavage	Lecher	lethed
kinase	knitch	kümmel	Ladino	lapped	laveer	lechwe	lether
kincob	knit up	kumpit	ladler	lapper	lavish	lecker	let lie
kindle	knives	kung fu	ladyfy	lappet	law-day	lectin	let-off
kindly	knobby	kunkur	laetic	lappie	lawful	lector	let-out
kind of	knolly	kurgan	lagena	lapser	lawing	ledged	let rip
kineme	knotty	Kurnai	lag-end	laptop	lawman	ledger	letted
kinety	know as	kurper	lagged	larder	lawmen	leegte	letter
king it	knower	kurtha	lagger	lardon	lawned	leetle	Lettic
kingly	know of	Kurukh	laggin	largen	lawyer	leeway	let wit
kinjal	knurly	kuruma	lagoon	largos	laxist	leftie	leucon
kinkey	kobang	Kurume	Lahnda	lariat	laxity	legacy	levade
kinkle	kobold	kurvey	laical	larker	Laxton	legate	levain
kipped	Kodiak	Kushan	Laïdes	Larmor	lay-bed	legato	levant
kipper	kokako	Kutani	laidly	larnax	lay-bys	leg-bye	Levant
kippin	kokila	kutcha	laid up	larrup	lay-day	legend	leveed
kipsie	kokopu	kutira	laithe	larvae	lay-fee	leggat	levers
Kirman	kolach	kuttar	lakish	larval	laying	legged	Levers
kirpan	Kolami	Kuvasz	Lakist	larynx	lay low	legger	levied
kirsch	Komodo	kvetch	Lakota	lascar	layman	legget	Levied
kirtan	konaki	kvutza	lalang	Lascar	laymen	legion	levier
kirtle	Kongos	kwacha	Lallan	lashed	lay off	legist	levies
kishke	kongsi	kwanga	lamaic	lasher	lay out	leglen	Levite
Kislev	konini	kwanza	lambda	lash-up	layout	leglet	levity
kismet	konjak	kybosh	Lambeg	lasket	Laysan	leg man	lewdly
kissar	koodoo	kyogen	lamber	lasque	lazier	legman	lexeme
kisser	koodos	Kyrgyz	lambie	lassie	lazily	legmen	Leyden
kitbag	kootie	laager	lamely	lassos	lazule	leg-pad	Leydig

liable	limner	litmus	loggia	louden	lupous	made up	maleic
liaise	limnic	litten	Logian	loudly	lurdan	madman	malgas
libate	limous	litter	logier	lounge	luring	madmen	Malian
libber	limper	little	logion	lourie	lurker	madras	Malibu
libbet	limpet	littly	log jam	louser	Lushai	Madras	malice
Lib Dem	limpid	lituus	log-log	louses	lusher	madtom	malign
libero	limply	Litvak	log-man	louver	lushly	maduro	Maliki
libido	limpsy	live in	log-off	louvre	Lusian	maenad	malism
Lib-Lab	linage	lively	log-out	lovage	lusory	Maffia	malist
libral	linden	livery	loined	love-in	luster	maffle	malkin
Libran	lineal	live to	loiter	lovely	lustly	magcon	mallam
Libyan	linear	livier	loligo	love-up	lustra	magged	mallee
lichee	line-up	living	Lolita	loveys	lustre	Maggid	mallei
lichen	lingam	livret	loller	loving	luteal	maggie	mallet
licken	lingel	livyer	lollop	lowboy	lutein	maggot	mallow
licker	linger	lizard	loment	low-cut	luting	magian	maloca
lictor	lingle	Lizzie	London	low-end	lutino	magilp	maloti
lidded	lingos	llanos	lonely	lowish	lutist	maglev	Malozi
lidden	lingot	Lloyd's	longan	low-key	lutite	magmas	malted
liddle	lingua	loaded	longer	low men	luvvie	magnet	malter
Liebig	linhay	loaden	longie	lownly	Luwian	magnon	maltha
lieder	linier	loader	longly	L-plate	luxate	magnox	maltol
liefly	lining	loadum	long on	lubber	luxury	Magnox	mambos
lieger	linish	load up	lontar	Lubish	Lyaeus	magnum	Mamluk
lie low	linked	loafer	loofah	lubric	lycaon	magpie	mammae
lie off	linker	loanee	loogan	Luccan	Lyceum	maguey	mammal
lierne	link up	loaner	looked	lucent	lychee	Magyar	mammee
lifter	linnet	loasis	looker	lucern	Lycian	mahant	mammer
lift-on	linsey	loathe	look-in	lucida	lycium	Mahdis	mammet
lift-up	Linson	loathy	lookit	Lucina	lyctid	mahout	Mammon
Lifuan	lintel	loaves	look on	Lucite	lyctus	Mahsud	mamoty
ligand	linter	lobate	look up	luckie	Lydian	mahwah	mampus
ligase	lintie	lobbed	loomer	lucuma	lydite	maidan	mamzer
ligate	linton	lobing	looney	lucumo	Lylian	maiden	manage
ligged	lionel	lobule	loonie	Ludian	lymphy	maigre	manaia
ligger	lionet	locale	looped	luetic	Lyngby	maihem	mañana
lights	lionly	locant	looper	lugged	lyrate	mailed	man-ape
lignin	lipase	locate	loop-in	luggee	lyrism	mailer	man-boy
lignum	lipoic	lochan	loosen	lugger	lyrist	mail-in	manche
ligula	lipoid	lochia	looser	luggie	lysate	maille	Manchu
ligule	lipoma	lochus	looter	lukiko	lysine	maimai	mancia
ligure	lipped	locked	lop-ear	lullay	lyxose	maimed	mancus
like as	lippen	locker	lopped	lumbar	Maasai	maimer	Mandan
likely	lipper	locket	lopper	lumber	mabele	Mainer	man-day
like so	lippet	lock in	loquat	lumens	macaco	mainly	mandil
liking	liquid	lock on	lorate	lumina	macana	Maioli	mandor
likuta	liquor	lock-up	lorcha	lumine	machan	Majlis	manege
lilied	lirate	locoed	lordly	lummox	machos	majoon	manège
lilies	Lisbon	locoes	loreal	lumped	Mackay	make do	maness
lilipi	lisper	locoum	Lorenz	lumpen	mackle	make in	manful
lilium	lissom	locule	lorica	lumper	macled	make it	mangel
Lillet	listed	loculi	lories	lunacy	macock	make of	manger
limail	listel	locust	loriot	lunary	macron	make on	mangey
limbal	listen	lodged	losing	lunate	macula	make up	mangle
limbed	lister	lodger	losset	lunged	macule	making	man-god
limber	litany	loerie	lostly	lunger	Madame	makoré	mangos
limbic	litchi	lofted	lost to	lungis	madcap	makuta	maniac
limbos	lither	lofter	lotion	lunker	madded	makutu	manify
limbus	lithia	loggat	lot-man	lunula	madden	malady	Manila
Limeys	lithic	logged	lotong	lunule	madder	Malaga	manioc
limier	Lithol	logger	lotted	lupine	maddle	malate	manism
limmer	lithos	logget	louche	lupoid	made of	Malawi	manito

manjak	marled	matter	medick	menton	micher	minify	mizzle
manjee	marler	mattie	medico	mentor	mickey	minima	mizzly
mankin	marlin	mature	medina	mentum	mickle	minimi	mnemic
man-mad	marmem	matzos	Medina	menudo	Micmac	mining	mnemon
mannan	marmot	maudle	medine	menuet	micron	minion	moaner
manned	maroon	maugre	Medise	menura	micros	minish	mobbed
manner	marque	mauler	Medism	menzil	mictic	minium	mobber
mannie	marram	mauley	medium	merbau	mid-age	minnie	mobbie
manoao	marred	maulvi	medius	mercer	mid-air	Minnie	mob cap
manool	marrer	mau-mau	Medize	merely	midday	minnow	mobile
manqué	marron	Mau Mau	medlar	merese	midden	Minoan	Möbius
man-rem	marrot	maumet	medley	merest	midder	minted	mob law
man-sty	marrow	maunch	medusa	mergee	middie	minter	mocamp
mantel	marshy	Maundy	meeken	merger	middle	Minton	mocker
mantic	Marsic	Mauser	meekly	mering	midear	minuet	mocket
mantid	martel	Mavors	meemie	merino	midget	minute	mock-up
mantis	marten	mawkin	meeten	merise	midgut	minyan	mocock
mantle	Martha	maxima	meeter	merkin	mid-leg	Minyan	mod con
Manton	martin	maxina	meetly	merled	mid-off	miombo	Model T
mantra	Martin	maxixe	meet up	merlin	midrib	miosis	modena
mantri	martyr	May-bug	megass	merlon	mid-sea	miotic	modern
mantua	marudi	mayday	Megger	Merlot	mid-sky	mirage	modest
manual	marula	May Day	megilp	merman	midway	miragy	modify
manuka	marvel	May dew	megohm	mermen	Miehle	mirror	modish
manure	marver	mayest	megrim	merops	mielie	misact	modius
manway	Masais	mayfly	mehari	merrie	mighty	misaim	module
manzil	masala	mayhap	mehtar	merula	mignon	miscue	moduli
Maoism	mascle	mayhem	meinie	mescal	mihrab	misdid	modulo
Maoist	mascon	maying	meisie	meself	mikado	misère	moffie
maomao	mascot	mayory	melano	meshed	Mikado	misery	moggie
Maoris	mashed	May-pop	melded	mesiad	milady	misfit	Moghul
Mao-tai	masher	maythe	melder	mesial	milage	mishap	mogote
map-net	mashie	mazame	melena	mesode	milden	mishit	mohair
map out	masked	mazard	Melian	messan	mildew	mishla	Mohave
mapped	masker	mazier	melick	messer	mildly	misken	Mohawk
mapper	maslin	mazily	meline	Messer	milieu	miskey	Mohock
maquis	masque	mazout	mellah	messin	miling	mislay	mohohu
Maquis	massed	mazuma	mellay	Messrs	milium	misled	moider
maraca	masser	meadow	mellow	mess-up	Milium	missal	moiety
marage	Massic	meager	melody	mestee	milken	missay	moiled
maraud	massif	meagre	meloid	metage	milker	missee	moiley
marble	Massim	mealer	melter	metake	milkie	missel	moisty
marbly	massoy	mealie	melton	Metaxa	milled	misset	Mojave
Marcan	mastax	meaner	melvie	meteor	miller	missie	moksha
marcel	masted	meanie	member	methel	Miller	missis	Molale
marcid	master	mean it	memoir	method	millet	missus	molary
marcor	mastic	meanly	memory	methos	Millon	misted	molded
marcot	matapi	measle	menace	methyl	milord	mister	molder
margay	matata	measly	ménage	métier	Milori	mistle	molest
margin	matico	meatal	menald	metope	milter	mistry	molies
Marial	matier	meatus	mendee	Metran	Milton	misuse	moline
Marian	matily	mecate	mender	metric	mimbar	mithan	moling
marina	matins	Meccan	mendhi	metrop	mimosa	mither	mollie
marine	matipo	Meckel	meneer	metros	Minaic	mitral	moloch
marish	matlow	medano	menhir	mettle	minbar	mitred	Moloch
Marist	mat-man	meddle	menial	Mewari	mincer	mitted	molten
marked	matoke	medfly	meninx	Mewati	minded	mitten	molter
marker	matric	mediae	mennal	mézair	Mindel	mixing	mombin
market	Matric	medial	mensal	mezuza	minder	mixite	moment
markka	matrix	median	mensch	miacid	Minean	Mixtec	momism
Markov	matron	Median	menses	mia-mia	minery	Mizpah	mommet
mark up	matted	Medici	mental	miasma	mingle	mizzen	mompei

momser	morkin	move it	multum	mutism	naiads	nebula	new boy
momzer	mormal	move on	mumble	mutter	naiant	nebule	new bug
monack	Mormon	move up	mummed	mutton	naïdes	nebulé	Newfie
monaul	mornay	moving	mummer	mutual	naïfly	nebuly	newing
Monday	Mornay	mowhay	mummia	mutuel	nailed	necked	newish
moneme	morose	mowing	mumper	mutule	nailer	necker	new law
moneys	morpho	mozzie	Munchi	mutuum	nail up	nectar	new man
mongan	morris	mozzle	Munich	muu-muu	namely	need-be	new one
monger	Morris	mpingo	munity	muvule	naming	needer	newsie
Mongol	morrow	Mr Chad	munshi	muvver	nanism	needle	newton
monial	morsel	Mrs Mop	Munshi	muzhik	nannie	needly	Newton
monied	mortal	mucate	munsif	muzzed	nanoid	needn't	nextly
monies	mortar	much as	muntin	muzzle	Nansen	nefast	next to
monish	Morton	muchly	muonic	my aunt	napalm	negate	ngaios
monism	morula	mucify	murage	my-dear	napery	neifty	Ngbaka
monist	mosaic	mucker	Murano	myelin	napkin	neinei	niacin
monkey	Mosaic	muck in	murder	myelon	Naples	nekton	Niamid
monkly	moseys	muckle	murein	my foot	napped	nelson	nibbed
monoao	moshav	muckna	murena	mygale	napper	Nelson	nibble
monody	mosker	muck-up	murine	my lady	nardoo	nembie	nibful
monoid	Moslem	mucoid	murmur	my life	nardus	Nemean	niblet
monops	mosque	mucosa	murphy	my lord	narial	Nenets	Nibmar
monose	Mossad	mucose	Murphy	my oath	narker	neo-con	nicely
montan	mossed	mucous	murram	myogen	nark it	neoned	Nicene
Montem	mosser	mud box	Murray	myopia	narrow	Nepali	nicety
moocha	mossie	mudcat	murrey	myopic	Nasara	nepeta	niched
moo-cow	mossoo	mud dab	murrha	myosin	nasion	nephew	nicher
moolah	mostly	mudder	musang	myosis	Nassau	nepman	nicish
mooley	mothed	muddie	muscae	myotic	nastic	Neread	nickar
moolvi	mother	muddle	muscat	myriad	nasute	nereid	nickel
moomba	motile	muddly	muscid	myrica	natant	Nereid	nicker
mooned	motion	mud eel	muscle	myrrhy	natica	nereis	nickey
mooner	motive	mud-hen	muscly	myrtle	nation	nerine	nicolo
moonga	motley	mud hog	museum	myself	native	Nerita	nidget
Moonie	motmot	Mudjur	musher	Mysian	natron	nerite	nidify
moon-up	motory	mud pie	mushie	Mysore	natter	nerium	niding
mootah	Motown	muduga	musico	mysost	nature	Nernst	nidiot
mooter	mottle	muesli	musing	mystic	naught	neroli	nid-nod
mopane	mottos	muffed	musion	mythic	nausea	nerval	nielli
mopery	Motuan	muffin	musive	mythoi	nautch	nerved	niello
mopier	motuca	muffle	musked	mythos	nautic	neshly	nievie
mopily	mouche	mugful	muskeg	mythus	Navaho	Nesite	niffer
mopish	mought	mugged	musket	my word	navaid	Nessus	nigger
Moplah	moujik	muggee	muskie	Myxine	Navajo	nester	niggle
mopoke	mouldy	mugger	musk ox	myxoid	naveta	nestle	niggly
mopped	*moulin*	mugget	muskwa	myxoma	navies	Nestor	nigguh
moppet	moulvi	muggle	Muslim	myzont	Naxian	netful	nighly
moppie	moundy	Mughal	muslin	nabbed	nay-say	nether	nights
morale	mourne	mukluk	musmon	nabber	naysay	net net	nighty
morass	mouser	muktuk	mussal	nabbie	Nazify	netted	nig-nog
morbid	mouses	muleta	mussel	nabism	Nazism	netter	nihang
moreen	mousey	mulier	must-be	nachas	nealie	nettle	Nikkei
Morenu	mousie	mulish	mustee	naches	neanic	nettly	nilgai
more of	mousle	mullah	muster	nachos	near by	net ton	nimbed
more so	mousmé	mullen	mustn't	nacket	nearby	neural	nimble
morgan	mousse	muller	mutant	nacred	near go	neuric	nimbly
Morgan	moutan	Muller	mutase	Na-Dene	nearly	neuron	nimbus
morgay	mouths	Müller	mutate	naevus	neaten	neuter	niminy
morgen	mouthy	mullet	mutely	nagana	neatly	New Age	nimmer
morgue	mouton	mulley	mutine	nagged	nebbuk	Newari	Nimrod
morion	movant	Mulozi	muting	nagger	neb-neb	Newark	nincom
morish	move in	multip	mutiny	naggle	nebris	New Art	nincum

ninety	non-com	Novial	nutter	oculus	oilcan	one-act	opaque
niobic	non-con	novice	Nutter	odd bod	oil-cup	one-arm	opelet
nipped	non-ego	novity	Nuzian	oddish	oildom	one-bar	opener
nipper	non-fat	no-vote	nuzzer	oddity	oil-gas	one day	open go
nipple	nonius	noways	nuzzle	odd job	oilier	on edge	openly
Nishga	non-net	Nowell	Nyanja	odd lot	oilily	Oneida	open up
Nissen	nonoic	nowhat	nybble	odd man	oilman	oneing	operon
nisses	nonose	nowhen	nympha	odd-odd	oilmen	one-man	ophite
nitery	non-use	no whit	nympho	odds-on	oil-nut	one-off	Ophite
nitric	noodle	nowise	nytril	odelet	oil out	one–one	ophrys
nitron	noodly	now now	oafish	odeums	oil pan	one-pip	opiate
nitryl	nooked	noyade	Oak-boy	Odinic	oil rig	one-two	opiism
nitwit	nookie	noyaux	oak-fly	odious	oil-way	one-way	opiner
Niuean	nooser	nozzle	oaklet	Odissi	Ojibwa	onfall	opioid
Nivose	Nootka	nritta	oak-web	odylic	okapis	on file	oppose
nix out	Noraid	nritya	oarage	oecist	OK-ness	on fire	oppugn
Noahic	Nordic	nuance	oar-lop	oedema	okoume	onflow	optant
no-ball	norite	nubbin	oarman	oekist	olamic	on foot	optate
nobber	normal	nubble	obduct	oeuvre	old age	on form	optics
nobble	norman	nubbly	obdure	of a day	old boy	on hand	optima
nobbly	Norman	Nubian	obeche	off-air	old dog	on heat	optime
nobbut	normed	nubile	obelus	off-cap	oldest	on high	option
nobler	Nornir	nuchal	oberek	offcut	old hat	on hire	opt out
nobody	Norroy	nuclei	obeyer	off day	old ice	on hold	opuses
nocake	Norway	nucule	object	offend	oldish	oniony	orache
nocent	nor yet	nuddle	objure	office	old lag	onlaid	oracle
no chop	nosema	nudely	oblata	offing	old law	on-lend	orally
noctua	nose-up	nudger	oblate	offish	old man	on life	orange
nodded	nosher	nudism	oblige	off-key	old pal	on-line	Orange
nodder	no shit	nudist	oblong	offlap	Old Peg	online	orator
noddle	no-show	nudity	oboist	offlet	Old Tom	on loan	orblet
no dice	nosh-up	nuffin	obolus	off-put	oleate	on mace	orb-web
nod off	no side	nuggar	obsess	off-set	olefin	on oath	orcein
nodose	nosier	nugget	obtain	offset	oleose	onrush	orchid
nodous	nosily	nullah	obtect	of hers	oleous	on sale	orchil
nodule	nosing	numbat	obtest	of late	O level	onsell	orchis
noduli	nosism	numbed	obtund	of mark	olfact	on show	ordain
noesis	no soap	number	obtuse	of mine	olingo	on side	ordeal
noetic	nosode	numbly	obvert	of name	olived	onside	ordure
Noetic	nossir	numdah	occamy	of note	oliver	on-site	Oregon
no fear	nostoc	numina	occult	of ours	Oliver	onsold	or else
no fool	nostos	numnah	occupy	OFSTED	olivet	on song	orenda
nogged	nostra	num-num	ocelli	oftens	ollamh	on spec	orfray
noggin	no such	nuncio	ocelot	of wont	olland	on suss	organa
no-good	notamy	nuncle	ochone	of yore	ollave	on tape	organy
no-iron	notary	nunlet	ochrea	ogdoad	omasum	on time	orgasm
no joke	notate	nuphar	Ockham	ogival	omelet	on tour	orgeat
no-jump	not bad	nuplex	o'clock	ogived	omened	onuses	orgiac
no less	notchy	nuragh	ocracy	Oglala	omenta	on view	orgies
no-load	not hay	nurser	octane	O grade	omertà	onward	orgone
nomade	nother	nursey	Octans	O'Grady	ometer	oocyst	oribis
nomady	notice	nursle	octant	ogress	omnify	oocyte	orient
no mean	notify	nutant	octave	ogrish	omnium	oodles	origin
nomina	no time	nutate	octavo	oh dear	onager	oogamy	oriole
nomism	notion	nut-cut	octode	Ohioan	on bail	oolite	Orisha
no more	not out	nuthin	octoic	ohmage	on call	oolith	orison
non-act	nougat	nutlet	octopi	oh well	oncome	oology	Orissi
nonage	nought	nutmeg	octose	oh yeah	oncost	oolong	Orkney
no-name	nounal	nut oil	octroi	oidium	on deck	oomiak	orl-fly
nonane	novate	nutria	octroy	oikist	ondine	oompah	orming
non-art	novell	nuts to	octuor	oil-box	on-ding	oorali	ormolu
nonary	novena	nutted	ocular	oil can	on duty	oozily	or more

ornate	outing	oxlike	paleae	Papago	Pasdar	Pawpaw	pegged
ornery	outjet	oxtail	Palekh	papain	pasear	paxwax	pegger
orobus	outjut	oxy-arc	palely	papaya	Pashto	pay bed	Pegity
orogen	outlaw	oxy-gas	paling	papery	*paskha*	paybob	peg-leg
orotic	outlay	oxygen	palish	papess	pass by	pay day	peg out
orphan	outlet	oxygon	palkee	papish	passed	payess	pegtop
Orphic	outlie	oxymel	pallah	papism	passée	pay for	Peguan
orpine	out-lot	oyster	Pallas	papist	passel	paynim	Peguer
orrery	outman	ozaena	palled	pappus	passer	pay off	Peigan
oscine	outnal	Ozalid	pallet	Papuan	passim	payola	Peirce
oscula	output	ozoned	pallia	papula	pass on	pay out	Peking
osiery	outran	ozoner	pallid	papule	pass up	payout	pelade
osmate	outray	ozonic	pallor	papyri	pastel	Pazand	pelage
osmics	outrig	pa'anga	palmar	parade	paster	pazazz	Peléan
osmium	outros	Pablum	palmed	paramo	pastie	pea-bug	pelham
osmole	outrow	paccay	palmer	parang	pastil	peachy	Pelham
osmose	outrun	pacier	palolo	paraph	pastis	pea-cod	pelike
osmund	out-run	pacify	palone	parcel	past it	peagle	Pelion
osprey	outsat	pacing	palpal	parded	pastor	pea-gun	pelite
ossein	outsee	packed	palpus	pardon	pastry	peahen	pellet
Ossete	outseg	packer	palter	parent	pataca	peaked	Pelman
ossify	outset	packet	paltry	parera	pataka	pealer	pelmet
ostend	outsin	packie	pampas	Pareto	patana	peanut	peloid
ostent	outsit	pack in	pamper	parget	patart	pea-pod	pelong
osteon	out-top	pack up	panace	pariah	patchy	pearly	pelota
ostial	outvie	Pac-Man	panada	Parian	patent	peasen	peltae
ostium	outwit	padauk	panama	paries	patera	peavey	pelter
ostler	ovally	padded	Panama	paring	patesi	pebble	peltry
Ostman	Ovambo	padder	panary	parisa	Pathan	pebbly	peludo
Ostmen	ovaria	paddle	pandan	parish	pathic	pechan	pelure
ostomy	ovator	pad eye	pandar	parity	pathos	peck at	pelves
ostrog	over-by	pad-nag	Pandee	parker	patiki	pecked	pelvic
Ostyak	overdo	padouk	pander	Parkes	patina	pecker	pelvis
Oswego	overgo	padsaw	pandit	parkie	patine	pecket	pencel
Othman	overly	Paduan	Paneth	parkin	patios	peckle	pencil
otiose	over to	paella	panfan	parkly	patois	pecten	pendle
otitic	ovibos	paeony	pan-fry	parlay	patrix	pectic	peneid
otitis	ovisac	paging	panfry	parley	patrol	pectin	Penest
Ottawa	ovonic	pagoda	panful	parnas	patron	pectus	penful
oubaas	ovular	Pahari	Pangan	parode	patted	pedage	pen-gun
oughta	owelty	paiche	pan-ice	parody	pattée	pedalo	penial
ouklip	owl bus	paigle	panisc	parole	patten	pedant	penide
ouncer	owlery	pai-hua	pankin	paroli	patter	pedate	penile
our kid	owl-fly	pai kau	pan-man	parore	pattle	pedder	penman
oursin	owlish	pailou	pan-mug	parous	patzer	peddle	Penman
ouster	owl jug	pained	pannam	parpen	paucal	pedion	penmen
outact	owl-ray	painty	panned	parrel	paulin	pedlar	penned
outage	oxalic	paired	pannum	parrot	paunch	pedway	penner
outarm	oxalis	pair up	pannus	parsec	pauper	peek-bo	pennet
out-ask	oxalyl	Paiute	Panoan	Parsee	pausal	peeled	penniä
outbid	ox-beef	pajala	pan out	parser	pavage	peeler	pennon
outbuy	oxbird	pakeha	pan-pie	parson	pavane	peenge	pen pal
outcry	ox cart	pakhal	panpot	partan	Pavian	peep-bo	*pensée*
out-cue	ox-eyed	pakihi	pantec	parted	paving	pee-pee	pensil
outdid	ox-foot	pakora	panter	parter	pavior	peeper	pentad
outeat	Oxford	pak pai	pantie	partly	pavise	peepul	Pentel
outfit	ox-gall	palace	pantle	parton	Pavlov	peerie	penton
outfly	oxgang	Palaic	pantos	parula	pawnee	peever	pentyl
out for	ox-head	palais	pantry	parure	Pawnee	peewee	penult
outfox	oxherd	palank	panyar	parvis	pawner	peewit	penury
outgas	oxhide	palapa	panzer	pascal	paw-paw	peg-bag	peonin
outgun	Oxisol	palate	papacy	Pascal	pawpaw	pegbox	people

pepful	phanal	Picene	pilose	pipped	planet	poddle	pommee
pepino	Phanar	pick at	pilous	pippie	plan on	podeon	pommel
peplos	pharos	picked	pilpul	pippin	Planté	podger	pommer
peplum	phaser	picker	pilule	pip-pip	plaque	podite	pommes
pepped	phases	picket	piment	pipsyl	plashy	podium	pommey
pepper	phasic	pickie	pimple	piqued	plasma	podley	Pommie
pepsin	phasis	pick in	pimply	piques	platan	podsol	Pomoan
peptic	phason	pickle	piñata	piquet	plated	Podunk	Pomona
Pequot	phasor	pick on	pinate	piracy	platen	podura	pompal
peract	phatic	pick up	pin-boy	pirate	plater	podzol	pomped
percid	phenic	picnic	pincer	piraya	platic	poetaz	pom-pom
percur	phenix	picong	pinche	pirned	player	poetic	pompom
perdie	phenol	picory	pindan	pirnie	play on	poetry	pompon
perfay	phenom	picral	pindar	pirrie	play up	poffle	ponask
perfin	phenon	picric	pinder	Pisces	pleach	poggle	poncey
period	phenyl	picryl	pineal	Pisgah	please	pogrom	poncho
perish	Philip	Pictor	Pineau	pisher	plebby	pointy	ponder
periti	Philly	picuda	pinene	pissed	pledge	poised	pondok
Perkin	phizog	piddle	pinery	pisser	pleiad	poiser	ponent
perk up	phlegm	piddly	pineta	piss on	Pleiad	poisha	pongal
Perlon	phloem	pidgin	pin-fit	piss-up	plenar	poison	pongee
Permic	phobia	piecen	pingao	pistia	plener	pokier	pongid
per mil	phobic	piecer	pinger	pistic	plenty	pokily	pongos
permit	phocid	pie-dog	pingle	pistil	plenum	poking	pongyi
pernio	phoebe	piedra	pingos	pistol	pleura	polack	ponies
Pernod	Phoebe	Piegan	pining	piston	pleuro	Polack	pontac
peroba	pholas	pieing	pinion	pitchi	plexal	polari	pontes
per pro	phoner	pielet	pinite	pitchy	plexor	polder	pontic
perron	phoney	pieman	pinken	pit dog	plexus	Polian	Pontic
persea	phonic	piemen	pinker	pithoi	pliant	police	pontil
Persic	phonon	pierce	pinkie	pithos	plical	policy	poodle
person	phooey	pierid	pinkly	pitied	pliers	poling	poonac
pertly	phoria	pieris	pinkos	pitier	plight	polish	Poonah
peruke	phossy	pietas	Pink 'Un	pities	plinth	Polish	pooped
peruse	photic	Piffer	pinlay	pitman	plisky	polite	poo-poo
Pesach	photog	piffle	pin-leg	Pitman	plissé	polity	poor do
pesage	photon	pig-bed	pin-man	pitmen	plodge	polka'd	poorly
Pesaro	photos	pig-bel	pinnae	pitpan	ploidy	polkas	pooter
peseta	phrase	pig-dog	pinnas	pit-pat	plombe	pollam	Pooter
pesewa	phrasy	pigeon	pinnay	pit-saw	plonko	pollan	pootle
peshwa	phreak	pigged	pinned	pitted	plotch	pollee	pop art
pester	pH-stat	piggie	pinner	pitter	plotty	pollen	Popean
pestle	phylae	piggin	pinnet	pit tip	plough	poller	popely
petard	phylic	piggle	pin oak	pituri	plover	pollex	popery
pet-day	phyllo	piglet	pinole	piupiu	plucky	polley	popess
petite	phylum	pignut	pinson	pixies	pluffy	pollie	pop-eye
petrel	physic	pig out	pintid	pizazz	plug in	polloi	pop fly
petrol	physio	pigpen	pintle	pizzle	plumed	polone	popgun
pe-tsai	phytal	pigsty	pintos	placee	plumet	Polong	popish
petted	phytic	pike on	pinule	placer	plummy	polony	Popish
petter	phytin	piking	Pinyin	placet	plumpy	Polony	popism
pettle	phytol	pilaff	pinyon	placid	plunge	polska	poplar
pewage	phyton	pilage	piolet	plagal	plural	polyad	poplin
pewdom	phytyl	Pilate	pionic	plague	plurry	polyol	pop off
pewful	piacle	pile up	piopio	plaguy	plushy	polype	pop-out
pewing	piaffe	pileus	pipage	plaice	pluton	polypi	popped
pewter	pianos	pilfer	pipe in	plaidy	pneuma	pomace	popper
peyote	piazza	pilger	pipery	plaint	poachy	pomade	poppet
peziza	pi-bond	piling	pipe up	planar	pocked	pomato	poppit
pfella	Picard	pillar	piping	planch	pocket	pomeis	popple
phakic	picaro	piller	pipkin	Planck	podded	pomelo	popply
phalli	picein	pillow	pip out	planer	podder	pomeys	popsie

pop-top	pottos	pricer	psocid	pungle	putter	quelea	raddle
porger	potzer	pricey	psyche	punier	puttoo	quelle	radeau
porion	pouchy	pricky	psycho	punily	puture	quench	radial
porism	poudre	priest	psylla	punish	puzzle	quetch	radian
porker	pouffe	primal	psy-ops	punkah	pycnic	queued	radios
porket	pounce	primed	psy-war	punker	pye-dog	queuer	radish
pornie	pounds	primer	PT boat	punkie	pyemia	queues	radium
porose	pourer	primly	pterin	punkin	pygarg	quiche	radius
porous	pouter	primos	ptisan	punned	pyjama	Quiché	radman
porret	powder	primus	ptooey	punner	pyjams	quilly	Radnor
porron	powwow	Primus	ptosis	punnet	pyknic	quince	radome
Porson	poxier	prince	ptotic	puntal	Pylian	quinch	radula
portal	Prague	prinky	ptygma	punter	pylori	Quincy	Raetic
portas	praise	priory	ptyxis	pupate	pyosis	quinia	raffee
ported	prance	priser	pubbed	pupped	pyrene	quinic	raffia
portée	prancy	prismy	pubble	puppet	pyrite	quinoa	raffle
porter	prankt	prison	public	Puppis	pyrola	quinol	rafter
portia	pranky	prissy	pucker	pupton	pyrone	quinsy	rag-bag
Portia	prasad	pritch	puckle	Purana	pyrope	quinte	ragbag
portly	pratal	privet	pudden	purdah	Pythic	quinti	ragged
porule	prater	prizer	pudder	Purdey	python	quinua	raggee
posada	pratie	prober	puddle	puréed	pyuria	quinze	ragger
poseur	praxis	probie	puddly	purées	pyx-box	quirky	raggie
poshly	prayer	probit	pueblo	purely	Qantas	quisby	raggle
posh up	pray-TV	Procne	puffer	purfle	Qatari	quisle	raging
posied	preach	Proddy	puffin	purgee	Q fever	quitch	raglan
posies	pre-act	profer	puff up	purger	qiblah	quite a	ragman
posish	pre-amp	profit	pug-dog	purify	qintar	quiver	ragmen
posnet	preamp	Progne	pugged	purine	Q meter	quizzy	rag-out
posser	precip	prolan	puggle	puriri	quadra	Qumran	ragout
posset	précis	proleg	puisne	purism	quadro	quokka	ragtag
possie	precog	prolix	pujari	purist	quaere	quorum	ragtop
possum	pre-cut	prolly	pukeko	purity	quagga	quotas	raguly
postal	precut	prolog	pukkah	purler	quaggy	quotee	rah-rah
postea	prefab	Prolog	pullen	purlin	quagma	quoter	raider
posted	prefer	promos	puller	purpie	quahog	quotha	railer
poster	prefix	prompt	pullet	purple	quaich	quotum	rail in
postie	preggo	pronto	pulley	purply	quaigh	qwerty	rainer
postil	preggy	pro-ode	pull in	purree	quails	QWERTY	raised
post-op	pre-law	propel	pull-on	purrer	quaint	rabate	raiser
Postum	prelim	proper	pull to	purser	quaiss	rabato	raisin
potage	pre-man	propho	pull up	pursue	quaite	rabbet	Rajput
pot-ale	pre-med	proppy	pullus	purvey	quaker	rabbin	rake in
potash	premed	propyl	pulpal	pusher	Quaker	rabbis	rakery
potato	pre-men	proser	pulper	push-in	qualmy	rabbit	rake up
pot-boy	premie	prosit	pulpit	push it	quango	rabble	raking
poteen	premio	prosty	pulque	Pushtu	quanta	rabies	rakish
potent	premix	protea	pulsar	push-up	Quapaw	raceme	ramada
potful	prenex	pro tem	pulsed	pusill	quarry	rachel	ramage
pot hat	prepay	protic	pulser	pussel	quarte	rachis	ram air
pother	preppy	proton	pultan	pusser	quarto	racial	rambai
pothos	preses	proved	pultun	puszta	quartz	racier	ramble
potion	pre-set	proven	pulwar	puteal	quasar	racily	ram-cat
potleg	presto	prover	pumice	put fly	quatre	racing	Ramean
pot-lid	pre-tax	Provie	pummel	putlog	quatro	racism	ramify
potman	pretor	Provos	pumped	put-off	quaver	racist	Ramism
pot off	pretty	prowed	pumper	put out	queach	rackan	Ramist
pot pie	prevue	pruner	punchy	put-put	queasy	racker	ram-jam
potsie	pre-war	prunus	puncta	putrid	Quebec	racket	ramjet
potted	preyer	prusik	puncti	putsch	queeny	rackle	rammed
potter	Priapi	prying	pundit	putted	queest	rack up	rammel
pottle	priced	pseudo	punger	puttee	quelch	racoon	rammer

rammle	ratbag	rebeck	redden	reflux	relier	report	retama
ramnas	rat-bat	rebend	redder	refold	relies	repose	retard
ramoon	rather	rebind	reddle	refoot	reline	repost	retell
ramose	Rathke	rebody	red dog	re-form	relish	repped	retene
ramous	ratify	reboil	red-ear	reform	relive	repros	retest
ramper	ratine	rebook	redeem	refuel	reload	repugn	re-time
ramrod	rating	reboot	red elm	refuge	reluct	repute	retina
ramtil	ration	rebore	red-eye	re-fund	relume	requit	retire
rancel	ratios	reborn	Red Fed	refund	remade	rerail	retold
rancho	ratite	reboso	red fin	re-fuse	remain	re-rate	retook
ranchy	ratlin	rebozo	red fir	refuse	remake	reread	retool
rancid	ratoon	rebrew	red fog	refute	remand	re-reel	retort
rancio	Ratrac	rebuff	red fox	regain	re-mark	reride	retoss
randan	rat-run	rebuke	red gum	regale	remark	re-rise	retour
randem	rattan	rebunk	red hat	regalo	remast	rerobe	retral
random	rat-tat	rebuoy	red-hot	regard	remede	re-roll	retree
ranger	ratted	rebury	redial	regent	remedy	re-roof	retrim
rangle	ratter	re-bush	red ink	reggae	remeet	resail	retrod
ranine	rattle	recall	red leg	regild	remeid	resait	retros
ranker	rattly	recant	red man	regime	remelt	resale	retted
ranket	ratton	re-case	red mud	régime	remind	resalt	retter
rankle	raunch	recast	Red Ned	Regina	remint	rescue	retube
rankly	rauque	recced	red oak	region	remise	reseal	retune
ransel	ravage	re-cede	redoes	Regius	remiss	reseat	returf
ransom	ravers	recede	redone	regive	remold	réseau	re-turn
ran-tan	ravery	recede	red-out	reg'lar	remora	resect	return
ranter	rave-up	recent	red rag	reglet	remord	reseda	retuse
ranula	ravine	recess	red-raw	regnal	remote	reseed	retype
raphae	raving	recipe	redraw	regret	remove	reseek	Reuben
raphia	ravish	recite	redrew	regrew	rempli	resell	re-urge
rapido	Rawang	reckon	red rot	regrow	remuda	resent	revamp
rapier	raw bar	recoal	red-top	regula	rename	reship	reveal
rapine	rawish	recoat	reduce	reguli	render	reside	revend
rapist	ray-fin	recock	reduct	regulo	renege	re-sign	revent
rap out	ray gun	recoct	reduit	rehang	rengas	resign	reverb
rapped	raylet	recode	redund	rehash	renish	resile	revere
rappee	razant	recoil	reebok	rehear	rennet	resing	Revere
rappel	razing	recoin	re-echo	reheat	rennin	resiny	revers
rappen	razzia	recopy	reechy	reheel	renown	resist	revert
rapper	razzle	record	reeded	rehome	rental	re-site	revery
raptly	reable	recork	reeden	rehung	rented	resite	revest
raptor	reachy	recoup	reeder	Reilly	renter	resize	review
raptus	reader	rectal	re-edit	reiter	renule	reskin	revile
rarefy	read-in	rectly	reefer	Reiter	renvoi	reslay	revise
rarely	read of	rector	reeler	reiver	reopen	resoil	revive
rarest	read up	rectos	re-emit	Rejang	repack	resold	revoke
rarify	reagin	rectum	reeper	reject	repaid	resole	revolt
rariki	realia	rectus	ree-raw	rejoin	repair	resorb	revote
raring	really	recumb	reesed	rekiss	repand	re-sort	revved
rarish	realty	recuse	reesle	reknit	repass	resort	rewake
rarity	reamer	redact	reesty	relade	repast	respin	reward
rasant	reaper	red ant	reeved	re-laid	repave	restem	rewarm
rascal	rearer	red ash	reezed	relaid	repeal	rester	rewash
rasher	reason	redate	reface	reland	repeat	restow	rewind
rashly	reasty	red bat	refect	relata	repent	rest up	rewire
raskol	reaver	red bay	refeed	relate	repick	result	reword
rasper	reback	red box	refill	relend	repine	resume	rework
rassle	rebake	red bud	refine	relent	replan	resumé	rewrap
raster	rebase	redbud	reflag	relevé	replay	résumé	Rexine
rastle	rebate	red bug	reflet	relict	replot	retail	Rexism
Rastus	rebato	redcap	reflex	relied	replum	retain	Rexist
rasure	re-beat	red cat	reflow	relief	repone	retake	reyoke

re-zero	riegel	roachy	rooter	rubbed	run low	sadden	salwar
rezone	riffle	roadeo	rootle	rubber	run mad	sadder	samaan
Rhages	rifled	roader	rootsy	rubble	runnel	saddle	samara
rhagon	rifler	roadie	rooves	rubbly	runner	Sadean	samba'd
rhebok	riggal	roamer	rope in	Rubens	runnet	sadful	sambal
rhenic	rigged	roaned	ropery	rubied	run off	sadism	sambar
rhesis	rigger	roarer	ropier	rubies	run-out	sadist	sambas
rhesus	riggot	roband	ropily	rubify	runrig	saeter	sambok
rhetic	righto	robbed	roping	rub off	runted	safari	Sambos
Rhetic	righty	robber	roquet	rub out	runway	safely	sambuk
rhetor	rigour	robbin	rorter	rubral	rupiah	safety	sambuq
rheumy	rig-out	Robert	rosace	rubric	rupial	Sagbag	sambur
rhexia	rilled	robing	rosary	ruched	rurban	sagely	samely
rhexis	rillet	Rob Roy	roscid	ruckle	ruscus	sagene	Samian
rhinal	Rilsan	robust	roscoe	ruckus	rushee	saggar	samiel
rhinos	rimaye	rochea	roseal	rudder	rushen	sagged	samier
Rhodes	rimier	rocher	rosery	ruddle	rusher	sagger	samite
rhodic	rim man	rochet	Roshis	rudely	rusine	sagina	samiti
rhombi	rimmed	rocker	rosied	rudery	russet	sagoin	samlet
rhotic	rimose	rocket	rosier	rudish	Russia	Sahara	sammen
Rhovyl	rimous	rococo	rosily	rudist	Russic	sahiba	sammie
rhumba	rimple	rodded	rosiny	rudite	Russki	said he	Samoan
rhymer	rinded	rodder	rosser	rueful	Russky	sailed	samosa
rhymic	rindle	rodent	rossie	rueing	rustic	sailer	sampan
rhythm	ringed	rodeos	roster	ruffed	rustle	sail in	sample
rhyton	ringer	rodham	rostra	ruffer	rustly	sailor	Samsam
Rialto	Ringer	rodlet	rotang	ruffle	rustre	saithe	Samsoe
ribald	ringie	rodman	rotary	ruffly	ruther	Saitic	Samson
riband	ring in	rodney	rotate	rufous	rutile	saiyid	sancho
ribbed	ringle	Rodney	rotche	rugate	rutted	Sakian	Sancho
ribber	ring up	roguer	rot-gut	rugged	ruttee	sakura	sancta
ribbit	rinser	Roland	rother	rugger	rutter	salaam	sandal
ribbok	Rinzai	roller	rotolo	ruggle	ruttle	salade	sandar
ribbon	Riojan	roll in	rottan	Rugian	Rwanda	salami	sanded
rib-eye	rioter	rollio	rotted	rugosa	Rylean	salary	sander
riblet	riotry	roll on	rotten	rugose	ryokan	Salian	sandhi
ribose	ripely	roll up	rotter	rugous	ryotti	salify	Sandow
Ricard	rip off	Romaic	rottle	rug-rat	Ryukyu	salina	sandur
richen	rip out	romaji	rotula	ruiner	Saanen	saline	sandyx
riches	ripped	Romani	rotund	rule in	Sabaic	Salish	sanely
richie	ripper	Romano	rouble	ruling	sabalo	salita	sangar
richly	ripple	Romany	roucou	rumaki	sabbat	saliva	sanies
ricker	ripply	Romeos	roughy	rumble	sabbed	sallee	sanify
ricket	Rippon	Romish	Rouman	rumbly	Sabean	sallet	sanity
rickey	riprap	Romney	rounce	rumdum	Sabian	sallow	sanjak
rickle	ripsaw	romper	rouncy	rum-jar	sabicu	salmis	Sankey
ricrac	rise to	romp in	roundy	rumkin	sabine	salmon	sannah
rictal	rise up	rondel	rouped	rummer	Sabine	saloon	sannup
rictus	rishis	rondos	rouper	rumour	sabkha	saloop	sanpro
ridded	rishon	ronins	rouser	rum pad	sabled	saltee	sansei
riddel	rising	roo-bar	rousie	rumped	sabred	salten	santal
ridden	risker	roodge	router	Rumper	sacate	salter	Santal
ridder	Risley	roofed	routhy	rumple	sachem	saltie	santir
riddle	risqué	roofer	roving	rumply	sachet	saltly	santon
rident	ritard	rooker	rowage	rumpot	sacked	saltus	Santos
ride-on	ritter	rookie	rowing	rumpus	sacken	saluki	Sanusi
ride up	ritual	rookus	row out	rum-tum	sacker	salute	sapele
ridged	Riu-kiu	roomed	rozzer	rundle	sacket	salver	sapful
ridgel	rivage	roomer	Rualla	run dry	sackie	salvia	saphie
ridger	rivery	roomie	Ruanda	runged	sacral	salvor	Sapiny
riding	rizzar	roomth	rubati	runkle	sacred	salvos	sapota
ridley	r month	rooted	rubato	runlet	sacrum	Salvos	sapour

sappan	saxony	sclera	scutal	secule	senary	sester	shamal
sapped	Saxony	scolex	scutch	secund	senate	sestet	shaman
sapper	sayall	scolia	scutel	secure	Sendai	seston	shamba
sapple	sayest	scoloc	scutty	sedate	sendal	Setine	shamer
sap-rot	saying	sconce	scutum	sedent	sendee	set net	shammy
sap-run	say nay	scoopy	scuzzy	sedged	sender	set off	shamus
sarang	say out	scopae	Scylla	sedile	send in	setose	shandy
sarape	say yea	scorch	scypha	seduce	sendle	set out	Shango
Sarcee	say yes	scorer	scyphi	seeded	send on	settee	shangy
sarcle	sayyid	scores	scythe	seedee	send up	setter	shanny
sardar	scabby	scoria	sea air	seeder	Seneca	settle	shanty
sarees	scaffy	scorse	sea-ape	see fit	senega	set-tos	shaped
sargus	scaife	scotch	sea-ash	see for	senhor	setule	shapen
saried	scalar	Scotch	sea bag	seegar	senile	severe	shaper
sarkar	scaled	scoter	sea-bat	seeing	senior	severy	shapka
sarlac	scaler	scotia	seabed	seeker	seniti	Sèvres	shapoo
sarnie	scaley	Scotic	sea-bug	seemer	senium	sewage	sharer
sarong	scalic	scotty	sea-cat	seemly	sennet	sewery	sharia
Sarouk	scally	Scouse	sea-cob	see off	sennit	sewing	Sharia
sarsen	scampi	scouth	sea cow	see out	señora	sewn-in	sharif
sartin	scance	scovan	sea dog	see red	senryu	sex act	sharka
sartor	scanty	scovel	sea-ear	see-saw	sensal	sex aid	sharky
sashay	scapus	scovin	sea-eel	seesee	Sen-Sen	sexfid	sharny
sashed	scarab	scowly	sea-egg	seethe	sensor	sexful	Sharps
sasine	scarce	scrape	sea fan	see you	sensum	sexier	sharpy
satang	scared	scrapy	sea-fir	Sefton	sentry	sexily	sharry
satara	scarer	scrawl	sea fog	seggie	Senufo	sexism	Shasta
sateen	scarfs	scraze	sea-fox	segoon	sepium	sexist	shaved
satiny	scarpe	screak	sea hen	segued	sepsis	sexpot	shaven
satire	scarry	scream	sea-hog	segues	septal	sextal	shaver
satnav	scarth	screed	sealed	seiche	septet	sextan	shavie
satori	scarus	screef	sealer	seidel	septic	sextar	shazam
satrap	scathe	screel	seaman	seiner	septum	sextet	sheafy
Saturn	scatty	screen	sea-mat	seised	sequel	sextic	sheath
saucer	scazon	screwy	sea-maw	seisin	sequin	sexton	sheave
Saudis	Sceaux	scribe	seamen	seized	serail	sextry	Shebat
sauger	scenic	scried	seamer	seizer	serang	sexual	sheela
saulie	scenty	scries	seamew	seizin	serape	Sézary	sheeny
Saumur	schelm	scrimp	Seanad	sejant	seraph	sferic	sheep-o
saurel	schema	script	seance	sejoin	seraya	Shabak	sheepy
sautéd	scheme	scrive	séance	sekere	serdab	shabby	sheety
savage	Schick	scrobe	sea oak	seldom	*serein*	shable	Sheika
Savage	Schiff	scroll	sea-owl	select	serene	shabti	sheikh
savant	schism	scroop	sea pen	selion	sereno	shacky	sheila
savate	schist	scrota	sea-pie	Seljuk	serial	shaded	shekel
savine	schitz	scruff	sea-pig	Selkup	Serian	shader	shelfs
saving	schizo	scrump	searce	seller	series	shadow	shelfy
savory	schlep	scrunt	search	sell-in	serine	shaduf	shelly
savour	school	scruto	sea-run	sell on	sermon	Shafii	Shelta
Sawbwa	schoon	scruze	season	sell up	Sernyl	shafty	shelty
sawder	schoot	scryer	seater	selsyn	serosa	shaggy	Shelty
sawfly	schorl	scubas	seaway	selves	serous	shahid	shelve
saw-gin	schout	scuddy	Sebago	Semang	serpaw	shaikh	shelvy
sawing	schuit	sculch	sebkha	semata	serrae	shaken	shenzi
saw-log	Schupo	sculpt	secant	semble	serran	shaker	she-oak
sawney	schuss	scummy	secede	seméed	serums	shakey	sherif
saw-pit	schuyt	scunch	secern	sememe	serval	shakos	Sherpa
saw-set	scient	scunge	secesh	Semite	server	Shakti	sherry
sawyer	sci-fic	scungy	Seckel	semmit	servos	shaley	sherut
saxaul	scilla	scurfy	second	Semple	sesame	shall I	sheugh
saxist	Sciote	scurry	secret	*sempre*	sesban	shalom	Shevat
saxman	sclaff	scurvy	sector	Semtex	seseli	shalot	shewel

shicer	shradh	sifter	sinker	skilly	sleyer	smelts	snippy
shield	shrank	sigher	sink in	skimpy	sliced	smeuse	snitch
shifta	shrape	sighty	sinned	skinch	slicer	smidge	snitty
shifty	shrdlu	siglum	sinner	skinny	slider	smilax	snivel
Shi'ism	shrewd	signal	sinnet	skip it	slight	smiler	snobby
Shiism	shriek	signed	sinter	skippy	slimly	smilet	Sno-cat
Shi'ite	shrift	signee	sintok	skirty	slimsy	smiley	snodly
Shiite	shrike	signer	Siouan	ski run	slinge	smirch	Snooks
shikar	shrill	signet	sipage	skiter	slinky	smirky	snoopy
shikho	shrimp	sign in	siphon	ski tow	slip-in	smitch	snoose
shikra	shrine	sign on	Sipibo	skiver	slip-on	smiter	snooty
shiksa	shrink	signor	siping	skivie	slippy	smithy	snoove
Shilha	shrive	sign up	sipped	skivvy	slip up	smoggy	snooze
shilpy	shroff	silage	sipper	ski-wax	slitch	smoked	snoozy
shimmy	shroud	silane	sippet	sklent	slithe	smoker	Snopes
shindy	shrove	silene	sipple	skolly	slithy	smokey	snorer
shined	Shrove	sileni	sirdar	Skraup	slitty	smokie	snorty
shiner	shruff	silent	sireen	skreek	sliver	smooch	snotty
shinny	shrunk	silica	Sirian	skreel	Sloane	smooge	snouch
Shinto	shtick	silked	sirkar	skrike	slobby	smooth	snouty
shinty	shtook	silken	sirrah	skuett	slogan	smouch	snubby
shippo	shtoom	silker	Sirrah	skunky	sloosh	smouse	snudge
shippy	shtuck	silkie	sirree	skutch	sloped	smriti	snuffy
Shiraz	shtumm	sillar	siskin	skycap	sloper	smudge	snugly
shirty	shufti	siller	sissoo	skyful	slopey	smudgy	snurge
shisha	shufty	siloes	sister	sky-god	sloppy	smugly	soaken
shit on	shut in	Silozi	sistra	skyish	sloshy	smutch	soaker
shitty	shut it	silure	sitcom	skyjam	slouch	smutty	soaper
shivah	shut to	silvan	sithen	Skylon	slough	Smyrna	soapie
shiver	shut up	silver	sit mum	skyman	slougi	snaggy	soarer
shivey	shyest	silvex	sit out	skyway	Slovak	snaily	sobbed
shivoo	shyish	simial	sitrep	slabby	sloven	snaith	sobber
shlump	shypoo	simian	sitten	slaggy	slower	snakey	so be it
shmear	sialic	simile	sitter	slaked	slowly	snap at	sobeit
shoaly	sialon	simkin	situal	slalom	slow-up	snap-in	sobful
shoddy	sibbed	simlin	situla	slangy	slubby	snap-on	sobole
shoder	sibred	simmer	Sivite	slanty	sludge	snappy	socage
shofar	siccan	simmon	Siwash	slap-up	sludgy	snap up	soccer
shoful	sicken	simnel	sixain	slashy	sluggy	snarer	social
shoggy	sicker	simony	six-gun	slatch	sluice	snarky	socius
shogun	sickie	simool	six-two	slater	sluicy	snarly	socked
shomer	sick-in	simoom	size up	slaver	slum it	snaste	socket
shonda	sickle	simoon	sizing	slavey	slummy	snatch	socman
shonky	sickly	simper	sizzle	Slavic	slumpy	snavel	Socred
shooed	sickos	simple	skaith	Slavon	slurry	snavle	sod-all
shoo-in	sicsac	simply	skance	slayer	slushy	snazzy	sodded
shoppe	sicula	sim-sim	skater	sleave	slutch	sneaky	sodden
shoppy	Sidamo	simson	skates	sleaze	slutty	sneath	sodger
shoran	Sidcot	simurg	skeigh	sleazo	sly dog	sneery	sodian
shorer	sidder	Sinaic	skelet	sleazy	slyest	sneeze	sodide
shorts	siddow	sin bin	skelly	sledge	slyish	sneezy	sodium
shorty	Siddur	Sindhi	skelvy	sleech	smahan	snelly	sod off
shotty	side-on	sindon	skerry	sleeky	smally	sniddy	sodoku
should	siding	sinewy	sketch	sleepy	smalts	Snider	sodomy
shouse	Siebel	sinful	skewed	sleety	smarmy	snidey	soever
shovel	sieger	singer	skewer	sleeve	smarty	snidge	soffit
shover	sienna	sing-in	ski-bob	sleeze	smatch	sniffy	soften
showed	sierra	single	skiddy	sleezy	smeary	snifty	softie
shower	siesta	singlo	skidoo	sleigh	smeech	snip at	softly
show in	siever	singly	Skidoo	sleugh	smeeth	sniper	sogged
show-me	sifaka	sing up	skiing	sleuth	smegma	snipes	soigné
show up	siffle	sinify	ski-ing	S level	smelly	snipey	soiled

soirée	sorner	spawny	splosh	squash	status	stitch	streak
solace	sorrel	spayad	splurt	squatt	staved	stithy	stream
solate	sorren	speary	spodic	squawk	staver	stiver	streck
soldan	sorrow	specie	spoilt	squdge	staves	stoach	streek
solder	sortal	specky	spoked	squdgy	Stavka	stocky	streel
sold on	sorted	speech	spoken	squeak	stayer	stodge	street
solely	sorter	speedo	sponge	squeal	stay in	stodgy	Strega
solemn	sortie	speedy	spongy	squeam	stay on	stogie	strene
solera	sort of	speiss	spooky	squill	stay-up	stoked	stress
soleus	so soon	spence	spoony	squint	steady	stoker	strewn
solidi	Sothic	spense	sporal	squire	steamy	stokes	striae
soling	sotted	sperma	Spörer	squirl	steboy	Stokes	strick
solion	sotter	sperms	sporty	squirm	steely	stoled	strict
solity	souari	spermy	sposhy	squirr	steepy	stolen	stride
sollar	soubah	sperse	spot on	squirt	steeve	stolid	strife
so long	soucar	spetch	spotty	squish	Stefan	stolon	strift
soloth	sought	spewer	spouse	Sranan	stelae	stomal	striga
soloti	souled	sphene	spousy	Stabex	stelar	stomas	strike
solute	souler	sphere	spouty	Stabit	stemma	stomia	strind
Solvay	soulie	sphery	sprack	stable	stemmy	stompy	Strine
solver	Soumak	sphinx	sprain	stably	stench	stoned	string
solvus	souper	spiced	sprang	staboy	stenog	stonen	stripe
Somali	source	spicer	sprawl	stacte	stenol	stoner	stript
so many	sourly	spicey	spread	stadda	stenos	stoney	stripy
sombre	sour on	spider	spreed	stadia	step-in	Stoney	strive
somite	souter	spiffy	sprees	stadic	step it	stooge	stroam
sommer	soviet	spigot	spreeu	staffs	step-on	stoopy	strobe
so much	Soviet	spiked	sprent	staged	steppe	stooth	strode
sonant	sovran	spiker	spring	stager	step up	stop by	stroil
sonata	sowans	spikey	sprink	stagey	stereo	stoper	stroke
sonder	sow bug	spilly	sprint	staggy	steric	stop-go	stroky
sonics	sowbug	spilth	sprite	stainy	sterks	stop in	stroll
sonnet	sowens	spinae	sprity	stairy	sterna	stop on	stroma
sonsie	so what	spinal	spritz	staker	Sterno	stoppo	stromb
sontag	sowing	spinar	sprong	stakey	sterny	stop up	strome
soogan	sowlth	spined	sprote	Stalag	sterol	storax	strong
soogee	sow-pig	spinel	sprout	stalch	sterro	storer	strool
soojee	sozzle	spinet	spruce	staler	steven	storey	stroud
sookey	spaced	spinks	spruik	stalky	stewed	stormy	stroup
sookie	spacer	spinny	spruit	stamen	stibic	stotty	strove
sooler	spacey	spinor	sprung	stance	stické	stound	strown
soon as	spader	spinto	sprunt	stanch	sticky	stoury	struck
sooner	spadix	spin-up	spryer	stanol	Sticky	stoush	struma
soonly	spammy	spiral	spryly	stanza	stieve	stoven	strung
soorma	spandy	spirea	spuddy	stanze	stiffy	stover	strunt
so or so	sparer	spired	spunky	stapes	stifle	stowce	struth
soothe	sparge	spirit	spurge	staple	stigma	stower	Stuart
Sophia	sparid	spital	spuria	starch	stilly	stow it	stubby
sophic	Sparks	spitty	spurii	starer	stilty	stract	stucco
sopite	sparky	spit up	spurry	starey	stinge	strafe	studio
sopped	sparry	spitzy	sputum	starko	stingo	straif	stuffy
sopper	sparse	spivvy	spydom	starry	stingy	straik	stuggy
sorage	sparth	splake	spyism	starve	stinko	strain	stumer
sorbet	sparus	splash	spy out	stases	stinky	strait	stumpy
sorbic	spasmi	spleen	squail	stasis	stinty	strake	stuns'l
sorbus	spasmy	spleet	squali	statal	stipel	straky	stunty
sordes	spatha	splice	squall	stated	stiper	strand	stupid
sordid	spathe	spliff	squama	stater	stipes	strass	stupor
sordor	spauld	spline	squame	Stater	stir in	strata	sturdy
sordun	spaver	splint	square	static	stir it	strath	sturks
sorely	spavie	splirt	squark	stator	stirps	strawn	styany
sorgho	spavin	splore	squary	statue	stir up	strawy	stylar

styler	Sullan	surtax	switch	tagged	tanger	tarsia	teapoy
stylet	sullen	survey	swivel	tagger	tangle	tarsus	tearer
stylos	sullow	surwan	swiver	taglet	tangly	tartan	tear-up
stylus	sulpha	Susian	swivet	tagrag	tangor	tartar	teasel
stymie	sultan	Susie-Q	swoony	taguan	tangos	Tartar	teaser
styrax	sultry	suslik	swoose	tahali	tangun	tarten	teaset
styrol	sumach	sussed	swoosh	tahina	Tangut	tartly	teated
styryl	sumbul	Sussex	swound	Tahiti	tanist	Tarvia	teazel
suable	summae	susurr	Sydney	tahsil	tanjib	Tarzan	teazle
suaeda	summar	sutile	syllab	taiaha	tanker	tasajo	Tebele
subbed	summat	sutler	syllid	t'ai chi	tanned	Tasian	techie
subbie	summed	suttee	sylphy	T'ai Chi	tanner	tasker	techno
sub-deb	summer	suttle	sylvae	taihoa	tannia	Taslan	teckel
subdue	summit	suture	sylvan	tailed	tannic	taslet	tecoma
sub-era	summon	Suzuki	sylvas	tailer	tannie	tassel	tectal
subfeu	sumner	Svarga	symbol	tail in	tannin	tasset	tectum
subgum	Sumner	svelte	syndic	tail on	tannoy	tassie	tedded
subito	sun arc	swaddy	syngas	tailor	Tannoy	Tassie	tedder
subjee	sunbed	swadge	syngen	tailye	Tanoan	tasted	Te Deum
sub-let	sunbow	swaged	synjet	taipan	tan-pit	taster	tedium
sublet	sundae	swager	synoil	taisch	tanrec	tatami	teedle
subman	Sunday	swallo	synroc	takahe	tantra	tatted	tee-hee
submen	sunder	swamis	syntax	take in	tan-vat	tatter	teemer
submit	sundew	swampy	syphon	take it	Tan war	tattie	teener
suborn	sun-dog	Swanee	Syriac	take on	Taoism	tattle	teensy
subsea	sundri	swanky	Syrian	take to	Taoist	tattoo	teenty
subset	sun-dry	swanny	syrinx	take up	taotai	taught	tee off
subtle	sundry	Swaraj	syrtis	taking	tapism	tauric	teepee
subtly	sungem	swardy	syrtos	takkie	taplet	Taurid	Teepol
suburb	sun-god	Swarga	syrupy	talbot	tap out	Taurus	teerer
subway	Sun Gun	swarri	system	talced	tappal	Tau Sug	teesoo
succah	sun-hat	swarry	syzygy	talcum	tapped	tauten	teetar
succor	sunhat	swarth	Szekel	talent	tapper	tautly	teetee
such as	sunken	swarty	Sze Yap	talion	tappet	tautog	teeter
sucken	sunker	swarve	tabard	talked	tap-tap	tavern	teethe
sucker	sunket	swashy	tabbed	talker	tap-too	tawdry	teethy
sucket	sunlet	swatch	tab key	talkie	tarada	tawhai	teevee
suck in	sunlit	swathe	tabled	talk-in	tarama	tawpie	Teflon
suckle	sunned	swaths	tabler	talk of	tarara	taxeme	Tegean
suck up	Sunnis	Swatow	tablet	talk to	tarata	taxied	tegmen
sudary	sunnud	swaver	tabnab	talk up	tar-box	taxies	tegula
sudden	sun-oil	swayed	taboos	tallow	tar-boy	taxine	telcos
Sudder	sun-ray	swayer	taboot	Talmud	tardon	taxman	tele-ad
sudser	sunset	sweaty	tabret	talook	targer	taxmen	teledu
sueded	suntan	swedge	Tabriz	talweg	target	taxwax	telega
Suevic	supawn	sweeny	tabued	tamale	Targui	Taylor	Telegu
suffer	superb	sweepy	tabule	Tamang	Targum	tchick	telial
suffix	sup gum	sweert	tachos	tamanu	tariff	tea bag	telium
Sufism	supine	sweety	tacker	tamari	taring	tea bar	tellen
sugary	supped	swelty	tacket	tamber	tariqa	tea-box	teller
suggan	supper	swerve	tackie	tamein	tarmac	tea boy	tellin
sugged	supple	sweven	tackle	tamely	Tarmac	tea-can	tellow
suited	supply	swifty	tactic	tamine	tarnal	teache	tellus
suiter	surely	swimmy	tactor	tammar	tarock	teacup	telome
suitor	surety	swines	tactus	Tammuz	tarpan	teagle	telson
sukiya	surfer	swinge	tadger	tampan	tar-pit	Teague	Teltag
Sukuma	surfie	swingy	Tadjik	Tampax	tarpon	teaman	Telugu
sulcal	Surlyn	swinny	taenia	tamper	tar-pot	teamer	Temiar
sulcus	surnai	swiper	Taffia	tampon	tarras	teanel	tempeh
sulham	surnap	swipey	tafone	tam-tam	tarred	tea oil	temper
suling	surrey	swirly	tag day	tan-bed	tarrow	tea pad	temple
sulker	Surrey	swishy	tag end	tandem	tarsal	teapot	tempos

tempus	tester	thewed	thyine	timous	titled	Tolman	top off
temura	testes	they'll	thymic	tinaja	titler	tolsel	top out
tenace	testis	they're	thymol	tincal	titman	Toltec	topped
tenant	teston	they've	thymus	tin can	titoki	toluic	topper
Tendai	tetany	Thibet	thyrse	tindal	ti-tree	toluol	toppie
tender	tetchy	thible	thyrsi	tinder	titter	toluyl	topple
tendon	tether	thicko	tibbin	tin ear	tittle	tolzey	topply
tenent	Tethys	thicky	Tibert	tineid	tittup	tomata	topset
tenner	tetrad	thieve	tibiae	tinful	titule	tomato	top ten
tennis	tetryl	thight	tibial	tinger	tityra	tombac	torchy
tennos	tetter	thingy	ticked	tingle	tjaele	tombic	torero
tenour	tettix	thinly	ticken	tingly	tmeses	tomboy	torfle
tenpin	Teuton	thiram	ticker	tin god	tmesis	tom-cat	Torgut
tenrec	tevish	thirst	ticket	tin hat	to a dot	tomcod	Tories
tensed	te-whit	thirty	tickey	tinier	to a man	tomial	tornal
tenser	tewhit	thitsi	tickle	tinily	to arms	tomium	tornus
tenson	tewtaw	thivel	tickly	tining	toasty	tommed	toroid
tensor	Texian	tholoi	tic-tac	tinker	to a tee	to-morn	torori
tented	Tex-Mex	tholos	Ticuna	tinkle	toa-toa	tomtit	torose
tenter	thaive	Thomas	tidbit	tinkly	to bits	tom-tom	torous
tenues	thakin	thorax	tiddle	tinman	to boot	to-name	torpex
tenuis	thakur	thoria	tiddly	tinned	tocher	tonant	torpid
tenure	thaler	thorny	tidier	tinner	tochis	toneme	torpor
tenuto	thalli	thoron	tidily	tinnet	to come	tone up	torque
tenzon	thamin	thorpe	tiding	tinnie	tocsin	Tongan	torret
tepary	Thamud	though	tie-bar	tinpot	to date	tonged	torrid
tepefy	thatch	thrack	tie-dye	tinsel	Todd-AO	tonger	torsel
tephra	that is	thrall	tieing	tinsey	todder	tongue	torsos
tepify	thawer	thrash	tienda	tinted	toddle	tonier	torten
teraph	the act	Thraso	tie-off	tinter	todger	tonify	tortes
terbia	theave	thrave	tie-pin	tipcat	todies	tonish	tortie
tercel	the axe	thrawn	tiepin	tipiti	toe box	tonist	torula
tercer	Theban	thread	tierce	tiplet	toecap	tonite	torvid
tercet	the Bar	threap	tiercé	tip off	toe-end	tonjon	Toryfy
tercio	the boy	threat	tiered	tipped	toeing	tonker	to seek
teredo	the Bye	threep	tierer	tippee	toe-out	tonlet	tosher
Terena	thecae	threne	tie rod	tipper	toe-rag	tonnel	tosser
terete	thecal	thresh	Tietze	tippet	toerag	tonner	toss in
tergal	The Day	threst	tie-wig	Tippex	toe-tip	tonsil	toss up
Tergal	the end	thrice	tiffin	Tipp-Ex	to-fall	tonsor	toston
tergum	the flu	thrift	tiffle	tipple	toffee	too bad	totara
termer	theine	thrill	tigery	tip-tap	togaed	tooler	t'other
termes	theirn	thring	tigger	tiptoe	togate	toolie	tother
termly	theirs	thrips	tiglic	tip-top	togged	tool up	to time
termon	theism	thrive	tiglon	tiptop	toggle	toonie	tot lot
termor	theist	throat	tignon	tipula	to hand	tooter	totora
ternal	the lot	throne	Tigray	tirade	to heel	toothy	totted
ternar	the man	throng	tigron	tirage	to home	tootle	totter
terpen	the Met	throve	tilery	tiring	Toidey	too-too	Tottie
terpin	thenal	thrown	tiling	tirlie	toiler	tootsy	tottle
terrae	thenar	thrump	tiller	tirrit	toilet	topass	toubab
terral	thence	thrums	tillet	tisane	toi-toi	topazy	toucan
Terran	the net	thrush	tillot	Tishri	tokkin	top-cut	touché
terrar	theory	thrust	Tilsit	tissue	to lack	top dog	touchy
terrer	there's	thulia	tilter	tiswas	Toledo	topees	toughe
terret	theses	thumby	tilt-up	tiswin	tolite	Top End	tought
territ	thesis	thumri	timbal	titbit	toller	top hat	toughy
terror	the Six	thurse	timber	titchy	tolley	Tophet	toupee
terser	the Ten	thusly	timbre	titely	toll in	tophus	toupet
tertia	thetic	thwack	timely	titfer	tol-lol	top-lit	tourer
Terran	thenal	throb					
testae	Thetis	thwart	timing	tither	tollon	topman	tourte
testee	the Way	thwite	timist	Titian	toll TV	topmen	Tourte

tousle	trendy	troppo	Tudric	turnel	two-one	unawed	unease
tously	trepan	tro-tro	tuffet	turner	two-ply	unbait	uneasy
touter	trepid	trotty	tufted	Turner	two-two	unbank	uneath
touzle	tressy	trotyl	tufter	turn in	two-way	unbare	unedge
towage	trevat	trough	tugged	turnip	Tyburn	unbark	UNESCO
toward	trevis	troupe	tugger	turn on	tycoon	unbelt	uneven
tow bar	triage	trouse	tuggle	turn to	tykish	unbend	uneyed
towery	tribal	trouts	tughra	turn up	tylose	unbent	unface
towhee	tricar	trouty	tugrik	turpid	Tylose	unbind	unfact
towing	Tricel	trover	tuille	turret	tymbal	unbitt	unfain
towkay	trichi	trowel	Tuinal	turron	tymber	unbody	unfair
townee	tricky	trowie	tuk-tuk	turrum	tympan	unbold	unfast
tow-net	tricot	truant	tulgey	turtle	typhon	unbolt	unfeed
townie	triduo	trucks	tulwar	turved	Typhon	unboot	unfelt
townly	triene	trudge	tumbak	turves	typhus	unborn	unfilm
to work	trifid	truest	tumble	Tuscan	typify	unbran	unfine
tow-row	trifle	true to	tumefy	tusche	typist	unbred	unfirm
towser	trigly	truing	tumour	tushed	tyrant	unbung	unfold
towzle	trigon	truish	tum-tum	tuskar	Tyrian	unburn	unfond
toxoid	tri-jet	truism	tumuli	tusked	Tyrode	unbury	unfool
toybox	triker	trumph	tumult	tusker	tystie	unbusy	unform
toy boy	trilby	trunch	tundra	tussac	uakari	uncage	unfree
toyboy	trillo	trusty	tune in	tussah	Ubangi	uncalm	unfurl
toy car	trimer	truths	tune up	tusser	uberty	uncart	ungain
toy dog	tri-mix	truthy	tunful	tussle	ubiety	uncase	ungave
to-year	trimly	try gun	Tungan	tutory	uckers	uncast	ungear
toyful	trinal	trying	Tungar	tutsan	udatta	unchid	ungild
toyish	triode	try out	Tungus	Tutsis	Udmurt	uncial	ungilt
toyman	triose	trypan	tung-yu	tuttis	Udsbud	unclad	ungird
trabea	triped	try-pot	tunica	tut-tut	uffish	unclay	ungirt
tracer	tripey	tsamma	Tunica	tu-whit	UFOish	unclew	ungive
tradal	tripla	tsetse	tuning	tu-whoo	Uganda	unclip	unglad
traded	triple	T-shirt	Tunker	tuxedo	uglier	unclog	unglue
trader	triply	tsk tsk	tunket	tuyere	uglify	unclue	ungone
tragal	tripod	Tsonga	tunned	tuyère	uglily	uncoat	ungood
tragic	tripos	tsores	tunnel	tvorog	Ugrian	uncock	ungrew
tragus	trippy	tsotsi	tunner	twaite	ugsome	uncoil	ungrow
traiky	tripus	T-strap	tupelo	twangy	uguisu	uncool	ungual
traily	Trique	tsuica	Tupian	tweedy	ujamaa	uncord	ungues
traist	triste	Tswana	tuplet	tweely	ulendo	uncork	unguis
trajet	tristy	T totum	tupped	tweeny	ullage	uncowl	ungula
tramal	trisul	Tuareg	tupsee	tweest	ulnage	uncurb	ungyve
trance	triton	tubage	turaco	tweeze	ulster	uncurl	unhair
tranky	Triton	tubbed	turban	twelve	Ulster	undead	unhand
tranny	trityl	tubber	turbeh	twenty	ultima	undeaf	unhang
trapes	triune	tubboe	turbid	twicer	ultimo	undear	unhasp
trappy	trivet	tubful	turbit	twiggy	umbery	undeep	unhead
trashy	trivia	tub-gig	turble	twilit	umbles	undern	unheal
trauma	trocar	tubing	turbos	twilly	umbone	undewy	unhear
travel	troche	Tubism	turbot	twiner	umboth	undies	unheld
travis	trochi	Tubist	Turcos	twinge	umbrae	undine	unhele
travoy	trogon	tubman	tureen	twingy	umbral	undock	unhelm
treaty	troika	tubule	Turfan	twinky	umbras	undoer	unhelp
treble	Trojan	tubuli	turfen	twinly	umbril	undoes	un-hero
trebly	trolly	Tucana	turgid	twirly	umfaan	undone	unhewn
trefid	Trombe	tuchun	turgor	twisel	umlaut	undraw	unhide
trefle	trompe	tucked	Turing	twisty	umpire	undrew	unhive
treflé	troner	tucker	turion	twitch	umteen	unduke	unholy
trek ox	troper	tucket	turkey	twitty	unable	undull	unhood
tremie	trophi	tuck in	Turkey	two-bit	unaker	unduly	unhook
tremor	trophy	tucuma	Turkic	two-egg	unakin	undust	unhoop
trench	tropic	Tudory	turned	twofer	unarch	undyed	unhope

unhung	unmown	unsnap	unwork	upsend	Usonan	varsal	verdet
unh-unh	unnail	unsnib	unworn	upsett	US pint	varved	verdin
unhurt	unneat	unsoft	unwrap	upshot	usuary	varvel	verdoy
unhusk	unnest	unsold	unyoke	upside	usurer	vassal	vergée
Uniate	unopen	unsole	uparch	upsoar	usward	vastly	verger
UNICEF	unpack	unsoul	upbank	upstay	Utahan	vat dye	verify
unific	unpaid	unsown	upbear	upstir	uterus	vatful	verily
unimer	unpass	unspan	upbeat	uptake	utmost	vat-man	verism
uniped	unpave	unspar	upbind	uptear	utopia	VATman	verist
unipod	unpeel	unsped	upboil	uptick	Utopia	VATmen	verity
unique	unpent	unspin	upbray	up till	utopic	vatted	vermes
unisex	unpick	unspit	upbuoy	uptime	U value	vaulty	vermil
unison	unpile	unspun	up-card	uptook	uvulae	vaunty	vermin
UNISON	unplug	Unstan	upcast	uptorn	uvular	vaward	vermis
unital	unpope	unstep	upcome	uptoss	vacant	V-block	vernal
united	unposh	unstow	upcurl	uptown	vacate	vealer	Verneh
uniter	unpray	unsued	updart	upturn	vacuum	vectis	vernix
unjoin	unprop	unsuit	update	upwaft	vading	vector	Verona
unjust	unrake	unsung	updraw	upwake	vadose	Vedism	verrel
unkard	unread	unsunk	upfill	upward	vagary	Vedist	versal
unkeen	unreal	unsure	upfold	upwarp	V-agent	veejay	versed
unkent	unredy	untack	upgang	upwash	vagile	vegete	verser
unkept	unreel	untame	upgaze	upwell	vagina	veggie	verset
unkind	unrein	untape	upgrow	upwind	vagous	Vehmic	versin
unking	unrent	unthaw	uphand	upwing	vagrom	V-eight	versor
unkink	unrest	untidy	uphang	up with	vahana	veigle	versos
unkiss	unrich	untied	upheap	upwith	vainly	veiled	versus
unknew	unrind	untile	upheld	uracil	Vaisya	veinal	vertex
unknit	unripe	untine	up helm	uraeus	vakeel	veined	vertic
unknot	unrobe	untire	uphill	Uralic	valent	veiner	vervet
unknow	unroll	untold	uphold	uramil	valeta	velate	vesica
unk-unk	unroof	untomb	uphroe	Urania	valgus	Velcro	vesper
unlace	unroot	untone	uphurl	uranic	valine	veleta	vessel
unlade	unrope	untorn	upkeep	Uranus	valise	vellon	vestal
unlaid	unrove	untrim	upknit	uranyl	Valium	vellum	vested
unlash	unrule	untrod	up land	uratic	vallar	velour	vestee
unlead	unruly	untrue	upland	urbane	valley	velure	vestry
unleaf	unrung	untuck	upleap	Urbino	vallum	velvet	vetchy
unleal	unruth	untune	uplift	urchin	valour	vendee	vetoer
unless	unsack	unturn	uplink	urease	valued	vender	vetoes
unlike	unsafe	unused	upload	uredia	valuer	vendor	ve-tsin
unlime	unsaid	unveil	uplong	ureide	values	vendue	vetted
unline	unsalt	unvest	uplook	uremia	valuta	veneer	vetter
unlink	unsane	unvote	upmost	ureter	valval	venene	vetust
unlive	unsawn	unware	upness	uretic	valvar	venery	vexing
unload	unseal	unwarp	up-pent	urgent	valved	Veneti	viable
unlock	unseam	unwary	upping	urinal	vamper	venger	viably
unloop	unseat	unweal	uppish	urning	vandal	venial	Viagra
unlord	unseen	unweft	uppity	urochs	vanish	Venice	viatic
unlost	unself	unwell	up-push	uronic	Vanist	Venite	viator
unlove	unsell	unwept	uprate	uropod	vanity	vennel	vibist
unluck	unsent	unwhig	uprear	ursine	vanner	venomy	Vibram
unlute	unsewn	unwill	uprend	urtica	Vannic	venose	vibrio
unmade	unsexy	unwily	uprest	urtite	vapory	venous	vicine
unmaid	unshed	unwind	uprise	urushi	vapour	vented	victim
unmake	unship	unwise	uprist	usable	Variac	venter	victor
unmask	unshod	unwish	uproar	usager	varied	ventil	vicuña
unmeek	unshoe	unwist	uproll	usance	varier	venule	vidame
unmeet	unshot	unwive	uproot	useful	varies	venust	videos
unmesh	unshut	unwont	uprose	useter	varlet	Vepsic	vidiot
unmild	unskin		uprush	us-ness	varoom	verbal	vidual
unmoor	unslip		upsara		varroa	verbid	vielle

Vienna	vittae	waboom	wampum	waspie	weirdo	whimmy	wilier
view as	Vittel	wacker	wampus	wasser	weirdy	whimsy	wilily
viewer	vivace	wackos	wanded	wasted	welded	whiner	will do
viewly	vivaed	wadded	wander	wastel	welder	whinge	willed
vigent	vivary	wadder	wandle	waster	welked	whingy	willer
vigoro	vively	waddle	wandoo	wastry	welkin	whinny	willet
vigour	vivers	waddly	wangan	watery	welled	whip in	willey
vihara	vivify	wade in	wangle	Watson	wellie	whip on	willie
Viking	vivres	wadies	wanhap	wattap	well-in	whippy	willow
vildly	vizard	wadmal	wanion	wattle	Welshy	whip up	will to
vilely	vizier	wadset	Wankel	Watusi	welted	whirly	willya
Vilene	vizsla	wafery	wanker	waught	welter	whirry	Wilson
vilify	vlakte	waffie	wankle	wavery	Wemyss	whisht	Wilton
vility	vocode	waffle	wanner	wavier	Wendic	whisky	wimble
villan	vocoid	waffly	want ad	wavies	we-ness	whited	wimmin
villus	vocule	wagged	wanted	wavily	wen jen	whiten	wimple
vineal	Vodian	wagger	wanter	wax-end	wen-yen	whitey	Wimpys
vinery	voguer	waggle	wanton	wax-eye	weren't	Whitey	wincer
vin fou	voguey	waggly	wapato	waxier	wessel	whizzo	wincey
vingty	voiced	waggon	wapiti	waxily	Wessex	whizzy	windas
vinify	voicer	Wagogo	wapper	waxing	wester	who-all	winded
vining	voided	Wahabi	wappie	wax-pod	westie	whoe'er	winder
vinney	voidee	wahine	wappit	wayang	Weston	wholly	windle
vinose	voider	wah-wah	waragi	waylay	wet bar	whomso	wind on
vinous	Volans	waiata	war bag	wayman	wet-bob	whoops	window
vintem	volant	wailer	warble	way off	wet fly	whoosh	wind up
vintry	volary	wainer	War Box	way-out	wether	whorer	winery
Vinyon	volcan	waiter	war cry	weaken	wet rot	whosis	Wingco
violer	volens	wait on	warday	weakie	wetted	whydah	winged
violet	volent	wait up	warded	weakly	wetter	why-not	winger
violin	volley	waiver	warden	wealth	wet way	Wiccan	winier
violon	volume	Wai-Wai	warder	weanel	whacko	wicked	wink at
vipoma	voluta	wakame	war-dog	weaner	whacky	wicker	winker
virago	volute	Wakash	warely	weanie	whaler	wicket	winkle
virent	volvox	wake to	warful	weapon	whales	wicopy	winner
vireos	vomica	wake-up	war gas	wearer	whally	widdle	winnow
virgal	vomity	waking	war-god	wear on	whammo	widely	winrow
virger	voodoo	Walach	warier	weasel	whammy	widger	winsey
virgie	vorago	Walian	warily	weaver	wharfs	widget	winter
virgin	vorant	waling	Waring	weazen	wharve	widgie	wintle
Virgos	vortex	walker	war-man	webbed	what ho	widish	wintry
virial	votary	Walker	warmer	web-fed	what if	wieldy	Wintun
virile	Vo-Tech	walk in	warmly	Webley	what of	wiener	wipe up
virino	voteen	walk it	warmth	wedded	whatso	wienie	wirble
virion	vote in	walk-on	warm up	wedeln	wheaty	wifely	wire in
viroid	voting	walk up	warner	wedged	wheely	Wiffle	wirier
virola	votive	wallah	warped	wedger	wheeze	wifish	wirily
virole	Votyak	walled	warper	wedgie	wheezy	wigeon	wiring
virose	vowess	waller	warple	weeded	whelky	wigged	wirrah
virous	vox pop	wallet	warred	weeder	whelve	wiggle	wisdom
virtue	voyage	wallie	warree	weekly	whenas	wiggly	wisely
visaed	voyeur	wallis	warren	weenie	whence	wighty	wisent
visage	vuelta	wallop	Warren	weeper	whenso	wiglet	wise to
viscid	Vulcan	wallow	warrer	weepie	wherry	wigsby	wished
viscin	vulgar	wallum	warsle	weeshy	wheyey	wig-wag	wisher
viscus	vulgus	walnut	warted	weever	whidah	wigwag	wishly
Vishnu	vulpic	walrus	wasabi	weevil	whiffy	wigwam	wissel
visile	vulval	walter	washed	wee-wee	whiles	wilder	Wistar
vision	vulvar	wamara	washen	wei ch'i	whilie	wildie	witchy
visual	vulvas	wamble	washer	weight	whilly	wildly	witful
vitric	Vynide	wambly	washin	Weimar	whilom	wilful	withal
vitrum	wabbit	wampee	wash up	weiner	whilst	wilgie	withen

wither	woomph	wrothy	yakuza	yen hop	yorker	zareba	zither
withes	woopie	wryest	yaller	yenned	Yorker	zariba	zlotys
within	worder	wubbit	yammer	yen-yen	Yorkie	zealot	zocalo
with it	wordly	wurley	Yankee	yeoman	Yoruba	zearat	zodiac
with us	worked	wurzel	Yanqui	yeomen	you-all	zeatin	zoftig
Witney	worker	wuther	yantra	yepsen	you bet	zebeck	Zogist
witted	work in	wu ts'ai	yaourt	yerbal	you lot	zebras	Zoilus
witter	work it	wyvern	yapped	yes-man	you see	zedonk	zombie
Wittig	work on	Xanadu	yapper	yes-men	youths	Zeeman	zonate
wittol	work to	X chair	yappet	yes sir	youthy	zenana	Zonian
wivern	work up	xenial	yaqona	yessir	yowler	Zendic	zoning
wizard	wormed	xenium	yarder	yessum	yow-yow	Zendik	zonite
woader	wormer	xeroma	Yardie	yester	yo-yoed	zenick	zonked
wobble	wornil	X-frame	yarely	yether	yo-yoer	Zenist	zonkey
wobbly	worrit	Xhosas	yarooh	Yezidi	yo-yoes	zenith	zonula
woeful	worsen	xoanon	yarran	yieldy	Y-plate	Zenker	zonule
Wogdon	worser	X-plate	yarrow	yikker	Y track	zephyr	zonure
woggle	worthy	x-rated	yatter	yipped	yttria	zereba	zooman
wolfer	wortle	X-rated	yaupon	yippee	yuckle	zeroth	zootic
wolver	woubit	xylary	yautia	yippie	Yukawa	zester	zorino
wolves	wounds	xylene	yaw-haw	Yishuv	yumpie	zeugma	zoster
wombat	woundy	xylose	yawler	Yizkor	yum-yum	ziarat	Zouave
wombed	wowser	xystus	yawner	ylidic	yuppie	ziczac	zounds
womble	wow-wow	yabber	yawper	yobbos	zacate	zigged	Zou-Zou
wompoo	wraith	yabbie	Yazidi	yogini	zaffre	zigzag	zoysia
wonder	wrap up	yachty	yclept	yogism	zaftig	zillah	zufolo
wongai	wrasse	yacker	Y cross	yogurt	zagged	Zimmer	Zuñian
wonner	wrathy	yaffle	yeared	yo-ho-ho	zaguan	zincic	Zurich
wonted	wraxle	Yagara	yearly	yoicks	zambra	zincos	zydeco
wonton	wreath	yah boo	yea-say	yoi-yoi	zambuk	Zindiq	Zydeco
wooded	wrench	Yahgan	yeasty	yoking	zander	zingel	zygite
wooden	wretch	Yahudi	yedder	Yokuts	zanier	zinger	zygoma
wooder	wriest	Yahveh	yeehaw	yolked	zanily	zinnia	zygote
woodie	wright	Yahweh	yeeuch	yomper	Zantac	zip bag	Zyklon
woodly	wristy	yakdan	ye gods	yom tov	Zapata	zip gun	zymase
woodsy	writee	Yakima	Yehudi	yonder	zap gun	zip-out	Zyrian
woofer	writer	yakked	yeller	yonker	zapote	zipped	Zythum
wooled	writhe	yakker	yellow	yonnie	zapped	zipper	
woolen	wroken	yakkha	yelper	yoo-hoo	zapper	zip-top	
woolly	wrongo	yaksha	Yemeni	yordim	zarape	zircon	

SEVEN LETTERS

Aaronic	abustle	acouchi	*ad litem*	agamous	airglow	al dente
abacist	abuttal	acquest	admiral	agarose	airhead	alecost
aback of	abutted	acquire	admirer	agelast	air-hole	ale-hoof
abacost	abutter	acquist	adnexal	ageless	airiest	alembic
Abaddon	abysmal	acreage	Adonian	age-long	air-kiss	alength
abalone	abyssal	acridid	adonize	age-mate	air lane	alerion
abandon	academe	acridly	adoptee	agendas	airless	alertly
abate of	academy	Acrilan	adopter	agendum	airlift	aleuron
abattis	Academy	acrobat	adorant	ageusia	air-lift	alewife
abature	Acadian	acrogen	adoring	aggrace	airlike	ale-wort
abaxial	acarine	acronym	adorner	aggrade	airline	alfalfa
Abbasid	acaroid	acrylic	adrenal	aggress	airlock	alfaqui
abdomen	acausal	actable	adulate	aggroup	airmail	alferez
abelian	accidie	act a lie	adulter	agilely	air mile	Alfisol
Abenaki	accinge	act-drop	adultly	agility	airmiss	alforja
abetted	acclaim	actinia	advance	agister	air-pipe	algebra
abetter	accompt	actinic	adverse	agistor	airplay	alginic
abettor	account	actinon	advised	agitant	airport	Ali Baba
abeyant	accrete	actress	advisee	agitate	air pump	alibied
abide by	accrual	act-tune	adviser	agitato	air rage	alidade
abiding	accrued	actuary	advisor	agnamed	air raid	alienee
abietic	accruer	actuate	advowee	agnatic	airship	alienor
abigail	accrues	act up to	aeolian	Agnoite	air-shot	aliform
ability	accurse	acushla	Aeolian	agnomen	air show	aliment
abiotic	accurst	acutely	aeonial	agnosia	airsick	alimony
a bit hot	accusal	acutest	aeonian	agnosic	airside	aliquot
abjurer	accused	acyclic	aerated	agonies	airtime	a little
ablator	accuser	acylate	aerator	agonise	air-time	alive oh
able for	ace-high	adagial	aerobat	agonism	airward	Al-kaaba
ableism	acerbic	adagios	aerobic	agonist	airwave	alkalic
abolish	acerbly	adamant	aerosol	agonize	ajutage	alkalis
abomasa	acerose	adamite	Aesopic	a good 'un	a kind of	alkanet
abortee	acetate	Adamite	aestive	agraffe	akvavit	alkanna
abortus	acetify	adangle	*aetatis*	agrapha	Aladdin	Alkoran
abought	acetone	adapter	a far cry	aground	alameda	alkoxyl
aboulia	acetous	adaptor	afar off	ahead of	Alamire	allayer
aboulic	Achaean	adaxial	a fat lot	a-height	à la mode	all ears
abrader	Achaian	adazzle	afeared	ahunger	alamort	alleged
Abraham	acharya	addenda	affable	ahungry	alanine	alleger
abreact	Achates	address	affably	aiblins	alapana	allegro
abreast	Acheron	adducer	affaire	aidable	Alaskan	allelic
abridge	achieve	adenine	*affairé*	aidance	Alastor	allergy
abroach	achiral	adenoid	affiant	aidless	albedos	alleyed
abscess	achylia	adenoma	affinal	aileron	albinos	all eyes
abscind	acicula	adeptly	affined	ailette	albitic	allgood
abscise	acid air	adherer	affixal	ailment	albumen	all hail
absciss	acid dye	adhibit	affixer	aim high	albumin	all-heal
abscond	acidify	adiabat	afflate	aimless	alcaide	allicin
absence	acidise	adipose	afflict	air-ball	alcalde	all-male
absinth	acidity	adipous	afforce	airbase	alcanna	allness
absolve	acidize	adivasi	affront	air-bell	alcayde	allonge
absorpt	acinous	Adivasi	afghani	air-cell	alcazar	all over
abstain	ack emma	adjoint	aflaunt	aircrew	alchemy	allower
abubble	aclinic	adjourn	aflower	airdrop	alchera	alloxan
a-burton	acolyte	adjudge	African	air-drop	alcohol	allseed
abusage	aconite	adjunct	against	airflow	Alcoran	all-star
abusive	acorned	adjutor	Aga Khan	airfoil	alcoved	all that

all this	amentum	anchusa	anodize	aphetic	Arabian	armlock
all-time	Amerind	ancient	anodyne	aphides	arabica	armoire
all told	Ameslan	ancilla	anoesis	aphonia	Arabise	armorer
allurer	Amharic	ancones	anoetic	aphonic	Arabism	armoury
alluvia	amiable	ancress	anomaly	aphotic	Arabist	armrest
all work	amiably	Andaman	anopsia	Apician	Arabize	army ant
allylic	amianth	andante	anormal	apiculi	arachis	arnatta
almadia	amidine	AND gate	anosmia	a-pieces	Aramaic	arnotto
almanac	amildar	andiron	anosmic	apishly	Aramean	arousal
almirah	aminded	and more	another	aplanat	araneid	arouser
almoign	amirate	and only	ansated	aplasia	Arapaho	arraign
almondy	ammeter	android	antacid	aplenty	araroba	arrange
almoner	ammonal	and so on	antapex	aplitic	aration	arrased
almonry	ammonia	and such	ant-bear	apnoeic	Arawaks	arrayal
almsfee	amnesia	and that	antbird	apocope	arbiter	arrayer
almsman	amnesic	anemone	antefix	apodeme	arblast	arrears
a load of	amnesty	anergic	ant eggs	apodous	arboral	arriage
aloetic	amniote	aneroid	antenna	apogamy	arboret	arrival
alonely	amoebae	aneurin	antheap	apogeal	arbutus	arriver
alongst	amoebas	a new one	ant-heap	apogean	arcaded	arrowed
aloofly	amoebic	angareb	anthill	apojove	Arcadia	arroyos
Alp-horn	amongst	angekok	Anthony	apology	Arcadic	arsenal
already	amoraic	angelet	anthrax	apolune	arcanum	arsenic
alright	amorino	angelic	anticly	apomict	archaic	art deco
Alsatia	amorist	angelin	antigen	apoplex	Archean	art form
al segno	Amorite	angelot	anti-god	apostil	archery	arthame
also-ran	amoroso	angelus	antilog	apostle	archeus	article
Altaian	amorous	angerly	antique	apothem	arch-foe	artisan
alterer	amorphy	Angevin	antlike	apparat	arching	artiste
althaea	amosite	anginal	ant-lion	apparel	archive	artizan
Althing	amotion	angioma	antonym	appeach	archlet	artless
althorn	amphora	Anglian	Antwerp	appease	archway	artsier
alto sax	amplest	anglice	anxiety	applaud	arc lamp	artsman
alumina	amplify	Anglify	anxious	applial	arc sine	artwork
alumnae	ampoule	Anglist	anybody	applied	arcuate	art work
alumnus	ampster	Angolan	any more	applier	ardency	arugula
alunite	amptman	angrier	anymore	applies	arduous	as a gift
alveary	ampulla	angrily	any road	appoint	areally	as a rule
alveole	amputee	anguine	any time	appress	areaway	ascarid
alveoli	amusing	anguish	anytime	apprise	arenite	ascaris
alyssum	amusive	angular	anyways	apprize	arenose	ascesis
amalgam	amylase	anhinga	anywhen	approof	areolae	ascetic
amasser	amylene	anilide	anywise	approve	areolar	ascitic
amateur	amyloid	aniline	apaches	appulse	Aretine	ascitic
amative	amylose	anility	Apaches	apraxia	arguing	asclent
amatory	anacard	animate	apagoge	apricot	argyria	ascribe
a matter	anaemia	animism	apanage	a priori	aridify	ascrive
amazing	anaemic	animist	aparejo	aproned	aridity	asepsis
ambages	anagoge	anionic	apatite	apropos	arietta	aseptic
ambassy	anagogy	aniseed	a peck of	aprotic	ariette	asexual
ambatch	anagram	anisole	apelike	apsidal	Arimasp	as far as
ambient	anality	annates	apeling	apsides	ariosos	ashamed
ambones	analogy	annatto	Apelles	apteryx	aripple	Ashanti
amboyna	analyse	annelid	apepsia	aptness	arkosic	A-shaped
ambries	analyst	annicut	apertly	Apulian	armband	Asherah
ambroid	analyze	annotto	aphakia	aquaria	arm-bone	ash-grey
ambs-ace	Anamese	annoyer	aphakic	aquatic	armfuls	ash-hole
ameboid	anapsid	annuity	aphasia	aquavit	armhole	ashiver
amender	anarchy	annular	aphasic	aqueous	armiger	ashling
amenity	anatase	annulet	aphelia	aquifer	armilla	ashtray
amental	anatomy	annulus	aphemia	aquiver	armless	ash tree
amentia	anchovy	anodise	aphesis	Arabdom	armlike	ashweed

ash-wood	Atebrin	audible	awarder	back-way	balling	barge in
Asianic	atelier	audibly	a wee bit	baclava	ballist	bar-girl
Asiarch	Atellan	audient	aweless	baconer	ballium	barilla
Asiatic	Atenism	audited	awesome	baculum	ballock	bar-keel
asinine	Aterian	auditor	awfully	bad call	balloon	barkeep
askance	at fault	aufgabe	awkward	bad coin	balls up	bar line
askaris	at first	augitic	awl-bird	bad debt	balmier	barmaid
asklent	at grade	augment	awlwort	baddest	balmily	barmier
AS level	at grass	augural	awnless	baddies	balneal	barmily
asocial	at grips	augurer	axe-head	baddish	baloney	barmkin
as of now	athanor	auguste	axially	bad form	balsamy	barmote
a sort of	at heart	aulnage	axillae	badland	Baluchi	Barnaby
asperge	atheise	aunties	axillar	badling	bambini	barneys
asperse	atheism	aurally	axinite	bad luck	bambino	barngun
asphalt	atheist	aureate	axinine	badmash	banally	barnlot
asphyxy	atheize	aureity	axolotl	bad mood	bandage	bar none
aspirer	atheous	aurelia	axoneme	badness	band-aid	barn owl
aspirin	athirst	aureola	Aymaras	bad news	Band-Aid	barocco
asprawl	athlete	aureole	azarole	bad show	bandbox	baronet
aspread	athrill	auricle	azelaic	baffler	bandeau	baroque
asquint	athrong	aurochs	Azilian	Baganda	bandied	Barotse
assagai	athwart	aurorae	azimuth	*bagarre*	bandier	barrace
assault	atingle	auroral	azotize	bagasse	bandies	barrack
assayer	atiptoe	auroras	Aztecan	bagfuls	banding	barrage
assegai	atishoo	auscult	azulene	baggage	bandits	barrico
assever	at issue	auslaut	azuline	baggier	bandlet	barrier
ass-head	at large	auspice	azurine	baggily	bandore	barring
asshole	at least	austere	azurite	bagging	bandsaw	bar-room
assizer	at night	austral	azygous	bag lady	band-saw	barruly
assizor	at nurse	autarch	Azymite	baglike	baneful	bar soap
asslike	atomies	autarky	baa-lamb	bagnios	bangled	bartsia
assuage	atomise	autobus	Baalism	bagpipe	bang off	barwood
assumer	atomism	autocar	Baalist	bagwash	bang out	barytes
assumpt	atomist	autocue	Baalite	bagworm	banjoes	barytic
assured	atomize	Autocue	babassu	Bahadur	banking	baryton
assurer	at pause	automat	babbitt	Baha'ism	banksia	bascule
assuror	at peace	autonym	Babbitt	Bahaism	banning	base hit
astable	at point	autopsy	babbler	Bahaist	bannock	baseman
astatic	at press	autumny	babiche	Bahiric	banquet	basenji
asteism	at quiet	auxesis	Babygro	bailage	banshee	base pay
astilbe	atresia	auxetic	babyish	baileys	banteng	bashful
astound	atresic	Avarian	babyism	bailiff	Banting	bashing
astrain	atretic	avarice	Babylon	baillie	banzuke	Bashkir
astrand	a trifle	ave-bell	babysit	bail out	baptise	bashlik
astream	atriums	avellan	Bacardi	bailout	baptism	basilar
astrict	at roost	avenger	baccate	bairnly	baptist	basilic
astride	atrophy	average	Bacchic	baittle	baptize	basinet
astroid	at sight	Avernal	Bacchus	baklava	baracan	Baskish
astylar	at speed	averred	Bachian	balance	Barbara	basmati
asudden	at squat	Avestan	bacilli	balcony	Barbary	Basotho
asunder	at stake	Avestic	backbar	baldies	barbate	basqued
as usual	at table	aviator	back emf	balding	barbell	bass-bar
atactic	attaboy	avicide	back-end	baldish	barbery	bassist
ataghan	attaché	avidity	backhoe	baldric	barbola	bassman
at a heat	attaint	avionic	backing	baleful	Barbour	bassoon
at a loss	attempt	avocado	backlit	bale out	barbule	bastard
at an end	at times	avodiré	backlog	baleout	barchan	bastide
at a push	attract	avoidal	back off	balkier	bar code	bastile
ataraxy	attrite	avoider	back out	ballade	bardies	bastion
at a time	at worst	avowant	back-pay	ballast	bardish	bastite
atavism	*auberge*	awaiter	back row	ballata	bardism	bateaux
at a word	auction	awake to	back-saw	ballboy	bargain	batfish

bat flea	bearpit	beer-jug	benison	betaken	bigness	Bismark
Bath bun	bear-pit	beer mat	benomyl	beta ray	bigoted	bismite
bathing	beastie	beer-off	benorth	betcher	bigotry	bismuth
bath mat	beastly	beeswax	benthic	Beth Din	big shot	bistort
bathtub	beatbox	beetled	benthos	bethink	big show	bistred
bath-tub	beatify	be fixed	benting	bethumb	big talk	bistros
bathyal	beating	be for it	benzene	bethump	big time	bitless
batiste	beatnik	beggary	benzine	betimes	big tree	bitonal
bat-mule	beat off	begging	benzoic	betitle	bike boy	bit part
batsman	beat out	beghard	benzoin	betoken	bikeway	bittern
batsmen	beaufin	begin at	benzole	betroth	bikkies	bittier
battels	beauish	begin on	benzoyl	betting	bilayer	bittily
battery	beau-pot	begloom	Beothuk	bettong	bilboes	bittock
battier	beavers	begonia	bepaint	betulin	bi-level	bitumen
battily	bebeeru	begorra	bequest	between	biliary	bitwise
batting	bebleed	begrace	be quick	betwixt	bilimbi	bivalve
battler	beblood	begrime	be quiet	bevilly	bilious	bivious
batture	be brief	beguile	bereave	bevvies	billard	bivouac
battuta	because	beguine	beretta	bewitch	billeté	bizarre
batwing	becharm	behight	bergylt	bezanty	billies	blabbed
bauchle	becloud	beignet	berhyme	bezique	billion	blabber
baudkin	becross	bejasus	be rid of	bez tine	billowy	blacken
Bauhaus	becrown	bejesus	Bermuda	bhangra	bilobed	blacker
bausond	bedding	bejewel	Bernese	bheesty	biltong	blackly
bauxite	bedevil	be judge	berried	Biafran	bimanal	black up
bavaroy	bedfast	beknave	berries	biasing	bi-media	bladder
baviaan	bedgown	belated	berserk	bias-ply	bimetal	blagged
bawcock	bedhead	Belauan	besaiel	biassed	bimodal	blagger
bawdier	bed-head	belcher	besaint	biaxial	bindery	blakeys
bawdily	bedight	beldame	besayle	bibasic	binding	blandly
bawl out	bedizen	Belgian	beseech	bibbing	binging	blanked
bawneen	bedload	belibel	beshade	bibbler	binning	blanket
bay leaf	Bedouin	believe	beshine	bib-cock	binocle	blankly
bayonet	bedpost	bellboy	beshrew	bibelot	biochip	blarney
bay salt	bedrest	bell-boy	besides	biblist	biocide	blasted
bay tree	bedrock	Belleek	besiege	bicycle	biodata	blaster
baywood	bedroll	bell-hop	beslave	bidarka	bioherm	blatant
bazooka	bedroom	bellied	besmear	biddery	biology	blather
be about	bedside	bellies	besmoke	biddies	biomass	blatter
beached	bedsock	bell jar	besouth	bidding	bionics	blawort
beadier	bedsore	bellman	bespake	bid fair	biotech	blaze up
beadily	bedtick	bellmen	bespeak	biennia	biotite	blazing
beading	bedtime	Bellona	bespeck	bifidly	biotope	bleakly
beadlet	be dying	bellows	bespell	bifilar	biotype	bleater
bead-rim	bee-balm	beloved	bespoke	bifocal	bipedal	bleeder
beagler	bee-bird	Beltane	besport	bifront	biplane	bleeper
beakful	beechen	belting	bespout	big band	bipolar	blellum
beamish	beefalo	beltman	bestain	big bang	biprism	blemish
beam sea	beefier	beltmen	bespeck	big bore	birchen	blender
beanbag	beefily	belt out	bestead	big deal	bircher	blesbok
bean-bag	beefing	beltway	best buy	bigener	Bircher	blessed
beanery	beef tea	belying	best end	Bigfeet	bird dog	blesser
be a pair	bee-glue	bemazed	bestest	Bigfoot	birdied	bless me
be a pulp	beehive	bencher	bestial	big game	birdies	blether
bear-cat	beeline	bendlet	bestick	biggest	birding	blewits
bearded	bee-moth	beneath	bestill	bigging	birdman	Blighty
beardie	been and	benefic	best man	biggish	biretta	blinder
bear-hug	beerage	benefit	bestorm	biggity	biriani	blindly
bearing	beer-boy	Benelux	bestrew	big-head	birling	blind me
bearish	beer gut	Bengali	be stuck	bighorn	biryani	blind to
bear off	beerier	benight	bestuck	big idea	biscuit	blinker
bear out	beerily	Benioff	betaine	big name	Bislama	blintze

blipped	boating	boluses	bordage	bow line	brassie	brisken
blister	boatman	bombard	bordure	bowline	brassil	brisket
blither	boatmen	bombast	boredom	bowling	brastle	briskly
blitter	Bobadil	bomb bay	Bornean	bowl out	brattle	bristle
bloated	bobajee	bombing	borneol	bowshot	bravado	bristly
bloater	bob a job	bomblet	bornite	bowtell	bravely	Bristol
blocker	bobance	bombora	boronia	bow wave	bravery	brisure
block in	bob a nob	bonaght	borough	bowyang	bravoes	Britain
block up	bobbery	bonanza	Borstal	boxcalf	bravura	British
Blondin	bobbies	bonasus	borstch	box coat	brawler	brittle
blooded	bobbing	bondage	bortsch	box-fish	brawner	brittly
bloomed	bobbish	bonding	boscage	boxfuls	brazier	britzka
bloomer	bobbled	bondman	boskage	box-haul	breachy	broaden
blooper	bobotie	bone-ash	Bosniac	boxiana	breaden	broadly
blossom	bobsled	bone dry	Bosnian	boxiest	breadth	brocade
blotchy	bob-sled	bone-oil	bosomed	box kite	breaker	brocard
blot out	bobstay	boneset	bosquet	boxlike	break in	brochan
blotted	bobtail	bonfire	bossage	boxroom	break of	brocked
blotter	bob-wire	bongoes	bossier	box-seat	break up	Brocken
blouson	Bocardo	boniest	bossily	box tree	breakup	brocket
blow-dry	bocasin	bonitos	bossism	boxwood	breasty	brockit
blowfly	boccaro	bonjour	boss-man	boycott	breathe	brodder
blowgun	bocking	bonkers	bostryx	boyhood	breathy	brodkin
blowier	bodeful	bonnail	Boswell	boykins	breccia	Broeder
blowing	bodikin	bonnier	botanic	boylike	brecham	broggle
blow job	body bag	bonnily	botargo	brabble	breeder	brogued
blow off	Boeotic	bontbok	botcher	braccio	breed in	broider
blow out	Boer War	bonzess	bothies	brachet	Breguet	broiler
blubbed	boffola	boobies	botling	brachia	brekker	broking
blubber	bogbean	boobook	bottine	bracing	brekkie	bromate
blucher	bog-bean	boodler	bottled	bracken	Bren gun	bromide
bludger	boggard	boogied	bottler	bracker	bretzel	bromine
blue bag	boggier	boogies	bottony	bracket	brevier	bromism
blue box	bogging	boohoos	botulin	bradawl	brevity	bromize
bluecap	boggler	bookend	boudoir	bradoon	brewage	bronchi
blue eye	bog-hole	book-end	boughed	bragged	brewery	broncho
blue fly	bog iron	bookful	boulder	bragger	brewing	broncos
bluegum	bog-land	booking	boulter	bragget	bribery	brooder
blueing	bog moss	bookish	bouncer	brahman	brickie	broomie
blueish	Bogomil	booklet	bounded	Brahman	brickle	brothel
blueism	bog pine	bookman	bounden	brahmic	bricole	brother
blue jay	bog-rush	bookmen	bounder	brahmin	bridler	brought
blue rod	bog-trot	book-shy	bound to	Brahmin	bridoon	browden
blue-sky	bogusly	Boolean	bound up	braider	briefly	brownie
blue tit	bogyman	boom box	bouquet	braid of	briered	Brownie
bluffer	bogymen	booming	bourbon	Braille	brigade	brownly
bluffly	Bohemia	boomlet	Bourbon	brained	brigand	browser
blunder	boilery	boonies	bourder	braless	brimful	bruchid
blunger	boiling	boorish	bourdon	bramble	brimmed	brucine
bluntly	boil-off	booster	bourock	brambly	brimmer	brucite
blur out	Bokhara	bootboy	bourrée	Bramley	brinded	bruckle
blurred	boleros	bootery	boutade	branchy	brindle	bruiser
blusher	boletus	bootleg	bow down	branded	Brinell	brulzie
bluster	bolivar	boot-top	bow-fast	brander	bringer	Brummie
boarder	bollard	booze-up	bow-hand	brangle	bring in	brumous
boardly	bollock	boozier	bowhead	bran-new	bring on	brushed
boarish	bologna	boozily	bowhunt	bran-pie	bring to	brusher
boaster	Bologna	bopping	bowlder	bran tub	bring up	brush up
boatage	boloney	bopster	bow-legs	brashly	brinish	brusque
boat-axe	Bolshie	boracic	bowless	brasque	brinjal	brustle
boat-fly	bolster	borasco	bowlful	brassed	brioche	brutely
boatful	bolting	Borazon	bowlful	brassey	briquet	brutify

brutish	bullous	burster	by a nose	caesura	calvish	canteen
brutism	bullpen	burthen	bycoket	cafe-bar	calvity	canthus
bruvver	bull-pup	bur-weed	bye-byes	café-bar	calyces	cantina
bruxism	bulrush	burying	bye-line	cagiest	calycle	canting
bubbler	bulwark	busbied	by force	cagoule	calypso	cantlet
bubonic	bumbaze	busbies	bygoing	cahoots	calyxes	cant off
buccaro	bumbler	buscarl	by golly	Cainite	calzone	cantred
buckeen	bumboat	bush-cat	by heart	Cairene	camaron	cantrip
buckeye	bum-boat	bush cow	by jingo	caisson	cambial	canvass
bucking	bummalo	bush-eel	byliner	caitiff	cambist	can wait
buckish	bumming	bush-fly	by night	cajeput	cambium	canzona
buckler	bumpety	bush hen	by order	cajoler	cambrel	canzone
buckoes	bumpier	bushido	by-place	cajuput	cambric	capable
buckram	bumpily	bushier	by right	cakelet	camelry	capably
buck-saw	bumping	bushies	Byronic	cake-mix	Camenes	cap-à-pie
bucolic	bumpkin	bushily	by sight	calabar	cameral	Cape Cod
buddied	bump off	bushing	byssine	calaber	Camford	Cape fox
buddies	bum-suck	bushman	by steam	calamus	cammock	capelet
budding	Bunbury	Bushman	by the by	calando	camoodi	capelin
budge up	buncher	bushmen	by-thing	calcify	Camorra	caperer
budless	buncoes	bush-pig	by turns	calcine	campana	capfuls
budworm	bundler	bush-rat	by water	calcite	Campari	Caphtor
buffalo	bundook	bush tea	bywater	calcium	camp bed	capital
buffish	bungler	bush-tit	by way of	calculi	camphor	capitan
buffoon	bunjara	busiest	bywoner	caldera	campier	capitao
bugaboo	bunk bed	busking	by wrong	caldron	campily	Capitol
bugbane	bunnies	bus lane	cabaret	calèche	camping	capless
bugbear	Bunraku	bussing	cabbage	calends	campion	caplike
bug-eyed	bunting	bus stop	cabbagy	calfish	campong	capouch
buggery	buoyage	bustard	cabbala	Caliban	camp out	capping
buggier	buoyant	bustier	Cabbala	caliber	camwood	caprate
buggies	burbler	bustler	cabbies	calibre	canakin	caprice
bugging	burdock	busy bee	cabined	caliche	canasta	caprine
bugloss	burdoun	butanol	cabinet	calicle	can bank	cap rock
bug-word	bureaus	butcher	Caboclo	calicos	can-buoy	caproic
bugwort	bureaux	butenyl	caboose	calinda	candela	caproyl
builder	burette	butlery	cabotin	calipee	candent	Capsian
build in	burgage	butment	cab-rank	caliper	candida	capsize
build on	burgeon	butt-end	ca'canny	caliver	candied	capstan
build up	burgess	buttery	ca' canny	callant	candies	capsule
built-in	burghal	but that	cachexy	call box	candiru	captain
built-up	burgher	but then	cacique	call-boy	candler	caption
buirdly	burghul	butties	cackler	call-day	can-dock	captive
bulblet	burglar	buttock	cacodyl	call for	candour	capture
bulbose	Burgund	buttons	cacoepy	calling	canella	capuche
bulbous	Burkitt	buttony	caconym	call off	cane-rat	carabid
bulimia	burlier	butt out	cadaver	callose	canezou	caracal
bulimic	burlily	but what	cad-bait	callous	canions	caracul
bulk-buy	Burmans	butyric	caddice	call out	cankery	caramba
bulkier	Burmese	buvette	caddied	calluna	cannach	caramel
bulkily	burn-bag	buxarry	caddies	calmant	cannery	caratch
bullace	Burnham	buyable	caddish	calomel	cannier	caravan
bull ant	burning	buy a pup	cadence	caloric	cannily	caravel
bullary	burnish	buy-back	cadency	calorie	canning	caraway
bullate	burn low	buy into	cadenza	calotte	cannula	carbene
bull-bat	burn off	buy over	cadgily	caloyer	canonic	carbide
bulldog	burnous	buy time	Cadmean	caltrap	canonry	carbine
bullied	burn out	buzzard	cadmium	caltrop	Canopic	car bomb
bullies	burp gun	buzz off	caducei	calumba	Canopus	carcake
bullion	bur-reed	buzz-saw	cad-worm	calumet	cantata	carcase
bullish	burrito	buzzwig	Caecias	calumny	Cantate	carcass
bullock	bursary	by and by	caesium	Calvary	cant-dog	car coat

carcoon	carry up	cat door	celeste	chalone	chassis	Chicano
cardecu	carsick	catechu	cellist	chaloth	chasten	chic-est
cardiac	cartage	catenae	Cellnet	chamade	chateau	chicken
cardial	cartful	catenas	cellule	chamber	château	chicory
cardies	cartman	cateran	celosia	chambré	chatted	chidden
cardoon	cart off	caterer	celsian	chamfer	chattel	chiding
carduus	cartoon	catfish	Celsius	chamiso	chatter	chiefly
care for	cart-rut	cat flap	cembalo	chamois	chayote	chiefry
careful	cart-way	cat foot	cenacle	champac	chazzan	chiffon
carezza	carvery	Cathari	censual	champer	cheapen	chigger
carfare	carve up	Cathars	censure	chancel	cheapie	chignon
carfuls	carving	cat-haul	centage	chancer	cheaply	chi-hike
cargoes	carvone	cathead	centaur	chancre	cheatee	chikara
cariama	car wash	cathect	centavo	changer	cheater	chikhor
Caribee	cascade	cathode	centile	channel	cheat on	Chilcat
caribou	cascara	cat-hole	centime	channer	chebule	childed
carices	caseate	catlick	céntimo	chanson	Chechen	childly
carinal	case law	catlike	centner	chanter	chechia	Chilean
carioca	case-oil	catling	central	chantey	checked	chiliad
cariole	caseous	catmint	centred	chantry	checker	Chilian
carious	casevac	cat's-ear	centric	chaotic	check in	Chilkat
caritas	cash box	cat's-eye	centrum	chapati	check on	chiller
carjack	cash cow	Catseye	century	chapeau	check-up	chillum
carking	cashier	cat show	cepheid	chaplet	Cheddar	chilver
carline	casinos	cat's-paw	Cepheus	chapman	cheeked	chime in
carling	Caspian	catsuit	ceramic	chapmen	cheeper	chimera
carlish	casquet	cat-tail	cerebra	chappal	cheerer	chimere
Carlism	cassada	cattalo	cereous	chapped	cheerio	chimney
Carlist	cassata	Cattern	ceresin	chappie	cheerly	chinchy
carload	cassava	cattery	cerotic	chappli	cheer up	Chindit
carmine	cassino	cattier	cerotin	chappow	cheetah	Chinese
carnage	cassiri	cattily	certain	chapter	cheetal	chinkle
Carnata	Cassius	catting	certify	charact	chelate	chinned
Carnian	cassock	cattish	cerumen	charade	Chelsea	chinook
carnify	cassone	catwalk	cervine	charged	chemise	Chinook
carnose	Castile	catydid	Cesolfa	chargee	chemism	chintzy
carnous	casting	caubeen	cessile	charger	chemist	chinwag
caroche	castled	caudate	cession	chargés	chequer	chin-wag
caroler	castlet	cauline	cesspit	charier	cherish	chip-axe
Carolin	cast net	caulker	cestode	charily	cheroot	chipped
Carolus	castock	cause of	cestoid	chariot	chervil	chipper
carosse	cast-off	caustic	ceviche	charism	chessel	chippie
carotic	cast out	cautery	Chablis	charity	chested	chirper
carotid	castral	caution	cha-cha'd	Charley	chester	chirrup
carotin	castrum	cavally	chacham	charlie	Chesvan	chitter
carouba	casuist	cavalry	cha-chas	Charlie	chetnik	chizzer
carouse	Catalan	cave art	Chadian	charmed	chevage	chlamys
carozzi	catalpa	caveman	chafery	charmer	chevied	chloral
car park	catapan	cavemen	chaffer	charnel	chevies	chloric
carpent	catarrh	cavetto	chafing	charpie	Cheviot	chobdar
carping	catasta	caviare	chagrin	charpoy	chevron	choc-bar
car pool	catawba	cayenne	chained	charqui	chewier	chochos
carport	catbird	cazerne	chaitya	charred	chewink	choc ice
carrack	catboat	CD video	chalaza	chartae	chew out	chocker
carried	catcall	cecitis	chalcid	charter	Chianti	Choctaw
carrier	catch-22	cedared	Chaldee	chase up	chiasma	choired
carries	catched	cedilla	chalder	chasing	Chibcha	choisya
carrion	catcher	cedrela	chalice	chasmal	chibouk	choke up
carroon	catch it	ceilidh	chalifa	chasmed	chicana	chokeys
carroty	catch on	ceiling	chalk up	chasmic	Chicana	chokier
carry it	catch up	celadon	challah	chasséd	chicane	chokies
carry-on	catchup	celesta	challis	Chassid	chicano	cholate

cholent	ciggies	claries	clogged	coastel	cohabit	comfily
cholera	ciliary	clarify	clogger	coaster	coherer	comfort
choline	ciliate	clarine	cloison	coating	cohibit	comfrey
chookie	cillery	clarion	Clootie	coaxial	coiffed	comical
chooser	Cimbric	clarity	clopped	cobbler	coignye	comital
chopine	cimelia	clarkia	close by	cob coal	coinage	comites
chopped	cindery	clasher	close in	cob-iron	coin box	comitia
chopper	cineast	clasper	closely	cob-loaf	coining	command
chorale	cineole	classer	close on	cob-meal	coition	commend
chordal	cingula	classes	close up	cob-nuts	cojuror	comment
chorded	Cinzano	classic	closing	cob pipe	cokeman	commère
chordee	cipolin	classis	closish	cocaine	cola nut	commish
choreal	Circean	class of	closure	coccoid	Colchic	commode
choregy	circled	clastic	clot-bur	cochlea	coldish	commons
choreic	circler	clatter	clothed	cockade	cold tap	commove
chorine	circlet	clauber	clothes	cockall	cold war	commune
chorion	circlip	claucht	clotted	cock-eye	cole tit	commute
chorist	circuit	claught	clotter	cockier	colibri	compact
chorizo	cirrose	clausal	cloture	cockies	colicin	compand
choroid	cirrous	clavate	clouted	cockily	colicky	company
chorten	cirsoid	clavier	clouter	cocking	colitis	compare
chortle	ciscoes	claw off	clovery	cockish	collage	compart
chouser	cissies	clayish	clubbed	cockler	collard	compass
chowder	cissoid	clay-pan	clubber	cockney	collate	compear
chrisom	cistern	cleaner	club car	cockpit	collect	compeer
Christy	cistron	cleanly	club-law	cockshy	colleen	compend
chromic	citable	cleanse	clubman	cock-shy	college	compère
chromyl	citadel	clean up	club-man	cocobay	collide	compete
chronal	cithara	clearer	clubmen	coconut	collier	compile
chronic	cithern	clearly	clued-up	cocopan	Collins	complex
chrysid	citizen	clear-up	clueing	cocotte	colloid	complot
chubbed	citrate	cleaved	Clumber	cocoyam	collude	componé
chucker	citrine	cleaver	clumper	coctile	colobus	compony
chuckie	citrous	clefted	Cluniac	coction	cologne	comport
chuck in	cittern	clement	clunker	cod-bait	Cologne	compose
chuck it	cityful	clerisy	clupeid	cod-bank	colonel	compost
chuckle	civilly	clerkly	cluster	codding	colonic	compote
chuck up	civvies	cleruch	clutter	coddler	colored	compter
chuddar	clabber	clethra	clypeal	codeine	colosse	compute
chuffed	clachan	cliched	clypeus	codetta	colossi	comrade
chugged	clacker	clichéd	clyster	codexes	coloury	Comtean
Chukchi	clacket	clicker	cnemial	codfish	colrake	Comtian
chumble	cladded	clicket	coachee	codices	colting	Comtism
chunder	cladism	cliency	coacher	codicil	coltish	Comtist
Channel	cladist	climate	co-adore	codilla	coluber	conacre
chunner	cladode	climber	coagent	codille	colugos	conatus
chunter	claggum	clinger	coagula	cod-line	colulus	con brio
churchy	claimer	clinker	coal-bed	codling	Columba	concave
churner	clamant	clinoid	coal-box	coehorn	columel	conceal
churrus	clamber	clipped	coal gas	coeliac	columna	concede
chutist	clammed	clipper	coalise	coenoby	comatic	conceit
chutney	clammer	clippie	Coalite	co-equal	combine	concent
chutter	clamour	cliquey	coalize	coequal	combing	concept
chylify	clamper	clitter	coalman	coercer	comb out	concern
chylous	clanger	clivers	coalmen	coexist	combust	concert
chymist	clanism	cloacae	coal oil	coffret	Comecon	conchae
chymous	Clapham	cloacal	coal-pit	cogence	comedic	conched
ciboria	clap-net	clobber	coal tar	cogency	comedic	conches
ciboule	clapped	clocher	coal tit	cognate	come for	conchie
cichlid	clapper	clocker	coaming	cognize	come off	concise
cidaris	clarain	clock in	coarsen	cog rail	come out	concoct
cieling	clarety	clodder	coastal	cog-wood	cometic	concord

Concord	contuse	cork oak	co-tidal	cowbird	crankly	criollo
concuss	convect	Corliss	cotinga	cow-camp	crankum	cripple
condemn	convene	cornage	cotland	cow chip	crank up	crispen
condign	convent	corn cob	cottage	cowfish	crannog	crisper
condole	convert	corneal	cottary	cow-fish	crapaud	Crispin
condone	convict	cornery	cottery	cow-flap	crap out	crisply
conduce	convoke	cornett	cottice	cow-gait	crapped	crissal
conduct	co-occur	corn-fed	cottier	cowgirl	crapper	crissum
conduit	cookery	cornice	cotting	cowhage	crappie	cristae
condyle	cookess	cornier	cottise	cow-hand	crasher	critter
confect	cooking	cornify	cottony	cow-heel	crassly	crizzle
confess	cookout	cornily	cot-town	cowherd	craunch	croaker
confide	cooktop	cornish	couchee	cowhide	craving	crocard
confine	coolant	Cornish	coucher	cow-hunt	crawler	crocean
confirm	cool bag	cornist	Couéism	cowitch	crazier	Crocean
conflab	cool box	corn-oil	Couéist	cow-lady	crazily	crochet
conflow	coolies	corn-row	Couette	cow-lick	creaght	Crocian
conflux	cooling	cornual	cougher	cowling	creamer	crocked
conform	coolish	cornute	cough up	cowpoke	creance	crocket
confuse	coon-can	cornuto	couguar	cow pony	creased	Croesus
confute	coon-dog	corolla	couldn't	cowries	creaser	crofter
congaed	coontie	coronae	couleur	co-write	creator	cro'jack
congeal	coopery	coronal	couloir	co-wrote	credent	crombec
congery	co-optee	coroner	coulomb	cowshed	creedal	Cronian
congest	co-owner	coronet	Coulomb	cow-shot	creeler	cronies
congius	copaiba	coronis	coulter	cow-skin	creeper	croodle
conical	copeman	corozos	council	cowslip	creepie	crooked
conidia	copepod	corpora	co-unite	cow-tail	creeshy	crooken
conifer	coperta	corrade	counsel	cow town	cremate	Crookes
coniine	co-pilot	correct	counter	cow-tree	cremona	crooner
conjoin	copilot	corrida	count on	coxcomb	Cremona	crop out
conjure	copious	corrode	country	coxless	crenate	cropped
conjury	coppery	corrody	count up	coyness	creosol	cropper
con moto	coppice	corrupt	coupled	coyotes	crepine	Cropper
connate	copping	corsage	coupler	cozener	crêping	croppie
connect	cop shop	corsair	couplet	crabbed	cresset	croquet
conning	copsole	corslet	coupure	crabber	crested	crosier
connive	copular	corsned	courage	crab-nut	cretize	crosser
connote	copulas	cortège	courant	crab-oil	crevice	crossly
conquer	copycat	cortina	courida	crab pot	crew-cut	crotala
consarn	copyism	co-ruler	courier	cracked	crewels	crotale
consent	copyist	corvina	courser	cracker	crewman	crottle
consign	coquina	corvine	courter	cracket	crewmen	croupal
consist	coquito	coryzal	courtly	crackle	cribbed	crouton
console	coracle	cosaque	couthie	crackly	cribber	croûton
consols	coranto	cosh boy	couthly	crack up	cribble	crowbar
consort	corbeau	coshery	couture	cradler	cricket	crow-boy
consult	corbeil	cosiest	couvade	cragged	crickey	crowder
consume	corcass	cosmism	couvert	craigie	cricoid	crowdie
contact	corcule	cosmist	covelet	cramble	Crimean	crow-hop
contain	cordage	Cossack	covered	cram-jam	crimine	crownal
contemn	cordate	costard	coverer	crammed	criminy	crowned
contend	cordial	costate	cover in	crammer	crimmer	crowner
content	cording	co-State	cover-up	crammle	crimper	crow-toe
contest	cordite	costean	coveted	cramped	crimple	crozier
context	cordoba	costing	coveter	crampet	crimson	crubeen
contoid	Cordtex	costive	cowardy	crampon	cringer	crucial
contort	corella	costrel	cow-baby	cramp up	cringle	crucian
contour	co-rival	costume	cowbail	cranage	crinite	crucify
contras	corkage	cot-case	cowbane	cranial	crinkle	crudded
control	corkier	coterie	cowbell	cranium	crinkly	cruddle
contund	corking	cothurn	cowbind	crankle	crinoid	crudely

crudify	culchie	curried	cyclian	damp-dry	Davidic	decayer
crudity	Culdean	currier	cycling	dampish	dawdler	decease
crueler	culling	curries	cyclise	damp off	dawning	deceive
cruelly	cullion	currish	cyclist	Danaert	dawn man	decency
cruelty	culotte	curship	cyclize	danaine	daybook	decener
cruiser	culpose	cursive	cycloid	danaite	day care	decibel
cruisie	culprit	cursory	cyclone	Danakil	day-dawn	decided
cruller	culrach	curtail	cyclops	dan buoy	day-girl	decider
crumble	culshie	curtain	Cyclops	dancing	dayless	decidua
crumbly	cultish	curtana	cydippe	dandier	day lily	decimal
crummie	cultism	Curtana	cylices	dandies	day-long	deciner
crumper	cultist	curtate	cymbalo	dandify	daylong	decking
crumpet	culture	curtesy	cymling	dandler	daymare	deckled
crumple	culvert	curtsey	cynical	Dane gun	daypack	declaim
crumply	Cumaean	curucui	Cynthia	Danelaw	day-peep	declare
crunchy	cumbent	curvant	cyperus	dangler	day room	declass
crunkle	Cumbric	curvier	cypraea	Daniell	daysack	decline
crunode	cumdach	curvity	cypress	Dankali	dayside	declive
crupper	cumquat	curvous	Cyprian	dankish	daysman	decoder
crusade	cumshaw	cushier	Cypriot	dannert	day-star	decolor
crusado	cumulet	Cushing	cypsela	danseur	day-tale	decorum
crusher	cumulus	cushion	cystine	Dantean	daytime	decreed
crusily	cuneate	Cushite	cystoid	daphnia	day trip	decreer
crustal	cunette	cusk-eel	cytisus	daphnin	daywork	decrees
crusted	cunning	cuspate	cytosol	dapifer	dazedly	decreet
cruzado	cup-cake	cusping	czardas	dapping	dazibao	decrial
cry-baby	cupcake	custard	czarina	dappled	dazzler	decried
cry back	cupfuls	custock	dabbing	dapsone	dead bat	decrier
cry down	cup hook	custode	dabbler	Darapti	dead end	decries
cryogen	Cupidon	custodi	dab hand	darbies	deadeye	decrown
cryonic	cuplike	custody	Dabitis	dare-all	deadish	decrypt
cryptal	cup-moss	custrel	dabster	dariole	dead man	decuman
cryptic	cupola'd	custron	dacitic	darkful	dead men	decuple
cryptos	cupping	cut a rug	dacoity	darkies	deadpan	decurve
crystal	cuprate	cutaway	dacryon	darkish	dead pay	Dedalic
cry wolf	cuprite	cut-away	Dadaism	darling	Dead Sea	deed-box
csardas	cuprous	cut back	Dadaist	darlint	dead set	deedful
C-shaped	cupular	cutback	daddies	Darling	deaf aid	deedily
C-spring	curable	cut dead	dafadar	darning	deafish	deep end
ctenoid	curaçao	cut down	daffier	dartman	deaf nut	deepest
cubbies	curaçoa	cuticle	daffily	dartoid	dealing	deep-fry
cubbing	curatic	cutikin	daggett	dart-sac	deanery	deeping
cubbish	curator	cut into	daggier	dasheen	deaness	deepish
cubhood	curbash	cutlass	dagging	Dashera	dearest	deep sea
cubical	curb-bit	cutlery	dag-lock	dashiki	deathly	deep-set
cubicle	curbily	cut-line	dago red	dashing	debacle	deep six
cubital	curcuma	cutling	Dagwood	dashpot	débâcle	deer fly
cubitus	curdler	cut loaf	Dahoman	Dassera	debaser	deerlet
cuckold	cure-all	cut moth	dailies	dastard	debater	defacer
cudbear	curette	cut open	dairies	dasturi	debauch	de facto
cuddies	curiara	cut-over	daisies	dasyure	debited	defamed
cudding	curiate	cut-rate	Dakotan	datable	debouch	defamer
cudeigh	curiosa	cutties	dalasis	datival	debride	default
cudweed	curioso	cutting	dallied	dattock	debrief	defease
cudwort	curious	cutwork	dallier	daubery	decadal	defence
cue ball	curlews	cutworm	dallies	daubing	decadic	defense
cue card	curlier	cuvette	damfool	Daulian	decagon	defiant
cuffing	curling	cyanate	dam-head	daunder	decalin	deficit
cui bono	currach	cyanide	damming	daunter	decamer	defiler
cuirass	curragh	cyanine	damn all	daunton	decanal	defined
cuisine	currant	cyanite	damnify	dauphin	decapod	definer
cuittle	current	cyathus	damosel	dauphin	decarch	deflate

deflect	demulce	despoil	dialyse	digging	dipolar	dismark
defocus	demurer	despond	dialyze	dighter	dippier	dismast
deforce	denarii	dessert	diamide	digital	dipping	dismiss
deframe	dendron	destain	diamine	diglyph	dipshit	dismute
defraud	denizen	De Stijl	diamond	dignify	Diptera	disnest
defrock	Denmark	destine	diandry	dignity	diptote	disobey
defrost	denning	destiny	diapase	digonal	diptych	disomic
defunct	densely	destock	diapasm	digoxin	dipylon	dispark
dégagée	densify	destool	diapery	digraph	diquark	dispart
degauss	density	destour	diapsid	digress	direful	dispend
deglaze	dentary	destroy	diarchy	digynic	dirempt	display
deglute	dentate	detente	diarial	dika fat	dirtier	dispone
degrade	dentine	détente	diarian	dilater	dirtily	dispope
dehisce	dentist	deterge	diaries	dilator	dirt-pie	disport
deicide	denture	determa	diarise	dildoes	disable	dispose
deictic	deodand	detinue	diarist	dilemma	disally	dispost
deified	deontic	detract	diarize	dillies	Disamis	dispute
deifier	de-orbit	detrain	diastem	dilling	disavow	disrank
deifies	depaint	detrude	diaster	dilruba	disband	disrate
deiform	*dépaysé*	deutzia	diasyrm	dilucid	disbark	disrobe
de-index	depetal	devalue	diaulos	diluent	disbody	disroof
Deipara	deplace	devance	diazine	dilutee	discage	disroot
deistic	deplane	develop	diazoma	diluter	discant	disrump
Deiters	deplete	deviant	dibasic	diluvia	discard	disrupt
deities	deplore	deviate	dibatag	Dimaris	discase	dissava
dekalin	deplume	devilet	dibbing	dimeric	discept	dissave
dekarch	deposal	devilry	dibbler	dimeter	discern	disseat
delaine	deposer	devious	dice-box	dimmest	discerp	dissect
delapse	deposit	devisee	diciest	dimming	discoes	dissent
Delasol	deprave	deviser	dickens	dimmish	discoid	dissert
delator	depress	devisor	dickeys	dimness	discord	dissing
delayed	deprive	devoice	dickier	dimpled	discuss	dissoul
delayer	depside	devolve	dickies	dimpsey	disdain	distaff
deleing	depthen	devoted	dictate	Dinaric	disease	distain
delible	deraign	devotee	diction	din-dins	disedge	distant
delight	derange	dewater	dictums	dine out	*diseuse*	distend
Delilah	Derbies	dewclaw	didache	dinette	disfame	distent
delimit	*de règle*	dew-claw	didakai	dingbat	disform	distich
deliver	derider	dewdrop	diddery	dingier	disgown	distort
delouse	derival	dewfall	diddler	dingily	disgulf	distune
Delphic	deriver	dewiest	diddums	dingoes	disgust	disturb
delphin	dermoid	dewless	didicoi	dinki-di	dishelm	distyle
deltaic	derrick	dew-pond	didymis	dinkier	dishful	diswood
deltoid	dertrum	dew-rake	die away	dinkies	dishier	ditcher
deluder	dervish	dew-worm	die-back	dinmont	dishing	dithery
demarch	descale	dextral	die-cast	dinnery	dish-mop	dittany
demency	descant	dextran	die down	dinning	dishome	ditties
démenti	descend	dextrin	die game	dinsome	dishorn	dittoes
demerge	descent	deyship	diehard	diocese	dish out	diurnal
demerit	deserve	dghaisa	die hard	diopter	dish-pan	dive-dap
Demerol	desight	dhrupad	die-link	dioptre	dishrag	dive-dop
demerse	desired	dhurrie	*dies non*	diorama	disject	diverge
demesne	deskill	diabase	dietary	diorite	disjoin	diverse
demigod	desk job	diabolo	diether	dioxane	disjune	divided
demi-hag	desk-man	diagram	diethyl	dioxide	disleaf	divider
demirep	desktop	diagrid	dietine	dip-head	dislike	diviner
demi-rep	desmans	dialect	dieting	diploid	dislimb	divisor
demi-sec	desmoid	dialing	dietist	diploma	dislimn	divorce
demoded	Desolre	dialist	diffide	diplont	dislink	divorcé
demonic	despair	dialled	diffuse	dipnoan	disload	divulge
demotic	despise	dialler	digamma	dipnoid	dislove	Divvers
demount	despite	diallyl	dig down	dipodia	dismail	divvies

dizzard	dog-tent	dotchin	dragoon	dronage	dualism	dunness
dizzier	dog-town	dottier	drag out	drongos	dualist	dunnies
dizzily	dogtrot	dottily	drag saw	dronish	duality	dunning
djibbah	dog-vane	dotting	drainer	drooler	dualize	dunnish
D-notice	dog-wolf	dottled	drapery	drooper	dualled	dunnock
do about	dogwood	dottrel	draping	drop-fly	duarchy	dunster
do a bunk	doitkin	doubler	drappie	droplet	dub-a-dub	duopoly
do a fade	Dolbyed	doublet	drastic	drop off	dubbing	duotone
do a flit	doldrum	doubter	dratted	drop out	dubiety	dupable
do a mike	doleful	doucely	draught	dropped	dubious	duppies
doatish	dolldom	doughty	drawbar	dropper	ducally	duppion
dobbing	dollied	Douglas	draw bit	drosera	duchess	durable
do brown	dollier	Doulton	draw-boy	droshky	duchies	durably
docetic	dollies	dourine	draw-hoe	drostdy	duck ant	duramen
docible	dolosse	dovecot	drawing	drought	duck egg	durance
dockage	dolphin	dovekie	drawish	droving	duckett	durmast
doddery	doltish	dovelet	drawler	drowner	duckies	duskier
dodecad	domaine	dowable	draw-net	drubbed	ducking	duskily
dodecyl	domelet	dowager	draw off	drubber	duckpin	duskish
dodgast	domical	dowdier	draw out	drucken	ductile	dustbin
dodgery	domicil	dowdily	drayage	drudger	ducting	dust-box
dodgier	dominee	dowfart	drayman	drugged	ductule	dust-cap
dodgily	dominie	dowless	draymen	drugger	duddery	dustier
dodging	domitic	downbow	dreaded	drugget	dudgeon	dustily
doe-eyed	donatee	down-dip	dreader	druggie	dudheen	dusting
doeskin	donator	downier	dreadly	Druidic	due date	dustman
dogbane	doncher	downily	dreamed	Druidry	duelled	dustmen
dogbolt	done for	downish	dreamer	drumble	dueller	dust off
dog cart	Donegal	down-lie	dream up	drum kit	dueness	dustoor
dogcart	dongola	downset	dredger	drumlin	duetted	dustpan
dog days	Dongola	downsun	dreeing	drummed	duffing	dustuck
dogeate	Don Juan	dowries	dreidel	drummer	dugongs	duteous
dogface	donkeys	do wrong	Dresden	drum out	dukedom	dutiful
dog-fall	donnard	doyenne	dresser	drungar	dulcian	duumvir
dogfish	donning	Doyenne	dress up	drunken	dulcify	Duvetyn
doggery	donnish	doyleys	dribble	Drusian	dulcite	dvandva
doggess	donship	doylies	dribbly	druther	dullard	dwarves
doggies	dontcha	dozened	driblet	dryadic	dullify	dwelled
dogging	doodler	dozener	driddle	dry-blow	dullish	dweller
doggish	doomful	dozenth	drier-up	dry-bulb	dulness	dwell on
doggone	doomily	doze off	drifter	dry cell	dulosis	dwindle
doggrel	do or die	doziest	driller	dry cure	dulotic	dyarchy
doghead	doorman	dozzler	drinker	dry dock	dulsome	dybbuks
dog-hole	doormat	drabant	drinkie	dry-eyed	dumbell	dyeable
dog-hook	doormen	drabber	drink in	dry-foot	dummied	dye-line
dog-iron	doorway	drabbet	drink to	dry fuck	dummies	dyester
dogless	doozies	drabble	drink up	dry hole	dummy up	dye-wood
doglike	dope out	drabler	drip-dry	dry land	dumpier	dyingly
dogling	dopiest	drachma	drip-mat	dryland	dumpily	dynamic
dog-meat	Doppler	drackly	drip pan	dry mass	dumpish	dynamos
dog-nail	do proud	dracone	dripped	dry milk	dumpoke	dynasty
dog on it	dorados	Dracula	dripple	dryness	dun-bird	dyslogy
dog-poor	dor-hawk	draftee	drive at	dry-salt	duncery	dysuria
dog-race	Dorking	drafter	drive-by	dry-shod	duncify	dysuric
dog rose	dorlach	drag act	drive-in	dry sink	duncish	each way
dogrose	dormant	drag ass	drive-on	dryster	dungeon	eagerly
dog's age	dormice	dragged	driving	dry suit	dung-fly	eanling
dog's-ear	dornick	dragger	drizzle	drywall	dung-pot	earache
dogskin	dornock	draggle	drizzly	dry-wash	Dunkard	earbash
dog sled	dos-à-dos	draggly	drogher	dry well	Dunkirk	ear-bash
dog-star	do-si-dos	dragnet	droguer	D-shaped	dunnage	ear-clip
dog-tail	dossier	drag-net	dromond	dualise	dunnart	eardrum

ear-flap	écorché	ejector	emblaze	enchase	engross	entrust
earfuls	ecotage	eke-name	emblema	encheer	enguard	entwine
earhole	ecoteur	ekistic	embloom	en clair	enhance	entwist
earldom	ecotone	elaidic	embolia	enclasp	enjewel	E-number
earless	ecotype	Elamite	embolic	enclave	enjoyer	envelop
earlier	ecstasy	elastic	embolus	enclavé	enlarge	envenom
earlike	ectasia	elastin	embosom	enclose	enliven	envious
ear lobe	ectasis	elation	embound	encloud	en masse	environ
ear-lock	ecthyma	elative	embowed	encoder	ennoble	envyful
early on	ectopia	elderly	embowel	encomia	ennuyéd	enweave
earmark	ectopic	eldress	embower	encover	Enochic	enwheel
earmuff	ectypal	Eleatic	embrace	encrini	enolase	enwiden
ear-muff	ecuelle	elector	embrave	encrown	enolate	enwound
earnest	edacity	Electra	embroil	encrust	enology	enzymic
earnful	edaphic	electro	embrown	encrypt	enomoty	epacrid
earning	edenite	eledone	embryon	endarch	enotist	epacris
ear-pick	edestin	elegant	embryos	endemic	enounce	eparchy
earplug	edgiest	elegiac	embused	endgame	enplane	epaxial
earring	edictal	elegies	emender	end-game	enprint	épéeist
earshot	edicule	elegise	emerald	end-gate	enquire	epeiric
ear-stud	edifice	elegist	emerods	end-leaf	enquiry	epergne
earthen	edified	elegize	emersed	endless	enrheum	ephebic
earthly	edifier	element	emetine	end line	enripen	ephedra
earth up	edifies	elenchi	Emilian	endlong	enrober	ephelis
ear-tuft	editing	elevate	eminent	endmost	enrough	ephoral
easeful	edition	elf-bolt	emirate	endnote	enround	epiboly
ease out	edit out	elf-dock	emitted	end-note	en route	epicarp
easiest	educate	elf-lock	emitter	endogen	ensaint	epicene
east end	educrat	elf-shot	emotion	endopod	enshell	epicism
East End	eel-fare	elinvar	emotive	endorse	ensient	epicist
eastern	eel-like	elision	empanel	endower	enslave	epicure
easting	eelpout	elitism	empathy	end-play	ensnare	epiderm
easy all	eelskin	élitism	empearl	endurer	ensnarl	epidote
eatable	eelworm	elitist	emperor	enduros	enstamp	epigeal
eat away	eeriest	élitist	empiric	end-user	enstool	epigean
eat crow	effable	elixate	emplace	endways	enstyle	epigene
eat dirt	effendi	ellagic	emplane	endwise	ensuant	epigone
ebb-tide	efforce	ellipse	employe	end zone	ensuing	epigoni
Eblaite	effulge	ell-wand	employé	enemata	en suite	epigram
ebonies	egality	elm tree	emplume	enemies	ensurer	epigyne
ebonist	egg-case	elmwood	emporia	energic	entases	epigyny
ebonite	egg cell	elocute	empower	energid	entasis	epilate
ebonize	egg cosy	Elohist	empower	enfeoff	entente	epiloia
ebriety	egg-flip	elsehow	empress	enfever	entente	epimera
ebriose	egghead	elusion	emprise	Enfield	enteral	epimere
ebrious	eggiest	elusive	emptier	enflame	enterer	epimyth
ecbatic	eggless	elusory	emptily	enflesh	enteric	epiotic
ecbolic	egg-plum	elution	empting	enforce	enter on	episode
eccrine	egg roll	eluvial	emption	enframe	enteron	episome
ecdysis	egg-yolk	eluvium	empyema	engaged	enthral	epistle
echelle	egoless	Elysian	emu-bush	engagee	enthuse	epitaph
echelon	egotise	Elysium	emulate	engager	enticer	epitaxy
échevin	egotism	elytral	emulous	engined	Entisol	epithem
echidna	egotist	elytron	emu-wren	English	entitle	epithet
echinus	egotize	Elzevir	enabler	englobe	entrail	epitome
echites	ego trip	emacity	enactor	engorge	entrain	epitomy
echoism	eidetic	emanant	enamour	engrace	entrant	epitope
eclipse	eidolon	emanate	enation	engraft	entreat	epizoic
eclogue	eikonal	embargo	enchafe	engrail	entries	epizone
ecocide	einkorn	embassy	enchain	engrain	entrism	epizoon
ecology	eirenic	embathe	enchant	engrasp	entrist	epochal
economy	eis wool	embered	encharm	engrave	entropy	eponymy

epoxide	esquire	evacuee	exition	eyesome	fall-off	fartlek
epsilon	essayer	evangel	exocarp	eyesore	fall out	Far West
epulary	essence	evanish	exoderm	eye-spot	fallout	fasciae
epurate	Essenic	evasion	exogamy	eyespot	falsary	fascial
epyllia	estamin	evasive	exolete	eye view	falsely	fascias
equable	estated	evenest	Exonian	eyewash	falsies	fascine
equably	esthete	evening	exordia	eyewear	falsify	fascism
equally	estival	even now	exordia	eye-wink	falsism	Fascism
equator	estoile	even-odd	exotica	eye-worm	falsity	fascist
equerry	estrade	even out	exotism	fabliau	falutin	Fascist
equiaxe	estrado	eventer	expanse	fabular	fameful	fashery
equinox	estreat	Everest	ex parte	face off	familia	fashion
erasion	estrich	evertor	expense	face out	famille	fast-day
erasive	estrous	eve-star	expiate	faceted	famulus	fast foe
erasure	estuary	evictee	expiree	facient	fanatic	fast ice
erectly	etaerio	evictor	expirer	factful	fan belt	fasting
erector	etagere	evident	explain	factice	fancier	fastish
E-region	etamine	evil day	explant	faction	fancies	fast one
erelong	etatism	evil eye	explode	factive	fancily	fatally
eremite	etatist	Evil One	exploit	factoid	fan club	fat-body
erenach	etchant	evirate	explore	factory	fanfare	fateful
erepsin	etching	evirato	exposal	factual	fanfoot	fat-face
erethic	eternal	evocate	exposer	factums	fanlike	fat farm
ergodic	Etesian	evolute	exposit	facture	fan mail	fat-head
ergoism	ethanal	evolver	expound	faculae	fannell	fatidic
ergoted	Ethanim	ewe lamb	express	facular	fannies	fatigue
ericoid	ethanol	ewe-neck	expulse	faculty	fanning	Fatihah
erineum	etheric	exacter	expunct	fadable	fan palm	Fatimid
erinnic	ethical	exactly	expunge	faddier	fantail	fatless
erinose	ethmoid	exactor	expurge	faddily	fantast	fatlike
Erinyes	ethoxyl	exalter	exscind	faddish	fantasy	fatling
eristic	ethylic	examine	exsolve	faddism	fanwise	fatness
erl-king	ethynyl	example	exsurge	faddist	fanzine	fatsoes
ermelin	Etonian	exarate	extense	fade-out	Fapesmo	fattest
ermined	Euboean	excerpt	externe	faecula	faraday	fattier
ermines	eucaine	excimer	extinct	fagging	Faraday	fatting
erosion	Euchite	excited	extract	faggoty	faradic	fattish
erosive	euclase	exciter	extrema	fahlerz	faraway	fattism
erotica	eucomis	exciton	extreme	fahlore	far-away	fattist
erotise	eucrasy	excitor	extrude	faience	far-back	fatuity
erotism	eucrite	exclaim	exudate	failing	farceur	fatuoid
erotize	eudemon	exclave	exurban	failure	farcied	fatuous
errable	eugenia	exclude	exurbia	fainter	farcify	faucial
errancy	eugenic	excreta	exuviae	faintly	far-come	faulter
erratic	eugenol	excrete	exuvial	fair dos	far-down	faunist
erratum	euglena	excurse	ex-votos	fairies	Far East	faunule
errhine	Euglena	excusal	eyeable	fairing	farebox	fauvism
erudite	eulogia	excuser	eyeball	fairish	far from	fauvist
escapee	eulogic	execute	eye bank	fair sex	far gone	faux pas
escaper	eunomia	exegete	eye-bath	fairway	farmery	fawning
escheat	eunomic	exempla	eyebath	faitour	farming	faxable
escribe	eupathy	exergue	eye-beam	falafel	farmost	fayence
escroll	euphony	ex facie	eye bolt	Falange	farness	fazenda
escuage	eupione	exhaust	eye-bree	Falasha	Faroese	fearful
escudos	euploid	exhibit	eyebrow	falbala	farrago	feaster
eserine	eupnoea	exhumer	eye-drop	falcate	farrant	feather
E-shaped	Euratom	exigent	eyefuls	faldage	farrash	feature
esotery	euripus	exilian	eyehole	fallacy	farrier	febrile
espadon	eustasy	exility	eyelash	fall due	farruca	feckful
esparto	eustele	exister	eyeless	fall for	farsakh	federal
esplees	eustyle	exitial	eyelike	fall guy	farsang	feebler
espouse	Eutopia	exiting	eye mask	falling	farther	feed-bag

feed dog	fervour	filacer	fire-red	flannel	flipped	flybane
feeding	Festino	filaree	firmish	flannen	flipper	fly-bird
feedlot	festive	filaria	firstly	flanque	flip-top	fly-blow
fee-farm	festoon	filbert	first up	flapped	flirter	fly-boat
feeling	fetcher	filcher	fir tree	flapper	fliting	fly-book
feel out	fetch up	filemot	fish-day	flare up	flitted	fly camp
feelthy	fetiche	file off	fishery	flasher	flitter	fly-dope
feering	fetidly	filiate	fish-eye	flashly	flivver	fly-fish
fee tail	fetlock	filibeg	fish-fry	flasket	floatel	fly-flap
Fehling	fettler	filicic	fishful	flasque	floater	fly-flat
feigner	feudary	filicin	fishgig	flat-cap	floccus	fly-half
feirily	feudist	fillies	fishier	flatcar	floe ice	fly high
felafel	feu duty	filling	fishify	flatlet	flogged	fly-hook
fellate	feu-farm	fill out	fishily	flat off	flogger	fly into
fellies	Feulgen	filmdom	fishing	flat out	flookan	fly-kick
felloes	feveret	filmier	fishnet	flat-pea	floorer	flyleaf
felonry	fewness	filmily	fish out	flatted	floozie	fly-line
felsite	feyness	filmset	fishpot	flatten	flopped	flyness
felspar	fiancée	Filofax	fissile	flatter	flopper	flyover
felting	fiascos	fimbria	fission	flattie	Floreal	fly page
felt pen	fibbery	finable	fissive	flat-top	floreat	fly-past
felt tip	fibbing	finagle	fissure	flaucht	Florida	fly-post
felucca	fibroid	finally	fistful	flaught	florist	flyting
felwort	fibroin	finance	fistula	flaunch	floruit	flytrap
feminal	fibroma	fin-back	fitched	flaunty	florula	fly-trap
feminie	fibrose	find for	fitchée	Flavian	flotage	fly upon
femoral	fibrous	find God	fitchet	flavine	flotant	fly-wire
fencing	fibster	finding	fitchew	flavone	flotsam	f-number
Fendant	fibulae	find out	fit fair	flavour	flounce	foamier
fen-fire	fibular	fine art	fitment	fleabag	flouncy	fobbing
fenland	fibulas	fine-cut	fitness	flea-bug	flouter	focally
fennish	fictile	fineish	fitters	fleapit	flowage	focused
fenster	fiction	finesse	fittest	flea-pit	flowery	focuser
feodary	fictive	finewed	fitting	flebile	flowing	focuses
feoffee	fidalgo	finfoot	fiumara	fledged	flubbed	fodient
feoffer	fiddler	fingery	fixable	fleeced	flubdub	fog bank
feoffor	fiddley	finical	fixed-do	fleecer	flue-gas	foggage
Ferangi	fideism	finicky	fixedly	fleecie	fluence	foggier
feretto	fideist	finikin	fixture	fleerer	fluency	foggily
Ferison	fidgety	finless	fizzier	fleetly	fluidal	fogging
ferling	fidibus	finlike	fizzily	Fleming	fluidic	foghorn
fermail	fiefdom	finnack	flaccid	flemish	fluidly	fog-horn
fermata	fielded	finnied	Flacian	Flemish	flukier	fog lamp
ferment	fielden	finning	flacker	fleshed	flukily	fogless
fermery	fielder	Finnish	flacket	fleshen	flummer	fogydom
fermion	fiendly	finnsko	flag day	flesher	flummox	fogyish
fermium	fiercer	fin-toed	Flag Day	fleshly	flunker	fogyism
fernery	fierier	fin-weed	flagged	fletton	flunkey	foiling
fern-owl	fierily	fiorite	flagger	fleuret	fluoric	foilist
ferrate	fifteen	fipenny	flaglet	fleuron	flusher	folacin
ferrety	fifthly	Firbolg	flagman	flexile	flusker	folding
ferrian	fifties	fir cone	flagmen	flexing	fluster	fold-out
ferried	figbird	firearm	flakier	flexion	fluting	foliage
ferrier	figging	firebox	flakily	flexure	flutist	foliate
ferries	fighter	firebug	flaking	flicker	flutter	foliole
ferrite	fig leaf	fire-bug	flamant	flighty	fluvial	foliose
ferroan	figment	firedog	flambés	flimmer	fluxion	folk art
ferrous	fig tree	firefly	flamfew	flinder	flyable	folkier
ferrule	figural	fireman	flaming	flinger	flyaway	folkish
ferryer	figured	firemen	flâneur	fling to	fly-away	folknik
fertile	figurer	fire-new	flanger	fling up	fly-back	folksay
fervent	figwort	fire-pan	flanker	flip-dog	fly ball	follies

fomites	foreset	foulard	Frelimo	fructan	furioso	gaishen
fondaco	foresty	fouling	fremdly	fructed	furious	gala day
fondant	foretop	foul off	fremmit	fruited	furison	galagos
fondish	for ever	foul out	Frenchy	fruiter	furless	Galahad
fondler	forever	foul tip	frescos	frumper	furlong	galanga
fontful	for fair	foumart	freshen	frumple	furmety	galatea
foodful	forfare	founded	fresher	frustum	furnace	galeate
foodies	forfeit	founder	freshet	F-shaped	furnage	galeeny
food web	forfend	foundry	freshly	FT Index	furnish	galenic
foolery	for free	four-ale	fresnel	fubsier	furrier	galette
fool hen	forgave	fourché	Fresnel	fucated	furring	Galibis
foolish	forgery	Fourier	fretful	fuchsia	furrowy	galilee
footage	forgett	foussie	fretish	fuck all	fur seal	galipot
footbed	forgive	foveate	fretsaw	fucking	further	gallack
foot boy	forgoer	foveola	fretted	fuck off	furtive	gallant
footing	forgone	fovilla	fretter	fucused	fuscous	gallate
footler	for hire	fowling	friable	fuddler	fuse box	galleas
foot-log	forkful	fowl pox	friarly	Fuegian	fusible	Gallego
footman	fork out	fowl-run	fribble	fuehrer	fusidic	galleon
footmen	for life	fox bane	Fridays	fuelled	fusilli	gallery
footpad	for long	fox-fire	Friesic	fueller	fusilly	galleys
foot-rot	forlorn	foxhole	friezer	fuel oil	fusogen	gall-fly
footsie	for love	fox-hunt	frigate	fuel rod	fussier	gallica
Footsie	for luck	foxiest	frigged	fugally	fussify	gallice
footway	formant	foxlike	frigger	fugging	fussily	galliot
foo yong	formate	fox-mark	friggle	fuguing	fussock	gallium
foozler	formful	fox moth	frighty	fuguist	fusspot	gallnut
fopling	formica	foxship	frilled	fulcral	fustian	gall-nut
foppery	Formica	fox skin	fringer	fulcrum	fustier	galloon
foppish	forming	foxtail	frippet	fulgent	fustily	gallous
forager	formose	foxtrot	frisado	full age	futchel	gallows
foramen	formula	foyaite	frisbee	fullery	futhorc	galoped
forayer	formule	fractal	Frisbee	full out	futtock	galopin
forbade	fornent	fracted	Frisian	full pay	futural	galumph
forbear	for nuts	fraenum	frisker	fulmine	fuzzbox	gambade
forbore	for once	fragile	frisket	fulness	fuzzier	gambado
forceps	forpine	frailly	frisson	fulsome	fuzzily	Gambian
for cert	for real	frailty	frisure	fulvous	gabbart	gambier
forcing	for rent	Fraktur	frit-fly	fumaric	gabbier	gambist
fordeal	forsake	frame-up	fritted	fumaryl	gabbing	gambler
fording	for sale	framing	fritter	fumbler	gabbler	gamboge
foreact	for show	franion	frizado	fumette	gabbros	gambrel
forearm	forslow	franker	frizzle	funckia	gabelle	game act
forebay	forsook	frankly	frizzly	functor	gabfest	game all
forebow	for sure	frantic	Froebel	funding	gablock	gamebag
forecar	for that	frapler	frogbit	funeral	gadding	Game Boy
foreday	forth of	frapped	frog-eye	funfair	gadgety	gamelan
foredge	forties	fratery	frogged	funfest	Gaditan	game law
fore-end	fortify	fratter	froglet	fungate	gadling	gametic
foregut	fortlet	fraught	frogman	fungoid	gadroon	gamiest
foreign	Fortran	fraying	frogmen	fungous	gadwall	gammier
forelay	fortune	frazzle	fronded	funicle	Gaekwar	gangdom
foreleg	forward	freckle	frontal	funkier	Gaeldom	ganging
foreman	forwent	freckly	fronted	funkily	gaffled	ganglia
foremen	forworn	freebie	front of	funnier	gaggery	gang-man
forepaw	fossane	freedom	fronton	funnily	gagging	gangrel
foreran	fossick	freeman	froughy	funster	gag-rein	gangsta
forerib	fossula	freemen	frounce	furbery	gagster	gang war
forerun	fouetté	freesia	frousty	furbish	gahnite	gangway
foresaw	fougade	freeway	froward	furcate	gainful	ganosis
foresay	foughty	freezer	frowner	furcula	gaining	gantlet
foresee	foujdar	freight	frowsty	furiant	gainsay	garbage

garbler	gazelle	gesnera	gimlety	gleeful	gnasher	goitred
garboil	gazette	gessoed	gimmick	gleeman	gnathal	go large
garfish	gearbox	gessoes	gingall	glenoid	gnathic	goldarn
garland	gearing	gestalt	gingery	gleying	gnatter	gold bug
garlits	geckoes	Gestapo	gingham	gliadin	gnawing	gold-dig
garment	geebung	gestate	gingili	glibber	gneissy	gold-eye
Garnett	Geechee	gestion	gingkos	glidder	gnocchi	goldish
garnish	geelbek	gesture	gin-mill	gliding	gnomish	golf bag
garotte	gee whiz	get a rat	ginning	glimmer	gnomist	golfdom
garpike	Gehenna	get away	ginseng	glimpse	gnostic	goliard
Gartner	geishas	getaway	giocoso	gliosis	Goa ball	Goliath
gas boat	geladas	get back	gipsies	glirine	Goa bean	gollies
gas coal	gelatin	get down	Gipsify	glissés	go about	gombeen
gaseity	gelding	get even	gipsire	glisten	goadman	gomerel
gaseous	gelidly	get hell	Gipsyfy	glister	go ahead	gonadal
gas fire	gelling	get hers	giraffe	glitchy	go aloft	gondola
gashful	Gemaric	get into	girasol	glitter	go along	gondole
gashion	gemfish	get laid	girding	gloater	Goanese	gongora
gas laws	geminal	get left	girdler	globate	goateed	gonnoff
gasless	Geminid	get lost	girldom	globoid	goat-fig	good and
gas main	gemlike	get on to	girleen	globose	goat-god	good-bad
gas mask	gemmary	get onto	girlies	globous	goatish	good buy
gasohol	gemmate	get over	girlish	globule	goat nut	goodbye
gas oven	gemmery	get sick	Gironde	glochid	goat-rue	good day
gas ring	gemming	get some	gisarme	glomera	gobbing	good-den
gassier	gemmule	getting	gittern	glommed	gobbler	good egg
gassing	gemsbok	get well	give ear	gloomth	Gobelin	good for
gasthof	genappe	get wind	give off	gloppen	gobioid	good God
gastral	general	ghaffir	give out	gloried	go blind	goodhap
gas trap	generic	gharana	give way	glories	go broke	goodies
gastric	genesis	gharial	gizzard	glorify	go close	gooding
gastrin	genetic	ghastly	gjetost	glory be	go crook	goodish
gas well	genette	gheraos	glacial	Glory Be	goddard	good job
gateaus	Genevan	gherkin	glacier	glossal	goddess	good man
gateaux	genever	ghettos	gladded	glosser	goddize	goodman
gateleg	genipap	ghilgai	gladden	glossic	godetia	goodmen
gateman	genista	ghillie	gladder	glottal	go-devil	good now
gatemen	genital	Ghilzai	gladdie	glottic	Godfrey	good oil
gate-net	genitor	ghoster	gladdon	glottis	godhead	good old
gateway	genizah	ghostly	glad eye	glow-fly	Godhead	gooeyly
Gathaic	genning	giantly	gladful	glowing	godhood	go off at
Gatling	Genoese	giantry	gladius	glozing	godless	goofier
gattine	genomic	giardia	gladwin	glucose	godlier	goofily
gauchos	genteel	gibbose	glaikit	glue ear	godlike	gooiest
gaudery	gentian	gibbous	glammed	glueing	godlily	goolies
gaudier	gentile	giblets	glamour	glue-pot	godling	goombah
gaudies	gentler	GI bride	glancer	gluiest	godness	goondie
gaudily	genuant	giddier	glander	glummer	godpapa	goonery
Gaulish	genuine	giddify	glandes	glumose	godsend	goonish
gauntly	geodesy	giddily	glareal	gluonic	godship	goopher
gauntry	geogeny	giddy-up	glaring	glutaei	God slot	goopier
gausses	geogony	gigging	glarney	gluteal	go Dutch	Goorkha
gauzier	geoidal	giggish	glassen	glutean	godward	goosery
gauzily	geology	giggler	glassie	gluteus	Godward	goosish
gavotte	Geordie	gigolos	Glauber	glutted	go Fante	gorcock
gawkier	georgic	gigster	glaucus	glutton	go-fever	gorcrow
gawkily	gerbera	gilbert	glaze in	glycine	go for it	Gordian
gawkish	gerenuk	gilding	glazier	glyoxal	goggled	Gorgios
gayness	germane	gillery	glazily	glyphic	goggler	goriest
gaysome	gertcha	gillion	glazing	glyptal	go hence	gorilla
gazania	gerusia	gill-net	gleaner	glyptic	go in for	go round
gazebos	Gerzean	gimbals	glebous	gnarled	going to	Gorsedd

goshawk	granola	grey eye	grottos	guipure	gutsily	Halacha
go short	grantee	grey fox	grouchy	guisard	guttate	Halakah
gosling	granter	greyhen	grouper	Guisian	guttery	halberd
go snips	Grantha	greyish	groupie	guising	Gut-tide	halbert
go spare	grantor	grey jay	grouser	Gujarat	gutting	halcyon
gossipy	granule	greylag	grousey	Gujerat	guttler	halesia
gossoon	grapery	grey oak	grouter	gulchin	Guyanan	half-cap
Gothick	graphic	grey-out	growbag	Gulf War	guzzler	half-cut
Gothish	grapnel	grey pea	growing	gullery	gwyniad	half-day
Gothism	grapple	grey tin	growler	gulleys	gyle-fat	half-ebb
go to bed	grasper	gribble	grown-up	gullies	gyle-tun	half-god
go to law	grassed	gricing	grow out	gullish	gymnast	half-joe
go to pot	grasser	gridded	grubbed	gumboil	gymnure	half-lap
go to sea	grassum	griddle	grubber	gumboot	gymslip	half-leg
go to war	gratify	grieved	grubble	gumdrop	gypping	half-man
gouache	gratiné	griever	Grubean	gummata	gypsous	half pay
goujons	grating	griffin	grudger	gummier	Gypsyfy	half-pie
Goulard	graunch	griffon	gruelly	gummily	gyrally	halfway
goulash	graupel	grifter	gruffly	gumming	gyrator	halfwit
go under	gravely	griggle	grufted	gummite	gyrinid	halibut
gourami	gravida	griller	grumble	gummous	gyronny	halidom
gourmet	gravies	grimace	grumbly	gumshoe	gytrash	Halifax
gout-fly	graving	grimful	grummel	gum thus	haarder	halitus
goutily	gravity	grimier	grummet	gum tree	habdabs	hall boy
goutish	gravlax	grimily	grumose	gum-wood	habitat	halling
go wrong	gravure	grimmer	grumous	gunboat	habitué	hallion
goyisch	grazier	grimpen	grumphy	gun crew	habitus	hallock
gozzard	grazing	grinder	grunion	gun-deck	habutai	halloes
grab bag	greaser	grindle	grunter	gunfire	hachure	halloos
grabbed	greaten	gringos	gruntle	gunibri	hackbut	hallway
grabber	greater	grinned	grushie	gunless	hackery	halogen
grabble	Greater	grinner	Gruyère	gunlock	hacking	halo hat
grabens	great go	grip car	gryphon	gun moll	hackler	halpace
gracile	greatly	griping	grysbok	gunnera	hacklet	haltere
grackle	greaved	gripman	G-string	gunnery	hackman	halting
gradate	greaves	gripped	guanaco	gunnies	hackney	halyard
gradely	Grecian	gripper	Guanche	gunning	hacksaw	Hamadan
gradine	grecing	gripple	guanido	gunplay	had best	hamated
gradual	Grecise	grisard	guanine	gunroom	haddock	ham-bone
grafter	Grecism	griskin	guanoes	gunship	had need	Hamburg
grained	Grecize	gristle	guarana	gunshot	hadrome	Hamitic
grainer	grecque	gristly	Guarani	gun-site	hafnium	hammada
gramash	Greekly	gritted	guarded	gun slip	Haganah	hammier
grammar	greener	gritter	guardee	gunwale	hag-boat	hammily
grampus	Greener	grizzle	guarder	gunyang	hagfish	hamming
granage	greeney	grizzly	guariba	guppies	haggard	Hamming
granary	greenie	groaner	guayule	gurgler	haggish	hammock
granate	greenly	Grobian	gubbins	gurnard	haggler	hamster
grandad	greenth	grocery	guddler	gurning	hagigah	hamular
grandam	greeter	grockle	gudgeon	gushier	hag-ride	hamulus
grandee	gregale	grogram	guerdon	gushily	hagship	hanaper
grandly	gregory	groined	guereza	gushing	hahnium	Hanbali
grandma	Gregory	Grolier	guesser	gussied	hair bag	hand-axe
grandpa	greisen	gromell	guesten	gussies	haircut	handbag
granfer	greking	grommet	Guianan	gustful	hairdos	handful
granger	gremial	grooved	guichet	gustier	hairier	handgun
granita	gremlin	groover	guiding	gustily	hairily	hand-hot
granite	gremmie	grossen	Guignol	gustoes	hairnet	handier
grannam	grenade	grosser	guilder	gutless	hair net	handily
grannie	grenado	grossly	guildry	gutling	hair oil	hand-jam
grannom	grey box	gross up	guillem	Gutnish	hairpin	handjob
grannum	greyers	Grotian	Guinean	gutsier	Haitian	handled

handler	harrier	haylage	heigh-ho	hereout	Hi-liter	hoecake
hand off	harries	hayloft	heinous	here's to	hillier	hoedown
hand out	harshen	hayrick	heirdom	heretic	hilling	hoe into
handout	harshly	hayride	heiress	heritor	hillman	Hofmann
handsaw	harslet	hayseed	heirmos	herling	hill-man	hogback
handsel	harvest	Haytian	heister	Hermaic	hillmen	hog-deer
handset	has-been	hayward	hei-tiki	herniae	hillock	hog-fish
hands-on	hashish	haywire	helibus	hernial	hilltop	hoggery
hands up	Hasidic	hazeled	helical	hernias	himself	hogging
handy to	Hasidim	hazelly	helices	hernsew	hindgut	hoggish
hangdog	hassock	haziest	helicon	heroify	hinging	hog-head
hanging	hastate	headage	Helicon	heroine	hinnies	hoglike
hangman	hastier	head boy	helipad	heroise	hip bath	hog-line
hangmen	hastily	headier	hell-box	heroism	hip bone	hogling
hang of a	hasting	headily	hell-cat	heroize	hip-hole	hog-mane
hang off	hatable	heading	helldog	heronry	hipless	hog plum
hang out	hatband	headlet	Hellene	herring	hipness	hogskin
hankies	hatchel	headman	hellful	herself	hippest	hogwash
Hansard	hatcher	headmen	hell-hag	hership	hippies	hogweed
hanuman	hatchet	head off	hellier	Heshvan	hippish	hog-wild
Hanuman	hateful	head sea	hellion	hessian	hip roof	hog-yoke
ha'pence	hatfuls	headset	hellish	Hessian	hip-shot	Hohokam
ha'penny	hatless	head tax	hellite	hessite	hipster	hoister
hapless	hats off	head-tie	helluva	hetaera	hip-tile	hokiest
haploid	hattery	headway	hellyon	hetaira	hircine	hokonui
haplont	Hattian	heal-all	helotry	heteros	hire car	Holbein
ha'p'orth	hatting	healing	helpful	heumite	hireman	holdall
happier	hattock	healthy	helping	heurism	hire out	holding
happify	hat-tree	heap big	help out	hexadic	hirsute	hold off
happily	hauberk	heaping	helxine	hexagon	hirudin	hold out
happing	haubitz	hearing	hemiola	hexamer	his nibs	holdout
haptics	haughty	hearken	hemline	hexapla	his-self	hold-out
haratch	haulage	hear out	hemlock	hexapod	hissing	hole-saw
harbour	haul ass	hear say	hemming	hexarch	hiss off	holiday
hard hat	haulier	hearsay	henbane	hexitol	histoid	holiest
hard hit	haul off	hearted	hen-clam	hexogen	histone	hollaed
hardier	haul out	hearten	hen-coop	hexosan	history	holland
hardily	haunchy	heathen	hencote	heyduck	histrio	hollies
hardish	haunted	heather	hen-hawk	hibachi	hit back	holloes
hard nut	haunter	heating	hennaed	hiccupy	hitcher	holmium
hard pad	hautboy	heave-ho	hennery	hickeys	hitch up	holm-oak
hardpan	hauteur	heave to	henpeck	hickory	hit home	holster
hard pan	have a go	heavier	henries	hidalgo	hit list	holy day
hard roe	have fun	heavily	hensure	Hidatsa	hit-mark	holy Joe
hard set	have got	heavy on	henwife	hideous	hitting	Holy Joe
hard-top	havener	Hebraic	hen yard	hide out	Hittite	holy oil
hardtop	have-not	Hebrean	heparin	hideout	hive off	Holy See
harelip	have out	heckler	hepatic	hiemate	hoarder	holy war
haricot	have pat	hectare	heppest	higgler	hoarier	homager
Harijan	haverel	hedging	hepster	highboy	hoarily	Homburg
harmala	have way	hedonic	heptane	high day	hoarsen	home boy
harmful	haviour	heedful	heptode	high-end	hoatzin	homeboy
harmine	hawbuck	heel bar	heptoic	high hat	hobbies	homeish
harmony	hawkbit	heel bug	heptose	high-key	Hobbism	home key
harmost	hawk-eye	heel cup	herbage	high men	Hobbist	home-lot
harness	hawkish	heeling	herbary	high old	hobbler	homelyn
harpies	hawk-owl	heeltap	herbier	high sea	hobnail	Homeric
harping	hay-band	heel-tap	herblet	high-set	hocheur	home run
harpist	hay-barn	heftier	herbose	high tea	Hock-day	homiest
harpoon	haybote	heftily	herbous	highway	hocused	hominid
Harrian	haycock	hegemon	herb tea	Hilaria	hodiern	Homoean
harried	hay-fork	hegumen	herd-boy	hilding	hoe-cake	homolog

homonym	hosiery	hugsome	hydrate	ictuses	imbrued	in a romp
honchos	hospice	Huichol	hydride	Idahoan	imbrues	in a ruck
honesty	hostage	huitain	hydrion	Idalian	imbrute	in a rush
honeyed	hostess	hulking	hydroid	ideally	imbuing	in a snap
Honiton	hostile	humanly	hydrops	identic	imburse	in a snit
honkers	hosting	hum-bird	hydrous	idiotic	imitate	in a sort
honkies	hostler	humbler	hyemate	idiotry	immense	in a spin
honoree	hot bath	humdrum	hygeian	idleman	immerge	in a spot
honorer	hot cake	humeral	hygeist	idlesse	immerse	in a tale
honyock	hotfoot	humerus	hygiene	idolise	immoral	inaugur
hood-end	hothead	humetty	hygroma	idolism	impaint	in a walk
hooding	hotline	humidly	hymenal	idolist	impaler	in a wink
hoodlum	hot line	humidor	hymenia	idolize	impalla	in a wood
hoodman	hotness	humming	hymnary	Idumean	impalsy	in a word
hoodoos	hot seat	hummock	hymnist	idyllic	impanel	in banco
Hookean	hot shoe	humoral	hymnody	iffiest	impasse	in bar of
hooklet	hotshot	humored	Hypalon	I for one	impaste	in being
hook-pin	hot spot	humpier	hyped up	igneous	impasto	in blank
hook-pot	hotspur	humpies	hyperon	igniter	impavid	in blood
hook rug	hot tear	hunched	hypnoid	ignitor	impeach	in bloom
hook-tip	hottest	hundred	hypogea	ignoble	impearl	inboard
hoolock	hotties	Hungary	hypogee	ignobly	imperil	inbound
hooping	hotting	hunkers	hyponym	ignorer	impetus	inbread
Hoosier	hottish	hunkier	hypoxia	iguanid	Impeyan	inbreak
hoot owl	hot tube	Hunnish	hypoxic	ijolite	impiety	inbreed
hop-back	hot well	hunting	hyraces	ikebana	impinge	in brief
hop-bind	hot wind	huntite	I ask you	I knew it	impious	inbring
hop-bine	hot-wire	hunt out	Iberian	ileitis	implant	in-build
hopbush	hot-work	hunt's-up	Icarian	iliacus	implead	inbuilt
hopeful	houbara	hurdler	iceberg	Iliadic	implied	inburst
hophead	Houdini	hurleys	ice-bird	iligant	implies	incense
hoplite	hougher	hurling	ice blue	Illanun	impling	in check
hoppety	houhere	Hurrian	ice-boat	illapse	implode	in chief
hopping	hoummos	hurried	ice-bolt	ill-bred	implore	incipit
hoppity	houngan	hurrier	ice-cold	illegal	implume	incisal
hop-pole	housing	hurries	ice cube	illegit	imposer	incised
hopsack	houting	hurry-up	icefall	ill fame	impound	incisor
hop-sack	hoverer	hurtful	ice-fall	illfare	impregn	inciter
hop-toad	howbeit	husband	ice fish	illicit	impresa	in class
hop tree	how come	hushaby	ice floe	illitic	imprese	inclave
hopyard	however	hushful	ice-foot	I'll live	impress	in clear
horizon	howling	hushion	Iceland	ill luck	imprest	incline
hormone	how many	huskier	iceless	illness	imprint	inclose
horn-bug	how much	huskies	ice milk	illocal	improve	include
hornero	Howship	huskily	Icenian	illogic	impulse	incluse
horn-fly	Hoxnian	husking	ice pack	illoyal	imputer	incomer
hornful	H-shaped	hussies	ice pail	illusor	I myself	Inconel
horn gap	Huastec	Hussite	ice pick	ill will	in a bind	inconnu
hornier	Hubbard	hussive	ice rink	ill wind	in a body	in court
hornify	hubbies	husting	ice show	Ilocano	inadept	incover
hornily	hubless	hustler	ice-wool	ilvaite	in-a-door	incrust
hornist	Hubshee	hut-like	ice-work	imagery	in a drip	incubus
hornito	huddler	hutment	ice-worm	imagine	in a funk	incudes
horn-mad	hueless	hutting	ichabod	imagism	in a glow	incurve
horn-man	huff-cap	Huygens	icicled	imagist	in a huff	indeedy
horn-owl	huffier	hyaenid	iciness	imamate	in aid of	in depth
horrent	huffily	hyaline	icky-boo	imbauba	in a mood	indexer
horrify	huffish	hyalite	iconism	imbiber	in and in	indexes
horsier	huffkin	hyaloid	iconize	imbongi	inanely	indican
horsily	hugeous	hydatid	icosane	imbosom	inanity	indices
hosanna	huggery	hydrant	icteric	imbound	in a oner	indicia
hose-net	hugging	hydrase	icterus	imbower	inaptly	indigos

inditer	infuser	in place	interne	Iranian	isotron	Jahvism
indolic	ingenio	in point	in there	Iranize	isotype	jai alai
indolyl	ingénue	in press	in-thing	Iraqize	isozyme	Jainism
in doors	ingoing	in prest	intimal	irately	Ispahan	Jainist
indoors	ingorge	in print	intoner	ireless	Israeli	Jaipuri
Indo-Pak	ingoted	in proof	in total	irenics	issuant	jalouse
indorse	Ingoush	inquest	in touch	Iricism	issuing	jamadar
in doubt	ingraft	inquiet	intrada	iridial	isthmic	Jamaica
indoxyl	in grain	inquire	in trade	iridian	isthmus	jam-full
indraft	ingrain	inquiry	in train	iridium	Istrian	jammier
indrawn	ingrate	in ruins	intrant	irisate	itacism	jamming
in drink	ingress	in scale	intreat	Irisher	itacist	jam on it
induced	Ingrian	inscape	introit	Irishly	Italian	jam-pack
inducer	in gross	insculp	in troth	Irishry	Italiot	Janeite
indulge	in-group	insecta	intrude	irksome	itchier	jangler
indulto	ingrown	insecty	intruse	iron age	itching	janitor
in dummy	inhabit	inseity	in trust	Iron Age	itemise	jankers
indusia	inhaler	insense	intrust	ironies	itemize	jannock
indwell	in haste	inshell	in truth	ironing	iterant	January
indwelt	inhaust	inshoot	intuent	ironise	iterate	Japlish
Indycar	in heart	in shore	in turns	ironist	itinera	japonic
inearth	inherit	inshore	in twain	ironize	it seems	Jap silk
inedita	inhiate	in short	intwine	iron law	it tells	jarfuls
ineptly	inhibin	insider	intwist	iron man	iulidan	jargoon
inequal	inhibit	in sight	inulase	iron ore	Ivicene	jarkman
inertia	in holes	insight	Inupiaq	iron out	Ivorian	jarldom
inertly	in-house	insigne	Inupiat	iron pan	ivoride	jarless
inesite	inhuman	insipid	in utero	irruent	ivoried	jarring
in evens	in irons	in small	inutile	isagoge	ivories	jasmine
inexact	initial	in smoke	in vacuo	isatoic	ivorine	jaspery
inexist	inition	insofar	invader	ischial	ivy-bush	javaite
in faith	injunct	in sooth	invalid	ischium	ivy-leaf	Java man
infancy	injured	in spate	inveigh	Isfahan	ivy tree	javelin
infanta	injurer	in-spawn	inverse	I-shaped	I wonder	jawbone
infante	injuria	inspeak	invigor	Ishmael	jabbers	jaw-hole
infarct	ink ball	inspect	invited	Isiacal	jabbing	jawless
in fault	ink-fish	inspire	invitee	isidial	jacamar	jawline
infauna	inkhorn	inspoke	inviter	isidium	jacinth	jaw-rope
infaust	inkiest	in sport	in vitro	Islamic	jackass	jaws wag
inferno	inkless	in spots	in vogue	isleman	jackdaw	jay-bird
infidel	inkling	install	in voice	isleted	jackeen	jaywalk
infield	in-kneed	instant	invoice	Ismaeli	jackleg	jazz age
in fieri	inkshed	in state	invoker	Ismaili	jackman	jazzier
infight	inkweed	instate	involve	isobath	Jack oak	jazzify
infimum	inkwell	instead	inwards	isocrat	jack off	jazzily
inflame	ink-well	in steam	in way of	isodose	Jack-pin	jazzman
in flank	inky cap	in stock	inweave	isoflor	jackpot	jazzmen
inflate	in large	in-store	in whelp	isogamy	jacksie	jealous
inflect	inlayer	instyle	in whole	isogeny	Jack tar	jeepers
in flesh	inlying	in style	inyanga	isogony	jacobin	jeepney
inflict	innards	insular	iodated	isogram	Jacobin	Jehovah
in focus	innerly	insulin	ion burn	isohyet	Jacobus	jejunal
in folio	innerve	insulse	ionizer	isolate	jaconet	jejunum
infolio	innings	insured	ionogen	isolato	jacuzzi	jellaba
in force	in no way	insurer	ionomer	isoline	Jacuzzi	jellied
inforce	inocula	insurge	ion pair	isonomy	jadedly	jellies
infract	inolith	inswing	ion spot	isopach	jadeite	jellify
inframe	in order	in tears	ion trap	isospin	j'adoube	jemadar
in front	inosate	integer	lo paean	isotely	Jagatai	jenever
in fruit	inosine	intense	ipomoea	isotone	jaggery	jennies
infulae	in pairs	interim	ipseity	isotope	jaggier	jeofail
in funds	in phase	in terms	iracund	isotopy	jagging	jeopard

Jericho
jerkier
jerkily
jerk off
jerquer
jerries
Jerries
jerseys
jessamy
jessant
Jessean
jestful
Jesuist
jetfoil
Jetfoil
jetties
jetting
jewelly
jewelry
jewfish
Jew plum
Jewries
Jew's ear
Jew's eye
Jezebel
jhuming
jibbing
jib-boom
jib-door
jiffies
jigaboo
jig-a-jig
jig-bore
jiggety
jigging
jiggish
jillion
jiltish
Jim Crow
jim-jams
jimmied
jimmies
Jimminy
jingall
jingler
jingoes
jittery
jive-ass
Joannes
jobbery
jobbing
jobbish
job-hunt
jobless
Jo block
job shop
jobster
job-type
jobwork
jockeys
jocular
Joe Blow

Joe Soap
jogging
jogtrot
jog-trot
John Doe
John hop
Johnson
joinant
joinder
joinery
joining
jointed
jointer
jointly
joisted
jokelet
jollier
jollies
jollify
jollily
jollity
jollyer
jonnick
jonquil
joss-man
jotting
joukery
joulean
journal
journey
journos
jouster
joyance
joyancy
Joycean
joyless
joyride
joysome
J-shaped
jubilee
Judaean
Judaise
Judaism
Judaist
Judaize
judcock
judgess
judging
judoist
jug band
jugfuls
jugging
juggins
juggler
jughead
juglone
jugular
jugulum
juicier
juicily
ju-jitsu
jujuism

ju-jutsu
jukebox
jukskei
jumbuck
jumelle
jump bid
jump-cut
jumpier
jumpily
jumping
jump jet
jump-off
juncoes
June bug
Jungian
jungled
juniper
junk art
junkman
Jupiter
jurally
jurator
juridic
jury box
jury-leg
juryman
jurymen
jury-rig
jussion
jussive
justice
justify
justing
just now
jutting
juvenal
Juvenal
kabaddi
kabbala
Kabbala
kaboura
kachina
Kaddish
kagoule
kahawai
kainite
kajaten
kakapos
kalashy
kalends
kalimba
Kalmuck
Kalmyks
kalpack
Kamares
kamassi
kamerad
kampong
kampung
kanchil
Kandyan
K'ang-Hsi

Kannada
kantele
Kantian
Kantism
Karaism
Karaite
karakia
karakul
karamat
karanga
karaoke
karezza
Karnata
karstic
karting
Kashgai
Kashgar
Kashmir
Kashrut
Kashube
Kassite
kasturi
Kaszube
kathode
katsura
Kattern
katydid
kayaked
kayaker
kaylied
Kazakhs
kazooer
kebbuck
kecksie
kedlock
keelage
keeling
keelman
keelson
keep-fit
keeping
keepnet
keep-net
keep nit
keep off
keep out
keertan
keester
Keftian
keg beer
keister
keitloa
kelping
ken-mark
kenning
kenosis
kenotic
Kentish
Kentuck
kerasin
keratin
kerbing

kercher
Keresan
kernite
kerogen
Kerries
kerseys
keruing
kerygma
kestrel
Keswick
ketchup
ketolic
ketonic
ketosis
ketotic
kettler
key-clog
key-cold
key grip
keyhole
keyless
key move
keynote
keyring
key-ring
keyster
keyword
khaddar
khakied
khalasi
khalifa
Khalkha
khamsin
khanate
khanjar
khanjee
Khedive
Khoisan
kibbler
kibbutz
kibitka
Kichaga
kick ass
kicking
kickish
kick off
kick out
kiddier
kiddies
kidding
kiddish
kiddush
kidling
kidneys
kidskin
kid-star
Kieffer
kierful
kiering
Kievian
kiewiet
Kikongo

Kikuchi
Kikuyus
kill-cow
killian
killick
killing
killjoy
killock
kill off
kill out
kiln-dry
kilnful
kilobit
kiloton
kilting
kimonos
kinchin
kindler
kindred
kinesic
kinesis
kinetic
kinetin
kinfolk
kingcup
kingdom
king-hit
Kingite
kinglet
King Log
king-nut
kingpin
kinkier
kinkily
kinkled
kinless
kinship
kinsman
kinsmen
Kipchak
kippage
kippeen
kipping
kip-shop
kipsies
Kirghiz
kirkman
kirkmen
Kirlian
kirmess
kirtled
kissage
kissing
kiss off
kistful
kitchen
kite bar
kite-man
kitenge
kithara
kithing
kitless

kitling
kitschy
kitties
kitting
kittles
Kiwanis
Klamath
klapper
Kleagle
Kleenex
kleruch
klezmer
klipbok
klipdas
klister
klompie
klonkie
klootch
knacker
knaidel
knapped
knapper
knarred
knavery
knavish
kneader
kneecap
kneeing
kneeled
kneeler
knee-pan
kneesie
knees-up
kneidel
Knesset
knicker
knitted
knitter
knittle
knobbed
knobber
knobble
knobbly
knocker
knock on
knock up
knoller
knopped
knopper
knotted
knotter
know-all
know how
knowing
Knoxian
knubble
knubbly
knuckle
knuckly
Knudsen
knurled
Kodaker

koi carp	lacecap	lambast	lap-join	Latvian	leaf-bud	legging
kokanee	Lacerta	lambent	Laplace	Laudian	leafery	leghorn
koklass	laciest	lambert	Lapland	Laudism	leaf-fat	Leghorn
kolkhoz	lacinia	Lambert	lapping	Laudist	leaf-gap	legible
komatik	lack for	Lambeth	Lappish	laugher	leafier	legibly
kombers	lacking	lambkin	lap robe	laugh-in	leaflet	leg-iron
komfoor	lackwit	lamboys	Lapsang	launder	leagued	legitim
kongoni	laconic	lamb-pie	Laputan	laundry	leaguer	legless
koniaku	lacquey	lamella	lap-weld	laurate	leagues	leg-over
Konkani	lactary	laminae	lapwing	lauroyl	leakage	leg-pull
kookier	lactase	laminal	larceny	Lausitz	leakier	leg-rest
kookily	lactate	laminar	larchen	lavabos	lea-land	leg-ring
kopdoek	lacteal	lamming	lard-ass	lave net	leangle	legroom
Koppite	lactone	lampern	lard oil	lavolta	leaning	leg-room
koradji	lactose	lampers	lardoon	law-book	leanish	leg-rope
Koranic	lacunae	lampful	largely	law-hand	lean-tos	leg-show
Koranko	lacunal	lamping	largess	lawless	leap day	leg side
Koranna	lacunar	lampion	largish	lawlike	leaping	leg slip
Koreish	lacunas	lampist	larkish	Law Lord	learned	leg spin
korhaan	Ladakhi	lamplet	Larnian	lawsuit	learner	leg trap
korowai	ladanum	lamplit	larnite	law term	learn up	legumen
Koshare	laddish	lamp oil	lasagne	lawting	leasing	legumin
kotatsu	ladette	lampoon	lashing	laxness	leather	leg work
kotwali	ladhood	lamprey	lashkar	layaway	leave be	legwork
koumiss	ladinos	lamster	lash out	lay away	leave go	leg-worm
kouprey	Ladinos	land-boc	lassock	lay back	Leavers	Leibniz
K ration	ladrone	land-end	lassoer	lay bare	leaving	leister
kremlin	ladybug	land-ice	lassoes	lay dead	Leboyer	leisure
kriegie	Lady Day	landing	lassy me	lay down	lechery	lemanry
krieker	ladydom	land-law	lastage	lay-edge	Lechish	lemmata
Krilium	lady-fly	ländler	last day	layered	lectern	lemming
krimmer	ladyish	landman	last end	layette	lection	Lemnian
krypton	ladykin	landmen	lasting	lay fast	lectric	lempira
krytron	Laetare	landnam	last lap	layflat	lecture	lemurid
Kuan Yin	lagarto	land-rat	last man	laygear	lecythi	lending
kufiyeh	lag bolt	land tax	last out	lay into	ledging	lengthy
kulchur	lagenar	land-tie	Latakia	laylock	leecher	lenient
kumquat	lagetto	land-war	latania	lay odds	lee helm	lenitic
kunzite	laggard	langite	latchet	lay open	lee-lone	lens cap
kurbash	lagging	langley	latch on	layover	leemost	lensing
Kurdish	lag-last	langsat	late cut	lay over	leerier	lenslet
kursaal	lag time	langued	late fee	lay pipe	leerily	lensman
Kushite	Lagting	languet	lateish	lay wait	leer man	lensmen
kuteera	lah-de-da	languid	latency	lazaret	lee-room	lensoid
Kutenai	laicise	languor	laterad	Lazarus	leervis	lentigo
Kuwaiti	laicism	laniary	lateral	laziest	lee side	lentisk
kwanzas	laicity	laniate	Lateran	lazy arm	leesome	lentoid
kwedini	laicize	lanista	latexes	lazy-bed	leeward	Leonese
kyanise	laidron	lankier	lathery	lazy dog	lee wave	leonine
kyanite	lairage	lankily	lathing	lazy eye	left arm	Leonine
kyanize	lairdie	lanolin	latices	lazyish	lefties	leopard
kylikes	lairdly	lantana	latimer	lazzaro	leftish	leotard
kyoodle	lakelet	lantern	Latiner	L-driver	leftism	leproma
labaria	Lalique	lanyard	Latinic	leacher	leftist	leprose
labarri	lallang	Laocoön	Latinly	lead-ash	legally	leprosy
labarum	Lallans	Laotian	Latinos	leading	legatee	leprous
labella	lalling	lap belt	latitat	leadman	legator	leptome
labiate	lamaism	lap desk	latosol	lead off	legatos	leptons
labored	Lamaism	lapfuls	latrant	lead out	leg bail	lesbian
labroid	lamaist	lap-held	latrine	lead-tin	leg-bone	Lesbian
laccase	Lamaist	lapilli	latteen	leafage	leggero	lessest
lacebug	lambada	lap-iron	lattice	leaf-bed	leggier	lessive

let-down	lie-down	linctus	listful	lockram	loonies	lowerer
let drop	lie over	lindane	listing	lock-saw	loopful	low gear
let fall	lie with	lindorm	lit crit	locoman	loopier	low keep
Lethean	life-day	lineage	literal	Locrian	loosely	lowland
let into	lifeful	Linear A	lithate	locular	loosish	lowlier
let know	life-gun	Linear B	lithely	loculus	lop down	low life
let pass	life net	lineate	lithian	locusta	lop-ears	low-life
let slip	lifeway	lineman	lithify	locutor	loppage	lowlife
let stew	lift-fan	linemen	lithium	lodging	lopping	lowlily
lettiga	lifting	line-out	lithoes	loftier	lopseed	low-loss
letting	lift off	line pin	lithoid	loftily	lop-wood	low mass
Lettish	lift-out	Lingala	lithops	lofting	loquent	low Mass
lettuce	lift-web	lingcod	litotes	logatom	lord-dom	lowmost
let walk	ligancy	lingoes	litster	logbook	lordful	lowness
leucine	ligging	lingual	littery	log-cock	Lord God	low-pass
leucite	lighted	Linguet	littler	logging	lording	low-rise
leucoma	lighten	lingula	littlie	loghead	lordlet	low tech
leucous	lighter	liniest	liturgy	logical	Lorelei	low tide
levancy	lightly	linkage	livable	logiest	Lorentz	lowveld
levator	light on	link-boy	lived-in	log-line	lorgnon	Low Week
leveche	light up	linking	livener	logroll	lorilet	loxodon
leveler	lignify	linkman	live oak	logwood	lorimer	loyally
levelly	lignite	linkmen	live out	log-work	loriner	loyalty
level up	lignose	link off	livered	loiasis	lorisid	lozened
leveret	lignous	link rod	lividly	Lollard	lormery	lozenge
Levitic	ligroin	linnaea	lixivia	lollies	lorries	lozengy
lewisia	ligular	Linnean	llanero	lolling	losable	L-shaped
lew-warm	Lihyani	linocut	lloydia	lollopy	lose bet	lubbard
lexemic	likable	linoxyn	loading	lombard	loselry	lubrify
lex fori	like fun	linsang	loaning	Lombard	lose out	lucanid
lexical	like ice	linseed	loather	Londony	lose way	lucarne
lexicon	like mad	lintern	loathly	loneful	lost wax	lucence
lex loci	like sin	linuron	lobbies	long ago	lot-lead	lucency
ley line	lilacky	lion-ant	lobbing	long arm	lot-mead	lucerne
Lezgian	lily pad	lioncel	lobbyer	longbow	lotment	lucible
liaison	lily-pot	lion dog	lobcock	long-day	lottery	lucidly
liangle	limaces	lioness	lobe-fin	long dog	lotting	lucifee
liassic	limaçon	lionise	lobelia	long ear	loudish	Lucifer
liatris	limbate	lionish	lobopod	longest	lounder	lucific
libbard	limb-bud	lionism	lobster	long-fed	lounger	lucivee
libelee	limbeck	lionize	lob-tail	long hop	louring	luckier
liberal	limbric	lip-deep	lobular	longing	louse up	luckily
liberty	limeade	lipemia	lobulus	long ink	lousier	luculia
Liberty	lime-ash	lipless	lobworm	longish	lousily	Luddism
libidos	limepit	liplike	locable	long leg	loutish	Luddite
library	lime-pot	lip-line	locally	long off	louvred	Luganda
librate	limiest	lipoate	locator	long pig	lovable	Lugbara
Librium	liminal	lippier	lochage	long-pod	lovably	luggage
licence	limited	lipping	lochial	long run	loveful	lugging
license	limiter	lip-read	lockage	long sea	love-lay	lughole
licheny	limites	lip-sync	lock-box	Long Tom	love-pat	lug-mark
lich-owl	limning	lip-work	Lockean	long ton	lovered	lugsail
licitly	Limoges	liquate	lockful	lonning	loverly	lug sole
lickety	limping	liquefy	Lockian	look big	loverly	Lugwari
licking	limpish	liqueur	locking	looking	lowance	lugworm
lick-log	limpkin	liquidy	Lockist	look out	lowball	Luiseño
lickpot	limulus	liquify	lockjaw	lookout	lowbell	lullaby
licuala	linable	lirella	lockman	look-see	low-born	Lullian
lidgate	linaloe	lisente	locknut	loo mask	low-bred	Lullism
lidless	linalyl	lisping	lock-nut	loomery	lowbrow	Lullist
lie-abed	linaria	lissoir	lock out	looming	low-bush	lumbago
lie back	Lincoln	lissome	lockout	loonier	low-down	lumeter

luminal	machete	mahmudi	malmsey	man-keen	marcato	mascled
Luminal	Machian	Mahomet	malonic	mankier	marcher	masculy
luminol	machila	mahonia	malonyl	mankind	march on	mashlum
lumpers	machine	mahorka	malpais	manless	Marconi	Mashona
lumpier	Machism	Mahound	maltase	manlier	maremma	mash-tub
lumpily	machree	mahseer	Maltese	manlike	maremme	Mas John
lumping	Machzor	maidish	maltier	manlily	Marengo	mask jug
lumpish	maclura	maidkin	malting	manling	margate	masoner
lump sum	macouba	mailbag	maltman	man-made	margent	masonic
lunaria	macramé	mail-box	maltose	manness	margosa	Masonic
lunated	maculae	mailbox	malt-tax	manning	marimba	masonry
lunatic	macular	mail-car	Malvern	mannish	marined	Masorah
luncher	macumba	mail-day	mamaloi	mannite	mariner	masquer
lunette	maddest	mailing	mamboes	mannose	marital	massage
lungful	madding	maillot	mamelle	man o'war	markhor	mass-day
lunulae	maddish	mailman	mamelon	manpack	marking	masseur
lunular	made for	mailmen	mamilla	man-rate	mark man	massify
lunulet	madeira	mail-out	mammary	man-rope	markman	massily
lupanar	Madeira	Mainite	mammies	mansard	mark off	massive
lupulin	made man	ma-in-law	mammock	manship	mark out	mass man
lurcher	madhead	mainour	mammoth	mansion	mark you	massula
lurgies	Madison	main sea	manacle	man-size	marline	mastaba
luridly	mad keen	maintop	managed	man's man	marlion	mastage
lurking	madling	mainway	managee	manteau	marlite	mastery
lushbum	mad mick	maistry	manager	manteca	marloes	mastiff
lustful	madness	maizena	manakin	mantled	marl-pit	mastika
lustier	Madonna	majesty	manatee	mantlet	marmite	masting
lustily	madoqua	makable	manbote	Mantoux	Marmite	mastman
lustral	Madrasi	Makasar	mancala	mantrap	maroela	mastoid
lustred	madroña	make for	manchet	mantric	maroodi	matador
lustrum	madroño	make hay	man cook	Mantuan	Marplan	matcher
luteous	Maduran	make off	mandala	manuary	marplot	matchet
lute-pin	madwort	make out	mandant	manumit	marquee	match up
luthern	maestri	make war	mandate	manurer	marquis	matelot
luthier	maestro	make way	Mandean	manurey	Marrano	mathern
Lutomer	Mae West	Makonde	Manding	manward	married	matiest
lutrine	maffick	Malabar	mandola	man-week	marrier	Matilda
luvvies	Mafiosi	malacca	mandora	manwise	marries	matinal
lychnis	Mafioso	Malacca	mandore	Manx cat	marring	matinee
lycopin	magadis	malacia	Mandrax	Manxman	Marrism	matinée
lycopod	magenta	malacon	mandrel	Manxmen	Marrist	matless
lyddite	maggoty	malagas	maneton	man-year	marrowy	matraca
lye corn	Maghreb	malaise	Manetti	many–one	marry up	matrass
lygaeid	Maghrib	malambo	mangeao	Maori PT	Marsala	matrist
lyingly	Maghzen	malanga	mangier	maormor	marshal	matross
Lyle gun	magical	malaria	mangily	map-fire	Marsian	mattery
lymphad	magmata	Malayan	mangler	mapless	martelé	matting
lyncean	magnate	Malayic	mangoes	mappery	martial	mattins
lyncher	magneto	malcoha	mangold	mapping	Martian	mattock
lynchet	magnify	malease	man-haul	mappist	Martini	mattoid
lyngorm	magnums	maleate	manhole	map-read	martlet	maturer
lynx-eye	magslip	maleesh	manhood	Mapuche	martyry	matweed
Lyonese	magsman	malefic	man-hour	marabou	Marwari	mat-work
lyrated	maguari	malicho	manhunt	Maranao	Marxian	matzoth
lyrical	mahaila	malimbi	manicou	maranta	Marxise	maudlin
macabre	mahaleb	Malines	manihot	marasca	Marxism	Maulana
macadam	Mahamad	Malinke	manikin	Maratha	Marxist	maul oak
macaque	mahatma	malison	manilla	Marathi	Marxite	maunder
macauco	Mahdism	malkoha	Manilla	marbled	Marxize	Maurist
macchia	Mahdist	mallard	manille	marbler	Mary Ann	mauryah
maceral	Mahican	malleus	maniple	marblet	Masarwa	Mauryan
machair	mah-jong	Malling	manitou	Marburg	mascara	mauther

mauvish	medalet	Mennecy	metrete	mileage	minibus	miskick
mavrone	meddler	Mennist	metrify	milfoil	minicab	Miskito
mawkish	medevac	men-only	metrist	miliary	minikin	misknow
mawseed	mediacy	menorah	mettled	milieus	minimal	mislead
mawther	mediant	Men's Lib	me-wards	milieux	minimax	mislear
mawworm	mediate	*mens rea*	mew gull	militia	minimum	mislike
maxilla	medical	mensual	Mexican	milk bar	minimus	misluck
maximal	medicos	menthol	mezuzah	milk cap	miniver	mismade
maximin	mediety	mention	mezzani	milk-cow	minivet	mismake
maximum	Medinal	meranti	Miaotse	milk dry	Min of Ag	mismark
maxwell	mediums	mercado	miasmal	milkful	Minorca	mismate
Maxwell	medivac	mercery	miasmas	milkier	minster	mismove
May-bird	medleys	merchet	miasmic	milkily	mintage	misname
May-blob	medulla	Mercian	micelle	milking	mintier	misnome
May-bush	medusae	mercies	Michael	milk-leg	mint par	misplay
maycock	medusal	mercury	michery	milkman	mint tea	misrate
mayduke	medusan	mereing	mickery	milkmen	minuend	misread
Mayfair	medusas	merinos	micrify	milk run	minuter	misrule
mayfish	meerkat	merisis	micrite	milksop	minutia	missaid
May game	meeting	merited	microbe	millage	minxish	misseem
May lady	megabit	Merkani	mid-aged	mill-dam	Miocene	missend
May lily	megapod	mermaid	mid-brow	mill-dog	Mipolam	missies
May morn	Megaric	Meroite	mid-calf	Millian	miracle	missile
mayoral	megaron	merrier	midcrop	millime	mirador	missing
maypole	megasea	merrill	midcult	milling	Miranda	mission
May-rose	megaton	merrily	middest	mill-ink	mirbane	missish
maythen	meioses	mersion	middies	million	Mirditë	missive
maythes	meiosis	mesarch	middle C	Millite	mirific	missort
mayweed	meiotic	mesaxon	middler	mill-ken	mirkier	miss out
May Week	mei ping	meseems	Mideast	millman	mirrory	misstay
mazagan	Meissen	meshing	midgern	mill-run	misally	misstep
Mazahua	melaena	meshuga	midibus	milordo	misbode	missuit
Mazatec	melamed	mesityl	midiron	milreis	misborn	mistake
Mazdean	mélange	mesodic	midland	Miltown	miscall	mistbow
mazedly	melanic	mesonic	Midland	Mimamsa	miscast	mistell
mazeful	melanin	mesquit	mid-life	mimesis	mischty	misterm
Mazhabi	melasma	message	midline	mimetic	mis-cite	mistery
maziest	melilot	mess-boy	midmost	mimical	miscode	mistful
mazurka	melisma	Messiah	midnoon	mimicry	miscook	mistico
mazzard	melissa	messier	Midrash	mimness	miscopy	mistier
meacock	melkbos	Messier	midriff	mimulus	misdate	mistily
meadowy	Melkite	messily	midship	minable	misdeal	mistime
mealier	mellite	messing	mid-shot	Minaean	misdeed	mist-net
mealman	mellowy	mess kit	midsole	minaret	misdeem	mistook
meander	melodia	mess tin	midterm	minchen	misdial	mistral
meanies	melodic	mestiza	midtown	mincing	misdoer	mistune
meaning	melonry	mestizo	midward	mindful	misdraw	mistype
mean sun	meltemi	mestome	midweek	mindset	misease	misuser
mearing	melting	metalaw	Midwest	mind-set	miserly	miswent
measled	membral	metaled	midwife	mind you	misfall	misword
measles	memento	metally	mid-wing	mine-car	misfame	misyoke
measure	menacer	metamer	midwive	mine-pig	misfare	Mitanni
meat-ant	menalty	methane	Miesian	mine-pit	misfell	mitchel
meat-axe	menazon	methene	miffish	mineral	misfile	mitella
meat-fly	mendang	methide	might-be	mine tin	misfire	mitered
meatier	mending	Methody	mightn't	minette	misgive	mitogen
meatily	mendong	Methuen	migrant	minever	mishear	mitosis
meatman	mendung	metical	migrate	mingier	Mishnah	mitotic
meat tea	menfolk	Metonic	mikados	mingily	Mishnic	mitring
Meccano	Ménière	metonym	milcher	mingler	mishook	mitzvah
Mechlin	menisci	me-tooer	mildewy	miniate	misjoin	mixable
meconin	menkind	metopic	mildish	minibar	miskeys	mix-down

mixdown	monarch	moorish	mothery	muddler	mumpish	mycelia
mixedly	monarda	Moorish	moth fly	Mudéjar	muncher	mycosis
mixed-up	Mondays	moorlog	mothier	mudfish	munchie	mycotic
mixible	mondial	moorman	Motilon	mudflap	mundane	myeloid
mixture	moneran	Moorman	motivic	mud-flat	muninga	myeloma
mizmaze	moneron	moor-pan	motlier	mudflat	munjeet	myiasis
mizzler	moneyed	mop fair	motored	mud-flow	munnion	mylodon
Moabite	moneyer	mophead	motoric	mudflow	Munsell	mynheer
moanful	mongrel	mopiest	MOT test	mudhead	muntjac	myoball
moaning	moniker	mopping	mottled	mudhole	muntjak	myocoel
mobbing	monilia	moraine	mottler	mudhook	muonium	myocyte
mobbish	monitor	moraled	mottoes	mudlark	muraena	myogram
mobbism	monkdom	morally	moucher	mud-lava	murally	myology
mob rule	monkery	morassy	mouflon	mudless	muramic	myomere
mobsman	monkeys	moratto	mouillé	mud-line	murexes	myoneme
mobster	monkish	morbose	moulage	mud-lump	muriate	myopism
Mochica	monkism	morbous	moulded	mud-mask	murices	myosote
mockage	monocle	morceau	moulder	mud pack	murkily	myotome
mockery	monocot	mordant	moulted	mudpout	murnong	myotomy
mock sun	monodic	mordent	moulter	mud pump	murrain	myotube
modally	monodon	Mordvin	mounted	mud room	murther	myrcene
mod cons	monoecy	moreish	mounter	mud-sill	muscari	myricin
modeler	monofil	morello	Mountie	mud wall	muscled	myricyl
modello	monolog	more meo	mourner	mud wasp	muscose	myronic
moderne	monomer	Moreote	mousaka	mud wing	muscous	myrosin
modesty	mononym	Moresca	mousery	mud-worm	Muscovy	myrrhed
modicum	monoped	Moresco	mousier	mudwort	museful	myrrhic
modiste	monopod	more suo	mousily	muezzin	musette	my stars
modular	monoski	moriche	mouthed	muffish	mush ice	mystery
modulus	monsoon	morille	mouther	muffler	mushier	mystify
moellon	monster	morinda	movable	Muganda	mushily	mytheme
mofette	montage	moringa	movably	mug book	mushlaw	mythify
Mogadon	Montagu	Moriori	move out	mugfuls	mushrat	mythist
mohajir	montane	Morisca	Moviola	muggier	musical	my watch
moharra	montero	Morisco	mowable	mugging	musiker	myxomas
Mohawks	monther	Morlach	mowburn	muggins	musk-bag	nabbing
Mohegan	monthly	morling	mow down	muggish	muskier	nacarat
Mohican	montuno	mormaor	Mozarab	muggler	muskrat	nacelle
moidore	monture	morning	mozetta	mugient	musquaw	nacrite
Moinian	moocher	morocco	mpingos	mug shot	mussuck	nacrous
moisten	moochin	moronic	Mpongwe	mugshot	mustang	naevoid
moistly	moodier	morphew	Mr Clean	mugwort	mustard	naffing
moither	moodily	morphia	Mr Fixit	mugwump	mustier	nagging
mojarra	moolvie	morphic	Mr Right	muhimbi	mustily	nagsman
moko fig	moonack	morphon	Mrs Mopp	mukhtar	mustine	Nahuatl
molasse	mooneas	morpion	mucigel	mulatta	must not	nailery
moldier	moon-eye	mortary	mucigen	mulatto	mutable	nail-rod
molding	moonier	mortice	muckier	mulesed	mutably	Nailsea
mole rat	moonily	mortify	mucking	mullein	mutagen	nail set
molimen	moonish	mortise	mucopus	mullion	mutator	naively
mollify	moonjah	morulae	mucosal	mullite	mutedly	naïveté
mollock	moonlet	morwong	mucosal	mullock	muttony	naivety
mollusc	moonlit	Mosaism	mudbank	mulmull	mutuary	naïvety
mollusk	moon-man	moscato	mud-bath	multure	Muzaked	nakedly
molossi	moon rat	Moselle	mudbath	mumbler	muzzier	nakerer
Molotov	moonset	moseyed	mud-crab	mu-meson	muzzily	nakhoda
Molucca	moorage	Mosotho	muddied	Mumetal	muzzled	Nalline
momenta	Mooress	moss-bag	muddier	mummery	muzzler	Namaqua
mommies	moor-hag	moss-hag	muddify	mummied	myalgia	namaste
monacid	moorhen	mossier	muddily	mummies	myalgic	name-day
monades	moor-ill	moss-oak	muddish	mummify	myalism	name-son
monadic	mooring	mostest	muddled	mumming	myalist	name-tag

nankeen	nebulas	nestler	nibbler	nobbily	noodler	not that
nannies	necking	netball	niblick	nobbins	nookery	not very
naology	necklet	net book	Niblung	nobbler	nooklet	noughty
naperer	neck-oil	net-cord	Nicaean	no-being	noology	noumena
nap hand	necktie	netfuls	niceish	noblest	noonday	nourice
naphtha	necrose	netlike	nice one	no-brand	nooning	nourish
napless	nectary	net-play	nicking	no can do	no other	nouther
nappies	neddies	netsman	nicotia	no class	Nootkan	nouveau
napping	needful	netsuke	nictate	no-'count	nopalry	novator
narcism	needier	netting	niddick	noctuid	no place	novella
narciss	needler	netwise	niduses	noctule	noplace	novelly
nardine	need-not	network	Nielsen	nocturn	Norfolk	novelty
narkier	Ne'erday	Neumann	niffier	nocuous	no-right	novolak
narrate	negater	neumata	niftier	noddies	norimon	nowaday
narthex	negaton	neurine	niftily	nodding	norland	nowcast
nartjie	negator	neurite	nigella	nodical	Norland	nowhere
narwhal	neglect	neuroid	niggard	no doubt	norther	no wight
nasally	négligé	neuroma	niggery	nodular	norward	no wiser
nascent	Negress	neurone	niggler	nodulus	nor'-west	nowness
nash-gab	Negrito	neurula	nighter	no end of	Norwich	now that
Nashiji	Negroes	neuston	nightie	no entry	nose-ape	now then
Naskapi	Negroid	neutral	night in	Noetian	nosebag	nowther
Nasmyth	negroni	neutron	nightly	no-fault	nose cap	noxious
Nasonov	neigher	Nevadan	nigrify	no-fines	no-see-em	N-shaped
Nasrani	neither	never so	nigrous	nogging	no-see-um	nuanced
nastier	nellies	New Ager	Nilotic	no-hoper	nose-fly	nucleal
nastily	nelumbo	new ball	Nimbies	noisier	nosegay	nuclear
nasutus	nematic	newborn	nimbler	noisily	nose job	nucleic
natalid	nemeses	new chum	nimiety	noisome	nose-rag	nuclein
Natchez	nemesia	new-come	nimious	no-knock	nosh bar	nucleon
natrium	nemesis	new deal	Nimonic	nol-pros	noshery	nucleus
nattery	nemmind	newelty	ninepin	nomades	nosiest	nuclide
nattier	nemoral	Newgate	ninnies	nomadic	no siree	nucloid
nattily	Neogene	new girl	ninthly	nomarch	no small	nuggety
natural	neology	new-laid	niobate	nombril	nostril	nullify
natured	neonate	New Left	niobian	nominal	nostrum	nulling
naughty	neo-Nazi	new look	niobium	nominee	no sweat	nullity
nauplii	neoteny	new math	niobous	nomisma	not a bit	numbles
Nauruan	neotype	new moon	Nipmuck	nonagon	notable	numeral
Naussie	Neozoic	newness	nippier	nonamer	notably	numeric
nautili	Nepalis	new poor	nippily	non-bank	not a few	numinal
Navahos	nephric	new rich	nipping	non-drip	not a rap	nummary
navally	nephron	newsboy	nippled	none the	not a sou	nummion
navarch	nepotal	newsful	nirvana	none too	notatin	nunatak
navarin	nepotic	newsier	nitchie	non-flam	notator	nunbird
navette	Neptune	newsily	nithing	non-hero	notched	nun-buoy
navvied	nerdish	newsman	nitinol	non-iron	notcher	nuncios
navvies	nerf-bar	newsmen	Nitinol	non-jury	notedly	nuncius
Navy Cut	neritic	new star	nit-pick	non-life	notelet	nundine
navy rum	nerkish	newtake	nitpick	non-past	notepad	nunhood
nayword	Neronic	new tick	nitrate	nonplus	note-row	nunlike
Nazidom	nervier	new town	nitrene	non-pros	not half	nunnery
Naziism	nervily	new wave	Nitrian	non-sane	nothing	nunnish
Ndebele	nervine	new year	nitride	non-sked	no-throw	nunship
near cut	nervose	New Year	nitrify	non-skid	noticer	nuntius
nearish	nervous	New York	nitrile	non-slip	notitia	nuptial
neatify	nervure	next man	nitrite	non-stop	not much	nursery
neatnik	Nessler	nexuses	nitrous	nonsuch	not once	nursing
nebbich	nest box	Ngbandi	nitweed	nonsuit	no-touch	nurture
nebbish	nest egg	Niagara	niveous	non-user	not over	nut-cake
nebulae	nestful	niaouli	Nizamut	non-word	no trump	nutcase
nebular	nesting	nibbing	Noachic	non-zero	not-self	nutgall

nut-hook	obovoid	odyssey	Ohm's law	old year	one-stop	open out
nutlike	obscene	Oedipal	oil bath	olearia	one-tail	open-pit
nut-meat	obscure	Oedipus	oil-berg	olefine	one-time	open sea
nut-pine	obsequy	oenomel	oil-bird	oligist	one with	open-toe
nutrice	observe	oersted	oilcake	olisbos	on faith	open-top
nutrify	obtrude	oestral	oil-drop	olitory	on-glaze	open war
nuttery	Ob-Ugric	oestrin	oil drum	olivary	onglaze	operand
nuttier	obverse	oestrum	oiled-up	olivine	on-glide	operant
nutting	obviate	oestrus	oiliest	Olmecan	ongoing	operate
nuttish	obvious	of a kind	oil lamp	ologist	on guard	opercle
nut tree	obvolve	of a size	oilless	Olonets	on leave	operose
nut-wood	ocarina	of a sort	oil-meal	oloroso	only not	ophitic
nylghau	occiput	off-axis	oil-mill	Olympic	only too	Ophitic
nyloned	Occitan	off base	oil-palm	Olympus	on offer	opiatic
nymphae	occlude	off beam	oil pool	omalgia	on order	Opimian
nymphal	occluse	off-bear	oil-rich	omander	on paper	opinion
nymphet	Oceania	offbeat	oil-ring	Omarian	on piece	opossum
nymphic	oceanic	off-bore	oil-sand	Omarite	on shore	oppidan
nymphon	Oceanid	offcast	oil-seed	omental	onshore	opposed
nymphos	ocellar	offcome	oilseed	omentum	on sight	opposer
Nyquist	ocellus	off-corn	oil-silk	omicron	onsight	opposit
Nyungar	ochroid	off duty	oilskin	ominous	on space	oppress
oak cist	ochrous	offence	oil-spot	omitted	on-stage	opsonic
oak fern	ockerer	offense	oil trap	omitter	onstead	opsonin
oak-gall	ocreate	offeree	oil well	ommatin	on tally	optable
oak land	octadic	offerer	oily wad	omneity	on terms	optical
oaklike	octagon	offeror	Ojibwas	omniana	on the go	optimal
oakling	octamer	off form	Okazaki	omnibus	ontical	optimum
oak moss	octapla	off from	Okhrana	omnific	on toast	opulent
oak tree	octarch	offhand	okimono	Omnopon	on top of	opuntia
oak wilt	octaval	officer	olation	omomyid	on track	opus Dei
oak-wood	octavic	off-line	old bean	on a bend	on trial	oralism
oak-worm	octavos	offline	Old Bill	on a dime	on trust	oralist
oarfish	octette	offload	old bird	on and on	on-verse	orality
oar-hole	October	off-peak	old boot	onanism	onwards	Oral Law
oarless	octofid	off-ramp	old cock	onanist	on watch	oral sex
oarlock	octonal	off-road	old days	on appro	onychia	oranged
oar-port	octoped	off-sale	old dear	on a roll	onymity	orangey
oarsman	octopic	offscum	old-face	on a wind	onymous	orarion
oarweed	octopod	off side	old firm	Onazote	oof-bird	oration
oatcake	octopus	offside	old fogy	on board	oofless	oratory
oat cell	octuple	off site	old gang	once-off	ooftish	oratrix
oatmeal	oculate	offskip	old girl	oncotic	ooh-la-la	orbicle
Oaxacan	oculism	off spin	old gold	on-drive	oolitic	orbital
Obanian	oculist	offtake	old hand	on earth	oophyte	orbitar
obconic	oddball	off-time	old lady	one-base	ooplasm	orbited
obelion	odd-even	offward	old land	one down	oospore	orbiter
obelise	oddling	off year	Old Left	one-eyed	ootheca	orbless
obelisk	oddment	oficina	old maid	onefold	opacate	orcanet
obelize	oddness	of right	old moon	one-girl	opacify	orchard
obertas	oddside	of sorts	oldness	one-inch	opacity	orcinol
obesely	odd-toed	of state	Old Nick	oneiric	opacous	ordered
obesity	odeling	oftener	Oldowan	one–many	opaline	orderer
obit-day	Odinism	oft-time	old rope	oneness	opalise	orderly
obitual	Odinist	of value	old rose	one of us	opalite	order up
obligee	odonate	of which	old salt	one-pipe	opalize	ordinal
obliger	odorant	of yours	old ship	one-ring	opaquer	ordinar
obligor	odorate	oghamic	old snow	onerous	open air	ordinee
oblique	odorise	o'goblin	oldster	oneself	open day	orebody
Oblomov	odorize	Ogopogo	old-time	one-shot	open-end	orectic
obloquy	odorous	ogreish	old town	one's man	open ice	oregano
obovate	odoured	Ogygian	old wife	one-step	opening	oreweed

organal	Ostmark	outlaid	outstep	overfar	oxalate	paeonic
organic	ostraca	outland	outswim	overfat	oxazine	paganry
organon	ostrich	outlast	out-take	overfit	oxazole	pageant
organum	Ostwald	outleap	out-talk	overfly	ox-berry	page-boy
organza	otalgia	outlier	out-tell	overfur	ox-biter	pageful
orgiast	otariid	outline	out-toil	overget	ox-blood	page-one
orience	otocyst	outlive	out-took	overgot	ox-fence	Pagetic
oriency	otolite	outlook	out-tray	overhie	Oxfordy	paginal
orifice	otolith	out loud	out-trot	overhit	ox-frame	pagurid
origami	otology	outlove	out-turn	overjet	oxhouse	Pahlavi
orignal	ototomy	outlung	outvote	overjoy	oxidant	Pah-utah
Orionid	ottoman	outmode	out-vote	overlap	oxidase	paideia
Orleans	Ottoman	outmost	outwait	overlay	oxidate	pailful
orogeny	ouabain	outness	outwale	overlie	oxidise	painful
orology	oughtn't	out of it	outwalk	overlip	oxidize	pa-in-law
oronoco	ouguiya	out-over	outwall	overlow	Oxonian	painted
Oropesa	Our Lady	outpace	outward	overman	oxonium	painter
orotate	Our Lord	outpart	outwash	overmen	oxyacid	paint-in
orotund	ourself	outpass	outwear	overnet	oxylith	pairing
Orphean	oustiti	outpeep	outweep	overold	oxyntic	pair-oar
Orphism	outback	outpeer	outwell	overpay	oxy-salt	pair off
Orphist	outbawl	outplan	outwent	overply	oxytone	paisano
orphrey	outbear	outplay	out West	overran	oxyuris	Paisley
orra man	outbent	outplot	outwick	overrun	oystery	pajamas
orright	outblot	outport	outwind	oversaw	Ozarker	pakapoo
orsedue	outbrag	outpost	outwing	oversay	ozonide	pak-choi
orterde	outburn	outpour	out with	oversea	ozonify	Pakhtun
orthian	outcamp	outpray	outwith	oversee	ozonise	paktong
orthite	outcant	outrace	outwood	overset	ozonize	palabra
ortolan	outcast	outrage	outwore	oversew	pabouch	palaced
Orvieto	outcome	outrail	outwork	oversow	pabulum	paladin
or worse	outcrop	outrake	outworn	oversum	pacable	palarie
osazone	outdare	outrang	outyell	overtax	pace car	palatal
Osborne	outdate	outrank	ovality	overtip	pace lap	palatic
oscines	outdoes	outrant	ovarial	overtly	paceman	Palauan
oscular	outdoor	outrate	ovarian	overtop	pacemen	Palaung
osculum	outerly	outread	ovaries	overuse	pachisi	palaver
Osetian	outface	outride	ovarium	overwet	pachuco	palazzo
osiered	outfall	outring	ovation	overwin	paciest	paletot
Osirian	outfast	outroar	overact	ovicell	pacific	palette
Osiride	outflew	outrode	over age	ovicide	package	Paleyan
Osmanli	outflow	outroll	overage	Ovidian	pack ice	palfrey
osmiate	outflux	outroom	over all	oviduct	packing	palikar
osmious	outfool	outroot	overall	oviform	packman	palinal
osmolal	outfoot	outrung	overarm	ovistic	packmen	Palissy
osmolar	outfort	outrush	overate	ovocyte	pack off	pallavi
osmosis	outgang	outsail	overawe	ovoidal	pack rat	pallial
osmotic	outgate	outsell	overbid	ovonics	pack-way	pallier
osmunda	outgive	outshew	overbow	ovulary	paction	palling
os penis	outglow	outshop	overbuy	ovulate	paddies	pallion
ospreys	outgoer	outshot	overcup	ovulite	Paddies	pallium
osselet	outgoes	outshow	overcut	Owenism	padding	palmary
osseous	outgone	outshut	overday	Owenist	paddler	palmate
Ossetic	outgrew	outside	overdid	Owenite	paddock	palm cat
ossicle	outgrow	outsing	overdog	owl-like	padlock	palmful
ossific	outgush	outsize	overdot	owl-moth	Padovan	*palmier*
ossuary	out-half	outsoar	overdry	owney-oh	pad-play	palmiet
osteoid	outhaul	outsold	overdub	own goal	padrone	palmily
osteoma	outhold	outsole	overdue	ownhood	pad room	palmist
osteria	outhowl	outspan	overdye	ownness	Padshah	palmite
ostiary	outjump	outspin	overeat	ownself	paedeia	palmito
ostiole	outkick	outstay	overegg	ownsome	paenula	palm off

palm oil	pantile	parlour	pasties	pay rise	pedlary	pennate
palmtop	pantine	parlous	pastily	payroll	pedocal	pennies
palmula	pantler	Parnate	pastime	*paysage*	Pedrail	pennill
palm wax	pantoic	parodic	pasting	pay slip	pedrero	pennine
palmyra	pantoyl	parolee	pastose	payslip	ped-xing	penning
palooka	papable	paronym	pasture	pay-tone	peeling	pen-pond
palpate	papally	parotic	patache	P-Celtic	Peelite	Penrose
palship	papaloi	parotid	patagia	pea-bean	peel off	pensile
palsied	papauma	parquet	patamar	Peabody	peeping	pension
palsies	pap-boat	parried	Patarin	pea-bone	peep-toe	pensive
palsify	paperer	parries	patball	pea-bulb	peerage	penster
palting	Paphian	parrock	pat-ball	pea-bush	peerdom	pen-tail
paludal	papilio	parroco	patcher	pea-coat	peeress	pentane
pamment	papilla	parroty	patch-up	peacock	peevish	pentene
pampano	papoose	Parsism	patella	pea-comb	pegasse	pentice
pampean	papoosh	parsley	patency	pea-crab	Pegasus	pentode
pampero	pappies	parsnip	patener	pea-dove	peg away	pentose
panacea	pappose	Partaga	pat hand	peafowl	peg doll	pentryl
panache	paprika	partake	pathlet	pea-grit	peg down	penuche
Panadol	pap test	partial	pathway	peak cap	pegging	penwork
Panagia	Pap test	partied	patient	peakier	peglike	peonage
Panaman	papulae	partier	patinas	peaking	Pehlevi	peopler
pan-Arab	papular	parties	patness	peakish	Peierls	pepless
pancake	papulas	partify	patonce	Peakrel	peladic	peppery
pan-Celt	papyrin	partile	patrial	pea-lamp	pelagic	peppier
Panchen	papyrus	parting	patrico	pea-meal	pelamyd	pep pill
pandean	parable	partita	patriot	pea-moth	Peléean	pepping
pandect	parader	partite	patrist	pearled	pelican	pep talk
pandoor	parador	partlet	patroon	pearler	pelisse	peptide
pandora	parados	Partlet	patsies	pearlet	pelitic	peptize
pandore	paradox	partner	pattern	Pearson	pellack	peptone
pandour	paragon	part off	patties	peasant	pellety	peracid
pandrop	paralic	partook	patting	peascod	Pellian	percale
paneity	paramos	part-own	paturon	pea-soup	pellock	percase
panfish	parangi	part-way	patwari	peat-ash	peloria	per cent
panfuls	Pará-nut	parvenu	pauchty	peatbog	peloric	percept
Pangaea	parapet	parvise	paucity	peatery	pelorus	perched
pangene	para red	paschal	paughty	peat-hag	peloton	percher
pangful	paraski	pascual	Paulian	peatman	peltast	perches
pangram	parasol	Pashtun	Pauline	pea tree	peltate	percoid
panical	paratha	pasquil	Paulist	pea-vine	Peltier	percuss
panicky	parboil	Pasquin	Paul-Pry	pebbled	pelting	per diem
panicle	parched	passade	paunchy	pébrine	pembina	perdure
panicum	pardner	passado	paviour	peccant	pemphis	pereion
Panjabi	pareira	passage	paviser	peccary	pemphix	perfect
panlike	parerga	passant	pavlova	peccavi	penaeid	perfidy
pan-loaf	pareses	pas seul	Pavulon	pecking	penally	perform
pannage	paresis	passing	pawkier	peckish	penalty	perfume
pannier	Paretan	passion	pawkily	peckled	penance	perfumy
panning	paretic	passive	pawl-rim	pectase	penates	perfuse
panocha	parfait	pass-key	paxilla	pectate	penatin	pergana
panoply	pargana	passkey	Paxolin	pectens	pendant	pergola
panoral	parging	pass law	payable	pectize	pendent	perhaps
panoram	parisis	passman	pay back	pectora	pending	periapt
panorpa	parison	pass off	payback	pectose	pendule	peridia
pan-pipe	parkade	pass out	pay-book	pectous	penfold	peridot
pansala	parkier	passway	pay dirt	pedagog	penguin	perigee
pansied	parking	paste-in	pay down	pedalos	penises	perigon
pansies	parkish	pastern	payload	peddler	penlike	perilla
Panslav	parklet	paste-up	payment	pedicab	pen-mate	periost
panther	parkway	Pasteur	paynize	pedicel	pen-name	perique
panties	parleys	pastier	pay over	pedicle	pennant	peritus

periwig	peytral	pianino	pigging	pine gum	pipping	Pittite
perjure	pfennig	pianism	piggish	pine nut	piquant	pituita
perjury	phaeton	pianist	pig-herd	pine-oil	piquing	pit-wood
perkier	phalanx	piannet	pightle	pinesap	piragua	pitying
perkily	phalera	pianola	pig-iron	pine tag	piranha	pivotal
perlite	phallic	Pianola	pig-jump	pine-top	piratic	pivoted
permain	phallin	Piarist	pig-lead	pinetum	pirogue	pixyish
Permian	phalloi	piaster	piglike	pin-eyed	Pirquet	pizzazz
permsec	phallos	piastre	pig-lily	pin-fire	pisatin	placage
permute	phallus	pibcorn	pigling	pinfold	piscary	placard
peroral	phantom	pibroch	pig meat	pinguid	Piscean	placate
perosis	Pharaoh	picador	pigment	pinguin	piscina	placebo
per pale	pharate	picarel	pigmies	pinhead	piscine	placing
perpend	pharynx	piccolo	pig-root	pin-high	pismire	placita
perplex	phase in	piceous	pig's ear	pinhole	pissant	placket
perrier	phasing	pickage	pigskin	pin-hook	pissing	placode
Perrier	phasmid	pickaxe	pigsney	pinions	piss off	placoid
perries	phellem	pickeer	pigtail	pinkeen	*pissoir*	placula
persalt	phememe	pickery	pigwash	pinkers	piss-pot	*plafond*
Perseid	phenate	pickier	pigweed	pink-eye	pisspot	plagium
Perseus	phenoxy	pickily	pikelet	pink gin	pisteur	plagued
Persian	Phidian	picking	pikeman	pinkily	pistole	plaguer
persico	Phillis	pickled	pikemen	pinking	pit-a-pat	plagues
persist	philtre	pickler	pilcher	pinkish	pit-bank	plaguey
persona	phinnoc	pickman	pilcorn	pinkoes	pit-bing	plaided
perspex	phizgig	pickney	pilcrow	pink tea	pit boss	plaidie
Perspex	phlegmy	pick off	pileate	pin-mark	pit-brow	plainer
pertain	phlomis	pick out	pilgrim	pinnace	pit bull	plainly
pertish	Phocian	picotee	pillage	pinnate	pitched	plaited
perturb	phocine	picquet	pill-bag	pinnies	pitcher	plaiter
peruked	Phoebus	picrate	pillbox	pinning	pitch in	planate
perusal	phoenix	picrite	pill-bug	pinnock	pitch on	planche
peruser	phonate	Pictish	pilling	pinnule	pitch up	planful
pervade	phone-in	picture	pillion	pin-pool	pit-coal	planing
pervert	phoneme	piculet	pillock	pin-rack	pit-comb	planish
peskier	phonics	piddler	pillory	pinsapo	piteous	planned
peskily	phonier	piddock	pillowy	pin seal	pitfall	planner
pessary	phonily	piebald	pillule	pinsons	pit-head	planont
petasma	phorate	pie-card	piloted	pin-spot	pithead	plantal
petasus	phorbol	pie-cart	pilotry	pintado	pit-heap	plantar
pet-cock	phoresy	piece on	Pilsner	pintail	pithful	planter
pet-food	Photian	piece up	pilular	pint pot	pith hat	Plantin
pet-form	photino	pie-eyed	pimelea	pin-tuck	pithier	planula
pet hate	photism	pie-face	pimelic	Pintupi	pithily	planxty
petiole	photo CD	pieless	pimento	pinweed	pit-hole	plapper
pet name	photoes	pierage	pi-mesic	pin-work	pith ray	plashet
petrary	photo op	pierced	pi-meson	pinworm	pitiful	plasmal
Petrean	phragma	piercer	pimping	Pinxter	pit-lamp	plasmic
petrify	phrasal	Pierian	pimpish	Pinxton	pitless	plasmid
Petrine	phraser	pierine	pimpled	pioneer	pitmans	plasmin
petroil	phrator	pierrot	pinaces	piosity	Pitman's	plasmon
petrous	phratry	pieties	pinacol	piously	pit-mirk	plaster
pet-shop	phrenic	pietism	pinball	pipe cot	Pitocin	plastic
pettier	phrenzy	pietist	pin-bone	pipeful	pit pair	plastid
pettily	phugoid	piffler	pincers	pipe-gun	pit pony	plateau
petting	physics	pig-boat	pinched	pipe-lay	pit prop	Plateau
pettish	physiog	pig-cote	pincher	pipeman	pit-sawn	platina
petunia	physios	pig-face	pincord	pip emma	pit silo	plating
Petzval	phytane	pigfish	pin-curl	piperic	pit stop	platoon
pewless	phytase	piggery	Pindari	piperly	pitting	platted
pew-rent	phytate	piggier	pin down	pipette	Pittism	platten
pewtery	piaffer	piggies	pin-dust	pipless	pittite	platter

platzel	plounce	podical	polygon	popping	pot-arch	Prakrit
plaudit	plouter	poditic	polyion	poppish	potassa	praline
play-act	plovery	podiums	polymer	pop-shop	potator	prancer
playbox	plowman	Podsnap	polynia	popsies	pot-ball	pranker
playboy	plowmen	podurid	polynya	pop star	pot-bank	prankle
play-day	plucked	podware	polyoma	popster	pot-boil	prasine
playful	plucker	poë-bird	polyped	popular	potcher	prating
play God	pluck up	Poesque	polypod	porched	pot clay	prattle
play hob	plugged	poetast	polypus	porcine	potence	pravity
playing	plugger	poetese	polyrod	porgies	potencé	prawner
playlet	plug-hat	poetess	Polytec	porifer	potency	Praxean
play off	plug off	poetics	polyyne	porkery	potfuls	pray for
play-pen	plugola	poetise	pomatum	porkier	pot-guts	praying
playpen	plug-tap	poetism	pomelos	porkies	pot-head	preachy
play pew	plumach	poetize	Pomerol	porkman	pothead	pre-Aids
play-way	plumage	po-faced	pomeron	pork pie	potheen	prebend
pleaded	plumash	poggled	pomfret	porphin	pot-herb	pre-book
pleader	plumate	poiesis	pommage	porrect	pothery	precary
pleased	plumber	poietic	pommelé	porrigo	pothole	pre-cast
pleaser	plumbet	poinder	Pommies	portage	pot-hook	precast
pleater	plumbic	pointed	pompano	portail	pot-kiln	precede
plebify	plumery	pointel	pompion	portate	pot-lace	precent
plectra	plum-fir	pointer	pomposo	Porteña	pot life	precept
plectre	plumier	point up	pompous	portend	pot-line	precess
pledgee	plummet	poisony	ponchos	portent	pot luck	precise
pledger	plumose	Poisson	pondage	portess	potluck	precoce
pledget	plumous	poitrel	pongelo	portico	pot-mess	pre-cook
pledgor	plumpen	pokable	pongier	porting	potoroo	precook
pleione	plumper	poke-boy	Pongola	portion	pot-oven	pre-cool
plenary	plum-pie	poke-net	ponhaus	portlet	potrero	precool
plenipo	plumply	poke-out	poniard	portman	pot-shot	precure
plenish	plum pox	pokiest	pontage	portray	pottage	predamn
plenist	plumula	polacca	pontiff	posable	pottery	pre-date
pleopod	plumule	polacre	pontile	posaune	pottier	predate
plereme	plunder	Polaris	pontine	poseuse	potties	predial
plerion	plunger	polarly	Pontine	posited	pottily	predict
pleroma	plunket	polaron	pontoon	positon	potting	predoom
plerome	Plunket	poldavy	poodler	possess	pot-work	pre-echo
plessor	pluries	pole-axe	poofter	postage	pouched	pre-edit
pleurae	plusage	poleaxe	Pooh-Bah	postbag	poulard	preemie
pleural	plushed	polecat	pool car	postbox	poulter	pre-empt
pleuric	plushly	poleman	poonask	post-boy	poultry	preener
pleuron	pluteal	polemic	poon oil	post-bus	pounced	preface
plexure	pluteus	polenta	poopsie	post-dam	pouncer	pre-fade
pliable	pluvial	polhode	poor box	post-day	pouncet	prefect
pliably	Pluvius	poligar	poor-cod	postdoc	poundal	pre-fine
pliancy	plywood	politer	poorish	posteen	pounder	prefire
plicate	pneumic	politic	poor law	postern	pouring	preform
Plinian	poacher	polizei	poor man	postfix	poussin	pre-head
plinker	pochard	polizia	popadam	post hoc	poustie	preheat
plodded	Pockels	polkaed	popadom	postica	pouting	prehend
plodder	pocketa	pollack	pop-call	posting	poverty	pre-Inca
ploiter	pockety	pollard	popcorn	postman	powdery	prelacy
plonker	pocosin	pollies	pope-day	postmen	powered	prelate
plopped	poculum	polling	popedom	post-oak	poxiest	prelect
plosion	podagra	pollock	pop-eyed	post-tax	poy-bird	preload
plosive	podalic	poll tax	pop-hole	posture	prabble	prelude
plotful	pod corn	pollute	popinac	post-war	practic	premier
plotted	podding	polo hat	poplexy	postwar	praeses	premise
plotter	poddish	poloist	popover	potable	praetor	premiss
plottie	podgier	polybag	poppied	potager	prairie	premium
plotzed	podgily	polyene	poppies	potamic	praiser	premove

prename	priapic	prodder	prosody	psyllid	pummelo	pussley
prender	Priapus	Proddie	prosoma	ptarmic	pumpage	pussums
prenoun	pribble	prodigy	prosper	pterion	pump gun	pustule
prenova	pribumi	prodrug	prossie	pteroic	pumpion	putamen
pre-oral	price up	produce	prostie	pteroma	pumpkin	put away
pre-pack	pricier	product	prosula	pteryla	pump-log	put back
prepack	pricily	proette	protean	ptyalin	pumpman	putcher
prepaid	pricing	profane	protect	pubbing	pump-rod	put down
prepare	pricked	profert	protégé	pubbish	pumpset	putidly
prepend	pricker	profesh	proteid	puberal	punalua	put it on
pre-plan	pricket	profess	protein	puberty	punched	put it to
preplan	prickle	proffer	protend	publish	puncher	putlock
prepone	prickly	profile	protest	pub rock	punch in	put over
prepose	pridian	pro-form	Proteus	pub-time	punch-up	putrefy
prepped	prigger	profuse	protext	puccoon	punctal	putteed
prepper	primacy	progeny	protide	pucelle	punctum	puttied
preppie	primage	progger	protist	puchero	pungent	putties
prepreg	primary	program	protium	puckaun	puniest	putting
prepuce	primase	project	protoma	puckery	Punjabi	puttock
prepupa	primate	prolate	protome	puckish	punkish	put upon
prequel	primely	pro-life	protyle	pudding	punning	put up to
prerupt	primero	proline	proudly	puddled	punster	putwary
presage	primine	prolong	provand	puddler	punt-gun	puzzler
pre-sell	priming	promise	provant	puddock	pupfish	pyaemia
present	primmed	prommer	provect	pudency	pupilar	pyaemic
preside	primmer	promote	provend	pudenda	puppies	pycnial
presign	primula	pronaoi	proverb	pudgier	pupping	pycnium
pre-soak	pringle	pronaos	prove up	pudgily	pup-tent	pygmean
pre-sold	printed	Pronase	provide	pueblos	pupunha	pygmoid
pressel	printer	pronate	provine	puerile	Puranic	pyjamas
presser	print in	pronely	proviso	puff box	Purbeck	py korry
pressie	priorly	*proneur*	provoke	puffery	purfled	pyloric
press-on	prior to	pronged	provost	puffick	purging	pylorus
pressor	prisage	pronoun	prowess	puffier	puritan	pyralid
press-up	priscan	pronuba	prowler	puffily	purlieu	pyramid
Prestel	Priscol	propale	proxeny	puffing	purloin	pyretic
prester	prisere	propane	proxies	puff-leg	purpled	pyrexia
prestos	prismal	propend	proximo	pugging	purport	pyrexic
presume	prismed	propene	prozoic	puggish	purpose	pyridyl
pretape	pristaf	prop-fan	prozone	puggled	purpura	pyrites
pre-teen	prithee	propham	prudent	puggree	purpure	pyritic
pretend	privacy	prophet	prudery	pug-mill	pursive	pyrogen
pre-term	private	propine	prudish	pug-nose	pursual	pyronin
preterm	privies	prop-jet	prunase	Pugwash	pursued	pyrosis
pretest	privily	prop-leg	pruning	pukatea	pursuer	pyrrhic
pretext	privity	prop man	prunted	pukekos	pursues	Pyrrhic
pretone	proavis	propone	prurigo	pulaski	pursuit	pyrrole
pretzel	proband	propose	prushun	pullery	purview	pyruvic
prevail	probang	propped	prussic	pulleys	push-car	Pythiad
prevene	probate	propper	prytany	Pullman	push fit	Pythian
prevent	probing	propria	psalmic	pull off	pushful	pyxides
preverb	probity	propyla	psalter	pull out	pushier	pyxidia
preview	problem	propyne	psammic	pull-tab	pushily	Qashgai
previse	pro bono	pro rata	pschent	pulpify	pushing	Q-Celtic
prevost	procain	pro-rate	pseudos	pulpous	push off	Q-switch
prewarn	procarp	prosaic	psionic	pulsant	push-out	qua-bird
pre-wash	proceed	pro shop	p-skhent	pulsate	push-pin	quacker
prewash	process	prosier	psychal	pulsion	push-pit	quackle
prewire	Procion	prosify	psychic	pulsive	pushrod	quadrat
prexies	proctor	prosily	psychon	pulvini	push-tow	quadric
prezzie	procure	prosing	psychos	pulvino	puss-cat	quaffer
Priamel	prodded	prosist	psykter	pumiced	pussies	quahaug

quakier	quilled	radiale	rallier	rasping	realign	rectify
quaking	quillet	radiant	rallies	ratable	realise	rection
qualify	quilter	radiata	ralline	ratafia	realism	rectory
quality	quinary	Radiata	Ramadan	rat-a-tat	realist	rectrix
quamash	quinate	radiate	Ramazan	ratatat	reality	rectums
quangos	Quinean	radical	rambler	ratchet	realize	recurve
quantal	quinine	radicel	ramekin	rate-cap	re-allot	recusal
quantic	quinion	radices	ramenas	ratfink	reallot	recycle
quantum	quinnat	radicle	ram home	rat-fish	realtor	red alga
quarely	quinoid	radioes	ram line	rat flea	reaming	Red Army
quarrel	quinone	radiole	rammies	rat-hare	reannex	red-back
quartal	quintal	radulae	ramming	rathest	reaping	red-bait
quartan	quintan	radular	rammish	rat-hole	re-apply	Red-bait
quarter	quintet	raffish	ramonda	ratlike	reapply	red ball
quartet	quintic	raffler	rampage	ratline	rear end	red-band
quartic	quipped	Raffles	rampant	ratling	reargue	red bark
quartos	quipper	raft-dog	rampart	rat pack	rearing	red bass
quartzy	quiring	rag bolt	rampick	rat race	reassay	red bean
Quashee	quirked	rag book	rampier	rat-tail	Réaumur	red beds
quassia	quirley	rag doll	rampike	ratteen	reawake	red belt
quatern	Quiteño	rageful	rampion	rattier	rebadge	red-bird
quatrin	quitted	rageous	rampire	rattily	rebater	red body
quattie	quitter	raggedy	rampway	ratting	re-beget	redbone
quavery	quittor	ragging	ram-raid	rattish	re-begin	red book
quayage	quivery	rag-head	Ramsden	rattler	Rebekah	red buck
quayful	qui vive	rag-lamp	ramsons	rat-trap	rebelly	red card
queachy	Quixote	rag-shop	ram-stam	raucity	rebirth	red cell
Quechua	quiz kid	ragtail	ramulet	raucous	rebloom	red cent
Queen At	quizzed	ragtime	ramulus	raunchy	reboant	red clay
queenie	quizzee	Ragusan	rancher	rauriki	reboard	redcoat
queen it	quizzer	ragweed	rancour	ravaged	rebound	red core
queenly	quizzes	ragworm	randier	ravager	rebrace	red-cowl
queerer	quoiter	ragwort	randily	ravelin	rebring	red crab
queerie	quomodo	railage	randing	ravelly	rebuild	red deal
queerly	quondam	rail-bus	rangier	ravener	rebuilt	red deer
queller	Quonset	rail-car	rangily	ravined	rebuker	reddest
quelles	quorate	railcar	rangled	ravioli	rebuses	redding
quemely	quotity	rail gun	rangoli	raw deal	recarry	reddish
querent	Quraysh	railing	Rangoon	raw edge	recatch	red drum
queried	rabanna	rallman	Rankine	raw feel	receder	red-eyed
querier	rabbit-o	railmen	ranking	rawhide	receipt	red fire
queries	rabbity	rail off	ransack	rawness	receive	redfish
querist	rabidly	railway	ranular	raw silk	recency	red flag
querken	rabinet	raiment	Ranvier	rayless	recense	red gold
quester	rabious	rainbow	rapable	Raynaud	rechase	red hake
questor	raccoon	rain-day	rape-oil	r-colour	recheat	red-hand
quetsch	race man	rain-fly	raphide	reacher	recheck	red hare
quetzal	racemed	rainful	rapider	reach to	recital	redhead
queuing	racemic	rain-god	rapidly	reactor	reciter	red heat
quibble	race off	rain-hat	raploch	readapt	reclaim	red kite
Quichua	raceway	rainier	rapping	readier	reclear	red lamp
quicken	rachial	rainily	Rappist	readily	reclimb	red land
quickie	Rachman	rain off	Rappite	reading	recline	Redland
quickly	raciest	rain-out	rapport	Reading	reclose	red lane
quiddle	rack-bar	rainout	rapture	readmit	reclude	red lead
quidlet	rackett	raising	rarebit	read off	recluse	redlegs
quids in	rackety	raisiny	rare gas	readopt	recluse	red line
quiesce	racking	raisure	rasceta	read-out	re-count	red loam
quieten	rackman	Rajpoot	raschel	ready-up	recount	red mass
quieter	racloir	rake-off	Raschig	reagent	re-cover	red meat
quietly	racquet	rake out	rashful	real ale	recover	red mite
quietus	raddled	rallied	rashing	realgar	recross	red moki

redneck	referee	related	replied	respire	retying	ribible
redness	refined	relater	replier	respite	reunify	ribitol
red-nose	refiner	relator	replies	respond	reunion	ribityl
redoubt	reflate	relatum	replumb	respray	reunite	ribless
redound	reflect	relaxed	repoint	restage	reutter	riblike
red pine	refloat	relaxer	reposal	restain	revalue	ribosyl
redpoll	refocus	relaxin	reposit	restamp	reveler	Ribston
redraft	reforge	relearn	repping	restant	revelry	ribwork
red rain	refound	release	repress	restart	revenge	ribwort
redrawn	refract	relevel	reprice	restate	revenue	ricasso
re-dress	refrain	reliant	reprime	rest day	reverer	rice-rat
redress	reframe	relieve	reprint	resteel	reverie	Richard
red-ripe	refresh	relievo	reprise	restful	reverse	richish
redrive	refroze	relight	reproof	restiff	reversi	Richter
red roan	refugee	reliner	re-prove	resting	reviler	ricinus
red rock	refugia	relleno	reprove	restive	revisal	rickets
red-root	refusal	remains	reptant	restock	reviser	rickety
red rose	refuser	remanet	reptile	restore	revisit	rickeys
redskin	refutal	remarch	repulse	restudy	revisor	ricksha
red snow	refuter	remarry	repunit	restuff	revival	ricotta
red soil	regalia	rematch	repurge	restyle	reviver	ridable
red spot	regally	remicle	reputed	resuing	revivor	ridding
red star	regatta	remiges	request	re-surge	revoice	riddler
Red Star	regauge	remixer	requiem	resurge	revoker	rideman
red-tail	Régence	remnant	require	reswear	revolte	ride-off
red tape	regency	remodel	requite	reswell	revolve	ride out
red-tapy	Reggeon	remorse	requote	retable	revving	rideout
red tide	regimen	remoter	reraise	retablo	rewaken	ridered
red titi	reginal	remould	reredos	retaken	reweave	ridging
reduced	reglaze	remount	re-route	retaker	reweigh	ridglet
reducer	regnant	removal	rescind	retaste	rewound	ridotto
redward	regorge	removed	rescore	reteach	rewrite	rid-work
redware	regosol	remover	rescous	rethink	rewrote	Riemann
red-weed	regrade	renable	rescued	retiary	Reynard	rietbok
red wind	regrant	renably	rescuee	reticle	rhabdom	Riffian
redwing	regrate	reneger	rescuer	retinae	Rhaetic	riffled
red wolf	regreet	renegue	rescues	retinal	rhamnus	riffler
red-wood	regress	renerve	reseize	retinas	rhatany	riflery
redwood	regrind	renewal	re-serve	retinol	Rhemish	rifling
Redwood	regroup	renewer	reserve	retinue	Rhemist	rifting
red worm	regulae	rentage	reshape	retinyl	rhenate	rigaree
reed-bed	regular	rent boy	reshoot	retiral	Rhenish	rigging
reed-cap	regulon	rent car	resiant	retired	rhenium	riggish
reedier	regulus	rentier	resider	retiree	rhizine	righten
re-edify	reheard	rentrée	residua	retirer	rhizoid	righter
reedily	rehouse	reoccur	residue	retitle	rhizome	right-ho
reeding	reified	reoffer	resilia	retouch	Rhodian	rightie
reed-man	reifier	reorder	resilin	re-trace	rhodium	rightly
reef net	reifies	repaint	resined	retrace	Rhodoid	right oh
reek-hen	reigner	repaper	resinic	retrack	rhodora	right on
re-elect	reimpel	repayer	resitol	retract	rhodous	right-up
reel-fed	rein-arm	rephase	reskill	retrain	rhombic	rigidly
reeling	reindue	repiece	reslash	retread	rhombus	Rig-veda
reel off	reinter	repiner	reslush	retreat	rhubarb	Rig-Veda
re-enact	Reisner	repique	resmelt	retrial	rhymist	rikishi
re-endow	reissue	replace	resolve	retrick	rhythmi	rilievo
re-enjoy	reitbok	replant	re-sound	retried	rhytina	Rilkean
re-enter	rejoice	replate	resound	retries	riantly	rilling
re-entry	rejoint	replead	respeak	retsina	ribband	rillock
re-equip	rejudge	replete	respect	rettery	ribbing	rimfire
re-erect	relabel	replevy	respell	retting	ribbony	rimiest
re-exist	relapse	replica	respelt	retwist	ribcage	rimland

rimless	road oil	Romanes	Roscius	row crop	rummage	Rydberg
rimming	road tax	Romanic	roseate	rowdier	rummery	ryebuck
rimpled	roadway	Romanly	rosebay	rowdily	rummest	rye-land
rimrock	roanoke	Romansh	rose-bed	row down	rummily	Ryeland
rim-shot	roaring	romaunt	rose bit	Rowland	rummish	ryepeck
ringent	roaster	Romayne	rose box	rowlock	rumness	rye-worm
ringing	robbery	Romberg	rosebud	row over	Rumpish	ryotwar
ringled	robbing	romneya	rose-bug	row-port	rum ship	Saadian
ringlet	robinet	rompier	rose-cut	royalet	rum shop	saaidam
ring-man	robinia	romping	rose-hip	royally	run amok	Saalian
ring-net	robotic	rompish	roselet	royalty	runanga	Sabaean
ring off	robotry	romulea	rosella	royal we	run away	Sabaism
ring rot	robusta	ronchus	roseola	rozella	runaway	Sabaoth
ringway	rock bar	rondeau	rose red	rub-a-dub	run-back	sabatia
rinsing	rock-bed	rondure	rosette	rubatos	run-boat	sabaton
Riot Act	rock-bun	rongeur	rosiest	rub away	runchie	sabayon
riot gun	rockery	ronquil	rosined	rubbedy	rundale	sabbath
riotous	rock fan	röntgen	rosiner	rubbery	rundlet	sabbing
ripcord	rock-hog	Röntgen	rosolic	rubbing	run down	sabella
rip cord	rockier	Rood day	rosolio	rubbish	run-down	saboted
ripener	rockily	roofage	rostral	rubbity	rundown	sabreur
ripieni	rocking	roofies	rostrum	rubbler	rune-row	sacaton
ripieno	rockish	roofing	rota cut	rub down	run-flat	saccade
rip into	Rockism	rooflet	rotamer	rubella	run hard	saccate
rip line	Rockite	roof rat	rotator	rubeola	run heel	saccoon
riposte	rocklet	roof tax	rotifer	Rubicon	run high	saccule
rippier	rockman	rooftop	rotisse	rubious	run idle	sackage
ripping	rock oak	rooi-aas	roto-tom	rubisco	run into	sackbut
rippled	rock-oil	rooibok	rottack	rub it in	run lace	sackful
rippler	rockoon	rooibos	rotting	rub over	runless	sacking
ripplet	rock out	rooi-els	rotular	rub-rail	run mute	sacklet
rip-stop	rodding	rooikat	rotulet	ruby-red	runnage	saclike
ripstop	rodless	rooinek	rotunda	ruching	runnier	sacring
rip tide	rodlike	rookery	rotundo	ruckman	running	sacrist
Ripuary	rod-mill	rookish	rouéism	ruction	run over	sacrums
risbank	rodster	rook-pie	roughen	ruddier	run riot	saddest
risible	roebuck	roomage	rougher	ruddily	run time	saddish
risibly	Roedean	roomful	roughie	ruddock	runting	saddler
riskful	roe-deer	roomier	rough it	rude boy	runtish	Sadeian
riskier	roe ring	roomily	roughly	ruderal	run upon	sad-iron
riskily	Rogallo	rooming	rough up	rudesby	run wild	saditty
risotto	roguery	roomlet	roulade	ruellia	ruption	sadness
rissala	roguish	roomthy	rouleau	ruffian	rupture	sad sack
rissole	Rohilla	roosted	rounded	Ruffini	rurally	safaris
Ritalin	roinish	rooster	roundel	ruffled	rusbank	Safavid
ritzier	roister	rootage	rounder	ruffler	rush-nut	safe bet
ritzily	rokelay	root-cap	round in	ruff out	Russell	safe hit
rivalry	Rolando	rooting	roundle	rufiyaa	russety	safener
rivered	roll bar	rootlet	roundly	rugging	Russian	safe sex
riveret	rollick	root out	round on	ruinate	Russify	saffian
riveted	rolling	root rot	round to	ruinous	Russkis	saffron
riveter	rollmop	ropable	round up	rulable	rustier	safrole
riviera	roll off	rope-end	rouping	rule off	rustily	saga boy
rivière	roll-out	rope-way	rousant	rule out	rusting	saga-man
rivulet	roll-top	ropeway	rousing	rullion	rustler	sagaris
roached	rollway	ropiest	rouster	Rumansh	rustred	sagathy
roadbed	roloway	rorqual	routine	rum baba	Ruthene	sagbend
road hog	Romaika	rortier	routing	rumbler	ruthful	sage hen
road kid	romaine	rosacea	routous	rumenal	ruttier	sage tea
roadman	Romalis	rosaker	rout out	Rumford	rutting	sagging
road map	romance	rosalia	rowable	rumices	ruttish	sagitta
roadmen	romancy	Roscian	rowboat	ruminal	Rwandan	sag pond

saguaro	salt-tax	sanitar	satchel	scabrid	schemas	scotale
sagwire	salukis	Sankhya	satiate	scaddle	schemer	Scotchy
Saharan	saluter	Santali	satiety	scaffie	schepen	scoters
Sahidic	salvage	santoor	satined	scaglia	scherzi	Scotify
Sahiwal	salvoes	santour	satinet	scalade	scherzo	Scotism
Sahrawi	samadhi	san ts'ai	satiric	scalded	schisma	Scotist
sahuaro	samango	sanxian	satisfy	scalder	schitzy	Scot Nat
sailage	Samanid	sanyasi	satrapy	scalene	schizos	scotoma
sail-arm	samarra	s-aorist	satsang	scaleni	schizzy	Scottie
sailing	Samarra	saouari	satsuma	scale up	schlepp	scourer
sail-off	sambaed	sapajou	satyral	scalier	schlich	scourge
saimiri	Samboes	saphead	satyric	scaling	schlock	Scouser
sainted	sambuca	saphena	satyrid	scalled	schlong	scouter
saintly	sambuke	sapient	saucery	scallet	schloss	Scouter
Saivism	Samburu	sap lath	saucier	scallom	schlump	scowder
Saivite	Samhain	sapless	saucily	scallop	schmear	scowler
Saktism	Sam Hill	sapling	Saudian	scallot	schmeck	scraggy
salable	Samhita	saponin	saunter	scalped	schmeer	scraich
salamis	samiest	Sapphic	saurian	scalpel	schmelz	scranch
salband	samisen	sappier	sauries	scalper	Schmidt	scranny
salchow	Samnite	sappily	sauroid	scamble	schmuck	scraper
sale day	samogon	sapping	sausage	scammed	schmutz	scrapie
salgram	samolus	sapples	sautéed	scammer	schnook	scrappy
salices	Samorin	saprobe	sautoir	scamper	schnorr	scratch
salicet	samovar	sapsago	savable	scandal	schnozz	Scratch
salicin	Samoyed	sapwood	savanna	scandia	scholar	scraugh
salicyl	sampler	Saracen	savante	Scanian	scholia	scrawly
salient	samsara	sarafan	savarin	scanmag	schooly	scrawny
saligot	samshoo	sarangi	save-all	scanned	schrund	screaky
Salique	samurai	sarazin	saveloy	scanner	schtook	screamy
salival	sanctum	sarcasm	save you	scantle	schtoom	screech
sallied	sanctus	sarcast	saviour	scantly	Schwann	screeve
sallier	Sandawe	sarcina	savoury	scapple	Schwarz	screigh
sallies	sandbag	sarcler	savvied	scapula	sciapod	screwed
Sallies	sand bar	sarcode	savvier	scaredy	sciatic	screwer
sallowy	sandbar	sarcoid	savvies	scare up	science	screw-in
salmiac	sand-bed	sarcoma	sawbill	scarfed	scirrhi	screw up
salmine	sand boa	sarcopt	sawbuck	scarier	scissel	scribal
salmons	sandbox	sarcous	sawdust	scarify	scissel	scriber
salmony	sandboy	Sardian	saw-file	scarily	scissor	scrieve
salpinx	sand-bur	sardine	sawfish	scarlet	sclaffy	scrimmy
salsify	sand cay	sardius	saw-gate	scaroid	scleral	scrimpy
sal soda	sand dab	sardony	sawlike	scarped	scoffer	scrinch
salsola	sand eel	sarinda	sawmill	scarper	scogger	scringe
saltant	sanders	sarissa	sawn-off	scarred	scolder	scritch
saltate	sandesh	Sarkese	saw wood	scarves	Scoline	scriven
salt-box	sandfly	sarkier	saw-wort	scatted	scolion	scroggy
salt-cat	sandhog	sarkily	saxeous	scatter	scollop	scrolly
saltern	sandier	sarking	saxhorn	scauper	scolops	scronch
saltery	sand key	sarment	Saxonic	scavage	scomber	scrooch
saltfat	sandlot	sartage	Saxonly	sceatta	scooper	Scrooge
salt hay	sandman	sash bar	sayable	scenery	scooter	scrotal
saltier	sand pie	sashimi	say over	scenist	scopine	scrotum
saltily	sandpit	sashing	Say's law	scenite	scoptic	scrouge
saltine	sand rat	sashoon	says you	scented	scopula	scroyle
salting	sanfoin	sash saw	say-well	scenter	scoriac	scrubby
saltire	Sangoan	sassaby	say when	scepsis	scoriae	scrub up
saltish	sangoma	sassier	Sazarac	scepter	scorify	scruffo
Saltoun	sangria	sassily	scabbed	sceptic	scoring	scruffy
salt pan	Sangria	Satanas	scabble	sceptre	scorner	scrummy
salt-pit	sanicle	satanic	scabies	schalet	scorper	scrumpy
salt sea	sanious		scabish	schappe	Scorpio	scrunch

scrungy	sea-girt	sea-ware	seguing	septate	set shot	shagetz
scrunty	Sea Goat	sea wasp	segundo	septime	setting	shagged
scruple	seagull	seaweed	seismal	septuor	settled	shagger
scrutty	sea hair	sea-wind	seismic	sequela	settler	shagitz
scudded	sea hare	sea-wing	Seistan	sequent	settlor	shag-rag
scudder	sea-hawk	sea-wise	seizing	sequoia	setwall	shahdom
scuddle	sea holm	sea-wolf	seizure	seraphs	sevener	shaheed
scuffer	seajack	sea-worm	selenic	Serbian	seventh	shaheen
scuffle	seakale	sea-worn	selfful	Sercial	seventy	Shaitan
sculler	sea-king	sebacic	selfish	serener	seven-up	shake-up
sculpin	sea lace	sebundy	selfism	serfage	several	shakier
scumbag	sea-lake	seceder	selfist	serfdom	Severan	shakily
scumber	sea lane	seclude	self-set	serfish	severer	shaking
scumble	sealant	secluse	self-sow	serging	seviche	shakudo
scummed	sea-lark	Seconal	selling	seriate	Seville	shallon
scummer	sea legs	seconde	sell off	sericin	sevruga	shallop
scunner	sealery	secondi	sell out	sericon	sewable	shallot
scupper	seal-fur	secondo	seltzer	seriema	sewaged	shallow
scuppet	sealift	secrecy	selvage	serifed	sewster	shallun
scurfer	sealike	secreta	sematic	seringa	sexagon	shalwar
scurred	sea lily	secrete	sememic	serious	sex bomb	shamash
scutage	sealine	sectary	semence	sero-pus	sex cell	shamble
scutate	sealing	sectile	semicha	serosal	sexfoil	shambly
scutter	sea lion	section	semi-det	serovar	sexhood	shambok
scuttle	sea loch	sectism	semigod	Serpens	sexiest	Shammar
scyphus	sea lock	sectist	semi-log	serpent	sexless	shammed
scytale	Sea Lord	secular	seminal	serpigo	sex life	shammel
scythed	sea-luce	securer	seminar	serpula	sexpert	shammer
scyther	sea-maid	sedanca	seminia	Serrano	sex role	shampoo
Scythic	sea-mall	sedated	semi-ped	serrate	sex shop	shandry
sea bass	sea-mark	sedging	semi-pro	serried	sextain	shanked
sea-bean	seamier	sedilia	semi-sub	Sertoli	sextans	shanker
sea-bear	sea mile	seducee	Semitic	servage	sextant	Shannon
sea-beat	seaming	seducer	senarii	servant	sextary	shapely
Seabees	sea-monk	seeable	senator	servery	sextern	shape up
sea beet	sea moss	see-city	senatus	serve up	sextile	shaping
sea belt	seamost	seed-bed	sencion	Servian	sextine	sharded
sea bird	sea-moth	seedbed	send for	service	sextole	shareef
seabird	sea-palm	seed-box	sending	servile	sextula	sharifa
sea-boat	sea-pike	seed fat	send off	serving	sextuor	sharker
sea-born	sea pink	seedful	Senecal	Servite	Seyfert	Shar Pei
sea-calf	seaport	seedier	Senecan	sesamum	sferics	sharpen
sea-clam	searcer	seedily	senecio	Sesotho	sfumato	sharper
sea coal	sea-reed	seeding	senesce	sessile	shabbed	sharpie
seacock	searing	seed-lac	senhora	session	Shabbim	sharply
sea-cook	sea room	seedlet	señores	sestina	shabble	sharrer
sea-coot	sea salt	seed-lip	sensate	sestine	shab-rag	Shastan
sea-crab	sea-sand	seedman	sensify	setaria	shacked	Shastra
sea-crow	seasick	seed set	sensile	set back	shackle	shastri
sea-dace	seaside	see here	sensing	setback	shackly	shatter
sea-duck	sea slug	see into	sensise	set back	shaddup	Shavian
Sea Dyak	sea-song	seeking	sensism	setback	shade of	shaving
sea-dyke	sea-star	seek out	sensist	set down	shad-fly	Shavuot
seafare	sea-time	see life	sensive	set fair	shadier	shawled
sea-fern	seating	seeming	sensize	setfast	shadily	shawlie
sea-fire	sea-toad	see over	sensory	set free	shadine	Shawnee
sea-fish	sea-town	seepage	sensual	Sethian	shading	sheared
seafood	sea turn	seeress	Senussi	Sethite	shadoof	shearer
sea-fowl	sea-view	seerpaw	sepetir	set menu	shadowy	sheathe
sea fret	sea wall	see-safe	sephira	setness	shafted	sheaths
sea-frog	seawant	see to it	seppuku	set over	shafter	sheaved
sea-gate	seaward	segment	septage	set sail	shag-bag	sheaves

shebang	shinner	short on	sibness	silicic	sinuous	sketchy
shebeen	Shinner	shot-bag	sibship	silicle	sinward	skewgee
shedded	shin-oak	shotgun	sice ace	silicon	sipeera	skewing
shedder	Shinola	shotman	Sichuan	siliqua	sipping	skiable
shed-rod	shin-pad	shot-put	sick-bag	silique	siratro	skiapod
sheened	Shinshu	shotted	sickbay	silk hat	siredon	skibbet
sheenly	ship-boy	shotten	sickbed	silkier	sirenic	ski-boat
sheered	shipful	shout at	sickish	silkily	sirenin	skidded
sheerly	Shipibo	shouter	sickled	silking	Sir John	skidder
sheeted	shiplap	shout-up	sickler	sillier	sirloin	skiddoo
shegetz	shipman	showbiz	sicknik	sillily	sirmark	skid-lid
Sheikha	shipmen	show-box	sickout	sillion	sirocco	skid-pan
sheitel	ship off	showery	sick pay	sillock	sirship	skid row
shekere	ship out	show for	sic-like	siltage	sirtaki	skidway
shellac	shipped	showier	Siculan	silumin	sissier	skiffle
shelled	shippen	showily	siddown	silurid	Sistine	ski jump
sheller	shipper	showing	side-arm	silurus	sistrum	skilful
shelter	shippon	showman	side-bar	silvern	sit back	ski lift
sheltie	ship-rat	showmen	side-bet	silvery	sit down	skilled
Sheltie	shipway	show off	side-box	silver Y	sitella	skillet
shelver	shirker	show out	side boy	silvics	sit-fast	ski-mask
shelves	shirred	shreddy	sidecar	simatic	sitient	skimmed
she-male	shirted	shrewly	side-car	simchah	sit over	skimmer
Shemite	Shirvan	shrieky	side cut	similar	sits vac	skimmia
sheogue	shisham	shright	sideman	similor	sit tall	skimped
Sherari	shitbag	shrilly	sideral	simious	sitting	skinful
sherbet	shit-hot	shrimps	sideway	simpkin	situate	skinker
Sherbro	shitted	shrimpy	siemens	simpler	sit-upon	skinkle
Sherden	shitten	shrined	Siemens	simplex	sit well	skinman
shereef	shitter	Shriner	Sienese	simular	sit with	skinned
sheriff	shittim	shritch	sierran	Sinaean	Sivaism	skinner
sherifi	shiveau	shrivel	sievert	sinapic	Sivaite	Skinner
Sherman	shivery	shriven	siftage	sinapyl	sivvens	skin-pop
Sherpas	shmatte	shriver	sifting	sincere	sixfoil	skintle
sherris	shochet	shroudy	sighful	Sindbis	sixfold	ski pole
she-wolf	shocker	shrubby	sighing	sinding	six-four	skipped
shiatsu	shoebox	shrug on	sighted	sine bar	six-inch	skipper
shicker	shoeing	shucker	sighter	sine die	six-pack	skippet
shiften	shoe-tie	shudder	sightly	Sinetic	sixsome	skipple
shifter	shoggle	shuddup	sigmate	sinewed	sixteen	skirlie
shih-tzu	shoneen	shuffle	sigmoid	singara	sixthly	skirret
shikara	shoofly	shuffly	signage	singing	sixties	skirted
shikari	shoo-fly	shuftis	signans	single-o	Sixtine	skirter
shikimi	shoogle	shuggle	signary	singlet	sizable	skitter
shikker	shoot at	shunned	signate	sing out	sizzler	skittle
shilloo	shootee	shunner	sign bit	singult	sjambok	skiving
Shilluk	shooter	shunter	sign for	Sinhala	Sjögren	skookum
shilpit	shoot up	shurrup	signify	sinical	skaldic	Skoptsi
shimada	shop boy	Shuswap	signing	Sinitic	skatist	skreigh
shimmed	shopful	shut-eye	sign off	sinkage	skatole	skulker
shimmer	shoplet	shut-off	signora	sinkful	skedded	skulled
Shin Bet	shopman	shutout	signore	sinking	skeeler	skuttle
shinbin	shopmen	shut out	signori	sinless	skeeter	skyball
shindig	shopped	shutter	signory	sinning	skegger	sky bear
shindle	shopper	shuttle	sign out	sinopia	skeiner	sky blue
shingle	shoppie	Shylock	Sikhism	Sinopic	skelder	sky-clad
shingly	shoring	shyness	Siksika	sinopie	skellum	skydive
Shingon	shorten	shyster	silajit	sinopis	skelper	sky-high
shinier	shortia	siamang	silence	sinople	skelter	sky-hook
shinily	shortie	Siamese	Silenic	sinsyne	skepful	skyhoot
shining	shortly	Siberia	silenus	sinuate	skepsel	skyjack
shinned	short of	sibling	Silesia	sinuose	skeptic	skylark

skyless	sleep in	slumism	snaggle	snouted	softies	songlet
skylike	sleep on	slummed	snaggly	Snovian	softish	songman
skyline	sleep up	slummer	snakily	snowcap	soft roe	sonhood
sky-path	sleeved	slummie	snakish	snowcat	soft rot	Soninke
skyphos	sleever	slumper	snap off	Snowcem	soft-top	sonless
sky-ride	sleight	slurbow	snap out	snow-fly	soft toy	sonlike
skysail	slender	slurper	snapped	snow gum	Sogdian	Sonoran
sky-ship	slewing	slurred	snapper	snow-ice	soggier	sonship
sky-sign	slicken	slusher	snarler	snowier	soggily	sonsier
skytale	slicker	slushie	snarl-up	snowily	soilage	soonish
sky-walk	slickly	slutchy	snatchy	snow job	soil air	soother
skywalk	slidden	slyness	snatter	snowman	soiling	soothly
skyward	slidder	smacker	snavvle	snowmen	soil map	sootier
sky wave	sliding	small ad	sneaked	snow owl	soilure	sootily
slabbed	slifter	smaragd	sneaker	snow pea	sojourn	Sophian
slabber	slighty	smarten	sneak-up	snow-ski	sokeman	Sophies
slab-hut	slimier	smartly	snecked	snozzle	solacer	sophism
slacken	slimily	smashed	snecket	snubbed	Solacet	sophist
slacker	slim jim	smasher	snedder	snubber	solanum	sophora
slackly	slimmed	smash-up	sneerer	snuffer	solaria	soppier
slack up	slimmer	smatter	sneezer	snuff it	solatia	soppily
slagged	slinger	smeared	snekkja	snuffle	soldado	sopping
slagger	slinker	smearer	Snellen	snuffly	soldier	soprani
slainte	slip of a	smectic	snibbed	snugger	sold out	soprano
slammed	slip off	smectis	snibble	snuggle	solebar	sorbate
slammer	slipped	smeddum	snicker	snuggly	Soledon	sorbent
slander	slipper	smelled	snicket	snuzzle	solicit	Sorbian
slanter	slipway	smeller	snickle	soakage	solider	sorbile
slantly	slither	smellie	snick-up	soaking	solidly	Sorbish
slap-dab	slitted	smelter	snidely	soakway	solidus	sorbite
slapped	slitter	smetana	snidery	so-and-so	soliped	sorbose
slapper	sliving	smicket	sniff at	Soanean	soliton	sorcery
slashed	Sloaney	smiddum	sniffer	soapbox	solodic	sordini
slasher	Sloanie	smidgen	sniffle	soapery	soloist	sordino
slather	slobber	smidgin	sniffly	soapier	Solomon	sorghum
slating	slob ice	smiling	snifter	soapily	Solonic	sorites
slatish	sloe-gin	smirker	snigged	soap-lye	solpuga	soritic
slatted	slogged	smitham	snigger	soap-nut	soluble	sororal
slatter	slogger	smither	sniggle	soarage	solunar	soroses
Slavdom	sloping	smiting	snipped	soaring	solvate	sorosis
slavery	slop out	smitten	snipper	sobbing	solvent	sorrier
slaveys	slopped	smocker	snippet	so being	Somalis	sorrily
Slavian	sloshed	smoke-ho	snirtle	soberer	Somasco	sorrowy
Slavise	slot car	smokery	snitter	soberly	somatic	sortied
slavish	slot man	smokier	snittle	socager	some day	sorties
Slavish	slotted	smokily	snobdom	soccage	someday	sorting
Slavism	slotter	smoking	snodger	sociate	some few	sort key
slavist	slouchy	smokish	snogged	society	somehow	sort out
Slavist	sloughi	smolder	snogger	sockeye	someone	so-soish
slavite	sloughy	smoochy	snooded	socking	someway	Sotadic
Slavize	Slovene	smoodge	snoodle	soda ash	somewhy	sotalol
slaying	slowish	smoothe	snooker	soda-pop	somitic	so there
slecken	slubbed	smother	snooper	sod corn	somnial	Sothiac
sledded	slubber	smudger	snoozer	sodding	sonance	so to say
sledder	sludger	smugger	snoozle	sodding	sonancy	sotting
sledger	slugged	smuggle	snoring	soddish	sondage	sottish
sleechy	slugger	smutchy	snorkel	soddite	Soneryl	sot-weed
sleeked	sluicer	smutted	snorker	Sodomic	songful	souffle
sleeken	slumber	smutter	snorter	Sod's law	Songhai	soufflé
sleeker	slumdom	snaffle	snortle	Sod's Law	song-hit	soulful
sleekly	slumgum	snagged	snot-rag	sofa bed	Songish	soulish
sleeper	slum gun	snagger	snotter	so far as	songket	sounder

Soundex	sparsed	spicket	splurgy	spurred	staffer	startle
soundly	Spartan	spicula	spodium	spurrer	stagery	startly
sound on	spartle	spicule	spoiled	spurrey	stagged	start on
soupçon	spasmed	spidery	spoiler	spurter	stagger	start up
soupier	spasmic	spiegel	Spokane	spurtle	staggie	starved
soupily	spastic	spieler	spondee	sputnik	stagier	starven
soup man	spathae	spignel	sponger	sputter	stagily	starver
sour gum	spathic	spikery	spongey	spyhole	staging	statant
souring	spatial	spikier	spongin	spy ring	staidly	statary
sourish	spa town	spikily	sponsal	spy-ship	stained	stately
sourock	spatted	spiking	sponson	spyship	stainer	statera
soursop	spattee	spiling	sponsor	squabby	staired	statice
sousing	spatter	spilite	spoofer	squacco	staithe	statics
souslik	spattle	spilled	spooked	squaddy	stalder	station
soutane	spatula	spiller	spooler	squalid	stalely	statism
southen	spatule	spillet	spooned	squally	stalest	statist
souther	spaulty	spinach	spooner	squalor	staling	stative
sovkhoz	spavied	spindle	spoorer	squalus	stalish	statued
sowable	spawned	spindly	sporont	squamae	stalked	stature
sowarry	spawner	spin-dry	sporran	squarer	stalker	statusy
sowback	speaker	spin-dye	sporter	squashy	stallar	statute
sow-back	speakie	spinier	sportly	squatly	staller	staumer
sowbane	speak of	spinner	sporule	squatty	stall-in	staunch
Sowetan	speak to	spinney	spot map	squawky	stalloy	stave in
Soxhlet	speak up	spinode	spotted	squeaky	stamina	staving
soybean	speared	spin off	spotter	squeamy	stammel	stay-bar
sozzled	spearer	spinone	spousal	squeege	stammer	stay for
spacial	spearer	spinose	spouted	squeeze	stamnos	stay-law
spacier	special	spinous	spouter	squeezy	stamper	Stayman
spacing	specify	spin out	spraing	squelch	stamp on	stay put
Spackle	specked	spinule	spraint	squench	stand by	stay-rod
spaddle	speckle	spiraea	sprawly	squidge	standby	St Cross
spadger	speckly	spirane	sprayer	squidgy	standee	stead of
spading	specter	spirant	sprayey	squiffy	standel	stealer
spadona	spectra	spirity	spray-on	squilla	stander	stealth
spaeman	spectre	spiroid	sprazer	squinch	stand in	steamed
spag bol	specula	spirtle	spready	squinny	stand on	steamer
spaller	speeded	spirula	spreagh	squinsy	stand to	steamie
spalted	speeder	spit-box	spreath	squinty	stand up	steam in
Spam can	speedos	spite of	sprenge	squiral	staniel	stearic
spancel	speed-up	spitful	spretty	squiret	stanine	stearin
Spandau	speeler	spitish	spriggy	squirmy	Stanley	stearyl
Spandex	spelder	spit-out	spright	squishy	stannel	steddle
spangle	spelled	spittal	springe	squitch	stannic	Stedman
spangly	speller	spitted	springy	squodgy	stanza'd	steeboy
spaniel	spelter	spitter	spritty	sraddha	stapled	steeled
Spanish	spelunk	spittle	sprucer	S-shaped	stapler	steenth
spanker	spencer	spittly	spryest	stabbed	starchy	steepen
spanned	spender	splashy	spud can	stabber	star-cut	steeper
spanner	sperage	splatch	spudded	stabile	stardom	steeple
span-new	sperate	spleeny	spudder	stabler	starful	steeply
sparely	spermal	splenic	spuddle	stabley	staring	steep-to
sparger	spermic	splenii	spulyie	stab-man	starken	steep-up
Sparine	sphagna	splicer	spumoni	stachys	starkly	steerer
sparing	sphecid	splinty	spumose	stacked	starlet	Steiner
sparker	spheges	split-up	spumous	stacker	starlit	stellar
sparkle	spheral	splodge	spunkie	stack up	star-map	stelled
sparkly	spheric	splodgy	spun out	staddle	starnie	Steller
sparoid	spicate	sploshy	spur-bow	staddow	starred	stem-cup
sparred	spicery	splotch	spur-dog	stadial	starrer	stem-fly
sparrer	spicier	splunge	spurion	stadium	starter	stemlet
sparrow	spicily	splurge	spurner	staffed	start in	stemmed

stemmer	stick up	stop-net	striola	stylish	sub-song	sui-mate
stemple	Stiegel	stop off	striped	stylism	subsume	suit bag
stemson	stifado	stop-off	striper	stylist	subtack	suiting
stenchy	stiffen	stopoff	stripey	stylite	sub-teen	sulcate
stencil	stiffly	stop one	strippy	stylize	subtend	sulfide
stengah	stifled	stop out	stritch	styloid	subtest	Suliote
Sten gun	stifler	stopped	strived	stylops	subtext	sulkier
Stensen	stigmal	stopper	striven	stymied	subtile	sulkily
stenter	stigmas	stopple	striver	stymies	subtler	sullage
stenton	stigmat	stop-tap	strobic	styptic	subtone	sullied
stentor	stiller	stopway	stroker	Stypven	subtype	sullies
Stentor	stilted	storage	stromal	styrene	subunit	sulphur
step-cut	stilter	storeys	strophe	Styrian	subvent	sultana
stepdad	Stilton	storial	stroppy	styrone	subvert	Sumatra
stepmum	stimies	storied	strowed	suantly	sub voce	sumless
Stepney	stimuli	storier	strudel	suasion	sub-zero	summage
step off	stinged	stories	strumae	suasive	subzero	summand
step out	stinger	storify	stubbed	suasory	subzone	summary
stepped	stingle	storken	stubber	suavely	succade	summate
stepper	stinker	stormer	stubble	suavity	succeed	summers
stepson	stinted	stotter	stubbly	subacid	succent	summery
stepway	stinter	stourly	stub-end	subadar	success	summing
sterane	stipend	stouten	stub-pen	sub-aqua	succory	Summist
stereos	stipple	stoutly	stuck-up	sub-arch	Succoth	summons
sterile	stipula	stowage	stud-box	subashi	succour	sumpter
sterlet	stipule	stowing	studded	sub-atom	succous	sunbake
sternad	stir-fry	stow-net	studdle	sub-base	succuba	sun-bath
sternal	stirpes	strafer	student	subbing	succubi	sunbeam
sterned	stirred	straint	Student	subcool	succumb	sun bear
sternly	stirrer	straked	studied	subdean	succuss	sunbelt
stern on	stirrup	stramin	studier	subdual	suck dry	sunbird
sternum	St Kilda	strange	studies	subduct	suck-egg	sunburn
steroid	St Leger	strap in	studios	subdued	sucking	sun club
stertor	stocked	strap-on	Studite	subduer	suckler	sun-cure
stetson	stocker	strappy	stufato	subdues	suck off	Sundays
Stetson	stock up	stratal	stuffed	sub-edit	sucrase	sun deck
stetted	stodger	stratum	stuffer	subedit	sucrier	sundial
Steuben	stogies	stratus	stuff it	suberic	sucrose	sun-disc
steward	stoical	strawed	stumble	suberin	suction	sundown
stewart	stoiter	strawen	stumbly	subfief	sudamen	sunfall
stew-bum	stomach	strayed	stummed	subform	Sudanic	sunfast
stewing	stomata	strayer	stummer	subfusc	sudaria	sunfish
stewpan	stomate	streaky	stumper	sub-head	Sudeten	sun gear
stewpot	stomion	streale	stumpie	subhead	Sudetic	Sun King
St Faith	stomium	streamy	stump up	subject	sudoral	sun-lamp
sthenia	stomper	streety	stun gas	subjoin	suedene	sunlamp
sthenic	stompie	strepie	stun gun	sublate	suedine	sunless
stibine	stone me	stretch	stunned	sublime	Suevian	sunlike
stibium	stonier	stretta	stunner	submenu	suevite	sunnier
stichic	stonify	stretto	stunted	submiss	suey pow	sunnies
stichoi	stonily	strewed	stunter	suboval	suffect	sunnily
stichos	stonker	strewer	stupefy	suboxic	suffete	sunning
stick at	stooker	strewth	stupent	sub-plot	suffice	Sunnism
stick by	stookie	striata	stupify	sub-rent	sufflue	Sunnite
sticker	stooled	striate	stupose	subring	Suffolk	sunrays
Stickie	stoolie	strider	sturine	sub rosa	suffuse	sunrise
stick in	stooper	stridor	Sturmer	subsalt	Sufiism	sun-roof
stickit	stoopid	striges	stutter	subsere	sufuria	sunroof
stickle	stoothe	strigil	Stygian	subside	sugared	sunroom
stick-on	stop-dog	striked	stylary	subsidy	suggest	sun-rose
stick to	stopgap	striker	styling	subsist	sugging	sunspot
stickum	stop log	stringy	stylise	subsoil	suicide	sunstar

sun-suit	swagger	swinger	syntony	Taffies	tallied	*tant pis*
sunsuit	swaggie	swing it	syntype	Tagalic	tallier	tantric
suntrap	swagman	swingle	synusia	Tagalog	tallies	tantrum
sunward	swagmen	Swinhoe	Syrette	Tagamet	tallish	tan-yard
sunways	Swahili	swinish	Syriasm	tag axle	tallith	tao-tieh
sunwise	Swakara	swinker	syringa	tagetes	tallowy	taovala
supping	swallow	swipper	syringe	taggant	tally-ho	tap-bolt
suppler	swamper	swipple	syrphid	taggeen	taloned	tapered
support	swanker	switchy	system D	tagging	talonid	taperer
suppose	swankey	swithen	systole	tag line	tal qual	tapetal
suppost	swankie	swither	systyle	tag-lock	taluses	tapetum
suprema	swanned	Switzer	taaibos	tagmeme	talwood	tap-hole
supreme	swanner	swizzes	tabanid	tag sale	tamable	tap-hose
suprême	swannie	swizzle	tabaret	tag-sore	tamarau	tapicer
supremo	Swansea	swollen	Tabasco	tag-tail	tamarin	tapioca
suramin	swapped	swooned	tabbies	tag team	tamasha	tap-kick
suranal	swapper	swooner	tabbing	tag-worm	tambala	tap-lash
surance	swarded	swooper	tabella	tail-bay	tamboti	tapless
surbase	swarmer	swooshy	tabetic	tail-end	tambour	tapping
surcoat	swarthy	sworded	tabific	tail fin	tambuti	taproom
surdity	swasher	sworder	tabinet	tail-fly	tame cat	tap root
surface	swather	swotted	tableau	tail gas	Tammany	tap shoe
surfacy	swathes	swotter	tablier	tail-ill	tammies	tapster
surf-bum	swatted	swy game	tablina	tailing	tampico	tap-tool
surf day	swatter	syconia	tabling	tailism	tamping	tar acid
surfeit	swattle	syconus	tabloid	taillie	tampion	taraire
surfing	sway-bar	sycosis	tabooed	tail off	tanager	Taranji
surfuse	swazzle	syenite	taborer	tailory	Tanagra	tar-baby
surgent	swearer	Sylheti	tab show	tail-pin	tanbark	tar ball
surgeon	swear in	syllabe	tabular	tail-rod	tandava	tar base
surgery	sweated	syllabi	taccada	tail-wag	tandoor	tarbush
surging	sweater	sylloge	tacenda	tainted	tandour	tardier
surlier	sweddle	sylphid	Taceval	Taiping	tangata	tardily
surlily	Swedish	Sylphon	tachism	Tairona	tangelo	tardity
surmise	Sweeney	Sylvian	tachist	takable	tangena	tardive
surname	sweeper	sylvine	ta chuan	take aim	tangent	tardyon
surpass	sweeten	sylvite	tachyon	take air	tanghin	tarheel
surplus	sweetie	Sylvius	tacitly	take-all	tanghier	tar kiln
surreal	sweetly	symmory	tackety	take ill	tangily	tarnish
surreys	swelled	symport	tackier	Takelma	tangled	tarocco
surtout	swelp me	symptom	tackily	take off	tangler	tarried
surveil	swelter	synagog	tacking	take out	tangoes	tarrier
surview	sweltry	synapse	tackled	taker-in	tangram	tarries
survive	swept-up	synaxis	tackler	taker-up	tanguin	tarring
suspect	swerver	syncarp	tack rag	takhaar	taniwha	tarrish
suspend	swidden	synchro	tacnode	Takulli	tankage	tarrock
suspire	swiften	syncope	Taconic	Talaing	tankard	tar sand
sussing	swifter	syndrum	tacouba	talaria	tank car	tar-seal
suss law	swiftie	synergy	tactful	talaric	tankful	Tarsian
sustain	swiftly	synform	tactics	talayot	tank top	tarsier
sutlery	swigged	synfuel	tactile	talcing	tanling	tartana
suttees	swigger	syngamy	tactily	talcked	tannage	tartane
sutural	swiggle	synnema	taction	talcose	tannaim	tartare
sutured	swigman	synodal	tactoid	talcous	tannase	Tartary
Svanian	swiller	synodic	tactual	talipes	tannate	tartier
svarita	swim-cap	synonym	tadpole	talipot	tannery	tartily
swabbed	swim-fin	synovia	Tadzhik	talk big	tanning	tartine
swabber	swimmer	syntagm	taeniae	talking	tannish	tartish
Swabian	swindle	syntaxy	taenias	talk out	tansies	tartlet
swacked	swinely	synteny	taenite	tallage	tantara	tar-weed
swaddle	swinery	synthon	taffeta	tallboy	tantivy	tar-wood
swagged	swing-by	syntone	taffies	tall hat	tantony	Tasaday

tastier	tear gas	tempery	ternate	Thammuz	theorbo	thinner
tastily	tearing	tempest	ternery	thanage	theorem	Thiokol
tasting	tearlet	tempête	ternion	thankee	theoric	thionic
tattery	tear-off	templar	terpane	thanker	theosis	thionyl
tattier	tearoom	Templar	terpene	thapsia	the outs	thirdly
tattily	tea rose	templed	terrace	thatchy	the Pale	thirsty
tatting	tea shop	templet	terracy	that lot	the pits	this lot
tattler	teashop	tempter	terrage	that one	the Pool	thistle
tattoos	teasing	tempura	terrain	that's it	therapy	thistly
tauhinu	teat-cup	tenable	terrane	that was	thereat	thither
taungya	tea-tent	tenacle	terrene	that way	thereby	thiuram
taunter	teatime	tenancy	terreno	thaught	the Reef	thivish
taupata	tea tray	ten-code	terrier	thawing	therein	tholoid
Taurean	tea-tree	tendant	terries	the arts	thereof	Thomism
taureau	tea-ware	tend bar	terrify	theater	thereon	Thomist
Taurian	techier	tendent	terrine	theatre	thereto	Thomson
taurine	techies	tendenz	tersely	the Axis	theriac	thorian
tavelle	technic	tendril	tersest	Thebaic	therian	thorite
taverna	tectrix	tendron	tertial	Thebaïd	thermae	thorium
tawhine	teddies	teneral	tertian	the Bard	thermal	thornen
tawhiri	tedding	tenfold	tertius	the Bear	thermic	thought
tawnier	Tedesco	ten-foot	tessera	the best	thermit	thratch
taxable	tedious	ten-four	Test Act	the big C	thermos	thraver
taxably	tee-heed	ten-inch	testacy	the bird	Thermos	thready
taxator	tee-hees	tenmoku	testata	the bomb	the Rock	threave
tax bite	teemful	tennies	testate	the bowl	theroid	three Rs
tax-book	teenage	tenoner	test ban	the boys	the ruck	threnoi
tax-cart	teenful	tensely	test bed	the cake	The Rump	threose
tax code	teenier	tense up	test-fly	thecate	the runs	thrifty
tax disc	teer-boy	tensify	testier	the chop	the sack	thrilly
taxemic	teetery	tensile	testify	thecium	Thesean	thrimsa
tax-free	teether	tension	testily	the clod	the Shop	thrinne
taxicab	Tegeate	tensity	testing	the coif	the tomb	thrived
taxi-cab	tegmina	tensive	test out	thecoma	the Turk	thriven
taxiing	tegular	ten-spot	test-pit	the cord	theurgy	thriver
taxiway	Tehrani	tentage	test rig	the cuts	the veil	throaty
taxless	teistie	tent-bed	testudo	the East	the West	thrombi
tax-loss	tektite	tent-fly	tetanal	the evil	the wild	through
taxogen	telamon	tentful	tetanic	the Fens	the Word	throw by
tax year	telecom	tenthly	tetanus	the flat	the Yard	throwed
taxying	telecon	tentily	tetched	the game	they say	thrower
tayassu	telefax	tenting	Tethyan	thegnly	thiamin	throw in
tazetta	Telefax	tentive	tetrode	the hell	thicken	throw on
tchaush	teleost	tent peg	tetrose	the High	thicket	throw to
tea-ball	telesis	tenuity	tetrous	the Hill	thickie	throw up
tea-bowl	teletex	tenuous	tettery	the hole	thickly	thrummy
teacake	Teletex	tenured	teuchat	the Horn	thickos	thruout
tea cart	Telinga	tenutos	tew-iron	the lads	thick 'un	thrutch
teacher	tell-all	ten-year	Texican	the Lamb	thieves	thruway
teach-in	tellies	Teochew	textile	the land	thigger	thrymsa
tea cosy	tellina	tepidly	text-man	the lane	thighed	thudded
tea-dust	telling	tequila	text-pen	the less	thiller	thuggee
tea girl	tell off	terbium	textual	the life	thimble	thujone
tea gown	tell out	terebic	textura	the line	thin air	Thulean
teahead	telogen	terebra	texture	the Mail	thin-cut	thulite
tea lady	telomer	teredos	thacker	the men's	thingly	thulium
tea leaf	telpher	tergite	Thakali	the Moor	thingum	thumbed
tealery	Telugus	Terital	thalami	the most	thinker	thumber
tealess	temblor	term-day	Thalian	The Nine	think-in	thumper
team-man	temenos	termini	thallic	the nuts	think on	thump-up
tear-cat	temmoku	termite	thallus	the Oaks	think up	thunder
tearful	tempera	ternary	thalweg	theolog	thinned	thurify

thus far	timbrel	titmice	toilful	tool-man	torrefy	tow-line
thutter	timeful	Titoism	toiling	too much	torrent	towline
thwaite	time hit	Titoist	toisech	toothed	torsade	town car
thymele	time lag	Titoite	tokamak	tooting	torsion	town-end
thymine	time off	titrant	Tokarev	tootsey	torteau	townful
thymoma	timeous	titrate	told out	tootsie	tortile	town gas
thyroid	time-out	tittery	Toledan	toparch	tortive	townify
thyrsus	time was	titties	Toledos	top-boot	Tortoni	townish
thyself	timider	tittupy	Toletan	topchee	tortrix	townlet
tiaraed	timidly	titular	tollage	topcoat	torture	townman
Tibetan	timolol	Tityrus	toll-bar	top copy	torulae	town-way
tiburon	timothy	tizzies	Tollens	top deck	toruses	towpath
tick-fly	timpani	Tlingit	tollent	top-down	torvity	tow rope
ticking	Timucua	toad bug	tolling	top edge	torvous	toxical
tickler	Timurid	toad-eat	tollman	top-full	Torydom	Toxodon
tick off	tinamou	toadery	tollway	top gear	Toryish	toyless
tidally	tinchel	toadied	toluene	top hand	Toryism	toylike
tiddler	tindery	toadies	to match	top-hole	Toryize	toy-shop
tiddley	tin fish	toadish	tomb bat	topiary	to scale	toyshop
tideful	tinfoil	toadlet	tombola	topical	to spare	toytown
tide-rip	tin foil	to a hair	tombolo	top kick	toss off	trabant
tideway	tingent	toaster	tomelet	topknot	tosspot	trabuch
tidiest	tinging	toastie	tomenta	top-land	tostada	tracery
tidings	tingler	to a turn	tomfool	topless	totally	trachea
tidling	tinhorn	to a wish	Tommies	top-line	to taste	trachle
tidying	tiniest	tobacco	tomming	topmast	tote bag	tracing
tie-back	tinkler	to-burst	tompion	topmost	tote box	tracker
tie-beam	tin-loaf	toby jug	Tompion	topness	totemic	track-in
tie belt	tinnery	tobyman	tom pung	top note	totient	track up
tie-bolt	tinnier	toccata	tonally	to point	Totonac	tractor
tie-clip	tinnies	toc emma	tone arm	toponym	tottery	tractus
tie down	tinnily	tocusso	tonearm	topping	totting	trade in
tie game	tinning	toddies	toneful	toppish	tot up to	trade on
tie into	tin pest	toddler	tonemic	topsail	touch at	trade up
tieless	tin-tack	to death	tonepad	topside	touched	trading
tie line	tinting	tod-hole	tone-row	topsman	toucher	traduce
tierced	tin-type	toe-boot	tonetic	topsoil	touch in	traffic
tiercel	tinware	toe clip	tonette	topspin	touch on	tragedy
tiercet	tipless	toehold	tonging	top view	touch up	traiked
tiering	tip loss	toe-hold	tongman	topwise	toughen	trailer
tiffany	tipping	toe jump	tongued	top-work	toughie	trained
Tiffany	tippler	toeless	tonguer	Toradja	tough it	trainee
tiffler	tipsier	toe loop	tongues	torched	toughly	trainer
tigerly	tipsify	toenail	tonguey	torcher	toughra	train on
tighten	tipsily	toe-puff	tonical	torchon	touladi	traipse
tightly	tipster	toe rake	toniest	tordion	toupeed	traitor
Tigrean	tiptoed	toe-ring	tonight	torenia	touraco	traject
tigress	tiptoes	toering	Tonkawa	tore-out	tourism	tra-la-la
tigrine	tipulid	toe shoe	ton-mile	toreros	tourist	tramcar
tigroid	tiredly	toe-spin	tonnage	torgant	Tournai	trammel
tiki bar	tisicky	toe wall	tonneau	torgoch	Tournay	trammer
tilapia	tissual	toffees	tonnish	torgsin	tournee	trammie
tilbury	tissuey	toffies	tonsure	torment	tourney	tramper
tile-ore	titania	toffish	tontine	tormina	tousing	trample
tillage	titanic	toftman	tool bag	tornada	tou ts'ai	tramway
tilleul	Titanic	togated	tool-bar	tornado	towable	tranced
tillite	tit-bell	toggery	tool-box	torpedo	towards	tranche
tilloid	tithing	togging	toolbox	torpefy	towaway	tranché
tilt cab	titivil	togless	toolies	torpent	tow-boat	traneen
tilt-top	titlark	togt boy	tooling	torqued	towered	trangle
timbale	titling	toheroa	tool kit	torques	towfish	tranked
timbred	titlist	to horse	toolkit	torquey	tow-head	trannie

transit	tribade	trisect	trueing	tucking	Turkdom	twin bed
transom	triblet	triseme	trueish	tuck-net	Turkery	twin-cam
tranter	tribual	trishaw	true rib	tuck-out	turkeys	twindle
trap-bat	tribune	trismus	truffle	Tudesco	Turkify	twingle
trap-cut	tribute	trisome	trugger	Tuesday	Turkish	twin-jet
trapeze	tricast	trisomy	trumeau	tuffite	Turkism	twinkie
trap-gun	triceps	tritaph	trumper	tuftily	Turkize	twinkle
trap-net	tricker	tritely	trumpet	tufting	Turkman	twinkly
trapped	trickle	tritide	trump up	tugboat	Turkmen	twin-law
trapper	trickly	tritish	truncal	tugging	turmoil	twinned
trap-shy	tricksy	tritium	truncus	tuition	turn-cap	twin set
trasher	triclad	tritoma	trundle	tule fog	turn dog	twinset
traumas	tricorn	tritone	trunked	tumbaga	turnery	twinter
travail	trident	triumph	trunker	tumbler	turning	twin-tub
travois	triduan	triunal	trunnel	tumbrel	turnipy	twirler
trawler	triduum	trivial	trusser	tumbril	turnkey	twisted
trayful	triffid	trivium	trustee	Tumbuka	turn off	twister
tray top	trifler	trizzie	truster	tumesce	turn out	twist in
treacle	trifold	Troadic	trustie	tumidly	turnout	twistle
treacly	triform	trochal	trutine	tummied	turn-pin	twistor
treaded	trigamy	trochee	try back	tummies	turn-row	twitchy
treader	trigged	trochus	try it on	tummler	turpeth	twitted
treadle	trigger	trodden	trypsin	tumular	turtler	twitten
treason	triglot	troland	tryptic	tumulus	turtlet	twitter
treatee	trigone	troller	try-sail	tunable	turving	twizzle
treater	trigram	trolley	trysail	tunably	tushery	two-bill
treddle	Trilene	trollop	tryster	tundish	tussive	two-body
tree boa	trilith	tromino	tsaddik	tuned in	tussock	two-cent
tree-cat	triller	trommel	ts'ao shu	tuneful	tussore	two-coat
tree fox	trillet	tronage	tsarate	tune off	tutania	two-eyed
treeful	trilobe	troolie	tsardom	tune out	tutelar	twofold
tree god	trilogy	trooper	tsarian	tung oil	tutenag	two-foot
tree pie	trimmed	troopie	tsarina	tunhoof	tutorer	two-four
tree rat	trimmer	tropane	tsarish	tunicae	tutorly	two-hand
treetop	trim tab	tropary	tsarism	Tunican	tutoyer	two-leaf
trefoil	trinary	tropery	tsarist	tunicin	tutress	two-line
trehala	trindle	trophic	tsarlet	tunicle	tutulus	two-meal
trekbok	tringle	tropine	tsatlee	tunnage	tuxedos	twoness
trekked	trinity	troping	tsatske	tunnery	twaddle	two-part
trekker	trinket	tropism	T-shaped	tunnies	Twaddle	two-pipe
trekkie	trinkle	tropone	tsimmes	tunning	twaddly	two-shot
trek net	trinkum	trot out	T-square	tun-pail	twanger	twosome
trek-tow	triobol	trotted	tsukuri	tupaiid	twangle	two-spot
trellis	triolet	trotter	tsunami	tupelos	Twankay	two-star
tremble	trioxan	trouble	Tswanas	tupping	twanker	two-step
trembly	tripack	troughy	tuatara	turacin	twattle	two-time
tremolo	tripart	trounce	tub-bass	turbary	tweaker	two-tone
trenail	tripery	trouper	tubbier	turbine	tweeded	twybill
trendle	triple-A	trouser	tubbily	turbots	tweedle	twyfold
trental	tripler	trouter	tubbing	turdine	tweeter	tychism
trepang	triplet	Trouton	tubbish	turdish	tweetle	tykhana
tressed	triplex	trowman	tubeful	turdoid	tweezer	Tylenol
tressel	triplum	truancy	tube top	turfdom	twelfth	tylopod
trestle	tripody	truce to	tub-fish	turfier	twelver	tylosin
Trevira	tripoli	trucial	tubfuls	turfing	twibill	tylosis
trey-bit	tripped	trucker	tubifex	turfite	twiddle	tylotic
triable	tripper	truckie	tub-size	turfman	twiddly	tympana
triacid	trippet	truckle	tubster	turfmen	twifold	tympani
triadic	tripple	trudgen	tubular	turgent	twigged	tympany
triarch	tripton	trudger	tubulin	turismo	twiggen	Tyndall
triatic	trireme	true bug	tubulus	turista	twiglet	Tynwald
tri-axle	trisazo	true fly	tuck box	Turkana	twilled	type-bar

typeset	unbeget	undated	un-Greek	unlaced	unpoise	unslate
typhoid	unbegot	undazed	ungreen	unladen	unposed	unslave
typhoon	unbegun	undealt	ungrown	unlamed	unpower	unslept
typhous	unbeing	undeify	unguard	unlatch	unprone	unsling
typical	unbless	underdo	unguent	un-Latin	unproud	unslung
tyranny	unblest	undergo	ungulae	unlawed	unpurse	unsmart
Tyroler	unblind	undevil	unguled	unlearn	unpushy	unsnare
tzarina	unblock	undight	ungyved	unleash	unqueen	unsnarl
Tzeltal	unblown	undinal	unhandy	unleave	unquick	unsneck
tzigane	unboned	undined	unhappy	unlegal	unquiet	unsober
tzimmes	unbonny	undoing	unhardy	unlevel	unquote	unsolid
tzolkin	unbored	undrape	unhaste	unlight	unquoth	unsonsy
Tzotzil	unborne	undrawn	unhasty	unlimed	unraced	unsorry
Tz'u Chou	unbosom	undress	unheard	unlined	unraked	unsound
uberous	unbound	undried	unheart	unlived	unrated	unspell
ubicity	unbowed	undrunk	unheedy	unliver	unravel	unspent
udaller	unbrace	undular	unhinge	unlocal	unready	unspied
uddered	unbraid	undying	unhired	unlodge	unreeve	unspike
ufology	unbrave	undyked	unhitch	unloose	unregal	unspilt
Ugandan	unbrick	uneager	unhoard	unloved	unright	unsplit
ugliest	unbuild	uneared	unhomed	unloyal	unrimed	unspoil
uht-song	unbuilt	unearth	unhoped	unlucid	unrisen	unspool
ukelele	unbulky	uneaten	unhorse	unlucky	unriven	unstack
ukulele	unburnt	unedged	unhosed	unlusty	unrivet	unstagy
ulcered	unburst	unended	unhouse	unmaker	unrobed	unstaid
ulexite	uncaged	unequal	unhuman	unmanly	un-Roman	unstall
ullaged	uncanny	unexact	uniaxal	unmarry	unroost	unstate
ulnager	unchain	unfaded	unibody	unmated	unroped	unsteek
Ultisol	uncharm	unfaith	unicell	unmeant	unrough	unsteel
ululant	unchary	unfamed	unicist	unmerry	unround	unstick
ululate	unchild	unfazed	unicity	unmeted	unroyal	unstill
Ulysses	unchoke	unfiled	unicode	unmined	unruled	unsting
Umayyad	uncinch	unfined	unicorn	unmixed	unsaint	unstock
Umbanda	uncinus	unfired	unidea'd	unmoist	unsated	unstout
umbella	uncited	unfitly	unideal	unmoral	unsaved	unstrap
umbilic	uncivic	unfitty	uniface	unmould	un-Saxon	unstrip
umbonal	uncivil	unfixed	unified	unmount	unscale	unstuck
umbones	unclamp	unflesh	unifier	unmoved	unscrew	unstuff
umbrage	unclasp	unflown	unifies	unmowed	unseely	unstung
Umbrian	unclean	unfound	uniflow	unnamed	unsense	unsunny
umbrose	unclear	unframe	uniform	unneedy	unsewed	unswear
umbrous	uncling	unfreed	unineme	unnerve	unsexed	unsweet
umpteen	uncloak	unfresh	uninemy	unnoble	unshape	unswell
umwhile	unclose	unfrock	unional	unnoted	unsharp	unswept
unacted	uncloud	unfroze	Unionic	unoften	unshawl	unswore
unadept	unclued	unfumed	unipole	unoiled	unshell	unsworn
unaided	uncoded	unfunny	unireme	unorder	unshent	untaken
unaimed	uncomfy	unfused	un-Irish	unowned	unshewn	untamed
unaired	uncoped	unfussy	unitard	unpaced	unshift	untaxed
unalert	uncouch	ungated	unitary	unpagan	unshiny	unteach
unalike	uncouth	ungaudy	unities	unpaged	unshoed	untense
unalism	uncover	ungazed	uniting	unpaint	unshook	untenty
unalist	uncowed	ungiddy	unition	unpaper	unshorn	unthink
unalive	uncramp	ungirth	unitise	unpared	unshout	untight
unanism	uncrest	ungiven	unitive	unpaved	unshown	untiled
unaptly	uncross	unglobe	unitize	unpeace	unshowy	untimed
unarmed	uncrown	unglove	unjaded	unperch	unsight	untired
unasked	uncruel	unglued	unjoint	unplace	unsilly	untitle
unaware	unction	ungodly	unjolly	unplain	unsinew	untoned
unawful	uncured	ungrace	unjuicy	unplait	unsized	untread
unbaked	uncurse	ungrate	unkempt	unplank	unskill	untried
unbated	undared	ungrave	unknown	unplume	unslain	untripe

untrite	uplight	uranium	vagancy	variole	venomed	vetoism
untruly	uplying	uranous	vaginae	various	venomer	vetoist
untruss	upmount	uredial	vaginal	varment	ventage	vetting
untrust	up north	uredium	vaginas	varmint	ventail	vettura
untruth	up-piled	urethra	vagitus	varnish	Ventile	vetusty
untuned	upraise	urgence	vagrant	varsity	venting	vexable
untwine	upright	urgency	vaguely	varying	ventose	vexedly
untwist	uprisal	uricase	vaguish	vascula	Ventose	vexilla
untying	uprisen	uridine	vainful	vaseful	vent-peg	viaduct
unurged	upriser	urinant	vaivode	vastily	ventrad	vialled
unurned	up-river	urinary	valance	vastity	ventral	viatica
unusual	upriver	urinate	Val-A-Pak	VATable	venture	vibrant
unvenom	upscale	urinous	valence	Vatican	venturi	vibrate
unvexed	upshift	urnfuls	valency	vatting	Venturi	vibrato
unvisor	upshoot	urodele	valeric	Vaudese	Venuses	vibrion
unvital	upsides	urogram	valeryl	Vaudois	Vepsian	vibrios
unvocal	upsilon	urology	valeted	vaulted	veranda	vice-god
unvoice	upskill	urotoxy	valetry	vaulter	verbage	viceroy
unvowed	upslope	ursinia	valiant	vaumure	verbena	vicinal
unwaged	upspeak	urucuri	validly	vaunter	verbify	vicious
unwaked	upstage	useable	vallate	vecchio	verbose	Vickers
unwares	upstair	useless	valleys	Vectian	verdant	victory
unwater	upstand	use-life	vallota	vedalia	Verdian	victrix
unwaxed	upstare	ushabti	valonia	Vedanta	verdict	victual
unweary	upstart	U-shaped	valpack	Veddoid	verdite	videnda
unweave	upstate	usherer	valuate	vedette	verdure	vidette
unwiped	upsteer	Usonian	valuing	veeboer	verglas	vidicon
unwitch	upstood	Ustashi	valvate	veering	veridic	vidimus
unwitty	upsurge	usually	valving	veganic	veriest	Vidonia
unwived	upswarm	usucapt	valvula	Veganin	verismo	viduage
unwoman	upsweep	usuress	valvule	vegetal	vermeil	viduity
unwooed	upswell	usurped	vamoose	vehicle	vermian	Vietnik
unworld	upswept	usurper	vampire	veiling	Vermont	viewing
unworth	upswing	utensil	vampish	veinier	vernage	vigogne
unwound	uptaken	uterine	vampyre	veining	Vernean	vigonia
unwoven	uptaker	utilise	vanadic	veinlet	verneuk	vihuela
unwrite	up-tempo	utility	vanadyl	veinous	vernier	villaed
unwrung	up there	utilize	vandola	veinule	veronal	villafy
unyoked	upthrew	Utopian	vandyke	velamen	verruca	village
unzoned	upthrow	Utopism	Vandyke	velaria	verruga	villain
up a tree	uptight	Utopist	vanessa	velaric	versant	villein
upblown	uptower	Utrecht	vanette	velated	Versene	villose
upbound	uptrend	utricle	vanilla	veldman	versify	villous
upbraid	up until	utterer	vanille	veld pig	versine	Vincent
upbreak	upvalue	utterly	Van John	veld rat	version	vin cuit
upbring	upwards	U-valley	van pool	velella	versute	vincula
upbuild	upwound	uveitis	vantage	veliger	vertant	vinegar
upburst	up yours	uxorial	vanward	velites	vertigo	vine-rod
upcatch	urachal	vaatjie	vapidly	vellumy	vervain	vinewed
upchuck	urachus	vacance	vaporer	velours	vesania	vin gris
upclimb	uraemia	vacancy	vapoury	velouté	vesical	vinnied
upclose	uraemic	vacatur	vaquero	velvety	vesicle	*vin rosé*
upcoast	Uralian	vaccary	varanid	venally	vespine	vintage
updater	uralite	vaccine	varanus	venatic	vespoid	vintner
upfield	Uralite	vacuist	variant	vendace	vestige	Vinylon
upfloor	uralium	vacuity	variate	Vendean	vesting	violate
upflung	Ural owl	vacuole	varicap	venefic	vestock	violent
up front	uranate	vacuome	varices	veneral	vestral	violine
upfront	Uranian	vacuous	variety	venerer	vesture	violist
upglide	uranism	vacuums	varimax	Venetic	vesuvin	violone
upgrade	uranist	V aerial	Varinas	V-engine	veteran	viperid
upheave	uranite	vagally	variola	venison	vetiver	viragos

virally	voivode	waggler	want for	washier	waygate	weirdie
virelay	volante	wagoner	wanting	washily	waylaid	weirdly
viremia	Volapük	wagonry	want-wit	washing	wayless	weirdos
virgate	volatic	wagtail	wapitis	Washita	waymark	weiring
Virgoan	volcano	Wahhabi	wappato	washman	way-port	welcome
virgula	volleys	waifish	wapping	wash-off	way-post	welding
virgule	voltage	wailful	waratah	wash out	wayside	welfare
viridin	voltaic	wailing	war baby	wash-out	way-stop	well-cut
viroled	Voltaic	wainage	war-bird	washout	wayward	well day
virosis	voluble	wainful	warbled	wash-pan	way-wise	well-fed
virtual	volubly	wainman	warbler	wash-pen	waywode	wellies
virtued	volumed	waipiro	Warburg	wash-pot	way-worn	wellish
visaged	volumen	waisted	Wardian	washrag	wazzock	well-man
visaing	volupty	waister	warding	washtub	weakish	well met
vis-à-vis	voluted	waiting	wardite	wash-way	Wealden	well-off
viscera	volutin	wait out	ward off	Waspdom	wealthy	we'll see
viscoid	vomited	waitron	war-drum	wasp-fly	wearier	well-set
viscose	vomiter	Wakamba	wareful	waspily	wearily	well-way
viscous	vomitus	wakeful	warehou	Waspily	wearing	well-won
visible	voodoos	wakeman	wareshi	waspish	wearish	welsher
visibly	voorbok	wakener	warfare	Waspish	wear off	Welsher
visited	vorlage	Walapai	war game	wassail	wear out	Welshry
visitee	votable	walkies	war-hawk	wassell	weasand	welting
visiter	vote off	walking	warhead	wastage	weather	wemless
visitor	vote out	walkist	war hero	wastery	weazeny	wencher
Visking	votress	Walkman	wariest	wastrel	web-beam	wendigo
visnomy	vouchee	walk off	warless	watcher	Webbian	Wendish
visored	voucher	walk out	warlike	watchet	webbing	Wepsian
vistaed	vouchor	walkout	warling	watch it	web-foot	wergeld
vis viva	Vouvray	walkway	warload	watch up	weblike	wershly
vitally	vowelly	wallaba	war loan	watered	web-nest	werwolf
vitamin	voyager	wallaby	warlock	waterer	webster	west end
vitarum	vriddhi	Wallace	warlord	water in	web-toed	West End
vitelli	vriesia	Wallach	warm-air	water-ox	web-work	western
vitenge	V-shaped	wall bar	warming	wattage	webwork	westing
vitiate	V-thread	wall bed	warmish	Watteau	web-worm	westlin
vitious	vugular	wall-box	warning	wattled	wedding	wetback
vitrain	vulgate	wall-eye	warnish	wave-hop	wedging	wet bulb
vitrify	Vulgate	wallful	warn off	wavelet	wedlock	wet dock
vitrine	vulpine	wallies	war-note	wave-off	weedery	wet fish
vitriol	vulture	walling	warpage	waverer	weedful	wetland
vitrous	Wabenzi	Walloon	warpath	waveson	weedier	wet look
vittate	wackily	wall-rib	warping	wavicle	weeding	wetness
vivaing	wackoes	wall rue	war poet	waviest	Wee Free	wet pack
vivaria	wadable	wall-tie	war-post	wax bath	Weejuns	wet rent
vivency	waddies	Walther	warrant	wax bean	weekday	wet-shod
viverra	wadding	waltzer	warring	waxbill	weekend	wetsuit
vividly	waddler	wambais	warrior	wax doll	weenier	wettest
vivific	wad hook	wameful	war risk	waxiest	weepier	wet time
vixenly	Wafdist	wandery	war road	wax jack	weepies	wetting
Viyella	wafered	wangler	war room	waxlike	weepily	wettish
vizored	waferer	wanhope	warship	wax moth	weeping	wetware
vocable	waffler	wanigan	warthog	wax palm	weep out	wet wing
vocably	waftage	wanluck	wartime	wax shot	weevily	whacked
vocalic	wafting	wannabe	war-torn	wax-tree	weftage	whacker
vocally	wafture	wanness	war-wolf	waxwing	weigela	whack-up
vocoder	wagedom	wannest	war work	waxwork	weighed	whalery
voetsek	Wagener	wannion	war-worn	way back	weigher	whaling
voguish	wagerer	wannish	war zone	waybill	weigh in	wham-bam
voicing	waggery	wanrest	washbag	way fare	weighty	whammed
voidage	wagging	wanruly	washday	wayfare	weigh up	whangee
voiture	waggish	wantage	washery	way-gang		whanger

wharfie	whippin	wide-cut	wine fly	with pup	Woolpit	wrecker
wharrow	whip-ray	widener	wine-god	witless	woolsey	wren-boy
Wharton	whipsaw	wideout	wine gum	witling	wool wax	Wrenean
wharves	whirled	widgeon	wine-pot	witloof	woomera	Wrenian
whate'er	whirler	widower	wine red	witness	woonerf	wrenlet
what for	whirred	widowly	winesap	wittier	Wooster	wren-tit
what fun	whisker	wielder	wine-vat	wittily	woozier	wrester
Whatman	whiskey	wifedom	wing-bar	witting	woozily	wrestle
whatnot	whisper	wiggery	wing-bow	wit-worm	wordage	wriggle
whatsit	whister	wigging	wing-bud	wizened	wordier	wriggly
what's up	whistle	wiggler	wing-dam	wobbler	wordily	wringer
whatten	whistly	wightly	winglet	woe is me	wording	wrinkle
what way	whitbed	wigless	wingman	woesome	wordman	wrinkly
wheaten	whitely	wig-tree	wingmen	wolf-cry	work-bag	wristed
wheedle	Whiteys	wild cat	wing nut	wolf cub	workbox	wrister
wheeled	whither	wildcat	wing rib	wolf-dog	workday	write in
wheeler	whiting	wild dog	wing-tag	wolfess	workful	write up
wheelie	whitish	Wildean	wing-tip	Wolfian	working	writhed
wheeple	Whitley	wilding	winiest	wolfing	workman	writhen
wheetle	whitlow	wildish	winking	wolfish	workmen	writher
wheezer	whitret	wild man	winkler	wolfkin	work off	writing
wheezle	Whitsun	wild oat	winless	wolf-net	work out	written
whelked	whitten	wild pig	winning	wolfram	workout	writter
whemmel	whitter	wild rye	winnock	wolvish	work-shy	wronger
whene'er	whittle	wiliest	win over	womanly	worktop	wrongly
whereas	whizgig	Wilkism	winsome	wommera	worlded	wrong'un
whereat	whiz-kid	Wilkite	winters	wonkier	worldly	Wrotham
whereby	whizzed	willful	wintery	wonkily	worm-eel	wrought
where'er	whizzer	William	wipe off	wonning	wormery	wrybill
wherein	whoever	willies	wipe-out	wooable	wormian	wryneck
whereof	wholely	willing	wire act	wood ant	wormier	wryness
whereon	wholism	willock	wire bar	wood-axe	worming	wry-tail
whereso	wholist	willowy	wire bed	woodcut	wormish	W-shaped
whereto	whommel	wilsome	wire-cut	woodeny	worm red	Würmian
wherret	whoness	wimbler	wired-in	wood-god	worn out	wussies
whether	whoofle	wimbrel	wireman	wood-hen	worried	wüstite
whetted	whoompf	wimpily	wiremen	woodier	worrier	Wyandot
whetten	whoopee	wimpish	wire-rim	wooding	worries	wych elm
whetter	whooper	wimpled	wire-tap	woodish	worsest	wyerone
wheyish	whoop-up	wimpler	wireway	woodlet	worship	wysiwyg
which-so	whopped	winceys	wiriest	wood-lot	worsted	WYSIWYG
whicker	whopper	wincher	wised-up	woodman	worth it	xanthan
whiddle	whorage	windage	wise guy	woodmen	wotcher	xanthic
whiffer	whorish	windbag	wise man	wood-oil	would-be	xanthin
whiffet	whorism	wind-egg	wise saw	wood-owl	woulder	Xavante
whiffle	whorled	wind gap	wishful	wood rat	wouldn't	Xenopus
Whiglet	whortle	windier	wishing	wood rot	wouldst	xerarch
while as	whoseso	Windies	wishmay	wood-saw	wounded	xerosis
whilere	who's who	windigo	Wishram	woodsia	wounder	Xiphias
whimper	whuffle	windily	wispier	wood-tar	woundly	xiphoid
whimsey	whummel	winding	wispily	wood-tin	wound up	xograph
whindle	whyever	wind off	wispish	woodwax	wourali	X-shaped
whinger	whyness	windore	wistful	woofits	wrangle	xylenol
whinier	wichert	windowy	wistiti	woofter	wrapped	xylitol
whining	Wichita	windrow	witched	woolder	wrapper	yabbies
whinner	Wickham	Windsor	witchen	wool-fat	wrassle	yachter
whip-hem	wicking	wind-tie	witcher	wool-hat	wrastle	yachtie
whipman	wickiup	wind-way	withers	woolled	wreaker	Yahvist
whip-pan	wickner	wine bar	withery	woollen	wreathe	Yahwism
whipped	wickyup	wine box	with God	woolman	wreaths	Yahwist
whipper	widdrim	wine-dot	withies	woolmen	wreathy	yakking
whippet	wide boy	winefat	without	wool-oil	wrecked	Yamasee

yam-bean	yeasted	yolk-bag	ywroken	zemeism	Zingano	zonking
yandied	yellowy	yolk-sac	zacaton	zemstvo	Zingari	zonular
yandies	yen hock	yonside	zagging	Zennist	Zingaro	zooidal
yangban	Yenisei	York gum	Zairean	Zenonic	zingier	zookers
yang-yin	yenning	Yorkish	Zairese	zeolite	zingily	zoology
Yankton	yen pock	Yorkist	Zairian	zephyry	Zionism	zooning
yapness	yen shee	Yoruban	Zairois	zeppole	Zionist	zoonomy
yappier	Yerkish	you hear	Zambian	zeranol	zip code	zootaxy
yapping	yes-girl	you know	Zamorin	zero day	Zip code	zootomy
yardage	yeshiva	younger	zanella	zeroing	ZIP code	zootype
yardang	yestern	youngly	zaniest	zeroize	zipless	zopissa
yard-arm	yetling	young 'un	Zapotec	zero-sum	zip-lock	zorilla
yardarm	yettlin	younker	zappier	zestful	zippier	zorille
yard-dog	yew tree	youthen	zapping	zestier	zippily	zorrino
yardful	Y-fronts	youthly	zarnich	zetetic	zipping	zostera
yarding	Yiddish	you wait	zealous	Ziebart	zizania	zoukish
yard-man	yielder	yperite	zebraed	Ziegler	zloties	Z-plasty
yardman	Yi-hsing	Y-shaped	zebrano	zigging	Zoilean	Z-shaped
Yarkand	yin-yang	yttrium	zebrina	zillion	Zoilism	Zulu hat
yashmak	yipping	Yucatec	zebrine	zinc-air	Zoilist	zygaena
Yavapai	yobbery	yukkier	zebroid	zincate	zoisite	zygosis
yaw axis	yobbish	Yukoner	zebrule	zincian	Zolaism	zygotic
yawnful	yobboes	yule-day	zecchin	zincite	Zolaist	zymogen
yawning	yoghurt	yule log	zedoary	zincode	Zöllner	zymosan
year-end	yohimbe	yummier	zelator	zincoes	zomboid	zymosis
yearner	yokable	yuppies	zelkova	zinc ore	zonally	zymotic
year-old	yoke-elm	yuppify	zelotic	zingana	zonated	zymurgy

EIGHT LETTERS

aandblom	absentee	achillea	actively	adoptive	affright
aardvark	absenter	Achilles	activism	adorable	affronty
aardwolf	absently	Achinese	activist	adorably	affusion
aasvogel	absinthe	achiness	activity	adorally	afghanis
abacuses	absolute	achingly	act of God	Adriatic	aflutter
a bad life	absolver	achromat	actorish	adrogate	Africana
abapical	absonant	achromic	actressy	adroitly	after all
abasedly	absorbed	acicular	actually	adscript	after-wit
abatable	absorber	aciculum	actuator	adularia	after you
abatised	absterge	acid drop	aculeate	adulator	agar-agar
abatises	absterse	acid head	acutance	adultery	agatized
abattoir	abstract	acidness	adamance	aduncity	agedness
a battuta	abstruse	acidosis	Adamical	aduncous	age group
abbacies	absurdly	acidotic	Adam's ale	advanced	agencies
abbatial	abundant	acid rain	adaption	advancer	agenesis
abdicant	abusable	acid rock	adaptive	advisory	agential
abdicate	abutilon	acid salt	addendum	advocaat	agentive
abditory	abutment	acid test	addicted	advocacy	age range
abducens	abutting	acid tide	addition	advocate	ageratum
abducent	academia	aciduria	additive	advowson	ages with
abductor	academic	acorn-cup	additory	aecidial	aggrieve
Aberdeen	acanthus	acorning	addorsed	aecidium	agiotage
aberrant	Accadian	acosmism	adducent	aedicule	agitator
aberrate	accaroid	acosmist	adductor	aegirine	agitprop
abessive	accentor	acoustic	adenitis	aegirite	aglimmer
abetment	accepted	acquaint	adenoids	aegrotat	aglisten
abetting	accepter	acquired	adenoidy	aeration	aglitter
abeyance	acceptor	acquiree	adenomas	aerially	aglycone
abhorred	accident	acquirer	adenylic	aeriform	agnathan
abhorrer	accolade	acreable	adequacy	aerobics	agnation
abidance	accolled	acre-foot	adequate	aerofoil	agnition
a bit much	accollée	acridian	adessive	aerogram	Agnoetae
abjectly	accorder	acridiid	a devil of	aerolite	agnostic
ablation	accoster	acridine	adherend	aerology	Agnus Dei
ablative	accouche	acridity	adherent	aeronaut	agonized
ableness	accoutre	acrimony	adhesion	aeronomy	a good cry
ablution	accredit	acroatic	adhesive	aerostat	a good few
abnegate	accroach	acrobacy	adhocery	Aesopian	a good one
abnormal	accruing	acrodont	adhocism	aesthete	a good sup
abomasum	accuracy	acrolect	Adivasis	aestival	a good way
aborally	accurate	acrolein	adjacent	a fair cop	agraphia
abordage	accursed	acrolith	adjudger	afebrile	agraphic
aborning	accusant	acromial	adjuster	affected	agraphon
abortion	accusing	acromion	adjutage	affecter	agrarian
abortive	accustom	acronych	adjutant	affeeror	agreeing
abounder	Aceldama	acrostic	adjuvant	afferent	agrestal
above all	acentric	acrylate	Adlerian	affiance	agrestic
above par	Acephali	act a part	ad libbed	affinity	agrimony
abrasion	acephaly	actiniae	admire to	affirmer	agrology
abrasive	aceramic	actinian	admiring	afflatus	agronome
abridger	acerbate	actinide	admitted	affluent	agronomy
abrogate	acerbity	actinism	admitter	affodill	ague-tree
abruptly	acervate	actinium	admonish	afforder	aguishly
abscisic	acescent	actinoid	adnation	afforest	a hell of a
abscissa	acetable	actional	adolesce	affrayed	A horizon
abseiler	achiever	activate	adoption	affrayer	aigrette

aiguille	alchemic	alley-oop	alterity	amortise	anechoic
airborne	Alcmanic	alleyway	although	amortize	anestrus
air brake	aldehyde	all-fired	altitude	amperage	anethole
air-brick	alder fly	all flesh	alto clef	amphibia	aneurine
airbrick	alderman	all found	alto horn	amphipod	aneurism
airbrush	aldermen	all fours	altruism	amphorae	aneurysm
air-burst	Alderney	all hands	altruist	amphoral	Angeleno
aircraft	aldoxime	alliable	aluminum	amphoras	angelica
airdrome	aleatico	alliance	alum-rock	amphoric	angelize
Airedale	aleatory	all in all	alum-root	amplexus	angerful
air ferry	ale-bench	all-in-one	alunogen	ampullae	anginoid
airfield	aleberry	allision	alveolar	ampullar	Anglican
air force	alehouse	all-might	alveolus	amputate	angriest
airframe	aleurone	all-night	amacrine	Amratian	angstrom
airified	Aleutian	allocate	amadavat	amuletic	ångström
airiness	alewives	allodial	amandine	amusable	angulate
airliner	alfresco	allodium	Amapondo	amusedly	angulous
Air Miles	Algerian	allogamy	amaracus	amusette	anhedral
airplane	Algerine	allomone	amaranth	amygdala	anhedron
air plant	algicide	allopath	amaretti	amygdale	anhydric
air power	algidity	allotted	amaretto	amygdule	aniconic
air rifle	alginate	allottee	amazedly	anabases	animalic
airscrew	algology	allotter	Amazonic	anabasis	animally
air-shaft	Algonkin	allotype	amberoid	anabatic	animated
airspace	algorism	allotypy	ambiance	anabolic	animater
air speed	alguacil	all-party	ambience	anaconda	animator
airspeed	alguazil	all right	ambition	anaerobe	aniridia
airstrip	alibiing	all round	ambivert	anaglyph	anisated
air-tight	Alicante	all-sorts	ambligon	anagogic	anisette
airtight	alienage	allspice	amblygon	analcime	ankerite
air-to-air	alienate	all the go	Ambonese	analcite	ankylose
air-twist	alienism	all there	ambrette	analecta	annalist
airwaves	alienist	alluring	ambrosia	analects	Annamese
airwoman	alighted	allusion	ambulant	analemma	Annamite
airwomen	alizarin	allusive	ambulate	analogic	annealer
akinesia	alkahest	alluvial	ambusher	analogon	annexion
akinetic	alkalide	alluvian	amelcorn	analogue	annexure
Akkadian	alkalify	alluvion	amenable	analyser	annotate
akosmism	alkaline	alluvium	amenably	analyses	announce
Alabaman	alkalize	allylene	American	analysis	annually
Alabarch	alkaloid	all yours	Amerikan	analytic	annulary
à la carte	alkermes	almagest	amethyst	anapaest	annulate
alacrity	alkoxide	almanack	amiantus	anaphase	annulene
à la daube	alkylate	almeirah	amicable	anaphora	annulled
à la reine	all along	almighty	amicably	anarchal	annulose
alarming	allanite	alms-deed	amidated	anarchic	anodizer
alarmism	allative	almsfolk	amissing	anasarca	anointer
alarmist	all at sea	aloe vera	amitosis	anathema	an old one
à la russe	All Black	alogical	amitotic	anatheme	anomeric
albacore	all-clear	alopecia	ammoniac	Anatolic	Anomoean
Albanian	allegate	alphabet	ammonify	anatomic	anomuran
albiness	allegory	alpha ray	ammonite	ancestor	anoretic
albinism	allegros	Alpinism	ammonium	ancestry	anorexia
albinoid	allelism	Alpinist	ammonoid	anchoret	anorexic
albitite	alleluia	Alsatian	amnesiac	and a half	anorthic
albitize	alleluya	alstonia	amnestic	andesine	Ansafone
alburnum	Allen key	altarage	amniotic	andesite	Anselmic
alcabala	allergen	altar boy	amoebean	Andorran	anserine
alcahest	allergic	altarist	amoeboid	androgen	anserous
alcatras	allerion	alterant	*amoretto*	anecdota	answerer
alcavala	alley cat	alter ego	amorosos	anecdote	Antabuse

anteater	aperient	apprizer	ardurous	arsedine	asperser
antecede	aperitif	approach	area code	arsehole	aspheric
antedate	aperture	approval	areca nut	arsenate	asphodel
antelope	aphanite	approver	Areopagi	arsenide	asphyxia
antennae	aphasiac	après-ski	argentic	arsenite	aspirant
antennal	aphelion	apricate	argentry	arsenous	aspirate
antennas	aphetism	apronful	arginase	arsonist	aspirins
antepast	aphetize	apterous	arginine	artefact	assailer
ante-post	aphicide	aptitude	Argonaut	arterial	Assamese
anterior	aphorise	apyretic	argosies	arteries	assassin
ante-room	aphorism	apyrexia	arguable	artesian	assemble
antetype	aphorist	aqualung	arguably	artfully	assembly
antevert	aphorize	aquanaut	arguendo	artifact	assenter
anthelia	aphthous	Aquarian	argufied	artifice	assentor
anthelix	apiarian	aquarist	argufier	artiness	asserter
anthemia	apiaries	aquarium	argufies	artistic	assertor
antheral	apiarist	Aquarius	argument	artistly	assessee
anthesis	apically	aquatile	Argus eye	artistry	assessor
antibody	apiculus	aquatint	argutely	art of war	Assidean
antidote	aplastic	aqueduct	Arianism	art paper	assiento
antiform	aplustre	aquiline	Arianize	artsiest	assignee
anti-grav	apoapsis	aquosity	Aridisol	art union	assigner
Antiguan	apocrine	arachide	aridness	arum lily	assignor
anti-hero	apodixis	arachnid	arightly	Aryanism	Assisian
anti-life	apodoses	Araldite	arillate	Aryanize	assister
anti-lock	apodosis	Aramaean	arisings	as a whole	assonant
antilogy	apograph	araneous	aristate	asbestos	assonate
antimere	Apolline	arapaima	Arkansan	ascender	as soon as
antimony	Apollyon	Arawakan	Arkansas	ascetism	assorted
antinode	apologia	a raw deal	ark shell	ascidian	assuager
antinomy	apologue	arbalest	Armagnac	ascocarp	assuming
antiphon	apomixes	arbitral	armament	asconoid	Assyrian
antipode	apomixis	Arbor Day	armature	ascorbic	astatine
antipole	apophony	arboreal	armazine	aseismic	asterion
antipope	apophyge	arboreta	armchair	as ever is	asterisk
antiqued	apoplexy	arborist	Armeniac	as good as	asterism
antiques	aporetic	arborize	Armenian	ash blond	asteroid
anti-self	apospory	arborous	Armenoid	ashimmer	asthenia
antisera	apostasy	arboured	arm in arm	ash-plant	asthenic
anti-tank	apostate	arbuscle	Arminian	ashplant	as though
antithet	apothegm	arcadian	armorial	ashy-grey	as-told-to
antitype	appalled	Arcadian	armories	Asian flu	astonied
antlered	appanage	arcading	armorist	Asianize	astonish
Antonian	apparent	arcanely	armoured	as I see it	astragal
Antonine •	appealer	arcanist	armourer	as it were	astrally
antonymy	appear as	Archaean	armozeen	ask after	astringe
ant-plant	appearer	archaise	arms race	ask for it	astucity
antrorse	appeaser	archaism	Army List	askingly	Asturian
ant's eggs	appellee	archaist	army worm	as long as	astutely
anudatta	appellor	archaize	aromatic	Asmonean	as well as
anybody's	appendix	archdean	arpeggio	as one man	asyndeta
anyplace	appetent	archduke	arquebus	asparkle	asystole
anything	appetise	archival	arranger	aspartic	Atabrine
anywhere	appetite	archlute	arrantly	A Special	at a guess
Anzac Day	appetize	arch-mime	arrestee	aspected	at anchor
aoristic	applause	archness	arrester	asperate	at a pinch
Apachean	apple-bee	archwise	arrestor	asperges	at a price
apagogic	apple-pie	arc light	Arretine	asperity	ataraxia
apastron	appliqué	arcology	arrive at	aspermia	ataraxic
apatheia	apposite	arcuated	arrogant	aspermic	at a touch
apathist	appraise	ardently	arrogate	asperous	at bottom

atenolol
at hazard
atheling
Athenian
atherine
atheroma
athetize
athetoid
athletic
Athonite
atlantal
atlantes
Atlantic
at length
at livery
at nights
atom bomb
atomical
atomiser
atomizer
atonally
atrament
at random
at reflux
atremble
atrocity
atrophic
atropine
atropism
atropous
a truce to
at sermon
at source
at strain
attacher
attacker
attar-gul
attemper
attendee
attender
attentat
attercop
attester
attestor
at the bar
at the end
at the top
Atticise
atticism
Atticist
Atticize
Attic wit
attiring
attitude
attorney
attritor
at whiles
atwitter
atypical
aubretia
aucupate

audacity
audience
audit ale
auditing
audition
auditive
auditory
auditual
augelite
au gratin
augurate
augurial
auguries
augurous
Augustal
Augustan
augustly
aularian
aulnager
auntship
auramine
aurelian
auricula
aurorean
Ausonian
austerer
Austrian
autarchy
autarkic
authorly
autistic
autobahn
autocade
autocode
autocrat
auto-da-fé
autogamy
autogiro
autogyro
autoharp
autoland
autology
autolyse
automacy
automata
automate
automath
autonomy
autopsic
autoptic
autosome
autotomy
autotype
autumnal
autunite
avadavat
availing
avanious
Ave Maria

aventail
aventure
averager
averment
averring
aversely
aversion
aversive
aviaries
aviation
aviatrix
avidious
avifauna
avionics
avocados
Avogadro
avoucher
avowable
avowedly
avulsion
awakener
awanting
awearied
aweather
awninged
aw-shucks
axiality
axillant
axillary
axiology
axle-tree
axolemma
axonemal
axoplasm
axostyle
aye-green
Ayrshire
ayurveda
azedarac
azotemia
azoturia
Aztec hop
baasskap
Baathism
Baathist
babelish
babelism
babelize
babirusa
babouche
babushka
baby beef
baby blue
baby boom
baby bust
baby-doll
baby face
baby-farm
baby food

Babygros
babyhood
babykins
baby-like
baby talk
Bacardis
baccarat
bacchant
Bacchant
bacchiac
bacchius
bachelor
bacillar
bacillus
backache
backband
back beat
backbeat
backbite
back-bond
backbone
back-cast
backchat
backcomb
backdate
back door
backdoor
back down
backdown
backdrop
backer-up
backfall
backfill
backfire
backflip
backhand
back-heel
backland
backlash
backless
back-lift
back-line
backlist
backmost
back on to
backpack
back pain
backrest
back room
back-rope
back seat
backside
back-spin
backspin
backstay
back-stop
backstop
back talk
backveld
backward
backwash

back-word
backyard
bacon fat
Baconian
bacteria
Bactrian
baculine
Badarian
bad blood
bad books
bad break
bad faith
badge-man
badgerer
badigeon
badinage
badlands
bad loser
badly off
bad mouth
bad penny
bad scran
Baedeker
baffling
baggager
baggiest
bagpiper
baguette
Bahamian
Bahraini
bailable
bail-bond
bail-dock
bailiery
bailment
bailsman
bailsmen
Bakelite
bake-meat
Baker day
bakeries
bakeware
Bakewell
bakingly
balanced
balancer
balanoid
bald coot
baldhead
bald ibis
baldness
baldpate
Balearic
balefire
baleless
Balinese
balinger
balkiest
ballader
balladic
balladry

ballahoo
ballahou
ball clay
ballcock
balletic
ball game
ballgirl
ball gown
ball hawk
ballista
ball-like
ballocks
ballonet
balloted
balloter
ballpark
ball-peen
ball-race
ballroom
ballyhoo
ballyrag
balmiest
balmoral
balneary
balsamic
baluster
bamboula
banality
banalize
banausic
bandanna
bandboxy
bandeaux
bandelet
banderol
bandfish
bandiest
banditry
banditti
bandlike
bandpass
bandsman
bandsmen
bandster
banewort
bangalow
bangster
bangstry
bangtail
banisher
banister
banjoist
banjolin
bankable
bank-barn
bank bill
bank book
bank card
bankerly
bank-full
bankless

banknote	baronial	bastardy	bearably	bee-biter	bell pull
Bank Rate	baronian	bastille	bear a bob	bee-bread	bell push
bankroll	baronies	Batavian	bearance	beech-oil	bell-rope
bankrupt	barostat	bateless	bear arms	bee dance	bell tent
banksian	barouche	bateleur	bear away	bee-eater	bell-wire
bankside	barrable	batement	bearbind	beefcake	bellwort
banksman	barracan	Batesian	bear date	beefiest	bellyful
bank vole	barragan	Bath chap	beardlet	beef loaf	belly-god
bannered	barragon	bath cube	bear down	beef-wood	be lost in
bannerer	barranca	bathetic	bear hard	beefwood	be lost on
banneret	barrator	bat-horse	bearherd	bee plant	be lost to
bannerol	barratry	bathotic	bearlike	beeregar	below par
banterer	Barr body	bathrobe	bear's ear	beer hall	Bel Paese
bantling	barrenly	bathroom	bearskin	beeriest	belt down
banxring	barrette	bat-money	bear tack	beerless	beltless
baptizer	barrulet	Batswana	bearward	beer pump	belt line
barathea	bar-stool	battalia	bear with	beeswing	be mother
Barbados	barterer	batteler	beastish	beetroot	be myself
barbaric	Barthian	battered	be at abay	beetster	bench-end
barbasco	bartizan	batterer	beatable	befallen	benchlet
barbecue	Bartlett	battiest	beat down	befitted	bendable
barberry	baryonic	batwoman	beaten-up	beflower	bend over
barbette	barytone	batwomen	beatific	befogged	bendwise
barbican	basaltic	baudekin	beatster	befriend	beneaped
barbicel	basanite	baudrons	beat time	befringe	Benedick
barbiers	bascinet	bauhinia	beat to it	befuddle	benefact
barbital	baseball	bauxitic	beauties	begetter	benefice
barbiton	baseband	Bavarian	beautify	beggarly	Bengalis
barbitos	baseborn	bawdiest	beavered	beginner	benignly
Barbizon	baselard	bayadère	be baking	begirdle	Beninese
barbless	baseless	bayberry	bebopper	begotten	benjamin
Barbudan	baseline	Bayesian	béchamel	begrease	Benjamin
barbwire	base load	Bay State	bechance	begrudge	bent brow
bar chart	basement	bdellium	Bechuana	beguiler	bento box
bardling	baseness	bdelloid	beclothe	be hard on	bentwood
bardship	base-pair	beach bum	become of	behave to	benzilic
bareback	base rate	bead-folk	becoming	behavior	benzoate
barefoot	basic dye	beadiest	becudgel	beheadal	benzylic
barehead	basicity	beadlike	be cut out	behemoth	be packed
bareness	basic pay	bead-roll	bedabble	behither	beplumed
baresark	basidium	beadsman	bedarken	beholden	bepommel
barflies	basilary	beadsmen	bedazzle	beholder	bepowder
Bargello	basilect	bead-tree	bed-cover	behovely	bepraise
bargeman	Basilian	bead-work	bedcover	be hung up	bepuzzle
barghest	basilica	beadwork	beddable	be in a wax	bequeath
bar-goose	basilisk	be afraid	be dear of	bejabers	berattle
bar graph	basinful	be agreed	bedeguar	bejesuit	berberis
baritone	basketry	be ailing	bedesman	belabour	berberry
barkless	basophil	beak-head	bedimmed	bel canto	berceuse
bark-tree	basquine	beak-iron	bedlinen	belfries	berdache
barmiest	Basquish	beakless	bedmaker	believer	bereaved
barm-skin	bassarid	beaklike	be down on	belittle	bergamot
barnacle	bass clef	beam-ends	be down to	Belizean	bergenia
Barnardo	bass drum	beamless	bedplate	bellbird	berghaan
barn-ball	bassette	beam-tree	bedrench	bell-buoy	berg wind
barn door	bassetto	bean ball	bedskirt	bell-cord	beriberi
barnyard	bass-horn	bean curd	bedstead	bell-cote	Berliner
barogram	bassinet	bean-meal	bedstock	belleric	Bermudan
barometz	bass viol	beanpole	bedstraw	bell-like	Bermudas
baronage	basswood	bean tree	bedtable	bell lyra	berthage
baroness	bastarda	bearable	bedwards	bellower	berthing

be rude to	Bible-box	billiard	Bismarck	blandish	blotting
beryllia	biblical	billiken	bistable	blankety	blow away
bescrawl	Biblical	billions	bistoury	blarneys	blow-back
bescreen	bibulous	billycan	bit by bit	blastema	blow-ball
be seated	bickerer	bilobate	bitchery	blast off	blowfish
beseemly	bicolour	bimanous	bitchier	blastoid	blowhard
be served	biconvex	bimanual	bitchily	blastula	blow-hole
beshadow	bicuspid	bimbashi	bite back	blatancy	blowhole
be shot of	bicycler	bimbette	bite-size	blaze out	blowiest
be shut of	bicyclic	binaries	bitingly	blazered	blowlamp
besieger	bid a bead	binaural	bitterly	blazoner	blow over
besilver	biddable	bindi-eye	bittiest	blazonry	blowpipe
beslaver	biddance	bind over	biunique	bleacher	blow upon
besmirch	biddy-bid	bindweed	bivalent	bleakish	blowzier
besmutch	bidental	bingeing	biweekly	blearier	blowzily
be soft on	bidibidi	bin liner	bixbyite	blearily	blubbery
besotted	biennale	binnacle	biyearly	bleeding	blubbing
besought	biennial	binomial	blabbing	bleeping	bluchers
bespoken	biennium	binormal	black ant	blencher	bludge on
bespread	bifacial	bio-assay	black art	Blenheim	bludgeon
besprent	bifidity	bioassay	black ash	blennies	blue baby
Bessemer	bifolium	biocidal	black box	blenniid	blueback
best girl	biforked	biogenic	blackboy	blesbuck	bluebell
bestiary	biformed	biologic	black bun	blessing	blue bice
bestness	bigamies	biometry	black cap	blighted	blue-bill
bestowal	bigamist	biomorph	blackcap	blighter	bluebird
bestower	bigamous	bionomic	black dog	blimbing	blue book
bestreak	Big Apple	biopsies	black eye	blimpery	blue-bush
bestrewn	bigarade	bioscope	blackfly	blimpish	blue-chip
bestride	Big Board	biotical	black fox	blindage	blue-coat
bestrode	big chief	biparous	black gum	blind god	blue crab
bestrown	Big Chief	biparted	black ice	blind gut	blue duck
beta plus	Big Daddy	biphasic	blacking	blinding	blue-eyed
beta test	big eater	biphenyl	black ink	blindish	bluefish
betatron	bigeminy	biplanar	blackish	blind pig	blue funk
betel-nut	biggonet	bi-racial	Black Jew	blinkard	blue gown
Bethesda	big house	biramose	blackleg	blinking	blue-grey
bethwack	big money	biramous	black man	blipping	blue hare
bethwine	big mouth	birching	black neb	blissful	blue hawk
betonies	big noise	birch-rod	black oak	blissout	Blue John
betrayal	bignonia	bird bath	black oil	blistery	blue laws
betrayer	big smoke	birdcage	black out	blithely	blue line
bevatron	big stick	bird call	blackout	blizzard	blue ling
bevelled	big stiff	birdless	black-pot	blockade	blue moon
beveller	big-timer	bird-life	black rat	blockage	blueness
beverage	big wheel	birdlike	Black Rod	blocking	blue-nose
Bevin boy	bijugate	birdlime	black tar	blockish	blue note
bewailer	bilabial	birdseed	black tea	block out	blue pill
bewigged	bilander	bird's-eye	black tie	block tin	blue roan
bewilder	bilberry	bird shot	black til	bloc vote	blue rock
be wise to	bile duct	birdsong	black tin	blondine	blue ruin
bewrayer	biliment	birdying	blacktop	blondish	blue spot
bezantee	bilinear	birretta	bladdery	bloodier	blue-wing
B horizon	billable	birthday	blagging	bloodily	bluff off
biannual	billeted	birthing	*blagueur*	blood red	bluntish
biassing	billetee	biscacha	blah-blah	blood-tub	blur over
biaswise	billeter	Biscayan	Blakeian	bloomers	blurrier
biathlon	billfish	biscuity	blamable	bloomery	blurring
bibacity	billfold	bisector	blameful	blooming	blushful
bibation	billhead	bisexual	blancoed	blossomy	blustery
bibition	billhook	bishoply	blancoes	blotless	boarding

boar-fish	bolt-hole	book-post	bouldery	brancher	brideman
boastful	boltless	book-rest	bouncier	branchia	bridging
boatable	bolt-rope	bookshop	bouncily	brandies	brief-bag
boat-bill	bombarde	book-wise	bouncing	brandise	briefing
boat-deck	bombilla	bookwork	boundary	brandish	brigalow
boatfuls	bomb-site	bookworm	bounding	brand new	brighten
boat-hook	bombykol	boom town	bounties	brangler	brightly
boatlift	bona fide	boondock	bountith	branlike	brim-full
boatload	bonallie	boongary	bourtree	brassage	brimless
boat neck	bona-roba	bootable	boutique	brassard	brimming
boat race	bonavist	bootakin	bouzouki	brass hat	brim over
boat-tail	bondager	boot camp	bovarism	brassica	brindled
boat-yard	bond-land	Boot Hill	bovarize	brassier	brine-pan
bobachee	bondmaid	boot-hose	bovinely	brassies	bring low
bob-apple	bondsman	bootikin	bowelled	brassily	bring off
bobbinet	bondsmen	bootjack	bowenite	bratchet	bring out
bobby pin	bone-ache	boot-lace	boweries	bratling	brisling
bobolink	bonefire	bootlace	bowlfuls	brat pack	bristols
bobskate	bonefish	bootless	bowl game	brattery	britchel
bobsy-die	bonehead	bootlick	bowl over	brattice	Britonic
bobwhite	bone idle	boot-tree	bowsprit	brattish	broacher
bocconia	bone-lace	boozeroo	box-cloth	braunite	broad-axe
bodement	bone lazy	booziest	box elder	brawnier	broadish
Bode's law	boneless	boracite	box pleat	brazenly	broadway
bode well	bone-meal	borassus	box score	braziery	broccoli
bodeword	bonemeal	Bordeaux	box-thorn	brazilin	brochure
bodiless	bone-seed	bordello	boyishly	bread bin	brodekin
bodingly	bone-yard	borderer	Boy Scout	breakage	broderer
Bodleian	bongrace	bord-land	boy's-love	breaking	broidery
body blow	bonhomie	borecole	boys' play	break off	brokenly
bodyhood	bonhomme	borehole	B-picture	break out	brollies
body shop	Boniface	boresome	brabbler	breakout	bromelia
bodysuit	boniform	boringly	bracelet	breasted	bromelin
body type	boniness	borrower	brachial	breathed	bromidic
body wave	bonitary	borrow of	brachium	breather	Brompton
bodywork	bonneted	boss-eyed	brackeny	breeches	bronchia
body wrap	bonnibel	bossiest	brackish	breeding	bronchus
Boehmist	bonniest	boss-ship	braconid	breed out	bronzite
boehmite	bonsense	boss-shot	bracteal	breeze up	brood-hen
Boeotian	bons mots	bostangi	bractlet	breezier	broodier
boffinry	bonspiel	bosthoon	Bradbury	breezily	broodily
bog berry	bontebok	botanise	braggart	breloque	brookite
bogeyman	bony fish	botanist	braggery	brennage	brooklet
boggiest	boob tube	botanize	bragging	bretelle	brotulid
bog onion	boobyish	botchery	brahminy	bretessy	brougham
Bohairic	boogaloo	boteroll	braiding	brethren	brouhaha
Bohemian	boohooed	botflies	brain-box	breveted	brow-band
bohereen	bookable	both laws	brainbox	breviary	browbeat
boil away	bookcase	both ways	brain-fag	brewster	browless
boil down	book club	botryoid	brainier	Brewster	brown ale
boil over	book-fell	botrytis	brainily	Briarean	brown bag
boistous	book-hand	bottle-oh	brainish	Briareus	brown eye
bold-face	bookkeep	bottomed	brain-pan	bribable	brown fat
boldface	bookland	bottomer	brainpan	brickbat	Brownian
boldness	bookless	bottomry	brakeman	brickish	browning
Bolivian	booklike	bottom up	brakemen	brick-red	Browning
bollocks	bookling	botulism	brake pad	bridally	brownish
bollworm	book-lung	bouffant	brake van	bridalty	Brownism
boloneys	bookmark	bough-pot	brakevan	bride-ale	Brownist
Bolshies	book name	boughten	Bramleys	bride-bed	brown job
bolt-head	book page	bouillon	branched	bride-cup	brown-out

brown owl	bull-dust	burritos	bylander	calabaza	calypsos
brown rat	bulletin	burrower	bylawman	caladium	calyptra
brown top	bullfrog	burr-pump	by my hand	calamari	camalote
browsing	bullgine	bursitis	by myself	calamary	cambiums
brow tine	bullhead	burst out	by nature	calambac	camboose
bruilzie	bull-horn	bushbaby	by-passer	calamine	Cambrian
bruising	bullhorn	bush-bean	by reason	calamint	cameleer
Brumaire	bull huss	bushbuck	by rights	calamite	cameline
brumbies	bull-kelp	bush burn	Byronism	calamity	camellia
Brummies	bull-neck	bushfire	by spurts	calandra	cameloid
bruncher	bull-nose	bushiest	by square	calanoid	camelote
brunette	bullocky	bushless	byssuses	calathus	camerate
brushite	bull-pine	bushline	by starts	calcanea	camerist
brush off	bullring	bushment	by-street	calcanei	camisado
Brussels	bullrout	bush-rope	by the bye	calcific	Camisard
brutally	bullrush	bush-sick	by the way	calciner	camisole
brutedom	bull's-eye	bushveld	by weight	calcitic	camomile
bryology	bullshit	bush-walk	caatinga	calcrete	camoudie
bryonies	bull-weed	business	caballer	calc spar	campagna
bryozoan	bull-whip	buskined	Cabernet	calcspar	campaign
bryozoon	bullwort	bust a gut	cabin boy	calc-tuff	camp-fire
B Special	bully boy	busteous	cabining	calculus	campfire
bubaline	bully off	bustiest	Cabistan	calendar	camphene
bubblier	bullyrag	bustious	cable car	calender	camphine
buccally	buln-buln	bustuous	cable-ese	calfhood	campiest
buccinum	bumbaste	busybody	cableway	calfless	camp it up
bucellas	bum-clock	busyness	caboceer	calflike	camp oven
buckaroo	bum fluff	busywork	caboched	calf love	campshed
buckbean	bummaree	butanoic	cabochon	calfskin	camp-site
buck-bush	bump-ball	butanone	caboodle	calibred	campsite
bucketed	bumpiest	butcher's	caboshed	calicoes	campuses
buck-horn	bump into	butchery	cabotage	caliduct	camshaft
buckhorn	bum's rush	butoxide	cabriole	calipash	camstone
buck-jump	bum steer	butteris	cachalot	caliphal	Canadian
buckle to	buncombe	butter up	cachexia	Calippic	canaille
Buckley's	bundle up	butt-head	cachucha	callable	canalise
buckling	bun fight	buttoned	cacodoxy	callaloo	canalize
buckshee	bungalow	button up	cacology	call away	Canarese
buckshot	bungarra	buttress	cactuses	call back	Canarian
buckskin	bunged up	butt weld	cadastre	call down	canaries
Buddhism	bung-hole	but which	caddying	call-girl	canaster
Buddhist	bungling	butylate	cadenced	call home	cancelli
buddleia	bunny-hug	butylene	caducean	calliard	cancrine
budgeree	bunodont	butyrate	caduceus	calliope	cancroid
budgerow	buntline	butyrous	caducity	calliper	candidly
budgeted	buoyancy	buy money	caducous	call note	candy ass
buff coat	Burberry	buzz-bomb	caecitis	callosal	candy bar
buffeted	burglary	buzz-word	caesious	call-over	candy-man
buggiest	burgonet	buzzword	caesural	callowly	cane toad
bughouse	burgrave	by chance	caesuras	call sign	cane-work
Buginese	burgundy	by choice	café noir	call time	Canfield
bugology	buriable	by-corner	caffeine	call upon	can-hooks
building	Burkinan	by deputy	cafuffle	calmness	canicule
bulberry	burletta	by design	cage bird	Calor gas	caninity
bulblike	burliest	by dint of	cageling	calories	canister
bulfinch	burnable	by-effect	cage-work	calotype	canities
bulkhead	burn away	by George	caginess	calvados	cankered
bulkiest	burn down	by halves	cajolery	calvaria	cannabis
bullated	Burnsian	by heaven	cake-hole	calx vive	cannella
bull-dike	burnside	by inches	cakewalk	calycine	cannelon
bulldoze	burnt-out	by itself	calabash	calycled	cannibal

canniest	caracara	carrozzi	casually	cavalier	cerclage
cannikin	caracole	carry-all	casualty	cavatina	cerebral
cannonry	caragana	carry-cot	catacomb	cavayard	cerebrum
cannulae	carangid	carrycot	catalase	caveatee	cerement
cannulas	carapace	carrying	catalyse	caveator	ceremony
canoeing	carbamic	carry off	catalyst	cave bear	cernuous
canoeist	carbamyl	carry out	catalyze	cave-fish	cerotate
canoness	carbinol	Carshuni	catamite	cavelike	cerulean
canonise	carbolic	carstone	catapult	caverned	cervelat
canonist	carbonic	cart-body	cataract	cavesson	cervical
canonize	carbonyl	cartfuls	catch-all	cavilled	cervices
canon law	carboxyl	cart-load	catchfly	caviller	Cesarean
canoodle	carburet	cartload	catchier	cavitary	Cesarian
canopied	carcajou	cartoony	catchily	cavitate	cessavit
canopies	carcanet	cart-road	catching	cavities	cesspipe
canorous	carceral	cart-shed	catch out	cavy-yard	cesspool
can skill	cardamom	cart tail	catechin	cayenned	Cestrian
canstick	cardamum	cart-whip	catechol	cecidium	cetacean
cantator	card case	carucage	category	cecropia	ceterach
cant-hook	card game	carucate	catenary	Celarent	cetology
canticle	cardigan	caruncle	catenate	celature	chabutra
cantikoy	cardinal	carve out	catenoid	celeriac	cha-chaed
cant-line	cardines	caryatid	cateress	celerity	chaconne
cantonal	cardioid	Casanova	catering	celibacy	chadless
cantoned	carditis	cascabel	Cathayan	celibate	chafe-wax
cantoris	card-room	casebook	cathedra	cellared	chaffron
cantrail	card vote	case-load	catheter	cellarer	Chagatai
canzonet	carefree	caseload	cathetus	cellaret	chagigah
Caodaism	careless	casemate	cathexes	cellated	chainlet
Caodaist	Carelian	casement	cathexis	cell-like	chainsaw
capacity	caretake	case-shot	cathodal	cellular	chain-saw
capeador	care-worn	case-weed	cathodic	cell wall	chair-bed
Cape cart	careworn	casework	catholic	cembalos	chair-car
capeline	cargador	case-worm	Catholic	cementer	chairman
capeskin	cargoose	cashable	cat-house	cementum	chairmen
Capetian	carillon	cash book	Catiline	cemetery	chalazae
Cape-weed	carinate	cash card	cationic	Cencibel	chalazal
capitana	caritive	cashcard	Catonian	cenobite	Chaldaic
capitano	carmined	cash crop	cat's-foot	cenotaph	Chaldean
capitate	carminic	cash desk	cat's-head	Cenozoic	chaldron
capitula	carnally	cash down	cat's-meat	censurer	chaliced
cap-money	Carnatic	cash flow	cat's-tail	censuses	chalkier
caponier	carnauba	cashless	catstick	centaury	chalk out
caponise	carneous	cashmere	cattiest	centavos	chalk-pit
caponize	carnifex	cash-sale	cattleya	centrale	challahs
capotted	carnival	cassette	Catullan	centring	chaloner
cap-paper	Carolean	Castalie	Caucasic	centrism	chalonic
capriole	Carolina	castanet	caucused	centrist	chaloupe
capriped	Caroline	cast away	caucuses	centrode	Chambéry
caproate	carolled	castaway	caudally	centroid	chambray
caprylic	caroller	cast down	caudated	centuple	champain
caprylyl	carotene	casteism	caudicle	cephalic	champers
capsicum	carousal	casteist	caudillo	cephalin	champion
capsizal	carousel	castelet	caught up	cephalon	chance on
capstone	carouser	castelry	cauldron	ceramics	chancery
capsular	carpeted	cast iron	caulicle	ceramist	chancier
captious	car phone	castling	causable	cerastes	chancily
capturer	carplike	cast lots	causally	ceration	chandler
capuchin	carriage	castrate	causerie	ceratite	change up
Capuchin	carriole	castrati	causeway	Cerberus	chanties
capybara	carritch	castrato	cautious	cercaria	chaology

chapatti	chemosis	chip shot	Christer	cingular	classier
chapbook	chempaka	chirayta	Christie	cingulum	classify
chapeaux	chemurgy	chiretta	Christly	cinnabar	classily
chapelry	chenille	chirpier	chromate	cinnamic	classism
chaperon	chequeen	chirpily	chromite	cinnamon	classist
chapiter	Cherokee	chirping	chromium	cinnamyl	class war
chaplain	cherries	chirrupy	chromone	cinqfoil	clattery
chapless	cherubic	chit-chat	chromous	cipherer	Claudian
chapping	cherubim	chittack	chrysene	Circinus	clausula
characin	Cheshire	chitties	chthonic	circlage	clavated
charcoal	chessman	chivalry	chubbier	circling	clavecin
chariest	chessmen	chloasma	chubbily	circuity	clavicle
charisma	chess set	chlorate	chuckler	circular	claviger
charlady	chestful	chloride	chuck off	circuses	claw back
charlock	chestier	chlorine	chuck out	circussy	claw-back
charmful	chestily	chlorite	chugging	cirriped	clawback
charming	chestnut	chloroma	chummage	Ciskeian	clawless
charring	cheverel	chlorous	chummery	cislunar	clawlike
Chartism	chewable	choanoid	chummier	cisterna	claylike
Chartist	chewiest	Choctaws	chummily	cis-trans	claymore
chasseur	chew over	choicely	chump end	cistvaen	clay pipe
chastely	Cheyenne	choirboy	chumship	citation	Clayton's
chastise	Chiantis	choirman	chunkier	citatory	cleading
chastity	chiasmus	choirmen	chupatti	citified	clean-cut
chastize	chiastic	choir nun	chupatty	citruses	cleanish
chasuble	Chibchan	choke off	churchly	city desk	clean out
chatelet	chicaner	chokidar	churinga	city farm	clean-run
chatline	Chicanos	chokiest	churlish	cityfied	cleanser
chatroom	chick-pea	choleric	churning	city gent	clearage
chat show	chickpea	choliamb	churn out	city hall	clear-air
chattery	chiefdom	chondrin	churn-owl	cityless	clear-cut
chattier	chiefess	choo-choo	chutneys	city page	clearing
chattily	chiffony	choosier	chutzpah	cityward	clearish
chatting	childbed	choosily	chylific	civet cat	clear off
chauffer	childish	chop-chop	chyluria	civil day	clear-out
chaunter	children	choppier	ciabatta	civilian	clearway
chawdron	chiliasm	choppily	cibarial	civilise	cleavage
cheapish	chiliast	chopping	cibarian	civility	cleavers
cheatery	chillier	chop suey	cibarium	civilize	clecking
chebulic	chillies	chopsuey	ciborium	civil law	cleft lip
checkers	chillily	choragic	cicatrix	civil war	cleidoic
check-nut	chill out	choragus	cicelies	clabbery	clematis
check off	chilopod	chorally	cicerone	clackety	clemency
check out	chimaera	chordate	ciceroni	cladding	clencher
checkout	chimeric	chording	cicisbeo	claimant	clergess
check sum	chimneys	chore-boy	ciderist	clambake	clergies
checksum	China ink	choregus	ciderkin	clammier	clerical
chedarim	Chinaman	choriamb	ci-devant	clammily	clerihew
chee-chee	Chinamen	C horizon	cigarito	clamming	clerkage
cheekier	China tea	chorused	ciliated	clangour	clerkdom
cheekily	chin-chin	choruses	Cilician	clannish	clerkess
cheerful	chinkara	chota peg	Cilicism	clanship	clerkish
cheerier	Chinkies	chouette	cimarron	clansman	cleruchy
cheerily	chinless	choultry	cimbalom	clansmen	cleveite
cheese it	Chinooks	chow-chow	Cimbrian	clap-dish	cleverer
cheesier	chins wag	chow mein	cimmaron	clapping	cleverly
cheewink	chipmunk	Chrisake	cinchona	claptrap	clew-line
chelator	Chippewa	chrismal	cincture	claqueur	cliental
cheliped	chippies	chrismon	cineaste	clarence	clientry
Chellean	chipping	Christed	cinéaste	clarinet	climatal
chemical	chip-shop	christen	cinerary	Clarisse	climatic

clinamen	Club Soda	cockerel	coiffure	colt foal	complect
clincher	clubster	cock-eyed	coigning	colthood	complete
clingier	clueless	cockiest	coinable	colubrid	complice
clinging	clumpier	cock-loft	coincide	Columban	complied
clinical	clumpish	cockneys	co-inhere	columbic	complier
clinkery	clumsier	cock's egg	coistrel	Columbus	complies
clinking	clumsily	cockspur	coke-oven	columnal	compline
clip-clop	clunkier	cocksure	colander	columnar	complish
clipping	clupeoid	cocktail	colation	columned	composal
cliquier	cly-faker	cocoanut	Colchian	Comanche	composed
cliquish	clypeate	cocobolo	cold bath	comatose	composer
cliquism	cnidocil	coco palm	cold call	combated	compotus
clitoral	coach-box	coco-plum	cold cuts	combater	compound
clitoris	coach-dog	cocorite	cold deck	comb-back	compress
cloaking	coachful	code book	cold feet	combined	comprise
clobiosh	coachman	code name	cold lead	combiner	compulse
clock off	coachmen	codiaeum	cold meat	combless	computer
cloddish	coaction	codified	coldness	comblike	computor
clodpate	coactive	codifier	cold-slaw	come away	computus
clodpole	coadjust	codifies	coldslaw	come back	comrogue
clodpoll	coagency	codology	cold snap	comeback	con amore
cloggier	coagment	codomain	cold sore	comedian	conarium
clogging	coagulin	co-domini	cold wave	comedies	conation
cloister	coagulum	codpiece	cold work	comedist	conative
clonally	coal dust	co-driver	colerake	come down	concause
clopping	coalesce	cod seine	coleseed	comedown	conceder
closable	coalface	cod's-head	coleslaw	come home	conceity
closed-in	coal fire	co-editor	colewort	come into	conceive
close off	coalfish	coeffect	coliform	comelier	concerti
close out	coal-hole	coelomic	coliseum	comelily	concerto
close-run	coalizer	coenurus	collagen	comeling	concetto
close-set	coal mine	coenzyme	collapse	come near	conchies
closeted	coalmine	coercion	collards	come over	conchoid
cloth-cap	coal-sack	coercive	collared	cometary	conclave
clothier	coal-seam	co-estate	collator	come true	conclude
clothing	coarsely	coevally	colleger	come upon	concrete
clotpole	coarsish	coextend	collider	comfiest	condense
clotting	coassume	cofactor	colliery	comfreys	condoler
clottish	coatless	coffered	collogue	comingle	condoner
cloudier	coatroom	cofferer	colloque	comitant	conducti
cloudily	coat-tail	cofferet	colloquy	comitial	condylar
cloudlet	coattest	coffined	colluder	comities	conelike
clownery	co-author	cogently	collyria	commando	conferee
clownish	cobaltic	cogitate	colobine	commence	conferva
cloyless	cobwebby	cognatic	colobium	commenda	confetti
cloysome	Coca-Cola	cognizee	coloboma	commerce	confider
clubbier	coccagee	cognizor	colonial	commoner	confined
clubbing	Cocceian	cognomen	colonies	commonly	confiner
clubbish	coccidia	cognosce	colonise	commonty	conflate
clubbism	coccyges	cognovit	colonist	communal	conflict
clubbist	coccyxes	cogueful	colonize	communer	confocal
club foot	cochleae	cog-wheel	colopexy	commuter	confound
club-haul	cochlear	cogwheel	colophon	comozant	confrère
clubland	cochlite	cohelper	colorant	compadre	confront
clublike	cockaded	coherent	coloring	compages	confused
clubmate	cockatoo	cohering	colossal	comparer	confuter
clubmoss	cock-bead	cohesion	colossus	compesce	congaing
club-root	cock-bill	cohesive	colotomy	compiler	congener
clubroot	cockboat	cohobate	coloured	compital	congiary
club-rush	cock crow	coiffeur	colourer	complain	conglobe
club soda	cockcrow	coiffing	colour in	compleat	Congoese

Congo pea	convulse	cordwain	corsetry	courtesy	cram-full
congrats	cony-fish	cordwood	Corsican	courtier	cramming
congress	conynger	core area	cortical	courtlet	cramoisy
Congreve	cony-wool	co-regent	cortices	court-man	crampoon
conicity	cooeeing	coreless	cortisol	couscous	crane-fly
conicoid	cooingly	core loss	corundum	cousinly	craneman
conidial	cookable	core time	corvette	cousinry	craniate
conidium	cookbook	core tool	Corybant	covalent	craniums
coniform	cook-camp	Corfiote	Corycian	covenant	crankier
conjoint	cookless	Coriolis	coryphée	Coventry	crankily
conjugal	cook-maid	corkiest	cosecant	coverage	crankous
conjunct	cookshop	corklike	cosherer	coverall	crankpin
conjurer	cookware	cork lino	cosiness	covercle	crannied
conjuror	coolabah	cork tree	cosmetic	covering	crannies
conniver	coolamon	corkwing	cosmical	coverlet	crap game
conodont	coolibah	corkwood	cosseted	co-versed	crappier
conoidal	cooliman	corn baby	costated	covertly	crapping
conoidic	coolness	corn-ball	costless	coveting	crashing
conquest	coonjine	corn beef	costlier	covetise	crash pad
conserve	coonskin	corn cake	costmary	covetous	crassula
consider	coon song	corn chip	cost-plus	covinous	crateful
consoler	co-optate	corn crib	cost push	cowardly	crateman
consommé	co-option	corneous	costumer	cowberry	crateral
conspire	co-optive	cornered	cosy up to	cow-cocky	cratonic
constant	co-ossify	cornerer	cot death	cow-heart	cravenly
constate	cop a plea	cornetcy	cotectic	cow-hitch	craw-craw
construe	copastor	cornetti	co-tenant	cow-horse	crawfish
consular	cophosis	cornetto	coterell	cow-house	crayfish
consulta	copiable	corn-flag	cot-house	cowl neck	craziest
consumed	coplanar	corn-husk	cotsetla	co-worker	crazy ant
consumer	copperas	corniced	Cotswold	co-writer	creakier
consumpt	copperer	corniche	cottaged	cow shark	creakily
contango	coppiced	cornicle	cottager	cow-wheat	cream bun
contempt	coprosma	corniest	cottagey	coxalgia	creamery
contessa	copulate	Corn Laws	cotterel	coxalgic	cream ice
continua	copyable	corn lily	cottoner	coxiness	creamier
continue	copybook	cornmeal	cotton on	coxswain	creamily
continuo	copydesk	corn-pipe	cotton to	cozenage	cream nut ·
contline	copy-edit	corn pone	cotton up	crabbier	cream off
contorni	copyhold	corn-rent	cotyloid	crabbily	cream tea
contorno	copyread	corn rose	couchant	crabbing	creatine
contract	coq au vin	cornrows	couching	crab-hole	creation
contrail	coquetry	corn silk	coughing	crablike	creative
contrair	coquette	corn smut	cough out	crabmeat	creatrix
contrary	coquitos	corn snow	could use	crab's-eye	creature
contrast	coracoid	cornuted	coulisse	crab tree	crebrity
contrate	coradgee	corn-worm	coumarin	crabwise	credence
con-trick	coraleta	coronach	countess	crabwood	credenda
contrite	coralled	coronary	counties	crackers	credenza
contrive	corallum	coronate	counting	cracking	credible
convener	coral pea	coronium	countour	crack-jaw	credibly
convenor	coral rag	coronoid	count out	crackled	credited
converge	coral-red	corporal	count ten	cracknel	creditor
converse	Coramine	corporas	coup-cart	crackpot	creeklet
conversi	cordelle	corpsman	coupling	cradling	creelful
convexly	cordiner	corpuses	couponed	craftier	creepage
conveyer	cordless	corridor	couraged	craftily	creepier
conveyor	cordlike	corrival	courante	craggier	creepily
convince	cordoned	corroder	courbash	craggily	creeping
convolve	cordovan	corselet	coursing	cragsman	cremator
convoyer	corduroy	corseted	court-day	cragsmen	crenated

crenelle	crossbar	crutched	cupidone	Cuthbert	cytosine
crenellé	crossbow	cruzados	cup of tea	cuticula	czarevna
creodont	cross bun	cruzeiro	cupolaed	cutinize	czaritsa
creolian	cross-cut	cry havoc	cupreous	cut it out	dabchick
creolise	cross fox	cryingly	cup shake	cutlings	dactylic
creolism	crossing	cryolite	cupulate	cut loose	dado-rail
creolist	crosslet	cryonics	curacies	cut no ice	Daedalic
creolize	cross-ply	cryopump	curaçoas	cut paper	daemonic
creosote	cross-sea	cryostat	curarine	cut-price	daffiest
crepitus	cross-tie	cryptand	curarize	cutpurse	daffodil
crescent	crossway	cryptate	curassow	cut short	daftness
crescive	crostini	cry quits	curatage	cuttable	dageraad
crespine	crotalum	cry uncle	curation	cuttanee	Dagestan
cresting	crotched	C Special	curative	cut-under	daggered
cresylic	crotchet	cubature	curatory	cutwater	daggiest
cretonne	crottels	cube root	curatrix	cutwithe	daimonic
crevasse	croucher	cubiform	curbless	cyanelle	dainteth
creviced	croupade	cubistic	curb roof	cyaneous	daintier
crew neck	croupier	cuboidal	curculio	cyanidin	daintify
cribbage	crousely	Cub Scout	curdlike	cyanogen	daintily
cribbing	crow-bait	cuckoldy	cureless	cyanosed	daintith
cribrose	crow-bill	cucumber	curlicue	cyanosis	daiquiri
cribwork	crowd out	cucurbit	curliest	cyanotic	dairying
Crichton	crowfoot	cuddikie	curlless	cyanuric	dairyman
crimeful	crown all	cuddlier	curl-pate	cyathium	dairymen
criminal	crown cap	cudgerie	curlycue	cybersex	daker-hen
crimpage	crowning	cuffless	currance	cycadean	Dalcroze
crimpily	crownlet	cuff link	currency	Cycladic	dalesman
crimsony	crown rot	cufuffle	curricle	cyclamen	dalesmen
cringing	crown saw	culching	cursedly	cycleway	dalmatic
crinière	crow step	cul-de-sac	curseful	cyclical	dal segno
crippler	cruciate	culicide	cursillo	cyclitis	Damascus
crispate	crucible	culicine	cursitor	cyclonic	damnable
crispier	crucifer	culinary	curtness	cyclopes	damnably
crispish	crucifix	culottes	curtseys	Cyclopes	damn-fool
cristate	cruddier	culpable	curtsies	cyclopia	damn well
criteria	crude oil	culpably	curvated	Cyclopic	Damocles
critical	crudités	cultigen	curvedly	cyclosis	damp down
critique	cruelest	cultivar	curveted	cydippid	dampener
crivvens	cruelled	cultrate	curviest	cylinder	dampness
croakier	crueller	cultural	cush-cush	cymatium	danalite
croakily	cruellie	cultured	cushiest	cynicism	dancette
Croatian	crumb-bum	culverin	cushiony	cynodont	dancetté
croceate	crumbier	cumacean	Cushitic	cynology	dandiest
crockard	crumblet	Cumanian	cusparia	cynosure	dandilly
crockery	crumhorn	cumarone	cuspated	cyprides	dandling
crocoite	crummier	cumberer	cuspidal	cyprinid	dandruff
crocuses	crummily	Cumbrian	cuspides	Cypriote	dandydom
crofting	crumpled	cumbrous	cuspidor	cypselae	dandyish
cromlech	crumpler	cum laude	cussedly	Cyrenaic	dandyism
cromorne	cruncher	cumulate	cuss word	Cyrenian	Danebrog
Cromwell	crunodal	cumulous	custardy	Cyrillic	Danegeld
cronyism	crusader	Cunarder	custodee	cysteine	dane-hole
crookdom	crush bar	cuneated	custodes	cystitis	danewort
crookery	crush-hat	cuneatic	customal	cystlike	dangling
crookish	crushing	cuniform	customer	cytaster	Danishry
crop-full	crush-pen	cunjevoi	custumal	cytidine	dankness
crop-mark	crustate	cupboard	cut a dash	cytisine	danseuse
crop-over	crustier	cupelled	cuteness	cytogamy	Danubian
cropping	crustily	Cup Final	cut glass	cytokine	Daphnean
crop-sick	crustose	cupidity	cutgrass	cytology	dapperly

Darbyite	dead lift	deceiver	defatted	demersal	depilate
daringly	deadlily	December	defeater	Demetian	depilous
Dark Ages	deadline	decemvir	defecate	demijohn	deplorer
dark blue	dead load	decenary	defector	demi-lion	depolish
dark days	deadlock	decennia	defender	demilune	deponent
darkener	dead loss	decenter	defensor	demister	deportee
darkfall	dead-melt	decently	deferent	demitted	depraver
darkling	deadness	decentre	deferral	demiurge	deprival
darkmans	dead shot	decidual	deferred	demobbed	deprived
darkness	dead time	decigram	deferrer	democrat	depriver
darkroom	dead well	decimate	defiance	demo-disc	depurate
darksome	dead wood	decipher	defilade	demolish	deputies
dark star	dead work	decision	definite	demoness	deputise
Dartmoor	de-aerate	decisive	deflater	demoniac	deputize
dart-moth	deafened	deck-beam	deflator	demonial	deration
dartrous	deaf mute	deck-hand	deflexed	demonian	Derby day
dash down	deafness	deckhand	deflower	demonise	Derby Day
dastardy	dealable	declared	defluent	demonish	derelict
data bank	dealbate	declarer	deforcer	demonism	de-rigged
database	deal-fish	déclassé	deforest	demonist	derision
datacoms	dealings	decliner	deformed	demonize	derisive
data link	deal with	declutch	deformer	De Morgan	derisory
data type	deanship	decohere	defrayal	demotion	derivate
datebook	dearborn	decolour	defrayer	dempster	derogate
dateless	dearie me	decorate	defreeze	demurely	derrière
date line	Dear John	decorous	defrost	demurest	descaler
date-mark	dearness	decouple	deftness	demurity	describe
date palm	deathbed	decrease	defusion	demurral	descried
date-plum	death cap	decrepit	degasify	demurred	descrier
date rape	death cup	decretal	degassed	demurrer	descries
datively	death-day	decuplet	degraded	demyship	descript
datolite	deathful	decurion	degrader	denarius	descrive
daturine	death-ray	decurved	degrease	denatant	deseeder
daubster	death row	decypher	dehorner	denature	deselect
daughter	death tax	Dedalean	dehorter	denazify	deserted
daunting	deaurate	dedendum	deicidal	dendrite	deserter
Davy lamp	debagged	dedicant	deionise	dendroid	desertic
dawn raid	debarred	dedicate	deionize	dene-hole	deserved
daybreak	debility	dedition	dejected	de-netted	deserver
day by day	debitage	dedolent	delation	deniable	designed
daydream	debiting	deedless	Delaware	denizate	designer
daylight	deblazon	deed poll	delectus	dennebol	desilver
day shift	debonair	deemster	delegacy	denotata	desirous
day-to-day	deboshed	deep-down	delegant	denotive	desition
dazzling	debruise	deepener	delegate	denounce	desk lamp
deaconry	debtless	deep-etch	deletion	Denshire	desolate
dead beat	debugged	deep kiss	delicacy	dentalia	despatch
deadbeat	debugger	deep-laid	delicate	dentally	despisal
dead body	debunker	deepmost	delirium	dentaria	despiser
deadbolt	debussed	deepness	delivery	dentated	despotat
dead-born	debutant	deep-read	Delphian	dentelle	despotic
dead cert	débutant	deepsome	delusion	denticle	destinal
dead duck	decadary	deep tank	delusive	dentinal	destrier
deadener	decadent	deer-ball	delusory	denudate	destruct
deadfall	decalage	deer-horn	delustre	deny bail	desyatin
dead-fire	decanate	deer-lick	demagogy	departed	detached
dead hand	decanter	deerlike	demander	departer	detailed
dead-head	decarchy	deer-park	démarche	depender	detailer
deadhead	decatize	deerskin	demented	depeople	detainee
dead heat	deceased	de-excite	dementia	depicter	detainer
deadlier	decedent	defamous	demerara	depictor	detassel
				demerger	

detecter	dial-bird	diecious	dioecism	discless	disponee
detector	diallage	diederik	Diogenes	disclike	disponer
deterred	dialling	diegesis	Diogenic	disclose	disponge
detester	diallist	diegetic	Dionysic	discolor	disposal
dethrone	dialogic	dieldrin	diopside	discount	disposed
detonate	dialogue	dielytra	dioptase	discover	disposer
detoxify	dial tone	dieresis	dioptric	discreet	dispread
detrital	dialyser	Dies irae	dioramic	discrete	disprize
detrited	dialyses	diestrum	dioritic	discrown	disproof
detritic	dialysis	dietetic	diphasic	discuses	disprove
detritus	dialytic	diffract	diphenyl	diseased	dispunct
detrusor	diamanté	diffuser	diplegia	disedify	dispunge
deuce ace	diameter	diffusor	diplexer	disembed	disputer
deucedly	dianetic	digamist	diploidy	disenact	disquiet
deuce set	dianthus	digamous	diploma'd	disendow	disrober
deuteric	diapalma	digenean	diplomat	disenjoy	disseise
deuteron	diapason	digenite	diplopia	disfaith	disseize
devalued	diapause	digester	diplopic	disflesh	disserve
devalues	diapente	diggings	diplopod	disfrock	dissever
devaster	diaphane	digitate	dippiest	disgavel	dissight
deverbal	diaphone	digitise	dip slope	disgorge	dissolve
deviable	diaphony	digitize	dipstick	disgrace	dissuade
deviance	diapiric	dihedral	dipteral	disgrade	distally
deviancy	diarchal	dihybrid	dipteran	disguise	distance
deviator	diarchic	dihydric	Dircaean	dishevel	distancy
devildom	diascope	dikaryon	directee	dishevel	distaste
deviless	Diaspora	diketone	directly	dishfuls	distinct
deviling	diaspore	Dilantin	director	dishiest	distract
devilish	diastase	dilatant	direness	dishoard	distrain
devilism	diastema	dilatate	dirgeful	dishonor	distrait
devilize	diastole	dilation	diriment	dishorse	distress
devilkin	diastral	dilative	dirt bike	dishouse	district
devilled	diastyle	dilatory	dirtiest	disinter	distrust
devil ray	diatomic	diligent	dirtless	disjoint	disunify
deviltry	diatonic	dill weed	dirt road	disjunct	disunion
devolute	diatreme	dillybag	dirty dog	diskette	disunite
Devonian	diatribe	dilution	dirtyish	diskless	disunity
devotion	diazepam	dilutive	disabled	disk pack	disvalue
devourer	diazinon	diluvial	disabuse	disliker	ditement
devoutly	diborane	diluvian	disagree	dislodge	ditheism
dewberry	dicacity	diluvium	disallow	disloyal	ditheist
dewiness	dicastic	dimerise	disannex	dismally	ditherer
dew point	dicentra	dimerize	disannul	dismarry	dithying
dew-snail	dichoree	dimerous	disapply	dismayer	ditty bag
dewy-eyed	dichotic	dimethyl	disarmer	dismoded	ditty box
dextrose	dichroic	Dimetian	disarray	dismount	diuresis
dextrous	Dickensy	diminish	disaster	Disneyfy	diuretic
dey-house	dickerer	diminute	disavail	disorder	divagate
dey-woman	dickhead	dimities	disbench	disowner	divalent
dhu stone	dickiest	diner-out	disboard	dispatch	dive-bomb
diabasic	dicky bow	dingbats	disbound	dispeace	diverger
diabetes	dicrotic	ding-dong	disbowel	dispense	diversly
diabetic	dictamen	ding down	disbrain	dispermy	diverter
diabolic	dictator	dinghies	disburse	disperse	divertor
diabolos	didactic	dingiest	discandy	dispetal	dividant
diacetic	didactyl	dinkiest	discette	dispiece	dividend
diaconal	didapper	Dinky car	discharm	dispirit	divi-divi
diaculum	diddicoy	dinky-die	discinct	displace	dividual
diagnose	didrachm	dinosaur	disciple	displant	divinely
diagonal	didymium	dintless	disclaim	displode	divinest
diagraph	didymous	diocesan	disclass	displume	divinify

divinise	doghouse	donation	*doublure*	downward	dreadful
divinity	dog-hutch	Donatism	doubtful	downwarp	dreamery
divinize	dog Latin	Donatist	doubting	downwash	dreamful
division	dog-leech	donative	douçaine	downwell	dreamier
divisive	dogmatic	donatory	doughboy	downwind	dreamily
divisory	do-gooder	donatrix	doughier	down with	dreamish
divorcee	dog's-bane	doneness	doughnut	downzone	drearier
divorcée	dogsbody	do no harm	doum-palm	Dowsabel	drearily
divorcer	dog-shore	do no less	douppion	doxology	dreggish
divulger	dogshore	do-nought	dourness	do you see	dreichly
dizygous	dog-sleep	Don Pedro	douzaine	doziness	drencher
dizziest	dog's life	don't-care	douzeper	drabbest	drengage
Dizzyite	dog's meat	don't-know	dovecote	drabbish	dressage
djellaba	dog's-nose	doolally	dove-eyed	drabbler	dressier
DNA virus	dog's-tail	doombook	dove grey	drabness	dressing
do a Melba	dog-stone	doom-ring	dove-hawk	dracaena	dress out
do a mooch	dog-stove	doomsday	dovelike	drachmae	dribbler
do battle	dog-tired	doomsman	doveling	drachmas	dribblet
dobchick	dog-tooth	doomster	dovetail	draconic	driftage
Docetism	dog-trick	doom-tree	dove tree	Draconid	drift-ice
Docetist	dogwatch	doorbell	dowdiest	draftier	drifting
dochmiac	dog-weary	door-case	dowdyish	draggier	drift-net
dochmius	dog-whelk	doorcase	dowdyism	dragging	drift-pin
docilely	dohickey	door head	dowelled	drag-hook	driftway
docility	do homage	door-knob	dowfness	drag-hunt	drilling
docimasy	Doketism	doorknob	Dow–Jones	drag-line	Drinamyl
docketed	doldrums	doorless	downbear	dragline	drinkery
dockland	dolerite	doornail	downbeat	dragoman	drinking
dockside	dolesome	doorpost	downcast	dragomen	drink off
docksman	dolichos	door-sill	downcome	dragonet	drip-drip
dockyard	do-little	doorsman	down east	drag race	drip-drop
doctoral	doll-baby	doorstep	downface	drag-rope	drip-feed
doctorer	dollhood	doorstop	downfall	dragsman	drippier
doctorly	dolliest	doorward	downfold	dragster	drippily
doctress	dolloped	dooryard	downhaul	drainage	dripping
doctrine	dollship	dopamine	down helm	drama-doc	drip tray
document	dolly-bag	dopchick	downhill	dramatic	drisheen
doddered	dolly mop	dope-ring	downhole	Drambuie	drivable
dodderel	dolly peg	dopester	down-home	drammock	drive off
dodderer	dolly pot	dopiness	downiest	dram-shop	drive out
dodecane	dolly-tub	dormancy	downland	dratting	driveway
dodgiest	dolmades	dormered	down lead	draughty	drollery
do dirt to	dolmenic	dormient	downless	Dravidic	drollish
Dodonean	dolomite	dormouse	downlike	drawable	dromical
do duty as	doloroso	dormy one	downlink	draw back	drone-bee
doegling	dolorous	dorsally	download	drawback	drone-fly
dogberry	domainal	do scathe	downmost	drawcard	drongoes
Dogberry	domanial	dosseret	downpipe	drawcord	droopier
dog-cheap	domelike	dotation	downplay	draw down	droopily
dog-daisy	Domesday	do the ton	downpour	drawdown	drop away
dog-eared	domestic	dotiness	downrate	draw-gate	drop back
dogeship	domicile	dotingly	downrush	draw-kiln	drop dead
dog-faced	dominant	dot plant	downside	draw-leaf	drop down
dog fence	dominate	dottable	downsize	draw-loom	drop goal
dogfight	domineer	dottered	Downsman	draw lots	drop-head
doggedly	dominial	dotterel	down time	drawn-out	drophead
doggerel	dominion	dottiest	downtime	draw rein	drop into
dog-goned	dominoed	douanier	down town	drawstop	drop-keel
dog-grass	dominoes	double up	downtown	draw-well	drop kick
dog-grate	Dom Pedro	doubling	downtrod	dray-cart	drop-leaf
doggy bag	donatary	doubloon	downturn	dray-road	dropless

droplike	dubbined	dumpiest	dynamist	eburnean	effluvia
drop-line	duberous	dumpling	dynamite	ecaudate	effusion
drop on to	dubitant	dumpoked	dynamize	Ecce Homo	effusive
dropping	dubitate	dumpster	dynastic	ecclesia	eftsoons
drop-ripe	Dubliner	dump tank	dynatron	ecdysial	egestion
drop-seed	Dubonnet	duncedom	dysgenic	ecdysone	egestive
drop shot	ducatoon	duncical	dyslalia	ecgonine	egg-bound
dropside	Duchenne	dun-diver	dyslexia	echinate	egg-crate
dropsied	duchesse	dungaree	dyslexic	echinite	egg cream
dropsies	duck arse	dung-cart	dyspathy	echinoid	egg-dance
drop-tank	duckbill	dung-fork	dyspepsy	echogram	egg-eater
drop test	duck-dive	dung-heap	dyspnoea	echoless	eggplant
dropwise	duck-hawk	dunghill	dystocia	eclectic	egg sauce
dropwort	duckling	dung-worm	dystonia	eclipser	eggshell
drop zone	duckmeat	dunnakin	dystonic	eclipsis	egg-slice
droughty	duck-mole	dunniken	dystopia	ecliptic	egg-spoon
drown out	duck's-egg	dunstone	dytiscid	eclogite	egg-timer
drowsier	duck-shot	duodecad	dytiscus	eclosion	egg-tooth
drowsily	duck soup	duodenal	Dzongkha	ecocidal	egg-whisk
drubbing	ducktail	duodenum	eagle eye	eco-label	egg white
drudgery	duck-walk	duologue	eagle owl	ecologic	ego-ideal
drug bust	duckweed	dupeable	eagle ray	economic	egoistic
druggery	ductible	duplexer	ear-biter	ecophene	egomania
druggies	ductless	duration	ear drops	Ecotopia	Egyptian
drugging	ductwork	durative	Earl Grey	ecstasis	E horizon
druggist	duelling	duskiest	earliest	ecstatic	eicosane
drugless	duellist	duskness	earlship	Ecthesis	eidently
Druidess	duetting	Dussehra	earlyish	ectoderm	eidolons
Druidism	duettino	dust-bath	earnings	ectoloph	eighteen
drumbeat	duettist	dust bowl	earphone	ecumenic	eighthly
drumfire	duffadar	dustcart	earpiece	edacious	eighties
drum fish	dukeling	dust-coat	ear-shell	eddyless	Einstein
drumhead	dukeship	dust down	earth god	eddy-wind	either-or
drum into	Dukhobor	dustheap	earthier	edentate	ejection
drumming	dulcetly	dustiest	earthily	edgeless	ejective
drum roll	dulciana	dustless	earth-man	edge-rail	ekistics
drunkard	dulcimer	dust-shot	earth-nut	edge-tool	elasipod
drunkery	dulcinea	dust-trap	earth-pig	edgeways	elastane
drunkish	dulcitol	Dutch act	earth-wax	edge well	elastase
drupelet	dull-head	Dutch cap	ease away	edgewise	elatedly
druzhina	dullness	Dutch hoe	easeless	edginess	elbowing
dry-clean	dumb ague	Dutchify	easement	edifying	elbow-pad
dry cough	dumb-bell	Dutchman	easiness	editress	el cheapo
dry death	dumb cane	Dutchmen	easterly	educable	Eldonian
dry-flied	dumb chum	dutiable	Eastlake	educated	Eldonine
dry-flies	dumb down	dutiless	eastland	educator	eldorado
dry goods	dumb-dumb	duty-free	eastmost	educible	El Dorado
dry joint	dumbhead	duty-paid	East Side	eduction	eldritch
dry light	dumb-iron	duxelles	eastward	eductive	election
dry-nurse	dumbness	dwarfish	East–West	eel-grass	elective
dry plate	dumb peal	dwarfism	east wind	eelgrass	electret
dry-point	dumb play	dwelling	easy-care	eel-spear	electric
dry prune	dumb show	dybbukim	easy game	eeriness	electron
dry scall	dumbshow	dye-house	easy meat	effecter	electros
dry shave	dum casta	dye laser	eateries	effector	electrum
dry slope	dumfound	dyer's oak	eat pussy	effendis	elegance
dry spell	dummerer	dyestuff	eau-de-Nil	efferent	elegancy
dry steam	dummkopf	dying god	eau-de-vie	efficacy	elegiast
dry-stone	dummy run	dynamics	Ebenezer	effigial	elenchus
drystone	dummy tit	dynamise	Ebionite	effigies	elenctic
dualling	dumosity	dynamism	ebullism	effluent	eleolite

Eleonora	eminency	encolour	enleague	enuresis	epistasy
elephant	emissary	encomium	enlistee	enuretic	epistler
eleusine	emissile	encrinal	enlister	envassal	epistoma
elevated	emission	encrinus	enmarble	envelope	epistyle
elevator	emissive	encroach	enmities	enviable	epitasis
elevener	emitting	encumber	enmuffle	enviably	epitaxis
eleventh	emmarble	encyclic	enneagon	environs	epitheca
elf-arrow	emmarvel	encypher	ennobler	envisage	epitomic
elf-shoot	Emmental	endamage	Enochian	envision	epitopic
Elgarian	emoticon	endanger	enormity	Enzedder	epitrite
elicited	empacket	endarken	enormous	enzootic	epitrope
elicitor	empanada	endemial	enquirer	éolienne	epizooty
eligible	empathic	endemism	enravish	eolithic	eponymic
eligibly	emphases	endermic	enricher	epanodos	eponymus
eliquate	emphasis	end grain	enrolled	ependyma	epopoeia
elk-hound	emphatic	end it all	enrollee	ephebeum	epsomite
ellipses	empierce	endocarp	ensample	ephectic	eptitude
ellipsis	employee	endoderm	ensconce	ephemera	epulotic
elliptic	employée	endoderm	enscroll	Ephesian	epyllion
elongate	employer	endogamy	ensearch	Ephesine	equaeval
eloquent	empocket	endogeny	ensemble	ephorate	equalise
elsewhen	empoison	endorsee	enshadow	epibiont	equalist
elsewise	empolder	endorser	ensheath	epiblast	equality
eludible	emporial	endosome	enshield	epibolic	equalize
eluviate	emporium	end-paper	enshrine	epically	equalled
emaciate	emptiest	endpaper	enshroud	epicalyx	equal pay
embalmer	emptying	end-piece	ensialic	epicedia	equation
embanker	empty set	end-plate	ensiform	epichile	equative
embattle	empurple	end point	ensigncy	epicotyl	equiaxed
Ember day	empyreal	end to end	ensilage	epicycle	equiform
Ember eve	empyrean	endurant	enslaver	epidemic	equinely
embetter	emu-apple	enduring	ensnarer	epidotic	equipage
embezzle	emulator	energies	ensphere	epidural	equipped
embitter	emulgent	energise	enswathe	epifauna	equipper
emblazer	emulsify	energize	entailer	epifocal	equiseta
emblazon	emulsion	enervate	entangle	epigamic	equitant
embodied	emulsive	enfeeble	entellus	epigenic	equities
embodier	emulsoid	enfetter	entemple	epigeous	equivoke
embodies	enaction	enfilade	entering	epigones	equivote
embolden	enactive	enflower	enthalpy	epigraph	Equuleus
embolism	enactory	enfolder	enthrone	epigynum	eradiate
embolium	enallage	enforcer	enticing	epilepsy	erasable
embolize	enanthic	enfrenzy	entirely	epilogue	Erasmian
embossed	enargite	engaging	entirety	epimeral	Erastian
embosser	enascent	engender	entities	epimeric	erectile
embracer	en brosse	engineer	entoderm	epimeron	erection
embryoid	encaenia	enginery	entoptic	epinasty	erective
embryoma	Encaenia	engirdle	entozoal	epinicia	eremitic
embusing	encavern	Englishy	entozoon	epiphany	eremurus
embussed	enceinte	engolden	entr'acte	epiphora	ereption
emendate	encentre	engorger	entrails	epiphyte	erethism
emergent	encharge	engouled	entrance	epiplasm	erewhile
emerited	enchaser	engraven	entreaty	epiploic	ergastic
emeritus	encipher	engraver	entrench	epiploon	ergative
emersion	encircle	engroove	entrepôt	epipubic	ergogram
emery bag	enclisis	enhancer	entresol	epipubis	ergotism
emetical	enclitic	enhearse	entropic	episcope	ericetal
emiction	enclosed	enheaven	entryism	episodal	Eridanus
emigrant	encloser	enjoiner	entryist	episodic	erigeron
emigrate	enclothe	enkindle	entryman	episomal	Eritrean
eminence	encoffin	enlarger	entryway	epispore	erminois

erodable	esthetic	eugenist	eventide	exemplar	exponent
erodible	estimate	euhedral	eventing	exemplum	exporter
erogenic	estivate	eulachon	even-toed	exequial	exposita
erotesis	Estonian	Eulerian	eventual	exequies	exposure
erotetic	estopped	eulogies	everdamp	exercise	expresso
erotical	estoppel	eulogise	evermore	exergual	expulser
errantly	estovers	eulogism	eversion	exertion	expunger
errantry	estrange	eulogist	eversive	exertive	exscribe
erringly	estriche	eulogium	everyday	ex gratia	extended
error bar	estridge	eulogize	every few	exhalant	extender
error box	estrogen	Eunomian	everyhow	exhibit A	extensor
errorist	esurient	eunuchry	Everyman	exhorter	exterior
eructate	eta patch	euonymus	every one	exhumate	external
eruction	eta prime	eupatrid	everyone	exigence	extispex
erumpent	et cetera	eupepsia	every way	exigency	extolled
eruption	etcetera	eupeptic	everyway	exigible	extoller
eruptive	etchable	euphenic	eviction	exiguity	extorter
eryngium	eternise	euphonia	evidence	exiguous	extrados
erythema	eternity	euphonic	evil days	exilarch	extra dry
erythrol	eternize	euphonon	evildoer	eximious	extra sec
escalade	ethanoic	euphoria	evil hour	existent	extremal
escalado	ethanoyl	euphoric	evilness	existing	extremum
escalate	ethenoid	euphotic	evincive	exit line	extrorse
escaline	etherate	euphrasy	evitable	exit poll	extruder
escallop	ethereal	euphuism	evocable	exit visa	extubate
escalope	etherean	euphuist	evocator	ex-libris	exultant
escapade	etherial	euploidy	evolvant	ex nihilo	exundant
escapism	etherify	eupnoeic	evolvent	exocrine	exuviate
escapist	etherise	Eurasian	evulgate	exoergic	ex-votive
escargot	etherism	Eurobond	evulsion	exogamic	eye-black
escarole	etherize	Eurocrat	exacting	exogenic	eyeblack
eschalot	Ethernet	European	exaction	exonumia	eyedness
eschewal	ethician	Eurozone	examinee	exophora	eyeglass
eschewer	ethicise	europium	examiner	exoplasm	eyeleted
escudero	ethicism	eurythmy	examplar	exorable	eye level
esculent	ethicist	eurytope	excamber	exorcise	eye-liner
Eskimoid	ethicize	Eusebian	excavate	exorcism	eyeliner
esoteric	ethidium	eusocial	excedent	exorcist	eye of day
espalier	ethionic	eustatic	excelled	exorcize	eye-patch
esparcet	Ethiopic	eustelic	exceptor	exordial	eyepatch
espartos	ethnarch	eutectic	exchange	exordium	eyepiece
especial	ethnical	eutrophy	exciplex	exospore	eye-rhyme
espiegle	ethnonym	euxenite	excision	exossate	eyes down
espousal	ethogram	evacuant	excitant	exoteric	eye-shade
espouser	ethology	evacuate	exciting	exotherm	eyesight
espresso	ethoxide	evadable	excitive	exotoxin	eyes left
Esquimau	ethylate	evaluate	excitory	expanded	eye-stalk
essayism	ethylene	evanesce	excitron	expander	eye-tooth
essayist	etiolate	evangile	excluder	expected	eyewater
essaylet	etiology	evasible	excretal	expecter	fabliaux
Essenian	Eton crop	eve-churr	excreter	expedite	fabulate
Essenism	Eton suit	evection	excursus	expelled	fabulist
essexite	Etrurian	even-aged	excuse me	expellee	fabulous
essoinee	Etruscan	evendown	excusive	expeller	faburden
essoiner	eucalypt	even-even	execrate	expender	façadism
essonite	eucharis	evenfall	executer	expertly	façadist
estancia	eucrasia	evenings	executor	expiable	face-ache
esteemer	eudaemon	even just	executry	expiator	face-bone
esterase	eudemony	evenness	exegeses	explicit	face card
esterify	Euganean	evensong	exegesis	exploder	face down
esthesis	eugenics	eventful	exegetic	explorer	faceless

face-lift	fall-pipe	fashious	feebless	fenchone	field pea
facelift	fall-rope	fastback	feeblest	fencible	fiendish
face mask	fall-trap	fastball	feebling	fenestra	fiercely
face pack	fall void	fast-boat	feeblish	feng shui	fiercest
face-play	fall zone	fast buck	feedable	fen sedge	fieriest
facetiae	false god	fastener	feed back	fen tiger	fife-rail
faceting	false key	fast food	feedback	feracity	fifth day
face up to	false leg	fasthold	feed cock	Feraghan	fiftieth
facially	false oat	fast land	feed crop	feretory	fiftyish
facilely	false rib	fast lane	feed high	fermatas	fight for
facility	falsetto	fastness	feed-pipe	fern ally	fighting
factious	faltboat	fast-talk	feed pump	fern-bird	fight off
factotum	falterer	fastuous	feed-room	fernland	fight out
faculous	fameless	fast-wind	feed-tank	Fernleaf	figuline
faddiest	familial	fatalism	feelable	fernless	figurant
fade away	familiar	fatalist	feel free	fernlike	figurate
fadeless	families	fatality	feel-good	fern-seed	figure on
fadingly	Familism	fat-faced	feel like	fernyear	figure up
Faeroese	Familist	fatherly	feel up to	ferocity	figurine
faggoted	famished	fathomer	fees tail	ferreous	figurist
faggoter	famously	fatigate	feetless	ferreted	filagree
fail-dyke	Fanagalo	fatigued	feigning	ferreter	filament
fail-safe	fancical	fatigues	feijoada	ferriage	filander
fainéant	fanciest	Fatimite	feistier	ferritic	filariae
fainness	fanciful	fatmouth	feistily	ferritin	filarial
faintest	fancy man	fatstock	Felapton	ferruled	filature
faintish	fan dance	fattener	feldspar	ferryage	filching
fair copy	fandango	fattiest	felicide	ferryman	file away
fair-face	fanfaron	fatty oil	felicity	ferrymen	file-fish
fair fall	fangless	faubourg	felinely	fervency	filefish
fair game	fanlight	faultful	felinity	fervidly	filially
Fair Isle	fantasia	faultier	fellable	festally	filicide
fairlead	fantigue	faultily	fellahin	festival	filiform
fair maid	faradaic	faulting	fellatio	fetation	filigree
fair name	faradism	faulture	fellator	fetching	Filipina
fairness	faradize	faunally	fellness	fetch out	Filipino
fair play	farcical	Faustian	fellowly	fetch way	filix mas
fair rent	farcy bud	fauterer	fell-wool	feticide	fillable
fairyism	farewell	fauteuil	felonies	fetterer	fill a gap
faithful	far-famed	favonian	felsitic	feudally	filleted
Faithist	far-flung	favoured	felstone	feverfew	filleter
fake book	far forth	favourer	feltlike	feverish	filliped
fakement	farinose	fayalite	feltness	feverous	filmable
Falashas	farmable	fealties	femalely	fewtrils	film buff
falcated	farm-hand	fearless	femality	fibre-tip	film clip
falchion	farmhand	fearsome	femalize	fibrilla	filmfest
falconer	farmhold	feasible	femerell	fibromas	film-goer
falconet	farm land	feasibly	feme sole	fibrosis	filmiest
falconry	farmwife	feast day	femicide	fibrotic	film pack
falderal	farmyard	feastful	feminine	Fichtean	film star
Faliscan	farnesol	feathery	feminise	fiddlier	film unit
fall away	faro bank	featness	feminism	fiddling	filterer
fall-back	farouche	featural	feminist	Fidelism	filthier
fall down	farragos	featured	feminity	Fidelist	filthify
fallfish	farriery	febrific	feminize	fidelity	filthily
fall flat	farthest	February	feminoid	fidgeted	filtrate
fallible	farthing	feckless	fen-berry	fidgeter	finagler
fallibly	fasciate	feculent	fenceful	fiducial	finalise
fall-leaf	fascicle	fedayeen	fence-row	field-bed	finalism
fall-line	fasciola	federacy	fenchane	field day	finalist
fall over	fascitis	federate	fenchene	fieldful	finality

finalize	fire pink	five-leaf	flatland	flimsily	flowerer
findable	fire-plug	fivesome	flatling	flincher	floweret
find a way	fireplug	five-star	flatmate	flinders	flow-line
find-spot	fire-raid	fixation	flatness	Flinders	flow pipe
fineable	fire-risk	fixative	flat-nose	flindosa	flubbing
fine arts	fire-room	fixature	flat-pack	fling mud	flue-cure
fine-draw	fire sale	fixed-doh	flat race	fling off	flue-dust
Fine Gael	fire-ship	fixed oil	flat rate	flintier	flueless
fine-hand	fireship	fixidity	flat spin	flintily	fluellen
fine lady	fireside	fizz-boat	flattery	flip-flap	fluently
fineless	fire-step	fizziest	flattest	flip-flop	flue pipe
fineness	fire trap	flabbier	flatties	flip jump	flue-stop
fineries	fire-tree	flabbily	flatting	flippant	flue-work
fine-spun	fire-walk	flackery	flattish	flipping	fluffier
fine-tune	fire wall	flag-boat	flat tyre	flip side	fluffily
fingered	fireweed	flag down	flatware	flirtier	fluidics
fingerer	firewood	flagella	flatwise	flirtish	fluidify
fingrigo	firework	flag-fall	flatworm	flitchen	fluidise
finicism	firm land	flagging	flaunter	flittern	fluidism
finished	firmness	flagless	flautino	flitters	fluidist
finisher	firmware	flag-list	flautist	flittery	fluidity
finish up	first aid	flag-pole	flavonol	flitting	fluidize
finitary	first day	flagpole	flavoury	flixweed	fluidram
finitely	first off	flag-rank	flawless	floatage	fluigram
finitise	First War	flagrant	flax-blue	float-cut	flukiest
finitism	fiscally	flag-root	flax-bush	floating	flummery
finitist	fishable	flagship	flax-comb	float-ore	flunkeys
finitize	fish-beam	flake out	flax-lily	floccose	flunkies
finitude	fish-bolt	flakiest	flax-seed	floccule	flunk out
finnesko	fish-bowl	flambeau	flaxseed	flocculi	fluorene
finnowed	fishbowl	flambéed	fleabane	flock-bed	fluorian
fin whale	fish cake	flame gun	flea bite	flogging	fluoride
fippence	fish farm	flamelet	flea-dock	flooding	fluorine
fippenny	fish-fork	flamenco	fleasome	floodlit	fluorite
fireable	fish-glue	flame out	fleawort	flood out	flurried
firearms	fish-hawk	flameout	fleckled	floorage	flurries
fire away	fish-hook	flamines	flection	flooring	flushing
fireback	fishiest	flamingo	fleecier	floor-mop	Flushing
fire-ball	fishless	flammant	fleecies	floozies	flush out
fireball	fishlike	flancard	fleecily	floppier	fluttery
fire-bird	fishling	Flanders	fleeting	floppily	flux-line
fire-bomb	fish-meal	flânerie	flesh-fly	flopping	fly a kite
firebomb	fishmeal	flapjack	fleshier	Flora day	fly-blown
fire-boot	fish pond	flapless	fleshing	florally	flyblown
firebrat	fish-pool	flapping	flesh out	Florence	fly-drive
fireclay	fishtail	flare-out	fleshpot	floreted	fly-eater
fire-cure	fish-tank	flash-dry	fletcher	floriate	fly frame
firedamp	fishwife	flash-gun	flexible	florican	fly-mould
fire door	fishworm	flashgun	flexibly	Floridan	fly-paper
fire exit	fissiped	flashier	flextime	floridly	fly-pitch
fire-eyed	fissural	flashily	flexuose	florigen	flysheet
fire-fang	fissured	flashing	flexuous	florikan	fly-speck
firefish	fistfuls	flash out	flexural	floscule	fly-spray
fire-fork	fistiana	flat arch	fleysome	flossied	fly-strip
fire hall	fistical	flat boat	flicflac	flossier	fly-swish
fire hose	fistmele	flatfish	flichter	flotilla	flyunder
fire-iron	fistulae	flat foot	flickery	flounder	flywheel
fireless	fistular	flatfoot	flighted	flourier	fly-whisk
fire-line	fistulas	flat-four	flighter	flourish	foalfoot
firelock	fitfully	flat-head	flimflam	flow-blue	foamback
fire-opal	fivefold	flat iron	flimsier	flowered	foamiest

foamless	foot-drop	foregoes	for keeps	foul play	free-born
fob-chain	footfall	foregone	for kicks	founding	freeborn
fob watch	foot-folk	forehand	forklike	fountain	free city
focaccia	foot-gear	forehead	fork over	fountful	freedman
focalise	foothill	forehear	forktail	four-ball	freedmen
focalize	foothold	forehock	formable	four-eyes	free fall
focusing	footless	forehold	formalin	fourfold	Freefone
focussed	footlike	foreknow	formally	four-foot	free-form
fodderer	footling	forelady	form book	four-four	free gift
fog-bound	footmark	forelaid	form drag	Fournier	free hand
fogbound	foot-muff	foreland	formedon	four-part	freehand
fogeydom	footnote	forelimb	formeret	four-post	freehold
fogeyish	foot pace	forelive	formerly	fourreau	free-kick
foggiest	foot page	forelock	formicid	fourrier	Free Kirk
foglight	footpath	forelook	formless	foursome	freelage
foie gras	foot-race	foremast	form-line	four-star	free list
foldable	footrest	foremean	for money	fourteen	freeload
fold away	foot-rope	foremilk	Formosan	fourthly	free love
foldaway	foot-rule	foremost	form-room	fowl pest	freeness
foldboat	footslog	forename	formulae	foxberry	free pass
folderol	footsore	forenoon	formular	fox-chase	free path
foldless	footstep	forensic	formulas	foxglove	free port
foliated	footsure	foreoath	form word	fox-grape	Freepost
foliator	footwall	forepart	formwork	foxhound	free rein
folivore	footwear	forepeak	forprise	foxiness	free soil
folk-club	footwell	foreplan	forrader	fox shark	free vote
folk epic	footwork	foreplay	forsaken	fox snake	freeware
folkfest	footworn	forerank	forsaker	frabjous	free will
folkiest	foralite	foreroom	for shame	fractile	freeze up
folkland	foramina	foresaid	forshape	fraction	freezing
folklore	for a song	foresail	for short	fracture	fremitus
folkmoot	forborne	foreseat	forsooth	fragment	Frencher
folk rock	force cup	foreseer	forspeak	fragrant	Frenchie
folksier	forcedly	foreshew	forspend	framable	Frenchly
folk song	forceful	foreship	forspoke	frame-saw	frenetic
folk tale	force-out	foreshot	forswear	frampold	frenulum
folk ways	forcible	foreshow	forswore	francisc	frenzied
folkways	forcibly	foreside	forsworn	francise	frenzies
follicle	fordable	foreskin	forthink	francium	frequent
folliful	fordless	foreslow	fortieth	francize	frescade
follower	forebear	forestal	fortress	frank-fee	frescoed
follow-on	forebode	forestay	fortuity	Frankish	frescoes
follow-up	forebody	forested	fortuned	franklin	freshish
fomenter	forecall	forester	fortyish	Franklin	freshman
Fomorian	forecame	forestry	forwards	frapping	freshmen
fondling	forecast	foretack	forweary	frascati	fresh-run
fondness	forecome	foretell	foryield	Frascati	Fresison
font-name	foredawn	foretime	forzando	fraudful	fretless
fontware	foredeck	foretold	fossette	fraughan	fretting
food call	foredoom	forewarn	fossiled	Fräulein	frettish
food-fish	foredoor	forewent	fosterer	fraxetin	fretwork
foodless	foredune	forewing	fostress	freakdom	Freudian
food-pass	fore-edge	foreword	Foucault	freakier	friaries
fool away	foreface	foreyard	fougasse	freakily	fribbler
foolscap	forefeel	forge-man	foughten	freakish	friction
foolship	forefend	forgiven	foul ball	freak-out	friended
football	forefoot	forgiver	foul copy	freckled	friendly
foot-bank	foregame	forinsec	foul-hook	free alms	Friesian
foot bath	foregate	forjudge	foul line	free ball	frigging
footbath	foregift	forkball	foulmart	freebase	frighted
foot-bone	foregoer	forkedly	foulness	freeboot	frighten

frigidly	fructify	full tilt	fusilier	gambades	garbless
frijoles	fructose	full-time	fusional	gambeson	garboard
frillery	frugally	full toss	fussiest	gambling	garcinia
frillier	fruitage	full vent	fustiest	gambroon	gardener
frilling	fruit bar	full word	futilely	game ball	gardenia
Frimaire	fruit-bat	fulminic	futility	game bird	gardyloo
fringing	fruitbat	fumarate	futilize	gamebook	garefowl
frippery	fruitery	fumarole	futurism	gamecock	garganey
frisette	fruit fly	fumaroyl	futurist	game fish	gargoyle
friskier	fruitful	fumed oak	futurity	game-fowl	garishly
friskily	fruit gum	fume hood	futurize	gamefowl	garlicky
frithing	fruitier	fumeless	fuzz-ball	gameless	garreted
frittata	fruitily	fumerole	fuzziest	gameness	garrison
fritting	fruition	fumigant	fuzzword	game park	garrotte
Friulian	fruitist	fumigate	gabbiest	game plan	Garry oak
frizzier	fruitive	fumingly	gabbroic	game show	Garshuni
frog-face	fruitlet	fumishly	gabbroid	gamesman	gartered
frog-fish	fruit set	fumitory	gable-end	gamesmen	gas alarm
frogfish	frumenty	funboard	gadabout	gamesome	gas black
froggery	frumious	function	Gadarene	gamester	gaselier
froggies	frumpier	fundable	gadflies	gaminess	gas field
frogging	frumpily	funerary	gadgetry	gammarid	gas-fired
froggish	frumpish	funereal	Gadhelic	gammiest	gas gland
frogland	frustrum	fungible	gadzooks	gammoner	gas-house
froglike	frustule	fungibly	gainable	Gandhian	gasified
frog-lily	frustums	funguses	gainings	Gandhist	gasifier
frogling	frutices	funiform	gainless	gandoura	gasifies
frog-spit	fubsiest	funk-hole	gainsaid	gang-bang	gasiform
froideur	fuchsine	funkiest	gain time	gang-cask	gaslight
frolicky	fuchsite	funkster	gaitered	gang-days	gas meter
from afar	fucoidal	funniest	galabiya	Gangetic	gasolene
from A to B	fuel cell	funny man	galactan	gang-gang	gasolier
from A to Z	fuel food	furacity	galactic	gangland	gasoline
from home	fuelless	furanose	galangal	ganglial	gaspacho
fromward	fuelling	furbelow	Galatian	gangliar	gas pedal
frondage	fuel tank	furcated	galaxies	ganglier	gas plant
frondent	fugacity	furcraea	galbanum	gangling	gas poker
frondeur	fughetta	furcular	galeated	ganglion	gassiest
frondlet	fugitate	furculum	Galenian	gang rape	gasteral
frondose	fugitive	furfural	Galenism	gangrene	*gasthaus*
frondous	fugleman	furfuran	Galenist	gang-shag	gas-tight
frontage	fuglemen	furfurol	Galician	gang show	gastraea
front end	fulcrate	furfuryl	Galilean	gangsman	gastrula
frontier	fulcrums	furibund	Galilean	gangster	gasworks
frontlet	Fulfulde	furlable	Gallegan	ganister	gate-bill
front man	fulgorid	fur-lined	galleria	gannetry	gate city
frontman	fulgural	furlough	gall-gnat	ganoidal	gatefold
frostier	full-back	furphies	galliard	gantline	gateless
frostily	full beam	furriery	galliass	gantlope	gatepost
frosting	full butt	furriest	Gallican	gantries	gate-ward
frost-nip	full cock	furriner	gallipot	Ganymede	gatherer
frothier	full face	furrowed	gallivat	gaolbird	gather up
frothily	full hand	furthest	gall-less	gape-seed	gauchely
frottage	full lock	furuncle	galloped	gape-worm	gaudiest
frotteur	full moon	fusarium	galloper	gapeworm	gaudy-day
frottola	fullness	fusarole	galloway	gapingly	Gaullism
frou-frou	full page	fuselage	Galloway	garaging	Gaullist
frowsier	full pelt	fuseless	galluses	garagist	gaumless
frowster	full sail	fusel oil	gall wasp	Garamond	gauntlet
frowzily	full stop	fuse wire	galopade	garancin	Gaussian
frozenly	full term	fusiform	galoping	garbanzo	gauziest

Gavel Act	geologic	ghostily	giveable	gliffing	glycolic
gavelled	geomancy	ghosting	give a fit	glimmery	Glyconic
gaveller	geometer	ghostish	give alms	glissade	glycosyl
gavelock	geometry	ghoulish	give away	glissant	gnashers
gawkiest	geophagy	giantess	giveaway	glistery	gnashing
gay Greek	geophone	giantish	give back	glittery	gnathion
gazeboes	geophyte	giantism	giveback	glitzier	gnatlike
gazement	geoponic	giantize	give best	glitzily	gnatling
gazoomph	Georgian	gibbeted	give down	gloaming	gnat-snap
gazpacho	geotaxis	gibbsite	give fits	globally	gnawable
gazumper	geranial	gibingly	give hell	globated	gneissic
gazunder	geraniol	gib-staff	give it to	globical	gnomical
gear down	geranium	giddiest	give odds	globular	gnomonic
gearless	gerardia	giff-gaff	give on to	globulin	goalball
geelhout	germanic	gift-book	give over	glomming	goal kick
Gelasian	Germanic	giftedly	give skin	gloomful	goalless
gelastic	Germanly	giftless	give suck	gloomier	goal-line
gelatine	germ bomb	gift shop	glabella	gloomily	goalpost
gelation	germ cell	giftware	glabrate	glooming	go around
geldable	germinal	gift-wrap	glabrous	gloriole	go-ashore
gelidity	Germinal	giftwrap	glaciate	glorious	Goa stone
gematria	germless	gigaflop	gladdest	glory-box	go astray
geminate	germ line	gigantic	gladding	glory-pea	goatfish
Geminian	gerocomy	gigglier	glad hand	glossary	goat-foot
geminous	Geronimo	gigglish	gladiate	glosseme	goathair
gemmeous	gerontic	gig-lamps	gladioli	glossier	goatherd
gemshorn	geropiga	gigmanic	gladless	glossily	goatlike
gemstone	gestagen	gildable	gladness	glossist	goatling
gendarme	gestogen	Gilderoy	glad rags	glove box	goat moth
gendered	gestural	gild over	gladsome	glovebox	goatskin
gene bank	gesturer	gill arch	glaistig	glove-fit	goat's-rue
gene flow	get about	gillaroo	glamming	glow-lamp	goat tang
gene pool	get a grip	gillenia	glamoury	glow plug	goat-weed
generant	get ahead	gill slit	glance at	glow-worm	go back on
generate	get a heat	gilt-edge	glanders	gloxinia	goblinry
generous	get along	gilt-head	glandule	glucagon	gobstick
genetics	get a rush	gilt-tail	glareose	glucaric	God-awful
genetrix	get going	giltwood	glareous	glucinum	God bless
Genevese	get ideas	gimcrack	glasnost	gluconic	godchild
Genevize	get in bad	gimmicky	glass eye	glucosan	God-given
genially	get out of	gin and it	glassful	glucosic	God grant
genitive	get rid of	gin berry	glassier	glueball	God knows
genitory	get round	gin-crawl	glassify	glue-like	godliest
geniture	gettable	gingerly	glassily	gluelike	godmamma
geniuses	get taped	gingival	glassine	glühwein	God's Acre
gennemic	get thank	gingkoes	Glassite	glummest	God's book
genoa jib	get there	ginglymi	glass-man	glumness	God's gift
genocide	Getulian	ginned up	glastick	glumpily	Godspeed
genotype	get where	gin rummy	glaucoma	glumpish	God squad
Genovese	get wired	gin sling	glaucose	glutaeus	godwards
gentilic	get wrong	Gioconda	glaucous	glutamic	Godwards
gentlest	gewgawed	giraffes	glaziery	glutaric	Goethean
gentrice	geyseric	giraffid	gleaming	glutenin	Goethian
gentrify	Ghanaian	girasole	gleaning	glutting	goethite
geodesic	ghastful	girlhood	glee club	gluttony	goffered
geodetic	ghawazee	girl-less	gleesome	glyceria	go-getter
geogenic	ghettoes	Girondin	glegness	glyceric	go halves
geognost	Ghiordes	girthing	gletcher	glycerin	Goidelic
geognosy	Ghoorkha	girth-web	glibbest	glycerol	goings-on
geogonic	ghostess	girtline	glibness	glyceryl	goitrous
geologer	ghost gum	gisement	gliddery	glycogen	Golconda

Goldbach	go off pop	graffiti	great pox	grimmest	grubbily
gold bloc	goofiest	graffito	great tit	grimness	grubbing
gold card	googlies	grainage	great toe	grimoire	grubhood
gold disc	gooiness	grainier	Great War	grinagog	grub-kick
gold dust	go on fire	graining	great wen	grindery	grub-worm
goldenly	go on tick	grain-pit	greedier	grinding	grudging
goldfish	goopiest	gralloch	greedily	grinning	grueller
gold foil	goose-cap	gramarye	greegree	griphite	gruesome
gold king	goose egg	gram-atom	Greekdom	gripless	gruffish
gold leaf	goosegog	gramercy	Greekery	gripping	gruiform
goldless	go places	grandada	Greekess	gripsack	grumbler
gold mine	go public	grand air	Greek god	Griselda	grumness
gold-rush	gorbelly	grandame	Greekish	griseous	grumphie
gold salt	gorgeous	grand cru	Greek key	grisette	grumpier
golf ball	gorgeret	granddad	greement	gris-gris	grumpily
golf cart	gorgerin	grandeur	greenery	grislier	grumpish
golf club	gorgonia	grandfer	green eye	grith-man	Grundies
golgotha	goriness	grand mal	green fat	gritless	grunting
golliwog	gormless	grandpop	green fee	grittier	gryphite
golloped	go see-saw	grandson	greenfly	grittily	guacharo
go long on	go soft on	granitic	Greenian	gritting	guaiacol
Gomarian	go sour on	grannies	greening	grizzled	guaiacum
Gomarist	gospeler	grant aid	greenish	grizzler	Guaicuru
gomashta	gossamer	granular	greenlet	groanful	guanacos
gombroon	gossiped	grapelet	green man	groaning	guanylic
gonadial	gossiper	grapheme	green tea	groggery	guarache
go native	gossipry	graphics	greeting	groggier	guaranty
gondolet	gossypol	graphite	greffier	groggily	guardant
Gondwana	go steady	grappier	Grelling	grog-shop	guard dog
gone away	Gothonic	grappler	Grenache	groining	guardful
gone coon	go to bits	grapsoid	Grenadan	gromwell	guardian
goneness	go to hell	grasping	Grenfell	groo-groo	guarding
gonfalon	go too far	grass box	Gretchen	groomish	Guaycuru
gonfanon	go to seed	grassier	grey area	groovier	Guelphic
gong-gong	go to show	grassing	grey-back	groovily	guéridon
gonidial	go to town	grass pea	grey-coat	grope out	guerilla
gonidium	go to work	grass ski	grey crow	grosbeak	Guernsey
gonoduct	gouge-bit	grateful	grey duck	groschen	Guesdism
gonopore	gourdful	gratiola	grey-eyed	gross out	Guesdist
good book	gourmand	grattage	grey fowl	gross sum	Guianese
good Book	goutweed	grattoir	greymail	gross ton	Guianian
goodbyes	governor	gratuity	grey mare	grottier	guidable
good debt	go wallop	gravamen	greyness	grottoed	guidance
good deed	gownsman	gravelly	grey pine	grottoes	guide dog
good doer	Goyesque	Gravette	grey seal	grounded	Guide Law
good-even	Graafian	gravific	grey wolf	grounder	guideway
good form	grabbing	*gravitas*	grid bias	groupage	guidguid
goodlier	grab-hook	graviton	gridelin	grouping	guileful
good luck	grab rail	grayling	gridiron	groupism	guiltier
good name	grace-cup	grazable	gridlock	groupist	guiltily
goodness	graceful	graziery	griefful	grouplet	guimauve
good show	gracilis	greasier	grievous	group sex	Guinness
good-time	gracioso	greasily	griffaun	grouting	Gujarati
good turn	gracious	great age	griggish	growable	Gujerati
goodwife	gradatim	great ape	Grignard	grow away	gulfweed
good will	gradient	great auk	grillade	grow down	gullable
goodwill	graduand	great big	grillage	growlery	gullible
good word	graduate	great day	grilling	Growmore	gullibly
goodyear	Graecise	Great Dog	grimacer	groyning	gull-like
goodyera	Graecism	great gun	Grimaldi	grubbery	gull-wing
goof-ball	Graecize	greatish	grimiest	grubbier	gulosity

gumbotil	habendum	half-door	handfast	hardball	Hasidism
Gummidge	hability	half-face	handfuls	hard-boil	hassocky
gummiest	habitant	half-hear	handgrip	hard case	hasteful
gummosis	habitate	half-hose	hand-held	hard cash	hastener
gumpheon	habitual	half-hour	handhold	hard clam	hastiest
gumption	habitude	half-inch	handhorn	hard coal	hatchery
gum resin	habs-nabs	half-jack	handicap	hard copy	hatchety
gum-water	hachures	half-life	handiest	hard core	hatching
gunfight	hacienda	half-lift	hand it to	hard-core	hatchway
gunk-hole	hackette	half-line	handless	hardcore	hateable
gun-layer	hackneys	half-mark	handline	hard disk	hateless
gunmaker	hackster	half-mast	handlist	hard doer	hate mail
gun-metal	hackwork	half-mile	handloom	hardener	Hathoric
gunmetal	Hadassah	half-moon	handmade	hard fact	hat-money
gunny bag	hadronic	half-move	handmaid	hard fern	hatstand
gunpoint	haematic	halfness	hand-mill	hardhack	hat-trick
gunpower	haematin	half note	hand over	hard-head	hauerite
gun-range	haere mai	half-pace	handover	hardhead	haulyard
gunsight	Hagarene	half-part	handpass	hardiest	haunched
gunsmith	hagberry	half-pass	hand-pick	hard-laid	haunting
gunstock	Haggadah	half-pike	handpump	hard line	haurient
gunstone	Haggadic	half-pint	handrail	hardline	hausfrau
gurdwara	hag-taper	half-shot	hand-sewn	hard luck	haustral
gurgeons	Hail Mary	half-slip	hands off	hard-meat	haustrum
Gurkhali	hair-ball	half-sole	handsome	hardness	haüynite
Gurmukhi	hairband	half-step	hand tool	hard-nose	have a few
guruship	haircare	half-term	handwork	hard porn	have a fit
gushiest	hair-cell	half-tide	handy for	hard rock	have a job
gusseted	hair clip	half-time	handyman	hard sell	have done
gustable	hair-cord	half-tone	handymen	hardship	have left
gustiest	hair-grip	halftone	hanepoot	hard soap	have legs
gut flora	hairgrip	half-wave	hangable	hard tack	haveless
gut-level	hairiest	half-word	hang a leg	hardtail	havelock
guts-ache	hair lace	half-year	hang back	hard tick	havenage
gut-shoot	hairless	haliotis	hangbird	hardware	have need
gutsiest	hairlike	hall door	hanger-on	hardwood	have pity
guttated	hairline	hallmark	hang fire	hard word	haversin
guttatim	hair-lock	hallmote	hang it up	harebell	have to be
guttered	hair moss	hallooed	hangment	harefoot	have to do
guttural	hair seal	hall tree	hangnail	harelike	havildar
Guyanese	hair-worm	hallucal	hang-nest	haremlik	havocked
guzzling	Halachic	halluces	hangover	hare-pipe	Hawaiian
Gwentian	Halafian	haloform	Hang Seng	hare's-ear	hawfinch
gyle-kier	Halalcor	haltered	hankerer	hare's fur	hawk-eyed
gymkhana	halalled	halteres	hanksite	harewood	hawklike
gymnasia	halation	halt sign	Hannibal	Hargrave	hawkmoth
gymnotus	haleness	halutzim	Hanukkah	hark back	hawk-nose
gynander	halesome	hamartia	haploidy	Harleian	hawkshaw
gynarchy	half-arse	hamerkop	happen-so	harlotry	hawkweed
gynobase	half-back	hammerer	happiest	harmless	hawthorn
gypseous	half-ball	hammiest	happy day	harmonic	hay fever
gypsy cab	half-beak	Hanafite	haptenic	haroseth	hayfield
Gypsydom	half-belt	hanaster	hapteron	harp seal	haymaker
gypsyish	half-blue	handball	haqueton	harridan	haystack
Gypsyish	half-boot	handbell	hara-kiri	harrower	hazarder
Gypsyism	half-bred	handbill	harangue	harrow in	hazardry
gyration	half-butt	handbook	harasser	harrumph	hazelnut
gyratory	half cock	handcart	harbinge	hartwort	haziness
gyrostat	half-dead	handclap	hard at it	haruspex	headache
habanera	half-deck	handcuff	hardback	Harveian	headachy
Habdalah	half-dime	hand down	hardbake	hash sign	head back

headband	heavy mob	hellweed	hereunto	high camp	hired man
head-butt	heavy oil	helmeted	hereupon	high card	hireless
head case	heavy wet	helminth	herewith	higher-up	hireling
headfast	hebdomad	helmless	herisson	high-five	his heels
headgear	hebetate	helmsman	heritage	high gear	Hispanic
head girl	hebetude	helmsmen	heritrix	high-hole	Hisperic
head-hunt	Hebraean	helotage	hermetic	high jump	hiss away
headhunt	Hebraise	helotism	hermitic	high kick	histerid
headiest	Hebraism	helotize	hermitry	highland	histioid
headlamp	Hebraist	helpable	herniary	high life	histogen
headland	Hebraize	helpless	Herodian	high-lone	histomap
headless	hecatomb	helpline	heroical	high-lows	historic
headline	hectical	help-mate	heroship	high mass	Histosol
headlock	hedgehog	helpmate	herpetic	High Mass	histrion
headlong	hedge-hop	helpmeet	herptile	highmost	his watch
headmost	hedge-pig	Helvetic	herseems	highness	hit a blot
head-note	hedgerow	helvolic	herstory	high-rise	hitch pin
headnote	hedonism	hemiopia	Hertzian	high-risk	hitherto
head noun	hedonist	hemiopic	her watch	high road	hit it off
head-race	heedless	hemipode	Hesiodic	high seas	hit squad
head-rail	heelaman	hemisect	hesitant	high sign	hit woman
headrest	heelball	hempland	hesitate	high spot	hit women
headroom	heel-bone	hempseed	hesperid	hightail	hoactzin
head-rope	heel grip	henchman	Hesperus	high-tech	hoarding
head-sail	heelless	henchmen	hetaerae	high tide	hoarhead
headsail	heel-lift	henequen	hetairai	high time	hoariest
headship	heel-post	hen-fruit	heuchera	highveld	hoarsely
headsman	heel-rope	hen house	heuretic	high wine	Hoastman
headsmen	heemraad	hennaing	hexagram	high wire	hobbitry
head-tire	heftiest	hen-party	hexanoic	highwood	hobbyism
headward	hegberry	hen-roost	hexaplar	hijacker	hobbyist
head wind	Hegelian	hepatica	hexapody	hilarity	hob-or-nob
headwind	Hegelism	hepatoma	hexatone	hill-folk	hock-cart
headword	hegemony	hepialid	hey jingo	hill fort	hockelty
headwork	heighten	heptagon	hiatuses	hilliest	hocklety
head-yard	heirless	heptamer	hibernal	hillocky	hock-shop
healable	heirloom	heptarch	hibiscus	hillside	Hocktide
healsome	heir male	heraldic	hiccough	himation	hocusing
hearable	heirship	heraldry	hiccuped	himseems	hocussed
hear hear	HeLa cell	herbaged	hic jacet	Hinayana	hodgepot
hear of it	helenium	herbaria	hickwall	hinderer	Hoffmann
hear tell	heliacal	herb beer	hidalgos	hind-head	hoggerel
heartful	helicity	herbiest	hiddenly	hindmost	hog-Latin
heartier	helicoid	herbless	hide away	hindside	hog louse
heartily	heliodon	herblike	hideaway	Hinduise	hogmanay
heart rot	heliodor	Hercules	hidebind	Hinduism	hog-maned
heat-drop	heliport	herd book	hideland	Hinduize	hog-nosed
heatedly	Helladic	herdsman	hideless	hindward	hog on ice
heathery	hell-bent	herdsmen	hideling	hindwing	hog's back
heath-hen	hell-born	Herdwick	hidlings	hingeing	hog-score
heat lamp	hell-bred	hereaway	hidrosis	hinge-pin	hogshead
heat pump	Hellenic	heredity	hidrotic	hinnible	hog-tight
heat rash	hell-fire	Hereford	hidy-hole	hip-boots	ho-ho bird
heat sink	hellfire	herefrom	hielaman	hip flask	hokiness
heat wave	hell-hole	heregeld	hierarch	hip joint	holdable
heatwave	hellicat	here goes	hieratic	hipparch	hold back
heavenly	hell-kite	herenach	hierurgy	hippuric	holdback
heaviest	hell-like	hereness	higgling	hippydom	hold dear
heavy bag	he'll live	here's how	highball	hiragana	hold down
heavyish	hell-ship	heresies	high-born	hircarra	holdfast
heavy man	hellward	heretoga	highbrow	hireable	hold good

hold hard	homespun	hoop pine	hotbrain	humanise	Hyde Park
hold over	homester	hoop ring	hotchpot	humanism	hydracid
hold pace	home town	hooroosh	hoteldom	humanist	hydranth
hold true	home unit	hoosegow	hotelier	humanity	hydrarch
hold with	homeward	hooshtah	hot flash	humanize	hydrated
holeable	homework	hopeless	hot flush	humanoid	hydrator
hole-card	homicide	hopingly	hothouse	humantin	hydremia
holiness	homilete	hop joint	hot metal	humblest	hydridic
holistic	homilies	hop-plant	hot money	humidify	hydrogel
hollaing	homilise	Horatian	hot pants	humidity	hydrogen
Hollands	homilist	Horlicks	hotplate	humified	hydromel
hollowly	homilite	hormonal	hot-press	humifies	hydronym
holly oak	homilize	hormonic	hot-short	humility	hydropic
holmgang	hominess	horn-band	hot-stove	hummable	hydropot
Holmgren	hominine	hornbeak	hot stuff	hummocky	hydropsy
holm tree	hominoid	hornbeam	hot water	humorise	hydroski
Holocene	homodont	hornbill	hound-dog	humorism	hydrosol
hologamy	homogamy	hornbook	hounding	humorist	hydrotic
hologram	homogene	horn cell	houndish	humorize	hydroxyl
holoptic	homogeny	hornfels	hour hand	humorous	hyena-dog
holotype	homology	horn-fish	hour-long	humoured	hyenaism
holozoic	homonymy	horniest	houseboy	humpback	hygienic
Holstein	homotopy	hornless	house dog	humpiest	hylicist
Holy City	homuncio	hornlike	housefly	humpless	hylology
holy fire	honchoes	hornpipe	houseful	humstrum	hylozoic
Holy Lamb	Honduran	hornpout	house-lot	humulone	hymeneal
Holy Land	honestly	horn-rims	houseman	humusify	hymenean
holy loaf	honewort	horn-ring	housemen	Hunanese	hymenial
Holy Mary	honey ant	horntail	house row	hundreds	hymenium
Holy Name	honey bag	hornwork	house-sit	hungered	hymn book
Holy Rood	honey bee	hornworm	housetop	hungerer	hymnless
holytide	honeybee	hornwort	hoveller	hungerly	hyoidean
Holy Week	honey-bun	horologe	hoverfly	hung-over	hyoscine
Holy Writ	honeybun	horology	how about	hungrier	hypaxial
Holy Year	honeydew	horopter	howdahed	hungrily	hypergol
home base	honeyish	horrible	howgozit	hunkiest	hypernym
home-bird	honey pot	horribly	howitzer	huntable	hyperope
homebody	honey sac	horridly	howl down	hunt away	hyperper
home-bred	honorand	horrific	how's life	huntaway	hyphaema
home-brew	honorary	horse ant	howsoe'er	hunt ball	hypnosis
home farm	honorial	horsebox	how's that	hunt down	hypnotic
home-felt	honourer	horse-car	huarache	huntress	hypocone
homegirl	hoodless	horsefly	hub brake	hunt riot	hypodigm
home help	hoodlike	horse-hoe	hubbuboo	huntsman	hypogamy
homeland	hoodooed	horseman	huck-bone	huntsmen	hypogeal
homeless	hoodwink	horsemen	huckster	Huon pine	hypogean
homelier	hoofless	horse-pox	huet-huet	hurcheon	hypogene
homelike	hoof-pick	horse-way	huff-duff	hurroosh	hypogeum
homelily	hook-bill	horsiest	huffiest	hurtless	hypogyny
homeling	hook-bolt	hortulan	hügelite	hurtsome	hyponome
home loan	hook-bone	hoseless	hugeness	hushabye	hyponymy
home-made	hooked on	hose-pipe	huggable	hushedly	hypopyon
homeobox	hookless	hosepipe	Huguenot	hush-hush	hyposmia
home perm	hooklike	hospital	hula hoop	huskanaw	hypothec
home port	hook-nose	hospitia	hula-hula	huskiest	hypotony
Homerist	hook shop	hospodar	hull down	hustings	hyraceum
Homerite	hook shot	hosteler	hully gee	Huweitat	hysteria
homeroom	hookworm	hostelry	hum and ha	Huxleyan	hysteric
home rule	hooligan	hostessy	humanely	hyacinth	iambical
homesick	hoop-back	hostless	humanics	Hyblaean	iambuses
homesite	hoop-iron	hot blast	humanify	hybodont	I am sorry

lapygian	idolater	immersed	in accord	indamine	infamize
iatrical	idolatry	imminent	in a creel	indazole	infamous
Ibicenco	idolizer	immingle	in action	Indebele	infantry
ibotenic	idoneity	immobile	inaction	indebted	infaunal
Ibsenish	idoneous	immodest	inactive	indecent	in favour
Ibsenism	idrialin	immolate	in a hurry	in defect	infector
Ibsenist	id ul-fitr	immortal	in and out	in demand	infectum
Ibsenite	idyllian	immotile	in a pause	indented	infecund
iceblink	idyllise	immotive	inarable	indenter	inferior
iceblock	idyllist	immunise	in armour	indentor	infernal
ice-bound	idyllize	immunity	in a sense	indesert	infernos
ice chest	iggerant	immunize	inasmuch	in detail	inferred
ice cream	Ignatian	impacted	in a trice	indevout	infilter
ice field	ignition	impactor	in a whiff	India ink	infinite
ice-front	ignitron	impaired	in a while	Indiaman	infinity
ice house	ignobler	impairer	in a whisk	Indiamen	infirmly
ice lolly	ignominy	impalace	in back of	Indianan	infixion
ice-piton	ignorant	impaling	in-basket	indicant	inflamer
ice plant	iguanian	impanate	inbreath	indicate	in flames
ice sheet	iguanoid	imparity	Inca dove	indicial	inflated
ice shelf	iimbongi	imparter	incalver	indicium	inflater
ice-skate	ijolitic	impedite	in camera	indictee	inflator
ice storm	Iliadist	impelled	in candle	indicter	inflexed
ice-water	illation	impeller	in care of	indigena	in-flight
ice-yacht	illative	impellor	in case of	indigene	inflight
ichoglan	ill blood	imperial	Inca tern	indigent	in flower
ichorous	I'll buy it	imperium	incensed	indigest	influent
ichthyic	ill-deedy	impetigo	incenser	indigoid	infolded
Ichthyol	ill-fated	impierce	incenter	indirect	informal
iconical	illigant	impinger	incentor	inditing	informed
icterine	illinium	impishly	incentre	indocile	informer
id al-adha	Illinois	impleach	inceptor	indolent	infra dig
I dare say	illiquid	impledge	in charge	Indology	infra-red
idealess	I'll say so	implicit	inchmeal	indrawal	infrared
ideal gas ,	ill-timed	implunge	inchoate	inducive	in fresco
idealise	ill-treat	impocket	in chorus	inductee	infringe
idealism	illumine	impolder	inchworm	inductor	infusion
idealist	illusion	impolicy	incident	indulged	infusive
ideality	illusive	impolite	in-circle	indulger	infusory
idealize	illusory	imponent	incision	induline	in future
ideation	illuvial	imporous	incisive	indument	ingather
idée fixe	Illyrian	importee	incisure	indurate	in grease
identify	Illyrism	importer	incitive	indusial	ingroove
identity	Illyrist	imposing	incitory	indusium	in-ground
ideogram	ilmenite	imposter	incivism	industry	ingrowth
ideology	imaginal	impostor	inclined	inedible	inguinal
idiocies	imaginer	imposure	incliner	inedited	inhalant
idiogram	imagines	impotent	in clover	in effect	inhalent
idiolect	imambara	imprimis	included	in effigy	inhauler
idiosome	imbecile	imprison	incoming	in embryo	inhearse
idiot box	imbolden	improper	in common	inequity	inheaven
idiotish	imbrices	improver	in convoy	inerrant	inherent
idiotism	imbruing	impudent	in course	inert gas	inhesion
idiotize	imitable	impugner	incourse	inertial	inhibine
idiotope	imitator	impunity	increase	inertion	in his way
idiotype	immanely	impurely	increate	in escrow	inhumane
idiozome	immanent	impurify	incubate	inessive	inhumate
idle away	immantle	impurist	incubous	in excess	inimical
idlehood	immarble	impurity	incumber	inexpert	iniquity
idleness	immature	I must say	incurred	in face of	initiand
idocrase	immember	in a blaze	indagate	infamies	initiate

in itself	insanely	interbed	intruder	iridious	Islamize
in its way	insanify	intercom	intubate	Irish elk	islander
injected	insanity	intercut	intuiter	Irishian	isleless
injector	inscient	interest	inturned	Irishism	islesman
injuries	inscribe	interior	in two ups	Irishize	Ismailis
inkberry	inscript	interlap	inundant	Irishman	is no more
ink block	inscroll	interlay	inundate	Irishmen	isobaric
inkiness	in season	intermit	in unison	Irish Sea	isocheim
inkstand	in secret	intermix	inurbane	Irish yew	isochore
in labour	insectan	internal	invalidy	ironbark	isochron
inlander	insecure	internee	invaried	iron blue	isocline
in league	inseeing	Internet	invasion	ironclad	isocolon
inleague	in series	Interpol	invasive	iron-clay	isocracy
in liquor	inserter	interred	invecked	Iron Duke	isocryme
in little	insertor	interrer	invected	iron gang	isogenic
in livery	insetted	interrex	inveigle	iron-grey	isogloss
inlooker	insetter	intersex	in velvet	iron hand	isogonal
inmostly	in sheets	intersow	inventar	iron-hard	isogonic
in motion	in shreds	intertex	inventer	iron hoof	isograft
in muster	in shtook	intertie	inventor	ironical	isograph
in my book	inside of	interval	in verity	iron lace	isohelic
in my mind	insignia	inter-war	inversed	iron lady	isoionic
innately	insignis	interwar	inverted	ironless	isolable
innatism	in sign of	in the air	inverter	iron-like	isolated
in nature	insister	in the bag	invertor	iron loss	isolator
in need of	insist on	in the can	investor	iron lung	isolexic
inner bar	insolate	in the ear	inviable	iron mask	isologue
inner ear	insolent	in the end	in view of	iron mike	isomeric
inner man	insomnia	in the log	invigour	iron-mold	isometry
in no case	insomuch	in theory	inviscid	iron-sand	isomorph
innocent	in spades	in the raw	invitant	iron-shot	isonomic
in no mood	in-sphere	in the red	inviting	Ironside	isophane
in no time	insphere	in the sun	invocant	iron tree	isophene
innovate	inspired	in the way	invocate	iron ware	isophone
in no wise	inspirer	inthrall	involute	ironware	isophote
innuendo	in spirit	inthrust	involved	ironweed	isopleth
inoculum	inspirit	intifada	involver	ironwood	isopodan
in orders	instable	intilted	in wake of	ironwork	isoprene
inornate	instance	intimacy	in want of	Iroquois	isospore
inosinic	instancy	intimate	inwardly	irrelate	isostasy
inositol	instinct	intimism	inwinter	irrigate	isostere
in pastel	institor	intimist	inworker	irrision	isothere
in person	instress	intimity	iodinate	irritant	isotherm
in pickle	in-stroke	intitule	iodoform	irritate	isotonic
in pieces	instruct	into fits	iodophor	irrorate	isotopic
in places	insulary	intonaco	iodyrite	irrumate	isotropy
in pocket	insulate	intonate	ion drive	Isabella	isotypic
in proper	insulter	intoneme	Ionicism	isagogic	isozooid
in public	in sunder	intonico	ionicity	Isaianic	isozymic
inputted	insurant	into play	Ionicize	isangoma	ispaghul
inputter	intaglio	intorted	ionizing	Isaurian	Israelis
inquirer	intaking	intra-day	ionogram	Iscariot	issuable
in quires	in tandem	intrados	iotacism	ischuria	issuably
in reason	intarsia	intrench	ipso jure	is he ever	issuance
in relief	integral	intrepid	irefully	Ishihara	isthmian
in retard	Intelsat	intrigue	irenarch	isidiate	itaconic
in return	intended	intrinse	irenical	isidioid	ITAR-Tass
in review	intender	intromit	irenicon	Islamise	itchiest
in revolt	intenser	intronic	Irgunist	Islamism	itch mite
inrolled	intently	introrse	Irianese	Islamist	itchweed
in room of	interact	intruded	iridesce	Islamite	I tell you

itemizer	Japanesy	Jew's harp	jovially	jury-mast	kedgeree
iterance	Japan ink	jib-sheet	jovialty	justicer	keek-keek
iterancy	Japanise	Jiffy bag	joy-bells	justness	keel-bill
it is said	Japanism	Jiffy pot	joyfully	jut-jawed	keelboat
it is told	Japanize	jig about	joy-house	juvenile	keelhaul
it is true	japanned	jig borer	joy juice	Kababish	keelless
it's a deal	Japanner	jiggerer	joyously	kabassou	keel-like
ivory-nut	Japan wax	jig plate	joyrider	Kabbalah	keenness
ivy-berry	Japhetic	jillaroo	joy-stick	kabeljou	keepable
I warrant	japishly	jim-dandy	joystick	Kabinett	keep away
Ixionian	japonica	jingbang	joy-wheel	Kabistan	keep back
jabberer	jararaca	jingoish	jubilant	kabloona	keep cave
jacitara	jargoner	jingoism	jubilate	kafenion	keep down
jackaroo	jargonic	jingoist	jubilean	kaffiyeh	keep fair
Jack bean	jarlship	jipijapa	jubilize	kailyard	keep from
Jack boat	jarosite	jiu-jitsu	Judahite	kaimakam	keep goal
jackboot	jasmined	jive talk	Judaical	kaka-beak	keep-left
Jack-bowl	jaspered	Joachism	Judaizer	kakariki	keep over
jackeroo	jasponyx	Joachist	judgment	kakemono	keep pace
jacketed	jaundice	jobation	judicial	Kakiemon	keep rank
jackfish	jauntier	job-coach	jugglery	kala-azar	keepsake
Jack-fish	jauntily	job horse	Jugoslav	kale-bell	keep shop
jack-line	Javanese	job house	jugulate	kalendar	keep step
Jack-pine	javanite	job press	juiciest	kale-runt	keep time
jack plug	Java plum	job-print	Julia set	kale-time	keep tune
Jack plug	jaws harp	job-share	julienne	kale-worm	keep with
Jack-roll	jawsmith	jobsheet	jumboism	kaleyard	keeshond
jackshay	jaw-tooth	jockette	jumboize	kalicine	keffiyeh
jackstay	Jaycette	jocosely	jumbo jet	kallidin	kelewang
jackyard	jazerant	jocosity	jumpable	Kalmucks	kelp crab
Jacobaea	jazziest	joctaleg	jump bail	kamacite	kelp-fish
Jacobean	jazz-rock	jocundly	jump ball	Kamakura	Kemalism
Jacobian	jealousy	jodhpurs	jump boot	kamikaze	Kemalist
Jacobite	jeepable	Joe Blake	jumped-up	Kanarese	kennedya
Jacobson	Jehovist	Johannes	jumpiest	Kanesian	kennetic
jacquard	jejunely	John boat	jump lead	kangaroo	kenspeck
jactance	jelloped	John Bull	jump-rock	kantikoy	Kentucky
jactancy	jelly bag	John Crow	jump rope	kaoliang	keratoma
jaculate	jelutong	Johndarm	jump seat	kaolinic	keratose
jacuzzis	jeopardy	John Dory	jump ship	Kapenaar	kerbside
jadeitic	jeremiad	johnnies	jump shot	Karabagh	kerchief
jaggedly	Jeremiah	joinable	jump suit	Karelian	Kermanji
jaggiest	jerepigo	joint box	jumpsuit	Karitane	kermesse
jagirdar	jerkiest	jointing	jump to it	Karnaugh	kernelly
jail-bait	jerk-line	joint-saw	jump turn	Karshuni	kerosene
jailbait	jeroboam	jointure	jump-weld	karstify	kerosine
jailbird	jerrican	joisting	junction	karsting	Kerr cell
jakealoo	jerrycan	jokeless	juncture	karyotin	Kerry cow
jalapeño	jerryism	jokesome	junk bond	Kashmiri	keskidee
jalopies	jerseyed	jokester	junketed	katakana	ketamine
jalousie	jerupiga	jokiness	junketer	katheter	ketazine
Jamaican	jessamin	jokingly	junk food	katonkel	ketimine
jambolan	jest-book	jolliest	junk mail	Katyusha	keto-acid
jamboree	Jesuitic	jolt-head	junk shop	kauri gum	keto-enol
Jamesian	Jesuitry	joltless	junkyard	kawakawa	ketonize
jammiest	jet black	Jonathan	Junonian	kayaking	ketoxime
jam-proof	jettison	jonglery	jurament	kayakist	keurboom
Janglish	jewelled	*jongleur*	Jurassic	kazachoc	key-block
janitrix	jeweller	Jonkanoo	juratory	kazooist	keyboard
janizary	Jewishly	journeys	juristic	Keating's	key-bugle
Japanese	jew's harp	jousting	jury-list	Keatsian	key money

keynoter	King high	knee-boot	korrigum	lactonic	lamenter
key-plate	kinghood	knee-boss	kourbash	lacunary	laminary
keypunch	kingklip	knee-deep	kouskous	lacunate	laminate
keystone	King Kong	knee-high	kowtower	lacunose	laminose
khaki bos	kingless	knee-hole	krameria	lad-bairn	laminous
khalasis	kinglike	kneehole	kratogen	laddered	lampless
khalassi	kingling	knee-jerk	kraw-kraw	ladified	lamp-post
Khaldian	king lory	kneelike	kreutzer	ladifies	lamppost
Khaskura	king post	kneeling	kromesky	ladleful	lampreys
Khedival	king rail	knee-roof	Kuchaean	ladle out	lampyrid
Khilafat	kin group	knickers	Kulinism	lad of wax	lancegay
Khoikhoi	kingship	knife-bar	Kurilian	lad's love	lancelet
Khurasan	king-side	knife-boy	Kuroshio	ladybird	lanceted
khus-khus	king-size	knifeful	kurtosis	lady-fern	land ahoy
kibitzer	kingsman	knife-man	kurumaya	ladyfied	land army
kickable	king's peg	knightly	kurveyor	ladyfish	land bank
Kickapoo	kingston	knitbone	Kushitic	ladyhood	land-bank
kick back	kingwood	knitchel	kvetcher	ladyless	landbank
kickback	kinkajou	knitting	Kwakiutl	ladylike	land-bred
kick-ball	kinkhost	knitwear	kyanitic	lady-love	land crab
kickball	kinkiest	knitwork	kymogram	Lady Luck	landfall
kick-down	kinkless	knobbing	kyphosis	Lady Muck	land-fast
kickseys	kinsfolk	knobbled	kyphotic	ladyship	landfill
kickshaw	kip house	knobbler	kyrielle	lady's man	land-floe
kicksies	kipperer	knoblike	Labadist	lady ware	land-folk
kickster	Kipsigis	knobwood	labdanum	lady wife	landform
kick-tail	kirkless	knocking	labelled	laen-land	land-fyrd
kick-turn	kirk-town	knock off	labeller	Laetrile	land girl
kidflick	kirkyard	knock out	labellum	lagander	landlady
kid-glove	kirn-baby	knockout	labially	Lag b'Omer	land legs
kidology	Kir-Shehr	knorhaan	labiated	lag fault	landless
Kilkenny	kiskadee	Knossian	lability	lagoonal	land line
killable	kissable	knot-head	labilize	lag phase	landline
killbuck	kissably	knot-hole	Laborism	Lagrange	landlord
killcrop	kiss away	knotless	laborous	laically	landmark
killdeer	kiss-curl	knottier	laboured	laicizer	land mass
kill-lamb	kissless	knottily	labourer	laid-back	land-mine
killogie	kistvaen	knotting	Labrador	laid work	landmine
kill-time	kitcheny	knotweed	laburnum	laitance	land-pike
kill zone	kitefish	knotwork	Lacanian	Lakeland	land-poor
kilobase	kite-mark	knowable	lace-fern	lakeless	landrace
kilobuck	Kitemark	know best	lacelike	lakeside	landrail
kilobyte	kithless	knuckled	lacerate	lake-weed	Landseer
kilogram	Kiwanian	knuckler	lacertid	lallygag	Land's End
kilovolt	Kjeldahl	knurling	lacewing	lamanism	land ship
kilowatt	Klansman	kohekohe	lacewood	lamantin	land-sick
kimonoed	Klansmen	koh-i-noor	lacework	lamasery	landside
Kim's game	Kleinian	kohlrabi	laciness	lambaste	landslip
kindless	klephtic	koinonia	lackaday	lambdoid	landsman
kindlier	kleywang	Kolarian	lackland	lambency	landsmen
kindlily	klipfish	kolinsky	Laconian	lambhood	land-take
kindling	klipkous	Kol Nidre	Laconise	lambkill	landward
kindness	Klondike	komitaji	laconism	lamblike	land-wash
kinesics	klystron	Komsomol	Laconize	lambling	land-wind
kinetics	knackery	kookiest	lacqueys	lamb's fry	land wire
kingbird	knallgas	Kootenai	lacrimal	lambskin	Langhans
kingbolt	knapping	koradjis	lacrosse	lame duck	lang-kale
king-carp	knapsack	korfball	lacrymal	lamellae	langlauf
king crab	knapweed	korimako	lactated	lamellar	Langmuir
king fern	knee-bend	koromiko	lacteous	lameness	langosta
kingfish	knee-bone	korrigan	lactogen	lamented	langrage

langsuir	laterite	lawyerly	leadwort	left bank	lens-work
lang syne	laterize	laxation	leaf beet	left-hand	lenticel
language	late-wake	laxative	leafbird	leftmost	lenticle
languish	late wood	layabout	leaf cast	leftness	Lent lily
lankiest	lathe-bed	lay an egg	leaf curl	leftover	Lent term
lankness	latherer	lay aside	leaf-fall	left turn	Lenz's law
lanneret	lath-nail	laybarge	leaf-flea	leftward	Leonberg
lanosity	lathyrus	lay clerk	leaf-frog	left-wing	lepidote
lanthana	latifund	lay elder	leaf-gold	legacies	leporine
lanthorn	Latinate	layer-cut	leafiest	legal aid	leprolin
lap-board	Latinise	layering	leaf-lard	legal cap	lepromin
lapelled	Latinish	layer-out	leafless	legalese	leptonic
lapicide	Latinism	layer pit	leaflike	legalise	Lesghian
lapidary	Latinist	layer vat	leaf node	legalism	les girls
lapidate	Latinity	lay gauge	leaf-roll	legalist	lessness
lapidify	Latinize	laylight	leaf-scar	legality	less than
lapidist	latitant	lay pipes	leaf-soil	legalize	let alone
lapillus	latitude	layshaft	leaf-spot	legal man	let blood
lap joint	Latonian	laystall	leaguing	legatary	let drive
lappeted	lattener	lay to wed	leaguite	legatine	lethally
Lapponic	latterly	lay vicar	leakance	legation	lethargy
lapsable	latticed	lay waste	leakiest	legative	let loose
lapstone	laudable	laywoman	lean-burn	leg-break	let me see
lap strap	laudably	laywomen	leanness	leg drive	lettable
lap-table	laudanum	lazarets	lean-over	legended	lettered
Laputian	laudator	Lazarist	lean upon	Legendre	letterer
larboard	laudible	Lazarite	leapable	legendry	letteret
larcener	laughful	laziness	leap-frog	legerity	lettrine
larch gum	laughing	lazulite	leapfrog	leggiero	lettrism
larderer	laugh off	lazurite	leap year	leggiest	lettrist
lardiner	laughter	lazy-back	learning	leg-guard	leucitic
largesse	launcher	lazyhood	learn off	legioned	leucoses
lark-heel	Laurasia	lazy-jack	learn out	legitime	leucosin
larksome	laureate	lazy-Jack	leasable	leg stump	leucosis
larkspur	Laurence	leachate	leaseman	legumina	leucotic
larrigan	lava bomb	leadable	leash law	leg woman	leukemia
larrikin	lava flow	lead-acid	leathern	Leibnitz	leukosin
larruped	lava-lava	lead away	leathery	Leishman	leukosis
larvated	lavatera	lead-back	leavable	leisured	levanter
laryngal	lavation	lead-bars	leave for	lemmatic	Levanter
larynges	lavatory	lead-burn	leave off	lemonade	levelism
lashed-up	lava tube	lead cell	leave out	lemonish	levelled
lashings	lava ware	lead comb	leavings	lemon law	leveller
lashless	lave-ears	leadenly	Lebanese	lemon oil	level off
lash rope	lavement	leadered	Lechitic	lemurian	level out
laspring	lavender	leaderly	lecithin	lemurine	leverage
last days	Laverack	lead flat	lectrice	lemuroid	leviable
last gasp	laverock	lead-free	lecturee	lenation	levigate
last home	laver-pot	leadless	lecturer	lendable	levirate
last name	lavishly	lead-line	lecythus	lengthen	levitant
last post	law agent	lead-mill	ledgment	lenience	levitate
last word	law court	lead-nail	leeangle	leniency	levodopa
latanier	lawcourt	lead-rope	lee-board	Leninism	levulose
latching	lawfully	lead shot	leeboard	Leninist	levyable
latchkey	lawgiver	leadsman	leechdom	Leninite	lewdness
latch-pan	law Latin	lead-spar	leechery	lenities	lewdster
lateener	law-maker	lead time	lee gauge	lenition	Lewis gun
late mark	lawmaker	lead-tree	leeriest	lenitive	Lewisian
latemost	lawn meet	lead-wash	leerness	leno loom	lewisite
lateness	lawn sand	lead wool	lee shore	lens hood	Lewisman
latently	Lawrence	leadwork	left-back	lensless	lexigram

liar dice	lifetime	limberly	linesmen	literati	lobbyist
libament	life-tree	limbless	line-wire	literato	lobeless
libation	life-vest	limblike	line-work	literose	lobelike
libatory	lifeward	limb-meal	ling-bird	litharge	lobeline
libeccio	life-work	lime-cast	lingerer	lithemia	loblolly
libelled	liftable	limekiln	lingerie	lithosol	lobotomy
libellee	liftback	limeless	linguine	lithsman	lobstick
libeller	lift down	Limenian	linguist	litigant	lobulate
libelous	lift-gate	limerick	lingular	litigate	local bus
liberate	liftless	Limerick	lingworm	litreage	localise
Liberian	lift-slab	lime-rock	liniment	litterer	localism
libretti	lift wire	lime-sink	linisher	little go	localist
libretto	ligament	lime soap	linking r	littlest	locality
licensed	liganded	lime-soda	link road	littling	localize
licensee	ligation	lime tree	linkspan	littlish	local pub
licenser	ligature	lime-twig	link-verb	littoral	location
licensor	ligeance	limewash	link-word	liturgic	locative
lichanos	lightage	lime-work	link-work	Litz wire	locellus
lichened	light air	limicole	Linnaean	liveable	Loch Fyne
lichenin	light-bob	liminary	linoleic	live bait	Lochlann
lich-gate	light-box	liminess	linolein	live-born	lochside
lich-path	light-day	limitary	linoleum	live coal	lockable
lick-hole	light due	limitate	Linotype	live down	locketed
licorice	lightful	limit bid	linstock	live it up	lockfast
lie about	light-gun	limit dog	lint-head	livelier	lock-knit
lie ahead	lighting	limiting	lion-head	livelily	lockless
lie along	lightish	limit man	lionhood	live load	lock on to
lie close	light-man	limnetic	lionizer	livelong	locksman
lie doggo	light oil	limnoria	lion-like	liveness	locksmen
liegedom	light out	limonene	lion's ear	liveried	lockspit
liegeman	light-pen	limonite	lionship	liveries	lock step
liegemen	light red	limonium	lipaemia	liverish	locofoco
Liégeois	ligneous	Limousin	lipaemic	liver pad	locomote
lie heavy	lignitic	limpidly	lip-brush	liver rot	loco-weed
lie in wed	ligulate	limpness	lip gloss	live up to	locution
lientery	Ligurian	limuloid	lipogram	liveware	locutory
lie to wed	likeable	linalool	lipoidal	live well	lodesman
lie under	likeably	linarite	liposome	live wire	lodestar
lie waste	like a log	linchpin	lippiest	live with	lodgment
lifebelt	like fury	lincture	lipsalve	liveyere	lodicule
lifeboat	like hang	lindworm	lipstick	lividity	loessial
lifebuoy	like hell	lineable	lip-strap	living-in	loftiest
life cord	likelier	lineally	Liptauer	livingly	loftsman
life form	likeness	linearly	liquesce	Livonian	log-board
life-hold	likening	line-boat	liquidly	lixivial	log cabin
lifeless	likesome	line-book	liquidus	lixivium	log canoe
lifelike	like that	line-bred	liration	lizardly	log flume
lifeline	like this	line-camp	liripipe	llaneros	log-house
life list	like well	line drop	lispound	load line	logician
lifelong	like wild	linefeed	lissomly	loadstar	logicise
life peer	likewise	line gale	listable	loaf-cake	logicism
life-raft	lilliput	line haul	listener	loaiasis	logicist
liferent	lily bell	lineless	listen in	loamless	logicize
life-ring	lily feet	line loss	listeria	loanable	logistic
life-save	lily-iron	linen tea	listless	loan-farm	logogram
life-size	lily-like	line pipe	list vote	loanword	logology
lifesome	lily-pond	line-ride	Lisztian	loathful	logotype
life span	lily-turf	line scan	litanies	loathing	log sheet
lifespan	lima bean	line-side	literacy	lobation	log table
life test	limacine	lineside	literary	lobby-gow	loiterer
life-tide	limation	linesman	literate	lobbyism	Lollardy

lollipop	long seas	loquence	love-pass	lumberer	lutidine
lolloped	long ship	loquency	love-play	lumberly	lutulent
lollygag	long shot	*loquitur*	lover boy	luminant	luxation
lomentum	longsome	lordless	lovering	luminary	luxmeter
Londoner	longspur	lordlier	love seat	luminate	luxuries
lone hand	long-stay	lordlike	lovesick	luminise	luxurist
lonelier	longstop	lordlily	lovesome	luminism	lycaenid
lonelily	long suit	lordling	love-song	luminist	lych-gate
loneness	long-tail	Lord Muck	love-tree	luminize	lycopene
lone pair	long-term	lordosis	love-vine	luminous	Lycurgan
lonesome	long-time	lordotic	lovingly	lump coal	lyke wake
lone star	long togs	lord over	low-alloy	lumpfish	lymphoid
lone wolf	*longueur*	Lord's day	low-class	lumpiest	lymphoma
long acre	long view	Lord's Day	Low Dutch	lumpless	lymphous
long bill	longwall	lordship	low enema	lump work	lynching
longbill	longward	loreless	lower jaw	lumpy jaw	lynch law
long blow	long wave	loricate	low-flung	lunabase	lynch mob
longboat	longways	lorikeet	low-grade	lunacies	lynchpin
long bone	longwise	lorisoid	low heels	luna moth	lynx-eyed
long card	long-wool	lornness	low-keyed	Luna Park	lynxlike
long cist	long word	Lorraine	Low Latin	lunar day	Lyonnais
long clam	lonicera	lorry-bus	low-level	lunarian	Lyonnese
long clay	look as if	lorry-hop	lowliest	lunarite	Lyonnois
long-coat	look back	loseable	lowlight	lunarium	lyophile
long date	look down	lose face	low-lived	lunation	lyophobe
long-dead	looker-in	lose time	low-lives	lunch box	lyrately
long dung	looker-on	lossless	low-lying	luncheon	lyra viol
long-ells	look good	lostness	low point	lung book	lyre-bird
longeron	look here	lost rock	low water	lungeing	lyre-tail
longeval	look like	lost soul	low-wines	lungeous	lyricise
long face	look over	lote-tree	low-yield	lungfish	lyricism
long firm	look sick	Lothario	loxodont	lungfuls	lyricist
long game	look up to	lotiform	loyalism	lungless	lyricize
longhair	looniest	lotus-eat	loyalist	lungworm	lyriform
longhand	loony-bin	Loucheux	loyalize	lungwort	lysarden
long haul	loop film	loud-hail	Loyolite	lunkhead	lysergic
longhead	loophole	loudness	lozenged	lunulate	lysogeny
long home	loopiest	lousiest	lozenger	Lupercal	lysopine
longhorn	loop jump	loveable	lubberly	lupulone	lysosome
long hour	loop-knit	love-bird	Lubecker	lurement	lysozyme
long John	loop-knot	lovebird	lubrical	Lurgi gas	lyzarden
long jump	loop-lace	lovebite	Lucanian	luringly	Macanese
long-legs	loop line	love bush	Lucchese	Lusatian	Macaoese
long lens	loop pile	love-curl	lucently	luscious	macaroni
long-life	loop-work	love-dart	lucernal	lushburg	macaroon
long line	loop-worm	loved one	Lucianic	lush drum	Macassar
long live	loop yarn	love game	lucidity	lush-head	Maccabee
long-lost	loose box	love-hate	luciform	lushness	maccoboy
long mark	loose end	love-knot	luckiest	lustered	macerate
long-moss	loose ice	Lovelace	luckless	lustiest	machinal
longneck	loosener	loveless	lucky-bag	lustless	machiner
longness	loosen up	lovelier	lucky dip	lustrate	machismo
long nine	loo table	love life	lucky him	lustring	macilent
long nose	lootable	lovelify	luculent	lustrous	mackerel
long odds	lop-eared	lovelike	Lucullan	lustrums	Mackinaw
long-play	lop-grass	lovelily	lucumony	lutanist	macropod
long pull	lophioid	loveling	luderick	lutecium	macruran
long rape	lopolith	lovelock	lug-chair	lutenist	maculate
long room	loppered	lovelorn	luggable	Lutetian	maculose
long rope	lopsided	love-mate	luggaged	lutetium	maculous
	lopstick	love nest	lukewarm	Lutheran	macushla

Madagass	mailable	make love	maltwort	mannitol	marginal
mad-apple	mail boat	make over	malvasia	man of God	margined
mad-brain	mailboat	make play	Mameluco	man of law	margrave
made dish	mail cart	make post	Mameluke	man of men	mariachi
Madeiran	mail drop	make room	mamillar	man-of-war	maribout
Madelung	mailgram	make sail	Mamma mia	man of wax	marigold
made mast	mailless	make sure	mammifer	manorial	marikina
maderize	maillots	make time	mammilla	manostat	marinade
made road	mailroom	make up to	mammitis	manpower	marinara
made wine	mailshot	make wing	mammogen	man-shift	marinate
mad Greek	mail-time	make with	Mam'selle	man-sized	marinise
madhouse	maimedly	make-work	managing	mansonia	Marinism
mad money	main beam	Makololo	man alive	mansuete	Marinist
madrigal	main body	makomako	man-child	manswear	marinize
madroños	main crop	maladies	manciple	mantelet	Mariotte
madstone	maincrop	maladive	man-crazy	mantical	mariposa
Madurese	main deck	mala fide	Mandaean	man-tiger	mariscal
madwoman	main dish	Malagash	Mandaite	mantiger	maritime
madwomen	main drag	Malagasy	mandamus	mantilla	marjoram
maeander	Maine Law	malamute	mandarin	mantises	markable
Maecenas	mainland	malapert	mandator	mantissa	mark-boat
maenadic	main line	malaprop	mandelic	mantling	mark down
maestoso	mainline	malarial	mandible	man to man	markdown
maestria	mainmast	malarian	Mandingo	man-trade	markedly
Maffiosa	mainpast	malarkey	Mandinka	manually	marketed
magadize	mainsail	Malawian	mandolin	manucode	marketer
magatama	mainstay	malaxate	mandorla	manumise	markless
magazine	main stem	Malayali	mandrake	manumize	marksman
magaziny	maintain	mal de mer	mandrill	manurial	marksmen
magdalen	main-ward	Malecite	man-eater	man-woman	mark time
Magellan	main yard	maledict	maneless	manyatta	marmoset
maggotry	maiolica	male fern	manerial	many-body	marocain
Maghribi	Maithili	malefice	maneuver	manyfold	Maronite
magic eye	Maitrank	malemute	manfully	many–many	marooner
magician	Maitreya	maleness	mangabey	manyness	marquess
magicked	majestic	malengin	manganic	manzello	marquise
magister	majolica	male pill	manganin	Maori bug	marriage
magmatic	Majorana	malgrace	Manganja	Maori dog	marrowed
magnesia	Majorcan	maligner	mangiest	Maoridom	marrying
magnesic	Majorism	malignly	mango-fly	Maori-hen	marry off
magnetic	Majorist	malihini	mangonel	maple key	marry out
magneton	majority	Malikite	mangrove	maple pea	Marshall
magnetos	major key	malinger	man-hater	map-maker	marsh gas
magnific	make a bag	Maliseet	maniacal	mappable	marsh hay
magnolia	make a bed	malistic	Manichee	maquette	marshier
Magosian	makeable	mallards	manicure	marabout	marshman
maharaja	make a bow	malleate	manifest	maracock	marsh tit
maharana	make a hit	mallecho	manifold	marantic	Marsilid
maharani	make a row	malleoli	maniform	marasmic	Martaban
Mahayana	make as if	malodour	Manipuri	marasmus	martagon
mah-jongg	make away	malonate	manistic	marathon	Martello
mahogany	makebate	Malorian	manitoka	marauder	Martenot
mahoitre	make down	Maloryan	mani wall	maravedi	martinet
Mahratta	make eyes	maltdust	mankiest	marbling	martynia
Mahratti	make fast	Malthoid	manliest	marcella	martyred
maidenly	make-game	maltiest	manna-ash	March fly	martyrly
maid-fish	make good	malt-kiln	manna-gum	marching	Mary Jane
maidhood	make-hawk	maltreat	mannered	march-man	Maryland
maidless	make head	malt shop	mannerly	Margaret	Mary lily
maidling	make it up	maltster	mannikin	margaric	Marymass
maieutic	makeless	maltworm	mannitic	margarin	marzipan

mascotry	maturest	meat-hook	melanite	menseful	messiest
mash note	maturity	meatiest	melanoid	men's room	messmate
mash-roll	matutine	meatless	melanoma	menstrua	mess-room
mason-bee	maumetry	meat loaf	melanose	mensural	messuage
Masonite	maundful	meat rack	melanous	menswear	mesteque
Mason jar	mausolea	meat-rail	Melchite	mentally	mestizos
Masorete	mauveine	meat safe	melilite	menthone	metaboly
Masorite	maverick	meatuses	melinite	menu card	metacism
massacre	maxillae	mechanic	melismas	mephitic	metacone
massager	maximand	mecholyl	melissic	mephitis	metadyne
mass-book	maximise	meconium	melissin	Mercator	metagram
masseter	maximist	medalist	melissyl	merchant	metal age
masseuse	maximize	medalize	melitose	merciful	metalate
massicot	maximums	medalled	melittin	Merckani	metaling
massless	Mayanist	medallic	melktert	mercuric	metalist
mass noun	mayapple	medially	melleous	mereness	metalize
massoola	May-apple	medianly	mellitic	merengue	metalled
Massorah	mayflies	mediated	mellowly	meresman	metallic
mast cell	mayordom	mediator	melodeon	meretrix	metamere
mast coat	mayoress	Medicaid	melodial	mergence	metamict
masterer	mayorlet	Medicare	melodies	mericarp	metanoia
masterly	May queen	medicate	melodion	meridian	metaphor
masthead	mazarine	Medicean	melodise	meringue	metarule
mastitis	Mazdaean	medicine	melodist	meristem	metasoma
mastless	Mazdaism	medieval	melodium	meristic	meta-talk
mastodon	Mazdaist	medimnus	melodize	meriting	metatony
mast-step	Mazdeism	mediocre	melomane	merit pay	Metatron
mast year	mazelike	meditant	melonist	merocele	metazoan
masurium	mazement	meditate	melon-oil	merogamy	metazoic
Matabele	mazer cup	mediumly	meltable	merogony	metazoon
matachin	maziness	medjidie	melt away	Meroitic	meteoric
matadora	M-capture	medullar	melt down	merriest	metewand
Mata Hari	McGuffin	medusoid	meltdown	merryman	meteyard
matamata	McIntosh	meekness	melt-spin	merry men	methanal
matchbox	McKenzie	meeterly	melusine	mersalyl	methanol
match-fit	*mea culpa*	meetness	membered	Mersenne	methinks
matehood	mead-hall	meet with	membrane	merwoman	methodic
mateless	meadowed	megabuck	mementos	merycism	methoxyl
matelote	meagrely	megabyte	memorate	mescalin	methylal
material	mealable	megacosm	memorial	Mesdames	methylic
matériel	mealiest	megadont	memoried	meshumad	metonymy
maternal	mealless	megaflop	memories	meshwork	me-tooism
mateship	meal moth	megalith	memorise	mesially	metopism
mat-grass	mealtide	megalopa	memorist	mesmeric	metreage
mathemeg	mealtime	megalops	memorize	mesnalty	metrical
mathesis	meal-worm	megapode	Memphian	mesocarp	metritic
mathetic	mealworm	Megarian	memsahib	mesoderm	metritis
Mathurin	mealy bug	megastar	menacing	mesoform	meunière
matiness	me-and-you	megaunit	Menapian	mesolabe	Mexicano
matrical	mean moon	megavolt	menarche	mesolect	mezereon
matrices	meanness	megawatt	mendable	mesomere	mezuzoth
matrixes	mean time	Meg Dorts	mendment	mesosome	mezzroll
matronal	meantime	Megillah	Menevian	mesotron	miasmata
matronly	mean tone	megimide	menhaden	mesozoan	mica flap
mattedly	mean well	meionite	menially	Mesozoic	Micawber
Matthean	measlier	meiosis I	meninges	mesozoon	micellar
mattress	measured	meiotaxy	meningic	mespilus	Michigan
maturant	measurer	Meissner	meniscal	mesquite	micritic
maturase	meatball	melamine	meniscus	Messapic	microamp
maturate	meat cube	Melanian	men-of-war	mess hall	microbic
maturely	meathead	melanism	menology	Messidor	microbus

microdot	Milky Way	minihole	misgiver	mistryst	modistic
micrurgy	millable	minimise	misgrown	misusage	modulate
midas fly	mill band	minimism	misguide	misvalue	mofussil
midbrain	mill bill	minimize	mishmash	miswrite	Mohammed
mid-cycle	mill-dust	mini-moke	Mishnaic	Mithraic	Moharram
middling	mill-hand	minimums	misinfer	miticide	mohonono
mid-earth	millhand	mini pill	misjudge	mitigant	mohoohoo
midfield	mill-head	minipill	miskeyed	mitigate	moieties
midnight	milliamp	minister	Miskitos	mitre box	moirette
mid-ocean	milliard	ministry	mislearn	mitt camp	moistful
midpoint	milliary	minneola	misliker	mittened	moistify
mid-range	millibar	minorate	misliver	mittimus	moistish
midships	millième	Minorcan	mislodge	mitzvoth	moisture
mid-spoon	milliner	Minoress	mismatch	mixed bag	mokaddam
midstead	millions	Minorite	mismated	mixed bed	moki-moki
mid-water	mill-pick	minority	mismetre	mixer tap	moko-moko
midwater	millpond	Minotaur	misnomer	Mixtecan	molality
midwives	mill-pool	minstrel	misogamy	mizen top	molarity
mightest	mill-post	mint-bill	misogyne	mnemonic	molassed
mightful	mill-race	mint cake	misogyny	Mobilian	molasses
mightier	mill-rind	mintiest	misology	mobilise	moldiest
mightily	mill-ring	mint mark	misorder	mobilism	Moldovan
mighty me	mill-sail	minueted	misplace	mobilist	mole-cast
migmatic	mill seat	minutely	misprint	mobility	molecule
mignonne	mill site	minutest	misprize	mobilize	mole-head
migraine	mill tail	minutial	misproud	mobocrat	molehill
migrator	mill town	minyanim	misquote	moccasin	moleskin
mijnheer	mill-weir	Miocenic	misroute	Mochican	molester
miladies	mill-work	miositic	misruler	mockable	molinary
Milanese	miltonia	Miquelet	missable	mock-bird	Molinism
milch cow	Miltonic	*mirepoix*	Miss Anne	mock croc	Molinist
mild beer	mimester	miriness	missense	mock lead	molleton
mildness	mimetism	mirkiest	misserve	mock moon	mollient
mile-mark	mimetite	mirliton	miss fire	moco-moco	Mollisol
milepost	mimiambi	mirrored	misshape	modalise	moll-shop
Milesian	mimicked	mirthful	missikin	modalism	mollusca
miliaria	mimicker	Mirzapur	missound	modalist	mollycot
militant	minacity	misagree	Missouri	modality	molossid
military	minatory	misalign	misspeak	modalize	molossus
militate	mince pie	misandry	misspell	modeless	Moluccan
milk bank	minchery	misanter	misspend	modeliar	molybdic
milk-bush	mind-cure	misapply	misspent	modeling	molysite
milk drop	mind-game	misaward	misspoke	modelist	momental
milk-duct	mindless	misbeget	miss-stay	modelled	momently
milkfish	mind-read	misbegin	misstate	modeller	momentum
milkiest	mineable	misbirth	misstyle	Modenese	monachal
milkless	mine dump	misbound	missworn	moderacy	monadism
milk line	mine host	miscarry	missyish	moderant	monadist
milk-loaf	mine-hunt	mischief	mistaken	moderate	Mona Lisa
milkmaid	mine-iron	miscible	mistaker	moderato	monamide
milk name	minerval	miscount	misteach	moderner	monamine
milkness	minestra	miscreed	misthink	modernly	monandry
milk-pail	mine-town	misdoing	mistiest	modestly	monarchy
milk room	mine-work	misdoubt	mistimed	modicity	monaster
milk-sick	mingiest	misdrive	mistitle	modified	monastic
milk-tree	minicell	misentry	mistless	modifier	monaural
milk-tube	mini-coat	miserere	mistlike	modifies	monaxial
milk-walk	Mini Disc	miseries	mistreat	modiolar	monazite
milk-warm	minidisk	misery me	mistress	modiolus	*mondaine*
milkweed	minigene	misfaith	mistrial	modishly	mondongo
milkwort	minigolf	misfield	mistrust	Modistae	Mondrian

monellin	monosemy	moot hall	Mortlake	mounseer	mudirieh
monensin	monosign	moot-hill	mortmain	mountain	mud-laden
monetary	monosome	mootness	mort-skin	mountant	mud pilot
monetise	monosomy	mop-board	mortuary	mounting	mud puppy
monetite	monotint	mopiness	Mosaical	mournful	mudslide
monetize	monotone	mopishly	mosasaur	mourning	mud snail
money-bag	monotony	mopper-up	moshavim	mouse-dun	mud snake
money box	monotype	mopstick	mosquito	mouse-ear	mudstone
money-man	monoxide	moquette	Mosquito	mousekin	mud trout
mongcorn	Monsieur	morainal	moss-back	mouselet	muff cock
Mongolic	monstera	morainic	moss-crop	mouse pox	muffetee
mongoose	Montague	moralise	moss horn	mousiest	muffling
monicker	Montanan	moralism	mossiest	moussaka	muga silk
monilial	monteith	moralist	mosslike	mouthful	muggiest
monistic	monte-jus	morality	moss opal	mouthier	mug-house
monition	Monterey	moralize	moss-peat	mouthily	mug's game
monitory	monticle	moral law	moss pink	mouth off	Muhammad
monitrix	Montilla	moralled	moss rose	mouth rot	Muharram
monk bond	monument	moration	moss-wood	moveable	muishond
monkeyfy	mood drug	moratory	Most High	move a peg	muisvoël
monkfish	moodiest	Moravian	most like	move away	mujtahid
Mon-Khmer	moodooga	morbidly	moteless	move into	mulattos
monkhood	moonball	morbific	motelier	moveless	mulberry
monk seal	moonbeam	morbilli	moteling	movement	mulching
monk-seam	moon boot	mordancy	mothball	move over	mule-bird
monk's gun	moon-cake	more like	mothered	moviedom	mule deer
monkship	mooncalf	morellos	motherer	movieola	mulesing
monk shoe	moon-dial	moreness	motherly	movingly	muleteer
monniker	moon-down	moreover	mothiest	mowburnt	muley cow
monoacid	moon-eyed	morepork	mothlike	moyen-âge	mulishly
monobloc	moon-face	Morescos	motility	mozzetta	mullered
monobuoy	moonfish	Moresque	motional	Mrs Thing	mulligan
monocarp	moongate	moribund	motivate	Mswahili	mullocky
monocled	mooniest	moriform	motivity	muchacha	mulloway
monocrat	moonless	morillon	mot juste	muchacho	multeity
monocule	moonlike	morindin	motliest	much less	multifid
monoculi	moon pool	Morlacco	Motorail	muchness	multimer
monocyst	moonrise	mormyrid	Motorama	mucilage	multiped
monocyte	moonseed	mormyrus	motor bus	mucinous	multiple
monodies	moonshee	mornings	motor car	muck-heap	multi-ply
monodist	moonshot	mornless	motor cop	muckiest	multiply
monodont	moonsiff	morn star	motordom	muckluck	multi-use
monogamy	moonwalk	Moroccan	motorial	muckrake	multi-way
monogeny	moonward	moroccos	motoring	muck soil	multurer
monogerm	moonwort	morology	motor inn	muckworm	mummy bag
monoglot	moon-year	moronism	motorise	mucky pup	muncheel
monogram	moor-bird	moronity	motorism	mucocele	munch out
monogyny	moorburn	morosely	motorist	mucoidal	mung bean
monohull	moor-coal	morosity	motorium	mucoitin	municipy
monokini	moorcock	morosoph	motorize	mucosity	muniment
monolith	moor-evil	Morphean	motorman	mucrones	munition
monology	moorfowl	morpheme	motormen	muculent	munyeroo
monomial	moor game	Morpheus	motorway	mud-brick	muralist
monomino	moor-head	morphine	mottling	mudbrick	muralled
monopody	moorland	morphing	moufflon	muddiest	Muranese
monopole	Moorpark	morphism	mouldery	muddle up	murchana
Monopole	moor-pout	morphoea	mouldily	mud fever	murderee
monopoly	moor-sick	mortally	moulding	mud fluid	murderer
Monoprix	moorsman	mortgage	mould oil	mud flush	murenger
monoptic	moose fly	mortific	moulinet	mudguard	murexide
monorail	mootable	mortiser	mound ant	mudirate	muriatic

muricate	mutinize	nail down	natatory	nearness	nembutsu
Muridism	mutinous	nail file	nathless	near-seal	Nemedian
muriform	mutterer	nail-gall	natiform	nearside	nemesism
muringer	muttoned	nail head	national	near-silk	nenuphar
murkness	mutually	nail-hole	natively	near upon	neoblast
murksome	muzziest	nailless	nativism	neatherd	neo-Latin
murmurer	myatonia	nailsick	nativist	neatness	neolocal
murphies	mycelial	nainsell	nativity	Nebbiolo	neologic
murrelet	mycelium	nainsook	nativize	nebulate	neomorph
murrhine	mycetoma	naissant	natterer	nebulise	neomycin
murrnong	mycetome	naked ape	nattiest	nebulist	neonatal
muscadel	mycology	naked bed	Natufian	nebulium	neo-Nazis
Muscadet	mydas fly	naked eye	naturise	nebulize	neon fish
muscatel	myelitic	nakhlite	naturism	nebulose	neon lamp
muscimol	myelitis	naloxone	naturist	nebulous	neon sign
muscling	myelomas	namaskar	naturize	neckband	neon tube
muscular	myelosis	nameable	naucrary	neck-beef	neophron
museless	mylodont	name-drop	naukrary	neck-bone	neophyte
musellim	mylonite	nameless	nauplial	neck-hole	neoplasm
mush-head	mylonize	name part	naupliar	necklace	neoprene
mushiest	myoblast	namesake	nauplius	neckless	Neorican
mushroom	myocomma	name-tape	nauseant	neckline	neotenic
musicale	myogenic	Namibian	nauseate	neck-lock	neotenin
music box	myograph	nanberry	nauseous	neck-rein	neoteric
musician	myokymia	nancy boy	nautical	neck-roll	Nepalese
musicker	myomeric	nannydom	nautilus	neck-vein	nepenthe
music-mad	myomorph	nannygai	navalism	neckwear	nephrite
musingly	myopathy	nannyish	navalist	neckweed	nephroid
musk-ball	myopical	Nantgarw	navarchy	necropsy	nephrops
musk deer	myoplasm	napellus	Navarran	necrosis	nepionic
musk duck	myositis	naphthol	navel-ill	necrotic	nepotism
muskeggy	myosotis	naphthyl	navicert	nectared	nepotist
musketry	myotatic	napiform	navicula	Ned Kelly	neptunic
muskiest	myotomic	napkined	naviform	needfire	Neronian
musklike	myotonia	napoleon	navigate	neediest	Neronize
Muskogee	myotonic	nappy pin	navy bean	needless	nerve gas
musk-rose	myriadth	narceine	navy blue	needment	nervelet
musk tree	myriapod	narcissi	Navy List	negation	nerve net
musk-wood	myristic	narcosis	navy plug	negative	nerve war
muskwood	myristin	narcotic	navy yard	negatory	nerviest
Muslimin	myristyl	narghile	Naxalism	negatron	nescient
muslined	myrmidon	naringin	Naxalite	negligee	neshness
muslinet	myronate	narkiest	nay-sayer	negligée	nestfuls
musquash	Mysoline	Narodnik	naysayer	Negretti	nestlike
mustache	Mysorean	narratee	Nazarean	Negrillo	nestling
mustardy	mystical	narrator	Nazarene	Negritic	net-layer
mustelid	mysticly	narrower	Nazarite	Negritos	netmaker
musterer	mystique	narrowly	Nazified	Negro dog	netsukes
muster in	mythical	nasalise	Nazifies	Negrodom	nettable
mustiest	mythless	nasalism	Nazirite	Negroish	nettling
mutation	myxedema	nasality	Ndebeles	Negroism	neumatic
mutative	myxinoid	nasalize	neap tide	Negro yam	neurally
mutchkin	myxomata	nascence	near-beer	neighbor	neuraxis
muteness	naartjie	nascency	nearctic	nektonic	neuritic
mute swan	nabobess	nasiform	Nearctic	Nelsonic	neuritis
muticous	nacreous	nasology	Near East	nelumbos	neuromas
mutilate	Naderism	nassella	near gale	nemacide	neuronal
mutillid	nag's-head	nastiest	near hand	nematode	neuronic
mutineer	nailable	Natalian	near home	nematoid	neuropil
mutinied	nail a lie	natality	near miss	Nembutal	neuroses
mutinies	nail bomb	natation	nearmost		neurosis

neurotic	nick-nack	Nixonian	non-licet	notalgia	nucellus
neuterly	nickname	Nixonite	non-metal	notalgic	nuciform
neutrino	nicotian	Noachian	non-moral	notarial	nucleant
Nevadian	nicotina	Noah's ark	non-party	notaries	nucleary
never-was	nicotine	Nobelist	non-polar	notarise	nuclease
new-baked	nicotize	nobelium	non-rigid	notarize	nucleate
new birth	nidation	nobility	non-sched	not at all	nucleoid
new blood	nidering	noble gas	nonsense	notation	nucleole
new-blown	nidicole	nobleman	non-stick	notative	nucleoli
new bread	nidified	noblemen	non-toxic	not-being	nuclidic
new broom	nidifies	noble rot	non-union	notchier	nudeness
newcomer	nidifuge	*noblesse*	nonuplet	notching	nude pact
New Delhi	nidorous	nobodies	non-usage	notebook	nugacity
newelled	nidulant	no bottle	non-voter	note card	nugation
new entry	niellist	nocturia	non-white	notecase	nugatory
Newlands	nielloed	nocturne	non-White	noteless	nuisance
New Light	nieveful	nodality	non-woven	not go far	nullable
newly-wed	niffiest	nodosity	no object	notified	null cone
Newmania	niff-naff	nodulate	noogenic	notifier	null link
new maths	Niflheim	nodulize	noontide	notifies	nullness
new-model	niftiest	nodulose	noontime	notional	numberer
New Model	Nigerian	nodulous	nopalery	not least	numb-fish
new money	niggling	noematic	nopaline	notornis	numb hand
New Negro	nigh-hand	noetical	no picnic	not quite	numbhead
new order	night bag	no-frills	normalcy	no trumps	numbness
New Right	night-box	no-go area	normally	not so bad	numeracy
newscast	nightcap	no-gooder	Normandy	not so hot	numerary
news desk	night eye	no-hitter	Norseman	not to say	numerate
newsgirl	night-fly	nohowish	Norsemen	noumenal	numerist
newshawk	night-hag	noiseful	northern	noumenon	numerous
newsiest	nightjar	noisette	northing	nounally	Numidian
newsless	nightman	noisiest	Northman	nounless	numinous
Newspeak	night off	no lack of	Northmen	nounness	nummular
newsreel	night out	no little	northpaw	nouveaux	numskull
news room	night owl	no longer	North Sea	nouvelle	nunation
newsroom	Nigritic	nomadise	norwards	Novatian	nunchaku
new-style	Nigrotic	nomadism	Norweyan	novation	nuncheon
New Style	nihilism	nomadize	noseband	noveldom	nunciate
new thing	nihilist	nomarchy	nose-clip	novelese	nundinal
new waver	nihility	no matter	nose-cone	novelise	nuppence
new woman	nil-grade	nominata	nosedive	novelish	nuraghic
New World	nimblest	nominate	nose door	novelism	nursling
New Year's	nimbused	nomistic	nose-down	novelist	nurtural
next-best	nimbuses	nomogram	nosehole	novelize	nurturer
next door	nine-eyed	nomology	nose leaf	novellas	nutation
nextness	ninefold	no mortal	noseless	November	nut brown
Nez Percé	nineteen	nonanoic	noseling	novenary	nut-crack
Nganasan	nineties	nonaries	nosepipe	novercal	nut-grass
Niam-Niam	Ninevite	non-Aryan	nose-ring	novitial	nuthatch
nibbanic	ning-nong	non-being	nosering	Novocain	nut-house
nibble at	ninjutsu	non-black	nose-tube	nowadays	nuthouse
nibbling	ninnyish	non-claim	nose-wipe	nowhence	nutmeggy
Nibelung	nippiest	non-count	nose-worm	nowheres	nutrient
niccolic	nitchevo	non-elect	noshable	no wonder	nutshell
niceling	nit-grass	non-empty	nosiness	nowtherd	nut-steak
niceness	nitrated	non-entry	nosology	n quadrat	nuttiest
niceties	nitriary	nonesuch	no sooner	nubecula	Nyamwezi
nice work	nitrogen	non-event	nostalgy	nubilate	nymphaea
Nichiren	nitrosyl	non-human	*nota bene*	nubility	nymphean
Nichrome	nitroxyl	non-ionic	not a bean	nubilous	nymphish
nickelic	nivation	nonjuror	not a hope	nucellar	nystatin

oafishly	occurred	of a truth	oil trade	Olympism	one while
oak-apple	oceanful	of course	oinochoe	omadhaun	one-woman
oakiness	Oceanian	of family	ointment	omelette	one-world
oat-grass	Oceanids	off and on	oiticica	omission	onhanger
oathable	oceanite	off-board	okey-doke	omissive	onion-fly
oat-plant	oceanity	off-brand	Okinawan	omitting	onion set
obduracy	ocean sea	off-break	Oklahoma	ommateal	on liking
obdurate	ocellate	offcomed	oknophil	ommateum	onliness
obeahism	ochreate	offcomer	old field	Ommayyad	onlooker
obeahman	ochreish	off-drive	old flame	omniform	only just
obedient	ochreous	offended	old fruit	omnitude	on my word
obeisant	ockerdom	offender	Old Glory	omnivore	on nights
obeyable	ockerism	offering	old guard	omnivory	onolatry
obeyance	ocnophil	off-gauge	Old Harry	omo-hyoid	onomancy
obituary	ocotillo	off-glide	Old Irish	omoplate	onomatop
objectee	octanoic	off-grain	Old Latin	omphalos	Onondaga
objector	octanoyl	off guard	Old Light	on a level	on pain of
oblately	octantal	officese	old-maidy	on and off	on parade
oblation	octapody	official	old money	on a plate	on parole
oblatory	octapole	offishly	Old Norse	on a slant	on points
obligant	octarchy	off-lying	old poker	on broach	on record
obligate	octaroon	off-piste	Old Saxon	on camera	on relief
obligato	octavian	off-pitch	old socks	once-born	on remand
obliging	octobass	off-price	Old South	once more	on screen
obliqued	octofoil	offprint	Oldspeak	onceness	on-screen
obliques	octonary	off-rhyme	old squaw	once-over	onscreen
oblivial	octopean	offscape	old stick	on change	onsetter
oblivion	octopian	offshoot	old story	on charge	on shares
oblongly	octopine	offshore	old-style	oncidium	on shikar
obnounce	octopoid	offsider	Old Style	oncogene	on stilts
obnoxity	octopole	off-stage	old sweat	oncolite	on stream
obrogate	octopush	off-track	old thing	oncology	on-street
obscurer	octoroon	off-verse	old-timer	oncoming	on strike
observer	octuplet	off-white	old times	oncosine	on supply
obsidian	octupole	of no name	old-timey	on course	on-target
obsolete	ocularly	of renown	Old Welsh	on credit	Ontarian
obstacle	oculated	of resort	old woman	on demand	on the air
obstruct	oddities	oftenest	old-world	one-acter	on the bit
obtainal	odd trick	of theirs	Old World	one-armed	on the bow
obtainer	Odinitic	oft-times	oleander	one-baser	on the bum
obtected	odiously	ogee arch	oleaster	one-berry	on the dot
obtemper	odometer	Oghuzian	olefiant	one by one	on the ebb
obtruder	odometry	ohmmeter	olefinic	one flesh	on the fly
obturate	odontoid	oil baron	olibanum	one-horse	on the gad
obtusely	odontome	oil-break	oligarch	one-idea'd	on the hip
obtusity	odourful	oilcloth	oligemia	one in six	on the hop
Ob-Ugrian	Odyssean	oilfield	oligomer	one-liner	on the jar
obvolute	odysseys	oil-fired	oligopod	one-night	on the job
Occamism	oeconomi	oil-gauge	oliguria	one-on-one	on the lam
Occamist	oecumene	oil-gland	oliguric	one or two	on the map
occasion	Oedipean	oiliness	oliphant	one-piece	on the mat
Occident	oenochoe	oil-paint	olive dun	one-place	on the nod
occluder	oenocyte	oil-paper	olive-fly	one's bark	on the pad
occlusal	oenology	oil-plant	olive oil	one's bite	on the pan
occlusor	Oerlikon	oil-press	olive pie	one's game	on the peg
occulter	oestrane	oil-shale	Olivetan	one-sided	on the run
occultly	oestriol	oil-shark	olivette	one's mark	on the sea
occupant	oestrone	oil slick	Olmecoid	one thing	on the sly
occupied	oestrous	oil spill	olorosos	one-to-one	on the tap
occupier	oestrual	oilstone	Olympiad	one-track	on the vag
occupies	of a piece	oil-tight	Olympian	onewhere	on the way

on thirds	operator	ordinant	osculate	outdress	outshove
on thorns	opercula	ordinary	osier bed	outdrink	outsider
on tiptoe	operetta	ordinate	Osmanlis	outdrive	outsight
ontogeny	operette	ordnance	osmicate	outer Bar	outsized
ontology	Ophelian	oreillet	osnaburg	outer ear	outskirt
on ullage	ophidian	ore-shoot	oso-berry	outer man	outsleep
on velvet	Ophitism	orfrayed	ossature	outfence	outsmart
on view of	ophiuran	organdie	Ossetian	outfield	outspeak
on wheels	ophiurid	organ-gun	Ossianic	outfight	outspeed
onymatic	opinicus	organise	ossicula	outflame	outspend
oofiness	opium den	organism	ossified	outflank	outstand
oogamete	Opium War	organist	ossifies	outflash	outstare
oogamous	opopanax	organity	osteitis	outflies	outstart
oogonial	oppilate	organize	ostinati	outfling	outstate
oogonium	opponens	organ-man	ostinato	outflung	outsteal
ookinete	opponent	organoid	ostomate	outflush	outstink
oolichan	opposing	orgasmal	ostracod	out front	outstood
oologist	opposite	orgasmic	ostracon	outfront	outstrip
oomycete	opposive	orgastic	ostreger	outfrown	outswear
oophoron	oppugner	orgonomy	Otaheite	outgases	outswell
oosphere	opsimath	orgulous	otarioid	outglare	outswing
oothecal	opsonize	oribatid	other man	outgoing	out-taken
ooze-calf	optation	orichalc	otiosely	out-group	out there
ooziness	optative	orielled	otiosity	outgrown	out-think
opacious	optic cup	oriental	otolitic	out-guard	out-throw
opacular	optician	oriented	otophone	outguess	out-trade
opal dirt	opticist	origanum	otoscope	out-Herod	out-trick
opalesce	opticity	original	ototoxic	outhouse	out-trump
opal ware	optimacy	orillion	otter-dog	outlaugh	outvalue
opaquely	optimate	orinasal	ottomans	outlawry	outvoice
opaquest	optimise	ormering	Ottomans	outlearn	out-voter
openable	optimism	ornament	Ottonian	outlying	outwards
open-arse	optimist	ornately	ought not	outmarch	outwatch
open bite	optimity	ornation	ouistiti	outmatch	outweary
open book	optimize	ornature	ouricury	outmoded	outweigh
opencast	optimums	ornithic	outargue	outmouth	outworld
open city	optional	orogenic	outbirth	outnoise	outwrite
open date	optotype	orometry	outblaze	out of bed	outyield
open door	opulence	oronasal	outbloom	out of key	ovalness
open-eyed	opuscula	orphancy	outblush	outpaint	Ovaltine
open file	opuscule	orphreys	outboard	out-place	ovariole
open fire	oracular	orpiment	outbound	outplace	ovaritis
open goal	oraculum	or rather	outbrave	outpoint	ovenbird
open line	oragious	Orrefors	outbreak	outpoise	oven-cook
open loop	orangery	orreries	outbreed	outpower	ovenette
open mind	orangish	orthesis	outbroke	outpsych	ovenware
open-neck	Orangist	orthicon	outbuild	outpunch	overaged
openness	oratoric	orthodox	outburst	outrager	overarch
open-plan	oratorio	orthoepy	outcarry	outrange	overbank
open-reel	oratress	orthopod	outcaste	outreach	overbark
open road	orbicule	orthosis	outcharm	outreign	overbear
open shop	orbitale	orthotic	outclass	outrider	overbeat
open-side	orbiting	orticant	outclimb	outright	overbend
open town	Orcadian	ortstein	outcrier	outrival	overbite
open ward	orchella	Ortygian	outcries	outscold	overblow
openwork	orchilla	Orvietan	outcross	outscore	overbody
operable	orchitis	oryzenin	outcurve	outshame	overboil
opera hat	ordainer	oscinine	outdance	outshine	overbold
operance	order man	oscitant	outdated	outshone	overbook
operancy	order pad	Oscotian	outdoors	outshoot	overboot
operatic	ordinand	osculant	outdream	outshout	overbore

overbrim	overhard	overrise	overwell	pacifico	palesman
overbrow	overhaul	overrode	overwent	pacified	palestra
overbull	overhead	overroll	overwind	pacifier	paleways
overbump	overheap	overroof	overwing	pacifies	palewise
overburn	overhear	overruff	overwise	pacifism	palfreys
overbusy	overheat	overrule	overwood	pacifist	palilogy
overcall	overhigh	oversail	overword	Pacinian	palimony
overcame	overhill	oversalt	overwork	packable	palinode
overcare	overhung	overseas	overworn	packager	palinody
overcast	overhunt	overseen	overwrap	packaway	palisade
overclad	overjump	overseer	overyear	pack-flat	palisado
overcloy	overkeep	overself	overzeal	pack it in	palladia
overcoat	overkill	oversell	ovicidal	pack-road	palladic
overcoil	overkind	over-shoe	ovicular	pack-sack	palliard
overcold	overking	overshoe	oviducal	packshot	palliate
overcome	overknee	overshot	oviposit	pack them	pallidly
overcook	overlade	overside	ovomucin	pad-cloth	palliest
overcool	overlaid	oversize	ovulator	Paddyism	palliums
overcrop	overlain	overslip	owleries	Padishah	pall-mall
overcrow	overland	overslow	owlglass	pad money	palmated
overcure	overlard	oversnow	owlishly	pad-steam	palm-ball
overdamp	overlate	oversoar	owl-light	padstone	palm-bird
overdear	overleaf	oversold	owl midge	paduasoy	palm crab
overdeck	overlean	oversoon	owl train	paeonies	palmella
overdoer	overleap	oversoul	own brand	pagandom	Palmerin
overdoes	overlier	overspan	own-label	paganise	palmette
overdo it	overline	overspin	own woman	paganish	palmetto
overdone	overling	overspun	oxalosis	paganism	palmfuls
overdoor	overlive	overstay	oxaluria	paganity	palm-grub
overdose	overload	overstep	oxathiin	paganize	palmiest
overdraw	overlock	oversway	oxazepam	pagehood	palmiped
overdrew	overlong	overswim	ox-botfly	pageship	palmitic
over ears	overlook	overt act	oxbow key	page-turn	palmitin
overeasy	overlord	overtake	Oxbridge	paginary	palm leaf
overface	overloud	overtalk	ox-fenced	paginate	palmlike
overfall	overloup	overtask	ox-harrow	pahoehoe	palm-lily
overfeed	overlove	overteem	oxidable	pailfuls	palm-play
overfell	over-many	overtell	oxidized	pain-free	palm-room
overfill	overmany	overtilt	oxidizer	painless	palm tree
overfilm	overmark	over time	oximeter	pain spot	palm-wasp
overfine	overmast	overtime	oximetry	paint box	palm wine
overfire	overmitt	overtire	ox-pecker	paintbox	palm-worm
overfish	overmost	overtoil	ox-tongue	paintier	palomino
overflew	overmuch	overtone	oxtongue	painting	palpable
overflow	overname	overtook	ox-warble	paint out	palpably
overfold	overnice	overtrap	oxyanion	paint-pot	palpebra
overfond	overpaid	overtrim	oxygenic	pair-bond	palpifer
overfree	overpark	overtrow	oxymeter	pair-feed	palpiger
overfull	overpass	overture	oxymoron	pair-mate	palstave
overgang	overpeer	overturn	oxyphile	pairment	palterer
overgave	overplay	overveil	oxytocic	pair-toed	palterly
overgaze	overplus	over vert	oxytocin	pairwise	paltrier
overgild	overpole	overview	oxytonic	Palamite	paludina
overgive	overrank	overwalk	oysterer	palander	paludine
overglad	overrash	overward	Ozarkian	palatial	paludism
overglut	overrate	overwarm	ozonizer	palatian	pamaquin
overgrew	overread	overwash	pabulary	palatine	pamperer
overgrow	overrent	overweak	pacation	palative	pamperos
overhair	overrich	overwear	pace-note	paleface	pamphlet
overhand	override	overween	pachalic	pale flax	panacean
overhang	overripe	overweep	pachinko	paleness	panached

panarchy	papalise	parashah	part-bred	pastoral	paxillar
panatela	papalism	parasite	parterre	pastorly	pay a call
pan-broil	papalist	paratomy	part fair	pastrami	pay claim
pancetta	papalize	paratype	part from	pastries	paynimry
panchama	Papal See	paravail	Parthian	pastural	pay phone
pancheon	paparchy	paravane	partiary	pasturer	payphone
Pancoast	papaship	par avion	partible	pat-a-cake	pay sauce
pancreas	paper bag	parawing	particle	patacoon	peaberry
panda car	paper boy	paraxial	partisan	patagial	pea-brain
pandanny	paper cup	parazoan	partitas	patagium	peaceful
pandanus	papering	parbreak	partizan	patch-box	peace-man
pandemic	paper man	parcener	partless	patchery	peacenik
panderer	paper run	parclose	part-load	patch fox	peachery
pandowdy	papillae	pardoner	partners	patchier	pea-chick
panegyry	papillar	pardon me	partness	patchily	peachier
paneless	papillon	parental	part-song	patching	peach-pip
paneling	papirosa	parented	part-time	pâte dure	peacocky
panelist	papisher	pareoean	part with	patellae	pea-flour
panelled	papistic	parergon	part-work	patellar	pea green
panel pin	papistly	Paretian	partyism	patentee	peak hour
panel saw	papistry	parfocal	party man	patently	peakiest
panel van	papulose	pargeted	parvenue	patentor	peak load
panforte	papulous	pargeter	parwanah	Paterian	pea-plant
pangeran	papyrosa	pargetry	parylene	paternal	pear drop
pangless	parabema	parhelia	parypate	pathetic	pearl ash
panglima	parabola	parhelic	pasch-egg	pathless	pearl-hen
Pangloss	parachor	parietal	pascuant	pathogen	pearlier
pangolin	paracone	parietes	pashadom	patience	pearling
pan-human	paradigm	parietin	pashalic	patiency	pearlish
panic bar	paradise	Parisian	pashmina	patinaed	pearlite
panicked	paradors	parkiest	pasilaly	patinate	pearmain
panicled	paradoxy	parkland	paspalum	patootie	pear tree
Paninean	paradrop	parklike	passable	patriate	pearwood
pan juice	paraffin	parlance	passably	patrices	peasanty
panmixia	paraffle	parlando	passalid	patronal	peasecod
pannikin	parafoil	parlleys	pass away	patronee	pea-shell
Pannonic	paraform	Parma ham	passback	patronly	pea-stake
panoptic	paragoge	Parmesan	passband	patronym	peat-coal
panorama	paragone	parodial	passbook	pattable	peatland
pan pipes	Paraguay	parodied	pass door	pattamar	peatmoss
panplain	parajump	parodies	passer-by	pattened	peat-reek
pan-Roman	parakeet	parodist	Passeres	patterer	peatship
pansophy	parakite	parodize	pass–fail	patterny	pea-viner
panstick	parallax	paroemia	pass-hemp	pattress	peccable
pansyish	parallel	parolein	passible	pattypan	peccancy
pantcoat	paralyse	paronymy	passival	patulent	peccavis
panterer	paralyze	paroquet	pass laws	patulous	peck horn
pantheon	parament	parosmia	passless	pauldron	peck mood
pantiled	paramese	parotoid	pass line	Paulista	pecorino
pantiler	par amour	Parousia	pass-mark	paunched	pectines
pantless	paramour	paroxysm	pass over	pauropod	pectoral
pantoate	paranete	parroted	Passover	pavement	peculate
pantofle	paranjah	parroter	pass play	pavilion	peculiar
pantonal	paranoia	parrotry	passport	pavisade	pedagogy
pantopod	paranoic	Parseval	password	pavisand	pedal bin
Pantopon	paranoid	parsonic	pastance	pavonian	pedal car
pantries	paraoxon	parsonly	pastiche	pavonine	pedalfer
pant suit	parapack	parsonry	pastiest	pawkiest	pedalier
panurgic	paraquat	partaken	pastille	pawl-bitt	pedalled
papabile	parasail	partaker	pastless	pawnable	pedaller
papacies	parasang	part-book	pastness	pawnshop	pedaloes

pedantic	penalize	Percaine	Pershing	Pfeiffer	phthalic
pedantry	penchant	per caput	personae	phacelia	phthises
pedately	pencraft	perceant	personal	phacopid	phthisic
peddling	pendency	perceive	personas	phalaena	phthisis
pederast	pendicle	percepta	perspire	phalange	phulkari
pedestal	pendular	perchery	perspiry	Phalange	phut-phut
pedicate	pendulum	perentie	persuade	phalaris	phylarch
pedicure	Penelope	perester	Pertelot	phallism	phyletic
pediform	penetral	perfecta	perthite	phalloid	phyllary
pedigree	penitent	perfecto	pertness	phantasm	phyllite
pediment	penknife	perflate	Perugian	phantast	phyllode
pedipalp	pen-light	perforce	perukier	phantasy	phyllody
pedology	penlight	perforin	Peruvian	Pharisee	phylloid
pedregal	pennated	perfumed	perverse	pharmacy	phyllome
peduncle	pennoned	perfumer	pervious	phase out	physalis
peekaboo	penn'orth	Pergonal	perylene	pheasant	physeter
peekapoo	penny-fee	periagua	Peshitta	phenagle	physical
peelable	penology	perianal	peskiest	phenetic	physicky
peep-hole	penseful	perianth	pessimal	phengite	physique
peephole	pen shell	periblem	pessimum	phenogam	piacular
peep-show	pensiful	pericarp	pesterer	phenolic	pia mater
peep-toed	penstock	pericope	pest-ship	phenylic	pianette
peerless	pentacle	pericyte	petaline	phialine	pianiste
peership	pentagon	periderm	petalism	philabeg	piassava
peesweep	pentamer	peridial	petalite	Phillips	piazzaed
peetweet	pentanol	peridium	petalled	philobat	piblokto
Pegasean	pentarch	periergy	petalody	philodox	picaroon
pegboard	Pentelic	perifuse	petaloid	Philomel	picayune
peggotty	pentitol	perigean	*pétanque*	Philonic	piccolos
peggy bag	Pentland	Périgord	petchary	philtrum	Picenian
peggy tub	Pentomic	perigyny	petechia	phimosis	pichurim
peg-house	pentosan	perijove	peterman	phimotic	piciform
peignoir	pent roof	perilled	petermen	phlegmon	pickable
Peircian	penumbra	perilous	Peternet	phloxine	pickerel
pejorate	penuries	perilune	Peter Pan	Phocaean	picker-up
pejorism	Penutian	perineal	Peterson	Phoebean	picketed
pejorist	penwiper	perineum	petiolar	phonemic	picketer
Pekinese	penwoman	periodic	petioled	phonetic	pickfork
pelagian	peonidin	perioral	petition	phoniest	pickiest
Pelagian	peperino	periotic	petitive	phononic	pickings
pelandok	peperite	perisarc	petit mal	phoresis	picklock
Pelasgic	peperoni	perisher	petitory	phoretic	pick-me-up
pelerine	peplumed	peritomy	petrific	phorminx	pick over
peliosis	peppered	perjured	petrolic	phormium	pick-pole
pellagra	pepperer	perjurer	petronel	phoronid	picksome
pelleted	pepper-up	perkiest	petrosal	phosgene	pickwick
pelleter	peppiest	perlitic	pettable	phosphor	picloram
pellicle	pep rally	permeant	pettedly	photoact	picnicky
pell-mell	peptidic	permease	pettiest	photofit	picoline
pellucid	peptidyl	permeate	pettifog	photogen	picritic
peloidal	peptizer	per mille	pettitoe	photo lab	Pictland
pelorism	peptogen	permuter	Petty Bag	photomap	pictural
pelorize	Pepuzian	Permutit	petty pan	Photomat	pictured
pelt-wool	Pepysian	pernancy	petulant	photonic	piddling
pelvises	peracute	peroneal	petuntse	photopic	pie-biter
Pembroke	perahera	peroneus	pew group	photo-set	piece-bag
pemmican	peramble	Peronism	pewterer	photoset	piece-dye
pemoline	per annum	Peronist	Peyerian	phrasing	piecener
penacute	per arsin	perorate	peyotism	phratric	piece out
penalise	perboric	peroxide	peyotist	phreatic	pie chart
penality	Perbunan	perseity	Pfalzian	Phrygian	piecrust

pied crow	pimentos	pinprick	pitchier	planking	playhour
pied duck	pimiento	pinscher	pitching	plankter	playland
Pied Monk	pimpling	pinswell	pitchman	planktic	playless
piedmont	pinacoid	pin-table	pitch-oil	plankton	playlist
piedness	pinacone	pint-size	pitch-ore	plank-way	playmake
pie-eater	pinafore	pin valve	pitch-out	planless	playmate
pie-faced	pinakoid	pin-wheel	pithiest	planning	playroom
pie graph	pinaster	pinwheel	pithless	planosol	play safe
pie-melon	pinboard	pipe away	pithlike	planster	playsome
pie-plant	pince-nez	pipe band	pith-tree	plantain	play-suit
piercing	pincette	pipe bomb	pitiable	plant-bug	playsuit
pier-head	pinch-bar	pipeclay	pitiably	planting	playtime
pierless	pinch-bug	pipe down	pitiless	plantlet	play upon
pie-wagon	pinch-gut	pipefish	Pitmanic	plant out	play up to
piffling	pinch-hit	pipefuls	pitmatic	plantula	pleached
piff-paff	pinching	pipeless	pit organ	plantule	pleading
pig along	pinch-off	pipelike	pittance	plan view	pleasant
pigeonry	pinch-out	pipeline	pit viper	plashily	pleasing
piggiest	pinch-run	pipe-rack	pivoting	plashing	pleasure
piggling	Pindaric	piperade	pivotman	plasmoid	plebania
pig Latin	Pindarry	piperine	pixelate	plasmoma	plebbish
pig louse	pine cone	pipe roll	pixie cap	plasteel	plebeian
pig-metal	pine-knot	pipe-stem	pixie hat	plastery	plectrum
pig-mould	pine land	pipe tree	pixie-led	plastify	Pleiades
pigsties	pineries	pipe-vine	pize-ball	plastome	plein-air
pig's wash	pine tree	pipework	pizzeria	plastral	plenarty
pigswill	pine vole	pipewort	placable	plastron	plentify
pikehead	pineweed	pipkrake	placably	platanna	pleonasm
pike-pole	pine wood	piquable	placater	platanus	pleoptic
pilaster	pinewood	piquance	placcate	platband	plethora
pilchard	ping-pong	piquancy	Place Act	plateaus	plethory
pile arms	pin-grass	piracies	place-bet	plateaux	plethron
pileated	pinguefy	pirastic	placebos	plateful	pleurisy
pile it on	ping-wing	piratess	placeman	platelet	pleurite
pileless	pin hinge	piriform	place mat	plate pie	plexuses
pilentum	pinioned	piri-piri	placemen	platform	pliantly
pile-shoe	pin joint	piripiri	placenta	platinic	plicated
pile-work	pink-foot	piroshki	placidly	platinum	plimsole
pilewort	pink gold	pirozhki	Placidyl	Platonic	plimsoll
pilferer	pink lady	pis aller	placitum	platting	Pliocene
piliated	pinkness	pisanite	plagiary	platypus	Pliofilm
pilidium	pinkroot	piscator	plaguily	platysma	pliosaur
piliform	pink slip	piscinae	plaguing	plaudite	pliotron
Pilipino	pink spot	piscinas	plaiding	plausive	plip-plop
pillager	Pinkster	pishashi	plain bob	Plautine	plodding
pillaloo	pinkwash	pishogue	plainful	playable	plombage
pillared	pink wine	pish-pash	plaining	play away	plopping
pillaret	pinkwood	pisiform	plainish	play back	plotless
pill head	pinledge	pisolite	plain man	playback	plot-line
pilliver	pin lever	pisolith	plain-saw	play ball	plottage
pillowed	pin money	pissabed	plaister	playbill	plotting
pill slab	pinnacle	piss away	plaiting	playbook	plotwise
pillwort	pinnated	piss down	plancher	play-debt	ploughed
pilosity	pinniped	pisshead	planchet	play down	plougher
pilotage	pinnular	piss-hole	plancier	play face	plough in
piloting	pinochle	piss-take	plane-bit	play fair	plowland
pilotism	pinoleum	pistacia	planeful	Playfair	pluckier
pilot jet	pin-paper	pistolet	planetal	playfere	pluckily
pilot-man	pin-patch	pitahaya	planetic	playgame	plucking
Pilsener	pin plate	pit canal	planform	playgirl	plug back
Piltdown	pinpoint	pitch-cap	plangent	playgoer	plug-cock
pilulous	Pinpoint	pitch for	plank bed	play high	plug flow

plug fuse	podgiest	polisher	polypite	poor show	Portland
plugging	podiatry	polish up	polypody	poortith	port-last
plug-hole	podiform	politely	polypoid	poor-will	portlier
plughole	podocarp	politest	polypore	popehood	portmote
plug-ugly	podocyte	politico	polypose	Pope Joan	portolan
plumaged	Podolian	politics	polypous	popeless	portrait
plumbago	podomere	politied	polyseme	popelike	portress
plumbane	pod razor	polities	polysemy	popeling	portsman
plumbate	pod shell	politize	polysome	pope's eye	port tack
plumb-bob	podzolic	polka dot	polysomy	Pope's eye	portuary
plumbean	Poe-esque	polkaing	polytene	popeship	Portugal
plumbery	poethood	pollable	polyteny	pop group	portulac
plumbian	poetical	poll-book	polytomy	popinjay	portunal
plumbing	poetizer	poll card	polytope	popishly	port wine
plumbism	poetless	poll deed	polytype	poplared	porulose
plumbite	poetling	pollenin	polytypy	poplolly	poseable
plumbous	poetship	poll-evil	polyuria	pop music	poshness
plum cake	pogonion	pollical	polyuric	popocrat	poshteen
plum duff	poignant	pollices	polyzoan	Popovets	positing
plumelet	Poincaré	pollinia	polyzoic	poppadam	position
plumeria	pointage	pollinic	polyzoon	poppadom	positive
plumetis	point bar	polliwog	pomander	Poppy Day	positron
plumetty	pointful	pollster	pomarine	pop-rivet	posology
plumiest	pointier	polluted	pomelled	Popsicle	possible
plumiped	pointing	polluter	pomerium	popskull	possibly
plumlike	pointlet	pollywog	pommellé	populace	postally
plummier	point man	polo coat	pommetty	populate	postbase
plummily	point net	polocyte	pomology	populism	post-boat
plumping	point out	poloidal	pompanos	populist	postcard
plumpish	pointrel	polo neck	Pompeian	populous	post-cart
plum tree	poisoner	Polonian	pompilid	pop-valve	postcode
plumular	Poitevin	polonies	pompless	pop-visit	postcure
plungeon	poke-nook	polonium	pomponed	poquosin	post-date
plunging	pokerish	Polonize	ponchoed	poristic	postdate
plunther	poke-root	polo-pony	ponderal	pork-chop	postdict
plurally	pokeweed	Polovtsy	ponderer	porkfish	post-echo
pluriarc	pokiness	polt-foot	pond-fish	porkiest	post-edit
plushier	Polabian	poltroon	pond life	porkling	postface
plushily	Polabish	Polwarth	pond-lily	porkwood	post-fine
plus sign	Polander	polyacid	pond-pine	porky-pie	postform
plus-twos	polar cap	polyadic	pondweed	porn-shop	post-free
plutonic	Polar cap	polyarch	ponerine	porocyte	post-girl
plutonyl	polarise	polybase	pongiest	porogamy	postgrad
Pluviose	polarity	polyclad	ponticum	poroporo	post-hole
pluvious	polarize	polydrug	pontifex	porosity	post-horn
Plyglass	Polaroid	Polyfoto	pontific	porously	posthuma
plymetal	pole-bean	polygala	pony-tail	porphyry	postical
Plymouth	pole-boat	polygamy	ponytail	porpoise	postiche
pnicogen	pole-jump	polygene	pooh-pooh	porridge	posticum
pnictide	poleless	polygeny	pool-ball	porridgy	post-lady
pochards	pole-mast	polyglot	pool hall	portable	postlude
pochette	polemise	polygram	pool room	portably	postmark
pocketed	polemist	polygyny	poolside	portales	post-mill
pocketer	polemize	polylogy	poonghie	Portaloo	post-note
pock-mark	pole-reed	polymath	poontang	portance	post-obit
pockmark	pole star	polymery	poop deck	port arms	post-oral
pockwood	polestar	polymict	poor-farm	porteous	post-paid
podagral	pole-trap	polyneme	Poor-Jack	portfire	postpone
podagric	poleward	polyopia	Poor John	porthole	postpose
podalgia	policies	polypary	poor man's	porticos	post rank
podargus	policing	polypide	poorness	porticus	post-road
podetium	poliosis	polypier	poor rate	portière	post room

post ship	Powindah	prehuman	prestore	prizable	propanal
post-sync	powwower	pre-ictal	presumer	prizeman	propanol
post-term	Powysian	prejudge	pretence	prizemen	propenal
post town	poxvirus	prelatic	pretense	proavian	propense
postural	Poynting	pre-Latin	pretonic	probable	propenyl
posturer	Pozidriv	prelatry	pretrain	probably	properly
posy ring	practice	prelimit	pretreat	procaine	property
potassic	practise	preluder	pretrial	proceeds	prophage
potation	*praecipe*	preludia	prettier	procello	prophase
potatoes	praedial	Preludin	prettify	prochain	prophecy
potatory	praefect	preludio	prettily	proclaim	prophesy
pot-au-feu	Praesepe	premerit	previous	Proclian	prophyll
pot-belly	Praguean	premiate	prevotal	procline	propiska
pot-board	Praguian	premiere	priapean	Procline	proplasm
pot-bound	Prairial	première	priapism	proclive	propless
pot-earth	prairied	premisal	Priapist	procural	propofol
potented	praise be	premiums	price-cut	procurer	propolis
potently	Pramnian	premolar	price out	prodding	proposal
potholed	pram-park	pre-moral	price tab	prodelta	proposed
potholer	prandial	premorse	price tag	prodigal	proposer
potholey	prankful	premotor	price war	prodnose	propound
pot-house	prankish	premoult	priciest	prodroma	propoxur
potlatch	praskeen	prenasal	prick-ear	prodrome	proppily
pot-metal	pratfall	prenatal	pricking	producer	propping
pot-paper	pratique	prentice	pricklet	proemial	proprium
pot plant	prat-kick	pre-order	prideful	profaner	prop-root
potreros	prattler	pre-owned	prie-dieu	profiler	prop wash
pot roast	prayable	preparer	priestly	profilin	prop-word
potsheen	prazosin	prep chef	priggery	profited	propylic
potsherd	preacher	prepense	priggish	profiter	propylon
pot-shoot	preach up	preppier	priggism	pro forma	prorogue
pot stand	preadapt	preppies	primally	profound	prosaism
potstick	pre-adult	prepping	primatic	profunda	prosaist
pot still	preamble	pre-print	primeval	profundi	proseman
potstone	pre-axial	preprint	primmest	progeria	prosiest
potterer	preboard	prepubes	primming	progeric	prosodia
pottiest	precaval	prepubic	primness	proggins	prosodic
pot-train	precinct	prepubis	primrose	prognose	prosopon
pot-water	precious	prepulse	primrosy	prograde	prospect
pot-woman	precipit	prepupal	princely	progress	prostate
poulaine	précised	prequark	princeps	prohibit	prostyle
pouldron	précises	pre-rinse	princess	pro-knock	protalus
poulette	preclose	pre-Roman	princock	prolapse	pro tanto
poultice	preclude	presager	printery	pro-lifer	protases
poundage	precurse	prescind	printing	prolific	protasis
pound-fee	predator	presence	print out	Prolixin	protatic
Poundian	predella	preserve	printout	prolixly	protease
pounding	Predmost	presider	print run	prologue	protégée
pound-net	pre-elect	Presidia	priorate	promisee	proteose
pound out	preening	presidio	prioress	promiser	protheca
pourable	pre-entry	presolar	priories	promisor	prothyle
poverish	pre-exist	press bed	priority	promotee	protidic
povidone	prefacer	press box	prisable	promoter	protocol
Povindah	preferee	press day	Priscian	promotor	protomer
power car	prefetch	press fit	prismane	prompter	protonic
power cut	prefixal	pressing	prismoid	promptly	protopod
power-egg	prefocus	pression	prisoned	promulge	protozoa
powerful	preggers	pressive	prisoner	pronator	protract
power law	pregnane	pressman	prissier	prong-hoe	protrude
power-net	pregnant	pressmen	prissily	pronotal	pro-tutor
power set	prehnite	pressure	pristane	pronotum	protypon
Powhatan	pre-human	prestige	pristine	pro or con	proudful

proudish
provable
provably
provedly
Provence
provenly
prove out
Proverbs
proviant
provided
provider
province
proviral
provirus
provisor
provisos
provoked
provoker
provosty
prowl car
proxemic
proxenus
proximad
proximal
proxy war
prudence
prudency
pruinose
prunable
prunasin
prunella
prunello
prurient
pruritic
pruritus
Prussian
Prutenic
pryddest
pryingly
prytanis
psalmist
psalmody
psaltery
psammite
psammoma
psellism
psephism
psephite
pseudery
pseudish
psilocin
psilosis
psilotic
psionics
psoralen
psychism
psychist
psychoid
psych out
psyllium
pteropod
pterotic

ptilinal
ptilinum
ptilosis
ptomaine
ptyalism
pubarche
pub crawl
pubertal
publican
Publican
publicly
pub lunch
pucellas
puckauly
puckeroo
puckerow
puckfist
pucklike
puckster
puddingy
puddling
pudendal
pudendum
pudgiest
pudibund
pudicity
puebloan
puffball
puffbird
puffiest
puffinry
puff pipe
puff port
puff-puff
puggaree
pugilant
pugilism
pugilist
Puginian
pug-nosed
puissant
Pulfrich
pulicose
pulicous
pulingly
Pulitzer
pullable
pull-back
pull-bell
pullbone
pull caps
pull-cord
pull-date
pull-down
pull foot
Pullmans
pull over
pullover
pull rank
pulmonic
pulmotor
pulperia

pulpiter
pulpitis
pulpitry
pulpitum
pulpless
pulpwood
pulsator
pulse jet
pulsific
pultrude
pulvilio
pulvinar
pulvinus
pumicite
pumpable
pump-down
pump iron
pumpless
pump room
pump ship
pump-tree
pump-well
punaluan
punch-bag
punchbag
puncheon
punchery
punchier
punchily
punching
punch out
punctate
punctual
punctule
puncture
punditry
pungence
pungency
Punic War
puniness
punisher
punition
punitive
punitory
Punjabis
punk chic
punkette
punk rock
punnable
Punt e Mes
punt-pole
pupa-case
puparial
puparium
pupation
pupiform
pupilage
pupil age
pupilage
pupilary
pupildom
pupillar

pupilled
pup joint
puppetry
puppy-dog
puppydom
puppy fat
puppyish
puppyism
purblind
purchase
purdahed
pure-bred
pure line
pure milk
pureness
pure pute
pure tone
purflewe
purfling
purgator
purified
purifier
purifies
puriform
puristic
Purkinje
purlieus
purparty
purplish
purposed
purposer
purpuric
purpurin
purse-bag
purseful
purse-net
purse-web
purslane
pursuant
pursuing
purulent
purveyor
purwanah
Puseyism
Puseyist
Puseyite
pushable
push-ball
push-bike
pushcart
push-down
push hold
pushiest
pushover
push pass
push-pull
push-shot
puss boot
puss moth
pussy cat
pustulan
pustular

put about
putanism
putative
putchock
put forth
put out of
putridly
put right
putterer
put to bed
put to sea
putt-putt
put under
put-up job
put-you-up
puzzlist
pycnogon
pycnosis
pyelitic
pyelitis
pygidial
pygidium
pygmaean
pygmy owl
pyinkado
pyjamaed
pyknosis
pyknotic
pylagore
pyoderma
pyranose
pyrazine
pyrazole
Pyrenean
pyrenoid
pyrexial
pyridine
pyriform
pyritify
pyritise
pyritize
pyritose
pyritous
pyrology
pyrolyse
pyrolyze
pyrosoma
pyroxene
pyroxyle
pyrrolic
pyruvate
pythonic
pyx-cloth
pyxidium
qaimaqam
qindarka
Quaalude
quackery
quackish
quackism
quadplex
quadrant

quadrate
quadriga
quadroon
quaestor
quagmire
quagmiry
quailery
quaintly
Quakerly
quakiest
qualmish
quandary
quandong
quantify
quantile
quantise
quantity
quantize
quaranty
quarrian
quarried
quarrier
quarries
quarrion
quarrons
quartern
quartile
quart-pot
quatorze
quatrain
quaverer
quay-punt
quayside
queasier
queasily
Quebecer
Quechuan
Quechuas
queen ant
queen bee
queen cat
queendom
queening
Queenite
queenlet
Queen Mum
queen-pin
queerdom
queer for
queerish
queerity
quencher
quenelle
quercine
querying
quesited
question
questman
queueing
quibbler
Quichean
quick fix

quickish	racegoer	rail-bird	ram-sammy	ratchety	real life
quick one	racemate	rail bond	Ramsauer	rateable	real line
quick-set	racemise	railcard	ramshack	rateably	real live
quickset	racemize	rail-head	ram's head	rate-card	realness
quiddany	racemose	railhead	ram's horn	rat-goose	real time
quiddity	racemous	raillery	ramulose	rat-house	re-anchor
quidnunc	race riot	railless	ramulous	raticide	reanneal
quietest	rachides	rail-line	ranalian	ratified	reanswer
quietish	rachilla	rail link	ranarian	ratifier	reapable
quietism	rachitic	railroad	ranch egg	ratifies	reap-hook
Quietism	rachitis	rail yard	ranchero	rational	reappear
quietist	racially	rain band	ranchito	rationes	rear-arch
Quietist	raciness	rainbird	ranchman	rat-racer	rear lamp
quietude	Racinian	rainbowy	randiest	rat-rhyme	rearmost
quillaja	racistic	rain-cape	Randlord	ratsbane	re-arouse
quilling	rack-deal	raincoat	randomly	rat-snake	rearrest
quill pen	racketed	rain crow	rangette	rat's tail	rear-view
quilting	racketer	rain date	range war	rattiest	rearward
quincunx	rack-rail	rain-door	rangiest	rattling	reascend
quindene	rack-rent	raindrop	rangiora	rattoner	reascent
quinella	raclette	rainfall	raniform	raurekau	reasoner
quiniela	Racovian	rain-fowl	rankness	rave it up	re-aspire
quinovic	radar map	rain frog	ranksman	Ravelian	reassail
quinsied	radar net	rainiest	ransomer	ravelled	reassert
quintain	radially	rainless	rapacity	raveness	reassess
quintile	radiance	rainsuit	rapakivi	ravening	reassign
quintole	radiancy	rain-tree	rape-cake	ravenous	reassort
quippery	radiated	rain-wash	rape-seed	ravingly	reassume
quipping	radiator	rainwear	rapeseed	ravisher	reassure
quippish	radicand	rain-worm	rap group	raw-boned	reattach
quipster	radicate	rainworm	raphanus	raw humus	reattack
Quirinal	radicule	rainy day	rapidest	Rawlplug	reattain
quirkier	radio cab	raisable	rapidity	raw umber	reawaken
quirkily	radio car	raisedly	rap music	ray fleck	re-become
quirkish	radio fix	raise hob	rapontic	Rayleigh	re-behold
quisling	radio ham	rajaship	rapparee	rayogram	rebeldom
quiteron	radio map	raja yoga	rap sheet	Rayonism	rebelled
quit rate	radio net	rake down	raptness	Rayonist	rebeller
quit-rent	radionic	rakehell	raquette	razor cut	rebellow
quitting	Radio One	rake over	rara avis	razor-man	reboiler
quivered	Radio Two	rakishly	rare bird	reabsorb	reborrow
quixotic	radiused	ralli car	rare book	reaccept	rebottle
quixotry	radiuses	rallying	rarefied	reaccess	rebranch
quiz game	radwaste	rallyist	rarefier	reach for	rebuffal
quiz show	raft-duck	Ramadhan	rareness	reaching	rebunker
quizzery	raftered	ramarama	rarified	reach rod	reburial
quizzing	raftsman	rambling	rarifies	reactant	reburied
quoad hoc	raftsmen	Ramboism	rarities	reaction	reburies
quoddity	ragabash	rambutan	rascally	reactive	rebuttal
quod vide	raga rock	ramentum	rascalry	readable	rebutted
quoining	rageless	Ramessid	rascasse	readably	rebutter
quotable	rag frame	ramicorn	rascette	readerly	rebutton
quotient	raggedly	ramified	rasgulla	readiest	Récamier
rabbeted	raggling	ramifies	rashling	readjust	recanter
rabbinic	ragingly	ramiform	rashness	read-only	recapped
rabbited	Ragnarok	ramillie	rasplike	read over	recapper
rabbiter	rag paper	Ramistic	Rasputin	readvise	recaptor
rabbitry	ragstone	ramosely	Rastaman	ready-mix	recceing
rabidity	ragtimer	rampager	rastered	reaffirm	receival
race card	ragtimey	rampancy	ratanhia	reagency	receiver
racecard	rag trade	rampiked	rataplan	reaginic	re-cement
race game	rag-wheel	rampsman	rat-arsed	realizer	recently

re-centre	redeemer	reed mace	regioned	relaxant	renogram
receptor	redefect	reed-mark	register	relaxing	renounce
recessed	redefine	reed pipe	registry	relaxity	renovate
rechange	redeless	reed-stop	regnancy	relay bid	renovize
recharge	redemand	reed-wren	regolith	relearnt	renowned
recidive	redeploy	reef flat	regrater	releasee	renowner
recision	redesign	reef knot	reground	releaser	rentable
reckless	redesman	reelable	regrowth	releasor	rent-a-car
reckling	red-faced	reel foot	regulate	relegate	rent-free
reckoner	red giant	reel-rall	reguline	relevant	rentless
reckon up	red gland	re-embark	rehallow	relexify	rent roll
recliner	red grass	re-embody	rehandle	reliable	rent-seck
reclothe	red–green	re-emerge	reharden	reliably	renumber
recoiler	Red Guard	re-employ	rehearse	reliance	renversé
Recollet	red-heart	re-enable	reheater	relicary	reobtain
recolour	red horse	re-engage	rehoboam	reliefer	reoccupy
recommit	redirect	re-engine	Rehoboth	relieved	reoffend
reconfer	redistil	re-enlist	Reichert	reliever	reopener
reconvey	redivide	re-excite	Reichian	religate	reordain
Recordak	red judge	re-expand	reigning	religion	reorient
recordal	red light	re-export	reignite	relisher	reovirus
recorder	red maple	refained	reillume	reloader	repairer
recouple	red mavis	refasten	reimbibe	relocate	repartee
recourse	red mulga	refereed	reimport	relucent	repealer
recovery	red noise	referees	reimpose	relumine	repeated
recradle	red-nosed	referend	reincite	remainer	repeater
recreant	red ochre	referent	reindeer	remanent	repelled
recreate	redolent	referral	reindict	remanned	repeller
rectally	red osier	referred	reinduce	remarker	repenter
rectenna	redouble	referrer	Reinecke	remarque	repeople
rectoral	Red Paint	refigure	reinette	remaster	reperuse
rectress	red panda	refinery	reinfect	remedial	repetend
recurred	red perch	refining	reinform	remedied	rephrase
recusant	Red River	refinish	reinfuse	remedies	repiqued
recycler	red route	refitted	reingulf	remember	repiques
redactor	Red Rover	reflexly	reinless	remiform	replacer
red adder	red sable	reflower	reinsert	remigate	repledge
red alder	red scale	refluent	reinsist	reminder	replevin
red alert	redshank	reforest	reinsman	remissly	replicar
redargue	red shift	reformat	reinstil	remittal	replicon
red-beard	redshift	reformed	reinsure	remitted	replight
red beech	red shirt	reformer	reinvade	remittee	replough
red biddy	red-short	refreeze	reinvent	remitter	replunge
red birch	redstart	refrozen	reinvest	remodify	repolish
red-blind	red steer	refugium	reinvite	remolade	reporter
red board	red-stone	refunder	Reissner	remotely	repotted
red bream	red tabby	re-fusion	reissued	remotest	repoussé
red-brick	red-taped	refusion	reissues	remotion	repreach
redbrick	red-tapey	refusnik	Reithian	remotive	reprieve
red cedar	reducing	regainer	rejected	remskoen	reprisal
red chalk	reduviid	regalian	rejectee	remurmur	reproach
Red China	red viper	regalism	rejecter	remuster	reproval
red coral	red-water	regalist	rejector	renature	reprover
red cross	redwater	regality	rejigged	renderer	republic
Red Cross	red wheat	regarder	rejigger	rendzina	repugner
reddenda	re-echoed	regasify	rejoicer	renegade	repulser
reddendo	re-echoes	regather	rejumble	renegado	repurify
red devil	reed-bird	regelate	rekindle	renegate	required
red Devon	reedbuck	regicide	relapser	reneguer	requirer
red dwarf	reediest	regifuge	relation	reniform	requital
red-eared	reedlike	regiment	relative	renitent	requiter
red earth	reedling	regional	relaunch	renminbi	re-reader

rere-arch	ressalah	reusable	rhonchus	rightish	rippling
re-record	rest-balk	revalued	Rhoosian	rightism	rip track
re-refine	rest-cure	revalues	rhopalia	rightist	riroriro
re-reform	rest gown	revealer	rhopalic	right now	rise time
re-relate	rest home	reveille	rho-theta	right off	rishitin
re-repeat	restitch	revelled	rhubarby	right out	riskiest
re-return	restless	reveller	rhymable	righty-ho	riskless
re-reveal	rest mass	revelous	rhymical	rigidify	risoluto
re-revise	restoral	revenant	rhyolite	rigidity	risorius
re-roller	restorer	revenger	rhythmed	rigidize	risottos
re-rubber	re-strain	revenuer	rhythmic	rigorism	riteless
resaddle	restrain	reverber	rhythmus	rigorist	ritenuto
resalute	restrict	reverend	ria coast	rigorous	ritornel
rescreen	restrike	reverent	ribaldry	Rig-vedic	ritratto
rescribe	restring	reverify	ribandry	rigwiddy	ritually
rescript	rest room	reversal	ribboned	rilievos	ritziest
rescuing	restroom	reverser	ribboner	rim-brake	rivaless
research	restruck	reversis	ribbonry	rim drive	rivality
reselect	restrung	reverter	rib-grass	rimeless	rivalize
reseller	resubmit	revestry	rib-joint	rimester	rivalled
resemble	resummon	revetted	ribosome	rim light	riveling
resenter	resupine	reviewal	ribozyme	rimosity	rivelled
reserved	resupply	reviewer	rib-roast	rimstone	riverain
reserver	resurgam	reviling	ribulose	rindless	river-bed
resetter	resurvey	revision	rice-bird	ring back	river-god
resettle	retailer	revisory	rice-bowl	ringbark	river gum
resident	retainer	revivify	rice milk	ringbolt	river hog
Residenz	retarded	revolted	ricercar	ringbone	riverine
residing	retardee	revolter	richesse	ring book	riverlet
residual	retarder	revolute	richness	ring-dial	riverman
residuum	retarget	revolver	richweed	ring-dove	river oak
resignal	retaught	revuette	ricketed	ring dyke	rivet gun
resigned	retemper	rewarder	ricketic	ringette	riveting
resignee	retender	rewarewa	rickrack	ring-fort	rivulose
resigner	rethatch	re-weight	rickshaw	ring gear	RNA virus
resilium	rethread	rewhiten	rickyard	ringhals	roadable
re-silver	rethrone	rewinder	ricochet	ringlead	road band
resinate	retiarii	reworker	riddance	ringless	road-book
resinify	reticent	rewriter	riddling	ringlety	road fund
resining	reticula	Reynolds	rideable	ringlike	road hand
resinize	reticule	rezoning	ride down	ring main	road-head
resinoid	retiform	rhabdite	ride high	ring-neck	road hump
resinous	retimber	rhabdoid	rideress	ring-pull	road kill
resister	retinene	Rhaetian	ride work	ring road	roadless
resistor	retinoid	rhagades	ridgelet	ring-rope	road show
resmooth	retinula	rhamnose	ridgeway	ringside	roadshow
resoften	retiracy	rhapsode	ridicule	ringspot	roadside
resolder	retiring	rhapsody	rid space	ringster	road sign
resolute	retorted	rheidity	Riesling	ringtail	roadsman
resolved	retorter	rhematic	rifampin	ring true	roadster
resolver	retrally	rheobase	rifeness	ring-walk	road test
resonant	retrench	rheogram	riffling	ring-wall	roadwork
resonate	retrieve	rheology	riff-raff	ringwise	roasting
resorcin	retroact	rheopexy	rifle-gun	ring-work	robeless
resorter	retrofit	rheostat	rifleman	ringworm	roborant
resource	retrorse	rhetoric	riflemen	rinkhals	robotics
respirit	Retrovir	rhinitis	riftless	riometer	robotise
resplend	returned	rhizopod	rift-sawn	riot gear	robotism
responsa	returnee	rhodinal	rigadoon	riparial	robotize
response	returner	rhodinol	rigatoni	riparian	robuster
respread	returnik	rhomboid	right arm	ripeness	robustic
respring	reuniter	rhonchal	rightful	ripienos	robustly

rocaille	roll-call	root-leaf	rosiness	rowdiest	rum booze
Rochelle	roll cast	rootless	rosining	rowdy-dow	rum go run
rocheted	roll feed	rootlike	rosin oil	rowdyish	rum-hound
rock-a-bye	rollicky	rootling	rosoglio	rowdyism	ruminant
rock alum	roll mark	root node	ros solis	rowelled	ruminate
Rockaway	roll-neck	root sign	Ross seal	row house	rummager
rock-bird	rollocks	root-weed	rostrate	rowiness	rumorous
rock bolt	roll over	root-worm	rostrums	royalise	rumoured
rock cake	roll rate	ropeable	rosulate	royalism	rumourer
rock cavy	rolwagen	rope-band	rosybill	royalist	rump-bone
rock coal	roly-poly	rope burn	rosy drop	royalize	rumpless
rock cook	Romagnol	rope down	Rotarian	royal oak	rumption
rock-dove	romancer	rope into	rotaries	rub along	rum start
rock duck	Romanese	ropelike	rotation	rubashka	rumti-too
rock-dust	Romanian	rope-roll	rotative	rubbaboo	run about
rocketed	Romanies	rope's end	rotatory	rubberdy	runabout
rocketer	romanise	rope-walk	rotavate	rubbishy	run after
rocketry	Romanish	rope-work	rotenone	rub-board	runagate
rock face	Romanism	rope-yard	rot-grass	rubby-dub	run along
rockfall	Romanist	rope-yarn	rotor arm	rubeanic	run a mile
rockfest	Romanity	ropiness	rototill	Rubenist	run a risk
rock-fill	romanize	roqueted	rotproof	rubeolar	rune-tree
rockfish	Roman law	*roquette*	rottener	rubeosis	run for it
rockfoil	romantic	rortiest	rottenly	rubicund	rungless
rock goat	Roman tub	rosalger	rotundly	rubidium	run metal
rock hair	Rome-scot	rosaline	roughage	rub noses	runnable
rock-hewn	Romeward	rosarian	rough cut	rubrical	runnered
rockiest	rompiest	rosaries	rough dab	rubstone	runner-up
rock jock	Romulian	rosarium	rough-dry	ruby-back	runniest
rockless	roncador	rose boss	rough-hew	ruby mine	runology
rocklike	rondache	rosebowl	roughies	ruby port	run out on
rockling	rondavel	rose bush	roughing	ruby-tail	run short
rock pile	rondeaux	rose comb	roughish	ruby zinc	ruralise
rock pool	rondelet	rose-drop	rough log	rucksack	ruralism
rock rose	rondelle	rose-fish	rough mix	ruddered	ruralist
rock-salt	rood-beam	rose-gall	rough-out	ruddiest	rurality
rock star	rood-loft	rose gold	rouleaus	rude joke	ruralize
rockster	roof bolt	rose-grub	rouleaux	rudeness	rush-bush
rock-weed	roofless	rose leaf	roulette	ruderate	rush hour
Rockwell	rooflike	roseless	rouncing	rudiment	rushlike
rock-wool	roofline	roselike	round-arm	rudistid	rush line
rock-work	roof-rack	roselite	roundeye	ruefully	rush-toad
rock worm	roof rail	rosemalt	rounding	rufflike	russeted
rock wren	roof-tile	rosemary	roundish	ruffling	Russniak
rodomont	roof-tree	rose-mole	roundlet	rugately	rust belt
roentgen	rooigras	rose nail	round log	Rugbeian	rustical
Roentgen	rooihout	roseolar	round lot	rug brick	rusticly
roe-stone	rook-worm	rosepath	round off	ruggedly	rustiest
roestone	roomette	rose pink	round out	rugosely	rustless
Rogatian	roomfuls	rose-rash	round pin	rugosity	rustle up
rogation	roomiest	rose rial	round-top	rugulose	rustling
Rogatist	roomless	roseries	roundure	ruinable	rusty dab
rogatory	room-mate	rose-root	rousable	ruinated	rutabaga
Rogerene	roorback	roseroot	rousette	ruinator	ruthenic
roitelet	roosting	rose show	rousting	ruleless	ruthless
Rolandic	root-ball	rose-spot	routeing	rule over	rutilant
role-play	root beer	rose tree	route man	ruleress	rutilous
rollable	rootedly	rosetted	routeman	Rumanian	Ruy Lopez
rollaway	rootfast	rose vine	routiner	rumänite	rye bread
roll axis	root gall	rosewood	rovingly	rum baron	ryegrass
roll back	root-hair	rose-work	row-barge	rumbelow	ryotwary
roll cage	root-knot	rosewort	row-de-dow	rumbling	Ryukyuan

Sabba-day	saginate	salt away	sand flea	saponify	satirism
sabbatia	sagittal	salt bath	sand goby	saponite	satirist
sabbatic	sago palm	salt beef	sand-hill	saponule	satirize
Sabellic	sag wagon	salt-burn	sandhill	saporous	satranji
sabellid	Sahaptin	saltbush	sand-hole	sapphire	satrapal
sabinene	Saharaui	salt-cake	sandiest	sapphism	satrapic
Sabinian	Sahelian	salt dome	sand-iron	sapphist	saturant
sabotage	sahibdom	salt fish	sandiver	sappiest	saturate
saboteur	sahib-log	salt flat	sand lark	saprobic	Saturday
sabre-cut	sahuaros	saltiest	sand leek	sapropel	saturnal
sabre leg	sailable	salt junk	sandlike	sapskull	saturnic
sabre saw	sail-boat	salt lake	sand lily	sap spout	satyress
sabulous	sailboat	saltless	sand-lime	sap-stain	satyrion
sac-à-lait	sailfish	salt lick	sandling	sapucaia	satyrish
sacbrood	sail into	saltlike	sand pear	saraband	saucebox
saccadic	sailless	salt mine	sand-pump	Saraband	saucepan
saccated	sail loft	saltness	sand-reed	Sarabite	sauciest
saccular	sailorly	salt plug	sand-rock	sarangis	saunders
sacculus	sailsman	salt-pond	sand-shoe	sarassin	sauropod
sacellum	sail wing	salt side	sandsoap	Saratoga	sausagey
sackable	sailyard	salt sore	sand sole	sarcelly	savagely
sackfuls	sainfoin	salt-weed	sand-star	sarcenet	savagery
sackless	saintdom	salt well	sand-trap	sarcodic	savagess
sacklike	saintess	saltwort	sand-tray	sarcomas	savagism
sack race	saintish	salutary	sandveld	sardelle	savannah
sack ship	sakabula	salvable	sand-wash	sardonic	saveable
sack suit	salacity	salvager	sand-wasp	sardonyx	save face
sack time	salad bar	salvific	sand wave	sargasso	savingly
sacraria	saladero	salvinia	sandwich	Sargonid	savories
sacredly	saladine	samarium	Sandwich	sarkiest	savorous
sacristy	salading	sambaing	sand-worm	Sar-Major	savourer
saddlery	salad-oil	samcloth	sandwort	saronged	Savoyard
Sadducee	salarian	same here	sandyish	Saronian	savviest
sadhuism	salariat	same like	sandy ray	sarpanch	sawbench
sadistic	salaried	sameness	saneness	sarplier	sawbones
sado-maso	salaries	samizdat	sangaree	sarrazin	sawdusty
Safaitic	saleable	Samnitic	Sangrado	sarsenet	saw-edged
safe area	saleably	samphire	sangrail	Sartrean	sawed-off
safe edge	sale ring	samplery	sanguine	Sarum use	sawflies
Safehand	saleroom	sampling	san-hsien	Sasanian	saw frame
safe-hold	Salesian	samsaric	sanidine	sasanqua	saw-grass
safekeep	salesman	samskara	sanified	sash cord	sawgrass
safe lamp	salesmen	Sam Slick	sanifies	sash-door	saw-horse
safe load	sales tax	samtchoo	sanitary	sashless	sawhorse
safeness	sale-yard	sanative	sanitate	sash tool	saw-shark
safe seat	salicine	sanatory	sanitise	Sassanid	sawtooth
safeties	Salic law	Sancerre	sanitize	Sassella	saw-wrest
safe-tray	salictum	sanctify	sannyasi	sassiest	saxatile
saffraan	salience	sanction	Sanscrit	sastruga	saxboard
saffrony	saliency	sanctity	sanserif	sastrugi	saxe blue
safranin	salinely	sanctums	sans-gêne	Satanise	Saxe blue
sagacity	salinity	sandarac	Sanskrit	Satanism	Saxondom
sagakomi	Salishan	sandbank	sans peur	Satanist	Saxonian
sagamité	salivant	sand-bath	Santa Ana	Satanity	Saxonise
sagamore	salivary	sand blow	santalin	Satanize	Saxonish
saganaki	salivate	sand boil	santalol	sateless	Saxonism
sagebush	sallower	sand-cast	santonin	satiable	Saxonist
sage cock	Sally-man	sand-club	santorin	satining	Saxonize
sage hare	salmonet	sand core	saperavi	satinize	sayonara
sageness	salmonid	sand crab	sap green	satin oil	say uncle
sageship	Salopian	sand dune	sapidity	satin-top	scabbard
sage-wood	salpicon	sand-fish	sapience	satirise	scabbier

scabbing	scentful	sclerose	scraggly	scrupler	sea eagle
scabbler	scenting	sclerous	scramble	scrutiny	seafarer
scabious	scent out	scoffery	scrambly	scuddick	sea-fever
scabland	sceptism	scofflaw	scramjet	scudding	sea-fight
scablike	sceptral	scoinson	scrammed	scuffing	sea-flood
scab-mite	sceptred	scolding	scrannel	scuffler	sea-floor
scabrous	schapska	scoleces	scraping	scuggery	sea front
scabweed	schedule	scolices	scraplet	scuggish	seafront
scacchic	Scheiner	scolytid	scrapped	scullery	seagoing
scaffold	schemata	scombrid	scrapper	scullion	sea-grape
scalable	scheming	scomfish	scrappet	sculptor	sea grass
scalawag	schemist	scone cap	scrapple	scumless	sea green
scald-hot	scherzos	scone-hot	scratchy	scummier	sea gypsy
scalding	Schiedam	scoopful	scrattle	scumming	sea heath
scale-bug	schiffli	scooping	scraunch	scungier	sea holly
scalenus	schiller	scoop-net	scrawler	scurfily	sea horse
scale-pan	schizoid	scoparin	screamer	scurfing	sea-hound
scaliest	schizont	Scophony	screechy	scurried	sea ivory
scallion	schliere	scopolin	screeder	scurrier	sea-jelly
scalprum	schlocky	scopulae	screed in	scurries	sealable
scamming	schmaltz	scorable	screener	scurrile	seal calf
scammony	schmatte	scorcher	screever	scurvied	sea lemon
scamping	schmooze	score-box	screw cap	scurvier	sea level
scampish	schmucky	score off	screw-die	scurvily	seal-hole
scandent	schnapps	score out	screw eye	scutated	sea-light
Scandian	scholard	scores of	screw fly	scutcher	sea-louse
scandium	scholion	scorious	screwier	scutella	seal ring
scanning	scholium	scornful	screwing	scuttled	sealskin
scansion	schooler	scorpene	screwish	scuttler	sea-lungs
scantier	schoolie	Scorpian	screw-pin	scutulum	Sealyham
scantily	schooner	scorpion	screw-tap	scuzzbag	seamanly
scantity	Schottky	Scorpios	screw top	scybalum	seamfree
scaphoid	schradan	Scorpius	scribble	scyphate	seamiest
scapulae	Schrader	scot-free	scribbly	scyphose	seamless
scapular	Schröder	Scotican	scribing	Scythian	sea-morse
scapulas	schryari	scotomas	scribism	scything	seamount
scarabee	sciaenid	scotomia	scriggle	Scythism	sea mouse
scarcely	sciagram	scotopia	scrimish	sea-acorn	seam-rent
scarcity	sciatica	scotopic	scrimped	sea-adder	seamster
scaredly	scienced	Scots fir	scrimply	sea-angel	seam weld
scareful	scienter	Scotsman	scripted	sea-arrow	sea-nymph
scare out	scilicet	Scotsmen	scripter	sea aster	sea onion
scarf pin	scimitar	Scots Nat	scriptor	sea-bathe	sea otter
scariest	scincoid	Scottice	scrofula	sea beach	sea-perch
scariose	sciolism	Scottify	scrogged	sea-beast	sea-piece
scarious	sciolist	Scottish	scroggin	sea-blite	sea-pilot
scarless	sciolous	scourger	scrolled	seaboard	seaplane
scarpine	scioness	Scourian	scroller	seaborne	sea poppy
scarping	scioptic	scouring	scrotums	sea-bound	sea-power
scarring	scirocco	scout bee	scrouger	sea bream	sea price
scatback	scirrhus	scout car	scrounge	sea cadet	sea purse
scathing	scissile	Scoutery	scroungy	sea-chest	seaquake
scattald	scission	scouting	scrubbed	sea-clerk	sea-raven
scattery	scissors	Scoutish	scrubber	sea-cliff	searcher
scattier	sciurine	Scoutism	scrubble	sea-cloth	search me
scattily	sciuroid	Scout Law	scrub jay	sea-coast	searobin
scatting	sclareol	scowbank	scrub oak	seacraft	sea-rover
scavager	sclereid	scrabble	scrub-tit	sea crust	seascape
scavenge	sclerema	Scrabble	scrumble	sea-cunny	Sea Scout
scenario	sclerite	scrag-end	scrum-cap	sea-daisy	sea shell
scenical	scleroid	scragged	scrumple	sea devil	seashell
scent-bag	scleroma	scragger	scrunchy	seadrome	seashore

sea-shrub	sedulous	Selenite	semi-open	septfoil	set of day
seasider	see about	selenium	semiosis	septimal	set piece
sea snail	see after	selenous	semiotic	septoria	set point
sea snake	see a wolf	Seleucid	semi-oval	septuple	set right
sea-snipe	seecatch	self-bias	semi-pros	sequelae	set scene
seasonal	seed ball	self-born	semi-ring	sequence	set screw
seasoner	seed bank	self-bred	Semitise	sequency	set scrum
sea speed	seed-bird	self-care	Semitism	sequined	Setswana
sea-stack	seed bull	self-ease	Semitist	seraglio	settable
sea-state	seed cake	self-good	Semitize	seraphic	settle in
sea-stick	seed-coat	self-hate	semitone	seraphim	settle up
sea stock	seed-corn	self-heal	semolina	seraphin	settling
sea-swine	seedcorn	self-help	semology	serenade	setulose
seat belt	seed down	selfhood	semplice	serenata	seven-day
seat-bone	seed-fish	self-hunt	sempster	serenely	severely
sea-thief	seed-head	selfless	sempstry	serenest	Severian
sea-thong	seediest	self-life	semuncia	serenise	severies
sea tiger	seed-leaf	self-loop	senarian	serenity	severish
seatless	seedless	self-lost	senarius	serenize	severity
seat-mate	seedlike	self-love	senatory	serfhood	Sevillan
seat-mile	seedling	self-made	sendable	serfship	sewaging
sea train	seed-plot	self-mass	send away	sergeant	sewellel
sea trial	seedsman	selfmate	send back	serially	sewerage
sea trout	seedsmen	selfness	send down	seriated	sewer-air
sea-valve	seed-time	self-pity	send word	seriatim	sewer rat
seawards	seed year	self-rule	senecios	sericite	sew-round
sea water	seedy toe	selfsame	sengreen	seriffed	sex-blind
seawater	seek dead	self-seed	Senhouse	serigala	sex crime
sea-weary	seemless	self-sown	senicide	serjeant	sex drive
seaweedy	seemlier	selfward	senilely	sermoner	sexenary
seawoman	seemlily	self-will	senility	sermonic	sexiness
sea wrack	seerlike	self-wise	senilize	serology	sexology
sebesten	seership	sellable	sennight	serosity	sexploit
Sebilian	see stars	sellette	señorita	serotine	sextette
secateur	segolate	selvaged	Senoussi	serotiny	sextolet
secesher	sego lily	selvagee	senseful	serotype	sextuple
Sechuana	segreant	selvedge	sensible	Serpasil	sextuply
secluded	seicento	semantic	sensibly	serpolet	sex-typed
secodont	seiching	semblant	sensific	serpulae	sexually
secondee	Seidlitz	sembling	sensoria	serpulid	sexupara
seconder	seif dune	semester	sensuism	serranid	sforzato
secondly	seigneur	semi-arid	sensuist	serrated	shabbier
secretin	seignior	semi-axis	sensuous	serratic	shabbify
secretly	seignory	semi-beam	sentence	serratus	shabbily
secretor	seine-net	semi-bold	sentient	servable	shabrack
sectator	seismics	semi-cell	sentinel	serve out	shackage
sectoral	seismism	semi-coke	sentries	servicer	shack-job
sectored	sei whale	semidine	sentry-go	servient	shackles
secundly	seizable	semi-dome	Senussia	servitor	shadblow
secundus	seized of	semiflex	sepaline	servo tab	shaddock
securely	sejugate	semi-hoop	sepalled	sesamoid	shades of
secure of	seladang	Sémillon	sepalody	sescuple	shadiest
security	selamlik	semilune	sepaloid	sesterce	shadower
sedately	seldseen	semi-main	separate	sestetto	shadowly
sedation	selected	semi-mute	separist	sestonic	shafting
sedative	selectee	seminary	Sephadex	set about	shagbark
sederunt	selectly	seminate	Sephardi	set a fire	shaggery
sedge-fly	selector	seminium	sepiment	set apart	shaggier
sediment	selenate	Seminole	septagon	set aside	shaggily
sedition	selenian	seminoma	septated	se-tenant	shagging
seducing	selenide	semi-nude	septenar	set forth	shagreen
sedulity	selenite	semi-opal	septette	setiform	shagroon

shahbanu	sheather	shift key	shocking	shotting	siallite
shakable	shedding	shift off	Shockley	should-be	Sibelian
shake-bag	she-devil	shigella	shoddier	shoulder	Siberian
shake off	shedhand	shiitake	shoddily	shouldn't	sibilant
shake out	shed roof	shikasta	shoebill	shout for	sibilate
shake-rag	shed-room	shikimic	shoe-deep	shouting	sibilous
shakiest	sheeling	shilling	shoehorn	shoveler	Sibiriak
shale oil	sheep-bot	shimmery	shoelace	shove-net	sibyllic
shalgram	sheep-bug	shimmied	shoe-last	shove off	Sicanian
shalloon	sheepcot	shimmies	shoeless	showable	sicarius
shamanic	sheep-dip	shimming	shoepack	show a leg	Siceliot
shambles	sheepdog	shim-sham	shoe-tree	showance	Sicilian
sham-damn	sheep-fly	shin bone	shofroth	show band	sick call
shamedly	sheepish	shindies	shogunal	showband	sickener
shameful	sheep-ked	shingled	shonkier	showboat	sickerly
shamiana	sheepman	shingler	shooting	show-card	sick flag
shamisen	sheep-pen	shingles	shootist	showcard	sickless
shammies	sheep pox	shiniest	shoot-off	showcase	sicklied
shamming	sheep-ree	shin-leaf	shoot-out	showdown	sicklier
shammock	sheep-rot	shinnery	shop-book	showerer	sicklily
shampoos	sheep-run	shinnied	shop-gaze	show flat	sickling
shamrock	sheet-fed	shinnies	shop girl	showfolk	sick list
shamyana	sheetful	shinning	shopless	showgirl	sickness
Shandean	sheet ice	shinties	shoplift	show home	sick note
shandies	sheeting	Shinwari	shopping	showiest	sickroom
Shangaan	sheetlet	ship a sea	shoppish	showjump	sidalcea
Shangana	sheikhly	shipless	shop talk	showreel	sida-weed
shanghai	Shekinah	shiplike	shop-worn	showroom	side arms
shanking	shelduck	shipload	shopworn	show tune	side band
shank-net	shelf cod	shipmate	shorebug	show wood	sideband
shannies	shelfful	shipment	shore fly	shrapnel	side bend
shanties	shelf ice	ship over	shore-gun	shredded	side-blow
shantung	shelf sea	shippage	shoreman	shredder	side-bone
shapable	shell-bit	shipping	shortage	shred-pie	sideburn
shapeful	shell egg	shipside	shortall	shrew-ash	side-coat
shape out	shell ice	ship time	short-arc	shrewdie	side-comb
sharable	shelling	ship-work	short-arm	shrewdly	side dish
Shararat	shell out	shipworm	short-ass	shrewish	side door
Shardana	sheltery	shipyard	short con	shrew-run	side drum
shareman	shelties	shiralee	short cut	shrieker	side-face
share-out	sheltron	shireman	short-day	shrieval	side-foot
sharkish	shelving	shire-oak	short dog	shrimped	side-head
shark-ray	Shemitic	shirring	short-eat	shrimper	sidehill
sharn-bud	shending	shirtier	short end	shrinker	side-hold
sharp end	shepherd	shirtily	short for	shrink on	sidekick
sharpish	shepster	shirting	shorties	shrouder	side lamp
sharp-set	Sherarat	shirt-jac	shortish	shrubbed	sidelamp
shashlik	Sheraton	shirt-pin	short leg	shrublet	side-land
shattery	Sherlock	shit-face	short rib	shrub oak	sideless
shauchle	sherries	shithead	short run	shrugged	sideline
shauchly	sherwani	shit-hole	short-set	shrug off	sideling
Shaviana	Shetland	shitless	short ton	shrunken	side lobe
Shavuoth	Shevuoth	shit-list	Shoshone	shuddery	side-lock
shawabti	shey-shey	shittier	shot-bush	shuffler	sidelong
shawling	shickery	shitting	shot-free	shunless	side-look
shawmist	shielded	shitwork	shot gold	shunning	side meat
shay-shay	shielder	shivaree	shot-hole	shunpike	side mill
sheading	shieling	shiverer	shot line	shuriken	side note
shealing	shiftful	Shiv Sena	shot-mark	shut down	side play
shearing	shiftier	shkotsim	Shotokan	shutdown	side pond
shearman	shiftily	shoading	shot-peen	shutting	side-post
sheathed	shifting	shoaling	shot rope	shuttler	sidereal

siderean	silicify	Sindhian	six-eight	skinnery	slangism
siderite	silicone	sinecure	sixpence	skinnier	slanting
side road	silicula	sine tone	sixpenny	skinning	slap bang
side-rope	siliquae	sine wave	sixscore	skin pass	slap-bass
side-scan	siliques	sinewous	sixtieth	skin test	slapdash
side seat	silkbark	sin-flood	sixtyish	skin worm	slaphead
sideshow	silkenly	sinfonia	sixty-six	skiogram	slapjack
side-slip	silk-fowl	sinfully	sizeable	skip bail	slapping
sidesman	silkiest	singable	sizeably	skipjack	slap shot
sidesmen	silklike	singeing	size-bone	ski-plane	slashing
side spin	silk moth	singhara	sizeless	skippery	slat-back
sidestep	silk road	singling	siziness	skipping	slateful
side suit	silk-tail	sing-sing	sizzling	skip-read	slattern
side-sway	silk-tree	singsing	skate key	skip-rope	slatting
side tone	silkweed	sing-song	skean-dhu	skip zone	slave ant
side trip	silkworm	singsong	skedding	skirmish	slavedom
side view	silky oak	singular	Skeeball	skirting	slave jib
sidewalk	sillabub	sinicize	skeelful	ski stick	slaverer
side-wall	silladar	sinigrin	skeeling	skittery	Slavonic
sideward	sillapak	sinister	skeeting	skittish	slayable
sideways	silliest	sinkable	skeletal	skittler	sleazier
side wind	sillikin	sink-hole	skeleton	skivvied	sleazily
sidewind	silly ass	sinnable	skelloch	skivvies	sledding
side-wing	silly-how	Sinn Fein	skelping	skokiaan	sledging
side-wipe	sillyism	sinogram	skerrick	skullcap	sleepery
sidewise	siloxane	sinology	skerries	skullery	sleepful
Sidneian	silphium	Sinology	sketcher	skunkdom	sleepier
Sidonian	silurian	sinuated	skew arch	skunkish	sleepily
siege gun	Silurian	sinumbra	skew-back	sky cloth	sleeping
sierozem	siluroid	sinusoid	skewback	skydiver	sleep-out
sieveful	silverer	Siphnian	skewbald	skylight	sleeveen
sieve map	silverly	siphonal	skew gear	skylined	sleeving
siffleur	silvical	siphoner	skewness	sky pilot	sleigher
Sigalert	silylate	siphonic	skiagram	skyrmion	sleighty
Sigatoka	simazine	sireless	Skiatron	skyscape	slendang
sight bar	simetite	sirename	skid beam	sky shade	slew-foot
sightful	similise	sirenian	skidding	skytrain	slew rate
sight gag	similize	sireship	skid mark	skywards	slew-rope
sighting	simoleon	siriasis	skid road	skywatch	slick ear
sightsee	simoniac	siscowet	skiffler	sky-write	slickens
sigmatic	Simonian	siserary	ski-jorer	slabbery	slidable
signable	simonise	sissiest	skilless	slabbing	slidably
signally	simonist	sissonne	skillful	slab-cake	sliddery
signator	Simonite	sissy bar	skilling	slabline	slide-bar
signatum	simonize	sissyish	skillion	slack-jaw	slideway
sign away	simperer	sisterly	skim milk	slack off	slifting
signifer	simplest	sit about	skimming	slaggier	slighten
signific	simplify	sitarist	skimpier	slagging	slighter
signless	simplism	sithence	skimpily	slag heap	slightly
signoria	simplist	sit-inner	skimping	slag-lead	slim cake
sign over	simpulum	sit loose	skincare	slagless	slime-eel
signpost	simuland	sitology	skin-deep	slag-wool	slimiest
silanize	simulant	sit shiva	skin-dive	slaister	slimline
Silastic	simulate	sittella	skin flap	slalomer	slimmest
silbador	simulfix	sitter-in	skinfold	slambang	slimming
silcrete	simulium	sit tight	skin-food	slam dunk	slimness
silenced	Sinaitic	situlate	skinfuls	slamdunk	sling-bag
silencer	sinapine	sit under	skin game	slamming	sling mud
silently	sinapism	sitz-bath	skinhead	slammock	sling off
Silesian	sin bosun	sitzmark	skinking	slangier	slinkier
silicate	sincerer	six by six	skinless	slangily	slinkily
silicide	sinciput	Six Clerk	skinlike	slangish	slip away

slip-case
slip face
slip form
slip-hook
slip-horn
slip into
slip-knot
slip-over
slipover
slippage
slippery
slippier
slipping
slip-rail
slip ring
slip road
slip-rope
slipshod
slip-shoe
slip-slap
slip-slop
slip-ware
slipware
slit drum
slit-eyed
slit gong
slithery
slit lamp
slitless
slittier
slitting
slobbery
slobbish
slob-land
sloe-eyed
sloganed
slogging
slope off
slop-over
sloppage
slop-pail
sloppery
sloppier
sloppily
slopping
slop-shop
slop-work
sloshier
sloshing
slot-back
slothful
slot hole
slot seam
slotting
slouched
sloucher
slovenly
slovenry
slow back
slow bell
slow burn
slow-down

slowdown
slow-drag
slow-foot
slowness
slow pass
slowpoke
slow-scan
slow time
slow-worm
slubbery
slubbing
sludging
slugabed
slug-fest
sluggard
slugging
sluggish
slug-horn
slughorn
slug-line
slumbery
slumland
slumless
slumlord
slummier
slumming
slummock
slump sum
slurries
slurrily
slurring
slushier
slushily
slushing
slush pit
sluttery
sluttish
slyboots
smack-dab
smacking
smallage
small-arm
small cap
small end
small fry
smallish
smallpox
smaltine
smaltite
smarmier
smarmily
smarties
smarting
smartish
smart set
smashery
smash hit
smashing
smear-dab
smearing
smectite
smeethly

smellage
smellier
smelling
smell out
smeltery
smidgeon
smig bait
smileful
smircher
smirkily
smirkish
smithers
smithery
Smithian
smithier
smithies
smocking
smoggier
smoggily
smogless
smokable
smoke box
smoke dry
smoke-hos
smoke out
smoke pot
smokiest
smoocher
smoodger
smoothen
smoother
smoothie
smoothly
smørbrød
smothery
smoulder
smudgier
smudgily
smuggery
smuggest
smuggish
smuggler
smugness
smut-ball
smut-mill
smuttier
smuttily
smutting
smythite
snack bar
snackery
snagging
snaggled
snailery
snailish
snake-bit
snake fly
snake oil
snake-pit
snap-back
snap bean
snap-bolt

snap-brim
snap head
snap-hook
snap-link
snap-lock
snappier
snappily
snapping
snappish
snap-ring
snapsack
snapshot
snapweed
snarkily
snarkish
snarlier
snarling
snarlish
snatcher
snatch it
snazzier
snazzily
sneak-box
sneakier
sneakily
sneaking
sneakish
sneaksby
sneerful
sneering
sneezing
snibbing
sniffier
sniffily
sniffing
sniffish
sniffler
sniff out
snifting
sniggery
snigging
sniggler
snipe eel
snipe fly
snippety
snippier
snippily
snipping
snip-snap
snitcher
snobbery
snobbess
snobbier
snobbily
snobbing
snobbish
snobbism
snobling
snogging
snooding
snoopery
snootful

snootier
snootily
snoozier
snore-off
snorting
snort out
snotnose
snottier
snottily
snoutish
snowball
snow-bank
snow bear
snow-belt
snowbird
snow boot
snow-clad
snowcock
snow-cold
snow-cone
snow crab
snowdrop
snowfall
snow flea
snow-hole
snowiest
snowless
snowlike
snow lily
snowline
snow-melt
snowpack
snowshoe
snow-slip
snow-tyre
snow vole
snow wolf
snow worm
snowyish
snowy owl
snubbing
snubbish
snub cube
snub nose
snuffbox
snuffier
snuffing
snuffler
snuffman
snuff out
snuggery
snuggest
snuggish
snuggler
snugness
soakaway
soak-hole
soak it to
so-and-sos
soapbark
soapiest
soap-lees

soapless
soaplike
soap-rock
soapsuds
soap-tree
soapweed
soapwort
soarable
soaraway
Soberano
soberest
soberize
Sobieski
Sobranye
sobriety
sob story
sob-stuff
so-called
sociable
sociably
socially
societal
Socinian
sockeroo
socketed
socketer
sockette
sock it to
sock-lamb
sockless
Socratic
soda-acid
soda alum
soda card
soda jerk
soda lake
soda lime
sodalist
sodalite
sodality
sodamide
soda pulp
soddenly
soddyite
sod house
sodomise
sodomist
sodomite
sodomize
sod widow
softback
softball
soft clam
soft coal
soft copy
soft-core
soft corn
soft crab
softener
soft food
soft-foot
soft hail

soft-head	Solignum	soothing	soup-bone	spanglet	specious
soft-land	solitary	soothsay	soupiest	Spaniard	speckled
soft line	solitude	sootiest	soup line	Spanishy	spectate
softling	solleret	sootless	sourball	spanking	spectral
soft loan	solodize	sophical	sour beef	span-long	spectred
softness	solonetz	soporose	sour crop	spanning	spectrin
soft rush	so long as	soporous	sourdine	span roof	spectrum
soft sell	Solonian	soppiest	sour dock	spanspek	specular
soft-shoe	solo stop	sopranos	soured on	spansule	speculum
soft soap	solpugid	Sorabian	sour mash	Spansule	speeched
soft sore	solstice	soralium	sourness	span wire	speecher
soft spot	solution	sora rail	sour plum	spanwise	speed bug
soft tack	solvable	sorbitan	sourpuss	span-worm	speed cop
soft tick	solvency	sorbitic	sour veld	sparable	speedful
software	Somalian	sorbitol	sourwood	sparaxis	speed hog
soft wart	somatism	sorcerer	soutache	spar-buoy	speedier
softwood	somatist	sordidly	southard	spar-deck	speedily
soggiest	somatize	soredial	southern	spare for	speedway
so help me	sombrely	soredium	southing	spare rib	speering
soil bank	sombrero	sorehead	southpaw	spargana	spekboom
soil-less	sombrous	Sorelian	Southron	sparhawk	spelaean
soilless	somebody	soreness	South Sea	spark-gap	spelding
soil mark	somedeal	Sörensen	souvenir	sparkish	spellful
soil pipe	somegate	soricine	souvlaki	sparkled	spelling
soil type	some hope	sororate	Sovietic	sparkler	spell out
soil wash	somerset	sororial	sovranly	sparklet	speltoid
solacing	sometime	sororise	sovranty	spark out	Spencean
solander	somewhat	sorority	sow-belly	sparling	spend-all
solandra	somewhen	sororize	sowbread	sparmate	spending
solanine	somewise	sorption	sow-drunk	sparring	spent tan
solar day	somnific	sorptive	sow-louse	sparrowy	spergula
solarise	so muckle	sorriest	sow-metal	sparsely	spermary
solarism	sonantal	sorrower	sow's-baby	sparsity	spermata
solarist	sonatina	sorryish	soya bean	spartina	spermine
solarium	sonerila	sortable	soya meal	spar tree	sperm oil
solarize	songbird	so soon as	soya milk	spasmous	spermous
solaster	songbook	Sotadean	soy frame	spasm war	Spetsnaz
solation	songfest	souchong	soy sauce	spatfall	sphagnum
solatium	song-form	soul bell	space age	spathose	sphecoid
sola topi	songless	soul-body	space bar	spathula	sphenoid
solderer	songlike	soul-cake	spaceful	spatiate	spherics
soldiery	song-plug	soul-case	space gun	Spätlese	spherify
solecism	song-post	Soul City	space lab	spatting	spheroid
solecist	songster	soul food	spaceman	spatular	spherule
solecize	sonicate	soulhood	spacemen	spavined	sphinges
soleless	Sonifier	soulical	space out	spawling	sphingid
solemnly	son-in-law	Souliote	spaceway	spawning	spianato
soleness	sonneted	soul kiss	spaciest	speak-box	spicated
solenium	sonnetry	soulless	spacious	speak for	spiccato
solenoid	sonny boy	soul-like	spadeful	speaking	spice bag
sole-tree	Sonny Jim	soul-mass	spade lug	speak out	spice-box
solfeggi	sonobuoy	soul mate	spademan	spear gun	spiciest
solidago	Son of God	soulmate	spadices	speargun	spicular
solidary	son of man	soul-scot	spadille	spearing	spiculum
solidate	sonogram	soul-shot	spadroon	spearman	spidered
solidest	sonolyse	soul-sick	spaewife	Spearman	spiderly
solidify	sonorant	sound-bow	spaggers	spearmen	spiffier
solidism	sonority	soundbox	spagyric	spear oak	spiffily
solidist	sonorous	soundful	spalding	speciate	spiffing
solidity	sonsiest	sounding	spalpeen	specific	spigelia
soliform	soonness	sound-law	spandrel	specimen	spiggoty
solifuge	soothful	sound off	spangler	speciose	spikelet

spikiest
spilitic
spillage
spilling
spillway
spinachy
spinally
spindled
spin-down
spin echo
spine-oak
spinette
spin flip
spiniest
spinifex
spiniken
spinless
spinnbar
spinnery
spinneys
spinning
spinodal
Spinozan
spin-scan
spin-spin
spinster
spinstry
spintext
spin wave
spiny eel
spiny rat
spiracle
spirally
spirated
spirelet
spirifer
spirilla
spirited
spirit up
spiritus
spirling
spitball
spit-curl
spiteful
spitfire
spit-jack
spitlock
spitskop
spitting
spittled
spittoon
spivvery
spivvish
splasher
splatchy
splatted
splatter
splendid
splenial
splenium
splenius
splenoid

splicing
splinder
splinter
split end
split-new
split pea
split pin
split run
splitter
splotchy
splutter
Spodosol
spoffish
spoilage
spoliate
spondaic
spondean
spondyle
spongier
spongily
sponging
spongoid
sponsion
spontoon
spoofery
spookery
spookier
spookily
spooking
spookish
spookist
spooming
spoon bow
spoonful
spoonier
spoonily
spoonish
spoonist
sporadic
sporonin
sporosac
sportful
sportier
sportily
sporting
sportive
sporular
spot-ball
spot kick
spot lamp
spotlamp
spotless
spot-list
spot news
spot test
spottier
spottily
spotting
spot-weld
spoucher
spousage
spout cup

spouting
sprackle
sprackly
spraddle
spragger
sprangle
sprangly
spratted
spratter
sprattle
sprauncy
sprawler
spray can
spray-dry
spray-gun
spraying
sprayman
spreader
spreckle
spreeish
Sprengel
spriggan
sprigged
sprigger
spriglet
springal
springer
springle
sprinkle
sprinter
spritely
sprittle
spritzer
sprocket
sprosser
sprottle
sprouted
sprouter
sprowsie
sprucely
spruce-up
spruiker
spruntly
spryness
spudding
spumante
spun gold
spunkier
spunkily
spun silk
spun yarn
spunyarn
spur-gall
spur-gear
spurious
spurless
spurlike
spur line
spurling
spur mark
spurreys
spurrier

spurries
spurring
spur road
spur-wing
sputtery
spyglass
spy plane
squabash
squabbed
squabble
squabbly
squab pie
squad car
squaddie
squadrol
squadron
squailer
squalene
squaller
squaloid
squamate
Squamish
squamose
squamous
squamule
squander
square go
squarely
square on
square up
squarish
squarson
squasher
squashes
squat tag
squatted
squatter
squattle
squawker
squaw-man
squeaker
squealer
squeamer
squeegee
squeezer
squegger
squelchy
squibbed
squibber
squidded
squidger
squid jig
squiffed
squiffer
squiggle
squiggly
squilgee
squinacy
squinted
squinter
squirage
squireen

squirely
squiress
squirish
squirism
squirmer
squirrel
squirter
squitter
squizzed
squizzle
squopper
stabbing
stablest
stabling
stablish
staccato
stackful
stack gas
stadiums
staffage
stag bush
stage box
stage-set
stag film
staggard
staggeen
staggers
staggery
stagging
stag head
stag-horn
stag-hunt
stagiary
stagiest
staglike
stagnant
stagnate
Stahlian
staining
stair-rod
stairway
stake-net
stake out
stalagma
stalking
stalklet
stallage
stallary
stall-fed
stalling
stallion
stallite
stall off
stallout
stalwart
Stamford
staminal
Stamp Act
stampage
stampede
stamping
stamp out

stamp war
stanchel
stancher
standage
standard
stand for
standing
standish
stand off
stand oil
stand out
standout
stand pad
stand pat
stand Sam
staneraw
stanhope
Stanhope
stanitza
stank-hen
stannary
stannate
stannite
stannous
stanzaed
stanzaic
stapedes
stapelia
star-beam
starched
starcher
starchly
star drag
stardust
stare-cat
starfish
stargaze
stargazy
starkers
starless
starlike
starling
starosta
starosty
starrier
starrily
starring
star ruby
starship
star-shot
startful
starting
startled
startler
start off
start out
star turn
starward
Star Wars
starwort
stasimon
statable

statedly	stellify	sticking	stockist	storable	strenkle
statelet	stelline	stick-jaw	stockman	storeman	strepent
statical	stelling	stick-lac	stockmen	storemen	Strepyan
staticky	stellini	stickler	stock-out	store pay	stressed
statolon	stellion	stick-man	stockout	storeyed	stressor
statuary	Stellite	stick out	stockpot	storiate	stretchy
statuefy	stem cell	stick-pin	stodgier	storkish	streusel
statural	stemflow	stickpin	stodgily	stormful	strewage
staumrel	stemless	stiction	stoechas	storm-god	strewing
Staunton	stemlike	stiff-arm	stoicise	stormier	striatal
stay-away	stem-line	stiffish	Stoicism	stormily	striated
stay-down	stemmata	stiff one	stoicize	storming	striatum
stay-hook	stemmery	stifling	stolidly	storm-jib	stricken
staylace	stemming	stigmata	stolones	Stormont	strickle
stayless	stem-post	stigmate	stolonic	Storting	strictly
stay over	stem root	stilbene	stolport	stotinka	stridden
staysail	stem rust	stilbite	Stolypin	stoupful	striddle
stay-ship	stem turn	stiletto	stomachy	stoutish	strident
stay-tape	stemware	stillage	stomapod	stowable	striffen
stay-wire	stenlock	still-air	stomatal	stow away	strigate
steadier	stenosed	stilling	stomatic	stowaway	striggle
steadily	stenosis	stillion	stomping	stow-ball	strigose
steading	stenotic	Stillson	stone-age	stow-boat	strigous
steadite	stenting	stilt bug	Stone Age	strabism	strike in
steady on	stent-net	stimulus	stone axe	straddle	strike up
stealage	step back	stingier	stone-bow	stradiot	striking
stealing	stepdame	stingily	stonecat	strafing	strimmer
stealthy	step down	stingray	stonefly	straggle	Strimmer
steam age	stephane	stinkard	stone-jug	straggly	stringed
steam-car	step into	stink-bug	stoneman	straight	stringer
steam fly	step iron	stink-cat	stone net	strain at	string up
steamier	stepless	stinkier	stone-pit	strained	strinkle
steamily	steplike	stinking	stone run	strainer	strip cup
steaming	step on it	stink-pot	stone-saw	strain up	stripier
steam tug	step over	stinkpot	stoniest	straiten	striping
steapsin	steppage	stintage	stonking	straitly	striplet
stearate	stepping	stinting	stooling	stramash	strip map
steatite	stepsire	stipites	stooping	strammel	stripped
steatoma	stepwise	stippled	stoop tag	stranded	stripper
Stechkin	stereome	stippler	stop a gap	stranger	striving
steel-bow	stericks	stipular	stop band	strangle	strobila
steelbow	sterigma	stipuled	stopbank	strap-end	strobile
Steel boy	sterling	stirless	stop bath	strapped	strobili
steelier	Sterling	Stirling	stop bead	strapper	strobing
steelify	sternful	stirring	stop-butt	strapple	stroddle
steeling	Sternist	stitchel	stopcock	stratege	stroking
steel pan	sternite	stitcher	stop dead	strategy	stroller
steel pen	sternman	stitch up	stop down	stratify	stromata
steenbok	sternson	St Kildan	stop-gate	stratose	strombus
steening	sternums	St Lucian	stop-knob	straught	stronger
steeping	sternway	St Monday	stop lamp	stravaig	strongly
steepish	stetting	stob-mill	stopless	strawboy	strong of
steepled	stewable	stoccado	stop list	straw-dry	strontia
steepler	stewarty	stocious	stop-lock	straw hat	strophae
steerage	stewpack	stockade	stop-loss	strawish	strophic
steering	stibious	stock-boy	stopover	straw man	stropped
steerman	stibnite	stock car	stoppage	streaked	strouter
steer-oar	sticcado	stock-hut	stopping	streaker	Strowger
steer off	stickage	stockier	stop sign	streamer	struck on
steevely	stickful	stockily	stop time	streeted	struggle
steeving	stickier	stocking	stop word	strelitz	strummed
stellate	stickily	stockish	stop-work	strength	strummer

strumose	sturgeon	subserve	sudorous	sumpitan	supinate
strumous	sturnoid	sub-shell	sudsable	sumption	supinely
strumpet	stylitic	subshrub	suedette	sum total	suppable
strung-up	stymying	subsidia	suet face	sun-baked	supplant
strutted	suasible	subsizar	sufferer	sun-bathe	supplely
strutter	subacute	subsolar	sufficer	sunbathe	supplest
stub-axle	subadary	subsonic	suffixal	sunbeamy	supplial
stubbard	subadult	subspace	sufflate	sun-blind	supplice
stubbier	subagent	substage	suffling	sunblind	supplied
stubbily	subahdar	substant	suffrage	sunblock	supplier
stubbing	Subarian	substorm	suffragi	sunbreak	supplies
stubbled	sub-basal	substyle	suffrago	sunburst	supposal
stubborn	sub-breed	subtalar	sugar-bag	sun-crack	supposed
stub-bred	Subbuteo	subtense	sugar-box	sun cream	supposer
stub-iron	subchela	Subtiaba	sugar-gum	sun-dance	suppress
stub-nail	subclass	subtidal	sugaring	Sundayed	suprafix
stub-tail	subcycle	subtilin	sugarish	sunderer	supremos
stub wing	subduing	subtilly	sugar pea	sun-dress	supremum
stub wire	subduple	subtilty	sugar rag	sundress	surbahar
stuccoer	subdural	subtitle	suggesta	sun-dried	surbased
stuccoes	subdwarf	subtlest	suicidal	sundries	surcease
stud-bolt	subequal	subtlety	sui juris	sundrops	surculus
stud book	suberane	subtlist	suitable	sungates	sure card
studding	suberate	subtonic	suitably	sungazer	sure find
stud farm	suberect	subtopia	suitcase	sunglass	sure-fire
stud-fish	suberize	subtotal	suit-hold	sungrebe	sureness
studious	suberone	subtract	suitlike	sunlight	sureties
stud-mare	suberose	subtribe	suit real	sunn hemp	surfable
stud-wall	suberous	subtrist	suitress	sunniest	surfaced
stud-work	sub-floor	subucula	suit-roll	Sunny Jim	surfacer
stuffage	subfloor	subulate	sukebind	sun-perch	surfbird
stuffbag	sub-frame	suburban	sukiyaki	sun plant	surf-boat
stuffier	subgenus	suburbia	sulcated	sun-print	surf-clam
stuffily	subgiant	sub verbo	sulculus	sun-scald	surf-coot
stuffing	subgrade	subverse	sulfamic	sunsetty	surf-duck
stultify	subgrain	subvital	sulindac	sunshade	surf-fish
stumbler	sub-group	subvocal	sulkiest	sun-shaft	surf-ride
stummick	subgroup	succinct	sullenly	sunshine	surgeful
stumming	subhuman	succinea	sulliage	sunshiny	surgency
stumpage	subimago	succinic	sulphane	sunspecs	surgical
stump bed	subitize	succinum	sulphate	sunstone	surhuman
stump-end	subjoint	succinyl	sulphide	sun visor	suricate
stumpier	subjugal	succubus	sulphite	sunwards	Suriname
stumpily	sub-lease	such a one	sulphone	sun-wheel	surliest
stumping	sublease	suchlike	sulphury	Supadriv	surmisal
stumpish	sublevel	suchness	sultanic	supellex	surmiser
stump leg	sublimer	suchwise	sultanry	superadd	surmount
Stundism	sublunar	suckable	sul tasto	superate	surplice
Stundist	submerge	suckener	sultrier	superbly	surprise
stunkard	submerse	suckered	sultrily	superego	surquidy
stunning	sub-nosed	suckerel	Sumatran	superfix	surrebut
stunpoll	suborder	sucker-up	sumbitch	superfly	surround
stunsail	suborned	suck-fish	sum check	superhet	surroyal
stunt man	suborner	suck-hole	Sumerian	superior	surtitle
stuntman	subovate	suckling	summable	superius	surucucu
stuntmen	suboxide	sucupira	summator	superloo	surveyal
stupeous	subphyla	Sudanese	summerly	superman	surveyor
stupider	subpoena	sudarium	summitry	supermen	survival
stupidly	subpolar	sudation	summoner	supernal	surviver
sturdied	subprior	sudatory	sumotori	super-rat	survivor
sturdier	sub-range	suddenly	sumphish	superset	suspense
sturdily	subsella	suddenty	sump-hole	supertax	Sussex ox

susumber	sweating	sybarite	synochal	tacsonia	take down
susurrus	sweat-rag	sycamine	synochus	tactical	take fire
suttinly	sweat rug	sycamore	synodite	tactless	take five
suzerain	Swede saw	sycomore	synonymy	tactosol	take from
Svedberg	sweenied	syconium	synopses	taeniate	take gate
Svengali	sweepage	syconoid	synopsis	taenioid	take heat
Sverdrup	sweeping	syenitic	synoptic	tafferel	take hold
swabbing	sweep-net	syllabic	synovial	taffrail	take-home
swaddler	sweet-bag	syllable	syntagma	tag along	take life
Swadeshi	sweet bay	syllabub	syntaxes	tagboard	take note
swaggery	sweetful	syllabus	syntaxic	taggable	take odds
swagging	sweet gum	sylphish	syntaxis	Taghairm	take over
swag lamp	sweeting	Sylvaner	syntenic	taglioni	takeover
swagsman	sweetish	sylvanly	syntexis	tagmemic	take part
swainish	sweet man	sylvanry	synthase	tagmosis	take post
Swainson	sweet pea	sylvatic	syntonic	tag strip	taker-off
swamp gas	sweetsop	symbiont	syphilis	tagua-nut	take root
swamphen	swell-box	symbiose	syphonic	Tahitian	take rust
swampier	swelldom	symbiote	Syriarch	Tahunian	take ship
swampish	swelling	symbolic	syringes	taiglach	take sick
swamp-oak	swellish	symmachy	syrinxes	tail-area	take silk
swamp ore	swellism	symmelia	systatic	tail away	take that
swan-dive	swell mob	symmetry	systemed	tail back	take vent
swan-drop	swift fox	sympathy	systemic	tailback	take wind
swanherd	Swiftian	sympatry	systolic	tail-bone	take wine
swankier	swiftlet	symphile	syzygial	tail boom	take wing
swankily	swigging	symphily	syzygies	tailcoat	take-with
swanking	swilling	symphony	syzygium	tail comb	takingly
swankpot	swill-tub	symplasm	Szechuan	tail cone	Taki-Taki
swanlike	swim fair	symplast	Szechwan	taileron	talapoin
swan-mark	swim-hole	symploce	tabarded	tail-flap	talcking
Swanndri	swimming	sympodia	tabby cat	tailgate	talcumed
swan-neck	swimmist	symposia	tableaux	tail-head	talented
swannery	swim-pool	sympotic	table-cut	tail lamp	tale-piet
swanning	swimsuit	synalgia	tableful	tailless	talesman
swan's egg	swimwear	synangic	table-hop	tail-like	talesmen
swan-shot	swindler	synanthy	table mat	tail male	talionic
swanskin	swine flu	synaphea	table top	tailored	talisman
swansong	swine-pox	synapses	tabletop	tailorly	talkable
swap fund	swine-sty	synapsid	tablette	tail-pipe	talk away
swap-hook	swingbin	synapsis	tablinum	tailpipe	talk back
swap meet	swingier	synaptic	tabooism	tail-pole	talkback
swapping	swinging	synarchy	Taborite	tail-race	talk down
swap shop	swing man	synastry	tabouret	tail-rope	talkfest
swartish	swing set	syncarpy	tabulary	tail-skid	talk over
swashing	Swissess	syncline	tabulate	tailspin	talk shop
swash way	switched	syncopal	tac-au-tac	tail unit	talk show
swastika	switchel	syncopic	T account	tail-walk	talk tall
swatchel	switcher	syncrude	tachinid	tailward	Tallensi
swathing	switch in	syncytia	tachisme	tail wind	talliate
swatting	switch-on	syndeses	Tacitean	tailwind	tallness
swayable	swizzled	syndesis	taciturn	tailwise	tallowed
sway-back	swizzler	syndetic	tack coat	tainture	tallower
swear off	swooning	syndeton	tack-duty	takeable	tall ship
swear out	swooping	syndical	tackiest	take a bow	tall talk
sweat-bee	sword-arm	syndrome	tackling	take a low	tallwood
sweat-box	sword-cut	synechia	tack-nail	take away	tally-hos
sweat fly	swording	synectic	tack room	take-away	tallying
sweatful	sword-law	synergic	tacksman	takeaway	tallyman
sweat-hog	sword-mat	synergid	tack weld	take back	tallymen
sweatier	sworn man	syngamic	taco chip	take boat	Talmudic
sweatily	swotting	syngraph	taconite	take care	talukdar

tamandua	tappable	tawdrily	teardown	telsonic	terai hat	tetrical
tamanoir	tap pants	tawniest	tear-drop	temerity	terakihi	tetrobol
tamarack	tap-rivet	tawny owl	teardrop	temerous	teraphim	tetrodon
tamarind	tap stock	taxation	tear duct	tempered	teratoid	tettered
tamarisk	tap water	taxative	tear into	temperer	teratoma	teuchter
tamarugo	taqueria	tax break	tear it up	Templary	terawatt	teucrium
Tamashek	tarakihi	tax-eater	tear-jerk	template	terebene	teuf-teuf
tambouki	Taranchi	taxemics	tearless	templify	Teresian	Teutonic
tamboura	Tarascan	tax exile	tearlike	temporal	teriyaki	textbook
tameable	tarbagan	tax haven	teasable	tempting	terminal	text file
tameless	tarboosh	taxiarch	tea-scrub	temulent	terminer	text-hand
tameness	tar-brush	taxi-boat	teaseler	tenacity	terminus	textless
Tamilian	tardiest	taxi-girl	tease out	tenacula	termitic	textuary
tamperer	targeted	taxinomy	techiest	tenaille	termless	textural
tamponed	targetry	taxi rank	tectonic	tenantry	termoner	textured
Tamworth	Targumic	taxi-ride	Teddy boy	tendance	term-time	thacking
Tanaiste	tarkashi	taxodium	teenaged	tendence	termwise	Thai silk
tandemer	tarlatan	taxonomy	teenager	tendency	terraced	thalamic
tandemly	tarnhelm	taxpayer	teenhood	tenderer	terrapin	thalamus
tandoori	tarogato	tax point	teeniest	tenderly	Terrapin	thalline
tanekaha	tar-paper	tax-taker	teensier	tendines	terraria	thallium
tangelos	Tarpeian	Tayacian	teenybop	Tenebrae	terrazzo	thalloid
tangency	tarragon	tayberry	tee shirt	tenebrio	terrella	thallose
tang-fish	tarriest	Tay–Sachs	teething	tenement	terrible	thallous
tangible	tarrying	T-bar lift	teetotal	Tenerife	terribly	Thamudic
tangibly	tarsioid	teaberry	teetotum	tenesmus	terrific	thanadar
tangiest	tarsitis	tea-billy	teguexin	ten-gauge	Terry Alt	Thanatos
tanglier	Tarskian	tea-board	tegument	tenon saw	tertiary	thanedom
tangling	tartanry	tea-bread	teichoic	tenorino	tertiate	thanewer
tangoist	tartaret	tea break	teiglach	tenorist	teru-tero	thankful
tan-house	tartaric	tea-brick	telecast	tenorite	Terylene	thank God
tanistry	Tartaric	tea caddy	telechir	tenoroon	terzetti	thanking
tankette	tartarin	tea chest	telecine	tenotomy	terzetto	thanks be
tank farm	Tartarly	teaching	telecoms	tenpence	tessella	thanks to
tankfuls	Tartarus	tea cloth	telefilm	tenpenny	tesserae	thank you
tankless	tartiest	tea dance	telegony	ten-pound	tesseral	thataboy
tank suit	tartness	tea fight	telegram	tensible	tessular	thataway
tank town	tartrate	tea glass	tele-lens	ten-speed	testable	thatched
tank trap	Tartuffe	tea green	telemark	tentacle	testamur	thatcher
tannable	tar-water	tea house	telepath	tent city	testator	that gate
tantalic	tarwhine	teal blue	teleport	tent club	testatum	that'll do
tantalum	task-work	tea-maker	teleseme	tent coat	test card	that long
tantalus	tasselly	team-boat	telestic	tent-door	test case	thatness
tantrism	tastable	team game	teletext	tentless	test-fire	that once
tantrist	taste bud	team-land	telethon	tentlike	testicle	that said
Taoistic	taste-cup	team-mate	teletype	ten to one	testiest	thaw-lake
tapaculo	tasteful	team race	Teletype	ten-to-two	test meal	thawless
tapadero	tastiest	teamsman	teleview	tent ring	test tube	the Apple
tapas bar	tattered	teamster	televise	tent-sack	testudos	thearchy
tap-borer	tattiest	team-talk	telework	tent show	test well	the Ashes
tap-dance	tattling	teamwork	tellable	tent town	tetanise	Theatine
tapeable	tattooed	tea olive	tell a lie	tentwise	tetanize	theatral
tape deck	tattooer	tea party	tell away	tentwort	tetanoid	theatric
tape hiss	tau cross	tea place	tell-tale	tenuious	tetchily	the Backs
tapeless	tau-staff	tea plant	telluric	tenurial	tetchous	thebaine
tape-line	tautness	tea plate	telomere	Ten Words	tetradic	the Beast
taper tap	tautomer	tearable	tellable	teocalli	tetragon	the bends
tapestry	tautonym	tear a cat	tell a lie	teosinte	Tetralin	the Blitz
tape-tied	taut ship	tear-arse	tell away	tephrite	tetramer	the Blues
tapeworm	taverner	tearaway	tell-tale	tepidity	Tetra Pak	the board
tap-house	tawdrier	tear bomb	telluric	teraflop	tetrapod	the brink
tapiroid		tear down	telomere	teraglin	tetrarch	the brute

the Buffs	thermics	thinnest	threaten	thwartly	tillable
the bumps	thermion	thinning	three-bar	thwittle	tillered
the Burse	thermite	thinnish	three-day	thyme-oil	tillicum
the chase	thermode	thin seam	three-one	thymitis	till-roll
the cloth	the Rolls	thin-sown	three-ply	thymosin	Tilsiter
the Coast	theropod	thin-spun	three-two	thyrsoid	tiltable
the Craft	the round	thin-worn	three-way	Tia Maria	tilt-boat
the Creed	the rules	thio-acid	threitol	tiarella	tilt-wing
the creep	the Salon	thioctic	threnode	Tiberian	tilt-yard
the Devil	thesauri	thionate	threnody	Tibetian	Timacuan
The Downs	the Shake	thionine	threshel	tibialis	timarchy
the drink	the shits	thiotepa	thresher	Ticinese	timariot
the Duchy	the Skins	thiourea	Thresher	tickameg	timbered
the enemy	the small	third age	thribble	tick-bean	timbrous
theetsee	the Smoke	third ear	thriller	tick-bird	time-ball
the Exile	the solid	third eye	thrimble	ticketed	time base
the faith	The Souls	third man	thrinter	ticketer	time-bill
the first	the South	third sex	thripple	tickling	time bomb
the Flood	the Speck	thirlage	throatal	ticklish	time code
the girls	thespian	thirster	throated	tick over	Timeform
the goods	Thespian	thirteen	throbbed	tick-seed	time-fuse
thegosis	Thetford	thirties	throbber	tick-tack	timeless
the hills	the thing	thisaway	thrombin	tick-tick	timelier
the House	thetical	this baby	thrombus	tick-tock	timelike
the Index	the Tombs	this bout	thronger	tidal air	time lock
the issue	the Tower	this gate	thropple	tiddlier	time-rate
theistic	the trots	this here	throstle	tide-boat	time slot
the jumps	theurgic	this is it	throttle	tideland	time span
the Kavir	the weeps	this life	throwing	tideless	time warp
the knife	the widow	this much	throw mud	tideline	timewise
the Lakes	thewless	thisness	throw off	tidemark	time-work
thelemic	thewness	this once	throw out	tide mill	time-worn
the Lords	the Yards	thistled	throw rug	tide over	time zone
thematic	thiamine	thiswise	thrumble	tidesman	timidest
the McCoy	thiazide	thole-pin	thrum cap	tidewave	timidity
theme pub	thiazine	Thompson	thrummed	tidiness	timoneer
the Mogul	thiazole	thoracal	thrummer	tie-break	Timorese
the mopes	thick-cut	thoraces	thruster	tie clasp	timorous
themself	thick ear	thoracic	thudding	tie match	tin-arsed
the night	thick end	thoraxes	thuggery	Tientsin	tincture
the North	thickety	thornier	thuggish	tie one on	tingeing
theocrat	thickish	thornily	thuggism	tiffined	tingible
theodicy	thickset	thorough	Thuggism	tiger-cat	tin-glass
theogony	thief ant	thoughty	thumbful	tiger-eye	tin-glaze
theology	thiefdom	thousand	thumb nut	tigerine	tinglier
theonomy	Thiersch	thowless	thumb-pad	tigering	tinglish
theorbos	Thiessen	Thracian	thumb-pin	tigerish	ting-tang
theories	thievery	thraldom	thumb-pot	tigerism	ting-ting
theorise	thieving	thralled	thumbs up	tiger-nut	tininess
theorism	thievish	thraneen	thumpety	tight-ass	tinkerer
theorist	thimbled	thranite	thumping	tight end	tinkling
theorize	thin-film	thrapple	thundery	tightish	tin-mouth
theosoph	thingamy	thrasher	thurible	tightwad	tinniest
theowdom	thingies	thraving	thurifer	tigridia	tinnitus
the peace	thingify	thraward	thurrock	Tigrinya	tin-panny
the pools	Thingman	thrawing	Thursday	Tigurine	tin plate
the pouts	think big	thrawnly	thus-gate	Tikopian	tinselly
the ranks	think box	threaded	thusness	tilefish	tinselry
therblig	think fit	threaden	thuswise	tile game	tinsmith
therefor	thinking	threader	thwacker	tile-kiln	tinsnips
theremin	think out	threadle	thwarter	tile-work	tin-stone
thereout	thinness	threaper	thwartle	tile-yard	tinstone

tintable	to a fault	tomatoey	top-graft	total sum	toxodont
tintless	to and fro	tombless	tophaike	total war	toxology
tint-tool	tobaccos	tombolos	top-heavy	tote fair	toymaker
tiny mind	to be sure	tombotie	Tophetic	totemism	trabeate
tippable	toboggan	tomentum	to pieces	totemist	tracheae
tippeter	Tobralco	Tom Jones	top-level	totemite	tracheal
tippy-toe	tochered	Tommy-bag	top light	tote road	trachean
tipsiest	tocology	tommy bar	top-liner	to the bad	tracheas
tip speed	todayish	Tommy-bar	toplofty	to the nth	tracheid
tipstaff	toddy cat	tommy-gun	top-notch	totitive	trachoma
tip-touch	to die for	tommy-rot	topology	totterer	trachyte
tiramisu	tod-tails	tommyrot	top onion	tottling	trackage
tired Tim	toe-board	Tommy-rot	toponium	tottlish	track-bed
tireless	toe brake	Tom-noddy	toponymy	totty-pot	trackbed
tiresome	toe-cover	tomogram	topotaxy	toucanet	tracking
tiringly	toe-crack	tomorrer	topotype	touch box	track-man
Tir-na-nog	toe-piece	tomorrow	top-score	touchier	trackman
Tironian	toe-plate	tom thumb	top-shell	touchily	trackmen
tirrivee	toe-strap	Tom Thumb	Topsider	touching	track rod
Tisha b'Av	toe to toe	to my mind	top-stone	touch off	trackway
tissular	to excess	tonalism	top table	touchous	tractate
titanate	to-flight	tonalist	top-water	touch-pad	tractile
Titaness	Tofranil	tonalite	top whack	tough guy	traction
titanian	together	tonality	top yeast	toughish	tractive
Titanian	Togolese	tone-deaf	toquilla	tough nut	tractlet
Titanism	tohu-bohu	tone down	torchère	touracos	tractrix
titanite	toileted	toneless	torchlit	tourdion	tradable
titanium	toiletry	tone poem	torch-man	tourelle	tradeful
titanous	toilette	tone poet	toreador	Tourette	trade gap
titchier	toilinet	ton-force	toreutic	touristy	trade off
tithable	toilless	tongkang	tor-grass	tour jeté	trade war
titheman	toilsome	tongsman	to rights	tourneys	traditor
tithe-pig	toil-worn	tonguing	Torinese	Tournois	traducer
titihoya	tokening	tonicity	tornadic	tournure	tragical
titivate	tokenism	tonology	tornados	tout seul	tragopan
titmouse	tokenist	tonstein	tornaria	tovarich	tragulid
tit-pipit	tokenize	tonsured	torn-down	tovarish	trailing
titrator	tokonoma	ton tight	tornillo	towardly	trail mix
titterer	Tok Pisin	toodle-oo	toroidal	towelled	trail-net
tittuped	Tokugawa	toolache	tor ouzel	towering	trailway
titty-bag	Tokyoite	tool-crib	torpidly	town ball	trainage
tittymeg	tolbooth	tool head	torquate	town-bull	traineau
titubant	tol-de-rol	toolless	torridly	town hall	trainful
titubate	tolerant	tool-mark	tortelli	town home	training
titulary	tolerate	tool-post	tortilla	townhood	trainman
tjanting	tolerize	toolroom	tortilly	townland	trainmen
tjurunga	tolidine	tool shed	tortious	townless	train-oil
tlachtli	tollable	tooraloo	tortoise	town plan	train set
Tlapanec	toll-bait	too right	Tortolan	Townsend	Trajanic
toadfish	toll call	toothful	tortuose	township	Traminer
toadflax	toll-dish	toothier	tortuous	townsman	tramless
toad-frog	toll-free	toothily	tortured	townsmen	tramline
toadless	toll gate	toothing	torturer	town-talk	trampdom
toadlike	toll-road	toothlet	torulose	townward	tramping
toad-lily	tollroad	tooth-mug	torulous	tow-plane	trampish
toadling	toloache	tootsies	tosafist	towplane	trampled
toad-rush	Toltecan	toparchy	toss oars	tow-start	trampler
toad's cap	toluylic	topazine	tosylate	toxaemia	tram-rail
toadship	tomahawk	top board	totalise	toxaemic	tram road
toad-spit	tomalley	top brass	totality	toxicant	tram silk
toadyish	tomatine	top dress	totalize	toxicity	tranchet
toadyism	tomatoes	top fruit	totalled	toxocara	trancing

trannies	trecento	tribunal	triology	troubler	tubbiest
tranquil	tre corde	tributor	trioxide	trouncer	tub chair
transact	tree-bear	tributyl	tripcock	troupial	tubchair
trans-bay	tree calf	trichina	tripedal	trousers	tube-feed
transect	tree-crab	trichite	triphane	trousies	tube-foot
transept	tree-crow	trichome	triplane	trout-fly	tubeless
transfer	tree cult	trichord	triplice	troutful	tube-lift
transfix	tree duck	trickery	triploid	trouting	tubelike
tranship	tree fern	trickful	tripodal	troutlet	tube line
transire	tree frog	trickier	Tripolye	trouvère	tubercle
transmew	treeless	trickily	trippage	truantly	tuberize
transmit	treelike	tricking	trippant	truantry	tuberose
transoid	tree line	trickish	trippery	truchman	tuberous
transude	tree-moss	tricklet	trippier	truckage	tube sock
transume	treenail	trick out	tripping	truckful	tube-well
trantery	tree ring	tricorne	trippist	trucking	tube worm
trap-ball	tree-rune	Tricouni	trippler	truckler	tubiform
trap boat	tree toad	tric-trac	tripsome	trucklot	tubipore
trap cage	tree wasp	tricycle	triptane	truckman	tubulate
trap-crop	trek Boer	tridacna	triptote	true bill	tubulose
trapdoor	trek-cart	tridecyl	triptych	true blue	tubulous
trapezia	trekking	Tridione	trip-wire	true-born	tubulure
trapezii	trembler	triennia	tripwire	true-bred	tub-wheel
trapfall	tremblor	triethyl	trisomic	true grit	tuckahoe
trap-hook	Tremcard	trifecta	tristeza	true leaf	tuck-away
traplike	tremella	trifling	tristful	true left	tuck-comb
trap-line	tremolos	trifocal	tristich	true love	tucked up
trap-nest	trencher	triforia	tristubh	trueness	tuck into
trappean	trendier	trigenic	trithing	truffled	tuck-mill
trapping	trendify	trigging	tritiate	truistic	tuck-rail
trappist	trendily	triglyph	tritical	trumeaux	tuck shop
Trappist	trending	trigness	tritonal	trumpery	tuco-tuco
trap-play	trendoid	trigonal	Tritonly	trumpety	tucutucu
trappoid	Trentine	trigonia	trit-trot	truncage	Tudesque
trap-rock	trephine	trigonid	triumvir	truncate	Tudorish
trap-shot	trepidly	trigonon	triunion	trunched	Tudorize
trap-tree	tresaiel	trigonum	triunity	trundler	Tuesdays
trapunto	tresance	trigraph	trizonal	trunkful	tuff-tuff
trap-yard	tresayle	trihedra	trochaic	trunking	tug-of-war
trash can	tresette	trilbied	trochili	trunnion	tug pilot
trashery	trespass	trilbies	trochlea	trussing	tuilette
trash-ice	tressure	trilemma	trochoid	truss-rod	tukutuku
trashier	trevalli	tri-level	troilism	trustful	tule wren
trashily	trevally	trilling	troilist	trustier	tullibee
trashman	triactor	trillion	troilite	trusties	tumandar
Traskite	triadism	trillium	trolleys	trustify	tumble up
trattles	trialism	trilobal	trollius	trustily	tumbling
trauchle	trialist	trilobed	trollopy	trusting	tumefied
traulism	triality	trimaran	trombone	truthful	tumefies
traverse	trialled	trimeric	trombony	truth set	tumidity
traverso	trial run	trimesic	troopial	try a fall	tummy bug
travesty	triangle	trimeter	trophied	tryingly	tumorous
trawl net	triapsal	trimmest	trophies	tryworks	tumoural
trayfuls	triarchy	trimming	tropical	tsarevna	tump-line
treacher	Triassic	trimness	troponin	tsaritsa	tump-tump
treading	triaxial	trimodal	trot-cosy	tsarship	tumulary
tread out	triazine	trimoric	trothful	tsessebi	tumulate
treasure	triazole	trimotor	trotteur	T-shirted	tumulous
treasury	tribally	trim-tram	trotting	tsitsith	tuna fish
treaties	tribasic	Trimurti	trottles	tsunamic	tuneable
treating	tribelet	trinklet	trottoir	tsunamis	tuneless
treatise	tribrach	trinodal	troubled	tubbable	tunesome

tunester	turn-tree	twistify	tyrosine	unarched	unbunged
tungsten	turn Turk	twist-off	Tyrrhene	unargued	unburden
tungstic	turpidly	twist tie	Tyrtaean	unartful	unburied
tung tree	turreted	twitched	Tysonian	unasking	unburies
Tungusic	turrible	twitchel	tzatziki	unatoned	unburned
tunicary	turrited	twitcher	tzitzith	unavowed	unburrow
tunicate	tuskless	twittery	Ubiquist	unawaked	unbutton
tunicked	tusklike	twitting	ubiquity	unawares	uncabled
tuniness	tussocky	twittish	uchimata	unbacked	uncalled
Tuniseen	tutelage	twit-twit	udderful	unbadged	uncandid
Tunisian	tutelary	two by two	uddiyana	unbaited	uncapped
Tunisine	tutorage	two-cycle	udometer	unbanded	uncaring
tunnyman	tutordom	two-eared	Ugaritic	unbanked	uncarved
tun tight	tutoress	two-edged	uglified	unbanned	uncashed
Tupamaro	tutorial	two-ended	uglifier	unbarbed	uncastle
tuppence	tutorize	two-faced	uglifies	unbarded	uncaught
tuppenny	Tuvaluan	two-field	ugliness	unbarked	uncaused
tu quoque	Tuvinian	two-holer	ugsomely	unbarred	unceiled
Turanian	tuxedoed	two hoots	Uigurean	unbarrel	uncellar
turanose	tuxedoes	two-horse	Uigurian	unbathed	uncement
turbaned	TV dinner	two-lined	uintaite	unbeaten	uncenter
turbidly	Twaddell	two parts	ulcerate	unbecome	uncentre
turbinal	twaddler	twopence	ulcerous	unbedded	unchancy
turbined	twa-grass	twopenny	uliginal	unbegged	uncharge
turbiner	Twainian	two-piece	ulterior	unbeheld	unchaste
turbines	twanging	two-rowed	ultimacy	unbelief	uncheery
turbocar	twangler	two-shear	ultimata	unbelted	unchewed
turbofan	twatchel	two-shoes	ultimate	unbended	unchoked
turbojet	twattler	two-sided	ultimity	unbenign	unchosen
Turcoman	tweedier	two-state	Ultonian	unbenumb	unchurch
turfiest	tweedily	two-teeth	ultraism	unbereft	uncially
turfless	tweedler	two-timer	ultraist	unbeseem	unciform
turf-line	tweeness	two times	ultra-red	unbiased	uncinate
turgency	tweezers	two-tooth	ululance	unbidden	uncipher
turgidly	twelvemo	Tychonic	Ulyssean	unbigged	unclench
Turinese	twenties	Tylorean	umbellar	unbishop	Uncle Ned
Turkmens	twentymo	Tylorian	umbelled	unbitted	Uncle Sam
Turkoman	twiddler	tympanal	umbellet	unbitten	Uncle Tom
Turk's cap	twiffler	tympanic	umbilici	unblamed	unclever
turlough	twiggage	tympanum	umble pie	unbloody	unclinch
Turlupin	twig-gall	type area	umbonate	unbobbed	unclosed
turmeric	twiggery	type-ball	umbrella	unbodied	unclothe
turnable	twigging	typecast	umbrette	unbodily	uncloudy
turn away	twilight	typeface	umpirage	unboiled	uncloven
turnaway	twilling	type-form	umpiress	unbolted	uncloyed
turn back	twin-bill	type-high	umptieth	unbonded	unclutch
turnback	twin-born	type site	umpty-ump	unbonnet	uncoated
turn-beam	twin city	type size	umquhile	unbooked	uncocked
turn-bolt	twinging	type test	unabated	unboring	uncoined
turncoat	twinhood	typhonic	unabused	unbottle	uncombed
turncock	twi-night	Typhonic	unaching	unbought	uncomely
turn down	twinkler	typified	una corda	unboyish	uncommon
turndown	twinleaf	typifier	unactive	unbraced	uncooked
turnkeys	twin-lens	typifies	unadored	unbreech	uncooled
turn-mark	twinling	typology	unaffied	unbribed	uncopied
turn over	twinning	tyramine	unafraid	unbridle	uncorked
turnover	twin-pair	tyrannic	unageing	unbright	uncosted
turnpike	twinship	tyrannis	unallied	unbroken	uncostly
turnsick	twin soul	tyre-iron	unamazed	unbuckle	uncouple
turnsole	twin-spot	tyreless	unamused	unbudded	uncovery
turnspit	twin town	Tyrolean	unanchor	unbudget	uncreate
turn tail	twistier	Tyrolese	unaneled	unbundle	unctuous

unculled	undersow	unfenced	ungutted	unionize	unlooped
uncumber	undertax	unfetter	unhabile	union nut	unloosen
uncurbed	undertie	unfilial	unhacked	unipivot	unlopped
uncurled	undertip	unfilled	unhailed	unipolar	unlorded
uncursed	undertow	unfirmly	unhaired	uniquely	unlordly
undamned	underuse	unfished	unhallow	uniquity	unlovely
undamped	under way	unfitted	unhalter	unironed	unloving
undaring	underway	unflawed	unhamper	unisonal	unmaiden
undarken	underwit	unfluted	unhanged	unissued	unmaimed
undarned	undesert	unfolded	unhappen	unitable	unmalted
undashed	undesire	unfolder	unharden	unit cell	unmanned
undation	undevout	unfooted	unharmed	unit cost	unmantle
undaubed	undieted	unforbid	unhatted	unitedly	unmapped
undazzle	undimmed	unforced	unheaded	unit load	unmarked
undecane	Undinism	unforged	unhealed	univalve	unmarred
undecent	undinted	unforgot	unhealth	universe	unmasked
undecide	undipped	unformal	unhearty	univocal	unmasker
undecked	undivine	unformed	unheated	un-Jewish	unmeetly
undecree	undoable	unfought	unhedged	unjoined	unmelted
undeemed	undocked	unfouled	unheeded	unjolted	unmended
undelete	undoctor	unframed	unhelmed	unjoyful	unmerged
undelved	undoffed	unfreeze	unhelped	unjoyous	unmighty
undenied	undoomed	un-French	unhemmed	unjudged	unmilked
undented	undotted	unfriend	unherded	unjustly	unmilled
underact	undouble	unfrozen	unheroic	unkeeled	unminded
under age	undraped	unfrugal	unhidden	unkenned	unminted
underage	undreamt	unfunded	unhinged	unkennel	unmissed
underarm	undriven	unfurred	unholier	unkilled	unmitred
underbed	undubbed	ungainly	unholily	unkilned	unmixing
underbid	undulant	ungalled	unholpen	unkindly	unmoaned
underbit	undulate	ungarter	unhomely	unkinged	unmocked
undercap	undulled	ungauged	unhonest	unkingly	unmodern
undercup	undulose	ungeared	unhooded	unkissed	unmodish
undercut	undulous	ungelded	unhooked	unknight	unmolten
underdip	undunged	ungenial	unhoping	unkosher	unmoored
underdog	undusted	ungentle	unhopped	unlanded	unmortal
underdot	unearned	ungently	unhorned	unlawful	un-Mosaic
underfed	uneasier	un-German	unhoused	unleaded	unmoving
underfit	uneasily	ungifted	unhulled	unleafed	unmuffle
under fog	unedible	ungilded	unhumble	unleared	unmuzzle
underfug	unedited	ungirded	unhunted	unlearnt	unnailed
underfur	unelated	ungiving	unhusked	unleased	unnapped
under-god	unending	ungladly	unhymned	unlevied	unnature
under God	unendued	unglazed	unialgal	unliable	unneeded
underhew	unenvied	ungloved	Uniatism	unlicked	unnimble
underjaw	unequals	ungnawed	uniaxial	unlidded	unnimbly
underlap	unerotic	ungoaded	unicycle	unlifted	unobeyed
underlay	unerring	ungolden	unifilar	unlikely	unopened
underlet	unespied	ungorged	unilobar	unliking	unordain
underlid	unevenly	ungotten	unimaged	unlimber	unpacked
underlie	unexotic	ungowned	unimbued	unlineal	unpacker
underlip	unfading	ungraced	unimodal	unlinked	unpained
underman	unfairly	ungraded	un-Indian	unliquid	unpaired
under one	unfallen	ungraven	uninemic	unlisted	unpalled
underpan	unfamous	ungrazed	uninfeft	unlively	unparted
underpay	unfanned	ungreasy	uninodal	unlivery	unpassed
underpin	unfarced	ungreedy	uninured	unliving	unpathed
underran	unfasten	unground	uninvite	unloaden	unpawned
underrun	unfather	unguided	union dye	unloader	unpaying
undersea	unfaulty	unguilty	unionise	unlocked	unpeeled
underset	unfeared	ungulate	unionism	unlonely	unpeered
undersky	unfelled	ungummed	unionist	unlooked	unpegged

unpeople	unringed	unsigned	unsurely	unversed	upgather
unperson	unrinsed	unsimple	unsurety	unvetted	upgrader
unphased	unripely	unsinful	unswathe	unviable	upgrowth
unphoney	unripped	unsinged	unswayed	unviewed	upheaval
unpicked	unrobbed	unsiphon	untackle	unvirtue	upheaver
unpinned	unrobust	unslaked	untagged	unvizard	upholder
unpitied	unrocked	unsleeve	untailed	unvoiced	up in arms
unplaced	unroofed	unsliced	untalked	unvulgar	uplander
unplaned	unrooted	unslough	untangle	unwalked	uplifter
unplayed	unrotted	unslowed	untanned	unwalled	uplooker
unpliant	unrotten	unsluice	untapped	unwaning	up-market
unplowed	unrouged	unsmoked	untarred	unwanted	upmarket
unplumed	unroused	unsmooth	untasked	unwanton	upper air
unpocket	unrouted	unsoaped	untasted	unwarded	upper-cut
unpoetic	unrubbed	unsocial	untaught	unwarily	uppercut
unpoised	unruffle	unsocket	untenant	unwarmed	upper dog
unpoison	unruined	unsodden	untended	unwarned	upperest
unpolish	unrulier	unsoiled	untender	unwarped	upper jaw
unpolite	unrusted	unsolder	untented	unwashed	upper ten
unpolled	unsacked	unsolemn	untested	unwashen	uppishly
unposted	unsacred	unsolved	untether	unwasted	uprising
unpraise	unsaddle	unsordid	unthatch	unwatery	uprootal
unprayed	unsafely	unsorted	unthawed	unwaving	uprooter
unpreach	unsafety	unsought	unthread	unwealth	uproused
unpretty	unsailed	unsouled	unthrift	unweaned	upsaddle
unpriced	unsained	unsoured	unthrone	unwebbed	upsetter
unpriest	unsalted	unspared	unthrown	unwedded	upsprang
unprimed	unscaled	unsphere	untidier	unweeded	upspring
unprison	unscared	unspiced	untidily	unweened	upstager
unprized	unschool	unspiked	untilled	unweight	upstairs
unprobed	unscored	unspoilt	untimber	unwelded	upstater
unprofit	unsealed	unspoken	untimely	unwemmed	up sticks
Unprofor	unseared	unsprang	untinged	unwetted	upstream
UNPROFOR	unseason	unspread	untinned	unwieldy	up street
unproper	unseated	unspring	untinted	unwifely	up-stroke
unproved	unsecret	unsprung	untipped	unwigged	upstroke
unproven	unseeded	unsquare	untiring	unwilful	upthrust
unpruned	unseeing	unstable	untithed	unwilled	uptilted
unpublic	unseemly	unstably	untitled	unwinged	up to date
unpulled	unseized	unstaled	untoiled	unwinter	uptowner
unpumped	unseldom	unstated	untombed	unwisdom	upturner
unpurged	unselect	unstayed	untoward	unwisely	upwardly
unquoted	unsensed	unsteady	untraced	unwished	uralitic
unrailed	unserene	unstitch	untraded	unwonted	uranitic
unraised	unserved	unstolen	untragic	unwooded	Urartian
unreally	unsettle	unstored	untrendy	unworded	urbanely
unreaped	unsexier	unstrain	untruism	unworked	urbanise
unreason	unsexual	unstream	untrusty	unwormed	urbanism
unrecked	unshaded	unstress	untucked	unworthy	urbanist
unregard	unshadow	unstrike	unturned	unyeaned	Urbanist
unreined	unshaken	unstring	ununited	unzipped	urbanite
unrepaid	unshamed	unstrong	unurgent	unzipper	urbanity
unrepair	unshaped	unstruck	unusable	up-a-daisy	urbanize
unrepose	unshapen	unstrung	unuseful	up-anchor	urbicide
unrested	unshared	unstuffy	unvalued	upas tree	urceolus
unretted	unshaved	unsubtle	unvamped	up a stump	urchinly
unrhymed	unshaven	unsubtly	unvaried	upbubble	uredines
unribbed	unshelve	unsucked	unveiled	up-choked	uredinia
unridden	unshrine	unsuited	unveiler	upcoming	ureilite
unriddle	unshroud	unsummed	unveined	upcurved	ureteral
unrifled	unsicker	unsunned	unvenged	updoming	ureteric
unrigged	unsifted	unsupped	unvented	upfurled	urethane

urethrae	vaginula	vaporous	veinulet	vergence	vibronic
urethral	vagotomy	vapoured	velamina	vergency	viburnum
urethras	vagotony	vapourer	velarise	verified	vicarage
Urfirnis	vagrance	vapulate	velarity	verifier	vicarate
urgently	vagrancy	varactor	velarium	verifies	vicaress
uric acid	vainness	varanian	velarize	veristic	vicariad
uridylic	Valaisan	vardapet	Velcroed	verities	vicarial
urnfield	valanced	vargueño	veld-kost	verjuice	vicarian
urobilin	vale-lily	variable	veldsman	*verligte*	vicarish
uroboric	Valencia	variably	velleity	vermetid	vicarism
uroboros	valerate	variance	vellinch	vermicle	vice-king
urochord	valerian	variator	velocity	vermined	viceless
urodaeum	valeting	variceal	velodyne	verminer	vice-like
urodelan	Valhalla	varicose	velveret	Vermoral	vicelike
urologic	valiance	variedly	velveted	vermouth	vicenary
uroscopy	valiancy	varietal	vena cava	vernally	vice ring
urostyle	validate	variform	venality	Verneuil	Vichyist
urotoxic	validity	varihued	venation	vernicle	Vichyite
uroxanic	valinche	variolar	vendable	Veronese	vicinage
Ursuline	Valiumed	variorum	vendetta	veronica	vicinism
urticant	Valkyrie	Variscan	*vendeuse*	verrucae	vicinity
urticate	valleyed	varistor	vendible	verrucas	Viconian
urushiol	Vallhund	varletry	venenose	verselet	victoria
usedness	valorise	varminty	venerate	verseman	Victoria
used-to-be	valorize	varnishy	venereal	versical	victorin
usefully	valorous	vartabed	Venerean	versicle	victress
use-money	valproic	vascular	Venerian	vertebra	Victrola
usership	Valsalva	vasculum	venerous	vertexes	videofit
usherdom	Valspeak	vasefuls	Venetian	vertical	video map
ustilago	valuable	Vaseline	vengeful	vertices	videotex
usufruct	valuably	vasiform	venially	verticil	Viennese
usurious	valuator	vasquine	venidium	Vertisol	Viet Cong
usurping	valvelet	vassalic	venogram	very good	Viet Minh
uteritis	valvifer	vassalry	venomous	very well	*vieux jeu*
Utilidor	valvular	vastness	venosity	vesalian	viewable
utilizer	vambrace	Vatinian	venously	vesicant	view card
Uto-Aztec	vampiric	vaultage	vent-hole	vesicate	viewdata
Utopiast	vamplate	vaulting	ventless	vesicula	viewless
utopiate	vanadate	vauntery	Ventolin	vesperal	viewport
utopical	vanadian	vauntful	ventouse	vespiary	viewsite
utriculi	vanadium	vaunting	venturer	vestiary	Vigenere
utterest	vanadous	vauntlay	venturis	vestless	vigilant
uver hand	vandalic	Vauxhall	Venusian	vestment	vigneron
uvermost	Vandalic	vavasory	venville	vestries	vignette
uvularia	vanessid	vavasour	veracity	vestuary	vignoble
uvularly	vanguard	veal calf	verandah	vestural	vigorish
uvulitis	vanillic	vectigal	veratria	vestured	vigorist
uxorious	vanillin	vectored	veratric	vesturer	vigorous
vaalhaai	vanillon	Vedantic	veratrum	Vesuvian	vildness
Vaalpens	vanillyl	veganism	verbally	Vesuvius	vileness
vacantly	vanisher	Vegemite	verbatim	vexation	vilified
vacation	vanities	vegetant	verbiage	vexatory	vilifier
vaccinal	vanitory	vegetate	verbless	vexillum	vilifies
vaccinee	Vanitory	vegetive	verboten	vexingly	vilipend
vaccinia	vanitous	Vegliote	verdancy	*via media*	villadom
vacherin	vanquish	vehement	Verdelho	viatical	villager
vacuolar	V antenna	veiledly	verderer	viaticum	villaget
vagabond	van't Hoff	veilless	verditer	vibrance	villagey
vagaries	vapidity	vein-gold	verdured	vibrancy	villainy
vagility	vaporise	veiniest	verdurer	vibrator	villakin
vaginant	vaporish	veinless	verecund	vibrioid	villatic
vaginate	vaporize	veinlike	vergaloo	vibrissa	vin blanc

vinchuca	visceral	voice box	waesucks	wall-hook	war-eagle
vincible	viscount	voiceful	Waffen SS	wall-hung	wareless
vincibly	viscuous	voidable	wafflike	wall-knot	wareness
vinculum	Visigoth	voidance	wage bill	wall-less	Warerite
vindaloo	visional	voidless	wageless	wall-nail	warfarin
vinegary	visioned	voidness	wager-cup	walloped	war fever
vine-hook	visioner	voilette	wage stop	walloper	warfront
vine leaf	visitant	voir dire	waggable	wallower	war-gamer
vineless	visiting	volantly	waggoner	wall pass	war grave
vine moth	vis major	volatile	wagonage	wall plug	war-guilt
vineries	Visqueen	volation	wagon-bed	wall-rock	warhorse
vine tree	visually	volatize	wagon box	Wallsend	War House
vine-wood	vital air	volcanic	wagonful	wall-side	wariness
vineyard	vitalise	volitant	wagon-lit	wall-tent	waringin
vinified	vitalism	volitate	wagon-man	wall-tree	warmable
vinifies	vitalist	volition	wagon-way	wall unit	warm bath
vin jaune	vitality	volitive	Wahabism	wall vase	warm boot
vinolent	Vitalium	volkswil	Wahabite	wall-walk	warm down
vino nero	vitalize	volleyer	wahoo elm	wall-wash	warmed-up
vinosity	vitamin A	volplane	waiflike	wall-work	warmer-up
vinously	vitamin B	Volscian	wailsome	wallwort	warmness
vin rouge	vitamin C	volsella	wainscot	wambling	warmouth
vintager	vitamin D	Volstead	waist-gun	wandered	warm over
vintnery	vitamin E	voltaism	wait-a-bit	wanderer	warm work
Vinylite	vitamin H	Volterra	wait-list	wanderoo	warpaint
vinylogy	vitamin K	volumina	waitress	Wandjina	war-party
violable	vitamin M	volution	waivable	wandsman	warp-beam
violater	vitamin P	volvelle	Wakashan	wangrace	warp-lace
violator	vitellin	volvulus	wakeless	wanhappy	war-plane
violence	vitellus	vomerine	wakerife	wan smile	warplane
violency	vitiator	vomit bag	Waldense	wantable	war-proof
violetta	vitiligo	vomiting	Waldeyer	want in on	warragal
viologen	vitreous	vomition	waldhorn	wantless	warranty
viomycin	vituline	vomitory	waldrapp	want list	warrener
viperine	vivacity	vomitous	wale-knot	wantoner	warrigal
viperish	vivarium	voodooed	walkable	wantonly	warspeak
viperous	viva voce	voorslag	walk-away	wanweird	war-steed
viraemia	viverrid	voracity	walk-back	wanwordy	wartless
viraemic	vividity	vortexes	walker-on	wanworth	wartlike
virement	vivified	vortical	walk good	wappered	war trial
virgated	vivifier	vortices	walk home	warbling	wartweed
virgater	vivifies	votaress	walk hots	war bride	wartwort
virginal	vivipary	votaries	walk into	war chest	war-weary
Virginia	vivisect	votarist	walk-mill	war cloud	war-whoop
virginly	vixenish	votation	walk over	warcraft	war widow
virgular	vizarded	vote bank	walkover	war crime	washable
viricide	vizcacha	vote down	walksman	ward aide	washaway
viridian	vizieral	voteless	walk tall	war dance	wash-ball
viridine	vizyless	voussoir	walk up to	wardatar	wash-bowl
viridity	Vlachian	vowelise	walk with	ward-book	washbrew
virilism	vocalese	vowelist	Walkyric	wardency	wash-coat
virility	vocalion	vowelize	Walkyrie	wardenry	wash-deck
virogene	vocalise	vowelled	Wallabee	warderer	wash-dirt
virology	vocalism	voyageur	Wallacea	war diary	wash-dish
virosome	vocalist	vulcanic	wallaroo	ward maid	wash down
virtuosa	vocality	vulgarly	walled-in	wardmote	washdown
virtuosi	vocalize	vulpinic	walled-up	wardress	washed up
virtuoso	vocation	vulsella	wall-eyed	wardrobe	washer-up
virtuous	vocative	vulvitis	wall-face	ward-room	wash-fast
virucide	Vodafone	Wachagga	wall fern	wardroom	wash-hand
virulent	vogesite	wadeable	wallfish	wardship	washiest
viscacha	Vogulian	wade into	wall game	wardsman	washland

wash-line	wave base	web-wheel	well-read	wheat-fly	whipster
wash-pool	wave down	Wechsler	well-room	wheatish	whip tail
washroom	wave drag	Wedgwood	Wellsian	wheedler	whiptail
wash-sale	waveform	weedhead	well then	wheelage	whipworm
wasplike	waveless	weed-hook	well-to-do	wheel bug	whirling
wastable	wavelike	weediest	well-tomb	wheel car	whirring
waste bin	wave-line	weedless	well-trap	wheel-dog	whiskery
wasteful	wave mark	weedling	well-used	wheeling	whiskeys
waste-way	wave-path	wee hours	well-wish	wheelman	whiskied
wastrife	wavering	weeklies	well with	wheel-map	whiskies
Wasukuma	wave trap	week-long	well-worn	wheelmen	whisking
watch-box	waviness	weeklong	Welsbach	wheel-ore	whispery
watch cap	wavingly	week-work	Welshman	wheel-pit	whistled
watchdog	Wavy Navy	weeniest	Welshmen	wheel-set	whistler
watch for	wax berry	weep-hole	werewolf	wheel-tax	white ant
watchful	waxberry	weepiest	Wernicke	wheezily	white ash
watchman	wax borer	weetless	Wesleyan	wheezing	white box
watchmen	wax-cloth	weet-weet	West Bank	whelpish	white boy
watch out	waxcloth	weft fork	westerly	whenever	whitecap
waterage	wax gland	wegotism	West Indy	whereout	white elm
water-ash	wax in age	wehrlite	westland	wherever	white-eye
water-bag	waxiness	Weichsel	Westmark	wherries	white fir
water bat	wax-light	weigh-bar	westmost	whetting	whitefly
water-bed	wax paper	weighing	West Nile	whey-face	white fox
waterbed	wax plant	weighman	west side	Whieldon	white-gum
water-boa	wax print	weigh off	West Side	whiffier	white-hat
waterbok	wayboard	weigh out	westward	whiffled	white-hot
water-boy	waybread	weirdies	west wind	whiffler	White Hun
water bug	way-chain	weirdish	wet dream	Whiggery	white leg
water bus	wayfarer	weirdity	wet-eared	Whiggess	white lie
water-cow	way-going	welcomer	wet lease	Whiggify	White man
water-dog	waygoose	weldable	wet meter	Whiggish	whitener
water elm	waylayer	weldless	wet-nurse	Whiggism	white oak
water-fly	way-leave	weldment	wet plate	Whigling	white oil
water gas	wayleave	weldmesh	wet shave	Whigship	white-out
water gum	way-point	weld pool	wet smack	Whillans	white owl
waterhen	waypoint	welladay	wet steam	whimbrel	whitepox
water ice	way train	well-aged	wettable	whimmery	white rat
waterily	way-wiser	well away	wet trade	whimpish	white rod
watering	wazirate	wellaway	wet-white	whimseys	white rot
waterish	weakener	well-baby	Weymouth	whimsies	white rum
water jug	weakfish	well-boat	whackier	whimsily	white tie
waterlog	weaklier	well-born	whacking	whim-wham	white tin
Waterloo	weakling	well-bred	whale-fin	whinchat	whitling
waterman	weak link	well-curb	whaleman	whiniest	whitster
watermen	weakness	well deck	whale oil	whinnied	whittler
water-net	weak side	well-dish	whammies	whinnies	Whit walk
water oak	weak spot	well-done	whamming	whinyard	whiz-bang
Water Pik	weanable	well-head	wharfage	whipbird	whizzing
water-pot	weanling	well-hole	wharfing	whip-club	whizz-kid
water rat	weaponed	well-hung	wharf-rat	whipcord	whodunit
water-ret	weaponry	well-kept	what else	whip-crop	whole lot
water-rot	wearable	well-kerb	whatever	whip hand	whole sum
water-ski	weariest	well-kick	what-like	whip-jack	whomever
waterway	weariful	well-knit	whatness	whiplash	whooping
watsonia	wear thin	well-like	what of it	whipless	whoopsie
watt-hour	wear well	well-lost	what size	whip-like	whopping
wattless	weaselly	well-made	what's new	whiplike	whoredom
wattling	weathery	well-near	what then	whip line	whoreson
Waughian	Weatings	wellness	what time	whipping	Whorfian
Waughism	weavable	well-nigh	what with	whip-roll	whorlbat
waveband	Weberian	well-paid	wheatear	whipship	whosever

whydunit	wind-blow	wink hard	wittiest	woodlark	word-book
wickeder	windburn	winkless	wittolly	woodless	wordbook
wickedly	wind-cone	winnable	wizardly	wood lily	word-deaf
wickered	wind down	winnower	wizardry	wood-meal	word-game
wickless	winder-up	winterer	wobblier	woodmote	wordiest
widdiful	windfall	winterim	wobbling	woodness	wordless
wide ball	wind farm	winterly	woefully	woodnote	wordlore
wide-band	wind gall	wintrier	woe is him	wood-opal	word mark
wide-body	wind-harp	wintrify	wolf call	woodpile	word-pair
wide-eyed	wind-hole	wintrily	wolf clan	wood pulp	wordplay
wideness	windiest	wipeable	wolf coat	wood-rock	word-sign
wide open	windlass	wipe down	Wolffian	woodruff	word size
widow-man	windless	wire-draw	wolf-fish	woodrush	wordsman
wieldier	windlike	wiredraw	wolf-head	wood sage	wordster
Wien's law	windling	wire edge	wolflike	wood-sear	word time
wifehood	wind load	wire-hair	wolfling	wood-sere	word-type
wifeless	windmill	wire into	wolf-moth	woodshed	word wrap
wifelike	windowed	wireless	wolf-note	wood shot	workable
wigglier	windpipe	wireline	wolf-pack	woodside	workably
wig-stand	windrock	wire-mark	wolfskin	woodsman	workaday
Wilcoxon	wind-rose	wire nail	wolf tree	woodsmen	work away
wild arum	wind-sail	wirepull	womandom	woodstar	workaway
wild boar	windsail	wire rope	womanise	wood-tick	work back
wildbore	wind-slab	wire wool	womanish	woodwall	workboat
wild card	windsock	wirework	womanism	woodward	workbook
wild deer	windster	wireworm	womanist	woodware	work camp
wild duck	wind-suck	wire-wove	womanity	woodwasp	work card
wildered	windsurf	wiriness	womanize	woodwind	workfare
wildfire	windward	wirrwarr	woman-man	wood-wing	work-flow
wildfowl	wine book	wiseacre	womb-like	wood wool	workfolk
wild goat	wine buff	wisehead	womblike	woodwork	work-hand
wild leek	wine-dark	wiselike	womenish	woodworm	workhead
wildlife	wine farm	wiseling	wonderer	woodwose	workless
wildling	wine lake	wiseness	wonderly	wood-wren	workload
wild mare	wine-lees	wishable	wondrous	woodyard	workmate
wildness	wineless	wishbone	wonkiest	wooingly	work over
wild oats	wine list	wish book	wontedly	wool-card	workover
wild pine	wine-palm	wishless	won't wash	wool-clip	work rate
wild rape	wine rack	wish-list	wood-acid	wool-comb	workroom
wild rice	wineries	wish-wash	wood-bill	woolding	works bus
wild silk	wineskin	wispiest	woodbind	wool-dyed	workshop
wild type	wine snob	wistaria	woodbine	wool-fell	worksite
wild vine	winesour	wisteria	Woodbury	Woolfian	worksome
wild well	wing-band	witch elm	woodchat	wool-hawk	work-team
Wild West	wing-beat	witchery	woodchip	woolleny	workwear
wild woad	wing-case	witch-hat	wood-chop	woollier	workwise
wildwood	Wing Chun	witching	wood-coal	woollily	workyday
wilfully	wing-clap	wit-craft	woodcock	wool-like	world-all
wiliness	wingding	witeless	Wood Cree	Woolmark	World Cup
wiliwili	wingedly	with calf	wood-dove	wool moth	worldful
willable	wing-fish	withdraw	wood-duck	wool-pack	worldish
will-form	wing-game	withdrew	woodenly	woolpack	worldlet
Williams	wing-half	with ease	wood-fire	woolsack	world-old
williwaw	wingless	withered	wood-free	Woolsack	world war
will-less	winglike	witherer	wood-frog	woolshed	worm-cast
willowed	wing root	withe-rod	wood grub	wool-skin	worm-gear
willsome	wing-sail	withhold	woodhack	wool team	worm-hole
willyart	wing-shot	with luck	wood-heap	Woolwich	wormhole
win again	wing span	withness	wood-hole	wool-work	wormiest
winchman	wingspan	with that	wood-ibis	woop woop	wormless
wind axis	wing-wall	withwind	woodiest	wooziest	wormlike
wind band	wink away	withy-bed	woodland	word-base	wormling

wormseed	wristily	yam-stick	Yogacara	Zenonian	zoogenic
worm-tube	wristlet	yanggona	yoghurty	zeolitic	zoogloea
wormwood	wrist-pin	Yang Shao	yokelish	Zephiran	zoolatry
worn-down	writable	Yank tank	yoke-mate	zephyrus	zoologer
wornness	write off	Yanomami	yoke-skey	Zeppelin	zoologic
worricow	write out	yappiest	yoke-toed	zeroable	zoomancy
worrited	writerly	yardbird	yoke-tree	zero-base	zoometry
worry out	writhing	yardland	Yokohama	zero beat	zoom lens
worse off	writhled	yard-rope	yokozuna	zero hour	zoomorph
worserer	wrizzled	yard sale	yolk duct	zero in on	zoom shot
worthful	wrongful	yardsman	yolkless	zero-rate	zoonosis
worthier	wrongous	yard-wand	yonderly	zero-zero	zoonotic
worthily	wry-faced	Yarkandi	York boat	zerumbet	zoophile
wouldest	wry-mouth	Yarmouth	youngest	zestiest	zoophily
would God	Wundtian	yarmulka	youngish	zetacism	zoophyte
woulding	wurtzite	yarmulke	younglet	zibeline	zooscopy
woundily	xanthate	yarn-beam	young man	Ziegfeld	zoosophy
wounding	xanthene	yarraman	yourself	ziggurat	zoosperm
wrackful	Xanthian	yataghan	youthful	zigzaggy	zoospore
wrangler	xanthine	yawmeter	youthify	zikkurat	zootomic
wrap coat	xanthism	yeanling	youthily	Zimbabwe	zootoxic
wrap it up	xanthoma	year-bird	ytterbia	zimbalom	zootoxin
wrap-over	xanthone	yearbook	yuffrouw	zinc grey	zoot suit
wrappage	xanthous	yearling	Yugoslav	zinc roof	zootypic
wrapping	Xantippe	year-long	Yukaghir	zingiber	zophorus
wrap reel	Xaverian	yearnful	yukiness	zingiest	zopilote
wrathful	xenogamy	yearning	yukkiest	Zionward	zos-grass
wrathily	xenolith	year-ring	yule-clog	Zipf's law	Z-plastic
wreakful	xenology	yea-sayer	yule even	zippered	zubrowka
wreathed	xenotime	yeastier	yule-tide	zippiest	zucchini
wreathen	xerocopy	yeastily	Yuletide	zircaloy	zugzwang
wreather	xerosere	Yeatsian	yummiest	zirconia	Zuricher
wreckage	xiphioid	yellowly	yuppyish	zirconic	zwieback
wreckful	xography	Yemenite	Yusufzai	zirconyl	zygaenid
wrecking	X-ray eyes	yen siang	Yuvaraja	zizyphus	zygodont
wrencher	X-ray tube	yeomanly	yuzbashi	zoanthid	zygology
Wrennery	xylidine	yeomanry	Zadokite	zodiacal	zygomata
wren-tail	xylocarp	yeowoman	zamindar	Zoellner	zygomere
wresting	Xylonite	yersinia	zampogna	zoetrope	zygonema
wrestler	xylotomy	yes and no	zaniness	zombiism	zygosity
wrest-pin	xylulose	Yes and No	zappiest	zonality	zygosome
wretched	yachting	yes siree	zarzuela	zonation	zygotene
wriggled	Yaghnobi	yestreen	zastruga	zoneless	Zylonite
wriggler	yahooism	yes-woman	zealless	zone-melt	zymodeme
wringing	yahrzeit	yield gap	zealotic	zone time	zymogram
wrinkled	yakitori	yielding	zealotry	zoochore	zymology
wrinklie	Yale lock	Yinglish	zebra eel	zoochory	
wrist-bag	yam house	yodelled	zemindar	zooecial	
wrist hit	yammerer	yodeller	zenithal	zooecium	

NINE LETTERS

Aaronical
Aaron's rod
abaciscus
abackward
a bad sport
a bad taste
abandoned
abandonee
abandoner
abasement
abashedly
abashless
abashment
abatement
abattises
abbotship
abdicable
abdicator
abdominal
abduction
abductive
abearance
abecedary
Abernethy
aberrance
aberrancy
abettance
abhorrent
abhorring
abidingly
abilities
abiogenic
a bit of fat
a bit thick
abjection
Abkhazian
ablatival
abnegator
abnormity
abnormous
abolisher
abolition
abominate
abondance
aborigine
ABO system
about-face
aboutness
about time
about-turn
Abrahamic
abrogable
abrogator
abruption
abscessed
abscision
abscissae

abscissas
absconder
absit omen
absorbent
absorbing
abstainer
abstinent
abstracta
absurdism
absurdist
absurdity
abuilding
abundance
abundancy
abusively
abysmally
Abyssinia
academese
academies
academism
Academism
Academist
acalculia
acanthine
acanthite
a cappella
acariasis
acaricide
acarology
acathisia
accedence
accension
accentual
acceptant
acception
acceptive
accessary
accession
accessory
accidence
accidious
accipiter
acclaimer
acclimate
acclivity
acclivous
accompany
accordant
according
accordion
account of
account to
accretion
accretive
accumbent
accusable
acellular

acephalic
acerebral
acervulus
acescence
acescency
acetabula
acetamide
acetifier
acetylate
acetylene
acetylide
achalasia
Acheulean
Acheulian
Achillean
achimenes
acholuric
aciculate
acidaemia
acid house
Acid House
acidified
acidifies
acidities
acidulate
acidulent
aciculous
aciniform
a-cock-bill
aconitine
a coon's age
acorn worm
acoustics
acquiesce
acquiring
acquittal
acquitted
acquitter
acridness
acritarch
acrobatic
acronymic
acropetal
acrophobe
acropolis
acrospire
activator
actorship
actualise
actualism
actualist
actuality
actualize
actual sin
actuarial
actuaries
actuation

aculeated
acuminate
a cut above
acuteness
acyclovir
acylation
adamantly
Adamesque
Adamitism
adaptable
adaptably
adderbolt
adderwort
addicting
addiction
addictive
addleness
addressed
addressee
addresser
addressor
adducible
adduction
adductive
ademption
adenoidal
adenomata
adenosine
adeptness
adeptship
a deuce of a
adherence
adherency
adhibited
ad hominem
adiabatic
adiaphora
Adi Granth
ad interim
adipocere
adipocyte
adiposity
adjacence
adjacency
adjection
adjective
adjournal
adjustive
adjutancy
adjutator
ad libbing
ad libitum
admeasure
adminicle
admirable
admirably
admiralty

Admiralty
admission
admissive
admitting
admixtion
admixture
admonitor
ad nauseam
adnominal
adoptable
adoration
adorative
adoringly
adornment
adpressed
adrenalin
adrogator
adsorbate
adsorbent
adstratum
adulation
adulatory
adulterer
adulthood
adultness
adumbrate
adunation
ad valorem
advance on
advantage
advection
advective
advenient
adventism
Adventism
adventist
Adventist
adventive
adventure
adverbial
adversary
adversely
adversity
advertent
advertise
advisable
advisably
advisedly
advocator
aedicular
aegophony
aeolienne
aeolipyle
aepyornis
aerialist
aeriality
aerobatic

aerodrome
aerolitic
aeromancy
aerometry
aeronomer
aeronomic
aerophagy
aerophobe
aerophone
aeroplane
aerospace
aerotrain
Aesopical
aesthesis
aesthetic
aestivate
aetheling
aethereal
aetiology
a fair deal
a fast buck
affecting
affection
affective
affectual
affidavit
affiliate
affirmant
affixture
afflation
afflicter
affluence
affluency
affluxion
affricate
affronted
affrontee
affronter
aflatoxin
aforehand
aforesaid
aforetime
a fortiori
Afrikaans
Afrikaner
after-born
after-care
aftercare
afterclap
aftercrop
after-damp
afterdamp
after dark
after-days
after-game
afterglow
afterlife

aftermath	airworthy	alignment	all square	amazingly	amphtrack
after meat	airy-fairy	alikeness	all the way	amazon ant	ampleness
aftermost	aisleless	alimental	all-ticket	Amazon ant	amplified
afterness	aitchbone	alimenter	allumette	Amazonian	amplifier
afternoon	aitchless	aliphatic	allurance	Amazonism	amplifies
after-pain	akathisia	aliteracy	alluviate	amazonite	amplitude
afterward	alabaster	aliterate	alluvious	ambagious	amputator
afterword	à la broche	aliveness	alluviums	ambassage	a mug's game
agapemone	alack-a-day	alkalosis	allwheres	amber-fish	amusement
agateware	alarmable	alkekengi	alma mater	ambergris	amusingly
agent noun	alarm-bell	all aboard	Alma Mater	amberjack	amusively
agentship	alarm bird	alla breve	almandine	ambiguity	amygdalin
age of gold	alarm call	allantoic	almandite	ambiguous	amylopsin
aggravate	alarm-post	allantoid	almond eye	ambisonic	anabiosis
aggregate	alaternus	allantoin	almond oil	ambitious	anabiotic
aggressor	albarello	allantois	almsgiver	amblyopia	anabolism
aggrieved	albatross	all-around	almshouse	amblyopic	anabranch
agistment	Albertine	all at once	almswoman	Amboinese	anachoret
agitating	albertite	All Blacks	aloneness	Amboynese	anaclasis
agitation	albescent	all comers	alongside	ambrosial	anacruses
agitative	albespine	allective	along with	ambrosian	anacrusis
aglyphous	albinoism	allegator	aloofness	Ambrosian	anaerobic
agnolotti	albinotic	allegedly	alpargata	ambrotype	Anaglypta
a gone coon	albititic	allegiant	alpenglow	ambulance	anaklasis
agonistes	alburnous	allegoric	alpenhorn	ambulator	analeptic
agonistic	alcarraza	allemande	alpenrose	ambuscade	analgesia
agonizing	alchemies	Allemanic	alpha plus	ambuscado	analgesic
agony aunt	alchemise	allenarly	alpha test	amendable	analogate
a good life	alchemist	all ends up	alpha wave	amendment	analogies
a good many	alchemize	allergies	Alpine fir	Amen glass	analogise
a good step	Alcmanian	allergist	alstonite	amenities	analogist
a good ways	alcoholic	alleviate	altarless	Amerasian	analogize
agreeable	Alcoranic	allicient	altar-tomb	Americana	analogous
agreeably	aldehydic	alligator	altarwise	Americani	analysand
agreeance	alder tree	all kind of	alterable	americium	analysans
agreement	Aldis lamp	all nature	altercate	ametropia	anamneses
agrestial	aleatoric	allocable	alter egos	ametropic	anamnesis
agriology	alecithal	allocator	alternant	amianthus	anandrous
agronomic	aleconner	allodiary	alternate	amidships	anaphoric
a hard case	ale firkin	allogenic	alternity	amino acid	anaplasia
ahistoric	ale gallon	allograft	altimeter	amissible	anaptyxis
à huis clos	Alemannic	allograph	altimetry	ammocoete	anarchial
ahungered	alembroth	allometry	altiplano	ammoniate	anarchism
aid-de-camp	aleph-null	allomorph	altissimo	ammonitic	anarchist
aid-prayer	alertness	allopathy	altricial	amnestied	anarchize
ailanthus	ale-taster	allopatry	aluminate	amnesties	anarthria
aimlessly	Alexander	allophane	aluminise	amniotomy	anastatic
air bridge	alfilaria	allophone	aluminium	amoralism	a nasty one
air-castle	Alfredian	allostery	aluminize	amoralist	anathemas
air-cooled	algarroba	allotment	aluminous	amorality	anatocism
air-filter	algebraic	allotrope	alum-stone	amorosity	Anatolian
air gunner	algebrist	allotropy	alveolate	amorously	anatomies
air letter	algedonic	allotting	amability	amorphism	anatomise
airmobile	Algonkian	allotypic	amanuense	amorphous	anatomist
air piracy	Algonquin	allowable	amaryllid	amourette	anatomize
air pirate	algorithm	allowably	amaryllis	ampersand	anatopism
air pistol	Alice band	allowance	amassment	amphibian	ancestral
air pocket	Alice blue	allowedly	amatorial	amphibium	anchorage
air potato	alicyclic	all-points	a matter of	amphibole	anchoress
airstream	alienable	all-seater	amaurosis	amphiboly	anchorite
air ticket	alienator	all serene	amaurotic	amphilogy	anchorman
air-vessel	alienness	all smiles	amazement	amphioxus	anchormen

anchoveta	animalize	antihelix	apologies	aprosopia	argentine
anchovies	animal oil	antiknock	apologise	apsidiole	Argentine
anchylose	animateur	Antillean	apologist	apyrexial	argentite
anciently	animation	antimeric	apologize	aqua birth	argentous
ancientry	animatism	antimonic	apomictic	Aqua Libra	argillite
ancillary	animistic	antinomic	apophatic	aquaplane	Argus-eyed
Andamaner	animosity	antinovel	apophonic	aqua regia	argy-bargy
andantino	anisogamy	antipasti	apophysis	aquarelle	Arhatship
andesitic	ankle-bone	antipasto	apoptosis	aquariums	arhythmic
and like it	ankle boot	antipathy	apoptotic	aqua vitae	Arianizer
andradite	ankle-ring	antiphony	apostatic	aquilegia	a right one
androecia	ankle sock	antipodal	apostolic	arabesque	Aristarch
androgyne	ankylosis	antipodes	apotheose	Arabicism	Arizonian
androgyny	ankylotic	antiquary	appalling	Arabicize	Arkansan
Andromeda	annectent	antiquate	appalment	arability	armadilla
androsace	annelidan	antiquing	Appaloosa	arabinose	armadillo
and things	annexable	antiquity	appanaged	arachidic	armed camp
anecdotal	annexment	antiscion	apparatus	arachnean	armillary
anecdotic	annotator	antiserum	apparency	arachnoid	armistice
anelastic	announcer	antitoxic	apparitor	Aragonese	Armorican
anemogram	annoyance	antitoxin	appealing	aragonite	armouring
anemology	annoyment	antitrade	appeasive	Arakanese	armstrong
aneuploid	annualize	anti-trust	appellant	araneidan	army corps
angel cake	annuitant	antitrust	appellate	arational	army lorry
angel dust	annuities	antivenin	appendage	araucaria	Arnoldian
angel-fish	annularly	antivenom	appendant	arbitrage	Arnoldism
angelfish	annulated	antiviral	appertain	arbitrary	Arnoldist
angel food	annulling	antivirus	appetence	arbitrate	aromatise
angelhood	annulment	ant-orchid	appetency	arbitress	aromatize
angelical	anodynous	ant-thrush	appetible	arboreous	arousable
angélique	anoestrus	anucleate	appetiser	arboretum	arpeggios
angelship	an old song	a number of	appetizer	arborical	arraigner
angel-skin	anomalies	anxieties	applauder	arbovirus	arrayment
angerless	anomalism	anxiously	apple-cart	archabbey	arrearage
angersome	anomalous	any old how	apple-head	archabbot	arrestive
angiogram	anomalure	à outrance	applejack	archaical	arrhythmy
angiology	anonymity	Apalachee	apple-peru	archaizer	arris-ways
angiomata	anonymous	apart from	apple tree	archangel	arriviste
angle-iron	anopheles	apartheid	appliable	archducal	arrogance
anglesite	anorectic	apartment	appliance	archduchy	arrogancy
angle-wing	anorthite	apartness	applicant	arch-enemy	arrow arum
anglewise	anovulant	apartotel	applicate	archeress	arrow-back
Anglicise	anoxaemia	apathetic	appliquéd	archetype	arrowhead
Anglicism	*anschluss*	aperiodic	appliqués	arch-fiend	arrowroot
Anglicist	Anselmian	apertness	appointed	archiater	arrow-slit
Anglicize	Antarctic	apertural	appointee	Archibald	arrow-wood
angostura	antefixal	apetalous	appointer	archilute	arrow worm
angriness	antelopes	aphanitic	appointor	archimage	arseniate
Anguillan	antelucan	apheresis	apportion	archimime	arsenical
anguished	antenatal	Aphrodite	appraisal	architect	arsenious
angularly	antennary	aphyllous	appraisee	archivist	arsesmart
angulated	antennule	apiculate	appraiser	archivolt	arsy-versy
angustura	anthelion	apishness	apprehend	archontic	art cinema
anhedonia	anthemion	aplanatic	approbate	archosaur	art editor
anhydride	anthology	apocentre	approve of	arc minute	artemisia
anhydrite	anthozoan	apocopate	April fool	arc second	arteriole
anhydrous	anthropic	Apocrypha	April Fool	Arctic fox	arteritis
anidrosis	anticline	apodictic	apriorism	arcuation	arthritic
animalise	anticodon	apoenzyme	apriorist	arduously	arthritis
animalism	antidoron	apogamous	apriority	arecoline	arthrodia
animalist	antidotal	apolarity	apronfuls	Areopagus	arthrodic
animality	antigenic	Apollonic	aprosexia	aretalogy	arthropod

arthrosis	assiduity	atlas moth	auld thief	auxiliary	baby grand
Arthurian	assiduous	at leisure	au naturel	auxospore	baby house
artichoke	assistant	at liberty	Aunt Sally	auxotroph	babyishly
articular	assistful	at longest	aureation	available	Babylonic
artificer	associate	atmometer	auric acid	availably	bacchanal
artillery	assonance	atomicity	aurichalc	availment	Bacchanal
artisanal	assort ill	atomistic	auricular	avalanche	bacchante
artlessly	assuasive	atonalism	auriscope	avalanchy	Bacchante
art object	assuetude	atonalist	aurorally	avascular	bacchants
arty-farty	assumable	atonality	auspicate	avengeful	baccharis
aryballos	assumedly	at one blow	auspicial	averagely	Bacharach
arytenoid	assumpsit	atonement	austenite	averrable	bacillary
as and when	assurance	at-oneness	austerely	Averroism	back-acter
asbestine	assuredly	at one time	austerest	Averroist	back-along
ascendant	assurgent	at peril of	austerity	avertable	back bench
ascendent	asthmatic	at present	autarchic	avertible	backbench
ascending	astrachan	atrocious	autarkies	avifaunal	backbiter
ascension	astraddle	atrophied	autarkist	avirulent	backboard
ascensive	astragali	atrophies	autecious	avisandum	backboned
ascertain	astrakhan	at seasons	authentic	avizandum	backcloth
ascetical	astrocyte	at soonest	authoress	avocation	back-court
ascitical	astrodome	attainder	authorial	avocatory	back-crawl
asclepiad	astrolabe	attempter	authoring	avoidable	back cross
Asclepiad	astrology	attendant	authorise	avoidably	backfield
asclepias	astronaut	attention	authorism	avoidance	back-flash
ascospore	astronomy	attentive	authority	avoidless	back-front
asexually	Astroturf	attenuate	authorize	avuncular	back-house
ashamedly	AstroTurf	attestant	autoclave	awakening	backlight
Ashantian	astucious	at the helm	autocracy	awardable	back-liner
ash blonde	a sure find	at the last	autocrime	awareness	back-pedal
Ashkenazi	as witness	at the most	autocross	awesomely	backpiece
ashlaring	asyllabic	Attic base	autocycle	awestruck	backplate
aside from	asymbolia	Attic salt	autofocus	awfulness	backsight
asininity	asymmetry	attingent	autogamic	a whale of a	back slang
ask no odds	asymptote	attorneys	autogenic	a whole lot	backslash
as of right	asyndetic	attractor	autograft	awkwardly	backslide
asomatous	asyndeton	attribute	autograph	axe-hammer	back-space
asparagus	as you were	attrition	autogyros	axial flow	backspace
aspartame	atacamite	attritive	autoicous	axiomatic	back stage
aspectful	at a gallop	attritted	autolatry	axle-tooth	backstage
aspectual	at a glance	at unaware	autolysin	axle tramp	backstair
aspergill	at a low ebb	at vantage	autolysis	Axminster	backstone
aspersion	at any cost	at war with	autolytic	axopodium	back-swing
aspersive	at any rate	aubergine	automaker	axotomous	back-sword
aspersoir	at a profit	aubrietia	automatic	ayatollah	backtrack
aspersory	ataractic	au courant	automaton	Aylesbury	backwards
asphalter	at a stroke	auctorial	autonomic	ayurvedic	back water
asphaltic	atavistic	audacious	autonomy	Ayurvedic	backwater
asphaltum	at command	audiogram	autophagy	azeotrope	backwoods
asphyctic	ateliosis	audiology	autopilot	azimuthal	bacterial
asphyxial	atemporal	audio tape	autopista	azo colour	bacterium
aspirator	atheistic	audiotape	Autoplate	azotaemia	bacterize
as regards	athematic	auditoria	autopsies	azotaemic	bacteroid
assailant	athenaeum	auditress	autoroute	Baagandji	bad breath
assaulter	atheology	auger-hole	autoscope	babacoote	bad cess to
assayable	athetesis	augmented	autoscopy	Babbittry	badgeless
assembler	athetosis	augmenter	autos-da-fé	baboonery	bad health
assentant	a thin time	augmentor	autosomal	baboonish	badminton
assertion	athletics	augurship	autotelic	baby bonus	bafflegab
assertive	at its best	augur well	autotoxic	baby buggy	bagatelle
assertory	Atjehnese	Augustine	autotoxin	Baby Buggy	bagginess
assession	Atlantean	aulacogen	autozooid	baby-faced	bag people

bagpiping	bandolero	Barnumese	battering	beatitude	be excused
bag-shaped	bandolier	barograph	battiness	be at pains	befalling
bahuvrihi	bandoline	barometer	battleaxe	*beau geste*	befitting
bailiwick	bandoneon	barometry	battlebus	beau ideal	befogging
bailliage	band-shell	baronetcy	battle-cry	beau idéal	before God
bain-marie	bandstand	barotropy	battology	beau monde	befortune
bairn-team	bandurria	bar person	baulk line	beauteous	begetting
bakeapple	bandwagon	barracker	bavaroise	beautiful	beggarism
bake blind	bandwidth	barracoon	bawdiness	*beaux arts*	beggingly
bakehouse	baneberry	barracuda	bay laurel	be avenged	beginning
bakestone	banefully	barrelage	bayoneted	beaver-dam	begin over
baking tin	Bangorian	barrelled	bay-whaler	be awake up	begin upon
baksheesh	banjolele	barretter	bay window	be a wake-up	begin with
Balaamite	banjulele	barricade	be about to	beblister	beglamour
balaclava	bankshall	barricado	beach ball	beblubber	beglerbeg
Balaclava	banner-cry	barrister	beachhead	because of	beg pardon
balalaika	bannerman	barrow-boy	beach plum	beccafico	begrutten
balancing	bannister	barrowful	beach-rock	become man	beguiling
balanitis	banqueted	Barrowist	beachside	be cooking	beguinage
balconied	banqueter	barry wavy	beachwear	becquerel	behaviour
balconies	banquette	bartender	beaconage	becripple	be herself
baldachin	Bantustan	basal body	bead-house	bedangled	be himself
baldaquin	banyan-day	baseboard	beadiness	bed-bottle	Behmenism
bald eagle	baptismal	base-court	beadledom	beddy-byes	beholding
baldicoot	baptistry	base level	bead-plant	be death on	behoveful
baldmoney	barathrum	base metal	bead sedge	bedfellow	be in a flap
Balearian	Barbadian	base-piece	beady-eyed	bediasite	beingness
balection	barbarian	bashfully	be a fool to	bedimming	being that
balefully	barbarise	basically	beak-sedge	bedjacket	be in stays
bale-goods	barbarism	basic salt	be all eyes	Bedlamite	be in touch
Balkanise	barbarity	basic slag	be all over	bedrabble	be in trade
Balkanize	barbarize	basifixed	beaminess	bedraggle	bejabbers
balladeer	barbarous	basifugal	beamingly	bedridden	belatedly
balladize	barbecued	basilical	bean caper	bed-settee	beleaguer
ball-court	barbecues	basilican	beaneries	bedsitter	belemnite
ballerina	barbitone	basipetal	beanfeast	bedspread	belemnoid
ballistae	barbotine	basketful	bean goose	bed-warmer	*bel esprit*
ballistic	barcarole	basketing	be annoyed	bed-wetter	believe me
ball joint	Barcelona	Basque cap	beanstalk	bedwetter	belittler
ballonnet	bar-coding	bas-relief	be any good	bedworthy	bell curve
ballooner	bare bones	bastinade	bear a hand	beech-fern	bell-glass
ballot box	barefaced	bastinado	bear a part	beechmast	bellhouse
balloting	bargainee	bastioned	bearberry	beech tree	bellicose
ballpoint	bargainer	bastonade	beardless	beechwood	bell metal
ball-proof	bargain on	batch loaf	beardlike	beefeater	bell-miner
ball valve	bargainor	bate an ace	beards wag	beefiness	bell-punch
balm-apple	bargander	Bath brick	bear fruit	beef olive	bell-skirt
balminess	bargepole	bath chair	bear-grass	beefsteak	bell tower
balsam fir	barkcloth	Bath chair	bearishly	bee-keeper	bellyache
balsa wood	barkeeper	bathhouse	Béarnaise	Beelzebub	bellyband
Balthazar	barleymow	Bath metal	bear's foot	bee martin	belly-flop
Baltimore	bar magnet	batholith	bear state	bee-master	bellyflop
Balzacian	barmaster	Bathonian	Bear State	bee orchid	bellyfuls
bamboozle	barmbrack	bath salts	beastings	be equal to	belly-wool
bandaging	barm cloth	Bath stone	beastlier	beer belly	belomancy
bandar-log	Barmecide	bath towel	beastlike	beer glass	belonging
banderole	barminess	bathwater	beat about	beerhouse	below deck
bandicoot	Barnabite	Bath white	be at a loss	beeriness	belt drive
bandiness	barnacled	bathybius	beatenest	beer money	belvedere
banditism	barnbrack	battalion	beatified	Beersheba	be missing
bandobast	barn dance	battening	beatifies	beestings	bemoisten
bandoleer	barnstorm	batteries	beating-up	beet sugar	bemonster

bemusedly	besprenge	bilge keel	birthwort	blackjack	blearness
be my guest	best bower	bilge-pump	bisection	black kite	blemisher
bench-hook	bestially	bilharzia	bishopdom	blacklead	blessedly
benchmark	bestirred	bilingual	bishopess	blacklist	blind coal
bench seat	best-known	biliously	bishopric	black lung	blind date
bench-stop	bestrewed	bilirubin	bismillah	blackmail	blind fish
bench test	be stuck on	biliteral	bismuthic	black mark	blindfold
bendiness	be sweet on	billabong	bismuthyl	black mass	blindless
benedight	beta decay	billander	bismutite	Black Mass	blindling
beneficed	beta waves	billboard	bisontine	black monk	blindness
benefited	betel-palm	bill-clerk	bitchiest	Black Monk	blind side
benempted	*bête noire*	billeting	biternate	black Moor	blind spot
Bengalese	bethought	billiards	bite-sized	blackness	blindworm
benighted	be through	billiment	bit-player	black pine	blinkered
benignant	be to blame	billionth	bit string	Black Pope	blink-eyed
benignity	betrothal	billycock	bitter end	blackrobe	blissless
benitoite	betrothed	billy goat	bitterish	black rust	blitheful
be nowhere	better off	bilocular	bitter-nut	black sage	blizzardy
Bensonian	bevel gear	bimonthly	bitter pit	black sand	blockader
Benthamic	bevelling	binderies	bittiness	black soil	block-book
benthonic	bevelment	Binet test	bivalence	black spot	blockhead
bentincks	bewitcher	binocular	bivalency	black swan	blockhole
bentonite	bewritten	binominal	bivallate	blacktail	block move
benzenoid	bez-antler	binomial	bivariate	black tang	block-ship
benzidine	bezesteen	binturong	biventral	black tern	blockship
be on about	bezoardic	biochemic	bivoltine	black titi	block vote
be one's age	Bhutanese	bioethics	bizarrely	black wash	blonde ray
be oneself	biathlete	biofouler	blab-mouth	blackwood	blondness
be on guard	biaxially	biogenous	blackback	Blackwood	blood-ally
be on wings	bibacious	biography	black ball	blade-bone	blood bank
bepatched	Bible belt	biohazard	blackball	bladeless	blood-bath
bepearled	Bible Belt	biohermal	black-band	bladelike	bloodbath
beplaster	Bible oath	biologise	black bass	blade-work	blood cell
berberine	bicameral	biologism	black bean	blaeberry	blood feud
Berberine	biconcave	biologist	black bear	blameable	blood-heat
be resting	bicyclist	biologize	black belt	blameably	bloodiest
berg adder	bidentate	biometric	black bent	blameless	blood-knot
bergander	bid fair to	bionomics	black bile	blandness	bloodless
berkelium	bienniums	biopoesis	blackbird	blank-book	bloodline
Berkshire	bifarious	biorhythm	black body	blanketed	blood-lily
Bermudian	bifilarly	biosensor	black book	blankness	blood-line
Bernician	biformity	biosocial	blackbuck	blank test	bloodline
Bernoulli	bifrontal	biosphere	blackbutt	blank wall	blood-lust
be rolling	bifronted	biostrome	black coal	Blanquism	bloodlust
berry-like	bifurcate	bipartite	blackcock	Blanquist	blood meal
berserker	bigarreau	bipedally	black damp	blarneyed	bloodroot
berserkly	Big Bertha	bipinnate	black disc	blaspheme	bloodshed
beryllium	big cheese	bipyramid	black drop	blasphemy	bloodshot
bescatter	big dipper	birch-bark	blackener	blast bomb	blood test
bescratch	bigeminal	birch beer	black-eyed	blastemal	bloodwite
beseeched	bigeneric	birch tree	blackface	blast-hole	bloodwood
beseecher	big-headed	birch-wine	blackfish	blast-pipe	bloodworm
be set fair	big league	birchwood	black flag	blastulae	blood-wort
besetment	big-ticket	birdbrain	blackfoot	blastular	bloomered
besetting	biguanide	bird's-foot	Blackfoot	blatantly	bloomless
be shook on	bijection	bird's nest	black game	blatterer	blossomed
beslobber	bijective	bird table	black gold	blaze away	blotchier
beslubber	bike chain	bird-watch	black hawk	blazingly	blow a fuse
be soppy on	bilabiate	birthmark	blackhead	bleachery	blow a kiss
bespangle	bilateral	birth pill	black heat	bleakness	blow-drier
bespatter	bilbergia	birth rate	black hole	blear-eyed	blow-dryer
bespeckle	bilboquet	birth-sign	black jack	bleariest	blowflies

blowtorch	body louse	boobyalla	bourgeois	brambling	breasting
blow trade	body odour	booby trap	bouvardia	branchery	breast job
blowziest	body-whorl	boogieing	Bovey coal	branchiae	breast-pin
blubberer	Boeotarch	book-craft	bovrilize	branchial	breathe in
Bluebeard	Bofors gun	bookishly	bovver boy	branching	breathful
blueberry	bog-butter	book-Latin	bow-backed	branchlet	breathier
blue-black	bog cotton	book-louse	bow-bearer	branch out	breathily
blue blood	bog-garden	bookmaker	bow-chaser	brandiron	breathing
blue crane	bogginess	book-plate	bowelless	brandling	brecciate
blue devil	bog myrtle	bookplate	bowerbird	brand-mark	Brechtian
blue-domer	bog orchid	bookshelf	bowhunter	brand name	breeching
bluegrass	bog spavin	bookstack	bowl along	brandreth	breezeway
blue-joint	bogusness	bookstall	bow-legged	brashness	breeziest
blue metal	bog violet	bookstore	bowler hat	brass band	bregmatic
blue mould	boiled egg	book token	Bow Street	brasserie	Brehon law
blue-mouth	boiled oil	book value	bowstring	brassiere	bressumer
blue-nosed	boilingly	boomerang	bow window	brassière	bretessed
Blue Peter	bold-faced	boomingly	Box and Cox	brassiest	Breton hat
blue-plate	boldfaced	boomslang	box camera	brass nail	Breton lai
blue point	bolection	boorishly	box canyon	brass rags	Bretwalda
blueprint	boliviano	bootblack	box clever	brass rule	breveting
blue rinse	Bollinger	boot-faced	box girder	brassware	brevetted
blue shark	Bolognese	bootmaker	Boxing Day	bratwurst	breweries
blue shift	Bolognian	bootstrap	box number	braveness	brewhouse
blue stone	bolometer	booziness	box office	brawniest	bribeable
bluestone	bolometry	borborygm	box spring	brazeless	bric-a-brac
blue water	Bolshevik	bordellos	box-turtle	brazen age	bricabrac
blue whale	bolsterer	bordereau	box-wallah	Brazilian	bric-à-brac
blue-white	Boltzmann	bore rigid	boycotter	Brazil nut	brick-dust
bluffness	bombachas	bore stiff	boyfriend	bread-corn	brick-kiln
blunderer	bombarder	boric acid	Boyle's law	bread-kind	brickwork
bluntness	bombardon	born-again	boy wonder	breadless	brickyard
blurriest	bombasine	Borrovian	brachiate	breadlike	bricolage
blushless	bombastic	borrowing	bracingly	breadline	bricoleur
blusterer	bombazine	borrow pit	brackened	bread roll	bride-cake
blutwurst	bombed-out	Borsalino	bracketed	bread-root	bride-lace
Boanerges	bomb-happy	Borussian	brackmard	breadthen	bridemaid
board foot	bombilate	boss about	bracteate	bread-tree	bridesman
board game	bombinate	bossa nova	bracteole	breakable	bride-to-be
boardroom	bomb-ketch	boss cocky	Brahmanic	break a leg	bridewell
boardwalk	bombproof	bossiness	brahminic	break a set	bridge-man
board-work	bombshell	Bostonese	Brahmoism	break away	bridle-bit
boat-cloak	bomb-sight	Bostonian	Brahmsian	breakaway	bridleway
boat-drill	bombsight	Boston ivy	brain-case	break-back	briefcase
boat-house	bomb squad	botanical	brain-cell	break bulk	briefless
boathouse	bona fides	botanizer	brain-dead	break crop	briefness
boatswain	bond paper	Botswanan	brainiest	break down	brier rose
boat-train	bondslave	bottle-age	brainless	breakdown	brigadier
boatwoman	bondstone	bottle-fed	brain-sand	break even	brigandry
bobarchee	bondwoman	bottle out	brain scan	breakfast	brightish
bobbin-net	bone-black	bottle-tit	brainsick	break in on	brillante
bobbishly	bone china	bottom dog	brainstem	break into	brilliant
bobby calf	bone-earth	bottom out	brainwash	break-line	brimstone
bobby wren	bone-tired	bottoms up	brainwave	breakneck	brimstony
bob-sleigh	bone weary	boudinage	brainwork	break open	bring back
bobsleigh	bonhomous	boulevard	brake disc	break rank	bring down
bobtailed	bonniness	bounciest	brake drum	break ship	bring over
bodacious	bon vivant	boundless	brake-pipe	break step	brininess
body-check	bon viveur	bounteous	brake shoe	break wind	brinjarry
body clock	bon voyage	bountiful	brakesman	breakwind	briquette
body count	boobialla	bouquetin	brakesmen	break with	briskness
bodyguard	booboisie	bourdonné	Bramantip	breast-fed	brislings

bristling	brown-nose	buff-stick	Burnsiana	by my troth	cafeteria
Britannia	brown pink	buffy coat	burnt cork	by no means	cafetière
Britannic	brown rice	bugger all	burrawang	by numbers	cageyness
Briticism	brown spar	bugger off	burrel-fly	by oneself	cailleach
Britisher	brown spot	buggy-ride	bursarial	by parcels	Cainozoic
Britishly	brown-tail	bug-hunter	bursaries	by-product	cairngorm
Britoness	brownwort	bugle-horn	bursiform	by request	cake-bread
brittlely	brow ridge	bugleweed	bur walnut	byrlawman	cake-slice
Brittonic	Brummagem	buildable	bus-driver	by seeming	calaboose
broadband	Brunswick	build down	bush basil	bystander	calabrese
broad bean	brushback	bulbiform	bushcraft	by stealth	Calabrian
broad-bill	brushfire	bulbosity	bushelful	by the book	calamanco
broad-brim	brushless	Bulgarian	bushelman	by the head	calandria
broad-brow	brushlike	Bulgarize	bushiness	by the hour	calavance
broadcast	brush over	bulgingly	bush poppy	by the lump	calcaneal
broad hint	brushware	bulkiness	bush shirt	by the mass	calcanean
broad-jump	brushwood	bullberry	bush vetch	by the rood	calcaneum
broad-leaf	brushwork	bull-diker	bushwhack	by the yard	calcaneus
broadleaf	brusquely	bulldozer	bustiness	bytownite	calcarate
broadloom	brutalise	bullfight	butadiene	Byzantian	calcarine
broadness	brutalism	bullfinch	but and ben	Byzantine	calcedony
broad seal	brutalist	bullimong	butcherer	cabaletta	calcicole
broadside	brutality	bullishly	butcherly	caballada	calcified
broadtail	brutalize	bull-nosed	buteonine	caballero	calcifies
broadwalk	brute fact	bull point	butlerage	caballine	calcifuge
broadways	brutehood	bull-snake	butleress	cabbalism	calcimine
broadwise	bruteness	bull's wool	butsecarl	cabbalist	calculate
brochette	brutishly	bull trout	butter-box	cab driver	calculous
broiderer	Brylcreem	bulltrout	butterbur	cabin crew	calendary
broken man	bryophyte	bully beef	buttercup	cabinetry	calendric
broken tea	Brythonic	bully tree	butterfat	cabin-mate	calendula
brokerage	bubble car	bumble-bee	butterfly	cablegram	calenture
brokeress	bubble gum	bumbledom	butteries	cable-laid	calescent
bromeliad	bubblegum	bum-fodder	butter-nut	cable's end	calf's foot
brominate	bubbliest	bumiputra	butternut	cabriolet	calibogus
bromoform	buccaneer	bumper car	butter-pat	cacao bean	calibrate
bromyrite	buccinoid	bumpiness	buttinsky	cacao tree	calico cat
bronchial	Bucentaur	bumpkinet	butt joint	cachectic	calicular
Bronze Age	buckboard	bumpkinly	buttocked	cacholong	caliphate
brood cell	buck-brush	bumpology	button-boy	caciquism	Calixtine
broodiest	buck dance	bump-start	button day	cacodemon	calla lily
brookable	bucketful	bumptious	button ear	cacodylic	call forth
brook char	bucketing	bum-sucker	buttoning	cacoethes	callidity
brooklime	buck fever	bunchy top	butty-gang	cacophony	Callippic
brookweed	buck-hound	Bundesrat	buxomness	cacuminal	callitrix
broom-corn	bucklered	Bundestag	by a canvas	cadastral	callosity
broomrape	bucko mate	bundobust	by a jugful	cadaveric	calloused
brothelly	Buck's Fizz	bungaloid	by all odds	caddie car	callously
brothelry	buck's horn	bunk-house	by analogy	caddis-fly	call quits
brotherly	buckstall	bunkhouse	by a street	caddishly	call truce
browallia	buckthorn	bunny girl	by default	cadential	calmative
brown alga	buck-tooth	buoyantly	by degrees	cadetship	calmingly
brown bear	buckwheat	burggrave	by force of	cadginess	calorific
brown belt	buckyball	burgh-bote	by herself	caduciary	calumnied
Brown Bess	bucolical	burgherly	by himself	caecilian	calumnies
brown-bill	buddy film	burghmote	by Jupiter	Caenozoic	Calvinian
brown coal	budgetary	burkundaz	by means of	Caen stone	Calvinise
brown-eyed	budgeteer	burlesque	by measure	caerulean	Calvinism
brown hare	budgeting	burliness	by mirrors	Caesarean	Calvinist
brown loaf	buffaloes	burn alive	by mistake	Caesarian	Calvinize
brown malt	buffet car	burningly	by my faith	Caesarism	calycular
brownness	buffeting	burnisher	by my sooth	Caesarist	calyx-tube

camarilla	cannonade	caravette	carolytic	cast about	catechism
Cambodian	cannon bit	carbamate	carpaccio	Castalian	catechist
Cambridge	cannoneer	carbamide	carpenter	cast an eye	catechize
camcorder	cannulate	carbanion	carpentry	cast aside	categorem
camel-back	canoe-like	carbazole	carpet-bag	casteless	categoric
camel-hair	canoe wood	carbolate	carpet-bed	castellan	caterwaul
camel-like	canonical	carbolize	carpeting	castellar	cat-footed
camelries	canonizer	carbonade	carpet-rod	castellet	Catharine
Camembert	canonries	carbonado	carpincho	caste mark	Catharism
cameo part	canonship	Carbonari	carpology	cast forth	Catharist
camera-eye	can-opener	carbonate	car pooler	cast gorge	catharses
cameraman	cantabile	carbonise	carrageen	castigate	catharsis
cameramen	cantaloup	carbonium	carriaged	castilian	cathartic
camera-shy	cantarist	carbonize	carronade	Castilian	cathectic
Camestres	cantation	carbon tax	carrousel	castle-nut	cathedral
camleteen	cantharis	carbuncle	carry away	cast loose	Catherine
campanero	cantharus	carbuncly	carry back	castoreum	catlinite
campanile	cantilena	carburise	carry over	castor oil	cat litter
campanist	cantingly	carburize	carry sail	castrator	catocalid
campanula	Cantonese	carcinoid	cartelise	Castroism	catoptric
campcraft	cantonize	carcinoma	cartelize	cast round	cat-tackle
Campeachy	cantorial	cardboard	Cartesian	cast steel	catteries
camper van	canvassed	cardiacal	carthamin	casualism	cattiness
camp-fever	canvasser	cardialgy	carthamus	casuality	cattishly
camphoric	capacious	card index	cart-horse	casuarina	cattle-dog
campiness	capacitor	cardphone	carthorse	casuistic	cattleman
camp-stool	caparison	card-sharp	cartilage	casuistry	cattlemen
campylite	Cape daisy	card-swipe	cartogram	catabatic	Catullian
Canaanite	Cape Dutch	card table	cartouche	catabolic	cat-witted
Canada Day	capellane	card trick	cartridge	cataclasm	Caucasian
Canada jay	Cape Malay	care-cloth	cart's tail	cataclysm	Caucasoid
Canadiana	Cape smoke	careenage	cart track	catalepsy	caucusing
canal boat	capillary	careerism	cartulary	catalexis	caudillos
canal rays	cap in hand	careerist	cartwheel	catalogue	cauldrife
canceleer	capitally	carefully	carvacrol	catalysed	caulicole
cancelled	capitated	caregiver	carveries	catalyser	causalgia
canceller	capitular	care label	caryatids	catalyses	causality
cancerate	capitulum	care-laden	caryopses	catalysis	causation
Cancerian	capo tasto	car engine	caryopsis	catalytic	causative
cancerous	capotasto	caressive	caseation	catamaran	causeless
candareen	capotting	caretaker	case-bound	catamenia	cautelous
candidacy	capriccio	cargo boat	case knife	catamount	cauteries
candidate	Capricorn	cargo cult	casemated	cat-and-dog	cauterise
candle-end	caprifoil	Caribbean	case study	cataphora	cauterize
candlelit	caprylate	cariosity	cashew nut	cataplasm	cautioner
Candlemas	capsaicin	carjacker	cash nexus	cataplexy	cavalcade
candle-nut	capsicine	Carlylean	cashpoint	catarrhal	cavallard
candy cane	cap sleeve	Carlylese	cash price	catasetum	cavalries
candytuft	capsomere	Carlylism	cash value	catatonia	cavendish
cane-brake	capsulate	Carmelite	Cassandra	catatonic	cavernous
cane chair	capsulise	carnalise	cassareep	catchable	cavewoman
cane-grass	capsulize	carnality	cassation	catch cold	cavewomen
cane-juice	captaincy	carnalize	Casseiver	catch crop	cavilling
canephora	captation	carnation	casserole	catch fire	ceanothus
cane sugar	captivate	carnelian	cassimere	catchiest	cease fire
cane-syrup	captivity	carnivore	Cassinese	catch-line	ceasefire
cane-trash	cap verses	carnivory	cassingle	catchline	ceaseless
canicular	carabidan	carnosity	Cassinian	catchment	cedar-bird
cankerous	carambola	carnotite	cassocked	catchpole	cedar tree
cannelure	carambole	carob tree	cassoulet	catchweed	cedarwood
canneries	carangoid	carolitic	cassowary	catchword	celandine
canniness	carapaced	carolling	Cassubian	catechise	celebrant

celebrate	cereopsis	chancroid	checklist	chieftain	chlorella
celebrity	certainly	chancrous	checkmate	chihuahua	chloritic
celery top	certainty	chandlery	check over	chilblain	chloropal
celestial	certified	changeful	check-rail	childcare	chlorosis
celestine	certifier	change leg	check-rein	childhood	chlorotic
Celestine	certifies	channelly	checkroom	childless	choak-full
celestite	certitude	chantable	check up on	childlike	chock-full
cellarage	cerussite	chanteuse	cheechako	childness	chocolate
cellaress	Cervantic	Chantilly	cheek-bone	childship	chocolaty
cellaring	cervisial	chantress	cheekbone	child-wife	choirgirl
cellarman	Cesolfaut	chantries	cheekiest	Chile pine	choke back
cellarway	cespitose	Chanukkah	cheeriest	chiliagon	choke-coil
cell block	cessation	chaotical	cheerless	chiliarch	choke-damp
celloidin	cetaceous	chaparral	cheese-fly	chilliest	choke down
cellotape	ceylanite	chapeless	cheeselip	chillness	choke-full
cellphone	Ceylonese	chaperone	cheesiest	chillsome	choke-pear
cellulate	ceylonite	chapleted	cheilitis	chime bars	choke-weed
cellulite	chabazite	chaprassi	chelation	chimerism	chokiness
celluloid	chabootra	Chap Stick	chelicera	chiminage	chokingly
cellulose	cha-cha-cha	charabanc	cheliform	china-blue	choleraic
cellulous	cha-chaing	character	chelonian	china clay	Chomskian
celsitude	chaetodon	charbroil	chemisorb	China-root	Chomskyan
Celticism	chafferer	charge cap	chemistry	China rose	chondrify
Celticist	chaffinch	chariness	chemurgic	china shop	chondrite
Celticize	chaffweed	chariotee	cheongsam	China silk	chondroid
Celtic Sea	Chagataic	chariotry	chequered	Chinatown	chondroma
cembalist	chain gang	charities	Cheremiss	China tree	chondrule
cementing	chain gear	charivari	Cherenkov	chinaware	choosiest
cementite	chainless	charlatan	cherimoya	chincapin	chop-house
cenematic	chainlike	charlotte	cherisher	chinch bug	chop logic
censorial	chain link	charmeuse	chernites	chinchona	choppered
censorian	chain-mail	charmless	chernozem	chincough	choppiest
centaurea	chain-pump	Charolais	cherry-bob	chinesery	chopstick
Centaurus	chain-shot	charoseth	cherry pie	chin music	chop sueys
centenary	chain-wale	chartered	cherry red	chinovnik	choragium
centenier	chain-work	charterer	chess-tree	chin-strap	choralism
centering	chairlady	Chartreux	chestiest	chinstrap	choralist
centesimo	chair-lift	charwoman	chevachee	chintzier	choral ode
centésimo	chairlift	charwomen	chevalier	chintzily	Choral Ode
centigram	chalazion	Charybdis	chevaline	chipboard	choriambi
centipede	chalcidid	chaseable	chevrette	Chipewyan	chorionic
centralia	chalcogen	chasséing	chevronel	chipolata	chorister
Centralia	chalkiest	chastener	chevronny	chirality	chorizont
centrally	chalk-line	chastiser	chevrotin	chirimoya	choroidal
centre bit	chalk talk	chatelain	chewiness	chirology	chorology
centreing	challenge	chatoyant	chew-stick	chironomy	chorusing
centrical	Chalybean	chatterer	Chian wine	chiropody	chowkidar
centriole	chalybite	chattiest	chiasmata	chirpiest	Chrissake
centumvir	chambered	chauffeur	chibouque	chirruped	Christian
centurial	chamberer	chaukidar	Chicagoan	chirurgic	Christies
centuried	chameleon	chavender	chicanery	chiselled	Christmas
centuries	chamfrain	chaw-bacon	chickadee	chiseller	chromatic
centurion	chamomile	chaw-stick	chickaree	chisel-toe	chromatid
ceraceous	chamosite	cheapener	Chickasaw	chi-square	chromatin
cerastium	champagne	cheapjack	chickling	chitinize	chromogen
ceratitic	champaign	cheapness	chickweed	chitinoid	chronical
cercarial	champ clos	cheatable	chicories	chitinous	chronicle
cercarian	champerty	checkable	chidingly	chitlings	chronique
cerebella	champlevé	checkered	chidlings	chivalric	chrysalid
cerebrate	chanceful	check into	chief good	chlamydia	chrysalis
cerecloth	chancelry	checkless	chiefless	chloracne	chrysanth
cereology	chanciest	check-list	chiefship	chlordane	chthonian

chubbiest	civically	clearcole	close upon	coat-stand	coenosarc
Chubb lock	civilized	clear-eyed	cloth ears	coaxially	coenzyme A
chuck-full	civilizee	clear grit	cloth-head	coaxingly	co-equally
chuck-hole	civilizer	clearness	cloud base	cobalamin	coequally
chummiest	civil list	clearskin	cloudiest	cobaltite	coercible
chump chop	Civil List	clear soup	cloud-land	cobaltous	coeternal
chunkiest	civilness	clearweed	cloudless	Cobdenism	coevality
chupattis	civil year	clearwing	cloudlike	Cobdenite	coffee bar
chuprassy	clack-dish	cleavable	clout-nail	co-brother	coffee cup
church-ale	cladistic	cleithral	clove pink	cobwebbed	coffee-pot
churchdom	cladogram	clemently	clown fish	cobweb law	coffee urn
churchlet	claimable	clepsydra	clownship	cocainism	coffer-dam
churchman	claimless	clergyman	cloyingly	cocainize	coffering
churchmen	clamantly	clergymen	clozapine	coccidian	coffining
church-owl	clamberer	clerkhood	clubbable	coccidium	co-founder
churingas	clammiest	clerkship	clubbiest	coccolith	cogitable
churnable	clamorous	cleverest	club class	coccygeal	cogitator
churn-milk	clamourer	cleverish	clubhouse	cochineal	cognately
churrasco	clamp down	clianthus	club-money	cochleate	cognation
ciabattas	clamp-down	clientage	clumpiest	cock-a-hoop	cognisant
cibarious	clampdown	clientele	clumsiest	Cockaigne	cognition
cicatrice	clam-shell	clifflike	clunkiest	cockateel	cognitive
cicatrise	clamshell	climactic	clustered	cockatiel	cognizant
cicatrize	clankless	climatize	clutch bag	cocked hat	cohabited
ciclatoun	clansfolk	climbable	cly-faking	cock-fight	cohabitee
cicutoxin	clapboard	climb down	clypeated	cockfight	cohabiter
cigarette	clap-bread	climb-down	cnidarian	cock-horse	cohabitor
cigarillo	clapmatch	climbdown	coachload	cockiness	coheiress
ciguatera	Clarendon	climb into	coach whip	cock-laird	coherence
ciliation	clareteer	cling film	coachwhip	cocklebur	coherency
ciliiform	clarified	clingfish	coachwood	cockle-hat	co-heritor
Cimmerian	clarifier	clingiest	coachwork	cock-light	coiffeuse
cinchonic	clarifies	clinician	coadapted	cockneyfy	coiffured
cincinnus	clarionet	clinquant	coadjutor	cock-penny	coin money
cinderous	classable	clipboard	coadunate	cockroach	Cointreau
cinematic	classical	clip joint	coagulant	cock robin	colcannon
cinephile	classiest	clippable	coagulase	cockscomb	colchicum
cineraria	classless	cliquiest	coagulate	cocksfoot	cold blood
cinereous	class-list	clitellar	coal black	cockshead	cold cream
Cingalese	classmate	clitellum	coalfield	cockshies	cold-finch
cingulate	class-noun	cloakless	coal-fired	cockshoot	cold frame
cinnamate	classroom	cloakroom	coal-heugh	cock-stand	cold front
cinquedea	clathrate	cloche hat	coal-house	cockswain	cold light
cipherdom	clatterer	clock-face	coalhouse	cockyolly	cold-short
circadian	claustral	clock golf	coalition	cocky's joy	cold start
circinate	claustrum	clockwise	coal-meter	cocoa bean	cold steel
circuiter	claviform	clockwork	coal miner	cocoa moth	cold store
circuitor	clay court	clodpated	coalminer	cocoa nibs	cold sweat
circuitry	clay slate	clog dance	coalmouse	cocoa tree	cold table
circulate	claystone	cloggiest	coal-owner	coco-de-mer	cold water
cirrhosis	claytonia	cloisonné	coal-works	coco fibre	colectomy
cirrhotic	cleanable	cloistral	co-aration	coco-grass	colemouse
cirriform	clean-bowl	closeable	coarbiter	cocoonery	colic-root
cirripede	clean down	close a gap	coarctate	code-named	coliphage
cisalpine	cleanlier	close call	coastland	coecilian	collagist
cispadane	cleanlily	closed-end	coastline	coeducate	collapsar
citharist	cleanness	close down	coastward	coelomate	collapsed
citizenly	cleanskin	close-knit	coastways	coelostat	collar day
citizenry	clearable	closeness	coastwise	coemption	collation
cityscape	clearance	close port	coat check	coenobite	collative
city state	clear away	close-reef	coat dress	coenobium	colleague
citywards	clear-cole	closeting	coat-money	coenocyte	collectar

collected	columbite	commonest	concocter	conjobble	continent
collector	columbium	commonise	concoctor	conjoined	continual
collegial	columella	commonish	concordat	conjoiner	continued
collegian	columnist	commonize	concourse	conjugacy	continuer
collegium	coma vigil	common law	concreate	conjugate	continues
Colleries	combatant	commorant	concreter	conjuress	continuos
collidine	combating	commotion	concubine	conjure up	continuum
colligate	combative	communard	concurred	conkering	contorted
collimate	comb-brush	communion	condemned	connately	contourné
collinear	combinate	communise	condenser	connation	contralto
collision	combining	communism	condictio	connected	contrasty
collocate	comb-jelly	communist	condignly	connecter	contrived
collodion	comboloio	community	condiment	connector	contriver
collogued	combretum	communize	condition	Connemara	contrôlée
collogues	comburent	commutate	condolent	connexion	contumacy
colloidal	come about	commutual	conducive	connexity	contumely
colloquia	come again	compactly	conductor	connivent	contusion
collotype	come along	compactor	conductus	connubial	contusive
collusion	come amiss	compactum	condyloid	conqueror	conundrum
collusive	come and go	compadres	condyloma	Conradian	convector
collusory	come apart	compander	cone-sheet	conscient	convenery
colluvial	come clean	companies	cone-shell	conscious	converger
colluvies	comedones	companion	conessine	conscribe	converser
colluvium	comeliest	compasser	Conestoga	conscript	conversus
collyrium	come loose	compelled	cone wheat	consensus	converted
Colly-west	come of age	compeller	confabbed	consenter	converter
colocynth	come off it	compendia	conferral	conserver	convertor
colometry	come-outer	competent	conferred	consignee	convexity
colonelcy	come-o'-will	complaint	conferrer	consigner	convictor
colonizer	come round	completer	confessee	consignor	convinced
colonnade	come short	complexly	confessio	consonant	convincer
colophony	comet-year	complexus	confessor	consonous	convivial
Coloradan	come under	compliant	confidant	consortia	convocate
colorific	comfiness	complicit	confident	conspirer	convolute
colossean	comforter	component	confiding	constable	cony-garth
colosseum	comically	composant	configure	constancy	co-obligor
Colossian	comic book	composite	confinity	constrain	cook-chill
colostomy	Cominform	composure	confirmed	constrict	cookeries
colostrum	Comintern	comprador	confirmee	construal	cookhouse
colourant	comitadji	computist	confirmer	construct	cookie jar
colour bar	commander	comradely	confirmor	construed	cook-shack
colour-box	commandos	comradery	confitent	construes	Cook's tour
colourful	commandry	con and pro	Confiteor	consulage	cook-stove
colouring	commencer	concausal	confiture	consulary	cool-house
colourise	commendam	concavely	confluent	consulate	coolie hat
colourist	commender	concavity	conformal	consuless	cool-store
colourize	commensal	concealer	conformer	consultee	cooperage
colour-man	commenter	conceited	confrater	consulter	cooperant
colour sup	comminate	conceiver	Confucian	consultor	co-operate
colourway	commingle	concenter	confusing	contactor	cooperate
colpotomy	comminute	concentre	confusion	contagion	co-optable
coltishly	commissar	conceptus	conga drum	contagium	copacetic
colt-pixie	committal	concerned	congenial	contained	coparceny
coltsfoot	committed	concerted	conger eel	container	co-partner
colt's tail	committee	concertos	congeries	contangos	copartner
colubrine	committer	concessor	Congolese	contemner	copasetic
columbary	commodate	conchitic	congruent	contemper	copepodan
columbate	commodify	concierge	Congruism	contender	copepodid
columbiad	commodity	conciliar	Congruist	contented	copestone
Columbian	commodore	concisely	congruity	contestee	copiapite
columbine	commonage	concision	congruous	contester	coping saw
Columbine	Common Era	concluder	conically	con thanks	copiously

copolymer
Copper Age
copper bit
copper-cut
copperish
copper-nob
copper ore
co-present
co-produce
coprolite
coprolith
coprology
coprozoic
copsewood
copyboard
copyright
coral fern
coral-like
coralline
corallita
corallite
coralloid
coral-pink
coral reef
coral-root
coral spot
coral tree
coral vine
coral-wood
coralwort
corbeille
corbelled
corbicula
cor blimey
corchorus
cord-drill
Cordelier
cord-grass
cordially
cordiform
co-regency
co-regnant
coreopsis
coriander
co-rivalry
corkiness
corkingly
corkscrew
cormorant
corn borer
cornbrash
corn-bread
cornbread
corncrake
corn dance
corn dolly
cornelian
cornemuse
corner-boy
corner-hit
corner-man
cornetist

cornfield
cornflake
cornflour
corn-house
cornicing
corniness
cornopean
corn poppy
corn-roast
corn salad
corn-shuck
corn snake
corn-stalk
cornstone
corn sugar
corn syrup
Cornubian
corollary
corolline
coronated
coroneted
coronilla
coroplast
corozo-nut
corpocrat
corporate
corporeal
corposant
corpulent
corpuscle
corralled
corrasion
correctly
corrector
correlate
corrodent
corrosion
corrosive
corrugate
corrupter
corruptly
corseting
corticate
corticene
corticine
corticoid
corticole
cortisone
coruscant
coruscate
corydalis
corymbose
coscoroba
coseismal
cosmogeny
cosmogony
Cosmoline
cosmology
cosmonaut
cosmorama
cosseting
cost clerk

costerdom
costering
costingly
costively
costliest
cost price
costumery
costumier
cotangent
cote-house
co-tenancy
cothurnal
cothurned
cothurnus
cotillion
cotonnade
cotter pin
cottonade
cotton gin
Cottonian
cottonize
cotton-rat
cotton-top
cotyledon
couchancy
couchette
Couéistic
cough away
cough down
cough drop
coulibiac
coulombic
coumarone
councilor
countable
countably
countback
count down
countdown
countless
count noun
countries
countrify
countryfy
countship
coup d'état
coup stick
courbette
courgette
court card
courteous
courtesan
courtezan
court fool
court-hand
court leet
Court leet
courtlier
courtlike
courtling
court roll
courtroom

courtship
court shoe
court week
courtyard
cousinage
cousiness
couturier
covalence
covalency
covariant
covellite
coverable
cover crop
cover girl
cover note
cover over
cover slip
cover-slut
coverture
covert way
covetable
covin-tree
cowabunga
cowardice
cowardize
cow-banger
cow-hocked
cow-keeper
cowl-staff
Cowperian
co-written
coxcombic
coxcombry
crab apple
crabbedly
crabbiest
crab-grass
crabgrass
crab louse
crab-stick
crab-stock
crack down
crackdown
crackhead
crackless
crackling
cracksman
cracksmen
cradle-cap
craftiest
craftless
craftsman
craftsmen
craftwork
crag-bound
craggiest
crammable
cramp-bone
cramp fish
cramp-iron
crampness
cramponny

cramp-ring
cranberry
cranelike
crane line
crane-neck
crank-axle
crankcase
crankiest
crankness
cranreuch
crape-fern
crape hair
crappiest
crapulent
crapulous
crash-dive
crash-halt
crash-land
crash-stop
crassness
cratefuls
craterlet
craterous
cravatted
cravingly
craziness
crazy bone
crazy-pave
creakiest
cream cake
cream-cups
cream horn
creamiest
creamlike
cream puff
cream soda
cream soup
creamware
creatable
creatress
creatural
crediting
creditrix
credulity
credulous
creedless
creepered
creep-hole
creepiest
creep up on
cremaster
cremation
crematory
crenation
crenature
crenelate
crenulate
creophagy
crêpeline
crêpe sole
crepitant
crepitate

crepitous
crêpoline
crepuscle
crescendi
crescendo
crestless
crest-line
cretinise
cretinism
cretinize
cretinoid
cretinous
crevicing
crewelist
crib-biter
cribellum
cricketed
cricketer
crimeless
crime wave
criminate
criminous
crimplene
Crimplene
crinoidal
crinoline
crinosity
crippling
crispiest
crispness
cristated
criterial
criterion
criticise
criticism
criticist
criticize
critiqued
critiques
croakiest
crocheted
crocheter
crocketed
crocodile
croisette
croissant
Crokerism
Cro-Magnon
Cromerian
crook-back
crookback
crookeder
crookedly
crookneck
crop-eared
croqueted
croquette
crosiered
crossable
cross-beak
cross-beam
cross-bill

crossbill	crudeness	cunctator	custodiam	cyphonism	damselfly
crossbred	cruellest	cuneiform	custodian	Cyprianic	danburite
cross-date	cruelling	cunicular	custodier	cyprinoid	danceable
cross-eyed	cruelness	cuniculus	customary	cyrtolite	dance band
cross-fade	cruelties	cunninger	custom car	cystalgia	dance-card
crossfire	cruiseway	cunningly	customise	cystidean	dance hall
cross-hair	crumbiest	cupbearer	customize	cystidium	dancehall
cross-head	crumblier	cupelling	custumary	cystiform	danceress
cross-jack	crumbling	cupferron	cut a caper	cystocarp	dancingly
cross-keys	crummiest	cup-fungus	cut across	cystocele	dandelion
cross-kick	crunchier	cup grease	cut and run	cystolith	dandiacal
crossless	crunchily	Cupid's bow	cutaneous	cystotomy	dandified
cross-line	crushable	cup lichen	cut a shine	Cytherean	dandifies
cross-link	crush-room	cup-marked	cut a swath	cytidylic	dandiprat
cross-lots	crustated	cuppiness	cut a tooth	cytocidal	dandruffy
crossness	crustiest	curb-chain	cut capers	cytokinin	dandy-cart
cross over	crustless	curb-plate	cutcherry	cytologic	dandyfunk
crossover	cruzeiros	curbstone	cut didoes	cytolysis	dandy-line
cross-pass	cry craven	curdiness	cuticular	cytolytic	dandyprat
cross-path	cry halves	curettage	cutis laxa	cytoplasm	dandy roll
cross-peen	cry harrow	curetting	cut it fine	cytosolic	danger man
crossroad	cryogenic	curfuffle	cut-out box	cytotoxic	dangerous
cross-ruff	cryoprobe	curialism	cut splice	cytotoxin	Danish axe
crosstalk	cryoscopy	curialist	cutter-bar	czarevich	Danish dog
cross the T	cry out for	curiosity	cut the rug	dachshund	Dannebrog
cross tide	cryptical	curiously	cut-throat	Dadaistic	Dantesque
cross-town	cryptogam	curliness	cutthroat	Daedalian	danthonia
cross-tree	cryptonym	curlingly	cuttingly	daffiness	Dantonist
crosswalk	ctenidial	curl-paper	cut up well	Daghestan	dapatical
crossways	ctenidium	curl-pated	Cuvierian	dailiness	daphnetin
crosswind	Cuba libre	curl the mo	cyanamide	Daily Mail	Dardanian
cross-wire	Cuban heel	curly kale	cyanicide	Daily News	daredevil
crosswise	cubbishly	currajong	cyanolabe	daintiest	dark horse
cross with	cubby hole	currawong	cyanurate	daiquiris	dark lines
crossword	cubically	currently	cybernate	dairy farm	darklings
crosswort	cubic foot	curricula	cyberpunk	dairy-free	dark space
Crostarie	cubicular	currishly	cybotaxis	dairymaid	darnation
crotaline	cubiculum	curry-comb	cycadeoid	daisy-bush	darned net
crotchety	cubic yard	cursillos	cyclamate	daisy-like	dartboard
croton oil	cuckoldom	cursively	cyclamens	daisy tree	Darwinian
crouchant	cuckoldry	cursorial	cycle clip	Dalai Lama	Darwinise
croustade	cuckoo bee	cursorily	cyclicity	dales folk	Darwinism
crowberry	cuckoo-bud	curtailer	cyclogiro	Daliesque	Darwinist
crow-eater	cuckquean	curtain-up	cycloidal	dalliance	Darwinize
crown cork	cucullate	curtal-axe	cyclonite	dally away	dashboard
crown fire	cuddliest	curtation	Cyclopean	Dalmatian	dashingly
crown full	cudgelled	curtilage	Cyclopian	Dalradian	dashlight
crown gall	cudgeller	curvation	cyclopoid	Daltonian	dastardly
crown land	cuirassed	curvature	Cyclopses	daltonism	dasypygal
crown lens	cuisinier	curve ball	cyclorama	Daltonize	data entry
crownless	culicidal	curveless	cyclothem	damascene	dataglove
crown rust	cullender	curvesome	cyclotomy	Damascene	data sheet
crow-quill	culminant	curveting	cyclotron	damaskeen	date-lined
crow's-foot	culminate	curvetted	cylindric	damnation	date stamp
crow's-nest	culs-de-sac	curviform	cymagraph	damnatory	datum-line
crucially	cultistic	curviness	cyma recta	damnified	dauntless
crucified	cultivate	curvingly	cymbalist	damnifies	davenport
crucifier	cultrated	cushiness	cymbidium	damningly	Davenport
crucifies	culturist	cushioned	cymbiform	damoiseau	Davidical
cruciform	cultus-cod	cusimanse	cymophane	dampishly	Davy Jones
cru classé	cumulated	cuspidate	cynegetic	damp-proof	day centre
cruddiest	cunabulum	custodial	cynically	damp squib	day-flower

day labour	debatably	declinate	defection	delineate	dentalise
day letter	debauched	declivity	defective	deliquium	dentality
Day of Doom	debauchee	declivous	defendant	deliriant	dentalium
day of rest	debaucher	decoction	defension	deliriate	dentalize
day return	debenture	decodable	defensist	delirious	dentation
day school	debitable	decoherer	defensive	deliverer	Denticare
day-spring	debit card	decollate	defensory	deliverly	denticule
dazedness	debiteuse	décolleté	deference	Delphinus	dentiform
deaconate	debit side	decomplex	deferment	delta plus	dentistry
deaconess	de Broglie	decompose	deferring	delta rays	dentition
dead-alive	debt-slave	decongest	defiantly	delta wing	denturist
dead broke	debugging	decontrol	deficient	deltidium	denyingly
dead drunk	debussing	decorated	definable	deltoidal	deoculate
dead horse	Debussyan	decorator	definably	demagnify	deodorant
dead house	debutante	découpage	definiens	demagogic	deodorise
deadliest	débutante	decoy-duck	definitor	demagogue	deodorize
deadlight	decachord	decoy ship	definitum	demandant	deoxidate
deadly sin	decadence	decreeing	deflation	demanding	deoxidize
dead march	decadency	decrement	deflector	demand-led	departure
dead point	decagonal	decretion	deflexion	demantoid	depascent
dead's part	decahedra	decretist	deflexure	demarcate	depasture
dead stock	decalcify	decretive	defluence	demeaning	dependant
deadstock	decalitre	decretory	defluvium	demeanour	dependent
dead water	Decalogue	decubital	defluxion	demements	depiction
dead white	decameric	decubitus	defocused	demention	depictive
deaf adder	decametre	decumbent	defoliant	demersion	depicture
deaf-blind	decanally	decuplate	defoliate	demesnial	depigment
deal board	decaploid	decurrent	deformity	demi-devil	depletion
deaminate	decapodan	decursive	defrauder	demi-glace	depletive
deaneries	decastyle	decussate	defroster	demi-gorge	deplumate
dean's list	decathlon	dedicated	defterdar	demi-lance	depoetize
dear heart	decaudate	dedicatee	degassing	*demi-monde*	depollute
dear knows	decayable	dedicator	degausser	demi-pique	deposable
death-bell	deceitful	deducible	degrading	demisable	deposited
death-bird	decencies	deduction	degreaser	demission	depositee
death blow	decennary	deductive	degree day	demitasse	depositor
deathblow	decenniad	deductory	degustate	demitting	depot ship
death camp	decennial	deep-drawn	dehiscent	demiurgic	depravity
death cell	decennium	deep field	dehydrase	demi-volte	deprecate
death duty	decentish	deep-fried	dehydrate	demnition	depredate
death-fire	deception	deep-fries	*Dei gratia*	demobbing	depressed
death-head	deceptive	deep-mined	deil a haet	demob suit	depressor
deathless	decertify	Deep South	deionizer	democracy	depriment
deathlier	decession	deep space	deiparous	demonical	depsidone
deathlike	decidable	deep-toned	deistical	demulcent	depth bomb
deathling	decidedly	deerberry	deityship	demurrage	depthless
death mask	deciduate	deer-brush	dejection	demurrant	depurator
death rate	deciduoma	deer-grass	Dekabrist	demurring	deputable
death roll	deciduous	deer-hound	Delasolre	demystify	deputator
death-sick	decilitre	deerhound	delay line	dendritic	derealize
deathsman	decillion	deer mouse	delectate	denervate	derepress
death-song	decimally	deer's hair	delegable	de-netting	de-rigging
death toll	decimator	deer-track	delegatee	denigrate	de rigueur
death trap	decimetre	defaecate	delegator	denitrate	derisible
deathward	deck cargo	defalcate	delftware	denitrify	derivable
death wish	deck-chair	defatting	delicious	den mother	dermatome
debagging	deckchair	defaulter	delictual	denominal	dermestid
deballast	deck class	defeatism	delighted	denotable	derogator
debarment	deck-house	defeatist	delighter	denotatum	derring-do
debarrass	declaimer	defeature	delignify	denouncer	derringer
debarring	declarant	defecated	delimited	*de nouveau*	descanter
debatable	déclassée	defecator	delimiter	denseness	descender

describer	detrition	diagnoses	dictatrix	dime novel	disablist
descripta	detrusion	diagnosis	dictature	dimension	disaccept
desecrate	deturpate	dialectal	didactive	dimensive	disaccord
desertify	deuce game	dialectic	diddledum	dime-store	disadvise
desertion	deuterate	dialogise	didelphid	dimidiate	disaffect
desert oak	deuteride	dialogism	diervilla	dimissory	disaffirm
desert rat	deuterium	dialogist	dieselise	dimorphic	disagreed
deserving	deutoxide	dialogize	dieselize	dim-witted	disagreer
desiccant	devaluate	dialoguer	diesel oil	Dinantian	disagrees
desiccate	devaluing	dial-plate	die-sinker	dine out on	disanchor
designata	devastate	dialysate	dietaries	ding-a-ling	disanoint
designate	developed	dialyzate	diet-bread	dinginess	disappear
designful	developer	diamagnet	diet-drink	dining car	disarming
designing	Devensian	diametral	dietetics	dinkum oil	disattire
desinence	devesture	diametric	dietician	dinothere	disavowal
desipient	deviation	diamidine	dietitian	dioecious	disbarred
desirable	deviative	diamonded	diet-sheet	dioestrus	disbelief
desirably	deviatory	diandrous	different	diogenite	disbranch
desireful	deviceful	Dianetics	difficile	Dionysiac	disbudded
desk-bound	devil a bit	dianoetic	difficult	Dionysian	disburden
desk diary	devil a one	diapering	diffident	diopsidic	disbursal
desmosome	devil bird	diaphanie	diffluent	dioptrics	disburser
desolater	devilfish	diaphonic	diffusant	Dioscuric	discalced
desolator	devilhead	diaphragm	diffusate	diosgenin	discarder
desorbent	devilhood	diaphysis	diffusely	dip candle	disc brake
despaired	devil-like	diapirism	diffusion	dip circle	discerner
despairer	devilling	diaristic	diffusive	dipeptide	discharge
desperado	devilment	diarrhoea	Digambara	diphthong	disciform
desperate	devil's bit	diascopic	digastric	diploidal	disclimax
despite of	devilship	diastasic	digenesis	diplomacy	disclosed
despoiler	devil's own	diastasis	digenetic	diplomaed	discloser
desponder	devil-wood	diastatic	digestant	diplomate	discoboli
despotism	deviously	diastolic	digestion	diplonema	discohere
despotist	devisable	diasystem	digestive	diplotene	discoidal
despotize	devitrify	diathermy	digitalin	dip needle	discolour
despumate	devonport	diathesis	digitalis	dipperful	discomfit
destinate	devotedly	diathetic	digitally	dip switch	discommon
destinies	dew-clawed	diatomite	digitated	DIP switch	discouple
destitute	dewlapped	diatonism	digitizer	dipterist	discourse
destroyer	Dexedrine	diazonium	digitoxin	dipterous	discovert
desuetude	dexterity	diazotize	diglossia	dipyramid	discovery
desultory	dexterous	diazotype	diglossic	direct dye	discreate
detailing	dextrally	dibstones	diglottic	direct hit	discredit
detail man	dextrorse	dicastery	dignified	direction	discumber
detection	dezincify	dicentric	dignifier	directive	discusser
detective	dhobi itch	dichasium	dignifies	directory	disdainer
detension	diablerie	dichogamy	dignitary	direct ray	disembark
detention	diablotin	dichoptic	dignities	directrix	disembody
detergent	diabolify	dichotomy	digraphic	direct tax	disemploy
determent	diabolise	dichroism	digresser	direfully	disenable
determine	diabolism	dichroite	diguanide	dirigible	disengage
deterrent	diabolist	dichromat	dihydrate	dirigisme	disentail
deterring	diabolize	dichromic	dika bread	dirigiste	disentomb
detersion	diacetate	dicky bird	dike-grave	dirt cheap	disesteem
detersive	diachrony	dicky seat	dilatable	dirtiness	disfavour
dethroner	diachylon	diclinism	dilatancy	dirt money	disfigure
detonator	diaclinal	diclinous	dilatator	dirt track	disflower
detorsion	diaconate	dicrotism	dilettant	dirt-wagon	disforest
detortion	diacritic	dictamnus	diligence	dirty look	disgorger
detracter	diactinic	dictation	dill-water	dirty pool	disgracer
detractor	diaeresis	dictative	dilutable	dirty word	disguisal
detriment	diaeretic	dictatory	dilutedly	dirty work	disguiser

dishallow	disrepair	diversify	dogmatist	door frame	downfield
dishcloth	disrepute	diversion	dogmatize	doorknock	downglide
dish-clout	disrupter	diversity	dognapper	door plate	downgrade
dish-cover	disruptor	diversive	do-goodery	door-stead	downiness
dish-faced	dissected	diverting	do-gooding	door-stone	downlight
dish it out	dissector	divertive	do-goodism	dope-fiend	downrange
dishonest	disseisee	divesture	dog-paddle	do penance	downright
dishonour	disseisin	dividable	dog-robber	dope-sheet	down-river
dishtowel	disseisor	dividedly	dogs of war	do poo-poos	downriver
dishwater	dissemble	divi-divis	dog's onion	dor-beetle	downscale
disimmure	dissensus	dividuity	dog's tooth	do right by	downshift
disimpale	dissenter	dividuous	dog's trick	dormition	downslope
disinfect	disshadow	divinator	dog trials	dormitive	down south
disinfest	disshroud	divisible	dog tucker	dormitory	downspout
disinform	dissident	divisibly	dog-violet	Dormobile	down-stage
disinhume	dissimile	divulgate	dog-winkle	doronicum	downstage
disinvent	dissipate	divulsion	Dolbyized	dorsality	downstair
disinvest	dissocial	divulsive	dolce vita	dorsiflex	downstart
disinvite	dissogeny	Dixiecrat	dolefully	doryphore	downstate
disjaskit	dissogony	Dixieland	dole queue	dosemeter	down-swept
disk drive	dissolute	dizygotic	doleritic	dosimeter	downswing
dislocate	dissolver	dizziness	dollar day	dosimetry	downthrew
dislustre	dissonant	djellabah	Dollardom	doss-house	downthrow
dismality	dissonate	do a mizzle	dollar gap	dot matrix	downtoner
dismalize	disspread	do any good	dollhouse	do to death	down tools
dismantle	dissuader	do a runner	dolloping	dot-stitch	down under
dismarble	dissunder	do a wee-wee	dolly-bird	dottiness	downwards
dismayful	distantly	Dobermann	dolomitic	double act	downweigh
dismember	distemper	dobsonfly	Dolophine	double axe	do wonders
dismissal	distenant	Dobsonian	dolorific	double bar	do wrong to
dismutase	disthrone	dock brief	dolostone	double bed	dowryless
disnature	distichal	docketing	dolphined	double-dig	do you hear
disobeyer	distilled	dock-glass	doltishly	double dip	do you mind
disoblige	distiller	doctorand	Domdaniel	double dot	dozedness
disoccupy	distingué	doctorate	dome-light	double-dye	draconian
disorient	distinguo	doctoress	domically	double-gee	draffsack
disparage	distraint	doctorial	dominance	doubleton	draftiest
disparate	distraite	doctorism	dominancy	double top	draftsman
disparish	disturbed	doctorize	dominator	doubtable	draftsmen
disparity	disturber	doctrinal	dominical	doubtless	drag-chain
dispauper	disulfide	docudrama	Dominican	douceness	draggiest
dispelled	disusance	doddering	Dominique	doucepere	drag-hound
dispeller	disvisage	doddypoll	domitable	douche-bag	dragomans
dispenser	diswarren	dodecagon	donkeydom	dough-face	dragoness
dispeople	ditchless	dodecamer	donkeyish	doughiest	dragonfly
dispermic	diterpene	dodgem car	donkeyman	doughtier	dragonish
dispersal	dithionic	dodginess	donnishly	doughtily	dragonism
disperser	dithizone	dod-rotted	donor card	Doukhobor	dragonize
displacer	dithyramb	do duty for	donorship	dovehouse	drag queen
displayer	ditrochee	dogaressa	do-nothing	Dover sole	drag-seine
displease	dittander	dog-clutch	doodlebug	dove's-foot	drag-staff
dispondee	dittanies	dog collar	doodle-doo	dowagerly	drag-strut
disponent	dittogram	dog-eat-dog	doohickey	dowdiness	drainable
dispose of	dittology	dog-fennel	doojigger	dowelling	draincock
disposure	diurnally	dogginess	doomfully	dower land	drainless
dispraise	diuturnal	doggishly	doominess	dowerless	drainpipe
disprofit	divalence	dog-headed	doom-laden	dowitcher	Dramamine
disproval	divalency	dog-legged	doomsayer	do without	dramatics
disputant	divellent	dog-lichen	doomwatch	down along	dramatise
disregard	divergent	dogmatics	do one's bit	downcoast	dramatism
disrelate	diverless	dogmatise	do one's nut	downcomer	dramatist
disrelish	diversely	dogmatism	door-cheek	downfault	dramatize

drapeable	driveller	duck's bill	Dutchland	earliness	echovirus
draperies	drive over	duck-shove	Dutch oven	early bird	ECHO virus
drape suit	drive-time	duck's meat	Dutch pink	early days	eclampsia
dratchell	drizzling	duckstone	Dutch roll	early wood	eclamptic
Dravidian	Dr Martens	ducted fan	Dutch rush	earnestly	eclectism
drawbench	droitural	ductility	Dutch tile	earringed	ecologist
drawerful	drollness	dude ranch	Dutch wife	earth-ball	economics
draw forth	dromedary	duffel bag	duteously	earth-born	economies
draw-knife	droningly	duffle bag	dutifully	earthfast	economise
drawlatch	droopiest	dufrenite	duty-bound	earthiest	economism
drawn work	drop a hint	dulcamara	duty cycle	earthlike	economist
draw-plate	drop-black	dulcified	duty visit	earthling	economize
draw-poker	drop-eared	dulcifies	dwarfling	earth-rise	eco-raider
draw-shave	drop-forge	dulcitone	dwarfness	earth-soul	ecosphere
draw-sheet	drop-light	dulcitude	dwarf star	earth-star	écossaise
draw steel	droppable	dulcorous	dwarf wall	earthstar	ecosystem
draw-table	droppings	dulocracy	dyarchies	earthward	ecphrasis
draw-works	drop-press	dumb barge	dyer's weed	earthwork	ecstasies
dray horse	drop scene	dumb blond	dyingness	earthworm	ecstasise
dreadless	drop scone	dumb cluck	dying oath	earwigged	ecstasize
dreadlock	drop short	dumbfound	dyke-grave	easefully	ectoblast
dreadness	dropsical	dumb piano	dyke-reeve	eastabout	ectocrine
dream away	dropstone	dummy teat	dynameter	eastbound	ectogenic
dreamboat	droshkies	dumpiness	dynamical	East Ender	ectomorph
dream-book	drotchell	dumpishly	dynamiter	Easter Day	ectoplasm
dream-hole	droughted	dump truck	dynamotor	Easter egg	ectoproct
dreamiest	drove road	dump valve	dynasties	easterner	ectropion
dreamland	drowsiest	duncehood	dyschezia	East India	ecumaniac
dreamless	drug abuse	dunce's cap	dyscrasia	East Sider	ecumenics
dreamlike	drug squad	duncishly	dyscrasic	eastwards	ecumenism
dream-time	drugstore	Dundonian	dysentery	easy as pie	ecumenist
dreamtime	Druidical	Dundreary	dysgenics	easy chair	edelweiss
dreariest	drum brake	dune buggy	dyslectic	easy-going	edibility
Dresdener	drum major	Dunkirker	dyspepsia	easygoing	edictally
dress coat	drumstick	dunnamany	dyspeptic	easy money	edificial
dress down	drum tower	Dunstable	dysphagia	easy-paced	editorial
dressiest	drunkenly	duodecimo	dysphasia	easy-peasy	education
dressmake	drunk tank	duodenary	dysphasic	easy rider	educative
dribbling	dry as dust	duopolies	dysphemia	easy terms	educatory
driftless	Dryasdust	duopolist	dysphonia	easy touch	Edwardian
drift mine	dry-blower	duplation	dysphoria	eau-de-Luce	Edwardine
driftweed	Drydenian	duple time	dysphoric	eau sucreé	effective
driftwood	Drydenish	duplexity	dysphotic	eavesdrop	effectual
drillable	drying-day	duplicate	dysplasia	Ebionitic	efficient
drill-book	drying oil	duplicity	dyspnoeal	ebriosity	effigiate
drill pipe	drylander	dupondius	dyspnoeic	ebulliate	efflation
drill-ship	dry matter	Dupuytren	dysthymia	ebullient	effluence
drill stem	dry-rotten	Duralumin	dysthymic	eccentric	effluvium
drinkable	dry-salter	dura mater	dystocial	ecchymoma	effluxion
drinkably	dry season	duricrust	dystopian	ecclesial	effortful
drink deep	dry shaver	duskiness	dystrophy	ecdysiasm	effulgent
drink down	dry valley	duskishly	dziggetai	ecdysiast	egg-beater
drink hail	dualistic	dusky titi	each other	echeveria	egg-carton
drinkless	dubbining	dust-cloth	eagerness	echiuroid	eggheaded
drip-dried	dubieties	dust cover	eagle-eyed	echograph	egg-shaped
drip-dries	dubiosity	dust devil	eagle-hawk	echoingly	egg-slicer
drip joint	dubiously	dustiness	eagle-wood	echolalia	eglantine
drippiest	dubitable	dust sheet	ealdorman	echolalic	egomaniac
dripstone	dubitably	dust storm	ear-basher	echometer	egotistic
driveable	duckboard	Dutch barn	earbasher	echo organ	egregious
drive-belt	duck decoy	Dutch doll	ear covert	echo verse	egression
drivelled	duck's arse	Dutch door	eared seal	echo-virus	egressive

egromancy	elocution	emotivism	end or mend	entamoeba	epidermic
eider-down	elocutory	emotivity	endorphin	entangler	epidermis
eiderdown	Elohistic	empathise	endoscope	entelechy	epidosite
eider duck	elongated	empathist	endoscopy	enterable	epifaunal
eidetiker	elopement	empathize	endosperm	enterally	epigramme
Eid ul-Adha	eloquence	empennage	endospore	enter into	epigraphy
Eid ul-Fitr	elsewhere	emphasise	endosteal	enteritis	epigynous
eigentone	Elsterian	emphasize	endosteum	entertain	epiklesis
eight ball	elucidate	emphysema	endostyle	enthymeme	epilation
eight days	elumbated	empicture	endotherm	entoblast	epileptic
eightfold	elusively	Empire Day	endotoxic	entoconid	epilimnia
eightieth	elutriate	empirical	endotoxin	entophyte	epilithic
eightsome	emanation	Empsonian	endowment	entoproct	epilobium
eighty-six	emanatist	emptiness	end result	entourage	epilogise
eirenicon	emanative	empty nest	endsville	entrammel	epilogist
eisegesis	emanatory	empty word	endungeon	entrapped	epilogize
either way	embargoes	empyreuma	endurable	entrapper	epimedium
ejaculate	embarrass	emulation	endurably	entrechat	epimerase
ejectment	embassade	emulative	endurance	entrecôte	epimerise
ekphrasis	embassage	emulgence	energetic	*entremets*	epimerism
elaborate	embassies	emulously	energizer	*entre nous*	epimerite
elaeolite	embattled	emunctory	energumen	entropion	epimerize
elastance	embayment	enactable	energy gap	entry form	epinastic
elastomer	embedment	enactment	*en famille*	enubilate	epineural
elatement	embellish	enamelled	enfeebler	enucleate	epinician
elaterite	Ember days	enameller	enflurane	enumerate	epinicion
elaterium	Embertide	enanthema	enfreedom	enunciate	epiphanic
elbow room	Ember week	encapsule	engarland	enveloped	epiphragm
Elder Edda	embezzler	encaustic	engineman	enverdure	epiphyses
elder hand	emblemize	enchanter	englacial	enviously	epiphysis
elderhood	emblossom	enchilada	Englander	envoyship	epiphytal
eldership	embossing	enchorial	Englisher	enwreathe	epiphytic
elder tree	embosture	encircler	Englishly	enwrought	epipodial
eldorados	embowment	enclosure	Englishry	enzymatic	epipodite
electable	embraceor	encomiast	engrailed	eotechnic	epipodium
electoral	embracery	encomiums	engraving	eparchies	epipteric
electress	embracive	encompass	engrosser	epaulette	epirogeny
Electress	embrangle	encounter	enhancive	ependymal	episcopal
electride	embrasure	encourage	enhearten	epeolatry	episcopic
electrify	embrazure	Encratite	enigmatic	ephedrine	episememe
electrize	embreathe	encrimson	enjealous	ephemerae	epistasis
electrode	embrigade	encrinite	enjoinder	ephemeral	epistatic
electroes	embrittle	encurtain	enjoyable	ephemeras	epistaxis
electuary	embrocado	end-around	enjoyably	ephemerid	epistemic
elegantly	embrocate	end-artery	enjoyment	ephemeris	epistoler
elegiacal	embroider	endearing	enkindler	ephemeron	epitapher
elemental	embroiler	endeavour	enlighten	ephialtes	epitaphic
elenchtic	embryonal	endeictic	enlivener	epibiotic	epitaxial
elephanta	embryonic	endemical	en passant	epicedial	epithelia
elephants	embryo sac	endenizen	*en pension*	epicedian	epitheted
Elers ware	embryotic	endlessly	enquiries	epicedium	epithetic
elevation	embussing	end-member	enquiring	epicenter	epitomise
elevatory	emendator	endocrine	enragedly	epicentre	epitomist
elevenses	emergence	endoergic	*en rapport*	epiclesis	epitomize
elfin-tree	emergency	endogamic	enrapture	epicormic	epizeuxis
elfin-wood	eminently	endogenic	enrolling	epicritic	epizootic
elf-locked	Emmenthal	endolymph	enrolment	epicurean	epochally
eliciting	emolliate	endomixis	ensaffron	Epicurean	eponymist
eliminant	emollient	endomorph	ensimatic	epicurish	eponymous
eliminate	emolument	endophora	ensorcell	epicurism	epoxidize
elixation	emotional	endophyte	enstatite	epicyclic	epoxy glue
ellipsoid	emotively	endoplasm	ensulphur	epidermal	epulation

epuration	escheator	etymology	even hands	excisable	existible
equaliser	escopette	eucalypti	even money	excise law	exit wound
equalizer	escortage	eucalypts	eventless	exciseman	ex-librism
equalling	Eskimo dog	eucaryote	eventuate	excisemen	ex-librist
equalness	Eskimo pie	eucentric	eve-of-poll	excitable	exocyclic
equal sign	esophagus	Eucharist	ever-being	excitably	exodermal
equatable	esophoria	Euclidean	everglade	excitancy	exodermis
equerries	esoterica	eudemonic	evergreen	excitedly	exodontia
equifinal	esoterism	eugenesic	ever-ready	excitonic	exoenzyme
equimolar	esotropia	eugenesis	eversible	exclaim at	ex officio
equipment	esperance	euglenoid	ever since	exclaimer	exogamous
equipoise	Esperanto	eukaryote	everybody	exclaim on	exogenous
equipping	espionage	eulogizer	every inch	exclosure	exolution
equirotal	esplanade	Eumenides	every last	excluding	exonerate
equisetum	espringal	eunuchism	everylike	exclusion	exophoria
equitable	Esquimaux	eunuchize	ever yours	exclusive	exophoric
equitably	esquiress	eunuchoid	every time	exclusory	exorcizer
equivalve	essayette	euphemise	everywhen	ex-convict	exordiums
equivocal	essayical	euphemism	every whit	excoriate	exosmosis
equivoque	Essenical	euphemist	evidently	excrement	exosphere
eradicant	essential	euphemize	evildoing	excretion	exostosed
eradicate	essenwood	euphenics	evil-liver	excretive	exostosis
era-making	establish	euphonies	evincible	excretory	exostotic
erasement	*estaminet*	euphonise	eviration	excubitor	exoticism
erbswurst	estampage	euphonism	evitation	exculpate	exotropia
erectable	estate car	euphonium	evocation	excurrent	expanding
erectness	estate tax	euphonize	evocative	excursion	expansile
ergograph	estimable	euphonous	evocatory	excursive	expansion
ergometer	estimably	euphorbia	evolution	excusable	expansive
ergometry	estimator	euphrasia	evolutive	excusably	expatiate
ergonomic	estoppage	euraquilo	evolvable	excusator	expectant
ergotized	estopping	eurhythmy	ewe-necked	execrable	expecting
eriometer	estradiol	euriballi	exactable	execrably	expective
erminites	estranged	Eurocracy	exactness	execrator	expedient
Ernestine	estranger	Euro-rebel	exactress	executant	expediter
erogenous	estuarial	Eurospeak	exaltedly	execution	expeditor
erosional	estuarian	eurytherm	examinant	executive	expellent
erosivity	estuaries	eurythmic	examinate	executory	expelling
eroticise	estuarine	eurytopic	exanimate	executrix	expensive
eroticism	esurience	Euskarian	exanthema	exegesist	experient
eroticist	esuriency	eusuchian	exaration	exegetics	expertise
eroticize	eternally	eutaxitic	exarchate	exegetist	expertize
erotology	ethanoate	eutectoid	Exarchist	exemplary	expiation
errand-boy	ethanolic	euthanasy	excambion	exemplify	expiatory
erratical	ethereous	euthanize	excarnate	exemptile	expiscate
erroneous	etherical	euthenics	excavator	exemption	explainer
errorless	ethically	eutherian	exceeding	exequatur	explanans
erstwhile	ethionine	euthyroid	excellent	exerciser	explanate
Ertebølle	Ethiopian	eutrophic	excelling	exercitor	expletive
eruciform	ethmoidal	Eutychian	excelsior	Exercycle	expletory
eruditely	ethnarchy	evacuable	excentral	exergonic	explicans
erudition	ethnicism	evacuator	excentric	exfoliate	explicate
erythemal	ethnicist	evadingly	except for	exhalable	explodent
erythrina	ethnicity	evagation	excepting	exhauster	exploitee
erythrine	ethnocide	evaginate	exception	exhibited	exploiter
erythrism	ethnogeny	evaluable	exceptive	exhibiter	explosion
erythrite	ethnology	evaluator	excerptor	exhibitor	explosive
erythroid	ethylenic	evangelic	excessive	exhumator	exponence
erythrose	etiquette	evaporate	exchanger	exigenter	exponency
escalator	Eton fives	evaporite	exchequer	exigently	exponible
escapable	etorphine	evasively	excipient	exilement	exposable
escape key	et sequens	even break	excipulum	existence	expositor

expounder	eyebrowed	faintness	fancy-free	fatuously	fermentum
expresser	eye-glassy	fair's fair	fancy-sick	fat-witted	fernbrake
expressly	eyeleting	fair-trade	fancy-work	faultiest	ferneries
expressor	eye-opener	fairwater	fandangle	faultless	fern-house
expressos	eye pencil	fairy cake	fandangos	fault-line	ferocious
expulsion	eyes front	fairy flax	fan heater	faunistic	ferrament
expulsive	eye-shadow	fairy gold	fan mussel	Faverolle	Ferrarese
expulsory	eyeshadow	fairyland	Fannie Mae	favourite	ferreting
expurgate	eye socket	Fairyland	fanny belt	fawningly	ferrocene
exquisite	eye splice	fairy-like	fanny pack	fearfully	ferryable
exsection	eyes right	fairy moss	fantailed	fearingly	ferryboat
exsertile	eye strain	fairy ring	fantasied	feathered	fertilely
exsertion	eyestripe	fairy rose	fantasise	featurely	fertilise
ex-service	Eyetalian	fairy tale	fantasist	febricula	fertility
exsiccate	Fabianism	fairy tern	fantasize	febrifuge	fertilize
exstrophy	Fabianist	fairy wren	fantasque	febrility	fervently
exsuccous	fabricant	faith cure	fantassin	Febronian	fervorous
exsuction	fabricate	faithless	fantastic	feckfully	fess point
exsurgent	fabulator	Falabella	fantastry	feculence	festilogy
extempore	face-brick	Falangism	faradaism	fecundate	festinate
extensile	face-cloth	Falangist	far afield	fecundify	festively
extension	facecloth	Falcidian	farandole	fecundity	festivity
extensity	face cream	falciform	fare stage	federally	festivous
extensive	face facts	faldstool	farmeress	feed a part	festology
extenuate	face-glass	Falernian	farmhouse	feed-floor	festucine
externate	face-guard	Faliscian	farmstead	feedstock	fetch away
externise	face out of	Falklands	far or near	feed-stuff	fetch down
externity	face paint	fall about	farragoes	feedstuff	fetichism
externize	face-piece	fallacies	farrantly	feed-water	fetidness
extirpate	face-plate	fallacion	far-seeing	fee-farmer	fetisheer
extispicy	faceplate	fallalery	far to seek	fee-faw-fum	fetishise
extolling	face-saver	fall apart	Far Wester	feel cheap	fetishism
extolment	facetious	fall-board	fasciated	feelingly	fetishist
extorsion	face value	fall-front	fascicled	feel small	fetishize
extorsive	faciation	fall in two	fascicule	fee simple	fetlocked
extortion	facsimile	fall money	fasciitis	feet first	fettucini
extortive	facticity	Fallopian	fasciolar	feignedly	feudalise
extracted	factional	fall out of	fascistic	feistiest	feudalism
extractor	factitive	fall short	Fascistic	Félibrism	feudalist
extradite	factivity	false card	fashioned	felicific	feudality
extrapose	factorage	false coin	fashioner	fellaheen	feudalize
extra time	factorial	false dawn	fast break	fellation	feudatory
extravert	factories	false face	fastening	fellatrix	*feu de joie*
extremely	factorise	false fire	fastidium	fell-field	fever heat
extremism	factorize	falsehood	fastigium	fell hound	fever tree
extremist	factotums	false keel	fast track	fellowess	fiat money
extremity	fact sheet	false move	fast train	felonious	Fibonacci
extremums	factually	falseness	fatalness	femineity	fibrefill
extricate	facultate	false step	fatefully	fenceless	fibreless
extrinsic	facultied	falsettos	fat-headed	fence post	fibriform
extrovert	faculties	falsework	fathogram	fence-shop	fibrillar
extrusile	facundity	falsified	fatidical	fenestrae	fibrinoid
extrusion	faddiness	falsifier	fatigable	fenestral	fibrinous
extrusive	faddishly	falsifies	fatiguing	Fenianism	fibrocyte
exuberant	fadeproof	falsities	family man	fenoterol	fibrolite
exuberate	fadmonger	falsified	famishing	fenugreek	fibromata
exudation	Fadometer	family man	fanatical	feoffment	fibrously
exudative	faggoting	famishing	fanciable	feracious	fictional
exultance	fagmaster	fanatical	fanciless	ferberite	fictively
exultancy	fainaigue	fanciable	fanciness	Feringhee	fiddle-bow
exululate	faineancy	fanciless	fancy cake	fermental	fiddliest
eyebright	faintless	fanciness		fermenter	fideistic

fidgetily	filter aid	fireplace	fixedness	flat-nosed	flood-lamp
fidgeting	filter-bed	fire-power	fixed odds	flattener	flood-mark
fidget pie	filter out	firepower	fixed star	flatten in	flood tide
fiduciary	filter tip	fireproof	fixed-wing	flatterer	floor lamp
field-book	filthiest	fire-stick	fizziness	flatulent	floorless
field boot	filtrable	fire-stone	fizzle out	flatwoods	floor plan
fieldfare	fimbriate	fire-storm	flabbiest	flaughter	floor show
field goal	finagling	firestorm	flabellum	flaunched	flop-eared
field-grey	financeer	firethorn	flaccidly	flaunting	flop-house
field hand	financial	fire-tongs	flacherie	flavonoid	flophouse
field mark	financier	fire-water	flagellar	flavorous	flopperoo
field rank	financist	firewater	flagellum	flavoured	floppiest
fieldsman	finchlike	firewoman	flageolet	flax-brake	floptical
fieldsmen	find fault	firmament	flagitate	flay-flint	floreated
field-test	find Jesus	first base	flagrance	flea-louse	floriated
field vole	find means	first-born	flagrancy	fléchette	floridean
fieldwork	find-place	first chop	flagstaff	fleckered	Floridian
fiendlike	findrinny	first coat	flagstone	fleckless	floridity
fierasfer	fine-drawn	first cost	flag-waver	fledgling	floristic
fieriness	fine grain	first-foot	flail-tank	fleeciest	floristry
fifteenth	fine print	first gear	flake tool	fleetness	florulent
fifth gear	fine rolls	first good	flakiness	fleshhood	floscular
fifth part	fine tuner	first hand	flambeaus	flesh-hook	flos ferri
fiftyfold	fin-footed	first lady	flambeaux	fleshiest	flossiest
fifty-nine	finger-dry	First Lady	flambéing	fleshings	floss silk
fightable	finger-end	first line	flame-cell	fleshless	flotation
fight back	fingerful	firstling	flameless	fleshlier	flouncing
fightback	fingering	first love	flamelike	flesh-meat	flour-bolt
fight down	fingertip	first mate	flamencos	fleshment	flouriest
fight fair	finialled	first name	flame test	fleshpots	flourishy
fig-leafed	finically	firstness	flame-trap	flesh side	flow chart
figmental	finicking	first oars	flame tree	flesh tint	flowerage
fig-parrot	finishing	first post	flame-ware	flesh-worm	flower bed
fig-pecker	finish off	first-rate	flamingly	fletching	flower-bug
figurable	Finlander	first slip	flamingos	flexility	flower-fly
figurally	Finnicize	fiscality	flammable	flexional	flowerful
figure out	finocchio	fish eagle	flammeous	flexitime	flowerily
figurette	fioritura	fisheries	flanchard	flight bag	flowering
file-shell	fioriture	fisherman	flanching	flightier	flowerpot
file snake	fir balsam	fishermen	Flandrian	flightily	flowingly
filiality	fire alarm	fishgarth	Flandrish	flight net	flow-meter
filiation	fireboard	fishiness	flannelly	flimsiest	flowmeter
filigrane	firebrand	fish-knife	flap-sight	fling down	flow sheet
filigreed	fire-break	fish louse	flap-table	fling open	flowsheet
Filipinos	firebreak	fish-plate	flap-valve	fling wide	flowstone
filler cap	fire-brick	fish-sauce	flareless	flint corn	fluctuant
filleting	firebrick	fish slice	flare-path	flintiest	fluctuate
filliping	fire coral	fish-sound	flare star	flintless	fluctuous
fillister	fire-crack	fissility	flashback	flintlock	flue-brush
filly-foal	firecrest	fist fight	flash bulb	flintwood	fluffiest
film badge	fire cross	fisticuff	flashbulb	flip chart	fluid dram
filmcraft	fire-drake	fistulate	flash burn	flippancy	fluid gram
film-going	fire drill	fistulose	flash card	flirtiest	fluidible
filminess	fire-eater	fistulous	flashcard	floatable	fluidizer
film-maker	fire-fight	fistycuff	flash-cube	float-boat	fluidness
film speed	firefight	fittingly	flashiest	floatsome	fluid vein
film stock	fireflies	fit to drop	flash lamp	flocculus	flukiness
film strip	fire-guard	five-a-side	flashless	flock-book	fluoboric
filmstrip	fireguard	five-lined	flashness	flockless	fluorated
filmy fern	firehouse	fivepence	flash over	flockmeal	fluoresce
filoplume	fire-irons	fivepenny	flash tube	floodable	fluorosis
filoselle	firelight	fixed idea	flash unit	floodgate	fluorspar

flushness	fool's mate	foreshock	formicine	fourpence	freestyle
flustered	footboard	foreshore	formolize	fourpenny	free throw
flustrate	footbrake	foresight	formosity	four-rowed	free trade
flutelike	foot-cloth	foreslack	form sheet	fourscore	free verse
flutterer	foot-fault	forespeak	formulaic	fourth day	free wheel
fluxional	footloose	forespend	formulary	four walls	freewheel
fluxmeter	footplate	forespent	formulate	four wheel	free world
fly agaric	foot-pound	forespoke	formulise	foveolate	freezable
fly-bitten	footprint	forestage	formulism	fox-hunter	freeze-dry
fly bridge	foot's pace	forestall	formulist	fractious	freeze out
fly-by-wire	footstalk	forest-bed	formulize	fraenulum	freighter
fly-cruise	footstall	forest fly	formylate	fragilely	fremdness
fly-fungus	footstone	forestful	for my part	fragility	French bed
flying-fox	footstool	forestial	for naught	fragrance	Frenchery
flying jib	foppishly	forestick	fornicate	fragrancy	French flu
fly orchid	forage cap	forest oak	for nought	frailness	French fry
fly screen	forasmuch	forestone	for-profit	frailties	Frenchify
fly stitch	for a spell	foretaste	forsythia	framboise	Frenchily
fly-strike	for a start	foreteach	fortalice	frameable	Frenchism
fly-tipper	forastero	forethink	Fortescue	frame drum	Frenchman
fly to arms	for a while	foretoken	forthcome	frameless	Frenchmen
flyweight	forbearer	foretooth	forthfare	frame work	French oak
foal-tooth	forbiddal	foreutter	forthward	framework	French pox
foaminess	forbidden	forewheel	forthwith	franchise	frequence
foamingly	forceable	forewoman	fortified	Francoist	frequency
focaccias	forceably	forewomen	fortifier	francolin	freshener
focusable	force down	foreworld	fortifies	frangible	fresh-find
focusless	force-feed	forewrite	fortitude	franglais	freshness
focussing	force-land	for fear of	fortnight	frankable	fretboard
foetation	forceless	forfeited	for toffee	frankfold	fretfully
foeticide	forcemeat	forfeiter	fortunate	frankness	friar-bird
fogginess	force-pump	forficate	forty acre	franticly	fribblish
fog signal	forcipate	forgather	forty-five	frascatis	fricassee
foil-borne	foreboder	forgeable	fortyfold	fratchety	fricative
foliation	forebrain	forgeries	forty-nine	fraternal	friending
foliature	forecabin	forgetful	forwander	fraudless	frightful
folic acid	fore-cited	forgetive	for want of	fraudsman	fright wig
foliolate	foreclose	forgetter	forwarder	fraudster	frigidity
folk-blues	forecourt	forgiving	forwardly	fraughted	frikkadel
folk dance	for effect	forgotten	fossicker	freakiest	frilliest
folkiness	forefield	forjeskit	fossilate	freak show	fringe net
folkloric	forefront	forjudger	fossildom	free agent	fripperer
folk music	foregoing	forkiness	fossilise	free bench	friskiest
folksiest	foreguess	fork lunch	fossilist	freeboard	frit-flies
folkweave	forehorse	for lack of	fossilize	free fight	frithborh
follicule	foreigner	for laughs	fossorial	free float	fritterer
following	foreignly	forlornly	fosterage	free grace	frivolity
follow out	forejudge	formalise	foul brood	free house	frivolled
food chain	fore-kamer	formalism	foul Fiend	free lance	frivoller
food cycle	foreknown	formalist	foul mouth	freelance	frivolous
food stamp	forenamed	formality	foul proof	free-liver	frizziest
foodstuff	forenight	formalize	foundling	free lunch	frock coat
food value	foreorder	formal sin	foundress	Freemason	frog-eater
fool about	forepiece	formamide	foundries	Freephone	frog-faced
fool along	foreplane	formation	foundrous	free place	frogmarch
fooleries	foreprise	formative	four-by-two	free-range	frogmouth
foolhardy	forereach	formatted	Fourcault	free sheet	frog-spawn
foolishly	forerider	form-board	four-cycle	free space	frogspawn
foolproof	foreright	form class	four-flush	free State	frog-stool
fool round	foreseize	form-genus	Four-H club	free stock	frolicked
fool's coat	foresheet	formicary	four-oared	freestone	frolicker
fool's gold	foreshine	formicate		free-style	from below

from now on	full blast	fusimotor	Galwegian	gas thread	genicular
from out of	full-blood	fusionist	gama grass	gastritis	geniculum
frondesce	full-blown	fusogenic	gamahuche	gastropod	genistein
frontager	full board	fussation	gambolled	gastrulae	genitalia
frontally	full-cream	fussiness	game-board	gastrular	genitival
front door	full dress	fustianed	game chips	gate array	Genoa cake
frontless	full drive	fustigate	game-piece	gatecrash	genocidal
front line	fullerene	fustilugs	game point	gatehouse	genophore
front page	full-faced	fustiness	game rhyme	gate-lodge	genotoxic
front room	full flood	fuzziness	gammadion	gate money	genotypic
frontsman	full-grown	gabardine	gamma plus	gate pulse	genteelly
frontward	full house	gabbiness	gamma rays	gate-stead	gentilise
frontways	full marks	gaberdine	Gammexane	gate-table	gentilism
frontwise	full pitch	gabionade	gammoning	gate valve	gentility
front yard	full point	gabionage	gandharva	gatewards	gentilize
frostbite	full-scale	gadgeteer	Gandhi cap	gathering	gentiness
frost-fish	full score	gadrooned	Gandhi-ism	gather out	gentle art
frostiest	full speed	Gaelicize	gang agley	gather way	gentleman
frostless	full steam	Gaeltacht	gangboard	gaucherie	gentlemen
frostlike	full-timer	Gaetulian	gang drill	gaudeamus	genuflect
frost-nail	fulminant	gainfully	gangliest	gaudiness	genuinely
frost-work	fulminate	gainsayer	ganglions	gaugeable	genu varum
frothiest	fulminous	gainstand	gangplank	gauleiter	geobotany
frowardly	fulsomely	galactase	gannister	gauntness	geocorona
frowsiest	fumarolic	galactose	gaolbreak	gauzelike	geodesist
frowstier	fumigator	gala dress	garbology	gauziness	geography
Fructidor	funambulo	gala night	gardenage	gavelkind	geologise
fructosan	fundament	galantine	gardenery	gavelling	geologist
fructuous	fundatrix	galenical	gardenful	Gawdelpus	geologize
frugality	fundiform	galingale	gardening	gawkiness	geomancer
frugivore	funebrial	gallabiya	gardenist	gay plague	geomantic
fruit-body	fungation	gallamine	garden pea	gay rights	geometric
fruit cake	fungicide	gallantly	garden-pot	gaze-hound	geometrid
fruitcake	fungiform	gallantry	garderobe	gazetteer	geomorphy
fruit-dove	fungology	gall-apple	garganeys	gazpachos	geoponics
fruiterer	fungosity	gallberry	gargarism	gear lever	georgette
fruit-farm	funicular	gallerian	garibaldi	gear shift	Georgiana
fruitiest	funiculus	galleried	garlandry	gearstick	georgical
fruitless	funkiness	galleries	garnished	gearwheel	geosphere
fruit loaf	funnelled	gallicise	garnishee	gee-string	geotactic
fruit tree	funnel-web	Gallicise	garnisher	Gelalaean	geotropic
fruit-wood	funniment	Gallicism	garniture	gelidness	gerfalcon
fruitwood	funniness	gallicize	garreteer	gelignite	geriatric
frumpiest	funny bone	Gallicize	garreting	gelsemine	germander
frusemide	funny-face	gallinazo	garrotter	gelsemium	germanely
frustrate	funny farm	gallingly	garrulity	gemellion	Germanify
fruticose	funny-ha-ha	gallinule	garrulous	geminally	Germanise
frying pan	furacious	Gallionic	Garryowen	geminated	Germanish
fuck about	furbisher	Gallipoli	gartering	gemmation	Germanism
fuel gauge	furcation	gallivant	gasconade	gemmology	Germanist
fuel-value	furfurous	galliwasp	gas cooker	*gemütlich*	Germanity
fugacious	furiosity	gallonage	gas-cooled	genealogy	germanium
Fulbright	furiously	gallooned	gas engine	generable	German ivy
fulfilled	furnished	gallopade	gas-fitter	generalia	Germanize
fulfiller	furnisher	galloping	gas helmet	generally	germanous
fulgently	furniture	gallstone	gasholder	generator	germarium
fulgorous	furriness	Galoisian	gas-mantle	generical	germicide
fulgurant	furtherer	Galtonian	gasometer	Genesitic	germinant
fulgurate	furtherly	galvanise	gasometry	genetical	germinate
fulgurite	further to	galvanism	gaspereau	geniality	germ layer
fulgurous	furtively	galvanist	gaspingly	genialize	germ plasm
full and by	fusillade	galvanize	gassiness	genically	gerundial

gerundive	giggliest	gladfully	globulite	go belly up	gonangium
Gesolreut	gigmanity	gladiator	globulous	go berserk	gondolier
gestation	gill cleft	gladiolus	glocalize	go-between	gone goose
gestative	gill cover	Gladstone	glochidia	gobletful	gongerine
gestatory	gill-flirt	glaikitly	glomerate	goblinize	gongorism
get abroad	gill plate	glaireous	glomerule	gobstruck	gongorist
get across	gill pouch	glamorize	glomeruli	Goclenian	goniatite
get around	gill raker	glamorous	gloomiest	go counter	gonococci
get-at-able	gilravage	glance ore	gloriette	go current	gonophore
get back at	Gilsonite	glandered	glorified	God-a-mercy	gonotheca
get better	gilt-edged	glandlike	glorifier	goddamned	go nowhere
get down to	gilt spurs	glandular	glorifies	God defend	gonozooid
get ground	gimballed	glareless	glory-hole	go decimal	go nuclear
get hold of	gimcracky	glariness	glory-tree	godemiche	gonyaulax
get in good	gimlet eye	glaringly	glossator	godfather	good buddy
get theirs	gimmer-hog	glass ball	glossiest	God forbid	good cause
get the nod	gimmickry	glass case	glossitis	God help me	good cheer
get the pip	gingerade	glass crab	gloss over	godliness	good fairy
get the rap	ginger ale	glass-dust	glost-fire	godmother	good faith
get the run	ginger-nob	glassener	glost oven	godparent	good grief
get to know	ginger nut	glassfuls	glottalic	God's blood	goodiness
get wind of	ginger-pop	glass-gall	gloveless	God's earth	goodliest
geyserite	ginglymus	glassiest	gloveress	God's penny	good liver
ghastlier	ginormous	glassless	glowingly	God's truth	good looks
ghastlily	gin-palace	glasslike	glow-light	Godwinian	good loser
ghazeeyeh	gin-soaked	glassware	gloze over	Godwinism	good money
ghettoise	giraffine	glass wool	glozingly	go eyes out	good night
ghettoize	giraffoid	glass work	gluconate	go forward	goodnight
ghost crab	girandole	glasswort	glucoside	goggle-box	good on you
ghosthood	girl guide	glaucodot	glueyness	goggle-eye	good sense
ghostless	Girl Guide	glaziness	glutamate	go haywire	good store
ghostlier	girlishly	gleamless	glutamine	going away	good stuff
ghostlike	girl scout	gleanings	glutinize	going-over	good thing
ghostlily	Girl Scout	glebe-land	glutinous	go it alone	good-timer
ghost moth	Girondism	gleditsia	glyceride	go it blind	good times
ghostship	Girondist	gleefully	glycerine	go-karting	good value
ghost town	Girtonian	glengarry	glycerole	goldarned	goodwives
ghost word	gitterner	Glenlivet	glycocoll	gold brick	good works
giant-cell	glenoidal	glycollic	goldbrick	goody-good
giant clam	give a back	glide bomb	glycolyse	goldcrest	gooeyness
gianthood	give about	glide into	Glyconean	golden age	go off well
giant-like	give again	glideless	glycoside	golden boy	goofiness
giantship	give a hand	glide path	glyoxylic	golden-eye	goofy foot
giant toad	give a miss	glide-twin	glyptical	goldeneye	go one's way
gibbed cat	give beans	glidingly	gnat-eater	golden key	goopiness
gibberish	give birth	glint-lake	gnathonic	golden rod	goosander
gibberose	give chase	glint-line	gnat's piss	goldenrod	goose-fair
gibbeting	give ear to	glissader	gnawingly	gold-fever	goosefoot
Gibbonian	give forth	glissandi	gneissoid	goldfield	goose-girl
gibbosity	give guard	glissando	gneissose	goldfinch	gooseherd
gibbously	give it a go	glitterer	gnomology	goldfinny	gooselike
Gibeonite	give law to	glitziest	gnomonics	gold medal	goose-neck
giblet pie	give mouth	globalise	gnostical	gold plate	goose-skin
Gibraltar	given name	globalism	Goa butter	goldsinny	goose-step
giddiness	givenness	globalist	go against	goldsmith	goosiness
gift-horse	giving-set	globalize	goal-mouth	Gold Stick	go over big
gift token	glabellae	globe-fish	goalmouth	golf links	go pillion
gigametre	glabellar	globelike	Goa powder	golf widow	gorblimey
gigantean	glacially	globe-trot	goatishly	Golgi body	gorbuscha
gigantise	glaciated	globosely	goat's foot	goliardic	gorgeaunt
gigantism	glaciered	globoside	go bananas	golloping	gorgonian
gigantize	glacieret	gladdener	globosity	go begging	gomphosis	gorgonise

gorgonize	granaries	gratingly	green lane	groomship	guard rail
goshawful	grandaddy	gratitude	green leek	groomsman	guard ring
gospelize	grand-aunt	gratulant	greenless	grooviest	guardroom
gospeller	grand coup	gratulate	greenling	gropingly	guardship
gossamery	grand duke	gravadlax	greenmail	grosgrain	guardsman
gossipdom	grandeval	gravamens	green meat	gros point	guardsmen
gossiping	grandiose	gravamina	greenness	grossness	guard's van
gossipred	grand jeté	graveless	green road	grossular	Guernseys
Gothamite	grand jury	gravelish	green room	grotesque	guerrilla
go the pace	grand lama	gravelled	greensand	grottiest	guessable
go the vole	grandmama	graveller	greens fee	grouch bag	guess-rope
Gothicise	grandness	gravel-pit	greensick	grouchier	guess-warp
Gothicism	grandpapa	graveness	green spot	grouchily	guess work
Gothicist	Grand Prix	graveside	greenweed	groundage	guesswork
Gothicize	grandsire	grave-trap	Greenwell	ground ash	guest beer
go through	grand slam	graveward	Greenwich	groundhog	guestless
go to court	grand tour	graveyard	greenwood	ground-ice	guest list
go to cuffs	graniform	gravidity	greenyard	grounding	guest-rope
go to earth	granitize	gravitate	greeshoch	ground ivy	guestship
go to glory	granitoid	gravitino	gregarian	groundnut	guestwise
go to grass	granivore	gravy boat	gregarine	groundout	Guevarism
go to press	granny-sit	graybeard	Gregorian	groundsel	Guevarist
go to roost	grantable	graywacke	Grenadian	groupment	guidebook
go to scale	grant bail	grazeable	grenadier	group rate	guideless
go to sleep	granulate	grease cup	grenadine	groupware	guideline
go to smash	granulite	grease gun	gressible	group work	guidepost
go to waste	granuloma	greasiest	grevillea	groveless	guide rope
gourdfuls	granulose	great-aunt	greybeard	grovelled	Guidonian
goutiness	granulous	Great Bear	grey birch	groveller	guildable
gouty-stem	grapelike	greatcoat	grey cells	growingly	guildhall
governess	Grape-Nuts	Great Dane	grey drake	grownness	guildship
go walkies	grape-shot	great deal	Grey Friar	grow out of	guildsman
go whistle	grapeshot	Great Fire	grey goose	grubbiest	guildsmen
go without	grape tree	great game	grey groat	grub-screw	guileless
gowpenful	grapevine	great-line	greyhound	grubstake	guillaume
Goyaesque	graphemic	greatness	grey nurse	grudgeful	guillemot
grabbable	graphical	Great Seal	grey scale	gruelling	guilloche
graceless	graphited	great ship	grey trout	gruffness	guiltiest
grace note	graphitic	great skua	greywacke	grumbling	guiltless
grace-wife	grappling	Great Week	grey whale	grumpiest	Guinea-hen
gracility	graspable	great year	griefless	Grundyish	Guineaman
gradation	graspless	greediest	grievance	Grundyism	guinea pig
gradatory	grass bird	Greek fire	grihastha	Grundyite	guitarist
grade line	grass carp	Greek fret	grill room	grunerite	Gujaratis
Gradgrind	grasserie	Greek gift	grimalkin	gruntling	Gulf State
gradience	grass frog	Greekless	griminess	guacamole	gulleries
gradually	grass hook	Greekling	Grimm's Law	guacharos	gulleting
graduated	grassiest	Greekness	grindable	guacomole	gully-hole
graduator	grassland	Greek to me	gripe's egg	Guadalupe	gulpingly
Grahamism	grassless	green alga	gripingly	guanidine	gum acacia
Grahamite	grasslike	greenback	grisaille	guanidino	gum arabic
grain-gold	grass moth	green bean	grisliest	guanosine	gumbo filé
grainiest	grass-plat	green belt	grist-mill	guarantee	gum dragon
grainless	grass poly	green card	grit-blast	guarantor	gum mastic
grain side	grassquit	green crop	gritstone	guardable	gummatous
graithing	grass tree	Greeneian	grittiest	guard band	gumminess
gram-force	grass-wren	green-eyed	grizzlier	guard-boat	gumptious
graminous	graticule	greenfeed	grocerdom	guard-book	gum-shield
grammatic	gratified	greengage	groceries	guard cell	gumshield
grampuses	gratifier	greenhead	grocering	guardedly	gum storax
Gram stain	gratifies	greenhorn	groggiest	guard hair	gumsucker
Granadine	gratinéed	Greenland	groomless	guardless	gun cotton

gun-lascar	haematoid	half-plane	handiwork	hard error	hastiness
Gunn diode	haematoma	half-plate	handlebar	hard graft	hatchback
gunpowder	haemocoel	half-price	hand-organ	hard-grass	hatch-boat
gun-runner	haemogram	half-rhyme	hand-press	hardheads	hatchling
gunrunner	haemolyse	half-round	handprint	hard-heart	hatchment
gunwale to	haemostat	half-sheet	hand round	hardiesse	hatefully
gurgitate	Haflinger	half-shell	hands down	hardihead	hatha yoga
Gurneyite	Haggadist	half-stuff	handshake	hardihood	hatha yogi
gurry sore	haggardly	half-title	handsomer	hardiment	hatted kit
gushiness	haggishly	half-track	handspaik	hardiness	haughtier
gushingly	hagiarchy	half-truth	handspike	hard-liner	haughtily
gustation	hagiology	half-value	handspoke	hardliner	Hau-hauism
gustative	hag-ridden	half-verse	hand-staff	hard lines	haulabout
gustatory	hagridden	half-world	handstand	hardly any	haunching
gustfully	hailstone	halieutic	hand-towel	hard money	haustella
gustiness	hailstorm	halitosis	handwrite	hard-nosed	*haut monde*
gut-bucket	hairbrush	halituous	handygrip	hard-paste	have a bath
gutlessly	haircloth	hall house	handy-work	hard sauce	have a care
gutsiness	hair crack	hallockit	hang about	hardshell	have a go at
guttation	hairdress	Hallow day	hang a jury	hardstone	have a leak
guttering	hairdrier	Hallowe'en	hang a left	hard stuff	have a mind
guttiform	hairdryer	hall-stand	hangarage	hard to get	have a pull
Guy Fawkes	hair-grass	hallstand	hangers-on	hard wheat	have a want
gymnasial	hairiness	Hallstatt	hang-glide	hard-wired	have a word
gymnasium	hairpiece	hall table	hang heavy	hare-brain	have got to
gymnastic	hair-point	halluciné	hang it all	hare's-foot	have had it
gynaeceum	hair shirt	halobiont	hang loose	hare's-tail	have ideas
gynaecoid	hair-sieve	halogenic	hang one on	hariolate	have in tow
gynobasic	hair-slide	halophile	hankering	Harlemese	have it out
gynocracy	hair-space	halophyte	Hanseatic	Harlemite	havenless
gynoecium	hairspray	halothane	Hanse town	harlequin	haver-cake
gynophore	hairstyle	halter top	hansom cab	harmaline	have right
Gypsyhood	hairy frog	haltingly	ha'pennies	harmattan	haversack
gypsy moth	halalling	hamadryad	haphazard	harmfully	Haversian
gypsy rose	halberded	hamadryas	haphtarah	harmonial	haversine
gypsywort	half-adder	hamamelis	haplessly	harmonica	have shame
gyrectomy	half an eye	hamartoma	haplology	harmonies	have wired
gyrfalcon	half-baked	Hamathite	haplontic	harmonise	have words
gyromancy	half-blood	hamburger	happening	harmonist	havocking
gyro-pilot	half board	hamfatter	happi-coat	harmonium	Hawcubite
gyropilot	half-bound	ham-fisted	happiness	harmonize	hawk-eagle
gyroplane	half-breed	ham-handed	happy days	harmotome	hawk-faced
gyroscope	half-caste	Hamletish	happy dust	harnessed	hawk-nosed
haberdash	half-court	Hamletism	happy hour	harnesser	hawksbill
habergeon	half-crown	Hamletize	happy land	harpooner	hawse-full
habitable	half-dozen	hammering	happy pair	harp-shell	hawse-hole
habitably	half-dress	hammerman	happy pill	harquebus	hawse-pipe
habitacle	half-eagle	hammer out	happy ship	harrateen	hawse-plug
habitancy	half-faced	hammer-toe	haranguer	Harrogate	hay asthma
habituate	half-flood	Hampshire	harbinger	Harrovian	haymaking
hacendado	half-frame	Hampstead	harborage	harrowing	hay-scales
hackamore	half-groat	hamstring	harbourer	harshness	hazardous
hackberry	half-hardy	hamstrung	Hardanger	Hartleian	hazard pay
hackerdom	half-heard	Hanbalite	hardboard	hartshorn	hazelwort
hackneyed	half hitch	handbasin	hard-bound	haruspicy	headboard
hack watch	half-James	handbrake	hard bread	harvester	head-chief
had better	half-light	handclasp	hard chine	harveyize	head-cloth
had rather	half-litre	handcraft	hard cover	Hashemite	headcount
Hadrianic	half-miler	hand cream	hardcover	hash-house	head-court
hadrosaur	half-naked	Handelian	hardening	Hashimoto	head-dress
haecceity	half-noble	handglass	harden off	Hasmonean	headdress
haematite	halfpenny	handiness	Harderian	hastilude	head first

headiness	Hebraical	hemstitch	heroinism	high-class	historify
headlight	Hebrewdom	hen-and-egg	heronries	High Court	historize
headliner	Hebrewess	hendiadys	heronshaw	High Dutch	hit and run
headlongs	Hebrewism	henpecked	heroology	high enema	hit a nerve
head louse	Hebrician	Henrician	herriment	higher-ups	Hitchcock
head-money	Hebridean	Henrietta	hesitance	high-flier	hitch-hike
headphone	heckberry	Henry Clay	hesitancy	high-flown	hitchhike
head-piece	hecogenin	Henry's law	hesitater	high-flyer	hit for six
headpiece	hectarage	hen's fruit	Hesperian	high-grade	Hitlerian
headscarf	hectogram	Hentenian	hesperiid	high heels	Hitlerism
headstall	hedge-bill	hepatical	hessonite	high jinks	Hitlerist
head start	hedge-bird	hepatitis	hesternal	high-keyed	Hitlerite
head-stave	hedgebote	heptaglot	Hesychast	high-level	hit-or-miss
headstock	hedgeless	heptanoic	hetaerism	highlight	hit parade
headstone	hedge-side	heptarchy	hetairism	high point	hit the hay
head voice	hedge-wood	Heracleid	heterodox	high-speed	hit wicket
headwards	hedgingly	heracleum	heteronym	high table	Hizbollah
headwater	hedrumite	heraldist	heteropod	high-toned	hoar frost
healingly	hedychium	herbalism	heterosis	high water	hoarhound
healthful	heedfully	herbalist	heterotic	high words	hoariness
healthier	heel-piece	herbalize	heuristic	hilarious	hoarstone
healthily	heel-plate	herbarise	hexacanth	hill-billy	hob-and-nob
hearkener	heffalump	herbarist	hexachord	hillbilly	Hobbesian
heartache	heftiness	herbarium	hexagonal	hill climb	hobgoblin
heartbeat	hegemonic	herbarize	hexahedra	hilliness	hobnailed
heartburn	heinously	herb-grace	hexameric	Himalayan	hobnobbed
heartfelt	heir-at-law	herbicide	hexameron	Himyarite	hobohemia
hearthrug	heliborne	herbivore	hexameter	hindberry	Hobthrush
hearth-tax	helically	herbivory	hexaploid	hindbrain	hockeyist
heartiest	helictite	herborise	hexastich	hinder end	Hock-money
heartland	heliogram	herborist	hexastyle	Hindooism	hocussing
heartless	heliostat	herborize	Hexateuch	hindrance	hodiernal
heartlike	heliotype	herb Paris	hexatomic	hindsight	hodmandod
heart-lung	heliozoan	herb water	hexatonic	hingeless	hodograph
heart-moth	hell-broth	hercogamy	hexestrol	hingewise	hodometer
heart-root	hell-diver	Herculean	hexuronic	hip girdle	hodoscope
heartsick	hellebore	Hercynian	hey presto	hip-length	hogbacked
heartsome	Hellenian	hercynite	Hezbollah	hippiedom	hog-badger
heartsore	Hellenise	herderite	hibakusha	hippocamp	hoggishly
heartwise	Hellenism	herd-grass	hibernate	hip pocket	hog peanut
heartwood	Hellenist	hereabout	Hibernian	hippocras	hog-sucker
heart-worm	Hellenize	hereafter	Hibernize	hippodame	hog-trough
heat death	hell-fired	here below	hiccuping	hippology	hohlflute
heath-bell	hell-gates	hereright	hiccup-nut	hippurite	hoi polloi
heath-bird	hell-hound	heretical	hickories	hired girl	hoist sail
heath-cock	hellishly	hereunder	hiddenite	hirsutism	hokeyness
heathenly	hell to pay	here we are	hidebound	hirundine	holandric
heathenry	Helmholtz	heritable	hideosity	hispanise	holarctic
heathered	helophyte	heritably	hideously	Hispanism	Holarctic
heath-fowl	helpfully	heritance	hidey-hole	Hispanist	hold aloof
heathland	Helvetian	heritress	Hieracite	hispanize	hold a plea
heathlike	hem and haw	herkogamy	hieracium	hispidity	hold at bay
heatproof	hemicycle	hermeneut	hierarchy	hissingly	hold cheap
heat-treat	hemihedry	hermetism	hieratite	Histadrut	hold court
heave down	hemiopsia	hermetist	hierodule	histamine	holderbat
heaviness	hemipenis	hermitage	hierogamy	histidine	hold forth
heavisome	hemiplegy	hermitess	hierogram	histogeny	hold hands
heavy-duty	Hemiptera	Hermitian	hierology	histogram	hold in fee
heavy spar	hemispasm	hermitish	high altar	histology	hold out on
heavy type	hemistich	hermitism	highboard	historian	hold pleas
hebdomade	hemitrope	herniated	high-brown	historied	hold serve
hebdomary	hemitropy	heroic age	high chair	histories	hold short

hold water	homiliary	hormogone	hot bottle	hugeously	hybridity
hole-in-one	homoclime	hormonize	hot button	hula skirt	hybridize
hole-proof	homocline	horned owl	hot chisel	hum and haw	hybridoma
holidayer	homodimer	horniness	Hotchkiss	humanhood	hybridous
holinight	homoeobox	horn poppy	hot-dipped	humanizer	hybrid tea
Hollander	homoeosis	horn-snake	hotdogged	humankind	hydantoin
Hollerith	homoeotic	hornstone	hotdogger	humanness	hydathode
holloware	homo faber	hornwrack	hot-headed	human race	hydraemia
holly blue	homogamic	horologer	hotheaded	human wave	hydraemic
holly fern	homograft	horologic	hot potato	humble-bee	hydraform
hollyhock	homograph	horometry	hot-rodder	humbugged	hydrangea
Hollywood	homologue	horoscope	hot shower	humbugger	hydrastis
Holmesian	homolysis	horoscopy	hot spring	humdinger	hydratase
holoaxial	homolytic	horridity	Hottentot	humectant	hydration
holocaine	homomorph	horrified	hound-fish	humectate	hydratuba
holocaust	homonymic	horrifies	hour-angle	humective	hydraulic
holocrine	homophile	horseback	hourglass	humic acid	hydraulis
holograph	homophobe	horse-balm	houseboat	humic coal	hydraulus
Holophane	homophone	horsebane	housebote	humidness	hydrazide
holophote	homophony	horsebean	house-burn	humiliate	hydrazine
holophyte	homoplasy	horse-boat	house call	hummeller	hydrazoic
holostean	homopolar	horse-colt	housecarl	hummingly	hydrazone
holotypic	homospory	horse-comb	housecoat	hummocked	hydriform
holy basil	homostyly	horse fair	house-flag	humongous	hydriodic
holy bread	homotherm	horse-fish	housefuls	humorsome	hydrocast
holy cross	homotopic	horse-foal	house-girl	hump bluey	hydrocele
holy Cross	homousian	horse-gear	household	humpiness	hydrocoel
Holy Ghost	homuncule	horsehair	house-hunt	hump speed	hydrocool
Holy Grail	homunculi	horse-head	housekeep	humungous	hydrofoil
holy grass	honey-bear	horsehide	housekept	hunchback	hydroform
holy laugh	honey-bird	horse-hoer	house-lamb	hundredal	hydrofuge
holy place	honeycomb	horse-hoof	houseleek	hundreder	hydrolase
holy souls	honey drop	horseless	houseless	hundredor	hydrolise
holystone	honey-flow	horselike	houseling	hundredth	hydrolith
holy water	honeyless	horse-load	housemaid	Hungarian	hydrology
Holy Write	honeymoon	horse-meat	housemate	hungriest	hydrolube
homacanth	honeysuck	horse-mill	houseroom	hunkerish	hydrolyse
home-baked	honeywort	horsemint	housewife	hunkerism	hydrolyst
homebuyer	honky-tonk	horse-nail	housework	hunky-dory	hydrolyze
homefolks	honorable	horseplay	houstonia	hunterman	hydronium
home-grown	honoraria	horse-plum	houyhnhnm	hurricane	hydronymy
home guard	honorific	horse-pond	hoverport	hurriedly	hydropath
Home Guard	honorless	horse race	howardite	hurry call	hydrophil
home-leave	Hoochinoo	horse's ass	how are you	hurtfully	hydroptic
homeliest	hood-mould	horse shit	how goes it	husbander	hydrosere
home-maker	hoodooism	horse-shoe	howlingly	husbandly	hydrosome
home movie	hoof stick	horseshoe	how's about	husbandom	hydrostat
homeopath	Hooke's law	horsetail	how say you	husbandry	hydrovane
homeostat	hook gauge	horsewhip	howsoever	hushfully	hydrowire
home-owner	hook-nosed	horsiness	howtowdie	hush money	hydroxide
homeowner	hoop skirt	hortation	hoydenish	hush-puppy	hydrozoan
home plate	hoop-snake	hortative	hübnerite	huskiness	hydrozoic
home range	hope chest	hortatory	hubristic	Hussitism	hydrozoon
homestall	hopefully	hortensia	huckaback	hustle-cap	hygiastic
homestead	hop-garden	hospitage	huckstery	hut-circle	hygienics
homestyle	hopper-car	hospitium	Hudson Bay	Hutterian	hygienist
home trade	hop-picker	hosteller	Hudsonian	Hutterite	hygrology
home truth	hop-pillow	hostilely	hue and cry	Huttonian	hygrostat
homewards	hopscotch	hostilise	huegelite	Huygenian	hylobatid
homeyness	hop the wag	hostility	huffiness	hybridise	hylozoism
homicidal	hordeolum	hostilize	huffingly	hybridism	hylozoist
homiletic	horehound	hot and hot	huffishly	hybridist	Hymettian

hymnaries	hypotonus	I know what	immensity	importune	incensory
hymnodies	hypsodont	Ilchester	immersion	imposable	incentive
hymnodist	Hyrcanian	ileectomy	immigrant	impostume	inception
hymnology	hysteroid	ileostomy	immigrate	imposture	inceptive
hyoid arch	iatrogeny	iliac vein	imminence	impotable	incessant
hyoid bone	Ibicencan	I like that	imminency	impotence	incidence
hyolithid	ibotenate	ill at ease	immission	impotency	incipient
hypacusis	ibuprofen	Illawarra	immixture	impounder	inciteful
hypakusis	ice-boater	ill-boding	immodesty	imprecate	inclement
hypallage	ice bucket	ill effect	immolator	imprecise	inclining
hypaspist	iced lolly	illegally	immorally	impressed	inclosure
hyperacid	ice-flower	illegible	immovable	imprinter	include in
hyperbola	ice hockey	illegibly	immovably	improbity	including
hyperbole	Icelander	ill-formed	immundity	impromptu	inclusion
hypercube	Icelandic	ill-gotten	immunizer	improving	inclusive
hyperemia	ice-master	ill health	immunogen	improvise	inclusory
hyperfine	ice-skater	ill humour	immusical	imprudent	incognita
hyperform	ichneumon	illiberal	immutable	impsonite	incognito
hypergamy	ichnology	illicitly	immutably	impudence	in-college
hypericum	ichthyoid	illimited	impaction	impudency	income tax
hyperonic	iconicity	Illinoian	impactite	impulsion	incommode
hyperopia	iconodule	ill-judged	impactive	impulsive	incompact
hyperopic	iconology	ill nature	impanated	impulsory	in company
hypertely	iconostas	illogical	impanator	impunible	incomplex
hypertext	icterical	ill-omened	impartial	impunibly	in concert
hyperweak	idealizer	ill-placed	impartite	impuritan	incondite
hypethral	ideal type	ill repute	impassion	imputable	in context
hyphenate	idée reçue	ill-suited	impassive	in a bad way	in control
hyphenism	identical	ill-taught	impatiens	in a big way	incorpsed
hyphenize	identikit	ill temper	impatient	inability	incorrect
hypinosis	Identikit	ill-thewed	impayable	in a canter	incorrupt
hypnoidal	ideograph	illuminer	impeacher	inactuate	in council
hypnology	ideologue	ill-willer	impeccant	in advance	in-country
hypnotise	ideomotor	ill-wisher	impedance	in a fright	increaser
hypnotism	ideophone	imageable	impedient	in a manner	increment
hypnotist	ideoplasm	imageless	impellent	in a moment	incrimson
hypnotize	idioblast	image tube	impelling	inamorata	incubator
hypobaric	idiograph	imaginary	impendent	inamorate	inculcate
hypoblast	idiolalia	imagining	impending	inamorato	inculpate
hypocaust	idiomatic	imaginist	imperator	inaneness	incumbent
hypoconid	idiopathy	imagistic	imperfect	inanimate	incunable
hypocotyl	idiophone	imbalance	imperious	inanities	incurable
hypocrise	idioplasm	imbecilic	impetrate	inanition	incurably
hypocrisy	idiot card	I'm blessed	impetuous	in any case	incurious
hypocrite	idiotical	imblossom	impicture	in a pelter	incurrent
hypoderma	idioticon	imbrangle	impieties	inaptness	incurring
hypogaeal	idiotypic	imbreathe	impinging	in arrears	incursion
hypogenic	idle wheel	imbricate	impiously	in a swivet	incursive
hypogeous	idolatric	imbroglio	impiteous	inaudible	incurvate
hypomania	idrialite	imbuement	implanter	inaudibly	indagator
hypomanic	if and when	imidazole	implement	inaugural	indecency
hypomorph	if he's a day	imino acid	impletion	in ballast	indecorum
hyponasty	ifs and ans	imitation	impliable	in between	in default
hypoploid	if you like	imitative	implicans	in blossom	in defence
hyporchem	ignitable	imitatrix	implicate	inbreathe	indelible
hyposarca	ignitible	immanacle	implicity	inbringer	indelibly
hypostome	ignoblest	immanence	impliedly	in cahoots	indemnify
hypostyle	ignorable	immanency	implosion	incapable	indemnity
hypotaxis	ignoramus	immediacy	implosive	incapably	indenting
hypotheca	ignorance	immediate	impluvium	incarnate	indention
hypotonia	ignorancy	Immelmann	impolitic	incaution	indenture
hypotonic	iguanodon	immensely	important	incendive	in despair

indexable	inerrable	infuriate	innocence	insetting	integrism
indexible	inerrancy	infusable	innocency	in several	integrist
indexical	inerratic	infusible	innocuity	inshallah	integrity
indexless	inertness	infusoria	innocuous	inshining	intellect
index-link	inerudite	in general	in no sense	in shivers	Intelpost
indialite	in essence	ingenious	innovator	inshore of	intendant
Indian cup	I never did	ingenuity	innoxious	inside job	intending
Indian fig	inevident	ingenuous	innuendos	inside out	intensate
Indianian	inexactly	ingestion	inoculant	insidious	intensely
Indian ink	inexpiate	ingestive	inoculate	insighted	intensest
Indianise	in extenso	inglenook	inoculist	in sight of	intensify
Indianism	inextinct	ingleside	inodorous	in silence	intension
Indianist	in extreme	ingliding	in one word	insincere	intensity
Indianize	infalling	ingluvial	inorderly	insinking	intensive
Indian red	infancies	ingluvies	in order to	insinuant	intention
Indian tea	infanteer	ingot iron	inorganic	insinuate	intentive
indicator	infantile	ingrained	inosinate	insipidly	inter alia
indicavit	infantine	ingrowing	inotropic	insipient	interbank
indicible	infantize	inhabited	in outline	insistent	intercede
indiction	infarcted	inhabiter	in passing	insistive	intercept
indigenal	in fashion	inhalator	in-patient	in so far as	intercity
indigence	infatuate	in harmony	in peril of	insolence	InterCity
indigency	infection	inharmony	in place of	insolency	intercool
indignant	infective	in harness	in point of	insoluble	intercrop
indignity	inferable	inherence	inpouring	insolubly	interdeal
indigotic	inferably	inherency	in private	insolvent	interdict
indigotin	inference	inherited	in process	insomniac	interdine
indirubin	inferible	inheritor	in profile	inspanned	interface
in disgust	inferring	inhibited	inputting	inspector	interfere
indispose	infertile	inhibiter	in quest of	inspirate	interfile
in dispute	infestive	inhibitor	inquietly	inspiring	inter-firm
individua	infidelic	in high gig	inquiline	in spirits	interflow
Indo-Aryan	infielder	inhumanly	inquinate	in spite of	interfold
indolence	in-fighter	in ill part	inquiries	installed	interfuse
Indophile	infighter	initially	inquiring	installer	intergrow
indraught	infigured	initiated	inquorate	instanter	interject
inducible	infilling	initiator	in reality	instantly	interknit
inductile	infinitum	injection	in reserve	instigate	interknot
induction	infirmary	injective	in right of	instilled	interlace
inductive	infirmity	in jig time	inrolling	instiller	interlaid
inductory	inflation	injurious	inrunning	institute	interlard
in due form	inflected	injustice	inruption	insuavity	interleaf
indulgent	inflexion	inland ice	inrushing	insuccess	interline
indulging	inflicter	inlandish	in saltire	insuffice	interlink
indumenta	inflictor	inland sea	insatiate	insularly	interlock
indurable	inflowing	in leaguer	insatiety	insulator	interlope
indusiate	influence	in-leakage	inscience	insulsity	interlude
indweller	influenza	inlet pipe	inscriber	insultant	interlune
in earnest	influxion	in light of	insecable	insulting	intermedi
inebriant	infolding	in line for	in secrecy	in support	interment
inebriate	infomania	in low keep	insectary	insurable	intermesh
inebriety	informant	in measure	insectile	insurance	intermine
inebrious	informity	in-migrant	insection	insurgent	intermont
in echelon	infortune	inner city	insectual	insurrect	in terms of
in eclipse	infractor	innermore	inselberg	in-swinger	internist
ineffable	infradian	innermost	insensate	inswinger	internode
ineffably	in fraud of	innerness	insequent	intaglios	interpage
inelastic	infringer	inner tube	inserting	in tatters	interplay
inelegant	in front of	innervate	insertion	integrand	interpole
in epitome	in full cry	innholder	insertive	integrant	interpose
ineptness	in full rig	inningses	in-service	integraph	interpret
inequable	infuriant	innkeeper	in session	integrate	interring

interrupt	intrinsic	ionogenic	Islamitic	isotypism	jacutinga
interseam	introduce	ionophore	island arc	isoxazole	jadedness
intersect	introject	ionosonde	island-hop	Israelite	jade-green
intersole	in trouble	ionotropy	islandman	issueless	jade-stone
Intertype	introvert	ion rocket	islomania	is the case	jaguarete
intervale	intrusion	ion source	Ismaelism	isthmuses	jailbreak
intervein	intrusive	*ipse dixit*	Ismaelite	itabirite	jaileress
intervene	intuition	*ipso facto*	Ismailian	itacistic	jail fever
intervent	intuitive	irascible	Ismailite	itaconate	jailhouse
intervert	intumesce	irascibly	isoallele	Italianly	jalapeños
interview	inturning	irateness	isobathic	italicise	jalousied
interweft	in two twos	iridocyte	isocercal	Italicism	jamabundi
interwind	Inuktitut	iridology	isochrony	italicize	jambalaya
interwork	inunction	iridotomy	isocitric	it beats me	jam-packed
interwove	inundatal	irisation	isoclinal	itchiness	janissary
intestacy	inurement	Irish bull	isoclinic	it depends	janitress
intestate	inurnment	Irish deer	isocratic	iteration	Jansenism
intestine	inusitate	Irish harp	isocrymal	iterative	Jansenist
in that way	inutility	Irish lace	isocyanic	itineracy	Januaries
in the buff	invadable	Irish moss	isoenzyme	itinerant	Japanesey
in the cart	invalided	Irishness	isogamete	itinerary	japanning
in the club	invalidly	Irish stew	isogamous	itinerate	Japan rose
in the dark	invariant	irksomely	isogeneic	itsy-bitsy	jargonaut
in the dice	invective	iron-bound	isogenous	itty-bitty	jargoneer
in the dock	inveigher	iron chink	isohaline	ivory-bill	jargonise
in the dust	inveigler	iron Chink	isohydric	ivory gate	jargonish
in the hole	invention	Iron Cross	isohyetal	ivory gull	jargonist
in the know	inventive	Iron Guard	isoimmune	ivory-like	jargonize
in the leaf	inventory	iron horse	isolating	ivory plum	jarringly
in the lump	inventrix	iron-mould	isolation	ivorytype	jarvey-car
in the main	Inverness	iron paper	isolative	ivorywood	jasperize
in the mass	inversely	Ironsides	isolectic	Ivy League	jasperoid
in the milk	inversion	ironsmith	isologous	ivy-leaved	jaundiced
in the mire	inversive	ironstone	isomerase	izimbongi	jauntiest
in the mood	invertant	ironworks	isomeride	jaborandi	jaw clutch
in the pink	invertase	Iroquoian	isomerise	jacaranda	jaw-fallen
in the rear	invertend	irradiant	isomerism	Jack-a-Lent	jay-hawker
in the road	investure	irradiate	isomerize	Jack-block	jaywalker
in the shit	invidious	irreality	isomerous	jack-chain	jazziness
in the soup	inviolacy	irregular	isometric	jacketing	jealously
in the suds	inviolate	irreption	isoniazid	Jack Frost	jeannette
in the swim	inviscate	irrigable	isooctane	jackfruit	jeeringly
in the team	invisible	irrigator	isopachic	Jack Ketch	Jelalaean
in the vein	invisibly	irriguous	isophenal	jackknife	jellified
in the wild	invitress	irritable	isophonic	Jack-light	jellifies
in the wind	invocable	irritably	isophotal	Jack Napes	jelly baby
in the yolk	involucel	irritancy	isophotic	jack plane	jelly bean
in thought	involucra	irritated	isoplasty	Jack plane	jellyfish
in token of	involucre	irritator	isopodous	Jack-screw	jelly-like
intonable	involuted	irrumator	isopolity	Jack shaft	jelly roll
intonator	in witness	irruption	isopropyl	Jack-sharp	Jennerian
intorsion	inworking	irruptive	isopycnal	jack snipe	jenneting
Intourist	inwreathe	Irvingism	isopycnic	jacksnipe	jenny-wren
in-transit	in writing	Irvingite	isorhythm	jackstaff	jequirity
intra-oral	inwrought	isagogics	isosceles	jackstone	jerboa-rat
in trellis	iodimetry	isallobar	isosmotic	jackstraw	jerkiness
intricacy	iodinized	ischaemia	isostatic	Jack-towel	jerkingly
intricate	iodometry	ischaemic	isosteric	Jacobinic	jerkwater
intrigant	iodophile	ischiadic	isotactic	jacopever	jerry-shop
intrigued	ion engine	ischiatic	isotheral	jacquerie	Jerseyman
intriguer	ionically	Isidorian	isotopism	jactation	Jersey tea
intrigues	ionizable	isinglass	isotropic	jaculator	Jerusalem

jessamine	jointedly	Julianist	Kaiserism	kennelled	killingly
jestingly	jointless	julienned	Kaiserist	Kensitism	kill ratio
Jesuitess	jointress	Juliet cap	kakemonos	Kensitite	kiln-dried
Jesuitise	joint-rule	jumboizer	kakkerlak	Kenticism	kiln-dries
Jesuitism	jointured	jumbo-size	kakotopia	kentledge	Kilner jar
Jesuitize	jointweed	jumby-bead	kalanchoe	Kenyanize	kilocycle
Jesus wept	jointworm	jumby-bean	kallitype	Keplerian	kilohertz
jetavator	joistless	jumby-bird	kalsilite	keratitis	kilojoule
jet engine	jokesmith	jumby-tree	kalsomine	keratosis	kilolitre
jet-lagged	jolleying	jumentous	kamachili	keratotic	kilometre
jet-setter	jollified	jump-about	kamagraph	kerb-crawl	kilotonne
jet stream	jollifies	jump blues	Kama Sutra	kerb drill	Kimeridge
Jew-baiter	jolliment	jumper ant	Kamchadal	kerbstone	kindliest
jewel-fish	jolliness	jumperism	Kamilaroi	kerfuffle	kinematic
jewellery	jollities	jumpiness	kanamycin	Kerguelen	kinescope
jewelling	jollopped	jumpingly	kankerbos	kermes oak	king cobra
jewel-weed	jolly boat	jump salty	kaolinise	kernelled	kingcraft
Jew-lizard	jolly-tail	jump spark	kaolinite	Kerry blue	king-devil
Jew's apple	joltiness	jump-start	kaolinize	ketogenic	kingdomed
Jews' stone	joltingly	junctural	kaparring	ketolysis	king-eider
Jew's trump	Jonsonian	Juneberry	karabiner	ketolytic	kingmaker
jib-headed	Jordanian	June grass	Karankawa	ketonemia	king prawn
jib-header	Jordanite	jungle cat	karanteen	ketonuria	king's blue
Jicarilla	Josephine	jungle gym	Karnataka	kettleful	king's evil
jigamaree	Josephism	jungle hen	karrozzin	key-colour	king's-hood
jig button	Josephite	jungle law	karst land	key-holder	king-sized
jill-flirt	Josephson	jungle rot	karyogamy	keyholder	king-snake
jingle-boy	joshingly	juniorate	karyogram	Keynesian	king's pawn
jitterbug	joss-house	juniority	karyology	keystroke	king's rook
jobcentre	joss stick	junkerdom	karyomere	khaki weed	king's ship
jobholder	Joule's law	junketeer	karyosome	khalifate	king's side
job-hopper	journalet	junketing	karyotype	Kharoshti	King Stork
job-hunter	journeyer	Junoesque	Kashubian	Khedivate	kininogen
jobmaster	joviality	juriballi	katabasis	Khedivial	kinkcough
job-office	jovialize	juridical	katabatic	Khorassan	kinkiness
job-sharer	jowlopped	jury-fixer	katabolic	Khotanese	kinoplasm
Job's tears	joy-flight	jurywoman	Katangese	kibbutzim	kinsmanly
jobsworth	joylessly	jurywomen	Kathakali	kick about	kinswoman
jockey-box	joy-popper	Jussiaean	Katharine	kick-boxer	kinswomen
jockey cap	jubilance	just about	katharsis	kick-pleat	kinzigite
jockeydom	jubilancy	justicial	Katherine	kick-stand	kipper-nut
jockstrap	jucundity	justiciar	Kat stitch	kickstand	kippersol
jockteleg	Judaistic	justified	Kavirondo	kick-start	kipper tie
jocularly	Judas goat	justifier	Keatsiana	kick-wheel	Kirbigrip
joculator	Judas-hole	justifies	keel-block	kiddie car	kirby-grip
jocundity	Judas kiss	juttingly	keel-bully	kiddingly	kirkwards
jodhpured	Judas tree	juvenilia	keelivine	kiddushin	Kissagram
Joe Bloggs	judgelike	juventude	keel-plate	kid-gloved	kiss hands
Joe Miller	judge-made	juxtapose	keelyvine	kidnapped	kissingly
Joe Public	judgement	Kaapenaar	keep a coil	kidnapper	kissogram
Johannean	judgeship	Kabardian	keep cases	kidney ore	kissproof
Johannine	judgingly	Kabardine	keep count	kid sister	kistbandi
Johannite	judgmatic	Kabbalism	keepering	kids' stuff	Kiswahili
Johansson	judicator	Kabbalist	keep faith	kiepersol	kitchener
John-apple	judiciary	kadaitcha	keep guard	kieserite	Kitchener
John Canoe	judicious	Kadhakali	keep house	kilderkin	kite-flyer
Johnny Raw	jug-handle	Kaffir pot	keep order	Killamook	kitschier
Johnny Reb	jug kettle	Kaffir tea	keep quiet	Killarney	kitschily
Johnswort	juice harp	Kafir harp	keep score	kill-crazy	kittenish
join hands	juiceless	kahikatea	keep store	kill-devil	Kittitian
join issue	juiciness	kaikomako	keep under	killer bee	kittiwake
joint bolt	juke-joint	kairomone	Kelly pool	killifish	kiwi fruit

Kizilbash	kraurotic	lady-clock	land cress	larkiness	launching
klapmatch	Krugerism	Ladyships	land drain	lark's heel	launchman
Kleenexes	Krugerite	lady's maid	landdrost	larmoyant	launch pad
klendusic	krummholz	lady-smock	land fever	larruping	launderer
klieg eyes	krummhorn	laevulose	land-flood	larvicide	laundress
klinostat	Kshatriya	lafayette	land force	larviform	laundries
Klondiker	kudzu vine	lager beer	land-gavel	larvikite	Laurasian
knackered	Ku Kluxism	lager lout	land grant	laryngeal	laurelled
knaveries	kundalini	laggardly	landgrave	lascivity	laurel oak
knaveship	kungu cake	laggingly	land-leech	laserdisc	lavaliere
knavishly	Kurdistan	lagniappe	land-loper	laserwort	lave-eared
kneadable	kurrajong	lag of duds	landloper	lashingly	lavendery
knee-board	kusimanse	lag of tide	land of Nod	lassitude	law centre
knee-brace	kymograph	lagomorph	landowner	lasso-cell	law-church
knee-holly	kynurenic	laid paper	landplane	last agony	law French
knee joint	labelling	lairdship	land-right	last-court	lawgiving
knee-piece	label-stop	lake-basin	Landrover	last ditch	law-keeper
knee-plate	labialise	Lake poets	landscape	lastingly	lawlessly
knickered	labialism	Lake Poets	land scrip	last night	law-making
knife-edge	labiality	lake trout	land-shark	last rites	lawn chair
knife-fish	labialize	lallation	landslide	last sleep	lawn edger
knifeless	labilizer	lamb-creep	land speed	last straw	lawnmower
knifelike	laborious	Lambegger	land-swell	last thing	lawn party
knife rest	laborsome	lambently	land-thief	last trump	lawn sieve
knife-work	labourage	lamb fries	land-value	last words	law office
knightage	labour day	lamb's ears	landwards	latch bolt	law of kind
knightess	Labour Day	Lamb shift	land-water	latchkeys	laws of war
kniphofia	labouring	lamb's-wool	land wheel	late comer	law-worthy
knob-nosed	labourism	lambswool	land yacht	latecomer	lay aboard
knobstick	Labourism	lamburger	Langobard	late hours	lay abroad
knock back	Labourist	lame-brain	langouste	late Latin	lay a ghost
knock cold	Labourite	lamebrain	languaged	Late Latin	lay before
knock down	labour spy	lamellate	langue d'oc	late-model	lay bishop
knocker-up	labyrinth	lamellose	languidly	late night	lay deacon
knock over	laccolite	lament for	laniaries	laterally	layer cake
knock wood	laccolith	laminable	lankiness	lateritic	layer tint
knotberry	lace-glass	laminaran	lanterloo	lathe-head	lay eyes on
knotgrass	lacemaker	laminaria	lanthanum	lather-boy	lay figure
knottiest	lacerable	laminarin	Laodicean	lathyrism	lay hold of
know about	lacertian	laminated	lapageria	laticlave	lay open to
knowingly	lacertine	laminator	lapideous	latimeria	layperson
know-it-all	lachrymal	lamington	lapidific	Latinical	lay reader
knowledge	laciniate	laminitis	Laplacian	Latinizer	lay rector
koala bear	lac insect	Lammas Day	Laplander	Latinless	lay sister
kobellite	lackeyism	lampadite	Lapponian	Latin rite	lay to rest
koenenite	lack-Latin	lampblack	Lapponoid	latitancy	lazaretto
koesister	laconicum	lampbrush	lapsarian	latration	lazarlike
Kohs block	lacquerer	lamper-eel	lapse rate	latreutic	lazulitic
kokerboom	lacrimals	lamp-house	lap-strake	latter-day	lazy-board
kok-saghyz	lactamase	lamplight	larbolins	latter end	lazybones
komatiite	lactamide	lampooner	larcenies	latterkin	lazy eight
komitadji	lactarium	lampshade	larcenist	latticing	Lazy Susan
konimeter	lactation	lamp shell	larcenous	laudanine	lazy-tongs
kookiness	lactifuge	lanarkite	larch tree	laudation	lazzarone
kopa Maori	lactocele	Lancaster	larchwood	laudative	leachable
Koreanize	lactonize	lance-jack	lardy-cake	laudatory	leaderene
kornelite	lactulose	lance-oval	Largactil	laughable	leaderess
Korsakoff	ladder way	lancewood	large-eyed	laughably	lead glass
koulibiac	ladies' man	lanciform	largeness	laugh away	lead glaze
kozatchok	ladlefuls	lancinate	large type	laugh down	lead-horse
krakowiak	Lady altar	land agent	larghetto	laugh-line	leadingly
kraurosis	lady-chair	landaulet	largition	laughsome	lead large

lead light	legalness	lettering	lie around	Lille lace	lion dance
lead ochre	legantine	letterset	lie fallow	lily liver	lion-heart
lead-paper	leg before	Leucadian	liegeless	lily white	Lions Club
lead-plant	leg-cutter	leucocyte	liege lord	limaceous	lion's foot
lead ratio	legendary	leucoderm	lienteric	limber-box	lion's leaf
lead-reins	legendist	leuconoid	Liesegang	Limburger	lion's tail
lead-screw	leger line	leucotome	lifeblood	lime green	lion-tawny
lead sheet	legginess	leucotomy	life cycle	Limehouse	lipidosis
lead story	legginged	leukaemia	life-force	lime juice	lip-labour
lead-swing	leg glance	leukaemic	lifefully	limelight	lipolysis
leaf-brown	legionary	leukocyte	life-giver	lime-punch	lipolytic
leaf green	legislate	Levallois	lifeguard	limestone	lipophile
leafiness	leg-puller	Levantine	life-plant	lime water	lipothymy
leafleted	leg theory	level down	life-saver	lime-works	lippitude
leaf-louse	leguleian	level-free	life-sized	limitable	lip-reader
leaf miner	leg warmer	levelling	lifestyle	limitedly	lipsticky
leaf mould	Leicester	levelness	life's work	limitless	lip-syncer
leaf-nosed	leiomyoma	level test	life-table	limnology	liquation
leaf-point	leisurely	level tube	life-while	limonitic	liquefied
leaf scald	leitmotif	leverwood	life-world	limousine	liquefier
leaf-scale	leitmotiv	leviathan	lift truck	limpidity	liquidate
leaf-spine	lemanless	levigator	lift valve	limpingly	liquidise
leaf-stalk	lemmatize	leviratic	lightable	limp wrist	liquidity
leaf-trace	lemniscus	levitator	lightboat	linamarin	liquidize
leakiness	lemon balm	Levitical	light bulb	linch-hoop	liquified
lean times	lemon curd	levulinic	light-buoy	Lincrusta	liquifies
lean years	lemon drop	levulosan	light cone	linea alba	liquorice
learnable	lemon-game	levy-money	light cord	line ahead	liquorish
learnedly	lemon sole	Lewis acid	lightener	lineality	liquorist
leaseback	lemon tree	Lewis base	light-fast	lineament	liquorous
leasehold	lemonwood	lexically	lightfast	line angle	lispingly
lease-lend	lend a hand	Leyden jar	lightfoot	linearise	Lissajous
leastways	lend an ear	Leylandii	light hand	linearity	listen for
leastwise	Lend-Lease	liability	light into	linearize	listening
leathered	lengthful	libellant	lightless	lineation	listen out
leathwake	lengthier	libelling	lightmans	line block	listerial
leave flat	lengthily	libellist	lightness	line-drawn	list price
leave from	lengthman	libellous	lightning	line-drive	literally
leave go of	lengthmen	libellula	lightship	line-fence	literatim
leave over	leniently	liberally	light show	line gauge	literator
leave up to	lenitable	liberator	lightsome	line graph	literatus
Leavisian	lens paper	liberties	lights out	line judge	lithaemia
Leavisite	Lenten pie	libertine	light-time	linenfold	lithaemic
lecherous	lenticule	libidinal	light trap	linen-hall	litheness
Leclanché	lentiform	librarian	light-well	linenless	lithesome
lectorate	lentiscus	libraries	lightwood	lineolate	lithiasis
lectotype	lentitude	libration	light year	line-rider	lithiated
lecturess	leotarded	libratory	lign-aloes	liner note	lithocyst
ledge-door	leprophil	libriform	lignified	line shaft	lithoidal
ledgeless	leprosery	licensure	lignifies	line space	lithology
ledgement	leprously	lichenism	ligniform	line-storm	Lithol red
leechlike	leptocaul	lichenist	ligularia	line-width	lithopone
leech-line	leptonema	lichenoid	ligulated	lingberry	lithosere
leech-rope	leptosome	lichenose	ligustrum	lingering	lithotint
leek-green	leptotene	lichenous	Lihyanite	lingually	lithotomy
leeriness	lespedeza	lich-house	like a shot	lingulate	lithotype
leeringly	Lesser Dog	lich-stone	like as not	linksland	Lithuanic
leewardly	lesser fry	licitness	like crazy	linograph	litigable
left bower	Lestrigon	lickerish	likeliest	linoleate	litigator
left field	lethality	lick-penny	like magic	linolenic	litigious
left flank	lethargic	lick whole	likkewaan	lintelled	litoptern
leftwards	letter box	lidocaine	lilangeni	lintwhite	litterbug

littering	localizer	long dress	loose rein	loving cup	lunar node
little auk	localness	long drink	loose shot	lowballer	lunar year
little-boy	local time	long-eared	loose smut	lowbeller	lunatical
Little Dog	local veto	longevity	lop and top	low-browed	lunch hour
little end	locatable	longevous	lopez-root	lowbrowed	lunchless
little Joe	locellate	long-faced	lophiodon	Low Church	lunch-room
little man	Lochinvar	long field	lophodont	low comedy	lunch-time
little old	locked jaw	long-fours	lop-rabbit	lowerable	lunchtime
little owl	lock horns	long glass	loquacity	lower case	Lundyfoot
little toe	lockjawed	long grass	loquently	lower deck	lung-fever
liturgies	locksmith	longhouse	lorazepam	lowermost	lung fluke
liturgise	locomotor	longicorn	Lord Derby	Lowestoft	lung-power
liturgism	loculated	longingly	lordliest	Low German	lunisolar
liturgist	locuplete	longitude	Lord Mayor	low-headed	lunitidal
liturgize	lodestone	long johns	lordships	low-income	lunulated
live-birth	lodgeable	long knife	Lordships	lowlander	lupinosis
live fence	lodgement	Long Knife	lorgnette	Lowlander	lupulinic
live in sin	lodge-pole	long-liner	loricated	lowlihead	luridness
liveliest	lodgerdom	long-lived	Lorrainer	lowliness	lurkingly
live on air	loftiness	Long March	lorry park	low-loader	lusophone
liverance	logaoedic	long metre	lose an eye	low-minded	lustering
liverleaf	logarithm	long-nosed	lose caste	low-necked	lustfully
liverless	log-basket	Longobard	lose count	low relief	lust-house
live rough	logginess	long price	lose flesh	low season	lustihead
Liverpool	logheaded	long purse	lose heart	Low Sunday	lustihood
liver spot	logically	long rains	lose touch	loxodrome	lustiness
liver-wing	logic bomb	long-range	lose track	loxodromy	lustreful
liverwort	logic gate	longshore	loss-maker	loyalness	lutaceous
liveryman	logistics	long-short	loss-proof	loyalties	luteinize
liverymen	log-normal	long sight	lost cause	lubricant	lutescent
live steam	logograph	long sixes	lost river	lubricate	Lutherism
livestock	logogriph	long straw	Lotharios	lubricity	Lutherist
live tally	logolatry	long-timer	lot-jumper	lubricous	lutulence
lividness	logomachy	long verse	Lotophagi	Lucianist	luxuriant
Livornese	logophile	long views	lotteries	lucidness	luxuriate
lixiviate	logothete	long vowel	lotus-bird	luciferin	luxurious
lixivious	logroller	long waist	lotus-land	luckiness	Lycaonian
load-and-go	logrunner	longwards	loud-mouth	luck-money	Lycurgean
loadberry	loincloth	long whist	loudmouth	lucrative	Lycurgian
loadspace	Lollardry	long-wings	loud pedal	Lucretian	lyme-grass
loadstone	lollingly	long years	lounge bar	lucubrate	lymphatic
loaf-bread	lolloping	look about	loup-garou	Lucullean	lymph node
loaf-eater	Lombardic	look after	louringly	Lucullian	lymphomas
loaferdom	London fog	look-ahead	louse-trap	Ludditism	Lyon Court
loaferism	London gin	look-alike	lousewort	ludicrous	lyophilic
loaf sugar	Londonian	lookalike	lousiness	Luftwaffe	lyophobic
loaminess	Londonish	look alive	loutishly	lullabied	lyotropic
Loamshire	Londonism	look askew	love-apple	lullabies	lyrically
loan-blend	London ivy	looker-out	love beads	lullingly	lysimeter
loan-money	Londonize	look round	love child	lumbering	lysogenic
loan-place	loneliest	look sharp	love feast	lumberman	lysosomal
loan shark	Lone Scout	look small	love-juice	lumbermen	lytically
loan-shift	longaeval	look smart	loveliest	lumbrical	macabrely
loathness	long-beard	looniness	love-light	lumbricus	macadamia
loathsome	longboard	loon pants	lovely and	luminaire	macaronic
lobectomy	long-chain	loose back	love match	luminance	Macartney
lobscouse	long chair	loose-fill	loverless	luminesce	Maccabean
Lob's pound	long cloth	loose fish	loverlike	luminizer	Maccabees
lobulated	long cross	loose head	love-scene	lumpiness	macédoine
local call	long-dated	loose-knit	love-spoon	lumpishly	macerator
localitis	long dozen	loose-leaf	love-story	lump sugar	MacGuffin
localized	long-drawn	looseness	love-token	lunarnaut	Machiavel

machinate	magnetize	make entry	malt-floor	manicotti	maranatha
machinery	magnetoid	make feast	malt-house	manifesto	Marangoni
machinist	magnetron	make fun of	malthouse	maninosay	marbleize
Machmeter	magnifico	make haste	maltiness	manipular	marcasite
macilence	magnified	make hay of	malt-maker	man-killer	marcassin
macilency	magnifier	make merry	malt sugar	manlihood	marcelled
macintosh	magnifies	make money	malvoisie	manlikely	March hare
MacIntosh	magnitude	make or mar	mamillary	manliness	march-land
MacKenzie	Magyarize	make peace	mamillate	manna-tree	March moth
mackerels	maharajah	make ready	mammalian	mannequin	marchpane
Maclaurin	maharanee	makeready	mammalogy	mannerise	march past
macrobian	maharishi	make sense	mammaries	mannerism	Marconist
macrocosm	Mahlerian	make shift	mamma's boy	mannerist	Marcusian
macrocyst	mahlstick	makeshift	mammering	mannerize	Mardi gras
macrocyte	Mahometan	make speed	mammiform	mannishly	Mardi Gras
macro lens	Mahometry	make sport	mammillar	mano a mano	mareogram
macrolide	maidenish	make terms	mammogram	Manoeline	mare's nest
macrology	maieutics	make tired	Mammondom	manoeuvre	mare's tail
macromere	mail coach	make use of	Mammonish	manometer	margarate
macropsia	mail cover	make water	Mammonism	manometry	margarine
macrurous	Mailmerge	make waves	Mammonist	man orchid	margarita
mactation	mail order	Malabaric	Mammonite	manorship	margarite
maculated	mail-rider	malachite	mammy-sick	manoscope	marginate
madam-shop	mail train	maladroit	man and boy	man-riding	margining
madarosis	main brace	mala fides	mananosay	mansarded	marialite
madcapery	mainferre	malagueña	man-at-arms	mansionry	Marianism
maddening	mainframe	Malagueña	Manchegan	manslayer	Marianist
mad-doctor	main guard	malagueta	mancipate	man's woman	Mariavite
madeleine	mainliner	malanders	Mancunian	manticism	marigraph
made-up tie	mainplane	malarious	mandarine	manticore	marihuana
mad-headed	mainprize	malathion	mandatary	Mantinean	marijuana
mad minute	main range	Malayalam	mandative	mantology	marimonda
madrepore	mainsheet	Malay fowl	mandatory	manualism	Mariology
madrilene	Maintenon	Malaysian	mandilion	manualist	maritally
Madrileño	maize-bird	Maldivian	mandoline	manubrial	Maritimer
maelstrom	maize-smut	maldonite	manducate	manubrium	marked man
maenadism	majesties	malebolge	man-eating	Manueline	marker pen
maestosos	major axis	maleffect	maned wolf	manurable	market day
maestrale	major-domo	male gauge	man enough	manurance	marketeer
magalogue	majorette	malegueta	man-for-man	Manxwoman	marketing
magaziner	major part	male organ	man Friday	Manxwomen	market man
maggot-pie	majorship	male rhyme	Man Friday	many a moon	Markovian
maghemite	major suit	male screw	manganate	many a time	marlberry
magianism	major term	malformed	manganese	manyogana	Marlovian
magically	majuscule	malgré lui	manganite	manyplies	marl slate
magic away	make a back	malic acid	manganoan	many-sided	marlstone
magicking	make a book	maliceful	manganous	many-where	marmalade
magic wand	make a face	malicious	mangel-fly	manzanita	marmalady
magistery	make after	malignant	mange mite	Maoriland	marmolite
magistral	make a fuss	malignify	mangerful	Maori oven	marmorate
Maglemose	make a head	malignity	mange-tout	Mapharsen	marmoreal
magmatism	make a mark	malleable	mangetout	maple beer	marmorean
magmatist	make a mess	malleably	manginess	maple bush	marquench
Magnaflux	make a move	mallee hen	mango-bird	maple leaf	Marquesan
magnesian	make a quid	mallemuck	mango-fish	maple tree	marquetry
magnesite	make a rise	malleolar	mango tree	maple-wood	Marranism
magnesium	make a show	malleolus	manhandle	map lichen	marriable
magnetics	make a step	Mallorcan	manhattan	map-making	marrowfat
magnetise	make a time	Malmaison	manhunter	map-reader	marrowsky
magnetism	make a waft	malpraxis	manically	map turtle	Marrucian
magnetist	make a work	maltalent	Manichean	maquisard	Marrucine
magnetite	make doubt	malt-combs	manichord	marabunta	marry into

marry well	mass-point	May-cherry	mediciner	melon-wood	mephitism
marshalcy	mass-ratio	mayflower	meditater	melonworm	merbromin
Marsh Arab	mastalgia	mayhappen	meditator	mélophone	mercaptan
marshbird	masterate	mayoralty	medium dry	melopoeia	mercatory
marshbuck	masterdom	mayorship	mediumism	melopoeic	mercement
marsh fern	masterful	mazedness	medullary	melphalan	mercenary
marsh frog	mastering	Mazzinian	meetinger	meltingly	merceries
marsh hawk	master key	mead-bench	mefenamic	melt water	mercerise
marshiest	master-man	meadowing	megacycle	Melungeon	mercerize
marshland	masticate	meadow rue	megadeath	memberess	merciable
marsh pink	mastigure	meadstead	megafauna	mementoes	merciless
marsh spot	mastoidal	mealberry	megahertz	Memnonian	merciment
marsh tern	matagouri	mealie-cob	megalopod	memoirist	mercurate
marsh worm	matchable	mealiepap	megamouth	memorable	mercurial
marshwort	match ball	mealiness	megaphone	memorably	Mercurian
marsh wren	match-book	mealy tree	megaphyll	memoranda	mercurous
marsquake	matchbook	meandered	megapolis	memorious	mercy-seat
marsupial	match-card	me and mine	megascope	memorizer	mereology
marsupian	matchcoat	meandrine	megashear	Memphitic	mere right
marsupite	match-head	meandrous	megaspore	menaceful	merestead
marsupium	matchless	meaningly	megastore	menadione	merestone
Martellos	matchlock	means–ends	megatonne	menagerie	merganser
martemper	matchmake	means test	meibomian	men-at-arms	merismoid
martially	match-play	mean to say	meiofauna	mendacity	merispore
martin-box	matchplay	meanwhile	meiosis II	Mendelian	meristele
martin bug	match race	mean white	mekometer	Mendelism	meritable
martineta	match-safe	mean White	melaleuca	Mendelist	meritedly
Martinism	match up to	measliest	melanemia	Mendelize	meritless
Martinist	matchwood	measurely	melanized	mendicant	merocrine
Martinmas	matelassé	measure up	melanosis	mendicate	merogonic
martyrdom	materiate	measuring	melanotic	mendicity	meroistic
martyrial	maternity	meat-flies	melanuria	mendipite	merostome
martyries	mateyness	meat-house	melanuric	mend or end	merozoite
martyrion	matfellon	meatiness	melaphyre	mengkuang	merriment
martyrise	matriarch	meat jelly	melastoma	men in blue	merriness
martyrish	matricide	meatotomy	melatonin	meningeal	merry hell
martyrize	matriclan	meat-wagon	melibiase	meningism	merrymake
marvelled	matricula	meat-works	melibiose	Menippean	Mertonian
marveller	matriline	mechanics	Meliboean	meniscate	mesangial
masculate	matriliny	mechanise	meliceris	meniscoid	mesangium
masculine	matrimony	mechanism	meliorate	Mennonist	mesaxonic
masculist	matronage	mechanist	meliorism	Mennonite	mescaline
mashallah	matronism	mechanize	meliorist	menologia	mescalism
masochism	matronize	mechoacan	meliority	menopause	mesentery
masochist	mattamore	meclozine	melismata	menseless	meshugaas
masonried	matterful	Mec Vannin	melituria	Menshevik	meshuggah
mason-wasp	matt paint	medallion	mellilite	mesmerian	mesmerian
mason-work	matutinal	medallise	mellitate	menstrual	mesmerise
Masoretic	maudlinly	medallist	mellotron	menstruum	mesmerism
massacrer	Maugrabee	medallize	melocoton	mensurate	mesmerist
massagist	Maugrabin	medal play	melodious	mental age	mesmerize
Massalian	maulstick	mediaeval	melodizer	mentalism	mesne lord
Massaliot	maunderer	median fin	melodrama	mentalist	mesoblast
mass-house	Mauritian	mediately	melodrame	mentality	mesocolic
Massilian	mausolean	mediation	melologue	mentalize	mesocolon
Massiliot	mausoleum	mediative	melomania	mental set	mesoconch
massiness	mawkishly	mediatize	melomanic	mentation	mesocracy
massively	maxillary	mediatory	melongena	menticide	mesogloea
massivity	maximally	mediatrix	melongerie	mentioned	mesomeric
mass media	maximizer	medicable	melon-hole	mentioner	mesomorph
Massorete	may as well	medically	melon pink	mentorial	mesonotum
mass-penny	May beetle	medicinal	melon-seed	mepacrine	mesopause

mesophase
mesophile
mesophyll
mesophyte
mesoscale
mesospore
mesotherm
mesotonic
mess about
messagery
Messalian
Messalina
messaline
Messapian
messenger
Messenian
Messianic
Messieurs
messiness
mestranol
metabasis
metabolic
metacarpi
metaconal
metaconid
metacryst
metagnome
metagnomy
metalaxyl
metalegal
metallide
metalline
metalling
metallise
metallist
metallize
metalloid
metalmark
metalogic
metalwork
metameric
metanotum
metaphase
metaphone
metaphony
metaplasm
metatarsi
metatonic
Metawileh
metaxylem
metecious
meteorise
meteorism
meteorite
meteorize
meteoroid
meteorous
meterless
meter maid
metestrus
metformin
methadone

methanate
methanoic
metheglin
methodise
Methodism
Methodist
methodize
methonium
methought
methoxide
methylate
methylene
methyl red
metoecism
metonymic
metreless
metricate
metrician
metricise
metricize
metric ton
metroland
metrology
metronome
metronymy
metroplex
metropole
Meursault
mevalonic
Mezentian
mezzanine
mezza voce
mezzotint
mianserin
miasmatic
micaceous
mica-slate
mica valve
Michelson
micky-mick
Micoquian
microbeam
microbial
microbian
microbody
microbore
microcard
Microcard
microchip
microcode
microcook
microcopy
microcosm
microcyst
microcyte
microfilm
microform
microglia
microgram
microinch
microlite
microlith

micrology
micromere
micromesh
micromole
micronize
micro-oven
micropore
micropsia
micropyle
microsome
microtext
microtine
microtome
microtone
microtron
microunit
microwatt
microwave
microweld
micturate
mid-circle
middle age
middle ear
middle leg
middleman
middlemen
middle rib
middle way
mid-heaven
midinette
Midlander
Midrashic
Midrashim
mid-season
mid-square
midstream
midsummer
midwicket
midwifely
midwifery
midwinter
mightiest
mightless
migmatite
migration
migrative
migratory
mild steel
mile-eater
miles away
milestone
milioline
miliolite
militance
militancy
militaria
milk fever
milk float
milk-glass
milk-house
milkiness
milk punch

milk ridge
milk round
milk shake
milk snake
milksoppy
milkstone
milk stout
milk sugar
milk-toast
milk tooth
milk train
milk-vetch
milk white
millboard
mill-clack
millenary
millenism
millenium
millennia
millepede
millepore
Millerian
millering
Millerism
millerite
Millerite
mill-horse
mill-house
milligram
millinery
millioned
millionth
millipede
millivolt
mill-lands
millocrat
mill-power
Mills bomb
mill-scale
mill-shaft
millstone
mill-wheel
milometer
Miltonian
Miltonise
Miltonism
Miltonist
Miltonize
miltwaste
mimiambic
mimically
mimicking
mimicries
minacious
minareted
minargent
minarichi
minced pie
mincemeat
minchiate
mincingly
mind-curer

mindfully
minefield
minelayer
Minervois
mine shaft
mine-stone
miniature
mini-break
minidress
minimally
minimizer
mining bee
Minipiano
mini-rugby
miniscule
miniskirt
ministrer
minitrack
Minkowski
Minnesong
Minnesota
minor axis
minor suit
minor term
minoxidil
mint-green
mint julep
mint price
mint sauce
mint-sling
mint state
minueting
minuscule
minus sign
minute-gun
minuteman
Minuteman
minutemen
Minutemen
minuterie
minutiose
minutious
minxishly
mirabelle
miracidia
mirligoes
mirrorize
mirthless
mirthsome
misadvice
misadvise
misallied
misallies
misassign
misaunter
misbecome
misbehave
misbelief
misbeseem
misbestow
mischance
mischancy

mischarge
mischieve
mischoice
mischoose
mis-cipher
miscolour
misconvey
miscopied
miscopies
miscreant
miscreate
misdecide
misdemean
misderive
misdesert
misdirect
misemploy
miserable
miserably
miserhood
misesteem
misfeasor
misfigure
misformed
misgiving
misgotten
misgovern
misgrowth
misguided
misguider
mishandle
mishanter
mishappen
Mishnical
misinform
misjudger
misleader
misleared
misliking
mislippen
misliving
mislocate
mismanage
misnumber
misoccupy
misogynic
misoneism
misoneist
misorient
misosophy
mispickel
mispraise
misprisal
misprizer
misquoter
misreader
misrecite
misreckon
misrelate
misrender
misrepeat
misreport

misscript	moderated	moneyless	monoptote	moor-grass	mosaicked
misshaped	moderator	moneywort	monopulse	moor-palms	Mosaic law
misshapen	moderatos	Mongolian	monorchid	moorpunky	Mosaic Law
missilery	modernise	Mongolise	monorchis	moorstone	moschatel
missiness	modernism	mongolism	monorheme	moose-bird	Moses boat
missional	modernist	Mongolize	monorhine	moose bush	moskeneer
missioned	modernity	Mongoloid	monorhyme	moose milk	Mosleyite
missioner	modernize	mongooses	monosemic	moosewood	mosquital
Miss Molly	modiation	mongrelly	monoskier	moose-yard	moss agate
Miss Nancy	modillion	monitress	monosomic	moot court	Mössbauer
misspeech	modularly	monkeyish	monosperm	moralizer	moss-berry
miss plant	modulator	monkeyism	monospore	moralless	moss green
Miss Right	Moeso-Goth	monkey-man	monostich	moralness	moss-grown
miss sahib	Moguntine	monkey-nut	monostome	moral play	moss-house
miss stays	moistener	monkey-pot	monotoned	moratoria	mossiness
mistemper	moistless	monkeypox	monotonic	morbidity	mossy horn
mister man	moistness	monkishly	monotower	morbility	mostlings
misthrive	molarized	Monk-Latin	monotreme	mordacity	mostwhere
mistified	molassied	monkshood	monotropa	mordantly	mot d'ordre
mistigris	Moldavian	monk's-seam	monotropy	mordicant	moth-borer
mistiness	moldavite	monk's shoe	monotypic	Morellian	moth-eaten
mistletoe	molecular	monoamine	monovular	Morescoes	mother hen
Mitannian	mole drain	monobasic	monoxylic	morganise	mothering
mitchella	molehilly	monoblast	monoxylon	Morganism	mother wit
Mithraeum	mole snake	mono-cable	Monroeism	Morganist	mothproof
Mithraism	molestful	monoceros	Monsignor	morganite	motivated
Mithraist	molestive	monochord	monsoonal	morganize	motivator
mitigable	molindone	monocline	mons pubis	morindone	moto-cross
mitigator	moll-heron	monocoque	monstrous	Mormondom	motocross
Mitnagged	mollified	monocracy	Montanian	Mormoness	motorable
mitre gear	mollifier	monocular	Montanism	Mormonish	motor area
mitrewort	mollifies	monoculus	Montanist	Mormonism	motor bike
mitriform	molluscan	monocycle	Montanize	Mormonist	motorbike
mitsumata	molluscum	monocytic	monthlies	Mormonite	motor boat
mitt joint	Mollweide	monodelph	month-long	Mormon war	motorcade
mixedness	mollyhawk	monodrama	month's man	mormoopid	motor camp
Mixmaster	mollymawk	monodromy	monticule	morningly	motor home
mixoploid	Molossian	monoecism	Montonero	morphemic	motorhome
mizen-mast	molossine	monogamic	monzonite	morphined	motorless
mizen-sail	molybdate	monogenic	moodiness	morphogen	motor root
mizen yard	molybdite	monograph	mood swing	morphonic	motor unit
mnemonics	molybdous	monoicous	moon-blind	morphosis	motor wind
mnemonist	mom-and-pop	monolater	moon buggy	Morrisian	mouchette
mnemonize	momentary	monolatry	moon-clock	Morrisite	mouldable
Moabitess	momentous	monolayer	moon-daisy	Morse code	mould-loft
Moabitish	monachise	monologic	moon-faced	morselize	mould-made
moa-hunter	monachism	monologue	moon flask	mortalism	mouldwarp
moanfully	monachize	monomachy	mooniness	mortality	mouldy fig
moaningly	monadical	monomania	mooningly	mortalize	mound-bird
mobbishly	monadnock	monomeric	moonlight	mortal sin	moundsman
mob-handed	monarchal	monometer	moon-month	mortar-bed	mountable
mobiliary	monarchic	monomyary	moon probe	mortarium	mountainy
mobilizer	monastery	mononymic	moonquake	mortcloth	mournival
mobocracy	Monastral	monophagy	moonraker	mortgagee	mousebird
mockeries	monatomic	monophone	moonscape	mortgager	mouse deer
mockernut	Mondayish	monophony	moonshine	mortgagor	mouse-fish
mock goose	monecious	monophyly	moonshiny	mortician	mouse hare
mockingly	money-back	monopitch	moonstomp	mortified	mouse-hawk
mock olive	moneybags	monoplane	moonstone	mortifier	mouse-hole
modelling	money-belt	monoploid	Moon's type	mortifies	mouse-hunt
modellist	money-bill	monopolar	moonwards	mosaicism	mouselike
model-room	money crop	monopsony	Moorcroft	mosaicist	mouseling

mouse moth	mugginses	murder log	mutilator	mystifies	narratory
mouseship	mujahedin	murder-man	mutoscope	mythicise	narratrix
mousetail	mujahidin	murder one	muttering	mythicism	narrow axe
mousetrap	mulattoes	murderous	mutton-fat	mythicist	narrow-cut
mousiness	mulctuary	murder rap	mutualise	mythicize	narrowest
mousseron	mule chest	muricated	mutualism	mythology	narrowish
moustache	mulga tree	murkiness	mutualist	mythomane	narrow way
Moustiers	mulga wire	murmuring	mutuality	myxamoeba	nasal bone
mouthable	muliebral	murmurish	mutualize	myxoedema	nascently
mouthfuls	mulierose	murmurous	mutuation	myxospore	naseberry
mouth glue	Müllerian	Murphy bed	muzziness	myxovirus	Nassanoff
mouth-harp	mullioned	murrained	my cabbage	myzostome	Nasserism
mouthiest	mullipuff	Murray cod	mycelioid	Nabataean	Nasserist
mouthless	mully-grub	musaceous	Mycenaean	Nabeshima	Nasserite
mouthpart	multicore	muscadine	mycobiont	nabobship	nastiness
mouth ring	multifoil	muscarine	mycologic	nache-bone	Natal lily
mouth root	multifold	muscicole	mycophage	nagelfluh	Natal plum
mouthwash	multifont	muscle car	mycophagy	naggingly	Natal sore
move about	multiform	muscle-man	mycophile	Nagualism	Natatores
move along	multigene	muscology	mycotoxin	Nahuatlan	natheless
move house	multigerm	muscovado	mycterism	nail brush	native cat
movie-goer	multihull	muscovite	myctophid	naileress	native dog
movie star	Multilith	Muscovite	mydriasis	nail-maker	native oak
Movietone	multipara	musefully	mydriatic	nail-plate	native son
moving day	multipath	museology	myelocele	nail punch	natrolite
moving-man	multiplet	museumish	myelocyte	naissance	nattiness
moving map	multiplex	mushiness	myelogram	naiveness	naturally
Moygashel	multipole	mushroomy	myelomata	naked boys	nature-god
Mozarabic	multi-role	mushy peas	myenteric	nakedness	naturelle
Mozartian	multi-task	musically	my guess is	nakhlitic	Naugahyde
Mr Charley	multitask	music book	mylohyoid	nalidixic	naughtier
mridangam	multi-tier	music case	mylonitic	namaycush	naughtily
Mr Justice	multitude	music hall	myocardia	name after	naumachia
Mrs Grundy	multi-user	musicless	myoclonic	name-check	nausea gas
Mr Speaker	multiwall	music-roll	myoclonus	name-child	nautilite
muck about	mumbudget	music-room	Myocrisin	name names	nautiloid
muck-a-muck	mumchance	music type	myofibril	name-plate	naval base
muckender	mum-figure	music-wire	myoglobin	nameplate	Navarrese
muckerish	mummeries	musketade	myologist	name-story	Navarrois
muckiness	Mummerset	musketeer	myomatous	Namierian	navelwort
muckraker	mummichog	musketoon	myoneural	Namierite	navicular
muck sweat	mummified	muskiness	myopathic	Namierize	navigable
mucky-muck	mummifies	musk melon	myoseptum	namma hole	navigably
mucolytic	mummiform	Muskogean	myriorama	nancified	navigator
mucronate	mum-mumble	musk plant	myristate	Nandi bear	naya paisa
mudaliyar	mummy-case	musk shrew	myrmecoid	nanny goat	naysasaid
mud-dauber	mummychog	Muslimism	myrmekite	nanometre	naysasays
muddiness	mummy-pits	musselled	myrmeleon	Nanticoke	Nazaritic
muddledly	mummy's boy	mussel mud	myrmicine	naphthene	Naziphile
muddledom	mumpsimus	mussiness	myrobalan	naphthous	nearabout
mud-hopper	mundanely	Mussolini	myrrh tree	Napierian	near money
mudlarker	mundanity	Mussulman	mystacial	napkining	near of kin
mud-logger	mundatory	mussurana	mystagogy	nappy rash	nearshore
mud minnow	mundungus	mustachio	mysterial	narcissus	near sight
mud-sucker	Municheer	mustafina	mysteries	narcolept	near thing
mud-turtle	municipal	mustanger	mysticete	narcotise	neat-house
muff diver	municipia	mustarder	mysticise	narcotism	neat's-foot
muffineer	municipio	musteline	mysticism	narcotist	nebenkern
muffin man	munjistin	muster out	mysticity	narcotize	Nebraskan
muffledly	murder bag	mustiness	mysticize	narratage	nebuliser
mugearite	murderess	must needs	mystified	narration	nebulizer
mugginess	murderish	mutagenic	mystifier	narrative	necessary

necessity	neologism	neurology	nickel bag	night-work	noiseless
neck-break	neologist	neuromast	nickelian	nigricant	noises off
neck-canal	neologize	neuromata	nickeline	Nigritian	noisiness
neckcloth	neo-Nazism	neuromere	nickelite	nigritude	noisomely
neckinger	Neonomian	neuropath	nickelled	nigrosine	no kidding
neck-piece	neon tetra	neurotomy	nickelous	Nile perch	nolle-pros
neck-towel	neopentyl	Neustrian	nicknamer	Nilometer	nomadical
neck-verse	neophilia	neuterdom	nickpoint	nilpotent	no-meaning
necrology	neophilic	neutrally	nick-stick	nimbu-pani	nomically
necrotise	neophobia	neutretto	nicotiana	Nimrodian	nominable
necrotize	neophobic	neutrinos	nicotined	nine-holes	nominally
necrotype	neoplasia	neutronic	nicotinic	ninepence	nominator
nectareal	neotenous	never a one	nictation	ninepenny	nominatum
nectarean	neoterism	never ever	nictitant	ninetieth	no mistake
nectarian	neotocite	never-fail	nictitate	ninetyish	nomocanon
nectaries	nepenthes	never fear	niddering	ninhydrin	nomocracy
nectarine	nephalism	never heed	niellated	ninth part	nomograph
nectarium	nepheline	Never Land	niffiness	nip bottle	non-access
nectarous	nepheloid	never mind	niff-naffy	nipcheese	non-action
needfully	nephology	nevermind	niftiness	nipperkin	nonameric
neediness	nephritic	nevermore	Niger seed	nippiness	nonce-word
needle-bug	nephritis	Newcastle	niggardly	nippingly	non-coding
needleful	nephrosis	new-collar	niggerdom	Nipponese	non compos
needle gap	nephrotic	new-create	niggerish	Nirvanist	non-concur
needle-gun	Neptunian	New Critic	niggerism	Nissen hut	non-driver
needle ice	Neptunism	new-fallen	nigger toe	Nissl body	nonentity
needleman	Neptunist	newfangle	night-bell	Nithsdale	none other
needs must	neptunite	new ground	nightbird	nit-picker	non-finite
Néel point	neptunium	New Jersey	night-blue	nitpicker	nongenary
Néel spike	neroli oil	Newmanism	night boat	Nitralloy	non-greasy
nefandous	nervation	Newmanite	night bolt	nitratine	nonillion
nefarious	nervature	Newmanize	night-cart	nitration	non-Jewish
negatival	nerve cell	Newmarket	nightclub	nitrified	nonjurant
neglecter	nerve-cord	newsagent	night-crow	nitrifier	nonjuring
neglector	nerve-knot	newsbreak	nightfall	nitrifies	nonleaded
negligent	nerveless	newsbrief	night-gear	nitro-acid	non-lethal
negotiant	nerve-path	news butch	nightglow	Nitrolime	non-linear
negotiate	nerve-ring	new school	nightgown	nitronium	non liquet
Negrillos	nerviness	newsflash	nighthawk	nitrosate	non-member
negritize	nervosity	news hound	night-herd	nitroxide	non-native
Negritude	nervously	newsiness	night-lamp	nitwitted	non-normal
negro-head	nescience	newspaper	night lark	Nivernois	non-object
Negroidal	nessberry	newsprint	nightless	Nixie tube	no nothing
Negroland	Nestorian	news-sheet	night-life	no-account	nonpareil
Negroness	net-fisher	news-stand	nightlife	Noachical	non-paying
Nehruvian	nether man	newswoman	night-line	nobbiness	non-person
neighbour	netminder	Newtonian	night-long	nobiliary	non placet
neisseria	net-player	Newtonist	nightmare	noble hawk	non-plural
Nelson eye	net profit	new towner	night-rail	nobleness	non-porous
Nelsonian	net system	new wavish	night-robe	Nobodaddy	non-profit
nelumbium	networker	New Yorker	night safe	no chicken	non-racial
nematogen	neuralgia	next of kin	night-side	no comment	non-random
nemertean	neuralgic	next world	night-soil	noctidial	non-reader
nemertine	neural net	Niagarian	nightspot	noctiluca	non-regent
nemophila	neuration	nialamide	night star	nocturnal	non-return
neocortex	neuraxial	nibble-nip	night-stop	noddingly	nonreward
neodamode	neuridine	nibble off	night-tide	noddy-shot	non-sexist
neodymium	neurinoma	niccolite	night-time	node point	non-sexual
neohexane	neuristor	niccolous	night-walk	nodulated	non-smoker
neolithic	neurocyte	nice as pie	nightward	no effects	non-tenure
neologian	neuroglia	nice Nelly	nightwear	no flies on	non-treaty
neologise	neurogram	nick-eared	night-wind	no-fly zone	non-united

non-valent	nose putty	nuisancey	nylon salt	obstinacy	Oddfellow
non-verbal	nose-thirl	nullibist	nymphaeum	obstinate	odd jobber
non-viable	nose trick	nullified	nymphalid	obstruent	odd-job man
non-voting	nose wheel	nullifier	nymphette	obstupefy	odd man out
non-worker	nosheries	nullifies	nymphical	obtention	odd parity
noodledom	nosophile	nullipara	nymphlike	obtrusion	odiferous
noodleism	nostalgia	nulliplex	nystagmic	obtrusive	odorosity
no offence	nostalgic	nullipore	nystagmus	obtundent	odorously
nook-shaft	no starter	nullisome	oak coffin	obturator	odourless
noologist	Nostratic	nullisomy	oak-pruner	obumbrate	oeconomus
noontimes	notabilia	nullities	oarswoman	obvention	oedematic
noosphere	not a cheep	null space	oast house	obversely	oedometer
Nootka fir	notaphily	number one	oat burner	obversion	oenanthic
nootropic	notarikon	number six	oat-celled	obvertend	oenanthol
no problem	not a speck	Number ten	obbligato	obviation	oenomancy
nordcaper	not a thing	Number Ten	obconical	obviative	oenomania
Nordicism	not at home	number two	obcordate	obviously	oenophile
Nordicist	not be in it	numbingly	obduction	occipital	oenothera
norlander	notchback	numbskull	obedience	occludent	oesophagi
normalise	notchiest	numerable	obediency	occlusion	oestrogen
normalism	notepaper	numerably	obeisance	occlusive	of an age to
normality	nothingly	numeraire	O be joyful	occultism	of a sudden
normalize	nothing to	numerator	obeliscal	occultist	of a surety
Normanise	nothosaur	numerical	obeseness	occupance	off-bearer
Normanism	notionary	numero uno	obfuscate	occupancy	off camera
Normanist	notionate	numinosum	objectant	occurrent	off-campus
Normanize	notionist	nummulary	objectify	occurring	off-centre
Normannic	not likely	nummuline	objection	occursion	off chance
normative	not much on	nummulite	objectise	oceanaria	off colour
normocyte	not nearly	nuncupate	objective	Oceanides	off course
Norseland	notochord	nunnation	objectize	ocean pout	off cutter
Norseness	notonecta	nunneries	objet d'art	oceanward	off-design
Northants	notoriety	nun's cloth	objicient	ocean wave	offendant
north-east	notorious	Nuremberg	objurgate	oceanwise	offending
North-East	not proven	nurse cell	obligable	ocellated	offensive
northerly	no-trumper	nurse-crop	obligator	ochlocrat	offerable
northland	nougatine	nurse-fish	obligedly	ocotillos	offertory
Northland	nourisher	nurse-frog	obligator	octachord	offhanded
northmost	nouvelles	nurseling	obliquely	octagonal	office boy
northness	Novachord	nursemaid	obliquing	octahedra	officeful
north pole	novelette	nurseries	obliquity	octameric	office-man
North Pole	novelness	nurse-tend	obliviate	octameter	officerly
North Star	novelties	nurse-tree	oblivious	octanoate	officiant
northward	Novembery	nursingly	oblongish	octaploid	officiary
north-west	novemdial	nurturant	obnoxiety	octastich	officiate
North-West	novendial	nutburger	obnoxious	octastyle	officinal
north wind	novennial	nut-butter	obreption	Octateuch	officious
Norway rat	noviciate	nut cutlet	obscenely	octave key	off-island
Norwegian	novilunar	nutjobber	obscenity	octennial	off-limits
nor'wester	novitiate	nutmegged	obscurant	octillion	offloader
nor'-wester	novocaine	nutriment	obscurely	Octobrist	off-pricer
nose ahead	Novocaine	nutrition	obscurity	octocoral	off-putter
nosebleed	nowhither	nutritive	obsecrate	octoploid	off ration
nose-candy	noxiously	nutriture	obsequent	octopodan	off-roader
nose drops	no you don't	nut runner	obsequial	octopodes	offsaddle
nose flute	nuclearly	nuts about	obsequies	octopuses	off-screen
nose-heavy	nucleated	nuts in May	observant	octostyle	off-season
nose of wax	nucleator	nuttiness	obsession	Octoteuch	off-shears
nose-paint	nucleolar	nut-weevil	obsessive	ocularist	offspring
nose paste	nucleolus	nux vomica	obsidious	oculiform	off-street
nose-piece	nucleonic	nuzzerana	obsolesce	oculistic	off-target
nose print	nugacious	nyctalope	obstetric	odalisque	off the air

off the bit	oligomery	one-suiter	on the road	operatize	orchestre
off the map	oligopoly	one-to-many	on the rope	opercular	orchideal
off theory	oliprance	one-upness	on the Rory	operculum	orchidist
off the peg	olive-back	one-valued	on the sick	operosely	orchotomy
offuscate	olive-bark	ongoingly	on the side	operosity	orderable
of its kind	olive drab	on holiday	on the skew	ophiolite	order arms
of one mind	olive-like	oniomania	on the spot	ophiology	order book
of oneself	olivenite	onion dome	on the spur	Ophiuchus	order form
of one's own	olive-plum	onion-like	on the take	ophiuroid	orderless
of purpose	Oliverian	onion-skin	on the tick	ophthalmy	orderlies
oftenness	olive tree	onlooking	on the tilt	opilionid	order mark
oftentime	olive-yard	onomastic	on the town	opiniated	order wire
of that ilk	ololiuqui	onomatopy	on the trot	opinional	ordinaire
of the year	ombrology	on one hand	on the turf	opinioned	ordinance
of treason	ombudsman	on one's arm	on the turn	opodeldoc	ordinator
ogee curve	ombudsmen	on one's day	on the wane	opponency	Oregonian
ogreishly	omegatron	on one's ear	on the wind	opportune	organ-bird
ohmically	ominously	on one side	on the wing	opposable	organdies
oikoumene	omissible	on one's own	on thin ice	oppressed	organelle
oil-beetle	ommatidia	on one's pat	ontically	oppressor	organette
oil burner	omnifocal	on one's tod	ontogenic	oppugnant	organetto
oil colour	omnirange	on one's way	ontologic	opsimathy	organical
oil-cooled	omophagia	on passage	on welfare	optically	organific
oiled-down	omophagic	on purpose	onymously	optic axis	organized
oiled silk	omphaloid	on receive	on your way	optic disc	organizer
oil engine	on a budget	on request	oogenesis	optic lobe	organless
oil heater	on account	onslaught	oogenetic	optimally	organ loft
oil-strike	on a charge	on stand-by	oological	optimific	organosol
oil string	onanistic	on station	ooplasmic	optimizer	organ pipe
oil switch	on a string	on the ball	Oort cloud	optometer	organ stop
oil tanker	on a sudden	on the bash	opacified	optometry	organzine
okey-dokey	on average	on the beam	opacifier	optomotor	orgiastic
Oklahoman	on balance	on the beer	opacifies	optophone	orgillous
Old Bailey	on benefit	on the bias	opal-agate	opulently	orientate
old boy net	onbethink	on the boil	opalesque	opuscular	orienteer
old codger	once again	on the case	opal glass	opuscules	orientite
Old French	oncogenic	on the club	open-armed	opusculum	orifacial
old fustic	oncolitic	on the cuff	open chain	oraculate	orificial
old Indian	oncologic	on the dead	open class	oraculous	oriflamme
old leaven	oncolysis	on the dole	open cover	orangeade	Origenism
old master	oncolytic	on the fang	open cycle	orange bat	Origenist
old school	oncometer	on the feed	open-ended	Orangeism	originant
old sledge	on deposit	on the fret	open-faced	Orangeman	originary
old soaker	on draught	on the game	open field	Orangemen	originate
old stager	one and all	on the hoof	open-heart	orange-oil	Orkneyman
old-wifish	one-design	on the hook	open house	orange-red	Orleanian
oleaceous	one-for-one	on the hour	open newel	orang-utan	Orleanism
olecranal	one-handed	on the jump	open range	orangutan	Orleanist
olecranon	one in five	on the lees	open score	orational	ornithine
oleic acid	one-legged	on the line	open shelf	orationer	ornithoid
olenellid	one-lunger	on the make	open-skies	oratorial	orobanche
oleograph	one moment	on the mark	open space	oratorian	orocratic
oleometer	one nation	on the mend	open stage	oratories	orofacial
oleoresin	one-old-cat	on the move	open-stock	oratorios	orography
olfaction	one-reeler	on the nail	open-tread	oratorize	orologist
olfactive	onerosity	on the nose	open water	orbicular	orometric
olfactory	onerously	on the outs	open woods	orbivirus	orotidine
oligaemia	one-seater	on the pill	operatics	orb-weaver	orphanage
oligaemic	one's Maker	on the piss	operating	orcharded	orphandom
oligarchy	one's needs	on the prod	operation	orchester	orphanise
oligistic	one's scene	on the rack	operatise	orchestic	orphanize
Oligocene	one's spies	on the rise	operative	orchestra	orpharion

Orphic egg	other than	out of play	oven-ready	over-large	overstood
orphreyed	otherways	out of rule	oven timer	overlarge	overstrew
Orpington	otherwise	out of step	over again	overlayer	overstudy
orris root	otoconium	out of sync	overalled	overlearn	overstuff
ortanique	otolithic	out of time	overaward	overlight	overswarm
or the like	otologist	out-of-town	overblown	overlying	oversweep
orthocone	otoplasty	out of true	overboard	overmatch	oversweet
orthodoxy	otorrhoea	out of tune	overborne	overmount	overswell
orthoepic	otoscopic	out of turn	overbound	overnight	overswing
orthoform	otter tail	out of wind	overbrood	overpaint	overtaker
orthology	ottocento	out of work	overbuild	overpedal	overterve
orthopter	oubliette	out-parish	overcarry	overpitch	overthink
orthoptic	oughtness	outplacer	overcatch	overplant	overthrew
orthostat	Ouled Nail	outporter	overcheck	overpoise	overthrow
orthotist	Our Father	outpreach	overcivil	overpower	overtired.
orthotone	ouroboros	outputter	overclimb	overpress	overtness
Orwellian	ourselves	outraging	overcloak	overprice	overtower
oscillate	out and out	outreason	overclose	overprint	over to you
oscitancy	outasight	outreckon	overcloud	overprize	overtrace
os frontis	out at feed	out-relief	overcomer	over proof	overtrade
osmanthus	outbacker	outréness	overcount	overproof	overtrain
osmic acid	out-basket	outridden	overcover	overproud	overtrawl
osmically	outbellow	outriding	overcreep	overpunch	overtread
osmometer	outbranch	outrigged	overcroft	overquick	overtrick
osmometry	outbrazen	outrigger	overcross	overrapid	overtrump
osmophile	outcoming	outrunner	overcrowd	overreach	overtrust
osmophore	out-county	outsearch	overcrust	overreact	over-under
osmundine	outcrying	out-sentry	overdated	overready	overvalue
osseously	outcurved	outsetter	overdraft	overrider	overvault
Ossianism	outdazzle	outshifts	overdrank	overright	overwatch
ossicular	outdoorsy	outshrill	overdrawn	overrigid	overwater
ossiculum	outermost	outside in	overdress	overripen	overweary
ossifrage	outerwear	outside of	overdried	overrisen	overweigh
osso bucco	outfitter	outskirts	overdrink	overroast	overwhelm
ossuaries	outgallop	outsource	overdrive	overruler	overworld
ostectomy	outgassed	outspoken	overdrove	oversales	overwound
ostension	outgiving	outsprang	overdrunk	overscore	overwrite
ostensive	outgrowth	outspread	overeager	oversexed	ovibovine
ostensory	outhauler	outspring	overearly	overshade	oviductal
ostentate	outhector	outstrain	overerupt	oversharp	oviferous
osteocyte	outhumour	outstream	overexert	overshine	ovigerous
osteoderm	out island	outstride	overfleet	overshoot	oviparity
osteology	outjockey	outstrike	overflies	overshort	oviparous
osteopath	outjuggle	outsucken	overfloat	oversight	ovivorous
osteotome	outlabour	out-thrown	overflood	oversized	ovomucoid
osteotomy	outlander	out-thrust	overflown	overskirt	ovotestis
ostinatos	outlet box	out-tongue	overflush	oversleep	ovulation
ostleress	outlinear	out-travel	overglaze	overslide	ovulatory
ostracion	outlustre	outwardly	overglide	overslung	owdacious
ostracise	outmaster	outwinter	overgloom	oversmoke	owlet-moth
ostracism	outnumber	out with it	overgorge	overspeak	owl monkey
ostracite	out of a hat	outworker	overgraze	overspeed	owl-parrot
ostracize	out of a job	Ovaherero	overgreat	overspend	owl-pigeon
ostringer	out of curl	ovalbumin	overhappy	overspill	ownerless
Ostrogoth	out of date	ovaliform	overhardy	overspoke	ownership
Oswego tea	outoffice	ovational	overharsh	overspray	oxacillin
other half	out of form	ovationed	overhaste	overstaff	oxazolone
otherkins	out of gear	oven-bread	overhasty	overstain	oxbow lake
other life	out of hand	oven-cloth	overhorse	overstand	ox-eye arch
otherness	out of line	oven-glass	overissue	overstate	Oxfordian
other some	out of love	oven glove	overjoyed	oversteer	Oxfordish
other such	out of luck	ovenproof	overladen	overstock	Oxfordism

oxidation	paillette	palmistry	panoramic	parabolic	paratroop
oxidative	painfully	palmitate	panorpoid	parabrake	parbuckle
oximetric	pain perdu	palm-print	pan-sexual	parachute	parcelize
oxybaphon	pain point	palm sugar	pansified	Paraclete	parcelled
oxygenase	pain-proof	palm swift	Panslavic	paraconid	parcenary
oxygenate	paintable	palm viper	pansophic	Pará cress	parc fermé
oxygenise	paintball	Palmyrene	pantagamy	paracrine	parcheesi
oxygenize	paint bomb	palominos	pantaleon	paradeful	parch mark
oxygenous	painterly	paloverde	pantalets	paradisal	parchment
oxy-helium	paintiest	palpation	pantaloon	paradisic	pardalote
oxyphilic	paintless	palpebral	pantdress	paradores	paregoric
oxytropis	paintress	palpiform	pantheism	paradoses	parenesis
oysterage	paint-root	palpitant	pantheist	paradosis	parentage
oyster bed	paint shop	palpitate	pantie leg	paradoxer	parentela
oystering	paintwork	palsgrave	pantihose	paradoxic	parenting
oysterish	pair-horse	Palsgrave	pantiling	parafango	parfilage
oyster-man	pair-oared	paltriest	pantingly	paraffiny	parfleche
oysterous	pair royal	Paludrine	Pantocain	parafovea	pargasite
ozocerite	Pakistani	palustral	pantology	paraglide	pargeting
ozokerite	Pakkawood	Pampangan	pantomime	paragnath	parge-work
ozonation	palace car	pampas cat	pantoufle	paragnost	parhelion
ozone hole	palaeosol	pampas fox	pantropic	paragogic	parhypate
ozoneless	palaestra	pampootie	pantryman	paragraph	pariah dog
pacemaker	palampore	panaceist	pantrymen	Pará grass	pariahdom
pace-stick	palankeen	Panama hat	pantskirt	paragutta	parichnos
pachycaul	palanquin	pan-Arabic	pants suit	paralalia	paring bee
pachyderm	Palantype	panatella	pantyhose	paralegal	pari passu
pachynema	palatable	Panatrope	paparazzi	paralexia	Paris blue
pachytene	palatably	pan-Celtic	paparazzo	paralexic	Paris club
pacifarin	palatally	panchayat	paperback	paralogia	parisonic
pacifical	palaverer	panchrony	paper-bank	paralysed	parity bit
packaging	pale-faced	pancosmic	paper-bark	paralyser	Parkerize
pack-cloth	Paleocene	pancratic	paper clip	paralyses	Parkesine
pack drill	Paleozoic	panderess	paper-coal	paralysis	parkwards
packed out	Palestine	panderism	paper doll	paralytic	parlatory
packet rat	paletoted	pandurate	paper-feed	paramatta	parleyvoo
pack-frame	palilalia	pandurina	paper game	paramedic	parlously
packhorse	Palladian	panegyric	paper girl	parameter	parlyaree
pack-house	palladium	panel-back	paperless	paramorph	parnassia
pack sheep	palladous	panel game	paper mill	paramount	parnassim
packstaff	Pallas cat	panelling	paper pulp	paramylum	Parnassus
pack-track	pallasite	panellist	paper-reed	paranasal	parochial
pack-train	palletise	panel show	paper sack	paranatal	parodical
pactional	palletize	panel wall	paper-spar	paranemic	paroecism
pactolian	palliasse	panel-work	paper tape	paranoiac	paroemiac
paddle-box	palliator	panettone	paper-thin	paranotal	paroicous
paddy-bird	pallidity	pan-German	paper town	paranotum	paromoeon
Paddyland	palmarian	panhandle	paper ware	paranymph	parosteal
Paddy mail	palmarosa	panic bolt	paper-wasp	parapatry	parotitic
pademelon	palmately	panicking	paperwork	parapegma	parotitis
pad mangle	palmation	pan-Ionian	papillary	parapeted	parqueted
pad-saddle	Palm Beach	panlectal	papillate	paraplane	parquetry
pad stitch	palm-borer	panlogism	papilloma	para-rhyme	parrakeet
paedagogy	palm civet	panmictic	papillose	parascend	parrhesia
paedarchy	Palm Court	panniered	papillote	parascene	parricide
paederast	palmellin	panniform	papillous	parasital	parr marks
paedogamy	palmettos	Pannonian	papulated	parasitic	parroting
pageantry	palm-heart	panograph	parabasal	paraskier	parrotism
page-paper	palm honey	panoistic	parabasis	parasoled	parrotize
page-proof	palminess	panoplied	parabiont	para-state	parrot-pea
paillasse	palmipede	panoplies	parabolae	parataxis	Parseeism
pailleted	palmister	panoramal	parabolas	parathion	parse-tree

parsimony	pasticcio	Paul Jones	pearlwort	pegmatite	pennanted
parsleyed	pastiness	paulownia	pear midge	pegmatoid	penniform
parsonage	pastorage	paunchier	peasantry	pegomancy	penniless
parsondom	pastorale	pauperage	pease-meal	pegtopped	penninite
parsoness	pastorali	pauperdom	pea-souper	peirastic	pennoncel
Parsonian	pastorate	pauperise	peat-house	Pekingese	penny ante
parsoning	pastosity	pauperism	peat-spade	Peking man	penny gaff
parsonish	pasturage	pauperize	pea-urchin	Pelasgian	pennyland
partaking	pasturing	pauperous	pea-weevil	pelecypod	penny pies
part hence	patch cord	paupiette	pebble-bed	Pelignian	penny post
parthenic	patchiest	pauseless	peccaries	pellagrin	penny wise
partially	patch lead	Pavlovian	peck order	pellet bow	pennywort
partified	patchouli	pawkiness	peck-right	pelleting	Penobscot
parti pris	patch-plug	pawn chain	Pecksniff	pelletise	pen-pusher
partition	patch reef	pawn storm	pecorinos	pelletize	penseroso
partitive	patch test	paxillose	pectinase	pellicule	pensioner
partogram	patchwork	pax Romana	pectinate	pellitory	pensively
part-owner	patellate	pay a score	pectineal	pellotine	penstemon
partridge	patent log	pay dearly	pectineus	Pelmanise	pentagram
part-timer	paternity	pay freeze	pectinite	Pelmanism	pentagrid
party boat	pathogeny	pay gravel	pectinous	Pelmanist	pen-tailed
party game	pathology	pay its way	pectolite	Pelmanize	pentalogy
party-goer	pathotype	Payloader	peculator	pelobatid	pentalpha
partyless	patiently	paymaster	pecuniary	pelophile	pentamery
party line	patinated	pay-off man	pecunious	peloriate	pentangle
partyness	patio door	pay packet	pedagogal	peltately	pentanoic
party plan	patio rose	paysagist	pedagogic	pelvic fin	pentapody
party-poop	patissier	pay toilet	pedagogue	pemphigus	pentarchy
party wall	patlander	pea-beetle	pedal boat	pempidine	pentarsic
party wire	Pat Malone	peaceable	pedal bone	penalties	pentathol
parvitude	Patmorean	peaceably	pedalling	pen and ink	Pentecost
Pascalian	Patna rice	peace camp	pedal note	Penbritin	penthouse
pas de chat	patriarch	peaceless	pedal pole	penceless	pentomino
pas de deux	patrician	peace pipe	pedantise	pencil box	Pentothal
pas glissé	Patrician	peace sign	pedantism	pencilled	pentoxide
paso doble	patricide	peace talk	pedantize	penciller	pentrough
passament	patriclan	peacetime	pedatifid	pendanted	penultima
pass check	patriline	pea-chafer	pede-cloth	pendently	penumbrae
pass-court	patriliny	peach-blow	pederasty	pendicler	penumbral
passement	patrimony	peacheroo	pediatric	Pendleton	penumbras
passenger	patriotic	peach fuzz	pedicator	pendragon	penurious
passepied	patristic	peachiest	pedicular	Pendragon	peperomia
passerine	patrol car	peach-palm	pedigreed	pendulant	pepperbox
passers-by	patrolled	peach tree	pediplain	pendulate	pepper gas
pass-guard	patroller	peacockly	pediplane	penduline	pepperina
passingly	patrolman	peacockry	pediunker	pendulous	peppering
passional	patrolmen	pea-combed	pedlarism	peneplain	pepperoni
passioned	patrology	pea-flower	pedocalic	penetrant	pepper pot
passivate	patronage	pea gravel	pedogenic	penetrate	Pepsi-Cola
passively	patronate	pea-jacket	pedologic	pen-friend	pepsinate
passivise	patroness	peakiness	pedomancy	penfriend	peptidase
passivism	patronise	pearl bulb	pedometer	pen holder	peptonise
passivist	patronite	pearl-bush	pedophile	penholder	peptonize
passivity	patronize	pearlfish	pedoscope	penicilli	Pepysiana
passivize	patterned	pearliest	pedotribe	penillion	peracarid
pass round	patterner	pearlitic	peduncled	peninsula	peracetic
pass water	patty-cake	pearlized	peel-house	penis-bone	peragrate
paste-down	paucality	pearl-like	peep-sight	penis-envy	perborate
pastelist	Paulician	pearl-opal	peer group	penistone	percaline
paste-over	Paulinism	pear-louse	peeringly	penitence	per capita
pasterned	Paulinist	pearl spar	peevishly	penitency	perceiver
paste-wash	Paulinize	pearlware	peg-legged	penknives	percenter

per centum	perisperm	perverted	phalangid	phlorizin	physicism
perceptum	perispore	perverter	phalanxed	phlyctena	physicist
perchance	peristome	peshmerga	phalanxes	phonation	physicked
perch-bolt	peristyle	peskiness	phalarope	phonatory	physic-nut
percheron	peritonea	pessaries	phalluses	phone bank	physisorb
perciform	peritrack	pessimise	phanariot	phone book	phytocide
percolate	peritreme	pessimism	phanotron	phonecard	phytogeny
per contra	peritrich	pessimist	phansigar	phonemics	phytolith
per curiam	peri-urban	pessimize	phantasma	phonetics	phytology
percussor	perjuries	pesterous	Pharaonic	phonetise	phytosaur
perdition	perkiness	pest-house	Pharisaic	phonetism	phytotomy
Père David	Perkinism	pesticide	pharmacal	phonetist	phytotron
peregrine	perlative	pestilent	Pharsalia	phonetize	Piagetian
pereiopod	perlemoen	pestology	pharyngal	phoney war	pia-matral
perennate	permalloy	Pétainism	pharynges	phoniness	pianistic
perennial	permanent	Pétainist	phase down	phonodisc	pianoless
perfecter	permeable	petalless	phaseless	phonofilm	pianolist
perfectly	permeance	petal-like	phase-lock	phonogram	piano roll
perfector	permeator	petalodic	phaseolin	phonolite	piano trio
perfectos	perminvar	petal ware	phase rule	phonology	piano wire
perfervid	permitted	petardeer	phasitron	phonotype	piazzetta
perfidity	permittee	petaurist	phellogen	phonotypy	Picassian
perfluent	permitter	petechiae	phenacite	phoronomy	Picco pipe
perforant	permutate	petechial	phenakite	phosphate	Picentine
perforate	permutite	peter-boat	phenazine	phosphene	piceworth
performer	pernettya	Peter-fish	Phenergan	phosphide	pickaback
perfumery	perniosis	petersham	phenetics	phosphine	pick a lock
perfusate	perorally	Petertide	phenetole	phosphite	pick-a-tree
perfusion	perorator	pethidine	Phenidone	phosphori	pickeerer
perfusive	perosmate	petillate	phenobarb	phossy jaw	pickerels
Pergamene	perovskia	petiolate	phenocopy	Photinian	picketing
pergunnah	peroxided	petiolule	phenogram	photo call	pickiness
periapsis	peroxidic	petit four	phenolase	photocall	pick-proof
peribolus	perpetual	petit jury	phenolate	photocell	pickpurse
periclase	perplexed	petrefact	phenology	photocopy	pickthank
Periclean	perradial	Petri dish	phenoloid	photoemit	picktooth
pericline	perrhenic	petrified	phenol red	photo-etch	pick-up arm
pericolic	perrotine	petrifies	phenomena	photogram	picnic ham
pericycle	persecute	Petrinism	phenotype	photolyse	picnicked
perifovea	persevere	petrogeny	phenoxide	photolyze	picnicker
Périgueux	persimmon	petrol cap	phenylate	photomask	picolinic
perihelia	persister	petroleum	phenylene	photonics	picrolite
perilling	personage	petrolize	phenytoin	photoplay	pictogram
perilymph	personate	petrology	pheromone	photoscan	pictorial
perimeter	person-day	petticoat	philander	photostat	picturing
perimetry	personify	pettiness	philately	Photostat	picturize
perimorph	personize	pettishly	philippic	phototube	pidginist
perinatal	personnel	petty cash	Philippic	phototype	pidginize
periodate	persuader	petty jury	philister	phrasally	piece down
periodize	Pertelote	petty whin	Philistia	phrenetic	piecemeal
perioecic	perthitic	petulance	phillyrea	phrenitic	piece-rate
periostea	pertinent	petulancy	philogyny	phrenitis	piecewise
peripatos	perturbed	phacoidal	philology	phthalate	piece-work
peripatus	perturber	phacolite	philomath	phthiocol	piecework
periphery	pertussal	phacolith	Philomela	phycology	pied goose
periphony	pertussis	Phaeacian	Philonian	phylarchy	Pied Piper
periplasm	perusable	phaenogam	Philonize	phyletism	pie-funnel
periproct	pervagate	phage type	philosoph	phyllitic	piepowder
perirenal	pervasion	phagocyte	phlebitic	phyllomic	pier glass
Periscian	pervasive	phagosome	phlebitis	phyllopod	pierrette
periscope	perveance	phalanger	phlogosis	phylogeny	pierrotic
perishing	pervenche	phalanges	phloretin	physician	pier-stake

pier-table
pietistic
pigeoneer
pigeonite
pigeon-pea
piggeries
piggishly
piggyback
piggy bank
pig-headed
pigheaded
Pig Island
pigmeater
pigmental
pigmented
pignerate
pignorate
pigtailed
piked horn
piked shoe
pikeperch
pikestaff
pilau rice
pile-drive
pilferage
pilgarlic
pilgrimed
pilgrimer
pillar box
pillarist
pillicock
pilloried
pillories
pillorize
pilomotor
pilonidal
pilot-bird
pilot-boat
pilot-coat
pilot fish
pilot hole
pilot lamp
pilotless
pilotship
pilot tone
pilot wire
pilpulist
pimientos
pimpernel
pinaceous
pinafored
pinarette
pinchable
pinchbeck
pin-cherry
pinch-fist
pinch-roll
pin clover
Pindarism
pinealoma
pineapple
pine-drops

pine-mouse
pine-snake
pine straw
piney wood
pinheaded
pinholder
pinholing
pin-hooker
pinjrapol
pink coral
Pinkerton
pinkiness
pink noise
pinko-grey
pink paper
pink-stern
pinnacled
pinnately
pinnation
pinnay oil
pinniform
pinnulate
PIN number
pinocytic
Pinot Noir
pin pallet
pin-setter
pin-stitch
pinstripe
pintadera
pintailed
Pinterish
pint glass
pint-sized
pint stoup
pin-tucked
pious hope
piousness
pipe berth
pipe dream
pipedream
pipe-fiend
pipe-layer
pipe-light
pipeliner
pipe major
pipe-metal
pipe organ
piperonal
piperonyl
piperoxan
pipesnake
pipe-still
pipe-stone
pipetting
piping hot
pipradrol
pipsqueak
piquantly
piquetist
piratedom
piratical

piripiris
piroplasm
pirouette
piscation
piscatory
piscicide
pisciform
piscinity
pishrogue
Pismo clam
pisolitic
piss about
piss-house
pissingly
piss-proud
piss-taker
pistachio
pistacite
pistareen
pistoleer
pistolled
piston pin
piston rod
pit-bottom
pit cavity
pitch axis
pitch-dark
pitchfork
pitch-hole
pitchiest
pitch into
pitch-knot
pitchlike
pitch-line
pitch-mark
pitch-opal
pitch pine
pitch-pipe
pitchpole
pitch shot
pitch tree
piteously
pitfalled
pithecian
pithecoid
pith fleck
pithiatic
pithiness
pitifully
pitometer
pitot head
pitot tube
Pitot tube
Pitressin
pit-sawyer
pit silage
pittancer
pitticite
pituicyte
pituitary
pituitous
Pituitrin

pityingly
pivotable
pivotally
pivot foot
pivot-hole
pivot word
pixie hood
pixie-like
pixie-path
pixie-pear
pixilated
pizotifen
pizzicati
pizzicato
placarder
placating
placation
placatory
placeable
place-book
place card
place-kick
placeless
placement
place name
placentae
placental
placentas
placidity
plackless
placoderm
placodont
placulate
plague pit
plague-rat
plain card
plain cook
plain hunt
plain jane
plain Jane
plainness
plainsman
plainsmen
plainsong
plain suit
plain text
plaintful
plaintiff
plaintile
plain time
plaintive
plain-work
plaitless
plait-work
planarian
planarity
planation
planching
Planckian
Planck law
plane away
planeload

planeness
planeside
planesman
planetary
plane time
planetoid
plane tree
plangency
planiform
planigale
planigram
planisher
plankless
plank-road
planktont
plankways
plankwise
Planorbis
plantable
plant-cane
plantless
plantlike
plantling
plantmilk
plantsman
plantsmen
planuloid
plaquette
plasma arc
plasmagel
plasma jet
plasmasol
plasmatic
plasmodia
plastered
plasterer
plasticky
plasticly
plastigel
plastique
plastisol
plateaued
platefuls
plateless
platelike
plate line
plate-mark
plate mill
plate rack
plate-rail
plate-roll
platinate
platinise
platinite
platinize
platinode
platinoid
platinous
platitude
Platonian
Platonise
Platonism

Platonist
Platonize
platytera
plausible
plausibly
plaustral
play about
play-actor
play along
play a part
play booty
play by ear
play-dough
played out
play false
playfight
playfully
playgoing
playgroup
play house
playhouse
play-lunch
playmaker
play smash
play-table
plaything
pleadable
plea-house
plea-in-bar
plea-in-law
pleasable
pleasance
pleasedly
please God
pleasured
pleasurer
plectrums
pleiomery
pleiotaxy
plenarily
plenarium
plenilune
plenitude
plenteous
plentiful
pleonexia
pleophony
pleoptics
plerionic
plethoric
pleuritic
pleuritis
plexiform
plexiglas
Plexiglas
plicately
plication
plicature
plightful
plinthite
plombière
ploration

plosional	pocketful	poke-salad	polyester	Pommyland	porphyrio
Plotinian	pocketing	polar bear	polyether	pomoerium	porrected
Plotinism	pocket rot	polar body	polygamic	pompadour	porringer
Plotinist	pockiness	polar hare	polygenic	pompholyx	Porsonian
Plotinize	pockmanty	polariton	polygonal	pompoleon	port-a-beul
plot-ratio	Pocomania	polarized	polygonic	pomposity	Portainer
plottable	podagrous	polarizer	polygonum	pompously	portalled
plough-boy	podginess	polar star	polygraph	ponderate	portatile
ploughman	podiatric	polarward	polygynic	ponderosa	portative
plowshare	podocytic	pole-horse	polyhedra	ponderous	porterage
pluckiest	podoscaph	pole-lathe	polyimide	pond snail	porteress
pluckless	podotheca	polemarch	polyionic	pontianak	portfolio
pluck side	podzolise	polemical	polylogue	pontoneer	portholed
plugboard	podzolize	pole-piece	polymathy	pontooner	porticoed
pluggable	poemscape	pole vault	polymeric	Pontypool	porticoes
plug gauge	poetaster	polewards	polymetre	poodle-cut	portional
plugged-in	poeticise	polianite	polymodal	poodle-dog	portioner
plug horse	poeticism	police box	polymorph	poodledom	portliest
plug riots	poeticize	police dog	polymythy	pool house	portolano
plumbagos	poeticule	policedom	polymyxin	pool shark	portolans
plumbeous	poet's poet	policeman	polyomino	poopnoddy	portrayal
plumbicon	pogey bait	policemen	polyonymy	poop scoop	portrayer
plumbless	pogie bait	Polisario	polyopsia	poop-sheet	portreeve
plumb line	pogo stick	polishing	polyorama	poop-stick	Port Salut
plumb rule	pogromist	polish off	polyphage	poor child	port-sider
plumeless	pohickory	politarch	polyphagy	poorhouse	Portuguee
plumelike	poignance	politburo	polyphant	poor loser	portulaca
plume moth	poignancy	politeful	polyphase	poor mouth	port watch
pluminess	poinciana	politesse	Polypheme	poor snake	port-winer
plummeted	poindable	political	polyphone	poor white	port-winey
plummiest	pointable	politicly	polyphony	poor White	posigrade
plumosite	point duty	politicos	polyphyly	Pooterish	possessed
plumosity	pointedly	poll-clerk	polypidom	pop artist	possessor
plumpness	pointelle	pollen-sac	polypifer	pop-bottle	possident
plunderer	pointiest	pollinary	polyploid	pope's head	poss-stick
plunge bed	point lace	pollinate	polypnoea	pope's nose	postalize
plunge cut	pointless	pollinise	polyporus	Poplarism	post-axial
pluralise	pointlike	pollinium	polyposis	Poplarist	postcaval
pluralism	point mass	pollinize	polyptych	popliteal	postcenal
pluralist	point shoe	poll-taker	polypuses	popocracy	post-coach
plurality	pointsman	pollucite	polysemia	Popperian	post crown
pluralize	pointsmen	pollutant	polysemic	Popperism	post-entry
plurative	pointwise	pollution	polysomal	poppet-leg	posterial
pluriform	point-work	pollutive	polysomic	poppycock	posterior
plurisign	poisonful	Pollyanna	polyspike	poppy-head	posterish
plus fours	poison gas	polonaise	polyspore	poppy-seed	posterist
plushette	poisoning	polo shirt	polyspory	popularly	posterity
plushiest	poison ivy	polo stick	polystely	porbeagle	posterize
plushness	poison oak	polyamide	polytenic	porcelain	post-exist
plutarchy	poisonous	polyamine	polythene	porchless	posthabit
plutocrat	poison pen	polyandry	polytonal	porcupine	post-haste
plutology	poitrinal	polyanion	polytonic	porcupiny	posthitis
Plutonian	poke-berry	polyantha	polytopic	pore water	post-horse
plutonism	poke-check	polyarchy	polytrope	poriferan	post-house
Plutonist	poke fun at	polybasic	polytypic	pork-eater	posticous
plutonium	pokelogan	polyblast	polyvinyl	pornocrat	post-ictal
plutonomy	poker back	polychord	polywater	porogamic	postilion
ply rating	poker chip	polyclone	polyxenic	poromeric	postnasal
pneograph	poker dice	polyconic	pomace-fly	porometer	post-natal
pneumatic	poker-face	polycrase	pomaceous	porphyria	postnatal
pneumonia	poker-work	polycross	pomewater	porphyric	postnatus
pneumonic	pokerwork	polyergus	pommelled	porphyrin	post-paper

postponer	pound sign	pre-action	preferent	presbyope	pretty-boy
postposit	*pourboire*	pre-adamic	preferred	presbyter	prettyish
post-rider	pour-point	preadvise	pre-feudal	presbytia	prettyism
post-tonic	pourpoint	pre-agonal	prefigure	prescaler	pretypify
postulant	poussette	pre-assign	prefixion	pre-school	prevailer
postulata	poutassou	preassume	prefixoid	preschool	prevail on
postulate	poutingly	preassure	pre-flight	prescient	prevalent
posturing	powder-bag	pre-atomic	preflight	prescreen	preventer
posturist	powder-box	preatomic	preformer	prescribe	preverbal
posturize	powdering	preattune	pregnable	prescript	prevernal
postvelar	powderize	prebendal	pregnance	pre-season	previable
postviral	powder keg	prebender	pregnancy	pre-select	previewer
postwoman	powder-man	prebiotic	prehallux	preselect	prevision
postwomen	powder rag	Preboreal	preheater	presenile	priapulid
potagerie	Powellise	precancel	pre-inform	presenium	priceable
potashery	Powellism	precancer	pre-intone	presentee	priceless
potassium	powellite	precative	prejacent	presenter	price list
potato-bug	Powellite	precatory	prejudger	presently	price-mark
potato-eye	Powellize	precedent	prejudice	presentor	price ring
potato-fly	power base	preceding	prelacies	preserval	price stop
potato pie	powerboat	precentor	prelatess	preserver	priciness
potato pit	power-dive	preceptee	prelatial	presexual	pricklier
potato rot	power game	preceptor	prelation	preshrink	prickling
potato set	powerless	precipice	prelatist	pre-shrunk	prick-mark
pot-boiler	power line	precisely	prelatize	president	prick-post
potboiler	power-load	precisian	prelature	presidial	prick-seam
pot-bunker	power-loom	précising	prelector	presiding	prick-song
pot cheese	power pack	precision	preludial	presidium	prick-spur
potentate	power play	precisive	preludise	Presidium	prickwood
potential	power pole	preclimax	preludium	pressable	prideless
potentize	power tool	precocene	preludize	press book	prie-dieux
pot-garden	power unit	precocial	prelusion	press card	priest-cap
pot-gutted	powldoody	precocity	prelusive	press-gang	priestdom
pothecary	pox-doctor	pre-coital	prelusory	press home	priestess
pot holder	pozzolana	precoital	premature	press lord	priggable
potholing	practical	preconise	premedial	press-mark	primacies
pot-hunter	practicum	preconize	premiumed	pressmark	Primacord
pot-licker	practised	precooler	premodify	press roll	primaeval
pot-likker	practiser	precordia	premonish	press-room	primality
pot-liquor	praenomen	precostal	premorbid	press show	primaries
pot of gold	praetexta	precursor	premortal	press stud	primarily
pot-pourri	praetoria	precystic	pre-mortem	pressured	primarize
potteries	pragmatic	predacity	premotion	press view	primatial
pottiness	Prague ham	predation	premunise	presswork	primavera
pottinger	praisable	predatory	premunize	press-yard	prime cost
pottle-pot	praisably	predefine	preneural	prestable	prime lens
pot-valour	praiseach	predesign	pre-notice	prestance	primeness
potwaller	praiseful	predicant	prenotion	prestigey	prime rate
pouchless	pranksome	predicate	preoccupy	prestress	primer DNA
pouchlike	prankster	predictor	preocular	presuming	prime-sign
poudrette	pratchant	predigest	pre-option	pretectal	prime time
Poujadism	pratement	*predikant*	preordain	pretectum	prime tone
Poujadist	prattling	predilect	preparate	pretenced	primidone
poulterer	prayerful	predorsal	prepartum	pretended	primigene
pound away	prayer mat	pre-echoes	prepatent	pretender	primipara
pound-boat	prayer-nut	pre-editor	preponder	pretensed	primitial
pound cake	prayer rug	pre-embryo	prepostor	preterist	primitive
pound coin	pray in aid	pre-emptor	prepotent	preterite	primordia
pound lock	preachier	pre-engage	preppiest	pretermit	primo uomo
pound-meal	preachify	pre-exilic	preputial	pretibial	primrosed
pound note	preachily	pre-expose	pre-reader	pretorian	primstaff
pound open	preaching	prefatory	pre-record	prettiest	primuline

princedom	procyonid	promising	pro re nata	protostar	pterygote
princekin	prodigies	promissor	prorogate	prototype	Ptolemaic
princelet	prodition	promittor	prorogued	protoxide	ptygmatic
principal	prodromal	promoting	prorogues	protozoal	pubescent
principes	prodromic	promotion	prosaical	protozoan	pubiotomy
principle	producent	promotive	prosateur	protozoic	public act
printable	productor	prompt box	proscenia	protozoon	public bar
print down	proembryo	prompting	proscribe	proudness	publicise
print hand	proenzyme	promptive	proscript	Proustian	publicist
printhead	proestrus	prompture	prosector	proustite	publicity
printless	pro-ethnic	promulger	prosecute	proveable	publicize
print-room	pro-family	pronation	Prose Edda	provedore	public law
print-shop	profanely	proneness	proselyte	Provençal	publisher
priorship	profanity	prongbuck	prose poem	provender	Puccinian
prismatic	professed	pronghorn	proseucha	provident	puckishly
prisonful	professor	pronounal	prosified	providing	puddening
prisoning	profferer	pronounce	prosifies	provision	pudginess
prisonize	profilist	Prontosil	prosimian	provisory	puerilely
prison-van	profilmic	pro-nuncio	prosiness	provocate	puerilism
prissiest	profiteer	prooemium	prosocial	provoking	puerility
privateer	profiting	proofless	prosodeme	provolone	puerperal
privately	profluent	proof load	prosodiac	provostal	puff-adder
privation	profugate	proof-read	prosodial	provostry	puffickly
privatise	profundal	proofread	prosodian	proxemics	puffiness
privatism	profundus	propagand	prosodion	proximate	puff-paste
privative	profusely	propagate	prosodist	proximity	puff piece
privatize	profusion	propagule	prosopyle	proxy vote	puftaloon
privilege	profusive	propanoic	prostatic	Prozymite	pug-engine
privities	progenote	propanone	prosthion	prudelike	pugillary
privy seal	progestin	propargyl	prostrate	prudently	pugnacity
prizeable	prognathy	propelled	protamine	pruderies	puissance
prizeless	prognoses	propeller	protandry	prudishly	pulicious
prize-list	prognosis	propellor	protanope	prune tree	pull about
prize ring	programme	propenoic	protargol	prurience	pull a face
proaction	proguanil	properdin	protarsal	pruriency	pull apart
proactive	projector	prophasic	protarsus	prussiate	pull a rock
pro and con	prolabium	prophetic	proteanly	prytaneum	pull-drive
probation	prolactin	propidium	protectee	psalm-book	pullicate
probative	prolamine	propinque	protector	psalmodic	pull round
probatory	prolapsus	propionic	proteinic	psaltress	pullulant
probeable	prolately	propionyl	protester	psammitic	pullulate
probingly	prolation	propodeum	protestor	psephitic	pull wires
probiotic	prolative	propodium	prothalli	pseudodox	pully-haul
probosces	prolepses	proponent	protheses	pseudoism	pulmonary
proboscis	prolepsis	Propontic	prothesis	pseudonym	pulmonate
procacity	proleptic	proposant	prothetic	pseudopod	pulp-canal
procedure	proletary	proposita	prothorax	pseudosex	pulpiness
proceeder	prolidase	propositi	prothyrum	psoriasis	pulpiteer
procerity	prolixity	propriate	protistan	psoriatic	pulpotomy
processal	prologist	propriety	protistic	psoroptic	pulp-stone
processor	prologize	propshaft	protocone	psychical	pulqueria
prochiral	prologued	proptosed	protocorm	psychonic	pulsatile
pro-choice	prologuer	proptosis	protoderm	psychoses	pulsation
proclisis	prologues	propugner	proto-form	psychosis	pulsative
proclitic	prolonged	propulsor	protogram	psychotic	pulsatory
proconsul	prolonger	propylaea	protogyny	ptarmical	pulse code
procreant	prolusion	propylene	protohaem	ptarmigan	pulseless
procreate	prolusory	propylite	protolith	pteridine	pulse-wave
proctitis	promazine	propylons	protology	pteropine	pulverise
procuracy	promenade	pro-rating	protonate	pterosaur	pulverize
procuress	promethea	proration	protonema	pterygium	pulverous
procurved	prominent	pro-rector	protopope	pterygoid	pulvillus

pulvinate	pursuable	pyorrhoea	quamoclit	quietener	racialist
pumiceous	pursuance	pyramidal	quantally	quietlike	racialize
pummelled	purulence	pyramidic	quantizer	quietness	raciation
pump-brake	purulency	pyramidon	quarryman	quiet-room	racing car
pump drill	push about	Pyramidon	quarrymen	quietsome	raciology
pump-water	push along	pyrethrin	quartered	quiet time	rackarock
punchable	push-and-go	pyrethrum	quarterer	quietuses	rack-block
punchayat	push-chain	pyrexical	quarterly	quillback	rack chain
punchball	pushchair	pyridoxal	quartette	quillwork	rack chase
punch bowl	push-cycle	pyridoxic	quartetto	quillwort	racked-out
punchbowl	pusher set	pyridoxol	quartzite	quinarian	racketeer
punch card	pusher-tug	pyritical	quartzose	quinarius	racketing
punchcard	pushfully	Pyroceram	Quasimodo	quindecim	rack mount
punchiest	pushiness	pyroclast	quaverous	quinidine	rack-punch
punchless	pushingly	pyrogenic	quay crane	quinoidal	rack-wheel
punch-line	push money	pyrograph	queasiest	quinoline	raconteur
punchline	push plate	pyrolatry	Quebecker	quinology	racoon dog
punch-mark	push-start	pyrolysis	Québecois	quinonoid	radar trap
punch-pull	pussyfoot	pyrolytic	quebracho	quinquina	radial-ply
punch tape	pussy hair	pyromancy	Queen-Anne	quintette	radiantly
punctated	pussy palm	pyromania	queen cake	quintuple	radiately
punctilio	pussy-toes	pyromanic	queen-cell	quintuply	radiating
punctuate	pussy-whip	pyrometer	Queen City	quinzaine	radiation
pungently	pustulate	pyrometry	queenfish	quiritary	radiative
puniceous	pustulous	pyromucic	Queen high	quiritian	radiature
punishing	put across	pyrophori	queenhood	quirkiest	radically
punningly	put at risk	pyrothere	queenless	quitclaim	radicchio
punt-about	putidness	pyrotoxin	queenlier	quite a few	radicular
pupariate	put in mind	pyroxenic	queenlike	quite some	radio buoy
pupillage	put paid to	pyroxylin	queen lily	quittance	radiocast
pupillary	put-putted	Pyrrhonic	Queen Mary	quiverful	Radio Five
pupilless	putrefied	pyrroline	queen post	quixotism	Radio Four
pupillize	putrefier	pythoness	queenship	quizzable	radiogram
pupil-room	putrefies	qinghaosu	queen-side	quizzical	radioland
pupilship	putridity	Q-spoiling	queen-size	Qumranite	radioless
puppeteer	putriform	quadrable	queen wasp	quoad hanc	radiology
puppetish	putrilage	quadratic	queer fish	quoad hunc	radionics
puppy foot	putschism	quadratus	queerness	quodlibet	radio star
puppyhood	putschist	quadrifid	quercetin	quotation	radiothon
puppy love	put them up	quadrille	querimony	quotative	radio wave
purchaser	put to rout	quadruped	querulist	quotidian	radiumize
pure-blood	putty-like	quadruple	querulity	rabatment	radius bar
pure quill	putty-root	quadruply	querulous	rabbeting	radiusing
purgation	put up with	quaesitum	queue-jump	rabbinate	radius rod
purgative	put wise to	quaffable	quibbling	rabbinise	radknight
purgatory	puzzle-box	quail-call	quickbeam	rabbinism	radon seed
purgeable	puzzledly	quail-dove	quick-clay	rabbinist	raffinate
puritanic	puzzledom	quail hawk	quickener	rabbinize	raffinose
purloiner	puzzle-peg	quail-pipe	quick-eyed	rabbiship	raffishly
puromycin	puzzolana	quaintish	quick-fire	rabbit-dog	rafflesia
purposely	Pybuthrin	Quakerdom	quickgold	rabbiting	raftering
purposive	pycnidial	Quakeress	quick kill	rabbitish	ragefully
purpurate	pycnidium	quaker gun	quick-knit	Rabelaism	rag picker
purpureal	pyelogram	Quakerish	quicklike	rabidness	ragpicker
purpurean	Pygmalion	Quakerism	quicklime	raceabout	rail fence
purpurite	pygomelus	quakingly	quick-look	racehorse	railinged
purringly	pygopagus	qualified	quickness	race-knife	rain-caped
purse-belt	pygostyle	qualifier	quicksand	race music	rain-charm
purse boat	pyococcal	qualifies	quick step	racetrack	rain check
purseless	pyococcus	qualitied	quickstep	rachidial	rain cloud
purse-pick	pyodermia	qualities	quick time	rachidian	rain dance
pursiness	pyodermic	qualmless	quiescent	racialism	rain gauge

rain-goose	rascality	read-write	reckoning	recumbent	redressal
raininess	Raskolnik	ready-made	reclaimer	recurrent	redresser
rainlight	rasophore	ready room	reclinate	recurring	redressor
rainmaker	raspatory	Reaganaut	reclusely	recursant	red riband
rain print	raspberry	Reaganism	reclusion	recursion	red ribbon
rainproof	rasp-house	Reaganite	reclusive	recursive	red setter
rain-slick	raspingly	realistic	recognise	recurvate	red sorrel
rain-stone	Rastafari	realities	recognize	recurvous	red spider
rainstorm	rasterise	realmless	recoinage	recusance	red squill
rainswept	rasterize	real money	recollate	recusancy	red-streak
rainwater	rat cheese	reanalyse	re-collect	redaction	red-tailed
raise Cain	ratcheted	reanimate	recollect	red anchor	red tangle
raised bog	ratemeter	reapplied	Recollect	red-backed	red-tapery
raised pie	ratepayer	reapplies	recombine	Red-baiter	red-tapish
raise hell	ratheness	reappoint	recomfort	red banner	red-tapism
raise sand	ratherest	rearguard	recommand	red bishop	red-tapist
Rajmahali	rathe-ripe	rear-horse	recommend	Red Branch	Red Terror
rakehelly	ratherish	rear light	recompact	redbreast	redthroat
rakeshame	rationale	rearmouse	recompose	red carpet	red thrush
ralli cart	rationate	rearousal	recompute	red caviar	red tombac
rambootan	rat-racing	rearrange	reconcile	Red Centre	reducible
ramellose	rat-tailed	rear sight	recondite	red clover	reducibly
rammishly	rat-tat-tat	rearsight	reconduct	red darnel	reductant
rampantly	rattening	rearwards	reconfine	reddendum	reductase
ramparted	rattiness	reasoning	reconfirm	reddishly	reduction
ram-raider	rattlebox	reassault	reconjure	reddition	reductive
ramuscule	raucously	reassurer	reconnect	red duster	redundant
rancellor	raunchier	reattempt	reconquer	redeliver	red vision
rancelman	raunchily	rebaptism	reconsign	redemptor	red willow
rancheria	rauwolfia	rebaptize	reconsult	red ensign	red-winged
rancheros	ravelling	rebatable	recontest	redeposit	red wrasse
ranchette	ravelment	rebbitzin	reconvene	redescend	reed-grass
ranch mink	raven-duck	rebelling	reconvert	redevelop	re-edifier
rancidity	raven-like	rebellion	reconvict	red fescue	reediness
ranciéite	raven-tree	rebel yell	reconvoke	red figure	re-edition
rancorous	ravishing	rebidding	record hop	red-footed	reed-organ
randiness	raw sienna	rebirther	recording	red godwit	reed relay
randkluft	ray blight	reblossom	recordist	red groper	re-educate
randomise	ray-finned	rebounder	Recordite	red grouse	reef heron
randomize	ray floret	rebreathe	recounter	red-handed	reef knoll
rangatira	ray-fungus	rebuilder	recoveree	red-headed	reef-point
rangeland	rayograph	rebukeful	recoverer	red howler	reefpoint
ranginess	Rayonnism	rebutment	recreance	redialled	reek penny
rank order	Ray's bream	rebutting	recreancy	Red Indian	re-embrace
rankshift	razor-back	recapping	recreator	redingote	re-enfeoff
ransacker	razorback	recaption	recrement	redivivus	re-enforce
ransackle	razorbill	recapture	recruital	red-legged	re-engrave
Ranterism	razor clam	recedence	recruiter	red menace	re-enslave
rantingly	razor edge	receiptor	rectangle	red monkey	re-entrant
rantipole	razor-fish	receiving	rectified	red mullet	re-entries
ranunculi	razor gang	recension	rectifier	red myrtle	reevesite
rapacious	razor plug	reception	rectifies	red-necked	re-examine
rap centre	razor wire	receptive	rectional	red nettle	re-express
rapid-fire	razzberry	recession	rectitude	redolence	refashion
rapidness	reachable	recessive	rectocele	redoubler	refection
rappelled	reachless	Rechabite	rectopexy	redoubted	refective
raptorial	reacquire	recharger	rectorate	red-pencil	refectory
rapturous	reactance	recharter	rectoress	red pepper	referable
rare earth	readathon	rechauffe	rectorial	red planet	reference
raree-show	readdress	réchauffé	rectories	Red Prince	referenda
rascaldom	readiness	recherché	rectorite	red rattle	referring
rascalism	readvance	recipient	rectrices	red reflex	refinable

refinance	rehearsal	remarries	replacive	resecrete	reswallow
refinedly	rehearser	Rembrandt	replanned	resection	retaliate
refitment	rehearten	remeasure	replaster	resembler	retardant
refitting	rehydrate	remediate	repleader	resentful	retardate
reflagged	Reichsrat	remigrate	repledger	resequent	retardive
reflation	Reichstag	remindful	replenish	reserpine	retardure
reflecter	reign mark	Remington	repletion	reservist	retentate
reflector	reign name	reminisce	replevied	reservoir	retention
reflex arc	reimburse	remissful	replevies	resetting	retentive
reflexion	reimmerge	remission	replicant	res gestae	retexture
reflexive	reimmerse	remissive	replicase	reshuffle	rethinker
refluence	reimplace	remissory	replicate	residence	rethought
refocused	reimplant	remitment	reply-paid	residency	rethunder
Reform Act	reimpress	remittent	reportage	residuary	retiarian
reformado	reimprint	remitting	reposeful	residuous	retiarius
reformate	reinclose	remixture	repositor	resignant	reticella
reformism	reindeers	remnantal	repossess	resilient	reticello
reformist	re infecta	remontant	repotting	resin-bush	reticence
refortify	reinflame	remontoir	reprehend	resinosis	reticency
refounder	reinflate	rémoulade	re-present	resin-weed	reticular
refractor	reinforce	removable	represent	resistant	reticulin
refreshen	reinhabit	renascent	repressed	resistent	reticulum
refresher	reinherit	rencontre	represser	resistful	retinally
refuelled	reinspect	rendering	repressor	resistive	retinence
refulgent	reinspire	render-set	repricing	resitting	retinitis
refurbish	reinstall	rendition	reprieval	resizable	retinular
refurnish	reinstate	renewable	reprimand	re-soluble	retiredly
refusable	reinsurer	renewedly	reprinter	resoluble	retorsion
refusenik	reissuing	renewment	reprobacy	resolvent	retortion
refutable	reiterant	renguerra	reprobate	resonance	retortive
refutably	reiterate	renitence	reprocess	resonator	retoucher
regal lily	rejection	renitency	reprocure	resorbent	retractor
regal moth	rejective	renneting	reproduce	respecter	retreaded
regardant	rejigging	renouncer	reprofile	respelled	retreader
regardful	rejoicing	renovator	reprogram	respirate	retreatal
regarding	rejoinder	renownful	reptation	responaut	retreater
regencies	relatable	rent party	reptilian	responder	retribute
re-genesis	relatival	rent table	republish	responser	retrieval
regentess	relaxedly	reoxidize	repudiant	responsor	retriever
Reggeized	relay race	repackage	repudiate	responsum	retrocede
reggeonic	relay rack	repairman	repugnant	ressaldar	retrodden
Regge pole	relearned	repairmen	repulsion	rest frame	retrodict
regicidal	relection	reparable	repulsive	restfully	retro-fire
regiminal	relegable	reparably	reputable	rest house	retroflex
regionary	relenting	repassage	reputably	restiform	retroject
regisseur	relevance	repassant	reputedly	restitute	retroussé
registral	relevancy	repayable	requalify	restively	retrovert
registrar	relic area	repayment	requester	rest level	retrusion
registree	relief map	repeat fee	requicken	restraint	return-day
registrer	relighted	repeating	requisite	restringe	returning
regosolic	religiose	repêchage	re-radiate	restudied	return key
regrading	religious	repellent	re-reading	restudies	reunified
regressor	reliquary	repelling	rere-brace	resubject	reunifies
regretful	reliquiae	repentant	re-release	resublime	reunion
regretted	relucence	repercuss	reremouse	resuggest	reutilise
regretter	relucency	reperform	re-resolve	resultant	reutilize
reguerdon	reluctant	reperfume	rerunning	resultful	revaluate
regulable	reluctate	reperible	resalable	resumable	revaluing
regularly	remainder	repertory	rescinder	resummons	revarnish
regulator	remanence	reperusal	rescoring	resurface	revelator
reguluses	remanning	repicture	rescuable	resurgent	revelling
rehearing	remarried	repiquing	rescue bid	resurrect	revelment

revelries	rhizotomy	ridiculer	riskiness	rockburst	Romantsch
reverable	rhizotron	riemskoen	risk money	rock candy	Romany chi
reverence	rhodamine	rifamycin	rissaldar	rock chuck	Romany rye
reversely	rhodanthe	riff-raffy	ritenutos	rock cress	Rome-penny
reversify	Rhodesian	rifle bird	ritodrine	rocker arm	Romewards
reversing	rhodonite	rifle shot	ritualise	rocker box	rommelpot
reversion	rhodopsin	rifomycin	ritualism	rockeries	rompingly
revertant	rhombogen	rift block	ritualist	rocketeer	rood goose
revetment	rhombuses	rigescent	rituality	rocketing	roof-brain
revetting	rhopalial	rightable	ritualize	rocket net	roof-climb
revibrate	rhopalium	right away	ritziness	rocket pad	roof light
revictual	rhotacise	right-back	rivalless	rock-flour	roof prism
revisable	rhotacism	right bank	rivalling	rock hound	roofscape
revisited	rhotacize	right-down	rivalries	rock-house	roof-slate
revivable	rhumb-line	righteous	rivalrous	rock hyrax	roof-water
revocable	rhymeless	right-hand	rivalship	rockiness	rooikrans
revocably	rhymester	rightless	river-bank	rock maple	rookeries
revokable	rhyolitic	right line	riverboat	rock melon	rook rifle
revolting	rhythmise	rightmost	river crab	rock music	room clerk
revoluble	rhythmist	rightness	river duck	rock 'n' roll	roominess
revolving	rhythmite	right side	river fish	rock ouzel	rooming-in
revulsant	rhythmize	right turn	riverless	rock pipit	roomstead
revulsion	rhytidome	rightward	river-like	rock pitch	Roosevelt
revulsive	ribanding	right-wing	riverside	rock plant	roost-cock
revusical	Ribandism	rigidness	riverward	rock-shaft	root-bound
rewardful	Ribandist	rigmarole	river-weed	rock-slide	root canal
rewarding	Ribandman	rigourism	riverwise	rock-solid	root-graft
rewhisper	ribavirin	rillettes	rix-dollar	rock-stone	root-house
rewirable	rib-bender	rime-frost	roach pole	rock tripe	rootiness
rewording	Ribbonism	rimestock	roadblock	rock waste	root-prune
reworking	Ribbonman	rimrocker	road brand	rock-water	rootstock
rewrapped	rib-digger	rind graft	roadcraft	rod and gun	root swell
rewriting	ribosomal	ring a bell	roadfarer	rodential	rooty-toot
rewritten	ribozymal	ring-bound	road-goose	rodentian	rope-a-dope
rhabditic	Ricardian	ring-canal	roadhouse	rodent-run	rope brown
rhabditid	rice-field	ringcraft	road metal	rodgersia	rope horse
rhabditis	rice-grain	ring-cross	roadscape	rodingite	rope-house
rhapontic	rice-grass	ring dance	road sense	rod puppet	rope-maker
rhapsodic	rice-paper	Ringerike	roadstead	Rodriguan	rope-sight
rhatanies	ricercare	ring false	road train	rogan josh	rope-trick
rhematize	ricercata	ring-fence	roaringly	rogueries	Roquefort
rheobasic	rice table	ring flash	roast beef	rogueship	roqueting
rheometer	rice-water	ring-frame	robber-fly	roguishly	Rorschach
rheometry	richardia	ring gland	robberies	roisterer	Rörstrand
rheophile	Richelieu	ringingly	Robertian	role model	rosaceous
rheophobe	rich rhyme	ringleted	Robertine	roller bit	rosary pea
rheophyte	ricketily	ring light	robin-chat	roller-gin	rose aphid
rheoscope	ricky-tick	ring-oiled	Robin Hood	rollicker	rose-apple
rheotaxis	ride again	ring oiler	robin huss	rollingly	rose-a-ruby
rhetorize	riderless	ring ouzel	robin-snow	Romagnese	rose-berry
rheumatic	ridership	ring round	robot bomb	Romagnola	rose-color
rheumatiz	ride rusty	ring shake	robotical	Roman alum	rosefinch
rhinarial	ride short	ringsider	robustest	romancing	rosemaled
rhinarium	ridgeback	ring-snake	rocambole	romancist	rose-noble
Rhineland	ridge-band	rinky-dink	roche alum	Romanesco	Rosenthal
Rhine wine	ridge-bone	rinky-tink	roche lime	Roman foot	roseolous
rhinology	ridgeling	riotously	Roche lobe	Romanizer	rose-point
rhipsalis	ridge pole	riparious	Roche zone	Roman mile	rosetting
rhizobial	ridge tent	rippingly	rock along	roman noir	rose water
rhizobium	ridge tile	Ripuarian	rock-basin	Roman nose	Rosinante
rhizocarp	ridge tree	rise above	rock-bound	romantism	rosin-back
rhizoidal	ridgewise	rising sun	rock brake	romantist	rosinweed

Rosminian	round hand	rubeoloid	rurbanism	sacrifice	saleratus
rosoglios	Roundhead	rubeolous	rurbanist	sacrilege	salesgirl
Rossinian	round heel	rubescent	Ruritania	sacristan	saleslady
Ross River	round meal	rubicelle	rushingly	sacristan	salesroom
Ross's gull	roundness	rubicate	rushlight	saddle-ass	sales talk
rostellar	round rape	rubrician	Ruskinese	saddle-bag	Salic code
rostellum	round seam	rubricism	Ruskinian	saddlebag	salicetum
rostrally	round shot	rubricist	Ruskinism	saddle-bar	salicylic
rostrated	roundsman	rubricity	Ruskinite	saddle bow	saliently
rosy cross	roundsmen	ruby glass	russeting	Sadducaic	saligenin
rosy finch	round text	rucervine	Russified	Sadducean	salinator
Rotameter	round trip	ruck-rover	Russifies	Sadducize	salitrose
rotascope	round turn	rudaceous	rust-brown	safari ant	salivaria
rotatable	roundward	rudbeckia	rusticate	safeguard	Sallee-man
Rotavator	roundways	rudder-bar	rusticism	safe house	sallowest
rotavirus	roundwise	ruddiness	rusticity	safe light	sallowish
rotochute	round wood	ruddleman	rusticize	safety cab	sally-hole
rotometer	roundworm	ruddy duck	rustiness	safety man	Sally Lunn
rotor disc	rousement	rue the day	rustproof	safety net	sally-port
rotor head	rousingly	rufescent	rutaceous	safety pin	sallyport
rotor ship	rout-chair	ruffianly	ruthenate	safety rod	salmon fry
Rotovator	route-goer	Rufflette	Ruthenian	safflower	salmonoid
rottenest	route taxi	rug-cutter	ruthenium	saffranon	salmon run
Rotten Row	routinary	rug-headed	ruthfully	safranine	Salomonic
rotundate	routineer	ruination	rutilated	sagaciate	saloon bar
rotundity	routinely	ruinosity	rye coffee	sagacious	saloon car
roughback	routinise	ruinously	rye whisky	sagapenum	saloonist
rough bent	routinish	rule-joint	sabadilla	sagebrush	salopette
rough calf	routinism	rule of law	Sabbathly	sage Derby	salpinges
roughcast	routinist	rule-right	Sabbatian	sage green	salsifies
rough coal	routinize	rulership	sabbatise	sagginess	salt a mine
rough coat	routously	rum butter	Sabbatism	sagittary	saltation
rough copy	roving eye	rum-cherry	sabbatize	sagittate	saltative
rough deal	rowan tree	rumenitis	Sabellian	sago-grass	saltatory
Rough Fell	rowdiness	ruminated	Sabianism	Sahaptian	salt cedar
rough file	rowelling	ruminator	sablefish	sahibhood	salt chuck
rough-hewn	row-galley	rumminess	sableness	Saigonese	salt-glaze
rough leaf	row matrix	rump steak	sabrewing	sailboard	salt grass
rough-lock	row vector	rum-runner	saccharic	sailcloth	salt horse
roughneck	Royal Anne	run across	saccharin	sail-fluke	salt-house
roughness	royal blue	run around	saccharum	sailmaker	saltiness
rough pâté	royal duke	run at tilt	sacciform	sailoress	salt marsh
rough ride	royal fern	runcinate	sacculate	sailor hat	saltpetre
rough seal	royal fish	rune-staff	sacerdoce	sailoring	salt spoon
roughshod	royal mast	rune-stave	sacerdocy	sailor-man	salt spray
roughsome	Royal Navy	run foul of	sachaline	sailor top	salt water
rough spin	royal road	run holder	sachemdom	sailplane	salt works
rough-tail	royal sail	run-in shed	sack chair	sainthood	salubrity
rough-tree	royal stag	run it fine	sackcloth	saintless	salumeria
rough work	royalties	runners-up	sack dress	saintlier	saluresis
rouletted	royetness	runner-ups	sack drill	saintlike	saluretic
Roumanian	rubber boa	runningly	Sack-friar	saintling	Salvarsan
Roumelian	rubber dam	run ragged	sack lunch	saint's day	salvation
rouncival	rubber ice	runrigged	sack paper	saintship	salvatory
round-arch	rubberise	run scared	sacrality	sakawinki	Samaritan
roundball	rubberize	run to meet	sacralize	salacious	Sam Browne
round clam	rubberoid	run to seed	sacrament	salad days	same again
round coal	rubbisher	Runyonese	sacrarium	salangane	same to you
round down	rubbishly	rupestral	sacred axe	salaryman	sameyness
roundelay	rub elbows	rupicapra	sacred cow	salarymen	Samoyedic
round fish	rubellite	rural dean	Sacred War	Saldanier	sample bag
round game	Rubensian	ruralness	sacred way	Salempore	sam-sodden

Samson fox	sapphiric	satisfier	scale-worm	sceptical	scioptric
Samsonian	sappiness	satisfies	scaliness	schapping	sciroccos
samsonite	sapraemia	satrapies	scallawag	schedular	scirrhoid
Samuelite	sapraemic	saturable	scalloped	scheduled	scirrhous
sanatoria	saprobity	saturated	scalloper	scheduler	scissorer
sanbenito	saprolite	saturator	scallywag	scheelite	scleritis
sanctoral	sapsucker	Saturdays	scalogram	schelling	sclerogen
sanctuary	Sarabaite	Saturnian	scalpette	schematic	sclerosed
sandalled	sarabande	saturniid	scalpless	Scherbius	sclerosis
sandarach	Saracenic	saturnine	scalp-lock	scherzino	sclerotal
sandblast	sarbacane	saturnism	scalpture	scherzino	sclerotia
sand-blind	sarcastic	satyrical	scalp yell	schilling	sclerotic
sand-clock	sarcelled	sauce-boat	scaly dove	Schilling	sclerotin
sand cloud	sarcocarp	sauceless	scaly-foot	schistose	scobiform
sand-crack	sarcocyst	saucer eye	scaly-tail	schistous	scold's bit
sand-devil	sarcoidal	saucerful	scamander	schlemiel	scolecite
sand drown	sarcolite	saucerian	scambling	schlenter	scolecoid
sandflies	sarcomata	saucerize	scammered	schlepped	scoliosis
sand-gaper	sarcomere	saucerman	scamperer	schlepper	scoliotic
sand-glass	sarcoptic	sauciness	scamphood	schlieren	scolopale
sand-grain	sarcoptid	saunterer	scannable	schmaltzy	scolopoid
sand-happy	sarcosine	Sauternes	scantiest	schmecker	scolytoid
sandiness	sarcosome	Sauvignon	scantling	schmutter	scombroid
sand lance	Sardinian	savagedom	scantness	schnapper	scoopfuls
sand-mason	sargassum	savage man	scapegoat	schnauzer	scoop neck
sand-mould	sarkiness	Savile Row	scapement	schnitzel	scoparius
sandpaper	Sarmatian	savonette	scaphopod	schnorkel	scopeless
sand perch	sartorial	savourily	scapolite	schnorrer	scopiform
sandpiper	sartorian	saw-billed	scapulary	schnozzle	scopoline
sand-plain	sartorius	saw-doctor	scarabaei	scholarch	scopperil
sand plant	sarvodaya	saw gourds	scaraboid	scholarly	scopulate
sand-shark	sash cramp	saw-handle	scare-babe	scholiast	scorbutic
sand-smelt	sash frame	sawmiller	scarecrow	Schönlein	scorbutus
sand-spout	saskatoon	saw the air	scare-head	school age	scorching
sandstock	sasquatch	saw-timber	scarf ring	schoolboy	score-book
sandstone	Sasquatch	Saxe paper	scarf-skin	schoolday	scorebook
sandstorm	sassafras	saxifrage	scarf-wise	schooldom	score-card
sand-table	Sassanian	saxitoxin	scarified	schoolery	scorecard
sand wedge	Sassenach	Saxon blue	scarifier	schoolful	score draw
sand yacht	sassiness	saxophone	scarifies	schooling	scoreless
sang-froid	sassolite	scabbiest	scariness	school-ma'm	scoreline
Sanhedrim	satanical	scagliola	scarp-bolt	schoolman	scorified
Sanhedrin	Satanship	scald-crow	scarpetti	schoolmen	scorifier
sanitaria	satedness	scald-fish	Scatchard	schorlite	scorifies
sanitizer	satellise	scald-head	scatheful	Schrammel	scoriform
sanjakate	satellite	scald milk	scatology	Schreiner	scorodite
sanjakbeg	satellize	scale-bark	scattered	Schroeder	scorpaena
sans façon	satelloid	scale-beam	scatterer	schvartze	scorpioid
sans serif	satiation	scale-blue	scattiest	schwartze	Scotch cap
santolina	satin bell	scale carp	scavagery	sciaenoid	Scotch egg
santonica	satin-bird	scale down	scavenage	sciagraph	Scotch elm
sapanwood	satinette	scale-fern	scavenger	sciamachy	Scotchery
sap-beetle	satinized	scale-fish	scazontic	sciatical	Scotch fir
sap-headed	satin-like	scale-leaf	scelerate	sciential	Scotchify
saphenous	satin moth	scaleless	scenarios	scientise	Scotchman
sapiently	satin spar	scalelike	scenarist	scientism	Scotchmen
sapodilla	satin wire	scale-moss	scene-dock	scientist	Scotch peg
sapogenin	satinwood	scalenous	scene-plot	scientize	Scoticise
saponaria	satirical	scale-roof	scene-room	scintilla	Scoticism
saponarin	satirizer	scalesman	scentless	sciomachy	Scoticize
saporific	satisfice	scalewise	scent tuft	sciomancy	scotomata
sapotoxin	satisfied	scale work	scent-wood	sciophyte	scotomize

scotophil
scotophor
Scots pine
scoundrel
scrabbled
Scrabbler
scraggier
scraggily
scragging
scramasax
scrambled
scrambler
scramming
scrapbook
scrap heap
scrapiana
scrap iron
scrappage
scrappier
scrappily
scrapping
scrapyard
scratched
scratcher
scrawling
scrawnier
screaking
screaming
screecher
screeding
screed off
screenage
screenful
screening
screwable
screw axis
screwball
screw-bean
screw-bolt
screw-down
screwed-up
screw gear
screw hook
screwiest
screw-jack
screwless
screw-nail
screw pile
screw pine
screw-pump
screw-rate
screwsman
screw tail
screw-wise
screw worm
scribable
scribbler
scribe-awl
scrimmage
scrimshaw
scrippage
scription

scriptory
scripture
scrivello
scrivener
scroddled
scroll bar
scrolling
scroll saw
scrounger
scrubbery
scrubbing
scrub-bird
scrubbish
scrub-fowl
scrubland
scrub pine
scrub suit
scrub tick
scrub-wren
scruffier
scruffily
scrum-half
scrummage
scrunchie
scrutable
scrutator
scrutoire
scuba-dive
sculpture
scummiest
scuncheon
scungiest
scurviest
scutation
scutcheon
scutellar
scutellum
scutiform
scybalous
scytheman
sea anchor
sea-angler
sea-animal
sea bamboo
sea barley
sea battle
sea-beaten
sea beggar
sea-bottle
sea breeze
sea-canary
sea change
sea-cradle
sea-crafty
sea dingle
sea dragon
seafaring
sea-farmer
sea-fisher
sea-flower
sea-insect
sea island

seajacker
sea jockey
sea-kindly
sealapack
sea-lawyer
sea league
sealeries
sealer jar
seal point
sealpoint
seal-stone
sea marker
seaminess
sea monkey
sea myrtle
sea-needle
sea-nettle
sea-orange
sea-parrot
sea-parson
sea-pigeon
sea-purple
sea radish
searchful
searching
sea rocket
sea-roving
sea-salted
sea-scurvy
sea seiche
sea shanty
sea-slater
seasoning
sea-sorrow
sea-spider
sea spurge
sea squirt
sea-strand
sea-sucker
Seatainer
sea-tangle
sea thrift
sea turtle
sea urchin
sea voyage
sea-walled
seawardly
sea-washed
seaweeded
seaworthy
sebaceous
secateurs
secernent
secession
seclusion
seclusive
secondary
second cut
second day
secondman
Second War
secretary

secretion
secretive
secretory
sectarial
sectarian
sectaries
sectarism
sectility
sectional
sectorial
secularly
secundine
securable
securance
sedentary
sedge-bird
seditious
seducible
seduction
seductive
seed-eater
seed-field
seediness
seed money
see double
seed-pearl
seedpearl
seed-plant
seedsnipe
seeing eye
seek after
seekingly
seemingly
seemliest
see much of
see of Rome
See of Rome
see reason
see things
Seger cone
segholate
segmental
segmented
segmenter
segregant
segregate
Seguridad
Sehna knot
Sehnsucht
seigneury
seigniory
seignoral
seine-boat
seismical
Seitz disc
selachian
selection
selective
selectman
selectron
selendang
selenious

selenitic
Seleucian
self-abuse
self-actor
self-aware
self-being
self-black
self-build
self-color
self-doubt
self-drive
self-exile
self-faced
self-field
self-given
self-glory
self-image
selfishly
self-lover
self-moved
self-noise
self-poise
self-pride
self-serve
self-study
self-timer
self-trust
self-twist
selfwards
self-worth
Seljukian
sellathon
Sellotape
sell short
Semainean
semanteme
semantics
semantron
semaphore
semblable
semblably
semblance
semeiosis
semen bank
semestral
Semi-Arian
semi-Bantu
semibreve
semi-broch
semicolon
semi-deity
semi-domed
semi-feral
semi-field
semi-final
semifinal
semi-fluid
semifluid
semi-globe
semi-grand
semi-group
semi-lunar

semilunar
semi-major
semi-metal
semi-minor
seminally
semi-nomad
semiology
semi-opera
semiotics
semi-plume
semi-prone
semi-rigid
Semi-Saxon
semi-smile
semi-solid
semi-steel
semi-sweet
semitonal
semitonic
semivowel
semi-works
sempitern
senatress
sendaline
Sendzimir
Seneca oil
senectude
senescent
seneschal
senhorita
seniority
sennachie
senocular
sensation
sensatory
senseless
sensillum
sensitise
sensitive
sensitize
sensorial
sensorily
sensorium
sensually
sentencer
sentience
sentiency
sentiment
sentition
sentry box
Senussian
separable
separably
separated
separator
separatum
Sephardic
Sephardim
Sepharose
sepiolite
septanose
septarian

septarium	serrefine	sewerless	shakefork	shaveling	shelf back
septation	serrulate	sexagenae	Shakeress	shavetail	shelffuls
September	servaline	sexagonal	shakerful	shawlless	shelf-life
septemfid	servantry	sex appeal	Shakerism	sheaf oats	shelf-like
septemvir	serveries	sexcapade	shake wave	shear flow	shelflike
septenary	Servetian	sex change	shakiness	shear-head	shelf-list
septenate	serve time	sexennial	Shakspere	shear-hulk	shelf mark
septennia	Servetist	sexennium	shallowly	shear-legs	shelf room
septicity	serviette	sexercise	shamaness	shearling	shell-back
septiform	servilely	sex factor	shamanism	shear mark	shellback
septimole	servilism	sexfoiled	shamanist	shear wave	shell bean
septotomy	servility	sex kitten	shamanize	sheat-fish	shell-bird
septuplet	servitrix	sexlessly	shamateur	sheathing	shell-duck
sepulcher	servitude	sex-linked	shambling	shebeener	Shelleyan
sepulchre	servo flap	sex maniac	shambolic	Shechinah	shellfire
sepulture	sessility	sex object	shambrier	sheddable	shellfish
sepurture	sessional	sex symbol	shameface	sheenless	shell game
sequacity	sessioner	sextoness	shamefast	sheep-back	shell-gold
sequencer	sesterces	sextuplet	shameless	sheep-bell	shell-heap
sequently	sestertii	sextuplex	sham fight	sheep-bush	shell-less
sequester	set abroad	sextupole	shampooed	sheep-camp	shell-like
sequestra	setaceous	sex typing	shampooer	sheepcote	shell-lime
sequinned	set afloat	sexual act	shanachie	sheepfold	shell pink
seraglios	set a lot by	sexualise	Shandyism	sheep-hook	shell rock
seraphine	set at ease	sexualism	shanghais	sheepkill	shell roof
seraskier	set at rest	sexuality	Shangri-La	sheeplike	shell-sand
Serbonian	set battle	sexualize	shank-bone	sheepling	shell suit
serenader	set copper	sexvalent	shantyman	sheep-mark	shell-type
sergeancy	set eyes on	sforzandi	Shaoshing	sheepmeat	shell-work
sergeanty	set fire to	sforzando	shapeable	sheepnose	shelterer
serialise	set foot in	sforzatos	shapeless	sheep-rack	shemozzle
serialism	set foot on	sgraffiti	shapelier	sheep's-bit	shenachie
serialist	set in hand	sgraffito	shape-note	sheep scab	she-oak net
seriality	set much by	shabbiest	sharashka	sheep's eye	shepstare
serialize	set on fire	shabbyish	shard-born	sheep-sick	sheriffry
seriately	set on foot	shackbolt	shareable	sheepskin	sheshbesh
seriation	set phrase	shackling	share-beam	sheep-tick	she's right
sericeous	set square	shad-belly	share-bone	sheepwalk	she's sweet
sericitic	set theory	shadberry	sharecrop	sheep-wash	shevelled
serigraph	setting-up	shade card	share shop	sheepwash	shewbread
serinette	settle bed	shade deck	sharesman	sheer-hulk	Shibayama
seriosity	set to work	shadeless	shareware	sheerlegs	shibuichi
seriously	set up shop	shade tree	sharifate	sheer-line	shickered
serjeancy	seven-bore	shadiness	sharifial	sheerness	shickster
serjeanty	seven days	shadow box	sharifian	sheer-plan	shield arm
sermonise	seven-eyes	shadowily	shark-bait	sheer-pole	shield-bud
sermonist	sevenfold	shadowing	shark-moth	sheer-rail	shield bug
sermonize	seven seas	shadowish	sharkskin	sheet bend	shieldbug
sermonoid	sevensome	shad-trout	sharpbill	sheet film	shielding
serogroup	seventeen	shaft-hole	sharpener	sheet-flow	shiftable
serologic	seventhly	shaftless	sharp-eyed	sheet iron	shiftiest
serositis	seventies	shaftment	sharpling	sheetless	shiftless
serotinal	seven year	shaftsman	sharpness	sheetlike	shift lock
serotonin	severable	shaggiest	sharp rush	sheet-mill	shift work
serotypic	severally	shaggy cap	sharpshin	sheet-pile	shikimate
serpentin	severalth	Shahaptan	sharp-shod	Sheetrock	shillaber
serpently	severalty	shahtoosh	sharpster	sheet-wash	shime-waza
serpentry	severance	shahzadah	sharp-tail	Sheffield	shimiyana
serranoid	Sevillana	shakeable	Shastraic	sheikhdom	shine away
serration	Sevillano	shake a leg	shatterer	sheld-duck	shine down
serrature	Sevillian	shake down	shavecoat	sheldrake	shineless
serrefile	sewee bean	shakedown	shavehook	shelducks	shine upon

shine up to	shogunate	shortstop	shrinkage	siderosis	silential
shin-guard	shonicker	short suit	shrink fit	siderotic	silentish
shininess	shonkiest	short-term	shroffage	siderurgy	silica gel
shiningly	shootable	short time	shroudage	side salad	silicated
Shintoism	shoot away	short-toed	shrouding	side-shoot	siliceous
Shintoist	shoot back	short view	shrubbage	side-split	silicious
shipboard	shoot down	shortwall	shrubbery	side-stick	silicosis
shipborne	shoot-'em-up	shortward	shrubless	side-swipe	silicotic
ship canal	shop-board	short wave	shrublike	sideswipe	siliquose
ship-craft	shop class	short wind	shrub rose	side table	siliquous
ship-fever	shopcraft	short-wool	shrugging	sidetrack	silkaline
ship money	shop floor	shot alloy	shubunkin	side valve	silk-gland
ship-of-war	shopfront	shot-blast	shuffling	sidewards	silk grass
shipowner	shop-house	shot-borer	shunnable	side-wheel	silkiness
shippable	shopocrat	shotcrete	shunt line	side-wiper	silkoline
ship plane	shopwoman	shot-drill	shut-knife	sieva bean	silk waste
shippound	shorebird	shot-firer	shuttance	sieve cell	silliness
ship-royal	shore-boat	shot-glass	shuttling	sievelike	siltation
ship's boat	shore crab	shot-group	sialidase	sieve tube	siltstone
shipshape	shoreface	shotmaker	siallitic	sighfully	silver age
ship's time	shore-fish	shot-metal	sialogram	sighingly	Silverblu
ship-to-air	shore lark	shot noise	sialolith	sightable	silver eel
shipwreck	shoreless	shot-pouch	sibilance	sight bill	silver-eye
shire-hall	shoreline	shotproof	sibilancy	sight feed	silver fir
shire-jury	shore-rope	shot-tower	sibilator	sight-hole	silver fox
shiremoot	shoreside	shout down	siblicide	sightless	silvering
shire-town	shoresman	shovelard	sibylline	sight line	silverish
Shirodkar	shoreward	shovelful	sibyllism	sight-read	silverite
shirtiest	shoreweed	shovel hat	Sibyllist	sightseer	silverize
shirtless	shore zone	shovelled	siccative	sight-sing	silver key
shirt stud	shorn lamb	shoveller	sice-point	sightsman	silver-tip
shirt-tail	short-arse	shovel-man	siciliana	sight tube	silvester
shite-hawk	short ball	showbizzy	siciliano	sigillary	silvicide
shitepoke	short bill	show cause	sick-berth	sigillate	simantron
shit-faced	shortcake	shower box	sickening	sigma-bond	simarouba
shit-house	short-coat	shower-cap	sickishly	sigmatism	Simeonite
shithouse	short date	show fight	sick leave	sigmoidal	similarly
shittiest	short dung	show forth	sicklemia	signal box	Simmental
shivering	shortened	show-glass	sicklemic	signalise	simmering
shlimazel	shortener	show house	sicklepod	signality	simo chart
shmegegge	shorten in	showiness	sickliest	signalize	simonious
shmendrik	shortfall	show-piece	sick nurse	signalled	simon-pure
shoal-mark	short fuse	showpiece	Sicyonian	signaller	Simon Pure
shoalness	short game	show-place	Siddonian	signalman	Simon Says
shockable	short gown	showplace	side-aisle	signalmen	simpatico
shock cone	short-hair	show round	sideboard	signal red	simpering
shock cord	shorthair	show sport	side chain	signaries	simple eye
shockedly	shorthand	show trial	side chair	signatary	simplesse
shock-head	short haul	show-woman	sidedness	signation	simpleton
shock test	short head	Shqipetar	side drift	signatory	simple vow
shock tube	shorthold	shragging	side entry	signature	simulacra
shock wave	shorthorn	shredding	sideguard	signboard	simulacre
shoddiest	short hour	shrewdish	side-horse	sign digit	simulated
shoddyism	short leet	shrewlike	side issue	significs	simulator
shoddyite	short list	shrew-mole	side lever	signified	simulcast
shoeblack	shortlist	shrieking	side-light	signifier	sincerely
shoe-brush	short mark	shriek out	sidelight	signifies	sincerest
shoemaker	shortness	shriek-owl	sidelings	signorial	sincerity
shoe-piece	short odds	shrike-tit	side order	signories	Sindebele
shoeshine	short-punt	shrillish	side-piece	signorina	sine curve
shoesmith	short seas	shrimpish	side plate	Sikkimese	sinewless
shoe-valve	short stop	shrimplet	sideritic	silent cop	sing along

singalong	skateable	sky border	Slavonism	sloganeer	small reed
singed cat	skatepark	sky burial	Slavonize	sloganize	small room
singingly	skate-sail	sky-colour	sleazebag	slop about	small sail
single cut	skedaddle	skydiving	sleaziest	slop basin	small shot
single tax	skeezicks	sky-farmer	sleekness	slope arms	small slam
singleton	skeletony	sky filter	sleep-away	slopehead	small talk
sing small	Skeltonic	sky-flower	sleepered	slope wash	small-time
singsongy	skeptical	skyjacker	sleep fast	slopeways	small-town
singulary	sketchier	skylarker	sleepiest	slopingly	small type
singultus	sketchily	skylounge	sleepless	sloppiest	smalt-blue
Sinhalese	sketching	sky-marker	sleep over	sloppy joe	smaragdus
sinistral	sketchist	sky-rocket	sleepover	sloshiest	smarmiest
sinlessly	sketch map	skyrocket	sleep sofa	sloth bear	smart alec
sinneress	sketch pad	sky screen	sleepwalk	slot-hound	smart-arse
sinningia	skew field	slab bacon	sleeve-cap	slot-meter	smart card
sinologue	skew-whiff	slab-sided	sleeve dog	slot racer	smartcard
Sinologue	skiagraph	slab-stone	sleeve gun	slot wedge	smartness
Sinophile	skiamachy	slackener	sleevelet	slot-wound	smartweed
Sinophobe	skiascope	slack hand	sleeve-nut	slouch hat	smasheroo
sinuately	skiascopy	slack lime	sleigh bed	slouchily	smatterer
sinuation	ski-bobber	slackness	slenderer	slouching	smear-case
sinuosely	skiddooos	slack rein	slenderly	Slovakian	smear test
sinuosity	ski-joring	slack-rope	sleuth-dog	Slovakish	smegmatic
sinuously	ski jumper	slackster	sliceable	Slovenian	smellable
sinusitis	skilfully	slack suit	slickered	Slovenish	smell a rat
siphonage	skill-less	slaggiest	slickness	slow-belly	smelliest
siphonate	skim-board	slag-glass	slickster	slowcoach	smell-less
siphonein	skimobile	slag notch	slideable	slow-hound	smilacina
siphonous	skimpiest	slakeless	slide-rest	slow loris	smileable
siphuncle	skin cream	slalomist	slide-rock	slow march	smileless
sippingly	skin depth	slammakin	slide rule	slow match	Smilesian
sirenical	skin diver	slanderer	slide-wire	slow track	smilingly
siren suit	skin-dried	slangiest	slidingly	slow virus	smith shop
Sir Garnet	skin-flick	slangster	slightish	slow wheel	smock-face
Siryenian	skinflint	slanguage	slime-ball	slug it out	smockless
sisal hemp	skin graft	slant-eyed	slime-flux	slug-nutty	smock-mill
sisserara	skin house	slant-eyes	sliminess	slug-snail	smock-race
sissified	skinniest	slant-line	sling-back	sluice-box	smoggiest
sissiness	skinny-dip	slantways	sling-cart	sluice-way	smokeable
sistering	skinny-rib	slantwise	sling pump	slumberer	smoke-ball
Sisyphean	skin-tight	slap-happy	slingshot	slumbrous	smoke-boat
Sisyphism	skintight	slapstick	slingsman	slummiest	smoke bomb
sitatunga	skin tonic	slash-hook	slinkiest	slummocky	smoke bush
sit-downer	skin trade	slash-pine	slip a disc	slump test	smoke-free
site value	skiograph	slate blue	slip-cased	slung shot	smoke-head
sit-me-down	skiomachy	slate club	slip-catch	slush-cast	smoke-hole
sitomania	skippable	slate grey	slip-coach	slush fund	smoke-jack
sitringee	skirt duty	slat fence	slip cover	slushiest	smokeless
situation	skirt-land	slatiness	slipe wool	slush-lamp	smoke-pole
situtunga	skirtless	slaughter	slip joint	slush pump	smoke ring
sit well on	skirtlike	slave-born	slip-noose	slut's wool	smoke-room
sitzkrieg	skirt soil	slave-fork	slippered	smackeroo	smoke-shop
Six Day War	Skokomish	slaveless	slippiest	smacksman	smoke tree
six-seater	Skoptsism	slavering	slip-plane	small arms	smokiness
sixteenmo	skotophil	slave ship	slip ratio	small beer	smoochier
sixteenth	Skraeling	Slavicist	slip sheet	small-bore	smoochily
sixth form	skrimshaw	Slavicize	slipstone	small-cell	smoothish
sixth part	skull-fish	slavishly	slittiest	small coal	smorzandi
sixtyfold	skull-less	Slavistic	slivovitz	small debt	smorzando
sixty-nine	skunk-bear	slavocrat	slobberer	small deer	smotherer
sizarship	skunk-bird	Slavonian	slob trout	small guts	smudge pot
size-stick	skunkweed	Slavonise	sloe-thorn	smallness	smudgiest

smuggling	snootiest	soap-stock	soil-creep	solvolyse	sorrel-top
smut-grass	snooziest	soapstone	soil group	Somaschan	sorriness
smut-hound	snore away	soap-suddy	soil phase	sombreros	sorrowful
smuttiest	snore-hole	soap-works	soil water	someplace	sorrowing
Smyrnaean	snoreless	soaringly	sojourner	something	sortation
Smyrniote	snoringly	sobbingly	sokemanry	sometimes	sortieing
snack food	snot-nosed	soberness	solaceful	sometimey	sortilege
snag-tooth	snottiest	sobriquet	solar apex	somewhere	sortilegy
snailfish	snout-face	sob sister	solar cell	somewhile	sortition
snail-horn	snoutless	soccer fan	solar hour	sommelier	sostenuto
snail-like	snout-moth	soccerite	solariums	somnolent	Sothiacal
snail mail	snowberry	socialise	solar lamp	Somocista	so to speak
snail-slow	snow-blind	socialism	solar mass	so much for	sottishly
snake bird	snow-blink	socialist	solar myth	so much the	sotto voce
snake eyes	snowboard	socialite	solar pond	Sonagraph	soubrette
snakefish	snowbound	sociality	solar pool	song cycle	soufrière
snake-head	snow-break	socialize	solar salt	songfully	soughless
snake hips	snow-broth	social war	solar time	song-motet	soul-force
snakelike	snow buggy	sociation	solar wind	song-perch	soulfully
snakeroot	snow bunny	sociative	solar year	songsmith	soul-house
snakeship	snow-camel	societary	soldering	sonically	soul music
snakeskin	snow-craft	societies	soldierly	sonicator	soul stuff
snakesman	snow-creep	sociogram	soldier on	sonic bang	sou markee
snakeweed	snow devil	sociolect	solemness	sonic boom	sound bite
snakewise	snowdrift	sociology	solemnify	sonic mine	sound boom
snakewood	snow-eater	sociopath	solemnise	sonneteer	sound card
snakiness	snowfield	socketing	solemnity	sonneting	sound cell
snakishly	snow finch	socket set	solemnize	sonnetize	sound-film
snap gauge	snowflake	Socotrine	solenette	son of a gun	sound gate
snaphance	snow-fleck	Socratean	solenodon	son of toil	sound head
snap out of	snow goose	Socratist	sole-plate	sonograph	sound-hole
snappable	snow grain	Socratize	solfatara	sonolysis	soundhole
snappiest	snow-grass	soda bread	solfeggio	sonolytic	soundless
snap-sound	snowiness	soda glass	solferino	sonometer	soundness
snare drum	snow-maker	soda nitre	solicited	sons-in-law	sound post
snareless	snow mould	soda water	solicitee	soon after	sound wave
snarliest	snow-mouse	sodbuster	solicitor	sooranjee	soup bunch
snazziest	snow plane	sodomitic	solidaire	sooterkin	soupiness
sneak-boat	snow plant	Soerensen	solid body	soothfast	soup plate
sneakered	Snow Queen	soft-board	solid fuel	sootiness	soup spoon
sneakiest	snowscape	soft brome	solidness	sooty tern	soup-stock
sneaksman	snowshoed	soft-cover	soliflual	sophianic	sour bread
sneck-band	snowshoer	soft drink	solifugid	sophister	sour cream
sneck-draw	snow-sleep	softening	soliloquy	sophistic	sour crout
sneeshing	snowstorm	softer sex	soli-lunar	sophistry	sourdough
sneeze gas	snow-water	soft focus	solipsism	sophomore	sour gourd
Snell's law	snow white	soft fruit	solipsist	soporific	sour grass
snelskrif	snub-nosed	soft goods	solipugid	soppiness	sour-sweet
snideness	snuff-dish	soft-grass	solitaire	sopranino	souteneur
sniffable	snuff film	soft maple	sollicker	sopranist	South Bank
sniffiest	snuffiest	soft-nosed	solmizate	sorb-apple	Southdown
sniggerer	snuffless	soft-paste	solodized	sorbitize	south-east
snipe bill	snuffling	soft pedal	soloistic	Sorbonist	South-East
snipe fish	snuff-mill	soft-shell	Solomonic	sorceress	southerly
snipiness	soakingly	soft sugar	solonchak	sorceries	Southeyan
snippiest	Soanesque	soft Tommy	solonized	sorcerize	southland
snivelled	soapberry	soft touch	solo whist	sorcerous	southmost
sniveller	soapboxer	soft wheat	solstitia	sordidity	southness
snobbiest	soap-house	sogginess	solutizer	sorediate	south pole
snob value	soapiness	soi-disant	Solutrean	soredioid	South Seas
snockered	soap opera	soil auger	Solutrian	sore point	south-side
Snohomish	soap-plant	soil class	solvation	soritical	southward

south-west	sparingly	speedboat	spikenard	spiritous	spokeless
South-West	spark ball	speed bump	spike-rush	spiritual	spoken for
south wind	spark coil	speed hump	spike-team	spirituel	spokesman
souvlakia	sparkless	speediest	spikiness	spirogram	spokesmen
souvlakis	sparklike	speed king	spillikin	spirogyra	spokewise
sou'wester	spark line	speedless	spill over	spiroidal	spoliator
sovereign	sparkling	speed-read	spillover	spirulina	spondylus
Sovietise	sparkover	speedster	spinal tap	spissated	sponge bag
Sovietism	spark plug	speed trap	spination	spit blood	spongeful
Sovietist	sparkplug	Speed-walk	spin a yarn	spit chips	spongeing
Sovietize	sparsedly	speedwell	spindlage	spiteless	spongelet
Sovnarkom	spar-stone	speedy cut	spindlier	spitework	spongeous
sow-backed	Spartanly	speldring	spindling	spit image	spongiest
sow-gelder	sparteine	spellable	spin-drier	spit it out	spongiole
soya sauce	Spartiate	spellbind	spindrift	spit-roast	spongiosa
space-ager	spasmatic	spell down	spin-dryer	spit-shine	spongiose
space club	spasm band	spelldown	spinebill	spitstick	spongious
spaceless	spasmodic	spellican	spinefoot	splashier	sponsalia
space lift	spasmogen	speluncar	spineless	splashily	sponsible
spacelike	spathodea	spelunker	spinelike	splash-net	spookiest
space-line	spatially	spendable	spine road	splash out	spoon-back
space mine	Spätleses	spent gnat	spinetail	splat-cool	spoon-bait
spaceport	spattered	spermatia	spin glass	splatting	spoonbill
space race	spatulate	spermatic	spin-house	splay-foot	spoon-feed
spacer gel	spatulose	spermatid	spiniform	spleenful	spoonfeed
spaceship	spatulous	sperm bank	spininess	spleenish	spoonfuls
space shot	speakable	sperm cell	spin label	splendent	spoon-hook
space-sick	speakably	speronara	spinnable	splendour	spooniest
spacesuit	speak-back	spew frost	spinnaker	splenetic	spoonless
space–time	speakeasy	spewiness	spinneret	splenitis	spoon-meat
space walk	speak fair	sphacelia	spinniken	splenosis	spoonwood
space warp	speak past	sphacelus	spin-orbit	spleuchan	spoonworm
space wave	speak with	sphagnose	spinorial	splice-bar	spoonyism
spaciness	spearfish	sphagnous	spinosely	splintage	sporangia
spacistor	spearhead	sphendone	spinosity	splintery	spore-case
spade-bone	spearlike	sphenotic	Spinozism	splinting	sporeling
spade-farm	spearmint	sphere gap	Spinozist	split-arse	sporidium
spadefish	spear-play	spherical	Spinozite	split beam	sporocarp
spade foot	spear side	spherular	spin-rinse	split-dose	sporocyst
spadefuls	spearsman	sphincter	spintrian	split-down	sporocyte
spadelike	spearwood	sphinxian	spinulate	split flap	sporogony
spadesman	spearwort	spicebush	spinulose	split gear	sporozoan
spade-tree	specially	spice-cake	spinulous	split-half	sporozoon
spadewise	specialty	spice mill	spiracles	split jeté	sportance
spadework	specie jar	spice rack	spiracula	split jump	sportfish
spae-craft	specified	spicewood	spiral arm	split mind	sportiest
spaghetti	specifier	spiciness	spirality	split page	sportless
spagyrist	specifies	spick-span	spiralize	split rail	sportling
Spam medal	speckless	spiculate	spiralled	split ring	sports car
spanaemia	speckling	spiderish	spiraloid	split shot	sports day
spanandry	spectacle	spider-leg	spirantal	split time	sportsman
Spanglish	spectator	spiderman	spiration	splitting	sportsmen
Spanishly	spectrous	spidermen	spireless	splittism	sportster
spareable	speculate	spiderweb	spiriform	splittist	sporulate
spareless	speculist	spiffiest	spirillar	splodgily	spot board
spareness	speech act	spigelian	spirillum	spluttery	spot check
spare part	speech day	spike-buck	spiritful	spodumene	spot level
spare time	speechful	spike-fish	spirit gum	spoilable	spotlight
spare tyre	speechify	spike heel	spiriting	spoil-five	spot meter
sparganum	speeching	spike-horn	spiritism	spoilless	spot-nosed
sparge arm	speechlet	spikelike	spiritist	spoilsman	spot plate
spargosis	speedball	spike-nail	spiritize	spoilsmen	spottiest

spousally	squashier	stackless	staminody	start over	steel-iron
spout-bath	squashily	stack-room	staminoid	star tulip	steel mill
spout-fish	squatness	stack-yard	stammerer	starvedly	steel tape
spout-hole	squat rack	stackyard	stampable	star-wheel	steel trap
spoutless	squattage	staddling	stamp book	statehood	steel wool
sprackish	squattest	stadhouse	stamp duty	stateless	steelwork
spratting	squattily	staffette	stampeder	statelily	steelyard
sprayable	squatting	staffless	stamp-mill	State line	steenbras
sprayed-on	squattish	staff-room	stanchion	statement	steenbuck
sprayless	squaw corn	staffroom	stand away	stateroom	steenkirk
spraylike	squaw duck	staff vine	stand back	Stateside	steentjie
spray zone	squawfish	stageable	stand buff	statesman	steep-down
spreading	squawk-box	stage door	stand down	state-wide	steephead
sprechery	squaw-root	stage hand	stand easy	staticize	steepness
spreckled	squaw-weed	stagehand	stander-by	stational	steerable
sprekelia	squeakery	stage hero	stand good	stationer	steerhide
sprigging	squeakier	stage left	stand high	statistic	steerling
sprightly	squeakily	stagelike	stand mute	statively	steersman
sprigtail	squeamish	stage name	stand on me	stativity	steersmen
springald	squeamous	stage play	stand over	statocone	stegomyia
spring bed	squeegeed	staggerer	standpipe	statocyst	stegosaur
springbok	squeegees	staghound	stand upon	statocyte	steinbock
spring-gun	squelcher	staginess	stand up to	statolith	steinkirk
springier	squencher	Stagirite	stand well	statuette	Steinmann
springily	squibbery	stag movie	stanhopea	statusful	Stelazine
springing	squibbing	stagnance	stannator	status quo	stellaria
springlet	squibbish	stagnancy	stapedial	statutory	stellated
sprinkler	squidding	stag-night	stapedius	staunchly	stellerid
spritsail	squid fish	stag-party	stapeliad	stave-wood	stellular
sprouting	squidgier	stag's head	staple gun	stay-awake	stem borer
spruce fir	squidgily	stag's horn	star-anise	Staybrite	stem-glass
spruce hen	squiffier	staidness	star-apple	stay-clean	St Emilion
spruce tea	squillion	stainable	star atlas	St Bernard	stemmatic
spunkiest	squinancy	stainless	starboard	steadfast	stem piece
spunkless	squint-eye	staircase	starburst	steadiest	stenchful
spur-rowel	squiralty	stair-foot	star chart	steadyish	Stenonian
spur royal	squirarch	stairhead	starchier	steady pin	stenosing
spur-wheel	squiredom	stairless	starchily	steak raid	stenotope
sputcheon	squirelet	stairlift	star cloud	stealable	stenotype
sputterer	squirmier	stair-step	star coral	steam bath	stenotypy
spymaster	squirt can	stairwell	star-delta	steam beer	stent-roll
squabbier	squirt gun	stake-boat	stare down	steam-bent	stepbairn
squabbish	squirting	stake-body	star-facet	steamboat	stepchild
squabbler	squishier	stalactic	star fruit	steam-coal	step-dance
squaddies	squitters	stalemate	stargazer	steam-cure	step fault
squadrism	Sri Lankan	staleness	star-grass	steam-heat	step-gable
squadrist	stabilate	Stalinise	staringly	steamiest	stephanic
squalidly	stabilise	Stalinism	starkness	steam iron	step motor
squalmish	stabilism	Stalinist	starlight	steamless	step-stool
squameous	stabilist	Stalinite	star-proof	steam line	step wedge
squamosal	stability	Stalinize	starquake	steamroll	steradian
squarable	stabilize	Stalinoid	starriest	steamship	stercoral
square cap	stable boy	stalkable	star route	steatitic	sterculia
square cut	stable-fly	stalk-eyed	starry ray	steatosis	sterilant
square hit	stableful	stalkless	starscape	steedless	sterilely
square law	stable lad	stalklike	star shell	steekgras	sterilise
square leg	stableman	stall-feed	star-shine	steel band	sterility
squareman	stablemen	stall seat	star-stone	steel-clad	sterilize
square off	staccatos	stall turn	start in on	steel drum	stern-boat
square pin	stachyose	stalworth	start-line	steel-face	sternebra
squarrose	stackable	staminate	startling	steelhead	stern-fast
squash bug	stack arms	staminode	startlish	steeliest	Stern Gang

stern-line	stimulate	stomachal	stop thief	straplike	strikable
sternmost	stingaree	stomached	stop valve	strap-line	strike off
sternness	sting-fish	stomacher	stopwatch	strappado	strike oil
stern-port	stingiest	stomachic	stop-water	strapping	strike out
sternpost	stingless	stomatose	store card	strap-rail	strike pay
stern-rail	stinglike	stomatous	store-farm	strap shoe	string art
stern tube	stink-bird	stompneus	storeroom	strap-work	string bed
stern-walk	stink bomb	stone-bark	storeship	strapwork	string cot
sternward	stinkeroo	stone-bass	storesman	strapwort	stringent
steroidal	stinkhorn	stone-blue	store-wide	Strasburg	stringful
Stetsoned	stinkiest	stone-boat	storey box	stratagem	stringier
stevedore	stinkweed	stonebuck	storiated	strategic	stringily
stewardly	stinkwood	stone-cast	storiette	strategus	stringing
stewardry	stintedly	stone-cell	storkling	stratiote	string man
stewartry	stintless	stonechat	stormable	straw boss	string out
stibophen	stipended	stone-coal	storm-area	strawless	string tie
stichical	stipiform	stone-cold	storm-bird	strawline	striolate
stick at it	stipitate	stone-crab	storm coat	strawneck	strip cell
stick-back	stippling	stonecrop	storm-cock	straw poll	strip club
stickball	stipulate	stone-dead	storm cone	straw ring	strip-down
stick bean	stipulode	stone-deaf	storm cuff	straw tick	stripiest
stick-bomb	stirabout	stone-delf	storm-door	straw vote	stripline
stick down	stir-crazy	stone-dust	storm-drum	straw wine	stripling
stick 'em up	stir-fried	stone-dyke	storm-flap	straw-work	strip-loin
sticker-up	stir-fries	stone face	stormiest	straw-worm	strip mall
stick fast	stirpital	stone-fall	stormless	straw yard	strip mill
stick free	stitchery	stonefish	storm-sail	strayaway	strip mine
stickiest	stitching	stoneless	storm-wave	stray-line	stripping
stick it on	stock-book	stonelike	storm wind	strayling	strip well
stickless	stock-card	stone-lily	stornello	streakier	strobilus
sticklike	stock cube	stone line	story book	streakily	strokable
stickling	stock dove	stone-mint	storyette	streaking	stroke oar
stick pigs	stock duck	stone pine	storyless	streaming	strolling
stick-slip	stockfish	stone ring	story-line	streamlet	stromatic
stick to it	Stockholm	stone-root	storyline	stream-tin	stromboid
stick up to	stockiest	stone-shot	stoss-side	stream-way	strong-arm
stickweed	stockinet	stonewall	stounding	streelish	strongbox
stick with	stockless	stoneware	stourness	street boy	strongers
stickwork	stock line	stoneweed	stoutness	streetcar	strongest
sticky dog	stocklist	stonework	stoveless	street dog	strong eye
sticky end	stock-lock	stonewort	stove-pipe	streetful	strongish
sticky-out	stockpile	stone-yard	stow-blade	street kid	strong man
stiffener	stock rail	stoniness	stow-board	streetlet	strongman
stiff-leaf	stockroom	stonkered	straddler	streetman	strongmen
stiff-neck	stock-size	stony-iron	straggler	street rod	strongyle
stiffness	stocktake	stoolball	straight-A	streetway	strontian
stigmaria	stock unit	stoop ball	strainful	strengite	strontium
stigmatic	stock up on	stoop crop	straining	strengthy	stroppier
stigmergy	stock-whip	stoothing	stranding	strenuity	stroppily
stilettos	stockwork	stop-and-go	strangely	strenuous	stropping
stillborn	stockyard	stop-block	strangled	stressful	structure
stilleite	stodgiest	stop-drill	strangler	stressman	struggler
still-head	stoep-room	stop-hound	strangles	stretcher	strumatic
still hunt	stoically	stop light	strangury	strewment	strumitis
still less	stokehold	stop-order	strap-bolt	striation	strumming
still life	stoke-hole	stoppable	strap-down	striature	strung-out
stillness	stokehole	stoppo car	strap-fork	striction	strutting
still room	Stokes' law	stop press	strap-game	stricture	strychnia
stiltedly	stole-fees	stop-ridge	strap-hang	stridence	strychnic
stilt heel	stolidity	stop-seine	strap iron	stridency	strychnos
stilt-root	stolonate	stop short	strap-laid	strifeful	stubbiest
stimulant	stolonial	stop-start	strapless	strigated	Stubbsian

stub-tenon	subahship	submucous	succourer	sulphamic	sunset law
stub track	subalpine	subnormal	succubous	sulphated	sun-spider
stuccador	subaltern	suboctave	succulent	sulphazin	sun-spring
stuccoist	subapical	subocular	succumber	sulphidic	sun spurge
stuckness	subaquean	subpatent	succursal	sulphinic	sunstroke
studental	subarctic	subphylum	suckening	sulphinyl	sunstruck
studentry	subastral	subpoena'd	sucker-cup	sulphonal	Sun Yat-sen
stud-groom	subatomic	subramose	sucking-up	sulphonic	superable
stud-horse	Sub-Boreal	subregion	suck-teeth	sulphonyl	superacid
stud-house	subbotnik	subrision	suctional	sulphured	superbike
studiable	sub-bottom	subrisive	suctorial	sulphuret	superbity
studiedly	sub-branch	subrogate	suctorian	sulphuric	superbomb
stud poker	subcaudal	subrotund	sudatoria	sulphuryl	Super Bowl
study hall	sub-cheese	subsample	sudoresis	Sulpician	supercede
stuff coat	sub-clause	subscribe	sudorific	sulpiride	supercity
stuff gown	subclause	subscript	suedehead	sultanate	supercoil
stuffiest	subclimax	subsecive	suede shoe	sultaness	supercool
stuffless	subcostal	subsellia	suet crust	sultanism	supercrat
stuffover	subdeacon	subserous	suet-faced	sultanize	superegos
stump-foot	subdivide	subsidies	Suez group	sultriest	superette
stumpiest	subdolous	subsiding	suffering	summaries	superfine
stump-jump	subdorsal	subsidise	suffixoid	summarily	superflow
stump mast	subduable	subsidium	suffixual	summarise	superflux
stumpnose	subduedly	subsidize	suffocate	summarist	superfuse
stump-tail	sub-editor	subsocial	Suffolker	summarize	supergene
stump word	subeditor	subsoiler	suffragan	summation	superglue
stump-work	subentire	substance	suffrutex	summative	supergrid
stuntedly	subereous	substract	suffusion	summer-day	superheat
stunt-head	subfactor	substrata	suffusive	summer egg	superhero
stuntness	subfamily	substrate	sugar beet	summering	superhive
stupefied	subfossil	substruct	sugarbird	summerish	supermale
stupefier	subgenera	substylar	sugar-bush	summerize	supermart
stupefies	subhedral	subsultus	sugar-camp	summing-up	supermind
stupidest	subiculum	subsystem	sugar cane	summiteer	supernate
stupidish	subincise	subtenant	sugar-coat	summonses	supernova
stupidity	subinfeud	subtenure	sugarless	summulist	superpose
stuporose	subjacent	subterete	sugar loaf	sump guard	super-race
stuporous	sub judice	subtilely	sugar-mite	sumptuary	super-real
sturdiest	subjugate	subtilise	sugar palm	sumptuous	supersede
stutterer	sublation	subtilism	sugar-pine	sun awning	supersign
style-book	sub-lessee	subtility	sugar-plum	sun-bathed	superstar
styleless	sub-lessor	subtilize	sugarplum	sunbather	supervene
stylidium	sub-lethal	subtitler	sugar sack	sun-bonnet	supervise
styliform	subletter	subtopian	sugar sand	sun-bright	superweak
stylishly	sublimate	subtribal	sugar snap	Sundanese	supinator
stylistic	sublimely	subtriple	sugar snow	Sundayish	suppering
stylitism	sublimest	subtropic	sugar soap	sundowner	suppliant
stylobata	sublimity	subulated	sugar-sops	sun filter	supply day
stylobate	sublimize	subungual	sugar-teat	sunfisher	supply-led
stylohyal	sublinear	subvassal	sugar-tree	sunflower	supporter
stylolite	sublunary	subversal	sugar vase	sun-grazer	supposing
stymieing	subluxate	subverter	suggester	sun-helmet	suppurate
styptical	submarine	subwarden	suggestor	sunk fence	supremacy
styrofoam	submaster	subwoofer	suggestum	sun-kissed	supremely
Styrofoam	submental	succedent	sugillate	sun lotion	supremity
styrolene	submerged	succeeder	suicidism	sun lounge	surcharge
suability	submicron	succentor	suikerbos	sunniness	surcingle
suasively	submissly	successor	suit at law	sunny side	surculose
suaveness	submittal	succinate	suit regal	sunrising	sure thing
suavities	submitted	succinite	suit royal	sun-scorch	surfacely
subaerial	submitter	succorant	sulciform	sunscreen	surfacing
subagency	submucosa	succotash	sulkiness	sun-seeker	surfboard

surfeited	swampiest	sweet papa	sword-belt	sympodial	syntaxial
surfeiter	swampland	sweet rush	swordbill	sympodium	Syntaxian
surf-grass	swamp lily	sweetshop	sword-cane	symposiac	syntectic
surficial	swamp-pink	sweet-sour	sword-case	symposial	synthalin
surf music	swamp rock	sweet spot	sword-fern	symposium	syntheses
surf-perch	swan goose	sweet talk	swordfish	synagogal	synthesis
surfusion	swanimote	sweet-veld	sword-hand	synagogue	synthetic
surgeless	swankiest	sweet wine	sword knot	synalepha	syntrophy
surgeoncy	swan plant	sweetwood	swordless	synangium	syphilide
surgeries	Swan River	sweet wort	swordlike	synanthic	syphilise
surge tank	swansdown	swellfish	sword lily	syncellus	syphilize
Surinamer	swan-upper	swell-head	swordplay	Synchromy	syphiloid
surliness	swan-white	swept-back	sword-side	synchrony	syphiloma
surmaster	Swarajist	swept-wing	swordsman	synchysis	syphonage
surmullet	swarm cell	Swiderian	swordsmen	syncitium	Syracusan
surpasser	swarthier	swift-foot	swordtail	synclinal	Syriacism
surpliced	swarthily	swiftness	sword-work	syncopate	Syrianize
surplus to	swartness	swimathon	swung dash	syncretic	syringeal
surprisal	swartzite	swimdress	swy school	syncytial	syringing
surprised	swash mark	swimgloat	sybaritic	syncytium	systaltic
surpriser	swash-work	swimmable	sycophant	syndactyl	systemise
surquidry	Swatantra	swimmeret	syllabary	syndicate	systemist
surreally	swatching	swindlery	syllabify	syndromic	systemize
surrejoin	swatchway	swine-back	syllabise	synechism	systoflex
surrender	sway-brace	swine-cote	syllabism	synechist	systrophe
surrendry	swayingly	swine-head	syllabize	synecious	taaffeite
surrogacy	swear pink	swineherd	syllabled	synectics	tabacosis
surrogate	swear word	swinehood	syllepses	synedrian	tabasheer
survivant	sweat-band	swine-hull	syllepsis	synedrion	tabbouleh
suscitate	sweatband	swing-back	sylleptic	synenergy	tabbyhood
Susianian	sweat-bath	swingball	syllogise	syneresis	tab collar
suspected	sweatered	swing-boat	syllogism	synergise	tabellion
suspecter	sweatiest	swingboat	syllogist	synergism	tablature
suspector	sweatless	swing-coat	syllogize	synergist	table bell
suspended	sweat-pore	swing-door	sylphlike	synergize	table-book
suspender	sweatshop	swingeing	sylvanite	syngameon	table desk
suspensor	sweat sock	swing-gate	sylvanity	syngamous	tablefuls
suspicion	sweatsuit	swing hand	sylvester	syngeneic	table game
Sussex cow	sweep away	swingiest	Sylvester	synizesis	table lamp
sustained	sweepback	swing-over	sylvinite	synizetic	tableland
sustainer	sweep hand	swing pass	symbioses	synkaryon	table-maid
sustenant	sweep-wire	swing room	symbiosis	synneusis	tablement
susuhunan	sweerness	swing-rope	symbiotic	synochous	table-plan
susurrant	sweet corn	swingster	symbolise	synodally	table ruby
susurrate	sweetcorn	swing-tail	symbolism	synodical	table salt
susurrous	sweetener	swing-tool	symbolist	synodsman	table talk
sutleress	sweet-eyed	swing-tree	symbolize	synoecism	table tape
sutteeism	sweet fern	swing vote	symbolled	synoecize	table-tomb
suturally	sweet flag	swing-wing	symbology	synoekete	tableware
Svanetian	sweet gale	swinishly	symmelian	synoicous	table wine
Svengalis	sweetikin	swipe card	symmetral	synonymic	tablewise
swaddling	sweet John	swipecard	symmetric	synopsise	tabularly
swag belly	sweetleaf	Swiss bank	sympathic	synopsize	tabulator
swaggerer	sweet life	Swiss file	sympatric	synoptist	tacamahac
Swahilize	sweet lime	Swiss roll	symphilic	synostose	tachylite
swainmote	sweetling	switching	symphonic	synovitis	tacitness
Swaledale	sweetlips	switchman	symphonie	synsacral	tackifier
swallower	sweetmart	switch off	symphylan	synsacrum	tackiness
swamp deer	sweetmeal	swivel eye	symphylid	syntactic	tack-money
swamp fire	sweetmeat	swivel-gun	symphyses	syntagmas	tactfully
swamp hare	sweet milk	swivelled	symphysis	syntagmic	tactician
swamp hook	sweetness	sword-bean	symplasma	syntaxeme	tacticity

tactilely	take aside	tangental	tarsalgia	Taylorism	telematic
tactility	take a step	tangerine	tarsotomy	Taylorize	telemeter
tactually	take a toll	tanginess	Tartarean	Tchambuli	telemetry
tae kwon do	take a toss	tangliest	Tartarian	Tchuktchi	telemotor
taeniasis	take a walk	tank wagon	tartarise	teaboardy	teleology
taffy pull	take a wife	tannaitic	tartarize	tea-broker	teleonomy
taft joint	take cover	tanneries	tartiness	teachable	teleosaur
tag and rag	take guard	tantadlin	tartronic	teachably	telepathy
tagmemics	take hands	tantalate	Tashi Lama	teacherly	telephone
tagnicati	take heart	Tantalean	tasimeter	teacupful	telephony
tag-phrase	take issue	tantalian	task force	tea garden	telephote
tahsildar	take it ill	Tantalian	task group	tea-kettle	telephoto
tail-block	take-leave	tantalise	Tasmanian	tea master	telepoint
tailboard	take place	tantalite	Tasmanoid	team-teach	teleprint
tail-drain	take roost	tantalize	tasselled	team vicar	telerobot
tail-ender	take shape	tantivies	tasseller	teapotful	telesales
tailer-out	take short	tant mieux	tasteable	tear apart	telescope
tailgater	take sides	Tanzanian	tasteless	tear-fault	telescopy
tail-grape	take stock	tanzanite	tastesome	tearfully	teleseism
tail-heavy	take to bed	Taoiseach	taste-test	tear-gland	telestich
tail-hound	take turns	tap-cinder	tastiness	tear sheet	teletyper
tail light	take water	tap-dancer	tastingly	tear-smoke	televisor
tailordom	Talbotype	tape-delay	tasto solo	tear-thumb	tell apart
tailoress	talc light	tape drive	tatami mat	teartness	tell a tale
tailoring	talcuming	tape-grass	tater-trap	teasel-bur	tellingly
tailorism	talegalla	tape punch	Tatianist	teashoppy	tellinite
tailorize	tale of woe	taper-lock	tattiness	teasingly	tell tales
tailpiece	taliation	taperness	tattooing	tea-taster	tell-truth
tailplane	talismans	taperwise	tattooist	tea-things	tellurate
tail-rhyme	talk about	tape-sizer	Tauberian	Tebilized	tellurian
tail rotor	talkathon	tapespond	Tauchnitz	technical	telluride
tail-screw	talkative	taphonomy	taunt-song	technicum	tellurion
tail-shaft	talking of	Tapleyism	tauricide	technique	tellurism
tail-slide	talking-to	tap-rooted	tauriform	tectiform	tellurite
tail-spine	talk round	tapstress	tauroboly	tectogene	tellurium
tailstock	talky-talk	tap wrench	taurodont	tectonics	tellurous
tail-valve	tall drink	tar and tig	tautology	tectonism	teloblast
tailwards	tall-grass	tarantass	tautonymy	tectonite	telomeric
tail-water	talliable	tarantism	Tavastian	tectonize	telophase
tail wheel	tall order	tarantula	tawdriest	tectorial	telotaxis
tailwheel	tallow-cut	taraxacin	tawniness	tectrices	temazepam
tainchell	tallow-dip	taraxacum	tawny port	teddy bear	temperate
taintless	tallowish	tar-barrel	taxaceous	Teddy girl	temperish
tai-otoshi	tallow-nut	tardiness	tax credit	tediously	temper-pin
tai-sabaki	tallow-top	tarentaal	tax-dodger	teenagery	tempietto
Taiwanese	tall poppy	Tarentine	tax dollar	teensiest	temporale
takamakie	tally card	tarentola	tax-eating	teenspeak	temporary
take aback	tally-hoes	targeteer	taxed cart	teeny-tiny	temporise
take a bath	Talmudism	targeting	taxed ward	Teeswater	temporize
take about	Talmudist	target man	tax-evader	tegmental	temptable
take a fall	talmudize	target pin	tax-exempt	tegmentum	tempt fate
take after	talookdar	targetted	taxi dance	tegularly	temptress
take a hint	talus cone	target-tug	taxidermy	Tehuelche	temulence
take a joke	tamarillo	Targumist	taximeter	teknonymy	temulency
take alarm	tambookie	Targumize	taxiplane	telamones	tenacious
take a leak	tambourer	tarmacked	taxi squad	telecomms	tenaculum
take amiss	tambourin	tarnation	taxi strip	teleferic	tenaillon
take apart	tamoxifen	tarpaulin	taxonomer	telegenic	tenancies
take a pull	tamponade	Tarragona	taxonomic	telegonic	ten a penny
take a punt	tamponage	tarriance	tax relief	telegraph	tenderest
take a risk	tamponing	tarriness	tax return	teleguide	tenderise
take a seat	tanalized	tarryhoot	Taylorise	teleiosis	tenderish

tenderize	termagant	test strip	thecodont	therapies	thingness
tenderpad	terminate	tête-à-tête	the common	therapist	thingummy
tendinous	terminism	*tête-bêche*	thecosome	therapsid	thing-word
tendonous	terminist	tetracene	the Deluge	Theravada	thinkable
tendrilly	termitary	tetractys	the Divine	the Reaper	thinkably
tenebrism	termiting	Tetradite	the dozens	thereaway	think back
tenebrist	term paper	tetragamy	the Eleven	therefore	think long
tenebrity	term-piece	tetraglot	the Empire	therefrom	think over
tenebrose	ternately	tetragram	the Fringe	thereinto	think-tank
tenebrous	terpenoid	tetraktys	theft-boot	there it is	think with
ten-eighty	terpineol	tetralogy	theftuous	thereness	thinnings
ten-finger	*terra alba*	tetrapody	the Garden	thereover	thin on top
ten-gallon	terracing	tetrarchy	the glassy	Theresian	thin space
Tennessee	terraform	tetrasome	thegnhood	thereunto	thioester
tennis arm	terraglia	tetrasomy	thegnship	thereupon	thio-ether
tennis net	terramara	tetrazole	the hounds	therewith	thionazin
tennis pro	terramare	tetromino	theileria	theriacal	thiophene
ten o'clock	terranean	tetroxide	the ladies	the rise of	third-best
tenonitis	terrarium	tetterous	the Ladies	thermally	third gear
tenor bell	terra rosa	Teutonise	the latest	thermical	third hand
tenor clef	terrazzos	Teutonism	the League	thermidor	third last
ten-seater	terrenely	Teutonist	thelemite	Thermidor	thirdness
tenseless	terrenity	Teutonize	the Litany	thermoset	third part
tenseness	terricole	textology	thelytoky	thermotic	third rail
ten signal	terrified	textorial	them and us	the road to	third-rate
tensility	terrifier	text paper	the man who	therology	third root
tensional	terrifies	textually	the mass of	thesaurus	third slip
tensioner	territory	texturing	thematize	the Scrubs	thirdsman
tensorial	terrorise	texturise	the matter	these days	thirstful
ten-strike	terrorism	texturize	theme park	the shakes	thirstier
tentacled	terrorist	thack-tile	theme song	the size of	thirstily
tentacula	terrorize	Thai stick	theme tune	the smalls	thirtieth
tentacule	terseness	thalamite	the missis	the sooner	thirtyish
tentative	tervalent	thalassic	the moment	the spit of	thirty-one
tent-cloth	Tervueren	thallious	then-a-days	the squits	thirty-six
tent dress	*terza rima*	Thamudite	the nation	the States	thirty-two
ten tenths	terzettos	thanatoid	theobroma	the sticks	this child
tent-flies	Tesla coil	thanehood	the occult	the Stores	this world
tenth Muse	tessaract	thane-land	theocracy	the street	thitherto
tenth part	tesselate	thaneship	theocrasy	the Sweeps	tholeiite
tenth-rate	tessellar	thankless	theogonic	the Tarmac	Thomistic
Tenthredo	tesseract	than usual	theolatry	thetatron	thong-weed
tenth wave	tesserate	thatching	the old sod	the Terror	Thorazine
tent-maker	tessitura	that's flat	theologal	the Twelve	thoriated
tentorial	testacean	that's that	theologer	theurgist	thornback
tentorium	testacies	that's what	theologic	the Usages	thornbill
tent-stake	testament	that there	theologue	the Virgin	thorn bush
ten-twenty	testation	thaumatin	theomachy	the waters	thorniest
tenuously	testatrix	the absurd	theomancy	they're off	thornless
teocallis	test chart	theandric	theomania	thickener	thornlike
tephigram	test-cross	the animal	theopathy	thick-film	thorn moth
tephritic	test drive	thearchic	theophagy	thickhead	thorntail
tephritid	test-frame	theatrics	theophany	thick-knee	thorn tree
tephroite	testified	theatrize	theorbist	thick-knit	thornveld
tepidness	testifier	the Baltic	theorboed	thickness	thornwood
teporingo	testifies	Thebesian	theoretic	thickskin	thorow-wax
teratogen	testimony	the best of	theorizer	thick-sown	thoughted
terceroon	testiness	the boards	theosophy	thieflike	thoughter
terebinth	test match	the Border	the plains	thigh bone	thousands
terebrant	test paper	the Broads	the Psalms	thigh-boot	thralldom
terebrate	test-piece	the Castle	the queen's	thigh roll	thrashing
Terentian	test pilot	the Circus	the Queens	thinghood	thrash out

thrasonic	thrustful	tiger-like	time study	tizziness	tonalitic
thread bag	thrusting	tiger lily	timetable	T-junction	Tonbridge
threadfin	thumb-band	tiger milk	time train	Tlaxcalan	toneburst
threadier	thumbless	tiger moth	time trial	toad-eater	toned-down
threading	thumbling	tiger's-eye	timidness	to a degree	tone-group
threadlet	thumb-lock	tiger-ware	timocracy	toadstone	tongue-bit
threatful	thumb-mark	tiger-wolf	Timor deer	toadstool	tonguelet
three ages	thumbnail	tiger-wood	Timor pony	to a nicety	tongue-pad
three-axis	thumb pick	tight back	timorsome	toast rack	tongue-tie
three-ball	thumb-ring	tight cask	timpanist	toastrack	tonically
three-body	thumb-rope	tightener	tinder-box	to a tittle	tonic wine
three-card	thumbtack	tight head	tinderbox	to a wonder	tonka bean
three-deck	thundered	tightness	tinder-dry	toccatina	Tonkinese
threefold	thunderer	tightrope	tin-enamel	Tocharian	tonograph
three-foot	thuringer	tight ship	tingliest	Tocharish	tonometer
three-four	Thursdays	tight spot	tin-hatted	today week	tonometry
three-line	Thurstone	tikinagun	tin helmet	toddy-bird	tonoplast
three-mast	thus and so	tiki torch	tinkerdom	toddy palm	tonotaxis
threeness	thwacking	tile-drain	tin-kettle	toddy-tree	to nothing
three-part	thwarting	tile-maker	tin Lizzie	toe-dancer	tonotopic
three-pile	thwart-saw	tile-sherd	tinned air	toe-ragger	tonsillar
threesome	Thyestean	tilestone	tinned dog	toe-rubber	tonsorial
three-spot	thylacine	till-alarm	tinniness	toe-weight	tonsurate
three-star	thylakoid	Tillamook	tin-opener	toftstead	ton weight
three-toed	thymallus	tillering	tinselled	togavirus	Tony award
threnetic	thymidine	tillerman	tin-stream	togidashi	toodle-pip
threnodes	thymocyte	tilt guard	tint-block	toilet bag	tool-house
threnodic	thyratron	tiltmeter	tintinnid	toilet box	tool-maker
threonine	thyristor	tilt rotor	tip-and-run	toileting	toolmaker
threshing	thyrocele	tilt-wheel	tip for tap	toilet set	tool steel
threshold	thyroidal	timber-dog	tipsiness	toilfully	toothache
thresh out	thyroidic	timber due	tipsy-cake	toilingly	toothachy
thriftier	thyronine	timbering	tip-tap-toe	tokenless	toothcarp
thriftily	thyrotomy	timber jam	tip-tilted	token ring	tooth-comb
thrilling	thyroxine	timberman	tiptoeing	token vote	toothcomb
throatful	Tiburtine	timbermen	tip-topper	Tokharian	toothiest
throatier	tick-a-tick	timber-toe	tiredness	tokoloshe	toothless
throatily	tick-borne	Timbuctoo	tiretaine	tolerable	toothlike
throating	ticket-day	time about	tire-woman	tolerably	tooth-mark
throatlet	ticketing	time check	tirshatha	tolerance	toothpick
throbbing	tick fever	time clock	tit and ass	tolerancy	tooth-pulp
throbless	tickicide	time-delay	titchiest	tolerator	toothsome
thrombose	tidal boat	time depth	tit for tat	tolerogen	toothwort
thronedom	tidal bore	time frame	tithe barn	tolguacha	toothy-peg
throppled	tidal flow	timefully	titheless	toll-booth	toot sweet
throttler	tidal wave	time-lapse	titillate	tollbooth	top banana
througher	tiddliest	timeliest	titivator	toll-house	top cutter
throughly	tiddy oggy	time limit	title deed	tol-lol-ish	top cymbal
throwable	tidelands	timenoguy	titleless	toll plaza	top dollar
throw a fit	tide table	time of day	title-page	toll-taker	top drawer
throw away	tidetable	timeously	title-part	Tolstoyan	topectomy
throwaway	tidewater	timepiece	title role	toluidine	top-flight
throw back	tie a can on	time-saver	titleship	tomatillo	top-hamper
throwback	tie and dye	time-scale	title song	tomboyish	top-hatted
throw down	tiercelet	timescale	titration	tomboyism	topiarian
throw-line	tierceron	time-share	tit-tat-toe	tombstone	topiaries
throw open	tiffanies	timeshare	tittivate	tomentose	topiarist
throw over	tiffining	time sheet	tittlebat	tomentous	topically
throwster	tiger barb	time-shift	tittuping	tommyhawk	top-loader
thrum-eyed	tigerfish	time slice	tittupped	tommy ruff	topminnow
thrumming	tigerhood	time–space	titubancy	Tommy-shop	topocline
thrumwort	tiger-iris	time-stamp	titularly	tomograph	topograph

topologic	to the last	townscape	Trafalgar	trapezial	tree onion
toponymic	to the life	townsfolk	tragedian	trapezing	tree peony
toposcope	to the lips	townwards	tragedies	trapezist	tree pipit
toposcopy	tother day	toxaphene	tragedist	trapezium	treescape
top people	to the skin	toxically	tragedize	trapezius	tree shrew
toppingly	to the wide	toxicosis	tragelaph	trapezoid	tree snake
top-sawyer	to this day	toxigenic	Tragerian	trap-hatch	tree swift
top scorer	to this end	toxocaral	traghetto	trap-house	tree trunk
top secret	Totonacan	toxophily	trailable	trap-light	trefoiled
top-stitch	totting-up	toxophore	trail arms	trap-match	tregetour
topstitch	touchable	Toynbeean	trail bike	trappings	trehalase
topsy-turn	touch-back	trabeated	trail boss	trap-point	trehalose
top-timber	touchback	trabecula	trail head	trapshoot	treillage
top twenty	touch base	traceable	trailless	trapskiff	trek chain
top-weight	touch down	traceably	trail-rope	trapstick	trek fever
torbanite	touchdown	traceless	trailside	trash fish	trek wagon
torch-fish	touch-hole	traceried	trainable	trashiest	trellised
torchless	touchiest	traceries	trainband	trash nail	trematode
torch lily	touch-kick	tracheary	train down	trash-rack	tremblant
torch race	touch-last	tracheate	trainless	trash rock	tremblier
torch song	touchless	tracheole	trainload	trashtrie	trembling
torchwood	touch-line	trachytic	train-mile	trattoria	tremissis
toreutics	touchline	track-ball	train-shed	traumatic	tremogram
tormented	touch-mark	trackball	trainsick	travailer	tremolant
tormentil	touch shot	track-boat	trainside	traveling	tremolist
tormentor	Touch Tone	track down	train-spot	travelled	tremolite
tormentry	touch-type	trackless	train-stop	traveller	tremorine
tornadoes	touch wood	track-line	traitress	traversal	tremulant
torpedoes	touchwood	track shoe	Trakehner	traversed	tremulate
torpefied	toughener	trackside	tralucent	traverser	tremulous
torpefies	tough luck	trackster	tramphood	travisher	trenchant
torpidity	toughness	track-suit	tram-plate	trawl-beam	trenchful
torpitude	tough shit	tracksuit	trample on	trawl-buoy	trenchman
torquated	Touretter	track with	trampling	trawl-head	trench-rat
torrefied	Tourettic	track-work	trampoose	trawl line	trendiest
torrefies	touristic	tractable	trancedly	trawl-warp	trendless
torridity	tournasin	tractably	tranceful	tray-buggy	trend line
torsional	tournedos	tractator	transaxle	tray stand	trendyism
tortillon	tournesol	tract home	Transcash	tray table	trepanger
tortrices	tournette	tractless	transcend	treachery	trepanned
tortricid	tourneyer	tradeable	transcode	treadless	trepanner
torturous	Tourte bow	trade book	transduce	treadmill	trepidant
torulosis	tourtière	trade card	transfect	treasurer	trepidate
Toryishly	Toussaint	trade down	transform	treatable	trepidity
to satiety	tout court	trade-last	transfuse	treatably	treponeme
tosheroon	towelette	tradeless	transgene	treatment	tressette
to speak of	towelhead	trade mark	transient	Trebbiano	triagonal
tosticate	towelling	trademark	transited	trebuchet	trial-bred
total heat	towel rail	trade name	translate	trebucket	trial heat
totalizer	towerless	trade-room	transmake	treddling	trial jury
totalling	towerlike	trade-sale	transmiss	tredrille	trialling
totalness	tow-headed	trade show	transmute	tree agate	triallist
totem pole	towing-net	tradesman	transomed	tree civet	trialogue
to the boil	town clerk	tradesmen	transonic	tree daisy	triangled
to the bone	town clown	trade term	transpire	tree deity	triannual
to the dogs	town crier	trade-test	transport	tree-goose	triathlon
to the east	town-guard	trade wind	transpose	tree heath	triatomic
to the echo	town house	tradition	trans-ship	tree house	triatomid
to the fore	towniness	traditive	transship	tree limit	triazolam
to the full	town-major	traditors	transtage	tree-louse	tribadism
to the good	town mayor	traducian	transumpt	tree lupin	tribalism
to the hilt	town mouse	traductor	trap-drums	tree mouse	tribalist

tribalize	trihedral	trochlear	trunk-hose	tumescent	turntable
tribeless	trihedron	trollopee	trunkless	tumidness	turn-under
tribeship	trihybrid	trombenik	trunk line	tummy-ache	turpitude
tribesman	trihydric	tron-pound	trunk main	tumorigen	turquoise
tribesmen	trijugate	troop-ship	trunk road	Tunbridge	turreting
tribology	trilineal	troopship	trunk-work	tunefully	turriform
tribulage	trilinear	troostite	truss-beam	tunesmith	Tuscanism
tribulate	trilithic	troparion	truss-hoop	tungstate	Tuscanize
tribunate	trilithon	trophaeum	trustable	tungstite	Tuscarora
Tribunite	trillions	trophy tax	trust deed	tungstous	tusk shell
tributary	trilobate	tropicana	trust fund	Tungusian	tussilago
tricenary	trilobite	tropistic	trustiest	tunicated	tussocked
trichinae	trilogies	tropology	trustless	tunicless	tussocker
trichinal	trimerous	tropolone	truth drug	tuning-key	tutiorism
trichitic	trimester	tropylium	truth game	tuning peg	tutiorist
trichogen	trimethyl	trothless	truthless	tunnelist	tutorhood
trichroic	trimetric	troubling	truthlike	tunnelled	tutorless
trichrome	Trimphone	troublous	trying-pot	tunneller	tutorship
trichuris	trinality	troughful	try-scorer	tunnel-net	twaa-grass
trickiest	Trinidado	troughing	try-square	tunnel-pit	twaddling
trickless	trinities	trouncing	Tsakonian	Tupamaros	twayblade
trickling	trinitrin	trousered	tsarevich	Tupinamba	tweediest
trickment	trinketry	trousseau	tsaricide	Tupperian	twelfthly
tricksier	trinomial	Trousseau	Tsimshian	Tupperism	twelvemos
tricksily	trionymal	troutless	tsugi ashi	turbaries	twentieth
tricksome	triparted	trout-lily	Tsukahara	turbidite	twentyish
trickster	tripelike	trout-line	tsurikomi	turbidity	twenty-one
triclinia	triplasic	troutling	tubbiness	turbinate	twenty-two
triclinic	triploidy	trowelful	tubectomy	turboprop	twice-born
tricolour	trip-madam	trowelled	tube dress	turbopump	twice-laid
tricosane	tripmeter	troweller	tube-nosed	turbulent	twice-told
Tricotine	tripoline	troxidone	tubercled	turcopole	twiddling
tricresyl	trippiest	truanting	tubercula	tureenful	twifallow
tricrotic	triptyque	truantism	tubercule	Turfanian	twig-borer
tricuspid	tripudist	truceless	tube skirt	turfiness	twilighty
tricycler	tripudium	truck crop	tube steak	turgidity	twin-birth
tricyclic	triquetra	truckload	tube train	turkeyhen	twin float
tridactyl	triradial	truck-shop	tub garden	turkey oak	twingeing
tridecane	triradius	truckster	tubicolar	Turkey red	twiningly
tridental	Trisagion	truck stop	tubificid	Turkey rug	twinkling
tridented	trisector	truckstop	tub-pulpit	Turkicize	twin plate
tridrachm	trisomy-21	truculent	tubularly	Turkishly	twin prime
tridymite	tristesse	true coral	tubulated	Turk's head	twin-screw
triecious	tritanope	true–false	tuckamore	turmoiler	twirligig
triennial	triteness	true lover	tucker-bag	turn about	twistable
triennium	tritheism	true-metal	tucker-box	turnabout	twistedly
trierarch	tritheist	true molar	tuck-plate	turn after	twisteroo
Triestine	tritheite	true north	tuck-point	turn again	twist grip
trieteric	tritiated	truepenny	tuck-seine	turnagain	twistical
trifacial	triticale	true right	Tudor rose	turn-bench	twistiest
trifolium	Tritoness	true topaz	tufaceous	Turnerian	twist knot
triforial	triturate	trump card	tug of love	Turnerism	twist-lock
triforium	triumphal	trumpeted	Tuileries	turnerite	twist pile
triformed	triumpher	trumpeter	tuitional	turnip-fly	twist yarn
trigamist	triumviri	trumpetry	tulip fire	turn loose	twitchety
trigamous	triumvirs	truncated	tulip-like	turn out of	twitchier
trigemini	trivalent	truncheon	tulip-root	turnpiker	twitchily
triggered	trivially	trunkback	tulip tree	turn round	twitterer
trigintal	tri-weekly	trunk-band	tulip-wood	turnround	two and two
trigonous	trocheize	trunk call	tulipwood	turn-screw	two a penny
trig point	trochilus	trunkfish	tumble-bug	turnstile	two-bagger
trigynous	trochleae	trunkfuls	tumble-dry	turnstone	two-bottle

two-by-four	uki-gatame	unannoyed	unbundler	uncongeal	underbear
two cheers	uki-otoshi	unanxious	unburning	uncontent	underbill
two-Chinas	Ukrainian	unapplied	unburthen	uncontrol	underbite
two-decker	ulcerated	unapropos	uncandour	unconvert	underbody
two-figure	uliginose	unaptness	uncannier	uncordial	underbred
two-fisted	uliginous	unarrayed	uncannily	uncorrect	underbrim
twofoldly	ulotrichy	unarrived	uncapping	uncorrupt	underburn
two-footed	Ulsterman	unashamed	uncareful	uncounted	underbush
two-forked	Ulstermen	unaskable	uncarried	uncoupled	undercard
two-handed	ultimatum	unassayed	unceasing	uncoupler	undercart
two-hander	ultracold	unassumed	uncentral	uncoursed	undercast
two-headed	ultradian	unassured	uncentred	uncourted	underclad
two-leaved	ultra-high	unattaint	uncertain	uncourtly	underclay
two-legged	ultrahigh	unattired	uncessant	uncouthie	underclub
two-lipped	ultrathin	unattuned	unchained	uncouthly	undercoat
two-old-cat	ululation	unaudited	unchalked	uncovered	under-cook
two-piecer	ululatory	unavenged	unchanged	uncoveted	undercook
two-seater	umbellate	unaverted	unchanted	uncracked	undercool
two-stroke	umbellule	unavoided	uncharged	uncramped	undercure
two-suiter	umbilical	unbaffled	uncharity	uncreased	underdamp
two-tailed	umbilicar	unbalance	uncharmed	uncreated	underdeck
two-thirds	umbilicus	unbandage	uncharnel	uncrested	underdone
two-valued	umbratile	unbanning	uncharred	uncrinkle	underdose
Tyburnian	umfundisi	unbaptise	uncharted	uncropped	underdraw
Tychonian	umpteenth	unbaptize	unchecked	uncrossed	underdrew
tycoonery	umpty-nine	unbarring	uncheered	uncrowded	underedge
tycoonish	umzimbeet	unbashful	unchidden	uncrowned	underface
tylectomy	unabashed	unbearded	unchilded	uncrumple	underfall
tympanist	unabating	unbearing	unchilled	uncrushed	underfeed
tympanums	unabiding	unbeguile	unchinked	unctional	underfeet
Tynesider	unability	unbeknown	unchipped	unculture	underfelt
type genus	unabraded	unbelieve	unchopped	uncunning	underfill
type-lever	unaccused	unbeloved	uncinated	uncurable	under fire
type metal	unactable	unbending	uncivilly	uncurdled	underflow
type-wheel	unadapted	unbethink	unclaimed	uncurious	under foot
typewrite	unadmired	unbewitch	unclarity	uncurling	underfoot
typhlitic	unadopted	unbiassed	unclasped	uncurrent	underfund
typhlitis	unadoring	unbigoted	unclassed	uncurried	undergang
typhoidal	unadorned	unbinding	unclassic	uncurtain	undergear
Typhonian	unadvised	unblasted	uncleaned	undamaged	undergird
typically	unaerated	unblended	uncleanly	unda maris	undergrad
typograph	unaffable	unblessed	uncleanse	undaunted	undergrip
typophile	unaffixed	unblinded	uncleared	undazzled	underhair
tyranness	unaidable	unblooded	unclearly	undebased	under hand
tyrannies	unaidedly	unbloomed	uncleaved	undebated	underhand
tyrannise	unalarmed	unblotted	unclerkly	undecagon	underhang
tyrannize	unaligned	unblunted	uncleship	undecayed	under-head
tyrannous	unallayed	unblurred	unclimbed	undeceive	underhive
tyrantess	unallowed	unbookish	unclipped	undecency	underhold
tyre chain	unalloyed	unbounded	uncloaked	undecided	underhole
tyre gauge	unaltered	unbraided	unclogged	undefaced	underhung
tyrocidin	unamended	unbranded	unclothed	undefiled	underided
tyromancy	unamiable	unbridged	unclotted	undefined	underived
ubication	unamiably	unbridled	unclouded	undelayed	underkeel
ubiquitin	unamorous	unbriefed	uncloying	undelight	underkill
ude-garami	unamusing	un-British	unclutter	undeluded	under-king
ude-gatame	unangelic	unbrother	unclerky	undenoted	underlaid
ufologist	unanimism	unbrought	uncoerced	underarch	underlain
Uganda kob	unanimist	unbruised	uncombine	under arms	underland
ugglesome	unanimity	unbrushed	uncomplex	under a vow	underlead
ugli fruit	unanimous	unbuckled	unconcern	underback	underleaf
Uitlander	unannexed	unbuilded	unconfine	underbark	underlier

underlife	undeserve	unexalted	ungodlike	unilineal	unlenited
underlift	undesired	unexcised	ungodlily	unilinear	unlighted
underline	undevious	unexcited	ungrafted	unimpeded	unlikable
underling	undevised	unexerted	ungranted	unincited	unlimited
under load	undignify	unexpired	ungrasped	unindexed	unliteral
underload	undiluted	unexposed	ungrassed	uninhumed	unlivable
underlook	undimpled	unextinct	ungreased	uninjured	unlived-in
under-lord	undivided	unfadable	un-Grecian	uninomial	unlocated
underlout	undivined	unfailing	ungreeted	uninsured	unlogical
undermass	undonnish	unfancied	ungrieved	uninvaded	unlosable
undermine	undoubted	unfarrant	ungritted	uninvited	unlovable
undermost	undowered	unfashion	ungroomed	uninvoked	unluckier
undernote	undrained	unfazable	ungrooved	uniocular	unluckily
under oath	undreaded	unfearful	ungrown-up	union down	unmakable
underpaid	undreamed	unfearing	ungrudged	Union flag	unmanacle
underpart	undressed	unfeather	unguarded	un-ionized	unmanaged
underpass	undresser	unfeeling	unguessed	unionized	unmangled
underpeep	undrilled	unfeigned	unguiform	union jack	unmanlike
underplay	undrowned	unfertile	ungulated	Union Jack	unmanning
under-plot	undrugged	unfestive	unhabited	union list	unmanured
underplot	undrunken	unfigured	unhandily	union pipe	unmarried
underpole	undulancy	unfitness	unhandled	union shop	unmartial
underprop	undulated	unfitting	unhappier	union suit	unmatched
underrate	undulator	unflanked	unhappily	union-wide	unmatured
under-read	undurable	unflecked	unharbour	uniovular	unmeaning
underread	unduteous	unfledged	unharmful	uniparous	unmeasure
underride	undutiful	unfleshed	unharming	uniplanar	unmeddled
underring	undyingly	unfleshly	unharness	unipotent	unmedical
underripe	undynamic	unflooded	unhassled	uniramous	unmelodic
underrobe	unearnest	unfloored	unhasting	uniserial	unmelting
underroof	unearthed	unflushed	unhatched	unisexual	unmenaced
underruff	unearthly	unflyable	unhaunted	un-Islamic	unmerited
under sail	uneaseful	unfocused	unhealthy	unisonant	unmetered
underseal	uneasiest	unfoolish	unheard-of	unisonous	unmindful
undersell	uneatable	unfortune	unhearing	Unitarian	unmingled
undershot	unechoing	unfounded	unheedful	unitarily	unminuted
underside	unedified	unfranked	unheeding	unitarism	unmixable
undersign	uneducate	unfraught	unhelpful	unitarist	unmixedly
undersize	uneffaced	unfreedom	unhelping	unitarity	unmonarch
underskin	unelastic	unfreeman	unheroism	unitively	unmoneyed
undersoil	unelbowed	unfretted	unholiest	unit price	unmorally
undersold	unelected	unfrosted	unholster	unit train	unmotived
undersong	unelegant	unfructed	unhonesty	unit trust	unmoulded
undersort	unemptied	unfuelled	unhopedly	univalent	unmounted
underspin	unenacted	unfunnier	unhopeful	universal	unmourned
undertake	unendowed	unfunnily	unhostile	unjarring	unmovable
undertide	unengaged	unfurnish	unhumanly	unjealous	unmovably
undertint	un-English	unfussily	unhumbled	unjointed	unmovedly
undertone	unenjoyed	ungainful	unhurried	unjustice	unmuddied
undertook	unentered	ungallant	unhurtful	unkedness	unmuscled
undertrod	unenticed	ungarbled	unhurting	unkemptly	unmusical
underturf	unenvious	ungarnish	unicelled	unkindled	unmuzzled
undervest	unequable	ungenteel	uniclinal	unkindred	unnatural
underwave	unequably	ungenuine	unicolour	unknitted	unneedful
underwear	unequally	unghostly	unicursal	unknotted	unnerving
underwent	unerrable	ungirdled	unicuspid	unknowing	unneutral
underwind	unerrancy	ungirthed	unifacial	unknown to	unnotable
underwing	unerupted	ungleaned	unifiable	unlasting	unnotched
underwire	unessayed	unglorify	uniformal	unlatched	unnoticed
underwood	unessence	unglossed	uniformly	unlatined	unobliged
underwool	unethical	unglutted	unignited	unleached	unobvious
underwork	unevolved	ungoddess	unijugate	unlearned	unoffered

unopening	unpuritan	unsavable	unsmelled	unsuiting	unvisored
unopposed	unpursued	unsavoury	unsmelted	unsullied	unvouched
unordered	unquailed	unsayable	unsmiling	unsuspect	unvoyaged
unorderly	unqualify	unscalped	unsmitten	unswaddle	unwakened
unorganic	unqueenly	unscanned	unsmoking	unsweeten	unwalking
unpacific	unquelled	unscarred	unsnapped	unswollen	unwarlike
unpainful	unquietly	unscathed	unsnuffed	untactful	unwarming
unpainted	unrallied	unscented	unsoberly	untainted	unwasting
unpalsied	unrattled	unscepter	unsolaced	untakable	unwatched
unpapered	unravaged	unsceptre	unsoldier	untamable	unwatered
unpartial	unrazored	unscience	unsoluble	untapered	unwealthy
unpassing	unreached	unscorned	unsonlike	untaxable	unwearied
unpatched	unreacted	unscoured	unsoothed	untelling	unweeting
unpatient	unreadily	unscraped	unsounded	untempted	unweighed
unpausing	unreading	unsecular	unsoundly	untenable	unwelcome
unpayable	unrealism	unsecured	unsparing	untenably	unwheeled
unpegging	unrealist	unseduced	unspawned	untenured	unwhipped
unpeopled	unreality	unseeable	unspecked	unthanked	unwillful
unperfect	unrealize	unseeking	unspelled	unthinned	unwilling
unperplex	unrebated	unseeming	unspilled	unthought	unwinding
unpervert	unrebuked	unselfish	unspliced	unthrifty	unwinking
unpetrify	unrecited	unselling	unspoiled	unthriven	unwishful
unphrased	unreduced	unsensual	unsported	unthumbed	unwishing
unpickled	unrefined	unserious	unspotted	untidiest	unwistful
unpierced	unrefuted	unservile	unsprayed	untighten	unwittily
unpiloted	unregular	unsetting	unspringy	untimeous	unwitting
unpinning	unrelated	unsettled	unspurred	untirable	unwomanly
unpiteous	unrelaxed	unsevered	unsquared	untoasted	unworking
unpitiful	unremoved	unsewered	unstabler	untoiling	unworldly
unpitying	unrenewed	unsexiest	unstacked	untongued	unworried
unplagued	unreplied	unshackle	unstaffed	untouched	unwounded
unplaited	unrescued	unshapely	unstained	untracked	unwrapped
unplanked	unreserve	unsheared	unstalked	untrained	unwreaked
unplanned	unresolve	unsheathe	unstamped	untrapped	unwreathe
unplanted	unrestful	unshelled	unstarred	untreated	unwrecked
unplastic	unresting	unshifted	unstarted	untrended	unwrested
unplaying	unretired	unshining	unstately	untressed	unwrinkle
unpleased	unrevised	unshipped	unstaunch	untrilled	unwritten
unpleated	unrevived	unshirted	unstaying	untrimmed	unwronged
unpledged	unrevoked	unshocked	unsteeled	untrodden	unwrought
unpliable	unridable	unshodden	unsteeped	untrusted	unzealous
unpliancy	unriddler	unshrined	unsterile	untumbled	unzipping
unplucked	unrigging	unshrived	unstiffen	untunable	up against
unplugged	unrightly	unshriven	unstifled	untunably	up and down
unplumbed	unripened	unshutter	unstilled	untuneful	up-and-over
unpointed	unripping	unsighing	unstinted	unturning	Upanishad
unpoliced	unrippled	unsighted	unstirred	untutored	uparching
unpolitic	unriveted	unsightly	unstocked	untwinned	upbraider
unpompous	unroasted	unsimilar	unstopped	untwisted	upbreathe
unpopular	unrounded	unsincere	unstopper	untypable	upbrought
unpotable	unroyally	unsinewed	unstoried	untypical	upbrushed
unpowered	unruffled	unsinking	unstrange	ununiform	upbuilder
unpraised	unrulable	unsinning	unstretch	unushered	up-channel
unprecise	unruliest	unskiable	unstriped	unusually	upconvert
unprepare	unrumpled	unskilful	unstudded	unuttered	up-country
unpressed	unsaddled	unskilled	unstudied	unvarying	upcurrent
unpricked	unsainted	unskimmed	unstuffed	unvaulted	updatable
unprickly	unsaintly	unskinned	unstylish	unveiling	updraught
unprinted	unsalable	unslacked	unsubdued	unvenomed	upfilling
unpromise	unsaluted	unsmartly	unsubject	unverdant	up for sale
unpropped	unsampled	unsmashed	unsuccess	unviolent	Uphaliday
unprovide	unsatiate	unsmeared	unsugared	unvisited	uphearted

upheaving
Up-Helly-Aa
uphoisted
upholster
up Jenkins
uplandish
uplift bra
uplifting
uplighter
upmanship
upon sight
upon trust
upper case
upper deck
upper hand
uppermost
upperwing
up-pricked
up-putting
uprightly
uprooting
ups-a-daisy
upsetting
upsidaisy
upsitting
upstander
upstartle
upswallow
upsy-daisy
up the ante
up the flue
up the line
up the pole
up the wall
up to putty
up to snuff
uptrained
upturning
upwards of
upwarping
upwelling
upwhirled
uraninite
uranology
uranotile
urataemia
urban myth
urceolate
urchin cut
urea cycle
ureameter
urea resin
uredinial
uredinium
ure of land
ureometer
ureotelic
Uriah Heep
uricaemia
uricaemic
uridrosis
urination

urine mark
urinology
urkingdom
urochrome
urodelous
urography
urokinase
urolagnia
urolagnic
urologist
urophilia
uropygial
uropygium
Ursa Major
Ursa Minor
urticaria
urticated
Uruguayan
usability
use-by date
uselessly
use the sea
usherette
usherless
ushership
usitative
usualness
usucapion
usucaptor
usurpress
uterotomy
utilities
utopianly
Utraquism
Utraquist
utricular
utriculus
utterable
utterance
utterless
uttermost
utterness
uvarovite
uvulatomy
uvulotomy
uxoricide
vaaljapie
vacancies
vacatable
vaccinate
vaccinial
vaccinist
vaccinium
vaccinoid
vacillant
vacillate
vacuolate
vacuously
vacuumize
vacuum wax
vade-mecum
vadiation

vagarious
vaginally
vaginitis
vagolytic
vagotonia
vagotonic
vagrantly
Vaishnava
Valaisian
Valencian
valencies
valentine
Valentino
valet-park
valiantly
validator
validness
Valkyrian
vallation
vallecula
valleyful
valley tan
valproate
Valsalvan
valuation
valuative
value-free
valueless
valvassor
valve head
valveless
valviform
valvotomy
vambraced
vampiness
vampirine
vampirish
vampirism
vampirize
vanadiate
vanadious
vanaspati
vance-roof
vandalise
vandalish
vandalism
vandalize
Van der Hum
Van Gelder
vanillaed
vanity bag
vanity-box
vanity set
Vannetais
van-pooler
vantbrace
Vanuatuan
vapidness
vaporable
vaporetti

vaporetto
vaporific
vaporizer
vapouring
vapourise
vapourish
vapourize
Varangian
variation
variative
varicella
varicosed
variegate
varieties
varietism
varietist
varifocal
variolate
variolist
variolite
varioloid
variolous
variously
variphone
variscite
vari-sized
varletess
varnished
varnisher
Varronian
varsities
Varsovian
varvelled
varyingly
vasectomy
vasomotor
vasovagal
vassalage
vassaldom
vassaless
vassalize
vastation
vastidity
vastitude
vatically
Vatican II
vaticinal
Veblenian
vectorial
vectoring
vectorise
vectorize
Vedantism
Vedantist
vee engine
vegetable
vegetally
vehemence
vehemency
vehicular
veininess
veinstone

vein-stuff
veld-craft
veldskoen
veld sores
vellicate
velocious
velodrome
velometer
velvet ant
velveteen
velveting
vendition
venditive
veneering
venerable
venerably
venerator
vengeable
vengeably
vengeance
veniality
venireman
venomness
venomsome
venospasm
ventiduct
ventifact
ventilate
ventosity
ventrally
ventricle
venturous
Venusberg
Venus clam
Venus' hair
veracious
verandaed
verapamil
veratrine
veratrole
verbalise
verbalism
verbalist
verbality
verbalize
verbal* led
verbascum
verberant
verberate
verbicide
verbosely
verbosity
verdantly
verdigris
verdurous
vergeress
Vergilian
vergobret
veridical
veritable
veritably
vermicide

vermicule
vermiform
vermifuge
vermilion
verminate
verminous
Vermonter
vernaccia
vernalise
vernality
vernalize
vernation
verneuker
veronique
verrucose
verrucous
versatile
verseless
versicule
versified
versifier
versifies
versional
vers libre
vertebrae
vertebral
verticity
Very light
vesicular
vespasian
vesselful
vestibula
vestibule
vestigial
vestigium
Vestinian
vestiture
vestryman
vestrymen
vetchling
vetoistic
vetturino
vexatious
vexedness
vexillary
viability
Via Crucis
viaducted
Via Lactea
viatorial
vibracula
vibraharp
vibrantly
vibraslap
vibratile
vibration
vibrative
vibratory
vibriones
vibrionic
vibriosis
vibrissae

vibrogram
vicariant
vicariate
vicariism
vicarious
vicarship
vicennial
Vicentine
vice-queen
viceregal
vicereine
viceroyal
vicesimal
vice squad
vice versa
viciously
vicontiel
victimage
victimise
victimize
Victorian
victories
victorine
victrices
victualer
videlicet
videodisc
video film
video game
videogram
video jock
videotape
videotext
vie en rose
vie intime
viewgraph
viewiness
viewphone
viewpoint
vigesimal
vigilance
vigilante
vignetter
Vikingism
villagery
villaless
Villanova
villiform
villosity
vimineous
vinaceous
Vincennes
vindemial
vindicate
vin du pays
vine black
vine louse
vine snake
vingerpol
vingt-et-un
vino cotto
vino crudo

vino dolce
vinolence
vinolency
vinometer
vino rosso
vino santo
vino secco
vino tinto
vinylogue
violation
violative
violatory
violently
violet bee
violet-ear
violetish
violet ray
violet tea
violinist
viosterol
viperfish
viper-like
viperling
viper-wine
viragoish
virescent
virgation
Virgilian
Virginian
virginity
virginium
virgin wax
Virgoulee
virialize
viricidal
virilized
virilocal
virologic
viropexis
virtually
virtuosic
virucidal
virulence
virulency
virus-like
visagiste
vis a tergo
viscerate
viscidity
viscidium
vis comica
viscosity
viscounty
viscously
Vishnuism
Vishnuite
visionary
visioning
visionist
visitable
visitador
visitator

visitress
visorless
vista-dome
visual aid
visualise
visualist
visuality
visualize
visual ray
vital heat
Vitallium
vitaminic
Vitaphone
vitellary
vitelline
vitiation
vitiosity
Vitreosil
vitrified
vitrifies
vitriform
vitrinite
vitriolic
Vitrolite
Vitruvian
vivacious
Vivaldian
vive le roi
viverrine
vivianite
vividness
vivifying
vivotoxin
vizierate
vizierial
vocabular
vocal cord
vocalized
vocalizer
vocal line
vocalness
vodkatini
vo-do-deo-do
vogue word
voice coil
voiceless
voice mail
voice-over
voice part
voice-tube
voice vote
voilà tout
voiturier
vol-au-vent
volcanian
volcanism
volcanist
volcanity
volcanoes
volkslied
volkspele
volte-face

Volterran
voltinism
voltmeter
volumetry
voluminal
voluntary
volunteer
vomitoria
von Gierke
voodooism
voodooist
voorloper
voracious
vorlaufer
vorticism
vorticist
vorticity
vorticose
vouchsafe
vowelless
vox humana
vox nihili
vox populi
voyeurism
voyeurist
Vulcanian
vulcanise
vulcanism
vulcanist
vulcanite
vulcanize
vulgar era
vulgarian
vulgarise
vulgarism
vulgarity
vulgarize
vulnerary
vulpanser
Vulpecula
vulpicide
vulpinism
vulsellum
vulturine
vulturish
vulturous
vulviform
wackiness
wadcutter
Wade–Giles
Wadhamite
wadsetter
wafer-iron
waferlike
wafer-thin
wage claim
wage drift
wagenboom
wager-boat
wage scale
wage slave
waggeries

waggishly
Wagnerian
Wagnerism
wagon boss
wagonette
wagon-head
wagon-load
wagonload
wagon-road
wagon-roof
wagon-tent
wagon-tree
wagon-yard
waifishly
wailfully
wailingly
waistband
waistcoat
waist-deep
waist-high
waistless
waistline
wait about
waitering
wait for it
waitingly
wait on God
wait state
wakefully
wake-robin
wakon-bird
Walachian
Walcheren
Waldenses
waldflute
wale-piece
walk about
walkabout
walkathon
walk a turn
walk-clerk
Walkerite
walk-march
walk on air
walk out on
walk-round
walk short
wallabies
Wallacean
wall-board
wallboard
wall brown
wall chart
wallchart
wall clock
wall cress
walled-off
Wallerian
walletful
wall-fruit
walloping
wallowish

wallpaper
wall-piece
wall-plate
wall-sided
wall space
wall-stone
Walpolian
Walpurgis
Walrasian
Walras' law
Waltonian
waltz king
wambenger
Wampanoag
wanchance
wanchancy
wandering
Wanderobo
wandought
wanked-out
wanthrift
wantonize
want out of
wapentake
Wapishana
Wappinger
war artist
warble fly
war bonnet
war damage
wardrober
ward round
ward-woman
war effort
warehouse
warfaring
war gaming
Warholian
war-kettle
warlockry
warmblood
warm front
warmonger
war museum
warm-water
warningly
War Office
war orphan
warp print
warp speed
warranted
warrantee
warranter
warrantor
war-saddle
wart-biter
wart-cress
wart snake
warty newt
war-worker
wash-basin
washbasin

washboard	water-cool	Watsonian	web offset	wellstead	wheat-corn
wash-brush	water-crow	wattle-eye	weddinger	well-sweep	wheat-duck
washcloth	water cure	wattmeter	wedgebill	well-taken	wheat germ
washed out	water deer	wave aside	wedge-form	well-timed	wheatgerm
washerman	water down	wave-bread	wedge-heel	well-tried	wheat-land
washers-up	water drum	wave cloud	wedgelike	well water	wheatless
wash-house	water-dust	wavefront	wedge-shoe	well-wheel	wheatmeal
washiness	waterfall	wave group	wedgetail	well-willy	wheedling
washing-up	water fern	wave guide	wedge tent	well woman	wheel-back
washplain	water flag	waveguide	wedgewise	well worth	wheelbase
washstand	water flea	wavellite	Wednesday	Welsh aunt	wheelless
wash-table	Waterford	wavemeter	weed-grown	Welshcomb	wheel-like
wash-water	waterfowl	wave-motor	weedicide	Welsh harp	wheel lock
washwoman	watergall	wave-power	weediness	Welsh main	wheel-made
Waspiness	watergate	waverider	weekender	Welshness	wheel-seat
waspishly	Watergate	waveshape	weeknight	Welsh wave	wheel slip
wasp-paper	water-gilt	wave-siren	weepiness	wenchless	wheelsman
wasp's nest	water-head	wave train	weepingly	wenchlike	wheelsmen
wasp-waist	water-hole	wax-billed	Wehrmacht	wend again	wheel-spin
wassailer	waterhole	wax candle	weighable	Wernerian	wheelspin
waste-book	water jump	wax-colour	weigh a ton	wernerite	wheel well
waste-cock	water-knot	wax flower	weigh-beam	werowance	wheelwise
waste-gate	water-laid	wax-insect	weigh down	Werterean	wheelwork
waste-heap	water-lane	wax-kernel	weigher-in	Werterism	wheely bin
waste heat	water-leaf	wax museum	weigh into	Wesleyism	whelphood
wasteland	waterless	wax myrtle	weighment	westabout	whelpless
wasteless	water lily	wax pocket	weightage	westbound	whelpling
wasteness	water-line	wax resist	weightier	west coast	whencever
waste-pile	waterline	wax tablet	weightily	West-ender	whensoe'er
waste pipe	water main	wayfaring	weighting	westering	whereaway
waste plug	watermark	way letter	weinkraut	westerner	wherefore
waste silk	water mass	waymarker	weird-like	westernly	wherefrom
waste-weir	water mica	way of life	weirdness	West India	whereinto
wastingly	water-mill	way-ticket	weirdsome	West Saxon	whereness
Waswahili	watermill	waywarden	welcomely	West Sider	whereunto
watchable	water-mite	waywardly	welcoming	westwards	whereupon
watchband	water-mole	wayzgoose	weld decay	wether hog	wherewith
watch-bell	water pipe	weakening	welfarism	wet season	wherryman
watch-bill	water polo	weaker sex	welfarist	Weyl group	wherrymen
watch-boat	water-pore	weak grade	wellanear	whackiest	whetstone
watch-care	water pump	weak-kneed	well aware	whakapapa	whey-cream
watch-case	water rail	weakliest	wellawins	whaleback	whey-faced
watch-fire	water rate	weak point	well-being	whale-bird	whichaway
watchfire	water ring	weald-clay	well-brick	whaleboat	whichever
watch hill	water-sail	wealdsman	well-built	whalebone	whichways
watchless	watershed	wealthful	well-cress	whale-feed	whiffiest
watch-list	waterside	wealthier	Wellerism	whale-food	whiffling
watch-mate	water silk	wealthily	well-found	whalehead	whillaloo
watch over	water-spot	wealth tax	well-grate	whalerman	whillywha
watch room	water-stop	weaponeer	well-grown	wharf-boat	whimberry
watchword	water taxi	wear-dated	well-house	wharfless	whimperer
watchwork	water tree	weariable	well-kempt	what about	whimsical
water-bath	water tube	weariless	well known	what a life	whinberry
water bear	water vine	weariness	well-liked	what and if	whingeing
water bird	water vole	wearingly	well-lined	what cheer	whininess
waterbird	water-wave	wearisome	well-loved	what gives	whiningly
waterbody	waterweed	weaselled	well-meant	what price	whinstone
water-buck	water-wolf	weatherly	well-oiled	whatsoe'er	whip-craft
water-bull	waterwork	weaver ant	well-order	what's what	whip-crane
Waterbury	water-worm	weaveress	well-point	what's with	whip-graft
water-butt	waterwort	weavingly	well-saved	wheat belt	whippable
water-cart	wathstead	web-footed	well spent	wheat-bird	whipper-in

whip-round	white monk	wide-scale	windhover	wirephoto	wolf's head
whip snake	White Monk	wide-where	windiness	wirescape	wolf's-milk
whipstaff	white mule	wide world	windingly	wire story	wolf-snake
whipstall	whiteness	widow-bird	winding up	wire wheel	Wollaston
whip-stick	whitening	widowered	windolite	wire-wound	wolverene
whipstock	white note	widowhood	window box	Wisconsin	wolverine
whirl-bone	white pine	widow's men	windowful	wisecrack	woman-body
whirligig	white port	widow-wail	windowing	wise woman	woman-born
whirlpool	White Raja	widthways	window tax	wish-dream	womanhead
whirl-puff	white rent	widthwise	windproof	wishfully	womanhood
whirlwind	white room	wiederkom	windrower	wishingly	woman-hour
whiskered	white rose	wieldable	wind-shake	wishtness	womanizer
whisk tail	white rust	wieldiest	wind shear	wispiness	womankind
whiskyish	white sage	Wiener dog	windstorm	wistfully	womanless
whisky mac	white sale	Wiffle bat	windswept	witch-ball	womanlike
whisperer	white-shoe	wiggliest	windthrow	witch-bowl	womanness
whistling	white-skin	wig-picker	wind-tight	witchetty	woman's man
White Army	white sock	wigwagged	wind-trunk	witch-hunt	womenfolk
whitebait	white soup	Wilburite	wineberry	witch-knot	womenkind
white bass	white spot	wildscape	wineglass	witchlike	women's lib
whitebeam	white titi	wild basil	wine-grape	witch-lock	wonder boy
white bear	whitewall	wild beast	wine-house	witch-mark	wonderful
white belt	white ware	wild goose	wine label	witch-post	wondering
white bird	whitewash	wild horse	wine lodge	witchweed	wonkiness
white book	whitewear	wild Irish	winemaker	witchwork	wood apple
white cane	whiteweed	wild pansy	wine-party	witereden	wood avens
white cell	whitewing	wild pitch	winepress	with a bang	woodbined
white clay	whitewood	wildscape	wing chair	with a bump	wood bison
white coal	white work	wild tansy	wing-cover	with a rush	woodblock
white coat	white worm	willemite	winged elm	with a will	wood-borer
whitecoat	whitherso	Willesden	wing-shell	with child	woodchuck
white comb	whittawer	willingly	wing-snail	with costs	woodcraft
white crow	whittling	will needs	wink-a-peep	withdrawn	wood-drake
white-damp	Whitworth	willowily	winkle-pin	withering	wooden cut
white deal	whizz-bang	willowish	Winnebago	witherite	wooden leg
white-eyed	whodunnit	willow oak	winningly	withernam	woodentop
whiteface	wholefood	willow tit	winsomely	withouten	wood fibre
white fish	whole gale	will-power	winterage	withstand	wood-fired
whitefish	whole-life	will to art	winter bud	with usury	wood-flour
white flag	whole meal	wilsomely	winter day	with young	wood-grain
white flux	wholemeal	Wilsonian	winter egg	withywind	woodhenge
white fuel	whole milk	Wilsonism	wintering	witlessly	wood-house
white goat	wholeness	Wilsonite	winterise	witnesser	woodhouse
white gold	whole note	Wiltshire	winterish	witteboom	woodiness
white grub	whole-rock	Wimbledon	winterize	wittering	wood-knife
white hake	wholesale	wimpiness	Winter War	witticism	woodlouse
Whitehall	wholesome	wimpishly	win the day	witticize	wood mouse
whitehead	whole-time	wincingly	wintriest	wittiness	wood nymph
white heat	wholewise	wind a horn	wipe-clean	wittingly	wood-paper
white hole	whoop-de-do	wind-bells	Wiradhuri	woadwaxen	wood-print
white hope	whoop it up	wind-blown	Wiradjuri	wobbegong	wood-pussy
white iron	whoo-whoop	wind-bound	wire birch	wobbliest	woodquest
White Lady	whore-hunt	windbound	wire brush	wobbygong	wood-reeve
white land	whore's egg	wind-brace	wire cable	woebegone	woods boss
white lead	whoreship	wind-break	wire cloth	woe betide	woods colt
whitelike	whore-shop	windbreak	wire-drawn	woe be to us	wood-screw
white lime	whorishly	wind-chest	wire-frame	wolfberry	woodscrew
white line	whosoever	wind-chill	wire gauge	wolfhound	wood-seary
white list	wickedest	wind-crust	wire gauze	wolfishly	woodsmoke
white loaf	wide-angle	wind-drift	wire-glass	wolframic	wood-snail
white meat	wide awake	wind force	wire grass	wolfsbane	wood-spell
white mica	wideawake	wind-gauge	wire house	wolf's claw	woodspite

wood stain	World Bank	wrestling	xylophone	yolk gland	Zetlander
wood-stork	world fair	wretchock	xylorimba	Yom Kippur	Zetlandic
wood-stove	worldhood	wriggling	yacht club	yonderway	zeuglodon
wood sugar	worldless	wrighting	yachtsman	Yorkshire	zeugmatic
woodwards	worldlier	wring-bolt	yachtsmen	Yoshiwara	zeunerite
woodwaxen	world-life	wrinklier	yacht-yard	you bet you	zigzagged
woody pear	worldlily	wrinklies	Yahwistic	you name it	zillionth
wool alien	world-line	wrinkling	yam potato	youngerly	zinc green
wool-blind	worldling	wristband	yamstchik	young-eyed	zincotype
wool-flock	world's end	wrist-bone	Yang–Mills	young fogy	zinc oxide
wool-grass	world-soul	wrist-drop	Yankee bet	young lady	zinc white
wool-house	world-view	wrist jerk	Yankeedom	younglike	Zinfandel
woolliest	worldward	wrist-play	Yankeeish	youngling	zinkenite
woollyish	worldwide	wrist-slap	Yankeeism	young lion	Zionistic
wool-pated	world-wise	wrist-work	Yankeeize	youngness	Zionwards
wool-press	worm-eaten	writative	Yanktonai	youngster	zippiness
wool-scour	wormeaten	write-back	yard-grass	Young Turk	zirconate
wool table	worm-eater	write down	yard of ale	yours ever	zirconian
wool-track	worm-fence	write-once	yardstick	you said it	zirconium
wool-wheel	worm grass	writeress	yarn count	youth camp	zitherist
Woolworth	worm-holed	writ large	yashmaked	youth club	Zolaesque
woomerang	worminess	wrongdoer	Yawelmani	youthhead	Zolaistic
wooziness	worm-shell	wrong-foot	yawniness	youthhood	zombified
Worcester	worm-snake	wronghead	yawningly	youthless	zone-level
word-blind	wormstall	wrongness	yea and nay	yrast line	zone plate
word-bound	worm-wheel	wrong side	year class	ytterbite	zoogamete
word-break	worriedly	wrong-slot	year-round	ytterbium	zoogloeal
word-class	worriment	wrong-wise	year's mind	Yucatecan	zoography
word-field	worrisome	wrought-up	yeast cake	yucca moth	zoo-keeper
word-final	worriting	wry-necked	yeastiest	yucca-palm	zookeeper
word-hoard	worry-guts	wulfenite	yeastless	yuckiness	zoologise
word-index	worry-wart	Wulfilian	yeastlike	Yung Chêng	zoologist
wordiness	worse luck	wunnerful	Yeibichai	Yunnanese	zoologize
word-magic	worsement	wuthering	yellow ant	yuppiedom	zoophilia
word order	worseness	Wyandotte	yellow boa	yuppie flu	zoophilic
word-paint	worst-case	wych hazel	yellow bob	yuppieism	zoophobia
word-salad	worthiest	Wyclifist	yellow box	yuppified	zoophorus
wordsmith	worthless	Wyclifite	yellow-boy	yuppifies	zoophytic
word-stock	wouldn't it	Xanthippe	yellow cat	zamacueca	zoosporic
word-watch	woundable	xanthomas	yellow dog	zamindari	zootechny
workalike	wound cork	xenoblast	yellowfin	Zanzibari	zootheism
workbench	woundedly	xenocracy	Yellow Hat	zapateado	zootomist
workerist	woundless	xenocryst	yellowish	Zapotecan	zoot-shirt
work ethic	wound wood	xenograft	yellow-leg	Zealander	zosterops
workforce	woundwort	xenolalia	yellow oat	zealotism	zucchetto
work group	wove mould	xenomania	yellow ore	zealously	zucchinis
workhorse	wowserish	xenophile	yellow yam	zebra fish	zumbooruk
workhouse	wowserism	xenophobe	yeomaness	zebra-wolf	Zwinglian
workingly	wrain-bolt	xeroderma	yerba maté	zebrawood	zygantrum
workmanly	wrangling	xerograph	yesterday	Zechstein	zygomatic
work of art	wrap party	xeromorph	yestereve	Zeitgeist	zygophore
work out of	wrapperer	xerophagy	Yggdrasil	Zeldovich	zygospore
workpiece	wrapround	xerophile	Yiddisher	Zendicism	zymogenic
workplace	wrathless	xerophily	yieldable	zeolitize	zymolysis
work point	wreakless	xerophyte	yieldless	zephyrean	zymolytic
worksheet	wreathing	xi hyperon	yield sign	zephyrous	zymometer
work-space	wreathlet	xiphoidal	Y junction	zero grade	zymophore
workspace	wreckfish	x-question	yobbishly	zero-graze	
work study	wreckfree	xylocaine	yodelling	zero-point	
work table	wreckling	xylocopid	Yogacarin	zero-power	
workwoman	wreck-wood	xylograph	yo-heave-ho	zero sound	
workwomen	wrenching	xylophage	yohimbine	zestfully	

TEN LETTERS

aardwolves
a bang-up job
Abbe number
abbreviate
abdication
abdominous
aberdevine
Aberdonian
aberrantly
aberration
abhorrence
abhorrible
abiogenist
abjectness
abjuration
ablatively
able-bodied
able rating
able seaman
abnegation
Abney level
abnormally
abominable
abominably
abominator
aboriginal
aborigines
abortional
abortively
abortorium
above board
above-cited
above price
above proof
above water
Abraham-man
abrasional
abreaction
abreactive
abridgment
abrogation
abruptness
abscission
absconsion
absent from
absentness
absinthium
absolutely
absolution
absolutise
absolutism
absolutist
absolutize
absolvable
absolvitor
absorbable
absorbance

absorbancy
absorbedly
absorbency
absorption
absorptive
abstemious
abstention
abstergent
abstersion
abstersive
abstinence
abstinency
abstracted
abstracter
abstractly
abstractor
abstractum
abstrusely
abstrusity
abstrusive
absurdness
abundantly
abusefully
Abyssinian
acacia tree
academical
acanthosis
acaricidal
acatalepsy
acausality
accelerate
accentuate
acceptable
acceptably
acceptance
acceptancy
acceptedly
accessible
accessibly
access road
access time
accidental
accidented
accidently
accipitral
accomplice
accomplish
accordable
accordance
accordancy
accordment
accostable
accoucheur
accountant
account day
account for
accounting

accredited
accrescent
accruement
accubation
accumulate
accuracies
accurately
accursedly
accusation
accusative
accusatory
accusingly
accustomed
acephalous
acerbities
acervation
acervuline
acetabulum
acetic acid
acetogenic
acetonuria
acetylator
acetylenic
acetyl silk
Achaemenid
Acherontic
achievable
achirality
achondrite
achromatic
achronical
acicularly
acidimetry
acidophile
a-cock-horse
acoelomate
acolythist
acorn shell
acotyledon
acoustical
acquainted
acquirable
acquitment
acquitting
acrimonies
acroamatic
acrobatics
acrobatism
acrolithic
acromegaly
acronychal
acronymize
acrophobia
acrophobic
across lots
acrostical
acroterial

acroterion
acrylamide
actability
act and deed
acting copy
acting part
acting play
actinolite
actionable
actionably
action-noun
action rear
action song
activation
active duty
active life
active list
activeness
active verb
activities
act of faith
act of grace
actomyosin
act one's age
act the fool
act the goat
actualness
acute angle
Adam-and-Eve
adamantane
adamantine
adamellite
Adamitical
a damn sight
Adam's apple
adaptation
adaptative
adaptitude
adaptively
adder-stone
Addisonian
additament
additional
additively
additivity
addle-brain
addressing
adenovirus
adequately
adequation
adequative
adherently
adhesively
adhibiting
adhibition
adiaphoron
adipose fin

adjectival
adjudgment
adjudicate
adjunction
adjunctive
adjuration
adjuratory
adjustable
adjustment
administer
admiration
admirative
admiringly
admissable
admissible
admittable
admittance
admittedly
admonisher
admonition
admonitory
adolescent
Adonis blue
adoptively
ad personam
adrenaline
adrenergic
adrogation
adroitness
adsorbable
adsorbtion
adsorption
adsorptive
Adullamite
adulterant
adulterate
adulteress
adulteries
adulterine
adulterize
adulterous
advance man
advantaged
adventurer
advertence
advertency
advertiser
advisement
advisories
advocatess
advocation
advocatory
adzuki bean
aeciospore
aedileship
aegophonic
aeolotropy

aerenchyma	afterpiece	albumenize	alleviator	altar-bread
aeriferous	aftershave	albuminoid	all-firedly	altar-cloth
aerobatics	after-shock	albuminous	All Hallows	altarpiece
aero-engine	aftershock	alchemical	alliaceous	altar-stone
aerogramme	aftersight	alchemilla	allicholly	altazimuth
aerography	aftertaste	alcheringa	alliciency	alteration
aeronautic	after-times	alchymical	alligation	alterative
aeronomist	aftertouch	alcoholate	all in a rush	alternance
aerophobia	afterwards	alcoholise	alliterate	alternator
aerosolize	after-world	alcoholism	all kinds of	altimetric
aerostatic	after-years	alcoholist	all-nighter	altisonant
aero-towing	agallochum	alcoholize	allocation	altivolant
aerotowing	agapanthus	alcoometer	allochthon	altogether
aeruginous	agency shop	Alcoranist	allocution	altruistic
Aeschylean	aggeration	aldermanic	allodially	alum-schist
aestivator	agglutinin	aldermanly	allogeneic	amalgamate
aetiologic	aggrandise	aldermanry	allometric	Amandebele
a fair shake	aggrandize	alderwoman	allopathic	amanuenses
a fair treat	aggravator	alderwomen	allopatric	amanuensis
a fat chance	aggregable	Alemannian	allophonic	amastigote
affability	aggression	Alemannish	allosteric	amateurish
affectable	aggressive	alexanders	allotheism	amateurism
affectedly	aghastness	Alfvén wave	allotropic	amatorious
affectless	agitatedly	algal bloom	allottable	amazedness
affeerment	agnominate	algebraist	all-overish	ambassador
affettuoso	agnostical	algebraize	alloy steel	ambidexter
affinities	agonic line	algolagnia	all-purpose	ambisexual
affinitive	agonizedly	algolagnic	all right by	ambisonics
affirmable	agonothete	algologist	all-rounder	ambivalent
affirmance	agony uncle	Algonquian	all-Russian	ambiverted
affixation	a good field	algorismic	all sorts of	ambosexual
affliction	a good sport	alienation	all the best	ambulacral
afflictive	a good while	alien-enemy	all the mode	ambulacrum
affluently	agoraphobe	alimentary	all the rage	ambulation
affordable	a great loss	alimentive	all the same	ambulative
affordably	agreeingly	a little wee	all the time	ambulatory
affrighted	agrimonies	alkalaemia	allurement	ambuscader
affrighten	agrologist	alkalinity	alluringly	ambushment
affrontive	agronomist	alkalinize	allusively	a measure of
Afghan coat	aguishness	alkaloidal	all-weather	ameliorate
aficionado	a hand's turn	alkylation	almacantar	ameloblast
aforetimes	a heap sight	alla marcia	almond cake	amen corner
afraidness	a-horseback	all-America	almond-eyed	amendatory
Africander	aid and abet	all and each	almond eyes	amenity bed
Africanise	aide-de-camp	all and some	almond milk	amercement
Africanism	aid fatigue	Allan Water	almond pink	amerciable
Africanist	air bladder	allargando	almond tree	Americanly
Africanity	air cushion	all-creator	alms-basket	Amerindian
Africanize	air-freight	all day long	almsgiving	amiability
Afrikander	air hostess	allegation	almucantar	amianthine
afrormosia	airmanship	allegeable	aloha shirt	ammoniacal
after a sort	Air Marshal	allegement	Aloha State	ammoniacum
afterbirth	air officer	allegiance	along about	ammoniated
aftercomer	Air Officer	allegiancy	alongshore	ammunition
aftergrass	akroterion	allegories	alpenstock	amoebiases
after-guard	alabastron	allegorise	alphabetic	amoebiasis
after-hours	alacritous	allegorism	alpha decay	amoebicide
after-image	alarm clock	allegorist	alphametic	amoebiform
after leech	alarmingly	allegorize .	alpha minus	amoebocyte
afterlight	alarm watch	allegretto	alpha waves	ampelopsis
afternoons	Albigenses	Allen screw	Alphonsine	ampere-hour
afterpains	albinistic	allergenic	Alpine rose	ampère-hour

ampere-turn	anchorless	anhidrosis	antibiotic	apart-hotel
amphibious	anchor-ring	anhidrotic	antibodies	aphaeresis
amphibolic	anchylosis	anhungered	anti-busing	aphaeretic
amphibrach	and all that	aniline dye	anti-choice	aphorismic
amphictyon	Andalusian	animadvert	Antichrist	aphoristic
amphigouri	andalusite	animalcule	antichthon	apiculture
amphimacer	Andaluzian	animatedly	anticipant	aplanatism
amphimixis	Andamanese	anisocoria	anticipate	apocalypse
Amphitryon	andantinos	anisotropy	anticlimax	Apocalypse
amphoteric	and knows it	ankle-biter	anticlinal	apocalypst
ampicillin	androcracy	ankylosaur	antidromic	apocarpous
ampliation	androecium	annalistic	anti-emetic	apochromat
ampliative	androgenic	annexation	antifreeze	apocryphal
amputation	androgynal	annihilate	antigorite	apodeictic
amygdaline	Andromedid	Anno Domini	anti-heroes	apolaustic
amygdaloid	androspore	annominate	antilogies	apolitical
amylolysis	androstane	annotation	antilogism	Apollinian
amylolytic	and so forth	annotative	antilopine	Apollonian
amyotrophy	and the like	annoyancer	antimasque	apologetic
anabaptise	and welcome	annoyingly	antimatter	apologizer
Anabaptism	anecdotage	annualized	antimonate	apophthegm
Anabaptist	anecdotist	annual ring	antimonial	apophyseal
anabaptize	anemochore	annularity	antimonian	apoplectic
anachronic	anemograph	annulation	antimonide	aposematic
anaclastic	anemometer	annullable	antimonite	aposporous
anacolutha	anemometry	annunciate	antinomian	apostasies
anadromous	anemophily	annuntiate	antinomies	apostatise
anagenesis	anemoscope	anodically	Antiochene	apostatism
anagenetic	anesthesia	anoestrous	Antiochian	apostatize
anaglyphic	aneuploidy	anogenital	antipathic	apostolate
anaglyptic	aneurismal	anointment	antiphonal	apostolize
anagogical	aneurysmal	anopheline	antiphoner	apostrophe
anal-erotic	angelicize	anorexiant	antiphonic	apothecary
analogical	angel-noble	answerable	antipodean	apothecial
analphabet	angelology	answerably	antiproton	apothecium
anal sadism	angel's eyes	answer back	antiquated	apotheoses
analysable	angel-shark	answerless	anti-racism	apotheosis
analyse out	angioblast	antagonise	anti-racist	apotropaic
analytical	angiosperm	antagonism	anti-Semite	Appalachee
anamnestic	angleberry	antagonist	antisepsis	apparelled
anamorphic	angledozer	antagonize	antiseptic	apparently
anapaestic	angle of lag	ante-bellum	antisocial	apparition
anapaestus	anglepoise	antecedent	antistatic	appealable
anaplastic	Anglepoise	antecessor	antitheism	appearance
anaptyctic	angler fish	antechapel	antitheist	appeasable
anarchical	Anglistics	ante-chapel	antitheses	appendaged
anarthrous	Anglo-Irish	antedating	antithesis	appendance
anasarcous	Anglo-Latin	anteflexed	antithetic	appendancy
anastigmat	Anglomania	antelopine	antitrades	appendence
anastomose	Anglophile	ante-mortem	antitragus	appendical
anastrophe	Anglophobe	antepartum	antivenene	appendices
anathemize	anglophone	antepenult	antlerless	appendicle
anatomical	Anglo-Roman	anteriorly	antler-moth	appendixes
anatomizer	Anglo-Saxon	ante-temple	antonymous	apperceive
anatropous	angora goat	antheridia	antorbital	appetition
ancestress	angora wool	anthomania	antrustion	appetitive
ancestrial	anguineous	anthophore	anvil cloud	appetizing
ancestries	angularity	anthracene	anxiolytic	applausive
ancestrula	angulation	anthracite	any time now	apple cider
anchoretic	angwantibo	anthracoid	anywhither	apple-green
anchor-hold	anharmonic	anthropoid	aortic arch	apple sauce
anchoritic	anhelation	antibiosis	apagogical	apple-woman

applianced
applicable
applicably
applicator
applotment
appointive
appositely
apposition
appositive
appraisive
appreciate
apprentice
approacher
approvable
approvance
approvedly
apron stage
apterygote
aqua fortis
aquamanile
aquamarine
aquarobics
aquatinter
a quick buck
aquiferous
arable land
arachis oil
arachnidan
arachnitis
araneology
Araucanian
araucarian
arbalester
arbitrable
arbitrager
arbitrated
arbitrator
arboretums
arboricide
arborvirus
arbor vitae
arc furnace
archaicism
archaicist
archaistic
archbishop
archdeacon
archegonia
archeology
archer fish
archetypal
arch-flamen
Archimedes
architrave
archonship
archontate
archpriest
arcologies
Arctic char
Arctic hare
Arctic skua
Arctic tern

arcubalist
arc welding
area bishop
arenaceous
arena stage
arenavirus
arenovirus
Areopagite
Argand lamp
argonautic
argumental
arguteness
argyrodite
Arimaspian
aristocrat
aristology
arithmancy
arithmetic
arles-penny
armadillos
Armageddon
armigerous
armipotent
armorially
armour-clad
armourless
arm the lead
arm-wrestle
aromatizer
arpeggione
arrear-band
arrestable
arrestment
arrhythmia
arrhythmic
arrogantly
arrogation
arrow-grass
arrowsmith
arse-kisser
arse-licker
arsenolite
art and part
arteriolar
artfulness
art gallery
arthralgia
arthrodial
articulacy
articulate
artificial
artisanate
artistical
artistlike
art nouveau
art therapy
arty-crafty
asafoetida
asarabacca
as a starter
asbestosis
ascariasis

ascendable
ascendance
ascendancy
ascendency
asceticism
ascidiform
ascogenous
ascogonium
ascomycete
as concerns
ascribable
ascription
ascriptive
asexuality
ashen-faced
ashipboard
Ashkenazic
Ashkenazim
ash of roses
Asiaticism
as it stands
aslantwise
aspalathus
asparagine
aspergilla
asperities
as per usual
asphaltene
asphaltite
aspherical
asphyxiant
asphyxiate
aspidistra
aspiration
aspiringly
Asquithian
assailable
assailment
assaultive
assemblage
assemblies
assembling
assentator
assentient
assentment
assertible
assertoric
assessable
assessment
asseverate
assibilate
assientist
assignable
assignably
assignment
assimilate
assishness
assistance
assistancy
ass-kissing
ass-licking
associable

associater
associator
assoilment
assonantal
assortment
assumingly
assumption
assumptive
assurgency
astarboard
asteriated
asteroidal
asthma herb
astigmatic
astonisher
astounding
astragalar
astragalus
astral body
astral lamp
astriction
astrictive
astringent
astrobleme
astrograph
astrohatch
astrolabic
astrolatry
astrologer
astrologic
astrometry
astronomer
astronomic
astrophile
astuteness
asymmetric
asymptotic
asyntactic
at all costs
at all hours
a tall order
at any price
at a pin's fee
at a premium
at a sitting
at a squeeze
at a stretch
at a tangent
at a venture
ateleiosis
ateleiotic
at farthest
at full cock
at full pelt
at full sail
at full tilt
at furthest
at gunpoint
Athabascan
at half cock
at half mast
Athanasian

Athapaskan
at high wish
athletical
at interest
at its worst
at long last
atmosphere
atomically
atomic bomb
atomic heat
atomic mass
atomic pile
at one's best
at one's ease
at one sweep
at one swoop
at outrance
atrabiliar
atramental
atraumatic
atrocities
attachable
attachment
attackable
attainable
attainment
attendance
attenuated
attenuator
attestable
attestator
at that rate
at the climb
at the least
at the money
at the point
at the ready
at the trail
at the wheel
at the worst
at this rate
Attic order
attirement
attornment
attractant
attraction
attractive
attritting
attunement
at unawares
at variance
at what time
atypically
auctioneer
Audenesque
audibility
audiogenic
audiometer
audiometry
audiophile
audit-house
auditorial

auditorily	autostrada	bacitracin	ballistics	barn-gallon
auditorium	autotheism	back-action	ball of fire	baroclinic
audit trail	autotheist	back-berand	balloonist	barometric
auger-shell	autotomize	backbiting	balneology	baron court
augmentive	autotrophe	backblocks	balsam pear	baronetage
auguration	autoxidize	back boiler	balustrade	baronetess
augustness	autumnally	back burner	bamboo-fish	baronetize
Auld Reekie	auxanogram	back-double	bamboozler	barotrauma
Aureomycin	auxochrome	back-fanged	banalities	barotropic
auriculate	auxotrophy	backfriend	banana bird	barracouta
auriferous	avant-garde	backgammon	Bananaland	barracudas
aurigation	avanturine	background	bananaquit	barramundi
aurivorous	avaricious	backhanded	banana skin	barratrous
auscultate	avengement	backhander	banana tree	barrel-fish
auspicious	avengeress	backing dog	banderilla	barrelling
austenitic	aventurine	backmarker	bandleader	barrenness
Australian	average out	back-marker	bandmaster	barrenwort
australite	aversation	back number	Band of Hope	barring-out
Australoid	averseness	backpacker	bandy-bandy	barterable
Australorp	aviculture	backsheesh	bangtailed	bartizaned
Austrasian	avidiously	backslider	banishment	bar tracery
austringer	avirulence	back-spacer	bank charge	barycentre
autarchies	avondbloem	backstairs	bank martin	barysphere
autarkical	avouchable	back-stitch	bankruptcy	baselessly
autecology	avouchment	backstitch	banqueteer	base-minded
authigenic	avunculate	backstreet	banqueting	base relief
authorized	awakenment	backstroke	Bantingism	base-runner
authorizer	award wages	back-to-back	banyan tree	bashawship
authorless	awkwardish	backvelder	Baphometic	basilectal
authorling	axe-breaker	backwardly	baptistery	Basilidian
authorship	axemanship	back-winter	baptizable	basil thyme
autochthon	axenically	bacterioid	Baralipton	basketball
autocratic	axinomancy	bacteruria	barasingha	basket-boat
autocrator	axiologist	bad bargain	Barbary ape	basket case
autodidact	axiomatize	bad company	barbecuing	basket fish
autoecious	Aylesburys	bad feeling	barbed wire	basket hilt
auto-erotic	azeotropic	badger game	barberries	basket meal
autogamous	azomethine	bad weather	barber-shop	basket star
autogenous	azoprotein	bafflement	Barbie doll	basketwork
autography	azygos vein	bafflingly	barbituric	basophilia
autoimmune	babblative	bagassosis	barcarolle	basophilic
autologous	babblement	baggage car	bardee grub	basse dance
autolysate	babblingly	baggage tag	bardolater	basse danse
automation	babe in arms	bag of bones	bardolatry	basset-horn
automatise	babesiasis	bagpudding	bare-backed	bass guitar
automatism	babesiosis	bagstuffer	barefooted	basso buffo
automatist	babiroussa	bail bandit	bare-footed	bassoonist
automatize	baby boomer	bailieship	barehanded	bass-relief
automatons	baby buster	bail-jumper	bareheaded	bastardize
automatous	baby-farmer	bains-marie	bargain for	bastillion
automobile	baby-jumper	bairn's part	bargeboard	bastnäsite
automotive	Babylonian	baked beans	barium meal	Bath Oliver
autonomies	Babylonish	baking soda	bark beetle	bathometer
autonomism	baby-minder	balance due	barkentine	bathometry
autonomist	baby powder	Balbriggan	barley-bird	bathymeter
autonomous	babysitter	balderdash	barley-bree	bathymetry
autophagic	baby walker	bald-headed	barley-corn	bat mitzvah
autoplasty	bacchantes	baldmoneys	barleycorn	batologist
autoptical	bacchantic	balibuntal	barley-hood	baton round
autorotate	Bacchantic	ballasting	barley-wine	batrachian
autoscopic	bachelorly	ball-buster	Barmecidal	battailous
autosexing	bacilluria	ball flower	bar mitzvah	Battenberg

battery hen	bed of roses	belly dance	be taken ill	bilocation
battledore	be done with	belly laugh	beta rhythm	bimanually
battlement	bed-wetting	belongings	be the end of	bimestrial
battleship	bedwetting	below decks	be the limit	bimetallic
baulkiness	beech-drops	below there	be to do with	bimodality
baum marten	beefburger	Belshazzar	be to praise	binary code
bawdy house	beef cattle	be master of	betrayment	binary form
bayberries	beef tomato	bemusement	better days	binary star
bayoneting	beef-witted	bench press	better half	binary tree
bay whaling	beehive-hat	bench-screw	betterment	binational
BBC English	bee-keeping	bench-table	betterness	binaurally
beach buggy	beer bottle	benedicite	better-to-do	Binitarian
beach front	beer cellar	Benedictus	betweenity	binoculars
beachfront	beer engine	benefactor	beudantite	binomially
beach-grass	beer garden	beneficent	be up to trap	binoxalate
beach-la-mar	beetle-back	beneficial	bevel wheel	binucleate
Beach-la-mar	beetle-head	benefiting	bewailable	biocenosis
beachwards	be even with	Beneventan	bewailment	biocentric
beadleship	beforehand	benevolent	be well left	biochemist
be a fool for	before long	Bengal kino	bewildered	biodegrade
be a hit with	before meat	benignancy	bewitchery	biodynamic
Beaker Folk	before time	bent double	bewitching	bioethical
beam engine	beforetime	Benthamism	beyond seas	biofouling
bean sprout	befoulment	Benthamite	be yourself	biogenesis
bearded tit	be free with	bentonitic	biannually	biogenetic
bear down on	befriender	*ben trovato*	Bible class	biographee
bear garden	be geared up	Benzedrine	Bible clerk	biographer
beargarden	beggarhood	benzhydrol	Bible paper	biographic
bear hard on	be great fun	benzpyrene	biblically	biological
bear in hand	behind bars	be on record	bibliology	biomedical
bear in mind	behindhand	be on the rag	bibliomane	biometrics
bearleader	behind line	be open with	bibliopegy	biomimetic
bear malice	behind time	be prepared	bibliopole	biomorphic
bear market	be hung up on	bequeathal	bibliopoly	bionically
be a skinner	be in hiding	bequeather	bibliothec	bionomical
beastliest	bejewelled	bergerette	bibulosity	bio-organic
be at a stand	be laughing	Bergsonian	bibulously	biophysics
beatifical	be left with	beribboned	bicultural	biopolymer
Beatrician	belemnitic	Berkeleian	bid against	bioscience
beat the air	Belgravian	Berlin blue	bidonville	biospheric
beat the bat	believable	Berlin wool	bid welcome	biotically
beat the gun	be like that	Berlin work	biennially	biparental
beat the rap	belladonna	Berliozian	bifacially	biparietal
Beaujolais	bell-animal	Bermuda rig	bifocalled	bipartisan
beautician	bellarmine	Bernardine	bigamously	bipedalism
beautified	bell-bottom	bescribble	Big Brother	bipedality
beautifier	bell-crater	beseeching	bigeminate	bipolarity
beautifies	*belle laide*	be set round	big-hearted	birational
beautiless	belletrism	besottedly	big-leaguer	birch-water
beauty spot	belletrist	besprinkle	big-mouthed	bird cherry
beaver lamb	bellflower	best friend	*bijouterie*	bird of Jove
beaver-tail	bell-hanger	bestialise	bikini line	bird of Juno
bêche-de-mer	bell-pepper	bestiality	bilberries	bird of prey
becomingly	bell-ringer	bestialize	bilge water	bird's-foots
be confined	bell-shaped	bestiaries	bilharzial	bird-strike
bedazement	bell-sleeve	bestirring	biliverdin	bird-witted
bedchamber	Bell's palsy	bestowment	bill and coo	Birmingham
bedclothes	bell-string	bestridden	billbergia	birthnight
be deceived	bell the cat	best-seller	billet-doux	birthplace
bedevilled	bell-topper	be stuck for	bill of fare	birthright
Bedlington	bell-wether	best wishes	bill of sale	birthstone
bed of nails	bellyacher	be sure that	billposter	bishop-bird

bishophood
bishoplike
bishop's cap
bismuthate
bismuthine
bissextile
bistouries
bisulphate
bitchiness
bite and sup
biting lice
bit of fluff
bit of goods
bit of rough
bit of skirt
bit of spare
bit of stuff
bitonality
bitten with
bitter bark
bitter beer
bitterling
bitterness
bitter pill
bitter-root
bitter sage
bitter-weed
bitter-wood
Bitumastic
bituminise
bituminize
bituminous
biuret test
bivouacked
biweeklies
bizarrerie
black alder
blackamoor
blackberry
black birch
blackboard
black bread
black cumin
Black Death
black earth
black-faced
blackflies
Black Friar
black frost
black grape
blackguard
black-heart
black house
black Irish
black ivory
black level
black light
black magic
Black Maria
black money
black-mouth
black olive

black plate
black power
Black Power
black sheep
blackshirt
blacksmith
black-snake
blacksnake
Black Stone
black stump
blackthorn
black tripe
black vomit
Black Watch
black water
black widow
bladder nut
blady grass
blamefully
blanchfarm
blanch over
blancmange
blandander
blanket bog
blanketeer
blanketing
blank verse
blanquette
blasphemer
blastocyst
blastoderm
blastodisc
blastomere
blastopore
blazonment
bleariness
bleary-eyed
bleatingly
bleed white
blenchfarm
blight-bird
blind alley
blind drunk
blindingly
blindlings
blind snake
blind tiger
blind trust
blissfully
blister-fly
blister gas
blistering
blitheness
blithering
blithesome
blitzkrieg
block-board
blockboard
block grant
blockhouse
blockishly
block party

block plane
blond beast
blonde lace
blood-borne
blood count
blood donor
blood eagle
blood fluke
blood group
blood-guilt
blood horse
bloodhound
bloodiness
blood money
blood royal
blood serum
blood sport
bloodstain
bloodstock
bloodstone
blood sugar
blood wagon
bloody flux
bloody hand
Bloody Mary
bloomeries
bloomerism
bloomingly
Bloomsbury
blotchiest
blottesque
blow a cloud
blow-by-blow
blowziness
bludgeoner
blue-bonnet
bluebottle
blue cheese
blue cohosh
blue-collar
blue dahlia
blue ensign
blue groper
blue ground
blue heeler
bluejacket
Bluemantle
blue monkey
blue murder
blue-pencil
blue riband
blue ribbon
blue-rinsed
blue runner
blue streak
blue tangle
bluethroat
bluetongue
bluff it out
bluishness
blurriness
blushingly

blustering
blusterous
board-wages
boastfully
boastingly
boat people
boat-shaped
bobbin lace
bobby socks
bobby-soxer
bob-periwig
Bob's-a-dying
bodiliness
body colour
body double
body search
body warmer
body weight
Boehmenism
Boehmenist
bog-blitter
bog iron ore
bog lemming
Bogomilian
Bogomilism
bog-trotter
bogtrotter
boiler room
boiler suit
boiler-tube
boiling hot
boil the pot
boisterous
boldacious
bolivianos
Bollandist
bollocking
boll-weevil
bolometric
Bolshevism
Bolshevist
Bolshevize
bolshiness
bolstering
bombardier
Bombay duck
bomb-vessel
bondholder
boneheaded
bone marrow
bone-setter
boneshaker
bone spavin
bonitarian
bonnethead
bonsai tree
bonus issue
bon vivants
bon viveurs
boobook owl
booby-hatch
booby prize

bookbinder
bookkeeper
bookmaking
bookmobile
book-muslin
book of fate
book of life
bookseller
book-trough
boondoggle
boosterism
bootlegger
bootlessly
bootlicker
borborygmi
borderland
borderline
boringness
borrow-head
borrow-hole
borsholder
bosselated
bossy-boots
bossyboots
Boswellian
Boswellism
Boswellize
Botany wool
bothersome
botryoidal
bottle bank
bottled gas
bottle-feed
bottle-head
bottleneck
bottlenose
bottle tree
bottom edge
bottom gear
bottom-land
bottomless
bottom line
bottommost
bottomried
bottomries
bough-house
bought deal
bougienage
Boulangism
Boulangist
bouleverse
bounce back
bounciness
bouncingly
boundaries
bountihead
bouquetier
Bourbonism
Bourbonist
bourgeoise
bournonite
bouts rimés

bovver boot	brazenness	bridgeward	brow antler	bulk buying
bow-compass	braziletto	bridgework	browbeater	bulkheaded
bowdlerise	Brazil wood	bridle-hand	brown argus	bullamacow
bowdlerism	breadboard	bridleless	Brown Betty	bull-and-cow
bowdlerize	breadcrumb	bridle path	brown bread	bulldog ant
bower-cable	breadfruit	bridle-rein	brown earth	bullet-head
bowie knife	bread-knife	bridle-road	browned off	bullet-tree
bowl-barrow	bread sauce	bridle-wise	brown goods	bull-fiddle
bow the knee	bread-stick	brigandage	brown hyena	bull-headed
box barrage	bread wheat	brigandine	brown-noser	bullionist
boxing ring	break a blow	brigandish	brown ochre	bull market
box of birds	break a fall	brigandism	brown paper	bull-necked
box spanner	break bread	brigantine	brown sauce	bullroarer
boyishness	break cover	brightener	Brown-shirt	bull thatch
boys in blue	break-dance	brightness	Brownshirt	bum-bailiff
braaivleis	break faith	brightsome	brown snake	bum-freezer
braceleted	break forth	brightwork	brownstone	bump and run
brachialis	break-front	brilliance	brown study	bumpkinish
brachiator	break of day	brilliancy	brown sugar	bump supper
brachiopod	break point	brimborion	brown trout	bum-sucking
brachylogy	break-point	bring about	bruisewort	bunch-berry
brachyuran	breakpoint	bring forth	brunch coat	bunch grass
bracketing	break ranks	bring round	brush aside	bunder-boat
bracteated	break shins	bring to bay	brusquerie	bungee cord
bradykinin	breakstone	bring under	brute force	bungee rope
bradypepsy	break water	Britannian	bryologist	bunglesome
bradyseism	breakwater	Britishism	bryophytic	bunglingly
braggingly	breastbone	broad arrow	bubble bath	bunya bunya
Brahmanism	breastfeed	broad-brush	bubblehead	Burberries
brahminism	breast-high	broadcloth	bubblement	burdensome
brainchild	breast-pump	broad gauge	bubble over	bureaucrat
brain coral	breast-wall	broad-piece	bubble pack	burgessdom
brain death	breastwise	broadscale	bubble wrap	burglaries
brain drain	breastwork	broadsheet	bubbly-jock	burglarise
brain fever	breathable	broadsword	bubonocele	burglarize
braininess	breathe out	Broca's area	buccinator	Burgundian
brainpower	breathiest	brocatelle	Bucephalus	burgundies
brain-stone	breathless	brocatello	Buchmanism	burlesqued
brainstorm	breath test	broken-down	Buchmanite	burlesquer
brain trust	breech baby	broken home	bucketfuls	burlesques
brake block	breechless	broken line	bucket seat	Burmese cat
brake fluid	breezeless	brokenness	bucket shop	burnet-moth
branchiate	breeziness	broken reed	buck-jumper	burnet rose
branchless	brekekekex	broken time	buckle down	burnt cream
branchlike	brent-goose	broken wind	Buddhahood	burnt ochre
branch-line	brevetting	bromic acid	Buddhistic	burnt taste
branch-work	breviaries	bronchiole	buddy movie	burnt umber
brandering	brick-built	bronchitic	budgerigar	bur-parsley
brand image	brick-earth	bronchitis	budget plan	burrow-duck
brandisher	brick-field	brontology	buffalo fly	burrow into
brandy ball	bricklayer	brontosaur	buffalo-nut	bursarship
brandy snap	brickmaker	bronzewing	buff arches	bursectomy
brandy-wine	bridegroom	broodiness	buffer area	burstproof
brassed off	bride price	broodingly	buffer stop	Buscot Park
brassiness	bridesmaid	brood patch	buffer zone	bushbabies
brass plate	bridgeable	brood pouch	buffet meal	bush canary
brass tacks	bridge a gap	brood queen	bufflehead	bush clover
brat packer	bridge-bote	brook trout	buffoonery	bushelfuls
bratticing	bridge-deck	broom-grass	buffoonish	bush-harrow
brave it out	bridgehead	broom-sedge	bufotenine	bush jacket
brawniness	bridgeless	broomstaff	bugologist	bush lawyer
brazen-face	bridge roll	broomstick	build round	bush league

Bushmanoid	cabin fever	calmodulin	cannibalic	capturable
bushmaster	cachinnate	calumniate	cannibally	carabineer
bush-ranger	cack-handed	calumnious	cannon ball	carabinier
bushranger	cacodaemon	calyculate	cannon-bone	caramelise
bush-shrike	cacodorous	cambric tea	cannon-shot	caramelize
bus shelter	cacodylate	camelopard	cannot wait	Carancahua
bus-spotter	cacography	camel's-hair	canoe birch	caravaneer
bus station	cacomistle	camel-thorn	can of worms	caravanned
bustlingly	cacophonic	cameo glass	canonicate	caravanner
busybodied	cactaceous	camera crew	canonicity	carbonados
busybodies	cadaverine	cameralism	canonistic	carbonator
busy Lizzie	cadaverous	cameralist	canophilia	carbon copy
butcheries	caddie cart	camera-work	Canopic jar	carbonizer
butlership	caddis-worm	camerawork	Cantabrian	carbonless
butterball	cadilesker	camerlingo	cantaloupe	carbonnade
butter-bean	caecostomy	Cameronian	cantatrice	carboxylic
butter-bump	Caerphilly	camouflage	canterbury	carbuncled
butter-bush	Caesar baby	campaigner	Canterbury	carcel lamp
butter dish	caespitose	campestral	canti fermi	carcinogen
butterfish	*café au lait*	campground	cantilever	carcinomas
butterless	caffeinism	camphorate	cantillate	cardboardy
buttermilk	Caffrarian	campimeter	canto fermo	cardholder
butter-tree	ca'ing whale	campimetry	cantonment	cardinally
butterwort	cajolement	camp-on busy	can't seem to	Cardiofunk
buttery-bar	cake of soap	Canaanitic	canvas-back	cardiogram
button-back	calamander	Canada bird	canvassing	cardiology
buttonball	calamaries	canalicule	canzonetta	cardmember
button-bush	calamitean	canary-bird	caoutchouc	card player
button-down	calamities	Canary sack	capability	carelessly
buttoned up	calamitous	canary-seed	capacitate	caressable
buttonhole	calaverite	cancellans	capacities	Care Sunday
buttonhook	calcareous	cancellate	capacitive	caricature
buttonless	calcarious	cancelling	Cape brandy	carination
button-like	calceolate	cancellous	Cape doctor	cariogenic
button-tree	calciferol	cancelment	Cape gannet	carjacking
button-wood	calcinable	cancer bush	Cape pigeon	Carmathian
by accident	calcitonin	cancer-root	Capernaite	carnallite
by all means	calcitrate	cancrinite	Cape salmon	carnassial
by a long way	calc-sinter	cancrizans	capillaire	Carolinian
by and large	calculable	candelabra	capitalise	carotenoid
by any means	calculably	candelilla	capitalism	Carpathian
by courtesy	calculated	candescent	capitalist	carpellary
by-election	calculator	candidness	capitalize	carpet-moth
by eminence	calculuses	candle-beam	capital sum	carpet-tack
by marriage	Caledonian	candle-fish	capitation	carphology
by one's will	caledonite	candle-tree	capitellum	carpopedal
by reason of	calendarer	candlewick	Capitolian	carpophore
by rotation	calendener	candle-wood	Capitoline	carpospore
by snatches	calescence	candy apple	capitulary	carragheen
byssinosis	calf-length	candy-assed	capitulate	carrier bag
byssinotic	calf's snout	candyfloss	capnomancy	carrying-on
bystanding	calibrator	candy-store	capo tastos	carry it off
by the dozen	caliciform	candy-sugar	cappuccino	Carthusian
by the great	calico-bush	cane-worker	capriccios	cartomancy
by the gross	caliginous	caniniform	capricious	cartonnage
by then that	call a truce	canker-rose	Capri pants	cartoonery
by the piece	calligraph	cankerworm	capsulated	cartoonish
by the stern	call it a day	canker-worm	capsulitis	cartoonist
by virtue of	callithrix	cannabinol	captainess	cartophily
by yourself	callowness	cannel-bone	captiously	cartwright
caballeros	call signal	cannel coal	captivater	caruncular
cabin class	call to mind	cannelloni	captivator	carwitchet

caryatides
cascarilla
case-bottle
case-harden
caseinogen
caseworker
cashew tree
Caspian Sea
Cassegrain
cassia tree
cassinette
Cassiopeia
cassolette
cassumunar
cast a clout
cast adrift
cast anchor
castaneous
cast around
cast ashore
castellany
castellate
cast-for-age
castigator
casting-net
castleward
castor bean
castration
castrative
cast stones
casualness
casual poor
casualties
casual ward
casus belli
catabolism
catabolite
catabolize
cataclases
cataclasis
catafalque
catagmatic
Catalanist
catalectic
cataleptic
catalogued
cataloguer
catalogues
Catalonian
catamenial
catananche
cataphatic
cataphoric
cataphract
cataractal
catarrhine
catarrhous
catastasis
catatoniac
catawampus
cat burglar
catch a cold

catch a crab
catchflies
catchiness
catchpenny
catch-title
catch-water
cat cracker
catechesis
catechetic
catechizer
catechumen
categorial
categories
categorise
categorize
catenarian
catenaries
catenation
catenulate
catheretic
cathode ray
catholicly
Catholicly
catholicon
Catholicos
catoptrics
catostomid
cat's cradle
cattle cake
cattle grid
cattle stop
caulescent
cauliflory
cause havoc
causidical
causticity
cautionary
cautiously
cavalierly
cavalryman
cavalrymen
cavitation
cavity wall
celebrated
celebrator
celebrious
celery pine
celery salt
cellar-book
cellobiose
cellophane
Cellophane
cellulated
cellulitic
cellulitis
cellulosic
Celtic nard
cemeterial
cemeteries
cenematics
censorable

censorship
censurable
centauries
centennial
centerfold
centesimal
centigrade
centilitre
centillion
centimetre
centipedal
centralise
centralism
centralist
centrality
centralize
centre back
centrefold
centre half
centre line
centremost
centricity
centrifuge
centriolar
centromere
centrosome
centuriate
cephalalgy
cephalitis
cephalopod
cerambycid
ceramicist
ceratohyal
cerebellar
cerebellum
cerebrally
ceremonial
ceremonies
Cerinthian
cerography
certiorari
certiorate
ceruminous
cervantite
cervicitis
cessionary
cetologist
Ceylon moss
chaetodont
chaffingly
Chagataian
chain drive
chain-plate
chain-smoke
chain snake
chain store
chain wheel
chair-borne
chair organ
chairwoman
chairwomen
chalcedony

chalcid fly
Chalcidian
chalcocite
chalkboard
chalk cliff
chalkiness
chalk-stone
challenged
challenger
chalybeate
Chamaeleon
chamberlet
chamber-lye
chamber pot
Chambertin
chamfering
chamositic
champagney
champertor
champignon
chanceable
chancellor
chanceries
chanciness
chandelier
changeable
changeably
change down
change ends
change eyes
change gear
changeless
changeling
changement
change note
change over
changeover
change step
channel cat
channelise
channelize
channelled
chaologist
chaparajos
chaparejos
chapelries
chaperonin
chap-fallen
chaplaincy
chaplainry
chaptalize
chapterman
characeous
charactery
Chardonnay
chargeable
charge-book
charge card
charge-hand
chargehand
chargeless
charioteer

charismata
charitable
charitably
charladies
Charles' law
Charles' Law
charleston
Charleston
charmingly
charmonium
Charollais
charophyte
chartreuse
chartulary
chasmogamy
chastelain
chasteness
chaste tree
chatelaine
chatellany
chattelism
chatterbox
chattermag
chattiness
Chaucerian
Chaucerism
chaud-froid
chaud-mellé
chauffeuse
chautauqua
chauvinism
chauvinist
cheapskate
checkerman
checkermen
check out of
checkpoint
check-stone
check-taker
check valve
cheddaring
cheekiness
cheek-pouch
cheek-tooth
cheerfully
cheerie-bye
cheeriness
cheeringly
cheesecake
cheese-head
cheese-mite
cheese-pare
cheesewood
cheesiness
cheirology
Chekhovian
cheliceral
Chelsea bun
Cheltonian
chemiatric
chemically
chemisette

chemotaxis	chinquapin	chorus girl	cinder-cone	Clark's crow
cheque-book	chintziest	chota hazri	Cinderella	clarschach
chequebook	chionodoxa	chowchilla	cinder path	clasp hands
cheque card	chip basket	christener	cine camera	clasp-knife
cherry-like	chip heater	Christhood	cinema-goer	classicise
cherry-pick	Chippewyan	Christless	cinematize	classicism
cherry plum	chippiness	Christlike	cinerarium	classicist
cherry tree	chirognomy	chromaffin	ciné-vérité	classicize
cherry wood	chirograph	chromatism	cinquefoil	classified
cherrywood	chiromancy	chromatoid	cipherable	classifier
chersonese	chironomic	chrome alum	Circassian	classifies
chess-apple	chironomid	chromosome	circensian	classiness
chessboard	chirpiness	chronicity	circle back	claudicant
chess-clock	chirruping	chronicler	circlewise	clavichord
chessylite	chirurgeon	chronogram	circuiteer	clavicular
chestiness	chirurgery	chronology	circuition	Claviolone
chestnutty	chisel-like	chrysaline	circuitous	clawed toad
chest voice	chiselling	chrysalize	circulable	claw hammer
chevesaile	chi-squared	chrysaloid	circularly	clayeyness
chevisance	chitarrone	chrysolite	circulator	clay pigeon
chevrotain	chit-chatty	chrysotile	circumcise	clean break
Chevy Chase	chitty-face	chrysotype	circumduce	clean hands
chewing gum	chivalrous	chubbiness	circumduct	clean house
chew the cud	chlamydiae	chuck-a-luck	circumflex	cleanliest
chew the fat	chlamydial	chucker-out	circumfuse	cleansable
chew the rag	chloramine	chuck-wagon	circummure	clean sheet
chicharron	chloridize	chuckwagon	circumoral	clean slate
chickenpox	chlorinate	chuckwalla	circumvent	clean sweep
Chief Rabbi	chlorinity	chukka boot	cire perdue	clearstory
chiffchaff	chloritize	chumminess	cismontane	clementine
chiffonier	chloritoid	chunkiness	cispontine	Clementine
chiffon pie	chloritous	chupatties	Cistercian	clerestory
chifforobe	chlorodyne	Church Army	citizeness	clergiable
child abuse	chloroform	church-bell	citizenish	clerically
childbirth	choanocyte	church-book	citric acid	cleromancy
child bride	chocaholic	churchgoer	citronella	clever Dick
Childermas	chockstone	churchless	citrulline	cleverness
childishly	chocoholic	churchlike	city editor	clew-garnet
childproof	chocolatey	church mode	City editor	click-clack
child's play	choiceness	church-rate	city father	clientship
child-woman	choir organ	church-scot	civil court	climatical
Chile hazel	choir stall	church-text	civil death	clinginess
Chile nitre	chokeberry	churchward	civilities	clingingly
chiliarchy	choke-berry	churchwise	civil state	clingstone
chiliastic	choke chain	church work	civil wrong	clinically
chilliness	cholagogue	churchyard	cladistics	clink-clank
chillingly	choliambic	Church year	cladoceran	clinkstone
chimaeroid	chondritic	churlishly	claim a foul	clinometer
chimerical	choose ends	churn-staff	clamminess	cliometric
chimney-bar	choosiness	cicatrices	clangorous	clioquinol
chimney pot	choosingly	cicatrizer	clanjamfry	clippingly
chimney-top	chop-fallen	Ciceronian	clankingly	clish-clash
chimpanzee	chopper-cot	cicisbeism	clannishly	clockmaker
China aster	choppiness	cider apple	clanswoman	clock radio
China berry	Chorasmian	cider press	clanswomen	clock tower
China crêpe	choregraph	cigaresque	clap eyes on	clock-watch
chinagraph	choreiform	cigarillos	clapped out	cloddishly
China grass	choreology	cigar plant	claptrappy	clodhopper
china plate	choriambic	cimeliarch	clarabella	clog-dancer
Chinawoman	choriambus	cimetidine	Clarenceux	clogginess
chinchilla	chorically	cinchonine	claret wine	cloistered
Chinese box	choropleth	cinchonism	clarichord	cloisterer

cloisterly
close as wax
closed book
closed door
closed loop
closed shop
close-range
close ranks
close shave
close-stool
close thing
closet play
cloth-bound
cloth-eared
clotheless
clothes-bag
clothes-peg
clothes-pin
cloudberry
cloudburst
cloud cover
cloudiness
cloudscape
clove-brown
clove hitch
cloven foot
cloven hoof
clover leaf
cloverleaf
clownishly
club-footed
cluelessly
clumsiness
cluster fly
Clydesdale
cnidoblast
coacervate
coach-built
coach-horse
coach house
coadjutant
coadjutrix
coagulable
coagulator
coal-bunker
coal-cellar
coalescent
coal-heaver
coal-master
coal mining
coalmining
coal of fire
coal-worker
coaptation
coarse fish
coarseness
coassessor
coastguard
coat armour
coat-hanger
coatimundi
coat of arms

coat of mail
cobalt blue
cobalt bomb
cobwebbery
cobweb bird
cobweblike
coccydynia
cochleated
cockabully
cockalorum
cockamamie
cockamaroo
cock-and-hen
cock a snook
cockatrice
cock-beaded
cockchafer
cockernony
cockleburr
cockmaster
cockneydom
cockneyess
cockneyish
cockneyism
cockneyize
cock-paddle
cock-sucker
cocksurely
cock-tailed
cock-teaser
cocky-leeky
coconut ice
coconut shy
codability
coddled egg
code number
codicology
codirector
codominant
codswallop
coeducator
coelacanth
coeliotomy
coenobitic
coenocytic
co-equality
coequality
coercitive
coercively
coercivity
coetaneous
coeternity
co-executor
coexistent
coffee bean
coffee cake
coffee mill
coffee nibs
coffee-room
coffee shop
coffee tree
coffin-bone

coffinless
coffin-nail
coffin-ship
cogitabund
cogitation
cogitative
cognisable
cognisance
cognizable
cognizably
cognizance
cognominal
cognoscent
co-guardian
cohabitant
cohabiting
coheirship
coherently
cohesively
cohibition
coincident
co-infinite
co-inherent
coking coal
co-labourer
co-latitude
colchicine
cold chisel
cold fusion
cold shower
cold turkey
colemanite
Coleoptera
coleoptile
coleorhiza
collar-beam
collar-bone
collarbone
collarette
collarless
collar of SS
collar-stud
collar-work
collatable
collateral
collection
collective
collegiate
collicular
colliculus
collieries
colligable
colligible
collimator
colloblast
collocable
collocutor
colloguing
collophane
colloquial
colloquies
colloquise

colloquist
colloquium
colloquize
colometric
colonially
colonnaded
colonnette
Coloradian
coloration
coloratura
colorature
colorectal
colossally
colossuses
colotomies
colourable
colourably
colour code
colour fast
colour film
colourizer
colourless
colour line
colour over
colour wash
colportage
colporteur
colposcope
colposcopy
coltsfoots
colt's tooth
columellar
columnated
column-inch
combattant
combinable
combinedly
comburgess
combustion
combustive
come abroad
come across
come-at-able
come before
come copper
comedienne
comedietta
come easy to
come-hither
come home to
come it over
comeliness
comestible
come to good
come to hand
come to life
come to mind
come to pass
come to rest
come to that
comfortful
comforting

comicality
comic opera
comic paper
comic strip
comitative
commandant
commandeer
commandery
commanding
commandite
commeasure
commentary
commentate
commercial
comminator
comminutor
commissary
commission
commissive
commissure
commitment
committing
commixtion
commixture
commodatum
commodious
commonable
commonalty
common cold
common form
common gull
commonhold
common hunt
common jury
common land
common mica
common name
commonness
common noun
common opal
common room
common salt
common seal
common sole
common suit
common tern
common time
common vole
common weal
commonweal
common year
commorancy
commorient
communally
communiqué
commutable
commutator
compact car
compaction
company car
company law
comparable

comparably
comparator
comparison
compassion
compassive
compass saw
compatible
compatibly
compatriot
compelling
compendium
compensate
competence
competency
competitor
compilator
complacent
complainer
complain of
complanate
complected
complement
completely
completion
completist
completive
completory
complexant
complexify
complexion
complexity
compliable
compliance
compliancy
complicacy
complicate
complicity
compliment
complotter
compluvium
composable
composedly
composed of
compositor
compositum
composture
compotator
compounded
compounder
compradore
comprehend
compresent
compressed
compressor
compromise
compulsion
compulsive
compulsory
computable
Comstocker
conalbumin
conatively

conceive of
concentric
conception
conceptive
conceptual
concerning
concertina
concertino
concertize
concession
concessive
concettism
concettist
conchiolin
conchoidal
conchology
conciliate
concinnate
concinnity
concinnous
concipient
conclavist
concludent
conclusion
conclusive
conclusory
concoction
concoctive
concordant
concrement
concretely
concretion
concretise
concretize
concubinal
concurrent
concurring
concursion
concussion
concussive
condensate
condensery
condensity
condescend
condignity
condolence
condonable
conducible
conducting
conduction
conductive
condurango
condylarth
coneflower
cone-in-cone
confabbing
confection
confederal
conference
conferment
conferring
confessant

confession
confidante
confidence
confidency
confinable
confinedly
confirmand
confiscate
conflation
confluence
conformism
conformist
conformity
confounded
confounder
confronter
confusable
confusedly
confusible
confutable
congeneric
congenital
congestion
congestive
conglobate
congregant
congregate
congruence
congruency
conhydrine
conicopoly
coniferous
conjecture
conjointly
conjugally
conjugated
conjunctly
conjurator
connatural
connecting
connection
connective
conniption
connivance
connivancy
connivence
conoidical
conqueress
conquering
conscience
consecrate
consectary
consension
consensual
consentant
consentive
consequent
conservate
considered
considerer
consignify
consilient

consimilar
consistent
consistory
consociate
consolable
consonance
consonancy
con sordino
consortion
consortism
consortium
conspectus
conspiracy
conspirant
constantan
Constantia
constantly
constative
constipate
constitute
constraint
constringe
construing
consuetude
consulship
consultant
consulting
consultory
consumable
consumedly
consummate
contact man
contagious
containing
contentful
contention
contentive
contentual
contestant
contextual
contexture
contiguity
contiguous
continence
continency
contingent
continuant
continuing
continuity
continuous
contortion
contour map
contraband
contrabass
contracted
contractee
contractor
contradict
contraflow
contrahent
contraltos
contrapose

contraries
contrarily
contravene
contrecoup
contre-jour
contribute
contritely
contrition
control key
controlled
controller
control rod
controvert
convalesce
convection
convective
convenable
convenance
convenient
convention
conventual
convergent
conversant
conversely
conversion
conversive
convertend
convertism
convertite
convertive
convex lens
convexness
conveyable
conveyance
conviction
convictism
convictive
convincing
convoluted
convoyance
convulsant
convulsion
convulsive
co-obligant
cooker hood
cooking top
cook's knife
cool-headed
cooperancy
cooperator
Cooper pair
cooper-shop
co-optation
co-optative
co-ordinate
coordinate
cop a packet
coparcener
copartnery
copepodous
Copernican
copper belt

copperhead	cornerback	cosmic dust	coupleteer	crab nebula
copper-knob	corner flag	cosmic rays	coupon bond	Crab nebula
copper loss	corner-kick	cosmodrome	coupon-free	crab plover
copper-nose	cornerless	cosmogenic	courageous	crab-spider
copperskin	corner shop	cosmogonic	course-book	crack a crib
copper wire	cornerwise	cosmopolis	coursebook	crackajack
co-presence	cornetcies	cosmoramic	course unit	crack-brain
co-producer	cornettist	co-specific	courseware	cracked-pot
coprolalia	corn-factor	Cossack hat	coursework	crack hardy
coprolitic	cornflower	Costa Rican	court-baron	crack house
copromania	corn-ground	costliness	court-craft	crackiness
co-promoter	corn-husker	costmaries	court dress	cradle-roof
coprophagy	Cornishman	cosy corner	courtesies	cradle song
coprophile	Cornishmen	cote-hardie	court-house	craft guild
coprophily	corn-popper	coterminal	courthouse	craftiness
copulation	cornstarch	cothurnate	courtierly	craft-union
copulative	cornucopia	cottage pie	courtliest	cragginess
copulatory	Coromandel	cotton belt	court-metre	craneflies
copy editor	coronalled	cotton-bush	court of law	cranesbill
copyholder	coronaries	cotton cake	court order	craniology
copyreader	coronation	cotton-fish	court party	craniotome
copy-taster	corpocracy	cotton lord	cousinhood	craniotomy
copy-typist	corporally	cotton-mill	Cousin Jack	crankiness
copywriter	corporator	cotton-seed	cousinship	crankshaft
coquelicot	corporeity	cottontail	couturière	crank-wheel
coquetries	corpulence	cotton tree	couverture	crap-artist
coquettish	corpulency	cottonweed	covalently	crapaudine
coquimbite	corpuscule	cottonwood	covariance	crapulence
coracoidal	corpus vile	cotton wool	covariancy	craquelure
coral-berry	corralling	cotton-worm	covenantal	crashingly
coral-plant	correction	couch grass	covenanted	crassitude
coral polyp	corrective	cough candy	covenantee	crater-lake
coral snake	correctory	cough sweet	covenanter	crater-like
coram nobis	corregidor	coulombian	covenantor	cravenness
cor anglais	correption	Coulomb law	coverchief	crawlingly ·
corbelling	correspond	coulometer	cover drive	crawl space
corbie-step	Corriedale	coulometry	covered way	crazy about
corbin-bone	corrigenda	coulterneb	cover-glass	creakiness
corded ware	corrigible	councillor	cover point	creakingly
cordelière	corrigibly	councilman	cover-shame	creameries
cordialise	corroboree	councilmen	cover story	creaminess
cordiality	corrodable	council tax	covert coat	cream sauce
cordialize	corrodiary	counselled	covertness	creatinine
cordierite	corrodible	counsellee	covetingly	creational
cordillera	corrosible	counsellor	covetously	creatively
cordon bleu	corrugator	counteract	covinously	creativity
corduroyed	corruptful	counterbid	cowardness	creaturely
cordwainer	corruption	counter-ion	cowberries	credential
corelation	corruptive	counterman	cow-catcher	creditable
corelative	corselette	counterspy	cowcatcher	creditably
core memory	corsetière	countertop	cow-creamer	credit card
coriaceous	corsetless	count heads	coweringly	Creditiste
Corinthian	Cortaillod	count noses	cow-hearted	credit note
cork-jacket	corticated	countryman	cow-parsley	creditress
corkscrewy	corybantic	countrymen	cow parsnip	credit sale
cork-tipped	coryneform	country put	Cowperitis	credit side
corn brandy	coryphaeus	count sheep	cowpuncher	credulence
corn circle	coryphodon	county hall	cowslipped	creepiness
corn-cockle	Cosa Nostra	county seat	cow-spanker	creepingly
corncockle	Coslettize	county town	coxopodite	creep-joint
corn dodger	cosmetical	coup de main	crabbiness	creep-mouse
corned beef	cosmically	coupleless	crab-harrow	crematoria

crenellate
crenulated
crêpe paper
crépinette
crescendos
crescented
crescentic
crested tit
cretaceous
crèvecoeur
crewel work
crib-biting
cribellate
cribriform
crick-crack
cricketana
cricket bag
cricket-bat
cricketing
crime sheet
criminally
criminator
crimpiness
cringeling
cringingly
crinkle-cut
crinolined
criosphinx
crippledom
crispation
crispature
crispbread
crispiness
criss-cross
critically
criticizer
criticling
critiquing
crocheting
crookedest
crooningly
crop circle
croqueting
cross-bench
crossbones
cross-breed
crossbreed
cross-check
cross-court
cross-dress
cross-grain
cross-guard
cross-hatch
cross-index
crossleted
cross-light
crossmatch
crosspatch
crosspiece
cross-point
cross-react
cross-refer

cross slide
cross-staff
cross the t's
crosstrees
cross-vault
cross wires
crotchless
crouchback
Crouch ware
crow-flower
crow-footed
crow garlic
crownation
crown conch
crown court
Crown Court
Crown Derby
crown ether
crown glass
crown graft
crown green
crown-piece
crown roast
crown vetch
crown wheel
cruciality
cruciation
cruelty man
cruet-stand
cruise ship
cruisewear
crumbiness
crumbliest
crumminess
crunchiest
crushingly
crustacean
crustation
crustiness
cryoconite
cryogenics
cryonicist
cryophorus
cryoscopic
cryosphere
cryptogram
cryptolect
cryptology
cryptozoic
cryptozoon
cry shame on
crystallic
crystallin
crystal set
ctenophore
cubby house
cubic nitre
cuboid bone
cuckoo-land
cuckoo pint
cuckoo scab
cuckoo spit

cuckoo wasp
cuculiform
cucullated
cucumiform
cuddleable
cuddlesome
cudgelling
cudgel-play
cuirassier
cuir-ciselé
culdoscope
culdoscopy
culicicide
culicifuge
culinarian
culinarily
cultically
cultivable
cultivator
cultriform
culturable
culturally
culverkeys
culvertage
Cumberland
cumberless
cumberment
cumbersome
cumbrously
cummerbund
cumulately
cumulation
cumulative
cumuliform
cunctation
cunctative
cunctatory
cundurango
cunningest
cup-and-ball
cup-and-cone
cup-and-ring
Cupid's dart
cup of assay
cuprea bark
curability
curate's egg
curatively
curatorial
curd cheese
curelessly
Curetonian
curiologic
curled kale
curly-wurly
curmudgeon
curmurring
currencies
curricular
curriculum
curry paste
cursedness

curtain-rod
curvaceous
curvedness
curvetting
Cushingoid
cuspidated
cussedness
custard pie
customable
customably
customizer
custom-made
cut a corner
cut a figure
cut-and-fill
cut a splash
cut corners
cut-offness
cut the knot
cuttle-bone
cuttlefish
cutty grass
cutty-stool
cut up rough
cyanic acid
cyanine dye
cyanogenic
cyanometer
cyanometry
cyanophyte
cyathiform
cybernetic
cyberspace
cybotactic
cycle track
cyclically
cyclo-cross
cyclograph
cyclometer
cyclometry
cyclopedia
cyclopedic
cycloramic
cyclostome
cyclostyle
cyclothyme
cyclotomic
cylindered
cylindrite
cylindroid
cylindroma
cymotrichy
cynegetics
cynophobia
Cyrenaican
cyrtometer
cystectomy
cystinosis
cystinotic
cystinuria
cystometer
cystometry

cystoscope
cystoscopy
cystostomy
cytochrome
cytologist
cytopathic
cytophilic
cytotropic
daffodilly
daggerhead
daggle-tail
Daguerrean
dahabeeyah
daily bread
daily dozen
daintihood
daintiness
dairy cream
daisy chain
daisy roots
daisy wheel
Dalton plan
damageable
damagement
damagingly
damascener
damask rose
damask work
dame school
damfoolery
damned well
damn my eyes
damp course
damselfish
damson plum
damson tree
dance-drama
dance floor
dance-house
dancercise
dandizette
dandy brush
dandy-horse
dandyishly
dandyzette
Danes' blood
dangerless
danger line
danger list
dangersome
danglement
Danish blue
dapperling
dapperness
dapple grey
daringness
Darjeeling
dark matter
Darling pea
darning-egg
dastardize
dasylirion

data-logger
data stream
date back to
date-cancel
datelessly
date-letter
daubréeite
daughterly
daunomycin
dauntingly
dauphinate
dauphiness
dawn chorus
daydreamer
day nursery
day of truce
day release
day tripper
dazzlement
dazzlingly
deaconhood
deacon-seat
deaconship
deactivate
dead-beaten
dead centre
dead colour
dead-end kid
dead letter
deadliness
deadlocked
dead nettle
deadpanned
dead ringer
dead-tongue
dead weight
de-aeration
deafferent
de-afforest
deaf-mutism
deaf-nettle
dealbation
dealership
dealkylate
deambulate
dear-bought
death adder
death agony
deathfully
death grant
death house
deathiness
death knell
deathliest
death-place
death's head
death squad
deathwards
death-watch
death-wound
deauration
debasement

debateable
debauchery
debentured
debilitate
debonairly
debouchure
debriefing
decadently
decagynous
decahedral
decahedron
Decalogist
decametric
decampment
decandrous
decangular
decapitate
decathlete
Decauville
deceivable
deceivably
decelerate
Decembrist
decempedal
decemviral
decentness
deceptible
deceptious
decigramme
decimalise
decimalism
decimalist
decimalize
decimation
decinormal
decipherer
decisional
decisively
decivilize
deckle edge
deck quoits
deck tennis
declarable
declarator
declaredly
declare war
declassify
declension
declinable
decollator
décolletée
decolonise
decolonize
decolorise
decolorize
decomposer
decompound
decompress
deconvolve
decorament
decoration
decorative

decorement
decorously
decreation
decree nisi
decreolize
decrepitly
decrescent
decretally
decryption
decumbence
decumbency
decurrence
decurrency
decussated
dedecorate
dedication
dedicative
dedicatory
deductable
deductible
deed of gift
de-emphasis
deep-bodied
deep-freeze
deep-frying
deep litter
deep-rooted
deep-seated
deep waters
deer-culler
deer forest
de-escalate
de-ethicize
defaceable
defacement
defalcator
defamation
defamatory
defeasance
defeasible
defeasibly
defecation
defectible
defeminize
defenceman
defendable
defendress
defenseman
defensible
defensibly
deferrable
deficiency
defilement
definement
definitely
definition
definitive
definitory
definitude
deflagrate
deflection
deflective

deflowerer
defocusing
defocussed
defoliator
deforciant
deformable
deformedly
defrayable
defrayment
defunction
defunctive
de Gaullism
degeneracy
degenerate
degradable
degreeless
degression
degressive
dehiscence
dehumanise
dehumanize
dehumidify
dehydrator
deiformity
deinothere
dejectedly
delaminate
Delawarean
Delawarian
del credere
delectable
delectably
delegacies
delegation
delegatory
Delhi belly
deliberant
deliberate
delicacies
delicately
deligation
delightful
delimitate
delimiting
delineable
delineator
delinquent
deliquesce
delirament
deliration
deliveress
deliveries
delocalise
delocalize
delphinine
delphinium
delphinoid
delta waves
deltiology
delucidate
deluginous
delusional

delusively
demagogism
demandable
demand note
demand pull
demarcator
dementedly
demi-cannon
demi-circle
demi-lancer
demi-ostage
demiourgos
demi-piqued
demissness
demobilise
demobilize
democratic
Democritic
demodectic
demodulate
Demogorgon
demography
demoiselle
demolisher
demolition
demonetise
demonetize
demoniacal
demonology
demoralise
demoralize
demoticist
demotivate
demureness
demurrable
denatation
denaturant
denaturize
dendriform
dendrogram
dendrology
denegation
denegatory
denigrator
denization
denominate
de nos jours
denotation
denotative
denotement
denouement
dénouement
densimeter
densometer
denticular
dentifrice
dentiscalp
denudation
denudative
denunciate
deobstruct
deodorizer

Deo gratias	derogatory	detectival	diagrammed	dig a pit for
deontology	derricking	detergency	diagraphic	digestedly
Deo volente	desalinate	determined	diagrydium	digestible
deoxidizer	desalinize	determiner	diakineses	digestibly
department	desaturate	deterrable	diakinesis	digger wasp
dependable	descendant	deterrence	dialectics	digitalise
dependably	descendent	detestable	dialogical	digitalize
dependance	descending	detestably	dialoguist	digitately
dependancy	descension	detonation	dialoguize	digitation
dependence	descensive	detonative	dialysable	digitiform
dependency	descramble	detoxicate	diamantine	digitorium
deperition	descriptor	detoxified	diamond-cut	diglottism
depilation	descriptum	detoxifies	diamondize	digression
depilatory	desecrator	detraction	diapedesis	digressive
deplorable	desert boot	detractive	diaphanous	dijudicate
deplorably	desert lark	detractory	diaphoneme	dikaryotic
deployment	desertless	detruncate	diaphorase	dilacerate
deplumated	desertness	devalorize	diaporesis	dilapidate
depolarise	desert rose	Devanagari	diarrhoeal	dilatation
depolarize	deservedly	devastator	diarrhoeic	dilatative
depopulate	deshabille	developing	diasceuast	dilatorily
deportable	*déshabille*	deviatoric	diaskeuast	dilemmatic
deportment	*déshabillé*	deviceless	diastaltic	dilettante
depositary	desiccator	devil dance	diathermal	dilettanti
depositing	desiderata	devil-devil	diathermic	diligently
deposition	desiderate	devilishly	diatribist	dilligrout
depository	designable	devil's club	diazeuctic	dill pickle
depositure	designator	devil's dirt	dibasicity	dilly-dally
depravedly	designatum	devil's dung	dichloride	dilucidate
deprecator	designedly	devil's dust	dichlorvos	diluteness
depreciate	designless	devil's grip	dichotomic	dilutional
depredator	designment	devil's guts	dichroitic	dime a dozen
depressant	desipience	devil's limb	dichromasy	dimetrodon
depressing	desipiency	devil's milk	dichromate	dimication
depression	desireless	deviltries	dickcissel	diminished
depressive	desiringly	devisement	Dickensian	diminisher
deprivable	desirously	devitalise	dicoumarin	diminuendi
depuration	desistance	devitalize	dicoumarol	diminuendo
depurative	desolately	devocalize	Dictaphone	diminution
depuratory	desolation	devolution	dictatress	diminutive
deputation	desolative	Devonshire	dictionary	dimorphism
deputative	desorption	devotement	Dictograph	dimorphous
deputyship	despairful	devotional	dictyosome	dim-sighted
deracinate	desperados	devourable	dicynodont	*Ding an sich*
derailleur	despicable	devourment	didactical	dingle-bird
derailment	despicably	devoutness	didascalic	dining hall
Derbyshire	despisable	dewberries	didgeridoo	dining room
deregister	despiteful	dewdropped	didjeridoo	dinner-bell
deregulate	despiteous	dextrality	didynamous	dinner-horn
derestrict	despondent	dextrorsal	did you ever	dinner lady
deridingly	desquamate	dhobi's itch	die-casting	dinnerless
derisively	dessiatine	diabetical	die-hardism	dinner-pail
derivately	destructor	diabolical	dielectric	dinner time
derivation	desudation	diacaustic	difference	dioestrous
derivative	detachable	diachronic	difficulty	Diogenical
dermatitis	detachedly	diaconicon	diffidence	dioptrical
dermatogen	detachment	diademated	diffidency	diorthosis
dermatosis	detainable	diagenesis	diffluence	diorthotic
dernier cri	detainment	diagenetic	diffusable	diotically
dernier mot	detectable	diaglyphic	diffusedly	Diotrephes
derogation	detectably	diagnostic	diffusible	diphonemic
derogative	detectible	diagonally	digammated	diphtheria

diphtheric
diphyletic
diphyllous
diphyodont
diplacusis
diplococci
diplodocus
diplograph
diploidion
diplomatic
diplophase
Dippel's oil
diprotodon
dipsomania
diptychous
directable
direct dial
direct mail
directness
Directoire
directress
directrice
direct rule
diremption
dirt-eating
dirt farmer
dirty Allan
dirty linen
dirty money
dirty trick
disability
disamenity
disanalogy
disanimate
disapparel
disappoint
disapprove
disarrange
disastrous
disbalance
disbarment
disbarring
disbelieve
disbenefit
disbudding
disburthen
discarnate
disc camera
discectomy
discerning
disc floret
dischargee
discharger
disc harrow
discipline
discipular
discission
disc jockey
disclaimer
disclosing
disclosure
discobolus

discomfort
discommend
discommode
discommons
discommune
discompose
disco music
disconcert
disconfirm
disconnect
discontent
discophile
discordant
discordful
discordous
discounsel
discounter
discourage
discourser
discoverer
discreeter
discreetly
discrepant
discrepate
discretely
discretion
discretive
discretize
disculpate
discursion
discursive
discursory
discussant
discussion
discussive
discutient
disdainful
diseasedly
diseaseful
diseconomy
diseducate
disembogue
disembosom
disembowel
disembroil
disempower
disenamour
disenchant
disendower
disengaged
disennoble
disenslave
disenthral
disentitle
disentrail
disentwine
disenvelop
disepalous
disfashion
disfeature
disfigurer
disfurnish

disgarland
disgarnish
disglorify
disgregate
disgruntle
disguising
disgustful
disgusting
dishabille
dish aerial
disharmony
dishearten
disherison
dishonesty
dishwasher
dishwatery
disimagine
disimprove
disincline
disinherit
disinhibit
disinvolve
disjection
disjointed
disjointly
dislikable
disloyally
disloyalty
dismalness
dismantler
dismission
dismissive
dismissory
Disneyland
disordered
disorderly
disorganic
disownment
disparager
dispassion
dispatcher
dispelling
dispensary
dispensate
dispensive
dispeopler
dispermous
dispersant
dispersion
dispersive
dispersoid
disphenoid
dispiteous
dispondaic
disponible
disposable
disposedly
dispositor
dispossess
dispraiser
disprovide
disputable

disputably
disputator
disqualify
disquieten
disquieter
disquietly
Disraelian
disrealize
disrespect
disruption
disruptive
disrupture
dissatisfy
dissceptre
dissection
dissective
disselboom
dissembler
dissension
dissenting
dissention
dissertate
disservice
dissheathe
dissidence
dissightly
dissilient
dissimilar
dissipated
dissipater
dissipator
dissociate
dissoluble
dissolubly
dissolvent
dissonance
dissonancy
dissuasion
dissuasive
distensile
distension
distichous
distillate
distillery
distilling
distilment
distinctly
distortion
distortive
distracted
distractor
distrainee
distrainer
distrainor
distraught
distressed
distribute
distringas
distruster
disturbant
disturbing
disulfiram

disulphide
disuniform
disutility
disyllabic
disyllable
ditchwater
ditch-water
ditheistic
dithematic
dithionate
dithionite
dithionous
ditriglyph
ditrigonal
ditrochean
dittograph
ditto marks
diurnal arc
diurnalist
diurnation
diuturnity
divagation
divaricate
dive-bomber
dive-dapper
divergence
divergency
divertible
divestment
dividually
divination
divinatory
divineness
divineress
diving bell
diving duck
diving suit
divinities
divinitize
divisional
divisively
divulgence
dizzyingly
do a swelter
do away with
dobby-weave
Dobos Torte
docibility
docimastic
dock-tailed
Doc Martens
do credit to
doctorally
doctor bird
doctor-fish
doctorhood
doctorship
doctrinary
doctrinate
doctrinism
doctrinist
documental

dodecanoic	doorkeeper	Douglasite	draught-net	drop astern
dodecarchy	door-to-door	doulocracy	draw a blank	drop down to
dog and bone	dope-runner	douzainier	draw breath	drop hammer
dogberries	Dorian mode	dove-colour	drawbridge	drop-handle
dog biscuit	dormer room	dove-flower	draw bridle	drop-letter
dog-bramble	Dorothy bag	dove-marble	Drawcansir	droppingly
dogfighter	dorsalmost	dove orchid	drawerfuls	drop serene
doggedness	Dorset Down	dovetailed	draw-gloves	drop-stroke
dog handler	dorsifixed	dovetailer	drawing-pad	drosometer
dog-leg hole	dosimetric	dovishness	drawing pin	drosophila
dogmatical	do the downy	do well to do	draw it mild	drossiness
dogmatizer	do the trick	dower chest	drawlingly	droughtily
dognapping	do things to	dower house	draw near to	drowningly
dogsbodies	dotishness	down and out	draw straws	drowsihead
dog's dinner	dot product	down at heel	drawstring	drowsiness
dog's letter	dotted line	down cellar	draw stumps	drowsy-head
dog's-tongue	dottrified	downcoming	dreadfully	drudgingly
dog-whipper	Douay Bible	down-coming	dreadingly	drug addict
Dolcelatte	double back	down-curved	dreadlocks	drug buster
dolesomely	double-bank	down-easter	dreamfully	druggister
do less than	double bass	downhiller	dreaminess	drug pusher
dollar area	double bill	down-market	dreamingly	Druid stone
dollarbird	double bind	downmarket	dreamscape	drumlinoid
dollar mark	double bond	downstairs	dream-world	drupaceous
dollar sign	double-book	downstater	dreamworld	druzhinnik
dollar spot	double chin	downstream	drearihead	dry battery
doll's house	double-crop	down-street	drearihood	dry-blowing
dolomitize	double cube	down-stroke	dreariment	dry canteen
dolorifuge	double date	downstroke	dreariness	dry-cleaner
dolorously	double-deck	down the pan	drearisome	dry farming
dolus bonus	double-dink	down timber	dredge-boat	dry Martini
dolus malus	double-dyed	down-to-date	dreikanter	dry measure
dome-headed	double-face	downtowner	dress house	dry monsoon
domestical	double flat	downwardly	dressiness	dry saltery
dominantly	doublefold	downy birch	dressmaker	dry shampoo
domination	double harp	dowsing rod	dress-sense	dual number
dominative	double-head	doxography	dress shirt	dubitation
dominatrix	double life	doxologies	Dreyfusard	dubitative
domineerer	double-lock	doxologize	drift apart	dub-skelper
Dominicker	doubleness	drabbiness	driftingly	duffel coat
Donald Duck	double-park	draconites	drift sight	duffle-coat
Donatistic	double play	dracontine	drill order	duke cherry
doner kebab	double reed	draegerman	drink-drive	dulcetness
Don Juanism	double-reef	drag-anchor	drinking up	dull-headed
donkey deep	double room	drag artist	drink-money	dullsville
donkey drop	double salt	dragginess	drink-taken	dull-witted
donkey-lick	double-shot	draggingly	drip coffee	dumb animal
donkey pump	double star	dragon arum	drippiness	dumb blonde
donkey vote	double stop	dragonfish	drivelling	dumb crambo
donkey work	double take	dragonnade	driven well	dumb friend
Donnybrook	double-talk	dragon root	driverless	dumbledore
Don Quixote	double team	dragon ship	drive shaft	dumb nettle
don't-carish	double time	dragon tree	driveshaft	dumb sheave
don't mind me	doubletree	drag-racing	driving box	dumbstruck
doodle-sack	double-wide	drainboard	drolleries	dumb waiter
doohickeys	doubtfully	drake's tail	dromomania	dumpy level
doomsaying	doubtingly	dramatical	droopiness	Dundee cake
do one's best	douc langur	dramaturge	droopingly	dunderhead
do one's dash	dough-baked	dramaturgy	droop-snoot	dunderpate
do one's duty	doughiness	draught ewe	drop a brick	dung-beetle
do one's face	doughtiest	draughtily	drop anchor	duniwassal
do one's head	Douglas fir	draughtman	drop asleep	dunnage bag

duodecimal	earth-light	ecstatical	eighty-nine	emblem book
duodecimos	earth-mover	ecthlipsis	eisteddfod	emblements
duodenitis	earthquake	ectodermal	ejaculator	embodiment
dupability	earthshine	ectogenous	ekistician	emboldener
duple ratio	earthwards	ectomorphy	elaborator	embolismic
duplicable	earth-woman	ectromelia	elasmosaur	embolismus
duplicator	ear-trumpet	Ecuadorian	elastician	embonpoint
durability	earwigging	ecumenical	elasticise	embossment
durational	ear-witness	eczematous	elasticity	embothrium
duratively	ease nature	edentulous	elasticize	embouchure
durativity	East Africa	edge-runner	elatedness	embowelled
Düreresque	Easter-dues	edge to edge	elbow chair	emboweller
dusky perch	easterlies	edible crab	elbow-joint	embrasured
dustbinman	Easter lily	edible frog	elderberry	embrighten
dust-colour	Easterling	edibleness	eldest hand	embroidery
dust jacket	Easter term	edifyingly	Eleaticism	embryogeny
Dutch feast	Eastertide	editionize	elecampane	embryology
Dutch light	Eastertime	editorship	electional	embryonary
Dutch lunch	Easter Week	educatable	electively	embryonate
Dutch metal	East German	edulcorate	electorate	embryotomy
Dutch treat	East Indian	Edwardiana	electorial	emendation
Dutch uncle	East Indies	effaceable	electrical	emendatory
Dutchwoman	East Riding	effacement	electrojet	emeraldine
Dutchwomen	eastwardly	effectible	electronic	emergently
duumvirate	easy does it	effectless	electrotin	Emersonian
dwarf elder	Easy Street	effectuate	elementary	emery board
dwarfishly	easy virtue	effeminacy	elephantic	emery cloth
dyeability	eat Chinese	effeminate	elephantry	emery paper
dyer's broom	eat dinners	effeminize	Eleusinian	emery wheel
dynamicist	eat one's hat	effervesce	elevatedly	emetically
dynamistic	eat the leek	effeteness	elevenfold	emigration
dynamitard	eaves-board	efficacity	eleven-plus	emigratory
dynastical	ebb and flow	efficience	eleventhly	emissaries
Dyophysite	Ebionitism	efficiency	eliminable	emissivity
Dyothelite	ebracteate	effleurage	eliminator	emmetropia
dypsomania	ebullience	effloresce	eliotropus	emmetropic
dysarthria	ebulliency	effortless	eliquation	emollience
dyscrasite	ebullition	effraction	elliptical	emparadise
dysenteric	eburnation	effrontery	elongation	empathetic
dysgraphia	ecce signum	effulgence	eloquently	empathetic
dysgraphic	ecchymosed	effusively	elsewhence	emphasizer
dyskinesia	ecchymoses	egg-coddler	elucidator	emphatical
dysphemism	ecchymosis	egg custard	elucubrate	emphyteuta
dysplastic	Eccles cake	egg tempera	elutriator	Empire City
dysprosium	ecclesiast	egocentric	eluviation	empire-line
dysprosody	echinoderm	egoistical	Elzevirian	empiricism
dystrophia	echinulate	egurgitate	emaciation	empiricist
dystrophic	echoically	Egypticity	emalangeni	emplastrum
each to each	echolocate	Egyptizing	emancipate	employable
eagle-stone	echopraxia	Egyptology	emancipist	employment
Eames chair	eclaircise	eicosanoic	emarginate	empoisoner
earbashing	eclectical	eicosanoid	emasculate	emulsified
early grave	eclipsable	eicosenoic	embalmment	emulsifier
early hours	ecliptical	eigenstate	embankment	emulsifies
early music	ecoclimate	eigenvalue	embarkment	enablement
early night	ecological	eighteenmo	embattling	enaliosaur
early riser	economical	eighteenth	embeddable	enamelling
ear-stopple	economizer	eighth note	ember-goose	enamellist
earth-board	ecotourism	eighth part	embitterer	enamelware
earthbound	ecotourist	eightpence	emblazoner	enamelwork
earth house	ecphonesis	eightpenny	emblazonry	enantiomer
earthiness	ecstasiate	eightyfold	emblematic	encampment

encasement	enfacement	entombment	epigastric	equanimous
encashable	*enfant gâté*	entomology	epigenesis	equestrial
encashment	enfleurage	entophytic	epigenetic	equestrian
encephalic	enfoldment	entrancing	epiglottal	equiatomic
encephalin	enforcedly	entrapment	epiglottic	equicrural
encephalon	enforcible	entrapping	epiglottis	equilibria
encephalos	engagement	en travesti	epigrapher	equilibrio
enchanting	engagingly	entreasure	epigraphic	equiparate
enchiridia	engarrison	entreaties	epileptoid	equipotent
encincture	engenderer	entrenched	epilimnion	equiradial
encomienda	engendrure	entryphone	epilogical	equi-signal
encourager	engineless	Entryphone	epimorphic	equitation
encrinital	engine room	enumerable	epineurium	equivalent
encrinitic	English elm	enumerator	epipelagic	equivocacy
encroacher	Englishism	enunciable	epiphanies	equivocate
encrustate	Englishize	enunciator	epiphanize	eradiation
encryption	Englishman	enveloping	epiphanous	eradicable
encyclical	Englishmen	environing	epipharynx	eradicated
encystment	engrossing	enwrapment	epiphonema	eradicator
endangerer	engulfment	enwrapping	epiphyllum	erectility
end by doing	enharmonic	enzymology	epiphyseal	eremitical
endearance	enhungered	eosinophil	epiphytous	Erewhonian
endearment	enigmatise	epagomenal	epipleural	ergastulum
endemicity	enigmatize	epagomenic	epiplocele	ergativity
endergonic	enjambment	epanaphora	episcleral	ergodicity
endingless	enjoinment	eparterial	episcopacy	ergonomics
end in smoke	enjoyingly	epaulement	episcopate	ergonomist
end moraine	enkephalin	epauletted	episcopize	ergonovine
endocarpic	enlacement	epeirogeny	episematic	ergophobia
endocervix	enlistment	epentheses	episiotomy	ergosphere
endocyclic	enlivening	epenthesis	episodical	ergosterol
endocytose	enmeshment	epenthetic	episomally	ergotamine
endodermal	enomotarch	epexegeses	epispastic	ergotoxine
endodermic	enormities	epexegesis	epistemics	eria cocoon
endodermis	enormously	epexegetic	episternal	ericaceous
endodontal	enough said	ephemerist	episternum	erosionist
endodontia	enquirable	ephemerons	epistolary	erotically
endodontic	enragement	ephemerous	epistolise	erotogenic
endoenzyme	enregister	Ephthalite	epistolist	erotomania
end of steel	enrichment	epiblastic	epistolize	errability
endogamous	ensanguine	epicanthic	epistrophe	erraticism
endogenous	enserfment	epicanthus	epitaphial	erubescent
endolithic	ensoulment	epicardiac	epitaphian	eructation
endomorphy	entailable	epicardial	epitaphize	eruptional
endophoric	entailment	epicardium	epithalamy	erysipelas
endophytic	enterclose	epicentral	epithecium	erythrasma
endorsable	enterocele	epichordal	epithelial	erythremia
endorsible	enterocyte	epiclastic	epithelium	erythritol
endoscopic	enterolith	epicondyle	epithetize	erythrosin
endosmosis	enterotomy	epicranial	epitomator	escadrille
endosmotic	enterprise	epicuticle	epitomical	escalation
endosulfan	enthraldom	epicycloid	epitomizer	escalatory
endothermy	enthronize	Epidaurian	epoch angle	escallonia
end product	enthusiasm	epideictic	eponychium	escalloped
end-scraper	enthusiast	epidemical	epoophoron	escape code
end-stopped	enticement	epidendrum	epoxy resin	escapeless
enduringly	enticingly	epidermoid	eprouvette	escapement
eneolithic	entincture	epididymal	Epsom salts	escape road
energetics	entireness	epididymis	equability	escapology
energy band	entireties	epidiorite	equational	escarpment
enervation	entitative	epidotized	equatorial	escartelee
enervative	entodermal	epigastria	equanimity	escharotic

eschatocol	euhemerist	every stick	exhaust gas	explicator
escheatage	euhemerize	everything	exhaustion	explicitly
eschewment	eukaryotic	everywhere	exhaustive	explodable
escritoire	eulogistic	evidential	exheredate	exploitage
escutcheon	eupatorium	evil spirit	exhibitant	exploitive
Eskimo roll	euphausiid	eviscerate	exhibiting	explorator
esoterical	euphemious	eviternity	exhibition	explosible
espacement	euphemizer	evolvement	exhibitive	exportable
espadrille	euphonical	evulgation	exhibitory	exposition
especially	euphonious	exacerbate	exhilarant	expositive
espressivo	euphorbium	exactingly	exhilarate	expository
esprit fort	euphoriant	exactitude	exhumation	expressage
essayistic	Euphratean	exaggerate	exigencies	expression
estanciero	euphuistic	exaltation	exiguously	expressive
estate duty	Eurafrican	examinable	exit permit	expressman
esterified	Eurasiatic	examinator	ex-meridian	expressway
esterifies	eurhythmic	exannulate	exobiology	expunction
esthiomene	Euripidean	exasperate	exocentric	expurgator
estimation	euroaquilo	exaspidean	exocuticle	exsanguine
estimative	Eurobabble	excalceate	exocytosis	exsibilate
estimatory	Eurocheque	ex cathedra	exocytotic	ex silentio
esuriently	euroclydon	excavation	exodontist	exsolution
etch figure	Eurodollar	excavatory	exogenetic	exspuition
Eteocretan	Euromarket	excecation	exoglossic	exsufflate
eternalise	Europeanly	exceedable	exomphalos	extemporal
eternalism	Eurosummit	excellence	exo-narthex	extendable
eternality	Eurovision	excellency	exorbitant	extendedly
eternalize	eurybathic	Excellency	exorbitate	extendible
eternities	euryhaline	exceptable	exorcistic	extensible
ethacrynic	euryhydric	exceptious	exospheric	extenuator
ethambutol	eurypterid	excerption	exoterical	exteriorly
ethanediol	eurythmics	excess fare	exothermal	exterior to
ethereally	Eustachian	excise duty	exothermic	externally
ethicalism	Euston Road	excisional	exotically	extinction
ethicality	euthanasia	excitation	exoticness	extinctive
ethnically	eutrapelia	excitative	expandable	extinguish
ethnologic	evacuation	excitatory	expandible	extirpator
ethologist	evacuative	excitement	expansible	extra cover
ethylamine	evaluation	excitingly	expatiater	extractant
ethyl ether	evaluative	excludable	expatiator	extracting
ethylidene	evanescent	excogitate	expatriate	extraction
etiolation	evangelise	excrescent	expectable	extractive
Eton collar	evangelism	excruciate	expectably	extractory
Eton jacket	evangelist	excursuses	expectance	extradural
etymologer	evangelize	excusatory	expectancy	extralegal
etymologic	evaporable	excuseless	expectedly	extramural
eucalyptic	evaporator	ex dividend	expedience	extraneity
eucalyptol	evaporitic	execration	expediency	extraneous
eucalyptus	even chance	execrative	expeditate	extricable
eucaryotic	even-handed	execratory	expedition	extrudable
euchlorine	evenliness	executable	expellable	extubation
eudaemonic	even parity	executancy	expendable	extuberant
eudaimonia	eventfully	exegetical	expendably	exuberance
eudemonics	even though	exemptible	expenditor	exuberancy
eudemonism	eventually	exenterate	experience	Exucontian
eudemonist	ever-during	exercitant	experiment	exulcerate
eudiometer	ever-living	Exeter hall	expertness	exultantly
eudiometry	every bit as	exfiltrate	expilation	exultation
eugenicist	every other	exhalation	expiration	exultingly
eugeocline	every penny	exhalative	expiratory	exumbrella
euglobulin	everyplace	exhalatory	explicable	exundation
euhemerism	every steek	exhalement	explicably	exurbanite

exuviation
eye-catcher
eye contact
eye-dialect
eyeglassed
eye-legible
eyelet hole
eye-opening
eye-service
eyespotted
eyestrings
eyewitness
fabricable
fabricator
Fabry–Pérot
fabulation
fabulosity
fabulously
face-fungus
facelessly
face powder
face-saving
face-symbol
face to face
faceworker
face-worker
facileness
facilitate
facilities
facinorous
facsimiled
fact-finder
factionary
factioneer
factionist
factiously
factitious
fact of life
factorable
factorship
factor VIII
factualism
factualist
factuality
Fade-Ometer
fadingness
faggot-iron
faggot vote
Fahrenheit
faint heart
faintingly
fair dinkum
fair enough
fairground
fair-haired
fair-minded
fair-spoken
fair-trader
fairy cycle
fairy-floss
fairy prion
fairy story

faithfully
falciparum
Falklander
fall aboard
fallacious
fall astern
fall back on
fall behind
fallen arch
fallenness
fall foul of
falling-out
fall in love
fall in with
fallow deer
fallowness
false alarm
false brome
false front
false issue
false jalap
false molar
false point
false scent
false start
false teeth
false topaz
falsettist
false whorl
famatinite
familiarly
familistic
family name
family room
family tree
famishment
famousness
fanaticise
fanaticism
fanaticize
fancifully
fancy bread
fancy dress
fancy goods
fancy-piece
fancy woman
fandangoes
fanglement
Fanny Adams
fantastico
fan-tracery
far and away
far and near
far and wide
far between
farcically
Far Eastern
far-fetched
farmerette
farouchely
far-sighted
Far Western

fasciation
fascicular
fasciculus
fascinated
fascinator
fascistoid
fashionist
fast asleep
fast bowler
Fastens-een
fast friend
fastidious
fastigiate
fasting-day
fast-twitch
fastuously
fast worker
fatalistic
fatalities
fatherhood
fatherland
fatherless
fatherlike
Father's Day
fathership
Father Time
fathomable
fathometer
fathomless
fatiguable
fat-soluble
fault-block
faultiness
Fauntleroy
fautorship
favourable
favourably
favouredly
favourless
fawn-colour
fax machine
fazendeiro
fearlessly
fearnought
fearsomely
feather-bed
feather-cut
featherfew
feathering
featherlet
featherman
feather ore
feat of arms
featurally
featurette
febrifugal
Februaries
februation
fecklessly
federalise
federalism
federalist

federalize
federation
federative
fed to death
feebleness
feeding-cup
feed-trough
feelingful
feel no pain
feet of clay
feigningly
feistiness
felicitate
felicities
felicitous
felix culpa
fellmonger
fellow-heir
fellowless
fellowlike
fellowship
fell walker
felon-grass
felony de se
felspathic
felt-tip pen
female fern
female hemp
femaleness
feme covert
feminality
femininely
femininist
femininity
feministic
fence-month
fenestella
fenestrate
fen-runners
fer de lance
feretories
fermentate
fermentive
ferntickle
ferocities
ferredoxin
ferric acid
ferricrete
ferro-alloy
fertilizer
fervidness
Fescennine
festerment
festoonery
fetch about
fetchingly
fetch-light
fetch round
fetiferous
fetterless
fetterlock
fettuccine

feuilleton
feverishly
feverously
fever pitch
fianchetto
Fianna Fáil
fiberboard
fiberglass
fible-fable
fibreboard
fibreglass
fibre-optic
fibrescope
fibrillary
fibrillate
fibrillose
fibrinogen
fibroblast
fibrogenic
fibrositic
fibrositis
fickleness
fictionary
fictioneer
fictionist
fictionize
fictitious
fiddle-back
fiddle-case
fiddle dock
fiddle-fish
fiddle-head
fiddler ray
fiddlewood
fidejussor
fiducially
field event
field glass
field guide
field mouse
field notes
fieldstone
fieldwards
fiendishly
fiend's limb
fierceness
fiery cross
fifth wheel
fifty-fifty
fight dirty
fightingly
fight it out
fight shy of
figuration
figurative
figurehead
figureless
filamented
filariases
filariasis
filariosis
file server

filialness
filibuster
filler hose
fillet weld
film colour
filmically
film-making
filmsetter
filopodial
filopodium
filterable
filter cake
filthiness
filtration
fimbriated
final cause
final drive
finalistic
finalities
final proof
find favour
find its way
fine tuning
finger bowl
finger food
finger-hole
finger lake
fingerless
finger-like
fingerling
finger-mark
fingermark
fingernail
finger-pick
fingerpick
finger-post
finger-ring
finger-snap
finger-wave
finicality
finishable
finish line
finishment
finish with
finiteness
finitistic
Finlandise
Finlandize
Finno-Ugric
fire blight
fire-eating
fire engine
fire escape
fire-hearth
fire-master
fire-office
fire-plough
fire-policy
fire-raiser
fire-ranger
fire screen
fire-shovel

fire-vessel
fire-walker
fire warden
fireworker
firing line
firing-step
first aider
first blood
first blush
first brush
First Cause
first-class
first comer
first cross
First Fleet
first floor
First Folio
first-fruit
first light
first mover
first night
first of all
first paeon
first-rater
First Reich
first sound
first table
first thing
first-timer
first water
First World
fiscal drag
fiscal year
fish-basket
fish-carver
fish-eaters
fisherfolk
fish-farmer
fish finger
fishing-fly
fishing rod
fish kettle
fish-ladder
fishmonger
fish poison
fish supper
fisticuffs
fisting cur
fistycuffs
fit as a flea
fitchet pie
fitfulness
fittedness
fit the bill
FitzGerald
five-corner
five-eighth
five-finger
five orders
fives-court
five-seater
five senses

fivestones
fixed focus
fixed point
flabbiness
flabellate
flaccidity
Flacianist
flagellant
flagellate
flagellist
flag-flying
flagginess
flagitious
flagrantly
flagstoned
flag-waving
flail chest
flail-joint
flail mower
flake-stand
flake-white
flak jacket
flamboyant
flamdoodle
flameproof
flame-proof
flamingoes
flanconade
Flanderkin
flangeless
flannelled
flapdoodle
flap-dragon
flapperdom
flapperish
flash-board
flash flood
Flash Harry
flash-house
flashiness
flashlight
flashpoint
flat bottom
flat-footed
flat-headed
flat racing
flattening
flatten out
flatteries
flattering
flatulence
flatulency
flatuosity
flavescent
flavourful
flavouring
flavourist
flawlessly
flax-hackle
flax-lilies
flea beetle
flea-bitten

flea-circus
flea collar
flea-hopper
flea market
fledgeless
fledgeling
fleeceable
fleecelike
fleece-wool
fleeciness
fleeringly
fleetingly
Flemish eye
flesh-brush
flesh-flies
fleshiness
fleshliest
flesh-quake
flesh tints
flesh wound
fleur-de-lis
fleur-de-lys
fleurettée
flexuosity
flexuously
flickering
flicker out
flick knife
flight call
flight crew
flight deck
flightiest
flightless
flight-line
flight path
flight plan
flight-shot
flight-test
flimsiness
fling aside
flint glass
flintiness
flint paper
flintstone
flippantly
flirtation
flitch beam
floatation
floatative
float-board
float glass
float-grass
floatingly
float-light
floatplane
float-stone
floccipend
flocculate
flocculent
flock paper
flooded box
flooded gum

flood-hatch
floodlight
flood plain
flood water
floorboard
floorcloth
floppiness
floppy disk
Flora dance
floral leaf
Florentine
flore pleno
florescent
floriation
floribunda
florideous
floridness
florilegia
floristics
flosculous
flote-grass
flounderer
flouriness
flourisher
floutingly
flower girl
flower head
flowerless
flower-like
flown cover
flow of soul
flue-boiler
fluffiness
flugelhorn
fluidified
fluidifies
fluid ounce
fluidounce
fluid ounce
flummeries
flunkeydom
flunkeyism
fluoborate
fluocerite
fluorescer
fluoridate
fluoridize
fluorinate
fluoroform
flurazepam
flurriedly
Flushinger
fluttering
fluvialist
fluviatile
fluviology
fluxionary
fluxionist
fly-by-night
flycatcher
fly-fishing
fly-flapper

fly in amber	for a change	forest tree	Fortune 500	franchisal
flying boat	forage crop	foresuffer	forty-eight	franchisee
flying bomb	forage-fish	foreteller	forty-fifth	franchiser
flying fish	for a giggle	forewarner	forty-first	franchisor
Flying Fish	for all that	for example	forty hours	Franciscan
flying jump	for all time	forfeiting	forty-niner	Franconian
flying leap	foraminate	forfeiture	forty-ninth	frangipane
flying mare	for a moment	forficated	forty-sixth	frangipani
flying ring	for a season	forge ahead	forty-third	fraternise
flying spot	for a surety	forgetness	forty winks	fraternity
flying suit	for a wonder	forgetting	forwearied	fraternize
flying wing	forbearant	forgettory	fossil fuel	fratricide
fly-pitcher	forbearing	forgivable	fosterable	fraudfully
fly-specked	forbidding	forgivably	fosterling	fraud squad
fly-swatter	force a card	forked head	foudroyant	fraudulent
fly the coop	forced move	forkedness	foul anchor	fraughtage
fly-tipping	forcedness	fork supper	foul befall	Fraunhofer
foamed slag	force field	fork-tailed	foul papers	fraxinella
foam flower	forcefully	forlornity	foul strike	freakiness
foam rubber	for certain	formalness	foundation	freakishly
focal plane	forcing pen	formal wear	founderous	freebooter
focal point	forcipated	formatting	foundryman	Free Church
fodderless	fordrunken	form-critic	fountained	free energy
foetalized	fore and aft	form factor	four-by-four	free-for-all
foeticidal	forebitter	formic acid	fourchette	free grower
foisonless	foreboding	formidable	four-colour	free-handed
fold-course	forebreast	formidably	four-figure	freeholder
foliaceous	forecaddie	formlessly	four-footed	free labour
foliar feed	forecaster	form letter	four-handed	freelancer
folie à deux	forecastle	form-master	Fourierism	free-living
foliferous	fore-elders	formulable	Fourierist	freeloader
folivorous	forefather	formula one	four-in-hand	free market
folk dancer	forefinger	formulator	four-letter	freemartin
folk guitar	foregainst	for my money	four o'clock	free pardon
folklorish	foreganger	for my share	four-parter	free period
folklorist	foregather	fornicator	four-poster	free school
folk memory	foreglance	for nothing	four-seater	free speech
folksiness	foreground	for openers	four-square	free spirit
folk singer	forehammer	forsakenly	four-stroke	free-spoken
follicular	forehanded	forshowing	fourteener	Free Stater
followable	forehander	forspeaker	fourteenth	freestyler
follow-spot	foreheaded	forsterite	fourth gear	free-tailed
follow suit	foreign aid	forswearer	fourth part	free-trader
fontanelle	foreignism	forte forte	fourth wall	free vector
font of type	foreignize	fortepiano	four-vector	free warren
foodaholic	foreintend	forte piano	four-winged	freewiller
foodoholic	foreladies	forthcomer	foveolated	freeze on to
fool around	foreloader	for the best	fowl plague	freeze over
foolometer	foremostly	for the jump	fox-hunting	freeze-thaw
fool's cress	foremother	for the rest	fox sparrow	freezingly
footballer	foreordain	for the ride	fox terrier	freightage
footbridge	forepassed	forthgoing	foxtrotted	freight car
foot-candle	foreperson	for this end	foxtrotter	freight ton
foot guards	forerunner	forthought	frabjously	fremescent
foot-licker	foreshadow	forthright	fractional	French bean
footlights	foresheets	fortissimi	fragmental	French blue
foot-locker	foresleeve	fortissimo	fragmented	French cuff
foot plough	forest fire	fortravail	fragranced	French door
foot-pounds	forest laws	fortuities	fragrantly	French grey
foot to foot	forestless	fortuitism	framboesia	French horn
footwarmer	forest park	fortuitist	frame house	French kiss
footy-footy	forestroke	fortuitous	frame story	French knot

Frenchlike	from on high	fumblingly	gallantize	Gartnerian
French loaf	from thence	fumigation	galleryite	gas bracket
French maid	from the way	fumigatory	galley-west	gas chamber
Frenchness	frondosely	fumishness	galleyworm	gasconader
French pink	frontality	functional	galley-yarn	gas guzzler
French roll	front bench	functorial	galliambic	gasifiable
French roof	frontignac	fund-holder	gallic acid	gas lighter
French seam	front money	fundholder	gallicizer	gasometric
frenziedly	front-pager	fund-raiser	galloglass	Gassendist
frequenter	frontstead	funduscopy	Gallophile	gas station
frequently	frontwards	funebrious	Gallophobe	gasteropod
fresh-baked	frostbound	funeralize	Gallo-Roman	gastralgia
fresh blood	frost crack	funeral urn	Gallup poll	gastralgic
fresh-faced	frost grape	funereally	galvanical	gastric flu
fresh out of	frost heave	fungaceous	galvanizer	gastrocele
freshwater	frostiness	fungicidal	Gambia kino	gastrolith
freshwoman	frothiness	fungitoxic	gambolling	gastrology
frettingly	frowningly	fungus-gnat	gamekeeper	gastronome
fretworked	frowstiest	funksticks	gamesomely	gastronomy
Freudianly	frowziness	funnel-like	gamestress	gastropexy
friability	frozen mitt	funnelling	gametangia	gastrotomy
fricandeau	frozenness	funniosity	game-tenant	gas turbine
fricasseed	fructified	funny money	game theory	gatekeeper
fricassees	fructifies	funny paper	gametocyst	gatelegged
fricatrice	frugalness	furanoside	gametocyte	gate of horn
frictional	fruitarian	furnishing	gametogeny	gatherable
Friedreich	fruitfully	furnish out	game warden	gather head
friendless	fruitiness	furosemide	gaminesque	Gatling gun
friendlier	fruit-juice	furrowless	gamma grass	gaucheness
friendlike	fruit-knife	furrow-like	gangbuster	gaudy-green
friendlily	fruit salad	furuncular	gangliated	gauging-rod
friendship	fruit salts	fusibility	gangliform	gaultheria
friezeless	fruit sugar	fusion bomb	ganglionic	gauntleted
frightened	frumpiness	fusion weld	gangrenous	gaylussite
frightener	frumpishly	fussbudget	gangsta rap	gazunderer
frightment	frustrable	fussocking	gannetries	gear change
Frigidaire	frustrater	fustanella	ganomalite	geiger tree
frigidness	frutescent	futileness	Gantt chart	geikielite
frigid zone	fruticetum	futureless	gap-toothed	geisha girl
frigorific	fuddy-duddy	future life	garage rock	gelatinase
frilliness	fugitation	futureness	garage sale	gelatinate
fringeless	fugitively	futuristic	garbage bin	gelatinise
fringe-tree	fulfilling	futurities	garbage can	gelatinize
fripperies	fulfilment	futurition	garden city	gelatinoid
friskiness	fuliginous	futurology	garden flat	gelatinous
frith-stool	full-bodied	fuzzy logic	gardenless	gemination
fritillary	full-bottom	fuzzy-wuzzy	garden path	geminative
frivolling	full chisel	gabblement	garden seat	genderless
frizziness	full colour	gabbroidal	gargantuan	genealogic
Froebelian	full growth	Gaditanian	gargoylism	genecology
Froebelism	full-length	gadolinite	garibaldis	generalate
froghopper	full nelson	gadolinium	garishness	generaless
frog orchid	full of shit	gadzookery	garlanding	generalise
frog's march	full-rigged	gaff-rigged	garlic pear	generalism
frolicking	full-rigger	gag-toothed	garnierite	generalist
frolicsome	full sister	Gaiety Girl	garnisheed	generality
from abroad	full-summed	gaillardia	garnishees	generalize
from a child	fulminator	gain-giving	garnishing	generation
from choice	fulmineous	gain ground	garnwindle	generative
from day one	fulminuric	galactonic	garrotting	generatrix
from memory	fulvescent	galia melon	garter belt	generosity
from nature	fumadiddle	galimatias	garter-blue	generously

Genesiacal	gesticular	gilt bronze	glasspaper	glyoxaline
genethliac	get a grip on	gimbal-ring	glass paper	glyoxylate
geneticism	get a hump on	gimmer-lamb	glass snail	glyphosate
geneticist	get a line on	gin and lime	glass snake	glyptodont
Geneva gown	get a load of	ginger beer	Glaswegian	gnamma hole
Geneva stop	get a load on	ginger lily	glauberite	gnashingly
genialness	get a move on	ginger-race	glauconite	gnathobase
geniculate	get clear of	ginger snap	gleaminess	gnomically
geniohyoid	get hitched	ginger wine	gleamingly	gnomologic
genius loci	Gethsemane	gingivitis	glebe-house	gnomonical
gentamicin	get in a flap	ginglyform	gleesomely	gnoscopine
genteelish	get in wrong	ginglymoid	gleization	gnosiology
genteelism	get it in one	gin pennant	glendoveer	gnosticise
genteelity	get knotted	Giottesque	gleyzation	Gnosticism
gentiledom	get nowhere	gippy tummy	glide-plane	gnosticize
gentilesse	get one's way	girdle-cake	glider bomb	gnotobiote
gentlefolk	get outside	girl Friday	glimmering	go a-begging
gentlehood	get round to	girlfriend	gliomatous	go-aheadism
gentleness	get stuck in	girly-girly	glitterati	goalkeeper
gentrified	get stuffed	gismondine	glitziness	goal-kicker
gentrifier	get the bird	gismondite	gloatingly	goal-minder
gentrifies	get the boot	give battle	globe daisy	goalminder
genu valgum	get the gate	give best to	globe tulip	go a long way
geobotanic	get the kirn	give change	globularly	goalscorer
geocentric	get the push	give fire to	glochidium	goal-tender
geochemist	get the ring	give ground	glomerular	goaltender
geocoronal	get the sack	give heed to	glomerulus	goat-footed
geocronite	get the swap	give it a fly	gloominess	goat's-beard
geodesical	get through	give or take	gloriation	goat's horns
geodetical	get to sleep	give rein to	gloriously	goat's-thorn
geodynamic	get unstuck	give rise to	glossarial	goatsucker
geognostic	get-up-and-go	give thanks	glossaries	goat willow
geographer	get up steam	give the gun	glossarist	gobemouche
geographic	get weaving	give to know	glossiness	gobsmacked
geological	Ghassulian	give tongue	glossology	gob-stopper
geometrize	ghastliest	give vent to	gloss paint	gobstopper
geomorphic	Ghibelline	glacé icing	glossy ibis	go critical
geophagist	ghost dance	glacialist	glottalize	God bless me
geophysics	ghostiness	glaciarium	glottology	God-fearing
geoponical	ghostliest	glaciation	Gloucester	Godfearing
geoscience	ghostology	glaciology	glove money	God help you
geotechnic	ghost story	glad-hander	glucosidal	go downhill
geotextile	ghost train	gladsomely	glucosidic	go down with
geothermal	ghost-write	Glagolitic	glucuronic	God save you
geothermic	ghoulishly	glamour boy	glucuronyl	God's wounds
geotropism	Giacobinid	glamourise	glumaceous	God willing
geratology	giant brain	glamourize	gluttoness	Godwottery
geriatrics	giant fibre	glance coal	gluttonise	go fly a kite
German band	giant order	glance over	gluttonish	go for broke
Germanical	giant panda	glancingly	gluttonize	goggle-dive
Germanizer	giant racer	glanderous	gluttonous	goggle-eyed
Germantown	giardiasis	glandiform	glycocalyx	go hard with
German wool	Gibson girl	glandulose	glycogenic	going on for
germicidal	gift coupon	glandulous	glycolipid	goings-over
germinable	giftedness	glass cloth	glycollate	going train
germinally	giggliness	glass coach	glycolysis	go it strong
germinator	Gilbertese	glass-faced	glycolytic	gold-beater
germ theory	Gilbertian	glass fibre	glycophyte	gold bridge
Geronomite	Gilbertine	glass-green	glycosidic	gold-digger
gerundival	gilded cage	glasshouse	glycosuria	golden ager
gestaltism	gill maggot	glassiness	glycosuric	golden alga
gestaltist	gilravager	glassmaker	glycuronic	golden calf

golden disc
golden girl
golden goal
Golden Horn
golden mean
golden mole
goldenness
golden orfe
golden rose
golden rule
golden seal
gold fringe
goldilocks
gold record
gold thread
goldwasser
Goldwynism
go lemony at
golf course
Golgi organ
Golgi stain
goliardery
goluptious
gombeen man
gondola car
go near to do
gongoozler
goniatitic
goniometer
goniometry
gonioscope
gonioscopy
gonococcal
gonococcus
gonorrhoea
gonotocont
good bearer
good fellow
good for you
Good Friday
good humour
good-liking
goodliness
good living
good-looker
good-morrow
good nature
good people
goody-goody
goofer dust
googolplex
go one's ways
go on record
go on the hop
gooseberry
goose bumps
goose-flesh
goosegrass
goose quill
goose-wings
gopher-hole
gopher wood

go platinum
gorbellied
gorblimeys
gorgeously
gorgoneion
Gorgonzola
gormandise
gormandize
gormlessly
gosh-darned
gospel oath
Gospel side
gospel-song
gossamered
gossiphood
go straight
go the limit
go the round
go the route
gothically
Gothically
gothicness
go to blazes
go to church
go together
go to ground
go to market
go to pieces
go to school
go to shrift
go to the bar
go to the mat
governable
governably
governance
governessy
government
grab handle
grab hold of
gracefully
graciosity
graciously
gradualism
gradualist
graduality
graduation
graffitied
graffitist
Graham's law
grainering
graininess
gramicidin
gramineous
grammarian
grammatist
gramophile
gramophone
Gram's stain
gram-weight
granadilla
grandchild
Grand Cross

grand-daddy
grand-ducal
grand duchy
grande dame
Grand Fleet
Grand Lodge
grandmamma
grand monde
Grand Mufti
grand-niece
grand opera
grandpappy
grand piano
grand scale
grand Sophy
Grands Prix
grandstand
grand style
grand total
grand-uncle
grangerism
grangerite
grangerize
granitical
granny bond
granny flat
granny knot
granophyre
grant-aided
grant-in-aid
granularly
granulated
granulator
granulitic
grapefruit
grape-paper
grape-stone
grape-sugar
graphemics
graphicacy
graphicate
graphitise
graphitize
graphitoid
graphology
graphotype
graph paper
graptolite
graspingly
grass-cloth
grasscloth
grass court
grass-finch
grass-green
grassiness
grass roots
grass skirt
grass snake
grass widow
grass-wrack
gratefully
gratifying

gratuities
gratuitous
grave-cloth
grave-goods
gravelling
gravel-rash
gravel-walk
grave-mound
graveolent
gravestone
Gravettian
gravewards
gravimeter
gravimetry
gravity-fed
gravy train
grease-ball
grease-band
greaseless
grease-trap
greasewood
greasiness
greasy pole
great Argus
Great Bible
great egret
great grief
great gross
great horse
great house
Great Lakes
great-niece
great organ
Great Power
Great Scott
great sheer
great-uncle
Grecianize
greediness
greedy-guts
Greek cross
green baize
Green Beret
green-blind
green brier
green cloth
Green Cloth
green drake
green earth
Greeneland
greenfield
greenfinch
greenflies
green goose
greenheart
green heron
greenhouse
green light
greenlight
Green Paper
Green Party
green plant

green pound
green salad
green sauce
greenshank
greenstick
greenstone
greenstuff
greensward
green thumb
gregarious
greisening
grenadilla
gressorial
grey market
grey matter
grey mullet
grey parrot
grey willow
gridlocked
grieveship
grievingly
grievously
griffinage
griffiness
griffinish
griffonage
Grignolino
grille-work
Grimaldian
Grimbarian
grimliness
grimthorpe
grind an axe
grind house
grindingly
grindstone
grinningly
gripe water
Gripe Water
grippingly
grisliness
grittiness
grizzliest
groaningly
groceteria
groggified
grogginess
grog-shanty
groove cast
grooveless
grooviness
Gros Michel
Gros Ventre
Grotianism
grottiness
grouchiest
ground arms
groundbait
ground-bait
ground ball
ground bass
ground crew

ground dove	guide-board	hackmatack	Hall effect	Hansardize
ground down	guided tour	hackneydom	hallelujah	Hanse-house
groundedly	guilefully	Hadley cell	Hall of Fame	haplophase
ground-fish	guillotine	Haeckelian	Hallowmass	happy event
ground game	guiltiness	haemanthus	Hallowtide	haptically
ground itch	Guinea corn	haematinic	halloysite	harassment
groundless	guinea fowl	haematitic	hall porter	harbourage
ground-line	Guinea-fowl	haematomas	halocarbon	hardbitten
groundling	Guinea worm	haematosis	halo effect	hard-boiled
ground loop	guitar-fish	haematuria	halogenate	hard cheese
groundmass	Gulf Stream	haematuric	halophilic	hard-done-by
ground-pine	gulli-gulli	haemocoele	halophytic	hard-earned
ground plan	gully-gully	haemolymph	halter neck	hard-fisted
ground rent	gum benzoin	haemolysin	Haman's ears	hard growan
ground rule	gumbo-limbo	haemolysis	hamber-line	hard-handed
ground-sill	gum juniper	haemolytic	hambro-line	hard-headed
groundsman	gummy shark	Hafflinger	hamesucken	hard-hitter
groundsmen	gum succory	hagiocracy	hammerbeam	hard labour
groundward	gunfighter	hagiolatry	hammer-blow	hardly ever
ground wave	gun-harpoon	hagiologic	hammerhead	hard mother
ground wood	gunkholing	hagioscope	hammer home	hard palate
groundwork	gunpowdery	hail shower	hammerless	hard-pushed
ground zero	gun-running	hair-powder	hammerlock	hard rubber
groupthink	gunrunning	hairspring	hammer-work	hard solder
grouse moor	gun shearer	hairstreak	hand-barrow	hard ticket
groutiness	gunslinger	hair-stroke	handedness	Hardyesque
grovelling	Guomindang	hakenkreuz	hand-gallop	hare-finder
growing bag	gurglingly	halberdier	handgunner	hare-lipped
growlingly	gurry-shark	halberdman	hand-habend	harelipped
growth area	gutterling	hale and how	handicraft	harem skirt
growth ring	gutter-tile	half a crown	handicuffs	harmlessly
growth zone	gutturally	half a dozen	hand in hand	harmonical
grubbiness	guzzle-guts	half an hour	hand-labour	harmonicon
grubstaker	gymnadenia	half-bottle	handleable	harmonious
Grub Street	gymnasiast	half-circle	handleless	harmonizer
grudgement	gymnasiums	half-cocked	handmaiden	Harmon mute
grudgingly	gymnastics	half-dollar	hand-me-down	harness cop
gruesomely	gymnosophy	half-duplex	hand of writ	harpooneer
grumpiness	gymnosperm	halfendeal	handpicked	harpoon gun
grumpishly	gynandrous	half-frames	handselled	harp-string
grunge rock	gyneocracy	half-galley	handshaker	harpy eagle
grunginess	gynocratic	half-guinea	hand signal	Harry groat
gruntingly	gynodioecy	half-headed	handsomely	Harry noble
guaiac test	gynophobia	half-hourly	handsomest	hartebeest
guanophore	gynophobic	half-hunter	handspring	haruspical
guaranteed	gyppy tummy	half-length	hand-to-hand	haruspices
guarantees	gypsophila	half-minute	handworked	Harvardian
guaranties	gypsophile	half-mooned	handworker	harvest-bug
guard-chain	gypsy winch	half nelson	handy-billy	harvestman
guardfully	gyrocopter	half-relief	handycuffs	harvestmen
guardhouse	gyroscopic	half-ringer	handy-dandy	hash browns
guardingly	gyrostatic	half-shaved	handy-sized	hastefully
Guarnerius	gyrotiller	half-sister	hang a right	hatcheller
Guatemalan	habiliment	half-stress	hang around	hatcheries
Guaycuruan	habilitate	half-timber	hanger-back	hatchet job
gubernator	habitation	half-topped	hang-glider	hatchet man
gudgeon pin	habitative	half-uncial	hanging day	haughtiest
guessingly	habit-shirt	half-volley	hanging lie	haunch-bone
guest house	habitually	half-witted	hangworthy	hauntingly
guestimate	hackbuteer	halfwitted	hanky-panky	haustellum
guest-night	hackbutter	half-yearly	Hannibalic	haustorial
Guggenheim	hack-hammer	hallabaloo	Hanoverian	haustorium

hautboyist
haute école
haut-relief
have a fly at
have a heart
have a nerve
have a point
have a shy at
have a smoke
have done it
have in mind
have in view
have it away
have it made
have mind of
have need of
have need to
have no idea
have no legs
have no peer
have no soul
have off pat
have scathe
have the pip
have the say
have to burn
have to wife
hawk-cuckoo
hawk's-beard
hawse-piece
hawser-laid
hazard side
Hazlittian
headbanger
head cheese
header-tank
headhunter
head-hunter
heading dog
headlessly
headlinese
headmaster
head office
head of hair
headspring
headsquare
headstrong
head-to-head
headwaters
health camp
health care
health club
health farm
health food
healthiest
healthless
healthsome
hearing aid
hear sermon
heart-block
heart-blood
heartbreak

heartening
heartfully
hear things
heartiness
heart of oak
heartquake
heart's-ease
heartsease
heart-spoon
heart-throb
heartthrob
heartwater
heart-whole
heat engine
heath-berry
heathendom
heathenish
heathenism
heathenize
heath-grass
heath-poult
heat-seeker
heat shield
heatstroke
heaven-born
heavenless
heavenlike
heaven-sent
heavenward
heavy-armed
heavy going
heavy metal
heavy swell
heavy water
hebdomadal
hebetation
Hebraistic
hecatomped
hectically
hectograph
hectolitre
hectometre
hedge-fence
hedgehoggy
hedge maple
hedonistic
heedlessly
heel-and-toe
hegemonist
Heidelberg
heightened
heightener
heil Hitler
heir female
heir in tail
heirs-at-law
Heisenberg
heliacally
helianthus
helicoidal
Heliconian
helicopter

heliograph
heliometer
heliometry
helioscope
heliotrope
helipterum
heli-skiing
hellacious
hellbender
hell-driver
Hellenizer
Hellespont
hellishing
hellraiser
hell-raiser
hell's angel
Hell's Angel
hell's bells
helmetless
helmet-like
helminthic
helmswoman
helplessly
hemelytron
hemi-acetal
hemianopia
hemianopic
hemibranch
hemicircle
hemicrania
hemidesmus
hemihedral
hemihedron
hemiplegia
hemiplegic
hemipteran
hemisphere
hemitropic
hemizygote
hemizygous
hemp-nettle
henceforth
henchwoman
hendecagon
hen harrier
hen-hearted
Henle's loop
henotheism
henotheist
henpeckery
hen-scratch
heortology
heparinise
heparinize
hepatitis A
hepatitis B
heptachlor
heptachord
heptagonal
heptahedra
heptameric
heptameter

heptarchal
heptarchic
heptastich
heptateuch
Heptateuch
heptathlon
heptatonic
Heraclitic
heraldical
herbaceous
Herbartian
herb bennet
herb-doctor
herb Gerard
herbicidal
herb mastic
herb Robert
hercogamic
herdswoman
hereabouts
here and now
hereditary
heresiarch
hereticate
heretofore
here you are
her indoors
heriotable
herky-jerky
Hermes seal
hermetical
hermit crab
hermithood
hermit ibis
hermitical
hermitship
herniation
herniotomy
Herodotean
heroically
heroi-comic
heron's-bill
herpolhode
Herrenvolk
Herrnhuter
hesitantly
hesitation
hesitative
hesitatory
Hesperides
hesperidia
hesperidin
Hessian fly
hetero-atom
heterocosm
heterocyst
heterodont
heterodoxy
heterodyne
heterogamy
heterogene
heterogeny

heterogony
heterology
heteronomy
heterosite
heterotaxy
heulandite
hew one's way
hexadecane
hexaemeron
hexagonous
hexahedral
hexahedron
hexahydric
hexamerism
hexamerous
hexametric
hexandrous
hexangular
hexaplaric
hexaploidy
hexavalent
hexoestrol
hexokinase
hexosamine
Hezbollahi
hiawaballi
hibernacle
hibernator
hibiscuses
Hib vaccine
hidden hand
hiddenmost
hiddenness
hide and hue
hide beetle
hiding-hole
hiera picra
hierarchal
hierarchic
hieratical
hierocracy
hieroglyph
hierograph
hierolatry
hierophant
hieroscopy
high and dry
high and low
highbinder
highbrowed
High Church
high colour
highermost
high-flying
high forest
High German
high ground
high-handed
high-headed
high-heeled
high-income
high-jumper

highlander	hit the pipe	Holy Father	homuncular	horse daisy
Highlander	hit the road	Holy League	homuncules	horse-drawn
high living	hit the roof	Holy Office	homunculus	horseflesh
high-minded	hit the sack	holy orders	Honest John	horseflies
high-octane	hit the silk	holy roller	honeybunch	horse guard
high places	hit the spot	Holy Spirit	honey chile	horse-laugh
high priest	hitty-missy	holy terror	honey-eater	horseleech
high relief	Hoabinhian	holy Willie	honeyeater	horse opera
high roller	hoar-headed	home and dry	honeyguide	horsepower
high school	hoarseness	homebodies	honey mouse	horse-racer
high season	hobbadehoy	home-brewed	honeystone	horse sense
high-souled	hobblebush	home-coming	honey-sweet	horse-shoer
high spirit	hobblingly	homecoming	honorarium	horse's neck
high street	hobby horse	homeliness	honourable	horse's tail
high-strung	hobnobbing	home-making	honourably	horsewoman
highwayman	hobohemian	Home Office	honourless	horsewomen
highwaymen	hocking ale	homeopathy	hooded crow	hose-in-hose
high yaller	Hock Monday	homeotherm	hooded seal	hospitable
high yellow	hocus-pocus	Homerology	hoodlumism	hospitably
Hilary term	hodden grey	home signal	hook and eye	hospitaler
hillwalker	hoddy-doddy	home thrust	hook-billed	hostelling
Himyaritic	hoddy-noddy	homeworker	hook-ladder	hostelries
hinderling	Hodegetria	homishness	hook stroke	hot-blooded
hindermost	hodgepodge	homme moyen	hootenanny	hot-brained
hindersome	hoernesite	homocercal	hopelessly	hot cathode
Hindustani	Hogan Mogan	homochromy	hop into bed	hotchpotch
hinterland	Hogarthian	homoclinal	Hopkinsian	hot cockles
hip-huggers	hog cholera	homocyclic	hopping mad	hot coppers
hip-hugging	Hogen Mogen	homodesmic	Hoppus foot	hot-desking
hipped roof	hog-killing	homoeomery	hopshackle	hotdogging
hippety-hop	hog's fennel	homoeopath	hop the twig	hot-presser
hippieness	hoity-toity	homo-erotic	Hopton wood	hot pursuit
hippocampi	hokey-cokey	homoerotic	hop trefoil	hotsy-totsy
Hippocrene	hokey-pokey	homogamety	horizontal	Hottentots
hippodrome	hold in play	homogamous	hormonally	hour-circle
hippogriff	hold it good	homogenate	horn beetle	house agent
hippogryph	hold out for	homogeneal	hornblende	housebound
hippomanes	hold the bag	homogenise	horned dace	housebreak
hippophagy	hold to bail	homogenize	horned frog	housebuyer
hippophile	holes-in-one	homogenous	horned lark	housecarle
hipsterism	hollabaloo	homokaryon	horned pout	house-clean
hirdy-girdy	Hollantide	homologate	horned toad	housecraft
hirondelle	hollow-eyed	homologise	hornet moth	house finch
hirudinean	hollow horn	homologize	hörnesite	houseflies
his and hers	hollowness	homologous	horn-rimmed	house guest
histaminic	hollow-ware	homomorphy	horn silver	house mouse
histiocyte	hollowware	homonymity	horography	house music
histogenic	holobranch	homonymous	horologion	house of God
histologic	holocarpic	homoousian	horologist	house party
histolysis	holoenzyme	Homoousion	horologium	house-place
histolytic	hologamete	homoousios	horoscopal	house plant
historical	hologamous	homophobia	horoscoper	house-proud
histrionic	holography	homophobic	horoscopic	house snake
hit-and-miss	holohedral	homophonic	horrendous	house style
hitch-hiker	holohedron	homoplasty	horridness	house-train
hitchhiker	holophrase	homopteran	horrifying	housewares
hithermost	holophytic	homorganic	horse-block	housewives
hitherside	holostylic	homosexual	horse brass	hovercraft
hitherward	holothuria	homostyled	horse-bread	hoverflies
Hitler's war	holus-bolus	homothally	horse-cloth	hoveringly
hit the deck	Holy Church	homozygote	horse-coper	hover-mower
hit the gong	Holy Family	homozygous	horse cubes	hovertrain

how do you do
howsomever
how's tricks
hubba-hubba
Hubble's law
huckle-back
huckle-bone
hucksterer
huddlement
huebnerite
hug-me-tight
hullabaloo
hully gully
humanation
human being
human chain
humaneness
humanistic
humanitary
humanities
humbleness
humblingly
humbuggery
humbugging
humdudgeon
humidified
humidifier
humidifies
humidistat
humidities
humid scall
humiliator
humming-top
humoresque
humoristic
humorously
humourless
humoursome
humpbacked
hump bridge
humusified
humusifies
hundredary
hunger-weed
hungriness
hungry rice
hunker down
hunting-box
hunting cat
hunting dog
Huntington
huntswoman
hunt the fox
hurdle race
hurdy-gurdy
hurly-burly
hurry along
hurrygraph
hurryingly
hurtlessly
hurtlingly
husbandman

husbandmen
Husserlian
hustlement
Hutchinson
hutch table
hyalinized
hyalinosis
hyaloplasm
hyaluronic
hyawaballi
hybridized
hybridizer
hydragogic
hydragogue
hydramnios
hydrastine
hydratable
hydraulics
hydrelaeon
hydrochore
hydrocrack
hydrogenic
hydrograph
hydrologic
hydrolysis
hydrolytic
hydromancy
hydromania
hydrometer
hydrometry
hydronymic
hydropathy
hydrophane
hydrophile
hydrophily
hydrophobe
hydrophone
hydrophyte
hydropical
hydroplane
hydroplant
hydroponic
hydropower
hydroscope
hydrospire
hydrotheca
hydrotical
hydrotreat
hydrotropy
hydroxylic
hydrozoate
hyetograph
hygrograph
hygrometer
hygrometry
hygrophile
hygrophyte
hygroscope
hylotheism
hymeneally
hymenopter
hymn of hate

hymnologic
hyoscyamia
hyoscyamus
hypabyssal
hypaethral
hypalgesia
hypalgesic
hypanthial
hypanthium
hyperacute
hyperaemia
hyperaemic
hyperalgic
hyperbaric
hyperbaton
hyperbolae
hyperbolas
hyperbolic
hyperdrive
hyperdulia
hyperdulic
hyperfocal
hypergluon
hypergolic
hypermedia
hypermorph
hyperoodon
hyperplane
hyperploid
hyperpnoea
hypersexed
hypersonic
hyperspace
hypertelic
hypertonia
hypertonic
hypertonus
hyperurban
hyphenated
hyphenless
hypnagogic
hypnogenic
hypnogogic
hypnotizer
hypoactive
hypoacusia
hypoacusis
hypocapnia
hypocapnic
hypocentre
hypocorism
hypocrisis
hypocrital
hypocritic
hypodermal
hypodermic
hypodermis
hypodorian
hypogamous
hypogeusia
hypogynous
hypolimnia

hypolydian
hypomaniac
hyponastic
hypophoria
hypophyses
hypophysis
hypoplasia
hypoploidy
hypostases
hypostasis
hypostatic
hypotactic
hypotenuse
hypothecal
hypotheses
hypothesis
hypothetic
hypoxaemia
hypsiconch
hypsodonty
hypsometer
hypsometry
hysteresis
hysteretic
hysterical
hystericky
iambically
iatrogenic
ice-breaker
ice dancing
Icelandish
ice machine
icemanship
ice-skating
ice station
ichthammol
ichthyosis
ichthyotic
icing sugar
iconically
iconoclasm
iconoclast
iconolater
iconolatry
iconomachy
iconometry
iconophile
iconoscope
icosahedra
I dare swear
iddingsite
ideal fluid
idealistic
idealities
ideational
idempotent
idem sonans
identified
identifier
identifies
identities
ideography

ideologies
ideologist
ideologize
ideophonic
idiolectal
idiopathic
idiot board
idiot light
idiot-proof
idolatress
idolatrize
idolatrous
idoloclast
idolothyte
I don't think
if anything
if I were you
if possible
ifs and ands
ifs and buts
if so be that
if you ask me
ignes fatui
ignicolist
igniferous
ignimbrite
ignipotent
ignivomous
ignobility
ignorantly
ignoration
ilang-ilang
ileocaecal
ill-advised
illaqueate
illatinate
illatively
illaudable
illaudably
I'll be bound
ill-behaved
ill-beloved
ill-defined
illegality
illegalize
ill feeling
ill-fitting
ill-founded
illinition
Illinoisan
illiteracy
illiterate
illiterati
ill-looking
ill-matched
ill-natured
illocality
illocution
I'll show you
ill-starred
ill success
illucidate

illuminant	immoralize	impresario	incandesce	inculpably
illuminate	immortally	impression	incantator	incumbence
illuminati	immortelle	impressive	incapacity	incumbency
illuminato	immoveable	impressure	Incaparina	incunabula
illuminise	immunities	imprimatur	incasement	incurrable
illuminism	immunology	imprisoner	incautious	incurrence
illuminist	immuration	improbable	incavation	indagation
illuminize	immurement	improbably	incendiary	in danger of
illuminous	impact test	improlific	incendiate	indebtment
illusional	impairment	impromptus	Inceptisol	indecently
illusively	impalement	improperly	incessable	indecision
illusorily	impalpable	improvable	incessably	indecisive
illustrate	impalpably	improvably	incessancy	indecorous
illuviated	impanation	improviser	incestuous	in defect of
ill-willing	imparadise	imprudence	in chancery	indefinite
image-maker	imparlance	imprudence	in charge of	indefinity
imaginable	imparsonee	impudently	inchastity	indelicacy
imaginably	impartable	impudicity	inch by inch	indelicate
imaginally	impartible	impugnable	inchoately	indevotion
imaginator	impartibly	impugnment	inchoation	indevoutly
imaginings	impartment	impuissant	inchoative	indexation
imbecilely	impassable	impulse buy	incidental	India House
imbecility	impassably	impunctate	incidently	in diameter
imbibition	impassible	impunitive	incinerate	Indian club
imbodiment	impassibly	impureness	incipience	Indian corn
imbreviate	impatience	impurities	incipiency	Indian file
imbricated	impatiency	imputation	incisiform	Indian hemp
imbroccata	impeccable	imputative	incisional	Indian lake
imbroglios	impeccably	*in absentia*	incisively	Indian meal
imbruement	impeccancy	inaccuracy	incitation	Indianness
I'm damned if	impediment	inaccurate	incitement	Indian path
imipramine	impeditive	inactivate	incivility	Indian pear
imitatress	impendence	inactively	inclemency	Indian pink
immaculacy	impendency	inactivity	inclinable	Indian pipe
immaculate	impenitent	inadaptive	includable	Indian poke
immanental	imperative	in addition	include out	Indian rice
immanently	imperatrix	inadequacy	includible	Indian shot
immanifest	imperially	inadequate	incoctible	Indian sign
immaterial	imperilled	inadhesive	incogitant	Indian teak
immaturely	impersonal	in a fashion	incognitos	Indian weed
immaturity	impervious	in a measure	incoherent	India paper
immeasured	impishness	inamoratos	incohesion	India proof
immemorial	implacable	in a morning	incohesive	indication
immergence	implacably	in-and-outer	incomeless	indicative
immersible	implicitly	in any event	incomplete	indicatory
immetrical	impolitely	in a pig's eye	in conclave	indicatrix
imminently	importable	inapparent	inconcrete	indicolite
immiscible	importance	inappetent	in conflict	indictable
immiscibly	importancy	inapposite	inconjunct	indictably
immiserate	importuner	inaptitude	inconstant	indictment
immittance	imposement	inarguable	incoronate	indigenise
immobilise	imposingly	inarguably	in course of	indigenist
immobilism	imposition	in arms with	incrassate	indigenity
immobility	impossible	inartistic	incredible	indigenize
immobilize	impossibly	in a twinkle	incredibly	indigenous
immoderacy	impostress	inaugurate	increscent	indigested
immoderate	impostrous	in bad order	incrustate	indigitate
immodestly	impotently	in bad stead	incubation	indignance
immolation	impoundage	in breach of	incubative	indignancy
immoralism	impoverish	inbreaking	incubatory	indigo-bird
immoralist	impregnant	inbreeding	inculcator	indigo blue
immorality	impregnate	in business	inculpable	indigolite

inspirator	inter-class	intervenor	intraneous	invitement
inspiredly	intercross	intervisit	intra-urban	invitingly
inspirited	interested	intervital	intra vires	invocation
inspissate	interfaith	intervocal	intravital	invocative
installant	interferer	intervolve	intrazonal	invocatory
installing	interferon	interweave	intrenched	involatile
instalment	interfluve	interwound	intrepidly	involucral
Instamatic	intergenic	interwoven	in triangle	involucrum
instantial	intergrade	interzonal	intrigante	involution
instantize	intergroup	intestinal	intriguant	involutory
instigator	interictal	in that case	intriguess	involvedly
instilling	interionic	in that view	intriguing	inwardness
instilment	interiorly	in the act of	introduced	in your face
in stitches	interior to	in the black	introducer	iodimetric
instituter	interlayer	in the blade	introgress	iodination
institutor	interleave	in the chips	introscope	iodization
in store for	interlevel	in the clear	introspect	iodometric
in strength	interloper	in the event	intrusive r	iodophilic
instructer	interlunar	in the field	intubation	ion chamber
instructor	intermarry	in the flesh	intuitable	ion etching
instrument	intermedia	in the frame	in two ticks	Ionian mode
insudation	intermedii	in the green	inundation	ionisation
insufflate	intermedin	in the issue	inurbanely	ionization
in suit with	intermewed	in the large	inurbanity	ionography
insularism	intermezzi	in the least	invaginate	ionosphere
insularity	intermezzo	in the money	invalidate	ionotropic
insularize	intermodal	in the night	invalid car	iproniazid
insulation	internally	in the nuddy	invaliding	Ipswichian
insulative	internment	in the pay of	invalidish	iracundity
insultable	internodal	in the pound	invalidism	Iranianist
insurgence	internship	in the pouts	invalidity	irefulness
insurgency	interocean	in the print	invaluable	irenically
insurrecto	interphase	in the right	invaluably	iridaceous
in sympathy	interplait	in the rough	invariable	iridectomy
intabulate	interplane	in the round	invariably	irideremia
intactness	interplant	in the shell	invariance	iridescent
intaglioes	interplead	in the straw	invariancy	iridodesis
intangible	interpoint	in the vague	inventable	iridosmine
intangibly	interpolar	in the way of	inventress	Irish green
integrable	interposal	in the white	inveracity	Irish horse
integrally	interposer	in the whole	inverecund	Irish point
integrated	interpubic	in the wilds	invertedly	Irish pound
integrator	interpulse	in the works	invertible	Irish Sweep
integument	interreges	in the world	invert soap	Irishwoman
intemerate	interregna	in the wrong	in very deed	Irishwomen
intemporal	interreign	inthronize	investable	iron-glance
intendance	interrenal	intimacies	investible	iron-handed
intendancy	interrogee	intimately	investment	iron-headed
intendedly	intershock	intimation	inveteracy	ironically
intendence	intershoot	intimidate	inveterate	iron maiden
intendency	interspace	intinction	invigilate	ironmaster
intendment	interstage	intolerant	invigorant	ironmonger
intenerate	interstate	intonation	invigorate	iron-sponge
intentness	interstice	intonement	invination	ironworker
interactor	intertidal	into pieces	invincible	irradiance
inter-agent	intertonic	intoxicant	invincibly	irradiancy
inter alios	intertrigo	intoxicate	inviolable	irradiated
interblend	intertwine	intractile	inviolably	irradiator
interbrain	intertwist	intragenic	inviolated	irrational
interbreed	interunion	intragroup	invirtuate	irregulate
interceder	interurban	in training	invitation	irrelation
interchain	intervener	intramural	invitatory	irrelative

irrelevant	isoseismal	jam session	jimson weed	judgematic
irreligion	isoseismic	janitorial	jimswinger	judgmental
irremeable	isosporous	Janus green	jingoistic	judication
irremeably	isosterism	Japan cedar	jinricksha	judicative
irresolute	isothermal	Japan earth	JK flip-flop	judicatory
irresolved	isothermic	Japanesery	jnana-marga	judicature
irreticent	isotropous	Japanesque	Joachimism	judicially
irreverend	Israelitic	Japan paper	Joachimist	*Jugendstil*
irreverent	issue of law	Japhethite	Joachimite	jugged hare
irrigation	I suppose so	japishness	job analyst	juggernaut
irrigative	Italianate	jardinière	jobbernowl	Juggernaut
irrigatory	Italianise	jargonelle	job-control	jugglement
irritament	Italianism	jar ramming	job-hopping	juggleress
irritating	Italianist	jasmine tea	job-sharing	jug-handled
irritation	Italianity	jasper-opal	jockey-boot	jugulation
irritative	Italianize	jasper-ware	jockey club	juice-joint
irroration	Italophile	jauntiness	jockey-coat	Julian Alps
irrumation	itinerancy	Java almond	jockeyship	Julian year
isabelline	it isn't done	Java canvas	jocoseness	jumble-bead
isatogenic	I told you so	Java pepper	jocosities	jumblement
Iscariotic	it's this way	javelineer	jocularity	jumble sale
isentropic	ivory black	javelin man	joe-pye weed	jumbomania
isethionic	ivory board	Javel water	John Dories	jumper stay
Ishmaelite	ivory-paper	jaw-breaker	johnny-cake	jumper suit
Isindebele	ivory tower	jaw-crusher	John Roscoe	jumper-wire
Islamicize	ivory-white	Jazzercise	Johnsonese	jump for joy
island-hill	ivy-garland	jealousies	Johnsonian	jumping rat
islandless	Ivy Leaguer	Jehosaphat	Johnsonism	jump jockey
Ismaelitic	jaborandis	Jehovistic	John Thomas	jump-master
isoallelic	jaboticaba	jejuneness	join action	jump the gun
isoantigen	jack-a-dandy	jelly-belly	join battle	junctional
isocaloric	jackanapes	jellygraph	joiner-work	Jungianism
isocephaly	Jack ashore	jelly paint	join forces	jungle cock
isocheimal	jackassery	jelly-plant	joint-grass	jungle fowl
isochronal	jackbooted	jeopardise	joint mouse	jungle-rice
isochronic	Jack curlew	jeopardize	joint-plane	junior dean
isochroous	jacketless	Jeremianic	joint-snake	junior miss
isocitrate	jackhammer	jerkin-head	joint stock	juniorship
isocyanate	Jack-ladder	jerry-build	joint-stool	juniper oil
isocyanide	jacklegged	jerry-built	jointuress	junk-bottle
isodynamic	Jack-merlin	Jersey blue	*jolie laide*	junk-dealer
isoenzymic	Jack Mormon	Jersey pine	Jollof rice	jurisprude
isoeugenol	jackrabbit	jestership	Jolly Roger	juristical
isoglossic	Jack's alive	Jesuitical	jolter-head	jury-fixing
isoglottal	Jack salmon	Jesuits' nut	jolt-headed	jury-rigged
isoglottic	Jack-socket	Jesuits' tea	Joshua tree	jury-rudder
isohalsine	jack socket	Jesus freak	jostlement	just as well
isokinetic	Jacksonian	jet-setting	journal-box	justiciary
isolatable	Jack the Lad	jet turbine	journalese	just in case
isoleucine	jackyarder	*jeu d'esprit*	journalise	just-in-time
isometrics	Jacobethan	Jew-baiting	journalism	just my luck
isomorphic	Jacobinism	jewel-block	journalist	just the job
isonitrile	Jacobinize	Jewishness	journalize	just too bad
iso-osmotic	Jacobitish	Jewish year	journeyman	Juvenalian
isopachous	Jacobitism	Jew's mallow	journeymen	juvenilely
isopachyte	jaculation	jib topsail	jovialness	juvenility
isopiestic	jaggedness	jigger coat	joyfulness	juvenilize
isoplastic	jaguarundi	jigger-mast	joyousness	juvescence
isoplethal	jailership	Jim Crowism	jubilantly	juxtaposit
isoprenoid	jamesonite	Jimmy Ducks	jubilarian	kabaragoya
isorrhythm	James Royal	Jimmy Grant	jubilation	kaempferol
isosbestic	Jamie Green	Jimmy Green	Judaically	kaersutite

kafferboom	kerb market	King's Guide	knight-head	laboursome
Kaffir beer	kerb weight	king's peace	knighthood	labour ward
kaffirboom	kerchiefed	King's Scout	knightlike	laccolitic
Kaffir corn	Kermanshah	king's spear	knightling	lace-border
Kaffir lily	kernelless	king's truce	knightship	lace lizard
Kaffir plum	Kerr effect	King Willow	knobbiness	lacemaking
Kaffir work	kerseymere	kinocilium	knobkerrie	lace-pillow
Kaffrarian	kerygmatic	kinspeople	knock about	laceration
Kafkaesque	ketohexose	Kiplingese	knockabout	lacerative
Kaiser roll	ketonaemia	Kiplingism	knock-kneed	lachenalia
kaisership	ketone body	Kiplingite	knock knees	lachrymary
Kaisership	kettledrum	Kiplingize	knockmeter	lachrymate
Kaiser's war	kettlefuls	Kiriwinian	knock silly	lachrymist
kaleyarder	kettle hole	kirkin-head	knock-stone	lachrymose
kalicinite	kettle lake	kirk-master	knock under	lachrymous
kallikrein	kettle-pins	Kirmanshah	knockwurst	laciniated
Kalmuckian	keyboarder	kiss better	knopkierie	lackadaisy
kamagraphy	key-drawing	kissing bug	knot-garden	lackey moth
Kamchatkan	keyhole saw	kissing kin	knot-stitch	lackeyship
Kampuchean	keypuncher	kiss my arse	knottiness	lacklustre
kangarooer	keystroker	kiss of life	know better	laconicism
Kantianism	khidmutgar	kiss the cup	know by name	lacquering
kaolinitic	khitmutgar	kiss the rod	knowledged	lactam ring
Kara-Kalpak	Khmer Rouge	kitchen-fee	know-little	lactescent
Karamojong	kibbutznik	kitchen tea	knuckle-bow	lactic acid
Karankawan	kick-boxing	kite-flying	knuckle-end	lactogenic
karaoke bar	kickshawed	kith and kin	Knudsen gas	lactometer
karate-chop	kicksorter	kitschiest	Kodiak bear	lactoscope
Karimojong	kick-the-can	kittenhood	koeksister	lactosuria
Karmathian	kick up a row	kittenlike	koettigite	lacustrian
Karrenfeld	kid brother	kittle-pins	kohlrabies	lacustrine
karst tower	kiddie-porn	klaberjass	kolbeckite	ladder-back
karyologic	kiddiewink	Klangfarbe	kolinskies	ladder fern
karyolysis	kidnapping	Klanswoman	kollergang	ladder-stop
karyolytic	kidney bean	Klanswomen	komatiitic	ladder-work
karyoplasm	kidney dish	klebsiella	kookaburra	ladies' room
karyotypic	kidney fern	klendusity	Korean pine	Lady chapel
Kashmirian	kidney worm	kleptocrat	Koreishite	ladyfinger
katabolism	kieselguhr	klieg light	kraft paper	lady-killer
keep a House	kiewietjie	klutziness	kratogenic	ladykiller
keep a tab on	killer cell	knackeries	Krebs cycle	lady orchid
keepership	kill or cure	knackwurst	Krems white	lady's horse
keep in play	Kilmarnock	knapsacked	krennerite	lady's laces
keep in with	kilometric	knave-bairn	kriegspiel	lady's smock
keep tabs on	kimberlite	knave noddy	Krishnaism	lady's waist
keep wicket	Kimmeridge	knee-action	kromeskies	Laestrigon
Kelvin's law	kinchin-lay	knee-braced	krugerrand	laevulinic
Kennel Club	kindliness	knee by knee	Ku Klux Klan	laevulosan
kennelling	kinematics	knee-halter	Kuomintang	lageniform
kennelmaid	kinetic art	knee-length	kurdaitcha	Lagrangian
kenoticism	kineticism	knee-rafter	kymography	lake-crater
kenoticist	kineticist	knee-timber	kynurenine	Lakelander
Kensington	kinetosome	knee to knee	Labarraque	Lake poetry
kenspeckle	King at Arms	knick-knack	labial pipe	lake salmon
Kentish rag	King Caesar	knickpoint	labiomancy	Lake school
Kentuckian	kingfisher	knife-blade	labiovelar	Lamarckian
Kenya Asian	king-hunter	knife-board	laboratory	Lamarckism
Kepler's law	kingliness	knife-edged	labour camp	lamaseries
keratinise	King of Arms	knife-guard	labouredly	lambdacism
keratinize	king parrot	knife-pleat	labour hero	lambdoidal
keratinous	king salmon	knife-point	labourless	lambrequin
keratotomy	King's Bench	knifepoint	labour-only	lamb's-tails

lamb-suckle	lantern-fly	laundermat	leaderless	legatorial
lamellated	lanternist	laundrette	leadership	Legendrian
lamentable	lantern-man	laundromat	leader tape	legibility
lamentably	lanthanide	Laundromat	lead glance	legionaire
laminagram	lanthanite	laundryman	leading dog	legionella
laminarian	lanthanoid	laundrymen	leading man	legislator
laminarize	lanuginose	laureation	lead pencil	legitimacy
lamination	lanuginous	laurelling	lead the van	legitimate
laminboard	laparotomy	Laurèntian	lead the way	legitimise
Lammas-land	lapidarian	laurustine	leaf-beetle	legitimism
lamp holder	lapidaries	lautermash	leaf blight	legitimist
lampoonery	lapidarist	lavatorial	leaf blotch	legitimity
lampoonist	lapidation	lavatories	leaf-cutter	legitimize
lamprey-eel	lapidicole	laver bread	leafcutter	leg-pulling
lamp-socket	Laplandish	Laves phase	leaf-folder	legrandite
Lancashire	lappet-moth	lavishment	leafhopper	legs eleven
lanceolate	lap winding	lavishness	leaf insect	leg-spinner
lance-snake	lardaceous	law-abiding	leafleteer	leguleious
lancet arch	lardy-dardy	law-borrows	leafleting	leguminose
lancet-fish	largamente	lawbreaker	leaf monkey	leguminous
land agency	large print	law-burrows	leaf-roller	Leibnizian
landammann	large-scale	lawfulness	leaf scorch	Leichhardt
land-battle	larghettos	lawkadaisy	leaf-shaped	leiotrichy
land breeze	larvicidal	lawkamercy	leaf-sheath	leishmania
land-bridge	laryngitic	lawn tennis	leaf spring	leisurable
land forces	laryngitis	law-officer	leap second	leisurably
landholder	lascivious	Law of Moses	lear-father	leisureful
land-hunger	Lassa fever	Lawrencian	least of all	lemmatical
land-hungry	last but one	lawrencium	leathering	lemniscate
landing net	last but two	Lawrentian	leatheroid	lemon grass
landing pad	last hurrah	Law Society	leave alone	lemon plant
landing run	last minute	lawsoniana	leave a mark	lemon thyme
land-jobber	last moment	law station	leave aside	lemuriform
land-junker	last resort	lawyer cane	leave it out	lengthened
landladies	Last Supper	lawyer-like	leavenless	lengthener
Land League	last things	lawyer's wig	leave out of	lengthiest
land-locked	late blight	lay a charge	leave-taker	length-mark
landlocked	late dinner	lay a ground	Lebensraum	lengthsman
land-looker	lateen sail	lay analyst	leberwurst	lengthways
landloping	latent heat	lay an eye on	lectionary	lengthwise
landlordly	latentness	laybacking	lectorship	lenitively
landlordry	latent root	lay brother	lecturette	lens turret
land-louper	lateral cut	lay claim to	ledeburite	lentamente
landlubber	lateralise	layer cloud	lederhosen	Lenten corn
landocracy	laterality	lay hands on	ledged door	Lenten face
land office	lateralize	lay in ashes	ledger-bait	Lenten fare
landowning	lateritize	laying mash	ledger book	Lenten-kail
landscaper	latest word	Laysan duck	ledger line	Lenten rose
land spring	latex paint	Laysan rail	ledger-pole	lenticular
land-stream	latifundia	Laysan teal	leechcraft	lentigines
landswoman	Latin cross	lay siege to	Lee–Enfield	lentivirus
långbanite	Latinesque	lay store by	Lee–Metford	Leonberger
Langerhans	Latinistic	lay to heart	left centre	leontiasis
langlaufer	latitation	lay to sleep	left-footed	leopard cat
langue d'oïl	lattermath	lazarettos	left-footer	leopardess
languisher	lattermost	lazar-house	left-handed	Leopardian
languorous	latter-will	lead astray	left-hander	leopard-man
laniferous	Laudianism	leadbeater	left-winger	leper-house
lanigerous	Laue method	lead bronze	legal eagle	lepidolite
lanosterol	laughingly	leadenness	legalistic	lepidopter
lansquenet	laugh track	leaden seal	legalities	leprechaun
lantern bug	laumontite	leaderette	legateship	leptocauly

leptomonad	liberty boy	lignoceric	linguister	litholatry
leptomonas	liberty cap	like a charm	linguistic	lithologic
leptoquark	liberty day	like a dream	linguistry	lithomancy
leptosomic	liberty man	like a leech	linkage map	lithomarge
leptospira	libidinous	like billy-o	linked list	lithophane
leptospire	Lib-Labbery	like blazes	linkedness	lithophany
lesbianism	librarious	like enough	lin-lan-lone	lithophile
lesseeship	librettist	likelihead	linnet-hole	lithophone
Lesser Asia	licensable	likelihood	linocutter	lithophyte
Lesser Bear	licentiate	likeliness	linography	lithoprint
lesser evil	licentious	like-minded	linolenate	lithotomic
lesserness	lichenized	liliaceous	linoleumed	lithotrite
Lesser Wain	lichenless	lilli-pilli	linotypist	lithotrity
lethal dose	licitation	lilly-pilly	linseed oil	Lithuanian
lethargize	Lieberkühn	lily flower	lion-hunter	litigation
let's face it	lie heavy on	lily-footed	lion's heart	litmus blue
letter bomb	lie in ruins	limaciform	lion's share	litmus test
letter-card	lie in state	limber hole	Lipizzaner	litterfall
letterform	lie leaguer	limber-neck	lipochrome	litter lout
lettergram	lieutenant	limberness	lipofuscin	Little Bear
letterhead	life-breath	limber pine	lipography	little-ease
letterless	life-estate	limber-rope	lipoidosis	little-girl
letter-wood	life-giving	limburgite	lipophobic	Little Lion
letter-word	Life Guards	lime-burner	lipothymic	Little Mary
let through	life jacket	lime-juicer	lipotropic	little neck
leucoblast	lifelessly	lime-squash	Lippes loop	littleness
leucocidin	life member	limicoline	Lippizaner	little ones
leucocytic	life-office	liminality	lip-service	little slam
leucoderma	life-policy	limitation	lip-syncing	little Turk
leucopenia	liferenter	limitative	lip-worship	littorinid
leucophore	life-saving	limited war	liquescent	liturgical
leucoplast	lifesomely	limit gauge	liquidator	live action
leucotaxin	life-spring	limit point	liquid drop	livelihood
leucotaxis	life-string	limitrophe	liquid fire	liveliness
leucotoxin	life tenant	limnograph	liquidiser	liver fluke
leukaemoid	life-writer	limnometer	liquidizer	liverishly
leukovirus	lift-bridge	limpet mine	liquidness	liver salts
lever frame	lift the leg	limpidness	liquorless	liverwurst
lever watch	ligamental	Lincolnian	lis pendens	live weight
levigation	light-armed	Lincoln imp	lissomness	living area
levitation	light bread	Lincoln Red	list broker	living dead
levitative	light curve	lincomycin	listenable	livingless
levy in mass	lightening	linearizer	listen good	livingness
lexicalize	lighterage	line astern	listlessly	living room
lexicology	lighterman	linebacker	list system	living wage
lexiconize	lightermen	line by line	litany-desk	living will
lexigraphy	light-grasp	line editor	literalise	lizardfish
Lexiphanes	light guide	line-ending	literalism	lizard-like
Lexiphanic	light horse	line finder	literalist	lizard-skin
ley farming	lighthouse	line-firing	literality	Lloyd's List
liableness	light meter	linen-panel	literalize	loaded down
libationer	light-money	linen-press	literarily	loaded with
libellulid	light of day	line of fire	literarism	load factor
liberalise	light o' love	line of life	literately	loading bay
liberalism	light organ	lineolated	literation	loading rod
liberalist	lightproof	linerboard	literatist	loadmaster
liberality	light-tight	line-riding	literature	loafer wolf
liberalize	light touch	liner train	literosity	loanholder
liberation	light value	line-squall	lithia-mica	loan-monger
liberative	light valve	lingualise	lithoclast	loan-office
liberatory	light water	lingualize	lithoglyph	loathingly
liberty act	lignocaine	linguiform	lithograph	lobe-finned

lobopodial	long corner	Lord Rector	Lubberland	lute-string
lobopodium	long drawer	Lord Warden	lubberlike	lutestring
lobotomies	long family	Lorentzian	lubber line	Lutine Bell
lobotomise	long figure	lorication	lubricator	luxuriance
lobotomize	long finger	lose ground	lubricious	luxuriancy
lobscouser	long-footed	lose height	luciferase	lycoperdon
lobsterish	longhaired	lose no time	Luciferian	lycopodium
lobster pot	long handle	lose the way	luciferous	Lydian mode
lobulation	long-headed	lose weight	lucifugous	lymphedema
local derby	long-horned	losing game	lucklessly	lymph gland
local group	long-jumper	loss-leader	lucubrator	lymphocyte
localistic	long-legged	loss-making	luculently	lymphokine
localities	long-lining	loss of face	ludibrious	lymphomata
local paper	long-living	loss of life	Ludolphian	lynchetted
local radio	long-lugged	lost labour	luff-tackle	lyophilise
local train	long-lunged	lost motion	luggage van	lyophilize
locational	long manure	Lost Tribes	lugubrious	lyre-flower
lock-and-key	long memory	lot and scot	lukewarmly	lyre-shaped
Lockeanism	long mirror	lotos-eater	lukewarmth	lyric drama
locked-coil	long-nebbed	lotus-eater	lumachelle	lyric stage
locker room	long-necked	loud hailer	lumber-camp	Lysenkoism
lock-keeper	long of life	loud-spoken	lumberjack	Lysenkoist
lock stitch	long pepper	loundering	lumber-port	lysigenous
lock-washer	long-player	lounge suit	lumber-raft	lysimachia
locomobile	long primer	louping-ill	lumber-room	lysogenize
locomotion	longshanks	louse-borne	lumbersome	maasbanker
locomotive	long sleeve	lovability	lumber town	macadamise
locomotory	longsomely	lovat green	lumber-yard	macadamize
loculament	long-spined	love affair	lumbricine	macaronies
locust bean	long-splice	lovelessly	lumbricoid	macaronism
locust-bird	long-staple	love letter	lumichrome	mace-bearer
locust tree	long stroke	lovelihead	lumiflavin	Macedonian
locutorium	long-tackle	loveliness	luminaries	maceration
Loddon lily	long-tailed	lovemaking	luminarism	macfarlane
lodemanage	long-termer	love-object	luminarist	Machangana
loganberry	long tongue	love-potion	lumination	machinable
logan-stone	long-winded	lover's knot	luminosity	machinator
loggerhead	look-and-say	lovers' lane	luminously	machine age
logicality	look around	lovers' tiff	lumisterol	machine-gun
logicalize	look babies	loveworthy	lumpectomy	Mach number
logical sum	look down on	lovey-dovey	lump of clay	mackintosh
logic-tight	look lively	lovingness	lumpsucker	Maconochie
logistical	look slippy	lowbrowism	luna cornea	macrocarpa
logography	loom the web	low-calorie	lunar cycle	macrocycle
logomaniac	loop aerial	low-country	lunar month	macrocytic
logophobia	loop-stitch	lower class	lunar orbit	macrofauna
logorrhoea	loop system	lower court	lunarscape	macromeric
logrolling	loose cover	Lower House	lunate bone	macrophage
Lollardism	loose-ended	lower sixth	lungs of oak	macrophyte
löllingite	loose order	lower world	lunkheaded	macropodid
Lombardian	loose scrum	low-melting	lurchingly	macro-scale
Lombardism	lop and crop	low opinion	lusciously	macroseism
Lombrosian	loperamide	low-pitched	Lushington	macrospore
London clay	lophiodont	low-powered	Lusitanian	maculation
lonelihood	lophophore	low profile	lustration	maculature
loneliness	lopolithic	low-residue	lustrative	Madagascan
lone ranger	lopsidedly	Lowryesque	lustratory	Madagascar
lonesomely	loquacious	low spirits	lustreless	madapollam
long-acting	Lord Bishop	low tension	lustreware	mad-brained
long barrow	lord it over	low to paper	lustrously	Madeira nut
long chalks	lordliness	loxodromic	luteolysis	Madonnaish
long chance	lordolatry	loyal toast	luteolytic	madreporic

Madura foot	Makasarese	Malpighian	man of mould	marination
maeandrine	make a House	Malta fever	man of sense	marine band
maeandrous	make a job of	malted milk	man of straw	marine blue
maedi-visna	make a match	Maltese cat	man of virtu	marine glue
magazinery	make amends	Maltese dog	manometric	marineland
magazinish	make a noise	Malthusian	manor house	marine soap
magazinist	make a point	malt liquor	manostatic	marine toad
Magellanic	make a raise	maltreater	manqueller	Mariolater
Magen David	make a shift	malt whisky	manservant	Mariolatry
Maghrebine	make a vaunt	malvaceous	man's estate	marionette
magicality	make-belief	Malvernian	mansionary	mariposite
magic glass	make bold as	malversate	manslaying	maritality
magistracy	make boot of	mamillated	mansuetude	markedness
magistrand	make eyes at	mammal-like	manteltree	marketable
magistrate	make game of	mammillary	mantically	marketably
Magna Carta	make its way	mammillate	mantletree	market-rate
magna opera	make it up to	mammogenic	mantlewise	market town
magnetical	make leeway	mammotroph	manucaptor	marking ink
magnetizer	make meat of	mammy wagon	manumitted	marking-nut
magnifical	make mock of	manageable	manumitter	markswoman
magnificat	make much of	manageably	manumotive	mark-vessel
magniloquy	make noises	management	manure-heap	markworthy
magnolious	make no sign	manageress	manuscript	marmennill
magnum opus	make or mend	managerial	many-headed	marquisate
magpie lark	make report	man and wife	many-valued	marrowbone
magpie moth	makeshifty	manavilins	many valved	marrowless
mahoganies	make the bag	Manchester	manzanilla	Marseilles
maidenhair	make the bed	manchineel	Maoritanga	Marshalate
maidenhead	make tracks	Manchurian	maple candy	marshaless
maidenhood	make up a bed	mancipable	maple-honey	marshalled
maidenlike	makeweight	mandevilla	maple sugar	marshaller
maiden name	malacology	mandibular	maple syrup	marshal-man
maiden over	malapertly	mandragora	mappemonde	marshalsea
maiden pink	malapropos	manducable	maquillage	marsh elder
maidenship	malaxation	manfulness	maraschino	marsh fever
Maid Marian	Malayanize	manganitic	marathoner	marsh grass
mail-armour	Malay apple	mangosteen	marble bone	marshiness
mailed fist	Malay tapir	maniacally	marble cake	marsh quail
maimedness	malconduct	Manichaean	marble gall	marsh tacky
main chance	malcontent	Manicheism	marble-wood	martellato
main clause	maldescent	manicurist	marcelling	martensite
main couple	maledicent	manifester	marcel wave	Martha Gunn
main course	malefactor	manifestly	marcescent	martial art
mainlander	maleficent	manifestos	marchantia	martialism
mainpernor	maleficial	manifolder	March brown	martialist
mainspring	maleic acid	manifoldly	March court	martiality
mainstream	malevolent	manifold to	march stone	martialize
main street	malfeasant	maniformly	Marcionist	martial law
Main Street	malgré tout	Manila hemp	Marcionite	martingale
maintained	maliferous	man-in-space	Marcomanni	martingana
maintainer	malignance	manipulate	marcottage	Martinware
maintainor	malignancy	man-midwife	mareograph	marvelling
maisonette	malingerer	manna-grass	marginalia	marvellous
maize-thief	mallardite	manna sugar	marginally	Marxianism
majestatic	malleation	mannerable	margin call	Marylander
majestical	mallee bird	mannerless	marginless	Mary Stuart
majestuous	mallee fowl	Mannesmann	margravate	Mary Warner
major-domos	malleiform	Mannlicher	margravial	marzacotto
Majoristic	mallenders	manoeuvrer	margravine	mascarpone
majorities	Mallorquin	man of blood	marguerite	masked ball
major piece	malodorous	man of ideas	Marheshvan	maskinonge
majuscular	malolactic	man of means	marigenous	mason's mark

masquerade
mass action
Massagetae
massasauga
mass defect
massecuite
mass effect
mass energy
masseteric
mass market
mass medium
mass-monger
mass number
mass-priest
mastectomy
master card
master hand
masterhood
masterless
mastermind
master race
mastership
master-work
masterwork
masterwort
masticable
masticator
mastic tree
mastiff bat
mastodonic
mastodynia
mastopathy
masturbate
mataeology
matchboard
match-maker
matchmaker
match-plane
match point
match-rifle
matchstick
materially
maternally
mathematic
mating call
matriarchy
matricaria
matricidal
matriculae
matricular
matrifocal
matrilocal
matriotism
matrocliny
Matronalia
matronhood
matronlike
matronship
matronymic
matterless
matter wave
maturation

maturative
matureness
matureness
maudlinism
maundering
Maundy coin
Maundy dish
mausoleums
mauvais pas
mauvais ton
mavourneen
maxilliped
maximalism
maximalist
maximality
Maxwellian
Maxwell law
Mayfairish
mayonnaise
McLuhanism
McNaughten
meadow bird
meadow foam
meadow frog
meadowland
meadowlark
meadowless
meadow vole
meagreness
meal-beetle
mealie meal
mealie rice
meal ticket
mealy-mouth
meandering
meaningful
mean-souled
mean square
measurable
measurably
measuredly
meat-headed
meat-market
meat-packer
meat ticket
mechanical
mechanizer
meconopsis
medal chief
medal round
meddlesome
meddlingly
media event
mediagenic
mediastina
mediatress
mediatrice
medicalize
medicament
medicaster
medication
medicative
Medici lace

medievally
mediocracy
mediocrist
mediocrity
meditation
meditative
medium rare
mediumship
medium shot
medium wave
medrinaque
medullated
medusa-fish
medusiform
meek mother
meerschaum
meet in with
meet the ear
meet the eye
mefloquine
megagamete
megalithic
megalocyte
megalosaur
megaphonic
megaripple
megascopic
meiofaunal
meiophylly
melanaemia
melanaemic
melancholy
Melanesian
Melanesoid
melanistic
melanocyte
melanoderm
melanosome
Melba sauce
Melba toast
Melburnian
melezitose
melianthus
meliorater
meliorator
melismatic
melizitose
mellophone
mellowness
melocactus
melodially
melomaniac
melon-shell
meloplasty
melting pot
Melvillean
Melvillian
member bank
memberless
membership
membranate
membranoid

membranous
membranula
memomotion
memorandum
memorative
memorially
memory bank
memory book
memory drug
memory drum
memory lane
memoryless
memory span
menacement
menacingly
menagerist
menarcheal
mendacious
mendicancy
mengkulang
mengovirus
meningioma
meningitic
meningitis
menologies
menologist
menopausal
menopausic
menorrhoea
Menshevism
Menshevist
menstruant
menstruate
menstruous
mensurable
mensurator
mental note
mental test
mental year
menu-driven
meperidine
mephenesin
mephitical
mepyramine
mercantile
mercaptide
merchandry
merchantry
mercifully
mercury arc
mercy sakes
meretrices
meridional
merismatic
meristelic
merit money
meritocrat
merogamete
merohedral
meromictic
meromyosin
merozygote

merry Greek
merrymaker
Merry Widow
Mertensian
mesenchyme
mesenteric
mesenteron
mesethmoid
meshugener
mesitylene
mesmerical
mesmerizer
mesocephal
mesoconchy
mesocratic
mesodermal
mesodorsal
mesogaster
mesogloeal
mesognathy
mesokurtic
mesolectal
mesolimbic
mesolithic
mesomerism
mesomorphy
mesophilic
mesophytic
mesopodium
mesorrhine
mesoscaphe
mesoscopic
mesosphere
mesostasis
mesothelia
mesothorax
mesovarium
message-boy
Messianism
mess jacket
metabiosis
metabiotic
metabolise
metabolism
metabolite
metabolize
metacarpal
metacarpus
metacentre
metacetone
metachrome
metaconule
metacyclic
meta-ethics
metagalaxy
metagnomic
metalation
metalepsis
metaleptic
metalleity
metallizer
metallurgy

metameride	Mezzofanti	midden cock	mill finish	minnarichi
metamerism	mezzo forte	midden fowl	mill-hopper	minnerichi
metamerous	mezzo piano	middle-aged	millilitre	Minnesotan
metanalyse	miargyrite	middle-ager	millimetre	minor canon
metaphonic	miarolitic	Middle Ages	millionary	minorities
metaphoric	mica-schist	middlebrow	millionism	minor piece
metaphrase	Michaelmas	middle deck	millionist	minstrelsy
metaphrast	Mickey Finn	Middle East	milliprobe	mint master
metaphysic	mickey-take	middle game	millocracy	mint parity
metaphysis	micklemote	middle life	millstream	minuscular
metaplasia	microatoll	middlemost	mill-stream	minute bell
metapodial	microbarom	middle name	millworker	minute-book
metapodium	microbiota	middleness	millwright	minute hand
metastably	microblade	middle rail	miltsiekte	minuteness
metastasis	microburin	middle-rank	mime artist	mirabilite
metastases	microburst	middle-rate	mimeograph	miracidial
metastasis	microcline	middle-road	mim-mouthed	miracidium
metastatic	microcrack	middle term	minatorily	miracle man
metatarsal	microcytic	middle-tone	minauderie	miraculize
metatarsus	microdrama	middleveld	minced meat	miraculous
metatheses	microdrive	Middle West	mind-bender	mirror carp
metathesis	microfauna	middlingly	Mindererus	mirror-like
metathetic	microfiche	mid-engined	mind-healer	mirror-work
metathorax	microflora	mid-feather	mindlessly	mirthfully
metempiric	microglial	midfielder	mind out for	mirthquake
meteoritic	micrograph	midi system	mind-reader	misaddress
methanogen	microgyria	midnightly	mine hunter	misapplied
methanolic	microimage	mid-oceanic	mine-laying	misapplies
methedrine	microlevel	midshipman	mineralise	misbelieve
Methedrine	microlight	midshipmen	mineralist	miscarried
methiocarb	microlitic	midsummery	mineralize	miscarries
methionine	microlitre	Midwestern	mineralogy	miscellany
methodical	micrologic	mightiness	mineraloid	mischanter
methodizer	micromania	migmatitic	mineral oil	misch metal
methodless	micromazia	migmatized	mineral rod	misclosure
methomania	micrometer	mignonette	mineral tar	miscompute
methoprene	micrometre	migraineur	mineral wax	misconceit
Methuselah	micrometry	migrainous	miner's inch	misconduct
methylator	micromolar	milecastle	miner's lung	miscontent
methyldopa	microphage	miliaceous	mine-sinker	miscounsel
meticulous	microphone	militantly	minestrone	miscreance
metoecious	microphony	militarily	mineworker	miscreancy
metoestrus	microphoto	militarise	mingimingi	miscreated
metoprolol	microphyll	militarism	mingle eyes	misdeliver
metre-angle	microphyte	militarist	minglement	misdeserve
metre psalm	microprint	militarize	mingle with	misdevoted
metrically	microprism	militation	Mingrelian	misdrawing
metrisable	microprobe	militiaman	miniaceous	miseducate
metrizable	micropylar	militiamen	mini-budget	misericord
metrocracy	micro-scale	milk-coffee	minikin pin	misery guts
Metroliner	microscope	milk powder	minimalism	misexecute
metrologic	microscopy	milk the ram	minimalist	misexplain
metromania	microseism	milled lead	minimality	misexpress
metronomic	microsleep	millefiore	minimalize	misfeature
metronymic	microslide	millegrain	mining-hole	misfortune
metropolis	microsomal	millennial	mining town	misimprove
mettlesome	microspore	millennian	miniseries	misincline
mevalonate	microstate	millennism	ministrant	misjoinder
Mexicanize	microstrip	millennium	ministrate	misleading
Mexican tea	microtherm	miller-moth	ministress	mismanager
Mexican War	microtonal	millesimal	ministries	mismeasure
mexiletine	Midas touch	millet-seed	mini-summit	misogamist

misogynism	mixty-maxty	Monarchian	monogenist	montelimar
misogynist	mizzen-mast	monarchies	monogenous	Montessori
misogynous	mizzen-sail	monarchise	monography	Montgomery
misologist	mizzen yard	monarchism	monogynist	month clock
misperform	mnemically	monarchist	monogynous	month's mind
misprision	mnemicness	monarchize	monohybrid	Montrealer
misreading	mnemonical	monastical	monohydric	monumental
misrecital	mobile home	monaurally	monoideism	monzonitic
missal book	mobocratic	Monday Club	monokaryon	moon-bounce
miss a trick	moccasined	Monégasque	monolithal	mooncalves
misseeming	mocha brown	monegenism	monolithic	moon-curser
missileman	mock-heroic	Monel metal	monologian	moon-flower
missiology	mock orange	monetarian	monologise	moonraking
missionary	mock privet	monetarily	monologist	moon-rocket
missionate	modacrylic	monetarism	monologize	moon-shaped
missioneer	modalistic	monetarist	monomaniac	moonshiner
missionist	modalities	moneymaker	monomerous	moonstruck
missionize	modal logic	money order	monometric	moonwalker
mission oak	mode-locked	money-power	monomictic	moose berry
Missisauga	modenature	money-saver	monophasic	mopane worm
Missourian	moderately	money-worth	monophonic	mophrodite
missourite	moderation	mongreldom	monoplegia	mopishness
misspender	moderatism	mongrelise	monoplegic	moral fibre
miss the bus	moderatist	mongrelism	monoploidy	moralistic
mistakable	modernizer	mongrelize	monopodial	moralities
mistakably	modern jazz	moniliasis	monopodium	moralizing
mistakenly	modernness	moniliform	monopodous	moral sense
mist-blower	modern side	monishment	monopolies	moral tutor
mist-flower	modifiable	monitorial	monopolise	morass-weed
misthought	modificand	monitories	monopolism	Morasthite
mistress it	modishness	monkey bars	monopolist	moratorium
mistressly	modularity	monkey-boat	monopolize	morbidness
mistruster	modularize	monkey-face	monopteral	morbillous
mistutored	modulation	monkey-rope	monopteros	morcellate
misventure	modulative	monkey suit	monorhinal	mordacious
miswriting	modulatory	monkliness	monorhymed	Mordvinian
mitch-board	Mohammedan	monk's bench	monosexual	more like it
mithridate	moissanite	monk's table	monosodium	more or less
mitigation	moist scall	monocarpic	monospermy	Moreton Bay
mitigatory	moist sugar	monocausal	monostable	morganatic
mitre-bevel	moisturise	monochroic	monostatic	morigerate
mitre block	moisturize	monochrome	monotheism	morigerous
mitre board	molariform	monochromy	monotheist	Morisonian
mitre-cramp	molendinar	monoclinal	monothetic	Mormon City
mitre joint	mole-plough	monoclinic	monotocous	morning-gun
mitre-plane	molinology	monoclonal	monotonely	morning tea
mitre-shell	moll-buzzer	monocormic	monotonise	morologist
mitre wheel	mollescent	monocratic	monotonist	moroseness
mitten crab	mollitious	monocrotic	monotonize	morphemics
mitt-reader	mollrowing	monoculist	monotonous	morphinism
Mittyesque	molluscoid	monoculous	monotropic	morphinist
mixed angle	molluscous	monocyclic	monotypous	morphodite
mixed blood	moll-washer	monocystic	monovalent	morphogeny
mixed bunch	molybdenum	monocystid	monoxenous	morpholine
mixed grill	moment-hand	monodactyl	monozygous	morphology
mixed media	monadiform	monodontal	Monsignori	morphoneme
Mix-Hellene	monadistic	monodromic	monsoonish	morris bell
mixing desk	monadology	monoecious	monstrance	Morris tube
mixohaline	Mona marble	monogamian	Montagnais	morrowless
mixologist	monandrous	monogamist	montagnard	morrow-mass
mixolydian	monarchess	monogamous	montbretia	Morse taper
mixoploidy	monarchial	monogenean	Monte Carlo	mortadella

mortadelle
mortal mind
mortarless
mortifying
mortuaries
mosaically
mosaic gold
mosaicking
mosaic work
mosasaurus
moscatello
Moscow mule
mosquitoes
mosquitoey
moss-backed
mossbunker
moss stitch
mother cell
mother-city
mother coal
motherhood
motherkins
motherland
motherless
motherlike
motherling
mother lode
mother love
mother's boy
Mother's Day
mother ship
mothership
mother's pet
mother's son
mother-to-be
motherwort
moth orchid
motionable
motionally
motionless
motion-work
motitation
motivation
motivative
motiveless
motleyness
motor coach
motor court
motor cycle
motorcycle
motor-drive
motor hotel
motor lodge
motor mouth
motormouth
motor nerve
motor sport
motor yacht
mottramite
mould-board
mouldiness
Moulinette

mountained
mountainet
mountebank
mount guard
mournfully
mourningly
mouse-eared
mouse-lemur
mousseline
moustached
moustachio
Mousterian
Mousteroid
mouth guard
mouthiness
mouthingly
mouth music
mouth organ
mouthpiece
moutonnéed
movability
movable-doh
movable rib
move in with
movelessly
movie-going
movie house
movie-maker
moving-coil
moving-iron
movingness
mower's mite
Mozambican
mozzarella
Mr Chairman
Mr Next-Door
Mrs Justice
mucedinous
much to seek
muciferous
mucigenous
muciparous
mucka-mucka
muckleness
muckraking
mucousness
mucronated
mud and stud
mud balance
muddle-head
muddlement
muddliness
muddlingly
mud-flinger
mudguarded
mud-logging
mud-skipper
mudskipper
mud-slinger
mud swallow
mud-thrower
mud volcano

muesli belt
muffin-face
muffle kiln
muff pistol
mugearitic
mugwumpery
mugwumpish
mugwumpism
Muhammadan
mujahideen
mulattress
mulberries
mule-driver
mule-headed
mule-killer
mule rabbit
muliebrity
mulishness
mullein tea
mullet-head
mulligrubs
multiaxial
multifidly
multiflash
multiflora
multifocal
multigrade
Multigraph
multilayer
multilevel
multimedia
multimeric
multimeter
multimodal
multi-party
multiphase
multiplane
multiplied
multiplier
multiplies
multipoint
multipolar
multisided
multi-stage
multistage
multi-track
multivalve
multiverse
multivious
multivocal
multocular
mumblement
mumblingly
mumbo-jumbo
mummy brown
mummy-cloth
Munchausen
mundane egg
municipium
munificent
munitioner
Muntz metal

muon number
mural crown
Muratorian
murderable
murder book
murder game
murder room
muriculate
Murphy's Law
Murray lily
Murray pine
muscardine
muscarinic
muscle cell
muscleless
muscle pull
muscle scar
muscovados
muscularis
muscularly
mushroomer
musical bow
musical box
musical ear
musicalise
musicality
musicalize
musical saw
music drama
musicianer
musicianly
musicology
music paper
music-shell
music stand
music stool
musk beetle
musket ball
musket shot
Muskhogean
musk mallow
musk orchid
musk turtle
mussel-bank
mussel crab
mussel duck
mussel plum
mussel rake
mustachios
mustard gas
mustard oil
mustard-pot
muster-book
muster-roll
mutability
mutagenize
mutarotate
mutassarif
mutational
mute button
mutessarif
muthafucka

mutilation
mutilative
mutinously
mutter over
mutton-bird
mutton chop
mutton-fish
mutton-head
mutton quad
mutual fund
mutualness
myasthenia
myasthenic
mycetocyte
mycetozoan
mycologist
mycophilic
mycoplasma
mycorrhiza
mycotrophy
myelinated
myeloblast
myelocoele
myelocytic
myelogenic
my lady wife
mylonitize
myoblastic
myocardiac
myocardial
myocardium
myoelastic
myofibroma
myogenesis
myographic
myological
myomectomy
myometrial
myometrium
myomorphic
myopically
myoplasmic
myosarcoma
my pleasure
myriadfold
myriapodal
myringitis
myriologue
myristicin
myrmekitic
myrtaceous
myrtle bird
myrtle wine
mysophobia
mystagogic
mystagogue
mysterioso
mysterious
mystery-bag
mystery man
mystically
mystifying

mythically
mythicizer
mythoclast
mythogenic
mythologem
mythologer
mythologic
mythomania
mythopoeia
mythopoeic
myxococcal
myxococcus
myxomatous
myxomycete
myzostomid
nabocklish
Nabokovian
nail-biting
nail enamel
nail-headed
nail-making
nail polish
nail-tailed
nail violin
naked force
naked truth
nalbuphine
nalorphine
naltrexone
namby-pamby
namelessly
name the day
nameworthy
nandrolone
nannyishly
nanosecond
naological
naphthalic
naphthenic
napkin ring
Napoleonic
nappy-liner
narcissine
narcissism
narcissist
narcolepsy
narcomania
narcotical
nard pistic
narratable
narratress
narrowback
narrow band
narrow boat
narrowcast
narrowness
narrow seas
nasal organ
nasologist
Nassauvian
nasturtium
natal cleft

natalities
natatorial
natatorium
nationally
nationalty
nationhood
nationwide
native bear
native-born
native bush
nativeness
native oven
native rock
nativistic
nativities
natron lake
natterjack
natty dread
natural day
natural gas
naturalise
naturalism
naturalist
naturality
naturalize
natural law
nature cure
nature food
natureless
nature poem
nature poet
nature walk
naturistic
naturopath
naughtiest
nauseating
nauseation
nauseously
nautch girl
nautically
nautiluses
naval brass
naval crown
navel-stone
naviculoid
navigation
Navy League
Nazarenism
Nazaritish
Nazaritism
Nazca lines
Nazi salute
Neapolitan
near at hand
neat cement
neat-handed
neatly shod
nebulosity
nebulously
neck-collar
neckercher
Necker cube

neck-spring
necrogenic
necrolatry
necrologue
necromance
necromancy
necrophile
necrophily
necrophobe
necropolis
necroscopy
nectar-bird
nectareous
nectarious
nectocalyx
needle-beam
needle beer
needle-book
needle-bush
needle-case
needle-cast
needlecord
needlefish
needlefuls
needle game
needle-lace
needle-like
needleloom
needle's eye
needlessly
needle time
needle-whin
needle-wood
needlework
need-to-know
ne'er-do-well
negational
negatively
negativism
negativist
negativity
negentropy
neglectful
neglecting
neglection
neglective
negligence
negligency
negligible
negligibly
negotiable
negotiable
negotiator
Negro cloth
Negrophile
Negrophobe
Negro's head
Negro State
Nelson cake
Nelsoniana
nematicide
nematocide

nematocyst
nematology
Nemean lion
nemesistic
nemocerous
neo-classic
neoclassic
neocyanine
neo-fascism
neo-fascist
neogenesis
neoglacial
neographic
neolocally
neological
neomorphic
neonatally
neontology
neopallial
neopallium
neopentane
neophiliac
neoplastic
neotechnic
neoterical
nephewship
nephometer
nephoscope
nephralgia
nephralgic
nephridial
nephridium
nephrocyte
nephrology
nephropexy
nephrotome
nephrotomy
nephsystem
nepotistic
nerve agent
nerve block
nerve fibre
nerve-force
nerve storm
Nesselrode
nesslerize
nesting box
net-drifter
net-fishing
nethermore
nethermost
nether vert
netherward
net-masonry
nettle beer
nettle-like
nettle-rash
nettlesome
nettle-tree
net tonnage
networking
neural arch

neural tube
neuraminic
neurectomy
neurilemma
neuroblast
neurocrine
neurogenic
neuroglial
neurolemma
neuromotor
neuronally
neuropathy
neuroplasm
Neuroptera
neurotoxic
neurotoxin
neuterness
neutralise
neutralism
neutralist
neutrality
neutralize
neutrodyne
never again
never-dying
never-never
New Academy
new arrival
New Dealish
New England
New English
newfangled
New Kingdom
New Leftist
New Mexican
new nothing
New Orleans
new realism
new realist
news agency
newscaster
news cinema
newsletter
newsmonger
newspapery
newsreader
news ticker
news-vendor
newsvendor
newsworthy
New Thought
New Worlder
new wrinkle
New York cut
New Yorkese
New Yorkish
New Zealand
next door to
next friend
nibblingly
Nicaraguan
nickel-iron

nickelized	night-spell	nodularity	non-utility	noteworthy
nickelling	nightstick	nodulation	non-vintage	not exactly
nickel note	night-stool	noegenesis	non-violent	not go nap on
nick of time	night-sweat	noegenetic	non-working	not half bad
nick-tailed	night-times	noise-maker	noogenesis	no thanks to
Nicobarese	nightwards	noise storm	noological	nothingism
Nicobarian	night watch	noisy miner	noon-flower	nothingist
Nicodemite	night-water	no man's land	noospheric	nothofagus
Nicolaitan	nigrescent	nom de plume	norbergite	nothomorph
nicol prism	nigromance	nomenclate	Norbertine	noticeable
Nicol prism	nihilistic	nomen nudum	Nordenfelt	noticeably
nicotinate	nihilities	nominalise	Nordhausen	notifiable
nicotinian	Nile lechwe	nominalism	normal form	not in order
nicotinise	nilly-willy	nominalist	normalizer	notionally
nicotinism	Nilo-Hamite	nominalize	normalness	notionless
nicotinize	Nilometric	nominately	Normanizer	not much cop
nidamental	nimbleness	nomination	normoblast	not one's day
nidderling	nimble Will	nominative	normocytic	notopodial
niddy-noddy	nincompoop	nomineeism	norsteroid	notopodium
nidicolous	nine-killer	nomography	northabout	not so dusty
nidificate	nine points	nomologist	northbound	not the less
nidifugous	nine-seater	nomothetic	north canoe	Nottingham
nidulation	nineteenth	non-abelian	North Downs	not to worry
nifedipine	nine-tenths	non-ability	northerner	not without
niffy-naffy	nine to five	non-aligned	northernly	noumenally
Niger-Congo	ninetyfold	non-capital	north light	nourishing
niggardize	nip and tuck	non-central	north-south	novaculite
nigger fish	Nipkow disc	nonchalant	Northumber	Novanglian
niggerhead	nippleless	non-citizen	northwards	novelesque
nigger luck	nipple-like	nonconform	Norway pine	novelistic
nigglingly	nipplewort	non-content	nose bot fly	novicehood
night adder	niridazole	noncurance	nose-bridge	noviceship
night-blind	Nissl stain	non-drinker	noselessly	novobiocin
night-bound	nit-picking	non-earning	nose-monkey	now and then
night chain	nitrazepam	non-elastic	nose tackle	nowanights
night-chair	nitric acid	non-essence	nose to nose	nowcasting
night class	Nitrochalk	non-ferrous	nose-to-tail	now or never
night clock	nitrofuran	non-fiction	nosocomial	nubiferous
night coach	nitro group	non-genital	nosography	nuciferous
night cream	nitrometer	nonjoinder	nosologist	nucivorous
nightdress	nitrophile	nonjurancy	nosophobia	nuclearism
night error	nitro-proof	non-logical	nosopoetic	nuclearist
night-glass	nitro-prove	non-morally	nostalgist	nuclearize
night heron	nitwittery	non-natural	Nostratian	nuclear sap
night horse	Nixonomics	non-nuclear	nostrility	nuclear war
night-house	Noah's Flood	nonny-nonny	nostrilled	nucleation
night-latch	no amount of	no-nonsense	no such luck	nucleonics
night light	Nobel prize	non-organic	nosy parker	nucleoside
nightmarey	Nobel Prize	non-patrial	Nosy Parker	nucleosome
night-night	nobilities	non-payment	notability	nucleotide
night nurse	noblemanly	non-playing	not a little	nuculanium
night or day	noble metal	nonplussed	not all that	nudibranch
night-piece	noblewoman	non-smoking	notaphilic	nulla-nulla
night-raven	noblewomen	non-soluble	notarially	nullibiety
night rider	nobody-crab	non-starter	notational	nullisomic
nightscape	nociceptor	non-stellar	not but what	nulliverse
night-scene	nocifensor	non-success	notch-house	numbedness
nightshade	no conjuror	non-summons	notchiness	numberable
night shift	nodal point	non-swimmer	not cricket	number-form
nightshirt	nodosarian	non-trivial	note-broker	numberless
night sight	nodosarine	nontronite	note-holder	number line
night snake	nod through	non-uniform	note-shaver	numbheaded

numeration	objectless	ocean spray	of a morning	old country
numerative	object love	ocean tramp	of even date	old crumpet
numerology	objectness	oceanwards	off balance	Old English
numerosity	object word	ochlocracy	offcasting	olde worlde
numerously	objets d'art	ochraceous	offenceful	old-fangled
numinosity	objuration	ochratoxin	offendable	Old Italian
numinously	oblateness	ochronosis	offendedly	Old Kingdom
numismatic	oblational	ochronotic	offer price	old-maidish
nummulated	obligately	ocnophilic	of few words	old-maidism
nummulitic	obligation	octadrachm	off-flavour	old-man bird
nummulitid	obligative	octaeteric	offhandish	old-mannish
numskulled	obligatory	octaeteris	office girl	Old Pals Act
nunciative	obligement	octagynous	office hymn	Old Pharaoh
nunciature	obligingly	octahedral	officeless	Old Scratch
Nupercaine	obliterate	octahedron	office wife	old soldier
nuptiality	Oblomovism	octamerism	officially	Old Stripes
nuptial pad	oblongness	octamerous	officiator	old-womanly
nurse-child	obnebulate	octandrous	offishness	old-womanry
nurse hound	obnubilate	octangular	off-licence	oleaginous
nurse-plant	oboe d'amore	octavalent	off one's dot	oleandrine
nurseryful	oboi d'amore	octave stop	off one's nut	oleiferous
nurseryman	obrogation	octodecimo	off-putting	oleography
nurserymen	obscurancy	octodrachm	off-roading	oleophilic
nurse shark	obscuredly	octofoiled	offset well	oleophobic
nurses' home	obsequence	octogenary	off-spinner	oleothorax
nursing bra	obsequious	octogynous	off the ball	oleraceous
nurturance	observable	octohedron	off the beam	olfactible
nutational	observably	octomerous	off the boil	oligarchic
nutcracker	observance	octonarian	off the cuff	oligoclase
nut factory	observancy	octonarius	off-the-face	oligoester
nutmeg-bird	obsidional	octopamine	off the hook	oligomeric
nutmeg tree	obsoletely	octoploidy	off the mark	oligomycin
nutritious	obsoletion	octopodous	off the pace	oligophagy
nutty slack	obsoletism	octopusher	off the rack	oligopsony
nyctalopia	obstacular	octovalent	off the reel	olistolith
nyctalopic	obstetrics	oculogyral	off-the-road	olivaceous
nyctinasty	obstinance	oculogyric	off the wall	olive crown
nympholept	obstinancy	oculomotor	off the wind	olive green
nystagmoid	obstructor	oculonasal	of like mind	olive-plant
oafishness	obtainable	odd and even	of no effect	Olonetsian
oak-barrens	obtainment	odditorium	of one piece	Omarianism
oaken towel	obtruncate	odd-pinnate	of one's will	ombrometer
oak-opening	obturation	odiousness	of one's word	ombrophile
oak-spangle	obtuseness	odontalgia	of some size	ombrophobe
oath-helper	obvelation	odontalgic	oftentimes	omega minus
obbligatos	obvolution	odontocete	of the blood	Omega point
obdurately	occasional	odontogeny	of the clock	omentopexy
obduration	occasioner	odontology	oh be joyful	ommatidial
obediently	occidental	odorimeter	oil-clothed	ommatidium
obeisantly	Occitanian	odorimetry	oil company	ommochrome
obeliscoid	occlusally	odoriphore	oil-gilding	omnibus box
obeliskoid	occultness	odynometer	oil of amber	omnificent
obituarial	occupation	oedematose	oil of roses	omnigenous
obituarian	occupative	oedematous	oil of spike	omnilucent
obituaries	occupiable	Oedipodean	oil of thuja	omnipotent
obituarily	occurrence	oenologist	oil of thyme	omniscient
obituarist	occurrency	oenomaniac	oil on water	omnivorous
obituarize	oceanarium	oenophilic	oil-painter	omophagist
objectable	ocean-basin	oesophagal	oilskinned	omphalitis
object-ball	ocean-going	oesophagus	Oireachtas	on a bowline
object code	oceanicity	oestradiol	Old Academy	on all fours
objectival	oceanology	of all loves	Old British	on all hands

on a platter	on the march	opera buffa	orcharding	orological
on approval	on the outer	opera cloak	orchardist	oropendola
on behalf of	on the prowl	opera house	orchardman	oropharynx
on business	on the queer	opera seria	orchardmen	orotundity
on campaign	on the quiet	operatable	orchestral	Oroya fever
once in a way	on the rails	operculate	orchestric	orphan drug
oncologist	on the rocks	operettist	orchideous	orphanhood
on commando	on the ropes	ophicleide	orchiopexy	orpheonist
oncosphere	on the scene	ophiolater	ordainment	Orphically
one and only	on the scent	ophiolatry	ordeal bean	orthoclase
one another	on the scoop	ophiolitic	order about	orthoconic
one at a time	on the shelf	ophiomancy	Order Order	orthodoxal
one fine day	on the skids	ophthalmia	order paper	orthodoxly
one-nighter	on the slate	ophthalmic	ordinaries	orthodrome
one-of-a-kind	on the sneak	opiniative	ordinarily	orthoepist
one or other	on the spree	opinionate	ordination	orthogonal
one-over-one	on the stuff	opinionist	ordinative	orthograde
one-plus-one	on the stump	opisometer	ordonnance	orthometry
one-sidedly	on the table	opisthotic	Ordovician	orthopedic
one-striper	on the tapes	opium dream	Oregon pine	orthophony
one-time pad	on the tapis	opium joint	oreography	orthophoto
one too many	on the tiles	opium poppy	organ clock	orthophyre
one-worlder	on the track	opossuming	organ-coral	orthopnoea
on good form	on the tramp	oppilation	organellar	orthopraxy
onion couch	on the twist	opposeless	organicism	Orthoptera
onion-grass	on the wagon	opposingly	organicist	orthoptere
onisciform	on the watch	oppositely	organicity	orthoptics
onlay graft	on the water	opposition	organic law	orthoptist
on my honour	on the way in	oppositive	organigram	orthotomic
on occasion	on the whole	oppression	organismal	orthotopic
onocentaur	ontogenist	oppressive	organismic	orthotropy
onomastics	ontologism	opprobrium	organistic	or whatever
on one's back	ontologist	oppugnable	organ-metal	or whenever
on one's feet	ontologize	oppugnance	organogeny	or wherever
on one's game	on transmit	oppugnancy	organogram	oryctology
on one's head	onwardness	optatively	organology	oscheocele
on one's jack	on your mark	optical art	organonomy	oscillator
on one's legs	onyx marble	optic angle	organ-point	oscitation
on one's mind	oophoritis	optic nerve	orguinette	osculation
on one's toes	oops-a-daisy	optic tract	orientable	osculatory
on schedule	oozlum bird	optimality	orientalia	Osiandrian
on the alert	opacimeter	optimistic	orientally	osmeterium
on the beach	opalescent	optionally	orientated	osmication
on the bench	opaqueness	option card	originally	osmiridium
on the blink	open access	optionless	originator	osmoceptor
on the block	open cheque	optometric	orimulsion	osmolality
on the books	open dating	opus magnum	Orimulsion	osmolarity
on the booze	open-handed	orache moth	orinasally	osmometric
on the brain	open letter	oracularly	Orion's belt	osmophilic
on the buroo	open market	orange-chip	orismology	osmophoric
on the cards	open-minded	orange dove	Orkney vole	osphradial
on the cheap	open-necked	orange lily	ornamental	osphradium
on the crook	open outcry	orange moth	ornamenter	ossiferous
on the cross	open prison	orange peel	ornateness	ostensible
on the dodge	open sandal	orangequit	orneriness	ostensibly
on the drink	open season	orangeries	ornithopod	osteoblast
on the fritz	open secret	orange-root	ornithosis	osteoclast
on the green	open sesame	orange tree	ornithotic	osteocolla
on the house	Open Sesame	orange-wood	orogenesis	osteologic
on the latch	open system	oratorical	orogenetic	osteolysis
on the level	open-topped	oratorship	orogenital	osteolytic
on the loose	openworked	orbiculate	orographic	osteomancy

osteometry
osteopathy
osteophyte
Ostpolitik
ostraceous
ostreiform
ostrichism
Oswego bass
othergates
otherguess
other place
other ranks
otherwhere
other woman
other world
otioseness
otological
otomycosis
ottava rima
otter-board
otter civet
otter-hound
otter-shell
otter shrew
otter-trawl
Ottomanism
Ottomanize
ouananiche
oudstryder
Ouidaesque
Ouija board
Our Saviour
out and away
out at heels
outbackery
outbalance
outblossom
outbreathe
outbreeder
outcasting
out-college
out-cricket
out-dooring
outdoorish
outdraught
outdweller
outer forme
Outer House
outer space
outer woman
outer world
outfielder
outflowing
outgassing
outgeneral
outglitter
outgrowing
outhousing
outjockeys
outlandish
outmeasure
outmigrant

outmodedly
out of blast
out of blood
out of court
out of doors
out of habit
out of heart
out of joint
out of order
out of phase
out of place
out of plumb
out of print
out of reach
out-of-round
out of scale
out of score
out of shape
out of sight
out of sorts
out-of-state
out of stock
out of taste
out of touch
out of truth
out of twist
out of whack
out on a limb
out-patient
outpatient
out-pension
outperform
outpouring
outpromise
out-quarter
outrageous
outrigging
outrightly
outs and ins
outscourer
outsetting
outsettler
outshining
outside job
outside man
outsiderly
outskirter
outsparkle
outstander
outstation
outstretch
outswagger
outsweeten
out-swinger
outswinger
out-thunder
out to grass
out to lunch
outvillain
outward man
outworking
outwrestle

outwrought
ouvrierism
Oval Office
ovariotomy
oven-bottom
overabound
overaction
overactive
overageing
over and out
overbelief
overbidder
overbitter
overbleach
overblouse
overboldly
overbought
overbridge
overbright
overbudget
overburden
overcanopy
overcharge
overchosen
overclothe
overcoated
overcolour
overcommit
overcooked
overcutter
overdaring
overdeepen
overdesign
overdesire
overdilute
overdosage
overdrawer
overeasily
overesteem
overexcite
overexpand
overexpose
overextend
overfavour
overflight
overfondly
overfulfil
overgovern
overgreedy
overground
overgrowth
overhanded
overhasten
overhearer
overhoused
overinform
over-insure
overinsure
overjacket
overkindly
overlabour
overlander

overlavish
overlaying
overlength
overliness
overlisten
overlocker
overlooker
overmantel
overmantle
overmaster
overmatter
overmickle
over-mighty
overmodest
overnicely
overnicety
overparted
overplease
overpraise
overpreach
overpunish
overrashly
overreckon
overrecord
over-refine
overrefine
overriding
overrunner
overshadow
overshroud
overslaugh
oversleeve
overspeech
overspread
overspring
oversprung
oversquare
overssized
overstayer
overstitch
overstorey
overstrain
overstream
overstress
overstrict
overstride
overstrike
overstring
overstrode
overstroke
overstrong
overstruck
overstrung
oversubtle
oversupply
overtaking
overtender
over the sea
over-the-top
over the way
overthrust
overthwart

overtopple
overtravel
overtumble
overturner
overviewer
overwander
overweight
overwinder
overwinter
overwisely
ovicapsule
oviposited
ovipositor
ovogenesis
ovogenetic
owlishness
owl monkeys
owl-swallow
oxalacetic
oxalic acid
Oxbridgean
ox-eye daisy
Oxford bags
Oxford blue
Oxford clay
Oxford Down
Oxford grey
Oxford shoe
Oxford weed
oxidizable
oxosteroid
oxprenolol
oxybromide
oxycephaly
oxygen acid
oxygenator
oxygen debt
oxygenless
oxygen mask
oxygen tent
oxymoronic
oxyphilous
oxyproline
oxy-propane
oxytonical
oyster-bank
oyster-boat
oyster-farm
oyster-fish
oyster-like
oyster loaf
ozone layer
ozonolysis
ozonolytic
ozonometer
ozonometry
ozonoscope
pace bowler
pacemaking
pace-setter
pachycauly
pacificate

pacificism	Paisleyite	pancratium	paperboard	paragaster
pacificist	palace coup	pancreatic	paperbound	parageusia
Pacific rim	Palaeocene	pancreatin	paper cable	paraglider
Pacific Rim	Palaeogene	pandectist	paper chain	paraglossa
pacifistic	palaeolith	pandemonic	paper-chase	paragneiss
pack animal	palaeopole	panegyrise	paperchase	paragnosis
packet-boat	palaeowind	panegyrist	paper cover	Paraguayan
packet ship	Palaeozoic	panegyrize	paper-faced	parahelium
packet soup	palaestral	panel board	paper guide	parakeelya
packing box	palaestric	panel fence	paper hanky	parakiting
pack-leader	palagonite	panel gauge	paperiness	paralipsis
pack-needle	palatalise	panel-house	paper-knife	paralleled
pack or peel	palatality	panel plane	paperknife	parallelly
pack-pedlar	palatalize	panel stamp	papermaker	paralogise
packsaddle	palateless	panel study	paper money	paralogism
pack-saddle	palatially	panel-thief	paper plate	paralogist
pack-straps	palatinate	panel truck	paper round	paralogize
pack them in	palatogram	Pangasinan	paper route	paralogous
packthread	paleaceous	pangenesis	paper shale	Paralympic
padded cell	Palermitan	pangenetic	paper-shell	paramagnet
paddle ball	palfrenier	panguingue	paper tiger	paramecium
paddle boat	palimpsest	panhandler	paper towel	paramedian
paddle-crab	palindrome	Panhard rod	paper-works	parametral
paddlefish	palisading	panic party	Papiamento	parametric
paddle foot	palisander	paniculate	papilionid	parametron
paddle-like	palladious	Panislamic	papillated	paramnesia
paddle-wood	pallasitic	pani-wallah	papillitis	paramnesic
Paddy Doyle	pall-bearer	panjandrum	papillomas	paramoudra
paddy field	pallbearer	pannier bag	papistical	paramouncy
paddymelon	pallescent	pannierman	papulation	paramyosin
paddy wagon	palliation	panography	papulosity	Paraná pine
Paddy wagon	palliative	panophobia	papyrology	paranormal
paddywhack	palliatory	panopticon	para-aortic	parapatric
pad the hoof	pallidness	panoramist	Parabellum	paraphasia
paederasty	palmaceous	panpsychic	parabiosis	paraphasic
paedeutics	palmatifid	pan-pudding	parabiotic	parapherna
paediatric	palm branch	pan-scourer	parablepsy	paraphilia
paedicator	palmchrist	Panslavism	parabolise	paraphilic
paedocracy	palmelloid	Panslavist	parabolist	paraphonia
paedophile	palmer-worm	pansophism	parabolize	paraphonic
paedotribe	palm-kernel	panspermia	paraboloid	paraphrase
Paelignian	Palm Sunday	pantalette	paracasein	paraphrast
paganistic	palm weevil	pantheress	para-church	paraphysis
pageanteer	palo blanco	pantherine	parachuter	paraplegia
page charge	palsy-walsy	pantherish	parade drum	paraplegic
page-galley	paltriness	pantie hose	parade ring	parapodial
page-turner	paludament	pantie raid	paradiddle	parapodium
pagination	palustrine	pantograph	paradingly	parapraxis
pagoda tree	palynology	pantologic	paradisaic	para-rescue
paideutics	pampas deer	pantometer	paradisean	paraselene
pailletted	pampelmoes	pantometry	paradisiac	parasexual
painkiller	pamphleted	pantomimic	paradisial	parasitise
painlessly	pamphletic	pantophagy	paradisian	parasitism
paintbrush	pan-African	pantoscope	paradoctor	parasitize
painted cup	Panamanian	pantothere	paradoxism	parasitoid
paint-frame	pan-and-tilt	pan-washing	paradoxist	parasol ant
paintiness	pan-Arabism	papal court	paradoxure	parastades
paint spray	Pancake Day	papal cross	paraenesis	parastatal
paint stick	pancake-ice	papal vicar	paraenetic	parastichy
paintstick	panchronic	papaverine	paraffinic	paratactic
pair of oars	pancosmism	papaverous	parafiscal	parathesis
Paisleyism	pancratist	paper birch	parafoveal	paratroops

paravisual	parramatta	pastorally	pave the way	pecker-head
paraxially	parricidal	pastorship	paving-tile	peckerwood
paraxylene	parrotbill	pastry-cook	pawnbroker	pectinated
parazonium	parrot-coal	pasturable	pawn-ticket	peculation
parcel bomb	parrot-fish	Patagonian	payability	peculative
parcel-gilt	parrotfish	Patavinian	pay-as-you-go	peculiarly
parcellate	parrot-like	Patavinity	Payne's grey	pedagogics
parcelling	parsley-bed	patch-board	pay-off line	pedagogism
parcel post	parson-bird	patchboard	pay station	pedagogist
parcel-wise	parsonhood	patchiness	pea-brained	pedalboard
parchmenty	parsonical	patch panel	Peace Corps	pedal cycle
pardonable	partakable	patchworky	peacefully	pedalferic
pardonably	parthenian	pâté maison	peacemaker	pedal point
pardon-bell	partialise	patentable	peace prize	pedal power
pardonless	partialism	patent roll	peach aphid	pedal straw
pareiasaur	partialist	Patent Roll	peach-black	pedantical
parenchyma	partiality	Pateresque	peach-bloom	pedanticly
parentally	partialize	paternally	peacherino	pedantries
parent cell	partial sum	pâte tendre	peachiness	pederastic
parentelic	participle	patha patha	peach Melba	pedestrial
parenteral	particular	pathematic	peach-stone	pedestrian
parenthood	partisanly	pathetical	peachy-keen	pede-window
parentless	partnering	pathfinder	peacockery	pediatrics
parents' day	partocracy	path length	peacock-eye	pedication
parent ship	partridges	path-master	Peacockian	pedicatory
parentship	parturiate	pathogenic	peacockish	pedicellar
par exemple	parturient	pathognomy	peacock ore	pedicelled
parfocally	party-liner	pathologic	peakedness	pediculous
pariah brig	party piano	pathotoxin	peak factor	pedicurist
Parian ware	parvenudom	patibulary	peak-to-peak	pedigerous
paribuntal	parvenuism	patibulate	Peano curve	pediluvium
pari-mutuel	parvovirus	patination	peanut worm	pedimental
Paris daisy	pas ciseaux	patisserie	pear-blight	pedimented
Paris green	pas d'action	patriality	pearl-berry	pedologist
parish mass	pasigraphy	patriarchy	pearl-diver	pedomotive
parish poor	Pasionaria	patriation	pearl-fruit	pedosphere
parish pump	pasquinade	patriciate	pearliness	pedotrophy
parish work	passageway	patricidal	pearl onion	peduncular
park course	passed pawn	patrilocal	pearl-perch	peely-wally
parking bay	passiflora	patrioteer	pearl-shell	peeping Tom
parking lot	passimeter	patriotess	pearlsides	peerie folk
parking tag	passionary	patriotism	pearl-stone	peerlessly
park-keeper	passionate	patristics	pearl-white	peer review
park-leaves	passionful	patrocliny	pearly king	pegmatitic
parliament	Passionist	patrolette	Pearly King	peg-tankard
parlour-car	passivator	patrolling	pearmonger	Peirce's Law
parmacetty	pass muster	patronizer	Pearsonian	pejoration
parmigiana	pass the hat	patronless	pear-sucker	pejorative
Parnassian	pasteboard	patronship	peasantess	Peking duck
Parnellism	paste grain	patronymic	peasantism	pelargonic
Parnellite	pastellist	pattawalla	peasantist	pelargonin
parodiable	pasteurise	patten-shoe	pease-brose	Pele's tears
parodistic	Pasteurism	patterning	pea-shooter	pellagrose
paroecious	pasteurize	patternise	peashooter	pellagrous
paronychia	paste-water	patternism	peau-de-soie	pelletable
paronymous	past future	patternist	pebble-dash	pellet bell
parovarian	pasticcios	patternize	pebble lens	pellet bomb
parovarium	pasticheur	patter-song	pebble tool	pelletizer
paroxysmal	pastillage	patulously	pebble-ware	pellet mill
paroxysmic	past master	Paulianist	peccadillo	pellicular
paroxytone	pastorales	Paul Revere	pêche Melba	pellucidly
parqueting	pastoralia	paunchiest	pecked line	peltmonger

pelvic arch
pelvic brim
pelvimeter
pelvimetry
pelycosaur
pemphigoid
pemphigous
penalty box
penannular
pencil beam
pencil case
pencil-line
pencilling
pencil mark
pendeloque
pendentive
Penelopean
Penelopize
penetrable
penetralia
penetrance
penetrator
pen-feather
penguinery
penicillia
penicillin
penicillus
peninsular
penitently
penmanship
pennatulid
penny-a-line
penny black
penny cress
penny-grass
penny plain
pennyroyal
penny Scots
penny stock
penny-stone
pennyworth
penologist
pen-pushing
pensionary
pensioneer
pension off
pentachord
pentagonal
pentahedra
pentalogue
pentameral
pentameric
pentameter
pentapedal
pentaploid
pentapolis
pentaprism
pentastich
pentastome
pentastyle
Pentateuch
pentathlon

pentatomid
pentatonic
pentimenti
pentimento
pentograph
pentosuria
pentosuric
pentstemon
penumbrous
peoplehood
people-king
peopleless
people's car
people's war
pepperbush
peppercorn
pepperette
pepperidge
pepper mill
peppermint
pepper-root
pepper soup
pepper tree
pepper-vine
pepperwood
pepperwort
pepsinogen
peptizable
peptolysis
peptolytic
peptonizer
peptonuria
peracetate
peralkalic
percentage
percentile
percentual
perception
perceptive
perceptron
perceptual
perchloric
percipient
percolator
perculsion
percurrent
percursory
percussion
percussive
perdricide
perdurable
perdurably
perdurance
père et fils
peremptory
perfect gas
perfection
Perfectist
perfective
perfervour
perficient
perfidious

perflation
perfoliate
perforable
perforated
perforator
perforce of
performing
pergelisol
periapical
periastral
periastron
pericardia
pericardic
pericentre
periclinal
periclinia
periculous
pericyclic
pericystic
peridental
peridermal
peridinian
peridotite
periegesis
perifoveal
perifusate
perifusion
perigonial
perigonium
perigynium
perigynous
perihaemal
perihelion
perikaryal
perikaryon
perilla oil
perilously
peril point
perimetral
perimetric
perimysium
perineural
periocular
periodical
periosteal
periosteum
peripatize
peripeteia
peripherad
peripheral
peripheric
periphonic
periphrase
periportal
peripteral
periscopic
perishable
perishably
perishless
perishment
peristomal
peristylar

peritectic
peritoneal
peritoneum
periungual
periwigged
periwinkle
perjurious
perlaceous
perlection
permafrost
permanence
permanency
permansive
permeation
permeative
permethrin
permillage
permirific
permission
permissive
permitting
Permo-Trias
permutable
Pernambuco
pernicious
pernickety
pernoctate
perofskite
peroration
peroratory
perovskite
peroxidase
peroxidize
peroxisome
perpension
perpetrate
perpetuana
perpetuate
perpetuity
perplexing
perplexity
perquisite
perrhenate
perruquier
per saltire
persecutee
persecutor
Persian cat
Persianist
Persianize
Persian red
Persian rug
persicaria
persiennes
persiflage
persifleur
persistent
persistive
personable
personably
personal ad
personalia

personally
personalty
personator
personeity
personhood
personkind
per stirpes
perstringe
persuading
persuasion
persuasive
pertinence
pertinency
perturbant
perturbate
perversely
perversion
perversity
perversive
peshwaship
Pestalozzi
pesterment
pestersome
pesticidal
pestilence
petaloidal
petechiate
Peter-penny
Peter's fish
petiteness
petitional
petitionee
petitioner
petit point
petits pois
Petrarchan
petrescent
petrogenic
petroglyph
petrograph
petrolatum
petrol blue
petrol bomb
petroleous
petrol head
petrolless
petrologic
petrol pump
Petronella
petrosilex
pets' corner
pettedness
pettichaps
petticoaty
petting zoo
petty canon
petty morel
petulantly
Petzval sum
pewterwort
phagedaena
phagocytic

phagosomal	philosophe	photophily	picket line	pilgriming
phalangeal	philosophy	photophore	picking peg	pilgrimise
phalangist	phlebogram	photo-print	pickpocket	pilgrimize
Phalangist	phlebology	photo-recce	pick-up tube	piliferous
phalangite	phlebotomy	photo-shock	picnic area	piligerous
phalangium	phlegmasia	photo shoot	picnickery	pillar-buoy
Phaleucian	phlegmatic	photostory	picnicking	pillar-file
phallicism	phlegmless	phototaxis	picnic meal	pillarless
phallocrat	phlegmonic	phototoxic	picric acid	pillar rose
phalloidin	phlogistic	phototroph	picrotoxin	pill-beetle
phanerogam	phlogiston	phototropy	pictograph	pilliwinks
phantasied	phlogopite	phragmites	pictorical	pillow-bere
phantasies	phocomelia	phrase book	Picts' house	pillow-book
phantasise	phocomelic	phraseless	picturable	pillowcase
phantasize	Phoenician	phrase name	picturedom	pillow lace
phantasmal	pholcodine	phrenology	picture hat	pillow lava
phantasmic	phone booth	phthisical	piece-goods	pillow-sham
phantastry	phonematic	phthisicky	piece-mould	pillowslip
Pharisaean	phone patch	phycobilin	piece-price	pillow sofa
Pharisaism	phoneyness	phycobiont	pie-counter	pillow talk
pharmacies	phonically	phylactery	pied-à-terre	pillow tank
pharmacist	phonogenic	phylarchic	Pied Friars	pillow-word
Pharsalian	phonograph	phyllodial	pie diagram	pill-popper
pharyngeal	phonolitic	phyllosome	piemontite	pill pusher
phascogale	phonologic	phyllotaxy	pierceable	pilocystic
phase angle	phonometer	phylloxera	piercement	pilot-bread
phase-array	phonometry	phylogenic	piercingly	pilot cable
phasemeter	phonotypic	Physeptone	pier-master	pilot chute
phaseollin	phorometer	physiatric	pier-mirror	pilot-cloth
phase space	phoronomic	physically	Piesporter	pilot-flame
phasically	phosgenite	physic-ball	piet-my-vrou	pilot house
pheasantry	phosphagen	physicking	piezometer	pilot light
phelloderm	phosphated	physiocrat	pig-boiling	pilot-major
phenacaine	phosphatic	physiology	pigeon drop	pilot snake
phenacetin	phosphinic	phytocidal	pigeongram	pilot valve
phenelzine	phosphonic	phytogenic	pigeon-hawk	pilot whale
phenformin	phosphoric	phytolacca	pigeon-hole	Piltdowner
phenocryst	phosphorus	phytometer	pigeonitic	pimento red
phenolized	phosphoryl	phytomonad	pigeon-loft	pimpmobile
phenologic	Photianism	phytophagy	pigeon pair	pinacocyte
phenomenal	Photianist	phytotoxic	pigeon-plum	pinacoidal
phenomenon	photically	phytotoxin	pigeon-post	pina colada
phenotypic	photodimer	pianissimi	pigeonries	pinacoline
pheromonal	photodiode	pianissimo	pigeon tick	pinacolone
philatelic	photo-essay	pianoforte	pigeon-toed	pince-nezed
Philippian	photoflash	piano organ	pigeon-weed	pincer-like
philippina	photoflood	piano score	pigeon-wing	pinchingly
Philippine	photogenic	piano stool	pigeon-wood	pinchpenny
Philippini	photograph	piano-tuner	piggy-wiggy	pinch-point
Philippise	photolitho	picaresque	pig-hunting	pinch-waist
Philippist	photolysis	picayunish	pig in a poke	pinch-wheel
Philippize	photolytic	Piccadilly	pigmentary	pincushion
Philistian	Photomaton	piccalilli	pig-sticker	pineal body
Philistine	photomesic	piccaninny	pigsticker	pine-barren
phillumeny	photomeson	piccoloist	pig-washing	pine beauty
philocynic	photometer	pichiciago	piked whale	pine-kernel
philologer	photometry	pichiciego	pilastered	pine lander
philologic	photomixer	pick a fight	pilastrade	pine linnet
philologue	photomural	pickaninny	pile-driver	pine-lizard
philomathy	photonovel	pick a thank	piledriver	pine marten
philopatry	photopathy	pick-cheese	pilgrimage	pine-needle
philopoena	photophile	picket-boat	pilgrimess	piney resin

pin-feather
pinguecula
pinguicula
pinguidity
pinguitude
pin-jointed
pink button
pink chaser
pink-collar
pink-footed
pink salmon
pink-washed
pinnatifid
pinnothere
pinocytose
pinosylvin
pinpointed
pinstriped
pinstriper
Pintsch gas
pioneerdom
pious fraud
piped music
pipelining
Pipe-Office
pipe-opener
piperazine
piperidine
pipe wrench
piping crow
pipperidge
pipsissewa
Piranesian
pirimicarb
pirouetter
piscifauna
pisolithic
piss artist
piss-cutter
piss-taking
pistachios
pistillary
pistillate
pistilline
pistillode
pistillody
pistilloid
pistolgram
pistol grip
pistol-hand
pistolling
pistol-shot
pistol-whip
piston-head
piston ring
piston slap
Pitcairner
pitch-black
pitch-brand
pitch curve
pitcherful
pitch-fibre

pitchiness
pitchmeter
pitch-penny
pitchstone
pit-headman
pitheciine
pith helmet
pithiatism
Pithiviers
pitilessly
pitot meter
pityriasis
pivotalism
pivotal man
pivot class
pivot-joint
pixelation
pixilation
pixillated
pizzicatos
place brick
place horse
place-money
placentary
place-value
placidness
placodioid
plagiarise
plagiarism
plagiarist
plagiarize
plagiosere
plague-flea
plagueless
plague pipe
plaguesome
plague spot
plainchant
plain flour
Plains Cree
plain tripe
plain weave
plait-dance
planarioid
planchette
Planck's law
plane chart
plane crash
planer-tree
planeshear
plane stock
plane-table
planetaria
planet cage
planetfall
planet-gear
planet-wide
plangently
plangorous
planholder
planimeter
planimetry

plank-owner
plank sheer
plank steak
planktonic
planlessly
planometer
planosolic
planospore
plansifter
plantation
planterdom
plant-louse
plashingly
plasma cell
plasmacyte
plasmagene
Plasmochin
plasmocyte
plasmodial
plasmodium
plasmogamy
plasmolyse
plasmolyte
plasmosome
plasmotomy
plastering
plasticate
plastician
plasticine
Plasticine
plasticise
plasticism
plasticity
plasticize
plastidome
plastidule
plastifier
plastogamy
plat du jour
plate count
plated wire
plate glass
platelayer
platemaker
plate metal
plate paper
platformed
platformer
Platformer
Platonical
platteland
platterful
platycodon
platymeria
platymeric
platypuses
plauditory
play-acting
play around
playboyish
playbroker
play-by-play

play-centre
play-doctor
playfellow
playground
play hookey
play it cool
playleader
playmonger
play possum
play scales
play school
playsomely
playstreet
play the ape
play the fox
play the hop
play the man
play the wag
play truant
playwright
playwriter
pleadingly
pleasanter
pleasantly
pleasantry
pleasaunce
pleasingly
pleasurist
plebeiance
plebeianly
plebiscita
plebiscite
pledgeable
pledge card
pleiomazia
pleiotropy
plenilunal
plenilunar
plenishing
plentitude
pleochroic
pleomastia
pleomorphy
pleonastic
pleonectic
plerematic
pleromatic
plerophory
plesiosaur
pleurodont
pleurotomy
pleximeter
plexometer
pliability
pliantness
plimsolled
pliosaurus
ploddingly
plonkingly
plottingly
ploughable
plough-alms

plough back
plough-beam
ploughbote
plough-foot
plough-gate
plough-gear
plough-head
plough-iron
plough-land
ploughland
plough-line
plough-shoe
plough-soil
plough-stot
plough-tail
pluck a rose
pluckiness
plug-drawer
plug nozzle
plug-switch
plug-uglies
plumassier
plum-colour
plummeting
plumminess
plum tomato
plunderage
plunderous
plunge bath
plunge pool
plungingly
pluperfect
pluralizer
plurimodal
plus-foured
plushiness
pluteiform
plutocracy
plutogogue
plutolater
plutolatry
plutomania
plutomanic
plutonomic
pluviosity
pneumatics
pneumatism
pneumatist
pneumatize
pneumocele
pneumogram
pneumotach
pochade box
pocketable
pocketbook
pocketfuls
pocket-hole
pocketless
pocket-like
pocket-size
pocket veto
pock-marked

pocomaniac	Police Motu	polygenous	pomiferous	porrection
podiatrist	police trap	polyglycol	pommelling	portacabin
podothecal	policlinic	polygonize	pomologist	portacaval
poena damni	policy loan	polygonous	Pomoranian	Portakabin
poetastery	policy-slip	polygraphy	pompelmous	portal vein
poetically	polioviral	polygynist	ponce about	portamenti
Poetic Edda	poliovirus	polygynous	pond-barrow	portamento
poeticizer	polishable	polyhalite	ponderable	port-crayon
poeticness	polishedly	polyhedral	ponderance	portcullis
poetry-book	Polishness	polyhedric	ponderancy	portentous
poetryless	politburos	polyhedron	ponderment	porterless
pogamoggan	politeness	polyhistor	pond-skater	porterlike
pogonotomy	politician	polyhybrid	pond slider	portership
pohutukawa	politicise	polyhydric	ponerology	portfolios
poignantly	politicize	polyketide	ponticello	portionary
poikilitic	politicked	polylectal	pontifical	portionist
poinsettia	polkamania	polylithic	pontifices	portliness
point angle	pollen-cell	polymastia	pony-engine	portocaval
point-blank	pollenless	polymastic	pony report	port of call
point block	pollen-tube	polymathic	poodle-fake	port of exit
point break	pollinator	polymerase	pooh-pooher	portolanos
pointed fox	pollinctor	polymeride	Pooh-sticks	Portuguese
point-event	polling day	polymerise	pools panel	positional
point focus	pollinical	polymerism	poor fellow	positioner
point group	poll parrot	polymerize	poor people	positively
pointleted	Poll-parrot	polymerous	poor relief	positivism
point of lay	poll-rating	polymethyl	poorshouse	positivist
point paper	pollutedly	polymetric	pop culture	positivity
pointy-head	polo collar	polymictic	Popemobile	positronic
Poiseuille	polocrosse	polymorphy	popishness	posnjakite
poisonable	polo-necked	Polynesian	poplar grey	possession
poison book	Polovtsian	polynomial	poplar hawk	possessive
poison-bulb	Poltalloch	polyocracy	poplinette	possessory
poison-bush	polyanthus	polyolefin	popocratic	postage due
poison pill	polyarchic	polyparies	poppet-head	postal card
poison-tree	polyatomic	polyphagia	popularise	postal code
poison vine	polybasite	polyphasic	popularish	postal note
poisonwood	polycarpic	Polyphemic	popularism	postal vote
Poissonian	polycation	Polyphemus	popularist	post-and-pan
Poisson law	polychaete	polyphenol	popularity	post-bellum
poke-bonnet	polycholia	polyphonic	popularize	post-chaise
poke-greens	polychoral	polyploidy	population	post-climax
poker-faced	polychrest	polypnoeic	populistic	postclitic
poke-sleeve	polychrome	polypodies	populously	post-coital
polar curve	polychromy	polypoidal	poriferous	post coitum
polarities	polyclimax	polyprotic	porismatic	post-common
polar light	polyclinic	polyrhythm	pork barrel	postcostal
polarogram	polyclonal	polysarcia	pork-pie hat	postcyclic
polar orbit	polycormic	polysemous	pornbroker	postdating
polar plant	polycotton	polysomaty	pornocracy	postdental
polatouche	polycyclic	polyspermy	pornograph	post-editor
pole-jumper	polycystic	polystelic	pornophile	post-exilic
polemicise	polydactyl	polytheism	porogamous	post factum
polemicist	polydipsia	polytheist	porousness	post festum
polemicize	polydymite	polythelia	porpentine	postholder
polemology	polyethene	polythetic	Porphyrian	posthumous
polemonium	polyethnic	polytocous	porphyries	postillate
poles apart	polygamist	polytomous	porphyrise	postillion
pole-screen	polygamize	polytropic	porphyrite	post-larval
policeable	polygamous	polytypism	porphyrize	postliminy
police bail	polygenism	polyvalent	porphyroid	postmaster
police boat	polygenist	Pomeranian	porraceous	postmature

postmedial	powder-like	prayer-bead	predecease	prenuptial
post-modern	powder-mill	prayer-bell	pre-decimal	pre-Oedipal
postmodern	powder-plot	prayer book	predeclare	pre-orbital
post-mortem	powder puff	prayer card	predestine	pre-package
post-ocular	powder room	prayer-desk	predestiny	prepalatal
post office	powder snow	prayer-flag	prediality	preparable
Post Office	power block	prayerless	predicable	preparator
post-partum	power board	prayer-mill	predicator	preparedly
post-runner	power brake	prayer-wall	prediction	prepayable
postscript	power cable	prayerwise	predictive	prepayment
post-season	power-crane	praying mat	predictory	prepensely
postulancy	power-drive	preachable	predispose	pre-planned
postulator	power élite	preach down	prednisone	prepollent
postulatum	powerfully	preacherly	pre-eminent	prepolymer
postverbal	powerhouse	preachiest	pre-emption	prepositor
potability	power level	preachment	pre-emptive	prepossess
potamogale	power plant	pre-adamite	preen gland	prepotence
potamology	powerplant	pre-adjunct	pre-English	prepotency
potash alum	power point	prealbumin	pre-exilian	preppiness
potato-bean	power train	preallable	prefashion	preprimate
potato-cake	pozzolanic	preallably	prefecture	pre-process
potato chip	practicant	preambular	preferable	preprocess
potato fern	practician	preamplify	preferably	pre-program
potato hook	practising	pre-animism	preference	preprogram
potato-ring	praecocial	pre-appoint	preferment	prep school
potato-trap	praecordia	pre-arrange	preferring	prepuberal
potato-vine	Praedesque	prearrange	prefixable	prepuberty
Potawatomi	praefervid	pre-baiting	prefixally	prepunched
pot-bellied	praelector	prebendary	prefixture	pre-qualify
pot bellies	praeludium	prebiology	preformism	prequalify
pot courage	praemunire	precarious	preformist	Pre-Raphael
potentiate	praepositi	precaution	prefrontal	pre-release
potentilla	praepostor	precedence	pregenital	prerequire
potentness	praeputium	precedency	preglacial	presageful
pot-furnace	praesidium	precentral	pregnantly	presbyopia
pot-hunting	Praesidium	precentrix	preharvest	presbyopic
pot-pourris	praetorial	preceptial	prehensile	presbytery
pot-shooter	praetorian	preception	prehension	prescience
pot-shotter	praetorium	preceptive	prehensive	pre-scoring
potter's rot	pragmatica	preceptory	prehistory	prescriber
potter wasp	pragmatics	preceptual	prehominid	presension
potty-chair	pragmatise	precession	pre-imagine	present-day
potty-train	pragmatism	preciosity	pre-incline	presential
pot-valiant	pragmatist	preciously	pre-Islamic	presentism
pot-walling	pragmatize	precipitin	prejudiced	presentist
pouch-mouth	prairie dog	Preclassic	prelatical	presentoir
Poulsen arc	prairie fox	preclusion	prelection	pre-service
pouncet-box	prairie hen	preclusive	prelingual	preserving
pound brush	praiseless	precocious	prelogical	presidence
pound close	praise name	precognise	preludious	presidency
pound-force	praise poem	precognize	premarital	presidiary
pound-house	praise poet	precompose	premaxilla	presignify
pound overt	praise song	preconcert	premedical	press agent
pound Scots	praisingly	precondemn	pre-meiotic	press baron
poundstone	praisseagh	precontour	pre-mention	press-board
powderable	pram-pusher	precordial	premiation	pressboard
powder base	prandially	precordium	pre-milking	press cloth
powder blue	prat digger	precurrent	premixture	press corps
powder-burn	prate-apace	precursive	premonitor	press flesh
powder-down	pratincole	precursory	prenatally	press-house
powder-horn	praxeology	predaceous	prenominal	pressingly
powderless	praxiology	predacious	pre-nuclear	press-money

press proof
pressurise
pressurize
prestation
prestellar
pre-stretch
presumable
presumably
presumedly
presuppose
presystole
pretendant
pretendent
pretending
pre-tension
pretension
pretensive
pretenture
prettified
prettifier
prettifies
prettiness
pretty much
pretty near
pretty well
prevailing
prevalence
prevalency
prevenance
prevenient
prevention
preventive
previously
prevocalic
prevoyance
prezygotic
price-fixed
price index
price point
prick-eared
prick-hedge
pricking-up
prickliest
pricklouse
prickly ash
prickly rat
prick-madam
prick punch
pridefully
priesthood
priestless
priestlike
priestling
priestship
priggishly
prima donna
prima facie
primaquine
primatical
primaveral
prime mover
primer fine

primevally
primiparae
primipilar
primipilus
primo buffo
primordial
primordian
primordium
primrosing
princehood
princelier
princelike
princeling
princeship
princessly
prince-wood
principate
principled
print chain
printeries
printfield
printmaker
print media
print order
print train
print union
print wheel
printworks
priorities
prioritise
prioritize
Priscoline
prismatoid
prismoidal
prison bars
prison-bird
prison camp
prison-crop
prisonment
prissiness
pristinely
private bar
private car
private eye
private law
private war
privatizer
privet hawk
privet-like
privileged
privy parts
privy purse
prize agent
prize court
prizefight
prize money
probenecid
problemist
procacious
procambial
procambium
procaryote

procedendo
procedural
proceeding
process ink
procession
processive
processual
prochloraz
pro-choicer
proclaimer
proclivity
procoelous
procreator
procrypsis
procryptic
proctalgia
proctology
proctorial
proctorize
procumbent
procurable
procurance
pro-curator
procurator
procurrent
procuticle
prodeltaic
prodigally
prodigious
producible
production
productive
profection
profession
proficient
profile cut
profitable
profitably
profitless
proflavine
profligacy
profligate
profluence
profluvium
profounder
profoundly
profulgent
profundity
progenitor
proglacial
proglottid
proglottis
prognathic
prognostic
programmed
programmer
progressor
pro hac vice
prohibited
prohibiter
prohibitor
prohormone

proinsulin
projectile
projection
projective
projecture
projicient
prokaryote
prokinesis
prokinetic
proleptics
proletaire
proletkult
prolixness
proloculus
prolocutor
prologizer
prologuing
prologuise
prologuize
prolongate
promenader
Promethean
promethium
prometryne
prominence
prominency
prominenti
promiscous
promiseful
promissive
promissory
promontory
promotable
promotress
prompt book
prompt-copy
promptness
prompt-note
prompt side
promptuary
promulgate
pronephric
pronephros
pronograde
pronominal
pronounced
pronouncer
pronucleus
pro-nuncios
prooestrus
proof-glass
proof-plane
proof-sheet
propachlor
propadiene
propagable
propaganda
propagator
propagular
propanidid
propanoate
propellant

propellent
propelling
propendent
propensely
propension
propensity
propeptide
proper name
properness
proper noun
Propertian
propertied
properties
prophecies
prophesied
prophesier
prophesies
prophetess
prophetism
prophylaxy
propionate
propitiate
propitious
proportion
proposable
propositum
propositus
propounder
propraetor
proprietor
pro-proctor
propulsion
propulsive
propulsory
propylaeum
propylitic
pro-ratable
proroguing
proruption
prosaicism
proscenium
prosciutto
proscriber
prosecutor
prose idyll
proseology
prose sense
prosilient
prosimious
prosodical
prosopylar
prospector
prospectus
prosperity
prosperous
prostanoic
prostatism
prosternal
prosternum
prostheses
prosthesis
prosthetic

Prostigmin	protrudent	pteromorph	pump-handle	push-towing
prostitute	protrusile	pterylosis	pump island	pussy posse
prostomial	protrusion	Ptolemaean	pumpkin pie	put a mock on
prostomium	protrusive	Ptolemaism	pump-primer	put-and-call
prostrator	proud flesh	Ptolemaist	punch board	put-and-take
protandric	proud-heart	puberulent	punch-drunk	put an end to
protanopia	provection	puberulous	punch graft	put a slur on
protanopic	proveditor	pubescence	punch-house	put a stop to
proteanism	provenance	publically	punchiness	putatively
protectant	proverbial	public bill	punch-press	put forward
protection	providable	public good	punctation	put in force
protective	providence	publicitor	punctiform	put it there
protectory	provincial	public life	punctiliar	putlog-hole
protectrix	provitamin	publicness	punctilios	put on an act
protegulum	provocable	public weal	punctually	put on a show
proteiform	provocator	pub theatre	punctuator	put on flesh
proteinase	provokable	puck-chaser	punctulate	put-putting
proteinoid	prowessful	puck-needle	Punic faith	putrescent
proteinous	proximally	pudding-bag	punishable	putrescine
pro tempore	prudential	pudding-pie	punishably	putridness
protension	pruriently	puddle-duck	punishment	put spurs to
protensity	Prussianly	puerperium	punitively	put store by
protensive	Przewalski	puffed rice	punk rocker	put through
protention	psalmodise	puffer fish	punto banco	putting-off
proteolyse	psalmodist	puffinosis	pupiparous	put to a vote
protervity	psalmodize	puff pastry	puppet-play	put to death
Protestant	psalterial	puff sleeve	puppet-show	put to grass
protestive	psalterian	pugilistic	puppyishly	put to shame
prothallia	psalteries	pugil stick	puppy-tooth	put to sleep
prothallus	psalterion	Puginesque	Purbeckian	putty-knife
prothetely	psalterium	pugnacious	purblindly	putty medal
protobiont	psammosere	puirt-a-beul	Purcellian	puzzlehead
protocolar	psephocrat	puissantly	purchasing	puzzlement
protocolic	psephology	pukka sahib	pure merino	puzzle-pate
protoconch	pseudandry	pulicosity	purging nut	puzzlingly
protoconid	pseudobulb	pull a boner	purinergic	pycnocline
protogenic	pseudocarp	pull a train	puritanise	pycnogonid
protograph	pseudocide	pulled wool	puritanism	pycnometer
protohuman	pseudocode	pull-hitter	puritanize	pycnospore
protologue	pseudocoel	pullovered	Purkinjean	pycnostyle
protolysis	pseudocyst	pull stakes	purlieu-man	pygmy-flint
protolytic	pseudodoxy	pull-stroke	purple haze	pygmy goose
protomeric	pseudogamy	pull-switch	purple lake	pyjama case
protonemal	pseudogene	pull the pin	purpleness	pyknolepsy
protopapas	pseudogley	pully-hauly	purple zone	pyocyanase
protophyll	pseudogout	pulmometer	purposeful	pyocyanine
protophyte	pseudology	pulmonaria	purse-pride	pyogenesis
protoplasm	pseudosoph	pulp-cavity	purse-proud	pyogenetic
protoplast	pseudostem	pulpectomy	purserette	pyracantha
protostele	psilocybin	pulpitical	pursership	pyramidate
protostome	psittacine	pulsatance	purse seine	pyramidion
prototroch	psittacism	pulsatilla	pursuantly	pyramidist
prototroph	Psyche knot	pulse-label	pursuivant	pyramidize
prototropy	psychiater	pulse radar	purtenance	pyranoside
prototypal	psychiatry	pulsimeter	purulently	pyrazoline
prototypic	psychicist	pultaceous	purveyance	pyrazolone
protovirus	psychogeny	pultrusion	puschkinia	pyrenocarp
protoxylem	psychogram	pulverable	push around	pyrethroid
protozoans	psychology	pulverizer	push-button	pyretology
protracted	psychopath	pulvinated	pushmobile	pyridazine
protractor	psychopomp	pummelling	push-stroke	pyridoxine
protreptic	pteranodon	pump-action	push things	pyrimidine

pyrochlore	qualup bell	quick-grass	radarscope	rain-doctor
pyrogallic	quandaries	quickhatch	radar-sonde	rainforest
pyrogallol	quangocrat	quick march	radar-track	rain jungle
pyrogenous	quantified	quick-match	radial axle	rainmaking
pyrography	quantifier	quicksandy	radial-flow	rain shadow
pyrologist	quantifies	quickthorn	radicalise	rain-shower
pyrolusite	quantitate	quick trick	radicalism	raise a dust
pyromaniac	quantities	quick water	radicality	raisedness
pyrometric	quantitive	quiddative	radicalize	raisin tree
pyromucate	quarantine	quiddities	radication	Rajasthani
pyrophoric	quarentene	quid pro quo	radicchios	rajpramukh
pyrophorus	quarkonium	quidsworth	radicellar	Rajya Sabha
pyrosphere	quarrelled	quiescence	radiculose	rakishness
pyrotechny	quarreller	quiescency	radio-assay	rally-cross
pyroxenite	quarrenden	quietistic	radioassay	rallycross
pyroxenoid	quarriable	quill drive	radiogenic	rallyingly
pyrrhichii	quarry tile	quinacrine	radiograph	ramblingly
Pyrrhonian	quartation	quinestrol	radio-label	Ramboesque
Pyrrhonism	quarterage	quingenary	radiolaria	ramfeezled
Pyrrhonist	quarter-boy	quinquefid	radiologic	ramificate
pyrrhonize	quarter day	quinsy-wort	radiolysis	rampacious
pyrrhotine	quarter-ill	quint major	radiolytic	rampageous
pyrrhotite	quartering	quint minor	radiometal	ram-raiding
Pythagoras	quarterman	quintuplet	radiometer	ramshackle
Pythagoric	quarter-saw	quirkiness	radiometry	ramshackly
pythiambic	quart major	quite other	radiopaque	ranch house
pythogenic	quartzitic	quit hold of	radiophare	ranch wagon
pythonical	quartz lamp	quiverfuls	radiophone	rancidness
pythonissa	quaternary	quizmaster	radiophony	randomizer
Qatabanian	quaternate	quiz-master	radiophoto	randomness
quack-quack	quaternion	quizzingly	radio range	random shot
quadrangle	quaternise	quoad sacra	radioscope	random walk
quadrantal	quaternity	rabbinical	radioscopy	range-plate
quadrantic	quaternize	rabbinship	radio shack	range-proof
Quadrantid	quatorzain	rabbit ball	radiosonde	rangership
quadraplex	quatrefoil	rabbit-fish	radiotelex	ranging-rod
quadratrix	queasiness	rabbit food	Radio Three	ranitidine
quadrature	queen conch	rabbit-foot	radiotoxic	ranivorous
quadrennia	queenliest	rabbit-like	radium beam	rank entire
quadriceps	queen olive	rabbit's ear	radium bomb	rannel-tree
quadriform	queenright	rabbit test	radium burn	rannygazoo
quadrilled	queen's head	rabblement	radium dial	ransomable
quadrilogy	queen-sized	rabble rout	raft-bridge	ransom-bill
quadripole	queen's lace	racecourse	rafterless	ransomless
quadrireme	Queensland	race memory	raft spider	ransom note
quadrivial	queen's pawn	race-reader	ragamuffin	ranterpike
quadrivium	queen's rook	race record	rag-chewing	rantle-tree
quadrumane	queen's-ware	race theory	rag content	ranunculin
quadrumvir	quenchable	race walker	raggedness	ranunculus
quadrupler	quenchless	rachiotomy	ragman roll	Raoult's law
quadruplet	quercitrin	Rachmanism	rah-rah girl	rappelling
quadruplex	quercitron	Rachmanite	railleries	rapping bar
quadrupole	quern-stone	racing flag	railroader	rapporteur
quaestuary	queryingly	racing form	rail timber	raptorious
quagginess	questingly	racing-line	railwayana	Rarotongan
quailfinch	questionee	racket-ball	railwaydom	rascallion
quaintness	questioner	racket-tail	railwayman	rasterizer
Quaker City	quick bread	rackleness	railwaymen	rat-catcher
Quaker Oats	quick-break	rack-master	railway rug	ratcheting
qualitated	quick death	rack-renter	rain bonnet	rate-buster
qualminess	quickening	raconteuse	rainbow boa	ratifiable
qualmishly	quick-firer	radar fence	raincoated	rationally

ration book	reasonable	reconsider	redialling	reflective
ration card	reasonably	recontinue	red iron ore	reflexible
rattle-bush	reasonless	recontract	rediscount	reflourish
rattle-head	reason will	recordable	rediscover	refocusing
rattle-jack	reassemble	record club	redissolve	refocussed
rattle-pate	reassembly	recordless	redistrict	reformable
rattletrap	reassertor	record type	redivision	Reform Club
rattle-weed	reassuring	recoupable	red jasmine	refractile
rattlingly	rebaptizer	recoupment	red lattice	refracting
raunchiest	rebatement	recoveries	red meerkat	refraction
raveningly	Rebeccaite	recreantly	Redmondism	refractive
ravenously	rebellious	re-creation	Redmondite	refractory
raven-stone	rebiddable	recreation	red morocco	refreshful
ravinement	rebirthing	recreative	red nucleus	refreshing
ravishment	reboundant	recrudency	redolently	refringent
rawinsonde	rebukeable	recrudesce	redoubling	refuelling
raw lobster	rebukingly	rectangled	red palm oil	refugeedom
ray diagram	rebuttable	rectorship	redressive	refugeeism
ray therapy	recallable	rectoscope	red rock-cod	refulgence
ray-tracing	recallment	rectoscopy	red sanders	refulgency
razor blade	recappable	recumbence	redshifted	refundable
razor-edged	recarriage	recumbency	red snapper	refundment
razor-grass	receivable	recuperate	red spinner	refuse bail
razor's edge	recentness	recurrence	red-spotted	refutation
razor-sharp	receptacle	recurrency	red stopper	refutative
razor-shell	receptible	recusation	reduceless	regainable
razor-slash	recercelée	recyclable	redundance	regainment
razzmatazz	rechristen	redactoral	redundancy	regalement
reablement	recidivate	red admiral	red warning	regalities
reaccustom	recidivism	red arsenic	red zinc ore	regardable
reach truck	recidivist	red atrophy	reed-and-tie	regardless
reacquaint	recidivous	red-bellied	reed dagger	regard ring
reactivate	recipience	red-blooded	reed switch	regelation
reactively	recipiency	red buckeye	reef-tackle	regeneracy
reactivity	reciprocal	red cabbage	re-election	regenerant
readership	recitalist	red campion	re-eligible	regenerate
reading age	recitation	Red Chamber	reel-to-reel	regent-bird
readjuster	recitative	red channel	re-emergent	regentship
readmitted	recivilize	red-cheeked	re-emission	reggaefied
read-mostly	recklessly	red-chested	re-emphasis	regicidism
readoption	reckonable	Red Chinese	re-enaction	regimental
ready-mixed	reclassify	red-cooking	re-enforcer	regionally
ready money	reclinable	red country	re-engineer	registered
reafferent	recogitate	red-crested	re-enlister	registerer
reafforest	recognitor	red-crossed	re-entrance	registrant
Reaganomic	recognizee	redcurrant	re-entrancy	registrary
realizable	recognizer	redecorate	Reeperbahn	registrate
realizably	recognizor	rededicate	re-erection	registries
reallocate	recoil gear	redeemable	re-evaluate	regnal year
reallotted	recoilless	redeemably	re-exchange	regolithic
real school	recoilment	redeemless	re-existent	regratress
real tennis	recolonise	redefector	re-exporter	regression
reanalysis	recolonize	redelivery	refainment	regressive
reappraise	recommence	red emperor	referendum	regretting
re-approach	recompense	redemption	referrible	regular guy
reap-silver	recomplete	redemptive	refillable	regularise
rear-facing	recompound	redemptory	refinement	regularity
reargument	recompress	redescribe	refineries	regularize
rear gunner	reconceive	red flannel	refiningly	regulation
rearmament	reconciler	red grouper	refixation	regulative
rear-vassal	recondense	red gurnard	reflagging	regulatory
rearwardly	reconquest	red herring	reflection	Rehobother

Reichsmark	remediless	repeatable	resarcelée	restenosis
reidentify	rememberer	repeatedly	reschedule	rest-harrow
reignition	remigation	repeatered	rescission	restlessly
reillumine	reminiscer	repeat mark	rescissory	restorable
reimburser	remissible	repeat sign	resealable	restrained
reim-kennar	remissness	repellence	researcher	restrainer
reimprison	remittable	repellency	resectable	restricted
reincrease	remittance	repentance	resediment	restrictee
reineckate	remittence	repersuade	resemblant	restrictor
reinforcer	remittency	repertoire	resembling	resultance
reinitiate	remobilize	répétiteur	resentment	resultless
reinscribe	remodelled	repetition	reservable	resumption
reinspirit	remodeller	repetitive	reservedly	resumptive
reinstator	remodified	repinement	resettable	resupinate
reinstruct	remodifies	repiningly	res extensa	resupplied
reinthrone	remonetise	replanning	Resh Galuta	resupplies
reintrench	remonetize	replicable	reshipment	resurgence
reinvasion	remoralize	replicably	residenter	retailment
reissuable	remorseful	replicator	residually	retainable
reiterance	remortgage	repolarize	resignedly	retainment
rejectable	remoteness	repopulate	resignment	retaliator
rejectment	remotivate	reportable	resilience	retardance
rejoiceful	removalist	report back	resiliency	retardancy
rejunction	removement	reportedly	resin canal	retardment
rejuvenant	remunerate	reposition	res integra	reticently
rejuvenate	Renaissant	repository	resistable	reticulate
rejuvenize	renal colic	repressing	resistance	reticulose
relabelled	renascence	repression	resistible	retinalite
relational	rencounter	repressive	resistless	retinulate
relatively	renderable	repressory	resmethrin	retired pay
relativise	rendezvous	reproacher	res nullius	retirement
relativism	rend the air	reprobance	resolidify	retiringly
relativist	renegadism	reprobater	resolutely	retouching
relativity	renegadoes	reprobator	resolution	retourable
relativize	renegation	reproclaim	re-solution	retractile
relaxation	renewalism	reproducer	resolutive	retraction
relaxative	renewalist	reprovable	resolutory	retractive
relay valve	renography	reptiliary	resolvable	retransfer
releasable	renominate	reptilious	resolvedly	retransmit
relegation	renovation	republican	resolvible	retraverse
relentless	renovative	repudiable	resonantly	retravirus
relentment	renownedly	repudiator	resonatory	retreatant
relevantly	renownless	repugnance	resorbence	retreatism
reliefless	rentalsman	repugnancy	resorcinol	retreatist
relief road	rent-charge	repurchase	resorcylic	retreative
relief roll	Rentenmark	repurified	resorption	retrencher
relief well	rent strike	repurifies	resorptive	retributor
relievable	renunciant	reputation	resounding	retrochoir
relievedly	renunciate	reputative	respectant	retrofocus
religation	reoccupied	requestman	respectful	retrograde
religioner	reoccupies	requiescat	respecting	retrogress
relinquish	reoccurred	requirable	respective	retrorsely
relishable	reorganise	requisitor	respirable	retrospect
relocation	reorganize	re-readable	respirator	retroverse
reluctance	repaganize	rereadable	respondent	retroviral
reluctancy	repaginate	rere-dorter	responsary	retrovirus
remand home	repairable	re-register	responsion	returnable
remarkable	reparation	rere-supper	responsive	return date
remarkably	reparative	re-revision	responsory	return fare
remarriage	reparatory	re-romanize	restaurant	return game
remediable	repatriate	resaleable	restaurate	returnless
remedially	repealable	resanctify	rest energy	return room

reundulate	rheophobic	Richardson	ringletted	robustness
reunionism	rheophytic	ricinoleic	ringmaster	Roche limit
reunionist	rheoscopic	rickettsia	ring-necked	rockabilly
reunitable	rheostatic	ricky-ticky	Ring of Fire	rock badger
revalidate	rheotactic	ricocheted	ring-opener	rock beauty
revalorize	rheotropic	ridability	ring pigeon	rock-bottom
revanchism	rhesus baby	riddlingly	ring plover	rocker foot
revanchist	rhetorical	ride a hobby	ring scaler	rocket-bomb
rev counter	rheumatics	ride and tie	ring-tailed	rocket ship
revealable	rheumatise	ride a tiger	ring-thrush	rocket sled
revealment	rheumatism	ride bodkin	ring velvet	rock garden
revegetate	rheumatize	ride cymbal	riot police	rock grouse
revelation	rheumatoid	ride herd on	rip and tear	rockhopper
revelative	Rhinegrave	ridge piece	rip current	Rockingham
revelatory	rhinestone	ridge stone	ripicolous	rock martin
revengeful	rhinobatid	ridgy-didge	ripping-saw	rock of ages
revenue tax	rhinoceral	ridiculize	rippleless	rock-pigeon
reverencer	rhinoceros	ridiculous	ripple mark	rock python
reverendly	rhinocerot	riding boot	ripple sole	rock rabbit
reverently	rhinophore	riding-coat	ripplingly	rock-ribbed
reverse bid	rhinophyma	riding-crop	rip-roaring	rock salmon
reversible	rhinoscope	riding-hood	ripsnorter	rocksteady
reversibly	rhinoscopy	riding lamp	risibility	rock stream
revertible	rhinovirus	riding sail	rising damp	rock-thrush
revestiary	rhizogenic	riebeckite	rising five	Rodinesque
reviewable	rhizomania	Riemannian	rising line	rogational
revigorate	rhizomorph	rifampicin	rising main	roghan josh
revilement	rhizophora	rifle-green	risky shift	roistering
revisiting	rhizophore	rifle range	ritardandi	roisterous
revitalise	rhizoplane	riflescope	ritardando	role player
revitalize	rhizoplast	rift timber	ritornelli	roll-collar
revivalism	rhodamine B	rift valley	ritornello	rolled gold
revivalist	rhodophyte	Riga balsam	Ritschlian	rolled oats
revivement	rhodoplast	rigescence	rittmaster	rollerball
revivified	rhomboidal	right about	ritual bath	roller-coat
revivifies	rhomboidei	right angle	river birch	roller tube
revivingly	rhumbatron	right bower	river-drift	roll-formed
revocation	rhyme royal	right field	river-drive	rollicking
revocatory	rhyme sheet	right flank	river-horse	rolling pin
revokeable	rhyodacite	rightfully	river pearl	roll latten
revolution	rhythmetic	right-lined	riverscape	roll-necked
revolvable	rhythmical	right of way	river-shrew	rollocking
revolvency	rhythmless	right on end	river snail	Rolls-Royce
revolvered	ribaldrous	right-sided	river stone	roll-up fund
rewardable	riband-fish	rightwards	river trout	roly-polies
rewardably	riband wave	right whale	riverwards	Romanaccio
rewardless	ribbon cane	rigidified	river-water	roman-à-clef
rewrapping	ribbon copy	rigidifies	rivetingly	romancical
rewrite man	ribbon-fern	rigoristic	road apples	Romanesque
rhabditoid	ribbonfish	rigorously	road bridge	Roman fever
rhabdocoel	ribbon-like	rijsttafel	road roller	Romanicist
rhabdolith	ribbonwood	Rimbaldian	roadroller	Romanistic
rhabdomere	ribbon worm	rinderpest	roadrunner	Roman-nosed
rhapsodies	rib-digging	ring-armour	road-tester	Romanowsky
rhapsodise	riboflavin	ring-billed	road tunnel	Roman snail
rhapsodist	ribophorin	ring-binder	roadworthy	romantical
rhapsodize	rib-tickler	ring burner	robber crab	Romany chal
Rhenish fan	Riccadonna	ringed dove	robberhood	rombowline
rheologist	rice-flower	ringed seal	robing room	Rome-runner
rheometric	rice powder	Ringelmann	roboticist	Romishness
rheopectic	rice stitch	ring finger	robotology	romper room
rheophilic	Richard Roe	ringleader	robustious	romper suit

rondeletia	rotativism	r selection	rum-running	Sabbath day
rongo-rongo	rotativist	rub-a-dub-dub	runability	Sabbath goy
Ronsardist	Rothschild	rubber band	run afoul of	sabbathize
rood-screen	rotiferous	rubber game	run against	sabbatical
roof garden	rotisserie	rubber heel	run a game on	sabota lark
rooibekkie	Rotissomat	rubberless	run and fell	sabretache
rooibos tea	rotor blade	rubberneck	run-and-read	sabretooth
rooirhebok	rotor cloud	rubber tree	run athwart	saccharase
room-ridden	rotorcraft	rubberware	run a voyage	saccharate
room-to-room	Rototiller	rubberwear	runcinated	saccharide
root-aorist	rottenness	rubbish bin	rune-ribbon	saccharify
root-balled	Rottweiler	rubbishing	Runge–Kutta	saccharine
root cellar	rotundness	rubbity-dub	run greenly	saccharize
root digger	Rouge Croix	rubble-work	runner bean	saccharoid
root doctor	rouge de fer	rubby-dubby	runnerless	saccharose
rootedness	rouge royal	Rubenesque	running dog	sacculated
root-fallen	Rouget cell	rubiaceous	running fit	sacerdotal
root ginger	rough-dried	rubicundly	running fix	sachemship
rootlessly	rough-dries	rubiginous	running ice	sackalever
root nodule	rough hound	Rubik's cube	running off	sack-bearer
rope-barrel	rough house	rubredoxin	running set	sackbutter
rope border	rough music	rubrically	run-of-river	sacred band
rope-dancer	rough-rider	rubricator	runologist	sacred book
rope ladder	rough scuff	ruby blende	run on a rail	sacred ibis
rope of sand	rough shoot	ruby copper	run the foil	sacredness
rope stitch	rough stuff	ruby silver	run the show	Sacred Writ
rope-walker	rough trade	ruby spinel	run through	sacrificer
roping-pole	rouletting	ruby-tailed	run to earth	sacrileger
roquelaure	Roumeliote	rubythroat	run to waste	sacristies
roriferous	round about	rucksacked	run-with-ram	sacroiliac
rosaniline	roundabout	rudder-bird	rupestrian	sacrosanct
roscoelite	round-armed	rudder-fish	rupturable	saddleback
rose acacia	round-armer	rudderless	Ruritanian	saddlebill
rose-beetle	round bilge	ruddy goose	rush candle	saddlebred
rose-chafer	round dance	ruderation	Russellian	saddle-gall
rose colour	round-eared	rudimental	Russellite	saddleless
rose copper	round-faced	Rudolphine	Russenorsk	saddle-like
rose-engine	roundhouse	ruefulness	russet coat	saddle-nose
rose-hopper	round-nosed	rufescence	Russia duck	saddle reef
rose linnet	round robin	ruffianage	Russian egg	saddleries
rose lintie	Round Table	ruffiandom	Russianise	saddle seat
rose madder	round towel	ruffianish	Russianism	saddle shoe
rose-maggot	round tower	ruffianism	Russianist	saddle-sore
rosemaling	rouseabout	ruffianize	Russianize	saddle-tank
rose-mallow	Rousseauan	rufter-hood	Russian tea	saddle tree
rose quartz	Roussillon	Rugby fives	Russonorsk	saddle vein
rose sawfly	roustabout	Rugby Union	Russophile	saddle wire
Rose Sunday	route march	rug-cutting	Russophobe	Sadducaean
rose-temple	route sheet	ruggedized	rust bucket	safari camp
rose-tinted	rove beetle	ruggedness	rust fungus	safari look
rose window	Rover Scout	rugulosity	rustically	safari park
Rosh Hodesh	rowan-berry	ruinatious	rusticater	safari suit
Rossby wave	rowdy-dowdy	rumblement	rusticness	safe-blower
Rossettian	rowing boat	rumble seat	rustic work	safe period
Ross's goose	rowing race	rumbullion	rustlingly	safety belt
rostellate	rowing tank	rumenotomy	rutheniate	safety boat
rostriform	royal burgh	rumfustian	ruthenious	safety bolt
rosy-billed	royal flush	rumination	Rutherford	safety film
Rotary club	royal icing	ruminative	ruthlessly	safety fuse
Rotary Club	royalistic	rumpsprung	rye whiskey	safety lamp
rotary-wing	royal jelly	rumpus room	Saarlander	safety play
rotational	royal paper	rumpy-pumpy	sabbath day	safety vent

safety zone	salt finger	sand plover	satellited	scale house
saffron bun	saltigrade	sand ripple	satellitic	scale of two
sage cheese	salt-making	sand shadow	satin paper	scalloping
sage grouse	salt meadow	sand-sucker	satin weave	scallopini
sage rabbit	salt rising	Sanfedista	satin white	scaloppine
saggar clay	salt shaker	Sanforized	satisficer	scammonies
sagination	salt spring	Sängerfest	satisfying	scandalise
sagittally	salt tablet	Sangiovese	satrapical	scandalize
sagittated	salubrious	sanguinary	saturation	scandalous
sago spleen	salutarily	sanguinely	saturnalia	scandaroon
sail-flying	salutation	sanguinity	Saturnalia	scanningly
sailmaking	salutatory	sanguinous	satyagraha	scansional
sail-needle	Salvadoran	Sanhedrist	satyagrahi	scansorial
sailor-fish	salverform	sanidinite	satyresque	scantiness
sailor knot	Salzburger	sanitarian	satyriasis	scapegrace
sailorless	samarskite	sanitarily	sauce-alone	scarabaeid
sailorship	sameliness	sanitarium	saucer bath	scarabaeus
sailor suit	Samian ware	sanitation	saucer-eyed	scaramouch
saintliest	sampaguita	San Luiseño	saucerfuls	scarcement
saintology	sample book	Sanocrysin	saucerless	scarceness
sakes alive	sample card	sans blague	sauerkraut	scarcities
salad cream	sample case	Sanskritic	sausage dog	scaredy-cat
salamander	sample room	sans nombre	Saussurean	scare rigid
salbutamol	Samson-fish	sans pareil	saussurite	scare stiff
sale of work	Samson post	sans phrase	Saut Basque	scarlatina
Salernitan	sanatarium	Santa Claus	savageness	scarlet day
sales clerk	sanatorium	Santa Maria	savageries	scarlet hat
sales drive	sanctified	Santobrite	savagerous	scarlet oak
sales pitch	sanctifier	saouari nut	save the day	scar tissue
saleswoman	sanctifies	sapiential	savingness	scatheless
saleswomen	sanctilogy	saponified	savings-box	scathingly
salicional	sanctimony	saponifier	saviouress	scatologic
salicylate	sanctioned	saponifies	Savonarola	scatomancy
salicylism	sanctioner	saporosity	Savonnerie	scattalder
salientian	sanctities	sappanwood	savourless	scatter-gun
saliferous	sanctitude	sapperment	savoursome	scattering
salifiable	sanctology	sapphirine	Savoy opera	scatter rug
salineness	sanctorale	saprogenic	sawmilling	scattiness
salivarian	sandal-foot	saprolitic	sawtoothed	scaturient
salivarium	sandalling	sapropelic	saw-whet owl	scavengery
saliva test	sandal tree	saprophile	saxicavous	scene-steal
salivation	sandalwood	saprophyte	saxicoline	scenically
sallenders	sandbagger	saproxylic	saxicolous	scent gland
sallowness	sand-barite	Saracenism	Saxon green	scent organ
salmagundi	sand-binder	Sarakatsan	Saxony blue	scent scale
salmanazar	sandcastle	Saramaccan	saxophonic	scepticise
Salmanazar	sand cherry	sarcococca	saxotromba	scepticism
salmon bass	sand dollar	sarcocolla	say a lot for	scepticize
salmonella	sanderling	sarcolemma	say ditto to	sceptredom
salmon-leap	sand filter	sarcophagi	say much for	schalstein
salmon pass	sand garden	sarcophagy	say that for	scheduling
salmon peal	sand goanna	sarcoplasm	say the word	schefflera
salmon pink	sand-groper	sarcopside	scabbarded	schematise
salon music	sandgrouse	sarcotesta	scabbiness	schematism
salonnière	sand-hiller	sarmentose	scabridity	schematist
saloon deck	sand-hopper	sarmentous	scabrously	schematize
saloon girl	Sandinista	sarracenia	scaffolder	schemeless
salopettes	sand lizard	sash weight	scala media	schemingly
saltarelli	sandlotter	sash window	scald-berry	schemozzle
saltarello	sand martin	Satanistic	scald cream	scherzandi
salt bridge	sand myrtle	Satanology	scale-board	scherzando
salt cellar	sandpapery	satchelled	scaledrake	scherzetto

Schiff base	scoria cone	screen dump	sculleries	sea spurrey
Schiff test	scoriation	screen grid	sculptress	sea-swallow
schipperke	scornfully	screenings	sculptural	seat-belted
schismatic	scorpaenid	screenless	sculpturer	sea thistle
schizocarp	scorpionic	screen pass	scumminess	sea trumpet
schizogony	scorpionid	screenplay	scurfiness	sea-unicorn
schizoidal	scortation	screen test	scurrility	sea-walling
schizoidia	scortatory	screen time	scurrilous	seborrhoea
schizotype	scorzalite	screwiness	scurviness	Secchi disc
schizotypy	scorzonera	screw-joint	scutellate	secernment
schlepping	scot and lot	screwmatic	scuttleful	secludedly
Schlieffen	Scotch cart	screw-plate	scuzziness	second Adam
schlimazel	Scotchgard	screw-press	scyphiform	second-best
schmegegge	Scotch kale	screw stock	scyphozoan	second chop
Schmeisser	Scotchlite	screw-stone	scytheless	second-foot
schmendrik	Scotch mist	screw valve	sea anemone	second gear
schnozzola	Scotchness	scribbling	sea-angling	second-hand
scholardom	Scotch rose	scribe-mark	sea-bathing	second home
scholarism	Scotch snap	scribeship	sea-biscuit	second last
scholastic	Scotch spur	scrimmager	sea blubber	second line
schoolable	Scotch tape	scrimshank	seaborgium	secondment
schooldays	Scotch yoke	scrip issue	sea-bristle	second name
school-days	scotometer	script girl	sea campion	secondness
schoolgirl	scotometry	scriptless	sea-captain	second-rate
school land	scotophase	scriptoria	sea-catfish	second self
schoolless	scotophily	script type	sea coconut	second slip
school-marm	scotoscope	scriptural	sea-farming	second wind
schoolmate	Scots-Irish	scriptured	sea-feather	secretaire
school milk	Scotswoman	scritch-owl	sea-fingers	secret life
schoolroom	Scotswomen	scrivenery	seafishery	secret list
school-ship	Scotticise	scrivening	sea-fishing	secretness
school time	Scotticism	scrobicule	sea-gherkin	sectionary
schoolward	Scotticize	scrofulide	sea horizon	sectionise
school year	Scottie dog	scrofulous	sea-keeping	sectionist
schorl rock	Scottishly	scrollable	sea lamprey	sectionize
Schwannoma	Scottishry	scroll back	sealed-beam	sector scan
sciagraphy	scout plane	scroll-bone	sealed book	secular arm
scientific	scovan lode	scroll-copy	sea-leopard	secularise
Scillonian	scowbanker	scroll-gall	sea lettuce	secularism
scimitared	scowdering	scroll-head	sealing wax	secularist
scindapsus	scowlingly	scroll salt	seamanlike	secularity
scintigram	scraggiest	scrollwork	seamanship	secularize
scintiscan	scraggling	scrubbable	seam bowler	secure arms
sciolistic	scraggy end	scrub board	seamlessly	securement
scissor-cut	scrambling	scrub-brush	sea-monster	secureness
scleriasis	scrape a leg	scrub-robin	seamstress	securiform
sclerified	scrap-metal	scrub round	seam welder	securities
scleromata	scrap paper	scruffiest	sea-officer	securitise
sclerosant	scrappiest	scrummager	sea passage	securitize
sclerosing	scratch hit	scrunch-dry	Sea Peoples	sedan chair
sclerotium	scratchier	scrunchies	sea-poacher	sedateness
sclerotize	scratchily	scrupulant	seaquarium	sedge-grass
sclerotome	scratching	scrupulist	searchable	sedimental
sclerotomy	scratch-mix	scrupulous	search coil	seditioner
scoffingly	scratch pad	scrutineer	sea returns	seducement
scoldingly	scratch-wig	scrutinies	seascapist	seducingly
scooterist	scrawniest	scrutinise	sea serpent	seductress
scopoletin	screechier	scrutinize	sea-service	sedulously
score a miss	screeching	scrutinous	seasonable	seed-cotton
scoreboard	screech owl	scuba-diver	seasonably	seed-furrow
score sheet	screenable	scuddiness	seasonally	seed parent
score under	screen door	scull about	seasonless	seed potato

seed stitch	self-rising	send word to	sermonical	severation
seed vessel	self-secure	Senecanism	sermonizer	severeness
seek repose	self-seeded	Senegalese	sermonneer	sewability
seem good to	self-seeder	senescence	serologist	sewage farm
seemlihead	self-seeker	senior year	serotinous	sexagenary
seemliness	self-slayer	sennegrass	serpentary	Sexagesima
see one's way	self-styled	sense datum	serpentile	sexangular
seersucker	self-system	sense organ	serpentine	sexational
see service	self-taught	sensitizer	serpentize	sexavalent
seethingly	self-willed	sensoriums	serpigines	sexduction
see through	self-wisdom	sensualise	serradilla	sex hormone
segmentary	sell-by date	sensualism	serrulated	sexivalent
segregable	Selsdon man	sensualist	sertanista	sex-limited
seguidilla	semantemic	sensuality	serum broth	sex-linkage
seicentist	semaphoric	sensualize	servantdom	sex offence
seignorage	sematology	sensuistic	serventism	sexologist
seignorial	semblative	sensuosity	service bus	sexpartite
seismicity	semeiology	sensuously	service car	sexploiter
seismogram	semeiotics	sentential	serviceman	sex-starved
seismology	semi-annual	sentiently	servicemen	sex therapy
sejunction	semi-chorus	Senussiite	serving-man	sextillion
seldomness	semicircle	senza bassi	servitress	sextonship
selectable	semicirque	separately	servo brake	sexual cell
selectness	semi-closed	separation	servo-motor	sexual role
selenodesy	semi-coking	separatism	servomotor	sexuparous
selenodont	semi-column	separatist	sessile oak	shabbiness
selenology	semi-desert	separative	sessionary	Shabbos-goy
Seleucidan	semi-direct	separatory	sessioneer	shabu-shabu
self-acting	semi-divine	separatrix	session man	shadow-cast
self-action	semi-double	septectomy	sestertium	shadowland
self-active	semiferine	septemfoil	sestertius	shadowless
self-binder	semi-fitted	septemviri	set abroach	shadow mask
self-colour	semi-formed	septenarii	set a copy to	shadow play
self-deceit	semi-lethal	septenary	set against	shadow test
self-denial	semi-liquid	septennate	set a stitch	shadow work
self-denied	semilunate	septennial	set forward	shaft-alley
self-denier	semi-mature	septennium	setiferous	shaft-drive
self-driven	seminarial	septically	setigerous	shaft grave
self-energy	seminarian	septicemia	set spurs to	shaft-horse
self-esteem	seminaries	septichord	set store by	shaganappi
self-exiled	seminarist	septicidal	settecento	shagginess
self-feeder	semination	septic tank	setterwort	shag-haired
self-formed	seminative	septillion	set the pace	shagreened
self-giving	seminology	septostomy	setting-dog	Shahanshah
self-hatred	semi-nudity	Septuagint	setting sun	shahbandar
self-helper	semi-opaque	sepulchral	settleable	shake hands
self-insure	semiotical	Sepulchran	settlement	shakuhachi
self-killed	semi-portal	sepultural	settlerdom	shallow end
selflessly	semiquaver	sequacious	settle with	shallow-fry
self-loader	semi-rotary	sequenator	set to music	shamefaced
self-loving	semi-savage	sequential	set up house	shamefully
self-motion	semi-sports	sequestral	seven-hilly	shame on you
self-motive	Semiticize	sequestrum	sevenpence	shandrydan
self-moving	semi-uncial	seralbumin	sevenpenny	shandygaff
self-murder	semi-weekly	Serbo-Croat	Seven Sages	shanghaied
self-opened	semotactic	sereneness	sevenscore	Shanks' mare
self-parody	sempstress	serenities	seven stars	shanty town
self-poised	senatorial	sergeantcy	seventieth	shape forth
self-praise	senatorian	serge denim	seventyish	shapeliest
self-raised	send abroad	serigraphy	Seven Words	Sharawaggi
self-rating	Senderista	serio-comic	severality	shard-borne
self-regard	send off for	sermonette	severalize	sharedness

shark-louse
sharp cedar
shattering
shaughraun
shavegrass
Shavianism
shea-butter
shear board
shear force
shear-grass
shear plane
shear steel
shearwater
sheathbill
sheath cell
sheath-fish
sheathless
shed master
shed-roofed
sheepberry
sheep-biter
sheep-crook
sheep-house
sheepishly
sheep-money
sheep's bane
sheep's foot
sheepshank
sheep's head
sheep-shear
sheet-block
sheet cable
sheet-flood
sheet glass
sheet metal
sheet music
sheldgoose
sheldrakes
shelf paper
shellacked
shell beach
shell-briar
shell cocoa
Shelleyana
Shelleyism
Shelleyite
shell-gland
shell-money
shell-mould
shell-mound
shell-plate
shellproof
shell-shock
shell-snail
shell steak
shelly-coat
shelterage
shelter leg
shenanigan
shepherded
shepherdly
shepherdry

sherardise
sherardize
sherbet dab
sheriffdom
sheriffing
sherry wine
she's apples
Shetlander
Shetlandic
shewelling
shibboleth
shield-back
shield fern
shieldless
shieldlike
shield-maid
shieldrake
shieldtail
shift dress
shiftening
shiftiness
shiftingly
shift-lever
shift-round
shift-stick
shift valve
shillelagh
shillibeer
shillooing
shingle cap
shingle-oak
Shinkansen
shin-tangle
ship-broken
shipbroker
ship-broker
ship burial
shipentine
ship-keeper
ship-ladder
ship-lapped
ship-letter
shipmaster
ship-repair
ship-rigged
ship's store
ship-timber
ship-to-ship
shipwright
shire-horse
shire-house
shire-reeve
shire-stone
shirt-dress
shirt-frill
shirt-front
shirtiness
shirtmaker
shirt-waist
shirtwaist
shish kebab
shit a brick

shit-eating
shit-kicker
shit-scared
shittiness
shiversome
shoaliness
shockingly
shock-mount
shockproof
shock stall
shock strut
shoddiness
shoddy-hole
shoe-buckle
shoe-flower
shoemaking
shoeshiner
shoestring
shoneenism
shonkinite
shoofly pie
shooldarry
shoot ahead
shoot a line
shoot craps
shoot it out
shopaholic
shop around
shop-bought
shop-finish
shop-fitter
shopfitter
shopkeeper
shoplifter
shopocracy
shoppiness
shop-soiled
shopwalker
shop window
shopworker
shore-based
shore break
shore-going
shore leave
shore party
shore seine
shorewards
short-arsed
short-assed
shortbread
short cards
short chain
short cloth
short-comer
short cross
shortcrust
short-dated
short drink
shortening
short field
short focus
short-fused

short grain
short-grass
short-hairs
short horse
short-lived
short metre
short order
short price
short-range
short score
short sight
short-stage
short story
short sword
short-timer
short title
short waist
shortwards
short whist
Shoshonean
shoshonite
shot effect
shot-firing
shotmaking
shot-peened
shot-putter
shot-window
shouldered
shoulder-in
shoutingly
shove-groat
shovelfuls
shovelhead
shovelling
shovelnose
shovel pass
showboater
shower-bath
shower head
showerless
shower-room
shower tree
shower unit
showground
showjumper
show-offish
show-people
show temper
show the way
show-window
shrewd-head
shrewdness
shrewishly
shrewmouse
Shrewsbury
shrievalty
shrillness
shrimp-boat
shrimplike
shrimp-pink
shrinkable
shrink film

shrink-ring
shrink-wrap
shrivelled
Shropshire
shroud-knot
shroud-laid
shroudless
shroudlike
shroud line
Shrovetide
shrug aside
Shtokavian
shuddering
shunt-wound
shut-out bid
shutter-bug
shutter-dam
shuttering
shuttle car
shut up shop
Shylockian
shystering
shysterism
sialagogue
sialogogue
sialomucin
Siamese cat
sibilantly
sibilation
sibilatory
sicca rupee
sicilianos
sicilienne
sick as a dog
sickerness
Sickertian
sickle-bill
sickle-cell
sickle hock
sickliness
sick-making
sick parade
side-branch
sideburned
side by side
sidecarist
side chapel
side effect
side glance
side-kicker
side-ladder
side-loader
side-pocket
sideration
sidereally
side-remark
side-result
siderocyte
siderolite
siderosome
siderostat
side-saddle

side-screen	silverless	singletree	skepticism	slashingly
side-stitch	silverlike	single-wide	sketchable	slate-black
side-stream	silverling	single-wire	sketch-book	slate-stone
side street	silver mail	sing-songed	sketchbook	slattering
side-stroke	silver orfe	singularly	sketchiest	slatternly
sidestroke	silver ring	sinisterly	skeuomorph	slaughtery
sideswiper	silver sand	sinistrous	Skevington	Slave Coast
side-taking	silverside	sinker-ball	skew bridge	slave-drive
sideways on	silvertail	sinkerless	skew chisel	slave-maker
sidewinder	silver thaw	sink or swim	skewer tree	Slave State
siege-piece	silver-tree	sinnership	skew system	slave trade
siege-train	silverware	Sinn Feiner	skiagraphy	slavocracy
Sierpinski	silverweed	sino-atrial	skiascopic	Slavophile
sieve plate	silver-work	sinography	skiddoooed	sleazeball
Sievers' law	silylation	sinologist	ski jumping	sleaziness
sight-board	similarity	Sinologist	skimmer hat	sleekstone
sight draft	similarize	Sinophilia	skimmingly	sleep a wink
sight-glass	similative	Sinophobia	skimpiness	sleepiness
sigillaria	similitude	sinsemilla	skim-plough	sleepingly
signal-book	simillimum	sin-shifter	skin a flint	sleep rough
signalling	simmer down	sinuatrial	skin-beater	sleep sound
signet ring	Simmerstat	sinus gland	skin beetle	sleep tight
sign-manual	simnel cake	sinusoidal	skin diving	sleep-waker
sign-writer	simoniacal	siphoneous	skin-drying	sleepyhead
signwriter	simple lens	sipunculan	skin effect	sleepy-head
silent heat	simpleness	sipunculid	skinflinty	sleepy-time
silentiary	simple time	sis-boom-bah	Skinner box	sleeve-fish
silentious	simplicial	sister cell	Skinnerian	sleeveless
silentness	simplicist	sister city	Skinnerism	sleeve link
silhouette	simplicity	Sister Dora	skinniness	sleeve note
silication	simplified	sisterhood	skin-search	sleigh bell
silicicole	simplifier	sister-hook	skin the cat	sleigh-ride
silicified	simplifies	sisterless	skippingly	slenderest
silicifies	simplistic	sisterlike	skirmisher	slenderise
siliconize	simulacral	sister ship	skirt-board	slenderize
siliculose	simulacrum	sistership	skirt-chase	slick paper
silk cotton	simulation	sister-wife	skirt-dance	slickstone
silk screen	simulative	sisymbrium	skittishly	slide-valve
silly billy	sincipital	sit heavy on	skittle-pot	slightness
silly house	sinecurism	sit loose to	skrimshank	slime mould
Silly putty	sinecurist	sit on brood	skunk works	slim volume
Silly Putty	sine qua non	sitophobia	sky fighter	sling chair
silo buster	sinfulness	sitosterol	skylighted	sling off at
silverback	Singhalese	sit pillion	sky marshal	sling-stone
silver band	singing arc	sit through	sky-parlour	slinkiness
silver bath	singing man	Sitwellian	sky-rockety	slinkingly
silver beet	singing saw	Sitwellism	skyscraper	slipperily
silverbill	single beer	Siwash camp	sky-surfing	slippering
silverbird	single-copy	Siwash duck	sky the wipe	slippiness
silver-bush	single-eyed	six-pounder	sky-writing	slip stitch
silver cord	single file	six-shooter	slacken off	slipstream
silver disc	single-foot	sixteenmos	slack water	slip-string
silver fern	single-hand	sixth sense	slag-hearth	slit-limpet
silverfish	singlehood	sixty-seven	slaked lime	slit pocket
silver foil	single-line	sizzlingly	slake water	slit trench
silver-fork	single malt	sjambokker	slammerkin	slitty-eyed
silver gilt	singleness	skateboard	slanderous	sloop of war
silver-grey	single reed	skate-leech	slanginess	slop bucket
silver king	single-reef	skedaddler	slangishly	sloppiness
silver lace	singles bar	skeletally	slangwhang	slopping-up
silver-lead	single-step	skeletonic	slantingly	slopseller
silver-leaf	single team	Skeltonian	slap-tongue	slop-worker

sloshiness
slot aerial
slothfully
slot-racing
slovenlike
Slovincian
slow bowler
slow cooker
slow motion
slow-twitch
slow-witted
sluggardly
sluggishly
slug pellet
sluice-fork
sluice-gate
sluice-head
slumber cap
slumberful
slumbering
slumber net
slumberous
slum burner
slumminess
slummocker
slurry seal
slushiness
slush-money
slush mould
sluttishly
smackering
Smalcaldic
small bower
small craft
small fruit
smallgoods
small hours
small mercy
small-pipes
small print
small-scale
small-sword
small-timer
smallwares
small world
small-yield
smaragdine
smaragdite
smarminess
smart aleck
smart alick
smart-arsed
smartingly
smart money
smart-mouth
smashingly
smattering
smear glaze
smeariness
smeethness
smell-feast
smelliness

smell of oil
smelteries
smirchless
smirkingly
smithcraft
smithereen
smitheries
Smithfield
smith's coal
smith's work
smock-faced
smock-frock
smoke alarm
smoke-black
smoke-dried
smoke-house
smoke-meter
smoke plant
smoke point
smoke shell
smokestack
smoke-stick
smoke-stone
smoke-wagon
Smokey Bear
smoking gun
smoochiest
smoothable
smooth-bore
smooth-head
smoothness
smooth newt
smooth talk
smooth tare
smørrebrød
smorzandos
smother-fly
smudge-fire
smudgeless
smudginess
smugglable
smut fungus
smuttiness
snaffle-bit
snail-fever
snailishly
snail-paced
snail's pace
snake dance
snake-fence
snake-gourd
snake house
snake juice
snakeology
snake plant
snake's head
snake-stone
snake story
snap-action
snap-beetle
snapdragon
snappiness

snappingly
snappishly
snap switch
snarkiness
snarlingly
snatchable
snatch-back
snatch crop
snazziness
sneak-guest
sneakiness
sneakingly
sneakishly
sneak thief
sneaky pete
sneeringly
sneezeweed
sneezewood
sneezewort
snick-snarl
sniffer dog
sniffiness
sniffingly
sniggering
snipe's-head
snipocracy
snippiness
snivelling
snob appeal
snobberies
snobbiness
snobbishly
snobocracy
snob-screen
snoopiness
snootiness
snooziness
snore-piece
snorkelled
snorkeller
snortingly
snottiness
snotty-nose
Snovianism
snowblower
snowcapped
snow-capped
Snowcemmed
snow course
Snowdonian
snow-grouse
snow-insect
snow-making
snowmaking
snowmobile
snow pellet
snow petrel
snow pigeon
snowplough
snow powder
snow roller
snow-snakes

snow-sports
snow-wreath
snowy egret
snubbiness
snubbingly
snubbishly
snuff-brown
snuff-gourd
snuffiness
snuffingly
snuff movie
snuff video
snuggeries
soaking pit
soaking wet
soap-boiler
soap-bubble
soap cerate
soap flakes
soap powder
soavemente
soberingly
sobersides
social cost
social evil
social fact
socializer
socialness
social unit
social wage
social work
societally
sociocracy
sociodrama
socio-legal
sociologic
sociometry
socionomic
sociopathy
sock chorus
sock cymbal
socketless
Socratical
soda bottle
sodalities
soda syphon
soddenness
sodium lamp
sodium pump
Sodom apple
Sodomitish
sod webworm
soetkoekie
soft answer
soft-boiled
soft cancer
soft centre
soften down
soft-footed
soft ground
soft-headed
soft hyphen

soft-lander
soft mother
softnomics
soft option
soft palate
soft sawder
soft-soaper
soft solder
soft-spoken
soft target
soft wicket
soft-wooded
soil catena
soil cement
soiled dove
soil mantle
soil sample
soil series
soil stripe
soil survey
sojourning
Soka Gakkai
solacement
solan goose
solanidine
solar flare
solar month
solar panel
solar power
solar still
soldanella
solderable
solderless
soldier ant
soldier-bug
soldieress
soldier-fly
soldieries
soldierize
solecistic
solemnizer
solemn mass
Solemn Mass
Solenhofen
solenocyte
solenoidal
solfataric
solicitant
soliciting
solicitous
solicitrix
solicitude
solid angle
solidarism
solidarist
solidarity
solid-drawn
solidified
solidifier
solidifies
solid newel
solid South

solids pump	sopping wet	spacebound	spattering	spermatize
solid state	sopraninos	space cabin	spatulated	sperm count
solifidian	sops-in-wine	space cadet	speakeress	spermicide
soligenous	sorbetière	spacecraft	speakerine	spermidine
solitaries	sordidness	space curve	speaker-key	spermoderm
solitarily	sore-headed	spacefarer	speak-house	spermogone
solivagant	sore throat	space flyer	speak ill of	spermology
Solochrome	sororicide	space frame	speakingly	sperm whale
Solomonian	sororities	space group	spear-grass	sphacelate
solonetzic	sorrel tree	space opera	spearminty	sphacelial
solstitial	sorrowless	space-order	spear-shaft	sphacelous
solstitium	sorrow song	spaceplane	specialise	sphalerite
solubilise	sortileger	space probe	specialism	sphenoidal
solubility	sostenutos	spacescape	specialist	sphereless
solubilize	Sothic year	space stage	speciality	sphericity
soluble RNA	soubriquet	spacewoman	specialize	spheriform
solutional	soucouyant	spacewomen	speciation	spherocyte
solvolysis	soughfully	spaciously	specie-room	spheroidal
solvolytic	soul-candle	spade beard	speciesism	spherosome
somatalgia	soul-doctor	spade-graft	speciesist	spherulite
somatocoel	soul-friend	spade-money	specifical	spheterize
somatogamy	soullessly	spade-press	speciosity	sphinxlike
somatology	soul-search	spade-wheel	speciously	spice-berry
somatotype	soul sister	spadiceous	spectacled	spice-plate
sombreness	sound-alike	spagyrical	spectacles	spiculated
sombreroed	soundalike	spallation	spectation	spider-band
somebodies	soundboard	spanandric	spectatory	spider-cell
somersault	sound check	spander-new	spectatrix	spider crab
somewhat as	soundcheck	spaniolate	spectrally	spider hole
somewhence	soundingly	spaniolize	spectredom	spider-hoop
somewheres	sound meter	Spanish elm	specularly	spider-like
somnambule	sound mixer	Spanish flu	speculator	spider lily
somnolence	sound print	Spanish fly	speech area	spider-line
somnolency	soundproof	Spanish nut	speech coil	spiderling
son and heir	soundscape	spankingly	speechless	spider mite
sonata form	sound shift	sparagmite	speech-song	spider-rest
Sonderbund	sound stage	sparge pipe	speed clock	spider's web
song-ballet	soundtrack	spark-erode	speed demon	spider-wasp
song-flight	sound truck	spark guard	speed freak	spider-work
songlessly	soup maigre	sparkiness	speediness	spiderwort
song period	soup-ticket	sparkishly	speed limit	spiflicate
song-school	sourcebook	sparmannia	speisesaal	spiked buck
songstress	sourceless	sparrow owl	speleology	spilitized
song thrush	source rock	sparseness	speleothem	spill blood
songwriter	sour cherry	Spartacism	spellbound	spill valve
sonication	sour grapes	Spartacist	spell-check	spinal cord
sonic speed	sour orange	spartakiad	spellingly	spin bowler
soniferous	sousaphone	Spartanism	spelunking	spindleage
sonorities	souterrain	Spartanize	Spencerian	spindleful
sonorosity	southabout	spasm music	Spencerism	spindliest
sonorously	southbound	spasmodism	Spencerite	spin doctor
sons of guns	South Devon	spasmodist	Spenserian	spinel ruby
soon or late	South Downs	spasmoneme	spermaceti	spine point
soon or syne	southerner	spasticity	spermaduct	spinescent
soothingly	southernly	spatangoid	spermagone	spinningly
soothsayer	southwards	spatchcock	spermalege	spinsterly
sooty mould	Sovietizer	spathulate	spermarium	spinstress
sophically	sovnarkhoz	spatialise	sperm-aster	spin tunnel
sophiology	sowthistle	spatialism	spermatise	spin vector
Sophoclean	Soyer stove	spatialist	spermatism	spiny mouse
sophomoric	spacearium	spatiality	spermatist	spiny shark
sophrosyne	space-borne	spatialize	spermatium	spiracular

spiraculum
spiral gear
spiralling
spiramycin
spirantize
spire-grass
spire-shell
spiritedly
spirit lamp
spiritless
spirit-like
spirituous
spirit-weed
spirograph
spirometer
spirometry
spissitude
spitballer
spitchcock
spitchered
spit cotton
spite fence
spitefully
spit-insect
spittle-bug
Spitzflöte
splacknuck
splanchnic
splashback
splash-dash
splash down
splashdown
splashiest
splash pool
splash-work
splash zone
splay fault
spleenless
spleenwort
splendidly
splenetive
splenocyte
splenology
splenotomy
splint-bone
splint-coal
split-brain
split-field
split graft
split hairs
split-image
split-level
split-phase
split shift
split stuff
split wheel
splutterer
spodomancy
spoilsport
spokenness
spokeshave
spokeslady

spoliation
spoliative
spoliatory
spondulick
spongeable
sponge bath
sponge cake
sponge crab
spongeless
spongelike
sponge tree
spongiform
sponginess
spongiosis
spongolite
spongology
sponsoress
sponsorial
spookiness
spool valve
spoon-bread
spoon canoe
spoon drain
spoondrift
spoonerism
spoonerize
spooniness
sporadical
sporangial
sporangium
spore print
Spörer's law
sporidiole
sporoblast
sporophore
sporophyll
sporophyte
sporozoite
sportfully
sportiness
sportingly
sportively
sportscast
sports coat
sports page
sports team
sportswear
spot effect
spot height
spotlessly
spotted dog
spotted gum
spotted ray
spottiness
spot-welder
spot zoning
spousehood
spouseless
sprauncier
spray-dried
spray-dries
spray-paint

spray tower
spreadable
spread head
spread-over
spreaghery
sprightful
spring-back
spring bolt
spring bows
springhaas
springhalt
spring hare
springhead
springiest
spring-jack
springless
springlike
spring line
springling
spring lock
spring rate
spring roll
springtail
spring tide
springtide
springtime
spring-wood
sprinkling
spritehood
sprocketed
sprout-land
spruce beer
spruceness
spruce pine
spud barber
spud wrench
spun-golden
spunkiness
spur blight
spurge hawk
spuriosity
spuriously
spur-winged
sputtering
spycatcher
squabasher
squabbiest
squabbling
squab-chick
squadronal
squadroned
squalidity
squall line
squamation
squamiform
squamosity
squamulose
squanderer
square away
square deal
square-eyed
square eyes

square foot
square-free
squarehead
square John
square meal
Square Mile
squareness
square pole
square root
square sail
square-tail
square-toed
square-toes
square up to
square wave
squarewise
square yard
squashable
squash bite
squashiest
squatarole
squat board
squaw-berry
squeakiest
squeezable
squeeze-box
squeeze toy
squeteague
squidgiest
squid-hound
squiffiest
squinch-owl
squint-eyed
squint-eyes
squirarchy
squirearch
squirehood
squireless
squirelike
squireling
squireship
squirmiest
squirrelly
squishiest
stabbingly
stabilator
stabiliser
stabilized
stabilizer
stable door
Stableford
stablefuls
stable girl
stable-lass
stablemate
stableness
stablisher
stab-stitch
stab stroke
stackfreed
stack-garth
stadholder

stadthouse
staff corps
staff nurse
staff-sling
stag beetle
stagecoach
stagecraft
stage right
staggering
stag-headed
stag-horned
stag-hunter
stagnantly
stagnation
stair-tower
stake-truck
stalactite
Stalag Luft
stalagmite
stalk borer
stalkiness
stall-board
stallenger
stall plate
stalwartly
stamineous
stamp-album
stamp and go
stamp hinge
stamp paper
Stancarist
stanchless
stand about
stand-alone
stand aloof
stand apart
standardly
stand aside
stand at bay
stand forth
stand guard
stand on end
standpoint
standstill
stand treat
stand up for
stannaries
stannotype
stanza-form
stanzaical
staphyloma
starbolins
star-bright
starch fish
starchiest
starchness
star-flower
staring mad
stark naked
starriness
starry-eyed
star stream

star-struck	steam navvy	stereobate	stigmergic	stone-brake
starstruck	steam organ	stereo card	stillatory	stone-brash
star system	steam point	stereogram	stillbirth	stonebreak
start a hare	steam power	stereology	still-house	stone-broke
starter set	steam radio	stereo pair	stillicide	stone canal
startingly	steam table	stereopsis	still lifes	stone-china
starvation	steam-tight	stereoptic	still-stand	stone-coral
starveling	steam train	Stereoscan	still water	stone-craft
stasiology	steel fixer	stereotaxy	stiltified	stone cream
state a case	steel frame	stereotomy	stimulable	stone-field
state-cabin	steeliness	stereotype	stimulancy	stoneflies
statecraft	steelworks	stereotypy	stimulator	stone fruit
stated case	steep-grass	sterically	stinginess	stone guard
State-house	steeple cup	sterilizer	stingingly	stonehatch
state of war	steep-water	sterlingly	stinkblaar	Stonehenge
State-paper	stellardom	sternalgia	stink gland	stone loach
State trial	stellately	sternal rib	stinkingly	stonemason
State visit	stellation	stern-board	stinkstone	stone river
statically	Steller jay	stern-chase	stipellate	stony-broke
staticisor	stelleroid	sterndrive	stipulator	stony coral
static line	stelliform	sterner sex	stirringly	stoopingly
staticness	stem family	stern-gland	stirrup-bar	stop-action
static test	stem ginger	stern-piece	stirrup cup	stop behind
static tube	stemmatics	sternsheet	stishovite	stop button
stationary	stem mother	stern speed	stitchbird	stop chords
station-day	stem sawfly	sternutory	stitchless	stop chorus
stationery	stem stitch	sternwards	stitch weld	stop-handle
stationman	stem-winder	stern-wheel	stitch-work	stop-motion
statistics	stench-pipe	stertorous	stitchwort	stop signal
statoblast	stench trap	stethogram	stob-thatch	stop-thrust
statocracy	stencilled	stevioside	stochastic	stop-volley
statolatry	stenciller	steward boy	stock-blind	store buyer
statoscope	Stengunner	stewardess	stock-board	storefront
statospore	stenograph	stiacciato	stock-brick	storehouse
statuarist	stenopaeic	stibialism	stock-frost	storiation
statueless	Stenorette	stichidium	stockhorse	storiology
statuesque	stenotherm	stichology	stockiness	stork's-bill
statutable	stenotopic	stickadove	stockinged	storm apron
statutably	stenotyper	stick chair	stockinger	storm-beach
statute law	stenotypic	stick dance	stockishly	stormbound
staurolite	stentorial	stick fixed	stock knife	storm choke
staurotide	stentorian	stick force	stockpiler	storm cloud
staverwort	step astray	stickiness	stock-proof	storm drain
stavesacre	step by step	stick it out	stock-purse	storm-finch
stay-at-home	step-dancer	stick one on	stock-rider	stormfully
stay-putter	stepfamily	stick shift	stock-route	storm-glass
stay shtoom	stepfather	sticktight	stock split	storminess
stay-stitch	step-gabled	stick up for	stock-still	storm-light
steadiment	stephanion	stickwater	stocktaker	storm-porch
steadiness	stephanite	sticky-back	stodge-full	stormproof
steady down	stepladder	stickybeak	stodginess	storm sewer
steak Diane	steplessly	sticky bomb	Stokes' line	storm surge
steak-house	step lively	sticky tape	stolen-wise	storm track
steakhouse	stepmother	stiff-arsed	stolidness	storm troop
steak knife	step-parent	stiffening	stomachful	storm-water
stealingly	step rocket	stifle-bone	stomatitic	storyboard
stealthful	stepsister	stiflingly	stomatitis	stout heart
stealthier	stercolith	stigmarian	stomatopod	stout party
stealthily	stercorary	stigmatise	stomochord	stove-grate
steamer rug	stercorate	stigmatist	stomodaeal	stow-master
steam gauge	stercorean	stigmatize	stomodaeum	strabismal
steaminess	stercorous	stigmatose	stomp dance	strabismic

strabismus
stracchino
Stracheyan
stragglier
straggling
straight A's
straighten
straightly
straight-up
strainable
strainedly
strainless
straitened
strait-lace
straitness
stramonium
strandflat
strand-line
Strandveld
strand-wolf
strap brake
strap hinge
strappados
Strasbourg
strategian
strategics
strategies
strategise
strategist
strategize
strathspey
stratified
stratifies
stratiform
stratocrat
stratotype
Straussian
stravaiger
strawberry
straw-blond
strawboard
straw braid
straw-death
straw paper
straw plait
stray field
streakiest
stream-flow
streamless
streamline
streamside
stream-tide
street arab
street Arab
street cred
street door
street drug
street girl
street-grid
street lamp
street name
street tree

streetward
streetwise
strelitzia
strengthen
strepitant
strepitoso
strepitous
stressable
stress-free
stressless
stress mark
stress test
stretching
stretch jet
stretch out
striaeform
strickenly
strictness
strictured
striddling
stridently
stridingly
stridulant
stridulate
stridulent
stridulous
strifeless
strike back
strike call
strike down
strike fire
strike home
strike-over
strike rate
strike root
strike-slip
strike upon
strike wide
strike zone
strikingly
strim-stram
string bass
string bean
stringency
stringendo
stringhalt
stringiest
stringless
stringlike
string-line
string vest
strinkling
striolated
strioscopy
stripagram
strip-chart
strip-graze
stripiness
strip joint
strip light
stripogram
strippable

strippeuse
strip-poker
strip steak
striptease
strivingly
strobe disc
strobe lamp
strobiloid
strobotron
stroganoff
Stroganoff
stroke book
stroke-haul
strokeless
stroke play
strokeplay
stroke-side
strokesman
stromateid
stromatous
strong-back
strong card
strong-eyed
strong gale
strong hand
strong head
stronghold
strong meat
strongness
strongroom
strong suit
strophical
strophiole
strophulus
stroppiest
structural
structured
struggle on
struggling
Struldbrug
strumatous
struthioid
struthious
strychnine
strychnism
stubbed-out
stubbiness
stubble-fed
stubble-rig
stubbornly
stub equity
stub-switch
studentess
studentish
studentize
studio flat
studiously
study group
stuffed owl
stuffiness
stultified
stultifier

stultifies
stumblebum
stump fence
stumpiness
stump plant
stump water
stunningly
stupefying
stupendous
stupidness
sturdiness
stylistics
stylograph
stylohyoid
stylolitic
stylometry
stylophone
stylopized
stypticity
suabe flute
suaveolent
subacidity
subacutely
sub-almoner
subangular
subaquatic
subaqueous
subarcuate
subaudible
subauditur
sub-calibre
sub-carrier
subcentral
subception
subchanter
subchelate
subclavian
subclavius
subcompact
subconical
subcordate
subcranial
subculture
subdeanery
subdialect
subdivider
subduction
subduement
subduingly
sub-element
subequally
subfuscous
subgeneric
subglacial
subglobose
sub-heading
subheading
subhumanly
subinfeoff
subintrant
subjacency
subjectify

subjectile
subjection
subjective
subjoinder
subjugable
subjugator
subkingdom
sublateral
sublattice
sublexemic
sublimable
sublimator
subliminal
sublingual
subliteral
subluminal
submariner
submarshal
submediant
submersion
submission
submissive
submitting
submontane
submucosal
subnascent
sub-nuclear
subnuclear
subodorate
sub-officer
suboptimal
sub-orbital
suborbital
subordinal
subpassage
subpoenaed
sub-prefect
subprogram
subreption
subreptive
subroutine
sub-Saharan
subscriber
subsection
subsellium
subsensual
subsequent
subserrate
subsessile
subshrubby
subsidence
subsidency
subsidiary
subsidizer
subsistent
subsolidus
subspecies
subspinous
substanced
substance P
substantia
sub-station

substation	sufferance	summer teal	superoxide	surf-riding
substellar	suffibulum	summer-tide	superpower	surf scoter
substitute	sufficient	summer time	super-royal	surgeoness
substratal	suffisance	summertime	superseder	surgically
substratum	suffragism	summer-tree	supersonic	Surinamese
subsultive	suffragist	summer wood	supersound	surjection
subsultory	sugarallie	summitless	superspace	surjective
subsumable	sugar-apple	summonable	superstate	surmisable
subsurface	sugar-baker	sumphishly	superstore	surmounted
subtangent	sugar-berry	sun balcony	supertonic	surnominal
subtenancy	sugar-candy	sun bittern	supertunic	surpassing
subterfuge	sugar daddy	sun compass	supervener	surplusage
subterrane	sugar-grass	Sunday best	supervisal	surprising
subterrene	sugar-house	Sunday face	supervisee	surrealism
subtertian	sugariness	Sundayfied	supervisor	surrealist
subtextual	sugar maple	sunderable	superwoman	surreality
subtilisin	sugarollie	sunderance	superwomen	Surrentine
subtleness	sugar-paper	Sunderland	supination	surreption
subtleties	sugar stick	sunderment	supineness	Surrey fowl
subtracter	sugar-tongs	sundriness	suppedanea	surrounder
subtractor	sugar-works	sun furnace	supper club	surveyable
subtrahend	suggestion	sunglasses	supperless	surveyance
subtropics	suggestive	sun-grazing	supper-time	survivable
subtypical	suicidally	sunk garden	supplanter	survivance
suburbanly	sui generis	sunk storey	supplejack	susception
suburbican	suit length	sun-lighted	supplement	susceptive
subvariety	suitorship	sun-lounger	suppleness	suscipient
subvention	suit-weight	sunlounger	suppletion	suspectful
subversion	sullenness	sun parlour	suppletive	suspension
subversive	sulphamate	sun-picture	suppletory	suspensive
succedanea	sulphamide	sunset home	suppliable	suspensoid
succeeding	sulphatase	sunsetting	suppliance	suspensory
successful	sulphatide	sunshining	suppliancy	suspicable
succession	sulphation	superalloy	supplicant	suspicious
successive	sulphinate	superaltar	supplicate	suspirious
succinctly	sulpho-acid	superbitch	supply base	Sussex fowl
succorance	sulphonate	superbness	supply drop	sustaining
succulence	sulphonium	superbrain	supply-side	sustenance
succussion	sulphosalt	supercargo	supportive	sustentate
succussive	sulphoxide	supercilia	supposable	sustention
such as it is	sulphurate	superclass	supposably	sustentive
suck around	sulphurise	supercross	supposedly	sutlership
suck-bottle	sulphurity	super-duper	suppressal	suturation
sucker-disc	sulphurize	superexalt	suppressed	suzerainty
sucker-fish	sulphurous	superexcel	suppresser	suzuribako
sucker-foot	sulphydric	super-extra	suppressor	Svetambara
sucking-pad	sulphydryl	superfecta	suprahuman	swage-block
sucralfate	sultan pink	superfluid	supralunar	swami-house
suction box	sultanship	supergiant	supraoptic	swamp angel
suction fan	sultriness	supergrass	suprapubic	swamp apple
suction gas	Sumerogram	supergroup	suprarenal	swamp buggy
suctorious	Sumerology	superheavy	supratidal	swamp fever
Sudan grass	summarizer	superhelix	supravital	swampiness
sudatories	summer bird	superhuman	surcharger	swamp quail
sudatorium	summer camp	superindue	sure as a gun	swamp robin
suddenness	summer duck	superionic	sure enough	swan flower
suede brush	summer-heat	superiorly	sure-footed	swan-hopper
suede-cloth	summer-land	superlunar	suretyship	swankiness
suede-shoed	summerless	supermanly	surfaceman	swan-maiden
suet-headed	summer-like	supermodel	surface-rib	swan mussel
sufferable	summer-long	supernally	surfactant	swan-necked
sufferably	summer's day	superorder	surfeiting	swanneries

Swan of Avon	swing Kelly	symphonies	synthetist	tailor-bird
swan-upping	swingle-bar	symphonise	synthetize	tailor-made
swarm-spore	swing-round	symphonism	Syntocinon	tailor-make
swarthiest	swing shift	symphonist	syntrophic	tailor-shad
swashingly	swing-swang	symphonize	syphilitic	tailorship
swash-plate	swing-wheel	symphyseal	syphilosis	tailor-wise
swashplate	swirl skirt	symphysial	syringeful	take a brief
swastikaed	swish-swash	symplasmic	systematic	take a chair
swatch-book	swish-swish	symplastic	systemizer	take a class
swath-board	Swiss chard	symplectic	systemless	take action
swayamvara	Swiss cream	symposiast	tabardillo	take advice
sway-backed	Swiss guard	symposiums	tabby weave	take a flyer
swear blind	Swiss steak	sympotical	tabernacle	take a knock
sweat blood	switchable	symptomize	table-board	take a level
sweat gland	switchback	synaereses	table-clock	take an oath
sweat-house	switch cane	synaeresis	tablecloth	take a smoke
sweatiness	switch deal	synaloepha	table-cover	take as read
sweatingly	switched-on	synanthous	table d'hôte	take breath
sweat it out	switcheroo	synaxarion	table jelly	take care of
sweat lodge	switchfoot	synaxarist	table knife	take charge
sweat pants	switchgear	syncarpous	table linen	take effect
sweatpants	switch gene	synchronal	table-money	take flight
sweatshirt	switch-girl	synchronic	tablemount	take fright
Swedish ivy	switch hook	Synclavier	table-music	take heed of
sweepingly	switch-horn	syncopated	table-plate	take in hand
sweepstake	switch-lamp	syncopator	tablescape	take in sail
sweet Alice	switch over	syncretise	table-shore	take it easy
sweet basil	switch tail	syncretism	tablespoon	take it slow
sweet bread	switchyard	syncretist	table-stone	take kindly
sweetbread	Switzeress	syncretize	table-water	taken aback
sweet-brier	swivel-eyed	syndactyly	tabloidese	take notice
sweet broom	swivel hips	synderesis	tabula rasa	take orders
sweet cumin	swivel-hook	syndicator	tabulation	take pity on
sweetening	swivelling	synecdoche	tabulatory	take refuge
sweet-grass	swooningly	synecology	tachograph	take sights
sweetheart	sword dance	synergetic	tachometer	take the air
sweetie-pie	sword grass	syngenesis	tachometry	take the bun
sweet Jesus	sword-proof	syngenetic	tachygraph	take the rap
sweet lemon	sword-sedge	syngnathid	tachykinin	take the rue
sweet mamma	sword-smith	synkinesis	tachymeter	take the sea
sweetmouth	swordstick	synkinetic	tachypnoea	take the sun
sweet music	sybaritish	synoecious	tachyscope	take the way
sweet Nancy	sybaritism	synonymies	tachyzoite	take to task
sweet olive	sycophancy	synonymise	taciturnly	take to wife
sweet sedge	Sydney-side	synonymist	tack-hammer	take up arms
sweetstuff	syllabuses	synonymity	tackle-fall	take up with
sweet tooth	syllogizer	synonymize	tackle-room	takhtrawan
sweet water	sylvestral	synonymous	tactically	takingness
swell-front	symbolatry	synoptical	tactlessly	Talbot's law
swellingly	symbolical	synostosis	tactuality	talc powder
swell-organ	symbolizer	synostotic	taeniacide	talc schist
swell-shark	symbolling	synovially	taeniafuge	talc window
sweltering	symmetries	syntactics	taeniodont	talebearer
swerveless	symmetrise	syntagmata	taffy apple	talentless
swim-feeder	symmetrize	syntaxemic	tagliarini	talent show
swimmingly	sympathies	syntaxical	tagraggery	talent-spot
swimsuited	sympathise	synteresis	tailcoated	tale of a tub
swine-cress	sympathist	synthesise	tail covert	taleteller
swine fever	sympathize	synthesist	tail female	talismanic
swing-chair	sympelmous	synthesize	tail-flower	talk down to
swing-glass	symphilism	synthetase	tail gunner	talk turkey
swingingly	symphilous	synthetise	tailorable	talkwriter

talky-talky	tariff wall	team spirit	Teller mine	tensometer
tallow-drop	tarmacadam	tea-planter	tellership	tentacular
tallow-face	tarmacking	tear bottle	telligraph	tentaculum
tallow tree	tarocchino	tear-jerker	telling-off	tenterhook
tallow-wood	Tarquinian	tearlessly	tellograph	tenth-value
tall timber	tarsectomy	tea-scented	telophasic	tent-master
tally-board	tarsonemid	tea-seed oil	telpherage	tent-pegger
tally clerk	tartareous	tea-service	temenggong	tent stitch
tally sheet	tartrazine	tea-tasting	temeritous	tenurially
tally-stick	tartronate	tea trolley	temerously	tepidarium
tallywoman	Tartuffian	tea yellows	temperable	teppan-yaki
Talmudical	Tartuffism	teaze-tenon	temperance	teratogeny
tamarillos	taskmaster	technetium	tempersome	teratology
tamboritsa	tassel-bush	technician	tempestive	terebellid
tambourine	tassel fish	technicise	Templardom	tergiverse
tamburitza	tasselling	technicism	templeless	termagancy
tameletjie	tassel-weed	technicist	temporalis	terminable
tame-poison	taste-blind	technicity	temporally	terminably
Tammanyism	taste blood	technicize	temporalty	terminalia
Tammanyite	tastefully	technocrat	temporizer	terminally
tandem axle	tat protein	technofear	temptation	terminator
tangential	tatpurusha	technology	temptingly	terminuses
tanglefoot	tattersall	technonomy	temulently	term-policy
tangle-legs	tattie-trap	tectogenic	tenability	term symbol
tanglement	tattle-tale	tectonical	tenantable	terne metal
tanglingly	tattlingly	teeny-weeny	tenantless	terne-plate
tank-buster	tauntingly	teeter-tail	tenantship	terpolymer
tank engine	tauromachy	teeth ridge	tendencies	terracette
tannic acid	tautologic	teetotaler	tendential	terracotta
tantalizer	tautomeric	teetotally	tenderable	terra firma
tantamount	tautonymic	tegumental	tender-eyed	Terramycin
Tantum ergo	tautophony	teichopsia	tenderfoot	terraneous
tap-changer	tautozonal	Tel Avivian	tenderizer	terrariums
tap-dancing	tawdriness	telecabine	tenderling	terra rossa
tape player	tawny eagle	telecamera	tenderloin	terreplein
tape reader	tawny pipit	telecaster	tenderness	terre-verte
tape-record	taxability	telechiric	tender spot	terrier-man
taperingly	tax bracket	telecobalt	tendinitis	territoria
tapescript	tax evasion	Telecopier	tendonitis	terrorizer
tapestried	taxflation	telegnosis	tendrillar	terrorless
tapestries	tax holiday	telegraphy	tendrilled	terror raid
taphonomic	taxi dancer	telemarket	tenebresce	Tersanctus
tapotement	taxidermal	telematics	tenebrific	tertiation
tap penalty	taxidermic	telemetric	tenebrious	tessellate
tappety-tap	taxi-driver	teleologic	tenemental	testaceous
tapping-bar	taxonomist	teleonomic	tenemented	test flight
tapping key	taxonomize	teleostean	tenementer	testicular
taradiddle	tax shelter	telepathic	tenmantale	test-market
Tarahumara	tayberries	telephoner	tennantite	test-retest
tarantella	T-bone steak	telephonic	Tennessean	test signal
tarantelle	Tcheremiss	telephotos	tennis ball	testudinal
tarantular	tchinovnik	teleprompt	tennis club	testudines
Tarantulle	T-connected	telepuppet	tennis knee	tetarteron
tarbooshed	teacherage	teleradium	tennis-play	tetchiness
tardigrade	teacheress	telerecord	tennis shoe	tetrabasic
targetable	tea-clipper	telescopic	tenotomies	tetracaine
target area	teacupfuls	telescreen	tenotomize	tetrachord
target cell	tea-drinker	televiewer	ten-pointer	tetracolon
target date	tea infuser	television	ten-pounder	tetracoral
target-rich	tea machine	televisual	tensegrity	tetradecyl
targetting	team player	teleworker	tensimeter	tetraethyl
tariffable	team rector	teliospore	tension bar	tetragnath

tetragonal	the classes	theophoric	think aloud	thread-mill
tetrahedra	the Commune	theopneust	thinkingly	thread vein
tetrameric	the Company	theorician	think-piece	thread-wire
tetrameter	thé complet	theosopher	think scorn	threadwork
tetramorph	the Creator	theosophic	think shame	threadworm
tetraploid	the Curragh	the Prophet	think twice	threatened
tetrapolis	The Customs	thereabout	thiochrome	threatener
tetrapylon	thé dansant	thereabove	thiocyanic	three balls
tetrarchic	the Descent	thereafter	thioindigo	three-eight
tetrasomic	the dickens	thereamong	thioketone	three-field
tetraspore	the dismals	thereanent	thiomersal	Three in One
tetrastich	the Eternal	therehence	thiopental	three parts
tetrastoon	the fair sex	thereright	thiophenol	threepence
tetrastyle	The Fifteen	thereunder	thiouracil	threepenny
tetrateuch	the Flemish	there you go	third-class	three-phase
tetrathlon	the Forties	thermalise	third floor	three-piece
tetratomic	the glad eye	thermalize	third flute	three-piled
tetterworm	the hard way	thermionic	third force	three-point
tetterwort	the heathen	thermistor	third house	threescore
teuthology	the heavens	Thermogene	third order	three-sixty
Teutomania	the icy mitt	thermogram	third party	three-space
Teutophile	the instant	thermology	third power	threnodial
Teutophobe	the insured	the r months	third-rater	threnodist
Texas fever	theistical	thermophil	Third Reich	thresh over
Texas Tower	the jitters	thermopile	third water	thriftiest
text editor	the likes of	thermostat	Third World	thriftless
text-letter	the low toby	thermotics	thirstiest	thrift shop
textualism	the Macedon	theromorph	thirstless	thriveless
textualist	the Mahatma	therophyte	thirteener	thrivingly
textuality	the Marches	the schools	thirteenth	throat-band
texturally	thematical	the shivers	thirty-five	throat-full
text-writer	theme music	thesis-play	thirtyfold	throatiest
T-formation	Themistian	the species	thirty-four	throat-lash
thack-board	themselves	Thessalian	thirty-nine	throatless
thack house	thenabouts	theta meson	this moment	throat-mane
thack-stone	thenardite	theta pinch	this or that	throat-pipe
Thailander	the nations	the Tempter	thistle cup	throat-wash
thalassian	thencefrom	the three R's	thixotropy	throatwort
thale cress	then-clause	thetically	tholeiitic	thromboses
thaliacean	theocrasia	the Tropics	tholos tomb	thrombosis
thalictrum	theocratic	the Twelfth	Thomsonian	thrombotic
thankfully	theodicaea	theurgical	thomsonite	throneless
thanksgive	theodicean	the visible	thorianite	throne room
thatchless	theodicies	the wee folk	thorn apple	throughout
thatch-palm	theodidact	the year dot	thorn-hedge	throughput
that's right	theodolite	the year one	thorniness	throughway
that will do	Theodosian	thiaminase	thorn-proof	throw about
the accused	Theodotian	thickening	thornproof	throw a look
thearchies	theogonies	thick-skull	Thorotrast	throw aside
theatrical	theogonist	thick space	thoroughly	throw-stick
the Balkans	the Old Dart	thick woods	thoughtful	thruppence
the big bird	theologate	thief-taker	thought-out	thruppenny
the big idea	theologian	thieveless	thoughtway	thrushlike
the big pond	theologies	thieveries	thousandth	thrutching
the big time	theologise	thievishly	thrawnness	thuddingly
the black ox	theologism	thill-horse	threadbare	thuggishly
the Borders	theologist	thimble-eye	thread-cell	thumb-cleat
the Borough	theologize	thimbleful	threadiest	thumb-flint
the Bye Plot	theomaniac	thimblerig	thread-lace	thumbikins
the cap fits	theopathic	thinginess	threadless	thumb index
the cassock	theophanic	thingumbob	threadlike	thumb paper
the Channel	theophobia	think again	thread mark	thumb piano

thumbpiece
thumbprint
thumbscrew
thumbs down
thumb-stall
thumb-stick
thumpingly
thunbergia
thunder-axe
thunder-box
thunderbox
thunderbug
thunder egg
thunderfly
thunderful
thunder-god
thundering
thunder-mug
thunderous
thunder run
thuribuler
Thuringian
thwartness
thwart-over
thwartship
thwartways
thwartwise
thymectomy
thymic acid
thymidylic
thyrohyoid
thyroideal
thyrotoxic
thysanuran
Tiahuanaco
Tibetology
tibiotarsi
ticker tape
ticket fine
ticketless
ticket tout
tickety-boo
tickle pink
ticklesome
tickle-tail
ticklishly
tick-tacker
tick typhus
ticky-tacky
tic-polonga
tidal basin
tidal river
tidal train
tiddlypush
tiddly suit
tiddlywink
tidewaiter
tidingless
tie-breaker
tie in knots
tie the knot
tiger-finch

tiger heron
tigerishly
tiger maple
tiger prawn
tiger shark
tiger-snake
tigrolysis
tillandsia
tiller-head
tillerless
tiller-rope
tiller soup
Tilley lamp
till-tapper
tilly-vally
tilt-hammer
timber-head
timberjack
timberland
timberless
timberline
timber tree
timber wolf
timber-work
timber-yard
timbreless
time-barred
time-course
time domain
time enough
time factor
time-fellow
timekeeper
time-killer
timelessly
timeliness
time-notice
time of life
time pencil
time policy
time's arrow
time-series
time-served
time-server
time signal
time-spirit
times table
time switch
time-taking
time thrust
time travel
time-waster
timocratic
timorously
tin-canning
tinctorial
tinder-like
tin disease
tinker-bird
tinktinkie

tinselling
Tinseltown
tin soldier
tintamarre
Tintometer
tin wedding
tin whistle
tip one's hat
tip-topmost
tirailleur
tirelessly
tiresomely
tiring-iron
tirocinium
tirra-lirra
tissue-bank
tissue type
tit and arse
Titanesque
titanosaur
tit-babbler
titbitical
tithingman
titillator
titivation
title entry
title fight
title-music
title-piece
titratable
titrimetry
tits and ass
tittupping
titty-totty
titubation
titularity
titulature
tit warbler
toad-headed
to a frazzle
to a miracle
to and again
to a proverb
toast Melba
to a surfeit
tobacco-box
tobacco fly
tobacco-man
Tobagonian
Tobin's tube
tobogganer
tobramycin
to capacity
Tocharian A
Tocharian B
tocher-band
tocher-good
tocherless
tocologist
tocopherol
toco toucan
toddlekins

toddy-ladle
toddy-stick
toe and heel
toe-curling
toe-dancing
toe of Italy
toe-tapping
toe the line
toffee-like
toffee-nose
Toggenburg
toggle-bolt
togt-ganger
to hospital
toilenette
toilet-case
toiletries
toilet roll
toilet-room
toilet soap
toilet tent
toilsomely
to infinity
tokay gecko
token booth
tokenistic
token money
tolazamide
tolazoline
tolerantly
toleration
tolfraedic
Tolkienian
toll bridge
toll-farmer
toll-keeper
tomahawker
tomatillos
tomato moth
tomato vine
tomato worm
Tom Collins
tomfoolery
tomfoolish
Tom o'Bedlam
tomography
tomorrower
Tom Pudding
tonalities
tonalitive
tone-colour
toned paper
tonelessly
tone-on-tone
tone sandhi
tongue-bang
tongue-fish
tongue-lash
tongueless
tonguelike
tongue-shot
tongue-slip

tongue-sole
tonguester
tongues wag
tongue-tied
tongue-work
tongue-worm
tonguiness
tonic major
tonic minor
tonic sol-fa
tonic spasm
tonic water
tonitruant
tonitruous
ton-mileage
tonofibril
tonometric
tonotactic
Tony Curtis
tool-holder
toolmaking
tool-pusher
too many for
too much for
to one's face
to one's feet
to one's hand
to one's head
to one's will
toothbrush
tooth fairy
tooth-glass
toothpaste
tooth-plate
tooth shell
to outrance
top and tail
topazolite
topgallant
tophaceous
top-heavily
Tophetical
topicality
topicalize
topknotted
Töpler pump
top-lighted
top-notcher
topogenous
topography
topoisomer
topologist
topologize
toponymist
toposcopic
topotactic
top-slicing
top-spinner
topsy-turvy
topsy-versy
torbernite
torchlight

tornado-pit	Tower pound	tragi-farce	transpolar	tree tomato
toroidally	towing hook	trail a pike	transposal	treillaged
torpedoist	towing line	trailerite	transposer	trek farmer
torpedoman	towing-path	trail-hound	transposon	trek netter
torpedo-net	towing-rope	trailingly	transprose	trekschuit
torpidness	Townsville	train crash	transputer	trellising
torporific	townswoman	train ferry	trans-shape	trembleuse
torrential	townswomen	train-guard	trans-sonic	trembliest
torrid zone	toxalbumin	traitoress	transudate	tremelloid
torsion bar	toxication	traitorism	transvalue	tremendous
tortellini	toxicology	traitorous	transvenom	tremograph
tortfeasor	toxiphobia	trajectile	transverse	tremolando
tortiously	toxophoric	trajection	trans-world	tremolitic
tortuosity	toxoplasma	trajectory	trap-cellar	tremolo arm
tortuously	toy library	trammelled	trapeziums	tremor disc
torturable	toy soldier	trammeller	trap-siding	tremorless
tos and fros	toy theatre	tramontana	trash-house	trenbolone
to some tune	trabaccolo	tramontane	trashiness	trenchancy
toss pillow	trabeation	trampoline	traumatise	trench boot
tosylation	trabeculae	tramp-tramp	traumatism	trench coat
totalistic	trabecular	trance-like	traumatize	trench feet
totemistic	trace-chain	trancelike	trautonium	trench foot
to the death	trace-horse	tranchette	travailous	trenchless
to the north	tracheated	tranexamic	travelator	trenchmore
to the point	tracheidal	tranquilli	travel card	trendiness
tother year	tracheitis	tranquillo	travelling	trepanning
to the skies	trachelate	tranquilly	travelogue	treponemal
to the south	tracheolar	transactor	travel-sick	trespasser
to the teeth	track-brake	transboard	traversely	trestle-bed
to the touch	tracker dog	transcribe	travertine	trevallies
to the winds	track event	transcript	travestied	triacetate
totipotent	tracklayer	transducer	travestier	triaconter
touch-and-go	tractarian	transearth	travesties	trial court
touchiness	Tractarian	transeptal	travolator	trial eight
touchingly	tractatule	transepted	trawlerman	triallelic
touch judge	tractility	transeunce	trawlermen	trial-piece
touch-me-not	tractional	transexual	traymobile	triandrous
touch panel	tractoring	transferee	tread-board	triangular
touch-paper	tractotomy	transferer	tread on air	Triangulum
touchpaper	Trade Board	transferor	tread water	triathlete
touch-piece	tradecraft	transgenic	treadwheel	triatomine
touch rugby	trade cycle	transgress	treasonous	triaxially
touchstone	trade paper	transhuman	treasuress	tribometer
tough pitch	trade plate	transience	treasuries	tribrachic
tough stuff	trade price	transiency	treatyless	trichiasis
tough titty	trade-route	transistor	treaty port	trichinous
Toulousain	tradesfolk	transiting	treble bell	trichocyst
Tourettism	trade union	transition	treble clef	trichogyne
touring car	trade waste	transitive	treble hook	trichology
tourmaline	traditores	transit man	trebleness	trichotomy
tournament	traduction	transitory	trecentist	trichroism
tourniquet	traductive	transitron	tree doctor	trichromat
tout simple	traffic cop	Transkeian	tree-feeder	trichromic
towability	traffic jam	translator	tree hoopoe	tricipital
towardness	trafficked	translucid	tree hopper	trickeries
tow-boating	trafficker	translunar	tree mallow	trick-frame
towel-gourd	tragacanth	transmural	tree martin	trickiness
towel-horse	tragedical	transmuted	tree medick	trickishly
tower block	tragedious	transmuter	tree of life	tricksiest
tower-cress	tragically	transocean	tree-oyster	trick wheel
toweringly	tragic flaw	transplace	treerunner	triclinium
tower karst	tragicomic	transplant	tree search	tricoccous

tricrotism	tripleness	trolley-car	trustingly	tundra swan
tricyclist	triple play	trolleyful	trust-stock	tunelessly
tridecylic	triple salt	trolleyman	truthfully	tuner-timer
tridentate	triple-tail	Trollopian	truth serum	tuning-cone
Tridentine	triple time	trollopish	truth squad	tuning fork
trienniums	triple tree	trombonist	truth table	tuning-wire
trierarchy	triplicate	tromometer	truth-value	tunnel-back
trifarious	triplicist	tron weight	try for size	tunnel-head
triflingly	triplicity	troop-horse	tryingness	tunnel-kiln
trifoliate	Tripolitan	troostitic	trypsinize	tunnel-like
trifurcate	tripperish	tropaeolin	tryptamine	tunnelling
trigeminal	trippiness	tropaeolum	tryptophan	Tupperware
trigeminus	trippingly	trophocyte	try-scoring	turbanless
trigesimal	tripsomely	trophogeny	tube curare	turbanwise
trigger man	trip switch	trophology	tube-flower	turbary pig
triglossia	tripudiant	trophonema	tube of flow	turbiditic
triglyphed	tripudiate	Trophonian	tuberation	turbidness
triglyphic	triquetrae	trophosome	tubercular	turbinated
trigonally	triquetral	tropically	tuberculin	turbodrill
trigonitis	triradiate	tropic bird	tuberculum	turbopause
trihedrons	trisection	tropologic	tuberiform	turboshaft
trihydrate	triseptate	tropopause	tuberosity	turbotrain
trilabiate	tri-service	tropophyte	tuberously	turbulence
trilaminar	triskelion	tropotaxis	tub gurnard	turbulency
trilateral	Tristanian	Trotskyism	tubicolous	Turcophile
trilineate	Tristanite	Trotskyist	tuboplasty	Turcophobe
trilingual	tristearin	Trotskyite	tub-thumper	turf-cutter
trilinguar	tristfully	troubadour	tubularian	turgescent
triliteral	tristichic	troubledly	tubularity	turgidness
trillibubs	tristylous	trouble man	tubulation	Turing test
trillingly	trisulcate	troughlike	tubulature	turkey-bush
trillionth	tritanopia	trousering	tubuliform	turkey-call
trilobitic	tritanopic	trousseaus	tuckerless	turkeycock
trilocular	triternate	trousseaux	tuck-stitch	turkey-corn
trimestral	triterpane	trout-perch	Tudoresque	turkey-gnat
trimmingly	triterpene	*trouvaille*	tuffaceous	Turkey hone
trimnasium	tritiation	trowelling	tuftaffeta	turkey-trot
trimonthly	triturable	troy weight	tufted duck	Turkey work
trimorphic	triturator	Trubenized	tuft-hunted	Turkish rug
tri-motored	triumphant	truce of God	tuft-hunter	turn around
Trinacrian	triumviral	truck frame	tug-boating	turnaround
trinacrite	triungulin	truck-house	tuitionary	turn a trick
trinkerman	triunities	truckle-bed	tularaemia	turn-bridge
trinoctial	trivalence	truck-store	tularaemic	turn bridle
trinocular	trivalency	truculence	tulip break	turnbroach
trinominal	trivialise	truculency	tulip-glass	turn-buckle
trioecious	trivialism	true for you	tumatakuru	turn-button
trio-sonata	trivialist	true to form	tumbledown	turn colour
tripartism	triviality	true to life	tumble-dung	turn-furrow
tripartite	trivialize	true to type	tumble home	turning-pin
trip-bucket	trochaical	truffle-dog	tumble-over	turning-saw
tripe-hound	trochanter	truistical	tumbler-cup	turnip-flea
tripeptide	trochiform	trumperies	tumblerful	turnip moth
trip-hammer	trochoidal	trumpeting	tumbleweed	turnip-tops
triphibian	trochotron	trumpet-lug	tumescence	turnip-wood
triphthong	troctolite	truncately	tumour-like	turn-plough
triphylite	troglobion	truncation	tumulation	turn signal
tripinnate	troglodyte	truncature	tumultuary	turns ratio
triplasian	trogloxene	trundle-bed	tumultuate	turn turtle
triple bond	trolley-bar	trunk-maker	tumultuous	turnverein
triple harp	trolley bus	trustfully	tunability	turpentine
triple jump	trolleybus	trustiness	tun-bellied	turpentiny

turtle-back	tympanitis	umbrellaed	unassorted	unborrowed
turtle-deck	tyndallize	umpireship	unassuaged	unbothered
turtle-dove	type basket	unabatable	unassuming	unbottomed
turtlehead	type-holder	unabatedly	unathletic	unbowelled
turtle-neck	typescript	unabridged	unatonable	unbranched
turtleneck	typesetter	unabsolved	unattached	unbreached
Turveydrop	typewriter	unabsorbed	unattacked	unbreathed
tut-mouthed	typhlosole	unacademic	unattained	unbreeched
tutorially	typhogenic	unaccented	unattended	unbribable
tuxedo sofa	typhomania	unaccepted	unattested	unbroached
tuzzy-muzzy	typhoonish	unaccursed	unavailing	unbrokenly
twanginess	typicality	unachieved	unavowable	unburdened
twangingly	typography	unacquaint	unavowedly	unburiable
tweediness	typologist	unacquired	unawakened	unburnable
Tweedledee	typologize	unactorish	unbackable	unbuttered
Tweedledum	typoscript	unactressy	unbailable	unbuttoned
tweet tweet	typothetae	unactuated	unbalanced	uncalcined
twelfth day	tyrannical	unadaptive	unbanished	uncalendar
Twelfth Day	tyrannizer	unaddicted	unbankable	uncandidly
twelfth man	tyrantship	unadjacent	unbaptized	uncanniest
twelve-bore	tyre-cement	unadjusted	unbarbered	uncanonise
twelvefold	tyrocinium	unadmiring	unbattered	uncanonize
twelve noon	tyrosinase	unadmitted	unbearable	uncanopied
twelve-note	Tyrrhenian	unadvanced	unbearably	uncaptious
twelve-tone	ubiquarian	unaffected	unbeatable	uncaptured
twenty-five	ubiquinone	unagitated	unbeatably	uncardinal
twentyfold	ubiquitary	unalarming	unbeautify	uncared-for
twenty-four	Ubiquitism	unalliable	unbecoming	uncaringly
twenty-nine	ubiquitous	unallotted	unbedimmed	uncarpeted
twiddly bit	ufological	unalluring	unbegotten	uncastable
twig-blight	ugsomeness	unaltering	unbeguiled	uncatholic
twigginess	uintathere	unamenable	unbeholden	uncautious
twig-pruner	ulceration	un-American	unbelieved	uncemented
twilighted	ulcerative	unamusable	unbeliever	uncensored
twin-bedded	ulotrichan	unanalysed	unbemoaned	uncensured
twin double	ulteriorly	unanalytic	unbendable	unchanging
twinflower	ultimacies	unanimated	unbeseemly	uncharming
twing-twang	ultimately	unannealed	unbesieged	unchastely
twi-nighter	ultimation	unannulled	unbesought	unchastity
twin sister	ultimative	unanointed	unbespoken	uncheerful
twist-drill	ultimatory	unanswered	unbestowed	uncheering
twistiness	ultimatums	unappalled	unbetrayed	unchildish
twistingly	ultrabasic	unapparent	unbettered	unchivalry
twitchiest	ultrafiche	unappealed	unbevelled	unchoosing
twittingly	ultraistic	unappeased	unbewailed	unchristen
two-address	Ultralente	unapprised	unbiasedly	unchristly
two figures	ultralight	unapproved	unbiblical	unchurched
two fingers	ultramafic	unarguable	unbiddable	unchurchly
two nations	ultra-short	unarguably	unbirthday	unciliated
two natures	ultrasonic	unarmoured	unbishoped	uncircular
two or three	ultrasound	unarranged	unblanched	uncivilise
two-pronged	Ultrasuede	unarrested	unblazoned	uncivility
two-sticker	*ultra vires*	unartfully	unbleached	uncivilize
two-striper	ultroneous	unartistic	unblenched	unclashing
two-tongued	ulvospinel	unascended	unblighted	uncleansed
two-wheeler	Umbandista	unasked-for	unblinking	unclerical
Tyburn tree	umbellated	unaspiring	unblissful	unclogging
tycoonship	umbellifer	unassailed	unbloodied	uncloister
tykishness	umbilicate	unasserted	unbloodily	unclosable
tylopodous	umboth duty	unassigned	unblushing	uncoffined
tympanites	umbracious	unassisted	unboastful	uncollated
tympanitic	umbrageous	unassoiled	unbonneted	uncoloured

uncombined	under-agent	undersexed	undisarmed	unenviable
uncomelily	underbelly	undersheet	undiseased	unenviably
uncommixed	underboard	undershirt	undisguise	unequalise
uncommonly	underbough	undershoot	undismayed	unequality
uncompared	underbrush	undershore	undisposed	unequalize
uncomposed	underbuild	undershrub	undisputed	unequalled
unconfined	undercarve	undersized	undistinct	unequipped
unconfused	underclass	underskirt	undiverted	unerringly
unconfuted	under-clerk	underslept	undivinely	unescorted
unconjugal	undercliff	underslung	undivorced	unesteemed
unconsoled	undercloak	undersound	undivulged	un-European
unconsumed	undercount	underspend	undoctored	unevenness
uncontrite	under cover	understaff	undogmatic	uneventful
unconveyed	undercover	understand	undomestic	unexacting
unconvince	undercreep	understate	undoneness	unexamined
uncopiable	undercroft	under steam	undoubtful	unexampled
uncorroded	undercrust	understeer	undoubting	unexcelled
uncorseted	under-devil	understock	undramatic	unexcepted
uncovenant	underdrain	understood	undrawable	unexciting
uncovetous	underdrawn	understory	undreading	unexecuted
uncreative	underdress	understudy	undrivable	unexistent
uncredited	underdrift	underswell	undrooping	unexisting
uncriminal	underdrive	undertaker	undubitate	unexpanded
uncrippled	underearth	underthing	undulately	unexpected
uncritical	under-fives	underthink	undulating	unexpended
uncrumbled	under-flame	undertoned	undulation	unexpiated
uncrumpled	underfloor	undertread	undulatory	unexplicit
unctuosity	underfocus	undertreat	undulously	unexploded
unctuously	underframe	undertrial	uneasiness	unexplored
uncultured	underglaze	undertrick	uneclipsed	unextended
uncumbered	undergrass	undertrump	uneconomic	unfaceable
uncustomed	under-grove	undertunic	unedifying	unfadingly
uncuttable	undergrowl	undervalue	uneducable	unfailable
undangered	undergrown	undervoice	uneducated	unfailably
undarkened	underjawed	under water	uneffected	unfainting
undazzling	underlayer	underwater	unegoistic	unfairness
undeadened	underlease	under weigh	unelectric	unfaithful
undebarred	underlever	underwhelm	unelevated	unfallible
undecaying	underlight	underwired	uneloquent	unfallowed
undeceived	underlinen	underworld	unembanked	unfamiliar
undeceiver	underlying	under wraps	unembodied	unfastened
undecipher	undermatch	underwrite	unembraced	unfathered
undecision	underminer	underwrote	unemphatic	unfatherly
undecisive	undernamed	undescried	unemployed	unfathomed
undeclared	underneath	undeserted	unenclosed	unfatigued
undeclined	under night	undeserved	unendeared	unfavorite
undefeated	undern-time	undesigned	unendingly	unfavoured
undefended	underpaint	undesiring	unendorsed	unfeasible
undefinite	underpants	undesirous	unenduring	unfeasibly
undeformed	underpitch	undestined	unenforced	unfeatured
undefrayed	underplant	undetached	unengaging	unfeigning
undegassed	underplate	undetailed	unenhanced	unfellowed
undegraded	underprice	undetected	unenjoying	unfeminine
undejected	underprint	undeterred	unenlarged	unfeminist
undelaying	underprize	undeviated	unennobled	unfettered
undemanded	under proof	undevoured	unenriched	unfighting
undeniable	underproof	undevoutly	unenrolled	unfilially
undeniably	underquote	undextrous	unentailed	unfillable
undeplored	underroast	undictated	unentangle	unfilleted
undepraved	underscore	undigested	unenthused	unfilmable
undeprived	underscrub	undiligent	unenticing	unfiltered
under-actor	underserve	undirected	unentitled	unfindable

unfingered
unfinished
unfirmness
unfishable
unflagging
unflurried
unfocussed
unfoldment
unfoliaged
unfoliated
unfollowed
unforcedly
unforcible
unforcibly
unfordable
unforeseen
unforetold
unforgiven
unforsaken
unfoughten
unfrequent
unfriended
unfriendly
unfrighted
unfruitful
unfunniest
unfurlable
unfurrowed
ungardened
ungartered
ungathered
ungenerous
ungenially
ungettable
ungimmicky
unglorious
ungoverned
ungraceful
ungracious
ungraithed
ungrateful
ungrounded
ungrudging
unguentary
unguentous
unguidable
unguidedly
unguiltily
unhabitual
unhallowed
unhaltered
unhampered
unhandsome
unhappiest
unharassed
unhardened
unharrowed
unhazarded
unhealable
unhearable
unheavenly
unhelpable

unhelpless
unheralded
unheroical
unhideable
unhindered
unhistoric
unholiness
unhollowed
unhomelike
unhonestly
unhonoured
unhouseled
unhumanise
unhumanize
unhumorous
unhuntable
unhurrying
unhygienic
uniaxially
unicameral
unicameral
unicentral
unicorn auk
unicyclist
unidentate
unifilarly
uniflorous
unifoliate
uniformise
uniformity
uniformize
unilabiate
unilateral
unilingual
uniliteral
unilobular
unilocular
unimagined
unimitable
unimitated
unimmersed
unimmortal
unimodular
unimpaired
unimparted
unimplored
unimposing
unimproved
unimpugned
unincensed
unincisive
unincluded
unindebted
unindented
unindicted
unindulged
uninfected
uninfested
uninflamed
uninformed
uninitiate
uninjected

uninnocent
uninominal
uninquired
uninspired
uninsulate
uninsulted
unintended
uninterest
uninterred
unintimate
uninuclear
uninvented
uninverted
uninvested
uninviting
uninvolved
Union House
unionistic
union joint
union screw
unipartite
uniplicate
unipolarly
uniqueness
uniseptate
uniseriate
unisonally
unisonance
unitedness
unit-factor
unit-holder
unitholder
unit-linked
unit matrix
univalence
univallate
univariant
univariate
university
univocalic
univocally
univoltine
unjacketed
unjoyfully
unjudicial
unjustness
unkillable
unkindness
unkinglike
unkinkable
unknighted
unknightly
unknitting
unknotting
unknowable
unlabelled
unlaboured
unladylike
unlamented
unlaudable
unlaunched
unlawfully

unleavened
unlectured
unlessened
unlessoned
unlettable
unlettered
unlevelled
unlicensed
unliftable
unlikeable
unlikelier
unlikeness
unlistened
unliterary
unliterate
unlittered
unliveable
unlockable
unloveable
unlovesome
unlovingly
unluckiest
unluminous
unlustrous
unmagnetic
unmaidenly
unmailable
unmakeable
unmanacled
unmanfully
unmanifest
unmannered
unmannerly
unmartyred
unmastered
unmatching
unmaterial
unmaternal
unmeasured
unmechanic
unmeddling
unmediated
unmeekness
unmeetable
unmeetness
unmellowed
unmemoried
unmendable
unmerciful
unmeriting
unmetalled
unmetallic
unmetrical
unmilitary
unmingling
unminished
unmirthful
unmiscible
unmissable
unmistaken
unmodified
unmolested

unmonastic
unmorality
unmortared
unmothered
unmotherly
unmoveable
unmovingly
unmurdered
unmuscular
unnameable
unnational
unneatness
unnoticing
unnotified
unnumbered
unnurtured
unobedient
unobjected
unobliging
unobscured
unobserved
unobtained
unoccupied
unoffended
unofficial
unopenable
unoperable
unoperated
unordained
unordinary
unoriental
unoriented
unoriginal
unorthodox
unossified
unoxidized
unpacified
unpackaged
unpalpable
unpampered
unparadise
unparallel
unpardoned
unparented
unpassable
unpastoral
unpastured
unpatented
unpathetic
unpeaceful
unpedantic
unpedestal
unpenitent
unpeppered
unperfumed
unperilous
unperished
unperjured
unpestered
unphonetic
unphysical
unpickable

unpillowed	unrealness	unrivalled	unsingable	unsummoned
unpitiable	unreasoned	unriveting	unsinister	unsupplied
unpitiably	unrebutted	unromantic	unsinkable	unsupposed
unplacable	unrecalled	unrousable	unsisterly	unsureness
un-Platonic	unreceived	unruinable	unsizeable	unsurfaced
unplayable	unreckoned	unruliness	unskillful	unsurgical
unplayably	unrecorded	unrummaged	unslakable	unsurmised
unpleasant	unredeemed	unruptured	unsleeping	unsurveyed
unpleasing	unreelable	unsackable	unslippery	unswayable
unpleasure	unreformed	unsafeness	unslipping	unswerving
unploughed	unrefusing	unsalaried	unslothful	unswinging
unplugging	unregarded	unsaleable	unsmirched	unsyllabic
unpoetical	unrejected	unsalutary	unsmokable	unsymbolic
unpoisoned	unrejoiced	unsalvable	unsmoothed	unsympathy
unpoliced	unrelative	unsanctify	unsmutched	untalented
unpolicied	unrelaxing	unsanguine	unsnapping	untameable
unpolished	unreleased	unsanitary	unsociable	untameness
unpolitely	unrelented	unsatiable	unsociably	untampered
unpolluted	unreliable	unsatiated	unsocially	untangible
unpopulate	unreliably	unsaturate	unsocketed	untappable
unpopulous	unrelieved	unsavoured	unsoftened	untasteful
unportable	unrelished	unscabbard	unsoldered	untearable
unpossible	unremarked	unscalable	unsolidity	untellable
unpowdered	unremedied	unsceptred	unsolvable	untellably
unpowerful	unremember	unschooled	unsonorous	untempered
unprecious	unremitted	unscorched	unsoothing	untempting
unprefaced	unrendered	unscottify	unspeaking	untenanted
unpregnant	unrenowned	unscourged	unspecific	untendered
unprepared	unrepaired	unscramble	unspeckled	untenderly
unprettily	unrepealed	unscreened	unspirited	unterraced
unpriestly	unrepeated	unscripted	unsporting	unterrific
unprincely	unrepelled	unscrubbed	unsqueezed	untestable
unprobably	unrepented	unsearched	unstablest	untethered
unproduced	unrepining	unseasonal	unstanched	unthankful
unprofaned	unreplaced	unseasoned	unstarched	unthatched
unprofited	unreplying	unseconded	unstartled	unthematic
unprolific	unreported	unseeingly	unstatable	unthinking
unpromised	unreposing	unseemlier	unstayable	unthrashed
unprompted	unreproved	unseizable	unsteadier	unthreaded
unprovable	unrequired	unselected	unsteadily	unthreshed
unprovided	unrequited	unsellable	unstinting	unthriving
unprovoked	unresented	unsensible	unstirring	unthronged
unpuckered	unreserved	unsensuous	unstitched	unthwarted
unpunctual	unresigned	unsentient	unstooping	unticketed
unpunished	unresisted	unshackled	unstopping	untidiness
unpurified	unresolved	unshadowed	unstraight	untillable
unpurposed	unrespited	unshakable	unstrained	untimbered
unquailing	unrestored	unshakenly	unstrapped	untiringly
unquarried	unretarded	unshapable	unstreaked	untithable
unquenched	unreticent	unsheathed	unstreamed	untogether
unquotable	unreturned	unshielded	unstressed	untouching
unransomed	unrevealed	unshingled	unstriated	untouristy
unraptured	unrevenged	unshipping	unstricken	untowardly
unrateable	unreverend	unshivered	unstringed	untradable
unratified	unreverent	unshoulder	unstripped	untrampled
unrationed	unreversed	unshowered	unstudious	untranquil
unravelled	unreviewed	unshrouded	unsublimed	untreasure
unraveller	unrewarded	unshuffled	unsuborned	untrenched
unravished	unrhythmic	unsilenced	unsufficed	untroubled
unreactive	unrideable	unsilvered	unsuffixed	untrueness
unreadable	unrightful	unsimplify	unsuitable	untrustful
unreadably	unripeness	unsinfully	unsuitably	untrusting
unrealized				

untruthful	unwritable	ureteritis	vaginismus	vaticinate
untuneable	unyielding	urethritis	vagrantize	vauclusian
unturbaned	unyouthful	urgentness	vail bonnet	vaudeville
unturnable	unzippered	urgicenter	Valdepeñas	vaultingly
untwisting	up a gum tree	uricosuric	valerianic	vauntingly
ununitable	up and about	uricotelic	validation	vavasories
unuplifted	up-and-comer	urinalyses	valleculae	Vegeburger
unusedness	up and doing	urinalysis	vallecular	vegetarian
unusefully	up-and-under	urinomancy	Valley Girl	vegetation
unusuality	upbraiding	urinometer	valley lily	vegetative
unutilized	upbringing	urinoscopy	valorously	vehemently
unvaluable	upbristled	urodynamic	value added	vehiculate
unvariable	up for grabs	urogenital	value-laden	veiledness
unvariably	upgradable	urographic	valve train	veld-cornet
unvariedly	uphillward	urological	valvulitis	veligerous
unveiledly	upholstery	uropoietic	vampire bat	velitation
unvendible	up in the air	urothelial	vampiredom	velocipede
unvenomous	upliftment	urothelium	vampirical	velocities
unventured	upon my life	urotropine	vanadinite	veltheimia
unveracity	upon my soul	uroxanthin	vancomycin	velutinous
unverified	upon my word	ursine seal	vancourier	velvet bean
unvigilant	upper class	urticarial	vanilla-pod	velvet crab
unvintaged	upper crust	urtication	vanishment	velvet-dock
unviolable	Upper House	usableness	vanitories	velvet duck
unviolated	upper sixth	usageaster	vanitously	velvetfish
unvirtuous	upper-stock	use and wont	vanity case	velvet-leaf
unvitiated	upper works	useful load	Vanity Fair	velvet-pile
unvolatile	uppishness	usefulness	vanity unit	velvet-worm
unvowelled	uppitiness	use the seas	vanquisher	venae cavae
unvulgarly	uproarious	usquebaugh	vapography	venational
unwalkable	upset price	ustulation	vaporiform	venatorial
unwandered	upsettable	usucapient	vaporosity	vendettist
unwareness	upside down	usucaption	vaporously	Venedotian
unwariness	upslope fog	usuriously	vapour-bath	veneration
unwashable	upstanding	usurpation	vapourless	venerative
unwatchful	upstirring	usurpative	vapour lock	venereally
unwavering	upsurgence	usurpatory	vapourware	venesector
unweakened	up the booay	usurpature	vapulation	venetianed
unweaponed	up the creek	usurpingly	varicellar	Venetianly
unwearable	up the river	utero-tubal	variciform	Venezuelan
unwearying	up the spout	utility man	varicocele	vengefully
unweighted	up the stick	utilizable	varicosity	venialness
unwellness	up to a point	Uto-Aztecan	variedness	venison pie
unwettable	up to no good	Utopianism	variegated	Venizelist
unwhitened	up to the bit	Utopianist	variegator	venoclysis
unwieldier	up to the hub	Utopianize	varietally	venography
unwieldily	upwardness	uvula trill	variformed	venomously
unwindowed	Ural-Altaic	uxoriality	variformly	venostasis
unwinnable	uralitized	uxoricidal	variolitic	ventilator
unwinnowed	Uranianism	uxorilocal	variometer	ventral fin
unwipeable	uranometry	uxoriously	varnishing	ventricose
unwiseness	uranophane	vacationer	vascularly	ventricous
unwithered	urban drift	vaccinator	vasculitic	ventricule
unwontedly	urbaneness	vacillancy	vasculitis	ventriculi
unwordable	urbanistic	vacillator	vase carpet	Venus's comb
unworkable	urbanology	vacuolated	vasoactive	Venus shell
unworkably	urceolated	vacuolized	vasomotion	verbalizer
unworthier	urchin fish	vacuum-pack	vassalship	verballing
unworthily	ureaplasma	vacuum pump	vas vasorum	verbal noun
unwrapping	Urecholine	vacuum tube	Vaticanism	verbicidal
unwrathful	uredosorus	Vagabondia	Vaticanist	Verdicchio
unwrinkled	uredospore	vagabondry	Vaticanize	verdictive

verge-board	vice-warden	vinho verde	vital power	voluptuary
vergerless	Vichy water	viniferous	vital spark	voluptuous
vergership	vicinities	vino blanco	vitaminise	volutation
veridicity	victimhood	vino locale	vitaminize	vomitories
verifiable	victimizer	vinologist	vitaminous	vomitorium
verifiably	victimless	vino tierno	vitrectomy	vortex ring
verkrampte	Victoriana	vinousness	vitremanie	vortically
vermicelli	victoriate	vintage car	vitreosity	vorticella
vermicular	victorious	vintneress	vitreously	vorticular
vermifugal	victualage	vinylidene	vitrescent	vortograph
Vermontese	victualled	vinylogous	vitriolize	vortoscope
vernacular	victualler	vinyl resin	vitrophyre	votability
Verner's Law	vicuña wool	violaceous	vituperant	Vote Office
verneukery	Vicwardian	viol d'amore	vituperate	vote-winner
verrucated	vidarabine	violescent	vituperous	votive mass
Versailles	video diary	violet-blue	vivificate	votive Mass
versecraft	videogenic	violet crab	viviparism	voussoired
verse drama	video nasty	violet wood	viviparity	vow-breaker
versed sine	videophile	viper-broth	viviparous	vowel-glide
versemaker	videophone	viperishly	vivisector	vowel-point
versicular	Vienna coup	viperously	vixenishly	vowel shift
versiculus	Vierendeel	viraginian	vizard-mask	voyageable
versifical	Vietnamese	viraginous	viziership	vulcanizer
versionist	Vietnamize	virescence	vlei loerie	vulgarizer
Vertebrata	view camera	virginally	vocabulary	vulgarness
vertebrate	viewership	virgin clay	vocabulist	vulnerable
vertically	viewfinder	virgin comb	vocal cords	vulnerably
verticilli	view halloo	virginhood	vocal folds	vulpicidal
Very pistol	viewlessly	virgin-like	vocalistic	vulvectomy
vesication	vigilantly	Virgin Mary	vocal score	waddlingly
vesicatory	vignetting	virgin wool	vocal tract	wading bird
vesiculate	vignettist	virialized	vocational	wading pool
vesiculose	vigorously	viridarium	vocatively	wafer-paper
vespertine	vigourless	virilizing	voce di gola	wafer-scale
vespiaries	vihuelista	viripotent	vociferant	waffle-iron
vestiarian	vilipender	virologist	vociferate	wage earner
vestiaries	villagedom	virtualism	vociferous	wage freeze
vestibular	villageful	virtualist	voetganger	wager of law
vestibulum	villaindom	virtuality	voicedness	waggonette
vestmental	villainess	virtueless	voice level	Wagner tuba
vestmented	villainies	virtuosity	voice of God	wagons-lits
vest-pocket	villainize	virtuously	voice-print	wagon train
vestry book	villainous	virulently	voiceprint	wagon-vault
vestry-room	villanella	vis a fronte	voice radio	wainscoted
veteran car	villanelle	viscerally	voicespond	wainwright
veterinary	Villanovan	viscometer	voiturette	waist-cloth
vetustness	villarette	viscometry	Volapükist	waist-rails
vexillator	villeinage	viscountcy	volatilise	wait and see
vibracular	Vincentian	Vishnuvite	volatility	wait-a-while
vibraculum	vin compris	visibility	volatilize	waiterlike
vibraphone	vindemiate	Visigothic	volitation	waiting-man
vibrograph	vin de table	visionally	volitional	waitperson
vibrometer	vindicable	visionless	volitorial	wait the day
vibrophone	vindicator	visitation	volleyball	wakerifely
vibroscope	vindictive	visitorial	Voltairean	wake-up call
vicariance	vinegar eel	visna-maedi	Voltairism	wake-up pill
vice-consul	vinegar-fly	visual axis	voltameter	wakey-wakey
vice-county	vinegarish	visualizer	volubility	Waldensian
vicegerent	vine-scroll	visual line	volumeless	walk-around
vice-legate	vine weevil	visuomotor	volumetric	walking day
vice-rector	vineyarded	vital force	volume unit	walking leg
vice-regent	vinho tinto	vitalistic	voluminous	walk in life

walk of life	war veteran	water gauge	wave-motion	weight gain
walk-on part	wash-basket	water glass	wave number	weightiest
Wallachian	wash-bottle	water-gruel	wave packet	weightless
wall-arcade	washerette	water-guard	wave period	weight loss
walla-walla	washer-wife	water-horse	waveringly	Weimaraner
Wallawalla	washeteria	water-house	wave-system	Weisswurst
wallbanger	washing bat	wateriness	wave theory	welcome mat
wall-barley	washing-day	waterishly	wave vector	welding rod
wall-border	washing-pan	water leech	waving base	well-bodied
wallflower	Washington	water lemon	wax and wane	well-bucket
wall garden	wash-kettle	water level	waxberries	well-chosen
wall lizard	wash-primer	waterlined	wax-cluster	well-decked
wall pepper	wash-trough	waterliner	waxed paper	well-decker
wall-pocket	wasp beetle	water-lungs	waxen image	well-earned
wall-poster	wassail-cup	watermelon	wax-pod bean	well enough
wall rocket	Wassermann	water meter	way-freight	well-faring
Wall Street	wastefully	water-mouse	way-outness	well fitted
wall-to-wall	wastel cake	water-mouth	way station	well-formed
wallwasher	waste mould	water nymph	weak ending	well-gotten
walnut tree	waste paper	water-organ	weak-handed	well-heeled
Walpoliana	waste water	water ouzel	weak-headed	well I never
Walt Disney	waste words	water pipit	weakliness	wellington
wambliness	wastreldom	water-plane	weak-minded	Wellington
wamblingly	watch below	water-power	weak moment	well-judged
wampumpeag	watch-chain	waterproof	weak sister	well-marked
wanderable	watch-charm	waterquake	wealthiest	well-meaner
wanderlust	watch-cloak	waterscape	wealthless	well-meated
wander plug	watchfully	water-screw	weanedness	well-padded
wander-year	watch-glass	watershoot	weaponized	well placed
wand flower	watch-guard	water shrew	weaponless	well-rested
wanking-pit	watch-house	watersider	weaponsman	well-shaped
wanrestful	watch-light	water-skier	wear a crown	well-shapen
wantedness	watchmaker	water slide	wearifully	well shrimp
wan-thriven	watch-night	watersmeet	wear motley	well-spaced
wantonness	watch-paper	water snake	wear willow	well-spoken
Wanyamwezi	watch-stand	water sport	wearyingly	wellspring
wapper-eyed	watch strap	waterspout	weaselling	well-spring
warble tone	watch-tower	water stoma	weaselship	well-suited
Warburgian	watchtower	water-stone	weasel word	well-tasted
War Cabinet	watch-wheel	water-table	weather bow	well to live
war college	water avens	water-thief	weather-box	well to pass
wardenship	water-based	water-thyme	weathering	well-turned
wardership	water beech	watertight	weatherize	well-willed
ward-heeler	water-bloom	water tower	weatherman	well-willer
war economy	Water Board	water wagon	weather map	well-wisher
war-hatchet	water-borne	waterwards	weathermen	well-wooded
warlordism	water-bough	water-waved	weaver-bird	well-worked
war machine	water-bound	water-wheel	web-machine	Welsh Black
warmed-over	water-brash	waterwheel	web-spinner	Welsh corgi
warm-headed	waterbrash	water wings	Websterian	Welsh hound
warming-pan	water break	water-witch	websterite	Welsh niece
warm sector	water-chute	waterworks	wedding day	Welsh onion
warmthless	water clerk	watery tomb	wedge shell	Welsh poppy
war of words	water-clock	Watteauish	Wednesdays	Welsh uncle
war pension	watercraft	wattlebird	weedkiller	Welsh Wales
warrandice	water crane	watt-second	week-to-week	Welshwoman
warranties	watercress	wave-action	Wegenerian	Welshwomen
warrantise	water drive	wave-change	weighboard	welt pocket
war refugee	water elder	wave energy	weigh-house	Wemba-wemba
Warrington	water-flood	wave filter	weigh-scale	Wendy house
warrioress	waterfront	wavelength	weigh-shaft	wentletrap
warriorism	Watergater	wavelessly·	weight belt	were-jaguar

Wertherian	wheezingly	white house	wickerwork	windfallen
Wertherism	whelk-stall	White House	wicket-gate	wind-fanner
we shall see	whenabouts	white level	wicket-keep	windflower
West Africa	when-issued	white light	Wicliffian	windjammer
West Banker	whensoever	white liver	Wicliffist	windlessly
West Briton	whereabout	white magic	wide-bodied	windmiller
westerlies	whereafter	white metal	wide-screen	windowless
westerling	whereanent	white money	widespread	window-like
westernise	where it's at	white mouse	widow-finch	window pane
Westernise	wheresoe'er	White Negro	widow-maker	window seat
westernism	whereunder	white night	widow's mite	window-shop
westernize	whey-butter	white noise	widow's peak	window sill
Westernize	whickering	white ox-eye	widow's walk	wind player
western man	whiggamore	White Paper	widow woman	windscreen
Western pug	Whiggishly	white perch	wifeliness	wind-shaken
West German	whimpering	white-point	Wife of Bath	windshield
West Indian	whimsiness	white-print	Wiffle ball	wind-sleeve
West Indies	whip aerial	white satin	wiggletail	Windsor Red
westlander	whippers-in	white sauce	wigwagging	Windsor tie
Westphalia	whippeteer	white scour	wild carrot	wind-spider
Westralian	whippiness	white shark	wildcatter	wind sprint
West Riding	whip-socket	white slave	wild cattle	wind-stream
westwardly	whip stitch	White slave	wild-caught	wind-sucker
wet bargain	whip the cat	whitesmith	wild cherry	windsurfer
wet blanket	whirl-about	white staff	wildebeest	wind tunnel
wet canteen	whirl-blast	white stick	wild endive	wind-vanner
wet cupping	whirlicote	white stock	wilderness	windwardly
wether head	whirlingly	white stone	wildflysch	wine-bibber
wether lamb	whirlybird	white stork	wildfowler	winebibber
wet monsoon	whiskerage	white stuff	wild garden	wine bottle
wet process	whiskified	white sugar	wild garlic	wine butler
wet through	whisky jack	whitethorn	wild ginger	wine cellar
wet-weather	whisky john	white trash	wild orange	wine-farmer
Weyl tensor	whisky-soda	white trout	wild radish	wine-gallon
whaleboned	whisky sour	white water	wild talent	wine-grower
whale louse	whispering	white whale	wild teasel	winemaking
whale shark	whist drive	white wheat	wild turkey	wine-porter
wharf crane	whistle for	white witch	Wilfridian	wine taster
wharfinger	white alder	whiting-mop	wilfulness	wine-vaults
whatabouts	whitebeard	Whitleyism	Wilhelmine	wine waiter
what a shame	white birch	Whitmanish	Williamite	wine writer
what is more	whiteboard	Whitmanism	will or nill	wing-bonnet
what matter	white brass	Whitmanite	willowherb	wing collar
whatsoever	white bread	Whitstable	willow leaf	wing covert
what's yours	whitebrick	Whitsun ale	willow-like	winged bean
wheat-grass	white cedar	Whitsun Day	willow tree	wingedness
wheatgrass	white death	Whit Sunday	willow-ware	wing-footed
wheatsheaf	white dwarf	whity-brown	willow weed	wing mirror
Wheat State	white-eared	whizzingly	willow wren	wing oyster
Wheatstone	white earth	whodunitry	will to live	wing-sheath
wheel brace	white egret	whole cloth	willy-nilly	wingspread
wheelchair	whiteflies	wholegrain	willy-willy	wing-stroke
wheel clamp	white friar	wholesaler	win and wear	win in a walk
wheel-cross	White Friar	wholescale	win by a head	Winstonian
wheel-horse	whitefront	whole-timer	winceyette	winter coat
wheel-house	white frost	wholewheat	winchester	winter duck
wheelhouse	white goods	whomsoever	Winchester	winter-feed
wheelie bin	white grape	whore-house	wind-broken	winter gnat
wheel-organ	White Guard	whorehouse	wind-burned	winter kill
wheel-plate	white-heart	whore's bird	wind chimes	winterless
wheel-press	white heron	whorl-grass	windedness	winter-long
wheeziness	white horse	wickedness	wind energy	winter-moth

winter ovum	woefulness	woodworker	world order	xanthation
winterpick	Wöhler test	woodwright	world-point	xanthistic
winter road	wolframate	woody plant	world power	xanthoderm
winter rose	wolframite	wool-bearer	world's fair	xanthomata
winter's day	wolf spider	wool-broker	world-weary	xanthopsia
winter teal	wolf's tooth	wool-carder	worm-burrow	xenarthral
winter-tide	wolf willow	wool cheque	worm-eating	xenobiosis
wintertide	Wolstonian	wool church	worm-killer	xenobiotic
wintertime	woman-child	wool-comber	worm-lizard	xenogamous
winter-weed	womanfully	wool-gather	worm-spring	xenogeneic
winter wren	woman-grown	wool-grower	worry along	xenogenous
win the kirn	womanishly	woollenize	worry beads	xenoglossy
win through	woman-power	woolliness	worryingly	xenolithic
wintriness	woman's page	woolly-bear	worry lines	xenologist
wiper blade	woman's work	woollybutt	worsenment	xenomaniac
wiping head	womb-to-tomb	woolly-head	worserment	xenophilia
wire basket	womenpower	woolly worm	worshipful	xenophobia
wire-cutter	women's page	woolmaster	worshipped	xenophobic
wire-drawer	women's room	wool-needle	worshipper	xenotropic
wiredrawer	women's wear	wool-packer	worthiness	xerography
wire-framed	womenswear	wool-roller	worth while	xeromorphy
wire ground	women's work	wool-shears	worthwhile	xerophilic
wire-guided	wonder-horn	wool-sorter	woundingly	xerophytic
wire-haired	wonderland	wool-staple	wraithlike	xerostomia
wirelessly	wonderment	wool-winder	wraparound	xiphopagus
wirepuller	wonder-work	wool-worker	wrappering	xiphosuran
wire-tapper	wondrously	Woolton pie	wrap-rascal	xiphosurid
wire-walker	wonga-wonga	Woosterish	wrathfully	X-irradiate
wire-worker	wontedness	Woosterism	wreak havoc	X-radiation
wirrasthru	wonton soup	word by word	wreathless	X-ray source
wishing-cap	wood barley	word-centre	wrest-block	X-ray vision
wishy-washy	wood betony	word-ladder	wrestle out	xyloglucan
witch alder	wood-boring	word length	wrest-plank	xylography
witch broom	wood-burner	wordlessly	wretcheder	xylophonic
witchcraft	wood-carpet	word-medial	wretchedly	xylotomist
witch dance	woodcarver	word method	wrinkliest	xylotomous
witch-grass	wood-copper	wordmonger	wrist-plate	yacht basin
witch hazel	woodcutter	wordsearch	wrist-watch	yaffingale
witchiness	wooden-head	word-square	wristwatch	Yagi aerial
witchingly	woodenness	word-symbol	writership	yaketty-yak
witch-mania	wooden pear	workaholic	writhingly	Yankee bond
witch-stone	wooden suit	work a point	writing bed	Yankee-land
withdrawal	woodenware	work-basket	writing-box	yarborough
withdrawer	woodgrouse	workerless	writing ink	yardlander
witherling	wood hoopoe	workfellow	writing pad	yard of land
withershin	woodlanded	work-harden	writing-pen	yardswoman
withholder	woodlander	workhoused	writ of aiel	Yarkand rug
within call	wood laurel	working day	wrongdoing	yarnwindle
within-door	wood millet	working man	wrongfully	yawing axis
within hail	woodmonger	working-out	wrongously	yawl-rigged
within land	woodpecker	working top	wrong scent	year by year
withinside	wood pigeon	work-master	wry-mouthed	yearnfully
with intent	woodpigeon	work-minded	Wulfrunian	yearningly
without end	wood-rabbit	workmonger	wunderkind	year-on-year
with reason	wood-ranger	workpeople	Wyattesque	yeastiness
with the sun	Wood's glass	work permit	Wycliffian	yedda braid
witness box	Wood's light	work scathe	Wycliffism	yellow-back
witnessing	wood sorrel	workshadow	Wycliffist	yellowback
wit-writing	wood spirit	work to rule	Wycliffite	yellow bean
wobbliness	woods-pussy	world-class	Wykehamist	yellow belt
wobbulated	wood-thrush	worldliest	Wykehamite	yellow bile
wobbulator	woodturner	world music	wyomingite	yellowbill

yellowbird	yeoman work	yourselves	Zhdanovist	zoographic
yellowcake	yerba buena	yours truly	zidovudine	zoolatrous
yellow card	yerba plant	youthfully	zigzaggery	zoological
yellow cell	yerba santa	youthiness	zigzagging	zoomelanin
yellow deal	yester-even	ytter earth	Zimbabwean	zoomorphic
yellow-eyed	yestermorn	yucca-borer	zinc blende	zoonomical
yellow-fish	yester-year	Yukon stove	zinc chrome	zoophagous
yellow flag	yesteryear	zabaglione	zinc-coated	zoophilism
yellowhead	Yiddishism	Zaghlulist	zinc finger	zoophilist
yellow jack	Yiddishist	Zambianize	zincograph	zoophilous
yellow Jack	yieldingly	zapateados	zinc yellow	zoosporous
yellow leaf	yield point	zearalanol	zipperhead	zootechnic
yellowlegs	yield table	zebra danio	zircon blue	zoothecium
yellow line	ylang-ylang	zebra finch	zoanthropy	zootomical
yellowness	yodization	zebra-plant	zodiac ring	zoot-suited
yellow pine	yoke-fellow	zemstvoist	zograscope	zoot-suiter
yellow rain	yotization	Zend-Avesta	*zollverein*	Zoroastric
yellow-root	you can talk	Zener cards	zombie-like	zucchettos
yellow rust	you can't win	Zener diode	zombiesque	zwitterion
yellow soap	you-know-who	Zengakuren	zonal index	zygocactus
yellow spot	youngberry	zephyr lily	zone centre	zygodactyl
yellow star	young blood	zero-coupon	zone fossil	zygologist
yellowtail	young entry	zero-energy	zone of fire	zygomycete
yellow ware	young flood	zero growth	zone-refine	zygosphene
yellow-wood	young fogey	zero option	zoocentric	zygosporic
yellow-wort	youngstock	zero rating	zoochorous	zymogenous
yeomanette	young thing	zerovalent	zooculture	zymologist
yeomanhood	young woman	zeuglodont	zoogeology	
yeomanries	your granny	Zhdanovism	zoographer	

ELEVEN LETTERS

Aaron's beard
abandonedly
abandonment
abandon ship
abashedness
Abbevillian
abbreviator
abdominally
abductively
abecedarian
abhorrently
abidingness
abiogenesis
abiological
abiotically
a bit and a sup
ablactation
ablutionary
abnormality
abnormalize
abolishable
abolishment
abomination
abortionist
aboundingly
above ground
aboveground
a box of birds
abracadabra
abridgeable
abridgement
abscondence
absentation
absenteeism
absent voter
absorbingly
absorptance
abstinently
abstraction
abstractive
absurdities
abusiveness
academician
academicism
academicize
acanthodian
acarologist
acatalectic
acataleptic
acaulescent
accelerandi
accelerando
accelerator
accentually
acceptation
acceptingly
accessaries

accessional
accessorial
accessorily
accessorise
accessorize
accipitrine
acclamation
acclamatory
acclimation
acclimatise
acclimatize
acclivities
acclivitous
accommodate
accompanied
accompanier
accompanies
accompanist
accordantly
accordingly
accoucheuse
accountable
accountably
accountancy
account book
accrediting
accrescence
accrescency
acculturate
acculturize
accumulator
accusatival
accustomary
acerbically
a certain age
acetanilide
acetate silk
acetoacetic
acetobacter
acetonaemia
acetylation
Achaemenian
acharnement
achievement
achondritic
achromatism
achromatize
achromatous
acicularity
acidimetric
acidization
acid of sugar
acidophilic
acidophilus
acid radical
acidulation
acidulously

acinaciform
acknowledge
aclinic line
acorn squash
a couple more
acoustician
acquiescent
acquiescing
acquirement
acquisition
acquisitive
acquittance
acraldehyde
acriflavine
acrimonious
acrocarpous
acrocentric
acromegalic
acropetally
a crow to pick
a crow to pull
acrylic acid
actinolitic
actinometer
actinometry
actinomycin
action front
action group
action point
active birth
active layer
active voice
actual grace
actualistic
actualities
actuarially
acumination
acupressure
acupuncture
acute accent
acute-angled
Adam's needle
adaptedness
adder's grass
adder's mouth
addititious
addressable
adenomatous
adhortation
adhortative
adiaphanous
adiaphorism
adiaphorist
adiaphorous
a dime a dozen
ad infinitum
adjectively

adjectivize
adjournment
adjudgement
adjudicator
adminicular
admiralship
Admiralties
admit to bail
adolescence
adolescency
adonization
Adoptionist
adorability
adrenal rest
adrenolytic
Adriatic Sea
adscription
adulterator
adumbration
adumbrative
advance copy
advancement
adventuress
adventurism
adventurist
adventurous
adverbially
adversarial
adversaries
adversative
adverseness
adversities
advertently
advertising
advertorial
advisedness
aeneolithic
aeolian harp
Aeolian harp
Aeolian mode
aeolotropic
aerobically
aerobiology
aerodynamic
aeroelastic
aerographer
aerological
aeronautics
aeroplanist
aerostatics
aerostation
Aesculapian
Aesculapius
aesthetical
aestivation
aeviternity
a fact of life

a far cry from
affectation
affectingly
affectional
affectioned
affectively
affectivity
affectually
affiliation
affiliative
affirmation
affirmative
affirmatory
afforcement
afformative
affranchise
affrication
affricative
affrightful
Afghan hound
aficionados
African hemp
Africanness
African teak
Afro-Asiatic
Afrocentric
afterburner
after-course
after-effect
after-growth
aftermarket
after-school
after sermon
against time
agamospermy
agathodemon
agelessness
Agent Orange
agglomerate
agglutinant
agglutinate
aggradation
aggrandizer
aggravating
aggravation
aggregately
aggregation
aggregative
aggrievance
aggrievedly
aggroupment
agile gibbon
agitatingly
agitational
aglomerular
agnosticism
agnus castus

agonistical
agonizingly
agony column
a good stitch
agoraphobia
agoraphobic
agrammatism
agrarianism
agriculture
agriologist
agriproduct
agrobiology
agronomical
ahead of time
ahistorical
aide-mémoire
aides-de-camp
aiguillette
ailurophile
ailurophobe
aimlessness
air corridor
aircraftman
aircraftmen
air-layering
airlessness
air mattress
airsickness
air terminal
air-to-ground
alabastrine
alamodality
a large order
albert chain
Albigensian
albugineous
albuminuria
albuminuric
alchemistic
alcohol-free
alcyonarian
alder kitten
aldermanity
alderperson
aldosterone
alembicated
aleuromancy
Alexandrian
alexandrine
Alexandrine
alexandrite
alexithymia
alexithymic
Alfvén speed
algebraical
alginic acid
algological
algorithmic
Alien Priory
alimentally
alisphenoid
a little bird

alizarin red
alkalescent
alkali metal
alkalimeter
alkalimetry
all-American
allantoides
allegorical
allegorizer
allegrettos
all-electric
allelomorph
alleluiatic
all ends over
alleviation
alleviative
alleviatory
All Fools' Day
alliterator
all manner of
alloantigen
allocentric
allodialism
allodialist
all of a piece
allogeneity
allogeneous
allographic
allomorphic
all one knows
allopathist
allophylian
allopurinol
allotropism
all outdoors
all-overness
all-powerful
All Souls' Day
all standing
all the while
all together
all to pieces
all-up weight
alluviation
all very well
almond paste
almonership
alongside of
alphabetise
alphabetize
alpha rhythm
altercation
alternately
alternating
alternation
alternative
altitudinal
altocumulus
alto-relievo
alto-rilievo
altostratus
alveolarity

amalgamable
amalgamater
amalgamator
amaranthine
amateurship
amativeness
amazingness
Amazon-stone
ambassadrix
ambiguities
ambiguously
ambilingual
ambitionist
ambitiously
ambivalence
ambivalency
ambiversion
amblygonite
ambrosially
amelanchier
ameliorator
amenability
amenorrhoea
amentaceous
amerciament
Amerenglish
American bar
American elk
American elm
Americanese
Americanise
Americanism
Americanist
Americanize
American tea
amethocaine
amethystine
amiableness
amicability
amici curiae
aminoacetic
amontillado
amorousness
amorphously
amortisable
amour propre
amphetamine
amphibolite
amphibology
amphictyony
amphidromic
amphimictic
amphipathic
amphiprotic
amphisbaena
Amphiscians
amplexicaul
amusingness
amusiveness
amyloidosis
amylopectin
amyotrophic

anachronism
anachronous
anacoluthia
anacoluthic
anacoluthon
anacreontic
anadiplosis
anaesthesia
anaesthesis
anaesthetic
anagnorisis
analogously
analysandum
analysation
analyticity
anaphylaxis
anaplerosis
anaplerotic
anarchistic
anastomoses
anastomosis
anastomotic
Anaxagorean
ancestorial
ancestrally
anchor plate
anchorwoman
anchorwomen
anchovy pear
ancientness
ancillaries
androconial
androconium
androcratic
androgynous
androsphinx
and then some
anecdotical
an eight days
anemometric
anemone fish
anencephaly
anfractuous
angelically
angelolatry
angelophany
angel-sleeve
angelus bell
angiography
angiomatous
angioplasty
angiotensin
Anglicanism
Anglicanize
Anglo-French
Anglo-Gallic
Anglo-Indian
Anglomaniac
Anglo-Norman
Anglophilia
Anglophobia
Anglophobic

anguishment
angwantibos
animal black
animalcular
animalistic
animatronic
animosities
aniseed tree
aniseikonia
aniseikonic
anisogamete
anisogamous
anisotropic
annabergite
annexionist
annihilable
annihilator
anniversary
annotatable
annunciator
anomalistic
anomalously
anonymously
anoplothere
anorthosite
anovulatory
answeringly
answerphone
antecedence
antecedency
antechamber
antecubital
anteflexion
antemundane
antenatally
antenniform
antenuptial
ante-orbital
antepagment
antependium
anteriority
anterograde
anteversion
antheridial
antheridium
antherozoid
anthocyanin
anthography
anthologies
anthologise
anthologist
anthologize
anthomaniac
Anthony Eden
anthracitic
anthracnose
anthracosis
anthracotic
anthranilic
antibilious
Antiburgher
anticathode

anticipator
anticodonic
anticyclone
anti-gravity
antigravity
anti-heroine
anti-Jacobin
antimasquer
antimoniate
antimonious
antinomical
anti-nuclear
antioxidant
antipathies
antipathist
antipathous
antiphonary
antiphonies
antiphrasis
antipyretic
antiquarian
antiquaries
antiquation
antiqueness
antiquities
antirrhinum
anti-Semitic
antispastic
antistrophe
antitetanic
antitetanus
antitypical
antonomasia
anxiousness
any amount of
any more than
any number of
any old thing
anything but
aortography
apartmental
apatosaurus
aphasiology
aphetically
aphrodisiac
apicultural
apocalyptic
apocopation
apocrisiary
apocynthion
apodictical
apodyterium
apogamously
Apollinaris
Apollonicon
apomorphine
aponeurosis
aponeurotic
apopetalous
apophyllite
aposiopesis
aposiopetic

apostatical
a posteriori
apostle-bird
apostlehood
apostleship
apostolical
apostrophic
apotheosise
apotheosize
Appalachian
appallingly
apparatchik
apparelling
apparelment
Appeal Court
appealingly
appearingly
appeasement
appellation
appellative
appertinent
appetencces
appetitious
apple brandy
apple-butter
apple of love
apple of Peru
apple-pie bed
application
applicative
applicatory
appliquéing
appointable
appointment
apportioner
appraisable
appreciable
appreciably
appreciator
apprehender
apprizement
approaching
approbation
approbative
approbatory
appropinque
appropriate
approvement
approvingly
approximant
approximate
appurtenant
apricot plum
apricot tree
aprioristic
apron-string
aptly enough
aquaculture
aquarellist
aquiculture
Arabian bird
Arabization

arachidonic
arachnoidal
arachnology
araliaceous
arbitrageur
arbitrament
arbitrarily
arbitration
arbitratrix
arbitrement
arboraceous
arboreality
arborescent
arboricidal
arborio rice
Arcadianism
archaeology
Archaeozoic
archaically
archangelic
arch-chanter
archdeanery
archdiocese
archduchess
archduchies
archdukedom
archegonial
archegonium
arch-enemies
archenteron
Archimedean
archipelago
architraved
arch-prelate
Arctic cisco
Arctic Ocean
arduousness
area bombing
area defence
areocentric
areopagitic
argentaffin
Argentinian
argle-bargle
argumentive
argy-bargied
argy-bargies
argyrophile
aristocracy
Aristotelic
arithmetize
arithmology
armalcolite
armed forces
armil sphere
Arminianism
Arminianize
armoured car
armour-plate
arms control
arm-twisting
aromaticity

arpeggiated
arraignment
arrangeable
arrangement
arrear-guard
arrentation
arrestation
arrestingly
arrhenotoky
arrow bamboo
arrow-headed
arrow of time
arse-kissing
arse-licking
arsenic acid
arsenicated
arse over tip
arse over tit
artefactual
artemisinin
arterialise
arterialize
arteriogram
arteriotomy
arthrodesis
arthropathy
articulable
articulated
articulator
artilleries
artillerist
artiodactyl
artisanship
artlessness
artsy-fartsy
arundineous
arytenoidal
asbestiform
ascensional
ascetically
ascititious
as cold as ice
a screw loose
as dry as dust
as easy as ABC
aseptically
a set of steps
ashamedness
ashamed to do
ash-coloured
Asiatically
as it happens
asking price
ask the banns
as like as not
as many again
as much again
as opposed to
aspect ratio
aspergillum
aspersorium
asphericity

aspheterism
asphyxiator
aspidistral
asportation
a sport of wit
a square deal
assafoetida
assassinate
assassin bug
assaultable
assay-master
assay office
assegai tree
assegai wood
assemblyman
assentation
assentingly
assertation
assertative
assertional
assertively
assertorial
asses' bridge
assessorial
assiduities
assiduously
assignation
assimilable
assimilator
Assiniboine
association
associative
associatory
assortative
assuagement
assubjugate
assuredness
Assyriology
assythement
as they speak
asthmatical
astigmatism
astonishing
as to the rest
astoundment
astringency
astrocytoma
astrography
astrologist
astrometric
astronomize
astroturfed
asyllabical
asymmetries
as you please
at a discount
at a distance
a tale of a tub
at all events
at all points
at a long stay
at a loose end

atelectasis
atelectatic
at every turn
at first hand
at full blast
at full speed
at handgrips
atheistical
atheologian
athleticism
Athole brose
athwartship
at intervals
at its height
Atlanticism
Atlanticist
at long range
at loose ends
atmospheric
atomic clock
atomic power
atomistical
atomization
atom smasher
at one's elbow
at one's heels
at one's peril
atrabiliary
atrabilious
atrociously
atropinized
attaché case
attachéship
attaintment
attemperate
attemptable
attemptible
attemptless
attentional
attentively
attenuation
attestation
attestative
at the back of
at the cost of
at the double
at the feet of
at the latest
at the minute
at the moment
at the outset
at the risk of
at the wicket
at the will of
attitudinal
attorneydom
attorneyism
attractable
attribution
attributive
attritional
auction room

auction sale
audaciously
audibleness
audio-active
audiologist
audiometric
audio typing
audio typist
audio-visual
audiovisual
auditoriums
auditorship
Auger effect
augmentable
Augustanism
Augustinian
aurichalcum
auricularly
auriculated
Aurignacian
aurora snake
auscultator
austereness
austerities
Australiana
Australioid
autarchical
authentical
author-craft
authorially
authorities
autocentric
autochthons
autochthony
autocracies
autocratism
autocratrix
auto-erotism
autogenesis
autogenetic
autographic
autokinesis
autokinetic
autological
automatical
automorphic
autonomical
autoplastic
autosoteric
auto-suggest
autotherapy
autotrophic
autumn tints
auxanometer
auxiliaries
auxochromic
auxotrophic
averageness
Averroistic
averruncate
avicularium
avocado pear

avocational
avoirdupois
awelessness
awesomeness
awestricken
awkwardness
a work of time
axe-grinding
axial vector
axiological
axiomatical
axisymmetry
axonometric
azeotropism
Azerbaijani
azimuthally
azoospermia
azotobacter
babu English
baby bouncer
baby-farming
babyishness
baby's breath
Bacchanalia
bacciferous
baccivorous
bachelordom
bachelorism
bachelorize
bacilliform
back and edge
back and fill
back-bencher
backbencher
backblocker
back country
backcountry
back-draught
back passage
back-payment
backroom boy
back-scatter
backscatter
backslapper
back-stabber
backswimmer
back to earth
back to front
backtracker
backup light
bacon beetle
bacteraemia
bacteraemic
bacterially
bactericide
bacteriocin
bacteriosis
bacteriuria
bad business
baddeleyite
Badger State
bad language

bad medicine
bad-tempered
baffle board
baffle plate
baggage room
bag of nerves
bag of tricks
bailer-shell
bailiffship
bail-jumping
Baily's beads
baked Alaska
baked potato
baker's bread
baker's dozen
baking sheet
balanceable
baldachined
bald cypress
baleen whale
balefulness
ballad metre
ballast-tank
ball-bearing
ball-breaker
balletomane
balloon-fish
balloon tyre
balloon vine
ballot paper
balls-aching
balm-cricket
balsam apple
balustraded
bamboo shoot
banana split
Banbury cake
bandboxical
bandoliered
bandy-legged
baneberries
Bangladeshi
bang on about
bankability
bank balance
banker's card
bankers' ramp
bank holiday
bank machine
bank manager
bank of issue
banksia rose
bank swallow
banteringly
banyan shirt
baptismally
baptistries
Barbaresque
barbarities
barbarously
barbastelle
barber's itch

barber's pole
barber's rash
barbiturate
barbola work
Bardolphian
barefacedly
bare-knuckle
bargain away
barge-couple
barge-course
bargemaster
Barisal guns
barkevikite
barking bird
barking deer
barley-break
barley sugar
barley water
barnstormer
barn swallow
baron-bailie
baronetcies
baron of beef
barouchette
barquentine
barracoutas
barramundis
barred umber
barrel-house
barrel-organ
barrel vault
barricading
barrier reef
barrow-wight
bar sinister
Bartholomew
barycentric
basaltiform
base on balls
base-running
bases-loaded
base-stealer
bashfulness
bashi-bazouk
basicranial
basifugally
basipetally
Baskerville
basket chair
basket-maker
basket weave
basket-woman
Basque beret
bastard balm
bastard wing
bastel-house
Bastille Day
bastle-house
bath essence
bathing suit
batholithic
bathometric

Bathurst bur
bathymetric
bathyscaphe
bathysphere
baton charge
batsmanship
battalia pie
battle array
battledress
battlefield
battle it out
battle royal
battle-wagon
battologize
Bayesianism
bay-windowed
be able to use
beachcomber
beach-master
be all thumbs
be all up with
be a match for
beam-compass
bean-counter
bean sprouts
bean trefoil
bearability
bear a faggot
bear a stroke
bear-baiting
bear company
bearded iris
beardedness
bearded seal
bear heavily
bearing-rein
bearishness
bear's breech
bear's garlic
bear's grease
bearskinned
bear the bell
bear witness
beastliness
beast of prey
be at college
beat the band
beat the gong
beat the meat
beat the wind
beat to a pulp
beau gregory
beaumontage
beauteously
beautifully
beauty queen
beauty salon
beauty sleep
beaverboard
Beaverboard
beaver cloth
be beknown of

bêches-de-mer
be concerned
bed and board
bedevilling
bedevilment
Bedford cord
bedizenment
bed-moulding
bedroom eyes
bedside book
bedside lamp
beech marten
beehive tomb
beer-parlour
beetle-brain
beetle drive
be expecting
befittingly
beggar-ticks
begging bowl
begin school
beguilement
beguilingly
be hard put to
behavioural
behemothian
be in the dark
be in the game
be in the race
be in the shit
belatedness
belaying-pin
beleaguerer
Belgian hare
believingly
bell-bottoms
bell captain
belle époque
bell-founder
bell-heather
bellicosity
belligerent
bellipotent
bellows-fish
bell-ringing
belly button
belly dancer
belly-timber
Belorussian
below ground
below stairs
be mates with
be mixed up in
benchership
bench-warmer
bend-leather
bend the head
bend the knee
Benedictine
benediction
benedictive
benedictory

benefaction
benefactive
benefactory
benefactrix
beneficence
beneficency
beneficiary
beneficiate
benefit-club
Beneventine
benevolence
Bengal light
Bengal tiger
benightment
benignantly
benignities
be nothing to
be no trouble
be not to know
be nuts about
benzene ring
benzoic acid
be of service
be one's speed
be on one's way
be on the land
be on your way
be ourselves
be plain with
be pushed for
be rained off
bereavement
Bergamasque
bergschrund
Berkeleyism
Berlin black
Berlin glove
Bernoullian
be rolling in
bertrandite
berylliosis
beryllonite
beseechment
beseemingly
Bessarabian
bessemerize
best friends
best-selling
be stuck with
beta blocker
be tempted to
betrothment
betting shop
betting slip
between-maid
betweenness
between-time
bevel square
bewhiskered
Bewick's swan
bewildering
bewitchment

beyond a joke
beyond doubt
beyond price
beyond words
bhakti-marga
bias binding
biauricular
Bible-banger
Bible-basher
bibliograph
biblioklept
bibliolatry
bibliomancy
bibliomania
bibliophile
bibliophily
bibliopolic
bibliotheca
bicarbonate
bicentenary
bicephalous
bicuspidate
bicycle clip
bicycle pump
biddability
bidialectal
biding-place
Biedermeier
bifariously
bifurcation
big business
bilaterally
bilberrying
bile pigment
bilinearity
biliousness
billets-doux
billiardist
billionaire
billitonite
bill of costs
bill of goods
billposting
billsticker
bilophodont
bimetallism
bimetallist
bimillenary
bimolecular
bimonthlies
bimorphemic
binary digit
binary scale
bindle-stiff
biocentrism
biochemical
bioclimatic
biocoenosis
biocoenotic
biodynamics
bio-electric
bio-engineer

bioengineer
bioethicist
biofeedback
biogenesist
biographies
biographist
biographize
biologistic
biomagnetic
biomedicine
biometrical
biophysical
biorhythmic
bioturbated
bipartitely
bipartition
bipyramidal
biquadratic
bird-banding
birdbrained
bird-fancier
bird-nesting
bird-ringing
bird-watcher
birdwatcher
birthday boy
birth father
birth mother
birth parent
birthweight
biscuit-like
bisexuality
bishopstool
bishop's weed
bishop's wort
Bismarckian
bite one's lip
bite the dust
bit of muslin
bits and bats
bits and bobs
bitter aloes
bitter-apple
bitter-cress
bitter-ender
bitter-gourd
bitter pecan
bitter-sweet
bitter-vetch
bivouacking
bizarreness
black Africa
Black Africa
black and tan
black arches
blackavised
black-backed
black beetle
blackbirder
black bottom
black-browed
black bryony

black butter	blind as a bat	body-builder	botanically	brank-ursine
black cattle	blind corner	bodybuilder	botanomancy	brass monkey
black cherry	blindfolded	body-centred	botheration	brattishing
black coffee	blindfolder	body politic	bottle-arsed	brazen-faced
black cohosh	blind hookey	body-popping	bottle-brush	brazen it out
blackfellow	blind nettle	body scanner	bottle-glass	bread basket
black-figure	blind stitch	body-servant	bottle-gourd	breadbasket
black ginger	blister pack	bog asphodel	bottle green	breadstuffs
black grouse	blithefully	bog rosemary	bottle-nosed	breadthless
black-headed	bloatedness	bog standard	bottle party	breadthways
black latten	blockade-man	bohemianism	bottom yeast	breadthwise
black letter	blockbuster	Bohemianism	boulder clay	breadwinner
black locust	block delete	boil a wallop	boulevarded	break a close
blackmailer	blockheaded	boiled shirt	bounce-flash	break a lance
black market	block heater	boiled sweet	boundedness	break-dancer
Black Monday	block system	boilermaker	bounden duty	breakfaster
black Muslim	blood-flower	boiler-plate	boundlessly	break ground
Black Muslim	blood-guilty	bokmakierie	bounteously	break the ice
black pepper	bloodlessly	bolt upright	bountifully	breast-board
black piedra	blood-letter	bombardment	bourgeoisie	breast-drill
black poplar	blood orange	bombastical	bourrée step	breastplate
black powder	blood plasma	bomb factory	boutonnière	breast shell
Black Prince	blood spavin	bombilation	bower-anchor	breast-wheel
black rubric	blood sports	bombination	bower-maiden	breathalyse
black scoter	bloodstream	bombproofer	boxer shorts	breathe upon
black spauld	bloodsucker	Bonapartism	boxing glove	breathiness
black spruce	bloodthirst	Bonapartist	box junction	brecciation
black squall	blood vessel	bonaventure	box-tortoise	bred and born
black velvet	bloody grave	bondmanship	Boys' Brigade	breech birth
black walnut	bloody shirt	bondservice	boysenberry	breech-block
bladder-fern	bloody sweat	bond-washing	brabblement	breeze-block
bladder-like	blossomless	bone breccia	brace and bit	brewsterite
bladder worm	blotting-pad	bone-seeking	brachiation	bribability
bladderwort	blow a gasket	*bonne bouche*	brachyodont	bricklaying
blaeberries	blow one's top	bonnet laird	brachyurous	brick-stitch
blamelessly	blow sky-high	bonnet-piece	bracingness	bridal suite
blameworthy	blow the gaff	bons vivants	bracteolate	bridge-house
blank cheque	blueberries	bons viveurs	bradycardia	Bridgettine
blanket bath	blue-blooded	bookbindery	braggadocio	bright spark
blanket coat	blue-cheeked	bookbinding	braggartism	brilliantly
blanket roll	blue-eyed boy	booking hall	Brahmanical	brindled gnu
blank flange	bluefin tuna	bookishness	brahmaputra	brine shrimp
blank window	blue-striped	bookkeeping	Brahmaputra	bring home to
blasphemies	blue tangles	book-learned	brahminical	bring to bear
blasphemous	blue vitriol	Book of Kings	brain damage	bring to book
blastematic	blue whiting	book of words	brainlessly	bring to heel
blast freeze	blunder away	bookselling	brainsickly	bring to life
blastocoele	blunderbuss	boom and bust	brains trust	bring to mind
blastogenic	blunderhead	boon service	brain-teaser	bring to pass
blastoporal	blunder upon	boorishness	brain tumour	bristle-bird
blastospore	B-lymphocyte	bootability	brake harrow	bristle-fern
blateration	boardsailer	boots and all	brake lining	bristle-like
blaze abroad	boardsailor	boot-topping	bralessness	bristletail
blaze a trail	board school	boracic acid	bramble-rose	bristle-worm
blazing star	boatbuilder	borborygmic	branchiated	Bristol milk
blearedness	boatmanship	borborygmus	branchiness	British Lion
blemishless	boat the oars	bordered pit	branchiopod	Britishness
blemishment	bob and weave	border print	brand leader	British warm
blepharitis	bob-sledding	born and bred	brand of Cain	brittleness
blessedness	bobsledding	borohydride	brandy punch	brittle-star
bless my soul	bodaciously	borough-town	brandy-toddy	broach spire
bleu celeste	Bodhisattva	bosom friend	branglement	broadcasted

broadcaster
Broad Church
broad-leaved
broadleaved
broad-minded
broadside on
Brobdingnag
brochantite
broken chord
broken field
broken heart
bromatology
bromidrosis
bromination
bronchially
bronchiolar
bronchocele
bronchogram
bronchotomy
brontothere
bronze medal
Brooklynese
brotherhood
brotherless
brothership
broth of a boy
brown-bagger
brown George
brucellosis
brush turkey
brusqueness
brutalities
brutishness
bryological
bryozoology
bubble-shell
buccinatory
buck-and-wing
bucket-wheel
buckler-fern
buck-passing
buck rarebit
buck-toothed
buck-washing
bucolically
buddy system
budge-barrel
buffalo bird
buffalo fish
buffalo robe
buffer state
buffer State
buff leather
bugger about
Buggins' turn
building lot
built on sand
bulbiferous
bulimarexia
bulimarexic
bulk carrier

bulk modulus
bull at a gate
bull-baiting
bulldog bond
bulldog clip
bulletproof
bullet train
bullfighter
bullishness
bull-mastiff
bullock-cart
bull-puncher
bull session
bullshitter
bull terrier
bull-whacker
bully pulpit
bumble-puppy
bumpologist
bumptiously
bunch-flower
Bunyanesque
buoyancy aid
buoyantness
buphthalmic
buphthalmos
burble point
bureaucracy
burgess oath
burgess-ship
burghership
burglarious
burgomaster
burlesquely
burlesquing
bur-marigold
burning bush
burning marl
burnt almond
burn to a chip
burnt sienna
burrows-town
bush-cricket
bush-leaguer
bushmanship
bush-ranging
bushwhacker
bushy-tailed
business end
businessman
businessmen
Butazolidin
butcher-bird
butcher blue
butcher meat
but me no buts
Butskellism
Butskellite
butter cloth
butter-cream
butterflies
butter-icing

butteriness
butter knife
butter-print
buttery-book
button-grass
buttonholer
button-mould
button-nosed
button-quail
button-stick
butyl rubber
butyraceous
butyric acid
butyrometer
buy gape-seed
buying spree
buy up a storm
by an eyelash
by any chance
by mischance
by one's guess
by ourselves
by piecemeal
byrlaw-court
Byronically
by that means
by the name of
by the side of
by this means
by this token
by wholesale
by your leave
Byzantinism
Byzantinist
caa'ing whale
cabbage-bark
cabbage-head
cabbage-like
cabbage moth
cabbage palm
cabbage rose
cabbage tree
cabbalistic
cabinet-work
cable length
cable stitch
cablevision
cacao butter
cachectical
cache memory
cacodoxical
cacographer
cacographic
cacophonies
cacophonous
caddis-flies
caddishness
cadmiferous
cadmium cell
Caesar salad
Caesar's wife
café society

cakes and ale
Calabar bean
calamancoes
calamistrum
calcarenite
calceolaria
calcicolous
calciferous
calcigerous
calcination
calculating
calculation
calculative
calculatory
calculiform
calefacient
calefaction
calefactive
calefactory
calendarial
calendrical
calibration
Californian
californite
californium
calisthenic
call a halt to
Callanetics
call changes
call cousins
calligraphy
calling card
calling hare
callipygian
callipygous
callistemon
call it quits
callitriche
call one's own
callosities
callousness
call the roll
call the tune
call the turn
call to order
calorically
calorimeter
calorimetry
calumniator
Calvinistic
calycanthus
calyculated
calypsonian
Camaldolese
Camaldolite
camaraderie
camel-spider
camera-ready
camera shake
camerawoman
Cameroonian
camomile tea

campaign wig
campaniform
campanology
campanulate
camphor tree
camphor-wood
camp-meeting
Canaanitish
Canada goose
Canadianism
Canadianize
canalicular
canaliculus
canary grass
cancellable
cancellated
cancerously
cancer stick
candelabras
candelabrum
candescence
candidature
candidiasis
candied peel
candleberry
candlelight
candlepower
candlestick
candy stripe
candystripe
canine tooth
cannabinoid
cannibalean
cannibalise
cannibalism
cannibalize
cannulation
canonically
canophilist
Canopic vase
cantharides
cantharidin
canting arms
capableness
capaciously
capacitance
cap and bells
Cape buffalo
Cape cowslip
Cape jasmine
Capernaitic·
capernoited
caper spurge
Cape sparrow
capillaries
capillarity
capillitium
capital gain
capital levy
capitalling
capital ship
capitulator

Cappadocian	carnificial	cataclysmal	cavernously	chain bridge
cappuccinos	carnivalite	cataclysmic	cavernulous	chain letter
capriccioso	carnivorous	catadromous	cavillation	chain-smoker
Capricornus	Carnot cycle	catallactic	ceaselessly	chain stitch
caprolactam	Carolingian	cataloguing	cecidiology	chairladies
capsulotomy	carol-singer	cataloguist	celebration	chairoplane
captaincies	carotid body	cataloguize	celebrative	chairperson
captainless	carpet dance	cat-and-mouse	celebratory	chalcedonic
captainship	carpet layer	cataplectic	celebrities	chalcophile
captivation	carpet-shark	cataractous	celestially	chalice vine
captivities	carpet shell	catastrophe	cellularity	chalk-stripe
carabideous	carpet-snake	catavothron	Celtiberian	challenging
carabiniere	carpogonial	catch a few z's	Celtic cross	chamaephyte
caravanette	carpogonium	catch hold of	cementation	chamberlain
caravanning	carrageenan	catch-phrase	cement mixer	chambermaid
caravan park	carriage dog	catchphrase	cenogenesis	chamber-tomb
caravan site	carriageway	catch-points	censureship	chameleonic
caraway seed	carrick bend	catch-stitch	centenarian	champerties
carbocyclic	carrier wave	catch the sun	centenaries	champertous
Carbonarism	carrion crow	catch-weight	centerboard	championess
carbonation	carryings-on	catchweight	centesimate	chancefully
carbonatite	carry the bat	catechetics	centigramme	chancellery
carbon black	carry the can	catechismal	centimetric	change front
carbon cycle	carry the day	catechistic	cent per cent	change hands
carbon fibre	carry weight	categorical	central bank	change-house
carbon paper	carsickness	cater-corner	centralizer	change of air
carbon steel	cartography	catercorner	centralness	channelling
car boot sale	cartophilic	cater-cousin	Central Park	chantarelle
carborundum	carunculate	caterpillar	Central Time	chanterelle
carboxylate	carvel-built	caterwauler	centreboard	chantership
carbuncular	carving-fork	cathartical	centre field	chanticleer
carburation	case grammar	cathedratic	centrepiece	chaos theory
carburetion	case history	catheterise	centre stage	chaotically
carburetted	case in point	catheterism	centrically	chaparreras
carburetter	cash-account	catheterize	centrifugal	*chapeau-bras*
carburettor	cashew apple	catholicate	centripetal	chapel royal
carbylamine	cashierment	catholicise	centrobaric	chaperonage
carcass meat	cash payment	Catholicism	centromeric	chapmanship
carcinology	cassiterite	catholicity	centumviral	charcuterie
carcinomata	cassowaries	catholicize	Centuriator	charged with
cardan joint	cast a slur on	Catholicize	cephalocele	charge-house
cardan shaft	castellated	catoptrical	cephalothin	charge nurse
Cardan's rule	caster sugar	cat-purchase	cerargyrite	charge sheet
cardinalate	caste-system	cat's pyjamas	cerebellums	charismatic
cardinalism	castigation	cat's whisker	cerebralism	charitarian
cardinalist	castigatory	cattishness	cerebralist	charitative
cardinality	Castile soap	cattle-egret	cerebration	charity ball
cardinalize	casting vote	cattle guard	cerebroside	charity walk
carding wool	castle-guard	cattle-truck	ceremonious	charlatanic
cardiograph	cast light on	cauliflower	cereologist	charlatanry
cardiospasm	castor sugar	causational	ceroplastic	Charles's Law
card-playing	castrensian	causatively	certain sure	charmlessly
card-sharper	cast the lead	causativity	certainties	charm school
carefulness	cast up gorge	caustically	certifiable	charnockite
caressingly	casual water	caustic bush	certifiably	charophytic
caressively	casuistical	caustic soda	certificate	chartaceous
caribou moss	catabaptist	caustic vine	Cesarewitch	chart-buster
caricatural	catabothron	caustic weed	cetological	chartbuster
carminative	catacaustic	cavalierish	chaetognath	charter-land
carnaptious	catachreses	cavalierism	chaff-cutter	charterless
carnationed	catachresis	cave dweller	chafing dish	Charter Mark
carnauba wax	cataclastic	cavernicole	chain armour	chart-topper

chase chorus
chasmogamic
chassisless
chastisable
chaulmoogra
check-action
check-string
Cheddar pink
cheek by jowl
cheer-leader
cheerleader
cheerlessly
cheeseboard
cheesecloth
cheese-flies
cheese-knife
cheesemaker
cheese pasty
cheese plant
cheese press
cheese salad
cheese scone
cheese straw
cheiranthus
chelicerate
cheliferous
Chelsea boot
Chelsea ware
chemicalize
chemin de fer
chemistries
chemotactic
chemotropic
chenopodium
chequer-wise
chequer-work
cherishable
cherishment
chernozemic
chestnut oak
cheval glass
chiaroscuro
chiastolite
chicaneries
chickabiddy
chicken feed
chicken-hawk
chicken Kiev
chicken mite
chicken-shit
chicken soup
chicken-weed
chicken wire
chieftaincy
chieftainry
chiffonnade
chikungunya
chilblained
child labour
child-minder
childminder
chill factor

chilli sauce
chillumchee
chimichanga
chimneyless
chimney-nook
china-closet
China orange
Chinese burn
Chinese copy
Chinese jute
Chinese leaf
Chinese wall
chinoiserie
chintziness
Chippendale
chirography
chirologist
chiromancer
chiromantic
chiropodist
chiropteran
chitterling
chitty-faced
chloanthite
chloric acid
chlorinator
chlorophyll
chlorophyte
chloroplast
chloroprene
chloroquine
chock-a-block
chocolatier
choirmaster
choir office
choir school
choir sister
choke cherry
choke-cymbal
choking coil
cholangitis
cholera belt
choler adust
cholesterin
cholesterol
cholinergic
chondrocyte
chondrodite
chondroitin
Chopinesque
chordophone
chordotonal
choreograph
chorography
choroid coat
choroiditis
choux pastry
chowderhead
chrismation
chrismatory
Christ-cross
christendie

Christendom
christening
Christiania
Christianly
Christingle
Christmases
Christmassy
Christology
Christ's sake
chrome green
chrome steel
chromic acid
chrominance
chromogenic
chromophile
chromophobe
chromophore
chromosomal
chronically
chronograph
chronologer
chronologic
chronometer
chronometry
chronoscope
chrysalides
chrysalises
chrysarobin
chrysoberyl
chrysocolla
chrysoidine
chrysomelid
chrysoprase
chuckawalla
chucklehead
churchgoing
church-grith
church-house
churchiness
churchmanly
church mouse
churchwoman
churchwomen
chyliferous
chylomicron
cicatricial
cicatricula
cicatrizant
ciconiiform
cigar flower
cigar-holder
cigar-shaped
ciliary body
cinchocaine
cinema organ
cinerariums
cinerary urn
cineritious
cinnabarine
cinnamon oil
cinquecento
Cinque Ports

circinately
circination
circle dance
circuitries
circularise
circularity
circularize
circular saw
circulation
circulative
circulatory
circumciser
circumlunar
circumpolar
circumsolar
circumspect
circumvolve
cirl bunting
cirriferous
cirrigerous
cisatlantic
cistophorus
citizenhood
citizenship
citronellal
citronellol
citrus fruit
City Company
city council
city fathers
city manager
city marshal
City marshal
city mission
city slicker
civic centre
civic-minded
civilianise
civilianize
civilizable
civil parish
civil rights
Civvy Street
cladogenous
claim-jumper
clairschach
clairvoyant
clamorously
clandestine
clapperclaw
clapper rail
class action
class-fellow
classically
classic race
classic tutu
class-leader
clathration
clavecinist
clavel-piece
clavicymbal
claw-and-ball

clay mineral
clean-limbed
cleanliness
clean-living
clean-shaven
clean ticket
clear-headed
clear-starch
clear the air
clear the way
clear-voiced
cleft palate
cleistogamy
clergy-house
clergywoman
clergywomen
clericalism
clericalist
clericality
clericalize
clerkliness
cleverality
clever-clogs
click beetle
client state
cliff-hanger
cliffhanger
climacteric
climatology
clinochlore
cliometrics
clipper ship
clockmaking
clodhopping
clog-almanac
close-carpet
close-fisted
close-handed
close-hauled
close-lipped
close season
closet drama
close to home
closet queen
closing time
clostridial
clostridium
clothesless
clothes line
clothes-moth
clothes-post
cloth-headed
cloth-miller
cloth of gold
cloth-worker
cloud-castle
cloudlessly
cloud seeder
cloud street
clouted shoe
clover-grass
cluster bomb

cluster pine	coffee-spoon	colonizable	commandment	compass rose
coadjutress	coffee stall	colonoscope	command post	compearance
coadunation	coffee table	colonoscopy	commandress	compellable
coagulation	coffin-joint	colorimeter	*comme il faut*	compendiate
coagulative	coffin-plate	colorimetry	commemorate	compendious
coalescence	coffin-stool	colostomies	commendable	compendiums
coalitioner	co-foundress	colouration	commendably	compensable
coal scuttle	cogenerated	colour atlas	commendador	compensator
coal-whipper	cogenerator	colour-blind	commendator	competently
coarctation	cognateness	colourfully	commend me to	competition
coat checker	cognitional	colour guard	commentator	competitive
coatimundis	cognitively	colour-index	commination	competitory
coaxial line	cognitivism	colouristic	comminatory	compilation
cobalt bloom	cognitivist	colour-light	comminution	compilatory
cobbler's wax	cognominate	colour-phase	commiserate	complacence
cobblestone	cognoscence	colour-plate	commissaire	complacency
coccidiosis	cognoscente	coltishness	commissural	complainant
coccinellid	cognoscenti	columbarium	committable	complaisant
coccosphere	cognoscible	columniated	committible	completable
Cochin China	cohortation	columniform	commodified	complexness
cock-a-leekie	coincidence	combat boots	commodifies	compliantly
cock-brained	co-inherence	combat dress	commodities	complicated
cockle-shell	co-inheritor	combatively	commonality	componentry
cockleshell	cold-blooded	combativity	common chord	comportment
cock one's eye	cold cathode	combination	common crier	comport with
cock one's hat	cold comfort	combinative	common field	compositely
cock sparrow	cold harbour	combinatory	common juror	composition
cock the ears	cold-hearted	combing wool	common maple	compositive
cock the nose	cold storage	combustible	common metre	compossible
cocky-leekie	cold warrior	combustibly	common murre	compostable
cocoa butter	coleopteran	come a gutser	commonplace	compost heap
coco matting	Coleridgian	come a purler	common pleas	compost pile
co-conscious	collaborate	come a stumer	common scold	compotation
coconut crab	collagenous	come between	common sense	compotatory
coconut milk	collapsible	come forward	common sewer	compound eye
coconut palm	collational	come in first	common shore	compresence
coconut tree	collectable	come in handy	common situs	compression
code-breaker	collectedly	come one's way	common snipe	compressive
codefendant	collect eyes	come over big	common stock	compressure
codependent	collectible	come short of	communalise	comprisable
codetermine	collegially	comet-finder	communalism	compromiser
codicillary	collegianer	come the acid	communalist	*compte rendu*
codling moth	collembolan	come through	communality	Comptometer
cod liver oil	collenchyma	come to a head	communalize	comptroller
co-education	colleterial	come to an end	communicant	compulsitor
coeducation	colligation	come to blows	communicate	compunction
coefficient	colligative	come to grief	communistic	compurgator
coelenteron	collimation	come to light	communities	computation
coelurosaur	collinearly	come to terms	commutation	computeracy
coenenchyme	collisional	comet-seeker	commutative	computerate
coercionist	collocation	come unstuck	compact disc	computerese
coessential	collocative	come-uppance	compactedly	computerise
coeternally	collocutory	come what may	compactness	computerist
co-executrix	colloidally	comfortable	compaginate	computerize
coexistence	colloquiums	comfortably	companioned	computistic
coextension	collusively	comfortless	comparatist	comradeship
coextensive	Collyridian	comfortress	comparative	Comstockery
co-favourite	colonelcies	comicalness	compare with	concamerate
coffee-berry	colonelling	comic relief	compartment	concatenate
coffee-break	colonelship	commandable	compassable	concave lens
coffee house	colonialism	Commandaria	compass card	concaveness
coffee-maker	colonialist	Commanderia	compassless	concealable

concealment
conceitedly
conceitless
conceivable
conceivably
concentrate
conceptacle
concernedly
concernment
concertante
concertanti
concert-goer
concert hall
concertina'd
concertinas
concertinos
concessible
conciliable
conciliarly
conciliator
conciseness
concitation
conclusible
concolorous
concomitant
concordable
concordance
concordancy
concordatum
concreative
concrescent
concubinage
concubinary
concurrence
concurrency
condemnable
condemnator
condensable
condensator
condensedly
condensible
condignness
condimental
condisciple
conditional
conditioned
conditioner
condolatory
condolement
condolingly
condominium
condonation
condottiere
conducement
conductance
conduct book
conductible
conductress
conduit-pipe
Condy's fluid
confabulate
confederacy

confederate
conferrable
conferrence
confessedly
confidently
confidingly
configurate
confineless
confinement
confirmable
confiscable
confiscator
conflagrant
conflagrate
conflictful
confliction
conflictive
conflictual
confluently
conformable
conformably
conformally
conformance
confusingly
confusional
confutation
confutative
congealable
congealment
congé d'élire
congee-house
congelation
congenerate
congenerous
congenially
congratters
congregated
congregator
congression
congressist
congressman
Congressman
congressmen
congruently
congruously
conicalness
conjectural
conjecturer
conjugality
conjugation
conjunction
conjunctiva
conjunctive
conjuncture
conjuration
connateness
connectable
connectedly
connectible
connectival
connexional
connoisseur

connotation
connotative
connubially
connumerate
conquerable
conquerless
consanguine
conscienced
consciously
consecrated
consecrator
consecution
consecutive
consentient
consequence
conservable
conservancy
conservator
considerate
considering
consignment
consilience
consistence
consistency
consolation
consolatory
consolatrix
consolement
consolidate
consolingly
consonantal
consonanted
consonantic
consonantly
consortiums
consortship
conspecific
conspicuity
conspicuous
conspirator
constabular
constellate
consternate
constipated
constituent
constituter
constitutor
constrained
constrainer
constricted
constrictor
construable
constructor
consultable
consultancy
consumerism
consumerist
consumingly
consummator
consumption
consumptive
contactable

contact lens
containable
containment
contaminant
contaminate
contango day
contemplant
contemplate
contenement
contentable
contentedly
contentious
contentless
contentment
content word
conterminal
contestable
contextless
continental
continently
contingence
contingency
continuable
continually
continuance
continuator
contorniate
contour line
contrabasso
contractant
contractile
contraction
contractive
contractual
contracture
contradance
contraposit
contraption
contrariant
contrariety
contrarious
contrastive
contratenor
contravener
contrayerva
contredanse
contretemps
contribuent
contributor
contrivable
contrivance
controlling
controlment
control room
control unit
controversy
contubernal
contumacity
conurbation
convalidate
convenience
conveniency

convential
conventicle
convergence
convergency
conversable
conversably
conversance
conversancy
conversible
convertible
convertibly
conveyancer
conveyorize
convictable
convincible
convivially
convocation
convolution
convolvulus
co-occurrent
cookery book
cook-general
cookie sheet
cool chamber
cooling-pond
cool tankard
co-operation
cooperation
co-operative
cooperative
Cooper's hawk
coordinator
Cootamundra
co-ownership
coparcenary
copiability
coping stone
copiousness
coplanarity
copper beech
copper-belly
copper Maori
copperplate
coppersmith
copper's nark
coppice-wood
coprocessor
copromaniac
coprophagia
coprophagic
coprophilia
coprophilic
copyability
copywriting
coquilla nut
coral insect
coral island
coralliform
coralloidal
coram judice
coram populo
corbel-stone

corbel-table	corymbiform	counter-mart	coxcombries	crêpe rubber
corbie-gable	corymbosely	countermine	coxopoditic	crepitation
corbie-steps	coryphodont	countermove	crabbedness	crepuscular
cordilleran	co-signatory	countermure	crab-catcher	crepusculum
cordwainery	cosmetician	counterpane	crab-fashion	crescentade
cordwaining	cosmeticize	counterpart	crack down on	crescentric
core sampler	cosmetology	counter-plea	cracked corn	crested newt
co-residence	cosmogonies	counterplot	crackedness	crestfallen
cork cambium	cosmogonist	counter-pole	cracker-bush	Creswellian
corn bunting	cosmography	counterpose	crackerjack	cribellated
corn-cob pipe	cosmologist	counter-roll	crack-headed	cricket-frog
corn ear worm	cosmonautic	counter-seal	crackle-ware	cricket-teal
cornerstone	cosmopolite	countersign	crack of dawn	crime-buster
corner throw	cosmothetic	countersink	crack of doom	crime writer
corn-husking	co-sovereign	counter-step	crack on sail	criminalise
corniculate	Cossack boot	countersunk	crack-voiced	criminalism
cornigerous	Cossack post	counter-tide	crack willow	criminalist
corn in Egypt	cost-benefit	counter-turn	cracovienne	criminality
corn parsley	cost-cutting	countertype	cradle-board	criminalize
corn spurrey	costingness	countervail	craftswoman	criminal law
cornucopian	costiveness	countervair	craftswomen	criminaloid
corn whiskey	costume play	counterview	craftworker	crimination
corollaries	cotemporary	counter-walk	crag and tail	criminative
corolla-tube	coterminous	counterwork	craggedness	criminatory
coronagraph	co-tidal line	countrified	cranberries	criminology
coronal bone	cotoneaster	country bred	crane-colour	criminously
coronership	cottage loaf	country club	crane-driver	crimson lake
coronograph	cotton candy	countryfied	crane-necked	crinigerous
corpocratic	cotton grass	country-folk	craniometry	crinkliness
corporality	cotton plant	country jake	craniopathy	cripplingly
corporately	cotton plush	country road	crape-myrtle	crithomancy
corporation	cotton-sedge	country rock	crappit-head	criticality
corporatism	cotton state	country seat	crapshooter	criticaster
corporatist	cotton twist	countryship	crapulosity	crochet hook
corporative	cotton waste	countryside	crash course	crocidolite
corporatize	couch potato	country town	crash cymbal	crocodilian
corporeally	Couette flow	country-wide	crash helmet	crocodiling
corporosity	coulometric	county court	crash-tackle	Cromwellian
corps d'élite	council-book	coup de grâce	crashworthy	crook-backed
corpse-light	council-fire	couple-close	crateriform	crookbacked
corpuscular	council flat	coupling-pin	crawling peg	crookedness
corpus juris	counselless	coupling-rod	crazy paving	Crookes tube
correctable	counselling	courageless	cream cheese	crop dusting
correctible	count-bishop	courteously	cream colour	cross-accent
correctness	countenance	courtesy cop	creamometer	cross-action
correctress	counter-arch	courtierism	cream sherry	cross-bearer
correlation	counterbass	court jester	creationism	cross-border
correlative	counter-bill	courtliness	creationist	crossbowman
corrigendum	counterblow	courtly love	creative art	crossbowmen
corroborant	counterbond	Court of Rome	creatorship	cross-corner
corroborate	counter-book	court tennis	credibility	cross-cousin
corrosively	counterbore	couscoussou	credit title	cross-cut saw
corrugation	counterbuff	Cousin Betty	credit union	cross-dating
corruptedly	counter-etch	cousin-in-law	credulously	cross-fenced
corruptible	counterfeit	covariation	cremasteric	cross-garnet
corruptibly	counter-fire	cover charge	crematories	cross-handed
corruptless	counterfoil	cover letter	crematorium	cross-legged
corruptness	counterfort	covert-baron	crème brûlée	cross-member
corruptress	counterglow	covert cloth	crenulation	cross-plough
cors anglais	counterlath	cowboy boots	creolistics	cross-rhythm
corticolous	countermand	cowslipping	creophagous	cross-saddle
coruscation	countermark	coxcombical	creosote oil	cross stitch

cross-street
cross swords
cross-tongue
cross-voting
crotcheteer
crouchingly
crouch start
crowberries
crowdedness
crowd of sail
crowd on sail
crowd-puller
Crown Agents
crown bowler
Crown colony
Crown Colony
crowned head
crown jewels
Crown Office
crown prince
Crown prince
crow's-footed
crow-stepped
crowstepped
crucialness
crucian carp
cruciferous
crucifixion
cruelty-free
cruise liner
crumbliness
crumple zone
crunchiness
crunchingly
crush stroke
crustaceous
cry cupboard
cry harrow on
cryobiology
cryonically
cryosurgery
cryotherapy
cryptically
cryptogamic
cryptogenic
cryptograph
cryptomeria
cryptophyte
cryptorchid
crystal axis
crystal ball
crystal form
crystal-like
crystalline
crystallise
crystallite
crystallize
crystalloid
ctenophoral
ctenophoran
ctenophoric
cubbishness

cub engineer
cubicalness
cub reporter
cuckoo clock
cuckoo's mate
cuckoo's meat
cucullately
cuir-bouilli
culicicidal
culmiferous
culmination
culpability
cultishness
cultivation
cultureless
culturology
culverineer
cum dividend
cumulonimbi
cunctatious
cunnilingue
cunnilingus
cunningness
cupellation
cup-mushroom
cup of estate
cupping-test
cuprammonia
cupriferous
cupro-nickel
curatorship
curb service
curettement
curialistic
curiosities
curiousness
curling iron
curling pins
curling rink
curl one's lip
curly endive
currant-tree
currentless
currentness
currishness
curry favour
curry powder
cursiveness
cursoriness
curtailment
curtail-step
curtain call
curtain fire
curtain-hook
curtainless
curtain line
curtain-rail
curtain-ring
curtain wall
curvilineal
curvilinear
cushionless

cushion-like
cushion star
cuspidation
customaries
customarily
custom-built
custom-house
customs duty
cut-and-cover
cut and dried
cut-and-paste
cut both ways
cutlass-fish
cut the melon
cutting-edge
cutting room
cut to pieces
cyanidation
cyanine blue
cyanophycin
cyanophytic
cybernation
cybernetics
cycadaceous
cycadophyte
cyclization
cycloalkane
cyclohexane
cyclopaedia
cycloplegia
cycloplegic
cyclosporin
cyclothymia
cyclothymic
cylinder oil
cylinder saw
cylindrical
cyma reversa
cynanthropy
cynological
cyperaceous
cypress-knee
cypress pine
cypress tree
cypress-vine
cypriniform
cyprinodont
cypripedium
cysticercus
cystoscopic
cystotomies
cytogenetic
cytological
cytomegalic
cytoplasmic
cytotropism
dactylogram
dactylology
Dagestan rug
dagger-board
daggerboard
dagger plant

dairy cattle
dairy farmer
daisy-cutter
dak-bungalow
dale and down
Dalecarlian
damask steel
dame's violet
damnability
Damoclesian
damper pedal
dampishness
damselflies
dance in a net
dancing girl
dandy roller
danger angle
danger money
dangerously
Daniell cell
daphne heath
dappled-grey
daredevilry
dark-adapted
dark current
dark glasses
dark lantern
Darling lily
darning-ball
darning-wool
Darwinistic
Darwin tulip
dashingness
data capture
daubréelite
dauntlessly
Davis Strait
dawn redwood
day after day
day and night
day labourer
days of grace
dazzle paint
de-accession
deaccession
deactivator
dead against
dead and gone
dead as a dodo
deadeningly
dead-hearted
deadpanning
dead soldier
dead to shame
deaf and dumb
deaf as a post
deafeningly
deamination
de-Anglicize
death duties
death-in-life
deathlessly

deathliness
death rattle
death throes
deattribute
debamboozle
debarbarize
debarkation
debasedness
debauchedly
debouchment
debridement
debs' delight
decadentism
decahedrons
decalcified
decalcifier
decalcifies
decalescent
decantation
decapeptide
decapitator
decapsulate
decarbonate
decarbonise
decarbonize
decarburize
decasualize
decaudation
deceitfully
deceivingly
decelerator
decemvirate
decennially
deceptively
decerebrate
decerniture
decidedness
deciduously
decillionth
decimo-sexto
deckle-edged
deckle strap
declamation
declamatory
declaration
declarative
declaratory
declination
declinatory
declinature
declivities
declivitous
decollation
décollement
décolletage
decolourant
decolourize
decommunize
decomposite
decondition
deconstruct
decorticate

decrepitate	degradingly	demon bowler	depravities	desperation
decrepitude	degranulate	demonianism	deprecation	despisement
decrescendo	degustation	demonically	deprecative	despisingly
decretalist	de haut en bas	demonocracy	deprecatory	despoilment
decretorial	dehonestate	demonolatry	depreciator	despondence
decuman gate	dehortation	demonomania	depredation	despondency
decumbiture	dehortative	demonstrate	depredatory	despumation
decurionate	dehortatory	demoralizer	depressedly	dessert fork
decurrently	dehydratase	Demosthenic	depressible	dessert wine
decursively	dehydration	demountable	deprivation	destabilise
decurvature	deictically	demutualize	deprivative	destabilize
decussately	deification	demyelinate	de profundis	de-Stalinize
decussation	deificatory	demystified	deprogramme	destination
dedentition	deistically	demystifies	depth charge	destitutely
dedicatedly	delabialize	demythicize	depth-finder	destitution
deductively	delafossite	denary scale	deracialize	destoolment
deductivism	delectation	dendritical	deraignment	destroyable
deductivist	deleterious	dendrologic	derangement	destructful
Deely-bobber	deliberator	dendrometer	derecognise	destruction
de-emphasise	deliciously	dendrophile	derecognize	destructive
de-emphasize	delightable	denervation	dereliction	destructure
deep-dish pie	delightedly	deniability	dermapteran	desulfurate
deep drawing	delightless	denigration	dermatology	desultorily
deepeningly	delightsome	denigratory	dermatoptic	desuperheat
deep-etching	delineation	denitration	dermoid cyst	detainingly
deep-fetched	delineative	denitrified	dermopteran	detectional
deep-freezer	delinquency	denitrifies	derring-doer	deteriorate
deep-milking	deliriously	denizenship	desacralize	determinacy
deep-mouthed	delitescent	denominable	descendable	determinans
deep therapy	deliverable	denominator	descendance	determinant
deerstalker	deliverance	dental floss	descendancy	determinata
deer-stealer	deliverness	dental nurse	descendence	determinate
defaecation	delivery van	dentary bone	descendible	determinism
defaillance	Della Robbia	dentellated	descloizite	determinist
defalcation	delphically	denticulate	descrambler	detestation
defatigable	delphinidin	dentigerous	describable	detractress
defectively	delphiniums	dentistical	description	detrainment
defence bond	delta rhythm	denumerable	descriptive	detribalise
defenceless	demagnetise	denumerably	desecration	detribalize
defence plea	demagnetize	denunciator	desecrative	detrimental
Defenderism	demagogical	denutrition	desegregate	deturpation
defensively	demagoguery	deny oneself	deselection	deuteranope
deferential	demand curve	deoxidation	desensitise	deuteration
defiantness	demand draft	deoxygenate	desensitize	deuterogamy
defibrinate	demandingly	deoxyribose	desert lemon	deutomerite
deficiently	demarcation	depasturage	deservingly	Deutschmark
definiendum	demarcative	depauperate	deserving of	devaluation
deflagrator	demarkation	depauperize	desexualise	devastating
defloration	dementation	dependently	desexualize	devastation
defocussing	demesmerize	depending on	desiccation	devastative
defoliation	demethylate	deperdition	desiccative	developable
deforcement	demi-bastion	dephlegmate	desiccatory	development
deformation	demigoddess	deploration	desideratum	deverbative
deformities	demi-pension	deploringly	designation	deviability
defraudment	democracies	deplumation	designative	deviational
defunctness	democratise	depoeticize	designatory	devil dancer
deglamorize	democratism	depolarizer	designingly	devil-dodger
deglutinate	democratize	depopulator	desilverize	devil's bones
deglutition	Democritean	deportation	desinential	devil's books
deglutitory	demodulator	depositable	desiredness	devil's dozen
degradation	demographer	depravation	desperadoes	devil's twine
degradative	demographic	depravement	desperately	deviousness

devirginate	dictatorial	diplococcus	discontinue	dismayingly
devitrified	dictatorily	diplohedral	discordance	dismembered
devitrifies	dictyostele	diplohedron	discordancy	dismemberer
devolvement	didacticism	diplomatese	discotheque	dismissable
devotedness	didactylous	diplomatise	discothèque	dismissible
devotionary	diddly-squat	diplomatist	discourager	dismutation
devotionist	die aborning	diplomatize	discourtesy	Disneyesque
devouringly	die like a dog	dip one's wick	discoveries	disobedient
Dewey system	die-stamping	dipper gourd	disc parking	disobliging
dexterously	die the death	diprotodont	discreation	disobstruct
dharmasutra	differentia	dipsomaniac	discredence	disordinate
Diabolonian	differently	dipterocarp	discredited	disorganise
diachronism	difficultly	dipyramidal	discreetest	disorganize
diachronous	diffidation	direct debit	discrepance	disparately
diacoustics	diffidently	direct-drive	discrepancy	disparities
diacritical	diffraction	direct grant	discriminal	disparition
diadelphous	diffractive	directional	discussable	dispartment
diagnosable	diffuseness	directively	discussible	dispatch box
diagnostics	diffusional	directivity	disdainable	dispatchful
diagonalize	diffusively	directorate	disembodied	dispendious
diagramming	diffusivity	directorial	disembodies	dispensable
dialectally	digestively	directories	disembogued	dispensator
dialectical	digital root	directrices	disembogues	dispensible
dialogician	digitigrade	direfulness	disemburden	dispersable
dialogistic	dignifiedly	dirndl skirt	disencumber	dispersedly
dialogue box	dignitaries	dirt-tracker	disentangle	dispersible
diamagnetic	diguanidine	dirty old man	disenthrone	displacency
diametrally	dihexagonal	disablement	disentrance	displayable
diametrical	dihybridism	disableness	disequality	display type
diamondback	dilapidated	disaccustom	disesteemer	displeasant
diamond-bird	dilapidator	disacquaint	disfunction	displeasing
diamond-like	dilatometer	disaffected	disgarrison	displeasure
diamond pane	dilatometry	disafforest	disgraceful	displicency
diamondwise	dilettantes	disagreeing	disgracious	disportment
diamorphine	diluvialist	disappearer	disgruntled	disposition
diaphaneity	diluvianism	disapproval	disguisedly	dispositive
diaphonemic	dimensional	disapprover	disgustedly	dispository
diaphoresis	dimensioned	disarmament	disharmonic	disprovable
diaphoretic	dimidiately	disarmingly	dishevelled	disputation
diapophysis	dimidiation	disassemble	dishonestly	disputative
diapositive	diminuendos	disassembly	dishonourer	disquantity
diarthrosis	diminutival	disavowable	dishumanize	disquieting
diastematic	dimorphemic	disbandment	disillusion	disquietude
diastrophic	dingleberry	disbeliever	disillusive	disquisitor
diasystemic	dining-chair	discalceate	disimprison	disregarder
diatessaron	dining table	discanonize	disinclined	disremember
diathermacy	dinner dance	discardable	disinfecter	disrobement
diathermous	dinner party	discardment	disinfector	dissectible
diatonicism	dinner-table	discernible	disinterest	disseminate
dicasterion	dinner wagon	discernibly	disinterred	disseminule
dichogamous	dinosaurian	discernment	disjointure	dissentient
dichotomies	dioeciously	discerption	disjunction	dissentious
dichotomise	Dionysiacal	discigerous	disjunctive	dissentment
dichotomist	Diophantine	disciplinal	disjuncture	dissepiment
dichotomize	dipeptidase	discipliner	dislikeable	dissertator
dichotomous	diphosphate	disclaimant	dislocation	dissimilate
dichromatic	diphtherial	discloister	dislocative	dissimulate
dichroscope	diphtheroid	discography	dislocatory	dissipation
Dickensiana	diphthongal	discolorate	dislodgment	dissipative
dicondylian	diphthongic	discomfited	disloyalist	dissociable
dicotyledon	diphycercal	discomfiter	dismal Jimmy	dissolutely
dictatorate	diplococcal	disconsider	dismayfully	dissolution

dissolutive
dissolvable
dissolvible
dissonantal
dissonantly
dissyllabic
dissyllable
dissymmetry
dissympathy
distaff side
Distalgesic
distantiate
distantness
distasteful
distempered
distemperer
distendedly
distensible
distillable
distinction
distinctive
distinguish
distomiasis
distortedly
distraction
distractive
distressful
distress-gun
distributee
distributor
distrustful
disturbance
disturbancy
disturbedly
disturnpike
disunionism
disunionist
disvaluable
disyllabize
diterpenoid
dithyrambic
dittography
divaricator
divellicate
divergement
divergently
divergingly
diverseness
diversified
diversifier
diversifies
diversiform
diversional
diversities
diverticula
divertingly
divestitive
divestiture
dividedness
dividuality
divine spark
diving board

divining rod
divisionary
divisionism
divisionist
divorceable
divorce case
divorceless
divorcement
divulgation
divulgement
do a line with
do a number on
dobsonflies
docetically
doch an doris
dockominium
dock-warrant
dockyard man
doctor-blade
doctorially
doctrinaire
doctrinally
documentary
documentize
dodder-grass
dodderiness
dodecahedra
dodecameric
dodecaphony
dodecastyle
dodge Pompey
dogfighting
doggerelize
doggishness
doggy-paddle
dog-handling
dogmatician
dog's-cabbage
dog's disease
dog's mercury
doily napkin
do justice to
dolabriform
dole-bludger
dolefulness
Dolly Varden
dolorimeter
dolphinfish
doltishness
domesticate
domesticism
domesticity
domesticize
domiciliary
domiciliate
domineering
Dominion day
domino paper
done to a turn
Donizettian
donkey derby
donkey Derby

donkey-stone
donkey stool
donnishness
do not seem to
do not want to
Donovan body
donovanosis
don't I know it
don't you know
doodly-squat
doomwatcher
do one's block
do one's scone
do one's stuff
do one's thing
door knocker
doorstepper
dormant tree
dormitories
dorsiferous
dorsiflexor
dos and don'ts
dot and go one
double agent
double album
double blank
double-blind
double bluff
double-bogey
double-check
double cream
double-cross
double-digit
double doors
double dummy
double Dutch
double eagle
double-edged
double-ender
double entry
double event
double-faced
double fault
double feast
double first
double fugue
double helix
double image
double quick
double rhyme
double sharp
double-sided
double-space
double-speak
doublespeak
double steal
doublethink
double tides
doubtlessly
doughtiness
dough-trough
Douglas pine

douroucouli
do well out of
do whoopsies
down-calving
down-channel
downconvert
down-country
downcurrent
down draught
downhearted
downlooking
down payment
downrightly
down-the-line
down the road
down-to-earth
downtrodden
downwarping
downwelling
downy mildew
doxographer
doxographic
doxological
doxorubicin
doxycycline
do your worst
dracunculus
draft dodger
draggle-tail
drag-hunting
dragon china
dragonflies
dragon's head
dragon's tail
drama critic
dramaticism
dramaticule
dramatistic
dramaturgic
dram-drinker
drape jacket
drastically
draught beer
draughtsman
draughtsmen
draught-tree
draw a bead on
drawing-book
drawing card
drawing room
drawn butter
dreadlessly
dreadlocked
dreadnought
dreamlessly
dream ticket
dream vision
dredging-box
dress agency
dress circle
dressing-box
dress length

dressmaking
dress parade
dress shield
dress weight
driblet cone
drift-anchor
drift-bottle
drift mining
drift-netter
drilling mud
drilling rig
drill string
drink-driver
drinker moth
drinks party
drip culture
dripping-pan
dripping wet
drivability
drive a quill
driver's test
drive system
driving axle
driving band
driving belt
driving iron
driving rain
driving seat
driving test
dromedaries
dromomaniac
drone-beetle
drop a curtsy
drop a stitch
drop curtain
drop-forging
drop initial
dropsically
drop-testing
drug peddler
drug traffic
drumbledore
drumlinized
drum machine
drum printer
drunkenness
drunkometer
dry diggings
dry gangrene
dry mounting
dry straight
dual control
dual-purpose
dubiousness
Dublin prawn
duchesse set
ducking-pond
dugout canoe
Duke of Yorks
dulcifluous
dull emitter
dumb animals

dumbfounder
dumper truck
dumpishness
duncishness
dunducketty
duopolistic
duple rhythm
duplication
duplicative
duplicature
duplicitous
durableness
durante vita
Durkheimian
duskishness
dust disease
dust-wrapper
dusty answer
dusty miller
Dutch cheese
Dutch clover
duteousness
dutifulness
duty officer
dwarf mallow
dyer's rocket
dynamically
dynamometer
dynamometry
dynasticism
dyscalculia
dysesthesia
dysfunction
dyslogistic
dyspareunia
dyspeptical
dysrhythmia
dysrhythmic
eager beaver
ear for music
Earl Marshal
early leaver
earn a living
earnestness
ear-piercing
earth almond
earth closet
earth colour
earthenware
earth hunger
earthliness
earth mother
earth-moving
earth pillar
earth tremor
easefulness
ease the helm
East African
east and west
east-by-north
East Coaster
Easter bunny

easternmost
Eastern Time
eating apple
eating-house
eating irons
eat one's tutu
eat salt with
eaves-trough
ebulliently
eccentrical
ecchondroma
ecclesiarch
echo chamber
echopractic
echo sounder
eclecticism
eco-friendly
econometric
economic man
economy-size
ectoblastic
ectogenesis
ectogenetic
ectomorphic
ectopically
ectopic beat
ectoplasmic
ectoplastic
ectoproctan
ectothermic
ectotrophic
ecumenicity
edaphically
eddy current
edible snail
edification
edificatory
editorially
educability
educational
edutainment
eff and blind
effectively
effectivity
effectually
efficacious
efficiently
effigiation
effigy mound
effortfully
effulgently
egalitarian
egg and bacon
egg-drop soup
Egg Saturday
eggshell-ful
egocentrism
ego-identity
egolessness
egomaniacal
egotistical
egregiously

Egyptianise
Egyptianism
Egyptianize
eidetically
eigenvector
eighteenmos
eight-seater
eight-square
Einsteinian
einsteinium
eisegetical
eisteddfods
ejaculation
ejaculative
ejaculatory
ejectamenta
eject button
ejector seat
elaborately
elaboration
elaborative
elaboratory
elastically
elasticated
elastic band
elasticized
elastic-side
elastomeric
Elastoplast
elbow grease
elbow-length
elbow-sleeve
elderflower
elderliness
election bun
electioneer
electorally
electorship
electricals
electric arc
electric eel
electric eye
electrician
electricise
electricity
electricize
electric ray
electrified
electrifier
electrifies
electrocoat
electrocute
electrocyte
electrofish
electroform
electroglow
electroless
electrolier
electrology
electrolyse
electrolyte
electrolyze

electron gun
electronics
electroplax
electro-slag
electrotype
electroweak
electuaries
elegiacally
elementally
elephant hut
elephantine
elephantoid
eleutherian
elevational
elevenpence
elevenpenny
elicitation
eligibility
elimination
eliminative
eliminatory
Elizabethan
ellipsoidal
ellipticity
elocutional
eloquential
elsewhither
elucidation
elucidative
elucidatory
elusiveness
elutriation
emanational
emancipator
emasculator
embarcadero
embarcation
embarkation
embarrassed
embellisher
emblematise
emblematist
emblematize
embolectomy
embowelling
embowerment
embraceable
embracement
embracingly
embracively
embrocation
embroiderer
embroilment
embryogenic
embryologic
embryonated
embryotoxic
Emerald Isle
emerald moth
emergencies
emery powder
emmenagogic

emmenagogue
emotionally
emotionless
emotiveness
empanelment
emperor moth
emperorship
emphyteusis
emphyteutic
empiecement
Empire State
empirically
emplacement
empleomania
empowerment
empty-handed
empty-headed
empty-nester
emulatively
emulsionise
emulsionize
enabling act
enamel paint
enamourment
enarthroses
enarthrosis
encapsidate
encapsulate
encaptivate
encarnadine
encarnalize
encased knot
encephaloid
enchainment
enchantedly
enchantment
enchantress
enchiridion
enchondroma
encomendero
encomiastic
encouraging
encrustment
enculturate
encumbrance
encystation
endaspidean
endearingly
endeavourer
endemically
endlessness
endocardial
endocardium
endocentric
endocranial
endocuticle
endocytosis
endocytotic
endodontics
endodontist
endogenesis
endogenetic

endoglossic
endometrial
endometrium
endomitosis
endomitotic
endomorphic
end one's days
endoplasmic
endopsychic
endorsation
endorsement
endoscopist
endospermic
endosteally
endothelial
endothelium
endothermic
endotrophic
end standard
enemy action
energetical
energy level
enfeoffment
enfleshment
enforceable
enforcement
enforcingly
enfranchise
engaged tone
engineering
engine house
englacially
English bond
English horn
English Miss
Englishness
English rose
engorgement
engraftment
engrammatic
engrossedly
engrossment
enhancement
enigmatical
enjambement
enlargement
enlightener
enlisted man
enlivenment
ennoblement
enolization
enorm lesion
enouncement
enquiringly
enragedness
enrichingly
ensepulchre
enslavement
ensnarement
entablature
entablement
enterocoele

enterocoely
enterocytic
enteropathy
enterostomy
enterotoxin
enteroviral
enterovirus
enterpriser
entertainer
enthralment
entitlement
entomologic
entomophagy
entoproctan
entrainment
entrance fee
entreatment
entrustment
entry permit
entwinement
enucleation
enumeration
enumerative
enunciation
enunciative
envelopment
enviability
enviousness
environment
enzymically
epanalepsis
epanaleptic
epanaphoral
epeirogenic
epenthesize
ephemerally
ephemerides
epicheirema
epicondylar
epicyclical
epidemicity
epidermical
epidiascope
epigastrium
epigenetics
epigrammist
epigraphist
epileptical
epilogistic
epimorphism
epinephrine
epipetalous
epiphyllous
epiphysitis
epiphytical
epiphytotic
epiplankton
episcopable
episcopalia
episcopally
episodicity
Epistle side

epistolizer
epitaxially
epithalamia
epithalamic
epithalamus
epithelioid
epithelioma
epitheliums
epithetical
epithymetic
epitrichial
epitrichium
epitrochoid
epoch-making
eponymously
epoxidation
equableness
equal rights
equatorward
equerryship
equiangular
equicaloric
equidistant
equiformity
equilateral
equilibrant
equilibrate
equilibrial
equilibrise
equilibrist
equilibrium
equilibrize
equinoctial
equipollent
equivalence
equivalency
equivocally
equivocator
eradication
eradicative
erasability
Erasmianism
Erastianism
eremacausis
eremejevite
ergatocracy
ergographic
ergometrine
eristically
erosiveness
erotogenous
erotomaniac
erratically
erraticness
erroneously
error circle
erubescence
eruditeness
eruditional
erysipeloid
erythematic
erythraemia

erythraemic
erythristic
erythrocyte
erythronium
erythropsia
escape hatch
escape shaft
escape speed
escape valve
escape wheel
escarbuncle
eschatology
escheatable
escheatment
esemplastic
Eskimo-Aleut
esotericism
esotericist
Esperantist
espieglerie
esquireship
essentially
establisher
estate agent
estate in fee
estate wagon
estrepement
estropiated
eteostichon
Eternal City
eternal life
eternalness
ethereality
etherealize
ethereal oil
etheromania
ethicalness
ethionamide
ethisterone
ethmoid bone
ethnobotany
ethnography
ethnologist
ethological
ethoxylated
Eton College
Etruscology
et sequentes
etymologies
etymologise
etymologist
etymologize
eubacterial
eubacterium
eucalyptian
Eucharistic
Euchologion
euchromatic
euchromatin
eudaemonism
eudaimonism
eudiometric

eugenically
eugeoclinal
eulogically
eunuch flute
eunuchoidal
eupepticity
euphemistic
euphonistic
eurhythmics
eurhythmist
Euro-African
Euro-Asiatic
Eurocentric
Euromissile
Europeanise
Europeanism
Europeanist
Europeanize
Euro-sceptic
euryphagous
eurythermic
euthanasiac
euthanasian
euthanatize
evagination
evanescence
Evangeliary
evangelical
evangelican
evangelizer
evanishment
Evans gambit
evaporation
evaporative
evasiveness
evening star
evening suit
eventlessly
eventration
eventuality
eventuation
ever-blessed
everlasting
evertebrate
every stitch
everywheres
evidentiary
evidentness
evil-looking
eviscerator
evocatively
evolutional
exaggerator
exaltedness
examination
examiningly
exasperated
exasperater
exasperator
excarnation
exceedingly
excellently

exceptional	exorbitance	exquisitely	factor eight	farinaceous
excerptible	exorbitancy	exquisitism	factor group	farkleberry
excessively	exoskeletal	exsangueous	factorially	farmer's lung
excitedness	exoskeleton	exsanguious	Factory Acts	farraginous
excitomotor	exostracize	exsiccation	factory farm	far-reaching
exclamation	exotericism	exsiccative	factory ship	fartherance
exclamative	exotericist	exstipulate	factory shop	farthermost
exclamatory	expansional	extemporary	facts of life	farthingale
exclusioner	expansively	extemporise	factualness	fasciculate
exclusively	expansivity	extemporize	facultative	fascinating
exclusivism	expatiation	extensional	faddishness	fascination
exclusivist	expatiative	extensively	fainéantism	fascinative
exclusivity	expatiatory	extenuation	fainting fit	fashionable
excogitator	expectantly	extenuative	fair-weather	fashionably
excommunion	expectation	extenuatory	fairy lights	fashionless
exconjugant	expectative	exteriorise	fairy martin	fast bowling
excoriation	expectingly	exteriority	faith healer	fast breeder
excorticate	expectorant	exteriorize	faithlessly	fast forward
excremental	expectorate	exterminate	faithworthy	fast neutron
excrescence	expediently	external ear	fall afoul of	fast reactor
excrescency	expeditious	externalise	fall-breaker	fata morgana
exculpation	expenditure	externalism	fallen angel	fat dormouse
exculpatory	expensively	externalist	fallen woman	fatefulness
excursional	experienced	externality	fall herring	father-in-law
excursively	experiencer	externalize	fallibilism	father right
excurvation	expiscation	externation	fallibilist	fatigueless
excystation	explainable	extirpation	fallibility	fatiguesome
ex-directory	explain away	extirpative	falling band	fatiguingly
executioner	explain into	extortioner	falling leaf	fatiloquent
executively	explanandum	extractable	falling star	fatuousness
executorial	explanation	extradition	fall short of	Faulknerian
exemplarily	explanative	extrapolate	fall through	fault-finder
exemplarism	explanatory	extravagant	false acacia	faultlessly
exemplarist	expletively	extravagate	false arrest	faunistical
exemplarity	explicandum	extravasate	false bottom	faussebraie
exemplified	explication	extremeness	false colour	favouritism
exemplifier	explicative	extremities	false gallop	fawningness
exemplifies	explicatory	extrication	false indigo	fearfulness
exencephaly	exploitable	extrinsical	false killer	fearnothing
exercisable	exploration	extroverted	false muster	feasibility
exfoliation	explorative	exuberantly	falsifiable	feather edge
exfoliative	exploratory	exululation	Falstaffian	feather-foil
exhaustedly	explorement	exumbrellar	falteringly	feather-head
exhaustible	exploringly	eyebrowless	familiarise	featherless
exhaustless	explosively	eye-catching	familiarism	feather-like
exhaust pipe	exponential	eye language	familiarity	feather palm
exhibitable	exportation	fabrication	familiarize	feather-pate
exhilarator	exposedness	fabricative	familistery	feathertail
exhorbitant	ex post facto	face-centred	family bible	featherwife
exhortation	expostulant	face flannel	family hotel	feather-work
exhortative	expostulate	face-lifting	fanatically	feature film
exhortatory	expoundable	face-painter	fanfaronade	featureless
ex hypothesi	expressedly	facetiously	fantabulous	febricitant
exinanition	expressible	facial angle	fantastical	Fechner's law
existential	expressless	facial nerve	fan the flame	fecundation
exoculation	express lift	facial sauna	fan vaulting	feed crusher
exoelectron	expressness	facilitator	Faraday cage	feed-forward
exogenously	expromissor	facing brick	Faraday's law	feeding-time
exoneration	expropriate	facioplegic	far-awayness	feeler gauge
exonerative	expulsatory	facsimilize	farcicality	feelingless
exonuclease	expurgation	fact-finding	farcy button	feel oneself
exorability	expurgatory	factionally	fare-you-well	feel one's way

feel strange
feignedness
feldspathic
feller-me-lad
fellow-me-lad
fell walking
feloniously
female child
female rhyme
female screw
femme fatale
fence lizard
fence-sitter
fender-stool
fenestrated
fennel-giant
feral pigeon
fer de lances
fergusonite
fermentable
Fermi energy
ferociously
ferricyanic
ferriferous
ferrimagnet
Ferris wheel
ferrocyanic
ferromagnet
ferruginous
ferruminate
ferry-bridge
fers de lance
fertileness
ferulaceous
ferventness
festinately
festination
festival-day
festiveness
festivities
festschrift
Festschrift
fetch around
fête galante
fetishistic
feudalistic
feudalities
feudatories
fibre optics
fibre-tipped
fibrillated
fibrinosity
fibro-cement
fibrocystic
fibroplasia
fibrousness
fictionally
fictiveness
fiddle-de-dee
fiddlededee
fiddler-back
fiddler crab

fiddlestick
fidejussory
fidgetiness
fidgetingly
fiduciaries
fiduciarily
field-cornet
field events
field hockey
field madder
field magnet
field sports
field system
field theory
fieldworker
fieri facias
fifteenthly
fifth column
fifty-fourth
fighting fit
fighting mad
fighting-top
fig-marigold
figure-dance
figured bass
figure of fun
filamentary
filamentose
filamentous
filet design
filet mignon
fille de joie
fillet steak
fill the bill
filmography
filmsetting
filter-paper
filthy lucre
fimbriation
final clause
final demand
financeable
financially
find against
fin de siècle
finding-list
find oneself
find one's way
find the lady
fine-grained
fines herbes
fine-weather
finger-board
fingerboard
finger glass
finger-paint
finger-plate
fingerprint
finger-stall
finger-stone
finger-tight
finicalness

finickiness
finickingly
Finno-Ugrian
fippenny bit
fipple flute
fir clubmoss
fire and flet
fire-balloon
fire-blanket
fire brigade
fire company
fire-control
firecracker
fire-curtain
fire-fighter
firefighter
fire-flaught
fire-hunting
fire hydrant
fire-lighter
firelighter
fire-raising
fire station
fire-walking
fire-watcher
fire-worship
firing party
firing-point
firing squad
firmamental
First Consul
first cousin
first-degree
first finger
first-footer
first-fruits
first lesson
first matter
first moment
first or last
first person
first school
first-sprung
first storey
first strike
first string
fiscal agent
fiscalities
fishability
fish-eye lens
fish-farming
fishing boat
fishing frog
fishing line
fissibility
fissionable
fission bomb
fissiparity
fissiparous
fissuration
fissure vein
fitted sheet

fittingness
fitting-room
fitting shop
fit to be tied
five-corners
five hundred
fixed income
flabbergast
flaccidness
flag-captain
flagellated
flagellator
flag-feather
flagitation
flag-officer
flag of truce
flag-station
flag-wagging
flak-catcher
flaky pastry
flamboyance
flamboyancy
flame nettle
flammulated
flannel-cake
flannelette
flannelling
flapmouthed
flapper vote
flash-freeze
flash memory
flash powder
flat-chested
flat-tummied
flatulently
Flaubertian
flauntingly
flavourless
flavoursome
flecklessly
Fleet Air Arm
fleet-footed
Fleet parson
Fleet Street
Flemish bond
Flemish coil
flesh colour
fleshliness
fleshmonger
Fletcherian
Fletcherism
Fletcherite
fletcherize
flexibility
flexionless
flexography
flickertail
flight-arrow
flightiness
flight-shaft
flimflammed
flimflammer

flinchingly
flip one's lid
flip one's wig
flip through
flirtatious
flitch-plate
floating rib
flocculence
flock-master
flock pigeon
flog to death
floor leader
floor-length
floor polish
floor-timber
floor-walker
floorwalker
floral dance
floral whorl
Florence oil
florescence
Florida moss
Florida room
floriferous
florilegium
floripondio
flour beetle
flourishing
flow diagram
flower-fence
floweriness
flower-piece
flower power
flower-spike
flowery dell
flowingness
flowing sail
fluctuation
fluid clutch
fluid drachm
flunkeyiana
fluorescein
fluorescent
fluorimeter
fluorimetry
fluorometer
fluorometry
fluoroscope
fluoroscopy
fluosilicic
flush-decker
flustration
flute player
flutter-mill
fluviometer
flux density
flying corps
flying field
flying horse
Flying Horse
flying jenny
flying-kites

flying lemur
flying mouse
flying shear
flying shore
flying speed
flying squad
flying squid
flying start
fly in pieces
fly-pitching
fly the track
foam plastic
focal length
foetiferous
folding door
foliage leaf
foliicolous
foliiferous
folk dancing
folliculate
folliculose
fomentation
fons et origo
foolhardier
foolhardily
foolishment
foolishness
fool's errand
football kit
foot breadth
foot-lambert
footmanship
footslogger
foot soldier
foot-washing
foppishness
for a full due
for a kick-off
for all I care
for all I know
foraminifer
forasmuch as
forbearance
forbiddance
forbiddenly
force a smile
forced march
force stroke
forcibility
for dear life
fore-against
fore-appoint
foreclosure
foredestine
foredestiny
forefeeling
forefighter
foreign body
foreignness
foremanship
forepurpose
forequarter

foreseeable
foreseeably
foreshorten
foresighted
foresignify
forespeaker
forestaller
forestation
forest devil
forest floor
forest-green
forethinker
forethought
fore-topmast
fore-topsail
for evermore
forevermore
foreverness
forewarning
forfeitable
forfeit bail
forficulate
forfoughten
forge-master
forgetfully
forget-me-not
forgettable
forgiveness
forgivingly
for God's sake
for instance
forlorn hope
forlornness
formability
formal cause
formalinize
formalistic
formalities
formational
formatively
form-history
formication
form quality
form-species
formularies
formularise
formularism
formularist
formularize
formulation
formulistic
formylation
fornication
fornicatrix
for one's life
for one's part
for one's sins
for one thing
for starters
Forstner bit
fortepianos
forthcoming

for the birds
for the money
for the nonce
for the use of
for the worse
fortifiable
fortissimos
fortnightly
fortunately
fortuneless
for twopence
forty-eighth
forty-footer
forty-seater
forty-second
forwardness
Fosbury flop
fossilation
fossil ivory
foster-child
foster-nurse
foul-mouthed
foundership
founder's kin
fountaineer
fountainous
fountain pen
four-channel
four figures
four-flusher
four hundred
four pounder
Fourth World
four-wheeled
four wheeler
fowl cholera
fox and geese
fox-coloured
fox squirrel
foxtail lily
foxtrotting
fractionary
fractionate
fractionise
fractionize
fractiously
fracturable
fragileness
fragmentary
fragmentise
fragmentize
fragrancies
frame aerial
frame of mind
Francomania
Francophile
Francophobe
francophone
frangipanis
Frankenthal
frankfurter

Franklinian
franklinite
frank-pledge
frantically
franticness
fraternally
fraternizer
fratricidal
fraudulence
fraudulency
free and easy
free company
free country
freedom ride
free-hearted
free library
Freemasonic
Freemasonry
free on board
free-quarter
free radical
free skating
freethinker
free thought
freeze-dried
freeze-dries
freeze-frame
freibergite
French brace
French bread
French chalk
French clock
French crown
French curve
French drain
French fries
Frenchified
Frenchifies
Frenchiness
French leave
French pleat
French sixth
French stick
French toast
French twist
French whisk
Frenchwoman
Frenchwomen
frenzy-fever
frequencies
frequentist
fresco secco
fresh breeze
fresnel lens
Fresnel lens
Fresnel unit
fretfulness
Freudianism
friableness
Friars Major
fricandeaus
fricandeaux

frictionize
friendliest
frigate bird
frightening
frightfully
frigidarium
frill lizard
fringilline
fritillaria
fritiniency
fritto misto
frivolities
frivolously
frock-coated
frock of mail
from nowhere
from scratch
from the dead
from way back
frondescent
frontal bone
frontal lobe
front burner
front-fanged
frontierism
frontlessly
front-loader
front matter
front office
frontolysis
frontolytic
front runner
frost-flower
frost pocket
froth-blower
frotteurism
frowardness
frowstiness
frozen limit
fructuously
frugivorous
fruit-bodies
fruit-grower
fruitlessly
fruit-picker
frustrating
frustration
frustrative
frutescence
fucoxanthin
fuel element
fugaciously
fulfillable
fulgentness
fulgurantly
fulgurating
fulguration
full as a bull
full as a goog
full as a tick
full-blooded
full brother

full-fledged
full-frontal
full-hearted
fulling-mill
full measure
full-mouthed
full of beans
fulminating
fulmination
fulminatory
fulminurate
fulsomeness
fume chamber
fummadiddle
funambulism
funambulist
fun and games
functionary
functionate
function key
fundamental
fundholding
fund-raising
funduscopic
funeral home
funeral pile
funeral pyre
fungibility
fungistasis
fungistatic
fungivorous
fungologist
fungus-midge
funny column
furaldehyde
furciferous
furiousness
furnishings
furnishment
furrow-slice
furthcoming
furtherance
furthermore
furthermost
furthersome
furtiveness
furunculous
fusible plug
fustigation
future shock
future state
gaberlunzie
gable-topped
gable-window
Gaboon viper
gaff topsail
gainfulness
gainstander
galactocele
galactoside
galanty show
galenically

gallanilide
gallantness
gallantries
gall bladder
gallery play
gallery tray
galley proof
galley slave
galliardize
Gallicanism
Gallicanist
gallimaufry
gallinacean
gallinipper
Gallomaniac
Gallophobia
gallotannin
gallousness
Gallovidian
Gallowegian
gallowglass
gallows-bird
gallows-tree
gally-beggar
Galois field
gambrel roof
gamekeeping
game licence
game of goose
game-playing
game reserve
games master
games theory
gametangium
gametically
gametogenic
gametophore
gametophyte
gaming house
gaming table
gamogenesis
gamogenetic
gander-month
Gandhiesque
gandy dancer
ganglioside
gang of three
gangsterdom
gangsterish
gangsterism
gang warfare
gangway seat
garam masala
garbologist
garden chair
garden cress
gardenesque
garden gnome
garden-house
garden party
garden snail
Garden State

garden stuff
Garibaldian
garlic bread
garlic press
garmentless
garnishment
Garrisonian
garrulously
garter snake
gas constant
gaseousness
gas equation
gas fittings
gas gangrene
gas kinetics
gas producer
gastrectomy
gastric mill
gastrocolic
gastrologer
gastromancy
gastronomer
gastronomic
gastropathy
gastropodan
gastroscope
gastroscopy
gastrostomy
gastrotomic
gastrotrich
gastrozooid
gatecrasher
gauge theory
gavelkinder
gay deceiver
gazing-stock
geanticline
gefilte fish
gegenschein
geitonogamy
gemmiferous
gemmiparity
gemmiparous
gemmologist
gendarmerie
genealogies
genealogise
genealogist
genealogize
genecologic
generalized
generalizer
generalness
general post
generalship
generically
genericness
gene therapy
genetically
genetic code
Geneva bands
Geneva Bible

Geneva cross
Geneva watch
geniculated
genitivally
genotypical
genteelness
gentianella
gentian root
gentilician
gentilitial
gentilitian
gentle craft
gentlemanly
gentlewoman
gentlewomen
genuflector
genuflexion
genuineness
geobotanist
geocentrism
geochemical
geodynamics
geomagnetic
geomantical
geomembrane
geometrical
geophysical
geopolitics
George Cross
George Medal
George-noble
geostrategy
geostrophic
geosyncline
geotechnics
geotectonic
German clock
germaneness
Germanicism
German ocean
German sixth
German-Swiss
germination
germinative
germ warfare
gerontocrat
gerontology
gerrymander
gerundially
gerundively
gestational
gestatorial
gesticulant
gesticulate
gestureless
get around to
get a shift on
get a sight of
get a spark up
get cracking
get done with
get even with

get in a twist
get one's blue
get one's call
get one's step
get religion
get the spike
get together
get worked up
ghastliness
ghostbuster
ghostliness
ghost-writer
giant fennel
giant hyssop
giant-killer
giant petrel
giant-powder
giant slalom
gibberellic
gibberellin
gibber-plain
gibbousness
Gideon bible
gift voucher
gigantesque
giganticide
gigantology
giggle-house
giggle-water
gigot sleeve
gilded youth
gild the lily
gild the pill
gillyflower
gimcrackery
gin and tonic
gingerbeery
gingerbread
ginger group
girdlestead
girlishness
Giuoco Piano
give a lead to
give and take
give a stop to
give a tumble
give birth to
give chase to
give faith to
give it a name
give it hot to
give leg bail
give lessons
give loose to
give offence
give oneself
give pause to
give place to
give the boot
give what for
give wings to
glabrescent

glacier mill	glutinosity	golden oldie	grade school	gratulatory
glacier snow	glutinously	golden perch	grade up with	grave accent
glade mallow	glycerinate	golden potto	gradiometer	gravedigger
gladfulness	glycocholic	golden share	gradualness	gravel-blind
gladioluses	glycophorin	Golden State	Graecomania	gravel court
Gladstonian	glycophytic	golden syrup	Graecophile	gravel voice
Gladstonism	glycosamine	gold reserve	Graeco-Roman	graven image
Gladstonite	glycosylate	Golgi method	grafting wax	Gravenstein
glaikitness	glycotropic	Goliath frog	grain colour	gravimetric
glamorously	glyphograph	gonadectomy	grain-cradle	graving dock
glamour girl	glyptically	go near doing	grain whisky	graving tool
glamour puss	gnat-catcher	gone gosling	graminology	gravitation
glance pitch	gnathobasic	gone to earth	grammalogue	gravitative
glaringness	gnathostome	gonfalonier	grammarless	gravity feed
glass-blower	gneissosity	gongoristic	grammatical	gravity wave
glass cutter	gnomologist	goniometric	gramophonic	greasepaint
glass-gazing	gnostically	gonioscopic	grandeeship	greaseproof
glassichord	gnotobiotic	gonorrhoeal	grandfather	greasy heels
glass lizard	go a bundle on	good company	grandfilial	great circle
glass-making	goal average	good evening	grandiflora	greatcoated
glass sponge	goalkeeping	good feeling	grandiosely	Great Dipper
Glastonbury	goal-kicking	good-hearted	grandiosity	great divide
glaucescent	go all the way	good heavens	grand manner	Great Divide
glaucomatic	go along with	good-looking	grand master	greaterness
glauconitic	goalscoring	good morning	grandmother	great laurel
glaucophane	goaltending	good-natured	grand-nephew	great-nephew
glazed frost	goatee beard	good success	grand old man	great primer
glazy humour	goatherdess	Good Templar	grandparent	Great Spirit
gleefulness	goatishness	go one better	grand siècle	great vassal
glengarries	go ballistic	goosefleshy	grangerizer	Grecian bend
glimmerless	Gobelin blue	goose-winged	graniferous	Grecian gift
glitter dust	gobemouches	goosishness	Granite City	Grecian knot
glitterless	goblinesque	go overboard	graniteware	Grecian nose
glitter rock	gobsmacking	gopher snake	granivorous	Greek chorus
globe-flower	go by default	Gopher State	granny's knot	Greek Church
globeflower	go by the book	Gordian knot	Granny Smith	greenbottle
globigerina	God Almighty	gormandizer	granny woman	green carder
globigerine	God bless you	gory details	granolithic	green cheese
globoseness	god-daughter	go somewhere	granophyric	green dragon
globularity	goddesshood	gospel music	Granth Sahib	green fallow
glochidiate	goddesslike	gospel-sharp	grants-in-aid	green ginger
Gloger's rule	goddess-ship	gospel truth	gran turismo	greengrocer
glomeration	godforsaken	gossipingly	granularity	greenkeeper
glomerulose	God-forsaken	Gothic novel	granulation	Greenlander
glossalalia	godlessness	go to college	granuliform	Greenlandic
glossematic	godlikeness	go-to-meeting	granulocyte	green linnet
glossolalia	go down a bomb	go to the dogs	grape-brandy	green magpie
glossolalic	God's country	go to the pack	graphematic	greenmailer
glossopetra	God's sonties	go to the wall	graphically	green manure
glottal stop	go end for end	go to the wars	graphic arts	green mealie
glottogonic	go great guns	go up in smoke	graphicness	green monkey
Glou-morceau	go in couples	go up the wall	graphomania	greenockite
glove puppet	going for one	gourmandise	graphometer	green oyster
gloweringly	going strong	gourmandism	graph theory	green pepper
glucosamine	go into orbit	gouvernante	grapple with	green plover
glucosidase	gold amalgam	governorate	graptolitic	green shoots
glucostatic	golden balls	go walkabout	grass-comber	green turtle
glucuronate	golden chain	go with a bang	grass-eating	Gresham's law
glucuronide	golden eagle	go with a roar	grass hockey	Gretna Green
glue-sniffer	golden goose	go with child	grasshopper	Grevy's zebra
glutathione	golden hello	gracelessly	grass skiing	greybearded
gluten bread	Golden Horde	gradational	gratulation	grey economy

grey gurnard	guest artist	haemocyanin	hammer drill	harmfulness
grey meerkat	guest-master	haemoglobin	hammer price	harmonistic
grey snapper	guest worker	haemophilia	hammer-smith	harmonogram
grey wethers	guide fossil	haemophilic	Hamming code	harness bull
griddle cake	Guide Guider	haemoptysis	hamstringed	harness cask
griffinhood	guildswoman	haemorrhage	hand and foot	harpsichord
grimgribber	guildswomen	haemorrhoid	hand-baggage	harrier-hawk
gripingness	guilelessly	haemostasis	handbagging	Harriet Lane
grippleness	guillotiner	haemostatic	hand-breadth	Harris tweed
grithbreach	guiltlessly	haemothorax	handfasting	Harrow drive
grizzly bear	Guinea grass	Haggadistic	hand grenade	harrowingly
grocer's itch	Guinea Negro	haggardness	handicapped	hart's tongue
grocer's port	Guinea peach	haggishness	handicapper	harum-scarum
Groenendael	Gulf Country	Hagiographa	hand in glove	harvestable
groom-porter	gullibility	hagiography	handkercher	harvest home
grooved ware	gum ammoniac	hagiologist	hand-knitted	harvestless
grotesquely	gum benjamin	hail the dool	hand of glory	harvest mite
grottoesque	gum sandarac	hairbreadth	handrunning	harvest moon
grouchiness	gun carriage	hairdresser	handselling	harzburgite
ground-cedar	gunslinging	hair lacquer	handshaking	hat-check boy
ground cover	gurgitation	hairpin bend	handsomeish	hatcheck boy
ground elder	gushingness	hair-raising	hand to mouth	hatchet-face
ground floor	gustatorial	hairstyling	handwriting	hatchet fish
ground frost	gustfulness	hairstylist	handwritten	hatchettine
ground glass	gut instinct	hair-trigger	hang by a hair	hatchettite
ground level	gutlessness	hairy-heeled	hang-gliding	hatchet work
ground-plate	gutta-percha	halcyon days	hang heavily	hatefulness
ground robin	gutter-blood	half a chance	hanging bird	hatlessness
groundsheet	gutter press	half a minute	hanging bowl	hatti-sherif
ground sloth	guttersnipe	half-and-half	hanging drop	haughtiness
ground speed	gutter-stick	half-baptize	hanging pawn	haughtonite
ground staff	gutturalism	half-binding	hanging wall	hauntedness
ground state	gutturality	half-blooded	hangmanlike	hausmannite
ground-swell	gutturalize	half-brother	hangmanship	haustellate
groundswell	gymnasiarch	half-century	hapaxanthic	have a bash at
groundwards	gymnastical	half-crowner	haphazardly	have a case on
groundwater	gynaecology	half-hearted	haphazardry	have a dash at
group theory	gynecologic	half holiday	haplessness	have a down on
groupuscule	gynogenesis	half-integer	haplography	have a hand in
growing zone	gynogenetic	half-landing	happy couple	have a lash at
grow into one	gynomonoecy	half measure	happy ending	have a lead on
grown-upness	gynostegium	half-sibling	happy family	have a look of
grow on trees	gypsiferous	half-starved	happy medium	have an eye to
growth curve	Gypsologist	half the time	haptoglobin	have a record
growth point	gyre-carline	half-volleys	harassingly	have a shower
growth stock	gyrocompass	halfway line	harbour-dues	have a show of
grozing-iron	gyro-horizon	hall bedroom	harbourless	have at heart
grudge fight	haberdasher	hallucinant	harbour seal	have eyes for
gruellingly	habituality	hallucinate	hard and fast	have heard of
grumblesome	habitualize	halobiontic	hard as nails	have it in for
grumblingly	habituation	halo-brimmed	hard-hearted	have it in one
gryllotalpa	habitudinal	halogenated	hard-hitting	have kittens
Guadeloupan	hackberries	halomethane	hard landing	have mercy on
guardedness	hacking coat	halomorphic	hard-mouthed	have pride in
guardianess	hadrosaurid	haloperidol	hard-pressed	have sex with
gubernation	haemangioma	halophilous	hardshelled	have the face
gubernative	haematocele	halter-break	hard-wearing	have the time
guelder rose	haematocrit	haltingness	hard-working	hawkishness
guerdonless	haematocyst	ham-fistedly	hardy annual	hazard light
Guernsey cow	haematoidin	ham-handedly	hare-brained	hazardously
guerrillero	haematology	Hamiltonian	Hare Krishna	hazel-grouse
guesstimate	haematomata	hammer-cloth	haricot bean	headbanding

headbanging	Hegelianize	heptavalent	hexametrize	high treason
headborough	hegemonical	Heracleidan	hexapeptide	high voltage
head-dresser	heightening	Heraclitean	hibernation	Highway Code
head-hunting	heinousness	herald-snake	Hibernicise	hilariously
headhunting	heiress-ship	herbiferous	Hibernicism	hill and dale
head of state	heir-general	herbivorous	Hibernicize	hill-billies
head of State	Heldentenor	herb of grace	hide-and-coop	hill of beans
headquarter	helichrysum	herb tobacco	hide-and-seek	hill station
head teacher	helicograph	herb Trinity	hideosities	hillwalking
healthfully	heliography	hereditable	hideousness	hip and thigh
healthiness	heliolithic	hereditably	hiding place	hippeastrum
health salts	heliometric	hereinafter	hiding power	hippiatrics
hearse-cloth	helioscopic	heresiology	hierarchies	hippishness
heart attack	heliostatic	heretically	hierarchise	hippoboscid
heartbroken	heliotroper	Her Majesty's	hierarchism	hippocampal
heart-cherry	heliotropic	hermeneutic	hierarchist	hippocampus
heart cockle	heliotropin	hermeticism	hierarchize	Hippocratic
hearth-money	helleborine	hermodactyl	hierocratic	hippologist
hearth-penny	helleborism	heroic verse	hierography	hippomobile
hearthstead	Hellenicize	heroineship	hieromonach	hippophobia
hearthstone	Hellenistic	heroization	Hieronymian	hippopotami
heartlessly	hellishness	hero-worship	hieronymite	hippotomist
heart of gold	hellraising	herpesvirus	High Admiral	hircocervus
heart's-blood	helmet-crest	herpetology	high as a kite	hire and fire
heart-shaped	helmet shell	herring-bone	highbrowish	hirsuteness
heart sounds	helminthoid	herringbone	highbrowism	Hispanicise
heart-struck	helpfulness	herring gull	high command	Hispanicism
heart-urchin	helping hand	herring-like	high country	Hispanicist
heat barrier	help oneself	herring-pond	higher court	Hispanicize
heathenesse	hemeralopia	Herschelian	higher plant	histiocytic
heather-bell	hemeralopic	hesperidium	highest good	histologist
heath-thrush	hemerythrin	Hessian boot	highfalutin	historiated
heat-seeking	hemianopsia	hetaerolite	high farming	historicise
Heaven knows	hemihydrate	heteracanth	high fashion	historicism
heavens hard	hemimorphic	heteroauxin	high finance	historicist
heavenwards	Hemingwayan	heteroclite	high-hearted	historicity
heave the log	hemiparesis	heterocycle	high holiday	historicize
heaving line	hemiparetic	heterodimer	high incomer	historiette
heavy-footed	hemiplegiac	heteroecism	high-jumping	histrionism
heavy-handed	hemipterous	heterogamic	high-kicking	hitherwards
heavy-headed	hemisection	heterogonic	highlandish	Hitleristic
heavyweight	hemispheral	heterograft	Highlandman	hit the booze
hebdomadary	hemisphered	heterolysis	Highlandmen	hit the skids
hebephrenia	hemispheric	heterolytic	highlighter	hit the trail
hebephrenic	hemitropism	heteromorph	high-melting	Hittitology
Hebraically	hendecarchy	heterophile	high old time	hoary marmot
heckelphone	heneicosane	heterophony	high opinion	hobble chain
hectic fever	Henle's layer	heteroploid	high-pitched	hobbledehoy
hectic flush	hepatectomy	heteropolar	high polymer	hobble skirt
hectogramme	hepatoscopy	heterospory	high-powered	hockey-stick
hectoringly	hepatotoxic	heterostyly	high profile	Hock Tuesday
hedge-doctor	hepatotoxin	heterotherm	high-quality	hoggishness
hedge-garlic	Hephaestian	heterotopia	high-ranking	hog in armour
hedge-hyssop	Hepplewhite	heterotopic	high sheriff	hog's pudding
hedge-priest	heptacosane	heterotroph	High Sheriff	hold against
hedge-school	heptadecane	heterousian	high spirits	hold hostage
hedging-bill	heptahedral	heuristical	high-stepper	hold one's own
hedonic tone	heptahedron	hexadecimal	high steward	hold one's way
hedonometer	heptamerous	hexagonally	High Steward	hold the baby
heedfulness	heptangular	hexahedrons	highstrikes	hold the fort
heel of Italy	heptarchies	hexahydrate	high-tensile	hold the line
Hegelianism	heptathlete	hexametrist	high tension	hold the ring

hold the sack	homothermic	horse-litter	human rights	hydrologist
hold to a draw	homozygotic	horse manure	human shield	hydrolysate
hold wedlock	Honduranean	horse-marine	Humboldtian	hydromantic
holey dollar	honest Injun	horse-master	humboldtine	hydromedusa
holiday camp	honest-to-God	horse mussel	humbuggable	hydrometeor
holiday home	honey badger	horse-pistol	humdrummery	hydrometric
hollandaise	honey bucket	horse racing	humdrumness	hydropathic
holler uncle	honeycombed	horseradish	humectation	hydrophilic
hollow heart	honey-flower	horse-walker	humeral veil	hydrophobia
holobenthic	honey-fuggle	horsfordite	humiliating	hydrophobic
holoblastic	honey fungus	Horst Wessel	humiliation	hydrophytic
holocaustal	honey-lipped	hose company	hummingbird	hydroponics
holocaustic	honey-locust	hospital bed	hunchbacked	hydroscopic
holoendemic	honeymooner	hospitalise	hundredfold	hydrosphere
holographic	honey-myrtle	hospitalism	hunger march	hydrostatic
holomorphic	honey possum	hospitality	hunt counter	hydrothorax
holophrasis	honeysucker	hospitalize	hunter's moon	hydrotropic
holothurian	honeysuckle	hospitaller	hunting-case	hydroxonium
Holsteinian	honorariums	hostageship	hunting crop	hydroxylase
Holy Rood Day	honour point	hostilities	hunting horn	hydroxylate
Holy Trinity	honours list	hot cross bun	hunting pink	hydroxyurea
home cooking	honour-trick	hot cupboard	hunt the hare	hydroxyzine
home-keeping	hooliganism	hotel-keeper	hunt the lady	hygrometric
homeostasis	Hooray Henry	hot-headedly	hurriedness	hygrophytic
homeostatic	Hooverville	hotheadedly	hurry-scurry	hygroscopic
homeothermy	hopefulness	hot-tempered	hurtfulness	hylomorphic
Homerically	hope I may die	houndstooth	hurtleberry	hylophagous
home science	hop hornbeam	houppelande	husbandhood	hylozoistic
Home Service	hop-o'-my-thumb	house arrest	husbandland	Hymenoptera
homesteader	hopper-barge	house-broken	husbandless	hymnography
home stretch	hopperdozer	house-buying	husbandlike	hymnologies
homicidally	hoppergrass	house church	husbandship	hymnologist
homiletical	Hopping Dick	house-father	hyacinthian	hyoscyamine
homiliaries	hopping-john	householder	hyacinthine	hyparterial
homocentric	hop the perch	householdry	hyaluronate	hyperactive
homoeomorph	hop the stick	house-hunter	hybrid swarm	hyperacusis
homoeopathy	horizon-blue	housekeeper	hydatidosis	hyperakusis
homoeotherm	horizonless	house lights	hydnocarpic	hyperbolism
homo-erotism	hormogonium	house martin	hydnocarpus	hyperbolist
homogametic	hormonology	housemaster	hydraelaeon	hyperbolize
homogeneate	horn antenna	house-mother	hydra-headed	hyperboloid
homogeneity	hornblendic	house of call	hydralazine	hyperborean
homogeneous	horned adder	House of Keys	hydrapulper	Hyperborean
homogenetic	horned cairn	house-parent	hydrargyria	hypercapnia
homogenized	horned grebe	house-sitter	hydrargyrum	hypercapnic
homogenizer	horned poppy	housesitter	hydrazinium	hypercharge
homographic	horned snake	housewifely	hydrazonium	hypercolour
homoiotherm	horned viper	housewifery	hydroborate	hypercolumn
homoiousian	hornswoggle	housewifish	hydrobromic	hypercritic
Homoiousion	horny-handed	housewright	hydrocarbon	hyperemesis
homolateral	horological	housing list	hydrochoric	hyperextend
homological	horribility	how-do-you-dos	hydrocooler	hypergamous
homologizer	horrifiedly	huckleberry	hydrocyanic	hypergelast
homomorphic	horripilant	hucksterdom	hydrofining	hypergeusia
homonuclear	horripilate	hucksteress	hydroformer	hyperinosis
homophonous	horrisonant	hucksterism	hydrogenase	hyperinotic
homoplastic	horror comic	hudibrastic	hydrogenate	hypermarket
homopterous	hors d'oeuvre	huffishness	hydrogen ion	hypermetric
Homo sapiens	horse-collar	Huguenotism	hydrogenite	hypermnesia
homosporous	horse-doctor	hullabaloos	hydrogenize	hypermnesic
homostylous	Horse Guards	human animal	hydrogenous	hypermobile
homothallic	horse-jockey	human nature	hydrography	hypermodern

hyperphagia	hypotenusal	if and only if	immediately	impignorate
hyperphagic	hypothallus	if you please	immediatism	impingement
hyperphoria	hypothecary	ignis fatuus	immediatist	impiousness
hyperphoric	hypothecate	ignition key	immedicable	implacental
hyperplasia	hypothecium	ignoble hawk	immedicably	implantable
hyperploidy	hypothermia	ignobleness	immelodious	implausible
hyperpnoeic	hypothermic	ignominious	immemorable	implausibly
hypersaline	hypothesise	ignoramuses	immenseness	implemental
hypersexual	hypothesist	ileocolitis	immensikoff	implementer
hypersomnia	hypothesize	ileostomies	immigration	implication
hypersomnic	hypothyroid	iliac artery	immigratory	implicative
hypersonics	hypotyposis	ill-affected	immitigable	imploration
hypersphere	hypsiconchy	illaqueable	immitigably	imploringly
hyperstatic	hypsochrome	ill-assorted	immobilizer	implosively
hypersthene	hypsography	I'll be damned	immodulated	impolitical
hypertensin	hypsometric	ill breeding	immomentous	impoliticly
hypertrophy	hysteresial	ill-disposed	immortalise	imponderous
hypertropia	hystericism	ill-equipped	immortalism	importantly
hyphenation	hysterotome	ill-favoured	immortalist	importation
hyphomycete	hysterotomy	ill-humoured	immortality	importunacy
hypnologist	hythergraph	illiberally	immortalize	importunate
hypnopaedia	iatraliptic	illicitness	immortified	importunely
hypnopaedic	Ibizan hound	illimitable	immunoassay	importunity
hypnopompic	Iceland gull	illimitably	immunogenic	impostorous
hypoacidity	Iceland moss	illimitedly	immunologic	imposturous
hypoalgesia	Iceland spar	ill-informed	impartation	impoundable
hypoblastic	ichneumoned	illiquidity	impartially	impoundment
hypobromite	ichnofossil	I'll learn you	impassioned	impractical
hypobromous	ichnography	ill-mannered	impassively	imprecation
hypocausted	ichthyolite	illogically	impassivity	imprecatory
hypocentral	ichthyology	ill-prepared	impatiently	imprecisely
hypochonder	ichthyornis	ill-tempered	impeachable	imprecision
hypochromia	ichthyosaur	illuminable	impeachment	impregnable
hypochromic	iconodulist	illuminance	impecuniary	impregnably
hypocrisies	iconography	illuminated	impecunious	impregnator
hypocycloid	iconometric	illuminator	impedimenta	impresarios
hypodiploid	iconophobia	illusionary	impenetrate	impressible
hypogastria	iconostases	illusionism	impenitence	impressment
hypogastric	iconostasis	illusionist	impenitency	*imprimatura*
hypoglossal	icosahedral	illustrated	imperatival	imprimitive
hypoglossus	icosahedron	illustrator	imperfectly	improbation
hypogonadal	icteritious	illustrious	imperforate	improbative
hypokinesis	icterogenic	illuviation	imperialise	improbities
hypokinetic	idempotence	illywhacker	imperialism	improperium
hypolimnial	identically	ilsemannite	imperialist	impropriate
hypolimnion	identic note	I'm a Dutchman	imperiality	impropriety
hypomorphic	ideogrammic	imaginarily	imperialize	improveable
hyponitrite	ideographic	imagination	imperilling	improvement
hyponitrous	ideokinetic	imaginative	imperiously	improvident
hypopharynx	ideological	Imam Bayildi	impermanent	improvingly
hypophyseal	ideoplastic	imbrication	impermeable	imprudently
hypoplastic	idioblastic	imbricative	impermeated	impugnation
hyposcenium	idioglossia	imbrutement	impersonate	impuissance
hypospadiac	idiographic	imbursement	impersonify	impulsively
hypospadial	idiomatical	imitability	impertinent	impulsivity
hypospadias	idiomorphic	imitational	imperturbed	inaccordant
hyposplenic	idiophoneme	imitatively	imperviable	inactivator
hypostasise	idiotically	immalleable	impetration	inadaptable
hypostasize	idiot savant	immanentism	impetrative	inadvertent
hypostatize	idling speed	immanentist	impetratory	inadvisable
hypotension	idolization	immantation	impetuosity	inadvisedly
hypotensive	idyllically	immarginate	impetuously	inadvisedly

inaesthetic	incoherence	independent	indulgingly	infinitival
in aggregate	incoherency	indesignate	in duplicate	infirmarian
in a great way	in cold blood	index finger	induplicate	infirmaries
inalienable	income group	index fossil	industrious	infirmation
inalienably	in command of	indexically	inebriation	infirmative
inalterable	incommodate	index-linked	in ecstasies	infirmities
inalterably	incommodity	index number	inedibility	in flagrante
inambitious	incompactly	Indian cedar	ineffective	inflammable
in a minor key	incompetent	Indian clubs	ineffectual	inflammably
inamissible	incompleted	Indian cress	inefficient	inflectable
inamoration	incompliant	Indian devil	inelaborate	inflictable
in-and-out boy	incomposite	Indianesque	inelegantly	influencive
in-and-out man	inconditely	Indian giver	ineloquence	influential
inanimately	in condition	Indian grass	ineluctable	infomercial
inanimation	inconfident	Indian Ocean	ineluctably	informality
in an instant	incongenial	Indian paint	inenarrable	informatics
in a nutshell	incongruent	India Office	inequitable	in formation
inappetence	incongruity	indiarubber	inequitably	information
inappetency	incongruous	India rubber	inequivalve	informative
in a small way	inconnected	indicanuria	inertialess	informatory
inattention	inconscient	indictional	inertia reel	informosome
inattentive	inconscious	indifferent	inescapable	infracostal
in at the kill	inconsonant	indigestion	inescapably	infrangible
inaugurator	inconstancy	indigestive	inessential	infrangibly
inauthentic	incontinent	indignantly	inestimable	infrequence
in authority	incorporate	indignation	inestimably	infrequency
in bad repair	incorporeal	indignatory	inevictable	infrigidate
in-betweener	incorrectly	indignities	inexactness	infructuose
incalescent	incorruptly	indigo finch	inexcitable	infructuous
incantation	incrassated	indigo plant	inexcusable	in full flood
incantatory	increasable	indigo snake	inexcusably	in full swing
incapacious	incredulity	indigo white	inexecution	infuriately
incapsulate	incredulous	indirection	inexhausted	infuriating
incarcerate	incremation	indirect tax	in existence	infuriation
incardinate	incremental	individuate	inexistence	ingathering
incarnadine	increpation	indivisible	inexpectant	ingenerable
incarnalize	incriminate	indivisibly	inexpedient	ingeniosity
incarnation	incrispated	Indo-African	inexpensive	ingeniously
incendivity	inculcation	Indo-Anglian	inexpertise	ingenuously
incensation	inculcatory	indoaniline	inexplosive	in good faith
incensement	inculpation	Indo-British	in facsimile	in good heart
incense tree	inculpative	Indo-Chinese	infangthief	in good store
incense-wood	inculpatory	indochinite	infanticide	in good voice
incensories	incunabular	Indo-Hittite	infantilise	ingrainedly
incentivize	incunabulum	Indo-Iranian	infantilism	ingratitude
incertitude	incuriosity	Indological	infantility	ingravidate
incessantly	incuriously	Indo-Malayan	infantilize	ingredience
in character	incurvation	indomitable	infantryman	Ingres paper
incinerator	incurvature	indomitably	infantrymen	ingurgitate
incipiently	Indanthrene	Indo-Pacific	infatuation	inhabitable
inclemently	indanthrone	indorsation	infectivity	inhabitance
inclination	indecencies	indorsement	infecundity	inhabitancy
inclinatory	indeciduous	indubitable	inferential	inhabitress
includingly	in deep water	indubitably	inferiority	inheritable
inclusively	indefinable	induced drag	infernality	inheritably
inclusivism	indefinably	inductional	infernalize	inheritance
inclusivist	indehiscent	inductively	infertility	inheritress
inclusivity	indemnified	inductivism	infestation	in her wisdom
incoercible	indemnifier	inductivist	infestivity	in his wisdom
incogitable	indemnifies	inductivity	infeudation	inhumanness
incognisant	indemnities	in due course	infieldsman	inimicality
incognizant	indentation	indulgently	infiltrator	inirritable

in isolation	inquisitive	instigative	intercooler	interrogate
initial line	inquisitory	instigatrix	intercostal	interrupted
initialling	in receipt of	instinctive	inter-county	interrupter
initiatress	in rehearsal	instinctual	intercourse	interruptor
injucundity	in rejoinder	institorial	intercrural	interseptal
injudicious	in residence	institorian	interdealer	intersertal
injuriously	in respect of	institution	interdental	intersexual
in justice to	in reversion	institutive	interdepend	intersocial
ink-blot test	insalubrity	institutrix	interdictor	intersperse
in measure as	insaturable	instreaming	interesting	intersphere
in medias res	inscenation	instruction	inter-ethnic	interspinal
in midstream	inscribable	instructive	interfacial	interstitia
in-migration	inscription	in substance	interfacing	inter-strain
in mimicry of	inscriptive	in such a wise	interfering	intersystem
in miniature	inscrutable	insufflator	interfinger	intertangle
in mothballs	inscrutably	insulin coma	interfluent	intertilled
innavigable	insculpture	insultation	interfluous	intertribal
inner circle	insectaries	insultingly	interfoliar	intervallic
inner planet	insectarium	insuperable	interfusion	interveinal
inner speech	insecticide	insuperably	intergrowth	interventor
inner-spring	insectivore	in support of	interiorise	interviewee
Inner Temple	insectivory	intagliated	interiority	interviewer
innervation	insectology	integralism	interiorize	interxylary
innocuously	in semblance	integralist	inter-island	intestation
innominable	inseminator	integrality	interjacent	in the basket
innoxiously	insensately	integration	interjector	in the case of
innumerable	insensitive	integrative	interleukin	in the clouds
innumerably	insentience	intellected	interlineal	in the face of
innutrition	inseparable	intelligent	interlinear	in the gift of
innutritive	inseparably	intelligize	interlingua	in the grease
inobnoxious	insertional	intemperate	interlining	in the grip of
inobservant	insertioned	intensation	interlobate	in the groove
inobtrusive	insessorial	intensative	interlocker	in the line of
inoculation	inseverable	intenseness	interlucent	in the making
inoculative	inseverably	intensified	interludial	in the middle
inodorously	in severalty	intensifier	intermeddle	in the name of
inoffensive	inside track	intensifies	intermedial	in the offing
inofficious	insidiously	intensional	intermedium	in the rattle
in one's blood	insincerely	intensities	interminate	in the saddle
in one's glory	insincerity	intensitive	intermingle	in the secret
in one's heart	insinuation	intensively	intermitted	in the sequel
in one's shirt	insinuative	intentional	internal ear	in the stream
in one's sleep	insinuatory	intentioned	internalise	in the street
in one's socks	insipidness	intentively	internality	in the upshot
in open court	insistently	interactant	internalize	in the wake of
inoperative	insistingly	interaction	internecine	intimidator
inopportune	insititious	interactive	internecive	intolerable
in order that	insomnolent	inter-agency	interneural	intolerably
inordinancy	insouciance	inter-allied	interneuron	intolerance
inorganized	inspectoral	interamnian	internuncio	into the wind
in paperback	inspectress	interannual	interplanar	intoxicator
in principal	inspiration	interatomic	interpolant	intoximeter
in principle	inspiratory	intercalary	interpolate	intra-atomic
in process of	inspiringly	intercalate	interpreted	intractable
in pursuit of	inspiriting	intercensal	interpreter	intractably
input-output	inspissator	interceptor	interracial	intradermal
inquilinism	instability	intercessor	interradial	intradermic
inquilinous	installment	interchange	interradius	intransient
inquination	instantiate	interchurch	interregnal	intra-ocular
inquiration	instatement	intercities	interregnum	intrapolate
inquiringly	instaurator	intercolumn	interrelate	intraracial
inquisition	instigation	intercommon	interrogant	intraspinal

intrathecal
intravenous
intraverbal
intrepidity
intricacies
intricately
intrinsical
intro-active
introductor
introessive
introflexed
intromitted
intromitter
introverted
intrudingly
intrusively
intuitional
intuitively
intuitivism
intuitivist
intumescent
in two shakes
inusitation
inutterable
invaccinate
invaginated
invalidness
invasionist
invectively
inventively
inventorial
inventoried
inventories
inventorize
inveracious
invertebral
invert sugar
in very sooth
investigate
investitive
investiture
inviability
invidiously
invigilator
invigorator
inviolately
inviscation
involucrate
involuntary
involutedly
involvement
iodargyrite
iodinatable
iodine value
iodomethane
iodoprotein
ion exchange
Ionic school
ionographic
ionophorous
ionospheric
ipecacuanha

I promise you
ipsilateral
Iraqization
iridescence
iridologist
iridoplegia
Irish bridge
Irish coffee
Irish Gaelic
Irish mantle
Irish potato
Irish setter
irksomeness
iron-binding
iron curtain
Iron Curtain
iron-hearted
iron jubilee
ironmongery
iron pyrites
iron rations
irradiation
irradiative
irradicable
irreceptive
irreclaimed
irrecusable
irrecusably
irredentism
irredentist
irreducible
irreducibly
irredundant
irreferable
irreflexion
irreflexive
irrefutable
irrefutably
irregularly
irregulated
irrelevance
irrelevancy
irreligious
irreluctant
irremissive
irremovable
irremovably
irreparable
irreparably
irresoluble
irretention
irretentive
irreticence
irreverence
irrevocable
irrevocably
irrevoluble
irritatedly
isadelphous
isallobaric
isapostolic
Iscariotism

isenthalpic
isethionate
isidiferous
Island Carib
isoantibody
isochimenal
isochronism
isochronous
isoclinally
isodiabatic
isodiaphere
isoelectric
isogeotherm
isolability
isolecithal
isomagnetic
isometrical
isometropia
isomorphism
isomorphous
isopropanol
isorhythmic
isotonicity
Israelitish
issue of fact
itacolumite
Italian hand
Italian iron
Italianizer
Italian pink
Italian roof
Italo-Celtic
Italophobia
itatartaric
itatartrate
it blows hard
itching ears
itching palm
itemization
iteratively
iteroparity
iteroparous
ithyphallic
ithyphallus
itineraries
itinerarium
itineration
it's your baby
it will serve
ivory-billed
ivy geranium
I want to know
jabberwocky
Jack and Jill
jackass brig
jackass-fish
jacket crown
Jack-fishing
Jack-hunting
Jack-pudding
Jack Russell
Jacky Winter

Jacobinical
Jacobitical
Jacob's staff
Jacqueminot
jactitation
jaggery palm
jaguarundis
Jamaicanism
jam tomorrow
janissaries
Jansenistic
Japan clover
Japanese ape
Japanese wax
Japan laurel
Japanolatry
Japanophile
Japan pepper
Japan quince
jargonesque
jargonistic
jarringness
jaunting car
Java sparrow
javelin fish
jaw-breaking
jealousness
Jeffrey pine
Jehoshaphat
jejunoileum
jejunostomy
jellied eels
jelly powder
jerboa-mouse
jerrymander
Jersey wagon
Jesuits' bark
jet aircraft
jimber-jawed
Jimmy Riddle
Jimmy the One
jingle shell
jitteriness
job analysis
job creation
joblessness
jockey-wheel
jocoserious
jocundities
jodhpur boot
John-a-dreams
John-Bullish
John-Bullism
John Citizen
John Collins
John Company
John Hancock
Johnsoniana
joie de vivre
join company
joint denial
jointedness

joint family
joint patent
joint-tenant
jolly fellow
jolt ramming
jolt-squeeze
Josephinism
josephinite
Joule effect
Joule–Kelvin
journal-book
journalizer
journey-work
jovicentric
Jovinianist
joylessness
Jubilee clip
Judaeophobe
Judaization
Judas-colour
Judas priest
Judas window
judgemental
judgemented
Judges' Rules
Judge's Rules
judiciality
judicialize
judiciaries
judiciously
jugular vein
jumper cable
jumper dress
jumper strut
jumping bean
jumping deer
jumping hare
jumping jack
jumping-pole
jumping seed
jumping-wire
jump Jim Crow
jump take-off
junction box
juncturally
jungle bunny
jungle fever
jungle green
jungle juice
jungle music
juridically
jurimetrics
just a minute
justice-seat
justiceship
justiciable
justifiable
justifiably
justify bail
just quietly
just-so story
just the same

juvenescent
juxta-marine
juxta-spinal
Kabardinian
Kabbalistic
kachina doll
Kaffir bread
Kaffir crane
Kaffir finch
Kaffir melon
Kaffir piano
Kalashnikov
kalkoentjie
kameeldoorn
kämmererite
kangaroo-dog
kangaroo-fly
kangaroo paw
kangaroo rat
Kara-Kirghiz
Karoo series
Kashmir goat
katabothron
katavothron
kedge anchor
kedgeree-pot
keelboatman
keepability
keep abreast
keep a corner
keep an eye on
keep a school
keep a secret
keep bad time
keep company
keep counsel
keeping-room
keep in shape
keep in touch
keep measure
keep one's bed
keep one's way
keep silence
keep track of
kefir grains
Kelvin scale
Kendal green
kenogenesis
Kentish crow
Kentish fire
Kentish tern
Kenya coffee
Kenyan Asian
Kepler's laws
keratectomy
keratoconus
keratoderma
keratolysis
keratolytic
keratometer
keratometry
keratophyre

kerb-crawler
kerb service
kern counter
kernicteric
kernicterus
Kernig's sign
ketogenesis
ketone group
ketopentose
ketosteroid
Kevenhuller
keyboardist
key industry
key of the sea
Keystone Kop
kick-and-rush
kick-starter
kick the beam
kidney graft
kidney-piece
kidney punch
kidney-stone
kidney table
kidney vetch
Kikuyu grass
Kilkenny cat
killer whale
killingness
killing-time
killing zone
kilocalorie
kilometrage
kilovoltage
kilowattage
kinderspiel
kind-hearted
kind payment
kindredness
kindredship
kinematical
kinesically
kinesiology
kinesthesia
kinetically
kinetochore
kinetodesma
kinetograph
kinetoplast
kinetoscope
King Charles
King Country
kingdom come
king of birds
king of kings
King of Kings
king penguin
king's bishop
King's bounty
King's colour
king's gambit
King's gambit
king's knight

king's ransom
king's silver
King's speech
king's yellow
king vulture
kinsmanship
Kiowa Apache
Kirk-session
kissability
kiss and tell
kissing-ball
kissing gate
kissing kind
kissing time
kiss-me-quick
kiss of death
kiss of peace
kiss the book
kiss the dirt
kiss the dust
kitchenable
kitchenette
kitchen-maid
kitchen-plot
kitchen roll
kitchen-sink
kitchenware
kite balloon
kitschiness
kittenishly
Klamath weed
Klein bottle
kleptocracy
kleptomania
Klinefelter
knapsacking
knavishness
kneecapping
knee-slapper
knee-strings
knicker yarn
knick-knacky
knife switch
knock for six
knock-me-down
knock on wood
knock rating
knock rotten
Knoevenagel
knottedness
knowability
know asunder
know by sight
knowingness
know-nothing
know too much
know who's who
knuckleball
knuckle-bone
knuckle-deep
knuckle down
knuckledust

knucklehead
knucklesome
Knudsen flow
kob antelope
koechlinite
koilonychia
Kondratieff
Koplik's spot
koringkriek
kornerupine
kreophagous
kulturkampf
Kulturkampf
kulturkreis
kulturstaat
Kupffer cell
kutnahorite
kwashiorkor
kymographic
labefaction
labia majora
labia minora
labiodental
laboriosity
laboriously
labour force
labouringly
labour pains
Labour Party
labour union
Labrador dog
Labradorian
labradorite
Labrador tea
labretifery
labyrinthal
labyrinthic
Lacanianism
laccolithic
lace curtain
laced valley
lacertilian
lacewing fly
lachrymator
laciniation
laconically
lacquer disc
lacquer tree
lacquerware
lacquer-work
lacrimation
lacrymation
lactalbumin
lactational
lactescence
lactiferous
lactobionic
lactochrome
lactoferrin
lactoflavin
lactophenol
ladder point

ladder-proof
ladder shell
ladder-truck
laddishness
ladies' cabin
ladies' chain
ladies' night
la dolce vita
Lady Macbeth
lady's finger
lady's mantle
Laffer curve
laggardness
laicization
lairdocracy
Lake Country
lake-dweller
lake herring
lake village
lalapaloosa
lalapalooza
lallygagged
lambda point
lamb's tongue
lamb succory
lamebrained
lamellicorn
lamelliform
lamentation
lamentingly
laminagraph
laminectomy
Lammas shoot
Lammas wheat
lammergeier
lammergeyer
lamp-chimney
lamplighter
lamprophyre
Lancastrian
lance-knight
lanceolated
lancepesade
lancet light
lancinating
land-grabber
landgravate
landgravine
landholding
landing-beam
landing card
landing-flap
landing gear
landing-wire
Land-leaguer
landlordism
land-marshal
land-measure
land of cakes
landscapist
land-service
landsknecht

land-steward	latrinogram	leading tone	leftishness	less and less
langbeinite	lattice beam	leading wind	left-leaning	lesser breed
Langobardic	lattice site	lead-papered	left luggage	lesser-known
langoustine	lattice wave	lead-plaster	left-wingery	lesser light
language lab	latticewise	lead-swinger	left-wingism	lesson-piece
languidness	lattice-work	lead the ring	legal beagle	lestobiosis
languish for	latus rectum	lead through	legal memory	lestobiotic
languishing	laubmannite	lead-vitriol	legal person	lethargical
laniariform	laudability	leaf blister	legal tender	lethiferous
lansfordite	laudanosine	leaf-cutting	legationary	let off steam
lantern fish	laudatorily	leaf gelatin	legendarily	let's-pretend
lantern jaws	laughing gas	leaflet raid	legerdemain	letter-paper
laparoscope	laughing owl	leaf-opposed	legibleness	letter-plate
laparoscopy	laughworthy	leaf protein	legionaries	letterpress
lap-dissolve	launderette	leaf shutter	legionnaire	letter-scale
lapidescent	Laura Ashley	leaf-tendril	legislation	letter-space
lapis lazuli	laurel-green	leaf-tobacco	legislative	lettuce-like
lap of honour	laurel-water	leaf warbler	legislatrix	leucocratic
Laporte rule	laurustinus	leafy spurge	legislature	leucodermic
lap portable	lavender bag	leaguer-lady	leglessness	leucomatous
larch sawfly	lavender oil	league table	leg-of-mutton	leucoplakia
lard-bladder	laver cutter	leal-hearted	Leidenfrost	leucopterin
large as life	lavishingly	lean against	leishmanial	leucorrhoea
large-handed	law and order	leaning-note	leishmanoid	leucotactic
large-minded	lawbreaking	lean mixture	Leisler's bat	leucotomies
large-souled	lawlessness	leap forward	leisureless	leucotomize
lark bunting	law merchant	leaping ague	leisurewear	leucotriene
lark sparrow	lawn-sleeved	leaping-head	lemming-like	leukaemogen
larrikinism	lawn sleeves	leaping time	lemon cheese	leukotriene
larviparous	law of effect	learnedness	lemon-colour	Levantinism
larvivorous	law of honour	learning set	lemon squash	levantinize
laryngismus	law of nature	leaseholder	lemon yellow	level-dyeing
laryngology	law of sewers	leatherback	lend wings to	level-headed
laryngotomy	Lawrentiana	leather-carp	lengthiness	leviathanic
LaserVision	lawrightman	leather-coat	lens coating	leviratical
lasiocampid	lay about one	leatherette	lentiginous	Levitically
last assizes	lay analysis	leather-head	Leonine City	lexigraphic
last evening	lay down arms	leatherleaf	leopard frog	lexotactics
last honours	layer colour	leather-like	leopard lily	*lex talionis*
lastingness	layer system	leatherneck	leopard moth	leycesteria
last morning	laying house	leatherwear	leopard seal	liabilities
last offices	lay in pledge	leatherwood	leopard-skin	libationary
last quarter	lay preacher	leave behind	leopard-tree	libellously
last the pace	Laysan finch	leave hold of	leopard-wood	liberal arts
latchkey kid	lay stress on	leave school	Lepidoptera	liberalizer
latch-string	lay together	leave-taking	lepidoptery	liberalness
late licence	lay weight on	leave to stew	lepidosiren	liberatress
latent image	lead balloon	leaving-shop	lepospondyl	libertarian
latent virus	lead bullion	lecanomancy	leprologist	liberticide
lateral line	lead-burning	Le Chatelier	lepromatous	libertinage
lateralward	lead captive	lecheguilla	leprophilia	libertinism
latera recta	lead chamber	lecherously	leprophobia	libertinous
lateritious	lead counsel	lechuguilla	leprosarium	Liberty Bell
latifundist	lead crystal	lecithinase	leprousness	liberty boat
latifundium	leadhillite	lectureship	leptodactyl	liberty bond
Latin Church	leader board	ledge-handle	leptokurtic	liberty hall
Latin letter	leading case	ledger space	leptomeninx	Liberty loan
Latin rights	leading edge	ledger-stone	leptorrhine	liberty-pole
Latin school	leading lady	leewardmost	leptospiral	Liberty ship
Latin square	leading mark	left-brained	Lesbian rule	liberty tree
latitudinal	leading note	left-fielder	lèse-majesté	liberum veto
latreutical	leading-rein	left for dead	lese-majesty	libidinally

librational
licenceless
lichenology
lickerishly
lickspittle
liederabend
Liederkranz
lie detector
lie like a log
lieutenancy
life and limb
lifeboatman
lifeboatmen
lifefulness
life history
life-in-death
lifemanship
life-or-death
life peerage
liferentrix
life science
life-support
life tenancy
life-writing
lift a finger
lifting beam
lifting body
lifting tape
lift the roof
ligamentary
ligamentous
ligand field
light a shuck
light-footed
light-handed
light-headed
light-heeled
light-limbed
light-minded
light-minute
Lightmonger
light-second
light-skirts
lightsomely
Light Sussex
lightweight
lignicolous
lignivorous
lignum aloes
lignum vitae
likeability
like another
like a streak
like it or not
Likert scale
like the wind
like winking
lilliputian
lily-livered
lily-trotter
limber-chain
limb of Satan

lime and hair
lime-rubbish
lime-sulphur
limitedness
limitlessly
limit switch
limnologist
limpingness
limp-wristed
linch-drawer
Lincolniana
Lincoln wool
Lindabrides
line abreast
linear motor
linebacking
line-casting
line drawing
line-filling
line-fishing
line manager
linen basket
linen-draper
linen duster
linen shower
line officer
line of force
line of march
line of metal
line of sight
line printer
line-soldier
line-spacing
lingenberry
lingeringly
lingoa geral
lingonberry
linguacious
lingua geral
Linguaphone
linguatulid
linguistics
link buttons
linocutting
linseed cake
linseed meal
lint-scraper
Linzertorte
lion-hearted
lionization
lion's turnip
lion tamarin
lipogenesis
lipomatosis
lipoprotein
liposarcoma
liposuction
lipotropism
liquefiable
liquescence
liquescency
liquidambar

liquidation
liquidities
liquid lunch
liquid paper
liquorishly
lirelliform
lisle thread
list-broking
listeriosis
literalizer
literalness
literaryism
lithia water
lithochrome
lithochromy
lithodipyra
lithodomous
lithofacies
lithogenous
lithography
lithologist
lithophagic
lithophanic
lithophytic
lithosphere
lithostatic
lithotomies
lithotomise
lithotomist
lithotomize
lithotripsy
lithotritic
lithotritor
litigiosity
litigiously
litmus paper
littérateur
little bitty
little death
little grebe
Little Horse
little house
little sheer
little skate
little woman
little-worth
liveability
live-bearing
live-for-ever
liver colour
live through
living chess
living death
living floor
living image
living space
lixiviation
lizard-green
lizard's tail
loadability
load draught
loading coil

loading dose
loaf of bread
loan capital
lo and behold
loathliness
loathsomely
lobectomies
loblolly bay
loblolly boy
lobotomized
lobster-boat
lobsterling
lobster moth
lobster-tail
local colour
localisable
localizable
local motion
local option
local talent
Lochaber-axe
lock forward
loco disease
locofocoism
Locrian mode
loculicidal
locum tenens
locus standi
locust-berry
locust-eater
locust years
locutionary
lodging-room
lodging turn
loellingite
lofting-iron
lofting pole
logarithmal
logarithmic
logging-rock
logical atom
logical form
logicalness
logical word
logistician
log-normally
logocentric
logodaedaly
log of claims
logographer
logographic
logogriphic
logomachies
logomachist
logopaedics
logorrhoeic
loiteringly
lollipop man
Lombard band
London broil
London plane
London pride

lonely heart
longanimity
longanimous
long-awaited
long clothes
longimanous
longingness
longinquity
long-keeping
long-lasting
long measure
Longobardic
long-playing
long purples
long-running
long service
longshoring
long-sighted
long-sleeved
long-sleever
long-tongued
long twelves
long-waisted
long weekend
long-woolled
look asquint
look daggers
looker-upper
looking-over
look one's age
look oneself
look the part
look through
loony-doctor
loop-the-loop
loose-bodied
loose cannon
loose change
loose-footed
loose-housed
loose-limbed
loose-lipped
loosestrife
lophobranch
lophophoral
lord and lady
Lord bless me
Lord Justice
Lord love you
Lord Marcher
Lord of hosts
logogriphic
Lord Provost
Lord's Prayer
Lord's Supper
Lords triers
Los Angeleno
lose courage
lose leather
lose one's rag
lose one's way
lose sight of
lose track of

lost weekend	Lydian stone	maggotiness	make and mend	mamelonated
lotophagous	Lyman series	magic bullet	make an end of	mamillation
loud-mouthed	Lyme disease	magic carpet	make a pass at	mammalogist
loudspeaker	lymphoblast	magic circle	make a puddle	mammaplasty
Louisianian	lymphocytic	Magic Marker	make a search	mammiferous
loutishness	lymphoedema	magic mirror	make a shot at	mammillated
louvre-board	lymphogenic	magic square	make a show of	mammography
lovableness	lymphopenia	magic stitch	make a splash	Mammonistic
love handles	lyonization	Maginot Line	make believe	Mammonitish
love-in-a-mist	lyricalness	magisterial	make certain	mammoplasty
low comedian	macadamizer	magisterium	make default	mammoth tree
lower fourth	Macassarese	Maglemosian	make friends	managership
lower orders	Macassar oil	Magna Charta	make history	man-bites-dog
lower school	machaerdont	magnanimity	make holiday	mancipation
lower second	machairodus	magnanimous	make light of	mancipatory
lowest terms	machicolate	magnateship	make off with	mandarinate
low fidelity	machicoulis	magnetician	make one's bow	mandarinism
low pressure	machinating	magnetotail	make one's way	mandataries
low-spirited	machination	magnifiable	make or break	mandatories
loxodromism	machine code	magnificent	make request	mandatorily
lozengewise	machine-head	magnificoes	make room for	mandibulary
lubber fiend	machineless	magnipotent	make scruple	mandibulate
lubber's hole	machine-like	magnoperate	make sense of	mandolinist
lubrication	machineries	magnum bonum	make sport of	manducation
lubricative	machine room	magpie diver	make strange	manducatory
lubritorium	machine shop	magpie goose	make the race	manganesian
Lucanian cow	machine tool	magpie-robin	make welcome	manganolite
lucratively	machine-wash	Maharashtri	make whoopee	mango-ginger
lucubration	machine word	maidservant	Malabar plum	mangrove fly
lucubratory	mackerel-fly	mailability	malabathrum	mangrove-hen
ludicrosity	mackereling	mail carrier	malacca cane	Manichaeism
ludicrously	mackerel sky	mailing list	Malacca cane	manifestant
lues venerea	macrobiotic	mailing shot	maladaptive	manifestive
luggageless	macrocosmic	maille noble	maladjusted	manifolding
lumbaginous	macrocyclic	Maimonidean	maladroitly	Manila cigar
lumber baron	macrofossil	main breadth	malapropian	manila paper
lumberingly	macrogamete	main chancer	malapropism	man in motion
lumber trade	macrophagic	main squeeze	malariology	manipulable
lumber-wagon	macrophytic	maintenance	malediction	manipulator
lumbricalis	macroscopic	maintopmast	maledictive	manlessness
lumbriculus	macrosmatic	maintopsail	maledictory	manlikeness
luminescent	macula lutea	maison close	malefaction	man-milliner
luminophore	maddeningly	maisonnette	malefically	man-mountain
lump-account	madder brown	maize-yellow	maleficence	manna-lichen
lumpishness	madefaction	major circle	male incense	manneristic
lunar module	Madeira cake	major league	malevolence	mannishness
lunatically	Madeira wine	major planet	malevolency	Mann–Whitney
lunch-dinner	made of money	make a bid for	malfeasance	manoeuvring
luncheon-car	made to order	make a figure	malfunction	man of action
lunette-shoe	Madonna blue	make a fist at	maliciously	man of honour
Lupercalian	madonna lily	make a fool of	malignantly	ma non troppo
lustfulness	Madonna lily	make a fuss of	malignation	manorialize
Lutheranise	Madras curry	make against	malignities	mansard roof
Lutheranism	madreporite	make a hash of	mallet-shoot	man-tailored
Lutheranize	madrigalian	make a hole in	malmsey wine	mantel clock
Lutyenesque	madrigalism	make a market	Malo-Russian	mantelletta
luxuriantly	madrigalist	make a meal of	malposition	mantelpiece
luxuriation	Madrilenian	make a mess of	malpractice	mantelplace
luxuriously	Maecenatism	make a mock of	Maltese lace	mantelshelf
lycanthrope	magazinedom	make a motion	malt extract	mantle fibre
lycanthropy	Magdalenian	make a muck of	malt spirits	mantlepiece
lychnoscope	magdalenism	make an ass of	malt vinegar	mantleshelf

mantua-maker	Marrucinian	materialize	meditullium	memorizable
manucaption	marry come up	material man	medium-dated	memory board
manuduction	Marseillais	maternalism	mediumistic	memory cycle
manuductory	Marshallese	mathematics	medium-pacer	memory trace
manufactory	Marshallian	mathematize	medium-range	menaccanite
manufacture	marshalling	matinée coat	medium-sized	menaphthone
manumission	marshalship	matinée idol	medley relay	menaquinone
manumitting	marshlander	matriarchal	Medusa's head	mendacities
Maorilander	marsh mallow	matriculant	meet halfway	mendelevium
Maori wrasse	marshmallow	matriculate	meet the case	mendication
map-measurer	marsh orchid	matrilineal	megaloblast	mend matters
maprotiline	marsh violet	matrilinear	megalomania	meneghinite
maraschinos	martensitic	matrimonial	megalomanic	meningocele
Marathonian	martial arts	matrimonies	megalopolis	meniscoidal
marbled newt	martialness	matter of law	megamachine	menorrhagia
marble-paper	martinetish	maudlin tide	meganucleus	menorrhagic
marble-stone	martinetism	Maundy money	megaphonist	menservants
marcescence	martin-house	Maundy purse	megastardom	mensuralist
marchership	Martiniquan	Mauretanian	megatherial	mensuration
march in a net	martyrology	Mauritanian	megatherian	mensurative
marchioness	marzipanned	mavrodaphne	megatherium	mental block
marconigram	masculinely	mawkishness	megatonnage	mentalistic
mare clausum	masculinise	mayonnaised	megavitamin	mentalities
mare liberum	masculinism	mayoralties	meiobenthic	mental nurse
marginalise	masculinist	McCarthyism	meiobenthos	mental ratio
marginalism	masculinity	McCarthyite	meiotically	mentholated
marginalist	masculinize	meadow brown	Mekhitarist	mentionable
marginality	masculinoid	meadow crake	melancholia	mentri besar
marginalize	maskelynite	meadow grass	melancholic	meprobamate
margination	masking tape	meadow mouse	melanoblast	mercapturic
margraviate	masochistic	meadow pipit	melanoderma	mercatorial
maria clausa	Masoretical	meadowsweet	melanophore	Mercatorial
maria libera	masquerader	meal-pennant	melanterite	mercenarian
mariculture	massiveness	mean anomaly	melioidosis	mercenaries
Marie Louise	mass meeting	meaningless	melioration	mercenarily
marinescape	mass-produce	meaningness	meliorative	mercenarism
marine store	mass society	mean streets	meliphagine	merchandise
marital rape	mastaba tomb	measureless	meliphagous	merchant-bar
marked price	masterbatch	measurement	mellaginous	merchantman
marker crude	master-class	meat-grinder	melliferous	merchantmen
market cross	masterclass	meat-packing	mellifluent	mercilessly
market-house	master clock	mechanician	mellifluous	mercuration
market maker	masterfully	mechanicism	mellisonant	mercurially
market mammy	master mason	mechanicist	mellivorous	mercury lamp
market overt	masterpiece	mechanistic	mellowspeak	mercury pool
market-peace	master's mate	mechanology	melodically	mercy flight
market place	master touch	Mechlin lace	melodiously	merdivorous
market price	mastication	medal ribbon	melon-cactus	Meredithian
market stall	masticatory	median strip	meloplastic	meretrician
marketstead	mastigoneme	mediastinal	melo-tragedy	merino sheep
market value	mastodontic	mediastinum	melpomenish	merit monger
market woman	mastoid bone	mediateness	meltability	meritocracy
Markov chain	mastoiditis	mediational	meltingness	meritorious
marlinspike	masturbator	mediatorial	membranella	merit rating
marmoreally	Matabele ant	medical hall	membraneous	merit system
maroon party	matchlessly	medicinable	memento mori	meroblastic
marquessate	matchmaking	medicinally	memorabilia	merocyanine
marqueterie	match-winner	medicine man	memorandums	merodiploid
marquisette	materialise	medievalise	Memorial Day	meromorphic
Marriage Act	materialism	medievalism	memorialise	Merovingian
marriage-bed	materialist	medievalist	memorialist	merry andrew
marron glacé	materiality	medievalize	memorialize	merry Andrew

merrymaking	metanephric	Micawberish	middle guard	mind one's eye
Merthiolate	metanephros	Micawberism	middle piece	mind the shop
mésalliance	metaphorist	Michelsberg	middle price	mineral blue
mesaortitis	metaphorize	Michigander	middlescent	mineral coal
mesencephal	metaphyseal	Michiganian	middle-sized	mineral grey
mesenchymal	metaphysial	Michurinism	middlestead	mineralizer
mesenterial	metaphysics	Michurinist	middle watch	mineralogic
mesenteries	metaplastic	Mickey Mouse	middle-water	mineral soil
meshuggenah	metapsychic	microampere	Middle White	mineral wool
mesoblastic	metascience	microbially	middle world	miner's right
mesocephali	metasequoia	microbicide	middle years	minesweeper
mesocyclone	metasomatic	micrococcal	middy blouse	miniaturise
mesogastric	Metastasian	micrococcus	mid-European	miniaturist
mesognathic	metastasise	microcolony	midlittoral	miniaturize
mesometrium	metastasize	microcopied	midnight sun	minifundism
mesomorphic	metasternal	microcopies	midsagittal	minifundist
mesonephric	metasternum	microcosmic	midship beam	minifundium
mesonephros	metatherian	microcyclic	midshipmite	minimal pair
mesopelagic	metathesize	microdegree	midwife toad	minimum wage
mesophyllic	metatrophic	microfaunal	might as well	ministerial
Mesopotamia	meteoristic	microfibril	migrational	ministrable
mesosalpinx	meteoritics	microfiches	migratorial	ministrator
mesosaprobe	meteorogram	microfilmer	mild-hearted	minnesinger
mesoseismal	meteoroidal	microfloppy	military age	Minnesinger
mesospheric	meteorolite	microfungus	militaryism	minor league
mesosternal	meteorology	microgamete	military law	minor orders
mesosternum	meteor swarm	micrography	milk-blooded	minor planet
mesosuchian	meteor trail	microgroove	milk-livered	minute-glass
mesothelial	meter-feeder	microinject	milk-parsley	minute steak
mesothelium	meter-reader	microlithic	milk pudding	minute-wheel
mesothermal	metethereal	micrologist	milk the bull	miogeocline
mesothermic	methacrylic	micromaniac	milk-thistle	miracle cure
mesothorium	methanation	micromastia	milkweed bug	miracle drug
message card	methenamine	micrometeor	milled board	miracle play
messageless	methicillin	micrometric	millenarian	mirifically
Messiahship	methimazole	micromodule	millenaries	mirror fugue
mesterolone	methisazone	micromotion	millenarism	mirror-glass
metabiology	Methodistic	Micronesian	millenarist	mirror image
metabolizer	methodology	micro-opaque	millenniums	mirror-plate
metacentric	method study	microphoned	Miller index	mirror scale
metachronal	methylation	microphonic	miller's soul	mirror stage
metachrosis	methyl green	microphytal	millet-grass	mirthlessly
meta-ethical	metoestrous	microporous	milliampere	misalliance
metafiction	metonymical	microreader	milligramme	misanthrope
metagenesis	metoposcopy	microrecord	millimetric	misanthropy
metagenetic	metre-candle	microscopic	millinerial	misarranged
metakinesis	metrication	microscreen	millionaire	misbecoming
metakinetic	metric psalm	microsecond	millionfold	misbegotten
metaldehyde	metric space	microsmatic	milliosmole	misbeholden
metalimnion	metric tonne	microsphere	millisecond	misbeliever
metalingual	metrisation	microswitch	Millon's test	miscarriage
metallicity	metrization	microtubule	milpa system	miscasualty
metallocene	metrolander	microvillar	Milquetoast	miscellanea
metallogeny	metrologist	microvillus	mimetically	mischiefful
metalloidal	metromaniac	micrurgical	mimographer	mischievous
metallurgic	metropolite	micturition	minaciously	mischristen
metalogical	metrostaxis	mid-Atlantic	mincingness	miscibility
metal thread	Mexican wave	middenstead	mind-bending	mis-citation
metalworker	mezzofantic	middle class	mind-blowing	misclassify
metamessage	Mezzogiorno	middle earth	mindfulness	misconceive
metamorphic	mezzotinter	middle eight	mind-healing	misconstrue
metanalysis	miasmically	middle genus	mind-numbing	miscreation

miscreative
misdecision
misdelivery
misdescribe
misdiagnose
misdivision
mise en scène
misemphasis
miserliness
misestimate
misfeasance
misfortuned
misfortuner
misfunction
misgoverned
misgovernor
misgrounded
misguidance
misguidedly
misidentify
misinclined
misinformer
misinstruct
misjudgment
mislocation
mismarriage
misperceive
mispersuade
mispleading
mispointing
misregister
misremember
misreporter
Miss America
misshapenly
missing link
missing mass
missishness
mississippi
miss one's tip
misspelling
miss the boat
mistakingly
mister wight
mistressing
mistrustful
mistrusting
mite society
Mithraicism
Mithraistic
mithridatic
Mithridatic
mitogenetic
mitotically
mitral valve
mitred abbey
mitred abbot
mitre-square
mix and match
mixed border
mixed-manned
mixed number

mixed school
mixing valve
mixolimnion
mixotrophic
mixtilinear
mnemonician
mnemotechny
mobbishness
mobile phone
mobilizable
Möbius strip
mobocracies
mock auction
mockingbird
mode-locking
model theory
moderantism
modern dance
modern Greek
modernistic
modern Latin
modificable
modificator
modillioned
modi vivendi
modus ponens
Moeso-Gothic
Mohini-attam
moisturizer
moko disease
mole-catcher
mole cricket
molecularly
molendinary
molestation
mollescence
mollifiable
mollycoddle
molly-dooker
Molucca balm
Molucca bean
Molucca crab
molybdenite
momentarily
momentously
monadically
monarchally
monarchical
monasterial
monasteries
monasticise
monasticism
monasticize
Monbazillac
monchiquite
money broker
money centre
money-clause
money cowrie
money-dealer
money flower
money for jam

money-jobber
moneylender
moneymaking
money market
money-monger
money spider
money supply
money's-worth
monitorship
monkey-apple
monkey-board
monkey bread
monkey-faced
monkey gland
monkey-house
monkeyishly
monkey's fist
monkeyshine
monkey trial
monkey trick
monkishness
Monmouth cap
monoblastic
monocarpous
monocentric
monochasial
monochasium
monochromat
monochromic
monochronic
monoclinous
monocracies
monocrystal
monocularly
monoculture
monocytosis
monodactyly
monodentate
monodically
monogastric
monogeneous
monogenesis
monogenetic
monoglacial
monogrammed
monographer
monographic
monohydrate
monolatrous
monolingual
monolithism
monolobular
monological
monologuise
monologuist
monologuize
monomorphic
monomyarian
Monongahela
mononuclear
monophagous
monophonous

monophthong
Monophysite
monopolizer
monopsonist
monopterous
monorhinous
monospermal
monospermic
monosporous
monostylous
monotechnic
Monothelism
Monothelite
monotically
monotonical
monotremate
monotrochal
monotrophic
monotropism
monovalence
monozygotic
Monseigneur
monstrosity
monstrously
mons Veneris
Montanistic
Montenegrin
montes pubis
Montgolfier
monthly rose
monticulose
Montpellier
moonlighter
moon-madness
moor-band pan
mooring-mast
mooring-post
Moorish idol
Moor macaque
mops and mows
moralizable
moratoriums
Moravianism
mordication
more and more
more by token
more majorum
morgenstern
moribundity
Morlacchian
Mormon Bible
Mormon State
Mormon trail
morning call
morning coat
morning-gift
morningless
morning line
morning room
morning star
morningtide
morological

moronically
morosophist
morphically
morphinated
morphogenic
morphologic
morphometry
morphonemic
morphophone
morphotropy
Morris chair
morris dance
mortal drunk
mortalities
mortarboard
mortar-piece
mortiferous
mortifiedly
mortise lock
mortmain act
Morton's foot
Morton's fork
mosasaurian
Moses basket
mosquito-bar
mosquito bee
mosquito net
moss campion
moss-cheeper
moss-trooper
mosstrooper
mossy-backed
mossy-cup oak
motherboard
Mother Bunch
mother-clove
mothercraft
mother earth
mother-house
mother image
mother-in-law
mother mould
mother-naked
Mother of God
mother plane
mother plant
mother queen
mother right
mother's help
mother's mark
mother's milk
mother's ruin
mother stone
mother water
moth mullein
mothproofer
motion study
motive power
motoneurone
motor cortex
motoring cap
motor racing

motor-sailer	multi-ethnic	muscularity	Myrmidonian	nasal concha
mottled calf	multifactor	muscularize	myrrhophore	nasalizable
mottled iron	multifidous	musculation	myrtle-berry	nasal meatus
mould-candle	multifloral	musculature	myrtle green	naseberries
mould-runner	multigravid	museography	mysteriarch	nasociliary
mountain air	multihulled	museologist	mystery play	nasogastric
mountain ash	multijugate	museum piece	mystery ship	nasopharynx
mountain bat	multilineal	mushroom hat	mystery tour	nasospinale
mountain cat	multilinear	musical film	mysticality	nationalise
mountain dew	multilithed	musicalness	mythography	nationalism
mountaineer	multilobate	musical ride	mythoheroic	nationalist
mountain man	multinomial	music centre	mythologian	nationality
mountainous	multi-occupy	musicianess	mythologies	nationalize
mountain rat	multiparity	musicogenic	mythologise	nation state
mountain tea	multiparous	musico-mania	mythologist	native heath
mouse and man	multipedous	musicophile	mythologize	native peach
mouse-colour	multiphased	music volute	mythomaniac	Native State
moustachial	multiphasic	muskellunge	mythopoeism	natriuresis
Moustierian	multiplanar	musket-arrow	mythopoeist	natriuretic
movableness	multiplaned	musketproof	mythopoesis	nattier blue
movable type	multiple-use	musk thistle	mythopoetic	Nattier blue
move a finger	multiplexer	mussel scalp	Mytilenaean	natural-born
movie camera	multiplexor	mussel-shell	myxamoeboid	natural food
movie-making	multipotent	mussitation	myxofibroma	natural fool
movie palace	multiracial	Mussolinian	myxomatized	natural horn
moving plant	multiserial	Mussolinism	myxomatosis	naturalizer
moving stair	multisonant	Mussulmanic	myxomycetan	natural life
moxibustion	multisonous	Mussulwoman	myxophycean	naturalness
Mozambiquer	multispiral	mustachioed	myxosarcoma	natural note
Mozartianly	multistable	mustard bush	naggingness	natural-sign
Mrs Next-Door	multi-storey	mustard seed	nail varnish	natural sine
much obliged	multistorey	mutableness	naked ladies	natural year
much the same	multivalent	mutagenesis	Namaqua dove	nature-faker
mucicarmine	multivalved	mutationist	nameability	nature-notes
muckle wheel	mumbo-jumbos	Mutt and Jeff	name-calling	nature print
mucociliary	mum's the word	mutteringly	name-dropper	nature strip
mucopeptide	mundaneness	mutualistic	name no names	nature study
mucoprotein	mundanities	mycological	Nancy Dawson	nature trail
mucoraceous	mundivagant	mycophagist	nannofossil	naturopathy
mucronulate	municipally	mycophagous	nanomachine	naughtiness
muddle along	munificence	mycoplasmal	Nantucketer	naughty bits
mud engineer	munitioneer	mycoplasmas	naphthacene	naupliiform
mud-slinging	murderously	mycoprotein	naphthalene	nauticality
mud-throwing	murder squad	mycorrhizae	naphthalize	naval stores
mud-wrestler	murmuration	mycorrhizal	naphthenate	navel-gazing
muffin-fight	murmuringly	mycotrophic	naplessness	navel orange
muffin-worry	murmurously	myelination	Napoleonism	navel string
muffishness	murmur vowel	myelogenous	Napoleonist	n-declension
muffling-box	muscardined	myelography	Napoleonize	Neanderthal
mule-driving	Muschelkalk	mygalomorph	narcissuses	neanthropic
mule-skinner	muscicapine	myocarditis	narcoleptic	near and near
mule-whacker	muscicolous	Myochrysine	narcomaniac	Near Eastern
mulga parrot	muscle-bound	myoelectric	narcoticism	near-sighted
mulierosity	muscle curve	myofilament	Narodnikism	near the bone
mullein moth	muscle fibre	myo-inositol	narrational	near the wind
mullein pink	muscle force	myriametric	narratively	neatherdess
mullein wave	muscle power	myriapodous	narrativity	neat's tongue
multangular	muscle sense	myringotome	narratology	necessarian
multi-access	muscle shirt	myringotomy	narratorial	necessaries
multicolour	muscologist	myriologist	narrow gauge	necessarily
multicuspid	Muscovy duck	myrmecobius	narrow goods	necessarium
multicyclic	Muscovy talc	myrmecology	nasal artery	necessitate

necessities
necessitous
necessitude
neck and crop
neck and neck
neckerchief
necking-cord
necrobiosis
necrobiotic
necrologies
necrologist
necromancer
necromantic
necrophilia
necrophilic
necrophobia
necrophobic
necroscopic
nectar-guide
nectarivore
needcessity
needfulness
needlecraft
needle fight
needle furze
needle-grass
needle match
needle paper
needlepoint
needle valve
needlewoman
needlewomen
need not have
ne'er the less
nefariously
negationist
neglectable
neglectedly
negligeable
negligently
negotiation
negotiatory
negotiatrix
Negrophobia
neighbourer
neighbourly
Nelson knife
Nelson touch
nemathecial
nemathecium
nematicidal
nematoblast
nematocidal
nematodirus
nematophore
nematozooid
neo-colonial
neocortical
neo-Georgian
neo-Hellenic
neo-linguist
neologistic

neonatology
Neoplatonic
neostigmine
neostriatal
neostriatum
neotechnics
neotectonic
neotenously
neothalamic
neothalamus
neotropical
nephelinite
nephelinize
nephologist
nephrectomy
nephroblast
nephrogenic
nephropathy
nephrostome
nephrostomy
nephrotoxic
nephrotoxin
ne plus ultra
Neptune's cup
nerve centre
nerve-doctor
nerve-ending
nervelessly
nervousness
nestle-chick
nestle-tripe
Netherlands
netherstock
netherwards
nether world
netherworld
net-practice
neural crest
neural plate
neural spine
neuraminate
neurapraxia
neurenteric
neurilemmal
neurocytoma
neurofibril
neurohaemal
neurohumour
neuroleptic
neurologist
neuromatous
neuropathic
neurophysin
neuropodial
neuropodium
neuropteran
neuroticism
neurotomies
neurotropic
neurotubule
neurulation
neutral axis

neutral-gear
neutralizer
neutron bomb
neutron star
neutropenia
neutrophile
never-ending
never-fading
never say die
New Age music
newbuilding
New Canadian
new Covenant
New Covenant
New Critical
new frontier
Newgate bird
New Humanism
New Humanist
New Jerseyan
new learning
Newman–Keuls
new potatoes
New Rightist
news butcher
newspapered
news theatre
New Year's Day
New Year's Eve
niacinamide
nice-looking
Nicene Creed
nickel-bloom
nickel brass
nickelodeon
nickel steel
nictitating
nictitation
Niderviller
Niersteiner
Nietzschean
Nigerianize
niggardness
niggerality
nigger brown
nigger cloth
nigger goose
nigger-stick
night and day
night-attire
night bomber
nightcapped
night-cellar
nightclubby
night effect
night-flower
night flying
nightgowned
night-herder
nightingale
nightmarish
night monkey

night-office
night parrot
night riding
night school
night-season
night-singer
night vision
night-walker
night-worker
nighty-night
nigrescence
nihilianism
nihil obstat
nikethamide
Nikkei index
Nile monitor
Nilo-Hamitic
Nilo-Saharan
Nimzo–Indian
Nimzowitsch
nine-to-fiver
ninety-three
Ningre Tongo
ninny-hammer
nipfarthing
nip in the bud
nirosatable
nitrate bath
nitric oxide
nitridation
nitrifiable
nitro-aerial
nitro-cotton
nitrogenase
nitrogenate
nitrogenize
nitrogenous
nitro-powder
nitrosamine
nitrosation
nitrous acid
nitty-gritty
noble liquid
noble-minded
noble savage
nobody's fool
nocardiosis
nociceptive
noctilucent
noctilucous
noctivagant
noctivagous
nocturnally
no fewer than
noise factor
noise filter
noiselessly
noisomeness
nolle-prosse
nomadically
nom de guerre
nomenclator

nomen dubium
nominatival
nomogenesis
nomographer
nomographic
nomological
noms de plume
nonagesimal
non-allergic
non-American
nonapeptide
non-apparent
non-attached
non-believer
non-Catholic
nonchalance
non-clerical
non-clinical
non-delivery
nondescript
non-election
non-elective
non-electric
nonentities
nonentitous
none the less
nonetheless
non-European
non-existent
non-existing
nonfeasance
non-invasive
non-linearly
non-literary
non-literate
non-magnetic
non-material
non-metallic
non-militant
non-military
non-negative
non-partisan
non-periodic
non-personal
non-physical
nonplussing
non-positive
non possumus
non-pressure
non-printing
non-provided
non-randomly
non-rational
non-reducing
non-resident
non-secretor
non-sensible
nonsensical
non-sequence
non sequitur
non-sexually
non-solvency

non-specific	nothing like	nuncupative	obscenities	odorousness
non-standard	nothingness	nuncupatory	obscuration	ods bodikins
non-syllabic	nothing to it	nundination	obscurement	odynophagia
non-thematic	nothosaurus	nun's veiling	obscureness	oecumenical
non-tropical	notice-board	nuptial mass	obscurities	oenological
non-unionist	noticeboard	Nuremberger	obsecration	oenophilist
non-unionize	notice paper	nurse-mother	observantly	oesophageal
non-vascular	notionalist	nursery word	observation	oestrogenic
non-verbally	not miss much	nurse-tender	observative	oestruation
non-violence	not much chop	nursing home	observatory	of a lifetime
non-volatile	not much in it	nurtureless	observingly	of all others
nook-shotten	notochordal	nutmeg-apple	obsessional	of all people
Nootka lupin	not one's line	nutmeg liver	obsessively	of all things
nordmarkite	notoriously	nutmeg melon	obsidianite	of an age with
Norfolk pine	not quite her	Nutmeg State	obsignation	of an evening
Norfolk reed	not up to much	nutrimental	obsignatory	of a suit with
normal fault	nought worth	nutritional	obsolescent	offbeatness
normalizing	noumenalism	nutritively	obstetrical	off-Broadway
Normanesque	noumenalist	nychthemera	obstinately	off-diagonal
Norman Saxon	noumenality	nyctinastic	obstination	offenceless
normatively	nourishable	nyctitropic	obstipation	offensively
normativism	nourishment	nyctophobia	obstriction	offertories
normativist	nouveau poor	nyctophonia	obstruction	offhandedly
normativity	nouvellette	Nymphenburg	obstructive	office block
North Africa	Nova Scotian	nympholepsy	obtemperate	office found
North Briton	Novatianism	nymphomania	obtenebrate	office hours
north by east	Novationist	nymphomanic	obtestation	office-house
north-easter	novelettish	oarsmanship	obtrusively	office party
northeaster	novelettist	oatmeal mush	obumbration	officerless
northerlies	Novemberish	oatmeal soap	obviousness	officerlike
northernism	now and again	obediential	Occam's razor	officership
northernize	nowhere near	obedientiar	occultation	officialdom
Northern Spy	nowhereness	obfuscation	occult blood	officialese
northlander	noxiousness	obfuscatory	occupancies	officialise
North Riding	noxious weed	object-glass	oceanariums	officialism
northwardly	nuclear atom	objectified	ocean stream	officiality
north-wester	nuclear bomb	objectifier	ochlocratic	officialize
northwester	nuclear club	objectifies	ochlophobia	officiation
Norway maple	nuclear-free	objectional	ochlophobic	officinally
no-score draw	nuclear fuel	objectivate	octadecanol	officiously
nose-glasses	nuclear pile	objectively	octagonally	off-islander
nose-nippers	nucleic acid	objectivise	octahedrite	off-licensed
nosographic	nucleolated	objectivism	octahedrons	off-licensee
nosological	nucleolinus	objectivist	octapeptide	off one's base
Nostradamic	nucleophile	objectivity	octave flute	off one's feed
Nostradamus	nucleoplasm	objectivize	octennially	off one's feet
no such thing	nucleosomal	object of art	octillionth	off one's game
not a bit of it	*nuée ardente*	object-world	octodecimos	off one's head
notableness	null and void	objet de luxe	octopartite	off one's oats
not a patch on	nullibicity	objet trouvé	octuplicate	offscouring
notaphilist	nullifidian	objurgation	oculogravic	offset litho
not a sausage	nulliparity	objurgative	odds and bobs	off the hooks
notationist	nulliparous	objurgatory	odds and ends	off the latch
not bat an eye	number board	oblationary	odds and sods	off the point
not care a fig	number-cloth	obligedness	odontoblast	off the press
notch effect	number opera	obliqueness	odontogenic	off the rails
notch filter	number plate	obliquitous	odontophore	off-the-shelf
not counting	numbers game	obliterator	odoriferant	off the track
note-cluster	numerically	oblivionize	odoriferous	off the watch
note-shaving	numismatics	obliviously	odorimetric	offuscation
not give a sod	numismatist	obnoxiously	odoriphoric	of good cheer
nothing in it	nuncupation	obsceneness	odorivector	of many words

of necessity
of no account
of the moment
of the name of
oillessness
oil of cloves
oil painting
oil platform
oil province
Old Believer
Old Catholic
Old Covenant
old identity
old-maidenly
Old Man River
old offender
Old Prussian
old religion
old retainer
old-spelling
old-standing
old Thirteen
old-womanish
old-womanism
old-worldish
oleographic
olfactorily
olfactorium
olfactronic
oligandrous
oligarchies
oligarchist
oligarchize
oligochaete
oligohaline
oligolectic
oligomerize
oligomerous
oligomictic
oligopolies
oligopolist
oligotrophy
oligotropic
olivary body
olive branch
olive button
olive-shaped
olive thrush
olla podrida
Olympianism
Olympic-size
ombrogenous
ombudswoman
ominousness
ommatophore
omni-antenna
omnibus book
omnifarious
omnificence
omniformity
omnilateral
omnilingual

omnipatient
omnipotence
omnipresent
omniscience
omnisciency
omphalocele
omphalotomy
on account of
onagraceous
on a sixpence
once or twice
onchocercal
on cloud nine
oncogenesis
oncological
one argument
one-coloured
one-downness
onefoldness
one-handedly
one in the eye
oneirocracy
oneiromancy
onerousness
one's own kind
one-storeyed
one's wits' end
on every hand
ongoingness
on horseback
onion-maggot
onion-twitch
on its merits
on no account
onomasticon
onomatology
on one's guard
on one's hands
on one's heels
on one's plate
on one's way in
on penalty of
on principle
on probation
on shipboard
on that score
on the back of
on the batter
on the bottle
on the bounce
on the button
on the carpet
on the chance
on the edge of
on the face of
on the fiddle
on the fuddle
on the ground
on the moment
on the parish
on the part of
on the pounce

on the square
on the stocks
on the street
on the stroke
on the view of
on the volley
on the wamble
on the way out
on this score
ontogenesis
ontogenetic
ontological
onychomancy
o'nyong-nyong
opalescence
open-and-shut
open circuit
open cluster
open college
open harmony
open-hearted
open housing
opening time
open-mouthed
open slather
open society
open texture
open the ball
open verdict
operability
operas buffa
operational
operatively
operculated
operoseness
ophicalcite
ophiologist
ophitically
opinionated
opinionator
opinionless
opinion poll
opobalsamum
opossum wood
opportunely
opportunism
opportunist
opportunity
opposedness
opposite sex
opprobriate
opprobrious
oppugnation
optical axis
optical disc
optical disk
optical flat
optical path
optic pencil
optic tectum
optionality
optionalize

opto-coupler
optokinetic
optometrist
oracle bones
oracularity
oraculously
oral history
oral society
orange grass
orange juice
Orange Lodge
orange pekoe
orange stick
orange-tawny
orange thorn
orang-outang
oratorially
orbicularis
orbicularly
orbiculated
Orcagnesque
orchestrate
orchestrina
orchestrion
orchidacity
orchid house
orchidology
orchidopexy
orchidotomy
orchiectomy
orderedness
ordered pair
orderliness
orderly book
orderly room
order to view
ordinary ray
ordnance map
Ordnance map
Oregon cedar
Oregon grape
organ-blower
organ-cactus
organically
organic soil
organisable
organistrum
organizable
organogenic
organonomic
organoscopy
organ-screen
orgiastical
oriel window
orientalise
orientalism
orientalist
orientality
orientalize
Oriental Jew
oriental rug
orientation

Origenistic
originality
original sin
origination
originative
Orion's hound
Orkney sheep
Orleanistic
ornamentist
ornithology
ornithopter
ornithosaur
orofacially
or otherwise
orphan virus
orris-powder
or something
orthocentre
ortho-cousin
orthodigita
orthodontia
orthodontic
orthodoxian
orthodoxies
orthodoxism
orthodoxist
orthodromic
orthoepical
orthogneiss
orthography
orthohelium
orthologous
orthometric
orthonormal
orthopaedic
orthophonic
orthophoria
orthophoric
orthophyric
orthopnoeic
orthopraxis
orthopteran
Orthopteron
orthoscopic
orthostatic
orthostichy
orthotropal
orthotropic
Osage orange
oscillating
oscillation
oscillatory
oscillogram
osmiophilic
osmotically
osmund royal
ostensively
ostensories
ostentation
osteoclasia
osteologist
osteopathic

osteophytic	outwardness	overpayment	oyster-grass	pair of steps
ostracoderm	ovariectomy	overpeopled	oyster-knife	pair of tongs
ostreaceous	oven-to-table	overpicture	oyster-piece	pair-skating
ostrich farm	over a barrel	overprecise	oyster-plant	palace guard
ostrich-fern	over a bottle	overproduce	oyster roast	palace hotel
ostrich-like	overachieve	overprotect	oyster-shell	palace style
Ostrogothic	over against	overreacher	oyster-tongs	palacewards
otherwheres	over and over	oversailing	oyster white	palaearctic
otherwhiles	overanxiety	oversparred	oyster-woman	Palaearctic
otitis media	overanxious	overspecify	ozoniferous	palaeofield
ototoxicity	overarching	oversteepen	ozonization	palaeoplain
out and about	overbalance	overstretch	ozonometric	palaeoslope
out-and-outer	overballast	overstudied	ozonoscopic	palaeosolic
out at elbows	overbearing	overstudies	ozonosphere	palaeothere
outbreathed	overblanket	overstuffed	Pacchionian	palagonitic
outbreeding	overbreathe	overtakable	pace-setting	palais glide
outbuilding	overburthen	overtedious	pachymeninx	Palais Royal
outcropping	overcareful	over the hill	pachysandra	palantypist
outdistance	overcasting	over the hump	pacifically	palato-velar
outdoorness	overcaution	over the moon	pacificator	palefrenier
outdoorsman	overchecked	over the odds	Pacific Time	Palestinian
outer planet	overclamour	overthought	pacifyingly	palindromic
outer suburb	overclosely	overthrowal	packability	palingenesy
outfighting	overclosure	overthrower	packageable	palmate newt
outflourish	overcoating	overtime ban	package deal	palmatiform
outjockeyed	overcomable	overtorture	package show	palmatisect
outline plan	overconcern	overtrample	package tour	palm-cabbage
out of action	overcorrect	overviolent	pack and peel	palmiferous
out of bounds	overcunning	overvoltage	packed cells	palm warbler
out of breath	over-curious	overweening	packed lunch	palpability
out of danger	overcurious	overwhelmer	packetarian	palpiferous
out of favour	overcurrent	overwilling	packing case	palpigerous
out of humour	overdevelop	overwrought	paddle board	palpitation
out of livery	overdraught	overzealous	paddle wheel	Palsgravine
out of period	overdryness	oviparously	paddock-hair	palynomorph
out of pocket	overeagerly	ovipositing	paddock-pipe	pampas grass
out of repair	overearnest	oviposition	Paddy Wester	pamphletary
out of season	overeducate	ovuliferous	paediatrics	pamphleteer
out of square	overexploit	oxalacetate	paediatrist	pamphleting
out-of-Stater	overfatigue	oxaloacetic	paedication	pamphletize
out of temper	overflowing	oxamniquine	paedodontic	pampiniform
out of the ark	overforward	oxazolidine	paedogamous	panagraphic
out of the red	overfraught	ox-eye tarpon	paedophilia	pan-American
out of the way	overfreight	Oxford cloth	paedophilic	pan-Anglican
out-of-towner	overgarment	Oxford frame	paedotrophy	Panathenaea
outposition	overglazing	Oxford Group	pageant-play	Panathenaic
outquencher	overgrazing	Oxford ochre	pageantries	pancake-bell
outriggered	overhanging	Oxford shirt	page printer	pancake coil
outside edge	overhastily	oxidability	pagoda stone	pancake race
outside lane	over-indulge	oxidational	pain barrier	pancake roll
outside line	overindulge	oxidatively	painfulness	Panchen Lama
outside loop	overknowing	oxidization	painkilling	pancratiast
outsideness	overlap nail	oxycephalic	painstaking	pancreatize
outsiderdom	overlapping	oxychloride	paintballer	pancultural
outsiderish	overlargely	oxygenation	paint-bridge	pancuronium
outsiderism	overlenient	oxygen lance	painted lady	pandean pipe
outside seat	overliberal	oxy-hydrogen	paint roller	pandemoniac
outsizeness	overlightly	oxyrhynchus	pair bonding	pandemonium
outsourcing	overmastery	oxysulphide	pairing-call	pandiagonal
outspokenly	overmeasure	oxytocinase	pair of cards	pandiatonic
outstanding	overnighter	oyster-brood	pair of hands	Pandora's box
outward form	overpartial	oyster drill	pair of stays	panduriform

panegyrical
panel beater
panel doctor
panel heater
panentheism
panentheist
pan-European
pangeometry
pan-Germanic
Panglossian
Panglossism
Panhellenic
panic attack
panic button
panic buying
panic-monger
panicmonger
panic-struck
paniculated
Panislamism
panne velvet
pannier tank
panographic
Panomphaean
pan-Orthodox
panpsychism
panpsychist
Panslavonic
pansophical
panspermism
pantaletted
pantalettes
pantalooned
Panthalassa
pantheistic
pantheology
panther-lily
panther piss
pantie-waist
pantile-lath
pantisocrat
Pantocrator
pantography
pantologist
pantometric
pantomimist
pantomogram
pantoscopic
pantothenic
pan-tropical
pants rabbit
pan-Turanian
panty girdle
Papal States
papal system
Papal Zouave
paperbacked
paper-cutter
paper flower
paper-hanger
paperhanger
paperknives

papermaking
paper napkin
paper-pusher
paper ribbon
paperweight
paper window
papier mâché
papilledema
papilliform
papillomata
papillosity
papoose-root
papovavirus
papyraceous
papyrograph
parabolanus
parabolical
Paracelsian
Paracelsist
paracentral
paracentric
paracetamol
parachordal
parachutage
parachutist
paracrystal
paradidymal
paradidymis
paradisical
paradoxical
paraffin oil
paraffin wax
paragastric
paragenesis
paragenetic
paragliding
paragogical
paragrapher
paragraphia
paragraphic
parahormone
paraldehyde
paraleipsis
parallactic
paralleling
parallelise
parallelism
parallelist
parallelity
parallelize
paralogical
Paralympics
paramedical
parametrial
parametrise
parametrium
parametrize
paramoecium
paramorphic
paramountcy
paramountly
paranucleus

paraparesis
parapet line
parapet wall
paraphernal
paraphiliac
paraphraser
paraphrasis
paraphrenia
paraphrenic
paraprotein
parapsychic
parasailing
parascender
parascience
paraselenae
parasitical
parasol pine
parasternal
parasuicide
parathecium
parathyroid
para-transit
paratrooper
paratrophic
paratyphoid
parcel paper
parcel shelf
parchedness
parchmenter
pare and burn
par éminence
parenchymal
parentalism
parentality
parent–child
parentcraft
parentheses
parenthesis
parenthetic
parenticide
parent-in-law
paresthesia
paretically
parfocality
parfocalize
parheliacal
parietal eye
paripinnate
parish altar
parish clerk
parishioner
Parisianism
Parisianize
parity check
parity digit
park-and-ride
parking deck
parking disc
parking lamp
park oneself
parlour game
parlour-maid

parlourmaid
parlour palm
parlousness
Parma violet
Parmenidean
parochially
parodically
parole board
paromomycin
paronomasia
paroophoron
parotid duct
parotiditis
paroxytonic
parquet work
parrot fever
parrot-finch
parrot-house
parrot mouth
parrot's bill
parrot snake
parrot tulip
parsley fern
parsley frog
parsleyworm
parson's nose
parson's-week
part company
parthenogen
partialness
partial tone
partial veil
partibility
participant
participate
participial
particolour
particulate
parting shot
parting tool
partitional
partitioned
partitioner
partitively
partnerless
partnership
part-payment
part-playing
part-singing
parturiency
parturition
part-writing
party-pooper
party popper
party spirit
party ticket
parvalbumin
parvanimity
paschal lamb
Paschaltide
Paschen body
pas de basque

pas de cheval
pasigraphic
passacaglia
passacaille
passage-bird
passage-boat
passage-hawk
passage-room
passage tomb
passage-work
pass a remark
pass current
passecaille
Passe Colmar
passengered
passibility
passing-bell
passingness
passing note
passing shot
passing show
passion-dock
passionless
passion play
Passiontide
Passion-tide
passion vine
Passion Week
passivation
passiveness
pass the buck
pass through
paste-bodied
pasteurella
pasteurizer
past oneself
pastophorus
pastoralism
pastoralist
pastorality
pastoralize
past perfect
past redress
pastureland
pataphysics
patchoulied
patch pocket
patchworker
pâte de verre
patelliform
patent house
patent-right
patent still
paternalism
paternalist
paternality
paternoster
pâte-sur-pâte
path-breaker
pathogenesy
pathogenous
pathognomic

pathography
pathologist
patienthood
patientless
patient Lucy
patientness
Patjitanian
patriarchal
patriarchic
patricianly
patrilineal
patrilinear
patrimonial
patrimonies
patriotical
Patriots' Day
patristical
patrologies
patrologist
patrol wagon
patronizing
patron saint
patroonship
patter flash
pattern-bomb
pattern book
pattern card
patternless
pattern room
patteroller
paucispiral
Paul–Bunnell
Paulinistic
Paul's betony
paunchiness
pauselessly
paving stone
pawnbrokery
pawnbroking
paxilliform
pay envelope
paying guest
paymistress
pay one's dues
pay one's scot
peace-keeper
peacekeeper
peacemaking
peacemonger
peace pledge
peach brandy
peacock blue
peacock-iris
peacock moth
pea-flowered
peak shaving
Peano axioms
peanut valve
pearl barley
pearl button
pearlescent
pearl-fisher

pearl millet
pearl mussel
pearl-oyster
pearl-powder
pearl-sinter
Pearly Gates
pearly queen
Pearly Queen
peasantries
pebble grain
pebble stone
pebble weave
peccability
peccadillos
peccaminous
peckishness
Peck's bad boy
pectinately
pectination
pectization
pectoral fin
peculiarism
peculiarity
peculiarize
pecuniarily
pecuniosity
pedagogical
pedagoguery
pedagoguish
pedagoguism
pedal origin
pedal-pusher
pedanticism
pedantocrat
pedestalled
pedestal mat
pedicellate
pediculated
pediculosis
pediocratic
pedogenesis
pedogenetic
pedological
pedunculate
peelability
peevishness
Pekingology
Peking opera
Peking robin
Pelagianism
Pelagianize
pelagically
pelargonium
Pelican flag
pellucidity
pelmatozoan
pelophilous
pelotherapy
Pelton wheel
pelvic floor
penalty area
penalty card

penalty goal
penalty kick
penalty line
penalty pass
penalty rate
penalty spot
pencil cedar
pencil skirt
pencil-stone
pending tray
pendulosity
pendulously
pendulum saw
penetralium
penetrating
penetration
penetrative
penguin suit
penicillate
penicillium
penicilloic
peninsulate
penitential
penniferous
pennilessly
penninerved
penniveined
penny-a-liner
penny arcade
penny loafer
pennyweight
penny-wisdom
penological
pen recorder
Penrose tile
pensionable
pensionably
pension book
pension fund
pensionless
pension plan
pensiveness
pentacyclic
pentadactyl
pentadecane
pentagamist
Pentagonese
Pentagonian
pentagonoid
pentagynous
pentahedral
pentahedron
pentahydric
pentamerism
pentamerous
pentamidine
pentandrous
pentangular
pentastomid
pentathlete
pentavalent
pentazocine

pentaconter
pentecostal
Pentecostal
pentecostys
penthemimer
pentlandite
penultimate
penuriously
people power
people's army
people's park
pepper dulse
pepper-grass
pepperiness
pepperminty
pepper-sauce
pepper steak
peptic gland
peptic ulcer
peptide bond
peptidergic
peptization
peracaridan
perambulate
perceivable
perceivance
perceptible
perceptibly
perchlorate
perchloride
percipience
percipiency
percolation
percolative
perduellion
perduration
peregrinate
peregrinity
perennation
perennially
perequation
perequitate
perestroika
perfectedly
perfectible
perfectness
perfervidly
perfoliated
perforation
perforative
performable
performance
perfumeless
perfumeries
perfunction
perfunctory
Pergamenian
perhexiline
pericardiac
pericardial
pericardium
pericarpial

pericarpium
pericentric
perichaetia
periclinium
pericranium
peridotitic
perigenital
periglacial
Périgordian
Perigordine
Périgord pie
perinatally
perinephric
perineurium
perinuclear
periodicity
periodic law
periodogram
periodontal
periodontia
periodontic
period piece
perionychia
periostitis
peripatetic
peripherial
peripheries
periphrases
periphrasis
periplasmic
periscopism
perishingly
peristalith
peristalsis
peristaltic
perisystole
peritectoid
perithecium
peritoneums
peritonitic
peritonitis
peritrophic
peritubular
perlocution
perlustrate
permanently
permanganic
permeameter
permissible
permissibly
permutation
pernavigate
peroxidatic
peroxide ion
peroxisomal
perpetrator
perpetually
perpetuance
perpetuator
perplexedly
persecution
persecutive

persecutory
persecutrix
perseverant
perseverate
Persian blue
Persian lamb
Persian silk
persistence
persistency
persnickety
personal bar
personalise
personalism
personalist
personality
personalize
personal law
personation
personative
personified
personifier
personifies
personology
persorption
perspective
perspicuity
perspicuous
perspirable
persuadable
persuasible
persulphate
pertainings
pertainment
pertinacity
pertinently
perturbable
perturbancy
perturbator
perturbedly
pervadingly
pervagation
pervaporate
pervasively
pervertedly
pervertible
pervicacity
pessimistic
pestiferous
pestilently
pest officer
pestologist
petal collar
pet aversion
Peter's pence
Peter's penny
petiolulate
petitionary
petit-maître
petits fours
Petrarchism
Petrarchist
Petrarchize

petrescence
petrodollar
petrofabric
petrography
petrol gauge
petrologist
pettability
petticoated
pettifogged
pettifogger
pettishness
petty-minded
petty school
petty spurge
Petzval lens
Peyer's patch
Pfund series
phaenogamic
phaeochrome
phaeophytin
phaethontic
phagedaenic
phagocytise
phagocytize
phagocytose
phainopepla
phalangitis
phalanstery
phallically
phallocracy
phallotoxin
phanerozoic
Phantasiast
phantasmata
phantastica
phantom limb
phantom pain
phantomship
Pharaoh's ant
Pharaoh's rat
Pharisaical
Phariseeism
pharyngitis
phase change
phellogenic
pheneticist
phenetidine
phenindione
phenol resin
phenomenism
phenomenist
phenotyping
phenoxazine
philanderer
philatelism
philatelist
philhellene
phillipsite
philodendra
philodespot
philogynist
philologian

philologise
philologist
philologize
philomathic
philopatric
philosemite
philosopher
philosophic
phlebograph
phlegmatism
phlegmonoid
phlegmonous
phlorrhizin
phoenix-like
phonational
phonematics
phonemicist
phonemicity
phonemicize
phone number
phone phreak
phonestheme
phonetician
phoneticise
phoneticism
phoneticist
phoneticize
phonic motor
phonic wheel
phonofiddle
phonography
phonologist
phonometric
phonophobia
phonotactic
phosphatase
phosphatide
phosphatize
phosphazene
phosphonate
phosphonium
phosphorane
phosphorate
phosphoreal
phosphorial
phosphorise
phosphorite
phosphorize
phosphorous
photoaction
photoactive
photocopied
photocopier
photocopies
photoeffect
photoenzyme
photo finish
photography
photoinduce
photoionize
photoisomer
photolabile

photomatrix
photometric
photomosaic
photo-offset
photopathic
photoperiod
photophilic
photophobia
photophobic
photoproton
photoreduce
photoresist
photosensor
photosetter
photosphere
photostable
photostatic
photosystem
phototactic
phototrophy
phototropic
photovisual
phragmosome
phrasal verb
phrase-maker
phraseogram
phraseology
Phrygian cap
phthalazine
phthiriasis
phycocyanin
phycologist
phycomycete
phyllocarid
phylloclade
phyllomania
phylloplane
phyllotaxis
physiatrist
physicalism
physicalist
physicality
physicalize
physicianer
physicianly
physiocracy
physiognomy
physiognosy
physiolater
physiolatry
physiologer
physiologic
physogastry
physostegia
physostigma
phytoalexin
phytobezoar
phytochrome
phytography
phytologist
phytosterol
piacularity

pianissimos
piano-action
piano nobile
piano player
Piastraccia
piccalillis
pichiciegos
pickelhaube
picket-house
pick holes in
picking-belt
picking-fork
picking-hole
pick-up truck
Pickwickian
pick-your-own
picnic chair
picnic lunch
picnic plate
picnic races
picnic table
pictography
pictorially
picture book
picture card
picture-goer
pictureless
picture rail
picture show
picturesque
picture tube
picture-wire
piebaldness
piece-broker
piece of arse
piece of cake
piece of gold
piece of meat
piece of tail
piece of work
piece-worker
Piedmontese
piedmontite
pieds-à-terre
pied wagtail
pie in the sky
Pierced Nose
pietistical
piezometric
pigeon-berry
pigeon-chest
pigeon grass
pigeon-holer
pigeon-house
pigeon's milk
piggishness
pig-headedly
pig-ignorant
Pig Islander
pigmentless
pignoration
pigsticking

pig's whisper	pirouettist	plane-tabler	plastogamic	pleiomerous
piledriving	piscatology	planetarian	plastometer	pleiophylly
pilfer-proof	piscatorial	planetarium	plastometry	pleiotropic
pilgrim city	piscivorous	Planet Earth	plate armour	Pleistocene
pill and poll	pisha paysha	plane the way	plate camera	plenilunary
pillar clock	piss and wind	planetismal	plate-clutch	plenipotent
pillar drill	pissasphalt	planetoidal	plate girder	plenteously
pillar plate	piss-elegant	planetology	platen press	plentifully
pillar-stone	pistolgraph	planet-wheel	plate number	plenum space
pillow-block	piston corer	planigraphy	plate pewter	pleochroism
pillow cover	piston drill	planimetric	plate-powder	pleocytosis
pillow-fight	pistonphone	planisphere	plateresque	pleomorphic
pillow mound	piston-valve	planispiral	plateworker	plerematics
pill peddler	pit aperture	planktology	platformate	plessimeter
pill-popping	pit-bottomer	plankton net	Platforming	plessimetry
pilocarpine	Pitcairnese	planoconvex	platinotype	pleurodynia
piloerector	pitch accent	planogamete	Platonicism	pleurolysis
pilotaxitic	pitch and pay	planography	Platonistic	pliableness
pilot burner	pitch-and-run	plano-miller	platter-face	plinth block
pilot driver	pitchblende	planospiral	platykurtic	pliosaurian
pilot engine	pitch-circle	Plantagenet	platymerism	ploshchadka
pilot-jacket	pitched roof	plant-animal	platypellic	plotting rod
pilpulistic	pitcherfuls	plant-beetle	platyrrhine	plough-point
pimento dram	pitcher-like	plant-cutter	platyrrhiny	plough-press
pimento tree	pitch-kettle	plantership	platyscopic	ploughshare
pinacotheca	pitch length	plant-feeder	playability	plough-staff
pinch-bottle	pitch the woo	planthopper	play-actress	plough-stilt
pinch effect	piteousness	plantigrade	play clothes	plough-stock
pinch-hitter	pitifulness	plantocracy	player-coach	plough under
pinch-roller	pit membrane	plantswoman	player-piano	plucked wool
pinch-runner	piton hammer	plantswomen	play for time	plug-bayonet
pin-dropping	pitot-static	plasmablast	play forward	plug tobacco
pineal gland	pit-planting	plasmacytic	playfulness	plumb a track
pinealocyte	pittosporum	plasmalemma	playing card	plumb jordan
pine-bud moth	pituitaries	plasmalogen	play it by ear	plumigerous
pine warbler	placability	plasmapause	play of words	plummetless
piney tallow	placatingly	plasma probe	play on a word	plum-pockets
pinguescent	place-holder	plasma sheet	play one's ace	plumptitude
pink disease	place-hunter	plasma torch	play on words	plum pudding
pink gilding	place-kicker	plasminogen	play-reading	plumularian
pinking-iron	placelessly	plasmoblast	play-the-ball	plunderbund
pink-sterned	placentitis	plasmodesma	play the fool	plunge basin
pinnatisect	place of arms	plasmolysis	play the game	plunge-churn
pinnywinkle	placer sheep	plasmolytic	play the jack	plunger mute
pinocytosis	placket-hole	Plasmoquine	play the Jack	plunger-pump
pinocytotic	plagal close	plasmotomic	play therapy	pluralistic
Pinteresque	plage region	plaster cast	play the wild	pluralities
pin the rap on	plagiarizer	plasterless	play through	pluriparity
pioneership	plagioclase	plaster-like	playwriting	pluriparous
pionization	plagiostome	plasterwork	plea bargain	pluripotent
pipe-cleaner	plagiotropy	plastically	plead guilty	pluriserial
pipe of peace	plague-house	plastic arts	pleasantest	plurivalent
piperaceous	plain dealer	plasticator	pleasedness	pluri-valued
piperitious	plain-headed	plastic bomb	pleasurable	plush-copper
pipe-stapple	plain people	plastic clay	pleasurably	plush-stitch
pipe the side	Plain People	plasticized	pleasureful	plush-velvet
pipe tobacco	plain sawing	plasticizer	plebeianism	Plutarchian
pipistrelle	plain sewing	plasticware	plebeianize	plutarchies
piquantness	plain-spoken	plastic wood	plebiscitum	plutocratic
Pirani gauge	plaintively	plastimeter	plecopteran	plutography
pirate-perch	plain turkey	plastiqueur	plectognath	plutologist
piratically	plait-stitch	plastochron	plectonemic	plutonomist

pluviograph
pluviometer
Plymouth gin
Plymouth Hoe
pneumatical
pneumatique
pneumatosis
pneumaturia
pneumectomy
pneumococci
pneumograph
pneumolysis
pneumonitic
pneumonitis
pocket beach
pocket knife
pocket money
pocket-mouse
pocket-piece
pocket-plums
pocket Venus
pocket-watch
pococurante
poddy-dodger
podophyllin
podophyllum
Podsnappery
Podsnappian
poena sensus
poeticality
poetization
Poets' Corner
pogonophore
poikilocyte
Poincaré map
point-action
point charge
point defect
point-device
pointed arch
pointedness
point ground
pointillism
pointillist
pointlessly
point number
point of sale
point of view
point source
point spread
poison elder
poison-green
poisonously
poison-plant
poison sumac
pokahickory
poke pudding
poker school
poker-worked
Poland water
polar circle
polarimeter

polarimetry
polarisable
polariscope
polarizable
polar lights
polarograph
polar vector
pole-finding
polemically
polemoscope
pole-vaulter
police court
police force
police judge
policemanly
police novel
police state
police State
police wagon
policewoman
policewomen
policy wheel
poliorcetic
Polish manna
Politbureau
politically
politicking
polka-dotted
pollen brush
pollen count
pollen fever
pollen grain
pollen index
pollen-plate
pollinarium
pollination
polling card
pollutional
Polovetsian
poltergeist
poltroonery
poltroonish
polyacrylic
polyallomer
polyandrian
polyandrist
polyandrium
polyandrous
polyangular
polyblastic
polycarpous
polycentric
polychaetan
polychromic
polycratism
polycrystal
polyculture
polydactyly
polydentate
polyenergid
polygamical
polygenesis

polygenetic
polyglacial
polyglottal
polyglottic
polygonally
polygrapher
polygraphic
polyhaploid
polyhedroid
polyhedrons
polyhedrous
polyhistory
polylingual
polyloquent
polymastism
polymerizer
polymicrian
polymignite
polymitosis
polymitotic
polymodally
polymorphic
polynuclear
polyonymous
polypectomy
polypeptide
polyphagous
polyphonies
polyphonist
polyphonous
polypropene
polysomatic
polyspermic
polysporous
polystyrene
polytechnic
polyterpene
polythionic
polytonally
polytopical
polytrichum
polytrophic
polyvalence
polyversity
polyvoltine
poly-wrapped
pomatorhine
pomegranate
Pomeranchuk
pomfret-cake
pomiculture
pommel horse
pomological
Pompeian red
composities
compousness
ponasterone
pond-culture
pond dogwood
ponderation
ponderosity
ponderously

pons Varolii
pontificate
pontificial
pony express
pony service
pony-trekker
Ponzi scheme
poodle cloth
poodle-faker
pool cathode
pool-measure
pools coupon
poor priests
pop festival
pop in and out
poplar-borer
poppet-valve
poppy-colour
poppy mallow
popularizer
popularness
population I
porcelainic
porcellanic
porcupinish
pork butcher
pork-chopper
pork-knocker
pornography
pornophobic
poroplastic
porosimeter
porosimetry
porphobilin
porphyritic
porridge ice
porriginous
portability
portal crane
portal frame
portal strut
portamentos
Portastudio
Port du Salut
porterhouse
porter's beer
porter's knot
portiforium
portionable
portionally
portionless
Port Jackson
Portlandian
portlandite
portmanteau
port of entry
portraitist
portraiture
portrayable
portrayment
positive ray
positronium

posological
possessible
possibilism
possibilist
possibility
postabdomen
post-abortal
post-abortum
postal meter
postal order
Postal Union
post-and-beam
post and pair
post-and-rail
post-axially
post captain
postcentral
post-chariot
postclassic
post-clypeus
postcranial
postdiction
post-entries
posteriorly
poster paint
poster paper
post eventum
post-exilian
postfrontal
postglacial
post-meiotic
post-mineral
postmitotic
post-natally
postnatally
postnominal
post-nuclear
post-nuptial
postorbital
postpalatal
postponable
postponence
post-primary
post-puberal
post-tension
Post Toastie
postulation
postulatory
post-village
postvocalic
potableness
potamogeton
potato-apple
potato-balls
potato-bogle
potato bread
potato crisp
potato-eater
potato flour
potato mould
potato onion
potato patch

potato-plant	prairie coal	preconceive	prematurely	presphenoid
potato-salad	prairie cock	preconquest	prematurity	press agency
potato scone	prairie dock	preconsider	premedicant	press-button
potato straw	prairie hawk	pre-contract	premedicate	press-forged
pot cupboard	prairie rose	precoracoid	premeditate	press number
potentially	prairie soil	pre-critical	premenstrua	press office
potentiator	prairie wolf	predatorily	premiership	press of sail
potestative	prairie wool	predecessor	premium bond	press revise
pot-layering	praisefully	prediabetes	Premium Bond	pressure-jet
pot marigold	praise-house	prediabetic	premodifier	pressure pad
potteringly	pralidoxime	predicament	premonition	Prester John
potter's clay	prat-digging	predication	premonitory	prestigeful
potter's lead	prattlement	predicative	premultiply	prestigious
pottery clay	Praxitelean	predicatory	premunition	prestissimo
pottery tree	prayer bones	predictable	premunitory	prestressed
potting shed	prayerfully	predictably	preoccupant	presumingly
potwalloper	prayer-group	predilected	preoccupied	presumption
pot-washings	prayer niche	prediluvian	preoccupies	presumptive
pot-wrestler	prayer plant	prediscover	pre-ordinate	presupposal
poule de luxe	prayer shawl	predoctoral	preparation	presynaptic
poult-de-soie	prayer-stick	predominant	preparative	presystolic
poultryless	prayer wheel	predominate	preparatory	prêt-à-porter
pound-breach	pray in aid of	predynastic	prepatellar	pretaxation
pound covert	praying band	pre-election	pre-planning	pre-teenager
pounded meat	praying-desk	pre-electric	prepollency	pretencedly
pound-keeper	preacheress	pre-eminence	pre-position	pretendedly
poundmaster	preacher-man	pre-eminency	preposition	pretentious
pound-weight	preachified	pre-emphasis	prepositive	pretergress
pour scorn on	preachifies	pre-emptible	prepotently	preterhuman
poverty line	preachiness	pre-existent	pre-prandial	preterition
poverty trap	pre-acquaint	pre-existing	preprandial	preteritive
powder-chest	pre-adamitic	pre-exposure	pre-pubertal	preterlegal
powder flask	preadaptive	prefatorial	prepubertal	preterminal
powder-house	preadmonish	prefatorily	prepunctual	pretty penny
powderiness	preambulary	prefectoral	pre-rational	prettyprint
powder paint	preambulate	prefectship	pre-register	prevalently
powder slope	pre-announce	prefectural	prerogative	prevaricate
power-broker	preaspirate	prefigurate	pre-Romantic	preventable
power centre	pre-assemble	prefinished	presagingly	preventible
power factor	pre-assembly	prefixation	presanctify	previsional
Powerformer	preaudience	pre-Freudian	presbycusis	price buster
power hitter	pre-bookable	pregalactic	presbyteral	price-fixing
powerlessly	Precambrian	pregnancies	prescapular	price leader
powerlifter	precatively	pre-graduate	pre-schooler	pricelessly
power-loader	precautious	prehensible	preschooler	price system
power outage	precedented	prehistoric	presciently	prickle-back
power-rating	precedently	pre-ignition	pre-selector	prickle-cell
power series	precellence	pre-indicate	preselector	prickliness
power shovel	precellular	pre-intimate	presenility	prickly heat
power stroke	preceptoral	pre-invasive	presentable	prickly pear
power supply	preceptress	preiotation	presentably	prick-stitch
Poynings' Law	precinctual	prejudicate	present arms	prick-sucker
practicable	precipitant	pre-judicial	pre-sentence	prick-teaser
practicably	precipitate	prejudicial	presentiate	pride and joy
practically	precipitous	prelanguage	presentient	pride of life
practice bar	preciseness	prelateship	presentment	Pride's Purge
Praenestine	precisional	prelibation	presentness	priestcraft
praepositor	preclinical	preliminary	preservable	priest-shire
praepositus	precognosce	prelimitate	preserve jar	priest's hole
praetorship	pre-coitally	preliteracy	presettable	prima donnas
pragmatical	precoitally	preliterate	presocratic	primal horde
pragmatizer	precompress	prelusively	pre-Socratic	primal scene

primariness
primary coil
primary wave
primateship
primatology
primigenial
primigravid
priming-hole
priming-iron
priming pump
priming-wire
primiparity
primiparous
primitively
primitivism
primitivist
primitivity
primitivize
primogenial
primo tenore
Primrose Day
primus motor
princeliest
prince royal
Prince Royal
prince's pine
princessdom
principally
printergram
printer's pie
printing out
printmaking
print-script
print-seller
prior charge
Priscillian
prismatical
prison-fever
prison-house
private army
private bank
private bill
private life
private line
privateness
private room
private view
private wire
privatistic
privatively
prize-giving
prize-master
prizewinner
prizeworthy
proactively
proactivity
pro-attitude
probabilify
probabilism
probabilist
probability
probasidium

probational
probationer
probatively
probingness
problematic
problemless
proboscidal
proboscides
procaryotic
processable
process heat
process lens
process-paid
process shot
prochain ami
prochronism
procidentia
proclaim war
proconsular
procreation
procreative
Procrustean
proctodaeal
proctodaeum
proctologic
proctorship
proctoscope
proctoscopy
procuration
procurative
procuratory
procuratrix
procurement
procyclical
prodelision
prodigality
prodigalize
prodigal son
prodigiosin
prodromatic
produceable
producer gas
productress
pro-European
profanation
profaneness
profanities
professedly
proficiency
profile drag
profile shot
profiterole
profoundest
profuseness
progenerate
progenitive
progenitrix
progeniture
progeny test
progestagen
progestogen
proglottids

prognathism
prognathous
programming
progression
progressist
progressive
prohibiting
prohibition
prohibitive
prohibitory
projectable
projectress
projicience
prokaryotic
prolateness
prolegomena
proleptical
proletarian
proletariat
proliferate
proliferous
prolificacy
prolificate
prolificity
proligerous
prolocution
prologuizer
prolongable
prolongedly
prolongment
promeristem
prominently
promiscuity
promiscuous
promise well
promisingly
promotional
promptitude
prompt table
promulgator
promycelial
promycelium
pronatalism
pronatalist
prooestrous
proof-reader
proofreader
proof spirit
proof strain
proof stress
proof theory
propafenone
propagandic
propagation
propagative
propagatrix
propamidine
propargylic
propatagial
propatagium
propellable
proper pride

proper psalm
property man
property tax
prop forward
prophesying
prophethood
prophetical
prophetless
prophetship
prophylaxis
propinquant
propinquate
propinquity
propinquous
propitiable
propitiator
propneustic
proposition
propranolol
propriation
proprietage
proprietary
proprieties
proprietory
proprietous
proprietrix
propugnator
propylidene
proquaestor
prorogation
prosaically
prosaicness
pros and cons
prosauropod
prosceniums
prosecution
prosecutive
prosecutrix
proselytess
proselytise
proselytism
proselytist
proselytize
proseminary
prosenchyma
prose poetry
prosiliency
prosiopesis
prosobranch
prosodiacal
prosopalgia
prospection
prospective
prostatitis
prosthetics
prosthetist
prostitutor
prostration
prostrative
protagonism
protagonist
Protagorean

protandrous
protanomaly
proteaceous
protectable
protectible
protectoral
protectress
protectrice
proteinosis
proteinuria
proteinuric
proteolipid
proteolysis
proteolytic
proterandry
proterogyny
Proterozoic
protestator
protest flag
protest vote
Protevangel
prothalamia
prothallial
prothallium
prothalloid
prothetelic
prothetical
prothoracic
prothrombin
protocercal
protocolist
protocolize
protocolled
protodeacon
protofibril
protogalaxy
protogynous
protolithic
protomartyr
protomerite
protonation
protonotary
protopathic
protopectin
protophilic
protoplanet
protopodite
protopterus
protoscolex
protostelic
protothetic
prototrophy
prototropic
prototyping
protractile
protraction
protrusible
protuberant
protuberate
provability
provenanced
provenience

providently
provinciate
Provins rose
provisional
provisioner
provisorily
provocation
provocative
provocatory
provokement
provokingly
provostship
proximately
proximation
prudentness
prudishness
Prufrockian
pruniferous
pruning hook
pruriginous
Prussianism
Prussianist
Prussianize
prussic acid
psalm-singer
psammophile
psammophyte
psephocracy
pseudergate
pseudocidal
pseudo-cleft
pseudocroup
pseudocubic
pseudo-event
pseudofovea
pseudograph
pseudokarst
pseudologer
pseudologia
pseudomonad
pseudomonas
pseudomorph
pseudonymic
pseudopodia
pseudoprime
pseudoscope
pseudoscopy
pseudostome
psilomelane
psionically
psittacosis
psittacotic
psophometer
psychagogic
psychagogue
psychedelia
psychedelic
psyche-glass
psychiatric
psychically
psychodrama
psychogenic

psychograph
psychologic
psycholytic
psychomancy
psychometer
psychometry
psychomotor
psychopathy
psychoplasm
psychostasy
psychotogen
pteridology
pterobranch
pterodactyl
pteropodous
ptilopaedic
ptochocracy
publicanism
publication
publicatory
public baths
public enemy
public house
publicistic
public libel
public order
public purse
public woman
public works
public wrong
publishable
publishment
puck carrier
puckishness
pudding face
pudding-head
pudding-time
pudding-wife
pudibundery
puerileness
puerilities
Puerto Rican
puff and blow
pulchritude
pull a stroke
pulley-block
pulley-wheel
pull leather
pull one's pud
pull strings
pull the plug
pull through
pullulation
pull up short
pulp-capping
pulpitarian
pulpousness
pulsatility
pulsational
pulveration
pulverulent
pumice stone

pumpability
pumpkin-head
pumpkin pine
pumpkinseed
pump-priming
pump-turbine
punch biopsy
punched card
punched tape
Punchinello
punching bag
punch-marked
punctilious
punctuality
punctuation
punctuative
punctulated
punishingly
punto in aria
pupariation
pupillarity
pupillogram
pupil-master
puppet-maker
puppet state
puppet-valve
puppy walker
Purbeck beds
purchasable
purchase tax
purdah glass
purdah party
purdah woman
pure and pute
pure-blooded
pure culture
pure science
purgatorial
purgatorian
purgatories
purging flax
purificator
puritanical
purple finch
purple gland
purple heart
purpleheart
purple heron
purple laver
purple osier
purple patch
purple prose
purple-shell
purportedly
purportless
purposeless
purpose-like
purpose-made
purposively
purposivism
purposivist
purpresture

purse-bearer
purse-cutter
purse-seiner
purse-string
pursiveness
pursuit race
Puseyitical
pushability
push-and-pull
push-bicycle
push-cyclist
pushfulness
pushingness
push moraine
push one's way
pushover try
push-process
push through
pussy-cat bow
pussy-footed
pussyfooter
pussy willow
pustulation
put a crimp in
put a match to
put in charge
put in motion
put in pledge
put in the pin
put it across
put on notice
put on the dog
put on weight
putrefiable
putrescence
putrescency
putrescible
putteringly
put the bee on
put the lid on
put the low to
put to flight
put together
put to rights
put to school
putty-colour
putty powder
put up a black
puzzle-pated
pyarthrosis
pycniospore
pycnometric
pyelography
pyeloplasty
pygmy glider
pygmy possum
pyjama party
pyknoleptic
pylorectomy
pylorospasm
pyramidally
pyramidated

pyramidical
pyramid-like
pyramid-rest
pyramid-spot
pyramid-text
pyramidwise
pyranometer
pyrargyrite
pyrobitumen
pyroclastic
pyrogallate
pyrogenetic
pyrographic
pyrogravure
pyrological
pyrophanite
pyrophorous
pyrotechnic
pyroxenitic
pyrrole ring
pyrrolidine
pyrrolidone
pyruvic acid
Pythagorean
pythagorise
pythagorize
Pythonesque
quacksalver
quadrangled
quadraphony
quadrathlon
quadratical
quadrennial
quadrennium
quadricycle
quadrillion
quadrumanal
quadrupedal
quadruplane
quadrupolar
quaestorial
quaestorian
quail-thrush
quaiss kitir
Quaker brown
Quakerishly
Quaker State
qualifiable
qualifiedly
qualitative
qualityless
quality mark
quality time
quantal part
quantum jump
quantum leap
quarrelling
quarrelsome
quarterback
quarter-bell
quarter-boat
quarter-boot

quarter-bred	quinquereme	radio beacon	Ranger Guide	read through
quarterdeck	quinquesect	radiocarbon	ranging-pole	re-advertise
quarter-evil	quinternion	radio-dating	Rangoon bean	readvertise
quarter-hour	quintillion	radio energy	rank and file	ready-to-wear
quarter-jack	quiritarian	radio galaxy	ransom money	ready-witted
quarter-Jack	quislingism	radiography	rant and rave	reafference
quarterland	quislingist	radio-iodine	rapaciously	Reaganesque
quarterlies	quislingite	radiolarian	rapier dance	Reaganomics
quarter-line	quitch-grass	radiolarite	rapping iron	reaggregate
quarter-moon	quit claim to	radioligand	rapscallion	real account
quarter note	quiveringly	radiolocate	rapturously	real essence
quarter peal	quizzically	radiologist	rarefaction	realignment
quarter pole	quodlibetal	radiolucent	rarefactive	realisation
quarter-race	quodlibetic	radiometric	rascalities	realization
quarter-tone	quotability	radio-opaque	Raschig ring	realizingly
quarter-wave	quota method	radiopacity	raspberries	re-allotment
quarter-wind	quota sample	radiophonic	Rasputinism	reallotment
quarto paper	quota system	radioscopic	Rastafarian	reallotting
quartz clock	quotational	radiovision	Rastafarism	really truly
quartz glass	quotidianly	raffishness	rataplanned	real of eight
quartz watch	rabbet plane	raggamuffin	ratatouille	realpolitik
quaveringly	rabbinistic	ragged right	rateability	reanimation
queen closer	rabbit berry	ragged robin	rate-capping	reapportion
queen hornet	rabbit brush	ragged staff	rathskeller	reappraisal
queenliness	rabbit drive	rag-merchant	ratiocinate	rear admiral
queen mother	rabbit fever	rah-rah skirt	rationalise	rear echelon
Queen's bench	rabbit-proof	railing-line	rationalism	rear its head
Queen's Bench	rabbit punch	railroad tie	rationalist	reascension
queen's conch	rabbit's foot	railwayless	rationality	reassertion
Queen's Guide	rabbit tooth	railway time	rationalize	reassociate
Queen's Scout	Rabelaisian	railway yard	rationative	reassurance
queen-stitch	race glasses	rainbow-bird	ration sheep	rebarbarize
queer-basher	race meeting	rainbow fish	rat kangaroo	rebarbative
queer screen	race suicide	rainbow-like	rat-tail-file	rebate plane
Queer Street	race walking	rain or shine	rattle-brain	reborrowing
querulously	racialistic	rainproofer	rattle-mouse	rebroadcast
questionary	racing demon	rain slicker	rattle-pated	rebuildable
questionist	raciologist	rainy season	rattlesnake	rebukefully
queue-jumper	rackan-crook	raise a ghost	raucousness	recalculate
queue theory	racket-court	raise a laugh	raunchiness	recalescent
quibblingly	racketiness	raised beach	ravanastron	recantation
quick-change	racket-press	raise up seed	Ravenscroft	recarbonate
quick-firing	racket sport	*raison d'être*	ravishingly	receive silk
quick-freeze	rack-jobbing	raking light	raw material	receptively
quick-loader	rack of bones	rallentandi	razor-backed	receptivity
quick-return	rack railway	rallentando	razor-billed	recessional
quicksilver	racquetball	ramanas rose	razzamatazz	recessively
quick-sticks	radar beacon	Raman effect	reaccession	recipiangle
quick-witted	radar picket	Rambouillet	reach-me-down	reciprocate
quid pro quos	radar screen	ramekin case	reactionary	reciprocity
quiescently	Radcliffian	ramgunshoch	reactionism	recirculate
quiet number	radiant flux	ramisection	reactionist	reclaimable
quill-driver	radiant heat	rammishness	reaction jet	reclamation
quilting bee	radiational	ramshackled	readability	reclination
quinazoline	radiatively	ranchslider	reader-aloud	recluseness
quincuncial	radical chic	rancorously	Reading beds	reclusively
quindecagon	radicalness	random error	reading-book	recognisant
quinhydrone	radical sign	randomicity	reading copy	recognition
quinine-tree	radical word	Raney nickel	reading-desk	recognitive
quinologist	radicellose	range beacon	reading room	recognitory
quinoxaline	radiculitis	range-change	readmission	recognizant
quinquennia	radioactive	rangefinder	readmitting	re-collected

recombinant	redoubtable	refrainment	relationary	repertorium
recombinase	redoubtably	refrangible	relationism	repetitious
recommencer	Red Republic	refreshener	relationist	replaceable
recommender	redressable	refreshment	relativizer	replacement
recommittal	redressment	refrigerant	relaxedness	replenisher
recommitted	red river hog	refrigerate	releasement	repleteness
reconditely	Red River jig	refringence	release note	repleviable
recondition	red rockfish	refringency	relentingly	replication
reconfigure	red sea bream	refulgently	reliability	replicative
reconnoitre	red squirrel	regardfully	Relic Sunday	replicatory
reconstruct	red tapeworm	regenerable	relief valve	reply coupon
record album	red-throated	regenerator	religionary	reportative
recordation	reductional	regerminate	religionism	reportorial
recordative	reductively	regimentary	religionist	report stage
record token	reductivism	regionalise	religionize	reposedness
recountable	reductivist	regionalism	religiosity	reposefully
recountless	reductorial	regionalist	religiously	repossessed
recoverable	redundantee	regionality	reliquaries	repossessor
recoverance	redundantly	regionalize	relishingly	representee
recoverless	reduplicate	register ton	relocatable	representer
recremental	red valerian	registrable	reluctantly	representor
recriminate	reed bunting	regium donum	reluctation	repressible
recruitable	reed-sparrow	regretfully	reluctivity	reprimander
recruitment	re-education	regrettable	remancipate	reprivatize
rectangular	reed warbler	regrettably	remediation	reproachful
rectifiable	reef-builder	regroupment	remembrance	reprobation
rectilineal	re-embroider	regular army	remigration	reprobative
rectilinear	re-emergence	regularizer	reminiscent	reprobatory
recultivate	re-emphasise	regulatable	remissively	reprogramme
recumbently	re-emphasize	regurgitant	remodelling	reprography
recuperable	re-enactment	regurgitate	remonstrant	reprovingly
recuperator	re-encounter	reharmonize	remonstrate	reptiliform
recurrently	re-endowment	Rehobothian	remorseless	Republic Day
recurringly	re-enjoyment	rehydration	removedness	Republicrat
recursively	re-equipment	reification	remunerable	republisher
recurvation	re-establish	reificatory	remunerator	repudiation
recurvature	re-existence	reincarnate	Renaissance	repudiative
redactional	re-expansion	reindeer-fly	renal cortex	repudiatory
redactorial	refashioner	reinfection	renal pelvis	repugnantly
redargution	refectioner	reinforcing	renegotiate	repullulate
red bandfish	refectorian	reingestion	renewedness	repulsively
red-breasted	refectories	reinoculate	Renoiresque	repurchaser
Red Brigades	referendary	reinsertion	renormalize	request stop
red children	referendums	reinstation	renosterbos	requirement
Red Crescent	referential	reinstitute	Renshaw cell	requisitely
redding-comb	refinedness	reinsurance	rentability	requisition
reddishness	reflectance	reintegrate	rent-charger	requisitory
redefection	reflexively	reinterment	rent-service	requotation
redetermine	reflexivity	reinterpret	reoccurring	re-radiation
redeveloper	reflexivize	reintroduce	reorganizer	re-recording
red-eye gravy	reflexology	reinvention	reorientate	resale price
red hardness	reflux valve	Reis Effendi	reoxidation	resarcelled
redhibition	refocillate	reiteration	reoxygenate	rescindable
redhibitory	refocussing	reiterative	repackaging	res cogitans
red-hot poker	re-formation	rejectament	repartition	res communis
rediffusion	reformation	rejectingly	repeat order	researchful
redirection	reformative	rejoicement	repellently	researchist
red ironbark	reformatory	rejoicingly	repellingly	resecretion
rediscovery	Reformatsky	rejuvenator	repentantly	resectional
red kangaroo	reformatted	rejuvenesce	repentingly	resegregate
red mangrove	reformeress	relabelling	repertorial	reselection
red orpiment	reformulate	relatedness	repertories	resemblance

resensitize	reticularly	revisionism	ricocheting	ritornellos
resentfully	reticulated	revisionist	ricochetted	ritournelle
resentingly	reticulitis	reviviscent	riddle-me-ree	Rittmeister
reservation	reticulosis	revoltingly	ride on a rail	ritual abuse
reserve bank	retinacular	rewardingly	ride pillion	ritual choir
reserve cell	retinaculum	rewrite rule	ride shotgun	ritualistic
residencies	retinispora	rhabarbarum	ride the fade	river-driver
residential	retinopathy	rhabdomancy	ride the gain	river gravel
resignalled	retinoscope	rhabdomeric	ride the line	river limpet
resignation	retinoscopy	rhabdomyoma	ride the rods	river mussel
resiliently	retinospora	rhabdovirus	ride to scale	river pirate
resinaceous	retinotopic	Rhaeto-Roman	ridge runner	river runner
resistantly	retired list	rhapidosome	riding habit	river salmon
resistively	retiredness	rhapsodical	riding-house	roach-backed
resistivity	retiring age	Rhenish wine	riding light	roadability
res judicata	retort pouch	rheological	riding rhyme	road breaker
res non verba	retort stand	rheomorphic	rifacimento	road company
resourceful	retractable	rheotropism	rigging-loft	road-hoggery
respectable	retractible	rhetorician	right-angled	road-hoggish
respectably	retransform	rhetoricize	right centre	road-holding
respectless	retranslate	rheumatical	right enough	road manager
respectuous	retransmute	rheumaticky	righteously	roadmanship
respiration	retransport	rhexigenous	right-footed	road-pricing
respiratory	retreatment	Rhinelander	right-handed	road sweeper
respite care	retribalize	Rhine maiden	right-hander	roaring game
resplendent	retribution	rhinestoned	right-minded	robber baron
respondence	retributive	rhinocerine	right of user	robe de style
respondency	retributory	rhinologist	rights issue	Robinocracy
responsible	retrievable	rhinoplasty	rights of man	Robinsonade
responsibly	retroaction	rhinorrhoea	right sphere	robotically
rest assured	retroactive	rhinoscopic	right-to-life	roboticized
restatement	retro-bulbar	rhipiphorid	right-to-work	robusticity
restfulness	retrocedent	rhizobially	right-winger	Roche's limit
rest his soul	retro-engine	rhizocarpic	right you are	rockaboogie
restiffness	retroflexed	Rhizoctonia	rigmarolery	rockahominy
restimulate	retrolental	rhizomatous	rigmarolish	rock and roll
restipulate	retro-rocket	rhizopodium	rigor mortis	rock-climber
restitution	retroverted	rhizopodous	rinforzando	rock-crusher
restitutive	return empty	rhizosphere	ring binding	rock crystal
restitutory	return match	Rhode Island	ring circuit	Rockefeller
restiveness	reupholster	rhodologist	ring complex	rocker panel
restoration	reusability	rhombohedra	ring counter	rocket plane
restorative	revaccinate	rhomboideus	ring culture	rocket range
restriction	revaluation	rhyme scheme	ringed perch	rocketsonde
restrictive	revealingly	rhynchosaur	ringed snake	rock glacier
restructure	revengeless	rhythmicise	ringingness	rock lobster
resubjugate	revengement	rhythmicity	ringing tone	rock 'n' roller
resultantly	revengingly	rhythmicize	ring of truth	rock pebbler
resultative	revenue bond	ribaudequin	ring spanner	rock-skipper
resurrector	reverbatory	ribbon chute	ring-straked	rock sparrow
resurrender	reverberant	ribbon grain	ring the bell	rock the boat
resuscitate	reverberate	ribbon-grass	ring the shed	rock wallaby
retaliation	reverential	ribbon plant	ring winding	rock warbler
retaliative	reverse arms	ribbon snake	riotousness	rock whiting
retaliatory	reverse fire	riboflavine	ripping cord	rodenticide
retardation	reverse gear	ribonucleic	ripple cloth	rodomontade
retardative	reversement	rib-roasting	ripple-fired	Rogation day
retardatory	reversional	rib-tickling	ripple-grass	Roger's blast
retelegraph	reversioner	Ricci tensor	riproarious	rogue's badge
retentional	revindicate	rice-bunting	ripsnorting	roguishness
retentively	revirescent	ricketiness	risk capital	role-playing
retentivity	revisionary	rickettsial	ritardandos	rollability

roller arena
rollerblade
Rollerblade
roller blind
roller-board
roller-coast
roller derby
roller Derby
roller disco
roller drier
roller skate
roller towel
roll-forming
rolling boil
rolling mill
roll-top desk
roll-your-own
Roman candle
Roman cement
Roman Empire
Romanensian
Roman father
roman-fleuve
Roman nettle
romanticise
romanticism
romanticist
romanticity
romanticize
Roman uncial
rompishness
roof pendant
rooibaadjie
rookus-juice
room-divider
room service
rooster comb
rooster tail
root-climber
root cutting
rope-dancing
ropemanship
rope-walking
roseate tern
rose blossom
rose-campion
rose-crystal
rose diagram
rose diamond
rose du Barry
rose gall-fly
Rosenmüller
rose-watered
Rosh Chodesh
Rosh Hashana
Rosicrucian
Rossettiana
rosso antico
Rotarianism
rotary blade
rotary press
rotary quern

rotary table
rotator cuff
rotogravure
rotten apple
rotten-stone
Rouge Dragon
rouge-et-noir
rouge flambé
rough as bags
rough bounds
roughcaster
rough-coated
rough collie
rough-footed
rough-handle
rough-legged
roughometer
rough-scaled
rough scruff
rough timber
rough tongue
round barrow
round-celled
roundedness
round-headed
round-heeled
Round Tabler
round timber
round-winged
Rousseauian
Rousseauish
Rousseauism
Rousseauist
Rousseauite
roust around
rover ticket
Rowland ring
Rowton house
royal assent
royal family
Royal Marine
Royal Maundy
royal octavo
royal plural
royal quarto
royal road to
royal tennis
Royston crow
rubber goods
rubberiness
rubber plant
rubber snake
rubber stamp
rubble-stone
rubefacient
rubefaction
rubelliform
Rubensesque
rubicundity
rubrication
ruby-dazzler
ruby wedding

rucksackful
ruddervator
ruddy plover
Rudesheimer
rudimentary
ruffed lemur
ruffian-like
ruffle shirt
Rugby League
rugby tackle
ruinousness
rule of court
rule of three
rule of thumb
Ruling Elder
rumble strip
rumbustical
rumbustious
rum cocktail
rum customer
rumgumption
rummage sale
rumour has it
run away with
run-downness
run-in groove
runnability
running back
running fire
running gear
running hand
running head
running iron
running jump
running knot
running mate
running moss
running rope
running shoe
running sore
running toad
runological
run the pikes
run to ground
runway light
run-with-bull
Runyonesque
rupicaprine
rupture a gut
rupturewort
rural school
ruridecanal
rush-bearing
rush-release
Ruskinesque
Russell body
Russia braid
Russian Bank
Russian bath
Russian Blue
Russian boot
Russian doll

Russianness
Russian pony
Russian vine
Russophobia
rust disease
rustication
ruthfulness
Sabbatarian
Sabbath lamp
Sabbathless
Sabbath loaf
Sabine's gull
saccharated
saccharined
sacculation
sacerdotage
sackclothed
sacramental
sacramentum
Sacred Blood
Sacred Heart
sacred music
sacred order
sacrificant
sacrificial
sacrilegist
sacring bell
saddle block
saddle brown
saddle-cloth
saddle-horse
saddle-house
saddle-joint
saddle point
saddle quern
saddle-shell
saddle tramp
Sadduceeism
Saengerfest
safe-breaker
safe conduct
safe deposit
safe keeping
safety-catch
safety chain
safety first
safety glass
safety match
safety paper
safety razor
safety valve
saffron cake
saffron plum
saffron rice
saffron-wood
sagaciously
sage sparrow
sagittal ray
Sagittarian
Sagittarius
sagittiform
sago pudding

sailboarder
sailing boat
sailing rule
sailing ship
sailorizing
sailor pants
sailor's knot
sailplaning
saintliness
Saint Monday
saintpaulia
salaciously
salad basket
salad burnet
salamandrid
sal ammoniac
saleability
salesladies
salesperson
salicaceous
salient pole
salinometer
salinometry
Salk vaccine
salmagundis
salmonberry
salmonellae
salmoniform
salmon louse
salmon stair
salmon trout
saloon rifle
salpingitis
sal-prunella
salsuginous
saltarellos
Saltash luck
saltational
saltatorial
salt-glazing
saltimbanco
saltimbocca
saltireways
saltirewise
saltishness
salt of lemon
salt of steel
salvability
Salvadorean
Salvadorian
salvageable
salvational
Salvationer
Salvatorian
Salve Regina
sal volatile
Samian earth
Samson's post
sanatoriums
Sancho Pedro
sanctionary
sanctioneer

sanctionism
sanctionist
sanctuaried
sanctuaries
sanctuarize
sanctus bell
sandblaster
sandbox tree
sand-casting
sand culture
Sandemanian
sand glacier
sandpaperer
sand-picture
sand-skipper
sand spurrey
sand-verbena
sandwich box
sandwich-man
sandwich-men
sandy blight
san fairy ann
sanguinaria
sanguineous
sanguine red
sanitariums
sanitary pad
sans-culotte
sansculotte
sansevieria
Sanskritist
Sanskritize
sans recours
saplessness
saplinghood
saponaceous
saponaretin
sapotaceous
saprobicity
saprobiotic
saprolegnia
saprophytic
Saracen corn
Saracenical
sarcastical
sarcoidosis
sarcolactic
sarcolemmal
sarcomatous
sarcophagal
sarcophagus
sardonicism
Sargasso Sea
sartorially
satanically
Satan monkey
Satanophany
satellitism
satin beauté
satin beauty
satin finish
satinflower

satin stitch
satin-walnut
satirically
satisfiable
satisfiedly
Satsuma ware
saturnalian
Saturnalian
saturnalias
saturninely
satyrically
satyromania
saucepanful
saucepan lid
sauerbraten
saurischian
Sauromatian
sausage curl
sausage meat
sausage roll
sausage-tree
save oneself
save the mark
save the tide
saving grace
savings bank
savings book
saviourhood
saviourship
savoir faire
Savonarolan
savouriness
savouringly
saw palmetto
Saxonically
saxophonist
say the truth
scabby mouth
scabby sheep
scaberulous
scaffoldage
scaffolding
scagliolist
scalability
scalar field
scalariform
scald-headed
scale armour
scale-blight
scale effect
scale factor
scale height
scale insect
scalene cone
scalenotomy
scale-stairs
scale-tailed
scale-winged
scalpriform
scaly lizard
scaly-tailed
scamblingly

Scamperdale
scandalized
scandalizer
scansionist
scapegoater
scapethrift
scapigerous
scapolitize
scapularies
scarabaeoid
scarabidoid
Scarborough
scare-buying
scaremonger
scare-quotes
scare tactic
scarlatinal
scarlet-bean
scarlet ibis
scarlet lady
scarlet rash
scatterable
scatter bomb
scatteredly
scattergood
scattergram
scatterling
scatter plot
scattershot
scelidosaur
scenarioize
scenography
scent-bottle
sceptically
sceptreless
schaalstein
scherzandos
schiacciato
schillerize
schismatist
schismatize
schism-house
schistosity
schistosome
schizanthus
schizocoele
schizocoely
schizogenic
schizogonic
schizotaxia
schizotaxic
schizothyme
schizotypal
schizotypic
schmaltzier
schnockered
Schoenflies
scholarhood
scholarlike
scholarship
scholiastic
school board

schoolchild
schoolcraft
schoolgirly
schoolhouse
school-marmy
schoolroomy
school shark
schoolwards
schottische
Schrödinger
Schubertiad
Schubertian
Schwabacher
sciagrapher
sciagraphic
sciatically
science book
science park
scientistic
Scientology
scincoidian
scintigraph
scintillant
scintillate
scintillous
sciophilous
scire facias
scirrhosity
scissor-bill
scissorbill
scissor-bird
scissor-kick
scissor-lift
scissor-tail
scissorwise
scleroblast
scleroderma
sclerometer
sclerophyll
Scleroscope
sclerotesta
sclerotinia
sclerotioid
sclerotised
sclerotitis
sclerotized
sclerotomal
sclerotomic
scolecodont
scolopender
scolopendra
scolopidium
scoop bonnet
scoop-necked
scopolamine
scopophilia
scopophilic
scorchingly
score points
score-reader
scoriaceous
scoring-book

scoring-card
scorpaenoid
scorpioidal
scorpion fly
Scotch argus
Scotch broth
Scotch catch
Scotch cuddy
Scotchiness
Scotch-Irish
Scotchprint
Scotchwoman
Scotchwomen
scotomatous
scotometric
scotophilic
scotophobia
Scotophobia
scotophobic
Scottishman
scoundrelly
scouring pad
scoutmaster
Scoutmaster
scragginess
scramble net
scraper ring
scrappiness
scrap screen
scratchable
scratch-back
scratch blue
scratch-coat
scratch dial
scratch hole
scratchiest
scratchings
scratchless
scratch-weed
scratch-work
scrawliness
scrawniness
screak of day
screaminess
screamingly
screechiest
screen actor
screen-perch
screen plate
screen porch
screen-print
screen saver
screw around
screw-capped
screwdriver
screwing die
screw-thread
scribacious
Scriblerian
scrimpiness
scrimshoner
scripophile

scripophily
scriptorial
scriptorium
scripturism
scripturist
scrive-board
scrobicular
scrofulitic
scroll-lathe
scrub-cutter
scrub turkey
scrub typhus
scruffiness
scrumminess
scrumptious
scrutinizer
scuba-diving
scufflingly
sculduddery
sculduggery
sculpturing
scuppernong
scurvy grass
scutcheoned
scutellated
scuttle-bone
scuttlebutt
scyphistoma
scyphostoma
Scythianism
sea bindweed
sea-blessing
sea-crawfish
sea cucumber
sea-daffodil
sea defences
sea elephant
sea-hedgehog
seakale beet
sea lavender
seal rookery
sea lungwort
seam bowling
sea milkwort
seamstering
seam welding
sea-pheasant
sea purslane
searchingly
searchlight
search party
sea sandwort
sea scorpion
seasickness
seasonality
season crack
sea starwort
sea-tortoise
sea-voyaging
sea wormwood
seborrhoeic
sebotrophic

secessional
seclusively
secondaries
secondarily
second cause
second-class
second floor
second front
second-guess
second-liner
second pedal
second rater
Second Reich
second sight
second sound
second speed
second table
second teeth
second thigh
second tooth
second water
Second World
secret agent
secretarial
secretariat
secretaries
secretional
secretively
sectile leek
sectionally
section head
section-line
section-mark
sectorially
sector-piece
secularizer
secundipara
sedentarily
sede vacante
sedimentary
seditionary
seditionist
seditiously
seductively
seeableness
see and serve
see daylight
seed crystal
seed orchard
see eye to eye
seeing-glass
see it coming
see little of
seemingness
seepage lake
see the light
see the world
segmentable
segmentally
segregation
segregative
seicentismo

seicentoist
seigneuress
seigneurial
seigniorage
seigniorial
seigniories
seine-netter
seismically
seismic wave
seismograph
seismologic
seismometer
seismometry
seismonasty
seismoscope
seize hold of
selaginella
selectional
selectively
selectivism
selectivist
selectivity
selectorate
selectorial
selenodetic
selenoscope
self-abandon
self-abasing
self-accused
self-adjoint
self-admired
self-analyst
self-assured
self-blimped
self-builder
self-centred
self-certify
self-closing
self-cocking
self-command
self-conceit
self-concern
self-content
self-control
self-created
self-culture
self-defence
self-delight
self-deluded
self-deluder
self-denying
self-despair
self-devoted
self-disgust
self-elected
self-evident
self-excited
self-feeding
self-feeling
self-fertile
self-finance
self-fluxing

selffulness
self-gravity
self-heating
self-imposed
self-induced
self-invited
selfishness
self-knowing
self-limited
self-loading
self-locking
self-mastery
self-mockery
self-mocking
self-neglect
self-opening
self-opinion
self-pitying
self-pleased
self-raising
self-reliant
self-relying
self-renewal
self-reproof
self-respect
self-sealing
self-seeding
self-seeking
self-service
self-serving
self-similar
self-starter
self-sterile
self-support
self-tapping
self-torment
self-torture
self-winding
self-wrought
selling race
sell oneself
sell the pass
sell-through
semantician
semanticism
semanticist
semanticity
semanticize
semaphorist
semasiology
semelparity
semelparous
sememically
semi-animate
semi-annular
semi-antique
semi-aquatic
semiaquatic
semicircled
semi-cursive
semi-display
semi-diurnal

semi-ellipse
semi-evening
semi-invalid
semi-lunated
semi-monthly
semi-nomadic
semiologist
semi-opacity
semiotician
semioticist
semi-palmate
semiquinone
semi-retired
semi-skilled
semi-skimmed
semispecies
semi-sterile
semitonally
semi-trailer
semi-tropics
semolexemic
semological
sempervivum
sempiternal
senate house
senatorship
send away for
send packing
send to grass
send to press
send to table
Seneca grass
senectitude
Senegambian
seneschalsy
seneschalty
senior class
senior tutor
sensational
sense aerial
sense-finder
senselessly
sensibilise
sensibility
sensibilize
sensiferous
sensigenous
sensitively
sensitivity
sensiveness
sensorially
Sensurround
sententiary
sententious
sentimental
sentinelled
separate off
separate out
sephirothic
sepiostaire
Sepoy Mutiny
septangular

septanoside
septavalent
septembrise
Septembrist
septembrize
septenaries
septenarius
septenniums
Septentrion
septicaemia
septicaemic
septiferous
septifragal
Septinsular
septivalent
Sepulchrine
sequentiary
sequestrant
sequestrate
Sequestrene
serendipity
serfishness
sergeancies
sericitized
sericulture
series-wound
serigrapher
serigraphic
serio-comedy
seriousness
serishtadar
sermonesque
sermonology
seroconvert
serological
serotherapy
serotine bat
serous gland
serpentaria
serpentinic
serpent-like
serpent-star
serpent-wand
serpiginous
serradillas
serrulation
servantless
servantship
serve and sue
serviceable
serviceably
service area
service book
service club
service flat
service game
serviceless
service line
service mark
service-pipe
service road
service tree

servileness
servile work
serving cart
serving dish
servitorial
servo system
sesquialter
sesquioxide
sesquipedal
sesquiplane
sessionally
setaceously
set an edge on
set a price on
set at naught
set at nought
set little by
set stocking
set the scene
set the stage
set the watch
setting coat
setting-pole
settledness
settling day
set to school
set well with
sevenfolded
seven-hilled
seven-league
seven-seater
seventeenth
seventh part
seventh wave
seventy-five
seventyfold
seventy-four
seventy-nine
severalfold
sewage grass
sewage works
sexadecimal
sexagesimal
sex criminal
sexdigitism
sexennially
sex instinct
sexlessness
sex offender
sexological
sex-reversal
sexsational
sextillions
sextodecimo
sexual organ
Seychellois
shackle-bolt
shackle-bone
shad-bellied
shadowgraph
shadowiness
shaft pillar

shake dancer
shake free of
Shakespeare
shakuhachis
shale shaker
shallowness
shallow-pate
sham Abraham
shamanistic
shamblingly
shamefastly
shamelessly
shameworthy
sham-operate
shanghaiing
shanks's mare
Shanks's mare
shanks's pony
Shanks's pony
shanty Irish
shape factor
shapelessly
shapeliness
shape memory
shape up well
shard-beetle
share-farmer
shareholder
share-milker
share-pusher
share tenant
shark's teeth
shark's tooth
shark-sucker
sharon fruit
sharp-tailed
sharp-witted
Shasta daisy
shatter belt
shatter cone
shatter-pate
shaver point
shaving foam
shawl collar
shear centre
shear stress
sheath dress
sheath knife
sheath skirt
shed light on
Sheela-na-gig
sheep-herder
sheep laurel
sheep-master
sheep-shears
sheep's heart
sheep-silver
sheep sorrel
sheer-strake
sheet anchor
sheet feeder
sheet-piling

shelf appeal
shellacking
shelled corn
shell-flower
shell-jacket
shell midden
shell-silver
shell-stitch
shelter belt
shelterdeck
shelter foot
shelter half
shelterless
shelter life
shelter tent
shelter tree
shelter wood
shepherd dog
shepherdess
shepherdize
sheriffalty
sheriffhood
sheriffship
sheriffwick
sheristadar
Sherlockian
sherry glass
sherry party
shield-board
shield-money
shiftlessly
shift system
shigellosis
shin-cracker
shingle bank
shingle-nail
shiningness
shining path
shin-plaster
shin-splints
Shintoistic
ship a stripe
ship biscuit
ship-breaker
shipbuilder
ship of fools
ship of State
shipping ore
ship's papers
ship's writer
shipton moth
ship-to-shore
shipyard eye
Shirburnian
shire-bishop
shire county
shire-ground
shirt blouse
shirt-button
shirt-cutter
shirt-jacket
shirtlifter

shirt of hair
shirt of mail
shirtsleeve
shit-stirrer
shittim wood
shiveringly
shockedness
shock-headed
shock troops
shock-worker
shoeing-horn
shoe leather
shonkinitic
shoot flying
shooting box
shooting war
shoot the cat
shoot the sun
shoot to kill
shop-breaker
shop-fitting
shopfitting
shopkeeping
shoplifting
shopping-bag
shop steward
shore dinner
shore-gunner
shore-hopper
shore patrol
short-acting
short ballot
short change
shortcoming
short corner
short-haired
short-handed
shorthander
short-headed
short-horned
short manure
short notice
short octave
short-period
short shorts
short shrift
short sleeve
short-spined
short-spoken
short square
short staple
Short Street
short-suited
short temper
short tennis
short-termer
short weight
short-winded
shoshonitic
shot-blaster
shot-peening
shot-putting

shot through	side-partner	silver medal	sinuousness	slate-pencil
shoulder bag	sidereal day	silver paper	sinus rhythm	slate-writer
shouldering	sideroblast	silver perch	siphonogamy	slatternish
shoulder pad	siderocytic	silver plate	siphuncular	slaughterer
shoulder pod	siderograph	silver-point	sipper-sauce	slaunchways
shoulder tab	sideropenia	silver print	sipunculoid	slaunchwise
shovelboard	sideropenic	silversides	sirocco oven	slave-bangle
shovel-penny	siderophile	silversmith	sister-block	slave-driver
show-and-tell	siderophore	silver spoon	sister-in-law	slave labour
showboating	side scraper	Silver State	sister tutor	slave market
shower-cloud	sidestepper	Silver Stick	Sitka spruce	slaveocracy
showeriness	side-wheeler	silversword	sitting duck	slaveringly
showerproof	Sierra Leone	silver tabby	sitting room	slave trader
shower stall	sift through	silver table	situational	slave worker
showjumping	sight cheque	silver trout	situationer	slavishness
showmanship	sight-holder	silver-white	sivatherium	Slavonicize
show of force	sightlessly	silvery pout	Six Counties	sledge-meter
show of hands	sightliness	Simonianism	sixteensome	sleep around
show oneself	sight-player	simperingly	sixteenthly	Sleeperette
show-stopper	sight-reader	simple feast	sixth-former	sleeper seat
show the flag	sight record	Simple Simon	sixty-fourmo	sleeper wall
show through	sight-screen	sincereness	skaapsteker	sleeping bag
show willing	sightseeing	sindonology	skate-barrow	sleeping car
shrew-stroke	sight-setter	sinews of war	skating rink	sleeplessly
shrew-struck	sight unseen	sinfonietta	skeletonian	sleep-shorts
shrew-tenrec	sightworthy	singability	skeletonise	sleep-talker
shrift-shire	sigillarian	Singaporean	skeletonize	sleep-waking
shrike vireo	sigillation	singer's node	skeleton key	sleepwalker
shrimp plant	sigmatropic	singing bird	Skeltonical	sleeve board
shrinkingly	sigmoidally	singing game	sketch-block	sleeve-valve
shrink-proof	signal plate	singing sand	sketchiness	sleigh-rider
shrivelling	signal tower	singing tree	skiagrapher	slenderness
shroud-brass	signatories	single-blind	skiagraphic	sleuth-hound
shrubberies	signaturist	single cream	skid-mounted	slice of life
shrubbiness	signifiable	single entry	skilfulness	slickenside
shrub mallow	significans	Single Grave	skilligalee	slick-licker
shruggingly	significant	single-horse	skim-coulter	slide guitar
shuddersome	significate	single-soled	skimmed milk	sliding door
shuffle beat	sign-painter	single-start	skimmer-cake	sliding keel
shufflewing	sign-vehicle	single stick	skimmington	sliding roof
shufflingly	signwriting	single-taxer	skin and bone	sliding rule
shut one's pan	silica glass	single track	skip-bombing	sliding seat
shutterless	silicic acid	single-tuned	skippership	slightingly
shutter weir	silicon chip	singularise	skirmishing	slim disease
shuttlecock	silicon iron	singularism	skirt-chaser	slimnastics
shuttleless	siliquiform	singularist	skirt-dancer	sling the bat
shuttle-race	silk snapper	singularity	skirt of beef	slip casting
sialectasis	silkworm gut	singularize	skirt patrol	slip edition
sialography	sillimanite	singulative	skulduggery	slipped disc
sialorrhoea	silly season	singultient	skull-buster	slipper bath
Siamese twin	silt-snapper	sinisterity	skullcapped	slipperette
Siberian jay	silverballi	sinistrally	sky-blue pink	slipper sock
Siberian tit	silver beech	sinistrorse	sky-coloured	slipperwort
siblingship	silverberry	sinking fund	Skye terrier	slippery dip
sibyllistic	silver birch	sinking sand	sky-scraping	slippery elm
sick benefit	silver blond	sink the wind	sky-shouting	slit sampler
sick cookery	silver bream	sinlessness	slant height	slit spirant
sickeningly	silver grain	sin-offering	slapdashery	sloop-rigged
sickishness	silveriness	sinological	slap-happily	sloothering
side-flowing	silver Latin	Sinological	slasher film	slope filter
side gallery	silver-lines	Sino-Tibetan	slash pocket	slopping-out
side-looking	silver maple	sinuosities	slate colour	sloth-monkey

slot machine
slotted line
slot winding
slouch-eared
slouchiness
slouchingly
slough grass
sloven-wagon
slow and sure
slow bowling
slow but sure
slow neutron
slow reactor
sluggardize
slug-setting
sluice-valve
slumber away
slumberland
slumberless
slumber room
slumbersome
slumberwear
slumgullion
smack-bottom
smack-smooth
Smalcaldian
small change
small circle
smallholder
small letter
small-minded
small stores
small wonder
smart-alecky
smarty-boots
smarty-pants
Smectymnuan
smellfungus
smilelessly
smilingness
smithereens
smithiantha
Smithsonian
smithsonite
Smith Square
smoke candle
smoked glass
smoked sheet
smoke helmet
smoke-jumper
smokelessly
smoke rocket
smokescreen
smoke-signal
smoke-tunnel
smoking room
smoky quartz
smoochiness
smooth-faced
smooth hound
smoothingly
smooth snake

smorgasbord
smotherable
smother crop
smother-kiln
snail darter
snail-flower
snake-doctor
snake feeder
snakes alive
snakishness
snap-brimmed
snapper-back
snapper fish
snapper grab
snap-shooter
snapshotter
snatch-block
snatch squad
sneck-drawer
sneezing gas
snickersnee
Snickometer
sniperscope
snob-cricket
snobocratic
snobography
snooze alarm
snorkelling
snotty-nosed
snout-beetle
snowberries
snow-blinded
snowboarder
snow bunting
snow cruiser
Snowdon lily
snow-dropper
snow leopard
snow machine
snowmobiler
snow panther
snow sparrow
snowy petrel
snowy plover
snuffliness
snufflingly
soak-the-rich
soapberries
soapbox cart
soap of glass
soapolallie
soarability
sober-minded
sociability
social climb
social élite
social ethic
socialistic
social order
social scale
social space
social whale

societarian
Socinianism
Socinianize
sociography
sociolectal
sociologese
sociologism
sociologist
sociologize
sociometric
sociopathic
sockdolager
soda biscuit
soda counter
soda cracker
soda process
soddishness
sodomitical
sod planting
so far so good
soft-centred
soft chancre
soft-focused
soft-hearted
soft landing
soft-shelled
soft-skinned
soft tissues
so help me God
soil climate
soil colloid
soil extract
soil polygon
soil profile
soil release
soil sampler
soil science
sojournment
solanaceous
solar energy
solar-heated
solarimeter
solar plexus
solar system
soldatesque
soldier bird
soldier-crab
soldier-fish
soldierhood
soldierlike
soldiership
sole-leather
solemncholy
solemnities
solemnsides
solenoglyph
solicitancy
solicitress
solid-bodied
solid colour
solid-hoofed
solid sender

solid system
soliflucted
soliloquies
soliloquise
soliloquist
soliloquize
solipsismal
solipsistic
solmisation
solmization
solo climber
solubilizer
Soluble blue
solutionist
solution set
solvability
solventless
somasteroid
somatically
somatic cell
somatogenic
somatomedin
somatoplasm
somatotonic
somatotopic
somesthetic
something of
somewhere in
somewhither
somnambular
somnambulic
somniculous
somniferous
somnolently
Somogyi unit
songfulness
Song of Songs
song-plugger
song sparrow
song stylist
songwriting
son of a bitch
Son of Heaven
soopolallie
soothfastly
soothsaying
sooty blotch
sophistical
sophistries
soporifical
soprano clef
Sorbo rubber
soroptimist
Soroptimist
sororicidal
sorrowfully
sorrowingly
sort program
sort routine
SOS redouble
soteriology
sottishness

soubrettish
sought after
soul brother
soul-catcher
soulfulness
sound as a nut
sound asleep
sound camera
sound effect
Soundex-code
sounding fit
sounding rod
soundlessly
sound-on-film
sound-ranger
sound stripe
sound system
soup and fish
soup kitchen
south-by-east
south-easter
southeaster
southerlies
southermost
southernism
southernize
southlander
southwardly
south-wester
southwester
sovereignly
sovereignty
Sovietology
sow one's oats
space charge
spacefaring
space flight
space heater
space helmet
spacelessly
space myopia
space needle
space rocket
spacer-plate
space-saving
space travel
spaceworthy
spade guinea
spade-shaped
spaghettini
span-counter
spandrelled
spangle gall
Spaniardize
Spanish comb
Spanish foot
Spanish goat
Spanish ibex
Spanish iris
Spanish lime
Spanish Main
Spanish moss

Spanishness
Spanish plum
Spanish tile
Spanish wood
spanker-boom
span loading
sparganosis
sparingness
sparklessly
sparklingly
sparrow-bill
sparrow-fart
sparrowhawk
sparrow-like
sparrow-tail
spasmatical
spasmodical
spasmogenic
spasmolysis
spasmolytic
spasmophile
spastically
spathaceous
spathulated
spatterdash
spatterdock
spatterware
spatulation
spatuliform
speakeasies
speakership
Speakership
speak evil of
speak well of
spear tackle
special area
special case
special jury
specialness
specialogue
specialties
special vert
specieshood
species pair
species-poor
species-rich
species rose
specifiable
specificate
specificity
specimen-box
specklessly
spectacular
spectatress
spectrality
spectrogram
spectrology
spectrotype
specularite
specular orb
speculation
speculatist

speculative
speculatory
speculatrix
speech chain
speech-house
speechified
speechifier
speechifies
speech sound
speed-bowler
speedometer
speed-reader
speedwriter
speedy trial
spelaeology
spellbinder
spelling-bee
spend a penny
spendthrift
Spenglerian
Spenglerism
spermacetic
spermatheca
spermatidal
spermatozoa
sperm candle
spermicidal
sperm morula
spermophile
spessartine
spessartite
sphacelated
sphaeridium
sphaerocone
sphagnum bog
sphairistic
sphenochasm
spherically
spherocytic
spherograph
spheroidism
spheroidize
spherometer
spheroplast
spherosomal
spherulitic
sphincteral
sphinctered
sphincteric
sphingosine
sphragistes
sphygmogram
sphygmology
sphyrelaton
spic and span
spiculation
spider conch
spider plant
spider-table
spider veins
spiderwebby
spider-wheel

spifflicate
spiflicated
spike-bozzle
spike Celtic
spike-fiddle
spiking curb
spill burner
spina bifida
spinach beet
spinach jade
spinach moth
spinal block
spinal canal
spin-allowed
spinal nerve
spinal shock
spin-bowling
spindle-back
spindle cell
spindleless
spindle side
spindle tree
spindle-wood
spine-basher
spinelessly
spinescence
spine-tailed
spiniferous
spinigerous
spin-lattice
spinning top
spinousness
Spinozistic
spinsterdom
spinsterial
spinsterian
spinsterish
spinsterism
spinulation
spiny lizard
spiraculate
spiral-bound
spiraliform
spirillosis
spiritistic
spirit level
spiritually
spiritualty
spirituelle
spirit world
spirketting
spirochaete
spirography
spirometric
spiroplasma
spitfire-jib
spitsticker
spittle-ball
Spitzenberg
splashboard
splashguard
splashiness

splash party
splashplate
splash-proof
splat-quench
splay-footed
splay-legged
spleen index
splendorous
splenectomy
spleniculus
splenorenal
splice-piece
splinter-bar
splinter bid
split beaver
split-minded
split pulley
split-screen
split second
split stitch
split stroke
split ticket
spokeswoman
spokeswomen
spondulicks
spondylitic
spondylitis
spondylosis
spondylotic
sponge-cakey
sponge cloth
sponge gourd
sponge-swamp
spongiology
sponsorship
spontaneity
spontaneous
spoon-backed
spoon-bender
spoon-billed
sporidesmin
sporidiolum
sporiferous
sporogenous
sporogonium
sporophytic
sportsmanly
sports shirt
sportswoman
sportswomen
sporulation
spotlighter
spotted deer
spotted dick
Spotted Dick
spottedness
spotted wilt
spot-welding
sprat-barley
spraunciest
sprawlingly
spray brooch

spray region
spread-adder
spread-eagle
spreadeagle
spreadingly
spreadsheet
sprightlily
sprig-tailed
spring a leak
spring a luff
springboard
spring-clean
spring fever
Springfield
spring grass
spring green
spring-house
springiness
springingly
spring onion
spring usher
spring water
sprinkingly
sprinklered
spritellier
spritualise
spud-bashing
spumescence
spurge olive
spur-leather
spying-glass
spy in the cab
spy in the sky
squail-board
squalidness
squander-bug
squandering
square-built
square dance
square drive
square perch
square piano
square serif
squarrosely
squarrulose
squash-berry
squashiness
squatterdom
squat thrust
squaw winter
squeakiness
squeamishly
squeeze bunt
squeeze lens
squeeze play
squeeze tube
squinny-eyed
squintingly
squirearchy
Squirearchy
squirocracy
squirrel-dog

squirrelish
squirrelled
squishiness
stab-and-drag
Stabat Mater
stab-culture
stabilitate
stable block
stacked head
stacked heel
stactometer
stadiometer
stadtholder
staff of life
staff system
staff writer
stage centre
stage design
stage effect
stage fright
stage-manage
stage-player
stage rights
stage school
stage-struck
stageworthy
stagflation
stagger-bush
staggerment
staggerwort
stag-hunting
staging area
staging post
stainlessly
stake a claim
stake-bodies
stake-driver
stakeholder
Stake of Zion
staktometer
stalactical
stalactitae
stalactital
stalactited
stalactites
stalactitic
stalagmitic
Stalinesque
Stalin organ
stalk switch
stall-holder
stallholder
stall-keeper
stall-reader
stall shower
stalwartism
Stambouline
stamp office
standardise
standardize
stand at abay
stand at ease

stand at stud
stand camera
stand in line
stand in with
stand neuter
stand of arms
stand-offish
standoffish
stand sentry
stand surety
stand-to-arms
staphylinid
Star Chamber
starchiness
starch-water
star-crossed
Stark effect
stark naught
star-lighted
star network
Star of David
star-studded
start button
starter home
star-thistle
starting-off
startlement
startlingly
star-tracker
start school
star vehicle
stasipatric
State-church
statelihood
stateliness
stately home
statemental
state-monger
state of life
state of play
State-prison
State rights
State school
state secret
statesmanly
stateswoman
state vector
static water
station-bill
station hand
station head
station-line
station pole
statistical
statoconium
stator blade
statuomania
status group
statute-book
statute fair
statute mile
statute-roll

statutorily
statuvolent
statuvolism
staunchness
staurolitic
stauroscope
stave church
stay-stomach
stay the pace
St Bruno lily
steadfastly
steady-going
steady state
steakburger
steak hammer
steal a match
stealthiest
steam boiler
steam-distil
steam engine
steamfitter
steam hammer
steam-heater
steam-jacket
steam-launch
steam-packet
steam plough
steam-raiser
steamroller
steam shovel
steam-vessel
stearic acid
steatopygia
steatopygic
steel-bender
steel driver
steel-framed
steel guitar
steelheader
steelworker
steeple-bush
steeplejack
steeplewise
steerage-way
steering box
steering-oar
steerswoman
stegosaurid
stegosaurus
Stella Maris
stellarator
Steller's jay
stellionate
stellularly
St Elmo's fire
stem-rooting
stem-winding
stencilling
Stender dish
Stendhalian
stenobathic
stenocardia

stenography
stenohaline
stenohydric
stenopodium
stenotyping
stenotypist
stentmaster
stentorious
step-bearing
stepbrother
step flaking
step forward
stephanotis
step-pyramid
step this way
stercobilin
stereoblock
stereograph
stereometer
stereometry
stereophony
stereophoto
stereoscope
stereoscopy
stereotaxic
stereotaxis
stereotyped
stereotyper
stereotypic
sterigmatic
sterile-male
stern-chaser
sternohyoid
sternutator
stethograph
stethometer
stethometry
stethophone
stethoscope
stethoscopy
stevedorage
stevedoring
stevengraph
Stevengraph
stewardship
stewing beef
stichometry
stick around
stick-figure
stick-handle
stick insect
stickleback
stick out for
stick-shaker
stiff-necked
stifle-joint
stilbestrol
still and all
stiltedness
stilt-heeled
stilt-plover
stimulating

stimulation
stimulative
stimulatory
sting-tailed
stink beetle
stinking bug
stinking gum
stinking yew
stipendiary
stipendless
stipitiform
stipulation
stipulative
stipulatory
stir a finger
stirrup bone
stirrup iron
stirrupless
stirrup pump
stirrup-vase
St John's wort
St Kilda wren
stock bowler
stockbroker
stock-father
stockholder
Stockholmer
stockinette
stocking cap
stocking-net
stockjobber
stockkeeper
stock market
stocktaking
stoepsitter
stoicalness
Stokes–Adams
Stokes' aster
Stolichnaya
stomach-ache
stomachfuls
stomachical
stomachless
stomach pump
stomach tube
stomach-worm
stomatology
stomp ground
stone circle
stone-colour
stone curlew
stonecutter
stone-getter
stone-ginger
stoneground
Stone Indian
stone marten
stone-plover
stoneroller
stone stripe
stonewaller
stonewashed

stone-weight	strap handle	strike hands	stultiloquy	subjectable
stoneworker	straphanger	strike lucky	stumblingly	subjectedly
stool-pigeon	strap-shaped	strike short	stump jumper	subjecthood
stoop labour	strata-bound	string along	stump-orator	subjectible
stop a packet	strata title	stringboard	stump-tailed	subjectless
stop-netting	strategetic	stringently	stun grenade	subjectship
Stoppardian	strategical	stringiness	stuntedness	subject-term
stop payment	stratocracy	string-piece	stupidities	subjugation
stopperless	stratopause	stringy-bark	stupor mundi	subjunction
stop short at	straw ballot	strionigral	Sturge–Weber	subjunctive
stop the show	straw basher	strioscopic	style critic	sublanguage
stop the tide	straw colour	striped bass	style-setter	sublethally
stop your gab	strawflower	striped tuna	styliferous	sublettable
storability	straw-hatter	strip-mining	stylishness	sublimation
storage cell	straw-needle	strip-search	stylization	sublimatory
storage life	straw-yellow	stripteaser	stylography	sublimeness
storage ring	streakiness	strobe light	stylometric	sublimified
storage unit	streak plate	strobe pulse	stylopodium	sublittoral
storage wall	streamingly	stroboscope	Stymphalian	subluminous
store-bought	streamlined	stroboscopy	stypticness	subluxation
store church	streamliner	strobotorch	Stypven time	submarginal
storekeeper	stream-works	Stroh violin	suasiveness	submergence
store the kin	street child	stroke-maker	subaerially	submergible
storm cellar	street cries	stromateoid	subagencies	submersible
storm centre	street fight	Strombolian	subarcuated	subminister
storm-collar	street floor	strong drink	sub-assembly	submissible
storm petrel	street-legal	strong force	Sub-Atlantic	submittable
storm-signal	street level	strongfully	subaudition	submultiple
storm-stayed	street light	strong grade	subaxillary	submunition
storm-system	street price	strong house	sub-basement	subordinacy
storm troops	streetproof	strong joint	subcategory	subordinary
storm window	streetscape	strong point	subcellarer	subordinate
story editor	street-smart	strong water	subcellular	subornation
storyteller	street style	strong woman	subclinical	subornative
stout fellow	street value	strong woods	subcontract	subpectoral
stove-enamel	strengthful	strongyloid	subcontrary	subpetiolar
stove lifter	strengthily	strontium-90	subcortical	subphonemic
stow-boating	strenuosity	stroppiness	subcritical	subprioress
straddle-bob	strenuously	struck joint	subcultural	subrational
straddle-bug	strep throat	structurate	subdeaconry	subregional
straggliest	stressed out	structurism	subdelegate	subrogation
straight-arm	stressfully	structurist	subdelirium	subscapular
straight-cut	stress grade	structurize	subdiaconal	subscribe to
straight eye	stress-group	struthonian	subdistrict	subscripted
straightish	stress-timed	struttingly	subdivision	subsemitone
straight job	stretchable	stubble-fire	subdivisive	subsensible
straight leg	stretch mark	stub-feather	subdolously	subsensuous
straight man	stretchneck	stub-mortise	subdominant	sub-sequence
straight off	strewn field	stub station	subduedness	subsequence
straight-out	strictarian	student card	sub-economic	subsequence
straight-run	strict tempo	studenthood	subfamilies	subserviate
straight tip	stride level	student lamp	subfraction	subservient
straightway	stridulator	studentless	subglabrous	subsistence
strain gauge	strigillate	student-like	subglobular	subspecific
strainingly	strike a blow	studentship	subgovernor	sub-standard
strainmeter	strike a line	studiedness	subgrouping	substandard
strait-laced	strike a path	studio couch	subharmonic	substantial
Straits-born	strike-bound	studio party	subhumanity	substantive
stramineous	strikebound	stud welding	subincision	substituend
Strangelove	strike-break	study circle	subirrigate	substituent
strangeness	strikebreak	stuffing box	subitaneous	substituted
strangulate	strike force	stultifying	subjacently	substituter

substration
substrative
subsumption
subsumptive
subtabulate
subtacksman
sub-teenager
subterminal
subthalamic
subthalamus
subtraction
subtractive
subtreasury
subtropical
subtruncate
subumbrella
suburbanise
suburbanism
suburbanite
suburbanity
suburbanize
suburbicary
subvertible
subvertical
subvocalize
succedaneum
successless
succinctory
succinimide
succourable
succourless
succulently
succumbency
such-and-such
such another
sucking-disc
sucking-fish
suction lift
suction pipe
suction pump
suction stop
sudden death
suede-footed
Suess effect
Suess wiggle
suet-brained
suet pudding
sufferingly
sufficience
sufficiency
sufficingly
suffixation
suffocating
suffocation
suffocative
Suffolk bang
suffraganal
suffragette
suffumigate
sugar-almond
sugar-baking
sugar-coated

sugar-fungus
sugar glider
sugar-loafed
sugar of lead
sugar of milk
sugar trough
suggestable
suggestible
sugillation
suicidality
suicide pact
suicidology
suitability
suitcaseful
suit of court
suit oneself
suit-service
suits my book
sulphanilic
sulphate ion
Sulphatriad
sulpholipid
sulphurator
sulphur bath
sulphureous
sulphuretum
sulphur-tree
sulphur tuft
sulphurweed
sulphydrate
sultanesque
summability
summariness
summational
summatively
summer apple
summer cloud
summer-dream
summer-field
summer grape
summer house
summeriness
summer lodge
summer-prune
summersault
summer snipe
summer stock
summer-tilth
summerwards
summit level
summonsable
summum bonum
sumptuosity
sumptuously
sum-totalize
Sunday child
Sunday joint
Sunday lunch
Sunday punch
sun-drenched
sunken fence
sunlessness

sunlighting
sunny side up
sun-painting
sun-scorpion
sunshine law
sun-stricken
suntan cream
superabound
superaerial
supercargos
super-charge
supercharge
supercilium
supercooled
super-de-luxe
superessive
superfamily
superfatted
superfemale
superficial
superficies
superfinely
superfluent
superfluity
superfluous
superfusate
superfusion
supergalaxy
superheated
superheater
superheroes
superimpose
superinduce
superinfect
superintend
superinvest
superioress
superiority
superjacent
superlative
superlunary
supermarine
supermarket
supermundal
supernatant
supernature
supernormal
superoctave
superscribe
superscript
supersedure
supersexual
supersonics
superstrata
superstrate
superstring
superstruct
supersubtle
supertanker
supervision
supervisory
suppedaneum

suppeditate
supper dance
suppliantly
supplicator
supply house
supply-teach
supportable
supportably
supportasse
support band
support cost
supportless
support line
supportress
supposition
suppositive
suppository
suppressant
suppression
suppressive
suppuration
suppurative
suprafacial
supralethal
supralineal
supralinear
supralunary
suprameatal
suprascript
suprasellar
supraspinal
suprasterol
supremacism
supremacist
Suprematism
suprematist
supremeness
surface blow
surface film
surfaceless
surface mail
surface-road
surface wave
surf-casting
surficially
surgeon-bird
surgeonfish
surgeonship
Surgicenter
surpassable
surprisable
surprisedly
surrebuttal
surrebutter
surrenderee
surrenderor
surrogation
surrounding
Sursum corda
surturbrand
surveillant
survival bag

survivalism
survivalist
survival kit
susceptance
susceptible
susceptibly
suscitation
suspectable
suspectuous
suspendible
suspenseful
suspensible
suspiration
sustainable
sustainably
sustainedly
sustainment
susurration
svarabhakti
swag-bellied
swagger cane
swagger coat
swallowable
swallow-dive
swallow fork
swallow-hole
swallow-kite
swallow-like
swallowtail
swallow-tick
swallowwort
swamp laurel
swamp plough
swamp privet
swamp rabbit
swan-hopping
swan-marking
sward-cutter
swarmer cell
swarthiness
swartrutter
swashbuckle
swath-turner
swear an oath
sweat equity
sweater girl
sweating pen
sweating-tub
Swede-basher
swede turnip
Swede turnip
sweet alison
sweet as a nut
sweet cherry
sweet cicely
sweet clover
sweet dreams
sweet fennel
sweet orange
sweet pepper
sweet potato
sweet rocket

sweet singer
sweet sultan
sweet violet
sweet yarrow
swee waxbill
swelled head
swell-headed
swept valley
swept volume
swift-footed
Swiftianism
swift-winged
swim-bladder
Swinburnian
swine-backed
swine's cress
swine's grass
swing bowler
swing-bridge
swingeingly
swingle-hand
swingletree
swing mirror
swing needle
swingometer
swing-ticket
swinishness
Swiss banker
Swiss cheese
Swiss-German
Swiss muslin
switch-blade
switchblade
switchboard
switch-grass
switch-knife
switch-plant
switch-tower
swivel chair
swollen head
swollenness
sword-bearer
sword-cutler
sword dancer
sword-in-hand
swordplayer
sybaritical
sycamore-fig
sycophantic
sycophantly
Sydneysider
syllabaries
syllabarium
syllabation
syllabicate
syllabicity
syllabified
syllabifies
sylleptical
syllogistic
sylvestrene
sylvestrian

Sylvestrian
symbolistic
symmetallic
symmetrical
sympathetic
sympathizer
sympetalous
symphonious
symphyllous
symplectite
sympodially
symposiarch
symptomatic
symptomless
synagogical
synapticula
synaptology
synaptosome
synchromesh
Synchromism
Synchromist
synchronise
synchronism
synchronist
synchronize
synchronous
synchro-swim
synchrotron
synclinally
syncopation
syncyanosis
syndesmosis
syndesmotic
syndicalism
syndicalist
syndicateer
syndication
syndiploidy
synecdochic
synechthran
synergistic
synesthesia
syngnathous
synodically
synonymical
synorogenic
synovectomy
synsemantic
synsepalous
syntactical
syntagmatic
syntaxially
syntectonic
synthesiser
synthesizer
synthetical
syntrophism
syphilology
syrup of figs
syssarcoses
syssarcosis
systematics

systematise
systematism
systematist
systematize
Szechuanese
Szechwanese
tabernacled
table-centre
table-decker
table-moving
table napkin
Table Office
table-rapper
table-screen
table stakes
table talker
table tennis
tabletopped
tablet paper
table-turner
taboparesis
tabular berg
tabular spar
tacheometer
tacheometry
tachometric
tachycardia
tachygraphy
tachypnoeic
tachysterol
taciturnity
tacking iron
tackle-block
tackle-house
tackling bag
tactfulness
tadpole-fish
taeniae coli
tagliatelle
tagmemicist
tag question
t'ai chi ch'uan
tail-bandage
tail-dragger
tail feather
tail general
tailor's tack
tail special
tail-spindle
tail-walking
taintlessly
take a chance
take a flight
take against
take a header
take a powder
take a tumble
take a view of
take a wicket
take by storm
take chances
take counsel

take-home pay
take in a reef
take it on one
take it out of
take it out on
take its toll
take leave of
take leave to
take lessons
take lightly
take offence
take on board
take one's way
take on trust
takeover bid
take pride in
take service
take station
take stock in
take stock of
take tea with
take the bent
take the cake
take the helm
take the piss
take the road
take the veil
take the word
take thought
take to heart
take trial of
take trouble
take warning
talebearing
talent scout
tale-telling
Taliacotian
talkatively
talking book
talking cure
talking drum
talking film
talking head
talking shop
talk through
tallow-faced
tallow shrub
tally system
Talmudistic
Talmud Torah
tambour desk
tambour hook
tambour-lace
tameability
Tamla Motown
Tammany Hall
tammie norie
tam-o'-shanter
tamper-proof
Tanganyikan
tangibility
tank circuit

tank-farming
tantalizing
tap-changing
tape guipure
tape machine
tape-measure
taphonomist
taphrogenic
tapping coil
tapping-hole
taradiddler
tarantulate
tarantulous
taratantara
Tarbuck knot
tare and tret
target organ
tarnishable
tar-pavement
tarradiddle
tarry-breeks
tarsoplasty
tartar sauce
Tartufferie
Tarzanesque
tassel-grass
tastelessly
tattie-bogle
tau particle
taurocholic
tautochrone
tautologies
tautologise
tautologism
tautologist
tautologize
tautologous
tautomerism
tautomerize
tautoousian
taxableness
tax gatherer
taxidermist
taxi service
taxonomical
Tchekhovian
tea-canister
tea ceremony
teachership
teacher's pet
teaching aid
teach school
tea district
tea-drinking
tea interval
tear and wear
tearfulness
tear-jerking
tear off a bit
tear-stained
teaspoonful
tea-strainer

technically	telopeptide	tergeminous	tetrarchate	the Die-hards
Technicolor	temerarious	termination	tetrarchies	the Divinity
technocracy	temperament	terminative	tetravalent	the Dominion
technofreak	temperately	terminatory	tetrazolium	The Elements
technologic	temperative	terministic	tetrazotize	the five wits
technophile	temperature	terminology	tetter-berry	the flower of
technophobe	temper-screw	termitaries	tettigoniid	theftuously
techno-speak	tempestuous	termitarium	Teutonicism	the game is up
tectibranch	temple block	termite-hill	Teutophobia	the glad hand
tectonician	temple mould	term of years	Texas Ranger	the glad mitt
tectosphere	tempo giusto	ternary form	textbookish	the greatest
tectospinal	temporalism	terpeneless	textile cone	the great wen
tediousness	temporalist	Terpsichore	text-picture	the hale ware
teeny-bopper	temporality	terra ignota	textureless	the half of it
teetotalish	temporalize	terraqueous	Thackerayan	the height of
teetotalism	temporaries	Terra Sienna	thalamotomy	the high toby
teetotalist	temporarily	terreneness	thalidomide	the infinite
teetotaller	tempo rubato	terrestrial	thallophyte	theirselves
tegestology	Tempranillo	terre-tenant	thanatology	the last rose
tegumentary	temptatious	terribility	thanatopsis	the length of
Tehuelchian	tenableness	terricoline	thank kindly	the long robe
Teilhardian	tenaciously	terricolous	thanklessly	the Lord's day
teknonymous	tenant right	terrigenous	thanksgiver	thelytokous
tektosphere	tendentious	territorial	thankworthy	the Main Plot
telebanking	tender-dying	Territorian	Thatcherism	the majority
telebetting	tender-eared	territories	Thatcherite	the man for me
telebroking	tender plant	territorium	that depends	the mind's eye
telecentric	tendon organ	terroristic	that is to say	the miseries
telecommand	tenebrionid	tertianship	that's an idea	the Missouri
telecommute	tenebrosity	tertium quid	that's the lot	the moon's age
telecontrol	tenementary	tessaraglot	that's torn it	the more part
telecottage	ten feet tall	tessellated	that was that	the Most High
telediphone	tennis court	testability	thaumatrope	the Mountain
telegrapher	tennis dress	testamental	thaumaturge	the Movement
telegraphic	tennis elbow	test batsman	thaumaturgy	the naked ape
telekinesis	Tennysonian	test-furnace	the Almighty	thenceafter
telekinetic	Tenon's space	testiculate	the ancients	thenceforth
telemeeting	tenorrhaphy	testimonial	theanthropy	the noble art
telemessage	ten out of ten	testimonies	the Atlantic	theobromine
teleologies	tenselessly	testimonium	theatre club	theocentric
teleologism	tensile test	testudinate	theatre-goer	theocracies
teleologist	tensiometer	tetanically	theatregoer	Theocritean
telepathise	tensiometry	tetanolysin	theatre-land	theodolitic
telepathist	tensionally	tetrachoric	theatreless	theogonical
telepathize	tensionless	tetracyclic	theatre-list	the old enemy
telephonist	tension wood	tetradactyl	theatre seat	the old story
teleprinter	tensor field	tetradecane	the Big Apple	theological
telerobotic	tensor force	tetradrachm	the Big Drink	theologizer
telescopist	tentability	tetragonous	the big smoke	the Olympics
Telescopium	tentaculate	tetragynous	the Big Three	theomachies
teleseismic	tentaculite	tetrahedral	the biter bit	theomachist
teleshopper	tentatively	tetrahedron	the Brethren	theomorphic
telesthesia	tent-pegging	tetrahydric	the bum's rush	theophagous
teletherapy	tent-trailer	tetralogies	the business	theophanies
televiewing	tent village	tetramerism	the Caudillo	theophanism
televisable	tenuousness	tetramerous	the Cenotaph	theophorous
tellings-off	tenure track	tetrandrous	The Chisholm	theorematic
tell the time	teonanacatl	tetraphonic	the cloister	theoretical
tell volumes	tephramancy	tetraplegia	the Corsican	theory-laden
telmatology	teratogenic	tetraplegic	the Creation	theosophies
telocentric	terbutaline	tetraploidy	the creature	theosophism
telodendron	terebration	tetrapodous	the Crescent	theosophist

theosophize	the wrong way	Thoreauvian	thrust-plane	tiller-chain
the other day	thickheaded	thorium-lead	thrust-shaft	tiller-lines
the other man	thick-leaved	thorny devil	thrust stage	tiller shoot
the outer bar	thick-lipped	thorough-pin	Thucydidean	timber beast
the Prophets	thicknesser	thorough-wax	thujaplicin	timber berth
the Psalmist	thick-witted	those kind of	thumb-bottle	timber drive
therapeusis	thieves' hole	those sort of	thumb-finger	timber-frame
Therapeutae	thigh-length	thoughtless	thumb-lancet	timber hitch
therapeutic	thigmotaxis	thoughtness	thumb-piston	timber-limit
theraphosid	thimblefuls	thought-read	thumb-sucker	time and tide
thereabouts	thimble-like	thought-wave	thunder-ball	time average
therebeside	thingamabob	thowthistle	thunder-bird	time-bargain
the Redeemer	thingamajig	thrasonical	thunderbird	time capsule
theretofore	thingliness	thread belay	thunderboat	time charter
theretoward	thingumabob	thread-board	thunderbolt	time deposit
therewithal	thingumajig	thread-guide	thunderclap	time-expired
therewithin	thingummies	threadiness	thunder-dint	timefulness
there you are	think back to	thread-paper	thunder-drop	timekeeping
theriolatry	think bubble	threatening	thunder-drum	time machine
theriomorph	thinking-box	threatfully	thunder-gust	time-payment
thermalling	Thinking Day	three-banded	thunderhead	time-serving
thermal unit	think it long	three cheers	thunderless	time-sharing
thermically	think it much	three-colour	thunder-pump	time-slicing
thermionics	think much of	three-corner	thuriferous	time-wasting
thermocline	think-tanker	three-decker	thus and thus	timocracies
thermoduric	thin red line	three-double	thwartingly	tin-bounding
thermograph	thin section	three-figure	thwart-ships	tinker's cuss
thermokarst	thin-skinned	threefoldly	thyme-leaved	tin-pan alley
thermolysin	thio-alcohol	three-footed	thymoleptic	Tin Pan Alley
thermolysis	thiocyanate	three-gaited	thymus gland	tinsmithing
thermolytic	thioguanine	three-handed	thyroiditis	tiny garment
thermometer	thiopentone	three-in-hand	thyrotropin	tip of the hat
thermometry	thiophanate	three-legged	thysanurous	tip one's mitt
thermonasty	thioredoxin	three-master	tibiotarsal	Tironensian
thermophile	third cousin	three-piecer	tibiotarsus	Tirthankara
thermophone	third-degree	three-seater	ticket-agent	tissue fluid
thermopower	Third Estate	three-square	ticket booth	tissue-lymph
Thermopylae	third eyelid	three-valued	ticking bomb	tissue paper
thermoscope	third finger	thriftiness	tickled pink	titanaugite
thermotaxic	third market	thrift store	tickle-grass	titanically
thermotaxis	third person	thrillingly	tickler coil	Titanically
thermotical	third stream	throatiness	tick pyaemia	titanothere
theropodous	thirstiness	throat-pouch	tick-tack-toe	Titianesque
Thersitical	thirty-eight	throat-strap	tick-trefoil	titillation
the same very	thirty-seven	throbbingly	tiddlywinky	titillatory
thesaurosis	thirty-three	thrombocyte	tie-breaking	title-holder
thesauruses	thirty-two-mo	thrombolite	Tiepolesque	tit magazine
these kind of	this and that	thromboxane	tierce major	titrimetric
these sort of	this evening	through-ball	tierce minor	tits and bums
the shoe fits	this instant	through-band	tie the rap on	titteringly
thesis-novel	this morning	through-bolt	tiger beetle	titty-bottle
the size of it	thistle-bird	through-deck	tiger-flower	T-lymphocyte
thesmothete	thistledown	throughfall	tiger-hunter	toad's cheese
Thespianism	thistle-head	throughflow	tiger-stripe	toad's eye tin
theta rhythm	thistle-like	through-gang	tight barrel	toad-stabber
the third sex	this-worldly	through-pass	tight corner	to advantage
the Troubles	thitherward	through-toll	tight-fisted	toast-colour
the unco guid	thixotropic	throw a punch	tight-lacing	toaster-oven
the very idea	thole amends	throw stones	tight-lipped	toastmaster
the very same	Thomistical	throw weight	tigroid body	tobacco dove
the wonder is	thoracotomy	thrust block	tile-hanging	tobacco-fish
the Writings	thoreaulite	thrust fault	till and frae	tobacco-leaf

tobaccoless	to one's shame	Totten trust	trades union	transfigure
tobacco lord	tooth-billed	totter-grass	tradeswoman	transfinite
tobacco moth	toothlessly	totteringly	tradeswomen	transfixion
tobacconist	tooth-marked	touch a nerve	trading post	transfluent
tobacco pipe	tooth powder	touch bottom	traditional	transformer
tobacco-root	toothsomely	touched gold	traditioned	transform up
tobacco-shop	top dressing	touch-finder	traditioner	transfusion
tobacco worm	topinambour	touch-in-goal	traducement	transfusive
to begin with	toplessness	touch-needle	trafficable	transglobal
Tobias night	toploftical	touch screen	trafficator	transhumant
Tobin bronze	topocentric	touch tablet	traffic cone	transiently
toboggan-cap	topographer	touch the ark	trafficking	transilient
tobogganing	topographic	touch-typing	traffic lane	transitable
tobogganist	topological	touch-typist	trafficless	transit camp
tocological	top one's part	tough-minded	traffic sign	transit-duty
toddlerhood	topping-lift	toujours gai	tragedienne	transitival
toddy-lifter	toppingness	tourbillion	tragédienne	transit-pass
toddy-tapper	top sergeant	tour de force	tragedietta	transit visa
toenadering	torch-bearer	touristical	trageremics	translatese
Toepler pump	torch-flower	tourist trap	Trager–Smith	translation
toffee apple	torch-holder	tous-les-mois	tragicality	translative
toffee-brown	torchon lace	tout compris	tragic irony	translatory
toffee-nosed	torch singer	tout de suite	tragicomedy	translatrix
toga virilis	tormentedly	tout le monde	trailbaston	translocase
toggle joint	tormentress	tow-coloured	trail-blazer	translocate
togt licence	tormentuous	Tower weight	trailblazer	translucent
toile de Jouy	tornado-lamp	to what avail	trailerable	translunary
toilet brush	Torontonian	towing light	trailer camp	transmarine
toilet-cover	torpedo boat	town council	trailer home	transmittal
toilet-glass	torpedo-body	townishness	trailer park	transmitted
toilet paper	torpedo-like	town marshal	trailer tent	transmitter
toilet table	torpedo tube	town meeting	trail-riding	transmortal
toilet-train	torque motor	town planner	train-bearer	transnature
toilet water	torrent-duck	townscaping	trained band	transnormal
tolbutamide	torrentuous	townspeople	traineeship	transocular
tolerablish	Torridonian	townsperson	training-day	transom-knee
tolerogenic	torsibility	toxicogenic	train-jumper	transpadane
toll and team	torsiograph	toxophilite	trainmaster	transparent
toll an entry	torsionally	toxoplasmic	train ticket	transphasor
Tom-and-Jerry	torsionless	toxoplasmin	traitorhood	transpierce
tomato juice	torsion test	trabeculate	traitorship	transponder
tomboyishly	torso-tosser	tracasserie	trammelling	transportal
tomentulose	torticollis	trace fossil	tranquility	transportee
Tommy-cooker	torturesome	tracelessly	tranquilize	transporter
tommy-gunner	torturously	tracheotomy	transaction	transposase
Tommy system	to shipboard	tracker ball	transalpine	transracial
Tommy talker	to start with	track events	trans-border	transsexual
tomographer	totalisator	track-laying	transcalent	transuranic
tomographic	totalizator	tracklement	transceiver	Transvaaler
tone cluster	total recall	tracklessly	transcreate	transversal
tone control	totemically	track record	transcriber	Transverter
tonemically	to the east of	track-suited	transdermal	transvestic
tonetically	to the height	track system	transductor	trap and ball
tongue thrum	to the letter	track-walker	transection	trap-drummer
tonic accent	to the marrow	tractorcade	transferase	trapeze-line
tonic-clonic	to the moment	tractor feed	transfer fee	trapeziform
tonological	tothersider	tradability	transfer ink	trapezoidal
to no purpose	to the tune of	trade-master	transferral	Trappistine
tonquin bean	to the west of	trade places	transferred	trap-shooter
tonsillitic	totipalmate	trade plates	transferrer	trascinando
tonsillitis	totipotence	trade school	transferrin	travel agent
tool-dresser	totipotency	trade secret	transfer RNA	travellable

traversable	tribulation	triplet code	trouser-clip	tub-thumpery
traverse-map	tribuneship	triple tiara	trouser-cuff	tub-thumping
traverse rod	tribunitial	triplet lily	trouserless	tubular tyre
Traxcavator	tribunitian	triquetrous	trouser suit	tucking-comb
treacheries	tributaries	trisepalous	trucidation	tucking-mill
treacherous	tributarily	tristichous	truck camper	Tudorbethan
tread on eggs	triceratops	tristimulus	trucklingly	tuft-hunting
tread-softly	trichinosis	trisyllabic	truck-master	tug aircraft
treasonable	trichomonad	trisyllable	truck system	tug at the oar
treasonably	trichomonal	tritagonist	truculently	tulipomania
treasurable	trichomonas	tritanomaly	true as steel	tulip poplar
treasury tag	trichopathy	tritheistic	true-hearted	tumble-dried
treble agent	trichophagy	Trito-Isaiah	true horizon	tumble-drier
treble rhyme	Trichoptera	tritonality	Trumanesque	tumble-dries
treckschuit	trichotomic	trituration	trumpet-bird	tumble-dryer
tree babbler	trichromasy	triumphally	trumpet call	tumbler-cart
treecreeper	trickle-down	triumphancy	trumpet-fish	tumblerfuls
tree cricket	tricksiness	triumphator	trumpet-leaf	tumbling-bay
tree diagram	tricoloured	triumph-gate	trumpetless	tumbling-box
tree network	tricolumnar	triumvirate	trumpet-lily	tumefacient
tree of Diana	triconodont	trivet table	trumpet-pipe	tumefaction
tree of Jesse	tricornered	trivializer	trumpet stop	tumescently
tree sparrow	tridecanoic	trivialness	trumpet-tree	tummelberry
tree surgeon	tri-dominium	Trobriander	trumpet-vine	tummy button
tree surgery	triennially	trochal disc	trumpet-weed	tumoricidal
tree swallow	trierarchal	trochophore	trump marine	tumorigenic
tree warbler	trifluralin	troglobiont	trump signal	tumour virus
tree-worship	trifoliated	troglodytic	truncheoned	tunableness
trefoliated	trifurcated	troglophile	trundle-head	tunefulness
trellis-work	triggerable	Trojan horse	trundle-tail	tungstenite
tremblement	trigger area	Trojan Horse	trunk-engine	tunica media
tremblingly	trigger fish	trolley-head	trunk murder	tuning meter
tremolo stop	triggerfish	trolley-pole	trunk-turtle	tuning-slide
tremulation	trigger-hair	trolley shop	trunnel-head	tunnel diode
tremulously	triggerless	trolley-wire	trunnel-hole	tunnel house
trenchantly	trigger tube	trolly-lolly	trust-buster	tunnel-vault
trencher cap	trihydrated	trombiculid	trustbuster	Tupi-Guarani
trencherful	trilobation	tropaeolin D	trustee bank	turban gourd
trencherman	trimellitic	trophobiont	trusteeship	turban shell
trenchermen	trimestrial	trophoblast	trustworthy	turbination
trench fever	trimetrical	trophogenic	truth to tell	turbiniform
trench-knife	Trimetrogen	tropholytic	trying-plane	turbocharge
trench mouth	trimming tab	trophophore	try it on with	turbo-diesel
trend-setter	trimorphism	trophoplasm	try one's hand	turboramjet
trendsetter	trimorphous	trophotaxis	try one's luck	turbosphere
trepanation	Trinidadian	trophozoite	trypanocide	turbulently
trepidation	Trinitarian	trophozooid	trypanosoma	Turcologist
trepidatory	Trinity term	trophy-money	trypanosome	turcopolier
trestle-tree	trinklement	tropicality	trypsinogen	Turgenevian
trestle-work	trinomially	tropicalize	T-shirt dress	turgescence
triadically	tripalmitin	tropomyosin	tubectomies	turgescency
trial lawyer	triparental	troposphere	tube-feeding	turkey-beard
trial trench	tripartisan	tropotactic	tuberculate	turkey-berry
triangulate	tri-personal	troth-plight	tuberculize	turkey-shoot
triantelope	tripetalous	trouble lamp	tuberculoid	Turkey stone
triaxiality	tripe velvet	troubleless	tuberculoma	Turkey wheat
triazine dye	triphibious	troublement	tuberculose	Turkish bath
tribalistic	triphyletic	troublesome	tuberculous	Turkishness
tribeswoman	triple agent	trouble spot	tube shelter	Turk's turban
tribeswomen	triple crown	troublously	tubiflorous	turn-and-bank
tribologist	triple point	trough fault	tubocornual	turn a profit
tribrachial	triple rhyme	trough shell	tub-preacher	turn-crowned

Turneresque	typewriting	unalienable	unblinkable	uncompanied
turning-mill	typewritten	unalienably	unblossomed	uncompelled
turnip-ghost	Typhoid Mary	unalienated	unbonneting	uncompleted
turnipology	typicalness	unallocated	unboundable	uncomplexed
turn of speed	typographer	unallowable	unboundedly	uncompliant
turn the cock	typographic	unalterable	unbreakable	uncomplying
turn the tide	typological	unalterably	unbreathing	unconcealed
turn to ashes	tyrannicide	unambiguity	unbrookable	unconceited
turpeth root	tyrannosaur	unambiguous	unbrotherly	unconceived
turret lathe	tyrannously	unambitious	unbudgeable	unconcerned
turret shell	tyroglyphid	unamendable	unbumptious	unconcerted
turtle-crawl	Tyrolean hat	unamplified	unburnished	unconcluded
turtle-grass	tyrosinemia	unanalogous	unburstable	unconcocted
turtle shell	tyrosinosis	unanimously	uncalcified	uncondemned
turtleshell	tyrothricin	unannotated	uncalled for	uncondensed
turtle-stone	tyuyamunite	unannounced	uncancelled	unconducive
Tuscan straw	Uganda Asian	unanswering	uncanniness	unconfessed
tussock land	uillean pipe	unanxiously	uncanonical	unconfident
tussock moth	ulcerogenic	unapostolic	uncanonized	unconfirmed
tussore moth	ulnar artery	unappealing	uncanvassed	unconformed
tussore-silk	ulotrichous	unapplauded	uncapacious	uncongealed
tutti-frutti	Ulsterwoman	unappointed	uncastrated	uncongenial
twaddlesome	Ulsterwomen	unarraigned	uncatalysed	unconnected
twaddle-toed	ulteriority	unarresting	uncatchable	unconquered
Twelfth-cake	*ultima Thule*	unashamedly	unceasingly	unconscious
twelfth part	ultrafidian	unaspirated	unceilinged	unconsented
twelve-gauge	ultrafilter	unassaulted	uncelestial	unconsigned
twelvemonth	ultramarine	unassertive	uncertainly	unconsonant
twelvepence	ultrametric	unattainted	uncertainty	unconstancy
twelvepenny	ultrasonics	unattempted	uncertified	unconsulted
twelve-toner	ultrastable	unattracted	uncertitude	unconsuming
twenty-eight	ultraviolet	unaugmented	unchainable	uncontained
twig-girdler	umbellately	unauthentic	unchambered	uncontented
twin brother	umbelliform	unavailable	unchartered	uncontested
twin crystal	umbilically	unavailably	unchastened	uncontrived
twin-engined	umbilicated	unavertable	unchastised	unconverted
twinkle roll	umbilicuses	unavertible	uncheckable	unconvicted
twinkle-toed	umboth tithe	unavoidable	uncheckered	unconvinced
twinklingly	umbriferous	unavoidably	unchequered	uncoroneted
twin paradox	unabashable	unawareness	uncherished	uncorrected
twin species	unabashedly	unballasted	unchildlike	uncorrupted
twist barrel	unabolished	unbarbarize	unchiselled	uncorruptly
twisted pair	unabrogated	unbarrelled	unchivalric	uncountable
twitch grass	unacclaimed	unbashfully	unchristian	uncountably
twitchiness	unaccordant	unbeauteous	uncinctured	uncount noun
two-and-eight	unaccounted	unbeautiful	uncivilised	uncourteous
two cultures	unaccusable	unbeclouded	uncivilized	uncourtlike
twofoldness	unadaptable	unbefitting	unclarified	uncouthness
two-handedly	unaddressed	unbeginning	unclassical	uncouthsome
twopenn'orth	unadjourned	unbeknownst	uncleanness	uncrackable
twopenny ale	unadmirable	unbelieving	unclearness	uncreatable
two-yearling	unadoptable	unbendingly	uncleavable	uncrossable
tympaniform	unadvisable	unbeneficed	unclimbable	uncrushable
tympanogram	unadvisably	unbenefited	uncloudedly	uncuckolded
tympanotomy	unadvisedly	unbeseeming	unclubbable	uncunningly
tympan sheet	unaesthetic	unbethought	uncluttered	uncuriously
Tyndall blue	unaffecting	unbetrothed	uncollected	uncurtailed
type-fallacy	unaffianced	unblameable	uncolonized	uncurtained
type founder	unafflicted	unblameably	uncomforted	uncushioned
type foundry	unaffronted	unblemished	uncommanded	uncustomary
typesetting	unagreeable	unblenching	uncommitted	undamnified
type species	unagreeably	unblindfold	uncompacted	undangerous

undauntable
undauntedly
undebauched
undecayable
undeceitful
undeception
undeceptive
undecidable
undecidedly
undecorated
undecylenic
undedicated
undefending
undefiledly
undefinable
undefinably
undefinedly
undeflected
undelayable
undelighted
undelivered
undemanding
undenatured
undenizened
undenounced
undeparting
undepending
undepressed
under a cloud
under-action
underactive
under a curse
under arrest
under a spell
underbearer
underbidder
underbitted
underbodice
underbodies
underbonnet
underbreath
underbridge
under-butler
under canvas
undercharge
underchosen
underclothe
undercolour
undercovert
undercutter
underdamper
underdogger
underemploy
underexpose
under-farmer
under favour
underground
undergrowth
underhammer
underhanded
underheaven
underhonest

underhorsed
underinsure
underinvest
underivable
underivedly
under-keeper
underlessee
underlimbed
underlining
underloaded
under-looker
undermanned
undermasted
under-master
under notice
underoccupy
underparted
underpraise
underreamer
underreckon
underrecord
under-report
underreport
underrun bar
underrunner
under-school
underseller
undersettle
under-sexton
undershorts
undersigned
undersleeve
underspread
understairs
understated
understater
understorey
understream
understrike
undertaking
undertenant
under the sod
under the sun
underthings
under threat
underthrust
undervaluer
under-vassal
under-viewer
under-warden
underweight
underwitted
under-worker
underwriter
undescended
undescribed
undeserving
undesigning
undesirable
undesirably
undespoiled
undestroyed

undeveloped
undeviating
undiagnosed
undignified
undilutedly
undisbanded
undiscerned
undisclosed
undiscussed
undisgraced
undisguised
undislodged
undispelled
undispensed
undispersed
undisplaced
undisproved
undissected
undissolved
undistilled
undistorted
undisturbed
undiverting
undividable
undividably
undividedly
undivinable
undivisible
undoubtable
undoubtably
undoubtedly
undrainable
undraperied
undreamable
undressable
undrinkable
undrinkably
undubitable
undubitably
undutifully
undyingness
unegotistic
unelaborate
unelectable
unembattled
unembezzled
unembroiled
unemotional
unempirical
unemptiable
unenamoured
unenchanted
unendearing
unendurable
unendurably
unenergetic
unenfeebled
unenjoyable
unenlivened
unentangled
unenterable
unenviously

unepiscopal
unequalable
unequal hour
unequalized
unequalness
unequitable
unequivocal
unescapable
unessential
unethically
unevidenced
unexamining
unexcavated
unexcitable
unexclusive
unexemplary
unexercised
unexhausted
unexhibited
unexistence
unexorcised
unexpanding
unexpansive
unexpectant
unexpensive
unexplained
unexploited
unexplosive
unexpounded
unexpressed
unextracted
unfailingly
unfalsified
unfaltering
unfanatical
unfantastic
unfashioned
unfatiguing
unfavorable
unfavourite
unfeathered
unfeelingly
unfeignedly
unfermented
unfittingly
unfixedness
unflappable
unflappably
unflattened
unflattered
unflavoured
unflinching
unforbidden
unforeknown
unforfeited
unforgeable
unforgetful
unforgiving
unforgotten
unformatted
unfortified
unfortunate

unfoundedly
unfractured
unfrenchify
unfreshness
unfructuous
unfulfilled
unfunniness
unfurnished
ungainfully
ungallantly
ungallantry
ungarmented
ungarnished
ungenerated
ungenteelly
ungentleman
unget-at-able
unglaciated
unglamorous
unglorified
ungodliness
ungospelled
ungraduated
ungraspable
ungratified
unguardedly
unguerdoned
unguessable
unguiculate
unguligrade
unhabitable
unhackneyed
unhandiness
unhappiness
unharboured
unhardiness
unharmfully
unharnessed
unharvested
unhazardous
unhealthful
unhealthier
unhealthily
unheartsome
unheedfully
unheedingly
unhelpfully
unheritable
unhingement
unhopefully
unhumanized
unhurriedly
unhusbanded
unicapsular
unicellular
unicolorate
unicolorous
unicoloured
unicorn bird
unicorn-fish
unicorn-root
unidiomatic

unification
unificatory
uniformally
uniformless
uniformness
unigeniture
unignorable
unignorably
unijunction
unilamellar
unilineally
unillumined
unimaginary
unimitative
unimmediate
unimodality
unimpeached
unimpededly
unimperious
unimportant
unimpressed
unimproving
unimpulsive
unincarnate
unincreased
unincubated
unindicated
unindulgent
unindurable
uninflected
uninforming
uninfringed
uningenious
uninhabited
uninhibited
uninitiated
uninjurious
uninnocence
uninquiring
uninscribed
uninspected
uninspiring
uninstalled
uninsulated
uninsurable
unintuitive
uninucleate
uninventive
uninvitedly
union-basher
union rustic
uniparental
unipersonal
unipolarity
unirrigated
unirritated
uniselector
uniserially
unisexually
unitive life
unitiveness
unitization

unity of time
universally
univocality
unjaundiced
unjudicious
unjustified
unkemptness
unkingdomed
unknowingly
unknownness
unlaborious
unlabouring
unlacquered
unlanguaged
unlaundered
unlearnable
unlearnedly
unlevelness
unliberated
unlightened
unlightsome
unlikeliest
unlimitable
unlimitedly
unliquefied
unlistening
unliterally
unlocalized
unlocatable
unlooked-for
unloverlike
unluckiness
unlucrative
unluxuriant
unluxurious
unmalicious
unmalignant
unmalleable
unmanliness
unmasculine
unmatchable
unmatchably
unmeaningly
unmeditated
unmelodious
unmemorable
unmemorably
unmentioned
unmercenary
unmeritable
unmeritedly
unmindfully
unmisgiving
unmitigable
unmitigably
unmitigated
unmixedness
unmockingly
unmodulated
unmoistened
unmolesting
unmollified

unmomentous
unmoralized
unmoralness
unmortgaged
unmortified
unmotivated
unmountable
unmurmuring
unmusically
unmutilated
unnaturally
unnavigable
unnavigated
unnecessary
unneedfully
unnervingly
unnourished
unnutritive
unobjective
unobnoxious
unobservant
unobserving
unobstinate
unobtrusive
unobviously
unoccupancy
unoffending
unofficered
unofficious
unoperating
unopposable
unoppressed
unorganized
unoriginate
unorthodoxy
unpadlocked
unpaintable
unpalatable
unpalatably
unpalliated
unparagoned
unparalyzed
unparcelled
unpardoning
unparriable
unpassioned
unpatriotic
unpatterned
unpausingly
unpeaceable
unpeaceably
unpedigreed
unpensioned
unperceived
unperfected
unperfectly
unperformed
unperishing
unpermanent
unpermitted
unperplexed
unpersuaded

unperturbed
unperverted
unpetrified
unpigmented
unpiteously
unpitifully
unpityingly
unplaceable
unplantable
unplastered
unplausible
unplausibly
unpleadable
unpleasable
unplumbable
unplundered
unpolarized
unpolemical
unpolitical
unpollarded
unpopularly
unpopulated
unportioned
unpossessed
unpractical
unpractised
unpraisable
unpreaching
unpredicted
unpreferred
unprescient
unpresented
unpreserved
unpresuming
unprevented
unprimitive
unprintable
unprintably
unprocessed
unprofessed
unprofiting
unprojected
unpromising
unprophetic
unprotected
unprovoking
unpublished
unpurchased
unputrefied
unqualified
unquickened
unquietness
unquivering
unransacked
unravelling
unravelment
unreachable
unreachably
unreadiness
unrealistic
unreasoning
unrecalling

unreceptive
unreclaimed
unrecounted
unrecovered
unrecruited
unrectified
unredressed
unreducible
unreflected
unrefracted
unrefrained
unrefreshed
unrefusable
unrefutable
unregardful
unregarding
unregretted
unregulated
unrehearsed
unrejoicing
unrelatable
unrelenting
unreligious
unreluctant
unremaining
unremittent
unremitting
unremovable
unrenewable
unrenounced
unrepayable
unrepentant
unrepenting
unrepressed
unreprieved
unreprinted
unrepugnant
unrepulsive
unreputable
unrequested
unrequisite
unrescinded
unresentful
unresenting
unresilient
unresisting
unrespected
unrestfully
unrestingly
unrestraint
unretentive
unretouched
unretracted
unretrieved
unreturning
unrevealing
unrevenging
unreverence
unrevivable
unrewarding
unrighteous
unromanized

unroughened
unrufflable
unsaintlike
unsandalled
unsatisfied
unsaturable
unsaturated
unsavourily
unscannable
unscattered
unsceptical
unscheduled
unscholarly
unscissored
unscrambler
unscratched
unscribbled
unscrutable
unseaworthy
unsectarian
unseductive
unseemingly
unseemliest
unsegmented
unselective
unselfishly
unsensitive
unsentenced
unseparated
unseriously
unsettledly
unseverable
unshakeable
unshakeably
unshapeable
unsharpened
unsharpness
unshattered
unsheltered
unshiftable
unshockable
unshockably
unshortened
unshovelled
unshrinking
unshunnable
unshuttered
unsightable
unskilfully
unslackened
unslakeable
unsmilingly
unsmothered
unsnubbable
unsoberness
unsocialist
unsociality
unsoldiered
unsoldierly
unsolicited
unsoundable
unsoundness

unspareable
unsparingly
unsparkling
unspeakable
unspeakably
unspecified
unspillable
unspiritual
unspoilable
unsponsored
unspottable
unspottedly
unsprinkled
unsqueamish
unsquelched
unstability
unstaidness
unstainable
unsteadfast
unsteadiest
unstiffened
unstillness
unstintedly
unstirrable
unstoppable
unstoppably
unstoppered
unstrapping
unstrategic
unstrenuous
unstressful
unstretched
unstudiedly
unstylishly
unsubduable
unsubjected
unsubmerged
unsubverted
unsucceeded
unsuccoured
unsuffering
unsulliable
unsupported
unsurpassed
unsurprised
unsuspected
unsuspended
unsuspicion
unsustained
unswallowed
unsweepable
unsweetened
unsyllabled
untaintable
untalkative
untarnished
unteachable
untechnical
untemptable
Untermensch
unterrified
untheorized

unthickened
unthinkable
unthinkably
unthriftily
untimeously
untinctured
unto oneself
untoothsome
untormented
untouchable
untouchably
untraceable
untraceably
untractable
untrainable
untravelled
untraversed
untreatable
untrembling
untremulous
untrimmable
untrumpeted
untrustable
untunefully
untwistable
untypically
ununiformed
ununiformly
ununionized
unupbraided
unusualness
unutterable
unutterably
unvarnished
unvaryingly
unvenerable
unventurous
unveracious
unversified
unviability
unvisitable
unvitrified
unvocalized
unvoluntary
unwandering
unwarranted
unwatchable
unweariable
unweariably
unweariedly
unweariness
unweathered
unwedgeable
unweetingly
unweighable
unwelcomely
unwelcoming
unwhispered
unwholesome
unwieldiest
unwillingly
unwinkingly

unwithdrawn
unwithering
unwithstood
unwitnessed
unwittingly
unwomanlike
unworkmanly
unworthiest
unwoundable
up against it
up-and-coming
up-and-downer
Upanishadic
upconverter
upgradation
upgradeable
upheavement
upholstered
upholsterer
upholstress
up one's alley
upon the tilt
upper circle
upper-crusty
upper fourth
upper-middle
upper school
upper second
upper storey
upper-tendom
Upper Voltan
upping-block
upright bass
uprightness
ups and downs
upsettingly
up shit creek
upstretched
upthrusting
uptightness
up to scratch
up to the chin
up to the ears
up to the hilt
up to the mark
upvaluation
uraniferous
uranium bomb
uranium lead
uranography
uranometria
uranoplasty
uranoscopus
urban blight
urban sprawl
urbiculture
urediospore
ureterocele
ureterotomy
urethrogram
urethrotome
urethrotomy

uriniferous
urinologist
urochordate
urodynamics
urogastrone
ursine sloth
urticaceous
urticarious
use immunity
uselessness
user-defined
user-hostile
usucaptable
uterine tube
utero-sacral
utilitarian
utility area
utility pole
utility room
utilization
Utopianizer
utraquistic
utricularia
uveoparotid
vacationist
vacation job
vaccination
vacillation
vacillatory
vacuolating
vacuolation
vacuousness
vacuum brake
vacuum-clean
vacuum flask
vacuum gauge
vacuum-tight
vagabondage
vagabondish
vagabondism
vagabondize
vaginal plug
vagotomized
Vaishnavism
Vaishnavite
valediction
valedictory
valence band
valence bond
Valentinian
vale of tears
valerianate
valeric acid
valinomycin
valleculate
valley-board
valley fever
Valleyspeak
valley train
vallisneria
valuational
value-system

value theory
valvulotomy
vampire trap
vampishness
Vanbrughian
vandalistic
van de Graaff
Vandemonian
van der Waals
vanguardism
vanguardist
vanilla bean
vanishingly
vanity basin
vanity press
vanity table
vaporimeter
vaporizable
vaporograph
vapour-proof
vapour trail
variability
variational
varicellous
variegation
variety shop
variformity
variolation
variousness
varnish-tree
varsovienne
vascularise
vascularity
vascularize
vasculature
vas deferens
vasectomies
vasectomise
vasectomize
vasodilator
vasopressin
vasopressor
Vatican City
vaticinator
vectitation
vector-borne
vector boson
vector field
vectorially
vectorscope
vector space
veer and haul
vegeculture
vegetablize
vehicle-mile
vehicle mine
vehicularly
Vehmgericht
vein-banding
veitchberry
velamentous
vellication

velocimeter
velocimetry
velt-marshal
velvet glove
velvet grass
velvetiness
velvet sauce
velvet sumac
venatically
Vendemiaire
vendibility
venditation
veneer crown
veneficious
venereology
venesection
Venetian red
Venice glass
Venn diagram
venographic
ventilation
ventilative
ventilatory
ventoseness
ventricular
ventriculus
ventriloque
ventriloquy
venturesome
venturously
Venus figure
Venus's basin
Venus's pride
veraciously
veratridine
verbalistic
verberation
verbigerate
verboseness
verd-antique
verdantness
verdigrised
verdureless
verecundity
veridically
verisimilar
vermiculate
vermiculite
vermiculose
vermiculous
vermination
verminicide
vermiparous
vermivorous
vernal glass
vernal grass
verruciform
verruculose
versatilely
versatility
verse anthem
versemonger

versicolour
versuteness
vertebrated
vertical fin
verticalise
verticalism
verticality
verticalize
verticillus
vertiginous
vesiculated
vesiculitis
vesper mouse
vespertinal
vestigially
vestimental
vesuvianite
vetoistical
vexatiously
vexillation
vexillology
Via Dolorosa
viaggiatory
via negativa
vibratility
vibrational
vibratoless
vibriocidal
vicar choral
vicariously
Vicar of Bray
vice admiral
vice-comital
vicegerence
vicegerency
viceregally
viceroyalty
viceroyship
vicey-versey
vichyssoise
viciousness
vicissitude
victimology
Victorianly
victory bond
victoryless
victory roll
victory sign
victualless
victualling
vicuña cloth
video arcade
video camera
videography
video piracy
video pirate
video-player
videorecord
video signal
vie de Bohème
Vienna paste
Vienna steak

Vienna white
vie romancée
viewability
vigesimally
vigilantism
vigogne yarn
vilifyingly
vilipensive
villagehood
villageless
village-like
village pump
villageress
villainizer
Villonesque
vinaigrette
vinblastine
vincibility
vincristine
vin de paille
vin d'honneur
vindication
vindicative
vindicatory
vine-dresser
vine-fretter
vinegarroon
vinegar worm
vineyarding
vineyardist
vinho branco
vinho da casa
viniculture
vin mousseux
vino de color
vino de pasto
vino maestro
vintage port
vintnership
viola d'amore
violational
viol da gamba
violentness
violet cream
violet shift
violet snail
violinistic
violoncello
viper's grass
virginalist
virginality
virgin birth
virgin honey
virgin metal
virgin queen
virgin widow
Virgouleuse
viridescent
virilocally
virogenesis
virogenetic
virological

virtual work
visceralize
viscerotome
viscerotomy
viscometric
viscosities
viscountess
viscounties
viscous flow
viscousness
visibleness
vis inertiae
visionaries
vision mixer
vision quest
Visitandine
visiting ant
visitorship
visive organ
visor-bearer
Vistavision
visual angle
visual field
visual point
visual range
viticulture
vitraillist
vitrescence
vitrescency
vitrescible
vitrifiable
vitriolated
vitrophyric
vituperable
vituperator
vivaciously
vivisection
vivisective
voce di petto
voce di testa
vociferance
vociferator
vodka gimlet
voice-figure
voicelessly
voidability
void and redd
voivodeship
volatile oil
volatilizer
volcanic ash
volcanicity
volcanology
volitionary
Volsteadism
voltaically
voltaic pile
voltammetry
volubleness
volume table
voluntaries
voluntarily

voluntarism	walking leaf	washer-drier	water-pepper	weather side
voluntarist	walking shoe	washer-dryer	water pistol	weather-tile
voluntative	walking tour	washer-upper	water pumper	weather-vane
Voortrekker	walk Matilda	washerwoman	water-shield	weathervane
voraciously	walk off with	washerwomen	water skater	weatherward
vortex sheet	walk out with	washing-bowl	water-souchy	weatherwise
vorticellid	walk Spanish	washing-line	water spider	weather-worn
vorticosely	walk through	washing soda	water-spirit	weaver finch
vortiginous	walk with God	wash its face	water-splash	weaver's knot
vote-catcher	wallaby-bush	wash-leather	water-stream	Webernesque
voting paper	Wallace line	Washo canary	water supply	Weber number
voting stock	wall-bearing	Washo zephyr	waterthrush	web-fingered
vowel colour	wall-bracket	waspishness	water tunnel	Weddell seal
vowel height	wallcreeper	wasp-waisted	water vapour	wedding band
vowel-laxing	wall hanging	wassail-bowl	water vessel	wedding-bush
vox angelica	wall-mounted	waste-basket	water violet	wedding cake
voyage royal	Wall of Death	wastebasket	water-waving	wedding-card
voyeuristic	wallowingly	waste breath	water-willow	wedding-knot
vulcanicity	walnut-shell	waste ground	water-worker	wedding list
vulcanizate	Walschaerts	wastel-bread	water yarrow	wedding ring
vulcanology	Waltonizing	wastethrift	watery grave	wedge-shaped
vulgarities	waltz-length	watch-keeper	Wathawurung	wedge-tailed
vulgar Latin	wampum snake	watchkeeper	Watteau back	weeding-hook
Vulgar Latin	wanderingly	watchmaking	Watteaulike	Wee Free Kirk
vulneraries	wand of peace	watch spring	wattled crow	weeknightly
vulpicidism	wanker's doom	water-bailie	wave changer	weeny-bopper
wage-earning	wantingness	water-bearer	wave machine	weeping-hole
wage economy	wappenschaw	Water-bearer	wave pattern	weequashing
wage one's law	war cemetery	water beetle	wave picture	Weichselian
wager-policy	war criminal	water betony	wave-surface	Weierstrass
wage slavery	ward-heeling	water-blinks	wave winding	weigh anchor
waggishness	ward-holding	water-bomber	wax-chandler	weighbridge
waggle dance	Ward-Leonard	water bottle	waxed jacket	weigh in with
wagon-master	ward of court	water bouget	wax-painting	weighmaster
wagon-wright	ward orderly	water budget	waywardness	weight-clock
Wailing Wall	war hospital	water-cannon	waywodeship	weight cloth
wainscoting	war hysteria	water-caster	weakest link	weightiness
wainscotted	warlessness	water closet	weak-hearted	weight-train
waistcoated	warm-blooded	watercolour	weak mixture	Weismannian
waist-gunner	war medicine	water-cooled	weak-sighted	Weismannism
waist-length	war memorial	water-cooler	wealthiness	Weissenberg
wait a minute	warm-hearted	watercourse	weapon-salve	welcome home
wait at table	war minister	water engine	weaponschaw	welcomeness
waiting game	warm the bell	water finder	weapon-smith	welcomingly
waiting list	warning bell	waterfowler	wearability	weldability
waiting-maid	warning-pipe	water garden	wear and tear	welding heat
waiting move	war of detail	water-gilder	wearilessly	welfare roll
waiting race	war of nerves	water hammer	wearisomely	welfare work
waiting room	warping-buoy	water heater	wear two hats	well advised
waiting time	warping-post	water hyssop	weary Willie	well and good
waitressing	warrantable	watering can	weasel-faced	well-behaved
wait the hour	warrantably	watering-pot	weasel-lemur	well-beloved
wakefulness	warrant card	water-jacket	weatherable	well-blooded
waking dream	warrantless	water-kelpie	weatherbitt	well-cistern
Waldenström	war reporter	Waterlander	weathercoat	well content
walk all over	war resister	water lizard	weathercock	well covered
walking bass	warriorship	waterlogged	weather deck	well-defined
walking dead	wart disease	waterlogger	weather-fend	well-dressed
walking doll	warts and all	Waterloo Cup	weather-gall	well-dresser
walking fern	washability	water-meadow	weathergirl	well-endowed
walking fish	wash-and-wear	water-miller	weather helm	well-fitting
walking lady	wash-drawing	water of life	weathermost	well-founded

well-groomed
well-looking
well-managed
well-matched
well-meaning
well-ordered
well-planned
well pleased
well-plucked
well-rounded
well-stacked
well-stocked
well-studied
well-thumbed
well-trodden
well-willing
well-wishing
well-wrought
Welsh cotton
Welsh dragon
Welsh Office
Welsh rabbit
Weltschmerz
welwitschia
wend one's way
Wensleydale
werewolfery
werewolfish
werewolfism
Wesleyanism
West African
west-by-north
West Coaster
west country
West Country
Western blot
Western boat
westernizer
westernmost
westernness
western roll
Western roll
Westminster
Westphalian
West-Pointer
wet diggings
wether sheep
wet one's clay
wet one's line
wet strength
wettability
whalebacked
whale-fisher
whaler shark
whalesucker
whangdoodle
wharf-lumper
Wharncliffe
what have you
whatsomever
what's trumph
what the hell

what you will
wheatflakes
wheedlingly
wheelbarrow
wheel-plough
wheel-window
wheel wobble
wheelwright
whelk-tingle
whensomever
whereabouts
wheresoever
wherewithal
whether or no
wheyishness
whichsoever
whiffle-ball
whiffletree
Whig history
whigmaleery
whimsically
whingeingly
whippersnap
whipping boy
whipping-top
whippletree
whipsy-derry
whiptail ray
whiskerando
whiskerless
whiskey jack
whisk-tailed
whisky money
whisky voice
whisperless
whistleable
whistle punk
Whistlerian
Whistlerism
whistle-stop
whistle-wood
whistlingly
White Africa
white-backed
Whiteboyism
white bronze
white bryony
whitecapper
Whitechapel
white clover
white coffee
white cohosh
white-collar
white ensign
White Father
whitefisher
white-footed
white ginger
white-haired
white-headed
white horses
White hunter

White Kaffir
white kerria
white knight
white letter
white-lipped
white matter
white-necked
White nigger
white nutmeg
white pepper
white plague
white poplar
white potato
White racism
White racist
white scours
White Sister
white spirit
white spruce
white squall
white squill
white-tailed
White Terror
whitethroat
white tombac
white-walled
white walnut
whitewasher
white willow
white window
white-winged
Whitgiftian
whitherward
whiting pout
whitishness
whitleather
whitlockite
Whitsuntide
Whittington
who-does-what
whole-colour
whole-hoofed
whole-length
whole number
wholesomely
whole-souled
whole-stitch
wholly-owned
whooper swan
whoremaster
whoremonger
whorishness
whorl-flower
whosesoever
wichuraiana
Wicked Bible
widdendream
widdershins
wide-ranging
widowerhood
widowership
widow's cruse

widow's weeds
Wiener Kreis
wiener roast
wienerwurst
wife-swapper
wigeon-grass
wildcatting
wildebeests
wildfowling
wild mustard
wild parsley
wild parsnip
wild tobacco
wild western
will and nill
williamsite
willingness
willow borer
willow-green
willowiness
will-worship
wilsomeness
wily beguile
wimpishness
windbaggery
windbagging
wind-bracing
windbreaker
windcharger
windcheater
wind-furnace
winding-hole
windingness
windjamming
windlestraw
wind machine
window-dress
window frame
window ledge
window plant
window scrim
window table
Windsor bean
Windsor blue
Windsor knot
Windsor soap
windsurfing
wind turbine
wine and dine
wineberries
winebibbing
wine-growing
wine steward
wine tasting
wine vinegar
wing-and-wing
winged words
wing-feather
wing flutter
wing formula
wing forward
wing loading

wingmanship
wing-walking
winnability
winningness
winning post
Winnipegger
winnow-cloth
win on points
winsomeness
winterberry
winter count
winter-crack
winter cress
winter grape
wintergreen
winter-house
winter midge
winter-proof
winter-proud
Winter's bark
winter sleep
winter snipe
winter-sport
wintersweet
winterwards
win the peace
wipe one's eye
wire-drawing
wiredrawing
wireless set
wire netting
wirepulling
wire service
wire-tapping
wire-walking
Wisconsinan
wisdom tooth
wisecracker
wisenheimer
wishfulness
wish I may die
wishing-well
wishtonwish
wish welcome
wistfulness
witch bottle
witch doctor
witches' brew
witchetties
witch-finder
witch-hopple
witch-hunter
witchmonger
witenagemot
with abandon
with an eye to
with a rattle
with a view of
with a view to
with damages
withdraught
withdrawing

witheringly
withershins
witherwrung
withholding
within board
within cry of
within doors
withinsides
within sight
within touch
with justice
with knobs on
with mirrors
without book
without door
without fail
withoutside
with-profits
with respect
withstander
with the wind
witlessness
witnessable
wobble-board
wobble plate
wobbulation
Wodehousian
wolfishness
wolf-madness
wolf whistle
wolvishness
woman doctor
womanliness
woman's woman
womanthrope
women's group
wonderfully
wonderingly
wonder rabbi
wonderstone
wood alcohol
wood anemone
wood buffalo
wood-burning
wood-butcher
woodcarving
wood-chopper
woodcreeper
woodcutting
wooden cross
wooden horse
wooden spoon
wooden walls
wood-leopard
woodmanship
Woodruff key
wood sanicle
wood-swallow
wood-turning
woodturning
wood vinegar
wood warbler

woodworking
woody tongue
wool-bearing
woolclasser
wool-clipper
wool-combing
woolly aphid
woolly indri
woolly lemur
wool-packing
wool-pulling
wool-stapler
word-catcher
word-finally
word for word
word-initial
wordmanship
word of mouth
word-painter
word-perfect
word-picture
word problem
word-process
words fail me
word-watcher
word-writing
workability
workaholism
workfulness
working copy
working girl
working load
working plan
workmanlike
workmanship
work of mercy
work release
work-sharing
workstation
work surface
work the tubs
work wonders
world-beater
world-famous
world-ground
worldliness
worldly-wise
worlds apart
World Series
world-spirit
worm-fishing
worried sick
worrisomely
worshipable
worshipless
worshipping
worsted work
worst-seller
worthlessly
wortle plate
woundedness
wound-stripe

wranglesome
wrapped up in
wrapper leaf
wreathingly
wrecking bar
wrecking car
wreck-master
wren-babbler
wrench fault
wren-warbler
wrestle down
wretchedest
wriggle-work
wrigglingly
wringing wet
wrinkleless
wrist clonus
wrist-length
writing-book
writing-case
writing desk
writing-lark
writ of error
wrong-headed
wronglessly
wrought iron
wunderkinds
Wurtz–Fittig
wyerone acid
Wykehamical
xanthelasma
xanthic acid
xanthinuria
xanthophore
xanthophyll
X chromosome
xenoantigen
xenobiology
xenoblastic
xenocrystal
xenocrystic
xenodochium
xenogenesis
xenoglossia
xenomorphic
xenophiliac
Xenophontic
xenotropism
xeranthemum
xerocopying
xerographic
xeromorphic
xerophilous
xerophytism
xerothermic
xiphopagous
X-radiograph
X-ray burster
xylocarpous
xylographer
xylographic
xylophagous

xylophonist
yacht broker
yachtswoman
yachtswomen
yackety-yack
Yagi antenna
Yankee State
yard-arm iron
yard-measure
Yarkand deer
yarn-spinner
Yarra-banker
Y chromosome
year of grace
yeas and nays
yeast powder
Yeddo spruce
yellow alert
yellow badge
yellow belle
yellow-belly
yellow birch
yellow cedar
yellow-cress
yellow earth
yellow elder
yellow fever
yellow fibre
yellow light
yellow metal
yellow ochre
yellow ox-eye
Yellow Pages
yellow perch
yellow peril
yellow robin
yellow sally
yellowshank
yellow shell
yellow snake
yellow topaz
yellow trout
yeoman bedel
Yeoman Usher
yersiniosis
yesternight
Yiddishkeit
yield stress
yobbishness
you and yours
you can't lose
you-know-what
Younger Edda
younger hand
youngership
young fustic
young master
young person
your servant
Your Worship
Youth Aliyah
youth centre

youth credit
youth hostel
youth leader
yttriferous
Yugoslavian
Yuwaalaraay
zealousness
zearalenone
zebra mussel
zebra spider
Zend-Avestan
Zener effect
zenith sweep
zenithwards
zenocentric
zenographic
zero-balance
zero gravity
zero tillage
zerovalency
zestfulness
zetetically
zigzag fence
zigzaggedly
zillionaire
Zimmer frame
zincography
zip fastener
zoantharian
zoanthropic
zoidogamous
zomotherapy
zonal fossil
zona radiata
zone defence
zone refiner
zone therapy
zoocultural
zoodynamics
zoomorphism
zoomorphize
zooplankter
zooplankton
zootechnics
zootheistic
Zoroastrian
Zuckerkandl
Zurich gnome
zygogenesis
zygogenetic
zygological
zygomorphic
zygotically
zymological
zymoplastic
zymosimeter
zymotechnic
zymotically

TWELVE LETTERS

abaft the beam
a barrel of fun
abbreviation
abbreviatory
abbreviature
abdominal leg
aberrational
abiding-place
a bite and a sup
a bit of no good
abnormalness
abolitionism
abolitionist
aboriginally
abortiveness
abortus fever
above measure
above oneself
above the line
above the salt
Abraham's barm
abscisic acid
absenteeship
absent-minded
absoluteness
absolute term
absolute unit
absolute zero
absolutistic
absorbedness
absorptivity
absquatulate
abstemiously
abstractable
abstractedly
abstractness
abstract noun
abstruseness
a button short
academically
academic year
acanthaceous
accelerandos
acceleration
accelerative
accelerogram
accentuation
access course
accessible to
acciaccatura
accidentally
acclimatizer
accommodable
accommodator
accompanable
accompanyist
accomplished

accomplisher
accordionist
accouchement
accouplement
accoutrement
accretionary
accroachment
accumulation
accumulative
accurateness
accursedness
accusatively
accusatorial
accustomedly
accustomed to
acetaldehyde
acetate fibre
acetoacetate
acetonitrile
Achilles heel
achlamydeous
achlorhydria
achlorhydric
acknowledged
acknowledger
acoustically
acoustic hood
acoustic lens
acoustic mine
acquaintance
acquiescence
acquiescency
acroamatical
acronychally
across the way
acrostically
a crow to pluck
acrylic resin
act counter to
actinometric
actinomycete
action-packed
action replay
active carbon
active matrix
actor-manager
adaptability
adaptational
adaptiveness
adder's tongue
addictedness
additionally
adequateness
Adessenarian
adhesiveness
adhesive tape
adjectitious

adjectivally
adjective dye
adjudication
adjudicative
adjudicature
adjunctively
adjutant bird
adminiculate
administrant
administrate
admonishment
admonitorial
admonitorily
adolescently
adorableness
a dose of salts
adrenal gland
adscititious
adsorptional
adsorptively
adulteration
adulterously
advance guard
advantageous
adventitious
Advent Sunday
adverbialize
advertise for
advisability
advocateship
aecidiospore
aero-allergen
aerodynamics
aeromagnetic
aeronautical
aerostatical
aesthetician
aestheticism
aestheticist
aestheticize
aetiological
affamishment
affectedness
affectionate
affinity card
afflictingly
afflictively
afforestable
affrightedly
affrightment
affrontingly
aforethought
African daisy
African peach
Afrikanerdom
Afrikanerism
Afrikanerize

Afro-American
afterburning
afternoon tea
afterthought
after you with
agalmatolite
agamogenesis
agamogenetic
age-hardening
agent-general
age of consent
age of puberty
ageostrophic
agglutinable
agglutinogen
aggregometer
aggressively
aggressivity
aggrievement
agnomination
agnostically
a good innings
a great one for
agreeability
agribusiness
agrichemical
agricultural
agrobusiness
agrochemical
agro-climatic
agroforestry
agro-industry
a high old time
aides-mémoire
ailurophobia
ailurophobic
air commodore
Air Commodore
air-cushioned
air-freshener
airmail paper
air-sea rescue
air-to-surface
alacritously
Aladdin's cave
Aladdin's lamp
albitization
alcaptonuria
alchemically
aldermanlike
aldermanship
alembication
alexipharmic
algebraicize
Alhambresque
alienability
a likely story

alimentation
alimentative
alive and well
alkalescence
alkalimetric
alkaline tide
alkalization
alkaptonuria
alkaptonuric
all-absorbing
alla cappella
all-alikeness
all and sundry
all-beauteous
all-embracing
All Hallow Eve
alligator gar
alligatoring
all-important
all-inclusive
alliteration
alliterative
all night long
alloantibody
all of a dither
all of a doodah
all of a sudden
all-or-none law
allotmenteer
allotropical
all-pervading
all-pervasive
all-roundness
All Saints' Day
all systems go
all to nothing
all to the good
alluringness
allusiveness
allyl plastic
Almain rivets
almightiness
alphabetical
alphabet soup
alphanumeric
Alpine chough
alstroemeria
alterability
altered chord
altitudinous
alto-rilievos
amalgamation
amalgamative
amateurishly
a matter of law
Amazon parrot
ambassadress
ambassadrice
ambidextrous
ambient music
ambisextrous
ambitionless

ambivalently
ambulance man
ambulatories
amelioration
ameliorative
amenableness
amenorrhoeal
amenorrhoeic
American aloe
American crow
American jute
Americanness
American plan
amicableness
amicus curiae
aminobenzoic
amino-plastic
amissibility
amitotically
ammonium alum
amontillados
amortisation
amortisement
amortization
a mouth to feed
amphibiously
amphibolitic
amphibrachic
amphicoelous
amphictyonic
amphidiploid
amphisbaenid
amphitheatre
amygdaloidal
Anabaptistic
anaerobiosis
anaesthetise
anaesthetist
anaesthetize
anagogically
anagrammatic
analogically
analphabetic
anal sadistic
analytically
anamorphosis
anaphylactic
anaplasmosis
anarchically
an arm and a leg
anastigmatic
anathematise
anathematism
anathematize
anatomically
an axe to grind
anchoritical
anchorpeople
anchorperson
anchovy-paste
anchovy toast
ancien régime

ancient Greek
ancient world
Andean condor
and no mistake
and otherwise
androcentric
androgenesis
androgenetic
androsterone
anecdotalism
anecdotalist
an ecstasy woe
anelasticity
anemographic
anemophilous
anencephalic
angelica tree
angiogenesis
angiographic
angiospermal
angle bracket
angle of pitch
Anglocentric
Anglo-Frisian
anguilliform
anhypostasia
anhypostasis
anhypostatic
aniline black
animadverter
animal rights
animatronics
anisaldehyde
anisocytosis
ankylosaurus
annihilation
annihilative
announcement
annunciation
annunciative
annunciatory
anonymuncule
anorexigenic
anorthoclase
anorthositic
anotherguess
another place
another story
antagonistic
antanaclasis
antebrachial
antecedental
antecedently
antediluvial
antediluvian
antemeridian
anteposition
anteprandial
anteriormost
anthelmintic
anthological
anthophilous

anthoxanthin
anthranilate
anthropogeny
anthropoidal
anthropolite
anthropology
anthroponymy
anthropotomy
anti-abortion
anti-aircraft
anticatholic
anticipation
anticipative
anticipatory
anticlerical
anticlinally
anticyclonic
antidiuretic
antifebrific
antifriction
anti-Gallican
antigenicity
antihysteric
antimacassar
antimalarial
antimoniated
anti-national
antiparallel
antiparticle
antipathetic
antiphonally
antipruritic
antirachitic
anti-Semitism
antisocially
antistrophic
antistrophon
antisymmetry
antitheistic
antithetical
anybody's game
anything like
Anzac biscuit
aoristically
Apache Indian
a painful lack
aperiodicity
apfelstrudel
aphidivorous
aphorismatic
aphoristical
apiculturist
a piece of cake
apocalyptist
apochromatic
apocryphally
Apollinarian
Apollinarist
apologetical
aposporously
apostle spoon
apostolicity

Apostolic See
apostrophise
apostrophize
apothecaries
apparatchiki
apparatchiks
apparentness
apparent time
apparitional
appassionate
appendectomy
appendicitis
appendicular
apperception
apperceptive
appetenccies
appetizingly
applaudingly
applausively
apple-cheeked
apple of Sodom
apple parings
apple strudel
appoggiatura
apportionate
appositeness
appositional
appositively
appraisement
appraisingly
appreciation
appreciative
appreciatory
apprehension
apprehensive
appressorium
approachable
approachless
approachment
approach road
appropriable
appropriator
approximator
appurtenance
a pretty penny
aptitude test
aquacultural
Arabian camel
Arabian horse
arachnophobe
araneologist
arbalestrier
arborescence
arborisation
arborization
archaeologic
archaeologue
archaeometry
archdeaconry
archdiocesan
archegoniate
archesporial

archesporium
archetypical
Archilochian
archinephric
archinephros
archipelagic
archipelagos
archiphoneme
architective
architecture
archosaurian
Arctic Circle
arcubalister
arcus senilis
arena theatre
aretalogical
arfvedsonite
Argand burner
Argentine ant
argentophile
argillaceous
argue the toss
argue well for
argumentator
argyrophilia
argyrophilic
aristocratic
aristolochia
aristologist
Aristophanic
Aristotelean
Aristotelian
arithmetical
arithmomania
arithmometer
armamentaria
Armenian bole
Armistice Day
armour-bearer
armour-plated
arm-wrestling
a rod in pickle
aromatherapy
aromatically
aromaticness
arpeggiation
arrhythmical
arrière-guard
arsenopyrite
arsphenamine
art-and-crafty
artesian well
arthrography
arthroplasty
articulately
articulation
articulative
articulatory
artificially
artilleryman
artillerymen
artistically

artist's proof
Aryanization
as best one can
as black as jet
as busy as a bee
Ascension Day
as clear as day
as clear as mud
Asclepiadean
ascomycetous
ascorbic acid
as dead as a nit
as dry as a chip
as good as gold
a show of hands
Ash Wednesday
ask a blessing
ask me another
a small matter
as often as not
aspartic acid
asphyxiation
aspirational
aspiringness
assassinator
assault craft
assembly line
assembly room
assembly shop
assertorical
asseveration
asseverative
assibilation
assification
assigneeship
assimilation
assimilative
assimilatory
assuefaction
as sure as a gun
as sure as fate
Asti spumante
a stone's throw
astonishable
astonishedly
astonishment
astoundingly
astringently
astrobiology
astrocompass
astrographic
a stroke above
astrolabical
astrological
astronautics
astronomical
astrophysics
asymmetrical
asymptomatic
asymptotical
asynchronous
at adventures

at all hazards
at all weapons
atamasco lily
at an easy rate
at arm's length
at a short stay
at close range
at death's door
at discretion
at first blush
at first brush
at first sight
at full length
at full strain
atheological
atheromatous
athlete's foot
athletically
athletic club
athwart-hawse
at knife-point
at knifepoint
Atlantic seal
Atlantic Time
atmospherics
at nought feet
atomic energy
atomic number
atomic theory
atomic volume
atomic weight
at one stretch
atrabilarian
at second hand
at short range
attemperator
at the hands of
at the heels of
at the mercy of
at the outside
at the point of
Attic dialect
attitudinise
attitudinize
attorneyship
attractively
attributable
at university
auction house
audio-lingual
audiological
auditorially
augmentation
augmentative
auld lang syne
Aulic Council
aurichalcite
auriferously
auscultation
auscultative
auscultatory
auspiciously

Austin Friars
Australasian
Australopith
Austrian pine
Austronesian
authenticate
authenticity
authigenesis
authorizable
auto-analysis
auto-antibody
autocatalyst
autochthonal
autochthones
autochthonic
autocritical
auto-destruct
autodidactic
autofocusing
autogenously
autohypnosis
autohypnotic
autoimmunity
automaticity
automobilism
automobilist
automobility
automorphism
autonomously
autoptically
autorotation
autosemantic
autotheistic
autotoxaemia
autotrophism
autoxidation
autumn crocus
auxanography
availability
avant-courier
avant-gardism
avant-gardist
avariciously
avascularity
a vengeance on
average out at
aviculturist
avitaminoses
avitaminosis
avocado green
Avogadro's law
award the palm
award-winning
awe-inspiring
a wink of sleep
awkward squad
axisymmetric
a year and a day
Azerbaijanis
babbitt metal
babe in Christ
babe of clouts

babingtonite
baby-blue-eyes
baby carriage
baby-snatcher
baccalaurean
Bacchanalian
bacchanalize
bachelorette
bachelor girl
bachelorhood
bachelorship
back and forth
backboneless
back-breaking
backgrounder
backhandedly
backing store
backing track
back-lighting
back of Bourke
back-pressure
backslapping
back-straight
back the field
back-to-nature
backwardness
backwoodsman
backwoodsmen
bacteriaemia
bactericidal
bacteriology
bacteriostat
bad conductor
baggage check
baggage claim
bag of mystery
bail bondsman
Bailey bridge
Bakewell tart
baking powder
Balaam basket
balance sheet
balance wheel
balancing act
ballade royal
ballad-monger
ball and chain
Ballan wrasse
ballet dancer
balletically
ballet-master
balletomania
ballistician
ballon d'essai
balloon frame
balloon glass
ballottement
ball-point pen
ballpoint pen
Balmer series
balm of Gilead
balneologist

balsam poplar
Balsam poplar
balustrading
Bananalander
bandersnatch
bandicoot rat
Bangladeshis
bang to rights
banker's order
banking-house
bankruptcies
bantamweight
Barbados lily
barbarically
Barbary sheep
bar billiards
Barcoo buster
bardolatrous
bare-knuckled
bargain price
baritone horn
barnstorming
barometrical
baroque music
baroreceptor
barratrously
barrier cream
barristerial
Bartlett pear
baselessness
base-stealing
Basic English
basidiospore
basisphenoid
basket clause
basket-hilted
basking shark
bass-baritone
basso-relievo
bastard title
bastard trout
batch process
bathing belle
bathochromic
bathroom tile
bathypelagic
battered baby
battered wife
battering ram
batting order
battleground
battlemented
battles royal
battleworthy
Baudelairean
baulk-cushion
Bayes' theorem
bayonet-grass
be a big boy now
be able to wait
be absorbed by
beachcombing

be after doing
beam-splitter
bean-bag chair
be apprised of
bearableness
bear-covering
bear evidence
be a ringer for
bearing metal
beast of ravin
be astute to do
beat a retreat
beat creation
beatifically
beat into fits
beat the clock
beat the drums
beat the Dutch
beaver meadow
becomingness
bedazzlement
bedding plane
bedding plant
be destined to
be determined
Bedfordshire
be displeased
bed of justice
bedroom farce
bedtime story
beef mountain
beer-swilling
bees and honey
Beethovenian
Beethovenish
beetle-backed
beetle-browed
before Christ
be for the best
befuddlement
beggarliness
beg one's bread
begrudgingly
behaviourism
behaviourist
be here to stay
be in derision
be in raptures
be in the chair
be in the right
be in the way of
be in two minds
Belgian block
believe you me
belittlement
belittlingly
bell-bottomed
belletristic
bell-founding
belligerence
belligerency
belly dancing

belly landing
below the belt
below the line
below the salt
belt conveyor
bench-warrant
bend sinister
bend the brows
bend the rules
benefactress
beneficently
beneficiaire
beneficially
benefit match
benevolently
Bengal quince
benjamin bush
benjamin-tree
be no relation
benzaldehyde
benzoquinone
be of no matter
be one's own man
be on the mooch
be poles apart
be pressed for
bepuzzlement
bequeathable
bequeathment
bergamot mint
Berkeley hunt
Bermuda cedar
Bermuda grass
Bermudian rig
beseechingly
beseemliness
besetting sin
be so good as to
besottedness
bespectacled
bestialities
beta particle
be the death of
be themselves
bet one's shirt
bet on the nose
be too many for
between-decks
between times
be upstanding
be up the flume
be well served
bewilderedly
bewilderment
bewitchingly
beyond a doubt
beyond belief
bibble-babble
Bible-banging
Bible-bashing
Bible-pounder
Bible-puncher

Bible-thumper
bibliography
bibliomaniac
bibliometric
bibliophilic
bibliopolist
bibliothecal
bibliothetic
bibulousness
bicameralism
bicentennial
bicycle chain
bide one's time
bikini briefs
bilateralism
bilaterality
bilharziasis
bilharziosis
bilification
bilingualism
bilinguality
billiard-ball
billingsgate
bill of health
bill of lading
bill of review
Bill of Rights
binary number
binary system
binary weapon
binocularity
biochemistry
biocoenology
biodiversity
bio-energetic
bioflavonoid
biogenically
biogeography
biographical
biohazardous
biologically
biomagnetism
biomechanics
biometrician
biophysicist
biorhythmics
bioscientist
biosynthesis
biosynthetic
bioturbation
bipinnatifid
birationally
bird's-eye view
bird's-nesting
bird-watching
birdwatching
birefringent
birth control
birthday book
birthday cake
birthday card
birthday girl

birthday suit
birthing pool
Bishops' Bible
bishop sleeve
bismuthinite
bismuth ochre
bitch goddess
bit of crumpet
bit on the side
bitter orange
biuniqueness
blabbermouth
black and blue
Black and Tans
blackberried
blackberries
blackbirding
Blackburnian
Black Country
blackcurrant
black diamond
black disease
black draught
black economy
black English
Black English
black-eye bean
blackguardly
black leopard
black mustard
black panther
Black Panther
black pudding
black quarter
black salsify
black-sterned
black tracker
black treacle
black truffle
black vulture
bladder senna
bladderwrack
blandishment
blank charter
blanket-piece
blanket stiff
blast furnace
blastocoelic
blastulation
blatherskite
bless my heart
bless the mark
bletherskate
blind tooling
blissfulness
blisteringly
blister pearl
blister steel
blithesomely
block booking
blockbusting
block diagram

blockheadism
blockishness
block letters
block release
blood and iron
blood-and-soil
blood brother
blood-letting
bloodletting
blood pudding
blood sausage
bloodshedder
bloodshotten
bloodstained
bloodsucking
bloodthirsty
bloody-minded
Bloody Monday
bloody murder
blow one's cool
blubberingly
blue asbestos
bluestocking
blue titmouse
blunderingly
blusteringly
blusterously
board of trade
boardsailing
boastfulness
boat-building
bobby-dazzler
bob-sleighing
bobsleighing
bodice-ripper
body-building
body language
body of Christ
body piercing
body-snatcher
body stocking
bog pimpernel
Bohr magneton
boiling point
boil the billy
boisterously
bomb disposal
bomber jacket
bona vacantia
bone-charcoal
Bonfire Night
bonne fortune
bonnet monkey
bonny-clabber
boogie-woogie
booking clerk
book learning
book-scorpion
Boolean logic
boor's mustard
bootblacking
boot-stocking

Border ballad	breakfasting	bronchophony	burton-tackle
border collie	break silence	bronchoscope	burying place
Border collie	break the bank	bronchoscopy	bus-conductor
boresomeness	break the pack	bronchospasm	bush-fighting
borosilicate	break through	bronco-buster	Bushman grass
borough-reeve	breakthrough	broncobuster	bush sickness
borrowed days	breast collar	brontophobia	business card
borrowed time	breast-plough	brontosaurus	businesslike
Botticellian	breast-pocket	bronze powder	business park
bottle-holder	breast-stroke	broom hickory	business suit
bottle-opener	breaststroke	brothel-house	busybodyness
bottle-washer	breastsummer	brother-in-law	butcher-boots
bottom dollar	breathalyser	brought to bed	butcher's bill
bottom drawer	breathe again	brown creeper	butcher's hook
bouillon cube	breathe short	brown holland	butcher's meat
boulangerite	breathlessly	Brownie Guide	butch haircut
boulderstone	breath of life	brownie point	butter-cooler
bounty hunter	breathtaking	Brownistical	buttercupped
bounty-jumper	breech action	brown mustard	butterfly bow
bouquet garni	breeches-buoy	brush wallaby	butterfly net
bourgeoisdom	breeches part	Brussels lace	butterfly nut
bourgeoisify	breech-loader	bubble memory	butterfly pea
bow and scrape	breed in and in	buccaneering	butter muslin
bow-compasses	breitschwanz	buccaneerish	butterscotch
bowhead whale	Brewster's law	buccolingual	buttery-hatch
bowler-hatted	brickfielder	Buckeye State	button-holder
bowling alley	brick-nogging	buck the tiger	buttress-root
bowling green	bridal wreath	Buddhistical	buyer's market
bow of promise	bride-chamber	budget buster	buyers' market
boxing weight	bridging loan	buffalo berry	buy the rabbit
boy-meets-girl	brigade-major	buffalo chips	by a long chalk
brachycephal	brigadier wig	buffalo grass	by contraries
brachygraphy	bright lights	buffle-headed	by courtesy of
brachylogies	brilliantine	build a sconce	by definition
brachypellic	bring forward	building line	Byelorussian
bracken-clock	bring through	building site	by entireties
bracket clock	bring to a head	building-term	by succession
brackishness	bring to grief	bulldog breed	by themselves
bradyseismic	bring to light	bulldog issue	by yourselves
Brahminy bull	bring to terms	bullen-bullen	cabbage white
Brahminy duck	bring up short	bullet-headed	cabin cruiser
Brahminy kite	brinkmanship	bullfighting	cabinet-maker
brain-damaged	bristle-grass	bull-headedly	cabinetmaker
brain scanner	Bristol board	bull-of-the-bog	cabinet organ
brain-twister	Bristol cream	bunch of fives	cabinet piano
brainwashing	Bristol glass	bunco-steerer	cabin-steward
bramble-berry	Bristol stone	bundle-sheath	cable pattern
brandenburgs	Britannicize	bungarotoxin	cable railway
brandy-bottle	British crown	bungee jumper	cable release
brandy butter	British Isles	bun in the oven	cachinnation
brandy-cherry	Britocentric	Bunsen burner	cachinnatory
brandy-pawnee	broadcasting	Buonapartist	cack-handedly
brass-monkeys	broad pennant	burdensomely	caco-magician
brass rubbing	broiler house	bureaucratic	cactus dahlia
brass section	broken-backed	burglar alarm	cadaverously
Braxton Hicks	broken colour	burial ground	caenogenesis
bread and milk	broken-winded	burn daylight	caenogenetic
bread and wine	broker-dealer	burn in effigy	cainogenesis
bread of trete	bromargyrite	burning-glass	cairn terrier
bread pudding	bromide paper	burn to a crisp	calabash tree
break contact	Bromo-Seltzer	burrowing owl	calamitously
break-dancing	bronchogenic	bursectomize	Calamity Jane

calcalkaline
calcitration
calcium oxide
calculatedly
calendar year
caliginosity
calisthenics
calligrapher
calligraphic
call into play
callisthenic
call of nature
call one's shot
call the shots
call to the bar
calorimetric
calumniation
calumniatory
calumniously
Calvary cross
cameralistic
camera lucida
camiknickers
campanologer
campanulated
camp fire girl
camp follower
campshedding
Canada balsam
canaliculate
canalization
canary yellow
cancellandum
cancellarian
cancellation
cancericidal
candid camera
candleholder
candle-waster
candy-striped
candystriped
candystriper
cane-coloured
cannon fodder
cannot choose
cannot resist
canonisation
canonization
canon regular
Cantabrigian
cantankerous
canterburies
cantharidean
cantharidize
cantilevered
cantillation
cantus firmus
can you beat it
capabilities
capacitation
capacitative
Cape anteater

Cape chestnut
Cape Coloured
Cape hyacinth
Cape marigold
Cape pondweed
Cape primrose
capercaillie
capercailzie
capillaceous
capital goods
capitalistic
Capitan Pasha
capitularies
capitulation
capitulatory
cap of liberty
capriciously
Capricornian
capstan lathe
captiousness
caput mortuum
caravanserai
carbohydrate
carbolic acid
carbolic soap
carbonaceous
carbon dating
carbonic acid
carbunculous
carburetting
carcinogenic
card-carrying
cardinal's hat
cardinalship
cardinal vein
cardinal wind
cardiography
cardiologist
carefreeness
carelessness
caricaturist
carillonneur
Carlovingian
Carlsbad plum
carnal member
Carolina duck
Carolina pink
Carolina rice
carol service
carol-singing
carpenter ant
carpenter bee
carpet-bagger
carpet-beater
carpet beetle
carpet knight
carpet square
Carpocratian
carpological
carriageable
carriage paid
carriwitchet

carry forward
carry one's bat
carry the baby
carry through
carry with one
carte blanche
Cartesianism
Carthaginian
cartographer
cartographic
cartoonishly
cartoon strip
cartophilist
cartouche-box
cartridge-box
cartridge-pen
carunculated
carving knife
case the joint
cash and carry
cash register
cassette deck
cassette tape
cast accounts
cast a stone at
castellation
casting couch
cast in the eye
castor action
cast stones at
cast the glove
casual pauper
casualty ward
catachrestic
catacoustics
catadioptric
catamountain
cataphoresis
cataphoretic
catastrophic
catch a packet
catch a Tartar
catch bending
catchingness
catch napping
catch sight of
catechetical
cathetometer
cathodically
catholically
Catholically
Catholic King
Catilinarian
cat o' mountain
cattle-lifter
cattle-plague
cattle-trough
caulking iron
cause célèbre
caustic plant
caution money
cautiousness

cavalier cuff
cavalry sword
cavalry twill
caveat emptor
cave painting
cedar waxwing
celestiality
celibatarian
cellar beetle
cell membrane
Celsius scale
Celtic fringe
cementitious
censoriously
centesimally
centillionth
central force
central lobby
centre circle
centre of mass
centre-second
centre spread
centrifugate
centrosphere
centumvirate
centuplicate
centuriation
century plant
cephalic vein
cephalometry
cephalopodal
cerebrotonic
ceremonially
cespititious
cessionaries
cestui que vie
cetane number
cetyl alcohol
chacma baboon
chaetigerous
chaffer words
chain printer
chairmanship
chaise longue
chaise lounge
chalcanthite
Chalcedonian
chalcedonies
chalcenteric
chalcogenide
chalcography
chalcolithic
chalcopyrite
chalicothere
chalk and talk
chalk drawing
chalk-striped
chamber music
chamber organ
championship
chance-medley
change-bowler

change colour
changelessly
change of gear
change of life
change of mind
change-ringer
changing room
Channel Fleet
channel-stone
chapel-master
chapel of ease
chapel of rest
chapelwarden
chaperonless
chaplaincies
chaplainship
Chaplinesque
chapter house
characterful
characterise
characterize
charcoal grey
charlatanism
Charles's Wain
charley horse
charmingness
charnel house
charnockitic
Charterhouse
charter-party
chart-topping
chassé croisé
chastisement
chastity belt
château in air
chattel slave
chattels real
chatteration
chatteringly
chaulmoogric
chauvinistic
checkerberry
checkerboard
check through
cheek to cheek
cheerfulness
cheeseburger
cheese-cutter
cheesemaking
cheesemonger
cheese-paring
cheiloplasty
chemical bond
chemiosmotic
chemokinesis
chemokinetic
chemotherapy
chemotropism
chequer-board
chequerboard
cherishingly
Cherokee rose

cherry-bounce
cherry brandy
cherry laurel
cherry picker
cherry tomato
cherubically
cherubimical
cherubinical
Cheshire acre
chesterfield
chest freezer
chestnutting
chestnut tree
chestnut wood
chest of viols
Cheviot sheep
Cheyne-Stokes
chicken brick
chicken gumbo
chicken-heart
chicken korma
chicken-liver
Chief Justice
Chief of Staff
chieftainess
child-bearing
childbearing
child benefit
child-centred
childishness
childminding
chiliahedron
chilli pepper
chilli powder
chimerically
chimney-board
chimney-money
chimney piece
chimney stack
chimney sweep
chimney swift
chimonanthus
China-watcher
Chinese anise
Chinese block
Chinese olive
Chinese white
chirognomist
chirographer
chirological
chiromantist
chiropractic
chiropractor
chiropterous
chivalresque
chivalrously
chlorapatite
chlorination
chloroformic
chloropicrin
chlorous acid
chocolate box

chokeberries
cholerically
chondrophore
chondrostean
choreography
choreologist
chorographer
chorographic
chorological
chorus-master
chosen people
chou moellier
chrematistic
chrestomathy
chrisom-cloth
Christian era
Christianise
Christianism
Christianity
Christianize
Christmas box
Christmas Day
Christmas Eve
Christophany
Christ's thorn
chromaticism
chromaticity
chromatogram
chromatology
chromatopsia
chrome yellow
chromic oxide
chromophilic
chromophobic
chromophoric
chromosphere
chronography
chronologies
chronologise
chronologist
chronologize
chronometric
chronotropic
chrysophanic
chrysopoetic
churchianity
Churchillian
church-litten
church-living
church parade
church school
churchwarden
churlishness
churnability
churrascaria
chylifactive
chymotrypsin
cigarette end
cigar-lighter
cilioretinal
cinchona bark
cinchonicine

cinematheque
cinéma-vérité
cinnamon bear
cinnamon fern
cinnamon rose
cinquefoiled
circuit board
circuit court
circuit judge
circuitously
circular loom
circularness
circular tour
circumcircle
circumcision
circumfluent
circumfluous
circumfusion
circumgyrate
circumjacent
circumjovial
circumjovian
circumnutate
circumscribe
circumscript
circumsphere
circumstance
circumvolute
cirrocumulus
cirrostratus
citification
citizens' band
city of refuge
civil defence
civilisation
civilization
civil liberty
civil servant
civil service
Civil Service
cladogenesis
cladogenetic
cladosporium
clairaudient
clair-obscure
clairvoyance
clairvoyante
clamjamphrie
clangorously
clannishness
clapboarding
clapperboard
claret colour
clarinettist
classicalism
classicalist
classicality
classicistic
classic races
classifiable
claudication
claustration

clavicembalo
clean and jerk
clean fingers
clear as a bell
clearing bank
clear-obscure
clear-sighted
clearstories
cleistogamic
clerk of works
clerodendrum
Cleveland bay
clever-clever
client-server
cliff-hanging
cliffhanging
cliff swallow
climatically
climbing-iron
clinker-built
clinographic
clipper-built
clippety-clop
cliquishness
clock-watcher
cloddishness
cloisterless
close borough
close-coupled
close-cropped
closed season
close-fitting
close-grained
close harmony
close-mouthed
close-quarter
cloth-binding
clothes-brush
clothes-drier
clothes horse
clothing-book
clothing-club
cloth of state
clotted cream
cloudberries
cloud chamber
cloud-hopping
cloud seeding
cloven-footed
cloven-hoofed
clover weevil
clownishness
club armchair
clubbability
club sandwich
cluelessness
coacervation
coachbuilder
coachmanship
coach station
coadaptation
coadventurer

coagulometer
coalitionism
coalitionist
coal measures
coal-merchant
coal-titmouse
coarse-fibred
coarticulate
coast disease
coast to coast
co-authorship
coaxial cable
cobalt glance
cobbler's awls
cobbler's pegs
cobweb spider
cocarcinogen
coccidiostat
cockeye pilot
cock-fighting
cockfighting
cock one's ears
cock one's nose
cock-shut time
cocksureness
cock-throwing
code-breaking
code of honour
codependency
codification
coelacanthid
coelenterate
coenobitical
coerciveness
coetaneously
coffin corner
cogeneration
cogitatively
cognoscitive
cohabitation
cohesiveness
coincidental
coincidently
coindication
co-inhabitant
coin-operated
cold compress
cold shoulder
coleopterist
coleopteroid
coleopterous
collaborator
collared dove
collaterally
collaudation
collectarium
collectively
collectivise
collectivism
collectivist
collectivity
collectivize

collectorate
collegiality
collegiately
collinearity
colliquative
collision-mat
collodionize
colloidality
collophanite
Collop Monday
colloquially
colluctation
collywobbles
cologne water
colombophile
colometrical
Colonel Blimp
colonisation
colonization
coloquintida
colorimetric
colour camera
colour-change
colour-filter
colourlessly
colour scheme
columbaceous
columbic acid
columniation
combat jacket
combinedness
combined pill
come a cropper
come across as
come a long way
come-by-chance
come into line
come into play
come it strong
come one's ways
come on strong
come tardy off
come to a point
come to naught
come to no good
come to nought
come to pieces
come to the top
comfortingly
Cominformist
commandingly
Command Paper
commemorator
commenceable
commencement
commendatary
commendation
commendatore
commendatory
commensalism
commensality
commensurate

commentaries
commentation
commercially
commiserable
commissarial
commissariat
commissaries
commissional
commissioned
commissioner
commit mayhem
committee man
commodiously
commonalties
Common Celtic
commonership
common factor
common ground
commonholder
common jackal
common laurel
common lawyer
common lizard
Common Market
commonplacer
common prayer
Common Prayer
common privet
common roller
common shrimp
common violet
commonwealth
communicable
communicably
communicator
Communion-cup
communionist
community tax
companionage
companionate
companion set
companion-way
companionway
compare notes
compartition
compass plane
compass-plant
compaternity
compatriotic
compellation
compellingly
compenetrate
compensation
compensative
compensatory
competitress
complacently
complainable
complaintive
complaisance
complanation
complemental

complementer
completeness
complete with
complexional
complexioned
complexities
complication
complicative
complimental
complimenter
componential
compo rations
composedness
compos mentis
compoundable
compound leaf
compoundness
compound time
compound word
comprecation
compressible
compulsative
compulsively
compulsorily
compunctious
compurgation
compurgatory
computer game
conceivement
concelebrant
concelebrate
concentrated
concentrator
concentrical
conceptional
conceptively
conceptually
concert grand
concertinaed
concertinist
concert party
concert pitch
concessional
concessioner
concessively
conchiferous
conchoidally
conchologist
conciliabule
conciliarism
conciliarist
conciliation
conciliative
conciliatory
conclamation
conclusively
concomitance
concomitancy
concordancer
concordantly
concordatory
concorporate

concremation
concrescence
concreteness
concupiscent
concurrently
condemnation
condemnatory
condemningly
condensation
condescender
conditionate
conductively
conductivity
conduct-money
conductorial
conduct sheet
conduplicate
confabulator
confectioner
confederator
conferential
confessional
confessorial
confidential
confinedness
confirmation
confirmative
confirmatory
confiscation
confiscatory
conflagrator
conformation
confoundable
confoundedly
confrontment
Confucianism
Confucianist
confusedness
confusticate
congeniality
congenitally
conglobation
conglobulate
conglomerate
conglutinate
congratulant
congratulate
congregation
congregative
congress boot
conic section
conidiophore
conjunctival
conjunctivas
conjure woman
conjurorship
connaturally
connectional
connectively
connectivity
conning tower
connubiality

conqueringly
conquistador
conscionable
conscionably
conscription
conscriptive
consecration
consecratory
consensually
consentience
consentingly
consequently
conservation
conservatism
conservatist
conservative
conservatize
conservatory
conservatrix
considerable
considerably
consignation
consistently
consistorial
consistorian
consistories
consociation
console table
consolidator
consonantism
conspiracies
conspiration
conspirative
conspiratory
constabulary
constatation
constipation
constituency
constitution
constitutive
constriction
constrictive
constringent
construction
constructive
consultation
consultative
consultatory
consummately
consummation
consummative
consummatory
contabescent
contact print
contact sheet
contact sport
contagionist
contagiously
containerise
containerize
contaminator
contemningly

contemplable
contemplator
contemporary
contemporize
contemptible
contemptibly
contemptuous
contentation
contentional
conterminate
conterminous
contestation
contextually
contignation
contiguously
contingently
continuality
continuation
continuative
continuities
continuously
contractable
contractedly
contractible
contractural
contractured
contract work
contradictor
contranatant
contrapuntal
contrariness
contrariwise
contribution
contributive
contributory
contriteness
contrivement
control board
control group
controllable
controllably
control panel
control tower
controverter
contumacious
contumelious
convalescent
convectional
convectively
convenership
conveniently
conventicler
conventional
conventioner
conventually
conversation
conversative
conveyancing
conveyor belt
convictively
convincement
convincingly

convivialist
conviviality
convolutedly
convulsional
convulsively
co-occurrence
cookie-cutter
cookie-pusher
cooking apple
cooking range
cooking-stove
cook the books
cooling tower
co-omnipotent
coordinately
coordination
coordinative
copolymerise
copolymerize
copper-fasten
copper glance
copper-headed
copper-nickel
co-production
coprophagous
coprophilous
co-proprietor
co-prosperity
copulatively
copy of verses
coquettishly
corduroy road
corelatively
core-sampling
co-respondent
corn chandler
corn crowfoot
corn exchange
corniche road
Cornish cream
Cornish pasty
corn marigold
corno inglese
corn on the cob
corn-shucking
corollaceous
coronal plane
coronary gold
coroner's jury
corporal oath
corporalship
corporealism
corporeality
corporealize
corpse-candle
cor pulmonale
corpusculous
corpus luteum
correctional
correctitude
correctively
correlatable

corresponder
corroborator
corruptively
Corsican pine
corticifugal
corticipetal
corticofugal
corticopetal
coscinomancy
cosmetically
cosmic string
cosmocentric
cosmogenetic
cosmogonical
cosmographer
cosmographic
cosmological
cosmonautics
cosmopolitan
costal pleura
costermonger
costing clerk
costlessness
cost of living
costume drama
costume piece
Cotswold lion
cottage ornée
cottage piano
cotton famine
cottonocracy
Cottonopolis
cotton-powder
cotton thread
cotton-woolly
cotyledonary
cotyledonous
cough mixture
Coulomb force
council-board
council-house
councilmanic
council of war
council-table
councilwoman
councilwomen
counsellable
countability
count against
countenanced
countenancer
counter-agent
counter-argue
counterblast
counter-charm
countercharm
countercheck
counter-claim
countercross
countercycle
counter-earth
counter-élite

counterforce
counterguard
counter lunch
countermarch
countermatch
counterminer
counter-offer
counter-order
counterpoint
counterpoise
counterproof
counterprove
counterpunch
counter-scale
counterscarp
countersense
countershaft
counterslope
counter-spell
counterstain
counter-tenor
counter-title
counter-trade
countervalue
counterweigh
countess-ship
counting-room
country dance
country house
country mouse
country music
country party
countrywoman
countrywomen
count the cost
count the days
county family
county school
coup de foudre
coupé de ville
coup the crans
courageously
courtesy call
courtiership
court-martial
court of guard
court plaster
cousin german
cousinliness
covalent bond
covering note
cover version
covetousness
cowardliness
Cowper's gland
coxswainless
coxswainship
crack a bottle
crack-brained
cracked wheat
crack the whip
cradle-rocker

cradle-scythe
cradle-snatch
craft-brother
craftsmaster
craftspeople
craftsperson
cranial index
cranial nerve
cranio-facial
craniologist
craniometric
cranioplasty
cranio-spinal
craniotomies
crapshooting
crash barrier
crash landing
crash the gate
creaking gate
cream cracker
creativeness
creaturehood
creatureship
credibleness
credit rating
creditworthy
creeping bent
creepy-crawly
cremationist
crematoriums
crème brûlées
crème caramel
crème de cacao
crème de noyau
crème fraiche
cremnophobia
crenellation
creolization
creosote bush
crêpe de Chine
crêpe Suzette
crepusculine
crepusculous
crescent moon
crescent roll
crested argus
cretaceously
crico-thyroid
Crimean shirt
crime-busting
crime fighter
criminal code
criminalness
cringingness
crise de nerfs
cristobalite
criteriology
critical mass
criticalness
critical path
critical size
criticizable

Cro-Magnon man
cromoglycate
Crookes glass
Crookes space
cross a cheque
cross and pile
cross-bedding
cross-bencher
cross-buttock
cross-channel
cross-connect
cross-country
cross-dresser
cross-examine
cross-grained
cross-handled
cross-heading
crossing over
cross-linkage
cross-posting
cross product
cross purpose
cross-reading
cross-section
cross-subsidy
crown bowling
crowned crane
Crown Gardens
crown-wearing
crucialities
crush barrier
cryoglobulin
cryopreserve
cry over spilt
cryptanalyst
cryptobiosis
cryptobiotic
cryptococcal
cryptogamist
cryptogamous
cryptography
cryptologist
cryptonymous
cry roast meat
crystal class
crystal clear
crystal-gazer
crystal glass
crystallitic
crystallizer
cubic content
cubistically
cucking-stool
cuckoo flower
cuckoo roller
cuckoo shrike
cuckoo wrasse
cucumber tree
cue and review
Culm Measures
culpableness
cultivatable

culture-bound
culture pearl
culture shock
cumber-ground
cumbersomely
cumbrousness
cumulatively
cumulonimbus
cunctipotent
cuneiformist
cunnilinctus
cupboard love
cupping-glass
cuprammonium
curarization
curativeness
curiological
curled mallow
curlie-wurlie
curling-stone
curling tongs
curl of the lip
curmudgeonly
currant borer
currant jelly
currency note
current asset
curve-fitting
curvifoliate
curvirostral
cushion-dance
custard apple
customizable
customs house
customs union
cut and thrust
cuticularize
cutinization
cut one's lucky
cut one's stick
cut on the bias
cut the cackle
cut the comb of
cutting grass
cutting horse
cyanochroite
cyanogenesis
cyanogenetic
cyanophilous
cyclodextrin
cyclonically
cyclopropane
cyclostomate
cylinder bore
cylinder head
cylinder lock
cylinder seal
cylindricity
cylindriform
cylindroidal
cymotrichous
cynocephalus

cystic artery
cysticercoid
cytochalasin
cytochemical
cytogenetics
cytoskeletal
cytoskeleton
cytotaxonomy
Czechoslovak
dabbling duck
dactylically
dactyloscopy
dactylozooid
daft as a brush
daggle-tailed
dairy factory
dairy-farming
Dalmatian dog
damaged goods
damask violet
damn your eyes
damson cheese
dance hostess
dance macabre
dance of death
Dance of Death
dance the hays
danger signal
Danish modern
Danish pastry
danse macabre
danseur noble
Darby and Joan
dariole mould
Dartmoor pony
Darwinianism
dassievanger
data terminal
datelessness
daughter atom
daughter cell
daughterhood
daughterless
daunorubicin
day blindness
daylight time
day of the week
deactivation
dead-and-alive
dead as mutton
dead-ball line
dead giveaway
de-adjectival
dead language
dead man's hand
Dead Sea apple
dead to rights
deaf-dumbness
de-alcoholize
dealkylation
deambulation
deambulatory

deanery synod
death-dealing
deathfulness
death-or-glory
death penalty
death warrant
debating club
debilitation
debilitative
debonairness
debt of honour
debt of nature
Debussyesque
decaffeinate
decalcomania
decalescence
decapacitate
decaphyllous
decapitalize
decapitation
decasyllabic
decasyllable
deceleration
December moth
decentralise
decentralist
decentralize
decentration
decidability
decimal place
decimal point
decimal scale
decipherable
decipherment
decisiveness
deckled-edged
declassified
declassifies
declensional
declinometer
decoloration
decommission
decomplement
decomposable
decomposible
decompressor
decongestant
decongestion
decongestive
deconsecrate
decontrolled
decoratively
decorousness
decorticator
decreasingly
decrescendos
dedicatorily
dedolomitize
deducibility
deep mourning
deer-coloured
de-escalation

de-excitation
defatigation
defenestrate
defensive end
defibrillate
deficiencies
definability
definiteness
definitional
definitively
deflagration
deflationary
deflationist
deflocculant
deflocculate
defraudation
degenerately
degeneration
degenerative
deglaciation
deglutitious
degree Kelvin
dehumidified
dehumidifier
dehumidifies
de-indexation
deionization
dejectedness
delamination
delayed shock
delegateship
delegitimize
Delian League
deliberately
deliberation
deliberative
delicateness
delicatessen
delightfully
delightingly
delimitation
delimitative
delinquently
deliquescent
delitescence
delitescency
deliver a jail
delivery room
Della Cruscan
deltiologist
delusiveness
demagnetizer
demand-driven
demembration
dementedness
demi-culverin
demilitarise
demilitarize
demi-mondaine
demineralise
demineralize
demi-toilette

democratical
democratizer
demodulation
demographics
demolishable
demolishment
demoniacally
demonization
demonologist
demonomaniac
demonopolise
demonopolize
demonstrable
demonstrably
demonstrator
demoralizing
Demosthenean
demotivation
denaturalise
denaturalize
denaturation
dendrologist
Denmark satin
den of thieves
denomination
denominative
denotational
denotatively
denouncement
densitometer
densitometry
denticulated
dentilingual
denuclearise
denuclearize
denudational
denumeration
denunciation
denunciative
denunciatory
deoch an doris
deontologist
deoperculate
deordination
departmental
depauperated
dependencies
depend upon it
dephlegmator
depilatories
depoliticise
depoliticize
depolymerise
depolymerize
depopularize
depopulation
depositaries
deposition
depositional
depositories
depravedness
depreciation

depreciative
depreciatory
depressingly
depressively
depressurise
depressurize
deproteinize
Deptford pink
depth of field
depth of focus
deputatively
deracination
deratization
deregulation
deregulatory
derelict land
derepression
derestricted
derisiveness
derivability
derivational
derivatively
dermabrasion
dermapterous
dermatophyte
dermographia
derogatively
derogatorily
desalination
desaturation
descendental
descensional
descent group
desensitizer
desertedness
desert island
deservedness
desideration
desiderative
designer drug
desirability
desirousness
desk sergeant
desolateness
desolatingly
despairfully
despairingly
despecialize
desperadoism
despitefully
despiteously
despoliation
despondently
despondingly
despotically
desquamation
desquamative
desquamatory
dessert apple
dessert-plate
dessertspoon
destroyingly

destructible
desulphurate
desulphurise
desulphurize
desultorious
desynonymize
detachedness
deteriorator
determinable
determinably
determinator
determinatum
determinedly
dethronement
detoxication
detractation
detractingly
detractively
detruncation
detumescence
deuteranomal
deuteranopia
deuteranopic
deuterostome
Deutsche Mark
developement
deviationism
deviationist
devil-in-a-bush
devilishness
devil-may-care
devil's matins
devil's needle
devil's tattoo
devil-worship
devolatilize
devotionally
dextrocardia
diabetogenic
diabolically
diadem monkey
diadem spider
diageotropic
diagrammatic
dialectician
dialecticism
dialectology
dialling code
dialling tone
dialogically
diamagnetism
diamond-drill
diamond-field
diamond frame
diamond-point
diamond snake
Diamond State
diaphanously
diapirically
diarthrodial
diastrophism
diathermancy

diatomaceous
diatonically
diazomethane
diazotizable
dibranchiate
dicarboxylic
dicatalectic
dichotomized
dichroiscope
dichromatism
Dickensianly
dictatorship
dictionaries
dictyostelic
didactically
diddle-diddle
die in harness
die in one's bed
diencephalic
diencephalon
die of illness
die on someone
diesel engine
dietetically
diethylamide
diethyl ether
Dietl's crisis
differentiae
differential
difficulties
diffusedness
diffusionism
diffusionist
digging-stick
digital clock
digitization
digladiation
dig oneself in
digressingly
digressional
digressively
Dijon mustard
dijudication
dilaceration
dilambdodont
dilapidation
dilatability
dilatational
dilatometric
dilatoriness
dilatory plea
dilettantish
dilettantism
dilettantist
dilly-dallied
dilly-dallier
dilly-dallies
dimensurator
dimerization
diminishable
diminishment
diminutively

dimmer switch
dingle-dangle
dingy skipper
dining saloon
dinner jacket
dioctahedral
Diogenes-crab
dioptrically
diphtheritic
diphtheritis
diphthongise
diphthongize
diploblastic
diplographic
diplomatical
diplostemony
dipole moment
dipyridamole
direct access
direct action
directedness
direct labour
direct method
direct object
directorship
direct speech
dirigibility
dirty weekend
disabilities
disaccharase
disaccharide
disaccordant
disadvantage
disaffection
disaffiliate
disaggregate
disagreeable
disagreeably
disagreement
disallowable
disallowance
disambiguate
disamenities
disanimation
disannulment
disapproving
disassembler
disassociate
disaster area
disastrously
disauthorize
disbursement
discarnation
disceptation
discerningly
discerptible
disciplehood
discipleship
disciplinant
disciplinary
disclamation
discographer

discolourate
discomfiting
discomfiture
discomforter
discommodate
discommodity
discommonize
discomposure
discongruity
disconnected
disconnecter
disconnexion
disconsolate
discontinued
discontinuee
discontinuer
discontinues
discontinuor
discordantly
discountable
discount rate
discount shop
discourteous
discoverable
discoverably
discoverture
discrediting
discreetness
discrepation
discreteness
discretional
discretively
discriminant
discriminate
disculpation
discursively
discursivity
discussional
discussively
disdainfully
diseasedness
disembarrass
disembellish
disemboguing
disenactment
disenchanter
disencourage
disendowment
disentrammel
disestablish
disfranchise
disgorgement
disgradation
disgregation
disguiseless
disguisement
disgustfully
disgustingly
dishabituate
disharmonise
disharmonize
dishevelling

dishevelment
dish of the day
dishonesties
disincarnate
disincentive
disinfectant
disinfection
disinflation
disingenuity
disingenuous
disinherison
disinherited
disinsectize
disintegrant
disintegrate
disintegrity
disinterment
disinterring
disintricate
disjointedly
disk emulator
dislodgement
dismayedness
dismissively
dismountable
disobedience
disorganizer
disorientate
dispatch-boat
dispatch case
dispauperize
dispensaries
dispensation
dispensative
dispensatory
dispensatrix
dispersivity
dispersonate
dispersonify
dispiritedly
dispiritment
dispiteously
displaceable
displacement
displeasance
displeasedly
disposedness
dispossessed
dispossessor
disprivilege
disprovement
disputatious
disqualified
disqualifies
disquietedly
disquietness
disquisition
disquisitive
disrecommend
disregardant
disregardful
disreputable

disreputably	diversionary	do nothing for	down-and-outer
disrespecter	diversionism	donothingism	downloadable
disreverence	diversionist	doodlebugger	Down syndrome
disruptively	diverticular	do one's utmost	down the drain
dissatisfied	diverticulum	dopaminergic	down the hatch
dissatisfies	divertimenti	doppelgänger	down the river
dissected map	divertimento	Doppler radar	down the track
disseisoress	divided skirt	Doppler shift	down the tubes
dissemblable	dividendless	Doppler width	downwardness
dissemblance	divine office	Dorcas basket	draconically
disseminator	diving beetle	dormer window	dracontiasis
dissenterism	diving petrel	dorsiflexion	draft dodging
dissentience	divinity calf	dorsiventral	drag one's feet
dissentingly	divinityship	dorsolateral	dragon's blood
dissertation	divinization	dorsoventral	dragon's teeth
dissertative	divisibility	Dostoevskian	drag the chain
disseverance	divisionally	do the dirty on	drainage tube
disseverment	division-bell	do the honours	drain the lees
dissimilarly	division sign	do the naughty	dramatically
dissimulator	divisiveness	dotted rhythm	dramaturgist
dissociality	do a hand's turn	Douay version	drapeability
dissocialize	doch an dorris	double-acting	draughtboard
dissociation	doctor's stuff	double-banked	draught horse
dissociative	doctrinalism	double-barrel	draught-house
dissolve away	doctrinalist	double-bitted	draughtiness
dissolvingly	doctrinarian	double boiler	draught-proof
dissuasively	doctrinarity	double bridle	drawback lock
dissymmetric	documentable	double-clutch	drawing-block
distance post	documentably	double dagger	drawing board
distemperate	document case	double-dealer	drawing-knife
distichously	docutainment	double-decked	drawing of tea
distillation	dodecahedral	double-decker	drawing paper
distillatory	dodecahedric	double digits	drawing-roomy
distilleries	dodecahedron	double-dipper	draw the cloth
distinctness	dodecandrous	double-figure	dreadfulness
distomatosis	dodecaphonic	double fleece	dreamfulness
distortional	doggerelizer	double-ganger	drenching-gun
distractedly	dogmatically	double-glazed	Dresden china
distractible	dog-tooth spar	double-handed	dressing case
distrainable	do-it-yourself	double-headed	dressing-comb
distrainment	dolesomeness	double header	dressing down
distraughtly	doll hospital	double hyphen	dressing gown
distressedly	dolly mixture	double-minded	dressing room
distributary	dolman sleeve	double nelson	drift-netting
distribution	dolorousness	double obelus	drinkability
distributism	dolphinarium	double paddle	drink-driving
distributist	Domain orator	double-ported	drinking-bout
distributive	dome fastener	double-queued	drinking-horn
disturbative	Domesday Book	double-spaced	drinking song
disturbingly	domesticable	double vision	drip-moulding
disutilities	domestically	double walled	drip painting
disvaluation	domesticator	double whammy	drivellingly
ditetragonal	domestic fowl	double yellow	drive-through
ditheistical	dominatrices	double-yolked	driving force
dithyrambist	dominical day	doubtful card	driving range
ditransitive	Dominicaness	doubtfulness	driving wheel
ditriglyphic	domino effect	doubtingness	droopingness
ditrigonally	domino theory	douceur de vie	drop a clanger
dittographic	donkey engine	doughnutting	drop back into
diuretically	donkey jacket	douroucoulis	drop-in centre
divaricately	donkey's years	Dover's powder	dropped scone
divarication	donor country	do violence to	dropping-well

dropping-zone	Easter Parade	Egyptologist	elliptically
drop the pilot	Easter Sunday	Eidophusikon	elocutionary
drosophilist	East Germanic	eighteenthly	elocutionist
drosophyllum	East Indiaman	eight-pounder	elocutionize
droughtiness	easy of access	eisteddfodau	elongational
drumbledrone	easy on the eye	eisteddfodic	elucubration
drunk as a lord	eat humble pie	Eisteddfodic	email ombrant
drunk-driving	eat one's terms	ejection seat	emanationism
drunken Helot	eat one's words	elasmobranch	emanationist
drying-closet	eau de Cologne	elasmosaurus	emancipation
Dryopithecus	eau de Javelle	elastic fibre	emancipative
dual-standard	eavesdropper	elastic limit	emancipatory
dubitatively	ebulliometer	elderberries	emargination
duchesse lace	ebullioscope	elder brother	emasculation
ducking-stool	ebullioscopy	Elder Brother	emasculative
duck's disease	eccentricity	electability	emasculatory
dufrenoysite	ecclesiastic	electiveness	embattlement
dulciloquent	ecclesiology	electrically	embeddedness
dumbstricken	echinococcus	electric blue	embezzlement
dumdum bullet	echinodermal	electric fire	embitterment
dumortierite	echolocation	electric hare	emblazonment
dunderheaded	echo-sounding	electrogenic	emblematical
dunghill cock	eclectically	electrolyser	embolisation
Dunmow flitch	eco-labelling	electrolysis	embolization
Dunstable way	ecologically	electrolytic	embouchement
duodecennial	econometrics	electromatic	embranchment
duodecimally	econometrist	electromeric	embroideress
duodenectomy	economically	electrometer	embroideries
duodenostomy	economic rent	electrometry	embroidering
durationless	economy class	electromotor	embryoid body
dust and ashes	economy drive	electron beam	embryologist
Dutch auction	eco-terrorism	electron lens	emerald green
Dutch bargain	eco-terrorist	electron pair	Emergicenter
Dutch courage	ecstatically	electron tube	emetic tartar
Dutch defence	ectoparasite	electronvolt	emigrant road
duty-free shop	ectoproctous	electro-optic	emolumentary
dwarfishness	ectrodactyly	electropaint	emotionalise
dynamic range	ecumenically	electrophile	emotionalism
dynamization	edging shears	electrophone	emotionalist
dynamometric	editorialise	electroplate	emotionality
dynastically	editorialist	electroplexy	emotionalize
dysaesthesia	editorialize	electroscope	empathically
dysgenically	educationese	electro-shock	emperor goose
dysphemistic	educationist	electrotonic	emphatically
dysteleology	edulcoration	electrotonus	emphaticness
each and every	Edwardianism	electrotyper	empoisonment
ear-defenders	effectuality	eleemosynary	Empty Quarter
earl palatine	effectuation	elementalism	empyreumatic
Earl Palatine	effeminately	elementarily	emulsifiable
early and late	effervescent	elementarity	enantiomeric
early closing	efficiencies	elephant-bird	enantiomorph
Early English	efflorescent	elephant fish	enantiopathy
early warning	effortlessly	elephant joke	enantiotropy
earned income	effronteries	elephant seal	enarthrodial
earnest money	effusiveness	elephant's ear	encephalitic
earn one's keep	egg and anchor	elevatedness	encephalitis
ear-splitting	eggs and bacon	eleventh part	enchantingly
earth-shaking	eggs Benedict	eligibleness	enchiridions
earth station	egoistically	elixir of life	enchondrosis
easel-picture	Egyptian bean	ellagitannin	encipherment
easterliness	Egyptian days	Ellingtonian	encirclement
Easter Monday	Egyptian lily	ellipsograph	enclitically

encloistered
encroachment
encrustation
encumberment
encumbrancer
encyclopedia
encyclopedic
endamagement
endangerment
endarteritis
endenization
endermically
en déshabillé
endless screw
endocarditic
endocarditis
endocervical
end of the line
end of the road
endogenously
endometritis
endomorphism
endonuclease
endoparasite
endoskeletal
endoskeleton
endosymbiont
endothelioma
endotracheal
endurability
enduringness
energization
enervatingly
enfeeblement
Enfield rifle
enfranchiser
engagingness
engenderment
engine driver
engineership
English flute
Englishwoman
Englishwomen
engrossingly
enharmonical
enhypostasia
enhypostatic
enjoyability
enjoy oneself
enliveningly
enophthalmos
enormousness
enshrinement
enspherement
enswathement
entablatured
entanglement
enter a caveat
enteric fever
enterobiasis
enterococcus
enterocoelic

enterokinase
enteropneust
enterotomies
enterprising
entertaining
enthronement
enthusiastic
enthymematic
entitatively
entomogenous
entomologist
entomologize
entoparasite
entoproctous
entoptically
entotympanic
entrammelled
entrance form
entrancement
entrancingly
entreatingly
entrenchment
entrepreneur
entropically
enviableness
envisagement
enzymologist
eosinophilia
eosinophilic
epexegetical
ephebiatrics
ephemeralism
ephemerality
epicureanism
Epicureanism
epicuticular
epicycloidal
epidemically
epidemiology
epididymides
epididymitis
epiglottitis
epigrammatic
epigraphical
epileptiform
epimorphosis
Epiphanytide
epiphenomena
epipterygoid
episcopacies
episcopalian
episcopalism
episcopality
episcopicide
episcotister
episiotomies
episodically
epistemology
epistolatory
episyllogism
epithalamial
epithalamium

epitheliosis
epitrochlear
eponymically
epoxide resin
equalitarian
equalization
equanimously
equatability
equationally
equatorially
equatorwards
equestrienne
equidistance
equifinality
equilibrator
equilibriate
equilibrious
equilibriums
equimultiple
equinumerous
equiparation
equipendency
equipollence
equipollency
equiprobable
equitability
equivalently
equivocality
equivocation
equivocatory
ergastoplasm
erratic block
erythematous
erythroblast
erythrocytic
erythrogenic
erythromycin
erythrophore
escape clause
escapologist
escutcheoned
Eskimo curlew
esoterically
espagnolette
esparto grass
especialness
essentialism
essentialist
essentiality
essentialize
essential oil
estrangement
eternity ring
eternization
ethanoic acid
ethanolamine
etherealness
etherization
etheromaniac
Ethiopianism
ethnocentred
ethnocentric

ethnogenesis
ethnographer
ethnographic
ethnohistory
ethnological
ethnoscience
ethosuximide
ethoxyethane
ethyl acetate
ethyl alcohol
ethylbenzene
etiquettical
etymological
etymologicon
Euboic talent
eucalyptuses
eucharistize
eudemonistic
eufunctional
euhemeristic
eunuchoidism
eupeptically
euphemiously
euphonically
euphoniously
euphorically
eurhythmical
Euro-American
Eurocentrism
Euro-currency
Euro-election
European plan
eurythermous
eustatically
euthyroidism
eutrophicate
Eutychianism
evanescently
evangelicity
evangelistic
evaporimeter
even-handedly
evening class
evening dress
evening paper
even Stephens
even-tempered
eventfulness
event horizon
eventide home
ever and again
ever-blooming
evergreen oak
everydayness
every man jack
every man Jack
everyone else
every so often
everywhither
evidentially
evil-speaking
evisceration

evolute curve
evolutionary
evolutionise
evolutionism
evolutionist
evolutionize
exacerbation
exactingness
exact science
exaggeration
exaggerative
exaggeratory
exalbuminous
examinership
exanthematic
exasperation
excalceation
excavational
Excellencies
excel oneself
excentricity
exceptionary
exchangeable
exchange rate
excitability
excited state
excitingness
excitomotory
exclaustrate
exclusionary
exclusionism
exclusionist
excogitation
excogitative
excruciating
excruciation
excursionary
excursionist
excursionize
excusability
executionary
executorship
exegetically
exencephalic
exenteration
exercise bike
exercise book
exercise yard
exercitation
exercitorian
exfiltration
exflagellate
exhaustingly
exhaustively
exheredation
exhibitional
exhibitioner
exhibitively
exhilaration
exhilarative
exiguousness
existibility

exobiologist
exoergically
exomologesis
exonormative
exopeptidase
exophthalmia
exophthalmic
exophthalmos
exophthalmus
exopterygote
exorbitantly
exorbitation
exorcistical
exorcization
exorcizement
exoterically
exothermally
exotic dancer
expansionary
expansion bit
expansion box
expansionism
expansionist
expatriation
expatriatism
expectancies
expectorator
expediential
expeditation
expeditioner
experiential
experimental
experimented
experimenter
expert system
explantation
explicitness
exploitation
exploitative
exponentiate
export reject
expositional
expositorily
expostulator
express clerk
expressional
expressively
expressivity
express rifle
express train
exprobration
expromission
expropriator
expulsionist
exsanguinate
ex-serviceman
ex-servicemen
exsibilation
exsufflation
exsufflicate
extemporizer
extendedness

extended-play
extensometer
exterminable
exterminator
exteroceptor
extinguisher
extortionary
extortionate
extortionist
extracranial
extractor fan
extraditable
extrahepatic
extralegally
extralimital
extralogical
extramarital
extramission
extramundane
extramurally
extra-musical
extraneously
extrapolable
extrapolator
extrasensory
extrasomatic
extra-special
extrasystole
extra-uterine
extravagance
extravagancy
extravaganza
extraversion
extraversive
extrinsicate
extrinsicism
extroversion
extroversive
extrovertish
exulceration
eye of a needle
eyes on stalks
fabulousness
facelessness
face-painting
face the facts
face the music
facilitation
facilitative
facilitatory
facsimileing
factionalise
factionalism
factionalist
factionalize
factiousness
factitiously
factorizable
factory floor
faggot-stitch
fail and divot
faint-hearted

faintishness
fair-mindedly
fairy penguin
fait accompli
faithfulness
faith healing
falcated teal
falcon-gentle
fallaciously
falling short
fall into line
fall like a log
fall together
fall to pieces
false bedding
false ceiling
false colours
false concord
false cypress
false economy
false gharial
false quarter
false vampire
false witness
falsificator
familiarizer
familiarness
family circle
family credit
family doctor
family living
Family of Love
famine prices
fancifulness
fanglomerate
fantasticate
faradization
fare thee well
far-sightedly
Farther India
Far Westerner
fasciculated
fascinatedly
fascioliasis
fashion house
fashion-paper
fashion piece
fashion plate
fast and loose
fastidiously
fastuousness
father figure
father-lasher
fatherliness
Father of lies
fathers-in-law
fathomlessly
fatigability
fatigue-dress
fatigue-party
fault breccia
fault-finding

faute de mieux	fibrinolytic	fireproofing	flippantness
favouredness	fibroadenoma	fireside chat	flirtational
favourite son	fibroblastic	fire-watching	flitter-mouse
fawn-coloured	fibrogenesis	first-aid post	floatability
fearlessness	fibrosarcoma	first and last	float-chamber
fearsomeness	fictionalise	first cellist	floating debt
feasibleness	fictionality	first century	floating dock
Feast of Fools	fictionalize	first edition	floating mill
feast of weeks	fictitiously	first-nighter	float process
feather-brain	fiddle-faddle	first officer	flocculation
feather-grass	fiddle-headed	first quarter	floor manager
featheriness	fiddle-string	first reading	Florence wine
feather-light	fidelity bond	first refusal	floriculture
feather-pated	*fidus Achates*	First Sea Lord	Florida water
febrifacient	field battery	fish and chips	florilegiums
Febronianism	field general	fishing story	flouring mill
fecklessness	field glasses	fit as a fiddle	flourishment
federalistic	field marshal	fitted carpet	floury miller
feeble-minded	Field Marshal	five-spice mix	flower-de-luce
feeing market	field-meeting	five-year plan	flower garden
feel one's feet	field mustard	fixed capital	flowering age
feel one's legs	field officer	flabelliform	flower of Jove
feel one's oats	field spaniel	flagellation	flower of wine
feel the pinch	fiendishness	flagellative	flower-pecker
feel wretched	fiftieth part	flagellatory	flower people
feet foremost	fighter cover	flagelliform	flowers of tan
feldspathoid	fighting cock	flagitiously	flowing sheet
felicitation	fighting fish	flagrantness	fluid extract
felicitously	fighting fund	flake culture	fluidization
fellow-travel	fighting talk	flamboyantly	fluidized bed
felon-setting	fighting trim	flamen dialis	flummadiddle
female condom	figurability	flame-thrower	fluoranthene
feminineness	figuratively	flammability	fluorapatite
femininistic	figure-caster	flammiferous	fluorescence
feminization	figure-dancer	flammivomous	fluoridation
fence-mending	figure skater	flammulation	fluorimetric
fence-sitting	filbert brush	flank forward	fluorination
fend and prove	filet de boeuf	flannelboard	fluorocarbon
fender bender	filibusterer	flannelgraph	fluorometric
fenestration	filter-feeder	flannel-mouth	fluoroscopic
fennel-flower	filter-tipped	flat-footedly	fluosilicate
Fermat number	finalization	flatteringly	fluphenazine
fermentation	final process	flavanthrone	flutteration
fermentative	finance house	flavoprotein	flutteringly
Fermi surface	financialist	flawlessness	flutter-wheel
fern crushing	find an office	fleece-picker	flying bridge
ferricyanide	finding-store	Fleet Admiral	flying change
ferrocyanide	find its level	fleet in being	flying circus
ferrugineous	find one's feet	fleetingness	flying coffin
fers-de-moline	find the means	Flemish horse	flying column
fertilizable	fine and dandy	flesh and fell	flying doctor
fetalisation	fine feathers	flexibleness	flying dragon
fetch a gutser	finely-strung	flexographic	flying façade
feudal system	finger-lickin'	flexor muscle	flying lizard
fever and ague	finger millet	flickeringly	flying picket
feverishness	finger puppet	flickermouse	flying saucer
fever therapy	fingle-fangle	flick through	flying school
fianchettoes	Finnish spitz	flight-number	flying tackle
fibrillation	fire and sword	flimflammery	fly into a rage
fibrilliform	fire-fighting	flimflamming	fly on the wall
fibrinolysin	fire-position	flindermouse	fly-the-garter
fibrinolysis	fire practice	flint-hearted	focalization

fodder-cheese	for Pete's sake	freethinking	fructivorous
folding doors	for pity's sake	freezing cold	fruitfulness
folding money	for reference	freezing rain	fruiting body
fold one's arms	forsakenness	freezing tool	fruit machine
foliage plant	for shortness	Freightliner	frumentation
folie du doute	forswornness	freight train	frumpishness
folkloristic	for the asking	French cotton	frustratedly
folk medicine	for the future	French endive	fuchsinophil
folliculated	for the life of	French letter	fuddy-duddies
folliculitis	for the love of	French polish	fuel-injected
follow-me-lads	for the moment	French sorrel	fugie-warrant
follow the sea	for the record	French turnip	fugitiveness
fondant icing	for the sake of	French window	fuliginosity
food additive	forthputting	frenetically	fuliginously
food for worms	forthrightly	frequentable	full-bottomed
foolhardiest	forthsetting	frequentness	fuller's earth
fool's parsley	fortieth part	fresh as paint	full throttle
football boot	fortuitously	freshmanship	fully-fledged
football pool	forty-seventh	Fresnel rhomb	fulminic acid
for account of	fossilizable	Freudian slip	fume cupboard
forbiddingly	foster-father	friar's balsam	funambulator
forced-choice	foster-mother	friars' balsam	functionally
forced labour	fouled anchor	fricandeaued	functionless
forcefulness	foul one's nest	frictionally	function word
force majeure	foundational	friction-ball	fungological
force the game	foundationer	frictionless	fungus-garden
force the pace	fountain-head	friendliness	funnel beaker
forcibleness	fountainhead	friendly fire	funniosities
forcing frame	fountainless	frigate-built	furfuraceous
fore-and after	four freedoms	frightenable	furnish forth
forebodement	Fourieristic	frightenedly	furniture van
forebodingly	fourpenny one	fringing reef	Further India
forecarriage	fourteenthly	Frisesomorum	furunculosis
forecastable	fourth estate	fritillaries	futilitarian
foreconceive	fourth finger	frolicsomely	futtock plate
forefatherly	Fourth of July	fromage blanc	futurologist
foreheadless	four-went-ways	fromage frais	fuzzy-wuzzies
foreign devil	fowling piece	from day to day	Gaelic coffee
foreign-going	fowl leucosis	from end to end	Gaelic League
foreign trade	fox and hounds	from out to out	gain a march on
forelock bolt	foxtail-grass	from overseas	gain ground on
forelock hook	fractionally	from strength	gain the ear of
forensically	fragmentally	from the first	galactagogue
forepleasure	fragmentizer	from the floor	galactosemia
forequarters	frame-breaker	from the heart	galacturonic
foresightful	francization	from tip to toe	Galbraithian
forestalment	Franck–Condon	from top to toe	Galilean moon
forest falcon	Francophilia	frondescence	gallery grave
forest marble	Francophobia	frondiferous	galley-packet
forest ranger	frangibility	frondoseness	galligaskins
forest red gum	frankalmoign	frontage road	gallinaceous
foretellable	Frankenstein	frontal crest	gallocyanine
for Gawd's sake	frankincense	front-bencher	Gallo-Romance
forgeability	fraternalism	frontbencher	gall-sickness
forked tongue	fraternities	frontierless	Galois theory
for lagniappe	fraudulently	frontiersman	Galsworthian
formaldehyde	freakishness	frontiersmen	galvanically
formalizable	freckle-faced	frontispiece	galvanic pile
formicarioid	free electron	front of house	galvanometer
formlessness	free-handedly	front passage	galvanometry
fornicatress	free of charge	front to front	galvanoscope
for one's pains	free-standing	fructiferous	galvanotaxis

game of chance
gamesmanship
gamesomeness
gametophoric
gametophytic
gamopetalous
gamophyllous
gamosepalous
gangliectomy
ganglionated
gang one's gate
ganophyllite
garden balsam
garden carpet
garden centre
gardener-bird
gardenership
Garden of Eden
garden privet
garden roller
garden suburb
garlic butter
garrison town
garter stitch
gasification
gas-permeable
Gastarbeiter
gastric fever
gastric juice
gastronomist
gastroplasty
gastropodous
gastroscopic
gastrulation
gateleg table
gate receipts
gathering cry
gather straws
Gavelkind Act
geanticlinal
Geissler tube
gelatigenous
gelatination
gelatiniform
gelatinously
gelatin paper
gemmological
genealogical
generability
general court
General Court
generalities
general staff
general store
General Synod
generational
generatively
generativism
generativist
generousness
gene splicing
genethliacal

genethliacon
genetic drift
geniculation
genioglossus
gennemically
genotoxicity
gentilitious
gentle falcon
gentle people
genuflection
genuflectory
geobotanical
geochemistry
geodesic dome
geodesic line
geodetically
geographical
geologically
geomagnetism
geomagnetist
geometrician
geophysicist
geoplanarian
geopolitical
geopotential
geoscientist
geosynclinal
geotechnical
Geraldton wax
geriatrician
Germanically
Germanomania
Germanophile
Germanophobe
German silver
germinal cell
gerontocracy
gerontophile
gerontophily
gesticulator
get a guernsey
get a Guernsey
get a handle on
get a hustle on
get a snitch on
get a wiggle on
get credit for
get hitched up
get one's eye in
get one's leave
get outside of
get-rich-quick
get rough with
get somewhere
get the best of
get the feel of
get the hang of
get the jump on
get the mitten
get the name of
get the needle
get the wind up

get with child
Ghibellinism
ghoulishness
giant noctule
giant sequoia
giant's stride
gibber gunyah
gibble-gabble
Gibraltarian
gift of the gab
gigantically
gigantomachy
gilding metal
gill filament
gin and orange
gingerliness
gingivectomy
Giorgi system
girder bridge
girting-place
give an edge to
give audience
give colour to
give credit to
give effect to
give in charge
give it the gas
give one's hand
give one's life
give one's word
give the elbow
give the guy to
give the lie to
give weight to
gizzard trout
glacial epoch
glacier burst
glaciologist
gladiatorial
gladiatorism
gladsomeness
Gladstone bag
glandiferous
glandulation
glass-blowing
glass ceiling
glass furnace
glass slipper
glassy humour
Glauber's salt
glaucescence
glaucomatous
glaucous gull
gleesomeness
gleification
glenohumeral
Glenurquhart
gliding-plane
glimmeringly
glioblastoma
glisteningly
glisteringly

glitteringly
gloaming-shot
global search
globe-thistle
globe-trotter
globigerinae
globigerinal
globigerinas
globularness
glockenspiel
glomerulitis
gloom and doom
gloriousness
glory be to God
glossatorial
glossography
glossolalist
glossologist
glossoplegia
glossopteris
glottal catch
glucoprotein
glue-sniffing
glutamic acid
glutethimide
gluttonously
glyceric acid
glycobiology
glycogenesis
glycogenetic
glycoprotein
glycyrrhizin
glyphography
glyptography
gnomonically
gnotobiology
gnotobiotics
go-aheadative
go and eat coke
goat-antelope
gobbledegook
gobbledygook
go by the board
go by the worse
go by the worst
God be thanked
God of the gaps
go down a storm
God's bodikins
God-surrogate
go for a burton
go glimmering
go hot and cold
going concern
go into action
go into detail
goitrigenous
gold blocking
Golden Fleece
Golden Friday
golden jackal
Golden Legend

golden number
golden oriole
golden plover
golden tettix
golden wattle
goldfish bowl
gold standard
Goliath crane
Goliath heron
gonadotropic
Gondwanaland
gone a million
good breeding
good clean fun
good creature
good-humoured
good riddance
Good Shepherd
good-tempered
good thinking
goody-goodies
go off at score
go one's own way
go one's rounds
go on the stage
go on the stump
gooseberries
goose pimples
go out of style
Gorbachevian
Gordon setter
gorgeousness
gormlessness
go shares with
gosling-green
gospel-singer
gossip column
gossip monger
go the knuckle
go to extremes
go to one's head
go to one's rest
go to the devil
go to the Devil
go to the front
go up in flames
go up the flume
go up the steps
governmental
governorship
go with a swing
gracefulness
graciousness
gradeability
grade cricket
graded school
Gradgrindery
gradient post
gradient wind
gradualistic
graduateship
Graecotrojan

grafting clay
grain leather
grallatorial
graminaceous
grammaticise
grammaticism
grammaticize
gram-molecule
Gram-negative
Gram-positive
Granary bread
grand duchess
Grand Guignol
grand inquest
grandisonant
Grandisonian
grandisonous
grand larceny
Grand Ole Opry
grandpappies
grand passion
grandstander
Granite State
granny annexe
granny bonnet
granny-sitter
granodiorite
granulocytic
grapeseed oil
graphic novel
graphitoidal
graphologist
graphomaniac
graspingness
grasshoppery
grass warbler
grass widower
gratefulness
gratifyingly
gratuitously
grave-clothes
gravel-voiced
grease monkey
Great Britain
Great Charter
Great Council
great-hearted
great hundred
great inquest
Great Malvern
great mullein
Great Pyramid
Great red spot
Great Russian
great thought
Grecian plait
Greek Cypriot
Greek Fathers
green alkanet
green channel
green fingers
greengrocery

Greenlandish
greenskeeper
green tobacco
green vitriol
gregariously
Grenzbegriff
grey antimony
grey eminence
grey kangaroo
greylag goose
grey squirrel
grievousness
griffinesque
grindability
grindle stone
grind to a halt
griseofulvin
grope one's way
gross tonnage
grossularite
grotesquerie
ground-cherry
ground-colour
groundedness
ground effect
Groundhog Day
groundkeeper
ground-laurel
groundlessly
ground parrot
ground roller
ground stroke
ground tackle
ground thrush
group captain
group dialect
group therapy
grovellingly
growing pains
growing point
growing stock
growth factor
grow together
grow whiskers
grudgingness
gruesomeness
Guadeloupean
Guadeloupian
guaiacum test
guanethidine
guardianless
guardianship
gubernacular
gubernaculum
Guernsey lily
guerrilla war
guessing game
guest-chamber
guest speaker
Guide's honour
guignolesque
guild-brother

guilefulness
guilt complex
Guinea flower
Guinea pepper
gumptionless
gunmetal blue
gunmetal grey
gunpowder tea
Gunter's chain
Gunter's scale
gurjun balsam
gutter-splint
Guy Fawkes day
gymnasiarchy
gymnosophist
gynaecocracy
gynaecologic
gynaecomazia
gynodioecism
gypsophilous
Gypsyologist
gyromagnetic
habeas corpus
haberdashery
habilimented
habilitation
habitability
habit-forming
habitualness
hack-and-slash
hacking cough
hackney coach
hackney horse
hadrosaurian
hadrosaurine
haematemesis
haematologic
haematoxylin
haemerythrin
haemodynamic
haemophilia B
haemophiliac
haemopoiesis
haemopoietic
haemorrhagic
haemosiderin
hagiographal
hagiographer
hagiographic
hagiolatrous
hagiological
haidingerite
haikal screen
hairdressing
hair follicle
hairlessness
hair mattress
hair of the dog
hair-restorer
hair's breadth
hair-splitter
half-integral

half-marathon	harmoniously	health resort	hell on wheels
half measures	harmonograph	hear a pin drop	hell's delight
half-mourning	harmonometer	heart and dart	hell's kitchen
half-seas-over	harquebusade	heart and soul	helmsmanship
half-timbered	harquebusier	heartbreaker	helplessness
halfway house	harrier-eagle	heart-burning	help-yourself
half-wittedly	harvest field	heart-disease	hemerocallis
hallowedness	harvest mouse	hearteningly	hemichordate
hallucinator	harvest queen	heart failure	hemimorphism
hallucinogen	hasenpfeffer	heartfulness	hemimorphite
hallucinosis	hasty pudding	heart of stone	hemiparasite
halogenation	hatchability	heart-rending	hemispheroid
halotrichite	hatchet-faced	heart-strings	hemp agrimony
hamartiology	hate campaign	heartstrings	henceforward
hammer-action	Haussmannize	heart to heart	henotheistic
hammer-harden	haute couture	heart-warming	heortologist
hammerheaded	haute cuisine	heat capacity	hepatisation
hammochrysos	have a crack at	heater-shaped	hepatization
hammock chair	have a crush on	heath-cropper	hepatomegaly
Hammond organ	have a derry on	heathenishly	hephthemimer
Hampshire hog	have a feel for	heather-bleat	heptahedrons
handclapping	have a fling at	heather honey	heptahydrate
handicapping	have a good arm	heave in sight	heptarchical
handie-talkie	have a good war	Heaven defend	Heracleitean
handkerchief	have a gust for	Heaven forbid	Heracleonite
hand over fist	have an eye for	heavenliness	heraldically
hand over hand	have a nice day	heavenly body	herb twopence
hand's-breadth	have a share in	heavenly host	Hercules' club
handsomeness	have a smack at	Heavens above	herd instinct
hanging guard	have a snout on	Heavens alive	herdsmanship
hanging judge	have a way with	heavy-hearted	here and there
hanging shelf	have a whack at	heavy petting	hereditament
hang one's head	have done with	heavy sleeper	hereditarian
hang out to dry	have got it bad	hebdomadally	hereditarily
hang the rap on	have it in mind	hebephreniac	hereinbefore
hang together	have no brow of	hecatompedon	heretication
hapaxanthous	have no choice	hectocotylus	heritability
happenchance	have no use for	hectographic	hermeneutics
happenstance	have no will of	hedenbergite	hermetically
happy as a clam	have one's will	hedge-creeper	hermetic seal
happy-go-lucky	have regard to	hedge-mustard	hermit thrush
happy release	have the ear of	hedge-parsley	heroicalness
happy warrior	have the heart	hedge sparrow	heroi-comical
haptotropism	have the law on	hedge trimmer	hero sandwich
hard currency	have the nerve	heebie-jeebie	hero's welcome
hard-favoured	have the right	heedlessness	herpes zoster
hard-featured	have the sense	height of land	herpetologic
hard feelings	have to do with	heir apparent	Hertzian wave
hard-headedly	have whiskers	hekistotherm	hesitatingly
hard-scrabble	Hawaian shirt	helianthemum	hesitatively
hard shoulder	head and front	helicoidally	heterauxesis
hard standing	headkerchief	heliocentric	heterocercal
hardstanding	headlongness	Heliogabalus	heteroclitic
hard swearing	headmasterly	heliographer	heterocyclic
Hare Krishnas	headmistress	heliographic	heterodesmic
harlequinade	head over ears	heliogravure	heteroduplex
harlequin bug	headquarters	heliotherapy	heteroecious
harlequin cup	head-shrinker	heliotropism	heterogamete
harlequinism	headshrinker	hellaciously	heterogamety
Harley Street	heads of state	hell and Tommy	heterogamous
harmlessness	headstrongly	Hellenophile	heterogeneal
harmonically	health centre	hellgrammite	heterogenist

heterogenous
heterogonous
heterography
hetero-immune
heterokaryon
heterologous
heteromerous
heteronomous
heteronymous
heteroousian
heteropathic
heterophasia
heterophilic
heterophonic
heterophoria
heterophoric
heterophylly
heteroplasia
heteroplasty
heteroploidy
heteropteran
heterosexism
heterosexist
heterosexual
heterosporic
heterostyled
heterothally
heterothermy
heterotrophy
heterozygote
heterozygous
he won't eat you
hexadecapole
hexahydrated
hexametrical
hexamitiasis
hexapetalous
hexasepalous
hexasyllabic
hexobarbital
hiatus hernia
hibernaculum
Hibernically
Hib infection
hidden agenda
hide one's face
hide one's head
hierarchical
hieratically
hierocracies
hieroglyphed
hieroglyphic
hierophantic
higher animal
higher orders
highfaluting
high fidelity
high-handedly
highly strung
high-mindedly
highmindedly
high pressure

high-reaching
high-security
high-sounding
high-spirited
high-stepping
high thinking
highty-tighty
highwaywoman
highwaywomen
Hilbert space
Hindoostanee
hindquarters
hippocentaur
Hippocratian
hippopotamic
hippopotamid
hippopotamus
hire purchase
Hispanically
hispaniolize
Hispanophile
hissing adder
histogenesis
histogenetic
histological
histoplasmin
historically
historicizer
historiology
histrionical
hitch and kick
Hitchcockian
hitching-post
hither and yon
Hitler salute
hit the bottle
hit the breeze
hit the bricks
hobnail liver
Hobson-Jobson
hodometrical
hognose snake
hoist the flag
Holbeinesque
hold harmless
hold one's hand
hold one's nose
hold the field
hold the stage
hold together
hold to ransom
holiday-maker
holidaymaker
holistically
hollow-ground
hollow square
Hollywoodean
Hollywoodish
Hollywoodism
Hollywoodize
holmquistite
holocephalan

holoparasite
holophrastic
holophyletic
holoplankton
holopneustic
Holy Alliance
Holy Cross Day
holy mackerel
holy of holies
Holy Saturday
Holy Thursday
home comforts
Home Counties
home from home
home industry
home language
homelessness
homeobox gene
homeothermal
homeothermic
Homerologist
home shopping
homesickness
homesteading
home straight
homing device
hominisation
hominivorous
hominization
homocaryotic
homochromous
homoeomerous
homoeomorphy
homoeopathic
homoeostasis
homogentisic
homoiomerous
homoiosmosis
homoiosmotic
homoiothermy
homokaryosis
homokaryotic
homolecithal
homologation
homomorphism
homomorphous
homonymously
homosexually
homothallism
homozygosity
honest broker
honey buzzard
honeycombing
honeycreeper
honey gilding
honey stomach
honeysuckled
honey-tongued
honnête homme
honoris causa
honour bright
honours of war

honour system
hood-moulding
Hooker's green
hootenannies
hopelessness
hopper-dredge
horizon glass
horizontally
horn arrester
hornblendite
horned helmet
horned lizard
horned sungem
hornlessness
Horn of Africa
horn of plenty
horometrical
horoscopical
horrendously
horribleness
horrifically
horrifyingly
horror-struck
hors concours
hors de combat
hors d'oeuvres
horse-breaker
horsebreaker
horse-eye bean
horsemanship
horseshoe bat
horse-soldier
horse-trading
horsiculture
horticulture
hortus siccus
hospital ball
hospital gown
hospital pass
hospital ship
hostess apron
host of heaven
hot gospeller
hot-shortness
Hottentot fig
Hottentot god
hound's-tongue
house and home
housebreaker
housebuilder
house colours
house-heating
householding
house-hunting
house-husband
housekeeping
house-manager
housemanship
house of cards
house officer
House of Lords
house-raising

house sparrow
house-surgeon
house-to-house
house-trained
house-warming
housey-housey
housie-housie
how about that
how's yourself
hubble-bubble
hucker-mucker
huckle-backed
hugger-mugger
human ecology
humane killer
humanistical
humanitarian
humanization
humble-jumble
humicubation
humification
humorousness
humourlessly
humoursomely
humpty-dumpty
Humpty-Dumpty
Hungarian cap
Hungary water
hunger-bitten
hunger strike
hunter-killer
hunter's green
hunter trials
hunting-lodge
hunting-shirt
hunting-watch
hunt saboteur
huntsman's cup
huntsmanship
hurdle racing
hurdy-gurdies
hurtlessness
hyacinth bean
hyalopilitic
hybridizable
hybrid vigour
hydatidiform
hydnocarpate
hydraulician
hydraulicity
hydraulic ram
hydrobiology
hydrocephaly
hydrochloric
hydrochorous
hydrocolloid
hydrocracker
hydrodictyon
hydrodynamic
hydro-extract
hydrofluoric
hydroformate

hydrogenator
hydrogen bomb
hydrogen bond
hydrogen-like
hydrogeology
hydrographer
hydrographic
hydrokineter
hydrokinetic
hydrological
hydrolysable
hydromedusan
hydronium ion
hydropathist
hydropathize
hydroperoxyl
hydrophanous
hydrophilous
hydrophobial
hydrophobist
hydrophobous
hydroponicum
hydroquinone
hydrosalpinx
hydrostatics
hydrotherapy
hydrothermal
hydrotreater
hydrotropism
hydroxide ion
hydrozincite
hyetographic
hygienically
hygrophilous
hylomorphism
hymenopteran
hymnographer
hypaesthesia
hypaesthetic
hyperacidity
hyperacousis
hyperalgesia
hyperalgesic
hyperbolical
hyperchromia
hyperchromic
hypercomplex
hypercorrect
hyperdiploid
hyperdulical
hyperendemic
hyperkinesia
hyperkinesis
hyperkinetic
hypermetrope
hypermorphic
hyperosmolar
hyperostosis
hyperostotic
hyperplastic
hyperpyretic
hyperpyrexia

hyperrealism
hyperrealist
hypersecrete
hyperspatial
hypersplenic
hypersthenia
hypersthenic
hypertension
hypertensive
hypertextual
hyperthermia
hyperthermic
hyperthyroid
hypertrophic
hypnoanalyst
hypnogenesis
hypnological
hypnotherapy
hypnotically
hypnotizable
hypoactivity
hypocellular
hypochlorite
hypochlorous
hypochondria
hypochondric
hypocoristic
hypocritical
hypodermatic
hypodiploidy
hypoeutectic
hypofunction
hypogastrium
hypognathous
hypogonadism
hypokalaemia
hypokalaemic
hypolimnetic
hypomochlion
hypophrygian
hypophyllous
hyposplenism
hypostatical
hyposulphite
hypothalamic
hypothalamus
hypothecator
hypothesizer
hypothetical
hypotonicity
hypotrichous
hypotrochoid
hypovolaemia
hypovolaemic
hypoxanthine
Hypsistarian
hypsithermal
hypsochromic
hypsographic
hysterectomy
hysterically
hysterogenic

hysteroscope
hysteroscopy
iambographer
iatrochemist
iatrophysics
Iceland poppy
ichnographic
ichnological
ichthyocolla
ichthyologic
ichthyophagi
ichthyophagy
iconoclastic
iconographer
iconographic
iconological
icosahedrons
idealization
ideationally
identifiable
identifiably
identity card
idiomaticity
Idiom Neutral
idiomorphism
idiopathetic
idiophonemic
idiosyncrasy
idiot savants
idolatrously
idoneousness
ignitability
ignitibility
ignition tube
iliac passion
ill-advisedly
ill-concealed
ill-conceived
illegalities
illegibility
illegitimacy
illegitimate
illiberalism
illiberality
illiberalize
illimitation
illiterately
illiterature
ill-naturedly
illogicality
ill-treatment
illuminating
illumination
illuminatism
illuminatist
illuminative
illuminatory
illuministic
illusiveness
illusoriness
illustration
illustrative

illustratory
ilmenorutile
image-breaker
image-worship
imaginal disc
imbecilitate
imbecilities
imbibitional
imitableness
immaculately
immaterially
immature soil
immeasurable
immeasurably
immemorially
immensurable
immersionism
immersionist
immethodical
immetrically
immiseration
immoderately
immoderation
immoralities
immortalizer
immovability
immune system
immunization
immunologist
immutability
impact crater
impact wrench
impartialist
impartiality
impassionate
impedimental
impenetrable
impenetrably
impenitently
imperatively
imperativism
imperativist
imperatorial
imperception
imperceptive
impercipient
imperfection
imperfective
imperforable
imperforated
imperialness
imperial pint
imperishable
imperishably
impermanence
impermanency
impersistent
impersonally
impersonator
impertinence
impertinency
imperviously

impetiginous
implantation
implicitness
impoliteness
imponderable
imponderably
importunator
imposingness
impostorship
impoverisher
impredicable
impregnation
impressional
impressively
imprevisible
imprisonable
imprisonment
improperness
impropriator
improsperous
improvership
improvidence
improvisator
impudentness
impulse clock
impunitively
impuritanism
impurity atom
imputability
imputatively
in a bad temper
inabstinence
inacceptable
inaccessible
inaccessibly
inaccuracies
inaccurately
inactivation
in a dead faint
inadequacies
inadequately
inadequation
inadmissible
inadmissibly
inadvertence
inadvertency
in a fair way to
in a family way
in a good light
in all but name
in all seeming
in-and-out work
inappeasable
inappellable
inapplicable
inapplicably
inappositely
in arrearages
inarticulacy
inarticulate
inartificial
in a sort of way

in attendance
in at the death
inaudibility
inauguration
inaugurative
inauguratory
inauspicious
in blanchfarm
incalculable
incalculably
incalescence
incandescent
incapability
incapacitant
incapacitate
incapacities
incarcerated
incarcerator
incatenation
incautiously
incendiaries
incendiarism
incense-cedar
incestuously
inchoateness
incidentally
incident room
incineration
incisiveness
incivilities
inclemencies
inclinometer
incoagulable
incogitantly
incogitative
incognisable
incognizable
incognizance
incoherently
incoincident
in commission
incommodious
in common with
incommutable
incommutably
incomparable
incomparably
incompatible
incompatibly
incompetence
incompetency
incompletely
incompletion
incompletive
incompliance
incompliancy
incomputable
incomunicado
inconcinnity
inconcludent
in conclusion
inconclusion

inconclusive
in conference
in confidence
inconfidence
inconformity
incongruence
inconscience
inconsequent
inconsidered
inconsistent
inconsolable
inconsolably
inconsonance
inconsonancy
inconstantly
inconsumable
in contention
incontinence
incontinency
incontinuity
incontinuous
inconvenient
incoronation
incorporable
incorporator
incorporeity
incorrigible
incorrigibly
incorrodible
incorruption
incrassation
increasement
increasingly
increditable
incriminator
incrustation
incubational
incumbencies
incunabulist
incurability
indebtedness
indecentness
indecisively
indeclinable
indeclinably
indecorously
indefeasible
indefeasibly
indefectible
indefectibly
indefensible
indefensibly
in defiance of
indefinitely
indefinition
indefinitive
indefinitude
indeformable
indehiscence
indelectable
indeliberate
indelibility

indelicacies
indelicately
independable
independence
independency
indeprivable
indetectable
indetectible
indetermined
indevoutness
index-linking
Indian almond
Indian madder
Indian mallow
Indian millet
Indian Mutiny
Indian physic
Indian potato
Indian runner
Indian summer
Indian turnip
Indian yellow
indicatively
indifference
indifferency
indigenously
indigestible
indigestibly
indigitation
indigoferous
indirect fire
indirectness
indirect rule
indiscipline
indiscreetly
indiscretion
indisputable
indisputably
indissoluble
indissolubly
indistinctly
indivertible
indivertibly
individually
individuated
indoctrinate
Indo-European
Indo-Gangetic
Indo-Germanic
indoleacetic
Indo-Pakistan
Indo-Scythian
inducibility
inductomeric
industrially
industry-wide
ineffability
ineffaceable
ineffaceably
inefficacity
inefficiency
inelasticity

ineliminable
ineloquently
inenubilable
inequal hours
inequalities
inequivalent
inequivalved
ineradicable
ineradicably
inerrability
inescutcheon
ineuphonious
inexactitude
inexecutable
inexhaustive
inexpectancy
inexpedience
inexpediency
inexperience
inexpertness
inexplicable
inexplicably
inexplorable
inexpressive
inexpugnable
inexpugnably
inexpungible
inextensible
inextirpable
inextricable
inextricably
infamousness
infanticidal
infant school
infatuatedly
infectiously
infelicities
infelicitous
inferability
infibulation
infidelities
infiltration
infiltrative
infinitation
infiniteness
infinitively
inflammation
inflammatory
inflatedness
inflationary
inflationism
inflationist
inflectional
informal vote
informedness
informercial
informidable
infotainment
infra-orbital
infrequently
infringement
infrustrable

infrustrably
infundibular
infundibulum
infusibility
infusoriform
ingemination
ingeneration
ingloriously
in good repair
ingratiating
ingratiation
ingratiatory
ingravescent
ingressively
inhabitation
inhalational
inhalatorium
inharmonious
inhibitingly
in holy orders
inhospitable
inhospitably
inhumanities
inhumorously
iniencephaly
inimicalness
iniquitously
initiatively
injudicially
injunctively
in league with
in like manner
in mistake for
in moderation
inner cabinet
inner Cabinet
inner reserve
Inniskilling
Innocents' Day
innovational
innovatively
innutritious
inobservable
inobservance
inobservancy
inoccupation
in one's favour
in one's regard
in one's senses
in one's sights
in one's sphere
in one's tracks
inoperculate
in opposition
inoppressive
inoppugnable
inordinately
inordination
inosculation
inostensible
inostensibly
in other words

inoxidizable
in particular
in perpetuity
in possession
in proper form
in proportion
inquartation
inquietation
inquire after
inquiry agent
inquisitress
in relation to
in retrospect
in revenge for
insalivation
insalubrious
insanitation
inscriptible
insectariums
insecticidal
insect-powder
insecureness
insemination
inseparately
in severality
in short order
insightfully
in silhouette
insimplicity
insolubilise
insolubility
insolubilize
insomnolence
insomnolency
insouciantly
inspectional
inspectorate
inspectorial
inspissation
installation
instauration
instillation
instinctless
institutress
instructible
instructress
instrumental
insubjection
insubmissive
in succession
insufferable
insufferably
insufficient
insufflation
insulin shock
insupposable
insurability
insurgencies
insurrection
in suspension
intabulation
intarissable

integral sign	intermeddler	interversion	intravitally
integumental	intermediacy	intervocalic	intrepidness
intellection	intermediary	interwovenly	intriguingly
intellective	intermediate	interwreathe	in triplicate
intellectual	interminable	interwrought	introducible
intelligence	interminably	in the balance	introduction
intelligency	intermission	in the bygoing	introductive
intelligible	intermissive	in the cause of	introductory
intelligibly	intermitotic	in the country	introflexion
intemperance	intermittent	in the event of	introgressed
intempestive	intermitting	in the extreme	introjection
inteneration	intermixable	in the general	introjective
interanimate	intermixedly	in the habit of	intromission
intercalator	intermixture	in the highest	intromittent
intercameral	intermontane	in the light of	intromitting
interception	internecinal	in the long run	intropulsive
interceptive	interneurone	in the mainour	introsuction
intercession	internuclear	in the midst of	introversion
intercessive	internuncial	in the morning	introversive
intercessory	internuncius	in the order of	introvertive
interchanger	internuptial	in the picture	intuitionism
interchapter	interoceanic	in the power of	intuitionist
intercoastal	interoceptor	in the running	intumescence
intercollege	interorbital	in the same box	invagination
intercommune	interosseous	in the shape of	invalidation
intercompany	interpellant	in the stead of	invasiveness
interconnect	interpellate	in the streets	inveiglement
interconvert	interpleader	in the teeth of	inverse ratio
intercranial	interplicate	in the thick of	invertebracy
intercurrent	interpluvial	in the train of	Invertebrata
interdiction	interpolable	in the weather	invertebrate
interdictive	interpolator	in this galley	inverted snob
interdictory	interpolymer	intimidating	investigable
interdiffuse	interpretant	intimidation	investigator
interdigital	interpretate	intimidatory	inveterately
interestedly	interpreting	intitulation	invigilation
interfemoral	interpretive	intolerantly	invigorating
interference	interregnums	intoleration	invigoration
interfertile	interrogatee	intonational	invigorative
interfluence	interrogator	intoxicating	invisibility
interfluvial	interruption	intoxication	invisible ink
interfulgent	interruptive	intoxicative	invisible man
intergeneric	interruptory	intracardiac	invitational
interglacial	intersectant	intracoastal	invitingness
interhalogen	intersection	intracranial	involutional
interimistic	intersegment	intragastric	involvedness
interinsular	intersensory	intraglacial	invulnerable
interjacency	inter-service	intrahepatic	invulnerably
interjection	interspersal	intralingual	invultuation
interjectory	interspinous	intralobular	in with a shout
interkinesis	interstadial	intramontane	iodine number
interlacedly	inter-station	intramundane	ion-exchanger
interlaminar	interstellar	intramurally	Ionic dialect
interlibrary	interstitial	intransigent	ionophoresis
interlineary	interstitium	intransitive	ionophoretic
interlineate	intertexture	intranuclear	ionospherist
interlingual	intertillage	intrapluvial	irascibility
interlinkage	intertissued	intrapreneur	iridectomize
interlobular	intertubular	intrapsychic	iridescently
interlocutor	intervallary	intraspecies	iridodonesis
intermarried	intervenient	intrauterine	Irish apricot
intermarries	intervention	intravaginal	Irish pennant

Irish terrier
Irish whiskey
ironicalness
ironing board
ironing cloth
iron mountain
irrationable
irrationally
irrealisable
irrealizable
irrebuttable
irreciprocal
irredeemable
irredeemably
irreductible
irredundance
irredundancy
irreflection
irreflective
irreformable
irrefragable
irrefragably
irregardless
irregenerate
irregularity
irrelatively
irrelevantly
irrelievable
irremediable
irremediably
irremissible
irremissibly
irrepairable
irrepassable
irrepealable
irrepealably
irrepentance
irreprovable
irreptitious
irresistable
irresistably
irresistance
irresistible
irresistibly
irresolutely
irresolution
irresolvable
irrespectful
irrespective
irrespirable
irresponsive
irreverently
irreversible
irreversibly
irrigational
irritability
irritatingly
irrotational
Iscariotical
Ishmaelitish
Ishmaelitism
I should smile

I should think
I should worry
Islamization
isoantigenic
isobarically
isobaric spin
isobilateral
isochromatic
isochronally
isochronical
isodiametric
isodynamical
isolated pawn
isolationism
isolationist
isomerically
isoperimeter
isoperimetry
isoprenaline
isoprene rule
isoprene unit
isotacticity
isothermally
isotonically
isotope shift
isotopically
isotopic spin
Italian earth
Italianesque
Italian paste
I tell you what
it is news to me
ivory-nut palm
I wouldn't know
Jack-a-lantern
jacket potato
jack-in-office
Jack-in-office
jack-in-the-box
Jack-in-the-box
Jack mackerel
jack-o'-lantern
Jack-o'-lantern
Jack-spaniard
Jacobean lily
Jacobitishly
Jacob's ladder
jacquard loom
jail-delivery
Jamaica ebony
Jamaican kino
James's powder
Japan current
Japanese deer
Japanese iris
Japanese rose
Japanese silk
Japanization
Japan lacquer
Japanologist
Japan varnish
jarovization

javelin-snake
Javelle water
Jeffersonian
jelly-bellied
je ne sais quoi
jenny spinner
jeremejevite
jerry-builder
Jesuitically
Jesus psalter
jet-propelled
jettisonable
jibber-jabber
jigger-tackle
jigsaw puzzle
Jimmy O'Goblin
Jimmy Skinner
Jimmy Woodser
Jindyworobak
jingle-jangle
job backwards
jockey pulley
jockey-sleeve
jockey spider
jocularities
John Crow nose
Johnny-jump-up
Johnson noise
joined patent
joint account
join the flats
joint-tenancy
joint venture
jolter-headed
jordan almond
Joule heating
Joule–Thomson
journalistic
journey-pride
journey-proud
journeywoman
joy of a planet
Judaeo-German
Judaeophobia
judgematical
Judgement Day
judicial duel
jug-and-bottle
jumping-board
jumping louse
jumping mouse
jumping shrew
jump the queue
junior school
jurisconsult
jurisdiction
jurisdictive
jurisprudent
juristically
Justice Clerk
Justicialism
Justicialist

justiciaries
justifyingly
Justinianian
Justinianist
juvenescence
juvenile lead
juvenile leaf
juvenileness
kachina dance
kaemmererite
Kaffirboetie
Kaffir orange
kainogenesis
kakistocracy
kaleidoscope
kanban system
kangaroo vine
karaoke music
Karitane baby
karyokinesis
karyokinetic
karyological
karyomitosis
karyomitotic
karyorrhexis
katharevousa
katharometer
katzenjammer
keeking-glass
Keene's cement
keep accounts
keep an eye out
keep good time
keep one's feet
keep one's head
keep one's legs
keep one's seat
keep one's word
keep the field
keep the house
keep the peace
keep together
Kelvin bridge
Kendal cotton
kentallenite
Kentish glory
keratectasia
keratinocyte
keratodermia
keratogenous
keratometric
keratoplasty
kerb-crawling
ketoacidosis
keto-compound
ketonization
kettle-bottom
kettle-holder
kettle of fish
kettle-stitch
Keynesianism
keypunchable

key signature	knee-trembler	ladder stitch	lantern-wheel
Khevenhuller	knick-knacket	ladylikeness	Laodiceanism
Khirbet Kerak	knife-grinder	Lady Mayoress	laparoscopic
kicking plate	knife machine	lady's cushion	laparotomies
kicking-strap	knife-pleated	lady's delight	laparotomize
kick the habit	knife-thrower	lady's slipper	lapidary-mill
kick up a stour	knight errant	lady's thistle	lapidicolous
kiddie sister	knightlihood	lady's tresses	lapis Armenus
kidney potato	knightliness	Lady Superior	lapis ollaris
kidney-shaped	knitting-case	lag of the tide	*lapsus calami*
kidney tubule	knitting-wire	laisser-aller	larch blister
killer-diller	knob-cone pine	laissez-aller	larder beetle
killikinnick	knock against	laissez-faire	larderellite
kilowatt-hour	knocking shop	Lake District	large calorie
Kimmeridgian	knowableness	lake-dwelling	large-hearted
kinaesthesia	knowledgable	lallapaloosa	Larmor radius
kinaesthesis	knowledge box	lallygagging	laryngealist
kinaesthetic	know the ropes	lamb's lettuce	laryngectomy
kindergarten	know the score	Lamentations	laryngophone
kindling-wood	knuckle-joint	laminability	laryngoscope
kinesiologic	knuckle under	laminagraphy	laryngoscopy
kinglessness	Knudsen gauge	Lammas growth	laryngospasm
king mackerel	Köchel number	lammervanger	lasagne verdi
king of beasts	koelreuteria	lampadedromy	lasciviously
king or Kaiser	Kommandatura	lampadomancy	laser printer
King's Counsel	Komodo dragon	lamprophyric	lasso-harness
king's cushion	Kremlinology	lamp standard	lasting power
King's English	Kriss Kringle	Lancasterian	latch circuit
King's Friends	Kromayer lamp	lancet window	latchings key
King's highway	kukumakranka	land-carriage	lateen mizzen
King's Proctor	kulturträger	land district	late in the day
King's Scholar	kupfernickel	land drainage	latent energy
kinnikinnick	kurchatovium	landgraviate	latent period
kin selection	Kyrie eleison	landing craft	lateral plate
kinship group	Labanotation	landing-light	lateralwards
Kiplingesque	labilization	landing place	laterisation
kirk-assembly	labiopalatal	landing stage	laterization
kirschwasser	laboratorial	landing strip	late-tackling
kitchen-diner	laboratories	Land-leaguism	laticiferous
kitchen Dutch	labouredness	landlessness	Latin America
Kitchener bun	labouring oar	landlordship	Latinization
kitchen-knave	labour in vain	landlubberly	Latin Quarter
kitchen-Latin	labour market	land-measurer	latitudinary
kitchen paper	labour of love	Land Registry	latitudinous
kitchen stove	labour-saving	land-surveyor	latter Lammas
kitchen-stuff	laboursomely	landward-bred	lattice frame
kitchen-wench	Labrador duck	Langmuir cell	lattice plane
kit furniture	Labrador spar	Langobardian	lattice point
kittle-cattle	labyrinthian	language area	laudableness
Klaas's cuckoo	labyrinthine	language arts	laughing crow
Klebs–Löffler	lacebark tree	language-game	laughing dove
kleptolagnia	Lachmann's law	languageless	laughing-game
kleptomaniac	lachrymation	*langue de chat*	laughing gull
kletterschuh	lachrymatory	Languedocian	laughterless
klinokinesis	lachrymosely	languishment	laughter-line
klinokinetic	lachrymosity	languorously	laugh to scorn
klipspringer	lacing course	lantern clock	launching pad
klydonograph	lacrimal bone	lantern-flies	launch window
knapsack pump	lactobionate	lantern-jawed	laundrywoman
knee-breeched	lactogenesis	lantern-light	laundrywomen
knee-breeches	lactonitrile	lantern-shell	laureateship
	lactoprotein	lantern slide	laurel-bottle

laurel-cherry
lavender-blue
lavender soap
law of nations
Law of Octaves
law of the land
law stationer
laxativeness
lay a finger on
lay communion
layer-pudding
layer shading
lay it on thick
lay one's bones
lay on the line
leachability
leadableness
leader stroke
leading-block
leading light
leading shoot
leading-staff
lead in prayer
leads and lags
lead the dance
leaflessness
leafless tree
leaning-stock
leap to the eye
learnability
learn by heart
learner plate
least squares
leather-bound
leathercloth
leatheriness
leather medal
leave a card on
leave-breaker
leave for dead
leave the room
lechenaultia
lectionaries
lecturership
ledger-tackle
leech-extract
Leech lattice
left and right
left defender
left half-back
left-handedly
left-hand rope
left-hand rule
left midfield
leftwardness
legacy-hunter
legal charity
legal fiction
legal holiday
legalitarian
legalization
legal opinion

legendary age
legislatress
legitimately
legitimation
legitimatise
legitimatize
leiophyllous
leiotrichous
Lemnian earth
lemon-scented
lemon verbena
lend colour to
lend itself to
lend one's ears
lenticellate
lenticulated
Leonardesque
leopard's bane
leopard snake
lepidomelane
lepidopteral
lepidopteran
leptocaulous
lepton number
Lesser Bairam
lesser diesis
Lestrigonian
let 'em all come
let oneself go
let oneself in
let-out clause
Letterer–Siwe
letter-office
letter-spaced
letter-weight
letter-writer
lettuce green
let well alone
leucoblastic
leucocytosis
leucopoiesis
leucopoietic
leucorrhoeal
Levalloisian
levallorphan
Levant storax
levelling rod
level one's aim
level pegging
levitational
Leviticalism
levorotatory
lex domicilii
lexicography
lexicologist
liberalistic
Liberal Party
liberticidal
liberty horse
libidinously
librarianess
library steps

licence plate
license plate
licentiation
licentiously
lichenometry
lichen planus
lichen-starch
lick creation
lickety-split
lick into fits
lick one's lips
lie down under
lie in one's way
lie in the dust
lie of the land
life-and-death
lifeguardman
life interest
lifelessness
lifelikeness
life sciences
life sentence
lifesomeness
lifting plate
lifting screw
lift one's eyes
lift one's game
lift one's hand
lift up the leg
light barrier
light-fixture
lightfulness
light-hearted
lighting plot
lightning box
lightning bug
lightning-rod
light quantum
light railway
light station
light-trapped
likeableness
like anything
like-mindedly
like old boots
like sardines
like the devil
like wildfire
limbic system
limb of the law
limited train
limnological
Lincolnesque
Lincoln green
Lincolnshire
linear search
line blanking
line-breeding
line-engraved
line-engraver
line-integral
line of battle

line of beauty
line of credit
line of vision
line regiment
line spectrum
line standard
lingua franca
lingual nerve
linguistical
linguodental
linoleic acid
lion-huntress
liquefacient
liquefaction
liquefactive
liqueur glass
liquid manure
liquid storax
liriodendron
listenership
listlessness
litaneutical
literalistic
literariness
lithifaction
lithogenesis
lithographer
lithographic
litholatrous
lithological
lithophagous
lithophilous
lithospermum
lithospheric
lithotomical
lithotripter
lithotriptic
lithotriptor
litter-basket
Little Africa
Little Dipper
little finger
little Hitler
little ice age
Little League
little master
little people
Littler's blue
little season
little tin god
littoral zone
liturgically
liturgiology
liveableness
liveable with
live and learn
liver-hearted
liverishness
Liverpudlian
liver sausage
liver-spotted
livery stable

live together
living fossil
living memory
lizard canary
lizard cuckoo
lizard orchid
loading gauge
load-shedding
load the bases
loan-sharking
lobeliaceous
loblolly pine
loblolly tree
lobster shift
lobster trick
local cluster
local content
localization
loci classici
locked groove
locking plate
locksmithery
locomotively
locum tenency
lodging house
loganberries
loggerheaded
logical truth
logic circuit
logic element
logistically
logocentrism
lollapaloosa
lollapalooza
lollipop lady
lomentaceous
London bridge
London purple
London rocket
London-shrunk
lonesomeness
long-and-short
long-distance
long division
long-drawn-out
longipennate
longitudinal
long-leaf pine
Longobardian
long rough dab
longshoreman
longshoremen
longsomeness
long-standing
long-tail pair
long trousers
long vacation
long-windedly
Lonsdale belt
looking-glass
look sideways
look who's here

loose-housing
loose-mouthed
loose-skinned
loose-tongued
lophophorate
lopsidedness
loquaciously
Lord Advocate
Lord bless you
Lord Ordinary
Lorentz force
Los Angelenos
lose interest
lose one's cool
lose one's grip
lose one's hair
lose one's head
lose one's life
lose one's mind
lose one's seat
lose one's wool
lose patience
lose the scent
losing battle
losing hazard
loss adjuster
lost property
lot attendant
lotaustralin
Lotharingian
lottery-wheel
lotus capital
loud and clear
loud and still
lounge lizard
loutrophoros
love-begotten
love-interest
lovelessness
love paramour
lovesickness
lovesomeness
love to pieces
Low-Churchism
Low Churchman
Low Countries
Lower Chamber
Lower Chinook
lower classes
lower pastern
lower regions
lower the boom
lower the tone
low frequency
low latitudes
low-molecular
low water mark
lubberliness
luce of the sea
Lucianically
lucklessness
Lucky Country

ludification
luffing crane
luggage check
lugubriosity
lugubriously
lukewarmness
lumber-jacket
lumbriciform
luminescence
luminiferous
luminousness
lumpectomies
lunar caustic
lunar-diurnal
lunar eclipse
lunar regular
luncheonette
luncheonless
luncheon meat
lungeing-ring
lurking-place
lusciousness
lustrousness
luteofulvous
luteotrophic
luteotrophin
Luxembourger
Luxemburgish
luxullyanite
lycanthropic
lychnoscopic
lying-in-state
lymphangioma
lymphangitis
lymphogenous
lymphography
lymphomatous
lymphotropic
lysergic acid
lysogenicity
Macaronesian
macaroni tool
macca-fat tree
machairodont
machiavellic
Machtpolitik
mackerel-back
mackerel-boat
mackerel gale
mackerel gull
mackintoshed
macrauchenia
macrobenthic
macrobenthos
macrobiotics
macrocephaly
macroclimate
macrocytosis
macroglossia
macrognathic
macronodular
macronucleus

macrophagous
macrophallic
macrophysics
macropterous
macrosegment
macroseismic
maculopapule
mad as a hatter
Madeira sauce
Mademoiselle
maderisation
maderization
Madonna braid
mad scientist
magic lantern
magic realism
magic realist
magistracies
magistrature
magma-chamber
magmatically
magnetically
magnetic disk
magnetic drum
magnetic flux
magnetic lens
magnetic mine
magnetic pole
magnetic tape
magnetisable
magnetizable
magnetograph
magnetogyric
magneto-ionic
magnetometer
magnetometry
magnetopause
magnetophone
magnifically
magnificence
magnificency
magniloquent
magnipotence
magnum opuses
Magnus effect
Mahometanism
maidening pot
maidening tub
maidenliness
maiden's blush
maiden speech
maid of honour
mainmortable
main sequence
maintainable
maintainment
maître d'hôtel
majestically
major general
majoritarian
majority rule
major prophet

Major Prophet	maloperation	manuscriptal	mastectomies
make a bad shot	Maltese cross	many moons ago	master-at-arms
make a bargain	maltodextrin	many's the time	Master Gunner
make a dash for	maltreatment	map butterfly	masterliness
make a day of it	Malvern water	map reference	masterly lode
make a fortune	malversation	marbled green	Master of Arts
make a habit of	mamenchisaur	marbled white	master-singer
make a merit of	mammalogical	marcasitical	mastersinger
make-and-break	mammary gland	marching band	master-spring
make an impact	mammillation	marching girl	master stroke
make a pig's ear	mammilliform	March meeting	master switch
make a play for	mammogenesis	Marcionitism	mastigophore
make a point of	mammographic	marconigraph	masturbation
make a study of	mammotrophic	Maréchal Niel	masturbatory
make a thing of	mammotrophin	mareographic	matador pants
make away with	man about town	marginal cost	matchbox bean
make ends meet	managemental	maricultural	match-winning
make free with	managerially	Marie Celeste	materializer
make good time	manatee-grass	marimbaphone	materialness
make it snappy	Manchu–Tungus	marine iguana	material noun
make little of	mandarin coat	marine stores	mathematical
make mischief	mandarin duck	Mariolatrous	mating season
make muckle of	mandarinship	Mariological	matriarchate
make no matter	mandarin vase	marionettish	matriarchies
make old bones	mandibulated	marionettist	matricentred
make one's gree	maneuverable	maritime pine	matrilateral
make one's mark	manganic acid	marked cheque	matrilineage
make one's soul	mangel beetle	market basket	matrilocally
make play with	mangel-wurzel	market garden	matrix number
make pleasant	mangrove crab	market hunter	matroclinous
make semblant	mangrove jack	market square	matronliness
make slight of	Manhattanese	marking board	matter of fact
make the arber	Manhattanite	marksmanship	matter of form
make the grade	manifestable	marline-spike	maturational
make the scene	manifestness	marmalade box	maudlin-drunk
make up leeway	manifoldness	marmalade cat	maunderingly
make wise to do	man in the moon	marmoraceous	Mauser action
malacologist	manipulandum	marriageable	mauvais sujet
malalignment	manipulation	marriage-ring	maximization
malapertness	manipulative	marriage-song	maximum price
malaria fever	manipulatory	married bliss	Maxwell demon
Malayan tapir	man-midwifery	married print	McLuhanesque
malaysianite	mannerliness	marrowskying	meadow beauty
Malaysianize	manoeuvrable	marrow squash	meadow fescue
malbehaviour	man-of-all-work	Marseillaise	meadow ground
malcontented	man of destiny	marsh harrier	mealy-mouthed
maldescended	man of feeling	marshmallowy	mealy pudding
maleducation	man of fortune	marsh treader	mealy redpoll
malefactress	man of leisure	marsh trefoil	mean business
malevolently	man of letters	marsh warbler	mean free path
malexecution	man of science	marsupialize	meaningfully
malformation	man-of-war fish	martagon lily	mean mischief
malignancies	manometrical	martial eagle	means and ways
malinfluence	mansion house	martinettish	mean sea level
Malinowskian	Mansion House	Martiniquais	means of grace
malleability	manslaughter	martyrolatry	mean solar day
malleableize	manteau-maker	marvellingly	measured mile
mallet finger	mantis shrimp	marvellously	measuredness
malnourished	mantle-cavity	marvel of Peru	measuring-cup
malnutrition	mantua-making	marzipanning	measuring jug
malocclusion	manufactural	masslessness	meat and drink
malodorously	manufacturer	mass spectrum	meatlessness

meat-offering
Mebyon Kernow
mecamylamine
mechanically
mechatronics
medallionist
medallion man
meddlesomely
mediatorship
medical board
medicamental
Medici collar
medicine ball
medicine line
medicine seal
medicine show
medicine tree
medicine wolf
mediocrities
mediocritize
mediopalatal
mediopassive
meditatingly
meditatively
medium bowler
medullary ray
meeting house
meeting-place
megacephalic
megalocardia
megalomaniac
megalomartyr
megalosaurus
megalosphere
megaphyllous
megatherioid
Meissen china
melancholiac
melancholies
melancholily
melancholise
melancholist
melancholize
melanization
melanocomous
melanocratic
melanodermia
melanodermic
mellifluence
melodic minor
melodramatic
melon-thistle
melted butter
melting-house
melting point
melt spinning
membrane-bone
membraneless
membraniform
membranology
memorability
memorializer

memorization
memory-belief
memory effect
ménage à trois
mendaciously
Mendelianism
mend one's pace
mend one's ways
men in buckram
meningococci
meniscectomy
menstruation
mental asylum
mental healer
mental health
menticulture
mercantilely
mercantilism
mercantilist
merchandiser
merchantable
merchant bank
merchanthood
merchant iron
merchantlike
merchant navy
merchant ship
mercifulness
mercurialism
mercurialist
mercuriality
mercurialize
meretricious
meridian line
meridian-mark
meridionally
meristematic
meristically
meritocratic
meroplankton
merosymmetry
merry as a grig
merry dancers
merry England
merry-go-round
merry-meeting
merry thought
mesarteritic
mesarteritis
mesatipellic
mescal button
mesenteritis
mesityl oxide
mesmerically
mesmerizable
mesne process
mesne profits
Meso-American
meso-appendix
mesocephalic
mesoconchous
mesogastrium

mesognathism
mesognathous
meso-inositol
mesokurtosis
mesometritis
mesomorphism
mesomorphous
meson factory
mesoplankton
Mesopotamian
mesosiderite
mesothelioma
mesothoracic
mesquite bean
message stick
Messeigneurs
messenger RNA
metacercaria
metachromasy
metachromism
metachronism
metacinnabar
metacontrast
metagalactic
metageometry
metagnathism
metagnathous
metalanguage
metal fatigue
metalimnetic
metalinguist
metallically
metallic bond
metallic soap
metallic yarn
metallogenic
metallophone
metallurgist
metalogician
metalworking
metamictness
metamorphise
metamorphism
metamorphize
metamorphose
metaphonized
metaphorical
metaphrastic
metaphysical
metapolitics
metapsychics
metapsychist
metasomatism
metasomatize
metathetical
metathoracic
metavolcanic
metempirical
meteorically
meteoritical
meteorograph
meteorolitic

meteorologic
meteoroscopy
meteor shower
methacholine
methacrylate
methanogenic
methanometer
methanotroph
methaqualone
methodically
methohexital
methotrexate
methoxychlor
methyl orange
methyl rubber
methyl violet
methysergide
meticulosity
meticulously
Metonic cycle
metoposcopic
metrological
metropolitan
metrorrhagia
metrorrhagic
Mexican brown
Mexican poppy
Meyerbeerian
mezzo-relievo
mezzo-rilievo
mezzo-soprano
mickey-taking
microammeter
microanalyst
microanatomy
microbalance
Microballoon
microbenthic
microbenthos
microbicidal
microbiology
microcapsule
microcephaly
microchemist
microcircuit
microclastic
microclimate
microcrystal
microcytosis
microdiorite
micro-element
microfilaria
microgranite
micrographer
micrographic
microgravity
microhabitat
micrological
micronodular
micronuclear
micronucleus
microphagous

microphonism
microphysics
micropipette
microprogram
micropterous
micropublish
microscopist
Microscopium
microsection
microsegment
microseismic
microspecies
microspheric
microsporous
microstylous
microsurgery
microtonally
microtubular
microvillous
microwavable
middle-ageing
middle course
middle finger
middle ground
middle-income
middle-length
middle period
middle-relief
middlescence
middle school
Middle States
Middle Temple
middleweight
middle wicket
middlingness
midnight blue
midnight mass
midship frame
Midsummer Day
mid-Victorian
Midwesterner
Milanese silk
mild-mannered
militariness
militaristic
military band
military drum
militiawoman
milk and honey
milk and water
milk for babes
milk purslane
milk-sickness
milkwood tree
millefeuille
Miller effect
miller's thumb
millesimally
milliammeter
milliardaire
millions fish
mill-mountain

Mill's Methods
Miltonically
miminy-piminy
minatoriness
mince matters
mind-boggling
mindlessness
mind one's hits
mind one's step
mind your back
mine-detector
mineragraphy
mineral black
mineral brown
mineral green
mineral jelly
mineralogist
mineral pitch
mineral water
mine-sweeping
mingle-mangle
minicomputer
minification
minimalistic
minimization
ministership
ministration
ministrative
minnow-fisher
minority debt
minor prophet
Minor Prophet
minstrelsies
miogeoclinal
Miquelet lock
miracle fruit
miraculously
mirror finish
mirror-writer
mirthfulness
misadventure
misaffection
misalignment
misanthropic
misapprehend
misattribute
misbehaviour
miscalculate
miscegenated
miscellanies
miscellanist
mischanceful
misconceiver
misconstruct
misdemeanant
misdemeanour
misdiagnosis
misdirection
miseducation
miserabilism
miserabilist
miserability

misexecution
misfit stream
misformation
misfortunate
misinformant
misinterpret
misjudgement
misknowledge
mislabelling
misleadingly
misogynistic
misorientate
misplacement
mispronounce
mispunctuate
misquotation
misrecollect
misrepresent
missel thrush
missiologist
missionaries
missionarize
mission house
mission stiff
Miss Milligan
misstatement
mistakenness
mistle thrush
mistranslate
mistreatment
mistresshood
mistressless
mistress-ship
mistrustless
mithridatise
mithridatism
mithridatize
mitochondria
mixed bathing
mixed company
mixed crystal
mixed doubles
mixed economy
mixed farming
mixed-traffic
mixtie-maxtie
mizen topmast
mizen topsail
mnemonically
mnemotechnic
Moabite stone
mobilisation
mobilization
modalization
model-drawing
moderateness
moderatorial
modern Greats
modernizable
modern school
modesty piece
modesty skirt

modification
modificative
modificatory
modi operandi
modus tollens
modus vivendi
moeritherium
moire antique
moistureless
molarization
mole-coloured
molecularity
mole fraction
molinologist
mollifyingly
molluscicide
mollycoddler
Molly Maguire
moloch gibbon
molybdomancy
momentaneity
momentaneous
monadelphous
monastically
mondo bizarro
monepiscopal
monetaristic
monetization
money changer
money-grubber
moneylending
money matters
money-spinner
Mongolian eye
monistically
monkey bridge
monkey-chaser
monkey engine
monkey flower
monkey island
monkey-jacket
monkey orchid
monkey parade
monkey-puzzle
monkey tricks
monkey wrench
monkeywrench
monk's rhubarb
monocellular
monochloride
monochromasy
monochromate
monochromist
monochromous
monoclinally
mono-coloured
monocularity
monocultural
monodelphian
monodisperse
monodramatic
monoeciously

monofilament	moralizingly	motor cyclist	mulberry tree
monogamistic	moral science	motorcyclist	mule-skinning
monogamously	moral support	motorization	mullein shark
monogenistic	moral victory	motor neurone	mullet-headed
monographist	morbilliform	motor scooter	mulligatawny
monohydrated	morcellation	motor vehicle	multi-angular
monoideistic	Morellianism	mottled umber	multicentral
monokaryotic	more's the pity	mouldability	multicentric
monolinguist	morigeration	mould-blowing	multichannel
monomaniacal	Mormon Church	mound-builder	multicircuit
monometallic	morning after	mound of Venus	multicostate
monomorphism	morning dress	mountain bike	multidentate
monomorphous	morning glory	mountain blue	multifaceted
mononucleate	morning paper	mountain cock	multifarious
monopetalous	morning watch	mountain duck	multiflorous
monophonemic	morphallaxis	mountain fern	multifoliate
monophyletic	morphiomania	mountain flax	multiformity
monophyllous	morphography	mountain goat	multiformous
monophyodont	morphologist	mountain hare	multigeneric
monophysitic	morphologize	mountain-high	multigravida
monopodially	morphomaniac	mountain land	multilaminar
monopolistic	morphometric	mountain lion	multilateral
monopsychism	morphology	mountain mint	multilayered
monoptically	morphophonic	mountain plum	multilingual
monorchidism	morphosyntax	mountain rice	multilobular
monosemantic	morphotactic	mountainside	multilocular
monosepalous	morphotropic	mountain snow	multiloquent
monosiphonic	morris dancer	Mountain Time	multimammate
monospecific	morrow-speech	mountainward	multimillion
monospermous	mortgageable	mountain wine	multinominal
monostichous	mortgage rate	Mount Everest	multinuclear
monostrophic	mortifyingly	Mountmellick	multiovulate
monosyllabic	mosquito-boat	mount of piety	multi-partism
monosyllable	mosquito-boot	mount of Venus	multi-partist
monosymmetry	mosquito coil	mournfulness	multipartite
monosynaptic	mosquito fish	mourning-band	multipinnate
monosystemic	mosquito hawk	mourning dove	multiple-disc
monotessaron	moss-trooping	mourning iris	multiple shop
monothalamic	most and least	mourning ring	multiple star
monotheistic	Most Reverend	mouse opossum	multiple twin
Monothelitic	Mother Church	mousquetaire	multiple-unit
monothematic	mother figure	moustache cup	multiplexing
monotonicity	mother-fucker	mouth-breeder	multiplexity
monotonously	motherfucker	mouthbrooder	multipliable
monotriglyph	mother-in-babe	mouth-filling	multiplicand
monozygosity	motherliness	mouth-to-mouth	multiplicate
Montagu shell	mother liquid	movable feast	multiplicity
Montbazillac	mother liquor	movable sheva	multiprogram
Montessorian	mother-loving	movelessness	multi-purpose
Monteverdian	Mother Nature	movie theatre	multiradiate
month by month	mothers-in-law	moving-target	multisection
monthly nurse	Mothers' Union	mucification	multiseptate
monticellite	mother tongue	mucilaginous	multi-tasking
monumentally	motionlessly	muck-spreader	multitasking
mood-altering	motivational	mucopurulent	multi-tracked
Moon Festival	motivelessly	mucormycosis	multi-tracker
Moorish gecko	moto perpetuo	muddle-headed	multivalence
moor-sickness	motor bicycle	mud in your eye	multivalency
moose pasture	motor-boating	mud-wrestling	multivallate
moral courage	motor caravan	muff coupling	multivariant
morality play	motor-coaster	Muggletonian	multivariate
moralization	motorcycling	mulberry-bird	multivarious

multiversity
multivoltine
multungulate
mumble-the-peg
mummy disease
mundane house
municipalise
municipalism
municipalist
municipality
municipalize
munificently
muniment deed
munitionette
munitionment
murdermonger
muriatic acid
murine typhus
muscovitized
museographer
museological
mushroom city
mushroom loaf
mushroom-ring
mushroom town
musical bumps
musical chime
musical clock
musical drive
musical sound
musicassette
music gallery
music-grinder
music-hallish
musicianship
music licence
musicography
musicologist
musico-phobia
music theatre
music therapy
musket powder
musk kangaroo
musk lorikeet
muskrat house
musk tortoise
Muslim League
musquash-root
mussel digger
mussel picker
Mussorgskian
Mussulmanism
mustang grape
muster-master
mutagenicity
mutarotation
mutationally
mutation mink
mutation rank
mutation rate
mutation stop
mutinousness

mutton-birder
mutton candle
mutton-fisted
mutton-headed
mutuatitious
muzzle-loader
mycetomatous
mycetophilid
mycoplasmata
my dear fellow
myelin sheath
myeloblastic
myelogenesis
myelographic
myelomatosis
my godfathers
mylohyoidean
mylonization
myochemistry
myofibrillar
myrmecochore
myrmecophile
myrmecophily
myrmecophyte
myrobalan nut
my sow's pigged
mystagogical
mystagoguery
mysteriously
mystery novel
mystery story
mystery woman
mysticalness
mystificator
mystifyingly
mythoclastic
mythogenesis
mythographer
mythographic
mythological
mythologizer
nail scissors
naive painter
naive realism
naive realist
namby-pambies
name-dropping
namelessness
nankeen cloth
nankeen heron
nanoplankton
Napier's bones
nap selection
narcissistic
narcissus fly
narcotically
Narragansett
narrowcasted
narrowcaster
narrow-minded
narrow squeak
nasalization

nasolacrimal
natalid organ
national bank
national debt
National Debt
national grid
nationalizer
nationalness
national park
native orange
native poplar
native potato
native quince
native turkey
native willow
nativity play
nativization
Natterer's bat
natural death
naturalesque
naturalistic
natural magic
natural order
natural parts
natural right
nature-faking
nature poetry
nature ramble
nature-spirit
naturopathic
nauseatingly
nauseousness
nautical mile
naval academy
naval brigade
naval officer
naval reserve
naval station
navigability
navigational
navy register
navy revolver
Nazariteship
Nazification
near infrared
near the heart
neat's-foot oil
neat's-leather
nebulization
nebulousness
nebulous star
neck and heels
necklace-tree
necktie party
necrological
necromantist
necrophagous
necrophiliac
necrophilism
necrophilist
necrophilous
necropolitan

necroscopies
nectareously
needle-and-pin
needle biopsy
needle roller
needle shower
needlessness
needleworker
neencephalic
neencephalon
negation-sign
negative glow
negativeness
negative pole
negative sign
negativistic
neglectfully
neglectively
negotiatress
Negro English
Negrophilism
Negrophilist
Negro tamarin
neighbouress
neighbouring
Nelson's blood
nematocerous
nematologist
nembutalized
neoclassical
Neo-Darwinian
Neo-Darwinism
Neo-Darwinist
neo-Hellenism
neon lighting
Neonomianism
neontologist
Neoplatonism
Neoplatonist
neosalvarsan
neotectonics
nephanalysis
nephelinitic
nephelometer
nephelometry
nephrologist
nephromixium
nephropathic
nephroptosis
Neptunianism
nerve impulse
nerve-patient
nerve-racking
nervous Nelly
nervous wreck
Nessler's tube
Nestorianism
Netherlander
Netherlandic
nether person
neurasthenia
neurasthenic

neurilemmoma
neuroanatomy
neurobiology
neuroblastic
neurocranium
neurofibroma
neurogenesis
neurogenetic
neurohormone
neurohumoral
neurological
neuropathist
neuropeptide
neuropterous
neuroscience
neurosensory
neurosurgeon
neurosurgery
neurotically
neurotrophic
neurotropism
neurypnology
neutralistic
neutral vowel
neutrophilic
never-ceasing
never-failing
nevertheless
never you fear
never you mind
New Criticism
new departure
New Englander
newfangledly
new-fashioned
Newfoundland
Newgate frill
Newgate novel
New Jersey tea
new of the moon
New Orleanian
news bulletin
news-gatherer
newslessness
newspaperdom
newspaperese
newspaperish
newspaperism
newspaperman
newspapermen
newsworthily
New Testament
New Thoughter
Newtonianism
Newtonically
New Zealander
next the heart
nice-nellyism
nichemanship
nickel nurser
nickel-plated
nickel silver

nicotinamide
niddle-noddle
nidification
Nigerian teak
Niger morocco
nigger heaven
night-adapted
nightclothes
nightclubber
night-commode
night crawler
night fighter
night-herding
nightie-night
night jasmine
night paddock
night-scented
night terrors
night-walking
night-watcher
nimble-footed
nimble-witted
nimbostratus
niminy-piminy
nine-nine-nine
nineteenthly
Nippon vellum
Nissl granule
nitrobenzene
nitromethane
nitromuriate
nitrophilous
nitrous oxide
no better than
noble science
nocking point
no-claim bonus
noctambulant
noctambulism
noctambulist
noctambulous
nocturnal arc
nodulization
no fixed abode
noise contour
noise limiter
nolens volens
nomadization
nomen agentis
nomenclative
nomenclature
nominalistic
nominal value
nomothetical
non-abstainer
non-addictive
non-admission
nonagenarian
non-alcoholic
non-alignment
non-ambiguous
non assumpsit

non-breakable
nonchalantly
non-Christian
non-combatant
non-committal
non-communist
non-Communist
non-conductor
non-contagion
non-cooperate
non-crossover
noncurantist
non-effective
non-efficient
non-emptiness
nonentitious
none-so-pretty
non-essential
none the worse
non-Euclidean
non-execution
non-executive
non-existence
non-explosive
non-fattening
non-fictional
non-flammable
non-inflected
non-intervene
non-intrusion
non-knowledge
non-linearity
non-logically
non-malignant
non-migratory
non-necessity
non-Newtonian
non-normality
non-obedience
non-objective
non-poisonous
non-political
non-reflexive
non-residence
non-resistant
non-resisting
non-scheduled
non-scientist
non-sectarian
non-segmental
non-selective
nonsense word
non-sensitive
non-technical
non-trivially
non-vanishing
non-violently
Noogoora burr
no question of
noradrenalin
nordmarkitic
norephedrine

Norfolk capon
normal forest
normalizable
normal saline
normal school
Norman French
Norman thrush
normlessness
normoblastic
normochromic
normotensive
normothermic
North African
North Britain
north country
North Country
north-eastern
Northern blot
northernmost
northernness
northern star
northern wren
Northumbrian
north-western
Norway spruce
noselessness
no such animal
notabilities
not an earthly
notarization
notary public
notationally
not care a cent
not care a chip
not care a hang
not care a snap
notch-bar test
notch-brittle
noteworthily
not give a damn
not give a hang
not give a shit
not have a clue
not having any
nothingarian
nothing doing
nothing for it
nothing loath
nothosaurian
notification
not if I know it
not in the book
not in the race
not much wiser
not one's scene
notoungulate
not to mention
not to speak of
not turn a hair
not worth a fig
nourishingly
nouveau riche

novelization
Novocastrian
nubbing-cheat
nuclear force
nuclear power
nuclear waste
nucleocapsid
nucleolonema
nucleophilic
nucleosidase
nucleotidase
nude contract
nugatoriness
nuisance raid
number-crunch
number theory
numerability
numerologist
numerousness
numinousness
numismatical
Nunc Dimittis
nursery class
nursery nurse
nursery rhyme
nursery slope
nut chocolate
nutritionist
nutritiously
nuts and bolts
nychthemeral
nychthemeron
nyctitropism
nyctohemeral
nympholeptic
nymphomaniac
obambulation
obdurateness
obedientiary
obedientness
Oberleutnant
obiter dictum
object choice
object-finder
objectionist
objectlessly
object lesson
object libido
object-matter
objet de virtu
oblanceolate
obligational
obligatorily
obligingness
oblique pedal
obliteration
obliterative
oblivescence
obliviscence
obmutescence
obnubilation
oboe da caccia

oboi da caccia
obreptitious
obscurantism
obscurantist
obscure vowel
obsequiously
Observantine
obsessionist
obsolescence
obsoleteness
obstacle race
obstetrician
obstreperous
obstructedly
occasionally
occasonalist
occidentally
occult spavin
occupational
oceanic crust
oceanisation
oceanization
oceanography
oceanologist
ochlocracies
ochlophobist
ochlospecies
octahedrally
octahedrical
octane number
octane rating
octave stanza
octogenarian
octopetalous
octosepalous
octosyllabic
octosyllable
oculo-agravic
odd-come-short
odontologist
odontophoral
oedematously
oesophagitis
of easy virtue
off at the nail
Offenbachian
offendedness
office-bearer
office junior
office of arms
office-seeker
office worker
officious lie
off one's block
off one's chump
off one's guard
off one's hands
off one's onion
off-puttingly
off-reckoning
off-the-course
off the record

of good family
of obligation
of the essence
of the order of
oidiomycosis
oil of juniper
oil of vitriol
oil on the fire
oil pollution
oil the wheels
oil to the fire
old-fashioned
old-field lark
old-field pine
Old Gentleman
Old Icelandic
old-maidenism
old-maidishly
old-man cactus
old man's beard
old moustache
Old Pretender
Old Ritualist
old school tie
Old Testament
old wives' tale
oleaginosity
oleaginously
oleander hawk
oleandomycin
oleoresinous
oleyl alcohol
olfactometer
olfactometry
olfactronics
oligarchical
oligocarpous
oligodynamic
oligopeptide
oligophagous
oligophrenia
oligopsonist
oligosaprobe
oligospermia
oligotrophic
olistostrome
Olympic games
Olympic Games
ombrological
ombrophilous
ombrophobous
ombrotrophic
omissibility
omnibus train
omnipotently
omnipresence
omnisciently
omnitemporal
omnitolerant
omnivorously
omphaloscopy
on a level with

on an even keel
on bended knee
once and again
once in a while
once too often
on cloud seven
oncogenicity
on commission
oncornavirus
one-and-thirty
one-arm bandit
one had best do
one-horse race
oneirocritic
oneiromancer
one jump ahead
one of the best
one of the boys
one's born days
one's cup of tea
one's ears burn
one's good lady
one-sidedness
one's luck is in
one's mind's eye
one's sun is set
one's writ runs
one-track mind
one-upmanship
on firm ground
on first blush
only-begotten
on occasion of
onomasiology
onomastician
onomatomania
onomatopoeia
onomatopoeic
on one's honour
on one's mettle
on one's pulses
on one's uppers
on one's way out
on security of
on sufferance
on the basis of
on the brink of
on the decline
on the faith of
on the high gig
on the horizon
on the kibes of
on the knocker
on the one hand
on the order of
on the outlook
on the point of
on the pretext
on the qui vive
on the rampage
on the rebound
on the schnozz

on the score of	optic chiasma	Orphan's Court	out in the cold
on the streets	optic measure	orphenadrine	outlandishly
on the track of	optic papilla	orthocephaly	outlaw strike
on the up and up	optic vesicle	orthoclastic	outmanoeuvre
on the up grade	optimization	orthodiagram	outmigration
on the upgrade	optoacoustic	orthodigital	outmodedness
on the wallaby	optometrical	orthodontics	out of conceit
on the warpath	oracularness	orthodontist	out of context
on this side of	orange-brandy	orthodoxical	out of control
ontotheology	orange-colour	orthodoxness	out of drawing
onus probandi	orange flower	orthoepistic	out of my sight
onychophagia	orange squash	orthoferrite	out of one's way
onychophoran	orange-yellow	orthogenesis	out of service
oophorectomy	Oratorianism	orthogenetic	out of spirits
open a door for	Oratorianize	orthognathic	out of the blue
open a gate for	oratorically	orthogonally	out of the milk
open-breasted	orbicularity	orthographer	out of the road
Open Brethren	orbiculately	orthographic	out of the swim
open compound	orbital index	orthokinesis	out of the true
open fracture	orchard grass	orthokinetic	out of the wood
open-handedly	orchard-house	orthomorphic	out of the wool
opening night	orchestrally	orthopaedics	out of winding
open interest	orchestra pit	orthopaedist	out on one's ear
open interval	orchestrator	orthopterist	out-pensioner
open juncture	orchestrelle	orthopteroid	outplacement
open learning	orchidaceous	orthopterous	outpocketing
open marriage	orchid cactus	orthorhombic	outrageously
open-mindedly	orchidectomy	orthotropous	outrightness
open one's ears	Order of Merit	orthovoltage	outscourings
open one's face	ordinariness	oryctologist	outside and in
open question	ordinary wine	Oscar-winning	outside cabin
open sandwich	organ-grinder	oscillatoria	outsidedness
open syllable	organicistic	oscillograph	outside track
opéra comique	organisation	oscillometer	outward bound
opera glasses	organistship	oscillometry	ovariotomies
opera recital	organization	oscilloscope	over-abundant
operatically	organizatory	osmoregulate	overabundant
operationism	organ of Corti	osmotic shock	overachiever
operationist	organogenist	ossification	overactivity
operatorship	organogenous	osteichthyan	overambition
ophiomorphic	organography	ostentatious	over and above
ophiophagous	organoleptic	osteoblastic	over-and-under
ophthalmitis	organologist	osteoclastic	overbearance
opinionation	orgasmically	osteogenesis	overbitterly
opinionative	orgastically	osteogenetic	overboldness
opinionnaire	orgiasticism	osteological	overcapacity
opisthodomos	oriental sore	osteomalacia	overcautious
opisthoglyph	orienteering	osteomalacic	overcoatless
opisthograph	original writ	osteopathist	overcomingly
opisthotonic	Orkney cheese	osteoporosis	overcompound
opisthotonos	ornamentally	osteoporotic	overcritical
opposability	ornithogalum	osteosarcoma	overcrowding
oppositeness	ornithologer	ostrich plume	over-delicacy
oppositional	ornithologic	other-worldly	overdelicacy
oppressingly	ornithomancy	otherworldly	over-delicate
oppressively	ornithophile	otosclerosis	overdelicate
opsonization	ornithophily	otosclerotic	overdramatic
optative mood	ornithoscopy	Ottoman Porte	overeasiness
optical bench	orogenically	ouster-le-main	overeffusive
optical fibre	orographical	outdatedness	overemphasis
optical glass	oro-rotundity	outfangthief	overengineer
optical sound	orphan asylum	outgoingness	overeruption

overestimate
over-exercise
overexercise
overexertion
overexposure
overfamiliar
overflourish
overflow pipe
overfondness
overfullness
overgenerous
overhand knot
overhydrated
over-inflated
overkindness
overlavishly
overlook bean
overlordship
overmodestly
overmodulate
overmuchness
overniceness
over one's head
over one's name
over-optimism
overoptimism
overpainting
overpersuade
overpopulate
overpowering
overpressure
overquantity
overreaction
overridingly
overrigorous
overripeness
oversampling
overseership
oversimplify
overspeaking
overspecific
oversprinkle
overstepping
overstrictly
oversubtlety
oversupplied
oversupplies
over-the-board
over the fence
over the limit
over the rails
overthrowing
overtrousers
overwatching
overwhelming
owl-butterfly
oxaloacetate
oxbow stirrup
Oxford chrome
Oxford Circus
Oxford hollow
Oxford School

Oxford Tracts
oxotremorine
oxyacetylene
oxycellulose
oxyluciferin
oxymyoglobin
oxyphosphate
oyster blenny
oyster-cellar
oyster-farmer
oyster-plover
oyster-shaped
oyster-veneer
pachycaulous
pachydermoid
pacification
pacificatory
Pacific Ocean
Pacific slope
packing-sheet
pack one's bags
paddle tennis
paddling pool
paddock-stone
paddock-stool
paedobaptism
paedobaptist
paedodontics
paedodontist
paedogenesis
paedogenetic
paedomorphic
paedophiliac
paganization
pagoda sleeve
paid holidays
paid-up member
painlessness
paintability
painted cloth
painted finch
painted grass
painted quail
paint the lily
pair of arrows
pair of gloves
pair of horses
pair of knives
pair of scales
pair of shears
pair of stairs
pair of wheels
palaeobotany
palaeocortex
palaeography
Palaeo-Indian
palaeolithic
palaeoniscid
palaeoradius
palatability
palatine bone
Palatine Hill

palato-dental
palatography
palatoplasty
Palestrinian
palette knife
palimbacchic
palimpsestic
palindromist
palingenesia
palingenesis
palingenetic
palinspastic
palisade cell
palisade-worm
Palladianism
Palladianize
palladiumize
palliatively
palma Christi
palmetto flag
palm-greasing
palmitic acid
palm squirrel
palo de hierro
palpableness
palsie-walsie
palynologist
pamperedness
Panathenaean
pan-Britannic
pan-Christian
panchromatic
pancreatitis
pancreozymin
pancytopenia
pandialectal
panel heating
panel painter
panel patient
pan-Germanism
pan-Germanist
pangrammatic
Panhellenism
Panhellenist
paniculately
panification
pannikin-boss
panpharmacon
panplanation
pan-sexualism
pan-sexuality
Panslavistic
pantaloonery
pantechnicon
pantellerite
panther juice
pantie-girdle
pantisocracy
pantographer
pantographic
pantological
pantomimical

pantomograph
pantophagist
pantothenate
Papanicolaou
paper-folding
paper-hanging
paper-machine
paper pattern
paper-pushing
paper-shelled
paper-stainer
paper-taffeta
Paphlagonian
papillectomy
papilloedema
papistically
papyriferous
papyrography
papyrologist
paraboliform
paraboloidal
parabronchus
paracellular
paracentesis
paracervical
parachronism
paraclinical
parade ground
paradigmatic
paradigm case
paradisaical
paradise-bird
paradise duck
paradise-fish
paradise-tree
paradisiacal
paradoxology
paraenetical
paraesthesia
paraesthetic
paraffinized
paraffin test
parafoveally
paraganglion
paragraphism
paragraphist
parahydrogen
paralanguage
paralipomena
parallel bars
parallel-park
parallel text
parallel turn
paralogistic
paralogously
paralysation
paralysingly
paramagnetic
parameterize
parametritic
parametritis
paramilitary

paramorphism	Parsonianism	pathographer	pedantocracy
paranatellon	parsonically	pathological	pedestal desk
paranoically	parson's table	patholopolis	pedestalling
paranormally	part exchange	patience-dock	pedestrianly
Paranthropus	Parthenopean	patio process	pedicellaria
paraphimosis	Parthian shot	pat on the back	pedicellated
paraphrastic	partial order	patriarchate	pediculicide
paraphyletic	partial umbel	patriarchess	Pedro Ximenez
paraphysical	participable	patriarchies	pedunculated
parapophysis	participator	patriarchism	peel one's eyes
parasagittal	particularly	Patriarchist	peerie pinkie
parascending	partisanship	patricentric	peerlessness
parasitaemia	partitioning	patricianism	peer pressure
parasite drag	partitionism	patrilateral	pejoratively
parasiticide	partitionist	patrilineage	pelargonidin
parasitology	partners desk	patrilocally	pelecypodous
parasphenoid	part of speech	Patripassian	pelican's foot
parasymbiont	partridge pea	patristicism	Pelican State
paratectonic	partycolored	patroclinous	pellucidness
paraterminal	party manners	patrological	pellucid zone
parathormone	party per bend	patronymical	pelvic girdle
parcellation	party per pale	patternation	pelvic thrust
parcel tanker	party per pile	pattern-paper	penalization
parchmentize	party-pooping	pattinsonize	penalty bench
pareiasaurus	pas de bourrée	patulousness	penalty bully
parenchymous	pas de ciseaux	Paulicianism	Penang lawyer
parenterally	pasque flower	pavor diurnus	pencil flower
parent-figure	passableness	pawn skeleton	pencil pusher
parenthesise	passage grave	pay-as-you-earn	*pendente lite*
parenthesize	passage-money	pay-off matrix	pendulum-ball
Parfait Amour	passed-master	pay on the line	pendulum-wire
Parian cement	passe-partout	peaceability	penetrameter
Parian marble	passepartout	peace-breaker	penetrometer
parietal bone	passibleness	peace economy	pen-feathered
parietal cell	passing place	peacefulness	penicillanic
parietal lobe	passionately	peace-keeping	penicilloate
paring-chisel	Passion cross	peacekeeping	penitent-form
Paris commune	passion fruit	peace-officer	penitentiary
parish church	passivizable	peach-blossom	penitentness
parish priest	pass one's lips	peach yellows	Pennsylvania
parish-rigged	passportless	Peacock Alley	penny-pincher
paristhmitis	pass the pikes	peacockishly	penny-postage
parisyllabic	past definite	peacock's tail	penny whistle
parking brake	pastern-joint	peanut butter	pen recording
parking light	Pasteur flask	pearlescence	pensifulness
parking meter	past historic	pearlessence	pensionaries
parking orbit	past mistress	pearl-fishery	pentagastrin
Parkinsonian	pastophorium	pearl-fishing	pentagonally
Parkinsonism	pastoralness	pearly whites	pentahedrons
parlour-house	past-pointing	peasant class	pentahydrate
paroccipital	past the chair	pease pudding	pentametrize
parochialism	pataphysical	pebble-dashed	pentapeptide
parochiality	pâté en croûte	pebble-lensed	pentapolitan
parochialize	patellectomy	peccadilloes	Pentateuchal
paroemiology	patent office	pecking order	pentose cycle
paronomastic	Patent Safety	Pecksniffery	People's Court
parotid gland	path-breaking	Pecksniffian	People's front
parquet floor	pathetically	Peclet number	People's Power
parrot's-perch	pathlessness	pectinaceous	pepper-caster
parsimonious	pathobiology	pectoral arch	peppered moth
parsley-piert	pathogenesis	pectoriloquy	pepper shaker
parsley sauce	pathogenetic	pedantically	peptide chain

peptidolysis
peptidolytic
peradventure
peraluminous
perambulator
perceptional
perceptively
perceptivity
perceptually
percipiently
percontation
percussively
percutaneous
peregrinator
peremptorily
perenniality
perestroikan
perfectation
perfect crime
perfectively
perfectivity
perfectivize
perfect pitch
perfidiously
perfoliation
performative
performatory
perfrication
pergameneous
periarterial
pericarditis
pericellular
pericemental
pericementum
perichaetial
perichaetium
perichaetous
perichoresis
periclinally
pericynthion
peridiastole
perigonadial
Perigourdine
perilousness
perimetrical
perinatology
periodic acid
periodically
periodograph
periodontics
periodontist
periodontium
periostracum
peripediment
peripherally
peripherical
periphrastic
perispomenon
peristrephic
perisystolic
peritrichate
peritrichous

periureteric
periurethral
perivascular
perivisceral
perjuriously
permaculture
permanentise
permanentize
permanent set
permanent way
permanganate
permeabilise
permeability
permeabilize
permissively
permissivism
permissivist
permittivity
perniciously
pernoctation
peroperative
perorational
peroxidation
peroxide bond
perpetration
perpetualism
perpetualist
perpetuality
perpetuation
perpetuative
perpetuities
perphenazine
perplexingly
perplexities
perquisition
persecutress
perseverance
perseverator
Persian berry
Persian green
Persian lilac
Persian sheep
Persian wheel
persistently
persistingly
persona grata
personalness
personalties
person-object
perspectival
perspicacity
perspiration
perspirative
perspiratory
persuadingly
persuasively
persulphuric
pertechnetic
pertinacious
perturbation
perturbative
perturbingly

Peruginesque
Peruvian bark
Peruvian lily
perverseness
perversities
pervicacious
perviousness
Pestalozzian
pestilential
pestological
petaliferous
Peterborough
Peter Pannish
Petersen grab
petitionable
petit treason
petrifaction
petrifactive
Petrobrusian
petrofabrics
petrogenesis
petrogenetic
petrographer
petrographic
petrol coupon
petrological
petrophysics
pettifoggery
pettifogging
petty average
petty officer
petty treason
Peutingerian
peyote button
phagedaenous
phagocytable
phagocytosis
phalaenopsid
phallocratic
phallophoria
phallophoric
phallophorus
phalloplasty
phanerogamic
phanerophyte
phantasmally
phantastical
Pharaoh hound
pharmaceutic
pharmacology
pharyngotomy
phase diagram
pheasantries
pheasant's eye
phellodermal
phenanthrene
phenetically
phenological
phenomenally
phenotypical
phentolamine
phenylacetic

Pherecratean
Pherecratian
Phi Beta Kappa
Philadelphia
philadelphus
philanthrope
philanthropy
philatelical
philathletic
philharmonic
philhellenic
philippinite
Philistinian
philistinish
philistinism
Philistinize
phillumenist
philobiblian
philobiblist
philodendron
philological
philosopheme
philosophess
philosophies
philosophise
philosophism
philosophist
philosophize
philotechnic
philotherian
phlebectasia
phlebography
phlebotomise
phlebotomist
phlebotomize
phlegmagogue
phlorizinize
phlyctenular
phoenicopter
phonaestheme
phonemically
phonetically
phonocamptic
phonographer
phonographic
phonological
phonometrics
phonotactics
phosphatemia
phosphatidic
phosphatidyl
phosphaturia
phosphaturic
phospholipid
phosphoresce
phosphoritic
Photinianism
photoallergy
photobiology
photocathode
photochemist
photochromic

photocollage	phyllotactic	pigeon-breast	pivotability
photocompose	phylogenesis	pigeon's blood	pivot bearing
photocontrol	phylogenetic	pigmentation	pivot grammar
photoconvert	physicalness	pigs might fly	placableness
photocurrent	physic garden	piked dogfish	place-betting
photodimeric	physicianess	Pilate's voice	placentation
photodynamic	physiocratic	pile-building	placentogram
photoelastic	physiognomic	pile dwelling	placentology
photoemitter	physiography	pillar-box red	place setting
photo-engrave	physiologist	pillion cloth	plagiaristic
photofission	physiologize	piloerection	plagioclimax
photogeology	physogastric	pilot balloon	plagiotropic
photographee	physostomous	pilot biscuit	plain bearing
photographer	phytobenthos	pilot carrier	plain buffalo
photographic	phytochemist	pilot episode	plain clothes
photogravure	phytogenesis	pilot officer	plain cooking
photokinesis	phytographic	Pilsner glass	plain dealing
photokinetic	phytohormone	pinchpennies	plain English
photometrist	phytological	pinealectomy	plain-hearted
photomontage	phytophagous	pineapple rum	plain hunting
photoneutron	phytophthora	pine grosbeak	plain sailing
photonuclear	phytosaurian	pine hawkmoth	Plains Indian
photo-oxidize	pia-arachnoid	pine overcoat	plain Spanish
photopigment	pianofortist	piney varnish	plains turkey
photopolymer	piano quartet	pinguedinous	plain weaving
photoprocess	piano quintet	pinguescence	plane sailing
photoproduct	pibble-pabble	pinhole borer	planetariums
photoprotein	Picassoesque	pink bollworm	planetesimal
photorealism	pickaninnies	pink cockatoo	planetologic
photorealist	pick a quarrel	pink-coloured	planet pinion
photorespire	pickerel frog	pink elephant	planigraphic
photoscanner	pickerel-weed	pink purslane	planispheric
photosensory	Pick's disease	pinnatifidly	planlessness
photo session	pick to pieces	pinpointable	planning gain
photosetting	pick up stakes	pip at the post	planoconcave
photospheric	pick up the tab	pipedreaming	planogametic
photosurface	picnic basket	pipe one's eyes	planographic
phototherapy	picnic ground	piping plover	planorbiform
phototrophic	picoplankton	piping shrike	plantain lily
phototropism	picornavirus	Pirandellian	plant hormone
phototypeset	pictographic	Pirandellism	plant kingdom
photovoltaic	pictorialism	pirate-stream	plasmacytoid
phragmoplast	pictorialist	piscicapture	plasmacytoma
phrase-marker	pictorialize	pisciculture	plasma engine
phraseograph	picture black	Piscis Volans	plasmalemmal
phreatophyte	picturedrome	pisiform bone	plasma sheath
phrenic nerve	picture frame	pistachio nut	plasmasphere
phrenicotomy	picturegraph	pistol-packer	plasmatocyte
phrenologist	Picturephone	pistol shrimp	plasmocytoma
phrenologize	picture-plane	piston engine	plasterboard
phrontistery	picture-space	pitch-and-putt	plaster saint
Phrygian mode	picture stage	pitch-and-toss	plastication
phthalic acid	piece by piece	pitch contour	plastic lymph
phthisiology	piece of eight	pitch control	plastic money
phycological	piece of flesh	pitcher plant	plastic paint
phycomycosis	piece of goods	pitching axis	plastocyanin
phylacteries	piece of water	pitch phoneme	plate-printer
phylarchical	piece-payment	pitch-plaster	plates of meat
phyletically	pied hornbill	pitch wickets	plate tracery
phyllodinous	piercingness	pitiableness	platform body
phyllopodium	pier-head jump	pitilessness	platform shoe
phyllosphere	piezo-crystal	pitter-patter	platform sole

platinum-blue
platinum disc
platitudinal
platonically
Platonically
Platonic body
Platonic year
Plattdeutsch
plattelander
platter-faced
platycephaly
platypussary
plausibility
play at see-saw
play ball with
playfighting
play for a fool
play hell with
playing field
play-material
play one's part
play opposite
play politics
playsomeness
play straight
play the field
play the whore
play with fire
plea of tender
pleasantness
pleasantries
pleasingness
pleasureless
pleasure-pain
plebbishness
plebeianness
plebiscitary
plecopterous
pleiochasium
pleiomorphic
pleiotropism
plenipotence
plenipotency
pleomorphism
plerocercoid
plesiosaurus
plessimetric
pleurisy-root
pleuronectid
Plimsoll line
Plimsoll mark
plinth course
ploddingness
plotlessness
plotting-book
plough-driver
plough-ground
plough-handle
plough-jogger
Plough Monday
plough-pattle
plough-wright

plumbaginous
plumbiferous
plum-coloured
plume-bearing
plume-thistle
plummer-block
plumpishness
plum-porridge
plumulaceous
plunger-valve
plural voting
pluriformity
plurilingual
pluriliteral
plurilocular
pluripotence
pluripotency
pluriseriate
plus ça change
plus juncture
plutocracies
plutological
pluviculture
pluviometric
Plymouth Rock
pneumaticity
pneumatocele
pneumatocyst
pneumatology
pneumococcal
pneumococcus
pneumocystis
pneumography
pneumothorax
pocket gopher
pocket passer
pocket-picker
pocket valley
poddy-dodging
poeticalness
poeticizable
poet laureate
Poet Laureate
pogonophoran
pogonotrophy
poikiloblast
poikiloderma
poikilotherm
poil de chèvre
point blanket
point contact
point d'esprit
pointfulness
pointing-bone
point-instant
point of appui
point of order
point of sight
point the bone
point-to-point
pointy-headed
poison oracle

poke one's head
poker-machine
polar diagram
polarimetric
polariscopic
polarization
polarography
polemologist
pole position
pole strength
police action
policeman fly
policemanish
police matron
police office
policeperson
police record
policyholder
policy-making
poliorcetics
polishedness
Polish marmot
politicalize
politicaster
pollakanthic
pollen basket
pollen parent
polling booth
polling clerk
pollutedness
Pollyannaish
Pollyannaism
polrumptious
polyacrylate
polyadically
polyanthuses
polyarchical
polybasicity
polycentrism
polychaetous
polychromism
polychromous
polydisperse
polyembryony
polyethylene
polygamistic
polygamously
polygenistic
polyglottism
polyglottous
polyhedrical
polyhedrosis
polyhistoric
polyisoprene
polymetallic
polymetrical
polymodality
polymolecule
polymorphean
polymorphism
polymorphous
polymyositis

polyneuritic
polyneuritis
polyoestrous
polyommatous
polypetalous
polypharmacy
polyphonical
polyphylesis
polyphyletic
polyphyllous
polyphyodont
polypiferous
polyploidize
polypneustic
polyreaction
polyrhythmic
polyribosome
polysaprobic
polysemantic
polysensuous
polysepalous
polyspermous
polysulphide
polysulphone
polysyllabic
polysyllable
polysymmetry
polysynaptic
polysyndeton
polysystemic
polytheistic
polytonalist
polytonality
polyurethane
pomacentroid
pommes frites
pompholygous
pons asinorum
Ponsonby rule
Pontiac fever
pontifically
pontificator
pony-trekking
poodle-faking
poop-ornament
poor relation
poor-spirited
poperyphobia
poplar beetle
poplar kitten
pop one's clogs
poppet-valved
poppy anemone
popular front
popular music
popular press
populational
population II
populousness
porcelainist
Porcelainite
porcelainize

porcelainous
porcellanite
porcellanous
porencephaly
pore pressure
pornographer
pornographic
porphyropsin
portableness
portal system
portcullised
porte-bouquet
porte cochère
porte-monnaie
portentously
porteous roll
porter's chair
porter's lodge
portmanteaus
portmanteaux
portrait-bust
portrait-lens
Port-Royalist
port-wine mark
positionally
position line
positiveness
positive pole
positive rays
positive sign
positivistic
possessional
possessioned
possessioner
possessively
possessorial
postage meter
postage stamp
postal ballot
post-alveolar
post-boarding
post-coitally
post-colonial
post-conquest
post-diluvial
post-diluvian
post-doctoral
postdoctoral
poster colour
posteriority
post exchange
post-existent
post-feminism
post-feminist
postfixation
post-Freudian
post-genitive
postgraduate
post-historic
posthumously
post-hypnotic
postillation

postliminary
postmaturely
postmaturity
postmeridian
postmistress
post-modifier
postmultiply
postneonatal
post-obit bond
post-obituary
postponement
postposition
postpositive
postprandial
post-pubertal
postscriptal
postscriptum
postsynaptic
post-tectonic
posture-maker
Posturepedic
potamologist
potato-beetle
potato blight
Potato Famine
potato masher
potato peeler
pot-companion
potentialise
potentiality
potentialize
potentiation
potentiostat
potichomania
potter's field
potter's lathe
potter's wheel
pottery mould
potwalloping
pouched mouse
poulard wheat
poultice-wise
pound and pint
pound-noteish
pound of flesh
pound one's ear
pouring cream
Poussinesque
poverty-grass
poverty level
poverty-plant
powder closet
powder colour
powdering-tub
powder monkey
power alcohol
power-broking
power-centred
power density
power failure
Powerforming
powerfulness

powerlifting
power loading
power package
power-sharing
power station
powers-that-be
power take-off
practicalism
practicality
practicalize
practice game
practitional
practitioner
pragmaticism
pragmatistic
Prague circle
Prague school
Prague Spring
prairie smoke
Prairie State
prairie wagon
praiseworthy
pralltriller
prankishness
pranksterism
praseodymium
prawn cracker
praxeologist
praxinoscope
prayer-carpet
prayerlessly
praying-shawl
preachership
pre-adamitism
preadmission
preamplified
preamplifier
pre-animistic
preassurance
pre-auricular
prebendaries
prebiologist
precalculate
precancerous
precantation
precariously
precautional
precedential
preceptorate
preceptorial
precessional
pre-Christian
preciousness
precious opal
precipitable
precipitance
precipitancy
precipitated
precipitator
precisianism
precisianist
precisionism

precisionist
precivilized
pre-classical
preclassical
preclusively
precociously
precognition
precognitive
pre-Columbian
pre-Communist
precondition
preconfigure
preconscious
predamnation
predecession
predesignate
predestinate
predetermine
predial tithe
predicatival
predictively
predictivity
predigestion
predilection
prediscovery
predisponent
prednisolone
predominance
predominancy
pre-eclampsia
pre-eclamptic
pre-embryonic
pre-emergence
pre-eminently
pre-emphasize
pre-emptioner
pre-emptively
pre-establish
pre-excellent
pre-existence
prefabricate
prefectorial
prefecturate
preferential
prefloration
prefoliation
preformation
preformative
preglacially
pregnability
pregnanediol
prehensility
prehistorian
pre-incarnate
pre-interpret
prejudgement
prejudicious
prelapsarian
prelingually
pre-makeready
premaritally
premaxillary

premeditated
premenarchal
premenopause
premenstrual
premenstruum
Premonstrant
premonstrate
premyelocyte
prenasalized
prentice hand
prenticeship
preoccupancy
pre-operation
preoperative
pre-opercular
pre-operculum
pre-ovulatory
preparedness
preplanetary
preponderant
preponderate
preponderous
preposterous
pre-processor
preprocessor
prepsychotic
pre-pubescent
prepubescent
prepyramidal
prereduction
pre-reflexive
prerequisite
prerogatived
presagefully
presbyterate
presbyteress
presbyterial
presbyterian
Presbyterian
presbyteries
presbyterion
presbyterism
presbyterium
prescribable
prescription
prescriptive
pre-selection
preselection
pre-selective
preselective
presensation
presensitize
presentation
presentative
presenteeism
presentiment
present value
present worth
preservation
preservative
preservatory
preserveress

preshrinkage
presidencies
presidentess
presidential
press attaché
Press Council
press cutting
pressed steel
press gallery
pressingness
press officer
press release
press to death
pressure-cook
pressure drag
pressure-feed
pressure head
pressure hold
pressure hull
pressure lamp
pressure mine
pressure sore
pressure suit
pressure tank
pressure-test
pressure tube
press-warrant
prestigiator
prestissimos
presumptious
presumptuous
pretenceless
Pretenderism
pretendingly
pretensively
preterlabent
pretermitted
pretonically
pretreatment
pretty fellow
pretty packet
pretty please
pretty-pretty
prevailingly
prevaricator
preveniently
preventative
preventional
preventively
preventorium
previousness
previsionary
price control
price-current
price-cutting
price shading
price support
pricking-iron
prickle-layer
prickly Moses
prickly poppy
prickly withe

pride of China
pride of India
pride of place
priestianity
priestliness
priestly code
priest-ridden
priggishness
primal father
primal scream
primary cause
primary group
primary radar
primer seisin
prime the pump
primevalness
primeval soup
primigravida
primogenital
primogenitor
primordially
primrose path
primulaceous
primuline red
primum mobile
Prince Albert
prince-bishop
princeliness
Prince Regent
prince's metal
Prince's metal
princess-ship
Princetonian
principal boy
principality
principal ray
printability
printer's mark
printer's ream
print spooler
print-through
prison editor
privateering
private hotel
private house
private means
private parts
private press
private wrong
privy chamber
privy council
Privy Council
privy members
prizefighter
prizewinning
proactivator
pro-anaphoral
pro and contra
probableness
probate court
probationary
problematise

problematist
problematize
problem child
proboscidean
proboscidian
probouleutic
procainamide
procarbazine
pro-cathedral
procedurally
process black
process chart
processional
processioner
process steam
process water
procès-verbal
prochirality
proclamation
proclamatory
proclivities
procoagulant
proconsulate
proctologist
proctorially
proctoscopic
proctotrupid
procyclidine
prodigiosity
prodigiously
producership
productional
productively
productivity
proembryonic
professional
professorate
professordom
professoress
professorial
professoriat
proficiently
profilograph
profilometer
profilometry
profit centre
profitlessly
profit margin
profit motive
profit-taking
profligately
profligation
profoundness
profundities
progenitress
progesterone
proglottides
prognostical
progradation
programmable
programmatic
projectional

projectively
projectivity
prolegomenal
prolegomenon
proletairism
proletariate
proliferator
prolifically
prolificness
prolongation
promastigote
prometaphase
promethazine
promised land
promontorial
promontoried
promontories
promontorium
prompt-script
promulgation
promyelocyte
pronominally
pronouncedly
pronunciable
pronunciator
proof-reading
propaedeutic
propagandise
propagandism
propagandist
propagandize
propagatress
propenseness
propensities
proper lesson
proper motion
propertyless
propheticism
prophylactic
propitiation
propitiative
propitiatory
propitiously
proportional
proportioned
proportioner
propoundment
propoundress
propoxyphene
proprietress
prop up the bar
proscribable
proscription
proscriptive
prose account
prosectorium
prosecutable
prose fiction
proselytizer
prosenchymal
prosiphonate
prosodically

prosopolepsy
prosopopoeia
prosopopoeic
prospectless
prospectuses
prospect well
prosperation
prosperously
prospicience
prostacyclin
prostitution
prosyllogism
protactinium
protatically
protectingly
protectional
protectively
protectorate
protectorial
protein shock
protensively
proteoglycan
proteroglyph
protestation
protestatory
protestingly
protest march
prothalamion
prothalamium
prothonotary
protistology
protocolling
proto-history
Proto-Hittite
protological
protomorphic
protonematal
protonmotive
protoplasmal
protoplasmic
protoplastic
Proto-Romance
protostellar
prototherian
protothetics
prototrophic
prototypical
protozoology
protractedly
protreptical
protrusively
protuberance
protuberancy
proud as Punch
proud-hearted
provableness
Provençalism
Provençalist
Provence rose
prove oneself
proverbially
prove too much

providential
province-wide
provincially
provisionary
provost guard
proxy sitting
prudentially
prunella salt
pruning-knife
Prussian blue
Prussian carp
Prussianizer
psammomatous
psammophilic
psephologist
pseudishness
pseudoallele
pseudo-Christ
pseudocrisis
pseudocumene
pseudocyesis
pseudo-entity
pseudofaeces
pseudogamous
pseudo-Gothic
pseudography
pseudohalide
pseudologist
pseudonymity
pseudonymous
pseudopodial
pseudopodium
pseudorabies
pseudorandom
pseudoscalar
pseudoscopic
pseudosexual
pseudouracil
pseudovector
psophometric
psychiatrics
psychiatrise
psychiatrist
psychiatrize
psychoactive
psychobabble
psychography
psycholeptic
psychologese
psychologies
psychologise
psychologism
psychologist
psychologize
psychomachia
psychometric
psychoneural
psychopathic
psychophysic
psychosexual
psychosocial
psychosphere

psychoticism
psychotropic
psychrometer
psychrometry
psychrophile
psychrotroph
pteridomania
pteridophyte
pteridosperm
pteropod ooze
pterosaurian
public figure
public health
public menace
public notary
public office
public orator
public school
public sector
public spirit
publish a will
Pucciniesque
pudding basin
pudding cloth
pudding-faced
pudding-grass
pudding-stone
puddle-jumper
puericulture
pugnaciously
puissantness
pull a fast one
pull-down menu
pull one's rank
pull one's wire
pull the wires
pull together
pull to pieces
pulpitically
pulque brandy
pulsed column
pulverizable
pulverizator
pulverulence
pumpernickel
punch forceps
Punchinellos
punching-ball
punctualness
punctulation
puncturation
punctureless
punitiveness
punkah-wallah
pupillograph
pupillometer
pupillometry
pupil teacher
puppeteering
puppet-master
puppet-player
puppyishness

Purbeck stone	pyritization	quarter-clock	quinquennial
purblindness	pyritohedral	quarter-final	quinquennium
purchaseable	pyritohedron	quarter-grain	quintangular
pure-breeding	pyroelectric	quarter-guard	quintessence
purification	pyrogenicity	quarter-horse	quintillions
purificatory	pyroligneous	quarter-light	quite another
Puritan spoon	pyromagnetic	quarter-miler	quit the scene
Purkinje cell	pyromaniacal	quartern loaf	quitting-time
purple airway	pyromorphite	quarter-piece	quixotically
purple martin	pyrophyllite	quarter-plate	quizzicality
purple urchin	pyrosulphate	quarter-point	quota quickie
purple wreath	pyrotartaric	quarter-round	quotationist
purpose-built	pyrotartrate	quarterstaff	rabbinically
purposefully	pyrotechnics	quarter-tonal	rabbit warren
Puseyistical	pyrotechnist	quarter-watch	rabble-rouser
pushmi-pullyu	pyroxmangite	quartz-locked	racemiferous
push one's luck	Pyrrhonistic	quasicrystal	racemization
pussyfootism	Pythian games	quasi-stellar	race theorist
put a damper on	pythonomorph	quaternarian	race-thinking
put a finger on	Quadragesima	quaternaries	rachischisis
put a jerk in it	quadraminium	quaternionic	rachitogenic
put a sock in it	quadrangular	quatrefoiled	racing driver
put behind one	quadraphonic	quattrocento	racing pigeon
put down roots	quadraplegia	Quebec heater	racketeering
put in the nips	quadrate-bone	Queen Anneish	racket-tailed
put into shape	quadrenniums	queen consort	Rackhamesque
put into words	quadriennium	queen dowager	rack mounting
put it on thick	quadrigamist	Queen Mary hat	radappertize
put money into	quadrillions	Queen of glory	radar plotter
put on a charge	quadrinomial	queen of night	radar scanner
put one across	quadriplegia	queen of tides	radial engine
put one's oar in	quadriplegic	queen pudding	radiant point
put on the line	quadrivalent	queen's bishop	radiant power
put on the spot	quadrominium	Queen's bounty	radiated mole
putrefacient	quadrophonic	queen scallop	radiation fog
putrefaction	quadrumanous	Queen's colour	radical right
putrefactive	quadrupedism	queen's flower	radicidation
put the acid on	quadruplegia	queen's gambit	radiesthesia
put the bite on	quaestorship	queen's knight	radiesthesic
put the boot in	Quaker collar	Queenslander	radiesthetic
put the make on	quaker-ladies	queen's pigeon	radio amateur
put the wind up	quaking aspen	Queen's Speech	radiobiology
put through it	quaking-grass	queen termite	radiochemist
putting green	qualificator	queer-bashing	radio contact
put to expense	quality paper	queerishness	radiodensity
put to silence	qualmishness	quench ageing	radio-element
put to the horn	quantifiable	querimonious	radiographer
put to the rout	quantitation	questionable	radiographic
put to the test	quantitative	questionably	radio horizon
put to the vote	quantitively	questionless	radioisotope
puzzle-headed	quantity mark	question mark	radio licence
puzzlingness	quantization	question time	radiological
Pygmalionism	quantum yield	question word	radiolucency
pyjama bottom	quaquaversal	quick-release	radio network
pyloroplasty	quarter-block	quick-sighted	radionuclide
pyonephrosis	quarter-bloke	quicksilvery	radio-opacity
pyramidology	quarter-blood	quill-coverts	radiophonics
pyramid shell	quarter-board	quill-feather	radio silence
pyrazinamide	quarter-bound	quilting hoop	radiosondage
pyrenomycete	quarter-breed	quinacridone	radio station
pyridoxamine	quarter-caste	quindecemvir	radiotherapy
pyritiferous	quarter-cleft	quinquenniad	radium needle

radius vector
radurization
ragamuffinly
ragged-hipped
ragged school
raggle-taggle
raglan sleeve
rags-to-riches
raiding party
railroad bull
railroad flat
railroadiana
railroad worm
rail-splitter
railway guide
railway hotel
railway novel
railway spine
rainbow smelt
rainbow snake
rainbow trout
raise a finger
raise its head
raise one's hat
raise the roof
raise the wind
raising-piece
raising-plate
rallentandos
Ramapithecus
ramblingness
rambunctious
ramentaceous
ramification
rampageously
ramshackling
random-access
random number
random sample
rangefinding
rank-and-filer
Rankine cycle
Rankine scale
rank outsider
ranunculuses
Raphaelesque
rapid transit
rapping plate
rarefication
raspberry jam
rataplanning
rat-bite fever
ratchet-wheel
rate constant
ratification
ratihabition
ratiocinator
ratio essendi
rationalizer
rationalness
rat-tail-grass
rat-tail spoon

rattle-headed
rauschpfeife
Ravenna grass
ravenousness
Rayleigh wave
ray treatment
razor-grinder
razzle-dazzle
reabsorption
reabsorptive
reacceptance
reaccumulate
reachability
reaction coil
reaction shot
reaction time
reaction wood
reactivation
readableness
readaptation
reading chair
reading clerk
reading-glass
readjustment
readminister
readmittance
reaffirmance
reagent grade
reagent paper
reallocation
real presence
reannexation
reapparition
reappearance
rearing-house
re-articulate
reasonlessly
reassemblage
reassessment
reassignment
reassimilate
reassortment
reassumption
reassuringly
reattachment
reattainment
rebelliously
recalcitrant
recalcitrate
recalescence
recapacitate
recapitalise
recapitalize
recapitulate
recategorize
receivership
recensionist
receptacular
receptionism
receptionist
receptitious
recessionary

rechargeable
recharge area
recharge well
recidivistic
recipiendary
reciprocally
reciprocator
reciting note
Reckitt's blue
recklessness
reclassified
reclassifies
recognisance
recognizable
recognizably
recognizance
re-collection
recollection
recollective
recombinable
recommission
recommitment
recommitting
recompensive
recomplicate
reconception
reconcilable
reconciliate
reconnection
reconnoitrer
reconsecrate
reconstitute
reconvention
reconversion
reconveyance
reconviction
recordership
record holder
record player
record sleeve
recovery room
recovery time
recovery ward
recreantness
recreational
recredential
recrudescent
rectosigmoid
recto-uterine
rectovaginal
recuperation
recuperative
Red Astrachan
red-blindness
red blood cell
red cobalt ore
red copper ore
red corpuscle
Red Delicious
redecoration
rededication
redefinition

redemptional
redemptioner
Redemptorist
redeployment
redeposition
red eyebright
red-eyed vireo
red-eye flight
redintegrate
red ironstone
rediscoverer
redissoluble
redistribute
Red Leicester
red-letter day
redoublement
red phalarope
Red River cart
Red Sandstone
red-shortness
reducibility
reductionism
reductionist
redundancies
red underwing
re-embarkment
re-embodiment
re-employment
re-engagement
re-enlistment
re-evaluation
re-excitation
re-expression
referability
referred pain
reflationary
reflationist
reflectingly
reflectional
reflectively
reflectivity
reflectorize
reflex camera
reflexogenic
reformatting
reform school
refoundation
refractility
refractively
refractivity
refractories
refractorily
refreshfully
refreshingly
refrigerated
refrigerator
refutability
regardlessly
regeneration
regenerative
regeneratory
regent oriole

regent parrot
Reggeization
regimentally
register book
register mark
register-ship
registraries
registration
reglementary
regressively
regressivity
regular canon
regulatively
rehabilitate
rehalogenize
rehydratable
Reichsthaler
reilluminate
reimbursable
reimposition
reimpregnate
reimpression
reinaugurate
reindeer moss
reingratiate
reinspection
reinstalment
reinvestment
reinvigorate
reiteratedly
rejectamenta
rejectionism
rejectionist
rejuvenation
rejuvenatory
relatability
relationally
relationless
relationship
relativeness
relativistic
relativitist
relay station
release agent
relentlessly
reliableness
relief agency
Relief Church
relieve guard
religionless
remainder man
remand centre
Rembrandtian
Rembrandtish
Rembrandtism
remedilessly
rememberable
rememberably
remembrancer
rememoration
remilitarize
remineralize

reminiscence
remonstrance
remonstrator
remorsefully
remote sensor
removability
remuneration
remunerative
remuneratory
Renaissancer
renal pyramid
renaturation
render homage
rendezvoused
rendezvouses
renegotiable
renewability
renomination
renounceable
renouncement
renovascular
Renshaw smash
rent of assise
renunciation
renunciative
renunciatory
reoccupation
reoccurrence
reordination
repagination
reparability
repatriation
repeat buying
repeat itself
repercussion
repercussive
reperforator
repetitional
repetitively
replantation
replevisable
replica plate
repopulation
repositories
repossession
repple depple
reprehension
reprehensive
reprehensory
representant
repressively
re-pressuring
repressurize
repristinate
reproachable
reproachless
reproducible
reproducibly
reproduction
reproductive
reproductory
reprogrammed

reprographer
reprographic
repromulgate
reptile house
republicanly
reputability
reputational
reputatively
reputed quart
requiem shark
requiescence
requiredness
rescuability
researchable
réseau rosacé
resectionist
resectoscope
Reserved List
reservedness
reserve grade
reserve price
resettlement
residentiary
residentship
residue class
resignalling
resignedness
resiniferous
resinography
resipiscence
resistlessly
resolubility
resoluteness
resolutioner
resolvedness
resoundingly
resourceless
respectfully
respectively
respirometer
respirometry
resplendence
resplendency
respondentia
responseless
response time
responsively
Responsivist
responsivity
responsorial
responsories
restauranter
restaurateur
restauration
resting place
restlessness
rest one's case
restrainable
restrainedly
restrengthen
restrictable
restrictedly

resubjection
resubmission
resumptively
resupination
resurrection
resurrective
resuscitable
resuscitator
retainership
retaining fee
retentionist
reticulately
reticulation
reticulocyte
retinopathic
retinoscopic
retired flank
retiringness
retort carbon
retractation
retractility
retranscribe
retransplant
retrenchment
retrieveless
retrievement
retrocedence
retrocession
retrocessive
retrodiction
retrodictive
retroduction
retroductive
retroflected
retroflexion
retrogradely
retrogradism
retrogradist
retrojection
retromingent
retropulsion
retropulsive
retrospectus
retrosternal
retroversion
return crease
return flight
return thanks
return ticket
reunionistic
reupholstery
revanchistic
revegetation
revelational
revengefully
reverberator
reverendship
reversal film
reverse angle
reverse fault
reverse lever
reverse plate

reverse video
reversionary
reversionist
revert to type
revirescence
revisitation
revivability
revivalistic
revivication
reviviscence
reviviscency
revocability
revolubility
revolutional
revolutioner
revulsionary
rhabdomancer
Rhadamanthus
rhamphotheca
rhenosterbos
rheomorphism
rheoreceptor
rhesus factor
rhesus monkey
rhetorically
rheumatology
rhinoceroses
rhinocerotic
rhinocerotid
rhinological
rhinopharynx
rhinoplastic
rhipidistian
rhizophagous
rhododendron
rhodomontade
rhombohedral
rhombohedric
rhombohedron
rhomboidally
rhopaloceral
rhyming slang
rhynchocoele
rhynchodaeum
rhynchostome
rhythmetical
rhythm guitar
rhythmically
rhythm method
rhythmometer
rhythmopoeia
rhytidectomy
ribble-rabble
ribbon figure
ribonuclease
Ricardianism
Richter scale
ricochetting
ride cushions
ride for a fall
ride one's luck
ride the rails

ride the stang
ride to hounds
ridiculosity
ridiculously
riding-master
riding school
riempiestoel
riffle beetle
rigging lines
right and left
right-fielder
rightfulness
right-hand man
right of abode
right of visit
right side out
right the helm
right-to-lifer
right-wingery
right-wingism
rigorousness
rig the market
rimming steel
ring armature
ring-building
ring dotterel
ringed plover
ringed thrush
ring fracture
ringing floor
ring-junction
ring pheasant
ringside seat
ringworm bush
ripple effect
ripple-marked
rip-roaringly
Rip Van Winkle
rise and shine
risk analysis
risk one's neck
Risorgimento
river-bottoms
river capture
river dolphin
river-driving
river herring
river lamprey
river of white
river running
roan antelope
roaring drunk
roaring trade
roasting-jack
roasting-spit
robber trench
Robertsonian
Robin-Hoodish
Robin-Hoodism
Robin ruddock
robotisation
robotization

robustiously
rock-climbing
rocker switch
rocketeering
rock festival
rock-hounding
rocking chair
rocking horse
rocking-stone
rock kangaroo
rock samphire
Rock scorpion
rockumentary
rococo stitch
rodenticidal
rodomontader
roebuck-berry
roentgen rays
Roentgen rays
Rogation Days
Rogationtide
Rogation week
roisteringly
role reversal
rollerblader
roller hockey
roller skater
roller steady
rolling drunk
rolling paper
rolling-press
rolling stock
rolling stone
roll in the hay
roll of honour
roll the bones
romaine crêpe
Roman balance
Roman holiday
romanization
Roman numeral
romantically
romanticness
Roman vitriol
roof of heaven
room at the top
rooming house
Roorkee chair
Rooseveltian
rootfastness
rootin' tootin'
rootlessness
root position
root pressure
rope-moulding
Rosary-Sunday
rose-breasted
rose cockatoo
rose-coloured
rose geranium
rose mahogany
rose of heaven

rose of Sharon
rose plantain
Rosetta stone
Rosetta Stone
rosette gauge
rosette plant
Rosh Hashanah
rostriferous
rotary beater
rotary camera
rotary cutter
rotary engine
rotary switch
rotationally
rote learning
rotten excuse
roughcasting
rough diamond
rough grazing
roughing pump
rough justice
rough passage
roundaboutly
round bracket
round herring
round-mouthed
round seizing
round-sheered
round the bend
round-tripper
rouse oneself
Rousseauvian
roving sailor
Rowland ghost
royal binding
royal demesne
Royal Society
royal warrant
rubber bridge
rubber bullet
rubber cement
rubber cheque
rubber-heeler
rubber johnny
rubber Johnny
rubbernecker
rubber-tapper
rubbing stone
Rube Goldberg
Rubens madder
rubification
rubinglimmer
rub one's hands
rub shoulders
ruby-throated
ruffed grouse
rugose mosaic
rulelessness
rule the roast
rule the roost
rumble-tumble
ruminatingly

ruminatively	saddle-galled	samprasarana	satyagrahist
rummage goods	saddle oyster	sanctanimity	satyric drama
rump and dozen	saddle-shaped	sanctifiable	satyromaniac
rumplessness	saddle-skirts	sanctificate	saucepanfuls
run a blockade	saddle stitch	sanctimonial	saucer-burial
run an eye over	Sadie Hawkins	sanctionable	sauce tartare
run counter to	sadistically	sanctionless	Saudi Arabian
run its course	safe and sound	sanctionment	Saudiization
running belay	safe as houses	sanding plate	saunteringly
running-board	safety factor	sand-moulding	sausage board
running brand	safety island	sand-painting	Sauveterrian
running fight	sage and onion	sandwich-boat	save one's face
running light	sage thrasher	sandwich cake	save one's hide
running mould	sailboarding	Sandwich tern	save one's neck
running noose	sail by the log	sand-yachting	save one's skin
running title	sailor collar	sanguiferous	save one's wind
running water	sailor-suited	sanguinarily	saving clause
run-of-the-mill	Sakellaridis	sanguinarine	Savi's warbler
run one's mouth	salad servers	sanguineness	saw-sharpener
run up against	salamandrian	sanguinolent	say a mouthful
ruptured duck	salamandrine	sanguivorous	say little for
ruralization	salamandroid	sanification	say one's beads
rush election	salamandrous	sanitariness	say one's piece
Russell fence	saleableness	sanitary belt	say something
Russell lupin	sale or return	sanitary ware	scabbard-fish
russet-coated	salesmanship	sanitization	scabbardless
Russian olive	salicologist	sansculottic	scabrousness
Russian sable	salient point	sansculottid	scaff and raff
Russian salad	salification	sans reproche	scaffold pole
rust-coloured	salinisation	santalaceous	scala tympani
rustproofing	salinization	sapientially	scale drawing
ruthenium red	sal mirabilis	sapindaceous	scale-pattern
ruthlessness	salmon-ladder	saponifiable	scale-reading
Sabbatianism	saloon-keeper	sapphire blue	scallop shell
sabbatically	saloon pistol	sapphire mink	scandalously
Sabellianism	Salpausselkä	saprobiology	scandal sheet
Sabin vaccine	salpiglossis	saprophagous	Scandinavian
sabre-bayonet	salpingogram	saprophilous	scanning coil
sabre-rattler	salpingotomy	saprophytism	scanning disc
sabre-toothed	salsolaceous	Saracen's corn	scanning line
saccadically	saltationism	Saracen's head	scanning spot
saccharinity	saltationist	sarcolactate	scapegoating
saccharinize	salt of sorrel	sarcomatosis	scapegoatism
saccharoidal	salt of tartar	sarcophagous	scaphocerite
sacerdotally	salt-spreader	sarcoplasmic	scaphoid bone
sacramentary	salt the books	sardar-bearer	scapular arch
sacrament day	salubriously	sardonically	scapulimancy
sacred circle	salutariness	Sardoodledom	scapulodynia
sacred egoism	salutational	sarong kebaya	scarfed joint
sacred number	salutatorian	sarrusophone	scarificator
sacred orders	salutatories	sarsaparilla	scarlet fever
sacred poetry	salutatorily	satanic abuse	scarlet macaw
sacred scarab	salutiferous	Satanophobia	scarlet snake
sacrificable	salvationism	satellitosis	scarlet whore
sacrificator	salvationist	satin de chine	scarlet woman
sacrifice bid	salvationize	satin leather	scathelessly
sacrilegious	salver-shaped	satirization	scatological
sacristaness	Samaritanism	satisfaction	scatophagous
sacro-iliitis	Samian letter	satisfactory	scatteration
sac-winged bat	Samosatenian	satisfyingly	scatterbrain
saddlebacked	Samothracian	satispassion	scatteringly
saddle bronco	sample bottle	saturability	scene-of-crime

scene-painter	scoring board	scyphiferous	secular abbot
scene-shifter	scoring-booth	scyphomedusa	secular canon
scene-stealer	scoring-paper	Scythian lamb	secular games
scenic artist	scornfulness	sea buckthorn	secularistic
Scenicruiser	scorpion fish	sea butterfly	secular plays
scenographer	scorpion-like	sea commander	secundum idem
scenographic	Scotch boiler	seafardinger	security risk
scent marking	Scotch coffee	sea-fisherman	sedge warbler
Scheherazade	Scotch cousin	sea hard-grass	sedimentable
Schellingian	Scotch pebble	sealed orders	seductionist
Schellingism	Scotch whisky	sealed source	sedulousness
schiller spar	Scotland Yard	seam-squirrel	seed dressing
schindylesis	Scotsmanship	sea-porcupine	seedling leaf
schismatical	Scottishness	search engine	seed metering
schistosomal	scoundreldom	searchership	see the back of
schizocarpic	scoundrelism	seaside finch	see what I mean
schizocoelic	scouring-rush	seaside grape	segmentalise
schizomycete	Scout's honour	season ticket	segmentalize
schizophrene	scrambled egg	secessionism	segmentation
schizorhinal	scramblingly	secessionist	seismography
schizostylis	scraperboard	secludedness	seismologist
schizothymia	scrap of paper	seclusionist	seismometric
schizothymic	scratch along	secobarbital	seismonastic
schmaltziest	scratchboard	seconda donna	seismoscopic
scholarchate	scratch-brush	second advent	selectionism
scholar's mate	scratch-build	secondary bow	selectionist
schoolboyish	scratch-grass	second ballot	seleniferous
school-divine	scratchiness	second banana	selenium cell
schoolfellow	scratchingly	second bottom	selenography
schoolkeeper	scratch paper	second coming	selenologist
school leaver	scratch sheet	second cousin	selensulphur
schoolmaster	scratch stock	second-degree	self-absorbed
school report	scratch video	Second Empire	self-accusing
schooner yawl	screechingly	second fiddle	self-activity
schorlaceous	screen editor	second finger	self-adhesive
Schottky line	screen-memory	second-handed	self-admiring
Schottky plot	screen-washer	second-hander	self-aligning
Schreinerize	screenwriter	Second Isaiah	self-analysis
Schroedinger	screw-steamer	second lesson	self-applause
sciatic nerve	screw-worm fly	second master	self-approval
sciatic notch	scribblative	second moment	self-assembly
scientifical	scribblement	second nature	self-begotten
scintigraphy	scribblingly	second person	self-betrayal
scintillator	scrimshander	second storey	self-boasting
scissiparity	scrimshanker	second strike	self-catering
scissiparous	scriptoriums	second string	self-centring
scissors hold	scripturally	second to none	self-changing
scissors-kick	scripturient	secretagogue	self-cleaning
scissor-tooth	scriptwriter	secret ballot	self-coloured
scitamineous	scrobiculate	secret police	self-conquest
sclerenchyma	scrophularia	secret weapon	self-contempt
sclerodermia	scrub wallaby	sectarianise	self-creation
sclerogenous	scrum machine	sectarianism	self-creative
sclerophylly	scrupulosity	sectarianize	self-critical
sclerotomies	scrupulously	sectionalise	self-deceived
scolopaceous	scrutinously	sectionalism	self-deceiver
scolopophore	sculpturally	sectionalist	self-deluding
scombrotoxic	scurrilities	sectionalize	self-delusion
scopophiliac	scurrilously	section-eight	self-destruct
scoptophilia	scutellation	Section Eight	self-devotion
score-reading	scutelliform	section house	self-distrust
scoring block	scuttled butt	sectoral horn	self-educated

self-effacing
self-election
self-elective
self-employed
self-enclosed
self-estimate
self-evidence
self-exciting
self-existent
self-exposure
self-financed
self-flattery
self-glorious
self-governed
self-homicide
self-hypnosis
self-identity
self-interest
self-involved
selflessness
self-limiting
self-loathing
self-luminous
self-managing
self-movement
self-murderer
self-oriented
self-policing
self-portrait
self-referral
self-reliance
self-reproach
self-revealed
self-reversal
self-righting
selfsameness
self-scrutiny
self-security
self-selected
self-shielded
self-starting
self-steering
self-violence
sell a dummy to
selling plate
selling point
selling price
sell the dummy
seltzer water
semantically
semeiologist
semelfactive
semi-annually
Semi-Arianism
semi-attached
semi-basement
semi-chemical
semicircular
semicylinder
semi-darkness
semi-deponent
semi-derelict

semi-detached
semidiameter
semi-finalist
semifinalist
semi-finished
semifluidity
semi-globular
semi-indirect
semi-infinite
semi-literacy
semi-literate
semi-metallic
seminal fluid
seminiferous
seminivorous
semi-official
semiological
semiotically
semi-palmated
semipalmated
semiparabola
semi-Pelagian
semi-precious
semiprecious
semi-rotatory
semi-sentence
semispheroid
Semitization
semi-tropical
semi-vitreous
sempervirent
sempiternity
senatorially
senior school
sensationism
sensationist
sense-content
sense-finding
sensibilizer
sensible heat
sensibleness
sensifacient
sensitometer
sensitometry
sensorimotor
sensualistic
sensuousness
sensu stricto
sentencehood
sentence-word
sententially
sentinelling
sentinel pile
sentinelship
senza sordini
separability
separateness
separatistic
Septembriser
Septembrizer
septemvirate
septennially

septicidally
septilateral
septipartite
septuagenary
Septuagesima
Septuagintal
sepulchrally
sequaciously
sequence book
sequence date
sequence shot
sequentially
sequestrable
sequestrator
seraphically
seraphicness
sergeant-fish
sergeantship
serializable
serial killer
serial number
serial rights
sericultural
serio-comical
serjeantship
sermonically
sero-immunity
seronegative
seropositive
seropurulent
serotaxonomy
serotonergic
serpentarium
Serpentarius
serpent eagle
serpent-green
serpenticide
serpenticone
serpentiform
serpentinely
serpentinise
serpentinite
serpentinize
serpentinous
serpent-stone
serum disease
servants' hall
serve at table
serve a writ on
serve the turn
service alley
service-berry
service court
service dress
service plate
servicewoman
servicewomen
serving-woman
servitorship
servo control
sesquialtera
sesquioxidic

sesquitertia
session clerk
set an example
set by the ears
set one's cap at
set one's teeth
set scrummage
set-theoretic
set the seal to
setting-stick
setting stuff
settling time
set to partner
Seven Sisters
seven-sleeper
severability
severance pay
sewage lagoon
sewing cotton
sexagenarian
sexcentenary
sex chromatin
sex surrogate
sex therapist
sextillionth
sextodecimos
sexton beetle
sextumvirate
sextuplicate
sexual system
Sezessionist
shade-bearing
shade maximum
shade-reading
shadow-boxing
shadowgraphy
shadow puppet
shadow-stitch
shadow stripe
shaft turbine
shaggy ink-cap
shaking palsy
shallow-pated
shamateurism
shamble-stave
shame culture
shamefacedly
shamefulness
Shanghainese
shank-painter
shape-changer
shaped charge
shape elastic
shaping knife
shareability
share capital
sharecropper
share economy
share-farming
shareholding
share-milking
share-pushing

shark-toothed
sharp eyespot
sharp-shinned
sharpshooter
sharp-sighted
sharp-tongued
shatter-brain
shatter crack
shatteringly
shatter-pated
shatter-proof
shatterproof
shatteryness
shauchliness
shaven latten
shaving brush
shaving cream
shaving horse
shaving stick
Shawnee salad
shebeen queen
sheep blowfly
sheep-dipping
sheepishness
sheep-nose-bot
sheep's fescue
sheep-shearer
sheepskinned
sheep-sleight
sheep's sorrel
sheep's tongue
sheet-almanac
sheet erosion
shelf company
shell company
shellcracker
shell-gritted
shell program
shell-shocked
shepherd king
shepherdless
shepherd's dog
shepherdship
shepherd's pie
Sheridaniana
sheriff clerk
sheriff court
sheriff's sale
Sherlockiana
Shetland lace
Shetland pony
Shetland wool
shield-bearer
shiftability
shiftfulness
shiftingness
shillingless
shilling-mark
shilly-shally
shimmeriness
shimmeringly
shimmy damper

shine through
shingle house
shingle slide
shining light
ship-breaking
shipbuilding
ship chandler
ship decanter
ship of burden
shipping-bill
shipping-note
ship-repairer
ship's biscuit
ship's company
ship's husband
Shirley poppy
shirtwaister
shockability
shock-brigade
shock-excited
shockingness
shocking pink
shock tactics
shock-testing
shock therapy
shock-workers
shoeing-smith
shoelessness
shoofly plant
shooting coat
shooting iron
shooting star
shoot one's wad
shoot the moon
shoot through
shopping cart
shopping list
shopping mall
shopping tray
shoppishness
shore-shooter
shore station
shore-whaling
short circuit
short-circuit
short clothes
short-coating
short commons
shorten sails
short fielder
short-grained
short measure
short-pitched
short-running
short service
short-sighted
short-sleeved
short-snorter
short-staffed
short-termism
short-termist
short-tongued

short-waisted
short-woolled
shot-blasting
shot in the arm
shoulder arms
shoulder-belt
shoulder-bone
shoulder-high
shoulder-knot
shoulderless
shoulder line
shoulder loop
shoulder mark
shoulder moth
shoulder note
shoulder-tuft
shoulder wing
shout the odds
shovel-hatted
shovel-plough
show business
show one's face
show one's hand
show one's head
show-stopping
shrewishness
shrievalties
shrift-father
shrike-thrush
shrike tyrant
shrinkage fit
shroud hawser
Shrove Monday
shrub trefoil
shudderingly
shuffle-board
shuffleboard
shunt circuit
shunt machine
shut one's face
shutter-blind
shutter speed
shuttle shell
shut your trap
sialographic
Siamese twins
Siberian crab
Siberian ibex
sick headache
sickle medick
sickle scaler
side reaction
sidereal time
sidereal year
siderochrome
siderography
siderophilin
siderostatic
siderurgical
side-splitter
side-wall tyre
side-whiskers

siege economy
sieve element
sighting shot
sigmoid colon
sigmoidicity
signal-caller
significance
significancy
significator
significatum
significavit
sign language
signpostless
sign stimulus
silage cutter
silanization
Silesian stem
silhouettist
silicicolous
siliciferous
silicon wafer
silk stocking
silk-throwing
silkworm moth
silver bridge
silver doctor
silver-glance
silver lining
Silver Office
silver poplar
silver salmon
silver screen
silver solder
silver string
silver thatch
silver tongue
silver wattle
silviculture
Simchat Torah
similarities
simoniacally
simple family
simple-minded
simplicistic
Simpson's rule
simulatively
Simultaneism
simultaneist
simultaneity
simultaneous
Sinanthropic
Sinanthropus
singableness
singing hinny
singing point
single-acting
single combat
single-decker
single-handed
single-hander
single market
single-minded

single parent
single-seater
single-source
single-valued
single-vision
single-wicket
singsong girl
singularness
sinicization
sinification
sinister bend
sinisterness
sinistrality
sinistrorsal
sinistrously
sinusoidally
sinus venosus
siphonaceous
siphonoglyph
siphonophore
siphonostele
siphonozooid
siphunculate
sir-reverence
sister german
sisterliness
sisters-in-law
sisyrinchium
site assembly
Sitka cypress
sit loosely on
situationism
situationist
six feet under
six of the best
sixty-fourmos
sixty per cent
sizzle cymbal
skateboarder
skeletal soil
skeleton army
skeleton crew
skeleton form
skeletonized
skeletonless
skeleton suit
skeleton weed
skeuomorphic
skew-symmetry
Skiddaw slate
skillion roof
skin friction
skin-grafting
skin magazine
skinnymalink
skipjack tuna
skipping rope
skip straight
skirt-dancing
skitteriness
skittishness
skittle-alley

skookum chuck
skookum house
skoptophilia
Skraup method
skrimshander
skull-busting
skullduggery
skull session
skunk cabbage
skunk currant
skutterudite
sky-scrapered
slabber-sauce
slack-twisted
slanderously
slangwhanger
slantingways
slapdashness
slash-and-burn
slash-burning
slasher movie
slate-writing
slatternness
slaughterdom
slaughtering
slaughterman
slaughterous
Slavonianize
Slavophilism
sledgehammer
sleeper agent
sleeper shark
sleepfulness
sleeping-pill
sleeping suit
sleep-talking
sleep through
sleepy-headed
Sleepy Hollow
sleepy lizard
sleeve-button
sleeve-garter
slender loris
slickensided
sliding scale
slip-carriage
slip of the pen
slip one's wind
slipper chair
slipperiness
slipper plant
slipper satin
slipper shell
slippery pole
slipshodness
slit-planting
slitting-mill
Sloane Ranger
slobber-chops
slop-clothing
slope circuit
slope current

slop-moulding
slothfulness
slot radiator
slotted spoon
slovenliness
slow handclap
slow puncture
sluggardness
sluggishness
slumbercoach
slumberously
slumber party
slum landlord
slumpflation
slush casting
sluttishness
small calorie
small capital
small-clothes
smallest room
small fortune
smallholding
small-mouthed
small pastern
small-townish
smart-aleckry
smash-and-grab
smatteringly
smell of roses
smoke concert
smoke goggles
smoke grenade
smoke-jumping
smoke Persian
smoker's cough
smoker's heart
smoking point
smoking stand
smooth blenny
smooth muscle
smooth-spoken
smooth tingle
smotheration
smotheringly
snaffle-mouth
snaggle-teeth
snaggle-tooth
snailishness
snail's gallop
snake charmer
snallygaster
snap-fastener
snappishness
snap-shooting
snap short off
snarling iron
sneak-current
sneak-hunting
sneakingness
sneak preview
sneck-drawing
snickeringly

snicker-snack
sniff the wind
snifter-valve
sniggeringly
snippetiness
snivellingly
snobbishness
snobographer
snollygoster
snook-cocking
snooperscope
snooze button
snowball tree
snowboarding
snow-dropping
snowdrop tree
snow-in-summer
snowmobiling
snow pheasant
snowshoe hare
snubbishness
snuff-dipping
soap-operatic
soboliferous
sociableness
social action
social centre
social change
social column
social credit
social gospel
social ladder
social status
social survey
social system
social weaver
social worker
sociobiology
sociocentric
sociodynamic
socioecology
sociological
socio-medical
sociometrist
socket outlet
Socratically
soda fountain
sodipotassic
sodium-cooled
sodopotassic
soft as a brush
soft currency
softly-softly
soft-shoulder
soil separate
soil sickness
soil solution
soixante-neuf
solar battery
solar eclipse
solar furnace
solar heating

solarisation
solarization
solar-powered
solar regular
soldier's wind
solecistical
solemniously
solicitation
solicitorial
solicitously
solidaristic
solid circuit
solid geology
solidifiable
solids-not-fat
solid stowing
solidungular
solidus curve
solifluction
soliloquizer
solitariness
solitary dodo
solitary wave
solitudinous
solo climbing
solodization
Solomon's seal
solonization
solstitially
soluble glass
solutionized
solvent abuse
somaesthesis
somaesthetic
somatisation
somatization
somatologist
somatopleure
somatostatin
somatotropic
somatotropin
somebody else
somersaulter
Somervillian
somnambulant
somnambulate
somnambulism
somnambulist
somniloquent
somniloquism
somniloquist
somnolescent
son et lumière
song and dance
song-grosbeak
songlessness
sonic barrier
sonochemical
son of the soil
sonorescence
sonorousness
soogee-moogee

soothingness
sophiologist
sophisticate
sophomorical
soporiferous
sorbefacient
sorediferous
soreheadedly
sorosilicate
sorry-go-round
sortilegious
Sothic period
soullessness
soul-sickness
sound archive
sound as a bell
sound barrier
sound channel
sounding-lead
sounding line
soundingness
sounding sand
sound picture
sound-ranging
Soundscriber
soupfin shark
soup-strainer
sousaphonist
South African
South America
Southcottian
south country
south-eastern
Southern Alps
Southern blot
Southern Cone
Southern Fish
southern hake
southernmost
southernness
southernwood
south sea rose
South Spainer
South Suffolk
Southumbrian
south-western
Sovietophile
Sovietophobe
sow the seed of
space blanket
space capsule
space chamber
space density
space fiction
space lattice
spacemanship
space physics
space shuttle
space station
space vehicle
spaciousness
spandrel wall

span-farthing
Spanish beard
Spanish broom
Spanish brown
Spanish cedar
Spanish dance
Spanish onion
Spanish sheep
Spanish topaz
Spanish tummy
Spanish white
spanner tight
spark chamber
spark counter
sparking coil
sparking plug
sparkishness
sparkleberry
sparrow-brain
sparrow-grass
sparrow's-fart
spasmophilia
spasmophilic
spatiography
spatteration
spatulamancy
speak daggers
speakerphone
speakingness
speaking stop
speaking-tube
speak volumes
spear-carrier
spear-running
spear thistle
special buyer
specialistic
specialities
specifically
specific heat
specific name
specificness
specimen-book
specimen page
speciousness
speck and span
speckled wood
specksioneer
spectatordom
spectatorial
spectatorism
spectral term
spectral type
spectre-lemur
spectrograph
spectrometer
spectrometry
spectrophone
spectroscope
spectroscopy
speech-centre
speechifying

speech island
speechlessly
speech-writer
Speedwriting
Speenhamland
speiss-cobalt
speleologist
spellbinding
spell-checker
spelling-book
spermathecal
spermaticide
spermatocide
spermatocyte
spermatology
spermatozoal
spermatozoan
spermatozoid
spermatozoon
spermogonium
spermologist
spew one's ring
sphacelation
sphagnum moss
sphairistike
sphenoid bone
sphericality
spheroidally
spheroidical
spherulitize
sphincterial
sphingolipid
sphygmograph
sphygmometer
sphygmometry
sphygmophone
sphygmoscope
spice-islands
spick and span
spider beetle
spider flower
spider-hunter
spider monkey
spider-naevus
spider orchid
spider-stitch
spiegeleisen
spiflication
spinach-green
spinal column
spinal marrow
spinal reflex
spina ventosa
spindle-berry
spindle cross
spindle fibre
spindle-shank
spindle-shell
spindle-whorl
spine-bashing
spine-chiller
spine-freezer

spine-tingler
spinnability
spinnbarkeit
spinning mule
spinsterhood
spinulescent
spiny dogfish
spiny lobster
spiral galaxy
spiral nebula
spiritedness
spirit fresco
spiritlessly
spirit of salt
spirit of wine
spirit-rapper
spiritualise
spiritualism
spiritualist
spirituality
spiritualize
spirituosity
spirochaetal
spirographic
spirolactone
Spitalfields
spit and image
spitefulness
spittle-staff
splash cymbal
splatterdash
splatterdock
splay-mouthed
splendacious
splendidness
splenic fever
splenisation
splenization
splenomegaly
splenotomies
splenunculus
splinter-deck
splish-splash
split bearing
split the atom
split the vote
split tin loaf
spoils system
spokespeople
spokesperson
sponge-finger
sponge rubber
spongiferous
spongioblast
spongologist
spoon-bending
spoon-fashion
sporadically
sporangiolum
sporodochium
sporogenesis
sportability

sportfishing
sportfulness
sporting girl
sportiveness
sport of kings
sport one's oak
sportscaster
sports centre
sports finder
sports ground
sports jacket
sportsperson
sports writer
spotlessness
spotted crake
spotted fever
spotted hyena
spouse-breach
Sprechgesang
Sprechstimme
sprightfully
spring barley
spring beauty
spring-beetle
spring collet
spring garden
spring greens
spring-loaded
spring peeper
spring salmon
spring squill
spring to mind
spriteliness
spritelliest
sprocket hole
sprocketless
spruce grouse
sprung rhythm
Spud Islander
spurge laurel
spurge nettle
spuriousness
spur valerian
sputteringly
spy satellite
spy strangers
squabblement
squab cushion
squacco heron
squamiferous
squamigerous
squanderlust
square dinkum
squared paper
square engine
square-headed
square Hebrew
square number
square-rigged
square-rigger
square-rooter
Squaresville

square thread
square wheels
squash tennis
squattocracy
squeaky clean
squeegee band
squid-jigging
squirarchies
squirearchal
squirrel cage
squirrel-corn
squirrel-fish
squirrel hake
squirrel-like
squirrelling
squirrel-tail
squish-squash
stabilimeter
stablishment
staccato mark
stackability
stacken-cloud
stacker crane
stack the deck
staddle-stone
staff college
staff officer
Stafford knot
stageability
stage manager
stage-playing
stage-setting
stage thunder
stage whisper
staggeringly
stagger-juice
stagger-tuned
stag-horn fern
stag-horn moss
stainability
stained glass
Stakhanovism
Stakhanovist
Stakhanovite
stalactiform
stalled cairn
stall for time
stalwartness
stammeringly
stamp booklet
stamping tube
stamp machine
stamp mealies
stanchion-gun
stand a chance
standard-bred
Standardbred
standard cell
standardizer
standard lamp
standard lens
standardless

standardness
standard time
standardwing
stand between
standing army
standing crop
standing dish
standing iron
standing joke
standing part
standing post
standing room
standing salt
standing wave
stand in stead
stand-off half
stand of pikes
stand the pace
Stanhope lens
Stanislavsky
Stanley crane
Stanley knife
stanniferous
stanzaically
stapedectomy
starchedness
star-cucumber
star prisoner
Stars and Bars
star sapphire
star-spangled
startability
start a family
starting gate
starting grid
starting line
starting post
stasigenesis
stasigenetic
State Council
statementing
state of grace
state pension
State pension
states-monger
statesperson
States rights
State trooper
static thrust
station agent
stationarily
stationarity
station break
station house
stationnaire
station-point
station-staff
station-wagon
statistician
statisticize
statogenesis
statuary vein

statuesquely	stercoration	stockbreeder	Straffordian
status-seeker	stereo-acuity	stockbroking	stragglingly
status symbol	stereo-camera	stock company	straight arch
status system	stereochrome	stock control	straight away
stave and tail	stereochromy	stock culture	straightaway
staying power	stereocilium	stockholding	straight-bred
stay-in strike	stereognosis	Stockholm tar	straight-edge
stay one's hand	stereography	stocking-foot	straightener
stay the night	stereoisomer	stockingless	straight face
St Bernard dog	stereologist	stocking mask	straight-line
steady-stater	stereometric	stocking-yarn	straight mute
steak tartare	stereophonic	stock-in-trade	straightness
steal the show	stereopticon	stockishness	straight peen
stealthfully	stereoscopic	stockjobbery	straight talk
stealthiness	stereotactic	stockjobbing	straight time
steamboating	stereotropic	stockmanship	straightways
steamboatman	sterilizable	stoechiology	straight wire
steamer-chair	sterling area	stoichometry	straightwise
steam turbine	sterlingness	stomach-achey	strain ageing
steam-whistle	sternocostal	stomach-tooth	strain a point
steatisation	stern-trawler	stomach upset	strainedness
steatization	sternutation	stoma patient	strain energy
steatopygial	sternutative	stomatodaeum	strainer arch
steatopygous	sternutatory	stone bramble	strainer post
steatorrhoea	sternwheeler	stone-crusher	strain-harden
steel drummer	stertorously	stone-dresser	strainlessly
steel furnace	stethography	stone-dusting	strainometer
steeplechase	stethometric	stone frigate	strait-jacket
steeple clock	stethoscoped	stone garland	straitjacket
steeple-house	stethoscopic	stone-heading	Strandlooper
steerability	Stevensonian	stonemasonry	strangerhood
steer clear of	St George's day	stone parsley	strangership
steering lock	stibocaptate	stone polygon	strange to say
steering post	stichometric	stonewalling	strange woman
steering sail	stichomythia	stony-hearted	stranglehold
stegosaurian	stichomythic	stoop and roop	strangle-weed
stellacyanin	stickability	stoop-gallant	strangulated
stellate hair	stick country	stop-and-frisk	strangullion
Stellenbosch	stick-fighter	stop-and-start	strangurious
Steller's duck	stick grenade	stop-cylinder	strap-handled
stelliferous	sticky wicket	stop one's ears	Stratfordian
stem analysis	stigmasterol	stop one's nose	straticulate
stem-christie	stigmatiform	stoppability	stratigraphy
stemmatology	stilboestrol	stopping rule	stratocirrus
stencil-plate	stiletto heel	stop the cable	stratocratic
stenocranial	still-fishing	stop the press	stratosphere
stenographer	stillicidium	store bullock	Stratovision
stenographic	stills camera	storiologist	Stravinskian
stenophagous	stillwellite	storm lantern	strawberries
stenothermic	stinging tree	storm shutter	straw-breadth
Stensen's duct	stinking bird	storm trooper	strawchopper
stentorianly	stinking fish	storm-warning	streak camera
step aerobics	stinking iris	stormy petrel	stream-anchor
stepdaughter	stinkingness	storytelling	streamlining
stepfamilies	stinking smut	stout-hearted	stream the log
step function	stinking weed	stove-pipe hat	street hockey
stepmotherly	stirrup pants	St Peter's fish	street-keeper
step on the gas	stirrup-strap	St Peter's keys	street people
step response	stir the blood	St Peter's wort	street person
Stercoranism	stitch in time	strabismally	street-porter
Stercoranist	stitch welder	strabismical	streets ahead
stercorarian	St John's bread	Stradivarius	street trader

street urchin
streetwalker
street warden
street worker
strengthener
strengthless
strepitation
strepsirhine
streptococci
streptolysin
streptomycin
streptosolen
Streptothrix
stressed skin
stress raiser
stress relief
stress-strain
stretcher fly
stretchiness
stretch marks
stricken hour
stride accent
stridulation
stridulatory
stridulously
strike a chord
strike a light
strike ground
strike it rich
strike me pink
striker-plate
striking-line
strikingness
string-course
string figure
stringhalted
string of tide
string-puller
string theory
strip cartoon
striped hyena
striped maple
striped mouse
striped pants
strip farming
strip-grazing
strip lynchet
stripped-down
strippergram
stripteasing
strobilation
strobiliform
stroboscopic
stroke-stitch
stromatolite
stromatolith
stromeyerite
strong-docked
strong-handed
strongheaded
strong-minded
strong stress

strongylosis
strontianite
strophanthin
strophanthus
strophiolate
structurally
strudel dough
strugglingly
strychninize
stubble-field
stubble-goose
stubble-quail
stubbornness
studding-sail
student grant
student nurse
Student's test
studio potter
studiousness
study-bedroom
stuffed olive
stuffed shirt
stump and rump
stump cricket
stump-grubber
stump-machine
stupefacient
stupefaction
stupefactive
stupefyingly
stupendously
sturdy beggar
sturgeon scow
stutteringly
stylistician
stylographic
stylometrics
stylometrist
subabdominal
subacuminate
subalternate
subalternity
subantarctic
subapostolic
subarachnoid
subarcuation
subarrhation
sub-brigadier
subcelestial
subcentrally
subcollector
subcommittee
subconscious
subconstable
subcontinent
subcutaneous
subdeaconate
sub-débutante
subdelirious
subdiaconate
subdialectal
subdividable

subdivisible
subduplicate
sub-editorial
subeditorial
suberization
subfeudation
subfeudatory
subglacially
subinfeudate
subintellect
subintroduce
subinvoluted
subjectional
subjectively
subjectivise
subjectivism
subjectivist
subjectivity
subjectivize
sublapsarian
Sublime Porte
subliminally
sublingually
submarine net
submaxillary
submergement
subminiature
submissively
subnormality
suboccipital
subopercular
suboperculum
suborbicular
subordinator
subpetiolate
sub-preceptor
subprincipal
subsatellite
subscribable
subscribe for
subscription
subscriptive
subsectioned
subsequently
subsequent to
subservience
subserviency
subsidiaries
subsidiarily
subsidiarity
subsizarship
subsonically
substantiate
substantival
substitution
substitutive
substitutory
substraction
substruction
substructure
subterranean
subterranity

subtopianize
subtreasurer
subumbrellar
subvassalage
subversively
subvertebral
subvocalizer
subway alumni
subway series
succedaneous
successfully
successional
successively
successivity
success story
succinctness
succinic acid
suck an orange
sucking louse
suck-it-and-see
suction plant
suction valve
Sudanization
sudanophilia
sudanophilic
sudoriferous
sudoriparous
sufficiently
sufflaminate
Suffolk latch
Suffolk punch
Suffolk Punch
Suffolk sheep
suffraganate
suffraganean
suffragistic
suffruticose
sugar-boilery
sugar-candied
sugar-candies
sugar daddies
sugar nippers
sugar-orchard
sugar snap pea
sugar the pill
sugar-weather
suggestively
suggestivity
suicide blond
suitableness
suitcasefuls
suit of dittos
suit one's book
sullied white
sulphidation
sulphocyanic
sulphonamide
sulphonation
sulphonylate
sulphuration
sulphur cycle
sulphuretted

sulphur match	superhighway	supranuclear	sweepingness
sulphurously	superhumanly	supraorbital	Sweet Adeline
sulphur print	superhumeral	suprarenalin	sweet alyssum
sulphur vivum	superiorship	suprascapula	sweet and sour
sultana grape	superlattice	suprasensual	sweetback man
sultana queen	superluminal	supraspecies	sweet calamus
Sumatran hare	supermanhood	supraspinous	sweet cassava
Sumerologist	supermassive	suprathermal	sweethearter
summarizable	supermullion	supravaginal	sweetishness
summary punch	supermundane	Supreme Being	sweet maudlin
summer-fallow	supernacular	Supreme Court	sweet-mouthed
summer master	supernaculum	sure-footedly	sweet pinesap
summer savory	supernatural	surface noise	sweet-scented
summer school	superorbital	surface paper	sweet sixteen
summer season	superordinal	surface-plate	sweet sorghum
summer squash	superorganic	surface speed	sweet-toothed
summer-weight	superovulate	surface-to-air	sweet trolley
summiteering	superplastic	surface water	sweet william
sumo wrestler	superposable	surge chamber	swellishness
sumphishness	superradiant	surgeon's knot	swelteringly
sun and planet	super-realism	surge voltage	swimmer's itch
Sunday dinner	super-realist	Suriname toad	swimming bath
Sunday driver	super-reality	surmountable	swimming-bell
Sunday letter	super-refined	surpassingly	swimming crab
Sunday's child	supersedable	surplice fees	swimming hole
Sunday school	supersedence	surplus value	swimmingness
sunken garden	supersensory	surprisingly	swimming pool
sunken storey	supersensual	surrealistic	swindle sheet
sunray pleats	supersession	surrejoinder	swine-chopped
sunshineless	supersessive	surroundings	swine's grease
sunshine roof	superspecies	surveillance	swing bowling
sunspot cycle	superstardom	survey course	swing Douglas
Sun Yat-senism	superstition	surveyorship	swinging boom
supellectile	superstratum	survivorship	swing the gate
superability	superterrene	susceptivity	swing the lead
superacidity	Super Tuesday	suspensively	Swiss cottage
superallowed	supervenient	suspensorial	switch-around
superambient	supervention	suspensorium	switch dealer
superannuate	supervoltage	suspiciously	switch dollar
superaqueous	superworldly	Sussex marble	switch-engine
superaudible	supplemental	sustainingly	switch-hitter
superaverage	supplementer	sustentacula	switch-tender
supercargoes	supplicantly	sustentation	swivel-bridge
supercarrier	supplication	sustentative	swizzle-stick
supercharged	supplicatory	svarabhaktic	swollen shoot
supercharger	supply-driven	swaggeringly	sword-bayonet
superciliary	supportative	swagger stick	sword dancing
supercilious	support group	swallow bobby	swordfishing
supercluster	supportingly	swallow's-nest	Sword of State
superconduct	supportively	swamp cabbage	sworn brother
supercurrent	support price	swamp cypress	sycamore moth
superelevate	suppositious	swamp sparrow	sycamore tree
supereminent	suppressedly	swamp wallaby	sycophantish
supererogant	suppressible	swamp warbler	sycophantize
supererogate	suprachoroid	swashbuckler	syenodiorite
superessence	supraciliary	sweat bullets	Sykes's monkey
superfluence	supracrustal	sweat cooling	syllabically
superfrontal	supraglacial	sweater-shirt	syllabicness
superglottal	supraliminal	sweating-room	Sylvester-eve
supergravity	supramaximal	Swedish drill	sylviculture
superhelical	supramundane	sweep-chimney	symblepharon
super-highway	supranatural	sweep-forward	symbolically

symbological
symbololatry
symmetallism
symmetallist
symmetrodont
sympathy card
symplasmatic
symposiastic
symptomatize
symptomology
synaesthesia
synaesthesis
synaesthetic
synanthropic
synapomorphy
synaptically
synapticular
synaptonemal
synaptosomal
synarthroses
synarthrosis
synchroflash
synchroneity
synchronical
synchronizer
synchroscope
synclinorium
syncretistic
syndactylism
syndactylous
syndesmology
syndiotactic
syndyotactic
synecdochism
synecologist
synergetical
synergically
syngenesious
synkinematic
synodic month
synonymously
synoptically
synoptophore
syntactician
syntacticist
synthesis gas
syntonically
syphiloderma
systematical
systematizer
systemically
tabernacular
table diamond
table licence
table manners
table-rapping
table-service
table-setting
table-tilting
table-top sale
table-turning
tabloidesque

tabulae rasae
tacheometric
tachycardiac
tachygenesis
tachygrapher
tachygraphic
tackle-porter
tactile value
tactlessness
taedium vitae
Tagliacotian
tail assembly
taillessness
tail of the eye
tailor's chair
tailor's chalk
tailor's dummy
tailor's twist
tail-twisting
Taka-diastase
take a fancy to
take a holiday
take a liberty
take a share in
take a shine to
take a sight at
take a whack at
take farewell
take for a ride
take it from me
take it on a lam
take kindly to
take no notice
take notice of
take occasion
take one's dick
take one's ease
take one's pick
take one's rest
take one's seat
take one's time
take one's will
take prisoner
take shipping
take the count
take the field
take the fifth
take the floor
take the knock
take the law of
take the stage
take the water
take together
take to pieces
take unawares
talcum powder
tale of terror
talipes varus
talismanical
talkee-talkee
talking blues
talking clock

talking point
tall oat-grass
tallow candle
tallow-topped
tamboo-bamboo
tambour-frame
tambourinist
tameableness
tamelessness
tandem garage
tangentially
tangent point
tangent screw
tangibleness
tangle-footed
tantalic acid
tape cassette
tape recorder
tape streamer
tapestry moth
tapestry-work
taphonomical
Tappertitian
tapsalteerie
taramasalata
Taranaki gate
Tardenoisian
tardigradous
target pistol
target theory
target tissue
tariff-reform
tarnowitzite
tarsorrhaphy
tartar emetic
tartare sauce
tartaric acid
taskmistress
tassel-flower
tassel-stitch
tastefulness
tauntingness
taurocholate
taurodontism
tauromachies
tautological
Tavastlander
tavern-keeper
tax allowance
tax avoidance
tax collector
tax deduction
tax exemption
taxing-master
tax inspector
tax-sheltered
tax threshold
Taylor system
teachability
teachers' aide
team handball
team ministry

team-teaching
tearlessness
tear one's hair
tear to shreds
teaspoonfuls
technetronic
technicalism
technicalist
technicality
technicology
technicolour
technobabble
technocratic
technography
technologies
technologism
technologist
technologize
technophilia
technophilic
technophobia
technophobic
technostress
tectocuticle
tectogenesis
tectogenetic
tectonically
tectospheric
teddy-bearish
teeing-ground
teensy-weensy
teeter-totter
teething ring
Teflon-coated
tektite field
telaesthesia
telaesthetic
telautograph
telecommuter
telecomputer
telegraph boy
telegraphese
telegraphist
telegraph key
telegraphone
teleguidance
telemarketer
teleological
teleoperator
telepathetic
telepherique
telephonable
telephone box
telephone pad
telephone set
telephone tag
telephone tap
telephonitis
telepolitics
telepresence
teleprompter
telerobotics

telescopical
teleshopping
telesoftware
teleteaching
teleutosorus
teleutospore
televisually
telharmonium
tell the truth
tell the world
telluric acid
Tellurometer
telodendrion
telolecithal
temerousness
temnospondyl
temperatured
tempestively
temple dancer
temporal bone
temporal lobe
temporalness
temporaneous
temptability
temptational
tempt fortune
temptingness
temulentness
tenant at will
tenant farmer
tendenzroman
tender annual
tender an oath
tender-footed
tender-minded
tenderometer
tenebrescent
ten-gallon hat
Tengmalm's owl
tennis-ground
tennis player
tennis racket
Tennysoniana
ten per center
tensiometric
tentaculated
tenuifolious
tenuirostral
ten-week stock
tequila plant
Tequistlatec
teratologist
teratomatous
tercentenary
terebenthene
terebinthina
terebinthine
terebratulid
terephthalic
tergiversate
term for years
terminalized

terminus a quo
termitophile
termolecular
terms of trade
terraced roof
terrace house
terra cognita
terraculture
terribleness
terrifically
terrificness
terrifyingly
terror-struck
tertiary road
tessellation
testamentary
testiculated
testosterone
test specimen
test the water
test-tube baby
testudinated
testudineous
tetanization
tetanus toxin
tetrachotomy
tetracycline
tetragonally
tetrahedrite
tetrahedrons
tetrahydrate
tetramorphic
tetraparesis
tetraparetic
tetrapolitan
tetrapterous
tetrapyrrole
tetrarchical
tetrastichic
tetrathionic
tetrodotoxin
teuthologist
Teutonically
Texas leaguer
textological
texture brick
textured yarn
thack and rape
Thackerayana
thalassaemia
thalassaemic
thalassocrat
thallic oxide
thallophytic
thankfulness
thank heavens
thanksgiving
thank-you-ma'am
that's the idea
that's the shot
that's your lot
thaumatology

thaumaturgic
thaumaturgus
the Admiralty
the Adversary
theanthropic
the Architect
the Argentine
the Atonement
theatregoing
theatre nurse
theatre of war
theatre organ
theatre party
theatrically
theatrocracy
theatrophone
the bee's knees
the big screen
theca externa
theca interna
the Captivity
the City of God
the clear grit
thecodontian
the Comforter
the Devil's job
the devil to do
the die is cast
the early bird
the fairer sex
the Fall of Man
the following
the Forty-five
the gentle art
the genus Homo
the Grand Turk
the hard stuff
the heroic age
the holy table
the Household
theileriasis
the invisible
theistically
the jury is out
the king's evil
the Lamb of God
the land knows
the land of nod
the land of Nod
the left bower
the long green
thematically
the Met Office
the multitude
then and there
Thénard's blue
the necessary
theocentrism
theocratical
the Old Reaper
the old regime
theologaster

theologician
theomorphism
Theopaschite
theopathetic
theophylline
theopneustic
theopolitics
theoretician
theoreticism
theoreticist
theorization
theosophical
the other side
the other week
the Peninsula
the Potteries
the provinces
the pure quill
therapeutics
therapeutist
thereagainst
the real McCoy
the real thing
there and then
thereinafter
there's a thing
therethrough
thermal cycle
thermal lance
thermal noise
thermal paper
thermal shock
thermal speed
thermic lance
Thermidorian
thermochromy
thermocouple
thermography
thermohaline
thermolabile
Thermolactyl
thermometric
thermonastic
thermophilic
thermoscopic
thermos flask
thermo-siphon
thermosphere
thermostable
thermostatic
thermotactic
thermotropic
the same story
the same to you
the second sex
the short robe
Thesmophoric
the softer sex
Thessalonian
the story goes
the Ten Tribes
the three Magi

the time of day
the tother day
theurgically
the very devil
the very thing
the ways of God
the weaker sex
the Windy City
the world over
the world's end
the worst kind
the young idea
thiacetazone
thiazolidine
thick and fast
thick and thin
thick-sighted
thick-skinned
thick-skulled
thick-tongued
thief-catcher
thieves' Latin
thievishness
thigh-slapper
thigmotactic
thigmotropic
thimbleberry
thimble-glass
thin blue line
think balloon
thinkingness
thinking part
think it scorn
think scorn of
think through
thiodiglycol
thioindigoid
thioridazine
thiosulphate
thirdborough
third country
third reading
Third Worlder
thirteenthly
thirty-two-mos
this long time
thistle crown
thistle-finch
thistle glass
thitherwards
thomsenolite
thoracically
thoracic cage
thoracic duct
thoracoscopy
thoracostomy
thorny oyster
thorogummite
thorough bass
thorough-bind
thoroughbred
thoroughfare

thoroughness
thorough post
thorough-sped
thoroughwort
thortveitite
thoughtcrime
thought-forms
thoughtfully
thought model
thought-saver
thought-world
thousandfold
thousand-legs
thowlessness
thread-cutter
thread-needle
threap-ground
three-address
three-cushion
three day week
three figures
three fourths
three monkeys
three-pounder
three-pronged
three-quarter
three-striper
three-tongued
three-wheeler
three wise men
thriftlessly
thrivingness
thrombectomy
thrombogenic
thrombolysis
thrombolytic
thrombopenia
thrombopenic
Throne Speech
throstle-cock
throttleable
throttle back
throughgoing
through-other
through-stone
throw a glance
throw a slur on
throw a wobbly
throw cushion
throw-forward
throwing-mill
throw light on
throw money at
throw one's eye
thrush-fungus
thrust vector
thrust washer
thuggishness
thumb-indexed
thunderation
thunder-blast
thundercloud

thunder-crack
thunder-flash
thunderflash
thunderingly
thunderlight
thunderously
thunder-plant
thunder-plump
thunder-sheet
thunder-snake
thunder stick
thunder-stone
thunderstorm
Thurberesque
thymectomize
thymiaterion
thymopoietin
thyroid gland
thyrotrophic
Tibeto-Burman
Tibetologist
ticket-holder
ticket office
ticket-porter
Ticklenburgs
ticklishness
tidal harbour
tiddledy-wink
tiddledywink
tiddlywinker
tidelessness
tide-surveyor
tiger bittern
tigerishness
tiger-striped
tight as a tick
tight-fitting
tile-drainage
till all hours
till doomsday
tilting rotor
timber-beetle
timber cruise
timber-doodle
timber-framed
timber-getter
timber-grouse
timber-jumper
timber-topper
time and again
time and a half
time constant
time-division
time exposure
time-honoured
timelessness
time-of-flight
time-resolved
time reversal
timocratical
timorousness
timothy grass

tinctorially
tingle-tangle
tinhorn sport
tinkle-tankle
tinmen's snips
tintinnabula
tip one's hands
tip the scales
tip the wink to
tiptoe around
tirelessness
tiresomeness
tirl at the pin
tissue typing
titaniferous
tithe-proctor
Titian-haired
titter-totter
tittle-tattle
titular abbot
titular saint
to admiration
toad-snatcher
toasting-fork
tobacco heart
tobacco house
tobacco plant
tobacco-pouch
tobacco-water
toddy-tapping
toe in the door
toffee hammer
toft and croft
togetherness
together with
toggle switch
to hell with it
toilet humour
toilet tissue
toilsomeness
to-infinitive
token economy
token payment
tolerability
toleratingly
tolerization
Tolkienesque
Tolstoyanism
tomfooleries
tomorrow week
tompot blenny
tone-deafness
tone dialling
tone language
tonelessness
tone-painting
tone-syllable
tongue-tacked
tonification
tonneau cover
tonofibrilla
tonofilament

tonsillotomy
tonsorialist
too late a week
to one's credit
to one's liking
tooth and nail
toothed whale
to perfection
top-fermented
top-heaviness
toploftiness
topochemical
top of the heap
top of the milk
top of the pops
topographist
topographize
toponomastic
topotactical
top-stitching
topstitching
topsy-turvily
toque macaque
torch-fishing
torch singing
torch-thistle
tormentingly
torpedo beard
torpedo juice
torque wrench
torrefaction
torrentially
Torricellian
torsionmeter
tortilla chip
tortoise core
tortoise-like
tortoise-pace
tortoise race
tortuosities
tortuousness
Tory democrat
toss a pancake
toss one's head
total eclipse
totalitarian
totalization
to that effect
to the north of
to the point of
to the purpose
tother school
to the south of
to this effect
touchability
touch-dancing
touched proof
touchingness
touch one's hat
touch the spot
tourist class
tourist track

tourmalinize
tournamental
tour operator
tours de force
tousle-haired
towardliness
tower mustard
Tower of Babel
town and tower
town planning
town twinning
toxicologist
toxigenicity
toxocariasis
toxophilitic
to your health
trabeculated
traceability
trace element
trace program
tracheophone
tracheoscopy
tracheostomy
trachomatous
tracing paper
tracing table
tracing-wheel
trackability
track athlete
track circuit
track-clearer
tracking shot
tractability
traction-load
tractoration
trade barrier
trade deficit
trade dispute
traded option
trade-edition
trade-English
trade journal
trade mission
tradescantia
tradespeople
tradesperson
trade surplus
trading floor
trading-house
trading-place
trading stamp
traditionary
traditionism
traditionist
traducianism
traducianist
Trafalgar Day
traffic court
traffic light
traffic-proof
traffic snarl
tragelaphine

tragicalness
tragic-comedy
tragicomical
trail-blazing
trailblazing
trailer-truck
trailing edge
trainability
training ship
training shoe
train-spotter
traitorously
trajectories
tralatitious
trampolinist
tranche de vie
tranquillise
tranquillity
tranquillize
tranquilness
transaminase
transaminate
transannular
transcalency
transcendent
transcension
trans-channel
transcribble
transcriptor
transcurrent
transdialect
transductant
transduction
transelement
transfashion
transfection
transferable
transfer-book
transfer case
transference
transfer line
transfer list
transferring
transfixedly
transfixture
transfluence
transfluvial
transformant
transformism
transformist
transfusible
transgenosis
transgressor
transhumance
transilience
transinsular
transitation
transitional
transitively
transitivise
transitivism
transitivity

transitivize
transitorily
transit-trade
translatable
translatress
translucence
translucency
transmigrant
transmigrate
transmission
transmissive
transmitting
transmogrify
transmontane
transmundane
transmutable
transnatural
transoceanic
transom-stern
transorbital
trans-Pacific
transpacific
transparence
transparency
transpeciate
transpicuous
transpirable
transplanter
transpontine
transportive
transposable
transqualify
transrhenane
trans-species
trans-stellar
transudation
transudatory
transumption
transumptive
transuranian
Transvaalian
transversary
transversely
transversion
transversive
transvestism
transvestist
transvestite
Trapezuntine
trap-shooting
traumatology
traumatropic
travel agency
travel bureau
travel folder
travelleress
traverse-book
traverse jury
travestiment
travesty role
treacle sleep
treadmilling

treason felon
treasonously
treasure hunt
treasureless
treasury bill
treasury-bond
treasury note
treasuryship
treatability
treaty Indian
treble chance
tree kangaroo
treelessness
tree of heaven
tree squirrel
trembler bell
tremendously
tremorlessly
trench-coated
trench mortar
trench-plough
trend-setting
trendsetting
trend-spotter
trend surface
trephination
trestle-board
trestle-table
triadelphous
trial balance
trial balloon
trial per pais
triangle moth
triangulable
triangularly
triangulated
triangulator
tribespeople
tribological
tribophysics
tribosphenic
Tribune group
tribute-money
tricentenary
trichiniasis
Trichinopoli
trichobezoar
trichogenous
trichologist
trichopathic
trichophagia
trichophobia
trichophytic
trichophyton
trichopteran
trichothecin
trichotomies
trichotomize
trichotomous
trichromatic
trichuriasis
trick-cycling

trick cyclist
trickeration
trickishness
trick or treat
trickstering
triclinarch
tridactylous
trident curve
tried and true
trienniality
Trifid Nebula
triflingness
trifoliolate
trifurcation
trigger-happy
trigger-plant
trigger-point
trigger price
trigger pulse
triglyceride
triglyphical
trigonelline
trigonometer
trigonometry
trigrammatic
trihemimeral
trihemimeris
trilaterally
trillionaire
trimeprazine
trimethoprim
trimethylene
trimming gear
trimming-tank
Trinity House
trinomialism
triode-hexode
trioeciously
tripartitely
tripartition
triphthongal
triple-decker
triple-headed
triple-header
triple-spaced
triplication
triplicities
tripos verses
trippingness
tripudiation
trismegistic
Tristanesque
tristfulness
triterpenoid
triumphalism
triumphalist
triumphantly
triumvirship
trivialities
trochanteral
trochanteric
trochosphere

troglobiotic
troglodytish
troglodytism
trolley-wheel
trolling pole
tromba marina
troop carrier
trophallaxis
trophic level
trophotropic
tropical year
tropological
troposcatter
tropospheric
troubledness
troublemaker
troubleshoot
trough garden
trouserettes
trouser-press
Trubetzkoyan
truck tractor
truck trailer
true-love knot
trumpet hypha
trumpet major
trumpet-mouth
trumpet-shell
trumpet-snail
trumpet style
trundle-wheel
trussing hoop
trust-busting
trust company
trustfulness
trustingness
trust officer
truthfulness
try a fall with
try masteries
try one's wings
trypaflavine
trypanocidal
trypanolysis
trypanolytic
trypanosomal
trypanosomic
trypanosomid
tryparsamide
tschermakite
tube-dwelling
tubercularly
tuberculated
tuberculosed
tuberculosis
tuberiferous
tuberization
tuberousness
tuberous root
tubocurarine
tubular bells
tuck position

tulipomaniac
tumble-action
tumbler-drier
tumbler-dryer
tumbler-glass
tumbling home
tumbling-mill
tumbu disease
tumultuation
tumultuously
tunelessness
tunica intima
tuning-hammer
tunnel effect
tunnel of love
tunnel vision
Tupi-Guaranis
turban squash
turban tumour
turbellarian
turbidimeter
turbidimetry
turbidometer
turbinectomy
turbocharger
turbostratic
Turcocentric
Turcophilism
Turkey carpet
turkey-fat ore
Turkey red oil
Turkey sponge
Turkish music
Turkish towel
turn a deaf ear
turn cat in pan
turning-lathe
turning point
turnip greens
turnip sawfly
turn of phrase
turn one's coat
turnpike gate
turnpike road
turn the trick
turn up trumps
turtle-backed
turtle-necked
tussie-mussie
tussock grass
tu-whit tu-whoo
Twelfth Night
twelve-seater
Twelve Tribes
twentyfourmo
twenty-seater
twenty-twenty
twilight area
twilight home
twilightless
twilight zone
twine-spinner

twisted-stalk
twitteration
twitteringly
two-facedness
twopenny post
two-way mirror
two-way street
Tyburn ticket
tychopotamic
tympanic bone
tympanometry
Tyndall meter
type approval
type-cylinder
type locality
type specimen
typhoid fever
typhoid state
typification
typographica
typographist
tyrannically
tyrannicidal
Tyrian purple
tyrosinaemia
ubiquitarian
ubiquitinate
ubiquitously
Ugandan Asian
uglification
Ugly American
ugly customer
ugly duckling
ullage rocket
ultimateness
ultramontane
ultramundane
ultraviolate
ultroneously
umbilication
umbrageously
umbrella bird
umbrella body
umbrella fund
umbrellaless
umbrella-like
umbrella pine
umbrella tree
unabsorbable
unacceptable
unacceptably
unacclimated
unaccredited
unaccustomed
unachievable
unacquainted
unacquirable
unactability
unadjectived
unadmonished
unadulterate
unadvertised

unaffectedly
unaffiliated
unaffordable
unaffrighted
unaggravated
unaggregated
unaggressive
unagitatedly
unalleviable
unalleviated
unalphabetic
unambivalent
unamiability
unanalogical
unanalysable
unanalytical
unanswerable
unanswerably
unapologetic
unapparelled
unappealable
unappealably
unappeasable
unappeasably
unappetising
unappetizing
unapproached
unarithmetic
unarticulate
unartificial
unascendable
unassailable
unassailably
unassignable
unassociable
unassociated
unassumingly
unastonished
unattackable
unattainable
unattainably
unattenuated
unattractive
unattributed
unauspicious
unauthorised
unauthorized
unavailingly
unbeautified
unbecomingly
unbefriended
unbegottenly
unbelievable
unbelievably
unbeneficial
unbenevolent
unbequeathed
unbetterable
unbewildered
unbiasedness
unbiological
unblinkingly

unbloodiness
unblushingly
unbreachable
unbreathable
unbridgeable
unbrokenness
unbuttressed
uncalculated
uncalendared
uncandidness
uncaringness
uncastigated
uncatalogued
uncatechized
uncelebrated
uncensorious
uncensurable
unchallenged
unchangeable
unchangeably
unchangingly
unchannelled
unchaperoned
uncharitable
uncharitably
unchasteness
uncheerfully
unchivalrous
unchristened
un-Christlike
unchronicled
unchurchlike
uncicatrized
uncinariasis
uncirculated
unclassified
Uncle Tommery
Uncle Tommish
Uncle Tommism
uncloistered
uncoagulable
uncoagulated
uncognizable
uncollegiate
uncombinable
uncome-at-able
uncomeliness
uncommenting
uncommercial
uncommonness
uncomparable
uncompelling
uncomplained
uncompounded
uncomprehend
uncompressed
uncomputable
unconceiving
unconcerning
unconfidence
unconfinable
unconfinedly

unconforming
unconformity
unconfounded
unconfronted
unconfusable
unconfusedly
unconfutable
unconjugated
unconnection
unconsecrate
unconsenting
unconsidered
unconsolable
unconsolably
unconstraint
unconsulting
unconsumable
unconsummate
uncontracted
uncontrolled
unconvenient
unconversant
unconversion
unconvincing
uncorrelated
uncorrigible
uncorruption
uncounselled
uncourageous
uncovenanted
uncreaturely
uncreditable
uncritically
uncriticized
unctuousness
uncultivable
uncultivated
unculturable
uncustomable
undamageable
undeceivable
undeciphered
undecisively
undeclarable
undeclinable
undecomposed
undecorative
undefeatable
undefendable
undefensible
undeflowered
undeformable
undegenerate
undeliberate
undelightful
undelighting
undemocratic
undemolished
undependable
underachieve
under-and-over
underbearing

underbellies
underblanket
under-builder
underclothed
underclothes
undercoating
under control
undercorrect
under cover to
undercurrent
underdoggery
underdrawing
undereducate
underfeature
underfilling
underfitness
underfooting
underframing
underfunding
undergarment
underhanging
under-hangman
under hatches
underivative
under-kingdom
underlayment
underleather
underlyingly
under-manager
under-marshal
undermeaning
undermeasure
under-officer
under one roof
under one's arm
underpayment
underpeopled
underperform
underpinning
underpitched
underpowered
underproduce
underpropper
under protest
under-servant
under-service
undersetting
under-sheriff
under-skinker
understaffed
understander
under-steward
understoreys
understories
understratum
understudied
understudies
undersucking
undersurface
under-teacher
undertenancy
under the rose

under the skin
under the wind
under the wire
underthought
undertrained
underutilise
underutilize
undervoltage
underworking
under-workman
underworldly
underwriting
underwritten
undesecrated
undeservedly
undesignated
undesignedly
undespairing
undetachable
undetectable
undetectably
undetermined
undigestible
undiligently
undiminished
undiplomatic
undiscerning
undischarged
undiscipline
undiscording
undiscovered
undiscursive
undisfigured
undislocated
undismantled
undismayable
undispatched
undisputable
undisputably
undisputedly
undisquieted
undissembled
undissipated
undissolving
undistracted
undistraught
undistressed
undisturbing
undivertible
undivertibly
undocumented
undogmatical
undoubtfully
undoubtingly
undramatical
undulatingly
uneconomical
unedifyingly
uneducatable
uneffaceable
unelaborated
uneloquently

unembittered
unemployable
unemployment
unencouraged
unencumbered
unendangered
unendingness
unenthralled
unenumerated
uneradicated
unerringness
uneschewable
uneuphonious
unevaporated
uneventfully
unexaminable
unexecutable
unexpectable
unexpectedly
unexplicable
unexplicitly
unexportable
unexpressive
unexpugnable
unexpurgated
unextenuated
unextirpated
unextricable
unfadingness
unfaithfully
unfamiliarly
unfastidious
unfathomable
unfathomably
unfatiguable
unfavourable
unfavourably
unfecundated
unfelicitous
unfemininity
unfertilised
unfertilized
unfinishable
unfittedness
unflaggingly
unflattering
unflickering
unforeboding
unforeseeing
unforewarned
unforgivable
unforgivably
unformalized
unformidable
unformulated
unfossilized
unfranchised
unfrequented
unfrequently
unfriendlier
unfriendship
unfrightened

unfruitfully
unfrustrable
unfulfilling
unfulfilment
unfunctional
ungainliness
ungarrisoned
ungenerosity
ungenerously
ungentleness
ungerminated
unglittering
ungovernable
ungovernably
ungracefully
ungraciously
ungratefully
ungregarious
ungrudgingly
unguaranteed
unguentarian
unguentarium
unguiculated
unhabituated
unhandsomely
unharmonious
unharmonized
unhealthiest
unhealthsome
un-Hellenized
unheroically
unhesitating
unhinderable
unhistorical
unhomeliness
unhoodwinked
unhospitable
unhumorously
unhydrolysed
unhyphenated
unhysterical
unicamerally
unicorn-plant
unicorn shell
unicorn's horn
unicorn whale
unidentified
unidolatrous
unifoliolate
uniformalize
uniformation
uniformities
unilaterally
unilinealism
unilingually
unillusioned
unimaginable
unimaginably
unimmergible
unimolecular
unimplicated
unimportance

unimportuned	unmarkedness	unpatronized	unquenchably
unimposingly	unmarketable	unpavilioned	unquestioned
unimpressive	unmasterable	unpenetrable	unravellable
unimprisoned	unmasticated	unpenetrated	unreactivity
unimprovable	unmeasurable	unperceiving	unrealisable
unincidental	unmeasurably	unperceptive	unrealizable
unindividual	unmechanical	unperforated	unreasonable
uninfectious	unmechanized	unperforming	unreasonably
uninfluenced	unmeddlesome	unperishable	unrebellious
uninitiation	unmeditative	unpermanency	unrebukeable
uninjectable	unmercifully	unpersuasive	unrecallable
uninoculated	unmethodical	unphysically	unreceivable
uninstructed	unmethodized	unpickupable	unreckonable
unintegrated	unmilitarily	unpicturable	unrecognized
unintendedly	unmiraculous	unpierceable	unreconciled
uninterested	unmirthfully	unpleasantly	unrecordable
unintermixed	unmistakable	unpleasantry	unredeemable
unintroduced	unmistakably	unpleasingly	unredeemably
uninvitingly	unmodernized	unpoetically	unreferenced
union-bashing	unmodifiable	unpoliceable	unreflecting
unionization	unmolestedly	unpolishable	unreflective
uniprocessor	unmusicality	unpoliteness	unreformable
unirradiated	unmyelinated	unpopularity	unrefreshing
unirritating	unmysterious	unpopularize	unregainable
unisegmental	unnaturalise	unportentous	unregeneracy
unisexuality	unnaturalism	unprecarious	unregenerate
unison string	unnaturality	unprejudiced	unregimented
unison-tuning	unnaturalize	unprelatical	unregistered
unitalicized	unnoteworthy	unpreparedly	unrejectable
Unitarianism	unnoticeable	unprescribed	unrelievable
unitary group	unnoticeably	unpretending	unrelievedly
United States	unnourishing	unprettiness	unremarkable
unit membrane	unnumberable	unprevailing	unremarkably
unity of place	unnutritious	unprincipled	unremembered
universalian	unobjectible	unprivileged	unremittedly
universalise	unobligingly	unproclaimed	unremorseful
universalism	unobsequious	unprocurable	unrepairable
universalist	unobservable	unproducible	unrepassable
universality	unobservance	unproductive	unrepealable
universalize	unobservedly	unprofitable	unrepeatable
universal set	unobstructed	unprofitably	unrepentance
universities	unobtainable	unprogrammed	unrepiningly
unjudicially	unoffendable	unpronounced	unreportable
unkerchiefed	unoffendedly	unpropertied	unreproached
unkindliness	unofficially	unpropitious	unreprovable
unlawfulness	unoppressive	unprosecuted	unrepublican
unlawyer-like	unoriginally	unprosperity	unrequitable
unlikelihood	unoriginated	unprosperous	unrequitedly
unlikeliness	unornamental	unprotestant	unresembling
unliquidated	unornamented	unprotesting	unreservedly
unlistenable	unorthodoxly	unprovidedly	unresistable
unliturgical	unoverlooked	unprovokable	unresistance
unlocomotive	unoverthrown	unprovokedly	unresistedly
unloveliness	unoxygenated	unprudential	unresistible
unlovingness	unpacifiedly	unpublicized	unresolvable
unlubricated	unparalleled	unpugnacious	unresolvedly
unmagnetized	unpardonable	unpulverized	unrespectful
unmaintained	unpardonably	unpunctuated	unrespecting
unmanageable	unpassionate	unpunishable	unrespective
unmanageably	unpasturable	unpunishably	unrespirable
unmanifested	unpatentable	unquantified	unresponsive
unmanumitted	unpatriotism	unquenchable	unrestrained

unrestricted
unretaliated
unreturnable
unreturnably
unrevealable
unreverenced
unreverently
unreviewable
unrhetorical
unrhythmical
unrightfully
unroadworthy
unruly member
unsacerdotal
unsacrificed
unsalubrious
unsanctified
unsanctioned
unsatisfying
unsaturation
unscandalous
unscholastic
unscientific
unscriptural
unscrupulous
unsculptured
unseamanlike
unsearchable
unsearchably
unseasonable
unseasonably
unseasonally
unsecularize
unseemliness
unsegregated
unsensitized
unsensualize
unsepulchred
unsepultured
unsettlement
unsheltering
unshrinkable
unsignatured
unsignifying
unsignposted
unsilicified
unslackening
unsleepingly
unslumbering
unsmoothable
unsocialized
unsolicitous
unspectacled
unsplittable
unsportingly
unsquandered
unstabilized
unstableness
unstanchable
unstatutable
unstatutably
unsteadiness

unsterilized
unstimulated
unstintingly
unstockinged
unstraitened
unstratified
unstrengthen
unstructured
unstruggling
unsubjugated
unsublimated
unsubmissive
unsubmitting
unsubscribed
unsubsidized
unsubstanced
unsuccessful
unsuccessive
unsufferable
unsufficient
unsuggestive
unsuperseded
unsupervised
unsuppliable
unsupportive
unsupposable
unsuppressed
unsurprising
unsurrounded
unsuspecting
unsuspicious
unsustaining
unswervingly
unsyncopated
unsystematic
untemptingly
untenability
untenantable
untenderness
unterminated
unterrifying
unthankfully
untheatrical
unthinkingly
unthoughtful
unthreatened
untimeliness
untouchingly
untowardness
untrammelled
untranslated
untransmuted
untruthfully
untumultuous
ununderstood
ununiformity
unupbraiding
unusefulness
unvaccinated
unvanquished
unveiledness
unventilated

unverbalized
unverifiable
unvictorious
unvindicated
unvindictive
unvirtuously
unvouchsafed
unvoyageable
unvulcanized
unvulnerable
unwantedness
unwashedness
unwatchfully
unwaveringly
unwearyingly
unweddedness
unwieldiness
unwontedness
unworshipful
unworshipped
unworthiness
unyieldingly
up and running
upbraidingly
upconversion
upland cotton
Upland cotton
upland plover
up one's sleeve
up one's street
upon my honour
upon occasion
upon straight
upon the books
Upper Chamber
Upper Chinook
upper classes
upper leather
upper regions
uproariously
uprootedness
upset stomach
up the Straits
up-to-dateness
up to one's ears
up to one's eyes
up to one's neck
up to the teeth
uranographer
uranographic
uranological
uranoplastic
uranothorite
urbanization
urbanologist
urban renewal
ureterectomy
ureterostomy
urethrometer
urethroscope
urethroscopy
Uriah Heepish

urinary tract
urinogenital
urobilinogen
urobilinuria
urochloralic
urolithiasis
uroporphyrin
ursine baboon
ursine howler
user-friendly
ustilaginous
usucapionary
usufructuary
usuriousness
uterovaginal
uterovesical
utility actor
utility curve
utility knife
utility truck
utterability
uxorilocally
uxoriousness
vacation home
vacation land
vacationland
vaccine lymph
vacuum bottle
vacuum-fitted
vacuum grease
vacuum-packed
vagabondical
vainglorious
valence quark
valence shell
Valenciennes
valent clause
valet parking
valetudinary
Vallombrosan
valorisation
valorization
valorousness
Valpolicella
valuableness
valuation law
value analyst
value calling
valued policy
value-neutral
vampirically
Van Allen belt
Vandiemonian
Vandyke beard
Vandyke brown
vanilla plant
vanilla sugar
vanity mirror
vanquishable
vanquishment
vantage-point
vaporability

vaporization
vaporousness
variable name
variableness
variationist
varicoloured
varied thrush
variety meats
variety store
variola major
variola minor
varnish sumac
varsity match
vasculotoxic
vasoactivity
vasodilating
vasodilation
vasodilatory
vasomotorial
Vaticanology
vaticination
vaticinatory
vaudevillian
vaudevillist
vaunt-courier
veduta ideata
vegecultural
vegetabilise
vegetability
vegetabilize
vegetable dye
vegetable oil
vegetable wax
vegetational
vegetatively
vegetivorous
veggie burger
vehiculation
vehiculatory
velarization
veld sickness
veldt-marshal
Velikovskian
velocipedist
velociraptor
velocity head
velvet carpet
velvet scoter
velvet sponge
venepuncture
venerability
Venetian blue
Venetian door
Venetian lace
vengefulness
venipuncture
venire de novo
venomousness
venous system
ventre à terre
ventricosity
ventriculite

ventripotent
ventromedial
Venture Scout
Venusbergian
Venus fly-trap
Venus flytrap
Venus's girdle
verbal action
verbalizable
verbenaceous
verderership
verecundness
veridicality
verification
verificatory
verisimilous
Verlainesque
vermiculated
vermiculture
vermilionize
vernacularly
vernis martin
versificator
vertebration
vertical keel
verticillate
verticillium
verumontanum
Very Reverend
vesicularity
vesiculation
vespertilian
vestal virgin
vestimentary
veterinarian
veterinaries
vibraharpist
vibraphonist
vibratiuncle
vibronically
vibrotactile
vicar-general
vice-consular
vice-governor
vicious cycle
Victorianism
Victorianist
Victorianize
Victoria plum
victoriously
victory point
videographer
videographic
video mapping
vie de château
Vienna Circle
vigintennial
vigintillion
vigorousness
vilification
village idiot
villagewards

villainously
vincibleness
vindemiation
vindicatress
vindictively
vinegar Bible
Vinegar Bible
vinegarishly
vinegar stick
vinicultural
vinification
vinolentness
vin ordinaire
vinous liquor
vinyl acetate
viola da gamba
viola pomposa
violaxanthin
violin spider
violoncellos
viperousness
Virgilianism
virgin forest
Virginia deer
Virginian sea
Virginia poke
Virginia rail
Virginia reel
virgin's bower
Virgin's spike
viridescence
virile member
virilescence
virilisation
virilization
virilocality
virtual focus
virtual image
virtuosoship
virtuousness
virulentness
viruliferous
visceral arch
visceral hump
viscerotonia
viscerotonic
viscoelastic
viscose rayon
viscosimeter
viscosimetry
viscountcies
viscountship
visible index
visible light
vision mixing
visitatorial
visiting-book
visiting card
visitors' book
visitors' list
visual acuity
visual binary

visual cortex
visualizable
visual purple
visuopsychic
visuosensory
visuospatial
visuotactual
vitalization
vital spirits
vitativeness
vitellogenin
vitellophage
viticultural
vitilitigate
vitreous body
vitreousness
vitrifaction
Vitruvianism
vituperation
vituperative
vituperatory
vituperously
vivification
viviparously
vixenishness
vocabularian
vocabularies
vocabularize
vocalization
vocationally
vocationless
vociferation
vociferative
vociferosity
vociferously
vodka martini
voice channel
voicefulness
voice leading
voice-printer
voidableness
volatileness
volatile salt
volcanically
volcanic bomb
volcanologic
volitionally
volitionless
Volksdeutsch
Volkspolizei
volley-firing
voltage clamp
voltammetric
volumetrical
voluminosity
voluminously
voluntariate
voluntaryism
voluntaryist
volunteerism
voluptuaries
voluptuously

vortex street	warping-frame	water strider	well-attended
vote-catching	warp knitting	water-swallow	well-balanced
vote of credit	warrant chief	water-tabling	well-becoming
votive tablet	warranty deed	water torture	well-breathed
vowel diagram	war to end wars	water-wagtail	well-breeched
vowel harmony	war-weariness	Watteauesque	well-deserved
vowel-quality	washer bottle	Watteau pleat	well-designed
vow of poverty	washing-house	wattled crane	well disposed
voyage policy	washing-place	waulking song	well-dressing
vulcanizable	washing-stand	wave analyser	well-educated
vulgarianism	washing-stock	wave equation	well-equipped
vulgar tongue	washing-stuff	wave function	well-favoured
wag-at-the-wall	Washingtonia	wave-offering	well-grounded
wagelessness	wash one's eyes	wave–particle	well I'm damned
wages council	wash one's head	waveringness	well-informed
Wagnerianism	wastefulness	wave velocity	wellingtonia
wagon-ceiling	wasting asset	way-going crop	well-intended
wagtail dance	watchability	way passenger	well-mannered
wah-wah effect	watch and ward	ways and means	well-ordering
wainscotting	watchfulness	weaponeering	well-pleasing
waistcoateer	watch-keeping	weapons-grade	well-prepared
waistcoating	watch-officer	wearifulness	well received
waiting-woman	watch-setting	wear the horns	well-tempered
wait one's turn	water bailiff	wear the pants	well-timbered
wakerifeness	water balance	weasel's snout	Welsh dresser
Waldorf salad	water-ballast	weasel-worded	Welsh rarebit
walk away from	water biscuit	weather-blate	Welsh terrier
walk away with	water blister	weatherboard	welterweight
walkie-talkie	water-boatman	weather-bound	Wernerianism
walk-in closet	water buffalo	weather chart	Wesleyanized
walking frame	Water-carrier	weather cycle	westerliness
walking party	water company	weather-glass	Western Front
walking-staff	water cracker	weather-house	Western Isles
walking stick	water-cricket	weatherology	Western Ocean
walking-sword	water cushion	weatherproof	Western Union
walking-wheel	water-diviner	weather-strip	West Germanic
walk the chalk	water-drinker	weatherstrip	West Highland
walk the plank	water figwort	weathertight	West-Indiaman
walk the wards	water-finding	weather-tiled	Westinghouse
wallaby-grass	waterfowling	weather-tiles	westwardmost
wallah-wallah	water-gilding	weather woman	Wetmore order
wallcovering	water hemlock	wedding-chest	wet one's pants
wall-eyed pike	watering hole	wedding group	wetting agent
wall painting	waterishness	wedding march	wet to the skin
Wall Streeter	Waterlandian	wedding night	whale-fishery
waltz Matilda	water lentils	wedding-party	whale-fishing
waltz off with	water lettuce	wedding-sheet	Wharton's duct
wandering Jew	Waterloo ball	Weeping Cross	whatever next
wanderluster	Waterloo blue	weeping myall	what is he like
wander-witted	watermanship	weightedness	what's cooking
Wankel engine	water-measure	weightlessly	what serves it
wantlessness	water milfoil	weightlifter	what's-her-face
warbler finch	water monitor	Weil's disease	what's-her-name
war communism	water opossum	weird sisters	what's in a name
wardrobe-room	water-parsnip	welcome wagon	what's the game
warehouseman	water-parting	welding steel	what's the odds
warehousemen	waterproofed	welding torch	wheat bulb fly
warmongering	waterproofer	welfare hotel	wheel and axle
warningfully	water-serpent	welfare state	wheel and deal
warning-piece	water soldier	well-adjusted	wheel balance
warning track	water-soluble	well-affected	wheelchaired
warning-wheel	water spaniel	well and truly	wheel landing

whencesoever
wheresomever
wherethrough
which is which
Whiggishness
while-you-wait
whimperingly
whimsicality
whimsy-whamsy
whip creation
whipperginny
whipping-girl
whipping post
whippoorwill
whip scorpion
whip-tom-kelly
whirly-whirly
whiskered bat
whiskey-water
whisky priest
whisperingly
white admiral
white arsenic
white balance
white-bellied
white-burning
white campion
white-crowned
white currant
white feather
white fingers
whitefishing
white-fronted
Whitehallese
Whitehallism
Whiteheadian
white-knuckle
white-livered
white mustard
white-on-white
whitepainter
white pelican
white pointer
white pomfret
white pudding
White Russian
white sanicle
white scourge
white slavery
White slavery
White's thrush
white stopper
white tea-tree
white-toothed
white truffle
white vitriol
white wagtail
whitewash gum
white wedding
white whiskey
Whitfieldian
whitherwards

whitlow-grass
Whitmanesque
who goes there
whole-earther
wholehearted
whole holiday
whoops-a-daisy
whortleberry
wibbly-wobbly
wicket-keeper
wicketkeeper
wide-reaching
wide receiver
wifelessness
wife-swapping
wiggle-waggle
wiggly-waggly
wild angelica
wild bergamot
wild chestnut
wild cinnamon
wild hyacinth
wild Irishman
wildlife park
wild marjoram
wild valerian
Wild West show
wild Williams
Wilhelminian
Williamsburg
will-o'-the-wisp
willow beauty
willow beetle
willow grouse
willow-leaved
willow myrtle
willy wagtail
willy-willies
Wilson's snipe
wimble-wamble
wimbly-wambly
win by a canvas
winding-sheet
windlessness
Windmill Hill
windmill-like
wind of change
window-screen
window-washer
wind-scorpion
Windsor brick
Windsor chair
wind-splitter
wind-stocking
windwardmost
windwardness
wine fountain
wineglassful
wing-adjutant
wing-clapping
winged oyster
winglessness

wing-shooting
win in a canter
winkle-picker
winning-chair
win one's spurs
winter annual
winter barley
winterbourne
winter cherry
winter-fallow
winter-flying
winter garden
Winterhalter
winterliness
winter packet
winter savory
winter sports
winter squash
winter-weight
wire mattress
wire recorder
wire-stitched
wire-stitcher
wire-strainer
wire stripper
Wisconsinite
wish-thinking
witches' broom
witch-hunting
witching hour
with a witness
withdrawable
withdrawment
witheredness
withholdable
withholdment
with impunity
within limits
within reason
withinside of
with interest
with one eye on
with one mouth
with one's will
with one voice
with open arms
without a name
without avail
without cease
without delay
without doors
without doubt
without limit
without price
without shame
without tears
with pleasure
with this view
witness-stand
Wolffian body
Wolffian duct
wollastonite

womanishness
woman of ideas
woman of means
woman of sense
woman's estate
woman's rights
woman trouble
women's libber
women's rights
wonder-monger
wonder-struck
wonder-worker
wondrousness
Woodburytype
wooden dagger
wood engraver
wooden-headed
wooden nutmeg
wooden tongue
wood hyacinth
woodmancraft
wood-pheasant
wool-classing
woolly-headed
woolly monkey
Woolworthian
word-category
word-deafness
word division
wordlessness
word-medially
word of honour
word-painting
wordsmanship
workableness
worker priest
work function
work furlough
working class
working hours
working lunch
working model
working order
working party
working space
working title
working woman
worklessness
work-mistress
work one's will
works council
World English
world history
world of words
world-ranking
world-shaking
worm charming
worm-conveyor
worm pipefish
worm's-eye view
wormwood-beer
worry oneself

worry through
worshipfully
worthfulness
Woulfe bottle
wound hormone
wranglership
wrathfulness
wreck-fishing
wrecking ball
Wrenaissance
wretchedness
wriggle out of
wrinkledness
wrinkle ridge
write out fair
write-protect
writer's block
writer's cramp
writing block
writing-board
writing paper
writing speed
writing-table
wrongfulness
wrong side out
wunderkinder
xanthelasmic
xanthic oxide
xanthochroic
xanthochroid
xanthomatous
xanthopterin
xanthorrhoea
xenoantibody

Xenophontean
xiphisternal
xiphisternum
X-irradiation
X-radiography
X-ray analysis
X-ray spectrum
xylobalsamum
xylographica
xylographist
Yankee Doodle
yellow baboon
yellow-billed
yellow George
yellow ground
yellowhammer
yellow-headed
yellow horned
yellow jacket
yellow jersey
yellow Monday
Yellow Monday
yellow pepper
yellow poplar
yellow rattle
yellow rocket
yellow-rumped
yellow streak
yellowthroat
yellow tissue
Yeoman Ushers
yeoman waiter
Yeoman Warder
yieldingness

Yindjibarndi
yo-heave-hoing
Yokohama fowl
Yom Kippur War
York shilling
Yorkshire fog
Yorkshireism
Yorkshireman
Yorkshiremen
Yorkshire pud
you don't say so
you never know
Young America
Young England
young-girlish
young hopeful
young-ladydom
young-ladyish
young manhood
young-mannish
you're another
your good self
you should see
youthfulness
yttrium metal
zamindarship
Zeeman effect
Zend-Avestaic
Zener voltage
zenith sector
zeolitically
zero-crossing
zeta function
zeugmatogram

Ziegfeld girl
Ziehl–Neelsen
zinc chloride
zinc chromate
zincographer
zincographic
zinc ointment
zinc sulphide
zonal defence
zone leveller
zone refining
zonule of Zinn
zoochemistry
zoochlorella
zoogeography
zoographical
zoologically
zoomagnetism
zoomechanics
zoomorphosed
zoopathology
zoophytology
zoosemiotics
zootomically
zooxanthella
zuppa di pesce
zuppa inglese
Zwinglianism
zwitterionic
zygapophysis
zygomorphism
zygomorphous
zygomycetous
zymotechnics

THIRTEEN LETTERS

Abbe condenser
Aberdeen Angus
abiogenically
abiologically
a bit of crumpet
abnormalities
aboriginality
abortifacient
about one's ears
above one's bend
above one's head
above reproach
Abraham's bosom
absence of mind
absolute music
absolute pitch
absolute value
absorbability
abstentionism
abstentionist
abstractional
abstractively
Abyssinian cat
Academy figure
accelerograph
accelerometer
acceptability
acceptilation
accessibility
accidentality
accident-prone
acclimatation
acclimatement
accommodating
accommodation
accommodative
accommodatory
accompaniment
accordingly as
account holder
accreditation
accretion disc
acculturation
acculturative
accustomation
acetaminophen
acetification
acetylcholine
aches and pains
achievability
achromaticity
achromatopsia
achromatopsic
acidification
acorn barnacle
acotyledonous
acquiescently

acquiescingly
acquired taste
acquisitional
acquisitively
acrimoniously
acrobatically
acronymically
across country
acrylonitrile
acting version
actinomorphic
actinomycosis
actinomycotic
actinotherapy
actino-uranium
actionability
action of a verb
active citizen
active service
active volcano
act of oblivion
Act of Sederunt
actual cautery
actualization
acupuncturist
adaptableness
Addressograph
a demon for work
adenoidectomy
adiabatically
adjustability
adjutant stork
admeasurement
admensuration
administrable
administrator
admirableness
admiralissimo
admissibility
admonishingly
Adnyamathanha
adrenal cortex
adrenalectomy
adsorbability
adult suffrage
advanced guard
advanced level
advantage game
adventuresome
adventurously
adversatively
advertisement
advisableness
aerial torpedo
aerobiologist
aerodynamical
aerogenerator

aesthetically
affectability
affenpinscher
affinity group
affirmatively
afflicted with
affordability
afforestation
affreightment
African pepper
African violet
African walnut
Afro-Caribbean
after a fashion
after the event
again and again
against nature
against the sun
agents-general
Age of Aquarius
agglomeration
agglomerative
agglutinating
agglutination
agglutinative
aggradational
aggravatingly
agonistically
a good day's work
a good question
agranulocytic
agreeableness
agree to differ
agriculturist
agrimensorial
agrobiologist
agronomically
aha experience
a hard row to hoe
a hundred to one
aides-mémoires
aircraftwoman
aircraftwomen
airs and graces
airworthiness
à la bonne femme
à la Florentine
à la fourchette
à la Portugaise
a laugh a minute
alchemistical
alcoholically
alcoholometer
alcoholometry
aldosteronism
alectryomancy
algebraically

a lion in the way
alisphenoidal
alkaline earth
alkaline metal
allegorically
allelomorphic
Allhallowmass
All Hallows' Day
Allhallowtide
alligator clip
alligator pear
alligator weed
all in a tremble
all in good time
allochthonous
all of a tremble
allowableness
all the day long
all-wheel drive
a long row to hoe
a losing streak
alpha and omega
Alpha and Omega
alphabetarian
alphabetiform
alpha globulin
alpha particle
alterableness
alternatingly
alternatively
altiplanation
aluminium foil
aluminization
aluminothermy
alveolar ridge
a matter of fact
a matter of form
ambassadorial
ambidexterity
ambiguousness
ambisexuality
ambisonically
ambitiousness
American cloth
American dream
American olive
American organ
American robin
American tiger
amitriptyline
amniocenteses
amniocentesis
amniotic fluid
amorphousness
amphibologies
amphidiploidy
amphiprostyle

amphisbaenian
amphitheatric
amplification
amplificatory
amplitudinous
amusement park
anachronistic
anaerobically
anagrammatise
anagrammatism
anagrammatist
anagrammatize
anal retention
anal-retentive
analysability
anaphorically
anaphrodisiac
anaphylactoid
anathematical
anathematizer
anatomization
anchorpersons
ancient Briton
Ancient Church
ancient lights
and all the rest
androdioecism
anecdotically
anencephalous
an eye for an eye
anfractuosity
angel food cake
angelicalness
angioneurotic
angiospermous
angle brackets
angle of attack
angle of repose
Anglicization
Anglo-American
Anglo-Catholic
Anglo-Normanic
Anglo-Saxondom
Anglo-Saxonism
angostura bark
angry young man
anharmonicity
animadversion
animalization
animal kingdom
animal spirits
anisometropia
anisometropic
annexationist
anniversaries
anniversarily
anomalousness
anonymousness
answerability
antenniferous
antepenultima
anterolateral

anthelminthic
anthocyanidin
anthophyllite
anthracothere
anthraquinone
anthropically
anthropogenic
anthropoid ape
anthropolatry
anthropologic
anthropometer
anthropometry
anthropomorph
anthropopathy
anthropophagi
anthropophagy
anthroposophy
anti-apartheid
anti-attrition
antibacterial
antichristian
anticlimactic
anticlinorium
anticlockwise
anticoagulant
anticoagulate
anti-communist
antigenically
antihistamine
antilogarithm
antimonic acid
antimony ochre
antinomianism
anti-personnel
antiphonaries
antipsychotic
antique-dealer
antiquitarian
antiresonance
antiscorbutic
antisocialism
antisociality
antispasmodic
antisymmetric
anybody's guess
anythingarian
apathetically
aperiodically
aphrodisiacal
apocalyptical
apocatastasis
apodictically
apokatastasis
apolausticism
apomictically
apoplectic fit
apoplectiform
Apostles' Creed
apostolically
apotelesmatic
appealability
appear in print

appellatively
appendiculate
apple-pie order
apple-polisher
Appleton layer
applicability
apportionable
apportionment
apprehensible
apprehensibly
appropinquate
appropinquity
appropriately
appropriation
appropriative
approximately
approximation
approximative
April Fool's Day
April Fools' Day
apron conveyor
aqueous humour
arabic numeral
Arabic numeral
arachnoiditis
arachnologist
arachnophobia
arachnophobic
arbitrariness
arboriculture
archaeography
archaeologian
archaeologise
archaeologist
archaeologize
archaeometric
archaeopteryx
archangelical
archbishopric
archdeaconess
archidiaconal
archimandrite
archipelagoes
archiphonemic
architectonic
architectress
architectural
archpresbyter
Arctic skipper
Ardington Wick
areolar tissue
areopagitical
argentiferous
argumentation
argumentative
aristocracies
aristocratism
aristocratize
aristological
arithmantical
arithmetician
arithmomaniac

armamentarium
armed bullhead
armed services
armour-plating
army of reserve
a roll in the hay
aromatization
arrhenotokous
arrière-pensée
arsenious acid
arseniuretted
art and mystery
artefactually
arteriography
arteriovenous
articled clerk
artificialism
artificiality
artificialize
arts and crafts
arty-and-crafty
arundinaceous
as a last resort
as bald as a coot
as bold as brass
ascending node
Ascensiontide
ascertainable
ascertainably
ascertainment
as deaf as a post
as far as it goes
as good as a play
as hard as nails
as heavy as lead
a shingle short
Ashkenazic Jew
a shot in the arm
ask for trouble
as large as life
as likely as not
as long as my arm
a small fortune
as meek as a lamb
asparagus fern
aspergillosis
a sport of terms
a sport of words
as right as rain
assassination
assault-at-arms
assault course
assembly rooms
assertibility
assertiveness
assertorially
assertory oath
assessionable
asset-stripper
assiduousness
assistantship
assisted place

associability
associateship
associational
associatively
associativity
as sure as death
Assyriologist
astereognosia
astereognosis
asthenosphere
as thin as a rail
as thin as a rake
as things stand
asthmatically
astonishingly
astral spirits
astrometrical
astronautical
astrophysical
astrotheology
at a full gallop
at a single heat
atavistically
at full stretch
atheistically
a tight squeeze
Atlantic Ocean
atlas vertebra
at loggerheads
atmospherical
at no allowance
atomic physics
atomic warfare
atomistically
at one's leisure
at one's own risk
at one's wits' end
atrabilarious
at right angles
atrociousness
at short notice
attainability
attemperament
attemperation
attention span
attentiveness
at the earliest
at the furthest
at the long last
at the same time
attitudinizer
attributively
a tub for a whale
auction bridge
auctioneering
audaciousness
audio cassette
Auger electron
aurora polaris
aurum mosaicum
Australianism
Australianize

Austrian brier
autecological
authentically
authenticator
authenticness
authoritarian
authoritative
authorization
autobiography
autocatalysis
autocatalytic
autocephalous
autochthonous
autodigestion
auto-eroticism
autographical
autohypnotism
auto-infection
auto-infective
automatically
autonomically
autoradiogram
autoxidizable
autumn equinox
autumn gentian
auxanographic
auxiliary verb
availableness
avalanche lily
Averroistical
a wipe in the eye
a woman's reason
a word and a blow
a worm will turn
axiologically
axiomata media
axiomatically
babbling brook
baby-snatching
baccalaureate
bachelor party
bachelor's hall
bachelor's wife
back-formation
back-scratcher
backwardation
backward point
bacteriocidal
bacteriologic
bacteriolysin
bacteriolysis
bacteriolytic
bacteriophage
bacterization
Bactrian camel
bad conscience
badger-baiting
bad-temperedly
Baedeker raids
bag and baggage
balance of mind
balance spring

Balkanization
ballistically
ball lightning
balloon-flower
balloon sleeve
ballroom dance
balneological
balneotherapy
balsamiferous
Balto-Slavonic
bamboo curtain
bamboozlement
Bank of England
bank statement
baptismal name
baptismal vows
baptism of fire
Barbados pride
barbarization
barbarousness
Barbary falcon
barbecue sauce
Barbour jacket
barefacedness
barfly jumping
bargain-hunter
barnacle goose
barnyard grass
baroclinicity
barrack square
barrel-chested
barrier method
bartonellosis
basal ganglion
bascule bridge
basibranchial
basic industry
basidiomycete
basioccipital
basso cantante
basso continuo
basso ostinato
basso profundo
bastard indigo
bastard-trench
bastardy order
bateleur eagle
bathing beauty
baton sinister
batrachotoxin
battle-cruiser
battlecruiser
battle fatigue
batwing sleeve
Bavarian cream
be a big girl now
beaked parsley
Beaker Culture
beam-compasses
beam in one's eye
bearded collie
bear repeating

bear suspicion
bear testimony
bear the stroke
bear witness to
beast of burden
be a stranger to
beat frequency
beat hell out of
beatification
beat the bounds
beat the pistol
beat the record
Beaufort scale
beauteousness
beautifulness
beauty contest
beauty parlour
be booked solid
be bound up with
be caught short
bed of sickness
bedside manner
beetle-crusher
before the beam
before the fact
before the mast
before the wind
be friends with
begging letter
beginner's luck
beginningless
begin the dance
begin the world
be hard put to do
be hard put to it
behave towards
behaviourally
behind the veil
behind the wire
be in a mood with
being-in-itself
be in the secret
believability
Belisha beacon
belles-lettres
belligerently
bellows-blower
bellows pocket
bellows to mend
belongingness
be lost without
below the chair
belt and braces
belt the bottle
benchmark test
benday process
bend one's elbow
beneath the sun
benedictional
beneficential
beneficiaries
beneficiation

benightedness
benign neglect
be nothing like
be off one's oats
be on the market
be possessed of
be quartered by
Berenice's Hair
Berkeleianism
Berlin pattern
Bermuda shorts
be rolling in it
beseemingness
beside oneself
beside the mark
be skin and bone
be snowed under
be spoiling for
be spoons about
best end of neck
be that as it may
be the making of
Beth Hamidrash
be through with
be torn between
betting office
between-whiles
bewilderingly
be with a person
beyond dispute
beyond example
beyond measure
beyond the pale
beyond the seas
beyond the veil
Bible-punching
Bible-thumping
bibliographer
bibliographic
bibliometrics
bibliothecary
bibliotherapy
bicentenaries
bidding prayer
bidimensional
bidirectional
big-headedness
big white chief
Bildungsroman
bimillenaries
binary fission
binary measure
binding energy
Binitarianism
biochemically
biocompatible
biodegradable
bio-electrical
bio-energetics
bioenergetics
biogeographer
biogeographic

biomechanical
biometrically
biophysically
biospeleology
biostatistics
biosynthesize
biosystematic
biotechnology
bipinnatisect
Bird of Freedom
bird of passage
bird sanctuary
bird's nest soup
birefringence
birthday party
biscuit barrel
bismuth glance
bite by the nose
bite one's nails
bite on granite
bite the bullet
bite the ground
bit of all right
bit-part player
bits and pieces
bitter cassava
black and white
black antimony
blackberrying
black bindweed
black-eyed bean
blackguardism
black mangrove
black mulberry
blacksmithery
blacksmithing
black-throated
bladder of lard
blamelessness
blanket finish
blanket flower
blanket stitch
blasphemously
blast freezing
blastogenesis
blastomycosis
blaze the trail
blear-eyedness
blear the eye of
bleeding heart
bleed like a pig
blended whisky
blennorrhagia
blepharoplast
blepharospasm
bless her heart
blind man's buff
blind stamping
blister-beetle
blister blight
blister copper
block capitals

block-faulting
block mountain
blood-curdling
blood-grouping
bloodlessness
blood pressure
blood relation
blood relative
bloodshedding
blood-vein moth
bloody warrior
Bloomfieldian
Bloomsburyite
Bloomsbury set
blotting paper
blow great guns
blow one's stack
blue beat music
blue-green alga
blue in the face
blunderheaded
board and board
boarding house
boatswain bird
bob's your uncle
Bob's your uncle
bodice-ripping
body corporate
body-snatching
boiled lobster
boil the kettle
bombastically
Bomber Command
bone turquoise
bony labyrinth
booking office
boon companion
booster rocket
boot and saddle
boraginaceous
bord and pillar
Border terrier
born in wedlock
boroughmonger
borrowed light
borrow trouble
botanographer
bougainvillea
bouillabaisse
boundary layer
boundary rider
boundary value
boundlessness
bounteousness
bountifulness
boustrophedon
bowel movement
bowler's wicket
bowling crease
bowstring hemp
box the compass
boysenberries

brachiosaurus
brachycephaly
brachydactyly
brachypterous
bracket fungus
brainlessness
brainstorming
braising steak
brake-cylinder
branchial arch
branchial tuft
branchiomeric
branch library
branch officer
brass farthing
brassicaceous
brave new world
brazen-facedly
breach of faith
bread and water
break and enter
breakfastless
breaking point
break one's duck
break one's fast
break one's head
break one's wind
break one's word
break short off
break the habit
break the mould
break to pieces
breast the tape
breathe freely
breathing-room
bred in the bone
Breeches Bible
breech-loading
breithauptite
brevet captain
breviloquence
Brewster angle
bridge-builder
bridge circuit
bridge of asses
bridge of boats
bridge passage
brilliantined
brimstone moth
brimstone-wort
bring into line
bring into play
bring to anchor
bring to effect
bring to market
bring to naught
bring to nought
bring to reason
bring up to date
Britannically
Briticisation
Briticization

British Empire
British Legion
broad ligament
broad-mindedly
broad spectrum
Broca's aphasia
Brock's benefit
broken-hearted
bromeliaceous
Brompton stock
bronchial tree
bronchiolitis
bronchography
bronchophonic
bronchorrhoea
bronchoscopic
brontosaurian
brother german
brother-in-arms
brotherliness
brotherly love
brothers-in-law
Brownie Guider
Browningesque
brown thrasher
brushed fabric
brush kangaroo
brutalitarian
brutalization
brute creation
brutification
bryologically
bryozoologist
bubble chamber
bubonic plague
budget account
buffalo clover
buffalo runner
building-block
building-brick
building-lease
bulbo-urethral
bulletin board
bullock's heart
bulrush millet
bumper sticker
bumptiousness
bungee jumping
burden of proof
bureaucracies
bureaucratise
bureaucratize
burghermaster
burglariously
Burgundy pitch
burial service
burn one's boats
burn one's ships
burn to a cinder
burnt offering
bursting point
burst its banks

burying beetle
burying ground
bush carpenter
bush cranberry
bush telegraph
business cycle
business hours
business lunch
business widow
businesswoman
businesswomen
business world
butcher's broom
butcher's knife
butobarbitone
butter-and-eggs
butter-fingers
butterfly bush
butterfly fish
butterfly kiss
butterfly nose
butterfly weed
button one's lip
button-through
butyrophenone
buy oneself out
buy on the stump
by acclamation
by all accounts
by analogy with
by appointment
by implication
by night and day
by word of mouth
cabbalistical
Cabernet Franc
cabinet-making
cabinetmaking
cable moulding
cacographical
cacophonously
cadmium yellow
Caesaro-papism
caespititious
calcification
calculability
calculatingly
calculational
calendar month
calico-printer
calligraphist
call into being
callisthenics
callithumpian
call to account
call to witness
calorifically
Calvinistical
Cambridge blue
camera lucidas
camera obscura
campaign trail

campanologist
campanularian
Campeachy wood
camphor laurel
campylobacter
Canada thistle
canaliculated
canary creeper
cancerousness
candidateship
candle-snuffer
Canes Venatici
canicular days
canicular year
canine madness
cannabis resin
cannibalistic
canonical hour
canonicalness
Canterbury hoe
cantonization
can you tie that
capaciousness
Cape buffaloes
Capernaitical
capitation fee
caprification
Captain Cooker
captivatingly
carbon dioxide
carboniferous
carbonization
carbonylation
carboxylation
carburization
carcinologist
carcinomatous
cardboard city
cardiac arrest
cardinalatial
cardinalitial
cardinal point
cardinal vicar
cardinal vowel
cardiographer
cardiographic
cardiological
careers master
cargo trousers
cariogenicity
Carnaby Street
carnal members
carnification
carnivalesque
carnivorously
carpenter-work
carpet bombing
carpet slipper
carpet sweeper
carriage clock
carriage trade
carrier pigeon

carrion-beetle
carrion flower
carrying-place
carrying trade
carte-de-visite
cartelization
cartilaginoid
cartilaginous
cartridge belt
cartridge-case
car washeteria
casement cloth
cash dispenser
Cassegrainian
Cassinian oval
cast a veil over
casting-bottle
castle-builder
castle in Spain
castle pudding
castor oil bean
casuistically
catalytically
catastrophism
catastrophist
catch at a straw
catchment area
catch on the hop
catch-question
catch the eye of
catch unawares
catechistical
catecholamine
catechumenate
categorematic
categorically
cater-cornered
cathartically
cathedral city
cat-o'-nine-tails
catoptromancy
cattle-rustler
catty-cornered
cattycornered
caustic potash
cauterization
cavernicolous
cayenne pepper
ceaselessness
celebrational
celery-top pine
celestial body
celestial pole
cellular phone
cellular plant
cellular radio
centesimation
Central Powers
centre fielder
centre forward
centrifugally
centripetally

cephalic index
cephalization
cephalometric
cephalopelvic
cephalopodous
cephalosporin
cephalothorax
cerebral palsy
cerebrospinal
ceremonialism
ceremonialist
ceremonialize
ceremonial law
ceremoniously
certification
certificatory
certified mail
certified milk
cervical smear
cervicofacial
Cetti's warbler
Chagas' disease
chain reaction
chair of estate
chaise longues
chalcenterous
chalcographer
chalcographic
chalcophanite
chalkhill blue
challengeable
challengingly
chamber-deacon
chamber-fellow
chamber of dais
chameleon-like
champ at the bit
chancelleries
chancel-screen
chance-medleys
chance one's arm
chancery court
changeability
changefulness
change of front
change of heart
change of scene
change-ringing
Channel Tunnel
chaparral cock
characterizer
characterless
character part
charge account
charge-capping
charge carrier
charge density
charity school
charity walker
charlatanical
charm bracelet
charmlessness

charter flight
charter member
Charter School
chartographer
chase one's tail
chasseur sauce
chateaubriand
Chattertonian
cheap and nasty
cheat the widdy
checkweighman
cheerlessness
cheese-skipper
cheiloplastic
chemical shift
chemisorption
chemoreceptor
chequered flag
Cherokee Strip
Chestertonian
chest-expander
chestnut brown
chevaleresque
chiaroscurist
Chickasaw plum
chicken-and-egg
chicken-breast
chickenburger
chieftaincies
chieftainship
child guidance
childlessness
childlikeness
child molester
children's hour
chilli relleno
chimney breast
chimney-corner
china-mark moth
China syndrome
Chinese puzzle
chinkerinchee
Chinook jargon
Chinook Jargon
chinook salmon
Chinook salmon
chiromantical
chi-square test
chitinization
chlamydomonas
chlamydospore
chlorocruorin
Chloromycetin
chocolate-boxy
chocolate chip
chocolate drop
chocolate-tree
choir practice
cholecystitis
cholera morbus
choo-choo train
chop and change

chopping-block
chopping-board
choral service
choral society
choreographer
choreographic
chorepiscopal
chorepiscopus
choripetalous
choristership
choroid plexus
choropleth map
chose in action
chowderheaded
chrestomathic
Christianable
Christianlike
Christian name
Christian year
Christmas bush
Christmas cake
Christmas card
Christmas rose
Christmas-tide
Christmas tree
Christologist
chromatically
chromatograph
chromatolysis
chromatophore
chrome leather
chrome tanning
chromium-plate
chromium steel
chromoprotein
chromosomally
chromosome map
chromospheric
chronobiology
chronographer
chronographic
chronological
chrysanthemum
chuck-farthing
chuckleheaded
Church Fathers
Churchilliana
churchmanlike
churchmanship
church service
chylification
cicatrization
Ciceronianism
cigarette card
cigarette-case
ciliary muscle
cinematically
cinematograph
cinnamon stone
cinnamon toast
cinquecentist
circumambages

circumambient
Circumcellion
circumduction
circumference
circumfluence
circumjacence
circumjacency
circumscriber
circumspectly
circumstanced
circumtabular
circumvallate
circumvention
civet de lièvre
civil aviation
civil engineer
civil marriage
cladistically
clairaudience
clairschacher
clairvoyantly
clamorousness
clandestinely
clandestinity
clankety-clank
clap on the back
clarification
clarificatory
classed growth
classlessness
claustrophobe
clavicembalos
claw the back of
clay ironstone
cleansing milk
clearance sale
clearing house
clear the coast
clear the decks
cleavage plane
cleavelandite
cleft sentence
clerical error
click language
climacterical
climactically
climatologist
climbing frame
climbing perch
clincher-built
cling together
clinical death
clinopinacoid
clinopyroxene
cliometrician
clish-ma-claver
cliticization
cloak-and-sword
clock-watching
cloister-garth
closed-circuit
closed society

close mourning
close one's ears
close one's eyes
close quarters
close the books
clothes-hanger
cloth of estate
cloth of silver
clouded yellow
cloudlessness
clubbableness
coach-building
coadjutorship
coagulability
coalification
coarse fishing
coarse-grained
coast of the sea
coast sickness
cobaltiferous
co-belligerent
cocainization
cochleariform
cock an eyebrow
cockatoo fence
cocker spaniel
Cockney School
cock-of-the-rock
cock-of-the-walk
cock-of-the-wood
cockspur grass
cockspur thorn
cocktail dress
cocktail-mixer
cocktail onion
cocktail party
cocktail stick
cock-throppled
co-consciously
coconut butter
codeterminant
codicological
co-educational
coeducational
coelacanthine
coenaesthesia
coenaesthesis
coercive force
coessentially
coextensively
coffee essence
coffee grinder
coffee grounds
coffee morning
cognate object
cognizability
cognomination
co-inheritance
cold as charity
cold-bloodedly
cold-heartedly
cold in the head

collaboration
collaborative
collard greens
collar of esses
collateralise
collaterality
collateralize
colleagueship
collectedness
collectorship
college living
College of Arms
collieshangie
colligability
collisionally
collisionless
collocability
collocational
colloquialism
colloquialist
colloquiality
colonial goose
colonoscopies
colourability
colourfulness
colour hearing
colouring book
colourization
column of route
Coma Berenices
combat fatigue
combativeness
combinability
combinational
combinatorial
combinatorics
combining form
combretaceous
come in one's way
come into force
come near doing
come out strong
come short home
come to a bad end
come to nothing
come to the fore
come up against
come up smiling
comfortlessly
comma bacillus
commandership
command module
commeasurable
commemoration
commemorative
commensurable
commensurably
commentitious
commercial art
commercialese
commercialise
commercialism

commercialist
commerciality
commercialize
commiseration
commiserative
commit suicide
commit to paper
commonalities
common carrier
common council
Common Council
common hamster
commonization
common-law wife
common opinion
common pompano
common sensory
common soldier
communalistic
communication
communicative
communicatory
Communion-rail
communitarian
communitorium
community home
communization
commutability
commutatively
commutativity
compactedness
compagination
companionable
companionably
companion-cell
companionhood
companionless
companionship
companion star
comparability
comparatively
comparativist
compartmental
compass course
compassionate
compass timber
compass window
compatibility
compatriotism
compendiously
competitioner
competitively
competitivity
complainingly
complementary
complex number
complicatedly
complimentary
Complutensian
compositeness
compositional
compositorial

compound fruit
compound order
compound umbel
comprehension
comprehensive
compressed air
compressional
compromission
comprovincial
Compton effect
computability
computational
computer-aided
computer virus
comrade-in-arms
comradeliness
concameration
concatenation
concavo-convex
concealed land
conceitedness
concentration
concentrative
concentricity
conceptionist
conceptualise
conceptualism
conceptualist
conceptualize
concernedness
concertinaing
concert master
concessionary
concessionist
conchological
concomitantly
concordantial
concrete mixer
concrete music
concrete verse
concretionary
concupiscence
concupiscible
condemned cell
condensed milk
condescending
condescension
conditionally
conduciveness
conducted tour
conductitious
conductometer
conductometry
conductor rail
conductorship
condylomatous
confabulation
confabulatory
confarreation
confectionary
confectionery
confederacies

confederation
confederative
confessionary
confessionist
confessorship
confidence man
confidingness
configuration
configurative
confiscatable
conflagration
conflagrative
confraternity
confrontation
confusability
conglomeratic
conglomerator
conglomeritic
congratulator
congressional
Congress Party
congresswoman
congresswomen
Congreve match
congruousness
conjecturable
conjecturally
conjugal rites
conjugate acid
conjugate axis
conjugate base
conjugational
conjunctional
conjunctively
conjunct proof
conjure doctor
connaturality
connaturalize
connectedness
connecting rod
Connemara pony
connotational
connotatively
connumeration
conquistadors
consanguineal
consanguinean
consanguinity
conscientious
consciousness
consecutively
consenescence
consentaneity
consentaneous
consequential
conservancies
conservatoire
conservatoria
conservatorio
considerately
consideration
consideringly

consimilarity
consistometer
consolamentum
consolidation
consolidatory
conspicuously
conspiratress
constableship
constablewick
Constantinian
constellation
constellatory
consternation
constituently
constrainable
constrainedly
constringency
constructible
consuetudinal
consul general
consultancies
consumer goods
consumeristic
consumptively
contabescence
contact flight
contact screen
container port
container ship
contamination
contaminative
contemplation
contemplative
contentedness
contentiously
contextualise
contextualism
contextualist
contextualize
continentally
contingencies
contingential
continualness
continuity man
contortionist
contrabandist
contrabassist
contra-bassoon
contraception
contraceptive
contractility
contractional
contractually
contradiction
contradictive
contradictory
contrafactual
contrafagotto
contrafissure
contraflexure
contralateral
contranatural

contrapuntist
contrariantly
contrariously
contrary terms
contrastingly
contrastively
contrate wheel
contravariant
contravention
contrectation
contributable
controversial
controversies
controversion
controvertist
convalescence
convalescency
convalidation
conventionary
conventioneer
conventionist
convent school
conversazione
conversionism
conversionist
convertiplane
convexo-convex
convocational
convolutional
convolvuluses
convulsionary
convulsionist
cool one's heels
cooperatively
cooperativity
co-partnership
copartnership
Copernicanism
copia verborum
copper-captain
copper pyrites
copper vitriol
co-precipitate
copying-pencil
copyrightable
coralligenous
core implement
co-religionist
coriander seed
Corinthianism
Corinthianize
corkscrew rule
corn buttercup
corner-forward
cornification
Cornish boiler
Cornish chough
Cornish engine
corno da caccia
coronagraphic
coronal suture
coronation mug

coronoid fossa
corporalities
corporate name
corporate town
corporational
corporativism
corps de ballet
corpse-reviver
Corpus Christi
corpusculated
corpus delicti
Correggiesque
correlational
correlatively
correlativity
correspondent
corresponding
corresponsive
corridor train
corrigibility
corroboration
corroborative
corroboratory
corrodability
corrodibility
corrosibility
corrosiveness
corruptedness
corruptionist
corticotropin
corymbiferous
cosignatories
cosmetologist
cosmochemical
cosmographies
cosmographist
cosmopolitism
co-sovereignty
cost-conscious
cost-effective
cost-efficient
costermongery
costly colours
co-trimoxazole
Cotswold sheep
cottage-bonnet
cottage cheese
cottage garden
cottier tenure
cotton batting
cotton flannel
cotton-picking
cotton-spinner
cotton-stainer
cotton-thistle
cough medicine
council estate
council school
countable noun
counteractant
counteraction
counteractive

counter-agency
counter-attack
counter-caster
counterchange
countercharge
counter-enamel
counter-extend
counter-faller
counterfeiter
counterfeitly
counterfleury
counter-gobony
counter-jumper
countermander
counter-marque
countermelody
counter-motion
counterpoison
counter-potent
counter-rhythm
counterrotate
counter-secure
counter-stroke
counterstroke
counterweight
counterworker
counting-frame
counting house
Count Palatine
country cousin
country-people
county borough
county council
county cricket
county library
coupling-reins
coupon-clipper
coup the creels
court bouillon
court circular
court cupboard
courteousness
courtesanship
courtesy light
courtesy title
Court of Appeal
Court of Arches
Court of Claims
court of record
court of review
courts martial
cousins german
covered bridge
cover one's feet
covert coating
covert feather
coxcombically
crab-apple tree
cracked up to be
cracker-barrel
cradle to grave
craftsmanship

cranberry bush
cranberry tree
crane-coloured
craniological
crapulousness
crash-helmeted
crazy like a fox
cream-coloured
cream of tartar
credence table
credentialled
creditability
credit account
credit squeeze
credulousness
creedlessness
creeping Jenny
creeping Jesus
creeping palsy
crème caramels
crème de cassis
crème de menthe
crèmes brûlées
crèmes caramel
Cremnitz white
crêpes Suzette
cribbage board
cribbage-faced
cricket ground
Crimean Gothic
crime-fighting
criminal court
criminalistic
criminal libel
criminologist
criminousness
crimson clover
critical angle
critical point
crocodile bird
crocodile clip
Crohn's disease
crop husbandry
cross-bearings
cross crosslet
cross-cultural
cross-division
cross-dressing
cross-examiner
cross-gartered
crossmatching
cross one's face
cross one's mind
cross one's path
crossover vote
cross-question
cross-reaction
cross-springer
cross the floor
crotchetiness
crow-blackbird
crowned pigeon

crown imperial
crowning glory
crown of thorns
crown princess
Crown princess
crudification
cruise control
cruise missile
cruiserweight
cruising speed
crustaceology
crusta petrosa
cry for the moon
cryobiologist
cryogenically
cryoturbation
cryptanalysis
cryptanalytic
cryptogrammic
cryptographer
cryptographic
cryptological
cryptozoology
crystal-gazing
crystalliform
crystallinity
crystallogeny
crystalloidal
crystal system
crystal violet
cuboctahedral
cuboctahedron
Cuisenaire rod
cultivability
cultured pearl
culturologist
Cumberland ham
Cumberland pig
cum grano salis
cummingtonite
cumulostratus
cuneiform bone
cupola furnace
curate's friend
curious-minded
currant tomato
Cursitor Baron
curtain-raiser
curvilinearly
cushion stitch
cushla-machree
custard marrow
custard powder
custodianship
customariness
custom clothes
customization
cut a wide swath
cut one's losses
cut the mustard
cut the painter
cyanoacrylate

cyanotrichite
cybernetician
cyberneticist
cycling lizard
cyclo-addition
cyclodialysis
cyclone cellar
cycloparaffin
cyclostrophic
cylinder-bored
cylinder press
cylindraceous
cylindrically
cynocephalous
cypress spurge
cytochemistry
cytogenetical
cytologically
cytomorphosis
cytopathology
dactyliomancy
dactylopodite
daddy-long-legs
daguerreotype
dairy products
damage control
damage-feasant
damnification
Damocles sword
dance barefoot
dancing-master
dancing-school
Dandie Dinmont
dandification
dangerous drug
dangerousness
Dano-Norwegian
Dark Continent
dark of the moon
Darling clover
Darling shower
darning-cotton
darning needle
darning-stitch
dastardliness
data processor
data retrieval
data structure
Daubenton's bat
daughterboard
daughter-in-law
daughter of Eve
dauntlessness
day care centre
dazzle-painted
dead and buried
dead as the dodo
dead man's bells
dead man's pedal
dead man's thumb
dead men's bells
dead men's shoes

dead reckoning
dead to the wide
deaf as an adder
Dean of Faculty
deathlessness
death sentence
death-stricken
deattribution
debating point
debauchedness
debenture bond
debt collector
decapsulation
decarboxylate
deceitfulness
decelerometer
decentralizer
deceptibility
deceptiveness
decerebration
deciduousness
decimal system
deck passenger
declamatorily
declaratively
declericalize
declinational
declivitously
decolouration
decompensated
decomposition
decompression
decompressive
deconcentrate
deconstructor
decontaminate
decontrolling
deconvolution
Decoration day
Decoration Day
decortication
decrepitation
decriminalise
decriminalize
dedecahedrons
deducibleness
deductibility
deep breathing
deep structure
defamiliarize
defeasibility
defectibility
defectiveness
defencelessly
defensibility
defensiveness
deferentially
deferred share
defervescence
defibrillator
defibrination
deflectometer

deforestation
deformability
deformational
deglutination
degradability
degradational
degranulation
degree Rankine
degrees of cold
dehonestation
dehydroacetic
dehydrogenase
dehydrogenate
dehydrogenize
deipnosophist
delayed action
delectability
deleteriously
Delian problem
deliciousness
delightsomely
delinquencies
deliquescence
deliquescency
deliriousness
deltoid muscle
demand deposit
demand feeding
dematerialise
dematerialize
demerara sugar
demeritorious
demethylation
demi-caractère
demineralizer
demiurgically
demographical
demolitionist
demonographer
demonolatrous
demonological
demon patience
demonstration
demonstrative
demonstratory
demyelination
demythologise
demythologize
denationalise
denationalize
denaturalizer
dendritically
dendrological
densitometric
dental formula
dentalization
dental surgeon
denticulation
deodorization
deontological
deoxygenation
depauperation

dependability
depersonalise
depersonalize
dephlegmation
dephosphorize
depicturement
deplorability
deprecatingly
deprecatively
deprecatorily
depressed area
depth-recorder
derationalize
derecognition
derequisition
derestriction
derivationist
dermatologist
dermatophytic
dermatoplasty
dermographism
descriptively
descriptivism
descriptivist
desegregation
desertization
desert the diet
desert varnish
deserve well of
deservingness
desirableness
desmognathous
desperateness
despicability
destituteness
destructional
destructively
desulphurizer
desultoriness
desuperheater
desynchronize
detachability
detail drawing
detectability
detectibility
detemporalize
deterioration
deteriorative
determinandum
determinantal
determinantia
determinately
determination
determinative
deterministic
detestability
detrimentally
deus ex machina
deuteragonist
deuteranomaly
deuterogamist
Deutero-Isaiah

deuteromerite
devastatingly
developmental
devil's own luck
devirgination
devolutionary
devolutionist
devotionalism
devotionalist
dexamethasone
dexterousness
dharmashastra
diabolization
diacatholicon
diachronistic
diacritically
diageotropism
diagnosticate
diagnostician
diagonal cloth
diagrammatize
dialectically
dialogistical
dial telephone
diametrically
diamondbacked
diamond-cement
diamond-shaped
diamond stitch
diamond willow
dianoetically
diaphonically
diaphragmatic
diaphragm down
diaphragm pump
diaphthoresis
diastatically
diathermanous
diathetically
diazo compound
diazotization
dice with death
dichlamydeous
dichoptically
dichotomously
dictatorially
dieffenbachia
dieselization
diffarreation
differentiate
differentness
difficileness
difficultness
diffractively
diffractogram
diffusibility
diffusiveness
digestibility
digestiveness
dig in one's toes
dig one's feet in
digressionary

dig the grave of
dihedral angle
dimensionally
dimensionless
dimension line
diminishingly
dimorphotheca
dim-wittedness
dinner service
dinner theatre
dioeciousness
Dionysiacally
Diotrephesian
diphenoxylate
diphenylamine
diphthongally
dipleidoscope
diplobacillus
diploid number
diplomatic bag
dipping-needle
dipsomaniacal
dipterologist
direct address
direct current
directionally
directionless
directiveness
direct mailing
direct oration
directorially
disaccordance
disadvantaged
disaffectedly
disaffirmance
disallegiance
disannexation
disappearance
disappointing
disapprovable
disarticulate
disassemblage
disaster movie
disburdenment
discapacitate
dischargeable
discharge lamp
discharge tube
disciplinable
discographies
discoloration
discolourment
discomforture
discommodious
discomposedly
disconcerting
disconcertion
disconformity
disconnection
discontentful
discontinuing
discontinuity

discontinuous
disconvenient
discount house
discount store
discourtesies
discovery well
discreditable
discreditably
discrepancies
discretionary
discriminable
discriminably
discriminator
discussionist
disembodiment
disembowelled
disemployment
disengagement
disentailment
disentombment
disestimation
disfavourable
disfavourably
disfellowship
disfiguration
disfigurement
disfiguringly
disfranchiser
disgracefully
disguisedness
dishabilitate
disharmonious
dishonourable
dishonourably
dish up the dirt
disillusioner
disinheriting
disinhibition
disinhibitory
disintegrable
disintegrator
disinterested
disintoxicate
disinvestment
disinvitation
disjunctively
dislikelihood
dismal Desmond
dismal science
dismantlement
dismemberment
disnaturalize
disobediently
disobligement
disobligingly
disoccupation
disordinately
disordination
disparagement
disparagingly
disparateness
dispassionate

dispatch rider
dispersedness
dispiritingly
displeasingly
disponibility
disposability
dispositional
dispositioned
dispositively
dispossession
dispraisingly
disproportion
dispunishable
disputatively
disquietingly
disregardable
disreputation
disrespectful
disruptionist
dissemblingly
dissemination
dissentaneous
dissepimental
dissepulchred
dissettlement
disseveration
dissimilarity
dissimilation
dissimilatory
dissimilitude
dissimulation
dissipativity
dissolubility
dissoluteness
dissymmetries
distantiation
distant signal
distastefully
distemperedly
disthronement
distinctively
distinguished
distinguisher
distortedness
distortionist
distractingly
distractively
distressfully
distressingly
distributable
distributress
district court
district nurse
distrustfully
disubstituted
disuniformity
dittographies
diurnal circle
diverging lens
divertibility
diverticulate
divertingness

divertisement
divide and rule
dividend yield
divine service
divinity fudge
divisibleness
divisionalise
divisionalize
division lobby
DNA polymerase
do a mischief to
do an ill turn to
do a person dirt
do a person good
Doctor Martens
doctor's orders
doctrinairism
documentalist
documentarian
documentaries
documentarily
documentarist
documentation
documentative
dodderingness
dodecahedrane
dodecaphonist
dogmatization
dog's breakfast
dolichocephal
dolichopellic
dollarization
doll's hospital
dolphinariums
Dome of Silence
domestication
domestic trade
domiciliation
domineeringly
dominical year
dominium utile
done to the wide
donothingness
don't mention it
do oneself well
do one's manners
Doppler effect
do reverence to
dormitory town
dotcom company
do the business
double-banking
double bassoon
double century
double-chinned
double coconut
double-crosser
double-dealing
double density
double digging
double-dipping
double feature

double figures
double-fronted
double glazing
double harness
double-hearted
double-jointed
double meaning
double obelisk
double or quits
double shuffle
double spacing
double tertian
double-tongued
double wedding
doubtlessness
Douglas's pouch
Douglas spruce
dovetail joint
Dow–Jones index
downconverter
downheartedly
Downing Street
downrightness
Down's syndrome
down the course
down to the wire
doxographical
doxologically
do you happen to
dracocephalum
draconic month
dracunculosis
draftsmanship
draggle-tailed
drainage basin
draining board
dramatic irony
dramatization
dramaturgical
drapery artist
draught-bridge
draught-screen
draughtswoman
draw a veil over
drawing-master
drawing-string
draw level with
draw one's steel
draw pig on pork
draw the badger
draw the line at
draw the stumps
dreadlessness
dreamlessness
dree one's weird
dress-carriage
dress-designer
dressed to kill
dress-improver
dressing-chest
dressing table
dribs and drabs

drill-sergeant
drink and drive
drinking water
drink-offering
drink one's fill
dripping crust
dripping toast
drive the green
drive-yourself
driving gloves
droopy drawers
dropping-field
drowned valley
drug addiction
drum majorette
Drummond light
drumstick tree
dryopithecine
dualistically
duchesse satin
duchesse-table
duchess sleeve
ductless gland
dulcification
dull the edge of
Dunkirk spirit
duplicability
Durham mustard
dusting powder
Dutch interior
Dutchman's pipe
dwelling house
dwelling place
dyed in the wool
dynamogenesis
dysfunctional
dysmenorrhoea
dyspeptically
early musician
earth sciences
Eastern Church
Eastern Empire
east-north-east
east-south-east
easy listening
easy on the eyes
eat its head off
eat like a horse
eat the bread of
eau de toilette
ebullioscopic
eccentrically
ecclesiolatry
ecclesiologic
echinopluteus
eco-geographic
econometrical
economization
ectopterygoid
ectrodactylia
ecumenicalism
ecumenicality

edge connector
Edict of Nantes
editor-in-chief
educatability
educated guess
educationally
effectiveness
effectualness
effervescence
effervescency
efficaciously
efficiency bar
efflorescence
egg flower soup
eggheadedness
egg on one's face
eggshell china
egocentricity
ego-psychology
egotistically
egregiousness
Egyptian black
Egyptian goose
Egyptian lotus
Egyptian onion
Egyptian wheel
Egyptological
eigenfunction
eight-day clock
eightsome reel
elaborateness
elanguescence
elasmotherium
elastic tissue
elder brethren
elder-sisterly
electioneerer
electoral roll
electric chair
electric fence
electric field
electric organ
electric razor
electric shock
electric storm
electric torch
electrization
electrocution
electrodeless
electrodermal
electrologist
electromagnet
electrometric
electromotive
electronic tag
electron shell
electro-optics
electrophilic
electrophonic
electrophorus
electroplaque
electroplater

electropolish
electroscopic
electro-silver
electrostatic
electrovalent
elegiac stanza
elephant grass
elephantiasis
elephant paper
elephant's foot
elephant shrew
eliminability
ellipsoidally
elocutionally
Elysian fields
Elysian Fields
embarrassedly
embarrassment
embellishment
embracingness
embranglement
embrittlement
embryogenesis
embryogenetic
embryological
embryonically
emerald cuckoo
emergency exit
Emersonianism
éminence grise
eminent domain
emotionlessly
emotive theory
emphysematous
empire builder
employability
empty calories
emulativeness
emulsion paint
enaliosaurian
enamouredness
enantiodromia
enantiomerism
enantiopathic
enantiotropic
encapsidation
encapsulation
encephalitis C
encephalocele
encephalogram
encomiastical
encompassment
encoppicement
encouragement
encouragingly
enculturation
enculturative
encyclopaedia
encyclopaedic
encyclopedian
encyclopedise
encyclopedism

encyclopedist
encyclopedize
endocrinology
end of the world
endolymphatic
endometriosis
endometriotic
endonormative
endoparasitic
endopeptidase
endopolyploid
endopterygote
endosymbiosis
endosymbiotic
endurableness
energetically
energumenical
enforcibility
engaged signal
engine-turning
English muffin
English setter
English walnut
enhypostatize
enigmatically
enjoyableness
enlightenment
ensorcellment
enteric-coated
enterocolitis
enterohepatic
enter one's head
enter one's mind
enterostomies
Entero-Vioform
entertainable
entertainment
enter the lists
entomological
entomophagous
entomophilous
entomostracan
entoparasitic
entrammelling
entrance wound
enumerability
enumeratively
environmental
enzymatically
enzymological
eosinophilous
epeirogenesis
epeirogenetic
ephemeralness
ephemeris time
epicondylitis
epidemiologic
epidermically
epidermolysis
epidotization
epigrammatise
epigrammatism

epigrammatist
epigrammatize
epileptically
epileptogenic
epimerization
epiphenomenal
epiphenomenon
epiphytically
epiplanktonic
epistemically
epithalamiums
epithetically
epitomization
epitrochoidal
epizootiology
epoxy-compound
Equality State
equestrianism
equianalgesic
equidifferent
equidistantly
equilibration
equilibristic
equimolecular
equipartition
equipollently
equiponderant
equiponderate
equipotential
equitableness
equity capital
equivocalness
equivoluminal
erase facility
ergonomically
eroticization
errand of mercy
erroneousness
erysipelatose
erysipelatous
erythrophobia
escallop-shell
escapological
eschatologist
eschatologize
escheatorship
eschscholtzia
esprit de corps
essentialness
establishable
establishment
estate-bottled
estates bursar
estimableness
estrangedness
etching ground
ethchlorvynol
ethnobotanist
ethnocentrism
ethnocultural
ethnohistoric
ethnolinguist

ethnomedicine
ethnophaulism
ethnosemantic
ethyl chloride
ethylene oxide
ethylenically
Etruscologist
eucalyptus oil
eucatastrophe
Eucharistical
eudiometrical
eugeosyncline
Euler's formula
euphausiacean
euphemistical
euphonization
Eurocommunism
Eurocommunist
European Court
Europocentric
Eurostrategic
eutectic point
eutectiferous
evangelically
evangelistary
evaporability
evaporatively
evasive action
evening breeze
evening prayer
evening school
eventlessness
eventualities
everlastingly
Everton toffee
everybody else
every which way
evocativeness
evolutionally
exaggeratedly
examinability
examinational
examinatorial
exanthematous
exasperatedly
excandescence
exceedingness
exceptionable
exceptionably
exceptionally
exceptionless
excess baggage
excessiveness
excess luggage
excess postage
exchange blows
exchange force
exchange paper
exchange value
exchequer bill
excisemanship
excitableness

exclamatorily
Exclusion Bill
exclusion zone
exclusiveness
exclusivistic
excommunicant
excommunicate
excortication
excrescential
excursion fare
excursiveness
excusableness
excuse oneself
exemplariness
exemplifiable
exhaustedness
exhaust stroke
exhibitionism
exhibitionist
exhortational
existentially
exobiological
ex-officio oath
exothermicity
expandability
expanded metal
expansibility
expansion bolt
expansion card
expansion slot
expansiveness
expectant heir
expectoration
expectorative
expedientness
expeditionary
expeditionist
expeditiously
expendability
expensiveness
explanatorily
explicatively
explicit faith
exploding wire
explorational
exploratively
exploratorium
exploring coil
explosibility
explosive bolt
explosiveness
exponentially
exportability
export surplus
expose oneself
expositionary
expostulation
expostulative
expostulatory
exposure meter
expressionism
expressionist

expropriation
expunctuation
expurgatorial
exquisiteness
exquisitively
exsanguineous
extemporarily
extendability
extendibility
extensibility
extensionally
extensionless
extensiveness
extenuatingly
exterior angle
extermination
exterminative
exterminatory
externalities
external world
externization
exteroceptive
exterritorial
extinguishant
extortionable
extracellular
extra-European
extragalactic
extrajudicial
extraliterary
extra-metrical
extraordinary
extrapolation
extrapolative
extrapolatory
extraposition
extrapunitive
extratropical
extravagantly
extravagation
extravasation
extravascular
extrinsically
extrospective
eyebrow pencil
fabricability
facetiousness
factorization
factor theorem
factory outlet
facultatively
faculty theory
fair and square
Fairlight Clay
fairy thimbles
faithlessness
fall from grace
fall into place
fall off a lorry
fall of the leaf
Fallopian tube
false asphodel

false position
false quantity
false relation
false scorpion
falsification
familiar angel
familiarities
family butcher
fanaticalness
fantastically
fantasticness
Faraday effect
far be it from me
fare indicator
farmer-general
farmhouse loaf
fasciculation
fascinatingly
Fascistically
fashion-monger
fashion victim
fat-headedness
fatiguability
faultlessness
faunistically
feast of reason
feather duster
feather-footed
feather-headed
feather stitch
feather-tailed
feather-tongue
feather-topped
featherweight
feature-length
featureliness
feature writer
fecundability
federationist
fed to the teeth
feeding bottle
feed the fishes
feel one's wings
fellow-citizen
fellow-feeling
fellow soldier
fellow subject
feloniousness
felt-tipped pen
feminine rhyme
femmes fatales
femoral artery
Fennoscandian
ferociousness
ferrimagnetic
ferroconcrete
ferroelectric
ferromagnetic
ferrosoferric
ferrumination
fertilisation
fertilization

fetch a compass
fetch and carry
fête champêtre
fetishization
feudalization
feuilletonist
fibrous tissue
fibrovascular
fiddle pattern
Fiddler's Green
fidepromissor
field bindweed
field-dressing
field emission
field equation
field fleawort
field hospital
field mushroom
field of honour
field of vision
field-preacher
field scabious
field strength
fifteenth part
fifteen-tonner
Fifth Monarchy
fifth position
fifty-year rule
fighter-bomber
fighting chair
fighting conch
fighting drunk
fighting-sails
fighting words
figure-casting
figure-flinger
figure of eight
figure of merit
figure skating
figure weaving
file in the foot
filibusterism
filing cabinet
filmographies
filterability
filter-feeding
filter-passing
final solution
financial year
find fault with
find one's level
find one's match
find one's way to
fine champagne
fine chemicals
fine gentleman
fineness ratio
fine-tooth comb
finger-breadth
finger-pillory
finishing-line
finnan haddock

fire insurance
fires of heaven
fire-swallower
first-classman
first-day cover
first language
first offender
first position
first sergeant
First World War
fisherman's rib
fishing vessel
fissiparously
fit like a glove
five o'clock tea
five positions
flagellantism
flagellomania
flame shoulder
Flanders brick
Flanders poppy
flannel flower
flashing point
flash in the pan
flatulentness
flauto piccolo
fleet marriage
Fleet marriage
flesh and blood
flesh-coloured
fleshing-knife
flight control
flight feather
flight officer
flinty-hearted
flirtatiously
flitter-winged
floating light
floating point
floating voter
floccillation
flood and field
floral diagram
floral formula
floral tribute
Florence flask
Florentine pie
floricultural
floristically
flounderingly
flourishingly
flowering fern
flowering rush
flowers of zinc
flow of spirits
flow structure
fluctuational
flummerdiddle
fluophosphate
fluorescently
flush lavatory
flutter-tongue

fluvioglacial
flying gurnard
flying machine
flying officer
Flying Officer
flying trapeze
fly on the wheel
fly-up-the-creek
focal distance
foetalization
fold one's hands
folk etymology
folkloristics
follow the drum
follow-through
food chemistry
food poisoning
food processor
foolhardiness
fool's paradise
football pools
foot in the door
foot passenger
for a certainty
for a constancy
for all seasons
for a long while
foramen magnum
foraminiferal
foraminiferan
forbiddenness
forced landing
force the issue
fore-and-aft cap
forecastingly
foreconscious
fore-end loader
foregrounding
foreign legion
Foreign Office
forejudgement
foreknowledge
foreordinance
foresightedly
forest wallaby
forget about it
forgetfulness
forget oneself
forgivingness
for good and all
fork-lift truck
formal concept
formalization
formationally
formation-rule
formativeness
form catalogue
form criticism
for mercy's sake
form-historian
formidability
form of address

formulaically
formulization
for once and all
for perpetuity
for preference
for that matter
forthbringing
for the account
for the present
fortification
fortitudinous
fortnightlies
fortunateness
fortune cookie
fortune hunter
Fortune's wheel
fortune-teller
forum shopping
fossiliferous
fossilization
foundationary
founder member
Fourier series
four-poster bed
fowl-paralysis
foxtail millet
fractionalise
fractionalism
fractionalist
fractionalize
fractionation
fractiousness
fragmentarily
fragmentation
frame dwelling
Franciscanism
frankmarriage
fraternal twin
freak of nature
free Communion
free companion
free selection
free to confess
freezing point
freezing works
French cricket
French defence
French disease
French kissing
French morocco
French mustard
French tickler
frequency band
frequentation
frequentative
fresh as a daisy
freshen the nip
fricandeauing
friction-brake
friction match
fridge-freezer
friend at court

friendly match
frighteningly
frightfulness
frilled lizard
fringe benefit
frivolousness
Froebel system
from head to toe
from here on out
from one's heart
from shipboard
from the cradle
from the word go
from wig to wall
frondescently
frontlessness
frontogenesis
frontogenetic
fructuousness
fruitarianism
fruit cocktail
fruitlessness
frumentaceous
frumentarious
frustratingly
fuddle one's cap
fuel injection
fugaciousness
fulfil oneself
full-bloodedly
fuller's teasel
full-fashioned
full-heartedly
full professor
fumble one's way
funambulation
funambulatory
functionalise
functionalism
functionalist
functionality
functionalize
functionaries
functionarism
function space
fundamentally
fungitoxicity
funipendulous
funny business
funny-peculiar
fur and feather
furnitureless
fussification
futtock shroud
future perfect
futurological
gain the wind of
galactorrhoea
galactosaemia
gallery forest
gallimaufries
Gallithumpian

gallows humour
galvanization
galvanometric
galvanoplasty
galvanoscopic
galvanotactic
galvanotropic
gamboge yellow
game-preserver
gametogenesis
gamma globulin
garden lettuce
garden produce
garden village
garden warbler
garlic-mustard
garnetiferous
garrulousness
garter-webbing
gas centrifuge
gasteromycete
gastrectomies
gastrocnemial
gastrocnemian
gastrocnemius
gastro-enteric
gastroenteric
gastronomical
gathering coal
gathering peat
gauge function
gauge pressure
gay liberation
Gay Liberation
gee whillikins
Geiger counter
gelatinizable
gemmiparously
gemmuliferous
genecological
general dealer
generalissima
generalissimo
generalizable
general pardon
general public
general reader
general strike
generation gap
generationism
genericalness
genethlialogy
genito-urinary
Genoese sponge
genotypically
genre painting
gentian bitter
gentian brandy
gentian spirit
gentian violet
gentlemanhood
gentlemanlike

gentlewomanly	girl about town	golden jubilee	granny's bonnet
geocentricity	girls together	golden-mouthed	granulomatous
geochemically	give a free hand	golden section	granulometric
geochronology	give an example	golden wedding	grape hyacinth
geodesic curve	give her the gun	Goliath beetle	grape-scissors
geological map	give offence to	gonadotrophic	graphemically
geometrically	give of oneself	gonadotrophin	graphicalness
geometric mean	give one's arm to	goniometrical	graphic artist
geometrideous	give one's heart	good afternoon	graphological
geomorphogeny	give the gate to	good for a laugh	grappling hook
geomorphology	give the mitten	good-for-nought	grappling iron
geophysically	give the sack to	Good King Henry	grasp at a straw
geopolitician	give thought to	good-naturedly	Grassmann's Law
Georgian green	glacial period	good neighbour	grass parakeet
geostationary	glacio-eustasy	good Samaritan	grass sickness
geotechnology	glaciofluvial	goody two-shoes	grass staggers
geotropically	glaciological	go one's own gait	graticulation
gephyrocercal	gladiatorship	goose barnacle	gratification
Germanization	glamorization	go over the wall	gratulatorily
German measles	glance one's eye	go over the wire	gravel culture
Germanophobia	Glauber's salts	Gordon Bennett	Graves' disease
German sausage	glenoid cavity	go the distance	Gravette point
germinability	glide-twinning	go the whole hog	gravimetrical
gerontocratic	gloaming sight	go the whole way	gravitational
gerontologist	globalization	go the wrong way	great and small
gerontophilia	global village	Gothic revival	greatcoatless
gerontophilic	global warming	go through with	Great Entrance
gerrymanderer	globe amaranth	go to one's heart	Greater Bairam
gerund-grinder	globe-trotting	governability	greater diesis
gesticulation	glocalization	governess cart	great-grandson
gesticulative	glorification	governing body	great kangaroo
gesticulatory	glossographer	governmentese	great majority
get a person off	glossological	government man	great omission
get a person out	glossophagine	go with the flow	great sessions
get a person wet	glottological	go with the tide	great sturgeon
get a rise out of	glow discharge	gracelessness	great unwashed
get a thing over	glucosinolate	gradationally	Great White Way
get in on the act	glucuronidase	grade crossing	Greek valerian
get it over with	glutinousness	gradual psalms	green amaranth
get off lightly	glycerination	graduate nurse	green copperas
get off the mark	glycerine tear	grain-elevator	green-fingered
get off to sleep	glycerokinase	graminivorous	greenhouse gas
get one's hand in	glycosylation	grammar school	Greenland dove
get one's own way	glyphographer	grammatically	green porphyry
get one's rag out	glyphographic	grammatolatry	greensickness
get on the brain	gnosiological	granddaughter	Greenwich Time
get on your bike	go a person's way	grandfatherly	greetings card
get square with	go-as-you-please	grandiloquent	gregarization
get the laugh on	goat and bee jug	grandiloquous	Gregory powder
get the message	Gobelin stitch	grandmasterly	grey manganese
get the picture	go by the name of	grandmaternal	grey marketeer
get the pricker	godfatherhood	grandmotherly	grey partridge
get the start of	godfathership	Grand National	grey phalarope
ghetto blaster	God forbid that	Grand Old Party	grieflessness
ghettoization	godless florin	grandparental	grief-stricken
ghostly father	godmothership	grandpaternal	grin and bear it
giant anteater	goffering iron	grand seigneur	grinding pains
giant kangaroo	go gangbusters	Grand Seignior	grinding-stone
gibber country	goggle-eye Jack	granger shares	grinding-wheel
gift of tongues	go into a huddle	granitization	groan inwardly
Giorgionesque	golden-crested	granny bashing	grody to the max
gird one's loins	golden hamster	granny glasses	grotesqueness

ground control
ground-hemlock
groundhog case
ground moraine
groundsel tree
groundskeeper
group dynamics
group genitive
group language
group marriage
group practice
group velocity
growing season
growth hormone
Grumbletonian
G-strophanthin
Guadalupe palm
guarantee fund
guardian angel
guard of honour
gubernatorial
guest of honour
guided missile
Guignet's green
guilelessness
guiltlessness
gum turpentine
gun microphone
Gunpowder Plot
gymnastically
gymnospermous
gynaecocratic
gynaecologist
gynaecomastia
gynandromorph
gynodioecious
gynomonoecism
Gypsy's warning
gyrofrequency
habeas corpora
habitableness
habit-training
haemarthrosis
haematidrosis
haematogenous
haematologist
haematomyelia
haematothorax
haemodialyser
haemodialysis
haemodynamics
haemorrhoidal
hairline crack
hair-splitting
hair-triggered
Haitian creole
hale and hearty
half-heartedly
half-sovereign
half the battle
half-timbering
hallucination

hallucinative
hallucinatory
halophosphate
ham-fistedness
ham-handedness
Hamito-Semitic
hammer-dressed
handcraftsman
handkerchiefs
handleability
hand-telescope
hang by a thread
hanging basket
hanging matter
hanging sleeve
hanging valley
Hang Seng index
hang up one's hat
hapax legomena
haphazardness
happy dispatch
happy families
happy landings
harbour master
hardenability
hard-heartedly
hard of hearing
hare and hounds
harlequin duck
harlequin fish
harlequin ring
harmonic minor
harmonisation
harmonization
harness-racing
harrowingness
Harry-long-legs
haruspication
harvest maiden
harvest-spider
hauling-ground
have a free hand
have a good mind
have a good time
have a regard to
have a time of it
have a word with
have by the ears
have designs on
have eyes to see
have good sport
have half a mind
have in a string
have itchy feet
have nothing on
have no time for
have one's eye on
have the care of
have the drop on
have the edge on
have the legs of
have the rags on

have the wind up
have the wood on
Hawaiian goose
Hawaiian shirt
hawthorn china
hay-home supper
hazardousness
heading-course
head over heels
head restraint
heads will roll
healthfulness
health officer
health physics
health service
health visitor
heap praises on
hear a bird sing
heartbreaking
heartbrokenly
hearth and home
hear the last of
heartlessness
heart-piercing
heartsickness
heart-stricken
heat-exchanger
Heath Robinson
heat-resistant
heat treatment
Heaven forfend
Heaven help you
heavenly fires
heave of the sea
heave the gorge
heavy-handedly
heavy hydrogen
heavy industry
hebdomadarian
Heberden's node
hecatontarchy
hectocotylize
hedge bindweed
hedge-clippers
hedgehog holly
heebie-jeebies
heel of the hand
heels over head
height to paper
heir designate
heir-portioner
heirs apparent
held in demesne
Heliogabalian
Hellenistical
Hellenization
Hellespontine
helminthiasis
helminthology
helter-skelter
hemerobaptist
hemicellulose

hemicolectomy
hemiparasitic
hemispherical
hemlock spruce
henceforwards
hepaticostomy
hepatomegalia
heptadecanoic
heptahydrated
heptametrical
heptasyllabic
hepthemimeral
heraldic tyger
Heralds' Office
herbarization
herborization
Hercegovinian
Hercules braid
heresiography
heresiologist
hereticalness
here we go again
heritage coast
heritage group
heritage trail
hermaphrodism
hermaphrodite
hermeneutical
herniorrhaphy
heroic couplet
herpes simplex
herpetologist
herring-choker
herring-gutted
Herzegovinian
heteroblastic
heterocarpous
heterochromia
heterochromic
heterochronic
heterogametic
heterogeneity
heterogeneous
heterogenesis
heterogenetic
heterographic
heterological
heteromorphic
heteronuclear
heteroplastic
heteropterous
heterostylism
heterostylous
heterothallic
heterothermic
heterotrophic
heterozygotic
heuristically
hexadactylism
hexadecimally
hexamethonium
hexamethylene

hexobarbitone
hey cockalorum
hide-and-go-seek
hieratic paper
hieroglyphist
hierogrammate
hierosolymite
high and mighty
High-Churchism
High Churchman
High Churchmen
High Constable
high explosive
high frequency
Highgate resin
Highland dress
Highland fling
Highland games
high latitudes
high-muck-a-muck
high opinion of
high priestess
high-thoughted
high water mark
hilariousness
Hildebrandine
Hippocratical
hippopotamian
hippopotamine
hispanization
histiocytosis
histochemical
histrionicism
hit a false note
hit the ceiling
hit the jackpot
Hittitologist
hobby-horsical
Hobson's choice
hoist one's flag
hold a brief for
hold aloof from
hold a torch for
hold in demesne
holding ground
hold it against
hold one's peace
hold one's serve
hold one's state
hole-and-corner
hole in the wall
holiday centre
hollow-cheeked
hollow-hearted
hollow-trunked
holluschickie
holoparasitic
holosericeous
Holy Communion
Holy Sacrament
Holy Scripture
Holy Sepulchre

homalographic
home economics
home economist
Home Secretary
homeward-bound
homiletically
homoeoblastic
homoeogeneous
homoeomorphic
homoeopathist
homo-eroticism
homogeneously
homoiothermic
homologically
homolographic
homoscedastic
homosexualist
homosexuality
honeycomb wall
honeydew melon
honorary canon
honorifically
honourability
honours course
honours degree
honours school
hook-and-ladder
Hooke coupling
hoop petticoat
Hopkinsianism
horizon mining
horizontal bar
horizontalism
horizontality
horizontalize
horrification
horripilation
horse-and-buggy
horse chestnut
horsefeathers
horse-foot crab
horsehair worm
horse mackerel
horse mushroom
horseshoe crab
horse sickness
horse traction
horticultural
Hosanna Sunday
hospital blues
hospital fever
hospital train
hospital trust
hot-air balloon
hot dark matter
hot-headedness
hotheadedness
hot laboratory
Hottentot fish
Hottentot's god
Hottentot's tea
houghmagandie

housebreaking
housebuilding
household book
household gods
household name
household word
houselessness
house longhorn
house magazine
housemistress
house of office
house of prayer
House of prayer
housewifeship
housing estate
housing scheme
howling baboon
howling monkey
hubristically
huckleberries
human equation
human interest
humiliatingly
humpback whale
hundredth part
hundredweight
hunger marcher
hunger striker
hungry forties
Huntingdonian
hunting ground
hunting spider
hurricane-bird
hurricane deck
hurricane lamp
hurricane wind
hush one's mouth
Hutchinsonian
hyalinization
hyaloclastite
hyaluronidase
hybridization
hydraulically
hydriodic acid
hydro-aromatic
hydrobiologic
hydroboration
hydrocephalic
hydrocephalus
hydrochloride
hydrodynamics
hydroelectric
hydrofracture
hydrogasifier
hydrogenation
hydrogenosome
hydrogenously
hydromagnetic
hydrometrical
hydroperoxide
hydrophobical
hydroponicist

hydrostatical
hydrosulphide
hydrosulphite
hydrotherapic
hydroxylamine
hydroxylation
hydroxylysine
hygrometrical
hygroscopical
hymenopterous
hyomandibular
hyperactivity
hyperbolicity
hyperboloidal
hypercellular
hypercritical
hyperdiploidy
hyperesthesia
hypereutectic
hyperfunction
hyperhidrosis
hyperkalaemia
hyperkalaemic
hyperlipaemia
hyperlipaemic
hypermetrical
hypermetropia
hypermetropic
hypermobility
hyperparasite
hyperphysical
hyperpolarize
hyperpyrexial
hypersalinity
hypersplenism
hypersthenite
hypertelorism
hypertonicity
hypertrophied
hypertrophous
hyperurbanism
hypervelocity
hyphenization
hyphomycetous
hypnoanalysis
hypnoanalytic
hypnotization
hypoaesthesia
hypobranchial
hypocalcaemia
hypocalcaemic
hypochondriac
hypochondrial
hypochondrium
hypochoristic
hypochromasia
hypochromatic
hypocycloidal
hypoeutectoid
hypoglycaemia
hypoglycaemic
hypolemniscus

hyponatraemia
hyponatraemic
hypophosphate
hypophosphite
hypopituitary
hyposecretion
hyposensitize
hypothecation
hypotheticate
hypothyroidic
hypotonically
hypotrichosis
hypsicephalic
hypsiconchous
hypsometrical
hyracotherium
hysteroscopic
hystricomorph
I am afraid that
I am yet to learn
iatrochemical
iatrogenicity
iatromechanic
iatrophysical
Ibero-American
ice-cream float
Iceland falcon
Iceland lichen
ichneumon wasp
ichnographies
ichthyologist
ichthyosaurus
iconographies
iconographist
iconometrical
icosahedrally
identicalness
identical twin
ideographical
ideologically
idiomatically
idiorrhythmic
idiosyncratic
idiots savants
if the shoe fits
if you must know
Ignatius's bean
ignominiously
ileocolostomy
illachrymable
Illawarra pine
I'll be jiggered
I'll be switched
ill-considered
ill-favouredly
ill-formedness
ill-humouredly
illimitedness
illocutionary
illogicalness
ill-temperedly
ill-thought-out

illuminometer
illusionistic
illustratable
illustriously
illustrissimo
image orthicon
imaginability
imaginariness
imaginatively
imagistically
imbalsamation
imitative arts
imitativeness
imitative word
immarcescible
immaterialise
immaterialism
immaterialist
immateriality
immaterialize
immatriculate
immediateness
immersion foot
immersion suit
immiscibility
immovableness
immunochemist
immunogenetic
immunological
immunotherapy
impact printer
impalpability
imparipinnate
impartibility
impassability
impassibility
impassionedly
impassionment
impassiveness
impatientness
impeccability
impecuniosity
impenetration
impenetrative
imperatorship
imperceivable
imperceivably
imperceptible
imperceptibly
impercipience
imperfectible
imperfectness
imperforation
imperformable
imperial eagle
imperialistic
imperiousness
impermanently
impermissible
impersonality
impersonation
imperspirable

impersuadable
impertinently
imperturbable
imperturbably
impetuousness
impignoration
implacability
implicational
implicatively
implicit faith
imploringness
implosiveness
impolitically
impoliticness
importunately
impossibilism
impossibilist
impossibility
impostumation
impracticable
impracticably
impractically
imprecatorily
impreciseness
impredicative
impregnatable
impreparation
impressionary
impressionism
Impressionism
impressionist
imprest system
improbability
improficiency
improgressive
impropriation
impropriatrix
improprieties
improvability
improvidently
improvisation
improvisatory
imprudentness
imp the wings of
impulse buying
impulse killer
impulsiveness
impurity level
imputation tax
imputrescence
imputrescible
in a brown study
in a cleft stick
inadventurous
inadvertently
in a fit state to
in a general way
in a good temper
inanimateness
in a person's lap
in a position to
inapplication

inappreciable
inappreciably
inappropriate
inarticulated
inattentively
incandescence
incantational
incapableness
incarceration
incarnational
incessantness
incidentalist
in circulation
incircumspect
inclinational
inclined plane
inclusion body
inclusiveness
incognoscible
incoherencies
incoincidence
incombustible
incomes policy
income support
incommiscible
incommodation
incommunicado
incompactness
in company with
incompetently
incompletable
incompossible
inconceivable
inconceivably
inconclusible
incondensable
incondensible
inconformable
incongruently
incongruities
incongruously
in conjunction
inconquerable
inconsciently
inconsciously
inconsecutive
in consequence
inconsequence
inconsiderate
inconsistence
inconsistency
inconsonantly
inconspicuous
inconstancies
inconstruable
incontaminate
incontestable
incontestably
incontestible
incontinently
in contumaciam
inconvenience

inconveniency
inconvertible
inconvertibly
inconvincible
incorporating
incorporation
incorporative
incorporeally
incorrectness
incorruptible
incorruptibly
incorruptness
incredibility
incredulously
incrementally
incriminating
incrimination
incriminatory
incubator bird
inculpability
incurableness
incuriousness
indefatigable
indefatigably
in deference to
indentureship
independently
indescribable
indescribably
indeterminacy
indeterminate
indeterminism
indeterminist
index register
Indian currant
Indian defence
Indian English
Indian fig tree
Indianization
Indianologist
Indian problem
Indian pudding
Indian saffron
Indian tobacco
indicator lamp
indifferently
indigo bunting
indiscernible
indiscernibly
indispensable
indispensably
indisposition
indissociable
indissuadable
indissuadably
indistinction
indistinctive
indisturbable
indisturbance
individualise
individualism
individualist

individuality
individualize
individuation
individuative
indoctrinator
Indo-Germanist
indoor cricket
Indo-Saracenic
induction coil
induction loop
inductiveness
induplication
in durance vile
industrialise
industrialism
industrialist
industrialize
industriously
ineducability
ineffableness
ineffectively
ineffectually
inefficacious
inefficiently
inegalitarian
inelaborately
inelastically
ineligibility
inequilateral
inequivalence
inevitability
inexclusively
inexhaustible
inexhaustibly
inexorability
inexpensively
inexperienced
in expiation of
inexplainable
inexpressible
inexpressibly
infallibilism
infallibilist
infallibility
infamous crime
infanticipate
infantilistic
infantilities
infant prodigy
infant teacher
infeasibility
infectiveness
inferentially
inferior ovary
inferribility
infiltrometer
in fine feather
infinitesimal
infinitivally
inflectedness
inflexibility
inflorescence

influenceable
influence line
influentially
informalities
informational
informatively
informatorily
infralittoral
inframarginal
infraspecific
infrigidation
infructuously
in full feather
infuriatingly
ingeniousness
ingenuousness
ingrain carpet
ingravescence
ingravidation
ingurgitation
in Heaven's name
inhibitedness
in high dudgeon
in high feather
in high spirits
inhomogeneity
inhomogeneous
in honour bound
inhospitality
iniencephalic
iniencephalus
inimitability
initial letter
in its entirety
injection well
injudiciously
injuriousness
ink-jet printer
inland revenue
inlet manifold
in-maintenance
innascibility
inner-directed
Inniskilliner
innocent party
in no condition
innocuousness
innovationist
innoxiousness
in obedience to
inobservation
inoculability
inoffensively
in one's element
in one's hearing
in one's opinion
in one's own name
in one's own time
inoperability
inopportunely
inopportunism
inopportunist

inopportunity
inorganically
in parenthesis
in perspective
in point of fact
in possibility
in Queer Street
inquiry office
inquisitional
inquisitively
inquisitorial
in reference to
in respect that
in restraint of
insatiability
inscriptional
insectiferous
insectivorous
insensateness
insensibility
insensitively
insensitivity
insertion gain
in short supply
inside country
inside forward
insidiousness
insignificant
insincerities
insinuatingly
insinuatively
in smooth water
insociability
insolubleness
insoluble soap
insolvability
in so many words
in some measure
inspection-car
inspectorship
inspirational
inspiritingly
instabilities
Instance Court
instantaneity
instantaneous
instantiation
instant replay
instinctively
instinctually
institutional
instructional
instructively
instrumentary
insubmergible
insubmersible
insubordinate
insubstantial
insufficience
insufficiency
insupportable
insupportably

insuppressive
insurpassable
insusceptible
intangibility
integrability
integrational
integumentary
intellectible
intelligenced
intelligencer
intelligently
intemperately
intensionally
intensive care
intensiveness
intentionally
intentiveness
interactional
interactively
interactivity
interalveolar
inter-American
interarterial
intercalarium
intercalation
intercalative
intercalatory
intercellular
interceptable
interceptible
interclavicle
intercolonial
intercolumnar
intercommoner
intercommunal
intercommuner
intercostally
intercropping
intercultural
intercurrence
interdentally
interdigitate
inter-dominion
interesterify
interest group
interestingly
interfacially
interfamilial
interferingly
interferogram
intergalactic
intergranular
interindustry
interior angle
interjectural
interlacement
interlamellar
interlaminate
interlanguage
interlardment
interlinearly
interlinguist

interlocation
interlocution
interlocutory
interlocutrix
interlopation
interlucation
interlunation
intermarriage
intermediator
intermetallic
intermittedly
intermittence
intermittency
intermodalism
intermountain
internal clock
internal exile
internal organ
internal rhyme
international
interneuronal
interoceptive
interoperable
interosculate
interparietal
interpellator
interpersonal
interpolation
interpolative
interpolatory
interposition
interpretable
interpretress
interproximal
interpunction
interquartile
interracially
interrelation
interrogation
interrogative
interrogatory
interruptable
interruptedly
interruptible
interscapular
intersidereal
interspecific
interspersion
interstratify
intersyllabic
intertropical
intervarietal
intervolution
in the abstract
in the concrete
in the course of
in the doghouse
in the employ of
in the extremes
in the majority
in the manner of
in the matter of

in the middle of
in the movement
in the nature of
in the negative
in the person of
in the pipeline
in the recovery
in the region of
in the same boat
in the same ship
in the shadow of
in the short run
in the smallest
in the spud line
in the swim with
in the throes of
in the vicinity
in the wind's eye
in the wrong box
in this context
into matchwood
into the ground
intoxicatedly
intra-arterial
intracapsular
intracellular
intracerebral
intracultural
intradermally
intra-European
intramuscular
intranational
intransigence
intransigency
intransitable
intransparent
intrapetiolar
intrapolation
intraregional
intraspecific
intratelluric
intrathecally
intrathoracic
intratropical
intravarietal
intravasation
intravascular
intravenously
intraversable
intricateness
intrinsically
introduceable
introductress
introgression
introgressive
intropunitive
introspection
introspective
introversible
intrusiveness
intuitionally
intuitiveness

inusitateness
invaccination
invariability
invectiveness
inventiveness
inventorially
invermination
Inverness cape
inverse square
inverted comma
inverted pleat
invertibility
investigation
investigative
investigatory
invidiousness
invincibility
inviolability
inviolateness
invisibleness
invita Minerva
involucellate
involuntarily
involutionary
inward-looking
iodine scarlet
ion propulsion
iontophoresis
iontophoretic
iota subscript
ipsilaterally
iridencleisis
iridocyclitis
iridodialysis
iris diaphragm
Irish American
Irishman's rise
iron bacterium
iron in the fire
ironmongeries
irrationalise
irrationalism
irrationalist
irrationality
irrationalize
irreciprocity
irreclaimable
irreclaimably
irrecognition
irrecoverable
irrecoverably
irrecuperable
irreflexivity
irrefrangible
irrefrangibly
irrelevancies
irreligionism
irreligionist
irreligiously
irremunerable
irreplaceable
irreplaceably

irrepleviable
irrepressible
irrepressibly
irresponsible
irresponsibly
irrestrictive
irretraceable
irretractable
irretrievable
irretrievably
irreverential
irrigationist
ischaemically
ischiorrhogic
isoagglutinin
isobarometric
isobathytherm
isocarboxazid
isochronously
isodimorphism
isodimorphous
isoelectronic
isogeothermal
isoionic point
isolatability
isolation camp
isomerization
isometrically
isomorphously
isophenomenal
isoproterenol
isostatically
isostructural
isothermobath
isotope effect
isotransplant
isotropically
Istrian marble
Italian garden
Italian millet
Italian stitch
italicization
itching powder
iterativeness
it is equal to me
it is whispered
it makes no odds
it remembers me
itsy-bitsiness
I will thank you
Ixionian wheel
jabberwockies
jackass barque
jackass-rigged
Jack cross-tree
Jack-in-a-bottle
Jack-in-the-bush
Jack-jump-about
Jacksonianism
Jack the Ripper
Jacob Evertsen
jakkalsbessie

Jamaica ginger
Jamaica pepper
Jamaica sorrel
janizary music
Jansenistical
Japanese anise
Japanese cedar
Japanese maple
Japanese paper
Japanese print
jargonization
jazzification
Jekyll and Hyde
jellification
jenny-long-legs
jerry-building
Jersey justice
Jerusalem pony
Jerusalem sage
jet propulsion
jeunesse dorée
jiggery-pokery
jingling match
Job's comforter
Johnny Crapaud
Johnny Newcome
Johnny penguin
Johnsonianism
jollification
Joseph and Mary
journal-letter
journey-weight
Judaeo-Spanish
judge advocate
judgementally
judgement debt
judgement-hall
judgement note
judgement-seat
Judge Ordinary
judge's marshal
judiciousness
Juggernautish
July high-flyer
July highflyer
jumping spider
jump in the lake
jump to the eyes
junction canal
junction diode
jungle-bashing
junior college
junior partner
junk jewellery
junk sculpture
Jupiter's beard
jurimetrician
jurisprudence
jury of inquiry
jury of matrons
justice in eyre
justiciarship

justification
justificative
justificatory
juvenile court
juxtaposition
juxtapositive
kachina dancer
kaleidoscopic
kangaroo apple
kangaroo court
kangaroo-grass
kangaroo mouse
kangaroo thorn
kaolinization
kapellmeister
Kate Greenaway
kathenotheism
katjiepiering
keeled scraper
keen as mustard
keep account of
keep an eye open
keep one's end up
keep one's peace
keep one's state
keep open house
keep the pledge
keep to oneself
Kelvin balance
Kenilworth ivy
Kennelly layer
Kensingtonian
Kentish plover
Kentucky Derby
Kentucky rifle
Kenyanization
Kepler problem
keratinolysis
keratinolytic
keratohyaline
keratomalacia
kermes mineral
kettledrummer
kettle moraine
keyhole limpet
Keystone State
khaki election
Khrushchevian
Khrushchevism
kick one's heels
kick the bucket
kick up a shindy
Kidderminster
kiddie brother
kidney machine
Killarney fern
killing bottle
killing-circle
Kilmarnock cap
kilogram-force
kilogram-metre
kind-heartedly

kindred spirit
kinematically
kinematograph
kinesiologist
kinetic energy
kinetic theory
kinetogenesis
kinetonucleus
King in Council
king of terrors
King's Attorney
King's Champion
King's evidence
King's Serjeant
King's shilling
Kingston valve
Kirchhoff's law
kiss goodbye to
kissing-comfit
kissing cousin
kiss-in-the-ring
kiss the ground
kist o' whistles
kitchen garden
Kitchen Kaffir
kitchen midden
kitchen police
Kitchen rudder
kitchen shower
kittenishness
kitty-cornered
Kjeldahl flask
knickerbocker
knick-knackery
knick-knackish
knife-throwing
knight marshal
knight-service
Knight Templar
knit one's brows
knock-on effect
knockout drops
knock sideways
knock spots off
knock together
know backwards
know inside out
knowledgeable
knowledgeably
knowledge base
knowledgeless
knowledgement
know like a book
know one's place
know one's stuff
know to speak to
know what's what
knuckleduster
knuckle timber
knuckle-walker
Knudsen number
Koch's bacillus

Komodo monitor
Krag–Jørgensen
Kremnitz white
Ku Klux Klanner
Kundalini yoga
labialization
laboriousness
labour brigade
Labour Weekend
labyrinth fish
labyrinthical
labyrinthitis
Lacedaemonian
lace-leaf plant
lachrymal vase
lachrymogenic
lackadaisical
lacrosse-stick
lactobacillus
lactoglobulin
lactonization
ladder polymer
ladies' fingers
Ladies' Gallery
Lady Bountiful
lady-in-waiting
lady of leisure
lady's bedstraw
lady's ear-drops
laevorotation
laevorotatory
laevotartaric
laevotartrate
lagophthalmia
lagophthalmic
lagophthalmos
laissez-passer
Lamarckianism
Lambeth degree
lambing season
lamb's quarters
lamellibranch
lamellipodium
laminagraphic
lampadephoria
lance corporal
lance-sergeant
land-community
landed plunger
landgraveship
landing ticket
land-measuring
land of promise
Land of the Free
landownership
land-surveying
language shift
langue de boeuf
languishingly
languish under
laparoscopies
laparoscopist

lappet-weaving
lapsus linguae
larch leaf cast
larding needle
larviposition
laryngealized
laryngectomee
laryngologist
laryngoscopic
laryngotomies
Last Judgement
latchkey child
latent partner
lateroflexion
lateroversion
Latin American
Latin language
latitudinally
latrine rumour
lattice energy
lattice filter
lattice girder
lattice window
laughableness
laughing death
laughing goose
laughing hyena
laughing stock
launching-ways
Launder-Ometer
lauryl alcohol
lavatory paper
lavatory style
lavender-water
Law Commission
law of averages
Lawson cypress
Laxton's Superb
lay by the heels
lay down the law
lay emphasis on
layer dressing
lay in the earth
lay on one's oars
lay on the table
lay the blame on
lazuli bunting
lead by the ears
lead by the nose
lead guitarist
leading-in wire
leading rating
leading seaman
leading-string
leading wheels
lead-pipe cinch
lead poisoning
leaf-arrowhead
leaf-butterfly
leafcutter ant
leafcutter bee
lean to one side

leap in the dark
learner driver
learning curve
learn the ropes
least chipmunk
leather beetle
leather-flower
leather-headed
leather-jacket
leatherjacket
leather-turtle
leave away from
leave it at that
leave standing
leave word with
lecherousness
lectisternium
left at the post
left-hand drive
left-hand screw
legal capacity
legate a latere
Legion disease
legislational
legislatively
legislatorial
leishmaniasis
leishmaniosis
Leishman stain
leisure centre
leisureliness
lemmatization
lemon-coloured
lemon geranium
lemon-squeezer
lend oneself to
lenticularity
lenticulation
lepidocrocite
lepidodendron
lepidopterist
lepidopterous
lepidosaurian
leptocephalic
leptocephalus
leptokurtosis
leptoprosopic
leptospirosis
leschenaultia
lesser noctule
lesser omentum
let a thing ride
let down gently
let George do it
lethal chamber
lethargically
let it go at that
letter-balance
letter-carrier
letter-founder
letter-heading
letter missive

letter-perfect
letter-quality
letters patent
lettre bâtarde
lettre de forme
lettre de somme
Letzeburgesch
leukaemogenic
Levant morocco
level crossing
level-headedly
levelling pole
lexicographer
lexicographic
lexicological
lexigraphical
Lexiphanicism
Liberal-Labour
liberationism
liberationist
liberty bodice
Liberty bodice
librarianship
library school
lichenicolous
lichenivorous
lichenologist
lichenometric
lickerishness
lick into shape
lick one's chops
Lieberkühnian
Liebfraumilch
lie down and die
lie on the gavel
lie on the table
lieutenancies
life assurance
Life Guardsman
life insurance
life-preserver
life scientist
lifting-bridge
lift one's elbow
lift one's hands
lift up the horn
light-demander
light-fastness
lightfastness
light-fingered
light-footedly
light-headedly
light horseman
light industry
light infantry
lighting tower
lightlessness
lightsomeness
lignification
lignitiferous
like a bad penny
like a millpond

like clockwork
like grim death
like lightning
like one o'clock
lily of the vale
limb-darkening
lime-marmalade
limestone fern
limitlessness
limnoplankton
Lincoln rocker
linear algebra
linearization
linear measure
line engraving
line-finishing
line-fisherman
line frequency
linen-armourer
linen-cupboard
line of country
line of defence
line of fortune
line one's purse
lingua francas
lingual ribbon
lingue franche
linguistician
linolenic acid
linsey-woolsey
lip microphone
lipodystrophy
lipogrammatic
lipolytically
liqueur brandy
liqueur whisky
liquid compass
liquid crystal
liquid measure
liquid starter
liquorice-root
liquorishness
listenability
listening post
list processor
literal-minded
literary agent
lithia-emerald
lithification
lithiophilite
lithontriptic
lithotripsies
litigiousness
little bittern
little-boy-lost
little Masters
Little Masters
little mastery
Little Red Book
Little Russian
little scarlet
little science

little theatre
liturgistical
live extempore
live in oneself
live like a lord
liver chestnut
liver-coloured
livery company
livery servant
live to oneself
living image of
living picture
living theatre
Lloyd-Georgian
loaded for bear
loading shovel
load-water-line
loathsomeness
loath-to-depart
Lobachevskian
lobster bisque
local exchange
local preacher
loculicidally
locum tenentes
locus ceruleus
lodge-pole pine
logarithmical
logical syntax
logistic curve
logit analysis
logodaedalist
logodiarrhoea
logographical
lollipop woman
Lombard Street
Londonization
long-acuminate
long-case clock
long-continued
longiloquence
longlivedness
long-sightedly
long-suffering
long-tailed mag
long-tailed tit
long time no see
look askance at
look daggers at
look forward to
look into space
loose coupling
lophotrichous
lord and master
lord-in-waiting
Lord love a duck
Lord of Misrule
Lord of Sabaoth
lord of the soil
lord paramount
Lord Privy Seal
Lords temporal

Lord Treasurer
lose one's block
lose one's heart
lose one's nerve
lose one's shirt
lose one's touch
lose one's voice
lose sleep over
lose touch with
lost in thought
Lotka–Volterra
lotus position
Louis-Philippe
lovers' quarrel
low-definition
lower one's eyes
lower one's flag
low-mindedness
low side window
low technology
lubricational
luck of the draw
lucrativeness
ludicrousness
Ludwig's angina
luggage locker
lumirhodopsin
lunar distance
lunatic asylum
lunatic fringe
lunisolar year
lupus vulgaris
luteinization
luxuriousness
lycanthropist
lymphadenitis
lymphoblastic
lymphocytosis
lymphomatosis
lymphopoiesis
lymphopoietic
lymphorrhagia
lymphosarcoma
macaronically
Macassar ebony
Macaulayesque
machiavellian
machiavellism
machiavellist
machicolation
machinability
machine finish
machine-gunner
machine-minder
machine-pistol
machine-tooled
mackerel shark
macroanalysis
macrocephalia
macrocephalic
macroclimatic
macrodiagonal

macro-economic
macroeconomic
macroglobulin
macromolecule
macronutrient
macrophysical
macroscopical
macrotrichium
maculopapular
Madagascarian
mad cow disease
made to measure
Madison Avenue
madreporarian
madrigalesque
maduromycosis
magazine cover
magazine story
magic mushroom
magisterially
magistratical
magnanimously
magnetic field
magnetic north
magnetic storm
magnetization
magnetometric
magnetomotive
magneto-optics
magnetosphere
magnetostatic
magnification
magnificently
magniloquence
magnitudinous
Magnolia State
Magyarization
Maharashtrian
mahogany birch
maiden-servant
maiden's wreath
maiden thought
maid of all work
Mainland China
mainstreeting
Maintenon chop
maison de passe
maison de santé
maison tolérée
maîtres d'hôtel
Majorana force
major-domoship
Major Mitchell
make account of
make a fine hand
make a fuss over
make a good fist
make a market of
make a martyr of
make a monkey of
make a muddle of
make an attempt

make an issue of
make a secret of
make a wry mouth
make expiation
make good cheer
make good speed
make in one's way
make mention of
make merry over
make no mistake
make nothing of
make one's début
make one's peace
make reprisals
make residence
make semblance
make the best of
make the domino
make the fur fly
make the most of
make the papers
make the riffle
make the rounds
make to measure
make tracks for
malabsorption
malacological
malacostracan
maladaptation
maladaptively
maladjustment
maladminister
maladroitness
malapropistic
malariologist
male menopause
malgovernment
maliciousness
Mallaby-Deeley
malleableness
malleo-incudal
malobservance
malt-distiller
Malthusianism
mammaliferous
manageability
managerialism
managerialist
Manchesterian
Manchesterism
Manchesterize
Mandelbrot set
manganapatite
manganese spar
manganiferous
mangold-wurzel
Manichaeistic
manifestation
manifestative
manifold paper
Manila cheroot
manipulatable

manneristical
man of his hands
man of pleasure
man of the cloth
man of the house
man of the match
man of the world
manufactories
many-sidedness
maple molasses
map projection
maraging steel
marbled beauty
marble orchard
march fracture
marching order
marconigraphy
Marek's disease
margin of error
margin release
mariculturist
marigold apple
marine biology
marine railway
marine science
marine trumpet
mariposa tulip
marketability
market economy
market shooter
marking cotton
marking stitch
marmalade plum
marmalade tree
marquois scale
mar resistance
marriage lines
marrons glacés
marrow pudding
marry a fortune
marsh marigold
marsh samphire
marsipobranch
marsupial bone
marsupial mole
Martello tower
martyrization
martyrologies
martyrologist
Marxistically
masculineness
mashie-niblick
massification
mass of requiem
Master Aircrew
master-builder
masterfulness
master mariner
masters-at-arms
master's degree
masticability
mastigophoric

mastoidectomy
Matara diamond
matchableness
matchboarding
match dissolve
matched orders
Mater Dolorosa
materfamilias
material cause
material clerk
materialistic
material thing
materia medica
maternalistic
mathematician
mathematicise
mathematicism
mathematicize
matinée jacket
matriculation
matriculatory
matrilineally
matrilocality
matrimonially
matrimony vine
matrix printer
matter subject
Matthew Walker
Matura diamond
mature economy
mature student
mauvaise honte
Maxwell's demon
May and January
meadow parsnip
meadow saffron
meals on wheels
mean deviation
meaninglessly
mean solar time
means-testable
measurability
measurelessly
measure swords
measuring cast
measuring tape
measuring worm
meat-and-potato
meat breakfast
meat poisoning
mechanicalism
mechanicalist
mechanicality
mechanicalize
mechanization
medial cadence
median section
mediastinitis
mediatization
medical garden
medical school
medicamentary

medicine chest
medicine glass
medicine lodge
medicine stamp
medicine woman
Medieval Greek
Medieval Latin
Mediterranean
medium bowling
medium close-up
meet one's Maker
meet one's match
meet-the-people
megacephalous
megakaryocyte
megaloblastic
megalocephaly
megalopolitan
megalosaurian
megalospheric
megastructure
meibomian cyst
Meistersinger
melamine resin
melancholious
melanogenesis
mellifluously
melodiousness
melodramatics
melodramatise
melodramatist
melodramatize
member country
membranaceous
membranogenic
membranophone
membrum virile
memorableness
memory mapping
Mendelssohnic
meningococcal
meningococcus
mensurability
mensurational
mental cruelty
mental healing
mental hygiene
mental illness
mental patient
menticultural
mento-vertical
Mercalli scale
mercenariness
mercerization
merchant fleet
merchant guild
mercilessness
mercurialness
Mercurochrome
mercury vapour
meridionality
merit increase

meritocracies
meritoriously
mermaid's purse
mescal buttons
mesencephalic
mesencephalon
mesmerization
mesmerizingly
mesocephalism
mesquite-grass
messengership
messenger wire
Messianically
mess of pottage
metabolically
metabolizable
metachromasia
metachromatic
metachronally
metafictional
metagrobolize
metal detector
metalliferous
metallization
metallochrome
metallochromy
metalloenzyme
metallography
metallurgical
metalogically
metamerically
metamorphoser
metamorphoses
metamorphosic
metamorphosis
metamorphotic
metaphosphate
metaphysician
metaphysicise
metaphysicize
metapolitical
metapsychosis
metarhodopsin
metastability
metasyncrisis
metasyncritic
metatarsalgia
metempiricism
metempiricist
metempsychose
metencephalic
metencephalon
met-enkephalin
meteoric stone
meteoriticist
meteorologist
methanoic acid
methapyrilene
methemoglobin
Methodistical
methodization
methodologies

methodologist
methohexitone
methyl alcohol
methylbenzene
methylene blue
metonymically
metoposcopist
metrification
metrizability
metronidazole
Mexican dollar
Mexican-Indian
Mexican orange
mezza-majolica
mezzo-rilievos
mezzo-sopranos
micellization
Mickey-mousing
micrencephaly
microanalyser
microanalysis
microaneurysm
microbiologic
microcellular
microcephalic
microcephalus
microchemical
microclimatic
microcomputer
microcosmical
microcracking
micro-economic
microeconomic
microfelsitic
microfilament
microfloppies
microfracture
microgranitic
micrographics
microhardness
microlighting
micrometeoric
micrometrical
micronization
micronutrient
micro-organism
microperthite
microphyllous
microphysical
microplankton
microporosity
microprinting
microscopical
microsurgical
microteaching
microtonality
microvascular
microwaveable
microwave oven
Middle Academy
Middle America
Middle Britain

Middle Eastern
Middle England
Middle English
Middle Kingdom
middle lamella
middle manager
middlemanship
middle passage
Middle Pointed
Middle Western
mid-life crisis
midnight feast
Midsummer's Day
might-have-been
migmatization
Mikimoto pearl
milieu therapy
military braid
military brush
military chest
Military Cross
Military Medal
milk chocolate
milk of almonds
milk of sulphur
milk the market
millennialism
millennialist
milliamperage
millionairess
millionairish
million-dollar
million-seller
millionth part
mill privilege
millstone grit
millwrighting
minaciousness
mind-bendingly
mind-blowingly
mind-expanding
mind-numbingly
mineragraphic
mineralizable
mineralogical
mineral purple
mineral tallow
mineral violet
mineral yellow
miner's disease
miner's lettuce
miniature golf
minikin string
ministerially
minster church
mint condition
mirror nucleus
mirror nuclide
mirror writing
mirthlessness
misadjustment
misallocation

misanthropise
misanthropist
misanthropize
misappreciate
misascription
misbecomingly
miscalculator
miscatalogued
miscegenation
miscellaneous
mischief-maker
mischief night
mischievously
miscomprehend
misconception
misconjecture
misconnection
misdoubtfully
misemployment
miserableness
misestimation
misexpression
misexpressive
misfunctional
misgovernance
misgovernment
misguidedness
misidentified
misidentifies
misimpression
mismanagement
misobservance
misperception
mispersuasion
misproportion
misshapenness
missiological
missionary box
Mississippian
missive letter
miss one's guess
mistletoe bird
mistresspiece
mistrustfully
mistrustingly
misunderstand
misunderstood
Mitchell grass
mitochondrial
mitochondrion
mixed blessing
mixed feelings
mixed language
mixed marriage
mixed metaphor
mixed-pressure
mix one's drinks
M'Naghten rules
mnemotechnics
moaning minnie
moaning Minnie
moccasin snake

model dwelling	monomolecular	morphonologic	mourning-piece
moderate a call	monomorphemic	morphophoneme	mourning widow
moderationist	mononucleated	morphophonics	mouse-coloured
moderatorship	mononucleosis	morphopoiesis	Moussorgskian
modern English	monophasicity	morphopoietic	moustacheless
modern history	monophthalmic	morphotactics	moustache tern
modernization	monophthongal	morphotropism	mouth-watering
modifiability	monophysitism	morris dancing	movable kidney
modus operandi	monopolizable	morselization	move mountains
moist gangrene	monopolylogue	mortality rate	moving average
moisture cream	Monopoly money	mort d'ancestor	moving picture
moisture meter	monopoly value	mortification	mowing-machine
molecular heat	monopsonistic	mortifiedness	muckle-mouthed
molinological	monosexuality	mosaic disease	muck-spreading
mollification	monosignative	mosquito fleet	mucocutaneous
mollificative	monosiphonous	mother-and-babe	muddle through
molluscicidal	monosyllabism	mother complex	Muhammadanism
molluscum body	monosymmetric	mother country	mulberry molar
momentariness	monothalamous	mother-fucking	mule-ear rabbit
moment of truth	Monothelitism	motherfucking	Müller-Thurgau
momentousness	monotocardian	Mother Hubbard	Mull of Kintyre
momentum space	monotonically	mother-of-pearl	multicellular
monachization	monotrematous	mother of thyme	multicoloured
monadological	monsoon forest	Mother Shipton	multicultural
Monarchianism	monstriferous	motion picture	multifilament
monarchically	monstrosities	motor accident	multifunction
Monday-clubber	monstrousness	motosensitive	multilamellar
Mondayishness	Montefiascone	mottled beauty	multilevelled
Monday morning	Montepulciano	mouldableness	multilinguist
monepiscopacy	montes Veneris	moulding-board	multilocation
money-grubbing	Montserratian	moulding-plane	multiloquence
money illusion	monumentalise	mountain avens	multimodalism
money-spinning	monumentalism	mountain chain	multinational
Mongolian fold	monumentality	mountain daisy	multi-negative
Mongolian spot	monumentalize	mountain devil	multi-partyism
Mongolization	mood-elevating	mountain ebony	multipersonal
monimolimnion	moon-blindness	mountain fever	multiple birth
monkeyishness	moonlight flit	mountain finch	multiple fruit
monkey-pod tree	mooring swivel	mountain green	multiple image
monoaminergic	mops and brooms	mountain heath	multiple ratio
monocarbonate	morale-booster	mountain maple	multiple shift
monocephalous	morality squad	mountainously	multiple store
monochromatic	moral majority	mountain pansy	multiplicable
monochromator	moral pressure	mountain pride	multiplicator
monocistronic	moral sciences	mountain quail	multiplicious
monocondylian	morbid anatomy	mountain range	multipolarity
monocotyledon	morbillivirus	mountain sheep	multi-position
monoculturist	more hispanico	mountains high	multi-positive
monodactylous	Moreton Bay fig	mountain slide	multipresence
monodialectal	Mormon cricket	mountain tiger	multiracially
monodramatist	morning coffee	mountain trout	multiserially
monoenergetic	morning prayer	mountainwards	multispectral
monogamically	morphallactic	mountain witch	multi-threaded
monogenically	morphemically	mountain zebra	multi-tracking
monoglyceride	morphinomania	mountebankery	multitudinism
monogrammatic	morphiomaniac	mountebankism	multitudinous
monographical	morphogenesis	mounting block	multivibrator
monohybridism	morphogenetic	mournful widow	multivocality
monomeniscous	morphographer	mourning bride	mumbo-jumboism
monometallism	morpholexical	mourning cloak	mummification
monometallist	morphological	mourning coach	Munchausenism
monomineralic	morphometrics	mourning-paper	municipal bond

municipalizer
Munsterlander
murder inquiry
murder mystery
murderousness
murder will out
murmurousness
murrhine glass
muscle current
muscle-flexing
muscle spindle
museographist
mushroom cloud
mushroom-coral
mushroom-faker
mushroom spawn
mushroom-stone
mushroom valve
musical chairs
musical comedy
music cassette
musicological
musquash house
mussel-cracker
mussel-crusher
mustard colour
mustard weevil
mutton quadrat
mutton snapper
mutualization
muzzle-loading
mycetophagous
mycobacterial
mycobacterium
mycologically
mycoplasmosis
mycotoxicosis
my grandmother
my noble friend
myoepithelial
myoepithelium
myringoplasty
myrmecologist
myrmecophagid
myrobalan plum
myrtle warbler
my sainted aunt
mysteriosophy
mystery writer
mystification
mystificatory
mythicization
mythification
mythopoetical
mytho-theology
myxobacterial
myxobacterium
myxoedematous
naked flooring
Namaqua grouse
namby-pambyism
name of the game

Namierization
naming of parts
nankeen cotton
nannoplankton
nape of the neck
Napoleonistic
narcomaniacal
narcotization
narrative line
narratologist
narrowcasting
narrow fabrics
Natal mahogany
national flour
National Front
national guard
National Guard
nationalistic
nationalities
National Party
National Trust
native fuchsia
native kumquat
native speaker
natural cosine
natural number
natural person
natural spirit
natural virtue
nature reserve
navicular bone
navigableness
navigation act
navigation law
Neanderthaler
Neapolitan ice
near one's heart
near-sightedly
nebular theory
necessariness
necessitarian
necessitation
necessitously
necklace shell
neck or nothing
necrotization
nectariferous
nectarivorous
nectocalycine
needle bearing
needle contest
needle-pointed
needless to say
nefariousness
negative-going
negative pedal
neglectedness
negligibility
negotiability
negrification
Negro minstrel
neighbourhead

neighbourhood
neighbourless
neighbour-like
neighbourship
nemathelminth
nematological
neocerebellar
neocerebellum
neoclassicism
neoclassicist
neoglaciation
neogrammarian
neo-linguistic
neolithically
neologization
neo-Malthusian
Neo-Melanesian
neonatologist
neontological
neo-plasticism
Neo-Synephrine
nephelometric
nephrectomize
nephridiopore
nephritic wood
nephrorrhaphy
nerve-deafness
nervelessness
nervous system
Netherlandian
Netherlandish
nether regions
network former
neuralgically
neural network
neuraminidase
neurapophysis
neurobiotaxis
neuroblastoma
neuro-effector
neuroelectric
neuroethology
neurofibrilla
neurofilament
neurohormonal
neuromuscular
neurone theory
neuronophagia
neurosurgical
neurosyphilis
neurotoxicity
neuter passive
neutral corner
neutral monism
neutral monist
neutron excess
neutron number
new Australian
New Australian
New Caledonian
New Englandish
New Englandism

newfanglement
newfangleness
Newgate school
New Journalism
New Journalist
new psychology
news-gathering
newsmongering
newspaperland
newspaperless
new technology
Newtown pippin
new world order
New Zealand ash
New Zealandism
New Zealand rug
New Zealand tit
Nicaragua wood
Nicene Council
nickel-and-dime
nickeliferous
nickelization
Nicolaitanism
nicotinic acid
niggardliness
nigger-shooter
night-blooming
nightclubbing
nightmarishly
night-primrose
night-wanderer
night-watching
night-watchman
nightwatchman
Nikkei average
Nile crocodile
nincompoopery
nincompoopish
Nine Days' Queen
nitrification
nitrile rubber
nitro compound
nitrofurazone
nitrogenation
nitrogen cycle
nitrogen fixer
nitroglycerin
nitromuriatic
nitroprusside
nitwittedness
nivellization
Nobel laureate
no-claims bonus
noctivagation
no great shakes
no great things
no holds barred
noiselessness
nolle prosequi
nomen actionis
nomenclatural
nominalizable

nominal ledger
nomologically
non-acceptance
non-advertence
non-aggression
non-allergenic
non-appearance
non-attachment
non-attendance
non-biological
non-centrality
non-classified
non-collegiate
non-compliance
non-compounder
non-condensing
non-conducting
nonconformism
Nonconformism
nonconformist
nonconformity
non-contagious
non-contingent
non-cooperator
nondescriptly
non-disclosure
non-evaluative
non-figurative
non-fulfilment
non-functional
non-homologous
non-infectious
non-intervener
non-membership
non-naturalism
non-naturalist
non-negotiable
non-observance
non-occurrence
non-orientable
non-parametric
non-perception
non-performing
non-persistent
non-physically
nonplussation
non-productive
non-randomness
non-regulation
non-residenter
non-resistance
non-returnable
non-scientific
nonsense verse
nonsensically
non-specialist
non-subscriber
non-successful
non-uniformity
non-verbalized
non-volatility
Nootka cypress

noradrenaline
noradrenergic
Norfolk Howard
Norfolk jacket
Norfolk plover
normalization
Norman English
Normanization
normativeness
normovolaemia
normovolaemic
North American
north and south
north-easterly
north-eastward
northerliness
northern canoe
Northern Crown
Northern Irish
North Germanic
North Islander
north-westerly
north-westward
nortriptyline
Norway haddock
Norway lemming
Norway lobster
Norwich school
nose-suspended
nosologically
nostalgically
not before time
not care a whoop
notch-planting
not come to much
not for a moment
not give a stuff
not go anywhere
not good enough
nothing to lose
no through road
noticeability
not made of salt
not miss a trick
not one's idea of
not on your life
notoriousness
not sufficient
not want to know
noun adjective
nouvelle vague
novel of terror
noviciateship
nuclear energy
nuclear family
nuclear fusion
nuclear isomer
nuclear weapon
nuclear winter
nucleogenesis
nucleohistone
nucleoplasmic

nucleoprotein
nuisance value
null character
nullification
null indicator
number-average
numbers racket
numerological
Numidian crane
numismatology
nuncupatively
nursery cannon
nursery garden
nursery school
nursery slopes
nursery stakes
nursing-father
nursing-mother
Nusselt number
nutmeg hickory
nutraceutical
nutritionally
nutritiveness
obedience test
obedientially
obedient plant
objectifiable
objectionable
objectionably
objectivation
objective lens
objectiveness
objectivistic
object of virtu
object program
objects clause
objurgatorily
obliquangular
oblique motion
oblique speech
oblique sphere
oblique stroke
obliviousness
obnoxiousness
observability
observational
observatories
obsessionally
obsessiveness
obstetrically
obstructingly
obstructively
obtainability
obtenebration
obtrusiveness
occasionalism
occasionality
occidentalise
occidentalism
occidentalist
occidentality
occidentalize

occipital bone
occipital lobe
occluded front
occupationist
oceanographer
oceanographic
oceanological
ocean pipefish
ochlocratical
octave coupler
octocentenary
octocorallian
oculist's stamp
Oddfellowship
odontoblastic
odontoglossum
odontological
odontophorous
odoriferously
odourlessness
odynometrical
oesophagocele
oesophagotomy
oestrogenized
oestrous cycle
of all the cheek
of all the nerve
of a parcel with
of a set purpose
of consequence
of evil presage
off and running
offencelessly
offensiveness
offhandedness
officer of arms
officiousness
off microphone
off one's own bat
off one's rocker
off one's rocket
off one's stroke
of little avail
of one's own head
of some account
of the nature of
of unsound mind
oil and vinegar
oil of lavender
oil one's tongue
oil the knocker
Olbers' paradox
old-age pension
old as the hills
old boy network
old clothes man
old-field birch
old-field mouse
old gooseberry
Old High German
old-maidenhood
old witch-grass

oleomargarine
oleo-pneumatic
olfactometric
oligarticular
oligochaetous
oligopolistic
oligosaprobic
oligosyllabic
olive-coloured
olive crescent
olive whistler
olivine basalt
Ollendorffian
Olympia oyster
ombudsmanship
omnibus volume
omnicompetent
omnipresently
omniprevalent
omnisubjugant
on a good wicket
on a person's top
on approbation
on bended knees
once and for all
once upon a time
onchocercosis
ondes martenot
one and another
one and the same
one for the book
one for the road
one-handedness
one in a million
oneiroscopist
one man one vote
one never knows
one-night stand
one's blood is up
one's level best
one's little all
one's name is mud
one's worse half
one-time-cipher
one way or other
on its own roots
onlie begetter
on oiled wheels
onomatologist
onomatopoeian
onomatopoeics
onomatopoesis
onomatopoetic
on one's account
on one's hunkers
on one's own hook
on pain of death
on solid ground
on tenterhooks
on the backhand
on the beam-ends
on the contrary

on the downside
on the face of it
on the forehand
on the gridiron
on the increase
on the pavement
on the pig's back
on the port tack
on the premises
on the safe side
on the scrounge
on the straight
on the strength
ontogenetical
ontogenically
ontologically
onychomycosis
onychophagist
opacification
open admission
open-bill stork
open-circuited
open classroom
open Communion
open community
open-endedness
open enrolment
open occupancy
open the door to
operating room
operationally
operativeness
ophthalmology
ophthalmotomy
opinionatedly
opisthobranch
opossum-shrimp
opportuneness
opportunistic
opportunities
oppositionary
oppositionist
opprobriously
optical centre
optical double
optical isomer
optical square
optic neuritis
opticokinetic
optic thalamus
optional extra
oral-formulaic
orange blossom
orange-quarter
orbital sander
orchard oriole
orchesography
orchestralist
orchestra seat
orchestration
orchidologist
orciprenaline

order of battle
order of the day
ordinal number
ordinary grade
ordinary level
ordinary scale
ordinary share
ordinary table
ordnance datum
organicalness
organogenesis
organogenetic
organographic
organological
organoplastic
organotherapy
orgiastically
orientability
orientalizing
oriental plane
oriental poppy
oriental topaz
orientational
Orient Express
orient oneself
originalities
original print
or I'm a Dutchman
orismological
ornamentalism
ornamentalist
ornamentality
ornamentalize
ornamentation
ornithischian
ornithologist
ornithologize
ornithopodous
oropharyngeal
orthocephalic
orthoepically
orthogenetics
orthognathism
orthognathous
orthogonality
orthogonalize
orthographies
orthographist
orthographize
orthohydrogen
orthologously
orthomorphism
orthophotomap
orthopinacoid
orthopoxvirus
orthoptically
orthopyroxene
orthosilicate
orthotectonic
oryctological
oscillography
oscillometric

oscilloscopic
os intermedium
Osiride column
Oslo breakfast
osmoregulator
ossiculectomy
ostensibility
ostensiveness
osteoclastoma
osteomyelitis
osteopetrosis
osteopetrotic
ostracization
ostreiculture
ostreoculture
ostreophagous
ostrobogulous
Ostyak Samoyed
Oswego biscuit
Otaheite apple
other-directed
otitis externa
otitis interna
otter-trawling
outblossoming
outdoor relief
outdoor things
outer garments
outing flannel
out like a light
outline stitch
out of a bandbox
out of all sight
out of harm's way
out of love with
out of one's hair
out of one's head
out of one's line
out of one's mind
out of one's road
out of one's time
out of one's tree
out of one's wits
out of position
out of practice
out of register
out of straight
out of the woods
out of training
outrecuidance
outriggerless
outsettlement
outspokenness
outstandingly
outward things
ovariectomies
ovariectomize
ovariotomized
over-abundance
overabundance
overambitious
over-anxiously

overanxiously
overattention
overbearingly
overcarefully
overcivilized
overcloseness
overcommitted
overconcerned
overconfident
overcredulity
overcredulous
over-curiosity
overcuriosity
overcuriously
overdecorated
overdetermine
overdischarge
overdispersed
overdramatise
overdramatize
overdraw check
overeagerness
overearnestly
over-elaborate
overelaborate
over-emotional
overemotional
overemphasise
overemphasize
overexcitable
overextension
overflowingly
overforwardly
overfurnished
overhastiness
overhead valve
overhydration
overinclusion
over-indulgent
overindulgent
over-insurance
overinsurance
overmasterful
overmastering
overofficious
overpopulated
overpotential
overprecision
over-prescribe
overprescribe
overpublicize
overqualified
overreadiness
overrunningly
oversaturated
oversensitive
oversharpness
overshot wheel
overstatement
overstimulate
overstitching
oversubscribe

over the sticks
overvaluation
overventilate
overvulcanize
overweeningly
overwhelmment
ovipositional
ovi-viviparous
ovoviviparity
ovoviviparous
owlet-nightjar
own-categories
owner-occupied
owner-occupier
oxalosuccinic
Oxford corners
Oxford marbles
Oxford mixture
Oxford ragwort
Oxford sausage
Oxford scholar
Oxford Scholar
ox-heart cherry
oxidizability
oystercatcher
oyster-farming
ozone-friendly
ozonification
pace tanti viri
packet network
packing needle
pack on all sail
padding stitch
paddle steamer
paddle-wheeler
Paddy's lantern
Paddy's lucerne
pad in the straw
paediatrician
paedomorphism
pageant master
page reference
page three girl
pain in the arse
pain in the neck
painstakingly
painted beauty
painterliness
painter's brush
painter's colic
Painter's Easel
pain threshold
paint stripper
pair-formation
pairing-season
pair of bellows
pair of colours
pair of pincers
Palaeo-Asiatic
palaeobiology
palaeobotanic
palaeoclimate

palaeocrystic
palaeocurrent
palaeoecology
palaeo-equator
palaeogeology
palaeographer
palaeographic
palaeogravity
palaeoniscoid
palaeontology
palaeopallial
palaeopallium
palaeospecies
palaeotechnic
palaeotherian
palaeozoology
palagonitized
palais de danse
palatableness
palatine uvula
palatographic
palatorrhaphy
paleanthropic
palimbacchius
palingenesian
palinspastics
palisade layer
palletization
Palmerstonian
Palmerstonism
Palmetto State
palpitatingly
palynological
palynomorphic
pampas flicker
pan-Africander
pan-Africanism
pan-Africanist
Panama disease
panatela cigar
pancake batter
panchromatize
panchronistic
pancratiastic
pandemoniacal
pandiculation
panegyrically
panel analysis
panel painting
panentheistic
pangrammatist
panharmonicon
panic stations
panic-stricken
panic-striking
pannier pocket
panoramically
pan-Protestant
panpsychistic
pansporoblast
Pantagruelian
Pantagruelism

Pantagruelist
pantheistical
pantisocratic
pantomography
papaveraceous
paper carriage
paper-fastener
paper mulberry
paper nautilus
paper shredder
paper streamer
papilliferous
papillomatous
papulo-vesicle
papyrographic
papyrological
parabolically
paracaseinate
paradigm shift
paradise apple
paradise crane
paradise stock
paradisically
paradoxically
paraganglioma
paragrammatic
paragraphical
para-influenza
parakeratosis
parakeratotic
paraleipomena
paralipomenon
parallax error
parallelistic
parallelogram
paralytically
paramagnetism
paramenstruum
paramountship
paramyoclonus
paramyxovirus
paranoiacally
paranormality
paraphernalia
paraphrasable
parapolitical
parapophysial
parapsoriasis
pararealistic
parascientist
parasexuality
parasitically
parasiticidal
parasitopolis
parasymbiosis
parasymbiotic
parasynthesis
parasynthetic
parasyntheton
paratragoedia
paravertebral
parcel-gilding

parcelization
parchment glue
parchment-lace
parchment-skin
pareiasaurian
parencephalon
parent company
parenthetical
parent–teacher
parepididymal
parepididymis
Pareto-optimal
pare to the bone
par excellence
parish council
parish lantern
parish pumpery
Parisian cloth
Parker's cement
parking ticket
Parkinson's law
parlementaire
parliamentary
parliamenteer
parliament man
Parnassianism
par of exchange
parotidectomy
par parenthèse
parrot disease
parrot-fashion
part and parcel
part brass rags
parthenocarpy
parthenogenic
parthenospore
participation
participative
participatory
participially
particle board
particoloured
particularise
particularism
particularist
particularity
particularize
partitionment
partition wall
partridge shot
partridge-wood
party politics
paschal candle
Paschen series
passage at arms
passage of arms
Passamaquoddy
passementerie
passenger-mile
passion flower
passion killer
passionlessly

Passion Sunday
passive smoker
passivization
passport photo
Pasteur effect
pastoral lease
pastoral staff
patentability
patent insides
patent leather
patent theatre
paterfamilias
paternalistic
paternity suit
paternity test
pathogenicity
pathognomical
pathognomonic
patriarchally
patriarchical
patricianship
patrilineally
patrilocality
patrimonially
patriotically
patripotestal
patronization
patronizingly
patte de velour
pattern-welded
pauperization
pavement-tooth
paxilliferous
pay-and-display
payback period
pay scot and lot
pay-television
peaceableness
peace dividend
peacelessness
peace-offering
peach leaf curl
peacock copper
peacock-flower
peacock throne
peak voltmeter
peanut brittle
peanut gallery
pearl-bordered
pearl of orient
peasant blouse
pebble-beached
pebble chopper
pebble culture
pebble-dashing
pebble glasses
pebble-grained
pebble hook-tip
pectoral quail
peculiarities
pedagogically
pedal clarinet

pedal keyboard
pedal wireless
pedantocratic
pedestal basin
pedestal table
pedestrianate
pedestrianise
pedestrianism
pedestrianize
pediculicidal
pedimentation
pediplanation
pedlar's French
pedogenetical
pedogenically
pedologically
pedunculation
pelican-flower
pellagragenic
pelletization
Peloponnesian
pelycosaurian
penalty clause
penalty double
penalty killer
pending basket
Pendragonship
pendulousness
pendulum-clock
pendulum swing
pendulum-wheel
peneplanation
penetrability
penetratingly
penetratively
penicillamine
penicillately
penicillation
penicilliform
penicillinase
peninsularity
peninsulation
penitentially
pennatulacean
pennilessness
Pennsylvanian
penny dreadful
penny-farthing
penny-pinching
pennyweighter
Penrose tiling
pentachloride
pentadelphous
pentahydrated
pentanoic acid
pentapetalous
pentasepalous
pentasyllabic
pentatonicism
penthemimeral
Pentland Crown
pentobarbital

penuriousness
Penzance brier
People's Bureau
people's choice
People's Palace
pepper-and-salt
peppered steak
peppermint gum
peppermint oil
peppermint-tea
peptidoglycan
peptizability
peptonization
peralkalinity
perambulation
perambulatory
perceivedness
perceptualize
percussion cap
percussion gun
percussionist
perdurability
perdu sentinel
peregrination
peregrinatory
peregrine tone
perennibranch
perfectionate
perfectionism
perfectionist
perfectionize
perfect square
perfervidness
perforant path
perfunctorily
periarteritis
periarticular
peribronchial
pericapillary
pericardotomy
perichondrial
perichondrium
peridiastolic
periglacially
perilymphatic
perimenopause
periodic table
periodisation
periodization
periodontally
periodontitis
periodontosis
perioperative
peripapillary
peripatetical
peripherality
peripheralize
perisaturnium
perishability
perisplenitis
perissodactyl
peritendineum

perityphlitis	phalansterian	phosphataemia	phycoerythrin
perivitelline	phallocentric	phosphate bond	phyllocladous
Perkin's purple	phanerogamous	phosphate rock	phyllophagous
perlustration	phantasmality	phosphogypsum	phylloquinone
permanent blue	Pharisaically	phosphokinase	phylogenetics
permanent wave	pharmaceutics	phospholipase	physical force
permeableness	pharmaceutist	phosphoretted	physicalistic
permineralize	pharmacognosy	phosphorylase	physical jerks
Permo-Triassic	pharmacologic	phosphorylate	physicianship
permselective	pharmacopoeia	phosphuretted	physiocracies
permutability	pharyngalized	photoacoustic	physiognomies
permutational	pharyngectomy	photoactivate	physiognomist
peroxide blond	pharyngoscope	photoactivity	physiognomize
peroxide group	phase contrast	photoaffinity	physiographer
perpendicular	phase inverter	photoallergic	physiographic
perpetualness	phase-splitter	photocatalyse	physiological
perplexedness	phase velocity	photocatalyst	physioplastic
perscrutation	phencyclidine	photochemical	physiotherapy
persecutional	phenmetrazine	photochromism	physisorption
perseverantly	phenobarbital	photocomposer	physoclistous
perseveration	phenolization	photocopiable	physostigmine
perseverative	phenol oxidase	photodetector	phytochemical
perseveringly	phenomenalise	photodimerize	phytoecdysone
Persian blinds	phenomenalism	photoejection	phytopathogen
Persian carpet	phenomenalist	photoelectric	phytoplankter
Persian walnut	phenomenality	photoelectron	phytoplankton
personalistic	phenomenalize	photoemission	phytosanitary
personalities	phenomenistic	photoemissive	phytotoxicant
personal space	phenomenology	photo-engraver	phytotoxicity
personal touch	phenothiazine	photofinisher	pianistically
personologist	phenoxyacetic	photogalvanic	piano concerto
perspectively	phenylalanine	photogeologic	pick and choose
perspectivism	phenylarsonic	photographica	picked dogfish
perspectivist	phenylene blue	photographist	pickle-herring
perspectivity	phenylephrine	photoisomeric	pick out of a hat
perspicacious	phenylmercury	photolability	pickpocketing
perspicuously	phenylpyruvic	photomagnetic	Pickwickianly
pertechnetate	Philadelphian	photonegative	picnic blanket
perthitically	philanthropic	photoperiodic	Picnic Society
pervaporation	philhellenism	photophoresis	picrochromite
pervasiveness	philhellenist	photophoretic	picrolichenic
pervertedness	Phillips curve	photophysical	picrolichenin
pestiferously	philobiblical	photopositive	picturability
pest of society	philodendrons	photoproduced	picture palace
Peter Grievous	philomathical	photoreaction	picture search
Petersen graph	philosophical	photoreceptor	picture signal
petite marmite	philosophizer	photorecovery	picturesquely
petrification	phlebographic	photoregulate	picture window
petrochemical	Phlegethontic	photoresistor	picturization
petro-currency	phlogisticate	photoresponse	pidgin English
petroleum coke	phonaesthesia	photoreversal	pidginization
petroliferous	phonaesthetic	photoscanning	piece of silver
petrolization	phonautograph	photosynthate	piece together
petrol lighter	phonematology	phototelegram	piecrust table
petrol station	phonemization	phototoxicity	pietistically
petrophysical	phonendoscope	photovoltaics	piezoelectric
petrotectonic	phonetization	phraseography	piezomagnetic
petticoatless	phoney-boloney	phraseologies	pigeon-chested
petticoat tail	phonocentrism	phraseologist	pigeon fancier
petty sessions	phonographist	phrenicectomy	pigeon-hearted
phaeophorbide	phonoreceptor	phrenological	pigging string
phagolysosome	phonus-bolonus	phycobilisome	pig-headedness

pigheadedness
pig in a blanket
pigmentocracy
pignut hickory
pig's breakfast
pilgrim-bottle
Pilgrim Father
pilgrim's shell
pillar-and-claw
pillar and room
pillar apostle
pill-millipede
pill-woodlouse
pilosebaceous
pinafore dress
pin connection
pineapple bomb
pineapple lily
pineapple weed
pinheadedness
pinhole camera
pink champagne
pink elephants
pinking shears
piroplasmosis
piscatorially
piscicultural
piss in the wind
pistol-packing
piston-engined
pit and gallows
pitch-accented
pitch-darkness
pitched battle
pitch-farthing
pitching-yeast
pitch it strong
pituitary body
placebo effect
place in the sun
placelessness
placentophagy
plagal cadence
plagiocephaly
plagioclastic
plagiogranite
plagiostomous
plagiotropism
plagiotropous
plain language
plain-speaking
plaintiveness
plain-wanderer
plaited stitch
plane-parallel
planetary gear
planetary hour
planetary year
planet carrier
planetography
planetologist
planification

planimetrical
plank-buttress
planktologist
planktonology
plantain-eater
planter's punch
plantsmanship
plasmacytosis
plasma-dynamic
plasmalogenic
plasmaspheric
plasmoblastic
plasmodesmata
plasmolysable
plasmolyticum
plaster-bronze
plaster jacket
plasterworker
plastic bronze
plastic bullet
plastochronic
plastoquinone
plateau basalt
plateau gravel
plate cylinder
platelet count
plate of silver
plate tectonic
platform party
platform plank
platform scale
platform-soled
platform stage
platform truck
platiniferous
platiniridium
platinization
platinum-black
platinum blond
platinum group
platinum metal
platitudinary
platitudinise
platitudinize
platitudinous
Platonic solid
platycephalic
platyhelminth
platykurtosis
plausibleness
player-manager
play for laughs
play for safety
play games with
play hard to get
play havoc with
playing-marble
play oneself in
play propriety
play the market
play the part of
play therapist

playwrighting
plead innocent
please oneself
please the pigs
pleasuredrome
pleasure-house
plebification
plectognathic
pleiophyllous
plenitudinous
plenteousness
plentifulness
plenum chamber
plerocephalic
plesiosaurian
plesiosauroid
plethorically
plethysmogram
pleurocarpous
pleurotyphoid
plotting board
plotting table
plough-bullock
ploughmanship
plumber's snake
plumbosolvent
plumed serpent
plumification
plum-puddinger
plunge cutting
plunkety-plunk
pluralization
plural society
pluripresence
plurisyllabic
plurisyllable
plutocratical
Plymouth china
Plymouth cloak
pneumatically
pneumatic duct
pneumatic tube
pneumatic tyre
pneumatolysis
pneumatolytic
pneumatometer
pneumatophore
pneumogastric
pneumographic
pneumonectomy
pneumonolysis
pocketability
pocket borough
pocket-picking
podzolization
poetical works
poeticization
poetic justice
poetic licence
poetry reading
poetry recital
Poets Laureate

pogonophorous
poikilosmosis
poikilosmotic
poikilothermy
Poincaré cycle
pointillistic
pointing-stick
pointlessness
point mutation
point of honour
points victory
poison-hemlock
poisonousness
Poisson's ratio
poke mullock at
poker patience
polar distance
polari-locular
polarographic
polecat ferret
polemological
policeman-bird
policemanlike
policemanship
police message
police officer
police science
police station
police-witness
policy science
poliomyelitic
poliomyelitis
politicalness
politicianism
pollakanthous
pollen analyst
pollen-chamber
pollen diagram
pollen profile
pollicitation
polliniferous
pollinigerous
pollinivorous
pollinization
polyacetylene
polyadelphous
polyarteritis
polyarthritic
polyarthritis
polyarticular
polybutadiene
polycarbonate
polycephalous
polychotomous
polychromasia
polychromasic
polychromatic
polycistronic
polycythaemia
polycythaemic
polydactylism
polydactylous

polydaemonism
polydispersed
polyembryonic
polyendocrine
polyethylenic
polygamically
polygenically
polygonaceous
polyhistorian
polykaryocyte
polymeniscous
polymerizable
polymethylene
polymolecular
polymorphemic
Polynesian rat
polynucleated
polypharmacal
polyphenylene
polyphosphate
polyphyletism
polypragmatic
polypropylene
polyprotodont
polyribosomal
polyserositis
polysomnogram
polysyllabism
polysynthesis
polysynthetic
polytechnical
polythalamous
Pomeranchukon
Pomeranian dog
pomiculturist
pomologically
Pompe's disease
pompier ladder
ponderability
ponderomotive
ponderousness
pontificality
pontification
pontoon bridge
Ponzo illusion
Poona painting
pooper scooper
poorly stocked
popping crease
poppy-coloured
population III
populationist
porcelain clay
porcellaneous
porcupine fish
porcupine-wood
porencephalic
porokeratosis
porokeratotic
porphyrinogen
porphyrinuria
porphyroblast

porphyroclast
portal bracing
Portland Place
Portland stone
portosystemic
portrait-stone
position angle
position paper
positive-going
positive logic
positive organ
possessionary
possessorship
possibilistic
possibilities
postabdominal
postalization
post-apostolic
post-auricular
post-Christian
post-classical
post-Communion
post-disseisin
post-emergence
poste restante
posteriormost
posterization
poster session
post-existence
postglacially
postlapsarian
postliminious
postman's knock
post-menarchal
postmenstrual
postmenstruum
post-modernism
postmodernism
post-modernist
postmodernist
postmodernity
postnuptially
post office box
post-office red
post-operative
postoperative
post-ovulative
post-ovulatory
postreduction
postscutellum
post-traumatic
post-treatment
postulational
postwar credit
potamological
potato creeper
potato disease
potato pancake
pot-belly stove
potential flow
potentialness
potential wall

potential well
potentiometer
potentiometry
potentization
Pott's fracture
pound for pound
pound sterling
poverty-struck
powder and shot
powder compact
powdering-gown
powdering-room
powder pattern
powdery mildew
power-assisted
power dressing
power industry
powerlessness
power-operated
power politics
power spectrum
power steering
pozzolanicity
practical joke
practicalness
practice-curve
praemunientes
praetorianism
pragmatically
prairie bottom
prairie-buster
prairie clover
prairie crocus
prairie falcon
prairie marmot
prairie oyster
prairie turnip
praisefulness
Prandtl number
praxeological
prayerfulness
prayer-meeting
pray extempore
praying mantis
preadaptation
preadmonition
pre-adolescent
preadolescent
preambulation
preambulatory
preanticipate
pre-aspiration
prebiological
precalculable
precarcinogen
precautionary
precautiously
precentorship
preceptorship
precinct house
precious blood
precious coral

precious metal
precious stone
precipitantly
precipitately
precipitation
precipitously
precogitation
preconception
preconization
precursorship
predatoriness
pre-delinquent
predestinator
predeterminer
predicability
predicamental
predicational
predicatively
predicativity
predictionism
predominantly
predominately
predominating
pre-engagement
prefabricator
prefatorially
preferability
preference bid
preferredness
prefiguration
prefigurative
prefigurement
preganglionic
pregenitality
pregeological
pregerminated
pregnancy test
prehistorical
pre-impregnate
pre-industrial
pre-intimation
preiotization
prejudication
prejudicially
prelectorship
preliminaries
preliminarily
pre-linguistic
prelinguistic
prematuration
prematureness
pre-medication
premedication
premeditation
premeditative
premenopausal
premillennial
premonitorily
premunization
preneoplastic
preoccupation
preoccupiedly

preordainment
pre-ordination
preparatively
preparatorily
prepare the way
preperception
prepolymerize
preponderance
preponderancy
prepositional
prepositively
prepositorial
prepossessing
prepossession
pre-preference
pre-production
preproduction
preprohormone
prepubescence
Pre-Raphaelism
Pre-Raphaelite
pre-reflective
presbytership
prescientific
prescriptible
presentiality
preserving jar
presidentship
press coverage
press-fastener
pressing board
press one's luck
press the flesh
press the point
pressure cabin
pressure gauge
pressure group
pressure plate
pressure point
pressure ridge
pressure-treat
prestigiation
prestigiously
presumingness
presumptively
pretendership
pretentiously
preteriteness
pretermission
pretermitting
preternatural
pretty-by-night
prettyprinter
prevarication
prevaricatory
preventionism
preventionist
prevocational
prevotal court
pricelessness
price movement
prick-me-dainty

prick one's ears
prick-shooting
priest's pintle
prima donna-ish
primal therapy
primary colour
primary oocyte
primary planet
primary school
primatologist
prime meridian
prime minister
Prime Minister
prime ministry
prime vertical
primigravidae
priming powder
primitive cell
primitiveness
primitivistic
primogenitary
primogenitive
primogeniture
primordialism
primordiality
primuline base
prince consort
Prince Consort
prince-elector
princely State
Prince of Peace
Prince of Wales
princess royal
Princess Royal
principal axis
principal girl
principalness
principalship
printed matter
printer buffer
Printers' Bible
printer's devil
printing-frame
printing-house
printing press
printing-sheet
printing union
print spooling
prismatically
prisoner of war
prisoners' bars
prisoner's base
prisoners' base
prison haircut
prisonization
privateersman
privateersmen
private income
private member
private number
private school
private sector

private treaty
privativeness
privatization
prizefighting
probabilistic
probabilities
probable cause
probable error
probationship
probativeness
problematical
problematique
problem column
procarcinogen
process camera
process cheese
processionary
processionist
processionize
process server
procès-verbaux
proclitically
proconsulship
procrastinate
proctological
procuratorial
producibility
productionize
product moment
profecticious
profectitious
professoriate
professorship
profile cutter
profilometric
profitability
profit and loss
profit-sharing
progenitorial
progestogenic
prognathously
prognosticate
programmatist
programme note
progressional
progressively
progressivism
progressivist
progressivity
prohibitively
projectionist
prolegomenary
prolegomenous
proleptically
proliferation
proliferative
proliferously
prolification
promenade deck
Prometheanism
prominent moth
promiscuously

promorphology
promotability
promotiveness
pronator teres
pronominalise
pronominalize
pronounceable
pronouncement
pronunciation
proof positive
proof strength
propagability
propagational
propanoic acid
propantheline
proparoxytone
propellerless
proper preface
prophetically
propinquitous
propiolactone
propionic acid
proportionate
propositional
propraetorial
propraetorian
proprietorial
proprietously
proprioceptor
proprio-spinal
propugnaculum
propulsion gun
propyl alcohol
propylenimine
prosaicalness
prosecutorial
prosification
prosopagnosia
prosopography
prospect-glass
prospectively
prostaglandin
prostatectomy
prostate gland
prosthodontia
protanomalous
protectionism
protectionist
protectorless
protectorship
proteinaceous
proteoclastic
proterandrous
proterogynous
Protestantdom
Protestantise
Protestantish
Protestantism
Protestantize
protest voting
prothetically
protoactinium

protochordate
protocultural
protodynastic
protofilament
protogalactic
Proto-Germanic
proto-historic
proto-language
proto-literate
proton donator
protonosphere
protriptyline
protruberance
protuberantly
proverbialism
proverbialist
proverbiality
proverbialize
Provident Club
providentness
provincialate
provincialise
provincialism
provincialist
provinciality
provincialize
provisionally
provisionless
provisionment
provocatively
provokingness
proximateness
proximity fuse
prudentialism
prudentialist
prudentiality
psammophilous
psephological
pseudisodomon
pseudoallelic
pseudo-archaic
pseudobedding
pseudobreccia
pseudobulbous
pseudo-concept
pseudodiploid
pseudohalogen
pseudoleucite
pseudological
pseudomorphic
pseudopatient
pseudoplastic
pseudo-problem
pseudoprophet
pseudoracemic
pseudo-science
pseudoseizure
pseudosematic
pseudosuchian
pseudouridine
psychagogical
psychanalysis

psychasthenia
psychasthenic
psychiatrical
psychic income
psychoanalyse
psychoanalyst
psychobabbler
psychobiology
psychocentric
psychodynamic
psychogenesis
psychogenetic
psychographer
psychographic
psychohistory
psychokinesis
psychokinetic
psychological
psychologizer
psychometrics
psychometrist
psychometrize
psychopathist
psychophysics
psychosomatic
psychostatics
psychosurgeon
psychosurgery
psychotechnic
psychotherapy
psychotically
psychotogenic
psychotrophic
psychrometric
psychrophilic
psychrosphere
pteridologist
pteridophytic
pterygoid bone
pterylography
ptygmatically
public analyst
public company
public holiday
public inquiry
publicization
public library
public opinion
public servant
public service
public utility
publish a libel
pudding course
pudding-headed
pudding-sleeve
Pulitzer Prize
pullet disease
pulmonary vein
pulse dialling
pulselessness
pulse pressure
pulse repeater

pulverization
pump attendant
pumped storage
pumpkin-headed
punching press
punch the clock
punctiliously
punctuational
punctus versus
punishability
punto a rilievo
pupillography
pupillometric
puppet-showman
Purbeck marble
purchase a writ
purchase-money
purchase price
pure and simple
puritanically
Purkinje fibre
purple emperor
purple grackle
purple passage
purposelessly
purposiveness
purpurogallin
push-button war
pusillanimity
pusillanimous
put a new face on
put a premium on
put a stopper on
put au fait with
put in the fangs
put in the shade
put in the wrong
put into effect
put one's face on
put one's feet up
put one's hand to
put one's mind to
put out of sight
put out to grass
put out to nurse
put pen to paper
put pressure on
putrilaginous
put the black on
put the flag out
put the hooks in
put to the blush
put to the sword
put to the torch
putty-coloured
put up one's hair
put up or shut up
put up the spout
pycnidiospore
pycnochlorite
pycnoconidium
pyelocystitis

pyramidically
pyrenocarpous
pyrheliometer
Pyribenzamine
pyriform fossa
pyrimethamine
pyrocellulose
pyrolytically
pyromagnetism
pyrophosphate
pyrosulphuric
pyrosynthesis
pyrosynthetic
pyrotechnical
pyroxferroite
pyrrolizidine
Pythagorician
quadragesimal
quadraphonics
quadratically
quadratojugal
quadrennially
quadridentate
quadrifoliate
quadrilateral
quadrilingual
quadriliteral
quadrillionth
quadrilocular
quadripartite
quadripinnate
quadrivalence
quadrivalency
quadrivoltine
quadrumvirate
quadrupartite
quadrupedally
quadruple time
quadruplicate
quadruplicity
Quaker meeting
qualification
qualificative
qualificatory
qualifiedness
qualitatively
qualitiedness
quality circle
quality factor
qualmlessness
quantophrenia
quantum number
quantum theory
quarantinable
quarrelsomely
quarter-finals
quarter-gunner
quartermaster
quarter-racing
Quartier Latin
Quartodeciman
quartz-halogen

quartziferous
quasi-contract
quasiparticle
quaternionist
quatre-couleur
queen excluder
Queen of the May
Queen's counsel
Queen's Counsel
queen's cushion
Queen's English
Queen's highway
Queensland nut
queen's pattern
Queen's Proctor
queen's pudding
queen staysail
queen's weather
querulousness
questionaries
questioningly
questionnaire
queue fourchée
quick-and-dirty
quick-tempered
quiet American
quiet as a mouse
quilting frame
quilting party
quincentenary
quincuncially
quingentenary
quinquagenary
Quinquagesima
quinquangular
quinquelobate
quinquenniums
quinquevalent
quinquevirate
quintillionth
quintuplicate
quizzicalness
quizzing-glass
quodlibetical
quota sampling
quotation mark
quotativeness
quotient group
rabbit-and-pork
rabbit tobacco
rabble-rousing
race condition
race relations
racialization
racing colours
rack and manger
rack-and-pinion
racy of the soil
radiant energy
radiant heater
radiant region
radiationally

radiation belt
radiation burn
radiationless
radical humour
radiesthesist
radiesthetist
radioactivate
radioactively
radioactivity
radiobiologic
radiochemical
radioisotopic
radiolocation
radio spectrum
radio-telegram
radioteletype
radiotoxicity
radium therapy
Raffaelle ware
Rafferty rules
rag-and-bone man
railroad guide
railway letter
rainbow cactus
rainbow runner
rainbow wrasse
raise one's eyes
raise the Devil
rake's progress
Raman spectrum
ramapithecine
ramentiferous
ramshackledom
ram's-horn snail
ranch bungalow
randomization
Rankine degree
rapaciousness
rapprochement
rapscallionly
rapturousness
rarefactional
raspberry cane
raspberry tart
rasterization
rateable value
ratiocination
ratiocinative
rational dress
rationalistic
rat-tail cactus
rattle-brained
Rayleigh limit
ray of sunshine
reaccommodate
reacquisition
reactionaries
reactionarily
reactive power
reader-printer
read one's shirt
ready reckoner

reaffirmation
reaggravation
reaggregation
realistically
realizability
realizational
realpolitiker
re-application
reapplication
reappointment
rear commodore
rearrangement
reasonability
reason of State
reassociation
Réaumur's scale
rebarbatively
rebroadcasted
rebroadcaster
rebukefulness
recalcitrance
recalcitrancy
recalculation
receiving barn
receiving line
receiving ship
receptibility
reception room
receptiveness
recessiveness
recess-printed
recharge basin
reciprocality
reciprocating
reciprocation
reciprocatory
recirculation
recirculatory
reclusiveness
recoil starter
recollectable
recombination
recommendable
recommunicate
recompensable
recomposition
recompression
recomputation
reconcentrado
reconcentrate
reconcilement
reconciliator
reconditeness
reconditioned
reconditioner
reconsignment
reconsolidate
reconstructed
reconstructor
record changer
recording head
record linkage

recoup oneself
recreationist
recrimination
recriminative
recriminatory
recrudescence
recrudescency
recrystallise
recrystallize
rectangularly
rectification
rectilinearly
rectitudinous
rectus in curia
recultivation
recursiveness
recyclability
recycling time
red-backed vole
red-back spider
red bishop bird
red dead-nettle
redding-stroke
redeemability
redeliverance
redescription
redevelopment
red hartebeest
red-headed smew
rediscoveries
redissolution
redissolvable
red jungle fowl
red phosphorus
red rag to a bull
Red Republican
Red Riding Hood
Red River fever
red sandalwood
red-shouldered
red spider mite
reducibleness
reducing agent
reductionally
reduction gear
reductiveness
reduplication
reduplicative
reduplicature
redwater fever
Redwood second
re-edification
reefing-jacket
re-eligibility
re-embarkation
re-enfeoffment
re-enforcement
re-entry permit
re-examination
re-exportation
refashionment
reference book

reference room
reference tube
referentially
refer to drawer
reflectometer
reflectometry
reflex copying
reflexibility
reflexiveness
reflexogenous
reflexologist
reflorescence
refocillation
reforestation
reformability
reformational
Reformational
reformatively
reformatories
Reform Judaism
reformulation
refractionist
refractometer
refractometry
refrigeration
refrigerative
refrigeratory
refurbishment
refurnishment
regardfulness
regermination
regimentation
regionalistic
regiospecific
register board
Register House
register plate
registrarship
regretfulness
regular clergy
regular fellow
regulator gene
regurgitation
reign of terror
reimbursement
reimmigration
reimportation
reincarnation
reincorporate
reinfestation
reinforcement
reinforce ring
reinoculation
reinstatement
reinstitution
reintegration
reintegrative
reinterpreted
reinterrogate
reinvestigate
reiteratively
rejection slip

rejuvenescent
relationality
relative pitch
relief pitcher
relieving arch
religiousness
remainder over
remancipation
remanufacture
remarkability
rematerialize
remeasurement
reminiscently
remissibility
remittance man
remonstrantly
remonstration
remonstrative
remonstratory
remorselessly
remote control
remote sensing
remythologize
renal dialysis
renationalise
renationalize
rendezvousing
renegotiation
renewal theory
renovationist
rental library
rent of ability
reorientation
reoxygenation
repairability
repealability
repeatability
repeating back
repeating coil
repeat oneself
repeat pattern
repetitionary
repetitiously
replenishment
replicability
replica method
replicatively
reportability
reportorially
reposefulness
reprecipitate
reprehensible
reprehensibly
representable
representment
repressionist
reproachfully
reproachingly
reproduceable
reprogramming
reprographics
reptiliferous

reptilivorous
republicanism
republicanize
republication
repugnatorial
repullulation
repulsiveness
requisiteness
requisitioner
rescue mission
resectability
resegregation
resentfulness
reserved seats
reservoir rock
resettability
residence city
residence time
residentially
resinographer
resinographic
resistibility
resistiveness
resolutionist
resolvability
resourcefully
respirability
respirometric
resplendently
restaurant car
restauranteur
restiform body
restimulation
restipulation
restoratively
restrainingly
restrictively
restrictivist
resublimation
resultant tone
resuscitation
resuscitative
retainability
retaining wall
retentiveness
retiary spider
reticular cell
reticulum cell
retinaldehyde
retirement age
retranslation
retransmitted
retributively
retributivism
retributivist
retroactively
retroactivity
retroanalysis
retrodictable
retrogression
retrogressive
retrospection

retrospective
returnability
return the lead
reunification
reutilization
revaccination
revelationist
revendication
reverberantly
reverberation
reverberative
reverberatory
reverentially
reversal speed
reverse-charge
reverse Polish
reverse thrust
reversibility
reversing mill
reviewability
revindication
revocableness
revoltingness
revolutionary
revolutionise
revolutionism
revolutionist
revolutionize
revolving door
revolving fund
rewardingness
Reye's syndrome
Rhadamanthine
Rhaeto-Liassic
Rhaeto-Romance
Rhaeto-Romanic
rhapsodically
rhematization
rheologically
rheoreceptive
rhesus macaque
rheumatically
Rhine daughter
rhizocephalan
rhizomorphous
Rhodes Scholar
rhodochrosite
rhombohedrons
Rhomboidal Net
rhopalocerous
rhotacization
rhyparography
rhythmicality
rhythmization
rhythm section
Ribbon Society
ribosenucleic
rice Christian
Richardsonian
Richard's pipit
rickety rosary
ride the blinds

ride the clutch
ridge cucumber
riffle-shuffle
rifle regiment
Riga rhine hemp
Riggs's disease
right defender
righteousness
right half-back
right-handedly
rightlessness
right midfield
right of common
right of search
Right Reverend
right-thinking
right triangle
ring blackbird
ring modulator
ripping-chisel
ripple control
ripple counter
ripple-flaking
riproariously
Risso's dolphin
rite of passage
Ritschlianism
ritualisation
ritualization
river bullhead
river-diggings
road allowance
robe de chambre
Robespierrist
robin's egg blue
robotomorphic
rob the spittle
rocambolesque
rock and roller
rocket chamber
rock mechanics
rock phosphate
Rocky Mountain
rodent officer
roentgenogram
roentgenology
rogue's gallery
rogues' gallery
rolled into one
roller bandage
roller bearing
roller coaster
rolling moment
rolling strike
roll-on roll-off
Roman Catholic
Roman hyacinth
romanticality
Roman wormwood
root and branch
root vegetable

Rorschach test
rose of Jericho
rose Pompadour
rose-water pipe
rotary cutting
rotary machine
rotary shutter
rotten borough
rotten-hearted
rough-and-ready
rough and round
rough-tonguing
round and round
round brackets
round the clock
round the twist
round-tripping
Rousseauesque
Rousseauistic
routinization
rowing machine
Rowland circle
Roxbury russet
Royal Air Force
royal antelope
royal peculiar
royal standard
royal straight
rubber-proofed
rubber-tapping
rub elbows with
rub of the green
rub on the green
rub resistance
ruddy shelduck
rude awakening
rudimentarily
ruffed bustard
rufous hornero
rugby football
ruggedization
Ruhmkorff coil
rule of the road
ruling passion
rumbustiously
runcible spoon
running battle
running stitch
run out of steam
run rings round
run the gamut of
rural delivery
rural district
rurbanization
Russell's viper
Russia leather
Russian ballet
Russian dinner
Russian stitch
russification
Russification
rustic bunting

rust-resistant
rustyback fern
rutherfordium
rye brome-grass
Sabba-day house
Sabbath candle
Sabbath school
sabbatization
sable antelope
sabre-rattling
saccharic acid
saccharimeter
saccharimetry
saccharolytic
saccharometer
saccharometry
sacerdotalism
sacerdotalist
sacerdotalize
sacralization
sacramentally
Sacred College
sacred concert
sacred history
sacred writing
sacrificially
sacring of mass
sacrosanctity
saddleback pig
saddle-blanket
saddle embolus
saddle feather
saddle-hackled
sado-masochism
sadomasochism
sado-masochist
sadomasochist
safety bicycle
safety curtain
safety deposit
safety-firster
safety harness
safety officer
saffron crocus
saffron-yellow
sagaciousness
sagittal crest
sailing course
sailing master
sailing orders
sailor's choice
Saint-Simonian
Saint-Simonist
salaciousness
salad dressing
salami tactics
Salam–Weinberg
sale-leaseback
sales engineer
salicylic acid
saliva ejector
salmon disease

salmonellosis
saloon theatre
salpingectomy
salpingolysis
salpingostomy
salt an account
salt-and-pepper
salted almonds
salt fingering
Salvation Army
Salvation Jane
Sam Browne belt
sample-and-hold
sampling error
sampling frame
sanctiloquent
sanctimonious
sanctionative
sandalwood oil
sand and canvas
sand-blindness
sand-hill crane
sandpaper tree
sand stargazer
sandwich-board
sandwich panel
sandy laverock
San Franciscan
sanitarianism
sanitary towel
sanitationist
sanitation man
Sankaracharya
San Pellegrino
sans cérémonie
sansculottish
sans-culottism
sansculottism
sansculottist
sansculottize
Santo Domingan
sapodilla plum
sarcastically
Sardanapalian
sargassum fish
Satanic school
satchel charge
satellite cell
satellite dish
satellite town
satellite vein
satellization
satiety centre
satin duchesse
satin sycamore
satiricalness
satisfiedness
Saturday night
Saturday penny
saucerization
Saussureanism
saussuritized

savannah grass
save-as-you-earn
save one's bacon
Savonius rotor
Savoy operetta
say for oneself
scalar product
scalding-house
scalene muscle
scalenohedral
scalenohedron
scaling-ladder
scallywaggery
scalping-knife
scaly anteater
scandalmonger
Scandihoovian
scanning field
scaphocephaly
scarabaeidoid
scarabaeiform
scarcity value
scarification
scarlet letter
scarlet runner
scatterometer
scavenger cell
scavenger hunt
scene shifting
scenic railway
schadenfreude
Schadenfreude
Scheele's green
Scheiner's halo
schematically
Schiff reagent
Schilling test
schinkenwurst
schistosomule
schizocarpous
schizocoelous
schizonticide
schizontocide
schizophrenia
schizophrenic
Schmidt camera
Schmidt number
Schoenbergian
scholarliness
scholasticate
scholasticism
schoolboyhood
school colours
schoolgirlish
school-marming
school-marmish
schoolmastery
school section
schoolteacher
schooner barge
Schottky diode
Schottky slope

Schrammel band
schreibersite
Schumannesque
Schumpeterian
Schwarzschild
Schwenkfelder
sciagraphical
scientificity
scientization
Scientologist
scientometric
scintigraphic
scintillantly
scintillating
scintillation
scintillogram
scintiscanner
scleractinian
scleroprotein
sclerotherapy
sclerotic bone
sclerotic ring
scolopendrine
scolopendrium
scoop the kitty
scorbutically
scorchingness
scorification
scorpion grass
scorpion senna
scorpion shell
Scotch bonnets
Scotch collops
Scotch pancake
Scotch terrier
Scotch thistle
scotomization
scouring paper
scouring-stone
scoutmasterly
scrambled eggs
scrambler bike
scrambling net
scrap merchant
scratched blue
scratch filter
scratch-mixing
screen current
screen editing
screen printer
screen voltage
screenwriting
screw-coupling
scrimmage line
scriptorially
scripturalism
scripturalist
scripturality
scripturalize
scriptureless
script-writing
scriptwriting

scrobiculated
scrofuloderma
scrumptiously
sculpturesque
scyphomedusan
scyphophorous
sea arrow-grass
sea breeziness
sea gooseberry
sea-kindliness
sealed verdict
seals of office
seam allowance
searchingness
search warrant
seaworthiness
sebaceous duct
seclusiveness
secondariness
secondary road
secondary wave
secondary wife
second chamber
second channel
second-guesser
second officer
second reading
second Redwood
Second Sea Lord
second service
second-sighted
secretary bird
secretaryship
secretiveness
secret members
secret service
secret society
sectorization
secular clergy
secundum artem
security check
security guard
sedentariness
sedge reedling
sedimentation
sedimentology
sedoheptulose
seductiveness
Seebeck effect
seek-no-further
segmentalizer
segregational
Seignette salt
seismic survey
seismographer
seismographic
seismological
selectionally
selection rule
selectiveness
selenocentric
selenographer

selenographic
selenological
self-abandoned
self-abasement
self-actualize
self-addressed
self-adjusting
self-adulation
self-analysing
self-appointed
self-asserting
self-assertion
self-assertive
self-assurance
self-assuredly
self-awareness
self-balancing
self-biography
self-centredly
self-cleansing
self-collected
self-communion
self-conceited
self-concerned
self-condemned
self-confessed
self-confident
self-confiding
self-conscious
self-contained
self-contented
self-convicted
self-criticism
self-deceitful
self-deceiving
self-deception
self-deceptive
self-defeating
self-defensive
self-denyingly
self-dependent
self-destroyer
self-diffusion
self-discovery
self-education
self-evidently
self-evolution
self-executing
self-existence
self-explained
self-fertility
self-fertilize
self-financing
self-flatterer
self-forgetful
self-governing
self-hypnotism
self-identical
self-important
self-improving
self-induction
self-inductive

self-indulgent
self-indulging
self-inflicted
self-insurance
self-judgement
self-knowledge
self-motivated
self-opiniated
self-opinioned
self-oscillate
self-parodying
self-pityingly
self-pollinate
self-pollution
self-possessed
self-propelled
self-quenching
self-recording
self-reference
self-referring
self-reflexive
self-regarding
self-regulated
self-reliantly
self-repugnant
self-restraint
self-revealing
self-righteous
self-sacrifice
self-satisfied
self-selecting
self-selection
self-shielding
self-slaughter
self-sterility
self-sufficing
self-surrender
self-sustained
seller's market
selling plater
semantic field
semasiologist
sematological
semi-automatic
semi-barbarian
semi-barbarism
semi-barbarous
semicarbazide
semicarbazone
semi-civilized
semi-classical
semiconductor
semi-conscious
semicylindric
semi-displayed
semi-empirical
semi-evergreen
semi-intensive
semi-invariant
semi-lunar bone
semi-monocoque
semi-nocturnal

Seminole horse
seminological
semiochemical
semi-palmation
semi-permanent
semi-permeable
semipermeable
semi-porcelain
semi-sterility
semi-synthetic
semisynthetic
Semito-Hamitic
semitonically
semi-vitrified
semologically
sempiternally
send to the wall
seneschalship
senior citizen
senior classic
senior college
senior officer
senior partner
senior service
sensationally
sensationless
senselessness
sense of beauty
sense of humour
sensibilities
sensitive fern
sensitiveness
sensitivities
sensitization
sensitometric
sensorineural
sententiosity
sententiously
sentimentally
sentimentless
senza ritenuto
separableness
separationism
separationist
septcentenary
septemfoliate
septentrional
septentrionic
septifragally
sequence space
sequentiality
sequesterment
sequestration
sequestrotomy
Serbo-Croatian
serendipitist
serendipitous
sergeant-at-law
Sergeant Baker
sergeant major
serialization
serial section

sericiculture
sericiculturist
serjeant-at-law
serodiagnosis
serofibrinous
serologically
serotaxonomic
Serpent-bearer
serpenticidal
serpentinitic
serpiginously
serum reaction
serum sickness
serve one's time
serve one's turn
serve-yourself
service charge
service module
service record
sesquialteral
sesquiterpene
sesquitertian
set by the heels
set measures to
set of bagpipes
set one's face to
set one's hand to
set one's seal to
set one's wits to
setting lotion
settlement day
settler's clock
settler's twine
Seven Sleepers
seventeenthly
seventh heaven
seven year itch
seven-year-vine
Seville orange
sewing machine
sexagesimally
sexationalism
sex attractant
sex chromosome
sexploitation
sexploitative
sexualization
shabby-genteel
shadelessness
shade-tolerant
shadow cabinet
shadow-casting
shadowgraphic
shadow picture
shadow-striped
shadow theatre
Shaftesburian
shaggy parasol
shake one's head
Shakespearean
Shakespearian
shake together

Shaking Quaker
shalwar-kameez
shamefastness
shamelessness
shammy leather
sham operation
shape an answer
shape-changing
shapelessness
sharp-featured
sharp practice
sharpshooting
sharp-wittedly
shear strength
sheep-shearing
sheep-smearing
Sheer Thursday
Sheikh-ul-Islam
shell concrete
shell-moulding
shepherd plaid
shepherd's club
shepherd's pipe
sherbet powder
Sheridanesque
sheriffalties
sheriff-depute
sheriff's clerk
sheriff's court
sherry cobbler
sherryvallies
Shetland sheep
shield-budding
shield of brawn
shield volcano
shifting pedal
shiftlessness
shift register
shimmy-foxtrot
shine and shade
shining armour
shining cuckoo
ship-brokerage
ship carpenter
ship in a bottle
ship of the line
shipping agent
shipping clerk
shipping fever
ship-repairing
ship's articles
ship's chandler
ship's corporal
ship's decanter
Shirley Temple
shockableness
shock absorber
Shockley diode
shock-mounting
shockproofing
shoddy dropper
shoebill stork

shoemaker's end
shoestring tie
shoofly rocker
shoot a profile
shooting brake
shooting break
shooting-glove
shooting-lodge
shooting match
shooting range
shooting stick
shoot one's bolt
shoot-the-chute
shoot the works
shop assistant
shop committee
shopkeeperish
shopkeeperism
shore platform
shore-shooting
short and sweet
short-breathed
short covering
short delivery
short division
short-eared owl
short of breath
short-tempered
short trousers
shot-hole borer
shot in the dark
shoulder blade
shoulder board
shoulder flash
shoulder joint
shoulder patch
shoulder-piece
shoulder plane
shoulder stand
shoulder strap
shouting match
shovel-stirrup
shove the queer
showdown poker
shower-bouquet
shower cubicle
shower curtain
show one's cards
show one's teeth
shredded wheat
shrew-hedgehog
shrike babbler
shrimp cracker
shrinkability
Shrove Tuesday
shuffle rhythm
shut one's mouth
shut the door on
shutting joint
sialoadenitis
Siberian crane
Siberian husky

Siberian tiger
sicca syndrome
sick as a parrot
sickle-feather
sick to death of
side frequency
sidereal clock
sideroblastic
siderographic
side-splitting
Siegfried Line
Sierra Leonean
Sierra Leonian
sieve analysis
sight distance
sightlessness
sigillography
sigmoid cavity
sigmoidectomy
sigmoidoscope
sigmoidoscopy
signalisation
signalization
signature dish
signatureless
signature tune
significantly
signification
significative
significatory
significatrix
sign the pledge
silent partner
silent whistle
siliciclastic
Silicon Valley
silly as a wheel
silver amalgam
silver jubilee
silver nitrate
silver plating
silver-pointed
silver service
silver-tongued
silver wedding
silvery arches
silvery gibbon
silvichemical
silvicultural
similar motion
simple-hearted
simple machine
simplex method
simulfixation
Sinanthropoid
sindonologist
single harness
single-hearted
single spacing
single-tasking
singularities
sin of omission

sintered glass
siphonapteran
siphonophoran
siphonostelic
siphunculated
sissification
sister keelson
sister nucleus
Sister of Mercy
sisters thread
sister uterine
Sistine Chapel
sit at the stern
sit on the fence
sitting member
sitting pretty
sitting target
sitting tenant
situationally
situation room
situs inversus
sixteenth note
sixteenth part
sixteen-tonner
skeletogenous
skeleton brass
skeleton clock
skeleton forme
skelpie-limmer
sketchability
skew-symmetric
skinny-dipping
skin potential
Skire Thursday
skirmishingly
skirting board
skunk porpoise
slab avalanche
slack adjuster
Slack-ma-girdle
slack variable
slanging match
slap and tickle
slap-happiness
slap in the face
slap on the back
slate-coloured
slaughterable
slave-bracelet
Slavification
Slavonization
sleeping giant
sleep-learning
sleeplessness
sleep like a log
sleep like a top
sleep movement
sleep-teaching
sleeve bearing
sleight of hand
slender-billed
slender-bodied

slick magazine
slide fastener
slide trombone
sliding hernia
sling one's hook
slip one's cable
slipper limpet
slipper-orchid
slippery hitch
slippery slope
slip the clutch
slit fricative
slobberhannes
sluice one's gob
slum clearance
slummockiness
slush moulding
smack one's lips
small capitals
small-for-dates
small-mindedly
small potatoes
small seraphim
small thanks to
smart-aleckism
smear campaign
smelling salts
smoke canister
smoked chicken
smoke detector
smoke-farthing
smokelessness
smokeless zone
smoking jacket
smoking pistol
smoothing iron
smooth-tongued
smothered mate
smother-tackle
smoulderingly
snaffle-bridle
snail-creeping
snake pipefish
snapper ending
snapping-point
sneak-thievery
snifting valve
snigging chain
snow-blindness
snow partridge
snowy mespilus
snuff-coloured
sober as a judge
sociable coach
social benefit
social climber
social comment
social compact
social control
social dialect
social disease
social drinker

social evening
social fascist
social history
socialisation
socialization
social process
social realism
social reality
social science
social service
social studies
socio-cultural
sociocultural
sociodramatic
socio-economic
sociolinguist
sociologistic
sock and buskin
socket spanner
Socratic irony
soda cellulose
soda-lime glass
sodium-amalgam
sodium nitrate
sodomitically
soft detergent
soft in the head
soft sculpture
soft-shell clam
soft-shell crab
software house
soil amendment
soil mechanics
soil scientist
solar constant
solderability
soldering iron
soldier beetle
soldier course
soldierliness
soldier orchid
soldier palmer
soldier's heart
solemnisation
solemnization
solenoid brake
solicitorship
solid geometry
solid solution
solidungulate
solidungulous
solifidianism
soliloquacity
solitary vireo
solubilizable
solutionizing
solution-treat
somatological
somatopleuric
somatopsychic
somatosensory
somatotrophic

somatotrophin
something else
something is up
something like
somethingness
somewhere else
somnambulance
somniferously
somnolescence
son Afro-Cubano
Song of Ascents
Song of Degrees
Song of Solomon
sonochemistry
son of the house
son of the manse
sonolytically
sons of bitches
sooner or later
soothfastness
soothsayeress
sooty mangabey
sophiological
sophistically
sophisticated
sophisticator
soporifically
sorbitization
sorrowfulness
sorting office
soul-searching
soul-sickening
sound and light
sound-boarding
sound engineer
sounding board
soundlessness
sound pressure
sound-symbolic
source program
South American
south and north
south-easterly
south-eastward
southerliness
southern beech
Southern Cross
Southern Crown
southern-fried
Southern Irish
Southern Ocean
South Islander
south-westerly
south-westward
sovereign good
sovereignship
sovereignties
Sovietization
sovietologist
Sovietologist
Sovietophobia
space-averaged

space industry
Space Invaders
space launcher
spacelessness
space medicine
space platform
space-reddened
space-sickness
space velocity
spade terminal
spaghetti bowl
spalding-knife
Spanish Armada
Spanish burton
Spanish dagger
Spanish garlic
Spanish guitar
Spanish squill
Spanish stitch
spanner wrench
span of control
spark-arrester
spark spectrum
sparks will fly
sparry iron ore
spasmodically
spatterdashed
speaker-hearer
speaking clock
speaking front
speak one's mind
speak the truth
speak together
Special Branch
special school
specificality
specification
specific cause
specimen shrub
speckled belly
speckled diver
speckled trout
specklessness
spectacle-case
spectacle clew
spectacled owl
spectacularly
spectatorship
spectinomycin
spectral class
spectral index
spectre-insect
spectrography
spectrometric
spectrophonic
spectroscopic
specular stone
speculatively
speculativism
speculum-metal
speechfulness
speech-reading

speech therapy
speed merchant
speleological
spelter solder
Spencerianism
spending money
spend the night
spermatically
spermatic cord
spermaticidal
spermatocidal
spermatogonia
spermatophore
spermatophyte
speromagnetic
sphericalness
spherical wave
spherocytosis
spheroidicity
sphingomyelin
sphygmography
sphygmometric
spider angioma
spider-catcher
spike lavender
spilitization
spill the beans
spindle-legged
spindle-shanks
spindle-shaped
spine-chilling
spine-freezing
spinelessness
spine-tingling
spinning-frame
spinning-house
spinning jenny
spinning wheel
spin-polarized
spinuliferous
spiny anteater
spiral balance
spiral binding
spiralization
spirit-rapping
spirits of salt
spirits of wine
spiritual home
spiritualized
spiritualizer
spiritualness
spirit varnish
spit and polish
spitting cobra
spitting image
spitting snake
splanchnology
splatter-faced
splendiferous
splenectomies
splenectomize
splenetically

splinter group	stabilimentum	state of the art	stereotypical
splinter party	stabilization	state of things	stereoviewing
splinter-proof	stab in the back	state prisoner	sterilisation
split decision	stacking fault	State prisoner	sterilization
split one's vote	stack the cards	States General	stern foremost
splutteringly	staff notation	statesmanlike	sternomastoid
spokesmanship	Staffordshire	statesmanship	sternopleural
spondylolysis	staff sergeant	States-righter	sternopleuron
spondylolytic	stagecoachman	stationary air	sternothyroid
sponge biscuit	stage director	stationmaster	steroidogenic
sponge mixture	stage-entrance	statistically	stethographic
sponge pudding	stage lighting	stato-acoustic	stethoscopist
spongiculture	stage presence	status anxiety	stet processus
spongiologist	staggering bob	status quo ante	St Germain pear
spongiopiline	stagger tuning	statute-barred	stickfast flea
spontaneously	stag-horn coral	statute labour	stick-fighting
spoonbill duck	stag-horn sumac	statute staple	stick-handling
Spörer minimum	stagnationist	statutory rape	sticking place
sporidiferous	stainlessness	stay-stitching	sticking point
sporonticidal	stain painting	stay the course	stick-in-the-mud
sporopollenin	staircase lock	St Bernard lily	stick out a mile
sporting house	stakebuilding	St Distaff's day	stick together
sporting woman	stalactitical	steadfastness	stiff as a poker
sport of nature	stalagmitical	steak au poivre	stiff-tail duck
sportsmanlike	stalagmometer	steal a march on	stiff upper lip
sportsmanship	Stalinization	steal the scene	stigmatically
sports section	stalking-horse	steam carriage	Still's disease
spotted orchid	staminiferous	steam cracking	stilpnomelane
spray refining	standard cable	steaming light	stimulability
spreadability	standard error	Stedman caters	stimulatingly
spreadingness	standard grade	steel bandsman	stinking cedar
spread oneself	Standard Grade	steeplechaser	stinking Roger
Sprengel's tube	stand in a sheet	steering wheel	stipendiaries
sprightliness	standing order	steersmanship	stirpiculture
spring balance	standing-place	steganography	stir the possum
spring cabbage	standing point	Steiner system	stitch welding
spring chicken	standing ropes	Stellwag's sign	St Lucie cherry
spring equinox	standing stone	stem succulent	St Luke's summer
spring fashion	stand-offishly	stenocephalic	stochasticity
spring herring	standoffishly	stenocrotaphy	stockbreeding
spritsail yard	stand sentinel	stenographist	stock exchange
sprocket-wheel	Stanford–Binet	Stensen's canal	Stock Exchange
spruce budworm	stanhope horse	stentoriously	stocking cloth
squandermania	Stanhope press	step-and-repeat	stocking-frame
square-bashing	stannary court	step out of line	stoicheiology
square bracket	Stanton number	steppe lemming	stoichiometry
square flipper	staphylococci	steppe polecat	Stokes' formula
square measure	starboard tack	stepping-stile	Stokes' theorem
square-pushing	star catalogue	stepping stone	stoloniferous
square-shooter	starch blocker	stercoraceous	stolonization
squashability	starch-reduced	stercorarious	stomachically
squash blossom	starfish plant	stereochemist	stomach muscle
squash rackets	star-nosed mole	stereocontrol	stomatiferous
squeaking sand	starting block	stereodiagram	stomatologist
squeamishness	starting-place	stereognostic	stomatoplasty
squeezability	starting point	stereographic	stomatoporoid
squeeze bottle	starting price	stereological	stomp one's feet
squeeze-pidgin	starting stall	stereophonics	stone-coloured
squinancy-wort	start to school	stereoplotter	stone pavement
squirarchical	stated account	stereoregular	stone the crows
squire of dames	statelessness	stereostatics	stop at nothing
squirrel grass	state of nature	stereotropism	stop consonant

stopping house
stopping-knife
stopping-place
stopping train
storage heater
storiological
storming-party
Stow-on-the-Wold
stracciatella
straight-ahead
straight angle
straight-armed
straight arrow
straight chain
straight drive
straight-eight
straight-faced
straight fight
straight flush
straight forth
straight goods
straight-grain
straight-laced
straight-lined
straight on end
straight razor
straightwards
strain at a gnat
straining-post
strain oneself
strain rosette
strandlooping
Strangelovean
strange matter
strangler tree
strangulation
strap railroad
Strasbourg pie
stratagemical
strategetical
strategically
stratigrapher
stratigraphic
stratocracies
stratocumulus
stratospheric
stratovolcano
Stravinskyite
strawberry pot
strawberry red
straw-coloured
straw potatoes
straw's breadth
streak culture
streak disease
streaming cold
stream the buoy
street chemist
street culture
street-orderly
street-sweeper
street village

streetwalking
strengthening
strenuousness
strepsipteran
streptocarpus
streptococcal
streptococcic
streptococcus
streptokinase
streptomycete
stressability
stress analyst
stress-breaker
stress contour
stress diagram
stress disease
stressfulness
stress mineral
stress-neutral
stress phoneme
stress-relieve
stretch a point
stretcher bond
stretcher case
stretch reflex
stria albicans
striatonigral
stricken field
strike a docket
strike-breaker
strikebreaker
strike-measure
strike me blind
strike the beam
strike through
striking force
striking-plate
striking price
striking-tache
Strindbergian
stringentness
string of tools
string-pulling
striopallidal
strip cropping
striped muscle
striped possum
striped squill
strip lighting
stripping film
striptease act
strobe-lighted
strobilaceous
strobilanthes
stroke-oarsman
stroke of state
stroke of State
stromatolitic
strong stomach
strong-wristed
strongyloides
strontia water

stroud blanket
structuralise
structuralism
structuralist
structurality
structuralize
structuration
structureless
structure plan
Struwwelpeter
stubble-jumper
studio theatre
stud-partition
stuffed monkey
stuffed pepper
stultifyingly
stultiloquent
stump-grubbing
Sturm und Drang
St Vitus's dance
stylagalmatic
style analysis
stylelessness
stylistically
stylopization
styptic pencil
suaviloquence
subadolescent
subastringent
sub-bituminous
subcategories
subcategorise
subcategorize
subclavicular
subcontractor
subcontraries
subcontrarily
subdeaconship
subdelegation
subdividingly
subdivisional
subdolousness
subeditorship
sub-elementary
subinhibitory
subinvolution
subirrigation
subjectedness
subject matter
subject-object
subjunctively
subjunctivity
sublacustrine
sub-lieutenant
sublimational
sub-linguistic
sublittorally
sub-machine gun
submandibular
submarine mine
submillimetre
submissionist

subordinaries
subordinately
subordination
subordinative
subpopulation
sub-postmaster
sub-post office
subprefecture
subreptitious
subsequential
subserviently
subsidization
subsistential
subsoil plough
subspeciation
substanceless
substantially
substantiator
substantively
substantivism
substantivist
substantivity
substantivize
substitutable
substructural
substructured
subtabulation
subterraneity
subterraneous
subtilisation
subtilization
subtriangular
subtriplicate
sub-underwrite
suburbicarian
subventionary
subventionize
subversionary
subversionist
succentorship
succenturiate
successionist
successlessly
successorship
sucker-bashing
sucking reflex
suckling-house
suck the monkey
suction dredge
suction stroke
suffering cats
sufficiencies
suffocatingly
suffraganeous
suffraganship
suffragettism
suffrutescent
suffumigation
sugar and honey
sugar aquatint
sugar-candyish
sugar squirrel

suggestionize
suggest itself
suicide clause
suicidologist
sulfamerizine
sulfanilamide
sulphadiazine
sulphamic acid
sulpharsenide
sulphocyanate
sulphonylurea
sulphur candle
sulphureously
sulphuric acid
sulphur shower
sulphur spring
sulphur-yellow
sul ponticello
sultana mother
sultana raisin
sultan's flower
summa cum laude
summarization
summation tone
summer boarder
summer cholera
summer country
summer cypress
summer-herring
summer kitchen
summer pruning
summer pudding
summer red-bird
summer sausage
summer tanager
summit meeting
sumptuousness
Sunday closing
Sunday painter
sundown doctor
Sunshine State
superabundant
super-achiever
superaddition
superannuable
superannuated
super-calender
supercalender
supercautious
supercavitate
supercollider
supercolossal
supercolumnar
supercomputer
supercontract
supercrescent
supercritical
superdominant
superelevated
supereloquent
supereminence
supereminency

superencipher
supererogator
superexchange
superfamilies
superfetation
superficially
superfineness
superfluidity
superfluities
superfluously
supergalactic
superhelicity
superhumanity
superhumanize
superintender
superior court
superior ovary
superlatively
supernational
supernormally
supernumerary
supernumerous
superordinary
superordinate
superorganism
superparasite
superpersonal
superphysical
superposition
superradiance
superrational
supersaturate
superscripted
supersensible
supersensuous
superstitious
superstructor
supersubtlety
supersymmetry
supertemporal
supervenience
suppeditation
supplantation
supplementary
supply teacher
support buying
support trench
suppositional
suppositories
suppressively
supra-axillary
suprachorioid
supracondylar
supralittoral
supranational
suprapersonal
suprascapular
suprasensible
suprasensuous
supraspecific
supraspinatus
supratemporal

Supreme Soviet
sure of oneself
surety of peace
surface-active
surface casing
surface-coated
surface-colour
surface effect
surprisedness
surprise-party
surreptitious
Surrey chicken
surrogate baby
surrogateship
surround sound
sursumduction
sursumversion
survivability
survival curve
survival value
suspender belt
suspense novel
suspension dot
suspicionless
Susquehannock
Sussex spaniel
sustentacular
sustentaculum
suttling-house
suxamethonium
Swainson's hawk
swallow a camel
swallow pigeon
swallow-tailed
swallow-winged
swamp mahogany
swamp pheasant
Swanee whistle
swashbuckling
sweating-house
Swedenborgian
Swedish modern
Swedish turnip
sweep the board
sweet chestnut
sweet marjoram
sweet nothings
sweet scabious
sweet-tempered
sweet-throated
sweetwood bark
swineherdship
swine's feather
swine's succory
swing both ways
swinge-buckler
switch dealing
switch-hitting
switching yard
switch selling
swivel shuttle
swollen-headed

sword-rattling
swordsmanship
sybaritically
sycamore maple
Sydney bluegum
syllabication
syllabization
syllable-count
syllable-timed
syllabub glass
sylleptically
syllogistical
syllogization
Sylow's theorem
Sylow subgroup
symbiotically
symbiotrophic
symbolic logic
symbolisation
symbolization
symbolography
symmetrically
symmetry group
sympathectomy
sympathetical
sympathoblast
sympathogonia
sympatholytic
sympatrically
symphalangism
symphonically
symphonic jazz
symphonic poem
symphoniously
symphysiotomy
sympiesometer
symptomatical
sympto-thermal
synallagmatic
synaposematic
synapticulate
synarthrodial
synchondroses
synchondrosis
synchronicity
synchronistic
synchronology
synchronously
syncretically
syndesmophyte
syndicalistic
synecdochical
synecological
synergistical
synodic period
synonymically
synovial joint
syntactically
syntactic foam
synthetically
syphilization
syphilophobia

syringobulbia
syringomyelia
systematician
systematicity
systemization
system program
systems design
tabes dorsalis
tableau vivant
table-mountain
table skittles
tablespoonful
tablet-weaving
taboparalysis
tachistoscope
tachyphylaxis
tacking-cotton
tackling dummy
tail-heaviness
tailor-fashion
tailor-herring
tailor's muscle
tail parachute
taintlessness
take a back seat
take account of
take a chance on
take a pleasure
take a thing ill
take exception
take in the rear
take it in turns
take its course
take liberties
take lying down
take one's leave
take one's lumps
take one's place
take on the chin
take-out double
take sanctuary
take seriously
take soundings
take suspicion
take the flings
take the ground
take the lid off
take the mickey
take the part of
take the pledge
take the plunge
take the salute
take the strain
take the waters
take to one's bed
take to the road
talent spotter
talipes valgus
talk a good game
talkativeness
talk of the town
talk one's way in

talk out of turn
talk poor-mouth
talk to oneself
tally-business
Talmudistical
talmudization
tamarind water
tambour-needle
tambour-stitch
tamper-evident
tangata whenua
tangentiality
tangoreceptor
tantalization
tantalizingly
tape cartridge
tape recording
tape recordist
tape transport
taphrogenesis
tar and feather
tarantula-hawk
target dialect
target program
tariff barrier
Tartarian lamb
Tartarian oats
Tasmanian wolf
tastelessness
Taunton turkey
tautologously
tautosyllabic
tax-deductible
taxonomically
taxonomic name
Taylorization
Tchaikovskian
teachableness
teach yourself
teapot tempest
tear to tatters
technical foul
technicalness
technicolored
technocomplex
technocracies
technographic
technological
tectocephalic
tectonisation
tectonization
tectonosphere
tectosilicate
tegestologist
tektosilicate
telautography
teleconverter
telediagnosis
telefacsimile
telegrammatic
telegraph pole
telemarketing

telencephalic
telencephalon
teleoperation
telephone bill
telephone book
telephone call
telephone dial
telephone girl
telephone pole
telephone poll
telephoto lens
teleportation
telerecording
telescope word
televangelism
televangelist
televisionary
television set
televisuality
Telinga potato
teller machine
tell me another
tell one's beads
telluric ochre
tellurous acid
temerariously
temperamental
temperateness
temperate zone
temper-brittle
tempest-tossed
tempestuously
temporalities
temporal power
temporariness
temporization
temporizingly
temptableness
tenaciousness
tenancy at will
tenant-righter
Tenby daffodil
tendentiously
tender-hearted
tender mercies
tendo Achilles
tenebrescence
tenebrousness
tenement house
ten-minute rule
Tennysonianly
Tenon's capsule
tenor clarinet
tenore robusto
tenosynovitis
tenpin bowling
tentaculiform
tentativeness
teratogenesis
teratological
tercentennial
terephthalate

tergiversator
term-catalogue
terminability
terminational
terminatively
terminologies
terminologist
termitologist
Terpsichorean
terraced house
Terra Japonica
terrestrially
terrible twins
terrification
territorially
terror-bombing
terrorization
Tertullianism
Tertullianist
testification
testificatory
testing ground
tetanospasmin
tetartohedral
tetartohedron
tetrachloride
tetradynamous
tetrahedrally
tetraparental
tetrapetalous
tetraquetrous
tetrasepalous
tetraspermous
tetrastichous
tetrasyllabic
tetrasyllable
tetrathionate
Teutonic cross
Teutonization
Texas longhorn
text processor
thalassocracy
thallium glass
thallous oxide
thanatologist
thanatophilia
thanatophobia
thanatophoric
thank goodness
thanklessness
thank-offering
thankworthily
Thatcheresque
Thathanabaing
that is as may be
that little lot
that's the stuff
thaumatolatry
thaumaturgist
theanthropism
theanthropist
Theatre of Fact

theatre sister
theatricalise
theatricalism
theatricality
theatricalize
the Authentics
the awkward age
the ayes have it
Thebaic marble
the Bard of Avon
Thebesian vein
the best part of
the blood royal
the city of Rome
the clean thing
the Crimean War
the daily grind
the dead ring of
the Depression
the deuce to pay
the devil to pay
the Disruption
the elements of
the five senses
the Five Wounds
the frozen mitt
the fur will fly
the gay science
the gentler sex
the good people
the great enemy
the Great Mogul
the Grim Reaper
the hell you say
the King's peace
the kiss of life
The Life Guards
the likelihood
the lion's mouth
the lion's share
the Lord's house
the Lord's table
the Lost Tribes
the main chance
thematization
the minute that
the Morasthite
the naked truth
thenceforward
the nick of time
the noes have it
the old country
theologically
Theophrastian
theoretically
theosophistic
the other night
the other place
the other thing
the other woman
the other world
the outer world

the penny drops
The Queen's Bays
therapeutical
thereinbefore
the right bower
theriomorphic
thermal motion
thermantidote
thermochemist
thermochromic
thermodynamic
thermo-elastic
thermoforming
thermogenesis
thermogenetic
thermographic
thermological
thermoneutral
thermonuclear
thermophilous
thermophysics
thermoplastic
thermos bottle
thermosetting
thermospheric
thermostatics
thermo-therapy
thermotropism
the rougher sex
the scene opens
these presents
the Shaky Isles
the social evil
the Soviet Zone
the spoken word
the sterner sex
the strength of
the Swan of Avon
theta activity
theta-function
The Temptation
the three kings
the tother year
the voice of God
the whole shoot
the whole story
thiabendazole
thickback sole
thick register
thick sandwich
Thiersch graft
thieves' market
thigmokinesis
thigmotropism
thimblerigger
thing in itself
thinkableness
think better of
think highly of
thinking-aloud
think little of
think straight

thiobacterium
thiocarbamate
thiocarbamide
thioglycollic
thiosulphuric
third position
Third Worldism
Third World War
thirst-country
thirtieth part
thirty-pounder
this afternoon
this day and age
this is the life
this little lot
thistle dollar
thistle funnel
thoracentesis
thoracolumbar
thoracoplasty
thorium series
thorough-brace
thorough-drain
thoroughgoing
thorough-paced
thorough-stone
thoughtlessly
thought police
thought-reader
thought reform
thought-stream
thousand-miler
thrasonically
thread-drawing
threat display
threateningly
three-cornered
three-day fever
three-line whip
threepenny bit
three per cents
three-quarters
thremmatology
threshing-mill
thrillingness
throat-cutting
throat halyard
thrombokinase
Throne of Grace
throstle frame
throttle-lever
throttle-valve
through-lounge
through-valley
throw a stone at
throwing-knife
throwing power
throwing-stick
throwing-table
throw stones at
throw together
thrush babbler

thrust bearing
thrust chamber
thrustfulness
thrust spoiler
thumb-fingered
thumb one's nose
thumb's breadth
thump a cushion
thunder-bearer
thunder-shower
thunderstormy
thunderstrike
thunderstroke
thunderstruck
thurification
thyroglobulin
thyroidectomy
thysanopteran
Tibetan cherry
Tibeto-Burmese
Tibeto-Chinese
tic douloureux
ticket barrier
ticket benefit
ticket chopper
ticket of leave
ticket-scalper
tickling stick
tick paralysis
tidal friction
tiddlywinking
tie the hands of
tight junction
tilting fillet
tilt mechanism
Tilt Yard guard
timber-cruiser
timber licence
timber rattler
time adverbial
time after time
time-and-motion
time-consuming
time out of mind
time ownership
time signature
time traveller
ting-a-ling-ling
ting-tang clock
tinman's solder
tintinnabular
tintinnabulum
tipitiwitchet
tippling-house
tip the balance
tirlie-whirlie
tissue culture
titanium oxide
titanium white
titillatingly
Titius–Bode law
tittle-tattler

titular bishop
toad-in-the-hole
toad-strangler
toast-and-water
toasting glass
toastmistress
tobacco beetle
tobacco-cutter
tobacconalian
tobacco streak
toboggan-chute
to coin a phrase
to distraction
toe-in-the-water
toga praetexta
toggle circuit
toggle-harpoon
to good purpose
to hell and gone
token estimate
token stoppage
tolerableness
tolerance dose
Toleration Act
tolerationism
tolerationist
toluidine blue
tomato pinworm
tomboyishness
to my knowledge
tone generator
tongue-in-cheek
tongue-lashing
tongue-twister
tonotopically
tonsillectomy
toothache tree
toothing-plane
toothlessness
toothsomeness
top dead centre
topknot pigeon
topochemistry
topographical
topoisomerase
topologically
topsy-turvydom
to put it mildly
torch-carrying
toreador pants
tornado-cellar
torpedo-bomber
Torrens system
tortoiseshell
Tory democracy
to say the least
to the backbone
to the contrary
to the eyeballs
totipotential
touchableness
touch football

touch of nature
touch of the sun
touch on the raw
touristically
town-traveller
toxicodendron
toxicological
toxoplasmosis
trabeculation
track and field
tracking error
track lighting
tractableness
Tractarianism
traction motor
traction wheel
trade discount
trade effluent
trade-language
trade magazine
tradesmanlike
tradesmanship
trade unionism
trade unionist
trade-weighted
trading estate
trading profit
traditionally
traditionless
traffic artery
traffic circle
traffic island
traffic-jammed
traffic lights
traffic police
traffic signal
traffic ticket
traffic warden
tragicomedies
trailer-sailer
trailing wheel
trail one's coat
trainsickness
train-spotting
trajectitious
tranquilliser
tranquillizer
transactional
transatlantic
transboundary
transcendence
transcendency
transcendible
transcortical
transcribable
transcribbler
transcriptase
transcription
transcriptive
transcultural
transcurrence
transfeminate

transfer mould
transfer orbit
transfer-paper
transferrable
transfigurate
transformable
transformance
transform down
trans-frontier
transfusional
transgredient
transgression
transgressive
transhumanate
transhumanize
transientness
trans-isthmian
transistorise
transistorize
transistor set
transit-circle
transitionary
transition fit
transitivizer
transit lounge
transketolase
translational
translatorese
transliterate
translocation
translucently
translucidity
transmarginal
transmaterial
transmembrane
transmigrator
transmissible
transmittable
transmittance
transmittancy
transmutation
transmutative
transnational
transom window
transparently
transpersonal
transpiration
transplendent
transportable
transportance
transport café
transport-ship
transposition
transpositive
transreceiver
transriverine
trans-shipment
transshipment
trans-Siberian
trans-specific
trans-synaptic
transthoracic

transurethral
transversally
transvestitic
Transylvanian
trapeze artist
trapezohedral
trapezohedron
traumatic acid
traumatically
traumatropism
traveller's joy
travelling bag
travelling rug
travel trailer
traverse-board
traverse-table
treacherously
tread a measure
tread the stage
treason felony
treasure chest
treasure-house
treasurership
Treasure State
treasure trove
Treasury bench
treatableness
treat like dirt
tree cranberry
tree of liberty
tree partridge
tree porcupine
tree structure
trellis stitch
trellis window
tremblingness
tremulousness
trencherwoman
trench warfare
trend analysis
Trendelenburg
trestle-bridge
trial and error
trial by battle
trial by combat
trial of the pyx
triamcinolone
triangularity
triangulately
triangulation
tribalization
triboelectric
tributariness
tricarboxylic
tricarpellary
tricentennial
trichological
trichopterous
trichothallic
trichothecene
trichromatism
trickle-charge

triconodontid	trunk-breeches	twilight shift	unapprehended
triethylamine	trunk dialling	twilight sleep	unappropriate
trifunctional	trunk murderer	twilight world	unarmed combat
trigger finger	trustlessness	twine-spinning	unarrestingly
trigonal quoin	trustworthily	twist and twirl	unarticulated
trigonometric	truth-function	twisted pillar	unascertained
trilateralism	truthlessness	twister's cramp	unashamedness
trilateralist	truthlikeness	twist the knife	unassaultable
trilaterality	try it on the dog	two-handedness	unassertively
trilateration	try one's hand at	two jumps ahead	unassimilable
trilingualism	tsutsugamushi	twopenny piece	unassimilated
triliteralism	tubal ligation	twopennyworth	unassuageable
triliterality	tuber cinereum	two-revolution	unatmospheric
trimerization	tubercularize	twos and threes	unattemptable
trimming-joist	tuberculation	two times table	unaugmentable
trimming wheel	tuberculiform	two-way stretch	unbashfulness
Trinity Sunday	tubular bridge	tympanometric	unbeautifully
trinucleotide	tubular vision	tympanoplasty	unbefittingly
tripersonally	tubulidentate	type facsimile	unbeginningly
triphibiously	tumbler pigeon	typographical	unbelievingly
tripinnatifid	tumbling stone	typologically	unbendingness
triple century	tumorigenesis	tyrannosaurus	unbeseemingly
triple spacing	turbidimetric	tyrannousness	unblemishable
triple vaccine	turbo-compound	Tyrrhenian Sea	unblessedness
triploblastic	turbo-electric	Ulsterization	unboundedness
tripoli polish	Turing machine	ultimate ratio	unbowdlerized
Tripolitanian	turkey-blossom	ultrafiltrate	unbreakfasted
trisaccharide	turkey buzzard	ultra-marathon	unbrotherlike
trisyllabical	Turkey leather	ultra-royalist	uncalculating
tritanomalous	turkey vulture	ultrasonicate	uncancellable
tritheistical	Turkicization	ultrasonogram	uncanonically
tritocerebral	Turkification	umbelliferous	uncatholicize
tritocerebrum	Turkish carpet	umbilical cord	unceasingness
tritubercular	Turkish coffee	umbrella field	unceremonious
triumfeminate	turmeric paper	umbrella plant	uncertainness
triumphal arch	turn end for end	umbrella stand	uncertainties
troglodytical	turn indicator	Umbrian school	uncertifiable
trolling motor	turning circle	Umbrian School	unchallenging
troop-carrying	turning radius	unabashedness	uncharismatic
trophallactic	turn inside out	unabbreviated	unchristianly
trophectoderm	turnip-cabbage	unabridgeable	uncinate gyrus
trophoblastic	turnip-lantern	unaccelerated	uncircumcised
trophonucleus	turn one's steps	unaccentuated	uncircumspect
trophotropism	turn on the heat	unaccompanied	uncivilizable
tropical month	turnover board	unaccountable	unclassically
tropical storm	turnpike trust	unaccountably	uncleanliness
tropocollagen	turn the corner	unadulterated	unclean spirit
troubadourish	turn the heat on	unadventurous	uncloudedness
trouble-making	turn the scales	unadvisedness	uncognoscible
troublemaking	turn the screws	unalcoholized	uncollectable
troublesomely	turn the tables	unamalgamated	uncomfortable
troublousness	turn to account	unambiguously	uncomfortably
trough battery	turpentine gum	unambitiously	uncommendable
trouser-suited	turpentine oil	un-Americanism	uncommendably
trumpeter swan	turpitudinous	unamiableness	uncommonplace
trumpet-flower	Turveydropian	unanimousness	uncompanioned
trumpet marine	twelvemonthly	unannihilated	uncompensated
trumpet medium	twelve-pounder	unanticipated	uncompetitive
trumpet seance	twentieth part	unappealingly	uncomplaining
trumpet-shaped	twenty-firster	unappointable	uncomplaisant
trumpet spiral	twilight house	unappreciable	uncomplicated
trumpet-tongue	twilight night	unappreciated	uncompromised

unconcealable
unconceitedly
unconceivable
unconceivably
unconcernedly
unconcernment
unconcludable
uncondensable
unconditional
unconditioned
unconflicting
unconformable
unconformably
uncongealable
unconjectured
unconnectedly
unconquerable
unconquerably
unconsciously
unconsecrated
unconsecutive
unconsidering
unconspicuous
unconstrained
unconstricted
unconstruable
unconstructed
unconsultable
unconsummated
uncontactable
uncontainable
uncontaminate
uncontentious
uncontestable
uncontestedly
unconversable
unconvertible
unconvincible
uncooperative
uncoordinated
uncopyrighted
uncorrectable
uncorruptedly
uncorruptible
uncorruptness
uncounterfeit
uncourteously
uncourtliness
uncreatedness
uncultivation
uncustomarily
undauntedness
undecapeptide
undecidedness
undefiledness
undefinedness
undegenerated
undeliberated
undeliverable
undenominated
undepreciated
underabundant

underachiever
underactivity
under a mistake
underbreeding
undercarriage
underclassman
underclothing
under colour of
under contract
undercovering
underdiagnose
underdoctored
underdrainage
undereducated
underemphasis
underemployed
underestimate
underexposure
under-falconer
underfunction
under-gardener
undergraduacy
undergraduate
undergrounder
underhandedly
underivedness
under-labourer
under-lordship
underminingly
undermodulate
under one's belt
under one's feet
under one's hand
under one's seal
underpainting
underplanting
under-prepared
underpropping
underresource
under-shepherd
understaffing
understanding
understatedly
understrapper
understrength
under the eye of
under the lee of
under the table
undescendable
undescribable
undescribably
undescriptive
undeservingly
undestroyable
undeterminate
undeviatingly
undiagnosable
undifferenced
undignifiedly
undiminishing
undiscernedly
undiscernible

undiscernibly
undisciplined
undiscoloured
undiscomfited
undiscouraged
undiscussable
undisguisable
undisguisedly
undishonoured
undispellable
undispensable
undissembling
undissociated
undissolvable
undistempered
undistinctive
undistributed
undistrustful
undisturbable
undisturbedly
undiversified
undividedness
undivorceable
undoctrinaire
undogmaticism
undomesticate
undulant fever
undulationist
undutifulness
unearthliness
uneasefulness
uneatableness
unelectrified
unemancipated
unemasculated
unembarrassed
unembellished
unembroidered
unemotionally
unencompassed
unencountered
unencouraging
unencumbering
unenforceable
un-Englishness
unenlightened
unentertained
unequivocable
unequivocably
unequivocally
unessentially
unestablished
unevangelical
unevangelized
unexaggerated
unexceptional
unexclusively
unexemplified
unexhaustible
unexpeditated
unexperienced
unexplainable

unexplainably
unexplanatory
unexploitable
unexpoundable
unexpressible
unfailingness
unfalsifiable
unfalteringly
unfamiliarity
unfashionable
unfashionably
unfeasibility
unfeelingness
unfeignedness
unfermentable
unflinchingly
unflourishing
unfluctuating
unforeseeable
unforethought
unforfeitable
unforgettable
unforgettably
unforgiveness
unforgivingly
unforthcoming
unfortunately
unfoundedness
unfriendliest
unfulfillable
ungainsayable
ungainsayably
ungenteelness
ungentlemanly
ungenuineness
ungeometrical
ungrammatical
ungual phalanx
unguardedness
unhealthfully
unhealthiness
unheedfulness
unhelpfulness
unhomogeneity
unhomogeneous
unhomogenized
unicameralism
unicameralist
unicorn beetle
uniflagellate
unilateralism
unilateralist
unilaterality
unilluminated
unillustrated
unimaginative
unimmediately
unimpassioned
unimpeachable
unimpeachably
unimportunate
unimpregnated

unimpressible
unincorporate
unincreasable
unindifferent
unindustrious
uninflammable
uninfluential
uninformative
uninhabitable
uninheritable
uninhibitedly
uninquisitive
uninspiringly
uninstructing
uninstructive
unintelligent
unintentional
unintercepted
uninteresting
unintermitted
uninterpreted
uninterrupted
unintimidated
unintuitively
uninventively
uniparentally
unitary matrix
unit character
United Kingdom
United Nations
unit of account
unity of action
Universal Aunt
universalizer
universal maid
universalness
universal time
Universal Time
universal veil
unjustifiable
unjustifiably
unkillability
unknowability
unknowingness
unladen weight
unlearnedness
unlimitedness
unlocalizable
unlovableness
unmacadamized
unmaliciously
unmarriedness
unmeaningness
unmelodiously
unmentionable
unmentionably
unmeritorious
unmindfulness
unmineralized
unministerial
unmisgivingly
unmistakeable

unmistrusting
unmitigatedly
unmixableness
unmonopolized
unmovableness
unmurmuringly
unmusicalness
unnameability
unnaturalized
unnaturalness
unnecessaries
unnecessarily
unneighboured
unneighbourly
unneutralized
unnourishable
unobliterable
unobliterated
unobservantly
unobstructive
unobtrusively
unobviousness
unofficerlike
unorganizable
unoriginality
unoriginately
unpasteurised
unpasteurized
unpatronizing
unpenetrating
unperceivable
unperceivably
unperceivedly
unperceptible
unperfectness
unperformable
unpermissible
unpersonified
unperspicuous
unpersuadable
unpersuadably
unperturbedly
unpetticoated
unphilosophic
unphysiologic
unpicturesque
un-pin-downable
unpitifulness
unplasticized
unpleasantish
unpleasurable
unpleasurably
unpliableness
unpolitically
unpolymerized
unpossibility
unpracticable
unpractically
unprecedented
unpredictable
unpredictably
unpremeditate

unpreoccupied
unpreparation
unpresentable
unpressurized
unpretentious
unpreventable
unpreventably
unpreventible
unproblematic
unproduceable
unprogressive
unproletarian
unpromisingly
unpromulgated
unprostituted
unprotectedly
unprovability
unprovisioned
unprovocative
unpublishable
unpublishably
unpunctuality
unpuncturable
unpurchasable
unpuritanical
unputdownable
unqualifiable
unqualifiedly
unquarrelsome
unquestioning
unquotability
unreadability
unreasoningly
unreceptivity
unreclaimable
unrecognition
unrecognizing
unrecollected
unrecommended
unrecompensed
unrecoverable
unrecruitable
unredressable
unregenerable
unregenerated
unrelatedness
unrelentingly
unreliability
unreligiously
unreluctantly
unremembrance
unremittingly
unremunerated
unrepentantly
unreplaceable
unreplenished
unrepresented
unreprievable
unreproachful
unreproaching
unresentfully
unresistingly

unrespectable
unresponsible
unrestingness
unretractable
unrighteously
unritualistic
unruffledness
unsacramental
unsaleability
unsalvageable
unsatisfiable
unsavouriness
unscandalized
unscholarlike
unscratchable
unscrutinized
unselectively
unselfishness
unself-knowing
unself-seeking
unsensational
unsententious
unsentimental
unsentinelled
unsequestered
unseriousness
unserviceable
unsettledness
unsewn binding
unshapeliness
unshatterable
unshrinkingly
unsightliness
unsight unseen
unsilenceable
unsinkability
unskilfulness
unslaughtered
unsmilingness
unsmotherable
unsociability
unsocial hours
unsoldierlike
unsolicitedly
unsolvability
unsophistical
unsparingness
unspecialized
unspectacular
unspeculative
unspiritually
unspontaneous
unspottedness
unstaunchable
unstereotyped
unstigmatized
unstimulating
unstreamlined
unstylishness
unsubduedness
unsubscribing
unsubstantial

unsubstituted
unsuitability
unsuperfluous
unsupportable
unsupportably
unsupportedly
unsurpassable
unsurpassably
unsurrendered
unsusceptible
unsuspectable
unsuspectedly
unsustainable
unsustainably
unswallowable
unsymmetrical
unsympathetic
untaintedness
untarnishable
untechnically
untenableness
unterminating
untheological
untheoretical
unthreatening
unthriftiness
untouchedness
untraditional
untransformed
untransmitted
untransparent
untransported
untravellable
untraversable
untremblingly
untrimmedness
untroublesome
untrustworthy
untunableness
untunefulness
ununiformness
unutilitarian
unvarnishedly
unvaryingness
unveraciously
unvitrifiable
unwarlikeness
unwarrantable
unwarrantably
unwarrantedly
unweariedness
unwelcomeness
unwhitewashed
unwholesomely
unwillingness
unwittingness
unwomanliness
unworkability
unworkmanlike
unworldliness
upgradability
upon one's heels

upon the back of
upperclassman
upsettingness
up to the elbows
up to the eyes in
up to the handle
up-to-the-minute
uralitization
uranium series
urban district
urediniospore
ureterography
urethrography
urethroscopic
uricacidaemia
urinary meatus
urinary system
ursine dasyure
user-definable
user interface
ustilagineous
uterine sister
utilitarianly
utility player
Utrecht velvet
uveoparotitis
vaccine damage
vacuolization
vacuum chamber
vacuum cleaner
vacuum forming
vagabond's skin
vagina dentata
valedictorian
valedictories
valedictorily
valeraldehyde
valiant beggar
validity check
valley of tears
Valliscaulian
value added tax
value analysis
value-for-money
valuelessness
value received
valvuloplasty
Van Allen layer
vandalization
Vansittartism
Vansittartite
vantage-ground
vapour barrier
vapour density
vapourishness
vapour tension
variationally
varicose veins
variety artist
vascular plant
vasodepressor
vasovasostomy

Vater's ampulla
Vater's papilla
vaulting horse
Vauxhall light
vector address
vectorization
vector product
vegetarianism
Velikovskyism
Velikovskyite
vendor placing
venerableness
venereologist
venetian blind
Venetian blind
Venetian chalk
Venetian cloth
Venetian glass
Venetian sumac
Venetian swell
Venetian whisk
veno-occlusive
ventriculitis
ventriloquial
ventriloquise
ventriloquism
ventriloquist
ventriloquize
ventriloquous
ventrolateral
venturesomely
venturousness
Venus's fly-trap
Venus's flytrap
veraciousness
verbalization
verbification
verbigeration
verdurousness
vergence angle
veridicalness
verifiability
verisimilarly
veritableness
vermiculation
vermilionette
vernacularise
vernacularism
vernacularist
vernacularity
vernacularize
vernal equinox
vernalisation
vernalization
vernier engine
verre églomisé
versatileness
versicoloured
versification
versificatory
vertical angle
vertical plane

vertical point
verticillated
vertiginously
vesicouterine
vesicovaginal
vesper sparrow
vessel element
vessel of paper
vexatiousness
vexillologist
vibrationally
vibrationless
vicariousness
Vicar of Christ
vicars-general
vice-admiralty
vice-consulate
vicegerencies
vice-president
vice-treasurer
vicious circle
vicious spiral
victimization
victimologist
Victoria Cross
victor ludorum
video cassette
videographics
video recorder
video terminal
vie d'intérieur
vie intérieure
Vienna sausage
Viennese waltz
vigintivirate
village burrow
villagisation
villagization
Villar y Villar
villein socage
vinca alkaloid
vindicability
vindicatingly
vindicatorily
vinegar mother
vinho corrente
viniculturist
vino corriente
vinyl chloride
viola bastarda
violoncellist
viperine snake
viper's bugloss
Virgilian lots
Virginia fence
virginiamycin
Virginian deer
Virginian poke
Virginia stock
virialization
virial theorem
virologically

virtual height
virtual memory
visceral brain
visceral cleft
visceral layer
visceral nerve
visceroptosis
viscerotropic
viscosimetric
visible speech
visionariness
visiting hours
visitor centre
visual agnosia
visual display
visualization
vital capacity
vitelligenous
vitelline duct
viticulturist
vitrification
vitrified fort
vitriolic acid
vitriolically
vivaciousness
vivisectional
vocal ensemble
vocationalise
vocationalism
vocationalize
vodka and tonic
voicelessness
voice-printing
voicespondent
volatilizable
volcanic glass
volcanologist
volcano rabbit
volitionality
Voltaireanism
volume control
volume-density
volumenometer
voluntariness
voluntaristic
von Willebrand
voraciousness
vortex turbine
vote of censure
vote on account
voting machine
vouchsafement
vowel mutation
vowel-quantity
vulcanisation
vulcanization
vulcanologist
vulgarisation
vulgarization
vulnerability
Wacker process
waffle stomper

wager of battle
wainscot chair
waistcoatless
wake-up service
Waldeyer's ring
walking corpse
walking-on part
walking-orders
walking papers
walking-rapier
walking-ticket
walk the boards
Wallace effect
walling hammer
wall newspaper
wall pennywort
walls have ears
Wall Streetish
Walsingham way
waltzing mouse
wamble-cropped
wandering cell
wandering fire
wandering star
wanderlusting
warbling vireo
Warburgianism
war department
Wardour Street
wardrobe trunk
war generation
warm-heartedly
warm reception
war resistance
wash-hand basin
wash-hand stand
washing powder
Washingtonian
Washington pie
wash one's brain
wash one's hands
waste disposal
waste-disposer
waste material
waste moulding
waste products
watch and watch
watching brief
watchlessness
watch one's back
watch one's step
watch the clock
water-breather
water caltrops
water chestnut
watercoloured
water-crowfoot
water-drinking
water-dropwort
water-flooding
water hyacinth
watering place

water-jacketed
waterlessness
water measurer
water moccasin
water mongoose
water-pheasant
water plantain
water pressure
waterproofing
water purslane
water sapphire
water scorpion
water softener
water starwort
water tortoise
water-vascular
water-witching
Watteau bodice
Watteau mantle
wattle and daub
wattled jacana
wave mechanics
waw conversive
wayfaring tree
way of business
way of the world
way of thinking
wayside pulpit
weak-kneedness
weapon-carrier
weaponization
weapons system
wearisomeness
wear the purple
wear the willow
weather-beaten
weather bureau
weather centre
weatherliness
Weatherometer
weather-tiling
weather window
wedding canopy
wedding-favour
wedding-finger
wedding knives
weed inspector
weekly boarder
week of Sundays
weeping willow
weighing-house
weightlifting
weight-watcher
Weight Watcher
Weinberg–Salam
welcome aboard
well-appointed
well-conducted
well-connected
well-developed
well-foundedly
Wellingtonian

well-knownness
well languaged
well-meaningly
well-nourished
well on one's way
well-organized
well-preserved
well-qualified
well-staircase
well-supported
well thought of
well-travelled
well-turned-out
Wernicke's area
Wessex culture
Western Church
Western Empire
Western saddle
west-north-west
West-of-England
west-south-west
wet-and-dry bulb
whaling-master
Wharton's jelly
what's your will
what the blazes
wheel-carriage
wheel-dwelling
wheel-engraved
wheeler-dealer
whenceforward
whereinsoever
where one lives
where's the fire
Whig historian
whimsicalness
whip into shape
whipping-bench
whipping cream
whipping-stock
whirling plant
whirling-table
whiskered tern
whistle-blower
whistle-speech
whistling duck
whistling kite
whistling moth
whistling-shop
whistling swan
white antimony
White backlash
white-bark pine
white-breasted
white cast iron
white-collared
white elephant
Whitefieldian
Whitefieldism
Whitefieldite
white-knuckled
white magnesia

white mahogany
white mangrove
white mulberry
whitepainting
white pipe tree
white ribboner
white sapphire
whitesmithery
whitesmithing
whitetail deer
white-throated
whitetip shark
whithersoever
wholesomeness
wholistically
whooping cough
whooping crane
whoremistress
wicket-keeping
wicketkeeping
widdy-widdy-way
wide-awakeness
wide brown land
wide of the mark
Widmanstätten
wife and mother
wild and woolly
wild gardening
wild liquorice
Wild Westerner
William Morris
will not hear of
willow gentian
willow-pattern
willow warbler
Wilson's petrel
Wiltshire Horn
winding engine
windmill grass
windmill plane
windmill plant
window cleaner
window display
window-dresser
window-shopper
window-trimmer
Windsor herald
wineglassfuls
wing-back chair
wing commander
winged thistle
winner-take-all
winning hazard
winning stroke
Winnipeg couch
winter aconite
winter bunting
winter country

winterization
winter jasmine
winter sleeper
wipe off the map
wire recording
wire-stitching
wire-stretcher
wiring diagram
witches' butter
witchetty bush
witchetty grub
witch flounder
witch of Agnesi
witch-smelling
with a bad grace
with a high hand
with all faults
with a siserary
with both hands
withdrawnness
with good grace
within an ace of
within cooee of
within earshot
within oneself
within reach of
with nothing on
with one accord
with open mouth
without a doubt
without gloves
without number
without reason
without result
withoutside of
with the stream
with the view of
with your leave
Wolffian ridge
Wolf–Rayet star
woman-movement
woman question
woman's righter
women's college
women's studies
wonderfulness
wonder-working
woodchip paper
wood engraving
wooden wedding
wood germander
wood-partridge
wood pimpernel
woodskin canoe
wool-blindness
wool-gathering
woollen-draper
woollen-witted

woolly mammoth
word a person up
word-blindness
word frequency
word geography
word-initially
wordmongering
word of command
word processor
Wordsworthian
worked to death
workhouse test
working dinner
work on tribute
work the oracle
world language
worldly-minded
worldly wisdom
wormwood water
worshippingly
worsification
worthlessness
worth one's salt
would-have-been
wound parasite
wraggle-taggle
wrapping paper
wreck of the sea
wrestling bout
wrist-slapping
writer's writer
writing-master
writing slider
writing-tablet
writ of besaiel
writ of inquiry
writ of summons
wrong-headedly
wrong way round
Württemberger
xanthochroism
xanthochromia
xanthochromic
xanthomatosis
xanthophyllic
xenoantigenic
xenobiologist
xenodiagnosis
xerodermatous
xerophthalmia
xerophthalmic
xiphiplastral
xiphiplastron
X-ray astronomy
xylographical
yachtsmanship
Yankee notions
Yarkand carpet

year after year
Yearly Meeting
year of Our Lord
year of the hare
Yeddo hawthorn
yellow admiral
yellow arsenic
yellow atrophy
yellow-bellied
yellow bunting
yellowfin sole
yellowfin tuna
yellow Geordie
yellowishness
yellow wagtail
yellow warbler
yellow warning
Yenisei-Ostyak
yeoman pricker
yeoman service
Yeoman Warders
yesterday's man
yield strength
yield the ghost
Yorkshire tyke
you and who else
you are welcome
young offender
Young's modulus
you should hear
yuppification
Zarathustrian
zebra crossing
zebra firefish
zenana mission
zenographical
zeolitization
zephyr gingham
zeta potential
zeugmatically
zigzag machine
zincification
Zinjanthropus
zinnober green
zodiacal light
Zöllner's lines
zona pellucida
zone levelling
zooflagellate
zoogeographer
zoogeographic
zooidiogamous
zooplanktonic
zoosporangium
zygapophyseal
zygodactylous
zygomatic arch
zygomatic bone

FOURTEEN LETTERS

a beam in one's eye
aberrationally
a bird in the hand
a bit of all right
abjuration oath
abjure the realm
abominableness
above and beyond
above suspicion
abrenunciation
absent-mindedly
absolutization
absorptiometer
absquatulation
abstemiousness
abstersiveness
abstractedness
abstractionism
abstractionist
acceptableness
accessibleness
accessory nerve
accidentalness
accompliceship
accomplishable
accomplishment
accordion pleat
accountability
accountantship
accumulatively
accusatorially
accustomedness
Achilles tendon
achondroplasia
achondroplasic
achromatically
achronological
acknowledgedly
acknowledgment
acquaintedness
across one's knee
across the board
actinide series
actinometrical
actio in distans
action painting
action research
action stations
active charcoal
active driveway
act of attainder
act of indemnity
Act of Supremacy
acupunctuation
adductor muscle

adenocarcinoma
adjacent angles
administration
administrative
administratrix
Admiralty Board
adoption agency
adrenal medulla
adrenocortical
adult education
advance booking
advanced degree
advantageously
Advent calendar
adventitiously
adverb of manner
Advocate-Depute
aerenchymatous
aerial cableway
aerial ping-pong
aerobiological
aerodynamicist
aeroelasticity
aerosolization
aesthesiometer
aetiologically
affair of honour
affectionately
affectlessness
a flea in one's ear
African cypress
Africanization
African pompano
after-knowledge
after-reckoning
after-sensation
against the hair
against the wall
aggrandization
aggrandizement
aggregate fruit
aggressiveness
agriculturally
agrobiological
agro-ecological
agro-industrial
agrotechnology
air-conditioned
air-conditioner
airing cupboard
Air Vice-Marshal
alcoholization
alcoholometric
alder buckthorn
Alexandrianism

alexipharmacon
Alfred the Great
alignment chart
alimentiveness
a lion in the path
alkalinization
all and singular
allegorization
allelomorphism
all in a day's work
all-in wrestling
alliterational
alliteratively
allodification
all one knows how
allopathically
allopatrically
allosterically
allotetraploid
all-overishness
all over the shop
all over the show
all there is to it
all-too-familiar
alphabetically
alphanumerical
alteration hand
altogetherness
altruistically
aluminium oxide
aluminothermic
amateurishness
ambassadorship
ambidextrously
ambrosia beetle
Ambrosian chant
ambulance woman
American Indian
American Legion
American marten
American plaice
American turtle
ammonification
ammonitiferous
amniotic cavity
amphiarthrosis
amphiarthrotic
amphibological
amylobarbitone
Anabaptistical
anachronically
anagrammatical
analogicalness
anamorphoscope
ancient demesne

ancient history
androdioecious
andromonoecism
angle of weather
Anglo-Gallicism
anhypostatical
annalistically
annular eclipse
annus mirabilis
answerableness
antagonistical
antagonization
antaphrodisiac
Antarctic Ocean
anthropologist
anthropologize
anthropometric
anthropopathic
anthropotomist
Anti-Birmingham
anticipatingly
anticipatively
anticipatorily
anticonvulsant
antidepressant
antidromically
anti-government
antihistaminic
antihysterical
antimacassared
antimetabolite
antimonarchist
antimony glance
antineoplastic
anti-odontalgic
antipathetical
antiperistasis
antiperspirant
antiphlogistic
antiphonically
antiquarianism
antiquarianize
antiscriptural
antiseptically
antisymmetrize
antisyphilitic
antithetically
anxiety complex
apartment block
apartment hotel
apartment house
aphoristically
apocalypticism
apologetically
apophthegmatic
apoplectically
appeal to Caesar
appendicectomy
apple of discord
apple of one's eye
apples and pears

applicableness
apply the brakes
appositionally
appreciatingly
appreciatively
apprehensively
apprenticehood
apprenticement
apprenticeship
approvableness
approved school
Arabian jasmine
Arabic numerals
arachnological
arbitratorship
arboricultural
archaeological
archaistically
archbishophood
archbishopship
archdeaconries
archdeaconship
archidiaconate
archiepiscopal
archipresbyter
archpriesthood
arenaceous rock
argentaffinoma
aristocratical
arithmetically
arithmetic mean
Ark of Testimony
armour-piercing
aromatherapist
arrhythmically
arrondissement
arterial system
article of faith
article of virtu
articulateness
artificialness
artificial silk
artillery plant
arty-craftiness
as a general rule
as clear as a bell
as crazy as a loon
a second opinion
as far as I can see
as fit as a fiddle
as God is my judge
as happy as a clam
as happy as Larry
Asiatic cholera
a smack in the eye
as mad as a hatter
as near as dammit
a sop to Cerberus
asparagus stone
as safe as houses
assertorically

asset-stripping
assimilability
as smart as paint
associationism
associationist
as the case may be
as the crow flies
asthenospheric
as the story goes
astragalomancy
astrochemistry
astrologically
astronomically
astrophysicist
as who should say
asymmetrically
asymptotically
asynchronously
a tap on the wrist
at a rate of knots
at daggers drawn
at equidistance
at full throttle
a thing of nought
Atlantic States
atomic mass unit
atomic particle
atomic spectrum
at one fell swoop
at one's disposal
at one's last gasp
at one's pleasure
atraumatically
atropinization
at swords' points
attainableness
attested cattle
attitude of mind
attitudinarian
attorn tenant to
attractiveness
audio frequency
audiometrician
audio secretary
auditory meatus
Augustinianism
aurora borealis
aurothiomalate
auspiciousness
Australian bear
Australianness
Australian teak
authentication
autobiographer
autobiographic
autocorrelator
autocratically
auto-erotically
autograph album
autolithograph
automatic pilot

automatization
autoradiograph
auto-suggestion
auto-suggestive
autotransplant
aux fines herbes
avariciousness
a will of one's own
a winning streak
a word to the wise
axiomatization
axis of symmetry
axisymmetrical
azidothymidine
babes in the wood
bachelor of arts
Bachelor of Arts
back-projection
backscattering
back-scratching
back-seat driver
bactericidally
bacteriologist
bacteriophobia
bacteriostasis
bacteriostatic
badminton court
baggage reclaim
balance of power
balance of trade
balloon barrage
ballpark figure
Balmoral tartan
banana republic
banded anteater
banged to rights
bangtail muster
banking parlour
banner headline
banqueting-hall
baptism of blood
Barbados cherry
barbituric acid
Bardfield oxlip
barefoot doctor
bargain and sale
bargain-hunting
bargaining chip
baroclinically
barometrically
barotropically
barrage balloon
barrel of laughs
barrister-at-law
baseball league
bastardization
bastard saffron
Batavian endive
bate one's breath
bathing costume
bathing-machine

bathorhodopsin
batsman's wicket
battering-train
batting average
be-all and end-all
be all the same to
bear and forbear
bear animalcule
bear comparison
bearded vulture
bear great state
Béarnaise sauce
beat generation
beatific vision
beat one's brains
beat one's breast
beat the drum for
beat to quarters
beat to the punch
beautification
bedroom slipper
bed-sitting room
beef to the heels
before one's eyes
before one's nose
before one's time
beg the question
behaviouralism
behaviouralist
behaviouristic
behind one's back
behind schedule
behind the times
being-for-itself
believe it or not
belladonna lily
belletristical
bells of Ireland
belted galloway
belt-tightening
benedictionary
beneficialness
benefit society
benzodiazepine
bergamot-orange
beside the point
Bessel function
best before date
better feelings
beyond question
beyond reproach
Bible Christian
bibliographies
bibliographise
bibliographize
bibliomaniacal
bid a person base
bidialectalism
big-heartedness
bilirubinaemia
billiard-marker

billiard saloon
bill of exchange
binary compound
Binet–Simon test
bioclimatology
biodegradation
bio-electricity
bio-engineering
bioengineering
biogenetically
biogeochemical
biographically
bioluminescent
biomathematics
biorhythmicist
biostatistical
biosystematics
biosystematist
bipartisanship
birch partridge
bird of paradise
Bismarckianism
bite the thumb at
bit of crackling
bitter-cucumber
bituminiferous
bituminization
bituminous coal
biuret reaction
black chameleon
black-eyed Susan
black guillemot
black horehound
black in the face
black manganese
black marketeer
black raspberry
black snakeroot
black stinkwood
black swallower
black turnstone
bladder-campion
blade-consonant
blank cartridge
blasting powder
blastomylonite
blaxploitation
bleaching-green
bleary-eyedness
Blenheim Orange
blepharoplasty
blessed thistle
blind as a beetle
blockade-runner
block and tackle
blocked letters
blond bombshell
blood poisoning
bloodthirstier
bloodthirstily
bloody-mindedly

blow hot and cold
blue marguerite
Blues and Royals
blue sowthistle
blue wildebeest
boa constrictor
boarding kennel
boarding school
board of control
boatswain's mate
boisterousness
Bologna sausage
bolometrically
boneless wonder
Book of Proverbs
borough council
borough-English
boroughmongery
borrowed plumes
bottom-dwelling
bottom falls out
botulinum toxin
bougainvillaea
bouncing castle
boundary umpire
bouquets garnis
Bourbon biscuit
bowdlerization
bowling average
Bowman's capsule
brachycephales
brachycephalic
Brackett series
bradymetabolic
brain-fever bird
brake parachute
branchial cleft
branchiomerism
branchiostegal
Bravais lattice
Brazilian tapir
bread and butter
bread and scrape
breadfruit tree
break-bone fever
break in shivers
break new ground
break one's heart
break the back of
break the ground
break the record
break the wicket
breathing-space
breathlessness
breathtakingly
breech delivery
breeder reactor
breeding ground
breeding season
bremsstrahlung
bridge-building

bright and early
Bright's disease
brightsomeness
brindled beauty
bring into being
bring up the rear
Bristol diamond
Bristol fashion
Britannia metal
British disease
British English
Britticisation
Brobdingnagian
Brocken spectre
broiler chicken
bronchiectasis
bronchodilator
bronze diabetes
brother uterine
brown haematite
Brownian motion
brownish-yellow
Brunswick green
brush discharge
Brussels carpet
Brussels sprout
buccolingually
Buckley's chance
buffer solution
bulimia nervosa
bull-headedness
bullock-puncher
bumper-to-bumper
bump of locality
bundle of nerves
Burchell's zebra
burdensomeness
bur in the throat
burnt to a cinder
burst in shivers
burst one's sides
bury the hatchet
bus-conductress
business person
busman's holiday
butter-fingered
butterfly valve
buttonball tree
button mushroom
buttonwood tree
buy a pig in a poke
by one's lonesome
by return of post
by the Lord Harry
by the same token
by the truckload
cabbage lettuce
cabbage-looking
Cabinet Council
cabinet pudding
cabinet scraper

cack-handedness
cadaverousness
cadence braking
caisson disease
calabash nutmeg
calamitousness
calamity-howler
calcaneocuboid
California Jack
call in evidence
call in question
calliper splint
call to the lot of
calorific value
calorimetrical
camera obscuras
campanological
campylotropous
Canadian French
canary-coloured
cannon-ball tree
canonical hours
cantaloup melon
cantankerously
can't be bothered
Canterbury bell
Canterbury tale
capacitatively
Cape gooseberry
Cape hartebeest
Cape hunting dog
capitalist road
capitalization
capriciousness
captain-general
captive balloon
capuchin monkey
caramelization
carbon monoxide
carboxylic acid
carcinogenesis
carcinological
carcinomatosis
Cardan's formula
cardiac passion
cardinal bishop
cardinal deacon
cardinal flower
cardinal humour
cardinal number
cardinal spider
cardinal virtue
cardiomyopathy
cardiovascular
carriage return
carry a torch for
cartes blanches
Cartesian devil
Cartesian diver
cartographical
cartoonishness

cartridge paper
cascara sagrada
case conference
casement window
cash on delivery
cassette player
castle-building
castle in the air
cast one's garter
castor oil plant
castrametation
cast the gorge at
casual labourer
catachrestical
catadioptrical
catastrophical
catch a likeness
catechetically
catechumenical
categorization
catenary bridge
cathedral glass
Catherine wheel
cathode ray tube
Catholic Herald
Cauchy sequence
Cauchy's theorem
caudal vertebra
caudate nucleus
cauliflower ear
cause and effect
causes célèbres
causewayed camp
caustic creeper
cedar of Lebanon
celestial globe
Celtic twilight
censoriousness
censurableness
centenarianism
Central America
central heating
centralisation
centralization
central locking
central reserve
centrifugality
centrifugalize
centrifugation
centrolecithal
centuplication
cercopithecoid
cerebral cortex
cerebrocentric
cestui que trust
ceteris paribus
Chagas's disease
chaises longues
chamber concert
chamber foreign
chamois leather

chancellorship
chances are that
Chandler wobble
changeableness
changelessness
change one's feet
change one's mind
change one's mood
change one's note
change one's skin
change one's tune
Channel Islands
channelization
chanson de geste
chaptalization
character actor
characterfully
characteristic
characterology
charcoal-burner
charcoal filter
charioteership
charitableness
charlotte russe
charm offensive
charter parties
Charter Society
chase the dragon
château-bottled
chattel slavery
checkerberries
cheese sandwich
chemical weapon
chemoautotroph
chemoreception
chemosynthesis
chemosynthetic
chemotherapist
chest of drawers
chest-protector
Chewings fescue
chicken à la King
chicken cholera
chicken-hearted
chicken-livered
Chief Constable
child allowance
child of the soil
child-resistant
Chilean jasmine
Chile saltpetre
chilli con carne
chimney swallow
chincherinchee
Chinese cabbage
Chinese lantern
Chinese laundry
Chinese New Year
chinless wonder
chitter-chatter
chivalrousness

chloral hydrate
chloridization
chloritization
chloromelanite
chlorophyllous
chloroplatinic
chlorothiazide
chlorpromazine
chocolate brown
chocolate-house
cholecystotomy
choledochotomy
cholelithiasis
cholinesterase
chondrocranium
chondrogenesis
chondrosarcoma
chorale prelude
chorda tendinea
choreographist
chorographical
chrestomathies
Christlikeness
Christmas carol
Christocentric
Christological
chromatic scale
chromatography
chromatophoric
chromodynamics
chronicle drama
chronobiologic
chronometrical
Church and State
church assembly
Church Congress
Church Covenant
Church Militant
Church Slavonic
churchwardenly
chute-the-chutes
cigarette-paper
cinematography
cineradiograph
cinnamaldehyde
circle of Willis
circuit-breaker
circuitousness
circular letter
circumadjacent
circumambience
circumambiency
circumambulate
circumbendibus
circumferentor
circumgyration
circumgyratory
circumlittoral
circumlocution
circumlocutory
circum-meridian

circumnavigate
circumnutation
circumposition
circumrotation
circumscissile
circumspection
circumspective
circumstantial
circumvolution
citizen's arrest
city missionary
civil commotion
civilizational
clapperdudgeon
claret-coloured
clasp one's hands
class-conscious
classical Latin
classification
classificatory
claustrophilia
claustrophobia
claustrophobic
clavicytherium
cleansing cream
clearance order
cleptoparasite
clerical collar
climatological
climb the ladder
clip the wings of
clitoridectomy
clitter-clatter
cloak-and-dagger
close communion
close Communion
closed interval
closed syllable
close the door on
close the door to
close to the bone
close to the wind
clothing coupon
cloth-yard shaft
clouded leopard
clove carnation
clutch at a straw
coarticulation
coasting vessel
cobalticyanide
co-belligerence
co-belligerency
cocarcinogenic
cochineal plant
cock-a-doodle-doo
cockatoo farmer
cock-of-the-north
cocksfoot grass
cocktail beetle
cocktail-shaker
coconut matting

coeliac disease
coessentiality
coetaneousness
coffee-coloured
cogitativeness
cognizableness
cognoscibility
co-guardianship
cohabitational
coign of vantage
coincidentally
cold dark matter
collapsibility
collectability
collective farm
collectiveness
collective noun
collectivistic
collector's item
college pudding
Colles' fracture
colometrically
colonel-general
Colonel-in-Chief
Colonial Office
Colorado beetle
colour fastness
colourlessness
colour-sergeant
combustibility
combustion-tube
come across with
come from behind
come full circle
come off the pill
come on the scene
come to the front
comfort station
comma butterfly
commandantship
command economy
commandingness
commensurately
commensuration
commentatorial
commissaryship
commissionaire
commit adultery
committee stage
committee woman
commit to memory
commit to prison
commodiousness
common alehouse
common caracara
common centaury
common criminal
common informer
common nuisance
common or garden
common property

common recovery
common ryegrass
commonsensible
commonsensibly
commonsensical
Common Sergeant
Common Serjeant
common shoveler
common toadfish
common valerian
Communion-cloth
Communion table
community chest
companion hatch
companion piece
company officer
comparableness
compassionable
compatibleness
compellability
compenetration
compensatingly
compensational
competitorship
complementally
complementizer
complexionally
complexionless
complimentally
compliment slip
composing-stick
compossibility
compound engine
compound raceme
comprehensible
comprehensibly
compromisingly
compulsatively
compulsiveness
compulsoriness
compunctiously
computer dating
concaulescence
concavo-concave
conceivability
concelebration
concentratedly
concentrically
conceptiveness
conceptualizer
concerti grossi
concerto grosso
concert pianist
concessionaire
concessiveness
conciliatorily
conclusiveness
concorporation
concrete poetry
concretization
concupiscently

condensability
condescendence
condescendency
conditionalism
conditionalist
conditionality
conductibility
conductimetric
conduction band
conductometric
conduplication
confessionless
confidence game
confidentially
confirmability
confirmatively
conformability
conformational
confoundedness
conglobulation
conglomeration
conglutination
congratulation
congratulative
congratulatory
congregational
congregationer
Congresspeople
Congreve rocket
conidiophorous
coniferization
conjecturality
conjugal rights
conjugate angle
conjugate focus
conjunctivitis
conjunct person
conjuring trick
connaturalness
connectibility
Connecticutter
conquistadores
consanguineous
consarcination
conscienceless
conservational
conservatively
conservativism
conservatories
conservatorium
consignificant
consistorially
consociational
consonant shift
conspiratorial
constabularies
constituencies
constitutional
constitutioned
constitutively
constitutivity

construability
constructional
constructively
constructivism
constructivist
consubstantial
consuetudinary
consulting room
consumer-driven
consummateness
consummatively
contact breaker
contact healing
contact process
contagiousness
container-grown
container-lorry
contemperature
contemporaries
contemporarily
contemptuously
conterminously
contiguousness
continental day
Continental day
continentalist
continentality
continentalize
continued story
continuity girl
continuousness
continuous wave
contour-chasing
contour feather
contrabandista
contract bridge
contractedness
contract killer
contradictable
contradictious
contradistinct
contragredient
contra-indicant
contra-indicate
contraindicate
contranatation
contraposition
contrapositive
contrapuntally
contra-rotating
contra-rotation
contrary-minded
contrary-to-fact
contra-seasonal
contrast medium
controlled drug
controllership
control surface
controvertible
contumaciously
contumeliously

convection cell
convection oven
conventionally
converging lens
conversational
convertibility
convexo-concave
convictiveness
convincingness
convolutionary
convulsiveness
Cooley's anaemia
Coolgardie safe
cooperationist
copper-bottomed
copper-fastened
copper sulphate
coproporphyrin
cops and robbers
Coptic Orthodox
coquettishness
coral-limestone
cord-ornamented
core curriculum
core vocabulary
Coriolis effect
corner cupboard
Corona Borealis
coronary artery
coronation oath
corporate image
corporate State
corporation tax
corpus callosum
corpuscularian
corpus striatum
Correggiescity
correspondence
correspondency
corrugated iron
corruptibility
corticosteroid
corticosterone
corticotrophic
corticotrophin
cosmochemistry
cosmographical
cosmologically
cosmopolitanly
cosmopolitical
cost accountant
cost accounting
cost-efficiency
cotemporaneity
cotemporaneous
Cotswold cheese
cotton-leaf worm
coumarone resin
council chamber
council-general
councillorship

counselor-at-law
counterbalance
counter-battery
counter-compony
counter-culture
counterculture
countercurrent
counterfactual
counterlathing
countermeasure
countermissile
counter-opening
counter-passant
counter-passion
counter-penalty
counterpuncher
counter-salient
countershading
countersubject
counting number
count one's beads
country dancing
county palatine
County Palatine
coupled columns
courageousness
course of nature
Court Christian
Court of Appeals
court of inquiry
Court of session
Court of Session
covering letter
cover the ground
cowardy custard
coxcombicality
Coxsackie virus
coyote diggings
cradle Catholic
cradle-snatcher
craft-conscious
cranberry jelly
creamery butter
creatureliness
credibility gap
creditableness
credit transfer
creepy-crawlies
crème Chantilly
crème de la crème
crème renversée
crickle-crackle
crime of passion
criminalistics
criminal lawyer
criminal record
criminological
criminous clerk
crinkle-crankle
crinkum-crankum
critical volume

crocodile tears
crook in one's lot
crook one's elbow
cross-buttocker
cross-countries
cross-fertilise
cross-fertilize
cross-fingering
cross-gartering
cross-infection
cross one's heart
cross-pollinate
cross-reference
cross-sectional
cross-subsidise
cross-subsidize
cross the path of
crouched burial
crown and anchor
Crown privilege
cruciverbalist
cruising radius
crumb structure
crushing stroke
cryobiological
cry one's eyes out
cryoprotectant
cryoprotection
cryoscopically
cryptococcosis
cryptogrammist
cryptographist
cryptoporticus
cryptorchidism
cryptovolcanic
crystal lattice
crystallizable
crystallize out
crystallogenic
crystallomancy
cucumber beetle
cucumber mosaic
cucurbitaceous
culture vulture
culturological
cumbersomeness
cumulativeness
cumulative vote
cumulonimbuses
curate-in-charge
curate's comfort
curiologically
current account
current affairs
current bedding
curricula vitae
curtain lecture
curvilinearity
cushion capital
cushion-thumper
cuss a person out

customary court
customs service
cut a person dead
cut one's teeth on
cut the throat of
cut-throat razor
cutthroat razor
cyanobacterium
cyanocobalamin
cyclomorphosis
cyclorrhaphous
cyclostomatous
cystic fibrosis
cytocentrifuge
cytogeneticist
cytophotometer
cytophotometry
dacryoadenitis
dacryocystitis
dactylographer
daffadowndilly
daffodil yellow
damfoolishness
dance of macabre
dance programme
dancing dervish
dancing-partner
dandelion clock
dark-adaptation
dark arches moth
darkling beetle
darning-machine
data processing
data protection
dative absolute
daughterliness
daughters-in-law
daylight saving
Day of Atonement
day of expiation
Day of Judgement
day of reckoning
dead man's handle
Dead Sea Scrolls
dead to the world
Dear John letter
death's head moth
debenture stock
debilitatingly
decapacitation
deceivableness
deceive oneself
de-Christianize
deciduous tooth
decimal coinage
decimalization
decivilization
declare oneself
declassifiable
declining years
decolonization

decolorization
decompensation
deconsecration
deconstruction
deconstructive
Decorated style
decorative arts
decorativeness
decree absolute
decreolization
deed of covenant
defeasibleness
defeminization
defence in depth
defenestration
defensibleness
deferentiality
defibrillation
definitionally
definitive host
definitiveness
deflocculation
degasification
degenerate code
degenerateness
degenerescence
degree absolute
degrees of frost
dehumanization
delaying action
delectableness
deliberateness
deliberatively
delightfulness
delocalization
demisemiquaver
demobilization
democratically
demolition ball
demonetization
demoralization
demoralizingly
demountability
denaturization
denazification
dendroclimatic
denominational
denominatively
dental mechanic
denumerability
depart from life
departmentally
dependableness
depigmentation
deplorableness
depolarization
deposit account
depot battalion
depreciatingly
depressingness
depressiveness

Derby porcelain
Derbyshire spar
deregistration
derivationally
derivativeness
derived fossils
dermatoglyphic
dermatographia
dermatological
dermatomycosis
dernier ressort
derogatoriness
desalinization
descending node
descriptionist
desert ironwood
desert pavement
desirelessness
desk dictionary
desophisticate
despairingness
despicableness
despiritualize
despitefulness
destructionist
desulphuration
detached retina
determinedness
detestableness
detoxification
detractiveness
devalorization
devaluationist
devil's advocate
devitalization
dexamphetamine
dextrorotation
dextrorotatory
dextrotartaric
dextrotartrate
diabolicalness
diachronically
diademed monkey
diagenetically
diagnostically
diagonalizable
diagonal matrix
diaheliotropic
dialectologist
diamantiferous
diamondiferous
diamond jubilee
diamond wedding
diaphototropic
diathermaneity
diathermically
dichotomically
dicotyledonous
dictation speed
die in one's boots
die in one's shoes

dielectrically
diesel-electric
differentiable
differentially
differentiator
different-sized
diffractometer
diffractometry
digestibleness
digestive gland
digestive tract
digger's delight
dig in one's heels
digitalization
digressiveness
dilemmatically
diluvial theory
dimensionality
diminutiveness
dingo on a person
dinoflagellate
diplographical
diplomatically
diplomatic copy
diplostemonous
dipterocarpous
dipterological
direct dialling
direct drilling
directionality
direct opposite
direct question
direct taxation
disaccommodate
disacknowledge
disaffiliation
disaffirmation
disaggregation
disambiguation
disapplication
disappointedly
disappointment
disapprobation
disapprobative
disapprobatory
disappropriate
disapprovingly
disarrangement
disassociation
disbelievingly
disciplinarian
disciplinarily
disciplinatory
discographical
discolouration
discombobulate
discomfortable
discomfortably
discommendable
discomposingly
disconcertedly

disconcertment
disconfirmable
disconformable
disconnectable
disconnectedly
disconsolately
disconsolation
discontentedly
discontentment
discontinuance
disconvenience
discount-broker
discountenance
discouragement
discouragingly
discourteously
discredibility
discretionally
discretiveness
discretization
discriminately
discriminating
discrimination
discriminative
discriminatory
discursiveness
disdainfulness
disedification
disembarkation
disemboguement
disembowelling
disembowelment
disempowerment
disenchantment
disencumbrance
disenfranchise
disengagedness
disenthralment
disentitlement
disequilibrate
disequilibrium
disestablisher
disforestation
disfurnishment
disgruntlement
disgustfulness
disgustingness
dishcloth gourd
disheartenment
disillusionary
disillusionise
disillusionize
disimpassioned
disimperialism
disimprovement
disincarcerate
disinclination
disincommodate
disincorporate
disinfestation
disinformation

disingenuously
disinheritance
disintegration
disintegrative
disinteresting
disjecta membra
disjointedness
dismissiveness
Disneyfication
disorderliness
disorientation
dispensability
dispensational
dispensatively
dispensatorily
dispersability
dispersibility
dispersiveness
dispersonalize
dispiritedness
dispiteousness
display cabinet
displeasurable
displeasurably
disputableness
disputatiously
disquietedness
disquisitional
disregardfully
disrespectable
disruptiveness
dissatisfiedly
dissertational
disserviceable
dissociability
dissuasiveness
dissymmetrical
distance runner
distemperature
distensibility
distortionless
distractedness
distraughtness
distressed area
distressedness
distress-rocket
distress signal
distributaries
distributional
distributively
distributivity
disulphide bond
disyllabically
dittany of Crete
divaricatingly
divergenceless
diverticulitis
diverticulosis
divertissement
divided highway
do a dishonour to

do a person out of
do a person proud
do a person stead
do a person wrong
Doctors' Commons
doctor's mandate
dodecasyllabic
dodecasyllable
dodge the column
dog in the manger
dogmaticalness
dog-tooth violet
do-it-yourselfer
dolce far niente
dolichocephali
dolichocephaly
dolomitization
dolphin-striker
domaine-bottled
domestic bursar
done to the world
don't-carishness
do one's business
do one's own thing
do one's possible
dormant partner
dormer bungalow
dorsoventrally
dor the dotterel
do something for
dot and carry one
double acrostic
double-breasted
double concerto
double cropping
double-declutch
double entendre
double exposure
double jeopardy
double knitting
double napoleon
double negative
double saucepan
double standard
double-stopping
double-stranded
doublet and hose
double-tonguing
doubting Thomas
downconversion
downhill of life
down in the dumps
down in the mouth
down one's street
down on one's luck
dracunculiasis
Drang nach Osten
draughtmanship
draughtsperson
drawing account
draw the longbow

dress-conscious
dress preserver
dress rehearsal
drift-indicator
drilling string
drinking-up time
drinking-vessel
drink like a fish
drink the waters
driver's license
drive the centre
drive to the wall
drive up the wall
driving licence
drop-handlebars
drop one's bundle
dropping-bottle
drunken driving
Dublin Bay prawn
duchesse sleeve
ducks and drakes
duelling pistol
duodeno-jejunal
duplicate ratio
duplicate whist
Dutch reckoning
dyed-in-the-grain
dyer's greenweed
dynamo-electric
dynamometer car
dysmenorrhoeal
dysmenorrhoeic
earn one's tucker
East Coast fever
Easter sittings
easy come easy go
eat oneself sick
eccentricities
ecclesiastical
ecclesiologist
echinococcosis
echocardiogram
ecocatastrophe
econometrician
economic growth
economy of scale
ectrodactylism
edible dormouse
editio princeps
educationalist
effectual grace
effeminateness
efficient cause
effortlessness
egalitarianism
eggbutt snaffle
egocentrically
Egyptian plover
eigenfrequency
eighteen-tonner
eight-leaf twill

eiusdem generis
elder-brotherly
elder statesman
Electra complex
electric charge
electric cooker
electric guitar
electric kettle
electric shaver
electrobiology
electrocautery
electrochemist
electrochromic
electrodeposit
electrodynamic
electrogenesis
electrokinetic
electrolytical
electromedical
electromyogram
electroneutral
electronically
electronic mail
electronograph
electron optics
electro-optical
electro-osmosis
electro-osmotic
electrophorese
electrostatics
electrosurgery
electrotechnic
electrotherapy
electrothermal
electrovalence
electrovalency
electroviscous
elegiac couplet
elementariness
elephant dugout
elephant's teeth
eleutheromania
Elizabethanism
ellipticalness
embankment wall
embarrassingly
emblematically
embryoniferous
embryotoxicity
emission nebula
emission theory
empathetically
emperor penguin
empire building
emprosthotonos
empyreumatical
emulsification
enamel painting
enantiomorphic
encephalitogen
encephalograph

encephalopathy
encounter group
encyclopaedism
encyclopaedist
encyclopedical
endarterectomy
endocrinologic
endodontically
endopolyploidy
endoscopically
endosmotically
endotracheally
enfant terrible
enforceability
enfranchisable
engagement ring
English disease
English English
Englishization
English mustard
English opening
English Psalter
engrossingness
enharmonically
enregistration
ensemble acting
ens realissimum
entepicondylar
enterogastrone
enterotoxaemia
enterprise zone
enterprisingly
entertainingly
enter the Church
enthronization
enthusiastical
entomopathogen
epexegetically
ephebiatrician
epichlorhydrin
epicontinental
epidemic typhus
epidemiologist
epididymectomy
epigenetically
epiglottiditis
epigrammatical
epigrammatizer
epigraphically
epistemologist
epistolography
epistolophobia
episyllogistic
epithelization
epizootiologic
equanimousness
equation of time
equiangularity
equinoctial day
equiponderance
equiponderancy

equivocatingly
ergastoplasmic
ergocalciferol
err on the side of
erythroblastic
erythrocytosis
erythropoiesis
erythropoietic
erythropoietin
escape velocity
eschatological
essence-peddler
establish a suit
esterification
estoppel in pais
eternalization
etherification
Ethiops martial
Ethiops mineral
ethnic minority
ethnobotanical
ethnographical
ethnohistorian
ethnologically
ethnosemantics
ethylene glycol
etymologically
Euclidean space
eugeosynclinal
Euler's constant
eulogistically
euphorbiaceous
euphuistically
Eurocentricity
Europarliament
Eusebian canons
Eustachian tube
eutrophication
evangelicalism
evangelicanism
evangelistical
evangelization
evaporated milk
evapotranspire
even-handedness
evening lychnis
evergreen hazel
everlasting pea
everywhere else
everywhereness
evolutionarily
evolutionistic
exacerbatingly
exaggeratingly
exaggeratively
exasperatingly
exceptionalism
exceptionality
exceptiousness
exclaim against
exclaustration

excluded middle
exclusion order
exclusive voice
excommunicable
excommunicator
excrementitial
excruciatingly
executioneress
executor dative
exflagellation
exhaustibility
exhaustiveness
exhereditation
exhilaratingly
existentialism
existentialist
exoatmospheric
exonucleolytic
exothermically
expansion board
expansionistic
expansion joint
expedientially
expense account
expergefaction
experienceable
experientalist
experientially
experimentally
explain oneself
exploitability
explosive rivet
exponentiation
expositionally
expressionless
expression-mark
expression-stop
expressiveness
express oneself
exsanguination
ex-servicewoman
ex-servicewomen
extemporaneous
extended burial
extended family
extensibleness
extensionality
extensor muscle
extinct volcano
extinguishable
extinguishment
extortionately
extracorporeal
extractability
extra-essential
extra-foraneous
extramaritally
extraneousness
extraordinaire
extra-parochial
extrapyramidal

extravagancies
extravehicular
extreme unction
face to faceness
face to face with
facinorousness
factitiousness
factor analysis
factor of safety
factory farming
factory trawler
faint-heartedly
fair-mindedness
fair-to-middling
fairy armadillo
fairy godmother
faits accomplis
fallaciousness
falling weather
fall into disuse
fall on deaf ears
fall on one's face
fall on one's feet
fall to the lot of
false hellebore
false pretences
false thorow-wax
falsifiability
fame and fortune
familiar spirit
Family Division
family likeness
family planning
family portrait
family skeleton
fancy franchise
fantasticality
fantastication
fantasy cricket
far-fetchedness
far-sightedness
farthingsworth
fashionability
fast and furious
fast friendship
fastidiousness
fatalistically
fatherlessness
father-long-legs
father of chapel
Father Superior
favourableness
feather-bedding
feather-brained
federalization
Federal Reserve
feeble-mindedly
feed check valve
feel the draught
feel the pulse of
feldspathoidal

felicitousness
fellow-commoner
fellow creature
fen-berrberries
fenestra ovalis
Fermat's theorem
fermentability
fermentescible
ferrimagnetism
ferromagnesian
ferromagnetism
ferroprussiate
Feynman diagram
fibrocartilage
fibrous protein
fictitiousness
fidei-commissum
field-artillery
field character
field-preaching
field telegraph
fifteen-pounder
fifth columnist
fighting chance
fighting-weight
fight up against
fight windmills
figurativeness
figure-floating
figure four trap
figure of speech
filio-pietistic
filling station
fill the stead of
finance company
finders keepers
find one's tongue
fine de la maison
finger alphabet
finger language
finger-pointing
finger's-breadth
finger spelling
finishing touch
Finlandisation
Finlandization
fire department
fire-discipline
fireless cooker
fire-worshipper
first intention
first principle
First Secretary
first-time buyer
fiscal engineer
Fischer–Tropsch
fisherman's bend
fisherman's knit
fisherman's knot
fisherman's tale
fish for oneself

fish out of water
fishtail burner
fissionability
fivepin bowling
flagellomaniac
flagitiousness
flag-lieutenant
flail harvester
flame-projector
flame-retardant
flat as a pancake
flat-footedness
flat-tail mullet
flauto traverso
flax-flower blue
flight envelope
flight recorder
flight sergeant
flight-shooting
flimflammeries
floating anchor
floating bridge
floating island
floating kidney
flocks and herds
flock wallpaper
flog a dead horse
floor exercises
floral envelope
Florence fennel
Florentine iris
floriculturist
flower children
flowering plant
flowerlessness
flow production
fluid amplifier
fluidification
fluid mechanics
fluoridization
fly honeysuckle
flying buttress
Flying Dutchman
Flying Fortress
Flying Scotsman
flying squadron
flying squirrel
fly in the face of
foam at the mouth
foetal distress
folk psychology
follow-my-leader
follow one's nose
follow the crowd
football coupon
for all one cares
for all the world
for a long season
foraminiferous
forbidden fruit
forbiddingness

forbid the banns
force one's voice
for Christ's sake
forcible-feeble
Forefathers' Day
forehandedness
foreign affairs
foreign service
foreordination
foreseeability
forest kangaroo
forest mahogany
forethoughtful
fore-topgallant
forgivableness
for good measure
for heaven's sake
forisfamiliate
Former Prophets
formidableness
for one's own hand
for the duration
for the hell of it
for the life of me
for the most part
for the soul of me
forthrightness
fortuitousness
fortune-hunting
fortune-telling
forward-looking
forward scatter
foundationless
foundation stop
founder's shares
founding father
founding member
four last things
four-leaf clover
four-letter word
four-on-the-floor
fourteenth part
fourteen-tonner
fourth position
four-wheel drive
fovea centralis
fractional note
fragrant orchid
fraternal order
fraternization
freedom fighter
free enterprise
free expression
free-handedness
freestone peach
freieslebenite
French Canadian
French dressing
French knickers
French lavender
French lungwort

French marigold
French mistress
French-polisher
French vermouth
frequency curve
freshwater flea
Fresnel biprism
frictionlessly
friction-murmur
friendlessness
friendly action
fringe medicine
frolicsomeness
from bad to worse
from head to foot
from side to side
from soup to nuts
from time to time
from wire to wire
from year to year
frontal assault
frontierswoman
frontierswomen
froth flotation
frozen shoulder
fructiferously
fructification
fuchsinophilia
fuchsinophilic
fuliginousness
full complement
full employment
full speed ahead
full steam ahead
fully-fashioned
functional food
fundamentalism
fundamentalist
fundamentality
funeral honours
funeral parlour
furfuraldehyde
furnished house
futuristically
futurity stakes
Gaelic football
gain the garland
galactocentric
galactophorous
galactopoiesis
galactopoietic
gall of the earth
galvanocautery
galvanoplastic
galvanotropism
game as Ned Kelly
gamma radiation
ganglionectomy
garboard strake
garden valerian
garnishee order

gastrovascular
gathering sound
gelatification
gelatinization
gelatinousness
geminate leaves
genealogically
general average
generalisation
generalissimos
generalization
general meeting
general-purpose
general service
general warrant
generativeness
generification
genethliacally
genetic profile
Geneva Protocol
geniculate body
gentleman-usher
gentrification
genuine article
geocentrically
geochronometry
geognostically
geographically
geological time
geomagnetician
geometrization
geomorphically
geomorphogenic
geopolitically
geosynchronous
geothermometer
German-American
German Catholic
Germanophilist
German shepherd
gerontological
gerontomorphic
get a person down
get a thing out of
get into trouble
get in touch with
get in wrong with
get it in the neck
get off one's bike
get oneself gone
get one's feet wet
get one's hands on
get one's leg over
get one's own back
get the best of it
get the better of
get the breeze up
get to first base
get to grips with
Gewürztraminer
gingerbread man

gingerbread nut
give a hare a turn
give credence to
give free rein to
give in marriage
give me strength
give occasion to
give one's love to
give one's mind to
give up the ghost
give us your fist
glacierization
glacio-eustatic
Gladstonianism
glandular fever
glanduliferous
glassification
global variable
globe artichoke
globe lightning
globus pallidus
Glorious Fourth
glory-of-the-snow
glossematician
glottalization
glucocorticoid
glucosidically
glyceraldehyde
glycogenolysis
glycogenolytic
glycolytically
glycosidically
goal difference
God bless my soul
God save the mark
God's own country
go for the doctor
go for the gloves
go into raptures
go into training
golden opinions
golden pheasant
golden samphire
golden triangle
gold of pleasure
Golgi apparatus
go like hot cakes
good conscience
good-fellowship
good-for-nothing
good-humouredly
good-temperedly
go off the handle
go on the streets
gooseberry eyes
gooseberry fool
go out of one's way
gopher tortoise
go separate ways
go to one's reward
go to the country

go to the trouble
governableness
governmentally
go with the times
grace and favour
gracious living
graduate school
gram-equivalent
grammaticality
grammaticalize
grammaticaster
grand battement
grandiloquence
grand inquistor
grandparentage
grand serjeanty
grandstand play
grandstand view
grangerization
granulocytosis
granulomatosis
graphic granite
graphitization
grappier cement
grasp the nettle
grass-widowhood
gratuitousness
graveyard cough
graveyard shift
graveyard watch
great attractor
great barracuda
great blue heron
Great Deliverer
greater omentum
great insertion
Grecian slipper
green-blindness
Green Cross code
greengroceries
green in one's eye
Greenland shark
Greenland whale
green sandpiper
gregariousness
Gregorian chant
Gregorian tones
griffon vulture
Grim the Collier
grist to the mill
ground-breaking
ground-fielding
ground-landlord
groundlessness
ground spearing
ground squirrel
group assurance
group insurance
growth industry
guild socialism
gull-billed tern

gurgeon stopper
gutter-crawling
gynaecological
gynomonoecious
gyroscopically
gyrostabilizer
gyro-stabilizer
gyrostatically
gyro-theodolite
haberdasheries
habitation site
haemagglutinin
haematological
haematophagous
haematopoiesis
haematopoietic
haematosalpinx
haemocytometer
haemolytically
haemosiderosis
hagiographical
halfpennyworth
half-wittedness
halfwittedness
hallelujah lass
hallucinogenic
hammer and tongs
handicraftsman
hand on the torch
hanging glacier
Hansen's disease
hapax legomenon
harassing agent
hard-headedness
hard-lying money
hardy perennial
harlequinesque
harlequin quail
harmonic motion
harmonic series
harmoniousness
harpsichordist
hate literature
have a concern in
have a soul above
have a thick skin
have a tile loose
have been around
have everything
have got it badly
have got it wired
have in contempt
have in derision
have it both ways
have no guts in it
have no words for
have one's hand in
have one's own way
have one's will of
have one too many
have on one's mind

have recourse to
have relation to
have the bulge on
have the goods on
have the grace to
have the guns for
have the hots for
have the laugh on
have the worse of
have to one's name
Hawaiian guitar
hawkbill turtle
hawk one's mutton
head for heights
head like a sieve
headmastership
head of the river
headstrongness
hear a person out
hearsay account
hearsay witness
heart-rendingly
hearts and minds
heart-searching
heat exhaustion
heathenishness
heather mixture
heath speedwell
heavenly-minded
heavens to Betsy
heavier-than-air
Heaviside layer
heavy breathing
heavy chemicals
hedonistically
heir of one's body
heliacal rising
Heligoland trap
hell for leather
helminthologic
help a person out
hemagglutinate
hemimetabolous
Hemingwayesque
hemispheroidal
hen and chickens
hentriacontane
heparinization
hepar sulphuris
hepaticologist
hepatocellular
hepatopancreas
hepatotoxicity
Heracliteanism
Heralds' College
Hercules beetle
Hercules powder
hereditability
hereditariness
here lies our way
heretoforetime

heritage centre
hermaphroditic
heroine-worship
hero-worshipper
herpetological
hesitation-form
hesitation-step
heteroaromatic
heterocaryotic
heterochromous
heterokaryosis
heterokaryotic
heteromorphism
heteromorphous
heteronomously
heterophyllous
heteropycnosis
heteropycnotic
heterosexually
heterospecific
heterosyllabic
heterothallism
heterotrophism
heterozygosity
hiccius doccius
hickery-pickery
hidden reserves
hierarchically
hieroglyphical
hierogrammatic
Hierosolymitan
High Commission
high-definition
high-handedness
Highland bonnet
Highland cattle
high-mindedness
highmindedness
high technology
Hindenburg line
hippopotamuses
histochemistry
histologically
histopathology
histoplasmosis
historicalness
historiography
histrionically
hit one in the eye
hobbledehoydom
hobbledehoyish
hobbledehoyism
hobnailed liver
Hofmann's violet
hoity-toityness
hold everything
hold in contempt
hold in derision
holding company
holding paddock
holding pattern

hold one's breath
hold one's ground
hold one's horses
hold one's tongue
hold on the slack
hold the clock on
hold the stirrup
hold up one's head
hole in the heart
holiday loading
holiday village
holier-than-thou
holo-alphabetic
holometabolous
holoparasitism
holoplanktonic
home missionary
homing instinct
homicidal mania
homme d'affaires
homoeomorphism
homoeomorphous
homoeoteleuton
homogenization
homoioteleuton
homophonically
homotransplant
honeycomb quilt
honeycomb tripe
honorary degree
honourableness
honours are even
hootchy-kootchy
horary question
horizontal dial
horizontalness
horned pondweed
horned screamer
horn spectacles
horrendousness
horror-stricken
horse-godmother
horse latitudes
horseshoe-vetch
horsewomanship
horticulturist
hospitableness
hostess trolley
hostile witness
hot and bothered
Hottentot bread
hot-water bottle
house detective
household bread
household stuff
housemaid's knee
House of Commons
House of Hanover
house of ill fame
House of Windsor
house physician

house-rent party
housing project
howling dervish
how the land lies
how the wind lies
Hubble constant
human geography
humanification
humanistically
human relations
human resources
humidification
humourlessness
humoursomeness
humpback bridge
humpback salmon
humpback sucker
hump-shouldered
humpty-dumpties
hundred-pounder
hung parliament
hunter-gatherer
hunting leopard
huntsman spider
hunt the slipper
hunt the thimble
hunt the whistle
hurdy-gurdy girl
hurricane force
hurricane-house
hyacinth of Peru
hyaluronic acid
hydatid disease
hydraulic brake
hydraulic organ
hydraulic press
hydrobiologist
hydrocarbonate
hydrocarbonous
hydrocephaloid
hydrocephalous
hydrocolloidal
hydrocortisone
hydrodynamical
hydro-explosion
hydro-extractor
hydrogenolysis
hydrogenolytic
hydrogeologist
hydrographical
hydrologically
hydrolytically
hydromagnetics
hydromechanics
hydronephrosis
hydronephrotic
hydrophilicity
hydrophobicity
hydropneumatic
hydroponically
hydrostatician

hydrotherapist
hydrothermally
hydrotreatment
hydroxonium ion
hydroxyapatite
hydroxybenzoic
hydroxyproline
hyetographical
hygroscopicity
hymnologically
hyperaesthesia
hyperaesthetic
hyperbolically
hyperbolic sine
hypercalcaemia
hypercalcaemic
hyper-Calvinism
hyper-Calvinist
hypercatharsis
hyperchromasia
hyperchromatic
hyperconscious
hypercriticism
hypercriticize
hypereutectoid
hyperexcitable
hyperextension
hypergeometric
hyperglycaemia
hyperglycaemic
hyperinflation
hyperirritable
hyperkeratosis
hyperkeratotic
hypermetabolic
hypernatraemia
hypernatraemic
hyperoxygenate
hyperparasitic
hyperphalangia
hyperpituitary
hypersecretion
hypersensitise
hypersensitive
hypersensitize
hypersexuality
hypersomnolent
hypersonically
hyperspherical
hyperthyroidic
hypertrichosis
hyperuricaemia
hyperuricaemic
hyperventilate
hypidiomorphic
hypnotherapist
hypo-allergenic
hypochondrical
hypochromicity
hypocritically
hypodermically

hypofunctional
hypomixolydian
hypophalangism
hypopharyngeal
hypophosphoric
hypophysectomy
hypostatically
hyposulphurous
hypothetically
hypothyroidism
hypotrachelium
hypsarrhythmia
hypsarrhythmic
hypsilophodont
hypsographical
hysterectomies
hysterectomise
hysterectomize
hysteresis loss
hysteretically
iatrochemistry
iatrogenically
iatromechanics
iatromechanist
iatrophysicist
I beg your pardon
Ibero-Caucasian
Ibicencan hound
iceberg lettuce
ichnographical
ichthyological
ichthyophagian
ichthyophagist
ichthyophagous
ichthyosaurian
icing on the cake
iconographical
I dare undertake
idealistically
identification
identificatory
identity crisis
identity matrix
identity parade
idiosyncrasies
idolatrousness
idols of the cave
if peradventure
I'll be seeing you
ill-conditioned
illegitimately
illegitimation
illegitimatize
illiberalities
illicit process
illimitability
illiterateness
illogicalities
I'll tell you what
illuminatingly
illustrational

illustratively
image converter
image dissector
image processor
imaginableness
Immaculate Lamb
immaculateness
immemorialness
immethodically
immetricalness
immiserization
immobilization
immoderateness
immovable feast
immune globulin
immune response
immunochemical
immunogenetics
immunoglobulin
impact strength
imparisyllabic
imparticipable
impassableness
impassibleness
impassionately
impeccableness
imperative mood
imperativeness
imperatorially
imperfect rhyme
imperial gallon
impermeability
impersonalness
imperturbation
imperviousness
implacableness
implausibility
implementation
imponderabilia
impossibleness
impoverishment
impracticality
impregnability
impressibility
impressionable
impressionably
impressionless
impressiveness
improbableness
improvableness
impulse turbine
inaccentuation
inaccurateness
inacquaintance
inadaptability
inadequateness
inadvisability
inagglutinable
inalienability
inalterability
inamissibility

in a person's arms
in a person's debt
in a person's name
inappositeness
inappreciation
inappreciative
inapprehension
inapprehensive
inapproachable
inarticulately
inarticulation
inartificially
inartistically
in a state of flux
in a thing's stead
inauspiciously
inauthenticity
incandescently
incapacitation
incarnationist
incautiousness
incendiary bomb
incestuousness
incivilization
incline one's ear
incommensurate
incommodiously
incommunicable
incommunicably
incompleteness
incomprehended
incompressible
inconclusively
inconditionate
inconsequently
inconsiderable
inconsiderably
inconsistently
incontrollable
incontrollably
inconveniently
incoordination
incorporeality
incorrectitude
incredibleness
incrementalism
incrementalist
inculpableness
indecipherable
indecisiveness
indecomposable
indecorousness
indefinability
indefiniteness
indeliberately
indeliberation
indemonstrable
indemonstrably
independencies
independentism
indestructible

indestructibly
indeterminable
indeterminably
Indian elephant
Indian plantain
indifferentism
indifferentist
indigenisation
indigenization
indigenousness
indirect object
indirect speech
indiscerptible
indiscoverable
indiscriminate
indisseverable
indisseverably
indissolublist
indistinctness
individualizer
indivisibility
Indo-Abyssinian
indoctrination
indoctrinatory
indomitability
Indo-Portuguese
indubitability
indubitatively
induction motor
industrial park
ineffectuality
ineluctability
inequalitarian
inertial system
inertia selling
inescapability
inessentiality
inevitableness
inexcitability
inexhaustively
inexorableness
inexplicitness
inexpressively
inextinguished
infallibleness
infant mistress
infectiousness
infelicitously
inflammability
inflammatorily
inflation-proof
inflectionally
inflectionless
infralapsarian
inframaxillary
infrangibility
infrasonically
infrastructure
infructescence
ingenerability
ingenerateness

ingloriousness
in good set terms
ingratiatingly
inhabitability
inhabitiveness
inharmoniously
inheritability
inheritance tax
inhumanitarian
inimitableness
iniquitousness
inirritability
initialization
inland ice sheet
in large measure
in loco parentis
in multiplicate
in my conception
innominate bone
innominate vein
innovativeness
Inns of Chancery
innumerability
in one fell swoop
in one's extremes
in one's mind's eye
in one's own right
inordinateness
inorganisation
inorganization
in peril of doing
in possession of
in preference to
inquisitorship
in receivership
insanitariness
insatiableness
inscrutability
inseparability
in sextuplicate
in shirtsleeves
insider dealing
insider trading
inside straight
insightfulness
insignificance
insignificancy
inspirationist
instalment plan
institutionary
instructorship
instrumentally
in succession to
insufficiently
insulating tape
insuperability
insuppressible
insurance agent
insurance stamp
insurmountable
insurmountably

insurrectional
intake manifold
intangibleness
integrationist
intellectively
intellectually
intelligential
intelligentsia
intempestively
intensionalist
intensionality
intentionalism
intentionalist
intentionality
interactionism
interactionist
interanimation
interarticular
interavailable
intercapillary
intercessional
intercessorial
intercommonage
intercommunion
intercommunity
interconnector
intercorrelate
interdefinable
interdependent
interdialectal
interdiffusion
interdigitally
inter-electrode
interestedness
interferential
interferometer
interferometry
interfertility
interfibrillar
interglandular
intergradation
interinfluence
interior design
interior-sprung
interjectional
interlineation
interlocutress
intermaxillary
intermediaries
intermediately
intermediation
intermigration
intermittently
intermittingly
intermolecular
internal energy
internal market
internal object
internal stress
Internationale
internment camp

interpalpebral
interpellation
interpenetrate
interplanetary
interpretation
interpretative
interpretively
interpunctuate
interpupillary
interruptingly
intersectional
intersegmental
intersexuality
interspersedly
interstitialcy
interstitially
intertrochlear
intertwinement
intertwiningly
intervalometer
interval signal
interventional
intervertebral
in the aggregate
in the ascendant
in the event that
in the family way
in the meanwhile
in the old school
in the process of
in the public eye
in the reckoning
in the short term
in this instance
intolerability
intonationally
into the bargain
into the discard
intoxicatingly
intra-abdominal
intracardially
intracisternal
intracranially
intractability
intracutaneous
intrafallopian
intramedullary
intramercurial
intramolecular
intransferable
intransigeance
intransigently
intransitively
intransitivity
intransitivize
intransparency
intrapulmonary
intrinsicality
introductorily
intromolecular
introspectable

introspectible
introsuscepted
intuitionalism
intuitionalist
intuitionistic
intussuscepted
intussusceptum
invaluableness
invariableness
Inverness cloak
inversion layer
investment bond
inveterateness
invigoratingly
invincibleness
inviolableness
invisible green
invitation card
iodimetrically
iodometrically
ionosphericist
ipsissima verba
Irish hurricane
Irish promotion
Irish wolfhound
Iron Chancellor
ironing blanket
ironstone china
irrecognisable
irrecognizable
irrecognizably
irrecollection
irreconcilable
irreconcilably
irreducibility
irreflectively
irrefutability
irregularities
irrelativeness
irrememberable
irremovability
irreparability
irreplevisable
irreproachable
irreproachably
irreproducible
irresoluteness
irrespectively
irresponsively
irrestrainable
irrestrainably
irrevocability
irrotationally
ischiatic notch
isentropically
Islamicization
island-mountain
island platform
island universe
isoagglutinate
isocalorically

isokinetically
isomorphically
isotopic number
Italian cypress
Italianization
Italian opening
it is my pleasure
jackass frigate
jackass penguin
Jack-by-the-hedge
Jack-in-the-green
Jack-in-the-hedge
Jack of the clock
Jacob's membrane
japaleño pepper
Japanese beetle
Japanese cherry
Japanese flower
Japanese garden
Japanese laurel
Japanese medlar
Japanese monkey
Japanese oyster
Japanese privet
Japanese quince
Japanese screen
Japanese vellum
jaune brilliant
jejuno-duodenal
jerboa kangaroo
Jerusalem cross
Jerusalem thorn
jeté en tournant
jeweller's putty
jeweller's rouge
jingling Johnny
jobbing builder
jobs for the boys
Johannisberger
John Barleycorn
joint adventure
joint committee
joint-stock bank
joker in the pack
joukery-pawkery
journal-bearing
judgematically
Judges' lodgings
Judicature Acts
judicial combat
judicial factor
judicial murder
judicial review
Julian calendar
junk playground
jurisdictional
Justice General
justiciability
justiciaryship
justifiability
juxta-articular

kaleyard school
kangaroo-beetle
Kaposi's sarcoma
karaoke machine
karstification
karyologically
karyotypically
Katyusha rocket
Kavirondo crane
keep a calm sough
keep a place warm
keep early hours
keep in suspense
keep one's chin up
keep one's figure
keep one's hair on
keep one's hand in
keep one's temper
keep one's wool on
keep on trucking
keep steeks with
keep to the house
Kepler's problem
keratinisation
keratinization
keratinophilic
kernel sentence
kerygmatically
keyhole surgery
keynote address
keystone effect
kick in the pants
Kierkegaardian
Kilkenny marble
killer instinct
Kimmeridge clay
Kimmeridge coal
kindergartener
kinetheodolite
kinetic heating
king and country
kingfisher blue
King James Bible
King's messenger
King's Messenger
Kiplingesquely
Kipp's apparatus
Kirk of Scotland
kirschenwasser
Kirschner value
kiss impression
kissing gourami
kit-cat portrait
kitchen cabinet
kitchen evening
kitchen-parlour
kite-photograph
kleptoparasite
knight bachelor
knight banneret
knight-errantry

knitting needle
knitting sheath
knock hell out of
knock into shape
knock on the head
know better than
knowledge-based
know-nothingism
know one's onions
know to one's cost
knuckle-walking
Koch postulates
Kohlrausch's law
kraak porselein
Kremlinologist
Ku Klux Klansman
Kupferschiefer
kyphoscoliosis
kyphoscoliotic
labour exchange
Labour Exchange
labour movement
laboursomeness
labyrinthiform
labyrinthodont
lachrymatories
ladies' carriage
Lady Chatterley
lady of pleasure
lady of the house
lady of the manor
lady of the night
lady's companion
lake settlement
lamellirostral
lamentableness
laminarization
lamprophyllite
Lancaster cloth
land-connection
landed interest
land on one's feet
lantern-flflies
lapidification
Lapland bunting
large intestine
large-mouth bass
larger than life
large-stomached
laryngofissure
laryngological
laryngopharynx
laryngoscopist
lasciviousness
last sacraments
Latakia tobacco
latent learning
lateralization
lateral moraine
lateritization
lath and plaster

latitudinarian
Latter-day Saint
Latter Prophets
lattice network
laughing matter
laughing-muscle
laughing thrush
Laura Ashleyish
laurel magnolia
lavatory humour
lavender cotton
law-abidingness
law of parsimony
law of the jungle
Lawson's cypress
lay at the door of
lay it on a person
lay it on the line
lay one's hands on
lay one's leg over
lead apes in hell
leading article
leading counsel
lead tetraethyl
lead to the altar
leaf-cutting ant
league football
lean-to building
learned journal
leather-hunting
leathery-turtle
leave no effects
leave of absence
leave well alone
lechatelierite
lecithotrophic
lecture circuit
lecture-recital
lecture theatre
left-handedness
left high and dry
legalistically
legerdemainist
leghaemoglobin
Legion of Honour
legislatorship
legitimateness
legitimization
leiomyosarcoma
leisure complex
lending library
leopard society
lepidotrichium
lepospondylous
leptocephalous
Lesser Antilles
lesser doxology
Lesser Doxology
Lesser Entrance
let a person know
let or hindrance

let out the links
letter by letter
lettering piece
letter of advice
letter of credit
letter of intent
letter of marque
letter of slains
letters missive
let the side down
let things slide
lettre de cachet
Levant wormseed
levelling-screw
levelling staff
lexicalization
lexical meaning
lex loci delicti
Leyland cypress
liaison officer
liberalization
Liberal Judaism
libertarianism
liberty cabbage
libidinousness
library binding
library edition
library science
licentiateship
licentiousness
lichenological
lick one's wounds
lie in one's teeth
lieutenantship
life expectancy
life membership
lift up one's eyes
lift up one's head
light-demanding
lighter-than-air
light flyweight
light-heartedly
lighting bridge
lighting-up time
light knotgrass
lightning chess
lightning-proof
lightning-stone
light pollution
lignocellulose
lignosulphonic
like it or lump it
like-mindedness
lilliputianize
limb of the Devil
limited company
limited edition
limited partner
limnologically
linear equation
line of business

line one's pocket
line-sequential
linguistically
lipogrammatist
liquidity ratio
liquid paraffin
liquid rheostat
liquorice-stick
liquorice vetch
listen to reason
list processing
literalization
literary agency
literary critic
literary editor
lithochromatic
lithographical
lithologically
little boys' room
little by little
Little Entrance
little-girl-lost
little green man
little magazine
little neck clam
Little's disease
little stranger
liturgiologist
live and let live
live by one's wits
live off the land
live on one's hump
liver of sulphur
livery cupboard
livery of seisin
living skeleton
living standard
Lloyd's Register
loan-collection
Lobel's catchfly
lobotomization
lobster Newburg
local authority
localizability
locomotiveness
locus classicus
locus of control
loft conversion
logical atomism
logical grammar
logical paradox
logical product
logical subject
Lombardy poplar
long-headedness
long in the tooth
longitudinally
Long Parliament
longs and shorts
longshore drift
long short story

long sufferance
long sweetening
long-tailed duck
long-tailed pair
long-tailed skua
long-windedness
look for trouble
looking-forward
look kindly upon
look to one's hits
loose-endedness
loquaciousness
Lord Chancellor
Lord God of hosts
Lord Lieutenant
Lord Mayor's Show
lord of regality
Lord of the Flies
lord of the manor
lord proprietor
lords and ladies
Lords of Session
Lords spiritual
Lord Woolton pie
Lorentz triplet
lose interest in
lose one's bottle
lose one's market
lose one's temper
lose one's tongue
lost generation
love in a cottage
love-in-idleness
loveworthiness
lovey-doveyness
loving kindness
lower criticism
lower intestine
lower one's guard
loxodromic line
Ludolph's number
lugubriousness
lumbar puncture
lumps of delight
Luxembourgeois
lycopodiaceous
lymphangiogram
lyophilization
lysogenization
macadamization
macaroni cheese
machinofacture
mackerel breeze
mackerel clouds
macrocephalous
macro-economics
macroeconomics
macro-economist
macro-evolution
macroevolution
macromolecular

macrosociology
macrostructure
madrigalianism
Maeterlinckian
magazine rights
magical realism
magical realist
magic-lanterned
magistrateship
magnesium flare
magnesium light
magnetic bottle
magnetic bubble
magnetic memory
magnetic mirror
magnetic moment
magnetic needle
magnetic stripe
magnetocaloric
magnetographic
magneto-optical
magnetospheric
magnetostatics
magniloquently
maidenhair fern
maidenhair tree
maiden plum tree
mails and duties
main-topgallant
maître de ballet
majesticalness
Majorana effect
major-generalcy
make a bonfire of
make a commotion
make a dead set at
make a fight of it
make a good job of
make allowances
make a mystery of
make a night of it
make a pig's ear of
make a poor mouth
make a present of
make a statement
make one's choice
make one's rounds
make relation to
make rings round
make so bold as to
make sweet music
make the round of
make the running
make the worst of
make up one's mind
Malabar spinach
malachite-green
malacostracous
malapportioned
malappropriate
malarrangement

Malayanization
Malay peninsula
malcontentedly
maldevelopment
maldistributed
male chauvinism
male chauvinist
male prostitute
malice prepense
malintegration
malmsey madeira
malnourishment
malobservation
malodorousness
malperformance
Malpighian body
malt-distillery
Maltese terrier
mamenchisaurus
mammillary body
mammilliferous
manageableness
managed economy
mandarin collar
mandarin jacket
mandarin orange
mandarin sleeve
mandelonitrile
manganese oxide
manganese steel
mangrove cuckoo
mangrove oyster
manifold writer
Manila tamarind
man in the street
manipulability
manipulatively
mannerlessness
man of the moment
man of the people
manometrically
man on the street
man's best friend
manslaughterer
manual alphabet
manual exercise
manufacturable
manuscriptural
Manx shearwater
marching orders
margaritaceous
margin of safety
marigold window
marine barracks
mariner portage
marketableness
market gardener
market research
marriage broker
marriage bureau
marriage market

marrow-stem kale
marry into money
marsh blackbird
marsh pennywort
marsupial mouse
martingale-stay
martyrological
marvellousness
masculine rhyme
Mason–Dixon Line
Mason–Dixon line
massage parlour
masseter muscle
mass production
Master in Lunacy
masterlessness
mastigophorous
mastoid process
material object
maternity dress
mathematically
matriarchalism
matrilineality
matrix sentence
matron of honour
matter of course
matter-of-factly
matter of record
Maunder minimum
Maundy Thursday
mauvaise langue
Maxwell's duiker
may it please you
McBurney's point
meadow cat's-tail
meadow mushroom
meal-worm beetle
mealy-mouthedly
meaningfulness
measurableness
mechanicalness
mechanical pulp
mechanical twin
mechanical zero
mechanocaloric
mechanomorphic
mechanotherapy
meddlesomeness
medicalization
medical officer
medicamentally
medicinal leech
medicine murder
meditativeness
medullary plate
megakaryoblast
megakaryocytic
megalocephalic
megalomaniacal
megascopically
megasporangium

megasporophyll
megastructural
Meissner effect
Melanchthonian
melanophlogite
melanovanadite
melt in the mouth
membra disjecta
membrane filter
membrification
mendaciousness
Mendelssohnian
mend one's fences
Men's Liberation
menstrual cycle
mensurableness
mental handicap
mento-Meckelian
Mephistopheles
mercantilistic
mercaptopurine
merchandisable
merchant banker
merchant marine
merchant prince
merchant seaman
merchant-tailor
mercury gilding
meretriciously
meridian circle
meroplanktonic
merosystematic
merry Christmas
mesaticephalic
Mesdemoiselles
mesoplanktonic
messenger cable
metabiological
metachromatism
metalinguistic
metallic thread
metallogenesis
metallogenetic
metallographer
metallographic
metallo-organic
metalloprotein
metamorphopsia
metamorphosize
metanephridial
metanephridium
metaphase plate
metaphorically
metaphosphoric
metaphysically
metapolitician
metapsychology
metascientific
metempirically
metempsychosic
metempsychosis

metensomatosis
meteoritically
meteorological
meteoroscopist
methaemoglobin
methanogenesis
methodicalness
methodological
meticulousness
metoclopramide
metoposcopical
metronomically
metropolitical
Mexicanization
Mexican Spanish
Mexican thistle
Michaelmas term
Michaelmas tide
microaerophile
microanatomist
microbarograph
microbiologist
microcephalism
microcephalous
microchemistry
microcircuitry
microcomputing
microcontinent
micro-economics
microeconomics
micro-economist
micro-electrode
micro-evolution
microevolution
microfibrillar
microinjection
micro-machining
micrometeorite
micrometeoroid
microminiature
microperthitic
microphthalmia
microphthalmic
microphthalmos
microprocessor
microprojector
micropulsation
microradiogram
microsporidian
microsporocyte
microstructure
microtechnique
microtrabecula
Middle American
middle-classdom
middle distance
Middle-European
middle-statured
midshipmanship
militarization
military orchid

military police
military school
military tenure
milking machine
milking-parlour
Milk of Magnesia
milkweed beetle
millenarianism
milling machine
millionairedom
millivoltmeter
Milroy's disease
mince the matter
mind-bogglingly
mind over matter
mineralization
mineralography
miniature score
minifloppy disk
mini-roundabout
ministerialism
ministerialist
minority report
miogeosyncline
miraculousness
mirror symmetry
misadventurous
misanthropical
misappellation
misapplication
misappropriate
misarrangement
misattribution
miscalculation
mischief-making
miscommunicate
miscomputation
misconjunction
misconsecrated
miscontentment
misdeclaration
misdescription
misdescriptive
misimprovement
misinformation
misinformative
misinstruction
misinterpreter
misleadingness
mismeasurement
misorientation
misperformance
mispunctuation
misremembrance
misrepresenter
misresemblance
missed abortion
missed approach
missionaryship
mission control
missive of lease

mistake one's man
mist propagator
mistranslation
Mittel-European
mixed technique
mobilizational
moccasin flower
mock auctioneer
mock turtle soup
modifiableness
modificability
modificational
modularization
modus decimandi
molecular layer
molecular sieve
molybdenum blue
momentaneously
moment-to-moment
money-mongering
money of account
money scrivener
mongrelization
monkey business
monkey on a stick
monobrominated
monocarpellary
monochromatise
monochromatism
monochromatist
monochromatize
monofunctional
monogamousness
monoglacialism
monoglacialist
monolingualism
monolithically
monomaniacally
mononucleotide
monophasically
monophonematic
monophonically
monophthongize
monopolization
monopropellant
monorail camera
monosaccharide
monosaccharose
monothetically
monotonousness
monotriglyphic
Monroe doctrine
Montagu's blenny
month of Sundays
Monumental City
moral certainty
moral cowardice
moralistically
morally certain
moral turpitude
morceau de salon

more power to you
more than enough
Moreton Bay pine
morganatically
morocco leather
morphinomaniac
morphometrical
morphophonemic
morphotectonic
mossy saxifrage
Most Honourable
mother-grabbing
mother language
motherlessness
mother of months
mothers' meeting
Mother Superior
mother tincture
motionlessness
motion sickness
motivationally
motivelessness
motor-ambulance
motor generator
motte-and-bailey
moulded breadth
mountain azalea
mountain beaver
mountaineering
mountain laurel
mountain linnet
mountain oyster
mountain parrot
mountain plover
mountain rescue
mountain sorrel
mountain system
mountain thrush
mount the ladder
mourning-brooch
mover and shaker
moving pavement
moving sidewalk
mucilaginously
mucomembranous
mucoperiosteum
mucous membrane
mucoviscidosis
muddleheadedly
Muhammadan blue
mulberry colour
Müllerian mimic
multarticulate
multi-articular
multidialectal
multi-electrode
multifactorial
multifariously
multifoetation
multilamellate
multilaterally

multilingually
multiple-access
multiple allele
multiple-aspect
multiple-choice
multiplication
multiplicative
multiplicities
multipotential
multiprocessor
multiracialism
multiracialist
multistability
multi-threading
multivallation
multiversities
municipal baths
municipalities
munificentness
munitions of war
muscatel raisin
musculofascial
museographical
mushroom anchor
mushroom colour
mushroom growth
musical glasses
musicalization
musico-dramatic
musk stork's-bill
mustard plaster
mutarotational
mutation theory
muzzle velocity
myelencephalic
myelencephalon
myeloblastosis
myelomonocytic
mylonitization
myohaemoglobin
myricyl alcohol
myrmecochorous
myrmecological
myrmecophagous
myrmecophilous
my service to you
mystagogically
mysteriousness
mystery of State
mythographical
mythologically
naked as a needle
name one's poison
nankeen kestrel
nanotechnology
Nansen passport
naphthaquinone
naphthenic acid
naphthoquinone
Napoleonically
Napoleonic Wars

narcoterrorism
narcoterrorist
narratological
narrow-mindedly
nasopharyngeal
national anthem
National Health
national income
national school
Native American
native tamarind
natural history
naturalization
natural liberty
natural numbers
natural pravity
natural science
natural spirits
natural tangent
natural trumpet
natural uranium
natural virtues
natural wastage
nature printing
naturistically
naval architect
navigation coal
Navy Department
Neanderthaloid
near-hysterical
near the knuckle
neat-handedness
Nebuchadnezzar
necessarianism
necessary house
necessary woman
necklace poplar
neck of the woods
necrologically
nectareousness
needle-threader
negative equity
negative growth
negative virtue
neglectfulness
negligibleness
negro-head beech
Negro spiritual
nematodiriasis
Nemean festival
neoclassically
neo-colonialism
neocolonialism
neo-colonialist
neocolonialist
nephritic stone
nephroblastoma
nephrotoxicity
nervous tension
nesslerization
nether garments

network theorem
neurapophyseal
neuroanatomist
neurobiologist
neurobiotactic
neuroendocrine
neurofibrillar
neurogenically
neuroglandular
neurologically
neuropathology
neuroretinitis
neuroscientist
neurosecretion
neurosecretory
neurotendinous
neutral-density
neutralization
neutron capture
neutron therapy
never-failingly
never-never land
Never Never Land
Newcastle Brown
Newcastle glass
newfangledness
Newfoundlander
new lease of life
new mathematics
new off the irons
news conference
newspaperishly
newspaperwoman
newsworthiness
New York dressed
New Zealand flax
nickel carbonyl
nicotinization
Nietzscheanism
nigger minstrel
night-blindness
night-flowering
night-wandering
nil desperandum
Nilotic monitor
nimble-fingered
nincompoopiana
nine days' wonder
nine men's morris
nineteenth hole
Nissl substance
nitrobacterium
nitrocellulose
nitrofurantoin
nitrogen-fixing
nitroglycerine
noctambulation
noise pollution
noisy scrub-bird
no leg to stand on
nomenclatorial

nomenclaturist
nominal account
nominal essence
nominalization
non-associative
non-barbiturate
non-belligerent
non-committally
non-communicant
non-compearance
non-competitive
nonconformance
non-conjunction
non-consequence
non-consumption
non-contentious
non-cooperation
non-destructive
non-dimensional
non-directional
non-disjunction
non-distinctive
non-electrified
non-exportation
non-importation
non-intelligent
non-intercourse
non-judgemental
non-ministerial
non-operational
non-participant
non-penetrative
non-performance
non-proficiency
non-proprietary
non-radioactive
non-rationality
non-referential
non-residential
non-restrictive
nonsensicality
non-significant
non-subscribing
non-substantial
norepinephrine
norethisterone
Norfolk spaniel
Norfolk terrier
Norman Conquest
Normandy butter
Normandy vellum
normoglycaemia
normoglycaemic
north-easterner
north-eastwards
northern lights
Northern Paiute
Northern States
north-north-east
north-north-west
north-westerner

north-westwards
Norwegian steam
Norwich terrier
nose suspension
not a blind bit of
not a dog's chance
not a hope in hell
not a pennyworth
notaries public
not ashamed to do
not bat an eyelid
not by a long shot
not care a bugger
not care a fig for
notch-sensitive
notch-toughness
note of addition
noteworthiness
not for the world
not get anywhere
not have a prayer
no thoroughfare
not if you paid me
not know from Eve
not move a muscle
not once or twice
not on your nelly
not the full quid
Nottingham lace
Nottingham reel
nouveaux riches
novel disseisin
novelistically
nuchal ligament
nuclear battery
nuclear fission
nuclearization
nuclear physics
nuclear-powered
nuclear reactor
nuclear warfare
nudibranchiate
nuisance ground
null hypothesis
null instrument
number-cruncher
numismatically
nundinal letter
Nuremberg rally
nursing officer
nutmeg-coloured
nutritionalist
nutritiousness
nymphomaniacal
Nyquist diagram
nystagmography
oak of Jerusalem
obdiplostemony
obedience class
obedience-train
obedience trial

Oberstleutnant
objective point
object language
objectlessness
oblate spheroid
obligativeness
obligatoriness
oblique oration
obliteratingly
obreptitiously
obsequiousness
observation car
obsessionalism
obsidional coin
obstacle course
obstreperously
obstructionary
obstructionism
obstructionist
occulting light
occupationally
occupation army
occupationless
occupation road
occurrence book
oceanic feeling
octocentennial
ocular spectrum
odd-come-shortly
odour-blindness
Oedipus complex
oenanthic ether
oesophagectomy
oesophagoscope
oesophagostomy
oestrogenicity
offer one's arm to
off-off-Broadway
off one's trolley
offset purchase
offshore island
off-the-shoulder
of public resort
of the essence of
of the first head
of the old school
oil on the flames
old-fashionedly
old-maidishness
old-man kangaroo
old man of the sea
old man saltbush
old woman's tooth
olfactory nerve
oligarchically
oligopsonistic
olivary nucleus
omnibus edition
omnicompetence
omnipercipient
omnium gatherum

omnivorousness
omphaloskepsis
on a full stomach
on a person's tail
onchocerciasis
one-armed bandit
one-dimensional
one-directional
one-downmanship
one had better do
oneirocritical
one of these days
one of the truest
one of the wisest
one of those days
one out of the box
one's better half
one's better self
one's blood boils
one's collocutor
one's finest hour
one's former self
one's number is up
one's Sunday best
one's teeth water
one with another
onomasiologist
onomatological
on one's beam-ends
on one's doorstep
on one's hind legs
on one's last legs
on one's occasion
on one's own terms
on the defensive
on the downgrade
on the down grade
on the high ropes
on the other hand
on the other part
on the pretext of
on the right foot
on the scrap heap
on the sidelines
on the subject of
on the telephone
on the wrong foot
oophorectomies
oophorectomize
Oort comet cloud
open-handedness
open-mindedness
open one's budget
open one's mind to
open subroutine
open university
Open University
open window unit
operating table
operationalise
operationalism

operationalist
operationality
operationalize
operations room
ophthalmic acid
ophthalmologic
ophthalmometer
ophthalmometry
ophthalmoscope
ophthalmoscopy
opiniativeness
opinionatively
opisthocoelian
opisthocoelous
opisthographic
opponent muscle
opposite number
opposite prompt
oppositionless
oppositiveness
oppressiveness
optical density
optical printer
optical scanner
optimalization
optimistically
optoelectronic
optometrically
orange-coloured
orange-strainer
orbitosphenoid
orchidectomize
Order in Council
orderly corpora
orderly officer
Order of the Bath
ordinal numeral
ordinary of arms
ordinary seaman
Ordnance Survey
organification
organismically
organizability
organizational
organized games
organometallic
organ-pipe coral
oriental carpet
oriental medlar
oriental stitch
ornithological
ornithomorphic
ornithophilist
ornithophilous
ornithosaurian
orogenetically
orographically
orohydrography
Orphean warbler
orthocephalous
orthochromatic

orthodiagraphy
Orthodox Church
orthoepistical
orthographical
orthomolecular
orthonormality
orthonormalize
orthophosphate
orthorrhaphous
orthoselection
orthotopically
ortolan bunting
oscillographic
osmometrically
osmoregulation
osmoregulatory
ostentatiously
osteoarthritic
osteoarthritis
osteoarthrosis
osteoarthrotic
osteochondroma
osteologically
osteosclerosis
ostreocultural
ostrich-feather
Otaheite orange
other fish to fry
otolaryngology
Ottomanization
outcountenance
out for the count
outlandishness
out of a clear sky
out of character
out of condition
out of one's depth
out of one's gourd
out of one's shell
out of one's sight
out of one's skull
out-of-roundness
out of the common
out of the window
out of this world
outperformance
outrageousness
outside forward
outward-bounder
outwash deposit
over-abundantly
overabundantly
overarticulate
overbitterness
overburdensome
overcapitalise
overcapitalize
overcautiously
overcommitment
overcommitting
overcompensate

overconfidence
overcorrection
overdispersion
overemployment
overenthusiasm
overestimation
overexcitement
overfamiliarly
overfavourable
overfulfilment
overgeneralise
overgeneralize
overgenerously
overgovernment
over-indulgence
overindulgence
overmodulation
over my dead body
over-optimistic
overoptimistic
over-particular
overparticular
overpersuasion
overpopulation
overpoweringly
overprivileged
overproduction
overprotection
overprotective
over-refinement
overrefinement
overrun oneself
oversaturation
overscrupulous
oversimplified
oversimplifier
oversimplifies
oversolicitous
oversolicitude
overspecialise
overspecialize
overstrictness
over the counter
overthoughtful
overwhelmingly
owe it to oneself
owlet-frogmouth
owl-faced monkey
oxalosuccinate
Oxford Movement
Oxford shirting
Oxford trousers
oxidation state
oxidizing agent
oxidoreductase
oxidoreduction
oxidoreductive
oxidulated iron
oxyhaemoglobin
oxymoronically
oyster mushroom

oyster toadfish
oyster-veneered
pachydermatous
Pacific halibut
Pacific pompano
pacifistically
package holiday
packet-switched
packing density
packing station
paddock-grazing
paedomorphosis
paint by numbers
painted bunting
painter's mussel
pair of bagpipes
pair of breeches
pair of knickers
pair of scissors
pair of trousers
pair production
palaeanthropic
palaeobiologic
palaeobotanist
palaeochemical
palaeoclimatic
palaeocortical
palaeoecologic
palaeogeologic
palaeographist
palaeolatitude
palaeomagnetic
palaeontologic
palaeopedology
palaeosalinity
Palaeo-Siberian
palaeostriatal
palaeostriatum
palaeotectonic
palaeothalamus
palaeotropical
palatalization
palato-alveolar
palato-quadrate
paleoanthropic
palmatipartite
palmetto thatch
pan-Americanism
pancake landing
Pancake Tuesday
panchronically
pancreatectomy
pan-diatonicism
panel technique
pan-Europeanism
panidiomorphic
pantisocratist
pantographical
pantomimically
pantomographic
pantopragmatic

pantoyltaurine
pan-Turanianism
papilionaceous
papillomatosis
papulo-erythema
papulo-pustular
papulo-squamous
parabiotically
Paracelsianism
parachute flare
paraconformity
paradiplomatic
paradisaically
paradisiacally
paradoxicality
parafollicular
paraganglionic
paragonimiasis
paragrammatism
parajournalism
parajournalist
paraleipomenon
paralinguistic
paraliturgical
parallel cousin
parallelepiped
parallel market
parallel-medium
parallelopiped
parallel rulers
parametrically
paramilitaries
paramount chief
parapatrically
paraphrastical
parapsychology
pararosaniline
parascientific
parasitization
parasitologist
paratactically
parcel delivery
parchment paper
pardonableness
parenchymatous
Parent's Charter
parents' meeting
pareschatology
pare to the quick
parietal pleura
parish magazine
parish register
Parisian matins
Parisian stitch
parity checking
parity of esteem
parliament-cake
parliament heel
parlour-boarder
Parmesan cheese
parodistically

paroemiography
paroemiologist
parole of honour
parsimoniously
pars intermedia
parthenocarpic
parthenogenone
partial counsel
partial denture
partial eclipse
partial product
partial valency
partial verdict
particularness
particular rule
partridge-berry
party political
passage-migrant
pass as sterling
pass in one's ally
passionateness
passive smoking
pasteurellosis
pasteurization
Pasteur pipette
pastille-burner
pastoral letter
past participle
past redemption
Patagonian cavy
Patau's syndrome
pâté de campagne
pâté de foie gras
patellofemoral
patent medicine
Paterson's curse
path difference
pathogenically
pathologically
patresfamilias
patriarchalism
patrilineality
patrimonialism
patriotic front
patronymically
patte de velours
pattern bombing
pattern darning
patternization
pattern-welding
pauciarthritis
pauciarticular
paucibacillary
pavement artist
pavor nocturnus
pay a compliment
pay for one's scot
pay reverence to
peacockishness
peak experience
pearly nautilus

peasant economy
pectinesterase
pectoral girdle
pectoral muscle
peculiar people
pedunculate oak
peeping Tommery
peer of the realm
Peltier cooling
penal servitude
penalty killing
pencil-and-paper
pendulum-spring
Penelope canvas
penetration aid
penicillin unit
penitentiaries
penny for the guy
penny-in-the-slot
Penrose diagram
Penrose process
pensionability
pentamethylene
pentatonically
Pentecostalism
Pentecostalist
pentobarbitone
People's Charter
people's theatre
peppercorn hair
peppercorn rent
peppercorn tree
peppermint-drop
peppermint lump
peppermint-tree
peptide linkage
percentage-wise
perceptibility
perceptiveness
perceptuo-motor
perchloric acid
percontatorial
percussion lock
percussiveness
percutaneously
perdurableness
Père David's deer
peremptoriness
perfect binding
perfect cadence
perfectibilian
perfectibilism
perfectibilist
perfectibility
perfectionment
perfectivation
perfectiveness
perfidiousness
perforated tape
performability
performance art

performance car
performatively
performatories
performing arts
perfunctionary
pericardectomy
pericardiotomy
pericementitis
perichondritis
periglaciation
perimenopausal
perimeter track
perimetrically
perinatologist
periodic system
periodontology
peripateticism
peripherically
periphrastical
periscope depth
periscopically
periscopic lens
perishableness
peristrephical
peritectically
peritelevision
peritoneoscopy
peritrichously
perlocutionary
permanent press
permanent tooth
permanent white
permissibility
permissiveness
perniciousness
pernicketiness
peroxosulphate
perpetual check
Persianization
Persian morocco
personableness
personal action
personal column
personal estate
personal injury
personal stereo
personificator
person of colour
personological
person-to-person
perspirability
persuadability
persuasibility
persuasiveness
Perthes disease
pertinaciously
perturbational
perturbatively
pervicaciously
pestilentially
Peter Pan collar

Peter principle
Peter Principle
petit battement
petit bourgeois
petite noblesse
petrochemistry
petrographical
petrol-electric
petroleum ether
petroleum jelly
petrologically
petrophysicist
petrosiliceous
petrotectonics
petty apartheid
petty bourgeois
petty constable
petty serjeanty
phagocytically
phagocytizable
phagolysosomal
phallocentrism
phantasmagoria
phantasmagoric
phantom circuit
pharmaceutical
pharmacologist
pharmacopoeial
pharmacopoeian
pharmacopolist
pharyngealized
pharyngotomies
phase converter
pheasant coucal
phenanthridine
phenanthroline
phenethicillin
phenobarbitone
phenosafranine
phenotypically
phenylbutazone
phenylene brown
phenylpyruvate
phenylthiourea
philanthropine
philanthropise
philanthropism
philanthropist
philanthropize
philanthropoid
philatelically
philologically
philosophaster
philosopheress
philosophistic
phlegmatically
phlegmaticness
phloroglucinol
phonematically
phonologically
phonoreception

phoronomically
phosphate glass
phosphodiester
phosphonitrile
phosphoprotein
phosphor bronze
phosphorescent
phosphoric acid
phosphorolysis
phosphorolytic
phosphoroscope
photoabsorbing
photoautotroph
photobiologist
photobleaching
photoblepharon
photocatalysis
photocatalytic
photochemistry
photocoagulate
photoconductor
photodecompose
photodetection
photoduplicate
photo-engraving
photoenzymatic
photofacsimile
photogenically
photogeologist
photogrammetry
photographable
photoinducible
photoinduction
photoinductive
photoinitiated
photoisomerism
photoisomerize
photolytically
photometrician
photonymograph
photo-oxidation
photo-oxidative
photoperiodism
photophthalmia
photophthalmic
photo-potential
photoradiogram
photorealistic
photoreception
photoreceptive
photoreduction
photoregulator
photo-reportage
photoreproduce
photoresistive
photosensitise
photosensitive
photosensitize
photostability
photostimulate
photosynthesis

photosynthetic
phototelegraph
phragmoplastic
phraseographic
phraseological
Phrygian bonnet
phthalocyanine
phthisiologist
phthisiophobia
phyllosilicate
phylogenetical
phylogenically
physical object
physical optics
physico-chemist
physiochemical
physiognomical
phytochemistry
phytogeography
phytopathology
phytosociology
piano accordion
piano reduction
piccaninny dawn
pick one's feet up
picoplanktonic
picture element
picture gallery
picture library
picture monitor
picturesquerie
picture theatre
picture-writing
piece of crumpet
pied flycatcher
pied kingfisher
pied woodpecker
pierced earring
piercement dome
piezomagnetism
piezoresistive
pigeon-breasted
pigeon-fancying
piggyback plant
pig in the middle
pile on the agony
Pilgrim Fathers
pilgrim's bottle
pillar and stall
pilot parachute
pincer movement
pinealectomize
pineapple fibre
pine carpet moth
pine lappet moth
pinkster flower
Pinkster flower
pinnated grouse
pinnatipartite
pin one's faith on
pin one's hopes on

pins and needles
pioneer species
piscicapturist
pisciculturist
piss and vinegar
pistachio green
pistilliferous
pistol-whipping
pit bull terrier
pitching moment
pituitary gland
placentiferous
placentography
placentologist
place of vantage
place of worship
plagiarization
plagiocephalic
plaguesomeness
plain chocolate
plain Dunstable
plain-heartedly
plains viscacha
plains-wanderer
Planck constant
Planck equation
plane-polarized
planetocentric
planetological
planet-stricken
planing-machine
planktological
plankton feeder
planktotrophic
planned economy
plan of campaign
plantation song
plant geography
plant pathology
plasmacellular
plasma dynamics
plasma membrane
plasmapheresis
plasmaphoresis
plasmodesmatal
plaster casting
plaster of Paris
plastic crystal
plasticization
plastic surgeon
plastic surgery
plate tectonics
platform rocker
platform sandal
platform tennis
platform ticket
platinocyanide
platino-iridium
platinum blonde
platinum metals
platinum sponge

platitudinizer
play a good stick
play a shell game
playback singer
play favourites
play for a sucker
play gooseberry
play it straight
playleadership
play the dickens
play the giddy ox
plea bargaining
plead not guilty
pleased as Punch
pleasurability
pleasure-ground
pleasuremonger
pleasure-seeker
plebiscitarian
plenary session
plenipotential
pleochroic halo
pleonastically
plesiomorphous
plethysmograph
pleurapophysis
pleurobranchia
plexiform layer
plough grinding
ploughing-match
plough the sands
pluck up courage
plug-compatible
plumber's friend
plumbosolvency
plum-in-the-mouth
plumose anemone
plunge grinding
plunge neckline
plural marriage
pluripotential
plurisegmental
plurisignative
plush-velveteen
plutocratizing
pluto-democracy
pluviculturist
pluviometrical
pneumatic drill
pneumatic-tyred
pneumatisation
pneumatization
pneumatologist
pneumatothorax
pneumoconiosis
pneumoconiotic
poacher's pocket
pocketableness
pocket expenses
pococuranteism
poet's narcissus

poikilitically
poikiloblastic
poikilocytosis
poikilothermal
poikilothermia
poikilothermic
point a finger at
point discharge
pointed blanket
point of station
point-policeman
point rationing
point-to-pointer
Poiseuille flow
Poiseuille's law
poison register
poke one's nose in
Polaris missile
polarizability
polar wandering
pole plantation
police informer
police positive
police reporter
Polish-American
Polish draughts
Polish notation
political novel
political trial
politicization
pollen analysis
pollen spectrum
polling station
polyacrylamide
polyalphabetic
polyautography
polybrominated
polycarpellary
polychromatism
polydispersity
polyelectronic
polyfunctional
polyglacialism
polyglacialist
polygonization
polygynandrous
polyhydramnios
polyisocyanate
polylingualism
polylithionite
polymenorrhoea
polymerization
polymorphously
polyneuropathy
polynomial time
polynucleotide
polyphonically
polyphosphoric
polypodiaceous
polyrhythmical
polysaccharide

polysyllabical
polytechnician
polytheistical
polythetically
polyunsaturate
polyvinylidene
pompano dolphin
Pontefract-cake
pontifical Mass
pontifical mass
pooh-pooh theory
poor man's orange
poor man's orchid
pop the question
popularity poll
popularization
populistically
porcelain shell
porcupine grass
pork-barrelling
porphyrization
porphyrogenita
porphyrogenite
portentousness
Port Jackson fig
Portland cement
Portland oolite
Portland powder
Portland spurge
positional play
position vector
positive column
posse comitatus
possessionless
possessive case
possessiveness
postacetabular
postal currency
posterolateral
posteroventral
postganglionic
post-industrial
postindustrial
post-infectious
postmastership
postmenopausal
post-millennial
postpositional
postpositively
postprandially
post-production
post-structural
potamoplankton
potash feldspar
potassium-argon
potato dumpling
potentiometric
potentiostatic
pounce commerce
powder magazine
powder one's nose

power breakfast
power frequency
power-political
practicability
practicalities
practical joker
practical nurse
pragmaticality
pragmatization
prairie-breaker
prairie chicken
prairie country
prairie rattler
prairie warbler
praiseworthily
prayerlessness
praying machine
preaching-cross
preaching friar
preaching-house
pre-adolescence
preadolescence
pre-anaesthetic
pre-appointment
pre-arrangement
prearrangement
prebendaryship
precalculation
precariousness
precatory words
precious metals
precipitinogen
precociousness
precommissural
pre-compression
preconsonantal
predaciousness
pre-delinquency
predesignation
predestinarian
predestinately
predestination
predeterminate
predictability
predictiveness
predisposition
pre-exponential
prefabrication
prefectorially
preferableness
preferentially
preferred share
preferred stock
pregermination
preglottalized
prehensiveness
pre-imagination
pre-impregnated
pre-incarnation
prejudiciously
premeditatedly

premenstrually
premillenarian
premonstration
prenegotiation
preoperational
preoperatively
preponderantly
preponderately
preponderation
preposterously
pre-publication
prepublication
prepunctuality
Pre-Raphaelitic
presbyterially
Presbyterianly
prescriptively
prescriptivism
prescriptivist
prescriptivity
presence of mind
presentability
presentational
presentimental
present oneself
preservability
president-elect
presidentially
presiding elder
press corrector
pressed for time
pressoreceptor
press secretary
press the button
pressure cooker
pressure vessel
pressurization
presumptuously
presupposition
pretensionless
pretensiveness
pretergression
prettification
prevailingness
prevailing wind
preventability
preventatively
preventibility
prevocalically
price-sensitive
prick and praise
prickly rhubarb
priest-in-charge
prima ballerina
primary feather
primary poverty
primary quality
primary teacher
primatological
primitive plane
primordial soup

Primrose League
primrose yellow
Prince Charming
princely States
prince's feather
Princess Regent
principal focus
principalities
principal parts
principal point
principledness
prinkum-prankum
printed circuit
printer plotter
printer-slotter
printing-office
prioritization
Priscillianism
Priscillianist
Priscillianite
prismatic layer
prison-breaking
prison sentence
prittle-prattle
private company
private inquiry
private patient
private service
private soldier
privileged debt
privileged deed
priviligentsia
pro aris et focis
probabiliorism
probabiliorist
probation order
pro bono publico
proboscidiform
proceleusmatic
processability
process control
processionally
prochlorophyte
procrastinator
Procrusteanism
procryptically
proctorization
procuratorship
prodigiousness
productibility
production line
production rule
productiveness
professionally
professionless
professorially
proficiency pay
profile machine
profitableness
profit à prendre
profitlessness

profligateness
progenitorship
progestational
prognosticable
prognostically
prognosticator
programme movie
programme music
progress-chaser
progressionism
progressionist
progress report
prohibited area
prohibitionary
prohibitionism
prohibitionist
projection lens
projection room
projection rule
projection test
projective test
proletarianise
proletarianism
proletarianize
prolocutorship
promise oneself
promissory note
promissory oath
prompt-critical
pronunciamento
proof-theoretic
propaedeutical
propagableness
propagandistic
proparoxytonic
propeller shaft
propenenitrile
proper fraction
propheticality
Prophet's flower
propitiatingly
propitiatorily
propitiousness
proportionable
proportionably
proportionally
proportionless
proportionment
propositionize
propraetorship
proprietorship
proprioception
proprioceptive
propyl aldehyde
propylene imine
proscriptively
prosencephalic
prosencephalon
prosopographer
prosopographic
prospectusless

prosperousness
prostatorrhoea
prosthetically
prosthodontics
prosthodontist
Protagoreanism
protectingness
protectiveness
protein plastic
protein therapy
proterogenesis
protest marcher
Protevangelium
prothonotaries
protistologist
protocanonical
protocontinent
proto-diasystem
Protogeometric
proto-historian
proton acceptor
proton-donating
protonospheric
protopetroleum
protoplanetary
protoplasmatic
protoporcelain
protoporphyria
protoporphyrin
protopresbyter
protospathaire
prototypically
protozoologist
protractedness
protrusiveness
proventricular
proventriculus
providentially
provincialship
Provisional IRA
provisionality
provost marshal
proximity talks
Prussian collar
Prutenic tables
pseudaesthesia
pseudarthrosis
pseudepigrapha
pseudisodomous
pseudo-catholic
pseudodipteral
pseudofracture
pseudomembrane
pseudomorphism
pseudomorphous
pseudoneurotic
pseudonymously
pseudopregnant
pseudoracemate
pseudorandomly
pseudo-rational

pseudoscorpion
pseudosymmetry
psilanthropism
psilanthropist
psychedelicize
psychoacoustic
psychoactivity
psychoanalysis
psychoanalytic
psychobiologic
psychochemical
psychocultural
psychodramatic
psychodynamics
psychogalvanic
psychogenetics
psychographics
psychohistoric
psycholinguist
psychologistic
psychometrical
psychoneurosis
psychoneurotic
psychopannychy
psychophonetic
psychophysical
psychopolitics
psychosexually
psychosocially
psychosomatics
psychosomatist
psychostatical
psychosurgical
psychrospheric
psychrotrophic
pteridological
pterodactyloid
public defender
public interest
publicity agent
public nuisance
public-spirited
puerperal fever
puffin crossing
pugilistically
pugnaciousness
puisne mortgage
Pullman kitchen
pull one's weight
pull the longbow
pull the strings
pulmobranchiae
pulmobranchial
punctuationist
punishableness
pupil barrister
pupillographic
pupillometrics
purchasability
purple amaranth
purple membrane

purple swamphen
purposefulness
purse and person
push the boat out
put a bold face on
put a good face on
put a person up to
put a person wise
put a slight upon
putative father
put it on the line
put it to a person
put off the scent
put on a good show
put on a pedestal
put on a poor show
put one's faith in
put one's hands on
put one's money on
put one's shirt on
put one's spoke in
put on the market
put on the screws
put out of the way
put out to tender
putrescibility
put the blocks on
put the breeze up
put the collar on
put the finger on
put the kibosh on
put the question
put the screws on
put the sleeve on
put the tin hat on
put the tin lid on
put up a good show
put up a poor show
pyelolithotomy
pyelonephritic
pyelonephritis
pyramidologist
pyramid selling
pyrenomycetous
pyridostigmine
pyriform muscle
pyritification
pyrobituminous
pyrogallic acid
pyrometallurgy
pyrometrically
pyrometric cone
pyrophosphoric
pyrotechnician
Pythagoreanism
quadragenarian
quadrangularly
quadrantanopia
quadrant method
quadrate muscle
quadrisyllable

quaking pudding
quality control
quantification
quantitatively
quantitativist
quantity theory
quaquaversally
quarantine flag
quart and tierce
quartan malaria
quarterbacking
quarter-binding
quarter century
quarter-gallery
quarter leather
quarter-pierced
quarter-pounder
quarter-section
quarter stretch
quartette table
quartetto table
Quaternitarian
quaternization
quattrocentist
Queen Anne's lace
Queen in Council
queening square
Queen of the West
Queen's Attorney
Queen's Champion
Queen's evidence
Queensland blue
Queensland hemp
Queensland sore
Queen's shilling
queen substance
quench-cracking
quercitron lake
questionlessly
question master
quiche Lorraine
quick on the draw
quick-reference
quick with child
quiescent sheva
quincentennial
quinquagesimal
quinquedentate
quinquefoliate
quinquelocular
quinquennially
quinquepartite
quinquesection
quintessential
quite something
quodlibetarian
quotidian fever
Rabelaisianism
Rachmaninovian
rack one's brains
radial symmetry

radial velocity
radiation frost
radiator grille
radicalization
radio announcer
radio astronomy
radioautograph
radiobiologist
radiochemistry
radioenzymatic
radio frequency
radiogenically
radiographical
radiologically
radio-resistant
radiosensitive
radiosensitize
radio-telegraph
radio-telemetry
radio-telephone
radio-telephony
radio telescope
radiotherapist
radius of action
Rafferty's rules
raft foundation
railway station
rainbow-serpent
rain pitchforks
rainwater goods
raise a blockade
raise an eyebrow
raise a standard
raise one's guard
raise one's voice
rambunctiously
rammelsbergite
rampageousness
ramshackleness
random variable
Rangoon creeper
rank difference
ranunculaceous
Raschig process
Rastafarianism
rate of exchange
ration strength
rat's-tail cactus
rat's-tail fescue
rat-tailed spoon
rattle one's dags
rattle the sabre
Rayleigh number
razor-billed auk
reaccumulation
reacquaintance
reactionaryism
reading-machine
read-only memory
read the riot act
read the Riot Act

reality-testing
realizableness
reaping-machine
reappraisement
rear projection
rear-view mirror
rear-wheel drive
reasonableness
reasonlessness
reassimilation
rebelliousness
recalcitrantly
recalcitration
recapacitation
recapitulation
recapitulative
recapitulatory
receiving order
reception class
reception order
recess printing
reciprocity law
recivilization
recoil particle
recollectively
recolonization
recombinant DNA
recommencement
recommendation
recommendatory
reconciliation
reconciliative
reconciliatory
reconfirmation
reconnaissance
reconsecration
reconstitution
reconstruction
reconstructive
record-breaking
recording angel
recording level
recoverability
recreationally
rectangularity
rectilinearity
recuperability
recurrence time
red-backed mouse
red-bloodedness
redeemableness
redintegration
redintegrative
redistillation
redistribution
redistributive
red-necked grebe
red precipitate
reductionistic
reed instrument
Reeves pheasant

refectory table
reference frame
reference group
reference level
reference-point
referentiality
reflectionless
reflectiveness
reflex klystron
reflexological
reformationist
Reformed Church
refractiveness
refractometric
refractoriness
refrangibility
refreshingness
refreshment bar
refugee capital
regardlessness
regasification
regeneratively
registered post
register office
registrability
registry office
regression line
regressiveness
regularization
regular octagon
regular soldier
regulator clock
rehabilitation
rehabilitative
reillumination
reimplantation
reinauguration
reindeer lichen
reinterpreting
reintroduction
reinvigoration
Rejection Front
rejuvenescence
relapsing fever
relational word
relativization
relaxation time
relentlessness
relexification
relief printing
relieve oneself
relinquishment
remain to be seen
remarkableness
Rembrandtesque
remedilessness
Remembrance Day
reminiscential
remobilization
remodification
remonetization

remoralization
remorsefulness
remuneratively
Renaissance man
renormalizable
reorganization
repetition work
repetitiveness
replaceability
replica plating
repolarization
reported speech
report progress
re-presentation
representation
representative
repressiveness
reprimandingly
repristination
reproductively
reproductivity
reprogrammable
repromulgation
repudiationist
repulsion motor
repurification
requisitionist
re-registration
reservationist
residentiaries
residual stress
resignationism
resignationist
resinification
resistanceless
resistlessness
resolving power
resonant cavity
resource centre
resource person
respectabilise
respectability
respectabilize
respectfulness
respect persons
responsibility
responsiveness
responsorially
restitutionism
restitutionist
rest on one's oars
restorationism
restorationist
restore in blood
restrainedness
restricted area
restrictedness
restrictionism
restrictionist
resurrectional
resurrectioner

retained object
retained profit
retention money
retinoblastoma
retirement home
retractability
retransmission
retransmitting
retributionist
retrievability
retrocognition
retrocognitive
retrodictively
retroductively
retrogradation
retroreflector
return envelope
return to nature
revalorisation
revalorization
revengefulness
Reverend Mother
reverification
reverse charges
reverse osmosis
reversing falls
reversing layer
reversing light
Revised Version
revitalization
revivification
revolving stage
rewardableness
Reynolds number
Reynolds stress
rheogoniometer
rhesus-negative
rhesus-positive
rhetoricalness
rheumatic fever
rheumatologist
rhinencephalic
rhinencephalon
rhinoceros bird
rhinoceros bush
rhinoceros horn
rhinosporidial
rhizocephalous
Rhode Island Red
rhopheocytosis
rhynchokinesis
rhynchokinetic
rhynchophorous
rhynchosaurian
rhynchosporium
rhyparographer
rhyparographic
rhythm and blues
ribbon-building
ribonucleoside
ribonucleotide

rich tea biscuit
rickety-rackety
riddle of claret
ridiculousness
right about-face
right about-turn
right ascension
right-hand drive
right-hand screw
right off the bat
rigidification
Ringer solution
ring in one's ears
ringmastership
ring the changes
ring the knell of
rise in the world
rise with the sun
Ritter's disease
river blindness
roadworthiness
roaring forties
roaring success
roast-beef plant
Robin Hood's barn
robin redbreast
Robinson Crusoe
robin's plantain
robustiousness
roche moutonnée
rocket larkspur
rocket launcher
roentgenograph
roentgenologic
roentgenoscope
roentgenoscopy
rogation flower
Rogation Sunday
rolling barrage
rolling chamber
romanceishness
Romanian stitch
romanticalness
roof of the mouth
roof of the world
root-mean-square
root of scarcity
rose leafhopper
rosette disease
rose-water still
Rosicrucianism
rostro-carinate
rostrocaudally
rotary printing
rough-and-tumble
rough breathing
rough greyhound
rough horsetail
roundaboutness
roundhouse kick
round on a person

round-the-houses
round the wicket
Rowland grating
Rowland's circle
royal abundance
Royal Engineers
Royal Sovereign
Royal Worcester
rubber solution
rubbing alcohol
rub the wrong way
ruddy sheldrake
ruddy turnstone
Rueping process
ruff and discard
Rules Committee
rules of the game
rumblegumption
Rump Parliament
run a person hard
run in the family
running account
running banquet
running bowline
running footman
running repairs
running rigging
run off one's feet
run one's own show
run the blockade
run the gauntlet
run the rule over
run with the ball
Rural Institute
rush one's fences
Russell paradox
Russianization
Russian scandal
Russian thistle
rust-resistance
Rydberg formula
Sabatier effect
Sabbatarianism
sabbaticalness
sabbatical year
sacchariferous
saccharimetric
saccharization
saccharomycete
sacramentalism
sacramentalist
sacramentality
sacramentarian
sacrament house
sacrament-money
sacrifice price
sacrilegiously
saddleback crow
saddleback gull
saddleback seal
saddle-coloured

saddle-grafting
saddle scabbard
saddle shoulder
saddle thrombus
safety-critical
safety engineer
saffron milk-cap
saffron-thistle
saleswomanship
saline solution
salinification
salinity crisis
Salisbury steak
salmon-coloured
saloon carriage
salpingography
salt of wormwood
salt-water taffy
salubriousness
salute the judge
same difference
sanctification
Sandemanianism
sandwich course
sanguification
sanguinariness
sanguinivorous
sanitary napkin
sansculotterie
Santa Gertrudis
saponification
sapphire quartz
sarcosporidial
sarcosporidium
satellite photo
satellite state
satellite State
satisfactorily
satisfiability
satisfyingness
satisfy oneself
saturated steam
saturation dive
saturnicentric
sausage balloon
sausage machine
savannah flower
savannah forest
savannah monkey
saved by the bell
save one's breath
save one's pocket
save the trouble
savings account
savings and loan
saw-scaled viper
saxifragaceous
say one thing for
scala vestibuli
scalogram board
scaly francolin

scandalization
scandalousness
scanning raster
scaphocephalic
scaphocephalus
scaphognathite
scared shitless
scaremongering
scarlatiniform
scarlet lychnis
scarlet tanager
scatterbrained
scatter cushion
scatter diagram
Schaumann's body
Scheduled Caste
Scheduled Tribe
Scheiner number
schematization
scheme of colour
Schering bridge
Schick-negative
Schick-positive
Schiff reaction
schismatically
schismogenesis
schistosomulum
schizonticidal
schizontocidal
schlockmeister
Schmitt trigger
schola cantorum
scholastically
scholasticized
schoolboyishly
school district
school-divinity
schoolgirlhood
schoolmasterly
schoolmistress
School of the Air
schoolteaching
Schottky defect
Schottky effect
Schottky theory
schreierpfeife
Schwenkfeldian
Schwyzertütsch
science fantasy
science fiction
scientifically
scientifiction
scientometrics
scintilla juris
scintillograph
scintillometer
scintillometry
scintilloscope
scintiscanning
sclerification
sclerophyllous

sclerotization
scobberlotcher
scolopophorous
scoop stretcher
score points off
scorpion orchid
scorpion-spider
Scotch asphodel
Scotch attorney
Scotch baronial
Scotch woodcock
Scott-connected
Scotticization
Scottification
Scottish-French
scouring powder
scoutmastering
scrape ceremony
scrape-trencher
scratch-brusher
scratching post
screaming eagle
screen printing
screw propeller
scribbleomania
scripturalness
scritch-scratch
scrofulodermia
Scroll of the Law
scroll painting
scrubbing-brush
scrupulousness
scrutinization
scurrilousness
sea-caterpillar
sea gilliflower
seamstress-ship
seaside sparrow
seasonableness
season cracking
sea stickleback
sebaceous crypt
sebaceous gland
secondary cause
secondary radar
secondary umbel
second blessing
second-handness
second language
second mortgage
second mourning
second pendulum
second position
second-rateness
second thoughts
Second World War
secret dovetail
sector analysis
sector scanning
secularisation
secularization

secular society
secundigravida
securitization
seditious libel
seedling blight
see something of
see the elephant
segmentability
segregationist
Seidlitz powder
seismic sea-wave
seismometrical
seismotectonic
self-abhorrence
self-abnegating
self-abnegation
self-abnegatory
self-absorption
self-accusation
self-accusatory
self-adjustment
self-admiration
self-advertiser
self-alienation
self-applauding
self-assessment
self-betterment
self-cancelling
self-censorship
self-compatible
self-complacent
self-conception
self-condemning
self-confidence
self-consistent
self-controlled
self-conviction
self-correcting
self-definition
self-defrosting
self-dependence
self-destroying
self-determined
self-diffidence
self-discipline
self-effacement
self-effacingly
self-employment
self-estimation
self-evaluation
self-evidencing
self-exaltation
self-excitation
self-experience
self-expression
self-expressive
self-fertilized
self-flattering
self-fulfilling
self-fulfilment
self-generating

self-government
self-hypnotized
self-immolation
self-importance
self-improvable
self-inductance
self-indulgence
self-infliction
self-interested
self-involution
self-ionization
self-justifying
self-limitation
self-liquidator
self-management
self-motivation
self-mutilation
self-partiality
self-pollinated
self-pollinator
self-possession
self-preserving
self-proclaimed
self-propelling
self-protection
self-protective
self-punishment
self-reflection
self-reflective
self-regulating
self-regulation
self-regulative
self-regulatory
self-repression
self-respectful
self-respecting
self-restrained
self-revelation
self-sacrificer
self-satisfying
self-similarity
self-subsistent
self-sufficient
self-suggestion
self-supporting
self-sustaining
self-sustenance
selfwilledness
semaphorically
semasiological
semi-autonomous
semicircularly
semiconducting
semiconduction
semiconductive
semi-convergent
semi-detachment
semi-diaphanous
semi-elliptical
semi-fabricated
semifabricator

semi-lunar valve
seminal vesicle
seminary priest
semi-occasional
semi-officially
semi-retirement
semispheroidal
Semitic-Hamitic
semnopithecine
semotactically
senatus consult
send of an errand
senile dementia
senior moralist
senior security
senior wrangler
sensationalise
sensationalism
sensationalist
sensationalize
sensationistic
sensitive brier
sensitive plant
sensory aphasia
sensualization
sentence adverb
sentimentalise
sentimentalism
sentimentalist
sentimentality
sentimentalize
separate school
septemdecenary
septuagenarian
sequaciousness
sequestrectomy
Serene Highness
sergeant-at-arms
sergeant-at-mace
Sergeant-at-mace
sergeant bugler
serial homology
serial symmetry
sericicultural
sericitization
series-parallel
serio-comically
serjeant-at-arms
serjeants-at-law
seroconversion
serodiagnostic
seropositivity
seroprevalence
serous membrane
serpentary root
serpentiferous
serpentine jade
serpentine rock
serum hepatitis
serve-and-volley
serve one's needs

serviceability
service ceiling
service measure
service-program
service routine
service station
servo-amplifier
servohydraulic
servo-mechanism
servomechanism
sesquialterate
sesquipedalian
sesquipedality
set oneself up as
set one's heart on
seven champions
Seven Last Words
seven-year apple
several fishery
several tenancy
sexcentenaries
sextuplication
sexual equality
sexual politics
seymouriamorph
shadowgraphist
shadowlessness
shadow quilting
shagbark walnut
shaggy-dog story
shake a loose leg
shake by the hand
shake hands with
shake one's elbow
shake one's sides
Shakespeariana
shamefacedness
Shanghailander
sharp as a needle
sharps and flats
shatter-brained
sheaf catalogue
shearing strain
shearing stress
shed the blood of
sheepdog trials
sheep's scabious
sheet lightning
Sheffer's stroke
Sheffield plate
shelf-catalogue
shell parrakeet
shepherd's check
shepherd's cress
shepherd's crook
shepherd's plaid
shepherd's purse
shepherd's staff
sheriff officer
Sherlock Holmes
shift character

shift end for end
shifting centre
shillingsworth
shilly-shallied
shilly-shallies
shilly-shallyer
shingle machine
shipping-master
shipping-office
ship's-carpenter
shock-absorbent
shock-absorbing
shock treatment
shooting-ground
shooting jacket
shooting season
shoot one's cuffs
shoot the breeze
shoot the chutes
shopping arcade
shopping centre
shore patrolman
shortlivedness
short-sightedly
short square leg
shotgun wedding
shot-hole fungus
shotten herring
shoulder charge
shouldered arch
shoulder-girdle
shoulder-height
shoulder-lappet
shoulder-length
shoulder period
shoulder season
shoulder stripe
shove-halfpenny
shovel and broom
shove one's oar in
show one's mettle
shrift-district
shrimp cocktail
shrinkage crack
shut one's eyes to
shut one's mind to
shutter release
shuttle bombing
shuttle service
sialolithiasis
Siamese fighter
Siberian weasel
sibling rivalry
sibling species
Sibylline books
sick and tired of
sickle-cell gene
side-of-the-mouth
siege mentality
Siemens furnace
Siemens process

sight liability
sigillographer
sigmoid flexure
sigmoidoscopic
signal strength
sign of the cross
sign of the times
silent majority
silicification
silicon carbide
siliconization
silk-stockinged
silk-tassel bush
silver-bell tree
silver pheasant
silver-printing
silver quandong
silversmithing
silver standard
silver sycamore
silviculturist
simple fracture
simple interest
simple interval
simple majority
simple-mindedly
simple pendulum
simple sentence
simplex tableau
simplification
simplificatory
simplistically
simultaneously
sindonological
Singapore sling
singe one's wings
single acrostic
single-breasted
single-handedly
single-mindedly
single standard
single-stranded
single suckling
singsong theory
sinking feeling
sin one's mercies
sins of the flesh
siphonapterous
siphonaxanthin
siphonoxanthin
sir-reverence of
sit at the feet of
sit in judgement
sit on one's hands
sit on the splice
sit on the throne
situationalism
situationalist
six o'clock swill
six-rowed barley
sixteen pounder

skate on thin ice
skeletal muscle
skiascopically
skimble-skamble
skin and blister
skin resistance
slack one's hands
slanderousness
slantindicular
slatternliness
slaughterhouse
slaughteringly
slaughterously
Slave of the Lamp
Slavonian grebe
sleeping beauty
Sleeping Beauty
sleeping lizard
sleeping-potion
sleep paralysis
sleepy sickness
sleeve-coupling
sleevelessness
slice of the cake
slide projector
sliding contact
slime bacterium
sling-back chair
slip-coat cheese
slipshoddiness
slip the painter
slope detection
slot television
sluggardliness
slumberousness
small-bourgeois
small intestine
small-mouth bass
small of the back
smelling bottle
smell of the lamp
smell of the shop
smell the ground
smoking concert
smooth flounder
smoothing plane
snaggle-toothed
snakebark maple
snapper sampler
snapping shrimp
snapping turtle
snatch one's time
snipper-snapper
snip-snap-snorum
snowflake curve
snowshoe rabbit
sociable plover
sociable weaver
social casework
social climbing
social contract

social democrat
social distance
social document
social drinking
social dynamics
social medicine
social mobility
social position
social register
social security
society of Jesus
Society of Jesus
sociobiologist
sociologically
socio-political
socio-religious
socio-technical
soda-mint tablet
sodium chloride
sodium lighting
soft-headedness
soil deficiency
soil exhaustion
soldier-termite
solecistically
solenoglyphous
solicitousness
solicitudinous
solid diffusion
solidification
solid injection
solifluctional
solitary thrush
solitudinarian
solubilization
solvent extract
solvolytically
someone or other
somewhere about
somnambulantly
somnambulation
somnambulistic
sonnet-sequence
soon afterwards
sooty albatross
sophistication
sophomorically
soporiferously
sordid dragonet
soreheadedness
soteriological
soul-destroying
sound as a pippin
sound generator
sound in damages
sounding rocket
sound-insulated
sound moderator
sound-symbolism
sound synthesis
source language

sourdough bread
south-easterner
south-eastwards
southern lights
Southern Paiute
Southern States
South Sea bubble
South Sea Bubble
South Sea scheme
south-south-east
south-southerly
south-south-west
south-westerner
south-westwards
Sovietological
space astronomy
space programme
space-reddening
space satellite
spaceship earth
space simulator
space telescope
space traveller
spacing machine
spaghetti house
spaghetti tongs
Spanish America
Spanish bayonet
Spanish bowline
Spanish dancing
Spanish Mission
Spanish needles
Spanish opening
spargefication
spark machining
spathic iron ore
spatial ability
spatialization
spatio-temporal
spatter rampart
spattling poppy
speak by the card
speak extempore
speak for itself
speaking skills
speak in tongues
speak like a book
speak out of turn
special edition
special effects
specialization
special licence
special partner
special pleader
special service
special verdict
specific charge
specific thrust
specific volume
spectacled bear
spectacle-glass

spectacularism
spectacularity
spectatorially
spectator sport
spectral series
spectrographer
spectrographic
spectrological
spectrometrist
spectroscopist
speechlessness
spellbindingly
spelling school
Spencer carbine
spermatiferous
spermatiophore
spermatization
spermatogonium
spermatophoric
spermatorrhoea
spermiogenesis
speromagnetism
sphere of action
spherical angle
spherical wedge
spheroplasting
sphincterotomy
sphygmographic
sphygmological
spinal puncture
spindle machine
spindle-shanked
spinning tunnel
spinous process
spin-stabilized
spinthariscope
spiny cocklebur
spiral cleavage
spirantization
spiritlessness
spiritual court
spiritualistic
spirituousness
spirochaetosis
spironolactone
spit and sawdust
spite and malice
spit in the eye of
splenic flexure
splice-grafting
splishy-splashy
split one's sides
split-skin graft
split the breeze
split the ticket
splitting field
sponge sandwich
sporadic E-layer
sporadic region
sporangiferous
sporangiophore

sporangiospore
sporotrichosis
sport-fisherman
sporting chance
sporting editor
sports medicine
spot commercial
spotted dogfish
spotted rat-fish
spread-eagleism
spread-eagleist
spreading adder
spreading-board
spreadsheeting
sprightfulness
spring mattress
spring training
sputter ion pump
squadron leader
squamocolumnar
square brackets
square-shooting
squatter pigeon
squeezableness
squelch circuit
squirearchical
squirrel-headed
squirrel monkey
stadial moraine
stadtholderate
stadtholderess
stage direction
stagflationary
stainless steel
stain-resistant
staircase shell
stalagmometric
stamp catalogue
stamp collector
stamped leather
stamped mealies
stamping ground
standard-bearer
standard candle
standardizable
standard-winged
stand corrected
standing-ground
standing orders
standing pillar
stand of colours
stand one's trial
stand the market
stand the racket
Stanislavskian
Stanley bustard
staphylococcal
staphylococcus
staphylomatous
starboard watch
starch hyacinth

star connection
stare into space
starfish flower
starlight scope
starting-handle
starting pistol
starting salary
starting-signal
start something
starvation diet
starve the crows
state an account
State education
state of affairs
State's attorney
State socialism
State socialist
stathmokinesis
stathmokinetic
static friction
static pressure
stationariness
stationary bike
stationary wave
Stationers' Hall
station-keeping
station pointer
statuary marble
statuesqueness
statutableness
steady from hare
steady the Buffs
steak and kidney
steal a marriage
steel engraving
steelification
steeplechasing
steeple-crowned
steering column
stegocephalian
Steller sea lion
Steller's sea cow
stellification
stentorophonic
stepped in years
stercoricolous
sterelminthous
stereochemical
stereoisomeric
stereometrical
stereomutation
stereo-plotting
stereoptically
stereoregulate
stereospecific
sterling silver
sternutatories
stertorousness
stethendoscope
stethoscopical
stibogluconate

stichometrical
stick-and-carrot
stick at nothing
stick in the mire
stick one's bib in
sticky-fingered
stigmatiferous
stigmatization
Stillson wrench
stilt sandpiper
stinging nettle
sting in the tail
stinking badger
stinking Willie
Stirling number
stir one's stumps
stirrup leather
stitchdown shoe
stochastically
stockbrokerage
stock character
stocking filler
stocking-masked
stocking stitch
stocking tights
stocking-weaver
stoichiometric
stomatogastric
stomatological
stone-cold sober
stopping effect
stopping-ground
storage battery
storage heating
storm and stress
storm in a teacup
stout-heartedly
strabismometer
strabismometry
straight-backed
straight driver
straight-haired
straightjacket
straight muscle
straight-necked
straight stitch
straight ticket
straining-frame
Straits Chinese
Strasbourg pâté
straticulation
stratification
stratigraphist
strawberry bass
strawberry bush
strawberry dish
strawberry leaf
strawberry mark
strawberry pear
strawberry roan
strawberry tree

straw in the wind
straw-splitting
stream function
street credible
street fighting
street lighting
streets ahead of
street-to-street
strengthlessly
strepsipterous
streptodornase
streptothricin
streptovaricin
streptozotocin
stress analysis
stress-breaking
stress fracture
stretchability
stretcher-party
stretch forming
stretching beam
stretching-bond
stretching-iron
stria atrophica
striated muscle
stridulousness
strike a balance
strike a bargain
strike a blow for
strike one's flag
striking-circle
string-coloured
strip-jack-naked
stroboscopical
stroke of genius
stroke of policy
stromatolithic
stromatoporoid
strong language
strong-man's-weed
strontium oxide
strophanthidin
Strouhal number
structural load
structuredness
strumpetocracy
strut one's stuff
stubble-burning
studentization
student teacher
student–teacher
studio portrait
stultification
stultificatory
stultiloquence
stumbling block
stupendousness
styloid process
subalternation
subatmospheric
subatomic level

subconsciously
subcontinental
subcontrariety
subcutaneously
subdisjunctive
subdistinction
subduction zone
suberification
subgenerically
subinfeudation
subinfeudatory
subjectability
subject-heading
subjective case
subjectiveness
subjectivistic
sub-lieutenancy
subliminal self
submerged tenth
submersibility
submicroscopic
submissiveness
subscribership
subsidiary goal
substance abuse
substantialise
substantialism
substantialist
substantiality
substantialize
substantiation
substantiative
substantivally
substitutional
substitutively
substitutivity
subtense method
subterraneanly
subterrestrial
sub-underwriter
subversiveness
successfulness
successionally
successionless
successiveness
Successor State
sucking-cushion
sucking stomach
suck the blood of
suck the hind tit
suction dredger
sufferance quay
suffice it to say
suggestibility
suggestio falsi
suggestiveness
suicide mission
suicide squeeze
sulfhemoglobin
sulphadimidine
sulphafurazole

sulphanilamide
sulphapyridine
sulphasalazine
sulphathiazole
sulphisoxazole
sulphonylation
sulphur dioxide
sulphurization
sulphurous acid
sulphurousness
summary offence
summation check
summer hyacinth
summer mastitis
summer quarters
summer resident
summer solstice
Sunflower State
sun in splendour
sunset industry
sunshine-yellow
superabundance
superabundancy
superadiabatic
superaffluence
superannuation
superannuitant
superb starling
supercargoship
supercelestial
superciliously
supercivilized
supercomputing
superconductor
superconscious
supercontinent
superelevation
supereminently
supererogation
supererogatory
superessential
superexcellent
superficialism
superficialist
superficiality
superficialize
superhelically
superhumanness
superimpending
superimposable
superincumbent
superinduction
superinfection
superintendent
superlapsarian
superlaryngeal
superluminally
supermanliness
supermarketeer
supermarketing
supermullioned

supermultiplet
supernaturally
supernormality
superoccipital
superovulation
superoxygenate
superphosphate
superpurgation
superradiantly
super-realistic
supersaturated
superscripting
superscription
supersensitive
supersensually
supersonically
superstitional
superstructive
superstructory
superstructure
supersubtilize
supersymmetric
superterranean
supervacaneous
supervisorship
supplementally
supplicatingly
supportability
supporting film
supportiveness
suppositionary
supposititiously
supposititious
suppressio veri
suppressor cell
suppressor gene
suppressor grid
suprachoroidal
supralapsarian
supramaxillary
supramolecular
supraoccipital
suprasegmental
supra-threshold
supreme pontiff
sure-footedness
surface blow-off
surface-printed
surface tension
surgeon general
Surgeon General
surgical spirit
Suriname cherry
Suriname poison
surpass oneself
surprise packet
surprisingness
surrender value
sursumvergence
susceptibility
susceptiveness

suspend payment
suspensiveness
suspiciousness
sustainability
sustained yield
swaddling-bands
swami jewellery
swamp sassafras
swan animalcule
Swan River daisy
swear like a lord
Swedish massage
Swedish masseur
sweet coltsfoot
sweeten the pill
sweet fenugreek
sweet galingale
sweetheart neck
sweetheart rose
sweet seventeen
swimming trunks
Swinburnianism
swine influenza
swinging-bridge
Swiss stone pine
sword of justice
sword-swallower
sworn to secrecy
symbolicalness
symbolo-fideism
symbolo-fideist
symmetricality
symmetric group
symmetrization
symmetrophobia
sympathetic ink
sympathicotony
sympathotropic
sympathy strike
symphysis pubis
symplectically
symptomatology
symptom complex
synaptogenesis
synchondrosial
synchronically
syncretistical
syncretization
synergetically
syngenetically
synonymousness
Synoptic Gospel
synsedimentary
syntax language
synthetic resin
syringe passage
Syrophoenician
systematically
system-building
system operator
systems analyst

system software
systems program
tabernacle-work
tableau curtain
tablespoonfuls
tabloidization
tabular iceberg
tachistoscopic
tacho-generator
tachygraphical
tachymetabolic
Taconic orogeny
Tahiti chestnut
tail-end Charlie
tailor-madeness
take a dim view of
take advantages
take a rise out of
take a slipper to
take by surprise
take delivery of
take farewell of
take fast hold of
take for granted
take holy orders
take in good part
take off one's hat
take one's chance
take one's choice
take oneself off
take one's flight
takeover bidder
take pleasure in
take possession
take precedence
take the biscuit
take the can back
take the edge off
take the gauge of
take the liberty
take the place of
take the trouble
take to one's legs
take to the boats
take up the glove
take up the slack
take up the torch
talismanically
talking machine
talking picture
tallow-chandler
tambourine dove
tangible assets
tank locomotive
tape reproducer
tapestry beetle
tapestry needle
tapestry-worker
tappity-tappity
tar and feathers
tarantula-juice

target audience
target language
tariff-reformer
taskmastership
Tasmanian cedar
Tasmanian devil
Tasmanian tiger
tassel hyacinth
tassel-pondweed
taste-blindness
tatterdemalion
tattersal check
tattle-tale grey
tautologically
tawny frogmouth
tea and sympathy
teacher edition
teaching fellow
tea-scented rose
technical hitch
technicalities
technification
techno-economic
technostressed
tectonophysics
tectonothermal
telangiectasis
telangiectatic
telautographic
teleconference
teleconnection
tele-evangelist
telegraph blank
telegraph board
telegraph plant
telemetrically
teleologically
telepathically
telephone booth
telephone kiosk
telephonically
telephonograph
telephotograph
teleprocessing
telescope-sight
telescopically
teletypesetter
teletypewriter
televangelical
televisionless
television tube
television-wise
tell it like it is
tell its own tale
telomerization
temporaneously
temporary tooth
temptationless
tenant paravail
tendo-synovitis
Tennysonianism

ten o'clock swill
tenore di grazia
tenure in capite
tequila sunrise
Tequistlatecan
teratogenicity
tercentenaries
terebinthinate
terebinthinous
tergiversation
tergiversatory
terminableness
terminal market
terminal string
terminal symbol
terminological
terminus ad quem
termitophagous
termitophilous
term of reproach
terotechnology
terra incognita
terra irredenta
terra ponderosa
terra sigillata
terrestriality
terrestrialize
terrible infant
territorialise
territorialism
territorialist
territoriality
territorialize
terror-stricken
terry towelling
tertian malaria
testamentarily
testimonialize
testing station
tetartohedrism
tetraalkyllead
tetrachotomous
tetracosactrin
tetractinellid
tetradactylous
tetraethyl lead
Tetragrammaton
tetrevangelium
Texas armadillo
text processing
thalamostriate
thalassography
thalassophobia
thanatological
that is news to me
thaumatropical
thaumaturgical
the age of reason
theatricalness
the Author of all
the beaten track

Thebesian valve
the bird is flown
the boy next door
theca folliculi
the Carabiniers
the child unborn
the Christ-child
the clean potato
the Emerald Isle
the English pale
the environment
the Eternal City
the facts of life
the far infrared
the fatal thread
the Five Nations
the Flowery Land
the frozen limit
the gate of death
the gentle craft
the great Author
the Great Divide
the Great Unpaid
the heart bleeds
the high command
the Hundred Days
the Incarnation
the Inquisition
the King's colour
the King's speech
the kiss of death
the laugh is on me
the life of Riley
the little woman
the Long Forties
the Lord's Prayer
the Lord's Supper
the Man Upstairs
the new celibacy
the noble savage
theocentricism
theocentricity
theocratically
Theodosian Code
the Old Dominion
theology of hope
the opposite sex
theosophically
the Philosopher
the public purse
the Queen's peace
therianthropic
the rich glutton
theriogenology
theriomorphism
thermal barrier
thermal imaging
thermal inertia
thermalization
thermal neutron
thermal printer

thermal reactor
thermal runaway
thermal springs
thermal storage
thermionically
thermochemical
thermochromism
thermodynamics
thermoelectric
thermo-junction
thermolability
thermomagnetic
thermometrical
thermophysical
thermoreceptor
thermoregulate
thermoremanent
thermotolerant
therocephalian
the roof falls in
the sinews of war
the Six Counties
the small screen
the sum of things
the two cultures
the vale of years
the whole shmear
the witch is in it
the world to come
thieves' kitchen
thieves' vinegar
thimble printer
thingification
things personal
think in terms of
think nothing of
thioglycollate
third-and-fourth
Third Programme
Third Secretary
third ventricle
thirteenth part
thirty-year rule
this mortal coil
thoracic cavity
thorny woodcock
thorough-lights
thorough-stitch
thought control
thoughtfulness
thoughtography
thought pattern
thought-reading
thousand island
thousand-jacket
thousandth part
threadbareness
three-card monte
three-card trick
three halfpence
three-halfpenny

three-letter man
threepenny nail
three-point turn
threshing floor
thrift industry
thriftlessness
thrombasthenia
thrombocytosis
thromboembolic
thromboplastic
thromboplastin
thrombosthenin
throne and altar
through-draught
through-ganging
through-passage
through-the-lens
through traffic
throw a veil over
throw oneself at
throw oneself on
throw overboard
throw the book at
throw the switch
thrust and parry
thrust reverser
thump the pulpit
thunder-bearing
thunder-blasted
thunderousness
thwacking-frame
thyro-arytenoid
thyroid hormone
thyrotoxicosis
thysanopterous
Tibetan mastiff
Tibetan spaniel
Tibetan terrier
Tiburtine stone
ticket-of-leaver
ticket-splitter
tickle the peter
tiddly-om-pom-pom
tie hand and foot
tilting furnace
timber carriage
time dilatation
time immemorial
time of one's life
time-travelling
tinhorn gambler
tintinnabulant
tintinnabulary
tintinnabulate
tintinnabulous
tissue-matching
title catalogue
title insurance
to a great extent
to a person's cost
to a person's face

tobacco-stopper
toilet-training
toing and froing
token-reflexive
tolerance level
tolerance limit
tolerogenicity
Tolman sweeting
Tom-and-Jerryism
tomato hornworm
tomfoolishness
tone separation
tongue-tiedness
tongue-twisting
to one's dying day
to one's own cheek
toothbrush tree
topgallant mast
topicalization
topochemically
topoinhibition
topologization
topotactically
topsy-turviness
topsy-turvyhood
torpedo-catcher
torpedo-netting
torsion balance
tortoise-beetle
torture chamber
to say nothing of
total abstainer
to tell the truth
to the bitter end
to the four winds
to the utterance
tough as leather
tower of silence
town councillor
toxin-antitoxin
tracheostomies
tracking weight
traction engine
traction splint
tractor-trailer
trade allowance
trade reduction
tradesman's door
trades unionist
trade-unionized
trading account
trading station
traditionalise
traditionalism
traditionalist
traditionality
traditionalize
Trafalgar chair
trafficability
traffic analyst
traffic calming

traffic control
traffic offence
traffic officer
traffic pattern
tragicomically
trailing vortex
training-school
traitorousness
transacetylase
transamination
transanimation
transcendental
transcendently
transcendingly
transconjugant
transductional
transempirical
transferential
transfer factor
transformation
transformative
transformer oil
transform fault
transfretation
transfusionist
transgressible
transitionally
transitiveness
transitoriness
Transjordanian
translationese
translatorship
transliterator
translocatable
transmigration
transmigrative
transmigratory
transmissional
transmissivity
transmit button
transmogrified
transmogrifier
transmogrifies
transparencies
transpeptidase
transpicuously
transplantable
transplendency
transplutonium
transpolitical
transportation
transportative
Transport House
transport-plane
transpulmonary
transsexualism
transsexualist
transsexuality
Transvaal daisy
transvaluation
transverbation

transversality
transverse axis
transverseness
transverse wave
transvesticism
transvestitism
trapdoor spider
trapeze harness
traumatization
traumatologist
traumatotropic
travel brochure
traveller's palm
traveller's tale
travelling wave
travel-sickness
traverse-survey
treacle mustard
tread the boards
tread under foot
treasure-flower
treat like a lord
tremendousness
treponematosis
treponemicidal
tricentenaries
trichinellosis
trichomoniasis
trichophytosis
trichotomously
trickle charger
tricontinental
Tridentine mass
tridimensional
tried and tested
trifacial nerve
trigger circuit
trigonocephaly
trihalomethane
trihedral angle
trihedral quoin
triiodomethane
trilateralness
trimethylamine
Trinitarianism
trinitrophenol
trinitrotoluol
trinkum-trankum
tripelennamine
tripersonalism
tripersonalist
tripersonality
triple acrostic
triple alliance
triple tonguing
tripperishness
triquetral bone
trisoctahedron
trisubstituted
trituberculate
triumphalistic

trivialization
Trivial Pursuit
trochlear nerve
troop the colour
trophoneurosis
tropical weight
tropic of Cancer
tropicopolitan
tropologically
trouble at t' mill
troubleshooter
trough of the sea
trouser-presser
true-lover's knot
Truman doctrine
trumpet creeper
trumpet-mouthed
trumpet pattern
trumpet-tongued
trussing needle
trustee process
trust territory
Trust Territory
truth-condition
try one's fortune
trypanosomatid
trypsinization
Tuatha Dé Danann
tubal pregnancy
tuberculin test
tumblification
tumbling-barrel
tumorigenicity
tumultuousness
tuner-amplifier
tunnel-visioned
turbogenerator
turf accountant
turkey-merchant
Turkish delight
Turkish slipper
Turkish tobacco
Turkoman carpet
turn a cartwheel
turn a deaf ear to
turn one's back on
turn one's girdle
turn one's hand to
turn on one's heel
turnpike sailor
turn up one's nose
turn up one's toes
turpentine-tree
turpentine weed
twiddle-twaddle
twingle-twangle
Twinkie defence
twistification
twist in the wind
twists and turns
twit in the teeth

two-backed beast
two-dimensional
two-pot screamer
tympanic cavity
tyndallization
type-psychology
tyrannicalness
ubiquitination
ubiquitousness
Ugandanization
ultimatization
ultimogeniture
ultracrepidate
ultrafidianism
ultramicrotome
ultramicrotomy
ultramontanism
ultramontanist
ultrasonically
ultrasonograph
ultrastructure
ultraviolation
ultroneousness
umbrageousness
umbrella bridge
Umklapp process
unacclimatized
unaccommodated
unaccomplished
unaccounted for
unaccustomedly
unacknowledged
unackowledging
unacquaintance
unadaptability
unadministered
unaffectedness
unaffectionate
unaggressively
unalterability
unambivalently
un-Americanized
unappetizingly
unappreciative
unapprehensive
unapproachable
unapproachably
unappropriated
unarithmetical
unartificially
unartistically
unaspiringness
unassumingness
unathletically
unattachedness
unattractively
unattributable
unattributably
unauthenticity
unauthorizedly
unavailability

unavoidability
unbearableness
unbecomingness
unbegottenness
unbureaucratic
unbusinesslike
uncertificated
unchangingness
uncheerfulness
unchivalrously
unchristianise
unchristianity
unchristianize
uncircumcision
uncivilization
unclassifiable
uncommissioned
uncommunicable
uncommunicated
uncompoundedly
uncomprehended
uncompromising
unconciliatory
unconditionate
unconfidential
unconfinedness
uncongeniality
unconscionable
unconscionably
unconservative
unconsiderable
unconsolidated
unconstructive
uncontaminated
uncontemplated
uncontemporary
uncontradicted
uncontrollable
uncontrollably
uncontrolledly
uncontroverted
unconventional
unconvincingly
uncorroborated
uncounsellable
uncountability
uncountenanced
uncourtierlike
uncrackability
uncriticizable
uncrystallized
undecidability
undecipherable
undecipherably
undecisiveness
undecomposable
undecompounded
undecorticated
undegenerating
undelightfully
undemonstrable

undemonstrated
undeniableness
underabundance
under bare poles
underbevelling
under command of
underdetermine
underdeveloped
underdiagnosis
underdispersed
undereducation
underemphasise
underemphasize
undergraduette
under-housemaid
underinsurance
underlineation
undermentioned
undernourished
under-occupancy
under-officered
underofficered
under penalty of
underperformer
underpetticoat
underpopulated
underprivilege
underqualified
underrehearsal
under-rehearsed
underrehearsed
under-represent
underrepresent
undersaturated
under-secretary
undersketching
understandable
understandably
understatement
understimulate
understrapping
undersubscribe
under suspicion
undertenancies
under the harrow
under the heel of
under the plough
under the wing of
under-treasurer
undertreatment
undervaluation
underwaistcoat
underworldling
undeservedness
undesirability
undestructible
undeterminable
undiminishable
undiscerningly
undiscontinued
undiscoverable

undiscoverably
undispatchable
undistractedly
undogmatically
undomesticated
undoubtfulness
undoubtingness
undramatically
undue influence
unearned income
uneconomically
uneducatedness
unelectability
unemphatically
unendurability
unenfranchised
unenlightening
unenterprising
unentertaining
unenthusiastic
unequilibrated
unetymological
uneuphoniously
uneventfulness
unexcitability
unexhilarating
unexpectedness
unexperimented
unextinguished
unfaithfulness
unfamiliarized
unfastidiously
unfatherliness
unfinishedness
unflappability
unflatteringly
unforeknowable
unforeseeingly
unfractionated
unfriendliness
unfruitfulness
ungenerousness
ungracefulness
ungraciousness
ungratefulness
ungroundedness
unhandsomeness
unharmoniously
unhesitatingly
unhistorically
unholy alliance
unhygienically
unhypocritical
unicellularity
unidentifiable
unidentifiably
unidimensional
unidirectional
unificationist
uniformitarian
uniformization

unilateralized
unilluminating
unillustrative
unimmortalized
unimolecularly
unimpressively
unincorporated
unindifference
unindifferency
unintellectual
unintelligence
unintelligible
unintelligibly
uninterestedly
unintermittent
unintermitting
uninterrogated
uninterruption
unintoxicating
uninvestigable
uninvestigated
union catalogue
union workhouse
Union Workhouse
United Brethren
United-Stateser
universal agent
universal donor
universalistic
universal joint
universitarian
unknowableness
unknown country
Unknown Soldier
Unknown Warrior
unletteredness
unliterariness
unmaidenliness
unmaintainable
unmalleability
unmannerliness
unmanufactured
unmarriageable
unmathematical
unmatriculated
unmeasuredness
unmerchantable
unmercifulness
unmetaphorical
unmetaphysical
unmethodically
unmotherliness
unnavigability
unnecessitated
unobligingness
unobstructedly
unornamentally
unostentatious
unpaintability
unpalatability
unparallelable

unparalleledly
unparallelness
unparticipated
unpassionately
unperceptively
unpersuasively
unphilosophize
unphotographed
unpleasantness
unpleasantries
unpleasingness
unpornographic
unpracticality
unpraiseworthy
unprecipitated
unprejudicedly
unpremeditated
unpreparedness
unprepossessed
unpresumptuous
unpretendingly
unprinceliness
unproblematize
unproductively
unprofessional
unprogrammable
unpropitiously
unproportional
unproportioned
unprosperously
unprotestingly
unprovableness
unprovidedness
unprovokedness
unquantifiable
unquestionable
unquestionably
unreadableness
unreciprocated
unrecognisable
unrecognizable
unrecognizably
unreconcilable
unreflectingly
unreformedness
unrefrigerated
unregenerately
unregeneration
unreliableness
unrelinquished
unrememberable
unremorsefully
unremunerative
unrenounceable
unreproachable
unreproducible
unreproductive
unrequitedness
unreservedness
unresolvedness
unrespectfully

unresponsively
unrestrainable
unrestrainably
unrestrainedly
unrestrictedly
unrhythmically
unrightfulness
unromantically
unsaleableness
unsatiableness
unsatisfaction
unsatisfactory
unsatisfyingly
unscripturally
unscrupulously
unshakeability
unshockability
unshoe-the-horse
unsociableness
unsociological
unsolvableness
unsophisticate
unspeakability
unspirituality
unspiritualize
unsplinterable
unstandardized
unstoppability
unstraightened
unstrengthened
unsubmissively
unsubstantiate
unsuccessfully
unsufficiently
unsuitableness
unsupercharged
unsuppressible
unsurmountable
unsurprisingly
unsuspectingly
unsuspiciously
unsympathizing
unsystematized
untameableness
unthankfulness
unthinkability
unthinkingness
unthoughtfully
untouchability
untowardliness
untractability
untranquillize
untransferable
untranslatable
untranslatably
untransmutable
untransplanted
untruthfulness
unupbraidingly
unutterability
unvanquishable

unvariableness
unvendibleness
unverbalizable
unvirtuousness
unwatchfulness
unwhisperables
unworkableness
unyieldingness
uproariousness
upside-down cake
up to one's neck in
up to one's tricks
up to the knocker
upwardly mobile
upward mobility
uranographical
urban guerrilla
urethral meatus
urinary bladder
use of the globes
user-orientated
user-unfriendly
uterine brother
utero-gestation
uteroplacental
utilitarianism
utilitarianize
utility program
utility routine
utility vehicle
utriculoplasty
vaccine-damaged
vaccine disease
vaccine program
vaccine therapy
vacuum abortion
vacuum activity
vaingloriously
valence grammar
Valencia almond
Valencia orange
valency grammar
Valentinianism
valerianaceous
valetudinarian
valetudinaries
vallate papilla
value judgement
vanilla essence
vanishing cream
vanishing point
vapour pressure
Varangian Guard
various reading
vasa deferentia
vascular bundle
vascular system
vasodilatation
vasomotorially
Vatican Council
Vaticanologist

vectored thrust
vector function
vegetable ivory
vegetable sheep
vegetationally
vegetationless
vegetative cell
vegetativeness
vegetative pole
velopharyngeal
velvet-painting
velvet tamarind
vending machine
venereological
Venetian carpet
Venetian School
Venetian window
ventriculogram
ventromedially
venture capital
Venus hairstone
verifiableness
verisimilitude
Verreaux's eagle
Verrocchiesque
vertical angles
vertical circle
vertical market
verticillaster
verticillation
vesicopustular
vesicoureteral
vesicoureteric
vespertilionid
vested interest
vestibular fold
vexillological
via affirmativa
vicar apostolic
vicar episcopal
vice-chancellor
vice-consulship
vice-legateship
vice-presidency
Victorian cycle
Victoria sponge
victoriousness
victrix ludorum
video amplifier
video frequency
video recording
video-telephone
Viennese coffee
Vietnamization
Villafranchian
villainousness
villein service
Vincent's angina
vindictiveness
vin doux naturel
vinho de consumo

viola da braccio
viola da gambist
violent profits
violet sea-snail
violetta marina
violino piccolo
Virginian quail
Virginian stock
Virgin Islander
virgin olive oil
virgin's garland
virial equation
virtual cathode
virtual reality
virtuous circle
visceral cavity
visceral pleura
viscerocranium
viscerotropism
viscose process
viscosity index
visible horizon
vision splendid
visiting fellow
visiting rights
visiting ticket
vitaminization
vitelline gland
vitelline layer
vitellogenesis
vitellogenetic
vitreous enamel
vitreous humour
vitreous lustre
vitreous silica
vitreous sponge
vitrifiability
vitriolization
vituperatively
viviparousness
vivisectionist
vociferousness
voice frequency
voicespondence
volatilization
volcaniclastic
volcanological
voltage divider
voltaic battery
volumetrically
voluminousness
voluntary-aided
Volunteer State
voluptuousness
vortex shedding
vouch to warrant
vowel gradation
vulcanological
vulgar fraction
vulnerableness
vulpine opossum

vulvovaginitis
wagtail warbler
waifs and strays
waiting problem
walk a chalk-line
walking catfish
walking funeral
walking machine
walking wounded
walk on crutches
walk one's rounds
walk the streets
walk with a stick
Walpurgis night
Walter Scottish
wandering hands
wandering nerve
want for nothing
wappenschawing
ward in Chancery
wardrobe master
warehouse party
war of attrition
warrantability
warrant dormant
warrant-officer
Wars of the Roses
war-substantive
wash and brush-up
washing machine
Washington clam
Washington lily
Wassermann test
Watch Committee
watch this space
water authority
water barometer
water bewitched
water-breathing
water chickweed
water chincapin
watercolourist
Waterford glass
water germander
water injection
water-insoluble
water on the knee
water pimpernel
water-privilege
waterproofness
water-repellent
water-resistant
watertightness
wattled lapwing
wave-mechanical
waw consecutive
waxen chatterer
weak-mindedness
weapons-carrier
weapon-training
wearing apparel

wear yellow hose
weatherability
weather balloon
weather-breeder
weathercockism
weather-cottage
weatherization
weatherproofed
weather prophet
weather station
wedding-garment
Wegener's theory
Weierstrassian
weighing-engine
weigh one's words
weight function
weightlessness
weight training
weight-watching
Weimar Republic
welfare benefit
welfare statism
well acquainted
well-documented
well-formedness
wellington boot
Wellington coat
well-maintained
well-structured
well thought out
Welsh clearwing
Weltanschauung
welter handicap
western hemlock
westernization
West Highlander
wet one's whistle
wet the other eye
whalebone whale
whaling station
what a vengeance
what countryman
what do you say to
what do you think
what-d'you-call-'em
what-d'you-call-it
what is your will
wheaten terrier
wheel balancing
wheel barometer
wheel-engraving
wheeler-dealing
wheel of fortune
wheel of Fortune
wheelwrighting
whiplash injury
whippersnapper
whiptail lizard
whistling eagle
whistling thorn
white blood cell

white butterfly
white chameleon
white Christmas
white corpuscle
white-headed boy
White Highlands
white horehound
white lightning
White man's grave
white merganser
white nickel ore
White supremacy
white-tailed gnu
whiting pollack
whittie-whattie
wholeheartedly
whole-tone scale
whoopee cushion
whortleberries
who the hangment
wide open spaces
widow bewitched
Wiedemann–Franz
wigs on the green
wild-goose chase
wild mignonette
wild snapdragon
wild strawberry
Wilhelmstrasse
William Morrisy
william-nilliam
will see about it
Winchester disk
wind and weather
wind-chill index
windfall profit
wind instrument
window dressing
window-envelope
windowlessness
window-trimming
Windsor uniform
Winebrennarian
winning-gallery
winning opening
winter daffodil
winter flounder
winter quarters
winter solstice
winter woollies
win the exchange
wish-fulfilling
wish-fulfilment
wishful thinker
wishy-washiness
witch-doctoring
witches' sabbath
with a good grace
with a heavy hand
with all reserve
with an even keel

with an ill grace
with a single eye
with a stick in it
with a vengeance
with a wet finger
with a whole skin
with difficulty
withdrawal slip
with effect from
with half a heart
withholding tax
within a cooee of
within an inch of
within the walls
with one eye shut
with one's tail up
without a murmur
without example
without more ado
without offence
without-profits
without remorse
without reserve
without scruple
with relation to
with the colours
Wittig reaction
woe worth the day
Wollaston prism
Wolverine State
woman about town
woman of fortune
woman of letters
woman of the town
woman-slaughter
woman's magazine
woman's movement
women's magazine
women's movement
Women's Movement
women's suffrage
wonder-stricken

woodchat shrike
wooden overcoat
wooden spoonist
woodland garden
wood strawberry
woollen-drapery
Worcesterberry
Worcester sauce
Worcestershire
word-internally
word processing
Wordsworthiana
worker-director
work experience
working capital
working classes
working drawing
working outline
working storage
working surface
work in progress
work like a charm
work one's ticket
works committee
world-weariness
worse than death
worshipfulness
worth one's while
worth's one's salt
worthwhileness
wring one's hands
wring the neck of
wrist-wrestling
writing cabinet
writ of tresaiel
xanthene colour
xenodiagnostic
xenophobically
xeroradiograph
xiphoid process
X-ray astronomer
X-ray department

yellow-breasted
yellow centaury
yellow oleander
yellow suckling
yellowtail scad
yellow toadflax
yeoman's service
yesterday's news
yoke-fellowship
Yorkshire chair
Yorkshirewoman
Yorkshirewomen
you bet your life
Young–Helmholtz
Young Pretender
you're telling me
you're the doctor
your little game
yours sincerely
Yours sincerely
yours to command
your university
youth and old age
youth hosteller
Zambianization
zebra angelfish
Zener breakdown
zenith distance
zero-derivation
zeta hypothesis
zeugmatography
zillah parishad
zingiberaceous
zooarchaeology
zoographically
zoological park
zoopraxography
Zoroastrianism
Zoroastrianize
zymogen granule
zymotechnology
zymotic disease

FIFTEEN LETTERS

Abbot of Unreason
a bone in her mouth
a bone in one's head
above the gangway
absolute alcohol
absorbent cotton
absorptiometric
abstracting from
acanthocephalan
accelerator card
accidental sharp
acclimatization
accommodatingly
accommodational
according to plan
accountableness
account rendered
accounts payable
acculturational
acculturization
a certain disease
acetic anhydride
acetyl coenzyme A
ace up one's sleeve
achlorophyllous
achondroplasiac
achondroplastic
acknowledgeable
acknowledgement
acoustic coupler
acquisitiveness
a crack of the whip
acrimoniousness
across the tracks
actinopterygian
action committee
action potential
activated carbon
activated sludge
active transport
act of contrition
Act of Parliament
Act of Settlement
Act of Toleration
Act of Uniformity
acupuncturation
acute rheumatism
Addison's disease
adenohypophysis
Adjutant General
administratress
Admiral of the Red
a drop in the ocean
adsignification
advanced studies
adventurousness
adverb of quality

advertisemental
Advocate-General
aerial torpedoed
aerial torpedoes
aerodynamically
affluent society
affranchisement
a fish out of water
African-American
African elephant
African mahogany
after first brush
against one's will
against the clock
against the grain
against the world
age of discretion
agglutinability
a gleam in one's eye
a glint in one's eye
agranulocytosis
agribusinessman
agribusinessmen
agriculturalist
a hair in one's neck
a hard nut to crack
ahead of one's time
a hundred per cent
Air Chief Marshal
air-conditioning
aircraft carrier
a kick in the teeth
algorithmically
alimentary canal
alive and kicking
all-accomplished
all along the line
all hell let loose
allotetraploidy
all over the place
all the night long
all the world over
a lot on one's plate
alphabetization
alternate angles
alternative fuel
alternativeness
aluminium bronze
aluminosilicate
a man and a brother
amaryllidaceous
a matter of course
a matter of record
ambassadorially
ambulance chaser
amende honorable
American cowslip

American English
Americanization
amicable numbers
a million dollars
amphiarthrodial
amphitheatrical
amusement arcade
anabolic steroid
anaesthesiology
anaesthetically
a nasty bit of work
ancient monument
ancylostomiasis
Andaman Islander
Anderson shelter
andromonoecious
androstenedione
angle of friction
angle of position
Anglo-vernacular
angular momentum
angular velocity
animal husbandry
animal magnetism
anisotropically
ankylostomiasis
annihilationism
annihilationist
annus horribilis
anomalistic year
anorexia nervosa
Antarctic Circle
antepenultimate
anteroposterior
anthropocentric
anthropogenesis
anthropological
anthropometrist
anthropomorphic
anthropopathism
anthropophagite
anthropophagous
anthroposophist
anthropotomical
anti-abortionist
antichristianly
anticlericalism
anticoagulation
antiferromagnet
anti-Gallicanism
antilogarithmic
antimonarchical
antimonious acid
antiperistaltic
antiphlogistian
Antiphlogistine
antisabbatarian

antisymmetrical
antitrinitarian
any port in a storm
apocalyptically
Apollinarianism
apophthegmatize
apparent horizon
appearance money
appendicularian
approachability
approbativeness
appropinquation
appropriateness
approximatively
apron-string hold
aqueous solution
arboriculturist
archaebacterial
archaebacterium
archaeomagnetic
archiepiscopacy
archiepiscopate
architectonical
architecturally
area linguistics
argumentatively
Aristotelianism
arithmetization
armed neutrality
armed to the teeth
armillary sphere
Arms of Patronage
arrest judgement
arterialization
artificial stone
artsy-and-craftsy
as a matter of fact
ascending letter
ascend the throne
asclepiadaceous
as dead as the dodo
as deaf as a beetle
as dry as a whistle
as dumb as a beetle
as easy as winking
as far as in me lies
as keen as mustard
ask for one's cards
a slice of the cake
as like as two peas
as long as your arm
asparagus beetle
a spit and a stride
as pretty as paint
assembly program
assimilationist
assisted passage
as sober as a judge
association book
associativeness
as sound as a roach
as the saying goes

astronavigation
Astronomer Royal
astronomical day
astrophysically
at a disadvantage
at all adventures
at close quarters
at cross purposes
Athanasian Creed
at heck and manger
atherosclerosis
atherosclerotic
athwart the hawse
Atlantic Charter
Atlantic pomfret
atmospherically
atomic structure
atrabiliousness
at rack and manger
at the crossroads
at the drop of a hat
at the first blush
at the instance of
Attorney-General
Attorney general
audience-chamber
Augustal Prefect
auricular finger
aurora australis
Australian crawl
Australian hazel
Australian Rules
authoritatively
autobiographies
autobiographist
autochthonously
autocorrelation
autocorrelogram
auto-destruction
auto-destructive
autogenetically
autograph-hunter
autographically
autolithography
autoplastically
autoradiography
autoschediastic
auto-suggestible
autotransformer
autotransfusion
autotrophically
autumnal equinox
auxiliary troops
aversion therapy
Avogadro's number
a wing and a prayer
awkward customer
Axminster carpet
bachelor's degree
background music
background noise
back on one's heels

back to square one
backward masking
bacteriological
Bahasa Indonesia
balaclava helmet
balance of nature
balance of terror
ballistic rocket
ballroom dancing
balsamic vinegar
Baltimore oriole
bargain basement
barking squirrel
barothermograph
Bartholomew fair
basal metabolism
basidiomycetous
basilar membrane
bastard mahogany
batch processing
batch production
Batesian mimicry
bathymetrically
bats in the belfry
battering-engine
Battersea enamel
bear away the bell
bear the blame for
beat all to sticks
beat a person to it
beaten at the post
beat the pants off
beat the tar out of
beat with the spit
beautiful people
beauty treatment
bed and breakfast
beefsteak fungus
beefsteak tomato
beer and skittles
be food for fishes
be food for powder
before the face of
before the letter
behind the scenes
be in at the finish
believe one's ears
Bell's inequality
below one's breath
below the gangway
bend someone's ear
beneath contempt
Benedictine rule
benefit of clergy
be one's own master
Bermuda triangle
Bermuda Triangle
beside the saddle
Bessemer process
between two fires
Beverley Minster
beyond exception

beyond one's grasp
bibliographical
bibliothecarial
bibliothecarian
bidirectionally
Bill of Exclusion
bill of mortality
bill of privilege
bimetallic strip
bind hand and foot
binocular vision
binomial theorem
bioavailability
biobibliography
biogeochemistry
biogeographical
biological clock
bioluminescence
biomechanically
biorhythmically
biosociological
biospeleologist
biostatistician
biostratigraphy
biotechnologist
birds of a feather
birthday honours
bishop suffragan
bite on the bullet
biting stonecrop
bituminous shale
black-coat worker
blackcurrant jam
Black Forest cake
black nightshade
black rhinoceros
black spleenwort
blackwater fever
black wildebeest
blameworthiness
blasphemousness
bleaching powder
Blenheim spaniel
blepharoplastic
blind baggage car
block signalling
blood-and-thunder
bloodthirstiest
Bloomsbury Group
bluegill sunfish
bluestockingism
blue vinny cheese
blunt instrument
board and lodging
Board of Ordnance
boatswain's chair
body-line bowling
bolt from the blue
bolt-uprightness
bonded warehouse
book of reference
Bordeaux mixture

Border Leicester
bore the pants off
Bornholm disease
born in the purple
borough surveyor
borrowed plumage
bottom-fermented
bottom of the heap
boustrophedonic
bowling analysis
Bow Street runner
bowstring-bridge
brachiocephalic
brachistochrone
brachycephalism
brachycephalous
brachydactylous
bradymetabolism
brake horsepower
braking distance
branchiobdellid
branchiostegite
branchiostegous
Brazilian nutmeg
breach of promise
bread of idleness
breaking of bread
break on the wheel
breath consonant
breathe one's last
breeding plumage
bricks and mortar
bring-and-buy sale
bring into effect
bring pressure on
bring to its knees
bristlecone pine
Britannia silver
British Standard
brittle fracture
broadly speaking
broad-mindedness
broken-heartedly
bronzed diabetes
bronze medallist
brothel creepers
brown rot disease
brushtail possum
Brussels griffon
bubble and squeak
building society
Burmese rosewood
burnet saxifrage
burning mountain
burn midnight oil
burn one's bridges
burn one's fingers
burst into flames
bury the tomahawk
business as usual
business studies
butter-and-egg man

butterfly blenny
butterfly flower
butterfly orchid
butterfly stroke
butter of almonds
by common consent
by fits and starts
by guess and by God
by hook or by crook
by process of time
by the grace of God
by these presents
by way of reprisal
cabbalistically
Cabinet minister
Cabinet Minister
cable television
calcium sulphate
Californian jack
call all to naught
call attention to
Calvinistically
candelabrum tree
cannibalization
cannot choose but
Canterbury bells
Cape Barren goose
Cape forget-me-not
Cape leaping hare
capillary action
capital gains tax
capitation grant
Capricorn beetle
captain's biscuit
captive audience
capture myopathy
carbonate of lime
carbonic acid gas
carcinogenicity
cardinal numeral
cardiopulmonary
career structure
carnal knowledge
carnivorousness
Carolina jasmine
carriage and pair
carriage forward
carriage release
Carrion's disease
carry conviction
carry the can back
carve for oneself
cash in one's chips
cask-conditioned
casting-director
cataclysmically
catch a glimpse of
catch-as-catch-can
catch one's breath
catch the fancy of
catechistically
categorematical

cathedral church
catheterization
Catholicization
cavity resonator
celestial sphere
cells of the brain
cellular blanket
Celtic spikenard
Centennial State
Central American
centrally-heated
centre of gravity
centre of inertia
cephalhaematoma
cephalochordate
cephalothoracic
cepheid variable
ceratobranchial
cerebrovascular
ceremoniousness
certified cheque
Ceylon satinwood
chamberlainship
change of address
change of clothes
change of scenery
change of the moon
Channel Islander
chanting goshawk
chapter and verse
character sketch
character string
charcoal biscuit
chargé d'affaires
charismatically
chattel interest
chattel mortgage
checking account
chemical warfare
chemico-physical
chemoautotrophy
chemotactically
chemotropically
chenopodiaceous
chess tournament
Chesterfieldian
Chian turpentine
chicken-breasted
chicken chasseur
chicken Maryland
chief technician
child of the manse
child psychology
Chinaman's chance
Chinese chequers
Chinese layering
Chinese whispers
chipping sparrow
chloramphenicol
chloroplatinate
chocolate mousse
cholangiography

cholecalciferol
cholecystectomy
cholera infantum
chondrification
choreographical
chorio-allantoic
chorio-allantois
choriocarcinoma
chorioretinitis
Christadelphian
Christian burial
Christmas flower
chromatographer
chromatographic
chronogrammatic
chronographical
chronologically
chuck in the towel
chuck-will's-widow
Church Catechism
Church of England
churchwardenism
churchwardenize
Churrigueresque
cigarette coupon
cigarette-holder
cinematographer
cinematographic
cinemicrography
cinephotography
cineradiography
circuit-training
circularization
circumambulator
circumferential
circumforaneous
circumgestation
circumincession
circumnavigable
circumnavigator
circumscribable
circumscription
circumspectious
circumspectness
circumstantiate
circumvallation
Citizen's Charter
civil government
civilianization
Clapham Junction
classical Arabic
classical ballet
classical guitar
cleansing tissue
clear a thing with
clear conscience
clear-headedness
clear one's throat
clericalization
Clerk of the Irons
Clerk of the Pells
clerk of the works

clingstone peach
close one's eyes to
close one's mind to
clotheslessness
cloud-cuckoo-land
cluster compound
coccolithophore
cocculus indicus
cochineal insect
cockneyfication
cock-of-the-plains
cocktail cabinet
cocktail sausage
co-consciousness
co-determination
codicologically
coequate anomaly
coextensiveness
coffee-table book
coherence theory
co-instantaneous
cold-bloodedness
cold-heartedness
cold obstruction
collaborate with
collaboratively
collared lemming
collared peccary
collateral issue
collective fruit
collector's piece
collegial church
collenchymatous
collision course
colonizationism
colonizationist
colour-blindness
colour constancy
coloured hearing
colouring matter
colour prejudice
combination laws
combination lock
combination oven
combination room
combination tone
combinatorially
combining weight
combustibleness
come back to earth
come down the pike
come down to cases
comedy of manners
come from nowhere
come home to roost
come into contact
come into one's own
come naturally to
come rain or shine
come the raw prawn
come to grips with
come to terms with

come to think of it
comfortableness
comity of nations
command language
commemoratively
commendableness
commentatorship
commercial docks
commercial space
commiseratingly
commiseratively
commissary court
commission agent
commit to writing
commodification
common gallinule
common knowledge
common-law lawyer
common logarithm
common merganser
common of pasture
common of piscary
commonplace book
commonplaceness
common sandpiper
common scrub-fowl
common twayblade
Commonwealth Day
communalization
communicability
communicational
communicatively
communistically
community centre
community charge
community leader
community spirit
community worker
commutativeness
companion-in-arms
companion ladder
company promoter
compartmentally
compassionately
compendiousness
competitiveness
compilation film
complementarily
complementarity
complementation
complex sentence
complicatedness
complimentarily
compliments slip
compositionally
compound machine
comprehendingly
comprehensively
comprehensivize
compressibility
computationally
computerization

computer program
computer science
conceivableness
concentric cable
conceptualistic
Concert of Europe
concert overture
concessionnaire
conchologically
condescendingly
conditional mood
condition-powder
condylarthrosis
confidence level
confidence limit
confidence trick
confidentiality
configurational
conformableness
confraternities
confrontational
congregationist
conical pendulum
conic projection
conjugationally
conjunctionally
conjunctiveness
connectionalism
Connemara marble
connoisseurship
connotative term
conscience money
conscientiously
conscriptionist
consecutiveness
consentaneously
consenting adult
consequentially
conservationist
conservation law
Conservative Jew
conservatorship
considerability
considerateness
consistory court
conspicuousness
constructionism
constructionist
consubstantiate
consumer durable
consumer society
consumptiveness
contemplatively
contemporaneity
contemporaneous
contemptibility
contempt of court
contentiousness
contingency fund
contingency plan
continuation day
contortuplicate

contraband of war
contraceptively
contractibility
contradictively
contradictorily
contrariousness
contrastiveness
contravallation
controllability
controversially
conus arteriosus
conus medullaris
convenience food
Conventicle Acts
conventionalise
conventionalism
conventionalist
conventionality
conventionalize
conversableness
conversationist
convolvulaceous
cool as a cucumber
cooperative farm
cooperativeness
co-precipitation
coracoid process
coral-root orchid
corbie messenger
cordon sanitaire
Corinthian brass
Corinthianesque
corno di bassetto
Corona Australis
coronoid process
corporate raider
corporation sole
correction fluid
correlativeness
correspondently
correspondingly
corroboratively
corrugated paper
corruptibleness
corrupt practice
corynebacterium
cosmic radiation
cosmochemically
cosmopolitanise
cosmopolitanism
cosmopolitanize
Cossack trousers
Costa Geriatrica
cost a person dear
cost-effectively
costermongerdom
costermongering
costoclavicular
cottage hospital
cottage industry
counsellor-at-law
counter-approach

counter-argument
counter-claimant
counter-coloured
countercultural
countercyclical
counter-evidence
counterfeitness
counter-flowered
counter-indicate
counterirritant
countermandable
countermovement
counterpart fund
counterposition
counter-pressure
counter-question
county corporate
Court of Audience
Court of Chancery
Court of Requests
couteau de chasse
Covenant of Grace
Covenant of Works
cover much ground
cover one's tracks
craniologically
crashworthiness
creation science
creature of habit
credit insurance
creeping barrage
creeping thistle
creep to the cross
cribriform plate
crime passionnel
criminalization
crissal thrasher
criteriological
critical damping
cross-connection
cross-culturally
crossing sweeper
crossopterygian
crossword puzzle
crude turpentine
crustaceologist
cry a person mercy
cry from the heart
cry one's heart out
cryoprecipitate
cryptanalytical
crypto-Calvinist
cryptozoologist
crystalliferous
crystalline lens
crystallisation
crystallization
crystallography
cry stinking fish
cry wolf too often
cubic centimetre
cuckoo in the nest

cultivatability
cultivation bank
cultural attaché
Cumberland sauce
cumulative error
curriculum vitae
Curse of Scotland
Cushing's disease
custos rotulorum
cut-and-come-again
cut one's eye-teeth
cutthroat weaver
cutting compound
cylindricalness
cylindro-conical
cytogenetically
cytomegalovirus
cytophotometric
Czechoslovakian
dacryoadenalgia
damp-proof course
dandelion coffee
dandelion greens
Dartford warbler
daughter element
daylight robbery
day of obligation
dead as a doornail
dead man's fingers
deafferentation
de-afforestation
de-Anglicization
Dean of peculiars
Dean of the Arches
decalcification
decarbonization
decarboxylation
decarburization
decartelization
decasualization
decemnovenarian
decertification
decimal fraction
decision problem
declamatoriness
declination axis
decolourization
decommunization
decomposability
decomposibility
deconcentration
deconstructible
decontamination
decontextualise
decontextualize
decrement of life
dedifferentiate
deed of variation
deep X-ray therapy
defencelessness
deferred annuity
deferred payment

deficit spending
definite article
definition in use
degenerationism
degenerationist
deglamorization
degree of freedom
dehydroascorbic
dehydrogenation
deindustrialize
delabialization
deleteriousness
delightsomeness
delignification
delirium tremens
deliver the goods
Della Cruscanism
delta connection
demagnetization
demagnification
dementia praecox
Democratic Party
democratization
demographically
demoiselle crane
demolition derby
demolition Derby
demolition order
demonologically
demonstrability
demonstrational
demonstratively
demutualization
demystification
demythicization
denitrification
dental hygienist
departmentalise
departmentalism
departmentalize
department store
depauperization
dephlogisticate
dephosphorylate
depleted uranium
depressor muscle
deprovincialize
depth psychology
deracialization
dermatoglyphics
dermatographism
dermatomyositis
dermatophytosis
desacralization
descant recorder
descriptiveness
desensitization
desertification
desilverization
dessertspoonful
destabilization
de-Stalinization

destroyer-escort
destroyer leader
destroying angel
destructibility
destructiveness
destructuration
detention centre
determinability
determinateness
determinatively
detribalization
deuteranomalous
developmentally
development area
devil-on-the-coals
devil-worshipper
devitrification
Devonshire cream
dezincification
diagonalization
diaheliotropism
dialectological
dialogistically
diamagnetically
diamondback moth
diamond crossing
diaphonemically
diaphototropism
diastereoisomer
dichotomization
dictatorialness
differentiation
digestive system
dig up the hatchet
diocesan council
Dionysian period
diphenhydramine
diplomatic corps
diplomatic pouch
direction-finder
director-general
disacquaintance
disadvantageous
disafforestment
disagreeability
disappearing act
disappointingly
disarticulation
discernibleness
discerptibility
discommendation
discommodiously
discomposedness
disconcertingly
disconfirmation
disconfirmatory
disconformities
discontinuation
discontinuously
discountenancer
discoverability
discovery method

discretionarily
disenchantingly
disentanglement
disenthronement
disgracefulness
dishabilitation
disharmoniously
dishearteningly
disillusionizer
disillusionment
disimprisonment
disinflationary
disinterestedly
disintoxication
disobligingness
disorderly house
disorganization
dispassionately
displaceability
displaced person
displacement ton
displeasingness
dispositionally
disproportional
disproportioned
disputativeness
disquisitionist
disreputability
disrespectfully
dissatisfaction
dissatisfactory
dissecting knife
dissimilarities
dissipationless
dissociableness
distastefulness
distemperedness
distinctiveness
distinguishable
distinguishably
distinguishedly
distinguishment
distractability
distractibility
distressfulness
distress warrant
distribution map
distributorship
district auditor
district heating
district visitor
distrustfulness
dithyrambically
diversification
dividend warrant
Divisional Court
division lobbied
division lobbies
doctrinarianism
dog's tooth violet
dolichocephalic
dollar diplomacy

domestic science
domestic servant
domestic service
domineeringness
dominical letter
done like a dinner
don't you forget it
doomsday machine
do one's damnedest
do one's heart good
do one's level best
do the other thing
double-barrelled
double-facedness
double indemnity
double or nothing
double pneumonia
double precision
Dow–Jones average
downheartedness
down to the ground
downy woodpecker
Doyenne du Comice
Dragon variation
drain to the dregs
dramatistically
dramaturgically
draught-excluder
draughtsmanship
draw in one's horns
drawn-thread-work
drawn-threadwork
draw the curtains
dream-vision poem
dressing forceps
dressing station
drinking problem
drogue parachute
droit de seigneur
droit du seigneur
drop one's aitches
drugstore cowboy
drunk as a fiddler
dry distillation
dual carriageway
dual personality
duchess potatoes
dumping syndrome
duple proportion
duplicate bridge
duplicitousness
durchkomponiert
Durham shorthorn
dusky cranesbill
Dutch elm disease
dynamic friction
dynamic pressure
dysfunctionally
dyslogistically
dysteleological
early retirement
earnings-related

earth connection
earthly paradise
earth-shattering
Easter-offerings
eat a person's salt
eat one's heart out
eat the wind out of
ecclesiasticism
ecclesiasticize
ecclesiological
echocardiograph
éclaircissement
eclipse of the sun
eclipsing binary
econometrically
economic geology
economic history
economic warfare
ectoplasmically
efficaciousness
efficiency audit
egg-and-spoon race
Egyptianization
Egyptian vulture
eighteen-pounder
ejaculatory duct
elastic stocking
election address
electrical storm
electric battery
electric blanket
electric circuit
electrification
electro-acoustic
electro-analysis
electrochemical
electrochromism
electrodialysis
electrodynamics
electrofocusing
electrogenicity
electrolysation
electromagnetic
electrometrical
electromyograph
electronegative
electronic flash
electronography
electrophoresis
electrophoretic
electroporation
electropositive
electroreceptor
electrostatical
electrosurgical
electrotechnics
Eleonora's falcon
eleutheromaniac
elevated railway
emancipationist
embarras de choix
embryologically

emotionlessness
empirio-critical
emulsifiability
enantiomorphism
enantiomorphous
encephalisation
encephalization
encephalography
encephalopathic
enchondromatous
encomiastically
endoatmospheric
endocrinologist
endonucleolytic
enforceableness
enfranchisement
Engelmann spruce
engineer's yeoman
English basement
English Canadian
English sickness
enlarge an estate
enlarge the heart
enlightenedness
entente cordiale
Entente Cordiale
enterohepatitis
enterotoxigenic
entomologically
entrench oneself
entrepreneurial
entrepreneurism
environmentally
epidemic cholera
epidemiological
epifluorescence
epipalaeolithic
epiploic foramen
Episcopal Church
episcopalianism
epistemological
epistolographic
epitheliomatous
equalitarianism
equation of state
equatorial mount
equatorial plate
equidimensional
equinoctial line
equinoctial year
equiponderation
equiprobability
equity draftsman
Erlenmeyer flask
erythromelalgia
escalator clause
escape committee
eternal triangle
etherealization
ethidium bromide
ethnic cleansing
ethnocentricism

ethnocentricity
ethnolinguistic
ethnomusicology
ethylenediamine
etymologization
Eucharistically
eudiometrically
euphemistically
Europeanization
evaporating dish
evening grosbeak
evening primrose
everlasting life
everlastingness
every now and then
exasperatedness
exceptionalness
exchangeability
exchange control
exclamation mark
exclamatoriness
exclusion clause
excommunication
excommunicative
excommunicatory
excrementitious
execute an estate
exemplification
exemplificative
exercise bicycle
exhaust manifold
exhibitionistic
exoerythrocytic
exonerate nature
expanded plastic
expanding bullet
expansion engine
expeditiousness
experientialism
experientialist
experimentalise
experimentalism
experimentalist
experimentalize
experimentation
experimentative
explanatoriness
exploded diagram
exponential time
expostulatively
express delivery
expressionistic
extemporariness
extemporization
extension course
extension ladder
exteriorization
externalization
exterritorially
extracellularly
extra-curricular
extracurricular

extrajudicially
extralinguistic
extraordinarily
extraprovincial
extrapunitively
extravascularly
extrinsic factor
extrinsic muscle
eyebrow tweezers
facts and figures
falling sickness
fall into one's lap
fall on hard times
fall on one's sword
fall over oneself
fall to one's share
fall to the ground
false conception
familiarization
family allowance
famous last words
fantasticalness
fantasy football
Faraday constant
fashionableness
Father Christmas
Father of History
feast of trumpets
feast one's eyes on
feathered friend
feather hyacinth
featherlessness
feather one's nest
feather-top grass
featurelessness
federal district
federal land-bank
feel in one's bones
feel oneself into
feel the weight of
fellow Christian
fellow-traveller
feminine caesura
fenestra rotunda
Fermi statistics
ferruginous duck
Fertile Crescent
feuilletonistic
Fibonacci number
Fibonacci series
fiddle-patterned
fideicommissary
fifth-generation
fight like billy-o
financial wizard
find in one's heart
finishing school
finishing stroke
fire certificate
fire in one's belly
first concoction
first derivative

first-generation
first intentions
first lieutenant
fisherman's story
fissiparousness
fissure eruption
fits of the mother
fix a person's fate
flash photolysis
flathead catfish
flavourlessness
flex one's muscles
flibbertigibbet
flight attendant
fling to the winds
flirtatiousness
floriferousness
flowering cherry
flowering willow
flower of the hour
fluorescent bulb
fluorescent lamp
fluoridationist
fly at higher game
flying phalanger
Flying Scotchman
fly off the handle
folding strength
folie de grandeur
folk-etymologize
follow the hounds
follow-the-leader
follow the plough
follow the string
fool's watercress
football stadium
foot-pound-second
forage-harvester
for all it is worth
forbidden ground
force the bidding
fore-appointment
foreground music
foreign exchange
foreign minister
Foreign Minister
forensic science
foresightedness
forget-me-not blue
for goodness' sake
forked lightning
form a government
formal education
formalinization
formation flying
formularization
for old sake's sake
for old times' sake
for one's name sake
for one's occasion
forthcomingness
for the first time

for the time being
Fortin barometer
forwarding agent
Foucault current
foul-mouthedness
foundation cream
foundation stone
four-dimensional
Fourier analysis
four-rowed barley
fourth dimension
fractionization
fragmentariness
fragmentization
Frankensteinian
franking machine
franklinization
Fraunhofer lines
free association
freedom of speech
Free Will Baptist
freezing-mixture
French artichoke
Frenchification
French partridge
friction welding
Friendly Society
frigate mackerel
frog in the throat
from first to last
from hand to mouth
from the ground up
from thenceforth
from the shoulder
from top to bottom
front-end loading
front-line states
front-wheel drive
frost shattering
führer principle
full-bloodedness
full-dress debate
full-heartedness
fulminating gold
functional group
functionalistic
fundamental bass
fundamental note
fundamental tone
funeral director
funeral expenses
fungistatically
funnel-web spider
furniture beetle
furniture polish
furor academicus
fused participle
futilitarianism
gaiety of nations
gain one's colours
Gainsborough hat
galactic equator

galvanic battery
gammon and patter
gasteromycetous
gastro-enteritis
gastroenteritis
gastronomically
gathering ground
Gaucher's disease
gauge invariance
gaze at one's navel
gelatin dynamite
General American
General Assembly
general delivery
general election
general hospital
general practice
gentleman-at-arms
gentleman farmer
gentleman friend
gentlemanliness
gentlewomanhood
gentlewomanlike
geochronologist
geochronometric
geomagnetically
geomorphologist
German cockroach
German cotillion
germinal vesicle
gesticulatingly
get a person's goat
get into one's head
get off the ground
get one's dander up
get one's head down
get one's rocks off
get one's skates on
get on with the job
get out from under
get out of the road
get the hell out of
get the measure of
get the worst of it
get-togetherness
get to windward of
get up to mischief
Gigantopithecus
gingerbread-palm
gingerbread-plum
gingerbread tree
give a person a fit
give a person best
give a person fits
give a person hell
give a person rats
give a person time
give it some welly
give it to a person
give my service to
give oneself airs
give oneself up to

give one's heart to
give one's regrets
give the finger to
give the game away
give the show away
glacio-eustatism
glass of antimony
glass-rope sponge
Gleichschaltung
globigerina ooze
globular cluster
Glorious Twelfth
glosso-laryngeal
gluconeogenesis
gluconeogenetic
gnathochilarium
gnathostomatous
Gobelin tapestry
God bless the mark
go down in history
go for the big spit
go for the jugular
gold-beater's skin
gold certificate
golden delicious
Golden Delicious
golden handcuffs
golden handshake
golden parachute
golden retriever
golden saxifrage
gonfaloniership
go off the deep end
go one better than
go out of one's head
gossip columnist
go to one's account
go to the scaffold
Götterdämmerung
go under the knife
government house
Government House
government issue
government paper
Government paper
governor-general
Governor-General
go without saying
go with the stream
graceless florin
graduated filter
grammaticalness
gramophonically
grandfatherhood
grandfatherless
grand horizontal
grandiloquently
Grand Inquisitor
grandmastership
grandmotherhood
grandmotherless
Grand Pensionary

granger railroad
granite-porphyry
grant-maintained
graphologically
gravimetrically
gravitationally
grease the fat pig
grease the fat sow
grease the palm of
grease the wheels
Greater Doxology
great-grandchild
great vowel shift
great white chief
great white egret
great white heron
great white shark
greenery-yallery
green revolution
green woodpecker
grenade-launcher
Grenadier Guards
greyhound-racing
Grignard reagent
grind the faces of
grist for the mill
groom of the stole
groom of the stool
groves of Academe
growth regulator
grumble and grunt
Guards battalion
guest appearance
gunner's daughter
gynaecocratical
gynandromorphic
Habeas Corpus Act
hackney carriage
hackney-chairman
hackney-coachman
haemagglutinate
haemoglobinuria
hairy in the heels
hairy woodpecker
half as much again
half-heartedness
hall of residence
hallucinatorily
hammer and sickle
hammerhead shark
Hamming distance
hand in one's chips
hand it to a person
hanging wardrobe
hang up one's boots
Hanseatic League
happy as a sandboy
hard-heartedness
hare and tortoise
hare's-foot clover
hark who's talking
harlequin beetle

harlequin smiler
harmonistically
harp on one string
Harrogate toffee
harum-scarumness
harvest festival
has no business to
hatched moulding
Haussmanization
have a bone to pick
have a good mind to
have a good stroke
have a person's ear
have a screw loose
have a slate loose
have a thing about
have a way with one
have been known to
have by the throat
have had enough of
have lost sight of
have money to burn
have no truck with
have one's heart in
have one's mansion
have one's moments
have one's way with
have the best of it
have the breeze up
have the dingbats
have the last word
have two left feet
have what it takes
hawksbill turtle
Hawthorne effect
health insurance
hearsay evidence
heartbreakingly
heating engineer
heaven of heavens
heavy-handedness
heir presumptive
heliacal setting
heliocentricism
heliometrically
heliotropically
Hellenistically
helminthologist
hemicryptophyte
hemicylindrical
hemispherectomy
hemispherically
hendecasyllabic
hendecasyllable
herb Christopher
Herculean labour
Hercules' Pillars
Hercynian Forest
heritage highway
hermaphroditism
hermeneutically
herring-bone gear

hesitation waltz
heterochromatic
heterochromatin
heterogeneously
heteromorphosis
heteroscedastic
heterosexuality
heterotopically
heuristic method
hexachloraphane
hexylresorcinol
hierogrammatist
higher criticism
higher education
Highland terrier
highly commended
high-muckety-muck
Himalayan balsam
Hippocratic oath
Hispanicization
histochemically
histocompatible
histopathologic
historic present
historiographer
historiographic
hit below the belt
Hitler moustache
hit the headlines
hit the high spots
hit the right note
hobbledehoyhood
Hodgkin's disease
Hofmann reaction
hold by the sleeve
hold one's service
hold one's whistle
holocrystalline
holographically
holosymmetrical
Holy Ghost flower
Holy Roman Empire
Homeric laughter
Homeric question
homochlamydeous
homogeneousness
homomorphically
honey locust tree
honeymoon couple
hooded merganser
hope against hope
horned syllogism
Horner's syndrome
hornet clearwing
horse and hattock
horseback-riding
horse-mastership
horseradish tree
horseshoe magnet
horticulturally
hospital corners
hospitality room

hospitalization
hot on the heels of
Hottentot cherry
Hottentot's bread
householdership
household troops
housemastership
housewifeliness
how the wind blows
how the world wags
Hubble's constant
hudibrastically
Hudsonian curlew
Hudsonian godwit
humanitarianism
Hungarian millet
Hungarian turnip
hurdy-gurdy house
Hurler's syndrome
hyaloid membrane
hybrid perpetual
hydraulic cement
hydraulic mining
hydrobiological
hydrobromic acid
hydrocyanic acid
hydrodynamician
hydrodynamicist
hydroelectrical
hydro-extraction
hydrogen cyanide
hydrogeological
hydromechanical
hydrometallurgy
hydrophobically
hydrops foetalis
hydrostatically
hydrosulphurous
hydrotropically
hydroxylapatite
hygrometrically
hygroscopically
hypercatalectic
hyperchromicity
hypercoagulable
hyperconjugated
hypercorrection
hypercritically
hyperdisyllable
hyperextensible
hyperfunctional
hyperinsulinism
hyperlipidaemia
hyperlipidaemic
hypermetabolism
hyperosmolality
hyperosmolarity
hyperparasitism
hyperphysically
hyperrhythmical
hypersomnolence
hyperspatiality

hyperthyroidism
hypnotizability
hypocellularity
hypochlorhydria
hypochlorhydric
hypochondriacal
hypochondriasis
hypochromatosis
hypocrateriform
hypomagnesaemia
hypomagnesaemic
hypoparathyroid
hypophosphorous
hypopituitarism
hypostasization
hypostatic union
hypostatization
hypothetication
hypoventilation
hypovitaminosis
hypsometrically
hysteresis curve
hysterica passio
hysteric passion
hystero-epilepsy
hystricomorphic
I am not concerned
iatromechanical
ice-cream parlour
ichthyodorulite
iconometrically
identifiability
identity element
ideographically
idiomorphically
idiosyncratical
idioventricular
idols of the tribe
if it comes to that
ignominiousness
ill-favouredness
illimitableness
illustriousness
image processing
imaginativeness
immatriculation
immeasurability
immedicableness
immersion heater
immoral earnings
immortalization
immortification
immunochemistry
immunocompetent
immunodeficient
immunodepressed
immunodiffusion
immunologically
impassionedness
impecuniousness
impenetrability
imperative logic

Imperial Majesty
imperial mammoth
imperial quarter
imperishability
imperscriptible
impertinentness
implicationally
implicativeness
imponderability
importunateness
impossibilitate
impossibilities
impracticalness
impredicability
impregnableness
imprescriptible
impressionistic
improgressively
improvidentness
improvisational
improvisatorial
inacceptability
inaccessibility
inadmissibility
in a great measure
in a large measure
in all conscience
in all likelihood
inamissibleness
inanimate nature
in a person's hands
in a person's mouth
in a person's place
in a person's stead
in a person's steps
in a person's train
inapplicability
inapprehensible
inappropriately
inattentiveness
Inauguration Day
inauthoritative
in black and white
incalculability
incidental music
incoagulability
incognizability
incommensurable
incommensurably
incommunicating
incommunicative
incommutability
incomparability
incompatibility
incomprehending
incomprehension
incomprehensive
incongruousness
inconnectedness
inconsecutively
inconsequential
inconsiderately

inconsideration
inconsistencies
inconsolability
inconspicuously
in contemplation
incorrigibility
increasableness
incredulousness
in debt to someone
indecent assault
indeed and indeed
indefeasibility
indefectibility
indefensibility
indefinableness
indemnification
indentation test
Independence Day
indeterminately
indetermination
indeterministic
Indian liquorice
Indian rope-trick
indifference map
indigestibility
indirect address
indirect passive
indisciplinable
indisputability
indissolubilist
indissolubility
indistinctively
indistinguished
indistributable
individualistic
individualities
indivisibleness
Indo-Europeanist
indomitableness
indubitableness
induced reaction
industriousness
ineffaceability
ineffectiveness
ineffectualness
inefficaciously
inexcusableness
inexpensiveness
inexplicability
inextensibility
inextricability
infanticipation
infantilization
infant mortality
infernal machine
infinite regress
infinitesimally
in fits and starts
inflammableness
informal patient
informationally
information room

informativeness
infrastructural
infundibuliform
infusorial earth
ingeminate peace
inheritableness
inhomogeneously
inhospitability
injudiciousness
in mint condition
in monosyllables
in no condition to
in no shape or form
innumerableness
inoffensiveness
in one's hip pocket
in one's own person
in one's right mind
inoperativeness
inopportuneness
in pride of grease
in prime of grease
in process of time
in quadruplicate
inquest of office
in quintuplicate
inquisitiveness
inquisitorially
in recompense for
in remembrance of
inscriptionless
inscrutableness
insensitiveness
inseparableness
in seventh heaven
insignificantly
insinuatingness
insinuativeness
inspection cover
inspirationally
instantaneously
institutionally
instructiveness
instrumentalism
instrumentalist
instrumentality
instrumentation
instrument board
instrument panel
insubordinately
insubordination
insubstantially
insurance broker
insurance policy
insurrectionary
insurrectionist
intellectualise
intellectualism
intellectualist
intellectuality
intellectualize
intelligibility

intemperateness
intensification
intention tremor
interactionally
intercellularly
intercessionary
interchangeable
interchangeably
interclavicular
intercollegiate
intercolumniary
intercomparison
interconnection
interconversion
interdependence
interdependency
interdigitation
interdiscipline
interestingness
interfascicular
interference fit
interferingness
interferometric
interfoliaceous
interglaciation
interim dividend
interindividual
interiorization
interjectionary
interlaboratory
interlacustrine
interlamination
interlinguistic
interminability
interminglement
intermodulation
internalization
internal revenue
internationally
interosculation
interparietally
interpersonally
interphalangeal
interpolability
interpolymerize
interpretership
interprovincial
interrogatingly
interrogational
interrogatively
interrogatories
interscholastic
intersentential
intersubjective
intertanglement
intertextuality
intertransverse
intertubercular
inter-university
interventionism
interventionist
intestinal flora

in the altogether
in the business of
in the first place
in the interest of
in the last resort
in the melting-pot
in the nick of time
in the presence of
in there pitching
in the same breath
in the vicinage of
in the vicinity of
in the wilderness
in this day and age
in time of drought
intolerableness
intonation curve
into the Ewigkeit
intracellularly
intracerebrally
intractableness
intraculturally
intra-epithelial
intrafascicular
intrafoliaceous
intra-linguistic
intramembranous
intramuscularly
intransigentism
intraperitoneal
intra-subjective
intravascularly
intrinsicalness
intrinsic factor
introjectionism
introjectionist
introspectively
introsusception
intrusive growth
intussusception
intussuscipiens
inverse spelling
investigational
investigatorial
investment trust
invisible export
invisible import
invisible mender
involuntariness
invulnerability
ion implantation
ionization gauge
ionospherically
ipecacuanha wine
Irish Australian
Irish blackguard
Irish martingale
Irish Sweepstake
irrationability
irrationalistic
irreconcilement
irreconcilable

irreconciliably
irredeemability
irreducibleness
irreductibility
irreflexiveness
irreformability
irrefragability
irreligiousness
irremovableness
irreparableness
irrepealability
irreprehensible
irrepresentable
irresistability
irresistibility
irretentiveness
irreverentially
irreversibility
irrevocableness
irrigation canal
irrotationality
I shouldn't wonder
island continent
is no oil painting
isoagglutinogen
isoelectrically
isoimmunization
isoperimetrical
isophane insulin
isotope dilution
isotransplanted
Italian quilting
Italian vermouth
it's a free country
jackass schooner
Jack in the basket
Jack-in-the-pulpit
jack of all trades
Jack of all trades
Jack of both sides
jagged chickweed
Japanese anemone
Japanese current
Japanese lacquer
Japanese lantern
Japanese macaque
Japanese spaniel
Japanese waltzer
japanned leather
jeepers creepers
Jeffersonianism
Jehovah's Witness
Jersey lightning
Jerusalem cherry
jewel in the crown
John-Bullishness
Johnny Head-in-Air
joint and several
join the banner of
join the majority
Jonathanization
journeyman clock

judge and warrant
judgement debtor
judicial torture
judiciary combat
jumping-off place
jumping-off point
junction railway
junior barrister
Jupiter's distaff
jurisprudential
justifiableness
juvenile hormone
juxtaglomerular
juxtapositional
kangaroo closure
kangaroo justice
katathermometer
keep a low profile
keep an eye peeled
keep company with
keep friends with
keep off the grass
keep one's balance
keep one's counsel
keep one's pants on
keep one's shirt on
keep one's station
Kentucky warbler
Kepler's equation
keratoacanthoma
kick a person's ass
kick the tar out of
kick up one's heels
killer submarine
kilogram calorie
kind-heartedness
King of the Castle
King of the Romans
king's bad bargain
King's quarantain
Kirghiz pheasant
kiss the pope's toe
kiss the Pope's toe
kitchen-gardener
kleptoparasitic
knickerbockered
knick-knackatory
knight commander
Knight of the Bath
knight of the post
knight of the road
knights bachelor
Knights Templars
knitting machine
knock all of a heap
know a thing or two
know from nothing
know-nothingness
know one's own mind
know where to find
knuckle sandwich
Koch's postulates

kymographically
labourer-in-trust
labour-intensive
labour relations
Labrador current
labradorescence
lachryma Christi
lackadaisically
lactoperoxidase
lacto-vegetarian
ladder-back chair
ladies' cloakroom
ladies-in-waiting
Lagrangian point
laissez-faireism
laissez-faireist
Lakeland terrier
lance bombardier
landed immigrant
land-measurement
landscape-marble
language loyalty
Laplace equation
Laplace operator
Lapland longspur
lapsang souchong
larch needle-cast
lares and penates
Larmor frequency
laryngotracheal
last but not least
latensification
latent ambiguity
lateral thinking
Latter-day Saints
lattice constant
laughing jackass
laugh like a drain
laugh out of court
Law Commissioner
law of continuity
law of mass action
law of succession
lay down one's arms
lay one's finger on
Laysan albatross
lay up in lavender
lazy daisy stitch
leading question
lead up the garden
League of Nations
learning machine
learn one's lesson
learn the hard way
least flycatcher
leather breeches
Leather-Stocking
leave in the lurch
ledger-millstone
legalitarianism
legal separation
leg before wicket

legislatorially
leg-of-mutton sail
Leninist–Marxist
lenticular cloud
lenticular gland
leopard-tortoise
lepidopterology
leptomeningitis
let a person blood
let daylight into
lethargicalness
let it all hang out
let one's hair down
letter of comfort
Letters of Orders
leukaemogenesis
level-headedness
leveraged buyout
lever escapement
Lewis machine-gun
lexicographical
lexicologically
lexicostatistic
lexigraphically
Liberal Democrat
Liberal Unionist
lichenification
lichen substance
lick the trencher
Liebig condenser
lie in one's throat
lie like a trooper
lie on the stomach
lie upon the wager
life-everlasting
life-threatening
lift coefficient
lift up one's hands
lift up one's voice
light-handedness
light-headedness
light microscope
light-mindedness
lightning beetle
lightning strike
light of one's life
light-scattering
lignocellulosic
lignosulphonate
like a dog's dinner
like a drowned rat
like a scalded cat
likelihood ratio
like the clappers
like thirty cents
lily of the valley
Lincoln Longwool
Lincolnshire Red
line-integration
line of flotation
line of scrimmage
linguistic atlas

linseed poultice
liquid petroleum
literary adviser
literary history
lithochromatics
lithonephrotomy
little chief hare
Little Englander
little girls' room
little or nothing
liturgiological
live dangerously
live one's own life
live over the shop
live with oneself
living daylights
living newspaper
loan translation
loaves and fishes
local government
local oscillator
Loch Ness monster
loco-descriptive
locomotor ataxia
lodger-franchise
logarithmically
logarithmic sine
logical addition
logographically
London shrinking
Longer Catechism
long-persistence
long-sightedness
long-sufferingly
longsufferingly
look the other way
look who's talking
lophobranchiate
Lord bless my soul
Lord Chamberlain
Lord High Admiral
lord-lieutenancy
lord proprietary
Lords Appellants
lords of creation
lose countenance
lose one's balance
lose one's heart to
lose the exchange
loudness control
loves' young dream
love's young dream
Lower California
lower one's sights
lower yield point
low-spiritedness
loxodromic curve
lues Boswelliana
Lulworth skipper
lumbrical muscle
luminosity curve
lump in the throat

luncheon voucher
lunisolar period
lute harpsichord
lymphadenectomy
lymphadenopathy
lymphatic system
lymphocytotoxic
lymphocytotoxin
lymphoedematous
lymphogranuloma
lymphoreticular
lyotropic series
McNaughten rules
machiavellianly
machine language
machine-readable
machine-washable
macrocosmically
macrolinguistic
macrophotograph
macroscopically
macrostructural
magazine section
Magellanic cloud
Magellanic Cloud
magistratically
magnanimousness
magnetic anomaly
magnetic compass
magnetic equator
magnetic termite
magnetizability
magnetochemical
magneto-electric
magnetotelluric
magnifying glass
main half-breadth
maintainability
maintenance dose
Maintenon cutlet
maison de couture
majoritarianism
majority carrier
majority verdict
make a beeline for
make a clean job of
make a conquest of
make a difference
make a difficulty
make a good fist at
make an example of
make an excursion
make a person's day
make a person sick
make a poor fist at
make a practice of
make a religion of
make a stranger of
make a thing about
make friends with
make life easy for
make light work of

make matchwood of
make mincemeat of
make one's manners
make out a case for
make shipwreck of
make short work of
make something of
make the best of it
make the money fly
malacopterygian
malaria parasite
malassimilation
malconformation
malconstruction
maldistribution
malice prepensed
malorganization
Malpighian layer
malpresentation
managed currency
Manchester goods
Manchester wares
Manchurian crane
Manchurian tiger
manganese bronze
manganese nodule
manganese-purple
manganese violet
mangel-wurzel fly
mangrove snapper
manic depression
manic-depressive
manifestational
manifestatively
manifest destiny
manneristically
manoeuvrability
manorialization
manslaughterous
manuscript paper
many a time and oft
maremma sheepdog
Marfan's syndrome
margaritiferous
marginalization
marine biologist
mariner's compass
mariner's portage
marine scientist
market potential
market socialism
marriageability
marriage licence
marriage payment
marriage portion
marshalling yard
marsh arrow-grass
marsh fritillary
martensitically
marvellous apple
Marxism-Leninism
Marxist-Leninism

Marxist-Leninist
Maryland chicken
masculinization
masochistically
mass observation
mass radiography
master-craftsman
master of beagles
Master of Misrule
Master of Science
material control
material culture
materialization
material science
mathematization
Matres Dolorosae
matriculability
matrix mechanics
mauvais coucheur
Maxwell equation
McNaughten rules
meadow buttercup
meadow soft-grass
meaninglessness
measurelessness
meat and potatoes
mechanical power
mechanistically
mechanochemical
mechano-electric
mechanomorphism
mechanoreceptor
medial malleolus
medical examiner
medical register
medieval history
medium frequency
medullary sheath
medulloblastoma
meet a person's eye
megachiropteran
megagametophyte
megalocephalous
megamillionaire
Meissner's plexus
melancholically
melissyl alcohol
mellifluousness
memorialization
memoria technica
mend one's manners
meningomyelitis
mental breakdown
mental defective
mentalistically
Mephistophelean
Mephistophelian
merchantability
merchant banking
merchant of death
merchant service
merchant stapler

mercurification
meritoriousness
merosymmetrical
merveille du jour
mesmerizability
messenger-at-arms
metagenetically
metageometrical
metal arc welding
metalinguistics
metallic circuit
metallothionein
metallurgically
metamathematics
metamictization
metaphysicality
metasomatically
metasyncritical
metempsychosist
methamphetamine
Methodistically
methods engineer
methylcellulose
methylphenidate
metropolitanate
metropolitanism
metropolitanize
Mexican-American
Mexican fruit fly
Mexican shilling
Mexican stand-off
mezzotint rocker
Michaelmas daisy
Michelson–Morley
microaerophilic
microanalytical
microangiopathy
microbiological
microcosmically
microcosmic salt
micro-electronic
microelectronic
microfilm reader
microfloppy disk
microfracturing
microgametocyte
microlinguistic
micromanipulate
micrometeoritic
micrometrically
micromillimetre
microphotograph
microphotometer
microphotometry
microprogrammer
microprojection
microradiograph
microscope slide
microscopically
microsporangium
microstructural
microtopography

microtrabecular
middle-age spread
middle-classness
middle-of-the-road
migratory locust
military academy
military attaché
military college
military honours
military service
military tribune
military two-step
millionaireship
Millionaires' Row
Minamata disease
mind one's P's and Q's
mineral charcoal
mineral dressing
mineralogically
mineralographic
miniature camera
miniaturization
minimal free form
minimum free form
minister general
Minister of State
minister premier
minority carrier
miogeosynclinal
miraculous berry
miraculous fruit
misappreciation
misapprehension
misapprehensive
misarticulation
misbecomingness
miscellaneously
mischaracterize
mischievousness
misconstruction
misdistribution
misintelligence
misproportioned
misrecollection
misregistration
mistletoe cactus
mist propagation
mistrustfulness
misunderstander
misvocalization
mite-borne typhus
mitochondrially
mixotrophically
mobile sculpture
mobile telephone
mock-nightingale
modernistically
modern languages
modulation index
moisten one's clay
moisture content
Moldo-Wallachian

molecular weight
molly cotton-tail
Molotov cocktail
molybdophyllite
moment of inertia
monadologically
monarcho-fascist
Monday fortnight
money for old rope
Mongolian hotpot
monkey orchestra
monkeywrenching
monochlamydeous
monochlorinated
monoconsonantal
monocrystalline
monodimensional
monographically
mono-substituted
monosyllabicity
monosymmetrical
monosymptomatic
mono-unsaturated
monounsaturated
Montagu's harrier
Monterey cypress
Montessorianism
month after month
montmorillonite
montmorillonoid
monumental mason
Moog synthesizer
moonlight lustre
mop the floor with
moral philosophy
moral psychology
Moral Rearmament
Moral Re-Armament
morning sickness
morphogenetical
morphographemic
morphographical
morphologically
morphophonemics
morphophonology
morphosyntactic
morphotectonics
Morrison shelter
mortise and tenon
mosquito-curtain
mosquito-netting
Mothering Sunday
mother of vinegar
motorway madness
mountain chicken
mountain-climber
mountain-folding
mountain gazelle
mountain gorilla
mountain hemlock
mountainousness
mountain panther

mountain railway
mountain ringlet
mounted infantry
mourning warbler
mousetrap cheese
mousseline glass
mousseline sauce
moustache-lifter
moustache monkey
moving staircase
much of a muchness
Muggletonianism
multi-articulate
multiculturally
multifunctional
multilateralism
multilateralist
multilateralize
multilingualism
multinationally
multi-occupation
multiple factors
multiple fission
multiprocessing
multiprogrammed
multitudinosity
multitudinously
murmur diphthong
muscovitization
muscular feeling
muscular stomach
musculoskeletal
musée imaginaire
musical director
musicologically
music to one's ears
musique concrète
mustard and cress
mustard-coloured
mutatis mutandis
mutton-leg sleeve
mutual induction
mutual insurance
mutualistically
myeloperoxidase
myenteric reflex
my learned friend
myoelectrically
myrmekitization
my sainted mother
mystery-religion
mythologization
naked as a jay-bird
nannoplanktonic
naphthalization
national holiday
nationalization
national product
National Lottery
National Savings
national service
national theatre

native companion
native cranberry
natural-coloured
natural language
natural religion
natural shoulder
natural theology
nature sanctuary
naughty nineties
nautical almanac
navigation light
near-sightedness
near ultraviolet
neat but not gaudy
necessitousness
necrobacillosis
necromantically
needle-and-thread
Néel temperature
Negro-Portuguese
neighbourliness
neoarsphenamine
Neo-Confucianism
neontologically
nephelinization
nephrolithiasis
nephrolithotomy
nephrosclerosis
neritic province
Nessler's reagent
nether millstone
network analyser
network analysis
network modifier
neurenteric cyst
neuroanatomical
neurobiological
neurodermatitis
neurodermatosis
neuroepithelial
neuroepithelium
neurohypophysis
neurolinguistic
neuropathologic
neurophysiology
neuropsychiatry
neuropsychology
neurosyphilitic
New Age traveller
New Commonwealth
New England aster
Newfoundland dog
New Frontiersman
Newgate Calendar
Newgate hornpipe
Newgate novelist
New Red Sandstone
New Zealand robin
nickel-in-the-slot
Nigerianization
Nightingale ward
night starvation

nineteen-pounder
nitrogen dioxide
nitrogen mustard
noble-mindedness
nobody's business
nomenclaturally
nomographically
non-attributable
non-attributably
non-availability
non-belligerence
non-belligerency
non-commissioned
non-committalism
non compos mentis
non-confidential
non-contagionist
non-contributory
nondescriptness
none the worse for
non-governmental
non-intelligence
non-interference
non-intervention
non-intoxicating
non-naturalistic
non-partisanship
non-prescription
non-productively
non-professional
non-profit-making
non-residentiary
nonsensicalness
non-significance
non-transferable
Norfolk dumpling
Norroy and Ulster
north-countryman
North countryman
north-countrymen
north-eastwardly
northern sea lion
north-westwardly
not anywhere near
not a proposition
not breathe a word
not care twopence
nothingarianism
nothing less than
not know from Adam
not much to look at
not once nor twice
not spare oneself
not the word for it
not unadjacent to
notwithstanding
not worth a button
nouvelle cuisine
now you're talking
nuclear emulsion
nuclear magneton
nuclear medicine

nuclear umbrella
nucleophilicity
nucleoprotamine
nucleosynthesis
nucleosynthetic
number crunching
numbered account
numerologically
numismatologist
Nuremberg trials
Nuremburg trials
nursery language
nystagmographic
obedientialness
objectification
objectivization
observationally
observation post
observation ward
obsidional crown
obstetrical toad
obstructiveness
obturator muscle
occasional cause
occasionalistic
occasional table
occidental topaz
occipitofrontal
occupation layer
oceanic province
oceanographical
ocellated turkey
ochlocratically
octocentenaries
octogenarianism
ocular dominance
odontoid process
odoriferousness
odour of sanctity
oestrogenically
official secrets
officina gentium
of foreign growth
of no consequence
of one's own accord
of one's own motion
of the first order
of the first water
of the same leaven
of understanding
oil a person's hand
oil of turpentine
old age pensioner
Old Commonwealth
Old Red Sandstone
old-womanishness
oligarchization
oligodendrocyte
oligodendroglia
oligohydramnios
oligomenorrhoea
oligomerization

oligonucleotide
oligosaccharide
omelette soufflé
omnidirectional
omnifariousness
on active service
on a person's track
once in a blue moon
on condition that
one-and-thirtieth
oneirocriticism
one over the eight
one's cake is dough
one's fingers itch
one's heart bleeds
one's heart breaks
one's mouth waters
one way or another
onomasiological
on one's high horse
on one's Jack Jones
on one's own ground
on speaking terms
on the back burner
on the foundation
on the ragged edge
on the right track
on the strength of
on the water wagon
on the wrong track
ontogenetically
on top of the world
onychogryphosis
open-heartedness
open one's heart to
operating profit
operating system
ophthalmologist
ophthalmometric
ophthalmoplegia
ophthalmoplegic
ophthalmoscopic
opinionatedness
opisthoglyphous
opisthognathous
opportunity cost
opprobriousness
optical activity
optical illusion
optically active
optical rotation
optic commissure
optimal foraging
optoelectronics
optokinetically
orange underwing
orange upperwing
orchestra stalls
orderly corporal
orderly sergeant
orders are orders
organizationist

organization man
organized labour
organogenically
organ-pipe cactus
orientalization
orientationally
original pravity
ornaments rubric
ornithorhynchus
orohydrographic
orthochromatize
orthodiagraphic
orthodontically
orthodromically
orthometrically
orthopaedically
orthopercussion
orthophosphoric
orthopsychiatry
orthostatically
Osgood–Schlatter
osmium tetroxide
osmotic pressure
osteochondritis
osteodystrophia
osteodystrophic
osteopathically
ostreoculturist
otolaryngologic
our first parents
Our Lady's psalter
outdoor pursuits
out of all measure
out of commission
out of one's senses
out of one's sphere
out of proportion
out of the picture
out of the running
out-of-the-wayness
outside interest
outsiderishness
ovarian follicle
overachievement
overambitiously
over and done with
overbearingness
overcarefulness
overcentralized
overconfidently
overcrowdedness
overcuriousness
overdevelopment
overearnestness
over-elaborately
overelaborately
over-elaboration
overelaboration
over-emotionally
overfamiliarity
overflowingness
overflow meeting

overforwardness
over head and ears
overmasteringly
overseas Chinese
oversensitivity
overstep the mark
overstimulation
oversusceptible
overventilation
overweeningness
Oxford marmalade
oxidation number
oxytetracycline
oyer and terminer
pacific blockade
packet switching
packing fraction
padder capacitor
padder condenser
Paddy's hurricane
painstakingness
painted terrapin
painted top-shell
painted tortoise
paint the town red
paired-associate
pair of compasses
pair of virginals
palaeencephalon
palaeoanthropic
palaeobiologist
palaeobotanical
palaeochemistry
palaeoecologist
palaeoethnology
palaeogeography
palaeogeologist
palaeographical
palaeohydrology
palaeointensity
palaeolimnology
palaeomagnetism
palaeomagnetist
palaeoneurology
palaeontography
palaeontologist
palaeopathology
palaeophytology
palaeostructure
palaeozoologist
palatine earldom
palato-maxillary
pale crêpe rubber
palynologically
pancreatization
pancreatography
panencephalitis
panophthalmitis
pan-Presbyterian
panselectionism
panselectionist
pantheistically

pantisocratical
pantothenic acid
paper-making wasp
papillary muscle
papulo-vesicular
parabolic spiral
paracrystalline
paradoxicalness
paragenetically
parageosyncline
paragraphically
paraheliotropic
parahippocampal
paralinguistics
parallelization
parallel parking
paralytic stroke
paramesonephric
parametric curve
paranitraniline
parasite fighter
parasiticalness
parasitic jaeger
parasitological
parasol mushroom
parasympathetic
paraventricular
parcels delivery
parchment-beaver
parchment-coffee
paregoric elixir
parenthetically
parfocalization
par for the course
Paris embroidery
parish communion
parish constable
parish Eucharist
parishionership
parliamentarian
parliamentarily
parliamentarism
Parliament clock
Parliament House
parochial school
paroemiographer
parrot-crossbill
parsonage teinds
parson's freehold
parthenogenesis
parthenogenetic
partial fraction
partial pressure
participational
particle physics
particularistic
particularities
Pascal's triangle
passenger pigeon
pass for sterling
pass in one's chips
passionlessness

passive immunity
passive-resister
pass one's eye over
passport control
pass round the hat
pass the hat round
pastoralization
past participial
paternoster lake
paternoster lift
paternoster line
pathetic fallacy
pathophysiology
patrimonial seas
patripassianism
pattern baldness
patterned ground
pattern practice
Patterson's curse
paulo-post-future
paurometabolous
pavement-pounder
pavement-toothed
pay off old scores
pay one's respects
peaches and cream
peacock pheasant
peacock's feather
Peano postulates
pebble prominent
pedogenetically
Pekingese stitch
pelican crossing
penalty shoot-out
pencil moustache
pencil sharpener
penetratingness
penetration twin
penetrativeness
pentaerythritol
pentanucleotide
people of the Book
Peoples of the Sea
people's republic
peppermint cream
peppermint-water
pepper saxifrage
peptic digestion
percentage point
perceptual-motor
percussion drill
peregrine falcon
perfect interval
perfectionation
perfectionistic
perfluorocarbon
performance bond
performance test
perfunctoriness
pergamentaceous
perianth segment
pericardiectomy

Périgord truffle
periodic decimal
perioesophageal
perioperatively
peripatetically
peristaltically
peristaltic pump
peritectic point
periventricular
Perkin synthesis
permanent magnet
permanganic acid
permissible dose
permselectivity
peroxosulphuric
perpendicularly
perpetual curate
perpetual motion
perpetuum mobile
per recte et retro
personal effects
personality cult
personalization
personal pension
personal pronoun
personal service
persona non grata
personification
perspectivistic
perspicaciously
perspicuousness
persuadableness
pessimistically
petition of right
Petition of Right
petits bourgeois
petrochemically
petticoat bodice
phaeochromocyte
phagocytability
phantasmagorian
Pharaoh's serpent
pharmacodynamic
pharmacogenetic
pharmacognosist
pharmacognostic
pharmacokinetic
pharmacological
pharmacotherapy
phase distortion
phase modulation
phenakistoscope
phenolphthalein
phenomenalistic
phenomenologist
phenylhydrazine
phenylhydrazone
phenylketonuria
phenylketonuric
philanthropical
philoprogeneity
philosophers' egg

philosophership
philosophically
philosophic wool
phonautographic
phonematization
phonemicization
phoneticization
phonocardiogram
phonologization
phonometrically
phonotactically
phosphatase test
phosphate island
phosphatization
phosphocreatine
phosphoglyceric
phosphonitrilic
phosphorescence
phosphorous acid
phosphorylation
phosphosilicate
phosphuranylite
photoabsorption
photoactivation
photobiological
photochemically
photoclinometry
photocoagulator
photoconducting
photoconduction
photoconductive
photoconversion
photodegradable
photodetachment
photodissociate
photoelasticity
photoelectrical
photoelectronic
photo-excitation
photofluorogram
photogoniometer
photogoniometry
photogrammetric
photoheliograph
photoionization
photojournalism
photojournalist
photolithograph
photolithotroph
photomacrograph
photomechanical
photometrically
photomicrograph
photomultiplier
photonegativity
photo-oxidizable
photopolymerize
photopositively
photopositivity
photoproduction
photoprotection
photoprotective

photoreactivate
photoregulation
photoresistance
photoresponsive
photoreversible
photosensitizer
photostationary
photosynthesise
photosynthesize
phototactically
phototelegraphy
photo-theodolite
phototopography
phototransistor
phototropically
phototypesetter
photozincograph
phrase-structure
phreatomagmatic
phrenologically
phreno-magnetism
phthisiological
physical culture
physicalization
physical science
physical therapy
physical torture
physico-chemical
physico-theology
physiographical
physiologically
physiopathology
physiotherapist
phytoagglutinin
phytochemically
phytoflagellate
phytogeographer
phytogeographic
phytopathogenic
phytoplanktonic
Pickering series
picket-pin gopher
picture magazine
picture-moulding
picture postcard
picturesqueness
pied-billed grebe
piezoelectrical
piezoresistance
pigeon guillemot
pigment printing
piliferous layer
pillow structure
pinking scissors
pin one's ears back
pinprick picture
pirate radio ship
pisciculturally
Piscis Austrinus
pitching machine
pitch the wickets
pitchy copper ore

pithecanthropic
Pithecanthropus
pit of the stomach
placenta praevia
plagiotropously
plain-spokenness
Planck's constant
Planck's equation
planetary nebula
planetary system
planimetrically
plantation crêpe
plant geographer
plasma frequency
plasmalemmasome
plasmal reaction
plasmodiophorid
plasmolytically
platform machine
platitudinarian
platitudinously
Platonistically
play a good game of
play a person foul
play a poor game of
play cat and mouse
play first fiddle
play first violin
play it for laughs
play off the stage
play the bear with
play third fiddle
play trumph about
Pleas of the Crown
pleasurableness
pleasure-cruiser
pleasure-seeking
plectonemically
pledge one's troth
pleiotropically
plenipotentiary
plethysmography
pleuropneumonia
plica circularis
plight one's troth
Plio-Pleistocene
plotting machine
ploughing engine
ploughman's lunch
ploughshare bone
plumed partridge
pluralistically
plurilingualism
plutocratically
pneumatic trough
pneumatological
Pneumatomachian
Pneumatomachist
pneumatotherapy
pneumonectomies
pneumonia blouse
pneumonic plague

pneumotachogram
pocket billiards
poetical justice
poikilothermous
Poincaré section
point discharger
point of no return
points rationing
point-to-pointing
poisoned chalice
poison pen letter
polar coordinate
polar flattening
polari-bilocular
police constable
police scientist
political animal
political asylum
political police
politzerization
polychlorinated
polychloroprene
polycrystalline
polydaemonistic
polydimensional
polyelectrolyte
polygenetically
polygon of forces
polygraphically
polyisobutylene
polyoxyethylene
polyphloisboian
polyplacophoran
polysomnography
polysyllabicity
polysymptomatic
polyunsaturated
polyvinyl acetal
pomatorhine skua
Pomeranian bream
Pontifex Maximus
poor boy sandwich
poor man of mutton
poor man's plaster
poor man's treacle
popular frontism
population curve
porcelain enamel
porcelain jasper
pork scratchings
porphobilinogen
porphyritically
porphyroblastic
porphyroclastic
Port Jackson pine
portmanteau word
portmantologism
portrait-gallery
portrait-painter
positional goods
position-finding
positive vetting

possession order
postage currency
post-consonantal
postoperatively
post-precipitate
post-synchronize
postulationally
postvocalically
potassium iodide
Potemkin village
potential energy
pottery-bark tree
poulter's measure
pour cold water on
poverty-stricken
powdering-closet
power-assistance
power of attorney
power-politician
power transistor
Poynting's vector
practicableness
praetorian guard
pragmaticalness
prairie-breaking
Prairie Province
prairie schooner
preachification
pre-acquaintance
pre-agricultural
pre-announcement
preapprehension
precancellation
precarcinogenic
precinct captain
precinct station
precipitability
precipitateness
precipitousness
preconceptional
predeterminable
predicamentally
predissociation
predominatingly
Prefect of Police
preference share
preference stock
prefiguratively
preformationism
preformationist
prehistorically
pre-implantation
pre-impregnation
prejudicialness
premeditatingly
premier minister
premodification
prenasalization
prenotification
prepositionally
prepositionless
prepossessingly

pre-professional
Pre-Raphaelitism
pre-recorded tape
preregistration
pre-reproductive
prerogative writ
Presbyterianism
Presbyterianize
prescriptionist
presence chamber
presentableness
presentationism
presentationist
preservationism
preservationist
presidentialism
presidentialist
presidents-elect
press conference
press correction
pressure casting
pressure chamber
pressure flaking
prestidigitator
prestigiousness
pretentiousness
preterimperfect
preternaturally
prevenient grace
price elasticity
prickly saltwort
prick up one's ears
pride of the world
priests-in-charge
prima ballerinas
primary election
primary evidence
primary industry
primary syphilis
Primitive Church
primitive circle
primitive colour
primitive groove
primitive streak
primitivization
Primrose Leaguer
principal clause
principal stress
print journalism
print journalist
prisoner of state
prisoner of State
prisoner's friend
private attorney
private language
private practice
private sentinel
privity of estate
privy councillor
privy counsellor
probationership
problematically

problem-oriented
proboscis monkey
procarcinogenic
processed cheese
procrastination
procrastinative
procrastinatory
professionalise
professionalism
professionalist
professionality
professionalize
professorialism
profibrinolysin
profile grinding
pro forma invoice
progenitiveness
prognostication
prognosticative
prognosticatory
programmability
progressive kiln
progressiveness
prohibitiveness
projection booth
projection fibre
projective plane
projective space
projective verse
prolate spheroid
proletarization
promiscuousness
promorphologist
pronunciability
Proper Bostonian
properispomenon
propheticalness
propidium iodide
propionaldehyde
proportionalism
proportionalist
proportionality
proportionately
propose marriage
propositionally
proprietary name
proprietary term
proprietorially
propylene glycol
propylitization
proselytization
prosenchymatous
prosobranchiate
prosopographies
prospectiveness
protection money
proteolytically
proteroglyphous
Protestant ethic
protestant flail
proto-historical
proton-accepting

protonephridial
protonephridium
protonotaryship
proto-scientific
protozoological
providentialism
provisionalness
provocation test
provocativeness
provocative test
proxime accessit
prunes and prisms
Prussian binding
Prussianization
Psalter of Cashel
psephologically
pseudaposematic
pseudepigraphal
pseudepigraphic
pseudo-Christian
pseudo-classical
pseudocoelomate
pseudohexagonal
pseudomalachite
pseudo-operation
pseudopotential
pseudopregnancy
pseudo-scientist
pseudo-statement
psychagogically
psychedelically
psychedelic rock
psychiatrically
psychoacoustics
psycho-aesthetic
psychobiography
psychobiologist
psychodiagnosis
psychodramatics
psychodramatist
psychodysleptic
psychoendocrine
psychogenically
psychogeography
psychogeriatric
psychohistorian
psychologically
psychometrician
psychopathology
psychophonetics
psychophysicist
psychopolitical
psychosexuality
psychosociology
psychostimulant
psychosynthesis
psychotechnical
psychotherapist
psychotogenesis
psychotomimetic
psychrotolerant
pteroylglutamic

pterygoid muscle
Ptolemaic system
public education
public ownership
public relations
public transport
publisher's cloth
pudding-pipe tree
pulchritudinous
pull a person's leg
pull by the sleeve
pull in one's horns
pull one's freight
pull one's pudding
pull one's punches
pull one's socks up
pullorum disease
pull the other one
pulmonary artery
pulmonary pleura
pulse modulation
punctiliousness
punctuation mark
punctus elevatus
punitive damages
purchasing power
pure mathematics
purple bacterium
purple copper ore
purple gallinule
purple moor-grass
purple sandpiper
purple sea urchin
purposelessness
push one's fortune
pusillanimously
puss in the corner
pussy-footedness
put a girdle about
put in one's pocket
put into practice
put one's back into
put one's finger on
put one's foot down
put one's foot in it
put on the buskins
put out of its pain
put out to pasture
put stuffing into
put the clock back
put the fluence on
put the helm aport
put the mockers on
put the squeeze on
put to one's shifts
put to the torture
pycnohydrometer
pygmy chimpanzee
pyloric stenosis
pyopneumothorax
pyramidal muscle
pyramidal orchid

pyramidal system
pyramidological
pyroclastic flow
pyroelectricity
pyrolytic carbon
pyrometamorphic
pyrophosphatase
pyrotechnically
quadragenarious
quadripartition
quadruplication
quantifiability
quantum increase
quarrelsomeness
quarterback club
quarterback sack
quarter-elliptic
quarter of an hour
quarter-repeater
quarter sessions
quarter-tonality
quatercentenary
quaternion group
Queen and country
queen of puddings
queen-of-the-night
Queensland maple
Queen's messenger
Queen's Messenger
quench hardening
questionability
quicker than scat
quick succession
quick-wittedness
quinalbarbitone
quincentenaries
quinquagenarian
quinquarticular
quintessentiate
quintuplication
rabbit-bandicoot
radioactivation
radio astronomer
radioautography
radiobiological
radiochemically
radio-controlled
radio-goniometer
radiogoniometer
radiogoniometry
radio-gramophone
radioheliograph
radioimmunology
radiolarian ooze
radiometrically
radio-protection
radio-resistance
radiosensitizer
radio-telegraphy
radio-telephonic
radio wavelength
radium emanation

railroad service
railway crossing
rainbow lorikeet
rain cats and dogs
raised-arm salute
raise one's hand to
raise one's sights
raise the siege of
raisins of the sun
range safety crew
rank correlation
Rankine's formula
rapid deployment
raspberry beetle
rational horizon
rationalization
rat-tailed maggot
rat-tailed radish
rattlesnake fern
rattlesnake root
rattlesnake weed
reactionariness
reaction chamber
reaction circuit
reaction pattern
reaction turbine
read-around ratio
re-advertisement
readvertisement
reafforestation
reaper-and-binder
reapportionment
rearguard action
rear its ugly head
rebarbarization
rebarbativeness
recarburization
receiver-general
receiver of wreck
reception centre
reciprocal cross
reciprocitarian
recitativo secco
recognizability
recollectedness
recombinational
reconcentration
reconcilability
reconfiguration
reconsideration
reconsolidation
reconstructable
reconstructible
reconvalescence
recoverableness
recreationalist
recrementitious
recruiting agent
rectified spirit
redaction critic
red-backed shrike
redemption yield

Redemptoristine
redetermination
red-headed wigeon
red-necked avocet
reds under the bed
reduce to silence
redundancy check
reduplicatively
red whortleberry
reed canary-grass
re-entering angle
re-establishment
reflexivization
reflux condenser
reformativeness
refortification
refracting angle
refractive index
refresher course
refrigeratories
regal walnut moth
regard one's navel
Regge trajectory
regionalization
regionary bishop
registered nurse
register tonnage
Regius professor
regression curve
regrettableness
rehearsal dinner
reimbursability
reincorporation
reindustrialise
reindustrialize
reinvestigation
relative address
relative density
releasing factor
relieving tackle
remand in custody
rememberability
remember oneself
Remembrancetide
remonstratingly
remorselessness
renal portal vein
render an account
renormalization
reopening clause
repeating circle
repetitiousness
reprecipitation
reprivatization
reproachfulness
reproducibility
Republican Party
required reading
requisitionally
rescue breathing
réseau ordinaire
resedimentation

reserve buoyancy
reserve currency
residence permit
residual current
residuary powers
resistentialism
resistentialist
resocialization
resonance energy
resonance hybrid
resourcefulness
respiratory tree
respiratory tuft
responsibleness
restrictiveness
resurrectionist
resurrectionize
resurrection man
resuscitability
reticular fibres
reticular system
reticular tissue
reticulocytosis
reticulosarcoma
retribalization
retroanalytical
retrogressional
retrogressively
retroperitoneal
retropharyngeal
retroreflective
retrospectively
retrotransposon
reverentialness
reversal process
reverse take-over
reverse takeover
revolutionaries
revolutionarily
revolutionology
revolving credit
rheumatological
rhinolaryngitis
rhinopharyngeal
rhombencephalic
rhombencephalon
rhyparographist
rhythmicization
ribbon cartridge
ribbon parachute
ribonucleic acid
Richardson's skua
riddle me a riddle
ride skimmington
ride the cushions
ride whip and spur
Riemann geometry
Riemann integral
rifle microphone
right-handedness
Right Honourable
right-mindedness

ring-a-ring o' roses
ring-tailed eagle
ring-tailed lemur
Rip-Van-Winkledom
Rip-Van-Winkleish
Rip-Van-Winkleism
rise with the lark
rising diphthong
risus sardonicus
ritualistically
road fund licence
roaring twenties
Robin Goodfellow
roche moutonnéed
rocket projector
roentgenography
roentgenologist
roentgenoscopic
Roger de Coverley
rogue and villain
Rolandic fissure
role-playing game
roly-poly pudding
romanticization
room temperature
Rossi–Forel scale
rotary converter
rotary egg-beater
Rotherham plough
rough green snake
roughly speaking
rough puff pastry
roundaboutation
round-shouldered
round-trip ticket
Rowland mounting
Royal Commission
Rubarth's disease
rubber fetishism
Rube Goldbergian
ruby anniversary
rudimentariness
ruler of the choir
rules of evidence
rumbustiousness
run a temperature
run interference
running headline
Russell's paradox
Russian dressing
Russian longhair
Russian roulette
Rutherford model
Rydberg constant
sabbatical river
Sabbatical river
sabre-toothed cat
sabretooth tiger
sacrifice market
saddleback shrew
saddle-stitching
saddling paddock

sado-masochistic
sadomasochistic
sage Derby cheese
sagittal section
sailor's farewell
sailor's pleasure
salamander-stove
salami technique
sales department
sales resistance
salicylaldehyde
salmon poisoning
salpingectomies
salpingographic
sancta sanctorum
sanctimoniously
sanguineousness
Sanskritization
sapphire wedding
saprophytically
satin flycatcher
satisfactionist
saturated diving
saturation point
savannah sparrow
save appearances
save one's longing
save one's own hide
scalene cylinder
scale of notation
scan-column index
Scandinavianism
Scandinavianize
scapolitization
scapular feather
scapulocoracoid
scarlet grosbeak
scarper the letty
scattering angle
scattering layer
scheduled flight
schillerization
schistosomiasis
schistosomicide
schizo-affective
Schmidt reaction
scholasticizing
school committee
school inspector
school-marmishly
schoolmastering
schoolmasterish
schoolmistressy
school of thought
schooner-frigate
Schopenhauerian
Schopenhauerism
Schopenhauerist
Schotten–Baumann
Schottky barrier
Schottky diagram
Schultz–Charlton

scientificality
scientistically
scimitar-babbler
scintillatingly
scintillography
scissors-grinder
sclerodermatous
Scotch Blackface
Scotchification
Scotch marmalade
Scott connection
Scottish terrier
scouring machine
scrape the barrel
scratched figure
scratch hardness
scratch one's head
scribaciousness
scribbling block
scribbling paper
scrivener's cramp
scrumptiousness
sculpturesquely
sea-island cotton
Sealyham terrier
sea oak coralline
seasick medicine
Second Adventist
secondary burial
secondary colour
secondary modern
secondary oocyte
secondary planet
second breakfast
second childhood
second-handiness
second honeymoon
second in command
second intention
second messenger
second secretary
Second Secretary
section sergeant
sector of a sphere
secular equation
secular humanism
secundogeniture
securities house
security analyst
security blanket
Security Council
sedan-chair clock
sedentarization
sedimentologist
see a person right
seek one's fortune
see the New Year in
seismic velocity
seismographical
seismologically
select committee
selenographical

selenologically
self-abandonment
self-advancement
self-advertising
self-affirmation
self-approbation
self-assuredness
self-capacitance
self-centredness
self-coincidence
self-complacence
self-complacency
self-confidently
self-consciously
self-consequence
self-consistency
self-constituted
self-containedly
self-containment
self-contentedly
self-contentment
self-cultivation
self-deliverance
self-deprecating
self-deprecation
self-deprecatory
self-destruction
self-destructive
self-determining
self-development
self-disciplined
self-dissociated
self-examination
self-explanatory
self-fertilizing
self-gratulation
self-gratulatory
self-gravitating
self-gravitation
self-importantly
self-improvement
self-indulgently
self-instruction
self-involvement
self-liquidating
self-liquidation
self-maintaining
self-maintenance
self-observation
self-opinionated
self-orientation
self-oscillating
self-oscillation
self-pollinating
self-pollination
self-portraiture
self-pronouncing
self-propagating
self-realisation
self-realization
self-referential
self-registering

self-reproachful
self-reproaching
self-righteously
self-sacrificial
self-sacrificing
self-satisfiedly
self-slaughtered
self-stimulation
self-subsistence
self-subsistency
self-substantial
self-sufficience
self-sufficiency
sell a person a pup
sell by the candle
Sellenger's round
semantic aphasia
semantic paradox
semicircularity
semi-crystalline
semicylindrical
semi-documentary
semi-empirically
semi-independent
semi-logarithmic
semi-manufacture
semi-Pelagianism
semi-permanently
semi-proletariat
semi-submersible
semi-transparent
senatorial order
Sendero Luminoso
send in an account
send round the hat
Seneca snakeroot
senior registrar
sense-experience
sensible horizon
sentence of death
sententiousness
sentimentalizer
separation order
septcentenaries
sequence dancing
sequestrotomies
serendipitously
sergeant-painter
sericiculturist
serjeants-at-arms
sero-sanguineous
serotherapeutic
serpentine front
serpentine stone
serpentine verse
serve the purpose
serve the stead of
serviceableness
service contract
service engineer
service industry
servomechanical

sesquicentenary
sesquioxidation
sesquiterpenoid
session musician
set a high value on
set one's sights on
set the clock back
settlement house
settle on the lees
settler's matches
seven deadly sins
seventeenth part
seventeen-tonner
sexagenarianism
sexual inversion
sexual selection
shaft horsepower
Shakespearianly
shake the midriff
Shannon's theorem
shape one's course
sharp-wittedness
shear-thickening
shelter magazine
shepherd's needle
sherbet fountain
sheriff's officer
shield cartilage
shield-nose snake
shift for oneself
shifting spanner
shift one's ground
shift-terminator
shilling shocker
ship of the desert
shipping tobacco
shirt-waist dress
shiver my timbers
shock excitation
shoe-billed stork
shoestring catch
shooting gallery
shopping trolley
shop-within-a-shop
shorten one's grip
shorten the arm of
shorthandedness
shorthand typist
short-headedness
Short Parliament
short sweetening
short-windedness
shotgun marriage
shot-hole disease
shoulder holster
shoulder-shotten
show a thing or two
show one's colours
shrinkage cavity
shrinking violet
shrink-resistant
shrunk in the wash

shuffle the cards
shut one's heart to
shuttle armature
Sibbald's rorqual
Siberian mammoth
Siberian pea-tree
Sicilian defence
Sicilian Vespers
Sicilian vespers
sickle-cell trait
sick man of Europe
sickness benefit
side-splittingly
side-stream smoke
Siemens producer
sigmoidoscopies
signal generator
significant form
significational
sign of the zodiac
silage harvester
silkworm disease
silky flycatcher
Silver Star medal
silvery marmoset
Simmonds' disease
simple structure
simply connected
simultanagnosia
sing another song
single-electrode
single pneumonia
sing the same song
singularization
sin of commission
sintered carbide
sister chromatid
situation comedy
situation ethics
situation report
six-and-thirtieth
sixty-fourth note
skeletonization
skim the cream off
sleeping draught
sleeping partner
sleeve Pekingese
slender mongoose
sling the hatchet
slip in the clutch
slip of the tongue
slog one's guts out
slotted armature
Slough of Despond
small-mindedness
smoke respirator
smooth breathing
snake in the grass
snap one's fingers
snow scorpion fly
soaked to the skin
social butterfly

social causation
social character
social Darwinism
social democracy
social geography
social insurance
socialistically
social ownership
social scientist
social secretary
social structure
sociobiological
socio-culturally
socioculturally
socioecological
socio-historical
sociolinguistic
sociometrically
sodium carbonate
sodium hydroxide
soft-centredness
soft furnishings
soft-heartedness
soft-shell turtle
soil association
soil conditioner
soil resistivity
solar prominence
soldier of Christ
solipsistically
Solomon Islander
solstitial point
solubility curve
somatologically
somatotopically
sonoluminescent
sooty shearwater
sophisticatedly
soprano recorder
sororal polygyny
sorry for oneself
soul-searchingly
sounding-balloon
sound insulation
source-criticism
South Africanism
south-eastwardly
Southern Baptist
Southern Comfort
south-westwardly
sow one's wild oats
spaceworthiness
spaghetti tubing
Spanish American
Spanish bluebell
Spanish chestnut
Spanish-Colonial
Spanish mackerel
Spanish omelette
Spanish windlass
spark telegraphy
sparring partner

spasmodicalness
spathose iron ore
spatial-temporal
speaker-listener
speak for oneself
speaking-machine
speaking-trumpet
speak of the devil
speak volumes for
special delivery
special interest
special pleading
special sessions
species richness
species-specific
specific disease
specific epithet
specific gravity
specific impulse
specific surface
speckled yellows
spectacled cobra
spectral tarsier
spectrochemical
spectroscopical
specular iron ore
speculativeness
speech community
speechification
speech pathology
speech stretcher
speech therapist
spelling checker
spermaceti whale
spermatogenesis
spermatogenetic
spes recuperandi
sphaerosiderite
spheroidal state
spheroidization
spherulitically
sphincter muscle
spike microphone
spill the blood of
spinifex texture
spinning machine
spinning process
spinning reserve
spinsterishness
spiral bevel gear
spiral stability
spiral staircase
spiritual courts
spiritual father
spirochaeticide
splanchnologist
splanchnomegaly
splanchnopleure
splendiferously
splenoportogram
splinter-netting
split infinitive

spoil a person for
spoilt for choice
spokeswomanship
spongioblastoma
spontaneousness
sporophytically
sporting picture
spotted redshank
sprain one's ankle
spreading factor
spread it on thick
spread one's wings
Sprengel air pump
spring snowflake
sprinkler system
spruce partridge
spur-of-the-moment
square the circle
squeeze an orange
squire of the body
stable companion
stadtholdership
stage management
stagnation point
stamp collecting
stamp collection
stand and deliver
standardization
standing ovation
standing rigging
stand-offishness
standoffishness
stand on ceremony
stand one's corner
stand one's ground
stand on one's head
stanhope phaeton
staphylorrhaphy
star of Bethlehem
starred question
Stars and Stripes
starvation wages
stasipatrically
State capitalism
State Department
State university
stationary point
stationary state
station-distance
station hospital
stationmistress
station-sergeant
statute merchant
statutes at large
statutory tenant
stealth aircraft
steal the picture
steamboat Gothic
steering compass
Stefan–Boltzmann
Steller's sea lion
stem-Christiania

stem-composition
Stensen's foramen
step on the toes of
stereochemistry
stereographical
stereoisomerism
stereoisomerize
stereologically
stereomonoscope
stereoselection
stereoselective
stereotaxically
stereotelescope
stereotypedness
stereotypically
steric hindrance
sternomaxillary
sternovertebral
steroidogenesis
Stevenson screen
sticking plaster
stick in one's craw
stick to one's guns
stick to one's last
stinkhorn fungus
stinking mayweed
stock and station
stockbroker belt
stocking stuffer
stomacher brooch
stone motherless
stop a person's way
stop-me-and-buy-one
stopping mixture
stopping station
stop the breath of
storage location
store-and-forward
stowage capacity
straddle carrier
straddle milling
straggle-brained
straight-facedly
straightforward
straight-grained
straight shooter
strain hardening
strait and narrow
straitlacedness
strait waistcoat
strange particle
stratagematical
stratagemically
stratigraphical
stratospherical
strawberry blite
strawberry blond
strawberry guava
strawberry perch
strawberry shrub
straw-necked ibis
stream of thought

street furniture
street jewellery
strephosymbolia
stress corrosion
stress-dilatancy
stretcher-bearer
stretcher strain
stretching-board
stretch one's legs
stretch receptor
stretch spinning
stretch the rules
stretch to the oar
stria gravidarum
stricken in years
strict Communion
strict liability
strike-slip fault
strike soundings
string along with
string orchestra
string telephone
striped squirrel
striped trousers
strongyloidosis
strontian yellow
structuralistic
structural steel
structurization
struggle meeting
stuckuppishness
studio apartment
studium generale
stump embroidery
Sturt's desert pea
stylographic pen
stylostatistics
subcommissioner
subdenomination
subintellection
subintelligitur
subject superior
sublapsarianism
sublimification
submarine canyon
submarine chaser
subordinateness
sub-postmistress
subreptitiously
subsequentially
subsidiary cells
subsistence crop
subsistence diet
subsistence wage
subspecifically
substance abuser
substantialness
substantia nigra
substantiveness
substantive verb
substitutionary
substratosphere

subterraneously
suburbanization
subvocalization
succession house
succession state
Succession State
successlessness
succinylcholine
succus entericus
sucking response
suck the hind teat
suction dredging
suction pressure
sufficient grace
sulcus of Rolando
sulphaemoglobin
sulphamethazine
Sulphamezathine
sulphate process
sulphinpyrazone
sulphureousness
sum and substance
summer and winter
summer complaint
summer diarrhoea
summer lightning
summer snowflake
sunrise industry
sunset provision
superabundantly
superadditional
supercavitation
superclustering
superconducting
superconduction
superconductive
superexaltation
superexcellence
superexcellency
superficial foot
superficialness
superfluousness
superheterodyne
superimposition
superindividual
superinducement
superintendence
superintendency
superior numbers
superlativeness
supermarket cart
supernaturalise
supernaturalism
supernaturalist
supernaturality
supernaturalize
supernumeraries
superordination
superplasticity
supersaturation
superstitionist
superstitiously

superstructural
superterraneous
supplementarily
supplementarity
supplementation
supply and demand
suppressibility
suppressor T cell
suprachiasmatic
supraclavicular
supradecompound
supranaturalism
supranaturalist
suprarelational
surface couching
surface-crossing
surface integral
surface printing
surgeons general
surrender to bail
surreptitiously
surrogate mother
surveyor-general
susceptibleness
suspense account
suspension point
sustaining pedal
Sutherland table
Swainson's thrush
swashbucklering
sweep second hand
sweet Fanny Adams
sweetheart plant
sweetlip emperor
swimming-bladder
swimming costume
swim with the tide
swine erysipelas
switch mechanism
switch-reference
sword-and-buckler
sword-and-sorcery
sword of Damocles
sycophantically
Sydenham's chorea
Sydney or the bush
syllabification
syllogistically
symbolic address
symbolical books
symbolistically
symmetricalness
sympathectomies
sympathetically
sympathicotonia
sympathicotonic
sympatho-adrenal
sympathogonioma
sympathomimetic
sympathy striker
symphonic ballet
symptomatically

synchronistical
synchronization
synchro receiver
syndical chamber
syndiotacticity
synecdochically
synecologically
synergistically
syntagmatically
syntectonically
systematic error
systematization
systemic grammar
systems analysis
systems operator
systems software
tableau curtains
table of contents
tachymetabolism
tacit relocation
Tahiti arrowroot
take a bit of doing
take advantage of
take a lot of doing
take a person up on
take a poor view of
take at advantage
take by the button
take exception to
take into account
take into custody
take it on the chin
take it or leave it
take knowledge of
take one's cue from
take one's eyes off
take one's leave of
take one's own life
take one's stand on
take service with
take some beating
take the bloom off
take the chill off
take the long view
take the shilling
take the view that
take the wraps off
take to one's bosom
take to one's heels
take wooden money
talk a person down
talk a person over
tallow-chandlery
tamper-resistant
tan a person's hide
tangent distance
tank transporter
target indicator
tarpaulin muster
tarragon vinegar
tarsometatarsal
tarsometatarsus

tattersall check
tautomerization
Tay–Sachs disease
teaching machine
tear oneself away
tear one's hair out
technical school
technologically
technostructure
tectonophysical
telegraph editor
telegraphically
telephone number
telephotography
teleradiography
telerobotically
telescope-driver
telescopic-rifle
telescopic sight
telestereoscope
telethermometer
tell its own story
temerariousness
temnospondylous
temperamentally
tempestuousness
tempt Providence
tenancy in common
Ten Commandments
tendentiousness
Tennessee marble
Tennessee walker
tensile strength
tentaculiferous
tent-caterpillar
teratocarcinoma
terebinthinated
terephthalamide
terminalization
terminal moraine
Territorial Army
terroristically
tertiary college
tetrabranchiate
tetrahexahedron
tetrahydrofuran
tetramerization
tetranucleotide
tetrasporangium
tetrasporophyte
tetrasyllabical
tetrazotization
Teutonic Knights
text linguistics
thalamocortical
thalassographic
thalassotherapy
thalidomide baby
thanatocoenosis
Thanksgiving Day
thankworthiness
that's more like it

the Antonine Wall
theatre workshop
the back of beyond
the Baltic States
the better part of
the bird has flown
the Book of Psalms
the breath of life
theca cell tumour
the change of life
the coast is clear
the common rustic
the Commonwealth
the Devil's own job
the Dircaean swan
the dreaded lurgy
the eleventh hour
the Encyclopedia
the end of the line
the end of the road
the eye of a needle
the Fatal Sisters
the fat of the land
the four freedoms
the girl next door
the Good Shepherd
the great assizes
the Gulf of Mexico
the Heavenly City
the herd instinct
the King's English
the late lamented
the man in the boat
the man in the moon
the Merry Monarch
the more's the pity
the nine worthies
the noble science
the Old Pretender
theorematically
theosophistical
the powers that be
the Principality
the Queen's colour
the Queen's speech
therapeutically
there is no saying
thermal analysis
thermal capacity
thermal velocity
thermionic valve
thermite process
thermite welding
thermochemistry
thermodynamical
thermo-halocline
thermo-hardening
thermomagnetism
thermoregulator
thermoremanence
thermosensitive
thermostability

the Scourge of God
the show must go on
the Six Dynasties
the soul of honour
the sport of kings
the Supreme Being
theta-phi diagram
the Three Estates
the three sisters
the Twelve Tables
the usual warning
the vast majority
the weaker vessel
the white feather
the whole boiling
the witching hour
the worse for wear
thickheadedness
Thiessen polygon
things of the mind
think for oneself
thinking subject
think on one's feet
think the world of
think twice about
thin on the ground
thin-skinnedness
third-generation
thirty-something
this day sennight
this-worldliness
thixotropically
Thomsen's disease
thoracicolumbar
thorough-draught
thoroughgoingly
thoughtlessness
threateningness
three-legged race
three musketeers
three-ring circus
thromboembolism
throttle control
through-composed
through the green
throw in one's hand
throw in the towel
throw one's hand in
throw one's tongue
throw the hatchet
thrust augmentor
thrust oneself in
thrust to the wall
thumbnail sketch
thumb one's nose at
thunderstricken
thyrocalcitonin
thyroidectomize
Tibetan antelope
Tibeto-Himalayan
ticket collector
ticket-splitting

tickle in the palm
tiddley-om-pom-pom
tiger salamander
tight corner tilt
tighten one's belt
till kingdom come
tilt at windmills
time of ignorance
time on one's hands
time-servingness
tinkling grackle
tip of the iceberg
tip over the perch
titanium dioxide
titanohaematite
titrimetrically
to a person's teeth
tobacco hornworm
tobacco whitefly
to be going on with
tocodynamometer
to have and to hold
tomographically
tongue-and-groove
tongue-depressor
tonsillectomies
too clever by half
too good to be true
too hot to hold one
to one's knowledge
top fermentation
topographically
torque converter
torsion pendulum
tossing the caber
total abstinence
totalitarianism
to the effect that
to the finger-ends
to the fingertips
to the last degree
to the manner born
to the right about
tough as old boots
tough-mindedness
toujours perdrix
tout au contraire
tower of strength
Townsend current
toxicologically
tracheotomy tube
tracking station
Trafalgar Square
traffic analysis
traffic engineer
tragico-farcical
trailing arbutus
training college
transactionally
transactivation
transcriptional
transelementate

trans-equatorial
transessentiate
transferability
transfer company
transfer machine
transfer-printed
transfiguration
transfigurative
transfigurement
transformerless
transgressively
transhistorical
transhumanation
transilluminate
transindividual
transistor radio
transition curve
transition metal
transition point
translatability
translationally
translation loan
translation wave
transliteration
translocational
transmissometer
transmutability
transmutational
transnationally
transparentness
transphenomenal
transplantation
transport number
transposability
transpositional
transpositively
transprovincial
trans-subjective
transubstantial
transverse colon
transverse flute
tranylcypromine
trapezoidal rule
traumatotropism
travel allowance
travelling crane
travelling stock
treacherousness
treasonableness
treasurableness
tree of knowledge
trembling poplar
triacontahedral
triacontahedron
trial by the media
trial of strength
triangular trade
trichinelliasis
trichloroacetic
trichloroethane
trichlorophenol
trick of the trade

trick-or-treating
trifluoperazine
trigeminal nerve
trigonocephalic
trigonometrical
Trincomalee wood
trinitrotoluene
Trinity Brethren
trip over oneself
tripping-circuit
trisyllabically
trochlear muscle
tropane alkaloid
trophectodermal
trophochromatin
tropical cyclone
tropicalization
troubadourishly
troubleshooting
troublesomeness
truant-inspector
true-heartedness
trumpet daffodil
trustee security
trust-investment
trustworthiness
truth-functional
try anything once
trypanosomiasis
try-your-strength
tuberculization
tuberculostatic
tufted hair-grass
tungsten carbide
tunica albuginea
tunica vaginalis
turban buttercup
Turkish crescent
Turkish trousers
turn a blind eye to
turn in one's grave
turn on a sixpence
turnover article
turn the tables on
turn to advantage
turnwrest plough
Turpentine State
turpentine still
tussore silkworm
twenty-four carat
twenty questions
twenty-something
twilight housing
twin carburettor
twin lamb disease
two-and-thirtieth
two pair of stairs
twopenny library
twopenny upright
two-up and two-down
typographically
typolithography

ubiquitarianism
ultimate Frisbee
ultimobranchial
ultracentrifuge
ultrafilterable
ultrafiltration
ultramicroscope
ultramicroscopy
ultramicrotomed
ultrasonication
ultrasonography
ultrastructural
umbilical artery
unacceptability
unaccommodating
unadulteratedly
unadventurously
unadvisableness
unalterableness
unambitiousness
unanalysability
unanswerability
unapostolically
unarchitectural
unargumentative
unascertainable
unassailability
unassertiveness
unattributively
unauthentically
unauthenticated
unauthoritative
unavailableness
unavoidableness
unbeauteousness
unbeautifulness
unbefittingness
unbeginningness
unbelievability
unbelievingness
unbeseemingness
unboiled lobster
unbrotherliness
uncategorizable
unceremoniously
unchallengeable
unchallengeably
unchangeability
uncharacterized
unchristianized
unchristianlike
unchronological
uncircumscribed
uncircumstanced
uncommunicating
uncommunicative
uncompanionable
uncompassionate
uncomplainingly
uncomplimentary
uncomprehending
uncomprehension

uncomprehensive
unconcernedness
uncondescending
unconditionally
unconjecturable
unconnectedness
unconscientious
unconsciousness
unconsequential
unconstrainable
unconstrainedly
uncontroversial
uncooperatively
uncopyrightable
uncorrespondent
uncorresponding
uncorruptedness
uncountable noun
uncoupling agent
uncourteousness
uncultivability
undangerousness
undefinableness
undemandingness
undemonstrative
undependability
under advisement
undercapitalise
undercapitalize
under compulsion
under correction
undercorrection
underdispersion
underemployment
underestimation
undergraduatish
underhandedness
underinvestment
under lock and key
undermodulation
underoccupation
under one's breath
under one's girdle
underpopulation
underprivileged
underproduction
undersaturation
under sentence of
understandingly
undersubscribed
under the aegis of
under the baton of
under the cloak of
under the counter
under the open sky
under the weather
undesirableness
undetectability
undischargeable
undisciplinable
undiscriminated
undisguisedness

undissemblingly
undistinguished
undisturbedness
unembarrassable
unemployability
unendurableness
unenlightenment
unequivocalness
unexceptionable
unexceptionably
unexceptionally
unexclusiveness
unfathomability
unforgivingness
unfortunateness
unfossiliferous
ungelatinizable
ungeneralizable
ungentlemanlike
ungovernability
ungrammatically
unhealthfulness
unimaginatively
unimprovability
uninformatively
uninhabitedness
uninhibitedness
unintelligently
unintentionally
uninterestingly
unintermittedly
uninterpretable
uninterruptable
uninterruptedly
uninterruptible
uninventiveness
unitary symmetry
United Provinces
United Statesman
universal bishop
universalizable
universalizably
unknowledgeable
unknown quantity
unlistenability
unmercenariness
unmetamorphosed
unmistakability
unmixed blessing
unmortifiedness
unnaturalizable
unnecessariness
unobjectionable
unobjectionably
unobliteratable
unobservability
unobtrusiveness
unorganizedness
unoriginateness
unpaintableness
unpalatableness
unparliamentary

unparticipating
unpatriotically
unpeaceableness
unperturbedness
unphilosophical
unphysiological
unpicturability
unpicturesquely
unpracticalness
unprecedentedly
unpremeditation
unprepossessing
unpretentiously
unproblematical
unprogressively
unpromisingness
unpronounceable
unpronounceably
unproportionate
unprotectedness
unprotestantize
unqualifiedness
unquestioningly
unreachableness
unrealistically
unrecommendable
unreconstructed
unrelentingness
unremittingness
unrepeatability
unrepresentable
unresistingness
unrevolutionary
unrighteousness
unsatisfiedness
unscholarliness
unseaworthiness
unselfconscious
unsensationally
unsentimentally
un-Shakespearian
unshrinkability
unsociable hours
unsophisticated
unspeakableness
unspectacularly
unspiritualness
unsportsmanlike
unstatesmanlike
unsteadfastness
unsubstantially
unsubstantiated
unsuperstitious
unsupportedness
unsuspectedness
unsymmetrically
unteachableness
unthinkableness
until such time as
until the present
untouchableness
untraceableness

untractableness
untraditionally
untransformable
untransmissible
untransportable
untreatableness
ununderstanding
unutterableness
unwholesomeness
up-and-comingness
upper atmosphere
Upper California
upper-middlebrow
upper yield point
uprighteousness
upside downwards
up the wooden hill
up to the eyebrows
use a person's name
usurp the place of
utility function
vacuum extractor
vacuum packaging
valence electron
valency electron
vandalistically
vanilla ice-cream
vanish into smoke
vanity publisher
variation method
varicella zoster
varicocelectomy
vascularization
vasculotoxicity
vasoconstrictor
Vater's corpuscle
Vatican roulette
vector potential
vegetable butter
vegetable garden
vegetable marrow
vegetable oyster
vegetable sponge
vegetable tallow
Velikovskianism
velocity profile
velvet copper ore
venereal disease
Venetian shutter
venographically
ventilation duct
ventriloquially
ventriloquistic
ventrolaterally
venturesomeness
Venus's hairstone
Venus's navelwort
verbal adjective
verbal diarrhoea
verbalistically
verbalizability
verdigris agaric

verge escapement
verificationism
verificationist
vertebral column
vertebrarterial
vertebrobasilar
verticalization
vertical take-off
vertical tasting
vertiginousness
very approximate
vesiculobullous
vestibular nerve
vestibulo-ocular
vestibulospinal
vestimentiferan
vibration damper
vice-chamberlain
vicissitudinous
Victorian Gothic
Victorian period
videoconference
Vienna schnitzel
Vienna Secession
vindicativeness
vintage festival
Virginia cowslip
Virginia creeper
Virginia opossum
Virginia tobacco
visceralization
viscoelasticity
viscometrically
visible spectrum
visiting fireman
visiting firemen
visualizability
vital statistics
vitamin B complex
vitriol of copper
Vitruvian scroll
vive la bagatelle
vivisectionally
Völkerwanderung
volume indicator
voluntary school
von Hippel–Lindau
voucher specimen
vouch to warranty
voyeuristically
vulnerabilities
vulturine parrot
wag one's finger at
waitress service
Walden inversion
walking delegate
walking dragline
walking sickness
walk in one's sleep
walk on eggshells
wallop in a tether
Wall Street crash

walrus moustache
wandering sailor
warm-bloodedness
warm-heartedness
warm-temperature
warning triangle
warrantableness
wash one's hands of
waste one's breath
watching-chamber
waterloggedness
Water of Ayr stone
water on the brain
water over the dam
water-resistance
water whorl-grass
weak interaction
wear the breeches
wear the trousers
wear to the stumps
weatherboarding
weathercock-like
weather forecast
Weber–Fechner law
wedge photometer
weeping capuchin
weighing machine
weighted average
weight for weight
well-conditioned
well-constructed
well-established
well-foundedness
well-intentioned
well-upholstered
Werdnig–Hoffmann
Werner's syndrome
West African teak
Western American
western red cedar
western sandwich
Westphalia bacon
wet from the press
wet the baby's head
whale acorn-shell
whatchamacallit
what's the betting
what's your poison
wheel animalcule
wheelbarrow race
whet one's whistle
Whipple's disease
whiptail wallaby
whirling dervish
whirling disease
whiskered auklet
whiskey-straight
whistle and flute
whistle-language
whistling kettle
whistling marmot
whistling thrush

White chauvinism
White chauvinist
White Cliffs opal
white dead-nettle
whited sepulchre
white embroidery
white maidenhair
white phosphorus
white rhinoceros
white sandalwood
wide area network
Wiener schnitzel
wild service tree
will-o'-the-wispish
willow ptarmigan
Wimmera ryegrass
Winchester fives
Winchester goose
Winchester quart
Winchester style
windscreen wiper
wipe a person's eye
wireless cabinet
wise man of Gotham
wishful thinking
witches' thimbles
with a difference
with a flying seal
with all one's soul
with bated breath
withdrawing room
wither on the vine
withholding rate
within arm's reach
within one's grasp
with life and limb
without ceremony
without question
without recourse
with reference to
Wittgensteinian
woman of pleasure
Women's Institute
Woodbury gravure
woodland caribou
woody nightshade
word association
word recognition
work double tides
work like a beaver
work like a nigger
work measurement
work one's arse off
work one's guts out
work one's passage
work one's tail off
world-historical
world literature
world without end
wormwood lecture
write oneself man
write-permit ring

writ of privilege
wrong-headedness
xanthine oxidase
xanthochromatic
xerographically
xeroradiography
xylographically
Yarmouth bloater
Yates' correction
yellow archangel
yellow cartilage

yellow pimpernel
yellow underwing
yeoman of signals
yield one's breath
yoko-shiho-gatame
you bet your boots
you'd be surprised
your corporosity
yours faithfully
Yours faithfully
you see what I mean

Yukawa potential
zenith telescope
zero-dimensional
zeugmatographic
Ziegfeld Follies
zodiac of the moon
zona fasciculata
zona glomerulosa
zona reticularis
zoogeographical
zygomatic muscle

SIXTEEN OR MORE LETTERS

a barrel of monkeys
a bee in one's bonnet
ablative absolute
able-bodied rating
able-bodied seaman
a bolt from the blue
absentee landlord
absent-mindedness
absolute humidity
absolute majority
Abyssinian banana
academic material
academic parlance
acanthopterygian
accelerator board
accessory mineral
access television
accommodationist
according to Hoyle
account executive
accounting period
accumulativeness
acquaintance rape
acquaintanceship
acroparaesthesia
actual bodily harm
a day after the fair
addition reaction
address oneself to
adjustment centre
Adjutant Generals
administratively
Admiral of the Blue
adrenalectomized
a drop in the bucket
advantageousness
adventitious root
aeromagnetometer
affectionateness
affiliation order
a foot in both camps
African blackwood
Afrikanerization
against the stream
agent provocateur
a hard act to follow
Alexandrine verse
a lick and a promise
alienation effect
alimentativeness
all gas and gaiters
all girls together
alligator snapper
alliterativeness
alpine strawberry
alternative birth
altitude sickness

a matter of opinion
ambidextrousness
American football
American John Dory
American woodcock
amoebic dysentery
Anabaptistically
anaesthetization
anagrammatically
a nasty bit of goods
anathematization
ancient historian
angle of incidence
Anglo-Catholicism
Angostura Bitters
animal liberation
annual aberration
anomalistic month
answering machine
answering service
antagonistically
anthropocentrism
anthropometrical
anthropomorphise
anthropomorphism
anthropomorphist
anthropomorphite
anthropomorphize
anthropomorphous
anthropopsychism
anthroposophical
antibody-negative
antichristianism
antichristianity
anticyclonically
anti-inflammatory
antipathetically
any other business
a piece of one's mind
a play within a play
a plum in one's mouth
apophthegmatical
apoplectic stroke
Apostolic Fathers
appendicectomies
appreciativeness
apprehensibility
apprehensiveness
approachableness
a price on one's head
archaeo-astronomy
archaeologically
archaeomagnetism
archiepiscopally
Archimedean drill
Archimedean screw
areal linguistics

aristocratically
arithmetic series
ark of the Covenant
Ark of the Covenant
army of occupation
aromatherapeutic
arranged marriage
arteriosclerosis
arteriosclerotic
articulated lorry
artificial kidney
artificial mother
artificial person
a run for one's money
as clear as crystal
as flat as a pancake
a shoulder to cry on
as near as a toucher
a song in one's heart
as pleased as Punch
as right as a trivet
assembly language
assistant manager
associationistic
as straight as a die
astro-archaeology
astrometeorology
astronomical unit
astronomical year
astrophotography
a thorn in one's side
a tiger in one's tank
atomic philosophy
at one's finger-ends
at one's fingertips
atrioventricular
at short intervals
at sixes and sevens
attendance centre
attesting witness
at the best of times
at the end of the day
attract attention
audience research
auditory scanning
auricular witness
Australian salmon
Australopithecus
authoritarianism
autobiographical
autoimmunization
auto-intoxication
autointoxication
autolithographic
automatic landing
automatic writing
autopsychography

autoradiographic
Avogadro constant
a whoop and a holler
bachelor's buttons
background heater
ballistic missile
ballyhoo of blazes
banded rudder-fish
Bangalore torpedo
Barbary partridge
barren strawberry
basement membrane
bathythermograph
bear a great stroke
beat about the bush
beat the hell out of
beat the shit out of
beautiful letters
behaviour pattern
behaviour therapy
behind the curtain
bells and whistles
Benedictine order
Benjamin's portion
Bermuda buttercup
best bib and tucker
between cup and lip
between ourselves
between the sheets
betwixt cup and lip
beyond comparison
biblical theology
bicycle-repair kit
bill of indictment
bill of quantities
bill of sufferance
bill of suspension
binary arithmetic
biocompatibility
biodegradability
biological mother
biospeleological
biostratigrapher
biostratigraphic
biosynthetically
biotechnological
bird-eating spider
bird's eye primrose
bird's-foot trefoil
birth certificate
birth control pill
black ipecacuanha
black nationalism
blackpoll warbler
black swallowwort
blackthorn winter
blast from the past
blind-man's holiday
blind with science
bloodthirstiness
blood transfusion
bloody-mindedness

blot one's copybook
blow one's socks off
blow the whistle on
bombardier beetle
bone of contention
born out of wedlock
boroughmongering
bottleneck guitar
bowels of the earth
Bow Street officer
brachycatalectic
Bramley's seedling
breach of the peace
bread and circuses
breakfast-service
breaking-strength
breath of fresh air
Brewster Sessions
brigadier general
bright young thing
Bristol porcelain
broderie anglaise
bronchopneumonia
bronchopulmonary
Brother of Charity
Brownian movement
brushed aluminium
builders' merchant
bull in a china shop
bumiputraization
bureaucratically
Burkitt's lymphoma
bursa of Fabricius
buttonhole stitch
cabbage butterfly
Caesarean section
calcium carbonate
calcium hydroxide
calcium phosphate
California condor
Californian holly
Californian poppy
call a spade a spade
calligraphically
call into question
call over the coals
calorimetrically
Camberwell Beauty
campanologically
Canadian pondweed
cantankerousness
canteen of cutlery
Canterbury gallop
cantilever bridge
capital-intensive
capitalistically
capitalist roader
capital territory
capita succedanea
cap of maintenance
captain-generalcy
caput succedaneum

carbon disulphide
carbon microphone
carbonyl chloride
cardiac glycoside
cardiac tamponade
cardinal-grosbeak
card up one's sleeve
Carolina allspice
carrying capacity
cartel of defiance
cartographically
caryophyllaceous
case of conscience
cassette recorder
catachrestically
catalytic cracker
catastrophically
Catholic Epistles
celestial equator
celestial horizon
cellulose acetate
central processor
centre of buoyancy
centre of pressure
centrifugal force
centripetal force
Chamber of Horrors
chamber orchestra
Champagne Charley
champing at the bit
change the subject
chaotic attractor
characterisation
characteristical
characterization
characterologist
character witness
chattels personal
chauvinistically
cheap and cheerful
Chelsea pensioner
chemical engineer
chemical reaction
chemiluminescent
chemoautotrophic
chemoprophylaxis
chemotherapeutic
chequered skipper
child-molestation
child pornography
children of Israel
Chiltern Hundreds
Chinese artichoke
chipping squirrel
chlordiazepoxide
chocolate biscuit
chocolate soldier
cholecystography
Chorlton-cum-Hardy
chorographically
Christianization
Christian Science

Christmas cracker
Christmas disease
Christmas present
Christmas pudding
chromic anhydride
chromolithograph
chronicle history
chronobiological
chronometrically
chryselephantine
church-government
church membership
Church of Scotland
churchwardenship
chymotrypsinogen
cigarette-lighter
cigarette machine
cinefluorography
cinematographist
cinemicrographic
cineradiographic
circle of position
circumambulation
circumambulatory
circumflex accent
circumlocutional
circumnavigation
circumspectively
circumstantially
Cities of the Plain
civil engineering
civil libertarian
clang association
clear-sightedness
Cleopatra's Needle
clerestory window
clerk of the cheque
Clerk of the Closet
clerk of the course
Clerk of the Scales
Clifden nonpareil
climatologically
clinical medicine
clitoridectomies
close one's heart to
clothes-conscious
clove gillyflower
clustered columns
coals to Newcastle
cobweb micrometer
coca-colonization
coccolithophorid
cock and bull story
cock one's eyebrows
codlings-and-cream
cognitive science
coitus reservatus
collaborationist
collateral bundle
collateral damage
collective memory
collectivization

College of Justice
collegiate church
collegiate Gothic
colorimetrically
colour supplement
colour television
combinatoriality
combine harvester
come into question
come into the world
come out in the wash
come to a sticky end
come to one's senses
come to the surface
come with a wet sail
commander-in-chief
commedia dell'arte
commensurability
commensurateness
commercial school
commissionership
Commodore-in-Chief
common astrologer
Common Councilman
common ground dove
common-law husband
commonsensically
common silverbill
common stork's-bill
commonwealth's-man
communal marriage
communicableness
community college
community service
community singing
companionability
compartmentalise
compartmentalize
compartmentation
complemental male
complex conjugate
complexification
compound fracture
compound interest
compound interval
compound pendulum
compound sentence
compression ratio
computer-friendly
computer graphics
computer language
computer literacy
computer-literate
computer-readable
concentratedness
concentric bundle
conceptualizable
conciliatoriness
conditional offer
conditions of sale
conference centre
confidentialness

configurationism
conformationally
congregationally
congressionalist
connective tissue
consanguineously
conscience clause
conscience-struck
conscionableness
conscious subject
conscript fathers
consequentialism
consequentialist
consequentiality
consequent points
conservation area
conservativeness
considerableness
consignification
consignificative
consolation prize
consolidated fund
Consolidated Fund
consolidationist
conspiracy theory
conspiratorially
constitutionally
constitutiveness
constructionally
construction camp
construction site
constructiveness
consubstantially
consumer research
consummativeness
contact herbicide
containerization
contemporariness
contemptibleness
contemptuousness
conterminousness
continental crust
continental drift
continental quilt
Continental roast
continental shelf
continental slope
contour ploughing
contraction joint
contradictiously
contra-indication
contraindication
contrapositively
contrary to nature
contra-seasonally
controversialism
controversialist
controversiality
contumaciousness
contumeliousness
convalescent home
convenience store

conversationally
conversation card
conversion factor
converter reactor
cooling-off period
cooperative store
Copernican system
Copernican theory
copolymerisation
copolymerization
copyright library
Corinthian bronze
Cornish moneywort
Coronation Street
corporealization
corpus cavernosum
corpus spongiosum
correspondential
corridor carriage
corridors of power
corrupt practices
cosmical constant
cosmographically
cost an arm and a leg
costume jewellery
cotton-boll weevil
counsel of despair
counter-clockwise
counterclockwise
counterculturist
countercurrently
counter-disengage
counter-embattled
counter-espionage
counter-extension
counterfactually
counterfeit crank
counter-influence
counter-intuitive
counter-offensive
counter-signature
countersignature
countervallation
Countess Palatine
country gentleman
county councillor
coupling constant
Court of Cassation
Court of Exchequer
court of peculiars
critical pressure
Crookes dark space
cross-correlation
cross-examination
cross-grainedness
cross one's fingers
crossover network
cross-pollination
crowd the mourners
cruciate ligament
crustaceological
cryopreservation

cryptobranchiate
cryptogrammatist
cryptozoological
crystalloblastic
crystallo-ceramie
crystallogenesis
crystallographer
crystallographic
crystals of tartar
cudgel one's brains
culpable homicide
cumulative voting
curve of striction
Cushing's syndrome
cuticularization
cut one's own throat
cyanamide process
cylindro-conoidal
cytoarchitecture
damage limitation
dance upon nothing
Danish blue cheese
Darby and Joan club
dark red silver ore
Davy Jones's locker
day of retribution
Day of the Covenant
deadly nightshade
dead-stick landing
deafening silence
death certificate
death-watch beetle
Debye temperature
decaffeinization
decapitalization
decentralization
declaration of war
declassification
dedolomitization
defence mechanism
deficit financing
definite integral
dehumidification
delegitimization
deliberativeness
demilitarization
demineralization
demonopolization
demonstrableness
demonstrationist
demonstratorship
denaturalization
dendrochronology
denominationally
dental technician
denuclearization
deoxyribonucleic
depalatalization
depoliticization
depolymerization
depressed classes
depressurization

deproletarianize
deproteinization
deputy lieutenant
descending letter
desophistication
despecialization
dessertspoonfuls
desulphurization
desynonymization
detective fiction
detention barrack
deteriorationist
determinableness
deuterocanonical
developmentalism
developmentalist
devil's coach-horse
devil's paintbrush
devolatilization
diabetes mellitus
diacetylmorphine
diagrammatically
dialect geography
dibenzanthracene
dies non juridicus
differential gear
differently abled
digestive biscuit
digital audio tape
dig up the tomahawk
dihydroxyacetone
diminishableness
diminishing glass
diphthongization
dip one's pen in gall
direction-finding
director-generals
direct proportion
disaccommodation
disafforestation
disagreeableness
disappropriation
discombobulation
disconnectedness
disconsideration
disconsolateness
discontentedness
discourteousness
discreditability
discriminability
discriminateness
discriminatingly
discriminatively
disembarrassment
disestablishment
disfranchisement
dishallucination
disheartenedness
disincarceration
disincorporation
disindividualize
disingenuousness

disinsectization
disintegratively
displacement pump
disposable income
disproportionate
disputatiousness
disqualification
disregardfulness
disreputableness
dissatisfiedness
dissymmetrically
distance learning
distinguishingly
distributionally
distributiveness
district attorney
disvulnerability
diverticulectomy
divine proportion
division of labour
Doctor of Civil Law
dogmatic theology
dolichocephalism
dolichocephalous
dolphin of the mast
domestic politics
domiciliary visit
dominium directum
donkey's breakfast
dot matrix printer
double Gloucester
double-mindedness
double refraction
double summertime
double yellow line
dovetail moulding
downwardly mobile
drama-documentary
dramatis personae
Dresden porcelain
dressmaker's dummy
drinking fountain
Droit of Admiralty
droplet infection
dropped handlebar
drown the shamrock
drumstick primula
dry behind the ears
duchesse potatoes
dull as ditchwater
duplex escapement
duplicato-dentate
Dutch nightingale
dynamic viscosity
East Indian walnut
eastward position
eccentric anomaly
ecclesiastically
echocardiography
eclipse of the moon
economies of scale
ectopic pregnancy

effectual calling
efficacious grace
eicosapentaenoic
eigenfrequencies
Eisenhower jacket
elastic cartilage
election petition
electoral college
electrician's tape
electricity meter
electro-acoustics
electrobiologist
electrochemistry
electrodynamical
electrogenic pump
electro-hydraulic
electrolytically
electromagnetism
electromigration
electromyography
electronographic
electro-oculogram
electro-optically
electropneumatic
electroreception
electroreduction
electrostriction
electrostrictive
electrosynthesis
electrotechnical
electrotherapist
electroviscosity
elegant variation
elementary school
elliptic geometry
embarkation leave
emission spectrum
emperor angel-fish
empirical formula
empirio-criticism
employment agency
employment office
enantiodromiacal
encephalitogenic
encephalographic
encephalopathies
encyclopedically
endocrinological
endotheliomatous
enemy of the people
engineering brick
English breakfast
English galingale
enough and to spare
enterochromaffin
entertainingness
enthusiastically
entomopathogenic
entrepreneurship
environmentalism
environmentalist
epeirogernically

epigrammatically
epiphenomenalism
epiphenomenalist
Epstein–Barr virus
expectative grace
expressionlessly
express messenger
Expurgatory Index
extemporaneously
extension bellows
external evidence
external relation
exterritoriality
extracorporeally
extra-essentially
extra-illustrated
extra-illustrator
extraordinary ray
extraterrestrial
extraterritorial
eyeball to eyeball
Fabry–Pérot etalon
facsimile edition
faint-heartedness
fall a sacrifice to
fall by the wayside
falling diphthong
fall into contempt
fall into oblivion
false bitter-sweet
false chanterelle
Faraday dark space
Faraday's constant
farthingale chair
fashion-conscious
fashion jewellery
feasibility study
Feast of Orthodoxy
feature programme
federal territory
feeble-mindedness
fellow countryman
fermentation lock
ferroelectricity
festival of lights
few and far between
fibroadenomatous
fictionalization
field-conventicle
Fifth-monarchy-man
fight to the finish
fight to the stumps
figure of four trap
finisher of the law
finishing touches
finite difference
fire and brimstone
fire extinguisher
first and foremost
first conjugation
first past the post
first things first

first triumvirate
fissure of Rolando
five o'clock shadow
flat-bottomed boat
flexible response
flibbertygibbety
flight lieutenant
flight refuelling
Florentine mosaic
Florentine stitch
flotsam and jetsam
flowering currant
flowers of sulphur
fluorimetrically
fluorometrically
fluorophotometer
fluorophotometry
fluoroscopically
fluviolacustrine
fly in the ointment
foam extinguisher
football hooligan
for all one is worth
forbidden degrees
for the love of Mike
for what it is worth
Foucault pendulum
foundation course
foundation member
foundation-school
Fourier transform
four-leaved clover
fourth-generation
frame of reference
Freedom of the Rule
French Revolution
frequency changer
frequency diagram
frequency polygon
fresh off the irons
from cover to cover
from force of habit
from month to month
from pillar to post
from space to space
fruits of the earth
Fulbright scholar
full dress uniform
fuming nitric acid
funicular polygon
funicular railway
further education
future contingent
galactic latitude
gammon and spinach
ganglion-blocking
gardener's garters
Garter King of Arms
gastric influenza
gastro-enterology
gastroenterology
gastro-intestinal

gastrointestinal
gastroscopically
genealogical tree
generalizability
general knowledge
genetic profiling
Geneva Convention
genitive absolute
gentleman of virtu
Gentleman's Relish
gentlemen farmers
geochronological
geographical mile
geographical pole
geological survey
geometrical ratio
geometric tracery
geomorphological
get away from it all
get one's hooks into
get one's knife into
get one's own back on
get one's teeth into
get to the bottom of
get up with the lark
girdle of chastity
give a miss-in-baulk
give a wide berth to
give full weight to
give to understand
glaciolacustrine
glosso-epiglottic
glosso-pharyngeal
glossopharyngeal
glottochronology
glove compartment
glucose phosphate
glycerophosphate
go-aheadativeness
go all unnecessary
golden maidenhair
goods and chattels
grey marketeering
groom of the ladder
guerrilla warfare
guiding telescope
guilty conscience
gunboat diplomacy
gutter journalism
gynaecologically
gynandromorphism
gynandromorphous
haematologically
haematoporphyrin
haemochromatosis
haemodynamically
haemoglobinaemia
hairline fracture
Hallelujah Chorus
hand and glove with
hand in one's checks
hanging committee

hanging indention
hanging paragraph
hang in the balance
hang up one's fiddle
happy-go-luckiness
harmonic analysis
harmonic function
haul over the coals
have for breakfast
have it one's own way
Hawking radiation
head and shoulders
hearsay knowledge
heart-lung machine
hearts-and-flowers
Heath-Robinsonish
Hebrew Scriptures
heiress-portioner
heirs presumptive
heliocentrically
heliographically
hell and high water
helmeted curassow
hepatolenticular
herbaceous border
hermaphroditical
herpetologically
hetero-agglutinin
heterosuggestion
heterotransplant
hexachloroethane
hieroglyphically
higgledy-piggledy
High Commissioner
highfalutination
histogenetically
histopathologist
hither and thither
hold a person's hand
holding operation
hold one's head high
hollandaise sauce
Holy Innocents' Day
home away from home
horseback opinion
horses for courses
horticulturalist
hospital gangrene
hostage to fortune
household effects
household science
housemaid's closet
House of Delegates
human engineering
hundred-per-center
hyaline cartilage
hydrochloric acid
hydrodynamically
hydroelectricity
hydro-engineering
hydrofluoric acid
hydroformylation

hydrogen peroxide
hydrogen sulphide
hydrographically
hydrometeorology
hydropericardium
hydrostatic press
hydrotherapeutic
hydrothermal vent
hydroxocobalamin
hygrothermograph
hyperbolic cosine
hyper-Calvinistic
hypercellularity
hyperchlorhydria
hyperchlorhydric
hyperchromatosis
hyperconjugation
hypercorrectness
hypergeometrical
hypermetamorphic
hyperoxygenation
hyperparathyroid
hyperpituitarism
hypersensitivity
hypertrophically
hyperventilation
hypervitaminosis
hypnotherapeutic
hypochlorous acid
hypochondriacism
hypocoristically
hypodermatically
hypophysectomize
hypophysiotropic
hypsilophodontid
hystero-epileptic
hysteron proteron
iatromathematics
iconoclastically
iconographically
icositetrahedron
identificational
idols of the market
illegal operation
image intensifier
immature cataract
immeasurableness
immunochemically
immunodeficiency
immunodepressant
immunodepression
immunodepressive
immunosuppressed
impenetrableness
imperceptibility
imperfect cadence
imperfectibility
imperial elephant
Imperial Highness
imperishableness
impermissibility
imperturbability

implementiferous
imponderableness
impracticability
improper fraction
imputrescibility
in a brace of shakes
inaccessibleness
in accordance with
in a class of its own
in all probability
in and out of season
in any shape or form
inappreciatively
inarticulateness
in a state of nature
inauspiciousness
incalculableness
incipient species
incognoscibility
incombustibility
incommensurately
incommodiousness
incomparableness
in comparison with
incompatibleness
incompletability
incomplete symbol
in compliance with
incompossibility
incomprehensible
incomprehensibly
inconceivability
inconclusiveness
in connection with
inconsequentness
inconsolableness
incontestability
incontrovertible
incontrovertibly
inconvertibility
incorrespondence
incorrespondency
incorrigibleness
incorruptibility
incubation period
indecent exposure
indeclinableness
indefatigability
indefeasibleness
indefensibleness
independent float
indescribability
Indian paintbrush
Indian restaurant
Indian tragacanth
indiarubber plant
indicator diagram
indigestibleness
indirect evidence
indirect lighting
indirect question
indiscernibility

indiscriminately
indiscrimination
indiscriminative
indispensability
indisputableness
indissolubleness
indoleacetic acid
induction furnace
induction heating
industrial action
industrial estate
industrial injury
industrial school
inegalitarianism
inertial guidance
inexhaustibility
inexplicableness
inexpressiveness
inexpugnableness
inextinguishable
inextinguishably
inferior meridian
in flagrant delict
influence peddler
information booth
inharmoniousness
inhospitableness
in huckster's hands
initial consonant
injection-moulded
injured innocence
inland navigation
in less than no time
innominate artery
in propria persona
insolubilization
inspector general
inspector of taxes
in spite of oneself
in statu pupillari
institutionalise
institutionalism
institutionalist
institutionalize
instrumentalness
insubstantiality
insufferableness
insufficientness
insulin treatment
insurance company
insurance premium
interpretability
interpretational
interpretatively
interpunctuation
interrelatedness
interrupted screw
intersegmentally
interstitial cell
interterritorial
intertestamental
interval training

interventricular
intervocalically
in the affirmative
in the driver's seat
in the first flight
in the lap of luxury
in the ordinary way
in the personage of
in the pudding club
in the same measure
in the second place
in this connection
intracisternally
intracontinental
intracutaneously
intraformational
intragastrically
intramolecularly
intransgressible
intrapericardial
intraventricular
introspectionism
introspectionist
inverisimilitude
inversely conical
inverse square law
inverted pendulum
inverted snobbery
inverted spelling
invisible exports
invisible imports
invisible mending
invulnerableness
inward investment
ionization energy
irreclaimability
irreconciliation
irreflectiveness
irremediableness
irrepressibility
irresistableness
irresistibleness
irresponsibility
irresponsiveness
irretrievability
irreversibleness
isoagglutination
isoagglutinative
isoelectric point
isolating barrier
Italian warehouse
it stands to reason
Jacobian function
Jamaica satinwood
Japanese knotweed
Japanese wisteria
Jerusalem letters
John Innes compost
Johnny-come-lately
jolterheadedness
Joule's equivalent
journalistically

journeys accounts
judgement summons
jumping-off ground
junior common room
junior high school
junior management
junior technician
jurisdictionally
Justinianian code
karyoplasplasmic
keep an eye skinned
keep a tight rein on
keep one's distance
keep one's eyes open
keep one's head down
keep one's trap shut
keep under one's hat
keep your pecker up
Kerry Blue terrier
kick the shit out of
kill with kindness
Kilmarnock bonnet
Kilmarnock willow
kinaesthetically
King Charles's head
King James Version
king's hard bargain
kiss and be friends
kitchen-gardening
kite's-foot tobacco
kleptoparasitism
kleptoparasitize
knight-errantship
Knight of Columbus
knight of the shire
knock the socks off
knock the tar out of
knowledgeability
knowledge factory
know the reason why
know the time of day
know what one likes
Krukenberg tumour
kulturgeschichte
Kurrichane thrush
laboratory animal
laboratory school
labouring classes
Labour of Hercules
Labrador feldspar
lackadaisicality
ladder tournament
Ladies' Aid Society
lady of easy virtue
Lagrange equation
laminated plastic
Lancashire hotpot
landscape painter
language planning
language-specific
lapis calaminaris
Laplace's equation

Laplace's operator
Laplace transform
Larmor precession
laryngealization
laser angioplasty
last thing at night
lateral malleolus
lattice leaf plant
lattice vibration
laugh one's head off
Laurentian Shield
law of gravitation
law of least action
lay hands on the ark
leaden fly-catcher
Leadenhall Street
Leader of the House
learning resource
leave the door open
left-hand marriage
left out in the cold
legal proceedings
legitimatization
lemon meringue pie
lenticular galaxy
lentiform nucleus
lesser of two evils
letter of attorney
letter of credence
letters avocatory
letters dimissory
Levitical degrees
lexicostatistics
Liberal Christian
Liberian calendar
life imprisonment
lift up the heart of
light-heartedness
light heavyweight
lignin sulphonate
like a bull at a gate
like a Cheshire cat
like a dose of salts
like a duck to water
like a house on fire
like a shag on a rock
like a ton of bricks
limited liability
limousine liberal
linen manufacture
line-of-battle ship
liqueur chocolate
listening gallery
literary-critical
literary executor
locomotive engine
logarithmic curve
logarithmic scale
loggerhead shrike
loggerhead turtle
logical necessity
logical operation

logical structure
loiter with intent
London particular
longitudinal wave
long-nosed potoroo
long-tailed jaeger
looking-glass carp
looking-glass land
Lord Chief Justice
Lord Commissioner
Lord Justice Clerk
Lorentz-covariant
Lorentz-invariant
lose one's bearings
lose one's stirrups
lost in the shuffle
love at first sight
love-lies-bleeding
lunar observation
lycopodium powder
lymphangiectasis
lymphangiography
lymphangiomatous
lyra glockenspiel
machiavellianism
macro-engineering
macro-instruction
macrolepidoptera
Macrolepidoptera
macrolinguistics
macrophotography
maestro di capella
magic chain-stitch
magistrates' court
magnesiochromite
magnetic meridian
magnetochemistry
magnetostriction
magnetostrictive
magnetotellurics
maintainableness
maintained school
maintenance order
Majorana particle
major-generalship
make an appearance
make both ends meet
make capital out of
make conversation
make no bones about
make no difference
maladministrator
malapportionment
malappropriation
Malayo-Polynesian
Malaysianization
malcontentedness
male-chauvinistic
male impersonator
malignant pustule
Malpighian tubule
mammographically

management buyout
managing director
Manchester cotton
Manchester School
mango-hummingbird
manifestationist
manipulativeness
man of distinction
man-of-the-worldish
maraschino cherry
marine-biological
marine scientific
market researcher
marriage articles
marriage guidance
marshmallow roast
marsupialization
masculine protest
mass spectrograph
mass spectrometer
mass spectrometry
mass spectroscope
Master in Chancery
Master of Requests
Master of the Horse
Master of the Rolls
master oscillator
material handling
maternal language
maternity benefit
matrimonial agent
matter of breviary
matter-of-factness
Matthew principle
Maxwell–Boltzmann
mayor of the palace
mealy-mouthedness
mean proportional
measurement cargo
mechanical stoker
mechanico-morphic
mechanochemistry
mechanoreception
mechanoreceptive
mechanosensitive
mediate inference
mediate knowledge
medical diathermy
mediocritization
Mediterraneanize
medium of exchange
medulla oblongata
meet one's Waterloo
melodramatically
melon-caterpillar
Member of Congress
members' enclosure
meningomyelocele
mental arithmetic
mental deficiency
mercantile marine
mercantile system

merchantableness
merchant-princely
merchant-venturer
mercurialization
mercury sublimate
meretriciousness
meridian altitude
meristematically
meritorious cause
mesembryanthemum
metabolic pathway
metabolizability
metallic tractors
metallocarborane
metallographical
metamathematical
meta-metalanguage
metaphrastically
meteorologically
methodologically
methylated spirit
methyl isocyanate
methyl salicylate
methylthiouracil
metropolitanship
metropolitically
Mexican overdrive
Michelangelesque
microcalorimeter
microcalorimetry
microchiropteran
microcirculation
microclimatology
microcontinental
microcrystalline
microelectronics
micro-electronics
micro-encapsulate
micro-engineering
micro-environment
microfiche reader
microfilamentous
microgametophyte
micrographically
microinstruction
microlepidoptera
Microlepidoptera
microlinguistics
micromanipulator
micrometeoroidal
micrometeorology
microminiaturize
microphotography
microphotometric
microprogramming
micropropagation
micropublication
microradiography
microsporidiosis
microtopographic
middle-aged spread
middle common room

middle distillate
middle linebacker
middle management
midsummer madness
militaristically
military hospital
milking shorthorn
mind-transference
mineral chameleon
ministering angel
minor determinant
minority movement
mirror embroidery
misanthropically
misappropriation
miscommunication
miscomprehension
misinterpretable
mispronunciation
mission furniture
mission statement
Miss Lonelyhearts
mistaken identity
misunderstanding
modal personality
model aircraft kit
molecular biology
momentaneousness
monarch butterfly
monetary targetry
monkey-puzzle tree
monkey's allowance
monoamine oxidase
monochromaticity
monocotyledonous
monoethanolamine
monopolistically
mono-substitution
monosyllabically
monotheistically
Montagu's sea-snail
Monte Carlo method
Monterey mackerel
montmorillonitic
moral inspiration
more often than not
more than ordinary
more than somewhat
morning-after pill
morphic resonance
morphologization
morphometrically
morphotactically
Mother Goose rhyme
moules bonne femme
mountain bluebird
mountain-building
mountain-climbing
mountain mahogany
mountain reedbuck
mountain sickness
mountain tortoise

mousseline-de-soie
moustached guenon
move the goalposts
move with the times
muddle-headedness
mulberry-coloured
Müllerian mimicry
mullion structure
multibillionaire
multicellularity
multiculturalism
multiculturalist
multidimensional
multidirectional
multidisciplined
multifactorially
multifariousness
multilateralness
multimillionaire
multiple exposure
multiplepoinding
multiple standard
multiplicability
multiplicational
multiplicatively
multiplier effect
multiplying-glass
multiprogramming
multituberculate
municipalization
mushroom-coloured
musical dramatist
musquash sealskin
muster-mastership
mutation pressure
mutual inductance
myasthenia gravis
myelographically
myelomeningocele
myricyl palmitate
myrmidon of the law
myrtle-of-the-river
nail to the counter
naked singularity
nanophanerophyte
nanotechnologist
narcissistically
narrow-mindedness
Nasmyth's membrane
National Assembly
National Covenant
national football
national minority
natural deduction
natural frequency
natural historian
naturalistically
natural logarithm
natural marmalade
natural resources
natural scientist
natural selection

navicular disease
Neapolitan medlar
Neapolitan violet
Neapolitan yellow
nearest neighbour
nearest one's heart
necessitarianism
neck-handkerchief
negative eugenics
negative evidence
negative feedback
negative geotaxis
negative instance
negative pregnant
negative quantity
negative transfer
negro-head tobacco
Negro Renaissance
neo-impressionism
neo-impressionist
neo-Malthusianism
neo-scholasticism
nepheline-syenite
nephrocalcinosis
nervous breakdown
Net Book Agreement
network structure
neurocirculatory
neurogenic theory
neurohypophysial
neurolinguistics
neuropathologist
neurophysiologic
neuropsychiatric
neurotransmitter
Newcastle disease
Newcastle pottery
Newfoundland fish
newspaper article
newspaper English
New Zealand falcon
New Zealand rabbit
New Zealand thrush
nightingale floor
Nilotic crocodile
Nirvana principle
nitrate reductase
nitrogen fixation
nitrogen narcosis
Nobel prizewinner
no-claims discount
no laughing matter
nonbiodegradable
non-chronological
non-communicating
non-contradiction
non-controversial
non-destructively
non-disjunctional
non-orientability
non-participating
non-proliferation

nonsense syllable
nonsensicalities
nonsensification
no questions asked
north-easternmost
north-east passage
northern hornworm
northwesternmost
north-west passage
notch-brittleness
note of admiration
nothing else for it
nothing of the kind
nothing of the sort
nothing to show for
not to be sneezed at
no two ways about it
nuclear chemistry
nuclear holocaust
nucleochronology
nucleophilically
nullificationist
nut milk chocolate
Nyquist criterion
oath of abjuration
Oath of Abjuration
oath of allegiance
obdiplostemonous
object complement
oblique ascension
observationalism
observationalist
obstreperousness
obstruction light
obturator foramen
occipital condyle
occipito-anterior
occipitotemporal
occupation bridge
occupation centre
occupation number
odium theologicum
oestrogenization
official birthday
official receiver
offshore islander
offshore purchase
oil of wintergreen
Old Contemptibles
old-fashionedness
old-fashioned rose
old Spanish custom
oligodendroglial
oligomenorrhoeic
on an empty stomach
on a silver platter
one of those things
one's better nature
one's gorge rises at
one's own resources
one way and another
onomatopoeically

on one's conscience
on one's own account
on pins and needles
on the front burner
on the right side of
on the stroke of one
on the windy side of
on the wrong side of
open-heart surgery
open the shoulders
operating theatre
ophthalmic artery
ophthalmological
ophthalmoscopist
opinionativeness
opisthographical
opisthopulmonate
opportunity State
opsonocytophagic
optical isomerism
optical pyrometer
oranges and lemons
order of Dannebrog
order of magnitude
Order of the Garter
organic chemistry
overplay one's hand
over-prescription
overreach oneself
overscrupulously
overshoot the mark
oversubscription
over the telephone
overwhelmingness
oviform limestone
ovigerous fraenum
oyster-shell scale
pachydermatously
padding capacitor
paired associates
paired comparison
pair of spectacles
palace revolution
palaeobathymetry
palaeocerebellar
palaeocerebellum
palaeodemography
palaeoecological
palaeo-equatorial
palaeogeographer
palaeogeographic
palaeogeological
palaeogeomorphic
palaeogeophysics
palaeolithologic
palaeontographer
palaeontological
palaeopathologic
palaeopedologist
palaeotopography
palaeozoological
palagonitization

palato-pharyngeal
palingenetically
palinspastically
pancreatectomize
Pantagruelically
pantographically
Pappenheimer body
para-aminobenzoic
paradigmatically
paradox of the liar
paraformaldehyde
parageosynclinal
paraheliotropism
parajournalistic
parallelepipedal
parallelogrammic
parallel tracking
paralysis agitans
paramagnetically
parameterization
paraphrasability
paraphrastically
paraprofessional
paraproteinaemia
parapsychologist
parautochthonous
parish councillor
parliamentaryism
parliamenteering
parochialization
parsimoniousness
partial involucre
particular estate
pass in one's checks
pass in one's marble
passive obedience
passive sacrifice
pass the time of day
pass to one's reward
Pasteur treatment
pastoral epistles
pastoral theology
paternoster-while
pathogenetically
pathophysiologic
patriarchal cross
patronal festival
pattern congruity
Pauline privilege
pay a compliment to
Paymaster General
peach-potato aphid
peacock butterfly
pearl everlasting
pebble spectacles
pedal steel guitar
peerless primrose
peine forte et dure
pellitory of Spain
Peloponnesian war
pendulum governor
penetration agent

people's democracy
peregrine praetor
perfectibilarian
perfidious Albion
perforation plate
performativeness
performing rights
periodical cicada
periodic function
period-luminosity
periodontoclasia
periphrastically
perish the thought
permanent pasture
permeabilization
permutation group
perpendicularity
perpetual spinach
perpetual student
persecution mania
Persian greyhound
personal computer
personal equation
personal property
personnel carrier
pertinaciousness
pervicaciousness
Peter Pannishness
petite bourgeoise
petitio principii
petrogenetically
petrographically
petroleum geology
petty bourgeoisie
Petzval condition
Peyronie's disease
phacoanaphylaxis
phalaris staggers
phallocentricity
phantasmagorical
phantom pregnancy
pharmaceutically
pharmacodynamics
pharmacogenetics
pharmacognostics
pharmacokinetics
pharyngalization
pharyngo-palatine
phenakistoscopic
phenolcarboxylic
phenomenological
phenylenediamine
philanthropinism
philanthropinist
philoprogenitive
philosopher's wool
philosophization
phlebothrombosis
phlebotomization
phlorizinization
phonetic alphabet
phonocardiograph

phonographically
phonograph record
phonophotography
phosphoglycerate
phosphoglyceride
phosphoinositide
phosphorescently
photoautotrophic
photochromoscope
photocoagulation
photocomposition
photoconductance
photodegradation
photoduplication
photodynamically
photoelectricity
photoelectronics
photofabrication
photofluorograph
photofluoroscope
photofluoroscopy
photogoniometric
photogrammetrist
photographically
photoheliography
photoheterotroph
photointerpreter
photokinetically
photolithography
photolitho offset
photolithotrophy
photoluminescent
photomacrography
photomicrography
photo opportunity
photoorganotroph
photoperiodicity
photopolarimeter
photopolarimetry
photoreactivable
photorespiration
photorespiratory
photosensitivity
photostereograph
photostimulation
photosynthesizer
phototelegraphic
phototherapeutic
phototopographer
phototopographic
phototrophically
phototypesetting
photovoltaically
photozincography
phraseologically
phycobiliprotein
phylogenetically
physical training
physico-chemistry
physiognomically
physiognomonical
physiopathologic

physiophilosophy
physio-psychology
phytopathologist
phytosociologist
pictorialization
picture frequency
picture-telephone
piezoelectricity
piezoresistivity
pigeon-woodpecker
piggy in the middle
pigtailed macaque
pillion passenger
pithecanthropine
pithecanthropoid
Pitman's Shorthand
pituitary extract
plagiaristically
plagiotropically
plain-heartedness
planishing hammer
planishing roller
planktonological
plankton recorder
plantation creole
plasma propulsion
plastic explosive
play fast and loose
play second fiddle
play second violin
play silly buggers
play the devil with
play the giddy goat
play to the gallery
pleased to meet you
plethysmographic
pleuro-peritoneal
pleuro-peritoneum
plunging neckline
plurisignatively
pluviometrically
Plymouth Brethren
pneumonectomized
pneumonoconiosis
pneumonoconiotic
pneumoperitoneum
pneumotachograph
poached-egg flower
pocket battleship
pocket calculator
poet-laureateship
poikilodermatous
poikilosmoticity
point of departure
point of reference
poke one's nose into
polarimetrically
polarizing filter
police dispatcher
police magistrate
policeman's helmet
police procedural

political economy
political hostess
politicalization
political offence
political refugee
political science
politico-economic
pollen mother cell
polychromatophil
polycondensation
polycotyledonous
polyelectrolytic
polygonal numbers
polymerizability
polymolecularity
polyoxymethylene
polyphyletically
polypseudonymous
polyrhythmically
polysomnographic
polysyllabically
polytheistically
polyvinyl acetate
polyvinyl alcohol
pommes allumettes
Pontifical Zouave
poor man's diggings
pop goes the weasel
poplar leaf-beetle
poplar lutestring
popular etymology
porcelainization
pornographically
portable computer
porterhouse steak
Port Jackson shark
Portuguese oyster
port-wine magnolia
positive definite
positive electron
positive eugenics
positive feedback
positive geotaxis
positive pressure
positive thinking
positive transfer
positivistically
posterolaterally
posteroventrally
post-modification
post-office bridge
post-reproductive
potassium cyanide
potential barrier
potential cautery
Poupart's ligament
poverty programme
powder metallurgy
powder-post beetle
power transformer
Poynting's theorem
pragmatistically

praiseworthiness
Prausnitz–Küstner
preaching-station
preamplification
preconsciousness
preconsideration
predatory pricing
predetermination
predeterminative
predial servitude
prelumirhodopsin
premeditatedness
premillennialism
premillennialist
Premonstratenses
Premonstratensis
preponderatingly
preposterousness
pre-revolutionary
prerogative court
prescriptibility
prescription drug
prescriptiveness
presensitization
presentationally
presentation copy
president-general
presiding officer
presignification
press into service
prestidigitation
prestidigitatory
presumption of law
presumptuousness
presuppositional
preterite-present
preternaturalism
preternaturalist
preterpluperfect
pretty as a picture
pretty-prettiness
previous question
prick in the garter
prickly glasswort
primary education
primary structure
primary treatment
Primate of England
prime-ministerial
Primitive Baptist
primitive lattice
primrose peerless
primus inter pares
Prince of Darkness
prince of the blood
principal section
printed circuitry
prior probability
prismatic compass
prisoner at the bar
prisoner's dilemma
private detective

private judgement
private residence
private secretary
probability curve
probation officer
probation service
problematization
proboscidiferous
process annealing
prochlorperazine
procurator fiscal
production number
product of inertia
professional foul
proficiency badge
progestationally
programmatically
programme company
programme picture
programme trading
progress of titles
Prohibition party
projectile anchor
projection welder
promenade concert
promorphological
pronounceability
pronunciation key
propargyl alcohol
propeller turbine
propelling pencil
propertylessness
property mistress
prophetic perfect
prophetic present
prophylactically
propositionalist
proprioceptively
propylthiouracil
proscriptiveness
proslambanomenos
prosodic analysis
prosopographical
prospecting claim
prosthaphaeresis
protected species
protection forest
protection racket
protective arrest
protochlorophyll
prototrophically
prototypographer
providentialness
Provident Society
proximity of blood
pseudepigraphous
pseudo-classicism
pseudocopulation
pseudoextinction
pseudomembranous
pseudomorphously
pseudoperipteral

pseudoperipteros
pseudoplasticity
pseudo-scientific
pseudoscopically
pseudostratified
psophometrically
psychiatric nurse
psychiatrization
psychic energizer
psychoacoustical
psycho-aesthetics
psychoanalytical
psychobiographer
psychobiographic
psychobiological
psychodiagnostic
psychogeographic
psychohistorical
psycholinguistic
psychologization
psychometrically
psychopathically
psychopathologic
psychophysically
psychophysiology
psychosomaticist
psychotechnology
psychotropically
pteroylglutamate
pterygoid process
pterygo-maxillary
public prosecutor
public-spiritedly
pudding in the oven
pull out of the fire
pull up by the roots
pull up one's stumps
pumpkinification
Punch-and-Judy show
punch-drunkenness
punctuationalism
punctuationalist
pupil-teachership
Purkinje's vesicle
purple granadilla
pursuit aeroplane
put a bold face on it
putative marriage
put heads together
put one's heart into
put out of one's mind
put the hard word on
put the skids under
put up the shutters
pyramidal numbers
Pyrenean sheepdog
pyrometallurgist
pyrometamorphism
quadraphonically
quadratic residue
quadricentennial
quadrupole moment

quality newspaper
quantificational
quantitativeness
quantity of estate
quantity surveyor
quantum chemistry
quantum mechanics
quarterback sneak
quarterly meeting
quarterly-pierced
quarter-partition
quarter-repeating
quasi-contractual
quatercentennial
Queckenstedt test
Queen Anne's bounty
queen-of-the-meadow
Queensberry rules
Queensland walnut
queen trigger fish
questionableness
quintessentially
rabbit-foot clover
radappertization
radial keratotomy
radiation counter
radiation pattern
radiation therapy
radiative capture
radiesthetically
radioactive waste
radioautographic
radio frequencies
radiogoniometric
radiographically
radioimmunoassay
radioimmunologic
radiolarian chert
radiolarian earth
radiosensitivity
radio-telegraphic
radiotherapeutic
ragtag and bobtail
Railway Institute
rainbow coalition
raise from the dead
raise its ugly head
raise one's glass to
raisins of Corinth
rambunctiousness
ramus communicans
rape crisis centre
rapid eye-movement
rap on the knuckles
rapture of the deep
raspberry vinegar
ratio cognoscendi
rat's-tail plantain
Rayleigh–Jeans law
razor strop fungus
reality principle
reap the whirlwind

recapitalization
recategorization
Received Standard
receive the spirit
receive the Spirit
receiving blanket
reciprocal course
reclassification
recoil escapement
recollectiveness
reconcilableness
reconstructional
recorded delivery
recording channel
recover the wind of
recovery position
recreation ground
recrystallizable
rectifying column
rectus et inversus
recurring decimal
recursion formula
red-breasted goose
red-light district
red-necked wallaby
Red Republicanism
red-throated diver
reduce to the ranks
reference library
refractory period
regal pelargonium
regent honeyeater
regimental colour
regiospecificity
Registrar General
registration mark
regular satellite
rehalogenization
re-identification
reign of terrorism
reincarnationism
reincarnationist
reintermediation
reinterpretation
relative humidity
relativistically
relieving officer
remainder theorem
remembrancership
remilitarization
remineralization
remote-controlled
removal of remains
remunerativeness
rend one's garments
renounce the world
reorganizational
repeating decimal
repertory company
replica technique
reprehensibility
representability

representational
representatively
representativity
reproachlessness
reproductiveness
reprographically
republican weaver
request programme
requisite variety
re-representation
rescue excavation
réseau à l'aiguille
residentiaryship
residual activity
residuary devisee
resist decoration
resolidification
resolutive clause
resonance capture
resonance chamber
resource industry
resourcelessness
respiratory tract
responsibilities
resting potential
restraint of trade
resurrection body
resurrection fern
retail price index
reticulate python
retinoscopically
retractile testis
retransformation
retransportation
retrogressionist
returning officer
reunificationist
revealed religion
reversing stratum
revival of letters
revolutioneering
rhabdomyosarcoma
Rhenish stoneware
rheumatoid factor
rhinoceros auklet
rhinoceros beetle
rhinolaryngology
rhinopharyngitis
rhinosporidiosis
Rhode Island White
rhynchocephalian
rhythm instrument
ribbon microphone
ride the lightning
ring-tailed possum
ring-tailed roarer
ring the changes on
rise from the ashes
rise from the ranks
river engineering
robin's pincushion
rocker-bottom foot

rock with laughter
rococo embroidery
roentgenkymogram
roentgenographic
roentgenotherapy
Rolando substance
Roman Catholicism
roof over one's head
roseate spoonbill
round-headed borer
roving commission
Rowland's mounting
royal Bengal tiger
Royal Institution
royal prerogative
rub shoulders with
rule of proportion
run into the ground
running on the spot
run off at the mouth
Russian bagatelle
Russian cigarette
Russian Easter egg
Russian wolfhound
saccharification
saccharimetrical
Sacrament Sabbath
sacrifice bidding
sacrificial anode
saddlebacked crow
saddleback jackal
saffron butterfly
Saint-Simonianism
sale and leaseback
sallow kitten moth
salvation history
same but different
sanctum sanctorum
sanitary engineer
sarcosporidiosis
Sardinian warbler
satellite country
satellite station
satisfaction note
satisfactoriness
saturable reactor
saturation diving
Saturday-to-Monday
saussuritization
savannah woodland
save out of the fire
save the phenomena
save the situation
scaly-bark hickory
scare the pants off
scarlet king-snake
scarlet pimpernel
scarlet rosefinch
scarlet tiger moth
scenographically
scentless mayweed
scheduled service

Schilder's disease
schismaticalness
schistosomicidal
schizophreniform
schlicht function
Schmidt telescope
schoolboyishness
school-leaving age
schoolmastership
schools broadcast
schools programme
Schweizerdeutsch
science-fictional
scientificalness
scientific method
scientifictional
scintillographic
scissors and paste
sclerenchymatous
Scotch warming-pan
Scottish baronial
scratch around for
screw dislocation
scribble-scrabble
scripture account
Scythian antelope
searcher of hearts
search high and low
seaweed marquetry
secondary feather
secondary poverty
secondary quality
secondary rainbow
secondary teacher
second-generation
second-handedness
second intentions
second lieutenant
Secretary-General
Secretary of State
secret as the grave
sectionalization
sedimentological
see a man about a dog
see a thing through
see off the new ball
see the light of day
segmentalization
segment of a circle
segment of a sphere
segregationalist
seismocardiogram
seize the open file
selection felling
selective realism
selective service
self-aggrandizing
self-annihilation
self-appreciation
self-condemnation
self-condensation
self-consistently

self-contemptuous
self-depreciation
self-depreciatory
self-dissociation
self-estrangement
self-flagellation
self-incompatible
self-inconsistent
self-opinionative
self-perpetuating
self-perpetuation
self-preservation
self-preservative
self-renunciation
self-satisfaction
self-sufficiently
self-transcending
sell a bill of goods
sell down the river
sell like hot cakes
sell one's life dear
semicircularness
semi-conservative
semidine reaction
semi-occasionally
semipermeability
semi-professional
semi-transparency
send in one's papers
send the hat around
senior common room
senior high school
senior management
sensationalistic
sense of direction
sentimentalistic
sentimental value
separate but equal
sequence of tenses
sergeant-majorish
Sermon on the Mount
seroepidemiology
serpentine marble
serpentinization
serve hand and foot
serve one's country
service reservoir
sesquicentennial
set little store by
set the kiln on fire
set-theoretically
seven-league boots
sewage irrigation
sex determination
sexual dimorphism
sexual harassment
sexual revolution
shake in one's shoes
Shakespearianism
shake the plum-tree
shearing strength
Sheehan's syndrome

shellbark hickory
shell transformer
sheriff principal
Shetland sheepdog
shifting keyboard
shiitake mushroom
shilling dreadful
shipping-articles
shirtsleeve order
shisha embroidery
shoestring fungus
shoestring potato
shortcrust pastry
Shorter Catechism
short-sightedness
shotgun formation
shoulder-of-mutton
shuttle diplomacy
Siberian purslane
Sibylline oracles
sick at the stomach
sick to the stomach
side-necked turtle
side-saddle flower
Sierra Leone peach
sight for sore eyes
signal-noise ratio
signal of distress
significance test
significant digit
significant other
silent dog whistle
silicoflagellate
silviculturalist
simple-mindedness
simultaneousness
singer-songwriter
single-lens reflex
single malt whisky
single-mindedness
sing the praises of
situations vacant
six and half a dozen
sixth-form college
size distribution
skeleton building
skirting radiator
slantindicularly
sleeping carriage
sleeping princess
sleeping sickness
sling one's hammock
slubberdegullion
small claims court
small is beautiful
small-still whisky
smell of the candle
smite hip and thigh
snakes and ladders
sociable grosbeak
social chauvinism
social conscience

social democratic
social-historical
socialist realism
socialist-realist
social morphology
social psychiatry
social psychology
social revolution
Society of Friends
socio-demographic
sociolinguistics
Socratic elenchus
soda-lime feldspar
sodium-vapour lamp
soil conservation
soldier of fortune
soldier's farewell
Solicitor-General
Solochrome cyanin
something chronic
something or other
sonoluminescence
soporiferousness
soprano saxophone
sound-conditioned
sound spectrogram
south-easternmost
southern hornworm
Southern Triangle
south-westernmost
sovereign pontiff
Sovietologically
space observatory
spaghetti western
Spanish influenza
Spanish toothpick
spark transmitter
spastic paralysis
spatio-temporally
speak with tongues
special constable
special intention
special plea-in-bar
specific activity
specific medicine
specific rotation
spectacled cayman
spectral analysis
spectrobolometer
spectrochemistry
spectroheliogram
spectrum analyser
spectrum analysis
speech physiology
speech recognizer
spendthriftiness
Spenserian stanza
spes successionis
sphaerocobaltite
sphincter control
sphingolipidosis
sphygmomanometer

sphygmomanometry
spick-and-spanness
spill one's guts out
spin polarization
spiny pocket-mouse
spiral divergence
spiral thickening
spirit duplicator
spiritual healing
spiritualization
spirituous liquor
spirochaeticidal
spirographically
Spithead pheasant
spit something out
spitting distance
splanchnocranial
splanchnocranium
splanchnological
splanchnopleuric
split personality
sporting of nature
spray steelmaking
square-shouldered
squeeze cementing
stag-horn calculus
Stammbaumtheorie
Standard American
standard of living
stand in the breach
stand up to the rack
stand widdershins
start withershins
state of emergency
State Scholarship
stationary motion
Stationery Office
statutory company
statutory holiday
statutory meeting
stay a person's hand
steganographical
Steinert's disease
stellate ganglion
stenographically
stepmotherliness
stepping-off place
step saver kitchen
stereochemically
stereocomparator
stereocontrolled
stereoelectronic
stereometrically
stereomicrograph
stereomicroscope
stereophonically
stereophotograph
stereoplanigraph
stereoradiograph
stereoregularity
stereoregulation
stereoscopically

stereospondylous
stereotactically
sterling balances
sternoclavicular
stethoscopically
Steward of England
stichometrically
stick one's chin out
stick one's neck out
stick-to-it-iveness
stinking camomile
stipple engraving
stock certificate
stock-gillyflower
stoichiometrical
Stonesfield slate
stopping distance
storefront church
stout-heartedness
stout trencherman
strain at the leash
strain every nerve
strange attractor
stratificational
stratified charge
strawberry blonde
strawberry clover
strawberry colour
strawberry tomato
strawberry weevil
streak photograph
strengthlessness
streptothricosis
stress relaxation
stretching-course
stretch one's wings
stretch the neck of
stretto maestrale
strictly speaking
strict settlement
strike a false note
strike all of a heap
strike an attitude
striking distance
striking platform
strip cultivation
strip development
stroboscopically
stroke of apoplexy
stroke of business
strolling players
strongheadedness
strong-mindedness
strong silent type
strongyloidiasis
struggle-for-lifer
strychninization
stubble your whids
stuff and nonsense
stuff of household
subcartilaginous
subconsciousness

subfractionation
subject catalogue
subjectification
submicroscopical
subordinated debt
subordinated loan
subordinationism
subordinationist
subscribe oneself
subscription book
subscriptionless
subsistence level
subsistence money
substitutability
substitutionally
substratum theory
succès de scandale
succession powder
sucrose phosphate
suffragistically
sulfaquinoxaline
sulphate-reducing
sulphur bacterium
sulphur butterfly
summer yellowbird
summit conference
sun-and-planet gear
Sunday observance
Sunday supplement
superaerodynamic
superciliousness
superconsciously
supercontraction
supercriticality
super-Dreadnought
supererogatorily
superessentially
superexcellently
superfecundation
superficialities
superficial metre
superintelligent
supernationalism
supernaturalness
superplastically
supersensitivity
superserviceable
superstitionless
supersubstantial
super-superlative
superterrestrial
supervacaneously
supervision order
supplementary arc
supply the stead of
support equipment
support stockings
supposititiousness
supposititiously
supranationalism
supranationality
suprasegmentally

supraterrestrial
supraventricular
surface chemistry
surface-condenser
surface structure
surface-to-surface
surrealistically
susceptibilities
suspend disbelief
suspended ceiling
suspension bridge
suspension-feeder
sustained-release
swaddling-clothes
Swainson's warbler
swallow prominent
swamp honeysuckle
sweating-sickness
sweat one's guts out
Swedenborgianism
Swedish whitebeam
sweet vernal grass
Swinhoe's pheasant
Swiss cheese plant
switch-blade knife
symbolic delivery
symmetry-breaking
sympathectomized
sympathetic magic
sympathetic nerve
sympathicotropic
sympathoblastoma
symptomatologist
synaesthetically
syncategorematic
synchondrosially
synchrocyclotron
synchronological
synchronous curve
synchronous motor
syndiotactically
synovial membrane
tabes mesenterica
table centrepiece
tagrag and bobtail
take a rain check on
take a running jump
take in one's stride
take off one's hat to
take one's medicine
take the gloves off
take the measure of
take the piss out of
take the sacrament
take to the heather
take to the streets
take up one's livery
take up the cudgels
take up the running
talk to a brick wall
teacher appraisal
teaching hospital

tear limb from limb
technical college
technical drawing
technocratically
tectonophysicist
teddy bears' picnic
teeming and lading
teeter on the brink
teething problems
teething troubles
teleconferencing
telecurietherapy
telephonographic
telephotographic
telespectroscope
temperature-chart
temperature-curve
Temple parliament
temple prostitute
temporaneousness
temporary captain
tender loving care
tender-mindedness
tephrochronology
terephthalic acid
terminal guidance
terminal juncture
terminal nosedive
terminal velocity
terminologically
terminus ante quem
terminus post quem
term of endearment
terms of reference
terotechnologist
terrain-following
terrestrial globe
territorial limit
tertiary industry
tertiary recovery
tertiary syphilis
testimonial match
textual criticism
thalamencephalon
thalidomide child
that makes two of us
that will be the day
the Age of Chivalry
the Alliance Party
the ancient regime
the Angelic Doctor
Theatre of Cruelty
the Bank of England
the Church visible
the Dark Continent
the end of the earth
the end of the world
the festive season
the Flowery Empire
the full treatment
the gift of tongues
the great majority

the great outdoors
the great unwashed
the higher command
the Holy Innocents
the Holy Sacrament
the Holy Sepulchre
the King's Serjeant
the lady of the lamp
the late Bronze Age
the life of the mind
the lion's provider
the Lord's Anointed
the Lords temporal
the Maid of Orleans
the Metaphysicals
the name of the game
theologian of hope
the one and the many
theophilanthrope
theophilanthropy
the other way about
the other way round
the present writer
the Queen's English
the real Simon Pure
there is no knowing
there is no telling
there lies your way
thermal agitation
thermal diffusion
thermal pollution
thermal radiation
thermanaesthesia
thermoacidophile
thermochemically
thermodynamicist
thermoelectrical
thermogravimetry
thermomechanical
thermometrically
thermo-multiplier
thermoneutrality
thermoplasticity
thermoregulation
thermoregulatory
thermostabilized
thermostatically
the seals of office
the Seven Years War
the short answer is
the Siege Perilous
the sky is the limit
the sovereign good
the story of my life
the talk of the town
theta temperature
the tender passion
the usual channels
Thevenin's theorem
the way of all flesh
the Way of the Cross
the whole caboodle

the worse for drink
thick as two planks
thick-billed murre
thick on the ground
thigmotactically
thinking distance
think nothing of it
think the better of
third conjugation
thirty-second note
this earthly round
thoracic vertebra
those were the days
thought-executing
thought-provoking
thousand-head kale
three-birds-flying
three-dimensional
three-halves power
three-quarter back
three wise monkeys
threshing machine
throat microphone
thrombocythaemia
thrombocytopenia
thrombocytopenic
thrombophlebitis
through passenger
throw cold water on
throw in one's chips
throw in the sponge
throw off the scent
throw oneself into
throw to the wolves
thumbnail scraper
thyroid cartilage
tibial tuberosity
ticket-of-leave man
tickle the ivories
tickle the midriff
time and time again
tintinnabulation
tintinnabulatory
tip a person a stave
titular character
to all appearances
to be reckoned with
toings and froings
tonic contraction
to outward seeming
topological space
torpedo destroyer
tortoiseshell cat
Tottenham Pudding
tourmalinization
tournedos Rossini
tracheary element
tracheobronchial
trackless trolley
traditionalistic
traffic policeman
traffic violation

tragi-catastrophe
train of carriages
tranquillization
transactionalist
transatlantician
transatlanticism
transcendentally
transcendentness
transcendingness
transconductance
transcontinental
transcriptionist
transcriptitious
transcrystalline
transculturation
transferable vote
transfer function
transfer moulding
transformability
transformational
transhydrogenase
transilluminator
transitional case
transitionalness
transition period
transitory action
transit passenger
translation table
transmethylation
transmigratively
transmissibility
transmission-gear
transmission line
transmission loss
transmutationist
transpeptidation
transportability
transportational
transposing organ
transposing piano
transubstantiate
transverse magnet
transverse suture
traveller's cheque
trente-et-quarante
triangle of forces
triangular number
triboelectricity
triboluminescent
trichotillomania
trick photography
typhoid condition
tyrant flycatcher
ultracentrifugal
ultracrepidarian
ultracrepidation
ultramicroscopic
ultrasonographer
unacceptableness
unaccomplishable
unaccountability
unaccustomedness

unacquaintedness
unaggressiveness
unanswerableness
unapologetically
unappealableness
unappeasableness
unassailableness
unattainableness
unattractiveness
unbelievableness
unchangeableness
uncharacteristic
uncharitableness
uncircumspection
uncircumstantial
unclaimed layaway
uncognoscibility
uncompoundedness
uncompromisingly
unconditionality
unconditionately
unconformability
unconstitutional
uncontradictable
uncontradictably
uncontrovertedly
uncontrovertible
uncontrovertibly
unconventionally
uncrystallizable
undemocratically
undenominational
underachievement
under a flying seal
underconsumption
underdevelopment
undernourishment
under observation
under pain of death
underperformance
under requisition
under-secretaries
understimulation
under the same roof
underutilization
undifferentiated
undiplomatically
undiscourageable
undiscriminating
undistinguishing
undistractedness
unecclesiastical
uneconomicalness
unenforceability
unenterprisingly
unentertainingly
unexperienceable
unextinguishable
unfashionability
unfathomableness
unfavourableness
ungovernableness

ungrammaticality
unhesitatingness
unidirectionally
unimaginableness
unimpeachability
unimpressibility
unimpressionable
unimpressiveness
unindividualized
unindustrialized
uninflammability
uninstructedness
unintellectually
uninterestedness
unintermittently
unintermittingly
United Free Church
universal compass
universal grammar
universalization
university member
university of life
unlawful assembly
unlawful homicide
unmanageableness
unmentionability
unmetaphorically
unmistakableness
unmodifiableness
unnoticeableness
unobsequiousness
unofficial member
unofficial strike
unoriginatedness
unostentatiously
unparalleledness
unpardonableness
unpassionateness
unperceptiveness
unperishableness
unpredictability
unprejudicedness
unpremeditatedly
unpresumptuously
unpretendingness
unprincipledness
unproductiveness
unprofessionally
unprofitableness
unpropitiousness
unprosperousness
unreasonableness
unreflectingness
unremuneratively
unrenormalizable
unrepresentative
unrespectability
unresponsiveness
unrestrainedness
unrestrictedness
unsatisfactorily
unsatisfyingness

unscientifically
unscrupulousness
unsearchableness
unseasonableness
unsentimentality
unsentimentalize
unserviceability
unsophistication
unsubmissiveness
unsubstantiality
unsuccessfulness
unsufficientness
unsusceptibility
unsuspectingness
unsuspiciousness
unsustainability
unsystematically
unsystematizable
unthoughtfulness
untranscendental
ununderstandable
ununderstandably
unwarrantability
up against the wall
upper middle class
upper pastern-bone
upper ten thousand
upward-compatible
urea-formaldehyde
ureterolithotomy
uroporphyrinogen
user-friendliness
user-programmable
uveoparotid fever
vacant possession
vacuum aspiration
vacuum deposition
vacuum extraction
vagabond's disease
vaingloriousness
Valdez Principles
value engineering
value-orientation
vanity publishing
vascular cylinder
vasoconstricting
vasoconstriction
vasoconstrictive
vectorcardiogram
vegetable gelatin
vegetable kingdom
vegetable sulphur
velocity of escape
velocity pressure
velvet revolution
Venice turpentine
venoconstriction
vent one's spleen on
ventriculoatrial
ventriculography
vermiform process
vertical thinking

vesiculopustular
vicarage tea party
vicar-generalship
vice-presidencies
vice-presidential
Victoria sandwich
victualling-house
vinaigrette sauce
viper in one's bosom
Virginia bluebell
Virginian cowslip
Virginian creeper
Virginian opossum
visiting lecturer
vive la différence
viviparous blenny
viviparous lizard
voice synthesizer
voltammetrically
voluntary patient
vote of confidence
vote with one's feet
Vulcanian Islands
vulpine phalanger
walking gentleman
walking on two legs
walking-stick palm
walk in the way with
walk the hospitals
war correspondent
wardrobe mistress
war establishment
warn off the course
war of the elements
warrant of fitness
washerwoman's itch
washerwoman's skin
waste-paper basket
water-intoxicated
water stick insect
way of looking at it
weaken the hands of
wear the petticoat
weatherproofness
weather-resistant
weather-stripping
weatherstripping
Weberian ossicles
wedding breakfast
wedding reception
week and week about
well-favouredness
well-proportioned
Welsh Nationalist
Wernicke's aphasia
Wernicke's disease
Wessex saddleback
western white pine
westward position
wet behind the ears
whale-headed stork
what the vengeance

Wheatstone bridge
wheel arrangement
whistle in the dark
white-eyed pochard
Whitehall Warrior
white information
white ipecacuanha
white iron pyrites
white-necked raven
white precipitate
White supremacism
White supremacist
white swallowwort
wholeheartedness
wooden-headedness

woolly rhinoceros
Wordsworthianism
working breakfast
working knowledge
worry oneself sick
wound tumour virus
xeroradiographic
xiphoid cartilage
Yankee jib topsail
yellowfin croaker
yellow phosphorus
yellow snapdragon
Yeoman of the Guard
Yeomen of the Guard
York–Antwerp rules

Yorkshire pudding
Yorkshire teacake
Yorkshire terrier
you know what I mean
young fellow-me-lad
young-gentlemanly
young grammarians
Zéphirine Drouhin
zigzag connection
zonal pelargonium
zooarchaeologist
zoological garden
zygomatic process
zymotechnologist

ENCYCLOPEDIC LISTS

HISTORY, POLITICS, AND WAR

RULERS OF ENGLAND
(with dates of reign)

Edwy or Eadwig	955–7	Henry VIII	1509–47
Edgar	959–75	Edward VI	1547–53
Edward the Martyr, St	975–8	Jane (Lady Jane Grey)	1553
Ethelred the Unready	978–1013	Mary I*	1553–8
Sweyn Forkbeard	1013–4	Philip*	1554–8
Ethelred the Unready	1014–6	Elizabeth I	1558–1603
Edmund Ironside	1016	James I	1603–25
Canute	1016–35	Charles I	1625–49
Harold I (Harefoot)	1035–40	The Commonwealth	1649–60
Hartacnut	1040–2	Oliver Cromwell	1653–8
Edward the Confessor, St	1042–66	Richard Cromwell	1658–9
Harold II	1066	Charles II	1660–85
William I (the Conqueror)	1066–87	James II	1685–8
William II (Rufus)	1087–1100	*William and Mary	1689–94
Henry I	1100–35	William III	1694–1702
Stephen	1135–54	Anne	1702–14
Henry II	1154–89	George I	1714–27
Richard I	1189–99	George II	1727–60
John	1199–1216	George III	1760–1820
Henry III	1216–72	George IV	1820–30
Edward I	1272–1307	William IV	1830–7
Edward II	1307–27	Victoria	1837–1901
Edward III	1327–77	Edward VII	1901–10
Richard II	1377–99	George V	1910–36
Henry IV	1399–1413	Edward VIII	1936
Henry V	1413–22	George VI	1936–52
Henry VI	1422–61; 1470–1	Elizabeth II	from 1952
Edward IV	1461–83		
Edward V	1483	* Indicates joint reign.
Richard III	1483–5		
Henry VII	1485–1509		

RULERS OF SCOTLAND
(with dates of reign)

Kenneth I (MacAlpine)	c. 844–58	Malcolm II	1005–34
Donald I	858–62	Duncan I	1034–40
Constantine I	862–77	Macbeth	1040–57
Aedh	877–8	Malcolm III	1057–93
Girac*	878–89	Donald III (Bane)	1093–4, 1094–7
Eocha*	878–89	Duncan II	1094
Donald II	889–900	Edgar	1097–1107
Constantine II	900–43	Alexander I	1107–24
Malcolm I	943–54	David I	1124–53
Indolphus	954–62	Malcolm IV	1153–65
Duff	962–6	William the Lion	1165–1214
Colin	966–71	Alexander II	1214–49
Kenneth II	971–95	Alexander III	1249–86
Constantine III	995–7	Margaret, Maid of Norway	1286–90
Kenneth III	997–1005	John Balliol	1292–6

RULERS OF SCOTLAND (cont.)
(with dates of reign)

(Edward I of England	1296–1306)	James III	1460–88
Robert I (Bruce)	1306–29	James IV	1488–1513
David II	1329–32	James V	1513–42
Edward Balliol	1332–56	Mary Stuart,	
David II (restored)	1356–71	Queen of Scots	1542–67
Robert II	1371–90	James VI of Scotland	1567–1625
Robert III	1390–1406	and I of England	1603–25
James I	1406–37		
James II	1437–60	* Indicates joint reign.	

PRIME MINISTERS OF THE UK
(with dates in office)

Sir Robert Walpole	1721–42	Earl Russell	1865–6
Earl of Wilmington	1742–3	Earl of Derby	1866–8
Henry Pelham	1743–54	Benjamin Disraeli	1868
Duke of Newcastle	1754–6	William Ewart Gladstone	1868–74
Duke of Devonshire	1756–7	Benjamin Disraeli	1874–80
Duke of Newcastle	1757–62	William Ewart Gladstone	1880–5
Earl of Bute	1762–3	Marquess of Salisbury	1885–6
George Grenville	1763–5	William Ewart Gladstone	1886
Marquess of Rockingham	1765–6	Marquess of Salisbury	1886–92
Earl of Chatham	1766–8	William Ewart Gladstone	1892–4
Duke of Grafton	1768–70	Earl of Rosebery	1894–5
Lord North	1770–82	Marquess of Salisbury	1895–1902
Marquess of Rockingham	1782	Arthur James Balfour	1902–5
Earl of Shelburne	1782–3	Sir Henry Campbell-Bannerman	1905–8
Duke of Portland	1783	Herbert Henry Asquith	1908–16
William Pitt	1783–1801	David Lloyd George	1916–22
Henry Addington	1801–4	Andrew Bonar Law	1922–3
William Pitt	1804–7	Stanley Baldwin	1923–4
Lord William Grenville	1806–7	Ramsay MacDonald	1924
Duke of Portland	1807–9	Stanley Baldwin	1924–9
Spencer Perceval	1809–12	Ramsay MacDonald	1929–35
Earl of Liverpool	1812–27	Stanley Baldwin	1935–7
George Canning	1827	Neville Chamberlain	1937–40
Viscount Goderich	1827–8	Winston Spencer Churchill	1940–5
Duke of Wellington	1828–30	Clement Attlee	1945–51
Earl Grey	1830–4	Sir Winston Spencer Churchill	1951–5
Viscount Melbourne	1834	Sir Anthony Eden	1955–7
Duke of Wellington	1834	Harold Macmillan	1957–63
Sir Robert Peel	1834–5	Sir Alec Douglas-Home	1963–4
Viscount Melbourne	1835–41	Harold Wilson	1964–70
Sir Robert Peel	1841–6	Edward Heath	1970–4
Earl Russell	1846–52	Harold Wilson	1974–6
Earl of Derby	1852	James Callaghan	1976–9
Earl of Aberdeen	1852–5	Margaret Thatcher	1979–90
Viscount Palmerston	1855–8	John Major	1990–7
Earl of Derby	1858–9	Tony Blair	from 1997
Viscount Palmerston	1859–65		

PRESIDENTS OF THE USA
(with dates in office)

1	George Washington	1789–97		23	Benjamin Harrison	1889–93
2	John Adams	1797–1801		24	(Stephen) Grover Cleveland	1893–7
3	Thomas Jefferson	1801–9		25	William McKinley	1897–1901
4	James Madison	1809–17		26	Theodore Roosevelt	1901–9
5	James Monroe	1817–25		27	William Howard Taft	1909–13
6	John Quincy Adams	1825–9		28	(Thomas) Woodrow Wilson	1913–21
7	Andrew Jackson	1829–37		29	Warren Gamaliel Harding	1921–3
8	Martin Van Buren	1837–41		30	Calvin Coolidge	1923–9
9	William Henry Harrison	1841		31	Herbert Clark Hoover	1929–33
10	John Tyler	1841–5		32	Franklin Delano Roosevelt	1933–45
11	James Knox Polk	1845–9		33	Harry S. Truman	1945–53
12	Zachary Taylor	1849–50		34	Dwight David Eisenhower	1953–61
13	Millard Fillmore	1850–3		35	John Fitzgerald Kennedy	1961–3
14	Franklin Pierce	1853–7		36	Lyndon Baines Johnson	1963–9
15	James Buchanan	1857–61		37	Richard Milhous Nixon	1969–74
16	Abraham Lincoln	1861–5		38	Gerald Rudolph Ford	1974–7
17	Andrew Johnson	1865–9		39	James Earl Carter	1977–81
18	Ulysses Simpson Grant	1869–77		40	Ronald Wilson Reagan	1981–9
19	Rutherford Birchard Hayes	1877–81		41	George Herbert Walker Bush	1989–93
20	James Abram Garfield	1881		42	William Jefferson Clinton	1993–2001
21	Chester Alan Arthur	1881–5		43	George Walker Bush	from 2001
22	(Stephen) Grover Cleveland	1885–9				

ROMAN EMPERORS
(with dates of reign)

Augustus	27 BC–AD 14	Balbinus	238	Constantine II	337–40
Tiberius	14–37	Maximus	238	Constans I	337–50
Caligula	37–41	Gordian III	238–44	Constantius II	337–61
Claudius	41–54	Philip	244–9	Magnentius	350–1
Nero	54–68	Decius	249–51	Julian	360–3
Galba	68–9	Hostilian	251	Jovian	363–4
Otho	69	Gallus	251–3	Valentinian I	364–75
Vitellius	69	Aemilian	253	Valens	364–78
Vespasian	69–79	Valerian	253–60	Procopius	365–6
Titus	79–81	Gallienus (joint rule)	253–68	Gratian	375–83
Domitian	81–96	Claudius II	268–9	Valentinian II	375–92
Nerva	96–8	Quintillus	269–70	Theodosius I	379–95
Trajan	98–117	Aurelian	270–5	Arcadius	395–408
Hadrian	117–38	Tacitus	275–6	Honorius	395–423
Antoninus Pius	138–61	Florian	276	Constantine III	407–11
Marcus Aurelius	161–80	Probus	276–82	Theodosius II	408–50
Lucius Verus	161–9	Carus	282–3	Constantius III	421–3
Commodus	180–92	Carinus	283–5	Valentinian III	423–55
Pertinax	193	Numerian	283–4	Marcian	450–7
Didius Julianus	193	Diocletian	284–305	Petronius Maximus	455
Septimius Severus	193–211	Maximian	286–305; 306–8	Avitus	455–6
Caracalla	211–7			Leo I	457–74
Geta	209–12	Constantius I	305–6	Majorian	457–61
Macrinus	217–8	Galerius	305–11	Libius Severus	461–7
Heliogabalus	218–22	Severus	306–7	Anthemius	467–72
Alexander Severus	222–35	Maxentius	306–12	Olybrius	472–3
Maximin I	235–8	Licinius	308–24	Julius Nepos	474–5
Gordian I	238	Maximin	310–3	Leo II	474
Gordian II	238	Constantine I (the Great)	312–37	Zeno	474–91
				Romulus Augustulus	475–6

*During the reign of Diocletian, the Roman Empire was divided and from then on sometimes had both a Western and an Eastern emperor.

WARS, BATTLES, AND CONFLICTS

Actium, Battle of	31 BC	Mexican War	1846–8
Agincourt, Battle of	1415	Midway Islands,	
American Civil War	1861–5	Battle of the	1942
Antietam, Battle of	1862	Napoleonic Wars	1805–15
Arbela, Battle of	331 BC	Nile, Battle of the	1798
Atlantic, Battle of the	1940–3	Omdurman, Battle of	1898
Ayacucho, Battle of	1824	Opium Wars	1839–42, 1856–60
Balaclava, Battle of	1854	Peloponnesian Wars	431–404 BC
Balkan Wars	1912–3	Peninsular War	1808–14
Boer War	1880–1, 1899–1902	Persian Wars	5th century BC
Bosnian Civil War	1992–5	Pharsalus, Battle of	48 BC
Boyne, Battle of the	1690	Princeton, Battle of	1777
Britain, Battle of	1940	Punic Wars	264–241 BC, 218–
Bulge, Battle of the	1944–5		201 BC, 149–146 BC
Bunker Hill, Battle of	1775	River Plate, Battle of the	1939
Cambrai, Battle of	1917	Russian Civil War	1918–21
Cerro Gordo, Battle of	1847	Russo-Japanese War	1904–5
Crimean War	1853–6	Sadowa, Battle of	1866
Culloden, Battle of	1746	Salamis, Battle of	480 BC
El Mansûra, Battle of	1250	Samnite Wars	343–341 BC, 316–
English Civil War	1642–9		314 BC, 298–290 BC
Erzurum, Battle of	1877, 1916	Second World War	1939–45
Falklands War	1982	Seven Years War	1756–63
First World War	1914–8	Sino-Japanese Wars	1894–5, 1937–45
Franco-Prussian War	1870–1	Six Day War	1967
French and Indian War	1754–63	Somme, Battle of the	1916
French Indochina War	1946–54	Spanish-American War	1898
French Wars of Religion	1562–98	Spanish Civil War	1936–9
Gallic Wars	58–51 BC	Stalingrad, Battle of	1942–3
Gettysburg, Battle of	1863	Tannenberg, Battle of	1914
Great Northern War	1700–21	Thirty Years War	1618–48
Gulf War	1991	Trafalgar, Battle of	1805
Hastings, Battle of	1066	Verdun, Battle of	1916
Hundred Years War	1337–1453	Vietnam War	1954–75
Iran-Iraq War	1980–8	War of 1812	1812–4
Issus, Battle of	333 BC	War of American	
Jena, Battle of	1806	Independence	1775–83
Jutland, Battle of	1916	War of the Austrian	
Korean War	1950–3	Succession	1740–8
Kosovo Conflict	1999	War of the Spanish	
Leyte Gulf, Battle of	1944	Succession	1701–14
Macedonian Wars	214–205 BC, 200–	Wars of the Roses	1455–85
	196 BC, 171–168	Waterloo, Battle of	1815
	BC, 149–148 BC	Xuzhou, Battle of	1949
Marathon, Battle of	490 BC	Yom Kippur War	1973
Marne, Battle of	1914	Ypres, Battle of	1914, 1915, 1917
Megiddo, Battle of	1469 BC, 1918		

MILITARY MEDALS

Air Force Cross (AFC)
Air Force Medal (AFM)
Albert Medal (AM)
Conspicuous Gallantry
  Medal (CGM)
Distinguished Flying Cross
  (DFC)

Distinguished Flying Medal
  (DFM)
Distinguished Service Cross
  (DSC)
Distinguished Service Medal
  (DSM)
George Cross (GC)
George Medal (GM)

Medal for Distinguished
  Conduct in the Field (DCM)
Military Cross (MC)
Military Medal (MM)
The Distinguished Service
  Order (DSO)
Victoria Cross (VC)

RANKS OF THE BRITISH AND AMERICAN ARMED FORCES

British Military Ranks

Army
Field Marshal
General
Lieutenant General
Major General
Brigadier
Colonel
Lieutenant Colonel
Major
Captain
Lieutenant
Second Lieutenant

Royal Navy
Admiral of the
  Fleet
Admiral
Vice Admiral
Rear Admiral
Commodore
Captain
Commander
Lieutenant
  Commander

Lieutenant
Sub Lieutenant
Midshipman

Royal Air Force
Marshal of the
  Royal Air Force
Air Chief Marshal
Air Marshal
Air Vice-Marshal
Air Commodore
Group Captain
Wing Commander
Squadron Leader
Flight Lieutenant
Flying Officer
Pilot Officer

American Military Ranks

Army and Air Force
Chief of Staff
General
Lieutenant General
Major General

Brigadier General
Colonel
Lieutenant Colonel
Major
Captain
First Lieutenant
Second Lieutenant

Navy
Chief of Naval
  Operations
Fleet Admiral
Admiral
Vice Admiral
Rear Admiral
Captain
Commander
Lieutenant
  Commander
Lieutenant
Lieutenant   junior
  grade (j.g.)
Ensign
Midshipman

WEAPONS

acoustic mine
airgun
air-to-air missile
AK-47
anti-aircraft gun
anti-ballistic-missile
anti-missile missile
anti-tank weapon
arbalest
arquebus
arrow
assault gun
assegai
atom- or A-bomb
automatic
axe
ballista
ballistic missile
battering ram
battleaxe
bayonet
bazooka
Big Bertha
bilbo
bill
blade
blockbuster
blowpipe
bludgeon
blunderbuss
Bofors gun

bolas
bolt
bombshell
boomerang
bow
bowie knife
brass cannon
brass knuckles
breech-loader
Bren gun
broadsword
Brown Bess
bullet
cannon
cannon royal
carbine
car bomb
catapult
cavalry sword
chopper
claymore
club
cluster bomb
Colt™
cordite
cosh
crossbow
cruise missile
cudgel
cutlass
dagger

dart
depth charge
dirk
double-barrelled gun
duelling pistol
dynamite
elephant gun
Enfield rifle
épée,
Exocet™
falchion
falconet
field gun
firebomb
flare
fléchette
flick knife
flintlock
flying bomb
foil
fowling piece
fragmentation bomb
fusil
Garand rifle or M-1
gas shell
Gatling gun
gelignite
gisarme
grenade
guided missile
gun

gun cotton
gunpowder
hackbut
halberd
hand grenade
handgun
hanger
harpoon
hatchet
heavy gun
howitzer
hydrogen- or H-bomb
incendiary bomb
intercontinental
  ballistic missile
javelin
jerid
kalashnikov
knife
knobkerrie
knuckleduster
kris
kukri
lance
landmine
lathi
letter bomb
Lewis gun
light machine-gun
limpet mine
longbow

WEAPONS (cont.)

lyddite
M-60 machine-gun
mace
machete
machine-gun
magazine rifle
magnetic mine
mangonel
matchlock
Maxim gun
Mills bomb
mine
mine-thrower
Minuteman
MIRV (multiple independently-targeted re-entry vehicle)
Molotov cocktail
mortar
musket
muzzle-loader
napalm
neutron bomb
nitroglycerine

nuclear bomb
panga
parang
partisan
Patriot™
pellet
petard
petrol bomb
pike
pistol
pistolet
plastic explosive
Polaris
poleaxe
pom-pom
quarterstaff
rapier
repeating rifle
Research Department Explosive or RDX
revolver
rifle
rocket
sabre
sawn-off shotgun

scimitar
Scud™ missile
semi-automatic
Semtex™
shell
shillelagh
shotgun
shrapnel
sidewinder
siege gun
single-barrelled gun
six-shooter
skean-dhu
sling
smoke bomb
smoothbore
spear
staff
star shell
stave
Sten gun
stick
stiletto
subgun
sub-machine gun

surface-to-air missile
surface-to-surface missile
swivel
sword
swordstick
throw-stick
time bomb
toledo
tomahawk
tommy-gun
torpedo
trebuchet
Trident
trinitrotoluene (TNT)
truncheon
Uzi
V-1
V-2
whiz-bang
Winchester™
woomera
woomerang
yataghan

HISTORICAL, POLITICAL, AND MILITARY FIGURES

Abbas, Ferhat (1899–1989) Algerian nationalist leader, President of the Algerian republic 1958–61

Abdul Hamid II (known as 'the Great Assassin' and 'the Red Sultan') (1842–1918) Sultan of the Ottoman Empire (1876–1909)

Abdullah, Sheikh Muhammad (known as 'the Lion of Kashmir') (1905–82) Nationalist leader in Kashmir

Abdullah ibn Hussein (1882–1951) king of Jordan 1946–51

Abdul Rahman, Tunku (1903–90) Malaysian statesman, Prime Minister of Malaya 1957–63 and of Malaysia 1963–70

Aberdeen, 4th Earl of (title of George Hamilton Gordon) (1784–1860) British Conservative statesman, Prime Minister 1852–5

Acheson, Dean Gooderham (1893–1971) American statesman

Adams, Gerard ('Gerry') (born 1948) Northern Irish Sinn Féin politician

Adams, John (1735–1826) American Federalist statesman, 2nd President of the US 1797–1801

Adams, John Quincy (1767–1848) American statesman, 6th President of the US 1825–9

Addams, Jane (1860–1935) American social reformer and feminist

Addington, Henry, 1st Viscount Sidmouth (1757–1844) British Tory statesman, Prime Minister 1801–4

Adenauer, Konrad (1876–1967) German statesman, first Chancellor of the Federal Republic of Germany 1949–63

Aeschines (c. 390–c. 314 BC) Athenian statesman and orator

Aga Khan, title of the imam or leader of the Nizari sect of Ismaili Muslims

Agricola, Gnaeus Julius (AD 40–93) Roman general and governor of Britain 78–84

Agrippa, Marcus Vipsanius (63–12 BC) Roman general

Ahern, Bertie (born 1954) Irish Fianna Fáil statesman, Taoiseach (prime minister) since 1997

Aitken, William Maxwell See BEAVERBROOK

Akbar, Jalaludin Muhammad (known as Akbar the Great) (1542–1605) Mogul emperor of India 1556–1605

Akhenaten (also Akhenaton) (14th century BC) Egyptian pharaoh of the 18th dynasty, reigned 1379–1362 BC

Akihito (born 1933) Emperor of Japan since 1989

Alaric (c. 370–410) king of the Visigoths

Albert, Prince (1819–61) consort to Queen Victoria

Albuquerque, Alfonso de (known as Albuquerque the Great) (1453–1515) Portuguese colonial statesman

HISTORICAL, POLITICAL, AND MILITARY FIGURES (cont.)

Alcibiades (*c.* 450–404 BC) Athenian statesman and general

Alexander, Harold (Rupert Leofric George), 1st Earl Alexander of Tunis (1891–1969) British Field Marshal and Conservative statesman

Alexander (known as Alexander the Great) (356–323 BC) king of Macedon 336–323

Alexander I (*c.* 1077–1124) king of Scotland

Alexander I (1777–1825) tsar of Russia

Alexander II (1198–1249) king of Scotland

Alexander III (1241–86) king of Scotland

Alexander III (1845–94) tsar of Russia

Alexander Nevsky (also Nevski) (canonized as St Alexander Nevsky) (*c.* 1220–63) Prince of Novgorod (1236–63) and Grand Prince of Vladimir (1252–63)

Alexander the Liberator (1818–81) tsar of Russia

Alfonso XIII (1886–1941) king of Spain 1886–1931

Alfred (known as Alfred the Great) (849–99) king of Wessex 871–99

Ali, Muhammad See MUHAMMAD ALI

Allenby, Edmund Henry Hynman, 1st Viscount (1861–1936) British soldier

Allende, Salvador (1908–73) Chilean statesman, President 1970–3

Allen, Ethan (1738–89) American soldier

Amenhotep I (16th century BC) Egyptian pharaoh, reigned 1546–1526

Amin, Idi (full name Idi Amin Dada) (born 1925) Ugandan soldier and head of state 1971–9

Amundsen, Roald (1872–1928) Norwegian explorer

Andrew, Prince, Andrew Albert Christian Edward, Duke of York (born 1960) second son of Elizabeth II

Andropov, Yuri (Vladimirovich) (1914–84) Soviet statesman, General Secretary of the Communist Party of the USSR 1982–4 and President 1983–4

Anne Boleyn See BOLEYN

Anne (1665–1714) queen of England and Scotland (known as Great Britain from 1707) and Ireland 1702–14

Anne of Cleves (1515–57) fourth wife of Henry VIII

Anne, Princess, Anne Elizabeth Alice Louise, the Princess Royal (born 1950) daughter of Elizabeth II

Antiochus III (known as Antiochus the Great) (*c.* 242–187 BC) Seleucid king

Antoninus Pius (86–161) Roman emperor 138–61

Antony, Mark (Latin name Marcus Antonius) (*c.* 83–30 BC) Roman statesman and general

Aquino, Corazón ('Cory') (born 1933) Philippine stateswoman, President 1986–92.

Aquitaine, Eleanor of See ELEANOR OF AQUITAINE

Arafat, Yasser (born 1929) Palestinian leader

Aragon, Catherine of See CATHERINE OF ARAGON

Aristides (known as Aristides the Just) (5th century BC) Athenian statesman and general

Arrow, Kenneth Joseph (born 1921) American economist

Artaxerxes I (died 425 BC) king of ancient Persia, reigned 464–425 BC

Arthur, traditionally king of Britain, historically perhaps a 5th or 6th-century Romano-British chieftain or general

Arthur, Chester Alan (1830–86) American Republican statesman, 21st President of the US 1881–5

Ashdown, Jeremy John Durham ('Paddy') (born 1941) British Liberal Democrat politician

Ashurbanipal, king of Assyria *c.* 668–627 BC

Asoka (died c. 232 BC) Indian emperor

Asquith, Herbert Henry, 1st Earl of Oxford and Asquith (1852–1928) British Liberal statesman, Prime Minister 1908–16

Assad, Hafiz al- (1928–2000) Syrian Baath statesman, President 1971–2000

Astor, Nancy Witcher Langhorne, Viscountess (1879–1964) American-born British Conservative politician

Atatürk, Kemal (born Mustafa Kemal; also called Kemal Pasha) (1881–1938) Turkish statesman and general, President of Turkey (1923–38)

Athelstan (895–939) king of England 925–39

Atkinson, Sir Harry (Albert) (1831–92) New Zealand statesman, Prime Minister 1876–7, 1883–4, and 1887–91

Attila (406–53) king of the Huns 434–53

Attlee, Clement Richard, 1st Earl Attlee (1883–1967) British Labour statesman, Prime Minister 1945–51

Augustus (born Gaius Octavianus; also called (until 27 BC) Octavian) (63 BC–AD 14) the first Roman emperor

Aung San (1914–47) Burmese nationalist leader

Aung San Suu Kyi (born 1945) Burmese political leader

Aurangzeb (1618–1707) Mogul emperor of Hindustan 1658–1707

Aurelian (Latin name Lucius Domitius Aurelianus) (*c.* 215–75) Roman emperor

Aurelius, Marcus (full name Caesar Marcus Aurelius Antoninus Augustus) (121–80) Roman emperor 161–80

Ayatollah Khomeini See KHOMEINI

Ayub Khan, Muhammad (1907–74) Pakistani soldier and statesman, President 1958–69

Azikiwe, (Benjamin) Nnamdi (1904–96) Nigerian statesman, President 1963–6

Babur (born Zahir al-Din Muhammad)

HISTORICAL, POLITICAL, AND MILITARY FIGURES (cont.)

(1483–1530) Mogul emperor of India *c.* 1525–30

Bacon, Francis, Baron Verulam and Viscount St Albans (1561–1626) English statesman and philosopher

Baden-Powell, Robert (Stephenson Smyth), 1st Baron Baden-Powell of Gilwell (1857–1941) English soldier and founder of the Boy Scout movement

Bader, Sir Douglas (Robert Steuart) (1910–82) British airman

Baffin, William (*c.* 1584–1622) English navigator and explorer

Bakunin, Mikhail (Aleksandrovich) (1814–76) Russian anarchist

Balboa, Vasco Núñez de (1475–1519) Spanish explorer

Baldwin, Stanley, 1st Earl Baldwin of Bewdley (1867–1947) British Conservative statesman, Prime Minister 1923–4, 1924–9, and 1935–7

Balfour, Arthur James, 1st Earl of Balfour (1848–1930) British Conservative statesman, Prime Minister 1902–5

Ball, John (died 1381) English rebel

Banda, Hastings Kamuzu (1906–97) Malawian statesman, Prime Minister 1964–94 and President 1966–94

Bandaranaike, Sirimavo Ratwatte Dias (1916–2000) Sinhalese stateswoman, Prime Minister of Sri Lanka 1960–5, 1970–7, and since 1994–2000

Barak, Ehud (born 1942) Israeli soldier and stateman, Prime Minister 1999–2001

Barbarossa, (born Khair ad-Din) (*c.* 1483–1546) Barbary pirate

Barbarossa See FREDERICK I

Bar-Cochba, Jewish leader of a rebellion in AD 132

Barents, Willem (died 1597) Dutch explorer

Barton, Sir Edmund (1849–1920) Australian statesman and jurist, first Prime Minister of Australia 1901–3

Batista, Fulgencio (full name Fulgencio Batista y Zaldívar) (1901–73) Cuban soldier and statesman, President 1940–4 and 1952–9

Bayard, Pierre du Terrail, Chevalier de (1473–1524) French soldier

Beale, Dorothea (1831–1906) English educationist

Beatty, David, 1st Earl Beatty of the North Sea and of Brooksby (1871–1936) British admiral

Beaverbrook, (William) Max(-well) Aitken, 1st Baron (1879–1964) Canadian-born British Conservative politician and newspaper proprietor

Becket, St Thomas à (*c.* 1118–70) English prelate and statesman

Begin, Menachem (1913–92) Israeli statesman, Prime Minister 1977–84

Belshazzar (6th century BC) last king of Babylon

Ben Bella, (Muhammad) Ahmed (born 1916) Algerian statesman, Prime Minister 1962–3 and President 1963–5

Beneš, Edvard (1884–1948) Czechoslovak statesman, Prime Minister 1921–2, President 1935–8 and 1945–8

Ben-Gurion, David (1886–1973) Israeli statesman, Prime Minister 1948–53 and 1955–63

Benn, Anthony (Neil Wedgwood) ('Tony') (born 1925) British Labour politician

Berenice (3rd century BC) Egyptian queen, wife of Ptolemy III

Beria, Lavrenti (Pavlovich) (1899–1953) Soviet politician and head of the secret police (NKVD and MVD) 1938–53

Bering, Vitus (Jonassen) (1681–1741) Danish navigator and explorer

Bernadotte, Folke, Count (1895–1948) Swedish statesman

Bernadotte, Jean Baptiste Jules (1763–1844) French soldier, king of Sweden (as Charles XIV) 1818–44

Bevan Aneurin ('Nye') (1897–1960) British Labour politician

Beveridge, William Henry, 1st Baron (1879–1963) British economist and social reformer, born in India

Bevin, Ernest (1881–1951) British Labour statesman and trade unionist

Bhutto, Benazir (born 1953) Pakistani stateswoman, Prime Minister 1988–90 and 1993–6

Bhutto, Zulfikar Ali (1928–79) Pakistani statesman, President 1971–3 and Prime Minister 1973–7

Biko, Stephen ('Steve') (1946–77) South African radical leader

Billy the Kid See BONNEY

Bismarck, Otto (Eduard Leopold) von, Prince of Bismarck, Duke of Lauenburg (known as 'the Iron Chancellor') (1815–98) German statesman

Black Prince (name given to Edward, Prince of Wales and Duke of Cornwall) (1330–76) eldest son of Edward III of England

Blair, Anthony Charles Lynton ('Tony') (born 1953) British Labour Prime Minister since 1997

Bligh, William (1754–1817) British naval officer

Bloody Mary, nickname of Mary I of England

Blum, Léon (1872–1950) French statesman, Prime Minister 1936–7, 1938, 1946–7

Blunt, Anthony (Frederick) (1907–83) British art historian, Foreign Office official, and Soviet spy

Boadicea See BOUDICCA

HISTORICAL, POLITICAL, AND MILITARY FIGURES (cont.)

Boethius, Anicius Manlius Severinus (*c.* 480–524) Roman statesman and philosopher

Bokassa, Jean Bédel (1921–96) Central African Republic statesman and military leader, President 1972–6, emperor 1976–9

Boleyn, Anne (1507–36) second wife of Henry VIII and mother of Elizabeth I

Bolger, James B(rendan) (born 1935) New Zealand statesman, Prime Minister 1990–7

Bolingbroke, surname of Henry IV of England

Bolívar, Simón (known as 'the Liberator') (1783–1830) Venezuelan patriot and statesman

Bonaparte (Italian, Buonaparte) See NAPOLEON

Bonney, William H. (Billy the Kid) (1859–81) American outlaw

Bonnie Prince Charlie See STUART

Boone, Daniel (*c.* 1734–1820) American pioneer

Borgia, Cesare (*c.* 1476–1507) Italian statesman

Borgia, Lucrezia (1480–1519) Italian noblewoman

Boris Godunov See GODUNOV

Bormann, Martin (1900–*c.* 1945) German Nazi politician

Botha, Louis (1862–1919) South African soldier and statesman, first Prime Minister of the Union of South Africa 1910–19

Botha, P(ieter) W(illem) (born 1916) South African statesman, Prime Minister 1978–84, State President 1984–9

Bothwell, 4th Earl of (title of James Hepburn) (*c.* 1536–78) Scottish nobleman and third husband of Mary, Queen of Scots

Boudicca (also Boadicea) (died AD 62) queen of the Britons, ruler of the Iceni tribe in eastern England

Bougainville, Louis Antoine de (1729–1811) French explorer

Bourguiba, Habib ibn Ali (born 1903) Tunisian nationalist and statesman, President 1957–87

Boutros-Ghali, Boutros (born 1922) Egyptian diplomat and politician, Secretary-General of the United Nations 1992–6

Bowie James ('Jim') (1799–1836) American frontiersman

Brandt, Willy (born Karl Herbert Frahm) (1913–92) German statesman, Chancellor of West Germany 1969–74

Branson, Sir Richard (born 1950) British businessman

Braun, Eva (1910–45) German mistress of Adolf Hitler

Brezhnev, Leonid (Ilich) (1906–82) Soviet statesman, General Secretary of the Communist Party of the USSR 1966–82 and President 1977–82

Bright, John (1811–89) English Liberal politician and reformer

Brown, John (1800–59) American abolitionist

Bruce James ('the Abyssinian') (1730–94), Scottish explorer

Bruce, Robert the See ROBERT THE BRUCE

Brundtland, Gro Harlem (born 1939) Norwegian Labour stateswoman, Prime Minister 1981, 1986–9, 1990–6

Bruton, John (Gerard) (born 1947) Irish Fine Gael statesman, Taoiseach (Prime Minister) 1994–7

Brutus, Marcus Junius (85–42 BC) Roman senator

Buchanan, James (1791–1868) American Democratic statesman, 15th President of the US 1857–61

Bukharin, Nikolai (Ivanovich) (1888–1938) Russian revolutionary activist and theorist

Bulganin, Nikolai (Aleksandrovich) (1895–1975) Soviet statesman, Chairman of the Council of Ministers (Premier) 1955–8

Buonaparte See NAPOLEON

Burgess, Guy (Francis de Moncy) (1911–63) British Foreign Office official and spy

Burghley, William Cecil, 1st Baron (1520–98) English statesman

Burgoyne John ('Gentleman Johnny') (1722–92) English general and dramatist

Burke, Edmund (1729–97) British man of letters and Whig politician

Burke, Robert O'Hara (1820–61) Irish explorer

Burke, William (1792–1829) Irish murderer

Burr, Aaron (1756–1836) American Democratic Republican statesman

Burton, Sir Richard (Francis) (1821–90) English explorer, anthropologist, and translator

Bush, George (Herbert Walker) (born 1924) American Republican statesman, 41st President of the US 1989–93

Bush, George Walker (born 1946) American Republican statesman, 43rd President of the US since 2001

Buss, Frances Mary (1827–94) English educationist

Bute, 3rd Earl of (title of John Stuart) (1713–92) Scottish courtier and Tory statesman, Prime Minister 1762–3

Buthelezi, Chief Mangosuthu (Gatsha) (born 1928) South African politician

Cabot, John (Italian name Giovanni Caboto) (*c.* 1450–*c.* 1498) Italian explorer and navigator

Cadbury, George (1839–1922) English cocoa and chocolate manufacturer and social reformer

Cade, John ('Jack') (died 1450) English rebel

Caesar See JULIUS CAESAR

HISTORICAL, POLITICAL, AND MILITARY FIGURES (cont.)

Calamity Jane (born Martha Jane Cannary) (*c.* 1852–1903) American frontierswoman

Caligula (born Gaius Julius Caesar Germanicus) (AD 12–41) Roman emperor 37–41

Callaghan, (Leonard) James, Baron Callaghan of Cardiff (born 1912) British Labour statesman, Prime Minister 1976–9

Cambyses (died 522 BC) son of Cyrus, king of Persia 529–522 BC

Campbell-Bannerman, Sir Henry (1836–1908) British Liberal statesman, Prime Minister 1905–8

Canmore, nickname of Malcolm III of Scotland

Canning, George (1770–1827) British Tory statesman, Prime Minister 1827

Canute (also Cnut) (died 1035) Danish king of England 1017–35, Denmark 1018–35, and Norway 1028–35

Capet, Hugh (or Hugo) (938–96) king of France 987–96

Capone Alphonse ('Al') (1899–1947) American gangster, of Italian descent

Caracalla (born Septimius Bassanius; later called Marcus Aurelius Severus Antoninus Augustus) (188–217) Roman emperor 211–17

Caratacus (also Caractacus) (1st century AD) British chieftain, son of Cunobelinus

Carnegie, Andrew (1835–1919) Scottish-born American industrialist and philanthropist

Carter, James Earl ('Jimmy') (born 1924) American Democratic statesman, 39th President of the US 1977–81

Cartier, Jacques (1491–1557) French explorer

Casanova, Giovanni Jacopo (full surname Casanova de Seingalt) (1725–98) Italian adventurer

Casement, Sir Roger (David) (1864–1916) Irish nationalist

Cassius, Gaius (full name Gaius Cassius Longinus) (died 42 BC) Roman general

Castle, Barbara (Anne), Baroness Castle of Blackburn (born 1911) British Labour politician

Castlereagh, Robert Stewart, Viscount (1769–1822) British Tory statesman

Castro, Fidel (born 1927) Cuban statesman, Prime Minister 1959–76 and President since 1976

Catherine de' Medici (1519–89) queen of France

Catherine II (known as Catherine the Great) (1729–96) empress of Russia, reigned 1762–96

Catherine of Aragon (1485–1536) first wife of Henry VIII

Catiline (Latin name Lucius Sergius Catilina) (*c.* 108–62 BC) Roman nobleman and conspirator

Cato, Marcus Porcius (known as Cato the Elder or Cato the Censor) (234–149 BC) Roman statesman, orator, and writer

Cavell, Edith (Louisa) (1865–1915) English nurse

Cavour, Camillo Benso, Conte di (1810–61) Italian statesman, Prime Minister 1852–9, 1860–1

Ceauşescu, Nicolae (1918–89) Romanian Communist statesman, first President of the Socialist Republic of Romania 1974–89

Cecil, William See BURGHLEY

Cetshwayo (also Cetewayo) (*c.* 1826–84) Zulu king

Chaka See SHAKA

Chamberlain, Joseph (1836–1914) British Liberal statesman

Chamberlain, (Arthur) Neville (1869–1940) British Conservative statesman, Prime Minister 1937–40

Champlain, Samuel de (1567–1635) French explorer and colonial statesman

Chandragupta Maurya (*c.* 325–297 BC) Indian emperor

Charlemagne (Latin Carolus Magnus Charles the Great) (742–814) king of the Franks 768–814 and Holy Roman emperor

Charles I (1500–58) king of Spain, reigned 1516–56 and Holy Roman emperor

Charles I (1600–49) king of England, Scotland, and Ireland, reigned 1625–49

Charles II (1630–85) king of England, Scotland, and Ireland, reigned 1660–85

Charles VII (1403–61) king of France 1422–61

Charles XII (also Karl XII) (1682–1718) king of Sweden 1697–1718

Charles, Prince, Charles Philip Arthur George, Prince of Wales (born 1948) heir apparent to Elizabeth II

Charles Martel (*c.* 688–741) Frankish ruler of the eastern part of the Frankish kingdom from 715 and the whole kingdom from 719

Chatham, 1st Earl of See PITT

Cheops (Egyptian name Khufu) (*fl.* early 26th century BC) Egyptian pharaoh of the 4th dynasty

Chiang Kai-shek (also Jiang Jie Shi) (1887–1975) Chinese statesman and general, President of China 1928–31 and 1943–9 and of Taiwan 1950–75

Chifley, Joseph Benedict (1885–1951) Australian Labor statesman, Prime Minister 1945–9

Childers, (Robert) Erskine (1870–1922) Irish writer and political activist, born in England

Chirac, Jacques (René) (born 1932) French statesman, Prime Minister 1974–6 and 1986–8 and President since 1995

Chou En-lai See ZHOU ENLAI

HISTORICAL, POLITICAL, AND MILITARY FIGURES (cont.)

Chrétien, (Joseph-Jacques) Jean (born 1934) Canadian Liberal statesman, Prime Minister since 1993

Christian, Fletcher (c. 1764–c. 1793) English seaman and mutineer

Churchill, Sir Winston (Leonard Spencer) (1874–1965) British Conservative statesman, Prime Minister 1940–5 and 1951–5

Cid, El (also the Cid) (born Rodrigo Díaz de Vivar), Count of Bivar (c. 1043–99) Spanish soldier

Clarendon, Earl of (title of Edward Hyde) (1609–74) English statesman and historian

Clark, Helen (born 1950) New Zealand Labour stateswoman, Prime Minister since 1999

Clark, William (1770–1838) American explorer

Claudius (full name Tiberius Claudius Drusus Nero Germanicus) (10 BC–AD 54) Roman emperor 41–54

Clausewitz, Karl von (1780–1831) Prussian general and military theorist

Cleisthenes (c. 570 BC–c. 508 BC) Athenian statesman

Clemenceau, Georges (Eugène Benjamin) (1841–1929) French statesman, Prime Minister 1906–9 and 1917–20

Cleopatra (also Cleopatra VII) (69–30 BC) queen of Egypt 47–30

Cleveland, (Stephen) Grover (1837–1908) American Democratic statesman, 22nd and 24th President of the US 1885–9 and 1893–7

Clinton, William Jefferson ('Bill') (born 1946) American Democratic statesman, 42nd President of the US (1993–2001)

Clive, Robert, 1st Baron Clive of Plassey (known as Clive of India) (1725–74) British general and colonial administrator

Clovis (465–511) king of the Franks 481–511

Cnut See CANUTE

Cobden, Richard (1804–65) English political reformer

Colbert, Jean Baptiste (1619–83) French statesman, chief minister to Louis XIV

Collins, Michael (1890–1922) Irish nationalist leader and politician

Columbus, Christopher (Spanish name Cristóbal Colón) (1451–1506) Italian-born Spanish explorer

Constantine (known as Constantine the Great) (c. 274–337) Roman emperor 312–37

Cook, Captain James (1728–79) English explorer

Cook, Thomas (1808–92) English founder of the travel firm Thomas Cook

Coolidge, (John) Calvin (1872–1933) American Republican statesman, 30th President of the US 1923–9

Corday, Charlotte (full name Marie Anne Charlotte Corday d'Armont) (1768–93) French political assassin

Coriolanus, Gaius (or Gnaeus) Marcius (5th century BC) Roman general

Cortés, Hernando (also Cortez) (1485–1547) first of the Spanish conquistadores

Cosimo de' Medici (known as Cosimo the Elder) (1389–1464) Italian statesman and banker

Crassus, Marcus Licinius ('Dives') (c. 115–53 BC) Roman politician

Crazy Horse (Sioux name Ta-Sunko-Witko) (c. 1849–77) Sioux chief

Crichton, James (known as 'the Admirable Crichton') (1560–c. 1585) Scottish adventurer

Crippen, Hawley Harvey (known as Doctor Crippen) (1862–1910) American-born British murderer

Crockett, David ('Davy') (1786–1836) American frontiersman, soldier, and politician

Croesus (6th century BC) last king of Lydia c. 560–546 BC

Cromwell, Oliver (1599–1658) English general and statesman

Cromwell, Thomas (c. 1485–1540) English statesman, chief minister to Henry VIII

Cumberland, William Augustus, Duke of (1721–65) English military commander

Cunard, Sir Samuel (1787–1865) Canadian-born British shipowner

Cunobelinus See CYMBELINE

Curtin, John (Joseph Ambrose) (1885–1945) Australian Labor statesman, Prime Minister 1941–5

Custer, George (Armstrong) (1839–76) American cavalry general

Cymbeline (also Cunobelinus) (died c. 42 AD) British chieftain

Cyrus (known as Cyrus the Great) (died c. 530 BC) king of Persia 559–530 BC

Cyrus (known as Cyrus the Younger) (died 401 BC) Persian prince

Da Gama, Vasco (c. 1469–1524) Portuguese explorer

Dalhousie, 1st Marquess of (title of James Andrew Broun Ramsay) (1812–60) British colonial administrator

Dampier, William (1652–1715) English explorer and adventurer

Danton, Georges (Jacques) (1759–94) French revolutionary

Darius I (known as Darius the Great) (c. 550–486 BC) king of Persia 521–486 BC

Darling, Grace (1815–42) English heroine

Darnley, Lord (title of Henry Stewart or Stuart) (1545–67) Scottish nobleman, second husband of Mary, Queen of Scots

David (died c. 962 BC) King of Judah and Israel c. 1000–c. 962 BC

David I (c. 1084–1153) king of Scotland, reigned 1124–53

HISTORICAL, POLITICAL, AND MILITARY FIGURES (cont.)

Dayan, Moshe (1915–81) Israeli statesman and general

Deakin, Alfred (1856–1919) Australian Liberal statesman, Prime Minister 1903–4, 1905–8, and 1909–10

Decius, Gaius Messius Quintus Trajanus (c. 201–51) Roman emperor 249–51

de Gaulle, Charles (André Joseph Marie) (1890–1970) French general and statesman, President 1959–69

de Klerk, F(rederik) W(illem) (born 1936) South African statesman, President 1989–94

Delors, Jacques (Lucien Jean) (born 1925) French socialist politician, president of the European Commission 1985–94

de' Medici, Catherine See CATHERINE DE' MEDICI

de Montfort, Simon See MONTFORT

Demosthenes (384–322 BC) Athenian orator and statesman

Deng Xiaoping (also Teng Hsiao-p'ing) (1904–97) Chinese Communist statesman

Derby, 14th Earl of (title of Edward George Geoffrey Smith Stanley) (1799–1869) British Conservative statesman, Prime Minister 1852, 1858–9, and 1866–8

de Valera, Eamon (1882–1975) American-born Irish statesman, Prime Minister (1932–48)

Diana, Princess (formally called Diana, Princess of Wales; born Lady Diana Frances Spencer) (1961–97) Former wife of Prince Charles

Dias, Bartolomeu (also Diaz) (c. 1450–1500) Portuguese navigator and explorer

Díaz, Porfirio (1830–1915) Mexican general and statesman, President 1877–80 and 1884–1911

Diocletian (full name Gaius Aurelius Valerius Diocletianus) (245–313) Roman emperor 284–305

Dionysius I (known as Dionysius the Elder) (c. 430–367 BC) ruler of Syracuse

Disraeli, Benjamin, 1st Earl of Beaconsfield (1804–81) British Tory statesman, of Italian Jewish descent; Prime Minister 1868 and 1874–80

Dollfuss, Engelbert (1892–1934) Austrian statesman, Chancellor of Austria 1932–4

Domitian (full name Titus Flavius Domitianus) (AD 51–96) Roman emperor 81–96

Douglas-Home, Sir Alec, Baron Home of the Hirsel of Coldstream (1903–95) British Conservative statesman, Prime Minister 1963–4

Dowding, Hugh (Caswall Tremenheere), Baron (1882–1970) British Marshal of the RAF

Drake, Sir Francis (c. 1540–96) English sailor and explorer

Dreyfus, Alfred (1859–1935) French army officer, of Jewish descent

Dubček, Alexander (1921–92) Czechoslovak statesman

Dudley, Robert, Earl of Leicester (c. 1532–88) English nobleman

Dulles, John Foster (1888–1959) American Republican statesman

Durham, John George Lambton, Earl of (1792–1840) British Whig statesman

Duvalier, François (known as 'Papa Doc') (1907–71) Haitian statesman, President 1957–71

Dzerzhinsky, Feliks (Edmundovich) (1877–1926) Russian Bolshevik leader, of Polish descent

Eadwig See EDWY

Earp, Wyatt (Berry Stapp) (1848–1929) American gambler and marshal

Eden, (Robert) Anthony, 1st Earl of Avon (1897–1977) British Conservative statesman, Prime Minister 1955–7

Edgar (944–75) king of England 959–75

Edinburgh, Duke of See PHILIP, PRINCE

Edmund Ironside, nickname of Edmund II of England

Edmund, St (born Edmund Rich) (c. 1175–1240) English churchman and teacher

Edmund the Martyr, St (c. 841–70) king of East Anglia 855–70

Edward I to VIII, kings of England

Edward, Prince, Edward Antony Richard Louis (born 1964) third son of Elizabeth II

Edward, Prince of Wales See BLACK PRINCE

Edward the Confessor, St (c. 1003–66) son of Ethelred the Unready, king of England 1042–66

Edward the Elder (c. 870–924) son of Alfred the Great, king of Wessex 899–924

Edward the Martyr, St (c. 963–78) son of Edgar, king of England 975–8

Edwy (also Eadwig) (died 959) king of England 955–7

Egbert (died 839) king of Wessex 802–39

Eichmann, (Karl) Adolf (1906–62) German Nazi administrator

Eisenhower Dwight David ('Ike') (1890–1969) American general and Republican statesman, 34th President of the US 1953–61

Elagabalus See HELIOGABALUS

El Cid See CID, EL

Eleanor of Aquitaine (c. 1122–1204) queen of France 1137–52 and of England 1154–89

Elgin, 8th Earl of (title of James Bruce) (1811–63) British colonial statesman

Elizabeth I (1533–1603) daughter of Henry VIII, queen of England and Ireland 1558–1603

Elizabeth II (born Princess Elizabeth Alexandra Mary) (born 1926) daughter of George VI, queen of the United Kingdom since 1952

Elizabeth, the Queen Mother (born Lady

HISTORICAL, POLITICAL, AND MILITARY FIGURES (cont.)

Elizabeth Angela Marguerite Bowes-Lyon) (born 1900) wife of George VI

Ellsworth, Lincoln (1880–1951) American explorer

Enver Pasha (1881–1922) Turkish political and military leader

Ericsson, Leif (also Ericson) (*fl. c.* 1000) Norse explorer, son of Eric the Red

Eric the Red (*c.* 940–*c.* 1010) Norse explorer

Eugénie (born Eugénia María de Montijo de Guzmán) (1826–1920) Spanish empress of France 1853–71 and wife of Napoleon III

Eyre, Edward John (1815–1901) British-born Australian explorer and colonial statesman

Fabius (full name Quintus Fabius Maximus Verrucosus, known as 'Fabius Cunctator') (died 203 BC) Roman general and statesman

Fahd ibn Abdul Aziz (born 1922) King and Prime Minister of Saudi Arabia since 1982

Fairfax, Thomas, 3rd Baron Fairfax of Cameron (1612–71) English Parliamentary general

Faisal I (1885–1933) king of Iraq, reigned 1921–33

Faisal II (1935–1958) king of Iraq, reigned 1939–58

Farnese, Alessandro, Duke of Parma (1545–92) Italian general and statesman

Farouk (1920–65) king of Egypt, reigned 1936–52

Fawkes, Guy (1570–1606) English conspirator

FDR, nickname of Franklin Delano Roosevelt

Ferdinand (known as Ferdinand of Aragon or Ferdinand the Catholic) (1452–1516) king of Castile 1474–1516 and of Aragon 1479–1516

Fillmore, Millard (1800–74) American Whig statesman, 13th President of the US 1850–3

Flinders, Matthew (1774–1814) English explorer

Foch, Ferdinand (1851–1929) French general

Ford, Gerald R(udolph) (born 1913) American Republican statesman, 38th President of the US 1974–7

Ford, Henry (1863–1947) American motor manufacturer

Forkbeard, Sweyn See SWEYN I

Forrest, John, 1st Baron (1847–1918) Australian explorer and statesman, Premier of Western Australia 1890–1901

Fox, Charles James (1749–1806) British Whig statesman

Francis I (1494–1547) king of France 1515–47

Franco, Francisco (1892–1975) Spanish general and statesman, head of state 1939–75

Frank, Anne (1929–45) German Jewish girl

Franz Josef (1830–1916) emperor of Austria 1848–1916 and king of Hungary 1867–1916

Fraser, (John) Malcolm (born 1930) Australian Liberal statesman, Prime Minister 1975–83

Frederick I (known as Frederick Barbarossa, 'Redbeard') (*c.* 1123–90) king of Germany and Holy Roman emperor 1152–90

Frederick II (known as Frederick the Great) (1712–86) king of Prussia 1740–86

Frederick William (known as 'the Great Elector') (1620–88) Elector of Brandenburg 1640–88

Frémont, John Charles (known as 'the Pathfinder') (1813–90) American explorer and politician

Freyberg, Bernard Cyril, 1st Baron Freyberg of Wellington and of Munstead (1889–1963) British-born New Zealand general

Friedman, Milton (born 1912) American economist

Frisch, Ragnar (Anton Kittil) (1895–1973) Norwegian economist

Frobisher, Sir Martin (*c.* 1535–94) English explorer

Froebel, Friedrich (Wilhelm August) (1782–1852) German educationist and founder of the kindergarten system

Fuad I (1868–1936) king of Egypt, reigned 1922–36

Fuchs, Sir Vivian (Ernest) (1908–99) English geologist and explorer

Fujimori, Alberto (Kenyo) (born 1939) Peruvian statesman, President (1990–2000)

Fulbright, (James) William (1905–95) American senator

Gaddafi, Mu'ammer Muhammad al (also Qaddafi) (born 1942) Libyan colonel, head of state since 1970

Gaitskell, Hugh (Todd Naylor) (1906–63) British Labour politician

Galba (full name Servius Sulpicius Galba) (*c.* 3 BC–AD 69) Roman emperor AD 68–9

Galbraith, John Kenneth (born 1908) Canadian-born American economist

Galtieri, Leopoldo Fortunato (born 1926) Argentinian general and statesman, President 1981–2

Gama, Vasco da See DA GAMA

Gandhi, Mahatma (born Mohandas Karamchand Gandhi) (1869–1948) Indian nationalist and spiritual leader

Gandhi, Indira (1917–84) Indian stateswoman, Prime Minister 1966–77 and 1980–4

Gandhi, Rajiv (1944–91) Indian statesman, Prime Minister 1984–9

Garfield, James A(bram) (1831–81) American Republican statesman, 20th President of the US March–September 1881

Garibaldi, Giuseppe (1807–82) Italian patriot and military leader

Garvey, Marcus (Mosiah) (1887–1940) Jamaican political activist and black nationalist leader

HISTORICAL, POLITICAL, AND MILITARY FIGURES (cont.)

Gates, William (Henry) ('Bill') (born 1955) US computer software entrepreneur
Gaulle, Charles de See DE GAULLE
Gaunt John of See JOHN OF GAUNT
Genghis Khan (1162–1227) the founder of the Mongol empire
George I to IV, kings of Great Britain and Ireland
George V, king of Great Britain and Ireland (from 1920 of the United Kingdom)
George VI, king of the UK
Geronimo (c. 1829–1909) Apache chief
Getty, Jean Paul (1892–1976) American industrialist
Giap, Vo Nguyen (born 1912) Vietnamese military and political leader
Gilbert, Sir Humphrey (c. 1539–83) English explorer
Giolitti, Giovanni (1842–1928) Italian statesman, Prime Minister five times between 1892 and 1921
Giscard d'Estaing, Valéry (born 1926) French statesman, President 1974–81
Gladstone, William Ewart (1809–98) British Liberal statesman, Prime Minister 1868–74, 1880–5, 1886, and 1892–4
Glendower, Owen (also Glyndwr) (c. 1354–c. 1417) Welsh chief
Gloriana, nickname of Elizabeth I of England and Ireland
Glyndwr See GLENDOWER
Göbbels See GOEBBELS
Godiva, Lady (died 1080) English noblewoman, wife of Leofric, Earl of Mercia
Godunov, Boris (1550–1605) tsar of Russia 1598–1605
Goebbels, (Paul) Joseph (also Göbbels) (1897–1945) German Nazi leader and politician
Goering, Hermann Wilhelm (1893–1946) German Nazi leader and politician
Gokhale, Gopal Krishna (1866–1915) Indian political leader and social reformer
Goldman, Emma (known as 'Red Emma') (1869–1940) Lithuanian-born American political activist
Gorbachev, Mikhail (Sergeevich) (born 1931) Soviet statesman, General Secretary of the Communist Party of the USSR 1985–91 and President 1988–91
Gordon, Charles George (1833–85) British general and colonial administrator
Gore, Albert ('Al') (born 1948) American Democrat statesman, Vice President of the US 1993–2001
Gracchus, Tiberius Sempronius (c. 163–133 BC) Roman tribune
Grafton, Augustus Henry Fitzroy, 3rd Duke of

(1735–1811) British Whig statesman, Prime Minister 1768–70
Grant, Ulysses S(impson) (born Hiram Ulysses Grant) (1822–85) American general and 18th President of the US 1869–77
Grenville, George (1712–70) British Whig statesman, Prime Minister 1763–5
Gresham, Sir Thomas (c. 1519–79) English financier
Grey, Charles, 2nd Earl (1764–1845) British statesman, Prime Minister 1830–4
Grey, Lady Jane (1537–54) queen of England 9–19 July 1553
Grey, Sir George (1812–98) British statesman and colonial administrator, Prime Minister of New Zealand 1877–9
Griffith, Arthur (1872–1922) Irish nationalist leader and statesman
Grimond, Joseph ('Jo'), Baron (1913–93) British Liberal politician
Grivas, George (Theodorou) (1898–1974) Greek-Cypriot patriot and soldier
Gromyko, Andrei (Andreevich) (1909–89) Soviet statesman, President of the USSR 1985–8
Guevara, Che (full name Ernesto Guevara de la Serna) (1928–67) Argentinian revolutionary and guerrilla leader
Guggenheim, Meyer (1828–1905) Swiss-born American industrialist
Gulbenkian, Calouste Sarkis (1869–1955) Turkish-born British oil magnate and philanthropist, of Armenian descent
Gustavus Adolphus (1594–1632) king of Sweden 1611–32
Hadrian (full name Publius Aelius Hadrianus) (AD 76–138) Roman emperor 117–38
Hague, William (Jefferson) (born 1961) British Conservative politician
Haig, Douglas, 1st Earl Haig of Bemersyde (1861–1928) British Field Marshal
Haile Selassie (born Tafari Makonnen) (1892–1975) emperor of Ethiopia 1930–74
Halifax, George Montagu Dunk, 2nd Earl of (1716–71) British Tory statesman
Hallowes, Odette (born Marie Céline) (1912–95) French heroine of the Second World War
Hamilcar (c. 270–229 BC) Carthaginian general and father of Hannibal
Hamilton, Alexander (c. 1757–1804) American Federalist politician
Hamilton, Lady Emma (born Amy Lyon) (c. 1765–1815) English beauty and mistress of Lord Nelson
Hammarskjöld, Dag (Hjalmar Agne Carl) (1905–61) Swedish diplomat and politician
Hammurabi (died 1750 BC) the sixth king of

HISTORICAL, POLITICAL, AND MILITARY FIGURES (cont.)

the first dynasty of Babylonia, reigned 1792–1750 BC

Hannibal (247–182 BC) Carthaginian general

Hardie, (James) Keir (1856–1915) Scottish Labour politician

Harding, Warren (Gamaliel) (1865–1923) American Republican statesman, 29th President of the US 1921–3

Hare, William (*fl.* 1820s) Irish murderer

Harefoot, Harold See HAROLD

Harmsworth, Alfred Charles William See NORTHCLIFFE

Harold I (known as Harold Harefoot) (died 1040) reigned 1035–40

Harold II (*c.* 1022–66) king of England 1066

Haroun-al-Raschid See HARUN AR-RASHID

Harris, Sir Arthur (Travers), 1st Baronet (known as 'Bomber Harris') (1892–1984) British Marshal of the RAF

Harrison, Benjamin (1833–1901) American Republican statesman, 23rd President of the US 1889–93

Harrison, William Henry (1773–1841) American Whig statesman, 9th President of the US, 1841

Harrod, Charles Henry (1800–85) English grocer and tea merchant

Harun ar-Rashid (also Haroun-al-Raschid) (763–809) fifth Abbasid caliph of Baghdad 786–809

Hasdrubal (died 207 BC) Carthaginian general

Hastings, Warren (1732–1818) British colonial administrator

Hathaway, Anne (*c.* 1557–1623) the wife of Shakespeare, whom she married in 1582

Hatshepsut (died 1482 BC) Egyptian queen of the 18th dynasty, reigned *c.* 1503–1482 BC

Havel, Václav (born 1936) Czech dramatist and statesman, President of Czechoslovakia 1989–92 and of the Czech Republic from 1993

Hawke, Robert James Lee ('Bob') (born 1929) Australian Labor statesman, Prime Minister 1983–91

Hawkins, Sir John (also Hawkyns) (1532–95) English sailor

Hayes, Rutherford B(irchard) (1822–93) American Republican statesman, 19th President of the US 1877–81

Heath, Sir Edward (Richard George) (born 1916) British Conservative statesman, Prime Minister 1970–4

Helena, St (AD *c.* 255–*c.* 330) Roman empress and mother of Constantine the Great

Heliogabalus (also Elagabalus) (born Varius Avitus Bassianus) (AD 204–22) Roman emperor 218–22

Hengist (died 488) semi-mythological Jutish leader

Henrietta Maria (1609–69) daughter of Henry IV of France, queen consort of Charles I of England

Henry (known as Henry the Navigator) (1394–1460) Portuguese prince

Henry I (Henry the Fowler) (*c.* 876–936) king of the Germans, reigned 919–36

Henry I (1068–1135) king of England, youngest son of William I, reigned 1100–35

Henry II (Saint Henry) (973–1024) king of the Germans, reigned 1002–24

Henry II (1133–89) king of England, reigned 1154–89

Henry III (1207–72) king of England, reigned 1216–72

Henry III to VII, kings of the Germans

Henry IV (Henry Bolingbroke) (1367–1413) king of England, reigned 1399–1413

Henry V (1387–1422) king of England, reigned 1413–22

Henry VI (1421–71) king of England, reigned 1422–61 and 1470–1

Henry VII (Henry Tudor) (1457–1509) king of England, reigned 1485–1509

Henry VIII (1491–1547) king of England, reigned 1509–47

Henry Bolingbroke See HENRY IV of England

Henry IV (known as Henry of Navarre) (1553–1610) king of France 1589–1610

Henry Tudor See HENRY VII of England

Hereward the Wake (11th century) semi-legendary Anglo-Saxon rebel leader

Herod Agrippa I (10 BC–AD 44) king of Judaea AD 41–4

Herod Agrippa II (AD 27–*c.* 93) king of (parts of) Palestine 50–*c.* 93

Herod Antipas (22 BC–AD 40) tetrarch of Galilee and Peraea 4 BC–AD 40

Herod the Great (*c.* 74–4 BC) ruler of Palestine, ruled 37–4 BC

Hess, (Walther Richard) Rudolf (1894–1987) German Nazi politician

Hickok, James Butler (known as 'Wild Bill Hickok') (1837–76) American frontiersman and marshal

Hicks, Sir John Richard (1904–89) English economist

Hill, Octavia (1838–1912) English housing reformer

Hillary, Sir Edmund (Percival) (born 1919) New Zealand mountaineer and explorer

Himmler, Heinrich (1900–45) German Nazi leader, chief of the SS (1929–45) and of the Gestapo (1936–45)

Hindenburg, Paul Ludwig von Beneckendorff und von (1847–1934) German Field Marshal and statesman, President of the Weimar Republic 1925–34

Hirohito (born Michinomiya Hirohito) (1901–89) emperor of Japan 1926–89

HISTORICAL, POLITICAL, AND MILITARY FIGURES (cont.)

Hiss, Alger (1904–96) American public servant and alleged spy

Hitler, Adolf (1889–1945) Austrian-born Nazi leader, Chancellor of Germany 1933–45

Ho Chi Minh (born Nguyen That Thanh) (1890–1969) Vietnamese Communist statesman, President of North Vietnam 1954–69

Hoffa, James Riddle ('Jimmy') (1913–c. 1975) American trade union leader

Holyoake, Sir Keith (Jacka) (1904–83) New Zealand National Party statesman, Prime Minister 1957 and 1960–72

Home of the Hirsel of Coldstream, Baron See DOUGLAS-HOME

Honecker, Erich (1912–94) East German Communist statesman, head of state 1976–89

Hoover, Herbert C(lark) (1874–1964) American Republican statesman, 31st President of the US 1929–33

Hoover, J(ohn) Edgar (1895–1972) American lawyer and director of the FBI 1924–72

Hoover, William (Henry) (1849–1932) American industrialist

Horsa See HENGIST

Hotspur, nickname of Sir Henry Percy

Howard, Catherine (c. 1521–42) fifth wife of Henry VIII

Howard, John (1726–90) English philanthropist and prison reformer

Howard, John (Winston) (born 1939) Australian Liberal statesman, Prime Minister from 1996

Hoxha, Enver (1908–85) Albanian statesman, Prime Minister 1944–54 and First Secretary of the Albanian Communist Party 1954–85

Hudson, Henry (c. 1565–1611) English explorer

Humboldt, Friedrich Heinrich Alexander, Baron von (1769–1859) German explorer and scientist

Hume, John (born 1937) Northern Irish SDLP politician

Husák, Gustáv (1913–91) Czechoslovak statesman, leader of the Communist Party of Czechoslovakia 1969–87 and President 1975–89

Hussein (ibn Talal) (also Husain) (1935–99) king of Jordan 1953–99

Hussein, Abdullah ibn See ABDULLAH IBN HUSSEIN

Hussein, Saddam (also Husain) (full name Saddam bin Hussein at-Takriti) (born 1937) Iraqi President from 1979

Hyde, Edward See CLARENDON

Ibarruri Gomez, Dolores (known as 'La Pasionaria') (1895–1989) Spanish Communist politician

Ibn Batuta (c. 1304–68) Arab explorer

ibn Hussein, Abdullah See ABDULLAH IBN HUSSEIN

Ikhnaton See AKHENATEN

Ine, king of Wessex 688–726

Iron Chancellor, nickname of Bismarck

Iron Duke, nickname of Wellington

Iron Lady, nickname of Margaret Thatcher

Isabella I (known as Isabella of Castile or Isabella the Catholic) (1451–1504) queen of Castile 1474–1504 and of Aragon 1479–1504

Isabella of France (1292–1358) daughter of Philip IV of France

Isocrates (436–338 BC) Athenian orator

Ito, Prince Hirobumi (1841–1909) Japanese statesman, Premier four times between 1884 and 1901

Ivan I (c. 1304–41) ruler of Russia, grand duke of Muscovy 1328–40

Jackson, Andrew (1767–1845) American general and Democratic statesman, 7th President of the US 1829–37

Jackson, Jesse (Louis) (born 1941) American politician and clergyman

Jackson, Thomas Jonathan (known as 'Stonewall Jackson') (1824–63) American general

Jack the Ripper (19th-century) unidentified English murderer

James, Jesse (Woodson) (1847–82) American outlaw

James I to VII, Stuart kings of Scotland

James I (1566–1625) son of Mary, Queen of Scots, king of Scotland (as James VI) 1567–1625, and of England and Ireland 1603–25

James II (1633–1701) king of England, Ireland, and (as James VII) of Scotland (1685–8)

Jaruzelski, Wojciech (born 1923) Polish general and Communist statesman, Prime Minister 1981–5, head of state 1985–9, and President 1989–90

Jefferson, Thomas (1743–1826) American Democratic Republican statesman, 3rd President of the US 1801–9

Jeffreys, George, 1st Baron (c. 1645–89) Welsh judge

Jehu (842–815 BC) king of Israel

Jellicoe, John Rushworth, 1st Earl (1859–1935) British admiral

Jenkins, Roy (Harris), Baron Jenkins of Hillhead (born 1920) English Labour and Social Democrat MP and scholar

Jervis, John, Earl St Vincent (1735–1823) British admiral

Jiang Jie Shi See CHIANG KAI-SHEK

Jiang Zemin (born 1926) Chinese Communist statesman

Jiménez de Cisneros, Francisco (also Ximenes de Cisneros) (1436–1517) Spanish statesman, regent of Spain 1516–17

HISTORICAL, POLITICAL, AND MILITARY FIGURES (cont.)

Jinnah, Muhammad Ali (1876–1948) Indian statesman and founder of Pakistan

Joan of Arc, St (known as 'the Maid of Orleans') (*c.* 1412–31) French national heroine

Joffre, Joseph Jacques Césaire (1852–1931) French Marshal

John (known as John Lackland) (1165–1216) son of Henry II, king of England 1199–1216

John I (known as John the Great) (1357–1433) king of Portugal, reigned 1385–1433

John III (known as John Sobieski) (1624–96) king of Poland 1674–96

John of Gaunt (1340–99) Duke of Lancaster

John Sobieski See JOHN III

Johnson, Andrew (1808–75) American Democratic statesman, 17th President of the US 1865–9

Johnson, Lyndon Baines (known as 'LBJ') (1908–73) American Democratic statesman, 36th President of the US 1963–9

Jones, John Paul (born John Paul) (1747–92) Scottish-born American naval officer

Josephine (born Marie Joséphine Rose Tascher de la Pagerie) (1763–1814) Empress of France 1796–1809

Juan Carlos (full name Juan Carlos Victor María de Borbón y Borbón) (born 1938) grandson of Alfonso XIII, king of Spain since 1975

Juárez, Benito Pablo (1806–72) Mexican statesman, President 1861–4 and 1867–72

Judas Maccabaeus (died *c.* 161 BC) Jewish leader

Jugurtha (died 104 BC) joint king of Numidia *c.* 118–104

Julian (known as the Apostate) (full name Flavius Claudius Julianus) (AD *c.* 331–63) Roman emperor 360–3, nephew of Constantine

Julius Caesar, Gaius (100–44 BC) Roman general and statesman

Justinian (Latin name Flavius Petrus Sabbatius Justinianus) (483–565) Byzantine emperor 527–65

Kádár, János (1912–89) Hungarian statesman, First Secretary of the Hungarian Socialist Workers' Party 1956–88 and Prime Minister 1956–8 and 1961–5

Kaiser Wilhelm See WILHELM II

Kalinin, Mikhail Ivanovich (1875–1946) Soviet statesman, head of state of the USSR 1919–46

Karl XII See CHARLES XII

Kaunda, Kenneth (David) (born 1924) Zambian statesman, President 1964–91

Keating, Paul (John) (born 1944) Australian Labor statesman, Prime Minister 1991–6

Kellogg, Will Keith (1860–1951) American food manufacturer

Kelly, Edward ('Ned') (1855–80) Australian outlaw

Kemal Pasha See ATATÜRK

Kennedy, Charles (Peter) (born 1959) British Liberal Democrat politican

Kennedy, Edward Moore ('Teddy') (born 1932) American Democratic politician

Kennedy, John F(itzgerald) (known as 'JFK') (1917–63) American Democratic statesman, 35th President of the US 1961–3

Kennedy, Robert F(rancis) (1925–68) American Democratic statesman

Kenneth I (known as Kenneth MacAlpine) (died 858) king of Scotland *c.* 844–58

Kenyatta, Jomo (*c.* 1891–1978) Kenyan statesman, Prime Minister of Kenya 1963 and President 1964–78

Keynes, John Maynard, 1st Baron (1883–1946) English economist

Khama, Sir Seretse (1921–80) Botswanan statesman, Prime Minister of Bechuanaland 1965 and President of Botswana 1966–80

Khan, Ayub See AYUB KHAN

Khatami, Mohammed (born 1943) Iranian political and religious leader, President from 1996

Khomeini, Ruhollah (known as Ayatollah Khomeini) (1900–89) Iranian Shiite Muslim leader

Khrushchev, Nikita (Sergeevich) (1894–1971) Soviet statesman, Premier of the USSR 1958–64

Khufu See CHEOPS

Kidd, William (known as Captain Kidd) (1645–1701) Scottish pirate

Kim Il Sung (born Kim Song Ju) (1912–94) Korean Communist statesman, first Premier of North Korea 1948–72 and President 1972–94

King, Martin Luther (1929–68) American Baptist minister and civil-rights leader

King, William Lyon Mackenzie (1874–1950) Canadian Liberal statesman, Prime Minister 1921–6, 1926–30, and 1935–48

Kissinger, Henry (Alfred) (born 1923) German-born American statesman and diplomat, Secretary of State 1973–7

Kitchener, (Horatio) Herbert, 1st Earl Kitchener of Khartoum (1850–1916) British soldier and statesman

Klerk, F. W. de See DE KLERK

Knut See CANUTE

Kohl, Helmut (born 1930) German statesman, Chancellor of the Federal Republic of Germany 1982–90, and of Germany 1990–8

Kosciusko, Thaddeus (or Tadeusz) (1746–1817) Polish soldier and patriot

Kossuth, Lajos (1802–94) Hungarian statesman and patriot

HISTORICAL, POLITICAL, AND MILITARY FIGURES (cont.)

Kosygin, Aleksei Nikolaevich (1904–80) Soviet statesman, Premier of the USSR 1964–80

Krishnamurti, Jiddu (1895–1986) Indian spiritual leader

Kropotkin, Prince Peter (1842–1921) Russian anarchist

Kruger, Stephanus Johannes Paulus (known as 'Oom (= uncle) Paul') (1825–1904) South African soldier and statesman

Krupp, Alfred (1812–87) German arms manufacturer

Kublai Khan (1216–94) Mongol emperor of China, grandson of Genghis Khan

Kumaratunga, Chandrika Bandaranaike (born 1945) Sri Lankan stateswoman, Prime Minister (1994) and President since 1994

Ladislaus I (canonized as St Ladislaus) (*c.* 1040–95) king of Hungary 1077–95

Ladislaus II (Polish name Władysław) (*c.* 1351–1434) king of Poland 1386–1434

Lafayette, Marie Joseph Paul Yves Roch Gilbert du Motier, Marquis de (also La Fayette) (1757–1834) French soldier and statesman

La Salle, René-Robert Cavelier, Sieur de (1643–87) French explorer

Laurier, Sir Wilfrid (1841–1919) Canadian Liberal statesman, Prime Minister 1896–1911

Law, (Andrew) Bonar (1858–1923) Canadian-born British Conservative statesman, Prime Minister 1922–3

Lee, Robert E(dward) (1807–70) American general

Leicester, Earl of See DUDLEY

Leichhardt, (Friedrich Wilhelm) Ludwig (1813–48) Australian explorer, born in Prussia

Leif Ericsson See ERICSSON

Lenin, Vladimir Ilich (born Vladimir Ilich Ulyanov) (1870–1924) the principal figure in the Russian Revolution and first Premier (Chairman of the Council of People's Commissars) of the Soviet Union 1918–24

Leo III (*c.* 680–741) Byzantine emperor 717–41

Leopold I (1790–1865) first king of Belgium 1831–65

Lepidus, Marcus Aemilius (died *c.* 13 BC) Roman statesman and triumvir

Lesseps, Ferdinand Marie, Vicomte de (1805–94) French diplomat

Leverhulme, 1st Viscount (born William Hesketh Lever) (1851–1925) English industrialist and philanthropist

Lewis, Meriwether (1774–1809) American explorer

Lie, Trygve Halvdan (1896–1968) Norwegian Labour politician, first Secretary-General of the United Nations 1946–53

Lin Biao (1908–71) Chinese Communist statesman and general

Lincoln, Abraham (1809–65) American Republican statesman, 16th President of the US 1861–5

Lin Piao See LIN BIAO

Liverpool, 2nd Earl of (title of Robert Banks Jenkinson) (1770–1828) British Tory statesman, Prime Minister 1812–27

Livingstone, Kenneth Robert ('Ken') (born 1945) British politician, Mayor of London since 2000

Llewelyn (also Llywelyn ap Gruffydd) (died 1282) prince of Gwynedd in North Wales

Lloyd George, David, 1st Earl Lloyd George of Dwyfor (1863–1945) British Liberal statesman, Prime Minister 1916–22

Llywelyn ap Gruffydd See LLEWELYN

Lorenzo de' Medici (known as Lorenzo the Magnificent) (1449–92) Italian statesman and scholar

Louis I to XVIII, kings of France

Louis I (known as Louis the Great) (1326–82) king of Hungary 1342–82 and of Poland 1370–82

Louis-Napoleon See NAPOLEON

Louis Philippe (1773–1850) king of France 1830–48

Ludendorff, Erich (1865–1937) German general

Ludwig I to III, kings of Bavaria

Luxemburg, Rosa (1871–1919) Polish-born German revolutionary leader

Lysander (died 395 BC) Spartan general

McAleese, Mary (Patricia) (born 1951) Irish politician, President from 1997

MacAlpine, Kenneth See KENNETH I

MacArthur, Douglas (1880–1964) American general

McCarthy, Joseph R(aymond) (1909–57) American Republican politician

Macbeth (*c.* 1005–57) king of Scotland 1040–57

Maccabaeus, Judas See JUDAS MACCABAEUS

MacDonald, Flora (1722–90) Scottish Jacobite heroine

Macdonald, Sir John Alexander (1815–91) Scottish-born Canadian statesman, Prime Minister 1867–73 and 1878–91

MacDonald, (James) Ramsay (1866–1937) British Labour statesman, Prime Minister 1924, 1929–31, and 1931–5

Machiavelli, Niccolò di Bernardo dei (1469–1527) Italian statesman and political philosopher

Mackenzie, Sir Alexander (1764–1820) Scottish explorer of Canada

McKinlay, John (1819–72) Scottish-born explorer

McKinley, William (1843–1901) American Republican statesman, 25th President of the US 1897–1901

HISTORICAL, POLITICAL, AND MILITARY FIGURES (cont.)

Maclean, Donald (Duart) (1913–83) British Foreign Office official and Soviet spy

McLeish, Henry (born 1948) Scottish Labour politician, First Minister of Scotland since 2000

Macmillan, (Maurice) Harold, 1st Earl of Stockton (1894–1986) British Conservative statesman, Prime Minister 1957–63

Macquarie, Lachlan (1762–1824) Scottish-born Australian colonial administrator

Madison, James (1751–1836) American Democratic Republican statesman, 4th President of the US 1809–17

Maecenas, Gaius (c. 70–8 BC) Roman statesman

Magellan, Ferdinand (Portuguese name Fernão Magalhães) (c. 1480–1521) Portuguese explorer

Maintenon, Marquise de (title of Françoise d'Aubigné) (1635–1719) mistress and later second wife of the French king Louis XIV

Major, John (born 1943) British Conservative statesman, Prime Minister 1990–7

Makarios III (born Mikhail Christodolou Mouskos) (1913–77) Greek Cypriot archbishop and statesman, President of the republic of Cyprus 1960–77

Malcolm I (died 954) king of Scotland, reigned 943–54

Malcolm II to IV, kings of Scotland

Malcolm X (born Malcolm Little) (1925–65) American political activist

Malenkov, Georgy (Maksimilianovich) (1902–88) Soviet statesman, born in Russia

Mandela, Nelson (Rolihlahla) (born 1918) South African statesman, President 1994–9

Mandelson, Peter (Benjamin) (born 1953) British Labour politician

Mandeville, Sir John (14th century) English nobleman

Man in the Iron Mask, a mysterious prisoner held in the Bastille and other prisons in 17th-century France

Manley, Michael (Norman) (1923–97) Jamaican statesman, Prime Minister 1972–80 and 1989–92

Mao Zedong (also Mao Tse-tung) (1893–1976) Chinese statesman, chairman of the Communist Party of the Chinese People's Republic 1949–76 and head of state 1949–59

Marat, Jean Paul (1743–93) French revolutionary and journalist

Marco Polo (c. 1254–c. 1324) Italian traveller

Marcus Aurelius See AURELIUS

Margaret, Princess, Margaret Rose (born 1930) only sister of Elizabeth II

Maria de' Medici See MARIE DE MÉDICIS

Maria Theresa (1717–80) Archduchess of Austria, queen of Hungary and Bohemia 1740–80

Marie Antoinette (1755–93) French queen, wife of Louis XVI

Marie de Médicis (Italian name Maria de' Medici) (1573–1642) queen of France

Marius, Gaius (c. 157–86 BC) Roman general and politician

Mark Antony See ANTONY

Marks, Simon, 1st Baron Marks of Broughton (1888–1964) English businessman

Marlborough, 1st Duke of (title of John Churchill) (1650–1722) British general

Marshall, George C(atlett) (1880–1959) American general and statesman

Martel, Charles See CHARLES MARTEL

Mary I (known as Mary Tudor) (1516–58) daughter of Henry VIII, reigned 1553–8

Mary II (1662–94) joint queen of England, Scotland and Ireland (1689–94)

Mary, Queen of Scots (known as Mary Stuart) (1542–87) daughter of James V, queen of Scotland 1542–67

Mary Stuart See MARY, QUEEN OF SCOTS

Mary Tudor See MARY I

Masaryk, Tomáš (Garrigue) (1850–1937) Czechoslovak statesman, President 1918–35

Mata Hari (born Margaretha Geertruida Zelle) (1876–1917) Dutch dancer and secret agent

Matilda (known as 'the Empress Maud') (1102–67) English princess, daughter of Henry I

Maximilian (full name Ferdinand Maximilian Joseph) (1832–67) emperor of Mexico 1864–7

Mazarin, Jules (Italian name Giulio Mazzarino) (1602–61) Italian-born French statesman

Mazzini, Giuseppe (1805–72) Italian nationalist leader

Mbeki, Thabo (born 1942) South African statesman, President since 1999

Médicis, Marie de See MARIE DE MÉDICIS

Meiji Tenno (born Mutsuhito) (1852–1912) emperor of Japan 1868–1912

Meir, Golda (born Goldie Mabovich) (1898–1978) Israeli stateswoman, Prime Minister 1969–74

Melbourne, William Lamb, 2nd Viscount (1779–1848) British Whig statesman, Prime Minister 1834 and 1835–41

Mellon, Andrew W(illiam) (1855–1937) American financier and philanthropist

Mendoza, Antonio de (c. 1490–1552) Spanish colonial administrator

Menes, Egyptian pharaoh, reigned c. 3100 BC

Menzies, Sir Robert Gordon (1894–1978) Australian Liberal statesman, Prime Minister 1939–41 and 1949–66

Messalina, Valeria (also Messallina) (AD c. 22–48) Roman empress, third wife of Claudius

Metternich, Klemens Wenzel Nepomuk

HISTORICAL, POLITICAL, AND MILITARY FIGURES (cont.)

Lothar, Prince of Metternich-Winneburg-Beilstein (1773–1859) Austrian statesman

Michelin, André (1853–1931) and **Édouard** (1859–1940) French industrialists

Mihailović, Dragoljub ('Draža') (1893–1946) Yugoslav soldier

Milošević, Slobodan (born 1941) Serbian politician, President of Serbia (1989–97) and of the Federal Republic of Yugoslavia (1997–2001)

Mirabeau, Honoré Gabriel Riqueti, Comte de (1749–91) French revolutionary politician

Mithridates VI (also Mithradates VI) (c. 132–63 BC) king of Pontus 120–63

Mitterrand, François (Maurice Marie) (1916–96) French statesman, President 1981–95

Mobutu, Sese Seko (full name Mobutu Sese Seko Kuku Ngbendu Wa Za Banga) (1930–97) Zaïrean statesman, President 1965–97

Moi, Daniel arap (born 1924) Kenyan statesman, President since 1978

Molotov, Vyacheslav (Mikhailovich) (born Vyacheslav Mikhailovich Skryabin) (1890–1986) Soviet statesman

Monash, Sir John (1865–1931) Australian general

Monck, George, 1st Duke of Albemarle (1608–70) English general

Monmouth, Duke of (title of James Scott) (1649–85) English claimant to the throne of England

Monroe, James (1758–1831) American Democratic Republican statesman, 5th President of the US 1817–25

Montcalm, Louis Joseph de Montcalm-Gozon, Marquis de (1712–59) French general

Montespan, Marquise de (title of Françoise-Athénaïs de Rochechouart) (1641–1707) French noblewoman

Montezuma II (1466–1520) Aztec emperor 1502–20

Montfort, Simon de (c. 1165–1218) French soldier

Montfort, Simon de, Earl of Leicester (c. 1208–65) English soldier, born in Normandy

Montgomery Bernard Law, 1st Viscount Montgomery of Alamein ('Monty') (1887–1976) British Field Marshal

Montrose, James Graham, 1st Marquess of (1612–50) Scottish general

Moore, Sir John (1761–1809) British general

Morgan, (Hywel) Rhodri (born 1939) Welsh Labour politician, First Secretary of Wales from 2000

Mortimer, Roger de, 8th Baron of Wigmore and 1st Earl of March (c. 1287–1330) English noble

Moses (fl. c. 14th–13th centuries BC) Hebrew prophet and lawgiver

Mosley, Sir Oswald (Ernald), 6th Baronet (1896–1980) English Fascist leader

Mountbatten, Louis (Francis Albert Victor Nicholas), 1st Earl Mountbatten of Burma (1900–79) British admiral and administrator

Mubarak, (Muhammad) Hosni (Said) (born 1928) Egyptian statesman, President since 1981

Mugabe, Robert (Gabriel) (born 1924) Zimbabwean statesman, Prime Minister 1980–7 and President since 1987

Muhammad, Mahathir (born 1925) Malaysian statesman, Prime Minister since 1981

Muhammad Ali (1769–1849) Ottoman viceroy and pasha of Egypt 1805–49, possibly of Albanian descent

Mujibur Rahman (known as Sheikh Mujib) (1920–75) Bangladeshi statesman, Prime Minister 1972–5 and President 1975

Muldoon, Sir Robert (David) (1921–92) New Zealand statesman, Prime Minister 1975–84

Mulroney, (Martin) Brian (born 1939) Canadian Progressive Conservative statesman, Prime Minister 1984–93

Murat, Joachim (c. 1767–1815) French general, king of Naples 1808–15

Murdoch, (Keith) Rupert (born 1931) Australian-born American publisher and media entrepreneur

Mussolini, Benito (Amilcaro Andrea) (known as 'Il Duce' = the leader) (1883–1945) Italian Fascist statesman, Prime Minister 1922–43

Mutsuhito See MEIJI TENNO

Nagy, Imre (1896–1958) Hungarian Communist statesman, Prime Minister 1953–5 and 1956

Nansen, Fridtjof (1861–1930) Norwegian Arctic explorer

Napoleon I (known as Napoleon; full name Napoleon Bonaparte) (1769–1821) Emperor of France 1804–14 and 1815

Napoleon II (known as the King of Rome) (1811–1832) Duke of Reichstadt

Napoleon III (known as Louis-Napoleon) (1808–73) Emperor of France 1852–70

Nasser, Gamal Abdel (1918–70) Egyptian colonel and statesman, Prime Minister 1954–6 and President 1956–70

Nebuchadnezzar (c. 630–562 BC) king of Babylon 605–562 BC

Necker, Jacques (1732–1804) Swiss-born banker

Nefertiti (also Nofretete) (fl. 14th century BC) Egyptian queen, wife of Akhenaten

Nehemiah (5th century BC) Hebrew leader who supervised the rebuilding of the walls of

HISTORICAL, POLITICAL, AND MILITARY FIGURES (cont.)

Jerusalem (*c.* 444) and introduced moral and religious reforms (*c.* 432)

Nehru, Jawaharlal (known as Pandit Nehru) (1889–1964) Indian statesman, Prime Minister 1947–64

Nelson, Horatio, Viscount Nelson, Duke of Bronte (1758–1805) British admiral

Nero (full name Nero Claudius Caesar Augustus Germanicus) (AD 37–68) Roman emperor 54–68

Nerva, Marcus Cocceius (AD *c.* 30–98) Roman emperor 96–8

Netanyahu, Benjamin (born 1949) Israeli Likud statesman, Prime Minister 1996–9

Neville, Richard See WARWICK

Nevsky See ALEXANDER NEVSKY

Newcastle, 1st Duke of (title of Thomas Pelham-Holles) (1693–1768) British Whig statesman, Prime Minister 1754–6 and 1757–62

Ne Win (born 1911) Burmese general and socialist statesman

Ney, Michel (1768–1815) French marshal

Ngata, Sir Apirana Turupa (1874–1950) New Zealand Maori leader and politician

Nicholas I and **II**, tsars of Russia

Nixon, Richard (Milhous) (1913–94) American Republican statesman, 37th President of the US 1969–74

Nkomo, Joshua (Mqabuko Nyongolo) (1917–99) Zimbabwean statesman

Nkrumah, Kwame (1909–72) Ghanaian statesman, Prime Minister 1957–60, President 1960–6

Nofretete See NEFERTITI

Noriega, Manuel (Antonio Morena) (born 1940) Panamanian statesman and general, head of state 1983–9

North, Frederick, Lord (1732–92) British Tory statesman, Prime Minister 1770–82

Northcliffe, 1st Viscount (title of Alfred Charles William Harmsworth) (1865–1922) British newspaper proprietor

Novotný, Antonín (1904–75) Czechoslovak Communist statesman, President 1957–68

Nyerere, Julius Kambarage (1922–99) Tanzanian statesman, President of Tanganyika 1962–4 and of Tanzania 1964–85

Oakley, Annie (full name Phoebe Anne Oakley Mozee) (1860–1926) American markswoman

Obote, (Apollo) Milton (born 1924) Ugandan statesman, Prime Minister 1962–6, President 1966–71 and 1980–5

O'Connell, Daniel (known as 'the Liberator') (1775–1847) Irish nationalist leader and social reformer

Octavian See AUGUSTUS

Offa (died 796) king of Mercia 757–96

O'Higgins, Bernardo (*c.* 1778–1842) Chilean

revolutionary leader and statesman, head of state 1817–23

Olaf I Tryggvason (969–1000) king of Norway, reigned 995–1000

Olaf II to V, kings of Norway

Old Hickory, nickname of Andrew Jackson

Old Pretender See STUART

Omar I (*c.* 581–644) Muslim caliph 634–44

Onassis, Aristotle (Socrates) (1906–75) Greek shipping magnate and international businessman

Onassis, Jacqueline Lee Bouvier Kennedy (known as 'Jackie O') (1929–94) American First Lady

Orange, William of See WILLIAM

Ortega, Daniel (full surname Ortega Saavedra) (born 1945) Nicaraguan statesman, President 1985–90

Orton, Arthur (known as 'the Tichborne claimant') (1834–98) English butcher

Osman I (also Othman) (1259–1326) Turkish conqueror, founder of the Ottoman (Osmanli) dynasty and empire

Oswald, Lee Harvey (1939–63) American alleged assassin of John F. Kennedy

Othman See OSMAN I

Otho, Marcus Salvius (AD 32–69) Roman emperor January–April 69

Otto I (known as Otto the Great) (912–73) king of the Germans 936–73, Holy Roman emperor 962–73

Owen, David (Anthony Llewellyn), Baron (born 1938) British politician

Owen, Robert (1771–1858) Welsh social reformer and industrialist

Pahlavi, Muhammad Reza (also known as Reza Shah) (1919–80) shah of Iran 1941–79

Pahlavi, Reza (born Reza Khan) (1878–1944) shah of Iran 1925–41

Paisley, Ian (Richard Kyle) (born 1926) Northern Irish clergyman and politician

Palme, (Sven) Olof (Joachim) (1927–86) Swedish statesman, Prime Minister 1969–76 and 1982–6

Palmerston, Henry John Temple, 3rd Viscount (1784–1865) British Whig statesman, Prime Minister 1855–8 and 1859–65

Pandit, Vijaya (Lakshmi) (1900–90) Indian politician and diplomat

Pankhurst, Mrs Emmeline (1858–1928), **Christabel** (1880–1958), and **(Estelle) Sylvia** (1882–1960) English suffragettes

Papineau, Louis Joseph (1786–1871) French-Canadian politician

Park, Mungo (1771–1806) Scottish explorer

Park Chung Hee (1917–79) South Korean statesman, President 1963–79

Parnell, Charles Stewart (1846–91) Irish nationalist leader

HISTORICAL, POLITICAL, AND MILITARY FIGURES (cont.)

Parr, Katherine (1512–48) sixth and last wife of Henry VIII

Pašić, Nikola (1845–1926) Serbian statesman

Pearson, Lester Bowles (1897–1972) Canadian diplomat and Liberal statesman, Prime Minister 1963–8

Peary, Robert Edwin (1856–1920) American explorer

Peel, Sir Robert (1788–1850) British Conservative statesman, Prime Minister 1834–5 and 1841–6

Peisistratus See PISISTRATUS

Pelham, Henry (1696–1754) British Whig statesman, Prime Minister 1743–54

Penn, William (1644–1718) English Quaker, founder of Pennsylvania

Perceval, Spencer (1762–1812) British Tory statesman, Prime Minister 1809–12

Percy, Sir Henry (known as 'Hotspur' and 'Harry Hotspur') (1364–1403) English soldier

Peres, Shimon (Polish name Szymon Perski) (born 1923) Israeli statesman, Prime Minister 1984–6 and 1995–6

Pérez de Cuéllar, Javier (born 1920) Peruvian diplomat, Secretary-General of the United Nations 1982–91

Pericles (*c.* 495–429 BC) Athenian statesman and general

Perón, Eva (full name María Eva Duarte de Perón; known as 'Evita') (1919–52) Argentinian politician

Perón, Juan Domingo (1895–1974) Argentinian soldier and statesman, President 1946–55 and 1973–4

Pestalozzi, Johann Heinrich (1746–1827) Swiss educational reformer

Pétain, (Henri) Philippe (Omer) (1856–1951) French general and statesman, head of state 1940–2

Peter I (known as Peter the Great) (1672–1725) tsar of Russia 1682–1725

Pheidippides (5th century BC) Athenian messenger

Philby, Harold Adrian Russell ('Kim') (1912–88) British Foreign Office official and spy

Philip I to **V**, kings of Spain

Philip I to **VI**, kings of France

Philip II of Macedon (382–336 BC) king of Macedon, father of Alexander the Great, reigned 359–336

Philip, Prince, Duke of Edinburgh (born 1921) husband of Elizabeth II

Photius (*c.* 820–*c.* 891) Byzantine scholar and patriarch of Constantinople

Pierce, Franklin (1804–69) American Democratic statesman, 14th President of the US 1853–7

Pilate, Pontius (died AD *c.* 36) Roman procurator of Judaea *c.* 26–*c.* 36

Pinkerton, Allan (1819–84) Scottish-born American detective

Pinochet, Augusto (full name Augusto Pinochet Ugarte) (born 1915) Chilean general and statesman, President 1974–90

Pisistratus (also Peisistratus) (*c.* 600–*c.* 527 BC) tyrant of Athens

Pitt, William (known as Pitt the Elder), 1st Earl of Chatham (1708–78) British Whig statesman

Pitt, William (known as Pitt the Younger) (1759–1806) British statesman, Prime Minister 1783–1801 and 1804–6

Pizarro, Francisco (*c.* 1478–1541) Spanish conquistador

Pocahontas (*c.* 1595–1617) American Indian princess, daughter of Powhatan (died 1618) an Algonquian chief in Virginia

Polk, James Knox (1795–1849) American Democratic statesman, 11th President of the US 1845–9

Polo, Marco See MARCO POLO

Pol Pot (born Saloth Sar) (1925–98) Cambodian Communist leader, Prime Minister 1976–9

Pompadour, Marquise de (title of Jeanne Antoinette Poisson; known as Madame de Pompadour) (1721–64) French noblewoman

Pompey (known as Pompey the Great; Latin name Gnaeus Pompeius Magnus) (106–48 BC) Roman general and statesman

Pompidou, Georges (Jean Raymond) (1911–74) French statesman, Prime Minister 1962–8 and President 1969–74

Ponce de León, Juan (*c.* 1460–1521) Spanish explorer

Porsenna, Lars (also Porsena) (6th century BC) legendary Etruscan chieftain

Powell, Colin (Luther) (born 1937) American general and Republican politician, Secretary of State from 2001

Powell, (John) Enoch (1912–98) British politician

Prescott, John (Leslie) (born 1938) British Labour politician

Primo de Rivera, Miguel (1870–1930) Spanish general and statesman, head of state 1923–30

Prince Albert, Prince Charles See ALBERT, PRINCE; CHARLES, PRINCE, ETC

Prince of Wales See CHARLES, PRINCE

Princes in the Tower, the young sons of Edward IV, namely **Edward, Prince of Wales** (born 1470) and **Richard, Duke of York** (born 1472), supposedly murdered in the Tower of London in or shortly after 1483

Princess Anne, Princess Diana See ANNE, PRINCESS; DIANA, PRINCESS, ETC

Prodi, Romano (born 1939) Italian statesman,

HISTORICAL, POLITICAL, AND MILITARY FIGURES (cont.)

Prime Minister of Italy 1996–8 and President of the European Commission since 1999

Profumo, John (Dennis) (born 1915) British Conservative politician

Pulitzer, Joseph (1847–1911) Hungarian-born American newspaper proprietor and editor

Pulu Tiglath-pileser III See TIGLATH-PILESER

Putin, Vladimir (born 1952) Russian statesman, President from 2000

Pyrrhus (*c.* 318–272 BC) king of Epirus *c.* 307–272

Qaddafi See GADDAFI

Rabin, Yitzhak (1922–95) Israeli statesman and military leader, Prime Minister 1974–7 and 1992–5

Radhakrishnan, Sir Sarvepalli (1888–1975) Indian philosopher and statesman, President 1962–7

Raffles, Sir (Thomas) Stamford (1781–1826) British colonial administrator

Rafsanjani, Ali Akbar Hashemi (born 1934) Iranian statesman and religious leader, President 1989–1996

Rahman See ABDUL RAHMAN, MUJIBUR RAHMAN

Rákosi, Mátyás (1892–1971) Hungarian Communist statesman, First Secretary of the Hungarian Socialist Workers' Party 1945–56 and Prime Minister 1952–3 and 1955–6

Raleigh, Sir Walter (also Ralegh) (*c.* 1552–1618) English explorer, courtier, and writer

Rameses See RAMSES

Ramses I to XI (also Rameses) Egyptian pharaohs

Ranjit Singh (known as 'the Lion of the Punjab') (1780–1839) Indian maharaja, founder of the Sikh state of Punjab

Rao, P(amulaparti) V(enkata) Narasimha (born 1921) Indian statesman, Prime Minister 1991–6

Rasputin, Grigori (Efimovich) (1871–1916) Russian monk

Ratana, Tahupotiki Wiremu (1873–1939) Maori political and religious leader

Reagan, Ronald (Wilson) (born 1911) American Republican statesman, 40th President of the US 1981–9

Red Baron, the See RICHTHOFEN

Redmond, John (Edward) (1856–1918) Irish politician

Rehoboam, king of ancient Israel *c.* 930–*c.* 915 BC

Reith, John (Charles Walsham), 1st Baron (1889–1971) Scottish administrator and politician, first director-general (1927–38) of the BBC

Revere, Paul (1735–1818) American patriot

Reynolds, Albert (born 1933) Irish Fianna Fáil statesman, Taoiseach (Prime Minister) 1992–4

Reza Shah See PAHLAVI

Rhodes, Cecil (John) (1853–1902) British-born South African statesman, Prime Minister of Cape Colony 1890–6

Ribbentrop, Joachim von (1893–1946) German Nazi politician

Richard I (known as Richard Coeur de Lion or Richard the Lionheart) (1157–99) king of England reigned 1189–99

Richard II (1367–1400) king of England, reigned 1377–99

Richard III (1452–85) king of England, reigned 1483–5

Richelieu, Armand Jean du Plessis (1585–1642) French cardinal and statesman

Richthofen, Manfred, Freiherr von (known as 'the Red Baron') (1882–1918) German fighter pilot

Riel, Louis (1844–85) Canadian political leader

Roberts, Frederick Sleigh, 1st Earl Roberts of Kandahar (1832–1914) British Field Marshal

Robert the Bruce (Robert I of Scotland) (1274–1329) king of Scotland, reigned 1306–29

Robespierre, Maximilien François Marie Isidore de (1758–94) French revolutionary

Robinson, Mary (Terese Winifred) (born 1944) Irish Labour stateswoman, President 1990–7

Rob Roy (born Robert Macgregor) (1671–1734) Scottish outlaw

Rockefeller, John D(avison) (1839–1937) American industrialist and philanthropist

Rommel, Erwin (known as 'the Desert Fox') (1891–1944) German Field Marshal

Roosevelt, (Anna) Eleanor (1884–1962) American humanitarian and diplomat

Roosevelt, Franklin D(elano) (known as FDR) (1882–1945) American Democratic statesman, 32nd President of the US 1933–45

Roosevelt, Theodore ('Teddy') (1858–1919) American Republican statesman, 26th President of the US 1901–9

Rosebery, 5th Earl of (title of Archibald Philip Primrose) (1847–1929) British Liberal statesman, Prime Minister 1894–5

Ross, Sir James Clark (1800–62) British explorer

Rothschild, Meyer Amschel (1743–1812) German financier

Rowntree, Benjamin Seebolm (1871–1954) English entrepreneur and philanthropist

Rupert, Prince (1619–82) English Royalist general, son of Frederick V, elector of the Palatinate, and nephew of Charles I

Russell, John, 1st Earl Russell (1792–1878) British Whig statesman, Prime Minister 1846–52 and 1865–6

Ryder, Sue, Baroness Ryder of Warsaw and

HISTORICAL, POLITICAL, AND MILITARY FIGURES (cont.)

Cavendish (1923–2000) English philanthropist

Sadat, (Muhammad) Anwar al- (1918–81) Egyptian statesman, President 1970–81

Saddam Hussein See HUSSEIN

Saladin (Arabic name Salah-ad-Din Yusuf ibn-Ayyub) (1137–93) sultan of Egypt and Syria 1174–93

Salazar, Antonio de Oliveira (1889–1970) Portuguese statesman, Prime Minister 1932–68

Salisbury, Robert Arthur Talbot Gascoigne-Cecil, 3rd Marquess of (1830–1903) British Conservative statesman, Prime Minister 1885–6, 1886–92, and 1895–1902

Sanger, Margaret (Higgins) (1883–1966) American birth-control campaigner

San Martín, José de (1778–1850) Argentinian soldier and statesman

Sargon II (died 705 BC) king of Assyria 721–705

Saul (11th century BC) (in the Bible) the first king of Israel

Savage, Michael Joseph (1872–1940) New Zealand Labour statesman,

Schindler, Oskar (1908–74) German industrialist

Schröder, Gerhard (born 1944) German statesman, Chancellor from 1998

Scipio Aemilianus (full name Publius Cornelius Scipio Aemilianus Africanus Minor) (c. 185–129 BC) Roman general and politician

Scipio Africanus (full name Publius Cornelius Scipio Africanus Major) (236–c. 184 BC) Roman general and politician

Scott, Sir Robert Falcon (1868–1912) English explorer and naval officer

Selcraig See SELKIRK

Selkirk, Alexander (also called Alexander Selcraig) (1676–1721) Scottish sailor

Selous, Frederick Courteney (1851–1917) English explorer, naturalist, and soldier

Senanayake, Don Stephen (1884–1952) Sinhalese statesman, Prime Minister of Ceylon 1947–52

Seneca, Lucius Annaeus (known as Seneca the Younger) (c. 4 BC–AD 65) Roman statesman, philosopher, and dramatist

Seneca, Marcus (or Lucius) Annaeus (known as Seneca the Elder) (c. 55 BC–c. AD 39) Roman rhetorician, born in Spain

Sennacherib (died 681 BC) king of Assyria 705–681

Severus, Septimius (full name Lucius Septimius Severus Pertinax) (146–211) Roman emperor 193–211

Seymour, Jane (c. 1509–37) third wife of Henry VIII and mother of Edward VI

Shabaka (known as Sabacon) (died 698 BC) Egyptian pharaoh of the 25th dynasty

Shackleton, Sir Ernest Henry (1874–1922) British explorer

Shaftesbury, Anthony Ashley Cooper, 7th Earl of (1801–85) English philanthropist

Shah, Reza See PAHLAVI

Shaka (also Chaka) (c. 1787–1828) Zulu chief

Shalmaneser III (died 824 BC) king of Assyria 859–824

Shamir, Yitzhak (Polish name Yitzhak Jazernicki) (born 1915) Israeli statesman, Prime Minister 1983–4 and 1986–92

Sharon, Ariel (born 1928) Israeli soldier and statesman, Prime Minister from 2001

Sherman, William Tecumseh (1820–91) American general

Shevardnadze, Eduard (Amvrosievich) (born 1928) Soviet statesman and head of state of Georgia from 1992

Shivaji (also Sivaji) (1627–80) Indian raja of the Marathas 1674–80

Sihanouk, Norodom (born 1922) Cambodian king 1941–55 and since 1993

Simnel, Lambert (c. 1475–1525) English pretender and rebel

Simpson, Wallis (née Wallis Warfield) (1896–1986) American wife of Edward, Duke of Windsor (Edward VIII)

Sitting Bull (Sioux name Tatanka Iyotake) (c. 1831–90) Sioux chief

Sivaji See SHIVAJI

Smith, Ian (Douglas) (born 1919) Rhodesian statesman, Prime Minister 1964–79

Smuts, Jan Christiaan (1870–1950) South African statesman and soldier, Prime Minister 1919–24 and 1939–48

Sobieski, John See JOHN III

Soliman See SULEIMAN I

Solomon, king of ancient Israel c. 970–c. 930 BC

Solon (c. 630–c. 560 BC) Athenian statesman and lawgiver

Solyman See SULEIMAN I

Somoza, Anastasio (full surname Somoza García) (1896–1956) Nicaraguan soldier and statesman, President 1937–47 and 1951–6

Spartacus (died c. 71 BC) Thracian slave and gladiator

Speke, John Hanning (1827–64) English explorer

Stalin, Joseph (born Iosif Vissarionovich Dzhugashvili) (1879–1953) Soviet statesman

Stanhope, Lady Hester Lucy (1776–1839) English traveller

Stanley, Sir Henry Morton (born John Rowlands) (1841–1904) Welsh explorer

Stephen (c. 1097–1154) grandson of William the Conqueror, king of England 1135–54

Stopes, Marie (Charlotte Carmichael)

HISTORICAL, POLITICAL, AND MILITARY FIGURES (cont.)

(1880–1958) Scottish birth-control campaigner

Stuart, Charles Edward (known as 'the Young Pretender' or 'Bonnie Prince Charlie') (1720–88) pretender to the British throne, son of James Stuart

Stuart, James (Francis Edward) (known as 'the Old Pretender') (1688–1766) pretender to the British throne, son of James II (James VII of Scotland)

Stuart, John McDouall (1815–66) Scottish explorer

Stuart, Mary See MARY, QUEEN OF SCOTS

Sturt, Charles (1795–1869) English explorer

Sucre, Antonio José de (1795–1830) Venezuelan revolutionary and statesman, President of Bolivia 1826–8

Suharto (born 1921) Indonesian statesman and general, President 1967–98.

Sukarno, Achmad (1901–70) Indonesian statesman, President 1945–67

Suleiman I (also Soliman or Solyman) (c. 1494–1566) sultan of the Ottoman Empire 1520–66

Sulla (full name Lucius Cornelius Sulla Felix) (138–78 BC) Roman general and politician

Sun King, nickname of Louis XIV of France

Sun Yat-sen (also Sun Yixian) (1866–1925) Chinese Kuomintang statesman, provisional President of the Republic of China 1911–12 and President of the Southern Chinese Republic 1923–5

Suzman, Helen (born 1917) South African politician, of Lithuanian Jewish descent

Sven See SWEYN I

Sweyn I (also Sven; known as Sweyn Forkbeard) (died 1014) king of Denmark c. 985–1014, ruler of England 1013–4

Taft, William Howard (1857–1930) American Republican statesman, 27th President of the US 1909–13

Talleyrand, Charles Maurice de (full surname Talleyrand-Périgord) (1754–1838) French statesman

Tambo, Oliver (1917–93) South African politician

Tamerlane (also Tamburlaine) (born Timur Lenk, 'lame Timur') (1336–1405) Mongol ruler of Samarkand 1369–1405

Tarquinius Priscus (anglicized name Tarquin) semi-legendary Etruscan king, reigned c. 616–c. 578 BC

Tarquinius Superbus (anglicized name Tarquin) semi-legendary Etruscan king, reigned c. 534–c. 510 BC

Tasman, Abel (Janszoon) (1603–c. 1659) Dutch navigator

Taylor, Zachary (1784–1850) American Whig statesman, 12th President of the US 1849–50

Teng Hsiao-p'ing See DENG XIAOPING

Thatcher, Margaret (Hilda), Baroness Thatcher of Kesteven (born 1925) British Conservative stateswoman, Prime Minister 1979–90

Themistocles (c. 528–462 BC) Athenian statesman

Theodora (c. 500–48) Byzantine empress, wife of Justinian

Theodoric (known as Theodoric the Great) (c. 454–526) king of the Ostrogoths 471–526

Theodosius I (known as Theodosius the Great; full name Flavius Theodosius) (c. 346–95) Roman emperor 379–95

Thesiger, Wilfred (Patrick) (born 1910) English explorer

Thomson, Roy Herbert, 1st Baron Thomson of Fleet (1894–1976) Canadian-born British newspaper proprietor and media entrepreneur

Tiberius (full name Tiberius Julius Caesar Augustus) (42 BC–AD 37) Roman emperor AD 14–37

Tichborne claimant See ORTON

Tiglath-pileser I to **III**, kings of Assyria

Timur See TAMERLANE

Tinbergen, Jan (1903–94) Dutch economist

Tito (born Josip Broz) (1892–1980) Yugoslav Marshal and statesman, Prime Minister 1945–53 and President 1953–80

Titus (full name Titus Vespasianus Augustus; born Titus Flavius Vespasianus) (AD 39–81) Roman emperor 79–81, son of Vespasian

Tojo, Hideki (1884–1948) Japanese military leader and statesman, Prime Minister 1941–4

Tone, (Theobald) Wolfe (1763–98) Irish nationalist

Torquemada, Tomás de (c. 1420–98) Spanish cleric and Grand Inquisitor

Toussaint L'Ouverture, Pierre Dominique (c. 1743–1803) Haitian revolutionary leader

Toynbee, Arnold (1852–83) English economist and social reformer

Trajan (Latin name Marcus Ulpius Traianus) (AD c. 53–117) Roman emperor 98–117

Trenchard, Hugh Montague, 1st Viscount of Wolfeton (1873–1956) British Marshal of the RAF

Trimble, (William) David (born 1944) Ulster Unionist politician, First Minister of Northern Ireland since 1998

Trotsky, Leon (born Lev Davidovich Bronstein) (1879–1940) Russian revolutionary

Trudeau, Pierre (Elliott) (1919–2000) Canadian Liberal statesman, Prime Minister of Canada 1968–79 and 1980–4

Trujillo, Rafael (born Rafael Leónidas Trujillo Molina; known as 'Generalissimo') (1891–1961) Dominican statesman, President

HISTORICAL, POLITICAL, AND MILITARY FIGURES (cont.)

of the Dominican Republic 1930–8 and
1942–52
Truman, Harry S. (1884–1972) American
Democratic statesman, 33rd President of the
US 1945–53
Tudjman, Franjo (1922–99) Croatian soldier
and statesman, President of independent
Croatia 1992–99
Tudor, Henry See HENRY VII of England
Tudor, Mary See MARY I of England
Turpin, Dick (1706–39) English highwayman
Tutankhamen (also Tutankhamun) (died c.
1352 BC) Egyptian pharaoh of the 18th
dynasty, reigned c. 1361–c. 1352 BC
Tuthmosis III (died c. 1450 BC) Egyptian
pharaoh of the 18th dynasty c. 1504–c. 1450
Tutu, Desmond (Mpilo) (born 1931) South
African clergyman
Tyler, John (1790–1862) American Whig
statesman, 10th President of the US 1841–5
Tyler, Wat (died 1381) English leader of the
Peasants' Revolt of 1381
Ulyanov, Vladimir Ilich See LENIN
Vajpayee, Atal Bihar (born 1926) Indian
statesman, President since 1998
Valera, Eamon de See DE VALERA
Valerian (Latin name Publius Licinius
Valerianus) (died 260) Roman emperor
253–60
Van Buren, Martin (1782–1862) American
Democratic statesman, 8th President of the
US 1837–41
Vancouver, George (1757–98) English
navigator
Vanderbilt, Cornelius (1794–1877) American
businessman and philanthropist
Vargas, Getúlio Dornelles (1883–1954)
Brazilian statesman, President 1930–45 and
1951–4
Velázquez de Cuéllar, Diego (c. 1465–1524)
Spanish conquistador
Verwoerd, Hendrik (Frensch) (1901–66) South
African statesman, Prime Minister 1958–66
Vespasian (Latin name Titus Flavius
Vespasianus) (AD 9–79) Roman emperor
69–79
Vespucci, Amerigo (1451–1512) Italian
merchant and explorer
Victor Emmanuel II (1820–78) ruler of the
kingdom of Sardinia 1849–61 and king of
Italy 1861–78
Victor Emmanuel III (1869–1947) king of Italy
1900–46
Victoria (1819–1901) queen of Great Britain
and Ireland 1837–1901 and empress of India
1876–1901
Villa, Pancho (born Doroteo Arango)
(1878–1923) Mexican revolutionary
Vitellius, Aulus (15–69) Roman emperor 69
Vivekananda, Swami (born Narendranath

Datta) (1863–1902) Indian spiritual leader
and reformer
Vladimir I (known as Vladimir the Great;
canonized as St Vladimir) (956–1015) grand
prince of Kiev 980–1015
Wade, George (1673–1748) English soldier
Waldheim, Kurt (born 1918) Austrian diplomat
and statesman; Secretary General of the
United Nations 1972–82 and President of
Austria 1986–92
Walesa, Lech (born 1943) Polish statesman,
President 1990–5
Wales, Prince of See CHARLES, PRINCE
Wallace, Sir William (c. 1270–1305) Scottish
national hero
Wallenberg, Raoul (1912–?) Swedish diplomat
Walpole, Sir Robert, 1st Earl of Orford
(1676–1745) British Whig statesman
Walsingham, Sir Francis (c. 1530–90) English
politician
Warbeck, Perkin (1474–99) Flemish claimant
to the English throne
Warren, Earl (1891–1974) American judge
Warwick, Earl of (title of Richard Neville;
known as 'the Kingmaker') (1428–71) English
statesman
Washington, Booker T(aliaferro) (1856–1915)
American educationist
Washington, George (1732–99) American
soldier and statesman, 1st President of the
US 1789–97
Webb, (Martha) Beatrice (née Potter)
(1858–1943) and **Sidney (James), Baron
Passfield** (1859–1947) English socialists,
economists, and historians
Weber, Max (1864–1920) German economist
and sociologist
Weizmann, Chaim (Azriel) (1874–1952) Israeli
statesman, President 1949–52
Wellington, 1st Duke of (title of Arthur
Wellesley; also known as 'the Iron Duke')
(1769–1852) British soldier and Tory
statesman, Prime Minister 1828–30 and 1834
Wenceslas (also Wenceslaus) (1361–1419)
king of Bohemia (as Wenceslas IV)
1378–1419
Whitlam, (Edward) Gough (born 1916)
Australian Labor statesman, Prime Minister
1972–5
Whittington, Sir Richard ('Dick') (died 1423)
English merchant and Lord Mayor of London
Wiesenthal, Simon (born 1908) Austrian
Jewish investigator of Nazi war crimes
Wilberforce, William (1759–1833) English
politician and social reformer
Wilhelm I (1797–1888) king of Prussia 1861–88
and emperor of Germany 1871–88
Wilhelm II (known as Kaiser Wilhelm)
(1859–1941) emperor of Germany
1888–1918, grandson of Queen Victoria

Wilhelmina (1880–1962) queen of the Netherlands 1890–1948

Willard, Emma (1787–1870) American educational reformer

William I (known as William the Conqueror) (*c.* 1027–87) the first Norman king of England, reigned 1066–87

William I (known as William the Lion) (1143–1214) grandson of David I, king of Scotland 1165–1214

William II (Rufus) (*c.* 1056–1100) king of England 1087–1100

William III and **IV,** kings of England

William, Prince, Arthur Philip Louis (born 1982) elder son of Prince Charles

William of Orange (1650–1702) joint king of Great Britain and Ireland 1689–1702

William Rufus See WILLIAM II

William the Conqueror See WILLIAM I

Wills, William John (1834–61) English explorer

Wilson, (James) Harold, Baron Wilson of Rievaulx (1916–95) British Labour statesman, Prime Minister 1964–70 and 1974–6

Wilson, (Thomas) Woodrow (1856–1924) American Democratic statesman, 28th President of the US 1913–21

Windsor, Duke of, title conferred on Edward VIII on his abdication in 1936

Wolfe, James (1727–59) British general

Wolsey, Thomas (known as Cardinal Wolsey) (*c.* 1474–1530) English prelate and statesman

Xerxes I (*c.* 519–465 BC) son of Darius I, king of Persia 486–465

Ximenes de Cisneros See JIMÉNEZ DE CISNEROS

Yamamoto, Isoroku (1884–1943) Japanese admiral

Yeltsin, Boris (Nikolaevich) (born 1931) Russian statesman, President of the Russian Federation 1991–9

Young Pretender, the See STUART

Zapata, Emiliano (1879–1919) Mexican revolutionary

Zenobia (3rd century AD) queen of Palmyra *c.* 267–272

Zhou Enlai (also Chou En-lai) (1898–1976) Chinese Communist statesman, Prime Minister of China 1949–76

Zhukov, Georgi (Konstantinovich) (1896–1974) Soviet military leader, born in Russia

Zia ul-Haq, Muhammad (1924–88) Pakistani general and statesman, President 1978–88

Zog I (full name Ahmed Bey Zogu) (1895–1961) Albanian statesman and king 1928–3999

RELIGION AND MYTHOLOGY

POPES FROM 1492
(with dates in office)

Alexander VI	1492–1503	Clement VIII	1592–1605	Clement XIII	1758–69
Pius III	1503	Leo XI	1605	Clement XIV	1769–74
Julius II	1503–13	Paul V	1605–21	Pius VI	1775–99
Leo X	1513–21	Gregory XV	1621–3	Pius VII	1800–23
Adrian VI	1522–3	Urban VIII	1623–44	Leo XII	1823–9
Clement VII	1523–34	Innocent X	1644–55	Pius VIII	1829–30
Paul III	1534–49	Alexander VII	1655–67	Gregory XVI	1831–46
Julius III	1550–5	Clement IX	1667–9	Pius IX	1846–78
Marcellus II	1555	Clement X	1670–6	Leo XIII	1878–1903
Paul IV	1555–9	Innocent XI	1676–89	Pius X	1903–14
Pius IV	1559–65	Alexander VIII	1689–91	Benedict XV	1914–22
Pius V	1566–72	Innocent XII	1691–1700	Pius XI	1922–39
Gregory XIII	1572–85	Clement XI	1700–21	Pius XII	1939–58
Sixtus V	1585–90	Innocent XIII	1721–4	John XXIII	1958–63
Urban VII	1590	Benedict XIII	1724–30	Paul VI	1963–78
Gregory XIV	1590–1	Clement XII	1730–40	John Paul I	1978
Innocent IX	1591	Benedict XIV	1740–58	John Paul II	from 1978

ARCHBISHOPS OF CANTERBURY
(with dates in office)

Augustine	597–604	Lyfing	1013–20
Laurentius	604–19	Æthelnoth	1020–38
Mellitus	619–24	Eadsige	1038–50
Justus	624–7	Robert of Jumièges	1051–2
Honorius	627–53	Stigand	1052–70
Deusdedit	655–64	Lanfranc	1070–89
Theodorus	668–90	Anselm	1093–1109
Beorhtweald	693–731	Ralph d'Escures	1114–22
Tatwine	731–4	William of Corbeil	1123–36
Nothelm	735–9	Theobald of Bec	1138–61
Cuthbeorht	740–60	Thomas à Becket	1162–70
Breguwine	761–4	Richard of Dover	1174–84
Jaenbeorht	765–92	Baldwin	1184–90
Æthelheard	793–805	Hubert Walter	1193–1205
Wulfred	805–32	Stephen Langton	1206–28
Feologild	832	Richard Grant (Wethershed)	1229–31
Ceolnoth	833–70	Edmund Rich	1233–40
Æthelred	870–89	Boniface of Savoy	1241–70
Plegmund	890–914	Robert Kilwardby	1272–8
Æthelhelm	914–23	John Pecham	1279–92
Wulfhelm	923–42	Robert Winchelsey	1293–1313
Oda	942–58	Walter Reynolds	1313–27
Ælfsige	959	Simon Mepham	1327–33
Beorhthelm	959	John Stratford	1333–48
Dunstan	960–88	John Offord	1348–9
Æthelgar	988–90	Simon Islip	1349–66
Sigeric Serio	990–4	Simon Langham	1366–8
Ælfric	995–1005	William Whittlesey	1368–74
Ælfheah	1005–12	Simon Sudbury	1375–81

ARCHBISHOPS OF CANTERBURY (cont.)
(with dates in office)

William Courtenay	1381–96	William Wake	1715–37
Thomas Arundel	1396–7	John Potter	1737–47
Roger Walden	1397–9	Thomas Herring	1747–57
Thomas Arundel (restored)	1399–1414	Matthew Hutton	1757–8
Henry Chichele	1414–43	Thomas Secker	1758–68
John Stafford	1443–52	Frederick Cornwallis	1768–83
John Kempe	1452–4	John Moore	1783–1805
Thomas Bourgchier	1454–86	Charles Sutton	1805–28
John Morton	1486–1500	William Howley	1828–48
Henry Deane	1501–3	John Sumner	1848–62
William Warham	1504–32	Charles Longley	1862–8
Thomas Cranmer	1532–55	Archibald Tait	1868–82
Reginald Pole	1555–8	Edward Benson	1883–96
Matthew Parker	1559–75	Frederick Temple	1896–1902
Edmund Grindal	1575–83	Randall Davidson	1903–28
John Whitgift	1583–1604	Cosmo Lang	1928–42
Richard Bancroft	1604–10	William Temple	1942–4
George Abbot	1611–33	Geoffrey Fisher	1945–61
William Laud	1633–45	Arthur Ramsey	1961–74
William Juxon	1660–3	Frederick Coggan	1974–80
Gilbert Sheldon	1663–77	Robert Runcie	1980–91
William Sancroft	1677–90	George Carey	from 1991
John Tillotson	1691–4		
Thomas Tenison	1694–1715		

SAINTS
(with feast dates)

Agnes of Bohemia	Mar. 2	Bridget of Sweden	Feb. 1
Agnes of Rome	Jan. 21	Bruno	Oct. 6
Aidan	Aug. 31	Campion	Dec. 1
Alban	June 22	Catherine (of Alexandria)	Nov. 25
Albertus Magnus	Nov. 15	Catherine of Siena	Apr. 29
Alexander Nevsky	Aug. 30, Nov. 23	Cecilia	Nov. 22
Aloysius	June 21	John Chrysostom	Jan. 27
Ambrose	Dec. 7	Clare of Assisi	Aug. 11
Andrew	Nov. 30	Clement of Alexandria	Dec. 5
Anne	July 26	Clement (of Rome)	Nov. 23
Anselm	Apr. 21	Columba	June 9
Anthony	Jan. 17	Crispin	Oct. 25
Anthony of Padua	June 13	Cuthbert	Mar. 20
Athanasius	May 2	Cyprian	Sept. 16, 26
Augustine (of Canterbury)	May 26	Cyril	Feb. 14
Augustine (of Hippo)	Aug. 28	Cyril of Alexandria	Feb. 9
Barnabas	June 11	David	Mar. 1
Bartholomew	Aug. 24	Denis	Oct. 9
Basil	Jan. 2, June 14	Dominic	Aug. 8
Bede	May 27	Dunstan	May 19
Benedict	July 11	Edmund	Nov. 16
Bernadette of Lourdes	Feb. 18	Edmund the Martyr	Nov. 20
Bernard	Aug. 20	Edward the Confessor	Oct. 13
Birgitta	Oct. 8	Edward the Martyr	Mar. 18
Bonaventura	July 15	Elizabeth	Nov. 5
Boniface	June 5	John Fisher	June 22
Bridget of Ireland	July 23	Francis of Assisi	Oct. 4

SAINTS (cont.)
(with feast dates)

Francis of Sales	Jan. 24	Mary Magdalene	July 22
Francis Xavier	Dec. 3	Matthew	Sept. 21
Geneviève	Jan. 3	Matthias	May 14 W. Ch., Aug.
George	Apr. 23		9 E. Ch.
Giles	Sept. 1	Michael	Sept. 29
Gregory of Nazianzus	Jan. 25 and 30 E.	Monica	Aug. 27
	Ch., Jan. 2 W. Ch.	Nicholas	Dec. 6
Gregory of Nyssa	Mar. 9	Olaf II	July 29
Gregory of Tours	Nov. 17	Oliver Plunket	July 11
Gregory the Great	Mar. 12	Oswald of York	Feb. 28
Helena	May 21 E. Ch., Aug.	Patrick	Mar. 17
	18 W. Ch.	Paul	June 29
Hilary	Jan. 13, Jan. 14 R.C.	Peter	June 29
	Ch.	Philip	June 6
Ignatius Loyola	July 31	Polycarp	Feb. 23
Irenaeus	Aug. 23 E. Ch., June	Sebastian	Jan. 20
	28 W. Ch.	Sergius	Sept. 25
Isidore of Seville	Apr. 4	Simeon Stylites	Jan. 5
James the Great	July 25	Simon	Oct. 28
James the Just	May 1	Stanislaus	Apr. 11
James the Less	Oct. 9 E. Ch., May 1	Stephen	Dec. 26 W. Ch., Dec.
	W. Ch.		27 E. Ch.
Jerome	Sept. 30	Stephen of Hungary	Sept. 2
Joan of Arc	May 30	Swithin	July 15
John of Damascus	Dec. 4	Teresa of Ávila	Oct. 15
John of the Cross	Dec. 14	Thérèse	Oct. 3
John the Baptist	June 24	Thomas	Dec. 21
John the Evangelist	Dec. 27	Thomas à Becket	Dec. 29
Joseph	Mar. 19	Thomas Aquinas	Jan. 28
Joseph of Arimathea	Mar. 17	Thomas More	June 22
Jude	Oct. 28	Timothy	Jan. 26, Jan. 22
Justin	June 1	Titus	Aug. 23 E. Ch., Feb.
Ladislaus I	June 27		6 W. Ch.
Lawrence	Aug. 10	Ursula	Oct. 21
Leo I	Feb. 18 E. Ch., Apr.	Valentine	Feb. 14
	11 W. Ch.	Vincent de Paul	July 19
Louis	Aug. 25	Vitus	June 15
Lucy	Dec. 13	Vladimir I	July 15
Luke	Oct. 18	Wenceslas	Sept. 28
Margaret	Nov. 16	Wilfrid	Oct. 12
Mark	Apr. 25		
Martha	July 29	E. Ch. = *Eastern Church*	
Martin	Nov. 11	R.C. Ch. = *Roman Catholic Church*	
Mary	Jan. 1 R.C. Ch., Mar.	W. Ch. = *Western Church*	
	25, Aug. 15, Sept. 8		

BIBLICAL CHARACTERS

Aaron (OT)	Barabas (NT)	Caiaphas (NT)	Enoch (OT)
Abel (OT)	Barabbas (NT)	Cain (OT)	Ephraim (OT)
Abraham (OT)	*Bartholomew *or*	Daniel (OT)	Esau (OT)
Absalom (OT)	Nathaniel (NT)	David (OT)	Esther (OT)
Adam (OT)	Bathsheba (OT)	Delilah (OT)	Eve (OT)
*Andrew (NT)	Belshazzar (OT)	Elijah (OT)	Ezekiel (OT)
Baal (OT)	Benjamin (OT)	Elisha (OT)	Gabriel (NT)

BIBLICAL CHARACTERS (cont.)

Gideon (OT)
Goliath (OT)
Herod Agrippa II (NT)
Herod Agrippa (NT)
Herod Antipas (NT)
Herod the Great (NT)
Hezekiah (OT)
Isaac (OT)
Isaiah (OT)
Ishmael (OT)
Israel (OT)
Jacob (OT)
James (NT)
*James the Greater (NT)
*James the Less (NT)
Jeremiah (OT)
Jesus (NT)
Jezebel (OT)

Job (OT)
*John (NT)
John the Baptist (NT)
Jonah (OT)
Jonathan (OT)
Joseph (NT)
Joseph of Arimathea (NT)
Joseph (OT)
Joshua (OT)
Judah (OT)
*Jude or Thaddeus (NT)
*Judas Iscariot (NT)
Lazarus (NT)
Lot (OT)
Luke (NT)
Mark (NT)
Martha (NT)

Mary Magdalene (NT)
Mary (NT)
Mary the Holy Mother (NT)
*Matthew or Levi (NT)
Matthias (NT)
Methuselah (OT)
Michael (NT)
Miriam (OT)
Moses (OT)
Nathan (OT)
Nebuchadnezzar (OT)
Nicodemus (NT)
Noah (OT)
Paul (Saul) (NT)
*(Simon) Peter (NT)
*Philip (NT)
Pontius Pilate (NT)

Rebekah (OT)
Ruth (OT)
Salome (NT)
Samson (OT)
Samuel (OT)
Sarah (OT)
Saul (PAUL) (NT)
Saul (OT)
Simon (NT)
Simon of Cyrene (NT)
*Simon the Canaanite (NT)
Solomon (OT)
Stephen (NT)
*Thomas (NT)
Timothy (NT)
Titus (NT)
* Indicates the twelve apostles.

BOOKS OF THE BIBLE

Old Testament
Genesis
Exodus
Leviticus
Numbers
Deuteronomy
Joshua
Judges
Ruth
Samuel I
Samuel II
Kings I
Kings II
Chronicles I
Chronicles II
Ezra
Nehemiah
Esther
Job
Psalms
Proverbs
Ecclesiastes

Song of Solomon
Isaiah
Jeremiah
Lamentations
Ezekiel
Daniel
Hosea
Joel
Amos
Obadiah
Jonah
Micah
Nahum
Habakkuk
Zephaniah
Haggai
Zechariah
Malachi

New Testament
Matthew
Mark
Luke

John
Acts
Romans
Corinthians I
Corinthians II
Galatians
Ephesians
Philippians
Colossians
Thessalonians I
Thessalonians II
Timothy I
Timothy II
Titus
Philemon
Hebrews
James
Peter I
Peter II
John I
John II
John III

Jude
Revelation

Apocrypha
Esdras I
Esdras II
Tobit
Judith
Additions to the Book of Esther
Wisdom of Solomon
Ecclesiasticus
Baruch
Letter of Jeremiah
Song of the Three Holy Children
Susanna
Bel and the Dragon
Prayer of Manasses
Maccabees I
Maccabees II

MONASTIC ORDERS

Antonians
Augustinian Hermits
Austin Friars
Barnabites
Benedictines
Bernardines
Black Friars
Black Monks
Blue Nuns
Bonhommes
Brethren of the
    Common Life
Brigittines
Brothers Hospitallers
Camaldolites
Canons Regular
Capuchins

Carmelites
Carthusians
Christian Brothers
Cistercians
Conceptionists
Conventuals
Culdees
Doctrinarians
Dominicans
Franciscans
Friars Minor
Friars Preachers
Gilbertines
Grey Friars
Grey Nuns
Hieronymites
Hospitallers

Ignorantines
Jacobins
Jesuits
Knights Templar
Marianists
Marists
Minims
Minorites
Norbertines
Oratorians
Passionists
Paulines
Piarists
Poor Clares
Poor Soldiers of the
    Temple
Praemonstratensians

Salesians
Servites
Sisters of Charity
Sisters of the Love of
    God
Sisters of the Sacred
    Cross
Somascans
Studites
Sylvestrines
Theatines
Trappists
Trinitarians
Ursulines
Visitandines
White Friars

RELIGIONS AND MAJOR DENOMINATIONS

Adventism
Amish
Anabaptism
ancestor-worship
Anglicanism
animism
Bahaism
Baptism
Brahmanism
Buddhism
cabbalism
cargo cult
Christianity
Christian Science
Confucianism
Congregationalism
Conservative
    Judaism
Druidism
Dutch Reformed
    Church
Eleusinianism

Evangelism
Gideons
Hare Krishna
Hasidism
Hinduism
Humanism
Islam
Ismaili Islam
Jainism
Jehovah's Witnesses
Judaism
Lamaism
Lutheranism
Mahayana
    Buddhism
Mazdaism
Messianic Judaism
Methodism
Mithraism
Moravianism
Norse
Orphism

Orthodox Judaism
Paganism
Parseeism
Pharisaism
Plymouth Brethren
Protestantism
Presbyterianism
Puritanism
Quakers
Rabbinism
Rastafarianism
Reconstructionism
Reform Judaism
Roman Catholicism
Sabaism
Saktism
Salvationism
Scientology ™
Seventh Day
    Adventism
Shaktism
Shamanism

Shia Islam
Shintoism
Sikhism
Sivaism
Spiritualism
Sufism
Sunni Islam
Tantrism
Taoism
Theravada
    Buddhism
Totemism
Unitarianism
Vedantism
Vishnuism
Voodoo
Wahabism
Yogism
Zande
Zen Buddhism
Zionism
Zoroastrianism

RELIGIOUS FESTIVALS
(with religion and date)

Epiphany	Christian	Jan.	Passover	Jewish	Mar., Apr.
Imbolc	Pagan	Jan.	Holi Mohalla	Sikh	Mar., Apr.
New Year	Chinese*	Jan., Feb.	Rama Naumi	Hindu	Mar., Apr.
Shrove Tuesday	Christian	Feb., Mar.	Ching Ming	Chinese*	Mar., Apr.
Ash Wednesday	Christian	Feb., Mar.	Baisakhi	Sikh	Apr.
Purim	Jewish	Feb., Mar.	Beltane	Pagan	Apr.
Mahashivaratri	Hindu	Feb., Mar.	Lailat ul-Isra wal		
Holi	Hindu	Feb., Mar.	Mi'raj	Islamic	Apr., May
Easter	Christian	Mar., Apr.	Lailat ul-Bara'h	Islamic	Apr., May

RELIGIOUS FESTIVALS (cont.)
(with religion and date)

Vesak	Buddhist	Apr., May	Succoth	Jewish	Sept, Oct.
Shavuoth	Jewish	May, June	Dusshera	Hindu	Oct.
Lailat ul-Qadr	Islamic	May, June	Samhain	Pagan	Oct.
Eid ul-Fitr	Islamic	May, June	Diwali	Hindu, Sikh	Oct., Nov.
Martyrdom of			Guru Nanak's		
Guru Arjan	Sikh	May, June	Birthday	Sikh	Nov.
Dragon Boat	Chinese*	June	Bodhi Day	Buddhist	Nov.
Festival			Christmas	Christian	Dec.
Summer Solstice	Pagan	June	Hanukkah	Jewish	Dec.
Dhammacakka	Buddhist	July	Winter Festival	Chinese*	Dec.
Eid ul-Adha	Islamic	July	Winter Solstice	Pagan	Dec.
Raksha Bandhan	Hindu	Aug.	Birthday of Guru		
Lammas	Pagan	Aug.	Gobind Singh	Sikh	Dec., Jan.
Janmashtami	Hindu	Aug., Sept.	Martyrdom of Guru		
Moon Festival	Chinese*	Sept.	Tegh Bahadur	Sikh	Dec., Jan.
Rosh Hashana	Jewish	Sept., Oct.			
Yom Kippur	Jewish	Sept., Oct.	Chinese* = *Chinese traditional religions.*		

GREEK GODS AND GODDESSES
(with Roman equivalent)

Aphrodite	Venus	Eros	Cupid	Iris	
Apollo		Eumenides		Nemesis	
Ares	Mars	or Furies		Nike	Victoria
Artemis	Diana	Gaia	Ge	Ouranos	Uranus
Asclepius	Aesculapius	Hades or Dis	Pluto	Pan	Faunus
Athene	Minerva	Hebe	Juventas	Persephone	Proserpine
Charites or	Aglaia,	Hecate		Poseidon	Neptune
Graces	Euphrosyne,	Helios	Sol	Rhea	Cybele
	Thalia	Hephaestus	Vulcan	Selene	Luna
Cronos	Saturn	Hera	Juno	Thanatos	Mors
Demeter	Ceres	Hermes	Mercury	Tuche	Fortuna
Dionysus	Bacchus	Hestia	Vesta	Zeus	Jupiter
Eos	Aurora	Hypnos	Somnus		

ROMAN GODS AND GODDESSES
(with Greek equivalent)

Aesculapius	Asclepius	Hecate	Hecate	Pluto	Hades
Apollo		Juno	Hera	Proserpine	Persephone
Aurora	Eos	Jupiter	Zeus	Saturn	Cronos
Bacchus	Dionysus	Juventas	Hebe	Sol	Helios
Ceres	Demeter	Lares and		Somnus	Hypnos
Cupid	Eros	Penates		Uranus	Ouranos
Cybele	Rhea	Luna	Selene	Venus	Aphrodite
Diana	Artemis	Mars	Ares	Vesta	Hestia
Faunus	Pan	Mercury	Hermes	Victoria	Nike
Fortuna	Tuche	Minerva	Athene	Vulcan	Hephaestus
Ge	Gaia	Mors	Thanatos		
Graces	Charites	Neptune	Poseidon		

THE NINE MUSES

Calliope (eloquence, epic poetry)
Clio (history)
Erato (lyric and love poetry)
Euterpe (music)
Melpomene (tragedy)
Polyhymnia (singing, rhetoric)
Terpsichore (dancing)
Thalia (comic and pastoral poetry)
Urania (astronomy)

RIVERS OF HADES

Acheron
Lethe

Phlegethon
Styx

THE LABOURS OF HERCULES

The Augean stables
The capture of Cerberus
The cattle of Geryon
The Ceryneian hind
The Cretan bull

The girdle of Hippolyte
The golden apples of the
  Hesperides
The Lernaean hydra
The mares of Diomedes

The Nemean lion
The Stymphalian birds
The wild boar of Erymanthus

CHARACTERS FROM GREEK AND ROMAN MYTHOLOGY

Achilles
Actaeon
Adonis
Aegisthus
Aeneas
Aeolus
Agamemnon
Ajax
Alcestis
Amazon
Andromache
Andromeda
Antigone
Arachne
Ariadne
Atalanta
Atlas
Atreus
Bellerophon
Boreas
Calypso
Cassiopeia
Castor
Centaurs
Cepheus
Cerberus
Charon
Charybdis

Chimera
Chiron
Chloe
Circe
Clytemnestra
Creon
Cyclops
Daedalus
Daphnis
Dido
Dryads
Electra
Endymion
Eteocles
Europa
Eurydice
Ganymede
Gorgons (Euryale,
  Medusa, Stheno)
Hamadryads
Harpies
Hector
Hecuba
Helen of Troy
Heracles (Hercules)
Hermaphroditus
Horae or Hours
Hydra

Icarus
Io
Iphicles
Iphigenia
Jason
Jocasta
Lamia
Lapiths
Maenads
Medea
Medusa
Menelaus
Midas
Minotaur
Naiads
Narcissus
Nestor
Niobe
Nymphs
Odysseus
Oedipus
Olympus
Oreads
Orestes
Orion
Orpheus
Pandora
Pasiphae

Patroclus
Pegasus
Penelope
Perseus
Phaethon
Philoctetes
Pollux
Polynices
Polyphemus
Priam
Prometheus
Remus
Rhea Silvia
Romulus
Satyrs
Scylla
Sibyls
Sirens
Sisyphus
Tantalus
Telemachus
Theseus
Thetis
Thyestes
Ulysses

EGYPTIAN GODS AND GODDESSES

Ament	Harmakhis	Min	Sebek
Ammon	Haroeris	Mont	Seker
Amon-Ra	Harsaphes	Mut	Sekhmet
Anhur	Harsiesis	Nefertum	Selket
Anquet	Hathor	Neheh	Sesheta
Anubis	Heket	Nekhebit	Seth *or* Set
Aten	Horus	Nephthys	Shai
Atum	Imhotep	Nun	Shu
Bast	Isis	Nut	Taueret
Behdety	Khensu	Osiris	Tefnut
Bes	Khepera	Ptah	Thoth
Buto	Khnum	Ra	Upuaut
Geb	Maat	Renenet	
Hapi	Mertseger	Renpet	
Harakhtes	Meskhent	Sati	

HINDU GODS AND GODDESSES

Aditi	Kama	Radha	Tvashtar
Agni	Kartikeya	Rama	Uma
Bhairavi	Krishna	Ravana	Ushas
Brahma	Kurma	Rudra	Vamana
Devi	Lakshmi	Sakti *or* Shakti	Varaha
Durga	Mara	Sarasvati	Varuna
Ganesha	Matsya	Savitar	Vata
Hanuman	Mitra	Shiva *or* Siva	Vishnu
Indra	Narasinha	Sita	Yama
Jagannatha *or*	Parvati	Skanda	
Juggernaut	Prajapati	Soma	
Kali	Puchan	Surya	

CELTIC GODS, GODDESSES, AND HEROES

Boann	Dana *or* Danu *or* Anu	Lêr	Ogma
Boanna, the	Dian Cecht	Ludd *or* Nudd	Ossian
Bran	Epona	Lugh	Pwyll
Brigit	Finn MacCool	Macha	Rhiannon
Cernunnos	Fomors	Manannan	Tuatha Dé Dannan
Dagda, the	Gobniu	Nuada	

NORSE MYTHOLOGY

Aesir – tribe of gods	Embla – first woman	Kvasir – god whose death
Alfheim – region of Asgard	Fenrir – wolf	created poetry
Asgard – home of the gods	Freyja – goddess of love	Loki – trickster god
Ask – first man	Freyr – protector of living	Midgard *or* Mannaheim –
Audumla – primeval cow	things	world of men
Aurgelmir – primeval giant	Frigga – wife of Odin	Mjollnir – Thor's hammer
Balder – god of the sun	Gerd – wife of Freyr	Muspelheim – realm of fire
Bifrost – rainbow bridge	Gungnir – Odin's spear	Niflheim – home of the dead
Brynhild – leader of the	Heimdal – guardian of Bifrost	Njord *or* Njorth – leader of
Valkyries	Hel – goddess of death	the Vanir
Buri – grandfather of Odin	Hoder – blind god	Norns (Urth, Verthandi,
Draupnir – Odin's magic ring	Jörmungand – serpent	Skuld) – Fates

NORSE MYTHOLOGY (cont.)

Odin *or* Wotan – chief god
Ragnarok – final battle
  between gods and giants
Sif – wife of Thor
Skidbladnir – magic ship
Sleipnir – Odin's eight-
  legged horse

Surt – lord of Muspelheim
Thor – god of thunder
Tyr – god of war
Valhalla – hall of the gods in
  Asgard
Valkyries – nine warrior
  goddesses

Vanir – gods of fertility
Vidar – son of Odin
Wayland Smith – lord of the
  elves
Yggdrasil – the Cosmic Tree
Ymir – giant from whose
  body the world was formed

ARTHURIAN LEGEND

Arthur – legendary British
  king
Avalon – paradise
Camelot – capital of Arthur's
  kingdom
Elaine – mother of Galahad
Excalibur – Arthur's sword
Fisher King – custodian of
  the Holy Grail
Galahad – knight

Gawain – knight
Guinevere – Arthur's wife
Holy Grail – used by Christ at
  the Last Supper
Iseult – lover of Tristram
Kay – Arthur's foster brother
Lancelot *or* Launcelot –
  knight
Lot – father of Gawain
Merlin – magician

Modred *or* Mordred – son of
  Morgan Le Fay
Morgan Le Fay – magician;
  Arthur's sister
Nineve – Lady of the Lake
Percival *or* Perceval – knight
Tristram – knight
Uther Pendragon – Arthur's
  father

GEOGRAPHY AND TRANSPORT

COUNTRIES OF THE WORLD
(with capital cities)

Afghanistan	Kabul	Dominican Republic	Santo Domingo
Albania	Tirana	Ecuador	Quito
Algeria	Algiers	Egypt	Cairo
Andorra	Andorra la Vella	El Salvador	San Salvador
Angola	Luanda	Equatorial Guinea	Malabo
Antigua and Barbuda	St John's	Eritrea	Asmara
Argentina	Buenos Aires	Estonia	Tallinn
Armenia	Yerevan	Ethiopia	Addis Ababa
Aruba	Oranjestad	Fiji	Suva
Australia	Canberra	Finland	Helsinki
Austria	Vienna	France	Paris
Azerbaijan	Baku	Gabon	Libreville
Bahamas, The	Nassau	Gambia, The	Banjul
Bahrain	Manama	Georgia	Tbilisi
Bangladesh	Dhaka	Germany	Berlin
Barbados	Bridgetown	Ghana	Accra
Belarus	Minsk	Greece	Athens
Belgium	Brussels	Grenada	St George's
Belize	Belmopan	Guatemala	Guatemala City
Benin	Porto Novo	Guinea	Conakry
Bhutan	Thimphu	Guinea-Bissau	Bissau
Bolivia	La Paz	Guyana	Georgetown
Bosnia-Herzegovina	Sarajevo	Haiti	Port-au-Prince
Botswana	Gaborone	Honduras	Tegucigalpa
Brazil	Brasilia	Hungary	Budapest
Brunei	Bandar Seri Begawan	Iceland	Reykjavik
		India	New Delhi
Bulgaria	Sofia	Indonesia	Djakarta
Burkina Faso	Ouagadougou	Iran	Tehran
Burundi	Bujumbura	Iraq	Baghdad
Cambodia	Phnom Penh	Ireland, Republic of	Dublin
Cameroon	Yaoundé	Israel	Jerusalem – de facto
Canada	Ottawa		
Cape Verde Islands	Praia	Italy	Rome
Central African Republic	Bangui	Ivory Coast	Yamoussoukro
Chad	N'Djamena	Jamaica	Kingston
Chile	Santiago	Japan	Tokyo
China	Beijing or Peking	Jordan	Amman
Colombia	Bogota	Kazakhstan	Astana
Comoros	Moroni	Kenya	Nairobi
Congo-Brazzaville	Brazzaville	Kiribati	Bairiki
Congo, Democratic Republic of – formerly Zaïre	Kinshasa	Korea, North	Pyongyang
		Korea, South	Seoul
		Kuwait	Kuwait City
Costa Rica	San José	Kyrgyzstan	Bishkek
Croatia	Zagreb	Laos	Vientiane
Cuba	Havana	Latvia	Riga
Cyprus	Nicosia	Lebanon	Beirut
Czech Republic	Prague	Lesotho	Maseru
Denmark	Copenhagen	Liberia	Monrovia
Djibouti	Djibouti	Libya	Tripoli
Dominica	Roseau	Liechtenstein	Vaduz

COUNTRIES OF THE WORLD (cont.)
(with capital cities)

Lithuania	Vilnius
Luxembourg	Luxembourg
Macedonia, Former	
Yugoslav Republic of	Skopje
Madagascar	Antananarivo
Malawi	Lilongwe
Malaysia	Putrajaya
Maldives	Male
Mali	Bamako
Malta	Valletta
Marshall Islands	Majuro
Mauritania	Nouakchott
Mauritius	Port Louis
Mexico	Mexico City
Micronesia	Kolonia
Moldova	Chişinău
Monaco	
Mongolia	Ulan Bator
Morocco	Rabat
Mozambique	Maputo
Myanmar – formerly	
Burma	Rangoon *or* Yangon
Namibia	Windhoek
Nauru	
Nepal	Kathmandu
Netherlands, The	Amsterdam
New Zealand	Wellington
Nicaragua	Managua
Niger	Niamey
Nigeria	Abuja
Norway	Oslo
Oman	Muscat
Pakistan	Islamabad
Palau	Koror
Panama	Panama City
Papua New Guinea	Port Moresby
Paraguay	Asunción
Peru	Lima
Philippines	Manila
Poland	Warsaw
Portugal	Lisbon
Qatar	Doha
Romania	Bucharest
Russia	Moscow
Rwanda	Kigali
St Kitts and Nevis	Basseterre
St Lucia	Castries
St Vincent and the Grenadines	Kingstown

Samoa – formerly Western Samoa	Apia
San Marino	San Marino
São Tomé and Principe	São Tomé
Saudi Arabia	Riyadh
Senegal	Dakar
Seychelles,The	Victoria
Sierra Leone	Freetown
Singapore	Singapore
Slovakia	Bratislava
Slovenia	Ljubljana
Solomon Islands	Honiara
Somalia	Mogadishu
South Africa	Pretoria
Spain	Madrid
Sri Lanka	Colombo
Sudan	Khartoum
Suriname	Paramaribo
Swaziland	Mbabane
Sweden	Stockholm
Switzerland	Berne
Syria	Damascus
Taiwan	Taipei
Tajikistan	Dushanbe
Tanzania	Dodoma
Thailand	Bangkok
Togo	Lomé
Tonga	Nuku'alofa
Trinidad and Tobago	Port of Spain
Tunisia	Tunis
Turkey	Ankara
Turkmenistan	Ashgabat
Tuvalu	Funafuti
Uganda	Kampala
Ukraine	Kiev
United Arab Emirates	Abu Dhabi
UK	London
USA	Washington, D.C.
Uruguay	Montevideo
Uzbekistan	Tashkent
Vanuatu	Vila
Vatican City	
Venezuela	Caracas
Vietnam	Hanoi
Yemen	Sana'a
Yugoslavia	Belgrade
Zambia	Lusaka
Zimbabwe	Harare

CAPITAL CITIES
(with countries)

Abu Dhabi	United Arab Emirates	Dodoma	Tanzania
Abuja	Nigeria	Doha	Qatar
Accra	Ghana	Dublin	Ireland, Republic of
Addis Ababa	Ethiopia	Dushanbe	Tajikistan
Algiers	Algeria	Freetown	Sierra Leone
Amman	Jordan	Funafuti	Tuvalu
Amsterdam	Netherlands, The	Gaborone	Botswana
Andorra la Vella	Andorra	Georgetown	Guyana
Ankara	Turkey	Guatemala City	Guatemala
Antananarivo	Madagascar	Hanoi	Vietnam
Apia	Samoa – formerly	Harare	Zimbabwe
	Western Samoa	Havana	Cuba
Ashgabat	Turkmenistan	Helsinki	Finland
Asmara	Eritrea	Honiara	Solomon Islands
Astana	Kazakhstan	Islamabad	Pakistan
Asunción	Paraguay	Jerusalem – *de*	
Athens	Greece	*facto*	Israel
Baghdad	Iraq	Kabul	Afghanistan
Bairiki	Kiribati	Kampala	Uganda
Baku	Azerbaijan	Kathmandu	Nepal
Bamako	Mali	Khartoum	Sudan
Bandar Seri Begawan	Brunei	Kiev	Ukraine
Bangkok	Thailand	Kigali	Rwanda
Bangui	Central African	Kingston	Jamaica
	Republic	Kingstown	St Vincent and the
Banjul	Gambia, The		Grenadines
Basseterre	St Kitts and Nevis	Kinshasa	Congo, Democratic
Beijing *or* Peking	China		Republic of –
Beirut	Lebanon		formerly Zaïre
Belgrade	Yugoslavia	Kolonia	Micronesia
Belmopan	Belize	Koror	Palau
Berlin	Germany	Kuwait City	Kuwait
Berne	Switzerland	La Paz	Bolivia
Bishkek	Kyrgyzstan	Libreville	Gabon
Bissau	Guinea-Bissau	Lilongwe	Malawi
Bogota	Colombia	Lima	Peru
Brasilia	Brazil	Lisbon	Portugal
Bratislava	Slovakia	Ljubljana	Slovenia
Brazzaville	Congo-Brazzaville	Lomé	Togo
Bridgetown	Barbados	London	UK
Brussels	Belgium	Luanda	Angola
Bucharest	Romania	Lusaka	Zambia
Budapest	Hungary	Luxembourg	Luxembourg
Buenos Aires	Argentina	Madrid	Spain
Bujumbura	Burundi	Majuro	Marshall Islands
Cairo	Egypt	Malabo	Equatorial Guinea
Canberra	Australia	Male	Maldives
Caracas	Venezuela	Managua	Nicaragua
Castries	St Lucia	Manama	Bahrain
Chişinău	Moldova	Manila	Philippines
Colombo	Sri Lanka	Maputo	Mozambique
Conakry	Guinea	Maseru	Lesotho
Copenhagen	Denmark	Mbabane	Swaziland
Dakar	Senegal	Mexico City	Mexico
Damascus	Syria	Minsk	Belarus
Dhaka	Bangladesh	Mogadishu	Somalia
Djakarta	Indonesia	Monrovia	Liberia
Djibouti	Djibouti	Montevideo	Uruguay

CAPITAL CITIES (cont.)
(with countries)

Moroni	Comoros	Santo Domingo	Dominican Republic
Moscow	Russia	São Tomé	São Tomé and
Muscat	Oman		Principe
Nairobi	Kenya	Sarajevo	Bosnia-Herzegovina
Nassau	Bahamas, The	Seoul	Korea, South
N'Djamena	Chad	Singapore	Singapore
New Delhi	India	Skopje	Macedonia, Former
Niamey	Niger		Yugoslav Republic
Nicosia	Cyprus		of
Nouakchott	Mauritania	Sofia	Bulgaria
Nuku'alofa	Tonga	St George's	Grenada
Oranjestad	Aruba	St John's	Antigua and Barbuda
Oslo	Norway	Stockholm	Sweden
Ottawa	Canada	Suva	Fiji
Ouagadougou	Burkina Faso	Taipei	Taiwan
Panama City	Panama	Tallinn	Estonia
Paramaribo	Suriname	Tashkent	Uzbekistan
Paris	France	Tbilisi	Georgia
Phnom Penh	Cambodia	Tegucigalpa	Honduras
Port-au-Prince	Haiti	Tehran	Iran
Port Louis	Mauritius	Thimphu	Bhutan
Port Moresby	Papua New Guinea	Tirana	Albania
Port of Spain	Trinidad and Tobago	Tokyo	Japan
Porto Novo	Benin	Tripoli	Libya
Prague	Czech Republic	Tunis	Tunisia
Praia	Cape Verde Islands	Ulan Bator	Mongolia
Pretoria	South Africa	Vaduz	Liechtenstein
Putrajaya	Malaysia	Valletta	Malta
Pyongyang	Korea, North	Victoria	Seychelles, The
Quito	Ecuador	Vienna	Austria
Rabat	Morocco	Vientiane	Laos
Rangoon *or* Yangon	Myanmar – formerly	Vila	Vanuatu
	Burma	Vilnius	Lithuania
Reykjavik	Iceland	Warsaw	Poland
Riga	Latvia	Washington, D.C.	USA
Riyadh	Saudi Arabia	Wellington	New Zealand
Rome	Italy	Windhoek	Namibia
Roseau	Dominica	Yamoussoukro	Ivory Coast
Sana'a	Yemen	Yaoundé	Cameroon
San José	Costa Rica	Yerevan	Armenia
San Marino	San Marino	Zagreb	Croatia
San Salvador	El Salvador		
Santiago	Chile		

CURRENCIES OF THE WORLD
(with countries)

afghani	Afghanistan
agora *pl.* -rot	Israel
at	Laos
austral *pl.* -ales	Argentina
baht	Thailand
baiza	Oman
balboa	Panama
ban *pl.* bani	Moldova, Romania
birr	Ethiopia
bolívar	Venezuela
boliviano	Bolivia
butut	The Gambia
cedi	Ghana
cent	Antigua and Barbuda, Australia, The Bahamas, Barbados, Belize, Canada, Cyprus, Dominica, Ecuador, Estonia, Ethiopia, Fiji, Grenada, Guyana, Jamaica, Kenya, Kiribati, Liberia, Malaysia, Malta, Marshall Islands, Mauritius, Micronesia, Namibia, Nauru, The Netherlands (until mid-2002), New Zealand, Palau, St Kitts and Nevis, St Lucia, St Vincent and the Grenadines, The Seychelles, Sierra Leone, Singapore, Solomon Islands, Somalia, South Africa, Sri Lanka, Suriname, Swaziland, Taiwan, Tanzania, Trinidad and Tobago, Tuvalu, Uganda, USA, Zimbabwe
cént	Peru
centas *pl.* -ai	Lithuania
centavo	Bolivia, Brazil, Cape Verde, Chile, Colombia, Cuba, Dominican Republic, El Salvador, Guatemala, Honduras, Mexico, Mozambique, Nicaragua, Philippines, Portugal (until mid-2002), São Tomé and Principe
centesimo *pl.* -mi	Italy (until mid-2002), San Marino, Vatican City
centésimo	Panama, Uruguay
centime	Algeria, Andorra, Belgium (until mid-2002), Benin,
centime (cont.)	Burkina Faso, Burundi, Cameroon, Central African Republic, Chad, Comoros, Congo, Democratic Republic of Congo-Brazzaville, Côte d'Ivoire, Djibouti, Equatorial Guinea, France, Gabon, Guinea, Guinea-Bissau, Haiti, Liechtenstein, Luxembourg, Madagascar, Mali, Monaco, Morocco, Niger, Rwanda, Senegal, Switzerland, Togo, Vanuatu
céntimo	Andorra, Costa Rica, Paraguay, Spain (until mid-2002), Venezuela
CFA franc	Benin, Burkina Faso, Central African Republic, Chad, Comoros, Congo-Brazzaville, Côte d'Ivoire, Equatorial Guinea, Gabon, Guinea-Bissau, Mali, Niger, Senegal, Togo
chetrum	Bhutan
chon	North Korea, South Korea
colón *pl.* colónes *or* colóns	Costa Rica, El Salvador
córdoba	Nicaragua
dalasi	The Gambia
Deutsche Mark *or* Deutschmark	Germany (until mid-2002)
dinar	Algeria, Bahrain, Iraq, Jordan, Kuwait, Libya, Macedonia, Sudan, Tunisia, Yugoslavia
dirham *or* dirhem	Libya, Morocco, Qatar, United Arab Emirates
dobra	São Tomé and Principe
dollar	Australia, The Bahamas, Barbados, Belize, Brunei, Canada, Equador, Fiji, Guyana, Jamaica, Kiribati, Liberia, Malaysia, Marshall Islands, Micronesia, Namibia, Nauru, New Zealand, Palau, Singapore, Solomon Islands, Taiwan, Trinidad and Tobago, Tuvalu, USA, Zimbabwe
dong	Vietnam

CURRENCIES OF THE WORLD (cont.)
(with countries)

drachma		kopeck, kopek,	
pl. -ae, -as	Greece (until mid-2002)	copeck or copek	Belarus, Russia
dram	Armenia	kopiyka	Ukraine
East Caribbean		koruna	Czech Republic, Slovakia
Dollar	Antigua and Barbuda,	krona	Sweden
East Caribbean		króna pl. -nur	Iceland
Dollar (cont.)	Dominica, Grenada, St	krone pl. kroner	Denmark, Norway
	Kitts and Nevis, St Lucia,	kroon pl. -ni	Estonia
	St Vincent and the	kuna pl. kune	Croatia
	Grenadines	kuruş or kurush	Turkey
escudo	Cape Verde, Portugal	kwacha	Malawi, Zambia
	(until mid-2002)	kwanza	Angola
euro	Austria, Belgium, Finland,	kyat	Myanmar
	France, Germany,	laari	Maldives
	Greece, Ireland, Italy,	lari	Georgia
	Luxmbourg, The	lats pl. lati	Latvia
	Netherlands, Portugal,	lek	Albania
	Spain	lempira	Honduras
eyrir pl. aurar	Iceland	leone	Sierra Leone
fen	China	lepton pl. -ta	Greece (until mid-2002)
filler	Hungary	leu pl. lei	Moldova, Romania
fils	Bahrain, Iraq, Jordan,	lev pl. leva	Bulgaria
	Kuwait, United Arab	lilangeni pl.	
	Emirates, Yemen	emalangeni	Swaziland
forint	Hungary	lipa	Croatia
franc	Andorra, Belgium (until	lira pl. lire	Italy (until mid-2002),
	mid-2002), Burundi,		Malta, San Marino,
	Comoros, Democratic		Turkey, Vatican City
	Republic of Congo,	lisente	Lesotho
	Côte d'Ivoire, Djibouti,	litas pl. litai	Lithuania
	France (until mid-2002),	loti pl. maloti	Lesotho
	Guinea, Liechtenstein,	luma	Armenia
	Luxembourg (until	lwei	Angola
	mid-2002), Madagascar,	manat	Azerbaijan, Turkmenistan
	Monaco, Rwanda,	marka	Bosnia Herzegovina
	Switzerland	markka	Finland
gopik	Azerbaijan	metical	Mozambique
gourde	Haiti	mil	Malta
groschen	Austria (until mid-2002)	millième	Egypt
grosz pl. groszy	Poland	millime	Tunisia
guaraní	Paraguay	möngö	Mongolia
guilder	The Netherlands (until	naira	Nigeria
	mid-2002), Suriname	nakfa	Eritrea
halala	Saudi Arabia	ngultrum	Bhutan
haler or halier		ngwee	Zambia
pl. haleru or		øre	Denmark, Norway
halierov	Czech Republic, Slovakia	öre	Sweden
hryvna		ouguiya	Mauritania
or hryvnya	Ukraine	pa'anga	Tonga
háo	Vietnam	paisa pl. paise	Bhutan, India, Nepal,
jiao	China		Pakistan
khoum	Mauritania	para	Macedonia, Yugoslavia
kina	Papua New Guinea	penni pl. -nia	
kip	Laos	or -nis	Finland
kobo	Nigeria	penny pl. pence	Republic of Ireland, UK

CURRENCIES OF THE WORLD (cont.)
(with countries)

peseta	Andorra, Spain (until mid-2002)	santimi	Latvia
		satang	Thailand
pesewa	Ghana	schilling	Austria (until mid-2002)
peso	Argentina, Chile, Colombia, Cuba, Dominican Republic, Mexico, Philippines, Uruguay	sen	Brunei, Cambodia, Indonesia, Japan, Malaysia
		sene	Samoa
		seniti	Tonga
pfennig *pl.* -nige	Germany (until mid-2002)	sent *pl.* senti	Estonia
piastre	Egypt, Lebanon, Syria	shekel *or* sheqel	Israel
poisha	Bangladesh	shilling	Kenya, Somalia, Tanzania, Uganda
pound	Cyprus, Egypt, Lebanon, Syria, UK	sol *pl.* soles	Peru
pul *pl.* puli *or* puls	Afghanistan	soum *pl.* soumy	Kyrgyzstan, Uzbekistan
pula	Botswana	stotin	Slovenia
punt	Republic of Ireland	stotinka *pl.* -inki	Bulgaria
pya	Myanmar	taka	Bangladesh
qindar *or*		tala	Samoa
qintar *pl.* -arka	Albania	tambala	Malawi
quetzal *pl.* -zales	Guatemala	tanga	Tajikistan
qursh	Saudi Arabia	tenesi	Turkmenistan
rand	South Africa	tenge	Kazakhstan
rappen	Liechtenstein, Switzerland	tetri	Georgia
real	Brazil	thebe	Botswana
rial	Iran, Oman	toea	Papua New Guinea
riel	Cambodia	tolar *pl.* -arji	Slovenia
ringgit	Malaysia	tugrik	Mongolia
riyal	Qatar, Saudi Arabia, Yemen	tyin	Kyrgyzstan, Uzbekistan
		vatu	Vanuatu
rouble	Belarus, Russia, Tajikstan	won	North Korea, South Korea
rufiyaa	Maldives	xu	Vietnam
rupee	Bhutan, India, Mauritius, Nepal, Pakistan, Seychelles, Sri Lanka	yen	Japan
		yuan	China
		zloty	Poland
rupiah	Indonesia		

ADMINISTRATIVE DIVISIONS OF ENGLAND
(with administrative centres)

*Avon	Bristol	Brighton and Hove	
Barking and Dagenham		Bristol	
Barnet		*Bromley*	
Barnsley		Buckinghamshire	Aylesbury
Bath and North East Somerset	Keynsham	Bury	
		Calderdale	Halifax
Bedfordshire	Bedford	Cambridgeshire	Cambridge
*Berkshire	Reading	*Camden*	
Bexley		Cheshire	Chester
Birmingham		*City of London*	
Blackburn with Darwen	Blackburn	*Cleveland	Middlesbrough
Blackpool		Cornwall	Truro
Bolton		Coventry	
Bournemouth		*Croydon*	
Bracknell Forest		*Cumberland	Carlisle
Bradford		Cumbria	Carlisle
Brent		Darlington	

ADMINISTRATIVE DIVISIONS OF ENGLAND (cont.)
(with administrative centres)

Derby		North Lincolnshire	Scunthorpe
Derbyshire	Matlock	*North Riding of Yorkshire	Northallerton
Devon	Exeter	North Somerset	Weston-
Doncaster			super-Mare
Dorset	Dorchester	North Tyneside	Wallsend
Dudley		Northumberland	Morpeth
Durham	Durham	North	
Ealing		Yorkshire	Northallerton
East Riding of Yorkshire	Beverley	Nottinghamshire	Nottingham
Enfield		Oldham	
Essex	Chelmsford	Oxfordshire	Oxford
Gateshead		Peterborough	
Gloucestershire	Gloucester	Plymouth	
*Greater London		Poole	
*Greater Manchester		Portsmouth	
Greenwich		Reading	
Hackney		Redbridge	
Halton	Widnes	Redcar and Cleveland	Redcar
Hammersmith and Fulham		Richmond Upon Thames	
Hampshire	Winchester	Rochdale	
Haringey		Rotherham	
Harrow		Rutland	Oakham
Hartlepool		St Helens	
Havering		Salford	
*Hereford and Worcester	Worcester	Sandwell	
Herefordshire	Hereford	Sefton	
Hertfordshire	Hertford	Sheffield	
Hillingdon		Shropshire	Shrewsbury
Hounslow		Slough	
*Humberside	Beverley	Solihull	
*Huntingdonshire	Huntingdon	Somerset	Taunton
Islington		Southampton	
Kensington and Chelsea		South Gloucestershire	Thornbury
Kent	Maidstone	Southend	
Kingston upon Hull		South Tyneside	South
Kingston-upon-Thames		Shields	
Kirklees	Huddersfield	Southwark	
Knowsley		*South Yorkshire	Sheffield
Lambeth		Staffordshire	Stafford
Lancashire	Preston	Stockport	
Leeds		Stockton-on-Tees	
Leicester		Stoke-on-Trent	
Leicestershire	Leicester	Suffolk	Ipswich
Lewisham		Sunderland	
Lincolnshire	Lincoln	Surrey	Kingston
Liverpool			Upon
Luton			Thames
Manchester			
Medway	Rochester	Sussex, East	Lewes
*Merseyside	Liverpool	Sussex, West	Chichester
Merton		Sutton	
Middlesbrough		Swindon	
Milton Keynes		Tameside	Ashton-
Newcastle upon Tyne			under-Lyne
Newham		Telford and Wrekin	Telford
Norfolk	Norwich	Thurrock	
Northamptonshire	Northampton	Tower Hamlets	
North-East Lincolnshire	Grimsby	Trafford	

ADMINISTRATIVE DIVISIONS OF ENGLAND (cont.)
(with administrative centres)

*Tyne and Wear	Newcastle upon Tyne	Wiltshire	Trowbridge
		Windsor and Maidenhead	
Wakefield		Wirral	Wallasey
Walsall		Wokingham	
Waltham Forest		Wolverhampton	
Wandsworth		Worcestershire	Worcester
Warrington		York	
Warwickshire	Warwick	*Yorkshire	
West Berkshire	Newbury		
*West Midlands	Birmingham		
Westminster			
*Westmorland	Kendal		
*West Riding of Yorkshire	Wakefield		
*West Yorkshire	Wakefield		
Wigan			
Wight, Isle of	Newport, IOW		

*Former or historic county.
Greater London unitary authorities are shown in italics.
Where no administrative centre is given, its name is identical to that of the authority it serves.

WELSH COUNTIES AND COUNTY BOROUGHS
(with administrative centres)

Anglesey	Llangefni	Monmouthshire	Cwmbran
Blaenau Gwent	Ebbw Vale	*Montgomeryshire	Welshpool
*Breconshire	Brecon	Neath and Port Talbot	Port Talbot
Bridgend		Newport	
*Caernarfonshire	Caernarfon	*Pembrokeshire	Haverfordwest
Caerphilly	Hengoed	Powys	Llandrindod Wells
Cardiff		*Radnorshire	Llandrindod Wells
*Cardiganshire	Aberystwyth	Rhondda-Cynon-Taff	Tonypandy
Carmarthenshire	Carmarthen	*South Glamorgan	Cardiff
Ceredigion	Aberaeron	Swansea	
*Clwyd	Mold	Torfaen	Pontypool
Conwy		Vale of Glamorgan	Barry
Denbighshire	Ruthin	*West Glamorgan	Swansea
*Dyfed	Carmarthen	Wrexham	
Flintshire	Mold		
*Glamorgan	Cardiff		
*Gwent	Cwmbran		
Gwynedd	Caernarfon		
*Merionethshire	Dolgellau		
Merthyr Tydfil			
*Mid Glamorgan	Cardiff		

*Former or historic county.
Where no administrative centre is given, its name is identical to that of the authority it serves.

SCOTTISH COUNCIL AREAS
(with administrative centres)

Aberdeen City	
Aberdeenshire	Aberdeen
Angus	Forfar
Argyll and Bute	Lochgilphead
*Argyll	Lochgilphead
*Ayr	
*Banff	
*Berwick	Duns
*Borders	Melrose
*Bute	Rothesay
*Caithness	Wick
*Central	Stirling
City of Edinburgh	
Clackmannanshire	Alloa
*Dumbarton	Dumbarton
Dumfries and Galloway	Dumfries
*Dumfries	
Dundee City	
East Ayrshire	Kilmarnock
East Dumbartonshire	Kirkintilloch
East Lothian	Haddington
East Renfrewshire	Glasgow
Falkirk	
Fife	Glenrothes
Glasgow City	
*Grampian	Aberdeen
Highland	Inverness
Inverclyde	Greenock
*Inverness	
*Kincardine	Stonehaven
*Kinross	
*Kirkcudbright	
*Lanark	Hamilton
*Lothian	Edinburgh

Midlothian	Dalkeith
Moray	Elgin
*Nairn	Nairn
North Ayrshire	Irvine
North Lanarkshire	Motherwell
Orkney Islands	Kirkwall
*Peebles	
Perth and Kinross	Perth
*Perth	
*Renfrew	Paisley
Renfrewshire	Paisley
*Ross and Cromarty	Dingwall
*Roxburgh	Newtown St. Boswells
Scottish Borders	Melrose
*Selkirk	
Shetland Islands	Lerwick
South Ayrshire	Ayr
South Lanarkshire	Hamilton
*Stirling	Stirling
*Strathclyde	Glasgow
*Sutherland	Golspie
*Tayside	Dundee
West Dumbartonshire	Dumbarton
Western Isles	Stornaway
West Lothian	Livingston
*Wigtown	Stranraer
*Zetland	Lerwick

*Former administrative division.
Where no administrative centre is given, its name is identical to that of the authority it serves.

COUNTIES AND DISTRICTS OF NORTHERN IRELAND
(with administrative centres)

Antrim	
Antrim, County	Belfast
Ards	Newtonards
Armagh	
Armagh, County	Armagh
Ballymena	
Ballymoney	
Banbridge	
Belfast City	
Carrickfergus	
Castlereagh	Belfast
Coleraine	
Cookstown	
Craigavon	
Derry City	
Down	Downpatrick
Down, County	Downpatrick
Dungannon	

Fermanagh	Enniskillen
Fermanagh, County	Enniskillen
Larne	
Limavady	
Lisburn	
Londonderry, County	Londonderry
Magherafelt	
Moyle	Ballycastle
Newry and Mourne	Newry
Newtownabbey	Ballyclare
North Down	Bangor
Omagh	
Strabane	
Tyrone, County	Omagh

Where no administrative centre is given, its name is identical to that of the authority it serves.

PROVINCES AND COUNTIES OF IRELAND
(with county towns)

Connacht	Galway				Kerry	Tralee
	Leitrim	Carrick-on-			Limerick	
		Shannon			Tipperary	Clonmel
	Mayo	Castlebar			Waterford	
	Roscommon					
	Sligo		Ulster		*Antrim	Belfast
					*Armagh	
Leinster	Carlow				Cavan	
	Dublin				Donegal	Lifford
	Kildare	Naas			*Down	Downpatrick
	Kilkenny				*Fermanagh	Enniskillen
	Laoighis *or*	Portlaoighise *or*			*Londonderry	
	Laois *or* Leix	Portlaoise			Monaghan	
	Longford				*Tyrone	Omagh
	Louth	Dundalk				
	Meath	Trim				
	Offaly	Tullamore				
	Westmeath	Mullingar				
	Wexford			*Indicates a county of Northern Ireland;		
	Wicklow			unmarked counties constitute the Republic		
				of Ireland.		
Munster	Clare	Ennis		*Where no county town is given, its name is*		
	Cork			*identical to that of the county it serves.*		

STATES OF THE USA
(with abbreviations and capitals)

Alabama	AL *or* Ala	Montgomery	New		
Alaska	AK *or* Alas	Juneau	Hampshire	NH	Concord
Arizona	AZ *or* Ariz	Phoenix	New Jersey	NJ	Trenton
Arkansas	AR *or* Ark	Little Rock	New Mexico	NM *or* N Mex	Santa Fe
California	CA *or* Cal	Sacramento	New York	NY	Albany
Colorado	CO *or* Colo	Denver	North Carolina	NC	Raleigh
Connecticut	CT *or* Conn	Hartford	North Dakota	ND *or* N Dak	Bismarck
Delaware	DE *or* Del	Dover	Ohio	OH	Columbus
Florida	FL *or* Fla	Tallahassee	Oklahoma	OK *or* Okla	Oklahoma
Georgia	GA	Atlanta			City
Hawaii	HA	Honolulu	Oregon	OR *or* Oreg	Salem
Idaho	ID *or* Ida	Boise	Pennsylvania	PA	Harrisburg
Illinois	IL *or* Ill	Springfield	Rhode Island	RI	Providence
Indiana	IN *or* Ind	Indianapolis	South Carolina	SC	Columbia
Iowa	IA	Des Moines	South Dakota	SD *or* S Dak	Pierre
Kansas	KS *or* Kan	Topeka	Tennessee	TN *or* Tenn	Nashville
Kentucky	KY *or* Ken	Frankfort	Texas	TX *or* Tex	Austin
Louisiana	LA	Baton Rouge	Utah	UT	Salt Lake City
Maine	ME	Augusta	Vermont	VT	Montpelier
Maryland	MD	Annapolis	Virginia	VA	Richmond
Massachusetts	MA *or* Mass	Boston	Washington	WA *or* Wash	Olympia
Michigan	MI *or* Mich	Lansing	West Virginia	WV *or* W Va	Charleston
Minnesota	MN *or* Minn	St Paul	Wisconsin	WI *or* Wis	Madison
Mississippi	MS *or* Miss	Jackson	Wyoming	WY *or* Wyo	Cheyenne
Missouri	MO	Jefferson			
		City	*District*		
Montana	MT *or* Mont	Helena	District of		
Nebraska	NE *or* Nebr	Lincoln	Columbia	DC	
Nevada	NV *or* Nev	Carson City			

STATES AND TERRITORIES OF AUSTRALIA
(with capitals)

New South Wales	Sydney	Northern Territory	Darwin
Queensland	Brisbane	Victoria	Melbourne
South Australia	Adelaide	Western Australia	Perth
Tasmania	Hobart		
Australian Capital Territory	Canberra – federal capital		

PROVINCES AND TERRITORIES OF CANADA
(with capitals)

Alberta	Edmonton	Ontario	Toronto
British Columbia	Victoria	Nunavut	Iqaluit
Manitoba	Winnipeg	Prince Edward Island	Charlottetown
New Brunswick	Fredericton	Quebec	Quebec
Newfoundland and Labrador	St John's	Saskatchewan	Regina
Northwest Territories	Yellowknife	Yukon Territory	Whitehorse
Nova Scotia	Halifax		

PROVINCES OF NEW ZEALAND

North Island
  Auckland
  Bay of Plenty
  Gisborne
  Hawkes Bay
  Manawatu-
    Wanganui
  Northland
  Taranaki
  Waikato
  Wellington

South Island
  Canterbury
  Marlborough
  Nelson
  Otago
  Southland
  Tasman
  West Coast
Islands
  Stewart Islands
  Chatham Islands

PROVINCES OF SOUTH AFRICA
(with capitals)

Eastern Cape	Bisho	Mpumalanga	Nelspruit
Free State	Bloemfontein	Northern	Pietersburg
Gauteng	Johannesburg	Northern Cape	Kimberley
KwaZulu/Natal	Ulundi	North-West	Mafikeng

AUSTRIAN STATES
(with capitals)

Burgenland	Eisenstadt	Tyrol	Innsbruck
Carinthia	Klagenfurt	Upper Austria	Linz
Lower Austria	St Pölten	Vienna	Vienna
Salzburg	Salzburg	Vorarlberg	Bregenz
Styria	Graz		

FRENCH REGIONS
(with capitals)

Alsace	Strasbourg	Languedoc-Roussillon	Montpellier
Aquitaine	Bordeaux	Limousin	Limoges
Auvergne	Clermont-Ferrand	Lorraine	Metz
Basse-Normandie	Caen	Midi-Pyrénées	Toulouse
Brittany (Bretagne)	Rennes	Nord-Pas-de-Calais	Lille
Burgundy (Bourgogne)	Dijon	Pays de la Loire	Nantes
Centre	Orléans	Picardie	Amiens
Champagne-Ardenne	Châlons-sur-Marne	Poitou-Charentes	Poitiers
Corsica (Corse)	Ajaccio	Provence-Alpes-Côte	
Franche-Comté	Besançon	d'Azur	Marseille
Haute-Normandie	Rouen	Rhône-Alpes	Lyon
Ile de France	Paris		

GERMAN STATES
(with capitals)

Baden-Württemberg	Stuttgart	West Pomerania	Schwerin
Bavaria	Munich	North Rhine-Westphalia	Düsseldorf
Berlin	Berlin	Rhineland-Palatinate	Mainz
Brandenburg	Potsdam	Saarland	Saarbrücken
Bremen	Bremen	Saxony	Dresden
Hamburg	Hamburg	Saxony-Anhalt	Magdeburg
Hessen	Wiesbaden	Schleswig-Holstein	Kiel
Lower Saxony	Hannover	Thuringia	Erfurt
Mecklenburg-			

ITALIAN REGIONS
(with capitals)

Abruzzo	L'Aquila	Molise	Campobasso
Basilicata	Potenza	Piedmont	Turin
Calabria	Catanzaro	Puglia	Bari
Campania	Naples	Sardinia	Cagliari
Emilia-Romagna	Bologna	Sicily	Palermo
Friuli-Venezia Giulia	Trieste	Trentino-Alto Adige	Trento
Lazio	Rome	Tuscany	Florence
Liguria	Genoa	Umbria	Perugia
Lombardy	Milan	Valle d'Aosta	Aosta
Marche	Ancona	Veneto	Venice

PORTUGUESE DISTRICTS
(with capitals)

Aveiro	Aveiro	Lisboa	Lisbon (Lisboa)
Beja	Beja	Portalegre	Portalegre
Braga	Braga	Porto	Porto
Bragança	Bragança	Santarém	Santarém
Castelo Branco	Castelo Branco	Setúbal	Setúbal
Coimbra	Coimbra	Viana do Castelo	Viana do Castelo
Évora	Évora	Vila Real	Vila Real
Faro	Faro	Viseu	Viseu
Guarda	Guarda		
Leiria	Leiria		

SPANISH REGIONS
(with capitals)

Andalusia	Seville	Catalonia	Barcelona
Aragon	Zaragoza	Extremadura	Mérida
Asturias	Oviedo	Galicia	Santiago de
Balearic Islands	Palma de Mallorca		Compostela
Basque Country	Vitoria	La Rioja	Longroño
Canary Islands	Las Palmas and	Madrid	Madrid
	Santa Cruz de	Murcia	Murcia
	Tenerife	Navarra	Pamplona
Cantabria	Santander	Valencia	Valencia
Castilla-La Mancha	Toledo	Ceuta	
Castilla-León	Valladolid	Melilla	

SWISS CANTONS
(with capitals)

Aargau	Aarau	Nidwalden	Stans
Appenzell Ausser-		Obwalden	Sarnen
Rhoden	Herisau	Sankt Gallen	Sankt Gallen
Appenzell Inner-Rhoden	Appenzell	Schaffhausen	Schaffhausen
Basel-Landschaft	Liestal	Schwyz	Schwyz
Basel-Stadt	Basel	Solothurn	Solothurn
Bern	Bern	Thurgau	Frauenfeld
Fribourg	Fribourg	Ticino	Bellinzona
Genève	Geneva	Uri	Altdorf
Glarus	Glarus	Valais	Sion
Graubünden	Chur	Vaud	Lausanne
Jura	Delémont	Zug	Zug
Luzern	Luzern	Zürich	Zürich
Neuchâtel	Neuchâtel		

RUSSIAN FEDERATION REPUBLICS
(with capitals)

Adygeya	Maikop	Karachai-Cherkessia	Cherkessk
Alania (or North Ossetia)	Vladikavkaz	Karelia	Petrozavodsk
Altai	Gorno-Altaisk	Khakassia	Abakan
Bashkortostan	Ufa	Komi	Syktyvkar
Buryatia	Ulan-Ude	Mari El	Yoshkar-Ola
Chechnya	Grozny	Mordovia	Saransk
Chuvashia	Cheboksary	Russia	Moscow
Dagestan	Makhachkala	Sakha	Yakutsk
Ingushetia	Nazran	Tatarstan	Kazan
Kabardino-Balkaria	Nalchik	Tuva	Kyzyl
Kalmykia	Elista	Udmurtia	Izhevsk

CITIES

Aachen	Alameda	Amman	Ardabil	Babel
Aalborg	Albacete	Amol	Arecibo	Babol
Aalen	Alba Iulia	Amoy	Arequipa	Babylon
Aalst	Albany	Amravati	Arezzo	Bacolod
Aarhus	Albuquerque	Amritsar	Argolis	Baghdad
Aba	Alcalá de	Amsterdam	Argos	Baguio
Abadan	Guadaira	Anaheim	Arles	Bahamas
Abbottabad	Alcalá de	Anápolis	Arlington	Bahawalpur
Abéché	Henares	Anchorage	Armagh	Baicheng
Aberdeen	Aleksandrovsk-	Anda	Armavir	Bakersfield
Abidjan	Sakhalinskiy	Anderson	Armidale	Balkh
Abilene	Aleppo	Andijon	Arnsberg	Baltimore
Åbo	Alessandria	Angarsk	Arta	Bamberg
Abu Dhabi	Alexandria	Angers	Arthur's Seat	Bandar
Abuja	Alexandroupolis	Angostura	Asahikawa	Lampung
Abydos	Algeciras	Ankara	Asansol	Bandung
Acapulco	Algiers	Annaba	Aschaffenburg	Bangalore
Accra	Alhambra	Ann Arbor	Aschersleben	Bangkok
Adana	Aligarh	Anniston	Asheville	Bangor
Adapazari	Alkmaar	Anqing	Ashgabat	Baniyas
Addis Ababa	Allahabad	Anshan	Ashquelon	Baoding
Adelaide	Allentown	Anshun	Assyria	Baoji
Adiyaman	Almaty	Antakya	Astana	Baoshan
Ado-Ekiti	Almelo	Antalya	Astrakhan	Baotou
Adrianopole	Almirante	Antananarivo	Asunción	Baracaldo
Afyon	Brown	Antioch	Aswan	Baranavichiy
Agadir	Almoravid	Anuradhapura	Asyut	Barcelona
Agra	Alost	Anvers	Athens	Bareilly
Ahlen	Alphen aan den	Anyang	Athínai	Barinas
Ahmadabad	Rijn	Aosta	Atlanta	Barquisimeto
Ahmadnagar	Alton	Aphrodisias	Attleboro	Barrie
Aintab	Altoona	Apollonia	Auburn	Barysaw
Aix-en-	Alwar	Appleton	Auckland	Basle
Provence	Amagasaki	Aqmola	Augsburg	Bastille
Ajmer	Amaravati	Aqtau	Aurora	Batman
Akashi	Amarillo	Aqtobe	Austin	Batna
Akita	Ambala	Aquila	Avignon	Baton Rouge
Akkad	Ambato	Aracajú	Avlona	Battambang
Akola	Amberg	Arad	Ayacucho	Batticaloa
Aksu	Amersfoort	Arak	Baalbek	Battle Creek

CITIES (cont.)

Baurú
Bayamo
Bayamón
Bayonne
Baytown
Beaverton
Bei'an
Beilhai
Beijing
Beirut
Bejaia
Belaya Tserkov
Belém
Belfast
Belfort
Belgaum
Belgorod
Bellary
Bellevue
Bellflower
Bellingham
Belo Horizonte
Belovo
Beltsy
Bengbu
Benha
Benoni
Benxi
Berezniki
Bergama
Bergen
Bergisch
 Gladbach
Berkeley
Berlin
Berne
Berry
Bethlehem
Beverly Hills
Bhagalpur
Bhiwandi
Bhopal
Bialystok
Bielefeld
Bikaner
Bilbao
Billings
Binghamton
Binzhou
Birmingham
Biscayne Bay
Bishkek
Blackfoot
Blagoveshchensk
Blantyre
Blida
Bloomington
Blumenau
Bobo-Dioulasso

Bochum
Bodrum
Bogotá
Bohemia
Boise
Bokaro Steel
 City
Bolan Pass
Bologna
Bombay
Bonampak
Bonn
Bordeaux
Borujerd
Bose
Bosra
Bossier City
Boston
Botou
Bottrop
Bouaké
Boulder
Bowling Green
Bradford
Braga
Braganza
Braila
Brandon
Brantford
Brasov
Bratislava
Bratsk
Brazzaville
Bremen
Brescia
Brest
Bridgeport
Brighton and
 Hove
Brisbane
Bristol
Brno
Brockton
Broken Arrow
Bromberg
Brookline
Brooklyn Park
Brownsville
Bruges
Brunswick
Brussels
Bryansk
Brzeg
Bucaramanga
Bucharest
Budapest
Buena Park
Buenos Aires
Buffalo

Bugis
Bujumbura
Bukhara
Bulawayo
Burbank
Burgas
Burgos
Burlington
Burnsville
Bushehr
Buzau
Byblos
Bytom
Byzantium
Cabimas
Cabinda
Cáceres
Cadiz
Caen
Cagayan de Oro
Cagliari
Caguas
Cairo
Calcutta
Calgary
Cali
Caloocan
Calvary
Camagüey
Camarillo
Cambridge
Campagna di
 Roma
Campina
 Grande
Campinas
Campos
Canandaigua
Candia
Cangzhou
Canterbury
Canton
Cape Coral
Capua
Caracas
Caracol
Carcassonne
Carchemish
Cariacica
Carniola
Carolina
Carthage
Casablanca
Castellón de la
 Plana
Catania
Caxias do Sul
Cebu
Cedar Rapids

Celaya
Ceske
 Budejovice
Chalcedon
Champs Elysées
Chan Chan
Chandigarh
Chandler
Chang'an
Changchun
Changde
Changji
Changzhi
Changzhou
Chaohu
Chaoyang
Charikar
Charjew
Charleroi
Charlesbourg
Charleston
Charlotte
Chattanooga
Chaudière Falls
Chavín de
 Huántar
Cheapside
Cheju
Chelmno
Chelyabinsk
Chemnitz
Chengde
Chengdu
Cherepovets
Cherkassy
Chernigov
Chernivtsi
Chernobyl
Chesapeake
Chester
Chiangmai
Chiba
Chicago
Chiclayo
Chicopee
Chicoutimi
Chifeng
Chigasaki
Chihuahua
Chillán
Chinatown
Chita
Choibalsan
Cholula
Chongqing
Chorzów
Christchurch
Chula Vista
Chuxiong

Chuzhou
Cicero
Cienfuegos
Cincinnati
Ciudad Bolivar
Ciudad
 Guayana
Ciudad Madero
Ciudad
 Obregón
Ciudad Victoria
Clarksville
Clearwater
Clermont-
 Ferrand
Cleveland
Cleveland
 Heights
Clifton
Clovis
Cluj-Napoca
Coblenz
Coburg
Cochabamba
Cognac
Coimbatore
Coimbra
College Station
Cologne
Colombo
Colón
Colonia
Colorado
 Springs
Colossae
Columbia
Columbus
Comilla
Concepción
Concord
Constantine
Constantinople
Constanza
Coon Rapids
Copán
Coral Springs
Córdoba
Corinth
Cork
Corona
Costa Mesa
Cotonou
Cottbus
Council Bluffs
Coventry
Cracow
Craiova
Ctesiphon
Cuenca

CITIES (cont.)

Cuiabá	Dubbo	Fayetteville	Guimaraes	Himeji
Curitiba	Dubrovnik	Feira de	Gujrat	Hino
Cuzco	Dubuque	Santana	Gulbarga	Hirakata
Dachau	Dukou	Flint	Guntur	Hiratsuka
Dali	Duluth	Florianópolis	Gwalior	Hirosaki
Dallas	Dum Dum	Fontana	Gyor	Hitachi
Damanhur	Dundee	Forest Lawn	Haarlemmer-	Ho Chi Minh
Damascus	Dunedin	Fort Lauderdale	meer	City
Dan	Dunfermline	Fort Smith	Habikino	Hollywood
Da Nang	Dunhua	Fort Wayne	Hachinohe	Bowl
Danbury	Duque de	Fort Worth	Hachioji	Hoorn
Danjiangkou	Caxias	Fountain Valley	Hadano	Huaibei
Danville	Durban	Frankenthal	Haeju	Huaihua
Daqing	Düren	Fredericksburg	Hagen	Huainan
Darbhanga	Durgapur	Fremont	Haicheng	Huaiyin
Darkhan	Durham	Fresno	Haining	Huambo
Dashhowuz	Dushanbe	Fujisawa	Hamadan	Huancayo
Daugavpils	Düsseldorf	Fuling	Hamamatsu	Huangshi
Davangere	Duyun	Fullerton	Hamburg	Hubli
Davao	Dzerzhinsk	Fürth	Hamhung	Hué
Davenport	East Orange	Gaborone	Hami	Huizhou
David	Eau Claire	Gabrovo	Hamilton	Hull
Daxian	Ech Chlef	Gainesville	Hamm	Hunjiang
Dayton	Ede	Galena	Hammond	Huntington
Daytona Beach	Edmond	Galveston	Hampton	Huntington
Dearborn	El Cajon	Garden Grove	Hancheng	Beach
Debrecen	Elea	Gary	Handan	Huntington Park
Decatur	Elgin	Gastonia	Hanzhong	Huntsville
Dehra Dun	Elis	Gath	Harappa	Hyderabad
Delhi	Elizabeth	Gaya	Hardwar	Ibadan
Delmenhorst	El Kef	Gera	Hasselt	Ibaraki
Denison	El Mansura	Germiston	Hastings	Ichihara
Denton	El Minya	Gerona	Haverhill	Ichikawa
Denver	El Paso	Gharyan	Hawthorne	Ichinomiya
Derbent	Ely	Ghaziabad	Hayward	Ife
Derby	Elyria	Ghent	Hebi	Ikeda
Des Moines	Encinitas	Gifu	Hechi	Ikeja
Dessau	Enschede	Gijón	Heerlen	Ilam
Detroit	Enshi	Glasgow	Hegang	Ilesha
Deventer	Enugu	Glendale	Heidelberg	Ilorin
Deyang	Ephesus	Gloucester	Heilbronn	Imperatriz
Dezhou	Epidaurus	Godoy Cruz	Helwan	Imperia
Dhaka	Erfurt	Gómez Palacio	Henderson	Independence
Dhanbad	Erie	Gorakhpur	Hengshui	Indore
Dharwar	Erlangen	Gordium	Hengyang	Ingolstadt
Dijon	Erode	Gorlovka	Herat	Innsbruck
Dinajpur	Escondido	Gotha	Hereford	Insein
Dispura	Espoo	Granada	Herne	Invercargill
Dodge City	Essen	Grand Prairie	Herning	Inverness
Doha	Esslingen	Grand Rapids	Hervey Bay	Iowa City
Donetsk	Euclid	Graz	Heshan	Ipoh
Dongchuan	Eugene	Great Falls	Hesperia	Irapuato
Dongguang	Evansville	Greeley	Heze	Irbid
Dongying	Ezhou	Greensboro	Hialeah	Iruma
Dordrecht	Fairbanks	Greenville	Higashimura-	Irvine
Dortmund	Fairfield	Gresham	yama	Irving
Douala	Faisalabad	Groznyy	High Point	Isesaki
Downey	Fargo	Guatemala City	Hikone	Istanbul
Dresden	Faridabad	Guayaquil	Hildesheim	Itami

CITIES (cont.)

Itanagar	Kaposvar	Komatsu	Liaoyuan	Manta
Ivanovo	Karaj	Konin	Liberec	Manzhouli
Iwaki	Karaklis	Koriyama	Lille	Maoming
Iwakuni	Karakorum	Korla	Lima	Maramba
Iwatsuki	Karamay	Koshigaya	Limoges	Mari
Iwo	Karbala	Kosice	Lincoln	Marib
Izmit	Kariya	Kostroma	Linfen	Matamoros
Jabalpur	Karviná	Koszalin	Linhai	Mathura
Jaboatão	Kashihara	Kota	Linhe	Matsubara
Jacobabad	Kashiwa	Kovrov	Linqing	Matsue
Jalalabad	Kassel	Kragujevac	Linxia	Matsumoto
Jamalpur	Kasugai	Kramatorsk	Linyi	Matsuyama
Jambi	Kasukabe	Kumagaya	Linz	Mayapan
Jamnagar	Kasur	Kumasi	Lishui	Mazar-e-Sharif
Janesville	Katowice	Kunming	Livermore	Medan
Jersey City	Katsuta	Kurashiki	Liverpool	Medellín
Jessore	Kaunas	Kure	Livonia	Medicine Hat
Jhansi	Kawachinagano	Kurgan	Lodi	Meerut
Jiamusi	Kawagoe	Kursk	Lodz	Meissen
Ji'an	Kawanishi	Kurume	London	Mei Xian
Jiangmen	Kawasaki	Kutaisi	Londrina	Meknès
Jiaojiang	Kazan	Kuytun	Long Beach	Melbourne
Jiaozou	Kecskemét	Kyongju	Longmont	Memphis
Jiaxing	Kediri	Kyoto	Longview	Mendoza
Jiayuguan	Kemerovo	Lafayette	Longyan	Merced
Jinchang	Kenner	Lagos	Lorain	Mérida
Jincheng	Kenosha	La Habra	Los Angeles	Mesa
Jingmen	Kerman	Lahti	Los Mochis	Metz
Jinhua	Kettering	Laiwu	Loudi	Miami
Jining	Key West	Lake Charles	Louisville	Mianyang
Jinshi	Khorramabad	Lakeland	Lowell	Miass
Jinzhou	Khulna	Lakewood	Lower Hutt	Michurinsk
Jishou	Kielce	La Mesa	Luanda	Midland
Jiujiang	Kimberley	Lancaster	Lubbock	Midwest City
Jixi	Kingston	Landshut	Lublin	Mildura
João Pessoa	Kirkuk	Langfang	Lubumbashi	Miletus
Joensuu	Kirovohad	Laohekou	Lucknow	Milpitas
Johannesburg	Kiryu	Laramie	Ludhiana	Minatitlán
Joinville	Kisangani	Largo	Lund	Minden
Joliet	Kisarazu	Larkana	Luohe	Minneapolis
Jujuy	Kislovodsk	Las Cruces	Lusaka	Minoo
Jundiaí	Kitakyushu	Las Vegas	Luzhou	Minsk
Kaduna	Kitami	Launceston	Lynchburg	Mirzapur
Kaesong	Kitchener	Laval	Lynn	Mishima
Kafr el Dauwar	Kitwe	Lawrence	Lynwood	Miskolc
Kafr el Sheikh	Kladno	Lawton	Ma'anshan	Mission Viejo
Kagoshima	Klagenfurt	Leeds	Macheng	Mississauga
Kaifeng	Klerksdorp	Lefkosia	Machida	Mitaka
Kaili	Knossos	Leicester	Macon	Mitla
Kairouan	Knoxville	Leipzig	Madrid	Miyakonojo
Kaiyuan	Kochi	Lengshuijiang	Madurai	Mmabatho
Kakamigahara	Kodaira	Lengshuitan	Magdeburg	Mobile
Kakogawa	Kofu	León	Mahabad	Modena
Kalamazoo	Koganei	Leshan	Mahilyou	Modesto
Kalisz	Kohima	Leverkusen	Mainz	Moe
Kaluga	Kokubunji	Levittown	Malegaon	Mogi das
Kalyan	Kolhapur	Lexington	Malmö	Cruzes
Kanazawa	Kolomna	Liaocheng	Manaus	Mohenjo-Daro
Kano	Komaki	Liaoyang	Manizales	Mombasa

CITIES (cont.)

Mönchen-gladbach	New Orleans	Orange	Pine Bluff	Rialto
Monclova	Newport Beach	Orebro	Pingdingshan	Richardson
Monroe	Newport News	Orem	Pingxiang	Richland
Montebello	New Rochelle	Orenburg	Pinsk	Rio Branco
Monterey	Newton	Orizaba	Piracicaba	Rio Cuarto
Monterey Park	New York	Orlando	Pisa	Riverside
Monterrey	Nicaea	Orsk	Pittsburgh	Rizhao
Montes Claros	Nice	Oruro	Plantation	Roanoke
Montpellier	Nicomedia	Osasco	Pleasanton	Rochester
Monza	Nicopolis	Osh	Pleven	Rockford
Mopti	Nieuwegein	Oshawa	Ploiesti	Rosetta
Moradabad	Nikopol	Oshkosh	Podolsk	Rotorua
Morelia	Nîmes	Oshogbo	P'ohang	Rotterdam
Mostar	Nimrud	Osijek	Poitiers	Royal Oak
Mosul	Nineveh	Oskmen	Poltava	Rubtsovsk
Moundou	Nishinomiya	Osnabrück	Pompano Beach	Rudnyy
Mountain View	Nizhnevartovsk	Ostia	Ponce	Ryazan
Mount Gambier	Nizhniy	Ostrava	Pontiac	Rybinsk
Mount Vernon	Novgorod	Ota	Popayán	Sabadell
Mozir	Noda	Otaru	Port Arthur	Sagamihara
Mudanjiang	Noginsk	Ouagadougou	Port St. Lucie	Saginaw
Multan	Norilsk	Oujda	Portsmouth	Saharanpur
Muncie	Norman	Oxford	Posadas	Saidpur
Münster	Norrköping	Oxnard	Potosí	Saigon
Murom	North Bay	Paderborn	Potsdam	St. Albans
Mycenae	Norwalk	Palembang	Prato	St. Catherines
Mykolayiv	Nova Iguaçu	Palm Bay	Pristina	Sainte-Foy
Naga City	Novgorod	Palmdale	Prokopyevsk	Saint John
Nagaoka	Novi Sad	Palmyra	Provo	St. Joseph
Nagasaki	Novokuznetsk	Palo Alto	Pskov	Saint-Laurent
Nagercoil	Novomoskovsk	Palu	Puente Alto	St. Louis
Nagoya	Novosibirsk	Pamplona	Putian	St. Petersburg
Nagpur	Nuevo Laredo	Panihati	Puyang	Sakai
Nakuru	Numazu	Pasay	Pyatigorsk	Sakura
Nalchik	Oak Ridge	Paterson	Qaraghandy	Salamanca
Namangan	Oberhausen	Patiala	Qinzhou	Salavat
Nanchong	Obihiro	Pavia	Qitaihe	Salem
Nanded	Oceanside	Pavlodar	Quanzhou	Salford
Nanping	Odawara	Pawtucket	Quezon City	Salt Lake City
Nantes	Odessa	Pécs	Qufu	Salvador
Nanyang	Ogaki	Pegu	Quilpué	Salzgitter
Naperville	Ogbomosho	Pella	Qum	Samara
Narbonne	Ogden	Pembroke Pines	Quzhou	Samaria
Nashua	Okara	Penza	Racine	Samarra
Nashik	Okayama	Pereira	Radom	Sanandaj
National City	Okazaki	Perm	Raipur	San Angelo
Nawabganj	Olathe	Pernik	Rajahmundry	San Antonio
Nawabshah	Olinda	Perpignan	Rajkot	San Bernardino
Ndola	Olomouc	Persepolis	Rancagua	San Bernardo
Nellore	Olsztyn	Perugia	Rangpur	San Diego
Nelson	Omaha	Petaling Jaya	Rapid City	San Francisco
Neubrandenburg	Omdurman	Peterborough	Rasht	San Jose
Neuquén	Ome	Petra	Ratisbon	San Luis
Neuss	Omiya	Petrópolis	Ravenna	San Mateo
Newark	Omsk	Pforzheim	Rawalpindi	San Miguel
New Britain	Omuta	Philadelphia	Redlands	Sanming
Newcastle upon Tyne	Onomichi	Phoenix	Rennes	Santa Ana
	Opole	Pico Rivera	Reno	Santa Clara
	Oral	Pietermaritzburg	Resita	Santarém

CITIES (cont.)

Santa Rosa	Sinuiju	Tempe	Vancouver	Xianyang
Santiago del	Sioux City	Temuco	Vanderbijlpark	Xiaogan
Estero	Sioux Falls	Terre Haute	Vantaa	Xichang
Santos	Siping	Thousand Oaks	Venlo	Xigaze
Sanya	Slavyansk	Thunder Bay	Ventura	Xilinhot
São Gonçalo	Slupsk	Tianshui	Vereeniging	Xingtai
Sapporo	Smolensk	Tiefa	Vicenza	Xintai
Sarajevo	Soka	Tieling	Vicksburg	Xinxiang
Sarapul	Solingen	Tikal	Victoria	Xinyang
Saratoga	Sorocaba	Tilburg	Vila Velha	Xinyu
Springs	Sosnowiec	Tiraspol	Villavicencio	Xinzhou
Saratov	Southampton	Tivoli	Vineland	Xuchang
Sardis	South Bend	Tlemcen	Virginia Beach	Yakeshi
Sargodha	Spokane	Toledo	Visalia	Yakima
Sarh	Stakhanov	Tomsk	Vitoria da	Yamagata
Sasebo	Staryy Oskal	Tongchuan	Conquista	Yamaguchi
Saskatoon	Stendal	Tonghua	Vitsyebsk	Yamato
Satu Mare	Sterlitamak	Tongliao	Vladikavkaz	Yambol
Savannah	Stockton	Tongling	Volgodonsk	Yangquan
Schenectady	Stralsund	Torrance	Volgograd	Yanji
Schwerin	Stuttgart	Torreón	Vologda	Yazd
Scranton	Subotica	Toulouse	Volzhskiy	Yelets
Seattle	Sudbury	Tours	Vorkuta	Yibin
Segovia	Suihua	Toyota	Voronezh	Yichang
Semarang	Suita	Traralgon	Votkinsk	Yingtan
Sendai	Suizhou	Trieste	Waco	Yining
Sétif	Sumy	Tromso	Walnut Creek	Yiyang
Seto	Sunderland	Troy	Waltham	Yokkaichi
Severodonetsk	Surgut	Truro	Wanxian	Yongzhou
Severodvinsk	Susa	Tucson	Warangal	Yonkers
Shakhty	Suzuka	Tula	Waterloo	York
Shangqiu	Syracuse	Tumen	Waukegan	Yoshkar-Ola
Shangrao	Syzran	Tunxi	Waukesha	Yuci
Shaoguan	Tábor	Tupelo	Weihai	Yueyang
Shaowu	Taegu	Tuscaloosa	Weinan	Yulin
Shaoxing	Tai'an	Tver	Wells	Yuma
Shaoyang	Taichung	Tyler	Wenzhou	Yuncheng
Shashi	Tainan	Tyumen	West Covina	Yuxi
Sheffield	Taipei	Uberaba	West Palm	Yuyao
Shenzhen	Taiping	Uberlandia	Beach	Zabrze
Shepparton	Taiyuan	Udaipur	Wheaton	Zahedan
Sherbrooke	Ta'iz	Uddevalla	Whittier	Zalantun
Shihezi	Takaoka	Ujjain	Windsor	Zamora
Shimizu	Takasaki	Ulanhot	Witten	Zanjan
Shimoga	Takatsuki	Ulan Ude	Wolfsburg	Zaria
Shiraz	Tamale	Ulhasnagar	Wolverhampton	Zhambyl
Shishou	Tambov	Ulm	Wonsan	Zhangye
Shiyan	Tangail	Ur	Worcester	Zhangzhou
Shizuishan	Tangshan	Uruapán	Wuhai	Zhaodong
Shreveport	Tanis	Utica	Wuppertal	Zhaotong
Shuangyashan	Tanta	Utrecht	Würzburg	Zhdanov
Shymkent	Tapachula	Utsunomiya	Wuxi	Zhoukou
Sialkot	Tarnów	Vacaville	Wuzhong	Zhuhai
Siena	Tarsus	Valencia	Wuzhou	Zhumadian
Silistra	Tartu	Valera	Xiangfan	Zhuzhou
Simbirsk	Tegucigalpa	Valledupar	Xiangtan	Zigong
Simi Valley	Tel Aviv	Vallejo	Xianning	Zlatoust

TOWNS

Aalsmeer
Aanekoski
Abbeville
Abbot's Langley
Aberdare
Abergele
Aberystwyth
Abilene
Abingdon
Abomey
Abydos
Achinsk
Adoni
Adria
Agadez
Agrinion
Aigues-Mortes
Airdrie
Aix-la-Chapelle
Aix-les-Bains
Ajka
Akjoujt
Aksum
Albany
Albena
Albertville
Albi
Albufeira
Albury
Alcobaça
Alcobendas
Alcoy
Aldeburgh
Aldershot
Aleksinac
Alfortville
Alloa
Almadén
Almetyevsk
Alnwick
Altamira
Altamura
Altay
Altenburg
Alton
Altötting
Altrincham
Amalfi
Ambleside
Amersham
Ames
Amesbury
Amityville
Amroha
Amstetten
Anaconda
Anadarko
Anantapur
Andover

Andújar
Ané ho
Anniston
Ansbach
Antequera
Antigonish
Antony
Antsirabe
Anzhero-
   Sudzhensk
Apeldoorn
Aranjuez
Ararat
Arlington
   Heights
Armentières
Arrah
Artigas
Arundel
Arusha
Arzamas
Asamankese
Ashby-de-la-
   Zouch
Ashford
Ashington
Aspen
Assisi
Athlone
Atlantic City
Aubervilliers
Auchterarder
Auchtermuchty
Augusta
Aurangabad
Aviemore
Avranches
Axminster
Aylesbury
Aylesford
Ayr
Ayutthaya
Baabda
Baalbek
Babahoyo
Bacau
Baccarat
Baden
Baden-Baden
Badulla
Baeza
Bafoussam
Baharampur
Bahraich
Baikonur
Baiyin
Bajram Curri
Bakewell
Bakhchisarai

Balakovo
Balashikha
Balboa
Balbriggan
Balkh
Ballina
Bamburgh
Bamenda
Banbury
Bangor
Banja Luka
Banqiao
Barahona
Barcelona
Barcelos
Bardolino
Bar-le-Duc
Barnsley
Barnstaple
Barrow
Basildon
Batala
Batalha
Batangas City
Bath
Bathurst
Battle
Bat Yam
Bayeux
Bayreuth
Beaconsfield
Bearsden
Beaumaris
Beaumes de
   Venise
Beaune
Bebington
Béchar
Beckenham
Bedford
Bedlington
Bedworth
Beenleigh
Beersheba
Beipiao
Belize City
Bellagio
Belleville
Bendigo
Berchtesgaden
Berenice
Berkhamsted
Bernkastel
Berwick-upon-
   Tweed
Bhadravati
Bhamo
Bharatpur
Bhatinda

Bhatpara
Bhiwani
Bhusawal
Bicester
Bideford
Bijapur
Bilaspur
Billund
Binche
Bingerville
Birchington
Birkenhead
Bishop's
   Stortford
Biskra
Bjorneborg
Blackburn
Blagoevgrad
Blair Atholl
Blaj
Blantyre
Blois
Boa Vista
Boca Raton
Bodmin
Bodrum
Bofors
Bognor Regis
Bogor
Bole
Bolsover
Bolton
Bongor
Boston
Botosani
Boulder
Bourg-en-
   Bresse
Bournemouth
Bracknell
Braintree
Brampton
Breda
Brentwood
Bridgend
Bridgwater
Bridlington
Brighouse
Brighton
Bristol
Brive-la-
   Gaillarde
Brixham
Broken Hill
Bromsgrove
Browning
Buckingham
Bude
Bukavu

Bukittinggi
Bundaberg
Bundoran
Burnley
Burton upon
   Trent
Bury
Bury St.
   Edmunds
Buxton
Caerphilly
Cairns
Cajamarca
Calama
Caltanisetta
Calvi
Camberley
Camborne
Cambridge
Cana
Capua
Cardigan
Carefree
Carlisle
Carlsbad
Carmel
Carrara
Cashel
Casper
Cassino
Castlebar
Catanzaro
Celje
Cerignola
Cesena
Cessnock
Cetinje
Chalatenango
Châlon-sur-
   Saône
Chambéry
Chamonix
Changshu
Chantilly
Charlestown
Chartres
Château-Thierry
Chatham
Cheb
Chelles
Chelmsford
Chesham
Chesterfield
Chichester
Chieti
Chinon
Cholula
Chorley
Christchurch

TOWNS (cont.)

Cîmpulung
Cirencester
Cleethorpes
Clonakilty
Cloncurry
Clonmel
Cluny
Coalport
Coatbridge
Cockermouth
Coff's Harbour
Colchester
Colditz
Coleraine
Colwyn Bay
Comayagua
Coober Pedy
Cookstown
Cooktown
Cootamundra
Copiapó
Corby
Cornwall
Corozal
Cosenza
Cowes
Cox's Bazar
Craigavon
Cranbourne
Crawley
Cremona
Crewe
Cristobál
Cuddapah
Cuernavaca
Cuneo
Curepipe
Curicó
Dakhla
Dalandzadgad
Dalkeith
Dangriga
Darlington
Darmstad
Dartford
Dartmouth
Dawson Creek
Deal
Deauville
Dehiwala
Delft
Denbigh
Deolali
Deva
Dewsbury
Dhahran
Dharamsala
Dhule
Diekirch

Dinant
Dinard
Dindigul
Dingwall
Diredawa
Divinópolis
Dobrich
Dolores Hidalgo
Doncaster
Dongsheng
Dornbirn
Douai
Douglas
Downend
Downpatrick
Droitwich
Duffel
Dumfries
Dundalk
Dunhuang
Dun Laoghaire
Dunmow
Duras
Durg
Durham
Earlston
Eastbourne
East Dereham
East Kilbride
East Lansing
Ebbw Vale
Eccles
Edam
Eger
Eidsvoll
Eilat
Eisenach
Ekibastuz
Elbasan
El Centro
Elche
Elda
El Djem
Elektrostal
El Escorial
Elgin
El Jadida
Elvas
Ennis
Ensenada
Entebbe
Epernay
Epping
Epsom
Epworth
Esch-sur-Alzette
Escuintla
Esquipulas
Essaouira

Estoril
Esztergom
Etawah
Etruria
Evesham
Evora
Evreux
Exmouth
Faenza
Faizabad
Falaise
Falkirk
Fall River
Falmouth
Famagusta
Farnborough
Farnham
Farrukhabad
Fátima
Feldkirch
Ferrara
Fianarantsoa
Fier
Firozabad
Flagstaff
Flin Flon
Flint
Flores
Foggia
Fontainebleau
Forlí
Forster-
 Tuncurry
Fort Collins
Fort William
Francistown
Frascati
Frauenfeld
Freiberg
Gadag
Gafsa
Gaillac
Galashiels
Gällivare
Galt
Gamlakarleby
Gander
Gandhinagar
Ganganagar
Garoua
Gateshead
Gattinara
Genk
Getafe
Gettysburg
Ghardaïa
Ghazni
Gillingham
Gitega

Glace Bay
Glastonbury
Glenrothes
Gneizeno
Godalming
Godhavn
Gomorrah
Gondar
Gondia
Gorazde
Gorgan
Görlitz
Gosport
Göttingen
Gouda
Gourock
Grafton
Gramsh
Grangemouth
Grantham
Grasse
Gravesend
Great Malvern
Great Yarmouth
Greifswald
Grevená
Grootfontein
Guarda
Guaymas
Gubbio
Guelph
Guéret
Guildford
Guise
Haddington
Ha'il
Hailar
Hakone
Halabja
Halden
Halesowen
Halifax
Hamilton
Hammamet
Hapur
Harlow
Harpers Ferry
Hartlepool
Hastings
Hatfield
Havant
Hawick
Heihei
Heinola
Helensburgh
Hengelo
Herculaneum
High Wycombe
Hillerod

Hilversum
Hitchin
Hof
Holguin
Hospet
Hotan
Houma
Hove
Hradec Králové
Huancavelica
Huangshan
Huánuco
Huddersfield
Huntingdon
Hwange
Idlib
Igualada
Ilkley
Imatra
Interlaken
Ioánnina
Ipswich
Iringa
Irvine
Iznik
Jackson
Jalgaon
Jalna
Jarrow
Järvenpää
Jedburgh
Jena
Jihlava
Jijiga
Jinja
Jipijapa
Jiuquan
Joliette
Jonquière
Jos
Kajaani
Kalgoorlie
Kalulushi
Kamakura
Kampen
Kankan
Kansk
Kanye
Kapfenberg
Karaikkudi
Kardhítsa
Kariba
Karlovac
Karlsruhe
Karlstad
Karnal
Karshi
Kashan
Kastoriá

TOWNS (cont.)

Kateríni	La Roche-sur-	Lytham Saint	Montbéliard	Nuneaton
Katihar	Yon	Anne's	Montélimar	Nyiregyháza
Kaufbeuren	La Serena	Macapá	Montreux	Oak Lawn
Kavieng	Latacunga	Macclesfield	Monywa	Oak Park
Keetmanshoop	Latina	Macerata	Moose Jaw	Oakville
Kendal	Latur	Machakos	Morecambe	Odienné
Kenilworth	Lausanne	Machala	Morogoro	Oldenburg
Kerava	Le Cannet	Mafra	Morpeth	Oldham
Kerkrade	Lecce	Magenta	Morristown	Olmos
Keswick	Le Creusot	Mahalapye	Morwell	Omagh
Kettering	Legnica	Maidenhead	Moshi	Onitsha
Khandwa	Leh	Maidstone	Motala	Orange
Kharagpur	Leiria	Maiduguri	Moulay Idriss	Orange Walk
Khaylitsa	Le Lamentin	Maikop	Moulins	Orapa
Khiva	Le Mans	Maitland	Mount Isa	Oristano
Khouribga	Lens	Malmédy	Mount Prospect	Orlova
Kidderminster	Leoben	Malmesbury	Mullingar	Ornsköldsvik
Kilifi	Leonding	Mandurah	Mutare	Orvieto
Kilkís	Les Abymes	Mandya	Muzzaffarnagar	Osorno
Killarney	Les Mureaux	Mantua	Muzzaffarpur	Otavalo
Kilmarnock	Letchworth	Manzini	Mwanza	Ottery St. Mary
Kineshma	Lethbridge	Maradi	Naas	Overland Park
King's Lynn	Leticia	Marbella	Nabeul	Paarl
Kinross	Lewes	Maroochydore	Nablus	Pagan
Kirkcaldy	Leyland	Maroua	Nadiad	Paignton
Kirkcudbright	Lichfield	Marsala	Nampula	Pailin
Kirkenes	Lifford	Masaya	Napa	Paisley
Kirkwall	Likasi	Mascara	Navan	Pakse
Kirriemuir	Limassol	Massa	Nazareth	Palm Beach
Kiruna	Limbe	Masvingo	Neath	Palmerston
Kitty Hawk	Limoux	Matera	Nerja	North
Klosterneuburg	Linares	Matlock	Newbury	Panipat
Kodok	Linlithgow	Maun	Newcastle	Paphos
Korhogo	Linköping	Mazatenango	under Lyme	Parbhani
Koudougou	Lisburn	Mbeya	Newmarket	Paris-Plage
Kourou	Lisdoonvarna	Mdina	New Plymouth	Pasig
Kouvola	Lismore	Medina	Newport	Passau
Kralendijk	Llandudno	Mégara	Newquay	Patan
Kraljevo	Llanelli	Mejicanos	Newton Abbot	Pau
Kranj	Llangollen	Melitopol	Newton Aycliffe	Pavlograd
Krasnyy Luch	Lobatse	Melk	Newton St.	Pazardzhik
Krefeld	Lockerbie	Melton	Boswells	Pec
Krosno	Logroño	Melton	Newtownabbey	Penzance
Krugersdorp	Loja	Mowbray	Neyshabur	Pervouralsk
Krusevac	Long Eaton	Melun	Ngaoundéré	Pesaro
Kusadasi	Lons-le-Saunier	Mende	Nijmegen	Peterlee
Kyustendil	Lorca	Meriden	Nitra	Pirmasens
La Ciotat	Loreto	Merthyr Tydfil	Nizamabad	Pitesti
Ladysmith	Los Alamos	Meru	Nkongsamba	Plauen
Lagos	Loughborough	Miami Beach	Nokia	Plymouth
Laguna Beach	Lourdes	Middlesbrough	Nome	Point-à-Pitre
La Jolla	Lowestoft	Milagro	Northallerton	Pokrovsk
La Laguna	Lubango	Milton Keynes	Northampton	Glazov
Lambersart	Lucca	Mödling	North Little	Polonnaruwa
Laon	Lüderitz	Mohács	Rock	Ponferrada
La Oroya	Lugano	Mold	North Shields	Pontefract
Laredo	Lugo	Molepolole	North Shields	Pontypool
Larnaca	Lushnje	Monastir	Norwich	Pontypridd
Larne	Luton	Moncton	Nottingham	Poole
			Novara	

TOWNS (cont.)

Porbandar	Rosenheim	Silver City	Szolnok	Veliko Turnovo
Portalegre	Rosyth	Simferopol	Tahoua	Vellore
Port Dickson	Rotherham	Sincelejo	Tamworth	Vénissieux
Port el Kantaoui	Rothesay	Sintra	Taree	Vercelli
Port Macquarie	Rotorua	Sion	Tarija	Verdun
Portmeirion	Rottweil	Sitka	Taroudant	Versailles
Portoviejo	Roubaix	Skegness	Tatabánya	Verviers
Port Sunlight	Rovaniemi	Skellefteå	Taunton	Veszprém
Port Talbot	Rugby	Skelmersdale	Taupo	Viana do
Potenza	Runcorn	Skokie	Tauranga	Castelo
Presov	Rustavi	Slavonsky Brod	Taza	Viborg
Preston	Sagar	Sliema	Telde	Vichy
Préveza	St. Andrews	Slough	Telford	Vidin
Prince George	St. Charles	Smederovo	Temirtau	Viedma
Princeton	St. Emilion	Sneek	Tennant Creek	Vila do Conde
Privas	St. Helens	Sodom	Teresina	Vila Real
Prizren	St. Helier	Sohag	Terni	Villach
Proddatur	Saint-Hubert	Solihull	Tetovo	Viña del Mar
Prome	St-Malo	Solikamsk	Tewantin	Viseu
Pucallpa	St-Nazaire	Sondrio	Thane	Viterbo
Puerto Plata	St. Peter Port	Sonoma	Thetford	Wadi Halfa
Pula	St-Quentin	Sonsonate	Thimphu	Wakefield
Puno	Salinas	Sopron	Thionville	Wallasey
Punta Gorda	Salisbury	Soria	Thun	Wallsend
Puqi	Sambalpur	Sorrento	Tiberias	Walsall
Puri	Sambhal	Southport	Tighina	Wangaratta
Purnia	Sangli ·	South Shields	Tijuana	Wantage
Qazvin	Sankt Pölten	Soyapango	Timimoun	Warrington
Qena	San Sebastian	Sozopol	Tindouf	Warrnambool
Queluz	Santa Barbara	Spa	Tiruppur	Warwick
Rabaul	Santa Maria	Spanish Town	Tokaj	Washington
Raichur	Sarasota	Sparks	Tombstone	Waterbury
Rajapalayam	Saumur	Spoleto	Torquay	Waterloo
Rambouillet	Sausalito	Sremska	Tourcoing	Watford
Rampur	Savannakhet	Mitrovica	Tralee	Weimar
Ramsgate	Savona	Stafford	Traun	Welkom
Randers	Sayama	Staines	Travnik	Wels
Ratlam	Scarborough	Stamford	Trim	Welwyn Garden
Rauma	Schwabach	Stavanger	Troon	City
Reading	Schweinfurt	Stellenbosch	Trowbridge	West Bromwich
Redcar	Scunthorpe	Stevenage	Tskhinvali	Westerham
Redding	Sedan	Steyr	Tübingen	Weston-super-
Redditch	Seinäjoki	Stockport	Tumkur	Mare
Redondo Beach	Seixal	Stockton-on-	Turpan	West Orange
Reigate	Selby	Tees	Tuticorin	Wethersfield
Remscheid	Selebi-Phikwe	Stornoway	Tuzla	Weymouth
Reus	Sensuntepeque	Strabane	Tychy	Whitby
Richmond	Seraing	Stretford	Udhagaman-	Whyalla
Richmond Hill	Sergiyev Posad	Stroud	dalam	Wichita Falls
Ringkøbing	Serowe	Struga	Udine	Wick
Ringsted	Sevenoaks	Strumica	Ulundi	Widnes
Riobamba	Sharpeville	Suceava	Urbino	Wiener
Río Tinto	Sheerness	Suhl	Vác	Neustadt
Rivera	Shibin el Kom	Sukhotal	Valenciennes	Wigan
Rochdale	Shrewsbury	Sunbury	Varadero	Williamsburg
Rochester	Siauliai	Sundsvall	Varazdin	Wilton
Rockingham	Sidi-bel-Abbès	Swakopmund	Varese	Winchester
Rohtak	Siegen	Swindon	Varna	Windsor
Ronda	Sikasso	Szekszárd	Vaslui	Winnetka

TOWNS (cont.)

Winona	Wolfsberg	Xánthi	Zadar	Zoetermeer
Winterthur	Woodstock	Xochimilco	Zagazig	Zouerate
Wisbech	Worksop	Yeovil	Zalaegerszeg	Zrenjanin
Wittenberg	Worms	Yorktown	Zielona Gora	Zwolle
Woking	Worthing	Youghal	Zinder	
Wokingham	Wrexham	Zaanstad	Zlin	

VILLAGES

Aberfoyle	Capo di Monte	Gort	Piltdown
Abu Simbel	Caprese	Gotham	Plassey
Agincourt	Michelangelo	Grasmere	Pompadour
Aihole	Carnac	Greenwich Village	Port Arthur
Albarracin	Catskill	Gretna Green	Prestonpans
Aldermaston	Cawdor	Gruyère	Quatre Bras
Aldwinkle	Cerne Abbas	Hallstatt	Ramillies
Alloway	Certaldo	Harlech	Rocamadour
Annapolis Royal	Chablis	Hattusas	Roquefort-sur-
Assen	Chavín de Huántar	Hell	Soulzon
Avebury	Chawton	Helpston	Rouffignac
Ayia Napa	Cheddar	Higher Walton	Rydal
Ayot St. Lawrence	Churchill	Hillsborough	San Simeon
Badminton	Clifden	Holne	Scone
Balaclava	Clouds Hill	Jerash	Selborne
Ballymahon	Clovelly	John o' Groats	Serowe
Ballymote	Cockburnspath	Karnak	Shaoshan
Balquhidder	Crécy	King's Cliffe	Silchester
Baniyas	Crosthwaite	Kinnesswood	Skara Brae
Bannockburn	Culloden	Lassa	Solferino
Barbizon	Dettingen	Laxton	St. David's
Battenberg	Dien Bien Phu	Lidice	Steventon
Beaulieu	Down Ampney	Lipizza	Stilton
Belsen	Downe	Llanfairpwll-	Sutton Courtenay
Bergamo	Dunmow	gwyngyllgo-	Ticonderoga
Bishopsbourne	Dunwich	gerychwyrn-	Tintagel
Bisley	East Bergholt	drobwllllan-	Tolpuddle
Blarney	East Budleigh	tysiliogogogoch	Tordesillas
Blenheim	East Coker	Longmen	Tremadoc
Bodhgaya	Eastwood	Malplaquet	Uffington
Bogazköy	Ecclefechan	Marengo	Waitangi
Borodino	Elis	Matmata	Walsingham
Borstal	Elstow	Mayerling	Warnham
Bournville	Eversley	Maynooth	Waterloo
Boys Town	Farndon	Monbazillac	West Malvern
Braemar	Flodden	Naseby	Westward Ho
Bramber	Folsom	Oberammergau	Widecombe-in-the-
Bray	Fort Raleigh	Oystermouth	Moor
Buchenwald	Fotheringhay	Palenque	Woburn
Callanish	Ganvie	Panmunjom	Yattenden
Camembert	Glamis	Passchendaele	Zelazowa Wola
Camperdown	Glynde	Pattaya	
Capernaum	Gorgonzola	Peenemunde	

OCEANS AND SEAS

Adriatic Sea
Aegean Sea
Andaman Sea
Antarctic Ocean
Arabian Sea
Arafura Sea
Aral Sea
Arctic Ocean
Atlantic Ocean
Azov, Sea of
Baltic Sea
Banda Sea

Barents Sea
Beaufort Sea
Bering Sea
Black Sea
Caribbean Sea
Caspian Sea
China Sea
Coral Sea
Dead Sea
East China Sea
Galilee, Sea of
Greenland Sea

Indian Ocean
Inland Sea
Ionian Sea
Irish Sea
Japan, Sea of
Java Sea
Kara Sea
Laptev Sea
Ligurian Sea
Marmara, Sea of
Mediterranean Sea
North Sea

Okhotsk, Sea of
Pacific Ocean
Red Sea
Ross Sea
Sargasso Sea
Savu Sea
South China Sea
Tasman Sea
Weddell Sea
White Sea
Yellow Sea

LAKES, LOCHS, AND LOUGHS
(with location)

Albert	Uganda, Democratic Republic of Congo	Ericht	Scotland
		Erie	Canada, USA
Aral Sea	Kazakhstan, Uzbekistan	Erne	Northern Ireland
Athabasca	Canada	Esthwaite	England
Awe	Scotland	Eyre	Australia
Baikal	Russia	Flathead	USA
Balaton	Hungary	Foyle	Ireland
Bala	Wales	Garda	Italy
Balkhash	Kazakhstan	Geneva	Switzerland, France
Bangweulu	Zambia	Grasmere	England
Bassenthwaite	England	Great Lake	USA, Canada; Australia
Bear	USA	Great Bear	Canada
Becharof	USA	Great Salt Lake	USA
Belfast	Northern Ireland	Great Slave	Canada
Breydon	England	Hawes Water	England
Buttermere	England	Hickling Broad	England
Caspian Sea	Iran, Russia, Azerbaijan, Kazakhstan, Turkmenistan	Huron	USA, Canada
		Ijsselmeer *or* Ysselmeer	The Netherlands
Celyn	Wales	Iliamna	USA
Central Park Lake	USA	Issyk-kul	Kyrgyzstan
Chad	Chad, Niger, Nigeria, Cameroon	Kara-Bogaz-Gol	Turkmenistan
		Kariba	Zambia, Zimbabwe
Champlain	USA	Katrine	Scotland
Chiemsee	Germany	Kivu	Democratic Republic of Congo, Rwanda
Clark	USA		
Clywedog	Wales	Koko Nor	China
Como	Italy	Kyoga *or* Kioga	Uganda
Coniston	England	Ladoga	Russia
Constance	Germany	Lake of the Woods	Canada
Corrib	Republic of Ireland	Leech	USA
Cwellyn	Wales	Léman	Switzerland, France
Dall	USA	Leven	Scotland
Derg	Republic of Ireland	Lochy	Scotland
Derwent Water	England	Lomond	Scotland
Dongting	China	Lop Nur *or*	
Edward	Uganda, Democratic Republic of Congo	Lop Nor	China
		Lucerne	Switzerland
Ennerdale	England	Maggiore	Italy, Switzerland

LAKES, LOCHS, AND LOUGHS (cont.)
(with location)

Malawi	Malawi, Tanzania, Mozambique
Manitoba	Canada
Maracaibo	Venezuela
Maree	Scotland
Martin	USA
Mask	Republic of Ireland
Menindee	Australia
Michigan	USA
Mille Lacs	USA
Mobutu	Uganda, Democratic Republic of Congo
Moosehead	USA
Naknek	USA
Nasser	Egypt
Natron	Tanzania
Neagh	Northern Ireland
Nemi	Italy
Ness	Scotland
Neusiedl	Austria, Hungary
Nicaragua	Nicaragua
Nipigon	Canada
Nu Jiang	China, Myanmar – formerly Burma
Nyasa *or* Nyassa	Malawi, Tanzania, Mozambique
Okeechobee	USA
Onega	Russia
Ontario	Canada, USA
Oulton Broad	England
Padarn	Wales
Pend Oreille	USA
Peipus	Russia, Estonia
Pontchartrain	USA
Poyang *or* P'o-yang	China
Pyramid	USA
Qinghai Hu	China
Rainy	USA
Rannoch	Scotland
Red Tarn	England
Ree	Republic of Ireland
Reindeer	Canada
Rudolf	Kenya, Ethiopia
Rutland	England
Rydal Water	England

Saimaa	Finland
St Clair	USA, Canada
St James's Park Lake	England
Salton Sea	USA
Serpentine, The	England
Strangford	Northern Ireland
Superior	USA, Canada
Tahoe	USA
Tana	Ethiopia
Tanganyika	Democratic Republic of Congo, Burundi, Tanzania, Zambia
Taupo	New Zealand
Tay	Scotland
Tegid	Wales
Teshekpuk	USA
Thirlmere	England
Titicaca	Peru, Bolivia
Tonle Sap	Cambodia
Torrens	Australia
Trasimeno	Italy
Tsana	Ethiopia
Tungting *or* Tung-t'ing	China
Turkana	Kenya, Ethiopia
Tustumena	USA
Ugashik	USA
Ullswater	England
Upper Klamath	USA
Urmia	Iran
Utah	USA
Van	Turkey
Vänern	Sweden
Victoria	Uganda, Tanzania, Kenya
Vierwaldstättersee	Switzerland
Volta	Ghana
Vyrnwy	Wales
Wast Water	England
Windermere	England
Winnebago	USA
Winnibigoshish	USA
Winnipeg	Canada
Yellowstone	USA

RIVERS
(with location)

Adda	Italy	Danube	Germany, Austria,
Adige	Italy		Romania, Hungary,
Adur	England		Slovakia, Bulgaria
Ain	France	Darling	Australia
Aire	England; France	Dart	England
Aisne	France	Dee	Scotland; Wales, England
Allan	Scotland; Syria	Demerara	Guyana
Aller	Spain; Germany	Derwent	England
Allier	France	Dnepr	Russia, Belarus, Ukraine
Aln	England	Dnestr	Ukraine, Moldova
Amazon	Peru, Brazil	Don	Russia; Scotland, England;
Amu Darya	Turkmenistan, Uzbekistan		France; Australia
Amur	Mongolia, Russia, China	Doon	Scotland
Angara	Russia	Dordogne	France
Annan	Scotland	Doubs	France, Switzerland
Araguaia	Brazil	Douro	Spain, Portugal
Arkansas	USA	Dove	England
Arno	Italy	Dovey	Wales
Arun	Nepal	Drava	Italy, Austria, Yugoslavia,
Assiniboine	Canada		Hungary
Athabasca	Canada	Duero	Spain
Aube	France	Durance	France
Avon	England	Dvina	Russia
Bann	Northern Ireland	Ebro	Spain
Beas	India	Eden	England, Scotland
Benue	Nigeria	Elbe	Germany, Czech Republic
Bermejo	Argentina	Emba	Kazakhstan
Bío-Bío	Chile	Ems	Germany, The
Brahmaputra	Tibet, India		Netherlands
Brent	England	Escaut	Belgium, France
Bug	Ukraine, Poland, Germany	Esk	Australia
Bure	England	Essequibo	Guyana
Camel	England	Euphrates	Iraq
Cam	England	Exe	England
Canadian	USA	Fal	England
Cauvery	India	Fly	Papua New Guinea
Chang Jiang	China	Forth	Scotland
Chao Phraya	Thailand	Fraser	Canada
Charente	France	Frome	Australia
Chari	Cameroon, Chad	Gambia	The Gambia, Senegal
Chenab	Pakistan	Ganges	India
Cher	France	Garonne	France
Churchill	Canada	Gironde	France
Cherwell	England	Glomma	Norway
Clutha	New Zealand	Godavari	India
Clyde	Scotland; Canada	Great Ouse	England
Colne	England	Guadalquivir	Spain
Coln	England	Han	China
Colorado	USA	Hawkesbury	Australia
Columbia	USA	Helmand	Afghanistan
Congo	Congo, Democratic	Hooghly	India
	Republic of Congo –	Hsi Chiang	China
	formerly Zaïre	Huang Ho	China
Cooper	Australia	Hudson	USA
Coppermine	Canada	Hunter	Australia
Coquet	England	Indus	India, Pakistan, China
Crouch	England	Irrawaddy	Myanmar – formerly
Damodar	India		Burma

RIVERS (cont.)
(with location)

Irtysh	China, Kazakhstan, Russia	Missouri	USA
Isis	England	Mole	England
Itchen	England	Monnow	England, Wales
James	USA; Australia	Moselle	Germany
Japurá	Brazil	Mureş	Romania, Hungary
Jordan	Israel, Jordan	Murray	Australia; Canada
Juba	Ethiopia, Somalia	Murrumbidgee	Australia
Jumna	India	Neckar	Germany
Juruá	Brazil	Negro	Spain; Brazil, Argentina,
Kafue	Zambia		Bolivia, Paraguay,
Kama	Russia		Uruguay, Venezuela
Kasai	Angola, Democratic	Neisse	Poland, Germany
	Republic of Congo –	Neman	Belarus, Lithuania
	formerly Zaïre	Niger	Nigeria, Mali, Guinea
Kolyma	Russia	Nile	Sudan, Egypt
Kuban	Russia	Ob	Russia
Kura	Turkey, Georgia,	Oder	Germany, Czech Republic,
	Azerbaijan		Poland
Kwa	Democratic Republic of	Ogooué	Gabon
	Congo – formerly Zaïre	Ohio	USA
Lachlan	Australia	Oise	France
Lagan	Northern Ireland	Orange	South Africa
Lahn	Germany	Orontes	Syria
Lea	England	Orwell	England
Lech	Germany, Austria	Otter	England
Lee	Republic of ireland	Ouse	England
Lena	Russia	Oxus	Turkmenistan, Uzbekistan
Liffey	Republic of Ireland	Paraguay	Paraguay
Limpopo	South Africa, Zimbabwe,	Paraná	Brazil
	Mozambique	Peace	Canada, USA
Lippe	Germany	Pearl	USA; China
Loddon	Australia; England	Pechora	Russia
Loire	France	Pecos	USA
Lot	France	Peel	Australia; USA
Lualaba	Democratic Republic of	Piave	Italy
	Congo – formerly Zaïre	Platte	USA
Lune	England	Po	Italy
Lüne	Germany	Potomac	USA
Maas	Netherlands	Purus	Brazil
Mackenzie	Australia	Putumayo	Ecuador
Madeira	Brazil	Rance	France
Magdalena	Colombia	Ravi	India, Pakistan
Main	Germany	Rede	England
Mamoré	Brazil, Bolivia	Red	USA
Manawatu	New Zealand	Rhine	Switzerland, Germany,
Marañón	Brazil, Peru		The Netherlands
Maritsa	Bulgaria	Ribble	England
Marne	France	Río Bravo	Mexico
Maros	Indonesia	Río de la Plata	Argentina, Uruguay
Medina	USA	Rio Grande	Jamaica
Medway	England	Ruhr	Germany
Mekong	Laos, China	Rur	Germany
Menderes	Turkey	Rye	England
Mersey	England	Saale	Germany
Meuse	France, Belgium	Saar	Germany, France
Minho	Spain, Portugal	Saguenay	Canada
Miño	Spain	Salado	Argentina; Cuba; Mexico
Mississippi	USA		

RIVERS (cont.)
(with location)

Salween	Myanmar – formerly Burma, China	Tamar	England
		Tarn	France
Saône	France	Tawe	Wales
Saskatchewan	Canada	Tawi	India
Scheldt	Belgium	Tay	Scotland
Seine	France	Tees	England
Senegal	Senegal	Tejo	Brazil
Severn	England	Tennessee	USA
Shannon	Republic of Ireland	Test	England
Shatt al-Arab	Iran, Iraq	Thames	England
Shenandoah	USA	Tiber	Italy
Slave	Canada	Ticino	Italy, Switzerland
Snake	USA	Tigris	Iraq, Turkey
Somme	France	Torridge	England
Songhua	Vietnam, China	Trent	England
Spey	Scotland	Tugela	South Africa
St John	Liberia; USA	Tunguska	Russia
St Lawrence	USA	Tweed	England, Scotland
Stour	England	Tyne	Scotland, England
Sungari	China	Ural	Russia, Kazakhstan
Susquehanna	USA	Ure	England
Sutlej	Pakistan, India, China	Uruguay	Uruguay, Brazil
Swale	England	Usk	Wales, England
Swannee or		Ussuri	China, Russia
Suwannee	USA	Vaal	South Africa
Syr Darya	Uzbekistan, Kazakhstan	Vienne	France
Taff	Wales	Vistula	Poland
Tagus	Portugal, Spain	Vltava	Czech Republic
Tajo	Spain	Volga	Russia; USA

MOUNTAINS
(with location)

Aconcagua	Argentina	Dykh-Tau	Russia
Annapurna	Nepal	Elbrus	Russia
Ararat	Turkey	Etna	Italy
Ben Nevis	Scotland	Everest	Nepal, Tibet
Bonete	Argentina	Fujiyama	Japan
Carrantuohill	Republic of Ireland	Huascarán	Peru
Chimborazo	Ecuador	Jaya	Indonesia
Citlaltépetl	Mexico	K2 or Godwin-Austen	India
Communism Peak	Tajikistan	Kanchenjunga	Nepal, India
Cotopaxi	Ecuador	Kenya	Kenya
Damavand	Iran	Kilimanjaro	Tanzania
Dufourspitze	Switzerland	Kinabalu	Malaysia

MOUNTAINS (cont.)
(with location)

Logan	Canada
McKinley	USA
Makalu I	Nepal, Tibet
Margherita	Democratic Republic of Congo – formerly Zaïre, Rwanda
Matterhorn	Switzerland, Italy
Mont Blanc	France, Italy
Muztag	China
Nanga Parbat	Pakistan
Ojos del Salado	Argentina, Chile
Pissis	Argentina
Pobedy	Kyrgyzstan
Popocatépetl	Mexico
Ras Dashen	Ethiopia
St Elias	USA, Canada
Scafell Pike	England
Slieve Donard	Northern Ireland
Snowdon	Wales
Tirich Mir	Pakistan
Tupungato	Argentina, Chile
Weisshorn	Switzerland

MOUNTAIN RANGES
(with location)

Alps	France, Switzerland, Italy, Austria, Liechtenstein
Altai	Kazakhstan, China, Mongolia
Andes	Venezuela, Colombia, Ecuador, Peru, Bolivia, Argentina, Chile
Apennine Hills	Italy
Appalachians	USA
Atlas Mountains	Morocco, Algeria, Tunisia
Balkan Mountains	Bulgaria
Bernese Alps	Switzerland
Black Mountains	Wales
Blue Mountains	Australia
Blue Ridge Mountains	USA
Brecon Beacons	Wales
Cairngorms	Scotland
Cambrian Mountains	Wales
Cantabrian Mountains	Spain
Carpathians	Czech Republic, Slovakia, Poland, Romania, Ukraine
Caucasus Mountains	Russia, Georgia, Azerbaijan, Armenia
Cévennes	France
Coast Mountains	Canada
Cumbrian Mountains	England
Dolomites	Italy
Drakensberg Mountains	South Africa, Lesotho
Flinders Range	Australia
Ghats Range	India
Golan Heights	Israel
Grampian Mountains	Scotland
Hamersley Range	Australia
Harz Mountains	Germany
Himalayas	China, India, Pakistan, Nepal, Bhutan
Hindu Kush	Afghanistan, Pakistan
Hoggar Mountains	Algeria
Jura Mountains	France, Switzerland
Kaikoura Ranges	New Zealand
Karakoram Range	Afghanistan, Pakistan, China, India
Kunlun Shan	China
Ladakh Range	India, Pakistan, China
MacDonnell Ranges	Australia
Middleback Ranges	Australia
Macgillicuddy's Reeks	Republic of Ireland
Mourne Mountains	Northern Ireland
Musgrave Ranges	Australia
North West Highlands	Scotland
Olympic Mountains	USA
Pamir Mountains	Tajikistan, China, Afghanistan
Pennines	England
Pindus Mountains	Greece, Albania
Pyrenees	France, Spain
Rocky Mountains or Rockies	USA, Canada
Sayan Mountains	Russia
Sierra Madre Range	Mexico
Sierra Morena Range	Spain
Sierra Nevada Range	USA
Smoky Mountains or Smokies	USA
Snowy Mountains	Australia
Taurus Mountains	Turkey
Tien Shan	Kyrgyzstan, China, Mongolia
Ural Mountains	Russia
Zagros Mountains	Iran

VOLCANOES
(with location)

Acatenango	Guatemala
Agung	Indonesia
Alcedo	Galapagos Islands, Ecuador
Ambrim	Vanuatu
Amburombu	Indonesia
Asama	Japan
Askja	Iceland
Aso	Japan
Atitlan	Guatemala
Awu	Indonesia
Bandai-san	Japan
Bárcena	Mexico
Bogoslof	USA
Buleng	Indonesia
Bulusan	Philippines
Cameroon	Cameroon
Capelinhos	Azores
Cerro Negro	Nicaragua
Chances Peak	Montserrat
Chimborazo	Ecuador
Cleveland	USA
Colima	Mexico
Coseguina	Nicaragua
Cotacachi	Ecuador
Cotopaxi	Ecuador
Demavend	Iran
Dempo	Indonesia
Didicas	Philippines
Dukono	Indonesia
El Misti	Peru
Erebus	Antarctica
Etna	Sicily, Italy
Fogo	Cape Verde
Fonualei	Tongas
Fuego	Guatemala
Fujiyama	Japan
Galeras	Colombia
Gamkonora	Indonesia
Gede	Indonesia
Great Sitkin	USA
Grimsvötn	Iceland
Guallatiri	Chile
Hekla	Iceland
Hibok Hibok	Philippines

Huainaputina	Peru
Hualalai	USA
Izalco	El Salvador
Jorullo	Mexico
Kaba	Indonesia
Katla	Iceland
Katmai	USA
Kerintji	Indonesia
Kilauea	USA
Kilimanjaro	Tanzania
Krakatau	Indonesia
Krakatoa	Indonesia
Laki	Iceland
Lascar	Chile
La Soufrière	Montserrat
Lassen	USA
Llaima	Chile
Long Island	Papua New Guinea
Lopevi	Vanuatu
Manam	Papua New Guinea
Marapi	Indonesia
Martin	USA
Mauna Kea	Hawaii, USA
Mauna Loa	Hawaii, USA
Mayon	Philippines
Meakan	Japan
Merapi	Indonesia
Mihara	Japan
Miyakejima	Japan
Momotombo	Nicaragua
Mount Saint Helens	USA
Myozin-syo	Japan
Ngauruhoe	New Zealand
Nila	Indonesia
Niuafo'ou	Tonga
Noyoe	Iceland
Nyamiagira	Democratic Republic of Congo
Nyiragongo	Democratic Republic of Congo
Okmok	USA

Ometepe	Nicaragua
O'shima	Japan
Osorno	Chile
Pacaya	Guatemala
Paloe	Indonesia
Paricutin	Mexico
Pavlof	USA
Pelée	Caribbean
Pinatubo	Indonesia
Poas	Costa Rica
Popocatapetl	Mexico
Puracé	Colombia
Puyehue	Chile
Rindjani	Indonesia
Rininahue	Chile
Ruapehu	New Zealand
Sabrina	Azores
Sangay	Ecuador
Sangeang	Indonesia
Santa Maria	Guatemala
Santorini	Greece
Semeru	Indonesia
Shishaldin	USA
Siau	Indonesia
Slamat	Indonesia
Soputan	Indonesia
Spurr	USA
Stromboli	Italy
Surtsey	Iceland
Taal	Philippines
Tacana	Guatemala
Tarawera	New Zealand
Ternate	Indonesia
Tjareme	Indonesia
Tokachi	Japan
Tongariro	New Zealand
Torbert	USA
Trident	USA
Tungurahua	Ecuador
Tupungatito	Chile
Unauna	Indonesia
Vesuvius	Italy
Villarrica	Chile
Vulcano	Italy
White Island	New Zealand
Yakedake	Japan

MOTORLESS VEHICLES

barouche	carry-all	dray	jaunting car	tarantass
bicycle	cart	droshky	landau	tilbury
brake	chaise	equipage	oxcart	trap
break	chariot	fiacre	phaeton	tricycle
britzka	clarence	fly	post-chaise	trishaw
brougham	coach	four-in-hand	prairie schooner	tumbril
buckboard	coach-and-four	gharry	rickshaw	Victoria
buggy	Conestoga	gig	rig	vis-à-vis
cab	wagon	hackney	rockaway	wagon
calash	covered wagon	hansom	spider phaeton	wagonette
Cape cart	curricle	hay-cart	stagecoach	wain
carriage	dog cart	haywain	sulky	wheelbarrow
carriole	drag	herdic	surrey	

MOTOR VEHICLES

ambulance	convertible	go-kart	motor caravan	snowmobile
armoured car	coupé	golf cart	off-roader	snowplough
articulated lorry	crash wagon	gritter	omnibus	soft top
automatic	*Am.*	hackney cab	open top	sports car
automobile	crawler tractor	half-track	people carrier	station wagon
beach buggy	delivery truck	hard top	*or* mover	steamroller
bloodmobile	digger	hatchback	public service	stock car
Am.	Dormobile™	hearse	vehicle *or* PSV	streetcar
bookmobile	double-decker	HGV	racing car	stretch
Am.	bus	hot hatch	rally car	limousine
bowser	dragster	hot rod	recreational	tanker
bubble car	DUKW *or* duck	JCB™	vehicle *or* RV	taxi
bulldozer	dune buggy	Jeep™	*Am.*	tourer
bus	dustcart	juggernaut	refrigerated van	tracklayer
cab	electric car	kart	removal van	tractor
cabriolet	estate	Land Rover™	roadster	trailer
camper	fire engine	limousine	runabout	tram
car	float	lorry	saloon	transporter
carryall *Am.*	fork-lift truck	low-loader	sedan *Am.*	trolleybus
car transporter	four-wheel	mammy wagon	semitrailer	truck
Caterpillar™	drive car	milk float	shooting brake	van
charabanc	garbage truck	Mini™	single-decker	wagon *or*
coach	*Am.*	mobile home	bus	waggon

VEHICLE PARTS

accelerator	brake	crankcase	flywheel	hood *Am.*
alternator	brake drum	cruise control	four-wheel	horn
anti-lock brake	brake light	cylinder	drive	hydraulic brake
anti-roll bar	bucket seat	cylinder head	freewheel	hydraulic
automatic	bumper	dashboard *or*	gate	suspension
choke	camshaft	dash	gauge	hypoid gear
automatic	carburettor	differential gear	gear	ignition
transmission	catalytic	disc brake	gearbox	ignition key
axle	converter	distributor	gear lever	indicator
bench seat	chassis	driving wheel	generator	manifold
blinker	clutch	drum brake	grille	mileometer
bodywork	connecting rod	fender *Am.*	hazard warning	monocoque
bonnet	cowl	filler cap	light	muffler
boot	crank	fluid drive	headlight	number plate

VEHICLE PARTS (cont.)

odometer *Am.*	rack-and-pinion	shift *Am.*	starter	tachograph
oil gauge	radial tyre	shock absorber	starter motor	tailpipe
overrider	radiator	sidelight	steering column	tail wheel
overrun brake	radius rod	silencer	steering gear	top gear
piston	reach	solenoid	steering wheel	tow bar
pneumatic tyre	reflector	spark plug	stick	track rod
power brakes	reverse	speedometer	stick shift *Am.*	transmission
power steering	running board	splashboard	stop light	winker
propeller shaft	shaft	sprag	suspension	wing

FAMOUS LOCOMOTIVES AND TYPES OF LOCOMOTIVE

Aerotrain	*Catch-Me-Who-Can*	Mikado	*Puffing Billy*
American Standard	Consolidation	Mistral	*Rocket*
Beyer-Garrett	*Flying Scotsman*	Mogul	*Royal George*
Big Boy	Fuel Foiler	*New Castle*	*Sans Pareil*
Blücher	Le Lyonnais	*Novelty*	Shuttle
Bullet train	*Locomotion*	Orient Express	Train à Grande
Capitole	*Mallard*	*Pioneer*	Vitesse *or* TGV

SHIPS AND BOATS

amphibious landing craft	DUKW *or* duck	mailboat	sailing ship
barge	E-boat	monkey-boat	sampan
battleship	factory ship	mosquito boat	school-ship
botel	flagship	motor-boat	sculler
bulk carrier	flat boat	narrow boat	shell
bumboat	freighter	oil tanker	ship's boat
cabin cruiser	galley	outboard	side-wheeler
cable ship	gig	outrigger	speedboat
canal boat	gondola	paddle boat	steamboat
canoe	houseboat	paddle steamer	steamship
cargo ship	hovercraft	passenger ship	sternwheeler
coal ship	hydrofoil	pilot boat	supertanker
collier	ice-boat	pinnace	surfboat
container ship	ice-breaker	pirogue	tanker
coracle	Indiaman	pontoon	tender
crabber	inflatable dinghy	powerboat	torpedo boat
cruiser	jet-boat	punt	tramp steamer
cruise ship	kayak	Q-ship	trawler
dinghy	keelboat	raft	troop carrier
dory	launch	randan	tugboat
dredger	lifeboat	revenue cutter	whaleboat
drifter	lighter	roll-on roll-off	wherry
	longboat	rowing boat	

SAILING SHIPS AND BOATS

barque	full-rigger	lugger	scow
barquentine	gaff cutter	man-of-war	shallop
brigantine	galleass	merchantman	skiff
caique	galleon	merchant ship	skipjack
caravel	galley	monohull	sloop
carrack	galliot	multihull	sloop of war
catamaran	hermaphrodite brig	nuggar	smack
catboat	hooker	outrigger	snekkja
clipper	in-rigger	pink	square-rigger
cutter	jolly boat	pinnace	tall ship
dhow	junk	polacre	tartan
dinghy	ketch	proa	trimaran
dragon boat	lateen	razee	windjammer
dromond	lighter	rigger	xebec
felucca	longboat	sabot	yacht
frigate	long-ship	schooner	yawl

NAUTICAL TERMS

aback	boltrope	dog watch	hull	quartermaster
abaft	boom	dolphin striker	jib	ratlines
abeam	boomkin	downhaul	kedge	rig
about-ship	bosun or bo's'n	easting	keel	Roaring Forties
admiral	bouse	euphroe	killick	scuppers
Admiralty mile	bow	fathom	knot	scuttle
aft	bowsprit	fid	landlubber	sea mile
ahoy	boxhaul	first watch	lanyard	shroud
alee	bridge	fore	larboard	splice
aloft	Bristol fashion	fore-and-aft	league	starboard
alow	bulkhead	forecastle or	lee	stem
amidships	bulwark	fo'c'sle	lubber's hole	stern
apeak	bunker	frap	marlinespike	sundowner
aport	bunt	freeboard	mate	superstructure
astern	burgee	futtock	middle watch	taffrail
athwartships	burton	gaff	moorings	tonnage
atrip	cable	galley	nautical mile	transom
avast	caulk	gam	orlop	truck
awash	clew	gangway	outhaul	vang
aweather	companion	garboard	pitching	veer
aweigh	companion-	grapnel	plimsoll line	vigia
ballast	ladder	gunwale	pontoon	wake
batten down	coxswain	gybe	poop	warp
beam	crowfoot	halyards	poppet	watch
becket	crow's nest	hatch	port	windlass
belay	Davy Jones'	hawse	prow	windward
berth	locker	hawser	purser	yardarm
bilge	deadlights	hold	quarter	yawing
bitt	deadweight	horse latitudes	quarterdeck	

PORTS

Aabenraa	Asunción	Bluefields	Cheboksary
Aalborg	Aveiro	Bodø	Cherkassy
Aalesund	Avilés	Boma	Chernigov
Abadan	Babruysk	Bombay	Chetumal
Abidjan	Bahía Blanca	Bône	Chicago
Abu Dhabi	Baku	Bonny	Chilung
Acapulco	Balikpapan	Bootle	Chimbote
Acre ·	Balkhash	Bordeaux	Chittagong
Adamstown	Ballina	Boulogne	Christiansted
Adelaide	Baltimore	Bratislava	Chukot
Aden	Bamberg	Brazzaville	Cienfuegos
Adria	Bandar Abbas	Brega	Cirebon
Agadir	Bandar Lampung	Bremen	Ciudad Bolivar
Aigues-Mortes	Banff	Bremerhaven	Civitavecchia
Ajaccio	Bangkok	Brest	Cleveland
Akashi	Bangor	Bridgeport	Coatzacoalcos
Akita	Banjarmasin	Bridgetown	Cóbh
Akranes	Banten	Bridlington	Cochin
Akrotiri	Bar	Brindisi	Cologne
Akureyri	Barahona	Brisbane	Colombo
Albany	Barcelona	Bristol	Colón
Aleksandrovsk-	Bari	Brownsville	Comodoro Rivadavia
Sakhalinskiy	Barisal	Buchanan	Conakry
Alexandretta	Barletta	Buenaventura	Concepción
Alexandria	Barrancabermeja	Buffalo	Concordia
Alexandroupolis	Barranquilla	Bunbury	Constanza
Algeciras	Barrow-in-Furness	Bundaberg	Cooktown
Algiers	Basra	Burgas	Copenhagen
Alicante	Bassein	Burnie	Coquimbo
Alleppey	Basse-Terre	Bushehr	Corinto
Almeria	Bastia	Bydgoszcz	Corpus Christi
Amalfi	Bata	Cadiz	Corrientes
Ambon	Batumi	Caesarea	Corunna
Ancona	Bay City	Cagliari	Cox's Bazar
Angoulême	Bayonne	Cagnes-sur-Mer	Cuddalore
Angra do Heroismo	Beaumont	Cairo	Cuttack
Annaba	Beihai	Calabar	Dahlak Islands
Antalya	Beira	Calais	Dakar
Antibes	Bejaïa	Calamata	Dalian
Antofagasta	Belém	Callao	Damietta
Antseranana	Belfast	Calvi	Da Nang
Antwerp	Belgrade	Camagüey	Dandong
Anzio	Belize City	Camden	Danzig
Aomori	Belle-Ile	Campeche	Dar es Salaam
Aqaba	Benguela	Canea	Darmstad
Aracajú	Benin	Cap Haïtien	Dartmouth
Arbroath	Berbera	Carrickfergus	Davao
Archangel	Berdyansk	Cartagena	Dhahran
Ardrossan	Berenice	Casablanca	Dieppe
Arecibo	Bergen	Castellón de la Plana	Díli
Arendal	Bharuch	Castries	Dinard
Arica	Bhavnagar	Catania	Dingle
Arkhangelsk	Biarritz	Cayenne	Djajapura
Arklow	Bideford	Cebu	Djibouti
Arrecife	Bilbao	Châlon-sur-Saône	Dniprodzerzhinsk
Aschaffenburg	Birkenhead	Changsha	Dnipropetrovsk
Ashdod	Bismarck	Charleston	Dordrecht
Assab	Bissau	Charlotte Amalie	Dortmund
Astrakhan	Bizerta	Châtellerault	Douala

PORTS (cont.)

Dover	Genoa	Huelva	Kineshma
Drammen	Georgetown	Hull	King's Lynn
Drogheda	George Town	Hydra	Kingston
Drouzhba	Geraldton	Ibiza	Kirkcaldy
Dubai	Ghent	Ifni	Kirkwall
Dublin	Gijón	Imabari	Kismayu
Dubrovnik	Gisborne	Immingham	Kitakyushu
Dundee	Giurgiu	Inchon	Klaipeda
Dunedin	Gladstone	Inhambane	Knoxville
Durban	Gomera	Ipswich	Kobe
Durrës	Gonaïves	Iquique	Kochi
East London	Gorzów Wielkopolski	Iquitos	Kompong Cham
Eilat	Gothenburg	Irún	Kompong Som
Elblag	Gourock	Iskenderun	Kota Kinabalu
Elizabeth	Grangemouth	Istanbul	Kotka
Ellesmere Port	Great Yarmouth	Izmir	Krasnodar
Encarnación	Greenock	Izmit	Kristiansand
Erie	Greenville	Jacksonville	Kristiansund
Esjberg	Grevenmacher	Jaffa	Kuching
Esmeraldas	Grimsby	Jaffna	Kurashiki
Essaouira	Guayaquil	Jakobstad	Kusadasi
Esztergom	Guaymas	Jamestown	Kushiro
Exmouth	Hachinohe	Jamnagar	Kuwait City
Fall River	Haeju	Jarrow	Kyrenia
Falmouth	Haifa	Jayapura	La Ceiba
Famagusta	Haikou	Jeddah	Lae
Fao	Haiphong	Jervis Bay Territory	Lagos
Fargo	Hakodate	Jiaojiang	La Paz
Faro	Halden	Jilin	La Plata
Fécamp	Halifax	Juneau	Larache
Felixstowe	Halmstad	Jyväskylä	Laredo
Fiume	Hamburg	Kagoshima	Larne
Flensburg	Hamilton	Kaliningrad	La Rochelle
Flushing	Hamina	Kaluga	Larvik
Folkestone	Hammerfest	Kampot	Las Palmas
Fortaleza	Hanau	Kamyshin	La Spezia
Frankfurt	Handa	Kankan	Latakia
Fray Bentos	Hanko	Kaohsiung	Lax
Fredericia	Härnösand	Karachi	Leeuwarden
Frederiksted	Hartlepool	Karlskrona	Leghorn
Fredrikstad	Harwich	Karlsruhe	Lerwick
Fremantle	Havana	Kaunas	Leticia
Freeport	Heilbronn	Kavála	Libreville
Fremantle	Helsingborg	Kazan	Liège
Fujairah	Helsinki	Keelung	Liepaja
Fukuoka	Heraklion	Keflavik	Limassol
Fukuyama	Hilo	Kelang	Limón
Funchal	Hobart	Kemi	Linea de la
Gabès	Ho Chi Minh City	Kenitra	Concepción
Galatz	Hodeida	Kenosha	Liverpool
Galle	Holyhead	Kerch	Lobito
Galveston	Honiara	Key West	Lomé
Galway	Honolulu	Kherson	London
Gao	Hook of Holland	Khorramshahr	Londonderry
Garoua	Horsens	Kiel	Lorain
Gävle	Horta	Kiev	Lorient
Gdańsk	Hrodna	Kigoma	Lowestoft
Gdynia	Hsinchu	Kimberley	Loyalty Islands
Geelong	Hué	Kimchaek	Luanda

PORTS (cont.)

Lübeck	Montreal	Nouadhibou	Pontianak
Ludwigshafen	Morecambe	Nouakchott	Poole
Luleå	Mossel Bay	Novorossiysk	Porbandar
Lüshun	Mostaganem	Nuuk	Pori
Lyons	Moulmein	Nyborg	Port Arthur
Macao	Mukalla	Nykøbing	Port Augusta
Maceió	Münster	Nykøping	Port-au-Prince
Machilipatnam	Murmansk	Oakland	Port Bell
Madras	Murom	Oban	Port Blair
Magdeburg	Muscat	Odense	Port Elizabeth
Magwe	Mykonos	Odessa	Port-Gentil
Mahajanga	Mymensingh	Oldenburg	Port Hedland
Mahón	Mytilene	Olympia	Port Kelang
Makhachkala	Nacala	Omsk	Portland
Malabo	Naestved	Oporto	Port Louis
Málaga	Nagasaki	Oran	Pôrto Alegre
Maldonado	Nagoya	Orange	Porto Novo
Malindi	Naha	Oranjestad	Port Pirie
Malmö	Nakhodka	Ordu	Port Rashid
Manado	Nakhon Sawan	Osaka	Port Said
Manama	Namibe	Osijek	Portsmouth
Manaus	Nampo	Ostend	Port Sudan
Mandalay	Nanaimo	Ostia	Port Sweetenham
Mangalore	Nantes	Otaru	Praia
Mannheim	Napier	Ouidah	Prince Rupert
Manzini	Naples	Oulu	Prome
Maracaibo	Narayanganj	Owendo	Pucallpa
Mar del Plata	Narbonne	Padang	Puerto Barrios
Mariehamn	Narvik	Pago Pago	Puerto Cortés
Mariupol	Nashville	Palembang	Puerto Montt
Marsala	Nassau	Palermo	Pula
Marseilles	Natal	Panaji	Puntarenas
Maryborough	Nauplia	Panchevo	Pusan
Masan	Návpaktos	Paramaribo	Pyrgos
Massawa	N'Djamena	Paraná	Qiqihar
Matamoros	Negombo	Patras	Quebec
Matanzas	Neijiang	Paysandú	Queen Charlotte
Matsuyama	Nellore	Pegu	Islands
Mazatlán	Nelson	Pekanbaru	Quilon
Mbandaka	Newark	Pelotas	Rabat
Mbini	New Bedford	Pemba	Rabaul
Memphis	New Caledonia	Pembroke	Rajshahi
Mersin	Newcastle	Pensacola	Ramsgate
Messina	New Hampshire	Peoria	Randers
Mexicali	Newhaven	Perth	Rangoon
Miami	New Orleans	Pesaro	Rashid
Middlesborough	New Plymouth	Peterhead	Rawson
Milford Haven	Newport News	Petropavlovsk	Recife
Milwaukee	New Providence	Petrozavodsk	Rethymnon
Minneapolis	Newry	Philadelphia	Reykjavik
Miyazaki	New York	Phnom Penh	Rhodes
Mocha	Niamey	Phuket	Richmond
Mogadishu	Niigata	Piacenza	Riga
Mohács	Niihama	Pietarsaari	Rijeka
Mokpo	Ningbo	Piraeus	Rio Gallegos
Mombasa	Niterói	Płock	Rio Grande
Monastir	Nizhniy Novgorod	Ponce	Rivne
Montego Bay	Nobeoka	Ponta Delgada	Rochefort-sur-Mer
Montevideo	Norrköping	Pontevedra	Rochester

PORTS (cont.)

Rockhampton
Rockingham
Rosario
Roscoff
Roskilde
Rosslare
Rostock
Rostov-on-Don
Rota
Rotterdam
Rouen
Ruse
Ryazan
Rybinsk
Safi
Saint-Denis
St. George's
Saint John
St. Louis
St-Malo
St-Nazaire
St. Petersburg
St. Tropez
Salem
Salerno
Salvador
Samara
Samsun
Sandakan
San Diego
San Juan
San Nicolas
San Sebastian
Santa Cruz de
  Tenerife
Santa Fe
Santander
Santarém
Santiago de Cuba
Santo Domingo
Santos
São Luis
Sarapul
Sasebo
Savannah
Seattle
Sebastapol
Ségou
Semarang
Semey
Seria
Sète
Setúbal

Seville
Shanghai
Shantou
Sharjah
Sheerness
Sibenik
Shimizu
Shizuoka
Sidon
Silistra
Sines
Sinop
Sinuiju
Sittwe
Skien
Skikda
Sligo
Smederovo
Smolensk
Sochi
Sousse
Southampton
South Shields
Stanley
Stavanger
Sterlitamak
Stockholm
Stockton
Stranraer
Strasbourg
Stuttgart
Suez
Sunderland
Sundsvall
Surat
Suva
Swakopmund
Swansea
Sydney
Syracuse
Szczecin
Szeged
Szolnok
Tacoma
Taganrog
Taichung
Takamatsu
Talcahuano
Tallinn
Tampa
Tampico
Tanga
Tangier

Tarragona
Tauranga
Tekirdağ
Tel Aviv
Tema
Thessaloníki
Thunder Bay
Thurso
Tianjin
Tilbury
Timaru
Toamasina
Tobruk
Togliatti
Tokushima
Tokyo
Tomakomai
Tomsk
Tonkin
Torre del Greco
Torun
Tottori
Toulon
Townsville
Trabzon
Tralee
Trapani
Trieste
Tripoli
Trois-Rivières
Troms
Trondheim
Tulsa
Tunis
Turku
Tuticorin
Tver
Tyre
Uddevalla
Ugarit
Ujung Pandang
Ullapool
Ulsan
Umeå
Ushuaia
Vaasa
Vác
Valdez
Valencia
Vallejo
Valletta
Vancouver
Varna

Västerås
Veracruz
Viana do Castelo
Vicksburg
Victoria
Vidin
Vientiane
Villahermosa
Visakhapatnam
Vitória
Volgograd
Volos
Vyatka
Walvis Bay
Wanganui
Weihai
Wellington
Wenzhou
Whangarei
Whitby
Willemstadt
Wilmington
Windsor
Wismar
Włocławek
Wollongong
Wonsan
Workington
Wroclaw
Wuhan
Wuhu
Xiamen
Yakutsk
Yalta
Yambol
Yantai
Yaroslavl
Yingkou
Yokkaichi
Yokohama
Yokosuka
Zadar
Zamboanga
Zeebrugge
Zhanjiang
Ziguinchor
Zonguldak
Zrenjanin

AIRCRAFT

aerodyne	cyclogiro	helicopter	pusher
Airbus™	dive bomber	interceptor	seaplane
airliner	drone	jet plane	swing-wing
amphibian	fighter	jumbo jet	taxiplane
autogiro	fighter-bomber	jump jet	triplane
biplane	flying boat	microlight	turbofan
bomber	freighter	multirole combat	turbojet
canard	glider	aircraft (MRCA)	turboprop
Concorde	gyrocopter	multiplane	
convertiplane	gyrodyne	night fighter	

INTERNATIONAL AIRPORTS
(with cities)

Arlanda	Stockholm	Leonardo da Vinci	
Ataturk	Istanbul	(Fiumicino)	Rome
Barajas	Madrid	Linate	Milan
Charles De Gaulle	Paris	Lindbergh Field	San Diego
Changi	Singapore	Logan	Boston
Chiang Kai-Shek	Taipei	Luis Muñoz Marin	San Juan
Cointrin	Geneva	McCarran	Las Vegas
Dorval	Montreal	Mirabel	Montreal
Douglas	Charlotte	Narita	Tokyo
Dulles	Washington	Ninoy Aquino	Manila
Echterdingen	Stuttgart	O'Hare	Chicago
Findel	Luxembourg	Okecie	Warsaw
Fornebu	Oslo	Orly	Paris
Gatwick	London	Pearson	Toronto
Hartsfield	Atlanta	St Paul	Minneapolis
Heathrow	London	Schiphol	Amsterdam
Helsinki-Vantaa	Helsinki	Sheremetyevo	Moscow
Hongqiao	Shanghai	Sky Harbor	Phoenix
Hopkins	Cleveland	Soekarno Hatta	Jakarta
John F. Kennedy	New York	Stansted	London
(Benito) Juarez	Mexico City	Subang	Kuala Lumpur
Kimpo	Seoul	Tegel	Berlin
King Khaled	Riyadh	Tullamarine	Melbourne
Kingsford Smith	Sydney	Wayne County	Detroit
La Guardia	New York		

SCIENCE AND TECHNOLOGY

UNITS OF MEASUREMENT

acre
air mile
ampere
amu
angstrom
are
astronomical unit
atmosphere
atomic mass unit
barleycorn
barrel
baud
becquerel
bel
bit
Board of Trade Unit
British thermal unit
bushel
butt
byte
cable
calorie
candela
candle
carat
cental
centiare
centner
chain
chronon
circular mil
cord
coulomb
cup
curie
cusec
cycle
dalton
daraf
darcy
day
decibel
degree
degree-day
denier

dioptre
dyne
electronvolt
em
en
epoch
erg
farad
faraday
fathom
fermi
firkin
foot
fresnel
furlong
gal
gallon
gamma
gauss
gilbert
gill
grade
grain
gram-atomic weight
gram *or* gramme
gram-molecular
  weight
gray
hank
henry
hertz
hogshead
Hoppus foot
horsepower
hour
hundredweight
inch
jansky
joule
kelvin
kilderkin
kilocycle
kilogram *or*
  kilogramme
kilometre

kiloton
kilowatt-hour
kip
knot
last
lea
league
light year
line
link
litre
lumen
lux
Mach number
magneton
maxwell
megaton
metre
mho
micrometre
micron
mil
mile
millibar
millimicron
minim
minute
mole
morgan
nail
nautical mile
neper
newton
nit
noggin
oersted
ohm
okta *or* octa
ounce
parsec
pascal
peck
perch
phon
phot

pica
pint
pipe
point
poise
pole
pound
poundal
puncheon
quart
quarter
quartern
quintal
rad
radian
rod
roentgen *or* röntgen
rood
rutherford
sabin
scruple
second
siemens
sievert
slug
span
steradian
stilb
stokes
stone
tesla
therm
tog
ton
tonne
torr
troy ounce
var
volt
watt
weber
x-unit
yard
year

CHEMICAL ELEMENTS
(with symbols)

actinium	Ac	hafnium	Hf	promethium	Pm
aluminium	Al	hassium	Hs	protactinium	Pa
americium	Am	helium	He	radium	Ra
antimony	Sb	holmium	Ho	radon	Rn
argon	Ar	hydrogen	H	rhenium	Re
arsenic	As	indium	In	rhodium	Rh
astatine	At	iodine	I	rubidium	Rb
barium	Ba	iridium	Ir	ruthenium	Ru
berkelium	Bk	iron	Fe	rutherfordium	Rf
beryllium	Be	krypton	Kr	samarium	Sm
bismuth	Bi	lanthanum	La	scandium	Sc
bohrium	Bh	lawrencium	Lr	seaborgium	Sg
boron	B	lead	Pb	selenium	Se
bromine	Br	lithium	Li	silicon	Si
cadmium	Cd	lutetium	Lu	silver	Ag
caesium	Cs	magnesium	Mg	sodium	Na
calcium	Ca	manganese	Mn	strontium	Sr
californium	Cf	meitnerium	Mt	sulphur	S
carbon	C	mendelevium	Md	tantalum	Ta
cerium	Ce	mercury	Hg	technetium	Tc
chlorine	Cl	molybdenum	Mo	tellurium	Te
chromium	Cr	neodymium	Nd	terbium	Tb
cobalt	Co	neon	Ne	thallium	Tl
copper	Cu	neptunium	Np	thorium	Th
curium	Cm	nickel	Ni	thulium	Tm
dubnium	Db	niobium	Nb	tin	Sn
dysprosium	Dy	nitrogen	N	titanium	Ti
einsteinium	Es	nobelium	Nb	tungsten or wolfram	W
erbium	Er	osmium	Os	uranium	U
europium	Eu	oxygen	O	vanadium	V
fermium	Fm	palladium	Pd	xenon	Xe
fluorine	F	phosphorus	P	ytterbium	Yb
francium	Fr	platinum	Pt	yttrium	Y
gadolinium	Gd	plutonium	Pu	zinc	Zn
gallium	Ga	polonium	Po	zirconium	Zr
germanium	Ge	potassium	K		
gold	Au	praseodymium	Pr		

ELEMENTARY PARTICLES

antielectron	kaon	proton
antineutron	lambda particle	psi particle
antiproton	lepton	quark
antiquark	meson	selectron
baryon	muon	slepton
boson	neutrino	squark
electron	neutron	tachyon
fermion	nucleon	tau particle
gluino	omega minus	wino
gluon	photino	W particle
graviton	photon	zino
hadron	pion	Z particle
Higgs boson	positron	

ROCKS AND MINERALS

Sedimentary Rocks

arenite
argillite
breccia
chalk
chert
claystone
coal
conglomerate
diatomaceous earth
dolomite
flint
ironstone
limestone
marl
mudstone
oolite
radiolarite
rag
rudite
sandstone
shale
siltstone
tillite

Metamorphic Rocks

amphibolite
eclogite
epidiorite
epidosite
gneiss
granulite
hornfels
marble
phyllite
psammite
pyroxenite
quartzite
schist
slate
verdite

Igneous Rocks

amygdaloid
andesite
anorthosite
aplite
basalt
diorite

dolerite
dunite
felsite
gabbro
granite
kimberlite
lamprophyre
lava
monzonite
obsidian
pegmatite
peridotite
phonolite
picrite
porphyry
pumice
rhyolite
syenite
tephrite
tonalite
trachyte
trap
tuff
variolite
vitrophyre

Minerals

anhydrite
anorthoclase
apatite
asbestos
augite
beryl
biotite
blackjack
borax
cassiterite
chalcopyrite
Chile saltpetre
chrysoberyl
cinnabar
corundum
diamond
dolomite
emery
euxenite
feldspar
fluorspar
fool's gold
fulgurite
galena

garnet
gypsum
haematite
halite
harmotome
hornblende
hyacinth
illite
ilmenite
kaolinite
lapis lazuli
malachite
marcasite
massicot
meerschaum
mica
molybdenite
mullite
oligoclase
opal
orthoclase
periclase
pitchblende
plagioclase
polybasite
pyrite
pyrites
quartz
realgar
rutile
saponite
sapphirine
scolecite
serpentine
siderite
sodalite
sphalerite
stannite
talc
thorite
topaz
tourmaline
tungstite
turquoise
vesuvianite
water sapphire
wolframite
zeolite
zincite
zircon

METAL ORES

anglesite	chalcocite	ironstone	siderite
argentite	chalcopyrite	limonite	smithsonite
arsenopyrite	chromite	litharge	stibnite
bauxite	copper pyrites	lodestone	tinstone
carnotite	cinnabar	magnetite	zinc blende
cassiterite	galena	mispickel	zincite
cerrusite	haematite	pitchblende	

GEOLOGICAL TIME

Cambrian period	Eocene epoch	Ordovician period	Pliocene epoch
Carboniferous	Holocene epoch	Palaeocene epoch	Precambrian era
period	Jurassic period	Palaeozoic era	Quaternary period
Cenozoic era	Mesozoic era	Permian period	Silurian period
Cretaceous period	Miocene epoch	Phanerozoic era	Tertiary period
Devonian period	Oligocene epoch	Pleistocene epoch	Triassic period

CLOUDS

altocumulus	cumulonimbus	noctilucent cloud
altostratus	cumulostratus	rain cloud
anvil cloud	cumulus	storm cloud
cirrocumulus	lenticular cloud	stratocumulus
cirrostratus	nimbostratus	stratus
cirrus	nimbus	thundercloud

WINDS
(with locations)

bise	Central Europe	mistral	Mediterranean
bora	Central Europe	monsoon	S Asia
buran	Central Asia	nor'wester	New Zealand
Cape doctor	South Africa	simoom or	
chinook	Rocky Mountains, USA	samiel	N Africa
etesian	E Mediterranean	sirocco	N Africa
Föhn or Foehn	Central Europe	southerly	
ghibli or gibli	N Africa	buster	SE Australia
harmattan	W Africa	tramontana	W Mediterranean
khamsin	Egypt	wet chinook	NW USA
levanter	W Mediterranean	williwaw	USA, Canada
meltemi	E Mediterranean		

CONSTELLATIONS
(with common names)

Andromeda		Lacerta	Lizard
Antlia	Air Pump	Leo	Lion
Apus	Bird of Paradise	Leo Minor	Little Lion
Aquarius	Water Bearer	Lepus	Hare
Aquila	Eagle	Libra	Balance or Scales
Ara	Altar	Lupus	Wolf
Aries	Ram	Lynx	
Auriga	Charioteer	Lyra	Lyre
Boötes	Herdsman or Bear Driver	Mensa	Table
		Microscopium	Microscope
Caelum	Chisel	Monoceros	Unicorn
Camelopardalis	Giraffe	Musca	Fly
Cancer	Crab	Norma	Level or Rule
Canes Venatici	Hunting Dogs	Octans	Octant
Canis Major	Great Dog	Ophiuchus	Serpent Bearer
Canis Minor	Little Dog	Orion	Hunter
Capricornus	Goat or Sea Goat	Pavo	Peacock
Carina	Keel	Pegasus	
Cassiopeia		Perseus	
Centaurus	Centaur	Phoenix	
Cepheus		Pictor	Painter's Easel
Cetus	Whale	Pisces	Fishes
Chamaeleon	Chameleon	Piscis Austrinus	Southern Fish
Circinus	Compasses	Puppis	Stern or Poop
Columba	Dove	Pyxis	Compass Box
Coma Berenices	Berenice's Hair	Reticulum	Net
Corona Australis	Southern Crown	Sagitta	Arrow
Corona Borealis	Northern Crown	Sagittarius	Archer
Corvus	Crow	Scorpius	Scorpion
Crater	Cup	Sculptor	
Crux (Australis)	Southern Cross	Scutum	Shield
Cygnus	Swan	Serpens	Serpent
Delphinus	Dolphin	Sextans	Sextant
Dorado	Swordfish or Goldfish	Taurus	Bull
Draco	Dragon	Telescopium	Telescope
Equuleus	Little Horse or Foal	Triangle	Triangulum
Eridanus	River	Triangulum Australe	Southern Triangle
Fornax	Furnace	Tucana	Toucan
Gemini	Twins	Ursa Major	Great Bear
Grus	Crane	Ursa Minor	Little Bear
Hercules		Vela	Sails
Horologium	Clock	Virgo	Virgin
Hydra	Sea Serpent	Volans	Flying Fish
Hydrus	Water Snake	Vulpecula	Fox
Indus	Indian		

PLANETS AND THEIR SATELLITES

Mercury	
Venus	
Earth	Moon
Mars	Phobos, Deimos
Jupiter	Metis, Adrastea, Amalthea, Thebe, Io, Europa, Ganymede, Callisto, Leda, Himalia, Lysithea, Elara, Ananke, Carme, Pasiphae, Sinope
Saturn	Pan, Atlas, Prometheus, Pandora, Epimetheus, Janus, Mimas, Enceladus, Tethys, Telesto, Calypso, Dione, Helene, Rhea, Titan, Hyperion, Iapetus, Phoebe
Uranus	Cordelia, Ophelia, Bianca, Cressida, Desdemona, Juliet, Portia, Rosalind, Belinda, Puck, Miranda, Ariel, Umbriel, Titania, Oberon, Caliban, Sycorax
Neptune	Naiad, Thalassa, Despina, Galatea, Larissa, Proteus, Triton, Nereid
Pluto	Charon

COMETS

Arend–Roland
Bennett
Biela
Borrelly
Bronsen–Metcalf
Comas Solá
Crommelin
Daylight Comet
Encke
Faye
Giacobini–Zinner
Grigg–Skiellerup
Hale–Bopp
Halley

Kohoutek
Kopff
Lexell
Olbers
Pons–Brooks
Pons–Winnecke
Schaumasse
Shoemaker–Levy
Stephan–Oterma
Tuttle
West
Westphal
Whipple

GALAXIES

Andromeda Galaxy
Black-eye Galaxy
Cartwheel Galaxy
Helix Galaxy
Large Magellanic
  Cloud *or* Nubecular
  Major
Milky Way Galaxy
Pinwheel Galaxy

Small Magellanic
  Cloud *or* Nubecular
  Minor
Sombrero Galaxy
Spindle Galaxy
Sunflower Galaxy
Triangulum Galaxy
Whirlpool Galaxy

COMPUTER TERMS

abort
access
accumulator
acoustic coupler
ADA
address
AI
ALGOL
algorithm
alphanumeric
analyzer

APL
Apple
Apple Mac
applications
  software
archive
ARPANET
artificial
  intelligence
assembler
assembly code

assembly language
authoring tool
backspace
backup
band printer
bandwidth
bar-code reader
barrel printer
batch processing
baud
BBS

belt printer
benchmark
beta test
binary
bit
bitmap
BITNET
block
boot
bootstrap
boot up

COMPUTER TERMS (cont.)

branch
bridge
browser
bubble-jet printer
bubble memory
buffer
bug
bulletin board
bus
byte
C
cache
CAD
CAL
CAM
carriage return
CD
CD-R
CD-ROM
central processing
  unit
chain printer
channel
character
chat room
chip
click rate
clock cycle
clock rate
COBOL
colour printer
command
common LISP
compact disc
compatibility
compile
compiler
COM port
compression
computer-aided
  design
computer-aided
  manufacture
coprocessor
copy
CORAL
counter
CPL
CPU
CR
cracker
crash
cryogenic memory
cursor

cybercommerce
cybernetics
cybersex
cyberspace
daisywheel printer
decimal
decompile
data
database
data processing
data tablet
debug
decode
delete
desktop publishing
digital versatile (or
  video) disc
digitizer
direct access
directory
disc or disk
diskette
display
dotcom company
dot-matrix printer
downgrade
download
downtime
drum printer
DTP
dump
DVD
dynamic memory
e-book
e-commerce
edit
electronic mail
email
emoticon
encryption
EPROM
erase
escape
Ethernet
expert system
ezine
field
file
file server
filter
fixed disc
flash memory
flat-bed plotter
floating-point

operation
FLOP
floppy disc
floptical disc
format
FORTH
FORTRAN
gibibyte
gig
gigabyte
Gopher
graphics
graphics user
  interface
GUI
halfword
handshake
hard disc
hardwire
hash
hashing
header
heartbeat
hexadecimal
hierarchical
  database
high-level language
home page
hot spot
HTML
hypertext
hypertext link
icon
impact printer
ink-jet printer
input
interface
Internet
Internet service
  provider
interpreter
intranet
ionographic printer
ISP
JANET
Java
Javascript
job
JOVIAL
joystick
key
keyboard
keypad
kibibyte

kilobyte
language
laptop
laser printer
light pen
line feed
line printer
LISP
login
LOGO
logoff
logon
logout
loop
Mac
Macintosh
MAClisp
macro
mailbox
mainframe
mebibyte
meg
megabyte
memory
menu
microcomputer
minicomputer
minidisc
modem
modulator-
  demodulator
monitor
motherboard
mouse
mulitmedia
multiplexer
multitasking
natural language
  processing
nesting
net
network
neural network
newline
node
notebook
OCR
octal
off-line
on-line
operating system
optical character
  recognition
optical disc

COMPUTER TERMS (cont.)

output
packet
palmtop
parallel port
parallel processor
parity
parser
Pascal
password
patch
PC
peripheral
personal computer
pixel
plotter
preprocessor
primary memory
printable character
printer
processor
program
memory
programmer
programming
programming
  language
PROLOG

PROM
queue
RAM
random-access
  memory
raster
read only memory
real time
record
register
relational database
repeater
robotics
ROM
router
save
scanner
screen saver
scroll
search engine
sector
semiconductor
  memory
serial port
SGML
SNOBOL
solid-state memory

sorting
sound card
source code
spelling checker
spider
spool
spreadsheet
sprite
star network
storage
supercomputer
system software
telnet
terminal display
text editor
time sharing
toolbar
toolbox
touchscreen
trackball
transceiver
transistor
Trojan horse
turnkey operation
upgrade
URL
Usenet

user-friendly
user interface
utility program
VBA
VDU
vector
video display unit
virus
Visual Basic
Visual Basic for
  Applications
volatile memory
WAN
wand
web
wide-area network
window manager
Word for Windows
WORDPERFECT
word processor
workstation
World Wide Web
write
WWW
WYSIWYG

MATHEMATICS TERMS

abscissa
addition
algebra
algorithm
aliquot part
analysis
antilogarithm
Apollonius' theorem
Argand diagram
arithmetic mean
arithmetic
  progression
array
associative law
asymptote
Banach space
base
Bayes' theorem
Bernoulli numbers
Bessel functions
binomial

binomial theorem
Boolean algebra
Briggsian logarithms
calculus
Cantor set
cardinal number
Cartesian coordin-
  ates
catastrophe theory
Cauchy sequence
chaos theory
Chinese remainder
  theorem
coefficient
common
  denominator
commutative law
complex number
conjugate
coordinate geometry
cosecant

cosine
cotangent
cube
cube root
decimal point
definite integral
de Moivre's formula
denominator
derivative
determinant
difference
differential calculus
differential equation
differentiation
digit
Diophantine
  equation
Dirichlet series
distributive law
division
divisor

eigenfunction
eigenvalue
eigenvector
equation
Eratosthenes, sieve
  of
Euclidean geometry
Euclid's axioms
Euler's constant
Euler's formula
expansion
exponent
exponential function
extrapolation
factor
factorial
Fermat's last
  theorem
Fibonacci numbers
field
formula

MATHEMATICS TERMS (cont.)

four-colour theorem
Fourier analysis
Fourier series
fractal
fractal set
fraction
function
fuzzy set
Galois group
game theory
Gaussian
 distribution
Gauss's theorem
geometric mean
geometric
 progression
Gödel numbers
googol
googolplex
gradient
Green's theorem
group
group theory
harmonic
 progression
Hermitian matrix
highest common
 factor
Hilbert space
Hilbert's problems
hyperbolic cosine
hyperbolic sine
hyperbolic tangent
identity
imaginary number
improper fraction
indefinite integral
inequality
infinitesimal calculus
integer
integral calculus
integrand
integration
intercept

interpolation
inverse
irrational number
iteration
Julia set
Klein bottle
Lagrange's theorem
Laplace operator
least squares
 method
Legendre poly-
 nomials
Leibniz's theorem
L'Hôpital's rule
Lie group
limit
linear equation
Lobachevskian
 geometry
locus
logarithm
long division
lowest common
 denominator
lowest common
 multiple
Maclaurin series
magic square
Mandelbrot set
Markov chain
matrix
mean
median
Mersenne numbers
midpoint theorem
Möbius strip
modulus
Monte Carlo method
multiple
multiplicand
multiplication
multiplier
Napierian logarithm
natural logarithm

natural numbers
Newton method
node
null hypothesis
number theory
numerator
operator
ordinal number
origin
parameter
partial derivative
Pascal's triangle
percentile
perfect number
perfect square
permutation
point of inflection
Poisson distribution
polar coordinates
polynomial
power
power series
prime number
product
proof
proper fraction
Pythagoras' theorem
quaternion
queuing theory
quotient
ratio
rational number
real number
reciprocal
recurring decimal
recursion
remainder
remainder theorem
repeating decimal
Riemannian
 geometry
ring
root
root-mean-square

Russell's paradox
scalar
secant
series
set
set theory
significant figure
Simpson's rule
simultaneous
 equations
sine
solution
square
square number
square root
stationary point
Stirling's
 approximation
Stokes' theorem
sub-group
subset
substitution
subtraction
sum
surd
tangent
Taylor series
tensor
transcendental
 function
transfinite number
transform
trigonometric
 function
unity
unknown
variable
vector
Venn diagram
vulgar fraction
whole number

SCIENTISTS, INVENTORS, AND PIONEERS

Abbe, Ernst (1840–1905) German physicist

Abel, Niels Henrik (1802–29) Norwegian mathematician

Adams, John Couch (1819–92) English astronomer

Agassiz, Jean Louis Rodolphe (1807–73) Swiss-born zoologist, geologist, and palaeontologist

Agnesi, Maria Gaetana (1718–99) Italian mathematician and philosopher

Airy, Sir George Biddell (1801–92) English astronomer and geophysicist

Alcock, Sir John William (1892–1919) English aviator

Aldrin, Edwin Eugene (known as 'Buzz') (born 1930) American astronaut

Alembert, Jean le Rond d' (1717–83) French mathematician, physicist, and philosopher

Alfvén, Hannes Olof Gösta (1908–95) Swedish astrophysicist

Alvarez, Luis Walter (1911–88) American physicist

Ampère, André Marie (1775–1836) French physicist

Anderson, Carl David (1905–91) American physicist

Anderson, Philip Warren (1923–96) American physicist

Andrews, Thomas (1813–85) Irish physical chemist

Ångström, Anders Jonas (1814–74) Swedish physicist and astronomer

Anthemius (known as Anthemius of Tralles) (6th century AD) Greek mathematician, engineer, and artist

Apollonius (known as Apollonius of Perga) Greek mathematician

Appleton, Sir Edward Victor (1892–1965) English physicist

Archimedes (c. 287–c. 212 BC) Greek mathematician

Aristarchus (known as Aristarchus of Samos) (3rd century BC) Greek astronomer

Arkwright, Sir Richard (1732–92) English inventor and industrialist

Armstrong, Edwin Howard (1890–1954) American electrical engineer

Armstrong, Neil (Alden) (born 1930) American astronaut

Arrhenius, Svante August (1859–1927) Swedish chemist

Aryabhata I, (476–c. 550) Indian astronomer and mathematician

Asimov, Isaac (1920–92) Russian-born American writer and scientist

Aston, Francis William (1877–1945) English physicist

Attenborough, Sir David (Frederick) (born 1926) English naturalist and broadcaster

Audubon, John James (1785–1851) American naturalist and artist

Auer, Carl, Baron von Welsbach (1858–1929) Austrian chemist

Austin, Herbert, 1st Baron Austin of Longbridge (1866–1941) British motor manufacturer

Avogadro, Amedeo (1776–1856) Italian chemist and physicist

Baade, (Wilhelm Heinrich) Walter (1893–1960) German-born American astronomer

Babbage, Charles (1791–1871) English mathematician, inventor, and pioneer of machine computing

Bacon, Roger (c. 1214–94) English philosopher, scientist, and Franciscan monk

Baer, Karl Ernest von (1792–1876) German biologist

Baeyer, Adolph Johann Friedrich Wilhelm von (1835–1917) German organic chemist

Baird, John Logie (1888–1946) Scottish pioneer of television

Bakewell, Robert (1725–95) English pioneer in scientific methods of livestock breeding and husbandry

Bakker, Robert T (born 1945) American palaeontologst

Banks, Sir Joseph (1743–1820) English botanist

Banting, Sir Frederick Grant (1891–1941) Canadian physiologist and surgeon

Barnard, Christiaan Neethling (born 1922) South African surgeon

Barnardo, Thomas John (1845–1905) Irish-born doctor and philanthropist

Bates, Henry Walter (1825–92) English naturalist

Bateson, William (1861–1926) English geneticist and coiner of the term genetics in its current sense

Batten, Jean (1909–82) New Zealand aviator

Beckmann, Ernst Otto (1853–1923) German chemist

Becquerel, Antoine-Henri (1852–1908) French physicist

Beeching, Richard, Baron (1913–85) English businessman and engineer

Behring, Emil Adolf von (1854–1917) German bacteriologist

Bell, Alexander Graham (1847–1922) Scottish-born American scientist and inventor

Benz, Karl Friedrich (1844–1929) German engineer and motor manufacturer

SCIENTISTS, INVENTORS, AND PIONEERS (cont.)

Bergius, Friedrich Karl Rudolf (1884–1949) German industrial chemist
Bernard, Claude (1813–78) French physiologist
Bernoulli, Daniel (1700–82) Swiss mathematician
Bernoulli, Jacques (1654–1705) Swiss mathematician
Bernoulli, Jean (1667–1748) Swiss mathematician
Bernoulli, Nicolas (1695–1726) Swiss mathematician
Berzelius, Jöns Jakob (1779–1848) Swedish analytical chemist
Bessel, Friedrich Wilhelm (1784–1846) German astronomer and mathematician
Bessemer, Sir Henry (1813–98) English engineer and inventor
Best, Charles Herbert (1899–1978) American-born Canadian physiologist
Bethune, Henry Norman (1890–1939) Canadian surgeon
Birdseye, Clarence (1886–1956) American businessman and inventor
Bjerknes, Vilhelm Frimann Koren (1862–1951) Norwegian geophysicist and meteorologist
Black, Joseph (1728–99) Scottish chemist
Blackett, Patrick Maynard Stuart, Baron (1897–1974) English physicist
Blanchard, Jean Pierre François (1753–1809) French balloonist
Blériot, Louis (1872–1936) French aviation pioneer
Blumenbach, Johann Friedrich (1752–1840) German physiologist and anatomist
Boas, Franz (1858–1942) German-born American anthropologist
Bohr, Niels Hendrik David (1885–1962) Danish physicist and pioneer in quantum physics
Boltzmann, Ludwig (1844–1906) Austrian physicist
Boole, George (1815–64) English mathematician
Bordet, Jules (1870–1961) Belgian bacteriologist and immunologist
Born, Max (1882–1970) German theoretical physicist and a founder of quantum mechanics
Bose, Sir Jagdis Chandra (1858–1937) Indian physicist and plant physiologist
Bose, Satyendra Nath (1894–1974) Indian physicist
Boucher de Perthes, Jacques (1788–1868) French archaeologist
Boulton, Matthew (1728–1809) English engineer and manufacturer
Boyle, Robert (1627–91) Irish-born scientist

Bradley, James (1693–1762) English astronomer
Bragg, Sir William Henry (1862–1942) English physicist, a founder of solid-state physics
Brahe, Tycho (1546–1601) Danish astronomer
Bramah, Joseph (1748–1814) English inventor
Brassey, Thomas (1805–70) English engineer and railway contractor
Braun, Karl Ferdinand (1850–1918) German physicist
Braun, Wernher Magnus Maximilian von (1912–77) German-born American rocket engineer
Breuil, Henri (Édouard Prosper) (1877–1961), French archaeologist
Brewster, Sir David (1781–1868) Scottish physicist
Bridgman, Percy Williams (1882–1961) American physicist
Briggs, Henry (1561–1630) English mathematician
Brindley, James (1716–72) pioneer British canal builder
Brisbane, Sir Thomas Makdougall (1773–1860) Scottish soldier and astronomer
Bronowski, Jacob (1908–74) Polish-born British scientist, writer, and broadcaster
Brown, Sir Arthur Whitten (1886–1948) Scottish aviator
Brunel, Isambard Kingdom (1806–59) English engineer
Brunel, Sir Marc Isambard (1769–1849) French-born British engineer
Buchan, Alexander (1829–1907) Scottish meteorologist
Buchner, Eduard (1860–1917) German organic chemist
Buckland, William (1784–1856) English geologist
Buffon, Georges-Louis Leclerc, Comte de (1707–88) French naturalist
Bunsen, Robert Wilhelm Eberhard (1811–99) German chemist
Byron, Augusta Ada See LOVELACE, COUNTESS OF
Calvin, Melvin (1911–97) American biochemist
Candolle, Augustin Pyrame de (1778–1841) Swiss botanist
Cannizzaro, Stanislao (1826–1910) Italian chemist
Cantor, Georg (1845–1918) Russian-born German mathematician
Carnot, Nicolas Léonard Sadi (1796–1832) French scientist
Carothers, Wallace Hume (1896–1937) American industrial chemist

SCIENTISTS, INVENTORS, AND PIONEERS (cont.)

Carrel, Alexis (1873–1944) French surgeon and biologist

Carson, Rachel (Louise) (1907–64) American zoologist

Carter, Howard (1874–1939) English archaeologist

Cartwright, Edmund (1743–1823) English engineer, inventor of the power loom

Cassini, Giovanni Domenico (1625–1712) Italian-born French astronomer

Cauchy, Augustin Louis, Baron (1789–1857) French mathematician

Cavendish, Henry (1731–1810) English chemist and physicist

Cayley, Arthur (1821–95) English mathematician and barrister

Cayley, Sir George (1773–1857) British engineer, the father of British aeronautics

Celsius, Anders (1701–44) Swedish astronomer, best known for his thermometer scale

Cerenkov See CHERENKOV

Chadwick, Sir James (1891–1974) English physicist

Chain, Sir Ernst Boris (1906–79) German-born British biochemist

Chamberlain, Owen (born 1920) American physicist

Chandrasekhar, Subrahmanyan (1910–95) Indian-born American astronomer

Chanute, Octave (1832–1910) French-born American aviation pioneer

Charcot, Jean-Martin (1825–93) French neurologist

Cherenkov, Pavel (Alekseevich) (also Cerenkov) (1904–90) Soviet physicist

Cherwell, Frederick Alexander Lindemann, 1st Viscount (1886–1957) German-born British physicist

Churchward, George Jackson (1857–1933) English railway engineer

Clausius, Rudolf (1822–88) German physicist, one of the founders of modern thermodynamics

Cochran, Jacqueline (1910–80) American aviator

Cockcroft, Sir John Douglas (1897–1967) English physicist

Cockerell, Sir Christopher Sydney (1910–99) English engineer

Cohn, Ferdinand Julius (1828–98) German botanist, a founder of bacteriology

Colt, Samuel (1814–62) American inventor

Compton, Arthur Holly (1892–1962) American physicist

Cooke, Sir William Fothergill (1806–79) English inventor

Copernicus, Nicolaus (Latinized name of Mikołaj Kopérnik) (1473–1543) Polish astronomer

Cort, Henry (1740–1800) English ironmaster

Coulomb, Charles-Augustin de (1736–1806) French military engineer

Courtauld, Samuel (1876–1947) English industrialist

Cousteau, Jacques-Yves (1910–97) French oceanographer and film director

Crawford, Osbert Guy Stanhope (1886–1957) British archaeologist

Crick, Francis Harry Compton (born 1916) English biophysicist

Crompton, Samuel (1753–1827) English inventor

Crookes, Sir William (1832–1919) English physicist and chemist

Culpeper, Nicholas (1616–54) English herbalist

Curie, Marie (1867–1934) Polish-born French physicist, pioneer of radioactivity

Curie, Pierre (1859–1906) French physicist, pioneer of radioactivity

Curtiss, Glenn (Hammond) (1878–1930) American air pioneer and aircraft designer

Cushing, Harvey Williams (1869–1939) American surgeon

Cuvier, Georges Léopold Chrétien Frédéric Dagobert, Baron (1769–1832) French naturalist

Daguerre, Louis-Jacques-Mandé (1789–1851) French physicist, painter, and inventor of the first practical photographic process

Daimler, Gottlieb (1834–1900) German engineer and motor manufacturer

Dale, Sir Henry Hallett (1875–1968) English physiologist and pharmacologist

Dalton, John (1766–1844) English chemist, the father of modern atomic theory

Dana, James Dwight (1813–95) American naturalist, geologist, and mineralogist

Dart, Raymond Arthur (1893–1988) Australian-born South African anthropologist and anatomist

Darwin, Charles (Robert) (1809–82) English natural historian and geologist, proponent of the theory of evolution by natural selection

Darwin, Erasmus (1731–1802) English physician, scientist, inventor, and poet

Davisson, Clinton Joseph (1881–1958) American physicist

Davy, Sir Humphry (1778–1829) English chemist, a pioneer of electrochemistry

Dawkins, Richard (born 1941) English biologist

de Broglie, Louis-Victor, Prince (1892–1987) French physicist

SCIENTISTS, INVENTORS, AND PIONEERS (cont.)

Debye, Peter Joseph William (1884–1966) Dutch-born American chemical physicist

Dedekind, Richard (1831–1916) German mathematician

de Duve, Christian René (born 1917) British-born Belgian biochemist

Dee, John (1527–1608) English alchemist, mathematician, and geographer

De Forest, Lee (1873–1961) American physicist and electrical engineer

de Havilland, Sir Geoffrey (1882–1965) English aircraft designer and manufacturer

de la Beche, Sir Henry Thomas (1796–1855) English geologist

Democritus (*c.* 460–*c.* 370 BC) Greek philosopher and scientist

Descartes, René (1596–1650) French philosopher, mathematician, and man of science

de Vries, Hugo (1848–1935) Dutch plant physiologist and geneticist

Dewar, Sir James (1842–1923) Scottish chemist and physicist

Diesel, Rudolf (Christian Karl) (1858–1913) French-born German engineer, inventor of the diesel engine

Diophantus (*fl.* prob. 250 AD) Greek mathematician

Dirac, Paul Adrian Maurice (1902–84) English theoretical physicist

Donkin, Bryan (1768–1855) English engineer

Doppler, Johann Christian (1803–53) Austrian physicist

Dunlop, John Boyd (1840–1921) Scottish inventor

Durkheim, Émile (1858–1917) French sociologist

Du Vigneaud, Vincent (1901–78) American biochemist

Earhart, Amelia (1898–1937) American aviator

Eastman, George (1854–1932) American inventor and manufacturer of photographic equipment

Eccles, Sir John Carew (1903–97) Australian physiologist

Eddington, Sir Arthur Stanley (1882–1944) English astronomer, founder of the science of astrophysics

Edison, Thomas (Alva) (1847–1931) American inventor

Egas Moniz, Antonio Caetano de Abreu Freire (1874–1955) Portuguese neurologist

Ehrlich, Paul (1854–1915) German medical scientist, one of the founders of modern immunology

Eiffel, Alexandre Gustave (1832–1923) French engineer

Einstein, Albert (1879–1955) German-born American theoretical physicist, founder of the theory of relativity, often regarded as the greatest scientist of the 20th century

Einthoven, Willem (1860–1927) Dutch physiologist

Ekman, Vagn Walfrid (1874–1954) Swedish oceanographer

Elton, Charles Sutherland (1900–91) English zoologist

Empedocles (*c.* 493–*c.* 433 BC) Greek philosopher, born in Sicily

Enders, John Franklin (1897–1985) American virologist

Epicurus (341–270 BC) Greek philosopher and scientist

Eratosthenes (*c.* 275–194 BC) Greek scholar, geographer, and astronomer

Ericsson, John (1803–89) Swedish engineer

Erlanger, Joseph (1874–1965) American physiologist

Esaki, Leo (born 1925) Japanese physicist

Euclid (*c.* 300 BC) Greek mathematician

Euler, Leonhard (1707–83) Swiss mathematician

Euler, Ulf Svante von (1905–83) Swedish physiologist, the son of Hans Euler-Chelpin

Euler-Chelpin, Hans Karl August Simon von (1873–1964) German-born Swedish biochemist

Evans, Sir Arthur (John) (1851–1941) English archaeologist

Evans-Pritchard, Sir Edward (Evan) (1902–73) English anthropologist

Fabre, Jean Henri (1823–1915) French entomologist

Fabricius, Johann Christian (1745–1808) Danish entomologist

Fahrenheit, Gabriel Daniel (1686–1736) German physicist

Faraday, Michael (1791–1867) English physicist and chemist

Fechner, Gustav Theodor (1801–87) German physicist and psychologist

Fermat, Pierre de (1601–65) French mathematician

Fermi, Enrico (1901–54) Italian-born American atomic physicist

Ferranti, Sebastian Ziani de (1864–1930) English electrical engineer

Ferrari, Enzo (1898–1988) Italian car designer and manufacturer

Fessenden, Reginald Aubrey (1866–1932) Canadian-born American physicist and radio engineer

Feynman, Richard Phillips (1918–88) American theoretical physicist

Fibonacci, Leonardo (known as Fibonacci of Pisa) (*c.* 1170–*c.* 1250) Italian mathematician

SCIENTISTS, INVENTORS, AND PIONEERS (cont.)

Fischer, Emil Hermann (1852–1919) German organic chemist

Fischer, Hans (1881–1945) German organic chemist

Fisher, Sir Ronald Aylmer (1890–1962) English statistician and geneticist

FitzGerald, George Francis (1851–1901) Irish physicist

Flamsteed, John (1646–1719) English astronomer

Fleming, Sir Alexander (1881–1955) Scottish bacteriologist

Fleming, Sir John Ambrose (1849–1945) English electrical engineer

Florey, Howard Walter, Baron (1898–1968) Australian pathologist

Fokker, Anthony Herman Gerard (1890–1939) Dutch-born American pioneer aircraft designer and pilot

Foucault, Jean Bernard Léon (1819–68) French physicist

Fourier, Jean Baptiste Joseph (1768–1830) French mathematician

Franck, James (1882–1964) German-born American physicist

Franklin, Benjamin (1706–90) American statesman, inventor, and scientist

Franklin, Rosalind Elsie (1920–58) English physical chemist and molecular biologist

Fraunhofer, Joseph von (1787–1826) German optician and pioneer in spectroscopy

Frazer, Sir James George (1854–1941) Scottish anthropologist

Frege, Gottlob (1848–1925) German philosopher and mathematician, founder of modern logic

Fresnel, Augustin Jean (1788–1827) French physicist and civil engineer

Frisch, Karl von (1886–1982) Austrian zoologist

Frisch, Otto Robert (1904–79) Austrian-born British physicist

Fuchs, (Emil) Klaus (Julius) (1911–88) German-born British physicist

Fulton, Robert (1765–1815) American pioneer of the steamship

Funk, Casimir (1884–1967) Polish-born American biochemist

Gabor, Dennis (1900–79) Hungarian-born British electrical engineer

Gagarin, Yuri (Alekseevich) (1934–68) Russian cosmonaut

Galen (full name Claudios Galenos; Latin name Claudius Galenus) (129–99) Greek physician

Galileo Galilei (1564–1642) Italian astronomer and physicist, one of the founders of modern science

Galois, Évariste (1811–32) French mathematician

Galton, Sir Francis (1822–1911) English scientist

Galvani, Luigi (1737–98) Italian anatomist

Gamow, George (1904–68) Russian-born American physicist

Gassendi, Pierre (1592–1655) French astronomer and philosopher

Gasser, Herbert Spencer (1888–1963) American physiologist

Gates, William (Henry) ('Bill') (born 1955) American computer entrepreneur

Gatling, Richard Jordan (1818–1903) American inventor

Gauss, Karl Friedrich (1777–1855) German mathematician, astronomer, and physicist

Gay-Lussac, Joseph Louis (1778–1850) French chemist and physicist

Geber (Latinized name of Jabir ibn Hayyan, c. 721–c. 815) Arab chemist

Geiger, Hans (Johann) Wilhelm (1882–1945) German nuclear physicist

Geikie, Sir Archibald (1835–1924) Scottish geologist

Gell-Mann, Murray (born 1929) American theoretical physicist

Gerard, John (1545–1612) English herbalist

Gibbs, Josiah Willard (1839–1903) American physical chemist

Gilbert, William (1544–1603) English physician and physicist

Glashow, Sheldon Lee (born 1932) American theoretical physicist

Goddard, Robert Hutchings (1882–1945) American physicist

Gödel, Kurt (1906–78) Austrian-born American mathematician

Goldmark, Peter Carl (1906–77) Hungarian-born American inventor and engineer

Goldschmidt, Victor Moritz (1888–1947) Swiss-born Norwegian chemist

Golgi, Camillo (1844–1926) Italian histologist and anatomist

Goodall, Jane (born 1934) English zoologist

Goodyear, Charles (1800–60) American inventor

Gould, Stephen Jay (born 1941) American palaeontologist

Graham, Thomas (1805–69) Scottish physical chemist

Gray, Asa (1810–88) American botanist

Greenfield, Susan (born 1950) British neurobiologist.

Gresley, Sir (Herbert) Nigel (1876–1941) British railway engineer

Grimaldi, Francesco Maria (1618–63) Italian Jesuit physicist and astronomer, discoverer of the diffraction of light

SCIENTISTS, INVENTORS, AND PIONEERS (cont.)

Guericke, Otto von (1602–86) German engineer and physicist

Haeckel, Ernst Heinrich (1834–1919) German biologist and philosopher

Hahn, Otto (1879–1968) German chemist, co-discoverer of nuclear fission

Haldane, J(ohn) B(urdon) S(anderson) (1892–1964) Scottish mathematical biologist

Hale, George Ellery (1868–1938) American astronomer

Hall, Charles Martin (1863–1914) American industrial chemist

Haller, Albrecht von (1708–77) Swiss anatomist and physiologist

Halley, Edmond (1656–1742) English astronomer and mathematician

Hamilton, Sir William Rowan (1806–65) Irish mathematician and theoretical physicist

Handley Page, Frederick See PAGE

Hargreaves, James (1720–78) English inventor

Harvey, William (1578–1657) English discoverer of the mechanism of blood circulation

Hawking, Stephen William (born 1942) English theoretical physicist

Haworth, Sir Walter Norman (1883–1950) English organic chemist

Heaviside, Oliver (1850–1925) English physicist and electrical engineer

Heisenberg, Werner Karl (1901–76) German mathematical physicist and philosopher, who developed a system of quantum mechanics based on matrix algebra

Helmholtz, Hermann Ludwig Ferdinand von (1821–94) German physiologist and physicist

Helmont, Joannes Baptista van (1577–1644) Belgian chemist and physician

Hero (known as Hero of Alexandria) (1st century) Greek mathematician and inventor

Herophilus (4th–3rd centuries BC) Greek anatomist, regarded as the father of human anatomy

Herschel, Sir (Frederick) William (1738–1822) German-born British astronomer, the father of stellar astronomy

Herschel, Sir John (Frederick William) (1792–1871) British astronomer and physicist, son of William Herschel

Hertz, Heinrich Rudolf (1857–94) German physicist and pioneer of radio communication

Hess, Victor Francis (born Victor Franz Hess) (1883–1964) Austrian-born American physicist

Hevesy, George Charles de (1885–1966) Hungarian-born radiochemist

Heyerdahl, Thor (born 1914) Norwegian anthropologist

Hilbert, David (1862–1943) German mathematician

Hill, Sir Rowland (1795–1879) British educationist, administrator, and inventor

Hinshelwood, Sir Cyril Norman (1897–1967) English physical chemist

Hipparchus (c. 170–after 126 BC) Greek astronomer and geographer, working in Rhodes

Hippocrates (c. 460–377 BC) the most famous of all physicians, of whom, paradoxically, almost nothing is known

Hodgkin, Sir Alan Lloyd (1914–98) English physiologist

Hodgkin, Dorothy (Crowfoot) (1910–94) British chemist

Hoe, Richard March (1812–86) American inventor and industrialist

Hollerith, Herman (1860–1929) American engineer

Holmes, Arthur (1890–1965) English geologist and geophysicist

Honda, Soichiro (1906–92) Japanese motor manufacturer

Hooke, Robert (1635–1703) English scientist

Hooker, Sir Joseph Dalton (1817–1911) English botanist and pioneer in plant geography

Hopkins, Sir Frederick Gowland (1861–1947) English biochemist, considered the father of British biochemistry

Howe, Elias (1819–67) American inventor

Hoyle, Sir Fred (born 1915) English astrophysicist, one of the proponents of the steady-state theory of cosmology

Hubble, Edwin Powell (1889–1953) American astronomer

Huggins, Sir William (1824–1910) British astronomer

Humboldt, Friedrich Heinrich Alexander, Baron von (1769–1859) German explorer and scientist

Hunter, John (1728–93) Scottish anatomist

Hutton, James (1726–97) Scottish geologist

Huxley, Sir Andrew Fielding (born 1917) English physiologist and grandson of Thomas Henry Huxley

Huxley, Sir Julian (1887–1975) English biologist and grandson of Thomas Henry Huxley

Huxley, Thomas Henry (1825–95) English biologist

Huygens, Christiaan (1629–95) Dutch physicist, mathematician, and astronomer

Hypatia (c. 370–415) Greek philosopher, astronomer, and mathematician

Ingenhousz, Jan (1730–99) Dutch scientist

SCIENTISTS, INVENTORS, AND PIONEERS (cont.)

Ipatieff, Vladimir Nikolaievich (1867–1952)
Russian-born American chemist

Issigonis, Sir Alec (Arnold Constantine)
(1906–88) Turkish-born British car designer

Jacobi, Karl Gustav Jacob (1804–51) German
mathematician

Jeans, Sir James Hopwood (1877–1946)
English physicist and astronomer

Jobs, Steven (Paul) (born 1955) American
computer entrepreneur

Johnson, Amy (1903–41) English aviator

Joliot, Jean-Frédéric (1900–58) French
nuclear physicist

Joule, James Prescott (1818–89) English
physicist

Jussieu, Antoine Laurent de (1748–1836)
French botanist

Kamerlingh Onnes, Heike (1853–1926) Dutch
physicist, who studied cryogenic
phenomena

Kekulé, Friedrich August (full name Friedrich
August Kekulé von Stradonitz) (1829–96)
German chemist

Kelvin, William Thomson, 1st Baron
(1824–1907) British physicist, professor of
natural philosophy at Glasgow 1846–95

Kendall, Edward Calvin (1886–1972)
American biochemist

Kennelly, Arthur Edwin (1861–1939)
American electrical engineer

Kepler, Johannes (1571–1630) German
astronomer

Kettering, Charles Franklin (1876–1958)
American automobile engineer

Kinsey, Alfred Charles (1894–1956) American
zoologist and sex researcher

Kirchhoff, Gustav Robert (1824–87) German
physicist, a pioneer in spectroscopy

Kitzinger, Sheila (Helena Elizabeth) (born
1929) English childbirth educator

Klaproth, Martin Heinrich (1743–1817)
German chemist, one of the founders of
analytical chemistry

Koch, Robert (1843–1910) German
bacteriologist

Krebs, Sir Hans Adolf (1900–81) German-born
British biochemist

Kroto, Sir Harold Walter (1900–81) British
chemist

Lagrange, Joseph Louis, Comte de
(1736–1813) Italian-born French
mathematician

Lamarck, Jean Baptiste de (1744–1829)
French naturalist, an early proponent of
organic evolution

Landau, Lev (Davidovich) (1908–68) Soviet
theoretical physicist, born in Russia

Langley, Samuel Pierpoint (1834–1906)
American astronomer and aviation pioneer

Langmuir, Irving (1881–1957) American
chemist and physicist

Laplace, Pierre Simon, Marquis de
(1749–1827) French applied mathematician
and theoretical physicist

Lavoisier, Antoine Laurent (1743–94) French
scientist, regarded as the father of modern
chemistry

Lawrence, Ernest Orlando (1901–58)
American physicist

Leakey, Louis (Seymour Bazett) (1903–72)
British-born Kenyan archaeologist and
anthropologist

Leblanc, Nicolas (1742–1806) French surgeon
and chemist

Leeuwenhoek, Antoni van (1632–1723) Dutch
naturalist

Le Verrier, Urbain (1811–77) French
mathematician

Lévi-Strauss, Claude (born 1908) French
social anthropologist

Liebig, Justus von, Baron (1803–73) German
chemist and teacher

Lilienthal, Otto (1848–96) German pioneer in
the design and flying of gliders

Lindbergh, Charles (Augustus) (1902–74)
American aviator

Lindemann, Frederick Alexander See
CHERWELL

Linnaeus, Carolus (Latinized name of Carl
von Linné) (1707–78) Swedish botanist,
founder of modern systematic botany and
zoology

Lippmann, Gabriel Jonas (1845–1921) French
physicist

Lister, Joseph, 1st Baron (1827–1912) English
surgeon, inventor of antiseptic techniques
in surgery

Lobachevski, Nikolai Ivanovich (1792–1856)
Russian mathematician

Locke, Joseph (1805–60) English civil
engineer

Lockyer, Sir (Joseph) Norman (1836–1920)
English astronomer

Lodge, Sir Oliver (Joseph) (1851–1940)
English physicist

Loewi, Otto (1873–1961) American
pharmacologist and physiologist, born in
Germany

Lorentz, Hendrik Antoon (1853–1928) Dutch
theoretical physicist

Lorenz, Konrad (Zacharias) (1903–89)
Austrian zoologist

Lovelace, Countess of (title of Augusta Ada
King neé Byron) (1815–52) English
mathematician

Lovell, Sir (Alfred Charles) Bernard (born
1913) English astronomer and physicist,
and pioneer of radio astronomy

SCIENTISTS, INVENTORS, AND PIONEERS (cont.)

Lovelock, James (Ephraim) (born 1919) English scientist

Lowell, Percival (1855–1916) American astronomer

Lyell, Sir Charles (1797–1875) Scottish geologist

Lysenko, Trofim Denisovich (1898–1976) Soviet biologist and geneticist

Mach, Ernst (1838–1916) Austrian physicist and philosopher of science

Malpighi, Marcello (c. 1628–94) Italian microscopist

Mandelbrot, Benoit (born 1924) Polish-born French mathematician

Mantell, Gideon Algernon (1790–1852) English geologist

Marconi, Guglielmo (1874–1937) Italian electrical engineer, the father of radio

Maury, Matthew Fontaine (1806–73) American oceanographer

Maxwell, James Clerk (1831–79) Scottish physicist

Mayr, Ernst Walter (born 1904) German-born American zoologist

Mead, Margaret (1901–78) American anthropologist and social psychologist

Medawar, Sir Peter (Brian) (1915–87) English immunologist and author

Meitner, Lise (1878–1968) Austrian-born Swedish physicist

Mendel, Gregor Johann (1822–84) Moravian monk, the father of genetics

Mendeleev, Dmitri (Ivanovich) (1834–1907) Russian chemist

Mercator, Gerardus (Latinized name of Gerhard Kremer) (1512–94) Flemish geographer and cartographer, resident in Germany from 1552

Messerschmidt, Wilhelm Emil ('Willy') (1898–1978) German aircraft designer and industrialist

Messier, Charles (1730–1817) French astronomer

Meyerhof, Otto Fritz (1884–1951) German-born American biochemist

Michelson, Albert Abraham (1852–1931) American physicist

Millikan, Robert Andrews (1868–1953) American physicist

Minkowski, Hermann (1864–1909) Russian-born German mathematician

Mitchell, R(eginald) J(oseph) (1895–1937) English aeronautical engineer

Moissan, Ferdinand Frédéric Henri (1852–1907) French chemist

Monod, Jacques Lucien (1910–76) French biochemist

Montgolfier, Joseph Michel (1740–1810) and **Jacques Étienne** (1745–99) French inventors

Moog, Robert (born 1934) American inventor

Morgan, Thomas Hunt (1866–1945) American zoologist

Morley, Edward Williams (1838–1923) American chemist

Morse, Samuel F(inley) B(reese) (1791–1872) American inventor

Mosander, Carl Gustaf (1797–1858) Swedish chemist

Moseley, Henry Gwyn Jeffreys (1887–1915) English physicist

Müller, Johannes Peter (1801–58) German anatomist and zoologist

Müller, Paul Hermann (1899–1965) Swiss chemist

Napier, John (1550–1617) Scottish mathematician

Nasmyth, James (1808–90) British engineer

Needham, Joseph (1900–95) English scientist and historian

Nernst, Hermann Walther (1864–1941) German physical chemist

Nervi, Pier Luigi (1891–1979) Italian engineer and architect

Neumann, John von (1903–57) Hungarian-born American mathematician and computer pioneer

Newcomen, Thomas (1663–1729) English engineer, developer of the first practical steam engine

Newlands, John Alexander Reina (1837–98) English industrial chemist

Newton, Sir Isaac (1642–1727) English mathematician and physicist

Nightingale, Florence (1820–1910) English nurse and medical reformer

Nobel, Alfred Bernhard (1833–96) Swedish chemist and engineer

Noether, Emmy (1882–1935) German mathematician

Nuffield, 1st Viscount (title of William Richard Morris) (1877–1963) British motor manufacturer and philanthropist

Oersted, Hans Christian (1777–1851) Danish physicist, discoverer of the magnetic effect of an electric current

Ohm, Georg Simon (1789–1854) German physicist

Omar Khayyám (died 1123) Persian poet, mathematician, and astronomer

Oort, Jan Hendrik (1900–92) Dutch astronomer

Opel, Wilhelm von (1871–1948) German motor manufacturer

Oppenheimer, Julius Robert (1904–67) American theoretical physicist

Ostwald, Friedrich Wilhelm (1853–1932) German physical chemist

SCIENTISTS, INVENTORS, AND PIONEERS (cont.)

Otis, Elisha Graves (1811–61) American inventor and manufacturer

Otto, Nikolaus August (1832–91) German engineer

Owen, Sir Richard (1804–92) English anatomist and palaeontologist

Page, Sir Frederick Handley (1885–1962) English aircraft designer

Pappus (known as Pappus of Alexandria) (*fl. c.* 300–350 AD) Greek mathematician

Paracelsus (born Theophrastus Phillipus Aureolus Bombastus von Hohenheim) (*c.* 1493–1541) Swiss physician

Parsons, Sir Charles (Algernon) (1854–1931) British engineer, scientist, and manufacturer

Pascal, Blaise (1623–62) French mathematician, physicist, and religious philosopher

Pasteur, Louis (1822–95) French chemist and bacteriologist

Pauli, Wolfgang (1900–58) Austrian-born American physicist who worked chiefly in Switzerland

Pauling, Linus Carl (1901–94) American chemist

Pavlov, Ivan (Petrovich) (1849–1936) Russian physiologist

Pearson, Karl (1857–1936) English mathematician, the principal founder of 20th-century statistics

Pelletier, Pierre-Joseph (1788–1842) French chemist

Perkin, Sir William Henry (1838–1907) English chemist and pioneer of the synthetic organic chemical industry

Perrin, Jean Baptiste (1870–1942) French physical chemist

Perthes, Jacques Boucher de See BOUCHER DE PERTHES

Petrie, Sir (William Matthew) Flinders (1853–1942) English archaeologist and Egyptologist

Pickering, William Hayward (born 1910) New Zealand-born American engineer

Pitt-Rivers, Augustus Henry Lane Fox (1827–1900) English archaeologist and anthropologist

Planck, Max (Karl Ernst Ludwig) (1858–1947) German theoretical physicist, who founded the quantum theory

Playfair, John (1748–1819) Scottish mathematician and geologist

Pliny (known as Pliny the Elder; Latin name Gaius Plinius Secundus) (23–79 AD) Roman natural historian

Poincaré, Jules-Henri (1854–1912) French mathematician and philosopher of science

Poisson, Siméon-Denis (1781–1840) French mathematical physicist

Porsche, Ferdinand (1875–1952) Austrian car designer

Prandtl, Ludwig (1875–1953) German physicist

Priestley, Joseph (1733–1804) English scientist and theologian

Proust, Joseph Louis (1754–1826) French analytical chemist

Prout, William (1785–1850) English chemist and biochemist

Ptolemy (2nd century) Greek astronomer and geographer

Raman, Sir Chandrasekhara Venkata (1888–1970) Indian physicist

Ramanujan, Srinivasa Aaiyangar (1887–1920) Indian mathematician

Ramón y Cajal, Santiago (1852–1934) Spanish physician and histologist

Ramsay, Sir William (1852–1916) Scottish chemist, discoverer of the noble gases

Ray, John (1627–1705) English naturalist

Rayleigh, John William Strutt, 3rd Baron (1842–1919) English physicist

Réaumur, René Antoine Ferchault de (1683–1757) French scientist

Regiomontanus, Johannes (born Johannes Müller) (1436–76) German astronomer and mathematician

Renault, Louis (1877–1944) French engineer and motor manufacturer

Rennie, John (1761–1821) Scottish civil engineer

Reuter, Paul Julius, Baron von (born Israel Beer Josaphat) (1816–99) German pioneer of telegraphy and news reporting

Richter, Charles Francis (1900–85) American geologist

Riemann, (Georg Friedrich) Bernhard (1826–66) German mathematician

Roe, Sir (Edwin) Alliott Verdon (1877–1958) English engineer and aircraft designer

Rolls, Charles Stewart (1877–1910) English motoring and aviation pioneer

Röntgen, Wilhelm Conrad (1845–1923) German physicist, the discoverer of X-rays

Royce, Sir (Frederick) Henry (1863–1933) English engine designer

Russell, Bertrand (Arthur William), 3rd Earl Russell (1872–1970) British philosopher, mathematician, and social reformer

Russell, Henry Norris (1877–1957) American astronomer

Rutherford, Sir Ernest, 1st Baron Rutherford of Nelson (1871–1937) New Zealand physicist

Ryle, Sir Martin (1918–84) English astronomer

SCIENTISTS, INVENTORS, AND PIONEERS (cont.)

Sagan, Carl (Edward) (1934–96) American astronomer

Salam, Abdus (1926–96) Pakistani theoretical physicist

Salk, Jonas Edward (1914–95) American microbiologist

Sanger, Frederick (born 1918) English biochemist

Savery, Thomas (known as 'Captain Savery') (c. 1650–1715) English engineer, constructor of the first practical steam engine

Scheele, Carl Wilhelm (1742–86) Swedish chemist

Schlick, Moritz (1882–1936) German philosopher and physicist

Schliemann, Heinrich (1822–90) German archaeologist

Schrödinger, Erwin (1887–1961) Austrian theoretical physicist

Schwann, Theodor Ambrose Hubert (1810–82) German physiologist

Seaborg, Glenn (Theodore) (1912–99) American nuclear chemist

Semmelweis, Ignaz Philipp (born Ignác Fülöp Semmelweis) (1818–65) Hungarian obstetrician who spent most of his working life in Vienna

Shannon, Claude Elwood (born 1916) American engineer

Shapley, Harlow (1885–1972) American astronomer

Sherrington, Sir Charles Scott (1857–1952) English physiologist

Shockley, William (Bradford) (1910–89) American physicist

Siemens, Ernst Werner von (1816–92) German electrical engineer

Sikorsky, Igor (Ivanovich) (1889–1972) Russian-born American aircraft designer

Sinclair, Sir Clive (Marles) (born 1940) English electronics engineer and entrepreneur

Singer, Isaac Merrit (1811–75) American inventor

Sloane, Sir Hans (1660–1753) English physician and naturalist

Smith, William (1769–1839) English land-surveyor and geologist

Snow, C(harles) P(ercy), 1st Baron Snow of Leicester (1905–80) English novelist and scientist

Soddy, Frederick (1877–1956) English physicist

Sopwith, Sir Thomas (Octave Murdoch) (1888–1989) English aircraft designer

Spallanzani, Lazzaro (1729–99) Italian physiologist and biologist

Spock, Benjamin McLane (known as Dr Spock) (1903–98) American paediatrician and writer

Stanier, Sir William (Arthur) (1876–1965) English railway engineer

Starling, Ernest Henry (1866–1927) English physiologist

Steller, Georg Wilhelm (1709–46) German naturalist and geographer

Steno, Nicolaus (Danish name Niels Steensen) (1638–86) Danish anatomist and geologist

Stephenson, George (1781–1848) English engineer, the father of railways

Stirling, James (1692–1770) Scottish mathematician

Stirling, Robert (1790–1878) Scottish engineer and Presbyterian minister

Struve, Otto (1897–1963) Russian-born astronomer

Swammerdam, Jan (1637–80) Dutch naturalist and microscopist

Swan, Sir Joseph Wilson (1828–1914) English physicist and chemist

Swedenborg, Emanuel (1688–1772) Swedish scientist, philosopher, and mystic

Szent-Györgyi, Albert von (1893–1986) American biochemist, born in Hungary

Szilard, Leo (1898–1964) Hungarian-born American physicist and molecular biologist

Talbot, (William Henry) Fox (1800–77) English pioneer of photography

Teilhard de Chardin, Pierre (1881–1955) French Jesuit philosopher and palaeontologist

Telford, Thomas (1757–1834) Scottish civil engineer

Teller, Edward (born 1908) Hungarian-born American physicist

Tereshkova, Valentina (Vladimirovna) (born 1937) Russian cosmonaut

Tesla, Nikola (1856–1943) American electrical engineer and inventor, born in what is now Croatia of Serbian descent

Thales (c. 624–c. 545 BC) Greek philosopher, mathematician, and astronomer

Theophrastus (c. 370–c. 287 BC) Greek philosopher and scientist

Thom, Alexander (1894–1985) Scottish expert on prehistoric stone circles

Thomson, Sir Joseph John (1856–1940) English physicist, discoverer of the electron

Thomson, Sir William See KELVIN

Tinbergen, Nikolaas (1907–88) Dutch zoologist

Tombaugh, Clyde William (1906–97) American astronomer

Tompion, Thomas (c. 1639–1713) English clock and watchmaker

SCIENTISTS, INVENTORS, AND PIONEERS (cont.)

Torricelli, Evangelista (1608–47) Italian mathematician and physicist

Townes, Charles Hard (born 1915) American physicist

Tradescant, John (1570–1638) English botanist and horticulturalist

Trevithick, Richard (1771–1833) English engineer

Tsiolkovsky, Konstantin (Eduardovich) (1857–1935) Russian aeronautical engineer

Tull, Jethro (1674–1741) English agriculturalist

Turing, Alan (Mathison) (1912–54) English mathematician

Tycho Brahe See BRAHE

Tyndall, John (1820–93) Irish physicist

Urey, Harold Clayton (1893–1981) American chemist

Van Allen, James Alfred (born 1914) American physicist

Van de Graaf, Robert Jemison (1901–67) American physicist

Vavilov, Nikolai (Ivanovich) (1887–*c.* 1943) Soviet plant geneticist

Vening Meinesz, Felix Andries (1887–1966) Dutch geophysicist

Verdon Roe, Sir Edwin Alliott See ROE

Vesalius, Andreas (1514–64) Flemish anatomist, the founder of modern anatomy

Vine, Frederick John (born 1939) English geologist

Virchow, Rudolf Karl (1821–1902) German physician and pathologist, founder of cellular pathology

Vitruvius (full name Marcus Vitruvius Pollio) (*fl.* 1st century BC) Roman architect and military engineer

Volta, Alessandro Giuseppe Antonio Anastasio, Count (1745–1827) Italian physicist

von Braun, Wernher Magnus Maximilian See BRAUN

von Neumann See NEUMANN

Waksman, Selman Abraham (1888–1973) Russian-born American microbiologist

Wallace, Alfred Russel (1823–1913) English naturalist

Wallis, Sir Barnes Neville (1887–1979) English inventor

Warburg, Otto Heinrich (1883–1970) German biochemist

Watson, James Dewey (born 1928) American biologist

Watson-Watt, Sir Robert Alexander (1892–1973) Scottish physicist

Watt, James (1736–1819) Scottish engineer

Wegener, Alfred Lothar (1880–1930) German meteorologist and geologist

Weinberg, Steven (born 1933) American theoretical physicist

Weismann, August Friedrich Leopold (1834–1914) German biologist, one of the founders of modern genetics

Welsbach, Carl Auer, Baron von See AUER

Werner, Abraham Gottlob (1749–1817) German geologist

Werner, Alfred (1866–1919) French-born Swiss chemist, founder of coordination chemistry

Westinghouse, George (1846–1914) American engineer

Wheatstone, Sir Charles (1802–75) English physicist and inventor

Wheeler, John Archibald (born 1911) American theoretical physicist

White, Gilbert (1720–93) English clergyman and naturalist

Whitehead, A(lfred) N(orth) (1861–1947) English philosopher and mathematician

Whitney, Eli (1765–1825) American inventor

Whittle, Sir Frank (1907–96) English aeronautical engineer, test pilot, and inventor of the jet aircraft engine

Wiener, Norbert (1894–1964) American mathematician

Wilkins, Maurice Hugh Frederick (born 1916) New Zealand-born British biochemist and molecular biologist

Wilson, Charles Thomson Rees (1869–1959) Scottish physicist

Wilson, Edward Osborne (born 1929) American social biologist

Wöhler, Friedrich (1800–82) German chemist

Wollaston, William Hyde (1766–1828) English chemist and physicist

Woodward, Robert Burns (1917–79) American organic chemist

Woolley, Sir (Charles) Leonard (1880–1960) English archaeologist

Wright, Orville (1871–1948) and **Wilbur** (1867–1912) American aviation pioneers

Yeager, Charles E(lwood) ('Chuck') (born 1923) American pilot

Young, Thomas (1773–1829) English physicist, physician, and Egyptologist

Zeiss, Carl (1816–88) German optical instrument-maker

Zeppelin, Ferdinand (Adolf August Heinrich), Count von (1838–1917) German aviation pioneer

Zworykin, Vladimir (Kuzmich) (1889–1982) Russian-born American physicist and television pioneer

MEDICINE

HUMAN BONES

ankle-bone
anvil
astragalus
backbone
breastbone
calcaneus
carpal
cheekbone
clavicle
collarbone
costa
cranium
cuboid
ethmoid
femur

fibula
floating rib
frontal bone
funny bone
hallux
hammer
heel bone
humerus
hyoid
ilium
incus
innominate
  bone
ischium
jawbone

kneecap
lunate bone
malleus
mandible
maxilla
metacarpal
metatarsal
nasal bone
navicular bone
occipital bone
parietal bone
patella
pelvis
phalanx
pisiform bone

pubis
rachis
radius
rib
sacrum
scaphoid
scapula
sesamoid bone
shin bone
shoulder blade
skull
sphenoid
spinal column
spine
stapes

sternum
stirrup
talus
tarsal
temporal bone
thigh bone
tibia
ulna
vertebra
vertebral
  column
vomer
wrist-bone
zygomatic bone

HUMAN MUSCLES

abdominal muscles
biceps
deltoid
gastrocnemius
gluteus
pectoral muscle
peroneal muscle
psoas

quadriceps
rhomboideus
sartorius
scalenus
soleus
splenius
trapezius
triceps

HUMAN GLANDS

Endocrine Glands

adrenal gland
corpus luteum
islets of Langerhans
ovary
parathyroid gland
pineal gland
pituitary gland
testis
thyroid gland

Exocrine Glands

Bartholin's gland
breast
Brunner's gland
buccal gland
Cowper's *or* bulbo-
  urethral gland
gastric gland
lacrimal gland
Lieberkühn's gland
liver
mammary gland
meibomian *or* tarsal
  gland
pancreas
parotid gland
preputial gland
prostate gland
salivary gland
sebaceous gland
sublingual gland
submandibular *or*
  submaxillary gland
sweat gland

PARTS OF THE HUMAN EYE

aqueous humour
blind spot
choroid
ciliary body
cone
conjunctiva
cornea
extrinsic muscle
eyeball
eyelash *or* cilium
eyelid *or* blepharon
  or palpebra
fovea
iris
lens

limbus
optic foramen
optic nerve
orbit
pupil
retina
rod
sclera
stroma
suspensory ligament
tarsal plate
tear glands (lacrimal
  glands)
vitreous humour

PARTS OF THE HUMAN EAR

auditory canal
auditory nerve
auricle *or* pinna
basilar membrane
cochlea
endolymph
Eustachian tube
hair cell

incus *or* anvil
inner ear
malleus *or* hammer
middle ear
organ of Corti
outer ear
perilymph
pinna *or* auricle

saccule
semicircular canal
stapes *or* stirrup
tectorial membrane
tympanic membrane *or* eardrum
utricle
vestibule

DISEASES AND MEDICAL CONDITIONS

acromegaly
actinomycosis
Addison's disease
AIDS
Alzheimer's disease
anaemia
anchylostomiasis
angina
anorexia nervosa
appendicitis
arthritis
asbestosis
Asperger's syndrome
asthma
autism
avitaminosis
beriberi
bilharzia
Bright's disease
bronchitis
brucellosis
bulimia nervosa
cancer
candidiasis
Chagas' disease
chickenpox
cholera
cirrhosis
clinical depression
coeliac disease
colitis
common cold
coronary heart disease
Creutzfeldt–Jakob disease
Crohn's disease
Cushing's disease
cyanosis

cystic fibrosis
cystitis
dengue
dermatitis
dhobi itch
diabetes
diphtheria
dysentery
Ebola fever
eczema
elephantiasis
emphysema
encephalitis
epilepsy
food poisoning
gastroenteritis
German measles
glandular fever
glaucoma
goitre
gonorrhoea
gout
Graves' disease
haemophilia
hepatitis
herpes
Hodgkin's disease
Huntington's chorea
hypertension
hyperthyroidism
impetigo
influenza
jaundice
kala-azar
Kaposi's sarcoma
Kawasaki disease
kwashiorkor
laryngitis
Lassa fever
legionnaires' disease

leprosy
leptospirosis
leukaemia
listeriosis
lupus
Lyme disease
malaria
measles
Ménière's disease
meningitis
motor neurone disease
mountain sickness
multiple sclerosis
mumps
Münchhausen's syndrome (by proxy)
muscular dystrophy
myalgic encephalitis (ME)
myasthenia gravis
narcolepsy
nephritis
osteoporosis
Paget's disease
Parkinson's disease
pellagra
peritonitis
phenylketonuria
plague
pneumoconiosis
pneumonia
poliomyelitis
porphyria
psittacosis
psoriasis
psychosis
rabies
Raynaud's disease

rheumatic fever
rheumatoid arthritis
rickets
ringworm
rubella (German measles)
St Vitus's dance
salmonella
scarlet fever
schizophrenia
scurvy
shingles
sickle-cell anaemia
silicosis
sinusitis
sleeping sickness
sleepy sickness
smallpox
spina bifida
sweating-sickness
Sydenham's chorea
syphilis
tetanus
thalassaemia
tonsillitis
toxic shock syndrome
toxoplasmosis
trachoma
tuberculosis
typhoid fever
typhus
venereal disease
Weil's disease
whooping cough
yaws
yellow fever

MEDICAL SPECIALITIES

anaesthetics
brain surgery
cardiology
chiropractic
chiropody
dentistry
dermatology
diagnostics
endocrinology
endodontics
ENT (ear, nose, & throat) medicine
epidemiology

exodontics
forensic pathology
gastroenterology
geriatrics
gerontology
gynaecology
haematology
heart surgery
immunology
nephrology
neurology
neurosurgery
nosology

obstetrics
oncology
ophthalmology
orthodontics
orthopaedics
osteology
otolaryngology
otology
otorhinolaryngology
paediatrics
paedodontics
pathology
periodontics

plastic surgery
podiatry
prosthodontics
radiology
radiotherapy
rheumatology
serology
surgery
teratology
urology
venereology

TYPES OF MEDICATION AND DRUG

anaesthetic
analgesic
antacid
anthelmintic
antibiotic
antibacterial
anticoagulant
anticonvulsant
antidepressant
antidote

antiemetic
antiepileptic
antifungal
antihistamine
anti-inflammatory
antipsychotic
antipyretic
antiseptic
antitussive
appetite suppressant

beta blocker
bronchodilator
decongestant
depressant
diuretic
emetic
expectorant
fungicide
immunosuppressive
laxative

muscle relaxant
nutraceutical
sedative
steroid
stimulant
tonic
tranquillizer
vasoconstrictor
vasodilator

SURGICAL OPERATIONS
(with description)

adenoidectomy	removal of adenoids	episiotomy	incision of vaginal opening
angioplasty	repair of blood vessel		
appendicectomy *or*		gastrectomy	removal of whole or part of stomach
appendectomy	removal of appendix		
arteriotomy	incision of artery	gastroplasty	repair of stomach
cheiloplasty	repair of lips	gastrostomy	opening of stomach
cholecystectomy	removal of gall bladder	gastrotomy	incision of stomach
cholecystotomy	incision of gall bladder	glossectomy	removal of all or part of tongue
colectomy	removal of colon		
colostomy	opening of colon	haemorrhoidectomy	removal of haemorrhoids
craniotomy	incision of skull		
cystectomy	removal of bladder	hepatectomy	removal of all or part of liver
cystoplasty	repair of bladder		
cystostomy	opening of bladder	hepaticostomy	opening of bile duct
cystotomy	incision of bladder	hysterectomy	removal of womb
dermatoplasty	repair of skin	hysterotomy	incision of womb
embolectomy	removal of blood clot	laparotomy	incision of abdomen
enterostomy	opening of small intestine	laryngectomy	removal of larynx
		laryngotomy	incision of larynx
enterotomy	incision of intestine	lithotomy	removal of kidney stone

SURGICAL OPERATIONS (cont.)
(with description)

lobectomy	removal of lobe of an organ	pleurotomy	incision of pleural membrane
lobotomy	incision of nerve fibres from frontal lobe of brain	pneumonectomy	removal of lung
		polypectomy	removal of polyp
lumpectomy	removal of breast tumour	prostatectomy	removal of prostate gland
		rhinoplasty	repair of nose
mammaplasty	reshaping of breast	salpingectomy	removal of fallopian tube
mastectomy	removal of breast		
myotomy	incision of muscle	salpingostomy	opening of fallopian tube
nephrectomy	removal of kidney		
nephrostomy	opening of kidney	splenectomy	removal of spleen
nephrotomy	incision of kidney	tenotomy	incision of tendon
neurectomy	removal of nerve	thoracoplasty	repair of thorax
neurotomy	incision of nerve	thoracotomy	incision of chest cavity
oesophagectomy	opening of oesophagus	thrombectomy	removal of blood clot
oophorectomy	removal of ovary	thymectomy	removal of thymus gland
orchidectomy	removal of testis		
orchidotomy	incision of testis	thyroidectomy	removal of all or part of thyroid gland
ostectomy	removal of bone		
osteotomy	incision of bone	tonsillectomy	removal of tonsils
ovariectomy	removal of ovary	tonsillotomy	incision of tonsil
ovariotomy	incision of ovary	tracheostomy	opening of windpipe
palatoplasty	repair of cleft palate	tracheotomy	incision of windpipe
pancreatectomy	removal of pancreas	ureterectomy	removal of ureter
pericardiectomy or		ureterostomy	opening of ureter
pericardectomy	removal of all or part of membrane around heart	ureterotomy	incision of ureter
		urethroplasty	repair of urethra
		urethrotomy	incision of urethra
pericardiotomy	incision of membrane around heart	vagotomy	incision of vagus nerve
		valvotomy	incision of heart valve
perineoplasty	repair of vaginal opening	varicotomy	excision of varicose vein
phalloplasty	repair of penis	vasectomy	removal of all or part of vas deferens
pharyngectomy	removal of pharynx		
phlebotomy	incision of vein		

THERAPIES

acupuncture
aromatherapy
art therapy
aversion therapy
balneotherapy
behaviour therapy
chiropractic
cognitive therapy
colour therapy
confrontation therapy
crystal therapy
drama therapy
electroconvulsive therapy
electroshock therapy
electrotherapy
family therapy

Gerson cure
Gestalt therapy
group therapy
homoeopathy
humanistic therapy
hydrotherapy
hypnotherapy
insulin shock therapy
mechanotherapy
megavitamin therapy
metrazol shock therapy
music therapy
narcotherapy
naturopathy
occupational therapy
osteopathy

play therapy
primal therapy
psychotherapy
rational-emotive therapy
recreational therapy
reflexology
regression therapy
relaxation therapy
release therapy
Rogerian therapy
sex therapy
shiatsu
shock therapy
sleep therapy
sound therapy

BRANCHES OF PSYCHOLOGY

abnormal psychology
Adlerian psychology
analytical psychology
animal psychology
apperceptionism
applied psychology
associationism
behaviourism
child psychology
clinical psychology
cognitive psychology
comparative psychology
configurationism
developmental psychology
educational psychology
ethology
experimental psychology

Freudianism
gestalt psychology
group psychology
Horneyan psychology
humanistic psychology
industrial and organizational
  psychology
introspection psychology
Jungian psychology
Lacanian psychology
metapsychology
neuropsychology
occupational psychology
parapsychology
Pavlovian psychology
physiological psychology
psychoanalysis

psychobiochemistry
psychobiography
psychobiology
psychodynamics
psychogenetics
psychography
psycholinguistics
psychometry
psychopathology
psychopharmacology
psychophysiology
Reichian psychology
Skinnerian psychology
social psychology
structuralism
Watsonian psychology

PHOBIAS

air travel	aerophobia	crowds	demophobia *or*
American people			ochlophobia
and things	Americophobia	dampness	hygrophobia
animals	zoophobia	darkness	scotophobia
bacteria	bacteriophobia	dawn	eosophobia
beards	pogonophobia	death	thanatophobia
beating	mastigophobia	depth	bathophobia
bed	clinophobia	dirt	mysophobia
bees	apiphobia	disease	pathophobia *or*
birds	ornithophobia		nosophobia
Black people		dogs	cynophobia
and things	Negrophobia	drink	potophobia
blood	haemophobia	drugs	pharmacophobia
blushing	erythrophobia	dust	koniophobia
body odour	bromidrosiphobia	electricity	electrophobia
bridges	gephyrophobia	enclosed places	claustrophobia
bullets	ballistophobia	English people	
cancer	carcinophobia	and things	Anglophobia
cats	ailurophobia	everything	panophobia *or*
childbirth	tocophobia		pantophobia
children	paedophobia	eyes	ommetaphobia
Chinese people		faeces	coprophobia
and things	Sinophobia	failure	kakorrhaphiaphobia
church	ecclesiophobia	fatigue	kopophobia
clouds	nephophobia	fear	phobophobia
coitus	coitophobia	feathers	pteronophobia
cold	cheimaphobia	fever	febriphobia
colour	chromophobia	fire	pyrophobia
comets	cometophobia	fish	ichthyophobia
constipation	coprostasophobia	floods	antlophobia
corpses	necrophobia	flowers	anthophobia
correspondence	epistolophobia	fog	homichlophobia
		food	cibophobia *or* sitophobia

PHOBIAS (cont.)

foreigners	xenophobia	loneliness	autophobia *or* ermitophobia
freedom	eleutherophobia	machinery	mechanophobia
French people and things	Francophobia *or* Gallophobia	magic	rhabdophobia
		marriage	gametophobia
fur	doraphobia	men	androphobia
German people and things	Germanophobia *or* Teutophobia	metal	metallophobia
		mice	musophobia
germs	spermophobia *or* bacteriophobia	microbes	bacillophobia *or* microbiophobia
ghosts	phasmophobia	mirrors	eisoptrophobia
giving birth to monsters	teratophobia	mites	acarophobia
		mobs	ochlophobia
God	theophobia	money	chrematophobia
gold	crysophobia *or* aurophobia	monsters	teratrophobia
		motion	kinetophobia
hair	trichophobia	music	musicophobia
heart disease	cardiophobia	names	onomatophobia
heat	thermophobia	narrowness	anginophobia
heaven	uranophobia	needles	belonephobia
hell	hadephobia *or* stygiophobia	new things	neophobia
		night	nyctophobia
heredity	patroiophobia	open places	agoraphobia
high buildings	batophobia	pain	algophobia
high places	acrophobia *or* hypsophobia	parasites	parasitophobia
		people	anthropophobia
home	oikophobia	philosophy	philosophobia
homosexuals	homophobia	pins	enetophobia
horses	hippophobia	places	topophobia
ice	cryophobia	pleasure	hedonophobia
ideas	ideophobia	poison	toxiphobia
idleness	thassophobia	politics	politicophobia
illness	nosophobia	The Pope	papaphobia
imperfection	atelophobia	poverty	peniaphobia
infinity	apeirophobia	precipices	cremnophobia
injury	traumatophobia	priests	hierophobia
inoculation	trypanophobia *or* vaccinophobia	punishment	poinephobia
		rabies	hydrophobophobia
insanity	lyssophobia *or* maniphobia	rail travel	siderodromophobia
		religious works of art	iconophobia
insects	entomophobia	reptiles	batrachophobia
insect stings	cnidophobia	responsibility	hypegiaphobia
Italian people and things	Italophobia	ridicule	katagelophobia
		rivers	potamophobia
itching	acarophobia	robbers	harpaxophobia
jealousy	zelotypophobia	ruin	atephobia
Jewish people and things	Judaeophobia	Russian people and things	Russophobia
justice	dikephobia	saints	hagiophobia
lakes	limnophobia	Satan	Satanophobia
leprosy	leprophobia	scabies	scabiophobia
lice	pediculophobia	Scottish people and things	Scotophobia
light	photophobia	sea	thalassophobia
lightning	astrapophobia	sex	erotophobia
lists	pinaciphobia *or* katastichophobia	shadows	sciophobia
		sharpness	acrophobia

PHOBIAS (cont.)

shock	hormephobia	teeth	odontophobia
sin	hamartophobia	telephone	telephonophobia
skin disease	dermatosiophobia *or*	thinking	phronemophobia
	dermatopathophobia	thirteen	triskaidekaphobia
sleep	hypnophobia	thunder	brontophobia *or*
slime	blennophobia		tonitrophobia *or*
small things	microphobia		keraunophobia
smell	olfactophobia *or*	time	chronophobia
	osmophobia	touch	haptophobia
snakes	ophidiophobia	travel	hodophobia
snow	chionophobia	tuberculosis	phthisiophobia
sound	acousticophobia	tyrants	tyrannophobia
sourness	acerophobia	vehicles	ochophobia
speech	lalophobia *or*	venereal	
	glossophobia *or*	disease	syphilophobia
	phonophobia	voids	kenophobia
speed	tachophobia	vomiting	emetophobia
spiders	arachnophobia	water	hydrophobia
standing	stasophobia	waves	cymophobia
stars	siderophobia	weakness	asthenophobia
stealing	kleptophobia	wind	anemophobia
string	linonophobia	women	gynophobia
sun	heliophobia	words	logophobia
swallowing	phagophobia	work	ergophobia
symmetry	symmetrophobia	worms	helminthophobia
taste	geumatophobia	writing	graphophobia
technology	technophobia		

PEOPLE IN MEDICINE AND PSYCHOLOGY

Addison, Thomas (1793–1860) English physician

Adler, Alfred (1870–1937) Austrian psychologist and psychiatrist

Anderson, Elizabeth Garrett (1836–1917) English physician

Arbuthnot, John (1667–1735) Scottish physician and writer

Banting, Sir Frederick Grant (1891–1941) Canadian physiologist and surgeon

Berger, Hans (1873–1941) German psychiatrist

Best, Charles Herbert (1899–1978) American-born Canadian physiologist

Binet, Alfred (1857–1911) French psychologist and pioneer of modern intelligence testing

Burt, Cyril Lodowic (1883–1971) English psychologist

Blumenbach, Johann Friedrich (1752–1840) German physiologist and anatomist

Browne, Sir Thomas (1605–82) English author and physician

Chauliac, Guy de (*c.* 1300–68) French physician

Dale, Sir Henry Hallett (1875–1968) English physiologist and pharmacologist

Dart, Raymond Arthur (1893–1988) Australian-born South African anthropologist and anatomist

Doll, Sir (William) Richard (Shaboe) (born 1912) English physician

Eccles, Sir John Carew (1903–97) Australian physiologist

Einthoven, Willem (1860–1927) Dutch physiologist

Eijkman, Christiaan (1858–1930) Dutch physician

Ellis, (Henry) Havelock (1859–1939) English psychologist and writer

Erlanger, Joseph (1874–1965) American physiologist

Euler, Ulf Svante von (1905–83) Swedish physiologist, the son of Hans Euler-Chelpin

Eysenck, Hans Jürgen (1916–97) German-born British psychologist

PEOPLE IN MEDICINE AND PSYCHOLOGY
(cont.)

Fechner, Gustav Theodor (1801–87) German physicist and psychologist

Florey, Howard Walter, Baron (1898–1968) Australian pathologist

Freud, Anna (1895–1982) Austrian-born British psychoanalyst, the youngest child of Sigmund Freud

Freud, Sigmund (1856–1939) Austrian neurologist and psychotherapist

Galen (full name Claudios Galenos; Latin name Claudius Galenus) (129–99) Greek physician

Galvani, Luigi (1737–98) Italian anatomist

Gasser, Herbert Spencer (1888–1963) American physiologist

Gilbert, William (1544–1603) English physician and physicist

Golgi, Camillo (1844–1926) Italian histologist and anatomist

Haller, Albrecht von (1708–77) Swiss anatomist and physiologist

Harvey, William (1578–1657) English discoverer of the mechanism of blood circulation and physician to James I and Charles I

Herophilus (4th–3rd centuries BC) Greek anatomist, regarded as the father of human anatomy

Hippocrates (*c.* 460–377 BC) the most famous of all physicians, of whom, paradoxically, almost nothing is known

Hodgkin, Sir Alan Lloyd (born 1914) English physiologist

Hunter, John (1728–93) Scottish anatomist

Huxley, Sir Andrew Fielding (born 1917) English physiologist and grandson of Thomas Henry Huxley

Jenner, Edward (1749–1823) English physician, the pioneer of vaccination

Jung, Carl (Gustav) (1875–1961) Swiss psychologist**Krafft-Ebing, Richard von** (1840–1902) German physician and psychologist

Klein, Melanie (1882–1960) Austrian-born psychoanalyst

Laing, R(onald) D(avid) (1927–89) Scottish psychiatrist

Landsteiner, Karl (1868–1943) Austrian-born American physician

Linacre, Thomas (*c.* 1460–1524) English physician and classical scholar

Lind, James (1716–94) Scottish physician

Macleod, John James Rickard (1876–1935) Scottish physiologist

Manson, Sir Patrick (1844–1922) Scottish physician, pioneer of tropical medicine

Mesmer, Franz Anton (1734–1815) Austrian physician

Moore, Francis (1657–*c.* 1715) English physician, astrologer, and schoolmaster

Müller, Johannes Peter (1801–58) German anatomist and zoologist

Nostradamus (Latinized name of Michel de Nostredame) (1503–66) French astrologer and physician

Osler, Sir William (1849–1919) Canadian-born physician and classical scholar

Owen, Sir Richard (1804–92) English anatomist and palaeontologist

Paracelsus (born Theophrastus Phillipus Aureolus Bombastus von Hohenheim) (*c.* 1493–1541) Swiss physician

Pavlov, Ivan (Petrovich) (1849–1936) Russian physiologist

Piaget, Jean (1896–1980) Swiss psychologist

Ramón y Cajal, Santiago (1852–1934) Spanish physician and histologist

Reed, Walter (1851–1902) American physician

Ross, Sir Ronald (1857–1932) British physician

Schwann, Theodor Ambrose Hubert (1810–82) German physiologist

Selye, Hans Hugo Bruno (1907–82) Austrian-born Canadian physician

Sherrington, Sir Charles Scott (1857–1952) English physiologist

Skinner, Burrhus Frederic (1904–90) American psychologist

Sloane, Sir Hans (1660–1753) English physician and naturalist

Spallanzani, Lazzaro (1729–99) Italian physiologist and biologist

Starling, Ernest Henry (1866–1927) English physiologist

Steno, Nicolaus (Danish name Niels Steensen) (1638–86) Danish anatomist and geologist

Sydenham, Thomas (*c.* 1624–89) English physician

Vesalius, Andreas (1514–64) Flemish anatomist, the founder of modern anatomy

Virchow, Rudolf Karl (1821–1902) German physician and pathologist, founder of cellular pathology

Watson, John Broadus (1878–1958) American psychologist, founder of the school of behaviourism

Wundt, Wilhelm (1832–1920) German psychologist

ANIMALS

MAMMALS

aardvark
aardwolf
agouti
ai
alpaca
angwantibo
anoa
ant bear
anteater
antelope
aoudad
ape
Arctic fox
Arctic hare
armadillo
ass
aurochs
axis deer
aye-aye
babirusa
baboon
Bactrian camel
badger
banteng
barbastelle
barking deer
bat
bear
beaver
bettong
bighorn
binturong
bison
black bear
blackbuck
blue fox
blue whale
boar
bobcat
bongo
bottlenose
brown bear
buffalo
bushbaby
bushbuck
cachalot
cacomistle
camel
cane rat
Cape buffalo
capuchin
  monkey
capybara

caracal
caribou
cat
catamount
cattle
cavy
chamois
cheetah
chevrotain
chickaree
chimpanzee
chinchilla
Chinese water
  deer
chipmunk
chiru
chital
cinnamon bear
civet
clouded leopard
coati
coatimundi
colobus
colugo
cony
cottontail
cougar
cow
coyote
coypu
crabeater seal
deer
deer mouse
desert rat
desman
dhole
dik-dik
dingo
dog
dolphin
donkey
dormouse
douroucouli
drill
dromedary
dugong
duiker
dziggetai
eland
elephant
elephant seal
elk
entellus

ermine
European bison
eyra
fallow deer
fennec
ferret
fieldmouse
fisher
flying fox
flying lemur
flying squirrel
fossa
foumart
fox
fruit bat
galago
gaur
gayal
gazelle
gelada
gemsbok
genet
gerbil
gerenuk
gibbon
giraffe
glutton
gnu
goat
goat antelope
golden cat
golden mole
gopher
goral
gorilla
grampus
grass monkey
grey squirrel
grey wolf
grison
grizzly bear
groundhog
ground squirrel
guanaco
guenon
guinea pig
gymnure
hairy hedgehog
hamadryas
hamster
harbour seal
hare
hartebeest

harvest mouse
hedgehog
hinny
hippopotamus
hippo
hog
honey badger
honey bear
hooded seal
horse
horseshoe bat
howler monkey
humpback
  whale
hutia
hyena
hyrax
ibex
impala
Indian elephant
indri
jackal
jackrabbit
jaguar
jaguarundi
jerboa
jumping mouse
kangaroo rat
kiang
killer whale
kinkajou
kit fox
klipspringer
kob
Kodiak bear
kudu
langur
lemming
lemur
leopard
leopard seal
liger
linsang
lion
llama
loris
lynx
macaque
manatee
mandrill
mangabey
mara
margay

markhor
marmoset
marmot
marten
meerkat
mink
mole
mole rat
mona monkey
mongoose
monkey
moon rat
moose
mouflon
mountain
  beaver
mountain cat
mountain goat
mountain lion
mountain sheep
mouse
mouse deer
mule
mule deer
muntjac
musk deer
musk ox
muskrat
musquash
narwhal
New World
  monkey
nilgai
noctule
nyala
ocelot
okapi
Old World
  monkey
olingo
onager
orang-utan
oribi
oryx
otter
otter shrew
ounce
ox
paca
pack rat
Pallas's cat
palm civet
pampas cat

MAMMALS (cont.)

panda	raccoon dog	sea lion	sun bear	water buffalo
pangolin	rat	sea otter	suslik	water rat
panther	ratel	sei whale	swine	water shrew
patas monkey	red deer	serotine bat	tahr	water vole
peccary	red fox	serow	tailless tenrec	weasel
Père David's	red squirrel	serval	takin	whale
deer	reedbuck	sheep	talapoin	white
pig	reindeer	shrew	tamandua	rhinoceros
pika	rhesus monkey	siamang	tamarin	white whale
pilot whale	rhinoceros	sifaka	tamarou	wild boar
pine marten	rhino	sika	tapir	wildcat
pipistrelle	right whale	silver fox	tarsier	wild dog
pocket gopher	roan antelope	sitatunga	tayra	wildebeest
pocket mouse	Rocky Mountain	skunk	tenrec	wisent
polar bear	goat	sloth	tiger	wolf
polecat	roe deer	sloth bear	tigon	wolverine
porcupine	rorqual	snow leopard	timber wolf	woodchuck
porpoise	royal antelope	snowshoe hare	titi	wood rat
potto	sable	solenodon	tree shrew	woolly monkey
pouched rat	sable antelope	souslik	unau	woolly
prairie dog	sabre-toothed	spectacled bear	urus	rhinoceros
prairie wolf	tiger	sperm whale	vampire bat	woolly spider
proboscis	saiga	spider monkey	vervet	monkey
monkey	saki	spiny dormouse	vicuña	yak
pronghorn	sambar	springbok	Virginia deer	zebra
puma	scaly anteater	springhaas	viscacha	zebu
pygmy	scaly-tailed	squirrel	vole	zorilla
hippopotamus	squirrel	squirrel monkey	walrus	
rabbit	sea cow	steinbok	wapiti	
raccoon or	sea elephant	stoat	warthog	
racoon	seal	stone marten	waterbuck	

BREEDS OF CAT

Abyssinian	Colourpoint	Korat	Siamese
American Shorthair	Shorthair	lilac-pointed	Singapura
American Wirehair	Cornish Rex	Maine Coon Cat	Smoke
Balinese	Cream	Malayan	Snowshoe
Birman	Cymric	Manx	Somali
Blue Burmese	Devon Rex	Norwegian Forest	Sphynx
blue-pointed	domestic longhair	Cat	Tabby
Bombay	domestic tabby	Ocicat	tabby-pointed
British Blue	Egyptian Mau	Oriental Shorthair	Tiffany
British Spotted	European Shorthair	Persian	Tonkinese
Burmese	Exotic Shorthair	Ragdoll	Tortoiseshell
Cameo	Havana	red-pointed	tortoiseshell-pointed
Chartreuse	Himalayan	Rex	Turkish Angora
Chinchilla	Japanese Bobtail	Russian Blue	Turkish Van
chocolate-pointed	Javanese	Scottish Fold	
	Kashmir	seal-pointed	

BREEDS OF DOG

Aberdeen terrier
affenpinscher
Afghan
Airedale terrier
akita
Alaskan malamute
Alsatian
Australian terrier
basenji
basset hound
beagle
Bearded Collie
Bedlington terrier
Belgian malinois
Bernese mountain
  dog
Bichon Frise
Black and Tan
  Coonhound
Blenheim spaniel
bloodhound
Border collie
borzoi
Boston terrier
Bouvier des Flandres
boxer
Briard
Brussels griffon
bulldog
bull mastiff
bull terrier
cairn terrier
Cavalier King
  Charles spaniel
chihuahua
chow
Clumber spaniel

cocker spaniel
collie
corgi
dachshund
Dalmatian
Dandie Dinmont
  terrier
deerhound
Dobermann pinscher
elk-hound
English setter
Eurasier
field spaniel
Finnish spitz
foxhound
fox terrier
Giant Schnauzer
golden retriever
Gordon setter
Great Dane
Great Pyrenees
greyhound
griffon
Groenendael
harrier
Hovawart
husky
Ibicencan hound
Ibizan hound
Irish setter
Irish terrier
Irish wolfhound
Ivicene
Istrian pointer
Jack Russell terrier
keeshond
kelpie

Kerry blue terrier
King Charles spaniel
Komondor
Kuvasz
Labrador retriever
laika
Lakeland terrier
Leonberger
Lhasa apso
Malamute
Maltese dog *or*
  terrier
Manchester terrier
mastiff
Mexican hairless
Newfoundland
Norfolk terrier
Norwegian elkhound
Norwich terrier
Old English
  sheepdog
otter hound
papillon
Pekinese
Pharaoh hound
pit bull terrier
pointer
Pomeranian
poodle
pug
puli
Pyrenean mountain
  dog
Pyrenean sheepdog
Pyrenean wolfhound
retriever
Rhodesian ridgeback

Rottweiler
St Bernard
saluki
Samoyed
schipperke
schnauzer
Scottish deerhound
Scottish terrier
Sealyham terrier
setter
Shetland sheepdog
shih-tzu
Siberian husky
Skye terrier
spaniel
spitz
springer spaniel
Staffordshire bull
  terrier
staghound
terrier
Tervuren
Tibetan terrier
tosa
vizsla
Weimaraner
Welsh corgi
Welsh hound
Welsh terrier
West Highland
  terrier
whippet
wirehaired fox terrier
Yorkshire terrier

BREEDS OF HORSE AND PONY

Andalusian
Anglo-Arab
Appaloosa
Arab
Ariègois
Asiatic Wild Horse
Barb
Bardigiano
Bashkir
Basuto pony
Breton
brumby
Budenny
Camargue

Caspian
Cleveland Bay
Clydesdale
Colorado Ranger
Comtois
Conestoga
Connemara pony
criollo
Czechoslovakian
  warmblood
Dales pony
Danish warmblood
Dartmoor pony
Dutch draught

Dutch warmblood
Exmoor pony
Falabella
Fell pony
Fjord
Friesian
Galiceño
Galloway
Gelderlander
Gotland
Hackney
Haflinger
Hanoverian
Highland pony

Holsteiner
Huçul
Hunter
Iceland pony
Indian Half-bred
Irish draught
Irish hunter
Jutland
Kabardin
Karabakh
Kathiawari
Kazakh
Konik
Landais

BREEDS OF HORSE AND PONY (cont)

Lippizaner
Lokai
Lundy Island
Mangalarga
Manipur pony
Mérens pony
miniature Shetland
Missouri fox-trotting
  horse
Morgan
Murgese
mustang
New Forest pony
Nonius
Noriker
Norwegian racing
  trotter

Oldenburger
Orlov trotter
Palomino
Paso Fino
Percheron
Peruvian Paso
Pinto
Pinzgauer
Plateau Persian
polo pony
pony of the
  Americas
Pottok
Quarter Horse
Rhinelander
Russ

Russian heavy
  draught
Russian warmblood
Sable Island
Saddlebred
Salerno
Schleswig
Shales horse
Shetland pony
Shire horse
Standardbred
Suffolk Punch
Swedish warmblood
Tarpan
Tartar pony
Tennessee walking
  horse

Tersk
thoroughbred
Timor
Trakehner
trotter
Viatka
Waler
warmblood
Welsh cob
Welsh Mountain
  pony
Württemberger
Yorkshire coach
  horse

POINTS OF A HORSE

cannon bone
cheek
chest
chestnut
chin groove
coffin bone
coronet
crest
croup

dock
elbow
ergot
feathers
fetlock
fetlock joint
flank
forearm
forelock

frog
gaskin
gullet
heel
hind quarters
hock
hoof
knee
loin

mane
navicular
  bone
pastern
pedal bone
point of hip
point of
  shoulder
poll

ribs
shank
sheath
shoulder
splint bone
stifle
tail
tendon
withers

BREEDS OF CATTLE

Aberdeen Angus
Africander
Andalusian
Australian Illawarra
  Shorthorn
Ayrshire
Bangus
Barrosã
Beefalo
Beef Shorthorn
Belgian Blue
Belted Galloway
Belted Welsh
Blonde d'Aquitaine
Brahman
British White
Brown Swiss
Charolais

Chianina
Danish Red
Devon
Dexter
Droughtmaster
Durham
Friesian
Galician Blond
Galloway
German Yellow
Guernsey
Hereford
Highland
Holstein-Friesian
Irish Moiled
Jamaica Hope
Jersey
Kerry

Kyloe
Limousin
Lincoln Red
Longhorn
Luing
Maine Anjou
Meuse-Rhine-Ijssel
Miranda
Mongolian
Murray Grey
N'Dama
Pinzgauer
Polled Hereford
Polled Welsh Black
Red-and-White
  Friesian
Red Poll
Red Ruby Devon

Romagnola
Santa Gertrudis
Shetland
Shorthorn
Simmental
South Devon
Sussex
Swedish Red-and-
  White
Texas Longhorn
Welsh Black
West Highland
White Galloway
White Park

BREEDS OF SHEEP

byssinian
Africander
Altai
Askanian
Australian Merino
Awassi
Berber
Bergamo
Beulah Speckled
Face
Biella
Blackface
Blackhead Persian
Black Welsh
Mountain
Bluefaced Leicester
Border Leicester
Bosnian Mountain
Brazilian Woolless
Campanian Barbary
Cannock Chase
Castlemilk Moorit
Caucasian
Cheviot
Chios
Clun Forest
Colbred
Columbia
Corriedale
Cotswold
Dales-Bred
Dartmoor
Derbyshire Gritstone
Devon Closewool
Devon Longwool

Dorper
Dorset Down
Dorset Horn
Dubrovnik
English Longwool
Exmoor Horn
French Blackheaded
Galway
Greek Zackel
Hampshire Down
Hebridean
Herdwick
Hill Radnor
Icelandic
Ile-de-France
Island Pramenka
Jacob
Karakachan
Karakul
Kent
Kerry Hill
Kivircik
Lacaune
Lacho
Lamon
Leicester
Lincoln Longwool
Llanwenog
Lleyn
Lonk
Lourdes
Manech
Manx Loghtan
Masai
Merino

Mongolian
Mug
Norfolk Horn
North Country
Cheviot
North Ronaldsay
Old Norwegian
Orkney
Oxford Down
Panama
Poll Dorset
Polwarth
Portland
Précoce
Radnor
Rambouillet
Red Karaman
Rhiw Hill
Romanov
Romeldale
Romney Marsh
Rough Fell
Ryeland
Sardinian
Scottish Blackface
Shetland
Shropshire
Sicilian
Soay
South Devon
Southdown
South Wales
Mountain
Spanish Merino
Suffolk

Swaledale
Swiss White Alpine
Swiss White
Mountain
Talavera
Targhee
Teeswater
Texel
Tibetan
Tsigai
Tyrol Mountain
Welsh Mountain
Wensleydale
Whiteface Dartmoor
Whiteface
Woodlands
Wicklow Mountain
Wiltshire Horn

Wild Sheep

aoudad
argali
barbary sheep
bharal
bighorn
blue sheep
dall sheep
mouflon
mountain sheep
urial
white sheep

BREEDS OF FOWL

Ancona	chicken	Campine	chicken
Andalusian	chicken	Cayuga	duck
Australorp	chicken	Chinese	goose
Aylesbury	duck	Cochin	chicken
Black East Indian	duck	Crested	duck
Black Norfolk	turkey	Crèvecour	chicken
Booted	bantam	Croad Langshan	chicken
Bourbon Red	turkey	Dorking	chicken
Brahma	chicken	Embden	goose
Brecon Buff	goose	Faverolle	chicken
Bresse	chicken	Frizzles	bantam
Broad-Breasted Bronze	turkey	Hamburgh	chicken
Broad-Breasted White	turkey	Houdan	chicken
Cambridge Bronze	turkey	Indian Game	chicken

BREEDS OF FOWL (cont.)

Indian Runner	duck	Pilgrim	goose
Ixworth	chicken	Plymouth Rock	chicken
Jersey Giant	chicken	Poland	chicken
Jubilee Indian Game	chicken	Redcap	chicken
Khaki Campbell	duck	Rhode Island Red	chicken
La Fleche	chicken	Roman	goose
Lakenfelder	chicken	Rosecomb	bantam
Lavender	guinea fowl	Rouen	duck
Leghorn	chicken	Rumpless	bantam
Magpie	duck	Scots Dumpy	chicken
Malay	chicken	Scots Grey	chicken
Malines	chicken	Sebastopol	goose
Mammoth Bronze	turkey	Sebright	bantam
Marans	chicken	Sicilian Buttercup	chicken
Marsh Daisy	chicken	Silkie	chicken
Modern Game	chicken	Spanish	chicken
Modern Langshan	chicken	Sultan	chicken
Muscovy	duck	Sumatra Game	chicken
Nankin	bantam	Sussex	chicken
Narragansett	turkey	Toulouse	goose
New Hampshire Red	chicken	Transylvanian Naked	
Nicholas	turkey	Neck	chicken
Norfolk Grey	chicken	Welsh Harlequin	duck
North Holland Blue	chicken	Welsummer	chicken
Old English Game	bantam	Whalesbury	duck
Orloff	chicken	White	guinea fowl
Orpington	chicken	White Austrian	turkey
Orpington	duck	White Holland	turkey
Pearl Grey	guinea fowl	Wyandotte	chicken
Phoenix	chicken	Yokohama	chicken

MARSUPIALS

bandicoot	kangaroo	pademelon	Tasmanian devil
bilby	koala bear	phalanger	thylacine
cuscus	marsupial mole	planigale	Tasmanian wolf
dalgyte	marsupial mouse	quokka	tree kangaroo
dasyure	marsupial rat	rabbit bandicoot	wallaby
flying phalanger	mouse opossum	rat kangaroo	wombat
hare wallaby	numbat	rat opossum	yapok
honey mouse	opossum	rock wallaby	

BIRDS

adjutant bird	auk	barbet	bird of paradise
albatross	auklet	barnacle goose	bittern
amadavat	avocet	barn owl	blackbird
anhinga	babbler	bateleur eagle	blackcap
antbird	bald eagle	bee-eater	black swan
Arctic tern	Baltimore oriole	bellbird	blue-bill

BIRDS (cont.)

bluebird
blue tit
boat-bill
bobolink
bobwhite
booby
bowerbird
brambling
brent-goose
broad-bill
brush turkey
budgerigar
bulbul
bullfinch
bunting
burrowing owl
bush tit
bush wren
bustard
butcher-bird
buzzard
Canada goose
canary
canvas-back
caracara
cardinal
carrion crow
cassowary
catbird
chaffinch
chat
chickadee
chicken
chiffchaff
chipping sparrow
chough
coal tit
cockatiel
cockatoo
coly
condor
coot
cormorant
corncrake
cowbird
crake
crane
crested tit
crocodile bird
crossbill
crow
cuckoo
cuckoo shrike
curassow
curlew
dabchick
darter
demoiselle crane
diamond-bird

dipper
diver
dove
duck
dunlin
dunnock
eagle
eagle owl
egret
eider duck
emperor penguin
emu
emu-wren
erne
fairy penguin
falcon
fantail
fernbird
fieldfare
finch
finfoot
firecrest
fish owl
flamingo
flicker
flower-pecker
flycatcher
francolin
friar-bird
frigate bird
frogmouth
fulmar
gadwall
gallinule
gannet
garganey
gnat-catcher
godwit
goldcrest
golden eagle
golden-eye
goldfinch
gooney bird
goosander
goose
goshawk
grackle
grassfinch
great tit
grebe
greenfinch
greenshank
greylag goose
griffon vulture
grosbeak
grouse
guillemot
gull
gyrfalcon

hammerhead
harlequin duck
harpy eagle
harrier
Hawaiian goose
hawfinch
hawk
hawk-owl
hedge sparrow
hen
heron
herring gull
hobby
honeycreeper
honeyeater
honeyguide
hooded crow
hoopoe
hoot owl
hornbill
horned owl
house martin
house sparrow
huia
hummingbird
ibis
jabiru
jacamar
jacana
jackdaw
jay
junco
kagu
kakapo
kea
kestrel
killdeer
kingbird
kingfisher
kinglet
kite
kittiwake
kiwi
knot
kookaburra
lammergeier
lanner
lapwing
lark
laughing jackass
laughing owl
laverock *Scot.*
lily-trotter
linnet
little owl
long-tailed tit
lorikeet
lory
lovebird

lyre-bird
macaw
magpie
mallard
manakin
mandarin duck
marabou stork
marsh harrier
martin
meadowlark
megapode
merganser
merlin
minivet
mistle thrush
mockingbird
Montagu's harrier
moorhen
Mother Carey's
    chicken
motmot
mourning dove
mousebird
Muscovy duck
mute swan
muttonbird
mynah bird
nene
nighthawk
night heron
nightingale
nightjar
noddy
notornis
nutcracker
nuthatch
oil-bird
oriole
ortolan
osprey
ostrich
ouzel
ovenbird
owl
owlet-frogmouth
oxpecker
oystercatcher
parakeet
parrot
partridge
peacock
peafowl
peewee
peewit
pelican
penguin
peregrine falcon
petrel
phalarope

BIRDS (cont.)

pheasant
phoebe
pigeon
pigeon-hawk
pilot bird
pintail
pipit
pipiwharauroa
plains-wanderer
plover
pochard
ptarmigan
puffin
pukeko
quetzal
rail
raven
razorbill
redhead
redpoll
redshank
redstart
redwing
reed-bird
reedling
reed warbler
rhea
rhinoceros bird
rice-bird
rifle bird
ring-dove
ring-necked
  pheasant
ring ouzel
roadrunner
robin
rock-dove
roller

rook
rosella
ruddy duck
ruff
sacred ibis
saddleback
sanderling
sand martin
sandpiper
sapsucker
scaup
scops owl
screamer
screech owl
scrub turkey
seagull
secretary bird
seriema
serin
shag
shearwater
sheathbill
shelduck
shoebill
shoveler duck
shrike
siskin
skimmer
skua
skylark
smew
snake bird
snipe
snow bunting
snow goose
snowy owl
song thrush
sparrow

sparrowhawk
spoonbill
starling
stilt
stonechat
stone curlew
stork
storm petrel
sunbird
sun bittern
swallow
swan
swiftlet
tailor-bird
takahe
tanager
tawny owl
teal
tern
thickhead
thornbill
thrasher
thrush
tinamou
titlark
titmouse
toucan
touraco
towhee
tragopan
treecreeper
trogon ·
tropicbird
tui
turkey
turkey vulture
turnstone
turtle-dove

twite
tyrant flycatcher
umbrella bird
vulture
wagtail
wallcreeper
warbler
wattlebird
waxbill
waxwing
weaver-bird
weaver finch
wheatear
whimbrel
whinchat
whip bird
whippoorwill
whistler
whitethroat
whooping crane
whydah
willet
willow warbler
woodchat
woodcock
woodcreeper
wood-duck
woodpecker
wren
wrybill
wryneck
yellowhammer
yellowhead
yellowlegs
zebra finch

REPTILES

adder
agama
alligator
alligator lizard
ameira
amphisbaena
anaconda
anole
asp
bandy-bandy
basilisk
bearded dragon
black snake
blind snake

blindworm
bloodsucker
boa constrictor
boomslang
box turtle
brown snake
bull snake
bushmaster
carpet python
caiman or cayman
chameleon
chuckwalla
cobra
cooter

copperhead
coral snake
corn snake
cottonmouth
crocodile
death adder
diamondback
  rattlesnake
diamondback
  terrapin
egg-eating snake
fence lizard
fer-de-lance
flying lizard

flying snake
frilled lizard
Gaboon viper
Galapagos giant
  tortoise
garter snake
gecko
gharial
giant tortoise
Gila monster
glass lizard
glass snake
goanna
gopher snake

REPTILES (cont.)

grass snake	lizard	rattlesnake	spitting cobra
green turtle	loggerhead turtle	reticulated python	taipan
harlequin snake	mamba	ribbon snake	terrapin
hawksbill turtle	mangrove snake	rinkhals	tiger snake
hognose snake	matamata	rock python	tokay
horned toad	milk snake	royal python	tortoise
horned viper	moccasin	Russell's viper	tree snake
iguana	moloch	sand lizard	tuatara
Indian python	monitor lizard	scalyfoot	turtle
Indigo snake	mugger	sea snake	vine snake
jungle runner	Nile crocodile	sidewinder	viper
king cobra	pit viper	skink	viviparous lizard
king snake	pond turtle	slider	wall lizard
Komodo dragon	puff-adder	slow-worm	wart snake
krait	python	smooth snake	water moccasin
leatherback	racer	snake	water snake
legless lizard	rainbow boa	snapping turtle	whip snake
legless skink	rat snake	soft-shelled turtle	worm lizard

AMPHIBIANS

axolotl	fire salamander	mud puppy	siren
bullfrog	frog	natterjack toad	smooth newt
caecilian	giant toad	newt	spade-foot toad
clawed toad	Goliath frog	olm	Suriname toad
Congo eel	hairy frog	platanna	tiger salamander
crested newt	hellbender	poison-arrow	toad
fire-bellied newt	horned toad	frog	tree frog
fire-bellied toad	midwife toad	salamander	

FISH

albacore	bichir	brisling	cichlid
alewife	billfish	buffalo fish	cisco
allis shad	bitterling	bullhead	climbing perch
amberjack	blackfish	bummalo	clingfish
anchovy	bleak	burbot	coalfish
anemone fish	blenny	butterfish	cobia
angelfish	blindfish	butterfly fish	cod
angel shark	blowfish	butterfly ray	coelacanth
angler fish	bluefish	candiru	conger eel
arapaima	blue shark	candlefish	cornetfish
archer fish	boarfish	capelin	crappie
argentine	Bombay duck	carp	croaker
bandfish	bonefish	carpet shark	crucian carp
barbel	bonito	catfish	cusk
barracuda	bonnethead	cavefish	cutlass fish
barramundí	bonnetmouth	char	dab
bass	bowfin	characin	dace
batfish	boxfish	chimaera	damselfish
beluga	bream	chub	danio
bib	brill	chum salmon	darter

FISH (cont.)

dealfish	hake	mudminnow	sailfish	stone bass
devil ray	half-beak	mudskipper	saithe	stonefish
discus	halibut	mullet	salmon	sturgeon
dogfish	hammerhead	mummichog	sand eel	sucker
dolphin-fish	shark	Murray cod	sandfish	sunfish
dorado	hatchetfish	muskellunge	sardine	surgeon fish
dory	herring	needlefish	sargassum fish	swordfish
dragonet	hogfish	nurse shark	sauger	swordtail
dragonfish	horse mackerel	oarfish	saury	tarpon
drum	houting	oilfish	sawfish	tautog
eagle ray	humpback	old wife	scad	tench
eel	salmon	opah	scat	tetra
eelpout	ice fish	orfe	scorpion fish	thornback
electric eel	ide	paddlefish	sculpin	threadfin
electric ray	jack	parrotfish	scup	thresher shark
elephant-snout	jewfish	pearlfish	sea bass	tigerfish
fish	John Dory	perch	sea bream	tiger shark
fighting fish	killifish	pickerel	sea horse	toadfish
filefish	kingfish	pike	sea perch	tomcod
firefish	kingklip	pikeperch	searobin	tommy ruff
flatfish	knifefish	pilchard	sea trout	toothcarp
flat-head	koi carp	pilot fish	sergeant-fish	tope
flounder	labyrinth fish	pipefish	shad	topminnow
fluke	lake trout	piranha	shanny	torpedo ray
flying fish	lamprey	plaice	shark	trevally
flying gurnard	lancetfish	pollack	sharksucker	triggerfish
four-eyed fish	lantern fish	pollan	sheatfish	trout
frogfish	leatherjacket	pomfret	sheepshead	trunkfish
garfish	lemon sole	pompano	shovelhead	tuna
garpike	ling	pope	shovelnose	turbot
glassfish	livebearer	porbeagle	shubunkin	twaite shad
globe-fish	lizardfish	porcupine fish	silverside	vendace
goatfish	loach	porgy	skate	viperfish
goby	lumpsucker	pout	skipjack tuna	wahoo
goldfish	lungfish	powan	skipper	walleye
goose-fish	mackerel	puffer fish	smelt	weakfish
gourami	madtom	pumpkinseed	smooth hound	weatherfish
grayling	mako	rabbitfish	snake mackerel	weever
grenadier	manta	rainbow trout	snapper	whale shark
groper	marlin	ratfish	snipe fish	whitebait
grunion	menhaden	ray	snook	whitefish
grunt	midshipman	redfin	sockeye salmon	white shark
gudgeon	miller's thumb	redfish	sole	whiting
guitarfish	minnow	remora	sparling	wirrah
gulper eel	molly	requiem shark	spadefish	wolffish
gunnel	monkfish	ribbonfish	spearfish	wrasse
guppy	moonfish	roach	sprat	x-ray fish
gurnard	Moorish idol	rockling	stargazer	yellow jack
gwyniad	moray eel	roughy	sterlet	yellowtail
haddock	mosquitofish	rudd	stickleback	zander
hagfish	mudfish	ruffe	stingray	zebra fish

INSECTS AND ARACHNIDS

alder fly
amazon ant
ambrosia beetle
ant
ant-lion
aphid
army ant
army worm
assassin bug
backswimmer
bark beetle
bedbug
bee
bee fly
beetle
bird-eating spider
black beetle
blackfly
black widow
blister beetle
bloodworm
blowfly
bluebottle
body louse
boll-weevil
bombardier beetle
booklouse
bookworm
borer
bot fly
bristletail
buffalo gnat
bug
bumble-bee
burying beetle
bush cricket
butterfly
cabbage root fly
caddis-fly
camel spider
capsid bug
cardinal spider
carpenter bee
carpet beetle
chafer
chigger
chinch bug
cicada
click beetle
cockchafer
cockroach
Colorado potato
  beetle
corn borer
cotton stainer
crab louse
crane-fly

cricket
croton bug
cuckoo-spit insect
cutworm
daddy longlegs
damselfly
darkling beetle
death-watch beetle
deer fly
devil's coach-horse
diadem spider
digger wasp
diving beetle
dobsonfly
dor-beetle
dragonfly
driver ant
drosophila
dung-beetle
earwig
elm bark beetle
false scorpion
fire ant
firebrat
firefly
flea
flea beetle
fly
froghopper
fruit fly
funnel-web spider
gadfly
gall midge
gall wasp
giant water bug
glow-worm
Goliath beetle
grain weevil
grasshopper
greenbottle
greenfly
ground beetle
ground bug
harlequin bug
harvestman
harvest mite
head louse
Hercules beetle
honey ant
honey bee
hornet
horntail
horsefly
housefly
hoverfly
hunting spider
huntsman spider

ichneumon
itch mite
jockey spider
June bug
katipo
katydid
ked
kissing bug
lacewing
lac insect
ladybird
lantern-fly
leaf beetle
leafcutter ant
leafcutter bee
leafhopper
leaf insect
leatherjacket
locust
louse
mason bee
May-bug
mayfly
mealworm
mealy bug
midge
mite
mole cricket
money spider
mosquito
moth
mygale
oil beetle
orb weaver
phylloxera
plant bug
plant hopper
pond-skater
potato beetle
potter wasp
praying mantis
raft spider
red ant
red-back
red bug
red spider mite
retiary spider
rhinoceros beetle
robber fly
rove beetle
sandfly
sawfly
scale insect
scarab
scorpion
scorpion fly
scorpion spider

screw-worm
sexton beetle
sheep ked
sheep tick
shield bug
silverfish
slave-making ant
snakefly
soldier beetle
Spanish fly
spider
spider mite
spider wasp
spittlebug
springtail
squash bug
stag beetle
stick insect
stink bug
stonefly
stylops
sun spider
tarantula
termite
thrips
tick
tiger beetle
tortoise beetle
trapdoor spider
tree hopper
tsetse fly
violin spider
warble fly
wasp
water beetle
water-boatman
water bug
water scorpion
water spider
water strider
webspinner
weevil
whip scorpion
whirligig
white ant
whitefly
white-tailed spider
wind scorpion
wireworm
wolf spider
wood borer
wood tick
woodwasp
woodworm

BUTTERFLIES AND MOTHS

Adonis blue
angle shades
apollo
argus
atlas moth
bagworm moth
birdwing
blue
brimstone butterfly
brown
burnet
burnished brass
cabbage white
Camberwell Beauty
cecropia moth
cinnabar moth
clearwing moth
clothes-moth
clouded yellow
codling moth
comma
copper
dagger

death's head
  hawkmoth
drinker
eggar
emerald
emperor moth
ermine
fritillary
fruit moth
gatekeeper
geometrid
goat moth
grayling
gypsy moth
hairstreak
hawkmoth
heath
io moth
lackey
lappet
large blue
leopard moth
lobster moth
luna moth

magpie moth
marbled white
meadow brown
merveille du jour
milkweed
monarch
morpho
Mother Shipton
mourning cloak
noctuid
nymphalid
oak eggar
orange-tip
owlet moth
painted lady
papilionid
peacock butterfly
peppered moth
plume moth
prominent
pug
purple emperor
puss moth
pyralid

red admiral
ringlet
satyrid
silk moth
silkworm moth
silver Y
skipper
speckled wood
sulphur
swallowtail butterfly
swift moth
tiger moth
tineid
tortoiseshell
tortrix
tussock moth
underwing
vapourer
wall brown
wax moth
white admiral
winter moth
yellow-tail

OTHER INVERTEBRATES

abalone
annelid worm
argonaut
ark shell
arrow worm
auger shell
bamboo worm
barnacle
beard worm
blood fluke
bootlace worm
bristle worm
centipede
Cestoda
chiton
clam
cockle
conch
cone shell
cone worm
cowrie
crab
crayfish
cuttlefish
earthworm
eelworm
feather duster

filaria
flatworm
fluke
giant clam
guinea worm
hairworm
hard-shell
heartworm
helmet shell
hermit crab
hookworm
horsehair worm
jellyfish
keyhole limpet
kidney worm
leech
limpet
liver fluke
lobster
lugworm
lungworm
millipede
mitre shell
money cowrie
murex
mussel
nautilus

nematode
nudibranch
octopus
olive shell
oyster
paddleworm
palolo worm
paper nautilus
parchment worm
peacock worm
peanut worm
pearly nautilus
periwinkle
piddock
pinworm
planarian
platyhelminth
Portuguese man of
  war
ragworm
razor shell
ribbonworm
roundworm
scallop
schistosome
sea anenome
sea cucumber

sea slug
sea urchin
shipworm
slipper shell
slug
snail
spider conch
squid
starfish
tapeworm
threadworm
tiger cowrie
tooth shell
top shell
triton shell
tubifex
tusk shell
venus clam
volute
wentletrap
whelk
whipworm
winkle
woodlouse
worm shell

SEASHELLS

abalone	flamingo tongue	nutmeg shell	sunset shell
angel wing	frog shell	nut shell	tellin
ark shell	furrow shell	olive	thorny oyster
auger	gaper	ormer	tiger cowrie
basket shell	giant clam	otter shell	tooth shell
bonnet	hard clam	oyster	top-shell
bubble shell	harp	oyster drill	tower shell
canoe shell	heart cockle	partridge shell	triton
carpet shell	helmet	pearly nautilus	triton's trumpet
carrier shell	hoof shell	pelican's foot	trough shell
cask shell	horn shell	pen shell	trumpet shell
chambered nautilus	horse mussel	periwinkle	tulip shell
chank	jewel box	pheasant shell	tun
clam	jingle shell	piddock	turban
coat-of-mail	junonia	pyramid shell	turkey wing
cockle	keyhole limpet	quahog	turret shell
cock's-comb oyster	lima	queen scallop	tusk shell
conch	limpet	razor-shell	umbrella shell
cone	lion's paw	rock shell	vase shell
cowrie	lucine	saddle oyster	venus
cup-and-saucer	marginella	scallop	Venus clam
date mussel	mitre	sea snail	violet sea snail
dog whelk	money cowrie	slipper limpet	volute
dove shell	moon shell	slit limpet	wedge shell
drill	murex	slit shell	wentletrap
drupe	mussel	spider conch	whelk
ear shell	nautilus	spindle shell	wing oyster
fig shell	necklace shell	spire shell	winkle
fighting conch	nerite	staircase shell	worm shell
file shell	Noah's ark	sundial	zebra mussel

YOUNG OF ANIMALS

calf	buffalo *or* camel *or* cattle *or* elephant *or* elk *or* giraffe *or* hartebeest *or* rhinoceros *or* seal *or* whale	filly	horse
		foal	horse *or* zebra
		fry	fish
		gosling	goose
cheeper	grouse *or* quail *or* partridge	joey	kangaroo
chick	chicken *or* hawk *or* pheasant	kid	antelope *or* goat *or* roedeer
colt	horse	kit	beaver *or* fox *or* weasel
cub	badger *or* bear *or* fox *or* leopard *or* lion *or* tiger *or* walrus *or* wolf	kitten	bobcat *or* cat *or* cougar *or* jackrabbit *or* skunk
		lamb	sheep
cygnet	swan	leveret	hare
duckling	duck	piglet	pig
eaglet	eagle	puppy	coyote *or* dog
elver	eel	tadpole	frog *or* toad
eyas	hawk	squab	pigeon
fawn	caribou *or* deer	whelp	dog *or* wolf

NAMES FOR MALE AND FEMALE ANIMALS

antelope	buck	doe	hare	buck	doe
badger	boar	sow	hartebeest	bull	cow
bear	boar	sow	horse	stallion	mare
bobcat	tom	lioness	impala	ram	ewe
buffalo	bull	cow	jackrabbit	buck	doe
camel	bull	cow	kangaroo	buck	doe
caribou	stag	doe	leopard	leopard	leopardess
cat	tom	queen	lion	lion	lioness
cattle	bull	cow	lobster	cock	hen
chicken	cock	hen	moose	bull	cow
cougar	tom	lioness	ox	bullock	cow
coyote	dog	bitch	peacock	peacock	peahen
deer	stag	doe	pheasant	cock	hen
dog	dog	bitch	pig	boar	sow
donkey	jackass	jennyass	rhinoceros	bull	cow
duck	drake	duck	seal	bull	cow
elephant	bull	cow	sheep	ram	ewe
ferret	jack	jill	swan	cob	pen
fish	cock	hen	tiger	tiger	tigress
fox	fox	vixen	weasel	boar	cow
giraffe	bull	cow	whale	bull	cow
goat	billygoat	nannygoat	wolf	dog	bitch
goose	gander	goose	zebra	stallion	mare

COLLECTIVE NAMES

Many are fanciful or humorous. They were taken up by Joseph Sturt in Sports & Pastimes of England (1801) *and by other antiquarian writers.*

army of caterpillars
bale of turtles
band of gorillas
bask of crocodiles
bellowing of bullfinches
bevy of roe deer *or* quails *or* larks *or* pheasants
bloat of hippopotami
brood of chickens
bury of rabbits
busyness of ferrets
cete of badgers
charm of finches
chattering of choughs
cloud of gnats
clowder of cats
congregation of plovers
covey of partridges
crash of rhinoceros
cry of hounds
descent of woodpeckers
desert of lapwings
dout of wild cats
down of hares
drift of swine
drove of horses *or* bullocks
erst of bees
exaltation of larks
flock of sheep

fluther of jellyfish
gaggle of geese on land
gam of whales
gang of elk
herd of cattle *or* elephants
hive of bees
hover of trout
kennel of dogs
kindle of kittens
knot of toads
labour of moles
leap *or* lepe of leopards
litter of kittens *or* pigs
mob of kangaroos
murder of crows
murmuration of starlings
muster of peacocks *or* penguins
mute of hares
obstinacy of buffalo
pace of asses
pack of hounds *or* grouse
paddling of ducks (on water)
pandemonium of parrots
parade of elephants
parcel of penguins
parliament of owls
pod of seals
pride of lions

rafter of turkeys
rookery of rooks
safe of ducks
sawt of lions
school of whales *or* dolphins *or* porpoises
siege of herons
shoal of fish
shrewdness of apes
skein of geese in flight
skulk of foxes
sloth of bears
smack of jellyfish
span of mules
spring of teal
stare of owls
string of horses
stud of mares
swarm of flies *or* bees
tiding of magpies
trip of goats
troop of baboons
turmoil of porpoises
turn of turtles
unkindness of ravens
watch of nightingales
yoke of oxen
zeal of zebras

PLANTS

TREES AND SHRUBS

acacia
alder
almond
apple
araucaria
arbutus
ash
aspen
assegai
balsa
banksia
banyan
baobab
bay tree
bebeeru
beech
belah
birch
blackthorn
bo tree
bottle-brush
bottle tree
box
buckthorn
cacao
calabash
camphor tree
cassia
cedar
champac
chestnut
coco-de-mer
coffee tree
coolabah
coral tree
corkwood
cornel
cypress
deodar
dhak
divi-divi
dogwood
dragon tree

eaglewood
ebony
elder
elm
eucalyptus
fever tree
fir
firethorn
flame tree
frangipani
fringe tree
Gaboon
gidgee
ginkgo
gomuti
guaiacum
guayule
gum tree
hawthorn
hazel
hickory
holly
hornbeam
iroko
ironwood
ivorywood
jacaranda
jarrah
jelutong
jojoba
Joshua tree
Judas tree
juniper
kaffirboom
kahikatea
kalmia
kamala
karri
kauri
kawakawa
kiaat
kingwood
koa

kowhai
kurrajong
lacquer tree
lantana
larch
laurel
lemonwood
Leylandii
lilac
lilly-pilly
lime
linden
logwood
macrocarpa
madroño
magnolia
mahogany
maidenhair tree
mako
mangrove
manna-ash
maple
matai
maté
may
mesquite
mimosa
mock orange
monkey puzzle
mulberry
myrtle
ngaio
nipa
nux vomica
oak
ocotillo
oleander
osier
pagoda tree
palm
palmyra
paulownia
peepul

pepper tree
pine
plane
pohutukawa
poplar
privet
pyinkado
pyracantha
quassia
quebracho
rain tree
redbud
redwood
rewarewa
rhododendron
ribbonwood
robinia
rosewood
rowan
rubber plant
sandalwood
sandarac
sandbox tree
sapele
sappanwood
saskatoon
sassafras
savin
sequoia
seringa
service tree
shagbark
shea
silk-cotton tree
simarouba
sneezewood
snowball tree
soapbark
sorb
sorrel tree
sourwood
spindle
spruce

stinkwood
strawberry tree
styrax
sumach *or*
  sumac
sycamore
tallow tree
tallow wood
tamarack
tamarind
tamarisk
tawa
teak
tea-tree
terebinth
thorn tree
thuja
toothache tree
totara
traveller's joy
tupelo
turpentine tree
umbrella tree
varnish tree
viburnum
walnut
wandoo
wattle
wayfaring tree
weigela
wellingtonia
whitebeam
wilga
willow
wine palm
witch hazel
yarran
yaupon
yew
ylang-ylang
yucca
zebrawood

FLOWERS

acanthus
acidanthera
aconite
African violet

agrimony
alkanet
alyssum
amaryllis

anemone
arrowroot
arum lily
asphodel

aspidistra
aster
aubrietia
avens

azalea
balsam
bedstraw
begonia

FLOWERS (cont.)

belladonna
bellflower
bindweed
bittersweet
black-eyed
  Susan
bladderwort
bleeding heart
bluebell
borage
bramble
broom
bryony
buddleia
bugle
bugloss
burdock
burnet
busy Lizzie
buttercup
butterwort
cactus
camellia
camomile
campion
candytuft
cardinal flower
carnation
carrion flower
catchfly
catmint
catnip
celandine
cheese plant
chickweed
Chinese lantern
chrysanthemum
cinquefoil
clematis
clove pink
clover
coltsfoot
columbine
comfrey
coneflower
convolvulus
cornflower
cotoneaster
cow parsley

cowpea
cowslip
cranesbill
crocus
crowfoot
cuckoo pint
cyclamen
daffodil
dahlia
daisy
dandelion
deadly
  nightshade
dead nettle
delphinium
dock
dropwort
duckweed
edelweiss
eglantine
evening
  primrose
eyebright
figwort
flax
fleabane
forget-me-not
forsythia
foxglove
freesia
fritillary
fuchsia
furze *or* gorse
gardenia
gentian
geranium
gillyflower
gladiolus
globe thistle
golden rod
goosefoot
groundsel
harebell
hawkweed
heather
hellebore
helleborine
hemlock
henbane

herb
  Christopher
herb Gerard
herb Paris
herb Robert
hibiscus
hogweed
hollyhock
honesty
honeysuckle
hop
houseleek
hyacinth
hydrangea
iris
japonica
jasmine
jonquil
kingcup
knapweed
knotgrass
laburnum
lady's finger
lady's slipper
lady's smock
lady's tresses
larkspur
lavender
lemon balm
lily
lily of the valley
lobelia
loosestrife
lords and ladies
lotus
lupin
mallow
marigold
may-apple
mayflower
mayweed
meadow saffron
meadowsweet
mignonette
milkwort
mint
mistletoe
moccasin
  flower

monkshood
montbretia
moonflower
morning glory
motherwort
mullein
narcissus
nasturtium
nettle
nightshade
orchid
oxlip
pansy
pasque flower
passion flower
pennyroyal
peony
peppermint
petunia
phlox
pimpernel
pink
pitcher plant
plantain
poinsettia
polyanthus
poppy
primrose
primula
ragged robin
ragwort
rhododendron
rock rose
rose
rosebay
rue
sage
St John's wort
salvia
samphire
saxifrage
scabious
shamrock
slipperwort
snakeroot
snapdragon
snowdrop
soapwort
Solomon's seal

sorrel
speedwell
spider plant
spikenard
spurge
stitchwort
stock
stonecrop
sundew
sunflower
sweet pea
sweet william
tansy
teasel
thistle
thorn apple
thyme
tiger lily
toadflax
touch-me-not
tradescantia
trefoil
tulip
twayblade
valerian
Venus flytrap
verbena
veronica
vervain
vetch
violet
wallflower
water lily
willowherb
wintergreen
wisteria
witchweed
wolfbane
wood sorrel
wormwood
woundwort
yarrow
yellow
  archangel
yucca
zinnia

PARTS OF A FLOWER

androecium
anther
bract
bractede

calyx
capitulum
carpel
carpophore

catkin
corolla
corymb
cyathium

cyme
filament
floret
glume

gynoecium
hypanthium
involucel
involucre

PARTS OF A FLOWER (cont.)

ladicule	ovule	placenta	sepal	stigma
lemma	palea	pollen	spadix	style
lip	panicle	pollen grain	spathe	tepal
monochasium	pedicel	pollinium	spike	umbel
nectary	peduncle	raceme	spikelet	
nucellus	petal	receptacle	spur	
ovary	pistil	rhachis	stamen	

GRASSES, SEDGES, AND RUSHES

bamboo	darnel	melick	spartina
barley	dog's-tail	millet	spear grass
beach grass	durra	oat	spelt
beard grass	elephant grass	oat-grass	spinifex
bent	esparto	orchard grass	squirrel-tail grass
Bermuda grass	feather grass	paddy	star grass
bluegrass	fescue	pampas grass	sugar cane
bristle grass	finger grass	panic	switch grass
brome	fiorin	papyrus	sword grass
broomcorn	fog	quack grass	tef
buffalo grass	foxtail	quaking grass	teosinte
bulrush	gama grass	quitch	timothy grass
bunch grass	hair-grass	redtop	tussock grass
canary grass	herd's-grass	reed	twitch grass
China grass	Indian corn	reed grass	vernal grass
cocksfoot	Indian rice	reed mace	wheat
cordgrass	Kentucky bluegrass	rice	wild oat
corn	lemon grass	rush	wild rice
cotton grass	lyme grass	rye	wire grass
couch grass	maize	ryegrass	woodrush
crabgrass	marram grass	sedge	Yorkshire fog
cutgrass	meadow grass	sorghum	zoysia

FUNGI AND ALGAE

agaric	bootlace fungus	chlorella	dog stinkhorn
amanita	bracket fungus	clouded agaric	dryad's saddle
amethyst deceiver	brain fungus	club foot	dulse
anabaena	bulgar	club fungus	ear fungus
anise cap	bull kelp	conferva	ear pick fungus
artist's fungus	butter cap	coral fungus	earth ball
bay bolete	Caesar's mushroom	coral-spot	earth fan
beefsteak fungus	cage fungus	cow-pat toadstool	earthstar
bird's-nest fungus	candle snuff fungus	cramp balls	earth tongue
black bulgar	carrageen	dead men's fingers	elf-cup
bladderwrack	caterpillar fungus	death cap	ergot
blewit	cauliflower fungus	deceiver	euglena
blusher	cep	desmid	fairy button
blushing bracket	Ceylon moss	destroying angel	fairy cakes
bolete	champignon	devil's bolete	fairy club
boletus	chanterelle	diatom	fairy-ring mushroom
bonnet	chicken of the woods	dinoflagellate	false chanterelle

FUNGI AND ALGAE (cont.)

false death cap
false morel
field mushroom
fire fungus
flame fungus
fly agaric
fucoid
fucus
funnel cap
ghost fungus
giant puffball
grisette
gulfweed
hedgehog fungus *or*
  mushroom
herald of the winter
honey fungus
horn of plenty
horsehair toadstool
  or mushroom
horse mushroom
ink cap
jelly babies
jelly fungus
jelly tongue
jew's ear
kelp

King Alfred's cakes
laminaria
laver
lawyer's wig
  mushroom
liberty cap
lorchel
meadow mushroom
milk cap
milk drop
miller
morel
nostoc
nullipore
oarweed
old man of the
  woods
orange-peel fungus
oyster mushroom
panther cap
parasol mushroom
parrot toadstool
peacock's tail
penny bun
plums and custard
poached egg fungus
poison pie

polypore
porcelain fungus
prince
puffball
redware
rockweed
russet shank
russula
sac fungus
saffron milkcap
St George's
  mushroom
sargassum
scarlet elf-cup
scarlet hood
sea lace
sea lettuce
sea tangle
seaware
sea wrack
shaggy inkcap
shaggy parasol
sickener
slippery jack
spike cap
spirogyra
spring amanita

stag's-horn fungus
stinkhorn
stinking parasol
stonewort
sulphur fungus
sulphur tuft
tawny grisette
toadstool
tough shank
truffle
tuckahoe
velvet cap
velvet foot
velvet shank
wax cap
weeping widow
witches' butter
wood blewit
wood hedgehog
wood mushroom
wood witch
wood woollyfoot
wrack
yellow brain fungus
yellow-staining
  mushroom *or*
  yellow stainer

ART, MUSIC, AND ENTERTAINMENT

ARTISTIC TERMS

abstract
academy
acrylic paint
air-brush
alla prima
allegory
anamorphosis
ancients
anti-cerne
aquarelle
aquatint
archaic
architectonic
armature
arricciato
arriccio
art nouveau
ashcan
assemblage
atelier
autograph
automatism
avantgarde
bamboccanti
barbizon
baroque
bauhaus
biedermeier
biomorphic
bistre
bitumen
bodegón
body
bozzetto
brush
brushwork
burin
bust
byzantine
cabinet
camaïeu
canvas
capriccio

caricature
carolingian
cartoon
caryatid
cast
chalk
charcoal
chiaroscuro
cire-perdue
cloisonnisme
collage
colourist
conté crayon
contrapposto
cosmati
counterproof
craquelure
cubism
dada
diptych
distemper
divisionism
drawing
drôlerie
drypoint
easel
eclecticism
ecorché
emulsion
engraving
etching
expressionism
fec
fecit
fëte champëtre
fixative
florentine
fresco
frottage
futurism
gesso
glaze
gothic

gouache
graffiti
grisaille
grotesque
ground
hatching
herm
illumination
illusionism
impasto
impressionism
imprimatura
inc
incidit
intaglio
intimisme
intonaco
kit-cat
kitsch
kore
kouros
landscape
limner
linocut
lithography
lost wax
maestà
mahlstick
mandorla
maquette
masterpiece
maulstick
medium
metalpoint
mezzotint
miniature
mobile
model
modello
monochrome
montage
morbidezza
mosaic

naive
naturalism
oil
op
palette
papiers collés
pastel
pastiche
patina
pencil
pentimento
perspective
picturesque
pietà
pigment
pleurant
pochade
pointillism
polyptych
pop
portraiture
pouncing
precisionism
predella
primitive
provenance
purism
putto
quadratura
quattrocento
realism
relief
renaissance
repoussé
repoussoir
retroussage
rococo
romanesque
salon
school
sculp
sculpsit
sculpture

scumble
secco
sepia
sfumato
sinopia
size
sketch
staffage
still life
stippling
stucco
style
stylization
stylus
superrealism
suprematism
surrealism
swag
symbolism
synthetism
tachisme
tempera
tenebrism
term
tesserae
tondo
trecento
triptych
trompe l'oeil
turpentine
tuscan
vanitas
varnish
veduta
venetian
verism
vorticism
wash
watercolour
woodcut
xylography

ART SCHOOLS AND STYLES

abstract art
abstract
  expressionism
action painting
Aesthetic Movement
art brut
art deco
arte povera
art informel
art nouveau
Arts and Crafts
  Movement
avant-garde
baroque
Blaue Reiter
Byzantine art
Camden School
classicism
cloisonnism
conceptual art
concrete art
constructivism
cubism
Dada

De Stijl
divisionism
environmental art
expressionism
fauvism
figurative art
Florentine school
folk art
futurism
grand manner
High Renaissance art
impressionism
International Gothic
intimisme
Islamic art
Jugendstil
junk art
kinetic art
kitsch
land art
magic realism
mannerism
metaphysical
  painting

minimalism
Minoan art
Mogul art
mozarabic art
naive art
naturalism
neoclassicism
neoexpressionism
neoimpressionism
neoromanticism
Neue Sachlichkeit
op art
orphism
Ottoman art
performance art
photorealism
plein-air painting
pointillism
pop art
postimpressionism
postmodernism
precisionism
Pre-Raphaelitism
primitive art

purism
Rayonism
realism
regionalism
Renaissance art
representational art
rococo
romanticism
Sienese school
socialist realism
social realism
suprematism
surrealism
symbolism
synchronism
synthetism
tachism
transavant-garde
Venetian school
verism
vorticism

ARCHITECTURAL TERMS

abacus
acanthus
annulet
anthemion
apophyge
architrave
Art Deco
Art Nouveau
astragal
atlas
baguette
banderole
baroque
bas-relief
Bauhaus
beaux-arts
billet
boss
brutalist
Byzantine
calotte
canephorae
capstone
Carolingian
cartouche
caryatid
cavetto
chevron
Churrigueresque
cinquecento

cinquefoil
classical
colossal
composite
congé
copestone
cordon
Corinthian
cornice
corona
coving
crocket
crownpiece
cusp
Cyclopean
cyma
dancette
Deconstructionism
dentil
De Stijl
dog-tooth
Doric
Early English
Early Renaissance
echinus
ectype
egg and anchor
egg and dart
egg and tongue
Egyptian

Empire
epistyle
facet
fascia
Federation
festoon
fillet
finial
flamboyant
flute
foil
foliation
fret
frieze
frontispiece
functional
gadroon
gorgerin
Gothic
Gothic Revival
Graeco-Roman
Grecian
Greek Revival
guilloche
gutta
head mould
headpiece
helix
herm
hood mould

hypotrachelium
Ionic
Islamic
lierne
listel
mannerist
medallion
medieval
Mesopotamian
metope
modernist
modillion
Moorish
Moresque
moulding
Mozarabic
Mudéjar
mullion
mutule
neck-mould
neoclassical
Norman
ogee
ovolo
Palladian
pendant
Perpendicular
polychromy
postmodernist
putto

ARCHITECTURAL TERMS (cont.)

quarter-round	rococo	stria	trefoil
quatrefoil	Roman	stucco	triglyph
quattrocento	Romanesque	taenia	Tuscan
quirk	rustication	talon	tympanum
quoin	Saracen	terminal	vaulting
reed	Saxon	torus	vernacular
reglet	scotia	tracery	vignette
Renaissance	scroll	transitional	volute
respond	splay	transom	zigzag

TYPES OF BUILDING

amphitheatre	convent	grange	mill	skyscraper	townhouse
aqueduct	cottage	greenhouse	monastery	stadium	triumphal
arena	dagoba	hangar	mosque	stockade	arch
barn	dome	house	pagoda	stupa	vault
basilica	folly	igloo	pavilion	talayot	viaduct
castle	fort	insula	Portakabin™	temple	villa
cathedral	fortress	keep	prison	thermae	warehouse
chapel	garage	maisonette	pyramid	tholos	windmill
chateau	geodesic	mansion	rath	tope	ziggurat
church	dome	mausoleum	sepulchre	tower	

FAMOUS BUILDINGS
(with location)

Acropolis	Athens
Alhambra	Granada, Spain
Blenheim Palace	Woodstock, England
Blue Mosque	Istanbul
British Museum	London
Buckingham Palace	London
Canary Wharf	London
Casa Milá	Barcelona
Chartres Cathedral	France
Chrysler Building	New York
Cologne Cathedral	Germany
Colosseum	Rome
Crystal Palace	London
Dome of the Rock	Jerusalem
Edinburgh Castle	Scotland
Eiffel Tower	Paris
Empire State Building	New York
Erechtheum or Erechtheion	Athens
Florence Cathedral	Italy
Forum Romanum	Rome
Galleria Vittorio Emanuele II	Milan
Golden Temple	Amritsar, India
Guggenheim Museum	New York
Guggenheim Museum	Bilbao
Hall of Supreme Harmony	Beijing
Hermitage, The	St Petersburg
Horyu-ji	Nara, Japan
Houses of Parliament	London
Jefferson Memorial	Washington
Jewish Museum	Berlin
John Hancock Center	Chicago
J. Paul Getty Museum	Malibu, California
King's College Chapel	Cambridge, England
Leaning Tower of Pisa	Italy
Louvre	Paris
Millennium Dome	London
Notre-Dame Cathedral	Paris
Pantheon	Rome
Parliament House	Vienna
Parthenon	Athens
Pennsylvania Station	New York
Pentagon	Arlington, Virginia
Petronas Towers	Kuala Lumpur
Pompidou Centre	Paris
President's Palace	Brasília
Pyramids	Egypt
Reichstag	Berlin
Reims Cathedral	France
Sacre Coeur	Paris
Sagrada Familia	Barcelona
St Basil's Cathedral	Moscow
Ste-Chapelle	Paris
St Mark's Cathedral	Venice

FAMOUS BUILDINGS (cont.)
(with location)

St Patrick's Cathedral	New York	Tower of London	England
St Paul's Cathedral	London	Transamerica Pyramid	San Francisco
St Peter's	Rome	Trans World Airways	
St Sophia	Istanbul	Terminal	New York
Sears Tower	Chicago	U.S. Capitol	Washington, D. C.
Sun Temple	Konarak, India	Versailles	Paris
Sydney Opera House	Australia	Westminster Abbey	London
Taj Mahal	Agra, India	White House	Washington, D. C.

THE MUSICAL SCALE IN TONIC SOL-FA

doh	ray	mi	fah	soh	lah	te

MUSICAL DIRECTIONS
(with translations)

a battuta	return to strict time	dal segno	from the sign
a cappella	unaccompanied	decrescendo	becoming quieter
accelerando	accelerating	dim(inuendo)	becoming quieter
adagietto	fairly slowly	dolente	sorrowfully
adagio	slowly	doppio	double
ad lib(itum)	at will	f(orte)	loudly
affettuoso	tenderly	fortissimo, ff	very loudly
agitato	agitated	giocoso	playfully
al fine	to the end	glissando	sliding
allargando	broadening	in modo di	in the manner of
allegretto	fairly lively	larghetto	fairly slowly
allegro	lively	largo	very slowly
al segno	as far as the sign	legato	tied, smoothly
amoroso	tenderly	leggiero	lightly
andante	moderately slow	lento	slowly
andantino	slightly faster than	maestoso	majestically
	andante	marcato	accented
animato	spirited	marcia	march
assai	very	meno mosso	slower pace
a tempo	in the original tempo	mezza voce	at half strength
attacca	continue without	mezzo	half
	stopping	mezzoforte, mf	fairly loudly
bis	repeat	moderato	moderately
calando	becoming quieter	molto	very
	and slower	morendo	dying away
cantabile	in a singing manner	mosso	fast
capriccioso	freely	moto	motion
coda	final part of a	nobilmente	nobly
	movement	non troppo	not too much
col legno	with stick of the bow	obbligato	not to be omitted
con amore	tenderly	ped	pedal
con brio	with vigour	pesante	heavily
con fuoco	fiery	pianissimo, pp	very soft
con sordino	with a mute	p(iano)	soft
cresc(endo)	becoming louder	più	more
da capo	from the beginning	pizz(icato)	plucked

MUSICAL DIRECTIONS (cont.)
(with translations)

poco	a little	sordino	mute
portamento	carrying one note into the next	sostenuto	sustained
		sotto voce	in an undertone
prestissimo	as fast as possible	staccato	detached
presto	very fast	stretto	in quicker time
rall(entando)	slowing down	stringendo	intensifying
ravvivando	quickening	subito	immediately
rinforzando, rfz	accentuated	tacet	instrument remains silent
rit(ardando)	slowing down		
ritenuto	more slowly	tempo	speed *or* beat
scherzando	playfully	ten(uto)	held
segno	sign	tutti	whole orchestra
semplice	simply	vivace	lively
sempre	always, throughout	vif	lively
senza	without	vivement	lively
sf(orzando), sfz	strongly accented	zoppa	syncopated

MUSICAL INSTRUMENTS

accordion	bumbass	cornu	euphonium
acoustic guitar	bumpa	courtaut	fandur
aeolian harp	buzz disk	cowbell	fiddle
alphorn	calliope	crook horn	fife
altohorn	carillon	crotals	fipple flute
angel chimes	castanets	crumhorn	flageolet
arpeggione	celeste	crwth	flexatone
atumpan	cello	cymbals	flugelhorn
auloi	chakay	cythara anglica	flute
autoharp	chang	da-daiko	French horn
bagpipe	changko	daibyoshi	gambang kaya
balalaika	chime	damaru	gansa gambang
bandoura	Chinese wood block	darabukka	gansa jongkok
banjo	chitarra battente	darbuk	geigenwerk
banjolele	chitarrone	dauli	glockenspiel
barrel drum	cimbalom	Deutsche schalmei	gong
barrel organ	cipactli	dhola	grand piano
baryton	cittern	didgeridoo	guqin
bassanello	clappers	dilruba	guitar
bass drum	clarinet	diplice	gusle
bass guitar	clarinet d'amore	diplo-kithara	handbell
bass horn	clave	djunadjan	harmonica
bassoon	clavichord	dobro	harmonium
bells	clavicor	dombak	harp
bird scarer	clavicytherium	double bass	harpsichord
bivalve bell	claviorgan	double bassoon	hawkbell
bodhran	cog rattle	doumdouba	heckelclarina
bombarde	componium	drum	heckelphone
bombardon	contrabass	dudelsack	heikebiwa
bongo drums	contrabassoon	dugdugi	helicon
bonnang	cor anglais	dulcimer	hi-hat cymbals
bouzouki	cornemuse	electric guitar	horn
bow harp	cornet	entenga	hu qin
buccina	cornett	enzenze	hula ipu
bugle	corno da caccia	erhu	hummel
bullroarer	cornopean	esraj	hurdy-gurdy

MUSICAL INSTRUMENTS (cont.)

hydraulis
jew's harp
jing hu
jingling Johnny
kalimba
kalungu
kamanje
kantele
kanteleharpe
kayageum
kazoo
kena
kenong
kendang
kettledrum
kithara
koboro
ko-kiu
komungo
könighorn
kora
koto
lamellaphone
likembe
lira
lirica
lirone
lithophone
lontar
lute
lyre
mandobass
mandocello
mandola
mandolin
mandolinetto
mandolone
maracas
marimba
masenqo
mayuri
mbira
mellophone
melodeon
melodica
metallophone
Moog ™ synthesizer
mouth organ
mrdamga
murumbu
musette
mu yü
nay
oboe
ocarina
octavin

o-daiko
okedo
ophicleide
organ
orpharion
orphica
o-tsuzumi
ottavino
p'ai pan
pandora
panhuéhuetl
panpipe
pianino
piano
pianoforte
pianola
piccolo
picco pipe
pien ch'ing
piffaro
pi nai
pipa
pipe
pochette
pommer
psaltery
pu-ilu
putorino
qin
ramkie
ranasringa
raspa
rattle
rauschpfeife
rebab
rebec
recorder
reshoto
rinchik
rommelpot
rote
ruan
sackbut
salpinx
sansa
santur
sanxian
sarangi
sarinda
sarod
saron
sarrusophone
saung-gauk
savernake horn
saw-thai
saxhorn

saxophone
saxotromba
saxtuba
saz
schrillpfeife
shaing
shaker
shakuhachi
shamisen
shanai
shawm
sheng
shiwaya
shô
shofar
side drum
sistrum
sitar
sleigh bells
slide trombone
slit drum
sona
sonajero
sopile
sordine
sordone
sousaphone
spike fiddle
spinet
spitzharfe
sralay
sringara
stamping tube
stock-and-horn
strumento di porco
stylophone
surbahar
surnaj
symphonium
synthesizer
syrinx
tabla
tabor
tallharpa
tambourine
tambura
tam-tam
tanpura
tar
teponaztli
terbang
theorbo
thumb piano
tibia
tiktiri
timbales

timpani
tin whistle
tlapanhuéhuetl
tlapiztali
tom-tom
totombito
triangle
triccaballacca
trombone
trumpet
tsuzumi
tuba
tubular bells
tudum
tumyr
tupan
turkish crescent
tympani
ukulele
valiha
vibraphone
vibra slap ™
vielle
vihuela
vina
viol
viola
viola bastarda
viola da gamba
viola d'amore
violetta
violin
violoncello
violone
virginal
whistle
whistle flute
wood block
Wurlitzer ™
xylophone
xylorimba
yangqin
yangum
yü
yueqin
yun lo
yun ngao
zampogna
zarb
zheng
zither
zobo
zummara
zurla
zurna

PEOPLE IN THE ARTS

Aalto, (Hugo) Alvar (Henrik) (1898–1976) Finnish architect and furniture designer

Adam, Robert (1728–92) Scottish architect

Adams, Ansel (Easton) (1902–84) American photographer

Albers, Josef (1888–1976) German-born American artist, designer, and teacher

Alberti, Leon Battista (1404–72) Italian architect, humanist, painter, and art critic

Albinoni, Tomaso (1671–1751) Italian composer

Allen, Woody (born Allen Stewart Konigsberg) (born 1935) American film director, writer, and actor

Allston, Washington (1779–1843) American landscape painter

Alma-Tadema, Sir Lawrence (1836–1912) Dutch-born British painter

Almodóvar, Pedro (born 1949) Spanish film director

Altdorfer, Albrecht (c. 1480–1538) German painter and architect

Altman, Robert (born 1925) American film director

Amati, Andrea (c. 1520–c. 1578) Italian violin maker

Amati, Antonio (c. 1550–1638) Italian violin maker

Amati, Girolamo (1551–1635) Italian violin maker

Amati, Nicolò (1596–1684) Italian violin maker

Anderson, Lindsay (Gordon) (1923–94) English film director

Anderson, Marian (1902–93) American operatic contralto

Andre, Carl (born 1935) American minimalist sculptor

Andrews, Dame Julie (born Julia Elizabeth Wells) (born 1935) English actress and singer

Angelico, Fra (born Guido di Pietro, monastic name Fra Giovanni da Fiesole) (c. 1400–55) Italian painter

Annigoni, Pietro (1910–88) Italian painter

Antonioni, Michelangelo (born 1912) Italian film director

Apelles (4th century BC) Greek painter

Appel, Karel (born 1921) Dutch painter, sculptor, and graphic artist

Arbus, Diane (1923–71) American photographer

Archipenko, Aleksandr (Porfirevich) (1887–1964) Russian-born American sculptor and painter

Armani, Giorgio (born 1934) Italian fashion designer

Armstrong, (Daniel) Louis (known as 'Satchmo') (1900–71) US jazz trumpeter and singer

Arne, Thomas (1710–78) English composer

Arnold, Sir Malcolm (Henry) (born 1921) English composer and trumpeter

Arp, Jean (also known as Hans Arp) (1887–1966) French painter, sculptor, and poet

Arrau, Claudio (1903–91) Chilean pianist

Artaud, Antonin (1896–1948) French actor, director, and poet

Ashcroft, Dame Peggy (Edith Margaret Emily) (1907–91) English actress

Ashkenazy, Vladimir (Davidovich) (born 1937) Russian-born pianist and conductor

Ashley, Laura (1925–85) Welsh fashion and textile designer

Ashton, Sir Frederick (William Mallandaine) (1904–88) British ballet-dancer and choreographer

Askey, Arthur (Bowden) (1900–82) English comedian and actor

Astaire, Fred (born Frederick Austerlitz) (1899–1987) American dancer, singer, and actor

Attenborough, Richard (Samuel), Baron Attenborough of Richmond-upon-Thames (born 1923) English film actor, producer, and director

Auerbach, Frank (born 1931) German-born British painter

Auric, Georges (1899–1983) French composer

Babbitt, Milton (Byron) (born 1916) American composer and mathematician

Bacall, Lauren (born 1924) American actress

Bach, Johann Sebastian (1685–1750) German composer

Bacharach, Burt (born 1929) American writer of popular songs

Bacon, Francis (1909–92) Irish painter

Baez, Joan (born 1941) American folk-singer

Bailey, David (born 1938) English photographer

Baker, Dame Janet (Abbott) (born 1933) English operatic mezzo-soprano

Baker, Josephine (1906–75) American dancer

Bakst, Léon (born Lev Samuilovich Rozenberg) (1866–1924) Russian painter and designer

Balanchine, George (born Georgi Melitonovich Balanchivadze) (1904–83) Russian-born American ballet-dancer and choreographer

Balcon, Sir Michael (1896–1977) English film producer

Balenciaga, Cristóbal (1895–1972) Spanish couturier

Ball, Lucille (1911–89) American comedienne

PEOPLE IN THE ARTS (cont.)

Bankhead, Tallulah (1903–68) American actress

Barber, Samuel (1910–81) American composer

Barbirolli, Sir John (Giovanni Battista) (1899–1970) English conductor, of Franco-Italian descent

Bardot, Brigitte (born 1934) French actress

Barenboim, Daniel (born 1942) Israeli pianist and conductor, born in Argentina

Barnum, P(hineas) T(aylor) (1810–91) American showman

Barrault, Jean-Louis (1910–94) French actor and director

Barry, Sir Charles (1795–1860) English architect

Barrymore, Ethel (1879–1959) American actress

Barrymore, John (1882–1942) American actor

Barrymore, Lionel (1878–1954) American actor

Bart, Lionel (1930–99) English composer and lyricist

Bartholdi, Frédéric-Auguste (1834–1904) French sculptor

Bartók, Béla (1881–1945) Hungarian composer

Bartolommeo, Fra (born Baccio della Porta) (c. 1472–1517) Italian painter

Baryshnikov, Mikhail (Nikolaevich) (born 1948) American ballet-dancer, born in Latvia of Russian parents

Basie, Count (born William Basie) (1904–84) American jazz pianist, organist, and bandleader

Baskerville, John (1706–75) English printer

Bateman, H(enry) M(ayo) (1887–1970) Australian-born British cartoonist

Bausch, Pina (born 1940) German choreographer

Bax, Sir Arnold (Edward Trevor) (1883–1953) English composer

Baylis, Lilian Mary (1874–1937) English theatre manager

Beardsley, Aubrey (Vincent) (1872–98) English artist and illustrator

Beaton, Sir Cecil (Walter Hardy) (1904–80) English photographer

Beatty, Warren (born Henry Warren Beaty) (born 1937) American actor, film director, and screenwriter

Bechstein, Friedrich Wilhelm Carl (1826–1900) German piano-builder

Beckmann, Max (1884–1950) German painter and graphic artist

Beecham, Sir Thomas (1879–1961) English conductor and impresario

Beethoven, Ludwig van (1770–1827) German composer

Behrens, Peter (1868–1940) German architect and designer

Beiderbecke, Bix (born Leon Bismarck Beiderbecke) (1903–31) American jazz musician and composer

Béjart, Maurice (born Maurice Jean Berger) (born 1927) French choreographer

Bell, Vanessa (1879–1961) English painter and designer

Bellini, Gentile (c. 1429–1507) Italian artist

Bellini, Giovanni (c. 1430–1516) Italian artist

Bellini, Jacopo (c. 1400–c. 1470) Italian artist

Bellini, Vincenzo (1801–35) Italian composer

Bennett, Sir Richard Rodney (born 1936) English composer

Benny, Jack (born Benjamin Kubelsky) (1894–1974) American comedian and actor

Berg, Alban (Maria Johannes) (1885–1935) Austrian composer

Bergman, (Ernst) Ingmar (born 1918) Swedish film and theatre director

Bergman, Ingrid (1915–82) Swedish actress

Berio, Luciano (born 1925) Italian composer

Berkeley, Busby (born William Berkeley Enos) (1895–1976) American choreographer and film director

Berkeley, Sir Lennox (Randall Francis) (1903–89) English composer

Berkoff, Steven (born 1937) English dramatist, director, and actor

Berlin, Irving (born Israel Baline) (1888–1989) Russian-born American songwriter

Berlioz, (Louis-)Hector (1803–69) French composer

Bernhardt, Sarah (born Henriette Rosine Bernard) (1844–1923) French actress

Bernini, Gian Lorenzo (1598–1680) Italian sculptor, painter, and architect

Bernstein, Leonard (1918–90) American composer, conductor, and pianist

Berry, Chuck (born Charles Edward Berry) (born 1931) American rock and roll singer, guitarist, and songwriter

Bertolucci, Bernardo (born 1940) Italian film director

Betterton, Thomas (1635–1710) English actor

Beuys, Joseph (1921–86) German artist

Bewick, Thomas (1753–1828) English artist and wood engraver

Binoche, Juliette (born 1964) French film actress

Birtwistle, Sir Harrison (Paul) (born 1934) English composer and clarinettist

Bizet, Georges (born Alexandre César Léopold Bizet) (1838–75) French composer

Blake, Peter (born 1932) English painter

Blake, William (1757–1827) English artist and poet

PEOPLE IN THE ARTS (cont.)

Blakey, Arthur ('Art') (1919–90), American jazz drummer

Bliss, Sir Arthur (Edward Drummond) (1891–1975) English composer

Bloch, Ernest (1880–1959) Swiss-born American composer, of Jewish descent

Blondin, Charles (born Jean-François Gravelet) (1824–97) French acrobat

Boccherini, Luigi (1743–1805) Italian composer and cellist

Bodoni, Giambattista (1740–1813) Italian printer

Bogarde, Sir Dirk (born Derek Niven van den Bogaerde) (1921–99) British actor and writer, of Dutch descent

Bogart, Humphrey (DeForest) (1899–1957) American actor

Bonnard, Pierre (1867–1947) French painter and graphic artist

Borodin, Aleksandr (Porfirevich) (1833–87) Russian composer

Borromini, Francesco (1599–1667) Italian architect

Bosch, Hieronymus (c. 1450–1516) Dutch painter

Botticelli, Sandro (born Alessandro di Mariano Filipepi) (1445–1510) Italian painter

Boucher, François (1703–70) French painter and decorative artist

Boulez, Pierre (born 1925) French composer and conductor

Boult, Sir Adrian (Cedric) (1889–1983) English conductor

Boulting, John (1913–85) and Roy (born 1913) English film producers and directors

Bourke-White, Margaret (1906–71) American photojournalist

Bow, Clara (1905–65) American actress

Bowie, David (born David Robert Jones) (born 1947) English rock singer, songwriter, and actor

Bowles, Paul (Frederick) (1910–99) American writer and composer

Boyce, William (1711–79) English composer and organist

Boyd, Arthur (Merric Bloomfield) (1920–99) Australian painter, potter, etcher, and ceramic artist

Boyer, Charles (1897–1977) French-born American actor

Brahms, Johannes (1833–97) German composer and pianist

Brain, Dennis (1921–57) English French-horn player

Bramante, Donato (di Angelo) (1444–1514) Italian architect

Branagh, Kenneth (Charles) (born 1960) English actor, producer, and director

Brancusi, Constantin (1876–1957) Romanian sculptor, who spent much of his working life in France

Brando, Marlon (born 1924) American actor

Brandt, Hermann Wilhelm ('Bill') (1904–83) German-born British photographer

Braque, Georges (1882–1963) French painter

Bream, Julian (Alexander) (born 1933) English guitarist and lute-player

Brel, Jacques (1929–78) Belgian singer and composer

Bresson, Robert (1907–99) French film director

Breughel See BRUEGEL

Bridge, Frank (1879–1941) English composer, conductor, and violist

Britten, (Edward) Benjamin, Lord Britten of Aldeburgh (1913–76) English composer, pianist, and conductor

Bronzino, Agnolo (born Agnolo di Cosimo) (1503–72) Italian painter

Brook, Peter (Stephen Paul) (born 1925) English theatre director

Brooks, Mel (born Melvin Kaminsky) (born 1927) American film director and actor

Brouwer, Adriaen (c. 1605–38) Flemish painter

Brown, Ford Madox (1821–93) English painter

Brown, James (born 1928) American soul and funk singer and songwriter

Brown, Lancelot (known as Capability Brown) (1716–83) English landscape gardener

Brubeck, David Warren ('Dave') (born 1920) American jazz pianist, composer, and bandleader

Bruce, Lenny (born Leonard Alfred Schneider) (1925–66) American comedian

Bruckner, Anton (1824–96) Austrian composer and organist

Bruegel, Jan Bruegel the Elder (1568–1625) Flemish artist

Bruegel, Pieter Bruegel the Elder (1525–69) Flemish artist

Bruegel, Pieter Bruegel the Younger (?1564–?1638) Flemish artist

Brunelleschi, Filippo (born Filippo di Ser Brunellesco) (1377–1446) Italian architect

Buffalo Bill (born William Frederick Cody) (1846–1917) American showman

Buñuel, Luis (1900–83) Spanish film director

Buonarroti, Michelangelo See MICHELANGELO

Burbage, Richard (c. 1567–1619) English actor

Burne-Jones, Sir Edward (Coley) (1833–98) English painter and designer

Burns, George (born Nathan Birnbaum) (1896–1996) American comedian

Burra, Edward (1905–76) English painter

PEOPLE IN THE ARTS (cont.)

Burton, Richard (born Richard Jenkins) (1925–84) Welsh actor

Busoni, Ferruccio (Benvenuto) (1866–1924) Italian composer, conductor, and pianist

Butler, Reginald Cotterell ('Reg') (1913–81) English sculptor

Butterfield, William (1814–1900) English architect

Buxtehude, Dietrich (c. 1637–1707) Danish organist and composer

Byrd, William (1543–1623) English composer

Caballé, Montserrat (born 1933) Spanish operatic soprano

Cage, John (Milton) (1912–92) American composer, pianist, and writer

Cage, Nicolas (born 1964) American film actor

Cagney, James (1899–1986) American actor

Caine, Sir Michael (born Maurice Micklewhite) (born 1933) English film actor

Caldecott, Randolph (1846–86) English graphic artist and watercolour painter

Calder, Alexander (1898–1976) American sculptor and painter

Callas, Maria (born Maria Cecilia Anna Kalageropoulos) (1923–77) American-born operatic soprano, of Greek parentage

Callicrates (5th century BC) Greek architect

Callow, Simon (born 1949) British actor and director

Calloway, Cab(ell) (1907–94) American jazz singer and bandleader

Cameron, James (born 1954) American film director and writer

Cameron, Julia Margaret (1815–79) English photographer

Camões, Luis (Vaz) de (also Camoëns) (c. 1524–80) Portuguese poet

Campbell, Mrs Patrick (née Beatrice Stella Tanner) (1865–1940) English actress

Campion, Jane (born 1954) New Zealand film director and screenwriter

Canaletto (born Giovanni Antonio Canale) (1697–1768) Italian painter

Canova, Antonio (1757–1822) Italian sculptor

Capability Brown See BROWN, LANCELOT

Capp, Al (born Alfred Gerald Caplin) (1909–79) American cartoonist

Capra, Frank (1897–1991) Italian-born American film director

Caravaggio, Michelangelo Merisi da (c. 1571–1610) Italian painter

Cardin, Pierre (born 1922) French couturier

Carmichael, Hoagy (born Howard Hoagland Carmichael) (1899–1981) American jazz pianist, composer, and singer

Carné, Marcel (1909–96) French film director

Carpaccio, Vittore (c. 1455–1525) Italian painter

Carr, Emily (1871–1945) Canadian painter and writer

Carracci, Agostino (1557–1602) Italian painter

Carracci, Annibale (1560–1609) Italian painter

Carracci, Ludovico (1555–1619) Italian painter

Carreras, José (born 1946) Spanish operatic tenor

Carrey, Jim (born 1962) Canadian-born American film actor

Carrington, Dora (de Houghton) (1893–1932) English painter

Carson, John William ('Johnny') (born 1925) American television personality

Carter, Elliott (Cook) (born 1908) American composer

Cartier-Bresson, Henri (born 1908) French photographer and film director

Caruso, Enrico (1873–1921) Italian operatic tenor

Casals, Pablo (also called Pau Casals) (1876–1973) Spanish cellist, conductor, and composer

Cash, Johnny (born 1932) American country music singer and songwriter

Caslon, William (1692–1766) English typographer

Cassatt, Mary (1844–1926) American painter

Casson, Sir Hugh (Maxwell) (1910–99) English architect

Cellini, Benvenuto (1500–71) Italian goldsmith and sculptor

Cézanne, Paul (1839–1906) French painter

Chabrol, Claude (born 1930) French film director

Chagall, Marc (1887–1985) Russian-born French painter and graphic artist

Chaliapin, Fyodor (Ivanovich) (1873–1938) Russian operatic bass

Chambers, Sir William (1723–96) Scottish architect

Chanel, Coco (born Gabrielle Bonheur Chanel) (1883–1971) French couturière

Chaney, Lon (full name Alonso Chaney) (1883–1930) American actor

Chaplin, Sir Charles Spencer ('Charlie') (1889–1977) English film actor and director

Charles, Ray (born Ray Charles Robinson) (born 1930) American pianist and singer

Chevalier, Maurice (1888–1972) French singer and actor

Chippendale, Thomas (1718–79) English furniture-maker and designer

Chirico, Giorgio de (1888–1978) Greek-born Italian painter

Chopin, Frédéric (François) (Polish name Fryderyk Franciszek Szopen) (1810–49) Polish-born French composer

Cibber, Colley (1671–1757) English actor, theatre manager, and dramatist

PEOPLE IN THE ARTS (cont.)

Clair, René (born René Lucien Chomette) (1898–1981) French film director

Clapton, Eric (born 1945) English blues and rock guitarist, singer, and composer

Claude Lorraine (also Lorrain) (born Claude Gellée) (1600–82) French painter

Cleese, John (Marwood) (born 1939) English comic actor and writer

Clift, (Edward) Montgomery (1920–66) American actor

Cline, Patsy (born Virginia Petterson Hensley) (1932–63) American country singer

Clouet, Jean (c. 1485–1541) and his son **François** (c. 1516–72) French painters

Cobain, Kurt (Donald) (1967–94) American rock singer, guitarist, and songwriter

Cochran, Sir C(harles) B(lake) (1872–1951) English theatrical producer

Cochran, Eddie (born Edward Cochrane) (1938–60) American rock and roll singer and songwriter

Cody, William Frederick See BUFFALO BILL

Cole, Nat King (born Nathaniel Adams Coles) (1919–65) American singer and pianist

Coleman, Ornette (born 1930) American jazz saxophonist, trumpeter, violinist, and composer

Collins, Joan (Henrietta) (born 1933) English actress

Coltrane, John (William) (1926–67) American jazz saxophonist and composer

Connery, Sir Sean (born Thomas Connery) (born 1930) Scottish actor

Connolly, Billy (born 1942) Scottish comedian and actor

Constable, John (1776–1837) English painter

Cook, Peter (Edward) (1937–94) English comedian and actor

Cooper, Gary (born Frank James Cooper) (1901–61) American actor

Cooper, Susan Vera ('Susie') (1902–95) English ceramic designer and manufacturer

Copland, Aaron (1900–90) American composer, pianist, and conductor, of Lithuanian descent

Copley, John Singleton (1738–1815) American painter

Coppola, Francis Ford (born 1939) American film director, writer, and producer

Corelli, Arcangelo (1653–1713) Italian violinist and composer

Corot, (Jean-Baptiste) Camille (1796–1875) French landscape painter

Correggio, Antonio Allegri da (born Antonio Allegri) (c. 1494–1534) Italian painter

Costa, Lúcio (1902–63) French-born Brazilian architect, town planner, and architectural historian

Costner, Kevin (born 1955) American film actor and director

Cotman, John Sell (1782–1842) English painter

Couperin, François (1668–1733) French composer, organist, and harpsichordist

Courbet, Gustave (1819–77) French painter

Courrèges, André (born 1923) French fashion designer

Coward, Sir Noel (Pierce) (1899–1973) English dramatist, actor, and composer

Cranach, Lucas (known as Cranach the Elder) (1472–1553) German painter

Crane, (Harold) Hart (1899–1932) American poet

Crane, Stephen (1871–1900) American writer

Crawford, Joan (born Lucille le Sueur) (1908–77) American actress

Crome, John (1768–1821) English painter

Crosby, Bing (born Harry Lillis Crosby) (1904–77) American singer and actor

Cruft, Charles (1852–1939) English showman

Cruikshank, George (1792–1878) English painter, illustrator, and caricaturist

Cruise, Tom (born Thomas Cruise Mapotter IV) (born 1962) American film actor

Cunningham, Merce (born 1919) American dancer and choreographer

Cusack, Cyril (1910–93) Irish actor

Cushing, Peter (1913–94) English actor

Czerny, Karl (1791–1857) Austrian pianist, teacher, and composer

Dadd, Richard (1817–86) English painter

Dalcroze See JAQUES-DALCROZE

Daldry, Stephen (born 1961) British theatre and film director

Dali, Salvador (1904–89) Spanish painter

Dallapiccola, Luigi (1904–75) Italian composer

Daubigny, Charles François (1817–78) French landscape painter

Daumier, Honoré (1808–78) French painter and lithographer

David, Jacques-Louis (1748–1825) French painter

Davies, Sir Peter Maxwell (born 1934) English composer and conductor

da Vinci, Leonardo See LEONARDO DA VINCI

Davis, Bette (born Ruth Elizabeth Davis) (1908–89) American actress

Davis, Miles (Dewey) (1926–91) American jazz trumpeter, composer, and bandleader

Day, Doris (born Doris Kappelhoff) (born 1924) American actress and singer

Dean, James (born James Byron) (1931–55) American actor

Debussy, (Achille) Claude (1862–1918) French composer and critic

de Falla, Manuel See FALLA

PEOPLE IN THE ARTS (cont.)

Degas, (Hilaire Germain) Edgar (1834–1917) French painter and sculptor

de Hooch, Pieter (also de Hoogh) (c. 1629–c. 1684) Dutch genre painter

de Kooning, Willem (1904–97) Dutch-born American painter

Delacroix, (Ferdinand Victor) Eugène (1798–1863) French painter

Delaunay, Robert (1885–1941) French painter

Delaunay-Terk, Sonia (1885–1979) Russian-born French painter and textile designer

de Lenclos, Ninon See LENCLOS

Delfont, Bernard, Baron Delfont of Stepney (born Boris Winogradsky) (1909–94) British impresario, born in Russia

Delibes, (Clément Philibert) Léo (1836–91) French composer and organist

Delius, Frederick (1862–1934) English composer, of German and Scandinavian descent

della Francesca See PIERO DELLA FRANCESCA

della Quercia, Jacopo (c. 1374–1438) Italian sculptor

della Robbia, Andrea (1435–1525) Italian sculptor

della Robbia, Giovanni (1469–c. 1529) Italian sculptor

della Robbia, Girolamo (1488–1566) Italian sculptor

della Robbia, Lucia (1400–82) Italian sculptor

del Sarto, Andrea See SARTO

de Maintenon See MAINTENON

de Mille, Cecil B(lount) (1881–1959) American film producer and director

de Montespan, Marquise de See MONTESPAN

Dench, Dame Judi(th Olivia) (born 1934) English actress

Deneuve, Catherine (born Catherine Dorléac) (born 1943) French actress

De Niro, Robert (born 1943) American actor

Denis, Maurice (1870–1943) French painter, designer, and art theorist

Depardieu, Gérard (born 1948) French actor

Deprez See DES PREZ

Derain, André (1880–1954) French painter

De Sica, Vittorio (1901–74) Italian film director and actor

des Prez, Josquin (also des Prés) (c. 1440–1521) Flemish composer

de Valois, Dame Ninette (born Edris Stannus) (1898–2001) Irish choreographer, ballet-dancer, and teacher

Diaghilev, Sergei (Pavlovich) (1872–1929) Russian ballet impresario

Dietrich, Marlene (born Maria Magdelene von Losch) (1901–92) German-born American actress and singer

Dimbleby, (Frederick) Richard (1913–65) English broadcaster

Dior, Christian (1905–57) French couturier

Disney, Walter Elias ('Walt') (1901–66) American animator and film producer

Dobell, Sir William (1899–1970) Australian painter

Doisneau, Robert (1912–94) French photographer

Dolin, Sir Anton (born Sydney Francis Patrick Chippendall Healey-Kay) (1904–83) English ballet-dancer and choreographer

Domingo, Placido (born 1941) Spanish-born tenor

Domino, Fats (born Antoine Domino) (born 1928) American pianist, singer, and songwriter

Donatello (born Donato di Betto Bardi) (1386–1466) Italian sculptor

Donizetti, Gaetano (1797–1848) Italian composer

Doré, Gustave (1832–83) French book illustrator

D'Oyly Carte, Richard (1844–1901) English impresario and producer

Drysdale, Sir Russell (1912–81) British-born Australian painter

Dubuffet, Jean (1901–85) French artist

Duccio (full name Duccio di Buoninsegna) (c. 1255–c. 1320) Italian painter

Duchamp, Marcel (1887–1968) French-born painter, sculptor, and art theorist

Dufay, Guillaume (c. 1400–74) French composer

Dufy, Raoul (1877–1953) French painter and textile designer

Du Maurier, George (Louis Palmella Busson) (1834–96) French-born cartoonist, illustrator, and novelist

Duncan, Isadora (1878–1927) American dancer and teacher

Dunstable, John (c. 1390–1453) English composer

du Pré, Jacqueline (1945–87) English cellist

Dürer, Albrecht (1471–1528) German painter and engraver

Durey, Louis (1888–1979) French composer

Duse, Eleonora (1858–1924) Italian actress

Dvořák, Antonín (1841–1904) Czech composer

Dylan, Bob (born Robert Allen Zimmerman) (born 1941) American singer and songwriter

Eakins, Thomas (1844–1916) American painter and photographer

Eastwood, Clint (born 1930) American film actor and director

Eisenstein, Sergei (Mikhailovich) (1898–1948) Soviet film director, born in Latvia

Elgar, Sir Edward (William) (1857–1934) British composer

PEOPLE IN THE ARTS (cont.)

Elgin, 7th Earl of (title of Thomas Bruce) (1766–1841) British diplomat and art connoisseur

El Greco (Spanish for 'the Greek'; born Domenikos Theotokopoulos) (1541–1614) Cretan-born Spanish painter

Ellington, Duke (born Edward Kennedy Ellington) (1899–1974) American jazz pianist, composer, and band leader

Ensor, James (Sydney), Baron (1860–1949) Belgian painter and engraver

Epstein, Sir Jacob (1880–1959) American-born British sculptor

Ernst, Max (1891–1976) German artist

Erté (born Romain de Tirtoff) (1892–1990) Russian-born French fashion designer and illustrator

Escher, M(aurits) C(orneille) (1898-1972) Dutch graphic artist

Evans, Dame Edith (Mary) (1888–1976) English actress

Evans, Gil (born Ian Ernest Gilmore Green) (1912–88) Canadian jazz pianist, composer, and arranger

Eyre, Sir Richard (born 1943) British theatre director

Fabergé, Peter Carl (1846–1920) Russian goldsmith and jeweller, of French descent

Fabriano, Gentile da See GENTILE DA FABRIANO

Fairbanks, Douglas (Elton) (born Julius Ullman) (1883–1939) American actor

Falla, Manuel de (1876–1946) Spanish composer and pianist

Fassbinder, Rainer Werner (1946–82) German film director

Fauré, Gabriel (Urbain) (1845–1924) French composer and organist

Fellini, Federico (1920–93) Italian film director

Fender, Leo (1907–91) American guitar-maker

Ferrier, Kathleen (1912–53) English contralto

Field, John (1782–1837) Irish composer and pianist

Fields, Dame Gracie (born Grace Stansfield) (1898–1979) English singer and comedienne

Fields, W. C. (1880–1946) American film actor

Fischer-Dieskau, Dietrich (born 1925) German baritone

Fitzgerald, Ella (1917–96) American jazz singer

Flaxman, John (1755–1826) English sculptor and draughtsman

Flynn, Errol (born Leslie Thomas Flynn) (1909–59) Australian-born American actor

Fokine, Michel (born Mikhail Mikhailovich Fokin) (1880–1942) Russian-born American dancer and choreographer

Fonda, Henry (1905–82) American actor

Fonda, Jane (born 1937) American actress

Fonda, Peter (born 1939) American actor

Fonteyn, Dame Margot (born Margaret Hookham) (1919–91) English ballet-dancer

Ford, Harrison (born 1942) American actor

Ford, John (born Sean Aloysius O'Feeney) (1895–1973) American film director

Forman, Milos (born 1932) Czech-born American film director

Formby, George (born George Booth) (1904–61) English comedian

Foster, Jodie (born 1962) American film actress

Foster, Sir Norman (Robert) (born 1935) English architect

Foster, Stephen (Collins) (1826–64) American composer

Fragonard, Jean-Honoré (1732–1806) French painter

Franck, César (Auguste) (1822–90) Belgian-born French composer

Franklin, Aretha (born 1942) American soul and gospel singer

Freud, Lucian (born 1922) German-born British painter, grandson of Sigmund Freud

Friedrich, Caspar David (1774–1840) German painter

Frink, Dame Elisabeth (1930–93) English sculptor and graphic artist

Frith, William Powell (1819–1909) English painter

Fry, Roger (Eliot) (1866–1934) English art critic and painter

Fuller, R(ichard) Buckminster (1895–1983) American designer and architect

Furtwängler, Wilhelm (1886–1954) German conductor

Fuseli, Henry (born Johann Heinrich Füssli) (1741–1825) Swiss-born British painter and art critic

Gable, (William) Clark (1901–60) American actor

Gabo, Naum (born Naum Neemia Pevsner) (1890–1977) Russian-born American sculptor

Gainsborough, Thomas (1727–88) English painter

Gallagher, Noel (born 1967) and his brother **Liam** (born 1969) British rock musicians

Gance, Abel (1889–1991) French film director

Garbo, Greta (born Greta Gustafsson) (1905–90) Swedish-born American actress

Garcia, Jerry (full name Jerome John Garcia) (1942–95) American rock singer and guitarist

Gardner, Ava (Lavinia) (1922–90) American actress

Garland, Judy (born Frances Gumm) (1922–69) American singer and actress

Garrick, David (1717–79) English actor, manager, and dramatist

PEOPLE IN THE ARTS (cont.)

Gaudí, Antonio (full surname Gaudí y Cornet) (1853–1926) Spanish architect

Gaudier-Brzeska, Henri (1891–1915) French sculptor

Gauguin, (Eugène Henri) Paul (1848–1903) French painter

Gaye, Marvin (1939–84) American soul singer and songwriter

Gehry, Frank O(wen) Canadian-born US architect

Gentile da Fabriano (c. 1370–1427) Italian painter

Géricault, (Jean Louis André) Théodore (1791–1824) French painter

Gershwin, George (born Jacob Gershovitz) (1898–1937) American composer and pianist, of Russian Jewish parentage

Getz, Stan (born Stanley Gayetsky) (1927–91) American jazz saxophonist

Ghiberti, Lorenzo (1378–1455) Italian sculptor and goldsmith

Ghirlandaio (born Domenico di Tommaso Bigordi) (c. 1448–94) Italian painter

Giacometti, Alberto (1901–66) Swiss sculptor and painter

Gibbons, Grinling (1648–1721) Dutch-born English sculptor

Gibbons, Orlando (1583–1625) English composer and musician

Gibbs, James (1682–1754) Scottish architect

Gibson, Mel (Columcille Gerard) (born 1956) American-born Australian actor and director

Gielgud, Sir (Arthur) John (1904–2000) English actor and director

Gigli, Beniamino (1890–1957) Italian operatic tenor

Gill, (Arthur) Eric (Rowton) (1882–1940) English sculptor, engraver, and typographer

Gillespie, Dizzy (born John Birks Gillespie) (1917–93) American jazz trumpet player, composer, and bandleader

Giorgione (also called Giorgio Barbarelli or Giorgio da Castelfranco) (c. 1478–1510) Italian painter

Giotto (full name Giotto di Bondone) (c. 1267–1337) Italian painter

Gish, Lillian (1896–1993) American actress

Glass, Philip (born 1937) American composer

Glazunov, Aleksandr (Konstantinovich) (1865–1936) Russian composer

Glinka, Mikhail (Ivanovich) (1804–57) Russian composer

Gluck, Christoph Willibald von (1714–87) German composer

Gobbi, Tito (1915–84) Italian operatic baritone

Godard, Jean-Luc (born 1930) French film director

Goes, Hugo van der (fl. c. 1467–82) Flemish painter, born in Ghent

Goldwyn, Samuel (born Schmuel Gelbfisz; changed to Goldfish then Goldwyn) (1882–1974) Polish-born American film producer

Goodman, Benjamin David ('Benny') (1909–86) American jazz clarinettist and bandleader

Goossens, Sir (Aynsley) Eugene (1893–1962) English conductor, violinist, and composer, of Belgian descent

Gordy, Berry Jr (born 1929) American record producer

Górecki, Henryk (Mikołaj) (born 1933) Polish composer

Gorky, Arshile (1904–48) Turkish-born American painter

Gould, Glenn (Herbert) (1932–82) Canadian pianist and composer

Gould, John (1804–81) English bird artist

Gounod, Charles François (1818–93) French composer, conductor, and organist

Goya (full name Francisco José de Goya y Lucientes) (1746–1828) Spanish painter and etcher

Grade, Lew, Baron Grade of Elstree (born Louis Winogradsky) (1906–98) British television producer and executive, born in Russia

Graham, Martha (1893–1991) American dancer, teacher, and choreographer

Grainger, (George) Percy (Aldridge) (1882–1961) Australian-born American composer and pianist

Grant, Cary (born Alexander Archibald Leach) (1904–86) British-born American actor

Grant, Duncan (James Corrow) (1885–1978) Scottish painter and designer

Grant, Hugh (John Mungo) (born 1960) British film actor

Granville-Barker, Harley (1877–1946) English dramatist, critic, theatre director, and actor

Grappelli, Stephane (1908–97) French jazz violinist

Greco, El See EL GRECO

Greenaway, Catherine ('Kate') (1846–1901) English artist

Greenaway, Peter (born 1942) English film director

Grenfell, Joyce (Irene Phipps) (1910–79) English entertainer and writer

Greuze, Jean-Baptiste (1725–1805) French painter

Grieg, Edvard (1843–1907) Norwegian composer, conductor, and violinist

PEOPLE IN THE ARTS (cont.)

Grierson, John (1898–1972) Scottish film director and producer

Griffith, D(avid) W(ark) (1875–1948) American film director

Grimaldi, Joseph (1779–1837) English circus entertainer

Gris, Juan (born José Victoriano Gonzales) (1887–1927) Spanish painter

Gropius, Walter (1883–1969) German-born American architect

Grosz, George (1893–1959) German painter and draughtsman

Grove, Sir George (1820–1900) English musicologist

Grünewald, Mathias (born Mathis Nithardt; also called Mathis Gothardt) (c. 1460–1528) German painter

Guardi, Francesco (1712–93) Italian painter

Guarneri, Giuseppe ('del Gesù') (1687–1744) Italian violin-maker

Guinness, Sir Alec (1914–2000) English actor

Gurney, Ivor (Bertie) (1890–1937) English poet and composer

Guthrie, Woody (born Woodrow Wilson Guthrie) (1912–67) American folk-singer and songwriter

Gwynn, Eleanor ('Nell') (1650–87) English actress

Haitink, Bernard (born 1929) Dutch conductor

Haley, William John Clifton ('Bill') (1925–81) American rock and roll singer

Hall, Sir Peter (born 1930) British theatre director

Hallé, Sir Charles (German name Karl Halle) (1819–95) German-born pianist and conductor

Hals, Frans (c. 1580–1666) Dutch portrait and genre painter

Hamada, Shoji (1894–1978) Japanese potter

Hammerstein, Oscar (full name Oscar Hammerstein II) (1895–1960) American librettist

Hammond, Dame Joan (1912–96) Australian operatic soprano, born in New Zealand

Hamnett, Katharine (born 1952) English fashion designer

Hancock, Tony (full name Anthony John Hancock) (1924–68) English comedian

Handel, George Frederick (born Georg Friedrich Händel) (1685–1759) German-born composer, resident in England

Handy, W(illiam) C(hristopher) (1873–1958) American blues musician

Hanks, Tom (Thomas J.) (born 1956) American film actor

Hardy, Oliver See LAUREL AND HARDY

Harlow, Jean (born Harlean Carpenter) (1911–37) American film actress

Harrison, George (born 1943) English rock and pop guitarist

Harrison, Sir Rex (born Reginald Carey Harrison) (1908–90) English actor

Hartnell, Sir Norman (1901–79) English couturier

Hawkins, Coleman Randolph (1904–69) American jazz saxophonist

Hawks, Howard (1896–1977) American film director, producer, and screenwriter

Hawksmoor, Nicholas (1661–1736) English architect

Hawthorne, Sir Nigel (born 1929) British actor

Hay, Will(iam Thomson) (1888–1949) English actor and comedian

Haydn, Franz Joseph (1732–1809) Austrian composer

Hayworth, Rita (born Margarita Carmen Cansino) (1918–87) American actress and dancer

Head, Edith (1907–81) American costume designer

Hearst, William Randolph (1863–1951) American newspaper publisher and tycoon

Helpmann, Sir Robert (Murray) (1909–86) Australian ballet-dancer, choreographer, director, and actor

Hendrix, Jimi (born James Marshall Hendrix) (1942–70) American rock guitarist and singer

Henri, Robert (1865–1929) American painter

Henze, Hans Werner (born 1926) German composer and conductor

Hepburn, Audrey (1929–93) British actress, born in Belgium

Hepburn, Katharine (born 1909) American actress

Hepplewhite, George (died 1786) English cabinet-maker and furniture designer

Hepworth, Dame (Jocelyn) Barbara (1903–75) English sculptor

Herzog, Werner (born Werner Stipetic) (born 1942) German film director

Hess, Dame Myra (1890–1965) English pianist

Hildegard of Bingen, St (1098–1179) German abbess, scholar, composer, and mystic

Hill, Benny (born Alfred Hawthorne) (1925–92) English comedian

Hindemith, Paul (1895–1963) German composer

Hirst, Damien (born 1965) British artist and sculptor

Hitchcock, Sir Alfred (Joseph) (1899–1980) English film director

Hitchens, Ivon (1893–1979) English painter

Hobbema, Meindert (1638–1709) Dutch landscape painter

PEOPLE IN THE ARTS (cont.)

Hockney, David (born 1937) English painter and draughtsman

Hoffman, Dustin (Lee) (born 1937) American actor

Hogarth, William (1697–1764) English painter and engraver

Hokusai, Katsushika (1760–1849) Japanese painter and wood-engraver

Holbein, Hans (known as Holbein the Younger) (1497–1543) German painter

Holiday, Billie (born Eleanora Fagan) (1915–59) American jazz singer

Holly, Buddy (born Charles Hardin Holley) (1936–59) American rock and roll singer, guitarist, and songwriter

Holst, Gustav (Theodore) (1874–1934) English composer, of Swedish and Russian descent

Homer, Winslow (1836–1910) American painter

Honegger, Arthur (1892–1955) French composer, of Swiss descent

Hooch, Pieter de See DE HOOCH

Hope, Bob (born Leslie Townes Hope) (born 1903) British-born American comedian

Hopkins, Sir Anthony (Philip) (born 1937) Welsh actor

Hopper, Edward (1882–1967) American realist painter

Hordern, Sir Michael (Murray) (1911–95) English actor

Horowitz, Vladimir (1904–89) Russian pianist

Horta, Victor (1861–1947) Belgian architect

Houdini, Harry (born Erik Weisz) (1874–1926) Hungarian-born American magician and escape artist

Howard, Leslie (born Leslie Howard Stainer) (1893–1943) English actor

Howard, Trevor (Wallace) (1916–88) English actor

Hughes, Howard (Robard) (1905–76) American industrialist, film producer, and aviator

Humperdinck, Engelbert (1854–1921) German composer

Humphries, (John) Barry (born 1934) Australian comedian

Hunt, (William) Holman (1827–1910) English painter

Huston, John (1906–87) American-born film director

Ictinus (5th century BC) Greek architect

Imhotep (*fl.* 27th century BC) Egyptian architect and scholar

Ingres, Jean Auguste Dominique (1780–1867) French painter

Irving, Sir Henry (born Henry Brodribb) (1838–1905) English actor-manager

Ives, Charles (Edward) (1874–1954) American composer

Ivory, James (born 1928) American film director

Jackson, Glenda (born 1936) English actress and politician

Jackson, Michael (Joe) (born 1958) American singer and songwriter

Jacopo della Quercia See DELLA QUERCIA

Jagger, Michael Philip ('Mick') (born 1943) English rock singer and songwriter

Jansens, Cornelius See JOHNSON

Jaques-Dalcroze, Émile (1865–1950) Austrian-born Swiss music teacher and composer

Jarman, Derek (1942–94) English film director

Jekyll, Gertrude (1843–1932) English horticulturalist and garden designer

Jewison, Norman (born 1926) Canadian film director and producer

John, Augustus (Edwin) (1878–1961) Welsh painter

John, Sir Elton (Hercules) (born Reginald Kenneth Dwight) (born 1947) English pop and rock singer, pianist, and composer

John, Gwen (1876–1939) Welsh painter

Johns, Jasper (born 1930) American painter, sculptor, and printmaker

Johnson, Cornelius (also Jansens) (1593–*c.* 1661) English-born Dutch portrait painter

Johnson, Robert (1911–38) American blues singer and guitarist

Jolson, Al (born Asa Yoelson) (1886–1950) Russian-born American singer, film actor, and comedian

Jones, Inigo (1573–1652) English architect and stage designer

Jones, Tom (born Thomas Jones Woodward) (born 1940) Welsh pop singer

Joplin, Janis (1943–70) American singer

Joplin, Scott (1868–1917) American pianist and composer

Jordaens, Jacob (1593–1678) Flemish painter

Josquin des Prez See DES PREZ

Kandinsky, Wassily (1866–1944) Russian painter and theorist

Kapoor, (Prithvi) Raj (1924–88) Indian actor and director

Karajan, Herbert von (1908–89) Austrian conductor

Karloff, Boris (born William Henry Pratt) (1887–1969) British-born American actor

Kauffmann, Angelica (also Kauffman) (1740–1807) Swiss painter

Kaye, Danny (born David Daniel Kominski) (1913–87) American actor and comedian

Kazan, Elia (born Elia Kazanjoglous) (born 1909) Turkish-born American film and theatre director

Kean, Edmund (1787–1833) English actor

PEOPLE IN THE ARTS (cont.)

Keaton, Buster (born Joseph Francis Keaton) (1895–1966) American actor and director

Keene, Charles Samuel (1823–91) English illustrator and caricaturist

Kelly, Gene (born Eugene Curran Kelly) (1912–96) American dancer and choreographer

Kelly, Grace (Patricia) (also called (from 1956) Princess Grace of Monaco) (1928–82) American film actress

Kemble, John Philip (1757–1823) English actor-manager, brother of Sarah Siddons

Kemble, Frances Anne ('Fanny') (1809–93) English actress

Kent, William (c. 1685–1748) English architect and landscape gardener

Kenton, Stan (born Stanley Newcomb) (1912–79) American bandleader, composer, and arranger

Kern, Jerome (David) (1885–1945) American composer

Khachaturian, Aram (Ilich) (1903–78) Soviet composer, born in Georgia

Kidman, Nicole (born 1967) Australian film actress

Kieslowski, Krzysztof (1941–96) Polish film director

King, B. B. (real name Riley B. King) (born 1925) American blues singer and guitarist

Kirchner, Ernst Ludwig (1880–1938) German expressionist painter

Klee, Paul (1879–1940) Swiss painter, resident in Germany from 1906

Klein, Calvin (Richard) (born 1942) American fashion designer

Klemperer, Otto (1885–1973) German-born conductor and composer

Klimt, Gustav (1862–1918) Austrian painter and designer

Kodály, Zoltán (1882–1967) Hungarian composer

Kooning, Willem de See DE KOONING

Korda, Sir Alexander (born Sándor Kellner) (1893–1956) Hungarian-born British film producer and director

Kreisler, Fritz (1875–1962) Austrian-born American violinist and composer

Kubrick, Stanley (1928–99) American film director, producer, and writer

Kurosawa, Akira (1910–98) Japanese film director

Laban, Rudolf von (1879–1958) Hungarian choreographer and dancer

Lalique, René (1860–1945) French jeweller

Lambert, (Leonard) Constant (1905–51) English composer, conductor, and critic

Lancaster, Burt(on Stephen) (1913–94) American film actor

Landseer, Sir Edwin Henry (1802–73) English painter and sculptor

Lang, Fritz (1890–1976) Austrian-born film director

Langtry, Lillie (born Emilie Charlotte le Breton) (1853–1929) British actress

Lassus, Orlande de (Italian name Orlando di Lasso) (c. 1532–94) Flemish composer

La Tour, Georges de (1593–1652) French painter

Lauder, Sir Harry (born Hugh MacLennan Lauder) (1870–1950) Scottish music-hall performer

Laughton, Charles (1899–1962) British-born American actor

Laurel and Hardy, Stan Laurel (born Arthur Stanley Jefferson) (1890–1965) and **Oliver Hardy** (1892–1957) American comedy duo

Lawrence, Sir Thomas (1769–1830) English painter

Leach, Bernard (Howell) (1887–1979) British potter, born in Hong Kong

Lean, Sir David (1908–91) English film director

Lebrun, Charles (1619–90) French painter, designer, and decorator

Le Corbusier (born Charles Édouard Jeanneret) (1887–1965) French architect and town planner, born in Switzerland

Lee, Ang (born 1954) Taiwanes film director

Lee, Bruce (born Lee Yuen Kam) (1941–73) American actor

Lee, Christopher (Frank Carandini) (born 1922) English actor

Lee, Gypsy Rose (born Rose Louise Hovick) (1914–70) American striptease artist

Lee, Spike (born Shelton Jackson Lee) (born 1957) American film director and actor

Léger, Fernand (1881–1955) French painter

Lehár, Franz (Ferencz) (1870–1948) Hungarian composer

Leibovitz, Annie (born 1950) American photographer

Leigh, Vivien (born Vivian Mary Hartley) (1913–67) British actress, born in India

Leighton, Frederic, 1st Baron Leighton of Stretton (1830–96) English painter and sculptor

Lely, Sir Peter (Dutch name Pieter van der Faes) (1618–80) Dutch portrait painter, resident in England from 1641

Lemmon, Jack (born John Uhler) (born 1925) American actor

Lennon, John (1940–80) English pop and rock singer, guitarist, and songwriter

Le Nôtre, André (1613–1700) French landscape gardener

Leonardo da Vinci (1452–1519) Italian painter, scientist, and engineer

PEOPLE IN THE ARTS (cont.)

Lewis, Jerry Lee (born 1935) American rock and roll singer and pianist

Liberace (full name Wladziu Valentino Liberace) (1919–87) American pianist and entertainer

Libeskind, Daniel (born 1946) Polish-born US architect

Lichtenstein, Roy (1923–97) American painter and sculptor

Ligeti, György Sándor (born 1923) Hungarian composer

Lind, Jenny (born Johanna Maria Lind Goldschmidt) (1820–87) Swedish soprano

Lindsay, Norman Alfred William (1879–1969) Australian artist

Lipchitz, Jacques (born Chaim Jacob Lipchitz) (1891–1973) Lithuanian-born French sculptor

Lippi, Filippino (c. 1457–1504) Italian painter, son of Fra Filippo Lippi

Lippi, Fra Filippo (c. 1406–69) Italian painter

Liszt, Franz (1811–86) Hungarian composer and pianist

Littlewood, (Maud) Joan (1914–91) English theatre director

Lloyd, Harold (Clayton) (1893–1971) American film comedian

Lloyd, Marie (born Matilda Alice Victoria Wood) (1870–1922) English music-hall entertainer

Lloyd Webber, Andrew, Baron (born 1948) English composer of musicals

Loach, Ken(neth) (born 1936) English film director

Loren, Sophia (born Sophia Scicolone) (born 1934) Italian actress

Lorrain, Claude See CLAUDE LORRAIN

Lorre, Peter (born Laszlo Lowenstein) (1904–64) Hungarian-born American actor

Lotto, Lorenzo (c. 1480–1556) Italian painter

Low, Sir David (Alexander Cecil) (1891–1963) British cartoonist, born in New Zealand

Lowry, L(aurence) S(tephen) (1887–1976) English painter

Lucas, George (born 1944) American film director, producer, and screenwriter

Lucas van Leyden (c. 1494–1533) Dutch painter and engraver

Lugosi, Bela (born Béla Ferenc Blasko) (1884–1956) Hungarian-born American actor

Lully, Jean-Baptiste (Italian name Giovanni Battista Lulli) (1632–87) French composer, born in Italy

Lumière, Auguste Marie Louis Nicholas (1862–1954) and Louis Jean (1864–1948) French inventors and pioneers of cinema

Lutosławski, Witold (1913–94) Polish composer

Lutyens, Sir Edwin (Landseer) (1869–1944) English architect

Lutyens, (Agnes) Elizabeth (1906–83) English composer

Lynch, David (born 1946) US film director and actor

Lynn, Dame Vera (born Vera Margaret Lewis) (born 1917) English singer

Lysippus (4th century BC) Greek sculptor

Mabuse, Jan (Flemish name Jan Gossaert) (c. 1478–c. 1533) Flemish painter

McCartney, Sir (James) Paul (born 1942) English pop and rock singer, songwriter, and bass guitarist

McKellen, Sir Ian British actor

Mackintosh, Sir Cameron (born 1946) British theatre producer

Mackintosh, Charles Rennie (1868–1928) Scottish architect and designer

Madonna (born Madonna Louise Ciccone) (born 1958) American pop singer and actress

Magritte, René (François Ghislain) (1898–1967) Belgian painter

Mahler, Gustav (1860–1911) Austrian composer, conductor, and pianist

Malevich, Kazimir (Severinovich) (1878–1935) Russian painter and designer

Malle, Louis (1932–95) French film director

Manet, Édouard (1832–83) French painter

Man Ray See RAY

Mansart, François (1598–1666) French architect

Mantegna, Andrea (1431–1506) Italian painter and engraver

Marceau, Marcel (born 1923) French mime artist

Markova, Dame Alicia (born Lilian Alicia Marks) (born 1910) English ballet-dancer

Marley, Robert Nesta ('Bob') (1945–81) Jamaican reggae singer, guitarist, and songwriter

Martin, Dean (born Dino Paul Crocetti) (1917–95) American singer and actor

Martin, Sir George (Leonard) (born 1926) English record producer

Martin, Steve (born 1945) American actor and comedian

Martini, Simone (c. 1284–1344) Italian painter

Marx, Chico (Leonard) (1886–1961) American comic actor

Marx, Groucho (Julius Henry) (1890–1977) American comic actor

Marx, Gummo (Milton) (1893–1977) American comic actor

Marx, Harpo (Adolph) (1888–1964) American comic actor

Marx, Zeppo (Herbert) (1901–1979) American comic actor

PEOPLE IN THE ARTS (cont.)

Masaccio (born Tommaso Giovanni di Simone Guidi) (1401–28) Italian painter

Mascagni, Pietro (1863–1945) Italian composer and conductor

Mason, James (Neville) (1909–84) English actor

Massine, Léonide Fëdorovich (born Leonid Fëdorovich Myassin) (1895–1979) Russian-born choreographer and ballet dancer

Masson, André (1896–1987) French painter and graphic artist

Matisse, Henri (Émile Benoît) (1869–1954) French painter and sculptor

Mayer, Louis B(urt) (born Eliezer Mayer) (1885–1957) Russian-born American film executive

Melba, Dame Nellie (born Helen Porter Mitchell) (1861–1931) Australian operatic soprano

Mendes, Sam(uel) (Alexander) (born 1965) British theatre and film director

Mendelssohn, Felix (full name Jakob Ludwig Felix Mendelssohn-Bartholdy) (1809–47) German composer and pianist

Menuhin, Yehudi, Baron (1916–99) American-born British violinist

Merchant, Ismail (born 1936) Indian film producer

Mercouri, Melina (born Anna Amalia Mercouri) (1925–94) Greek actress and politician

Mercury, Freddy (born Frederick Bulsara) (1946–91) British rock singer, born in Zanzibar

Messiaen, Olivier (Eugène Prosper Charles) (1908–92) French composer

Meyerbeer, Giacomo (born Jakob Liebmann Beer) (1791–1864) German composer

Michelangelo (full name Michelangelo Buonarroti) (1475–1564) Italian sculptor, painter, architect, and poet

Michelozzo (full name Michelozzo di Bartolommeo) (1396–1472) Italian architect and sculptor

Mies van der Rohe, Ludwig (1886–1969) German-born architect and designer

Milhaud, Darius (1892–1974) French composer

Millais, Sir John Everett (1829–96) English painter

Miller, (Alton) Glenn (1904–44) American jazz trombonist and bandleader

Millet, Jean (François) (1814–75) French painter

Milligan, Spike (born Terence Alan Milligan) (born 1918) British comedian and writer, born in India

Mills, Sir John (Lewis Ernest Watts) (born 1908) English actor

Mingus, Charles (1922–79) American jazz bassist and composer

Minton, Thomas (1765–1836) English pottery and china manufacturer

Miró, Joan (1893–1983) Spanish painter

Mitchell, Joni (born Roberta Joan Anderson) (born 1943) Canadian singer and songwriter

Mitchum, Robert (1917–97) American actor

Modigliani, Amedeo (1884–1920) Italian painter and sculptor, resident in France from 1906

Moholy-Nagy, László (1895–1946) Hungarian-born American painter, sculptor, and photographer

Mondrian, Piet (born Pieter Cornelis Mondriaan) (1872–1944) Dutch painter

Monet, Claude (1840–1926) French painter

Monk, Thelonious (Sphere) (1917–82) American jazz pianist and composer

Monroe, Marilyn (born Norma Jean Mortenson, later Baker) (1926–62) American actress

Montagna, Bartolommeo Cincani (*c.* 1450–1523) Italian painter

Monteverdi, Claudio (1567–1643) Italian composer

Montez, Lola (born Marie Dolores Eliza Rosanna Gilbert) Irish dancer

Moore, Dudley (Stuart John) (born 1935) English actor, comedian, and musician

Moore, Henry (Spencer) (1898–1986) English sculptor and draughtsman

Moreau, Jeanne (born 1928) French actress

Morecambe, Eric (born John Eric Bartholomew) (1926–84) English comedian

Morisot, Berthe (Marie Pauline) (1841–95) French painter

Morland, George (1763–1804) English painter

Morris, William (1834–96) English designer, craftsman, poet, and socialist writer

Morrison, James Douglas ('Jim') (1943–71) American rock singer

Morrison, Van (full name George Ivan Morrison) (born 1945) Northern Irish singer, songwriter, and musician

Morton, Jelly Roll (born Ferdinand Joseph La Menthe Morton) American jazz pianist, composer, and band leader

Moses, Anna Mary (known as Grandma Moses) (1860–1961) American painter

Moussorgsky See MUSSORGSKY

Mozart, (Johann Chrysostom) Wolfgang Amadeus (1756–91) Austrian composer

Mucha, Alphonse (born Alfons Maria) (1860–1939) Czech painter and designer

Muir, Jean (Elizabeth) (1933–95) English fashion designer

Munch, Edvard (1863–1944) Norwegian painter and engraver

PEOPLE IN THE ARTS (cont.)

Murillo, Bartolomé Esteban (*c.* 1618–82) Spanish painter

Murnau, Friedrich W. (1889–1931) German film director

Mussorgsky, Modest (Petrovich) (also Moussorgsky) (1839–81) Russian composer

Myron (*fl. c.* 480–440 BC) Greek sculptor

Nash, John (1752–1835) English town planner and architect

Nash, Paul (1889–1946) English painter and designer

Neill, Sam (born Nigel John Dermot) (born 1947) New Zealand actor

Nelson, Willie (born 1933) American country singer and songwriter

Newman, Barnett (1905–70) American painter

Newman, Paul (born 1925) American actor and film director

Nicholson, Ben (1894–1982) English painter

Nicholson, Jack (born 1937) American actor and director

Nielsen, Carl August (1865–1931) Danish composer

Niemeyer, Oscar (born 1907) Brazilian architect

Nijinsky, Vaslav (Fomich) (1890–1950) Russian ballet-dancer and choreographer

Nilsson, (Märta) Birgit (born 1918) Swedish operatic soprano

Niro, Robert De See DE NIRO

Noble, Adrian (born 1950) British theatre director

Nolan, Sir Sidney Robert (1917–93) Australian painter

Norman, Jessye (born 1945) American operatic soprano

Novello, Ivor (born David Ivor Davies) (1893–1951) Welsh composer, actor, and dramatist

Noverre, Jean-Georges (1727–1810) French choreographer and dance theorist

Nunn, Trevor (born 1940) British theatre director

Nureyev, Rudolf (1939–93) Russian-born ballet-dancer and choreographer

Nyman, Michael (born 1944) English composer

Offenbach, Jacques (born Jacob Offenbach) (1819–80) German composer, resident in France from 1833

O'Keeffe, Georgia (1887–1986) American painter

Oldfield, Bruce (born 1950) English fashion designer

Olivier, Laurence (Kerr), Baron Olivier of Brighton (1907–89) English actor and director

Ono, Yoko (born 1933) American musician and artist, born in Japan

Opie, John (1761–1807) English painter

Orbison, Roy (1936–88) American singer and composer

Orcagna (born Andrea di Cione) (*c.* 1308–68) Italian painter, sculptor, and architect

Orff, Carl (1895–1982) German composer

Ostade, Adriaen van (1610–85) Dutch painter and engraver

O'Toole, (Seamus) Peter (born 1932) Irish-born British actor

Ozawa, Seiji (born 1935) Japanese conductor

Pachelbel, Johann (1653–1706) German composer and organist

Pacino, Al(fred) (born 1940) American film actor

Paderewski, Ignacy Jan (1860–1941) Polish pianist, composer, and statesman, Prime Minister 1919

Paganini, Niccolò (1782–1840) Italian violinist and composer

Palestrina, Giovanni Pierluigi da (*c.* 1525–94) Italian composer

Palissy, Bernard (*c.* 1510–90) French potter

Palladio, Andrea (1508–80) Italian architect

Palmer, Samuel (1805–91) English painter and etcher

Paltrow, Gwyneth (born 1972) US film actress

Paolozzi, Sir Eduardo (Luigi) (born 1924) Scottish artist and sculptor, of Italian descent

Park, Nick (born 1958) English animator

Parker, Charles Christopher ('Charlie'; known as 'Bird' or 'Yardbird') (1920–55) American saxophonist

Parmigianino (also Parmigiano) (born Girolano Francesco Maria Mazzola) (1503–40) Italian painter

Parry, Sir (Charles) Hubert (Hastings) (1848–1918) English composer

Pärt, Arvo (born 1935) Estonian composer

Parton, Dolly (Rebecca) (born 1946) American singer and songwriter

Pasolini, Pier Paolo (1922–75) Italian film director and novelist

Pathé, Charles (1863–1957) French film pioneer

Paul, Les (born Lester Polfus) (born 1915) American guitarist and inventor of the solid-body electric guitar

Pavarotti, Luciano (born 1935) Italian operatic tenor

Pavlova, Anna (Pavlovna) (1881–1931) Russian dancer, resident in Britain from 1912

Paxton, Sir Joseph (1801–65) English gardener and architect

PEOPLE IN THE ARTS (cont.)

Pears, Sir Peter (1910–86) English operatic tenor

Peck, (Eldred) Gregory (born 1916) American actor

Pei, I(eoh) M(ing) (born 1917) American architect, born in China

Penderecki, Krzysztof (born 1933) Polish composer

Peterson, Oscar (Emmanuel) (born 1925) Canadian jazz pianist and composer

Petipa, Marius (Ivanovich) (1818–1910) French ballet-dancer and choreographer, resident in Russia from 1847

Pevsner, Antoine (1886–1962) Russian-born French sculptor and painter

Pfeiffer, Michelle (born 1957) American film actress

Phidias (5th century BC) Athenian sculptor

Phiz (pseudonym of Hablot Knight Browne) (1815–82) English illustrator

Piaf, Edith (born Edith Giovanna Gassion) (1915–63) French singer

Picasso, Pablo (1881–1973) Spanish painter, sculptor, and graphic artist, resident in France from 1904

Pickford, Mary (born Gladys Mary Smith) (1893–1979) Canadian-born American actress

Piero della Francesca (1416–92) Italian painter

Piper, John (1903–92) English painter and decorative designer

Piranesi, Giovanni Battista (1720–78) Italian engraver

Pisan, Christine de See DE PISAN

Pisano, Andrea (c. 1290–c. 1348) and **Nino**, his son (died c. 1368) Italian sculptors

Pisano, Nicola (c. 1220–c. 1278) and **Giovanni**, his son (c. 1250–c. 1314) Italian sculptors

Pissarro, Camille (1830–1903) French painter and graphic artist

Pizan, Christine de See DE PISAN

Poitier, Sidney (born 1924) American actor and film director

Polanski, Roman (born 1933) French film director, of Polish descent

Pollaiuolo, Antonio (c. 1432–98) and Piero (1443–96) Italian sculptors, painters, and engravers

Pollock, (Paul) Jackson (1912–56) American painter

Polyclitus (5th century BC) Greek sculptor

Pontormo, Jacopo da (1494–1557) Italian painter

Porter, Cole (1892–1964) American songwriter

Poulenc, Francis (Jean Marcel) (1899–1963) French composer

Poussin, Nicolas (1594–1665) French painter

Powell, Michael (Latham) (1905–90) English film director, producer, and screenwriter

Praxiteles (mid-4th century BC) Athenian sculptor

Preminger, Otto (Ludwig) (1906–86) Austrian-born American film director

Presley, Elvis (Aaron) (1935–77) American rock-and-roll and pop singer

Previn, André (George) (born 1929) German-born American conductor, pianist, and composer

Prez, Josquin des See DES PREZ

Price, Vincent (1911–93) American actor

Priscian (full name Priscianus Caesariensis) (6th century AD) Byzantine grammarian

Prokofiev, Sergei (Sergeevich) (1891–1953) Russian composer

Puccini, Giacomo (1858–1924) Italian composer

Pugin, Augustus Welby Northmore (1812–52) English architect, theorist, and designer

Purcell, Henry (1659–95) English composer

Puttnam, Sir David (Terence) (born 1941) English film director

Quant, Mary (born 1934) English fashion designer

Quercia, Jacopo della See DELLA QUERCIA

Rachmaninov, Sergei (Vasilevich) (1873–1943) Russian composer and pianist, resident in the US from 1917

Rackham, Arthur (1867–1939) English illustrator

Raeburn, Sir Henry (1756–1823) Scottish portrait painter

Rambert, Dame Marie (born Cyvia Rambam) (1888–1982) British ballet-dancer, teacher, and director, born in Poland

Rameau, Jean-Philippe (1683–1764) French composer, musical theorist, and organist

Ramsay, Allan (1713–84) Scottish portrait painter

Rank, J(oseph) Arthur, 1st Baron (1888–1972) English industrialist and film executive, founder of the Rank Organization

Raphael (Italian name Raffaello Sanzio) (1483–1520) Italian painter and architect

Rattle, Sir Simon (Denis) (born 1955) English conductor

Rauschenberg, Robert (born 1925) American artist

Ravel, Maurice (Joseph) (1875–1937) French composer

Ray, Man (born Emmanuel Rudnitsky) (1890–1976) American photographer, painter, and film-maker

Ray, Satyajit (1921–92) Indian film director

Redding, Otis (1941–67) American soul singer

Redford, (Charles) Robert (born 1936) American film actor

PEOPLE IN THE ARTS (cont.)

Redgrave, Corin (born 1939) English actor

Redgrave, Lynn (born 1943) English actress

Redgrave, Sir Michael (1908–85) English actor

Redgrave, Vanessa (born 1937) English actress

Redon, Odilon (1840–1916) French painter and graphic artist

Reed, Sir Carol (1906–76) English film director

Reed, Lou (full name Lewis Allan Reed) (born 1942) American rock singer, guitarist, and songwriter

Reich, Steve (born 1936) American composer

Reinhardt, Django (born Jean Baptiste Reinhardt) (1910–53) Belgian jazz guitarist

Reinhardt, Max (born Max Goldmann) (1873–1943) Austrian theatre director and impresario

Rembrandt (full name Rembrandt Harmensz van Rijn) (1606–69) Dutch painter

Renoir, (Pierre) Auguste (1841–1919) French painter

Renoir, Jean (1894–1979) French film director, son of Auguste

Repton, Humphry (1752–1818) English landscape gardener

Resnais, Alain (born 1922) French film director

Respighi, Ottorino (1879–1936) Italian composer

Reynolds, Sir Joshua (1723–92) English painter

Ribera, José (or **Jusepe**) **de** (known as 'Lo Spagnoletto', 'the little Spaniard') (c. 1591–1652) Spanish painter and etcher, resident in Italy from 1616

Rice, Sir Tim(othy Miles Bindon) (born 1944) English lyricist and entertainer

Rich, Buddy (born Bernard Rich) (1917–87) American jazz drummer and bandleader

Richard, Sir Cliff (born Harry Roger Webb) (born 1940) British pop singer, born in India

Richardson, Sir Ralph (David) (1902–83) English actor

Rie, Lucie (1902–95) British potter, born in Austria

Riefenstahl, Leni (full name Bertha Helene Amalie Riefenstahl) (born 1902) German film-maker and photographer

Rigg, Dame Diana (born 1938) British actress

Riley, Bridget (Louise) (born 1931) English painter

Rimsky-Korsakov, Nikolai (Andreevich) (1844–1908) Russian composer

Rivera, Diego (1886–1957) Mexican painter

Robbia See DELLA ROBBIA

Robbins, Jerome (1918–98) American ballet-dancer and choreographer

Roberts, Julia (born 1967) American film actress

Robeson, Paul (Bustill) (1898–1976) American actor and singer

Robey, Sir George (born George Edward Wade) (1869–1954) British comedian and actor

Robinson, Edward G. (born Emanuel Goldenberg) (1893–1972) Romanian-born American film actor

Robinson, (William) Heath (1872–1944) English cartoonist and illustrator

Robinson, Smokey (born William Robinson) (born 1940) American soul singer and songwriter

Robson, Dame Flora (1902–84) English actress

Rockwell, Norman (Percevel) (1894–1978) American illustrator

Roddenberry, Gene (full name Eugene Wesley Roddenberry) (1921–91) American television producer and scriptwriter

Rodgers, Richard (Charles) (1902–79) American composer

Rodin, Auguste (1840–1917) French sculptor

Rodrigo, Joaquin (1902–99) Spanish composer

Roeg, Nicholas (Jack) (born 1928) English film director

Rogers, Ginger (born Virginia Katherine McMath) (1911–95) American actress and dancer

Rogers, Richard (George), Baron Rogers of Riverside (born 1933) British architect, born in Italy

Romberg, Sigmund (1887–1951) Hungarian-born American composer

Romney, George (1734–1802) English portrait painter

Rooney, Mickey (born Joseph Yule Jr.) (born 1920) American actor

Rosa, Salvator (1615–73) Italian painter and etcher

Roscius (full name Quintus Roscius Gallus) (died 62 BC) Roman actor

Ross, Diana (born 1944) American pop and soul singer

Rossellini, Roberto (1906–77) Italian film director

Rossetti, Dante Gabriel (full name Gabriel Charles Dante Rossetti) (1828–82) English painter and poet

Rossini, Gioacchino Antonio (1792–1868) Italian composer

Rothko, Mark (born Marcus Rothkovich) (1903–70) American painter, born in Latvia

Rouault, Georges (Henri) (1871–1958) French painter and engraver

Rousseau, Henri (Julien) (known as 'le

PEOPLE IN THE ARTS (cont.)

Douanier', 'the customs officer')
(1844–1910) French painter

Rousseau, (Pierre Étienne) Théodore
(1812–67) French painter

Rowlandson, Thomas (1756–1827) English
painter, draughtsman, and caricaturist

Rubbra, (Charles) Edmund (1901–86) English
composer and pianist

Rubens, Sir Peter Paul (1577–1640) Flemish
painter

Rubinstein, Anton (Grigorevich) (1829–94)
Russian composer and pianist

Rubinstein, Artur (1888–1982) Polish-born
American pianist

Ruisdael, Jacob van (also Ruysdael)
(c. 1628–82) Dutch landscape painter

Ruskin, John (1819–1900) English art and
social critic

Russell, Ken (born Henry Kenneth Alfred
Russell) (born 1927) English film director

Rutherford, Dame Margaret (1892–1972)
English actress

Ruysdael See RUISDAEL

Saint Laurent, Yves (Mathieu) (born 1936)
French couturier

Saint-Saëns, (Charles) Camille (1835–1921)
French composer, pianist, and organist

Salieri, Antonio (1750–1825) Italian composer

Sansovino, Jacopo Tatti (1486–1570) Italian
sculptor and architect

Sargent, John Singer (1856–1925) American
painter

Sargent, Sir (Henry) Malcolm (Watts)
(1895–1967) English conductor and
composer

Sarto, Andrea del (born Andrea d'Agnolo)
(1486–1531) Italian painter

Sassoon, Vidal (born 1928) English hairstylist

Satie, Erik (Alfred Leslie) (1866–1925) French
composer

Scarlatti, (Pietro) Alessandro (Gaspare)
(1660–1725) Italian composer

Scarlatti, (Giuseppe) Domenico (1685–1757)
Italian composer

Schiaparelli, Elsa (1896–1973) Italian-born
French fashion designer

Schiele, Egon (1890–1918) Austrian painter
and draughtsman

Schoenberg, Arnold (1874–1951) Austrian-
born American composer

Schönberg, Claude-Michel (born 1944)
French composer of musicals

Schubert, Franz (1797–1828) Austrian
composer

Schulz, Charles (1922–2000) American
cartoonist

Schumann, Robert (Alexander) (1810–56)
German composer

Schütz, Heinrich (1585–1672) German
composer and organist

Schwarzenegger, Arnold (born 1947)
Austrian-born American film actor

**Schwarzkopf, Dame (Olga Maria) Elisabeth
(Friederike)** (born 1915) German-born
British soprano

Scorsese, Martin (born 1942) American film
director

Scott, Sir George Gilbert (1811–78) English
architect

Scott, Ridley (born 1939) English film director

Scriabin, Aleksandr (Nikolaevich) (also
Skryabin) (1872–1915) Russian composer
and pianist

Searle, Ronald (William Fordham) (born
1920) English artist

Seeger, Pete (born 1919) American folk
musician and songwriter

Segovia, Andrés (1893–1987) Spanish
guitarist and composer

Sellers, Peter (1925–80) English comic actor

Selznick, David O(liver) (1902–65) American
film producer

Seurat, Georges Pierre (1859–91) French
painter

Seymour, Lynn (born 1939) Canadian ballet-
dancer

Shankar, Ravi (born 1920) Indian sitar player
and composer

Shankar, Uday (1900–77) Indian dancer

Sharp, Cecil (James) (1859–1924) English
collector of folk-songs and folk-dances

Shearer, Moira (full name Moira Shearer
King) (born 1926) Scottish ballet-dancer and
actress

Sher, Sir Anthony (born 1951) British actor,
born in South Africa

Shostakovich, Dmitri (Dmitrievich) (1906–75)
Russian composer

Sibelius, Jean (born Johan Julius Christian
Sibelius) (1865–1957) Finnish composer

Sickert, Walter Richard (1860–1942) British
painter, of Danish and Anglo-Irish descent

Siddons, Sarah (née Kemble) (1755–1831)
English actress

Signac, Paul (1863–1935) French neo-
impressionist painter

Simon, Paul (born 1942) American singer and
songwriter

Sinatra, Frank (full name Francis Albert
Sinatra) (1915–98) American singer and
actor

Sisley, Alfred (1839–99) French impressionist
painter, of English descent

Skryabin See SCRIABIN

Smetana, Bedřich (1824–84) Czech composer

Smith, Bessie (1894–1937) American blues
singer

PEOPLE IN THE ARTS (cont.)

Smith, David (Roland) (1906–65) American sculptor

Soane, Sir John (1753–1837) English architect

Soderbergh, Steven (born 1963) American film director

Solti, Sir Georg (1912–97) Hungarian-born British conductor

Sondheim, Stephen (Joshua) (born 1930) American composer and lyricist

Sousa, John Philip (1854–1932) American composer and conductor

Soutine, Chaim (1893–1943) French painter, born in Lithuania

Spector, Phil (born 1940) American record producer

Speer, Albert (1905–81) German architect and Nazi government official

Spence, Sir Basil (Unwin) (1907–76) British architect, born in India

Spencer, Sir Stanley (1891–1959) English painter

Spielberg, Steven (born 1947) American film director and producer

Spode, Josiah (1755–1827) English potter

Springsteen, Bruce (born 1949) American rock singer, songwriter, and guitarist

Stainer, Sir John (1840–1901) English composer

Stanford, Sir Charles (Villiers) (1852–1924) British composer, born in Ireland

Stanislavsky, Konstantin (Sergeevich) (born Konstantin Sergeevich Alekseev) (1863–1938) Russian theatre director and actor

Starr, Ringo (born Richard Starkey) (born 1940) English rock and pop drummer

Stella, Frank (Philip) (born 1936) American painter

Stewart, James (Maitland) (1908–97) American actor

Stewart, Rod(erick David) (born 1945) English rock singer and songwriter

Stieglitz, Alfred (1864–1946) American photographer

Stirling, Sir James (born 1926) English architect

Stockhausen, Karlheinz (born 1928) German composer

Stokowski, Leopold (1882–1977) British-born American conductor, of Polish descent

Stone, Oliver (born 1946) American film director, screenwriter, and producer

Stradivari, Antonio (c. 1644–1737) Italian violin-maker

Strasberg, Lee (born Israel Strassberg) (1901–82) American actor, director, and drama teacher, born in Austria

Strauss, Johann (known as Strauss the Elder) (1804–49) Austrian composer

Strauss, Johann (known as Strauss the Younger) (1825–99) Austrian composer

Strauss, Richard (1864–1949) German composer

Stravinsky, Igor (Fyodorovich) (1882–1971) Russian-born composer

Streep, Meryl (born Mary Louise Streep) (born 1949) American actress

Streisand, Barbra (Joan) (born 1942) American singer, actress, and film director

Stubbs, George (1724–1806) English painter and engraver

Sullivan, Sir Arthur (Seymour) (1842–1900) English composer

Sutherland, Graham (Vivian) (1903–80) English painter

Sutherland, Dame Joan (born 1926) Australian operatic soprano

Swanson, Gloria (born Gloria May Josephine Svensson) (1899–1983) American actress

Tailleferre, Germaine (1892–1983) French composer and pianist

Tallis, Thomas (c. 1505–85) English composer

Tange, Kenzo (born 1913) Japanese architect

Tansen (c. 1500–89) Indian musician and singer

Tarantino, Quentin (Jerome) (born 1963) American film director, screenwriter, and actor

Tarkovsky, Andrei (Arsenevich) (1932–86) Russian film director

Tati, Jacques (born Jacques Tatischeff) (1908–82) French film director and actor

Tatum, Arthur ('Art') (1910–56) American jazz pianist

Tavener, Sir John (born 1944) British composer

Taylor, Dame Elizabeth (born 1932) American actress, born in England

Tchaikovsky, Pyotr (Ilich) (1840–93) Russian composer

Te Kanawa, Dame Kiri (Janette) (born 1944) New Zealand operatic soprano, resident in Britain since 1966

Telemann, Georg Philipp (1681–1767) German composer and organist

Tempest, Dame Marie (born Mary Susan Etherington) (1864–1942) English actress

Temple, Shirley (latterly Shirley Temple Black) (born 1928) American child star

Teniers, David (known as David Teniers the Younger) (1610–90) Flemish painter

Tenniel, Sir John (1820–1914) English illustrator and cartoonist

Terry, Dame (Alice) Ellen (1847–1928) English actress

Theodorakis, Mikis (born 1925) Greek composer

PEOPLE IN THE ARTS (cont.)

Thompson, Emma (born 1959) English actress and screenwriter

Thomson, Tom (full name Thomas John Thomson) (1877–1917) Canadian painter

Thorndike, Dame (Agnes) Sybil (1882–1976) English actress

Thorvaldsen, Bertel (also Thorwaldsen) (c. 1770–1844) Danish neoclassical sculptor

Tiepolo, Giovanni Battista (1696–1770) Italian painter

Tiffany, Louis Comfort (1848–1933) American glass-maker and interior decorator

Tintoretto (born Jacopo Robusti) (1518–94) Italian painter

Tippett, Sir Michael (Kemp) (1905–98) English composer

Titian (Italian name Tiziano Vecellio) (c. 1488–1576) Italian painter

Tortelier, Paul (1914–90) French cellist

Toscanini, Arturo (1867–1957) Italian conductor

Toulouse-Lautrec, Henri (Marie Raymond) de (1864–1901) French painter and lithographer

Tracy, Spencer (1900–67) American actor

Truffaut, François (1932–84) French film director

Turner, J(oseph) M(allord) W(illiam) (1775–1851) English painter

Turner, Tina (born Anna Mae Bullock) (born 1939) American rock and soul singer

Tussaud, Madame (née Marie Grosholtz) (1761–1850) French founder of Madame Tussaud's waxworks, resident in Britain from 1802

Uccello, Paolo (born Paolo di Dono) (c. 1397–1475) Italian painter

Ulanova, Galina (Sergeevna) (1910–98) Russian ballet-dancer

Ustinov, Sir Peter (Alexander) (born 1921) British actor, director, and dramatist, of Russian descent

Utamaro, Kitagawa (born Kitagawa Nebsuyoshi) (1753–1806) Japanese painter and printmaker

Utrillo, Maurice (1883–1955) French painter

Valentino, Rudolph (born Rodolfo Guglielmi di Valentina d'Antonguolla) (1895–1926) Italian-born American actor

Valois, Dame Ninette de See DE VALOIS

Vanbrugh, Sir John (1664–1726) English architect and dramatist

van de Velde, Adriaen (1636–72) Dutch painter

van de Velde, Esaias (c. 1591–1630) Dutch painter

van de Velde, Henri (Clemens) (1863–1957) Belgian architect, designer, and teacher

van de Velde, Willem van de Velde the Elder (1611–93) Dutch painter

van de Velde, Willem van de Velde the Younger (1633–1707) Dutch painter

Van Dyck, Sir Anthony (also Vandyke) (1599–1641) Flemish painter

Van Eyck, Jan (c. 1370–1441) Flemish painter

Van Gogh, Vincent (Willem) (1853–90) Dutch painter

van Leyden, Lucas See LUCAS VAN LEYDEN

Varèse, Edgar(d) (1883–1965) French-born American composer

Vasarely, Viktor (1908–97) Hungarian-born French painter

Vasari, Giorgio (1511–74) Italian painter, architect, and biographer

Vaughan, Sarah (Lois) (1924–90) American jazz singer and pianist

Vaughan Williams, Ralph (1872–1958) English composer

Velázquez, Diego Rodríguez de Silva y (1599–1660) Spanish painter

Velde, van de See VAN DE VELDE

Venturi, Robert (Charles) (born 1925) American architect

Verdi, Giuseppe (Fortunino Francesco) (1813–1901) Italian composer

Vermeer, Jan (1632–75) Dutch painter

Veronese, Paolo (born Paolo Caliari) (c. 1528–88) Italian painter

Victoria, Tomás Luis de (1548–1611) Spanish composer

Vigée-Lebrun, (Marie Louise) Élisabeth (1755–1842) French painter

Vignola, Giacomo Barozzi da (1507–73) Italian architect

Vigo, Jean (1905–34) French film director

Villa-Lobos, Heitor (1887–1959) Brazilian composer

Vinci, Leonardo da See LEONARDO DA VINCI

Visconti, Luchino (full name Don Luchino Visconti, Conte di Modrone) (1906–76) Italian film and theatre director

Vitruvius (full name Marcus Vitruvius Pollio) (fl. 1st century BC) Roman architect and military engineer

Vivaldi, Antonio (Lucio) (1678–1741) Italian composer and violinist

Vlaminck, Maurice de (1876–1958) French painter and writer

von Sternberg, Josef (1894–1969) Austrian-born American film director

Vuillard, (Jean) Édouard (1868–1940) French painter and graphic artist

Wagner, (Wilhelm) Richard (1813–83) German composer

Wajda, Andrzej (born 1929) Polish film director

Waller, Fats (born Thomas Wright Waller)

PEOPLE IN THE ARTS (cont.)

(1904–43) American jazz musician and songwriter

Walton, Sir William (Turner) (1902–83) English composer

Warburg, Aby (Moritz) (1866–1929) German art historian

Warhol, Andy (born Andrew Warhola) (c. 1928–87) American painter, graphic artist, and film-maker

Waterhouse, Alfred (1830–1905) English architect

Waters, Muddy (born McKinley Morganfield) (1915–83) American blues singer and guitarist

Watteau, Jean Antoine (1684–1721) French painter, of Flemish descent

Watts, George Frederick (1817–1904) English painter and sculptor

Wayne, John (born Marion Michael Morrison; known as 'the Duke') (1907–79) American actor

Weber, Carl Maria (Friedrich Ernst) von (1786–1826) German composer

Webern, Anton (Friedrich Ernst) von (1883–1945) Austrian composer

Wedgwood, Josiah (1730–95) English potter

Weill, Kurt (1900–50) German composer, resident in the US from 1935

Weissmuller, John Peter ('Johnny') (1904–84) American swimmer and actor

Welles, (George) Orson (1915–85) American film director and actor

West, Benjamin (1738–1820) American painter, resident in Britain from 1763

West, Mae (1892–1980) American actress and dramatist

Weyden, Rogier van der (French name Rogier de la Pasture) (c. 1400–64) Flemish painter

Whistler, James (Abbott) McNeill (1834–1903) American painter and etcher

Wilder, Billy (born Samuel Wilder) (born 1906) American film director and screenwriter, born in Austria

Wilkie, Sir David (1785–1841) Scottish painter

Williams, Hank (born Hiram King Williams) (1923–53) American country singer and songwriter

Williams, John (Christopher) (born 1941) Australian guitarist and composer

Winslet, Kate (born 1975) British film actress

Winterhalter, Franz Xavier (1806–73) German painter

Wolf, Hugo (Philipp Jakob) (1860–1903) Austrian composer

Wonder, Stevie (born Steveland Judkins Morris) (born 1950) American singer, songwriter, and musician

Wood, Sir Henry (Joseph) (1869–1944) English conductor

Wood, Natalie (1938–81) American actress

Worth, Charles Frederick (1825–95) English couturier, resident in France from 1845

Wren, Sir Christopher (1632–1723) English architect

Wright, Frank Lloyd (1869–1959) American architect

Wyatt, James (1746–1813) English architect

Wynette, Tammy (born Tammy Wynette Pugh) (1942–98) American country singer

Xenakis, Iannis (1922–2001) French composer and architect, of Greek descent

Yamasaki, Minoru (1912–86) American architect

Young, Neil (Percival) (born 1945) Canadian singer, songwriter, and guitarist

Zanuck, Darryl F(rancis) (1902–79) American film producer

Zappa, Frank (1940–93) American rock singer, musician, and songwriter

Zeffirelli, Franco (born Gianfranco Corsi) (born 1923) Italian film and theatre director

Zeuxis (fl. late 5th century BC) Greek painter, born at Heraclea in southern Italy

Ziegfeld, Florenz (1869–1932) American theatre manager

Zinnemann, Fred (1907–97) Austrian-born American film director

Zoffany, Johann (c. 1733–1810) German-born painter, resident in England from 1758

Zurbarán, Francisco de (1598–1664) Spanish painter

LITERATURE

LITERARY TERMS

absurdism
acmeism
aestheticism
allegory
alliteration
alliterative verse
ambiguity
anachronism
anapaest
anthropomorphism
assonance
Augustan
ballad
bathos
beat generation
blank verse
Bloomsbury group
burlesque
caesura
caricature
catharsis
classicism
cliché
conceit
couplet
courtly love
dactyl
Dadaism
deconstruction
denouement
diction
didacticism
doppelgänger
eclogue
elegy
elision
end stopping
enjambement
epic
epic simile
epigram
episodic
epistle
epistolary novel
epitaph
epithalamium *or*
  epithalamion

euphemism
euphony
euphuism
exemplum
existentialism
expressionism
eye rhyme
fable
fabliau
feminine ending
first person narrative
foot
free indirect style
free verse
futurism
genre
Georgian poets
Gongorism
Gothicism
Gothic novel
half rhyme
Harlem Renaissance
heptameter
hermeticism
heroic couplet
hexameter
Horatian ode
hubris
hyperbole
hypotaxis
iamb
ictus
imagery
imagism
interior monologue
internal rhyme
irony
kenning
Lake poets
lament
leitmotiv *or* leitmotif
limerick
Liverpool poets
lyric
magic realism
malapropism
mannerism

masculine ending
medievalism
metaphor
metaphysical poets
metonymy
metre
Miltonic sonnet
minimalism
mock heroic
modernism
monody
monometer
motif
Movement, the
myth
naturalism
negative capability
nemesis
neoclassicism
neorealism
objective correlative
objectivity
octameter
omniscient narrator
onomatopoeia
oxymoron
paradox
pararhyme
parataxis
parody
pastoralism
pathetic fallacy
pathos
pentameter
personification
Petrarchan sonnet
picaresque
Pléiade, la
postmodernism
post-structuralism
pre-Raphaelitism
pre-Romanticism
primitivism
prosody
prosopopoeia *or*
  prosopopeia
quatrain

realism
Renaissance
  humanism
reported speech
rhetoric
rhyme
Romanticism
Russian formalism
satire
scansion
sentimentality
sibilance
simile
socialist realism
social realism
sonnet
spondee
Spoonerism
stanza
stream of
  consciousness
stress
structuralism
Sturm und Drang
style
subjectivity
subplot
surrealism
syllable
symbolism
synechdoche
tetrameter
theme
third person
  narrative
tragedy
tragicomedy
transcendentalism
trimeter
trochee
ubi sunt
verismo
vorticism

TITLES OF WELL-KNOWN NOVELS
(with authors)

A Christmas Carol (Charles Dickens)
A Clockwork Orange (Anthony Burgess)
A Connecticut Yankee in King Arthur's Court (Mark Twain)
Adam Bede (George Eliot)
A Dance to the Music of Time (Anthony Powell)
A Day in the Life of Ivan Denisovitch (Alexander Solzhenitsyn)
A Dry White Season (André Brink)
A Farewell to Arms (Ernest Hemingway)
Age of Iron (J. M. Coetzee)
Agnes Grey (Anne Brontë)
A High Wind in Jamaica (Richard Hughes)
A Kind of Loving (Stan Barstow)
Alice's Adventures in Wonderland (Lewis Carroll)
All the Pretty Horses (Cormac McCarthy)
A Man of Property (John Galsworthy)
Amelia (Henry Fielding)
American Pastoral (Philip Roth)
A Modern Comedy (John Galsworthy)
And Then There Were None (Agatha Christie)
Animal Farm (George Orwell)
Anna Karenina (Leo Tolstoy)
Anna of the Five Towns (Arnold Bennett)
A Passage to India (E. M. Forster)
A Pocket Full of Rye (Agatha Christie)
A Portrait of the Artist as a Young Man (James Joyce)
A Room with a View (E. M. Forster)
Around the World in Eighty Days (Jules Verne)
A Sentimental Journey (Laurence Sterne)
A Severed Head (Iris Murdoch)
As I Walked Out One Midsummer Morning (Laurie Lee)
A Spell in Winter (Helen Dunmore)
A Suitable Boy (Vikram Seth)
A Tale of Two Cities (Charles Dickens)
A Town like Alice (Nevil Shute)
At Swim-Two-Birds (Flann O'Brien)
Barchester Towers (Anthony Trollope)
Barnaby Rudge (Charles Dickens)
Beau Geste (P. C. Wren)
Behind the Scenes at the Museum (Kate Atkinson)
Ben Hur (Lew Wallace)
Between the Acts (Virginia Woolf)
Billy Liar (Keith Waterhouse)
Black Beauty (Anna Sewell)
Bleak House (Charles Dickens)
Brave New World (Aldous Huxley)
Brideshead Revisited (Evelyn Waugh)
Bridget Jones's Diary (Helen Fielding)
Brighton Rock (Graham Greene)
Burmese Days (George Orwell)

Cakes and Ale (W. Somerset Maugham)
Cal (Bernard MacLaverty)
Camilla (Fanny Burney)
Cancer Ward (Alexander Solzhenitsyn)
Candide (Voltaire)
Cannery Row (John Steinbeck)
Captain Corelli's Mandolin (Louis de Bernières)
Casino Royale (Ian Fleming)
Castle Rackrent (Maria Edgeworth)
Catch-22 (Joseph Heller)
Cat's Eye (Margaret Atwood)
Cecilia (Fanny Burney)
Changing Places (David Lodge)
Chéri (Colette)
Children of the New Forest (Captain Marryat)
Chocolat (Joanne Harris)
Chocky (John Wyndham)
Cider with Rosie (Laurie Lee)
Clarissa (Samuel Richardson)
Clayhanger (Arnold Bennett)
Cold Comfort Farm (Stella Gibbons)
Coningsby (Benjamin Disraeli)
Coral Island (R. M. Ballantyne)
Cousin Bette (Honoré De Balzac)
Cranford (Mrs Gaskell)
Crime and Punishment (Fyodor Dostoevsky)
Crotchet Castle (Thomas Love Peacock)
Cry, the Beloved Country (Alan Paton)
Daisy Miller (Henry James)
Daniel Deronda (George Eliot)
David Copperfield (Charles Dickens)
Death on the Nile (Agatha Christie)
Decline and Fall (Evelyn Waugh)
Disgrace (J. M. Coetzee)
Doctor Zhivago (Boris Pasternak)
Dombey and Son (Charles Dickens)
Don Quixote (Miguel de Cervantes)
Dracula (Bram Stoker)
Dr Jekyll and Mr Hyde (Robert Louis Stevenson)
Dr No (Ian Fleming)
Emma (Jane Austen)
Erewhon (Samuel Butler)
Eustace and Hilda (L. P. Hartley)
Evelina (Fanny Burney)
Far From the Madding Crowd (Thomas Hardy)
Felicia's Journey (William Trevor)
Fever Pitch (Nick Hornby)
Finnegans Wake (James Joyce)
For Whom the Bell Tolls (Ernest Hemingway)
Frankenstein (Mary Shelley)
Franny and Zooey (J. D. Salinger)
G (John Berger)
Gigi (Colette)
Glenarvon (Lady Caroline Lamb)

TITLES OF WELL-KNOWN NOVELS (cont.)
(with authors)

Goldfinger (Ian Fleming)
Gone with the Wind (Margaret Mitchell)
Goodbye, Mr Chips (James Hilton)
Goodbye to Berlin (Christopher Isherwood)
Gormenghast (Mervyn Peake)
Great Expectations (Charles Dickens)
Gulliver's Travels (Jonathan Swift)
Guy Mannering (Walter Scott)
Harry Potter and the Chamber of Secrets (J.K. Rowling)
Harry Potter and the Goblet of Fire (J.K. Rowling)
Harry Potter and the Philosopher's Stone (J.K. Rowling)
Harry Potter and the Prisoner of Azkaban (J.K. Rowling)
Hard Times (Charles Dickens)
Headlong Hall (Thomas Love Peacock)
Heat and Dust (Ruth Prawer Jhabvala)
Herzog (Saul Bellow)
Holiday (Stanley Middleton)
Hotel du Lac (Anita Brookner)
How Green Was My Valley (Richard Llewellyn)
How Late it was, How Late (James Kelman)
How Many Miles to Babylon? (Jennifer Johnston)
I Claudius (Robert Graves)
In a Free State (V. S. Naipaul)
In Chancery (John Galsworthy)
Ivanhoe (Walter Scott)
Jacob Faithful (Captain Marryat)
Jacob's Room (Virginia Woolf)
Jane Eyre (Charlotte Brontë)
John Halifax, Gentleman (Mrs Craik)
Joseph Andrews (Henry Fielding)
Jude the Obscure (Thomas Hardy)
Just-So Stories (Rudyard Kipling)
Keep the Aspidistra Flying (George Orwell)
Kenilworth (Walter Scott)
Kidnapped (Robert Louis Stevenson)
King Solomon's Mines (Henry Rider Haggard)
Kipps (H. G. Wells)
Lady Chatterley's Lover (D. H. Lawrence)
Lark Rise to Candleford (Flora Thompson)
Last Orders (Graham Swift)
Les Misérables (Victor Hugo)
Life and Times of Michael K (J. M. Coetzee)
Little Dorrit (Charles Dickens)
Little Lord Fauntleroy (Frances Hodgson Burnett)
Little Women (Louisa M. Alcott)
Live and Let Die (Ian Fleming)
Liza of Lambeth (W. Somerset Maugham)
Lolita (Vladimir Nabokov)
London Fields (Martin Amis)

Lord of the Flies (William Golding)
Lorna Doone (R. D. Blackmore)
Lost Horizon (James Hilton)
Love, Again (Doris Lessing)
Love in a Time of Cholera (Gabriel García Márquez)
Love Story (Erich Segal)
Lucky Jim (Kingsley Amis)
Madame Bovary (Gustave Flaubert)
Malone Dies (Samuel Beckett)
Mansfield Park (Jane Austen)
Martin Chuzzlewit (Charles Dickens)
Metamorphosis (Franz Kafka)
Middlemarch (George Eliot)
Midnight's Children (Salman Rushdie)
Moby Dick (Herman Melville)
Moll Flanders (Daniel Defoe)
Molloy (Samuel Beckett)
Money (Martin Amis)
Monsieur Beaucaire (Booth Tarkington)
Moon Tiger (Penelope Lively)
Mr Midshipman Easy (Captain Marryat)
Mrs Dalloway (Virginia Woolf)
Murder on the Orient Express (Agatha Christie)
My Brother Jonathan (Francis Brett Young)
Nana (Émile Zola)
Nicholas Nickleby (Charles Dickens)
Nice Work (David Lodge)
Nightmare Abbey (Thomas Love Peacock)
Nights at the Circus (Angela Carter)
Nineteen Eighty-Four (George Orwell)
North and South (Mrs Gaskell)
Northanger Abbey (Jane Austen)
Northern Lights (Philip Pullman)
Offshore (Penelope Fitzgerald)
Of Mice and Men (John Steinbeck)
Oliver Twist (Charles Dickens)
One Hundred Years of Solitude (Gabriel García Márquez)
On the Road (Jack Kerouac)
Oranges Are Not the Only Fruit (Jeanette Winterson)
Orlando (Virginia Woolf)
Oscar and Lucinda (Peter Carey)
Our Lady of the Flowers (Jean Genet)
Our Man in Havana (Graham Greene)
Our Mutual Friend (Charles Dickens)
Out of the Silent Planet (C. S. Lewis)
Paddy Clarke Ha Ha Ha (Roddy Doyle)
Pamela (Samuel Richardson)
Paradise (Toni Morrison)
Paradise News (David Lodge)
Peregrine Pickle (Tobias Smollett)
Persuasion (Jane Austen)
Phineas Finn (Anthony Trollope)
Pincher Martin (William Golding)

TITLES OF WELL-KNOWN NOVELS (cont.)
(with authors)

Plague (Albert Camus)
Point Counter Point (Aldous Huxley)
Porgy (Du Bose Heyword)
Portnoy's Complaint (Philip Roth)
Possession (A. S. Byatt)
Prester John (John Buchan)
Pride and Prejudice (Jane Austen)
Rabbit at Rest (John Updike)
Rabbit is Rich (John Updike)
Rabbit Redux (John Updike)
Rabbit, Run (John Updike)
Raffles (E. W. Hornung)
Rasselas (Samuel Johnson)
Reading in the Dark (Seamus Deane)
Rebecca (Daphne Du Maurier)
Remembrance of Times Past (Marcel Proust)
Rites of Passage (William Golding)
Robinson Crusoe (Daniel Defoe)
Rob Roy (Walter Scott)
Rogue Justice (Geoffrey Household)
Rogue Male (Geoffrey Household)
Room at the Top (John Braine)
Roxana (Daniel Defoe)
Sacred Hunger (Barry Unsworth)
Saville (David Storey)
Schindler's Ark (Thomas Keneally)
Scoop (Evelyn Waugh)
Sense and Sensibility (Jane Austen)
She (Henry Rider Haggard)
Shirley (Charlotte Brontë)
Silas Marner (George Eliot)
Smiley's People (John Le Carré)
Something to Answer For (P. H. Newby)
Sons and Lovers (D. H. Lawrence)
Sorrell and Son (Warwick Deeping)
Staying On (Paul Scott)
Strait is the Gate (André Gide)
Swallows and Amazons (Arthur Ransome)
Sybil (Benjamin Disraeli)
Tarka the Otter (Henry Williamson)
Tender is the Night (F. Scott Fitzgerald)
Tess of the d'Urbervilles (Thomas Hardy)
The Adventures of Huckleberry Finn (Mark Twain)
The Adventures of Sherlock Holmes (Arthur Conan Doyle)
The Adventures of Tom Sawyer (Mark Twain)
The Ambassadors (Henry James)
The Amber Spyglass (Philip Pulman)
The Beautiful and Damned (F. Scott Fitzgerald)
The Big Sleep (Raymond Chandler)
The Blue Lagoon (H. de Vere Stacpoole)
The Bone People (Keri Hulme)
The Bride of Lammermoor (Walter Scott)

The Brothers Karamazov (Fyodor Dostoevsky)
The Castle of Otranto (Horace Walpole)
The Catcher in the Rye (J. D. Salinger)
The Chimes (Charles Dickens)
The Chrysalids (John Wyndham)
The Color Purple (Alice Walker)
The Conservationist (Nadine Gordimer)
The Country Girls (Edna O'Brien)
The Cricket on the Hearth (Charles Dickens)
The Day of the Triffids (John Wyndham)
The Devils (Fyodor Dostoevsky)
The Devils of Loudun (Aldous Huxley)
The Diary of a Nobody (G. and W. Grossmith)
The Elected Member (Bernice Rubens)
The Emperor of Ice Cream (Brian Moore)
The English Patient (Michael Ondaatje)
The Fall (Albert Camus)
The Family of Pascal Duarte (Camilo José Cela)
The Famished Road (Ben Okri)
The First Circle (Alexander Solzhenitsyn)
The Forsyte Saga (John Galsworthy)
The French Lieutenant's Woman (John Fowles)
The Ghost Road (Pat Barker)
The Go-Between (L. P. Hartley)
The God of Small Things (Arundhati Roy)
The Golden Bowl (Henry James)
The Golden Notebook (Doris Lessing)
The Good Soldier Schweik (Jaroslav Hašek)
The Grapes of Wrath (John Steinbeck)
The Great Gatsby (F. Scott Fitzgerald)
The Gulag Archipelago (Alexander Solzhenitsyn)
The Handmaid's Tale (Margaret Atwood)
The Heart of Midlothian (Walter Scott)
The Heroes (Charles Kingsley)
The History Man (Malcolm Bradbury)
The History of Henry Esmond (William Makepeace Thackeray)
The History of Mr Polly (H. G. Wells)
The History of Pendennis (William Makepeace Thackeray)
The Hobbit (J. R. R. Tolkien)
The Honourable Schoolboy (John Le Carré)
The Hound of the Baskervilles (Arthur Conan Doyle)
The Idiot (Fyodor Dostoevsky)
The Innocence of Father Brown (G. K. Chesterton)
The Invisible Man (H. G. Wells)
The Island of Doctor Moreau (H. G. Wells)
The Jungle Book (Rudyard Kipling)
The Kraken Wakes (John Wyndham)
The Last of the Mohicans (James Fenimore Cooper)

Literature

TITLES OF WELL-KNOWN NOVELS (cont.)
(with authors)

The Last Tycoon (F. Scott Fitzgerald)
The Lion, the Witch, and the Wardrobe (C. S. Lewis)
The Lonely Passion of Judith Hearne (Brian Moore)
The Long Goodbye (Raymond Chandler)
The Lord of the Rings (J. R. R. Tolkien)
The Lost World (Arthur Conan Doyle)
The Magus (John Fowles)
The Man in the Iron Mask (Alexandre Dumas)
The Memoirs of Sherlock Holmes (Arthur Conan Doyle)
The Midwich Cuckoos (John Wyndham)
The Mill on the Floss (George Eliot)
The Moon and Sixpence (W. Somerset Maugham)
The Moonstone (Wilkie Collins)
The Mysteries of Udolpho (Mrs Radcliffe)
The Mysterious Affair at Styles (Agatha Christie)
The Mystery of Edwin Drood (Charles Dickens)
The Naked and the Dead (Norman Mailer)
The Naked Lunch (William S. Burroughs)
The Name of the Rose (Umberto Eco)
The Old Curiosity Shop (Charles Dickens)
The Old Devils (Kingsley Amis)
The Old Man and the Sea (Ernest Hemingway)
The Outsider (Albert Camus)
The Pickwick Papers (Charles Dickens)
The Picture of Dorian Gray (Oscar Wilde)
The Pilgrim's Progress (John Bunyan)
The Plumed Serpent (D. H. Lawrence)
The Portrait of a Lady (Henry James)
The Prime of Miss Jean Brodie (Muriel Spark)
The Prisoner of Zenda (Anthony Hope)
The Private Memoirs and Confessions of a Justified Sinner (James Hogg)
The Professor (Charlotte Brontë)
The Rainbow (D. H. Lawrence)
The Red Badge of Courage (Stephen Crane)
The Remains of the Day (Kazuo Ishiguro)
Thérèse Raquin (Émile Zola)
The Return of the Native (Thomas Hardy)
The Riddle of the Sands (Erskine Childers)
The Rose and the Ring (William Makepeace Thackeray)
The Satanic Verses (Salman Rushdie)
The Scarlet Letter (Nathaniel Hawthorne)
The Scarlet Pimpernel (Baroness Orczy)
The Screwtape Letters (C. S. Lewis)
The Sea, The Sea (Iris Murdoch)
The Secret Agent (Joseph Conrad)
The Secret Garden (Frances Hodgson Burnett)
The Siege of Krishnapur (J. G. Farrell)

The Silmarillion (J. R. R. Tolkien)
The Silver Spoon (John Galsworthy)
The Subtle Knife (Philip Pullman)
The Tenant of Wildfell Hall (Anne Brontë)
The Thirty-Nine Steps (John Buchan)
The Three Musketeers (Alexandre Dumas)
The Time Machine (H. G. Wells)
The Tin Drum (Günter Grass)
The Trumpet Major (Thomas Hardy)
The Unbearable Lightness of Being (Milan Kundera)
The Vicar of Wakefield (Oliver Goldsmith)
The Warden (Anthony Trollope)
The War of the Worlds (H. G. Wells)
The Water-Babies (Charles Kingsley)
The Waves (Virginia Woolf)
The White Company (Arthur Conan Doyle)
The White Monkey (John Galsworthy)
The Wind in the Willows (Kenneth Grahame)
The Wings of the Dove (Henry James)
The Woman in White (Wilkie Collins)
The Woodlanders (Thomas Hardy)
Things Fall Apart (Chinua Achebe)
Three Men in a Boat (Jerome K. Jerome)
Through the Looking-Glass (Lewis Carroll)
Tinker, Tailor, Soldier, Spy (John Le Carré)
Titus Alone (Mervyn Peake)
Titus Groan (Mervyn Peake)
Tom Brown's Schooldays (Thomas Hughes)
Tom Jones (Henry Fielding)
To the Lighthouse (Virginia Woolf)
Treasure Island (Robert Louis Stevenson)
Trilby (George Du Maurier)
Tristram Shandy (Laurence Sterne)
Twenty Thousand Leagues Under the Sea (Jules Verne)
Two Years Before the Mast (Richard Henry Dana)
Ulysses (James Joyce)
Uncle Tom's Cabin (Harriet Beecher Stowe)
Under the Greenwood Tree (Thomas Hardy)
Vanity Fair (William Makepeace Thackeray)
Vice Versa (F. Anstey)
Villette (Charlotte Brontë)
Voss (Patrick White)
War and Peace (Leo Tolstoy)
Waverley (Walter Scott)
Westward Ho! (Charles Kingsley)
What Maisie Knew (Henry James)
Wives and Daughters (Mrs Gaskell)
Women in Love (D. H. Lawrence)
Wuthering Heights (Emily Brontë)
Zadig (Voltaire)
Zuleika Dobson (Max Beerbohm)

CHARACTERS FROM WELL-KNOWN WORKS OF FICTION
(with titles and authors)

Abbeville, Horace (*Cannery Row*, John Steinbeck)

Abel (*Middlemarch*, George Eliot)

Ablewhite, Godfrey (*The Moonstone*, Wilkie Collins)

Abrams Moss (*The History of Pendennis*, William Makepeace Thackeray)

Addenbrooke, Bennett (*Raffles*, E. W. Hornung)

Adler, Irene (*The Adventures of Sherlock Holmes*, Arthur Conan Doyle)

Aisgill, Alice (*Room at the Top*, John Braine)

Aitken (*Prester John*, John Buchan)

Akela (*The Jungle Book*, Rudyard Kipling)

Alibi, Tom (*Waverley*, Walter Scott)

Allan-a-Dale (*Ivanhoe*, Walter Scott)

Allworthy, Squire (*Tom Jones*, Henry Fielding)

Andrews, Joseph (*Joseph Andrews*, Henry Fielding)

Angelica (*The Rose and the Ring*, William Makepeace Thackeray)

Angstrom, Harry (*Rabbit, Run*, John Updike)

Apollyon (*The Pilgrim's Progress*, John Bunyan)

Aramis (*The Three Musketeers*, Alexandre Dumas)

Armitage, Jacob (*The Children of the New Forest*, Captain Marryat)

Arrowpoint (*Daniel Deronda*, George Eliot)

Aslan (*The Lion, the Witch, and the Wardrobe*, C. S. Lewis)

Athos (*The Three Musketeers*, Alexandre Dumas)

Ayesha (*She*, Henry Rider Haggard)

Bagheera (*The Jungle Book*, Rudyard Kipling)

Bagster (*Middlemarch*, George Eliot)

Baloo (*The Jungle Book*, Rudyard Kipling)

Barrymore (*The Hound of the Baskervilles*, Arthur Conan Doyle)

Bede, Adam (*Adam Bede*, George Eliot)

Beesley (*Lucky Jim*, Kingsley Amis)

Belladonna (*Vanity Fair*, William Makepeace Thackeray)

Bennet, Catherine (*Pride and Prejudice*, Jane Austen)

Bennet, Elizabeth (*Pride and Prejudice*, Jane Austen)

Bennet, Jane (*Pride and Prejudice*, Jane Austen)

Bennet, Lydia (*Pride and Prejudice*, Jane Austen)

Bennet, Mary (*Pride and Prejudice*, Jane Austen)

Bessie (*Jane Eyre*, Charlotte Brontë)

Bingley, Charles (*Pride and Prejudice*, Jane Austen)

Binkie, Lady Grizzel (*Vanity Fair*, William Makepeace Thackeray)

Black Dog (*Treasure Island*, R. L. Stevenson)

Blake, Franklin (*The Moonstone*, Wilkie Collins)

Bloom, Leopold (*Ulysses*, James Joyce)

Bloom, Molly (*Ulysses*, James Joyce)

Bones, Captain Billy (*Treasure Island*, Robert Louis Stevenson)

Booby, Sir Thomas (*Joseph Andrews*, Henry Fielding)

Bovary, Emma (*Madame Bovary*, Gustave Flaubert)

Brandon, Colonel (*Sense and Sensibility*, Jane Austen)

Brangwen, Gudrun (*The Rainbow, Women in Love*, D. H. Lawrence)

Brangwen, Ursula (*The Rainbow, Women in Love*, D. H. Lawrence)

Brocklehurst (*Jane Eyre*, Charlotte Brontë)

Brooke, Dorothea (*Middlemarch*, George Eliot)

Bruff (*The Moonstone*, Wilkie Collins)

Bulbo, Prince (*The Rose and the Ring*, William Makepeace Thackeray)

Bulstrode, Nicholas (*Middlemarch*, George Eliot)

Butler, Rhett (*Gone with the Wind*, Margaret Mitchell)

Cackle (*Vanity Fair*, William Makepeace Thackeray)

Captain Flint (*Swallows and Amazons*, Arthur Ransome)

Carraway, Nick (*The Great Gatsby*, F. Scott Fitzgerald)

Casaubon, Rev. Edward (*Middlemarch*, George Eliot)

Cass, Eppie (*Silas Marner*, George Eliot)

Casy, Rev. Jim (*The Grapes of Wrath*, John Steinbeck)

Caulfield, Holden (*The Catcher in the Rye*, J. D. Salinger)

Chainmail (*Crotchet Castle*, Thomas Love Peacock)

Challenger, Professor (*The Lost World*, Arthur Conan Doyle)

Chant, Mercy (*Tess of the D'Urbervilles*, Thomas Hardy)

Christian (*The Pilgrim's Progress*, John Bunyan)

Churchill, Frank (*Emma*, Jane Austen)

Clack, Drusilla (*The Moonstone*, Wilkie Collins)

Clare, Angel (*Tess of the D'Urbervilles*, Thomas Hardy)

Collins, Rev. William (*Pride and Prejudice*, Jane Austen)

CHARACTERS FROM WELL-KNOWN WORKS OF FICTION (cont.)
(with titles and authors)

Conroy, Gabriel ('The Dead', *Dubliners*, James Joyce)
Crawfurd, David (*Prester John*, John Buchan)
Crimsworth, William (*The Professor*, Charlotte Brontë)
Crusoe, Robinson (*Robinson Crusoe*, Daniel Defoe)
Cuff, Sergeant (*The Moonstone*, Wilkie Collins)
Cypress, Mr (*Nightmare Abbey*, Thomas Love Peacock)
Dalloway, Clarissa (*Mrs Dalloway*, Virginia Woolf)
Danvers, Mrs (*Rebecca*, Daphne du Maurier)
Darcy, Fitzwilliam (*Pride and Prejudice*, Jane Austen)
d'Artagnan (*The Three Musketeers*, Alexandre Dumas)
Dashwood, Henry (*Sense and Sensibility*, Jane Austen)
Dean, Ellen (*Wuthering Heights*, Emily Brontë)
Deans, Effie (*The Heart of Midlothian*, Walter Scott)
Deans, Jeanie (*The Heart of Midlothian*, Walter Scott)
De Bourgh, Lady Catherine (*Pride and Prejudice*, Jane Austen)
Dedalus, Simon (*A Portrait of the Artist as a Young Man*, *Ulysses*, James Joyce)
Dedalus, Stephen (*A Portrait of the Artist as a Young Man*, *Ulysses*, James Joyce)
Despair, Giant (*The Pilgrim's Progress*, John Bunyan)
De Winter, Maximilian (*Rebecca*, Daphne du Maurier)
Dixon, James (*Lucky Jim*, Kingsley Amis)
Doone, Lorna (*Lorna Doone*, R. D. Blackmore)
Dracula, Count (*Dracula*, Bram Stoker)
Dumbledore, Professor (the *Harry Potter* series, J. K. Rowling)
Durbeyfield, Tess (*Tess of the D'Urbervilles*, Thomas Hardy)
Eager, Rev. Cuthbert (*A Room with a View*, E. M. Forster)
Earnshaw, Catherine (*Wuthering Heights*, Emily Brontë)
East (*Tom Brown's Schooldays*, Thomas Hughes)
Easy, John (*Mr Midshipman Easy*, Captain Marryat)
Eeyore (*Winnie the Pooh*, A. A. Milne)
Everdene, Bathsheba (*Far from the Madding Crowd*, Thomas Hardy)
Eyre, Jane (*Jane Eyre*, Charlotte Brontë)
Fairfax, Jane (*Emma*, Jane Austen)
Fairfax, Mrs (*Jane Eyre*, Charlotte Brontë)

Fairlie, Frederick (*The Woman in White*, Wilkie Collins)
Fauntleroy, Lord Cedric Errol (*Little Lord Fauntleroy*, Frances Hodgson Burnett)
Fawn, Lord Frederic (*Phineas Finn*, Anthony Trollope)
Ffoulkes, Sir Andrew (*The Scarlet Pimpernel*, Baroness Orczy)
Finn, Huckleberry (*The Adventures of Huckleberry Finn*, *The Adventures of Tom Sawyer*, Mark Twain)
Finn, Phineas (*Phineas Finn*, Anthony Trollope)
Flanders, Moll (*Moll Flanders*, Daniel Defoe)
Flashman (*Tom Brown's Schooldays*, Thomas Hughes)
Forsyte, Fleur (*The Forsyte Saga*, John Galsworthy)
Forsyte, Irene (*The Forsyte Saga*, John Galsworthy)
Forsyte, Jolyon (*The Forsyte Saga*, John Galsworthy)
Forsyte, Jon (*The Forsyte Saga*, John Galsworthy)
Forsyte, Soames (*The Forsyte Saga*, John Galsworthy)
Fox, Brer (*Uncle Remus*, Joel Chandler Harris)
Frankenstein, Victor (*Frankenstein*, Mary Wollstonecraft Shelley)
Friday (*Robinson Crusoe*, Daniel Defoe)
Gatsby, Major Jay (*The Great Gatsby*, F. Scott Fitzgerald)
George (*Three Men in a Boat*, Jerome K. Jerome)
Geste, Beau (*Beau Geste*, P. C. Wren)
Glover, Catherine (*The Fair Maid of Perth*, Walter Scott)
Goodfellow, Robin (*St Ronan's Well*, Walter Scott)
Gordon, Squire (*Black Beauty*, Anna Sewell)
Granger, Hermione (the *Harry Potter* series, J. K. Rowling)
Grantly, Bishop of Barchester (*The Warden*, *Barchester Towers*, Anthony Trollope)
Gray, Dorian (*The Picture of Dorian Gray*, Oscar Wilde)
Grimes (*The Water-Babies*, Charles Kingsley)
Gulliver, Lemuel (*Gulliver's Travels*, Jonathan Swift)
Gunn, Ben (*Treasure Island*, Robert Louis Stevenson)
Hagrid (the *Harry Potter* series, J. K. Rowling)
Hands, Israel (*Treasure Island*, Robert Louis Stevenson)
Hannay, Richard (*The Thirty-Nine Steps*, John Buchan)

CHARACTERS FROM WELL-KNOWN WORKS OF FICTION (cont.)
(with titles and authors)

Harker, Jonathan (*Dracula*, Bram Stoker)
Harker, Minna (*Dracula*, Bram Stoker)
Harman, Joe (*A Town like Alice*, Nevil Shute)
Hatch, Bennet (*The Black Arrow*, Robert Louis Stevenson)
Hawkins, Jim (*Treasure Island*, Robert Louis Stevenson)
HCE (Humphrey Chimpden Earwicker) (*Finnegans Wake*, James Joyce)
Hearne, Judith (*The Lonely Passion of Judith Hearne*, Brian Moore)
Heathcliff (*Wuthering Heights*, Emily Brontë)
Hentzau, Rupert of (*The Prisoner of Zenda*, Anthony Hope)
Holmes, Mycroft (*The Return of Sherlock Holmes*, Arthur Conan Doyle)
Holmes, Sherlock (*The Adventures of Sherlock Holmes, The Hound of the Baskervilles*, etc., Arthur Conan Doyle)
Hornblower, Horatio (The *Hornblower* series, C. S. Forester)
Humpty-Dumpty (*Through the Looking-Glass*, Lewis Carroll)
Hunca Munca (*The Tale of Two Bad Mice*, Beatrix Potter)
Hur, Judah (*Ben Hur*, Lew Wallace)
Hyde, Edward (*Dr Jekyll and Mr Hyde*, Robert Louis Stevenson)
Indian Joe (*The Adventures of Tom Sawyer*, Mark Twain)
Ivanhoe, Wilfred, Knight of (*Ivanhoe*, Walter Scott)
Jabberwocky (*Alice Through the Looking-Glass*, Lewis Carroll)
Jackanapes (*Jackanapes*, Juliana H. Ewing)
Jeeves (*Thank you, Jeeves*, P. G. Wodehouse)
Jekyll, Henry (*Dr Jekyll and Mr Hyde*, Robert Louis Stevenson)
Jim, Lord (*Lord Jim*, Joseph Conrad)
Jones, Bridget (*Bridget Jones's Diary*, Helen Fielding)
Jones, Tom (*Tom Jones*, Henry Fielding)
Judy (*Wee Willie Winkie*, Rudyard Kipling)
K, Michael (*Life and Times of Michael K*, J. M. Coetzee)
Kanga (*Winnie the Pooh*, A. A. Milne)
Keeldar, Shirley (*Shirley*, Charlotte Brontë)
Kim (*Kim*, Rudyard Kipling)
Kipps, Arthur (*Kipps*, H. G. Wells)
Knightly, George (*Emma*, Jane Austen)
Ladislaw, Will (*Middlemarch*. George Eliot)
Lamb, Leonard (*Middlemarch*, George Eliot)
Lampton, Joe (*Room at the Top*, John Braine)
Latimer, Darsie (*Redgauntlet*, Walter Scott)
Laurence, Theodore (*Little Women*, Louisa M. Alcott)
Laurie (*Little Women*, Louisa M. Alcott)

Lawless (*The Black Arrow*, Robert Louis Stevenson)
Lector, Hannibal (*Red Dragon, The Silence of the Lambs, Hannibal*, Thomas Harris)
Lee, Lorelei (*Gentlemen Prefer Blondes*, Anita Loos)
Legree, Simon (*Uncle Tom's Cabin*, Harriet Beecher Stowe)
Leicester, Earl of (*Kenilworth*, Walter Scott)
Leigh, Captain Sir Amyas (*Westward Ho!*, Charles Kingsley)
Lessways, Hilda (*The Clayhanger Trilogy*, Arnold Bennett)
Lestrade of Scotland Yard (*A Study in Scarlet*, Arthur Conan Doyle)
Linton, Edgar (*Wuthering Heights*, Emily Brontë)
Lockwood (*Wuthering Heights*, Emily Brontë)
Lydgate, Tertius (*Middlemarch*, George Eliot)
Maccrotchet (*Crotchet Castle*, Thomas Love Peacock)
MacGregor, Robin (*Rob Roy*, Walter Scott)
Major, Major (*Catch-22*, Joseph Heller)
Manson, Dr Andrew (*The Citadel*, A. J. Cronin)
March, Amy (*Little Women*, etc., Louisa M. Alcott)
March, Beth (*Little Women*, etc., Louisa M. Alcott)
March, Jo (*Little Women*, etc., Louisa M. Alcott)
March, Meg (*Little Women*, etc., Louisa M. Alcott)
March Hare, The (*Alice's Adventures in Wonderland*, Lewis Carroll)
Marchmain, Teresa (*Brideshead Revisited*, Evelyn Waugh)
Marchmain, Earl of Brideshead (*Brideshead Revisited*, Evelyn Waugh)
Marchmain, Lady Cordelia (*Brideshead Revisited*, Evelyn Waugh)
Marchmain, Lady Julia (*Brideshead Revisited*, Evelyn Waugh)
Marchmain, Lord Sebastian (*Brideshead Revisited*, Evelyn Waugh)
Markham, Gilbert (*The Tenant of Wildfell Hall*, Anne Brontë)
Marner, Silas (*Silas Marner*, George Eliot)
Marple, Jane (*A Pocket Full of Rye*, Agatha Christie)
Mauleverer, Lord (*Cranford*, Mrs Gaskell)
Mercy (*The Pilgrim's Progress*, John Bunyan)
Merrilies, Meg (*Guy Mannering*, Walter Scott)
Messala (*Ben Hur*, Lew Wallace)
Michael, Duke of Strelsau (*The Prisoner of Zenda*, Anthony Hope)

CHARACTERS FROM WELL-KNOWN WORKS OF FICTION (cont.)
(with titles and authors)

Mitty, Walter (*The Secret Life of Walter Mitty*, James Thurber)

Mock Turtle, The (*Alice's Adventures in Wonderland*, Lewis Carroll)

Mole, Mr (*The Wind in the Willows*, Kenneth Grahame)

Montmorency, The Dog (*Three Men in a Boat*, Jerome K. Jerome)

Moore, Mrs (*A Passage to India*, E. M. Forster)

Moreau, Dr (*The Island of Dr Moreau*, H. G. Wells)

Morel, Paul (*Sons and Lovers*, D. H. Lawrence)

Morgan, Angharad (*How Green Was My Valley*, Richard Llewellyn)

Morgan, Huw (*How Green Was My Valley*, Richard Llewellyn)

Moriarty, Dean (*On the Road*, Jack Kerouac)

Moriarty, Professor James (*Memoirs of Sherlock Holmes*, Arthur Conan Doyle)

Morland, Catherine (*Northanger Abbey*, Jane Austen)

Mowgli (*The Jungle Book*, Rudyard Kipling)

Napoleon (*Animal Farm*, George Orwell)

Nash, Richard (Beau) (*Monsieur Beaucaire*, Booth Tarkington)

Nutkin, Squirrel (*The Tale of Squirrel Nutkin*, Beatrix Potter)

O'Ferrall, Trilby (*Trilby*, George du Maurier)

O'Hara, Kimball (*Kim*, Rudyard Kipling)

O'Hara, Scarlett (*Gone with the Wind*, Margaret Mitchell)

Olifaunt, Nigel (*The Fortunes of Nigel*, Walter Scott)

Omnium, Duke of (Family name Palliser) (The 'Palliser' series, Anthony Trollope, The 'Barsetshire' series, Angela Thirkell)

Otter, Mr (*The Wind in the Willows*, Kenneth Grahame)

Owl (*Winnie the Pooh*, A. A. Milne)

Palliser, Lady Glencora (*Phineas Finn*, Anthony Trollope)

Palliser, Plantagenet (*Phineas Finn*, Anthony Trollope)

Paradise, Sal (*On the Road*, Jack Kerouac)

Pendennis, Arthur (Pen) (*Pendennis*, William Makepeace Thackeray)

Pennyfeather, Paul (*Decline and Fall*, Evelyn Waugh)

Pickle, Peregrine (*Peregrine Pickle*, Tobias Smollett)

Piggy (*Lord of the Flies*, William Golding)

Piglet, Henry Pootel (*Winnie the Pooh*, A. A. Milne)

Pinkie (*Brighton Rock*, Graham Greene)

Poirot, Hercule (*The Mysterious Affair at Styles*, etc., Agatha Christie)

Polly, Alfred (*The History of Mr Polly*, H. G. Wells)

Poole, Grace (*Jane Eyre*, Charlotte Brontë)

Porgy (*Porgy*, Du Bose Heywood)

Porthos (*The Three Musketeers*, Alexandre Dumas)

Potter, Harry (the *Harry Potter* series, J. K. Rowling)

Proudie, Dr (*Framley Parsonage* and other 'Barsetshire' novels, Anthony Trollope)

Proudie, Mrs (*Framley Parsonage* and other 'Barsetshire' novels, Anthony Trollope)

Puck (Robin Goodfellow) (*Puck of Pook's Hill*, Rudyard Kipling)

Punch (*Wee Willie Winkie*, Rudyard Kipling)

Quantock, Mrs Daisy (*Queen Lucia*, E. F. Benson)

Quatermain, Allan (*King Solomon's Mines*, Henry Rider Haggard)

Quirk, Thady (*Castle Rackrent*, Maria Edgeworth)

Rabbit (*Winnie the Pooh*, A. A. Milne)

Rabbit, 'Brer' (*Uncle Remus*, Joel Chandler Harris)

Rabbit, The White (*Alice's Adventures in Wonderland*, Lewis Carroll)

Raffles, A. J. (*Raffles* series, E. W. Hornung)

Ralph (*Lord of the Flies*, William Golding)

Rama (Tiger Tiger) (*The Jungle Book*, Rudyard Kipling)

Ramsay, Mr (*To the Lighthouse*, Virginia Woolf)

Ramsay, Mrs (*To the Lighthouse*, Virginia Woolf)

Randall, Rebecca (*Rebecca of Sunnybrook Farm*, Kate D. Wiggin)

Rassendyll, Rudolf (*The Prisoner of Zenda*, Anthony Hope)

Rattler, Martin (*Martin Rattler*, R. M. Ballantyne)

Ready, Masterman (*Masterman Ready*, Captain Marryat)

Rebecca (*Rebecca*, Daphne du Maurier)

Rebecca (*Rebecca of Sunnybrook Farm*, Kate D. Wiggin)

Redgauntlet, Sir Arthur Darsie (*Redgauntlet*, Walter Scott)

Red King (*Through the Looking-Glass*, Lewis Carroll)

Red Knight (*Through the Looking-Glass*, Lewis Carroll)

Red Queen (*Through the Looking-Glass*, Lewis Carroll)

Reed, Mrs (*Jane Eyre*, Charlotte Brontë)

CHARACTERS FROM WELL-KNOWN WORKS OF FICTION (cont.)
(with titles and authors)

Remus, Uncle (*Uncle Remus* series, Joel Chandler Harris)
Ridd, John (*Lorna Doone*, R. D. Blackmore)
Rikki-Tikki-Tavi (*The Jungle Book*, Rudyard Kipling)
Rivers, St John (*Jane Eyre*, Charlotte Brontë)
Robsart, Amy (*Kenilworth*, Walter Scott)
Rochester, Bertha (*Jane Eyre*, Charlotte Brontë)
Rochester, Edward Fairfax (*Jane Eyre*, Charlotte Brontë)
Roo (*Winnie the Pooh*, A. A. Milne)
Roxana (*Roxana*, Daniel Defoe)
Ryder, Charles (*Brideshead Revisited*, Evelyn Waugh)
St Bungay, Duke of (*Phineas Finn*, Anthony Trollope)
St Clare, Evangeline (Little Eva) (*Uncle Tom's Cabin*, Harriet Beecher Stowe)
Sambo (*Just So Stories*, Rudyard Kipling)
Sanders (Sandi) (*Sanders of the River*, Edgar Wallace)
Sawyer, Tom (*The Adventures of Tom Sawyer*, Mark Twain)
Seal, Basil (*Put Out More Flags*, Evelyn Waugh)
Shandy, Tristram (*Tristram Shandy*, Laurence Sterne)
Sharp, Rebecca (Becky) (*Vanity Fair*, William Makepeace Thackeray)
Shelton, Richard (*The Black Arrow*, Robert Louis Stevenson)
Shere Khan (Lungri) (*The Jungle Book*, Rudyard Kipling)
Shipton, Mother (*The Luck of Roaring Camp*, Bret Harte)
Silver, Long John (*Treasure Island*, Robert Louis Stevenson)
Slope, Rev. Obadiah (*Barchester Towers*, Anthony Trollope)
Sloth (*The Pilgrim's Progress*, John Bunyan)
Smith, Winston (*Nineteen Eighty-Four*, George Orwell)
Smollet, Captain (*Treasure Island*, Robert Louis Stevenson)
Snowe, Lucy (*Villette*, Charlotte Brontë)
Sorrel, Hetty (*Adam Bede*, George Eliot)
Sorrell, Kit (*Sorrell and Son*, Warwick Deeping)
Southdown, Earl of (*Vanity Fair*, William Makepeace Thackeray)
Square (*Tom Jones*, Henry Fielding)
Starkadder, Judith (*Cold Comfort Farm*, Stella Gibbons)
Starkadder, Old Mrs (*Cold Comfort Farm*, Stella Gibbons)
Svengali (*Trilby*, George du Maurier)

Tarka (*Tarka the Otter*, Henry Williamson)
Temple, Miss (*Jane Eyre*, Charlotte Brontë)
Thatcher, Becky (*The Adventures of Tom Sawyer*, Mark Twain)
Thorne, Dr Thomas (*Doctor Thorne*, Anthony Trollope)
Thorpe, Isabella (*Northanger Abbey*, Jane Austen)
Thwackum (*Tom Jones*, Henry Fielding)
Thumb, Tom (*The Tale of Two Bad Mice*, Beatrix Potter)
Tiddler, Tom (*Adam's Opera*, Clemence Dane)
Tiger Lily (*Peter Pan*, J. M. Barrie)
Tiggy-Winkle, Mrs (*The Tale of Mrs Tiggy-Winkle*, Beatrix Potter)
Tilney, Henry (*Northanger Abbey*, Jane Austen)
Tinker Bell (*Peter Pan*, J. M. Barrie)
Tittlemouse, Mrs Thomasina (*The Tale of Mrs Tittlemouse*, Beatrix Potter)
Toad, Mr (*The Wind in the Willows*, Kenneth Grahame)
Tom (*The Water-Babies*, Charles Kingsley)
Tom, 'Uncle' (*Uncle Tom's Cabin*, Harriet Beecher Stowe)
Topsy (*Uncle Tom's Cabin*, Harriet Beecher Stowe)
Trelawney, Squire (*Treasure Island*, Robert Louis Stevenson)
Troy, Sergeant Francis (*Far from the Madding Crowd*, Thomas Hardy)
Trumpington, Lady (*The Virginians*, William Makepeace Thackeray)
Tulliver, Maggie (*The Mill on the Floss*, George Eliot)
Tulliver, Tom (*The Mill on the Floss*, George Eliot)
Turner, Jim (Captain Flint) (*Swallows and Amazons*, Arthur Ransome)
Tweedledee (*Through the Looking-Glass*, Lewis Carroll)
Tweedledum (*Through the Looking-Glass*, Lewis Carroll)
Twitchett, Mrs Tabitha (*The Tale of Tom Kitten*, Beatrix Potter)
Umpopa (*King Solomon's Mines*, Henry Rider Haggard)
Uncas (*The Last of the Mohicans*, James Fennimore Cooper)
Valiant-For-Truth (*The Pilgrim's Progress*, John Bunyan)
Vane, Harriet (*Strong Poison*, Dorothy L. Sayers)
Vane, Lady Isabel (*East Lynne*, Mrs Henry Wood)

CHARACTERS FROM WELL-KNOWN WORKS OF FICTION (cont.)
(with titles and authors)

Verinder, Lady Julia (*The Moonstone*, Wilkie Collins)

Violet Elizabeth (*Just William*, Richmal Crompton)

Virginian, The (*The Virginian*, Owen Wister)

Voldemort, Lord (the *Harry Potter* series, J. K. Rowling)

Walker, John (*Swallows and Amazons*, Arthur Ransome)

Walker, Roger (*Swallows and Amazons*, Arthur Ransome)

Walker, Susan (*Swallows and Amazons*, Arthur Ransome)

Walker, Titty (*Swallows and Amazons*, Arthur Ransome)

Walker, Vicky (*Swallows and Amazons*, Arthur Ransome)

Water Rat (Ratty) (*The Wind in the Willows*, Kenneth Grahame)

Waverley, Edward (*Waverley*, Walter Scott)

Western, Mrs (*Tom Jones*, Henry Fielding)

Western, Sophia (*Tom Jones*, Henry Fielding)

Western, Squire (*Tom Jones*, Henry Fielding)

Weston, Mrs (*Emma*, Jane Austen)

Whiteoak (family) (*The Whiteoak Chronicles*, Mazo de la Roche)

White-Tip (*Tarka the Otter*, Henry Williamson)

Whittier, Pollyanna (*Pollyanna*, Eleanor H. Porter)

Wilkes, Ashley (*Gone with the Wind*, Margaret Mitchell)

Wilkes, India (*Gone with the Wind*, Margaret Mitchell)

William (*Just William*, Richmal Crompton)

Williams, Percival William (*Wee Willie Winkie*, Rudyard Kipling)

Willoughby, John (*Sense and Sensibility*, Jane Austen)

Wimsey, Lord Peter Death Bredon (*Whose Body?*, Dorothy L. Sayers)

Winnie-the-Pooh (Edward Bear) (*Winnie-the-Pooh*, A. A. Milne)

Wolf, 'Brer' (*Uncle Remus*, Joel Chandler Harris)

Woodhouse, Emma (*Emma*, Jane Austen)

Woodhouse, Isabella (*Emma*, Jane Austen)

Wooster, Bertie (*Thank You, Jeeves*, etc., P. G. Wodehouse)

Worldly-Wiseman (*The Pilgrim's Progress*, John Bunyan)

Yossarian, Captain John (*Catch-22*, Joseph Heller)

CHARACTERS FROM THE NOVELS OF CHARLES DICKENS
(with novels)

Adams, Jack (Dombey and Son)
Akershem, Sophronia (Our Mutual Friend)
Allen, Arabella (The Pickwick Papers)
Allen, Benjamin (The Pickwick Papers)
Anne (Dombey and Son)
Ayresleigh, Mr (The Pickwick Papers)
Badger, Dr Bayham (Bleak House)
Badger, Laura (Bleak House)
Badger, Malta (Bleak House)
Badger, Matthew (Bleak House)
Badger, Quebec (Bleak House)
Badger, Woolwich (Bleak House)
Bagstock, Major (Dombey and Son)
Bailey, Benjamin (Martin Chuzzlewit)
Bailey, Captain (David Copperfield)
Baillie, Gabriel (The Pickwick Papers)
Balderstone, T. (Sketches by Boz)
Bamber, Jack (The Pickwick Papers)
Bangham, Mrs (Little Dorrit)
Bantam, Angelo Cyrus (The Pickwick Papers)
Baps (Dombey and Son)
Barbara (The Old Curiosity Shop)
Barbary, Miss (Bleak House)
Bardell, Mrs Martha (The Pickwick Papers)
Bardell, Tommy (The Pickwick Papers)
Barker, Phil (Oliver Twist)
Barkis (David Copperfield)
Barley, Clara (Great Expectations)
Barney (Oliver Twist)
Barnwell, B. B. (Martin Chuzzlewit)
Barton, Jacob (Sketches by Boz)
Barton, Mrs (Sketches by Boz)
Bates, Charley (Oliver Twist)
Bedwin, Mrs (Oliver Twist)
Begs, Mrs Ridger (David Copperfield)
Belling, Master (Nicholas Nickleby)
Belvawney, Miss (Nicholas Nickleby)
Berinthia (Dombey and Son)
Bet, Betsy (Oliver Twist)
Betsey, Jane (Dombey and Son)
Betsy (The Pickwick Papers)
Bitzer (Hard Times)
Blackpool, Stephen (Hard Times)
Blimber, Dr (Dombey and Son)
Blotton (The Pickwick Papers)
Bobster, Cecilia (Nicholas Nickleby)
Bobster, Mr (Nicholas Nickleby)
Boffin, Henrietta (Our Mutual Friend)
Boffin, Nicodemus (Our Mutual Friend)
Boldwig, Captain (The Pickwick Papers)
Bonney (Nicholas Nickleby)
Bounderby, Josiah (Hard Times)
Boythorn, Lawrence (Bleak House)
Brass, Sally (The Old Curiosity Shop)
Brass, Sampson (The Old Curiosity Shop)
Bravassa, Miss (Nicholas Nickleby)
Bray, Madeline (Nicholas Nickleby)

Bray, Walter (Nicholas Nickleby)
Brick, Jefferson (Martin Chuzzlewit)
Briggs (Dombey and Son)
Brogley (Dombey and Son)
Brooker (Nicholas Nickleby)
Browdie, John (Nicholas Nickleby)
Brown, Alice (Dombey and Son)
Brown, Mrs (Dombey and Son)
Brownlow, Mr (Oliver Twist)
Budden, Alexander August (Sketches by Boz)
Budden, Amelia (Sketches by Boz)
Budden, Octavius (Sketches by Boz)
Bullamy (Martin Chuzzlewit)
Bullseye (Oliver Twist)
Bumble (Oliver Twist)
Bunsby, Captain (Dombey and Son)
Buzuz, Sergeant (The Pickwick Papers)
Calton (Sketches by Boz)
Carker, Harriet (Dombey and Son)
Carker, James (Dombey and Son)
Carker, John (Dombey and Son)
Carton, Sydney (A Tale of Two Cities)
Casby, Christopher (Little Dorrit)
Charley (David Copperfield)
Cheeryble, Charles (Nicholas Nickleby)
Cheeryble, Frank (Nicholas Nickleby)
Cheeryble, Ned (Nicholas Nickleby)
Cheggs, Alick (The Old Curiosity Shop)
Chester, Edward (Barnaby Rudge)
Chester, Sir John (Barnaby Rudge)
Chick, John (Dombey and Son)
Chick, Louisa (Dombey and Son)
Chickweed, Conkey (Oliver Twist)
Chillip, Dr (David Copperfield)
Chivery, John (Little Dorrit)
Chollop, Hannibal (Martin Chuzzlewit)
Chuckster (The Old Curiosity Shop)
Chuffey (Martin Chuzzlewit)
Chuzzlewit, Anthony (Martin Chuzzlewit)
Chuzzlewit, Diggory (Martin Chuzzlewit)
Chuzzlewit, George (Martin Chuzzlewit)
Chuzzlewit, Jonas (Martin Chuzzlewit)
Chuzzlewit, Martin (Martin Chuzzlewit)
Chuzzlewit, Mrs Ned (Martin Chuzzlewit)
Chuzzlewit, Toby (Martin Chuzzlewit)
Clare, Ada (Bleak House)
Clark (Dombey and Son)
Clarke (The Pickwick Papers)
Claypole, Noah (Oliver Twist)
Cleaver, Fanny (Our Mutual Friend)
Clennam, Arthur (Little Dorrit)
Clive (Little Dorrit)
Clubber, Sir Thomas (The Pickwick Papers)
Cluppins (The Pickwick Papers)
Cly (A Tale of Two Cities)
Codger, Mrs (Martin Chuzzlewit)
Codlin, Thomas (The Old Curiosity Shop)

CHARACTERS FROM THE NOVELS OF CHARLES DICKENS (cont.)
(with novels)

Compeyson (Great Expectations)
Conway, General (Barnaby Rudge)
Cooper, Augustus (Sketches by Boz)
Cooper, Mrs (Sketches by Boz)
Copperfield, Clara (David Copperfield)
Copperfield, David (David Copperfield)
Corney, Mrs (Oliver Twist)
Crackit, Toby (Oliver Twist)
Craddock, Mrs (The Pickwick Papers)
Cratchit, Belinda (A Christmas Carol)
Cratchit, Bob (A Christmas Carol)
Cratchit, Tiny Tim (A Christmas Carol)
Crawley, Young Mr (The Pickwick Papers)
Creakle (David Copperfield)
Crewler, Mrs (David Copperfield)
Crewler, Rev Horace (David Copperfield)
Crewler, Sophy (David Copperfield)
Crimple, David (Martin Chuzzlewit)
Cripples, Mr (Little Dorrit)
Crookey (The Pickwick Papers)
Crowl (Nicholas Nickleby)
Crummles, Ninetta (Nicholas Nickleby)
Crummles, Vincent (Nicholas Nickleby)
Crumpton, Miss Amelia (Sketches by Boz)
Crumpton, Miss Maria (Sketches by Boz)
Cruncher, Jeremiah (A Tale of Two Cities)
Cruncher, Jerry (A Tale of Two Cities)
Crupp, Mrs (David Copperfield)
Crushton, Hon Mr (The Pickwick Papers)
Curdle (Nicholas Nickleby)
Cutler, Mr (Nicholas Nickleby)
Cutler, Mrs (Nicholas Nickleby)
Cuttle, Captain Ned (Dombey and Son)
Dadson (Sketches by Boz)
Daisy, Solomon (Barnaby Rudge)
Darnay, Charles (A Tale of Two Cities)
Dartle, Rosa (David Copperfield)
D'Aulnais (A Tale of Two Cities)
David (Nicholas Nickleby)
Dawes, Mary (Dombey and Son)
Dawkins, Jack (Oliver Twist)
Dedlock, Sir Leicester (Bleak House)
Dedlock, Volumnia (Bleak House)
Defarge, Madame (A Tale of Two Cities)
Dennis, Ned (Barnaby Rudge)
Dibabs, Mrs (Nicholas Nickleby)
Dingo, Professor (Bleak House)
Dingwall, M. P. (Sketches by Boz)
'Dismal Jimmy' (The Pickwick Papers)
Diver, Colonel (Martin Chuzzlewit)
Dodson (The Pickwick Papers)
Dolloby (David Copperfield)
Dombey, Fanny (Dombey and Son)
Dombey, Florence (Dombey and Son)
Dombey, Louisa (Dombey and Son)
Dombey, Paul (Dombey and Son)
Donny, Mrs (Bleak House)

Dorker (Nicholas Nickleby)
Dorrit, Amy (Little Dorrit)
Dorrit, Edward (Little Dorrit)
Dorrit, Fanny (Little Dorrit)
Dorrit, Frederick (Little Dorrit)
Dorrit, William (Little Dorrit)
Dowler, Captain (The Pickwick Papers)
Doyce, Daniel (Little Dorrit)
Drood, Edwin (Edwin Drood)
Drummle, Bentley (Great Expectations)
Dubbley (The Pickwick Papers)
Dumps, Nicodemus (Sketches by Boz, The Pickwick Papers)
Edmunds, John (The Pickwick Papers)
Estella (Great Expectations)
Evans, Jemima (Sketches by Boz)
Evenson, John (Sketches by Boz)
Fagin (Oliver Twist)
Feeder (Dombey and Son)
Feenix (Dombey and Son)
Fibbitson, Mrs (David Copperfield)
Finching, Mrs Flora (Little Dorrit)
Fips, Mr (Martin Chuzzlewit)
Fizkin, Horatio (The Pickwick Papers)
Flamwell, Mr (Sketches by Boz)
Fledgeby, Old (Our Mutual Friend)
Fledgeby, Young (Our Mutual Friend)
Fleming, Agnes (Oliver Twist)
Flintwinch, Affery (Little Dorrit)
Flintwinch, Ephraim (Little Dorrit)
Flintwinch, Jeremiah (Little Dorrit)
Flite, Miss (Bleak House)
Fogg (The Pickwick Papers)
Foliar (Nicholas Nickleby)
Gabelle, Theophile (A Tale of Two Cities)
'Game Chicken', The (Dombey and Son)
Gamp, Mrs Sarah (Martin Chuzzlewit)
Gargery, Biddy (Great Expectations)
Gargery, Joe (Great Expectations)
Gargery, Pip (Great Expectations)
Garland, Abel (The Old Curiosity Shop)
Garland, Mr (The Old Curiosity Shop)
Garland, Mrs (The Old Curiosity Shop)
Gashford (Barnaby Rudge)
Gaspard (A Tale of Two Cities)
Gay, Walter (Dombey and Son)
Gazingi, Miss (Nicholas Nickleby)
General, Mrs (Little Dorrit)
George, Mr (Bleak House)
George (The Pickwick Papers)
George (The Old Curiosity Shop)
Gilbert, Mark (Barnaby Rudge)
Gills, Solomon (Dombey and Son)
Gordon, Lord George (Barnaby Rudge)
Gowan, Harry (Little Dorrit)
Gradgrind, Louisa (Hard Times)
Gradgrind, Thomas (Hard Times)

CHARACTERS FROM THE NOVELS OF CHARLES DICKENS (cont.)
(with novels)

Graham, Mary (Martin Chuzzlewit)
Granger, Edith (Dombey and Son)
Green, Tom (Barnaby Rudge)
Gregsbury (Nicholas Nickleby)
Gride, Arthur (Nicholas Nickleby)
Gridley (Bleak House)
Grimwig (Oliver Twist)
Grip (Barnaby Rudge)
Groves, 'Honest' James (The Old Curiosity Shop)
Grudden, Mrs (Nicholas Nickleby)
Gunter (The Pickwick Papers)
Guppy, William (Bleak House)
Haggage, Dr (Little Dorrit)
Hardy, Mr (Sketches by Boz)
Haredale, Emma (Barnaby Rudge)
Haredale, Geoffrey (Barnaby Rudge)
Haredale, Reuben (Barnaby Rudge)
Harmon, John (Our Mutual Friend)
Harris, Mrs (Martin Chuzzlewit)
Harthouse, James (Hard Times)
Havisham, Miss (Great Expectations)
Hawdon, Captain (Bleak House)
Hawk, Sir Mulberry (Nicholas Nickleby)
Headstone, Bradley (Our Mutual Friend)
Heep, Uriah (David Copperfield)
Hexam, Charlie (Our Mutual Friend)
Hexam, Jesse (Our Mutual Friend)
Hexam, Lizzie (Our Mutual Friend)
Heyling, George (The Pickwick Papers)
Higden, Betty (Our Mutual Friend)
Hominy, Major (Martin Chuzzlewit)
Hortense (Bleak House)
Howler, Rev M. (Dombey and Son)
Hugh (Barnaby Rudge)
Jaggers (Great Expectations)
Janet (David Copperfield)
Jarley, Mrs (The Old Curiosity Shop)
Jarndyce, John (Bleak House)
Jellyby, Caddy (Bleak House)
Jellyby, Mrs (Bleak House)
Jellyby, Peepy (Bleak House)
Jingle, Alfred (The Pickwick Papers)
Jinkins (Martin Chuzzlewit)
Jo (Bleak House)
Jobling, Dr John (Martin Chuzzlewit)
Jobling, Tony (Bleak House)
Joe (The Pickwick Papers)
Johnson, Mr (Nicholas Nickleby)
Jones, Mary (Barnaby Rudge)
Jorkins (David Copperfield)
Jowl, Mat (The Old Curiosity Shop)
Jupe, Cecilia (Hard Times)
Kags (Oliver Twist)
Kedgick, Captain (Martin Chuzzlewit)
Kenwigs, Morleena (Nicholas Nickleby)
Kettle, La Fayette (Martin Chuzzlewit)

Kitterbell, Charles (Sketches by Boz).
Knag, Miss (Nicholas Nickleby)
Krook (Bleak House)
La Creevy, Miss (Nicholas Nickleby)
Lammle, Alfred (Our Mutual Friend)
Langdale (Barnaby Rudge)
Larkins, Mr (David Copperfield)
Leeford, Edward (Oliver Twist)
Lenville (Nicholas Nickleby)
Lewsome (Martin Chuzzlewit)
Lightwood, Mortimer (Our Mutual Friend)
Lillyvick (Nicholas Nickleby)
List, Isaac (The Old Curiosity Shop)
Littimer (David Copperfield)
Lobbs, Maria (The Pickwick Papers)
Lobbs, 'Old' (The Pickwick Papers)
Lorry, Jarvis (A Tale of Two Cities)
Losberne (Oliver Twist)
Lucas, Solomon (The Pickwick Papers)
Lumley, Dr (Nicholas Nickleby)
Lupin, Mrs (Martin Chuzzlewit)
MacStinger, Mrs (Dombey and Son)
Magnus, Peter (The Pickwick Papers)
Magwitch, Abel (Great Expectations)
Malden, Jack (David Copperfield)
Malderton, Mr (Sketches by Boz)
Mallard (The Pickwick Papers)
Manette, Dr (A Tale of Two Cities)
Manette, Lucie (A Tale of Two Cities)
Mann, Mrs (Oliver Twist)
Mantalini, Mr (Nicholas Nickleby)
Marchioness, The (The Old Curiosity Shop)
Marley, Jacob (A Christmas Carol)
Marton (The Old Curiosity Shop)
Mary Anne (David Copperfield)
Mary (The Pickwick Papers)
Matthews (Nicholas Nickleby)
Maylie, Harrie (Oliver Twist)
Maylie, Mrs (Oliver Twist)
Maylie, Rose (Oliver Twist)
Meagles (Little Dorrit)
Mealy (David Copperfield)
Mell, Charles (David Copperfield)
Merdle, Mr (Little Dorrit)
Micawber, Wilkins (David Copperfield)
Miff, Mrs (Dombey and Son)
Miggs, Miss (Barnaby Rudge)
Mills, Julia (David Copperfield)
Milvey, Rev Frank (Our Mutual Friend)
Minerva (The Pickwick Papers)
Minus (Sketches by Boz)
Mivins (The Pickwick Papers)
Moddle, Augustus (Martin Chuzzlewit)
Molly (Great Expectations)
Morfin (Dombey and Son)
Mould (Martin Chuzzlewit)
Mowcher, Miss (David Copperfield)

CHARACTERS FROM THE NOVELS OF CHARLES DICKENS (cont.)
(with novels)

Mullet, Professor (Martin Chuzzlewit)
Murdstone, Edward (David Copperfield)
Murdstone, Jane (David Copperfield)
Mutanhed, Lord (The Pickwick Papers)
Nadgett (Martin Chuzzlewit)
Nancy (Oliver Twist)
Nandy, John Edward (Little Dorrit)
Neckett, Charlotte (Bleak House)
Neckett, Emma (Bleak House)
Neckett, Tom (Bleak House)
Nickleby, Godfrey (Nicholas Nickleby)
Nickleby, Kate (Nicholas Nickleby)
Nickleby, Nicholas (Nicholas Nickleby)
Nickleby, Ralph (Nicholas Nickleby)
Nipper, Susan (Dombey and Son)
Noakes, Percy (Sketches by Boz)
Noggs, Newman (Nicholas Nickleby)
Nubbles, Christopher (The Old Curiosity Shop)
Nupkins, George (The Pickwick Papers)
O'Bleary (Sketches by Boz)
Old Barley (Great Expectations)
Omer (David Copperfield)
Pancks (Little Dorrit)
Pardiggle, Francis (Bleak House)
Pardiggle, O. A. (Bleak House)
Parsons, Gabriel (Sketches by Boz)
Pawkins, Major (Martin Chuzzlewit)
Peak (Barnaby Rudge)
Pecksniff, Charity (Martin Chuzzlewit)
Pecksniff, Mercy (Martin Chuzzlewit)
Pecksniff, Seth (Martin Chuzzlewit)
Peggotty, Clara (David Copperfield)
Peggotty, Daniel (David Copperfield)
Peggotty, Ham (David Copperfield)
Peggotty, Little Em'ly (David Copperfield)
Pell, Solomon (The Pickwick Papers)
Peps, Dr Parker (Dombey and Son)
Perch (Dombey and Son)
Perker (The Pickwick Papers)
Phunky (The Pickwick Papers)
Pickwick, Samuel (The Pickwick Papers)
Pilkins, Dr (Dombey and Son)
Pinch, Ruth (Martin Chuzzlewit)
Pinch, Tom (Martin Chuzzlewit)
Pipchin, Mrs (Dombey and Son)
Pipkin, Nathaniel (The Pickwick Papers)
Pirrip, Philip (Great Expectations)
Plornish, Thomas (Little Dorrit)
Pocket, Herbert (Great Expectations)
Pocket, Matthew (Great Expectations)
Pocket, Sarah (Great Expectations)
Podsnap, Georgiana (Our Mutual Friend)
Podsnap, Mr (Our Mutual Friend)
Pogram, Elijah (Martin Chuzzlewit)
Potatoes (David Copperfield)
Pott, Minverva (The Pickwick Papers)

Price, 'tilda (Nicholas Nickleby)
Priscilla (Bleak House)
Pross, Miss (A Tale of Two Cities)
Pross, Solomon (A Tale of Two Cities)
Pumblechook (Great Expectations)
Quale (Bleak House)
Quilp, Daniel (The Old Curiosity Shop)
Quinion (David Copperfield)
Raddle, Mr (The Pickwick Papers)
Raddle, Mrs (The Pickwick Papers)
Riah (Our Mutual Friend)
Riderhood, Pleasant (Our Mutual Friend)
Riderhood, Roger (Our Mutual Friend)
Rigaud, Monsieur (Little Dorrit)
Rouncewell, Mrs (Bleak House)
Rudge, Barnaby (Barnaby Rudge)
Rudge, Mary (Barnaby Rudge)
Rugg, Anastasia (Little Dorrit)
St Evremonde, Marquis De (A Tale of Two Cities)
St Evremonde, Marquise De (A Tale of Two Cities)
Sampson, George (Our Mutual Friend)
Sawyer, Bob (The Pickwick Papers)
Scadder, Zephaniah (Martin Chuzzlewit)
Scadgers, Lady (Hard Times)
Scaley (Nicholas Nickleby)
Scott, Tom (The Old Curiosity Shop)
Scrooge, Ebenezer (A Christmas Carol)
Sharp (David Copperfield)
'Shiny William' (The Pickwick Papers)
Sikes, Bill (Oliver Twist)
Simmons, Beadle (Sketches by Boz)
Simmons, William (Martin Chuzzlewit)
Skewton, Hon Mrs (Dombey and Son)
Skiffins, Miss (Great Expectations)
Skimpole, Arethusa (Bleak House)
Skimpole, Harold (Bleak House)
Skimpole, Kitty (Bleak House)
Skimpole, Laura (Bleak House)
Skittles, Sir Barnet (Dombey and Son)
Skylark, Mr (David Copperfield)
Slammer, Dr (The Pickwick Papers)
Sleary, Josephine (Hard Times)
Sloppy (Our Mutual Friend)
Slumkey, Hon Samuel (The Pickwick Papers)
Slurk (The Pickwick Papers)
Slyme, Chevy (Martin Chuzzlewit)
Smallweed, Bartholomew (Bleak House)
Smallweed, Joshua (Bleak House)
Smallweed, Judy (Bleak House)
Smiggers, Joseph (The Pickwick Papers)
Smike (Nicholas Nickleby)
Smorltork, Count (The Pickwick Papers)
Snagsby (Bleak House)
Snawley (Nicholas Nickleby)
Snevellici, Miss (Nicholas Nickleby)

CHARACTERS FROM THE NOVELS OF CHARLES DICKENS (cont.)
(with novels)

Snobb, The Hon (Nicholas Nickleby)
Snodgrass, Augustus (The Pickwick Papers)
Snubbin, Sergeant (The Pickwick Papers)
Sowerberry (Oliver Twist)
Sownds (Dombey and Son)
Sparkler, Edmund (Little Dorrit)
Sparsit, Mrs (Hard Times)
Spenlow, Dora (David Copperfield)
Spottletoes, Mrs (Martin Chuzzlewit)
Squeers, Fanny (Nicholas Nickleby)
Squeers, Wackford (Nicholas Nickleby)
Squod, Phil (Bleak House)
Stagg (Barnaby Rudge)
Stareleigh, Justice (The Pickwick Papers)
Startop (Great Expectations)
Steerforth, James (David Copperfield)
Stiggins (The Pickwick Papers)
Strong, Dr (David Copperfield)
Stryver, C. J. (A Tale of Two Cities)
Summerson, Esther (Bleak House)
Sweedlepipe, Paul (Martin Chuzzlewit)
Sweet William (The Old Curiosity Shop)
Swiveller, Richard (The Old Curiosity Shop)
Tacker (Martin Chuzzlewit)
Tamaroo, Miss (Martin Chuzzlewit)
Tapley, Mark (Martin Chuzzlewit)
Tappertit, Simon (Barnaby Rudge)
Tattycoram (Little Dorrit)
Taunton, Mrs (Sketches by Boz)
Tibbs, Mrs (Sketches by Boz)
Tigg, Montague (Martin Chuzzlewit)
Tippin, Lady (Our Mutual Friend)
Tisher, Mrs (Edwin Drood)
Tite-Barnacle, Clarence (Little Dorrit)
Tite-Barnacle, Ferdinand (Little Dorrit)
Tite-Barnacle, Junior (Little Dorrit)
Tite-Barnacle, Lord Decimus (Little Dorrit)
Tite-Barnacle, Mr (Little Dorrit)
Todgers, Mrs (Martin Chuzzlewit)
Toodle (Dombey and Son)
Toots, Mr P. (Dombey and Son)
Tottle, Watkins (Sketches by Boz)
Tox, Miss (Dombey and Son)
Trabb (Great Expectations)
Traddles, Tom (David Copperfield)
Trent, Frederick (The Old Curiosity Shop)
Trent, Nellie (The Old Curiosity Shop)
Trimmer, Mr (Sketches by Boz)
Trott, Alexander (Sketches by Boz)
Trotter, Job (The Pickwick Papers)
Trotwood, Betsey (David Copperfield)

Trundle (The Pickwick Papers)
Tuggs, Charlotte (Sketches by Boz)
Tuggs, Joseph (Sketches by Boz)
Tuggs, Simon (Sketches by Boz)
Tulkinghorn (Bleak House)
Tupman, Tracy (The Pickwick Papers)
Tupple (Sketches by Boz)
Turveydrop, Prince (Bleak House)
Twist, Oliver (Oliver Twist)
Varden, Dolly (Barnaby Rudge)
Varden, Gabriel (Barnaby Rudge)
Veneering, Anastasia (Our Mutual Friend)
Veneering, Hamilton (Our Mutual Friend)
Venus, Mr (Our Mutual Friend)
Verisopht, Lord Frederick (Nicholas Nickleby)
Vholes (Bleak House)
Von Koeldwethout (Nicholas Nickleby)
Vuffin (The Old Curiosity Shop)
Wackles, Jane (The Old Curiosity Shop)
Wackles, Melissa (The Old Curiosity Shop)
Wackles, Sophie (The Old Curiosity Shop)
Wade, Miss (Little Dorrit)
Walker, Mick (David Copperfield)
Wardle, Emily (The Pickwick Papers)
Wardle, Isabella (The Pickwick Papers)
Wardle, Mr (The Pickwick Papers)
Wardle, Rachel (The Pickwick Papers)
Waterbrook (David Copperfield)
Watkins (Nicholas Nickleby)
Watty (The Pickwick Papers)
Wegg, Silas (Our Mutual Friend)
Weller, Sam (The Pickwick Papers)
Weller, Tony (The Pickwick Papers)
Wemmick (Great Expectations)
Westlock, John (Martin Chuzzlewit)
Wickfield, Agnes (David Copperfield)
Wickfield, Mr (David Copperfield)
Wickham, Mrs (Dombey and Son)
Wilfer, Bella (Our Mutual Friend)
Wilfer, Lavinia (Our Mutual Friend)
Wilfer, Reginald (Our Mutual Friend)
Willet, Joe (Barnaby Rudge)
Willet, John (Barnaby Rudge)
Winkle, Nathaniel (The Pickwick Papers)
Witherden, Mr (The Old Curiosity Shop)
Withers (Dombey and Son)
Wititterly, Julia (Nicholas Nickleby)
Woodcourt, Allan (Bleak House)
Wopsle (Great Expectations)
Wrayburn, Eugene (Our Mutual Friend)

TITLES OF WELL-KNOWN PLAYS
(with playwrights)

Abigail's Party (Mike Leigh)
Accidental Death of An Anarchist (Dario Fo)
A Cuckoo in the Nest (Ben Travers)
A Day in the Death of Joe Egg (Peter Nichols)
A Doll's House (Henrik Ibsen)
After the Fall (Arthur Miller)
All For Love (John Dryden)
All God's Chillun Got Wings (Eugene O'Neill)
All My Sons (Arthur Miller)
All's Well That Ends Well (William Shakespeare)
Amadeus (Peter Shaffer)
A Man For All Seasons (Robert Bolt)
American Buffalo (David Mamet)
A Midsummer Night's Dream (William Shakespeare)
Amy's View (David Hare)
Androcles and the Lion (G. B. Shaw)
Andromaque (Jean Racine)
An Ideal Husband (Oscar Wilde)
An Inspector Calls (J. B. Priestley)
An Italian Straw Hat (Eugène Labiche)
Anna Christie (Eugene O'Neill)
Antigone (Sophocles, Jean Anouilh)
Antony and Cleopatra (William Shakespeare)
Arcadia (Tom Stoppard)
Arms and the Man (G. B. Shaw)
Arsenic and Old Lace (Joseph Kesselring)
Art (Yasmina Reza)
A Streetcar Named Desire (Tennessee Williams)
As You Like It (William Shakespeare)
A Taste of Honey (Shelagh Delaney)
Athalie (Jean Racine)
Aureng-Zebe (John Dryden)
A Woman of No Importance (Oscar Wilde)
Barefoot in the Park (Neil Simon)
Bartholomew Fair (Ben Jonson)
Billy Liar (Willis Hall and Keith Waterhouse)
Blithe Spirit (Noël Coward)
Blood Wedding (Federico García Lorca)
Broken Glass (Arthur Miller)
Caesar and Cleopatra (G. B. Shaw)
Candida (G. B. Shaw)
Captain Brassbound's Conversion (G. B. Shaw)
Caste (T. W. Robertson)
Cat on a Hot Tin Roof (Tennessee Williams)
Cavalcade (Noël Coward)
Charley's Aunt (Brandon Thomas)
Chips With Everything (Arnold Wesker)
Closer (Patrick Marber)
Copenhagen (Michael Frayn)
Coriolanus (William Shakespeare)
Cymbeline (William Shakespeare)
Dancing at Lughnasa (Brian Friel)
Dangerous Corner (J. B. Priestley)

Death of a Salesman (Arthur Miller)
Design for Living (Noël Coward)
Dr Faustus (Christopher Marlowe)
Duel of Angels (Jean Giraudoux)
Edward II (Christopher Marlowe)
Electra (Sophocles)
Endgame (Samuel Beckett)
Entertaining Mr Sloane (Joe Orton)
Faust (Goethe)
Five Finger Exercise (Peter Shaffer)
Flare Path (Terence Rattigan)
French Without Tears (Terence Rattigan)
Galileo (Bertolt Brecht)
Ghosts (Henrik Ibsen)
Glengarry Glen Ross (David Mamet)
Golden Boy (Clifford Odets)
Hamlet, Prince of Denmark (William Shakespeare)
Haunting Julia (Alan Ayckbourn)
Happy Days (Samuel Beckett)
Hay Fever (Noël Coward)
Heartbreak House (G. B. Shaw)
Henry IV [Parts 1 and 2] (William Shakespeare)
Henry V (William Shakespeare)
Henry VI [Parts 1, 2, and 3] (William Shakespeare)
Henry VIII (William Shakespeare)
Hobson's Choice (Harold Brighouse)
I Am a Camera (John van Druten)
Inadmissible Evidence (John Osborne)
Indian Ink (Tom Stoppard)
Journey's End (R. C. Sherriff)
Julius Caesar (William Shakespeare)
Jumpers (Tom Stoppard)
Juno and the Paycock (Sean O'Casey)
King John (William Shakespeare)
King Lear (William Shakespeare)
Krapp's Last Tape (Samuel Beckett)
Lady Windermere's Fan (Oscar Wilde)
Le Misanthrope (Molière)
Look Back in Anger (John Osborne)
Loot (Joe Orton)
Love For Love (William Congreve)
Love's Labour's Lost (William Shakespeare)
Macbeth (William Shakespeare)
Major Barbara (G. B. Shaw)
Man and Superman (G. B. Shaw)
Marriage À La Mode (John Dryden)
Measure For Measure (William Shakespeare)
Medea (Euripides)
Moonlight (Harold Pinter)
Mourning Becomes Electra (Eugene O'Neill)
Much Ado About Nothing (William Shakespeare)
Murder in the Cathedral (T. S. Eliot)
Noises Off (Michael Frayn)

TITLES OF WELL-KNOWN PLAYS (cont.)
(with playwrights)

Oedipus Rex (Sophocles)
Oleanna (David Mamet)
Othello (William Shakespeare)
Pandora's Box (Frank Wedekind)
Pericles (William Shakespeare)
Perkin Warbeck (John Ford)
Peter Pan (J. M. Barrie)
Phèdre (Jean Racine)
Pillars of Society (Henrik Ibsen)
Plenty (David Hare)
Present Laughter (Noël Coward)
Private Lives (Noël Coward)
Pygmalion (G. B. Shaw)
Quality Street (J. M. Barrie)
Racing Demon (David Hare)
Richard II (William Shakespeare)
Richard III (William Shakespeare)
Ring Round the Moon (Jean Anouilh)
Romanoff and Juliet (Peter Ustinov)
Romeo and Juliet (William Shakespeare)
Rookery Nook (Ben Travers)
Roots (Arnold Wesker)
Rosencrantz and Guildenstern Are Dead
  (Tom Stoppard)
Ross (Terence Rattigan)
Saint Joan (G. B. Shaw)
Separate Tables (Terence Rattigan)
Serious Money (Caryl Churchill)
She Stoops to Conquer (Oliver Goldsmith)
Sizwe Bansi is Dead (Athol Fugard)
Steaming (Nell Dunn)
Strife (John Galsworthy)
Suddenly Last Summer (Tennessee Williams)
Tamburlaine the Great (Christopher
  Marlowe)
Tartuffe (Molière)
The Acharnians (Aristophanes)
The Adding Machine (Elmer Rice)
The Admirable Crichton (J. M. Barrie)
The Alchemist (Ben Jonson)
The American Dream (Edward Albee)
The Anatomist (James Bridie)
The Apple Cart (G. B. Shaw)
The Bacchae (Euripides)
The Balcony (Jean Genet)
The Bankrupt (Alexander Ostrovsky)
The Barretts of Wimpole Street (Rudolf
  Besier)
The Beaux' Stratagem (George Farquhar)
The Birds (Aristophanes)
The Birthday Party (Harold Pinter)
The Broken Heart (John Ford)
The Broken Jug (Heinrich Von Kleist)
The Browning Version (Terence Rattigan)
The Caretaker (Harold Pinter)
The Caucasian Chalk Circle (Bertolt Brecht)
The Cherry Orchard (Anton Chekhov)

The Circle (W. Somerset Maugham)
The Cocktail Party (T. S. Eliot)
The Comedy of Errors (William Shakespeare)
The Constant Wife (W. Somerset Maugham)
The Contrast (Royall Tyler)
The Corn is Green (Emlyn Williams)
The Country Girl (Clifford Odets)
The Critic (Richard Brinsley Sheridan)
The Crucible (Arthur Miller)
The Deep Blue Sea (Terence Rattigan)
The Devil's Disciple (G. B. Shaw)
The Devils (John Whiting)
The Doctor's Dilemma (G. B. Shaw)
The Duchess of Malfi (John Webster)
The Dumb Waiter (Harold Pinter)
The Family Reunion (T. S. Eliot)
The Fire-Raisers (Max Frisch)
The Frogs (Aristophanes)
The Ghost Sonata (August Strindberg)
The Gift of the Gorgon (Peter Shaffer)
The Glass Menagerie (Tennessee Williams)
The Good-Natured Man (Oliver Goldsmith)
The Government Inspector (Nikolai Gogol)
The Hostage (Brendan Behan)
The Iceman Cometh (Eugene O'Neill)
The Importance of Being Earnest (Oscar
  Wilde)
The Jew of Malta (Christopher Marlowe)
The Lady's Not For Burning (Christopher Fry)
The Lark (Jean Anouilh)
The Linden Tree (J. B. Priestley)
The Madness of George III (Alan Bennet)
The Magistrate (Pinero)
The Maid's Tragedy (Francis Beaumont and
  John Fletcher)
The Master Builder (Henrik Ibsen)
The Matchmaker (Thornton Wilder)
The Merchant of Venice (William
  Shakespeare)
The Merry Wives of Windsor (William
  Shakespeare)
The Miser (Molière)
The Mousetrap (Agatha Christie)
The Old Bachelor (William Congreve)
The Philanderer (G. B. Shaw)
The Plough and the Stars (Sean O'Casey)
The Revenger's Tragedy (Cyril Tourneur)
The Rivals (Richard Brinsley Sheridan)
The Romans in Britain (Howard Brenton)
The Room (Harold Pinter)
The School For Scandal (Richard Brinsley
  Sheridan)
The School For Wives (Molière)
The Seagull (Anton Chekhov)
The Second Mrs Tanqueray (Pinero)
The Secret Rapture (David Hare)
The Shadow of a Gunman (Sean O'Casey)

TITLES OF WELL-KNOWN PLAYS (cont.)
(with playwrights)

The Spanish Tragedy (Thomas Kyd)
The Suppliant Women (Aeschylus)
The Taming of the Shrew (William Shakespeare)
The Tempest (William Shakespeare)
The Trojan Women (Euripides)
The Two Gentlemen of Verona (William Shakespeare)
The Weir (Conor McPherson)
The White Devil (John Webster)
The Wild Duck (Henrik Ibsen)
The Winslow Boy (Terence Rattigan)
The Winter's Tale (William Shakespeare)
This Happy Breed (Noël Coward)
Three Sisters (Anton Chekhov)
Three Tall Women (Edward Albee)
Timon of Athens (William Shakespeare)
'Tis Pity She's a Whore (John Ford)

Titus Andronicus (William Shakespeare)
Top Girls (Caryl Churchill)
Translations (Brian Friel)
Travesties (Tom Stoppard)
Troilus and Cressida (William Shakespeare)
Twelfth Night (William Shakespeare)
Two Noble Kinsmen (William Shakespeare and John Fletcher)
Uncle Vanya (Anton Chekhov)
Under Milk Wood (Dylan Thomas)
Venice Preserved (Thomas Otway)
Volpone (Ben Jonson)
Waiting For Godot (Samuel Beckett)
What Every Woman Knows (J. M. Barrie)
What the Butler Saw (Joe Orton)
Who's Afraid of Virginia Woolf? (Edward Albee)
Women Beware Women (Thomas Middleton)

CHARACTERS FROM THE PLAYS OF WILLIAM SHAKESPEARE
(with plays)

Aaron (Titus Andronicus)
Achilles (Troilus and Cressida)
Adam (As You Like It)
Adriana (The Comedy of Errors)
Aegeon (The Comedy of Errors)
Aemilia (The Comedy of Errors)
Agamemnon (Troilus and Cressida)
Agrippa (Julius Caesar, Antony and Cleopatra)
Ajax (Troilus and Cressida)
Alarbus (Titus Andronicus)
Albany, Duke of (King Lear)
Alonso (The Tempest)
Angelo (Measure for Measure)
Anne (Richard III)
Antiochus (Pericles)
Antipholus (The Comedy of Errors)
Antonio (The Merchant of Venice, The Tempest)
Antony (Julius Caesar, Antony and Cleopatra)
Ariel (The Tempest)
Armado (Love's Labour's Lost)
Arviragus (Cymbeline)
Audrey (As You Like It)
Aufidius (Coriolanus)
Aguecheek, Sir Andrew (Twelfth Night)
Banquo (Macbeth)
Baptista (The Taming of the Shrew)
Bardolph (1 Henry IV, 2 Henry IV, Henry V, The Merry Wives of Windsor)

Bassanio (The Merchant of Venice)
Bassianus (Titus Andronicus)
Beatrice (Much Ado About Nothing)
Belarius (Cymbeline)
Belch, Sir Toby (Twelfth Night)
Benedick (Much Ado About Nothing)
Benvolio (Romeo and Juliet)
Bernardo (Hamlet)
Berowne (Love's Labour's Lost)
Bertram (All's Well That Ends Well)
Bianca (The Taming of the Shrew, Othello)
Blunt (2 Henry IV)
Bolingbroke, Henry [Henry IV] (Richard II)
Bottom (A Midsummer Night's Dream)
Brabantio (Othello)
Brutus (Julius Caesar, Coriolanus)
Calchas (Troilus and Cressida)
Caliban (The Tempest)
Cambridge (Henry V)
Capulet (Romeo and Juliet)
Cassio (Othello)
Celia (As You Like It)
Cesario (Twelfth Night)
Charmian (Antony and Cleopatra)
Chiron (Titus Andronicus)
Clarence, George, Duke of (3 Henry VI, Richard III)
Claudio (Much Ado About Nothing, Measure for Measure)
Claudius (Hamlet)
Cleon (Pericles)

CHARACTERS FROM THE PLAYS OF WILLIAM SHAKESPEARE (cont.)
(with plays)

Cleopatra (Antony and Cleopatra)
Cloten (Cymbeline)
Cominius (Coriolanus)
Cordelia (King Lear)
Cornelius (Hamlet)
Cornwall, Duke of (King Lear)
Corin (As You Like It)
Coriolanus (Coriolanus)
Costard (Love's Labour's Lost)
Cressida (Troilus and Cressida)
Cymbeline (Cymbeline)
Demetrius (Titus Andronicus, A Midsummer
  Night's Dream, Antony and Cleopatra)
Dennis (As You Like It)
Desdemona (Othello)
Diana (All's Well That Ends Well)
Diomedes (Antony and Cleopatra, Troilus
  and Cressida)
Dionyza (Pericles)
Dogberry (Much Ado About Nothing)
Don Pedro (Much Ado About Nothing)
Donalbain (Macbeth)
Douglas (1 Henry IV)
Dromio (The Comedy of Errors)
Dumain (Love's Labour's Lost)
Duncan (Macbeth)
Edgar (King Lear)
Edmund (King Lear)
Edward IV (2 Henry VI, 3 Henry VI)
Elbow (Measure for Measure)
Elizabeth (Henry VI, Richard III)
Emilia (Othello)
Enobarbus (Antony and Cleopatra)
Eros (Antony and Cleopatra)
Escalus (Measure for Measure)
Fabian (Twelfth Night)
Falstaff (1 Henry IV, 2 Henry IV, The Merry
  Wives of Windsor)
Ferdinand (Love's Labour's Lost, The
  Tempest)
Feste (Twelfth Night)
Fleance (Macbeth)
Florizel (The Winter's Tale)
Flute (A Midsummer Night's Dream)
Fortinbras (Hamlet)
Frederick (As You Like It)
Froth (Measure for Measure)
Fulvia (Antony and Cleopatra)
George, Duke of Clarence (Henry VI, Richard
  III)
Gertrude (Hamlet)
Glendower, Owen (1 Henry IV)
Gloucester, Earl of (King Lear)
Gloucester, Richard, Duke of (2 Henry VI, 3
  Henry VI, Richard III)
Goneril (King Lear)
Gonzalo (The Tempest)

Gratiano (The Merchant of Venice, Othello)
Grey (Henry V)
Guiderius (Cymbeline)
Guildenstern (Hamlet)
Hal [Henry V] (1 Henry IV)
Hamlet (Hamlet)
Hecate (Macbeth)
Hector (Troilus and Cressida)
Helenus (Troilus and Cressida)
Helena (A Midsummer Night's Dream, All's
  Well That Ends Well)
Helicanus (Pericles)
Henry IV (Richard II, 1 Henry IV, 2 Henry IV)
Henry V (1 Henry IV, 2 Henry IV, Henry V)
Henry VI (1 Henry VI, 2 Henry VI, 3 Henry VI)
Henry VIII (Henry VIII)
Henry, Earl of Richmond [Henry VII] (Richard
  III)
Hermia (A Midsummer Night's Dream)
Hermione (The Winter's Tale)
Hero (Much Ado About Nothing)
Hippolyta (A Midsummer Night's Dream)
Horatio (Hamlet)
Hortensio (The Taming of the Shrew)
Hotspur (1 Henry IV)
Iachimo (Cymbeline)
Iago (Othello)
Imogen (Cymbeline)
Iras (Antony and Cleopatra)
Isabella (Measure for Measure)
Jacques (As You Like It)
Jaquenetta (Love's Labour's Lost)
Jessica (The Merchant of Venice)
Juliet (Romeo and Juliet, Measure for
  Measure)
Julius Caesar (Julius Caesar)
Katherina (The Taming of the Shrew)
Katherine (Henry V, Love's Labour's Lost)
Laertes (Hamlet)
Lafew (All's Well That Ends Well)
Laurence, Friar (Romeo and Juliet)
Lavinia (Titus Andronicus)
Lear (King Lear)
Leontes (The Winter's Tale)
Lepidus (Julius Caesar, Antony and
  Cleopatra)
Longaville (Love's Labour's Lost)
Lorenzo (The Merchant of Venice)
Lucentio (The Taming of the Shrew)
Luciana (The Comedy of Errors)
Lucius (Titus Andronicus)
Lysander (A Midsummer Night's Dream)
Lysimachus (Pericles)
Macbeth (Macbeth)
Macbeth, Lady (Macbeth)
Macduff (Macbeth)
Macduff, Lady (Macbeth)

CHARACTERS FROM THE PLAYS OF WILLIAM SHAKESPEARE (cont.)
(with plays)

Malcolm (Macbeth)
Malvolio (Twelfth Night)
Mamillius (The Winter's Tale)
Marcellus (Hamlet)
Margaret (2 Henry VI, 3 Henry VI, Richard III)
Maria (Love's Labour's Lost, Twelfth Night)
Mariana (Measure for Measure, All's Well That Ends Well)
Marina (Pericles)
Mark Antony (Julius Caesar, Antony and Cleopatra)
Martius (Titus Andronicus)
Menenius (Coriolanus)
Mercutio (Romeo and Juliet)
Miranda (The Tempest)
Montague (Romeo and Juliet)
Mortimer (1 Henry IV)
Mutius (Titus Andronicus)
Nerissa (The Merchant of Venice)
Nym (Henry V, The Merry Wives of Windsor)
Oberon (A Midsummer Night's Dream)
Octavia (Antony and Cleopatra)
Octavius, Caesar (Julius Caesar, Antony and Cleopatra)
Oliver (As You Like It)
Olivia (Twelfth Night)
Ophelia (Hamlet)
Orlando (As You Like It)
Orsino (Twelfth Night)
Osric (Hamlet)
Oswald (King Lear)
Othello (Othello)
Pandarus (Troilus and Cressida)
Paris (Troilus and Cressida)
Parolles (All's Well That Ends Well)
Patroclus (Troilus and Cressida)
Paulina (The Winter's Tale)
Percy (1 Henry IV)
Perdita (The Winter's Tale)
Pericles (Pericles)
Peto (2 Henry IV)
Petruchio (The Taming of the Shrew)
Phebe (As You Like It)
Philoten (Pericles)
Pinch (The Comedy of Errors)
Pisanio (Cymbeline)
Pistol (2 Henry IV, Henry V, The Merry Wives of Windsor)
Poins (1 Henry IV, 2 Henry IV)
Polixenes (The Winter's Tale)
Polonius (Hamlet)
Pompey (Measure for Measure, Antony and Cleopatra)
Portia (The Merchant of Venice)
Posthumous (Cymbeline)
Priam (Troilus and Cressida)
Prospero (The Tempest)

Proteus (The Two Gentlemen of Verona)
Puck (A Midsummer Night's Dream)
Quickly, Mistress (1 Henry IV, 2 Henry IV, The Merry Wives of Windsor)
Quince (A Midsummer Night's Dream)
Quintus (Titus Andronicus)
Regan (King Lear)
Richard II (Richard II)
Richard III (2 Henry VI, 3 Henry VI, Richard III)
Richard, Duke of Gloucester [Richard III] (Richard III)
Richmond, Henry, Earl of [Henry VII] (2 Henry VI, 3 Henry VI, Richard III)
Roderigo (Othello)
Romeo (Romeo and Juliet)
Rosalind (As You Like It)
Rosaline (Love's Labour's Lost)
Rosencrantz (Hamlet)
Rumour (2 Henry IV)
Saturninus (Titus Andronicus)
Scroop (Henry IV)
Sebastian (The Tempest, Twelfth Night)
Shallow, Justice (2 Henry IV, The Merry Wives of Windsor)
Shylock (The Merchant of Venice)
Sicinius (Coriolanus)
Silence (2 Henry IV)
Silvius (As You Like It)
Slender (The Merry Wives of Windsor)
Sly, Christopher (The Taming of the Shrew)
Snout (A Midsummer Night's Dream)
Snug (A Midsummer Night's Dream)
Solinus (The Comedy of Errors)
Stephano (The Tempest)
Tamora (Titus Andronicus)
Tearsheet, Doll (2 Henry IV)
Thasia (Pericles)
Theseus (A Midsummer Night's Dream)
Titania (A Midsummer Night's Dream)
Titus (Titus Andronicus)
Touchstone (As You Like It)
Trinculo (The Tempest)
Troilus (Troilus and Cressida)
Tybalt (Romeo and Juliet)
Ulysses (Troilus and Cressida)
Verges (Much Ado About Nothing)
Vincentio (Measure for Measure, The Taming of the Shrew)
Viola (Twelfth Night)
Violenta (All's Well That Ends Well)
Voltimand (Hamlet)
Volumnia (Coriolanus)
William (As You Like It)

THEATRICAL TERMS

above
act
act drop
actor
actor-manager
actress
ad lib
advertisement
  curtain
agent
alienation effect
amphitheatre
anti-masque
apron
arc light
arena
aside
asphaleian system
assistant stage
  manager (ASM)
audition
auditorium
author's night
backcloth
backing flat
backstage
balcony
barn door shutter
barrel
batten
below
benefit
bespeak
  performance
blackout
blocking
blue
boards
boat truck
book
book ceiling
book flat
book wing
boom
border
border light
box office
box set
bridge
bristle trap
built stuff
business
busk
buskin
call
call board
call boy
call door
carpenter's scene

carpet cut
carriage-and-frame
  system
catastrophe
catwalk
cauldron trap
ceiling-cloth
cellar
centre stage
chariot-and-pole
  system
chorus
circle
circuit
cloth
clouding
collective creation
colour wheel
command
  performance
composite setting
corner trap
corsican trap
coryphaeus
cothurnus
counterweight
  system
critic
crush bar
cue
curtain
curtain call
curtain-raiser
curtain set
cut-cloth
cyclorama
designer
detail scenery
deus ex machina
deuteragonist
dimmer
diorama
director
diseuse
double take
downstage
drag artist
dramatis personae
drapery setting
dress circle
dress rehearsal
dressing room
drop
drum-and-shaft
  system
dumb show
elevator
encore
enter

epilogue
exit
falling flap
fan effect
female impersonator
flat
flexible staging
flies
flipper
float
floodlight
flying effect
flyman
follow spot
footlight
footlights trap
formal stage
fox wedge
foyer
fresnel spot
frontcloth
front of house
gaff
gallery
gauze
gel
general utility
ghost glide
glory
gobo
gods
grave trap
green room
grid
grooves system
ground row
gypsy
halls
ham
hand-props
hand worked house
heavy
hoist
house
house light
impresario
improvisation
incidental music
inner stage
inset
in the round
iris
jackknife stage
jornada
juvenile
knockabout
kuppelhorizont
lashline
laterna magica

leg
leko
libretto
light batten
light console
lighting
light pipe
limelight
linsenscheinwerfer
lobsterscope
low comedian
LX
lycopodium
make-up
manager
manet
marionette
mask
masking piece
masque
matinée
mezzanine floor
mime
mise en scène
multiple setting
mummer
noises off
odeum
off-broadway
off-off-broadway
off stage
old man
old woman
olio
on stage
open stage
orchestra
orchestra pit
pageant lantern
panorama
paradiso
parallel
pass door
pepper's ghost
perch
periaktoi
pinspot
pipe
pipe batten
pit
platform
platform stage
playbill
plot sheet
portal opening
producer
profile board
profile spot
projector

THEATRICAL TERMS (cont.)

prologue
promenade
promenade
  production
prompt book
prompter
prompt side
prop
property
proscenium arch
proscenium border
proscenium doors
protagonist
puppet
quick-change room
rain box
rake
reflector
rehearsal
rep
repertory
resting
return
revolving stage
revue
rise-and-sink
rod-puppet
roll ceiling
rope house
rose
rostrum
run
rundhorizont

runway
saddle-iron
safety curtain
sand-cloth
scene
scene dock
scenery
sciopticon
scissor cross
scrim
scruto
sea row
set
set piece
set waters
show portal
sightline
silicon controlled
  rectifier
sill iron
simultaneous setting
skene
sky border
sky cloth
sky dome
slapstick
slips
slip stage
slote
sock
soubrette
sound effects
spieltreppe

spot bar
spotlight
stage
stage brace
stage cloth
stage crew
stage direction
stage door
stage-door keeper
stage lighting
stage manager (SM)
stage rake
stage setting
stalls
star trap
stereopticon
stichomythia
stock company
strip light
strobe light
supernumerary
switchboard
synchronous winch
  system
tableau
tabs
tail
teaser
technical rehearsal
throwline
thunder run
thundersheet
thyristor

toggle
top drop
tormentor
touring company
transformation
  scene
transparency
trap
traveller
traverse curtain
tree border
trickwork
tritagonist
truck
tumbler
understudy
unities
upper circle
upstage
utility
valance
vamp trap
visor
wagon stage
walk-on
wardrobe
water rows
wind machine
wings
word rehearsal

WRITERS, PHILOSOPHERS, AND SCHOLARS

Abelard, Peter (1079–1142) French scholar, theologian, and philosopher

Achebe, Chinua (born Albert Chinualumgu) (born 1930) Nigerian novelist, poet, short-story writer, and essayist

Addison, Joseph (1672–1719) English poet, dramatist, essayist, and Whig politician

Adorno, Theodor Wiesengrund (born Theodor Wiesengrund) (1903–69) German philosopher, sociologist, and musicologist

AE, pseudonym of George William RUSSELL

Aelfric (c. 955–c. 1020) Anglo-Saxon writer

Aeschylus (c. 525–456 BC) Greek tragic dramatist

Aesop (6th century BC) Greek storyteller

Agnesi, Maria Gaetana (1718–99) Italian philosopher and mathematician

Akhmatova, Anna (pseudonym of Anna Andreevna Gorenko) (1889–1966) Russian poet

Alain-Fournier (pseudonym of Henri-Alban Fournier) (1886–1914) French novelist

Alarcón, Pedro Antonio de (1833–91) Spanish novelist

Alarcón y Mendoza, Juan Ruiz de (1581–1639) Spanish dramatist

Albee, Edward Franklin (born 1928) American dramatist

Albertus Magnus, St (known as 'Saint Albert the Great') (c. 1200–80) German bishop, philosopher, and Doctor of the Church

Alcaeus (6th century BC) Greek lyric poet

Alcott, Louisa May (1832–88) American novelist

Aldiss, Brian W(ilson) (born 1925) English novelist and critic

WRITERS, PHILOSOPHERS, AND SCHOLARS (cont.)

Aldus Manutius (Latinized name of Teobaldo Manucci; also known as Aldo Manuzio) (1450–1515) Italian scholar, printer, and publisher

Algren, Nelson (Abraham) (1909–81) American novelist

Althusser, Louis (1918–90) French philosopher

Amis, Sir Kingsley (1922–95) English novelist and poet

Amis, Martin (Louis) (born 1949) English novelist, son of Kingsley Amis

Anacreon (6th century BC) Greek lyric poet

Anaxagoras (c. 500–428 BC) Greek philosopher

Anaximander (c. 610–c. 546 BC) Greek philosopher

Anaximenes (6th century BC) Greek philosopher

Andersen, Hans Christian (1805–75) Danish writer

Andrić, Ivo (1892–1975) Serbian writer

Angelou, Maya (born 1928) American novelist and poet

Anouilh, Jean (1910–87) French dramatist

Anselm of Canterbury, St (c. 1033–1109) Italian theologian and philosopher, archbishop, and Doctor of the Church

Apollinaire, Guillaume (pseudonym of Wilhelm Apollinaris de Kostrowitzki) (1880–1918) French poet

Apollonius (known as Apollonius of Rhodes) (3rd century BC) Greek poet

Apuleius (2nd century AD) Roman writer and rhetorician

Archilochus (8th or 7th century BC) Greek poet

Arendt, Hannah (1906–75) German-born American philosopher and political theorist

Ariosto, Ludovico (1474–1533) Italian poet

Aristarchus (known as Aristarchus of Samothrace) (c. 217–145 BC) Greek critic and grammarian

Aristippus (known as Aristippus the Elder) (late 5th century BC), Greek philosopher

Aristophanes (c. 450–c. 385 BC) Greek comic dramatist

Aristotle (384–322 BC) Greek philosopher and scientist

Arnold, Matthew (1822–88) English poet, essayist, and social critic

Ascham, Roger (1515–68) English scholar and writer

Asimov, Isaac (1920–92) Russian-born American writer and scientist

Asturias, Miguel Ángel (1899–1974) Guatemalan novelist

Atwood, Margaret (Eleanor) (born 1939) Canadian novelist, poet, critic, and short-story writer

Aubrey, John (1626–97) English antiquarian and author

Auden, W(ystan) H(ugh) (1907–73) British-born poet

Austen, Jane (1775–1817) English novelist

Austin, John (1790–1859) English jurist

Austin, John Langshaw (1911–60) English philosopher

Averroës (1126–98) Spanish-Arabian philosopher

Avicenna (Arabic name ibn-Sina) (980–1037) Persian-born Islamic philosopher and physician

Awdry, Reverend W(ilbert) V(ere) (1911–97) English writer of children's stories

Ayckbourn, Sir Alan (born 1939) English dramatist

Ayer, Sir A(lfred) J(ules) (1910–89) English philosopher

Bagehot, Walter (1826–77) English economist and journalist

Bainbridge, Dame Beryl (born 1934) British novelist

Baldwin, James (Arthur) (1924–87) American novelist

Ballantyne, R(obert) M(ichael) (1825–94) Scottish writer

Ballard, J(ames) G(raham) (born 1930) British novelist and short-story writer, born in China

Balzac, Honoré de (1799–1850) French novelist

Banks, Iain (born 1954) Scottish novelist

Barbour, John (c. 1320–95) Scottish poet and prelate

Barker, George (Granville) (1913–91) English poet

Barrett, Elizabeth See BROWNING

Barrie, Sir J(ames) M(atthew) (1860–1937) Scottish dramatist and novelist

Barth, John (Simmons) (born 1930) American novelist and short-story writer

Barth, Karl (1886–1968) Swiss Protestant theologian

Barthes, Roland (1915–80) French writer and critic

Bates, H(erbert) E(rnest) (1905–74) English novelist and short-story writer

Baudelaire, Charles (Pierre) (1821–67) French poet and critic

Baudrillard, Jean (born 1929) French sociologist and cultural critic

WRITERS, PHILOSOPHERS, AND SCHOLARS (cont.)

Baxter, James K(eir) (1926–72) New Zealand poet, dramatist, and critic

Beaumarchais, Pierre Augustin Caron de (1732–99) French dramatist

Beaumont, Francis (1584–1616) English dramatist

Beauvoir, Simone de See DE BEAUVOIR

Beckett, Samuel (Barclay) (1906–89) Irish dramatist, novelist, and poet

Beckford, William (1759–1844) English writer and collector

Beerbohm, Sir Henry Maximilian ('Max') (1872–1956) English caricaturist, essayist, and critic

Beeton, Mrs Isabella Mary (1836–65) English writer on cookery

Behan, Brendan (Francis) (1923–64) Irish dramatist and poet

Behn, Aphra (1640–89) English novelist and dramatist

Bell, Currer, Ellis, and Acton, pseudonyms used by Charlotte, Emily, and Anne BRONTË

Bell, Gertrude (1868–1926) English archaeologist and writer

Belloc, (Joseph) Hilaire (Pierre René) (1870–1953) French-born British writer, historian, and poet, of French–British descent

Bellow, Saul (born 1915) Canadian-born American novelist, of Russian Jewish descent

Bennett, Alan (born 1934) English dramatist and actor

Bennett, (Enoch) Arnold (1867–1931) English novelist, dramatist, and critic

Bentham, Jeremy (1748–1832) English philosopher and jurist

Bentley, Edmund Clerihew (1875–1956) English journalist and novelist

Bergerac See CYRANO DE BERGERAC

Bergson, Henri (Louis) (1859–1941) French philosopher

Berkeley, George (1685–1753) Irish philosopher and bishop

Berlin, Sir Isaiah (1909–97) Latvian-born British philosopher

Bertillon, Alphonse (1853–1914) French criminologist

Besant, Annie (1847–1933) English theosophist, writer, and political campaigner

Betjeman, Sir John (1906–84) English poet

Betti, Ugo (1892–1953) Italian dramatist, poet, and short-story writer

Bierce, Ambrose (Gwinnett) (1842–c. 1914) American writer

Bishop, Elizabeth (1911–79) American poet

Blackmore, R(ichard) D(oddridge) (1825–1900) English novelist and poet

Blackstone, Sir William (1723–80) English jurist

Blackwood, Algernon (Henry) (1869–1951) English writer

Blake, William (1757–1827) English poet and artist

Blixen, Karen (Christentze), Baroness Blixen-Finecke (*née* Dinesen; also known by the pseudonym of Isak Dinesen) (1885–1962) Danish novelist and short-story writer

Bloomfield, Leonard (1887–1949) American linguist

Blunden, Edmund (Charles) (1896–1974) English poet and critic

Blunt, Anthony (Frederick) (1907–83) British art historian, Foreign Office official, and Soviet spy

Blyton, Enid (1897–1968) English writer of children's fiction

Boccaccio, Giovanni (1313–75) Italian writer, poet, and humanist

Boileau, Nicholas (full surname Boileau-Despréaux) (1636–1711) French critic and poet

Boldrewood, Rolf (pseudonym of Thomas Alexander Browne) (1826–1915) Australian novelist

Böll, Heinrich (Theodor) (1917–85) German novelist and short-story writer

Bolt, Robert (Oxton) (1924–95) English dramatist and screenwriter

Bond, Edward (born 1934) English dramatist

Borges, Jorge Luis (1899–1986) Argentinian poet, short-story writer, and essayist

Borrow, George (Henry) (1803–81) English writer

Boswell, James (1740–95) Scottish author and biographer

Bowen, Elizabeth (Dorothea Cole) (1899–1973) British novelist and short-story writer, born in Ireland

Bowles, Paul (Frederick) (born 1910) American writer and composer

Boz, pseudonym used by Charles DICKENS in his *The Pickwick Papers* and contributions to the Morning Chronicle

Bradbury, Malcolm (Stanley) (1932–2000) English novelist, critic, and academic

Bradbury, Ray (Douglas) (born 1920) American writer of science fiction

Braille, Louis (1809–52) French educationist

Braine, John (Gerard) (1922–86) English novelist

WRITERS, PHILOSOPHERS, AND SCHOLARS (cont.)

Brecht, (Eugen) Bertolt (Friedrich)
(1898–1956) German dramatist, producer,
and poet

Breton, André (1896–1966) French poet,
essayist, and critic

Bridges, Robert (Seymour) (1844–1930)
English poet and literary critic

Brink, André (born 1935) South African
novelist, short-story writer, and dramatist

Brodsky, Joseph (born Iosif Aleksandrovich
Brodsky) (1940–96) Russian-born American
poet

Brontë, Charlotte (1816–55), **Emily** (1818–48),
and **Anne** (1820–49), English novelists

Brooke, Rupert (Chawner) (1887–1915)
English poet

Brookner, Anita (born 1928) English novelist
and art historian

Brooks, Cleanth (1906–94) American teacher
and critic

Browning, Elizabeth Barrett (1806–61)
English poet

Browning, Robert (1812–89) English poet

Bruno, Giordano (1548–1600) Italian
philosopher

Buber, Martin (1878–1965) Israeli religious
philosopher, born in Austria

Buchan, John, 1st Baron Tweedsmuir
(1875–1940) Scottish novelist and
statesman

Buck, Pearl S(ydenstricker) (1892–1973)
American writer

Bulwer-Lytton See LYTTON

Bunin, Ivan (Alekseevich) (1870–1953)
Russian poet and prose-writer

Bunting, Basil (1900–85) English poet and
journalist

Bunyan, John (1628–88) English writer

Burgess, Anthony (pseudonym of John
Anthony Burgess Wilson) (1917–93) English
novelist and critic

Burke, Edmund (1729–97) Irish politician,
philosopher, and writer

Burke, John (1787–1848) Irish genealogical
and heraldic writer

Burnett, Frances (Eliza) Hodgson (1849–1924)
British-born American novelist

Burney, Frances ('Fanny') (1752–1840)
English novelist

Burns, Robert (1759–96) Scottish poet

Burroughs, Edgar Rice (1875–1950) American
novelist and writer of science fiction

Burroughs, William S(eward) (1914–97)
American novelist

Burton, Sir Richard (Francis) (1821–90)
English explorer, anthropologist, and
translator

Butler, Samuel (1835–1902) English novelist

Butler, Samuel ('Hudibras') (1612–80) English
poet

Byatt, A(ntonia) S(usan) (born 1936) English
novelist and literary critic

Byron, George Gordon, 6th Baron
(1788–1824) English poet

Caedmon (7th century) English poet and
monk

Calderón de la Barca, Pedro (1600–81)
Spanish dramatist and poet

Caldwell, Erskine (Preston) (1903–87)
American novelist and short-story writer

Callimachus (*c.* 305–*c.* 240 BC) Greek poet and
scholar

Calvino, Italo (1923–87) Italian novelist and
short-story writer, born in Cuba

Camões, Luis (Vaz) de (also Camoëns)
(*c.* 1524–80) Portuguese poet

Campbell, (Ignatius) Roy(ston Dunnachie)
(1901–57) South African poet

Campbell, Thomas (1777–1844) Scottish
poet

Camus, Albert (1913–60) French novelist,
dramatist, and essayist

Canetti, Elias (1905–94) Bulgarian-born
British writer

Čapek, Karel (1890–1938) Czech novelist and
dramatist

Capote, Truman (born Truman Streckfus
Persons) (1924–84) American writer

Carlyle, Thomas (1795–1881) Scottish
historian and political philosopher

Carnap, Rudolf (1891–1970) German-born
American philosopher

Carr, Emily (1871–1945) Canadian writer and
painter

Carroll, Lewis (pseudonym of Charles
Lutwidge Dodgson) (1832–98) English
writer

Carter, Angela (1940–92) English novelist and
short-story writer

Cartland, Dame (Mary) Barbara (Hamilton)
(born 1901) English writer

Cary, (Arthur) Joyce (Lunel) (1888–1957)
English novelist

Cather, Willa (Sibert) (1876–1974) American
novelist and short-story writer

Catullus, Gaius Valerius (*c.* 84–*c.* 54 BC)
Roman poet

Cavafy, Constantine (Peter) (born
Konstantinos Petrou Kavafis) (1863–1933)
Greek poet

Céline, Louis-Ferdinand (pseudonym of
Louis-Ferdinand Destouches) (1894–1961)
French novelist

WRITERS, PHILOSOPHERS, AND SCHOLARS (cont.)

Cervantes, Miguel de (1547–1616) (full surname Cervantes Saavedra) Spanish novelist and dramatist

Champollion, Jean-François (1790–1832) French Egyptologist

Chandler, Raymond (Thornton) (1888–1959) American novelist

Chapman, George (c. 1560–1634) English poet and dramatist

Chateaubriand, François-René, Vicomte de (1768–1848) French writer and diplomat

Chatterton, Thomas (1752–70) English poet

Chaucer, Geoffrey (c. 1342–1400) English poet

Cheever, John (1912–82) American short-story writer and novelist

Chekhov, Anton (Pavlovich) (1860–1904) Russian dramatist and short-story writer

Chesterton, G(ilbert) K(eith) (1874–1936) English essayist, novelist, and critic

Chomsky, (Avram) Noam (born 1928) American theoretical linguist and political activist

Chopin, Kate (O'Flaherty) (1851–1904) American novelist and short-story writer

Chrétien de Troyes (12th century) French poet

Christie, Dame Agatha (1890–1976) English writer of detective fiction

Churchill, Caryl (born 1938) English dramatist

Cicero, Marcus Tullius (106–43 BC) Roman statesman, orator, and writer

Clare, John (1793–1864) English poet

Clarke, Sir Arthur C(harles) (born 1917) English writer of science fiction

Clarke, Marcus (Andrew Hislop) (1846–81) British-born Australian writer

Clemens, Samuel Langhorne See TWAIN

Clough, Arthur Hugh (1819–61) English poet

Cobbett, William (1763–1835) English writer and political reformer

Cocteau, Jean (1889–1963) French dramatist, novelist, and film director

Coetzee, J(ohn) M(axwell) (born 1940) South African novelist

Coleridge, Samuel Taylor (1772–1834) English poet, critic, and philosopher

Colette (born Sidonie Gabrielle Claudine) (1873–1954) French novelist

Collins, (William) Wilkie (1824–89) English novelist

Compton-Burnett, Dame Ivy (1884–1969) English novelist

Comte, Auguste (1798–1857) French philosopher, one of the founders of sociology

Conan Doyle See DOYLE

Conegliano, Emmanuele See DA PONTE

Confucius (Latinized name of K'ung Fu-tzu = 'Kong the master') (551–479 BC) Chinese philosopher

Congreve, William (1670–1729) English dramatist

Connolly, Cyril (Vernon) (1903–74) English writer

Conrad, Joseph (born Józef Teodor Konrad Korzeniowski) (1857–1924) Polish-born British novelist

Cookson, Dame Catherine (Anne) (1906–98) English writer

Cooper, James Fenimore (1789–1851) American novelist

Corelli, Marie (pseudonym of Mary Mackay) (1855–1924) English writer of romantic fiction

Corneille, Pierre (1606–84) French dramatist

Coward, Sir Noel (Pierce) (1899–1973) English dramatist, actor, and composer

Cowper, William (1731–1800) English poet

Crabbe, George (1754–1832) English poet

Crane, (Harold) Hart (1899–1932) American poet

Crane, Stephen (1871–1900) American writer

Crichton, Michael (born 1942) US novelist and screenwriter

Croce, Benedetto (1866–1952) Italian philosopher

Crompton, Richmal (pseudonym of Richmal Crompton Lamburn) (1890–1969) English writer

Cronin, A(rchibald) J(oseph) (1896–1981) Scottish novelist

Cudlipp, Hugh, Baron Cudlipp of Aldingbourne (1913–98) British newspaper editor

cummings, e(dward) e(stlin) (1894–1962) American poet and novelist

Cynewulf (late 8th–9th centuries) Anglo-Saxon poet

Cyrano de Bergerac, Savinien (1619–55) French soldier, duellist, and writer

Dahl, Roald (1916–90) British writer, of Norwegian descent

Dana, Richard Henry (1815–82) American adventurer, lawyer, and writer

d'Annunzio, Gabriele (1863–1938) Italian novelist, dramatist, and poet

WRITERS, PHILOSOPHERS, AND SCHOLARS (cont.)

Dante (full name Dante Alighieri) (1265–1321) Italian poet

Da Ponte, Lorenzo (born Emmanuele Conegliano) (1749–1838) Italian poet and librettist

Daudet, Alphonse (1840–97) French novelist and dramatist

David, Elizabeth (1913–92) British cookery writer

Davies, W(illiam) H(enry) (1871–1940) English poet

Davies, (William) Robertson (1913–95) Canadian novelist, dramatist, and journalist

Day Lewis, C(ecil) (1904–72) English poet and critic

de Beauvoir, Simone (1908–86) French existentialist philosopher and novelist

de Bernières, Louis (born 1954) British novelist

Defoe, Daniel (1660–1731) English novelist and journalist

Deighton, Leonard Cyril ('Len') (born 1929) English novelist

Dekker, Thomas (c. 1570–1632) English dramatist and novelist

de la Mare, Walter (John) (1873–1956) English poet and novelist

de la Roche, Mazo (1879–1961) Canadian novelist

de Maupassant, Guy See MAUPASSANT

de Pisan, Christine (also de Pizan) (c. 1364–c. 1430) Italian writer, resident in France from 1369

De Quincey, Thomas (1785–1859) English essayist and critic

Derrida, Jacques (born 1930) French philosopher

de Sade, Marquis See SADE

Descartes, René (1596–1650) French philosopher, mathematician, and man of science, often called the father of modern philosophy

de Spinoza, Baruch See SPINOZA

de Staël, Mme (née Anne Louise Germaine Necker) (1766–1817) French novelist and critic

de Troyes, Chrétien See CHRÉTIEN DE TROYES

Dickens, Charles (John Huffam) (1812–70) English novelist

Dickinson, Emily (Elizabeth) (1830–86) American poet

Diderot, Denis (1713–84) French philosopher, writer, and critic

Dinesen, Isak See BLIXEN

Diogenes (c. 400–c. 325 BC) Greek philosopher

Dionysius of Halicarnassus (1st century BC) Greek historian, literary critic, and rhetorician

Dodgson, Charles Lutwidge See CARROLL

Donatus, Aelius (4th century) Roman grammarian

Donne, John (1572–1631) English poet and preacher

Doolittle, Hilda (known as H. D.) (1886–1961) American poet

Dos Passos, John (Roderigo) (1896–1970) American novelist

Dostoevsky, Fyodor Mikhailovich (also Dostoyevsky) (1821–81) Russian novelist

Douglas, Lord Alfred (Bruce) (1870–1945) English poet

Dowson, Ernest (Christopher) (1867–1900) English poet

Doyle, Sir Arthur Conan (1859–1930) Scottish novelist

Doyle, Roddy (born 1958) Irish novelist

Drabble, Margaret (born 1939) English novelist

Draco (7th century BC) Athenian legislator

Dreiser, Theodore (Herman Albert) (1871–1945) American novelist

Dryden, John (1631–1700) English poet, dramatist, and critic

Du Bois, W(illiam) E(dward) B(urghardt) (1868–1963) American writer and political activist

Du Fu See TU FU

Dumas, Alexandre (known as Dumas père) (1802–70) French novelist and dramatist

Du Maurier, Dame Daphne (1907–89) English novelist,

Dunbar, William (c. 1456–c. 1513) Scottish poet

Dunne, John William (1875–1949) English philosopher

Duras, Marguerite (pseudonym of Marguerite Donnadieu) (1914–96) French novelist, film director, and dramatist

Durrell, Gerald (Malcolm) (1925–95) English zoologist and writer, brother of Lawrence Durrell

Durrell, Lawrence (George) (1912–90) English novelist, poet, and travel writer

Eco, Umberto (born 1932) Italian novelist and semiotician

Edgeworth, Maria (1767–1849) Irish novelist, born in England

Ehrenburg, Ilya (Grigorevich) (1891–1967) Russian novelist and journalist

Elia, pseudonym adopted by Charles LAMB in his *Essays of Elia* (1823) and *Last Essays of Elia* (1833)

WRITERS, PHILOSOPHERS, AND SCHOLARS (cont.)

Eliot, George (pseudonym of Mary Ann Evans) (1819–80) English novelist
Eliot, T(homas) S(tearns) (1888–1965) American-born British poet, critic, and dramatist
Elton, Ben (born 1959) British dramatist, novelist, and comedian
Éluard, Paul (pseudonym of Eugène Grindel) (1895–1952) French poet
Emerson, Ralph Waldo (1803–82) American philosopher and poet
Empson, Sir William (1906–84) English poet and literary critic
Engels, Friedrich (1820–95) German socialist and political philosopher, resident chiefly in England from 1842
Ennius, Quintus (239–169 BC) Roman poet and dramatist
Epictetus (c. 55–c. 135 AD) Greek philosopher
Erasmus, Desiderius (Dutch name Gerhard Gerhards) (c. 1469–1536) Dutch humanist and scholar
Erastus (Swiss name Thomas Lieber; also called Liebler or Lüber) (1524–83) Swiss theologian and physician
Euripides (480–c. 406 BC) Greek dramatist
Evelyn, John (1620–1706) English diarist and writer
Farquhar, George (1678–1707) Irish dramatist
Farrell, J(ames) G(ordon) (1935–79) English novelist
Farrell, J(ames) T(homas) (1904–79) American novelist
Faulkner, William (1897–1962) American novelist
Ferlinghetti, Lawrence (Monsanto) (born Lawrence Ferling) (born 1919) American poet and publisher
Feuerbach, Ludwig (Andreas) (1804–72) German materialist philosopher
Feydeau, Georges (1862–1921) French dramatist
Fichte, Johann Gottlieb (1762–1814) German philosopher
Fielding, Helen (born 1958) British novelist and humorous writer
Fielding, Henry (1707–54) English novelist
Fitzgerald, Edward (1809–83) English scholar and poet
Fitzgerald, F(rancis) Scott (Key) (1896–1940) American novelist
Flaubert, Gustave (1821–80) French novelist and short-story writer
Flecker, James (Herman) Elroy (1884–1915) English poet
Fleming, Ian (Lancaster) (1908–64) English novelist

Fletcher, John (1579–1625) English dramatist
Fo, Dario (born 1926) Italian dramatist
Ford, Ford Madox (born Ford Hermann Hueffer) (1873–1939) English novelist and editor
Ford, John (1586–c. 1639) English dramatist
Forester, C(ecil) S(cott) (pseudonym of Cecil Lewis Troughton Smith) (1899–1966) English novelist
Forster, E(dward) M(organ) (1879–1970) English novelist and literary critic
Forsyth, Frederick (born 1938) English novelist
Foucault, Michel (1926–84) French philosopher
Fowles, John (Robert) (born 1926) English novelist
Foxe, John (1516–87) English religious writer
Frame, Janet (Paterson) (born 1924) New Zealand novelist
France, Anatole (pseudonym of Jacques-Anatole-François Thibault) (1844–1924) French writer
Francis, Richard Stanley ('Dick') (born 1920) English jockey and writer
Franklin, (Stella Maria Sarah) Miles (1879–1954) Australian novelist
Frege, Gottlob (1848–1925) German philosopher and mathematician, founder of modern logic
Friedan, Betty (born 1921) American feminist and writer
Fromm, Erich (1900–80) German-born American psychoanalyst and social philosopher
Frost, Robert (Lee) (1874–1963) American poet
Fry, Christopher (Harris) (born 1907) English dramatist
Frye, (Herman) Northrop (1912–91) Canadian literary critic
Fuentes, Carlos (born 1928) Mexican novelist and writer
Fugard, Athol (born 1932) South African dramatist
Galsworthy, John (1867–1933) English novelist and dramatist
García Lorca See LORCA
García Márquez, Gabriel (born 1928) Colombian novelist
Gardner, Erle Stanley (1899–1970) American novelist and short-story writer
Gaskell, Mrs Elizabeth (Cleghorn) (1810–65) English novelist
Gassendi, Pierre (1592–1655) French astronomer and philosopher

WRITERS, PHILOSOPHERS, AND SCHOLARS (cont.)

Gay, John (1685–1732) English poet and dramatist

Genet, Jean (1910–86) French novelist, poet, and dramatist

Geoffrey of Monmouth (*c.* 1100–*c.* 1154) Welsh chronicler

Gibbon, Edward (1737–94) English historian

Gibbon, Lewis Grassic (pseudonym of James Leslie Mitchell) (1901–35) Scottish writer

Gibran, Khalil (also Jubran) (1883–1931) Lebanese-born American writer and artist

Gide, André (Paul Guillaume) (1869–1951) French novelist, essayist, and critic

Gilbert, Sir W(illiam) S(chwenck) (1836–1911) English dramatist and librettist

Ginsberg, Allen (1926–97) American poet

Gissing, George (Robert) (1857–1903) English novelist

Gobineau, Joseph Arthur, Comte de (1816–82) French writer and anthropologist

Godwin, William (1756–1836) English social philosopher and novelist

Goethe, Johann Wolfgang von (1749–1832) German poet, dramatist, and scholar

Gogol, Nikolai (Vasilevich) (1809–52) Russian novelist, dramatist, and short-story writer, born in Ukraine

Golding, Sir William (Gerald) (1911–93) English novelist

Goldsmith, Oliver (1728–74) Irish novelist, poet, essayist, and dramatist

Goncharov, Ivan (1812–91) Russian novelist

Goncourt, Edmond de (1822–96) and **Jules de** (1830–70) French novelists and critics

Gordimer, Nadine (born 1923) South African novelist and short-story writer

Gorky, Maxim (pseudonym of Aleksei Maksimovich Peshkov) (1868–1936) Russian writer and revolutionary

Grahame, Kenneth (1859–1932) Scottish-born writer of children's stories, resident in England from 1864

Gramsci, Antonio (1891–1937) Italian political theorist and activist

Grass, Günter (Wilhelm) (born 1927) German novelist, poet, and dramatist

Graves, Robert (Ranke) (1895–1985) English poet, novelist, and critic

Gray, Thomas (1716–71) English poet

Greene, (Henry) Graham (1904–91) English novelist

Greer, Germaine (born 1939) Australian feminist and writer

Grey, Zane (born Pearl Grey) (1872–1939) American writer

Grimm, Jacob (Ludwig Carl) (1785–1863) and **Wilhelm (Carl)** (1786–1859) German philologists and folklorists

Grisham, John (born 1955) American novelist

Grosseteste, Robert (*c.* 1175–1253) English churchman, philosopher, and scholar

Grotius, Hugo (Latinized name of Huig de Groot) (1583–1645) Dutch jurist and diplomat

Gunn, Thom (full name Thomson William Gunn) (born 1929) English poet

Habermas, Jürgen (born 1929) German social philosopher

Haeckel, Ernst Heinrich (1834–1919) German biologist and philosopher

Haggard, Sir Henry Rider (1856–1925) English novelist

Hakluyt, Richard (*c.* 1552–1616) English geographer and historian

Hall, (Marguerite) Radclyffe (1883–1943) English novelist and poet

Hammett, (Samuel) Dashiell (1894–1961) American novelist

Hamsun, Knut (pseudonym of Knut Pedersen) (1859–1952) Norwegian novelist

Han Suyin See SUYIN

Hardy, Thomas (1840–1928) English novelist and poet

Harris, Frank (born James Thomas Harris) (1856–1931) Irish writer

Harris, Thomas (born 1940) American novelist

Harte, (Francis) Bret (1836–1902) American short-story writer and poet

Hartley, L(eslie) P(oles) (1895–1972) English novelist

Hauptmann, Gerhart (1862–1946) German dramatist

Hašek, Jaroslav (1883–1923) Czech novelist and short-story writer

Hawthorne, Nathaniel (1804–64) American novelist and short-story writer

Hazlitt, William (1778–1830) English essayist and critic

H. D., pseudonym of Hilda DOOLITTLE

Heaney, Seamus (Justin) (born 1939) Irish poet

Hegel, Georg Wilhelm Friedrich (1770–1831) German philosopher

Heidegger, Martin (1889–1976) German philosopher

Heine, (Christian Johann) Heinrich (1797–1856) German poet

Heller, Joseph (1923–99) American novelist

Hellman, Lillian (Florence) (1907–84) American dramatist

WRITERS, PHILOSOPHERS, AND SCHOLARS (cont.)

Hemingway, Ernest (Miller) (1899–1961) American writer

Henry, O (pseudonym of William Sidney Porter) (1862–1910) American short-story writer

Heraclitus (c. 500 BC) Greek philosopher

Herbert, George (1593–1633) English metaphysical poet

Herbert, Sir A(lan) P(atrick) (1890–1970) English writer and politician

Herodotus (known as 'the Father of History') (5th century BC) Greek historian

Herrick, Robert (1591–1674) English poet

Herriot, James (pseudonym of James Alfred Wight) (1916–95) English short-story writer and veterinary surgeon

Herzl, Theodor (1860–1904) Hungarian-born journalist, dramatist, and Zionist leader

Hesiod (c. 700 BC) Greek poet

Hesse, Hermann (1877–1962) German-born Swiss novelist and poet

Heyer, Georgette (1902–74) English novelist

Highsmith, Patricia (born Patricia Plangman) (1921–95) American writer of detective fiction

Hite, Shere (born 1942) American feminist

Hobbes, Thomas (1588–1679) English philosopher

Hoffmann, E(rnst) T(heodor) A(madeus) (1776–1822) German novelist, short-story writer, and music critic

Hofmannsthal, Hugo von (1874–1929) Austrian poet and dramatist

Hogg, James (1770–1835) Scottish poet and novelist

Hölderlin, (Johann Christian) Friedrich (1770–1843) German poet

Holinshed, Raphael (died c. 1580) English chronicler

Holmes, Oliver Wendell (1809–94) American physician and writer

Homer (8th century BC) Greek epic poet

Hood, Thomas (1799–1845) English poet and humorist

Hopkins, Gerard Manley (1844–89) English poet

Horace (full name Quintus Horatius Flaccus) (65–8 BC) Roman poet of the Augustan period

Horkheimer, Max (1895–1973) German philosopher and sociologist

Hornby, Nick (born 1957) British novelist

Hornung, Ernest William (1866–1921) English novelist

Housman, A(lfred) E(dward) (1859–1936) English poet and classical scholar

Hughes, Edward James ('Ted') (1930–98) English poet

Hughes, (James Mercer) Langston (1902–67) American writer

Hugo Victor(-Marie) (1802–85) French poet, novelist, and dramatist

Hume, David (1711–76) Scottish philosopher, economist, and historian

Hurston, Zora Neale (1901–60) American novelist

Husserl, Edmund (Gustav Albrecht) (1859–1938) German philosopher

Huxley, Aldous (Leonard) (1894–1963) English novelist and essayist

Hypatia (c. 370–415) Greek philosopher, astronomer, and mathematician

Ibsen, Henrik (1828–1906) Norwegian dramatist

Illich, Ivan (born 1926) Austrian-born American educationist and writer

Ionesco, Eugène (1912–94) Romanian-born French dramatist

Iqbal, Sir Muhammad (1875–1938) Indian poet and philosopher, generally regarded as the father of Pakistan

Irving, Washington (1783–1859) American writer

Isherwood, Christopher (William Bradshaw) (1904–86) British-born American novelist

Ishiguro, Kazuo (born 1954) Japanese-born British novelist

Jacobs, William Wymark (1863–1943) English short-story writer

Jalal ad-Din ar-Rumi (also called Mawlana) (1207–73) Persian poet and Sufi mystic

James, Clive (Vivian Leopold) (born 1939) Australian television personality, writer, and critic

James, C(yril) L(ionel) R(obert) (1901–89) Trinidadian historian, journalist, political theorist, and novelist

James, P(hyllis) D(orothy), Baroness (born 1920) English writer of detective fiction

James, Henry (1843–1916) American-born British novelist and critic

James, William (1842–1910) American philosopher and psychologist, brother of Henry James

Jarry, Alfred (1873–1907) French dramatist

Jean Paul (pseudonym of Johann Paul Friedrich Richter) (1763–1825) German novelist

Jerome, Jerome K(lapka) (1859–1927) English novelist and dramatist

Jespersen, (Jens) Otto (Harry) (1860–1943) Danish philologist, grammarian, and educationist

WRITERS, PHILOSOPHERS, AND SCHOLARS (cont.)

Johnson, Samuel (known as Dr Johnson) (1709–84) English lexicographer, writer, critic, and conversationalist

Jones, Daniel (1881–1967) British linguist and phonetician

Jong, Erica (Mann) (born 1942) American poet and novelist

Jonson, Benjamin ('Ben') (1572–1637) English dramatist and poet

Joyce, James (Augustine Aloysius) (1882–1941) Irish writer

Jubran, Khalil See GIBRAN

Juvenal (Latin name Decimus Junius Juvenalis) (*c.* 60–*c.* 140) Roman satirist

Kafka, Franz (1883–1924) Czech novelist, who wrote in German

Kaiser, Georg (1878–1945) German dramatist

Kalidasa (5th century AD) Indian poet and dramatist

Kant, Immanuel (1724–1804) German philosopher

Karadžić, Vuk Stefanović (1787–1864) Serbian writer, grammarian, lexicographer, and folklorist

Kawabata, Yasunari (1899–1972) Japanese novelist

Keats, John (1795–1821) English poet

Keller, Helen (Adams) (1880–1968) American writer, social reformer, and academic

Kempe, Margery (*c.* 1373–*c.* 1440) English mystic

Keneally, Thomas (Michael) (born 1935) Australian novelist

Kerouac, Jack (born Jean-Louis Lebris de Kérouac) (1922–69) American novelist and poet, of French-Canadian descent

Kesey, Ken (Elton) (born 1935) American novelist

Kierkegaard, Søren (1813–55) Danish philosopher

King, Stephen (Edwin) (born 1947) American novelist

Kingsley, Charles (1819–75) English novelist and clergyman

Kipling, (Joseph) Rudyard (1865–1936) English novelist, short-story writer, and poet

Knox, Ronald Arbuthnott (1888–1957) English theologian and writer

Koestler, Arthur (1905–83) Hungarian-born British novelist and essayist

Kotzebue, August von (1761–1819) German dramatist

Kundera, Milan (born 1929) Czech novelist

Kung Fu-tzu See CONFUCIUS

Kyd, Thomas (1558–94) English dramatist

la Barca, Pedro Calderón de See CALDERÓN DE LA BARCA

La Bruyère, Jean de (1645–96) French writer and moralist

Lacan, Jacques (1901–81) French psychoanalyst and writer

Laclos, Pierre (-Ambroise-François) Choderlos de (1741–1803) French novelist

La Fontaine, Jean de (1621–95) French poet

Lagerlöf, Selma (Ottiliana Lovisa) (1858–1940) Swedish novelist

Lamartine, Alphonse Marie Louis de (1790–1869) French poet, statesman, and historian

Lamb, Charles (1775–1834) English essayist and critic

Lampedusa, Giuseppe Tomasi de (1896–1957) Italian novelist

Landor, Walter Savage (1775–1864) English poet and essayist

Langland, William (*c.* 1330–*c.* 1400) English poet

Larkin, Philip (Arthur) (1922–85) English poet

La Rochefoucauld, François de Marsillac, Duc de (1613–80) French writer and moralist

Laurence, (Jean) Margaret (1926–87) Canadian novelist

Lawrence, D(avid) H(erbert) (1885–1930) English novelist, poet, and essayist

Lawrence, T(homas) E(dward) (known as Lawrence of Arabia) (1888–1935) British soldier and writer

Layamon (late 12th century) English poet and priest

Leacock, Stephen (Butler) (1869–1949) Canadian humorist and economist

Lear, Edward (1812–88) English humorist and illustrator

Le Carré, John (pseudonym of David John Moore Cornwell) (born 1931) English novelist

Leconte de Lisle, Charles Marie René (1818–94) French poet

Lee, Laurie (1914–97) English writer

Lee, (Nelle) Harper (born 1926) American novelist

Le Fanu, (Joseph) Sheridan (1814–73) Irish novelist

Leibniz, Gottfried Wilhelm (1646–1716) German rationalist philosopher, mathematician, and logician

Leonard, Elmore (John) (born 1925) American writer of thrillers

Lerner, Alan J(ay) (1918–86) American lyricist and dramatist

WRITERS, PHILOSOPHERS, AND SCHOLARS (cont.)

Lesage, Alain-René (1668–1747) French novelist and dramatist

Lessing, Doris (May) (born 1919) British novelist and short-story writer, brought up in Rhodesia

Lessing, Gotthold Ephraim (1729–81) German dramatist and critic

Levi, Primo (1919–87) Italian novelist and poet

Lewis, Cecil Day See DAY LEWIS

Lewis, C(live) S(taples) (1898–1963) British novelist, religious writer, and literary scholar

Lewis, (Harry) Sinclair (1885–1951) American novelist

Lewis, (Percy) Wyndham (1882–1957) British novelist, critic, and painter, born in Canada

Li Bo See LI PO

Liddell Hart, Sir Basil Henry (1895–1970) British military historian and theorist

Li Po (also Li Bo, Li T'ai Po) (AD 701–62) Chinese poet

Li T'ai Po See LI PO

Littré, Émile (1801–81) French lexicographer and philosopher

Livy (Latin name Titus Livius) (59 BC–AD 17) Roman historian

Llosa, Mario Vargas See VARGAS LLOSA

Locke, John (1632–1704) English philosopher, a founder of empiricism and political liberalism

Lodge, David (John) (born 1935) English novelist and academic

London, Jack (pseudonym of John Griffith Chaney) (1876–1916) American novelist

Longfellow, Henry Wadsworth (1807–82) American poet

Longinus (*fl.* 1st century AD) Greek scholar

Lorca, Federico García (1898–1936) Spanish poet and dramatist

Loti, Pierre (pseudonym of Louis Marie Julien Viaud) (1850–1923) French novelist

Lovelace, Richard (1618–57) English poet

Lowell, Amy (Lawrence) (1874–1925) American poet

Lowell, James Russell (1819–91) American poet and critic

Lowell, Robert (Traill Spence) (1917–77) American poet

Lowry, (Clarence) Malcolm (1909–57) English novelist

Lucan (Latin name Marcus Annaeus Lucanus) (AD 39–65) Roman poet, born in Spain

Lucretius (full name Titus Lucretius Carus) (*c.* 94–*c.* 55 BC) Roman poet and philosopher

Lukács, György (1885–1971) Hungarian philosopher, literary critic, and politician

Luther, Martin (1483–1546) German Protestant theologian, the principal figure of the German Reformation

Lycurgus (9th century BC) Spartan lawgiver

Lydgate, John (*c.* 1370–*c.* 1450) English poet and monk

Lyly, John (*c.* 1554–1606) English prose writer and dramatist

Lyotard, Jean-François (1924–98) French philosopher and literary critic

Lytton, 1st Baron (born Edward George Earle Bulwer-Lytton) (1803–73) British novelist, dramatist, and statesman

McCarthy, Mary (Therese) (1912–89) American novelist and critic

Macaulay, Dame (Emilie) Rose (1881–1958) English novelist and essayist

Macaulay, Thomas Babington, 1st Baron (1800–59) English historian, essayist, and philanthropist

McCarthy, Cormac (born 1933) American novelist

McCullers, (Lula) Carson (1917–67) American writer

MacDiarmid, Hugh (pseudonym of Christopher Murray Grieve) (1892–1978) Scottish poet and nationalist

McGonagall, William (1830–1902) Scottish poet

Mackenzie, Sir (Edward Montague) Compton (1883–1972) English novelist, essayist, and poet

Maclean, Alistair (1922–87) Scottish novelist

McLuhan, (Herbert) Marshall (1911–80) Canadian writer and thinker

MacNeice, (Frederick) Louis (1907–63) Northern Irish poet

McPherson, Conor (born 1972) Irish dramatist

Maeterlinck, Count Maurice (1862–1949) Belgian poet, dramatist, and essayist

Mahfouz, Naguib (born 1911) Egyptian novelist and short-story writer

Mailer, Norman (born 1923) American novelist and essayist

Maimonides (born Moses ben Maimon) (1135–1204) Jewish philosopher and Rabbinic scholar, born in Spain

Malamud, Bernard (1914–86) American novelist and short-story writer

Malherbe, François de (1555–1628) French poet

Mallarmé, Stéphane (1842–98) French poet

Malory, Sir Thomas (??1400–1471) English writer

WRITERS, PHILOSOPHERS, AND SCHOLARS (cont.)

Malraux, André (1901–76) French novelist, politician, and art critic

Mamet, David (born 1947) American dramatist and screenwriter

Mandelstam, Osip (Emilevich) (also Mandelshtam) (1891–1938) Russian poet

Mann, Thomas (1875–1955) German novelist and essayist

Manning, Olivia (Mary) (1908–80) English novelist

Mansfield, Katherine (pseudonym of Kathleen Mansfield Beauchamp) (1888–1923) New Zealand short-story writer

Manzoni, Alessandro (1785–1873) Italian novelist, dramatist, and poet

Marcuse, Herbert (1898–1979) German-born American philosopher

Mare, Walter de la See DE LA MARE

Marinetti, Filippo Tommaso (1876–1944) Italian poet and dramatist

Marlowe, Christopher (1564–93) English dramatist and poet

Márquez, Gabriel García See GARCÍA MÁRQUEZ

Marryat, Frederick (known as Captain Marryat) (1792–1848) English novelist

Marsh, Dame Ngaio (Edith) (1899–1982) New Zealand writer of detective fiction

Martial (Latin name Marcus Valerius Martialis) (AD c. 40–c. 104) Roman epigrammatist, born in Spain

Martineau, Harriet (1802–76) English writer

Marvell, Andrew (1621–78) English poet

Marx, Karl (Heinrich) (1818–83) German political philosopher and economist, resident in England from 1849

Masefield, John (Edward) (1878–1967) English poet and novelist

Mason, A(lfred) E(dward) W(oodley) (1865–1948) English novelist

Massinger, Philip (1583–1640) English dramatist

Matthew Paris See PARIS, MATTHEW

Maugham, (William) Somerset (1874–1965) British novelist, short-story writer, and dramatist

Maupassant, (Henri René Albert) Guy de (1850–93) French novelist and short-story writer

Mauriac, François (1885–1970) French novelist, dramatist, and critic

Mawlana See JALAL AD-DIN AR-RUMI

Mayakovsky, Vladimir (Vladimirovich) (1893–1930) Soviet poet and dramatist, born in Georgia

Meleager (fl. 1st century BC) Greek poet

Melville, Herman (1819–91) American novelist and short-story writer

Menander (c. 342–292 BC) Greek dramatist

Mencius (Latinized name of Meng-tzu or Mengzi, 'Meng the Master') (c. 371–c. 289 BC) Chinese philosopher

Mencken, H(enry) L(ouis) (1880–1956) American journalist and literary critic

Meng-tzu See MENCIUS

Mengzi See MENCIUS

Meredith, George (1828–1909) English novelist and poet

Middleton, Thomas (c. 1570–1627) English dramatist

Mill, John Stuart (1806–73) English philosopher and economist

Miller, Arthur (born 1915) American dramatist

Miller, Henry (Valentine) (1891–1980) American novelist

Millett, Katherine ('Kate') (born 1934) American feminist

Milne, A(lan) A(lexander) (1882–1956) English writer of stories and poems for children

Milton, John (1608–74) English poet

Mishima, Yukio (pseudonym of Hiraoka Kimitake) (1925–70) Japanese writer

Mitchell, Margaret (1900–49) American novelist

Mitford, Nancy (Freeman) (1904–73) and her sister **Jessica (Lucy)** (1917–96) English writers

Molière (pseudonym of Jean-Baptiste Poquelin) (1622–73) French dramatist

Mommsen, Theodor (1817–1903) German historian

Montaigne, Michel (Eyquem) de (1533–92) French essayist

Montesquieu, Baron de La Brède et de (title of Charles Louis de Secondat) (1689–1755) French political philosopher

Montessori, Maria (1870–1952) Italian educationist

Montgomery, Lucy Maud (1874–1942) Canadian novelist

Moore, George (Augustus) (1852–1933) Irish novelist

Moore, G(eorge) E(dward) (1873–1958) English philosopher

Moore, Thomas (1779–1852) Irish poet and musician

More, Sir Thomas (canonized as St Thomas More) (1478–1535) English scholar and statesman, Lord Chancellor 1529–32

Morrison, Toni (full name Chloe Anthony Morrison) (born 1931) American novelist

Muir, Edwin (1887–1959) Scottish poet and translator

Munro, H(ector) H(ugh) See SAKI

WRITERS, PHILOSOPHERS, AND SCHOLARS (cont.)

Murdoch, Dame (Jean) Iris (1919–99) British novelist and philosopher, born in Ireland

Murray, (George) Gilbert (Aimé) (1866–1957) Australian-born British classical scholar

Murray Les (full name Leslie Allen Murray) (born 1938) Australian poet

Musil, Robert (1880–1942) Austrian novelist

Nabokov, Vladimir (Vladimorovich) (1899–1977) Russian-born American novelist and poet

Nader, Ralph (born 1934) American lawyer and reformer

Naipaul, V(idiadhar) S(urajprasad) (born 1932) Trinidadian novelist and travel writer of Indian descent, resident in Britain since 1950

Narayan, R(asipuram) K(rishnaswamy) (1906–2001) Indian novelist and short-story writer

Nash, (Frederic) Ogden (1902–71) American poet

Nashe, Thomas (1567–1601) English pamphleteer, prose writer, and dramatist

Neill, A(lexander) S(utherland) (1883–1973) Scottish teacher and educationist

Nennius (*fl. c.* 800) Welsh chronicler

Neruda, Pablo (born Ricardo Eliezer Neftalí Reyes) (1904–73) Chilean poet and diplomat

Nesbit, E(dith) (1858–1924) English novelist

Newby, (George) Eric (born 1919) English travel writer

Nietzsche, Friedrich Wilhelm (1844–1900) German philosopher

Nin, Anaïs (1903–77) American writer

O'Brien, Edna (born 1932) Irish novelist and short-story writer

O'Brien, Flann (pseudonym of Brian O'Nolan) (1911–66) Irish novelist and journalist

O'Casey, Sean (1880–1964) Irish dramatist

Occam, William of See WILLIAM OF OCCAM

Ockham, William of See WILLIAM OF OCCAM

O'Connor, (Mary) Flannery (1925–64) American novelist and short-story writer

Odets, Clifford (1906–63) American dramatist

Omar Khayyám (died 1123) Persian poet, mathematician, and astronomer

Ondaatje, (Philip) Michael (born 1943) Canadian writer, born in Sri Lanka

O'Neill, Eugene (Gladstone) (1888–1953) American dramatist

Orczy, Baroness Emmusca (1865–1947) Hungarian-born British novelist

Ortega y Gasset, José (1883–1955) Spanish philosopher

Orton, Joe (born John Kingsley Orton) (1933–67) English dramatist

Orwell, George (pseudonym of Eric Arthur Blair) (1903–50) British novelist and essayist

Osborne, John (James) (1929–94) English dramatist

Otway, Thomas (1652–85) English dramatist

Ouida (pseudonym of Marie Louise de la Ramée) (1839–1908) English novelist

Overbury, Sir Thomas (1581–1613) English writer and courtier

Ovid (full name Publius Ovidius Naso) (43 BC–AD c 17) Roman poet

Owen, Wilfred (1893–1918) English poet

Paglia, Camille (Anna) (born 1947) American cultural critic

Pagnol, Marcel (1895–1974) French dramatist, film director, and writer

Paine, Thomas (1737–1809) English political writer

Palgrave, Francis Turner (1824–97) English critic and poet

Panini (lived some time between 7th and 4th centuries BC) Indian grammarian

Paris, Matthew (*c.* 1199–1259) English chronicler and Benedictine monk

Parker, Dorothy (Rothschild) (1893–1967) American humorist, literary critic, short-story writer, and poet

Parmenides (*fl.* 5th century BC) Greek philosopher

Pascal, Blaise (1623–62) French mathematician, physicist, and religious philosopher

Pasolini, Pier Paolo (1922–75) Italian film director, poet, and novelist

Passos, John Dos See DOS PASSOS

Pasternak, Boris (Leonidovich) (1890–1960) Russian poet, novelist, and translator

Pater, Walter (Horatio) (1839–94) English essayist and critic

Patmore, Coventry (Kersey Dighton) (1823–96) English poet

Paton, Alan (Stewart) (1903–88) South African writer and politician

Pausanias (2nd century) Greek geographer and historian

Pavese, Cesare (1908–50) Italian novelist, poet, and translator

Paz, Octavio (1914–98) Mexican poet and essayist

Peacock, Thomas Love (1785–1866) English novelist and poet

Peake, Mervyn (Laurence) (1911–68) British novelist, poet, and artist, born in China

Peirce, Charles Sanders (1839–1914) American philosopher and logician

WRITERS, PHILOSOPHERS, AND SCHOLARS (cont.)

Pepys, Samuel (1633–1703) English diarist and naval administrator

Perelman, S(idney) J(oseph) (1904–79) American humorist and writer

Perrault, Charles (1628–1703) French writer

Petrarch (Italian name Francesco Petrarca) (1304–74) Italian poet

Petronius Gaius (known as Petronius Arbiter) (died AD 66), Roman writer

Philo Judaeus (also known as Philo of Alexandria) (*c.* 15 BC–AD *c.* 50) Jewish philosopher of Alexandria

Pindar (*c.* 518–*c.* 438 BC) Greek lyric poet

Pinero, Sir Arthur Wing (1855–1934) English dramatist and actor

Pinter, Harold (born 1930) English dramatist, actor, and director

Pirandello, Luigi (1867–1936) Italian dramatist and novelist

Plath, Sylvia (1932–63) American poet

Plato (*c.* 429–*c.* 347 BC) Greek philosopher

Plautus, Titus Maccius (*c.* 250–184 BC) Roman comic dramatist

Pliny (known as Pliny the Younger; Latin name Gaius Plinius Caecilius Secundus) (*c.* 61–*c.* 112) Roman senator and writer

Plotinus (*c.* 205–70) Philosopher, probably of Roman descent, the founder and leading exponent of Neoplatonism

Plutarch (Latin name Lucius Mestrius Plutarchus) (*c.* 46–*c.* 120) Greek biographer and philosopher

Poe, Edgar Allan (1809–49) American short-story writer, poet, and critic

Polybius (*c.* 200–*c.* 118 BC) Greek historian

Ponte, Lorenzo Da See DA PONTE

Pope, Alexander (1688–1744) English poet

Popper, Sir Karl Raimund (1902–94) Austrian-born British philosopher

Porphyry (born Malchus) (*c.* 232–303) Neoplatonist philosopher

Porter, Katherine Anne (1890–1980) American short-story writer and novelist

Porter, Peter (Neville Frederick) (born 1929) Australian poet, resident chiefly in England since 1951

Potter, Dennis (Christopher George) (1935–94) English television dramatist

Potter, (Helen) Beatrix (1866–1943) English writer of children's stories

Pound, Ezra (Weston Loomis) (1885–1972) American poet and critic

Powell, Anthony (Dymoke) (born 1905) English novelist

Pratchett, Terry (born 1948) British novelist

Prévost d'Exiles, Antoine-François (known as Abbé Prévost) (1696–1763) French novelist

Priestley, J(ohn) B(oynton) (1894–1984) English novelist, dramatist, and critic

Pritchett, Sir V(ictor) S(awdon) (1900–97) English writer and critic

Procopius (*c.* 500–*c.* 562) Byzantine historian, born in Caesarea in Palestine

Propertius, Sextus (*c.* 50–*c.* 16 BC) Roman poet

Proudhon, Pierre Joseph (1809–65) French social philosopher and journalist

Proust, Marcel (1871–1922) French novelist, essayist, and critic

Pullman, Philip (born 1946) British novelist

Pushkin, Aleksandr (Sergeevich) (1799–1837) Russian poet, novelist, and dramatist

Pym, Barbara (Mary Crampton) (1913–80) English novelist

Pynchon, Thomas (Ruggles) (born 1937) American novelist

Pyrrho (*c.* 365–*c.* 270 BC) Greek philosopher

Pythagoras (known as Pythagoras of Samos) (*c.* 580–500 BC) Greek philosopher

Quasimodo, Salvatore (1901–68) Italian poet

Queen, Ellery (pseudonym of **Frederic Dannay**, 1905–82, and **Manfred Lee**, 1905–71) American writers of detective fiction

Quincey, Thomas De See DE QUINCEY

Quine, Willard Van Orman (born 1908) American philosopher and logician

Quintilian (Latin name Marcus Fabius Quintilianus) (AD *c.* 35–*c.* 96) Roman rhetorician

Rabelais, François (*c.* 1494–1553) French satirist

Racine, Jean (1639–99) French dramatist

Radcliffe, Mrs Ann (1764–1823) English novelist

Rand, Ayn (born Alissa Rosenbaum) (1905–82) American writer and philosopher, born in Russia

Ransom, John Crowe (1888–1974) American poet and critic

Ransome, Arthur (Michell) (1884–1967) English novelist

Rattigan, Sir Terence (Mervyn) (1911–77) English dramatist

Rawls, John (born 1921) American philosopher

Reade, Charles (1814–84) English novelist and dramatist

Remarque, Erich Maria (1898–1970) German-born American novelist

Renan, (Joseph) Ernest (1823–92) French historian, theologian, and philosopher

WRITERS, PHILOSOPHERS, AND SCHOLARS (cont.)

Renault, Mary (pseudonym of Mary Challans) (1905–83) British novelist, resident in South Africa from 1948

Rendell, Ruth (Barbara), Baroness (born 1930) English writer of detective fiction and thrillers

Reza, Yasmina (born 1960) French dramatist

Rhys, Jean (pseudonym of Ella Gwendolen Rees Williams) (1890–1979) British novelist and short-story writer, born in Dominica

Richards, I(vor) A(rmstrong) (1893–1979) English literary critic and poet

Richardson, Samuel (1689–1761) English novelist

Richler, Mordecai (born 1931) Canadian novelist

Rilke, Rainer Maria (pseudonym of René Karl Wilhelm Josef Maria Rilke) (1875–1926) Austrian poet, born in Bohemia

Rimbaud, (Jean Nicholas) Arthur (1854–91) French poet

Robbe-Grillet, Alain (born 1922) French novelist

Rochester, 2nd Earl of (title of John Wilmot) (1647–80) English poet and courtier

Roget, Peter Mark (1779–1869) English scholar

Rolland, Romain (1866–1944) French novelist, dramatist, and essayist

Rossetti, Christina (Georgina) (1830–94) English poet

Rossetti, Dante Gabriel (full name Gabriel Charles Dante Rossetti) (1828–82) English painter and poet

Rostand, Edmond (1868–1918) French dramatist and poet

Roth, Philip (Milton) (born 1933) American novelist and short-story writer

Rousseau, Jean-Jacques (1712–78) French philosopher and writer, born in Switzerland

Rowe, Nicholas (1674–1718) English dramatist

Rowling, J(oanne) K(athleen) (born 1965) British children's writer

Ruiz de Alarcón y Mendoza, Juan (1580–1639) Spanish dramatist, born in Mexico City

Runyon, (Alfred) Damon (1884–1946) American author and journalist

Rushdie, (Ahmed) Salman (born 1947) Indian-born British novelist

Russell, Bertrand (Arthur William), 3rd Earl Russell (1872–1970) British philosopher, mathematician, and social reformer

Russell, George William (known as AE) (1867–1935) Irish poet and writer

Ryle, Gilbert (1900–76) English philosopher

Saadi See SADI

Sachs, Hans (1494–1576) German poet and dramatist

Sackville-West, Victoria Mary ('Vita') (1892–1962) English novelist and poet

Sade, Donatien Alphonse François, Comte de (known as the Marquis de Sade) (1740–1814) French writer and soldier

Sadi (also Saadi) (born Sheikh Muslih Addin) (*c.* 1213–*c.* 1291) Persian poet

Sagan, Françoise (pseudonym of Françoise Quoirez) (born 1935) French novelist, dramatist, and short-story writer

Said, Edward W(adi) (born 1935) American critic and writer, born in Palestine

Sainte-Beuve, Charles Augustin (1804–69) French critic and writer

Saint-Exupéry, Antoine (Marie Roger de) (1900–44) French writer and aviator

Saint-Simon, Claude-Henri de Rouvroy, Comte de (1760–1825) French social reformer and philosopher

Saint-Simon, Louis de Rouvroy, Duc de (1675–1755) French writer

Saki (pseudonym of Hector Hugh Munro) (1870–1916) British short-story writer, born in Burma

Salinger, J(erome) D(avid) (born 1919) American novelist and short-story writer

Sallust (Latin name Gaius Sallustius Crispus) (86–35 BC) Roman historian and politician

Sand, George (pseudonym of Amandine-Aurore Lucille Dupin, Baronne Dudevant) (1804–76) French novelist

Santayana, George (born Jorge Augustin Nicolás Ruiz de Santayana) (1863–1952) Spanish philosopher and writer

Sappho (early 7th century BC) Greek lyric poet

Sartre, Jean-Paul (1905–80) French philosopher, novelist, dramatist, and critic

Sassoon, Siegfried (Lorraine) (1886–1967) English poet and writer

Saussure, Ferdinand de (1857–1913) Swiss linguistics scholar

Sayers, Dorothy L(eigh) (1893–1957) English novelist and dramatist

Scaliger, Joseph Justus (1540–1609) French scholar

Scaliger, Julius Caesar (1484–1558) Italian-born French classical scholar

Schiller, (Johann Christoph) Friedrich (von) (1759–1805) German dramatist, poet, and writer

Schlegel, August Wilhelm von (1767–1845) German poet, critic, and translator

Schopenhauer, Arthur (1788–1860) German philosopher

WRITERS, PHILOSOPHERS, AND SCHOLARS (cont.)

Schreiner, Olive (Emilie Albertina) (1855–1920) South African novelist

Schumacher, E(rnst) F(riedrich) (1911–77) German economist

Scott, Sir Walter (1771–1832) Scottish novelist and poet

Seneca, Lucius Annaeus (known as Seneca the Younger) (c. 4 BC–AD 65) Roman statesman, philosopher, and dramatist

Shaffer, Sir Peter (born 1926) British dramatist

Shakespeare, William (also known as 'the Bard (of Avon)') (1564–1616) English dramatist

Shaw, George Bernard (1856–1950) Irish dramatist and writer

Shelley, Mary (Wollstonecraft) (1797–1851) English writer, wife of Percy Bysshe Shelley

Shelley, Percy Bysshe (1792–1822) English poet

Sheridan, Richard Brinsley (1751–1816) Irish dramatist and Whig politician

Shute, Nevil (pseudonym of Nevil Shute Norway) (1899–1960) English novelist

Sidney, Sir Philip (1554–86) English poet and soldier

Sillitoe, Alan (born 1928) English writer

Simenon, Georges (Joseph Christian) (1903–89) Belgian-born French novelist

Simon, (Marvin) Neil (born 1927) American dramatist

Simonides (c. 556–468 BC) Greek lyric poet

Sinclair, Upton (Beall) (1878–1968) American novelist and social reformer

Singer, Isaac Bashevis (1904–91) Polish-born American novelist and short-story writer

Sitwell, Dame Edith (Louisa) (1887–1964) English poet

Skelton, John (c. 1460–1529) English poet

Smith, Adam (1723–90) Scottish economist and philosopher

Smith, Stevie (pseudonym of Florence Margaret Smith) (1902–71) English poet and novelist

Smith, Sydney (1771–1845) English Anglican churchman, essayist, and wit

Smollett, Tobias (George) (1721–71) Scottish novelist

Snorri Sturluson (1178–1241) Icelandic historian and poet

Snow, C(harles) P(ercy), 1st Baron Snow of Leicester (1905–80) English novelist and scientist

Socrates (469–399 BC) Greek philosopher

Solzhenitsyn, Alexander (Russian name Aleksandr Isaevich Solzhenitsyn) (born 1918) Russian novelist

Sontag, Susan (born 1933) American writer and critic

Sophocles (c. 496–406 BC) Greek dramatist

Southey, Robert (1774–1843) English poet and writer

Soyinka, Wole (born 1934) Nigerian dramatist, novelist, and critic

Spark, Dame Muriel (born 1918) Scottish novelist

Spencer, Herbert (1820–1903) English philosopher and sociologist

Spender, Sir Stephen (1909–95) English poet and critic

Spengler, Oswald (1880–1936) German philosopher

Spenser, Edmund (c. 1552–99) English poet

Spillane, Mickey (pseudonym of Frank Morrison Spillane) (born 1918) American writer

Spinoza, Baruch de (or Benedict) (1632–77) Dutch philosopher, of Portuguese Jewish descent

Staël, Mme de See DE STAËL

Statius, Publius Papinius (AD c. 45–96) Roman poet

Steele, Sir Richard (1672–1729) Irish essayist and dramatist

Stein, Gertrude (1874–1946) American writer

Steinbeck, John (Ernst) (1902–68) American novelist

Steiner, Rudolf (1861–1925) Austrian philosopher, founder of anthroposophy

Stendhal (pseudonym of Marie Henri Beyle) (1783–1842) French novelist

Sterne, Laurence (1713–68) Irish novelist

Stevens, Wallace (1879–1955) American poet

Stevenson, Robert Louis (Balfour) (1850–94) Scottish novelist, poet, and travel writer

Stoker, Abraham ('Bram') (1847–1912) Irish novelist and theatre manager

Stoppard, Sir Tom (born Thomas Straussler) (born 1937) British dramatist, born in Czechoslovakia

Stowe, Harriet (Elizabeth) Beecher (1811–96) American novelist

Strabo (c. 63 BC–AD c. 23) historian and geographer of Greek descent

Strachey, (Giles) Lytton (1880–1932) English biographer

Strindberg, (Johan) August (1849–1912) Swedish dramatist and novelist

Suckling, Sir John (1609–42) English poet, dramatist, and Royalist leader

Suetonius (full name Gaius Suetonius Tranquillus) (AD c. 69–c. 150) Roman biographer and historian

WRITERS, PHILOSOPHERS, AND SCHOLARS (cont.)

Surtees, Robert Smith (1805–64) English journalist and novelist

Suyin, Han (pseudonym of Elizabeth Comber) (born 1917) Chinese-born British writer and doctor

Swedenborg, Emanuel (1688–1772) Swedish scientist, philosopher, and mystic

Swift, Jonathan (known as Dean Swift) (1667–1745) Irish satirist, poet, and Anglican cleric

Swinburne, Algernon Charles (1837–1909) English poet and critic

Symons, Julian (Gustave) (1912–94) English writer of detective fiction

Synge, (Edmund) J(ohn) M(illington) (1871–1909) Irish dramatist

Tacitus (full name Publius, or Gaius, Cornelius Tacitus) (AD c. 56–c. 120) Roman historian

Tagore, Rabindranath (1861–1941) Indian writer and philosopher

Tannhäuser, (c. 1200–c. 1270) German poet

Tate, Nahum (1652–1715) Irish dramatist and poet, resident in London from the 1670s

Tennyson, Alfred, 1st Baron Tennyson of Aldworth and Freshwater (1809–92) English poet

Terence (Latin name Publius Terentius Afer) (c. 190–159 BC) Roman comic dramatist

Thackeray, William Makepeace (1811–63) British novelist, born in Calcutta

Thales (c. 624–c. 545 BC) Greek philosopher, mathematician, and astronomer, of Miletus

Theocritus (c. 310–c. 250 BC) Greek poet, born in Sicily

Thespis (6th century BC) Greek dramatic poet

Thomas, Dylan (Marlais) (1914–53) Welsh poet

Thomas, (Philip) Edward (1878–1917) English poet

Thomas, R(onald) S(tuart) (1913–2000) Welsh poet and clergyman

Thompson, Flora (Jane) (1876–1947) English writer

Thompson, Francis (1859–1907) English poet

Thomson, James (1700–48) Scottish poet

Thoreau, Henry David (1817–62) American essayist and poet

Thrale, Mrs Hester Lynch (latterly Hester Lynch Piozzi) (1741–1821) English writer

Thucydides (c. 455–c. 400 BC) Greek historian

Thurber, James (Grover) (1894–1961) American humorist and cartoonist

Tibullus, Albius (c. 50–19 BC) Roman poet

Tillich, Paul (Johannes) (1886–1965) German-born American theologian and philosopher

Tolkien, J(ohn) R(onald) R(euel) (1892–1973) British novelist and academic, born in South Africa

Tolstoy, Leo (Russian name Count Lev Nikolaevich Tolstoi) (1828–1910) Russian writer

Toynbee, Arnold (Joseph) (1889–1975) English historian

Traherne, Thomas (1637–74) English prose writer and poet

Trevor, William (pseudonym of William Trevor Cox) (born 1928) Irish novelist and short-story writer

Trollope, Anthony (1815–82) English novelist

Troyes, Chrétien de See CHRÉTIEN DE TROYES

Tu Fu (AD 712–70) Chinese poet

Tulsidas (c. 1543–1623) Indian poet

Turgenev, Ivan (Sergeevich) (1818–83) Russian novelist, dramatist, and short-story writer

Twain, Mark (pseudonym of Samuel Langhorne Clemens) (1835–1910) American novelist and humorist

Tzara, Tristan (born Samuel Rosenstock) (1896–1963) Romanian-born French poet

Ulpian (Latin name Domitius Ulpianus) (died c. 228), Roman jurist, born in Phoenicia

Updike, John (Hoyer) (born 1932) American novelist, poet, and short-story writer

Uttley, Alison (1884–1976) English writer

Valéry, (Ambroise) Paul (Toussaint Jules) (1871–1945) French poet, essayist, and critic

Vanbrugh, Sir John (1664–1726) English architect and dramatist

Van der Post, Sir Laurens (Jan) (1906–96) South African explorer and writer

Vargas Llosa, (Jorge) Mario (Pedro) (born 1936) Peruvian novelist, dramatist, and essayist

Varro, Marcus Terentius (116–27 BC) Roman scholar and satirist

Vaughan, Henry (1621–95) Welsh poet

Veblen, Thorstein (Bunde) (1857–1929) American economist and social scientist

Vega, Lope de (full name Lope Felix de Vega Carpio) (1562–1635) Spanish dramatist and poet

Velleius Paterculus (c. 19 BC–AD c. 30) Roman historian and soldier

Vergil See VIRGIL

Verlaine, Paul (1844–96) French poet

Verne, Jules (1828–1905) French novelist

Vicente, Gil (c. 1465–c. 1536) Portuguese dramatist and poet

Vico, Giambattista (1668–1744) Italian philosopher

Vidal, Gore (born Eugene Luther Vidal) (born 1925) American novelist, dramatist, and essayist

WRITERS, PHILOSOPHERS, AND SCHOLARS (cont.)

Vigny, Alfred Victor, Comte de (1797–1863) French poet, novelist, and dramatist

Villon, François (born François de Montcorbier or François des Loges) (1431–??1463) French poet

Vine, Barbara, pseudonym used by Ruth RENDELL

Virgil (also Vergil) (Latin name Publius Vergilius Maro) (70–19 BC) Roman poet

Voltaire (pseudonym of François-Marie Arouet) (1694–1778) French writer, dramatist, and poet

Vonnegut, Kurt (born 1922) American novelist and short-story writer

Wain, John (Barrington) (1925–94) English writer and critic

Walker, Alice (Malsenior) (born 1944) American writer and poet

Wallace, (Richard Horatio) Edgar (1875–1932) English novelist, short-story writer, and journalist

Walpole, Sir Hugh (Seymour) (1884–1941) British novelist

Walton, Izaak (1593–1683) English writer

Ward, Mrs Humphry (*née* Mary Augusta Arnold) (1851–1920) English writer and anti-suffrage campaigner

Warren, Robert Penn (1905–89) American poet, novelist, and critic

Watts, Isaac (1674–1748) English hymn-writer and poet

Waugh, Evelyn (Arthur St John) (1903–66) English novelist

Webb, (Gladys) Mary (1881–1927) English novelist

Webster, John (*c.* 1580–*c.* 1625) English dramatist

Wedekind, Frank (1864–1918) German dramatist

Weil, Simone (1909–43) French essayist, philosopher, and mystic

Wells, H(erbert) G(eorge) (1866–1946) English novelist

Welsh, Irvine (born 1959) Scottish novelist

Welty, Eudora (born 1909) American novelist, short-story writer, and critic

Wesker, Arnold (born 1932) English dramatist

West, Dame Rebecca (born Cicily Isabel Fairfield) (1892–1983) British writer, born in Ireland

Wharton, Edith (Newbold) (1862–1937) American novelist and short-story writer, resident in France from 1907

White, Patrick (Victor Martindale) (1912–90) Australian novelist, born in Britain

White, T(erence) H(anbury) (1906–64) British novelist, born in India

Whitehead, A(lfred) N(orth) (1861–1947) English philosopher and mathematician

Whitman, Walt (1819–92) American poet

Whittier, John Greenleaf (1807–92) American poet and abolitionist

Wiesel, Elie (full name Eliezer Wiesel) (born 1928) Romanian-born American human-rights campaigner, novelist, and academic

Wilcox, Ella Wheeler (1850–1919) American poet, novelist, and short-story writer

Wilde, Oscar (Fingal O'Flahertie Wills) (1854–1900) Irish dramatist, novelist, poet, and wit

Wilder, Thornton (Niven) (1897–1975) American novelist and dramatist

William of Occam (also Ockham) (*c.* 1285–1349) English philosopher and Franciscan friar

Williams, Tennessee (born Thomas Lanier Williams) (1911–83) American dramatist

Williams, William Carlos (1883–1963) American poet, essayist, novelist, and short-story writer

Williamson, Henry (1895–1977) English novelist and wildlife writer

Wilson, Sir Angus (Frank Johnstone) (1913–91) English novelist and short-story writer

Wilson, Edmund (1895–1972) American critic, essayist, and short-story writer

Wittgenstein, Ludwig (Josef Johann) (1889–1951) Austrian-born philosopher

Wodehouse, Sir P(elham) G(renville) (1881–1975) British-born writer

Wolfe, Thomas (Clayton) (1900–38) American novelist

Wolfe, Tom (full name Thomas Kennerley Wolfe Jr) (born 1931) American writer

Wollstonecraft, Mary (1759–97) English writer and feminist, of Irish descent

Wood, Mrs Henry (née Ellen Price) (1814–87) English novelist

Woolf, (Adeline) Virginia (née Stephen) (1882–1941) English novelist, essayist, and critic

Wordsworth, Dorothy (1771–1855) English diarist, sister of William Wordsworth

Wordsworth, William (1770–1850) English poet

Wren, P(ercival) C(hristopher) (1885–1941) English novelist

Wyatt, Sir Thomas (1503–42) English poet

Wycherley, William (*c.* 1640–1716) English dramatist

Wyndham, John (pseudonym of John Wyndham Parkes Lucas Beynon Harris) (1903–69) English writer of science fiction

WRITERS, PHILOSOPHERS, AND SCHOLARS (cont.)

Xenophanes (*c.* 570–*c.* 480 BC) Greek philosopher

Xenophon (*c.* 435–*c.* 354 BC) Greek historian, writer, and military leader

Yeats, W(illiam) B(utler) (1865–1939) Irish poet and dramatist

Yevtushenko, Yevgeni (Aleksandrovich) (born 1933) Russian poet

Yourcenar, Marguerite (pseudonym of Marguerite de Crayencoeur) (1903–87) French writer

Zeno (known as Zeno of Elea) (*fl.* 5th century BC) Greek philosopher

Zeno (known as Zeno of Citium) (*c.* 335–*c.* 263 BC) Greek philosopher, founder of Stoicism

Zola, Émile (Édouard Charles Antoine) (1840–1902) French novelist and critic

SPORT AND GAMES

SPORTS AND SPORTING ACTIVITIES

aeroball
aerobatics
aikido
airgun shooting
air racing
Alpine climbing
Alpine combined event
Alpine skiing
American football *or* gridiron
angling
archery
association football *or* soccer
asymmetric bars
athletics
Australian rules football
autocross
badminton
ballooning
bandy
baseball
basketball
beagling
beam
bear baiting
biathlon
big-game fishing
blood sports
bobsleigh racing
bouldering
boules *or* boccie
bowling
boxing
bullfighting
bunji jumping
caber tossing
Canadian 5-pin bowling
Canadian canoe racing
Canadian football
canoeing
canoe polo
canoe sailing
canoe slalom racing
canoe sprint racing
carom billiards
caving
clay pigeon shooting
climbing
coarse fishing
cock fighting
coursing
court handball
cricket

croquet
cross bow archery
cross-country skiing *or*
   Nordic skiing
crown-green bowls
curling
cycle racing
darts
darts cricket
darts football
decathlon
deerstalking
discus
diving
downhill racing
down-the-line shooting
drag racing
dressage
English billiards
equestrianism
Eton wall game
falconry
fell running
fencing
ferreting
field archery
field events
field hockey
figure skating
flat-green bowls
flat racing
floor exercises
fly-fishing
football
fox hunting
freefall
free pistol shooting
freestyle skiing
French cricket
Gaelic football
game fishing
giant slalom
gliding
golf
greyhound racing
grouse shooting
gymkhana
gymnastics
hammer
handball
hang-gliding
haphido

harness horseracing
heptathlon
high bar *or* horizontal bar
high jump
hiking
hillwalking
horizontal bar *or* high bar
horseracing
horseshoe pitching
hurdles
hurling
ice climbing
ice-dancing
ice hockey
jai alai *or* pelota
javelin
jet skiing
judo
jujitsu
kabaddi
karate
karting
kayaking
kendo
kenipo
kick boxing
kiting
korfball
kung fu
lacrosse
langlauf
laser sailing
lawn tennis
long-distance running
long jump
luge
marathon
martial arts
match fishing
middle-distance running
mink hunting
modern pentathlon
moto-cross
motorcycle racing
motor racing
mountain biking
mountaineering
mountain running
netball
Nordic combined event
Nordic skiing *or* cross-
   country skiing

SPORTS AND SPORTING ACTIVITIES (cont.)

off-piste skiing
offshore yacht racing
Olympic French shooting
orienteering
otter hunting
parachuting
paragliding
parallel bars
parascending
pato
pelota *or* jai alai
petanque
pheasant shooting
pigeon racing
pigeon shooting
ping-pong *or* table tennis
pistol shooting
point-to-point
pole vault
polo
pommel horse
pool
potholing
powerboat racing
puissance
racquetball
rally cross
rambling
rapid-fire pistol shooting
relay racing
rhythmic gymnastics
rifle shooting
rings
rock climbing
rodeo
roller blading
roller derby
roller hockey
roller hockey
roller skating
roller skiing
rough shooting

rounders
rowing
rugby fives
rugby league
rugby union
running game target
  shooting
sailplaning
scrambling
scuba diving
sculling
sea fishing
sepak takrow
sharpshooting
shinty
shooting
short board sailing
short tennis
short-track speed skating
shot put
showjumping
sidecar racing
skateboarding
skeet shooting
skibob racing
ski-jumping
ski-mountaineering
skittles
skydiving
slalom
sled-dog racing
snooker
snorkelling
snowboarding
soccer *or* association football
softball
speedball
speed-skating
speedway
spelunking
sports aerobics
sprint

squash *or* squash rackets
steeplechase
stock-car racing
stoolball
super-G
surfing
swimming
synchronized swimming
table tennis *or* ping-pong
tae kwon do
tang soo do
target archery
team handball
tennis
tenpin bowling
Thai boxing
three-day event
tobogganing
track events
trampolining
trapshooting
triathlon
triple jump
trotting
tug of war
tumbling
underwater diving
vault
volleyball
volleyball
walking
water polo
water sports
weightlifting
white water rafting
wildfowling
wild water racing
windsurfing
winter sports
wrestling
yacht racing

SPORTING TERMS

abseil
ace
advantage
albatross
alley
arabesque
arena
away
back crawl
backhand

back heel
back pass
backstroke
batsman
batter
belay
bell
birdie
blade
blitz

block
bogey
bowler
breaststroke
bully off
bunker
butterfly
by-ball
bye
by-line

cannon
cartwheel
catcher
centre back
centre fielder
centre forward
centre half
chequered flag
chicane
coach

conversion
corner
count
course
court
cover point
cox
crawl
cross bar
cue

SPORTING TERMS (cont.)

curl
dead ball
dead heat
defence
deuce
dive
division
doubles
draw
dribble
drive
drop ball
drop goal
drop kick
drop shot
dummy
dunk
eagle
end
end zone
en rappel
épée
extra cover
extra time
fairway
false start
fault
feint
fielder
field goal
final
flanker back
flick
foil
follow-through
forehand
forward pass
Fosbury flop
foul
frame
free ball
free hit
free kick
freestyle
front crawl
fullback
full time

fumble
give and go
goal
goal attack
goal defence
goal difference
goalkeeper
goal kick
goal line
goal post(s)
goal shooter
golden goal
halfback
half-time
half volley
handball
handicap
hat trick
heat
high feet
high tackle
home goal
home leg
home run
home straight
infielder
injury time
inside left
inside right
karabiner
kickoff
kiss shot
knockout or k.o.
lap
left back
left centre-back
left defenseman
left fielder
left forward
left half
left hook
left wing
left wing-back
let
linebacker
line-out
linesman

links
lob
man-to-man
  marking
midfield
miscue
nominated ball
nose guard
obstruction
offence
offside
offside trap
onside
on the ropes
out
outfielder
outside left
outside right
overhead kick
own goal or o.g.
pacemaker or
  pacer
par
parry
pass
peel off
penalty
penalty corner
penalty flick
penalty kick
penalty shoot-
  out
penalty spot
photo finish
piste
pitcher
pit lane
piton
pit stop
pivot
place kick
playoff
pocket
pole position
possession
post
pot

promotion
prusiking
puck
push
put-in
putt
qualify
quarter
quarterback
quarterfinal
race
racket
rally
rank(ing)
rappel
raquet
referee
regatta
relegation
replay
reserves
return game
right back
right centre-
  back
right
  defenseman
right fielder
right forward
right half
right hook
right wing
right wing-back
ruck
running back
sabre
save
scissors kick
scoop
scrum
scrum half
scrummage
scull
seed
serve
short corner
shortstop

shuttlecock or
  shuttle
sidestroke
silver
slalom
slam dunk
slip-streaming
somersault
spar
speech play
split end
springboard
sprint
stanchion
stand-off half
starting blocks
starting pistol
stoppage time
striker
stroke
substitute
sudden death
sweeper
tackle
tailback
tee off
three quarter
through-ball
throw-in
tight end
time-out
toe-poke
touchdown
touching ball
touchline
try
tuck
uppercut
volley
wide receiver
wildcard
wing
wing attack
wing back
wing defence
wing forward
zonal defence

ATHLETIC EVENTS

biathlon
cross-country run
decathlon
discus
fell run
half-marathon
hammer throw
heptathlon
high jump
110m hurdles
400m hurdles
hurdling
javelin
long-distance race
long jump
marathon
middle-distance race
modern pentathlon
pole vault
50m race
100m race
200m race
400m race
800m race
1,500m race
1-mile race

5,000m race
10,000m race
relay
400m relay
1,600m relay
shotput
sprint
steeplechase
3,000m steeplechase
tetrathlon
tossing the caber
triathlon
triple jump
tug-of-war
20km walk
50km walk
women's 80m
  hurdles
women's 100m
  hurdles
women's 200m
  hurdles
women's 3,000m
  race

GYMNASTIC EVENTS

asymmetric bars
beam
floor exercises
high bar
horse vault
parallel bars
pommel horse
rhythmic gymnastics
rings
side horse vault
sports aerobics
trampolining
tumbling

TROPHIES, AWARDS, AND EVENTS
(with sport)

Admiral's Cup	sailing	European Champions' Cup	football,
African Nations Cup	football		basketball
Air Canada Silver Broom	curling	European Championships	football
All-England (Wimbledon)		European Cup-Winners' Cup	football
Championships	tennis	European Super Cup	football
All-Ireland Championship	Gaelic football,	Federation Cup	tennis
	hurling	FA (Football Association)	
Alpine Championships	skiing	Challenge Cup	football
America's Cup	sailing	FA Charity Shield	football
Ashes	cricket	FIFA (International	
Australian Open	tennis	Federation of Association	
Badminton Horse Trials	equestrian	Football) World Cup	football
Boat Race	rowing	Five Nations' Championship	rugby
British Open Championship	golf, snooker	Football League	
Camanachd Association		Championship	football
Challenge Cup	shinty	Football League Cup	football
Cambridge Blue		Formula One Drivers' World	
Cheltenham Gold Cup	horse racing	Championship	motor racing
Classics	horse racing	French Open	tennis
Coca Cola (League) Cup	football	Full Cap	football, rugby
Commonwealth Games	athletics	Gillette Cup	cricket
Cornhill Test	cricket	Golden Boot Award	football
Davis Cup	tennis	Gorden International Medal	curling
Daytona 500	motor racing	Grand National	greyhound
Derby	horse racing		racing
English Greyhound Derby	greyhound	Grand National Steeplechase	horse racing
	racing	Grand Prix	motor racing

TROPHIES, AWARDS, AND EVENTS (cont.)
(with sport)

Grand Slam	tennis
Guinness Trophy	tiddlywinks
Harmsworth Trophy	powerboat racing
Henley Royal Regatta	rowing
Highland Games	
IBF (International Boxing Federation) Championships	boxing
Icy Smith Cup	ice hockey
Indianapolis 500 or Indy 500	motor racing
International Championship	bowls
International Cross-country Championship	athletics
International Inter-city Industrial Fairs Cup	football
Iroquois Cup	lacrosse
Isle of Man TT	motorcycle racing
Jules Rimet Trophy	football
King George V Gold Cup	equestrian
Kinnaird Cup	fives
Le Mans 24-Hour Race	motor racing
Lombard Rally	motor racing
Lonsdale Belt	boxing
Macrobertson International Shield	croquet
Man of the Match	cricket, football
Marathon	athletics
Middlesex Sevens	rugby union
Milk Race	cycling
Monte Carlo Rally	motor racing
Most Valuable Player	American football, basketball
National Coarse Championship	angling
National Hunt Jockey Championship	horse racing
National Westminster Bank Trophy	cricket
Nordic Championships	skiing
Oaks	horse racing
Olympic Games	
One Thousand Guineas	horse racing
Open Croquet Championship	croquet
Oxford Blue	
Palio	horse racing
PFA (Professional Footballers' Association) Footballer of the year	football
PFA Manager of the Year	football
Premier League Championship	football

Prudential World Cup	cricket
Queen Elizabeth II Cup	equestrian
RAC Tourist Trophy	motor racing
Rose Bowl	American football
Royal Hunt Cup	horse racing
Rugby League Challenge Cup	rugby league
St Leger	horse racing
SFA (Scottish Football Association) Cup	football
South American Championship	football
Stanley Cup	ice hockey
Strathcona Cup	curling
Sudirman Cup	badminton
Superbowl	American football
Super Cup	handball
Swaythling Cup	table tennis
Test Series	cricket, rugby union
Tour de France	cycling
Triple Crown	rugby union
Two Thousand Guineas	horse racing
Uber Cup	badminton
UEFA (Union of European Football Associations) Cup	football
Uniroyal World Junior Championships	curling
US Masters	golf
US Open	tennis, golf
US PGA (Professional Golf Association) Championships	golf
Walker Cup	golf
Wightman Cup	sailing
Wimbledon	tennis
Wingfield Skulls	rowing
World Bowl	American football
World Championship	snooker
WBA (World Boxing Association) Championships	boxing
WBC (World Boxing Council) Championships	boxing
World Club Championship	football
World Cup	football
World Masters Championships	darts
World Series	baseball
Yellow Jersey	cycling

STADIUMS AND VENUES
(with main sporting event)

Aintree	horse racing
Anaheim Stadium, California	baseball
Anfield, Liverpool	football
Ascot	horse racing
Azteca Stadium, Mexico City	Olympics, football
Belfry, The	golf
Belmont Park, Long Island	horse racing
Bernabau Stadium, Madrid	football
Big Four Curling Rink	curling
Brands Hatch	motor racing
Brooklands	motor racing
Caesar's Palace, Las Vegas	boxing
Cardiff Arms Park	rugby union
Celtic Park, Glasgow	football
Central Stadium, Kiev	football
Cleveland Municipal Stadium	baseball
Corporation Stadium, Calicur	cricket
Croke Park, Dublin	Gaelic football, hurling
Crucibal, Sheffield	snooker
Crystal Palace	athletics
Daytona International Speedway	motor racing, motor cycling
Eden Gardens, Calcutta	cricket
Edgbaston	cricket
Epsom Downs	horse racing
Forum, The	gymnastics
Francorchamps, Belgium	motor racing
Goodison Park, Liverpool	football
Hampden Park, Glasgow	football
Headingley	cricket
Heysel Stadium, Brussels	football
Highbury, London	football
Hillsborough, Sheffield	football
Ibrox, Glasgow	football
Lahore	cricket
Landsdowne Road, Dublin	rugby union
Lenin Stadium, Moscow	football
Lords Cricket Ground	cricket
Louisiana Superdome	most sports
Maracana Stadium, Brazil	football
Meadowbank	athletics
Memorial Coliseum, Los Angeles	most sports
Moor Park, Rickmansworth	golf
Munich Olympic Stadium	athletics, football
Murrayfield	rugby union
Newlands, Cape Town	cricket, rugby union
Newmarket	horse racing
Nou Camp, Barcelona	football
Odsal Stadium, Bradford	rugby league
Old Trafford, Manchester	cricket, football
Olympic Stadium, Berlin	athletics, football
Oval, The	cricket
Royal and Ancient Golf Club of St Andrews	golf
San Siro, Milan	football
Senayan Main Stadium, Jakarta	cricket
Shanghai Stadium	gymnastics
Silverstone	motor racing
Stahov Stadium, Prague	gymnastics
Texas Stadium	most sports
Twickenham	rugby union
Villa Park, Birmingham	football
Wembley Conference Centre	darts
Wembley Stadium	football, rugby
White City	greyhound racing
White Hart Lane, London	football
Wimbledon	tennis
Windsor Park, Belfast	football

UK FOOTBALL CLUBS

Aberdeen	Birmingham City	Burnley	Colchester United
Airdrieonians	Blackburn Rovers	Bury	Coventry City
Albion Rovers	Blackpool	Cambridge United	Cowdenbeath
Aldershot	Bolton Wanderers	Cardiff City	Crewe Alexandra
Alloa	Bournemouth	Carlisle United	Crusaders
Arbroath	Bradford City	Celtic	Crystal Palace
Ards	Brechin City	Charlton Athletic	Darlington
Arsenal	Brentford	Chelsea	Derby County
Aston Villa	Brighton & Hove Albion	Chester City	Doncaster Rovers
Ayr United	Bristol City	Chesterfield	Dumbarton
Barnsley	Bristol Rovers	Clyde	Dundee
Berwick Rangers		Clydebank	Dundee United

UK FOOTBALL CLUBS (cont.)

Dunfermline Athletic
East Fife
East Stirlingshire
Everton
Exeter City
Falkirk
Forfar Athletic
Fulham
Gillingham
Glenavon
Glentoran
Grimsby Town
Halifax Town
Hamilton
  Academical
Hartlepool United
Heart of Midlothian
Hereford United
Hibernian
Huddersfield Town
Hull City
Ipswich Town
Kilmarnock
Larne

Leeds United
Leicester City
Leyton Orient
Lincoln City
Linfield
Liverpool
Luton Town
Manchester City
Manchester United
Mansfield Town
Meadowbank Thistle
Middlesbrough
Millwall
Montrose
Morton
Motherwell
Newcastle United
Northampton Town
Norwich City
Nottingham Forest
Notts County
Oldham Athletic
Oxford United
Partick Thistle

Peterborough United
Plymouth Argyle
Portsmouth
Port Vale
Preston North End
Queen of the South
Queen's Park
Queen's Park
  Rangers
Raith Rovers
Rangers
Reading
Rochdale
Rotherham United
Scarborough
Scunthorpe United
Sheffield United
Sheffield
  Wednesday
Shrewsbury Town
Southampton
Southend United
Stenhousemuir
Stirling Albion

St Johnstone
St Mirren
Stockport County
Stoke City
Stranraer
Sunderland
Swansea City
Swindon Town
Torquay United
Tottenham Hotspur
  or Spurs
Tranmere Rovers
Walsall
Watford
West Bromwich
  Albion
West Ham United
Wigan Athletic
Wimbledon
Wolverhampton
  Wanderers or
  Wolves
Wrexham
York City

EUROPEAN FOOTBALL CLUBS
(with country)

AC Milan	Italy	CSKA Moscow	Russia
AEK Athens	Greece	Duisburg	Germany
AIK Stockholm	Sweden	Dynamo Kiev	Ukraine
Ajax	The Netherlands	Ekeren	Belgium
Amadora	Portugal	Español	Spain
Anderlecht	Belgium	Farense	Portugal
AS Roma	Italy	FC Bruges	Belgium
Atalanta	Italy	FC Volendam	The Netherlands
Atlético de Bilbao	Spain	Feyenoord	The Netherlands
Atlético de Madrid	Spain	Fiorentina	Italy
Auxerre	France	Fortuna Sittard	The Netherlands
Barcelona	Spain	Galatasaray	Turkey
Bastia	France	Hajouk Split	Croatia
Bayer Leverkusen	Germany	Hamburg	Germany
Bayern Munich	Germany	Hansa Rostock	Germany
Benfica	Portugal	IFK Gothenburg	Sweden
Boavista	Portugal	Inter Milan	Italy
Bologna	Italy	Internazionale	Italy
Bordeaux	France	JC Kerkrade	The Netherlands
Borussia Dortmund	Germany	Juventus	Italy
Borussia		Karlsruhe	Germany
Mönchengladbach	Germany	Lazio	Italy
Braga	Portugal	Legia Warsaw	Poland
Brann Bergen	Germany	Le Havre	France
Brondby	Denmark	Lille	France
Cagliari	Italy	Lyons	France
Cologne	Germany	Marseilles	France

EUROPEAN FOOTBALL CLUBS (cont.)
(with country)

Metz	France	Royal Antwerp	Belgium
Monaco	France	Salzburg	Austria
Montpellier	France	Sampdoria	Italy
Munich	Germany	Setubal	Portugal
Nantes	France	Sevilla	Spain
Napoli	Italy	Slavia Prague	Czech Republic
Nice	France	Spartak Moscow	Russia
Olympiakos	Germany	Sparta Prague	Czech Republic
Panathinaikos	Germany	Sporting Gijón	Spain
Paris Saint Germain	France	Sporting Lisbon	Portugal
Parma	Italy	Standard Liège	Belgium
Perugia	Italy	Steaua Bucharest	Romania
Piacenza	Italy	Strasbourg	France
Porto	Portugal	Tilburg	The Netherlands
PSV Eindhoven	The Netherlands	Utrecht	The Netherlands
Racing Santander	Spain	Valencia	Spain
Rapid Vienna	Austria	Verona	Italy
Real Madrid	Spain	VFB Stuttgart	Germany
Real Sociedad	Spain	Vicenza	Italy
Real Zaragoza	Spain	Vitesse Arnhem	The Netherlands
RKC Waalwijk	The Netherlands	Werder Bremen	Germany

AMERICAN FOOTBALL TEAMS

Atlanta Falcons	Indianapolis Colts	New York Jets
Buffalo Bills	Kansas City Chiefs	Philadelphia Eagles
Chicago Bears	Los Angeles Raiders	Phoenix Cardinals
Cleveland Browns	Los Angeles Rams	Pittsburgh Steelers
Dallas Cowboys	Miami Dolphins	San Diego Chargers
Denver Broncos	Minnesota Vikings	San Francisco 49ers
Detroit Lions	New England Patriots	Seattle Seahawks
Green Bay Packers	New Orleans Saints	Tampa Bay Buccaneers
Houston Oilers	New York Giants	Washington Redskins

BASEBALL TEAMS

Atlanta Braves	Detroit Tigers	Philadelphia Phillies
Baltimore Orioles	Kansas City Royals	Pittsburgh Pirates
Boston Red Sox	Los Angeles Dodgers	St Louis Browns
Brooklyn Dodgers	Milwaukee Braves	St Louis Cardinals
California Angels	Minnesota Twins	San Francisco Giants
Chicago Cubs	New York Giants	Texas Rangers
Chicago White Sox	New York Mets	Toronto Blue Jays
Cincinnati Reds	New York Yankees	Washington Senators
Cleveland Indians	Oakland Athletics	

CRICKETING TERMS AND EXPRESSIONS

all-rounder
bail
batsman *or*
  batswoman
beamer
body-line
bosie
bouncer
boundary
bowler
bye
century
chinaman
cover
cow-shot
crease
cut
daisy-cutter
deep square leg
duck
fielder
fine leg

flipper
googly
golden duck
gully
hat-trick
hit wicket
hook
how's that! *or*
  howzat!
innings
in-swinger
late cut
leg before wicket
  (l.b.w.)
leg bye
leg glance
leg-side fielder
leg slip
leg spin
leg-theory bowling
long hop
long leg

long off
long on
longstop
maiden
mid-off
mid-on
mid-wicket
no-ball
non-striker
offside fielder
off spin
out-swinger
over
overthrow
reverse sweep
reverse swing
run
scorer
seamer
shooter
short leg
sight-screen

silly mid-off
silly mid-on
silly point
slips
Snickometer™
square cut
square leg
sticky dog
sticky wicket
stonewalling
striker
stumped
sweep
test match
third man
ton
top-spinner
twelfth man
umpire
wicket
wicketkeeper
yorker

GOLFING TERMS

ace
addressing the ball
albatross
backswing
baff
birdie
bisque
blaster
bogey
brassie
bunker
bye
caddie
dead ball

divot
dog-leg hole
dormy
downswing
driver
driving iron
dubbed shot
eagle
fairway
flagstick
follow-through
fore!
forecaddie
green

handicap
hanging ball
hole-high ball
hole in one
iron
lofted shot
mashie iron
midiron
niblick
nineteenth hole
par
pin
pitch and putt
putter

recovery shot
rough
rub of the green
sand shot
sclaff
spot putting
tee
tee off
trap
upswing
water hazard
wedge
wood shot

FENCING TERMS

blade
corps à corps
counterattack
counter-riposte
coupé
cutover
electrical foil

en garde *or* on guard
épée
feint
flèche
foil
foil button
foil grip

foil guard
guard
lunge
mask
parry
piste
remise

riposte
running attack
sabre
supination
touch
touché

GAMES

Aunt Sally
bagatelle
beetle
bingo
blind man's buff
bumble-puppy
catch
cat's cradle
charades
Chinese whispers
conkers
consequences
cowboys and Indians
crambo
craps
curling
darts
diabolo
dominoes
ducks and drakes
dumb crambo

fan-tan
fivestones
follow-my-leader
forfeits
fox and geese
grandmother's
    footsteps
hangman
hazard
hide-and-seek
hoopla
hopscotch
hunt the slipper
hunt the thimble
I spy
it
jacks
jackstraws
jukskei
keno
kickean

leapfrog
liar dice
lotto
mah-jong
marbles
murder in the dark
musical chairs
nim
noughts and crosses
pachinko
paintball
pall-mall
pass the parcel
piggy
pig in the middle
pinball
pin the tail on the
    donkey
pitch-and-toss
poker dice
postman's knock

prison base
quoits
roulette
sardines
shove-halfpenny
shovelboard
Simon Says
spillikins
spin the bottle
swy
tag
taw
tick-tack-toe
tiddlywinks
tig
tipcat
trap-ball
twenty questions
two-up

BOARD GAMES

backgammon
checkers *Am.*
chess
Chinese chequers
Chinese chess
Cluedo™
draughts
fox and geese

go
gobang
goose
halma
kono
ludo
mancala
merrill

Monopoly™
pachisi
peggotty
Pictionary™
race game
Risk™
salta
Scrabble™

shogi
snakes and ladders
solitaire
steeplechase
Trivial Pursuit™
uckers
wari
wei ch'i

COMPUTER GAMES
(mostly tradenames)

Adventure
Asteroids
Donkey Kong
Doom
Flight Simulator

Freecell
Myst
Odyssey
Pac-Man
Pong

Quake
Sim City
Sonic the Hedgehog
Space Invaders
Spacewar

Super Mario
    Brothers
Tetris
Tomb Raider
Worms

CARD GAMES

all fours	chemin de fer	lansquenet	pitch	slapjack
auction bridge	cinch	loo	poker	snap
baccarat	coon-can	lottery	pontoon	snip-snap-
banker	comet	matrimony	Pope Joan	snorum
basset	cribbage	Michigan	primero	solitaire *Am.*
beggar-my-	Dom Pedro	monte	quadrille	speculation
neighbour	duplicate bridge	muggins	quinze	spite and
belote	écarté	nap	red dog	malice
bezique	euchre	Newmarket	reverse	strip Jack naked
blackjack	fan-tan	noddy	rouge et noir	thirty-one
Black Maria	faro	old maid	rubber bridge	three-card
blind poker	five hundred	ombre	ruff	monte
Boston	forty-five	Pam	rummy	tredrille
brag	gleek	panguingue	Russian Bank	twenty-five
bridge	happy families	patience	Sancho Pedro	vingt-et-un
California jack	hearts	pedro	scopa	vint
canasta	high-low	Pelmanism	seven-up	whipperginny
Canfield	imperial	penny ante	sixty-six	whist
cassino	klaberjass	pinochle	skat	
cheat	Klondike	piquet	skin	

SPORTSPEOPLE

Abrahams, Harold (Maurice) (1899–1978) English athlete

Agassi, André (born 1970) American tennis player

Agostini, Giacomo (born 1944) Italian racing motorcyclist

Alekhine, Alexander (born Aleksandr Aleksandrovich Alyokhin) (1892–1946) Russian-born French chess player

Ali, Muhammad See MUHAMMAD ALI

Andretti, Mario (Gabriele) (born 1940) Italian-born American motor-racing driver

Ashe, Arthur (Robert) (1943–93) American tennis player

Atherton, Michael Andrew (born 1968) English cricketer

Ballesteros, Severiano ('Sevvy') (born 1957) Spanish golfer

Banks, Gordon (born 1937) English footballer

Bannister, Sir Roger (Gilbert) (born 1929) British middle-distance runner and neurologist

Beamon, Robert ('Bob') (born 1946) American athlete

Beckenbauer, Franz (born 1945) German footballer and manager

Becker, Boris (born 1967) German tennis player

Beckham, David (born 1975) English footballer

Berra, Yogi (born Lawrence Peter Berra) (born 1925) American baseball player

Best, George (born 1946) Northern Irish footballer

Border, Allan (Robert) (born 1955) Australian cricketer

Borg, Björn (Rune) (born 1956) Swedish tennis player

Bosanquet, Bernard James Tindall (1877–1936) English all-round cricketer

Botham, Ian (Terence) (born 1955) English all-round cricketer

Boycott, Geoffrey (born 1940) English cricketer

Brabham, Sir John Arthur ('Jack') (born 1926) Australian motor-racing driver

Bradman, Sir Donald George ('Don') (1908–2001) Australian cricketer

Bruno, Frank(lin Ray) (born 1961) English boxer

Budge, John Donald ('Don') (1915–2000) American tennis player

Busby, Sir Matt(hew) (1909–94) Scottish-born footballer and football manager

Campbell, Donald (Malcolm) (1921–67) English motor-racing driver and holder of world speed records, son of Sir Malcolm Campbell

Campbell, Sir Malcolm (1885–1948) English motor-racing driver and holder of world speed records

SPORTSPEOPLE (cont.)

Cantona, Eric (born 1966) French footballer

Capablanca, José Raúl (1888–1942) Cuban chess player

Carling, Will(iam David Charles) (born 1965) English Rugby Union player

Carson, William Hunter Fisher ('Willie') (born 1942) Scottish jockey

Cawley, Evonne (Fay) (née Goolagong) (born 1951) Australian tennis player

Chappell, Gregory Stephen ('Greg') (born 1948) Australian cricketer

Charlton, John ('Jack') (born 1935) English footballer and manager, brother of Bobby Charlton

Charlton, Sir Robert ('Bobby') (born 1937) English footballer, brother of Jack Charlton

Chichester, Sir Francis (Charles) (1901–72) English yachtsman

Christie, Linford (born 1960) Jamaican-born British sprinter

Clay, Cassius See MUHAMMAD ALI

Coe, Sebastian (born 1956) British middle-distance runner and Conservative politician

Comaneci, Nadia (born 1961) Romanian-born American gymnast

Compton, Denis (Charles Scott) (1918–97) English cricketer

Connolly, Maureen Catherine (known as 'Little Mo') (1934–69) American tennis player

Connors, James Scott ('Jimmy') (born 1952) American tennis player

Cooper, Sir Henry (born 1934) English boxer

Cowdrey, (Michael) Colin, Baron (1932–2000) English cricketer

Cruyff, Johan (born 1947) Dutch footballer and football manager

Culbertson, Ely (1891–1955) American bridge player

Curry, John (Anthony) (1949–94) English ice-skater

Dalglish, Kenneth Mathieson ('Kenny') (born 1951) Scottish footballer and manager

Davenport, Lindsay (born 1976) American tennis player

Davis, Joe (1901–78) and his brother, **Fred** (born 1913) English billiards and snooker players

Davis, Steve (born 1957) English snooker player

Dean, Christopher See TORVILL AND DEAN

Dempsey, William Harrison ('Jack') (1895–1983), American boxer

Devoy, Susan (born 1954) New Zealand squash player

DiMaggio, Joseph Paul ('Joe') (1914–99) American baseball player

Di Stefano, Alfredo (born 1926) Argentinian-born Spanish footballer

D'Oliveira, Basil (Lewis) (born 1931) British cricketer and coach, born in South Africa

Edberg, Stefan (born 1966) Swedish tennis player

Edwards, Gareth (Owen) (born 1947) Welsh Rugby Union player

Edwards, Jonathan (David) (born 1966) English athlete

Eusebio (full name Ferraira da Silva Eusebio) (born 1942) Mozambican-born Portuguese footballer

Evert, Christine Marie ('Chris') (born 1954) American tennis player

Faldo, Nicholas Alexander ('Nick') (born 1957) English golfer

Fangio, Juan Manuel (1911–95) Argentinian motor-racing driver

Ferguson, Alex(ander Chapman) (born 1941) Scottish football manager and footballer

Finney, Thomas ('Tom') (born 1929) English footballer

Fischer, Robert James ('Bobby') (born 1943) American chess player

Fittipaldi, Emerson (born 1946) Brazilian motor-racing driver

Foreman, George (born 1948) American boxer

Fosbury, Richard (born 1947) American high jumper

Fraser, Dawn (born 1937) Australian swimmer

Frazier, Joseph ('Joe') (born 1944) American boxer

Gascoigne, Paul (known as 'Gazza') (born 1967) English footballer

Gavaskar, Sunil Manohar (born 1949) Indian cricketer

Gehrig, Henry Louis ('Lou') (1903–41), American baseball player

Gibson, Althea (born 1927) American tennis player

Grace, W(illiam) G(ilbert) (1848–1915) English cricketer

Graf, Stephanie ('Steffi') (born 1969) German tennis player

Greaves, James ('Jimmy') (born 1940) English footballer

Gretzky, Wayne (born 1961) Canadian ice-hockey player

Gunnell, Sally (Jane Janet) (born 1966) English athlete

Hadlee, Sir Richard (John) (born 1951) New Zealand cricketer

SPORTSPEOPLE (cont.)

Hailwood, Mike (full name Stanley Michael Bailey Hailwood) (1940–81) English racing motorcyclist

Hakkinen, Mika (1900–78) Finnish motor-racing driver

Hamilton, Sir Charles (1900–78) New Zealand inventor and motor-racing driver

Hendry, Stephen (Gordon) (born 1969) Scottish snooker player

Heyhoe-Flint, Rachel (born 1939) English cricketer

Hill, Damon (born 1960) English motor-racing driver, son of Graham Hill

Hill, (Norman) Graham (1929–75) English motor-racing driver

Hinault, Bernard (born 1954) French racing cyclist

Hobbs, Sir John Berry ('Jack') (1882–1963) English cricketer

Hussain, Nasser (born 1968) English cricketer, born in India

Hutton, Sir Leonard ('Len') (1916–90) English cricketer

Imran Khan See KHAN, IMRAN

Indurain, Miguel (born 1964) Spanish cyclist

Jacklin, Antony ('Tony') (born 1944) English golfer

John, Barry (born 1945) Welsh Rugby Union player

Johnson, Earvin (known as 'Magic Johnson') (born 1959) American basketball player

Johnson, Jack (1878–1946) American boxer

Jones, Marion (born 1976) American sprinter and long-jumper

Jones, Robert Tyre ('Bobby') (1902–71) American golfer

Jordan, Michael (Jeffrey) (born 1963) American basketball player

Kapil Dev (full name Kapil Dev Nikhanj) (born 1959) Indian cricketer

Karpov, Anatoli (born 1951) Russian chess player

Kasparov, Gary (born Gary Weinstein) (born 1963) Azerbaijani chess player, of Armenian Jewish descent

Keegan, (Joseph) Kevin (born 1951) English footballer and manager

Khan, Imran (full name Imran Ahmad Khan Niazi) (born 1952) Pakistani cricketer

Khan, Jahangir (born 1963) Pakistani squash player

King, Billie Jean (born 1943) American tennis player

Korbut, Olga (born 1955) Soviet gymnast, born in Belarus

Korchnoi, Viktor (Lvovich) (born 1931) Russian chess player

Lara, Brian (Charles) (born 1969) West Indian cricketer

Larwood, Harold (1904–95) English cricketer

Lauda, Nikolaus Andreas ('Niki') (born 1949) Austrian motor-racing driver

Laver, Rodney George ('Rod') (born 1938) Australian tennis player

Law, Denis (born 1940) Scottish footballer

Lendl, Ivan (born 1960) Czech-born tennis player

Lewis, Denise (born 1972) British heptathlete

Lewis, Frederick Carleton ('Carl') (born 1961) American athlete

Lewis, Lennox (born 1965) British boxer

Liddell, Eric (1902–45) British athlete and missionary, born in China

Lillee, Dennis (Keith) (born 1949) Australian cricketer

Lineker, Gary (Winston) (born 1960) English footballer

Liston, Sonny (born Charles Liston) (1932–70) American boxer

Louis, Joe (born Joseph Louis Barrow) (1914–81) American boxer

McEnroe, John (Patrick) (born 1959) American tennis player

Mansell, Nigel (born 1954) English motor-racing driver

Maradona, Diego (Armando) (born 1960) Argentinian footballer

Marciano, Rocky (born Rocco Francis Marchegiano) (1923–69) American boxer

Matthews, Sir Stanley (1915–2000) English footballer

Merckx, Eddy (born 1945) Belgian racing cyclist

Montana, Joe (known as 'Cool Joe') (born 1956) American football player

Moore, Robert Frederick ('Bobby') (1941–93) English footballer

Moses, Ed(win Corley) (born 1955) American athlete

Moss, Sir Stirling (born 1929) English motor-racing driver

Muhammad Ali (born Cassius Marcellus Clay) (born 1942) American boxer

Navratilova, Martina (born 1956) Czech-born American tennis player

Nepia, George (1905–86) New Zealand Rugby Union player

Nicklaus, Jack (William) (born 1940) American golfer

Norman, Gregory John ('Greg') (born 1955) Australian golfer

Owen, Michael (born 1979) English footballer

Owens, Jesse (born James Cleveland Owens) (1913–80) American athlete

SPORTSPEOPLE (cont.)

Palmer, Arnold (Daniel) (born 1929) American golfer

Pelé (born Edson Arantes do Nascimento) (born 1940) Brazilian footballer

Perry, Frederick John ('Fred') (1909–95), British-born American tennis player

Piggott, Lester (Keith) (born 1935) English jockey

Player, Gary (born 1936) South African golfer

Prost, Alain (born 1955) French motor-racing driver

Puskas, Ferenc (born 1927) Hungarian footballer

Ramsey, Sir Alf(red Ernest) (1920–99) English footballer and manager

Ranjitsinhji Vibhaji, Kumar Shri, Maharaja Jam Sahib of Navanagar (1872–1933) Indian cricketer and statesman

Redgrave, Sir Steve (born 1962) British oarsman

Rhodes, Wilfred (1877–1973) English cricketer

Richards, Sir Gordon (1904–86) English jockey

Richards, Viv (born Isaac Vivian Alexander Richards) (born 1952) West Indian cricketer

Robinson, Sugar Ray (born Walker Smith) (1920–89) American boxer

Ruth, Babe (born George Herman Ruth) (1895–1948) American baseball player

Sampras, Pete (born 1971) American tennis player

Schumacher, Michael (born 1969) German motor-racing driver

Seles, Monica (born 1973) American tennis player, born in Yugoslavia

Senna, Ayrton (1960–94) Brazilian motor-racing driver

Shankly, William ('Bill') (1913–81) Scottish-born football manager and footballer

Sheene, Barry (born Stephen Frank Sheene) (born 1950) English racing motorcyclist

Shilton, Peter (born 1949) English footballer

Simpson, O(renthal) J(ames) (born 1947) American football player, actor, and celebrity

Sobers, Sir Garfield St Aubrun ('Gary') (born 1936) West Indian cricketer

Spassky, Boris (Vasilyevich) (born 1937) Russian chess player

Spitz, Mark (Andrew) (born 1950) American swimmer

Stewart, Jackie (born John Young Stewart) (born 1939) British motor-racing driver

Thompson, Daley (born 1958) English athlete

Todd, Mark James (born 1956) New Zealand equestrian

Torvill and Dean, Jayne Torvill (born 1957) and **Christopher (Colin) Dean** (born 1958) English ice-skaters

Trevino, Lee (Buck) (known as 'Supermex') (born 1939) American golfer

Trueman, Frederick Sewards ('Fred') (born 1931) English cricketer

Tyson, Michael Gerald ('Mike') (born 1966) American boxer

Wade, (Sarah) Virginia (born 1945) English tennis player

Walker, John (born 1952) New Zealand athlete

Weissmuller, John Peter ('Johnny') (1904–84) American swimmer and actor

Williams, J(ohn) P(eter) R(hys) (born 1949) Welsh Rugby Union player

Williams, Serena (born 1982) and her sister **Venus** (born 1980), American tennis players

Wisden, John (1826–84) English cricketer

Woods, Eldrick ('Tiger') (born 1975) American golfer

Wright, William Ambrose ('Billy') (1924–94) English footballer

Zatopek, Emil (1922–2000) Czech long-distance runner

FOOD AND DRINK

COOKERY TERMS

baking
barbecuing
boiling
braising
broiling
casseroling
charbroiling
coddling

curing
currying
deep-frying
fricasseeing
frying
grilling
marinating
oven-roasting

parboiling
pickling
poaching
pot-roasting
roasting
sautéeing
scrambling
simmering

smoking
spit-roasting
steaming
stewing
stir-frying
toasting

HERBS

angelica
anise
basil
bay leaf
bergamot
borage
camomile
chervil
chicory

chives
comfrey
dill
fennel
fenugreek
lavender
lemon mint
lovage
marjoram

mint
oregano
parsley
peppermint
pot-herb
rosemary
rue
saffron
sage

savory
sesame
sorrel
spearmint
sweet cicely
tarragon
thyme

SPICES

allspice
black pepper
capers
caraway seeds
cardamom
cassia
cayenne pepper

chilli
cinnamon
cloves
coriander
cumin
curcuma
five spices

garam masala
garlic
ginger
ginseng
green pepper
juniper berries
mace

mustard
nutmeg
paprika
pimento
turmeric
vanilla
white pepper

CHEESES

Ami du Chambertin
Beaufort
Bel Paese
blue brie
blue cheese
blue vinney
Boursin
Brie
Caerphilly
Cambozola
Camembert

Cantal
Chaumes
Cheddar
Cheshire
chèvre
Churnton ™
Colby
cottage cheese
cream cheese
curd cheese
Danish blue

Derby
Dolcelatte
double Gloucester
Dunlop
Edam
Emmental
feta
fromage frais
Gervais
gjetost
Gloucester

Gorgonzola
Gouda
grana
Gruyère
halloumi
Ilchester
Jarlesburg
Lancashire
Leicester
Liederkranz
Limburger

CHEESES (cont.)

Liptauer
Livarot
mascarpone
Monterey
Monterey Jack
mozzarella
Neufchâtel
Oka
Parmesan
pecorino

Port Salut
provolone
quark
Reblochon
Red Leicester
Reggiano
ricotta
Romano
Roquefort
Sage Derby

Saint Agur
Sainte Honoré
Saint Nectaire
Samsoe
Stilton
stracchino
Swiss cheese
taleggio
Tillamook
Tilsit

Tomme de Savoie
tvorog
vacherin
Vignotte
Wensleydale
Wiltshire
Windsor
Windsor Red

BEANS AND PEAS

adzuki bean
bean sprout
black-eyed bean
broad bean
butter-bean
chickpea
flageolet

French bean
garden pea
haricot bean
horse bean
kidney bean
lentil
lima bean

mangetout
mung bean
pea-bean
petit pois
pinto bean
red bean
runner bean

scarlet runner
soya bean
split pea
string bean
sugar pea
sugar snap pea
wax-pod bean

VEGETABLES

artichoke
asparagus
aubergine
avocado pear
bamboo shoots
bean
beet
beetroot
breadfruit
broccoli
Brussels sprout
cabbage
calabrese
capsicum
cardoon
carrot
cassava

cauliflower
celeriac
celery
chard
chayote
chervil
chicory
Chinese
 cabbage
Chinese leaves
collard
corn on the cob
courgette
cress
cucumber
curly kale
dishcloth gourd

eggplant
endive
fennel
gherkin
gourd
gumbo
Jerusalem
 artichoke
kale
kohlrabi
leek
lentil
lettuce
mangetout
manioc
marrow
marrow squash

mustard
okra
onion
orache
oyster plant
pak-choi
parsnip
pea
pepper
pimiento
potato
pumpkin
radish
rutabaga
salsify
savoy
scallion

scorzonera
sea kale
shallot
spinach
spinach beet
squash
succory
swede
sweet corn
sweet potato
taro
tomato
turnip
water chestnut
watercress
yam
zucchini *Am.*

TYPES OF PASTA

agnolotti	farfalle	noodles	spaghettini
annellini	farfalline	orecchiette	spaghettone
bigoli	fettucce	paglia e fieno	stelline
bucatini	fettuccine	pappardelle	tagliatelle
cannelloni	fidelini	penne	tagliolini
capelli	fusilli	pipe	taglioni
cappelletti	gramigna	ravioli	tortellini
conchiglie	lasagne	rigatoni	tortelloni
cravattine	linguine	risoni	tortiglioni
ditali	lumache	rotelle	trenette
ditalini	macaroni	rotini	tuffoloni
ditaloni	manicotti	spaghetti	vermicelli

DESSERTS

Apfelstrudel	crême caramel	junket	stewed fruit
apple charlotte	crêpes Suzette	kissel	suet pudding
apple pie	crumble	Knickerbocker Glory	summer pudding
baked Alaska	custard	Mississippi mud pie	sundae
baklava	dairy ice cream	mousse	tapioca
banana split	death by chocolate	pandowdy	tipsy-cake
banoffi pie	egg custard	pavlova	tiramisu
bavaroise	entremets	peach Melba	treacle tart
Black Forest gateau	Eve's pudding	plum pudding	trifle
blancmange	floating island	rice pudding	upside-down
bread-and-butter	fool	roly-poly	pudding
pudding	fresh fruit	semolina	Viennoise
Brown Betty	fruit cup	shoofly pie *Am.*	[pudding]
cabinet pudding	fruit flan	sorbet	water ice
cajeta	fruit salad	soufflé	whip (gooseberry
charlotte russe	granita	sponge pudding	whip)
Christmas pudding	ice cream	spotted dick	yogurt
cobbler	jam tart	spumoni	zabaglione
compote	jelly	steamed pudding	

CAKES

almond cake	Dundee cake	Madeira cake	seedcake
angel cake	Eccles cake	madeleine	shortcake
baba	éclair	marble cake	simnel cake
Bakewell tart	fairy cake	meringue	sponge cake
baklava	flapjack	millefeuille	strudel
bannock	frangipane	muffin	Swiss roll
Battenburg	fruit cake	pancake	teacake
brownie	gateau	pandowdy	tipsy-cake
cheesecake	Genoa cake	parkin	torte
cruller	gingerbread	pavlova	upside-down cake
cupcake	hoecake	plum cake	Victoria sponge
Danish pastry	koeksister	pound cake	wedding cake
devil's food cake	kuchen	queen cake	yule log
doughnut	ladyfinger	rock cake	
drop scone	lardy-cake	scone	

FRUITS AND NUTS

alligator pear	crab apple	mandarin	redcurrant
almond	cranberry	mango	salmonberry
ananas	currant	mangosteen	sapodilla
apple	damson	medlar	satsuma
apricot	date	melon	service-berry
areca nut	dewberry	minneola	sharon fruit
avocado	durian	monkey-nut	sloe
babaco	elderberry	mulberry	sour cherry
bael	fig	muscat	sour gourd
bakeapple	filbert	musk melon	sour orange
banana	genipap	nectarine	sour plum
betel-nut	gooseberry	nipa	soursop
bilberry	gourd	olive	spice-berry
blackberry	granadilla	orange	star-apple
blackcurrant	grape	palm nut	star fruit
blueberry	grapefruit	passion fruit	strawberry
boysenberry	greengage	pawpaw	sweet chestnut
Brazil nut	groundnut	peach	sweetsop
breadfruit	grugru nut	peanut	tamarillo
breadnut	guava	pear	tamarind
bullace	hackberry	pecan	tangelo
burrawang nut	hazelnut	persimmon	tangerine
butternut	huckleberry	pineapple	tayberry
carambola	ivory-nut	pine nut	tomato
carob	jackfruit	pippin	tree tomato
cashew	jujube	pistachio	Ugli fruit™
cherry	kaki	plantain	walnut
chestnut	kiwi fruit	plum	watermelon
chinaberry	kumquat	pomegranate	white currant
citron	lemon	pomelo	white walnut
clementine	lime	prickly pear	whortleberry
cob-nut	loganberry	quandong	winter cherry
coconut or cocoanut	longan	Queensland nut	youngberry
coffee nut	loquat	quince	
cola nut	lychee	rambutan	
costard	macadamia nut	raspberry	

BREAD

bagel	bun	grissini	pumpernickel
baguette	ciabatta	hallah	roll
bap	corn bread	méteil bread	rusk
bara brith	cottage loaf	muffin	rye bread
black bread	croissant	nan bread	schnecken
bloomer	ficelle	pan loaf	soda bread
bread stick	focaccia	pitta bread	split tin
bridge roll	French bread	plait	stollen
brioche	garlic bread	potato bread	unleavened bread
brown bread	gluten bread	pretzel	wholemeal bread

CEREALS

arborio rice	burghul	Indian millet	rice
barley	Comolino rice	maize	semolina
Basmati rice	corn	méteil	sorghum
blé	cracked wheat	millet	spelt
bran	durra	oats	wild rice
buckwheat	durum wheat	Patna rice	
bulgur	froment	pearl barley	

SAUCES

aillade	bread	espagnole	poivrade
aïoli	Breton	financière	Provençal
Albufera	Cambridge	genevoise	Reform
allemande	caper	génoise	Robert
andalouse	caramel	hollandaise	romaine
anglaise	cardinal	lyonnaise	Roquefort
apple	Chambertin	Madeira	royale
aurore	Chambord	maltaise	Russian
banquière	Chantilly	marinière	soy
bâtarde	chasseur	mint	suprême
béarnaise	Chateaubriand	Mornay	sweet-and-sour
Beauharnais	chaud-froid	mousseline	tartare
béchamel	Chivry	mustard	tomato
Bercy	chocolate	Nantua	tortue
bolognaise	Choron	napolitaine	velouté
Bontemps	Colbert	normande	white
bordelaise	cranberry	onion	Worcestershire
bourguignonne	Cumberland	oyster	
brandade	dijonnaise	parsley	

COCKTAILS AND MIXED DRINKS

Alexander	commodore	julep	planter's punch
angel's kiss	corpse reviver	kir	posset
apple car	daiquiri	knickerbocker	prairie oyster
apple jack	elephant's ear	maiden's prayer	punch
archbishop	fallen angel	Manhattan	raki
beachcomber	fine and dandy	martini	rum collins
beadle	fix	merry widow	sangria
bee's knees	fizz	mint julep	screwdriver
between the sheets	flip	moonlight	sidecar
bishop	gin and it	mulled ale	sour
black maria	gin sling	mulled wine	toddy
black velvet	gimlet	negus	Tom Collins
bloody Mary	grog	night cap	Waldorf
Buck Jones	Harvey Wallbanger	nog	wassail bowl
Bucks fizz	high ball	old-fashioned	white gin sour
champagne buck	horse's neck	pina colada	white lady
churchwarden	John Collins	pink lady	whiz bang

WINES AND VARIETIES OF GRAPES

Aleatico	Chianti	Malvasia Bianca	Riesling
Aligoté	Chinon	Mammolo	Rioja
Aloxe-Corton	Cinsaut	Mandelaria	Rivesaltes
Alsace	Claret	Manseng	Romanée-Conti
Amontillado	Colombard	Manzanilla	Rosé
Bandol	Corton-Charlemagne	Margaux	Saint-Emilion
Barbaresco	Côte-Rôtie	Marsala	Saint Estephe
Barbera	Côtes-de-Provence	Marsanne	Saint Julien
Barolo	Côtes-du-Rhône	Martini	Sancerre
Barsac	Côtes-du-Roussillon	Médoc	Sangiovese
Beaujolais	Côtes-du-Ventoux	Mercurey	Santenay
Beaune	Côtes-du-Vivarais	Merlot	Saumur
Blanc Fumé	Crémant	Meunier	Sauternes
Blanquette de	Crépy	Meursault	Sauvignon Blanc
Limoux	Crozes-Hermitage	Monbazillac	Savigny-lès-Beaune
Bordeaux	Dolcetto	Montagny	Sémillon
Bourgueil	Dubonnet	Montepulciano	Sherry
Brouilly	Entre-Deux-Mers	Montilla	Shiraz or Syrah
Bual	Falerno	Montlouis	Sylvaner
Bull's Blood	Fino	Montrachet	Tavel
Burgundy	Fitou	Morey-Saint-Denis	Tempranillo
Byrrh	Frangy	Mosel	Tocai Friulano
Cabernet Franc	Fumé Blanc	Moselle	Tokay
Cabernet Sauvignon	Furmint	Mourvedre	Trebbiano
Cahors	Gaillac	Müller-Thurgau	Valençay
Campari	Gamay	Muscadelle	Valpolicella
Carignan	Gevrey-Chambertin	Muscadet	Verdejo
Cassis	Gewürztraminer	Muscat	Verdelho
Chablis	Gigondas	Nebbiolo	Verdello
Chambolle-Musigny	Graves	Nuits-Saint-Georges	Verdicchio
Champagne	Grenache	Orvieto	Verduzzo
Chardonnay	Grignolino	Pauillac	Vermentino
Chassagne-	Grüner Veltliner	Pinotage	Vermouth
Montrachet	Haut Poitou Wines	Pinot Blanc	Vernaccia
Château d'Yquem	Hermitage	Pinot Gris	Vin de Paille
Château Haut-Brion	Hock	Pinot Noir	Vinho Verde
Château Lafite	Kerner	Pommard	Vin Jaune
Château Latour	Lacrima Christi	Port	Viognier
Château Margaux	Lambrusco	Pouilly-Fuissé	Volnay
Château Mouton-	Madeira	Pouilly-Fumé	Vosne-Romanée
Rothschild	Málaga	Retsina	Vouvray
Chenin Blanc	Malbec	Richebourg	Zinfandel

BEERS

ale	ice beer	pale ale
bitter	keg beer	porter
bottled beer	lager	real ale
brown ale	low-alcohol beer	steam-brewed beer
canned beer	lite	stout
draught beer	mild	strong ale

CHAMPAGNE MEASURES

magnum = 2 bottles
jeroboam = 2 magnums
rehoboam = 3 magnums
methuselah = 4 magnums

salmanazar = 6 magnums
balthazar = 8 magnums
nebuchadnezzar = 10 magnums

MISCELLANEOUS

BIRTHSTONES
(with month)

garnet	Jan.	ruby	July
amethyst	Feb.	sardonyx	Aug.
bloodstone	Mar.	sapphire	Sept.
diamond	Apr.	opal	Oct.
emerald	May	topaz	Nov.
pearl	June	turquoise	Dec.

SIGNS OF THE ZODIAC
(with dates)

Aries	Mar. 21 – Apr. 19	Libra	Sept. 23 – Oct. 23
Taurus	Apr. 20 – May 20	Scorpio	Oct. 24 – Nov. 21
Gemini	May 21 – June 21	Sagittarius	Nov. 22 – Dec. 21
Cancer	June 22 – July 22	Capricorn	Dec. 22 – Jan. 19
Leo	July 23 – Aug. 22	Aquarius	Jan. 20 – Feb. 18
Virgo	Aug. 23 – Sept. 22	Pisces	Feb. 19 – Mar. 20

WEDDING ANNIVERSARIES

paper	1st	lace	13th
cotton	2nd	ivory	14th
leather	3rd	crystal	15th
fruit *or* flowers	4th	china	20th
wood	5th	silver	25th
iron	6th	pearl	30th
wool *or* copper	7th	coral	35th
bronze *or* pottery	8th	ruby	40th
pottery *or* willow	9th	sapphire	45th
tin *or* aluminium	10th	gold	50th
steel	11th	emerald	55th
silk *or* linen	12th	diamond	60th

GEMSTONES AND SEMI-PRECIOUS STONES

agate	carbuncle	fire-opal	moss agate	sardonyx
almandine	carnelian	garnet	greenstone	topaz
amber	cat's-eye	hawk's-eye	onyx	tourmaline
amethyst	chalcedony	hyacinth	opal	turquoise
aquamarine	corundum	jade	plasma	zircon
bloodstone	diamond	jasper	ruby	
cairngorm	emerald	lapis lazuli	sapphire	

FABRICS AND FIBRES

acetate	crinoline	linsey-woolsey	sailcloth
acrylic	Dacron™	long cloth	sarsenet
alpaca	damask	Lycra™	sateen
angora	denim	Mackinaw *Am.*	satin
astrakhan	doeskin	mackintosh	say
baize	Donegal tweed	madras	serge
brocade	drill	Malines	sharkskin
brocatelle	duffel	marocain	sheer
buckram	dungaree	Marseilles	shoddy
bunting	faille	matting	silk
burlap	felt	melton	stammel
calico	flannel	microfibre	stockinet
cambric	flannelette	mohair	suede
camel hair	gabardine	moire	swansdown
Canton crepe	gauze	moleskin	tabaret
canvas	Georgette crepe	mousseline	tabby
cashmere	gingham	muslin	tapestry
challis	gossamer	nankeen	tarpaulin
chambray	grenadine	netting	Terylene™
cheesecloth	gunny	nylon	ticking
chenille	haircloth	oiled silk	toile
cheviot	Harris tweed	organdie	towelling
chiffon	hemp	organza	tricot
chinchilla	herringbone	Orlon™	Tricotine
chino	hessian	Paisley	tulle
chintz	hopsack	panne velvet	tweed
coconut matting	horsehair	piqué	twill
coir	huckaback	plaid	velour
cord	jacquard	plush	velvet
corduroy	jean	polyester	velveteen
cotton	jersey	poplin	vicuña
crepe	jute	polyvinyl chloride	viscose
crepe-back satin	lamé	(PVC)	webbing
crepe de Chine	leatherette™	rayon	wool
crimplene™	linen	sackcloth	worsted

SEWING TECHNIQUES

appliqué
basting
binding
couching
crocheting
cutwork
darning
drawn-work
embroidery
facing

faggoting
fine-drawing
gathering
laid work
mitring
needlepoint
overcasting
overlocking
oversewing
patchwork

pleating
quilting
ruching
ruffling
scalloping
shirring
smocking
topstitching
tucking
whitework

SEWING STITCHES

backstitch
blanket stitch
blind stitch
buttonhole stitch
chain stitch
cross stitch
crow's foot

feather stitch
Florentine stitch
French knot
gros point
hemstitch
herringbone stitch
kettle stitch

lazy daisy stitch
lock stitch
needlepoint
overstitch
petit point
running stitch
satin stitch

stay stitch
stem stitch
tack
tailor's tack
tent stitch
topstitch
whip-stitch

KNITTING TERMS

argyle
bawneen (wool)
Berlin (wool)
cable stitch
chain
crochet
double knitting

Fair Isle
fingering (wool)
fisherman
foundation
garter stitch
graft
increase

intarsia
moss stitch
plain stitch
purl stitch
raschel
ribbing
shell-stitch

slip-stitch
stocking stitch
trellis stitch
warp
worsted
yarn

KNOTS

bend
Blackwall hitch
bow
bowknot
bowline
bowline on the bight
carrick bend
cat's-paw
clove hitch
diamond knot
Englishman's tie
figure-of-eight knot
fisherman's bend

fisherman's knot
granny knot
half hitch
hangman's knot
harness hitch
hawser-bend
Hercules knot
hitch
loop-knot
love-knot
Matthew Walker
mesh knot
overhand knot

prusik
reef knot
rolling hitch
round turn and two
   half hitches
running bowline
running knot
sailor's knot
sheepshank
sheet bend
shroud-knot
slip-knot
square knot

surgeon's knot
thumb knot
timber hitch
true-love knot
Turk's head
wall-knot
wale-knot
water-knot
weaver's knot
Windsor knot

CLOTHING AND FOOTWEAR

all-in-one
alpine hat
ankle boot
anklet
anorak
apron
apron tunic
Ascot
baboosh
babushka
baby bonnet
baldric
ball dress
balloon skirt
Balmoral
bandanna
bandeau
bandoleer
bandore
basinet
basque
bath robe
bathing cap
bathing costume
bathing suit
battle jacket
beanie
bearskin
beaver
bed jacket
bed socks
bell skirt
belt
beret
beretta
bib
bib-and-brace
bicorn
bikini
billicock
blazer
bloomer dress
bloomers
blouse
blouse coat
blousette
blouson
boater
bobby socks
bodice
body
body coat
body warmer
boiled shirt
bolero
bonnet
boob tube
boot
bootee

boudoir cap
bowler
box cape
box coat
boxer shorts
boxers
bra
braces
brassière
breeches
breton
briefs
brigandine
broadbrim
brogue
Brunswick
bucket tops
burka
burnoose
burnous
busby
bush jacket
business suit
buskin
cabriolet
caftan
calash
camise
camisole
camouflage suit
cancan dress
canvas shoe
cape
cape collar
cappa
cardigan
cardinal
cargo trousers
cassock
cavalier boot
chalwar
chaplet
chaps
chasuble
chatelaine
chemise
chemise dress
chemise frock
chemisette
Chesterfield
chevron
chinos
chukker shirt
cloak
cloche
clog
coachman's coat
coat
coat dress

coat shirt
cobcab
cocked hat
combination
combing jacket
coolie coat
coolie hat
cornet
corona
coronel
coronet
corselet
corset
corset bodice
corset cover
cossack
cossack cap
cottage bonnet
cottage cloak
coverall
coverchief
cowboy boots
cowboy hat
cowl
coxcomb
cravat
crinoline
culotte
cummerbund
cutaway
dance dress
daps
deerstalker
derby
dhoti
dickey
dinner dress
dinner jacket
dinner suit
divided skirt
djellaba
dog collar
domino
doublet
drawers
dress clothes
dress coat
dress plaid
dress shirt
dress shoe
dress suit
dressing gown
dressing jacket
duck-bill
duffel coat
dungarees
dunstable
dust coat
duster

dutch cap
earcap
earmuff
eclipse tie
elevator shoes
empire skirt
espadrilles
Eton cap
Eton jacket
evening dress
evening gown
evening shoes
evening skirt
everett
faldetta
fanchon
fedora
fez
flannels
flatcap
flying suit
forage cap
frock
frock coat
G string
gabardine
gaberdine
gaiter
galligaskin
galoshes
gamashes
gansey
gansy
garibaldi
garment
garter
gaucho
gauntlet
Glengarry
glove
gown
grass skirt
greatcoat
Guernsey
gum boot
gum shoe
gym shoe
habit
half slip
half-hose
halter
harem skirt
hat
Hawaiian skirt
helmet bonnet
helmet cap
hennin
hobble skirt
homburg

CLOTHING AND FOOTWEAR (cont.)

hood	necklace	rubbers	stomacher
hose	nightcap	ruff	stovepipe hat
hosiery	nightdress	ruffle	string glove
house coat	nightgown	running shoe	string tie
hula skirt	nightshirt	Russian boot	string vest
hunting boot	Norfolk jacket	sabot	sugar-loaf hat
Inverness	opera cloak	sabotine	suit
jack boot	opera hat	Sam Browne belt	sultane
jacket	overalls	sandal	sun hat
jama	overblouse	sari	sun suit
jamah	overcoat	sarong	sunbonnet
jeans	overdress	sash	surplice
jellies	overgaiter	scarf	suspender-belt
jerkin	overshirt	Scotch bonnet	suspenders
jersey	overshoe	service cap	swagger coat
jockey cap	overskirt	shalwar	sweat shirt
jodhpur	Oxford bags	shawl	sweater
judo coat	Oxfords	shift	swim suit
jump suit	Panama hat	shimmy	T-shirt
jumper	pantalets	shirt	tabard
jupon	pantaloons	shirtwaist	tail coat
kepi	panties	shirtwaister	tailleur
kilt	pants	shoe	tailored suit
kimono	panty girdle	shooting jacket	tails
kirtle	panty hose	shorts	tam
kittel	parka	shovel hat	tam-o'shanter
knee breeches	pashmina	silk hat	tamise
knickerbockers	pea jacket	singlet	tank top
knickers	pedal pushers	ski boot	tarboosh
knitwear	peg-top	skirt	tea gown
leggings	peignoir	skull cap	teddy
leotard	petticoat	slacks	teddybear coat
loafers	picture hat	sleeping suit	ten-gallon hat
loincloth	pierrot	slip	tent dress
lounge suit	pillbox	slip-over	thigh boot
lumberjack jacket	pilot coat	slipper	thong
mandarin coat	pinafore	sloppy joe	three-piece
mantilla	pinner	slouch hat	tiara
mantle	pith helmet	smock	tights
mantua	plimsolls	smoking jacket	toga
maxi	plus fours	snap-brim hat	top boot
mess jacket	poke bonnet	sneakers	top coat
middy	polonaise	snood	top hat
middy blouse	poncho	snowshoe	topee
midi	pork pie hat	sock	topi
mini	pullover	sombrero	topper
mitt	pumps	sou'wester	toque
mitten	puttee	soutane	toquette
mobcap	pyjamas	sporran	trainers
moccasin	quaker bonnet	sport shirt	trench coat
monkey jacket	quaker hat	sports clothes	trencher
morning dress	raglan	sports coat	trews
mother hubbard	reefer	sports jacket	tricorn
muff	riding habit	sportswear	trilby
muffler	riding hood	step-in	trouserettes
mufti	robe	stock	trousers
mule	roll-on	stocking	trunk-hose
neckcloth	rompers	stocking cap	trunks
neckerchief	rubber apron	stole	tunic

CLOTHING AND FOOTWEAR (cont.)

tunicle
turban
tutu
tuxedo
tweeds
twin set
two-piece
Tyrolean hat
Ulster
underclothes

underclothing
undergirdle
underpants
undershirt
underskirt
undervest
underwear
undies
veil
vest

waistcoat
walking shoe
watch coat
watteau
wedding gown
wedding veil
wedgies
wellingtons
wimple
windbreaker

windcheater
Windsor tie
wing collar
wing tie
woolly
wrap
wrapper
Y-fronts
yashmak
zoot suit

CERAMICS

agate-ware
Arita ware
Berlin ware
bisque
bone china
Castleford ware
Castor ware
champlevé
Chantilly ware
Chelsea porcelain
Ch'ing porcelain
cloisonné
Coalport
creamware
Crown Derby
Delft

Dresden china
earthenware
eggshell china
faience
fine china
fired porcelain
flatware
hard-paste
hollowware
Imari ware
ironstone
jasper ware
Kakiemon ware
Kutani ware
Limoges
maiolica *or* majolica

Meissen ware
mezza-maiolica
Ming ware
Nabeshima ware
Nanking ware
Parian porcelain
porcelain
porcelain enamel
queen's ware
raku
Rockingham ware
Royal Doulton
Royal Worcester
salt-glaze
Satsuma porcelain
semi-porcelain

Seto ware
Sèvres
soft-paste porcelain
Spode ware
stone china
stoneware
Staffordshire ware
Sung ware
Talavera ware
Tang ware
Ting ware
Toft ware
Vincennes ware
Wedgwood
Worcester

TYPES AND STYLES OF FURNITURE

Bauhaus
bentwood
bombé
boulle
cabriole
Chippendale

Duncan Phyfe
Empire
Gothic Revival
Hepplewhite
inlaid
Jacobean

Louis Quatorze
Louis Quinze
Louis Seize
Louis Treize
Queen Anne
Regency

reproduction
rustic
Scandinavian
Shaker
Sheraton

COLOUR NAMES

absinthe	carmine	grey	old rose
Alice blue	carnation	gris	olive
alizarin	carnelian	gun metal	olive brown
amaranth	carrot	hazel	olive drab
amber	castano	heather	olive green
amethyst	cerise	henna	onyx
apple green	cerulean	hyacinth	opal
apricot	chalk white	ice blue	orange
aquamarine	chamois	Indian ochre	Oxford blue
argent	champagne	Indian red	oyster pink
aubergine	charcoal grey	Indian yellow	parchment
auburn	chartreuse	indigo	peach
aureus	châtaine	iron brown	peacock blue
avocado	cherry	iron yellow	pea green
azo yellow	chestnut	Italian pink	pearl
azure	Chinese red	ivory	pearl grey
baby blue	Chinese white	jacinth	pepper-and-salt
baby pink	chocolate	jade	peridot
battleship grey	chrome	jaune	periwinkle blue
beige	chrome green	jet	petrol blue
bianco	chrome red	jonquil	phthalo green
biscuit	chrome yellow	khaki	pillar-box red
black	cinnamon	lamp black	pine green
blackberry	citron	lapis lazuli	pink
blanc	claret	lavander	pistachio
blau	cobalt blue	leaf green	platinum
bleu	cochineal	lemon yellow	plum
blonde	cocoa	lilac	poppy red
blood red	coffee	lime green	powder blue
blue	congo red	Lincoln green	primrose
blue-black	copper	liver brown	Prussian blue
blue-green	coral	logwood brown	puce
bottle green	cornflower	madder	purple
braun	cream	magenta	racing green
brick red	crimson	mahogany	raisin
bronze	cyan	maize	raspberry
brown	cyclamen	marigold	raw sienna
brun	Delft blue	maroon	raw umber
brunette	dove grey	mauve	red
Brunswick green	drab	melon	red brown
buff	duck-egg blue	midnight blue	red lead
burgundy	dun	mignonette	red ochre
burnet	eau de nil	milk white	robin's-egg blue
burnt almond	ebon	mint green	rose
burnt sienna	ebony	moss green	rose madder
burnt umber	emerald	mother-of-pearl	rouge
cadet blue	flake white	mulberry	rot
cadet grey	flame orange	mushroom	royal blue
cadmium orange	flame red	mustard	ruby
cadmium red	flaxen	nacarat	russet
cadmium yellow	flesh pink	Naples yellow	sable
caeruleus	forest green	navy blue	saffron
café au lait	fuchsia	neutral	salmon pink
Cambridge blue	garnet	Nile blue	sand
camel	ginger	Nile green	sandalwood
canary yellow	gold	noir	sap green
capucine	golden	ochre	sapphire
caramel	green	oeillet	scarlet
cardinal red	grenadine	off-white	Scheele's green

COLOUR NAMES (cont.)

schwartz
sea blue
sea green
sepia
shocking pink
shrimp
sienna
silver
sky blue
slate
snow white
solferino

spring green
strawberry blonde
strawberry pink
tan
tangerine
teak
teal
tea rose
terracotta
terra verde
terre vert
Thénard's blue

titanium white
titian
topaz
tortoise shell
turquoise
Tyrian purple
ultramarine
umber
Vandyke brown
verde
verdigris
vermillion

vert
violet
viridian
walnut
white
white lead
white zinc
yellow
yellow ochre

NAMES

BOYS' NAMES

Aaron	Alger	Archy	Bas	Botolph
Abdul	Algernon	Armand	Basie	Botulf
Abdullah	Algie	Armando	Basil	Boyce
Abe	Algy	Armin	Bastian	Boyd
Abel	Ali	Arnaud	Bat	Brad
Abner	Alick	Arnie	Baz	Bradley
Abraham	Alistair	Arnold	Beau	Bram
Abram	Allan	Art	Ben	Bramwell
Adair	Allen	Artemas	Benedick	Brandan
Adal	Allistair	Artemus	Benedict	Brandon
Adam	Allister	Arthur	Benet	Brendan
Adamnan	Alonzo	Artie	Benito	Brent
Adamu	Aloysius	Arturo	Benjamin	Bret
Adolf	Alphonse	Arty	Benji	Brett
Adolph	Alphonso	Asa	Bennet	Brian
Adolphe	Alphonsus	Asher	Bennett	Brice
Adolphus	Alun	Ashley	Benny	Brock
Adrian	Alured	Assim	Bentley	Broderick
Aeneas	Alvah	Athelstan	Berenger	Bruce
Ahmad	Alvar	Athol	Berkeley	Bruno
Ahmed	Alvie	Atom	Bernard	Bryan
Aidan	Alvin	Auberon	Bernardo	Bryce
Ainsley	Alvis	Aubert	Bernhard	Bryn
Ainslie	Alwyn	Aubrey	Bernie	Bud
Ajay	Amadou	August	Berny	Burt
Al	Ambrose	Augustin	Bert	Buster
Alain	Amos	Augustine	Berthold	Byron
Alan	Amyas	Augustus	Bertie	Cadel
Alaric	Ananda	Aulay	Bertram	Cadell
Alasdair	Anatoly	Austen	Bertrand	Cadwallader
Alastair	Ancel	Austin	Bethel	Caesar
Alban	André	Avery	Beverley	Cai
Albany	Andreas	Axel	Bevis	Caius
Alberic	Andrew	Aylmer	Bez	Cal
Albert	Andy	Aylwin	Bill	Caleb
Alden	Aneirin	Azariah	Billie	Callum
Aldhelm	Aneurin	Baldwin	Billy	Calum
Aldis	Angel	Balthasar	Bing	Calvin
Aldo	Angelo	Balthazar	Bjorn	Cameron
Aldous	Angus	Barclay	Blaine	Camillus
Aldred	Ansel	Barnabas	Blair	Campbell
Aldus	Ansell	Barnaby	Blaise	Caractacus
Aldwin	Anselm	Barnard	Blake	Caradoc
Aldwyn	Anthony	Barnet	Blane	Caradog
Alec	Anton	Barney	Blase	Carey
Aled	Antonio	Baron	Boaz	Carl
Alex	Antony	Barrett	Bob	Carleton
Alexander	Anwar	Barrie	Bobbie	Carlo
Alexis	Aquila	Barrington	Bobby	Carlos
Alf	Archelaus	Barron	Bonar	Carlton
Alfie	Archer	Barry	Boniface	Carol
Alfonso	Archibald	Bart	Boris	Carolus
Alfred	Archie	Bartholomew	Botolf	Carter

BOYS' NAMES (cont.)

Cary	Cormac	Deryk	Edom	Farquhar
Casey	Cornelius	Des	Edward	Farran
Caspar	Corney	Desmond	Edwin	Farren
Cassim	Cosimo	Dewi	Edwyn	Feargus
Cecil	Cosmo	Dexter	Egbert	Felix
Cedric	Courtenay	Diarmait	Eldon	Ferdinand
Cedrych	Courtney	Diarmid	Eldred	Fergie
Cerdic	Craig	Diarmuid	Eleazar	Fergus
Ceri	Crispian	Dick	Eli	Fernando
Chad	Crispin	Dickie	Elias	Fidel
Chandler	Crystal	Dickon	Elihu	Finlay
Charles	Cuddie	Dicky	Elijah	Fitzroy
Charley	Cuddy	Digby	Eliot	Fletcher
Charlie	Curt	Diggory	Ellery	Florian
Charlton	Curtis	Dillon	Elliot	Floyd
Chas	Cuthbert	Dion	Ellis	Fluellen
Chauncey	Cy	Dionysius	Elmer	Flurry
Chauncy	Cyprian	Dirk	Elton	Fortunatus
Chay	Cyril	Dominic	Elvin	Francesco
Chester	Cyrus	Dominick	Elvis	Francis
Chris	Dafydd	Don	Elwyn	Francisco
Christian	Dai	Donal	Emanuel	Franco
Christie	Dale	Donald	Emery	Frank
Christmas	Damian	Donny	Emil	Frankie
Christopher	Damien	Donovan	Emile	Franklin
Christy	Damon	Doran	Emlyn	Fraser
Chrystal	Dan	Dorian	Emmanuel	Frasier
Chuck	Daniel	Doug	Emrys	Frazer
Ciaran	Danny	Dougal	Enoch	Fred
Clarence	Dante	Dougie	Enos	Freddie
Clark	Darby	Douglas	Eoghan	Freddy
Claud	Darcy	Drew	Ephraim	Frederic
Claude	Darrel	Drogo	Eppie	Frederick
Claudius	Darrell	Duane	Erasmus	Fredric
Clayton	Darren	Dud	Eric	Fredrick
Cledwyn	Darryl	Dudley	Erik	Fulbert
Clem	Daryl	Dugald	Erle	Gabriel
Clement	Dave	Duggie	Ern	Gaius
Cliff	David	Duke	Ernest	Gamaliel
Clifford	Davy	Duncan	Ernie	Gareth
Clifton	Dean	Dunstan	Errol	Garfield
Clint	Declan	Durand	Esau	Garnet
Clinton	Dee	Dustin	Esme	Garret
Clive	Del	Dwayne	Esmond	Garrick
Clyde	Delbert	Dwight	Ethan	Garry
Clym	Delroy	Dylan	Ethelbert	Garth
Cole	Den	Eamon	Ethelred	Gary
Colin	Denholm	Eamonn	Eugene	Gaspar
Colley	Denis	Earl	Eustace	Gavin
Colm	Dennis	Earnest	Evan	Gawain
Colum	Denny	Eben	Evander	Gaylord
Columba	Denys	Ebenezer	Evelyn	Gaz
Conan	Denzil	Ed	Everard	Gene
Conn	Derby	Eddie	Ewan	Geoff
Connor	Derek	Eddy	Ewen	Geoffrey
Conor	Dermot	Eden	Ezekiel	Geordie
Conrad	Derrick	Edgar	Ezra	George
Constant	Derry	Edmond	Fabian	Georgie
Constantine	Deryck	Edmund	Faron	Geraint

BOYS' NAMES (cont.)

Gerald	Hamlyn	Hughie	Jarred	Judd
Gerard	Hammond	Hugo	Jarrod	Jude
Gerrard	Hamnet	Humbert	Jarvis	Jules
Gerry	Hamo	Humph	Jason	Julian
Gershom	Hamon	Humphrey	Jasper	Julius
Gervais	Hank	Husain	Javed	Junior
Gervase	Hannibal	Hussein	Jawaharlal	Justin
Gerwyn	Hans	Huw	Jay	Jyoti
Gethin	Hardy	Hyman	Jed	Kamal
Gib	Harley	Hymie	Jedidiah	Kane
Gideon	Harold	Hywel	Jeff	Karl
Gidon	Haroun	Iain	Jefferson	Karol
Gil	Harrison	Ian	Jeffery	Kay
Gilbert	Harry	Ibrahim	Jeffrey	Keir
Giles	Hartley	Ichabod	Jem	Keith
Gillean	Harun	Idris	Jemmy	Kelvin
Gillian	Harvey	Ifor	Jeremiah	Ken
Gilroy	Hashim	Ignatius	Jeremias	Kendal
Glen	Hassan	Igor	Jeremy	Kendall
Glyn	Hayden	Ike	Jermaine	Kenelm
Godfrey	Haydon	Imran	Jerome	Kenneth
Godwin	Heath	Ingram	Jerry	Kenny
Goldwin	Heber	Inigo	Jess	Kenred
Goldwyn	Hector	Iolo	Jesse	Kenrick
Gordon	Hedley	Iorwerth	Jesus	Kent
Graeme	Henri	Ira	Jethro	Kentigern
Graham	Henry	Irvin	Jillian	Kenton
Grahame	Herb	Irvine	Jim	Kester
Grant	Herbert	Irving	Jimmy	Kevin
Granville	Herbie	Irwin	Joachim	Khaled
Grayburn	Hercules	Isa	Job	Khalid
Greg	Hereward	Isaac	Jocelyn	Khurshid
Gregor	Herman	Isaiah	Jock	Kieran
Gregory	Hermann	Isidore	Joe	Kilroy
Grenville	Hervé	Israel	Joel	Kim
Griffith	Hervey	Ithel	Joey	Kimball
Grover	Hew	Itzhak	Johannes	Kimberley
Guido	Hezekiah	Ivan	John	Kimberly
Gunter	Hieronymus	Ives	Johnnie	King
Gunther	Hilary	Ivo	Johnny	Kingsley
Gus	Hillary	Ivor	Johnston	Kirby
Gussie	Hippolytus	Izaak	Jolyon	Kirk
Gustaf	Hiram	Jabez	Jon	Kit
Gustav	Hob	Jack	Jonah	Kofi
Gustave	Hobart	Jackie	Jonas	Kris
Gustavus	Holden	Jacky	Jonathan	Krishnan
Guy	Homer	Jacob	Jools	Kurt
Gwilym	Honor	Jacques	Jordan	Kyle
Gwylim	Honour	Jacqui	Joscelin	Kyren
Gwyn	Hopi	Jago	José	Laban
Gwynfor	Horace	Jahangir	Joseph	Lachlan
Gyles	Horatio	Jake	Josh	Lambert
Hadrian	Horry	James	Joshua	Lance
Hal	Howard	Jamie	Josiah	Lancelot
Ham	Howel	Jamshed	Josias	Lanty
Hamil	Howell	Jan	Jotham	Larry
Hamilton	Hubert	Japhet	Juan	Lars
Hamish	Huey	Japheth	Judah	Launce
Hamlet	Hugh	Jared	Judas	Launcelot

BOYS' NAMES (cont.)

Lauren	Lyndon	Mick	Nicol	Parry
Laurence	Lynn	Mickey	Nicolas	Pascal
Lauri	Madoc	Micky	Nigel	Pascoe
Laurie	Magnus	Mike	Nik	Pat
Lawrence	Malachi	Milburn	Niles	Patrick
Lawrie	Malachy	Miles	Ninian	Paul
Layton	Malcolm	Milo	Noah	Pedro
Lazarus	Malise	Milton	Noam	Pelham
Leander	Mallory	Mitch	Noel	Perce
Lee	Malory	Mitchell	Nolan	Perceval
Leigh	Malvin	Mohammed	Norbert	Percival
Leighton	Manasses	Mohandas	Norm	Percy
Lemuel	Manfred	Montagu	Norman	Peregrine
Len	Manley	Montague	Norris	Perry
Lennox	Manny	Monte	Norton	Pete
Leo	Manohar	Montgomery	Nowell	Peter
Leofric	Mansel	Monty	Nye	Phil
Leoline	Mansur	Morarji	Obadiah	Philemon
Leon	Manuel	Moray	Oberon	Philibert
Leonard	Manus	Mordecai	Octavian	Philip
Leopold	Marc	Morgan	Octavius	Phillip
Leroi	Marcel	Morris	Odo	Phineas
Leroy	Marcellus	Mort	Ogden	Phinehas
Les	Marco	Mortimer	Olaf	Pierre
Leslie	Marcus	Morty	Olav	Piers
Lester	Mario	Moses	Olave	Piet
Levi	Marius	Moshe	Oliver	Pip
Lew	Mark	Moss	Olivier	Piran
Lewis	Marmaduke	Mostafa	Ollie	Poldie
Lex	Marshall	Motilal	Omar	Prescott
Liam	Martin	Muhammad	Onuphrius	Preston
Lincoln	Marty	Muir	Orlando	Prince
Lindsay	Martyn	Mungo	Orrell	Quentin
Lionel	Marvin	Murdoch	Orson	Quincy
Llewellyn	Marvyn	Murray	Orval	Quinn
Llewelyn	Mat	Murtagh	Orville	Quintin
Lloyd	Matt	Myles	Osbert	Rab
Lonnie	Matthew	Myron	Osborn	Rabbie
Loren	Matthias	Napoleon	Osborne	Radcliff
Lorenzo	Maurice	Nat	Oscar	Rafael
Lori	Max	Nathan	Osho	Rafe
Lorin	Maximilian	Nathanael	Osmond	Rainer
Lorn	Maxwell	Nathaniel	Osmund	Rajiv
Lorne	Maynard	Neal	Ossie	Ralph
Lou	Meirion	Ned	Ossy	Ramlal
Louie	Mel	Neddie	Oswald	Ramon
Louis	Melford	Neddy	Oswin	Ramsay
Lovell	Melville	Nehemiah	Otho	Ramsey
Lowell	Melvin	Neil	Otis	Ranald
Lucas	Melvyn	Neill	Otto	Randal
Lucian	Meredith	Nelson	Owain	Randall
Lucien	Merlin	Nevil	Owen	Randolph
Lucius	Merrion	Neville	Ozzie	Randy
Ludo	Merton	Newton	Pablo	Raoul
Ludovic	Merv	Niall	Paddy	Raphael
Luke	Mervin	Nicholas	Padraig	Rashid
Luther	Mervyn	Nick	Palmer	Ray
Lyle	Micah	Nicky	Paolo	Raymond
Lyn	Michael	Nicodemus	Parker	Raymund

BOYS' NAMES (cont.)

Rayner	Russell	Simon	Thomas	Walter
Raynor	Ruud	Sinclair	Thorley	Ward
Reg	Ryan	Sitaram	Thornton	Warner
Reggie	Sacha	Sly	Thurstan	Warren
Reginald	Sacheverell	Sol	Thurston	Warwick
René	St John	Solly	Tim	Washington
Reuben	Salamon	Solomon	Timmy	Wat
Rex	Salman	Spencer	Timothy	Wayne
Reynard	Salvador	Stafford	Titus	Wendell
Reynold	Salvatore	Stan	Tobias	Wesley
Rhys	Sam	Stanford	Toby	Wilbert
Riccardo	Sammy	Stanislaus	Todd	Wilbur
Rich	Sampson	Stanley	Tolly	Wilf
Richard	Samson	Stephen	Tom	Wilfred
Richie	Samuel	Steve	Tommy	Wilfrid
Rick	Satyendra	Steven	Tony	Will
Ricki	Saul	Stevie	Torquil	Willard
Ricky	Saxon	Stew	Travers	William
Rik	Scott	Stewart	Travis	Willie
Rikki	Seamus	Stirling	Trefor	Willis
Roald	Sean	Stu	Trev	Willoughby
Rob	Seb	Stuart	Trevor	Willy
Robbie	Sebastian	Subhas	Tristan	Wilmer
Robert	Sefton	Sunil	Tristram	Wilmot
Robin	Selby	Swithin	Troy	Win
Rod	Selwyn	Syd	Tudor	Windsor
Roddy	Septimus	Sydney	Turlough	Winfred
Roderick	Serge	Syed	Ty	Winfrid
Rodger	Sergei	Sylvanus	Tyrone	Winnie
Rodney	Sergio	Sylvester	Ulric	Winston
Rodolph	Sergius	Taffy	Ulysses	Winthrop
Rodrigo	Seth	Talal	Upton	Woodrow
Roger	Seumas	Talbot	Urban	Wyatt
Roland	Seward	Taliesin	Uriah	Wybert
Rolf	Sextus	Tam	Valentine	Wyndham
Rollo	Seymour	Tancred	Valery	Wynford
Rolly	Shamus	Tariq	Vaughan	Wynn
Rolph	Shane	Tarquil	Vaughn	Wynne
Roly	Shannon	Tarquin	Vere	Wystan
Ron	Shaun	Taylor	Vernon	Xavier
Ronald	Shaw	Ted	Vic	Yehudi
Ronnie	Shawn	Teddie	Vick	Yossef
Rory	Sheldon	Teddy	Victor	Yusuf
Ross	Shelley	Tel	Vijay	Yves
Rowan	Shem	Terence	Vin	Zachariah
Rowland	Sheridan	Terrence	Vince	Zacharias
Roy	Sholto	Terri	Vincent	Zachary
Royal	Sid	Terry	Vinnie	Zack
Royston	Sidney	Tertius	Virgil	Zak
Rudi	Siegfried	Tex	Vitus	Zane
Rudolf	Sigismund	Thaddeus	Wade	Zechariah
Rudolph	Sigmund	Theo	Wal	Zedekiah
Rudy	Silas	Theobald	Waldo	Zeke
Rufus	Silvanus	Theodore	Wallace	Zephaniah
Rupert	Silvester	Theodoric	Wallis	Zoran
Russ	Sim	Theophilus	Wally	
Russel	Simeon	Thom	Walt	

GIRLS' NAMES

Abanya	Alix	Anstice	Beatrice	Bonny
Abbie	Allegra	Anthea	Beatrix	Branwen
Abby	Allie	Antoine	Beattie	Brenda
Abigail	Allison	Antoinette	Beatty	Bride
Ada	Ally	Antonia	Bebe	Bridget
Adela	Alma	Antonina	Becky	Bridie
Adelaide	Aloisia	Antonnia	Bedelia	Brighid
Adele	Aloysia	Anwen	Bee	Brigid
Adeline	Alphonsina	Anya	Bel	Brigit
Adina	Althea	Anyetta	Belinda	Brigitta
Adriana	Alva	Aphra	Bell	Brigitte
Adrianne	Alvie	Apollonia	Bella	Briony
Adrienne	Alvina	Appolina	Belle	Brita
Agatha	Amalia	April	Benita	Britannia
Aggie	Amalie	Arabella	Berenice	Britt
Agnes	Amanda	Araminta	Bernadette	Brona
Agneta	Amaryllis	Aramintha	Bernadina	Bronwen
Agnetha	Amata	Ariadne	Bernardina	Bronwyn
Aileen	Amber	Ariane	Bernardotta	Brunetta
Ailsa	Amelia	Arianna	Bernice	Bryony
Aimee	Amicia	Arlene	Bernie	Caitlin
Aine	Amina	Arletta	Berny	Cal
Ainsley	Aminta	Arline	Berry	Cameron
Ainslie	Amy	Armina	Berta	Camilla
Aisha	Anaïs	Artemisia	Bertha	Camille
Aisling	Anastasia	Ashley	Beryl	Candace
Aislinn	Andie	Asma	Bess	Candice
Aithne	Andrea	Aspasia	Bessie	Candida
Alabama	Andrée	Astra	Bessy	Candy
Alana	Aneira	Astrid	Beta	Canice
Alanna	Angel	Athena	Beth	Caprice
Alannah	Angela	Athene	Bethan	Cara
Alberta	Angelica	Audra	Bethany	Carey
Albertina	Angelina	Audrey	Bethia	Carina
Albertine	Angeline	Augusta	Betsy	Carita
Albina	Angelique	Augustina	Bette	Carla
Albinia	Angharad	Aurea	Bettina	Carleen
Albreda	Angie	Aurelia	Bettrys	Carlene
Alda	Anis	Aureole	Betty	Carlotta
Aldith	Anita	Auriel	Beulah	Carly
Aldreda	Ann	Aurora	Beverley	Carlyn
Aledwen	Anna	Ava	Beverly	Carmel
Alethea	Annabel	Aveline	Bianca	Carmela
Aletta	Annabella	Averil	Biddy	Carmelita
Alex	Annabelle	Avice	Billie	Carmen
Alexa	Annalisa	Avis	Bina	Carol
Alexandra	Annaple	Avril	Birdie	Carola
Alexandria	Anne	Ayesha	Birgit	Carole
Alexandrina	Anneliese	Aziza	Birgitta	Carolina
Alexia	Annette	Bab	Bithica	Caroline
Alexis	Annice	Babette	Blanch	Carolyn
Alfreda	Annie	Babs	Blanche	Carrie
Ali	Annika	Barbara	Blodwen	Cary
Alia	Annis	Barbie	Blodyn	Caryl
Alice	Annora	Barbra	Blossom	Carys
Alicia	Anona	Basma	Blythe	Casey
Alina	Anouska	Bathsheba	Bobbie	Cass
Aline	Anselma	Bea	Bonita	Cassandra
Alison	Anstey	Beata	Bonnie	Cassie

GIRLS' NAMES (cont.)

Cat	Cindy	Danette	Dorinda	Elvie
Cath	Cis	Daniella	Doris	Elvina
Catharine	Ciss	Danielle	Dorita	Elvira
Catherine	Cissie	Daph	Dorothea	Em
Cathleen	Cissy	Daphne	Dorothy	Emanuela
Cathy	Claire	Darcy	Dorrie	Emeline
Catrin	Clara	Darlene	Dot	Emelyn
Catrina	Clarabel	Davida	Dottie	Emerald
Catriona	Clare	Davina	Dreda	Emilia
Caz	Claribel	Davinia	Dulcie	Emily
Cecile	Clarice	Dawn	Dymphna	Emma
Cecilia	Clarinda	Deanna	Dympna	Emmanuela
Cecilie	Clarissa	Deanne	Eartha	Emmeline
Cecily	Clarrie	Deb	Easter	Emmie
Ceinwen	Claudette	Debbie	Eda	Ena
Celeste	Claudia	Deborah	Eden	Enid
Celestina	Claudine	Debra	Edie	Erica
Celestine	Clem	Dede	Edina	Erika
Celia	Clemence	Dee	Edith	Erin
Celina	Clemency	Deirdre	Edna	Ermintrude
Celine	Clementia	Delia	Edwina	Ermyntrude
Ceri	Clementina	Delilah	Effie	Ernestine
Ceridwen	Clementine	Della	Eileen	Eryl
Cerys	Cleo	Delma	Eiluned	Esme
Chandrika	Cleopatra	Delphine	Eilwen	Esmeralda
Charis	Clodagh	Delwen	Eily	Estella
Charissa	Clotilda	Delwyn	Eira	Estelle
Charity	Colette	Delyth	Eirian	Esther
Charlene	Colina	Demelza	Eithne	Ethel
Charley	Colleen	Denise	Elain	Etheldreda
Charlie	Columbina	Dennie	Elaine	Ethelinda
Charlotte	Columbine	Dervla	Eldreda	Ethne
Charmaine	Concepta	Deryn	Eleanor	Etta
Charmanay	Concetta	Desdemona	Eleanora	Ettie
Charmian	Connie	Desiree	Elena	Etty
Chattie	Constance	Di	Eleonora	Eudora
Cher	Constancy	Diamond	Elfreda	Eugenia
Cherelle	Constantia	Diana	Elfrida	Eugenie
Cherie	Cora	Diane	Elined	Eulalia
Cherry	Coral	Dianne	Elinor	Eulalie
Cheryl	Coralie	Dilys	Elisabeth	Eunice
Chloe	Cordelia	Dina	Elise	Euphemia
Chris	Corinna	Dinah	Elisha	Eustacia
Chrissie	Corinne	Dione	Elissa	Eva
Chrissy	Cornelia	Dionne	Eliza	Evadne
Christa	Courtenay	Dionysia	Elizabeth	Evangelina
Christabel	Courteney	Dodie	Ella	Evangeline
Christian	Courtney	Doll	Elle	Eve
Christiana	Cressida	Dolly	Ellen	Evelina
Christiania	Crystal	Dolores	Ellie	Eveline
Christie	Cynthia	Dominica	Elma	Evelyn
Christina	Cytherea	Dominique	Eloisa	Evie
Christine	Daff	Donna	Eloise	Evita
Christmas	Dagmar	Dora	Elroy	Evonne
Christy	Daisy	Dorcas	Elsa	Fabiana
Ciara	Dale	Doreen	Elsie	Faith
Cicely	Damaris	Dorette	Elspeth	Fan
Cilla	Dana	Doria	Elspie	Fanny
Cinderella	Dani	Dorice	Eluned	Farah

GIRLS' NAMES (cont.)

Faron	Gaynor	Gwen	Horatia	Jan
Farran	Gemma	Gwenda	Horry	Jancis
Farren	Genevieve	Gwendolen	Hortense	Jane
Fatima	Genevra	Gwendoline	Hortensia	Janet
Faustina	Georgette	Gwendolyn	Howard	Janetta
Fay	Georgia	Gwenllian	Hulda	Janette
Faye	Georgiana	Gwladys	Huldah	Janey
Felicia	Georgie	Gwyn	Hyacinth	Janice
Felicity	Georgina	Gwynedd	Hyacintha	Janie
Fenella	Geraldine	Gwyneth	Hylda	Janine
Fern	Gerda	Gwynneth	Hypatia	Janis
Ffyona	Geri	Hadassah	Ianthe	Jansis
Fidelia	Germaine	Hagar	Ida	Jasmine
Fifi	Gerry	Haidee	Idonea	Jay
Finola	Gert	Halcyon	Ife	Jayleen
Fiona	Gertie	Hannah	Ilma	Jayne
Fionnghuala	Gertrude	Harriet	Ilona	Jean
Fionnuala	Ghislaine	Harriette	Ilse	Jeanette
Flavia	Gilberta	Hasna	Iman	Jeanie
Fleur	Gilbertine	Hattie	Imani	Jeanne
Flo	Gilda	Hatty	Immy	Jeannette
Flora	Gill	Haya	Imogen	Jeannie
Florence	Gillian	Hayley	Ina	Jeannine
Floretta	Gina	Hazel	Indira	Jemima
Flossie	Ginette	Heather	Inez	Jemma
Flower	Ginevra	Hebe	Ingeborg	Jen
Floy	Ginger	Hedda	Ingrid	Jenifer
Fortune	Ginny	Hedwig	Iola	Jenna
Foster	Gisela	Hedy	Iolanthe	Jennie
Fran	Giselle	Heidi	Iona	Jennifer
Franca	Gita	Helen	Irene	Jenny
Frances	Glad	Helena	Iris	Jeri
Francesca	Gladys	Helene	Irma	Jess
Francie	Glenda	Helewise	Isa	Jessamine
Francine	Glenis	Helga	Isabel	Jessamyn
Francisca	Glenna	Héloïse	Isabella	Jessica
Frankie	Glenys	Hennie	Isabelle	Jessie
Frannie	Glinys	Henny	Isadora	Jewel
Franny	Gloria	Henrietta	Iseult	Jill
Freda	Glory	Henriette	Ishbel	Jillian
Frederica	Glynis	Hepsey	Isla	Jinny
Frederika	Golda	Hepsie	Ismay	Jo
Fredrica	Goldie	Hepsy	Isobel	Joan
Fredrika	Grace	Hepzibah	Isolde	Joanna
Freya	Gracie	Hermia	Ita	Joanne
Frieda	Grainne	Hermione	Ivah	Jocasta
Gabbie	Grania	Hester	Ivy	Jocelyn
Gabby	Greta	Hetty	Jacinta	Jodi
Gabi	Gretchen	Heulwen	Jacintha	Jodie
Gabriella	Gretel	Hilary	Jackie	Jody
Gabrielle	Griselda	Hilda	Jacky	Johanna
Gaby	Grizel	Hildegard	Jacoba	Joleen
Gaenor	Grizzel	Hildegarde	Jacobina	Jolene
Gail	Guendolen	Hillary	Jacqueline	Joni
Gale	Guinevere	Hippolyta	Jacquelyn	Jonquil
Garnet	Gulielma	Holly	Jacquetta	Jonti
Gay	Gus	Honora	Jacqui	Joscelin
Gaye	Gussie	Honoria	Jade	Josepha
Gayle	Gusta	Hope	Jael	Josephine

GIRLS' NAMES (cont.)

Josette	Kirsty	Libby	Luce	Marcelle
Josie	Kit	Liddy	Lucetta	Marcia
Joss	Kitty	Liesel	Lucette	Marcie
Joy	Kristen	Liesl	Lucia	Marcy
Joyce	Kristin	Lil	Luciana	Margaret
Juanita	Kristina	Lila	Lucie	Margareta
Judi	Kristine	Lilac	Lucille	Margaretta
Judith	Kula	Lili	Lucina	Margarita
Judoc	Kylie	Lilian	Lucinda	Margarita
Judy	Laetitia	Lilias	Lucky	Marge
Julia	Lalage	Lilith	Lucrece	Margie
Juliana	Lalla	Lilla	Lucretia	Margo
Julianne	Lana	Lillah	Lucrezia	Margot
Julie	Laraine	Lillian	Lucy	Marguerita
Julienne	Larissa	Lillias	Luella	Marguerite
Juliet	Larraine	Lillie	Lulu	Maria
Juliette	Laura	Lily	Lydia	Mariabella
Julitta	Lauraine	Lina	Lyn	Mariam
June	Laureen	Linda	Lynda	Mariamne
Justina	Laurel	Lindsay	Lynette	Marian
Justine	Lauren	Lindsey	Lynn	Marianne
Kara	Laurencia	Lindy	Lynne	Marie
Karen	Laurentia	Linette	Lynnette	Mariel
Karin	Lauretta	Linnet	Lynzi	Marietta
Karina	Laurette	Lisa	Lyra	Mariette
Kate	Lauri	Lisbeth	Mabel	Marigold
Kath	Laurie	Lise	Mabella	Marika
Katharine	Laurina	Lisette	Mabelle	Marilyn
Katherine	Laurinda	Lita	Mable	Marina
Kathleen	Lavena	Liz	Maddie	Marion
Kathryn	Laverne	Liza	Maddy	Marisa
Kathy	Lavina	Lizanne	Madeleine	Marissa
Katie	Lavinia	Lizbeth	Madelina	Marita
Katrina	Lea	Lizzie	Madeline	Marjorie
Katrine	Leah	Lizzy	Madge	Marla
Katy	Leanne	Llinos	Madonna	Marlene
Kay	Lee	Lois	Mae	Marlin
Kaz	Leigh	Lola	Maeve	Marlyn
Keeley	Leila	Lolita	Magda	Marni
Kelda	Leilah	Lolly	Magdalen	Marnie
Kellie	Lela	Lora	Magdalena	Marsha
Kelly	Lena	Loraine	Magdalene	Marta
Kendra	Lennie	Loreen	Maggie	Martha
Keren	Lenny	Loren	Magnolia	Marti
Kerenhappuch	Lenore	Loretta	Mahala	Martie
Keri	Leona	Lorette	Mahalah	Martina
Kerri	Leonie	Lori	Mahalia	Martine
Kerrie	Leonora	Lorinda	Maidie	Marty
Kerris	Les	Lorn	Mair	Mary
Kerry	Lesley	Lorna	Maire	Maryam
Keturah	Lesli	Lorraine	Mairin	Matilda
Kezia	Leslie	Lottie	Maisie	Mattie
Keziah	Leta	Lotty	Malvina	Matty
Khaleda	Letitia	Lou	Mamie	Maud
Kim	Lettice	Louella	Mandy	Maude
Kimberley	Lettie	Louisa	Manuela	Maudie
Kimberly	Letty	Louise	Mara	Maura
Kirby	Liana	Lu	Marah	Maureen
Kirsten	Lianne	Lucasta	Marcella	Mavis

GIRLS' NAMES (cont.)

Maxine	Mirabel	Nicola	Patty	Raina
May	Mirabella	Nicole	Paula	Raine
Meave	Mirabelle	Nicolette	Paulette	Raiyah
Meg	Miranda	Nikki	Pauline	Ramani
Megan	Miriam	Nina	Peace	Ramona
Meggie	Mirvat	Ninette	Pearl	Raphaela
Meggy	Miryam	Nita	Pearlie	Raquel
Meghan	Mitzi	Noele	Peg	Raymonde
Mehala	Mo	Noeleen	Peggy	Rebecca
Mehalah	Modesty	Noeline	Pen	Rebekah
Mehalia	Moira	Noelle	Penelope	Regina
Mehetabel	Moll	Nola	Penny	Reine
Mehitabel	Molly	Nona	Pepita	Rena
Meirion	Mona	Nora	Perdita	Renata
Mel	Monica	Norah	Peronel	Rene
Melania	Monique	Noreen	Perpetua	Renée
Melanie	Morag	Norma	Peta	Renie
Melba	Morna	Nova	Petra	Rhea
Melicent	Morwenna	Nuala	Petrina	Rhian
Melinda	Moyna	Nyree	Petronella	Rhiannon
Meliora	Moyra	Octavia	Petronilla	Rhoda
Mélisande	Muna	Odette	Petula	Rhona
Melisent	Muriel	Odile	Phebe	Rhonda
Melissa	Myfanwy	Odilia	Phemie	Rhonwen
Melloney	Myra	Oenone	Phil	Ria
Melodie	Myrna	Olga	Philadelphia	Rica
Melody	Myrtilla	Oliff	Philippa	Ricarda
Melva	Myrtle	Olive	Phillida	Richmal
Melvina	Mysie	Olivet	Phillipa	Rika
Mercedes	Nada	Olivia	Phillippa	Rina
Mercia	Nadia	Ollie	Phillis	Rita
Mercy	Nadine	Olwen	Philomena	Roberta
Meredith	Nahum	Olwyn	Phoebe	Robina
Meriel	Nan	Olympia	Phyllida	Robyn
Merilyn	Nance	Ona	Phyllis	Rochelle
Merle	Nancy	Oona	Pia	Roisin
Merrilyn	Nanette	Oonagh	Pippa	Roma
Merrion	Nanny	Opal	Pleasance	Romaine
Merry	Naomi	Ophelia	Poll	Rona
Meryl	Nat	Oriana	Polly	Ronalda
Meta	Natalia	Oriel	Pollyanna	Ronna
Mia	Natalie	Ottilia	Poppy	Ronnette
Michaela	Natasha	Ottilie	Portia	Ros
Michele	Nawal	Owena	Primrose	Rosa
Michelle	Nell	Ozzy	Prisca	Rosabel
Mignon	Nellie	Pam	Priscilla	Rosabella
Milborough	Nelly	Pamela	Prissy	Rosabelle
Mildred	Nerina	Pamelia	Pru	Rosaleen
Millicent	Nerissa	Pandita	Prudence	Rosalia
Millie	Nerys	Pandora	Prue	Rosalie
Milly	Nessa	Pansy	Prunella	Rosalind
Mima	Nessie	Parthenia	Queena	Rosalinda
Mimi	Nest	Pascale	Queenie	Rosaline
Mina	Nesta	Pat	Queeny	Rosalyn
Minerva	Netta	Patience	Rachael	Rosamond
Minna	Nettie	Patricia	Rachel	Rosamund
Minnie	Neva	Patsy	Rae	Rosanna
Minty	Nichola	Patti	Raelene	Rosanne
Mira	Nicky	Pattie	Rafaela	Rose

GIRLS' NAMES (cont.)

Roseann	Shari	Sukey	Tilly	Vilma
Roseanna	Sharon	Susan	Timothea	Vina
Roseanne	Sharron	Susanna	Tina	Vinny
Roseline	Shauna	Susannah	Tirzah	Viola
Roselyn	Shaz	Susanne	Tisha	Violet
Rosemarie	Sheba	Susie	Toni	Violetta
Rosemary	Sheelagh	Suzanna	Tonia	Violette
Rosetta	Sheena	Suzanne	Tonya	Virginia
Rosie	Sheila	Suzette	Topanga	Vita
Rosina	Sheilah	Suzy	Topsy	Viv
Rosita	Shelagh	Svetlana	Toru	Viva
Roslyn	Shelley	Sybella	Totty	Vivia
Rowan	Shelly	Sybil	Tracey	Vivian
Rowena	Shena	Sybilla	Tracy	Viviana
Roxana	Sherri	Sylvia	Tricia	Vivien
Roxane	Sherry	Sylvie	Trina	Vivienne
Roxanna	Sheryl	Tabitha	Tris	Walburga
Roxanne	Shirl	Talitha	Trisha	Wallis
Roxy	Shirley	Tallulah	Trissie	Wanda
Ruby	Shona	Tamar	Trix	Wendy
Ruth	Shushana	Tamara	Trixie	Wilfreda
Ruthie	Shushanna	Tamasine	Trudi	Wilfrida
Sabina	Sian	Tammy	Trudie	Wilhelmina
Sabrina	Sib	Tamsin	Trudy	Willa
Sadie	Sibbie	Tania	Tryphena	Williamina
Saffron	Sibby	Tanith	Tyra	Wilma
Sal	Sibella	Tansy	Ulrica	Win
Salena	Sibilla	Tanya	Ulrika	Winefred
Salina	Sibyl	Tara	Una	Winifred
Sally	Sibylla	Tatiana	Unity	Winnie
Salome	Sidonia	Tegan	Ursula	Winnifred
Sam	Sidony	Tegwen	Val	Wynn
Samantha	Síle	Temperance	Valda	Wynne
Sammy	Silvana	Teresa	Valentina	Xanthe
Sanchia	Silvia	Terri	Valentine	Xenia
Sandie	Simona	Terry	Valeria	Yasmin
Sandra	Simone	Tess	Valerie	Yolanda
Sandy	Síne	Tessa	Vanda	Yvette
Santha	Sinead	Tessie	Vanessa	Yvonne
Sapphire	Siobhan	Tetty	Vashti	Zana
Sara	Siri	Thea	Velda	Zandra
Sarah	Sisley	Thelma	Velma	Zara
Sarai	Sissie	Theodora	Venetia	Zareen
Saranna	Sissy	Theodosia	Venus	Zarina
Sarina	Sonia	Theophania	Vera	Zein
Sarita	Sonja	Theophila	Verena	Zelda
Sarra	Sonya	Theresa	Verity	Zelma
Scarlet	Sophia	Thérèse	Verna	Zena
Scarlett	Sophie	Theresia	Verona	Zenobia
Seana	Sophronia	Thirsa	Veronica	Zillah
Selena	Sophy	Thirza	Véronique	Zinnia
Selina	Sorcha	Thomasina	Vi	Zita
Selma	Stacey	Thomasine	Vicki	Zoë
Senga	Stacy	Thora	Vicky	Zohra
Septima	Stefanie	Thyone	Victoria	Zola
Seraphina	Stella	Thyra	Victorine	Zora
Serena	Stephanie	Tibby	Vida	Zorah
Shani	Stevie	Tiffany	Vijaya	Zoulika
Shannon	Sue	Tilda	Vikki	Zuleika

ABBREVIATIONS

A

a acceleration; are(s) (metric measure of land); atto- (prefix indicating 10^{-18}, as in **am**, attometre); the first vertical row of squares from the left on a chessboard

a. acre(s); address; age; alto; amateur; anno (Latin: in the year); answer; ante (Latin: before)

a 2 a due (Italian: for two (voices or instruments))

A absolute (temperature); ace; adenine; adenosine; adult (former certification); Advanced (in **A level**); affinity; ammeter (in circuit diagrams); ampere(s); area; an arterial road (as in **A1, A40**, etc.); assault (in **A-day**); atom(ic) (as in **A-bomb**); austral (monetary unit of Argentina); Austria; mass number; nucleon number; ten (in hexadecimal notation); a blood group or its associated antigen; the highest mark or grade for work; managerial, professional (occupational grade); a musical note or key; a standard paper size; a universal affirmative categorical proposition

Å angstrom unit

A. academy; acre(s); adjutant; admiral; alto; America(n); annual; answer; April; assistant; associate; August

A1 (in Lloyd's Register) ships maintained in good and efficient condition

A3 a standard paper size, 297 × 420 mm

A4 a standard paper size, 210 × 297 mm

A5 a standard paper size, 148 × 210 mm

āa ana (Greek: of each; specifying quantities of ingredients in prescriptions)

a.a. after arrival; always afloat

AA administrative assistant; Alcoholics Anonymous; American Aviation (aircraft); anti-aircraft; Architectural Association; Augustinians of the Assumption; author's alteration; Automobile Association; a certificate issued for a ship stating that all crew matters are in order; a film not be shown to a child under 14 unless accompanied by an adult; a size of battery or cell

AA1 a very high quality rating for credit

AAA Amateur Athletic Association; anti-aircraft artillery; Australian Association of Accountants; Automobile Association of America; the highest quality rating for credit

AA&QMG Assistant Adjutant and Quartermaster-General

AAC Army Air Corps

AACR Anglo-American Cataloguing Rules

AAE American Association of Engineers

AAEE Aircraft and Armament Experimental Establishment

AAFCE Allied Air Forces in Central Europe

AAG Assistant Adjutant-General

AAM air-to-air missile

AAMI age-associated memory impairment

A & A additions and amendments

A&AEE Aeroplane and Armament Experimental Establishment

A & C addenda and corrigenda

A&E Accident and Emergency (department of a hospital)

a&h accident and health

a&i accident and indemnity

A & M Ancient and Modern (hymn book)

A & N Army and Navy (Club *or* Stores)

A & P advertising and promotion; (New Zealand) Agricultural and Pastoral (Association, Show, etc.)

A & R artists and repertoire *or* repertory (as in **A & R man**)

a&s accident and sickness

AAP affirmative action programme; Australian Associated Press

a.a.r. against all risks

AASC Australian Army Service Corps

A'asia Australasia

AAT alpha-1-antitrypsin (treatment for cystic fibrosis)

ab. abridgment

a/b airborne

Ab astatine (originally called alabamine; *see under* At)

AB Aberdeen; able-bodied seaman; airborne; Alberta (Canada); ammonia for bees (applied for stings); antiballistic (missile); (USA) Bachelor of Arts (Latin *Artium Baccalaureus*); a human blood group containing A and B antigens

ABA Amateur Boxing Association; Antiquarian Booksellers' Association; Australian Bankers' Association

abbrev. abbreviation

ABC Advance Booking Charter (airline ticket); airway, breathing, circulation (in first aid); American Broadcasting Company; Argentina–Brazil–Chile; atomic, biological, and chemical (weapons or warfare); Audit Bureau of Circulation; Australian Broadcasting Commission

ABCA Army Bureau of Current Affairs

abd. abdicate(d); abdomen; abdominal

ABD all but dissertation (of a candidate reading for a higher degree); average body dose (of radiation)

ABE acetone–butanol–ethanol (solvent)

abf absolute bloody final (drink)

abl. ablative

ABM antiballistic missile

ABO a blood group system based on the presence or absence of antigens A and B

A-bomb atom bomb

Abp Archbishop

ABP arterial blood pressure

abr. abridge(d); abridgment

ABRC Advisory Board for the Research Councils

ABRV advanced ballistic re-entry vehicle

abs. abstract

ABS acrylonitrile–butadiene–styrene (type of plastic); Antiblockiersystem (in **ABS brake**; German: antilocking system); Australian Bureau of Statistics

abse. re. absente reo (Latin: the defendant being absent)

abs. re. absente reo

abstr. abstract(ed)

abt about

ABTAC Australian Book Trade Advisory Committee

abv. above

a.c. alternating current; ante cibum (Latin: before meals; in prescriptions)

a/c account; account current

Ac acetyl (ethanoyl) group; actinium

AC air conditioning; Air Corps; Alcohol Concern (a charity); alternating current; analogue computer; ante Christum (Latin: before Christ); Appeal Case(s); appellation contrôlée; Assistant Commissioner; Athletic Club; Companion of the Order of Australia

A/C account; account current; air conditioning; aircraftman

ACA Australian Consumers' Association

ACAA Agricultural Conservation and Adjustment Administration

acac acetylacetonate ion (used in formulae)

acad. academy

ACAS Advisory Conciliation and Arbitration Service; Assistant Chief of Air Staff

ACB Australian Cricket Board

acc. accelerate; acceleration; acceptance; accepted; accompanied (by);

accompaniment; according (to); account; accountant; accusative

ACC (New Zealand) Accident Compensation Corporation; accumulator; acute cardiovascular collapse; Agricultural Credit Corporation Ltd; Anglican Consultative Council

acce. acceptance

accel. accelerando (Italian; with increasing speed)

ACCM Advisory Council for the Church's Ministry

accom. accommodation

accred. accredited

acct. account(ing); accountant

accum. accumulative

ACD acid citrate dextrose (as in **ACD solution**)

AC/DC alternating current/direct current; bisexual

ACDS Assistant Chief of Defence Staff

ACE advanced cooled engine; Advisory Centre for Education; Allied Command Europe; angiotensin-converting enzyme (as in **ACE inhibitor**); (Member of the) Association of Conference Executives

ACER Australian Council for Educational Research

ACET Aids care, education, and treatment

ACF Army Cadet Force

ACG Assistant Chaplain-General

ACGS Assistant Chief of the General Staff

ACh acetylcholine

ACH automated clearing house

ack. acknowledge; acknowledgment

ACK acknowledgment

ack-ack anti-aircraft (World War I phonetic alphabet for AA)

ackgt acknowledgment

ACM Air Chief Marshal; air combat manoeuvring

a.c.n. all concerned notified

ACNS Assistant Chief of Naval Staff

ACORD Advisory Council on Research and Development

ACORN A Classification of Residential Neighbourhoods (directory); automatic checkout and recording network

ACOS Assistant Chief of Staff

ACOST Advisory Council on Science and Technology

ACP African, Caribbean, and Pacific (countries)

acpt. acceptance

ACR audio cassette recorder

ACRE Action with Rural Communities in England

ACRS Accelerated Cost Recovery System

ACS Additional Curates Society; advanced communications system; automated confirmation service

ACSEA Allied Command South East Asia

a/cs pay. accounts payable

a/cs rec. accounts receivable

act. acting; active; actor; actual; actuary

ACT advance corporation tax; Australian Capital Territory; Australian College of Theology

actg acting

ACTH adrenocorticotrophic hormone

ACTU Australian Council of Trade Unions

ACV actual cash value; air-cushion vehicle

ACW aircraftwoman

ACWS aircraft control and warning system

ad advertisement; (North America) advantage

a.d. after date; ante diem (Latin: before the day); autograph document

AD accidental damage; active duty; air defence; Algerian dinar (monetary unit; *see also under* DA); anno Domini (Latin: in the year of the Lord); Art Director; assembly district; Assistant Director; Australian Democrat(s); average deviation; Dame of the Order of Australia

A/D analog–digital (conversion)

ADA a programming language (after Ada Lovelace (1815–52), British mathematician)

adag. adagio

Adapt Access for Disabled People to Arts Today

ADAS Agricultural Development and Advisory Service; automatic data acquisition system

A-day assault day

ADB accidental death benefit; African Development Bank; Asian Development Bank

ADC advanced developing country; aide-de-camp; Aid to Dependent Children; analogue-to-digital converter; Assistant District Commissioner

ADCM Archbishop of Canterbury's Diploma in Church Music

ADC(P) personal aide-de-camp to HM the Queen

add. add *or* let there be added (in prescriptions; Latin *adde or addantur*); addendum; addition(al); address(ed)

ADD airstream direction detector

addl additional

addn addition

addsd addressed

ADEME Assistant Director, Electrical and Mechanical Engineering

ADF (Australia) approved deposit fund; Asian Development Fund; Australian Defence Force; automatic direction finder

ad fin. ad finem (Latin: at *or* near the end)

ADFManc Art and Design Fellow, Manchester

ADFW Assistant Director of Fortifications and Works

ADG Assistant Director-General

ADGB Air Defence of Great Britain

ADGMS Assistant Director-General of Medical Services

ADH antidiuretic hormone; Assistant Director of Hygiene

ADHD attention deficit and hyperactivity disorder

ADI acceptable daily intake (of a toxic substance in food)

ad inf. ad infinitum (Latin: to infinity)

ad init. ad initium (Latin: at the beginning)

ad int. ad interim (Latin: in the meantime)

adj. adjacent; adjective; adjoining; adjoint; adjourned; adjudged; adjunct; adjustment; adjutant

ADJAG Assistant Deputy Judge Advocate-General

adjt adjutant

Adjt-Gen Adjutant-General

ADL Ada design language

ad lib. ad libitum (Latin: according to pleasure, i.e. freely)

ad loc. ad locum (Latin: at the place)

adm. administration; administrative; administrator; admission; admitted

Adm. Admiral; Admiralty

admin. administration; administrator

ADMS Assistant Director of Medical Services

ADN Yemen

ADNS Assistant Director of Nursing Services

ADOS Assistant Director of Ordnance Services

ADP adenosine diphosphate; automatic data processing

ADR alternative dispute resolution; American Depository Receipt

a.d.s. autograph document signed

ADS&T Assistant Director of Supplies and Transport

ADST approved deferred share trust

ADTS Automated Data and Telecommunications Service

adv. advance; adverb(ial); adversus (Latin: against); advertisement; advertising; advice; advise; adviser; advisory; advocate

Adv. Advent; Advocate

ad val. ad valorem (Latin: according to value)

advb adverb

ADVS Assistant Director of Veterinary Services

advt advertisement

ADWE&M Assistant Director of Works, Electrical and Mechanical

ADX automatic digital exchange

ae. aetatis (Latin: at the age of; aged)

AE account executive; age exemption; agricultural engineer(ing); Air Efficiency Award; American English; George Russell, 1867–1935, Irish poet; (in Lloyd's Register) third-class ships

AEA Atomic Energy Authority

AEAF Allied Expeditionary Air Force

AE & P Ambassador Extraordinary and Plenipotentiary
AEC additional extended coverage; Agricultural Executive Council; (USA) Atomic Energy Commission
AECCG African Elephant Conservation Coordinating Group
AeE Aeronautical Engineer
AEEU Amalgamated Engineering and Electrical Union (formed from merger of AEU and EETPU)
AEF Allied Expeditionary Force
A-effect alienation effect
a.e.g. ad eundem gradum (Latin: to the same degree)
AEGIS Aid for the Elderly in Government Institutions
AEI American Express International
AEM Air Efficiency Medal
aeq. aequalis (Latin: equal)
AER Army Emergency Reserve
AERE Atomic Energy Research Establishment (Harwell)
AERO Air Education and Recreation Organization
aeron. aeronautical; aeronautics
aet. aetatis (Latin: at the age of; aged)
AEU Amalgamated Engineering Union (formerly AUEW; see AEEU)
AEU(TASS) Amalgamated Engineering Union (Technical, Administrative, and Supervisory Section)
AEW airborne early warning (aircraft)
a.f. advanced freight; audiofrequency
Af afgháni (monetary unit of Afghanistan)
Af. Africa(n); Aruban florin (monetary unit of Aruba)
AF Académie Française (French literary academy); across flats (used in denoting sizes of nuts, as in ½AF); air force; Anglo-French; audiofrequency; autofocus
A/F as found (in auction catalogues)
AFA (Scotland) Associate of the Faculty of Actuaries
AFAM Ancient Free and Accepted Masons
AFB (USA) Air Force Base
AFC Air Force Cross; automatic flight control; automatic frequency control
AFCENT Allied Forces in Central Europe (of NATO)
AFDS Air Fighting Development Squadron
aff. affiliate(d); affix
afft affidavit
Afg. Afghanistan
AFG Afghanistan
Afgh. Afghanistan
AFHQ Allied Force(s) Headquarters
AFI American Film Institute
AFIA (Australia) Associate of the Federal Institute of Accountants
AFL-CIO American Federation of Labor and Congress of Industrial Organizations

AFM Air Force Medal; atomic force microscope; audiofrequency modulation
AFP alpha-fetoprotein
Afr. Africa(n)
AFr. Anglo-French
AFR accident frequency rate (in industry)
AFRASEC Afro-Asian Organization for Economic Cooperation
AFRC Agricultural and Food Research Council
aft. after; afternoon
AFTN Aeronautical Fixed Telecommunications Network
AFV armoured fighting vehicle
ag. agent; agreement; agriculture
Ag silver (Latin argentum)
Ag. August
AG Adjutant-General; (Germany) Aktiengesellschaft (public limited company; plc); Attorney-General
Aga Aktiebolaget Gasackumulator (cooker)
AGARD Advisory Group for Aerospace Research and Development (in NATO)
AGC (USA) advanced graduate certificate; automatic gain control
agcy agency
agd agreed
AgE Agricultural Engineer
AGH Australian General Hospital
agit. agitatum (Latin: shaken)
Agitprop Agitpropbyuro (Soviet bureau in charge of agitation and propaganda)
AGM air-to-ground missile; annual general meeting
agr. agricultural; agriculture; agriculturist
AGR advanced gas-cooled reactor
AGRA Army Group Royal Artillery
agric. agricultural; agriculture; agriculturist
agron. agronomy
AGSM Australian Graduate of the School of Management
agst against
agt agent; agreement
a.g.w. actual gross weight
AGWI Atlantic, Gulf, West Indies
agy agency
a.h. aft hatch; ampere-hour
AH anno Hegirae (Latin: in the year of the Hegira; in the Muslim calendar); Antwerp–Hamburg coastal ports
AHA Australian Hotels Association
AH & FITB Agricultural, Horticultural, and Forestry Industry Training Board
AHAUS Amateur Hockey Association of the United States
AHC Accepting Houses Committee
AHF antihaemophilic factor
AHG antihaemophilic globulin
AHH aryl hydrocarbon hydroxylase (used in tobacco research)
AHQ Air Headquarters; Army Headquarters
a.i. ad interim (Latin: for the meantime)

AI Amnesty International; Army Intelligence; artificial insemination; artificial intelligence
AIC Agricultural Improvement Council
AICC All India Congress Committee
AID acute infectious disease; artificial insemination (by) donor
AIDA attention, interest, desire, action (of the customer)
Aids acquired immune deficiency syndrome
AIF Australian Imperial Forces
AIG Adjutant Inspector-General
AIH artificial insemination (by) husband
AIM Australian Institute of Management
AIR All India Radio
AJA American of Japanese ancestry; Australian Journalists' Association
AJAG Assistant Judge Advocate-General
AJC Australian Jockey Club
AK Alaska; automatic Kalashnikov (rifle); Knight of the Order of Australia
a.k.a. also known as
al. alcohol(ic); alia (Latin: other things)
a.l. allotment letter; autograph letter
Al aluminium
AL Alabama; Albania; Anglo-Latin; St Albans
Ala alanine
Ala. Alabama
ALA all letters answered
Alap as low as practicable (describing radiation doses or levels)
Alara as low as reasonably achievable (describing radiation doses or levels)
Alas. Alaska
alb. albumin
Alb. Albania(n); Alberta
ALBM air-launched ballistic missile
alc. alcohol
ALCM air-launched cruise missile
ALCS Authors' Lending and Copyright Society
Ald. Alderman
ALE additional living expense
A level Advanced level
ALF Animal Liberation Front; Arab Liberation Front (Iraq)
ALFSEA Allied Land Forces South-East Asia
alg. algebra(ic)
Alg. Algeria(n)
Algol algorithmic language
ALI Argyll Light Infantry
ALICE Autistic and Language-Impaired Children's Education
ALJ Australian Law Journal
alk. alkali
ALM audiolingual method (in teaching a foreign language)
ALP Australian Labor Party
ALS autograph letter signed

al seg. al segno (Italian: to the sign)

alt. alteration; alternate; alternative; alternator; altimeter; altitude; alto

ALT alanine aminotransferase

Alta. Alberta

alt. dieb. alternis diebus (Latin: every other day)

alt. hor. alternis horis (Latin: every other hour)

alt. noct. alternis noctibus (Latin: every other night)

ALU arithmetic and logic unit

alum. aluminium

am attometre(s)

a.m. amplitude modulation; ante meridiem (Latin: before noon)

a/m above mentioned

Am americium

Am. America(n)

AM air mail; Albert Medal; amplitude modulation; ante meridiem; assistant manager; (USA) Master of Arts (Latin *Artium Magister*); Member of the Order of Australia

AMA Assistant Masters Association; Australian Medical Association

Amb. Ambassador; ambulance

AMC Agricultural Mortgage Corporation Ltd

AMDG ad majorem Dei gloriam (Latin: to the greater glory of God; the Jesuit motto)

amdt amendment

Amex American Express

AMF Australian Military Forces

AMG Allied Military Government

AMGOT Allied Military Government of Occupied Territory (in World War II)

AMI acute myocardial infarction

AMMA Assistant Masters' and Mistresses' Association

AMORC Ancient Mystical Order Rosae Crucis (Rosicrucians)

amort. amortization

amp. ampere; amplified; amplifier

AMP adenosine monophosphate; Australian Mutual Provident Society

Amraam advanced medium-range air-to-air missile

AMS American Musicological Society; army medical services; Assistant Military Secretary; automatic music search

amt amount

AMT airmail transfer

AMTE Admiralty Marine Technology Establishment

AMTRI Advanced Manufacturing Technology Research Institute

amu atomic mass unit

AMVETS American Veterans (of World War II and subsequent wars)

an. anno (Latin: in the year)

a.n. above named

An actinon

AN acid number; Anglo-Norman; antenatal

A/N advice note

ANA All Nippon Airways; Article Number Association

anal. analogous; analogy; analysis; analytic

anat. anatomical; anatomy

anc. ancient

ANC African National Congress; Army Nurse Corps

anch. anchored

AND and (from its sense in logic, as in **AND gate, AND operation**); Andorra

ANF atrial natriuretic factor

Angl. Anglican; Anglicized

Anh. Anhang (German: appendix; of a book, etc.)

anhyd. anhydrous

anim. animato (Italian: in a lively manner)

ann. annals; anni (Latin: years); annual; annuity

anniv. anniversary

anon. anonymous(ly)

ANOVA analysis of variance

ANS autonomic nervous system

ANSI American National Standards Institute

ant. antenna; anterior; antonym

Ant. Antarctica

ANTA Australian National Travel Association

anthrop. anthropological; anthropology

antilog antilogarithm

antiq. antiquarian; antiquity

ANU Australian National University

ANZ Australia and New Zealand Banking Group

ANZAAS Australian and New Zealand Association for the Advancement of Science

Anzac Australian and New Zealand Army Corps (in World War I)

ANZUS Australia, New Zealand, and the United States (referring to the security alliance between them)

AO Australian Opera; Officer of the Order of Australia

A/O account of; and others

AOA Air Officer in charge of Administration

AOB any other business

AOC Air Officer Commanding; appellation (d'origine) contrôlée (French: controlled place of origin; wine classification)

AOCB any other competent business

AOD Army Ordnance Department

AOER Army Officers' Emergency Reserve

AOH Ancient Order of Hibernians

A-OK (USA) all (systems) OK

AONB area of outstanding natural beauty

a/or and/or

AOR adult-oriented rock; album-oriented rock

a.p. additional premium; ante prandium (Latin: before a meal; in prescriptions); author's proof

Ap. apostle

AP additional premium; adjective phrase; (USA) Air Police; (Spain)

Alianza Popular (Popular Alliance; political party); average payable

APB all-points bulletin (police alert); Auditing Practices Board

APC armoured personnel carrier

APD Army Pay Department

APEC Asia-Pacific Economic Cooperation Conference

APEX Advance-Purchase Excursion (reduced airline or rail fare)

APH antepartum haemorrhage

API American Petroleum Institute; application programmer interface

APIS Army Photographic Intelligence Service

API scale American Petroleum Institute scale (for measuring the specific gravity of petroleum products)

APL A Programming Language

APLA Azanian People's Liberation Army

APM Assistant Provost-Marshal

apmt appointment

APO Armed Forces Post Office

Apoc. Apocalypse; Apocrypha(l)

app. apparatus; apparent(ly); appendix (of a book); applied; appointed; apprentice; approved; approximate(ly)

appar. apparatus; apparent(ly)

appd approved

appl. appeal; applicable; applied

appro approval

approx. approximate(ly)

APPU Australian Primary Producers' Union

appx appendix (of a book)

Apr. April

APR Accredited Public Relations Practitioner; annual percentage rate (of interest)

APS (Australia) Aborigines' Protection Society

APSE Ada programming support environment

apt. apartment

APT advanced passenger train; alum-precipitated (diphtheria) toxoid

APTC Army Physical Training Corps

APU acute psychiatric unit (of a prison, etc.); Assessment of Performance Unit (body monitoring pupil performance)

aq. aqua (Latin: water); aqueous

AQ accomplishment quotient; Administration and Quartering

aq. bull. aqua bulliens (Latin: boiling water)

aq. cal. aqua calida (Latin: warm water)

aq. com. aqua communis (Latin: tap water)

aq. dest. aqua destillata (Latin: distilled water)

aq. ferv. aqua fervens (Latin: hot water)

aq. frig. aqua frigida (Latin: cold water)

AQMG Assistant Quartermaster-General

aq. pur. aqua pura (Latin: pure water)

aq. tep. aqua tepida (Latin: tepid water)

ar. arrival; arrive(s) *or* arrived

a.r. all risks; anno regni (Latin: in the year of the reign)

Ar argon; aryl group

Ar. Arabia(n); Arabic; Aramaic

AR accomplishment ratio; account receivable; analytical reagent; Anna Regina (Latin: Queen Anne); annual return; Arkansas; Army Regulations; Autonomous Region

Arab. Arabia(n); Arabic

Aram. Aramaic

arb. arbitrager; arbitration; arbitrator

arc. arcato *or* coll'arco (Italian: with the bow)

ARC Aeronautical Research Council; Agricultural Research Council (now the AFRC); Aids-related complex; Archaeological Resource Centre (York); Architects' Registration Council

ARCA Associate of the Royal Cambrian Academy

arccos arc (inverse) cosine

arccosec arc (inverse) cosecant

arccot arc (inverse) cotangent

arch arc (inverse) hyperbolic cosine

arch. archaic; archaism; archery; archipelago; architect; architectural; architecture

Arch. Archbishop

archaeol. archaeology

Archbp Archbishop

Archd. Archdeacon; Archduke

archit. architecture

archt. architect

ARCIC Anglican/Roman Catholic International Commission

arcos arc (inverse) cosine

arcsec arc (inverse) secant

arcsin arc (inverse) sine

arctan arc (inverse) tangent

ARCUK Architects' Registration Council of the United Kingdom

ARE Admiralty Research Establishment; Arab Republic of Egypt

ARF acute respiratory failure

Arg arginine

Arg. Argentina; Argentine

ARICS Professional Associate of the Royal Institution of Chartered Surveyors

Ariz. Arizona

Ark. Arkansas

Arm. Armenia(n); Armoric(an)

ArM Master of Architecture (Latin *Architecturae Magister*)

ARM Australian Republican Movement

ARMS Action for Research into Multiple Sclerosis

arp. arpeggio

ARP air-raid precautions

ARPANET Advanced Research Projects Agency Network

arr. arrangement; arranged (by); arrival; arrive(s); arrived

ARR accounting rate of return

arsech arc (inverse) hyperbolic secant

arsh arc (inverse) hyperbolic sine

arsinh arc (inverse) hyperbolic sine

art. article; artificial; artillery

artanh arc (inverse) hyperbolic tangent

arth arc (inverse) hyperbolic tangent

arty artillery

ARV American (Standard) Revised Version

As arsenic

As. Asia(n); Asiatic

AS Advanced Supplementary (in **AS level**); al segno (Italian: to the sign); Anglo-Saxon; antisubmarine

A/S account sales; Advanced Supplementary (in **A/S level**); after sight; alongside

ASA Advertising Standards Authority; Amateur Swimming Association; Army Sailing Association; Australian Society of Accountants

a.s.a.p. as soon as possible

ASAT antisatellite (interceptor)

asb. asbestos

ASBM air-to-surface ballistic missile

ASBSBSW Amalgamated Society of Boilermakers, Shipwrights, Blacksmiths, and Structural Workers

Asc. Ascendant

ASC Administrative Staff College, Henley; altered state of consciousness

ASCAB Armed Services Consultant Approval Board

ASCAP American Society of Composers, Authors, and Publishers

ASCII American Standard Code for Information Interchange

ASD Armament Supply Department

ASDE Airport Surface Detection Equipment

ASE American Stock Exchange

ASH Action on Smoking and Health

ASI airspeed indicator

ASIO Australian Security Intelligence Organization

ASL American Sign Language

A/S level Advanced Supplementary level

ASM air-to-surface missile

Asn asparagine

ASN army service number

ASO Air Staff Officer

Asp aspartic acid

ASP (USA) Anglo-Saxon Protestant

ASPAC Asian and Pacific Council

ass. assembly; assistant; association

ASSC Accounting Standards Steering Committee

assn association

assoc. associate(d); association

ASSR Autonomous Soviet Socialist Republic

asst assistant

asstd assorted

assy assembly

Assyr. Assyrian

AST aspartate aminotransferase; Atlantic Standard Time; automated screen trading

ASTC Administrative Service Training Course

ASTM American Society for Testing Materials

astr. astronomer; astronomical; astronomy

astrol. astrologer; astrological; astrology

astron. astronomer; astronomical; astronomy

ASU Arab Socialist Union

ASV American Standard Version

ASVU Army Security Vetting Unit

ASW antisubmarine work

ASWDU Air Sea Warfare Development Unit

ASWE Admiralty Surface Weapons Establishment

at. atmosphere; atomic

At ampere-turn (unit); astatine; (a member of the) Auxiliary Territorial Service

AT achievement test; alternative technology; antitank; Atlantic Time; attainment target

ATA Air Transport Auxiliary

ATAF Allied Tactical Air Force

ATB advanced technology bomber; all-terrain bike

ATC air-traffic control; Air Training Corps; Air Transport Command; Art Teacher's Certificate; authorization to copy (of software); automatic train control

ATCRBS Air Traffic Control Radar Beacon System

ATD Art Teacher's Diploma

ATE automatic test equipment

a tem. a tempo (Italian: in time)

Atl. Atlantic

ATL actual total loss; adult T-cell leukaemia

atm atmosphere (unit of pressure)

atm. atmospheric

ATM automated teller machine

ATN arc tangent; augmented transition network

at. no. atomic number

ATO Ammunition Technical Officer (bomb-disposal officer in the RAOC); assisted takeoff

A to J (New Zealand) Appendices to Journals (of the House of Representatives or Parliament)

ATOL Air Travel Organizers' Licence

ATP adenosine triphosphate; automatic train protection

ATPL(A) Airline Transport Pilot's Licence (Aeroplanes)

ATPL(H) Airline Transport Pilot's Licence (Helicopters)

ATS automated trade system; Auxiliary Territorial Service (in World War II)

att. attached; attention; attorney
ATT antitetanus toxoid
Att-Gen. Attorney-General
attn attention; for the attention of
attrib. attribute; attributed (to); attribution; attributive(ly)
atty. attorney
Atty.-Gen. Attorney-General
ATV all-terrain vehicle
at. wt. atomic weight
Au gold (Latin *aurum*)
AU angstrom unit; astronomical unit
AUA agricultural unit of account (in the EC)
AUC ab urbe condita *or* anno urbis conditae (Latin: (in the year) from the founding of the city; indicating years numbered from the founding of Rome); Australian Universities Commission
aud. audit; auditor
AUEW Amalgamated Union of Engineering Workers
aug. augmentative; augmented
Aug. August
AULLA Australasian Universities Language and Literature Association
AUM air-to-underwater missile
AUP Aberdeen University Press
Aus. Australia(n); Austria(n)
AUS Australia
Aust. Australia(n); Austria(n)
Austral. Australasia; Australia(n)
aut. autumn
auth. author(ess); authority; authorize(d)
Auth. Ver. Authorized Version (of the Bible)
auto. automatic; automobile; automotive
autobiog. autobiographical; autobiography
aux. auxiliary
AUX auxiliary verb
av. avenue; average; avoirdupois
a.v. ad valorem (Latin: according to value)
Av. Avenue
AV acid value; ad valorem (Latin: according to value); Artillery Volunteers; atrioventricular (as in **AV bundle, AV node**); audio-visual; Authorized Version (of the Bible)
AVA audiovisual aids
AVC additional voluntary contribution (in pension schemes); automatic volume control
AVD Army Veterinary Department
avdp. avoirdupois
ave. avenue
avg. average
AVI audio visual interleaved
AVLA Audio Visual Language Association
AVLIS atomic vapour laser isotope separation
AVM Air Vice-Marshal
avn aviation
avoir. avoirdupois
AVR Army Volunteer Reserve

AVRO A. V. Roe and Co
a.w. actual weight; all water
AW Articles of War
AWA Amalgamated Wireless (Australasia) Ltd
AWACS airborne warning and control system
AWB (South Africa) Afrikaner Weerstandsbeweging (right-wing political party); Australia Wool Board
AWC Australian Wool Corporation
AWE Atomic Weapons Establishment
AWJ Arizona
AZT azidothymidine (drug used in treating Aids)

B

b the second vertical row of squares from the left on a chessboard
b. bag; bale; ball; base; brother; bass; billion; bloody (euphemism); book; born; bowled by; breadth; bye
B baht (Thai monetary unit); balboa (Panamanian monetary unit); baryon number; Belgium; Birmingham; bishop; black (indicating the degree of softness of lead in a pencil; also in **BB, double black, etc.);** bolívar (Venezuelan monetary unit; *see also under* Bs); (USA) bomber (as in **B-52**); boron; breathalyzer (as in **B-test**); eleven (in hexadecimal notation); magnetic flux density; secondary road (as in **B405**, etc.); susceptance; administrative, professional (occupational grade); a blood group or its associated antigen; a musical note or key; a standard paper size; something of secondary importance or interest (as in **B-film, B-road**)
B. Bachelor (in academic degrees); bass; bay; Bible; billion; book; breadth; British
B4 a standard paper size, 250 × 353 mm
B5 a standard paper size, 176 × 250 mm
Ba barium
BA Bachelor of Arts; bank acceptance; Bath; British Academy; British Airways; British Association (for the Advancement of Science); British Association (pitch of screw thread, as in **4BA**)
BAA British Airports Authority
BAAB British Amateur Athletic Board
BAAF British Agencies for Adoption and Fostering
BAAL British Association for Applied Linguistics
BAAS British Association for the Advancement of Science
BABIE British Association for Betterment of Infertility and Education
Bac. (France) baccalauréat (school examination)
BAc Bachelor of Acupuncture

BAC biologically active compound(s); blood-alcohol concentration; British Aircraft Corporation; Business Archives Council
BACAT barge aboard catamaran
BAcc Bachelor of Accountancy
BACM British Association of Colliery Management
BACO British Aluminium Company Ltd
BACS Bankers' Automated Clearing Service
bact. bacteria(l)
bacteriol. bacteriological; bacteriology
BADA British Antique Dealers' Association
BAe British Aerospace
BAE Bachelor of Aeronautical Engineering; Bachelor of Arts in Education; (USA) Bureau of Agricultural Economics
BAEA British Actors' Equity Association
BA(Econ) Bachelor of Arts in Economics
BA(Ed) Bachelor of Arts in Education
BAED Bachelor of Arts in Environmental Design
BAFO British Air Forces of Occupation
BAFTA British Academy of Film and Television Arts
BAGA British Amateur Gymnastics Association
BAgEc Bachelor of Agricultural Economics
BAgr Bachelor of Agriculture
BAgrSc Bachelor of Agricultural Science
BAHOH British Association for the Hard of Hearing
BAI Bachelor of Engineering (Latin *Baccalaureus Artis Ingeniariae*)
BAIE British Association of Industrial Editors
BA(J) Bachelor of Arts in Journalism
bal. balance
BAL blood-alcohol level; British anti-lewisite (dimercaprol; antidote to war gas and metal poisoning)
ball. ballast
BALPA British Airline Pilots' Association
Balt. Baltic
BAM Bachelor of Applied Mathematics; Bachelor of Arts in Music
BAMA British Aerosol Manufacturers' Association
b. and b. bed and breakfast
B & C building and contents
B & D bondage and discipline
B&FBS British and Foreign Bible Society
B and S brandy and soda
B&W black and white
BAO Bachelor of Arts in Obstetrics
BAOMS British Association of Oral and Maxillo-Facial Surgeons
BAOR British Army of the Rhine

bap. baptized

BAPC British Aircraft Preservation Council

BAppArts Bachelor of Applied Arts

BAppSc(MT) Bachelor of Applied Science (Medical Technology)

bapt. baptism; baptized

Bapt. Baptist

bar. barometer; barometric; barrel (container or unit of measure); barrister

Bar. baritone

BAR Browning Automatic Rifle

BARB Broadcasters' Audience Research Board

BARC British Automobile Racing Club

BArch Bachelor of Architecture

BArchE Bachelor of Architectural Engineering

barg. bargain

barit. baritone

Bart. Baronet

Bart's St Bartholomew's Hospital, London

BAS Bachelor in Agricultural Science; Bachelor of Applied Science

BASc Bachelor of Agricultural Science; Bachelor of Applied Science

BASC British Association for Shooting and Conservation

BASCA British Academy of Songwriters, Composers, and Authors

Basic beginners' all-purpose symbolic instruction code (programming language); British-American scientific international commercial (in **Basic English**)

BASMA Boot and Shoe Manufacturers' Association and Leather Trades Protection Society

BASW British Association of Social Workers

batt. battery

Bav. Bavaria(n)

b.b. ball bearing; bearer bonds

BB bail bond; bed and breakfast; Blackburn; Blue Book (the HMSO publication *UK National Accounts*); B'nai B'rith (Jewish international society); Boys' Brigade; Brigitte Bardot (1934– , French film actress); double black (indicating a very soft lead pencil)

BBA Bachelor of Business Administration; Big Brothers of America; born before arrival; British Bankers' Association; British Board of Agreement

BBB treble black (indicating a very soft lead pencil)

BBBC British Boxing Board of Control

BBC British Broadcasting Corporation

BBFC British Board of Film Censors

bbl. barrel (container or unit of measure for oil, etc.)

BBMA British Brush Manufacturers' Association

BBQ barbecue

BBS Bachelor of Business Science; bulletin board system

BBSF British Brain and Spine Foundation

BBV Banco Bilbao Vizcaya (Spanish bank)

b.c. basso continuo; blind copy

BC Bachelor of Chemistry; Bachelor of Commerce; bank clearing; bankruptcy court; Battery Commander; before Christ (following a date); bills for collection; blood consumption; borough council; British Coal; British Columbia

BCA (New Zealand) Bachelor of Commerce and Administration; British Chiropractic Association

BCAP British Code of Advertising Practice

BCAR British Civil Airworthiness Requirements

BCAS British Compressed Air Society

b.c.c. blind carbon copy; body-centred cubic

BCC British Coal Corporation; British Council of Churches

BCCI Bank of Credit and Commerce International

BCD binary-coded decimal; blue compact dwarf (type of star)

BCE Bachelor of Chemical Engineering; Bachelor of Civil Engineering; before common era (following a date; the non-Christian equivalent of BC); Board of Customs and Excise

BCF billion cubic feet; British Chess Federation; British Cycling Federation

BCG bacille Calmette–Guérin (antituberculosis vaccine)

BCh Bachelor of Surgery (Latin *Baccalaureus Chirurgiae*)

BCL Bachelor of Civil Law

BCM British Commercial Monomark

BCMF British Ceramic Manufacturers' Federation

BCMG Birmingham Contemporary Music Group

BCMS Bible Churchmen's Missionary Society

BCNZ Broadcasting Corporation of New Zealand

BCom Bachelor of Commerce

BComSc Bachelor of Commercial Science

BCPL Basic Computer Programming Language

BCS Bachelor of Chemical Science; Bachelor of Commercial Science; Bengal Civil Service; British Cardiac Society; British Computer Society

BCSA British Constructional Steelwork Association

BCURA British Coal Utilization Research Association

BCYC British Corinthian Yacht Club

bd board; bond; bound; bundle

b.d. bill(s) discounted

b/d brought down

Bd baud; Board; Boulevard

BD Bachelor of Divinity; Bahrain dinar (monetary unit); Bangladesh; bill(s) discounted; Bradford; Bundesrepublik Deutschland (Federal Republic of Germany)

B/D bank draft; bill(s) discounted; brought down

BDA Bachelor of Domestic Arts; Bachelor of Dramatic Art; British Deaf Association; British Dental Association; British Diabetic Association

Bde Brigade

BDes Bachelor of Design

bd.ft. board foot (measure of timber)

b.d.i. both dates included

BDI (Germany) Bundesverband der Deutschen Industrie (Federal Association of German Industry)

bdl. bundle

bdrm bedroom

bds boards; bundles

BDS Bachelor of Dental Surgery; Barbados; British Driving Society

BDSc Bachelor of Dental Science

b.d.v. breakdown voltage

b.e. bill of exchange

Be beryllium

Bé Baumé (temperature scale)

BE Bachelor of Education; Bachelor of Engineering; Bank of England; Barkhausen emission; best estimate; bill of exchange; British Element; British Empire

BEA British East Africa; British Epilepsy Association

BEAB British Electrical Approvals Board

BEAMA (Federation of) British Electrotechnical and Allied Manufacturers' Associations

BEAS British Educational Administration Society

BEc Bachelor of Economics

BEC Building Employers' Confederation

BECTU Broadcasting, Entertainment, and Cinematograph Technicians Union (formed by amalgamation of BETA with ACTT)

BEd Bachelor of Education

Beds Bedfordshire

BEE Bachelor of Electrical Engineering

BEF British Equestrian Federation; British Expeditionary Force (in World Wars I and II)

BEI Banque européenne d'investissement (French: European Investments Bank)

Bel. Belgian; Belgium

Belg. Belgian; Belgium

BEM British Empire Medal; bug-eyed monster

BEMA British Essence Manufacturers' Association; Business Equipment Manufacturers' Association

BEMAS British Education Management and Administration Society

BEME Brigade Electrical and Mechanical Engineer

Benelux Belgium, Netherlands, Luxembourg (customs union)
Beng. Bengal(i)
BEng Bachelor of Engineering
BEngr Bachelor of Engraving
BEO Base Engineer Officer
Berks Berkshire
BES Bachelor of Engineering Science; Biological Engineering Society; British Ecological Society; Business Expansion Scheme
BESO British Executive Service Overseas
BEST British Expertise in Science and Technology (database)
bet. between
BEUC Bureau européen des unions de consommateurs (French: European Bureau of Consumers' Unions)
BeV (USA) billion electronvolts
BEXA British Exporters Association
bf brief
b.f. bloody fool; bold face
b/f brought forward
BF Bachelor of Forestry; Banque de France (Bank of France); Belgian franc; bloody fool; body fat; breathing frequency
B/F brought forward
BFA Bachelor of Fine Arts
BFBS British and Foreign Bible Society
BFI British Film Institute
BFMIRA British Food Manufacturing Industries' Research Association
b.f.o. beat-frequency oscillator
BFPO British Forces Post Office
BFr Belgian franc
BFSS British Field Sports Society
bg bag
b/g bonded goods
BG Bulgaria
BGCS Botanic Gardens Conservation Secretariat
BGenEd Bachelor of General Education
BGS Brigadier General Staff; British Geological Survey; British Geriatrics Society; British Goat Society
Bh bohrium
BH Belize (formerly British Honduras); black hole; Bournemouth
B/H bill of health
B'ham Birmingham
BHE Bachelor of Home Economics
B'head Birkenhead
BHF British Heart Foundation
bhp brake horsepower
BHRA British Hydromechanics' Research Association
BHRCA British Hotels, Restaurants, and Caterers' Association
BHS British Home Stores; British Horse Society
Bi bismuth
Bib. Bible; Biblical
bibl. bibliographer; bibliographical; bibliography
BIBRA British Industrial Biological Research Association

BICERI British Internal Combustion Engine Research Institute
b.i.d. bis in die (Latin: twice a day; in prescriptions)
BID Bachelor of Industrial Design
BIE Bachelor of Industrial Engineering
BIEE British Institute of Energy Economics
BIF British Industries Fair
BIFFEX Baltic International Freight Futures Exchange
BIFU Banking, Insurance, and Finance Union
BIH Bureau international de l'heure (French: International Time Bureau)
BIIBA British Insurance and Investment Brokers' Association
BIM British Institute of Management
biog. biographic(al); biography
biol. biological; biology
BIOS basic input-output system
BIR British Institute of Radiology
BIS Bank for International Settlements; British Interplanetary Society
BISF British Iron and Steel Federation
BISFA British Industrial and Scientific Film Association
BISPA British Independent Steel Producers' Association
BISRA British Iron and Steel Research Association
bit binary digit
BJ Bachelor of Journalism; bubblejet (printer)
BJSM British Joint Services Mission
bk backwardation; bank; book
Bk berkelium
bkcy bankruptcy
bkg banking
bkpt bankrupt
bks barracks; books
BKSTS British Kinematograph, Sound, and Television Society
bl barrel (container or unit of measure)
bl. bale; black; blue
b.l. bill of lading; breech-loading (rifle)
BL Bachelor of Law; Bachelor of Literature; Barrister-at-Law; bill lodged; bill of lading; Bloch lines; Bolton; British Leyland; British Library
B/L bill of lading
BLA Bachelor of Landscape Architecture; Bachelor of Liberal Arts; British Liberation Army
bldg building
BLESMA British Limbless Ex-Servicemen's Association
BLEU Belgo-Luxembourg Economic Union
BLit Bachelor of Literature
BLitt Bachelor of Letters (Latin Baccalaureus Litterarum)
blk black; block; bulk
BLL Bachelor of Laws
BLOX block order exposure system
BLS Bachelor of Library Science

BLT bacon, lettuce, and tomato (sandwich)
Blvd Boulevard
b.m. board measure (measurement of wood)
BM Bachelor of Medicine; Bachelor of Music; base metal; benchmark; bone marrow; brigade major; British Monomark; British Museum
BMA British Medical Association
BMC British Medical Council; British Motor Corporation
BME Bachelor of Mechanical Engineering; Bachelor of Mining Engineering; Bachelor of Music Education; benign myalgic encephalomyelitis
BMedSci Bachelor of Medical Science
BMEO British Middle East Office
BMet Bachelor of Metallurgy
BMetE Bachelor of Metallurgical Engineering
BMEWS ballistic missile early-warning system
BMH British Military Hospital
BMI body-mass index; Broadcast Music Incorporated
BMJ British Medical Journal
BMM British Military Mission
BMR basal metabolic rate
BMRA Brigade Major Royal Artillery
BMS Bachelor of Marine Science
BMT basic motion time-study
BMus Bachelor of Music
BMW Bayerische Motorenwerke (German: Bavarian Motor Works)
BMX bicycle motocross
bn bassoon; battalion; billion
Bn Baron; Battalion
BN Bachelor of Nursing; bank note; Brighton
BNAF British North Africa Force
BNEC British National Export Council
BNF Backus–Naur form; British Nuclear Fuels (Limited)
BNFC British National Film Catalogue
bnkg banking
BNOC British National Oil Corporation; British National Opera Company
BNP Banque nationale de Paris (French: National Bank of Paris)
BNS buyer no seller
BNSc Bachelor of Nursing Science
BNSC British National Space Centre
BNTA British Numismatic Trade Association
BNurs Bachelor of Nursing
b.o. back order; branch office; broker's order; buyer's option
b/o brought over
BO body odour; box office
B/O brought over; buyer's option
BOA British Olympic Association; British Orthopaedic Association
BOAC British Overseas Airways Corporation
BOC British Oxygen Corporation

BOCE Board of Customs and Excise

Bod. Bodleian Library (Oxford)

BOD biochemical oxygen demand

BOF beginning of file

B of E Bank of England

BoJ Bank of Japan

Bol. Bolivia(n)

BOLTOP better on lips than on paper (written on the back of envelopes containing love letters)

BONUS Borrower's Option for Notes and Underwritten Standby

bor. borough

bos'n boatswain

BOSS (South Africa) Bureau of State Security

bot. botanic(al); botany; bottle; bought

BOT beginning of tape (in **BOT marker**); Board of Trade (now part of DTI)

BOTB British Overseas Trade Board

BOT marker beginning of tape marker

bp below proof (of alcohol density); bills payable; boiling point

bp. baptized; birthplace

Bp Bishop

BP Bachelor of Pharmacy; Bachelor of Philosophy; (Robert) Baden-Powell (1857–1941, founder of the Boy Scout movement; barometric pressure; basis point; before present (following a number of years); blood pressure; boiling point; British Petroleum; British Pharmacopoeia

B/P bills payable

BPA Bachelor of Professional Arts; British Paediatric Association

BPAS British Pregnancy Advisory Service

BPC British Pharmaceutical Codex

BPE Bachelor of Physical Education

b.p.f. bon pour francs (French: value in francs)

BPG Broadcasting Press Guild

BPH Bachelor of Public Health

BPharm Bachelor of Pharmacy

BPhil Bachelor of Philosophy

bpi bits per inch

BPIF British Printing Industries' Federation

bpm beats per minute

BPMF British Postgraduate Medical Federation

bps bits per second

BPS British Pharmacological Society

BPsS British Psychological Society

b.pt. boiling point

bpy bipyridine (used in formulae)

Bq becquerel

br. branch; bronze; brother

b.r. bank rate; bills receivable

Br birr (Ethiopian monetary unit); Bombardier; bromine; Brother; Bugler

Br. Branch; Breton; Britain; British

BR blink reflex; Brazil; British Rail; Bromley

B/R bills receivable

BRA Brigadier Royal Artillery; British Records Association; British Rheumatism and Arthritis Association

BRAD British Rates and Data (publications directory)

Braz. Brazil(ian)

BRCS British Red Cross Society

BRE Bachelor of Religious Education; Building Research Establishment

b. rec. bills receivable

Brig. Brigadier

Brig. Gen. Brigadier General

Brit. Britain; British

BRM British Racing Motors

BRMA British Rubber Manufacturers' Association

BRMCA British Ready-Mixed Concrete Association

BRN Bahrain

BRNC Britannia Royal Naval College

bro. brother

brom. bromide

bros. brothers

BRS British Road Services

BRU Brunei

bs bags; bales

b.s. balance sheet; bill of sale

Bs bolívars; boliviano (Bolivian monetary unit)

BS Bachelor of Surgery; Bahamas; Bibliographical Society; bill of sale; Biochemical Society; Bristol; British Standard (indicating the catalogue or publication number of the British Standards Institution); British Steel plc; Budgerigar Society; building society; bullshit

B/S bill of sale; bill of store

BSA Bachelor of Science in Agriculture; Bachelor of Scientific Agriculture; body surface area; Boy Scouts' Association

BSAA Bachelor of Science in Applied Arts

BSAdv Bachelor of Science in Advertising

BSAE Bachelor of Science in Aeronautical Engineering; Bachelor of Science in Agricultural Engineering

BSAgr Bachelor of Science in Agriculture

BSB British Satellite Broadcasting; British Standard brass (type of screw thread)

BSBA Bachelor of Science in Business Administration

BSBI Botanical Society of the British Isles

BSBus Bachelor of Science in Business

BSc Bachelor of Science

BSC Bachelor of Science in Commerce; British Steel Corporation; British Sugar Corporation; Broadcasting Standards Council

BScA Bachelor of Science in Agriculture

BScApp Bachelor of Applied Science

BSCC British Society of Clinical Cytology

BSCE Bachelor of Science in Civil Engineering

BSChE Bachelor of Science in Chemical Engineering

BScD Bachelor of Dental Science

BSc(Dent) Bachelor of Science in Dentistry

BSc(Econ) Bachelor of Science in Economics

BSc(Ed) Bachelor of Science in Education

BSc(Hort) Bachelor of Science in Horticulture

BScMed Bachelor of Medical Science

BSc(Nutr) Bachelor of Science in Nutrition

BScSoc Bachelor of Social Sciences

BSD Bachelor of Science in Design; British Society of Dowsers

BSE Bachelor of Science in Education; Bachelor of Science in Engineering; bovine spongiform encephalopathy

BSEc Bachelor of Science in Economics

BSEE Bachelor of Science in Electrical Engineering; Bachelor of Science in Elementary Education

BSEIE Bachelor of Science in Electronic Engineering

BSEM Bachelor of Science in Engineering of Mines

BSES Bachelor of Science in Engineering Sciences; British Schools Exploring Society

BSF Bachelor of Science in Forestry; British Salonica Force; British Standard fine (type of screw thread)

BSFA British Science Fiction Association

BSFM Bachelor of Science in Forestry Management

BSFor Bachelor of Science in Forestry

BSFS Bachelor of Science in Foreign Service

BSFT Bachelor of Science in Fuel Technology

BSGE Bachelor of Science in General Engineering

BSH British Society of Hypnotherapists

BSHA Bachelor of Science in Hospital Administration

BSHE Bachelor of Science in Home Economics

BSHyg Bachelor of Science in Hygiene

BSI British Standards Institution

BSIA British Security Industry Association

BSIE Bachelor of Science in Industrial Engineering

BSIS Business Sponsorship Incentive Scheme

BSJ Bachelor of Science in Journalism

BSJA British Show Jumping Association

BSkyB British Sky Broadcasting (formed by merger of BSB with Sky Television)

Bs/L bills of lading

BSL Bachelor of Sacred Literature; Bachelor of Science in Linguistics

BSLS Bachelor of Science in Library Science

BSM Bachelor of Sacred Music; Bachelor of Science in Medicine; British School of Motoring

BSME Bachelor of Science in Mechanical Engineering; Bachelor of Science in Mining Engineering

BSMet Bachelor of Science in Metallurgy

BSMetE Bachelor of Science in Metallurgical Engineering

BSMT Bachelor of Science in Medical Technology

BSN Bachelor of Science in Nursing

BSNS Bachelor of Naval Science

BSocSc Bachelor of Social Science

BSOT Bachelor of Science in Occupational Therapy

BSP Bachelor of Science in Pharmacy; British Standard pipe (type of screw thread); business systems planning

BSPA Bachelor of Science in Public Administration

BSPE Bachelor of Science in Physical Education

BSPH Bachelor of Science in Public Health

BSPT Bachelor of Science in Physical Therapy

BSRA British Ship Research Association

BSRT Bachelor of Science in Radiological Technology

BSS Bachelor of Secretarial Science; Bachelor of Social Science; basic safety standards; British Standards Specification

BSSc Bachelor of Social Science

BSSE Bachelor of Science in Secondary Education

BSSO British Society for the Study of Orthodontics

BSSS Bachelor of Science in Secretarial Studies; Bachelor of Science in Social Science

BST Bachelor of Sacred Theology; bovine somatotrophin; British Summer Time

B/St bill of sight

BSU bench scale unit

BSW British Standard Whitworth (type of screw thread)

bt bought

Bt Baronet; brevet

BT Bachelor of Teaching; Bachelor of Theology; behaviour therapy; Belfast; benign tumour; British Telecom

BTA British Theatre Association; British Tourist Authority (formerly British Travel Association)

BTB breakthrough bleeding

BTC British Transport Commission

BTCh Bachelor of Textile Chemistry

BTCV British Trust for Conservation Volunteers

BTE Bachelor of Textile Engineering

BTEC Business and Technician Education Council

BTech Bachelor of Technology

BTEX benzene, toluene, ethylbenzene, and xylene (solvents)

BTG British Technology Group

bth bath(room)

BTh Bachelor of Theology

BTHMA British Toy and Hobby Manufacturers' Association

BThU British thermal unit

btl. bottle

btm bottom

BTN Brussels Tariff Nomenclature

BTP Bachelor of Town Planning

btry battery

BTS British Telecommunications Systems

Btss Baroness

Btu British thermal unit

BTU Board of Trade unit; (USA) British thermal unit

BTW by the way (used in electronic mail)

bty battery

bu. bushel(s)

Bu butyl group (in formulae)

BUAV British Union for the Abolition of Vivisection

Bucks Buckinghamshire

bul. bulletin

Bulg. Bulgaria(n)

bull. bulletin

BUNCH Burroughs, Univac, NCR, Control Data, Honeywell (computer manufacturers)

BUPA British United Provident Association (health-insurance company)

bur. buried

Bur. Burma

BUR Burma

bus. business

bush. bushel

b.v. book value

BV bene vale (Latin: farewell); Blessed Virgin (Latin *Beata Virgo*); blood volume

BVA British Veterinary Association

BVetMed Bachelor of Veterinary Medicine

BVM Bachelor of Veterinary Medicine; Blessed Virgin Mary (Latin *Beata Virgo Maria*)

BVMS Bachelor of Veterinary Medicine and Surgery

b/w black and white

BW biological warfare; black and white; body weight; bonded warehouse; British Waterways

B/W black and white

BWA Baptist World Alliance

BWG Birmingham Wire Gauge

BWI British West Indies

BWM British War Medal

BWR boiling-water reactor

BWV Bach Werke-Verzeichnis (German: Catalogue of Bach's Works; precedes the catalogue number of a work by J. S. Bach)

bx box

b.y. billion years

BYOB bring your own beer (booze, *or* bottle)

Byz. Byzantine

Bz benzene (in formulae)

C

c centi- (prefix indicating 10^{-2}, as in **cm**, centimetre); concentration; constant; cubic (in **cc**, cubic centimetre); specific heat capacity; speed of light in a vacuum; the third vertical row of squares from the left on a chessboard

c. canine (tooth); caput (Latin: chapter); carat; carbon (paper); case; cathode; caught; cent(s); centavo(s); centime(s); centre; century; chairman; chairwoman; chapter; child; church; circa (Latin: about; preceding a date); city; colt; contralto; copyright; cousin; cycle(s)

c/- (Australia, New Zealand) care of (in addresses)

C Cambrian; capacitance; carbon; Carboniferous; (USA) cargo transport (specifying a type of military aircraft, as in **C-5**); Celsius (in **°C**, degree Celsius; formerly degree centigrade); centre (of stage); century; cocaine; cold (water); Command Paper (prefix to serial number, 1870–99). *See also under* Cd; Cmd; Cmnd; Companion (in British Orders of Chivalry); coulomb; crown (a standard paper size; *see under* C4; C8); Cuba; cytidine; cytosine; heat capacity; hundred; molecular concentration; a programming language (developed from B); a musical note or key

C. Cape (on maps); Catholic; Celtic; clubs; Conservative; Corps; council; counter-tenor; county

C1 supervisory, clerical (occupational grade)

C2 skilled manual (occupational grade)

C3 a low standard of physical fitness; hence inferior (originally a military grade)

C4 Channel Four; crown 4to (a standard paper size, 7½ × 10 in)

C5 Channel Five

C8 crown 8vo (a standard paper size, 5 × 7½ in)

ca. carcinoma; circa

c.a. capital asset; coll' arco (Italian: with the bow)

Ca calcium

CA California; Carlisle; Central America; Chartered Accountant; Chief Accountant; civil aviation; clean air; coast artillery; commercial agent; Consular Agent; Consumers' Association; Controller of Accounts; Cooperative Agreement; County Alderman; current assets

C/A capital account; credit account; current account

CAA Civil Aviation Authority; Clean Air Act

CAAV Central Association of Agricultural Valuers

cab. cabin

CAB Citizens' Advice Bureau; Commonwealth Agricultural Bureaux

CABEI Central American Bank for Economic Integration

CABG coronary artery bypass graft(ing)

CABS coronary artery bypass surgery

CACM Central American Common Market

CAD cash against documents; computer-aided design; coronary artery disease

CADCAM computer-aided design, computer-aided manufacturing

CADMAT computer-aided design, manufacturing, and testing

CADS computer-aided design system

CAE (Australia) College of Advanced Education; computer-aided engineering

CAER Conservative Action for Electoral Reform

CAF charities aid fund; cost and freight

CAI computer-aided instruction

cal calorie

cal. calendar; calibre

Cal kilocalorie

Cal. California

CAL computer-aided learning

calc. calculate(d)

Calif. California

Caltech California Institute of Technology

Cam. Cambridge

CAM communication, advertising, and marketing (as in **CAM Foundation**); computer-aided manufacture

Camb. Cambridge

Cambs Cambridgeshire

CAMC Canadian Army Medical Corps

cAMP cyclic AMP (adenosine 3′-5′-phosphate)

CAMRA Campaign for Real Ale

CAMS Certificate of Advanced Musical Study

CAMW Central Association for Mental Welfare

can. canon; canto

Can. Canada; Canadian; Canon(ry)

CAN customs-assigned number

canc. cancellation; cancelled

c & b caught and bowled (by)

c & c carpets and curtains

c & d collection and delivery

C & E Customs and Excise

c & f cost and freight

C & G City and Guilds

c & i cost and insurance

C & I commerce and industry

c & m care and maintenance

C & W country and western (music)

Cant. Canterbury; Canticles

Cantab. Cantabrigiensis (Latin: of Cambridge; used with academic awards)

Cantuar. Cantuariensis (Latin: (Archbishop) of Canterbury)

CANUS Canada–United States

cap. capacity; capiat (Latin: let him take; in prescriptions); capital; capitalize; capital letter; capitulum or caput (Latin: chapter or heading)

CAP Common Agricultural Policy (in the EC); computer-aided production

CAPE Clifton Assessment Procedures for the Elderly

caps. capital letters; capsule

Capt. Captain

car. carat

c.a.r. compounded annual rate (of interest)

CAR Central African Republic; compound annual return

carb. carbon; carbonate

Card. Cardinal

CARD Campaign Against Racial Discrimination

CARE Christian Action for Research and Education; Cooperative for American Relief Everywhere; Cottage and Rural Enterprises

CARICOM Caribbean Community and Common Market

CARIFTA Caribbean Free Trade Area

carn. carnival

carp. carpentry

carr. fwd carriage forward

CAS Chief of Air Staff; collision avoidance system

ca. sa. capias ad satisfaciendum (a writ of execution)

CASE computer-aided software engineering; Confederation for the Advancement of State Education; Cooperative Awards in Science and Engineering

casevac casualty evacuation

CASI Canadian Aeronautics and Space Institute

cat. catalogue; catamaran; catechism; category

CAT Centre for Alternative Technology; chloramphenicol acetyl transferase (as in **CAT assay**); clear-air turbulence; College of Advanced Technology; computer-aided teaching; computer-aided testing; computer-aided trading; computer-aided typesetting; computerized axial tomography

Catal. Catalan

Cath. Cathedral; Catholic

CATI computer-assisted telephone interviewing

CATS credit accumulation transfer scheme

CATV cable television; community antenna television

caus. causative

cav. caveat

Cav. cavalry

CAV curia advisari vult (Latin: the court wishes to consider it; used in law reports when the judgment was given after the hearing)

c.b. cash book; centre of buoyancy (of a boat, etc.)

c/b caught and bowled

Cb columbium

CB Cambridge; Cape Breton (Canada); carbon black; centre back (of stage); chemical and biological (weapons or warfare); Citizens' Band; Companion of the (Order of the) Bath; confined to barracks; county borough

CBA cost benefit analysis

CBC Canadian Broadcasting Corporation; Central Buying Company; complete blood count; County Borough Council

CBD cash before delivery; central business district

CBE Commander of the Order of the British Empire

CBEL Cambridge Bibliography of English Literature

CBI Confederation of British Industry

CBIM Companion of the British Institute of Management

CBiol Chartered Biologist

CBL computer-based learning

CBNS Commander British Navy Staff

CBOE Chicago Board of Options Exchange

CBOT Chicago Board of Trade

CBR chemical, bacteriological, and radiation (weapons or warfare)

CBS (USA) Columbia Broadcasting System; Confraternity of the Blessed Sacrament

CBSA Clay Bird Shooting Association

CBSI Chartered Building Societies Institute

CBSO City of Birmingham Symphony Orchestra

CBT computer-based training

c.b.u. completely built-up (of goods for immediate use)

CBW chemical and biological warfare

CBX company branch (telephone) exchange

CBZ carbobenzloxy

cc carbon copy; cubic centimetre(s)

cc. chapters

c.c. carbon copy; contra credit; cubic centimetre(s)

CC City Council; City Councillor; civil commotion; civil court; closed circuit (transmission); collision course; colour correction; Companion of the Order of Canada; company commander; County Clerk; County Commissioner; County Council; County Court; cricket club

C–C carbon–carbon (as in **C–C bond**)

CCA current-cost accounting

CCAB Consultative Committee of Accountancy Bodies

CCAHC Central Council for Agricultural and Horticultural Cooperation

CCB (South Africa) Civil Cooperation Bureau

CCBI Council of Churches for Great Britain and Ireland

CCBN Central Council for British Naturism

CCC Central Criminal Court; Commodity Credit Corporation; County Cricket Club; Customs Cooperation Council

CCCI command, control, communications, and intelligence

CCCP Soyuz Sovietskikh Sotsialisticheskikh Respublik (Russian: Union of Soviet Socialist Republics)

CCD Central Council for the Disabled; charged-coupled device

CCE Chartered Civil Engineer

CCF Combined Cadet Force; congestive cardiac failure

CCFD complementary cumulative frequency distribution

CCFM Combined Cadet Forces Medal

CCFP Certificate of the College of Family Physicians

CCG Control Commission for Germany

CCGT combined-cycle gas turbine

CCHE Central Council for Health Education

CChem Chartered Chemist

CCHMS Central Committee for Hospital Medical Services

CCIA Commission of the Churches on International Affairs

CCITT Comité consultatif international télégraphique et téléphonique (French: International Telegraph and Telephone Consultative Committee)

CCJ Circuit Court Judge; Council of Christians and Jews

CCM caffeine clearance measurement

c.c.p. cubic close-packed

CCP Chinese Communist Party; Code of Civil Procedure; Court of Common Pleas

CCPR Central Council of Physical Recreation

CCR cassette camera recorder

CCRA Commander Corps of Royal Artillery

CCRE Commander Corps of Royal Engineers

CCREME Commander Corps of Royal Electrical and Mechanical Engineers

CCRSigs Commander Corps of Royal Signals

CCS casualty clearing station

CCSU Council of Civil Service Unions

CCTA Central Computer and Telecommunications Agency

CCTS Combat Crew Training Squadron

CCTV closed-circuit television

CCU coronary care unit

CCV control-configured vehicle

ccw. counterclockwise

CCW Curriculum Council for Wales

cd candela; cord

c.d. carried down; cash discount; cum dividend (i.e. with dividend)

Cd cadmium; Command Paper (prefix to serial number, 1900–18). *See also under* C; Cmd; Cmnd

CD Canadian Forces Decoration; certificate of deposit; Civil Defence; civil disobedience; closing date; compact disc; Conference on Disarmament (of the UN); contagious disease; Corps Diplomatique (French: Diplomatic Corps)

C/D consular declaration

CDA Copper Development Association

CDC Control Data Corporation (computer manufacturers)

CDE compact disc erasable; Conference on Confidence- and Security-Building and Disarmament in Europe (as in **CDE treaty**)

c.d.f. cumulative distribution function

cd fwd carried forward

CDH congenital dislocation of the hip

CDI compact-disc interactive

CDipAF Certified Diploma in Accounting and Finance

c. div. cum dividend (i.e. with dividend)

CDM cold dark matter (as in **CDM theory**)

Cdn Canadian

CDN Canada

cDNA complementary DNA

Cdo Commando

CDP Committee of Directors of Polytechnics

Cdr Commander

CD-R compact-disc recordable

CDRA Committee of Directors of Research Associations

Cdre Commodore

CD-ROM compact disc read-only memory

CDS Chief of the Defence Staff

CDSO Companion of the Distinguished Service Order

CDT (USA and Canada) Central Daylight Time; Craft, Design, and Technology (a subject on the GCSE syllabus)

CDTV Commodore Dynamic Total Vision; compact-disk television

CDU Christlich-Demokratische Union (Christian Democratic Union; German political party)

CDV CD-video (compact-disc player); Civil Defence Volunteers; current domestic value

c.e. caveat emptor (Latin: let the buyer beware); compass error

Ce cerium

CE Chemical Engineer; Chief Engineer; Christian Endeavour; Christian Era (following a date); Church of England; Civil Engineer; Common Entrance; Common Era (following a date); Communauté européenne (French: European Community, EC; now often used in place of CEE); Corps of Engineers; Council of Europe

CEA Central Electricity Authority; Cinematograph Exhibitors Association; Combustion Engineering Association; Confédération européenne de l'agriculture (French: European Confederation of Agriculture)

CED Committee for Economic Development

CEDO Centre for Educational Development Overseas

CEDR Centre for Dispute Resolution

CEE Communauté économique européenne (French: European Economic Community; *see also under* CE)

CEED Centre for Economic and Environment Development

CEGB Central Electricity Generating Board

CEI Council of Engineering Institutions

CEIR Corporation for Economic and Industrial Research

cel. celesta

Celt. Celtic

CEMA Council for Economic Mutual Assistance; Council for the Encouragement of Music and the Arts

CEMR Council of European Municipalities and Regions

CEMS Church of England Men's Society

cen. central; century

CEN Comité européen de normalisation (French: European Standardization Committee)

CENELEC Comité européen normalisation électrotechnique (French: European Electrotechnical Standardization Committee)

CEng Chartered Engineer

cent. centavo; centesimo; centigrade; central; centum (Latin: hundred); century

CENTAG Central (European) Army Group (in NATO)

CENTO Central Treaty Organization

CEO Chief Executive Officer

CER (Australia and New Zealand) Closer Economic Relations

CERG Conservative European Reform Group

CERL Central Electricity Research Laboratories

CERN Conseil européen pour la recherche nucléaire (French: European Organization for Nuclear Research; now called European Laboratory for Particle Physics)

cert. certificate(d); certification; certified; certify

CERT Charities Effectiveness Review Trust

Cert Ed Certificate in Education

CertHE Certificate in Higher Education

certif. certificate

CES Christian Evidence Society

CEST Centre for Exploitation of Science and Technology

Cestr. Cestrensis (Latin: (Bishop) of Chester)

CET Central European Time; Common External Tariff; Council for Educational Technology
cet. par. ceteris paribus (Latin: other things being equal)
CETS Church of England Temperance Society
Ceyl. Ceylon
cf. calfskin; compare (Latin *confer*)
c.f. cantus firmus (Latin: fixed song); carried forward; cost and freight
Cf californium
Cf. Confessions
CF Canadian Forces; Cardiff; carriage forward; Chaplain to the Forces; Comorian franc (monetary unit of Comoros); compensation fee; conventional fractionation radiotherapy; cost and freight; crystal field (as in **CF theory**); cystic fibrosis
CFA Canadian Field Artillery; Communauté financière africaine (French: African Financial Community, as in **CFA franc**); Council for Acupuncture
CFAF CFA (Communauté financière africaine) franc
CFC chlorofluorocarbon; Common Fund for Commodities (in the UN)
c.f.d. cubic feet per day
CFD computational fluid dynamics
CFE Central Fighter Establishment; College of Further Education; Conventional Forces in Europe (as in **CFE treaty**)
c.f.h. cubic feet per hour
CFI cost, freight, and insurance
c.f.m. cubic feet per minute
CFM Cadet Forces Medal; chlorofluoromethane
CFO Central Forecasting Office; Chief Financial Officer
CFP Common Fisheries Policy (of the EC); Communauté financière du Pacifique (French: Pacific Financial Community)
CFPF CFP (Communauté financière du Pacifique) franc
CFR Commander of the Order of the Federal Republic of Nigeria; commercial fast reactor; Co-operative Fuel Research (Committee) (as in **CFR engine**)
c.f.s. cubic feet per second
CFS Central Flying School; chronic fatigue syndrome
CFT complement fixation test
CFTC (USA) Commodity Futures Trading Commission
cg centigram(s); centre of gravity
CG Captain-General; Captain of the Guard; centre of gravity; coastguard; Coldstream Guards; Consul-General
CGA colour graphics adapter; Community of the Glorious Ascension; Country Gentlemen's Association
CGBR Central Government Borrowing Requirement
cge carriage
CGE Conservative Group for Europe

CGH Cape of Good Hope
CGI City and Guilds Institute; computer graphics interface
CGLI City and Guilds of London Institute
cgm centigram(s)
CGM Conspicuous Gallantry Medal
cgo cargo
CGRM Commandant-General of the Royal Marines
cgs centimetre, gram, second (in **cgs units**)
CGS Chief of General Staff
CGT capital-gains tax
CGT-FO (France) Confédération général du travail–force ouvrière (General Confederation of Labour–Workers' Force)
ch cosh
ch. chain (unit of measure; crochet stitch); chaldron; chaplain; chapter; charge(s); check; chestnut; cheval-vapeur (French: horsepower); chief; child(ren); church
c.h. candle hour(s); central heating; court house; custom(s) house
Ch. Chaldean; Chaldee; Champion; Chancellor; China; Chinese; Chirurgiae (Latin: of surgery; in academic degrees); Church
CH Chester; Companion of Honour; corporate hospitality; custom(s) house; Switzerland (French *Confédération Helvétique*)
C/H central heating
Chal. Chaldaic; Chaldean
Chamb. Chamberlain
Chan. Chancellor; Chancery
chap. chaplain; chapter
CHAPS Clearing House Automatic Payments System
char. character; charter
CHAR Campaign for Homeless People (originally Campaign for the Homeless and Rootless)
charact. characterize
ChB Bachelor of Surgery (Latin *Chirugiae Baccalaureus*)
CHB Companion of Honour of Barbados
CHC child health clinic; Community Health Council
ChD Doctor of Surgery (Latin *Chirugiae Doctor*)
Ch. D. Chancery Division
CHD coronary heart disease
CHDL computer hardware description language
ChE Chemical Engineer
CHE Campaign for Homosexual Equality
chem. chemical(ly); chemist(ry)
ChemE Chemical Engineer
Ches. Cheshire
ch. fwd charges forward
chg. charge
Ch. hist. Church history
Chin. China; Chinese
CHINA Come home, I need action (on letters)
CHIPS Clearing House Inter-Bank Payments System
CHIRP Confidential Human Incidence Reporting Programme

(pilots' comments on safety trends)
Ch. J. Chief Justice
Chl chlorophyll (as in **Chl a**)
ChLJ Chaplain of the Order of St Lazarus of Jerusalem
chm. chairman; checkmate
ChM Master of Surgery (Latin *Chirurgiae Magister*)
choc. chocolate
chor. choral; chorus
CHP combined heat and power (energy use)
ch. pd charges paid
ch. ppd. charges prepaid
chq. cheque
CHQ Corps Headquarters
Chr. Christ; Christian(ity); Chronicles
chron. chronicle; chronological(ly); chronology
Chron. Chronicles
chs chapters
CHSA Chest, Heart, and Stroke Association
CHSC Central Health Services Council
c.h.w. constant hot water
Ci curie
CI Channel Islands; Chief Inspector; Colour Index; combustion index; compression-ignition (as in **CI engine**); continuous improvement (in management); contrast index; Côte d'Ivoire (Ivory Coast); (Imperial Order of the) Crown of India
C³I command, control, communications, and intelligence
CIA (USA) Central Intelligence Agency; Chemical Industries' Association
CIAgrE Companion of the Institution of Agricultural Engineers
CIAL Corresponding Member of the International Institute of Arts and Letters
CIArb Chartered Institute of Arbitrators
CIB Central Intelligence Board; Chartered Institute of Bankers; (New Zealand) Criminal Investigation Branch
CIBSE Chartered Institution of Building Services Engineers (formerly Chartered Institute of Building Services, **CIBS**)
CIC Commander-in-Chief
Cicestr. Cicestrensis (Latin: (Bishop) of Chichester)
CICHE Committee for International Cooperation in Higher Education
CICI Confederation of Information Communication Industries
CID Committee for Imperial Defence; Council of Industrial Design; Criminal Investigation Department
Cie Compagnie (French: Company; Co.)
CIE Commission internationale de l'éclairage (French: International Commission on Illumination; ICI); Companion of the Order of the Indian Empire (former honour);

(Ireland) Córas Iompair Éireann (Irish Gaelic: Transport Organization of Ireland)

c.i.f. cost, insurance, and freight (as in **c.i.f. contract**)

c.i.f.c. cost, insurance, freight, and commission

c.i.f.c.i. cost, insurance, freight, commission, and interest

c.i.f.e. cost, insurance, freight, and exchange

CIFE Colleges and Institutes for Further Education

c.i.f.i. cost, insurance, freight, and interest

CIGasE Companion of the Institute of Gas Engineers

CIGS Chief of the Imperial General Staff

CIH Certificate in Industrial Health

CII Chartered Insurance Institute

CIM China Inland Mission; Commission for Industry and Manpower; computer input on microfilm; computer-integrated manufacture

CIMA Chartered Institute of Management Accountants

CIMarE Companion of the Institute of Marine Engineers

CIMechE Companion of the Institution of Mechanical Engineers

CIMEMME Companion of the Institute of Mining Electrical and Mining Mechanical Engineers

CIMGTechE Companion of the Institution of Mechanical and General Technician Engineers

CIN cervical intraepithelial neoplasia (in grading cervical smears)

C-in-C Commander-in-Chief

CIO (USA) Congress of Industrial Organizations

CIOB Chartered Institute of Building

CIPA Chartered Institute of Patent Agents

CIPFA Chartered Institute of Public Finance and Accountancy

CIPM Commission internationale des poids et mesures (French: International Committee on Weights and Measures); Companion of the Institute of Personnel Management

CIPS Choice in Personal Safety (organization)

CIPW Cross, Iddings, Pirsson, Washington (rock classification; named after its devisers)

cir. circa; circular; circulation; circumference

CIR Commission on Industrial Relations

circ. circa; circular; circulation; circumcision; circumference

circum. circumference

CIRIA Construction Industry Research and Information Association

CIS combined-injury syndrome; Commonwealth of Independent States (the former Soviet republics)

CISAC Centre for International Security and Arms Control

CISC complex instruction-set computer

CIS–COBOL compact interactive standard COBOL

CISL Confédération internationale des syndicats libres (French: International Confederation of Free Trade Unions)

CISTI Canadian Institute for Scientific and Technological Information

cit. citation; cited; citizen; citrate

CIT (New Zealand) Central Institute of Technology; Chartered Institute of Transport

CITES Convention on International Trade in Endangered Species

CIU Club and Institute Union

civ. civil; civilian

CIV City Imperial Volunteers

CIWF Compassion in World Farming

CJ Chief Justice

CJA Criminal Justice Act

CJD Creutzfeldt–Jakob disease

CJM Congregation of Jesus and Mary

ck cask; check; cook

CKD completely knocked down (i.e. in parts; of goods for sale)

ckw. clockwise

cl centilitre(s)

cl. claim; clarinet; class; classification; clause; clearance; clergy(man); clerk; close; cloth

c.l. carload; cum laude (Latin: with praise)

c/l cash letter

Cl chlorine

CL civil law; common law; Sri Lanka (formerly Ceylon)

CLA Country Landowner's Association

class. classic(al); classification; classified

clav. clavier

cld called; cleared

CLIMAP Climate: Long-range Interpretation, Mapping, and Prediction (international project)

CLit Companion of Literature

CLJ Commander of the Order of St Lazarus of Jerusalem

Cllr Councillor

clo. clothing

CLP Constituency Labour Party

CLPT computer language(s) for the processing of text

CLR computer-language recorder

CLRAE Conference of Local and Regional Authorities of Europe

CLT computer-language translator

clvd clavichord

cm centimetre(s)

c.m. carat métrique (French: metric carat); causa mortis (Latin: by reason of death); common metre; court martial

cM centimorgan

Cm curium

CM carboxymethyl (in **CM-cellulose**); Certificated Master; Chelmsford; church mission(ary); command module (spacecraft);

common metre; Congregation of the Mission; Corresponding Member; Master of Surgery (Latin *Chirurgiae Magister*); Member of the Order of Canada

CMA Canadian Medical Association; Communication Managers' Association

CMAC Catholic Marriage Advisory Council

CMB Central Midwives Board (superseded by UKCC)

CMC Conservation Monitoring Centre

CMChM Master of Surgery

Cmd Command Paper (prefix to serial number, 1919–56). *See also under* C; Cd; Cmnd

CMD common metre double; conventional munitions disposal (type of bomb disposal)

Cmdr Commander

Cmdre Commodore

CMEA Council for Mutual Economic Assistance (i.e. COMECON)

CMF Central Mediterranean Force; Commonwealth Military Forces

CMG Companion of the Order of St Michael and St George

CMI cell-mediated immunity; computer-managed instruction

cml commercial

CML chronic myelocytic leukaemia

CMLJ Commander of Merit of the Order of St Lazarus of Jerusalem

Cmnd Command Paper (prefix to serial number since 1957). *See also under* C; Cd; Cmd

CMOS complementary metal oxide semiconductor

Cmpn Companion

CMS Certificate in Management Studies; Church Missionary Society; conversational monitor system

CMV cytomegalovirus

CN Canadian National (Railway)

C/N carbon–nitrogen (in **C/N ratio**); cover note; credit note

CNAA Council for National Academic Awards

CNAR compound net annual rate

CNC computer numerical control

CND Campaign for Nuclear Disarmament

CNES Centre national d'études spatiales (French space agency)

CNF Commonwealth Nurses' Federation

CNG compressed natural gas

CNI Companion of the Nautical Institute

CNN Cable News Network; Certified Nursery Nurse

CNO Chief Nursing Officer; Chief of Naval Operations

cnr corner

CNR Canadian National Railway

CNRS (France) Centre national de la recherche scientifique (National Centre for Scientific Research)

CNS central nervous system

c.o. complains of

c/o care of; carried over

Co cobalt
Co. Coalition; Colorado; Company; County
CO Cabinet Office; cardiac output; Colchester; Colombia; Colorado; combined operations; Commanding Officer; Commonwealth Office (now part of the FCO); conscientious objector; criminal offence; Crown Office; current oscillations
C/O cash order; certificate of origin
CoA coenzyme A
COA change of address
coad. coadjutor
Cobol common business-oriented language
COC combined oral contraceptive
coch. cochleare (Latin: spoonful)
coch. amp. cochleare amplum (Latin: heaped spoonful)
coch. mag. cochleare magnum (Latin: tablespoonful)
coch. med. cochleare medium (Latin: dessertspoonful)
coch. parv. cochleare parvum (Latin: teaspoonful)
COCOM Coordinating Committee for Multinational Export Controls
COCOMO constructive cost model
c.o.d. cash on delivery
Cod. codex
COD cash on delivery; chemical oxygen demand; (USA) collect on delivery; Concise Oxford Dictionary
CODAN carrier-operated device anti-noise
CODASYL Conference on Data Systems Languages
codec coder-decoder
Codesh Convention for a Democratic South Africa
co-ed coeducational
CoEnCo Committee for Environmental Conservation
C of A Certificate of Airworthiness
C of C Chamber of Commerce
C of E Church of England; Council of Europe
C of I Church of Ireland
C of M Certificate of Maintenance
C of S Chief of Staff; Church of Scotland
cog. cognate
CoG centre of gravity
COGB certified official government business
COHSE Confederation of Health Service Employees (former trade union)
COI Central Office of Information
col. collect(ed); collector; college; collegiate; colonial; colour(ed); column
Col. Colombia(n); Colonel; Colorado; Colossians
COL computer-oriented language; cost of living
coll. collateral; colleague; collect(ed); collection; collector; college; collegiate; colloquial(ism); collyrium (eyewash)
collab. collaboration (with)
collat. collateral(ly)

collect. collective(ly)
colloq. colloquial(ly); colloquialism
coll'ott. coll'ottava (Italian: in octaves)
collr collector
Colo. Colorado
Coloss. Colossians
cols columns
Col-Sergt Colour-Sergeant
com. comedy; comic; commerce; commercial; commission(er); committee; common(ly); commune; communication(s)
Com. Commander; Commissioner; Committee; Commodore; Communist
COM computer output on microfilm
COMA Committee on Medical Aspects of Food Policy
COMAL common algorithmic language
comb. combination; combining; combustion
Comdg Commanding
Comdr Commander
Comdt Commandant
COMECON Council for Mutual Economic Assistance
Comet Committee for Middle East Trade
COMEX (USA) Commodity Exchange (New York)
Cominform Communist Information Bureau
COMINT communications intelligence
Comintern Communist International
coml commercial
comm. commentary; commerce; commercial(ly); committee; commonwealth; communication
commem. commemoration
Commissr Commissioner
Commn Commission
Commnd Commissioned
Commy Commissary
COMO Committee of Marketing Organizations
comp. companion; comparative; compare; compensation; compilation; compiled; compiler; complete; composition; compositor; compound(ed); comprehensive; comprising
Comp Companion (of an institution; as in **CompIMechE**, Institution of Mechanical Engineers)
compar. comparative; comparison
Comp-Gen Comptroller-General
compo. composition
Comr Commissioner
comsat communications satellite
Com. Ver. Common Version (of the Bible)
Comy-Gen Commissary-General
con. concerto; conclusion; conjunx (Latin: wife); connection; consolidate(d); continue(d); contra (Latin: against); convenience; conversation

Con. Conformist; Conservative; Consols; Consul; contralto
conc. concentrate(d); concentration; concerning; concerto
con. cr. contra credit
cond. conductor
conf. confection; confer (Latin: compare); conference; confessor
Confed. Confederacy; Confederate; Confederation
cong. congius (Latin: gallon); congregation(ist)
Cong. Congregational(ist); Congress; Congressional
con. inv. consular invoice
conj. conjugation; conjunction; conjunctive
conn. connect(ed); connection; connotation
Conn. Connecticut
cons. conservation; conserve; consigned; consignment; consolidated; consonant; constable; constitution(al); construction; consul; consult(ing)
Cons. Conservative; Conservatoire; Constable; Constitution; Consul
con. sec. conic section
Conserv. Conservatoire
consgt consignment
Consols consolidated annuities
const. constable; constant; constitution
constr. construct(ion); construe
cont. container; containing; contents; continent(al); continue(d); continuo; contra (Latin: against); contract; contraction; control(ler)
contd continued
contemp. contemporary
contg containing
contr. contract(s); contracted; contraction; contralto; contrary; contrast(ed); control(ler)
contr. bon. mor. contra bonos mores (Latin: contrary to good manners)
contrib. contributing; contribution; contributor
CONUS continental United States
conv. convention(al); convertible
Conv. Convocation
co-op. cooperative
cop. copper; copyright(ed)
Cop. Copernican; Coptic
COP coefficient of performance
COPA Comité des organisations professionnelles agricoles de la CE (French: Committee of Agricultural Organizations in the EC)
COPD chronic obstructive pulmonary disease
Copec Conference on Christian Politics, Economics, and Citizenship
Copt. Coptic
COPUS Committee on the Public Understanding of Science
cor. corner; cornet; coroner; corpus (Latin: the body); correct(ed); correction; correlative; correspondence; correspondent; corresponding

Cor. Corinthians

CORE (USA) Congress of Racial Equality

CORGI Confederation for Registration of Gas Installers

Cor. Mem. Corresponding Member

Corn. Cornish; Cornwall

corol. corollary

Corp. Corporal; Corporation

corr. correct(ed); correction; corrective; correspond(ent); correspondence; corresponding; corrupt(ed); corruption

correl. correlative

corresp. correspondence

Corresp. Mem. Corresponding Member

Cor. Sec. Corresponding Secretary

cos cosine

c.o.s. cash on shipment

Cos. Companies; Counties

COS cash on shipment; Charity Organization Society; Chief of Staff

COSA Colliery Officials and Staffs Association

cosec cosecant

cosech hyperbolic cosecant

cosh hyperbolic cosine

COSHH Control of Substances Hazardous to Health

CoSIRA Council for Small Industries in Rural Areas

COSLA Convention of Scottish Local Authorities

cosmog. cosmography

COSPAR Committee on Space Research

Coss. Consules (Latin: Consuls)

COSSAC Chief of Staff to Supreme Allied Commander

cot cotangent

cotan cotangent

COTE Committee for the Accreditation of Teacher Education

coth hyperbolic cotangent

COV covariance; crossover value

covers coversed sine

Coy. company

cp. compare

c.p. candlepower

CP Canadian Pacific (Railway); Canadian Press; (formerly, in South Africa) Cape Province; change point; chemically pure; Chief Patriarch; Clerk of the Peace; College of Preceptors; colour printing (as in **CP filter**); Command Post; commercial paper; Common Pleas; Common Prayer; Communist Party; Community Programme (employment scheme); corporal punishment; Court of Probate

CPA (USA) Certified Public Accountant; Chartered Patent Agent; claims payable abroad; Commonwealth Parliamentary Association

CPAC Consumer Protection Advisory Committee

CPAG Child Poverty Action Group

CPAS Church Pastoral Aid Society

CPB Communist Party of Britain

CPC Clerk of the Privy Council; clinicopathological conference; Communist Party of China; Conservative Political Centre

cpd compound

CPGB Communist Party of Great Britain

c.p.h. cycles per hour

CPH Certificate in Public Health

CPhys Chartered Physicist

cpi characters per inch

Cpl Corporal

CPL Commercial Pilot's Licence

CPM Colonial Police Medal

CP/M Control Program Monitor

CPO Chief Petty Officer; compulsory purchase order; County Planning Officer

CPP current purchasing power (in **CPP accounting**)

CPR Canadian Pacific Railway; cardiopulmonary resuscitation

CPRE Council for the Protection of Rural England

CPRS Central Policy Review Staff

cps characters per second; cycles per second

CPS Centre for Policy Studies; cents per share; Crown Prosecution Service; Custos Privati Sigilli (Latin: Keeper of the Privy Seal)

CPSA Civil and Public Services Association (clerical civil servants' union)

CPSU Communist Party of the Soviet Union

CPsychol Chartered Psychologist

CPU central processing unit; Commonwealth Press Union

CQ charge of quarters

CQSW Certificate of Qualification in Social Work

cr. credit(or); crown

Cr chromium; Councillor

CR Carolina Regina (Latin: Queen Caroline); Carolus Rex (Latin: King Charles); carriage return; carrier's risk; cash receipts; Civis Romanus (Latin: Roman citizen); Community of the Resurrection; company's risk; complete regression; conditioned reflex; Costa Rica (abbrev. or IVR); credit report; critical ratio; Croydon; current rate; Custos Rotulorum (Latin: Keeper of the Rolls)

CRA Commander of the Royal Artillery

CRAC Careers Research and Advisory Centre

CRAeS Companion of the Royal Aeronautical Society

CRAMRA Convention on the Regulation of Antarctic Mineral Resource Activities

CRASC Commander of the Royal Army Service Corps

CRC camera-ready copy; Cancer Research Campaign; Community Relations Council; cyclic redundancy check

CRCP Certificant of the Royal College of Physicians

CRCS Certificant of the Royal College of Surgeons

CRE Commander of the Royal Engineers; Commercial Relations and Exports; Commission for Racial Equality

cres. crescendo

Cres. Crescent (in street names)

CRF capital recovery factor

CRIB Current Research in Britain (publication)

crim. criminal

crim. con. criminal conversation (i.e. adultery)

crit. critic; critical(ly); criticism

CRMF Cancer Relief Macmillan Fund

CRMP Corps of Royal Military Police

CRNCM Companion of the Royal Northern College of Music

CRO cathode-ray oscilloscope; community relations officer; Criminal Records Office

CRP (India) Central Reserve Police

CRT cathode-ray tube; composite rate tax

cryst. crystalline; crystallography

cs. case

c.s. capital stock

c/s cases; cycles per second

Cs caesium

CS capital stock; Chartered Surveyor; Chemical Society; Chief of Staff; Christian Science; Civil Service; Clerk to the Signet; Court of Session; Czechoslovakia; CS gas

C/S cycles per second

CSA Child Support Agency; Confederate States of America

CSB Bachelor of Christian Science; chemical stimulation of the brain

CSBM Confidence- and Security-Building Measures

csc cosecant

CSC Civil Service Commission; Congregation of the Holy Cross; Conspicuous Service Cross (replaced by the DSC)

CSCE Conference on Security and Cooperation in Europe

CSD Chartered Society of Designers; Civil Service Department; Cooperative Secretaries Diploma

CSE Certificate of Secondary Education (replaced by General Certificate of Secondary Education, GCSE)

CSEU Confederation of Shipbuilding and Engineering Unions

CSF cerebrospinal fluid; colony-stimulating factor (as in **G-CSF**, granulocyte CSF)

CSG Companion of the Order of the Star of Ghana

CS gas a tear gas (surname initials of its US inventors, Ben Carson and Roger Staughton)

CSI compact source iodide (as in **CSI lamp**); Companion of the Order of the Star of India

CSIRO Commonwealth Scientific and Industrial Research Organization (Australia)

CSM cerebrospinal meningitis; Committee on Safety of Medicines; Company Sergeant-Major

CSO Central Statistical Office; Chief Scientific Officer; Chief Signal Officer; Chief Staff Officer; colour separation overlay; community service order

CSP Chartered Society of Physiotherapists; Civil Service of Pakistan; Council for Scientific Policy

CSR combat-stress reaction

CSS Certificate in Social Service; (member of the) Congregation of the Holy Ghost (Sanctus Spiritus); Holy Ghost Father; Council for Science and Society

CSSB Civil Service Selection Board

CSSR Congregatio Sanctissimi Redemptoris (Latin: Congregation of the Most Holy Redeemer; Redemptorists)

CST (USA) Central Standard Time

CSTI Council of Science and Technology Institutes

CStJ Commander of the Most Venerable Order of the Hospital of St John of Jerusalem

CSU catheter specimen of urine; Christlich-Soziale Union (Christian Social Union; German political party); Civil Service Union

CSV community service volunteer

CSYS (Scotland) Certificate of Sixth Year Studies

ct carat; caught; cent; court; crate

ct. centum (Latin: hundred); certificate

Ct. Connecticut; Count; (or **Ct**) countertenor; Court

CT cable transfer; Canterbury; cell therapy; (USA) Central Time; computerized tomography (as in **CT scanner**); Connecticut; corporation tax; counter trade

CTC city technology college; Commando Training Centre; crushing, tearing, and curling (machine); Cyclists' Touring Club

CText Chartered Textile Technologist

CTF coal-tar fuels

ctge cartage; cartridge

CTL constructive total loss

CTM computerized tomographic myelography

ctn carton; cotangent

CTO cancelled to order (of postage stamps)

CTOL conventional takeoff and landing

ctr. centre

CTR controlled thermonuclear research

cts centimes; cents; certificates; crates

CTS Catholic Truth Society; computerized tomographic scanner

CTT capital-transfer tax

CTV cable television; Canadian Television Network Limited

CTZ control traffic zone (around an aerodrome or airport)

cu. cubic

Cu copper (Latin *cuprum*)

CU Cambridge University; close-up

cub. cubic

CUF common university fund

cum. cumulative

cum div. cum dividend (i.e. with dividend)

cum. pref. cumulative preference (shares)

CUNA Credit Union National Association

CUP Cambridge University Press; Cuban peso (monetary unit)

cur. currency; current

cur. adv. vult curia advisari vult

curt. current (i.e. this month)

CUSO Canadian University Services Overseas

CUTS Computer Users' Tape System

c.v. cheval-vapeur (French: horsepower); curriculum vitae

CV calorific value; cardiovascular; Common Version (of the Bible); convertible; Coventry; (Canada) Cross of Valour; curriculum vitae

2CV 2 cheval-vapeur (deux chevaux; two-horsepower French car)

CVA cerebrovascular accident

CVCP Committee of Vice-Chancellors and Principals (of the Universities of the United Kingdom)

c.v.d. cash versus documents

CVD chemical vapour deposition

CVEsc escudo (monetary unit of Cape Verde)

CVI common variable immunodeficiency

CVJ constant velocity joint (in vehicles)

CVO Commander of the Royal Victorian Order

C.voc. colla voce (Italian: with the voice; instruction to accompanist)

CVS cardiovascular system; chorionic villus sampling; Council of Voluntary Service

CVSNA Council of Voluntary Service National Association

CVT constant variable transmission (in vehicles)

cw. clockwise

c.w. carrier wave

CW chemical weapons; Cockcroft–Walton (as in **CW generator**); continuous wave(s) (as in **CW radar**; also indicating Morse code, as in **CW speed**); Crewe; Curie–Weiss (in **CW law**)

CWA Crime Writers' Association

CWGC Commonwealth War Graves Commission

Cwlth Commonwealth

c.w.o. cash with order

CWO Chief Warrant Officer

CWS Cooperative Wholesale Society; Court Welfare Service

cwt hundredweight

cx cervix

cy capacity; currency; cyanide (in formulae); cycle(s)

CY calendar year; Cyprus

cyc. cyclopedia

cyl. cylinder; cylindrical

Cym. Cymric

Cys cysteine

Cz Cenozoic

CZ Canal Zone

Czech. Czechoslovak; Czechoslovakia(n)

D

d day; deci- (prefix indicating 0.1, as in **dB**, decibel); deuteron; dextrorotatory (as in *d*-**tartaric acid**); diameter; doh (in tonic sol-fa); relative density; thickness; a small increment in a given variable or function (as in dy/dx); the fourth vertical row of squares from the left on a chessboard

d. dam (in animal pedigrees); date; daughter; day; deciduous; degree; delete; depart(s); diameter; died; dime; dinar(s); dividend; dollar(s) (symbol **$**); dose; drachma(s); penny *or* pennies (Latin *denarius*)

D absorbed dose (of radiation); dalasī (Gambian monetary unit); defence (in **D notice**); deuterium; diameter; dinar (Tunisian monetary unit); dong (Vietnamese monetary unit); drag; electric flux density; five hundred; Germany; the first derivative of a function (in **D operator**); an optically active compound having a configuration related to dextrorotatory glyceraldehyde (as in **D-glucose**); a musical note or key

D. December; (USA) Democrat(ic); Deus (Latin: God); diamonds; Director; doctor; Dominus (Latin: God *or* Christ); Don (Spanish title); Duchess; Duke; Dutch

da deca- (prefix indicating 10, as in **dam**, decametre)

d/a days after acceptance; documents against acceptance

Da dalton(s)*

D/a deposit account; discharge afloat

DA Dartford; deed of arrangement; delayed action (bomb); dinar (Algerian monetary unit); Diploma in Anaesthesia; Diploma in Art; direct action; (USA) District Attorney; doesn't answer; duck's arse (hairstyle)

D/A days after acceptance; deposit account; digital-to-analogue; documents against acceptance (as in **D/A bill**)

DAA&QMG Deputy Assistant Adjutant and Quartermaster-General

DAAG Deputy Assistant Adjutant-General

DA&QMG Deputy Adjutant and Quartermaster-General

DAB digital audio broadcasting

DAc Doctor of Acupuncture

DAC Development Assistance Committee (of the OECD); digital-to-analogue converter

DACG Deputy Assistant Chaplain-General

DAD Deputy Assistant Director (as in **DADMS**, Deputy Assistant Director of Medical Services; **DADOS**, Deputy Assistant Director of Ordnance Services; **DADQ**, Deputy Assistant Director of Quartering; **DADST**, Deputy Assistant Director of Supplies and Transport)

DADG Deputy Assistant Director General (as in **DADGMS**, Deputy Assistant Director General of Medical Services)

DAdmin Doctor of Administration

DAE Dictionary of American English

DAFS Department of Agriculture and Fisheries for Scotland

DAG Deputy Adjutant-General

DAGMAR defining advertising goals for measured advertising results

DAgr Doctor of Agriculture

Dak. Dakota

dal decalitre(s)

dam decametre(s)

DAMS Deputy Assistant Military Secretary

Dan. Daniel; Danish

D&AD Designers and Art Directors Association

D&B discipline and bondage

D & C dilatation and curettage (of the uterus)

d and d drunk and disorderly

D & D death and dying

D and V diarrhoea and vomiting

d.a.p. documents against payment

DAP distributed array processor

DAP&E Diploma in Applied Parasitology and Entomology

DAppSc Doctor of Applied Science

DAQMG Deputy Assistant Quartermaster-General

DAR Daughters of the American Revolution

DArt Doctor of Art •

d.a.s. delivered alongside ship

DASc Doctor of Agricultural Science(s)

dat. dative

DAT dementia of the Alzheimer type; digital audio tape

DATEC Art and Design Committee, Technician Education Council

Datel data telex (data transmission service)

DATV digitally assisted television

dau. daughter

DAvMed Diploma in Aviation Medicine

DAX Deutsche Aktienindex (German share price index)

d.b. double bass

dB decibel(s)

Db dobra (monetary unit of São Tomé and Príncipe); dubnium

DB Bachelor of Divinity (Latin *Divinitatis Baccalaureus*); daybook; delayed broadcast; (Germany) Deutsche Bundesbank (German Federal Bank); Domesday Book

dBA decibel A (decibels above reference noise, adjusted: unit for measuring noise)

DBA Doctor of Business Administration; doing business as

DBC Deaf Broadcasting Council

DBE Dame Commander of the Order of the British Empire

DBib Douay Bible

dbk drawback

dbl. double

DBMS database management system

DBO Diploma of the British Orthoptic Board

DBS direct broadcast(ing by) satellite

DC da capo (Italian: from the head; i.e. repeat from the beginning); Daughters of Charity of St Vincent de Paul; de Candolle (indicating the author of a species, etc.); Detective Constable; direct current; District Commissioner; district council; District of Columbia (abbrev. *or* postcode); Doctor of Chiropractic; documents (against) cash; Douglas Commercial (aircraft, as in **DC10**); down centre (of stage)

D/C deviation clause

DCAe Diploma of the College of Aeronautics

DCAS Deputy Chief of the Air Staff

DCB Dame Commander of the Order of the Bath

DCC digital compact cassette; Diploma of Chelsea College

DCE data-communication equipment; domestic credit expansion

DCF discounted cash flow

DCG Deputy Chaplain-General

DCGS Deputy Chief of the General Staff

DCh Doctor of Surgery (Latin *Doctor Chirurgiae*)

DCH Diploma in Child Health

DChD Doctor of Dental Surgery

DChE Doctor of Chemical Engineering

DCI Detective Chief Inspector; double column inch (in advertisements)

DCL Doctor of Civil Law

DCLI Duke of Cornwall's Light Infantry

DCLJ Dame Commander of the Order of St Lazarus of Jerusalem

DCM Diploma in Community Medicine; Distinguished Conduct Medal

DCMG Dame Commander of the Order of St Michael and St George

DCnL Doctor of Canon Law

DCO Duke of Cambridge's Own (regiment)

DComm Doctor of Commerce

DCP Diploma in Conservation of Paintings; Diploma in Clinical Pathology

DCPath Diploma of the College Pathologists

DCR Diploma of the College of Radiographers (as in **DCR(MU)**, medical ultrasound; **DCR(NM)**, nuclear medicine; **DCR(R)**, diagnostic radiography; **DCR(T)**, radiotherapy)

DCrim Doctor of Criminology

DCS Deputy Chief of Staff; Deputy Clerk of Sessions; digital camera system; Doctor of Christian Science; Doctor of Commercial Sciences

DCSO Deputy Chief Scientific Officer

DCT Doctor of Christian Theology

DCVO Dame Commander of the Royal Victorian Order

dd dated; delivered

d.d. days after date; delayed delivery; delivered dock; demand draft; dry dock; today's date (Latin *de dato*)

D/d days after date; delivered

DD damage done; demand draft; direct debit; dishonourable discharge; Doctor of Divinity; Duchenne dystrophy; Dundee

D/D demand draft; dock dues

DDA Dangerous Drugs Act

D-Day Day Day (the specified day, i.e. 6 June 1944, for the Allied invasion of Europe)

DDC Dewey Decimal Classification (of library books); dideoxycytidine (Aids treatment); direct digital control

DDD deadline delivery date

DDE dynamic data exchange

DDGAMS Deputy Director-General, Army Medical Services

DDI dideoxyinosine (Aids treatment)

DDL data description language(s); Deputy Director of Labour

DDM Diploma in Dermatological Medicine

DDME Deputy Director of Mechanical Engineering

DDMI Deputy Director of Military Intelligence

DDMOI Deputy Director of Military Operations and Intelligence

DDMS Deputy Director of Medical Services

DDMT Deputy Director of Military Training

DDNI Deputy Director of Naval Intelligence

DDO Diploma in Dental Orthopaedics; District Dental Officer

DDPH Diploma in Dental Public Health

DDPR Deputy Director of Public Relations

DDPS Deputy Director of Personal Services

DDR Deutsche Demokratische Republik (German Democratic Republic *or* East Germany; now part of Germany); Diploma in Diagnostic Radiology

DDRA Deputy Director, Royal Artillery

DDRD Deputy Directorate of Research and Development

dd/s delivered sound

DDS Dewey Decimal System (library-book classification); Director of Dental Services; Doctor of Dental Science; Doctor of Dental Surgery

DDSD Deputy Director of Staff Duties

DDSM (USA) Defense Distinguished Service Medal

DDST Deputy Director of Supplies and Transport

DDT dichlorodiphenyltrichloro-ethane (insecticide)

DDVP dimethyldichlorovinyl phosphate (dichlorvos; insecticide)

DDWE&M Deputy Director of Works, Electrical and Mechanical

d.e. double entry

DE Delaware; Department of Employment (now part of the DfEE); Derby; Doctor of Engineering

Dea. Deacon

DEA Department of Economic Affairs (former UK government department)

deb. debenture; debit

dec. deceased; declaration; declension; decrease; decrescendo (Italian; decrease loudness)

Dec. December

decd deceased

decl. declension

DEconSc Doctor of Economic Science

decresc. decrescendo (Italian; decrease loudness)

ded. dedicate(d); dedication

DEd Doctor of Education

def. defective; defence; defendant; deferred; definite; definition

DEFCON defence readiness condition

deft. defendant

deg. degree

DEHA di-2-ethylhexyl adipate (plasticizer in clingfilm)

DEI Dutch East Indies (former name for Indonesia)

del. delegate; delete

Del. Delaware

deld. delivered

deleg. delegate

dem. demand; demurrage

Dem. (USA) Democrat(ic)

DEME Directorate of Electrical and Mechanical Engineering

DEMS defensively equipped merchant ships

DemU (Northern Ireland) Democratic Unionist

den. denier

Den. Denmark

DEn Department of Energy

DEN District Enrolled Nurse

DEng Doctor of Engineering

DEngS Doctor of Engineering Science

denom. denomination

dent. dental; dentist(ry)

DEOVR Duke of Edinburgh's Own Volunteer Rifles

dep. depart(s); departure; deponent; depose(d); deposit; depot; deputy

DEP Department of Employment and Productivity

dept department

dept. deputy

der. derivation; derivative

Derby. Derbyshire

deriv. derivation; derivative; derive(d)

DERL derived emergency reference level (of radiation)

Des. Designer

DES data encryption standard; Department of Education and Science

desc. descendant

DesRCA Designer of the Royal College of Art

destn destination

det. detach; detachment; detail; determine; detur (Latin: let it be given)

Det Detective (as in **Det Con**, Detective Constable; **Det Insp**, Detective Inspector; **Det Sgt**, Detective Sergeant; **Det Supt**, Detective Superintendent)

DET diethyltryptamine (hallucinogenic drug)

Deut. Deuteronomy

DEW distant early-warning (as in **DEW line**; network of radar stations)

df. draft

d.f. dead freight

DF Defender of the Faith; direction finder; Djibouti franc (monetary unit); Doctor of Forestry

DFA Doctor of Fine Arts

DFC Distinguished Flying Cross

DfEE Department for Education and Employment

DFHom Diploma of the Faculty of Homeopathy

DFLS Day Fighter Leaders' School

DFM Distinguished Flying Medal

dft defendant; draft

dg decigram(s)

DG Deo gratias (Latin: thanks be to God); Director-General; Dragoon Guards; Dumfries

DGAA Distressed Gentlefolks Aid Association

DGAMS Director-General, Army Medical Services

DGEME Director-General, Electrical and Mechanical Engineering

DGMS Director-General of Medical Services

DGMT Director-General of Military Training

DGMW Director-General of Military Works

DGNPS Director-General of Naval Personal Services

DGO Diploma in Gynaecology and Obstetrics

DGP Director-General of Personnel

DGPS Director-General of Personal Services

DGS Diploma in Graduate Studies

Dh dirham (monetary unit of United Arab Emirates)

DH dead heat; Department of Health; dirham (Moroccan monetary unit); Doctor of

Humanities; Durham

DHA District Health Authority

Dhc Doctor honoris causa (honorary doctorate)

DHL Doctor of Hebrew Letters; Doctor of Humane Letters

DHMSA Diploma in the History of Medicine (Society of Apothecaries)

DHQ district headquarters

DHSS Department of Health and Social Security (former government department, now split into the DoH and DSS)

DHumLit Doctor of Humane Letters

DHyg Doctor of Hygiene

di. diameter

Di didymium

DI Department of the Interior; Detective Inspector; donor insemination

dia. diameter

diag. diagram

dial. dialect(al)

diam. diameter

DIANE Direct Information Access Network for Europe

DIAS Dublin Institute of Advanced Sciences

DIC Diploma of Membership of the Imperial College of Science and Technology (London)

dict. dictation; dictator; dictionary

dicta. dictaphone

DICTA Diploma of Imperial College of Tropical Agriculture

diff. differ; difference; different; differential

dig. digest (book or summary); digit(al)

DIG Deputy Inspector-General

DIH Diploma in Industrial Health

dil. dilute(d)

DIL dual in-line (as in **DIL switch**)

dim. dimension; diminuendo; diminutive

Din dinar (Yugoslavian monetary unit)

DIN Deutsches Institut für Normung (German national standards organization; as in **DIN connector**, etc.)

DIng Doctor of Engineering (Latin Doctor Ingeniariae)

dinky double income, no kids (used of couples)

dio. diocese

dioc. diocesan; diocese

dip. diploma

Dip Diploma (in degrees and qualifications)

DIP dual in-line package

DipAD Diploma in Art and Design

DipAe Diploma in Aeronautics

DipASE Diploma in Advanced Study of Education, College of Preceptors

DipAvMed Diploma of Aviation Medicine, Royal College of Physicians

DipBA Diploma in Business Administration

DipBS Diploma in Fine Art, Byam Shaw School

DipCAM Diploma in Communication, Advertising, and Marketing of CAM Foundation

DipCD Diploma in Child Development; Diploma in Civic Design

DipCE Diploma in Civil Engineering

DipChemEng Diploma in Chemical Engineering

DipCom Diploma in Commerce

DipEcon Diploma in Economics

DipEd Diploma in Education

DipEl Diploma in Electronics

DipESL Diploma in English as a Second Language

DipEth Diploma in Ethnology

DipFD Diploma in Funeral Directing

DipFE Diploma in Further Education

DipGSM Diploma in Music, Guildhall School of Music and Drama

DipHA Diploma in Hospital Administration

DipHE Diploma in Higher Education

DipHum Diploma in Humanities

dipl. diploma; diplomat(ic)

DipLA Diploma in Landscape Architecture

DipLib Diploma of Librarianship

DipM Diploma in Marketing

DipMet Diploma in Metallurgy

DipN Diploma in Nursing

DipNEd Diploma in Nursery School Education

DipPharmMed Diploma in Pharmaceutical Medicine

DipREM Diploma in Rural Estate Management

DipSoc Diploma in Sociology

DipTA Diploma in Tropical Agriculture

DipT&CP Diploma in Town and Country Planning

DipTech Diploma in Technology

DipTh Diploma in Theology

DipTP Diploma in Town Planning

DipTPT Diploma in Theory and Practice of Teaching

dir. direct(ed); direction; director; dirham

DIR developer inhibitor release

dis. discharge; discount

disb. disbursement

disc. discount; discover(ed)

dismac digital scene-matching area correlation sensors

dist. distant; distinguish(ed); district

distr. distribution; distributor

DistTP Distinction in Town Planning

DIT double income tax (in **DIT relief**)

div. divide(d); dividend; division; divorce(d)

DIY do-it-yourself

DJ dinner jacket; disc jockey; Doctor of Law (Latin *Doctor Juris*)

DJAG Deputy Judge Advocate-General

DJI (USA) Dow Jones Index

DJIA (USA) Dow Jones Industrial Average

DJS Doctor of Juridical Science

DJT Doctor of Jewish Theology

DJur Doctor of Law (Latin *Doctor Juris*)

dk dark; deck; dock

DK Denmark

Dkr krone (monetary unit of Denmark and Greenland)

dkyd dockyard

dl decilitre(s)

DL Darlington; Deputy Lieutenant; diesel; down left (of stage)

D/L demand loan

DLC Diploma of Loughborough College; down left centre (of stage)

dld. delivered

DLES Doctor of Letters in Economic Studies

DLI Durham Light Infantry

DLit Doctor of Literature

DLitt Doctor of Letters (Latin *Doctor Litterarum*)

DLittS Doctor of Sacred Letters

DLJ Dame of Justice of the Order of St Lazarus of Jerusalem

DLO dead letter office; Diploma in Laryngology and Otology; dispatch (money payable) loading only

dlr dealer

DLR Docklands Light Railway

DLS Doctor of Library Science

dly daily

dm decimetre(s)

DM Daily Mail; Deutschmark (German monetary unit); direct mail; Doctor of Medicine

DMA Diploma in Municipal Administration; direct memory access

DMAC duobinary multiplexed analogue component

D-mark Deutschmark

DMC district medical committee

DMD Doctor of Medical Dentistry; Duchenne muscular dystrophy

DME Diploma in Mechanical Engineering

DMet Doctor of Metallurgy

DMI Director of Military Intelligence

DMin Doctor of Ministry

DMJ Diploma in Medical Jurisprudence

DMJ(Path) Diploma in Medical Jurisprudence (Pathology)

DML Doctor of Modern Languages

DMLJ Dame of Merit of the Order of St Lazarus of Jerusalem

DMO Director of Military Operations; district medical officer

DMR Diploma in Medical Radiology

DMRD Diploma in Medical Radiological Diagnosis

DMRE Diploma in Medical Radiology and Electrology

DMRT Diploma in Medical Radiotherapy

DMS Diploma in Management Studies; Director of Medical Services; Doctor of Medical

Science; Doctor of Medicine and Surgery

DMSO dimethylsulphoxide (used in ointments)

DMSSB Direct Mail Services Standard Board

DMT dimethyltryptamine (hallucinogenic drug); Director of Military Training

DMU decision-making unit (within an organization); directly managed unit (of NHS hospitals)

DMus Doctor of Music

DMZ demilitarized zone

DN debit note; de novo (Latin: from the beginning); Diploma in Nursing; Doncaster

DNA deoxyribonucleic acid; District Nursing Association

DNB Dictionary of National Biography

DNC distributed numerical control

DNE Diploma in Nursing Education; Director of Naval Equipment

DNF did not finish (of competitors in a race)

DNI Director of Naval Intelligence

DNOC dinitro-*o*-cresol (pesticide)

DNR do not resuscitate

DNS Department for National Savings

do. ditto

DO deferred ordinary (shares); delivery order; Diploma in Ophthalmology; Diploma in Osteopathy; direct object; direct order; dissolved oxygen; Doctor of Optometry; Doctor of Osteopathy

DOA dead on arrival

DOAE Defence Operational Analysis Establishment (of the Ministry of Defence)

d.o.b. date of birth

DObstRCOG Diploma of the Royal College of Obstetricians and Gynaecologists

doc. document(s)

Doc. Doctor

DOC Denominazione di Origine Controllata (Italian: name of origin controlled; Italian wine classification); District Officer Commanding

DocEng Doctor of Engineering

DOCG Denominazione di Origine Controllata Garantita (Italian: name of origin guaranteed controlled; Italian wine classification)

DOE Department of the Environment; depends on experience (referring to salary in job advertisements); Director of Education

DoH Department of Health

DOHC double overhead camshaft

DOI Department of Industry

dol. dolce (Italian: sweetly; i.e. gently); dollar

DOL Doctor of Oriental Learning

dom. domain; domestic; dominant; dominion

Dom. Dominica; Dominican; Dominus (Latin: Lord)

DOM Deo Optimo Maximo (Latin: to God, the best, the greatest); dirty old man; Dominican Republic

DOMS Diploma in Ophthalmic Medicine and Surgery

DON Diploma in Orthopaedic Nursing

DORA Defence of the Realm Act (1914)

Dors. Dorset

DOrth Diploma in Orthodontics

DOS Director of Ordnance Services; disk operating system; Doctor of Ocular Science

DoT Department of Transport

DOT digital optical tape

dow. dowager

DOW died of wounds

doz. dozen

d.p. directione propria (Latin: with proper direction; in prescriptions); direct port

DP data processing; delivery point; disabled person; displaced person; duty paid

D/P documents against payment

DPA Diploma in Public Administration; discharged prisoners' aid

DPB deposit pass book

DPCM differential pulse code modulation

DPD Data Protection Directive; Diploma in Public Dentistry

DPEc Doctor of Political Economy

DPed Doctor of Pedagogy

DPh Doctor of Philosophy

DPH Diploma in Public Health; Director of Public Health

DPhil Doctor of Philosophy

DPhysMed Diploma in Physical Medicine

dpi dots per inch

dpl. diplomat

DPM data-processing manager; Diploma in Psychological Medicine

DPMI DOS Protected Mode Interface

DPP deferred payment plan; Director of Public Prosecutions

DPR Data Protection Register; Director of Public Relations

DPS Director of Personal Services; Director of Postal Services; dividend per share; Doctor of Public Service

dpt department; deposit; depot

DPT diphtheria, pertussis (whooping cough), tetanus (in **DPT vaccine**)

DPW Department of Public Works

dr debtor; dram

dr. debit; drachm; drachma; draw(n); drawer

Dr Director; Doctor; drachma (Greek monetary unit); Drive (in street names)

DR (USA) Daughters of the Revolution; dead reckoning; dining room; Diploma in Radiology; down right (of stage); dry riser (pipe with attachment for fireman's hose)

D/R deposit receipt

DRAC Director, Royal Armoured Corps

DRAM dynamic random-access memory

DRAW direct read after write

DRC Diploma of the Royal College of Science and Technology, Glasgow; down right centre (of stage)

DRCOG Diploma of the Royal College of Obstetricians and Gynaecologists

DRCPath Diploma of the Royal College of Pathologists

DRD Diploma in Restorative Dentistry

DRDW direct read during write

DRE Director of Religious Education; Doctor of Religious Education

Dr ing Doctor of Engineering

Dr jur Doctor of Laws

DRM Diploma in Radiation Medicine

DRO disablement resettlement officer

DrOecPol Doctor of Political Economics (Latin *Doctor Oeconomiae Politicae*)

DRP dividend reinvestment plan

Dr rer. nat. Doctor of Natural Science

DRS Diploma in Religious Studies

DRSAMD Diploma of the Royal Scottish Academy of Music and Drama

DRSE drug-related side effects

d.s. date of service; daylight saving; days after sight; day's sight; document signed

DS dal segno (Italian: (repeat) from the sign); debenture stock; Detective Sergeant; Directing Staff; Doctor of Science; Doctor of Surgery; Down's syndrome; driver seated (in **DS vehicle**)

DSA Diploma in Social Administration

DSAC Defence Scientific Advisory Council

DSAO Diplomatic Service Administration Office

DSc Doctor of Science

DSC Distinguished Service Cross; Doctor of Surgical Chiropody

DSCHE Diploma of the Scottish Council for Health Education

DScMil Doctor of Military Science

DSD Director of Staff Duties

DSDP Deep-Sea Drilling Project

DSL Doctor of Sacred Letters

DSM Distinguished Service Medal; Doctor of Sacred Music

DSO (Companion of the) Distinguished Service Order

DSocSc Doctor of Social Science(s)

d.s.p. decessit sine prole (Latin: died without issue)

d.s.p.l. decessit sine prole legitima (Latin: died without legitimate issue)

DSR debt service ratio; dynamic spatial reconstructor

Dss Deaconess

DSS Department of Social Security; Director of Social Services; Doctor of Holy Scripture (Latin *Doctor Sacrae Scripturae);* Doctor of Social Science

DSSc Diploma in Sanitary Science

DSSL document style specification language

DST Daylight Saving Time; deep-sleep therapy; Director of Supplies and Transport; Doctor of Sacred Theology; Double Summer Time

DStJ Dame of Justice of the Order of St John of Jerusalem

dstn destination

D. Surg. Dental Surgeon

DSW Doctor of Social Welfare

DT Daily Telegraph; (USA) detective; Dorchester (Dorset)

DTA Diploma in Tropical Agriculture

d.t.b.a. date to be advised

DTCD Diploma in Tuberculosis and Chest Diseases

d.t.d. detur talis dosis (Latin: let such a dose be given)

DTD Diploma in Tuberculous Diseases; document type definition

DTE data terminal equipment

DTech Doctor of Technology

DTh Doctor of Theology

DTH Diploma in Tropical Hygiene

DTI Department of Trade and Industry

DTIC dacarbazine (anticancer drug)

DTL diode-transistor logic; down the line (in shooting)

DTM Diploma in Tropical Medicine

DTMH Diploma in Tropical Medicine and Hygiene

DTp Department of Transport

DTP desktop publishing

DTPA diethylenetriaminepenta-acetic acid (diagnostic aid)

DTPH Diploma in Tropical Public Health

DTR double taxation relief

DT's delirium tremens

Du. Duke; Dutch

DU depleted uranium; Doctor of the University; duodenal ulcer

Dunelm. Dunelmensis (Latin: (Bishop) of Durham)

DUniv Doctor of the University

dup. duplicate

DUP (Northern Ireland) Democratic Unionist Party

Dur. Durham

DUV damaging ultraviolet (radiation)

DV Deo volente (Latin: God willing); Douay Version (of the Bible)

DVA Diploma of Veterinary Anaesthesia

DV&D Diploma in Venereology and Dermatology

DVD Digital video (or versatile) disk

DVH Diploma in Veterinary Hygiene

DVLA Driver and Vehicle Licensing Authority

DVLC Driver and Vehicle Licensing Centre (Swansea)
DVM Doctor of Veterinary Medicine
DVMS Doctor of Veterinary Medicine and Surgery
DVR Diploma in Veterinary Radiology
DVS Doctor of Veterinary Surgery
DVSc Doctor of Veterinary Science
d.w. dead weight
DW dock warrant
DWA driving without awareness
d.w.c. deadweight capacity
dwr drawer
dwt pennyweight
d.w.t. deadweight tonnage
DX daylight exposure (indicating that the speed of a film can be set automatically in a suitably equipped camera); long-distance
dy. delivery
Dy dysprosium
DY Benin (formerly Dahomey); dockyard; Dudley
Dyd. Dockyard
dz. dozen
DZ Algeria; drop zone

E

e electromotive; electron; electron charge; positron (in **e**⁺); the transcendental number 2.718 282... ; the fifth vertical row of squares from the left on a chessboard
e. eldest; engineer(ing); Erlang (unit of traffic intensity)
E earth (indicating the terminal in an electrical circuit); east(ern); east London; Ecstasy (hallucinogenic drug); electric field strength (light ital. in nonvector equations; bold ital. in vector equations); electromotive force; emalangeni (sing. lilangeni; monetary unit of Swaziland); energy; E-number (EC-approved code number of a food additive, as in **E200**); exa- (prefix indicating 10^{18}, as in **EJ**, exajoule); illuminance; (ital.; *or* **E$_e$**) irradiance; Spain; Young modulus; casual workers (occupational grade); a musical note or key; a universal negative categorical proposition
E. Earl; Egypt(ian); England; English
ea. each
EA East Anglia; enterprise allowance
EAA Edinburgh Architectural Association
EAC East African Community
EACSO East African Common Services Organization
EAGGF European Agricultural Guidance and Guarantee Fund (in the EC)
EAK (East Africa) Kenya
EAN European Academic Network
e. & e. each and every
E & OE errors and omissions excepted (on invoice forms)
e.a.o.n. except as otherwise noted
EAP East Africa Protectorate; English for academic purposes

EARN European Academic and Research Network
EAROM electrically alterable read-only memory
EAS equivalent air speed
EAT (East Africa) Tanzania
EAU (East Africa) Uganda
EAW Electrical Association for Women
EAZ (East Africa) Tanzania (Zanzibar; *see also under* EAT)
EB electricity board; Encyclopaedia Britannica
EBC English Benedictine Congregation
EBCDIC extended binary-coded decimal-interchange code
e-beam electron beam
EBM expressed breast milk
EbN east by north
EBNF extended BNF (Backus normal form)
E-boat Enemy War Motorboat (German torpedo boat in World War II)
Ebor. Eboracensis (Latin: (Archbishop) of York)
EBR electron-beam recording
EBRD European Bank for Reconstruction and Development
EbS east by south
EBU English Bridge Union; European Broadcasting Union
EBV Epstein–Barr virus
EC East Caribbean; East Central London; east coast; Ecuador; emergency commission; Engineering Corps; Established Church; (Canada) Etoile du Courage (French: Star of Courage); European Community (now often used in place of EEC)
ECA Economic Commission for Africa (UN agency); Educational Centres Association
ECAFE Economic Commission for Asia and the Far East
eccl. ecclesiastic(al)
Eccles. Ecclesiastes
ecclesiast. ecclesiastical
Ecclus. Ecclesiasticus
ECD estimated completion date
ECE Economic Commission for Europe (UN agency)
ECFMG Educational Council for Foreign Medical Graduates
ECG electrocardiogram
ECGD Export Credits Guarantee Department
ECLAC Economic Commission for Latin America and the Caribbean (UN agency)
ECM electronic countermeasure(s) (for jamming enemy signals, destroying guided missiles, etc.)
ECMA European Computer Manufacturers' Association (Geneva)
ecol. ecological; ecology
econ. economical; economics; economy
ECOSOC Economic and Social Council (of the UN)
ECOVAST European Council for the Village and Small Town

ECOWAS Economic Community of West African States
ECP Euro-commercial paper
ECPA Electric Consumers Protection Act (1986)
ECR electronic cash register
ECS European Communications Satellite
ECSC European Coal and Steel Community
ECT electroconvulsive therapy; emission-computerized tomography
ecu European Currency Unit (in the EC)
ECU English Church Union
Ecua. Ecuador
ed. edited; edition; editor; education
Ed. Editor
ED effective dose (as in **ED$_{50}$**, mean effective dose); Efficiency Decoration; equivalent dose (of radiation); European Democrat; ex dividend
EdB Bachelor of Education
EDB ethene dibromide (antiknock agent and soil fumigant)
EDC Economic Development Committee; Engineering Design Centre; European Defence Community; expected date of confinement
EdD Doctor of Education
EDE effective dose equivalent (of radiation)
EDF European Development Fund
EDG European Democratic Group
Edin. Edinburgh
edit. edited; edition; editor
EdM Master of Education
EDM electronic distance measurement
edn edition
EDP electronic data processing
EDR (Japanese) Electronic Dictionary Research
EdS Education Specialist
EDS Electronic Data Systems Corporation
EDT (USA, Canada) Eastern Daylight Time
educ. educated; education; educational
EDV end-diastolic volume
EE Early English; Eastern Electricity; electrical engineer(ing); errors excepted
EEA European Economic Area
EE & MP Envoy Extraordinary and Minister Plenipotentiary
EEB European Environmental Bureau
EEC European Economic Community
EEF Egyptian Expeditionary Force; Engineering Employers' Federation
EEG electroencephalogram
EEIBA Electrical and Electronic Industries Benevolent Association
EEMS enhanced expanded memory specification
EENT eye, ear, nose, and throat

EEO equal employment opportunity

EER energy–efficiency ratio

EEROM electrically erasable read-only memory

EET Eastern European Time

EETPU Electrical, Electronic, Telecommunications, and Plumbing Union

EETS Early English Text Society

EEZ exclusive economic zone

EF elongation factor

EFA European Fighter Aircraft

EFCE European Federation of Chemical Engineering

EFI electronic fuel injection (of car engines)

EFIS electronic flight-information system

EFL English as a foreign language; external financial limit

EFM electronic fetal monitor

EFT electronic funds-transfer

EFTA European Free Trade Association

EFTPOS electronic funds-transfer at point of sale

EFTS electronic funds-transfer system

e.g. exempli gratia (Latin: for example)

Eg. Egypt(ian); Egyptology

EGA enhanced graphics adapter

EGF epidermal growth factor

EGM extraordinary general meeting

EGmbH (Germany) Eingetragene Gesellschaft mit beschränkter Haftung (registered limited company)

EGR earned growth rate; exhaust gas recirculation (as in **EGR valve**)

Egypt. Egyptian

eh. ehrenhalber (German: honorary)

EH Edinburgh

EHF extremely high frequency

EHO Environmental Health Officer

EHT extra-high tension

EHV extra-high voltage

EI East Indian; East Indies; exposure index

EIA Engineering Industries Association; environmental impact analysis; Environmental Investigation Agency; exercise-induced asthma

EIB European Investment Bank

EICS East India Company's Service

EIEE early infantile epileptic encephalopathy

E-in-C Engineer-in-Chief

EIS Educational Institute of Scotland; environmental impact statement; executive information system

EISA extended industry standard architecture

EIU Economist Intelligence Unit

ELA electronic learning aid

ELBS English Language Book Society

ELDO European Launcher Development Organization (now part of ESA)

elec. electric(al); electricity; electronic

elem. element(s); elementary

elev. elevation

ELF extremely low frequency

ELISA enzyme-linked immunosorbent assay

Eliz. Elizabethan

ELR exceptional leave to remain (for four years in the UK; granted to asylum-seekers)

ELT English language teaching (for foreign students)

ELV expendable launch vehicle

e.m. electromagnetic

EM Earl Marshal; Edward Medal; electromagnetic; electromotive; electronic mail; electron microscope; Engineer of Mines; enlisted man

EMA European Monetary Agreement

email electronic mail

EMBO European Molecular Biology Organization

embryol. embryology

EMCOF European Monetary Cooperation Fund

EME East Midlands Electricity

EMet Engineer of Metallurgy

emf electromotive force

EMG electromyogram

EMI Electric and Musical Industries

Emp. Emperor; Empire; Empress

EMP electromagnetic pulse

EMR electromagnetic radiation

EMS emergency medical service; European Monetary System; expanded memory specification

emu electromagnetic unit

EMU economic and monetary union (within the EC); extravehicular mobility unit

en ethylenediamine (used in formulae)

EN Enfield; Enrolled Nurse

ENB English National Ballet

enc. enclosed; enclosure

Enc. Brit. Encyclopaedia Britannica

encl. enclosed; enclosure

ency. encyclopedia

ENE east-northeast

ENEA European Nuclear Energy Agency

eng. engine; engineer(ing); engraved; engraver; engraving

Eng. England; English

ENG electronic news gathering (in TV broadcasting)

EN(G) Enrolled Nurse (General) (formerly SEN)

Eng. hn English horn

engin. engineer(ing)

engr engineer; engraver

engr. engrave(d); engraving

ENIAC Electronic Numerical Integrator and Calculator (first electronic calculator)

enl. enlarge(d); enlargement; enlisted

EN(M) Enrolled Nurse (Mental)

EN(MH) Enrolled Nurse (Mental Handicap)

ENO English National Opera

Ens. ensemble; Ensign

ENSA Entertainments National Service Association (in World War II)

ENT ear, nose, and throat

entom. entomological; entomology

Ent. Sta. Hall entered (registered) at Stationers' Hall (requirement to secure copyright on books before 1924)

env. envelope; environs

e.o. ex officio

EO Equal Opportunities; Executive Officer; executive order

EOB end of block; Executive Office Building

EOC end of cycle; Equal Opportunities Commission

EOD end of data (computing code); explosive ordnance disposal

EOE equal opportunity employer; errors and omissions excepted (on invoice forms); European Options Exchange

EOF end of file

EOJ end of job

e.o.m. end of the month

EOPH Examined Officer of Public Health

EOQC European Organization for Quality Control

EOR end of record

EORTC European Organization for Research on Treatment of Cancer

EOT end of tape (as in **EOT marker**); end of transmission

e.p. en passant

Ep. Epistle

EP estimated position; extended-play (gramophone record)

EPA eicosapentaenoic acid (cholesterol-reducing fatty acid)

EPC easy-processing channel (in **EPC black**, filler in rubber compounding); European Patent Convention

EPCOT Experimental Prototype Community of Tomorrow (Florida)

EPG electropalatogram; Eminent Persons Group

Eph. Ephesians

EPI Eysenck Personality Test

EPIC European Prospective Investigation into Cancer

Epiph. Epiphany

EPIRB emergency position indicator radio beacon

Epis. Episcopal(ian); Epistle

EPM electron-probe microanalysis

EPNdB effective perceived noise decibels

EPNS electroplated nickel silver

EPO erythropoietin; European Patent Office

EPOS electronic point of sale (as in **EPOS terminal, EPOS system**)

EPP European People's Party; executive pension plan

EPR electron paramagnetic resonance (as in **EPR spectroscopy**)

EPROM erasable programmable read-only memory

e.p.s. earnings per share

EPT early pregnancy test; excess profits tax

EPU European Payments Union

eq. equal; equation; equivalent

EQ educational quotient; equivalence (as in **EQ gate**)

EQC external quality control

eqn equation

eqpt equipment

equiv. equivalent

er elder

Er erbium

ER Eastern Region (British Rail); Eduardus Rex (Latin: King Edward); efficiency report; Elizabeth Regina (Latin: Queen Elizabeth); emergency room

ERA Electrical Research Association; (USA) Equal Rights Amendment

ERC Economic Research Council; Electronics Research Council

ERCP endoscopic retrograde cholangiopancreatography

ERD Emergency Reserve Decoration

ERDF European Regional Development Fund

Erf electrorheological fluid

ERG electrical resistance gauge; electroretinogram

ERI Edwardus Rex et Imperator (Latin: Edward King and Emperor)

ERM Exchange Rate Mechanism

Ernie electronic random number indicating equipment (premium-bond computer)

ERP European Recovery Programme

ERS earnings-related supplement; emergency radio service; emergency response system

ERT excess retention tax

ERTS Earth Resources Technology Satellite

ERV English Revised Version (of the Bible)

ERW enhanced radiation weapon

Es einsteinium

ES Education Specialist; El Salvador

ESA European Space Agency

ESB electrical stimulation of the brain

Esc escape key; escudo (Portuguese monetary unit)

ESCAP Economic and Social Commission for Asia and the Pacific (UN agency; formerly ECAFE)

Esd. Esdras

Esda electrostatic deposition analysis (as in **Esda test**)

ESE east-southeast

ESF European Science Foundation

ESG Education Support Grant; English Standard Gauge

ESL English as a second language

ESN educationally subnormal

ESNS educationally subnormal, serious

ESOL English for speakers of other languages

ESOP employee share-ownership plan

esp. especially; espressivo (Italian: expressively)

ESP English for specific purposes; extrasensory perception

ESPRIT European strategic programme for research and development in information technology

Esq. esquire (in correspondence)

ESR erythrocyte sedimentation rate

ESRC Economic and Social Research Council (formerly SSRC); Electricity Supply Research Council

ESRIN European Space Research Institute (Italy)

ESRO European Space Research Organization (now part of ESA)

Ess. Essex

Esso Standard Oil (phonetic spelling of SO)

est. establish(ed); estate; estimate(d); estimation; estuary

Est. Established

EST (USA, Canada) Eastern Standard Time; electroshock therapy

estab. establish(ed); establishment

Esth. Esther

esu electrostatic unit

ESU English-Speaking Union

Et ethyl (used in formulae)

ET (USA) Eastern Time; (Arab Republic of) Egypt; Employment Training (for the unemployed); ephemeris time; extraterrestrial

ETA estimated time of arrival; Euzkadi ta Askatsuna (Basque: Basque Nation and Liberty; nationalist organization)

et al. et alibi (Latin: and elsewhere); et alii (Latin: and others)

etc. et cetera (Latin: and other things)

ETD estimated time of departure; extension trunk dialling

ETF electronic transfer of funds

Eth. Ethiopia(n); Ethiopic

ETH Ethiopia

ethnol. ethnology

ETI estimated time of interception; extraterrestrial intelligence

ETR estimated time of return

et seq. et sequens (Latin: and the following)

ETSU Energy Technology Support Unit (of the Department of Energy)

ETUC European Trade Union Confederation

et ux. et uxor (Latin: and wife)

ETV educational television

ety. etymological; etymologist; etymology

Eu europium

EUA European unit of account

EUDISED European Documentation and Information Service for Education

Eur. Europe(an)

Euratom European Atomic Energy Community

Eur Ing European Engineer

EUROM European Federation for Optics and Precision Mechanics

EUV extreme ultraviolet

EUW European Union of Women

eV eingetragener Verein (German: registered society); electronvolt

EV English Version (of the Bible); exposure value

EVA ethene and vinyl acetate (copolymers); extravehicular activity

evan. evangelical; evangelist

e.w. each way (betting)

EW electronic warfare

EWO Educational Welfare Officer; European Women's Orchestra

ex. examination; examine(d); example; except(ed); exception; exchange; excluding; excursion; execute(d); executive; express; extra

Ex. Exodus

EX Exeter

exam. examination

ex aq. ex aqua (Latin: from water)

ex b. ex bonus (without bonus)

exc. excellent; except; excepted; exception; excursion

Exc. Excellency

ex cap. ex capitalization (without capitalization)

exch. exchange; exchequer

excl. exclamation; exclamatory; excluding; exclusive

ex cp. ex coupon (without the interest on the coupon)

exd examined

ex div. ex dividend (without dividend)

exec. executive; executor

exes expenses

ex int. ex interest (without interest)

ex lib. ex libris (Latin: from the books of)

ex n. ex new (of shares)

EXNOR exclusive-NOR (as in **EXNOR gate**)

Exod. Exodus

ex off. ex officio (Latin: by right of office)

exor executor

EXOR exclusive-OR (as in **EXOR gate**)

exp exponential

exp. expenses; experiment(al); expire(d); export(ed); exporter; express

expt experiment

exptl experimental

exr executor

exrx executrix

exs expenses

ext. extension; extent; external(ly); extinct; extra; extract

EXTEND Exercise Training for the Elderly and/or Disabled

exx examples; executrix

Ez. Ezra
EZ easy
Ezek. Ezekiel
Ezr. Ezra.

F

f fah (in tonic sol-fa); femto- (prefix indicating 10⁻¹⁵, as in **fm**, femtometre); f-number (ratio of the focal length of a lens to its aperture, as in **f8**); focal length; forte (Italian; loudly); frequency; fugacity; function (as in *f);* the sixth vertical row of squares from the left on a chessboard

f. fathom(s); female; feminine; filly; fine; folio; following (page); foot; foul; franc(s); guilder (monetary unit of the Netherlands)

F Fahrenheit (in °F, degree Fahrenheit); false; farad(s); Faraday constant; fast (on a clock or watch regulator); (USA) fighter (specifying a type of military aircraft, as in **F-106**); filial generation (as in **F₁**, first generation); fluorine; f-number (as in **F4**; *see under* f); force; franc (monetary unit of various countries); France; Helmholtz function; a musical note or key; a spectral type

F. fathom(s); Federation; female; feminine; filly; fine; folio; foul

f.a. fanny adams; free alongside; freight agent

FA Faculty of Actuaries; fanny adams; field artillery; Football Association

f.a.a. free of all averages

FAA Film Artists' Association; Fleet Air Arm

FAB fuel-air bomb

fac. facsimile; factor; factory; faculty

f.a.c. fast as can (be)

FACE field artillery computer equipments

facs. facsimile

FACT Federation Against Copyright Theft

FAD flavin adenine dinucleotide

FAE fuel-air explosive(s)

Fah. Fahrenheit

FAI Fédération aéronautique internationale (French: International Aeronautical Federation); Football Association of Ireland

fam. familiar; family

FAM Free and Accepted Masons

F & AP fire and allied perils

f & d freight and demurrage

f & f fixtures and fittings

F and Gs folded and gathered pages

f & t fire and theft

FANY First Aid Nursing Yeomanry

f.a.o. finish all over; for the attention of

FAO Food and Agriculture Organization (of the UN)

FAP fixed action pattern

f.a.q. fair average quality; free alongside quay

FAR free (of claim) for accident reported

FARE Federation of Alcoholic Rehabilitation Establishments

FARELF Far East Land Forces

f.a.s. free alongside ship

FAS fetal alcohol syndrome; free alongside ship

FAST Federation Against Software Theft

fath. fathom

fax facsimile transmission

FB foreign body

FBA Federation of British Artists; fluorescent brightening agent (used in detergents)

FBI (USA) Federal Bureau of Investigation

FBL flight-by-light (aircraft control system)

FBO for the benefit of

FBT fringe benefit tax

FBu Burundi franc (monetary unit)

FBU Fire Brigades Union

FBW fly-by-wire

f.c. follow copy

FC (Australia) Federal Cabinet; fieri curavit (Latin: the donor directed this to be done; on gravestones and other monuments); Football Club

fcap foolscap

FCAR free of claim for accident reported

FCB file control block

f.c.c. face-centred cubic

FCD First Chief Directorate (of the KGB)

FCEC Federation of Civil Engineering Contractors

FCIA Foreign Credit Insurance Association

f. co. fair copy

FCO Foreign and Commonwealth Office

fcp. foolscap

fcs francs

FCS Federation of Conservative Students

FCU fighter control unit

f.d. focal distance; free delivery

FD Fidei Defensor (Latin: Defender of the Faith (Henry VIII); e.g. on British coins); free-delivered (at docks)

FDF Food and Drink Federation

FDM frequency-division multiplexing

FDO for declaration (purposes) only

FDP (Germany) Freie Demokratische Partei (Free Democratic Party)

FDR Franklin Delano Roosevelt (1882–1945, US president 1933–45)

Fe iron (Latin *ferrum*)

FE Far East; further education

FEAF Far East Air Force

Feb February

fec. fecit (Latin: (he or she) made it; on works of art next to the artist's name)

FEC Foreign Exchange Certificate (tourist currency used in China; compare RMB)

Fed. Federal(ist); Federated; Federation

FED Federal Reserve System

FEER fundamental equilibrium exchange rate

FEL free-electron laser

fem. female; feminine

FEM finite-element method

FEP fluorinated ethene propene (a plastic)

FET field-effect transistor

ff fecerunt (Latin: (they) made it; on works of art next to the artists' names); folios; following (pages, lines, etc.); fortissimo (Italian; very loudly)

f.f. fixed focus

FF Fianna Fáil (Irish Gaelic: warriors of Ireland; Irish political party); field force

f.f.a. free from alongside (ship)

FFA (Scotland) Fellow of the Faculty of Actuaries

FFC Foreign Funds Control

fff fortississimo (Italian; as loudly as possible)

FFF Free French Forces

FFHC Freedom from Hunger Campaign

FFI Finance for Industry; French Forces of the Interior

FFPS Fauna and Flora Preservation Society

FFr French franc

f.f.s.s. full-frequency stereophonic sound

ffy faithfully

f.g. fully good

FG Fine Gael (Irish Gaelic: tribe of the Gaels; Irish political party)

FGA foreign general average

f.g.f. fully good, fair

FH fetal heart; family history

FHB family hold back

FHH fetal heart heard

FHNH fetal heart not heard

FHR fetal heart rate

FI Falkland Islands; flow injection

FIA full interest admitted

Fiat Fabbrica Italiana Automobili Torino (Italian Motor Works in Turin)

fib. fibula

f.i.b. free into barge; free into bunker

FIBOR Frankfurt Inter-Bank Offered Rate

Fid. Def. Fidei Defensor

FIDE Fédération internationale des échecs (French: International Chess Federation)

fi. fa. fieri facias (writ of execution; Latin: have it done)

FIFA Fédération internationale de football association (French: International Federation of Association Football)

FIFO first in first out

fig. figurative(ly); figure(s)

FILO first in last out

FIMBRA Financial Intermediaries, Managers, and Brokers Regulatory Association

fin. finance; financial; finis (Latin: the end); finish

Fin. Finland; Finnish

f.i.o. for information only

fir. firkin

FIRA Furniture Industry Research Association

FIS Family Income Supplement; free into store

f.i.t. free of income tax

FJI Fiji

FK Falkirk

Fkr Faroese krone (monetary unit)

fl. floor; flores (Latin: flowers; powdered form of a drug); floruit (Latin: flourished; indicates the period of greatest activity of a person whose birth and death dates are not known); fluid; flute; (Netherlands) guilder (from its former name *florin*)

Fl. Flanders; Flemish

FL Flight Lieutenant; Florida; Liechtenstein

Fla. Florida

fld field

fl. dr. fluid dram

Flem. Flemish

FLN (Algeria) Front de Libération Nationale (French: National Liberation Front)

flops floating-point operations per second (a measure of computer power, as in **Mflops**, megaflops)

flor. floruit

fl oz fluid ounce

fl. pl. flore pleno (Latin: with double flowers)

FLQ (Canada) Front de Liberation du Québec (French: Quebec Liberation Front)

flst. flautist

Flt Flight

F/Lt Flight Lieutenant

Flt Cmdr Flight Commander

Flt Lt Flight Lieutenant

Flt Off. Flight Officer

Flt Sgt Flight Sergeant

fm fathom(s); femtometre(s); from

f.m. frequency modulation

Fm fermium

FM facilities management; Field Marshal; frequency modulation

FMB Federation of Master Builders

FMCG fast-moving consumer goods

FMD foot and mouth disease

FMG franc (monetary unit of Madagascar)

Fmk markka (Finnish monetary unit)

fml formal

FMN flavin mononucleotide

FMS flight-management systems

FNCO Fleet Naval Constructor Officer

fo. folio

f/o for orders

FO Field Officer; Flying Officer; Foreign Office (now part of the FCO); forward observer

FOB free on board

FoC father of the (trade-union) chapel

FOC free of charge; free of claims

FOD free of damage

FOE Friends of the Earth

FOFA follow-on forces attack

FOH front of house

FOIA (USA) Freedom of Information Act

FOIC Flag Officer in charge

fol. folio; follow(ed); following

folg. following

foll. followed; following

FONA Flag Officer, Naval Aviation

FONAC Flag Officer, Naval Air Command

FOQ free on quay

for. foreign(er); forestry

FOR free on rail

Ford (Kenya) Forum for the Restoration of Democracy (political party)

FOREST Freedom Organization for the Right to Enjoy Smoking Tobacco

fort. fortification; fortified

Fortran formula translation (a programming language)

f.o.s. free on ship; free on station

f.o.t. free of tax

f.o.w. first open water; free on wagon

FOX Futures and Options Exchange (in **London FOX**)

fp forte-piano (Italian; loud (then) soft); freezing point

f.p. fine paper; flash point; freezing point; fully paid (of shares)

FP fire policy; floating policy; freezing point; fully paid (of shares)

FPA Family Planning Association; free of particular average

FPC Family Practitioner Committee; fish protein concentrate

FPO field post office

fps feet per second; foot-pound-second (as in **fps units**); frames per second

fr. fragment; franc(s); from

f.r. folio recto (Latin: on the right-hand page)

Fr Brother (Latin *Frater*); Father; francium

Fr. France; Frau (German: Mrs); Friday

FR Faroe Islands; Federal Republic; freight release

F/R folio reference

Fra Brother (Italian *frate*)

FRA forward rate agreement

FRAME Fund for the Replacement of Animals in Medical Experiments

FRBS Fellow of the Royal Society of British Sculptors

FRC Financial Reporting Council

FRCD floating-rate certificate of deposit

freq. frequent(ly); frequentative

FRES Federation of Recruitment and Employment Services

FRG Federal Republic of Germany

Fri. Friday

FRIH (New Zealand) Fellow of the Royal Institute of Horticulture

Fris. Frisian

Frl. Fräulein (German: Miss)

FRN floating-rate note

FRO fire risk only

front. frontispiece

Frs. Frisian

FRS (USA) Federal Reserve System; Fellow of the Royal Society

FRSA Fellow of the Royal Society of Arts

FRSAI Fellow of the Royal Society of Antiquaries of Ireland

FRSC Fellow of the Royal Society of Chemistry (formerly FCS; FRIC)

FRSE Fellow of the Royal Society of Edinburgh

FRSH Fellow of the Royal Society for the Promotion of Health

FRSL Fellow of the Royal Society of Literature

FRSM Fellow of the Royal Society of Medicine

FRSNZ Fellow of the Royal Society of New Zealand

FRST Fellow of the Royal Society of Teachers

FRSTM&H Fellow of the Royal Society of Tropical Medicine and Hygiene

frt freight

FS field security

FSH follicle-stimulating hormone

FSMC Freeman of the Spectacle-Makers' Company

FSO Foreign Service Officer

FSR Field Service Regulations

ft feint; fiat (Latin: let there be made); foot; fort

ft. fortification

Ft forint (Hungarian monetary unit); Fort

FT Financial Times

FTA (Index) Financial Times Actuaries Share Index

FTAM file transfer, access, and management

FTASI Financial Times Actuaries All-Share Index

FTAT Furniture, Timber, and Allied Trades Union

FTC flying training command; Full Technological Certificate (of City and Guilds Institute)

fth. fathom

FT (Index) Financial Times Ordinary Share Index

ft-lb foot-pound

FT Ord Financial Times (Industrial) Ordinary Share Index

ft/s feet per second

FTS flying training school

FTSE 100 Financial Times Stock Exchange 100 Index

FTZ free-trade zone

fur. furlong(s)

fut. future; futures

f.v. fishing vessel; folio verso (Latin: on the reverse (i.e. left-hand) page)

FVP flash vacuum pyrolysis

FVRDE Fighting Vehicle Research and Development Establishment
FWCC Friends' World Committee for Consultation
fwd forward
f.w.d. four-wheel drive; front-wheel drive
f.w.t. fair wear and tear
FY Blackpool
FYC Family and Youth Concern
FYI for your information

G

g acceleration of free fall; gallon(s); gaseous (as in $H_2O(g)$); gluon; gram(s); grav; the seventh row of vertical squares from the left on a chessboard
g. geographical (as in **g. mile**); guilder(s); guinea(s)
G conductance; gauss; (Australia, USA) general exhibition (certification); giga- (prefix indicating 10^9, as in **GHz** (gigahertz), or (in computing) 2^{30}); Glasgow; gourde (Haitian monetary unit); grand (1000 pounds or dollars); gravitational constant; guanine; guanosine; guarani (Paraguayan monetary unit); shear modulus; a musical note or key
G. German(y); good; Gulf (on maps, etc.)
G3 Group of Three (most powerful western economies)
G5 Group of Five (nations that agreed to exchange-rate stabilization)
G7 Group of Seven (leading industrial nations)
G10 Group of Ten (nations lending money to the IMF)
G24 Group of Twenty Four (industrialized nations)
G77 Group of Seventy Seven (developing countries)
g.a. general average
Ga gallium
Ga. Georgia
GA Gaelic Athletic (Club); Gamblers Anonymous; general agent; General American; General Assembly (of the UN); general average; Geographical Association; Geologists' Association; Georgia; goal attack
GAA (Ireland) Gaelic Athletic Association
GAB general arrangements to borrow (in the IMF)
GABA gamma-aminobutyric acid (a neurotransmitter)
GAFTA Grain and Free Trade Association
GAI Guild of Architectural Ironmongers
gal gallon(s)
Gal. Galatians
gall. gallon
galv. galvanic; galvanize(d)
G&AE general and administrative expense
G and O gas and oxygen (in anaesthetic)

G & S Gilbert and Sullivan
G & T gin and tonic
GAR Grand Army of the Republic (in the American Civil War)
GATT General Agreement on Tariffs and Trade
gaz. gazette; gazetteer
Gb gilbert
GB Great Britain (abbrev. or IVR)
GBA Alderney
GBE (Knight or Dame) Grand Cross of the Order of the British Empire
GBG Guernsey
GBH grievous bodily harm
GBJ Jersey
GBM Isle of Man
g.b.o. goods in bad order
GBS George Bernard Shaw (1856–1950, Irish-born dramatist and critic)
GBZ Gibraltar
GC George Cross
GCA Girls' Clubs of America; ground-controlled approach; Guatemala
GCB (Knight or Dame) Grand Cross of the Order of the Bath
GCBS General Council of British Shipping
GCC Gas Consumers Council; Gulf Cooperation Council
GCD greatest common divisor
GCE General Certificate of Education
GCF greatest common factor
GCH (Knight) Grand Cross of the Hanoverian Order
GCHQ Government Communications Headquarters
GCI ground-controlled interception
GCIE (Knight) Grand Commander of the Order of the Indian Empire
GCLJ Grand Cross of St Lazarus of Jerusalem
GCLH Grand Cross of the Legion of Honour
GCM Good Conduct Medal; greatest common measure; greatest common multiple
GCMG (Knight or Dame) Grand Cross of the Order of St Michael and St George
GCON Grand Cross of the Order of the Niger
GCSE General Certificate of Secondary Education
GCSG (Knight) Grand Cross of the Order of St Gregory the Great
GCSI (Knight) Grand Commander of the Order of the Star of India
GCSJ (Knight) Grand Cross of Justice of the Order of St John of Jerusalem
GCStJ (Bailiff or Dame) Grand Cross of the Most Venerable Order of the Hospital of St John of Jerusalem
GCVO (Knight or Dame) Grand Cross of the Royal Victorian Order
gd good; grand-daughter; ground
Gd gadolinium
GD goal defence; Grand Duke
GDBA Guide Dogs for the Blind Association

GDC General Dental Council
Gdns Gardens
GDP gross domestic product
GDR German Democratic Republic (East Germany; now part of Germany)
gds goods
Ge germanium
GEC (UK) General Electric Company
GED general educational development
GEF Global Environment Facility (of the World Bank)
gen. gender; genealogy; general(ly); generic; genitive; genus
Gen. General; Genesis; Geneva
geneal. genealogy
genit. genitive
Genl General
geod. geodesy; geodetic
geog. geographer; geographic(al); geography
geol. geologic(al); geologist; geology
geom. geometric(al); geometry
ger. gerund(ive)
Ger. German(y)
Gerbil Great Education Reform Bill (1988)
Ges. Gesellschaft (German: company or society)
Gestapo Geheime Staatspolizei (German: secret state police; in Nazi Germany)
GeV gigaelectronvolt(s)
GF Guinean franc
GFOFs geared futures and options and funds
GFR German Federal Republic
GFS Girls' Friendly Society
GG Girl Guides; Governor General
gge garage
g.gr. great gross (144 dozen)
GH Ghana; growth hormone
GHOST global horizontal sounding technique (for collecting atmospheric data)
GHQ General Headquarters
GHz gigahertz
gi. gill (unit of measure)
Gi gilbert
GI galvanized iron; gastrointestinal; generic issue; (Royal) Glasgow Institute (of the Fine Arts); (USA) government issue (hence, a US serviceman)
Gib. Gibraltar
GIFT gamete intrafallopian transfer (for assisting conception)
GIGO garbage in, garbage out
GIMechE Graduate of the Institution of Mechanical Engineers
GINO graphical input output (for computer graphics)
GIP glazed imitation parchment (a type of paper)
Gk Greek
GK goalkeeper
GKC G(ilbert) K(eith) Chesterton (1874–1936, British journalist and author)

gl. gill (unit of measure); glass; gloss

g/l grams per litre

GL Gloucester; Grand Luxe (of a car)

4GL fourth-generation language

glam greying, leisured, affluent, married

Glam. Glamorgan

Glas. Glasgow

GLC gas–liquid chromatography; Greater London Council (abolished 1986); ground-level concentration (of radioactive material)

GLCM ground-launched cruise missile

gld. guilder

Gln glutamine

Glos Gloucestershire

gloss. glossary

glt gilt

Glu glutamic acid

Gly glycine

gm gram

g m gram metre

GM Geiger–Müller (as in **GM counter**); general manager; General Motors Corporation; genetically modified; geometric mean; George Medal; grant maintained

G-man (USA) Government man (an FBI agent)

g.m.b. good merchantable brand

GMB General, Municipal, Boilermakers (trade union; formerly GMBATU; GMWU); Grand Master (of the Order) of the Bath

GMBE Grand Master of the Order of the British Empire

GmbH (Germany) Gesellschaft mit beschränkter Haftung (private limited company; Ltd)

Gmc Germanic

GMC general management committee; General Medical Council; Guild of Memorial Craftsmen

GMIE Grand Master of the Order of the Indian Empire

GMKP Grand Master of the Knights of St Patrick

GMMG Grand Master of the Order of St Michael and St George

GMP Grand Master of the Order of St Patrick

g.m.q. good merchantable quality

GMS grant-maintained status

GMSI Grand Master of the Order of the Star of India

GMST Greenwich Mean Sidereal Time

GMT Greenwich Mean Time

GMW gram-molecular weight

gn. guinea

GNC General Nursing Council (replaced by UKCC)

gnd ground

GNP gross national product

Gnr Gunner

gns guineas

GNVQ General National Vocational Qualification

GO General Office(r); general order

g.o.b. good ordinary brand

GOC General Officer Commanding

GOC-in-C General Officer Commanding-in-Chief

GOE General Ordination Examination

GOM Grand Old Man

GOP (USA) Grand Old Party (the Republican Party)

Gosplan Gos(udarstvennaya) Plan(ovaya Comissiya) (Russian: State Planning Commission)

GOT glutamatic oxaloacetic transaminase (renamed aspartate aminotransferase, AST)

Goth. Gothic

Gov. government; governor

Govt government

gox gaseous oxygen

gp group

GP Gallup Poll; general pause; general practitioner; general purpose; Gloria Patri (Latin: glory be to the Father); graduated pension; Grand Prix

GPALS Global Protection Against Limited Strikes (reduced SDI programme)

Gp Capt Group Captain

gpd gallons per day

gph gallons per hour

GPI general paralysis of the insane

GPM gallons per minute

GPMU Graphical, Paper, and Media Union (formed by merger of NGA and SOGAT)

GPO General Post Office

GPR ground-penetrating radar

GPS gallons per second; (Australia) Great Public Schools (indicating a group of mainly nonstate schools, and of sporting competitions between them)

GPT glutamic pyruvic transaminase (renamed alanine aminotransferase, ALT); Guild of Professional Toastmasters

GPU General Postal Union; Gosudarstvennoye Politicheskoye Upravlenie (Russian: State Political Administration; Soviet state security system, 1922–23)

GQ general quarters

gr. grade; grain (the unit); gram; gross

Gr. Grecian; Greece; Greek

GR gamma ray; general relativity; Georgius Rex (Latin: King George); Greece; Gulielmus Rex (Latin: King William)

grad. graduate(d)

gram. grammar(ian); grammatical

GRC General Research Corporation

GRE Guardian Royal Exchange Assurance Group

gro. gross (unit of quantity)

grp group

grs grains; gross

gr. t. gross ton

GRU Glavnoye Razvedyvatelnoye Upravleniye (Russian: Central Intelligence Office)

gr. wt. gross weight

gs. guineas

g.s. grandson

GS General Secretary; general service; General Staff; goal shooter; grammar school

GSA Girls' Schools Association; Glasgow School of Art

GSC gas–solid chromatography

g.s.m. good sound merchantable (quality)

GSM general sales manager; (Member of the) Guildhall School of Music and Drama

GSO General Staff Officer

GSP glass-fibre strengthened polyester; Good Service Pension

GSR galvanic skin reflex

GSS Government Statistical Service

GST Greenwich Sidereal Time

g-st garter-stitch

gt gilt; great

gt. gutta (Latin: a drop)

GT gas turbine; gauge theory; Gran Turismo (Italian: grand touring; sports car)

Gt Brit. Great Britain

GTC (Scotland) General Teaching Council; good till cancelled

gtd guaranteed

GTI Gran Turismo Injection (sports car)

GTO Gran Turismo Omologata (Italian: certified for grand touring; of sports cars)

GTS gas turbine ship

GU genitourinary; Guam; Guildford

guar. guarantee(d)

Guat. Guatemala

gui. guitar

GUI Golfing Union of Ireland; graphic user interface

Guin. Guinea

Gulag Glavnoye Upravleniye Lagerei (Soviet prison and labour camp system)

GUM (Russia) Gosudarstvenni Universalni Magazin (Universal State Store)

GUT grand unified theory

GUY Guyana

g.v. gravimetric volume

GV (France) grande vitesse (fast goods train)

gvt government

GVW gross vehicle weight

GW gigawatt(s); guided weapons (as in **GW cruiser**)

GWR Great Western Railway

Gy gray

gyn. gynaecological; gynaecology

H

h heat transfer coefficient; hecto- (prefix indicating 100, as in **hm**, hectometre); height; hour; Planck constant; specific enthalpy; a small increment; the eighth vertical row of squares from the left on a chessboard

h. harbour; hard(ness); height; high; horizontal; horn; hour; hundred; husband

H enthalpy; hard (indicating the degree of hardness of lead in a pencil; also in **HB**, hard black; **HH , double hard; etc.);** henry(s); heroin; histamine receptor (in **H₁**, **H₂**; used in specifying types of antihistamines); Hungary; hydrogen; magnetic field strength

H. halfpage; Harbour; hardness; hearts; herbaceous; hospital; hydrant

ha hectare

h.a. hoc anno (Latin: in this year)

Ha hahnium (element 105)

HA hardy annual; Harrow; Health Authority; heavy artillery; Highway(s) Act; Historical Association

HAA heavy anti-aircraft; hepatitis-associated antigen

HA & M Hymns Ancient and Modern

Hab. Habakkuk

HAC Honourable Artillery Company

HAF Hellenic Air Force

Hag. Haggai

HAI hospital-acquired infection

H. & B. Humboldt and Bonpland (indicating the authors of a species, etc.)

h & c hot and cold (water)

Hants Hampshire

h. app. heir apparent

HARCVS Honorary Associate of the Royal College of Veterinary Surgeons

HART (New Zealand) Halt All Racist Tours (antiracist sports organization)

Harv. (USA) Harvard University

HAT housing action trust

HB hard-black (on pencils; indicating medium-hard lead); hardy biennial

H.B. & K. Humboldt, Bonpland, and Kunth (indicating the authors of a species, etc.)

HBC high breaking capacity; Hudson's Bay Company

HBIG hepatitis B immunoglobulin

HBLV human B-lymphotropic virus

HBM Her Britannic Majesty

H-bomb hydrogen bomb

HBP high blood pressure

HBV hepatitis B virus

h.c. honoris causa (Latin: for the sake of honour; honorary); hot and cold (water)

h/c held covered

HC Heralds' College; High Church; Highway Code; Holy Communion; House of Commons

H/C held covered

HCAAS Homeless Children's Aid and Adoption Society

hcap handicap

HCBA Hotel and Catering Benevolent Association

HCF highest common factor; Honorary Chaplain to the Forces

HCFC hydrochlorofluorocarbon

HCH hexachlorocyclohexane (an insecticide)

HCI human–computer interface

HCIMA Hotel Catering and Institutional Management Association

HCM His Catholic Majesty

hcp handicap

h.c.p. hexagonal close-packed

HCSA Hospital Consultants and Specialists Association

hd hand; head

h.d. heavy duty; hora decubitus (Latin: at bedtime)

HD Hodgkin's disease; Huddersfield; hydrogen-deuterium

HDA (Australia) Hawkesbury Diploma in Agriculture

hdbk handbook

HDD head-down display; Higher Dental Diploma

HDipEd Higher Diploma in Education

hdkf handkerchief

HDL high-density lipoprotein

HDLC high-level data link control (a communications protocol)

hdlg handling

HDP high-density polyethylene

hdqrs headquarters

HDR hot dry rock (in **HDR energy**)

HDTV high-definition television

hdwd hardwood; headword

He helium

HE higher education; high explosive; His Eminence; His Excellency; horizontal equivalent

HEAO High Energy Astronomy Observatory

Heb. Hebrew (language); Hebrews

HEC (école des) hautes études commerciales (French: (college of) higher commercial studies); Higher Education Corporation

HEH His Exalted Highness

HEIC Honourable East India Company

HEICS Honourable East India Company's Service

heir app. heir apparent

heir pres. heir presumptive

HEO Higher Executive Officer; highly elliptic-inclined orbit (as in **HEO satellite**)

HEOS high-elliptic-inclined-orbit satellite

HEP human error probability

her. heraldic; heraldry

herp. herpetologist; herpetology

Herts Hertfordshire

hex hexadecimal (notation)

hex. hexachord; hexagonal

hf half

Hf hafnium

HF hard firm (on pencils; indicating hard lead); high frequency

HFA hydrofluoroalkane

HFARA Honorary Foreign Associate of the Royal Academy

hf. bd. half binding

HFC high-frequency current; hydrofluorocarbon

HFRA Honorary Foreign Member of the Royal Academy

hg hectogram(s)

Hg mercury (Latin *hydrargyrum*)

HG Harrogate; High German; His Grace; Home Guard; Horse Guards

HGG hypogammaglobulinaemia

hGH human growth hormone

hgt height

HGTAC Home Grown Timber Advisory Committee

HGV heavy goods vehicle

HGW heat-generating waste

hh hands (height measurement for horses)

HH double hard (on pencils; indicating very hard lead); Herbig–Haro (in **HH object**); (Member of the) Hesketh Hubbard Art Society; His Highness; His Holiness (title of the Pope)

HHA half-hardy annual; Historic Houses Association

HHB half-hardy biennial

hhd hogshead

HHH treble hard (on pencils; indicating very hard lead)

HHNK hyperglycaemic hyperosmolar nonketoacidotic coma (in diabetes)

H-Hour Hour Hour (i.e. the specified time at which an operation is to begin)

HHP half-hardy perennial

HHS (USA) Department of Health and Human Services (replaced HEW)

HI Hawaii; Hawaiian Islands; hearing impaired; hic iacet (Latin: here lies; on gravestones)

HIDB Highlands and Islands Development Board

hi-fi high fidelity

HIH His Imperial Highness

hilac heavy-ion linear accelerator

HILAT high-latitude (in **HILAT satellite**)

HIM His Imperial Majesty

Hind. Hindi; Hindu; Hindustan(i)

His histidine

HIS hic iacet sepultus *or* sepulta (Latin: here lies buried; on gravestones)

hist. histology; history

HIV human immunodeficiency virus (the cause of AIDS)

HJ hic jacet (Latin: here lies; on gravestones); Hilal-e-Jurat (Pakistani honour)

HJS hic jacet sepultus *or* sepulta (Latin: here lies buried; on gravestones)

HK Hong Kong (abbrev. *or* IVR); House of Keys (Manx Parliament)

HKJ (Hashemite Kingdom of) Jordan

hl hectolitre(s)

HL House of Lords

HLA human lymphocyte antigen (as in **HLA system**)

HLD Doctor of Humane Letters

HLI Highland Light Infantry

HLW high-level (radioactive) waste

hm hectometre(s)

HM hazardous material; headmaster; Her Majesty

HMA Head Masters' Association; high-memory area

HMAS Her Majesty's Australian Ship

HMC Headmasters' Conference; Hospital Management Committee; Household Mortgage Corporation

HMCA Hospital and Medical Care Association

HMCIC Her Majesty's Chief Inspector of Constabulary

HMCN Her Majesty's Canadian Navy

HMCS Her Majesty's Canadian Ship

HMF Her Majesty's Forces

HMG Her Majesty's Government

HMHS Her Majesty's Hospital Ship

HMI Her Majesty's Inspector (of schools); human–machine interface

HMIED Honorary Member of the Institute of Engineering Designers

HMIP Her Majesty's Inspectorate of Pollution

HMNZS Her Majesty's New Zealand Ship

HMOCS Her Majesty's Overseas Civil Service

HMP hoc monumentum posuit (Latin: (he or she) erected this monument)

HMS Her Majesty's Service; Her Majesty's Ship

HMSO Her Majesty's Stationery Office

HMV His Master's Voice (gramophone-record company)

hn horn

HNC Higher National Certificate

HND Higher National Diploma

ho. house

Ho holmium

HO habitual offender; head office; Home Office

HoC House of Commons

HoD head of department

H of C House of Commons

H of K House of Keys

H of L House of Lords

H of R (USA) House of Representatives

Hol Holocene

HOLLAND hope our love lasts and never dies

hon. honorary; honourable

Hon Honorary (in titles, as in **HonFInstP**, Honorary Fellow of the Institute of Physics); Honorary Member (in titles, as in **HonRCM**, Honorary Member of the Royal College of Music); Honourable (title)

Hond. Honduras

hons honours

Hon. Sec. Honorary Secretary

HOOD hierarchical object-oriented design

Hook. (Sir William) Hooker (indicating the author of a species, etc.)

Hook. fl. Hooker fils (Sir Joseph Hooker, son of Sir William Hooker; indicating the author of a species, etc.)

hor. horizon; horizontal

horol. horology

hort. horticultural; horticulture

Hos. Hosea

hosp. hospital

hp horsepower

h.p. hire purchase

HP hardy perennial; Hemel Hempstead; (USA) Hewlett–Packard (electronics and computing manufacturer); high performance; high power; hire purchase; house physician; Houses of Parliament

hpch. harpsichord

HPk Hilal-e-Pakistan (Pakistani honour)

HPP high-pressure polyethylene

HPV human papilloma virus

HQ headquarters

HQA Hilal-i-Quaid-i-Azam (Pakistani honour)

hr hour

Hr Herr (German: Mr, Sir)

HR heart rate; Hereford; Home Rule(r); (USA) House of Representatives

HRCA Honorary Royal Cambrian Academician

HRE Holy Roman Emperor

HRGI Honorary Member of the Royal Glasgow Institute of the Fine Arts

HRH Her Royal Highness

HRHA Honorary Member of the Royal Hibernian Academy

HRI Honorary Member of the Royal Institute of Painters in Water Colours

HRIP hic requiescit in pace (Latin: here rests in peace; on gravestones)

Hrn Herr(e)n (German: Messrs, Sirs)

HROI Honorary Member of the Royal Institute of Oil Painters

HRP human remains pouch

hrs hours

HRSA Honorary Member of the Royal Scottish Academy

HRSW Honorary Member of the Royal Scottish Water Colour Society

HRT hormone replacement therapy

h.s. hoc sensu (Latin: in this sense); hora somni (Latin: at bedtime)

Hs hassium

HS hic sepultus or sepulta (Latin: here is buried; on gravestones); high school; Home Secretary

HSA human serum albumin

HSC Health and Safety Commission; Higher School Certificate (replaced by GCE A level)

HSDU hospital sterilization and disinfection unit

HSE Health and Safety Executive; hic sepultus est (Latin: here lies buried; on gravestones)

HSH Her Serene Highness

HSI human–system interface

HSM Her Serene Majesty

HSSU hospital sterile supply unit

HST Hawaii Standard Time; high-speed train; Hubble Space Telescope

HSV herpes simplex virus

ht height

HT half time; Hawaii Time

5-HT 5-hydroxytryptamine

HTLV human T-cell lymphotropic virus

HTML hypertext mark-up language

Hts Heights (in place names)

HTV Harlech Television

HU Hull

HUAC House (of Representatives) Un-American Activities Committee

HUD head-up display

Hugo Human Genome Organization

hum. human; humanities (classics); humorous

HUMINT human intelligence (espionage activities)

HUMV human light vehicle

Hung. Hungarian; Hungary

Husat Human Science and Advanced Technology Research Institute

h.v. high velocity

HV health visitor; high velocity; high voltage

HVA Health Visitors' Association (trade union; now a section of the MFS)

HVAC heating, ventilation, air conditioning; high-voltage alternating current

HVCert Health Visitor's Certificate

HVDC high-voltage direct current

HVP hydrolysed vegetable protein

h.w. hit wicket

h/w herewith

HW hazardous waste; high water; hot water

HWM high-water mark

HX Halifax

hy heavy

hyg. hygiene

hyp. hypotenuse; hypothesis; hypothetical

Hz hertz

I

i the imaginary number $\sqrt{-1}$

i. incisor (tooth); interest; intransitive

I electric current; inti (Peruvian monetary unit); iodine; isospin quantum number; Italy; luminous intensity; one; radiant intensity; a particular affirmative categorial statement

I. Iesus (Latin: Jesus); Imperator (Latin: Emperor); Imperatrix (Latin: Empress); Independence; Independent; Infidelis (Latin: unbeliever, infidel); Institute; International; Ireland; Island

i.a. in absentia (Latin: while absent)

Ia. Iowa

IA Indian Army; information anxiety; Institute of Actuaries; Iowa

IA5 International Alphabet, Number 5

IAA indoleacetic acid (plant hormone); International Advertising Association

IAAF International Amateur Athletic Federation

IAAS Incorporated Association of Architects and Surveyors

IAC Institute of Amateur Cinematographers

IACP International Association of Chiefs of Police

IACS International Annealed Copper Standard

IADR International Association for Dental Research

IAEA International Atomic Energy Agency

IAF Indian Air Force; Indian Auxiliary Force

IAGB & I Ileostomy Association of Great Britain and Ireland

IAHM Incorporated Association of Headmasters

IALA International Association of Lighthouse Authorities

IAM Institute of Administrative Management; Institute of Advanced Motorists; Institute of Aviation Medicine

IAMC Indian Army Medical Corps

IAO Incorporated Association of Organists

IAOC Indian Army Ordnance Corps

IAPS Incorporated Association of Preparatory Schools

IAPSO International Association for the Physical Sciences of the Oceans

IARF International Association for Religious Freedom

IARO Indian Army Reserve of Officers

IARU International Amateur Radio Union

IAS immediate access store; Indian Administrative (formerly Civil) Service; indicated air speed

IASS International Association for Scandinavian Studies

IAT International Atomic Time

IATA International Air Transport Association

IATUL International Association of Technological University Libraries

IAU International Association of Universities; International Astronomical Union

IAWPRC International Association on Water Pollution Research and Control

ib. ibidem

IB in bond; International Bank (for Reconstruction and Development); invoice book

IBA Independent Broadcasting Authority; indole 3-butyric acid (rooting compound); International Bar Association

IBB Invest in Britain Bureau

IBBR interbank bid rate

IBD inflammatory bowel disease

IBEL interest-bearing eligible liability

IBF International Badminton Federation; International Boxing Federation

IBG Institute of British Geographers

IBI invoice book inwards

ibid. ibidem (Latin: in the same place; indicating a previously cited reference to a book, etc.)

IBiol Institute of Biology

IBM International Business Machines (Corporation; computer manufacturer)

IBMBR interbank market bid rate

IBO invoice book outwards

IBRD International Bank for Reconstruction and Development (the World Bank)

IBRO International Bank Research Organization; International Brain Research Organization

IBS Institute of Bankers in Scotland

IBTE Institution of British Telecommunications Engineers

i/c in charge (of); in command

IC identity card; Iesus Christus (Latin: Jesus Christ); immediate constituent; Imum Coeli (the lowest point on the ecliptic below the horizon); integrated circuit; internal-combustion (engine)

ICA ignition control additive (for motor vehicles); Institute of Chartered Accountants in England and Wales; Institute of Contemporary Arts; International Coffee Agreement; International Colour Authority; International Cooperation Administration; International Council on Archives; International Cyclist Association

ICAA Invalid Children's Aid Association

ICAEW Institute of Chartered Accountants in England and Wales

ICAI Institute of Chartered Accountants in Ireland

ICAO International Civil Aviation Organization

ICAS Institute of Chartered Accountants of Scotland

ICBM intercontinental ballistic missile

ICBN International Code of Botanical Nomenclature

ICBP International Council for Bird Preservation

ICC International Chamber of Commerce; International Convention Centre (Birmingham); International (formerly Imperial) Cricket Conference

ICCA International Cocoa Agreement

ICCH International Commodities Clearing House

ICCPR International Covenant on Civil and Political Rights (of the UN)

ICCROM International Centre for Conservation at Rome

ICD International Classification of Diseases (WHO publication)

Ice. Iceland(ic)

ICE ice, compress, elevation (treatment for limb bruises); Institution of Civil Engineers; internal-combustion engine

ICED International Council for Educational Development

ICEF International Federation of Chemical, Energy, and General Workers' Unions

Icel. Iceland(ic)

IC engine internal-combustion engine

ICER Industry Council for Electronic Equipment Recycling

ICES International Council for the Exploration of the Sea

ICF inertial-confinement fusion; International Canoe Federation

ICFTU International Confederation of Free Trade Unions

ICHCA International Cargo Handling Co-ordination Association

IChemE Institution of Chemical Engineers

ichth. ichthyology

ICI Imperial Chemical Industries; International Commission on Illumination

ICIDH International Classification of Impairments, Disabilities, and Handicaps (WHO publication)

ICJ International Commission of Jurists; International Court of Justice

ICL International Computers Ltd

ICM Institute for Complementary Medicine; Institute of Credit Management; International Confederation of Midwives

ICMS International Centre for Mathematical Sciences (Edinburgh)

ICN Infection Control Nurse; International Council of Nurses

ICNA Infection Control Nurses' Association

ICNB International Code of Nomenclature of Bacteria

ICNCP International Code of Nomenclature of Cultivated Plants

ICNV International Code of Nomenclature of Viruses

ICO Islamic Conference Organization

ICOM International Council of Museums

ICOMOS International Council of Monuments and Sites

ICorrST Institution of Corrosion Science and Technology

ICP intracranial pressure

ICPO International Criminal Police Organization (Interpol)

ICR intelligent character recognition

ICRC International Committee of the Red Cross

ICRF Imperial Cancer Research Fund

ICRP International Commission on Radiological Protection

ICRU International Commission on Radiation Units (and Measurements)

ICS Indian Civil Service; Institute of Chartered Shipbrokers; International Chamber of Shipping; investors' compensation scheme

ICSA Institute of Chartered Secretaries and Administrators

ICSH interstitial-cell-stimulating hormone

ICSID International Council of Societies of Industrial Design

ICSLS International Convention for Safety of Life at Sea

ICSU International Council of Scientific Unions (in UNESCO)

ICU intensive care unit

ICW Institute of Clerks of Works of Great Britain; International Congress of Women; interrupted continuous waves

ICWA Institute of Cost and Works Accountants

ICZN International Code of Zoological Nomenclature

id. idem (Latin: the same)

Id. Idaho

ID Idaho; identification; inside diameter; Intelligence Department; intradermal; Iraqi dinar (monetary unit)

IDA International Development Association; Islamic Democratic Association

IDB illicit diamond buying; Internal Drainage Board

IDC industrial development certificate

IDD insulin-dependent diabetes; international direct dialling

IDDD international direct distance dial(ling)

IDDM insulin-dependent diabetes mellitus

IDF International Dental Federation

IDMS integrated data-management system

IDN in Dei nomine (Latin: in God's name)

IDP integrated data processing; International Driving Permit

IDRC International Development Research Centre

IDS Income Data Services; Industry Department for Scotland; Institute of Development Studies

IDV International Distillers and Vintners

i.e. id est (Latin: that is); inside edge

IE Indo-European (languages)

IEA Institute of Economic Affairs; Institution of Engineers, Australia; International Energy Agency

IEC industrial energy conservation; International Electrotechnical Commission

IED improvised explosive device

IEDD improvised explosive device disposal (type of bomb disposal)

IEE Institution of Electrical Engineers

IEEIE Institution of Electrical and Electronics Incorporated Engineers

IEHO Institution of Environmental Health Officers

IEI Institution of Engineers of Ireland

IEME Inspectorate of Electrical and Mechanical Engineering

IEng Incorporated Engineer

IERE Institution of Electronic and Radio Engineers

IES Indian Educational Service; Institution of Engineers and Shipbuilders in Scotland

IET interest equalization tax

IExpE Institute of Explosives Engineers

IF initiation factor; interferon; intermediate frequency

IFA independent financial adviser

IFAC International Federation of Automatic Control

IFAD International Fund for Agricultural Development (of the UN)

IFALPA International Federation of Air Line Pilots' Associations

IFAW International Fund for Animal Welfare

IFC International Finance Corporation; (USA and Canada) International Fisheries Commission

IFCTU International Federation of Christian Trade Unions (now called World Confederation of Labour, WCL)

IFE intelligent front end

iff if and only if

IFF Identification, Friend or Foe (radar identification system)

IFGO International Federation of Gynaecology and Obstetrics

IFIP International Federation for Information Processing

IFL International Friendship League

IFLA International Federation of Library Associations

IFMC International Folk Music Council

IFORS International Federation of Operational Research Societies

IFP (South Africa) Inkatha Freedom Party

IFPI International Federation of the Phonographic Industry

IFR instrument flying regulations

IFRB International Frequency Registration Board

IFS Indian Forest Service; International Federation of Surveyors; Irish Free State

Ig immunoglobulin (as in **IgA**, **IgE**, **IgG**)

IG Ilford; Indo-Germanic (languages); Inspector General; Instructor in Gunnery

IGasE Institution of Gas Engineers

IGD illicit gold dealer

IGF insulin-like growth factor

IGFA International Game Fish Association

IGM International Grandmaster

ign. ignite(s); ignition; ignotus (Latin: unknown)

IGS independent grammar school

IGU International Gas Union; International Geographical Union

IGY International Geophysical Year (1.7.57 to 31.12.58)

IH iacet hic (Latin: here lies; on gravestones)

IHC (New Zealand) intellectually handicapped child

IHD International Hydrological Decade (1965–74); ischaemic heart disease

IHF International Hospitals Federation

IHospE Institute of Hospital Engineering

ihp indicated horsepower

IHS Jesus (Greek ΙΗΣΟΥΣ)

IHSM Institute of Health Services Management

IHT Institution of Highways and Transportation

IIAC Industrial Injuries Advisory Council

IIAS International Institute of Administrative Sciences

IIB Institut international des brevets (French: International Patent Institute)

iid independent identically distributed (of random variables)

IID insulin-independent diabetes

IIEP International Institute of Educational Planning

3i Investors in Industry

IIL integrated injection logic

IIM Institution of Industrial Managers

IInfSc Institute of Information Scientists

IIP International Ice Patrol

IIR isobutylene-isoprene rubber

IIS International Institute of Sociology

IISS International Institute of Strategic Studies

IIT Indian Institute of Technology

IKBS intelligent knowledge-based system

IL Illinois; Institute of Linguists; interleukin (as in **IL-1**, **IL-2**); Israel

ILA International Law Association; International Longshoremen's Association

ILC International Law Commission (of the UN)

ILEA Inner London Education Authority

ILEC Inner London Education Committee

ill. illustrate(d); illustration

Ill. Illinois

illus. illustrate(d); illustration; illustrator

ILN Illustrated London News

ILO International Labour Organization (of the UN)

ILP Independent Labour Party

ILR independent local radio

ILS instrument landing system

ILTF International Lawn Tennis Federation

ILU Institute of London Underwriters

ILW intermediate-level waste

IM Indian Marines; International Master; intramuscular

IMA Institute of Mathematics and its Applications; International Music Association; Irish Medical Association

IMarE Institute of Marine Engineers

IMARSAT International Maritime Satellite Organization

IMC Institute of Management Consultants; Institute of Measurement and Control; instrument meteorological conditions

IMCO Intergovernmental Maritime Consultative Organization (of the UN)

IMEA Incorporated Municipal Electrical Association

IMechE Institution of Mechanical Engineers

IMINT image intelligence (gained from aerial photography)

IMF International Monetary Fund

IMG International Management Group

IMGTechE Institution of Mechanical and General Technician Engineers

IMinE Institution of Mining Engineers

IMINT image intelligence (gained from aerial photography)

imit. imitate; imitation; imitative

IMM Institution of Mining and Metallurgy

IMMTS Indian Mercantile Marine Training Ship

IMO International Maritime Organization; International Meteorological Organization; International Miners' Organization

imp. imperative; imperfect; imperial; impersonal; import(ed); important; importer; impression; imprimatur; imprint

Imp. Imperator (Latin: Emperor); Imperatrix (Latin: Empress); Imperial

IMP International Match Point

imper. imperative

imperf. imperfect; imperforate (of stamps)

impers. impersonal

impf. imperfect

impv. imperative

IMRO Investment Management Regulatory Organization

IMS Indian Medical Service; Information Management System; Institute of Management Services; International Musicological Society

IMT International Military Tribunal

IMU International Mathematical Union

IMunE Institution of Municipal Engineers (now part of the Institution of Civil Engineers)

IMW Institute of Masters of Wine

in inch(es)

in. inch(es)

In indium

IN Indiana; Indian Navy

INAO (France) Institut national des appellations d'origine des vins et eaux-de-vie (body controlling wine production)

inbd inboard (on an aircraft, boat, etc.)

Inbucon International Business Consultants

inc. include(d); including; inclusive; income; incomplete; incorporate(d); increase

Inc. Incorporated (after names of business organizations; US equivalent of Ltd)

INCA International Newspaper Colour Association

incl. include(s); included; including; inclusive

incog. incognito

incorp. incorporated; incorporation

INCPEN Industry Committee for Packaging and the Environment

incr. increase(d); increasing

in d. in dies (Latin: daily)

ind. independence; independent; index; indicative; indirect(ly); industrial; industry

Ind. Independent; India(n); Indiana; Indies

IND India; in nomine Dei (Latin: in God's name)

indef. indefinite

indic. indicating; indicative; indicator

indiv. individual

induc. induction

ined. ineditus (Latin: unpublished)

inf. infantry; inferior; infinitive; influence; information; infra (Latin: below)

INF intermediate-range nuclear forces (as in **INF treaty**)

infin. infinitive

infl. influence(d)

INH isonicotinic acid hydrazide (isoniazid; antituberculosis drug)

init. initial(ly); initio (Latin: in the beginning)

INLA Irish National Liberation Army

in lim. in limine (Latin: at the outset)

in loc. in loco (Latin: in place of)

in loc. cit. in loco citato (Latin: in the place cited (in text))

in mem. in memoriam (Latin: to the memory (of))

inorg. inorganic

in pr. in principio (Latin: in the beginning)

INR independent national radio (as in **INR licence**); Index of Nursing Research

INRI Iesus Nazarenus Rex Iudaeorum (Latin: Jesus of Nazareth, King of the Jews)

ins. inches; inspector; insulate(d); insulation; insurance

INS International News Service

INSA Indian National Science Academy

INSEA International Society for Education through Art

INSEAD Institut européen d'administration des affaires (French: European Institute of Administrative Affairs)

INSET in-service training

insol. insoluble

insp. inspect(ed); inspection; inspector

inst. instant (this month); instantaneous; institute; institution; instrument(al)

InstAct Institute of Actuaries

InstBE Institution of British Engineers

InstE Institute of Energy

instl. installation

InstMM Institution of Mining and Metallurgy

instn institution

InstP Institute of Physics

InstPet Institute of Petroleum

InstPI Institute of Patentees and Inventors

instr. instructor; instrument(al)

InstR Institute of Refrigeration

InstSMM Institute of Sales and Marketing Management

InstT Institute of Transport

int. intelligence; interest; interim; interior; internal; international; interpret(er); introit

int. al. inter alia (Latin: among other things)

Intelsat International Telecommunications Satellite Consortium

intens. intensifier; intensive

inter. intermediate

interj. interjection

internat. international

Interpol International Criminal Police Organization

interrog. interrogate; interrogation; interrogative

intl international

intr. intransitive

intro. introduce; introduction; introductory

INTUC Indian National Trade Union Congress

INucE Institution of Nuclear Engineers

inv. invent(ed); invention; inventor; invoice

invt. inventory

IO intelligence officer

I/O input/output

IOB Institute of Bankers (renamed Chartered Institute of Bankers, CIB); Institute of Building (renamed Chartered Institute of Building, CIOB)

IOC International Olympic Committee

IOCU International Organization of Consumers' Unions

IoD Institute of Directors

IODE (Canada) Imperial Order of Daughters of the Empire

IOF Independent Order of Foresters

I of E Institute of Export

I of M Isle of Man

IOGT International Order of Good Templars

IoJ Institute of Journalists

IOM Indian Order of Merit; Isle of Man

IOOF Independent Order of Oddfellows

IOP input/output processor; Institute of Painters in Oil Colours

IoS The Independent on Sunday

IOSCO International Organization of Securities Commissions

IOU I owe you

IOW Isle of Wight

IP in-patient; Ipswich

IPA Institute of Practitioners in Advertising; International Phonetic Alphabet; International Phonetic Association; International Publishers' Association

IPC International Polar Commission; International Publishing Corporation

IPCC Intergovernmental Panel on Climatic Change (of the UN)

IPCS Institution of Professional Civil Servants

IPD (Scotland) in praesentia dominorum (Latin: in the presence of the Lords (of Session))

IPE Institution of Plant Engineers; Institution of Production Engineers; International Petroleum Exchange

IPFA (Member or Associate of the Chartered) Institute of Public Finance and Accountancy

IPHE Institution of Public Health Engineers

IPI Institute of Patentees and Inventors; International Press Institute

IPlantE Institution of Plant Engineers

IPM Institute of Personnel Management

IPP intermittent positive pressure (ventilation)

IPPA Independent Programme Producers' Association

IPPF International Planned Parenthood Federation

IPPR Institute for Public Policy Research

IPPS Institute of Physics and the Physical Society

IPPV intermittent positive-pressure ventilation

IPR Institute of Public Relations

IProdE Institution of Production Engineers

ips inches per second; instructions per second

IPS inches per second; Indian Police Service; Indian Political Service; Institute of Purchasing and Supply

IPT Institute of Petroleum Technologists

IPTS International Practical Temperature Scale

IPU Inter-Parliamentary Union

i.q. idem quod (Latin: the same as)

IQ intelligence quotient

IQA Institute of Quality Assurance

IQS Institute of Quantity Surveyors

i.r. inside radius

Ir iridium

Ir. Ireland; Irish

IR information retrieval; infrared (radiation); Inland Revenue; international registration; Iran; Iranian rial (monetary unit); isoprene rubber

IRA Irish Republican Army

IRAD Institute for Research on Animal Diseases

Iran. Iranian

IRBM intermediate-range ballistic missile

IRC Industrial Reorganization Corporation

Ire. Ireland

IREE(Aust) Institution of Radio and Electronics Engineers (Australia)

IRF International Rowing Federation

IRFB International Rugby Football Board

Iris infrared intruder system

IRIS International Research and Information Service

IRL Republic of Ireland

IRM innate releasing mechanism

IRN Independent Radio News

IRO Inland Revenue Office; International Refugee Organization

IRPA International Radiation Protection Association

IRQ interrupt request; Iraq

IRR internal rate of return

irreg. irregular(ly)

IRRI International Rice Research Institute

IRRV Institute of Revenues, Rating, and Valuation

IRTE Institute of Road Transport Engineers

Is. Isaiah; Island(s); Isle(s)

IS Iceland; International Society of Sculptors, Painters, and Gravers

Isa. Isaiah

ISA industry standard architecture; International Sociological Association; International Standard Atmosphere (formerly Interim Standard Atmosphere)

ISAM indexed sequential access method

ISBA Incorporated Society of British Advertisers

ISBN International Standard Book Number

ISC Imperial Service College (Haileybury); Indian Staff Corps; intermittent self-catheterization

ISCE International Society of Christian Endeavour

ISCh Incorporated Society of Chiropodists

ISCM International Society for Contemporary Music

ISCO Independent Schools Careers Organization

ISD international subscriber dialling

ISDN Integrated Services Digital Network

ISE Indian Service of Engineers; Institution of Structural Engineers; International Stock Exchange of the UK and the Republic of Ireland Ltd

ISF International Shipping Federation

ISI International Statistical Institute; Iron and Steel Institute

ISIS Independent Schools Information Service

ISJC Independent Schools Joint Council

ISK króna (Icelandic monetary unit)

isl. island; isle

ISM Incorporated Society of Musicians

ISME International Society for Musical Education

ISMRC Inter-Services Metallurgical Research Council

ISO Imperial Service Order; International Standards Organization (International Organization for Standardization)

ISP Institute of Sales Promotion; International Study Programme; Internet service provider

ISPEMA Industrial Safety (Personal Equipment) Manufacturers' Association

ISQ in statu quo (Latin: in the same state; unchanged)

ISR information storage and retrieval

ISRO International Securities Regulatory Organization

iss. issue

ISSN International Standard Serial Number

IST Indian Standard Time; Institute of Science Technology

ISTC Institute of Scientific and Technical Communicators; Iron and Steel Trades' Confederation

ISTD Imperial Society of Teachers of Dancing

isth. isthmus

IStructE Institution of Structural Engineers

ISU International Seamen's Union

ISV International Scientific Vocabulary; independent software vendor

ISVA Incorporated Society of Valuers and Auctioneers

ISWG Imperial Standard Wire Gauge

It. Italian; Italy

IT ignition temperature; information technology; International Table (in **IT calorie**)

i.t.a. initial teaching alphabet

ITA Independent Television Authority (superseded by the IBA)

ITAI Institution of Technical Authors and Illustrators

ital. italic

Ital. Italian

ITALY I trust and love you

ITB Industry Training Board; International Time Bureau

ITC Independent Television Commission; International Tin Council; International Trade Centre

ITE Institute of Terrestrial Ecology

ITEME Institution of Technician Engineers in Mechanical Engineering

ITF International Tennis Federation; International Trade Federations; International Transport Workers' Federation

ITI Institute of Translation and Interpreting

ITMA Institute of Trade Mark Agents; It's That Man Again (BBC radio series)

ITN Independent Television News

ITO International Trade Organization

ITS Industrial Training Service; International Trade Secretariat

ITT International Telephone and Telegraph Corporation

ITTF International Table Tennis Federation

ITU intensive therapy unit; International Telecommunication Union (of the UN); International Typographical Union

ITV Independent Television

IU immunizing unit; international unit(s)

IUA International Union of Architects

IUB International Union of Biochemistry

IUCD intrauterine contraceptive device

IUCN International Union for the Conservation of Nature and Natural Resources

IUCW International Union for Child Welfare

IUD intrauterine death; intrauterine (contraceptive) device

IUGG International Union of Geodesy and Geophysics

IUGR intrauterine growth retardation

IUGS International Union of Geological Sciences

IUHPS International Union of the History and Philosophy of Science

IULA International Union of Local Authorities

IUMI International Union of Marine Insurance

IUPAC International Union of Pure and Applied Chemistry

IUPAP International Union of Pure and Applied Physics

IUPS International Union of Physiological Sciences

IUTAM International Union of Theoretical and Applied Mechanics

i.v. increased value; intravenous(ly); invoice value

IV intravenous(ly); Inverness; invoice value

IVA individual voluntary arrangement (in bankruptcy proceedings)

IVB invalidity benefit

IVC inferior vena cava

IVF in vitro fertilization

IVP intravenous pyelogram

IVR international vehicle registration

IVS International Voluntary Service

IWA Inland Waterways Association

IWC International Whaling Commission

IWEM Institution of Water and Environmental Management (formerly IPHE; IWPC)

IWGC Imperial War Graves Commission (now Commonwealth War Graves Commission)

IWPC Institute of Water Pollution Control

IWW Industrial Workers of the World; International Workers of the World

IY Imperial Yeomanry

IYRU International Yacht Racing Union

IZ I Zingari (cricket club)

IZS insulin zinc suspension (diabetes treatment).

J

j current density

J angular momentum; current density; jack; Japan; joule(s); magnetic polarization; mechanical equivalent of heat

J. Jacobean; January; Jesus; Journal; Judge; July; June; Justice

Ja. January

JA Jamaica; joint account; Judge Advocate; Justice of Appeal

Jaat joint air attack team

Jac. Jacobean

JACT Joint Association of Classical Teachers

Jafo just another fucking observer

JAG Judge Advocate General

JAL Japan Airlines

Jam. Jamaica; James

Jan January

j. & w.o. jettisoning and washing overboard

JANET Joint Academic Network

Jap. Japan(ese)

JAP (USA) Jewish American Princess

Jas. James

JAT Jugoslovenski Aero-Transport (Yugoslav Airlines)

JATO jet-assisted takeoff

Jav. Java(nese); javelin

JBCNS Joint Board of Clinical Nursing Studies

JC Jesus Christ; Julius Caesar; jurisconsult (legal adviser; jurist)

JCB Bachelor of Canon Law (Latin *Juris Canonici Baccalaureus*); Bachelor of Civil Law (Latin *Juris Civilis Baccalaureus*); Joseph Cyril Bamford (excavating machine; named after its manufacturer)

JCC Junior Chamber of Commerce

JCD Doctor of Canon Law (Latin *Juris Canonici Doctor*); Doctor of Civil Law (Latin *Juris Civilis Doctor*)

JCI Junior Chamber International

JCL job-control language; Licentiate in Canon Law (Latin *Juris Canonici Licentiatus*); Licentiate in Civil Law (Latin *Juris Civilis Licentiatus*)

JCP Japan Communist Party

JCR junior common room (in certain universities)

JCS Joint Chiefs of Staff; Journal of the Chemical Society

jct. junction

JCWI Joint Council for the Welfare of Immigrants

jd joined

JD Doctor of Laws or Jurisprudence (Latin *Jurum*

Doctor); Jordan dinar (monetary unit); Julian date; juvenile delinquent

JDipMA Joint Diploma in Management Accounting Services

Jer. Jeremiah

JESSI Joint European Submicron Silicon Initiative

JET Joint European Torus (Culham, Oxfordshire)

JETP Journal of Experimental and Theoretical Physics

J/F journal folio

JFET junction field-effect transistor

JFK John Fitzgerald Kennedy (US president (1961–63) or airport)

j.g. junior grade

JHS Jesus Hominum Salvator (Latin: Jesus Saviour of Men)

jic just in case

JICTAR Joint Industry Committee for Television Advertising Research

JIT just-in-time (manufacturing method)

JJ Judges; Justices

Jl. journal; July

JLP Jamaica Labour Party

JMB Joint Matriculation Board

jn join; junction; junior

jnc. junction

j.n.d. just noticeable difference

jnl journal

jnlst journalist

jnr junior

JNR Japanese National Railways

jnt joint

JNTO Japan National Tourist Organization

jnt stk joint stock

JO job order; Journal Officiel (French: Official Gazette); junior officer

Jon. Jonah

Josh. Joshua

jour. journeyman

JOVIAL Jules' own version of international algorithmic language (named after Jules Schwarz, computer scientist)

JP jet propulsion; Justice of the Peace

JPS jet-propulsion system(s)

Jr Junior

JR Jacobus Rex (Latin: King James)

JRC Junior Red Cross

JSB joint-stock bank

JSD Doctor of Juristic Science

JSDC Joint Service Defence College

JSLS Joint Services Liaison Staff

JSP Japan Socialist Party

JSPS Japan Society for the Promotion of Science

JSSC Joint Services Staff College

J-stars joint surveillance and targeting acquisition radar system

jt joint

Jt Ed. Joint Editor

JTIDS Joint Tactical Information Distribution Systems

jtly jointly

Jud. Judges; Judith

Abbreviations

JUD Doctor of Canon and Civil Law (Latin *Juris Utriusque Doctor*)

judgt judgment

JUGFET junction-gate field-effect transistor

Jul. July

Jun. June; junior

junc. junction

Junr junior

JurD Doctor of Law (Latin *Juris Doctor*)

jurisd. jurisdiction

jurisp. jurisprudence

jus. justice

JV joint venture

jwlr jeweller

j.w.o. jettisoning and washing overboard

JWV Jewish War Veterans

Jy July

K

k Boltzmann constant; kilo- (prefix indicating 1000, as in **km**, kilometre; *or* (in computing) 1024, as in **kbyte**, kilobyte); thermal conductivity; a unit coordinate vector

k. (USA) karat; king; knit

K bulk modulus; Cambodia; carrying capacity (as in **K-strategist**); equilibrium constant; kaon; kelvin(s); kilo-; kina (monetary unit of Papua New Guinea); king; kip (Laotian monetary unit; *see also under* KN); Kirkpatrick (preceding a number in Ralph Kirkpatrick's catalogue of Domenico Scarlatti's works); Köchel (preceding a number in Ludwig von Köchel's catalogue of Mozart's works); (Zambian) kwacha (monetary unit; *see also under* MK); kyat (Burmese monetary unit); potassium (Latin *kalium*); one thousand

K. King; knit

K9 canine (K9 dogs; army dogs)

KA Kilmarnock; Knight of St Andrew, Order of Barbados

Kan. Kansas

k & b kitchen and bathroom

KANU Kenya African National Union

KAR King's African Rifles

kb kilobar(s); kilobase(s)

KB kilobyte; King's Bench; king's bishop; Knight Bachelor; knit into back of stitch; knowledge base

kbd keyboard

KBE Knight Commander of the Order of the British Empire

kbp kilobase pair

KBP king's bishop's pawn

KBS Knight of the Blessed Sacrament; knowledge-based system

kbyte kilobyte

kc kilocycle

KC Kansas City; Kennel Club; King's College; King's Counsel; Knight Commander; Knights of Columbus

kcal kilocalorie(s)

KCB Knight Commander of the Order of the Bath

KCC (Knight) Commander of the Order of the Crown, Belgium and the Congo Free State

K cell killer cell

KCH King's College Hospital (London); Knight Commander of the Hanoverian Order

KCHS Knight Commander of the Order of the Holy Sepulchre

KCIE Knight Commander of the Order of the Indian Empire

KCLJ Knight Commander of the Order of St Lazarus of Jerusalem

KCMG Knight Commander of the Order of St Michael and St George

kcs kilocycles per second

Kčs koruna (monetary unit of the Czech Republic and Slovakia)

KCSA Knight Commander of the Military Order of the Collar of St Agatha of Paterna

KCSG Knight Commander of the Order of St Gregory the Great

KCSI Knight Commander of the Order of the Star of India

KCSJ Knight Commander of the Order of St John of Jerusalem (Knights Hospitaller)

KCSS Knight Commander of the Order of St Silvester

KCVO Knight Commander of the Royal Victorian Order

KD kiln dried; knock down (at an auction sale); knocked down (of goods for sale); Kuwaiti dinar (monetary unit)

KDC knocked-down condition (of goods)

KDG King's Dragoon Guards

KE kinetic energy

KEAS knots equivalent airspeed

KEH King Edward's Horse

Ken. Kentucky

KEO King Edward's Own

keV kiloelectronvolt(s)

kg keg; kilogram(s)

KG Knight of the Order of the Garter

KGB Komitet Gosudarstvennoi Bezopasnosti (Russian: Committee of State Security)

KGCB Knight Grand Cross of the Bath

Kgs Kings

KH Knight of the Hanoverian Order

KHC Honorary Chaplain to the King

KHDS Honorary Dental Surgeon to the King

KHNS Honorary Nursing Sister to the King

KHP Honorary Physician to the King

KHS Honorary Surgeon to the King; Knight of the Order of the Holy Sepulchre

kHz kilohertz

KIA killed in action

KIAS knots indicated airspeed

K-i-H Kaisar-i-Hind (Emperor of India; medal)

KIO Kuwait Investment Office

kJ kilojoule(s)

KJ knee jerk

KJV King James Version (of the Bible)

KKK Ku Klux Klan

KKt king's knight

KKtP king's knight's pawn

KL Kuala Lumpur

KLH Knight of the Legion of Honour

KLJ Knight of the Order of St Lazarus of Jerusalem

KLM Koninklijke Luchtvaart Maatschappij (Royal Dutch Airlines)

KLSE Kuala Lumpur Stock Exchange

km kilometre(s)

KM Knight of Malta

KMT Kuomintang (Chinese Nationalist Party)

kn knot; krona (Swedish monetary unit; *see also* SKr); krone (Danish or Norwegian monetary unit; *see also* Dkr; NKr)

KN king's knight; kip (Laotian monetary unit)

KNP king's knight's pawn

Knt Knight

KO knock out

KOC Kuwait Oil Company

K of C Knights of Columbus

Komintern Communist International (Russian *Kom(munistícheskii) Intern(atsionál)*)

KORR King's Own Royal Regiment

KOSB King's Own Scottish Borderers

KOYLI King's Own Yorkshire Light Infantry

KP king's pawn; Knight of the Order of St Patrick

KPD Kommunistische Partei Deutschlands (German Communist Party)

kph kilometres per hour

KPM King's Police Medal

KPNLF Khmer People's National Liberation Front

KPU Kenya People's Union

kr. krona (Swedish monetary unit; *see also* SKr); króna (Icelandic monetary unit; *see also* ISK); krone (Danish or Norwegian monetary unit; *see also* Dkr; NKr)

Kr krypton

KR King's Regiment; King's Regulations; king's rook

KRL knowledge representation language (in artificial intelligence)

KRP king's rook's pawn

KRRC King's Royal Rifle Corps

KS Kansas; Kaposi's sarcoma; King's Scholar

KSC Knight of St Columba

KSG Knight of the Order of St Gregory the Great

KSh Kenya shilling (monetary unit)

KSJ Knight of the Order of St John of Jerusalem (Knights Hospitaller)

KSLI King's Shropshire Light Infantry

KSS Knight of the Order of St Silvester

KSSU KLM, SAS, Swissair, UTA (international airline organization)

KStJ Knight of the Order of St John of Jerusalem (Knights Hospitaller)

kt (USA) karat; kilotonne(s); knot

Kt knight

KT Kingston-upon-Thames; Knight (of the Order) of the Thistle; Knight Templar

Kt Bach. Knight Bachelor

Ku kurchatovium (element 104)

kV kilovolt(s)

KV Köchel Verzeichnis (German: Köchel catalogue; see under K)

kVAr kilovar(s)

kVp kilovolts, peak (applied across an X-ray tube)

kW kilowatt(s)

KW Kirkwall, Orkney

kWh kilowatt hour(s)

KWIC key word in context (as in **KWIC index**)

KWOC key word out of context (as in **KWOC index**)

KWP Korean Workers' Party

KWT Kuwait

ky. kyat (Burmese monetary unit; see also under K)

Ky. Kentucky

KY Kentucky; Kirkaldy; Kol Yisrael (Israeli broadcasting station)

KZ killing zone.

L

l laevorotatory (as in *l*-**tartaric acid**); lah (in tonic sol-fa); length; lightning; liquid (as in H$_2$O(l)); litre(s)

l. lake; law; leaf; league; left; length; line (of written matter); link; low; pound (Latin *libra*; symbol: £)

L angular momentum; Avogadro constant; fifty; inductor; language (as in L$_1$, first language; L$_2$, second language); latent heat; learner (driver; on British motor vehicles); lempira (Honduran monetary unit); length; lift; light (in **L-chain** of an immunoglobulin molecule); litre(s); live (on electric plugs); Liverpool; longitude; luminance; Luxembourg; radiance; an optically active compound having a configuration related to laevorotatory glyceraldehyde (as in **L-lactic acid**)

L. Lady; Lake; large; late; law; League; left or (in the theatre) stage left; lethal; liber (Latin: book); Liberal; Licentiate (in degrees, etc.); Lieutenant; line (of written matter); link; Linnaeus (indicating the author of a species, etc.); lira or (pl.) lire (Italian monetary unit; see also Lit) Loch; locus (Latin: place); Lodge (fraternal); London; Lough; low; pound (Latin *libra*; symbol: £)

La lanthanum

La. Lane; Louisiana

LA Lancaster; large aperture; Latin America(n); law agent; Legislative Assembly; Library Association; Literate in Arts; Liverpool Academy; local agent; local authority; Los Angeles; Louisiana

LAA light anti-aircraft

lab. laboratory; labourer

Lab. Labour; Labrador

LAC leading aircraftman; Licentiate of the Apothecaries' Company; London Athletic Club

LACSA Lineas Aéreas Costarricenses (Costa Rican Airlines)

LACSAB Local Authorities' Conditions of Service Advisory Board

LACW leading aircraftwoman

LAD language acquisition device

ladar laser detection and ranging

L. Adv. Lord Advocate

LAFTA Latin American Free Trade Association

LAH Licentiate of the Apothecaries' Hall (Dublin)

LAI leaf area index

LAIA Latin American Integration Association (formerly LAFTA)

LAK lymphokine-activated killer (in **LAK cell**; used in cancer treatment)

lam. laminate(d)

Lam. Lamarck (indicating the author of a species, etc.); Lamentations

LAMDA London Academy of Music and Dramatic Art

LAMSAC Local Authorities' Management Services and Computer Committee

LAN Linea Aérea Nacional (de Chile) (Chilean national airlines; Lan Chile); local-area network

Lancs Lancashire

L & NWR London and North-Western Railway

L & SWR London and South-Western Railway

L & YR Lancashire and Yorkshire Railway

lang. language

Lantirn low-altitude navigation and targeting infrared system

LAO Laos; Licentiate in the Art of Obstetrics

Lap. Lapland

LAPT London Association for the Protection of Trade

LAR Libya

LARSP Language Assessment, Remediation, and Screening Procedure

LAS London Archaeological Service

laser light amplification by stimulated emission of radiation

LASER London and South Eastern Library Region

LASH lighter aboard ship

lat. latitude

Lat. Latin

LATS long-acting thyroid stimulator

LAUTRO Life Assurance and Unit Trust Regulatory Organization

LAV light armoured vehicle; Lineas Aéreas Venezolanas (Venezuelan Airlines); lymphadenopathy-associated virus (original name for the Aids virus, HIV)

LAX Los Angeles international airport

lb pound(s) (weight; Latin *libra*)

l.b. landing barge; leg bye

LB Liberia; light bomber; local board

LBA late booking agent (euphemism for ticket tout)

LB & SCR London, Brighton, and South Coast Railway

LBC London Broadcasting Company

L/Bdr Lance-Bombardier

lbf pound-force

LBJ Lyndon Baines Johnson (1908–73, US president 1963–69)

LBO leveraged buyout

LBS London Business School

LBV Late Bottled Vintage (of port wine)

lbw leg before wicket

l.c. left centre; letter of credit; loco citato (Latin: in the place cited; textual annotation); lower case

LC Cross of Leo; landing craft; Legislative Council; letter of credit; (USA) Library of Congress; line crosser (a defector); Lord Chamberlain; Lord Chancellor

LCAD London Certificate in Art and Design

LCB left centre back (of stage); London Convention Bureau; Lord Chief Baron

LCC leadless chip carrier; life-cycle cost(ing); London Chamber of Commerce; London County Council (superseded by the Greater London Council, GLC)

LCD liquid-crystal display; lowest common denominator

LCDT London Contemporary Dance Theatre

LCE London Commodity Exchange

LCF lowest common factor

LCh Licentiate in Surgery (Latin *Licentiatus Chirurgiae*)

LCJ Lord Chief Justice

LCL less-than-container load; Licentiate in Canon Law

LCM London College of Music; lowest common multiple

LCN load classification number

L-Col Lieutenant-Colonel

L-Corp. Lance-Corporal

LCP Licentiate of the College of Preceptors; liquid-crystal polymer; London College of Printing

L/Cpl Lance-Corporal

LCPS Licentiate of the College of Physicians and Surgeons

LCSP London and Counties Society of Physiologists

LCST Licentiate of the College of Speech Therapists

LCT landing craft tank

LCV Licentiate of the College of Violinists

ld lead; load

l.d. legal dose

Ld Limited (company); Lord (title)

LD Lady Day; Laus Deo (Latin: Praise be to God); learning-disabled; lethal dose (as in **LD$_{50}$**, median lethal dose); Liberal and Democratic; Libyan dinar (monetary unit); Licentiate in

Divinity; Llandrindod Wells; London Docks; Low Dutch

LDC less-developed country

LDDC London Docklands' Development Corporation

ldg landing; loading

Ldg Leading (rank)

Ldge Lodge

L.d'H. Légion d'Honneur

LDiv Licentiate in Divinity

LDL low-density lipoprotein

LDN less-developed nation

Ldp Lordship

LDP (Japan) Liberal-Democratic Party; London daily price

LDPE low-density polyethylene (used in packaging materials)

ldr leader

lds loads

LDS Latter-day Saints; laus Deo semper (Latin: praise be to God for ever); Licentiate in Dental Surgery

LDSc Licentiate in Dental Science

LDV Local Defence Volunteers (Home Guard)

Le leone (monetary unit of Sierra Leone)

LE Egyptian pound (monetary unit); Leicester; London Electricity; lupus erythamatosus

lea. league; leather; leave

LEA Local Education Authority

LEAP Life Education for the Autistic Person

LEB London Electricity Board

LEC Local Enterprise Company

lect. lecture(r)

LED light-emitting diode

leg. legal; legate; legation; legato (Italian: bound; i.e. smoothly); legislation; legislative; legislature

Leics Leicestershire

Leip. Leipzig

LEM lunar excursion module

LEPRA Leprosy Relief Association

LES Liverpool Engineering Society

LETS Local Employment and Trade System

Leu leucine

Lev. Leviticus

lex. lexicon

lexicog. lexicographer; lexicographical; lexicography

lf light face

l.f. ledger folio

Lf limit of flocculation (in toxicology)

LF low frequency

LFBC London Federation of Boys' Clubs

LFCDA London Fire and Civil Defence Authority

lg long

lg. large

LG Lady Companion of the Order of the Garter; Life Guards; Low German

lge large

LGer Low German

LGk Late Greek

LGM Little Green Men

LGr Late Greek

LGSM Licentiate of the Guildhall School of Music

LGTB Local Government Training Board

lgth length

lg tn long ton

LGU Ladies' Golf Union

LGV Large Goods Vehicle

l.h. left half; left hand(ed)

LH left hand(ed); Light Horse; luteinizing hormone

LHA Lord High Admiral

lhb left halfback

LHC Lord High Chancellor

l.h.d. left-hand drive

LHD Doctor of Humanities or of Literature (Latin *Litterarum Humaniorum Doctor*)

LHeb Late Hebrew

LH-RH luteinizing-hormone-releasing hormone

LHS left hand side

LHSM Licentiate of the Institute of Health Services Management

LHT Lord High Treasurer

Li lithium

LI Light Infantry; Long Island (New York)

LIAB Licentiate of the International Association of Book-Keepers

lib. liber (Latin: book); liberty; librarian; library; libretto

Lib. Liberal

LIBA Lloyd's Insurance Brokers' Association

lib. cat. library catalogue

Lib Dem Liberal Democrat

LIBID London Inter-Bank Bid Rate

LIBOR London Inter-Bank Offered Rate

Lic. Licentiate (in degrees, etc.)

LIC linear integrated circuit

LicAc Licentiate of Acupuncture

LICeram Licentiate of the Institute of Ceramics

LicMed Licentiate in Medicine

LICW Licentiate of the Institute of Clerks of Works

lidar light detection and ranging

Lieut Lieutenant

Lieut-Col Lieutenant-Colonel

Lieut-Com Lieutenant-Commander

Lieut-Gen Lieutenant-General

Lieut-Gov Lieutenant-Governor

LIFFE London International Financial Futures and Options Exchange

LIFireE Licentiate of the Institution of Fire Engineers

LIFO last in, first out

LILO last in, last out

lim. limit

LIM linear-induction motor

LIMEAN London Inter-Bank Mean Rate

lin. lineal; linear

linac linear accelerator

Lincs Lincolnshire

ling. linguistics

lin-log linear-logarithmic

Linn. (Carolus) Linnaeus (1707–78, Swedish botanist)

LIOB Licentiate of the Institute of Building

LIP life insurance policy

LIPM Lister Institute of Preventive Medicine

LIPS logical inferences per second

liq. liquid; liquor

LISM Licentiate of the Incorporated Society of Musicians

LISP list processing (a programming language)

lit. literal(ly); literary; literature; litre(s); little

Lit lira (Italian monetary unit)

LitB Bachelor of Letters or Literature (Latin *Litterarum Baccalaureus*)

lit. crit. literary criticism

LitD Doctor of Letters or Literature (Latin *Litterarum Doctor*)

lith. lithograph(y)

Lith. Lithuania(n)

litho. lithograph(ic); lithography

lithol. lithology

Lit. Hum. Litterae Humaniores (Latin: the humanities; classics course at Oxford University)

LittB Bachelor of Letters or Literature (Latin *Litterarum Baccalaureus*)

LittD Doctor of Letters or Literature (Latin *Litterarum Doctor*)

LittM Master of Letters or Literature (Latin *Litterarum Magister*)

liv. st. livre sterling (French: pound sterling)

LJ Lord Justice

lkge leakage

ll. leaves; leges (Latin: laws); lines (of written matter)

l.l. loco laudato (Latin: in the place quoted)

LL Late Latin; Law Latin; Lebanese pound (monetary unit); linear-linear; Llandudno; Lord-Lieutenant; Low Latin

LL. lines (of written matter); Lords

LLA Lady Literate in Arts

LLB Bachelor of Laws (Latin *Legum Baccalaureus*)

LLCM Licentiate of London College of Music

LLCO Licentiate of the London College of Osteopathy

LLD Doctor of Laws (Latin *Legum Doctor*)

Llds Lloyd's

LLE low-level exposure (to radiation)

LLL Licentiate in Laws

LLM Master of Laws (Latin *Legum Magister*)

LLNW low-level nuclear waste

LLRW low-level radioactive waste

LLW low-level (radioactive) waste

lm lumen

Lm Maltese lira (monetary unit)

LM Licentiate in Medicine; Licentiate in Midwifery; long metre; Lord Mayor; lunar module

LMC Local Medical Committee

LMCC Licentiate of the Medical Council of Canada

LMD long metre double
LME London Metal Exchange
LMed Licentiate in Medicine
LMP last menstrual period
LMR liquid-metal reactor; London Midland Region
LMRCP Licentiate in Midwifery of the Royal College of Physicians
LMRSH Licentiate Member of the Royal Society for the Promotion of Health
LMRTPI Legal Member of the Royal Town Planning Institute
LMS Licentiate in Medicine and Surgery; local management of schools; London Mathematical Society; London, Midland and Scottish Railway; London Missionary Society; loss of memory syndrome
LMSSA Licentiate in Medicine and Surgery of the Society of Apothecaries
LMT length, mass, time; local mean time
LMVD (New Zealand) Licensed Motor Vehicle Dealer
LMX London Market Excess of Loss (at Lloyd's)
ln natural logarithm
Ln Lane (in place names)
LN Lincoln
LNat Liberal National
LNER London and North Eastern Railway
LNG liquefied natural gas
LO liaison officer
LOB Location of Offices Bureau
loc. locative
loc. cit. loco citato
loco. locomotion; locomotive
L of C lines of communication
L of N League of Nations
LOFT low-frequency radio telescope
log logarithm
log. logic(al)
LOI lunar orbit insertion
Lond. London
Londin. Londiniensis (Latin: (Bishop) of London)
long. longitude
Lonrho London Rhodesian
l.o.p. line of position
loq. loquitur (Latin: he speaks)
LORCS League of Red Cross and Red Crescent Societies
LOS loss of signal
lot. lotion
Lot Polskie Linie Lotnicze (Polish Air Lines)
LOX liquid oxygen
l.p. long primer (a size of printer's type); low pressure
Lp Lordship
LP Labour Party; large paper (edition of a book); life policy; Limited Partnership; long-playing (of a gramophone record); Lord Provost; low pressure; lumbar puncture
L/P letterpress; life policy
LPC Lord President of the Council
LPG liquefied petroleum gas

LPh Licentiate in Philosophy
LPLC low-pressure liquid chromatography
lpm lines per minute
LPO London Philharmonic Orchestra
L'pool Liverpool
LPS London Philharmonic Society; Lord Privy Seal
LPSO Lloyd's Policy Signing Office
Lpz. Leipzig
LQ letter quality (of printed output)
lr lower
Lr lawrencium
LR Lloyd's Register (of Shipping)
LRAD Licentiate of the Royal Academy of Dancing
LRAM Licentiate of the Royal Academy of Music
LRB London Residuary Body (in local government)
LRC London Rowing Club
LRCM Licentiate of the Royal College of Music
LRCP Licentiate of the Royal College of Physicians
LRCPE Licentiate of the Royal College of Physicians of Edinburgh
LRCPI Licentiate of the Royal College of Physicians of Ireland
LRCPSGlas Licentiate of the Royal College of Physicians and Surgeons of Glasgow
LRCS Licentiate of the Royal College of Surgeons of England
LRCSE Licentiate of the Royal College of Surgeons of Edinburgh
LRCSI Licentiate of the Royal College of Surgeons in Ireland
LRCVS Licentiate of the Royal College of Veterinary Surgeons
LREC Local Research Ethics Committee
LRPS Licentiate of the Royal Photographic Society
LRSC Licentiate of the Royal Society of Chemistry
LRSM Licentiate of the Royal Schools of Music
LRT light rail transit; London Regional Transport
LRTI lower respiratory tract infection
LRV lunar roving vehicle
l.s. left side; letter signed; locus sigilli (Latin: the place of the seal); lump sum
LS Leading Seaman; Leeds; Lesotho; Licentiate in Surgery; Linnean Society; locus sigilli; London Sinfonietta; long shot; Syrian pound (monetary unit)
LSA Licence in Agricultural Sciences; Licentiate of the Society of Apothecaries
LS&GCM Long Service and Good Conduct Medal
l.s.c. loco supra citato (Latin: in the place before cited)
LSd Sudanese pound (monetary unit)
LSD least significant digit; lysergic acid diethylamide (hallucinogenic drug)

L.S.D. librae, solidi, denarii (Latin: pounds, shillings, pence)
LSE London School of Economics and Political Science
L-Sgt Lance-Sergeant
LSHTM London School of Hygiene and Tropical Medicine
LSI Labour and Socialist International; large-scale integration
LSJ London School of Journalism
LSO London Symphony Orchestra
LSS life-support system
LST landing ship (for) tank(s) or transport; local standard time
LSZ (New Zealand) limited speed zone
lt light
l.t. local time; long ton
Lt Lieutenant; Light
LT lawn tennis; Licentiate in Teaching; London Transport; low tension; Turkish lira (monetary unit)
LTA Lawn Tennis Association; lighter than air (of an aircraft)
LT & SR London, Tilbury, and Southend Railway
LTB London Tourist Board
Lt-Cdr Lieutenant-Commander
LTCL Licentiate of Trinity College of Music, London
Lt-Col Lieutenant-Colonel
Lt-Com Lieutenant-Commander
Ltd Limited (after the name of a private limited company)
Lt-Gen Lieutenant-General
Lt-Gov Lieutenant-Governor
LTh Licentiate in Theology
LTH luteotrophic hormone
LTI Licentiate of the Textile Institute
Lt Inf. Light Infantry
LTM Licentiate in Tropical Medicine
LTOM London Traded Options Market
LTP long-term potentiation
ltr letter; lighter
LTTE (Sri Lanka) Liberation Tigers of Tamil Eelam
l/u laid up
Lu lutetium
LU Liberal Unionist; loudness unit; Luton
LUC London Underwriters Centre
LUG local users group
LUNCO Lloyd's Underwriters Non-Marine Claims Office
LUOTC London University Officers' Training Corps
Luth. Lutheran
Lux. Luxembourg
LuxF Luxembourg franc (monetary unit)
lv. leave (of absence, as from military duty); livre (French: book)
Lv lev (Bulgarian monetary unit)
LV left ventricle; licensed victualler; luncheon voucher
LVA Licensed Victuallers' Association

LVLO Local Vehicle Licensing Office

LVO Lieutenant of the Royal Victorian Order

Lw lawrencium

LW long-wave; low water

LWL length (at) waterline (of a ship); load waterline

LWM low water mark

LWRA London Waste Regulation Authority

LWT London Weekend Television

lx lux

LXX Septuagint (from its 70 translators)

l.y. light year

Lys lysine

M

m magnetic moment; mass; me (in tonic sol-fa); meta (as in *m*-dichlorobenzene); metre(s); milli- (prefix indicating 1/1000 (i.e. 10^{-3}), as in **mm**, millimetre); million

m. maiden (over); male; mare; mark(s); married; masculine; medicine; meridian; meridies (Latin: noon); meridional; mile(s); (USA, Canada) mill(s) (monetary unit); minim (liquid measure); minute(s); misce (Latin: mix); molar (tooth); month; moon

M em; loti (monetary unit of Lesotho; pl. maloti); luminous exitance; Mach (followed by a number); magnetization; Malta; Manchester; mass, especially molar mass; (Australia) mature audience (certification); medium (size); mega- (prefix indicating one million, as in **MW**, megawatt; *or* (in computing) 2^{20}, as in **Mbyte**, megabyte); metal (in a chemical formula, as in **MOH**); million; minim (liquid measure); moment of a force; motorway (as in **M1**, **M4**, etc.); radiant exitance; thousand; the middle term of a syllogism

M. Magister (Latin: Master); Majesty; Manitoba; Marquess; Marquis; Master (in titles); Medieval; Member (in titles); metronome; mezzo *or* mezza (Italian: half); Middle; militia; Monday; Monsieur (French: Mr *or* Sir); Mountain

m/a my account

mA milliampere(s)

Ma Mach number

MA Massachusetts; Master of Arts; mental age; Military Academy; military assistant; mobility allowance; Morocco

MAA Manufacturers' Agents Association of Great Britain; master-at-arms

MAAF Mediterranean Allied Air Forces

MAAT Member of the Association of Accounting Technicians

Mac. Maccabees (books of the Apocrypha)

MAc Master of Accountancy

MAC multiplexed analogue components

MACE Member of the Association of Conference Executives; Member of the Australian College of Education

Maced. Macedonia(n)

mach. machine(ry); machinist

MACM Member of the Association of Computing Machines

MAD magnetic anomaly detection; major affective disorder; mutual assured destruction

Madag. Madagascar

MADO Member of the Association of Dispensing Opticians

MAE Master of Aeronautical Engineering; Master of Art Education; Master of Arts in Education

MA(Ed) Master of Arts in Education

MAEE Marine Aircraft Experimental Establishment

MAFF Ministry of Agriculture, Fisheries, and Food

mag. magazine; magnesium; magnet(ic); magnetism; magneto; magnitude; magnum

Mag. Magyar

MAgEc Master of Agricultural Economics

MAgr Master of Agriculture

MAI Master of Engineering (Latin *Magister in Arte Ingeniaria*)

MAIB Marine Accident Investigation Branch

maj. major; majority

Maj Major

Maj-Gen Major-General

Mal. Malachi; Malay(an)

MAL Malaysia

MALD Master of Arts in Law and Diplomacy

MAMEME Member of the Association of Mining Electrical and Mechanical Engineers

man. management; manual(ly)

Man. Manila; Manitoba

Manch. Manchester

mand. mandolin

M & B May and Baker (pharmaceutical company); mild and bitter (beer); Mills and Boon (publisher of romantic fiction)

M & E music and effects

Man. Dir. Managing Director

M&S Marks & Spencer plc

Manit. Manitoba

manuf. manufacture(d); manufacturer; manufacturing

MANWEB Merseyside and North Wales Electricity Board

MAO Master of Obstetric Art; monoamine oxidase

MAOI monoamine oxidase inhibitor (antidepressant)

MAOT Member of the Association of Occupational Therapists

MAP Ministry of Aircraft Production

MAPsS Member of the Australian Psychological Society

mar. marimba; maritime; married

Mar. March

MAR Master of Arts in Religion

MARAC Member of the Australasian Register of Agricultural Consultants

marc. marcato (Italian: marked; i.e. each note emphasized)

MARC machine-readable cataloguing

March. Marchioness

MArch Master of Architecture

marg. margin(al)

mar. insce. marine insurance

Marq. Marquess; Marquis

MARV manoeuvrable re-entry vehicle

mas. masculine

MASc Master of Applied Science

MASC Member of the Australian Society of Calligraphers

MASCAM masking-pattern adaptive sub-band coding and multiplexing

MASCE Member of the American Society of Civil Engineers

maser microwave amplification by stimulated emission of radiation

MASH (USA) mobile army surgical hospital

Mass. Massachusetts

mat. matinée

MAT marine, aviation, and transport; Master of Arts in Teaching

MATh Master of Arts in Theology

maths. mathematics

MATS Military Air Transport Service

MATSA Managerial Administrative Technical Staff Association

Matt. Matthew

MATV master antenna television

Mau Re Mauritian rupee (monetary unit)

MAusIMM Member of the Australasian Institute of Mining and Metallurgy

max. maxim; maximum

mb millibar(s)

m.b. misce bene (Latin: mix well)

MB Bachelor of Medicine (Latin *Medicinae Baccalaureus*); Manitoba; mark of the Beast; (Canada) Medal of Bravery; megabyte

MBA Master of Business Administration

MBAcA Member of the British Acupuncture Association

mbar millibar(s)

MBASW Member of the British Association of Social Workers

m.b.c. maximum breathing capacity

MBC metropolitan borough council; municipal borough council

MBCS Member of the British Computer Society

MBD minimal brain dysfunction

MBE Member of the Order of the British Empire

MBG microemulsion-based gel

mbH mit beschränkter Haftung (German: with limited liability)

MBHI Member of the British Horological Institute

MBIFD Member of the British Institute of Funeral Directors

MBKSTS Member of the British Kinematograph, Sound, and Television Society

MBO management buyout; management by objectives

MBOU Member of the British Ornithologists' Union

MBP mean blood pressure

MBPICS Member of the British Production and Inventory Control Society

MBPsS Member of the British Psychological Society

MBSc Master of Business Science

MBT main battle tank; mean body temperature

Mbyte megabyte

m/c machine; motor cycle

MC Master of Ceremonies; Master of Surgery (Latin *Magister Chirurgiae*); Member of Council; Military Cross; Missionaries of Charity; Monaco; Monte Carlo

M/C Manchester

MCA Management Consultants' Association; micro channel architecture; monetary compensatory amount(s)

MCAM Member of the CAM Foundation

MCB Master in Clinical Biochemistry; memory control block; miniature circuit breaker; multiple-cratering bomblets

MCBSI Member of the Chartered Building Societies Institute

MCC Manchester Computer Centre; Marylebone Cricket Club; member of the county council; metropolitan county council

MCCD RCS Member in Clinical Community Dentistry of the Royal College of Surgeons

MCD Master of Civic Design; Movement for Christian Democracy

MCE Master of Civil Engineering

MCFP (Canada) Member of the College of Family Physicians

MCG Melbourne Cricket Ground

MCGA multicolour graphics array

MCh Master of Surgery (Latin *Magister Chirurgiae*)

MCHC mean cell haemoglobin concentration

MChD Master of Dental Surgery (Latin *Magister Chirurgiae Dentalis*)

MChE Master of Chemical Engineering

MChemA Master in Chemical Analysis

MChOrth Master of Orthopaedic Surgery (Latin *Magister Chirurgiae Orthopaedicae*)

MChS Member of the Society of Chiropodists

mchy machinery

MCIBSE Member of the Chartered Institution of Building Services Engineers

MCIM Member of the Chartered Institute of Marketing

MCIOB Member of the Chartered Institute of Building

MCIS Member of the Institute of Chartered Secretaries and Administrators (formerly Chartered Institute of Secretaries)

MCIT Member of the Chartered Institute of Transport

MCL Master of Civil Law

MClSc Master of Clinical Science

MCMES Member of the Civil and Mechanical Engineers' Society

MCom Master of Commerce

MCommH Master of Community Health

MConsE Member of the Association of Consulting Engineers

MCOphth Member of the College of Ophthalmologists

MCP male chauvinist pig; Member of Colonial Parliament; Member of the College of Preceptors

MCPA 2-methyl-4-chlorophenoxy-acetic acid (used in herbicides)

MCPB 4-(2-methyl-4-chlorophen-oxy)butanoic acid (weedkiller)

MCPP Member of the College of Pharmacy Practice

MCPS Mechanical Copyright Protection Society; Member of the College of Physicians and Surgeons

MCR middle common room (in certain universities)

MCS Madras Civil Service; Malayan Civil Service; Military College of Science

MCSEE Member of the Canadian Society of Electrical Engineers

MCSP Member of the Chartered Society of Physiotherapy

MCST Member of the College of Speech Therapists

MCT mainstream corporation tax; Member of the Association of Corporate Treasurers

MCU medium close-up

Md mendelevium

Md. Maryland

M/d months after date

MD Doctor of Medicine (Latin *Medicinae Doctor*); main droite (French: right hand); malicious damage; managing director; mano destra (Italian: right hand); Maryland; memorandum of deposit; mentally deficient; Middle Dutch; military district; mini-disc (in sound recording); musical director

MDA methylenedioxyampheta-mine (hallucinogenic drug; love drug *or* ice); methylenedioxymeth-amphetamine (hallucinogenic drug; Ecstasy); monochrome display adaptor; Muscular Dystrophy Association

M-day (USA) mobilization day

MDC metropolitan district council; more developed country

MDentSc Master in Dental Science

MDes Master of Design

MDHB Mersey Docks and Harbour Board

mdise merchandise

Mdlle Mademoiselle (French: Miss)

Mdm Madam

MDMA methylenedioxymeth-amphetamine (hallucinogenic drug; Ecstasy)

Mdme Madame (French: Mrs)

mdnt midnight

MDP Mongolian Democratic Party

MDR minimum daily requirement

MDS Master of Dental Surgery

MDSc Master of Dental Science

mdse merchandise

MDT (USA) Mountain Daylight Time

MDu Middle Dutch

Me Maine (USA); Messerschmitt (German aircraft); methyl (used in formulae)

ME Maine; marine engineer(ing); Master of Education; Master of Engineering; mechanical engineer(ing); Medway; Middle East(ern); Middle English; military engineer; mining engineer(ing); Most Excellent (in titles); myalgic encephalomyelitis

MEAF Middle East Air Force

meas. measure

MEB Midlands Electricity Board

MEc Master of Economics

MEC Member of the Executive Council; Middle East Command

MECAS Middle East Centre for Arab Studies

mech. mechanical(ly); mechanics; mechanism

MECI Member of the Institute of Employment Consultants

MECO main engine cut off

MEcon Master of Economics

med. medical; medicine; medieval; medium

Med. Mediterranean

MEd Master of Education

MED minimum effective dose

Medit. Mediterranean

med. jur. medical jurisprudence

MedScD Doctor of Medical Science

MEF Middle East Force

meg megabyte

MEIC Member of the Engineering Institute of Canada

MELF Middle East Land Forces

mem. member; memento (Latin: remember); memoir(s); memorandum; memorial

MENCAP Royal Society for Mentally Handicapped Children and Adults

MEng Master of Engineering

MEO Marine Engineering Officer

MEP (Sri Lanka) Mahajana Eksath Peramuna (People's United Front); Master of Engineering Physics; mean effective pressure; Member of the European Parliament

MEPA Master of Engineering and Public Administration

mer. meridian; meridional

merc. mercantile; mercury

MERLIN Multi-Element Radio-linked Interferometer Network (UK)

Messrs Messieurs (French: gentlemen *or* sirs; used in English as pl. of Mr; *see also under* MM)

met. metallurgical; metallurgist; metallurgy; metaphor; metaphysics; meteorological (as in **met. office**); meteorology; metronome; metropolitan

Met methionine; Metropolitan Opera House (New York); Metropolitan Police

metal. metallurgical; metallurgy

metaph. metaphor(ical); metaphysical; metaphysics

MetE Metallurgical Engineer

meteorol. meteorological; meteorology

Meth. Methodist

MetR Metropolitan Railway (London)

MeV megaelectronvolt(s)

Mex. Mexican; Mexico

MEX Mexico

MEXE Military Engineering Experimental Establishment

Mez mezzo-soprano

mf mezzo forte (Italian; moderately loudly)

mF millifarad(s)

MF machine finish(ed) (of paper); Master of Forestry; medium frequency; melamine–formaldehyde (as in **MF resin**); Middle French; multifrequency

M/F male or female (in advertisements)

MFA Master of Fine Arts

MFARCS Member of the Faculty of Anaesthetists of the Royal College of Surgeons

MFC Mastership in Food Control

MFCM Member of the Faculty of Community Medicine

mfd manufactured

mfg manufacturing

MFH Master of Foxhounds

MFHom Member of the Faculty of Homeopathy

MFlem Middle Flemish

MFLOPS million floating-point operations per second

MFM modified frequency modulation

MFN most favoured nation (in trade agreements)

MFOM Member of the Faculty of Occupational Medicine

MFPA Mouth and Foot Painting Artists

mfr. manufacture; manufacturer

MFr Middle French

m. ft. mistura fiat (Latin: let a mixture be made; in prescriptions)

MFV motor fleet vessel

mg milligram(s)

Mg magnesium

MG machine glazed (of paper); machine gun; main gauche

(French: left hand); Major-General; make good; Morris Garages (sports car; named after its original manufacturer); myasthenia gravis

MGA Major-General in charge of Administration

MGB Ministerstvo Gosudarstvennoi Bezopasnosti (Russian: Ministry of State Security; Soviet secret police, 1946–54); motor gunboat

MGC Machine Gun Corps

MGDS RCS Member in General Dental Surgery of the Royal College of Surgeons

MGGS Major-General, General Staff

MGI Member of the Institute of Certificated Grocers

MGk Medieval Greek

M. Glam Mid Glamorgan

MGM Metro-Goldwyn-Mayer (film studio)

MGO Master General of the Ordnance; Master of Gynaecology and Obstetrics

Mgr Manager; Monseigneur (French: my lord); Monsignor

MGr Medieval Greek

Mgrs Managers; Monsignors

mgt management

mH millihenry(s)

MH Master of Horse; (USA) Medal of Honor

MHA (Australia, Canada) Member of the House of Assembly; Methodist Homes for the Aged

MHCIMA Member of the Hotel Catering and Institutional Management Association

MHD magnetohydrodynamics

MHE Master of Home Economics

MHG Middle High German

MHK (Isle of Man) Member of the House of Keys

M.Hon. Most Honourable

MHR (USA, Australia) Member of the House of Representatives

MHRA Modern Humanities Research Association

MHRF Mental Health Research Fund

MHS message-handling system

MHW mean high water (of tides)

MHz megahertz

mi. mile; (USA, Canada) mill(s) (monetary unit)

MI Michigan; Military Intelligence; mounted infantry; myocardial infarction

MI5 Military Intelligence, section five (British counterintelligence agency)

MI6 Military Intelligence, section six (British intelligence and espionage agency)

MIA Master of International Affairs; missing in action

MIAA&S Member of the Incorporated Association of Architects and Surveyors

MIAeE Member of the Institute of Aeronautical Engineers

MIAgrE Member of the Institution of Agricultural Engineers

MIAM Member of the Institute of Administrative Management

MIBF Member of the Institute of British Foundrymen

MIBiol Member of the Institute of Biology

MIBritE Member of the Institution of British Engineers

MIB(Scot) Member of the Institute of Bankers in Scotland

Mic. Micah

MICE Member of the Institution of Civil Engineers

MICEI Member of the Institution of Civil Engineers of Ireland

MICFor Member of the Institute of Chartered Foresters

Mich. Michaelmas; Michigan

MIChemE Member of the Institution of Chemical Engineers

MICorrST Member of the Institution of Corrosion Science and Technology

MICR magnetic-ink character recognition

microbiol. microbiology

micros. microscopist; microscopy

MICS Member of the Institute of Chartered Shipbrokers

mid. middle

Mid. Midshipman

MIDAS missile defence alarm system

Middx Middlesex

MIDI musical instrument digital interface

Mid. Lat. Middle Latin

MIDPM Member of the Institute of Data Processing Management

MIE(Aust) Member of the Institution of Engineers, Australia

MIED Member of the Institution of Engineering Designers

MIEE Member of the Institution of Electrical Engineers

MIEI Member of the Institution of Engineering Inspection

MIE(Ind) Member of the Institution of Engineers, India

MIES Member of the Institution of Engineers and Shipbuilders, Scotland

MIEx Member of the Institute of Export

MIExpE Member of the Institute of Explosives Engineers

MIF migration inhibition factor

MIFA Member of the Institute of Field Archaeologists

MIFF Member of the Institute of Freight Forwarders

MIFireE Member of the Institute of Fire Engineers

MiG Mi(koyan and) G(urevich) (Soviet jet fighter; named after its designers)

MIG metal-inert gas (as in **MIG welding**)

MIGasE Member of the Institution of Gas Engineers

MIGeol Member of the Institution of Geologists

MIH Master of Industrial Health; Member of the Institute of Housing

MIHort Member of the Institute of Horticulture

MIHT Member of the Institution of Highways and Transportation

MIIM Member of the Institute of Industrial Managers

MIInfSc Member of the Institute of Information Sciences

mil. military; militia

MIL Member of the Institute of Linguists

MILGA Member of the Institute of Local Government Administrators

milit. military

MILocoE Member of the Institution of Locomotive Engineers

MIM Member of the Institute of Metals

MIMarE Member of the Institute of Marine Engineers

MIMC Member of the Institute of Management Consultants

MIMechE Member of the Institution of Mechanical Engineers

MIMGTechE Member of the Institution of Mechanical and General Technician Engineers

MIMI Member of the Institute of the Motor Industry

MIMinE Member of the Institution of Mining Engineers

MIMM Member of the Institution of Mining and Metallurgy

MIMunE Member of the Institution of Municipal Engineers (now amalgamated with the Institution of Civil Engineers)

min minimum; minute(s)

min. mineralogical; mineralogy; minim (liquid measure); minimum; mining; minor; minute(s)

Min. Minister; Ministry

MIND National Association for Mental Health

mineral. mineralogical; mineralogy

Minn. Minnesota

Min. Plen. Minister Plenipotentiary

MInstAM Member of the Institute of Administrative Management

MInstBE Member of the Institution of British Engineers

MInstD Member of the Institute of Directors

MInstE Member of the Institute of Energy

MInstEnvSci Member of the Institute of Environmental Sciences

MInstMC Member of the Institute of Measurement and Control

MInstME Member of the Institution of Mining Engineers

MInstMM Member of the Institution of Mining and Metallurgy

MInstP Member of the Institute of Physics

MInstPet Member of the Institute of Petroleum

MInstPI Member of the Institute of Patentees and Inventors

MInstPkg Member of the Institute of Packaging

MInstPS Member of the Institute of Purchasing and Supply

MInstR Member of the Institute of Refrigeration

MInstRA Member of the Institute of Registered Architects

MInstT Member of the Institute of Transport

MInstTM Member of the Institute of Travel Managers in Industry and Commerce

MInstWM Member of the Institute of Wastes Management

MINucE Member of the Institution of Nuclear Engineers

MIOSH Member of the Institution of Occupational Safety and Health

m.i.p. mean indicated pressure

MIP marine insurance policy; maximum investment plan; Member of the Institute of Plumbing; monthly investment plan

MIPA Member of the Institute of Practitioners in Advertising

MIPM Member of the Institute of Personnel Management

MIPR Member of the Institute of Public Relations

MIProdE Member of the Institution of Production Engineers

MIPS million instructions per second

MIQ Member of the Institute of Quarrying

MIRAS mortgage interest relief at source

MIREE(Aust) Member of the Institution of Radio and Electronics Engineers (Australia)

MIRT Member of the Institute of Reprographic Technicians

MIRTE Member of the Institute of Road Transport Engineers

MIRV multiple independently targeted re-entry vehicle

MIS management information system; Member of the Institute of Statisticians

misc. miscellaneous; miscellany

MISD multiple instruction (stream), single data (stream)

Miss. Mission; Missionary; Mississippi

mist. mistura (Latin: mixture)

MIStructE Member of the Institution of Structural Engineers

MITA Member of the Industrial Transport Association

MITD Member of the Institute of Training and Development

MITE Member of the Institution of Electrical and Electronics Technician Engineers

MITI (Japan) Ministry of International Trade and Industry

MITT Member of the Institute of Travel and Tourism

Mitts minutes of telecommunications traffic

MIWEM Member of the Institution of Water and Environmental Management

MJ megajoule(s)

MJI Member of the Institute of Journalists

MJS Member of the Japan Society

MJur Magister Juris (Latin: Master of Law)

mk mark

Mk mark (type of car)

MK Malawi kwacha (monetary unit); Milton Keynes

mks marks; metre kilogram second (as in **mks units**)

mkt market

ml millilitre(s)

ml. mail

ML Licentiate in Medicine (Latin *Medicinae Licentiatus*); Master of Law(s); Medieval Latin; Motherwell; motor launch

MLA Master of Landscape Architecture; Member of the Legislative Assembly

MLC Meat and Livestock Commission; (India, Australia) Member of the Legislative Council

MLCOM Member of the London College of Osteopathic Medicine

MLD minimal lethal dose

MLF multilateral (nuclear) force

MLG Middle Low German

MLitt Master of Letters (Latin *Magister Litterarum*)

Mlle Mademoiselle (French: Miss)

MLO military liaison officer

MLR minimum lending rate; Modern Language Review

MLS Master of Library Science

MLSO Medical Laboratory Scientific Officer

MLW mean low water (of tides)

mm millimetre(s)

m.m. made merchantable; mutatis mutandis (Latin: with the necessary changes)

MM Maelzel's metronome (indicating the tempo of a piece); Majesties; Martyrs; Master Mechanic; Master of Music; mercantile marine; Messieurs (French: gentlemen *or* sirs; used in French as pl. of M (Monsieur); *compare* Messrs); Military Medal

MMA Metropolitan Museum of Art

MMB Milk Marketing Board

MMC Monopolies and Mergers Commission

MMD (Zambia) Movement for Multiparty Democracy

MMDS multipoint microwave distribution system

Mme Madame (French: Mrs)

MME Master of Mechanical Engineering; Master of Mining Engineering; Master of Music Education

MMechE Master of Mechanical Engineering

MMed Master of Medicine

MMedSci Master of Medical Science

MMet Master of Metallurgy

MMetE Master of Metallurgical Engineering

mmf magnetomotive force

mmHg millimetre(s) of mercury (unit of pressure)
MMin Master of Ministry
MMM (Canada) Member of the Order of Military Merit
3M Minnesota Mining and Manufacturing Company
MMR measles, mumps, rubella (in **MMR vaccine**)
MMS Marine Meteorological Services; Member of the Institute of Management Services
MMSA Master of Midwifery of the Society of Apothecaries
MMSc Master of Medical Science
MMU memory management unit
MMus Master of Music
MMusEd Master of Musical Education
mn. midnight
Mn manganese; Modern (of languages)
MN Merchant Navy; Minnesota
MNA Master of Nursing Administration; Member of the National Assembly (of Quebec)
MNAD Multinational Airmobile Division (of NATO)
MNC multinational company
MnE Modern English
MNE multinational enterprise
MNECInst Member of the North East Coast Institution of Engineers and Shipbuilders
mng managing
mngmt management
mngr manager
MnGr Modern Greek
MNI Member of the Nautical Institute
MNR marine nature reserve; Mozambique National Resistance
MNurs Master of Nursing
mo. moment; month
m.o. mail order; modus operandi; money order
m-o months old
Mo molybdenum
Mo. Missouri; Monday
MO mail order; manually operated; mass observation; Master of Obstetrics; Medical Officer; military operations; Missouri; modus operandi; money order
MO&G Master of Obstetrics and Gynaecology
MOBS multiple-orbit bombardment system (nuclear-weapon system)
MoC mother of the (trade-union) chapel
mod. moderate; moderato (Italian; at a moderate tempo); modern; modulus
MoD Ministry of Defence
modem modulator demodulator
mod. praes. modo praescripto (Latin: in the manner directed)
Mods Honour Moderations (at Oxford University)
MOEH Medical Officer for Environmental Health
MOH Master of Otter Hounds; Medical Officer of Health

MOI Ministry of Information
mol mole(s)
mol. molecular; molecule
MOL manned orbital laboratory
mol. wt. molecular weight
m.o.m. middle of month
MOMI Museum of the Moving Image
mon. monastery; monetary
Mon. Monday
Mont. Montana
mor. morocco
Mor. Moroccan; Morocco
MOR middle-of-the-road
MORI Market and Opinion Research Institute (as in **MORI poll**)
morn. morning
morph. morphological; morphology
mor. sol. more solito (Latin: in the usual manner; in prescriptions)
mos. months
MOT Ministry of Transport (usually referring to the road-vehicle test, as in **MOT certificate**)
MOVE Men Over Violence (association for wife batterers)
movt movement
MOW (New Zealand) Ministry of Works; Movement for the Ordination of Women
MOX mixed oxide (as in **MOX fuel**)
mp melting point; mezzo piano (Italian; moderately softly)
m.p. melting point
MP Member of Parliament; Metropolitan Police; Military Police(man); Mounted Police(man)
MPA Master of Professional Accounting; Master of Public Administration; Master Printers Association; Member of the Parliamentary Assembly of Northern Ireland
MPBW Ministry of Public Building and Works
MPC maximum permissible concentration
MPD maximum permissible dose
MPE Master of Physical Education; maximum permissible exposure (to radiation)
MPEA Member of the Physical Education Association
mpg miles per gallon
MPG main professional grade (teacher's basic salary)
mph miles per hour
MPh Master of Philosophy
MPH Master of Public Health
MPhil Master of Philosophy
MPIA Master of Public and International Affairs
MPLA Movimento Popular de Libertação de Angola (Portuguese: Popular Movement for the Liberation of Angola)
MPO management and personnel office; Metropolitan Police Office
MPP Member of the Provincial Parliament (of Ontario)

MPRISA Member of the Public Relations Institute of South Africa
MPRP Mongolian People's Revolutionary Party (communists)
MPS Medical Protection Society; Member of the Philological Society; Member of the Physical Society; mucopolysaccharide (as in **MPS disease**)
MPsyMed Master of Psychological Medicine
MQ metol-quinol (photographic developer)
Mr Mister
MR magnetic resonance (as in **MR scanner**); Master of the Rolls; mate's receipt; motivation(al) research; municipal reform
MRA Moral Rearmament
MRAC Member of the Royal Agricultural College
MRACP Member of the Royal Australasian College of Physicians
MRACS Member of the Royal Australasian College of Surgeons
MRAeS Member of the Royal Aeronautical Society
MRAIC Member of the Royal Architectural Institute of Canada
MRAS Member of the Royal Asiatic Society
MRBM medium-range ballistic missile
MRBS Member of the Royal Botanic Society
MRC Medical Research Council
MRCA multirole combat aircraft
MRCGP Member of the Royal College of General Practioners
MRC-LMB Medical Research Council Laboratory of Molecular Biology
MRCO Member of the Royal College of Organists
MRCOG Member of the Royal College of Obstetricians and Gynaecologists
MRCP Member of the Royal College of Physicians
MRCPA Member of the Royal College of Pathologists of Australia
MRCPath Member of the Royal College of Pathologists
MRCPE Member of the Royal College of Physicians of Edinburgh
MRCPGlas Member of the Royal College of Physicians and Surgeons of Glasgow
MRCPI Member of the Royal College of Physicians of Ireland
MRCPsych Member of the Royal College of Psychiatrists
MRCS Member of the Royal College of Surgeons
MRCSE Member of the Royal College of Surgeons of Edinburgh
MRCSI Member of the Royal College of Surgeons of Ireland
MRCVS Member of the Royal College of Veterinary Surgeons
MRD machine-readable dictionary
MRe Mauritian rupee (monetary unit)
MRE Master of Religious Education; meal, ready to eat;

Microbiological Research Establishment

MRG Minority Rights Group

MRGS Member of the Royal Geographical Society

MRH Member of the Royal Household

MRHS Member of the Royal Horticultural Society

MRI magnetic resonance imaging; Member of the Royal Institution

MRIA Member of the Royal Irish Academy

MRIAI Member of the Royal Institute of the Architects of Ireland

MRIC Member of the Royal Institute of Chemistry

MRIN Member of the Royal Institute of Navigation

MRINA Member of the Royal Institution of Naval Architects

MRIPHH Member of the Royal Institute of Public Health and Hygiene

MRM mechanically recovered meat (in food processing)

MRMetS Member of the Royal Meteorological Society

mRNA messenger RNA

MRO Member of the Register of Osteopaths

MRP manufacturers' recommended price

MRPharmS Member of the Royal Pharmaceutical Society

Mrs Mistress (title of a married woman)

MRS magnetic resonance spectroscopy

MRSA methicillin-resistant *Staphylococcus aureus*

MRSC Member of the Royal Society of Chemistry (formerly MRIC)

MRSH Member of the Royal Society for the Promotion of Health

MRSL Member of the Royal Society of Literature

MRSM Member of the Royal Society of Medicine; Member of the Royal Society of Musicians of Great Britain

MRSPE Member of the Royal Society of Painter-Etchers and Engravers

MRSPP Member of the Royal Society of Portrait Painters

MRST Member of the Royal Society of Teachers

MRTPI Member of the Royal Town Planning Institute

MRUSI Member of the Royal United Service Institution

MRV multiple re-entry vehicle

MRVA Member of the Rating and Valuation Association

ms manuscript; millisecond(s)

m.s. mail steamer

m/s metre(s) per second; months after sight

m/s² metre(s) per second squared

Ms Miss *or* Mrs (unspecified)

MS mail steamer; mano sinistra (Italian: left hand); manuscript; Master of Surgery; Mauritius;

medium shot; memoriae sacrum (Latin: sacred to the memory of; on gravestones); milestone; minesweeper; Mississippi; multiple sclerosis

MSA Master of Science in Agriculture; Member of the Society of Apothecaries; Mineralogical Society of America

MS&R Merchant Shipbuilding and Repairs

MSArch Master of Science in Architecture

MSAutE Member of the Society of Automobile Engineers

MSBA Master of Science in Business Administration

MSBus Master of Science in Business

MSc Master of Science

MSC Manchester Ship Canal; Manpower Services Commission

MScA Master of Science in Agriculture

MSc(Arch) Master of Science in Architecture

MScD Master of Dental Science

MSChE Master of Science in Chemical Engineering

MSCI Index Morgan Stanley Capital International World Index

MSD Doctor of Medical Science

MSDent Master of Science in Dentistry

MS-DOS MicroSoft Disk Operating System

MSE Member of the Society of Engineers

MSEd Master of Science in Education

MSEE Master of Science in Electrical Engineering

MSEM Master of Science in Engineering Mechanics

MSF Manufacturing, Science, and Finance (Union); Master of Science in Forestry; Médecins sans frontières (French: Doctors Without Frontiers; charitable organization)

MSG monosodium glutamate (food additive)

Msgr Monseigneur (French: my lord); Monsignor

MSH Master of Staghounds

MSHE Master of Science in Home Economics

MSHyg Master of Science in Hygiene

MSI medium-scale integration

MSIAD Member of the Society of Industrial Artists and Designers

MSIE Master of Science in Industrial Engineering

MSINZ Member of the Surveyors' Institute of New Zealand

MSJ Master of Science in Journalism

MSL mean sea level

MSM Master of Sacred Music; Meritorious Service Medal

MSME Master of Science in Mechanical Engineering

MSN Master of Science in Nursing

MSO Member of the Society of Osteopaths

MSocSc Master of Social Science(s)

MSPE Master of Science in Physical Education

MSPH Master of Science in Public Health

MSPhar Master of Science in Pharmacy

MSQ managing service quality

MSR Member of the Society of Radiographers; missile-site radar

MSS manuscripts; Master of Social Science; Master of Social Service; Member of the Royal Statistical Society

MSTD Member of the Society of Typographic Designers

Mstr Master

MSU midstream (specimen of) urine

MSW magnetic surface wave(s); medical social worker

MSY maximum sustainable yield (of a natural resource)

mt. megaton

m.t. metric ton(s)

Mt meitnerium; metical (monetary unit of Mozambique); Mount; Mountain

MT mail transfer; mean time; mechanical transport; Montana; motor tanker; motor transport

M/T empty (used on gas cylinders); mail transfer

MTA Music Trades' Association

MTAI Member of the Institute of Travel Agents

MTB motor torpedo boat

MTBE methyl *t*-butyl ether (lead-free antiknock petrol additive)

MTC Mechanized Transport Corps

MTCA Ministry of Transport and Civil Aviation

MTD Midwife Teacher's Diploma

MTech Master of Technology

MTEFL Master in the Teaching of English as a Foreign Language

mtg meeting; mortgage

mth month

MTh Master of Theology

mtn motion

MTO made to order

Mt Rev Most Reverend (title of archbishop)

Mts Mountains; Mounts

MTS Master of Theological Studies

MU Musicians' Union

MUF maximum usable frequency

MUFTI minimum use of force tactical intervention

MUGA multiple-gated arteriography (as in **MUGA scan**)

mun. municipal(ity)

MUniv Master of the University

mus. museum; music(al)

MusB Bachelor of Music (Latin *Musicae Baccalaureus*)

MusD Doctor of Music (Latin *Musicae Doctor*)

MusM Master of Music (Latin *Musicae Magister)*

mv mezza voce (Italian: half voice; i.e. softly)

m.v. market value; mean variation; motor vessel

mV millivolt(s)

MV megavolt(s); merchant vessel; motor vessel; muzzle velocity (of firearms)

MVB Bachelor of Veterinary Medicine

MVD Doctor of Veterinary Medicine; Ministerstvo Vnutrennikh Del (Russian: Ministry of Internal Affairs; Soviet police organization, 1946–60)

MVEE Military Vehicles and Engineering Establishment

MVL motor-vehicle licence

MVO Member of the Royal Victorian Order

MVSc Master of Veterinary Science

mW milliwatt(s)

MW Malawi; Master of Wine; medium wave; megawatt(s); molecular weight; Most Worshipful; Most Worthy

MWeldI Member of the Welding Institute

Mx maxwell; Middlesex

my million years (following a number)

MY motor yacht

myc. mycological; mycology

MYOB mind your own business

MYRA multiyear rescheduling agreement

myst. mystery

myth. mythological; mythology

N

n amount of substance; en; indefinite number; nano- (prefix denoting 10^{-9}, as in **nm**, nanometre); neutron; normal (i.e. unbranched, as in **n-butane**); n-type (semiconductor)

n. name; natus (Latin: born); nephew; net; neuter; new; nominative; noon; note; noun; number

N en; knight; naira (Nigerian monetary unit); neutral; newton(s); ngultrum (monetary unit of Bhutan; *see also under* Nu); nitrogen; north(ern); north London; Norway; nuclear (as in **N-weapon**); nucleon; substitution on a nitrogen atom (as in **N-phenylhydroxylamine**)

N. National(ist); navigation; Navy; New; Norse; north(ern); November

n/a not applicable; not available

Na sodium (Latin *natrium*)

NA Netherlands Antilles; new account; Nomina Anatomica (Latin: Anatomical Names; official anatomical terminology); North America(n)

N/A new account; no account; not available

n.a.a. not always afloat

NAAFI Navy, Army, and Air Force Institutes

NAAS National Agricultural Advisory Service

NAB National Advisory Body for Public Sector Higher Education; National Assistance Board (former government department); National Australia Bank

NABC National Association of Boys' Clubs

NABS National Advertising Benevolent Society

NAC National Advisory Council; National Agriculture Centre; National Association for the Childless

NACAB National Association of Citizens Advice Bureaux

NACCB National Accreditation Council for Certification Bodies

NACNE National Advisory Committee on Nutrition Education

NACODS National Association of Colliery Overmen, Deputies, and Shotfirers

NACOSS National Approved Council for Security Systems

NACRO National Association for the Care and Resettlement of Offenders

NAD nicotinamide adenine dinucleotide; no abnormality detected

NADEC National Association of Development Education Centres

NADFAS National Association of Decorative and Fine Arts Societies

NADGE NATO Air Defence Ground Environment

NADH a reduced form of NAD (H is the symbol for hydrogen)

NADP nicotinamide adenine dinucleotide phosphate

NADW North Atlantic deep water

NAEA National Association of Estate Agents

NAEW NATO Airborne Early Warning

NA f. Netherlands Antillean guilder (monetary unit)

NAFTA New Zealand and Australia Free Trade Agreement; North American Free Trade Agreement

NAGC National Association for Gifted Children

Nah. Nahum

Nahal (Israel) No'ar Halutzi Lohem (Hebrew: Pioneer and Military Youth)

NAHAT National Association of Health Authorities and Trusts

NAHT National Association of Head Teachers

NAI nonaccidental injury

NAIRU nonaccelerating inflation rate of unemployment

NAITA National Association of Independent Travel Agents

NAK negative acknowledgment

NALGO National and Local Government Officers' Association (former trade union)

N. Am. North America(n)

NAMAS National Measurement and Accreditation Service

NAMCW National Association of Maternal and Child Welfare

NAMH National Association for Mental Health (now called MIND)

NAMMA NATO MRCA Management Agency

NAMS (USA) national air-monitoring sites

NAND not AND (as in **NAND gate, NAND operation**)

N&P National and Provincial (building society)

N and Q notes and queries

NAO National Audit Office

NAPF National Association of Pension Funds

naph. naphtha

NAPO National Association of Probation Officers (trade union)

NAPT National Association for the Prevention of Tuberculosis

NAS naval air station; Noise Abatement Society

NASA (USA) National Aeronautics and Space Administration

NASDA (Japan) National Space Development Agency

NAS/UWT National Association of Schoolmasters/Union of Women Teachers

nat. national(ist); natural; natus (Latin: born)

N. At. North Atlantic

NATFHE National Association of Teachers in Further and Higher Education

natl national

NATLAS National Testing Laboratory Accreditation Scheme

NATO North Atlantic Treaty Organization

NATS National Air Traffic Services

nat. sc. natural science(s)

NATSOPA National Society of Operative Printers, Graphical and Media Personnel (formerly National Society of Operative Printers and Assistants)

naut. nautical

nav. naval; navigable; navigation; navigator

NAV net asset value (of an organization)

Nav.E. Naval Engineer

navig. navigation; navigator

NAVSAT navigational satellite

NAWC National Association of Women's Clubs

NAWO National Alliance of Women's Organizations

NAYC Youth Clubs UK (formerly National Association of Youth Clubs)

NAYT National Association of Youth Theatres

Nazi Nationalsozialisten (German: National Socialist)

nb no ball; nota bene (Latin: note well)

Nb niobium

NB New Brunswick (Canada); North Britain (i.e. Scotland); nota bene (Latin: note well)

NBA Net Book Agreement; North British Academy

NBC National Book Council; (USA) National Broadcasting Company; nuclear, biological, and chemical (of weapons or warfare)

NbE north by east

NBG no bloody good

NBI National Benevolent Institution

NBK National Bank of Kuwait

NBL National Book League (formerly Council); not bloody likely

NBPI National Board for Prices and Incomes

NBR nitrile-butadiene rubber

NBRI National Building Research Institute

NBS Newcastle Business School

NBV net book value (of an asset)

NbW north by west

NC National Certificate; National Curriculum; New Church; nickel–cadmium (of electric cells); no charge; North Carolina (abbrev. or postcode); numerical control or numerically controlled (as in **NC machine**)

N/C new charter; no charge

NCA National Certificate of Agriculture; National Childminding Association; National Cricket Association

NCB National Children's Bureau; National Coal Board (now British Coal Corporation, BCC); no claim bonus

NCBW nuclear, chemical, and biological warfare

NCC National Computing Centre; National Consumer Council; National Curriculum Council; Nature Conservancy Council

NCCI National Committee for Commonwealth Immigrants

NCCJ National Conference of Christians and Jews

NCCL National Council for Civil Liberties (now called Liberty)

n.c.d. no can do

NCDAD National Council for Diplomas in Art and Design

NCDL National Canine Defence League

NCET National Council for Educational Technology

NCI New Community Instrument

NCLC National Council of Labour Colleges

NCNC National Convention of Nigeria and the Cameroons; National Convention of Nigerian Citizens (political party)

NCO noncommissioned officer

NCP National Car Parks Ltd; (Australia) National Country Party (now called National Party)

NCPS noncontributory pension scheme

NCR National Cash Register (Company Ltd); no carbon required (of paper)

NCRL National Chemical Research Laboratory

NCSC (Australia) National Companies and Securities Commission

NCSE National Council for Special Education

NCT National Chamber of Trade; National Childbirth Trust

NCU National Communications Union; National Cyclists' Union

NCV no commercial value

NCVCCO National Council of Voluntary Child Care Organizations

NCVO National Council for Voluntary Organizations

NCVQ National Council for Vocational Qualifications

NCW National Council of Women (of Great Britain)

n.d. no date; not drawn

Nd neodymium

ND Naturopathic Diploma; neutral density; no date; North Dakota (abbrev. or postcode)

N-D Notre-Dame (French: Our Lady; in church names, etc.)

NDA National Diploma in Agriculture

N. Dak. North Dakota

NDB nondirectional beacon

ndc National Defence College

NDC National Dairy Council

NDCS National Deaf Children's Society

NDD National Diploma in Dairying; National Diploma in Design

NDE near-death experience

NDH National Diploma in Horticulture

NDIC National Defence Industries Council

NDN National District Nurse Certificate

NDP National Democratic Party (of various countries); net domestic product; (Canada) New Democratic Party

NDPS National Data Processing Service

NDSF National Diploma of the Society of Floristry

NDU Nursing Development Unit

n.e. not exceeding

n/e new edition; no effects (i.e. no funds)

Ne neon

NE Naval Engineer; Nebraska; Newcastle; new edition; New England; no effects (i.e. no funds); northeast(ern); nuclear energy

N/E new edition; no effects (i.e. no funds); not entered

NEAC New English Art Club

NEAF Near East Air Force

NEARELF Near East Land Forces

Neb. Nebraska

NEB National Enterprise Board; New English Bible

NEBSS National Examinations Board for Supervisory Studies

n.e.c. not elsewhere classified

NEC National Executive Committee; National Exhibition Centre (Birmingham); (Japan) Nippon Electric Company

NECCTA National Educational Closed Circuit Television Association

NECInst North East Coast Institution of Engineers and Shipbuilders

NEDC National Economic Development Council; North East Development Council

NEDO National Economic Development Office

NEEB North Eastern Electricity Board

neg. negative(ly); negligence

NEG negative (in transformational grammar)

Neh. Nehemiah

NEH National Endowment for the Humanities

NEL National Engineering Laboratory

nem. con. nemine contradicente (Latin: no-one opposing; unanimously)

N. Eng. northern England

n.e.p. new edition pending

Nep. Neptune (planet)

NEQ nonequivalence (as in **NEQ gate**)

NERC Natural Environment Research Council

n.e.s. not elsewhere specified

Neth. Netherlands

n. et m. nocte et mane (Latin: night and morning; in prescriptions)

neurol. neurological; neurology

Nev. Nevada

Newf. Newfoundland

New M New Mexico

New Test. New Testament

n.f. noun feminine

NF National Front; Newfoundland; no funds; Norman French (language)

NFBTE National Federation of Building Trades Employers

NFC National Freight Consortium

NFCO National Federation of Community Organization

Nfd Newfoundland

NFD Newfoundland; no fixed date

NFDM nonfat dry milk

NFER National Foundation for Educational Research

NFFO nonfossil-fuel obligation (for electricity companies)

NFFPT National Federation of Fruit and Potato Trades

NFHA National Federation of Housing Associations

NFL (USA, Canada) National Football League

Nfld Newfoundland

NFMS National Federation of Music Societies

NFS National Fire Service; network file service; not for sale

NFSE National Federation of Self-Employed (and Small Businesses)

NFT National Film Theatre

NFU National Farmers' Union

NFWI National Federation of Women's Institutes

NG New Guinea; nitroglycerine; no good; Nottingham
NGA National Graphical Association
NGC New General Catalogue (prefixed to a number to designate a Catalogue object)
NGk New Greek
NGNP nominal gross national product
NGO (India) nongazetted officer; nongovernmental organization
NGS nuclear generating station
NGTE National Gas Turbine Establishment
NGU nongonococcal urethritis
NGV natural-gas vehicle
NH New Hampshire (abbrev. or postcode); northern hemisphere
NHBC National House-Building Council
NHBRC National House-Builders' Registration Certificate
N.Heb. New Hebrew; New Hebrides
NHG New High German
NHI National Health Insurance
NHK Nippon Hōsō Kyōkai (Japan Broadcasting Corporation)
NHR National Housewives Register
NHS National Health Service
NHTPC National Housing and Town Planning Council
Ni nickel
NI National Insurance; Native Infantry; Northern Ireland; North Island (New Zealand)
NIAB National Institute of Agricultural Botany
NIACRO Northern Ireland Association for the Care and Resettlement of Offenders
NIAE National Institute of Agricultural Engineering
NIAID National Institute of Allergy and Infectious Diseases
Nibmar no independence before majority African rule
NIBSC National Institute for Biological Standards Control
NIC National Incomes Commission; National Insurance contribution; newly industrialized country; Nicaragua
NiCad nickel–cadmium (battery)
NICAM near-instantaneous companded audio multiplex (for digital coding of audio signals)
NICEC National Institute for Careers Education and Counselling
NICG Nationalized Industries Chairmen's Group
NICRA Northern Ireland Civil Rights Association
NICS Northern Ireland Civil Service
NICU neonatal intensive care unit
NID National Institute for the Deaf; (India) National Institute of Design; Naval Intelligence Division; Northern Ireland District
NIDD non-insulin-dependent diabetes
NIES Northern Ireland Electricity Service

NIESR National Institute of Economic and Social Research
NIF note issuance facility
NIHCA Northern Ireland Hotels and Caterers Association
NIHE (Ireland) National Institute for Higher Education
NII Nuclear Installations Inspectorate
Nikkei Nihou Keizi Shimbun (share index on Tokyo Stock Exchange)
NILP Northern Ireland Labour Party
nimby not in my back yard (indicating liberals, reformers, etc., in principle but not in practice)
NIMH National Institute of Medical Herbalists
NIMR National Institute for Medical Research
NINO no inspector, no operator (system)
Nip. Nippon(ese)
N. Ir. Northern Ireland
NIR Nauchno-Issledovatel'skaya Rabota (Russian colour-television system); nonionizing radiation
NIRC National Industrial Relations Court
N. Ire. Northern Ireland
NIREX Nuclear Industry Radioactive Waste Executive
NIS new Israeli shekel (monetary unit)
NISTRO Northern Ireland Science and Technology Regional Organization
NISW National Institute for Social Work
NIT negative income tax
NJ New Jersey (abbrev. or postcode)
NK natural killer (as in **NK cell**); not known
NKC natural killer cell
NKGB Narodny Komissariat Gosudarstvennoi Bezopasnosti (Russian: People's Commissariat of State Security; Soviet agency, 1943–46)
NKr Norwegian krone (monetary unit)
NKVD Narodny Komissariat Vnutrennikh Del (Russian: People's Commissariat of Internal Affairs; Soviet agency, 1934–46)
NKz new kwanza (Angolan monetary unit)
n.l. new line; non licet (Latin: it is not permitted); non liquet (Latin: it is not clear)
NL National Liberal; Netherlands; New Latin; (Australia) no liability (after the name of a public limited company; equivalent to plc); north latitude
NLC National Liberal Club
NLCS North London Collegiate School
NLD (Burma) National League for Democracy
NLF National Liberal Federation; National Liberation Front; National Loans Fund

NLLST National Lending Library for Science and Technology
NLP natural language processing; neurolinguistic programming
NLQ near letter quality
NLS National Library of Scotland
n.l.t. not later than; not less than
NLW National Library of Wales
NLYL National League of Young Liberals
nm nanometre(s)
n.m. nautical mile(s); nonmetallic; noun masculine
N/m no mark(s) (on a bill of lading)
NM New Mexico (abbrev. or postcode); nuclear medicine
N. Mex. New Mexico
n mile nautical mile
NMP net material product
n.m.t. not more than
NMU National Maritime Union
NMW national minimum wage (as in **NMW policy**)
NN Northampton
NNE north-northeast
NNEB National Nursery Examination Board
NNHT Nuffield Nursing Homes Trust
NNI noise and number index (to evaluate aircraft noise)
NNMA Nigerian National Merit Award
NNOM Nigerian National Order of Merit
NNP net national product
NNR National Nature Reserve
NNT nuclear nonproliferation treaty
NNW north-northwest
no. north(ern); number (from Italian numero)
n.o. not out
No nobelium
No. north(ern); number (from Italian numero)
NO naval officer
n.o.c. not otherwise classified
NOC National Olympic Committee; not otherwise classified
NOCD not our class, dear
noct. nocte (Latin: at night)
NODA National Operatic and Dramatic Association
NODC non-OPEC developing country
n.o.i.b.n. not otherwise indexed by name
n.o.k. next of kin
nol. pros. nolle prosequi (Latin: do not prosecute; procedure for ending criminal proceedings)
nom. nominal; nominative
noncom. noncommissioned
Noncon. Nonconformist
non obst. non obstante (Latin: notwithstanding)
non pros. non prosequitur (Latin: he does not prosecute; former judgment in favour of defendant)
non seq. non sequitur (Latin: (a statement that) does not follow logically)

n.o.p. not otherwise provided (for)

NOP National Opinion Poll; not our publication

Nor. Norman; north; Norway; Norwegian

NOR not OR (as in **NOR gate**, **NOR operation**)

NORAD North American Air Defense Command

Norf. Norfolk

norm. normal

Norm. Norman

Northants Northamptonshire

Northd Northumberland

Norvic. Norvicensis (Latin: (Bishop) of Norwich)

Norw. Norway; Norwegian

NORWEB North Western Electricity Board

n.o.s. not otherwise specified

Nos. numbers (from Italian *numeros*)

NOT not (from its sense in logic, as in **NOT gate**, **NOT operation**)

NOTAR no-tail rotor (of an aircraft)

NOTB National Ophthalmic Treatment Board

Nottm Nottingham

Notts Nottinghamshire

nov. novel(ist); novice

Nov. November

NOX nitrogen oxide(s)

np new paragraph; new pence

n.p. net personalty; net proceeds; new paragraph; nisi prius (Latin: unless previously); nonparticipating; no place of publication given; no printer; no publisher; normal pitch; not paginated

Np neper; neptunium

NP national park; National Power plc; neuropsychiatric; neuropsychiatry; Newport; Notary Public; noun phrase

NPA National Park Authority; Newspaper Publishers' Association

NPC no-player character (in the game Dungeons and Dragons)

NPD Nationaldemokratische Partei Deutschlands (German: National Democratic Party; neo-Nazis); new product development; north polar distance

n.p.f. not provided for

NPF (Syria) National Progressive Front

NPFA National Playing Fields Association

NPG National Portrait Gallery

NPK nitrogen, phosphorus, and potassium (in fertilizers; from the chemical symbols of these elements)

NPL National Physical Laboratory (Teddington, Middlesex)

n.p.n.a. no protest for nonacceptance

n.p. or d. no place or date

n.p.p. no passed proof

NPP nuclear power plant

NPS nuclear power source; nuclear power station

NPT non-proliferation treaty

NPU not passed urine

NPV net present value; no par value (of shares)

NPW nuclear-powered warship

NQOC not quite our class

nr near

NR natural rubber; Norwich

NRA National Recreation Area; National Rifle Association; National Rivers Authority; nuclear-reaction analysis

NRC National Research Council

NRCC National Research Council of Canada

NRD National Register of Designers

NRDC National Research Development Corporation

NRDS neonatal respiratory distress syndrome

NREM non-rapid eye movement (as in **NREM sleep**)

NRM (Uganda) National Resistance Movement

NRMA (Australia) National Roads and Motorists Association

NROTC Naval Reserve Officer Training Corps

NRP nuclear reprocessing plant

NRPB National Radiological Protection Board

NRR Northern Rhodesia Regiment

NRs Nepalese rupee (monetary unit)

NRT net registered tonnage

NRV net realizable value

ns nanosecond(s); (Graduate of the Royal) Naval Staff (College, Greenwich)

n.s. near side; not specified; not sufficient (funds)

n/s nonsmoker; not sufficient (funds)

NS National Service; National Society; new series; Newspaper Society; New Style (method of reckoning dates); nonsmoker; not significant; Nova Scotia; nuclear ship

NSA National Skating Association

NSAID nonsteroidal anti-inflammatory drug

NSB National Savings Bank

NSC National Safety Council; National Sporting Club

NSCR National Society for Cancer Relief

NSF not sufficient funds; Nuclear Structure Facility (Daresbury, Cheshire)

NSG nonstatutory guidelines (concerning the National Curriculum)

NSHEB North of Scotland Hydroelectric Board

NSL National Sporting League

NSM new smoking material; nonstipendiary minister

NSPCC National Society for the Prevention of Cruelty to Children

n.s.p.f. not specially provided for

NSRA National Small-bore Rifle Association

NSU nonspecific urethritis

NSW New South Wales

n.t. net terms; net tonnage

NT (Ireland) National Teacher; National Theatre; National Trust; New Testament; Northern Territory (Australia); no-trump(s); Nurse Teacher

NTA net tangible assets

NTB nontariff barrier

NTD not top drawer

NTDA National Trade Development Association

NTG North Thames Gas

Nth North

NTI noise transmission impairment

NTP normal temperature and pressure

NTS National Trust for Scotland; not to scale

NTVLRO National Television Licence Records Office

nt. wt. net weight

n.u. name unknown

Nu ngultrum (monetary unit of Bhutan)

NU natural uranium; number unobtainable

NUAAW National Union of Agricultural and Allied Workers

NUCPS National Union of Civil and Public Servants

NUCUA National Union of Conservative and Unionists Associations

NUFLAT National Union of Footwear, Leather, and Allied Trades (now amalgamated with the NUHKW to form the National Union of Knitwear, Footwear, and Apparel Trades)

NUHKW National Union of Hosiery and Knitwear Workers

NUI National University of Ireland

NUIW National Union of Insurance Workers

NUJ National Union of Journalists

NUJMB Northern Universities Joint Matriculation Board

num. number; numeral(s)

Num. Numbers

NUM National Union of Mineworkers

NUMAST National Union of Marine, Aviation, and Shipping Transport Officers

numis. numismatic(s)

NUPE National Union of Public Employees (former trade union)

NUR National Union of Railwaymen

NUS National Union of Seamen; National Union of Students

NUT National Union of Teachers

NUTG National Union of Townswomen's Guilds

NUTGW National Union of Tailors and Garment Workers (now amalgamated with the GMB)

NUTN National Union of Trained Nurses

NUU New University of Ulster

NV (Netherlands) Naamloze Vennootschap (after the name of a company; equivalent to plc); Nevada; New Version; nonvintage (of wine, etc.); nonvoting (shares)

N/V nonvintage (of wine etc.); no value

NVG night-vision goggles

NVI nonvalue indicator (type of postage stamp)

NVM Nativity of the Virgin Mary

NVQ National Vocational Qualification

NW net worth; northwest(ern); northwest London

NWFP North-West Frontier Province (Pakistan)

NWP North-Western Province (India)

n. wt. net weight

NWT Northwest Territories (Canada)

NY New York (abbrev. *or* state postcode)

NYC New York City

NYD not yet diagnosed

NYMT National Youth Music Theatre

NYO National Youth Orchestra

NYOS National Youth Orchestra of Scotland

NYP not yet published

NYT National Youth Theatre

NZ New Zealand (abbrev. *or* IVR)

NZBC New Zealand Broadcasting Corporation

N. Zeal. New Zealand

NZEFIP New Zealand Expeditionary Force in the Pacific (in World War II)

NZEI New Zealand Educational Institute

NZIA New Zealand Institute of Architects

NZLR New Zealand Law Reports

NZMA New Zealand Medical Association

NZPA New Zealand Press Association

NZRFU New Zealand Rugby Football Union

NZRN New Zealand Registered Nurse.

O

o ortho (as in **o-cresol**)

o. octavo; old; only; order

O opium; oxygen; pint (Latin *octarius*); a blood group; a particular negative categorical proposition

O. Ocean; octavo; October; oculus (Latin: eye); Oddfellows; Office; Ohio; old; order (of knighthood, etc.); Orient; Osten (German: east); ouest (French: west)

o/a on account (of); on or about

OA objective analysis; office automation; Officier d'Académie (French: Officer of the Academy; award for services in education); old account; operational analysis; osteoarthritis; overall

OAA Outdoor Advertising Association of Great Britain

o.a.d. overall depth

o.a.h. overall height

OAM Medal of the Order of Australia

O & C Oxford and Cambridge (Schools Examination Board)

O & M organization and method(s)

O & O Oriental and Occidental Steamship Company

OAO one and only; Orbiting Astronomical Observatory

OAP old age pension(er)

OAPEC Organization of Arab Petroleum-Exporting Countries

OAR (of the) Order of Augustinian Recollects

OAS on active service; Organization of American States

OASIS optimal aircraft sequencing using intelligent systems

OAU Organization of African Unity

ob. obiit (Latin: (he *or* she) died); obiter (Latin: incidentally); oboe; observation; obstetric(s)

o.b. ordinary building (grade; of timber)

o/b on or before (preceding a date)

Ob. Obadiah

OB off Broadway; old bonded (whisky); old boy; Order of Barbados; order of battle; ordinary business (in life-assurance policies); outside broadcast

OBA optical bleaching agent (in detergents)

Obad. Obadiah

obb. obbligato (Italian: obligatory)

obdt obedient

OBE Officer of the Order of the British Empire; out-of-the-body experience

ob-gyn obstetrics–gynaecology

OBI Order of British India

obit. obituary

obj. object(ive); objection

obl. oblique; oblong

OBM Ordnance benchmark

Obogs on-board oxygen-generating system

ob. ph. oblique photograph(y)

obs. obscure; observation; observatory; observe(d); obsolete

obsc. obscure

obscd obscured

obstet. obstetric(s); obstetrician

obstn obstruction

OBU One Big Union

o.c. on centre; only child; open charter; opere citato

o/c officer commanding; overcharge

Oc. Ocean

OC Officer Commanding; operating characteristic; operations centre; oral contraceptive; (Officer of the) Order of Canada; original cover; overseas country

OCA Old Comrades Association

O.Carm. Order of Carmelites

O.Cart. Order of Carthusians

Oc.B/L ocean bill of lading

occ. occasion; occasional(ly); occident(al); occupation; occurrence

OCD obsessive compulsive disorder; Ordo Carmelitarum

Discalceatorum (Latin: (of the) Order of Discalced Carmelites; Discalced Carmelite Fathers)

oceanog. oceanography

OCF Officiating Chaplain to the Forces

OCR optical character recognition; Ordo Cisterciensium Reformatorum (Latin: (of the) Order of Reformed Cistercians; Trappists)

OCS (USA) Officer Candidate School

OCSO Order of Cistercians of the Strict Observance (Trappists)

oct. octave; octavo

Oct October

OCTU Officer Cadet Training Unit

OCU Operational Conversion Unit

o.d. oculus dexter (Latin: right eye); olive drab; outer diameter

OD oculus dexter (Latin: right eye); officer of the day; Old Dutch (language); olive drab; ordinary seaman; Ordnance datum (standard sea level of the Ordnance Survey); ordnance department; organization development; outer diameter; overdose

O/D on deck; on demand; overdraft

ODA Operating Department Assistant; Overseas Development Administration (formerly Ministry of Overseas Development, ODM)

ODan Old Danish

ODAS Ocean Data Station

ODC Order of Discalced Carmelites

ODESSA Organisation der SS-Angehörigen (German: Organization of SS members)

ODI Overseas Development Institute

ODM Ministry of Overseas Development

ODV eau de vie (French: cognac)

o.e. omissions excepted

Oe oersted

OE Old English (language)

OEA Overseas Education Association

OECD Organization for Economic Cooperation and Development

OED Oxford English Dictionary

OEEC Organization for European Economic Cooperation (superseded by OECD)

OEM original equipment manufacturer

OES Order of the Eastern Star

OF Oddfellows; oil-filled; oil-fired; old-face (type); Old French (language); Order of the Founder (of the Salvation Army); oxidizing flame

OFA oncofetal antigen

O factor oscillation factor

off. offer(ed); office; officer; official; officinal

OFFER Office of Electricity Regulation

OFGAS Office of Gas Supply

OFLOT Office of the National Lottery

OFM Order of Friars Minor (Franciscans)

OFMCap. Order of Friars Minor Capuchin (Franciscan order)

OFMConv. Order of Friars Minor Conventual (Franciscan order)

OFr Old French

OFR Order of the Federal Republic of Nigeria

OFris Old Frisian

OFS Orange Free State

OFT Office of Fair Trading

OFTEL Office of Telecommunications

OFWAT Office of Water Services

o.g. original gum; own goal

OG Officer of the Guard; ogee; original gum

OGael Old Gaelic

OGL open general licence

OGM ordinary general meeting

Ogpu Obyedinyonnoye Gosudarstvennoye Politicheskoye Upravleniye (Russian: United State Political Administration; Soviet state security system, 1923–34)

OGS Oratory of the Good Shepherd

OH Ohio

OHC overhead cam

OHG Old High German

OHMS On Her Majesty's Service

OHN occupational health nurse

OHNC occupational health nursing certificate

OHP overhead projector

OHS occupational health service; open-hearth steel

OHV overhead valve

OIC officer in charge

OIr Old Irish

OIt Old Italian

OJ Order of Jamaica

OJT on-the-job training

OK all correct (from *orl korrect*, phonetic spelling); Oklahoma

OKH Oberkommando der Heeres (German Army High Command, World War II)

Okla. Oklahoma

ol. oil (Latin *oleum*)

Ol. Olympiad

OL oculus laevus (Latin: left eye); Oldham; Old Latin; on-line; operating licence; (Officer of the) Order of Leopold

Old Test. Old Testament

OLE object linking and embedding

O level Ordinary level (replaced by GCSE)

OLG Old Low German

o.m. old measurement

OM old man; optical microscopy; Order of Merit; organic matter

OMC operation and maintenance costs

OMCS Office of the Minister for the Civil Service

OMI Oblate(s) of Mary Immaculate

OMM (Canada) Officer of the Order of Military Merit

omn. hor. omni hora (Latin: every hour)

OMO one-man operator *or* operation (of buses)

o.n. omni nocte (Latin: every night)

ON octane number; Old Norse; Ontario; (Jamaica) Order of the Nation

ONC Ordinary National Certificate; Orthopaedic Nursing Certificate

OND Ophthalmic Nursing Diploma; Ordinary National Diploma

ONF Old Norman French

ONG organisation non-gouvernementale (French: nongovernmental organization)

o.n.o. or near(est) offer

Ont. Ontario

ONZ Order of New Zealand

o/o on order

O/o offers over

OO once-over (i.e. a preliminary inspection)

OOD object-oriented design; officer of the day; officer of the deck

OOL object-oriented language

OON Officer of the Order of the Niger

OOP object-oriented programming

OOT out of town

OOW officer of the watch

op. opera (Latin: works); operation; operator; opposite; optical; opus (Latin: a work; *see also* Op.)

o.p. opposite prompt side (i.e. actor's right); out of print; overproof (of alcohol)

Op. Opus (preceding a number; indicating a piece by a particular composer)

OP observation post; old prices; open policy; opposite prompt side (i.e. actor's right); Ordo Praedicatorum (Latin: (of the) Order of Preachers; Dominicans); osmotic pressure; other people; out of print; outpatient; overproof (of alcohol)

op-amp operational amplifier

op art optical art

OPAS Occupational Pensions Advisory Service

OPB Occupational Pensions Board

OPC ordinary Portland cement

op. cit. opere citato (Latin: in the work cited; used in textual annotations)

OPCON operational control

OPCS Office of Population Censuses and Surveys

OPEC Organization of Petroleum-Exporting Countries

OPers Old Persian

OPEX operational, executive, and administrative personnel (in the UN)

ophthal. ophthalmic; ophthalmologist; ophthalmology

OPM (USA) other people's money; output per man

o.p.n. ora pro nobis (Latin: pray for us)

OPO one-person operator *or* operation (of buses)

opp. opuses; opposed; opposite; opposition

OPP oriented polypropene (in **OPP film**, used for packaging)

OPQ occupational personality questionnaire

OPr Old Provençal

OPruss Old Prussian

ops. operations

OP's other people's (as in **OP's cigarettes**)

opt. optative; optical; optician; optics; optimal; optimum; optional

OQ Officer of the National Order of Quebec

or. orange; orient(al)

o.r. owner's risk

OR official receiver; operational requirement; operational research; or (from its sense in logic, as in **OR gate**, **OR operation**); Oregon; other ranks; owner's risk

Oracle optional reception of announcements by coded line electronics (teletext service of Independent Television)

o.r.b. owner's risk of breakage

orch. orchestra(l); orchestrated by

ord. ordain(ed); order; ordinal; ordinance; ordinary; ordnance

o.r.d. owner's risk of damage

ordn. ordnance

Ore. Oregon

org. organic; organization; organized

orig. origin; original(ly); originate(d)

ORL otorhinolaryngology (ear, nose, and throat specialty; ENT)

ornithol. ornithological; ornithology

OROM optical read-only memory

ors. others

ORS Operational Research Society

ORSL Order of the Republic of Sierra Leone

Orth. Orthodox (religion)

o.s. oculus sinister (Latin: left eye); old series; only son; outside (measurement)

o/s out of stock; outsize (of clothing); outstanding

Os osmium

OS oculus sinister (Latin: left eye); Old Saxon (language); Old School; Old Style (method of reckoning dates); operating system; Ordinary Seaman; Ordnance Survey; out of stock; outsize (of clothing)

OS/2 Operating System/2 (produced by IBM and Microsoft)

OSA Order of St Augustine (Augustinians)

OSB Order of St Benedict (Benedictines)

osc (graduate of) overseas staff college

OSC Order of St Clare (Poor Clares)

OSCAR Orbital Satellites Carrying Amateur Radio; Organization for Sickle Cell Anaemia Research

OSD Order of St Dominic (Dominicans)

OSE operational support equipment

OSF Open Software Foundation; Order of St Francis (Franciscans)

OSFC Order of St Francis, Capuchin
O/Sig Ordinary Signalman
OSl Old Slavonic
OSM Order of the Servants of Mary (Servites)
OSNC Orient Steam Navigation Company
OSO orbiting solar observatory
o.s.p. obiit sine prole (Latin: died without issue)
OSp Old Spanish
O.SS.S Ordo Sanctissimi Salvatoris (Latin: (of the) Order of the Most Holy Saviour; Bridgettines)
O.SS.T Ordo Sanctissimae Trinitatis Redemptionis Captivorum (Latin: (of the) Order of the Most Holy Trinity for the Redemption of Captives; Trinitarians)
OST (USA) Office of Science and Technology
osteo. osteopath(ic)
OStJ Officer of the Order of St John of Jerusalem
OSU Order of St Ursula (Ursulines)
OSUK Ophthalmological Society of the United Kingdom
OT occupational therapy; Old Testament; operating theatre; (Australia) Overland Telegraph (from Adelaide to Darwin); overtime
OTB (USA) off-track betting
OTC Officers' Training Corps; one-stop-inclusive tour charter; Organization for Trade Cooperation; over the counter (as in **OTC market** (in securities); **OTC medicines**); oxytetracycline (an antibiotic)
OTE on-target earnings (for a salesman)
OTEC ocean thermal-energy conversion
OTeut Old Teutonic
OTH over the horizon (as in **OTH radar**)
OTS opportunities to see
ott. ottava (Italian: octave)
OTT over the top (i.e. excessive)
OTU operational training unit
OTurk Old Turkish
OU Open University; Oxford University
OUDS Oxford University Dramatic Society
OUP (Northern Ireland) Official Unionist Party; Oxford University Press
OURT Order of the United Republic of Tanzania
ov. overture
o.v.c. other valuable consideration (in contract law)
o.v.n.o. or very near offer
Ovra Opera di vigilanza e di repressione dell'anti-fascismo (Italian secret police of the Fascist regime)
O/W oil in water (emulsion)
OX Oxford
Oxbridge Oxford and Cambridge (Universities; regarded collectively)

OXFAM Oxford Committee for Famine Relief
Oxon Oxfordshire (Latin *Oxonia*); Oxoniensis (Latin: of Oxford)
oz ounce(s) (Italian *onza*)
oz T troy ounce.

P

p electric dipole moment; momentum (bold ital. in vector equations); para (as in **p-cresol**); penny; piano (Italian; softly, quietly); pico- (prefix indicating 10^{-9} as in **ps**, picosecond); pressure; proton; p-type (semiconductor)
p. page; part; participle; partim (Latin: in part); pass(ed); passing showers; past; per (Latin: by, for); person; pint; pipe; pius (Latin: holy); population; post (Latin: after); primus (Latin: first); pro (Latin: for, in favour of); purl
P four hundred; parity; parking (on road signs); pawn; peta- (prefix indicating 10^{-15} as in **PJ**, petajoule); pharmacy (on medicines obtained without a prescription from a pharmacy); phosphate; phosphorus; poise; polynomial (referring to a class of formal languages recognizable in polynomial time); Portugal; Post Office (on maps); power; pressure; proprietary (product); pula (monetary unit of Botswana)
P. Papa (Latin: Pope); Pastor; pater (Latin: father); pedal; Père (French: Father); perennial; populus (Latin: people); post; President; Priest; Prince; Progressive (party, movement, etc.); prompt side (i.e. the actor's left)
P45 a form relating to unemployment benefit issued by the DSS
pa. past
p.a. participial adjective; per annum; press agent
p/a personal account
Pa pascal; protactinium
Pa. Pennsylvania
PA Paisley; Pakistan Army; Panama; particular average; Pennsylvania; pernicious anaemia; personal accident; personal account; personal allowance; personal appearance; personal assistant; Pierre Allain (climbing boot; named after its inventor); Piper Aircraft (as in **PA-28**); political agent; Post Adjutant; power amplifier; power of attorney; press agent; Press Association; private account; programme assistant; public address (system); publicity agent; Publishers Association; purchasing agent
PABA *p*-aminobenzoic acid
PABX private automatic branch exchange
pac passed (final examination of the) advanced class (of the Military College of Science)
Pac. Pacific
PAC Pan-African(ist) Congress; Public Accounts Committee; put-

and-call (option)
P-A-C parent, adult, child (in transactional analysis)
PACE Police and Criminal Evidence Act (1984); Protestant and Catholic Encounter
PACT Producers' Alliance for Cinema and Television
PaD Pennsylvania Dutch
PAD passive air defence
p. ae. partes aequales (Latin: equal parts)
PaG Pennsylvania German
PAg Professional Agronomist
PAGB Proprietary Association of Great Britain
PAICV (Cape Verde) Partido Africano da Independencia de Cabo Verde (Portuguese: African Party for the Independence of Cape Verde)
Pak. Pakistan(i)
Pak Re Pakistan rupee (monetary unit)
pal. palaeography; palaeontology
Pal. Palace; Palestine
PAL phase alternation line
palaeontol. palaeontology
pam. pamphlet
Pan. Panama
PAN peroxyacetyl nitrate (atmospheric pollutant); polyacrylonitrile (polymer)
P&E plant and equipment
P & F chart point-and-figure chart
P & L profit and loss
P & O Peninsular and Oriental (Steamship Company)
P&OSNCo Peninsular and Oriental Steam Navigation Company
p & p postage and packing
PAO Prince Albert's Own (regiment); public affairs officer
par. paragraph; parallel; parenthesis; parish
Par. Paraguay
PAR perimeter acquisition radar; phased-array radar; precision approach radar; programme analysis review
para. paragraph
par. aff. pars affecta (Latin: (to the) part affected)
paren. parenthesis
parens. parentheses
Parl. Parliament; parliamentary
parl. proc. parliamentary procedure
Parly Sec. Parliamentary Secretary
part. participle; particular; partner(ship)
PAS public-address system
PASCAL a programming language (named after Blaise Pascal (1623–62), French philosopher, mathematician, and physicist)
pass. passage; passenger; passim (Latin: here and there throughout); passive
pat. patent(ed)
PAT preauthorized automatic transfer; Professional Association of Teachers

patd patented

path. pathological; pathology

Pat. Off. Patent Office

pat. pend. patent pending

PAU Pan American Union

PAX private automatic exchange

PAYE pay as you earn (income tax); pay as you enter

payt payment

PAYV pay as you view

Pb lead (Latin *plumbum)*

PB pass book; personal best; Pharmacopoeia Britannica (Latin: British Pharmacopoeia); phenobarbitone; plastic-bonded; Plymouth Brethren; power brakes; Prayer Book; purl into back of stitch

PBA poor bloody assistant

PBAB please bring a bottle

PBB polybrominated biphenyl (toxic constituent of plastics, etc.)

PBI poor bloody infantry(man)

pbk paperback (book)

PBM permanent benchmark; play by mail (of games)

PBR payment by results

PBS Public Broadcasting Service

PBX private branch exchange

pc parsec

pc. piece; price

p.c. per cent; postcard; post cibum (Latin: after meals; in prescriptions)

PC Panama Canal; Parish Council(lor); Parliamentary Commissioner (ombudsman); Past Commander; (Ireland) Peace Commissioner; perpetual curate; personal computer; Plaid Cymru; Police Constable; (USA) politically correct; polycarbonate; polypropylene carbonate (plastic); Post Commander; potentially correct; Prince Consort; printed circuit; Privy Council(lor); process control; (Canada) Progressive Conservative; propositional calculus; propylene carbonate

P/C petty cash; price(s) current

PCB petty cash book; polychlorinated biphenyl (toxic constituent of plastics, etc.); printed-circuit board; private car benefits

PCC parochial church council; Press Complaints Commission

PCE Postgraduate Certificate of Education

P-Celtic one of two main groups of languages that developed from Common Celtic. *See also* Q-Celtic

pcf pounds per cubic foot

PCFC Polytechnics and Colleges Funding Council

pci pounds per cubic inch

PCL printer control language

pcm per calendar month

PCM phase-contrast microscope; photochemical machinery; protein-calorie malnutrition; pulse-code modulation

PCMO Principal Colonial Medical Officer

PCN personal communications network

PCOD polycystic ovary disease

p-code an intermediate language designed as the target language for UCSD Pascal

PCP pentachlorophenol (wood preservative); phencyclohexyl-piperidine (the drug phencylidine; angel dust); pneumonia (complication of Aids); prime commercial paper

pcs. pieces; prices

PCS (Scotland) Principal Clerk of Session

pct per cent

PCTE portable common tool environment

p.c.u. passenger car unit

pd paid; passed

p.d. per diem (Latin: daily); post-dated; potential difference

Pd palladium

PD per diem (Latin: daily); Pharmacopoeia Dublinensis (Latin: Dublin Pharmacopoeia); (USA) Police Department; port dues; postal district; preventive detention; probability of detection; (Ireland) Progressive Democrat(s); progressive disease; property damage; public domain (software)

P/D price–dividend (in **P/D ratio**)

PDA personal digital assistant

PDGF platelet-derived growth factor

pdl poundal

PDL page description language; poverty datum line

PDM physical distribution management

PDN public data network

PDPA People's Democratic Party of Afghanistan

pdq pretty damn quick

PDR People's Democratic Republic; price–dividend ratio

PDRA postdoctoral research assistant

P/D ratio price–dividend ratio

PDS Parkinson's Disease Society

PDSA People's Dispensary for Sick Animals

PDT Pacific Daylight Time; personal development technology

PDTC Professional Dancer's Training Course Diploma

p.e. personal estate; printer's error

PE personal effects; Peru; Peterborough; Pharmacopoeia Edinburgensis (Latin: Edinburgh Pharmacopoeia); phase-encoded (of tape format); physical education; plastic explosive; polyeth(yl)ene; Port Elizabeth (South Africa); potential energy; Presiding Elder; printer's error; probable error; procurement executive; Protestant Episcopal

P/E price–earnings (in **P/E ratio**)

PEA Physical Education Association of Great Britain and Northern Ireland

PEC photoelectric cell

ped. pedal; pedestal; pedestrian

PEDir Director of Physical Education

PEI (Canada) Prince Edward Island

pen. peninsula(r)

Pen. Peninsula

PEN International Association of Poets, Playwrights, Editors, Essayists, and Novelists

PEng Member of the Society of Professional Engineers

Penn. Pennsylvania

Pent. Pentecost

PEP peak envelope power; personal equity plan; political and economic planning

per. percentile; period; person

Per. Persia(n)

PER price–earnings ratio; Professional and Executive Recruitment

PERA Production Engineering Research Association of Great Britain

per an. per annum (Latin: yearly)

P/E ratio price–earnings ratio

perc. percussion

per con per contra (Latin: on the other side)

perf. perfect; perforated; perforation; performed (by)

perp. perpendicular

per pro. per procurationem

pers. person; personal(ly); perspective

Pers. Persia(n)

pert. pertaining

PERT project evaluation and review technique

Peruv. Peruvian

PEST Political, Environmental, Social, and Technological (framework for analysing these aspects of a business environment); Pressure for Economic and Social Toryism (left-wing Conservative group)

pet. petroleum

Pet. Peter

PET polyeth(yl)ene terephthalate (plastic used in food packaging); positron-emission tomography (as in **PET scan**); potentially exempt transfer

PETN pentaerythritol tetranitrate (explosive)

PETRAS Polytechnic Educational Technology Resources Advisory Service

Petriburg. Petriburgensis (Latin: (Bishop) of Peterborough)

petrog. petrography

petrol. petrology

PEX a discounted airline fare (probably a back formation from APEX, advance-purchase excursion)

pf pfennig (German currency); piano (instrument; from *pianoforte)*

pf. perfect; preferred (stock); proof

p.f. piano e forte (Italian; soft and then loud); più forte (Italian; louder); pro forma (invoice)

pF picofarad(s)

PF Patriotic Front; Procurator-Fiscal

PFA Professional Footballers' Association; pulverized fuel ash

pfc passed flying college (in the RAF)

PFC polychlorinated fluorocarbon (synthetic resin)

pfd preferred

pfg pfennig (German currency)

PFLO Popular Front for the Liberation of Oman

PFLP Popular Front for the Liberation of Palestine

PFP Partnership for Peace; personal financial planning

pg. page

p.g. paying guest; proof gallon (of alcohol)

Pg. Portugal; Portuguese

PG parental guidance (certification); paying guest; postgraduate; prostaglandin (as in **PGE₁**, etc.)

PGA Professional Golfers' Association

PGCE Postgraduate Certificate of Education

PG Cert Postgraduate Certificate

PG Dip Postgraduate Diploma

PgDn page down (on a keyboard)

PGDRS psychogeriatric dependency rating scale

PGF polypeptide growth factor

PGL persistent generalized lymphadenopathy (a stage of Aids)

PGM precision-guided munition

PGR (Australia) parental guidance recommended (certification); psychogalvanic response

PgUp page up (on a keyboard)

ph phot(s)

ph. phase

pH potential of hydrogen ions (measure of acidity or alkalinity)

Ph phenyl group (in formulae); Philosophy (in degrees)

PH Perth; public health

PHAB Physically Handicapped and Able-Bodied

phar. pharmaceutical; pharmacist; pharmacopoeia; pharmacy

PharB Bachelor of Pharmacy (Latin *Pharmaciae Baccalaureus*)

PharD Doctor of Pharmacy (Latin *Pharmaciae Doctor*)

PharM Master of Pharmacy (Latin *Pharmaciae Magister*)

pharmacol. pharmacology

PhB Bachelor of Philosophy (Latin *Philosophiae Baccalaureus*)

PHC Pharmaceutical Chemist; primary health care

PhD Doctor of Philosophy (Latin *Philosophiae Doctor*)

Phe phenylalanine

PHE Public Health Engineer

PHI permanent health insurance

phil. philological; philology; philosopher; philosophical; philosophy

Phil. Philadelphia; Philharmonic; Philippians; Philippines

Philem. Philemon

Phil. I. Philippine Islands

philol. philological; philology

philos. philosopher; philosophical; philosophy

Phil. Trans. Philosophical Transactions of the Royal Society

of London

PhL Licentiate in Philosophy

PHLS Public Health Laboratory Service

PhM Master of Philosophy (Latin *Philosophiae Magister*)

PhmB Bachelor of Pharmacy

phon. phonetics; phonology

phot. photograph(ic); photographer; photography

photom. photometry

phr. phrase

phren. phrenological; phrenology

phys. physical(ly); physician; physicist; physics; physiological; physiology

phys. ed. physical education

physiol. physiological; physiologist; physiology

p.i. professional indemnity (policy)

PI parainfluenza virus; Philippine Islands; private investigator

PIA Pakistan International Airlines Corporation; Personal Investment Authority

PIARC Permanent International Association of Road Congresses

PIB Prices and Incomes Board (superseded by NBPI)

PIBOR Paris Interbank Offered Rate

pic. piccolo; pictorial

PIC programmable interrupt controller

PID pelvic inflammatory disease; personal identification device; prolapsed intervertebral disc (slipped disc)

PIDS primary immune deficiency syndrome

PIE Proto-Indo-European (language)

PIH pregnancy-induced hypertension

PIK payment in kind

pil. pilula (Latin: pill; in prescriptions)

PILL programmed instruction language learning

PILOT programmed inquiry, learning, or teaching

PIM personal information manager

PIMS profit impact of market strategy

p-i-n p-type, intrinsic, n-type (semiconductor)

PIN personal identification number (used, with cash or credit card, to access computer-based bank accounts, etc.)

pinx. pinxit (Latin: (he *or* she) painted it)

PIPPY person inheriting parent's property

PIRA Paper Industries Research Association

PITCOM Parliamentary Information Technology Committee

pixel picture element

pizz. pizzicato (Italian: pinched *or* plucked)

p.j. pyjama

PJ Presiding Judge; Probate Judge; pyjama

pk pack; package; park; peak; peck (unit)

pK potential of *K* (symbol for the dissociation constant; a measure of the strength of acids)

PK Pakistan; personal knowledge; Prausnitz-Kustner (as in **PK test**); psychokinesis

pkg. package

PKI Partai Komunis Indonésia (Indonesian Communist Party)

pkt packet; pocket

pkwy (USA) parkway

pl. place; plate; platoon; plural; pole (measure)

Pl. Place (in street names)

PL Paymaster Lieutenant; Pharmacopoeia Londiniensis (Latin: Pharmacopoeia of London); Plimsoll line (on a ship); Plymouth; Poet Laureate; Poland; Primrose League; product liability; product licence (on labels of medicinal products); programming language (as in **PL/I**, **PL/M**, etc.); public law; public library

PL/I Programming Language I

p.l.a. passengers' luggage in advance

PLA (China) People's Liberation Army; Port of London Authority

plat. plateau; platoon

PLATO programmed logic for automatic teaching operation

plc public limited company (following the name of a company)

PLC product life cycle; public limited company (following the name of a company)

Plen. Plenipotentiary

plf plaintiff

PLG private/light goods (vehicle)

PLI President of the Landscape Institute

PLM Paris–Lyons–Mediterranean (Railway)

PL/M Programming Language for Microcomputers

PLO Palestine Liberation Organization

PLP Parliamentary Labour Party

PLR public lending right

PLSS personal life-support system

pltf plaintiff

PLU people like us

Pluna Primeras Líneas Uruguayas de Navegación Aérea (Uruguayan airline)

plup. pluperfect

plur. plural; plurality

PL/Z Programming Language Zilog

pm. premium

p.m. post meridiem (Latin: after noon); postmortem (examination)

Pm promethium

PM particular metre; Past Master (of a fraternity); Paymaster; Police Magistrate; Postmaster; post meridiem; postmortem (examination); Prime Minister; Provost Marshal

PMA papillary, marginal, attached (gingivitis; in **PMA index**); paramethoxyamphetamine (hallucinogenic drug); personal military assistant; polymethyl acrylate (synthetic polymer)

PMBX private manual branch exchange

PMC Personnel Management Centre

PMG Paymaster General; Postmaster General; Provost Marshal General

p.m.h. per man-hour

PMH previous medical history

pmk postmark

PML probable maximum loss

PMO Principal Medical Officer

PMRAFNS Princess Mary's Royal Air Force Nursing Service

PMS premenstrual syndrome; President of the Miniature Society

pmt payment

PMT photomechanical transfer; premenstrual tension

PMX private manual exchange

pn p-type n-type semiconductor (as in **pn junction**)

p.n. please note; promissory note; proton number

PN postnatal; promissory note; pseudonoise (as in **PN sequence**); psychoneurotic

PNA Psychiatric Nurses Association

PNB Philippine National Bank

PNdB perceived noise decibel(s)

PNEU Parents' National Educational Union

PNG Papua New Guinea (abbrev. or IVR)

PNI psychoneuroimmunology

pnp p-type n-type p-type semiconductor (as in **pnp transistor**)

PNS parasympathetic nervous system

PNV (Spain) Partido Nacional Vasco (Basque Nationalist Party)

pnxt pinxit (Latin: he or she) painted it)

p.o. per os (Latin: by mouth; in prescriptions)

Po polonium

PO parole officer; personnel officer; petty officer; Philharmonic Orchestra; pilot officer; Portsmouth; postal order; Post Office

POA primary optical area (in graphic design); Prison Officers' Association (trade union)

POB Post Office Box

POC port of call

POD pay(ment) on delivery; Pocket Oxford Dictionary; port of debarkation

POE port of embarkation; port of entry

poet. poetic(al); poetry

POETS day Friday (piss off early tomorrow's Saturday)

POEU Post Office Engineers Union

P. of W. Prince of Wales

POGO Polar Orbiting Geophysical Observatory

pol. political; politics

Pol. Poland; Polish

POL petroleum, oil, and lubricants

pol. econ. political economy

polit. political; politics

POM prescription-only medicine

POMEF Political Office Middle East Force

Ponsi person of no strategical importance

Ponti person of no tactical importance

POO Post Office order

pop. popular(ly); population

POP plaster of Paris; point of purchase; Post Office preferred (size of envelopes, etc.); printing-out paper; proof of purchase

p.o.r. pay(able) on receipt; pay on return; port of refuge

Port. Portugal; Portuguese

pos. position; positive

POS point of sale

poss. possession; possessive; possible; possibly

POSSLQ (USA) person of the opposite sex sharing living quarters

Possum patient-operated selector mechanism (phonetic spelling of POSM)

POST Parliamentary Office of Science and Technology; point-of-sales terminal (in supermarkets, etc.)

posth. posthumous(ly)

pot. potassium; potential; potentiometer

POUNC Post Office Users' National Council

POV point of view

POW Prince of Wales; prisoner of war

pp past participle; per procurationem (Latin: by authority of; in correspondence, used by signatory on behalf of someone else); pianissimo (Italian; very quietly)

pp. pages

p.p. parcel post; per person; per procurationem; post-paid; post prandium (Latin: after a meal; in prescriptions); prepaid; privately printed

PP parcel post; parish priest; Past President; Patres (Latin: Fathers); pellagra-preventive (in **PP factor**, former name for the vitamin nicotinic acid); polyprop(yl)ene; prepositional phrase

PPA Periodical Publishers' Association; Pre-School Playgroups Association

ppb parts per billion

PPB paper, printing, and binding; party political broadcast; planning-programming-budgeting (system)

PPBS planning-programming-budgeting system

PPC Patres Conscripti (Latin: Conscript Fathers, members of the Roman Senate); pour prendre congé (French: to take leave); progressive patient care

PPCLI Princess Patricia's Canadian Light Infantry

ppd post-paid; prepaid

PPD purified protein derivative (of tuberculin)

PPE personal protective equipment; philosophy, politics, and economics (course at Oxford University)

pph. pamphlet

PPH post-partum haemorrhage

PPI plan-position indicator; policy proof of interest

PPInstHE Past President of the Institute of Highway Engineers

PPIStructE Past President of the Institution of Structural Engineers

PPITB Printing and Publishing Industry Training Board

PPL Phonographic Performance Limited

ppm pages per minute; parts per million; pulse per minute

PPM peak programme meter

PPMA Produce Packaging and Marketing Association

PPN public packet network

ppp pianississimo (Italian; as quietly as possible)

PPP Pakistan's People's Party; personal pension plan; private patients plan; purchasing power parity

PPPS post post postscriptum (Latin: third postscript)

ppr present participle

PPR printed paper rate (of postage)

PPRA Past President of the Royal Academy

PPRBA Past President of the Royal Society of British Artists

PPRBS Past President of the Royal Society of British Sculptors

PPRE Past President of the Royal Society of Painter-Etchers and Engravers

p.pro. per procurationem

PPROI Past President of the Royal Institute of Oil Painters

PPRTPI Past President of the Royal Town Planning Institute

PPS Parliamentary Private Secretary; pelvic pain syndrome; post postscriptum (Latin: further postscript); (Australia) prescribed payments system; Principal Private Secretary

PPSIAD Past President of the Society of Industrial Artists and Designers

ppt. precipitate

PPTA (New Zealand) Post-primary Teachers Association

PPU Peace Pledge Union

pq previous question

PQ parliamentary question; Province of Quebec

pr pair; paper; power

pr. present; price; print(ed); printer; printing; pronoun

p.r. per rectum (Latin: by the rectum)

Pr praseodymium; propyl group (in formulae)

Pr. Priest; Prince; Provençal

PR parliamentary report; payroll; percentile rank; personal representative; photographic reconnaissance; Populus Romanus (Latin: the Roman people); Pre-Raphaelite; press release; Preston; prize ring; profit rate; proportional representation; public relations; Puerto Rican; Puerto Rico

PRA President of the Royal Academy; (USA) Public Roads Administration

PRB Pre-Raphaelite Brotherhood

PRBS President of the Royal Society of British Sculptors

PRC People's Republic of China

PRCS President of the Royal College of Surgeons

PRE President of the Royal Society of Painter-Etchers and Engravers

Preb. Prebend(ary)

prec. preceding

pred. predicate

pref. preface; prefatory; preferably; preference; preferred; prefix

prelim. preliminary

prem. premium

prep. preparation; preparatory; preposition

PREPP Post-Registration Education and Practice Project (for establishing standards of nursing practice)

pres. present (time); presidency; presidential; presumed

Pres. Presbyter(ian); President

pret. preterite

prev. previous(ly)

PRF pulse repetition frequency

PRHA President of the Royal Hibernian Academy

PRI Plastics and Rubber Institute; President of the Royal Institute of Painters in Water Colours

PRIA President of the Royal Irish Academy

PRIAS President of the Royal Incorporation of Architects in Scotland

PRIBA President of the Royal Institute of British Architects

prim. primary; primitive

prin. principal; principle

Prin. Principal

print. printing

PRISA Public Relations Institute of South Africa

priv. private; privative

p.r.n. pro re nata (Latin: as the situation demands; in prescriptions)

pro. profession(al)

Pro proline

Pr.O Press Officer

PRO Public Record Office; public relations officer

prob. probable; probably; problem

proc. procedure; proceedings; process

Proc. Proceedings; Proctor

prod. produce(d); producer; product; production

prof. profession(al)

Prof. Professor

prog. prognosis; program; programme; progress; progressive

Prog. Progressive (party, movement, etc.)

PROI President of the Royal Institute of Oil Painters

PROLOG programming in logic (a programming language)

prom. promontory

PROM programmable read-only memory

pron. pronominal; pronoun; pronounce(d); pronunciation

PRONED Promotion of Non-Executive Directors

prop. proper(ly); property; proposition; proprietary; proprietor

PROP Preservation of the Rights of Prisoners

propr proprietor

PRORM Pay and Records Office, Royal Marines

pros. prosody

Pros. Atty Prosecuting Attorney

Prot. Protectorate; Protestant

pro tem. pro tempore (Latin: for the time being)

prov. proverb; proverbial(ly); province; provincial; provisional

Prov. Provençal; Provence; Proverbs; Province; Provost

prox. proximo (Latin: in the next (month))

prox. acc. proxime accessit (Latin: (he or she) came nearest; next in order of merit to the winner)

PRP profit- related pay

prs pairs

PRs Pakistan rupee (monetary unit)

PRS Performing Right Society Ltd; President of the Royal Society

PRSA President of the Royal Scottish Academy; Public Relations Society of America

PRSE President of the Royal Society of Edinburgh

PRSH President of the Royal Society for the Promotion of Health

PRSW President of the Royal Scottish Water Colour Society

PRT petroleum revenue tax

PRUAA President of the Royal Ulster Academy of Arts

Prus. Prussia(n)

PRWA President of the Royal West of England Academy

PRWS President of the Royal Society of Painters in Water Colours

ps passed school of instruction (of officers); picosecond(s); postscript

ps. pieces; pseudonym

Ps positronium

Ps. (Book of) Psalms; Psalm

PS paddle steamer; Parliamentary Secretary; passenger steamer; Pastel Society; Permanent Secretary; phrase structure; Police Sergeant; polystyrene; postscript; power steering; private secretary; Privy Seal; prompt side (i.e. the actor's left); (Australia) public service (equivalent to the civil service)

psa Graduate of RAF Staff College

Psa. (Book of) Psalms; Psalm

PSA Petty Sessions Area; pleasant Sunday afternoon; President of the Society of Antiquaries; (Australia) Prices Surveillance Authority; Property Services Agency; prostatic specific antigen; (New Zealand) Public Service Association

p's and q's manners (phonetic spelling of p(lea)se and (than)k you's)

PSB (Japan) Postal Savings Bureau

PSBR public sector borrowing requirement

psc passed staff college

PSD Petty Sessional Divison

PSDR public sector debt requirement

PSE Pacific Stock Exchange; pale soft exudate (in meat processing); Pidgin Sign English; psychological stress evaluator (lie detector)

pseud. pseudonym

psf pounds per square foot

PSG phrase-structure grammar

PSHFA Public Servants Housing Finance Association

psi pounds per square inch

PSI Policy Studies Institute

psia pounds per square inch, absolute

PSIAD President of the Society of Industrial Artists and Designers

psid pounds per square inch, differential

psig pounds per square inch, gauge

PSIS Permanent Secretaries Committee on the Intelligence Services

PSK phase shift keying

PSL private-sector liquidity; public-sector loan(s)

psm passed school of music (Certificate of the Royal Military School of Music)

PSMA President of the Society of Marine Artists

PSNC Pacific Steam Navigation Company

PSO personal staff officer; Principal Scientific Officer

PSP phenolsulphonphthalein (in **PSP test** for kidney function)

Pss Psalms

PSS Packet Switch Stream (PPN of British Telecom); postscripts

PSSC Personal Social Services Council

psso pass slipped stitch over

PST (USA, Canada) Pacific Standard Time

PSTN public switched telephone network

PSV public service vehicle

PSW psychiatric social worker

psych. psychological; psychology

psychoanal. psychoanalysis

psychol. psychological; psychologist; psychology

pt part; patient; payment; pint (abbrev. or symbol); point (abbrev. or in printing) symbol); port

pt. preterite

p.t. part time; past tense; pro tempore (Latin: for the time being)

Pt platinum; Point (in place names); Port (in place names)

PT (USA) Pacific Time; (USA) patrol torpedo (in **PT boat**); physical therapy; physical training; physiotherapist; postal telegraph; post town; pupil teacher; purchase tax

Pta peseta (Spanish monetary unit)

PTA Parent–Teacher Association; Passenger Transport Authority

PT boat (USA) patrol torpedo boat

PTC percutaneous transhepatic cholangiography; phenylthiocarbamide (referring to the inherited ability to taste it); plasma thromboplastin component

PTCA percutaneous transluminal coronary angioplasty

Pte Private; (India, etc.) private limited company (after company name; equivalent to Ltd)

PTE Passenger Transport Executive

PTFE polytetrafluoroeth(yl)ene

ptg printing

PTI physical training instructor; Press Trust of India; public tool interface

PTM pulse-time modulation

PTN pay through the nose; public telephone network (of British Telecom); public transportation network

PTO please turn over; power takeoff; public telecommunications operator; Public Trustee Office

ptp past participle

pts parts; payments; pints; points; ports

Pts. Portsmouth

PTS Philatelic Traders' Society

ptsc passed technical staff college

PTSD post-traumatic stress disorder

PTT Postal, Telegraph, and Telephone Administration

Pty (Australia, South Africa, etc.) Proprietary (after a company name; equivalent to Ltd)

p.u. paid up

Pu plutonium

PU passed urine; pick-up; polyurethane

pub. public; publican; publication; publish(ed); publisher; publishing

pubd published

pub. doc. public document

publ. public; publication; publicity; published; publisher

pubn publication

pubr publisher

pulv. pulvis (Latin: powder)

PUO pyrexia (fever) of unknown origin

pur. purchase(r)

PUS Permanent Undersecretary

PUVA psoralen ultraviolet A (treatment for psoriasis)

p.v. per vaginam (Latin: by the vagina)

PV petite vitesse (French: goods or slow train)

PVA polyvinyl acetate (synthetic resin); polyvinyl alcohol

PVC polyvinyl chloride (synthetic resin)

PVD peripheral vascular disease

PVF polyvinyl fluoride (synthetic resin)

PVP polyvinyl pyrrolidone (synthetic resin)

PVS persistent vegetative state; postviral syndrome (myalgic encephalomyelitis)

PVSM (India) Param Vishishc Seva Medal

Pvt. Private

p.w. per week

PW policewoman; prisoner of war; public works

PWA person with Aids

PWD Public Works Department

PWE Political Welfare Executive

PWLB Public Works Loan Board

pwt pennyweight

px Pedro Ximénez (grape; referring to sweet wines and sherries)

PX please exchange; (USA) Post Exchange (army or navy retail store); private exchange

pxt pinxit (Latin: (he or she) painted it)

py pyridine (used in formulae)

PY Paraguay

pyo pick your own (fruit, etc.)

PZI protamine zinc insulin (diabetes treatment)

PZS President of the Zoological Society

Q

q quark; quintal (100 kg)

q. quaere (Latin: inquire); quaque (Latin: every); quart; quarter; quarterly; query; question; quire

Q quality (in **Q factor**); quantity of heat; queen; quetzal (Guatemalan monetary unit); the highest level of security according to the Nuclear Regulatory Commission (as in **Q clearance**)

Q. quarterly; Quartermaster; quarter-page (in advertisement placing); Quarto (Shakespeare manuscript); Quebec; Queen; question; (Sir Arthur Thomas) Quiller-Couch (1863–1944, British writer)

QA quality assurance

QAB Queen Anne's Bounty

QAIMNS Queen Alexandra's Imperial Military Nursing Service

QAM quadrature amplitude modulation

Q & A question and answer

Qantas Queensland and Northern Territory Aerial Service (Australian national airline)

QARANC Queen Alexandra's Royal Army Nursing Corps

QARNNS Queen Alexandra's Royal Naval Nursing Service

QB Queen's Bench; queen's bishop

QBD Queen's Bench Division

QBI quite bloody impossible

QBP queen's bishop's pawn

QC quality control; Quartermaster Corps; Queen's Counsel

Q-Celtic one of two main groups of languages developed from Common Celtic. See also P-Celtic

QCVSA Queen's Commendation for Valuable Service in the Air

q.d. quaque die (Latin: every day)

q.d.s. quater in die sumendus (Latin: to be taken four times a day)

q.e. quod est (Latin: which is)

QE2 Queen Elizabeth II (passenger liner)

QED quantum electrodynamics; quod erat demonstrandum (Latin: which was to be proved)

QEF quod erat faciendum (Latin: which was to be done)

QEH Queen Elizabeth Hall (London)

QEI quod erat inveniendum (Latin: which was to be discovered or found out)

QEO Queen Elizabeth's Own

QF quick-firing

QFD quantum flavourdynamics

QFSM Queen's Fire Service Medal for Distinguished Service

QGM Queen's Gallantry Medal

q.h. quaque hora (Latin: every hour)

QHC Queen's Honorary Chaplain

QHDS Queen's Honorary Dental Surgeon

QHNS Queen's Honorary Nursing Sister

QHP Queen's Honorary Physician

QHS Queen's Honorary Surgeon

QI quartz–iodine (in **QI lamp**)

q.i.d. quater in die (Latin: four times a day)

QISAM queued indexed sequential access method

QKt queen's knight

QKtP queen's knight's pawn

ql quintal (100 kg)

q.l. quantum libet (Latin: as much as you please; in prescriptions)

QL query language

Qld Queensland

qlty quality

qly quarterly

qm. quomodo (Latin: by what means)

q.m. quaque mane (Latin: every morning; in prescriptions)

QM quantum mechanics; Quartermaster; Queen's Messenger

QMAAC Queen Mary's Army Auxiliary Corps

QMC Quartermaster Corps

Q. Mess. Queen's Messenger

QMG Quartermaster-General

Qmr Quartermaster

QMS Quartermaster Sergeant

q.n. quaque nocte (Latin: every night; in prescriptions)

QN queen's knight

QNI Queen's Nursing Institute

QNP queen's knight's pawn

qnt. quintet

QO qualified officer

QOOH Queen's Own Oxfordshire Hussars

Q(ops) Quartering (operations)

q.p. quantum placet

QP queen's pawn

q.pl. quantum placet (Latin: as much as seems good; in prescriptions)

QPM Queen's Police Medal

QPR Queen's Park Rangers (football club)

qq. questions

Qq. Quartos (Shakespeare manuscripts)

qq. hor. quaque hora (Latin: every hour; in prescriptions)

qq.v. quae vide (Latin: which (words, items, etc.) see; textual cross reference)

qr. quarter; quarterly; quire

QR queen's rook; quick response; riyal (monetary unit of Qatar)

QRIH Queen's Royal Irish Hussars

QRP queen's rook's pawn

qrs quarters

QRV Qualified Valuer, Real Estate Institute of New South Wales

q.s. quantum sufficit (Latin: as much as will suffice; in prescriptions); quarter section (of land)

QS quadraphonic-stereophonic (of audio equipment); quantity surveyor; quarter sessions; Queen's Scholar

QSM (New Zealand) Queen's Service Medal

QSO quasistellar object (i.e. a quasar); (New Zealand) Queen's Service Order

QSS quasistellar source

QSTOL quiet short takeoff and landing

qt quart

qt. quantity; quartet

q.t. quiet (as in **on the q.t.**)

qtly quarterly

qto quarto

QTOL quiet takeoff and landing

qtr quarter

qty quantity

qu. quart; quarter; quarterly; queen; query; question

quad. quadrant; quadraphonic; quadrilateral; quadruplicate

qualn qualification

quango quasi-autonomous nongovernmental organization

quar. quarter; quarterly

quasar quasistellar object

quat. four (Latin *quattuor*; in prescriptions)

Que. Quebec

ques. question

quint. quintuplicate

quor. quorum

quot. quotation

quotid. quotidie (Latin: daily)

q.v. quantum vis (Latin: as much as you wish); quod vide (Latin: which (word, item, etc.) see; textual cross reference)

QWERTY a standard keyboard in English-speaking countries (from the first six of the upper row of keys on a typewriter)

QWL quality of work(ing) life

qy query

R

r internal resistance; radius; radius vector; ray (in tonic solfa)

r. radius; railway; rain; range; rare; received; recipe; recto; replacing; residence; resides; right; rises; river; road; rod (unit of length); rouble; rubber; ruled; run(s); rupee

R eighty; molar gas constant; a radical (in formulae, as in **ROH**); radius; rand (South African monetary unit); ratio; Réaumur (temperature scale); resistance; (Australia, USA) restricted (certification); reverse (on selector mechanism of vehicle with automatic transmission); roentgen; rook; rough (in **R-form** of a bacterial colony)

R. rabbi; Radical; radius; railway; rector; Regiment; Regina (Latin: Queen); registered; Regius; regular (clothing size); Republican; reserve; response (in Christian liturgy); Respublica (Latin: Republic); Rex (Latin: King); right *or* (in the theatre) stage right; River; road; rouble; Royal; Rue (French: street)

Ra radium

RA Argentina; Rear-Admiral; Royal Academy; Royal Artillery

R/A refer to acceptor (on a bill of exchange)

RAA Regional Arts Association; Royal Academy of Arts

RAAF Royal Australian Air Force; Royal Auxiliary Air Force

RAAMC Royal Australian Army Medical Corps

Rabb. Rabbinic(al)

RABDF Royal Association of British Dairy Farmers

RABI Royal Agricultural Benevolent Institution

RAC Royal Agricultural College; Royal Armoured Corps; Royal Automobile Club

RACE Research and Development in Advanced Communication Technologies for Europe

RACGP Royal Australian College of General Practitioners

RAChD Royal Army Chaplains' Department

RACI Royal Australian Chemical Institute

RACO Royal Australian College of Ophthalmologists

RACOG Royal Australian College of Obstetricians and Gynaecologists

RACP Royal Australasian College of Physicians

RACS Royal Arsenal Cooperative Society; Royal Australasian College of Surgeons

rad radian

rad. radiator; radical; radius; radix

Rad. Radical

RAD Royal Academy of Dancing

RADA Royal Academy of Dramatic Art

radar radio detection and ranging

RADAR Royal Association for Disability and Rehabilitation

RADC Royal Army Dental Corps

RADIUS Religious Drama Society of Great Britain

RAdm Rear-Admiral

RAE Royal Aerospace (formerly Aircraft) Establishment; Royal Australian Engineers

RAEC Royal Army Educational Corps

RAeroC Royal Aero Club of the United Kingdom

RAeS Royal Aeronautical Society

RAF Royal Air Force

RAFA Royal Air Forces Association

RAFBF Royal Air Force Benevolent Fund

RAFG Royal Air Force Germany

RAFRO Royal Air Force Reserve of Officers

RAFVR Royal Air Force Volunteer Reserve

RAHS Royal Australian Historical Society

RAI Radiotelevisione Italiana (Italian broadcasting corporation; originally Radio Audizioni Italiane); Royal Anthropological Institute

RAIA Royal Australian Institute of Architects

RAIC Reception of Adults into the (Catholic) Church; Royal Architectural Institute of Canada

rall. rallentando (Italian: becoming slow)

r.a.m. relative atomic mass

RAM random-access memory; (Member of the) Royal Academy of Music

RAMC Royal Army Medical Corps

RAN Royal Australian Navy

R & A Royal and Ancient (Golf Club, St Andrews)

R & B rhythm and blues

r. & c.c. riot and civil commotion

R & D research and development

R & I Regina et Imperatrix (Latin: Queen and Empress); Rex et Imperator (Latin: King and Emperor)

R & M reliability and marketing

R & R rescue and resuscitation; rest and recreation; rock and roll

R&VA Rating and Valuation Association

RANR Royal Australian Naval Reserve

RANVR Royal Australian Naval Volunteer Reserve

RAOB Royal Antediluvian Order of Buffaloes

RAOC Royal Army Ordnance Corps

RAP Regimental Aid Post

RAPC Royal Army Pay Corps

RAPID Register for the Ascertainment and Prevention of Inherited Diseases

RAR Royal Australian Regiment

RARDE Royal Armament Research and Development Establishment

RARO Regular Army Reserve of Officers

RAS Royal Agricultural Society; Royal Asiatic Society; Royal Astronomical Society

RASC Royal Army Service Corps (now called Royal Corps of Transport, RCT)

RASE Royal Agricultural Society of England

RATO rocket-assisted takeoff

RAuxAF Royal Auxiliary Air Force

RAVC Royal Army Veterinary Corps

RAX rural automatic exchange

Rb rubidium

RB reconnaissance bomber (aircraft; as in **RB-57**); Republic of Botswana; Rifle Brigade; Royal Ballet

RBA (Member of the) Royal Society of British Artists

RBC red blood cell; red blood (cell) count; Royal British Colonial Society of Artists

RBE relative biological effectiveness (of radiation)

RBK&C Royal Borough of Kensington and Chelsea

rbl. rouble

RBNA Royal British Nurses' Association

RBS Royal Society of British Sculptors

RBSA (Member of the) Royal Birmingham Society of Artists

RBT random breath testing

RBY Royal Bucks Yeomanry

RC red (blood) cell; Red Cross; reinforced concrete; Reserve Corps; resin-coated (as in **RC paper**); resistor-capacitor; Roman Catholic; Taiwan (Republic of China)

RCA Central African Republic; Radio Corporation of America; (Member of the) Royal Cambrian Academy; (Member of the) Royal Canadian Academy of Arts; Royal College of Art

RCAC Royal Canadian Armoured Corps

RCAF Royal Canadian Air Force

RCamA (Member of the) Royal Cambrian Academy

RCAMC Royal Canadian Army Medical Corps

RCB right centre back (of stage)

RCB(CG) Republic of the Congo

RCC Roman Catholic Church

rcd received

RCD Regional Cooperation for Development (association of Asian countries); residual current device

RCDS Royal College of Defence Studies

RCGP Royal College of General Practitioners

RCH Republic of Chile

RCHA Royal Canadian Horse Artillery

RCHM Royal Commission on Historical Monuments

RCM radar countermeasures; regimental court martial; Royal College of Midwives; (Member of the) Royal College of Music

RCMP Royal Canadian Mounted Police (formerly Royal Northwest Mounted Police, RNWMP)

RCN Royal Canadian Navy; Royal College of Nursing

RCNC Royal Corps of Naval Constructors

RCNR Royal Canadian Naval Reserve

RCNT Registered Clinical Nurse Teacher

RCNVR Royal Canadian Naval Volunteer Reserve

RCO Royal College of Organists

RCOG Royal College of Obstetricians and Gynaecologists

RCP Royal College of Physicians

RCPath Royal College of Pathologists

RCPE Royal College of Physicians, Edinburgh

RCPI Royal College of Physicians of Ireland

RCPSG Royal College of Physicians and Surgeons of Glasgow

RCPsych Royal College of Psychiatrists

rcpt receipt

RCR Royal College of Radiologists

RCS Royal College of Science; Royal College of Surgeons of England; Royal Commonwealth Society; Royal Corps of Signals

RCSB Royal Commonwealth Society for the Blind

RCSE Royal College of Surgeons of Edinburgh

RCSI Royal College of Surgeons in Ireland

rct receipt; recruit

RCT remote control transmitter (for TV operation, etc.); Royal Corps of Transport

rcvr receiver

RCVS Royal College of Veterinary Surgeons

rd rendered; road; round; rutherford

r.d. relative density

Rd Road

RD récemment dégorgé (French: recently disgorged; referring to wines having a longer ageing period on their first cork); refer to drawer (on a cheque); Royal Dragoons; Royal Naval and Royal Marine Forces Reserve Decoration; Rural Dean; (New Zealand) Rural Delivery

RDA Rassemblement Démocratique Africain (French: African Democratic Rally; political party); recommended dietary allowance (of nutrients); Royal Defence Academy

RD&D research, development, and demonstration

RD&E research, development, and engineering

RDAT rotary-head digital audio tape

RDB Research and Development Board

RDBMS relational database management system

RDC Royal Defence Corps; Rural District Council

RDF radio direction finder; (USA) Rapid Deployment Force; Royal Dublin Fusiliers

RDI Royal Designer for Industry (of the Royal Society of Arts)

RDS radio data system (for automatic tuning of receivers); respiratory distress syndrome; Royal Drawing Society; Royal Dublin Society

RDT&E research, development, testing, and engineering

RDV rendezvous

RDX Research Department Explosive (cyclonite)

Re Reynolds number; rhenium; rupee (Indian monetary unit; see also Rs)

RE Reformed Episcopal; religious education; Right Excellent; Royal Engineers; Royal Exchange; Royal Society of Painter-Etchers and Engravers

REACH Retired Executives' Action Clearing House

react research education and aid for children with potentially terminal illness

Rear-Adm. Rear-Admiral

rec. receipt; recipe; record(ed); recorder; recording; recreation

REC regional electricity company

recd received

recit. recitative

recon. recondition

REconS Royal Economic Society

recpt receipt

recryst. recrystallized

rec. sec. recording secretary

rect. receipt; rectangle; rectangular

Rect. Rector(y)

red. redeemable; reduce(d); reduction

redox reduction–oxidation

Red R Register of Engineers for Disaster Relief

redupl. reduplicate; reduplication

ref. refer(red); referee; reference; reform(ed); refrigerated ship

Ref. Ch. Reformed Church

refl. reflect(ion); reflective; reflexive

Ref. Pres. Reformed Presbyterian

refrig. refrigeration; refrigerator

Ref. Sp. Reformed Spelling

reg. regiment; region; register(ed); registrar; registration; registry; regular(ly); regulation; regulator

Reg. Regent; Regina (Latin: Queen)

regd registered

Reg-Gen. Registrar-General

Reg. Prof. Regius Professor

regr. registrar

Regt Regent; Regiment

rel. relating; relation; relative(ly); release(d); relié (French: bound); religion; religious; reliquiae (Latin: relics)

rel. pron. relative pronoun

rem roentgen equivalent man (former unit of radioactivity)

rem. remark(s)

REM rapid eye movement (as in **REM sleep**)

REME Royal Electrical and Mechanical Engineers

remitt. remittance

REN ringer equivalence number

REngDes Registered Engineering Designer

rep. repair; repeat; repetatur (Latin: let it be repeated; in prescriptions); report(ed); reporter; representative; reprint

Rep. (USA) Representative; Republic; (USA) Republican

REPC Regional Economic Planning Council

repr. represented; representing; reprint(ed)

repro. reproduction

rept receipt; report

Repub. Republic; (USA) Republican

req. request; require(d); requisition

RERO Royal Engineers Reserve of Officers

res. research(er); reserve(d); residence; resident; reside(s); resigned; resolution

RES Royal Entomological Society of London

resp. respective(ly); respondent

ret. retain; retire(d); return(ed)

retd retained; retired; returned

R. et I. Regina et Imperatrix (Latin: Queen and Empress); Rex et Imperator (Latin: King and Emperor)

rev. revenue; reverse(d); review(ed); revise(d); revision; revolution; revolving

Rev. Revelation; Reverend; Review

rev. a/c revenue account(s)

Revd Reverend

Rev. Stat. Revised Statutes

Rev. Ver. Revised Version (of the Bible)

rf. rinforzando (Italian: reinforcing)

r.f. radio frequency

Rf rufiyaa (monetary unit of Maldives); rutherfordium

RF radio frequency; reconnaissance fighter (aircraft; as in **RF-4E**); research foundation; Rwanda franc (monetary unit)

RFA Royal Field Artillery; Royal Fleet Auxiliary

RFC Royal Flying Corps; Rugby Football Club

RFH Royal Festival Hall (London)

RFI radio-frequency interference

RFN Registered Fever Nurse

RFQ request for quotation

RFS Registry of Friendly Societies; Royal Forestry Society

RFU Rugby Football Union

RG Reading

RGA Royal Garrison Artillery

RGB red green blue (as in **RGB signals**)

RGG Royal Grenadier Guards

RGI Royal Glasgow Institute of the Fine Arts

RGJ Royal Green Jackets

RGN Registered General Nurse (formerly SRN)

RGNP real gross national product

RGO Royal Greenwich Observatory (now in Cambridge)

RGS Royal Geographical Society

RGSA Royal Geographical Society of Australasia

Rgt Regiment

r.h. right hand(ed)

Rh rhesus (factor) (as in **Rh positive**); rhodium

RH Redhill; Republic of Haiti; right hand(ed); Royal Highness

RHA Royal Health Authority; Road Haulage Association; Royal Hibernian Academy; Royal Horse Artillery

RHAS Royal Highland and Agricultural Society of Scotland

RHB Regional Hospital Board

r.h.d. right-hand drive (of a motor vehicle)

rheo. rheostat

rhet. rhetoric(al)

RHF Royal Highland Fusiliers

RHG Royal Horse Guards

RHHI Royal Hospital and Home for Incurables (Putney)

RHistS Royal Historical Society

RHM Ranks Hovis McDougall

RHR Royal Highland Regiment (Black Watch)

RHS Royal Highland Show; Royal Historical Society; Royal Horticultural Society; Royal Humane Society

RHV Registered Health Visitor

RI Railway Inspectorate; Regina et Imperatrix (Latin: Queen and Empress); reinsurance; religious instruction; Republic of Indonesia; Rex et Imperator (Latin: King and Emperor); Rhode Island (abbrev. or postcode); Rotary International; Royal Institution

RIA Royal Irish Academy

RIAA Recording Industry Association of America

RIAF Royal Indian Air Force

RIAI Royal Institute of the Architects of Ireland

RIAM Royal Irish Academy of Music

RIAS Royal Incorporation of Architects in Scotland

RIASC Royal Indian Army Service Corps

RIB rigid-hull inflatable boat

RIBA Member of the Royal Institute of British Architects; Royal Institute of British Architects

RIBI Rotary International in Great Britain and Ireland

RIC Royal Institute of Chemistry (now called Royal Society of Chemistry, RSC); Royal Irish Constabulary

RICA Research Institute for Consumer Affairs

RICE rest, ice, compression, elevation (for treating sports injuries)

RICS Royal Institution of Chartered Surveyors

RIE recognized investment exchange; Royal Indian Engineering (College)

RIF reduction in force; Royal Inniskilling Fusiliers

RIFF resource interchange file format

RIIA Royal Institute of International Affairs

RIM Islamic Republic of Mauritania; Royal Indian Marines

RIN Royal Indian Navy

RINA Royal Institution of Naval Architects

RINVR Royal Indian Naval Volunteer Reserve

RIOP Royal Institute of Oil Painters

RIP raster input processor; requiescat in pace (Latin: may (he, she, *or* they) rest in peace)

RIPA Royal Institute of Public Administration

RIPH&H Royal Institute of Public Health and Hygiene

RIrF Royal Irish Fusiliers

rit. ritardando (Italian: holding back); ritenuto (Italian: held back)

riv. river

RJ road junction

RK radical keratotomy (used in treatment of shortsightedness); religious knowledge

RKO (USA) Radio-Keith-Orpheum (film studio, now broadcasting company)

RL Republic of Lebanon; Rugby League

RLO returned letter office (formerly dead letter office, DLO)

RLPO Royal Liverpool Philharmonic Orchestra

RLPS Royal Liverpool Philharmonic Society

Rls rial (monetary unit of Iran)

RLS Robert Louis Stevenson (1850–94, Scottish writer)

RLSS Royal Life Saving Society

rly railway

rm ream; room

RM Madagascar; Registered Midwife; Reichsmark (former German currency); Resident Magistrate; Romford; Royal Mail; Royal Marines

RMA Royal Marine Artillery; Royal Military Academy (Sandhurst; formerly Woolwich); Royal Musical Association

RMB (China) renminbi (Chinese: people's money (the currency used by the indigenous population); *compare* FEC, Foreign Exchange Certificate)

RMCM (Member of the) Royal Manchester College of Music

RMCS Royal Military College of Science

RMedSoc Royal Medical Society, Edinburgh

RMetS Royal Meteorological Society

RMFVR Royal Marine Forces Volunteer Reserves

RMI Resource Management Initiative (for the NHS)

RMIT Royal Melbourne Institute of Technology

RMLI Royal Marine Light Infantry

r.m.m. relative molecular mass

RMM Republic of Mali

RMN Registered Mental Nurse

RMO resident medical officer

RMP Royal Military Police

RMPA Royal Medico-Psychological Association

rms root mean square

RMS root mean square; Royal Mail Service; Royal Mail Ship; Royal Microscopical Society; Royal Society of Miniature Painters

RMSM Royal Military School of Music

RMT National Union of Rail, Maritime, and Transport Workers (formed by amalgamation of the NUR with the NUS)

Rn radon

RN (USA) Registered Nurse; Republic of Niger; Royal Navy

RNA ribonucleic acid; Royal Naval Association

RNAS Royal Naval Air Service; Royal Naval Air Station

RNase ribonuclease

RNAY Royal Naval Aircraft Yard

R 'n' B rhythm and blues

RNBT Royal Naval Benevolent Trust

RNC Royal Naval College

RNCM (Member of the) Royal Northern College of Music

rnd round

RND Royal Naval Division

RNEC Royal Naval Engineering College

RNIB Royal National Institute for the Blind

RNID Royal National Institute for the Deaf

RNLI Royal National Lifeboat Institution

RNLO Royal Naval Liaison Officer

RNMDSF Royal National Mission to Deep Sea Fishermen

RNMH Registered Nurse for the Mentally Handicapped

RNPFN Royal National Pension Fund for Nurses

R 'n' R rock and roll

RNR Royal Naval Reserve

RNS Royal Numismatic Society

RNSA Royal Naval Sailing Association

RNSC Royal Naval Staff College

RNT Registered Nurse Tutor; Royal National Theatre

RNTNEH Royal National Throat, Nose, and Ear Hospital

RNVR Royal Naval Volunteer Reserve

RNVSR Royal Naval Volunteer Supplementary Reserve

RNXS Royal Naval Auxiliary Service

RNZAC Royal New Zealand Armoured Corps

RNZAF Royal New Zealand Air Force

RNZIR Royal New Zealand Infantry Regiment

RNZN Royal New Zealand Navy

RNZNVR Royal New Zealand Naval Volunteer Reserve

ro. recto; roan

r.o. run out

RO Radio Orchestra; receiving office(r); receiving order; record(s) office; regimental order; relieving officer; returning officer; rial Omani (monetary unit of Oman); Romania

ROA record of achievement; return on assets

ROC Royal Observer Corps

ROCE return on capital employed

ROE return on equity; Royal Observatory, Edinburgh

ROF Royal Ordnance Factory

R of O Reserve of Officers

ROG receipt of goods

ROI return on investment; (Member of the) Royal Institute of Oil Painters

ROK Republic of Korea

rom. roman (type)

Rom. Roman; Romance *or* Romanic (languages); Romania(n); Romans

ROM read-only memory

Rom. Cath. Roman Catholic

RONA return on net assets

ROP run of paper (as in **ROP printing**)

RORC Royal Ocean Racing Club

ro-ro roll-on/roll-off (ferry)

ROSE Research Open Systems in Europe

ROSLA raising of school-leaving age

RoSPA Royal Society for the Prevention of Accidents

rot curl (of a function)

rot. rotating; rotation

ROU Republic of Uruguay

Rp rupiah (Indonesian monetary unit)

RP Received Pronunciation; recommended price; Reformed Presbyterian; Regimental Police(man); Regius Professor; reply paid; reprint(ing); República Portuguesa (Republic of Portugal); Republic of the Philippines; return (of) premium; Révérend Père (French: Reverend Father); (Member of the) Royal Society of Portrait Painters

RPB recognized professional body

RPC Royal Pioneer Corps

RPE Reformed Protestant Episcopal

RPG report program generator; rocket-propelled grenade; role-playing game

RPI retail price index

rpm revolutions per minute

RPM reliability performance measure; resale price maintenance

RPMS Royal Postgraduate Medical School

RPN reverse Polish notation

RPO Royal Philharmonic Orchestra

RPR (France) Rassemblement pour la République (French: Rally for the Republic; Gaullists)

rps revolutions per second

RPS Royal Philharmonic Society; Royal Photographic Society

RPSGB Royal Pharmaceutical Society of Great Britain

rpt repeat; report

RPV remotely piloted vehicle

RQ regraded quality (of tyres); request for quotation; respiratory quotient

RQMS regimental quartermaster sergeant

RR Right Reverend; Rolls-Royce

RRC (Lady of the) Royal Red Cross

RRF Royal Regiment of Fusiliers

rRNA ribosomal RNA

RRP recommended retail price

RR. PP. Révérends Pères (French: Reverend Fathers)

3 Rs reading, (w)riting, and (a)rithmetic

RRS Royal Research Ship

r.s. right side

Rs rupees

RS Received Standard (English); Reformed Spelling; respiratory system; Revised Statutes; Royal Scots; Royal Society

RSA Republic of South Africa; Rivest, Shamir, and Adelman (denoting a method of encryption, as in **RSA cipher**, **RSA system**); Royal Scottish Academy; Royal Society for the Encouragement of Arts, Manufactures, and Commerce; Royal Society of Arts

RSAA Royal Society for Asian Affairs

RSAD Royal Surgical Aid Society

RSAF Royal Small Arms Factory

RSAI Royal Society of Antiquaries of Ireland

RSAMD Royal Scottish Academy of Music and Drama

RSAS Royal Surgical Aid Society

RSC Royal Shakespeare Company; Royal Society of Canada; Royal Society of Chemistry; Rules of the Supreme Court

RSCDS Royal Scottish Country Dance Society

RSCJ Religiosae Sacratissimi Cordis Jesus (Latin: Nuns of the Most Sacred Heart of Jesus; Sacred Heart Society)

RSCM Royal School of Church Music

RSCN Registered Sick Children's Nurse (formerly SRCN)

RSD Royal Society of Dublin

RSE Received Standard English; Royal Society of Edinburgh

RSF Royal Scots Fusiliers

RSFSR Russian Soviet Federative Socialist Republic

RSG rate-support grant; regional seat of government (in civil defence)

RSGB Radio Society of Great Britain (amateur radio operators)

RSGS Royal Scottish Geographical Society

RSH Royal Society for the Promotion of Health

RSHA Reichssicherheitshauptamt (Reich Security Central Office; in Nazi Germany)

RSI repetitive strain injury

R. Signals Royal Corps of Signals

RSJ rolled-steel joist

RSL (Australia) Returned Services League; Royal Society of Literature

RSLA raising of school-leaving age

RSM regimental sergeant major; Republic of San Marino; Royal School of Mines; Royal Society of Medicine; Royal Society of Musicians of Great Britain

RSMA Royal Society of Marine Artists

RSME Royal School of Military Engineering

RSNC Royal Society for Nature Conservation

RSNZ Royal Society of New Zealand

RSO Radio Symphony Orchestra; railway sorting office; resident surgical officer; Royal Scottish Orchestra; rural suboffice

RSocMed Royal Society of Medicine

RSPB Royal Society for the Protection of Birds

RSPCA Royal Society for the Prevention of Cruelty to Animals

RSPP Royal Society of Portrait Painters

RSRE Royal Signals and Radar Establishment (formerly Royal Radar Establishment, RRE)

RSS Fellow of the Royal Society (Latin *Regiae Societatis Socius*); Royal Statistical Society

RSSA Royal Scottish Society of Arts

RSSPCC Royal Scottish Society for the Prevention of Cruelty to Children

RSTM&H Royal Society of Tropical Medicine and Hygiene

RSUA Royal Society of Ulster Architects

RSV Revised Standard Version (of the Bible)

RSVP répondez s'il vous plaît (French: please reply)

RSW (Member of the) Royal Scottish Society of Painters in Water Colours

rt right

RT radio telegraph; radio telephone; received text

RTBA rate to be agreed

RTC (India) Road Transport Corporation; Round Table Conference

rte route

RTE Radio Telefis Éireann (Gaelic: Irish Radio and Television); real-time execution

Rt Hon. Right Honourable

RTITB Road Transport Industry Training Board

RTL real-time language; resistor-transistor logic

rtn return

rtng returning

RTO railway transport officer

RTOL reduced takeoff and landing

RTPI Royal Town Planning Institute

RTR Royal Tank Regiment

Rt Rev. Right Reverend

RTS Religious Tract Society; Royal Television Society; Royal Toxophilite Society

RTT radioteletype

RTU returned to unit

RTYC Royal Thames Yacht Club

RTZ Rio Tinto Zinc Corporation Limited

Ru ruthenium

RU Republic of Burundi; Roussel-Uclaf (French pharmaceutical company; in **RU-486**, abortion pill); Rugby Union

RUA Royal Ulster Academy of Painting, Sculpture, and Architecture

RUBISCO RuBP carboxylase

RUC Royal Ulster Constabulary

RUF revolving underwriting facility

RUG restricted users group

RUI Royal University of Ireland

RUKBA Royal United Kingdom Beneficent Association

rumpie rural upwardly mobile professional

RUR Royal Ulster Regiment

RURAL Society for the Responsible Use of Resources in Agriculture and on the Land

Rus. Russia(n)

RUSI Royal United Services Institute for Defence Studies (formerly Royal United Service Institution)

Russ. Russia(n)

r.v. random variable; rendezvous

RV rateable value; rendezvous; Revised Version (of the Bible)

RVC Royal Veterinary College

RVCI Royal Veterinary College of Ireland

RVSVP répondez vite, s'il vous plaît (French: please reply quickly)

RW right of way; Right Worshipful; Right Worthy

RWA (Member of the) Royal West of England Academy; Rwanda

RWAFF Royal West African Frontier Force

r.w.d. rear-wheel drive

RWF Royal Welch Fusiliers

RwFr Rwanda franc

RWS (Member of the) Royal Society of Painters in Water Colours

rwy railway

ry railway

RYA Royal Yachting Association

RYS Royal Yacht Squadron

RZSScot Royal Zoological Society of Scotland

S

s second(s); secondary (isomer; as in **s-butyl alcohol**); soh (in tonic sol-fa); solid (as in **NaCl(s)**); strange (a quark flavour)

s. school; section; see; semi-; series; sets; shilling; sign(ed); sine (Latin: without); singular; sinister (Latin: left); sire; small; snow; society; solidus (Latin: shilling); solo; son; soprano (instrument); spherical; steamer; stem; stratus (cloud); substantive; succeeded; sun(ny)

s/ sur (French: on; in place names)

S entropy; Schilling (Austrian monetary unit); seven; Sheffield; siemens; signå; Silurian; slow (on a clock or watch regulator); small (size); south(ern); sucre (Ecuadorian monetary unit); sulphur; Sweden

S. Sabbath; sable; sacral (of vertebrae); Saint; satisfactory; Saturday; Saxon; School; Sea; segno (Italian: sign); Senate; sentence; September; sepultus (Latin: buried); series; ship; signature; Signor (Italian: Mr); Socialist; Society; Socius (Latin: Fellow; in titles); soprano (voice); south(ern); spades; sun; Sunday

sa. sable

s.a. secundum artem (Latin: by skill); semiannual; sex appeal; sine anno (Latin: without date; undated); subject to approval

Sa samarium

SA Salvation Army; seaman apprentice; semiannual; sex appeal; Society of Antiquaries; Society of Arts; Society of Authors; Soil Association; South Africa(n); South America(n); South Australia(n); Sturmabteilung (German: storm troopers; Nazi terrorist militia); Swansea

S/A subject to acceptance

SAA small arms ammunition; South African Airways; systems application architecture

SAAB Svensk Aeroplan Aktiebolag (Swedish aircraft and car company)

SAAF South African Air Force

SAAFA Special Arab Assistance Fund for Africa

Sab. Sabbath

SAB Society of American Bacteriologists

SABC South African Broadcasting Corporation

Sabena Société anonyme belge d'exploitation de la navigation aérienne (Belgian World Airlines)

sac qualified at a small-arms technical long course

SAC Senior Aircraftman; (USA) Strategic Air Command

SACEUR Supreme Allied Commander Europe

SACLANT Supreme Allied Commander Atlantic

SACSEA Supreme Allied Command, SE Asia

SACW Senior Aircraftwoman

SAD   seasonal affective disorder
SAE   self-addressed envelope; stamped addressed envelope
SAEF   Stock Exchange Automatic Execution Facility
S. Afr.   South Africa(n)
S.Afr.D.   South African Dutch
SAGB   Spiritualist Association of Great Britain
SAGE   (USA, Canada) semiautomatic ground environment
SAH   Supreme Allied Headquarters
SAIDS   simian acquired immune deficiency syndrome
SAL   South Arabian League
SALR   South African Law Reports
SALT   Strategic Arms Limitation Talks
salv.   salvage
Salv.   Salvador
Sam.   Samaritan; Samuel
S. Am.   South America(n)
SAM   surface-to-air missile
Samar.   Samaritan
SAMC   South African Medical Corps
S. Amer.   South America(n)
san.   sanitary
SAN   styrene–acrylonitrile (polymer)
sand.   sandwich
S&F   stock and fixtures
S&H   shipping and handling (charges)
S & M   sadism and masochism; stock and machinery
s & s   sex and shopping (type of popular fiction)
SANDS   Stillbirth and Neonatal Death Society
s. & s.c.   sized and supercalendered (of paper)
S & T   Salmon & Trout Association
Sane   Schizophrenia – A National Emergency
sanit.   sanitary; sanitation
SANROC   South African Non-Racial Olympics Committee
Sans.   Sanskrit
sapfu   surpassing all previous foul-ups
s.a.p.l.   sailed as per list (i.e. Lloyd's List)
Sar.   Sardinia(n)
SAR   search and rescue; Sons of the American Revolution
SARAH   search and rescue homing (radar system); surgery assistant robot acting on the head (in brain surgery)
Sarl.   (France, Belgium, Luxembourg, Switzerland) société à responsabilité limitée (private limited company; Ltd)
SARSAT   search and rescue satellite-aided tracking
Sarum.   Sarumensis (Latin: (Bishop) of Salisbury)
SAS   Scandinavian Airline System; Special Air Service
SASC   Small Arms School Corps
Sask.   Saskatchewan
SASO   Senior Air Staff Officer

sat.   saturate(d)
Sat.   Saturday; Saturn
SAT   Senior Member of the Association of Accounting Technicians; South Australian Time; standard assessment task
SATB   soprano, alto, tenor, bass
SATRO   Science and Technology Regional Organization
SATS   South African Transport Services
S. Aus.   South Australia(n)
s.a.v.   stock at valuation
SAVAK   (Iran) Sāzmān-i-Attalāt Va Amnīyat-i-Keshvar (National Security and Intelligence Organization, 1957–79)
sax.   saxophone
Sax.   Saxon; Saxony
SAYE   save as you earn (savings scheme)
sb.   substantive
s.b.   single-breasted; small bore (rifle)
Sb   antimony (Latin *stibium*)
SB   Sam Browne (military officer's belt and strap); short bill (of exchange); simultaneous broadcast(ing); Special Branch (of police); stillborn; stretcher bearer
SBA   sick-bay attendant; standard beam approach
SBAA   Sovereign Base Areas Administration
SBAC   Society of British Aerospace Companies (formerly Aircraft Constructors)
SBC   single-board computer
SbE   south by east
SBM   single buoy mooring
SBN   Standard Book Number (replaced by ISBN)
SBP   systolic blood pressure
SBR   styrene–butadiene rubber
SBS   sick-building syndrome; Special Boat Service
SBStJ   Serving Brother of the Order of St John of Jerusalem
SBU   strategic business unit
SbW   south by west
sc   small capitals; (student at the) staff college
sc.   scale; scene; science; scientific; scilicet (namely *or* that is; from Latin *scire licet*); screw; scruple (unit of weight); sculpsit (Latin: (he *or* she) carved this)
s.c.   salvage charges; small capitals; supercalendered (of paper)
s/c   self-contained
Sc   scandium
Sc.   Scotch; Scots; Scottish
SC   same case; (Australia, New Zealand) School Certificate; Security Council (of the UN); self-contained; Senatus Consultum (Latin: decree of the Senate); Senior Counsel; Sessions Cases; Signal Corps; social club; South Carolina (abbrev. *or* postcode); Special Constable; staff college; Staff Corps; (Canada) Star of Courage; supercalendered (paper); Supreme Court
SCA   sickle-cell anaemia

Scand.   Scandinavia(n)
SCAO   Senior Civil Affairs Officer
SCAP   Supreme Command Allied Powers
SCAPA   Society for Checking the Abuses of Public Advertising
s. caps   small capitals
ScB   Bachelor of Science (Latin *Scientiae Baccalaureus*)
SCB   Solicitors Complaints Bureau
ScBC   Bachelor of Science in Chemistry
ScBE   Bachelor of Science in Engineering
SCBU   special-care baby unit
s.c.c.   single column centimetre
SCC   Sea Cadet Corps
SCCL   Scottish Council for Civil Liberties
ScD   Doctor of Science (Latin *Scientiae Doctor*)
SCDA   Scottish Community Drama Association
SCDC   Schools Curriculum Development Committee
ScDHyg   Doctor of Science in Hygiene
ScDMed   Doctor of Science in Medicine
SCE   Scottish Certificate of Education
SCF   Save the Children Fund; Senior Chaplain to the Forces
scfh   standard cubic feet per hour
scfm   standard cubic feet per minute
SCG   Sydney Cricket Ground
SCGB   Ski Club of Great Britain
sch.   scholar; school; schooner
Sch.   Schilling (Austrian monetary unit); School
sched.   schedule
scherz.   scherzando (Italian: playful, humorous)
SchMusB   Bachelor of School Music
schol.   scholar; scholarship
sci.   science; scientific
SCID   severe combined immunodeficiency disease
sci. fa.   scire facias (Latin: that you cause to know)
sci-fi   science fiction
scil.   scilicet
SCIT   Special Commissioners of Income Tax
SCL   Student in Civil Law
ScM   Master of Science (Latin *Scientiae Magister*)
SCM   State Certified Midwife (replaced by RM, Registered Midwife); Student Christian Movement
ScMHyg   Master of Science in Hygiene
SCOBEC   Scottish Business Education Council
SCONUL   Standing Conference of National and University Libraries
Scot.   Scotch (whisky); Scotland; Scottish
ScotBIC   Scottish Business in the Community

SCOTEC Scottish Technical Education Council

SCOTVEC Scottish Vocational Education Council

SCOUT Shared Currency Option Under Tender

SCP single-cell protein (in food technology)

SCPS Society of Civil and Public Servants

scr. scrip; scruple (unit of weight)

SCR senior common room (in a university); silicon-controlled rectifier

Script. Scriptural; Scripture(s)

SCSI small computer systems interface

SCUA Suez Canal Users' Association

scuba self-contained underwater breathing apparatus

sculp. sculpsit; sculptor; sculptural; sculpture

SCWS Scottish Co-operative Wholesale Society

sd sailed; sewed (of books); signed; sound

s.d. safe deposit; semidetached; sense datum; short delivery; sine die (Latin: without a day (being fixed)); standard deviation

SD Doctor of Science (Latin *Scientiae Doctor*); salutem dicit (Latin: (he *or* she) sends greeting); sea-damaged; semi-detached; senile dementia; Senior Deacon; sequence date; short delivery; Sicherheitsdienst (German: Security Service; in Nazi Germany); sight draft; South Dakota (abbrev. *or* postcode); special delivery; staff duties; standard deviation; structural description (in transformational grammar); Swaziland

S/D sight draft

SDA Scottish Development Agency; Scottish Diploma in Agriculture; Seventh Day Adventists; Social Democratic Alliance

S. Dak. South Dakota

SDAT senile dementia of the Alzheimer type

S-DAT stationary digital audio tape

SDC Society of Dyers and Colourists

SDD Scottish Development Department; subscriber direct dialling

SDF Social Democratic Federation

SDI Strategic Defense Initiative (US Star Wars programme)

SDIO (USA) Strategic Defense Initiative Office

SDLP (Northern Ireland) Social Democratic and Labour Party

SDO subdivisional officer

SDP Social Democratic Party; social, domestic, and pleasure

SDR special drawing right(s)

SDS sodium dodecyl sulphate (detergent); (Germany) Sozialistischer Deutscher Studentenbund (Federation of Socialist Students); (USA) Students for a Democratic Society

SDT Society of Dairy Technology

s.e. standard error

Se selenium

SE Society of Engineers; southeast(ern); southeast London; Standard English; Stirling engine; stock exchange

SEAC School Examination and Assessment Council; South-East Asia Command; Standard Eastern Automatic Computer

SEALF South-East Asia Land Forces

SEAQ Stock Exchange Automated Quotations

SEATO Southeast Asia Treaty Organization (1954–77)

sec secant

sec. second (of time or an angle); secondary; secretary; section; sector; secundum (Latin: according to)

SECAM séquentiel couleur à mémoire (colour-television broadcasting system developed in France)

SECC Scottish Exhibition and Conference Centre

Sec. Gen. Secretary General

sec. leg. secundum legem (Latin: according to law)

sec. reg. secundum regulam (Latin: according to rule)

sect. section

secy secretary

sed. sedative; sediment

SED Scottish Education Department; shipper's export declaration

sedt sediment

SEEB Southeastern Electricity Board

seg. segment

SEG socioeconomic grade

seismol. seismological; seismology

sel. select(ed); selection

sem. semester; semicolon

Sem. Seminary; Semitic

s.e.(m.) standard error (of the mean)

SEM scanning electron microscope

semp. sempre (Italian: always)

Sen. Senate; Senator; Senior

SEN special educational needs; State Enrolled Nurse

Senr Senior

SEO Society of Education Officers

sep. sepal; separable; separate(d); separation

Sep. September; Septuagint

SEPM Society of Economic Palaeontologists and Mineralogists

sepn separation

SEPON Stock Exchange Pool Nominees Ltd

Sept. September; Septuagint

seq. sequel; sequence; sequens (Latin: the following (one)); sequente (Latin: and in what follows); sequitur (Latin: it follows)

seq. luce sequenti luce (Latin: the following day; in prescriptions)

seqq. sequentia (Latin: the following (ones)); sequentibus (Latin: in the following places)

ser. serial; series; sermon; service

Ser serine

SERA Socialist Environment and Resources Association

Serb. Serbia(n)

SERC Science and Engineering Research Council (formerly SRC)

Serg. Sergeant

Serj. Serjeant

SERPS State Earnings-Related Pension Scheme

SERT Society of Electronic and Radio Technicians

serv. servant; service

SES Singapore Stock Exchange

SESDAQ Stock Exchange of Singapore Dealing and Automated Quotation System

SESI Stock Exchange of Singapore Index

SESO Senior Equipment Staff Officer

sess. session

SET selective employment tax (1966–73)

SETI search for extraterrestrial intelligence

sett. settembre (Italian: September)

sev. several

sf sforzando (Italian; strongly accented)

s.f. science fiction; sinking fund; sub finem (Latin: towards the end)

Sf Suriname guilder (monetary unit)

SF Finland; San Francisco; science fiction; signal frequency; sinking fund; Sinn Fein

SFA Scottish Football Association; sweet Fanny Adams (i.e. nothing)

SFC specific fuel consumption (of jet engines)

SFInstE Senior Fellow, Institute of Energy

sfm surface feet per minute

SFO Serious Fraud Office; Superannuation Funds Office

sfp sforzato-piano (Italian; strong accent, followed immediately by soft)

SFr Swiss franc

SFT supercritical fluid technology

SFTCD Senior Fellow, Trinity College Dublin

SFU suitable for upgrade (on airline tickets)

sfz sforzando

sg. singular

s.g. specific gravity

Sg seaborgium

SG Secretary General; ship and goods; singular (in transformational grammar); Society of Genealogists; Solicitor General; Stevenage; Surgeon General

SGA (Member of the) Society of Graphic Art

SGBI Schoolmistresses' and Governesses' Benevolent

Institution
sgd signed
SGF Scottish Grocers' Federation
SGHWR steam-generating heavy-water reactor
S. Glam South Glamorgan
SGML standard generalized markup language
SGP Singapore
Sgt Sergeant
SGT Society of Glass Technology
Sgt Maj. Sergeant Major
sh. share; sheep; sheet; shilling
s.h. second-hand
SHA Secondary Heads Association; sidereal hour angle; Special Health Authority
SHAEF Supreme Headquarters Allied Expeditionary Forces
Shak. William Shakespeare (1564–1616, English dramatist and poet)
SH&MA Scottish Horse and Motormen's Association
SHAPE Supreme Headquarters Allied Powers Europe (of NATO)
S/HE Sundays and holidays excepted
SHEX Sundays and holidays excepted
Sh.F. shareholders' funds
SHF superhigh frequency
SHHD Scottish Home and Health Department
SHM simple harmonic motion
SHO Senior House Officer
shoran short-range navigation
shp shaft horsepower (of an engine)
SHP single-flowered hardy perennial (rose)
shpg shipping
shpt shipment
shr. share(s)
sht sheet
SHT single-flowered hybrid tea (rose)
shtg. shortage
s.h.v. sub hac voce (Latin: under this word)
s.i. sum insured
Si silicon
SI Sandwich Islands (former name for Hawaii); Shetland Isles; South Island (New Zealand); (Order of the) Star of India; Staten Island (New York); styrene–isoprene (polymer); Système International (d'Unités; French: International System of Units; in **SI unit(s)**)
SIA Society of Investment Analysts; Spinal Injuries Association
SIAD Society of Industrial Artists and Designers (now called Chartered Society of Designers, CSD)
Sib. Siberia(n)
SIB Securities and Investments Board; self-injurious behaviour; Shipbuilding Industry Board
SIBOR Singapore Inter-Bank Offered Rate
sic. siccus (Latin: dry)

Sic. Sicilian; Sicily
SIC Standard Industrial Classification
SID sudden ionospheric disturbance
SIDS sudden infant death syndrome (cot death)
SIESO Society of Industrial and Emergency Service Officers
sig. signal; signature; signetur (Latin: let it be written *or* labelled)
Sig. signā (Latin: write; in prescriptions, preceding instructions to be written on the label for the patient's use); Signor (Italian: Mr); Signore (Italian: Sir)
SIG special-interest group
sig. fig. significant figures
SIGINT signals intelligence (gathering network)
sig. n. pro. signa nomine proprio (Latin: label with the proper name)
sim. similar(ly); simile
SIM Société internationale de musicologie (French: International Musicological Society)
SIMA Scientific Instrument Manufacturers' Association of Great Britain; system for identifying motivated abilities
SIMC Société internationale pour la musique contemporaine (French: International Society for Contemporary Music)
SIMCA Société industrielle de mécanique et carrosserie automobiles (French car manufacturers)
SIME Security Intelligence Middle East
SIMG International Society of General Medicine (Latin *Societas Internationalis Medicinae Generalis*)
SIMM single in-line memory module
sin sine
SinDrs Doctor of Chinese
sing. singular
sinh hyperbolic sine
SINS ship's inertial navigation system
SIO serial input/output
SIPO serial in, parallel out
SIPRI Stockholm International Peace Research Institute
SIS Secret Intelligence Service (MI6)
sit. sitting room; situation
SITA Société internationale de télécommunications aéronautiques (French: International Society of Aeronautical Telecommunications)
SITC Standard International Trade Classification
SITPRO Simpler Trade Procedures Board (formerly Simplification of International Trade Procedures)
sit. vac. situation vacant
SIW self-inflicted wound
SJ Society of Jesus; supersonic jet
SJA St John Ambulance (Brigade *or* Association)
SJAA St John Ambulance Association

SJAB St John Ambulance Brigade
SJC (USA) Supreme Judicial Court
SJD Doctor of Juristic Science (Latin *Scientiae Juridicae Doctor*)
sk sack
SK Saskatchewan; Stockport
skid *see* SCID
s.k.p.o. slip one, knit one, pass slipped stitch over
SKr Swedish krona (monetary unit)
Skt Sanskrit
s.l. salvage loss; sine loco (Latin: without place (of publication))
SL Serjeant-at-Law; Slough; Solicitor-at-Law; source language; south latitude
SLA Symbionese Liberation Army
SLAC Stanford Linear Accelerator Center
SLADE Society of Lithographic Artists, Designers, Engravers, and Process Workers
SLAET Society of Licensed Aircraft Engineers and Technologists
SLAM standoff land-attack missile
s.l.a.n. sine loco, anno, vel nomine (Latin: without place, year, name (of printer))
SLAR side-looking airborne radar
SLAS Society for Latin American Studies
S. Lat. south latitude
Slav. Slavonian; Slavonic
SLBM submarine-launched ballistic missile
SLC Stanford Linear Collider (at SLAC)
SLCM sea- launched cruise missile
sld sailed; sealed; sold
SLD self-locking device; Social and Liberal Democrats
s.l. et a. sine loco et anno (Latin: without place and year (of publication))
S level Special (formerly Scholarship) level
SLF Scottish Landowners' Federation
SLIM South London Industrial Mission
Slipar short light pulse alerting receiver (in an aircraft)
SLORC (Burma) State Law and Order Restoration Council
s.l.p. sine legitime prole (Latin: without lawful issue)
SLP Scottish Labour Party
SLR satellite laser ranging; self-loading rifle; single-lens reflex (camera)
SL Rs Sri Lanka rupee (monetary unit)
Slud salivate, lachrymate, urinate, defecate (effects of chemical weapons)
sly southerly
sm. small
s-m sadomasochism
Sm samarium
SM Master of Science (Latin *Scientiae Magister*); sadomasochism; sales manager; sanctae memoriae (Latin: of holy memory); Sergeant Major; short

metre; silver medal(list); Society of Miniaturists; Staff Major; stage manager; Submarine Duties; Sutton (Surrey)

SMATV satellite (formerly small) master antenna television

SMB Bachelor of Sacred Music

SMBG self-monitoring of blood glucose (for diabetics)

SMC Scottish Mountaineering Club

sm. caps. small capitals

SMD Doctor of Sacred Music; senile macular degeneration; short metre double

SME Sancta Mater Ecclesia (Latin: Holy Mother Church); Suriname

SMERSH Smert Shpionam (Russian: death to spies; section of KGB)

SMHO (Malta) Sovereign Military Hospitaller Order

Smith. Inst. Smithsonian Institution (Washington, DC)

SMLE short magazine Lee-Enfield (rifle)

SMM Master of Sacred Music; Sancta Mater Maria (Latin: Holy Mother Mary)

SMMT Society of Motor Manufacturers and Traders Ltd

SMO Senior Medical Officer; Sovereign Military Order

SMON subacute myelo-opticoneuropathy

s.m.p. sine mascula prole (Latin: without male issue)

SMP statutory maternity pay

SMR standard Malaysian rubber; standard metabolic rate

SMRTB Ship and Marine Requirements Technology Board

s.n. secundum naturam (Latin: according to nature, naturally); sine nomine (Latin: without name); sub nomine (Latin: under a specified name)

Sn tin (Latin *stannum*)

SN Senegal; Swindon

S/N signal-to-noise (in **S/N ratio**); stress-number (in **S/N curve**)

SNA systems network architecture

snafu situation normal, all fouled up

SNAP systems for nuclear auxiliary power

SNB sellers no buyers

SNCB Société nationale des chemins de fer belges (Belgian National Railways)

SNCC (USA) Student Nonviolent (later National) Coordinating Committee

SNCF (France) Société nationale des chemins de fer français (state railway authority or system)

SND Sisters of Notre Dame

SNG substitute natural gas

SNH Scottish National Heritage

SNIF short-term note issuance facility

SNIG sustainable noninflationary growth

SNO Scottish National Orchestra (renamed Royal Scottish Orchestra, RSO); Senior Naval Officer

SNOBOL a programming language designed for text manipulation

SNP Scottish National Party

Snr Senior

SNR signal-to-noise ratio; Society for Nautical Research; supernova remnant

s 'n' s sex and shopping (type of popular fiction)

SNTS Society for New Testament Studies

SNU solar neutrino unit

so. south(ern)

s.o. seller's option; shipping order; substance of (specifying weight of paper)

So. south(ern)

SO Scientific Officer; Signal Officer; Southampton; special order; Staff Officer; standing order; Stationery Office; suboffice; Symphony Orchestra

S/O shipowner

SOA state of the art

SOAP subjective, objective, analysis, plan (method of compiling patients' records)

SOB silly old bastard; son of a bitch

soc. socialist; society; sociology

Soc. Socialist; Society

SocCE(France) Société des ingénieurs civils de France (Society of Civil Engineers of France)

sociol. sociological; sociologist; sociology

SOCO scene-of-crime officer (in the police)

SOCS Society of County Secretaries

socy society

SODAC Society of Dyers and Colourists

SODEPAX Committee on Society, Development, and Peace

SOE Special Operations Executive (in World War II); state-owned enterprise

SOED Shorter Oxford English Dictionary

SOF sound on a film

SOFFEX Swiss Options and Financial Futures Exchange

S of F Ltd Society of Floristry Limited

S. of S. Secretary of State; Song of Songs

S. of Sol. Song of Solomon

SOGAT Society of Graphical and Allied Trades

sol. solicitor; soluble; solution

s.o.l. shipowner's liability

Sol. Solicitor; Song of Solomon

SOLACE Society of Local Authority Chief Executives

Sol. Gen. Solicitor General

soln solution

solr solicitor

Som. Somerset

SOM Society of Occupational Medicine

Som.Sh. Somali shilling (monetary unit)

sonar sound navigation and ranging

sop. soprano

SOP standard operating procedure; sum of products (in **SOP expression**)

SoR sale or return

s.o.s. si opus sit (Latin: if necessary; in prescriptions)

SOS save our souls (also, the clearest letters to transmit and receive in Morse code); Secretary of State

SOSc Society of Ordained Scientists

SoSh Somali shilling (monetary unit)

sost. sostenuto (Italian: sustained)

SOTS Society for Old Testament Study

Sou. south(ern)

sov. sovereign

SOV subject-object-verb (in **SOV language**)

sowc senior officers' war course

Soweto Southwestern Townships (South Africa)

sp. special; species; specific; specimen; spelling; spirit

s.p. self-propelled; sine prole (Latin: without issue); starting price

Sp. Spain; Spaniard; Spanish

SP Salisbury; Self-Propelled (Antitank Regiment); shore patrol; starting price (odds in a race); submarine patrol; supra protest

SpA (Italy) società per azioni (public limited company; plc)

SPAB Society for the Protection of Ancient Buildings

Sp. Am. Spanish American

Span. Spaniard; Spanish

Sp. Ar. Spanish Arabic

SPARC scalable processor architecture

SPC stored-program control (as in **SPC exchange**)

SPCK Society for Promoting Christian Knowledge

SPD Salisbury Plain District; Sozialdemokratische Partei Deutschlands (Social Democratic Party of Germany)

SPDA single-premium deferred annuity

SPE Society for Pure English

spec. special(ly); specific(ally); specification

specif. specifically; specification

SPECT single photon emission computed tomography

SPF sun protection factor (of sunscreening preparations)

SPG Society for the Propagation of the Gospel; Special Patrol Group

SPGB Socialist Party of Great Britain

sp. gr. specific gravity

sp. ht specific heat

spirit. spiritoso (Italian: in a spirited manner)

s.p.l. sine prole legitima (Latin: without legitimate issue)

SPLA Sudan People's Liberation Army

s.p.m. sine prole mascula (Latin: without male issue)

SPMO Senior Principal Medical Officer

SPNM Society for the Promotion of New Music

SPOD Sexual Problems of the Disabled (department of the Royal Association for Disability and Rehabilitation)

sport. sporting

spp. species (plural)

SPQR Senatus Populusque Romanus (Latin: the Senate and People of Rome); small profits and quick returns

spr. spring

Spr Sapper

SPR Society for Psychical Research

SPRC Society for the Prevention and Relief of Cancer

SPREd Society of Picture Researchers and Editors

SPRL Society for the Promotion of Religion and Learning

s.p.s. sine prole supersite (Latin: without surviving issue)

SPS syndiotactic polystyrene (a plastic)

SPSO Senior Principal Scientific Officer

spt seaport

SPTL Society of Public Teachers of Law

SPUC Society for the Protection of the Unborn Child

SPURV self-propelled underwater research vehicle

sq staff qualified

sq. sequence; sequens; squadron; square

Sq. Squadron; Square (in place names)

SQ sick quarters; stereophonic-quadraphonic (of audio equipment)

SQA software quality assurance

sq cm square centimetre(s)

sqd squad

sqdn squadron

Sqdn Ldr Squadron Leader

sq ft square feet

sq in square inch(es)

sq km square kilometre(s)

SQL standard query language; structured query language

sq m square metre(s)

sq mi square mile(s)

sq mm square millimetre(s)

sqn squadron

Sqn Ldr Squadron Leader

sqq. sequentia

sq yd square yard

sr steradian

Sr Senhor (Portuguese: Mr, Sir); Senior (after a name); Señor (Spanish: Mr, Sir); Sir; Sister (religious); strontium

SR Saudi riyal (Saudi Arabian monetary unit); Saunders Roe (aircraft); Seychelles rupee (monetary unit); Society of Radiographers; (USA) Sons of the Revolution; Southern Railway (now Region); Special Reserve;

Sunderland

S/R sale or return

Sra Senhora (Portuguese: Mrs); Señora (Spanish: Mrs)

SRA Squash Rackets Association

SRAM short-range attack missile; static random access memory

SR & CC strikes, riot, and civil commotion

SRBC sheep red blood cell(s)

SRBM short-range ballistic missile

SRC Science Research Council; Students' Representative Council

SRCh State Registered Chiropodist

SRCN State Registered Children's Nurse

SRG Strategic Research Group (marketing research company)

SRHE Society for Research into Higher Education

SRI Sacrum Romanum Imperium (Latin: Holy Roman Empire)

SRIS Science Reference Information Service

SRls Saudi riyal (monetary unit of Saudi Arabia)

SRN State Registered Nurse

sRNA soluble RNA

SRNA Shipbuilders and Repairers National Association

SRO self-regulatory organization; (USA) single-room occupancy (as in **SRO hotel**); standing room only; Statutory Rules and Orders; Supplementary Reserve of Officers

SRP State Registered Physiotherapist; suggested retail price

SRS Fellow of the Royal Society (Latin Societatis Regiae Sodalis)

SRSA slow-reacting substance A (of anaphylaxis)

Srta Senhorita (Portuguese: Miss); Señorita (Spanish: Miss)

SRU Scottish Rugby Union

SRY Sherwood Rangers Yeomanry

ss. sections; semis (Latin: half; in prescriptions); subsection

s.s. screw steamer; sensu stricto (Latin: in the strict sense); senza sordini (Italian: without mutes); steamship

SS Sacra Scriptura (Latin: Holy Scripture); Saints; Schutzstaffel (German: protection squad; Nazi paramilitary organization); Secretary of State; secret service; security service; social security; Southend-on-Sea; steamship; Straits Settlements; Sunday school

S/S steamship

SSA Society of Scottish Artists; standard spending assessment (in local government)

SSAC Social Security Advisory Committee

SSAE stamped self-addressed envelope

SSAFA Soldiers', Sailors', and Airmen's Families Association

SSAP Statement of Standard Accounting Practice

SSBN strategic submarine, ballistic nuclear

SSC Scottish Ski Club; Sculptors' Society of Canada; (India) Secondary School Certificate; Short Service Commission; Society of the Holy Cross (Latin Societas Sanctae Crucis); (Scotland) Solicitor before the Supreme Court; Species Survival Commission

SSD Doctor of Sacred Scripture (Latin Sacrae Scripturae Doctor); Social Services Department

SS.D Sanctissimus Dominus (Latin: Most Holy Lord; the pope)

SSE south-southeast

SSEB South of Scotland Electricity Board

S-SEED symmetric self-electro-optic-effect device

SSEES School of Slavonic and East European Studies (University of London)

SSF single-seater fighter (aircraft); Society of St Francis

S/Sgt Staff Sergeant

SSHA Scottish Special Housing Association

SSI Scottish Symphony Orchestra; site of scientific interest; small-scale integration; Social Services Inspectorate; Society of Scribes and Illuminators

SSJE Society of St John the Evangelist

SSM Society of the Sacred Mission; surface-to-surface missile

SSN severely subnormal; Standard Serial Number

SSO Senior Scientific Officer; Senior Supply Officer

ssp. subspecies

SSP statutory sick pay

SSPCA Scottish Society for the Prevention of Cruelty to Animals

SSPE subacute sclerosing panencephalitis

sspp. subspecies (plural)

SS.PP. Sancti Patres (Latin: Holy Fathers)

SSR secondary surveillance radar; Soviet Socialist Republic

SSRC Social Science Research Council

SSS standard scratch score

SSSI site of special scientific interest

SSStJ Serving Sister, Order of St John of Jerusalem

SST Society of Surveying Technicians; supersonic transport

SSTA Scottish Secondary Teachers' Association

SSW south-southwest

st. stanza; state; statute; stem; stet; stitch; stone (weight); strait; street; strophe; stumped by

s.t. short ton; steam trawler

St Saint; stokes

St. Statute; Strait; Street

ST septic tank; (Hubble) Space Telescope; speech therapist; spring tide; Standard Time; Stoke-on-Trent; Summer Time

sta. station

Sta Santa (Italian, Spanish, Portuguese: Saint (female))
STA Sail Training Association
stab. stabilization; stabilizer; stable
stacc. staccato
Staffs Staffordshire
STAGS Sterling Transferable Accruing Government Securities
START Strategic Arms Reduction Talks
stat. statics; statim (Latin: immediately; in prescriptions); stationary; statuary; statue; statute
STB Bachelor of Sacred Theology (Latin *Sacrae Theologiae Baccalaureus*)
stbd starboard
STC Senior Training Corps; Short-Title Catalogue; (India) State Trading Corporation
std standard; started
STD Doctor of Sacred Theology (Latin *Sacrae Theologiae Doctor*); sexually transmitted disease; (New Zealand) subscriber toll dialling; subscriber trunk dialling
Ste Sainte (French: Saint (female))
Sté société (French: company; Co.)
STE Society of Telecom Executives (trade union)
STEM scanning transmission electron microscope
sten. stenographer; stenography
Sten Shepherd and Turpin (inventors), Enfield (in **Sten gun**)
steno. stenographer; stenographic; stenography
STEP Special Temporary Employment Programme
ster. stereophonic; stereotype; sterling
St. Ex. Stock Exchange
stg sterling
stge storage
Sth South
STh Scholar in Theology
STI Straits Times Index (of the Singapore Stock Exchange)
STIM scanning transmission ion microscope
stip. stipend; stipendiary
stk stock
STL Licentiate in Sacred Theology (Latin *Sacrae Theologiae Licentiatus*)
stlg sterling
STM Master of Sacred Theology (Latin *Sacrae Theologiae Magister*); scanning tunnelling microscope; short-term memory
STMS short-term monetary support (within the EMS)
stmt statement
stn station
STOL short takeoff and landing
S to S ship to shore
stp standard temperature and pressure
STP Professor of Sacred Theology (Latin *Sacrae Theologiae Professor*); scientifically treated petroleum (an oil substitute; refers colloquially to a hallucinogenic drug); standard temperature and

pressure
str steamer
str. straight; strait; street; strings; stroke (oar); strong
stratig. stratigraphy
strd stranded
string. stringendo (Italian; intensifying)
STRIVE Society for the Preservation of Rural Industries and Village Enterprises
Sts Saints
STS Scottish Text Society
STSO Senior Technical Staff Officer
st. st. stocking stitch
STUC Scottish Trades Union Congress
stud. student
STV Scottish Television; single transferable vote
SU Scripture Union; special unitary (group; as in SU_3); strontium unit (of radioactive strontium)
sub. subeditor; subito (Italian: immediately, suddenly); subject; submarine; subordinated; subscription; substitute; suburb(an); subway
sub-ed. subeditor
subj. subject; subjective(ly); subjunctive
Sub-Lt Sub-Lieutenant
subs. subsidiary; subsistence
subsc. subscription
subsp. (pl. **subspp.**) subspecies
subst. substantive(ly); substitute
suc. successor
suff. sufficient; suffix
Suff. Suffolk; Suffragan
sum. sumat *or* sumendum (Latin: let him take *or* let it be taken; in prescriptions); summer
SUM surface-to-underwater missile
Sun. Sunday
SUNY State University of New York
sup supremum
sup. superfine; superior; superlative; supine (noun); supplement(ary); supply; supra (Latin: above); supreme
sup. ben. supplementary benefit
Sup. Ct Superior Court; Supreme Court
super. superfine; superior; supernumerary
superl. superlative
supp. supplement(ary)
Supp. Res. Supplementary Reserve (of officers)
supr. superior; supreme
Supt Superintendent
supvr supervisor
sur. surplus
surg. surgeon; surgery; surgical
surv. survey; surveying; surveyor
Surv. Gen. Surveyor General
Sus. Susanna (in the Apocrypha)
SUT Society for Underwater Technology
s.v. sailing vessel; side valve; sub verbo (Latin: under the word *or* heading); surrender value

Sv sievert
SV Sancta Virgo (Latin: Holy Virgin); Sanctitas Vestra (Latin: Your Holiness); stroke volume (of an engine)
svc. service
SVD swine vesicular disease
svgs savings
S-VHS super-VHS
SVO subject-verb-object (in **SVO language**)
s.v.p. s'il vous plaît (French: if you please)
s.v.r. spiritus vini rectificatus (Latin: rectified spirit of wine; in prescriptions)
SVS still-camera video system
s.vv. sub verbis (Latin: under the words or headings)
Sw. Sweden; Swedish
SW shipper's weight; short wave; small women (clothing size); South Wales; southwest(ern); southwest London
S/W software
SWA Namibia (formerly South West Africa)
Swab. Swabia(n)
SWA(L)K sealed with a (loving) kiss (on envelopes)
SWANU South West Africa National Union
SWAPO South-West Africa People's Organization
S/WARE software
SWCI software configuration item
SWEB South Wales Electricity Board; Southwest Electricity Board
Swed. Sweden; Swedish
SWET Society of West End Theatre
SwF Swiss franc (monetary unit)
SWG standard wire gauge
SWIE South Wales Institute of Engineers
SWIFT Society for Worldwide Interbank Financial Transmission
Swing Sterling warrant into gilt-edged stock
Switz. Switzerland
SWLA Society of Wildlife Artists
SWOT strengths, weaknesses, opportunities, and threats (of a new product)
SWPA South-West Pacific Area
SWR standing-wave ratio
SWRB Sadler's Wells Royal Ballet (now the Royal Ballet)
Swtz. Switzerland
Sx Sussex
SX Sundays excepted
Sy. supply; Surrey
SY Seychelles; Shrewsbury; steam yacht
SYB The Statesman's Year-Book
Syd. Sydney
SYHA Scottish Youth Hostels Association
syl. syllable; syllabus
sym. symbol; symphonic; symphony; symptom
symp. symposium
syn. synonym(ous); synonymy
sync synchronization

synd. syndicate; syndicated
synop. synopsis
synth. synthesizer
syr. syrup
Syr. Syria(n); Syriac
SYR Syria
syst. system
sz. size

T

t Student's t distribution; te (in tonic sol-fa); tertiary (isomer; as in **t-butane**); tonne(s)
t. taken (from); tare; teaspoon(ful); tempo; tempore (Latin: in the time of); tenor; tense; territory; thunder; time; ton(s) or tonne(s); town; township; transit; transitive; troy; tun
T kinetic energy; ribosylthymine; tera- (prefix indicating 10^{12} as in **TJ**, terajoule); tesla(s); thymine; torque; trainer (aircraft; as in **T-37**); tritium
T. tablespoon(ful); tace (Italian: be silent); telephone; tenor; Territorial; Territory; Testament; Thursday; time; Tuesday
Ta tantalum
TA Taunton; telegraphic address; temporary admission; Territorial Army; transactional analysis; Translators Association; travelling allowance
TAA Territorial Army Association; Trans-Australia Airlines
TA&VRA Territorial Auxiliary and Volunteer Reserve Association
tab. table (list or chart); tablet; tabulation; tabulator
TAB tabulator (on a typewriter); (Australia, New Zealand) Totalizator Administration Board; typhoid, paratyphoid A, paratyphoid B (vaccine)
TAC The Athletics Congress
TACAN tactical air navigation
TACV tracked air-cushion vehicle
TADA taking and driving away (police use)
Tads target acquisition and designation sight
TAF Tactical Air Force
TAFE technical and further education
tafu things are fouled up
tafubar things are fouled up beyond all recognition
TALISMAN Transfer Accounting Lodgement for Investors and Stock Management
tal. qual. talis qualis (Latin: average quality)
Tam. Tamil (language)
TAM Television Audience Measurement (as in **TAM rating**)
Tamba Twins and Multiple Births Association
tan tangent
T&AFA Territorial and Auxiliary Forces Association
T & AVR Territorial and Army Volunteer Reserve
T & E tired and emotional (i.e. drunk); travel and entertainment;

trial and error
t. & g. tongued and grooved
T & G Transport and General Workers' Union
t. & p. theft and pilferage
t. & s. toilet and shower
TANS Territorial Army Nursing Service (now merged with QARANC)
TANU Tanganyika African National Union
TAP Transportes Aéreos Portugueses (Portuguese Airlines)
TAPS Trans-Alaska Pipeline System
TARO Territorial Army Reserve of Officers
Tas. Tasmania(n)
TAS torpedo antisubmarine (course); true air speed
TASI time-assignment speech interpolation
Tasm. Tasmania(n)
Tass Telegrafnoye Agentsvo Sovetskovo Soyuza (Soviet news agency)
TAT thematic apperception test; tired all the time
TAURUS Transfer and Automated Registration of Uncertified Stock
TAVR Territorial and Army Volunteer Reserve (1967–79)
TAVRA Territorial Auxiliary and Volunteer Reserve Association
tax. taxation
t.b. trial balance; tubercle bacillus; tuberculosis
Tb terbium
TB torpedo boat; training board; Treasury bill; trial balance; tuberculosis
t.b.a. to be advised; to be agreed; to be announced
TBC time-based corrector
TBD torpedo-boat destroyer
TBF Teachers Benevolent Fund
TBG thyroxine-binding globulin
TBI throttle-body injection; total body irradiation
t.b.l. through back of loop
TBM tactical ballistic missile; tunnel-boring machine
TBO time between overhauls; total blackout
tbs. tablespoon(ful)
TBS talk between ships (radio apparatus); tight building syndrome
TBT tributyl tin (used in marine paints)
tc. tierce (organ stop)
Tc technetium
TC Tax Cases; traveller's cheque; tre corde (Italian: three strings; i.e. release soft pedal); (Trinidad and Tobago) (Order of the) Trinity Cross; Trusteeship Council (of the UN); tungsten carbide; twin carburettors (on motor vehicles)
TCA tricarboxylic acid (in **TCA cycle**); trichloroacetic acid (herbicide); tricyclic antidepressant (drug)
TCB tetrachlorobiphenyl

TCBM transcontinental ballistic missile
TCCB Test and County Cricket Board
TCD Trinity College, Dublin
TCDD tetrachlorodibenzodioxin (dioxin; environmental pollutant)
TCE trichloroeth(yl)ene (solvent)
tcf trillion cubic feet (measure of natural gas)
TCF Temporary Chaplain to the Forces; Touring Club de France
TCNQ tetracyanoquinodimethane
TCP transmission control protocol; trichlorophenylmethyliodisalicyl (an antiseptic)
TCPA Town and Country Planning Association
TD Galashiel's; tank destroyer; tardive dyskinesia; (Ireland) Teachta Dála (Gaelic: Member of the Dáil); technical drawing; Territorial (Efficiency) Decoration (in the Territorial Army); trust deed; Tunisian dinar (monetary unit)
TDA 2,4-toluene diamine (possible carcinogen released by breast implants)
TDC Temporary Detective Constable; top dead centre
TDL tunable diode laser
TDMA time-division multiple access
TDN total digestible nutrients
TDR Treasury deposit receipt
TDRSS tracking and data-relay satellite system
t.d.s. ter die sumendum (Latin: be taken three times a day; in prescriptions)
TDS tabular data stream
t/e twin-engined
Te tellurium
TEAC Technical Educational Advisory Council
TEC Training and Enterprise Council
tech. technical(ly); technician; technology
Tech(CEI) Technician (Council of Engineering Institutions)
technol. technological; technology
TEE Trans-Europe Express (train)
TEF toxicity equivalence factor
TEFL teaching (of) English as a foreign language
tel. telegram; telegraph(ic); telephone
TEL tetraethyl lead (petrol additive)
telecom. telecommunication(s)
teleg. telegram; telegraph(ic); telegraphy
telex teleprinter exchange
tel. no. telephone number
TEM Territorial Efficiency Medal
TEMA Telecommunications Engineering and Manufacturing Association
temp. temperate; temperature; temporary; tempore (Latin: in the time of)
Templar tactical expert mission-planner (military computer)

ten. tenor; tenuto (Italian: held, sustained)

Tenn. Tennessee

TENS transcutaneous electrical nerve stimulation

TeolD Doctor of Theology

TEPP tetraethyl pyrophosphate (pesticide)

ter. terrace; territory

terat. teratology

TERCOM terrain contour matching

term. terminal; termination

terr. terrace; territorial; territory

TES thermal-energy storage; Times Educational Supplement

TESL teaching (of) English as a second language

TESOL teaching of English to speakers of other languages

Tessa Tax-Exempt Special Savings Account

TET Teacher of Electrotherapy

TEU twenty-foot equivalent unit

Teut. Teuton(ic)

TEWT tactical exercise without troops

Tex. Texan; Texas

text. rec. textus receptus (Latin: the received text)

TF Telford; Territorial Force

TFAP Tropical Forestry Action Plan

TFD thin-film detector

tfr transfer

TFR Territorial Force Reserve

TFSC Turkish Federated State of Cyprus (Turkish *Kibris*)

TFW tactical fighter wing

TFX tactical fighter experimental (aircraft)

tg tangent

t.g. type genus

TG temporary gentleman; thank God; Togo; transformational-generative (grammar); transformational grammar

TGAT Task Group on Assessment and Testing

T-gate ternary selector gate

TGEW Timber Growers England and Wales Ltd

TGF transforming growth factor

TGI Target Group Index

TGIF thank God it's Friday

T-group training group

TGV (France) train à grande vitesse (high-speed passenger train)

TGWU Transport and General Workers' Union

Th thorium

Th. Thursday

TH Territory of Hawaii

ThB Bachelor of Theology (Latin *Theologicae Baccalaureus*)

THC tetrahydrocannabinol (cannabis component); (New Zealand) Tourist Hotel Corporation

ThD Doctor of Theology (Latin *Theologicae Doctor*)

THD total harmonic distortion (in sound recording)

theat. theatrical

THELEP Therapy of Leprosy

theol. theologian; theological; theology

theor. theorem; theoretical

theos. theosophical; theosophist; theosophy

therap. therapeutic(s)

therm. thermometer

thermom. thermometer; thermometry

THES Times Higher Education Supplement

Thess. Thessalonians

THF Trusthouse Forte plc

THI temperature–humidity index

ThL Theological Licentiate

ThM Master of Theology (Latin *Theologiae Magister*)

thou. thousand

thr. through

Thr threonine

THR total hip replacement

ThSchol Scholar in Theology

Thurs. Thursday

THWM Trinity (House) high-water mark

THz terahertz

Ti titanium

TI thermal imaging

TIA transient ischaemic attack

TIBOR Tokyo InterBank Offered Rate

TIC taken into consideration (of an offence); total inorganic carbon (in chemical analysis)

t.i.d. ter in die (Latin: three times a day; in prescriptions)

TIE theatre in education

TIG tungsten inert gas (welding)

TIGR Treasury Investment Growth Receipts (type of bond)

TIH Their Imperial Highnesses

Tim. Timothy

TIM transient intermodulation distortion (in sound recording)

timp. timpani

TIMS The Institute of Management Sciences

TINA there is no alternative (usually referring to Margaret Thatcher)

tinct. tincture

TIP terminal interface processor

TIR Transport International Routier (French: International Road Transport; on continental lorries)

tit. title

Tit. Titus

TJ talk jockey; triple jump

tk tank; truck

Tk taka (monetary unit of Bangladesh)

TKO technical knockout

tkt ticket

t.l. total loss; trade list

Tl thallium

TL target language; thermoluminescent (as in **TL-dating**); total loss; transmission line; Turkish lira (monetary unit)

T/L time loan; total loss

TLA three-letter abbreviation

TLC tender loving care; thin-layer chromatography; total lung

capacity; (Australia) Trades and Labour Council

TLG Theatrical Ladies' Guild

t.l.o. total loss only

TLR Times Law Reports; twin-lens reflex

TLS Times Literary Supplement; typed letter, signed

TLWM Trinity (House) low-water mark

t.m. true mean

Tm thulium

TM trademark; transcendental meditation; trench mortar

TMA Theatrical Management Association; Trans-Mediterranean Airways (Lebanese national airline); trimellitic acid

TMD theatre missile defence

TMJ temporomandibular joint (as in **TMJ syndrome**)

TMMG Teacher of Massage and Medical Gymnastics

TMO telegraph(ic) money order

tn ton; town; train

TN Tennessee; Tonbridge; Tunisia

TNC Theatres National Committee; transnational corporation

TNF theatre nuclear forces; tumour necrosis factor

tng training

TNM tumour (size), (lymph) node (involvement), metastasis (in **TNM classification**)

T-note Treasury note

tnpk. turnpike

TNT 2,4,6-trinitrotoluene (explosive)

t.o. turnover

TO table of organization; telegraph office; Transport Officer; turn over (page)

T/O turnover

Tob. Tobit

Toc H Talbot House (obsolete telegraphic code for its initials; original headquarters of the movement)

TOE theory of everything

TOEFL test(ing) of English as a foreign language

TOFC trailer on flat car (type of freight container)

tom. tomato; tomus (Latin: volume)

tonn. tonnage

TOO time of origin; to order only

TOP technical office protocol; temporarily out of print

TOPIC Teletext Output Price Information Computer

topog. topographer; topographical; topography

TOPS Training Opportunities Scheme

TOSD Tertiary Order of St Dominic

Toshiba Tokyo Shibaura Denki KK (Japanese corporation)

tot. total

TOTC time-on-target computation (military computer)

TOTP Top of the Pops (television programme)

TOW tube-launched optically tracked wire-guided (antitank missile)

toxicol. toxicological; toxicologist; toxicology

tp township; troop

t.p. teaching practice; title page

TP third party; toilet paper; (formerly, in South Africa) Transvaal Province; trigonometric point; turning point

TPA tissue plasminogen activator

TPC (Australia) Trade Practices Commission

tpd tons per day

tph tons per hour

tpi teeth per inch; tracks per inch; turns per inch

TPI tax and price index; threads per inch; tons per inch (immersion); (Australia) totally and permanently incapacitated; Tropical Products Institute

tpk. turnpike

TPM tons per minute

TPN total parenteral nutrition

Tpr Trooper

TPR temperature, pulse, respiration

tpt trumpet

TQ tel quel (exchange rate); Torquay; total quality (quality control)

TQM total quality management

tr. tinctura (Latin: tincture); trace; train; transaction; transitive; translate(d); translation; translator; transpose; transposition; treasurer; treble; trill; troop; trust; trustee

TR tempore regis or reginae (Latin: in the time of the king or queen); tons registered; transmit–receive (as in **TR switch**); Truro; trust receipt; Turkey

TRACE test equipment for rapid automatic checkout evaluation

trad. tradition(al)

trans. transaction; transfer(red); transit; transitive; translate(d); translation; translator; transparent; transport(ation); transpose; transverse

transcr. transcribed (by or for); transcription

transf. transferred

transl. translate(d); translation; translator

transp. transport(ation)

trav. traveller; travels

trbn. trombone

TRC Thames Rowing Club

TRDA Timber Research and Development Association

treas. treasurer; treasury

tree. trustee

trem. tremolando (Italian: trembling); tremulant (device in an organ)

TRF tuned radio frequency

TRH Their Royal Highnesses

TRIC Television and Radio Industries Club

trid. triduum (Latin: three days; in prescriptions)

trig. trigonometric(al); trigonometry

trike trichloroeth(yl)ene (solvent)

Trin. Trinity

tripl. triplicate

triple A anti-aircraft artillery

TRJ turboramjet (engine)

trlr trawler

TRM trademark

tRNA transfer RNA

TRO temporary restraining order

trop. tropic(al)

Trp troop; tryptophan

TRRL Transport and Road Research Laboratory

trs. transfer; transpose; trustees

Truron. Truronensis (Latin: (Bishop) of Truro)

t.s. turbine ship; twin screw

TS Cleveland; tasto solo (Italian: one key alone; in figured-bass playing); Theosophical Society (in England); tough shit; training ship; Treasury Solicitor; tub-sized (paper); typescript

TSA The Securities Association Ltd; total surface area; Training Services Agency (now called Training Agency)

TSB Trustee Savings Bank

tsc passed a Territorial Army course in staff duties

TSD Tertiary of St Dominic

TSE Tokyo Stock Exchange; Toronto Stock Exchange; transmissible spongiform encephalopathy

T.Sgt Technical Sergeant

TSh Tanzanian shilling (monetary unit)

TSH Their Serene Highnesses; thyroid-stimulating hormone

tsi tons per square inch

TSO Trading Standards Officer

tsp. teaspoon(ful)

TSR terminate and stay resident (program)

TSS toxic shock syndrome; twin-screw steamer; typescripts

TSSA Transport Salaried Staffs' Association

TSW Television South West

TT technical training; teetotal(ler); telegraphic transfer; Tourist Trophy (races); Trinidad and Tobago; Trust Territories (abbrev. or postcode); tuberculin-tested (as in **TT milk**)

TTB tetragonal tungsten bronze

TTBT Threshold Test Ban Treaty

TTC technical training centre

TTF Timber Trade Federation

TTFN ta-ta for now

TTL through the lens; to take leave; transistor-transistor logic; (Zimbabwe) tribal trust land

TTS teletypesetter

Tu. Tuesday

TU toxic unit; trade union; traffic unit; training unit; transmission unit; Tupolev (aircraft; as in **TU-104**)

TUC Trades Union Congress

Tues. Tuesday

TUG Telephone Users' Group

TULRA Trade Union and Labour Relations Act (1974)

Turk. Turkey; Turkish

TV television

TVEI Technical and Vocational Educational Initiative

Tvl Transvaal

TVO tractor vaporizing oil

TVP textured vegetable protein (a meat substitute)

TVR television rating

TVRO television receive only (type of antenna)

TW travelling wave (in **TW antenna**); Twickenham

TWA Thames Water Authority; time-weighted average; Trans-World Airlines

TWh terawatt hour(s)

TWIMC to whom it may concern

twocky take without owner's consent (of a person who takes away a car without the owner's consent)

TX Texas

Ty Territory

typ. typographer; typographic(al); typography

typh. typhoon

typo. typographer; typographic(al); typography

typw. typewriter; typewriting; typewritten

Tyr tyrosine

U

u instantaneous potential difference; up (a quark flavour); a velocity component or speed

u. uncle; unit; unsatisfactory; upper

U potential difference; rate of heat loss (measured in British thermal units; in **U value**, a measure of insulating power); universal (certification); upper class (of characteristics, language habits, etc.; also in **non-U**); uracil; uranium; uridine; you (from phonetic spelling, as in **IOU**, **while U wait**)

U. Union; Unionist; unit; United; University; unsatisfactory; upper

U/a underwriting account

UAB Unemployment Assistance Board

UAE United Arab Emirates

UAM underwater-to-air missile

u. & l.c. upper and lower case

UAR United Arab Republic (1958–71)

UARS upper-atmosphere research satellite

UART universal asynchronous receiver/transmitter

UAU Universities Athletic Union

UB Southall

UB40 the index card used for unemployment benefit

UBI Understanding British Industry (organization)

U-boat a German submarine during the World Wars (German Unterseeboot)

UBR Uniform Business Rate

u.c. una chorda; upper case

u/c undercharge

UC una corda (Italian: on one string; i.e. use soft pedal); under construction; undercover; upcast shaft; up centre (of stage); Upper Canada; uterine contraction

U$_c$ universal, particularly suitable for children (certification)

UCATT Union of Construction, Allied Trades, and Technicians

UCBSA United Cricket Board of South Africa

UCCA Universities Central Council on Admissions

UCET Universities Council for Education of Teachers

UCH University College Hospital (London)

UCITS Undertakings for Collective Investment in Transferable Securities

UCMSM University College and Middlesex School of Medicine

UCNS Universities' Council for Nonacademic Staff

UCR unconditioned reflex

UCS unconditioned stimulus

UCTA United Commercial Travellers' Association (now part of the MSF union)

UCW Union of Communication Workers

u.d. ut dictum (Latin: as directed; in prescriptions)

UDA Ulster Defence Association

UDC universal decimal classification; Urban Development Corporation; Urban District Council

UDF Ulster Defence Force; (South Africa) Union Defence Force; (South Africa) United Democratic Front

UDI unilateral declaration of independence

UDM Union of Democratic Mineworkers

UDN ulcerative dermal necrosis (fish disease)

UDR Ulster Defence Regiment

UE (New Zealand) university entrance (examination)

UEA University of East Anglia

UED University Education Diploma

u.e.f. universal extra fine (screw)

UEFA Union of European Football Associations

UF United Free (Church, of Scotland); urea–formaldehyde (as in **UF resin**)

UFAW Universities Federation for Animal Welfare

UFC United Free Church (of Scotland); University Funding Council

UFF Ulster Freedom Fighters

UFO unidentified flying object

UFT unified field theory

UHB urban haute bourgeoisie

UHF ultrahigh frequency

UHT ultra-heat-treated (as in **UHT milk**); ultrahigh temperature

UHV ultrahigh vacuum

u.i. ut infra (Latin: as below)

u/i under instruction

UIL United Irish League

UIT unit investment trust

UJ Union Jack; universal joint

UJC Union Jack Club (London)

UJD Utriusque Juris Doctor (Latin: Doctor of Civil and Canon Law)

UK United Kingdom

UK(A) United Kingdom Allcomers

UKA United Kingdom Alliance

UKAC United Kingdom Automation Council

UKADGE United Kingdom Air Defence Ground Environment

UKAEA United Kingdom Atomic Energy Authority

UKAPE United Kingdom Association of Professional Engineers

UKCC United Kingdom Central Council for Nursing, Midwifery, and Health Visiting

UKCIS United Kingdom Chemical Information Service

UKCOSA United Kingdom Council for Overseas Students' Affairs

UKCSBS United Kingdom Civil Service Benefit Society

UKDA United Kingdom Dairy Association

UKFBPW United Kingdom Federation of Business and Professional Women

UKgal UK gallon

UKIAS United Kingdom Immigrants' Advisory Service

UKISC United Kingdom Industrial Space Committee

UKLF United Kingdom Land Forces

UKMF(L) United Kingdom Military Forces (Land)

UKMIS United Kingdom Mission

UKOOA United Kingdom Offshore Operators Association

UKPIA United Kingdom Petroleum Industry Association Ltd

Ukr. Ukraine; Ukrainian

UKSLS United Kingdom Services Liaison Staff

UKSMA United Kingdom Sugar Merchant Association Ltd

UL up left (of stage)

ULC up left centre (of stage)

ULCC ultralarge crude carrier (oil tanker)

ULCI Union of Lancashire and Cheshire Institutes

ULF ultralow frequency

ULMS underwater long-range missile system

ULSEB University of London School Examinations Board

ult. ultimate(ly); ultimo (Latin: in the last (month); in correspondence)

ULT United Lodge of Theosophists

ULV ultralow volume (as in **ULV sprayer)**

u/m undermentioned

UM Mauritanian ouguiya (monetary unit)

UMB upper memory block

UMDS United Medical and Dental Schools

UMIST University of Manchester Institute of Science and Technology

UMNO United Malays (later Malaysia) National Organization

UMT universal military training

UN United Nations

UNA United Nations Association

unab. unabridged

unacc. unaccompanied

unattrib. unattributed

unauthd unauthorized

unb. unbound

UNBRO United Nations Border Relief Operation

UNC United Nations Command

UNCAST United Nations Conference on the Applications of Science and Technology

UNCDF United Nations Capital Development Fund

UNCED United Nations Conference on Environment and Development

UNCIO United Nations Conference on International Organization

UNCITRAL United Nations Commission on International Trade Law

unclas. unclassified

UNCLE United Network Command for Law Enforcement (fictional organization in TV series 'The Man from UNCLE')

UNCLOS United Nations Conference on the Law of the Sea

UNCSTD United Nations Conference on Science and Technology for Development

UNCTAD United Nations Conference on Trade and Development

UNDP United Nations Development Programme

UNDRO United Nations Disaster Relief Organization

UNECA United Nations Economic Commission for Asia

UNEF United Nations Emergency Force

UNEP United Nations Environment Programme

UNESCO United Nations Educational, Scientific, and Cultural Organization

UNFAO United Nations Food and Agriculture Organization

UNFICYP United Nations (Peace-Keeping) Force in Cyprus

UNFPA United Nations Fund for Population Activities

ung. unguentum (Latin: ointment)

UNHCR United Nations High Commissioner for Refugees

UNIA (USA) Universal Negro Improvement Association

UNICEF United Nations Children's Fund (formerly United Nations International Children's Emergency Fund)

UNIDO United Nations Industrial Development Organization

UNIFIL United Nations Interim Force in Lebanon

UNIP (Zambia) United National Independence Party

UNISIST Universal System for Information in Science and

Technology

Unit. Unitarian(ism)

UNITA União Nacional para a Independência Total de Angola (Portuguese: National Union for the Total Independence of Angola)

UNITAR United Nations Institute for Training and Research

univ. universal(ly); university

Univ. Universalist; University

UNIVAC universal automatic computer

UNIX a type of computer operating system

UNO United Nations Organization

unpub. unpublished

UNREF United Nations Refugee Emergency Fund

UNRISD United Nations Research Institute for Social Development

UNRRA United Nations Relief and Rehabilitation Administration

UNRWA United Nations Relief and Works Agency

UNSCOB United Nations Special Committee on the Balkans

UNSCOP United Nations Special Committee on Palestine

UNTAC United Nations Transitional Authority for Cambodia

up. underproof (of alcohol); upper

UP United Party (esp. in South Africa); United Presbyterian; United Press (news agency); University Press; Uttar Pradesh (formerly United Provinces)

UPC Uganda People's Congress; United Presbyterian Church; universal product code (bar code)

UPI United Press International

UPNI Unionist Party of Northern Ireland

UPR unearned premiums reserve

UPS uninterruptible power supply (to computers, etc.)

UPU Universal Postal Union (UN agency; formerly General Postal Union, GPU)

UPUP Ulster Popular Unionist Party

uPVC unplasticized polyvinyl chloride

UR unconditioned reflex; up right (of stage)

URC United Reformed Church; up right centre (of stage)

URI upper respiratory infection

URTI upper respiratory tract infection

URTU United Road Transport Union

Uru. Uruguay(an)

u.s. ubi supra (Latin: where (mentioned *or* cited) above); ut supra (Latin: as above)

u/s unserviceable; useless

US ultrasound scanning; Undersecretary; United States; United States highway (as in **US66**)

U/S unserviceable; useless

USA United States Army; United States of America (abbrev. *or* IVR)

USAF United States Air Force

USC Ulster Special Constabulary; United Somali Congress

USCL United Society for Christian Literature

USDAW Union of Shop, Distributive, and Allied Workers

USgal US gallon

USh Uganda shilling (monetary unit)

USI United Service Institution

USIA United States Information Agency

USM underwater-to-surface missile; unlisted securities market

USN United States Navy

USO (USA) United Service Organization

US of A United States of America

USP unique selling proposition (of a product); United States Pharmacopeia

USPG United Society for the Propagation of the Gospel (formerly SPG)

USR Universities' Statistical Record

USS United States Senate; United States Ship; United States Steamer

USSR Union of Soviet Socialist Republics

usu. usual(ly)

USW ultrashort wave

Ut. Utah

UT unit trust; universal time; Utah

U/T under trust

UTA Unit Trust Association

UTC Coordinated Universal Time (French *universel temps coordonné*); University Training Corps

Utd United

ut dict. ut dictum (Latin: as directed; in prescriptions)

utend. utendus (Latin: to be used)

U3A University of the Third Age

UTI urinary-tract infection

ut inf. ut infra (Latin: as below)

UTS ultimate tensile strength

ut sup. ut supra (Latin: as above)

UU Ulster Unionist

UUM underwater-to-underwater missile

UUUC United Ulster Unionist Coalition

UUUP United Ulster Unionist Party

UV ultraviolet

UV-A ultraviolet radiation of wavelength 320–380 m

UV-B ultraviolet radiation of wavelength 280–320 m

UVF Ulster Volunteer Force

U/W under will; underwriter

UWC Ulster Workers' Council

UWIST University of Wales Institute of Science and Technology

UWT Union of Women Teachers (now merged with NAS/UWT)

ux. uxor (Latin: wife)

UXB unexploded bomb

V

v instantaneous voltage; velocity; a velocity component *or* speed

v. valve; vein; ventral; verb(al); verse; version; verso; versus; very; via; vice (Latin: in place of); vide (Latin: see); village; violin; virus; vision; vocative; voice; volume; von (German: of; in names)

V electric potential; five; luminous efficiency; potential difference; potential energy; vanadium; Vatican City; verb (in transformational grammar); Vergeltungswaffe (German: reprisal weapon, as in **V-1** and **V-2**, World War II missiles); victory (as in **V-Day**, **V-sign**); volt; volume (capacity); types of aircraft

V. Venerable; version; Very (in titles); Via (Italian: street); Vicar; Vice (in titles); Viscount; Volunteer(s)

V1 Vergeltungswaffe 1

V2 Vergeltungswaffe 2

va viola

v.a. value analysis; verb active; verbal adjective

Va. Virginia (USA)

VA value-added; value analysis; (USA) Veterans' Administration; Vicar Apostolic; Vice-Admiral; (Order of) Victoria and Albert; Virginia; visual acuity

VAB vehicle assembly building (of NASA)

vac. vacancy; vacant; vacation; vacuum

VAD Voluntary Aid Detachment

VADAS voice-activated domestic appliance system

V-Adm Vice-Admiral

val. valley; valuation; value(d)

Val valine

van advantage

V&A Victoria and Albert Museum

V & V verification and validation

var. variable; variant; variation; variety; variometer; various

VAR visual aural range

Varig (Empresa de) Viação Aérea Rio Grandense (Brazilian airline)

var. lect. varia lectio (Latin: a variant reading)

Vascar visual average speed computer and recorder

VASP Viaçao Aérea São Paulo (Brazilian airline)

Vat. Vatican

VAT value-added tax

v. aux. auxiliary verb

VAV variable air volume (in **VAV** (air-conditioning) **system**)

VAX virtual address extension (range of computers manufactured by DEC)

VAX/VMS the standard operating system for VAX processors.

vb verb(al)

VB verbal constituent (in transformational grammar)

V bomber various types of aircraft (named after the types Victor, Vulcan, and Valiant)

vc. cello (from *violoncello*)

VC venture capital; Vice-Chairman; Vice-Chancellor; Vice-Consul; Vickers Commercial (aircraft, as in

VC10); Victoria Cross; Viet Cong; vital capacity
VCAS Vice-Chief of the Air Staff
VCDS Vice-Chief of the Defence Staff
VCE variable-cycle engine
VCGS Vice-Chief of the General Staff
VCH Victoria County History (reference book)
vcl. cello (from *violoncello*)
VCNS Vice-Chief of the Naval Staff
VCO (India) Viceroy's Commissioned Officer
VCPI virtual control program interface
VCR video-cassette recorder; visual control room (at an airfield)
v.d. various dates
VD venereal disease; Victorian Decoration; Volunteer Decoration (formerly awarded in the Territorial Army or the Royal Naval Volunteer Reserve)
V-Day Victory Day
VDC Volunteer Defence Corps
v. dep. verb deponent
VDH valvular disease of the heart
VDI virtual device interface
VDJ video disc jockey
VDQS vin délimité de qualité supérieure (French; superior-quality wine classification)
VDR video-disc recording
VDRL venereal disease research laboratory (in **VDRL test**, for syphilis)
VDT visual display terminal
VDU visual display unit
VE Victory in Europe (in **VE Day**, 8 May 1945)
VEB Volkseigener Betrieb (German: People's Concern; state-owned company)
veg. vegetable; vegetation
veh. vehicle; vehicular
vel. vellum; velocity
Ven. Venerable; Venetian; Venezuela(n); Venice
ver. verse; version
VERA vision electronic recording apparatus
verb. et lit. verbatim et literatim (Latin: word for word and letter for letter)
verb. sap. verbum sapienti satis (Latin: a word is enough to the wise)
vers versed sine
vers. version
vert. vertical
Very Rev. Very Reverend
ves. vespere (Latin: in the evening; in prescriptions); vessel
vet. veteran; veterinarian; veterinary
vet. sci. veterinary science
vet. surg. veterinary surgeon
v.f. very fair
VF ventricular fibrillation; Vicar Forane; video frequency; voice frequency
VFA (Australia) Victorian Football Association

VFL (Australia) Victorian Football League
VFM value for money (audit)
VFT (Australia) very fast train
VFW (USA) Veterans of Foreign Wars
v.g. verbi gratia (Latin: for example); very good
VG very good; Vicar General
VGA video graphics array
v.g.c. very good condition
VHC very highly commended
VHD video high density (system)
VHE very high energy
VHF very high frequency
VHP (India) Vishwa Hindu Parishad (militant Hindu group)
VHS Video Home System
VHT very high temperature
v.i. verb intransitive; vide infra (Latin: see below)
VI Vancouver Island; Virgin Islands
VIASA Venezolana Internacional de Aviácion, SA (Venezuelan International Airways)
vib. vibraphone
vic. vicar; vicarage; vicinity
Vic. Victoria (Australia)
VIC Victoria Institute of Colleges
Vice-Adm. Vice-Admiral
vid. vide (Latin: see)
VID virtual image display
vil. village
VIP very important person
VIR Victoria Imperatrix Regina (Latin: Victoria, Empress and Queen)
Virg. Virginia (USA)
v. irr. verb irregular
vis. visibility; visual
Vis. Viscount
visc. viscosity
VISTA Volunteers in Service to America
viz videlicet (Latin: namely; *z* is medieval Latin symbol of contraction)
VJ (Australia) Vaucluse Junior (yacht); Victory over Japan (in **VJ Day**, 15 Aug. or 2 Sept. 1945); video jockey
v.l. varia lectio (Latin: a variant reading)
VL Vulgar Latin
VLBW very low birth weight
VLCC very large crude carrier (oil tanker)
vle violone (double-bass viol)
VLF very low frequency
VLLW very low-level (radioactive) waste
vln violin
VLR very long range (aircraft); Victoria Law Reports
VLSI very large-scale integration
VM Victory Medal; Virgin Mary; virtual machine
V-Mail (USA) victory mail
VM/CMS virtual machine, conversational monitor system
VMD Doctor of Veterinary Medicine (Latin *Veterinariae Medicinae Doctor*)

VMH Victoria Medal of Honour (awarded by the Royal Horticultural Society)
VMS virtual machine system
vn violin
v.n. verb neuter
VN Vietnam (abbrev. *or* IVR)
vo. verso
VO very old (of brandy, whisky, etc.); Veterinary Officer; (Royal) Victorian Order
VOA Voice of America
voc. vocative
vocab. vocabulary
vocat. vocative
voc-ed vocational education
vol. volcano; volume; voluntary; volunteer
vols volumes
VOP very oldest procurable (of brandy, port, etc.)
VOR very-high-frequency omnirange *or* omnidirectional radio range (navigation aid)
vox pop vox populi (Latin: voice of the people)
v.p. verb passive
VP verb phrase (in transformational grammar); Vice-President; Vice-Principal; vita patris (Latin: during the life of his father)
VPP (India) value payable post; Volunteer Political Party
VPRP Vice-President of the Royal Society of Portrait Painters
VQMG Vice-Quartermaster-General
v.r. variant reading; verb reflexive
VR variant reading; velocity ratio; Victoria Regina (Latin: Queen Victoria); virtual reality; voltage regulator; Volunteer Reserve
VRAM video random access memory
VRD Royal Naval Volunteer Reserve Officers' Decoration
v. refl. verb reflexive
V. Rev. Very Reverend
VRI Victoria Regina et Imperatrix (Latin: Victoria, Queen and Empress)
VRO vehicle registration office
vs. versus
v.s. vide supra (Latin: see above)
VS Veterinary Surgeon; volti subito (Italian: turn over quickly)
VSB vestigial sideband
VSI vertical speed indicator
V-sign victory sign
VSO verb-subject-object (as in **VSO language**); very superior old (of brandy, port, etc.); Voluntary Service Overseas
VSOP very special old pale (of brandy, port, etc.)
VSR very special reserve (of wine)
V/STOL vertical and short takeoff and landing (aircraft)
v.t. verb transitive
Vt Vermont
VT variable time (as in **VT fuse**); vatu (monetary unit of Vanuatu); ventricular tachycardia; Vermont
VTC Volunteer Training Corps

VTE vicarious trial and error
VTO vertical takeoff (aircraft)
VTOL vertical takeoff and landing (aircraft)
VTR videotape recorder
VU volume unit (as in **VU meter**)
Vul. Vulgate
vulg. vulgar(ly)
vv. verbs; verses; (first and second) violins; voices; volumes
v.v. vice versa
VVO very very old (of brandy, port, etc.)
VW Very Worshipful; Volkswagen
v.y. various years

W

w a velocity component
w. water; week; weight; white; wicket; wide; width; wife; win; with; won; word
W load; tungsten (formerly wolfram); water closet; WC; watt; weight; Weigle (in **W reactivation**); west(ern); west London; winter loading (on load line); women's (clothing size); won (South Korean monetary unit); work
W. Wales; Warden; Wednesday; Welsh; Wesleyan; west(ern); white; wide; widow(er); widowed
WA Warrington; Washington (state); West Africa(n); Western Australia; with average
WAAAF Women's Auxiliary Australian Air Force
WAAC Women's Army Auxiliary Corps
WAAF Women's Auxiliary Air Force; Women's Auxiliary Australian Air Force
WAC (USA) Women's Army Corps (in World War II)
WACC World Association for Christian Communications
WAF with all faults; (USA) Women in the Air Force
W. Afr. West Africa(n)
WAG (West Africa) Gambia
WAGBI Wildfowl Association of Great Britain and Ireland
WAGGGS World Association of Girl Guides and Girl Scouts
WAIS Wechsler Adult Intelligence Scale
WAIS-R Wechsler Adult Intelligence Scale – Revised
Wal. Walloon
WAL (West Africa) Sierra Leone
WAN (West Africa) Nigeria; wide-area network
W & S whisky and soda
W & T wear and tear
WAP wireless applications protocol
war. warrant
War. Warwickshire
WARC World Administrative Radio Conference; World Alliance of Reformed Churches
Warks Warwickshire
Wash. Washington
WASP (USA) white Anglo-Saxon Protestant; (USA) Women Airforce Service Pilots
WAT weight, altitude, temperature (as in **WAT curves**); word association test
WATFOR University of Waterloo Fortran (Fortran compiler)
W. Aus. Western Australia
WAVES Women Accepted for Volunteer Emergency Service
w.b. water ballast; waybill; westbound; wool back
Wb weber
WB Warner Brothers (Pictures, Incorporated); waveband; waybill; Wechsler–Bellevue (Intelligence Scale)
WBA West Bromwich Albion (Football Club); World Boxing Association
WBC white blood cell; white blood (cell) count; World Boxing Council
WBF World Bridge Federation
WbN west by north
w.b.s. without benefit of salvage
WbS west by south
w.c. water closet; without charge
WC water closet; Wesleyan chapel; west central London
WCC World Council of Churches
W/Cdr Wing Commander
WCEU World Christian Endeavour Union
WCL World Confederation of Labour
WCT World Championship Tennis
WCTU (USA, Canada) Women's Christian Temperance Union
wd ward; warranted; wood; word; would
w/d warranted
WD (Windward Islands) Dominica; War Department; Watford; Works Department
W/D withdrawal
WDA writing-down allowance
WDC Woman Detective Constable
WDM wavelength division multiplex
WDS Woman Detective Sergeant
WDV written-down value
w/e weekend; week ending
WEA Royal West of England Academy; Workers' Educational Association
Wed. Wednesday
Weds. Wednesday
w.e.f. with effect from
WEFT wings, engine, fuselage, tail
WEN Women's Environmental Network
WES Women's Engineering Society
WES/PNEU Worldwide Education Service of Parents' National Educational Union
Westm. Westminster
WET West(ern) European Time
WEU Western European Union (for defence policy)
wf wrong fount
WF Wakefield
WFA White Fish Authority
w factor will factor
WFC World Food Council
w.fd wool forward
WFEO World Federation of Engineering Organizations
wff well-formed formula
WFP World Food Programme (of the FAO)
WFSW World Federation of Scientific Workers
WFTU World Federation of Trade Unions
w.fwd wool forward
WG (Windward Islands) Grenada; water gauge; weight guaranteed; W(illiam) G(ilbert) Grace (1848–1915, English cricketer); wire gauge; Working Group
WGA Writers' Guild of America
WGC Welwyn Garden City
Wg/Cdr Wing Commander
W. Ger. West German(y); West Germanic (language group)
W. Glam. West Glamorgan
WGmc West Germanic (language group)
wh. white
W h watt hour(s)
WH withholding
WHA World Hockey Association
w.h.b. wash-hand basin
whf. wharf
WhF Whitworth Fellow
WHO World Health Organization
whs. warehouse
WhSch Whitworth Scholar
whsle wholesale
whs. rec. warehouse receipt
whs. stk warehouse stock
w.i. when issued
WI West Indian; West Indies; Wisconsin; Women's Institute
WIA wounded in action
WICA Warsaw International Consumer Association
wid. widow(er)
Wigorn. Wigorniensis (Latin: (Bishop) of Worcester)
wilco will comply (in radio communications, etc.)
Wilts Wiltshire
WIMP weakly interacting massive particle; windows icons menus pointers
W. Ind. West Indian; West Indies
Wind. I. Windward Islands
Wing Cdr Wing Commander
wint. winter
WIP work in progress
WIPO World Intellectual Property Organization
Wis. Wisconsin
WISC Wechsler Intelligence Scale for Children
WISC-R Wechsler Intelligence Scale for Children – Revised
Wisd. Wisdom of Solomon
WITA Women's International Tennis Association
Wits. Witwatersrand
WIZO Women's International Zionist Organization
WJC World Jewish Congress
WJEC Welsh Joint Education Committee

wk weak; week; work

Wk Walk (in place names)

WKB Wentzel–Kramers–Brillouin (as in **WKB solution** of the Schrödinger equation)

wkly weekly

wks weeks

wkt wicket

WL (Windward Islands) St Lucia; wagon-lit (French: sleeping car); water line; wavelength

WLA Women's Land Army

wld would

WLF Women's Liberal Federation

wl fwd wool forward

WLHB Women's League of Health and Beauty

WLM Women's Liberation Movement

W. long. west longitude

WLR Weekly Law Reports

W/M weight or measurement

WMA Working Mothers' Association; World Medical Association

WMC Working Men's College

WMCIU Working Men's Club and Institute Union Ltd

wmk watermark

WMO World Meteorological Organization

WN Wigan

WNA winter North Atlantic loading (on load line)

WNO Welsh National Opera

WNP Welsh Nationalist Party

WNW west-northwest

w.o. walkover; written order

w/o without; written off

WO War Office; Warrant Officer; welfare officer; wireless operator; written order

w.o.b. washed overboard

w.o.c. without compensation

WOC(S) waiting on cement (to set)

WOF (New Zealand) Warrant of Fitness (for vehicles)

W/offr welfare officer

w.o.g. with other goods

Worcs Worcestershire

WORM write once read many (times)

WOSB War Office Selection Board

WOW waiting on weather; Women Against the Ordination of Women

w.p. weather permitting; word processing

Wp. Worship; Worshipful

WP weather permitting; White Paper; word processing; working pressure

WPA Western Provident Association; World Pool-Billiard Association

WPB wastepaper basket

WPBSA World Professional Billiards and Snooker Association

WPC Woman Police Constable

WPESS within pulse electronic sector scanning (in **WPESS sonar**)

WPI wholesale price index; World Press Institute

w.p.m. words per minute

WPMSF World Professional Marathon Swimming Federation

wpn weapon

WPPSI Wechsler Preschool and Primary Scale of Intelligence

WPT Women's Playhouse Trust

w.r. warehouse receipt; war risk

WR warehouse receipt; Wassermann reaction; Western Region; Willelmus Rex (Latin: King William); Wolf–Rayet (in **WR stars**); Worcester

WRAAC Women's Royal Australian Army Corps

WRAAF Women's Royal Australian Air Force

WRAC Women's Royal Army Corps

WRAF Women's Royal Air Force

WRANS Women's Royal Australian Naval Service

WRC Water Research Centre

WRI Women's Rural Institute

WRNS Women's Royal Naval Service

wrnt warrant

w.r.o. war risks only

WRP Worker's Revolutionary Party

w.r.t. with respect to

WRU Welsh Rugby Union

WRVS Women's Royal Voluntary Service (formerly WVS)

WS Walsall; Western Samoa; West Saxon; wind speed; (Scotland) Writer to the Signet

WSCF World Student Christian Federation

WSPU Women's Social and Political Union

WSTN World Service Television News

WSTV World Service Television

WSW west-southwest

wt weight

WT wireless telegraphy

WTA winner takes all; Women's Tennis Association

wtd warranted

WTN Worldwide Television News

WTO Warsaw Treaty Organization

WTS Women's Transport Service (now amalgamated with FANY)

WUF World Underwater Federation

WUS World University Service

WV (Windward Islands) St Vincent and the Grenadines; West Virginia; Wolverhampton

W. Va. West Virginia

WVS Women's Voluntary Service

WW wall-to-wall (in estate agency); warehouse warrant; Who's Who; World War

WW1 World War One (1914–18)

WW2 World War Two (1939–45)

WWF Worldwide Fund for Nature (formerly World Wildlife Fund)

WWMCCS World Wide Military Command and Control System

WWSSN worldwide standard seismograph network

WWSU World Water Ski Union

WWW World Weather Watch (of the WMO); World Wide Web

WX women's extra-large (clothing size)

Wy. Wyoming

WY Wyoming

Wyo. Wyoming

WYSIWYG what you see (on the screen) is what you get (from the printer)

X

x the basic number of chromosomes in a genome; a Cartesian coordinate (usually horizontal, as in **x-axis**); any card other than an honour; cross (as in **x-cut**, **x'd out**); ex; extra; an algebraic variable

X adults only (former certification, still used in **X-rated**, **X-rating**); beer strength (in **XX**, **XXX**, etc.); choice (on a ballot paper); Christ (from Greek letter X (chi), representing *ch*); Cross (as in **King's X**); error; experiment(al); exposure dose; extra; a halogen (as in **MgX**); a kiss; the location of a place or point on a map, diagram, etc; his mark; reactance; ten; any unknown, unspecified, or variable thing, factor, number, or person; X-ray; a sex chromosome in humans and most animals (as in **X chromosome**, **X-linked**, **XYY syndrome**)

xa ex all (without any benefits)

xb ex bonus (i.e. without bonus shares)

XBT expendable bathythermograph

xc ex capitalization (without capitalization); ex coupon (without the interest on the coupon)

XC (USA, Canada) cross-country (in **XC skiing**)

x.c.l. excess current liabilities

xcp ex coupon

xd ex dividend (without dividend)

XDR extended dynamic range (of cassettes)

Xe xenon

x-height typesize of lower-case letters excluding ascenders and descenders (from the height of the lower-case x)

xi ex interest (without interest)

XL extra large (clothing size)

Xmas Christmas

XML extensible mark-up language

XMS extended memory specification

xn ex new (without right to new shares)

Xn Christian

Xnty Christianity

XO executive officer; a cognac of superior quality

XOR exclusive-OR (as in **XOR gate**)

XP Christ *or* Christianity (from X (chi) and P (rho), the first two letters of the Greek word for Christ); express paid

XPS X-ray photoelectron spectroscopy

xq cross-question

xr ex rights (without rights)

XR X-ray(s)
X-ray electromagnetic radiation of very short wavelength
x ref. cross reference
XRF X-ray fluorescence
x.rts ex rights (without rights)
xs expenses
Xt Christ
Xtian Christian
Xty Christianity
xw ex warrants (without warrants)
X-Windows a precisely defined form of windowing mechanism developed by MIT
xyl. xylophone

Y

y a Cartesian coordinate (usually vertical, as in **y-axis**); an algebraic variable
y. yard; year; young; youngest
Y admittance; yen (Japanese monetary unit); Yeomanry; YMCA, YWCA, YMHA, or YWHA; yttrium; yuan (Chinese monetary unit; see also RMB); Yugoslavia; a sex chromosome of humans and most animals (as in **Y chromosome**, **Y-linked, XYY syndrome**)
YA York–Antwerp (Rules); (USA) young adult
YAC yeast artificial chromosome(s)
YACC yet another compiler-compiler
YAG yttrium–aluminium garnet
YAR York–Antwerp Rules
YAS Yorkshire Agricultural Society
Yb ytterbium
YB yearbook
YC Young Conservative
YC&UO Young Conservative and Unionist Organization
YCNAC Young Conservative National Advisory Committee
yd yard
YD Yemeni dinar (monetary unit)
yds yards
YE Your Excellency

yeo. yeoman; yeomanry
YER yearly effective rate (of interest)
YES Youth Employment Service; Youth Enterprise Scheme
YFC Young Farmers' Club
YHA Youth Hostels Association
YHANI Youth Hostels Association of Northern Ireland
YIG yttrium–iron garnet
YM YMCA
YMCA Young Men's Christian Association
YMHA Young Men's Hebrew Association
y.o. yarn over; year(s) old (following a number)
YO York
YOB year of birth
YOP Youth Opportunities Programme (replaced by Youth Training Scheme, YTS)
Yorks Yorkshire
YP young prisoner
YPTES Young People's Trust for Endangered Species
yr year; younger; your
yrbk yearbook
YRls Yemen riyal (monetary unit)
yrs years; yours (in correspondence)
yt yacht
YT Yukon Territory
y.t.b. yarn to back
YTD year to date
y.t.f. yarn to front
YTS Youth Training Scheme
YU Yugoslavia
Yugo. Yugoslavia
yuppie young urban professional
YV Venezuela
YVFF Young Volunteer Force Foundation
YWCA Young Women's Christian Association
YWHA Young Women's Hebrew Association

Z

z a Cartesian coordinate (as in **z-axis**); an algebraic variable
z. zero; zone
Z impedance; proton number; Zambia; a sex chromosome in birds and some insects
Z. zero (as in **Z-day**); zone
ZA South Africa
ZANU Zimbabwe African National Union
ZANU (PF) Zimbabwe African National Union (Patriotic Front)
ZAPU Zimbabwe African People's Union
Z-car a police patrol car (from zulu, radio call sign)
ZE Lerwick
Zech. Zechariah
Zeep zero-energy experimental pile
ZEG zero economic growth
Zeph. Zephaniah
ZETA zero-energy thermonuclear apparatus
ZFGBI Zionist Federation of Great Britain and Ireland
ZI zone of interior
ZIF zero insertion force (in **ZIF socket**)
ZIFT zygote intrafallopian transfer (treatment for infertility)
zip (USA) zone improvement plan (in **zip code**, US postcode)
Zl zloty (Polish monetary unit)
Zn zinc
zod. zodiac
zool. zoological; zoologist; zoology
ZPG zero population growth
Zr zirconium
ZS Zoological Society
ZST zone standard time
ZW Zimbabwe
zz zigzag
Zz. ginger (Latin zingiber)